Holy Bible

Presented to

By

Date

HOLY BIBLE

KING JAMES VERSION

King James Version Bible Large Print Compact Edition

PO Box 1599, Vereeniging, 1930, RSA

Produced with the assistance of The Livingstone Corporation, an e-Christian company (www.Livingstone.Corp.com).

Cover designed by Christian Art Publishers

Printed in China

ISBN 978-1-4321-1733-7 KJV034
ISBN 978-1-4321-1734-4 KJV035
ISBN 978-1-4321-1792-4 KJV070
ISBN 978-1-4321-1793-1 KJV071
ISBN 978-1-4321-1956-0 KJV082
ISBN 978-1-4321-1957-7 KJV083
ISBN 978-1-4321-3300-9 KJV131
ISBN 978-1-4321-3301-6 KJV132
ISBN 978-1-4321-3389-4 KJV155
ISBN 978-1-64272-865-1 KJV171
ISBN 978-1-64272-927-6 KJV206
ISBN 978-1-64272-928-3 KJV207
ISBN 978-1-63952-252-1 KJV232
ISBN 978-1-63952-674-1 KJV249
ISBN 978-1-63952-675-8 KJV250
ISBN 978-0-638-00276-8 KJV266

24 25 26 27 28 29 30 31 32 33 – 32 31 30 29 28 27 26 25 24 23

THE NAMES AND CANONICAL ORDER
OF ALL THE

BOOKS OF THE OLD AND NEW TESTAMENTS

THE NAMES AND ALPHABETICAL ORDER
OF ALL THE
BOOKS OF THE OLD AND NEW TESTAMENTS

THE
OLD TESTAMENT

THE FIRST BOOK OF MOSES

CALLED

GENESIS

1 In the beginning God created the
heaven and the earth.
2 And the earth was without form,
and void; and darkness *was* upon the
face of the deep. And the Spirit of God
moved upon the face of the waters.
3 And God said, Let there be light:
and there was light.
4 And God saw the light, that *it was*
good: and God divided the light from
the darkness.
5 And God called the light Day, and
the darkness he called Night. And the
evening and the morning were the first
day.
6 And God said, Let there be a firmament in the midst of the waters, and let
it divide the waters from the waters.
7 And God made the firmament, and
divided the waters which *were* under
the firmament from the waters which
were above the firmament: and it was
so.
8 And God called the firmament
Heaven. And the evening and the
morning were the second day.
9 And God said, Let the waters under
the heaven be gathered together unto
one place, and let the dry *land* appear:
and it was so.
10 And God called the dry *land*
Earth; and the gathering together of
the waters called he Seas: and God saw
that *it was* good.
11 And God said, Let the earth bring
forth grass, the herb yielding seed, *and*
the fruit tree yielding fruit after his
kind, whose seed *is* in itself, upon the
earth: and it was so.
12 And the earth brought forth grass,
and herb yielding seed after his kind,
and the tree yielding fruit, whose seed
was in itself, after his kind: and God
saw that *it was* good.
13 And the evening and the morning
were the third day.
14 And God said, Let there be lights
in the firmament of the heaven to
divide the day from the night; and let
them be for signs, and for seasons, and
for days, and years:
15 And let them be for lights in the
firmament of the heaven to give light
upon the earth: and it was so.
16 And God made two great lights;
the greater light to rule the day, and
the lesser light to rule the night: *he
made* the stars also.
17 And God set them in the firmament of the heaven to give light upon
the earth,
18 And to rule over the day and over
the night, and to divide the light from
the darkness: and God saw that *it was*
good.
19 And the evening and the morning
were the fourth day.
20 And God said, Let the waters bring
forth abundantly the moving creature
that hath life, and fowl *that* may fly
above the earth in the open firmament
of heaven.
21 And God created great whales,
and every living creature that moveth,
which the waters brought forth abundantly, after their kind, and every
winged fowl after his kind: and God
saw that *it was* good.

22 And God blessed them, saying, Be fruitful, and multiply, and fill the waters in the seas, and let fowl multiply in the earth.

23 And the evening and the morning were the fifth day.

24 And God said, Let the earth bring forth the living creature after his kind, cattle, and creeping thing, and beast of the earth after his kind: and it was so.

25 And God made the beast of the earth after his kind, and cattle after their kind, and every thing that creepeth upon the earth after his kind: and God saw that *it was* good.

26 And God said, Let us make man in our image, after our likeness: and let them have dominion over the fish of the sea, and over the fowl of the air, and over the cattle, and over all the earth, and over every creeping thing that creepeth upon the earth.

27 So God created man in his *own* image, in the image of God created he him; male and female created he them.

28 And God blessed them, and God said unto them, Be fruitful, and multiply, and replenish the earth, and subdue it: and have dominion over the fish of the sea, and over the fowl of the air, and over every living thing that moveth upon the earth.

29 And God said, Behold, I have given you every herb bearing seed, which *is* upon the face of all the earth, and every tree, in the which *is* the fruit of a tree yielding seed; to you it shall be for meat.

30 And to every beast of the earth, and to every fowl of the air, and to every thing that creepeth upon the earth, wherein *there is* life, *I have given* every green herb for meat: and it was so.

31 And God saw every thing that he had made, and, behold, *it was* very good. And the evening and the morning were the sixth day.

2 Thus the heavens and the earth were finished, and all the host of them.

2 And on the seventh day God ended his work which he had made; and he rested on the seventh day from all his work which he had made.

3 And God blessed the seventh day, and sanctified it: because that in it he had rested from all his work which God created and made.

4 These *are* the generations of the heavens and of the earth when they were created, in the day that the LORD God made the earth and the heavens,

5 And every plant of the field before it was in the earth, and every herb of the field before it grew: for the LORD God had not caused it to rain upon the earth, and *there was* not a man to till the ground.

6 But there went up a mist from the earth, and watered the whole face of the ground.

7 And the LORD God formed man *of* the dust of the ground, and breathed into his nostrils the breath of life; and man became a living soul.

8 And the LORD God planted a garden eastward in Eden; and there he put the man whom he had formed.

9 And out of the ground made the LORD God to grow every tree that is pleasant to the sight, and good for food; the tree of life also in the midst of the garden, and the tree of knowledge of good and evil.

10 And a river went out of Eden to water the garden; and from thence it

was parted, and became into four
heads.
11 The name of the first *is* Pison: that
is it which compasseth the whole land
of Havilah, where *there is* gold;
12 And the gold of that land *is* good:
there *is* bdellium and the onyx stone.
13 And the name of the second river
is Gihon: the same *is* it that compasseth
the whole land of Ethiopia.
14 And the name of the third river *is*
Hiddekel: that *is* it which goeth toward
the east of Assyria. And the fourth river
is Euphrates.
15 And the LORD God took the man,
and put him into the garden of Eden to
dress it and to keep it.
16 And the LORD God commanded
the man, saying, Of every tree of the
garden thou mayest freely eat:
17 But of the tree of the knowledge of
good and evil, thou shalt not eat of it:
for in the day that thou eatest thereof
thou shalt surely die.
18 And the LORD God said, *It is* not
good that the man should be alone; I
will make him an help meet for him.
19 And out of the ground the LORD
God formed every beast of the field,
and every fowl of the air; and brought
them unto Adam to see what he would
call them: and whatsoever Adam called
every living creature, that *was* the
name thereof.
20 And Adam gave names to all cattle, and to the fowl of the air, and to
every beast of the field; but for Adam
there was not found an help meet for
him.
21 And the LORD God caused a deep
sleep to fall upon Adam, and he slept:
and he took one of his ribs, and closed
up the flesh instead thereof;
22 And the rib, which the LORD God
had taken from man, made he a woman,
and brought her unto the man.
23 And Adam said, This *is* now bone
of my bones, and flesh of my flesh: she
shall be called Woman, because she
was taken out of Man.
24 Therefore shall a man leave his
father and his mother, and shall cleave
unto his wife: and they shall be one
flesh.
25 And they were both naked, the
man and his wife, and were not
ashamed.

3 Now the serpent was more subtil
than any beast of the field which
the LORD God had made. And he said
unto the woman, Yea, hath God said, Ye
shall not eat of every tree of the
garden?
2 And the woman said unto the serpent, We may eat of the fruit of the
trees of the garden:
3 But of the fruit of the tree which *is*
in the midst of the garden, God hath
said, Ye shall not eat of it, neither shall
ye touch it, lest ye die.
4 And the serpent said unto the
woman, Ye shall not surely die:
5 For God doth know that in the day
ye eat thereof, then your eyes shall be
opened, and ye shall be as gods, knowing good and evil.
6 And when the woman saw that the
tree *was* good for food, and that it *was*
pleasant to the eyes, and a tree to be
desired to make *one* wise, she took of
the fruit thereof, and did eat, and gave
also unto her husband with her; and he
did eat.
7 And the eyes of them both were
opened, and they knew that they *were*
naked; and they sewed fig leaves
together, and made themselves aprons.

8 And they heard the voice of the LORD God walking in the garden in the cool of the day: and Adam and his wife hid themselves from the presence of the LORD God amongst the trees of the garden.

9 And the LORD God called unto Adam, and said unto him, Where *art* thou?

10 And he said, I heard thy voice in the garden, and I was afraid, because I *was* naked; and I hid myself.

11 And he said, Who told thee that thou *wast* naked? Hast thou eaten of the tree, whereof I commanded thee that thou shouldest not eat?

12 And the man said, The woman whom thou gavest *to be* with me, she gave me of the tree, and I did eat.

13 And the LORD God said unto the woman, What *is* this *that* thou hast done? And the woman said, The serpent beguiled me, and I did eat.

14 And the LORD God said unto the serpent, Because thou hast done this, thou *art* cursed above all cattle, and above every beast of the field; upon thy belly shalt thou go, and dust shalt thou eat all the days of thy life:

15 And I will put enmity between thee and the woman, and between thy seed and her seed; it shall bruise thy head, and thou shalt bruise his heel.

16 Unto the woman he said, I will greatly multiply thy sorrow and thy conception; in sorrow thou shalt bring forth children; and thy desire *shall be* to thy husband, and he shall rule over thee.

17 And unto Adam he said, Because thou hast hearkened unto the voice of thy wife, and hast eaten of the tree, of which I commanded thee, saying, Thou shalt not eat of it: cursed *is* the ground for thy sake; in sorrow shalt thou eat *of* it all the days of thy life;

18 Thorns also and thistles shall it bring forth to thee; and thou shalt eat the herb of the field;

19 In the sweat of thy face shalt thou eat bread, till thou return unto the ground; for out of it wast thou taken: for dust thou *art*, and unto dust shalt thou return.

20 And Adam called his wife's name Eve; because she was the mother of all living.

21 Unto Adam also and to his wife did the LORD God make coats of skins, and clothed them.

22 And the LORD God said, Behold, the man is become as one of us, to know good and evil: and now, lest he put forth his hand, and take also of the tree of life, and eat, and live for ever:

23 Therefore the LORD God sent him forth from the garden of Eden, to till the ground from whence he was taken.

24 So he drove out the man; and he placed at the east of the garden of Eden Cherubims, and a flaming sword which turned every way, to keep the way of the tree of life.

4 And Adam knew Eve his wife; and she conceived, and bare Cain, and said, I have gotten a man from the LORD.

2 And she again bare his brother Abel. And Abel was a keeper of sheep, but Cain was a tiller of the ground.

3 And in process of time it came to pass, that Cain brought of the fruit of the ground an offering unto the LORD.

4 And Abel, he also brought of the firstlings of his flock and of the fat thereof. And the LORD had respect unto Abel and to his offering:

5 But unto Cain and to his offering he
had not respect. And Cain was very
wroth, and his countenance fell.
6 And the LORD said unto Cain, Why
art thou wroth? and why is thy countenance fallen?
7 If thou doest well, shalt thou not be
accepted? and if thou doest not well,
sin lieth at the door. And unto thee
shall be his desire, and thou shalt rule
over him.
8 And Cain talked with Abel his
brother: and it came to pass, when they
were in the field, that Cain rose up
against Abel his brother, and slew him.
9 And the LORD said unto Cain, Where
is Abel thy brother? And he said, I
know not: *Am* I my brother's keeper?
10 And he said, What hast thou done?
the voice of thy brother's blood crieth
unto me from the ground.
11 And now *art* thou cursed from the
earth, which hath opened her mouth to
receive thy brother's blood from thy
hand;
12 When thou tillest the ground, it
shall not henceforth yield unto thee
her strength; a fugitive and a vagabond
shalt thou be in the earth.
13 And Cain said unto the LORD, My
punishment *is* greater than I can bear.
14 Behold, thou hast driven me out
this day from the face of the earth; and
from thy face shall I be hid; and I shall
be a fugitive and a vagabond in the
earth; and it shall come to pass, *that*
every one that findeth me shall slay me.
15 And the LORD said unto him,
Therefore whosoever slayeth Cain, vengeance shall be taken on him sevenfold. And the LORD set a mark upon
Cain, lest any finding him should kill
him.
16 And Cain went out from the presence of the LORD, and dwelt in the land
of Nod, on the east of Eden.
17 And Cain knew his wife; and she
conceived, and bare Enoch: and he
builded a city, and called the name of
the city, after the name of his son,
Enoch.
18 And unto Enoch was born Irad:
and Irad begat Mehujael: and Mehujael
begat Methusael: and Methusael begat
Lamech.
19 And Lamech took unto him two
wives: the name of the one *was* Adah,
and the name of the other Zillah.
20 And Adah bare Jabal: he was the
father of such as dwell in tents, and *of
such as have* cattle.
21 And his brother's name *was* Jubal:
he was the father of all such as handle
the harp and organ.
22 And Zillah, she also bare Tubal-cain, an instructer of every artificer in
brass and iron: and the sister of Tubal-cain *was* Naamah.
23 And Lamech said unto his wives,
Adah and Zillah, Hear my voice; ye
wives of Lamech, hearken unto my
speech: for I have slain a man to my
wounding, and a young man to my hurt.
24 If Cain shall be avenged sevenfold,
truly Lamech seventy and sevenfold.
25 And Adam knew his wife again;
and she bare a son, and called his name
Seth: For God, *said she*, hath appointed
me another seed instead of Abel, whom
Cain slew.
26 And to Seth, to him also there was
born a son; and he called his name
Enos: then began men to call upon the
name of the LORD.

5 This *is* the book of the generations
of Adam. In the day that God
created man, in the likeness of God
made he him;
2 Male and female created he them;
and blessed them, and called their
name Adam, in the day when they were
created.
3 And Adam lived an hundred and
thirty years, and begat *a son* in his own
likeness, after his image; and called his
name Seth:
4 And the days of Adam after he had
begotten Seth were eight hundred
years: and he begat sons and daughters:
5 And all the days that Adam lived
were nine hundred and thirty years:
and he died.
6 And Seth lived an hundred and five
years, and begat Enos:
7 And Seth lived after he begat Enos
eight hundred and seven years, and
begat sons and daughters:
8 And all the days of Seth were nine
hundred and twelve years: and he died.
9 And Enos lived ninety years, and
begat Cainan:
10 And Enos lived after he begat
Cainan eight hundred and fifteen
years, and begat sons and daughters:
11 And all the days of Enos were nine
hundred and five years: and he died.
12 And Cainan lived seventy years,
and begat Mahalaleel:
13 And Cainan lived after he begat
Mahalaleel eight hundred and forty
years, and begat sons and daughters:
14 And all the days of Cainan were
nine hundred and ten years: and he
died.
15 And Mahalaleel lived sixty and
five years, and begat Jared:
16 And Mahalaleel lived after he
begat Jared eight hundred and thirty
years, and begat sons and daughters:
17 And all the days of Mahalaleel
were eight hundred ninety and five
years: and he died.
18 And Jared lived an hundred sixty
and two years, and he begat Enoch:
19 And Jared lived after he begat
Enoch eight hundred years, and begat
sons and daughters:
20 And all the days of Jared were
nine hundred sixty and two years: and
he died.
21 And Enoch lived sixty and five
years, and begat Methuselah:
22 And Enoch walked with God after
he begat Methuselah three hundred
years, and begat sons and daughters:
23 And all the days of Enoch were
three hundred sixty and five years:
24 And Enoch walked with God: and
he *was* not; for God took him.
25 And Methuselah lived an hundred
eighty and seven years, and begat
Lamech:
26 And Methuselah lived after he
begat Lamech seven hundred eighty
and two years, and begat sons and
daughters:
27 And all the days of Methuselah
were nine hundred sixty and nine
years: and he died.
28 And Lamech lived an hundred
eighty and two years, and begat a son:
29 And he called his name Noah, saying, This *same* shall comfort us concerning our work and toil of our hands,
because of the ground which the LORD
hath cursed.
30 And Lamech lived after he begat
Noah five hundred ninety and five
years, and begat sons and daughters:

31 And all the days of Lamech were seven hundred seventy and seven years: and he died.

32 And Noah was five hundred years old: and Noah begat Shem, Ham, and Japheth.

6 And it came to pass, when men began to multiply on the face of the earth, and daughters were born unto them,

2 That the sons of God saw the daughters of men that they *were* fair; and they took them wives of all which they chose.

3 And the LORD said, My spirit shall not always strive with man, for that he also *is* flesh: yet his days shall be an hundred and twenty years.

4 There were giants in the earth in those days; and also after that, when the sons of God came in unto the daughters of men, and they bare *children* to them, the same *became* mighty men which *were* of old, men of renown.

5 And GOD saw that the wickedness of man *was* great in the earth, and *that* every imagination of the thoughts of his heart *was* only evil continually.

6 And it repented the LORD that he had made man on the earth, and it grieved him at his heart.

7 And the LORD said, I will destroy man whom I have created from the face of the earth; both man, and beast, and the creeping thing, and the fowls of the air; for it repenteth me that I have made them.

8 But Noah found grace in the eyes of the LORD.

9 These *are* the generations of Noah: Noah was a just man *and* perfect in his generations, *and* Noah walked with God.

10 And Noah begat three sons, Shem, Ham, and Japheth.

11 The earth also was corrupt before God, and the earth was filled with violence.

12 And God looked upon the earth, and, behold, it was corrupt; for all flesh had corrupted his way upon the earth.

13 And God said unto Noah, The end of all flesh is come before me; for the earth is filled with violence through them; and, behold, I will destroy them with the earth.

14 Make thee an ark of gopher wood; rooms shalt thou make in the ark, and shalt pitch it within and without with pitch.

15 And this *is the fashion* which thou shalt make it *of*: The length of the ark *shall be* three hundred cubits, the breadth of it fifty cubits, and the height of it thirty cubits.

16 A window shalt thou make to the ark, and in a cubit shalt thou finish it above; and the door of the ark shalt thou set in the side thereof; *with* lower, second, and third *stories* shalt thou make it.

17 And, behold, I, even I, do bring a flood of waters upon the earth, to destroy all flesh, wherein *is* the breath of life, from under heaven; *and* every thing that *is* in the earth shall die.

18 But with thee will I establish my covenant; and thou shalt come into the ark, thou, and thy sons, and thy wife, and thy sons' wives with thee.

19 And of every living thing of all flesh, two of every *sort* shalt thou bring into the ark, to keep *them* alive with thee; they shall be male and female.

20 Of fowls after their kind, and of cattle after their kind, of every creeping thing of the earth after his kind,

two of every *sort* shall come unto thee,
to keep *them* alive.
21 And take thou unto thee of all food
that is eaten, and thou shalt gather *it* to
thee; and it shall be for food for thee,
and for them.
22 Thus did Noah; according to all
that God commanded him, so did he.

7 And the LORD said unto Noah,
Come thou and all thy house into
the ark; for thee have I seen righteous
before me in this generation.
2 Of every clean beast thou shalt take
to thee by sevens, the male and his
female: and of beasts that *are* not clean
by two, the male and his female.
3 Of fowls also of the air by sevens,
the male and the female; to keep seed
alive upon the face of all the earth.
4 For yet seven days, and I will cause
it to rain upon the earth forty days and
forty nights; and every living substance
that I have made will I destroy from off
the face of the earth.
5 And Noah did according unto all
that the LORD commanded him.
6 And Noah *was* six hundred years
old when the flood of waters was upon
the earth.
7 And Noah went in, and his sons, and
his wife, and his sons' wives with him,
into the ark, because of the waters of
the flood.
8 Of clean beasts, and of beasts that
are not clean, and of fowls, and of every
thing that creepeth upon the earth,
9 There went in two and two unto
Noah into the ark, the male and the
female, as God had commanded Noah.
10 And it came to pass after seven
days, that the waters of the flood were
upon the earth.
11 In the six hundredth year of Noah's
life, in the second month, the seventeenth day of the month, the same day
were all the fountains of the great deep
broken up, and the windows of heaven
were opened.
12 And the rain was upon the earth
forty days and forty nights.
13 In the selfsame day entered Noah,
and Shem, and Ham, and Japheth, the
sons of Noah, and Noah's wife, and the
three wives of his sons with them, into
the ark;
14 They, and every beast after his
kind, and all the cattle after their kind,
and every creeping thing that creepeth
upon the earth after his kind, and every
fowl after his kind, every bird of every
sort.
15 And they went in unto Noah into
the ark, two and two of all flesh, wherein *is* the breath of life.
16 And they that went in, went in
male and female of all flesh, as God
had commanded him: and the LORD
shut him in.
17 And the flood was forty days upon
the earth; and the waters increased,
and bare up the ark, and it was lift up
above the earth.
18 And the waters prevailed, and
were increased greatly upon the earth;
and the ark went upon the face of the
waters.
19 And the waters prevailed exceedingly upon the earth; and all the high
hills, that *were* under the whole heav-
en, were covered.
20 Fifteen cubits upward did the
waters prevail; and the mountains were
covered.
21 And all flesh died that moved
upon the earth, both of fowl, and of
cattle, and of beast, and of every creeping thing that creepeth upon the earth,
and every man:

22 All in whose nostrils *was* the
breath of life, of all that *was* in the dry
land, died.
23 And every living substance was
destroyed which was upon the face of
the ground, both man, and cattle, and
the creeping things, and the fowl of the
heaven; and they were destroyed from
the earth: and Noah only remained
alive, and they that *were* with him in
the ark.
24 And the waters prevailed upon the
earth an hundred and fifty days.

8 And God remembered Noah, and
every living thing, and all the cattle
that *was* with him in the ark: and God
made a wind to pass over the earth, and
the waters asswaged;
2 The fountains also of the deep and
the windows of heaven were stopped,
and the rain from heaven was
restrained;
3 And the waters returned from off
the earth continually: and after the end
of the hundred and fifty days the
waters were abated.
4 And the ark rested in the seventh
month, on the seventeenth day of the
month, upon the mountains of Ararat.
5 And the waters decreased continually until the tenth month: in the tenth
month, on the first *day* of the month,
were the tops of the mountains seen.
6 And it came to pass at the end of
forty days, that Noah opened the window of the ark which he had made:
7 And he sent forth a raven, which
went forth to and fro, until the waters
were dried up from off the earth.
8 Also he sent forth a dove from him,
to see if the waters were abated from
off the face of the ground;
9 But the dove found no rest for the
sole of her foot, and she returned unto
him into the ark, for the waters *were* on
the face of the whole earth: then he put
forth his hand, and took her, and pulled
her in unto him into the ark.
10 And he stayed yet other seven
days; and again he sent forth the dove
out of the ark;
11 And the dove came in to him in the
evening; and, lo, in her mouth *was* an
olive leaf pluckt off: so Noah knew that
the waters were abated from off the
earth.
12 And he stayed yet other seven
days; and sent forth the dove; which
returned not again unto him any more.
13 And it came to pass in the six hundredth and first year, in the first *month*,
the first *day* of the month, the waters
were dried up from off the earth: and
Noah removed the covering of the ark,
and looked, and, behold, the face of the
ground was dry.
14 And in the second month, on the
seven and twentieth day of the month,
was the earth dried.
15 And God spake unto Noah, saying,
16 Go forth of the ark, thou, and thy
wife, and thy sons, and thy sons' wives
with thee.
17 Bring forth with thee every living
thing that *is* with thee, of all flesh, *both*
of fowl, and of cattle, and of every
creeping thing that creepeth upon the
earth; that they may breed abundantly
in the earth, and be fruitful, and multiply upon the earth.
18 And Noah went forth, and his sons,
and his wife, and his sons' wives with
him:
19 Every beast, every creeping thing,
and every fowl, *and* whatsoever creepeth upon the earth, after their kinds,
went forth out of the ark.

20 And Noah builded an altar unto
the LORD; and took of every clean beast,
and of every clean fowl, and offered
burnt offerings on the altar.
21 And the LORD smelled a sweet
savour; and the LORD said in his heart, I
will not again curse the ground any
more for man's sake; for the imagination of man's heart *is* evil from his
youth; neither will I again smite any
more every thing living, as I have done.
22 While the earth remaineth, seed-
time and harvest, and cold and heat,
and summer and winter, and day and
night shall not cease.

9 And God blessed Noah and his
sons, and said unto them, Be
fruitful, and multiply, and replenish the
earth.
2 And the fear of you and the dread of
you shall be upon every beast of the
earth, and upon every fowl of the air,
upon all that moveth *upon* the earth,
and upon all the fishes of the sea; into
your hand are they delivered.
3 Every moving thing that liveth shall
be meat for you; even as the green herb
have I given you all things.
4 But flesh with the life thereof,
which is the blood thereof, shall ye not
eat.
5 And surely your blood of your lives
will I require; at the hand of every
beast will I require it, and at the hand
of man; at the hand of every man's
brother will I require the life of man.
6 Whoso sheddeth man's blood, by
man shall his blood be shed: for in the
image of God made he man.
7 And you, be ye fruitful, and multiply; bring forth abundantly in the
earth, and multiply therein.
8 And God spake unto Noah, and to
his sons with him, saying,
9 And I, behold, I establish my covenant with you, and with your seed after
you;
10 And with every living creature that
is with you, of the fowl, of the cattle,
and of every beast of the earth with
you; from all that go out of the ark, to
every beast of the earth.
11 And I will establish my covenant
with you; neither shall all flesh be cut
off any more by the waters of a flood;
neither shall there any more be a flood
to destroy the earth.
12 And God said, This *is* the token of
the covenant which I make between me
and you and every living creature that
is with you, for perpetual generations:
13 I do set my bow in the cloud, and it
shall be for a token of a covenant
between me and the earth.
14 And it shall come to pass, when I
bring a cloud over the earth, that the
bow shall be seen in the cloud:
15 And I will remember my covenant,
which *is* between me and you and every
living creature of all flesh; and the
waters shall no more become a flood to
destroy all flesh.
16 And the bow shall be in the cloud;
and I will look upon it, that I may
remember the everlasting covenant
between God and every living creature
of all flesh that *is* upon the earth.
17 And God said unto Noah, This *is*
the token of the covenant, which I have
established between me and all flesh
that *is* upon the earth.
18 And the sons of Noah, that went
forth of the ark, were Shem, and Ham,
and Japheth: and Ham *is* the father of
Canaan.
19 These *are* the three sons of Noah:
and of them was the whole earth over-
spread.

20 And Noah began *to be* an husbandman, and he planted a vineyard:
21 And he drank of the wine, and was
drunken; and he was uncovered within
his tent.
22 And Ham, the father of Canaan,
saw the nakedness of his father, and
told his two brethren without.
23 And Shem and Japheth took a garment, and laid *it* upon both their shoulders, and went backward, and covered
the nakedness of their father; and their
faces *were* backward, and they saw not
their father's nakedness.
24 And Noah awoke from his wine,
and knew what his younger son had
done unto him.
25 And he said, Cursed *be* Canaan; a
servant of servants shall he be unto his
brethren.
26 And he said, Blessed *be* the LORD
God of Shem; and Canaan shall be his
servant.
27 God shall enlarge Japheth, and he
shall dwell in the tents of Shem; and
Canaan shall be his servant.
28 And Noah lived after the flood
three hundred and fifty years.
29 And all the days of Noah were nine
hundred and fifty years: and he died.

10 Now these *are* the generations of
the sons of Noah, Shem, Ham,
and Japheth: and unto them were sons
born after the flood.
2 The sons of Japheth; Gomer, and
Magog, and Madai, and Javan, and
Tubal, and Meshech, and Tiras.
3 And the sons of Gomer; Ashkenaz,
and Riphath, and Togarmah.
4 And the sons of Javan; Elishah, and
Tarshish, Kittim, and Dodanim.
5 By these were the isles of the
Gentiles divided in their lands; every
one after his tongue, after their families, in their nations.
6 And the sons of Ham; Cush, and
Mizraim, and Phut, and Canaan.
7 And the sons of Cush; Seba, and
Havilah, and Sabtah, and Raamah, and
Sabtecha: and the sons of Raamah;
Sheba, and Dedan.
8 And Cush begat Nimrod: he began
to be a mighty one in the earth.
9 He was a mighty hunter before the
LORD: wherefore it is said, Even as
Nimrod the mighty hunter before the
LORD.
10 And the beginning of his kingdom
was Babel, and Erech, and Accad, and
Calneh, in the land of Shinar.
11 Out of that land went forth Asshur,
and builded Nineveh, and the city
Rehoboth, and Calah,
12 And Resen between Nineveh and
Calah: the same *is* a great city.
13 And Mizraim begat Ludim, and
Anamim, and Lehabim, and Naphtuhim,
14 And Pathrusim, and Casluhim,
(out of whom came Philistim,) and
Caphtorim.
15 And Canaan begat Sidon his firstborn, and Heth,
16 And the Jebusite, and the Amorite,
and the Girgasite,
17 And the Hivite, and the Arkite,
and the Sinite,
18 And the Arvadite, and the
Zemarite, and the Hamathite: and
afterward were the families of the
Canaanites spread abroad.
19 And the border of the Canaanites
was from Sidon, as thou comest to
Gerar, unto Gaza; as thou goest, unto
Sodom, and Gomorrah, and Admah,
and Zeboim, even unto Lasha.

20 These *are* the sons of Ham, after their families, after their tongues, in their countries, *and* in their nations.

21 Unto Shem also, the father of all the children of Eber, the brother of Japheth the elder, even to him were *children* born.

22 The children of Shem; Elam, and Asshur, and Arphaxad, and Lud, and Aram.

23 And the children of Aram; Uz, and Hul, and Gether, and Mash.

24 And Arphaxad begat Salah; and Salah begat Eber.

25 And unto Eber were born two sons: the name of one *was* Peleg; for in his days was the earth divided; and his brother's name *was* Joktan.

26 And Joktan begat Almodad, and Sheleph, and Hazar-maveth, and Jerah,

27 And Hadoram, and Uzal, and Diklah,

28 And Obal, and Abimael, and Sheba,

29 And Ophir, and Havilah, and Jobab: all these *were* the sons of Joktan.

30 And their dwelling was from Mesha, as thou goest unto Sephar a mount of the east.

31 These *are* the sons of Shem, after their families, after their tongues, in their lands, after their nations.

32 These *are* the families of the sons of Noah, after their generations, in their nations: and by these were the nations divided in the earth after the flood.

11 And the whole earth was of one language, and of one speech.

2 And it came to pass, as they journeyed from the east, that they found a plain in the land of Shinar; and they dwelt there.

3 And they said one to another, Go to, let us make brick, and burn them throughly. And they had brick for stone, and slime had they for morter.

4 And they said, Go to, let us build us a city and a tower, whose top *may reach* unto heaven; and let us make us a name, lest we be scattered abroad upon the face of the whole earth.

5 And the LORD came down to see the city and the tower, which the children of men builded.

6 And the LORD said, Behold, the people *is* one, and they have all one language; and this they begin to do: and now nothing will be restrained from them, which they have imagined to do.

7 Go to, let us go down, and there confound their language, that they may not understand one another's speech.

8 So the LORD scattered them abroad from thence upon the face of all the earth: and they left off to build the city.

9 Therefore is the name of it called Babel; because the LORD did there confound the language of all the earth: and from thence did the LORD scatter them abroad upon the face of all the earth.

10 These *are* the generations of Shem: Shem *was* an hundred years old, and begat Arphaxad two years after the flood:

11 And Shem lived after he begat Arphaxad five hundred years, and begat sons and daughters.

12 And Arphaxad lived five and thirty years, and begat Salah:

13 And Arphaxad lived after he begat Salah four hundred and three years, and begat sons and daughters.

14 And Salah lived thirty years, and begat Eber:

15 And Salah lived after he begat Eber four hundred and three years, and begat sons and daughters.

16 And Eber lived four and thirty years, and begat Peleg:

17 And Eber lived after he begat Peleg four hundred and thirty years, and begat sons and daughters.

18 And Peleg lived thirty years, and begat Reu:

19 And Peleg lived after he begat Reu two hundred and nine years, and begat sons and daughters.

20 And Reu lived two and thirty years, and begat Serug:

21 And Reu lived after he begat Serug two hundred and seven years, and begat sons and daughters.

22 And Serug lived thirty years, and begat Nahor:

23 And Serug lived after he begat Nahor two hundred years, and begat sons and daughters.

24 And Nahor lived nine and twenty years, and begat Terah:

25 And Nahor lived after he begat Terah an hundred and nineteen years, and begat sons and daughters.

26 And Terah lived seventy years, and begat Abram, Nahor, and Haran.

27 Now these *are* the generations of Terah: Terah begat Abram, Nahor, and Haran; and Haran begat Lot.

28 And Haran died before his father Terah in the land of his nativity, in Ur of the Chaldees.

29 And Abram and Nahor took them wives: the name of Abram's wife *was* Sarai; and the name of Nahor's wife, Milcah, the daughter of Haran, the father of Milcah, and the father of Iscah.

30 But Sarai was barren; she *had* no child.

31 And Terah took Abram his son, and Lot the son of Haran his son's son, and Sarai his daughter in law, his son Abram's wife; and they went forth with them from Ur of the Chaldees, to go into the land of Canaan; and they came unto Haran, and dwelt there.

32 And the days of Terah were two hundred and five years: and Terah died in Haran.

12 Now the LORD had said unto Abram, Get thee out of thy country, and from thy kindred, and from thy father's house, unto a land that I will shew thee:

2 And I will make of thee a great nation, and I will bless thee, and make thy name great; and thou shalt be a blessing:

3 And I will bless them that bless thee, and curse him that curseth thee: and in thee shall all families of the earth be blessed.

4 So Abram departed, as the LORD had spoken unto him; and Lot went with him: and Abram *was* seventy and five years old when he departed out of Haran.

5 And Abram took Sarai his wife, and Lot his brother's son, and all their substance that they had gathered, and the souls that they had gotten in Haran; and they went forth to go into the land of Canaan; and into the land of Canaan they came.

6 And Abram passed through the land unto the place of Sichem, unto the plain of Moreh. And the Canaanite *was* then in the land.

7 And the LORD appeared unto Abram, and said, Unto thy seed will I give this land: and there builded he an altar unto the LORD, who appeared unto him.

8 And he removed from thence unto a mountain on the east of Beth-el, and pitched his tent, *having* Beth-el on the west, and Hai on the east: and there he builded an altar unto the LORD, and called upon the name of the LORD.

9 And Abram journeyed, going on still toward the south.

10 And there was a famine in the land: and Abram went down into Egypt to sojourn there; for the famine *was* grievous in the land.

11 And it came to pass, when he was come near to enter into Egypt, that he said unto Sarai his wife, Behold now, I know that thou *art* a fair woman to look upon:

12 Therefore it shall come to pass, when the Egyptians shall see thee, that they shall say, This *is* his wife: and they will kill me, but they will save thee alive.

13 Say, I pray thee, thou *art* my sister: that it may be well with me for thy sake; and my soul shall live because of thee.

14 And it came to pass, that, when Abram was come into Egypt, the Egyptians beheld the woman that she *was* very fair.

15 The princes also of Pharaoh saw her, and commended her before Pharaoh: and the woman was taken into Pharaoh's house.

16 And he entreated Abram well for her sake: and he had sheep, and oxen, and he asses, and menservants, and maidservants, and she asses, and camels.

17 And the LORD plagued Pharaoh and his house with great plagues because of Sarai Abram's wife.

18 And Pharaoh called Abram, and said, What *is* this *that* thou hast done unto me? why didst thou not tell me that she *was* thy wife?

19 Why saidst thou, She *is* my sister? so I might have taken her to me to wife: now therefore behold thy wife, take *her*, and go thy way.

20 And Pharaoh commanded *his* men concerning him: and they sent him away, and his wife, and all that he had.

13 And Abram went up out of Egypt, he, and his wife, and all that he had, and Lot with him, into the south.

2 And Abram *was* very rich in cattle, in silver, and in gold.

3 And he went on his journeys from the south even to Beth-el, unto the place where his tent had been at the beginning, between Beth-el and Hai;

4 Unto the place of the altar, which he had made there at the first: and there Abram called on the name of the LORD.

5 And Lot also, which went with Abram, had flocks, and herds, and tents.

6 And the land was not able to bear them, that they might dwell together: for their substance was great, so that they could not dwell together.

7 And there was a strife between the herdmen of Abram's cattle and the herdmen of Lot's cattle: and the Canaanite and the Perizzite dwelled then in the land.

8 And Abram said unto Lot, Let there be no strife, I pray thee, between me and thee, and between my herdmen and thy herdmen; for we *be* brethren.

9 *Is* not the whole land before thee? separate thyself, I pray thee, from me: if *thou wilt take* the left hand, then I will go to the right; or if *thou depart* to the right hand, then I will go to the left.

10 And Lot lifted up his eyes, and
beheld all the plain of Jordan, that it
was well watered every where, before
the LORD destroyed Sodom and
Gomorrah, *even* as the garden of the
LORD, like the land of Egypt, as thou
comest unto Zoar.
11 Then Lot chose him all the plain of
Jordan; and Lot journeyed east: and
they separated themselves the one
from the other.
12 Abram dwelled in the land of
Canaan, and Lot dwelled in the cities of
the plain, and pitched *his* tent toward
Sodom.
13 But the men of Sodom *were* wicked
and sinners before the LORD exceedingly.
14 And the LORD said unto Abram,
after that Lot was separated from him,
Lift up now thine eyes, and look from
the place where thou art northward,
and southward, and eastward, and
westward:
15 For all the land which thou seest,
to thee will I give it, and to thy seed for
ever.
16 And I will make thy seed as the
dust of the earth: so that if a man can
number the dust of the earth, *then*
shall thy seed also be numbered.
17 Arise, walk through the land in the
length of it and in the breadth of it; for
I will give it unto thee.
18 Then Abram removed *his* tent, and
came and dwelt in the plain of Mamre,
which *is* in Hebron, and built there an
altar unto the LORD.

14 And it came to pass in the days of
Amraphel king of Shinar, Arioch
king of Ellasar, Chedorlaomer king of
Elam, and Tidal king of nations;
2 *That these* made war with Bera king
of Sodom, and with Birsha king of
Gomorrah, Shinab king of Admah, and
Shemeber king of Zeboiim, and the
king of Bela, which is Zoar.
3 All these were joined together in
the vale of Siddim, which is the salt sea.
4 Twelve years they served Chedorlaomer, and in the thirteenth year
they rebelled.
5 And in the fourteenth year came
Chedorlaomer, and the kings that *were*
with him, and smote the Rephaims in
Ashteroth Karnaim, and the Zuzims in
Ham, and the Emims in Shaveh
Kiriathaim,
6 And the Horites in their mount Seir,
unto El-paran, which *is* by the wilderness.
7 And they returned, and came to
En-mishpat, which *is* Kadesh, and
smote all the country of the Amalekites,
and also the Amorites, that dwelt in
Hazezon-tamar.
8 And there went out the king of
Sodom, and the king of Gomorrah, and
the king of Admah, and the king of
Zeboiim, and the king of Bela (the
same *is* Zoar;) and they joined battle
with them in the vale of Siddim;
9 With Chedorlaomer the king of
Elam, and with Tidal king of nations,
and Amraphel king of Shinar, and
Arioch king of Ellasar; four kings with
five.
10 And the vale of Siddim *was full of*
slime-pits; and the kings of Sodom and
Gomorrah fled, and fell there; and they
that remained fled to the mountain.
11 And they took all the goods of
Sodom and Gomorrah, and all their
victuals, and went their way.
12 And they took Lot, Abram's brother's son, who dwelt in Sodom, and his
goods, and departed.

13 And there came one that had
escaped, and told Abram the Hebrew;
for he dwelt in the plain of Mamre the
Amorite, brother of Eshcol, and brother of Aner: and these *were* confederate
with Abram.
14 And when Abram heard that his
brother was taken captive, he armed
his trained *servants*, born in his own
house, three hundred and eighteen,
and pursued *them* unto Dan.
15 And he divided himself against
them, he and his servants, by night, and
smote them, and pursued them unto
Hobah, which *is* on the left hand of
Damascus.
16 And he brought back all the goods,
and also brought again his brother Lot,
and his goods, and the women also, and
the people.
17 And the king of Sodom went out to
meet him after his return from the
slaughter of Chedorlaomer, and of the
kings that *were* with him, at the valley
of Shaveh, which *is* the king's dale.
18 And Melchizedek king of Salem
brought forth bread and wine: and he
was the priest of the most high God.
19 And he blessed him, and said,
Blessed *be* Abram of the most high
God, possessor of heaven and earth:
20 And blessed be the most high God,
which hath delivered thine enemies
into thy hand. And he gave him tithes
of all.
21 And the king of Sodom said unto
Abram, Give me the persons, and take
the goods to thyself.
22 And Abram said to the king of
Sodom, I have lift up mine hand unto
the LORD, the most high God, the possessor of heaven and earth,
23 That I will not *take* from a thread
even to a shoelatchet, and that I will
not take any thing that *is* thine, lest
thou shouldest say, I have made Abram
rich:
24 Save only that which the young
men have eaten, and the portion of the
men which went with me, Aner, Eshcol,
and Mamre; let them take their portion.

15 After these things the word of
the LORD came unto Abram in a
vision, saying, Fear not, Abram: I *am*
thy shield, *and* thy exceeding great
reward.
2 And Abram said, Lord GOD, what
wilt thou give me, seeing I go childless,
and the steward of my house *is* this
Eliezer of Damascus?
3 And Abram said, Behold, to me thou
hast given no seed: and, lo, one born in
my house is mine heir.
4 And, behold, the word of the LORD
came unto him, saying, This shall not be
thine heir; but he that shall come forth
out of thine own bowels shall be thine
heir.
5 And he brought him forth abroad,
and said, Look now toward heaven, and
tell the stars, if thou be able to number
them: and he said unto him, So shall
thy seed be.
6 And he believed in the LORD; and he
counted it to him for righteousness.
7 And he said unto him, I *am* the
LORD that brought thee out of Ur of the
Chaldees, to give thee this land to
inherit it.
8 And he said, Lord GOD, whereby
shall I know that I shall inherit it?
9 And he said unto him, Take me an
heifer of three years old, and a she goat
of three years old, and a ram of three
years old, and a turtledove, and a young
pigeon.

10 And he took unto him all these, and divided them in the midst, and laid each piece one against another: but the birds divided he not.

11 And when the fowls came down upon the carcases, Abram drove them away.

12 And when the sun was going down, a deep sleep fell upon Abram; and, lo, an horror of great darkness fell upon him.

13 And he said unto Abram, Know of a surety that thy seed shall be a stranger in a land *that is* not theirs, and shall serve them; and they shall afflict them four hundred years;

14 And also that nation, whom they shall serve, will I judge: and afterward shall they come out with great substance.

15 And thou shalt go to thy fathers in peace; thou shalt be buried in a good old age.

16 But in the fourth generation they shall come hither again: for the iniquity of the Amorites *is* not yet full.

17 And it came to pass, that, when the sun went down, and it was dark, behold a smoking furnace, and a burning lamp that passed between those pieces.

18 In the same day the LORD made a covenant with Abram, saying, Unto thy seed have I given this land, from the river of Egypt unto the great river, the river Euphrates:

19 The Kenites, and the Kenizzites, and the Kad-monites,

20 And the Hittites, and the Perizzites, and the Rephaims,

21 And the Amorites, and the Canaanites, and the Girgashites, and the Jebusites.

16 Now Sarai Abram's wife bare him no children: and she had an handmaid, an Egyptian, whose name *was* Hagar.

2 And Sarai said unto Abram, Behold now, the LORD hath restrained me from bearing: I pray thee, go in unto my maid; it may be that I may obtain children by her. And Abram hearkened to the voice of Sarai.

3 And Sarai Abram's wife took Hagar her maid the Egyptian, after Abram had dwelt ten years in the land of Canaan, and gave her to her husband Abram to be his wife.

4 And he went in unto Hagar, and she conceived: and when she saw that she had conceived, her mistress was despised in her eyes.

5 And Sarai said unto Abram, My wrong *be* upon thee: I have given my maid into thy bosom; and when she saw that she had conceived, I was despised in her eyes: the LORD judge between me and thee.

6 But Abram said unto Sarai, Behold, thy maid *is* in thy hand; do to her as it pleaseth thee. And when Sarai dealt hardly with her, she fled from her face.

7 And the angel of the LORD found her by a fountain of water in the wilderness, by the fountain in the way to Shur.

8 And he said, Hagar, Sarai's maid, whence camest thou? and whither wilt thou go? And she said, I flee from the face of my mistress Sarai.

9 And the angel of the LORD said unto her, Return to thy mistress, and submit thyself under her hands.

10 And the angel of the LORD said unto her, I will multiply thy seed exceedingly, that it shall not be numbered for multitude.

11 And the angel of the LORD said unto her, Behold, thou *art* with child, and shalt bear a son, and shalt call his

name Ishmael; because the LORD hath heard thy affliction.

12 And he will be a wild man; his hand *will be* against every man, and every man's hand against him; and he shall dwell in the presence of all his brethren.

13 And she called the name of the LORD that spake unto her, Thou God seest me: for she said, Have I also here looked after him that seeth me?

14 Wherefore the well was called Beer-lahai-roi; behold, *it is* between Kadesh and Bered.

15 And Hagar bare Abram a son: and Abram called his son's name, which Hagar bare, Ishmael.

16 And Abram *was* fourscore and six years old, when Hagar bare Ishmael to Abram.

17 And when Abram was ninety years old and nine, the LORD appeared to Abram, and said unto him, I *am* the Almighty God; walk before me, and be thou perfect.

2 And I will make my covenant between me and thee, and will multiply thee exceedingly.

3 And Abram fell on his face: and God talked with him, saying,

4 As for me, behold, my covenant *is* with thee, and thou shalt be a father of many nations.

5 Neither shall thy name any more be called Abram, but thy name shall be Abraham; for a father of many nations have I made thee.

6 And I will make thee exceeding fruitful, and I will make nations of thee, and kings shall come out of thee.

7 And I will establish my covenant between me and thee and thy seed after thee in their generations for an everlasting covenant, to be a God unto thee, and to thy seed after thee.

8 And I will give unto thee, and to thy seed after thee, the land wherein thou art a stranger, all the land of Canaan, for an everlasting possession; and I will be their God.

9 And God said unto Abraham, Thou shalt keep my covenant therefore, thou, and thy seed after thee in their generations.

10 This *is* my covenant, which ye shall keep, between me and you and thy seed after thee; Every man child among you shall be circumcised.

11 And ye shall circumcise the flesh of your foreskin; and it shall be a token of the covenant betwixt me and you.

12 And he that is eight days old shall be circumcised among you, every man child in your generations, he that is born in the house, or bought with money of any stranger, which *is* not of thy seed.

13 He that is born in thy house, and he that is bought with thy money, must needs be circumcised: and my covenant shall be in your flesh for an everlasting covenant.

14 And the uncircumcised man child whose flesh of his foreskin is not circumcised, that soul shall be cut off from his people; he hath broken my covenant.

15 And God said unto Abraham, As for Sarai thy wife, thou shalt not call her name Sarai, but Sarah *shall* her name *be*.

16 And I will bless her, and give thee a son also of her: yea, I will bless her, and she shall be *a mother* of nations; kings of people shall be of her.

17 Then Abraham fell upon his face,
and laughed, and said in his heart,
Shall *a child* be born unto him that is
an hundred years old? and shall Sarah,
that is ninety years old, bear?
18 And Abraham said unto God, O
that Ishmael might live before thee!
19 And God said, Sarah thy wife shall
bear thee a son indeed; and thou shalt
call his name Isaac: and I will establish
my covenant with him for an everlasting covenant, *and* with his seed after
him.
20 And as for Ishmael, I have heard
thee: Behold, I have blessed him, and
will make him fruitful, and will multiply him exceedingly; twelve princes
shall he beget, and I will make him a
great nation.
21 But my covenant will I establish
with Isaac, which Sarah shall bear unto
thee at this set time in the next year.
22 And he left off talking with him,
and God went up from Abraham.
23 And Abraham took Ishmael his
son, and all that were born in his house,
and all that were bought with his
money, every male among the men of
Abraham's house; and circumcised the
flesh of their foreskin in the selfsame
day, as God had said unto him.
24 And Abraham *was* ninety years
old and nine, when he was circumcised
in the flesh of his foreskin.
25 And Ishmael his son *was* thirteen
years old, when he was circumcised in
the flesh of his foreskin.
26 In the selfsame day was Abraham
circumcised, and Ishmael his son.
27 And all the men of his house, born
in the house, and bought with money of
the stranger, were circumcised with
him.

18 And the LORD appeared unto him
in the plains of Mamre: and he
sat in the tent door in the heat of the
day;
2 And he lift up his eyes and looked,
and, lo, three men stood by him: and
when he saw *them*, he ran to meet
them from the tent door, and bowed
himself toward the ground,
3 And said, My Lord, if now I have
found favour in thy sight, pass not away,
I pray thee, from thy servant:
4 Let a little water, I pray you, be
fetched, and wash your feet, and rest
yourselves under the tree:
5 And I will fetch a morsel of bread,
and comfort ye your hearts; after that
ye shall pass on: for therefore are ye
come to your servant. And they said, So
do, as thou hast said.
6 And Abraham hastened into the
tent unto Sarah, and said, Make ready
quickly three measures of fine meal,
knead *it*, and make cakes upon the
hearth.
7 And Abraham ran unto the herd,
and fetcht a calf tender and good, and
gave *it* unto a young man; and he hasted to dress it.
8 And he took butter, and milk, and
the calf which he had dressed, and set
it before them; and he stood by them
under the tree, and they did eat.
9 And they said unto him, Where *is*
Sarah thy wife? And he said, Behold, in
the tent.
10 And he said, I will certainly return
unto thee according to the time of life;
and, lo, Sarah thy wife shall have a son.
And Sarah heard *it* in the tent door,
which *was* behind him.

11 Now Abraham and Sarah *were* old
and well stricken in age; *and* it ceased
to be with Sarah after the manner of
women.
12 Therefore Sarah laughed within
herself, saying, After I am waxed old
shall I have pleasure, my lord being old
also?
13 And the LORD said unto Abraham,
Wherefore did Sarah laugh, saying,
Shall I of a surety bear a child, which
am old?
14 Is any thing too hard for the LORD?
At the time appointed I will return
unto thee, according to the time of life,
and Sarah shall have a son.
15 Then Sarah denied, saying, I
laughed not; for she was afraid. And he
said, Nay; but thou didst laugh.
16 And the men rose up from thence,
and looked toward Sodom: and
Abraham went with them to bring
them on the way.
17 And the LORD said, Shall I hide
from Abraham that thing which I do;
18 Seeing that Abraham shall surely
become a great and mighty nation, and
all the nations of the earth shall be
blessed in him?
19 For I know him, that he will command his children and his household
after him, and they shall keep the way
of the LORD, to do justice and judgment; that the LORD may bring upon
Abraham that which he hath spoken of
him.
20 And the LORD said, Because the cry
of Sodom and Gomorrah is great, and
because their sin is very grievous;
21 I will go down now, and see whether they have done altogether according
to the cry of it, which is come unto me;
and if not, I will know.
22 And the men turned their faces
from thence, and went toward Sodom:
but Abraham stood yet before the
LORD.
23 And Abraham drew near, and said,
Wilt thou also destroy the righteous
with the wicked?
24 Peradventure there be fifty righteous within the city: wilt thou also
destroy and not spare the place for the
fifty righteous that *are* therein?
25 That be far from thee to do after
this manner, to slay the righteous with
the wicked: and that the righteous
should be as the wicked, that be far
from thee: Shall not the Judge of all the
earth do right?
26 And the LORD said, If I find in
Sodom fifty righteous within the city,
then I will spare all the place for their
sakes.
27 And Abraham answered and said,
Behold now, I have taken upon me to
speak unto the Lord, which *am but*
dust and ashes:
28 Peradventure there shall lack five
of the fifty righteous: wilt thou destroy
all the city for *lack of* five? And he said,
If I find there forty and five, I will not
destroy *it*.
29 And he spake unto him yet again,
and said, Peradventure there shall be
forty found there. And he said, I will
not do *it* for forty's sake.
30 And he said *unto him*, Oh let not
the Lord be angry, and I will speak:
Peradventure there shall thirty be
found there. And he said, I will not do
it, if I find thirty there.
31 And he said, Behold now, I have
taken upon me to speak unto the Lord:
Peradventure there shall be twenty
found there. And he said, I will not
destroy *it* for twenty's sake.

32 And he said, Oh let not the Lord be
angry, and I will speak yet but this
once: Peradventure ten shall be found
there. And he said, I will not destroy *it*
for ten's sake.
33 And the LORD went his way, as soon
as he had left communing with
Abraham: and Abraham returned unto
his place.

19 And there came two angels to
Sodom at even; and Lot sat in the
gate of Sodom: and Lot seeing *them*
rose up to meet them; and he bowed
himself with his face toward the
ground;
2 And he said, Behold now, my lords,
turn in, I pray you, into your servant's
house, and tarry all night, and wash
your feet, and ye shall rise up early, and
go on your ways. And they said, Nay;
but we will abide in the street all night.
3 And he pressed upon them greatly;
and they turned in unto him, and
entered into his house; and he made
them a feast, and did bake unleavened
bread, and they did eat.
4 But before they lay down, the men
of the city, *even* the men of Sodom,
compassed the house round, both old
and young, all the people from every
quarter:
5 And they called unto Lot, and said
unto him, Where *are* the men which
came in to thee this night? bring them
out unto us, that we may know them.
6 And Lot went out at the door unto
them, and shut the door after him,
7 And said, I pray you, brethren, do
not so wickedly.
8 Behold now, I have two daughters
which have not known man; let me, I
pray you, bring them out unto you, and
do ye to them as *is* good in your eyes:
only unto these men do nothing; for
therefore came they under the shadow
of my roof.
9 And they said, Stand back. And they
said *again*, This one *fellow* came in to
sojourn, and he will needs be a judge:
now will we deal worse with thee, than
with them. And they pressed sore upon
the man, *even* Lot, and came near to
break the door.
10 But the men put forth their hand,
and pulled Lot into the house to them,
and shut to the door.
11 And they smote the men that *were*
at the door of the house with blindness,
both small and great: so that they wearied themselves to find the door.
12 And the men said unto Lot, Hast
thou here any besides? son in law, and
thy sons, and thy daughters, and whatsoever thou hast in the city, bring *them*
out of this place:
13 For we will destroy this place,
because the cry of them is waxen great
before the face of the LORD; and the
LORD hath sent us to destroy it.
14 And Lot went out, and spake unto
his sons in law, which married his
daughters, and said, Up, get you out of
this place; for the LORD will destroy this
city. But he seemed as one that mocked
unto his sons in law.
15 And when the morning arose, then
the angels hastened Lot, saying, Arise,
take thy wife, and thy two daughters,
which are here; lest thou be consumed
in the iniquity of the city.
16 And while he lingered, the men
laid hold upon his hand, and upon the
hand of his wife, and upon the hand of
his two daughters; the LORD being merciful unto him: and they brought him
forth, and set him without the city.
17 And it came to pass, when they
had brought them forth abroad, that he

said, Escape for thy life; look not behind thee, neither stay thou in all the plain; escape to the mountain, lest thou be consumed.
18 And Lot said unto them, Oh, not so, my Lord:
19 Behold now, thy servant hath found grace in thy sight, and thou hast magnified thy mercy, which thou hast shewed unto me in saving my life; and I cannot escape to the mountain, lest some evil take me, and I die:
20 Behold now, this city *is* near to flee unto, and it *is* a little one: Oh, let me escape thither, (*is* it not a little one?) and my soul shall live.
21 And he said unto him, See, I have accepted thee concerning this thing also, that I will not overthrow this city, for the which thou hast spoken.
22 Haste thee, escape thither; for I cannot do any thing till thou be come thither. Therefore the name of the city was called Zoar.
23 The sun was risen upon the earth when Lot entered into Zoar.
24 Then the LORD rained upon Sodom and upon Gomorrah brimstone and fire from the LORD out of heaven;
25 And he overthrew those cities, and all the plain, and all the inhabitants of the cities, and that which grew upon the ground.
26 But his wife looked back from behind him, and she became a pillar of salt.
27 And Abraham gat up early in the morning to the place where he stood before the LORD:
28 And he looked toward Sodom and Gomorrah, and toward all the land of the plain, and beheld, and, lo, the smoke of the country went up as the smoke of a furnace.
29 And it came to pass, when God destroyed the cities of the plain, that God remembered Abraham, and sent Lot out of the midst of the overthrow, when he overthrew the cities in the which Lot dwelt.
30 And Lot went up out of Zoar, and dwelt in the mountain, and his two daughters with him; for he feared to dwell in Zoar: and he dwelt in a cave, he and his two daughters.
31 And the firstborn said unto the younger, Our father *is* old, and *there is* not a man in the earth to come in unto us after the manner of all the earth:
32 Come, let us make our father drink wine, and we will lie with him, that we may preserve seed of our father.
33 And they made their father drink wine that night: and the firstborn went in, and lay with her father; and he perceived not when she lay down, nor when she arose.
34 And it came to pass on the morrow, that the firstborn said unto the younger, Behold, I lay yesternight with my father: let us make him drink wine this night also; and go thou in, *and* lie with him, that we may preserve seed of our father.
35 And they made their father drink wine that night also: and the younger arose, and lay with him; and he perceived not when she lay down, nor when she arose.
36 Thus were both the daughters of Lot with child by their father.
37 And the firstborn bare a son, and called his name Moab: the same *is* the father of the Moabites unto this day.
38 And the younger, she also bare a son, and called his name Ben-ammi: the same *is* the father of the children of Ammon unto this day.

20 And Abraham journeyed from
thence toward the south country,
and dwelled between Kadesh and Shur,
and sojourned in Gerar.
2 And Abraham said of Sarah his
wife, She *is* my sister: and Abimelech
king of Gerar sent, and took Sarah.
3 But God came to Abimelech in a
dream by night, and said to him,
Behold, thou *art but* a dead man, for
the woman which thou hast taken; for
she *is* a man's wife.
4 But Abimelech had not come near
her: and he said, Lord, wilt thou slay
also a righteous nation?
5 Said he not unto me, She *is* my sister? and she, even she herself said, He
is my brother: in the integrity of my
heart and innocency of my hands have
I done this.
6 And God said unto him in a dream,
Yea, I know that thou didst this in the
integrity of thy heart; for I also withheld thee from sinning against me:
therefore suffered I thee not to touch
her.
7 Now therefore restore the man *his*
wife; for he *is* a prophet, and he shall
pray for thee, and thou shalt live: and if
thou restore *her* not, know thou that
thou shalt surely die, thou, and all that
are thine.
8 Therefore Abimelech rose early in
the morning, and called all his servants,
and told all these things in their ears:
and the men were sore afraid.
9 Then Abimelech called Abraham,
and said unto him, What hast thou done
unto us? and what have I offended
thee, that thou hast brought on me and
on my kingdom a great sin? thou hast
done deeds unto me that ought not to
be done.
10 And Abimelech said unto
Abraham, What sawest thou, that thou
hast done this thing?
11 And Abraham said, Because I
thought, Surely the fear of God *is* not in
this place; and they will slay me for my
wife's sake.
12 And yet indeed *she is* my sister;
she *is* the daughter of my father, but
not the daughter of my mother; and she
became my wife.
13 And it came to pass, when God
caused me to wander from my father's
house, that I said unto her, This *is* thy
kindness which thou shalt shew unto
me; at every place whither we shall
come, say of me, He *is* my brother.
14 And Abimelech took sheep, and
oxen, and menservants, and womenservants, and gave *them* unto Abraham,
and restored him Sarah his wife.
15 And Abimelech said, Behold, my
land *is* before thee: dwell where it
pleaseth thee.
16 And unto Sarah he said, Behold, I
have given thy brother a thousand
pieces of silver: behold, he *is* to thee a
covering of the eyes, unto all that *are*
with thee, and with all *other*: thus she
was reproved.
17 So Abraham prayed unto God: and
God healed Abimelech, and his wife,
and his maidservants; and they bare
children.
18 For the LORD had fast closed up all
the wombs of the house of Abimelech,
because of Sarah Abraham's wife.

21 And the LORD visited Sarah as he
had said, and the LORD did unto
Sarah as he had spoken.
2 For Sarah conceived, and bare
Abraham a son in his old age, at the set
time of which God had spoken to him.

3 And Abraham called the name of his son that was born unto him, whom Sarah bare to him, Isaac.

4 And Abraham circumcised his son Isaac being eight days old, as God had commanded him.

5 And Abraham was an hundred years old, when his son Isaac was born unto him.

6 And Sarah said, God hath made me to laugh, *so that* all that hear will laugh with me.

7 And she said, Who would have said unto Abraham, that Sarah should have given children suck? for I have born *him* a son in his old age.

8 And the child grew, and was weaned: and Abraham made a great feast the *same* day that Isaac was weaned.

9 And Sarah saw the son of Hagar the Egyptian, which she had born unto Abraham, mocking.

10 Wherefore she said unto Abraham, Cast out this bondwoman and her son: for the son of this bondwoman shall not be heir with my son, *even* with Isaac.

11 And the thing was very grievous in Abraham's sight because of his son.

12 And God said unto Abraham, Let it not be grievous in thy sight because of the lad, and because of thy bondwoman; in all that Sarah hath said unto thee, hearken unto her voice; for in Isaac shall thy seed be called.

13 And also of the son of the bondwoman will I make a nation, because he *is* thy seed.

14 And Abraham rose up early in the morning, and took bread, and a bottle of water, and gave *it* unto Hagar, putting *it* on her shoulder, and the child, and sent her away: and she departed, and wandered in the wilderness of Beer-sheba.

15 And the water was spent in the bottle, and she cast the child under one of the shrubs.

16 And she went, and sat her down over against *him* a good way off, as it were a bowshot: for she said, Let me not see the death of the child. And she sat over against *him*, and lift up her voice, and wept.

17 And God heard the voice of the lad; and the angel of God called to Hagar out of heaven, and said unto her, What aileth thee, Hagar? fear not; for God hath heard the voice of the lad where he *is*.

18 Arise, lift up the lad, and hold him in thine hand; for I will make him a great nation.

19 And God opened her eyes, and she saw a well of water; and she went, and filled the bottle with water, and gave the lad drink.

20 And God was with the lad; and he grew, and dwelt in the wilderness, and became an archer.

21 And he dwelt in the wilderness of Paran: and his mother took him a wife out of the land of Egypt.

22 And it came to pass at that time, that Abimelech and Phichol the chief captain of his host spake unto Abraham, saying, God *is* with thee in all that thou doest:

23 Now therefore swear unto me here by God that thou wilt not deal falsely with me, nor with my son, nor with my son's son: *but* according to the kindness that I have done unto thee, thou shalt do unto me, and to the land wherein thou hast sojourned.

24 And Abraham said, I will swear.

25 And Abraham reproved Abimelech because of a well of water, which Abimelech's servants had violently taken away.

26 And Abimelech said, I wot not who hath done this thing: neither didst thou tell me, neither yet heard I *of it*, but to day.

27 And Abraham took sheep and oxen, and gave them unto Abimelech; and both of them made a covenant.

28 And Abraham set seven ewe lambs of the flock by themselves.

29 And Abimelech said unto Abraham, What *mean* these seven ewe lambs which thou hast set by themselves?

30 And he said, For *these* seven ewe lambs shalt thou take of my hand, that they may be a witness unto me, that I have digged this well.

31 Wherefore he called that place Beer-sheba; because there they sware both of them.

32 Thus they made a covenant at Beer-sheba: then Abimelech rose up, and Phichol the chief captain of his host, and they returned into the land of the Philistines.

33 And *Abraham* planted a grove in Beer-sheba, and called there on the name of the LORD, the everlasting God.

34 And Abraham sojourned in the Philistines' land many days.

22 And it came to pass after these things, that God did tempt Abraham, and said unto him, Abraham: and he said, Behold, *here* I *am*.

2 And he said, Take now thy son, thine only *son* Isaac, whom thou lovest, and get thee into the land of Moriah; and offer him there for a burnt offering upon one of the mountains which I will tell thee of.

3 And Abraham rose up early in the morning, and saddled his ass, and took two of his young men with him, and Isaac his son, and clave the wood for the burnt offering, and rose up, and went unto the place of which God had told him.

4 Then on the third day Abraham lifted up his eyes, and saw the place afar off.

5 And Abraham said unto his young men, Abide ye here with the ass; and I and the lad will go yonder and worship, and come again to you.

6 And Abraham took the wood of the burnt offering, and laid *it* upon Isaac his son; and he took the fire in his hand, and a knife; and they went both of them together.

7 And Isaac spake unto Abraham his father, and said, My father: and he said, Here *am* I, my son. And he said, Behold the fire and the wood: but where *is* the lamb for a burnt offering?

8 And Abraham said, My son, God will provide himself a lamb for a burnt offering: so they went both of them together.

9 And they came to the place which God had told him of; and Abraham built an altar there, and laid the wood in order, and bound Isaac his son, and laid him on the altar upon the wood.

10 And Abraham stretched forth his hand, and took the knife to slay his son.

11 And the angel of the LORD called unto him out of heaven, and said, Abraham, Abraham: and he said, Here *am* I.

12 And he said, Lay not thine hand upon the lad, neither do thou any thing unto him: for now I know that thou fearest God, seeing thou hast not withheld thy son, thine only *son* from me.

13 And Abraham lifted up his eyes, and looked, and behold behind *him* a ram caught in a thicket by his horns: and Abraham went and took the ram, and offered him up for a burnt offering in the stead of his son.

14 And Abraham called the name of that place Jehovah-jireh: as it is said *to* this day, In the mount of the LORD it shall be seen.

15 And the angel of the LORD called unto Abraham out of heaven the second time,

16 And said, By myself have I sworn, saith the LORD, for because thou hast done this thing, and hast not withheld thy son, thine only *son*:

17 That in blessing I will bless thee, and in multiplying I will multiply thy seed as the stars of the heaven, and as the sand which *is* upon the sea shore; and thy seed shall possess the gate of his enemies;

18 And in thy seed shall all the nations of the earth be blessed; because thou hast obeyed my voice.

19 So Abraham returned unto his young men, and they rose up and went together to Beer-sheba; and Abraham dwelt at Beer-sheba.

20 And it came to pass after these things, that it was told Abraham, saying, Behold, Milcah, she hath also born children unto thy brother Nahor;

21 Huz his firstborn, and Buz his brother, and Kemuel the father of Aram,

22 And Chesed, and Hazo, and Pildash, and Jidlaph, and Bethuel.

23 And Bethuel begat Rebekah: these eight Milcah did bear to Nahor, Abraham's brother.

24 And his concubine, whose name *was* Reumah, she bare also Tebah, and Gaham, and Thahash, and Maachah.

23

And Sarah was an hundred and seven and twenty years old: *these were* the years of the life of Sarah.

2 And Sarah died in Kirjath-arba; the same *is* Hebron in the land of Canaan: and Abraham came to mourn for Sarah, and to weep for her.

3 And Abraham stood up from before his dead, and spake unto the sons of Heth, saying,

4 I *am* a stranger and a sojourner with you: give me a possession of a buryingplace with you, that I may bury my dead out of my sight.

5 And the children of Heth answered Abraham, saying unto him,

6 Hear us, my lord: thou *art* a mighty prince among us: in the choice of our sepulchres bury thy dead; none of us shall withhold from thee his sepulchre, but that thou mayest bury thy dead.

7 And Abraham stood up, and bowed himself to the people of the land, *even* to the children of Heth.

8 And he communed with them, saying, If it be your mind that I should bury my dead out of my sight; hear me, and intreat for me to Ephron the son of Zohar,

9 That he may give me the cave of Machpelah, which he hath, which *is* in the end of his field; for as much money as it is worth he shall give it me for a possession of a buryingplace amongst you.

10 And Ephron dwelt among the children of Heth: and Ephron the Hittite answered Abraham in the audience of the children of Heth, *even* of all that went in at the gate of his city, saying,

11 Nay, my lord, hear me: the field give I thee, and the cave that *is* therein, I give it thee; in the presence of the sons of my people give I it thee: bury thy dead.

12 And Abraham bowed down himself before the people of the land.

13 And he spake unto Ephron in the audience of the people of the land, saying, But if thou *wilt give it*, I pray thee, hear me: I will give thee money for the field; take *it* of me, and I will bury my dead there.

14 And Ephron answered Abraham, saying unto him,

15 My lord, hearken unto me: the land *is worth* four hundred shekels of silver; what *is* that betwixt me and thee? bury therefore thy dead.

16 And Abraham hearkened unto Ephron; and Abraham weighed to Ephron the silver, which he had named in the audience of the sons of Heth, four hundred shekels of silver, current *money* with the merchant.

17 And the field of Ephron, which *was* in Machpelah, which *was* before Mamre, the field, and the cave which *was* therein, and all the trees that *were* in the field, that *were* in all the borders round about, were made sure

18 Unto Abraham for a possession in the presence of the children of Heth, before all that went in at the gate of his city.

19 And after this, Abraham buried Sarah his wife in the cave of the field of Machpelah before Mamre: the same *is* Hebron in the land of Canaan.

20 And the field, and the cave that *is* therein, were made sure unto Abraham for a possession of a buryingplace by the sons of Heth.

24 And Abraham was old, *and* well stricken in age: and the LORD had blessed Abraham in all things.

2 And Abraham said unto his eldest servant of his house, that ruled over all that he had, Put, I pray thee, thy hand under my thigh:

3 And I will make thee swear by the LORD, the God of heaven, and the God of the earth, that thou shalt not take a wife unto my son of the daughters of the Canaanites, among whom I dwell:

4 But thou shalt go unto my country, and to my kindred, and take a wife unto my son Isaac.

5 And the servant said unto him, Peradventure the woman will not be willing to follow me unto this land: must I needs bring thy son again unto the land from whence thou camest?

6 And Abraham said unto him, Beware thou that thou bring not my son thither again.

7 The LORD God of heaven, which took me from my father's house, and from the land of my kindred, and which spake unto me, and that sware unto me, saying, Unto thy seed will I give this land; he shall send his angel before thee, and thou shalt take a wife unto my son from thence.

8 And if the woman will not be willing to follow thee, then thou shalt be clear from this my oath: only bring not my son thither again.

9 And the servant put his hand under the thigh of Abraham his master, and sware to him concerning that matter.

10 And the servant took ten camels of the camels of his master, and departed; for all the goods of his master *were* in his hand: and he arose, and went to Mesopotamia, unto the city of Nahor.

11 And he made his camels to kneel
down without the city by a well of
water at the time of the evening, *even*
the time that women go out to draw
water.
12 And he said, O LORD God of my
master Abraham, I pray thee, send me
good speed this day, and shew kindness
unto my master Abraham.
13 Behold, I stand *here* by the well of
water; and the daughters of the men of
the city come out to draw water:
14 And let it come to pass, that the
damsel to whom I shall say, Let down
thy pitcher, I pray thee, that I may
drink; and she shall say, Drink, and I
will give thy camels drink also: *let the
same be* she *that* thou hast appointed
for thy servant Isaac; and thereby shall
I know that thou hast shewed kindness
unto my master.
15 And it came to pass, before he had
done speaking, that, behold, Rebekah
came out, who was born to Bethuel, son
of Milcah, the wife of Nahor, Abraham's
brother, with her pitcher upon her
shoulder.
16 And the damsel *was* very fair to
look upon, a virgin, neither had any
man known her: and she went down to
the well, and filled her pitcher, and
came up.
17 And the servant ran to meet her,
and said, Let me, I pray thee, drink a
little water of thy pitcher.
18 And she said, Drink, my lord: and
she hasted, and let down her pitcher
upon her hand, and gave him drink.
19 And when she had done giving
him drink, she said, I will draw *water*
for thy camels also, until they have
done drinking.
20 And she hasted, and emptied her
pitcher into the trough, and ran again
unto the well to draw *water*, and drew
for all his camels.
21 And the man wondering at her
held his peace, to wit whether the LORD
had made his journey prosperous or
not.
22 And it came to pass, as the camels
had done drinking, that the man took a
golden earring of half a shekel weight,
and two bracelets for her hands of ten
shekels weight of gold;
23 And said, Whose daughter *art*
thou? tell me, I pray thee: is there room
in thy father's house for us to lodge in?
24 And she said unto him, I *am* the
daughter of Bethuel the son of Milcah,
which she bare unto Nahor.
25 She said moreover unto him, We
have both straw and provender enough,
and room to lodge in.
26 And the man bowed down his
head, and worshipped the LORD.
27 And he said, Blessed *be* the LORD
God of my master Abraham, who hath
not left destitute my master of his
mercy and his truth: I *being* in the way,
the LORD led me to the house of my
master's brethren.
28 And the damsel ran, and told *them*
of her mother's house these things.
29 And Rebekah had a brother, and
his name *was* Laban: and Laban ran
out unto the man, unto the well.
30 And it came to pass, when he saw
the earring and bracelets upon his sister's hands, and when he heard the
words of Rebekah his sister, saying,
Thus spake the man unto me; that he
came unto the man; and, behold, he
stood by the camels at the well.
31 And he said, Come in, thou blessed
of the LORD; wherefore standest thou
without? for I have prepared the house,
and room for the camels.

32 And the man came into the house:
and he ungirded his camels, and gave
straw and provender for the camels,
and water to wash his feet, and the
men's feet that *were* with him.
33 And there was set *meat* before him
to eat: but he said, I will not eat, until I
have told mine errand. And he said,
Speak on.
34 And he said, I *am* Abraham's servant.
35 And the LORD hath blessed my
master greatly; and he is become great:
and he hath given him flocks, and
herds, and silver, and gold, and menservants, and maidservants, and camels,
and asses.
36 And Sarah my master's wife bare a
son to my master when she was old: and
unto him hath he given all that he hath.
37 And my master made me swear,
saying, Thou shalt not take a wife to my
son of the daughters of the Canaanites,
in whose land I dwell:
38 But thou shalt go unto my father's
house, and to my kindred, and take a
wife unto my son.
39 And I said unto my master,
Peradventure the woman will not follow me.
40 And he said unto me, The LORD,
before whom I walk, will send his angel
with thee, and prosper thy way; and
thou shalt take a wife for my son of my
kindred, and of my father's house:
41 Then shalt thou be clear from *this*
my oath, when thou comest to my kindred; and if they give not thee *one*, thou
shalt be clear from my oath.
42 And I came this day unto the well,
and said, O LORD God of my master
Abraham, if now thou do prosper my
way which I go:
43 Behold, I stand by the well of
water; and it shall come to pass, that
when the virgin cometh forth to draw
water, and I say to her, Give me, I pray
thee, a little water of thy pitcher to
drink;
44 And she say to me, Both drink
thou, and I will also draw for thy camels: *let* the same *be* the woman whom
the LORD hath appointed out for my
master's son.
45 And before I had done speaking in
mine heart, behold, Rebekah came
forth with her pitcher on her shoulder;
and she went down unto the well, and
drew *water*: and I said unto her, Let me
drink, I pray thee.
46 And she made haste, and let down
her pitcher from her *shoulder*, and said,
Drink, and I will give thy camels drink
also: so I drank, and she made the camels drink also.
47 And I asked her, and said, Whose
daughter *art* thou? And she said, The
daughter of Bethuel, Nahor's son,
whom Milcah bare unto him: and I put
the earring upon her face, and the
bracelets upon her hands.
48 And I bowed down my head, and
worshipped the LORD, and blessed the
LORD God of my master Abraham,
which had led me in the right way to
take my master's brother's daughter
unto his son.
49 And now if ye will deal kindly and
truly with my master, tell me: and if
not, tell me; that I may turn to the right
hand, or to the left.
50 Then Laban and Bethuel answered
and said, The thing proceedeth from
the LORD: we cannot speak unto thee
bad or good.

51 Behold, Rebekah *is* before thee,
take *her*, and go, and let her be thy
master's son's wife, as the LORD hath
spoken.
52 And it came to pass, that, when
Abraham's servant heard their words,
he worshipped the LORD, *bowing himself* to the earth.
53 And the servant brought forth jewels of silver, and jewels of gold, and
raiment, and gave *them* to Rebekah: he
gave also to her brother and to her
mother precious things.
54 And they did eat and drink, he and
the men that *were* with him, and tarried all night; and they rose up in the
morning, and he said, Send me away
unto my master.
55 And her brother and her mother
said, Let the damsel abide with us *a
few* days, at the least ten; after that she
shall go.
56 And he said unto them, Hinder me
not, seeing the LORD hath prospered my
way; send me away that I may go to my
master.
57 And they said, We will call the
damsel, and enquire at her mouth.
58 And they called Rebekah, and said
unto her, Wilt thou go with this man?
And she said, I will go.
59 And they sent away Rebekah their
sister, and her nurse, and Abraham's
servant, and his men.
60 And they blessed Rebekah, and
said unto her, Thou *art* our sister, be
thou *the mother* of thousands of mil-
lions, and let thy seed possess the gate
of those which hate them.
61 And Rebekah arose, and her damsels, and they rode upon the camels,
and followed the man: and the servant
took Rebekah, and went his way.
62 And Isaac came from the way of
the well Lahai-roi; for he dwelt in the
south country.
63 And Isaac went out to meditate in
the field at the eventide: and he lifted
up his eyes, and saw, and, behold, the
camels *were* coming.
64 And Rebekah lifted up her eyes,
and when she saw Isaac, she lighted off
the camel.
65 For she *had* said unto the servant,
What man *is* this that walketh in the
field to meet us? And the servant *had*
said, It *is* my master: therefore she took
a vail, and covered herself.
66 And the servant told Isaac all
things that he had done.
67 And Isaac brought her into his
mother Sarah's tent, and took Rebekah,
and she became his wife; and he loved
her: and Isaac was comforted after his
mother's *death*.

25 Then again Abraham took a wife,
and her name *was* Keturah.
2 And she bare him Zimran, and
Jokshan, and Medan, and Midian, and
Ishbak, and Shuah.
3 And Jokshan begat Sheba, and
Dedan. And the sons of Dedan were
Asshurim, and Letushim, and
Leummim.
4 And the sons of Midian; Ephah, and
Epher, and Hanoch, and Abida, and
Eldaah. All these *were* the children of
Keturah.
5 And Abraham gave all that he had
unto Isaac.
6 But unto the sons of the concubines,
which Abraham had, Abraham gave
gifts, and sent them away from Isaac his
son, while he yet lived, eastward, unto
the east country.

7 And these *are* the days of the years of Abraham's life which he lived, an hundred threescore and fifteen years.

8 Then Abraham gave up the ghost, and died in a good old age, an old man, and full *of years*; and was gathered to his people.

9 And his sons Isaac and Ishmael buried him in the cave of Machpelah, in the field of Ephron the son of Zohar the Hittite, which *is* before Mamre;

10 The field which Abraham purchased of the sons of Heth: there was Abraham buried, and Sarah his wife.

11 And it came to pass after the death of Abraham, that God blessed his son Isaac; and Isaac dwelt by the well Lahai-roi.

12 Now these *are* the generations of Ishmael, Abraham's son, whom Hagar the Egyptian, Sarah's handmaid, bare unto Abraham:

13 And these *are* the names of the sons of Ishmael, by their names, according to their generations: the firstborn of Ishmael, Nebajoth; and Kedar, and Adbeel, and Mibsam,

14 And Mishma, and Dumah, and Massa,

15 Hadar, and Tema, Jetur, Naphish, and Kedemah:

16 These *are* the sons of Ishmael, and these *are* their names, by their towns, and by their castles; twelve princes according to their nations.

17 And these *are* the years of the life of Ishmael, an hundred and thirty and seven years: and he gave up the ghost and died; and was gathered unto his people.

18 And they dwelt from Havilah unto Shur, that *is* before Egypt, as thou goest toward Assyria: *and* he died in the presence of all his brethren.

19 And these *are* the generations of Isaac, Abraham's son: Abraham begat Isaac:

20 And Isaac was forty years old when he took Rebekah to wife, the daughter of Bethuel the Syrian of Padan-aram, the sister to Laban the Syrian.

21 And Isaac intreated the LORD for his wife, because she *was* barren: and the LORD was intreated of him, and Rebekah his wife conceived.

22 And the children struggled together within her; and she said, If *it be* so, why *am* I thus? And she went to enquire of the LORD.

23 And the LORD said unto her, Two nations *are* in thy womb, and two manner of people shall be separated from thy bowels; and *the one* people shall be stronger than *the other* people; and the elder shall serve the younger.

24 And when her days to be delivered were fulfilled, behold, *there were* twins in her womb.

25 And the first came out red, all over like an hairy garment; and they called his name Esau.

26 And after that came his brother out, and his hand took hold on Esau's heel; and his name was called Jacob: and Isaac *was* threescore years old when she bare them.

27 And the boys grew: and Esau was a cunning hunter, a man of the field; and Jacob *was* a plain man, dwelling in tents.

28 And Isaac loved Esau, because he did eat of *his* venison: but Rebekah loved Jacob.

29 And Jacob sod pottage: and Esau came from the field, and he *was* faint:

30 And Esau said to Jacob, Feed me, I pray thee, with that same red *pottage*;

for I *am* faint: therefore was his name
called Edom.
31 And Jacob said, Sell me this day
thy birthright.
32 And Esau said, Behold, I *am* at the
point to die: and what profit shall this
birthright do to me?
33 And Jacob said, Swear to me this
day; and he sware unto him: and he
sold his birthright unto Jacob.
34 Then Jacob gave Esau bread and
pottage of lentiles; and he did eat and
drink, and rose up, and went his way:
thus Esau despised *his* birthright.

26 And there was a famine in the
land, beside the first famine that
was in the days of Abraham. And Isaac
went unto Abimelech king of the
Philistines unto Gerar.
2 And the LORD appeared unto him,
and said, Go not down into Egypt; dwell
in the land which I shall tell thee of:
3 Sojourn in this land, and I will be
with thee, and will bless thee; for unto
thee, and unto thy seed, I will give all
these countries, and I will perform the
oath which I sware unto Abraham thy
father;
4 And I will make thy seed to multiply
as the stars of heaven, and will give
unto thy seed all these countries; and
in thy seed shall all the nations of the
earth be blessed;
5 Because that Abraham obeyed my
voice, and kept my charge, my commandments, my statutes, and my laws.
6 And Isaac dwelt in Gerar:
7 And the men of the place asked *him*
of his wife; and he said, She *is* my sister: for he feared to say, *She is* my wife;
lest, *said he*, the men of the place
should kill me for Rebekah; because
she *was* fair to look upon.
8 And it came to pass, when he had
been there a long time, that Abimelech
king of the Philistines looked out at a
window, and saw, and, behold, Isaac
was sporting with Rebekah his wife.
9 And Abimelech called Isaac, and
said, Behold, of a surety she *is* thy wife:
and how saidst thou, She *is* my sister?
And Isaac said unto him, Because I
said, Lest I die for her.
10 And Abimelech said, What *is* this
thou hast done unto us? one of the
people might lightly have lien with thy
wife, and thou shouldest have brought
guiltiness upon us.
11 And Abimelech charged all *his*
people, saying, He that toucheth this
man or his wife shall surely be put to
death.
12 Then Isaac sowed in that land, and
received in the same year an hundredfold: and the LORD blessed him.
13 And the man waxed great, and
went forward, and grew until he
became very great:
14 For he had possession of flocks,
and possession of herds, and great store
of servants: and the Philistines envied
him.
15 For all the wells which his father's
servants had digged in the days of
Abraham his father, the Philistines had
stopped them, and filled them with
earth.
16 And Abimelech said unto Isaac, Go
from us; for thou art much mightier
than we.
17 And Isaac departed thence, and
pitched his tent in the valley of Gerar,
and dwelt there.
18 And Isaac digged again the wells
of water, which they had digged in the
days of Abraham his father; for the
Philistines had stopped them after the

death of Abraham: and he called their names after the names by which his father had called them.

19 And Isaac's servants digged in the valley, and found there a well of springing water.

20 And the herdmen of Gerar did strive with Isaac's herdmen, saying, The water *is* ours: and he called the name of the well Esek; because they strove with him.

21 And they digged another well, and strove for that also: and he called the name of it Sitnah.

22 And he removed from thence, and digged another well; and for that they strove not: and he called the name of it Rehoboth; and he said, For now the LORD hath made room for us, and we shall be fruitful in the land.

23 And he went up from thence to Beer-sheba.

24 And the LORD appeared unto him the same night, and said, I *am* the God of Abraham thy father: fear not, for I *am* with thee, and will bless thee, and multiply thy seed for my servant Abraham's sake.

25 And he builded an altar there, and called upon the name of the LORD, and pitched his tent there: and there Isaac's servants digged a well.

26 Then Abimelech went to him from Gerar, and Ahuzzath one of his friends, and Phichol the chief captain of his army.

27 And Isaac said unto them, Wherefore come ye to me, seeing ye hate me, and have sent me away from you?

28 And they said, We saw certainly that the LORD was with thee: and we said, Let there be now an oath betwixt us, *even* betwixt us and thee, and let us make a covenant with thee;

29 That thou wilt do us no hurt, as we have not touched thee, and as we have done unto thee nothing but good, and have sent thee away in peace: thou *art* now the blessed of the LORD.

30 And he made them a feast, and they did eat and drink.

31 And they rose up betimes in the morning, and sware one to another: and Isaac sent them away, and they departed from him in peace.

32 And it came to pass the same day, that Isaac's servants came, and told him concerning the well which they had digged, and said unto him, We have found water.

33 And he called it Shebah: therefore the name of the city *is* Beer-sheba unto this day.

34 And Esau was forty years old when he took to wife Judith the daughter of Beeri the Hittite, and Bashemath the daughter of Elon the Hittite:

35 Which were a grief of mind unto Isaac and to Rebekah.

27 And it came to pass, that when Isaac was old, and his eyes were dim, so that he could not see, he called Esau his eldest son, and said unto him, My son: and he said unto him, Behold, *here am* I.

2 And he said, Behold now, I am old, I know not the day of my death:

3 Now therefore take, I pray thee, thy weapons, thy quiver and thy bow, and go out to the field, and take me *some* venison;

4 And make me savoury meat, such as I love, and bring *it* to me, that I may eat; that my soul may bless thee before I die.

5 And Rebekah heard when Isaac spake to Esau his son. And Esau went to the field to hunt *for* venison, *and* to bring *it*.

6 And Rebekah spake unto Jacob her son, saying, Behold, I heard thy father speak unto Esau thy brother, saying,

7 Bring me venison, and make me savoury meat, that I may eat, and bless thee before the LORD before my death.

8 Now therefore, my son, obey my voice according to that which I command thee.

9 Go now to the flock, and fetch me from thence two good kids of the goats; and I will make them savoury meat for thy father, such as he loveth:

10 And thou shalt bring *it* to thy father, that he may eat, and that he may bless thee before his death.

11 And Jacob said to Rebekah his mother, Behold, Esau my brother *is* a hairy man, and I *am* a smooth man:

12 My father peradventure will feel me, and I shall seem to him as a deceiver; and I shall bring a curse upon me, and not a blessing.

13 And his mother said unto him, Upon me *be* thy curse, my son: only obey my voice, and go fetch me *them*.

14 And he went, and fetched, and brought *them* to his mother: and his mother made savoury meat, such as his father loved.

15 And Rebekah took goodly raiment of her eldest son Esau, which *were* with her in the house, and put them upon Jacob her younger son:

16 And she put the skins of the kids of the goats upon his hands, and upon the smooth of his neck:

17 And she gave the savoury meat and the bread, which she had prepared, into the hand of her son Jacob.

18 And he came unto his father, and said, My father: and he said, Here *am* I; who *art* thou, my son?

19 And Jacob said unto his father, I *am* Esau thy firstborn; I have done according as thou badest me: arise, I pray thee, sit and eat of my venison, that thy soul may bless me.

20 And Isaac said unto his son, How *is it* that thou hast found *it* so quickly, my son? And he said, Because the LORD thy God brought *it* to me.

21 And Isaac said unto Jacob, Come near, I pray thee, that I may feel thee, my son, whether thou *be* my very son Esau or not.

22 And Jacob went near unto Isaac his father; and he felt him, and said, The voice *is* Jacob's voice, but the hands *are* the hands of Esau.

23 And he discerned him not, because his hands were hairy, as his brother Esau's hands: so he blessed him.

24 And he said, *Art* thou my very son Esau? And he said, I *am*.

25 And he said, Bring *it* near to me, and I will eat of my son's venison, that my soul may bless thee. And he brought *it* near to him, and he did eat: and he brought him wine, and he drank.

26 And his father Isaac said unto him, Come near now, and kiss me, my son.

27 And he came near, and kissed him: and he smelled the smell of his raiment, and blessed him, and said, See, the smell of my son *is* as the smell of a field which the LORD hath blessed:

28 Therefore God give thee of the dew of heaven, and the fatness of the earth, and plenty of corn and wine:

29 Let people serve thee, and nations bow down to thee: be lord over thy brethren, and let thy mother's sons bow down to thee: cursed *be* every one that curseth thee, and blessed *be* he that blesseth thee.

30 And it came to pass, as soon as Isaac had made an end of blessing Jacob, and Jacob was yet scarce gone out from the presence of Isaac his father, that Esau his brother came in from his hunting.

31 And he also had made savoury meat, and brought it unto his father, and said unto his father, Let my father arise, and eat of his son's venison, that thy soul may bless me.

32 And Isaac his father said unto him, Who *art* thou? And he said, I *am* thy son, thy firstborn Esau.

33 And Isaac trembled very exceedingly, and said, Who? where *is* he that hath taken venison, and brought *it* me, and I have eaten of all before thou camest, and have blessed him? yea, *and* he shall be blessed.

34 And when Esau heard the words of his father, he cried with a great and exceeding bitter cry, and said unto his father, Bless me, *even* me also, O my father.

35 And he said, Thy brother came with subtilty, and hath taken away thy blessing.

36 And he said, Is not he rightly named Jacob? for he hath supplanted me these two times: he took away my birthright; and, behold, now he hath taken away my blessing. And he said, Hast thou not reserved a blessing for me?

37 And Isaac answered and said unto Esau, Behold, I have made him thy lord, and all his brethren have I given to him for servants; and with corn and wine have I sustained him: and what shall I do now unto thee, my son?

38 And Esau said unto his father, Hast thou but one blessing, my father? bless me, *even* me also, O my father. And Esau lifted up his voice, and wept.

39 And Isaac his father answered and said unto him, Behold, thy dwelling shall be the fatness of the earth, and of the dew of heaven from above;

40 And by thy sword shalt thou live, and shalt serve thy brother; and it shall come to pass when thou shalt have the dominion, that thou shalt break his yoke from off thy neck.

41 And Esau hated Jacob because of the blessing wherewith his father blessed him: and Esau said in his heart, The days of mourning for my father are at hand; then will I slay my brother Jacob.

42 And these words of Esau her elder son were told to Rebekah: and she sent and called Jacob her younger son, and said unto him, Behold, thy brother Esau, as touching thee, doth comfort himself, *purposing* to kill thee.

43 Now therefore, my son, obey my voice; and arise, flee thou to Laban my brother to Haran;

44 And tarry with him a few days, until thy brother's fury turn away;

45 Until thy brother's anger turn away from thee, and he forget *that* which thou hast done to him: then I will send, and fetch thee from thence: why should I be deprived also of you both in one day?

46 And Rebekah said to Isaac, I am weary of my life because of the daughters of Heth: if Jacob take a wife of the daughters of Heth, such as these *which are* of the daughters of the land, what good shall my life do me?

28 And Isaac called Jacob, and blessed him, and charged him,

and said unto him, Thou shalt not take
a wife of the daughters of Canaan.
2 Arise, go to Padan-aram, to the
house of Bethuel thy mother's father;
and take thee a wife from thence of the
daughters of Laban thy mother's brother.
3 And God Almighty bless thee, and
make thee fruitful, and multiply thee,
that thou mayest be a multitude of
people;
4 And give thee the blessing of
Abraham, to thee, and to thy seed with
thee; that thou mayest inherit the land
wherein thou art a stranger, which God
gave unto Abraham.
5 And Isaac sent away Jacob: and he
went to Padan-aram unto Laban, son of
Bethuel the Syrian, the brother of
Rebekah, Jacob's and Esau's mother.
6 When Esau saw that Isaac had
blessed Jacob, and sent him away to
Padan-aram, to take him a wife from
thence; and that as he blessed him he
gave him a charge, saying, Thou shalt
not take a wife of the daughters of
Canaan;
7 And that Jacob obeyed his father
and his mother, and was gone to Padan-
aram;
8 And Esau seeing that the daughters
of Canaan pleased not Isaac his father;
9 Then went Esau unto Ishmael, and
took unto the wives which he had
Mahalath the daughter of Ishmael
Abraham's son, the sister of Nebajoth,
to be his wife.
10 And Jacob went out from Beer-
sheba, and went toward Haran.
11 And he lighted upon a certain
place, and tarried there all night,
because the sun was set; and he took of
the stones of that place, and put *them*
for his pillows, and lay down in that
place to sleep.
12 And he dreamed, and behold a lad-
der set up on the earth, and the top of
it reached to heaven: and behold the
angels of God ascending and descending on it.
13 And, behold, the LORD stood above
it, and said, I *am* the LORD God of
Abraham thy father, and the God of
Isaac: the land whereon thou liest, to
thee will I give it, and to thy seed;
14 And thy seed shall be as the dust
of the earth, and thou shalt spread
abroad to the west, and to the east, and
to the north, and to the south: and in
thee and in thy seed shall all the families of the earth be blessed.
15 And, behold, I *am* with thee, and
will keep thee in all *places* whither
thou goest, and will bring thee again
into this land; for I will not leave thee,
until I have done *that* which I have
spoken to thee of.
16 And Jacob awaked out of his sleep,
and he said, Surely the LORD is in this
place; and I knew *it* not.
17 And he was afraid, and said, How
dreadful *is* this place! this *is* none other
but the house of God, and this *is* the
gate of heaven.
18 And Jacob rose up early in the
morning, and took the stone that he
had put *for* his pillows, and set it up *for*
a pillar, and poured oil upon the top of
it.
19 And he called the name of that
place Beth-el: but the name of that city
was called Luz at the first.
20 And Jacob vowed a vow, saying, If
God will be with me, and will keep me
in this way that I go, and will give me
bread to eat, and raiment to put on,

21 So that I come again to my father's
house in peace; then shall the LORD be
my God:
22 And this stone, which I have set *for*
a pillar, shall be God's house: and of all
that thou shalt give me I will surely give
the tenth unto thee.

29 Then Jacob went on his journey,
and came into the land of the
people of the east.
2 And he looked, and behold a well in
the field, and, lo, there *were* three
flocks of sheep lying by it; for out of
that well they watered the flocks: and a
great stone *was* upon the well's mouth.
3 And thither were all the flocks gathered: and they rolled the stone from the
well's mouth, and watered the sheep,
and put the stone again upon the well's
mouth in his place.
4 And Jacob said unto them, My
brethren, whence *be* ye? And they said,
Of Haran *are* we.
5 And he said unto them, Know ye
Laban the son of Nahor? And they said,
We know *him*.
6 And he said unto them, *Is* he well?
And they said, *He is* well: and, behold,
Rachel his daughter cometh with the
sheep.
7 And he said, Lo, *it is* yet high day,
neither *is it* time that the cattle should
be gathered together: water ye the
sheep, and go *and* feed *them*.
8 And they said, We cannot, until all
the flocks be gathered together, and *till*
they roll the stone from the well's
mouth; then we water the sheep.
9 And while he yet spake with them,
Rachel came with her father's sheep:
for she kept them.
10 And it came to pass, when Jacob
saw Rachel the daughter of Laban his
mother's brother, and the sheep of
Laban his mother's brother, that Jacob
went near, and rolled the stone from
the well's mouth, and watered the flock
of Laban his mother's brother.
11 And Jacob kissed Rachel, and lifted up his voice, and wept.
12 And Jacob told Rachel that he *was*
her father's brother, and that he *was*
Rebekah's son: and she ran and told
her father.
13 And it came to pass, when Laban
heard the tidings of Jacob his sister's
son, that he ran to meet him, and
embraced him, and kissed him, and
brought him to his house. And he told
Laban all these things.
14 And Laban said to him, Surely
thou *art* my bone and my flesh. And he
abode with him the space of a month.
15 And Laban said unto Jacob,
Because thou *art* my brother, shouldest
thou therefore serve me for nought?
tell me, what *shall* thy wages *be*?
16 And Laban had two daughters: the
name of the elder *was* Leah, and the
name of the younger *was* Rachel.
17 Leah *was* tender eyed; but Rachel
was beautiful and well favoured.
18 And Jacob loved Rachel; and said,
I will serve thee seven years for Rachel
thy younger daughter.
19 And Laban said, *It is* better that I
give her to thee, than that I should give
her to another man: abide with me.
20 And Jacob served seven years for
Rachel; and they seemed unto him *but*
a few days, for the love he had to her.
21 And Jacob said unto Laban, Give
me my wife, for my days are fulfilled,
that I may go in unto her.
22 And Laban gathered together all
the men of the place, and made a feast.
23 And it came to pass in the evening,
that he took Leah his daughter, and

brought her to him; and he went in
unto her.
24 And Laban gave unto his daughter
Leah Zilpah his maid *for* an handmaid.
25 And it came to pass, that in the
morning, behold, it *was* Leah: and he
said to Laban, What *is* this thou hast
done unto me? did not I serve with thee
for Rachel? wherefore then hast thou
beguiled me?
26 And Laban said, It must not be so
done in our country, to give the younger
before the firstborn.
27 Fulfil her week, and we will give
thee this also for the service which thou
shalt serve with me yet seven other
years.
28 And Jacob did so, and fulfilled her
week: and he gave him Rachel his
daughter to wife also.
29 And Laban gave to Rachel his
daughter Bilhah his handmaid to be
her maid.
30 And he went in also unto Rachel,
and he loved also Rachel more than
Leah, and served with him yet seven
other years.
31 And when the LORD saw that Leah
was hated, he opened her womb: but
Rachel *was* barren.
32 And Leah conceived, and bare a
son, and she called his name Reuben:
for she said, Surely the LORD hath
looked upon my affliction; now therefore my husband will love me.
33 And she conceived again, and bare
a son; and said, Because the LORD hath
heard that I *was* hated, he hath therefore given me this *son* also: and she
called his name Simeon.
34 And she conceived again, and bare
a son; and said, Now this time will my
husband be joined unto me, because I
have born him three sons: therefore
was his name called Levi.
35 And she conceived again, and bare
a son: and she said, Now will I praise
the LORD: therefore she called his name
Judah; and left bearing.

30 And when Rachel saw that she
bare Jacob no children, Rachel
envied her sister; and said unto Jacob,
Give me children, or else I die.
2 And Jacob's anger was kindled
against Rachel: and he said, *Am* I in
God's stead, who hath withheld from
thee the fruit of the womb?
3 And she said, Behold my maid
Bilhah, go in unto her; and she shall
bear upon my knees, that I may also
have children by her.
4 And she gave him Bilhah her handmaid to wife: and Jacob went in unto
her.
5 And Bilhah conceived, and bare
Jacob a son.
6 And Rachel said, God hath judged
me, and hath also heard my voice, and
hath given me a son: therefore called
she his name Dan.
7 And Bilhah Rachel's maid conceived again, and bare Jacob a second
son.
8 And Rachel said, With great wres-
tlings have I wrestled with my sister,
and I have prevailed: and she called his
name Naphtali.
9 When Leah saw that she had left
bearing, she took Zilpah her maid, and
gave her Jacob to wife.
10 And Zilpah Leah's maid bare
Jacob a son.
11 And Leah said, A troop cometh:
and she called his name Gad.
12 And Zilpah Leah's maid bare
Jacob a second son.

13 And Leah said, Happy am I, for the daughters will call me blessed: and she called his name Asher.

14 And Reuben went in the days of wheat harvest, and found mandrakes in the field, and brought them unto his mother Leah. Then Rachel said to Leah, Give me, I pray thee, of thy son's mandrakes.

15 And she said unto her, *Is it* a small matter that thou hast taken my husband? and wouldest thou take away my son's mandrakes also? And Rachel said, Therefore he shall lie with thee to night for thy son's mandrakes.

16 And Jacob came out of the field in the evening, and Leah went out to meet him, and said, Thou must come in unto me; for surely I have hired thee with my son's mandrakes. And he lay with her that night.

17 And God hearkened unto Leah, and she conceived, and bare Jacob the fifth son.

18 And Leah said, God hath given me my hire, because I have given my maiden to my husband: and she called his name Issachar.

19 And Leah conceived again, and bare Jacob the sixth son.

20 And Leah said, God hath endued me *with* a good dowry; now will my husband dwell with me, because I have born him six sons: and she called his name Zebulun.

21 And afterwards she bare a daughter, and called her name Dinah.

22 And God remembered Rachel, and God hearkened to her, and opened her womb.

23 And she conceived, and bare a son; and said, God hath taken away my reproach:

24 And she called his name Joseph; and said, The LORD shall add to me another son.

25 And it came to pass, when Rachel had born Joseph, that Jacob said unto Laban, Send me away, that I may go unto mine own place, and to my country.

26 Give *me* my wives and my children, for whom I have served thee, and let me go: for thou knowest my service which I have done thee.

27 And Laban said unto him, I pray thee, if I have found favour in thine eyes, *tarry: for* I have learned by experience that the LORD hath blessed me for thy sake.

28 And he said, Appoint me thy wages, and I will give *it*.

29 And he said unto him, Thou knowest how I have served thee, and how thy cattle was with me.

30 For *it was* little which thou hadst before I *came*, and it is *now* increased unto a multitude; and the LORD hath blessed thee since my coming: and now when shall I provide for mine own house also?

31 And he said, What shall I give thee? And Jacob said, Thou shalt not give me any thing: if thou wilt do this thing for me, I will again feed *and* keep thy flock:

32 I will pass through all thy flock to day, removing from thence all the speckled and spotted cattle, and all the brown cattle among the sheep, and the spotted and speckled among the goats: and *of such* shall be my hire.

33 So shall my righteousness answer for me in time to come, when it shall come for my hire before thy face: every one that *is* not speckled and spotted among the goats, and brown among the

sheep, that shall be counted stolen with me.

34 And Laban said, Behold, I would it might be according to thy word.

35 And he removed that day the he goats that were ringstraked and spotted, and all the she goats that were speckled and spotted, *and* every one that had *some* white in it, and all the brown among the sheep, and gave *them* into the hand of his sons.

36 And he set three days' journey betwixt himself and Jacob: and Jacob fed the rest of Laban's flocks.

37 And Jacob took him rods of green poplar, and of the hazel and chesnut tree; and pilled white strakes in them, and made the white appear which *was* in the rods.

38 And he set the rods which he had pilled before the flocks in the gutters in the watering troughs when the flocks came to drink, that they should conceive when they came to drink.

39 And the flocks conceived before the rods, and brought forth cattle ringstraked, speckled, and spotted.

40 And Jacob did separate the lambs, and set the faces of the flocks toward the ringstraked, and all the brown in the flock of Laban; and he put his own flocks by themselves, and put them not unto Laban's cattle.

41 And it came to pass, whensoever the stronger cattle did conceive, that Jacob laid the rods before the eyes of the cattle in the gutters, that they might conceive among the rods.

42 But when the cattle were feeble, he put *them* not in: so the feebler were Laban's, and the stronger Jacob's.

43 And the man increased exceedingly, and had much cattle, and maidservants, and menservants, and camels, and asses.

31 And he heard the words of Laban's sons, saying, Jacob hath taken away all that *was* our father's; and of *that* which *was* our father's hath he gotten all this glory.

2 And Jacob beheld the countenance of Laban, and, behold, it *was* not toward him as before.

3 And the LORD said unto Jacob, Return unto the land of thy fathers, and to thy kindred; and I will be with thee.

4 And Jacob sent and called Rachel and Leah to the field unto his flock,

5 And said unto them, I see your father's countenance, that it *is* not toward me as before; but the God of my father hath been with me.

6 And ye know that with all my power I have served your father.

7 And your father hath deceived me, and changed my wages ten times; but God suffered him not to hurt me.

8 If he said thus, The speckled shall be thy wages; then all the cattle bare speckled: and if he said thus, The ringstraked shall be thy hire; then bare all the cattle ringstraked.

9 Thus God hath taken away the cattle of your father, and given *them* to me.

10 And it came to pass at the time that the cattle conceived, that I lifted up mine eyes, and saw in a dream, and, behold, the rams which leaped upon the cattle *were* ringstraked, speckled, and grisled.

11 And the angel of God spake unto me in a dream, *saying*, Jacob: And I said, Here *am* I.

12 And he said, Lift up now thine eyes, and see, all the rams which leap upon the cattle *are* ringstraked, speckled, and grisled: for I have seen all that Laban doeth unto thee.

13 I *am* the God of Beth-el, where thou anointedst the pillar, *and* where thou vowedst a vow unto me: now arise, get thee out from this land, and return unto the land of thy kindred.

14 And Rachel and Leah answered and said unto him, *Is there* yet any portion or inheritance for us in our father's house?

15 Are we not counted of him strangers? for he hath sold us, and hath quite devoured also our money.

16 For all the riches which God hath taken from our father, that *is* ours, and our children's: now then, whatsoever God hath said unto thee, do.

17 Then Jacob rose up, and set his sons and his wives upon camels;

18 And he carried away all his cattle, and all his goods which he had gotten, the cattle of his getting, which he had gotten in Padan-aram, for to go to Isaac his father in the land of Canaan.

19 And Laban went to shear his sheep: and Rachel had stolen the images that *were* her father's.

20 And Jacob stole away unawares to Laban the Syrian, in that he told him not that he fled.

21 So he fled with all that he had; and he rose up, and passed over the river, and set his face *toward* the mount Gilead.

22 And it was told Laban on the third day that Jacob was fled.

23 And he took his brethren with him, and pursued after him seven days' journey; and they overtook him in the mount Gilead.

24 And God came to Laban the Syrian in a dream by night, and said unto him, Take heed that thou speak not to Jacob either good or bad.

25 Then Laban overtook Jacob. Now Jacob had pitched his tent in the mount: and Laban with his brethren pitched in the mount of Gilead.

26 And Laban said to Jacob, What hast thou done, that thou hast stolen away unawares to me, and carried away my daughters, as captives *taken* with the sword?

27 Wherefore didst thou flee away secretly, and steal away from me; and didst not tell me, that I might have sent thee away with mirth, and with songs, with tabret, and with harp?

28 And hast not suffered me to kiss my sons and my daughters? thou hast now done foolishly in *so* doing.

29 It is in the power of my hand to do you hurt: but the God of your father spake unto me yesternight, saying, Take thou heed that thou speak not to Jacob either good or bad.

30 And now, *though* thou wouldest needs be gone, because thou sore longedst after thy father's house, *yet* wherefore hast thou stolen my gods?

31 And Jacob answered and said to Laban, Because I was afraid: for I said, Peradventure thou wouldest take by force thy daughters from me.

32 With whomsoever thou findest thy gods, let him not live: before our brethren discern thou what *is* thine with me, and take *it* to thee. For Jacob knew not that Rachel had stolen them.

33 And Laban went into Jacob's tent, and into Leah's tent, and into the two maidservants' tents; but he found *them* not. Then went he out of Leah's tent, and entered into Rachel's tent.

34 Now Rachel had taken the images,
and put them in the camel's furniture,
and sat upon them. And Laban
searched all the tent, but found *them*
not.
35 And she said to her father, Let it
not displease my lord that I cannot rise
up before thee; for the custom of
women *is* upon me. And he searched,
but found not the images.
36 And Jacob was wroth, and chode
with Laban: and Jacob answered and
said to Laban, What *is* my trespass?
what *is* my sin, that thou hast so hotly
pursued after me?
37 Whereas thou hast searched all my
stuff, what hast thou found of all thy
household stuff? set *it* here before my
brethren and thy brethren, that they
may judge betwixt us both.
38 This twenty years *have* I *been* with
thee; thy ewes and thy she goats have
not cast their young, and the rams of
thy flock have I not eaten.
39 That which was torn *of beasts* I
brought not unto thee; I bare the loss of
it; of my hand didst thou require it,
whether stolen by day, or stolen by
night.
40 *Thus* I was; in the day the drought
consumed me, and the frost by night;
and my sleep departed from mine eyes.
41 Thus have I been twenty years in
thy house; I served thee fourteen years
for thy two daughters, and six years for
thy cattle: and thou hast changed my
wages ten times.
42 Except the God of my father, the
God of Abraham, and the fear of Isaac,
had been with me, surely thou hadst
sent me away now empty. God hath
seen mine affliction and the labour of
my hands, and rebuked *thee* yesternight.

43 And Laban answered and said
unto Jacob, *These* daughters *are* my
daughters, and *these* children *are* my
children, and *these* cattle *are* my cattle,
and all that thou seest *is* mine: and
what can I do this day unto these my
daughters, or unto their children which
they have born?
44 Now therefore come thou, let us
make a covenant, I and thou; and let it
be for a witness between me and thee.
45 And Jacob took a stone, and set it
up *for* a pillar.
46 And Jacob said unto his brethren,
Gather stones; and they took stones,
and made an heap: and they did eat
there upon the heap.
47 And Laban called it Jegar-
sahadutha: but Jacob called it Galeed.
48 And Laban said, This heap *is* a witness between me and thee this day.
Therefore was the name of it called
Galeed;
49 And Mizpah; for he said, The LORD
watch between me and thee, when we
are absent one from another.
50 If thou shalt afflict my daughters,
or if thou shalt take *other* wives beside
my daughters, no man *is* with us; see,
God *is* witness betwixt me and thee.
51 And Laban said to Jacob, Behold
this heap, and behold *this* pillar, which
I have cast betwixt me and thee;
52 This heap *be* witness, and *this* pillar *be* witness, that I will not pass over
this heap to thee, and that thou shalt
not pass over this heap and this pillar
unto me, for harm.
53 The God of Abraham, and the God
of Nahor, the God of their father, judge
betwixt us. And Jacob sware by the fear
of his father Isaac.
54 Then Jacob offered sacrifice upon
the mount, and called his brethren to

eat bread: and they did eat bread, and tarried all night in the mount.

55 And early in the morning Laban rose up, and kissed his sons and his daughters, and blessed them: and Laban departed, and returned unto his place.

32 And Jacob went on his way, and the angels of God met him.

2 And when Jacob saw them, he said, This *is* God's host: and he called the name of that place Mahanaim.

3 And Jacob sent messengers before him to Esau his brother unto the land of Seir, the country of Edom.

4 And he commanded them, saying, Thus shall ye speak unto my lord Esau; Thy servant Jacob saith thus, I have sojourned with Laban, and stayed there until now:

5 And I have oxen, and asses, flocks, and menservants, and womenservants: and I have sent to tell my lord, that I may find grace in thy sight.

6 And the messengers returned to Jacob, saying, We came to thy brother Esau, and also he cometh to meet thee, and four hundred men with him.

7 Then Jacob was greatly afraid and distressed: and he divided the people that *was* with him, and the flocks, and herds, and the camels, into two bands;

8 And said, If Esau come to the one company, and smite it, then the other company which is left shall escape.

9 And Jacob said, O God of my father Abraham, and God of my father Isaac, the LORD which saidst unto me, Return unto thy country, and to thy kindred, and I will deal well with thee:

10 I am not worthy of the least of all the mercies, and of all the truth, which thou hast shewed unto thy servant; for with my staff I passed over this Jordan; and now I am become two bands.

11 Deliver me, I pray thee, from the hand of my brother, from the hand of Esau: for I fear him, lest he will come and smite me, *and* the mother with the children.

12 And thou saidst, I will surely do thee good, and make thy seed as the sand of the sea, which cannot be numbered for multitude.

13 And he lodged there that same night; and took of that which came to his hand a present for Esau his brother;

14 Two hundred she goats, and twenty he goats, two hundred ewes, and twenty rams,

15 Thirty milch camels with their colts, forty kine, and ten bulls, twenty she asses, and ten foals.

16 And he delivered *them* into the hand of his servants, every drove by themselves; and said unto his servants, Pass over before me, and put a space betwixt drove and drove.

17 And he commanded the foremost, saying, When Esau my brother meeteth thee, and asketh thee, saying, Whose *art* thou? and whither goest thou? and whose *are* these before thee?

18 Then thou shalt say, *They be* thy servant Jacob's; it *is* a present sent unto my lord Esau: and, behold, also he *is* behind us.

19 And so commanded he the second, and the third, and all that followed the droves, saying, On this manner shall ye speak unto Esau, when ye find him.

20 And say ye moreover, Behold, thy servant Jacob *is* behind us. For he said, I will appease him with the present that goeth before me, and afterward I will see his face; peradventure he will accept of me.

21 So went the present over before him: and himself lodged that night in the company.

22 And he rose up that night, and took his two wives, and his two womenservants, and his eleven sons, and passed over the ford Jabbok.

23 And he took them, and sent them over the brook, and sent over that he had.

24 And Jacob was left alone; and there wrestled a man with him until the breaking of the day.

25 And when he saw that he prevailed not against him, he touched the hollow of his thigh; and the hollow of Jacob's thigh was out of joint, as he wrestled with him.

26 And he said, Let me go, for the day breaketh. And he said, I will not let thee go, except thou bless me.

27 And he said unto him, What *is* thy name? And he said, Jacob.

28 And he said, Thy name shall be called no more Jacob, but Israel: for as a prince hast thou power with God and with men, and hast prevailed.

29 And Jacob asked *him*, and said, Tell *me*, I pray thee, thy name. And he said, Wherefore *is* it *that* thou dost ask after my name? And he blessed him there.

30 And Jacob called the name of the place Peniel: for I have seen God face to face, and my life is preserved.

31 And as he passed over Penuel the sun rose upon him, and he halted upon his thigh.

32 Therefore the children of Israel eat not *of* the sinew which shrank, which *is* upon the hollow of the thigh, unto this day: because he touched the hollow of Jacob's thigh in the sinew that shrank.

33 And Jacob lifted up his eyes, and looked, and, behold, Esau came, and with him four hundred men. And he divided the children unto Leah, and unto Rachel, and unto the two handmaids.

2 And he put the handmaids and their children foremost, and Leah and her children after, and Rachel and Joseph hindermost.

3 And he passed over before them, and bowed himself to the ground seven times, until he came near to his brother.

4 And Esau ran to meet him, and embraced him, and fell on his neck, and kissed him: and they wept.

5 And he lifted up his eyes, and saw the women and the children; and said, Who *are* those with thee? And he said, The children which God hath graciously given thy servant.

6 Then the handmaidens came near, they and their children, and they bowed themselves.

7 And Leah also with her children came near, and bowed themselves: and after came Joseph near and Rachel, and they bowed themselves.

8 And he said, What *meanest* thou by all this drove which I met? And he said, *These are* to find grace in the sight of my lord.

9 And Esau said, I have enough, my brother; keep that thou hast unto thyself.

10 And Jacob said, Nay, I pray thee, if now I have found grace in thy sight, then receive my present at my hand: for therefore I have seen thy face, as though I had seen the face of God, and thou wast pleased with me.

11 Take, I pray thee, my blessing that is brought to thee; because God hath dealt graciously with me, and because I

have enough. And he urged him, and he
took *it*.
12 And he said, Let us take our journey, and let us go, and I will go before
thee.
13 And he said unto him, My lord
knoweth that the children *are* tender,
and the flocks and herds with young
are with me: and if men should over-
drive them one day, all the flock will
die.
14 Let my lord, I pray thee, pass over
before his servant: and I will lead on
softly, according as the cattle that goeth
before me and the children be able to
endure, until I come unto my lord unto
Seir.
15 And Esau said, Let me now leave
with thee *some* of the folk that *are* with
me. And he said, What needeth it? let
me find grace in the sight of my lord.
16 So Esau returned that day on his
way unto Seir.
17 And Jacob journeyed to Succoth,
and built him an house, and made
booths for his cattle: therefore the
name of the place is called Succoth.
18 And Jacob came to Shalem, a city
of Shechem, which *is* in the land of
Canaan, when he came from Padan-
aram; and pitched his tent before the
city.
19 And he bought a parcel of a field,
where he had spread his tent, at the
hand of the children of Hamor,
Shechem's father, for an hundred pieces of money.
20 And he erected there an altar, and
called it El-elohe-Israel.

34 And Dinah the daughter of Leah,
which she bare unto Jacob, went
out to see the daughters of the land.
2 And when Shechem the son of
Hamor the Hivite, prince of the country, saw her, he took her, and lay with
her, and defiled her.
3 And his soul clave unto Dinah the
daughter of Jacob, and he loved the
damsel, and spake kindly unto the
damsel.
4 And Shechem spake unto his father
Hamor, saying, Get me this damsel to
wife.
5 And Jacob heard that he had
defiled Dinah his daughter: now his
sons were with his cattle in the field:
and Jacob held his peace until they
were come.
6 And Hamor the father of Shechem
went out unto Jacob to commune with
him.
7 And the sons of Jacob came out of
the field when they heard *it*: and the
men were grieved, and they were very
wroth, because he had wrought folly in
Israel in lying with Jacob's daughter;
which thing ought not to be done.
8 And Hamor communed with them,
saying, The soul of my son Shechem
longeth for your daughter: I pray you
give her him to wife.
9 And make ye marriages with us,
and give your daughters unto us, and
take our daughters unto you.
10 And ye shall dwell with us: and the
land shall be before you; dwell and
trade ye therein, and get you possessions therein.
11 And Shechem said unto her father
and unto her brethren, Let me find
grace in your eyes, and what ye shall
say unto me I will give.
12 Ask me never so much dowry and
gift, and I will give according as ye shall
say unto me: but give me the damsel to
wife.

13 And the sons of Jacob answered Shechem and Hamor his father deceitfully, and said, because he had defiled Dinah their sister:

14 And they said unto them, We cannot do this thing, to give our sister to one that is uncircumcised; for that *were* a reproach unto us:

15 But in this will we consent unto you: If ye will be as we *be*, that every male of you be circumcised;

16 Then will we give our daughters unto you, and we will take your daughters to us, and we will dwell with you, and we will become one people.

17 But if ye will not hearken unto us, to be circumcised; then will we take our daughter, and we will be gone.

18 And their words pleased Hamor, and Shechem Hamor's son.

19 And the young man deferred not to do the thing, because he had delight in Jacob's daughter: and he *was* more honourable than all the house of his father.

20 And Hamor and Shechem his son came unto the gate of their city, and communed with the men of their city, saying,

21 These men *are* peaceable with us; therefore let them dwell in the land, and trade therein; for the land, behold, *it is* large enough for them; let us take their daughters to us for wives, and let us give them our daughters.

22 Only herein will the men consent unto us for to dwell with us, to be one people, if every male among us be circumcised, as they *are* circumcised.

23 *Shall* not their cattle and their substance and every beast of theirs *be* ours? only let us consent unto them, and they will dwell with us.

24 And unto Hamor and unto Shechem his son hearkened all that went out of the gate of his city; and every male was circumcised, all that went out of the gate of his city.

25 And it came to pass on the third day, when they were sore, that two of the sons of Jacob, Simeon and Levi, Dinah's brethren, took each man his sword, and came upon the city boldly, and slew all the males.

26 And they slew Hamor and Shechem his son with the edge of the sword, and took Dinah out of Shechem's house, and went out.

27 The sons of Jacob came upon the slain, and spoiled the city, because they had defiled their sister.

28 They took their sheep, and their oxen, and their asses, and that which *was* in the city, and that which *was* in the field,

29 And all their wealth, and all their little ones, and their wives took they captive, and spoiled even all that *was* in the house.

30 And Jacob said to Simeon and Levi, Ye have troubled me to make me to stink among the inhabitants of the land, among the Canaanites and the Perizzites: and I *being* few in number, they shall gather themselves together against me, and slay me; and I shall be destroyed, I and my house.

31 And they said, Should he deal with our sister as with an harlot?

35 And God said unto Jacob, Arise, go up to Beth-el, and dwell there: and make there an altar unto God, that appeared unto thee when thou fleddest from the face of Esau thy brother.

2 Then Jacob said unto his household, and to all that *were* with him, Put away the strange gods that *are* among you,

and be clean, and change your garments:
3 And let us arise, and go up to Beth-
el; and I will make there an altar unto
God, who answered me in the day of my
distress, and was with me in the way
which I went.
4 And they gave unto Jacob all the
strange gods which *were* in their hand,
and *all their* earrings which *were* in
their ears; and Jacob hid them under
the oak which *was* by Shechem.
5 And they journeyed: and the terror
of God was upon the cities that *were*
round about them, and they did not
pursue after the sons of Jacob.
6 So Jacob came to Luz, which *is* in
the land of Canaan, that *is*, Beth-el, he
and all the people that *were* with him.
7 And he built there an altar, and
called the place El-beth-el: because
there God appeared unto him, when he
fled from the face of his brother.
8 But Deborah Rebekah's nurse died,
and she was buried beneath Beth-el
under an oak: and the name of it was
called Allon-bachuth.
9 And God appeared unto Jacob
again, when he came out of Padan-
aram, and blessed him.
10 And God said unto him, Thy name
is Jacob: thy name shall not be called
any more Jacob, but Israel shall be thy
name: and he called his name Israel.
11 And God said unto him, I *am* God
Almighty: be fruitful and multiply; a
nation and a company of nations shall
be of thee, and kings shall come out of
thy loins;
12 And the land which I gave
Abraham and Isaac, to thee I will give
it, and to thy seed after thee will I give
the land.
13 And God went up from him in the
place where he talked with him.
14 And Jacob set up a pillar in the
place where he talked with him, *even* a
pillar of stone: and he poured a drink
offering thereon, and he poured oil
thereon.
15 And Jacob called the name of the
place where God spake with him, Beth-
el.
16 And they journeyed from Beth-el;
and there was but a little way to come
to Ephrath: and Rachel travailed, and
she had hard labour.
17 And it came to pass, when she was
in hard labour, that the midwife said
unto her, Fear not; thou shalt have this
son also.
18 And it came to pass, as her soul
was in departing, (for she died) that she
called his name Ben-oni: but his father
called him Benjamin.
19 And Rachel died, and was buried
in the way to Ephrath, which *is* Beth-
lehem.
20 And Jacob set a pillar upon her
grave: that *is* the pillar of Rachel's
grave unto this day.
21 And Israel journeyed, and spread
his tent beyond the tower of Edar.
22 And it came to pass, when Israel
dwelt in that land, that Reuben went
and lay with Bilhah his father's concubine: and Israel heard *it*. Now the sons
of Jacob were twelve:
23 The sons of Leah; Reuben, Jacob's
firstborn, and Simeon, and Levi, and
Judah, and Issachar, and Zebulun:
24 The sons of Rachel; Joseph, and
Benjamin:
25 And the sons of Bilhah, Rachel's
handmaid; Dan, and Naphtali:
26 And the sons of Zilpah, Leah's
handmaid; Gad, and Asher: these *are*

the sons of Jacob, which were born to
him in Padan-aram.
27 And Jacob came unto Isaac his
father unto Mamre, unto the city of
Arbah, which *is* Hebron, where
Abraham and Isaac sojourned.
28 And the days of Isaac were an hundred and fourscore years.
29 And Isaac gave up the ghost, and
died, and was gathered unto his people,
being old and full of days: and his sons
Esau and Jacob buried him.

36 Now these *are* the generations of
Esau, who *is* Edom.
2 Esau took his wives of the daughters of Canaan; Adah the daughter of
Elon the Hittite, and Aholibamah the
daughter of Anah the daughter of
Zibeon the Hivite;
3 And Bashemath Ishmael's daughter,
sister of Nebajoth.
4 And Adah bare to Esau Eliphaz;
and Bashemath bare Reuel;
5 And Aholibamah bare Jeush, and
Jaalam, and Korah: these *are* the sons
of Esau, which were born unto him in
the land of Canaan.
6 And Esau took his wives, and his
sons, and his daughters, and all the
persons of his house, and his cattle, and
all his beasts, and all his substance,
which he had got in the land of Canaan;
and went into the country from the face
of his brother Jacob.
7 For their riches were more than that
they might dwell together; and the land
wherein they were strangers could not
bear them because of their cattle.
8 Thus dwelt Esau in mount Seir:
Esau *is* Edom.
9 And these *are* the generations of
Esau the father of the Edomites in
mount Seir:
10 These *are* the names of Esau's
sons; Eliphaz the son of Adah the wife
of Esau, Reuel the son of Bashemath
the wife of Esau.
11 And the sons of Eliphaz were
Teman, Omar, Zepho, and Gatam, and
Kenaz.
12 And Timna was concubine to
Eliphaz Esau's son; and she bare to
Eliphaz Amalek: these *were* the sons of
Adah Esau's wife.
13 And these *are* the sons of Reuel;
Nahath, and Zerah, Shammah, and
Mizzah: these were the sons of
Bashemath Esau's wife.
14 And these were the sons of
Aholibamah, the daughter of Anah the
daughter of Zibeon, Esau's wife: and
she bare to Esau Jeush, and Jaalam,
and Korah.
15 These *were* dukes of the sons of
Esau: the sons of Eliphaz the firstborn
son of Esau; duke Teman, duke Omar,
duke Zepho, duke Kenaz,
16 Duke Korah, duke Gatam, *and*
duke Amalek: these *are* the dukes *that*
came of Eliphaz in the land of Edom;
these *were* the sons of Adah.
17 And these *are* the sons of Reuel
Esau's son; duke Nahath, duke Zerah,
duke Shammah, duke Mizzah: these *are*
the dukes *that came* of Reuel in the
land of Edom; these *are* the sons of
Bashemath Esau's wife.
18 And these *are* the sons of
Aholibamah Esau's wife; duke Jeush,
duke Jaalam, duke Korah: these *were*
the dukes *that came* of Aholibamah
the daughter of Anah, Esau's wife.
19 These *are* the sons of Esau, who *is*
Edom, and these *are* their dukes.
20 These *are* the sons of Seir the
Horite, who inhabited the land; Lotan,
and Shobal, and Zibeon, and Anah,

21 And Dishon, and Ezer, and Dishan: these *are* the dukes of the Horites, the children of Seir in the land of Edom.

22 And the children of Lotan were Hori and Hemam; and Lotan's sister *was* Timna.

23 And the children of Shobal *were* these; Alvan, and Manahath, and Ebal, Shepho, and Onam.

24 And these *are* the children of Zibeon; both Ajah, and Anah: this *was* *that* Anah that found the mules in the wilderness, as he fed the asses of Zibeon his father.

25 And the children of Anah *were* these; Dishon, and Aholibamah the daughter of Anah.

26 And these *are* the children of Dishon; Hemdan, and Eshban, and Ithran, and Cheran.

27 The children of Ezer *are* these; Bilhan, and Zaavan, and Akan.

28 The children of Dishan *are* these; Uz, and Aran.

29 These *are* the dukes *that came* of the Horites; duke Lotan, duke Shobal, duke Zibeon, duke Anah,

30 Duke Dishon, duke Ezer, duke Dishan: these *are* the dukes *that came* of Hori, among their dukes in the land of Seir.

31 And these *are* the kings that reigned in the land of Edom, before there reigned any king over the children of Israel.

32 And Bela the son of Beor reigned in Edom: and the name of his city *was* Dinhabah.

33 And Bela died, and Jobab the son of Zerah of Bozrah reigned in his stead.

34 And Jobab died, and Husham of the land of Temani reigned in his stead.

35 And Husham died, and Hadad the son of Bedad, who smote Midian in the field of Moab, reigned in his stead: and the name of his city *was* Avith.

36 And Hadad died, and Samlah of Masrekah reigned in his stead.

37 And Samlah died, and Saul of Rehoboth *by* the river reigned in his stead.

38 And Saul died, and Baal-hanan the son of Achbor reigned in his stead.

39 And Baal-hanan the son of Achbor died, and Hadar reigned in his stead: and the name of his city *was* Pau; and his wife's name *was* Mehetabel, the daughter of Matred, the daughter of Mezahab.

40 And these *are* the names of the dukes *that came* of Esau, according to their families, after their places, by their names; duke Timnah, duke Alvah, duke Jetheth,

41 Duke Aholibamah, duke Elah, duke Pinon,

42 Duke Kenaz, duke Teman, duke Mibzar,

43 Duke Magdiel, duke Iram: these *be* the dukes of Edom, according to their habitations in the land of their possession: he *is* Esau the father of the Edomites.

37 And Jacob dwelt in the land wherein his father was a stranger, in the land of Canaan.

2 These *are* the generations of Jacob. Joseph, *being* seventeen years old, was feeding the flock with his brethren; and the lad *was* with the sons of Bilhah, and with the sons of Zilpah, his father's wives: and Joseph brought unto his father their evil report.

3 Now Israel loved Joseph more than all his children, because he *was* the son of his old age: and he made him a coat of *many* colours.

4 And when his brethren saw that their father loved him more than all his brethren, they hated him, and could not speak peaceably unto him.

5 And Joseph dreamed a dream, and he told *it* his brethren: and they hated him yet the more.

6 And he said unto them, Hear, I pray you, this dream which I have dreamed:

7 For, behold, we *were* binding sheaves in the field, and, lo, my sheaf arose, and also stood upright; and, behold, your sheaves stood round about, and made obeisance to my sheaf.

8 And his brethren said to him, Shalt thou indeed reign over us? or shalt thou indeed have dominion over us? And they hated him yet the more for his dreams, and for his words.

9 And he dreamed yet another dream, and told it his brethren, and said, Behold, I have dreamed a dream more; and, behold, the sun and the moon and the eleven stars made obeisance to me.

10 And he told *it* to his father, and to his brethren: and his father rebuked him, and said unto him, What *is* this dream that thou hast dreamed? Shall I and thy mother and thy brethren indeed come to bow down ourselves to thee to the earth?

11 And his brethren envied him; but his father observed the saying.

12 And his brethren went to feed their father's flock in Shechem.

13 And Israel said unto Joseph, Do not thy brethren feed *the flock* in Shechem? come, and I will send thee unto them. And he said to him, Here *am I*.

14 And he said to him, Go, I pray thee, see whether it be well with thy brethren, and well with the flocks; and bring me word again. So he sent him out of the vale of Hebron, and he came to Shechem.

15 And a certain man found him, and, behold, *he was* wandering in the field: and the man asked him, saying, What seekest thou?

16 And he said, I seek my brethren: tell me, I pray thee, where they feed *their flocks*.

17 And the man said, They are departed hence; for I heard them say, Let us go to Dothan. And Joseph went after his brethren, and found them in Dothan.

18 And when they saw him afar off, even before he came near unto them, they conspired against him to slay him.

19 And they said one to another, Behold, this dreamer cometh.

20 Come now therefore, and let us slay him, and cast him into some pit, and we will say, Some evil beast hath devoured him: and we shall see what will become of his dreams.

21 And Reuben heard *it*, and he delivered him out of their hands; and said, Let us not kill him.

22 And Reuben said unto them, Shed no blood, *but* cast him into this pit that *is* in the wilderness, and lay no hand upon him; that he might rid him out of their hands, to deliver him to his father again.

23 And it came to pass, when Joseph was come unto his brethren, that they stript Joseph out of his coat, *his* coat of *many* colours that *was* on him;

24 And they took him, and cast him into a pit: and the pit *was* empty, *there was* no water in it.

25 And they sat down to eat bread: and they lifted up their eyes and looked, and, behold, a company of Ishmeelites came from Gilead with

their camels bearing spicery and balm and myrrh, going to carry *it* down to Egypt.

26 And Judah said unto his brethren, What profit *is it* if we slay our brother, and conceal his blood?

27 Come, and let us sell him to the Ishmeelites, and let not our hand be upon him; for he *is* our brother *and* our flesh. And his brethren were content.

28 Then there passed by Midianites merchantmen; and they drew and lifted up Joseph out of the pit, and sold Joseph to the Ishmeelites for twenty *pieces* of silver: and they brought Joseph into Egypt.

29 And Reuben returned unto the pit; and, behold, Joseph *was* not in the pit; and he rent his clothes.

30 And he returned unto his brethren, and said, The child *is* not; and I, whither shall I go?

31 And they took Joseph's coat, and killed a kid of the goats, and dipped the coat in the blood;

32 And they sent the coat of *many* colours, and they brought *it* to their father; and said, This have we found: know now whether it *be* thy son's coat or no.

33 And he knew it, and said, *It is* my son's coat; an evil beast hath devoured him; Joseph is without doubt rent in pieces.

34 And Jacob rent his clothes, and put sackcloth upon his loins, and mourned for his son many days.

35 And all his sons and all his daughters rose up to comfort him; but he refused to be comforted; and he said, For I will go down into the grave unto my son mourning. Thus his father wept for him.

36 And the Midianites sold him into Egypt unto Potiphar, an officer of Pharaoh's, *and* captain of the guard.

38 And it came to pass at that time, that Judah went down from his brethren, and turned in to a certain Adullamite, whose name *was* Hirah.

2 And Judah saw there a daughter of a certain Canaanite, whose name *was* Shuah; and he took her, and went in unto her.

3 And she conceived, and bare a son; and he called his name Er.

4 And she conceived again, and bare a son; and she called his name Onan.

5 And she yet again conceived, and bare a son; and called his name Shelah: and he was at Chezib, when she bare him.

6 And Judah took a wife for Er his firstborn, whose name *was* Tamar.

7 And Er, Judah's firstborn, was wicked in the sight of the LORD; and the LORD slew him.

8 And Judah said unto Onan, Go in unto thy brother's wife, and marry her, and raise up seed to thy brother.

9 And Onan knew that the seed should not be his; and it came to pass, when he went in unto his brother's wife, that he spilled *it* on the ground, lest that he should give seed to his brother.

10 And the thing which he did displeased the LORD: wherefore he slew him also.

11 Then said Judah to Tamar his daughter in law, Remain a widow at thy father's house, till Shelah my son be grown: for he said, Lest peradventure he die also, as his brethren *did*. And Tamar went and dwelt in her father's house.

12 And in process of time the daughter of Shuah Judah's wife died; and Judah was comforted, and went up unto his sheepshearers to Timnath, he and his friend Hirah the Adullamite.

13 And it was told Tamar, saying, Behold thy father in law goeth up to Timnath to shear his sheep.

14 And she put her widow's garments off from her, and covered her with a vail, and wrapped herself, and sat in an open place, which *is* by the way to Timnath; for she saw that Shelah was grown, and she was not given unto him to wife.

15 When Judah saw her, he thought her *to be* an harlot; because she had covered her face.

16 And he turned unto her by the way, and said, Go to, I pray thee, let me come in unto thee; (for he knew not that she *was* his daughter in law.) And she said, What wilt thou give me, that thou mayest come in unto me?

17 And he said, I will send *thee* a kid from the flock. And she said, Wilt thou give *me* a pledge, till thou send *it*?

18 And he said, What pledge shall I give thee? And she said, Thy signet, and thy bracelets, and thy staff that *is* in thine hand. And he gave *it* her, and came in unto her, and she conceived by him.

19 And she arose, and went away, and laid by her vail from her, and put on the garments of her widowhood.

20 And Judah sent the kid by the hand of his friend the Adullamite, to receive *his* pledge from the woman's hand: but he found her not.

21 Then he asked the men of that place, saying, Where *is* the harlot, that *was* openly by the way side? And they said, There was no harlot in this *place*.

22 And he returned to Judah, and said, I cannot find her; and also the men of the place said, *that* there was no harlot in this *place*.

23 And Judah said, Let her take *it* to her, lest we be shamed: behold, I sent this kid, and thou hast not found her.

24 And it came to pass about three months after, that it was told Judah, saying, Tamar thy daughter in law hath played the harlot; and also, behold, she *is* with child by whoredom. And Judah said, Bring her forth, and let her be burnt.

25 When she *was* brought forth, she sent to her father in law, saying, By the man, whose these *are*, *am* I with child: and she said, Discern, I pray thee, whose *are* these, the signet, and bracelets, and staff.

26 And Judah acknowledged *them*, and said, She hath been more righteous than I; because that I gave her not to Shelah my son. And he knew her again no more.

27 And it came to pass in the time of her travail, that, behold, twins *were* in her womb.

28 And it came to pass, when she travailed, that *the one* put out *his* hand: and the midwife took and bound upon his hand a scarlet thread, saying, This came out first.

29 And it came to pass, as he drew back his hand, that, behold, his brother came out: and she said, How hast thou broken forth? *this* breach *be* upon thee: therefore his name was called Pharez.

30 And afterward came out his brother, that had the scarlet thread upon his hand: and his name was called Zarah.

39 And Joseph was brought down to Egypt; and Potiphar, an officer of Pharaoh, captain of the guard, an

Egyptian, bought him of the hands of the Ishmeelites, which had brought him down thither.

2 And the LORD was with Joseph, and he was a prosperous man; and he was in the house of his master the Egyptian.

3 And his master saw that the LORD *was* with him, and that the LORD made all that he did to prosper in his hand.

4 And Joseph found grace in his sight, and he served him: and he made him overseer over his house, and all *that* he had he put into his hand.

5 And it came to pass from the time *that* he had made him overseer in his house, and over all that he had, that the LORD blessed the Egyptian's house for Joseph's sake; and the blessing of the LORD was upon all that he had in the house, and in the field.

6 And he left all that he had in Joseph's hand; and he knew not ought he had, save the bread which he did eat. And Joseph was *a* goodly *person*, and well favoured.

7 And it came to pass after these things, that his master's wife cast her eyes upon Joseph; and she said, Lie with me.

8 But he refused, and said unto his master's wife, Behold, my master wotteth not what *is* with me in the house, and he hath committed all that he hath to my hand;

9 *There is* none greater in this house than I; neither hath he kept back any thing from me but thee, because thou *art* his wife: how then can I do this great wickedness, and sin against God?

10 And it came to pass, as she spake to Joseph day by day, that he hearkened not unto her, to lie by her, *or* to be with her.

11 And it came to pass about this time, that *Joseph* went into the house to do his business; and *there was* none of the men of the house there within.

12 And she caught him by his garment, saying, Lie with me: and he left his garment in her hand, and fled, and got him out.

13 And it came to pass, when she saw that he had left his garment in her hand, and was fled forth,

14 That she called unto the men of her house, and spake unto them, saying, See, he hath brought in an Hebrew unto us to mock us; he came in unto me to lie with me, and I cried with a loud voice:

15 And it came to pass, when he heard that I lifted up my voice and cried, that he left his garment with me, and fled, and got him out.

16 And she laid up his garment by her, until his lord came home.

17 And she spake unto him according to these words, saying, The Hebrew servant, which thou hast brought unto us, came in unto me to mock me:

18 And it came to pass, as I lifted up my voice and cried, that he left his garment with me, and fled out.

19 And it came to pass, when his master heard the words of his wife, which she spake unto him, saying, After this manner did thy servant to me; that his wrath was kindled.

20 And Joseph's master took him, and put him into the prison, a place where the king's prisoners *were* bound: and he was there in the prison.

21 But the LORD was with Joseph, and shewed him mercy, and gave him favour in the sight of the keeper of the prison.

22 And the keeper of the prison committed to Joseph's hand all the prisoners that *were* in the prison; and whatsoever they did there, he was the doer *of it*.

23 The keeper of the prison looked not to any thing *that was* under his hand; because the LORD was with him, and *that* which he did, the LORD made *it* to prosper.

40 And it came to pass after these things, *that* the butler of the king of Egypt and *his* baker had offended their lord the king of Egypt.

2 And Pharaoh was wroth against two *of* his officers, against the chief of the butlers, and against the chief of the bakers.

3 And he put them in ward in the house of the captain of the guard, into the prison, the place where Joseph *was* bound.

4 And the captain of the guard charged Joseph with them, and he served them: and they continued a season in ward.

5 And they dreamed a dream both of them, each man his dream in one night, each man according to the interpretation of his dream, the butler and the baker of the king of Egypt, which *were* bound in the prison.

6 And Joseph came in unto them in the morning, and looked upon them, and, behold, they *were* sad.

7 And he asked Pharaoh's officers that *were* with him in the ward of his lord's house, saying, Wherefore look ye *so* sadly to day?

8 And they said unto him, We have dreamed a dream, and *there is* no interpreter of it. And Joseph said unto them, *Do* not interpretations *belong* to God? tell me *them*, I pray you.

9 And the chief butler told his dream to Joseph, and said to him, In my dream, behold, a vine *was* before me;

10 And in the vine *were* three branches: and it *was* as though it budded, *and* her blossoms shot forth; and the clusters thereof brought forth ripe grapes:

11 And Pharaoh's cup *was* in my hand: and I took the grapes, and pressed them into Pharaoh's cup, and I gave the cup into Pharaoh's hand.

12 And Joseph said unto him, This *is* the interpretation of it: The three branches *are* three days:

13 Yet within three days shall Pharaoh lift up thine head, and restore thee unto thy place: and thou shalt deliver Pharaoh's cup into his hand, after the former manner when thou wast his butler.

14 But think on me when it shall be well with thee, and shew kindness, I pray thee, unto me, and make mention of me unto Pharaoh, and bring me out of this house:

15 For indeed I was stolen away out of the land of the Hebrews: and here also have I done nothing that they should put me into the dungeon.

16 When the chief baker saw that the interpretation was good, he said unto Joseph, I also *was* in my dream, and, behold, *I had* three white baskets on my head:

17 And in the uppermost basket *there was* of all manner of bakemeats for Pharaoh; and the birds did eat them out of the basket upon my head.

18 And Joseph answered and said, This *is* the interpretation thereof: The three baskets *are* three days:

19 Yet within three days shall Pharaoh lift up thy head from off thee,

and shall hang thee on a tree; and the
birds shall eat thy flesh from off thee.
20 And it came to pass the third day,
which was Pharaoh's birthday, that he
made a feast unto all his servants: and
he lifted up the head of the chief butler
and of the chief baker among his servants.
21 And he restored the chief butler
unto his butlership again; and he gave
the cup into Pharaoh's hand:
22 But he hanged the chief baker: as
Joseph had interpreted to them.
23 Yet did not the chief butler remember Joseph, but forgat him.

41 And it came to pass at the end of
two full years, that Pharaoh
dreamed: and, behold, he stood by the
river.
2 And, behold, there came up out of
the river seven well favoured kine and
fatfleshed; and they fed in a meadow.
3 And, behold, seven other kine came
up after them out of the river, ill
favoured and leanfleshed; and stood by
the *other* kine upon the brink of the
river.
4 And the ill favoured and leanfleshed kine did eat up the seven well
favoured and fat kine. So Pharaoh
awoke.
5 And he slept and dreamed the second time: and, behold, seven ears of
corn came up upon one stalk, rank and
good.
6 And, behold, seven thin ears and
blasted with the east wind sprung up
after them.
7 And the seven thin ears devoured
the seven rank and full ears. And
Pharaoh awoke, and, behold, *it was* a
dream.
8 And it came to pass in the morning
that his spirit was troubled; and he sent
and called for all the magicians of
Egypt, and all the wise men thereof:
and Pharaoh told them his dream; but
there was none that could interpret
them unto Pharaoh.
9 Then spake the chief butler unto
Pharaoh, saying, I do remember my
faults this day:
10 Pharaoh was wroth with his servants, and put me in ward in the captain of the guard's house, *both* me and
the chief baker:
11 And we dreamed a dream in one
night, I and he; we dreamed each man
according to the interpretation of his
dream.
12 And *there was* there with us a
young man, an Hebrew, servant to the
captain of the guard; and we told him,
and he interpreted to us our dreams; to
each man according to his dream he did
interpret.
13 And it came to pass, as he interpreted to us, so it was; me he restored
unto mine office, and him he hanged.
14 Then Pharaoh sent and called
Joseph, and they brought him hastily
out of the dungeon: and he shaved
himself, and changed his raiment, and
came in unto Pharaoh.
15 And Pharaoh said unto Joseph, I
have dreamed a dream, and *there is*
none that can interpret it: and I have
heard say of thee, *that* thou canst
understand a dream to interpret it.
16 And Joseph answered Pharaoh,
saying, *It is* not in me: God shall give
Pharaoh an answer of peace.
17 And Pharaoh said unto Joseph, In
my dream, behold, I stood upon the
bank of the river:
18 And, behold, there came up out of
the river seven kine, fatfleshed and

well favoured; and they fed in a meadow:
19 And, behold, seven other kine
came up after them, poor and very ill
favoured and leanfleshed, such as I
never saw in all the land of Egypt for
badness:
20 And the lean and the ill favoured
kine did eat up the first seven fat kine:
21 And when they had eaten them up,
it could not be known that they had
eaten them; but they *were* still ill
favoured, as at the beginning. So I
awoke.
22 And I saw in my dream, and,
behold, seven ears came up in one
stalk, full and good:
23 And, behold, seven ears, withered,
thin, *and* blasted with the east wind,
sprung up after them:
24 And the thin ears devoured the
seven good ears: and I told *this* unto
the magicians; but *there was* none that
could declare *it* to me.
25 And Joseph said unto Pharaoh,
The dream of Pharaoh *is* one: God hath
shewed Pharaoh what he *is* about to do.
26 The seven good kine *are* seven
years; and the seven good ears *are*
seven years: the dream *is* one.
27 And the seven thin and ill favoured
kine that came up after them *are* seven
years; and the seven empty ears blasted with the east wind shall be seven
years of famine.
28 This *is* the thing which I have spoken unto Pharaoh: What God *is* about
to do he sheweth unto Pharaoh.
29 Behold, there come seven years of
great plenty throughout all the land of
Egypt:
30 And there shall arise after them
seven years of famine; and all the
plenty shall be forgotten in the land of
Egypt; and the famine shall consume
the land;
31 And the plenty shall not be known
in the land by reason of that famine
following; for it *shall be* very grievous.
32 And for that the dream was doubled unto Pharaoh twice; *it is* because
the thing *is* established by God, and
God will shortly bring it to pass.
33 Now therefore let Pharaoh look
out a man discreet and wise, and set
him over the land of Egypt.
34 Let Pharaoh do *this*, and let him
appoint officers over the land, and take
up the fifth part of the land of Egypt in
the seven plenteous years.
35 And let them gather all the food of
those good years that come, and lay up
corn under the hand of Pharaoh, and
let them keep food in the cities.
36 And that food shall be for store to
the land against the seven years of
famine, which shall be in the land of
Egypt; that the land perish not through
the famine.
37 And the thing was good in the eyes
of Pharaoh, and in the eyes of all his
servants.
38 And Pharaoh said unto his servants, Can we find *such a one* as this *is*,
a man in whom the Spirit of God *is*?
39 And Pharaoh said unto Joseph,
Forasmuch as God hath shewed thee all
this, *there is* none so discreet and wise
as thou *art*:
40 Thou shalt be over my house, and
according unto thy word shall all my
people be ruled: only in the throne will
I be greater than thou.
41 And Pharaoh said unto Joseph,
See, I have set thee over all the land of
Egypt.
42 And Pharaoh took off his ring from
his hand, and put it upon Joseph's

hand, and arrayed him in vestures of fine linen, and put a gold chain about his neck;

43 And he made him to ride in the second chariot which he had; and they cried before him, Bow the knee: and he made him *ruler* over all the land of Egypt.

44 And Pharaoh said unto Joseph, I *am* Pharaoh, and without thee shall no man lift up his hand or foot in all the land of Egypt.

45 And Pharaoh called Joseph's name Zaphnath-paaneah; and he gave him to wife Asenath the daughter of Poti-pherah priest of On. And Joseph went out over *all* the land of Egypt.

46 And Joseph *was* thirty years old when he stood before Pharaoh king of Egypt. And Joseph went out from the presence of Pharaoh, and went throughout all the land of Egypt.

47 And in the seven plenteous years the earth brought forth by handfuls.

48 And he gathered up all the food of the seven years, which were in the land of Egypt, and laid up the food in the cities: the food of the field, which *was* round about every city, laid he up in the same.

49 And Joseph gathered corn as the sand of the sea, very much, until he left numbering; for *it was* without number.

50 And unto Joseph were born two sons before the years of famine came, which Asenath the daughter of Poti-pherah priest of On bare unto him.

51 And Joseph called the name of the firstborn Manasseh: For God, *said he*, hath made me forget all my toil, and all my father's house.

52 And the name of the second called he Ephraim: For God hath caused me to be fruitful in the land of my affliction.

53 And the seven years of plenteousness, that was in the land of Egypt, were ended.

54 And the seven years of dearth began to come, according as Joseph had said: and the dearth was in all lands; but in all the land of Egypt there was bread.

55 And when all the land of Egypt was famished, the people cried to Pharaoh for bread: and Pharaoh said unto all the Egyptians, Go unto Joseph; what he saith to you, do.

56 And the famine was over all the face of the earth: And Joseph opened all the storehouses, and sold unto the Egyptians; and the famine waxed sore in the land of Egypt.

57 And all countries came into Egypt to Joseph for to buy *corn*; because that the famine was *so* sore in all lands.

42 Now when Jacob saw that there was corn in Egypt, Jacob said unto his sons, Why do ye look one upon another?

2 And he said, Behold, I have heard that there is corn in Egypt: get you down thither, and buy for us from thence; that we may live, and not die.

3 And Joseph's ten brethren went down to buy corn in Egypt.

4 But Benjamin, Joseph's brother, Jacob sent not with his brethren; for he said, Lest peradventure mischief befall him.

5 And the sons of Israel came to buy *corn* among those that came: for the famine was in the land of Canaan.

6 And Joseph *was* the governor over the land, *and* he *it was* that sold to all the people of the land: and Joseph's brethren came, and bowed down them-

selves before him *with* their faces to
the earth.
7 And Joseph saw his brethren, and
he knew them, but made himself
strange unto them, and spake roughly
unto them; and he said unto them,
Whence come ye? And they said, From
the land of Canaan to buy food.
8 And Joseph knew his brethren, but
they knew not him.
9 And Joseph remembered the
dreams which he dreamed of them, and
said unto them, Ye *are* spies; to see the
nakedness of the land ye are come.
10 And they said unto him, Nay, my
lord, but to buy food are thy servants
come.
11 We *are* all one man's sons; we *are*
true *men*, thy servants are no spies.
12 And he said unto them, Nay, but to
see the nakedness of the land ye are
come.
13 And they said, Thy servants *are*
twelve brethren, the sons of one man in
the land of Canaan; and, behold, the
youngest *is* this day with our father,
and one *is* not.
14 And Joseph said unto them, That *is*
it that I spake unto you, saying, Ye *are*
spies:
15 Hereby ye shall be proved: By the
life of Pharaoh ye shall not go forth
hence, except your youngest brother
come hither.
16 Send one of you, and let him fetch
your brother, and ye shall be kept in
prison, that your words may be proved,
whether *there be any* truth in you: or
else by the life of Pharaoh surely ye *are*
spies.
17 And he put them all together into
ward three days.
18 And Joseph said unto them the
third day, This do, and live; *for* I fear
God:
19 If ye *be* true *men*, let one of your
brethren be bound in the house of your
prison: go ye, carry corn for the famine
of your houses:
20 But bring your youngest brother
unto me; so shall your words be verified, and ye shall not die. And they did
so.
21 And they said one to another, We
are verily guilty concerning our brother, in that we saw the anguish of his
soul, when he besought us, and we
would not hear; therefore is this distress come upon us.
22 And Reuben answered them, saying, Spake I not unto you, saying, Do
not sin against the child; and ye would
not hear? therefore, behold, also his
blood is required.
23 And they knew not that Joseph
understood *them*; for he spake unto
them by an interpreter.
24 And he turned himself about from
them, and wept; and returned to them
again, and communed with them, and
took from them Simeon, and bound
him before their eyes.
25 Then Joseph commanded to fill
their sacks with corn, and to restore
every man's money into his sack, and to
give them provision for the way: and
thus did he unto them.
26 And they laded their asses with
the corn, and departed thence.
27 And as one of them opened his
sack to give his ass provender in the
inn, he espied his money; for, behold, it
was in his sack's mouth.
28 And he said unto his brethren, My
money is restored; and, lo, *it is* even in
my sack: and their heart failed *them*,

and they were afraid, saying one to
another, What *is* this *that* God hath
done unto us?
29 And they came unto Jacob their
father unto the land of Canaan, and
told him all that befell unto them; saying,
30 The man, *who is* the lord of the
land, spake roughly to us, and took us
for spies of the country.
31 And we said unto him, We *are* true
men; we are no spies:
32 We *be* twelve brethren, sons of our
father; one *is* not, and the youngest *is*
this day with our father in the land of
Canaan.
33 And the man, the lord of the country, said unto us, Hereby shall I know
that ye *are* true *men*; leave one of your
brethren *here* with me, and take *food*
for the famine of your households, and
be gone:
34 And bring your youngest brother
unto me: then shall I know that ye *are*
no spies, but *that* ye *are* true *men: so*
will I deliver you your brother, and ye
shall traffick in the land.
35 And it came to pass as they emptied their sacks, that, behold, every
man's bundle of money *was* in his sack:
and when *both* they and their father
saw the bundles of money, they were
afraid.
36 And Jacob their father said unto
them, Me have ye bereaved *of my children*: Joseph *is* not, and Simeon *is* not,
and ye will take Benjamin *away*: all
these things are against me.
37 And Reuben spake unto his father,
saying, Slay my two sons, if I bring him
not to thee: deliver him into my hand,
and I will bring him to thee again.
38 And he said, My son shall not go
down with you; for his brother is dead,
and he is left alone: if mischief befall
him by the way in the which ye go, then
shall ye bring down my gray hairs with
sorrow to the grave.

43 And the famine *was* sore in the
land.
2 And it came to pass, when they had
eaten up the corn which they had
brought out of Egypt, their father said
unto them, Go again, buy us a little
food.
3 And Judah spake unto him, saying,
The man did solemnly protest unto us,
saying, Ye shall not see my face, except
your brother *be* with you.
4 If thou wilt send our brother with
us, we will go down and buy thee food:
5 But if thou wilt not send *him*, we
will not go down: for the man said unto
us, Ye shall not see my face, except your
brother *be* with you.
6 And Israel said, Wherefore dealt ye
so ill with me, *as* to tell the man whether ye had yet a brother?
7 And they said, The man asked us
straitly of our state, and of our kindred,
saying, *Is* your father yet alive? have ye
another brother? and we told him
according to the tenor of these words:
could we certainly know that he would
say, Bring your brother down?
8 And Judah said unto Israel his
father, Send the lad with me, and we
will arise and go; that we may live, and
not die, both we, and thou, *and* also our
little ones.
9 I will be surety for him; of my hand
shalt thou require him: if I bring him
not unto thee, and set him before thee,
then let me bear the blame for ever:
10 For except we had lingered, surely
now we had returned this second time.
11 And their father Israel said unto
them, If *it must be* so now, do this; take

of the best fruits in the land in your
vessels, and carry down the man a present, a little balm, and a little honey,
spices, and myrrh, nuts, and almonds:
12 And take double money in your
hand; and the money that was brought
again in the mouth of your sacks, carry
it again in your hand; peradventure it
was an oversight:
13 Take also your brother, and arise,
go again unto the man:
14 And God Almighty give you mercy
before the man, that he may send away
your other brother, and Benjamin. If I
be bereaved *of my children*, I am
bereaved.
15 And the men took that present,
and they took double money in their
hand, and Benjamin; and rose up, and
went down to Egypt, and stood before
Joseph.
16 And when Joseph saw Benjamin
with them, he said to the ruler of his
house, Bring *these* men home, and slay,
and make ready; for *these* men shall
dine with me at noon.
17 And the man did as Joseph bade;
and the man brought the men into
Joseph's house.
18 And the men were afraid, because
they were brought into Joseph's house;
and they said, Because of the money
that was returned in our sacks at the
first time are we brought in; that he
may seek occasion against us, and fall
upon us, and take us for bondmen, and
our asses.
19 And they came near to the steward
of Joseph's house, and they communed
with him at the door of the house,
20 And said, O sir, we came indeed
down at the first time to buy food:
21 And it came to pass, when we
came to the inn, that we opened our
sacks, and, behold, *every* man's money
was in the mouth of his sack, our
money in full weight: and we have
brought it again in our hand.
22 And other money have we brought
down in our hands to buy food: we cannot tell who put our money in our
sacks.
23 And he said, Peace *be* to you, fear
not: your God, and the God of your
father, hath given you treasure in your
sacks: I had your money. And he
brought Simeon out unto them.
24 And the man brought the men into
Joseph's house, and gave *them* water,
and they washed their feet; and he gave
their asses provender.
25 And they made ready the present
against Joseph came at noon: for they
heard that they should eat bread there.
26 And when Joseph came home,
they brought him the present which
was in their hand into the house, and
bowed themselves to him to the earth.
27 And he asked them of *their* welfare, and said, *Is* your father well, the
old man of whom ye spake? *Is* he yet
alive?
28 And they answered, Thy servant
our father *is* in good health, he *is* yet
alive. And they bowed down their
heads, and made obeisance.
29 And he lifted up his eyes, and saw
his brother Benjamin, his mother's son,
and said, *Is* this your younger brother,
of whom ye spake unto me? And he
said, God be gracious unto thee, my
son.
30 And Joseph made haste; for his
bowels did yearn upon his brother: and
he sought *where* to weep; and he
entered into *his* chamber, and wept
there.

31 And he washed his face, and went out, and refrained himself, and said, Set on bread.

32 And they set on for him by himself, and for them by themselves, and for the Egyptians, which did eat with him, by themselves: because the Egyptians might not eat bread with the Hebrews; for that *is* an abomination unto the Egyptians.

33 And they sat before him, the firstborn according to his birthright, and the youngest according to his youth: and the men marvelled one at another.

34 And he took *and sent* messes unto them from before him: but Benjamin's mess was five times so much as any of theirs. And they drank, and were merry with him.

44 And he commanded the steward of his house, saying, Fill the men's sacks *with* food, as much as they can carry, and put every man's money in his sack's mouth.

2 And put my cup, the silver cup, in the sack's mouth of the youngest, and his corn money. And he did according to the word that Joseph had spoken.

3 As soon as the morning was light, the men were sent away, they and their asses.

4 *And* when they were gone out of the city, *and* not *yet* far off, Joseph said unto his steward, Up, follow after the men; and when thou dost overtake them, say unto them, Wherefore have ye rewarded evil for good?

5 *Is* not this *it* in which my lord drinketh, and whereby indeed he divineth? ye have done evil in so doing.

6 And he overtook them, and he spake unto them these same words.

7 And they said unto him, Wherefore saith my lord these words? God forbid that thy servants should do according to this thing:

8 Behold, the money, which we found in our sacks' mouths, we brought again unto thee out of the land of Canaan: how then should we steal out of thy lord's house silver or gold?

9 With whomsoever of thy servants it be found, both let him die, and we also will be my lord's bondmen.

10 And he said, Now also *let* it *be* according unto your words: he with whom it is found shall be my servant; and ye shall be blameless.

11 Then they speedily took down every man his sack to the ground, and opened every man his sack.

12 And he searched, *and* began at the eldest, and left at the youngest: and the cup was found in Benjamin's sack.

13 Then they rent their clothes, and laded every man his ass, and returned to the city.

14 And Judah and his brethren came to Joseph's house; for he *was* yet there: and they fell before him on the ground.

15 And Joseph said unto them, What deed *is* this that ye have done? wot ye not that such a man as I can certainly divine?

16 And Judah said, What shall we say unto my lord? what shall we speak? or how shall we clear ourselves? God hath found out the iniquity of thy servants: behold, we *are* my lord's servants, both we, and *he* also with whom the cup is found.

17 And he said, God forbid that I should do so: *but* the man in whose hand the cup is found, he shall be my servant; and as for you, get you up in peace unto your father.

18 Then Judah came near unto him,
and said, Oh my lord, let thy servant, I
pray thee, speak a word in my lord's
ears, and let not thine anger burn
against thy servant: for thou *art* even as
Pharaoh.
19 My lord asked his servants, saying,
Have ye a father, or a brother?
20 And we said unto my lord, We have
a father, an old man, and a child of his
old age, a little one; and his brother is
dead, and he alone is left of his mother,
and his father loveth him.
21 And thou saidst unto thy servants,
Bring him down unto me, that I may set
mine eyes upon him.
22 And we said unto my lord, The lad
cannot leave his father: for *if* he should
leave his father, *his father* would die.
23 And thou saidst unto thy servants,
Except your youngest brother come
down with you, ye shall see my face no
more.
24 And it came to pass when we came
up unto thy servant my father, we told
him the words of my lord.
25 And our father said, Go again, *and*
buy us a little food.
26 And we said, We cannot go down: if
our youngest brother be with us, then
will we go down: for we may not see the
man's face, except our youngest brother *be* with us.
27 And thy servant my father said
unto us, Ye know that my wife bare me
two *sons*:
28 And the one went out from me,
and I said, Surely he is torn in pieces;
and I saw him not since:
29 And if ye take this also from me,
and mischief befall him, ye shall bring
down my gray hairs with sorrow to the
grave.
30 Now therefore when I come to thy
servant my father, and the lad *be* not
with us; seeing that his life is bound up
in the lad's life;
31 It shall come to pass, when he
seeth that the lad *is* not *with us*, that
he will die: and thy servants shall bring
down the gray hairs of thy servant our
father with sorrow to the grave.
32 For thy servant became surety for
the lad unto my father, saying, If I bring
him not unto thee, then I shall bear the
blame to my father for ever.
33 Now therefore, I pray thee, let thy
servant abide instead of the lad a bondman to my lord; and let the lad go up
with his brethren.
34 For how shall I go up to my father,
and the lad *be* not with me? lest peradventure I see the evil that shall come on
my father.

45 Then Joseph could not refrain
himself before all them that
stood by him; and he cried, Cause every
man to go out from me. And there stood
no man with him, while Joseph made
himself known unto his brethren.
2 And he wept aloud: and the
Egyptians and the house of Pharaoh
heard.
3 And Joseph said unto his brethren,
I *am* Joseph; doth my father yet live?
And his brethren could not answer him;
for they were troubled at his presence.
4 And Joseph said unto his brethren,
Come near to me, I pray you. And they
came near. And he said, I *am* Joseph
your brother, whom ye sold into Egypt.
5 Now therefore be not grieved, nor
angry with yourselves, that ye sold me
hither: for God did send me before you
to preserve life.

6 For these two years *hath* the famine
been in the land: and yet *there are* five
years, in the which *there shall* neither
be earing nor harvest.
7 And God sent me before you to
preserve you a posterity in the earth,
and to save your lives by a great deliverance.
8 So now *it was* not you *that* sent me
hither, but God: and he hath made me
a father to Pharaoh, and lord of all his
house, and a ruler throughout all the
land of Egypt.
9 Haste ye, and go up to my father,
and say unto him, Thus saith thy son
Joseph, God hath made me lord of all
Egypt: come down unto me, tarry not:
10 And thou shalt dwell in the land of
Goshen, and thou shalt be near unto
me, thou, and thy children, and thy
children's children, and thy flocks, and
thy herds, and all that thou hast:
11 And there will I nourish thee; for
yet *there are* five years of famine; lest
thou, and thy household, and all that
thou hast, come to poverty.
12 And, behold, your eyes see, and the
eyes of my brother Benjamin, that *it is*
my mouth that speaketh unto you.
13 And ye shall tell my father of all
my glory in Egypt, and of all that ye
have seen; and ye shall haste and bring
down my father hither.
14 And he fell upon his brother
Benjamin's neck, and wept; and Benjamin wept upon his neck.
15 Moreover he kissed all his brethren, and wept upon them: and after
that his brethren talked with him.
16 And the fame thereof was heard in
Pharaoh's house, saying, Joseph's brethren are come: and it pleased Pharaoh
well, and his servants.
17 And Pharaoh said unto Joseph,
Say unto thy brethren, This do ye; lade
your beasts, and go, get you unto the
land of Canaan;
18 And take your father and your
households, and come unto me: and I
will give you the good of the land of
Egypt, and ye shall eat the fat of the
land.
19 Now thou art commanded, this do
ye; take you wagons out of the land of
Egypt for your little ones, and for your
wives, and bring your father, and come.
20 Also regard not your stuff; for the
good of all the land of Egypt *is* yours.
21 And the children of Israel did so:
and Joseph gave them wagons, according to the commandment of Pharaoh,
and gave them provision for the way.
22 To all of them he gave each man
changes of raiment; but to Benjamin he
gave three hundred *pieces* of silver, and
five changes of raiment.
23 And to his father he sent after this
manner; ten asses laden with the good
things of Egypt, and ten she asses laden
with corn and bread and meat for his
father by the way.
24 So he sent his brethren away, and
they departed: and he said unto them,
See that ye fall not out by the way.
25 And they went up out of Egypt,
and came into the land of Canaan unto
Jacob their father,
26 And told him, saying, Joseph *is* yet
alive, and he *is* governor over all the
land of Egypt. And Jacob's heart fainted, for he believed them not.
27 And they told him all the words of
Joseph, which he had said unto them:
and when he saw the wagons which
Joseph had sent to carry him, the spirit
of Jacob their father revived:

28 And Israel said, *It is* enough; Joseph my son *is* yet alive: I will go and see him before I die.

46

And Israel took his journey with all that he had, and came to Beer-sheba, and offered sacrifices unto the God of his father Isaac.

2 And God spake unto Israel in the visions of the night, and said, Jacob, Jacob. And he said, Here *am* I.

3 And he said, I *am* God, the God of thy father: fear not to go down into Egypt; for I will there make of thee a great nation:

4 I will go down with thee into Egypt; and I will also surely bring thee up *again*: and Joseph shall put his hand upon thine eyes.

5 And Jacob rose up from Beer-sheba: and the sons of Israel carried Jacob their father, and their little ones, and their wives, in the wagons which Pharaoh had sent to carry him.

6 And they took their cattle, and their goods, which they had gotten in the land of Canaan, and came into Egypt, Jacob, and all his seed with him:

7 His sons, and his sons' sons with him, his daughters, and his sons' daughters, and all his seed brought he with him into Egypt.

8 And these *are* the names of the children of Israel, which came into Egypt, Jacob and his sons: Reuben, Jacob's firstborn.

9 And the sons of Reuben; Hanoch, and Phallu, and Hezron, and Carmi.

10 And the sons of Simeon; Jemuel, and Jamin, and Ohad, and Jachin, and Zohar, and Shaul the son of a Canaanitish woman.

11 And the sons of Levi; Gershon, Kohath, and Merari.

12 And the sons of Judah; Er, and Onan, and Shelah, and Pharez, and Zerah: but Er and Onan died in the land of Canaan. And the sons of Pharez were Hezron and Hamul.

13 And the sons of Issachar; Tola, and Phuvah, and Job, and Shimron.

14 And the sons of Zebulun; Sered, and Elon, and Jahleel.

15 These *be* the sons of Leah, which she bare unto Jacob in Padan-aram, with his daughter Dinah: all the souls of his sons and his daughters *were* thirty and three.

16 And the sons of Gad; Ziphion, and Haggi, Shuni, and Ezbon, Eri, and Arodi, and Areli.

17 And the sons of Asher; Jimnah, and Ishuah, and Isui, and Beriah, and Serah their sister: and the sons of Beriah; Heber, and Malchiel.

18 These *are* the sons of Zilpah, whom Laban gave to Leah his daughter, and these she bare unto Jacob, *even* sixteen souls.

19 The sons of Rachel Jacob's wife; Joseph, and Benjamin.

20 And unto Joseph in the land of Egypt were born Manasseh and Ephraim, which Asenath the daughter of Poti-pherah priest of On bare unto him.

21 And the sons of Benjamin *were* Belah, and Becher, and Ashbel, Gera, and Naaman, Ehi, and Rosh, Muppim, and Huppim, and Ard.

22 These *are* the sons of Rachel, which were born to Jacob: all the souls *were* fourteen.

23 And the sons of Dan; Hushim.

24 And the sons of Naphtali; Jahzeel, and Guni, and Jezer, and Shillem.

25 These *are* the sons of Bilhah, which
Laban gave unto Rachel his daughter,
and she bare these unto Jacob: all the
souls *were* seven.
26 All the souls that came with Jacob
into Egypt, which came out of his loins,
besides Jacob's sons' wives, all the souls
were threescore and six;
27 And the sons of Joseph, which
were born him in Egypt, *were* two souls:
all the souls of the house of Jacob,
which came into Egypt, *were* threescore and ten.
28 And he sent Judah before him
unto Joseph, to direct his face unto
Goshen; and they came into the land of
Goshen.
29 And Joseph made ready his chariot, and went up to meet Israel his
father, to Goshen, and presented himself unto him; and he fell on his neck,
and wept on his neck a good while.
30 And Israel said unto Joseph, Now
let me die, since I have seen thy face,
because thou *art* yet alive.
31 And Joseph said unto his brethren,
and unto his father's house, I will go up,
and shew Pharaoh, and say unto him,
My brethren, and my father's house,
which *were* in the land of Canaan, are
come unto me;
32 And the men *are* shepherds, for
their trade hath been to feed cattle;
and they have brought their flocks, and
their herds, and all that they have.
33 And it shall come to pass, when
Pharaoh shall call you, and shall say,
What *is* your occupation?
34 That ye shall say, Thy servants'
trade hath been about cattle from our
youth even until now, both we, *and* also
our fathers: that ye may dwell in the
land of Goshen; for every shepherd *is*
an abomination unto the Egyptians.

47 Then Joseph came and told
Pharaoh, and said, My father and
my brethren, and their flocks, and their
herds, and all that they have, are come
out of the land of Canaan; and, behold,
they *are* in the land of Goshen.
2 And he took some of his brethren,
even five men, and presented them
unto Pharaoh.
3 And Pharaoh said unto his brethren, What *is* your occupation? And they
said unto Pharaoh, Thy servants *are*
shepherds, both we, *and* also our
fathers.
4 They said moreover unto Pharaoh,
For to sojourn in the land are we come;
for thy servants have no pasture for
their flocks; for the famine *is* sore in
the land of Canaan: now therefore, we
pray thee, let thy servants dwell in the
land of Goshen.
5 And Pharaoh spake unto Joseph,
saying, Thy father and thy brethren are
come unto thee:
6 The land of Egypt *is* before thee; in
the best of the land make thy father
and brethren to dwell; in the land of
Goshen let them dwell: and if thou
knowest *any* men of activity among
them, then make them rulers over my
cattle.
7 And Joseph brought in Jacob his
father, and set him before Pharaoh: and
Jacob blessed Pharaoh.
8 And Pharaoh said unto Jacob, How
old *art* thou?
9 And Jacob said unto Pharaoh, The
days of the years of my pilgrimage *are*
an hundred and thirty years: few and
evil have the days of the years of my
life been, and have not attained unto
the days of the years of the life of my
fathers in the days of their pilgrimage.

10 And Jacob blessed Pharaoh, and went out from before Pharaoh.

11 And Joseph placed his father and his brethren, and gave them a possession in the land of Egypt, in the best of the land, in the land of Rameses, as Pharaoh had commanded.

12 And Joseph nourished his father, and his brethren, and all his father's household, with bread, according to *their* families.

13 And *there was* no bread in all the land; for the famine *was* very sore, so that the land of Egypt and *all* the land of Canaan fainted by reason of the famine.

14 And Joseph gathered up all the money that was found in the land of Egypt, and in the land of Canaan, for the corn which they bought: and Joseph brought the money into Pharaoh's house.

15 And when money failed in the land of Egypt, and in the land of Canaan, all the Egyptians came unto Joseph, and said, Give us bread: for why should we die in thy presence? for the money faileth.

16 And Joseph said, Give your cattle; and I will give you for your cattle, if money fail.

17 And they brought their cattle unto Joseph: and Joseph gave them bread *in exchange* for horses, and for the flocks, and for the cattle of the herds, and for the asses: and he fed them with bread for all their cattle for that year.

18 When that year was ended, they came unto him the second year, and said unto him, We will not hide *it* from my lord, how that our money is spent; my lord also hath our herds of cattle; there is not ought left in the sight of my lord, but our bodies, and our lands:

19 Wherefore shall we die before thine eyes, both we and our land? buy us and our land for bread, and we and our land will be servants unto Pharaoh: and give *us* seed, that we may live, and not die, that the land be not desolate.

20 And Joseph bought all the land of Egypt for Pharaoh; for the Egyptians sold every man his field, because the famine prevailed over them: so the land became Pharaoh's.

21 And as for the people, he removed them to cities from *one* end of the borders of Egypt even to the *other* end thereof.

22 Only the land of the priests bought he not; for the priests had a portion *assigned them* of Pharaoh, and did eat their portion which Pharaoh gave them: wherefore they sold not their lands.

23 Then Joseph said unto the people, Behold, I have bought you this day and your land for Pharaoh: lo, *here is* seed for you, and ye shall sow the land.

24 And it shall come to pass in the increase, that ye shall give the fifth *part* unto Pharaoh, and four parts shall be your own, for seed of the field, and for your food, and for them of your households, and for food for your little ones.

25 And they said, Thou hast saved our lives: let us find grace in the sight of my lord, and we will be Pharaoh's servants.

26 And Joseph made it a law over the land of Egypt unto this day, *that* Pharaoh should have the fifth *part*; except the land of the priests only, *which* became not Pharaoh's.

27 And Israel dwelt in the land of Egypt, in the country of Goshen; and they had possessions therein, and grew, and multiplied exceedingly.

28 And Jacob lived in the land of
Egypt seventeen years: so the whole
age of Jacob was an hundred forty and
seven years.
29 And the time drew nigh that Israel
must die: and he called his son Joseph,
and said unto him, If now I have found
grace in thy sight, put, I pray thee, thy
hand under my thigh, and deal kindly
and truly with me; bury me not, I pray
thee, in Egypt:
30 But I will lie with my fathers, and
thou shalt carry me out of Egypt, and
bury me in their buryingplace. And he
said, I will do as thou hast said.
31 And he said, Swear unto me. And
he sware unto him. And Israel bowed
himself upon the bed's head.

48 And it came to pass after these
things, that *one* told Joseph,
Behold, thy father *is* sick: and he took
with him his two sons, Manasseh and
Ephraim.
2 And *one* told Jacob, and said,
Behold, thy son Joseph cometh unto
thee: and Israel strengthened himself,
and sat upon the bed.
3 And Jacob said unto Joseph, God
Almighty appeared unto me at Luz in
the land of Canaan, and blessed me,
4 And said unto me, Behold, I will
make thee fruitful, and multiply thee,
and I will make of thee a multitude of
people; and will give this land to thy
seed after thee *for* an everlasting possession.
5 And now thy two sons, Ephraim and
Manasseh, which were born unto thee
in the land of Egypt before I came unto
thee into Egypt, *are* mine; as Reuben
and Simeon, they shall be mine.
6 And thy issue, which thou begettest
after them, shall be thine, *and* shall be
called after the name of their brethren
in their inheritance.
7 And as for me, when I came from
Padan, Rachel died by me in the land of
Canaan in the way, when yet *there was*
but a little way to come unto Ephrath:
and I buried her there in the way of
Ephrath; the same *is* Beth-lehem.
8 And Israel beheld Joseph's sons,
and said, Who *are* these?
9 And Joseph said unto his father,
They *are* my sons, whom God hath
given me in this *place*. And he said,
Bring them, I pray thee, unto me, and I
will bless them.
10 Now the eyes of Israel were dim for
age, *so that* he could not see. And he
brought them near unto him; and he
kissed them, and embraced them.
11 And Israel said unto Joseph, I had
not thought to see thy face: and, lo, God
hath shewed me also thy seed.
12 And Joseph brought them out
from between his knees, and he bowed
himself with his face to the earth.
13 And Joseph took them both,
Ephraim in his right hand toward
Israel's left hand, and Manasseh in his
left hand toward Israel's right hand,
and brought *them* near unto him.
14 And Israel stretched out his right
hand, and laid *it* upon Ephraim's head,
who *was* the younger, and his left hand
upon Manasseh's head, guiding his
hands wittingly; for Manasseh *was* the
firstborn.
15 And he blessed Joseph, and said,
God, before whom my fathers Abraham
and Isaac did walk, the God which fed
me all my life long unto this day,
16 The Angel which redeemed me
from all evil, bless the lads; and let my
name be named on them, and the name
of my fathers Abraham and Isaac; and

let them grow into a multitude in the
midst of the earth.
17 And when Joseph saw that his
father laid his right hand upon the
head of Ephraim, it displeased him:
and he held up his father's hand, to
remove it from Ephraim's head unto
Manasseh's head.
18 And Joseph said unto his father,
Not so, my father: for this *is* the firstborn; put thy right hand upon his head.
19 And his father refused, and said, I
know *it*, my son, I know *it*: he also shall
become a people, and he also shall be
great: but truly his younger brother
shall be greater than he, and his seed
shall become a multitude of nations.
20 And he blessed them that day, saying, In thee shall Israel bless, saying,
God make thee as Ephraim and as
Manasseh: and he set Ephraim before
Manasseh.
21 And Israel said unto Joseph,
Behold, I die: but God shall be with you,
and bring you again unto the land of
your fathers.
22 Moreover I have given to thee one
portion above thy brethren, which I
took out of the hand of the Amorite
with my sword and with my bow.

49 And Jacob called unto his sons,
and said, Gather yourselves
together, that I may tell you *that* which
shall befall you in the last days.
2 Gather yourselves together, and
hear, ye sons of Jacob; and hearken
unto Israel your father.
3 Reuben, thou *art* my firstborn, my
might, and the beginning of my
strength, the excellency of dignity, and
the excellency of power:
4 Unstable as water, thou shalt not
excel; because thou wentest up to thy
father's bed; then defiledst thou *it*: he
went up to my couch.
5 Simeon and Levi *are* brethren;
instruments of cruelty *are in* their
habitations.
6 O my soul, come not thou into their
secret; unto their assembly, mine honour, be not thou united: for in their
anger they slew a man, and in their
selfwill they digged down a wall.
7 Cursed *be* their anger, for *it was*
fierce; and their wrath, for it was cruel:
I will divide them in Jacob, and scatter
them in Israel.
8 Judah, thou *art he* whom thy brethren shall praise: thy hand *shall be* in
the neck of thine enemies; thy father's
children shall bow down before thee.
9 Judah *is* a lion's whelp: from the
prey, my son, thou art gone up: he
stooped down, he couched as a lion, and
as an old lion; who shall rouse him up?
10 The sceptre shall not depart from
Judah, nor a lawgiver from between his
feet, until Shiloh come; and unto him
shall the gathering of the people *be*.
11 Binding his foal unto the vine, and
his ass's colt unto the choice vine; he
washed his garments in wine, and his
clothes in the blood of grapes:
12 His eyes *shall be* red with wine,
and his teeth white with milk.
13 Zebulun shall dwell at the haven of
the sea; and he *shall be* for an haven of
ships; and his border *shall be* unto
Zidon.
14 Issachar *is* a strong ass couching
down between two burdens:
15 And he saw that rest *was* good, and
the land that *it was* pleasant; and
bowed his shoulder to bear, and became
a servant unto tribute.
16 Dan shall judge his people, as one
of the tribes of Israel.

17 Dan shall be a serpent by the way, an adder in the path, that biteth the horse heels, so that his rider shall fall backward.

18 I have waited for thy salvation, O LORD.

19 Gad, a troop shall overcome him: but he shall overcome at the last.

20 Out of Asher his bread *shall be* fat, and he shall yield royal dainties.

21 Naphtali *is* a hind let loose: he giveth goodly words.

22 Joseph *is* a fruitful bough, *even* a fruitful bough by a well; *whose* branches run over the wall:

23 The archers have sorely grieved him, and shot *at him*, and hated him:

24 But his bow abode in strength, and the arms of his hands were made strong by the hands of the mighty *God* of Jacob; (from thence *is* the shepherd, the stone of Israel:)

25 *Even* by the God of thy father, who shall help thee; and by the Almighty, who shall bless thee with blessings of heaven above, blessings of the deep that lieth under, blessings of the breasts, and of the womb:

26 The blessings of thy father have prevailed above the blessings of my progenitors unto the utmost bound of the everlasting hills: they shall be on the head of Joseph, and on the crown of the head of him that was separate from his brethren.

27 Benjamin shall ravin *as* a wolf: in the morning he shall devour the prey, and at night he shall divide the spoil.

28 All these *are* the twelve tribes of Israel: and this *is it* that their father spake unto them, and blessed them; every one according to his blessing he blessed them.

29 And he charged them, and said unto them, I am to be gathered unto my people: bury me with my fathers in the cave that *is* in the field of Ephron the Hittite,

30 In the cave that *is* in the field of Machpelah, which *is* before Mamre, in the land of Canaan, which Abraham bought with the field of Ephron the Hittite for a possession of a buryingplace.

31 There they buried Abraham and Sarah his wife; there they buried Isaac and Rebekah his wife; and there I buried Leah.

32 The purchase of the field and of the cave that *is* therein *was* from the children of Heth.

33 And when Jacob had made an end of commanding his sons, he gathered up his feet into the bed, and yielded up the ghost, and was gathered unto his people.

50 And Joseph fell upon his father's face, and wept upon him, and kissed him.

2 And Joseph commanded his servants the physicians to embalm his father: and the physicians embalmed Israel.

3 And forty days were fulfilled for him; for so are fulfilled the days of those which are embalmed: and the Egyptians mourned for him threescore and ten days.

4 And when the days of his mourning were past, Joseph spake unto the house of Pharaoh, saying, If now I have found grace in your eyes, speak, I pray you, in the ears of Pharaoh, saying,

5 My father made me swear, saying, Lo, I die: in my grave which I have digged for me in the land of Canaan, there shalt thou bury me. Now therefore let me go up, I pray thee, and bury my father, and I will come again.

6 And Pharaoh said, Go up, and bury thy father, according as he made thee swear.

7 And Joseph went up to bury his father: and with him went up all the servants of Pharaoh, the elders of his house, and all the elders of the land of Egypt,

8 And all the house of Joseph, and his brethren, and his father's house: only their little ones, and their flocks, and their herds, they left in the land of Goshen.

9 And there went up with him both chariots and horsemen: and it was a very great company.

10 And they came to the threshingfloor of Atad, which *is* beyond Jordan, and there they mourned with a great and very sore lamentation: and he made a mourning for his father seven days.

11 And when the inhabitants of the land, the Canaanites, saw the mourning in the floor of Atad, they said, This *is* a grievous mourning to the Egyptians: wherefore the name of it was called Abel-mizraim, which *is* beyond Jordan.

12 And his sons did unto him according as he commanded them:

13 For his sons carried him into the land of Canaan, and buried him in the cave of the field of Machpelah, which Abraham bought with the field for a possession of a buryingplace of Ephron the Hittite, before Mamre.

14 And Joseph returned into Egypt, he, and his brethren, and all that went up with him to bury his father, after he had buried his father.

15 And when Joseph's brethren saw that their father was dead, they said, Joseph will peradventure hate us, and will certainly requite us all the evil which we did unto him.

16 And they sent a messenger unto Joseph, saying, Thy father did command before he died, saying,

17 So shall ye say unto Joseph, Forgive, I pray thee now, the trespass of thy brethren, and their sin; for they did unto thee evil: and now, we pray thee, forgive the trespass of the servants of the God of thy father. And Joseph wept when they spake unto him.

18 And his brethren also went and fell down before his face; and they said, Behold, we *be* thy servants.

19 And Joseph said unto them, Fear not: for *am* I in the place of God?

20 But as for you, ye thought evil against me; *but* God meant it unto good, to bring to pass, as *it is* this day, to save much people alive.

21 Now therefore fear ye not: I will nourish you, and your little ones. And he comforted them, and spake kindly unto them.

22 And Joseph dwelt in Egypt, he, and his father's house: and Joseph lived an hundred and ten years.

23 And Joseph saw Ephraim's children of the third *generation*: the children also of Machir the son of Manasseh were brought up upon Joseph's knees.

24 And Joseph said unto his brethren, I die: and God will surely visit you, and bring you out of this land unto the land which he sware to Abraham, to Isaac, and to Jacob.

25 And Joseph took an oath of the children of Israel, saying, God will surely visit you, and ye shall carry up my bones from hence.

26 So Joseph died, *being* an hundred and ten years old: and they embalmed him, and he was put in a coffin in Egypt.

THE SECOND BOOK OF MOSES

CALLED

EXODUS

1 Now these *are* the names of the
children of Israel, which came into
Egypt; every man and his household
came with Jacob.
2 Reuben, Simeon, Levi, and Judah,
3 Issachar, Zebulun, and Benjamin,
4 Dan, and Naphtali, Gad, and Asher.
5 And all the souls that came out of
the loins of Jacob were seventy souls:
for Joseph was in Egypt *already*.
6 And Joseph died, and all his brethren, and all that generation.
7 And the children of Israel were
fruitful, and increased abundantly, and
multiplied, and waxed exceeding
mighty; and the land was filled with
them.
8 Now there arose up a new king over
Egypt, which knew not Joseph.
9 And he said unto his people, Behold,
the people of the children of Israel *are*
more and mightier than we:
10 Come on, let us deal wisely with
them; lest they multiply, and it come to
pass, that, when there falleth out any
war, they join also unto our enemies,
and fight against us, and *so* get them up
out of the land.
11 Therefore they did set over them
taskmasters to afflict them with their
burdens. And they built for Pharaoh
treasure cities, Pithom and Raamses.
12 But the more they afflicted them,
the more they multiplied and grew.
And they were grieved because of the
children of Israel.
13 And the Egyptians made the children of Israel to serve with rigour:
14 And they made their lives bitter
with hard bondage, in morter, and in
brick, and in all manner of service in
the field: all their service, wherein they
made them serve, *was* with rigour.
15 And the king of Egypt spake to the
Hebrew midwives, of which the name
of the one *was* Shiphrah, and the name
of the other Puah:
16 And he said, When ye do the office
of a midwife to the Hebrew women,
and see *them* upon the stools; if it *be* a
son, then ye shall kill him: but if it *be* a
daughter, then she shall live.
17 But the midwives feared God, and
did not as the king of Egypt commanded them, but saved the men children
alive.
18 And the king of Egypt called for
the midwives, and said unto them, Why
have ye done this thing, and have saved
the men children alive?
19 And the midwives said unto
Pharaoh, Because the Hebrew women
are not as the Egyptian women; for
they *are* lively, and are delivered ere
the midwives come in unto them.
20 Therefore God dealt well with the
midwives: and the people multiplied,
and waxed very mighty.
21 And it came to pass, because the
midwives feared God, that he made
them houses.
22 And Pharaoh charged all his people, saying, Every son that is born ye
shall cast into the river, and every
daughter ye shall save alive.

2 And there went a man of the house
of Levi, and took *to wife* a daughter
of Levi.

2 And the woman conceived, and bare a son: and when she saw him that he *was a* goodly *child*, she hid him three months.

3 And when she could not longer hide him, she took for him an ark of bulrushes, and daubed it with slime and with pitch, and put the child therein; and she laid *it* in the flags by the river's brink.

4 And his sister stood afar off, to wit what would be done to him.

5 And the daughter of Pharaoh came down to wash *herself* at the river; and her maidens walked along by the river's side; and when she saw the ark among the flags, she sent her maid to fetch it.

6 And when she had opened *it*, she saw the child: and, behold, the babe wept. And she had compassion on him, and said, This *is one* of the Hebrews' children.

7 Then said his sister to Pharaoh's daughter, Shall I go and call to thee a nurse of the Hebrew women, that she may nurse the child for thee?

8 And Pharaoh's daughter said to her, Go. And the maid went and called the child's mother.

9 And Pharaoh's daughter said unto her, Take this child away, and nurse it for me, and I will give *thee* thy wages. And the woman took the child, and nursed it.

10 And the child grew, and she brought him unto Pharaoh's daughter, and he became her son. And she called his name Moses: and she said, Because I drew him out of the water.

11 And it came to pass in those days, when Moses was grown, that he went out unto his brethren, and looked on their burdens: and he spied an Egyptian smiting an Hebrew, one of his brethren.

12 And he looked this way and that way, and when he saw that *there was* no man, he slew the Egyptian, and hid him in the sand.

13 And when he went out the second day, behold, two men of the Hebrews strove together: and he said to him that did the wrong, Wherefore smitest thou thy fellow?

14 And he said, Who made thee a prince and a judge over us? intendest thou to kill me, as thou killedst the Egyptian? And Moses feared, and said, Surely this thing is known.

15 Now when Pharaoh heard this thing, he sought to slay Moses. But Moses fled from the face of Pharaoh, and dwelt in the land of Midian: and he sat down by a well.

16 Now the priest of Midian had seven daughters: and they came and drew *water*, and filled the troughs to water their father's flock.

17 And the shepherds came and drove them away: but Moses stood up and helped them, and watered their flock.

18 And when they came to Reuel their father, he said, How *is it that* ye are come so soon to day?

19 And they said, An Egyptian delivered us out of the hand of the shepherds, and also drew *water* enough for us, and watered the flock.

20 And he said unto his daughters, And where *is* he? why *is* it *that* ye have left the man? call him, that he may eat bread.

21 And Moses was content to dwell with the man: and he gave Moses Zipporah his daughter.

22 And she bare *him* a son, and he called his name Gershom: for he said, I have been a stranger in a strange land.

23 And it came to pass in process of time, that the king of Egypt died: and the children of Israel sighed by reason of the bondage, and they cried, and their cry came up unto God by reason of the bondage.

24 And God heard their groaning, and God remembered his covenant with Abraham, with Isaac, and with Jacob.

25 And God looked upon the children of Israel, and God had respect unto *them*.

3 Now Moses kept the flock of Jethro his father in law, the priest of Midian: and he led the flock to the backside of the desert, and came to the mountain of God, *even* to Horeb.

2 And the angel of the LORD appeared unto him in a flame of fire out of the midst of a bush: and he looked, and, behold, the bush burned with fire, and the bush *was* not consumed.

3 And Moses said, I will now turn aside, and see this great sight, why the bush is not burnt.

4 And when the LORD saw that he turned aside to see, God called unto him out of the midst of the bush, and said, Moses, Moses. And he said, Here *am* I.

5 And he said, Draw not nigh hither: put off thy shoes from off thy feet, for the place whereon thou standest *is* holy ground.

6 Moreover he said, I *am* the God of thy father, the God of Abraham, the God of Isaac, and the God of Jacob. And Moses hid his face; for he was afraid to look upon God.

7 And the LORD said, I have surely seen the affliction of my people which *are* in Egypt, and have heard their cry by reason of their taskmasters; for I know their sorrows;

8 And I am come down to deliver them out of the hand of the Egyptians, and to bring them up out of that land unto a good land and a large, unto a land flowing with milk and honey; unto the place of the Canaanites, and the Hittites, and the Amorites, and the Perizzites, and the Hivites, and the Jebusites.

9 Now therefore, behold, the cry of the children of Israel is come unto me: and I have also seen the oppression wherewith the Egyptians oppress them.

10 Come now therefore, and I will send thee unto Pharaoh, that thou mayest bring forth my people the children of Israel out of Egypt.

11 And Moses said unto God, Who *am* I, that I should go unto Pharaoh, and that I should bring forth the children of Israel out of Egypt?

12 And he said, Certainly I will be with thee; and this *shall be* a token unto thee, that I have sent thee: When thou hast brought forth the people out of Egypt, ye shall serve God upon this mountain.

13 And Moses said unto God, Behold, *when* I come unto the children of Israel, and shall say unto them, The God of your fathers hath sent me unto you; and they shall say to me, What *is* his name? what shall I say unto them?

14 And God said unto Moses, I AM THAT I AM: and he said, Thus shalt thou say unto the children of Israel, I AM hath sent me unto you.

15 And God said moreover unto Moses, Thus shalt thou say unto the children of Israel, The LORD God of your fathers, the God of Abraham, the God of Isaac, and the God of Jacob, hath sent me unto you: this *is* my name for ever, and this *is* my memorial unto all generations.

16 Go, and gather the elders of Israel together, and say unto them, The LORD God of your fathers, the God of Abraham, of Isaac, and of Jacob, appeared unto me, saying, I have surely visited you, and *seen* that which is done to you in Egypt:

17 And I have said, I will bring you up out of the affliction of Egypt unto the land of the Canaanites, and the Hittites, and the Amorites, and the Perizzites, and the Hivites, and the Jebusites, unto a land flowing with milk and honey.

18 And they shall hearken to thy voice: and thou shalt come, thou and the elders of Israel, unto the king of Egypt, and ye shall say unto him, The LORD God of the Hebrews hath met with us: and now let us go, we beseech thee, three days' journey into the wilderness, that we may sacrifice to the LORD our God.

19 And I am sure that the king of Egypt will not let you go, no, not by a mighty hand.

20 And I will stretch out my hand, and smite Egypt with all my wonders which I will do in the midst thereof: and after that he will let you go.

21 And I will give this people favour in the sight of the Egyptians: and it shall come to pass, that, when ye go, ye shall not go empty:

22 But every woman shall borrow of her neighbour, and of her that sojourneth in her house, jewels of silver, and jewels of gold, and raiment: and ye shall put *them* upon your sons, and upon your daughters; and ye shall spoil the Egyptians.

4 And Moses answered and said, But, behold, they will not believe me, nor hearken unto my voice: for they will say, The LORD hath not appeared unto thee.

2 And the LORD said unto him, What *is* that in thine hand? And he said, A rod.

3 And he said, Cast it on the ground. And he cast it on the ground, and it became a serpent; and Moses fled from before it.

4 And the LORD said unto Moses, Put forth thine hand, and take it by the tail. And he put forth his hand, and caught it, and it became a rod in his hand:

5 That they may believe that the LORD God of their fathers, the God of Abraham, the God of Isaac, and the God of Jacob, hath appeared unto thee.

6 And the LORD said furthermore unto him, Put now thine hand into thy bosom. And he put his hand into his bosom: and when he took it out, behold, his hand *was* leprous as snow.

7 And he said, Put thine hand into thy bosom again. And he put his hand into his bosom again; and plucked it out of his bosom, and, behold, it was turned again as his *other* flesh.

8 And it shall come to pass, if they will not believe thee, neither hearken to the voice of the first sign, that they will believe the voice of the latter sign.

9 And it shall come to pass, if they will not believe also these two signs, neither hearken unto thy voice, that thou shalt take of the water of the river, and pour *it* upon the dry *land*: and the water which thou takest out of the river shall become blood upon the dry *land*.

10 And Moses said unto the LORD, O
my Lord, I *am* not eloquent, neither
heretofore, nor since thou hast spoken
unto thy servant: but I *am* slow of
speech, and of a slow tongue.
11 And the LORD said unto him, Who
hath made man's mouth? or who
maketh the dumb, or deaf, or the seeing, or the blind? have not I the LORD?
12 Now therefore go, and I will be
with thy mouth, and teach thee what
thou shalt say.
13 And he said, O my Lord, send, I
pray thee, by the hand *of him whom*
thou wilt send.
14 And the anger of the LORD was
kindled against Moses, and he said, *Is*
not Aaron the Levite thy brother? I
know that he can speak well. And also,
behold, he cometh forth to meet thee:
and when he seeth thee, he will be glad
in his heart.
15 And thou shalt speak unto him,
and put words in his mouth: and I will
be with thy mouth, and with his mouth,
and will teach you what ye shall do.
16 And he shall be thy spokesman
unto the people: and he shall be, *even*
he shall be to thee instead of a mouth,
and thou shalt be to him instead of
God.
17 And thou shalt take this rod in
thine hand, wherewith thou shalt do
signs.
18 And Moses went and returned to
Jethro his father in law, and said unto
him, Let me go, I pray thee, and return
unto my brethren which *are* in Egypt,
and see whether they be yet alive. And
Jethro said to Moses, Go in peace.
19 And the LORD said unto Moses in
Midian, Go, return into Egypt: for all
the men are dead which sought thy life.
20 And Moses took his wife and his
sons, and set them upon an ass, and he
returned to the land of Egypt: and
Moses took the rod of God in his hand.
21 And the LORD said unto Moses,
When thou goest to return into Egypt,
see that thou do all those wonders
before Pharaoh, which I have put in
thine hand: but I will harden his heart,
that he shall not let the people go.
22 And thou shalt say unto Pharaoh,
Thus saith the LORD, Israel *is* my son,
even my firstborn:
23 And I say unto thee, Let my son go,
that he may serve me: and if thou
refuse to let him go, behold, I will slay
thy son, *even* thy firstborn.
24 And it came to pass by the way in
the inn, that the LORD met him, and
sought to kill him.
25 Then Zipporah took a sharp stone,
and cut off the foreskin of her son, and
cast *it* at his feet, and said, Surely a
bloody husband *art* thou to me.
26 So he let him go: then she said, A
bloody husband *thou art*, because of
the circumcision.
27 And the LORD said to Aaron, Go
into the wilderness to meet Moses. And
he went, and met him in the mount of
God, and kissed him.
28 And Moses told Aaron all the
words of the LORD who had sent him,
and all the signs which he had commanded him.
29 And Moses and Aaron went and
gathered together all the elders of the
children of Israel:
30 And Aaron spake all the words
which the LORD had spoken unto
Moses, and did the signs in the sight of
the people.

31 And the people believed: and
when they heard that the LORD had
visited the children of Israel, and that
he had looked upon their affliction,
then they bowed their heads and worshipped.

5 And afterward Moses and Aaron
went in, and told Pharaoh, Thus
saith the LORD God of Israel, Let my
people go, that they may hold a feast
unto me in the wilderness.
2 And Pharaoh said, Who *is* the LORD,
that I should obey his voice to let Israel
go? I know not the LORD, neither will I
let Israel go.
3 And they said, The God of the
Hebrews hath met with us: let us go, we
pray thee, three days' journey into the
desert, and sacrifice unto the LORD our
God; lest he fall upon us with pestilence, or with the sword.
4 And the king of Egypt said unto
them, Wherefore do ye, Moses and
Aaron, let the people from their works?
get you unto your burdens.
5 And Pharaoh said, Behold, the people of the land now *are* many, and ye
make them rest from their burdens.
6 And Pharaoh commanded the same
day the taskmasters of the people, and
their officers, saying,
7 Ye shall no more give the people
straw to make brick, as heretofore: let
them go and gather straw for themselves.
8 And the tale of the bricks, which
they did make heretofore, ye shall lay
upon them; ye shall not diminish *ought*
thereof: for they *be* idle; therefore they
cry, saying, Let us go *and* sacrifice to
our God.
9 Let there more work be laid upon
the men, that they may labour therein;
and let them not regard vain words.
10 And the taskmasters of the people
went out, and their officers, and they
spake to the people, saying, Thus saith
Pharaoh, I will not give you straw.
11 Go ye, get you straw where ye can
find it: yet not ought of your work shall
be diminished.
12 So the people were scattered a-
broad throughout all the land of Egypt
to gather stubble instead of straw.
13 And the taskmasters hasted *them*,
saying, Fulfil your works, *your* daily
tasks, as when there was straw.
14 And the officers of the children of
Israel, which Pharaoh's taskmasters
had set over them, were beaten, *and*
demanded, Wherefore have ye not fulfilled your task in making brick both
yesterday and to day, as heretofore?
15 Then the officers of the children of
Israel came and cried unto Pharaoh,
saying, Wherefore dealest thou thus
with thy servants?
16 There is no straw given unto thy
servants, and they say to us, Make
brick: and, behold, thy servants *are*
beaten; but the fault *is* in thine own
people.
17 But he said, Ye *are* idle, *ye are* idle:
therefore ye say, Let us go *and* do sacrifice to the LORD.
18 Go therefore now, *and* work; for
there shall no straw be given you, yet
shall ye deliver the tale of bricks.
19 And the officers of the children of
Israel did see *that* they *were* in evil
case, after it was said, Ye shall not min-
ish *ought* from your bricks of your daily
task.
20 And they met Moses and Aaron,
who stood in the way, as they came
forth from Pharaoh:

21 And they said unto them, The LORD look upon you, and judge; because ye have made our savour to be abhorred in the eyes of Pharaoh, and in the eyes of his servants, to put a sword in their hand to slay us.

22 And Moses returned unto the LORD, and said, Lord, wherefore hast thou *so* evil entreated this people? why *is* it *that* thou hast sent me?

23 For since I came to Pharaoh to speak in thy name, he hath done evil to this people; neither hast thou delivered thy people at all.

6 Then the LORD said unto Moses, Now shalt thou see what I will do to Pharaoh: for with a strong hand shall he let them go, and with a strong hand shall he drive them out of his land.

2 And God spake unto Moses, and said unto him, I *am* the LORD:

3 And I appeared unto Abraham, unto Isaac, and unto Jacob, by *the name of* God Almighty, but by my name JEHOVAH was I not known to them.

4 And I have also established my covenant with them, to give them the land of Canaan, the land of their pilgrimage, wherein they were strangers.

5 And I have also heard the groaning of the children of Israel, whom the Egyptians keep in bondage; and I have remembered my covenant.

6 Wherefore say unto the children of Israel, I *am* the LORD, and I will bring you out from under the burdens of the Egyptians, and I will rid you out of their bondage, and I will redeem you with a stretched out arm, and with great judgments:

7 And I will take you to me for a people, and I will be to you a God: and ye shall know that I *am* the LORD your God, which bringeth you out from under the burdens of the Egyptians.

8 And I will bring you in unto the land, concerning the which I did swear to give it to Abraham, to Isaac, and to Jacob; and I will give it you for an heritage: I *am* the LORD.

9 And Moses spake so unto the children of Israel: but they hearkened not unto Moses for anguish of spirit, and for cruel bondage.

10 And the LORD spake unto Moses, saying,

11 Go in, speak unto Pharaoh king of Egypt, that he let the children of Israel go out of his land.

12 And Moses spake before the LORD, saying, Behold, the children of Israel have not hearkened unto me; how then shall Pharaoh hear me, who *am* of uncircumcised lips?

13 And the LORD spake unto Moses and unto Aaron, and gave them a charge unto the children of Israel, and unto Pharaoh king of Egypt, to bring the children of Israel out of the land of Egypt.

14 These *be* the heads of their fathers' houses: The sons of Reuben the firstborn of Israel; Hanoch, and Pallu, Hezron, and Carmi: these *be* the families of Reuben.

15 And the sons of Simeon; Jemuel, and Jamin, and Ohad, and Jachin, and Zohar, and Shaul the son of a Canaanitish woman: these *are* the families of Simeon.

16 And these *are* the names of the sons of Levi according to their generations; Gershon, and Kohath, and Merari: and the years of the life of Levi *were* an hundred thirty and seven years.

17 The sons of Gershon; Libni, and
Shimi, according to their families.
18 And the sons of Kohath; Amram,
and Izhar, and Hebron, and Uzziel: and
the years of the life of Kohath *were* an
hundred thirty and three years.
19 And the sons of Merari; Mahali
and Mushi: these *are* the families of
Levi according to their generations.
20 And Amram took him Jochebed
his father's sister to wife; and she bare
him Aaron and Moses: and the years of
the life of Amram *were* an hundred and
thirty and seven years.
21 And the sons of Izhar; Korah, and
Nepheg, and Zichri.
22 And the sons of Uzziel; Mishael,
and Elzaphan, and Zithri.
23 And Aaron took him Elisheba,
daughter of Amminadab, sister of
Naashon, to wife; and she bare him
Nadab, and Abihu, Eleazar, and
Ithamar.
24 And the sons of Korah; Assir, and
Elkanah, and Abiasaph: these *are* the
families of the Korhites.
25 And Eleazar Aaron's son took him
one of the daughters of Putiel to wife;
and she bare him Phinehas: these *are*
the heads of the fathers of the Levites
according to their families.
26 These *are* that Aaron and Moses, to
whom the LORD said, Bring out the
children of Israel from the land of
Egypt according to their armies.
27 These *are* they which spake to
Pharaoh king of Egypt, to bring out the
children of Israel from Egypt: these *are*
that Moses and Aaron.
28 And it came to pass on the day
when the LORD spake unto Moses in the
land of Egypt,
29 That the LORD spake unto Moses,
saying, I *am* the LORD: speak thou unto
Pharaoh king of Egypt all that I say
unto thee.
30 And Moses said before the LORD,
Behold, I *am* of uncircumcised lips, and
how shall Pharaoh hearken unto me?

7 And the LORD said unto Moses, See,
I have made thee a god to Pharaoh:
and Aaron thy brother shall be thy
prophet.
2 Thou shalt speak all that I command thee: and Aaron thy brother shall
speak unto Pharaoh, that he send the
children of Israel out of his land.
3 And I will harden Pharaoh's heart,
and multiply my signs and my wonders
in the land of Egypt.
4 But Pharaoh shall not hearken unto
you, that I may lay my hand upon
Egypt, and bring forth mine armies,
and my people the children of Israel,
out of the land of Egypt by great judgments.
5 And the Egyptians shall know that I
am the LORD, when I stretch forth mine
hand upon Egypt, and bring out the
children of Israel from among them.
6 And Moses and Aaron did as the
LORD commanded them, so did they.
7 And Moses *was* fourscore years old,
and Aaron fourscore and three years
old, when they spake unto Pharaoh.
8 And the LORD spake unto Moses
and unto Aaron, saying,
9 When Pharaoh shall speak unto
you, saying, Shew a miracle for you:
then thou shalt say unto Aaron, Take
thy rod, and cast *it* before Pharaoh, *and*
it shall become a serpent.
10 And Moses and Aaron went in
unto Pharaoh, and they did so as the
LORD had commanded: and Aaron cast
down his rod before Pharaoh, and
before his servants, and it became a
serpent.

11 Then Pharaoh also called the wise men and the sorcerers: now the magicians of Egypt, they also did in like manner with their enchantments.

12 For they cast down every man his rod, and they became serpents: but Aaron's rod swallowed up their rods.

13 And he hardened Pharaoh's heart, that he hearkened not unto them; as the LORD had said.

14 And the LORD said unto Moses, Pharaoh's heart *is* hardened, he refuseth to let the people go.

15 Get thee unto Pharaoh in the morning; lo, he goeth out unto the water; and thou shalt stand by the river's brink against he come; and the rod which was turned to a serpent shalt thou take in thine hand.

16 And thou shalt say unto him, The LORD God of the Hebrews hath sent me unto thee, saying, Let my people go, that they may serve me in the wilderness: and, behold, hitherto thou wouldest not hear.

17 Thus saith the LORD, In this thou shalt know that I *am* the LORD: behold, I will smite with the rod that *is* in mine hand upon the waters which *are* in the river, and they shall be turned to blood.

18 And the fish that *is* in the river shall die, and the river shall stink; and the Egyptians shall lothe to drink of the water of the river.

19 And the LORD spake unto Moses, Say unto Aaron, Take thy rod, and stretch out thine hand upon the waters of Egypt, upon their streams, upon their rivers, and upon their ponds, and upon all their pools of water, that they may become blood; and *that* there may be blood throughout all the land of Egypt, both in *vessels of* wood, and in *vessels of* stone.

20 And Moses and Aaron did so, as the LORD commanded; and he lifted up the rod, and smote the waters that *were* in the river, in the sight of Pharaoh, and in the sight of his servants; and all the waters that *were* in the river were turned to blood.

21 And the fish that *was* in the river died; and the river stank, and the Egyptians could not drink of the water of the river; and there was blood throughout all the land of Egypt.

22 And the magicians of Egypt did so with their enchantments: and Pharaoh's heart was hardened, neither did he hearken unto them; as the LORD had said.

23 And Pharaoh turned and went into his house, neither did he set his heart to this also.

24 And all the Egyptians digged round about the river for water to drink; for they could not drink of the water of the river.

25 And seven days were fulfilled, after that the LORD had smitten the river.

8 And the LORD spake unto Moses, Go unto Pharaoh, and say unto him, Thus saith the LORD, Let my people go, that they may serve me.

2 And if thou refuse to let *them* go, behold, I will smite all thy borders with frogs:

3 And the river shall bring forth frogs abundantly, which shall go up and come into thine house, and into thy bedchamber, and upon thy bed, and into the house of thy servants, and upon thy people, and into thine ovens, and into thy kneadingtroughs:

4 And the frogs shall come up both on thee, and upon thy people, and upon all thy servants.

5 And the LORD spake unto Moses,
Say unto Aaron, Stretch forth thine
hand with thy rod over the streams,
over the rivers, and over the ponds, and
cause frogs to come up upon the land of
Egypt.
6 And Aaron stretched out his hand
over the waters of Egypt; and the frogs
came up, and covered the land of
Egypt.
7 And the magicians did so with their
enchantments, and brought up frogs
upon the land of Egypt.
8 Then Pharaoh called for Moses and
Aaron, and said, Intreat the LORD, that
he may take away the frogs from me,
and from my people; and I will let the
people go, that they may do sacrifice
unto the LORD.
9 And Moses said unto Pharaoh,
Glory over me: when shall I intreat for
thee, and for thy servants, and for thy
people, to destroy the frogs from thee
and thy houses, *that* they may remain
in the river only?
10 And he said, To morrow. And he
said, *Be it* according to thy word: that
thou mayest know that *there is* none
like unto the LORD our God.
11 And the frogs shall depart from
thee, and from thy houses, and from thy
servants, and from thy people; they
shall remain in the river only.
12 And Moses and Aaron went out
from Pharaoh: and Moses cried unto
the LORD because of the frogs which he
had brought against Pharaoh.
13 And the LORD did according to the
word of Moses; and the frogs died out
of the houses, out of the villages, and
out of the fields.
14 And they gathered them together
upon heaps: and the land stank.
15 But when Pharaoh saw that there
was respite, he hardened his heart, and
hearkened not unto them; as the LORD
had said.
16 And the LORD said unto Moses, Say
unto Aaron, Stretch out thy rod, and
smite the dust of the land, that it may
become lice throughout all the land of
Egypt.
17 And they did so; for Aaron
stretched out his hand with his rod, and
smote the dust of the earth, and it
became lice in man, and in beast; all
the dust of the land became lice
throughout all the land of Egypt.
18 And the magicians did so with
their enchantments to bring forth lice,
but they could not: so there were lice
upon man, and upon beast.
19 Then the magicians said unto
Pharaoh, This *is* the finger of God: and
Pharaoh's heart was hardened, and he
hearkened not unto them; as the LORD
had said.
20 And the LORD said unto Moses,
Rise up early in the morning, and stand
before Pharaoh; lo, he cometh forth to
the water; and say unto him, Thus saith
the LORD, Let my people go, that they
may serve me.
21 Else, if thou wilt not let my people
go, behold, I will send swarms *of flies*
upon thee, and upon thy servants, and
upon thy people, and into thy houses:
and the houses of the Egyptians shall
be full of swarms *of flies*, and also the
ground whereon they *are*.
22 And I will sever in that day the
land of Goshen, in which my people
dwell, that no swarms *of flies* shall be
there; to the end thou mayest know
that I *am* the LORD in the midst of the
earth.

23 And I will put a division between
my people and thy people: to morrow
shall this sign be.
24 And the LORD did so; and there
came a grievous swarm *of flies* into the
house of Pharaoh, and *into* his servants' houses, and into all the land of
Egypt: the land was corrupted by reason of the swarm *of flies*.
25 And Pharaoh called for Moses and
for Aaron, and said, Go ye, sacrifice to
your God in the land.
26 And Moses said, It is not meet so to
do; for we shall sacrifice the abomination of the Egyptians to the LORD our
God: lo, shall we sacrifice the abomination of the Egyptians before their eyes,
and will they not stone us?
27 We will go three days' journey into
the wilderness, and sacrifice to the
LORD our God, as he shall command us.
28 And Pharaoh said, I will let you go,
that ye may sacrifice to the LORD your
God in the wilderness; only ye shall not
go very far away: intreat for me.
29 And Moses said, Behold, I go out
from thee, and I will intreat the LORD
that the swarms *of flies* may depart
from Pharaoh, from his servants, and
from his people, to morrow: but let not
Pharaoh deal deceitfully any more in
not letting the people go to sacrifice to
the LORD.
30 And Moses went out from Pharaoh,
and intreated the LORD.
31 And the LORD did according to the
word of Moses; and he removed the
swarms *of flies* from Pharaoh, from his
servants, and from his people; there
remained not one.
32 And Pharaoh hardened his heart
at this time also, neither would he let
the people go.

9 Then the LORD said unto Moses, Go
in unto Pharaoh, and tell him, Thus
saith the LORD God of the Hebrews, Let
my people go, that they may serve me.
2 For if thou refuse to let *them* go,
and wilt hold them still,
3 Behold, the hand of the LORD is
upon thy cattle which *is* in the field,
upon the horses, upon the asses, upon
the camels, upon the oxen, and upon
the sheep: *there shall be* a very grievous murrain.
4 And the LORD shall sever between
the cattle of Israel and the cattle of
Egypt: and there shall nothing die of all
that is the children's of Israel.
5 And the LORD appointed a set time,
saying, To morrow the LORD shall do
this thing in the land.
6 And the LORD did that thing on the
morrow, and all the cattle of Egypt
died: but of the cattle of the children of
Israel died not one.
7 And Pharaoh sent, and, behold,
there was not one of the cattle of the
Israelites dead. And the heart of
Pharaoh was hardened, and he did not
let the people go.
8 And the LORD said unto Moses and
unto Aaron, Take to you handfuls of
ashes of the furnace, and let Moses
sprinkle it toward the heaven in the
sight of Pharaoh.
9 And it shall become small dust in all
the land of Egypt, and shall be a boil
breaking forth *with* blains upon man,
and upon beast, throughout all the land
of Egypt.
10 And they took ashes of the furnace, and stood before Pharaoh; and
Moses sprinkled it up toward heaven;
and it became a boil breaking forth
with blains upon man, and upon beast.

11 And the magicians could not stand
before Moses because of the boils; for
the boil was upon the magicians, and
upon all the Egyptians.
12 And the LORD hardened the heart
of Pharaoh, and he hearkened not unto
them; as the LORD had spoken unto
Moses.
13 And the LORD said unto Moses,
Rise up early in the morning, and stand
before Pharaoh, and say unto him, Thus
saith the LORD God of the Hebrews, Let
my people go, that they may serve me.
14 For I will at this time send all my
plagues upon thine heart, and upon thy
servants, and upon thy people; that
thou mayest know that *there is* none
like me in all the earth.
15 For now I will stretch out my hand,
that I may smite thee and thy people
with pestilence; and thou shalt be cut
off from the earth.
16 And in very deed for this *cause*
have I raised thee up, for to shew *in*
thee my power; and that my name may
be declared throughout all the earth.
17 As yet exaltest thou thyself against
my people, that thou wilt not let them
go?
18 Behold, to morrow about this time
I will cause it to rain a very grievous
hail, such as hath not been in Egypt
since the foundation thereof even until
now.
19 Send therefore now, *and* gather
thy cattle, and all that thou hast in the
field; *for upon* every man and beast
which shall be found in the field, and
shall not be brought home, the hail
shall come down upon them, and they
shall die.
20 He that feared the word of the
LORD among the servants of Pharaoh
made his servants and his cattle flee
into the houses:
21 And he that regarded not the word
of the LORD left his servants and his
cattle in the field.
22 And the LORD said unto Moses,
Stretch forth thine hand toward heav-
en, that there may be hail in all the
land of Egypt, upon man, and upon
beast, and upon every herb of the field,
throughout the land of Egypt.
23 And Moses stretched forth his rod
toward heaven: and the LORD sent thunder and hail, and the fire ran along
upon the ground; and the LORD rained
hail upon the land of Egypt.
24 So there was hail, and fire mingled
with the hail, very grievous, such as
there was none like it in all the land of
Egypt since it became a nation.
25 And the hail smote throughout all
the land of Egypt all that *was* in the
field, both man and beast; and the hail
smote every herb of the field, and
brake every tree of the field.
26 Only in the land of Goshen, where
the children of Israel *were*, was there no
hail.
27 And Pharaoh sent, and called for
Moses and Aaron, and said unto them, I
have sinned this time: the LORD *is* righteous, and I and my people *are* wicked.
28 Intreat the LORD (for *it is* enough)
that there be no *more* mighty thunderings and hail; and I will let you go, and
ye shall stay no longer.
29 And Moses said unto him, As soon
as I am gone out of the city, I will
spread abroad my hands unto the LORD;
and the thunder shall cease, neither
shall there be any more hail; that thou
mayest know how that the earth *is* the
LORD'S.

30 But as for thee and thy servants, I
know that ye will not yet fear the LORD
God.
31 And the flax and the barley was
smitten: for the barley *was* in the ear,
and the flax *was* bolled.
32 But the wheat and the rie were not
smitten: for they *were* not grown up.
33 And Moses went out of the city
from Pharaoh, and spread abroad his
hands unto the LORD: and the thunders
and hail ceased, and the rain was not
poured upon the earth.
34 And when Pharaoh saw that the
rain and the hail and the thunders were
ceased, he sinned yet more, and hardened his heart, he and his servants.
35 And the heart of Pharaoh was
hardened, neither would he let the
children of Israel go; as the LORD had
spoken by Moses.

10 And the LORD said unto Moses,
Go in unto Pharaoh: for I have
hardened his heart, and the heart of his
servants, that I might shew these my
signs before him:
2 And that thou mayest tell in the
ears of thy son, and of thy son's son,
what things I have wrought in Egypt,
and my signs which I have done among
them; that ye may know how that I *am*
the LORD.
3 And Moses and Aaron came in unto
Pharaoh, and said unto him, Thus saith
the LORD God of the Hebrews, How
long wilt thou refuse to humble thyself
before me? let my people go, that they
may serve me.
4 Else, if thou refuse to let my people
go, behold, to morrow will I bring the
locusts into thy coast:
5 And they shall cover the face of the
earth, that one cannot be able to see
the earth: and they shall eat the residue of that which is escaped, which
remaineth unto you from the hail, and
shall eat every tree which groweth for
you out of the field:
6 And they shall fill thy houses, and
the houses of all thy servants, and the
houses of all the Egyptians; which neither thy fathers, nor thy fathers' fathers
have seen, since the day that they were
upon the earth unto this day. And he
turned himself, and went out from
Pharaoh.
7 And Pharaoh's servants said unto
him, How long shall this man be a snare
unto us? let the men go, that they may
serve the LORD their God: knowest thou
not yet that Egypt is destroyed?
8 And Moses and Aaron were brought
again unto Pharaoh: and he said unto
them, Go, serve the LORD your God: *but*
who *are* they that shall go?
9 And Moses said, We will go with our
young and with our old, with our sons
and with our daughters, with our flocks
and with our herds will we go; for we
must hold a feast unto the LORD.
10 And he said unto them, Let the
LORD be so with you, as I will let you go,
and your little ones: look *to it*; for evil
is before you.
11 Not so: go now ye *that are* men,
and serve the LORD; for that ye did
desire. And they were driven out from
Pharaoh's presence.
12 And the LORD said unto Moses,
Stretch out thine hand over the land of
Egypt for the locusts, that they may
come up upon the land of Egypt, and
eat every herb of the land, *even* all that
the hail hath left.
13 And Moses stretched forth his rod
over the land of Egypt, and the LORD
brought an east wind upon the land all
that day, and all *that* night; *and* when it

was morning, the east wind brought the
locusts.
14 And the locusts went up over all
the land of Egypt, and rested in all the
coasts of Egypt: very grievous *were
they*; before them there were no such
locusts as they, neither after them shall
be such.
15 For they covered the face of the
whole earth, so that the land was darkened; and they did eat every herb of
the land, and all the fruit of the trees
which the hail had left: and there
remained not any green thing in the
trees, or in the herbs of the field,
through all the land of Egypt.
16 Then Pharaoh called for Moses
and Aaron in haste; and he said, I have
sinned against the LORD your God, and
against you.
17 Now therefore forgive, I pray thee,
my sin only this once, and intreat the
LORD your God, that he may take away
from me this death only.
18 And he went out from Pharaoh,
and intreated the LORD.
19 And the LORD turned a mighty
strong west wind, which took away the
locusts, and cast them into the Red sea;
there remained not one locust in all the
coasts of Egypt.
20 But the LORD hardened Pharaoh's
heart, so that he would not let the children of Israel go.
21 And the LORD said unto Moses,
Stretch out thine hand toward heaven,
that there may be darkness over the
land of Egypt, even darkness *which*
may be felt.
22 And Moses stretched forth his
hand toward heaven; and there was a
thick darkness in all the land of Egypt
three days:
23 They saw not one another, neither
rose any from his place for three days:
but all the children of Israel had light
in their dwellings.
24 And Pharaoh called unto Moses,
and said, Go ye, serve the LORD; only let
your flocks and your herds be stayed:
let your little ones also go with you.
25 And Moses said, Thou must give us
also sacrifices and burnt offerings, that
we may sacrifice unto the LORD our
God.
26 Our cattle also shall go with us;
there shall not an hoof be left behind;
for thereof must we take to serve the
LORD our God; and we know not with
what we must serve the LORD, until we
come thither.
27 But the LORD hardened Pharaoh's
heart, and he would not let them go.
28 And Pharaoh said unto him, Get
thee from me, take heed to thyself, see
my face no more; for in *that* day thou
seest my face thou shalt die.
29 And Moses said, Thou hast spoken
well, I will see thy face again no more.

11 And the LORD said unto Moses,
Yet will I bring one plague *more*
upon Pharaoh, and upon Egypt; afterwards he will let you go hence: when he
shall let *you* go, he shall surely thrust
you out hence altogether.
2 Speak now in the ears of the people,
and let every man borrow of his neighbour, and every woman of her neighbour, jewels of silver, and jewels of
gold.
3 And the LORD gave the people
favour in the sight of the Egyptians.
Moreover the man Moses *was* very
great in the land of Egypt, in the sight
of Pharaoh's servants, and in the sight
of the people.

4 And Moses said, Thus saith the LORD, About midnight will I go out into the midst of Egypt:

5 And all the firstborn in the land of Egypt shall die, from the firstborn of Pharaoh that sitteth upon his throne, even unto the firstborn of the maidservant that *is* behind the mill; and all the firstborn of beasts.

6 And there shall be a great cry throughout all the land of Egypt, such as there was none like it, nor shall be like it any more.

7 But against any of the children of Israel shall not a dog move his tongue, against man or beast: that ye may know how that the LORD doth put a difference between the Egyptians and Israel.

8 And all these thy servants shall come down unto me, and bow down themselves unto me, saying, Get thee out, and all the people that follow thee: and after that I will go out. And he went out from Pharaoh in a great anger.

9 And the LORD said unto Moses, Pharaoh shall not hearken unto you; that my wonders may be multiplied in the land of Egypt.

10 And Moses and Aaron did all these wonders before Pharaoh: and the LORD hardened Pharaoh's heart, so that he would not let the children of Israel go out of his land.

12 And the LORD spake unto Moses and Aaron in the land of Egypt, saying,

2 This month *shall be* unto you the beginning of months: it *shall be* the first month of the year to you.

3 Speak ye unto all the congregation of Israel, saying, In the tenth *day* of this month they shall take to them every man a lamb, according to the house of *their* fathers, a lamb for an house:

4 And if the household be too little for the lamb, let him and his neighbour next unto his house take *it* according to the number of the souls; every man according to his eating shall make your count for the lamb.

5 Your lamb shall be without blemish, a male of the first year: ye shall take *it* out from the sheep, or from the goats:

6 And ye shall keep it up until the fourteenth day of the same month: and the whole assembly of the congregation of Israel shall kill it in the evening.

7 And they shall take of the blood, and strike *it* on the two side posts and on the upper door post of the houses, wherein they shall eat it.

8 And they shall eat the flesh in that night, roast with fire, and unleavened bread; *and* with bitter *herbs* they shall eat it.

9 Eat not of it raw, nor sodden at all with water, but roast *with* fire; his head with his legs, and with the purtenance thereof.

10 And ye shall let nothing of it remain until the morning; and that which remaineth of it until the morning ye shall burn with fire.

11 And thus shall ye eat it; *with* your loins girded, your shoes on your feet, and your staff in your hand; and ye shall eat it in haste: it *is* the LORD's passover.

12 For I will pass through the land of Egypt this night, and will smite all the firstborn in the land of Egypt, both man and beast; and against all the gods of Egypt I will execute judgment: I *am* the LORD.

13 And the blood shall be to you for a token upon the houses where ye *are*: and when I see the blood, I will pass over you, and the plague shall not be upon you to destroy *you*, when I smite the land of Egypt.

14 And this day shall be unto you for a memorial; and ye shall keep it a feast to the LORD throughout your generations; ye shall keep it a feast by an ordinance for ever.

15 Seven days shall ye eat unleavened bread; even the first day ye shall put away leaven out of your houses: for whosoever eateth leavened bread from the first day until the seventh day, that soul shall be cut off from Israel.

16 And in the first day *there shall be* an holy convocation, and in the seventh day there shall be an holy convocation to you; no manner of work shall be done in them, save *that* which every man must eat, that only may be done of you.

17 And ye shall observe *the feast of* unleavened bread; for in this selfsame day have I brought your armies out of the land of Egypt: therefore shall ye observe this day in your generations by an ordinance for ever.

18 In the first *month*, on the fourteenth day of the month at even, ye shall eat unleavened bread, until the one and twentieth day of the month at even.

19 Seven days shall there be no leaven found in your houses: for whosoever eateth that which is leavened, even that soul shall be cut off from the congregation of Israel, whether he be a stranger, or born in the land.

20 Ye shall eat nothing leavened; in all your habitations shall ye eat unleavened bread.

21 Then Moses called for all the elders of Israel, and said unto them, Draw out and take you a lamb according to your families, and kill the passover.

22 And ye shall take a bunch of hyssop, and dip *it* in the blood that *is* in the bason, and strike the lintel and the two side posts with the blood that *is* in the bason; and none of you shall go out at the door of his house until the morning.

23 For the LORD will pass through to smite the Egyptians; and when he seeth the blood upon the lintel, and on the two side posts, the LORD will pass over the door, and will not suffer the destroyer to come in unto your houses to smite *you*.

24 And ye shall observe this thing for an ordinance to thee and to thy sons for ever.

25 And it shall come to pass, when ye be come to the land which the LORD will give you, according as he hath promised, that ye shall keep this service.

26 And it shall come to pass, when your children shall say unto you, What mean ye by this service?

27 That ye shall say, It *is* the sacrifice of the LORD's passover, who passed over the houses of the children of Israel in Egypt, when he smote the Egyptians, and delivered our houses. And the people bowed the head and worshipped.

28 And the children of Israel went away, and did as the LORD had commanded Moses and Aaron, so did they.

29 And it came to pass, that at midnight the LORD smote all the firstborn in the land of Egypt, from the firstborn of Pharaoh that sat on his throne unto the firstborn of the captive that *was* in the dungeon; and all the firstborn of cattle.

30 And Pharaoh rose up in the night, he, and all his servants, and all the Egyptians; and there was a great cry in Egypt; for *there was* not a house where *there was* not one dead.

31 And he called for Moses and Aaron by night, and said, Rise up, *and* get you forth from among my people, both ye and the children of Israel; and go, serve the LORD, as ye have said.

32 Also take your flocks and your herds, as ye have said, and be gone; and bless me also.

33 And the Egyptians were urgent upon the people, that they might send them out of the land in haste; for they said, We *be* all dead *men*.

34 And the people took their dough before it was leavened, their kneading-troughs being bound up in their clothes upon their shoulders.

35 And the children of Israel did according to the word of Moses; and they borrowed of the Egyptians jewels of silver, and jewels of gold, and raiment:

36 And the LORD gave the people favour in the sight of the Egyptians, so that they lent unto them *such things as they required*. And they spoiled the Egyptians.

37 And the children of Israel journeyed from Rameses to Succoth, about six hundred thousand on foot *that were* men, beside children.

38 And a mixed multitude went up also with them; and flocks, and herds, *even* very much cattle.

39 And they baked unleavened cakes of the dough which they brought forth out of Egypt, for it was not leavened; because they were thrust out of Egypt, and could not tarry, neither had they prepared for themselves any victual.

40 Now the sojourning of the children of Israel, who dwelt in Egypt, *was* four hundred and thirty years.

41 And it came to pass at the end of the four hundred and thirty years, even the selfsame day it came to pass, that all the hosts of the LORD went out from the land of Egypt.

42 It *is* a night to be much observed unto the LORD for bringing them out from the land of Egypt: this *is* that night of the LORD to be observed of all the children of Israel in their generations.

43 And the LORD said unto Moses and Aaron, This *is* the ordinance of the passover: There shall no stranger eat thereof:

44 But every man's servant that is bought for money, when thou hast circumcised him, then shall he eat thereof.

45 A foreigner and an hired servant shall not eat thereof.

46 In one house shall it be eaten; thou shalt not carry forth ought of the flesh abroad out of the house; neither shall ye break a bone thereof.

47 All the congregation of Israel shall keep it.

48 And when a stranger shall sojourn with thee, and will keep the passover to the LORD, let all his males be circumcised, and then let him come near and keep it; and he shall be as one that is born in the land: for no uncircumcised person shall eat thereof.

49 One law shall be to him that is homeborn, and unto the stranger that sojourneth among you.

50 Thus did all the children of Israel; as the LORD commanded Moses and Aaron, so did they.

51 And it came to pass the selfsame day, *that* the LORD did bring the children of Israel out of the land of Egypt by their armies.

13 And the LORD spake unto Moses, saying,

2 Sanctify unto me all the firstborn, whatsoever openeth the womb among the children of Israel, *both* of man and of beast: it *is* mine.

3 And Moses said unto the people, Remember this day, in which ye came out from Egypt, out of the house of bondage; for by strength of hand the LORD brought you out from this *place*: there shall no leavened bread be eaten.

4 This day came ye out in the month Abib.

5 And it shall be when the LORD shall bring thee into the land of the Canaanites, and the Hittites, and the Amorites, and the Hivites, and the Jebusites, which he sware unto thy fathers to give thee, a land flowing with milk and honey, that thou shalt keep this service in this month.

6 Seven days thou shalt eat unleavened bread, and in the seventh day *shall be* a feast to the LORD.

7 Unleavened bread shall be eaten seven days; and there shall no leavened bread be seen with thee, neither shall there be leaven seen with thee in all thy quarters.

8 And thou shalt shew thy son in that day, saying, *This is done* because of that *which* the LORD did unto me when I came forth out of Egypt.

9 And it shall be for a sign unto thee upon thine hand, and for a memorial between thine eyes, that the LORD's law may be in thy mouth: for with a strong hand hath the LORD brought thee out of Egypt.

10 Thou shalt therefore keep this ordinance in his season from year to year.

11 And it shall be when the LORD shall bring thee into the land of the Canaanites, as he sware unto thee and to thy fathers, and shall give it thee,

12 That thou shalt set apart unto the LORD all that openeth the matrix, and every firstling that cometh of a beast which thou hast; the males *shall be* the LORD's.

13 And every firstling of an ass thou shalt redeem with a lamb; and if thou wilt not redeem it, then thou shalt break his neck: and all the firstborn of man among thy children shalt thou redeem.

14 And it shall be when thy son asketh thee in time to come, saying, What *is* this? that thou shalt say unto him, By strength of hand the LORD brought us out from Egypt, from the house of bondage:

15 And it came to pass, when Pharaoh would hardly let us go, that the LORD slew all the firstborn in the land of Egypt, both the firstborn of man, and the firstborn of beast: therefore I sacrifice to the LORD all that openeth the matrix, being males; but all the firstborn of my children I redeem.

16 And it shall be for a token upon thine hand, and for frontlets between thine eyes: for by strength of hand the LORD brought us forth out of Egypt.

17 And it came to pass, when Pharaoh had let the people go, that God led them not *through* the way of the land of the Philistines, although that *was* near; for God said, Lest peradventure the people repent when they see war, and they return to Egypt:

18 But God led the people about, *through* the way of the wilderness of the Red sea: and the children of Israel went up harnessed out of the land of Egypt.

19 And Moses took the bones of Joseph with him: for he had straitly sworn the children of Israel, saying, God will surely visit you; and ye shall carry up my bones away hence with you.

20 And they took their journey from Succoth, and encamped in Etham, in the edge of the wilderness.

21 And the LORD went before them by day in a pillar of a cloud, to lead them the way; and by night in a pillar of fire, to give them light; to go by day and night:

22 He took not away the pillar of the cloud by day, nor the pillar of fire by night, *from* before the people.

14

And the LORD spake unto Moses, saying,

2 Speak unto the children of Israel, that they turn and encamp before Pi-hahiroth, between Migdol and the sea, over against Baal-zephon: before it shall ye encamp by the sea.

3 For Pharaoh will say of the children of Israel, They *are* entangled in the land, the wilderness hath shut them in.

4 And I will harden Pharaoh's heart, that he shall follow after them; and I will be honoured upon Pharaoh, and upon all his host; that the Egyptians may know that I *am* the LORD. And they did so.

5 And it was told the king of Egypt that the people fled: and the heart of Pharaoh and of his servants was turned against the people, and they said, Why have we done this, that we have let Israel go from serving us?

6 And he made ready his chariot, and took his people with him:

7 And he took six hundred chosen chariots, and all the chariots of Egypt, and captains over every one of them.

8 And the LORD hardened the heart of Pharaoh king of Egypt, and he pursued after the children of Israel: and the children of Israel went out with an high hand.

9 But the Egyptians pursued after them, all the horses *and* chariots of Pharaoh, and his horsemen, and his army, and overtook them encamping by the sea, beside Pi-hahiroth, before Baal-zephon.

10 And when Pharaoh drew nigh, the children of Israel lifted up their eyes, and, behold, the Egyptians marched after them; and they were sore afraid: and the children of Israel cried out unto the LORD.

11 And they said unto Moses, Because *there were* no graves in Egypt, hast thou taken us away to die in the wilderness? wherefore hast thou dealt thus with us, to carry us forth out of Egypt?

12 *Is* not this the word that we did tell thee in Egypt, saying, Let us alone, that we may serve the Egyptians? For *it had been* better for us to serve the Egyptians, than that we should die in the wilderness.

13 And Moses said unto the people, Fear ye not, stand still, and see the salvation of the LORD, which he will shew to you to day: for the Egyptians whom ye have seen to day, ye shall see them again no more for ever.

14 The LORD shall fight for you, and ye shall hold your peace.

15 And the LORD said unto Moses, Wherefore criest thou unto me? speak

unto the children of Israel, that they go forward:

16 But lift thou up thy rod, and stretch out thine hand over the sea, and divide it: and the children of Israel shall go on dry *ground* through the midst of the sea.

17 And I, behold, I will harden the hearts of the Egyptians, and they shall follow them: and I will get me honour upon Pharaoh, and upon all his host, upon his chariots, and upon his horsemen.

18 And the Egyptians shall know that I *am* the LORD, when I have gotten me honour upon Pharaoh, upon his chariots, and upon his horsemen.

19 And the angel of God, which went before the camp of Israel, removed and went behind them; and the pillar of the cloud went from before their face, and stood behind them:

20 And it came between the camp of the Egyptians and the camp of Israel; and it was a cloud and darkness *to them*, but it gave light by night *to these*: so that the one came not near the other all the night.

21 And Moses stretched out his hand over the sea; and the LORD caused the sea to go *back* by a strong east wind all that night, and made the sea dry *land*, and the waters were divided.

22 And the children of Israel went into the midst of the sea upon the dry *ground*: and the waters *were* a wall unto them on their right hand, and on their left.

23 And the Egyptians pursued, and went in after them to the midst of the sea, *even* all Pharaoh's horses, his chariots, and his horsemen.

24 And it came to pass, that in the morning watch the LORD looked unto the host of the Egyptians through the pillar of fire and of the cloud, and troubled the host of the Egyptians,

25 And took off their chariot wheels, that they drave them heavily: so that the Egyptians said, Let us flee from the face of Israel; for the LORD fighteth for them against the Egyptians.

26 And the LORD said unto Moses, Stretch out thine hand over the sea, that the waters may come again upon the Egyptians, upon their chariots, and upon their horsemen.

27 And Moses stretched forth his hand over the sea, and the sea returned to his strength when the morning appeared; and the Egyptians fled against it; and the LORD overthrew the Egyptians in the midst of the sea.

28 And the waters returned, and covered the chariots, and the horsemen, *and* all the host of Pharaoh that came into the sea after them; there remained not so much as one of them.

29 But the children of Israel walked upon dry *land* in the midst of the sea; and the waters *were* a wall unto them on their right hand, and on their left.

30 Thus the LORD saved Israel that day out of the hand of the Egyptians; and Israel saw the Egyptians dead upon the sea shore.

31 And Israel saw that great work which the LORD did upon the Egyptians: and the people feared the LORD, and believed the LORD, and his servant Moses.

15 Then sang Moses and the children of Israel this song unto the LORD, and spake, saying, I will sing unto the LORD, for he hath triumphed gloriously: the horse and his rider hath he thrown into the sea.

2 The LORD *is* my strength and song,
and he is become my salvation: he *is*
my God, and I will prepare him an
habitation; my father's God, and I will
exalt him.
3 The LORD *is* a man of war: the LORD
is his name.
4 Pharaoh's chariots and his host hath
he cast into the sea: his chosen captains
also are drowned in the Red sea.
5 The depths have covered them: they
sank into the bottom as a stone.
6 Thy right hand, O LORD, is become
glorious in power: thy right hand, O
LORD, hath dashed in pieces the enemy.
7 And in the greatness of thine excellency thou hast overthrown them that
rose up against thee: thou sentest forth
thy wrath, *which* consumed them as
stubble.
8 And with the blast of thy nostrils
the waters were gathered together, the
floods stood upright as an heap, *and*
the depths were congealed in the heart
of the sea.
9 The enemy said, I will pursue, I will
overtake, I will divide the spoil; my lust
shall be satisfied upon them; I will
draw my sword, my hand shall destroy
them.
10 Thou didst blow with thy wind, the
sea covered them: they sank as lead in
the mighty waters.
11 Who *is* like unto thee, O LORD,
among the gods? who *is* like thee, glorious in holiness, fearful *in* praises, doing
wonders?
12 Thou stretchedst out thy right
hand, the earth swallowed them.
13 Thou in thy mercy hast led forth
the people *which* thou hast redeemed:
thou hast guided *them* in thy strength
unto thy holy habitation.
14 The people shall hear, *and* be
afraid: sorrow shall take hold on the
inhabitants of Palestina.
15 Then the dukes of Edom shall be
amazed; the mighty men of Moab,
trembling shall take hold upon them;
all the inhabitants of Canaan shall melt
away.
16 Fear and dread shall fall upon
them; by the greatness of thine arm
they shall be *as* still as a stone; till thy
people pass over, O LORD, till the people
pass over, *which* thou hast purchased.
17 Thou shalt bring them in, and
plant them in the mountain of thine
inheritance, *in* the place, O LORD,
which thou hast made for thee to dwell
in, *in* the Sanctuary, O Lord, *which* thy
hands have established.
18 The LORD shall reign for ever and
ever.
19 For the horse of Pharaoh went in
with his chariots and with his horsemen
into the sea, and the LORD brought
again the waters of the sea upon them;
but the children of Israel went on dry
land in the midst of the sea.
20 And Miriam the prophetess, the
sister of Aaron, took a timbrel in her
hand; and all the women went out after
her with timbrels and with dances.
21 And Miriam answered them, Sing
ye to the LORD, for he hath triumphed
gloriously; the horse and his rider hath
he thrown into the sea.
22 So Moses brought Israel from the
Red sea, and they went out into the
wilderness of Shur; and they went
three days in the wilderness, and found
no water.
23 And when they came to Marah,
they could not drink of the waters of
Marah, for they *were* bitter: therefore
the name of it was called Marah.

24 And the people murmured against Moses, saying, What shall we drink?

25 And he cried unto the LORD; and the LORD shewed him a tree, *which* when he had cast into the waters, the waters were made sweet: there he made for them a statute and an ordinance, and there he proved them,

26 And said, If thou wilt diligently hearken to the voice of the LORD thy God, and wilt do that which is right in his sight, and wilt give ear to his commandments, and keep all his statutes, I will put none of these diseases upon thee, which I have brought upon the Egyptians: for I *am* the LORD that healeth thee.

27 And they came to Elim, where *were* twelve wells of water, and threescore and ten palm trees: and they encamped there by the waters.

16 And they took their journey from Elim, and all the congregation of the children of Israel came unto the wilderness of Sin, which *is* between Elim and Sinai, on the fifteenth day of the second month after their departing out of the land of Egypt.

2 And the whole congregation of the children of Israel murmured against Moses and Aaron in the wilderness:

3 And the children of Israel said unto them, Would to God we had died by the hand of the LORD in the land of Egypt, when we sat by the flesh pots, *and* when we did eat bread to the full; for ye have brought us forth into this wilderness, to kill this whole assembly with hunger.

4 Then said the LORD unto Moses, Behold, I will rain bread from heaven for you; and the people shall go out and gather a certain rate every day, that I may prove them, whether they will walk in my law, or no.

5 And it shall come to pass, that on the sixth day they shall prepare *that* which they bring in; and it shall be twice as much as they gather daily.

6 And Moses and Aaron said unto all the children of Israel, At even, then ye shall know that the LORD hath brought you out from the land of Egypt:

7 And in the morning, then ye shall see the glory of the LORD; for that he heareth your murmurings against the LORD: and what *are* we, that ye murmur against us?

8 And Moses said, *This shall be*, when the LORD shall give you in the evening flesh to eat, and in the morning bread to the full; for that the LORD heareth your murmurings which ye murmur against him: and what *are* we? your murmurings *are* not against us, but against the LORD.

9 And Moses spake unto Aaron, Say unto all the congregation of the children of Israel, Come near before the LORD: for he hath heard your murmurings.

10 And it came to pass, as Aaron spake unto the whole congregation of the children of Israel, that they looked toward the wilderness, and, behold, the glory of the LORD appeared in the cloud.

11 And the LORD spake unto Moses, saying,

12 I have heard the murmurings of the children of Israel: speak unto them, saying, At even ye shall eat flesh, and in the morning ye shall be filled with bread; and ye shall know that I *am* the LORD your God.

13 And it came to pass, that at even the quails came up, and covered the

camp: and in the morning the dew lay
round about the host.
14 And when the dew that lay was
gone up, behold, upon the face of the
wilderness *there lay* a small round
thing, *as* small as the hoar frost on the
ground.
15 And when the children of Israel
saw *it*, they said one to another, It *is*
manna: for they wist not what it *was*.
And Moses said unto them, This *is* the
bread which the LORD hath given you to
eat.
16 This *is* the thing which the LORD
hath commanded, Gather of it every
man according to his eating, an omer
for every man, *according to* the number
of your persons; take ye every man for
them which *are* in his tents.
17 And the children of Israel did so,
and gathered, some more, some less.
18 And when they did mete *it* with an
omer, he that gathered much had nothing over, and he that gathered little had
no lack; they gathered every man
according to his eating.
19 And Moses said, Let no man leave
of it till the morning.
20 Notwithstanding they hearkened
not unto Moses; but some of them left
of it until the morning, and it bred
worms, and stank: and Moses was
wroth with them.
21 And they gathered it every morning, every man according to his eating:
and when the sun waxed hot, it melted.
22 And it came to pass, *that* on the
sixth day they gathered twice as much
bread, two omers for one *man*: and all
the rulers of the congregation came
and told Moses.
23 And he said unto them, This *is that*
which the LORD hath said, To morrow *is*
the rest of the holy sabbath unto the
LORD: bake *that* which ye will bake *to
day*, and seethe that ye will seethe; and
that which remaineth over lay up for
you to be kept until the morning.
24 And they laid it up till the morning, as Moses bade: and it did not stink,
neither was there any worm therein.
25 And Moses said, Eat that to day;
for to day *is* a sabbath unto the LORD: to
day ye shall not find it in the field.
26 Six days ye shall gather it; but on
the seventh day, *which is* the sabbath,
in it there shall be none.
27 And it came to pass, *that* there
went out *some* of the people on the
seventh day for to gather, and they
found none.
28 And the LORD said unto Moses,
How long refuse ye to keep my commandments and my laws?
29 See, for that the LORD hath given
you the sabbath, therefore he giveth
you on the sixth day the bread of two
days; abide ye every man in his place,
let no man go out of his place on the
seventh day.
30 So the people rested on the seventh day.
31 And the house of Israel called the
name thereof Manna: and it *was* like
coriander seed, white; and the taste of
it *was* like wafers *made* with honey.
32 And Moses said, This *is* the thing
which the LORD commandeth, Fill an
omer of it to be kept for your generations; that they may see the bread
wherewith I have fed you in the wilderness, when I brought you forth from the
land of Egypt.
33 And Moses said unto Aaron, Take a
pot, and put an omer full of manna
therein, and lay it up before the LORD,
to be kept for your generations.

34 As the LORD commanded Moses, so Aaron laid it up before the Testimony, to be kept.

35 And the children of Israel did eat manna forty years, until they came to a land inhabited; they did eat manna, until they came unto the borders of the land of Canaan.

36 Now an omer *is* the tenth *part* of an ephah.

17 And all the congregation of the children of Israel journeyed from the wilderness of Sin, after their journeys, according to the commandment of the LORD, and pitched in Rephidim: and *there was* no water for the people to drink.

2 Wherefore the people did chide with Moses, and said, Give us water that we may drink. And Moses said unto them, Why chide ye with me? wherefore do ye tempt the LORD?

3 And the people thirsted there for water; and the people murmured against Moses, and said, Wherefore *is* this *that* thou hast brought us up out of Egypt, to kill us and our children and our cattle with thirst?

4 And Moses cried unto the LORD, saying, What shall I do unto this people? they be almost ready to stone me.

5 And the LORD said unto Moses, Go on before the people, and take with thee of the elders of Israel; and thy rod, wherewith thou smotest the river, take in thine hand, and go.

6 Behold, I will stand before thee there upon the rock in Horeb; and thou shalt smite the rock, and there shall come water out of it, that the people may drink. And Moses did so in the sight of the elders of Israel.

7 And he called the name of the place Massah, and Meribah, because of the chiding of the children of Israel, and because they tempted the LORD, saying, Is the LORD among us, or not?

8 Then came Amalek, and fought with Israel in Rephidim.

9 And Moses said unto Joshua, Choose us out men, and go out, fight with Amalek: to morrow I will stand on the top of the hill with the rod of God in mine hand.

10 So Joshua did as Moses had said to him, and fought with Amalek: and Moses, Aaron, and Hur went up to the top of the hill.

11 And it came to pass, when Moses held up his hand, that Israel prevailed: and when he let down his hand, Amalek prevailed.

12 But Moses' hands *were* heavy; and they took a stone, and put *it* under him, and he sat thereon; and Aaron and Hur stayed up his hands, the one on the one side, and the other on the other side; and his hands were steady until the going down of the sun.

13 And Joshua discomfited Amalek and his people with the edge of the sword.

14 And the LORD said unto Moses, Write this *for* a memorial in a book, and rehearse *it* in the ears of Joshua: for I will utterly put out the remembrance of Amalek from under heaven.

15 And Moses built an altar, and called the name of it Jehovah-nissi:

16 For he said, Because the LORD hath sworn *that* the LORD *will have* war with Amalek from generation to generation.

18 When Jethro, the priest of Midian, Moses' father in law, heard of all that God had done for Moses, and for Israel his people, *and* that the LORD had brought Israel out of Egypt;

2 Then Jethro, Moses' father in law, took Zipporah, Moses' wife, after he had sent her back,

3 And her two sons; of which the name of the one *was* Gershom; for he said, I have been an alien in a strange land:

4 And the name of the other *was* Eliezer; for the God of my father, *said he, was* mine help, and delivered me from the sword of Pharaoh:

5 And Jethro, Moses' father in law, came with his sons and his wife unto Moses into the wilderness, where he encamped at the mount of God:

6 And he said unto Moses, I thy father in law Jethro am come unto thee, and thy wife, and her two sons with her.

7 And Moses went out to meet his father in law, and did obeisance, and kissed him; and they asked each other of *their* welfare; and they came into the tent.

8 And Moses told his father in law all that the LORD had done unto Pharaoh and to the Egyptians for Israel's sake, *and* all the travail that had come upon them by the way, and *how* the LORD delivered them.

9 And Jethro rejoiced for all the goodness which the LORD had done to Israel, whom he had delivered out of the hand of the Egyptians.

10 And Jethro said, Blessed *be* the LORD, who hath delivered you out of the hand of the Egyptians, and out of the hand of Pharaoh, who hath delivered the people from under the hand of the Egyptians.

11 Now I know that the LORD *is* greater than all gods: for in the thing wherein they dealt proudly *he was* above them.

12 And Jethro, Moses' father in law, took a burnt offering and sacrifices for God: and Aaron came, and all the elders of Israel, to eat bread with Moses' father in law before God.

13 And it came to pass on the morrow, that Moses sat to judge the people: and the people stood by Moses from the morning unto the evening.

14 And when Moses' father in law saw all that he did to the people, he said, What *is* this thing that thou doest to the people? why sittest thou thyself alone, and all the people stand by thee from morning unto even?

15 And Moses said unto his father in law, Because the people come unto me to enquire of God:

16 When they have a matter, they come unto me; and I judge between one and another, and I do make *them* know the statutes of God, and his laws.

17 And Moses' father in law said unto him, The thing that thou doest *is* not good.

18 Thou wilt surely wear away, both thou, and this people that *is* with thee: for this thing *is* too heavy for thee; thou art not able to perform it thyself alone.

19 Hearken now unto my voice, I will give thee counsel, and God shall be with thee: Be thou for the people to God-ward, that thou mayest bring the causes unto God:

20 And thou shalt teach them ordinances and laws, and shalt shew them the way wherein they must walk, and the work that they must do.

21 Moreover thou shalt provide out of all the people able men, such as fear God, men of truth, hating covetousness; and place *such* over them, *to be* rulers of thousands, *and* rulers of hundreds, rulers of fifties, and rulers of tens:

22 And let them judge the people at all seasons: and it shall be, *that* every great matter they shall bring unto thee, but every small matter they shall judge: so shall it be easier for thyself, and they shall bear *the burden* with thee.

23 If thou shalt do this thing, and God command thee *so*, then thou shalt be able to endure, and all this people shall also go to their place in peace.

24 So Moses hearkened to the voice of his father in law, and did all that he had said.

25 And Moses chose able men out of all Israel, and made them heads over the people, rulers of thousands, rulers of hundreds, rulers of fifties, and rulers of tens.

26 And they judged the people at all seasons: the hard causes they brought unto Moses, but every small matter they judged themselves.

27 And Moses let his father in law depart; and he went his way into his own land.

19 In the third month, when the children of Israel were gone forth out of the land of Egypt, the same day came they *into* the wilderness of Sinai.

2 For they were departed from Rephidim, and were come *to* the desert of Sinai, and had pitched in the wilderness; and there Israel camped before the mount.

3 And Moses went up unto God, and the LORD called unto him out of the mountain, saying, Thus shalt thou say to the house of Jacob, and tell the children of Israel;

4 Ye have seen what I did unto the Egyptians, and *how* I bare you on eagles' wings, and brought you unto myself.

5 Now therefore, if ye will obey my voice indeed, and keep my covenant, then ye shall be a peculiar treasure unto me above all people: for all the earth *is* mine:

6 And ye shall be unto me a kingdom of priests, and an holy nation. These *are* the words which thou shalt speak unto the children of Israel.

7 And Moses came and called for the elders of the people, and laid before their faces all these words which the LORD commanded him.

8 And all the people answered together, and said, All that the LORD hath spoken we will do. And Moses returned the words of the people unto the LORD.

9 And the LORD said unto Moses, Lo, I come unto thee in a thick cloud, that the people may hear when I speak with thee, and believe thee for ever. And Moses told the words of the people unto the LORD.

10 And the LORD said unto Moses, Go unto the people, and sanctify them to day and to morrow, and let them wash their clothes,

11 And be ready against the third day: for the third day the LORD will come down in the sight of all the people upon mount Sinai.

12 And thou shalt set bounds unto the people round about, saying, Take heed to yourselves, *that ye* go *not* up into the mount, or touch the border of it: whosoever toucheth the mount shall be surely put to death:

13 There shall not an hand touch it, but he shall surely be stoned, or shot through; whether *it be* beast or man, it shall not live: when the trumpet soundeth long, they shall come up to the mount.

14 And Moses went down from the mount unto the people, and sanctified the people; and they washed their clothes.

15 And he said unto the people, Be ready against the third day: come not at *your* wives.

16 And it came to pass on the third day in the morning, that there were thunders and lightnings, and a thick cloud upon the mount, and the voice of the trumpet exceeding loud; so that all the people that *was* in the camp trembled.

17 And Moses brought forth the people out of the camp to meet with God; and they stood at the nether part of the mount.

18 And mount Sinai was altogether on a smoke, because the LORD descended upon it in fire: and the smoke thereof ascended as the smoke of a furnace, and the whole mount quaked greatly.

19 And when the voice of the trumpet sounded long, and waxed louder and louder, Moses spake, and God answered him by a voice.

20 And the LORD came down upon mount Sinai, on the top of the mount: and the LORD called Moses *up* to the top of the mount; and Moses went up.

21 And the LORD said unto Moses, Go down, charge the people, lest they break through unto the LORD to gaze, and many of them perish.

22 And let the priests also, which come near to the LORD, sanctify themselves, lest the LORD break forth upon them.

23 And Moses said unto the LORD, The people cannot come up to mount Sinai: for thou chargedst us, saying, Set bounds about the mount, and sanctify it.

24 And the LORD said unto him, Away, get thee down, and thou shalt come up, thou, and Aaron with thee: but let not the priests and the people break through to come up unto the LORD, lest he break forth upon them.

25 So Moses went down unto the people, and spake unto them.

20 And God spake all these words, saying,

2 I *am* the LORD thy God, which have brought thee out of the land of Egypt, out of the house of bondage.

3 Thou shalt have no other gods before me.

4 Thou shalt not make unto thee any graven image, or any likeness *of any thing* that *is* in heaven above, or that *is* in the earth beneath, or that *is* in the water under the earth:

5 Thou shalt not bow down thyself to them, nor serve them: for I the LORD thy God *am* a jealous God, visiting the iniquity of the fathers upon the children unto the third and fourth *generation* of them that hate me;

6 And shewing mercy unto thousands of them that love me, and keep my commandments.

7 Thou shalt not take the name of the LORD thy God in vain; for the LORD will not hold him guiltless that taketh his name in vain.

8 Remember the sabbath day, to keep it holy.

9 Six days shalt thou labour, and do all thy work:

10 But the seventh day *is* the sabbath of the LORD thy God: *in it* thou shalt not do any work, thou, nor thy son, nor thy daughter, thy manservant, nor thy maidservant, nor thy cattle, nor thy stranger that *is* within thy gates:

11 For *in* six days the LORD made heaven and earth, the sea, and all that in them *is*, and rested the seventh day: wherefore the LORD blessed the sabbath day, and hallowed it.

12 Honour thy father and thy mother: that thy days may be long upon the land which the LORD thy God giveth thee.

13 Thou shalt not kill.

14 Thou shalt not commit adultery.

15 Thou shalt not steal.

16 Thou shalt not bear false witness against thy neighbour.

17 Thou shalt not covet thy neighbour's house, thou shalt not covet thy neighbour's wife, nor his manservant, nor his maidservant, nor his ox, nor his ass, nor any thing that *is* thy neighbour's.

18 And all the people saw the thunderings, and the lightnings, and the noise of the trumpet, and the mountain smoking: and when the people saw *it*, they removed, and stood afar off.

19 And they said unto Moses, Speak thou with us, and we will hear: but let not God speak with us, lest we die.

20 And Moses said unto the people, Fear not: for God is come to prove you, and that his fear may be before your faces, that ye sin not.

21 And the people stood afar off, and Moses drew near unto the thick darkness where God *was*.

22 And the LORD said unto Moses, Thus thou shalt say unto the children of Israel, Ye have seen that I have talked with you from heaven.

23 Ye shall not make with me gods of silver, neither shall ye make unto you gods of gold.

24 An altar of earth thou shalt make unto me, and shalt sacrifice thereon thy burnt offerings, and thy peace offerings, thy sheep, and thine oxen: in all places where I record my name I will come unto thee, and I will bless thee.

25 And if thou wilt make me an altar of stone, thou shalt not build it of hewn stone: for if thou lift up thy tool upon it, thou hast polluted it.

26 Neither shalt thou go up by steps unto mine altar, that thy nakedness be not discovered thereon.

21

Now these *are* the judgments which thou shalt set before them.

2 If thou buy an Hebrew servant, six years he shall serve: and in the seventh he shall go out free for nothing.

3 If he came in by himself, he shall go out by himself: if he were married, then his wife shall go out with him.

4 If his master have given him a wife, and she have born him sons or daughters; the wife and her children shall be her master's, and he shall go out by himself.

5 And if the servant shall plainly say, I love my master, my wife, and my children; I will not go out free:

6 Then his master shall bring him unto the judges; he shall also bring him to the door, or unto the door post; and his master shall bore his ear through with an aul; and he shall serve him for ever.

7 And if a man sell his daughter to be a maidservant, she shall not go out as the menservants do.

8 If she please not her master, who hath betrothed her to himself, then shall he let her be redeemed: to sell her unto a strange nation he shall have no power, seeing he hath dealt deceitfully with her.

9 And if he have betrothed her unto his son, he shall deal with her after the manner of daughters.

10 If he take him another *wife*; her food, her raiment, and her duty of marriage, shall he not diminish.

11 And if he do not these three unto her, then shall she go out free without money.

12 He that smiteth a man, so that he die, shall be surely put to death.

13 And if a man lie not in wait, but God deliver *him* into his hand; then I will appoint thee a place whither he shall flee.

14 But if a man come presumptuously upon his neighbour, to slay him with guile; thou shalt take him from mine altar, that he may die.

15 And he that smiteth his father, or his mother, shall be surely put to death.

16 And he that stealeth a man, and selleth him, or if he be found in his hand, he shall surely be put to death.

17 And he that curseth his father, or his mother, shall surely be put to death.

18 And if men strive together, and one smite another with a stone, or with *his* fist, and he die not, but keepeth *his* bed:

19 If he rise again, and walk abroad upon his staff, then shall he that smote *him* be quit: only he shall pay *for* the loss of his time, and shall cause *him* to be thoroughly healed.

20 And if a man smite his servant, or his maid, with a rod, and he die under his hand; he shall be surely punished.

21 Notwithstanding, if he continue a day or two, he shall not be punished: for he *is* his money.

22 If men strive, and hurt a woman with child, so that her fruit depart *from her*, and yet no mischief follow: he shall be surely punished, according as the woman's husband will lay upon him; and he shall pay as the judges *determine*.

23 And if *any* mischief follow, then thou shalt give life for life,

24 Eye for eye, tooth for tooth, hand for hand, foot for foot,

25 Burning for burning, wound for wound, stripe for stripe.

26 And if a man smite the eye of his servant, or the eye of his maid, that it perish; he shall let him go free for his eye's sake.

27 And if he smite out his manservant's tooth, or his maidservant's tooth; he shall let him go free for his tooth's sake.

28 If an ox gore a man or a woman, that they die: then the ox shall be surely stoned, and his flesh shall not be eaten; but the owner of the ox *shall be* quit.

29 But if the ox were wont to push with his horn in time past, and it hath been testified to his owner, and he hath not kept him in, but that he hath killed a man or a woman; the ox shall be stoned, and his owner also shall be put to death.

30 If there be laid on him a sum of money, then he shall give for the ransom of his life whatsoever is laid upon him.

31 Whether he have gored a son, or have gored a daughter, according to this judgment shall it be done unto him.

32 If the ox shall push a manservant or a maidservant; he shall give unto their master thirty shekels of silver, and the ox shall be stoned.

33 And if a man shall open a pit, or if a man shall dig a pit, and not cover it, and an ox or an ass fall therein;

34 The owner of the pit shall make *it* good, *and* give money unto the owner of them; and the dead *beast* shall be his.

35 And if one man's ox hurt another's, that he die; then they shall sell the live ox, and divide the money of it; and the dead *ox* also they shall divide.

36 Or if it be known that the ox hath used to push in time past, and his owner hath not kept him in; he shall surely pay ox for ox; and the dead shall be his own.

22 If a man shall steal an ox, or a sheep, and kill it, or sell it; he shall restore five oxen for an ox, and four sheep for a sheep.

2 If a thief be found breaking up, and be smitten that he die, *there shall* no blood *be shed* for him.

3 If the sun be risen upon him, *there shall be* blood *shed* for him; *for* he should make full restitution; if he have nothing, then he shall be sold for his theft.

4 If the theft be certainly found in his hand alive, whether it be ox, or ass, or sheep; he shall restore double.

5 If a man shall cause a field or vineyard to be eaten, and shall put in his beast, and shall feed in another man's field; of the best of his own field, and of the best of his own vineyard, shall he make restitution.

6 If fire break out, and catch in thorns, so that the stacks of corn, or the standing corn, or the field, be consumed *therewith*; he that kindled the fire shall surely make restitution.

7 If a man shall deliver unto his neighbour money or stuff to keep, and it be stolen out of the man's house; if the thief be found, let him pay double.

8 If the thief be not found, then the master of the house shall be brought unto the judges, *to see* whether he have put his hand unto his neighbour's goods.

9 For all manner of trespass, *whether it be* for ox, for ass, for sheep, for raiment, *or* for any manner of lost thing, which *another* challengeth to be his, the cause of both parties shall come before the judges; *and* whom the judges shall condemn, he shall pay double unto his neighbour.

10 If a man deliver unto his neighbour an ass, or an ox, or a sheep, or any beast, to keep; and it die, or be hurt, or driven away, no man seeing *it*:

11 *Then* shall an oath of the LORD be between them both, that he hath not put his hand unto his neighbour's goods; and the owner of it shall accept *thereof*, and he shall not make *it* good.

12 And if it be stolen from him, he shall make restitution unto the owner thereof.

13 If it be torn in pieces, *then* let him bring it *for* witness, *and* he shall not make good that which was torn.

14 And if a man borrow *ought* of his neighbour, and it be hurt, or die, the owner thereof *being* not with it, he shall surely make *it* good.

15 *But* if the owner thereof *be* with it, he shall not make *it* good: if it *be* an hired *thing*, it came for his hire.

16 And if a man entice a maid that is not betrothed, and lie with her, he shall surely endow her to be his wife.

17 If her father utterly refuse to give her unto him, he shall pay money according to the dowry of virgins.

18 Thou shalt not suffer a witch to
live.
19 Whosoever lieth with a beast shall
surely be put to death.
20 He that sacrificeth unto *any* god,
save unto the LORD only, he shall be
utterly destroyed.
21 Thou shalt neither vex a stranger,
nor oppress him: for ye were strangers
in the land of Egypt.
22 Ye shall not afflict any widow, or
fatherless child.
23 If thou afflict them in any wise,
and they cry at all unto me, I will surely
hear their cry;
24 And my wrath shall wax hot, and I
will kill you with the sword; and your
wives shall be widows, and your children fatherless.
25 If thou lend money to *any of* my
people *that is* poor by thee, thou shalt
not be to him as an usurer, neither shalt
thou lay upon him usury.
26 If thou at all take thy neighbour's
raiment to pledge, thou shalt deliver it
unto him by that the sun goeth down:
27 For that *is* his covering only, it *is*
his raiment for his skin: wherein shall
he sleep? and it shall come to pass,
when he crieth unto me, that I will
hear; for I *am* gracious.
28 Thou shalt not revile the gods, nor
curse the ruler of thy people.
29 Thou shalt not delay *to offer* the
first of thy ripe fruits, and of thy
liquors: the firstborn of thy sons shalt
thou give unto me.
30 Likewise shalt thou do with thine
oxen, *and* with thy sheep: seven days it
shall be with his dam; on the eighth day
thou shalt give it me.
31 And ye shall be holy men unto me:
neither shall ye eat *any* flesh *that is*
torn of beasts in the field; ye shall cast
it to the dogs.

23 Thou shalt not raise a false
report: put not thine hand with
the wicked to be an unrighteous witness.
2 Thou shalt not follow a multitude to
do evil; neither shalt thou speak in a
cause to decline after many to wrest
judgment:
3 Neither shalt thou countenance a
poor man in his cause.
4 If thou meet thine enemy's ox or his
ass going astray, thou shalt surely bring
it back to him again.
5 If thou see the ass of him that
hateth thee lying under his burden,
and wouldest forbear to help him, thou
shalt surely help with him.
6 Thou shalt not wrest the judgment
of thy poor in his cause.
7 Keep thee far from a false matter;
and the innocent and righteous slay
thou not: for I will not justify the wicked.
8 And thou shalt take no gift: for the
gift blindeth the wise, and perverteth
the words of the righteous.
9 Also thou shalt not oppress a stranger: for ye know the heart of a stranger,
seeing ye were strangers in the land of
Egypt.
10 And six years thou shalt sow thy
land, and shalt gather in the fruits
thereof:
11 But the seventh *year* thou shalt let
it rest and lie still; that the poor of thy
people may eat: and what they leave
the beasts of the field shall eat. In like
manner thou shalt deal with thy vineyard, *and* with thy oliveyard.
12 Six days thou shalt do thy work,
and on the seventh day thou shalt rest:
that thine ox and thine ass may rest,

and the son of thy handmaid, and the stranger, may be refreshed.

13 And in all *things* that I have said unto you be circumspect: and make no mention of the name of other gods, neither let it be heard out of thy mouth.

14 Three times thou shalt keep a feast unto me in the year.

15 Thou shalt keep the feast of unleavened bread: (thou shalt eat unleavened bread seven days, as I commanded thee, in the time appointed of the month Abib; for in it thou camest out from Egypt: and none shall appear before me empty:)

16 And the feast of harvest, the firstfruits of thy labours, which thou hast sown in the field: and the feast of ingathering, *which is* in the end of the year, when thou hast gathered in thy labours out of the field.

17 Three times in the year all thy males shall appear before the Lord GOD.

18 Thou shalt not offer the blood of my sacrifice with leavened bread; neither shall the fat of my sacrifice remain until the morning.

19 The first of the firstfruits of thy land thou shalt bring into the house of the LORD thy God. Thou shalt not seethe a kid in his mother's milk.

20 Behold, I send an Angel before thee, to keep thee in the way, and to bring thee into the place which I have prepared.

21 Beware of him, and obey his voice, provoke him not; for he will not pardon your transgressions: for my name *is* in him.

22 But if thou shalt indeed obey his voice, and do all that I speak; then I will be an enemy unto thine enemies, and an adversary unto thine adversaries.

23 For mine Angel shall go before thee, and bring thee in unto the Amorites, and the Hittites, and the Perizzites, and the Canaanites, the Hivites, and the Jebusites: and I will cut them off.

24 Thou shalt not bow down to their gods, nor serve them, nor do after their works: but thou shalt utterly overthrow them, and quite break down their images.

25 And ye shall serve the LORD your God, and he shall bless thy bread, and thy water; and I will take sickness away from the midst of thee.

26 There shall nothing cast their young, nor be barren, in thy land: the number of thy days I will fulfil.

27 I will send my fear before thee, and will destroy all the people to whom thou shalt come, and I will make all thine enemies turn their backs unto thee.

28 And I will send hornets before thee, which shall drive out the Hivite, the Canaanite, and the Hittite, from before thee.

29 I will not drive them out from before thee in one year; lest the land become desolate, and the beast of the field multiply against thee.

30 By little and little I will drive them out from before thee, until thou be increased, and inherit the land.

31 And I will set thy bounds from the Red sea even unto the sea of the Philistines, and from the desert unto the river: for I will deliver the inhabitants of the land into your hand; and thou shalt drive them out before thee.

32 Thou shalt make no covenant with them, nor with their gods.

33 They shall not dwell in thy land, lest they make thee sin against me: for

if thou serve their gods, it will surely be
a snare unto thee.

24 And he said unto Moses, Come
up unto the LORD, thou, and
Aaron, Nadab, and Abihu, and seventy
of the elders of Israel; and worship ye
afar off.
2 And Moses alone shall come near
the LORD: but they shall not come nigh;
neither shall the people go up with
him.
3 And Moses came and told the people all the words of the LORD, and all
the judgments: and all the people
answered with one voice, and said, All
the words which the LORD hath said will
we do.
4 And Moses wrote all the words of
the LORD, and rose up early in the
morning, and builded an altar under
the hill, and twelve pillars, according to
the twelve tribes of Israel.
5 And he sent young men of the children of Israel, which offered burnt
offerings, and sacrificed peace offerings of oxen unto the LORD.
6 And Moses took half of the blood,
and put *it* in basons; and half of the
blood he sprinkled on the altar.
7 And he took the book of the covenant, and read in the audience of the
people: and they said, All that the LORD
hath said will we do, and be obedient.
8 And Moses took the blood, and
sprinkled *it* on the people, and said,
Behold the blood of the covenant,
which the LORD hath made with you
concerning all these words.
9 Then went up Moses, and Aaron,
Nadab, and Abihu, and seventy of the
elders of Israel:
10 And they saw the God of Israel:
and *there was* under his feet as it were
a paved work of a sapphire stone, and
as it were the body of heaven in *his*
clearness.
11 And upon the nobles of the children of Israel he laid not his hand: also
they saw God, and did eat and drink.
12 And the LORD said unto Moses,
Come up to me into the mount, and be
there: and I will give thee tables of
stone, and a law, and commandments
which I have written; that thou mayest
teach them.
13 And Moses rose up, and his minister Joshua: and Moses went up into the
mount of God.
14 And he said unto the elders, Tarry
ye here for us, until we come again unto
you: and, behold, Aaron and Hur *are*
with you: if any man have any matters
to do, let him come unto them.
15 And Moses went up into the
mount, and a cloud covered the mount.
16 And the glory of the LORD abode
upon mount Sinai, and the cloud covered it six days: and the seventh day he
called unto Moses out of the midst of
the cloud.
17 And the sight of the glory of the
LORD *was* like devouring fire on the top
of the mount in the eyes of the children
of Israel.
18 And Moses went into the midst of
the cloud, and gat him up into the
mount: and Moses was in the mount
forty days and forty nights.

25 And the LORD spake unto Moses,
saying,
2 Speak unto the children of Israel,
that they bring me an offering: of every
man that giveth it willingly with his
heart ye shall take my offering.
3 And this *is* the offering which ye
shall take of them; gold, and silver, and
brass,

4 And blue, and purple, and scarlet, and fine linen, and goats' *hair*,

5 And rams' skins dyed red, and badgers' skins, and shittim wood,

6 Oil for the light, spices for anointing oil, and for sweet incense,

7 Onyx stones, and stones to be set in the ephod, and in the breastplate.

8 And let them make me a sanctuary; that I may dwell among them.

9 According to all that I shew thee, *after* the pattern of the tabernacle, and the pattern of all the instruments thereof, even so shall ye make *it*.

10 And they shall make an ark *of* shittim wood: two cubits and a half *shall be* the length thereof, and a cubit and a half the breadth thereof, and a cubit and a half the height thereof.

11 And thou shalt overlay it with pure gold, within and without shalt thou overlay it, and shalt make upon it a crown of gold round about.

12 And thou shalt cast four rings of gold for it, and put *them* in the four corners thereof; and two rings *shall be* in the one side of it, and two rings in the other side of it.

13 And thou shalt make staves *of* shittim wood, and overlay them with gold.

14 And thou shalt put the staves into the rings by the sides of the ark, that the ark may be borne with them.

15 The staves shall be in the rings of the ark: they shall not be taken from it.

16 And thou shalt put into the ark the testimony which I shall give thee.

17 And thou shalt make a mercy seat *of* pure gold: two cubits and a half *shall be* the length thereof, and a cubit and a half the breadth thereof.

18 And thou shalt make two cherubims *of* gold, *of* beaten work shalt thou make them, in the two ends of the mercy seat.

19 And make one cherub on the one end, and the other cherub on the other end: *even* of the mercy seat shall ye make the cherubims on the two ends thereof.

20 And the cherubims shall stretch forth *their* wings on high, covering the mercy seat with their wings, and their faces *shall look* one to another; toward the mercy seat shall the faces of the cherubims be.

21 And thou shalt put the mercy seat above upon the ark; and in the ark thou shalt put the testimony that I shall give thee.

22 And there I will meet with thee, and I will commune with thee from above the mercy seat, from between the two cherubims which *are* upon the ark of the testimony, of all *things* which I will give thee in commandment unto the children of Israel.

23 Thou shalt also make a table *of* shittim wood: two cubits *shall be* the length thereof, and a cubit the breadth thereof, and a cubit and a half the height thereof.

24 And thou shalt overlay it with pure gold, and make thereto a crown of gold round about.

25 And thou shalt make unto it a border of an hand breadth round about, and thou shalt make a golden crown to the border thereof round about.

26 And thou shalt make for it four rings of gold, and put the rings in the four corners that *are* on the four feet thereof.

27 Over against the border shall the rings be for places of the staves to bear the table.

28 And thou shalt make the staves *of* shittim wood, and overlay them with gold, that the table may be borne with them.

29 And thou shalt make the dishes thereof, and spoons thereof, and covers thereof, and bowls thereof, to cover withal: *of* pure gold shalt thou make them.

30 And thou shalt set upon the table shewbread before me alway.

31 And thou shalt make a candlestick *of* pure gold: *of* beaten work shall the candlestick be made: his shaft, and his branches, his bowls, his knops, and his flowers, shall be of the same.

32 And six branches shall come out of the sides of it; three branches of the candlestick out of the one side, and three branches of the candlestick out of the other side:

33 Three bowls made like unto almonds, *with* a knop and a flower in one branch; and three bowls made like almonds in the other branch, *with* a knop and a flower: so in the six branches that come out of the candlestick.

34 And in the candlestick *shall be* four bowls made like unto almonds, *with* their knops and their flowers.

35 And *there shall be* a knop under two branches of the same, and a knop under two branches of the same, and a knop under two branches of the same, according to the six branches that proceed out of the candlestick.

36 Their knops and their branches shall be of the same: all it *shall be* one beaten work *of* pure gold.

37 And thou shalt make the seven lamps thereof: and they shall light the lamps thereof, that they may give light over against it.

38 And the tongs thereof, and the snuffdishes thereof, *shall be of* pure gold.

39 *Of* a talent of pure gold shall he make it, with all these vessels.

40 And look that thou make *them* after their pattern, which was shewed thee in the mount.

26 Moreover thou shalt make the tabernacle *with* ten curtains *of* fine twined linen, and blue, and purple, and scarlet: *with* cherubims of cunning work shalt thou make them.

2 The length of one curtain *shall be* eight and twenty cubits, and the breadth of one curtain four cubits: and every one of the curtains shall have one measure.

3 The five curtains shall be coupled together one to another; and *other* five curtains *shall be* coupled one to another.

4 And thou shalt make loops of blue upon the edge of the one curtain from the selvedge in the coupling; and likewise shalt thou make in the uttermost edge of *another* curtain, in the coupling of the second.

5 Fifty loops shalt thou make in the one curtain, and fifty loops shalt thou make in the edge of the curtain that *is* in the coupling of the second; that the loops may take hold one of another.

6 And thou shalt make fifty taches of gold, and couple the curtains together with the taches: and it shall be one tabernacle.

7 And thou shalt make curtains *of* goats' *hair* to be a covering upon the tabernacle: eleven curtains shalt thou make.

8 The length of one curtain *shall be* thirty cubits, and the breadth of one

curtain four cubits: and the eleven curtains *shall be all* of one measure.
9 And thou shalt couple five curtains by themselves, and six curtains by themselves, and shalt double the sixth curtain in the forefront of the tabernacle.
10 And thou shalt make fifty loops on the edge of the one curtain *that is* outmost in the coupling, and fifty loops in the edge of the curtain which coupleth the second.
11 And thou shalt make fifty taches of brass, and put the taches into the loops, and couple the tent together, that it may be one.
12 And the remnant that remaineth of the curtains of the tent, the half curtain that remaineth, shall hang over the backside of the tabernacle.
13 And a cubit on the one side, and a cubit on the other side of that which remaineth in the length of the curtains of the tent, it shall hang over the sides of the tabernacle on this side and on that side, to cover it.
14 And thou shalt make a covering for the tent *of* rams' skins dyed red, and a covering above *of* badgers' skins.
15 And thou shalt make boards for the tabernacle *of* shittim wood standing up.
16 Ten cubits *shall be* the length of a board, and a cubit and a half *shall be* the breadth of one board.
17 Two tenons *shall there be* in one board, set in order one against another: thus shalt thou make for all the boards of the tabernacle.
18 And thou shalt make the boards for the tabernacle, twenty boards on the south side southward.
19 And thou shalt make forty sockets of silver under the twenty boards; two sockets under one board for his two tenons, and two sockets under another board for his two tenons.
20 And for the second side of the tabernacle on the north side *there shall be* twenty boards:
21 And their forty sockets *of* silver; two sockets under one board, and two sockets under another board.
22 And for the sides of the tabernacle westward thou shalt make six boards.
23 And two boards shalt thou make for the corners of the tabernacle in the two sides.
24 And they shall be coupled together beneath, and they shall be coupled together above the head of it unto one ring: thus shall it be for them both; they shall be for the two corners.
25 And they shall be eight boards, and their sockets *of* silver, sixteen sockets; two sockets under one board, and two sockets under another board.
26 And thou shalt make bars *of* shittim wood; five for the boards of the one side of the tabernacle,
27 And five bars for the boards of the other side of the tabernacle, and five bars for the boards of the side of the tabernacle, for the two sides westward.
28 And the middle bar in the midst of the boards shall reach from end to end.
29 And thou shalt overlay the boards with gold, and make their rings *of* gold *for* places for the bars: and thou shalt overlay the bars with gold.
30 And thou shalt rear up the tabernacle according to the fashion thereof which was shewed thee in the mount.
31 And thou shalt make a vail *of* blue, and purple, and scarlet, and fine twined linen of cunning work: with cherubims shall it be made:

32 And thou shalt hang it upon four pillars of shittim *wood* overlaid with gold: their hooks *shall be of* gold, upon the four sockets of silver.

33 And thou shalt hang up the vail under the taches, that thou mayest bring in thither within the vail the ark of the testimony: and the vail shall divide unto you between the holy *place* and the most holy.

34 And thou shalt put the mercy seat upon the ark of the testimony in the most holy *place*.

35 And thou shalt set the table without the vail, and the candlestick over against the table on the side of the tabernacle toward the south: and thou shalt put the table on the north side.

36 And thou shalt make an hanging for the door of the tent, *of* blue, and purple, and scarlet, and fine twined linen, wrought with needlework.

37 And thou shalt make for the hanging five pillars *of* shittim *wood*, and overlay them with gold, *and* their hooks *shall be of* gold: and thou shalt cast five sockets of brass for them.

27 And thou shalt make an altar *of* shittim wood, five cubits long, and five cubits broad; the altar shall be foursquare: and the height thereof *shall be* three cubits.

2 And thou shalt make the horns of it upon the four corners thereof: his horns shall be of the same: and thou shalt overlay it with brass.

3 And thou shalt make his pans to receive his ashes, and his shovels, and his basons, and his fleshhooks, and his firepans: all the vessels thereof thou shalt make *of* brass.

4 And thou shalt make for it a grate of network *of* brass; and upon the net shalt thou make four brasen rings in the four corners thereof.

5 And thou shalt put it under the compass of the altar beneath, that the net may be even to the midst of the altar.

6 And thou shalt make staves for the altar, staves *of* shittim wood, and overlay them with brass.

7 And the staves shall be put into the rings, and the staves shall be upon the two sides of the altar, to bear it.

8 Hollow with boards shalt thou make it: as it was shewed thee in the mount, so shall they make *it*.

9 And thou shalt make the court of the tabernacle: for the south side southward *there shall be* hangings for the court *of* fine twined linen of an hundred cubits long for one side:

10 And the twenty pillars thereof and their twenty sockets *shall be of* brass; the hooks of the pillars and their fillets *shall be of* silver.

11 And likewise for the north side in length *there shall be* hangings of an hundred *cubits* long, and his twenty pillars and their twenty sockets *of* brass; the hooks of the pillars and their fillets *of* silver.

12 And *for* the breadth of the court on the west side *shall be* hangings of fifty cubits: their pillars ten, and their sockets ten.

13 And the breadth of the court on the east side eastward *shall be* fifty cubits.

14 The hangings of one side *of the gate shall be* fifteen cubits: their pillars three, and their sockets three.

15 And on the other side *shall be* hangings fifteen *cubits*: their pillars three, and their sockets three.

16 And for the gate of the court *shall be* an hanging of twenty cubits, *of* blue, and purple, and scarlet, and fine twined linen, wrought with needlework: *and* their pillars *shall be* four, and their sockets four.

17 All the pillars round about the court *shall be* filleted with silver; their hooks *shall be of* silver, and their sockets *of* brass.

18 The length of the court *shall be* an hundred cubits, and the breadth fifty every where, and the height five cubits *of* fine twined linen, and their sockets *of* brass.

19 All the vessels of the tabernacle in all the service thereof, and all the pins thereof, and all the pins of the court, *shall be of* brass.

20 And thou shalt command the children of Israel, that they bring thee pure oil olive beaten for the light, to cause the lamp to burn always.

21 In the tabernacle of the congregation without the vail, which *is* before the testimony, Aaron and his sons shall order it from evening to morning before the LORD: *it shall be* a statute for ever unto their generations on the behalf of the children of Israel.

28 And take thou unto thee Aaron thy brother, and his sons with him, from among the children of Israel, that he may minister unto me in the priest's office, *even* Aaron, Nadab and Abihu, Eleazar and Ithamar, Aaron's sons.

2 And thou shalt make holy garments for Aaron thy brother for glory and for beauty.

3 And thou shalt speak unto all *that are* wise hearted, whom I have filled with the spirit of wisdom, that they may make Aaron's garments to consecrate him, that he may minister unto me in the priest's office.

4 And these *are* the garments which they shall make; a breastplate, and an ephod, and a robe, and a broidered coat, a mitre, and a girdle: and they shall make holy garments for Aaron thy brother, and his sons, that he may minister unto me in the priest's office.

5 And they shall take gold, and blue, and purple, and scarlet, and fine linen.

6 And they shall make the ephod *of* gold, *of* blue, and *of* purple, *of* scarlet, and fine twined linen, with cunning work.

7 It shall have the two shoulderpieces thereof joined at the two edges thereof; and *so* it shall be joined together.

8 And the curious girdle of the ephod, which *is* upon it, shall be of the same, according to the work thereof; *even of* gold, *of* blue, and purple, and scarlet, and fine twined linen.

9 And thou shalt take two onyx stones, and grave on them the names of the children of Israel:

10 Six of their names on one stone, and *the other* six names of the rest on the other stone, according to their birth.

11 With the work of an engraver in stone, *like* the engravings of a signet, shalt thou engrave the two stones with the names of the children of Israel: thou shalt make them to be set in ouches of gold.

12 And thou shalt put the two stones upon the shoulders of the ephod *for* stones of memorial unto the children of Israel: and Aaron shall bear their names before the LORD upon his two shoulders for a memorial.

13 And thou shalt make ouches *of* gold;

14 And two chains *of* pure gold at the
ends; *of* wreathen work shalt thou
make them, and fasten the wreathen
chains to the ouches.
15 And thou shalt make the breastplate of judgment with cunning work;
after the work of the ephod thou shalt
make it; *of* gold, *of* blue, and *of* purple,
and *of* scarlet, and *of* fine twined linen,
shalt thou make it.
16 Foursquare it shall be *being* doubled; a span *shall be* the length thereof,
and a span *shall be* the breadth thereof.
17 And thou shalt set in it settings of
stones, *even* four rows of stones: *the
first* row *shall be* a sardius, a topaz, and
a carbuncle: *this shall be* the first row.
18 And the second row *shall be* an
emerald, a sapphire, and a diamond.
19 And the third row a ligure, an
agate, and an amethyst.
20 And the fourth row a beryl, and an
onyx, and a jasper: they shall be set in
gold in their inclosings.
21 And the stones shall be with the
names of the children of Israel, twelve,
according to their names, *like* the
engravings of a signet; every one with
his name shall they be according to the
twelve tribes.
22 And thou shalt make upon the
breastplate chains at the ends *of* wreathen work *of* pure gold.
23 And thou shalt make upon the
breastplate two rings of gold, and shalt
put the two rings on the two ends of the
breastplate.
24 And thou shalt put the two wreathen *chains* of gold in the two rings
which are on the ends of the breastplate.
25 And *the other* two ends of the two
wreathen *chains* thou shalt fasten in
the two ouches, and put *them* on the
shoulderpieces of the ephod before it.
26 And thou shalt make two rings of
gold, and thou shalt put them upon the
two ends of the breastplate in the border thereof, which *is* in the side of the
ephod inward.
27 And two *other* rings of gold thou
shalt make, and shalt put them on the
two sides of the ephod underneath,
toward the forepart thereof, over
against the *other* coupling thereof,
above the curious girdle of the ephod.
28 And they shall bind the breastplate by the rings thereof unto the
rings of the ephod with a lace of blue,
that *it* may be above the curious girdle
of the ephod, and that the breastplate
be not loosed from the ephod.
29 And Aaron shall bear the names of
the children of Israel in the breastplate
of judgment upon his heart, when he
goeth in unto the holy *place*, for a
memorial before the LORD continually.
30 And thou shalt put in the breastplate of judgment the Urim and the
Thummim; and they shall be upon
Aaron's heart, when he goeth in before
the LORD: and Aaron shall bear the
judgment of the children of Israel upon
his heart before the LORD continually.
31 And thou shalt make the robe of
the ephod all *of* blue.
32 And there shall be an hole in the
top of it, in the midst thereof: it shall
have a binding of woven work round
about the hole of it, as it were the hole
of an habergeon, that it be not rent.
33 And *beneath* upon the hem of it
thou shalt make pomegranates *of* blue,
and *of* purple, and *of* scarlet, round
about the hem thereof; and bells of
gold between them round about:

34 A golden bell and a pomegranate, a golden bell and a pomegranate, upon the hem of the robe round about.

35 And it shall be upon Aaron to minister: and his sound shall be heard when he goeth in unto the holy *place* before the LORD, and when he cometh out, that he die not.

36 And thou shalt make a plate *of* pure gold, and grave upon it, *like* the engravings of a signet, HOLINESS TO THE LORD.

37 And thou shalt put it on a blue lace, that it may be upon the mitre; upon the forefront of the mitre it shall be.

38 And it shall be upon Aaron's forehead, that Aaron may bear the iniquity of the holy things, which the children of Israel shall hallow in all their holy gifts; and it shall be always upon his forehead, that they may be accepted before the LORD.

39 And thou shalt embroider the coat of fine linen, and thou shalt make the mitre *of* fine linen, and thou shalt make the girdle *of* needlework.

40 And for Aaron's sons thou shalt make coats, and thou shalt make for them girdles, and bonnets shalt thou make for them, for glory and for beauty.

41 And thou shalt put them upon Aaron thy brother, and his sons with him; and shalt anoint them, and consecrate them, and sanctify them, that they may minister unto me in the priest's office.

42 And thou shalt make them linen breeches to cover their nakedness; from the loins even unto the thighs they shall reach:

43 And they shall be upon Aaron, and upon his sons, when they come in unto the tabernacle of the congregation, or when they come near unto the altar to minister in the holy *place*; that they bear not iniquity, and die: *it shall be* a statute for ever unto him and his seed after him.

29 And this *is* the thing that thou shalt do unto them to hallow them, to minister unto me in the priest's office: Take one young bullock, and two rams without blemish,

2 And unleavened bread, and cakes unleavened tempered with oil, and wafers unleavened anointed with oil: *of* wheaten flour shalt thou make them.

3 And thou shalt put them into one basket, and bring them in the basket, with the bullock and the two rams.

4 And Aaron and his sons thou shalt bring unto the door of the tabernacle of the congregation, and shalt wash them with water.

5 And thou shalt take the garments, and put upon Aaron the coat, and the robe of the ephod, and the ephod, and the breastplate, and gird him with the curious girdle of the ephod:

6 And thou shalt put the mitre upon his head, and put the holy crown upon the mitre.

7 Then shalt thou take the anointing oil, and pour *it* upon his head, and anoint him.

8 And thou shalt bring his sons, and put coats upon them.

9 And thou shalt gird them with girdles, Aaron and his sons, and put the bonnets on them: and the priest's office shall be theirs for a perpetual statute: and thou shalt consecrate Aaron and his sons.

10 And thou shalt cause a bullock to be brought before the tabernacle of the congregation: and Aaron and his sons

shall put their hands upon the head of the bullock.

11 And thou shalt kill the bullock before the LORD, *by* the door of the tabernacle of the congregation.

12 And thou shalt take of the blood of the bullock, and put *it* upon the horns of the altar with thy finger, and pour all the blood beside the bottom of the altar.

13 And thou shalt take all the fat that covereth the inwards, and the caul *that is* above the liver, and the two kidneys, and the fat that *is* upon them, and burn *them* upon the altar.

14 But the flesh of the bullock, and his skin, and his dung, shalt thou burn with fire without the camp: it *is* a sin offering.

15 Thou shalt also take one ram; and Aaron and his sons shall put their hands upon the head of the ram.

16 And thou shalt slay the ram, and thou shalt take his blood, and sprinkle *it* round about upon the altar.

17 And thou shalt cut the ram in pieces, and wash the inwards of him, and his legs, and put *them* unto his pieces, and unto his head.

18 And thou shalt burn the whole ram upon the altar: it *is* a burnt offering unto the LORD: it *is* a sweet savour, an offering made by fire unto the LORD.

19 And thou shalt take the other ram; and Aaron and his sons shall put their hands upon the head of the ram.

20 Then shalt thou kill the ram, and take of his blood, and put *it* upon the tip of the right ear of Aaron, and upon the tip of the right ear of his sons, and upon the thumb of their right hand, and upon the great toe of their right foot, and sprinkle the blood upon the altar round about.

21 And thou shalt take of the blood that *is* upon the altar, and of the anointing oil, and sprinkle *it* upon Aaron, and upon his garments, and upon his sons, and upon the garments of his sons with him: and he shall be hallowed, and his garments, and his sons, and his sons' garments with him.

22 Also thou shalt take of the ram the fat and the rump, and the fat that covereth the inwards, and the caul *above* the liver, and the two kidneys, and the fat that *is* upon them, and the right shoulder; for it *is* a ram of consecration:

23 And one loaf of bread, and one cake of oiled bread, and one wafer out of the basket of the unleavened bread that *is* before the LORD:

24 And thou shalt put all in the hands of Aaron, and in the hands of his sons; and shalt wave them *for* a wave offering before the LORD.

25 And thou shalt receive them of their hands, and burn *them* upon the altar for a burnt offering, for a sweet savour before the LORD: it *is* an offering made by fire unto the LORD.

26 And thou shalt take the breast of the ram of Aaron's consecration, and wave it *for* a wave offering before the LORD: and it shall be thy part.

27 And thou shalt sanctify the breast of the wave offering, and the shoulder of the heave offering, which is waved, and which is heaved up, of the ram of the consecration, *even* of *that* which *is* for Aaron, and of *that* which is for his sons:

28 And it shall be Aaron's and his sons' by a statute for ever from the children of Israel: for it *is* an heave offering: and it shall be an heave offering from the children of Israel of the

sacrifice of their peace offerings, *even* their heave offering unto the LORD.

29 And the holy garments of Aaron shall be his sons' after him, to be anointed therein, and to be consecrated in them.

30 *And* that son that is priest in his stead shall put them on seven days, when he cometh into the tabernacle of the congregation to minister in the holy *place*.

31 And thou shalt take the ram of the consecration, and seethe his flesh in the holy place.

32 And Aaron and his sons shall eat the flesh of the ram, and the bread that *is* in the basket, *by* the door of the tabernacle of the congregation.

33 And they shall eat those things wherewith the atonement was made, to consecrate *and* to sanctify them: but a stranger shall not eat *thereof*, because they *are* holy.

34 And if ought of the flesh of the consecrations, or of the bread, remain unto the morning, then thou shalt burn the remainder with fire: it shall not be eaten, because it *is* holy.

35 And thus shalt thou do unto Aaron, and to his sons, according to all *things* which I have commanded thee: seven days shalt thou consecrate them.

36 And thou shalt offer every day a bullock *for* a sin offering for atonement: and thou shalt cleanse the altar, when thou hast made an atonement for it, and thou shalt anoint it, to sanctify it.

37 Seven days thou shalt make an atonement for the altar, and sanctify it; and it shall be an altar most holy: whatsoever toucheth the altar shall be holy.

38 Now this *is that* which thou shalt offer upon the altar; two lambs of the first year day by day continually.

39 The one lamb thou shalt offer in the morning; and the other lamb thou shalt offer at even:

40 And with the one lamb a tenth deal of flour mingled with the fourth part of an hin of beaten oil; and the fourth part of an hin of wine *for* a drink offering.

41 And the other lamb thou shalt offer at even, and shalt do thereto according to the meat offering of the morning, and according to the drink offering thereof, for a sweet savour, an offering made by fire unto the LORD.

42 *This shall be* a continual burnt offering throughout your generations *at* the door of the tabernacle of the congregation before the LORD: where I will meet you, to speak there unto thee.

43 And there I will meet with the children of Israel, and *the tabernacle* shall be sanctified by my glory.

44 And I will sanctify the tabernacle of the congregation, and the altar: I will sanctify also both Aaron and his sons, to minister to me in the priest's office.

45 And I will dwell among the children of Israel, and will be their God.

46 And they shall know that I *am* the LORD their God, that brought them forth out of the land of Egypt, that I may dwell among them: I *am* the LORD their God.

30 And thou shalt make an altar to burn incense upon: *of* shittim wood shalt thou make it.

2 A cubit *shall be* the length thereof, and a cubit the breadth thereof; foursquare shall it be: and two cubits *shall be* the height thereof: the horns thereof *shall be* of the same.

3 And thou shalt overlay it with pure
gold, the top thereof, and the sides
thereof round about, and the horns
thereof; and thou shalt make unto it a
crown of gold round about.
4 And two golden rings shalt thou
make to it under the crown of it, by the
two corners thereof, upon the two sides
of it shalt thou make *it*; and they shall
be for places for the staves to bear it
withal.
5 And thou shalt make the staves *of*
shittim wood, and overlay them with
gold.
6 And thou shalt put it before the vail
that *is* by the ark of the testimony,
before the mercy seat that *is* over the
testimony, where I will meet with thee.
7 And Aaron shall burn thereon sweet
incense every morning: when he dress-
eth the lamps, he shall burn incense
upon it.
8 And when Aaron lighteth the lamps
at even, he shall burn incense upon it, a
perpetual incense before the LORD
throughout your generations.
9 Ye shall offer no strange incense
thereon, nor burnt sacrifice, nor meat
offering; neither shall ye pour drink
offering thereon.
10 And Aaron shall make an atonement upon the horns of it once in a year
with the blood of the sin offering of
atonements: once in the year shall he
make atonement upon it throughout
your generations: it *is* most holy unto
the LORD.
11 And the LORD spake unto Moses,
saying,
12 When thou takest the sum of the
children of Israel after their number,
then shall they give every man a ransom for his soul unto the LORD, when
thou numberest them; that there be no
plague among them, when *thou* numberest them.
13 This they shall give, every one that
passeth among them that are numbered, half a shekel after the shekel of
the sanctuary: (a shekel *is* twenty
gerahs:) an half shekel *shall be* the
offering of the LORD.
14 Every one that passeth among
them that are numbered, from twenty
years old and above, shall give an offering unto the LORD.
15 The rich shall not give more, and
the poor shall not give less than half a
shekel, when *they* give an offering unto
the LORD, to make an atonement for
your souls.
16 And thou shalt take the atonement
money of the children of Israel, and
shalt appoint it for the service of the
tabernacle of the congregation; that it
may be a memorial unto the children of
Israel before the LORD, to make an
atonement for your souls.
17 And the LORD spake unto Moses,
saying,
18 Thou shalt also make a laver *of*
brass, and his foot *also of* brass, to wash
withal: and thou shalt put it between
the tabernacle of the congregation and
the altar, and thou shalt put water
therein.
19 For Aaron and his sons shall wash
their hands and their feet thereat:
20 When they go into the tabernacle
of the congregation, they shall wash
with water, that they die not; or when
they come near to the altar to minister,
to burn offering made by fire unto the
LORD:
21 So they shall wash their hands and
their feet, that they die not: and it shall
be a statute for ever to them, *even* to

him and to his seed throughout their generations.

22 Moreover the LORD spake unto Moses, saying,

23 Take thou also unto thee principal spices, of pure myrrh five hundred *shekels*, and of sweet cinnamon half so much, *even* two hundred and fifty *shekels*, and of sweet calamus two hundred and fifty *shekels*,

24 And of cassia five hundred *shekels*, after the shekel of the sanctuary, and of oil olive an hin:

25 And thou shalt make it an oil of holy ointment, an ointment compound after the art of the apothecary: it shall be an holy anointing oil.

26 And thou shalt anoint the tabernacle of the congregation therewith, and the ark of the testimony,

27 And the table and all his vessels, and the candlestick and his vessels, and the altar of incense,

28 And the altar of burnt offering with all his vessels, and the laver and his foot.

29 And thou shalt sanctify them, that they may be most holy: whatsoever toucheth them shall be holy.

30 And thou shalt anoint Aaron and his sons, and consecrate them, that *they* may minister unto me in the priest's office.

31 And thou shalt speak unto the children of Israel, saying, This shall be an holy anointing oil unto me throughout your generations.

32 Upon man's flesh shall it not be poured, neither shall ye make *any other* like it, after the composition of it: it *is* holy, *and* it shall be holy unto you.

33 Whosoever compoundeth *any* like it, or whosoever putteth *any* of it upon a stranger, shall even be cut off from his people.

34 And the LORD said unto Moses, Take unto thee sweet spices, stacte, and onycha, and galbanum; *these* sweet spices with pure frankincense: of each shall there be a like *weight*:

35 And thou shalt make it a perfume, a confection after the art of the apothecary, tempered together, pure *and* holy:

36 And thou shalt beat *some* of it very small, and put of it before the testimony in the tabernacle of the congregation, where I will meet with thee: it shall be unto you most holy.

37 And *as for* the perfume which thou shalt make, ye shall not make to yourselves according to the composition thereof: it shall be unto thee holy for the LORD.

38 Whosoever shall make like unto that, to smell thereto, shall even be cut off from his people.

31 And the LORD spake unto Moses, saying,

2 See, I have called by name Bezaleel the son of Uri, the son of Hur, of the tribe of Judah:

3 And I have filled him with the spirit of God, in wisdom, and in understanding, and in knowledge, and in all manner of workmanship,

4 To devise cunning works, to work in gold, and in silver, and in brass,

5 And in cutting of stones, to set *them*, and in carving of timber, to work in all manner of workmanship.

6 And I, behold, I have given with him Aholiab, the son of Ahisamach, of the tribe of Dan: and in the hearts of all that are wise hearted I have put wisdom, that they may make all that I have commanded thee;

7 The tabernacle of the congregation, and the ark of the testimony, and the mercy seat that *is* thereupon, and all the furniture of the tabernacle,

8 And the table and his furniture, and the pure candlestick with all his furniture, and the altar of incense,

9 And the altar of burnt offering with all his furniture, and the laver and his foot,

10 And the cloths of service, and the holy garments for Aaron the priest, and the garments of his sons, to minister in the priest's office,

11 And the anointing oil, and sweet incense for the holy *place*: according to all that I have commanded thee shall they do.

12 And the LORD spake unto Moses, saying,

13 Speak thou also unto the children of Israel, saying, Verily my sabbaths ye shall keep: for it *is* a sign between me and you throughout your generations; that *ye* may know that I *am* the LORD that doth sanctify you.

14 Ye shall keep the sabbath therefore; for it *is* holy unto you: every one that defileth it shall surely be put to death: for whosoever doeth *any* work therein, that soul shall be cut off from among his people.

15 Six days may work be done; but in the seventh *is* the sabbath of rest, holy to the LORD: whosoever doeth *any* work in the sabbath day, he shall surely be put to death.

16 Wherefore the children of Israel shall keep the sabbath, to observe the sabbath throughout their generations, *for* a perpetual covenant.

17 It *is* a sign between me and the children of Israel for ever: for *in* six days the LORD made heaven and earth, and on the seventh day he rested, and was refreshed.

18 And he gave unto Moses, when he had made an end of communing with him upon mount Sinai, two tables of testimony, tables of stone, written with the finger of God.

32 And when the people saw that Moses delayed to come down out of the mount, the people gathered themselves together unto Aaron, and said unto him, Up, make us gods, which shall go before us; for *as for* this Moses, the man that brought us up out of the land of Egypt, we wot not what is become of him.

2 And Aaron said unto them, Break off the golden earrings, which *are* in the ears of your wives, of your sons, and of your daughters, and bring *them* unto me.

3 And all the people brake off the golden earrings which *were* in their ears, and brought *them* unto Aaron.

4 And he received *them* at their hand, and fashioned it with a graving tool, after he had made it a molten calf: and they said, These *be* thy gods, O Israel, which brought thee up out of the land of Egypt.

5 And when Aaron saw *it*, he built an altar before it; and Aaron made proclamation, and said, To morrow *is* a feast to the LORD.

6 And they rose up early on the morrow, and offered burnt offerings, and brought peace offerings; and the people sat down to eat and to drink, and rose up to play.

7 And the LORD said unto Moses, Go, get thee down; for thy people, which thou broughtest out of the land of Egypt, have corrupted *themselves*:

8 They have turned aside quickly out
of the way which I commanded them:
they have made them a molten calf,
and have worshipped it, and have sacrificed thereunto, and said, These *be* thy
gods, O Israel, which have brought thee
up out of the land of Egypt.
9 And the LORD said unto Moses, I
have seen this people, and, behold, it *is*
a stiffnecked people:
10 Now therefore let me alone, that
my wrath may wax hot against them,
and that I may consume them: and I
will make of thee a great nation.
11 And Moses besought the LORD his
God, and said, LORD, why doth thy
wrath wax hot against thy people,
which thou hast brought forth out of
the land of Egypt with great power, and
with a mighty hand?
12 Wherefore should the Egyptians
speak, and say, For mischief did he
bring them out, to slay them in the
mountains, and to consume them from
the face of the earth? Turn from thy
fierce wrath, and repent of this evil
against thy people.
13 Remember Abraham, Isaac, and
Israel, thy servants, to whom thou swarest by thine own self, and saidst unto
them, I will multiply your seed as the
stars of heaven, and all this land that I
have spoken of will I give unto your
seed, and they shall inherit *it* for ever.
14 And the LORD repented of the evil
which he thought to do unto his people.
15 And Moses turned, and went down
from the mount, and the two tables of
the testimony *were* in his hand: the
tables *were* written on both their sides;
on the one side and on the other *were*
they written.
16 And the tables *were* the work of
God, and the writing *was* the writing of
God, graven upon the tables.
17 And when Joshua heard the noise
of the people as they shouted, he said
unto Moses, *There is* a noise of war in
the camp.
18 And he said, *It is* not the voice of
them that shout for mastery, neither *is*
it the voice of *them that* cry for being
overcome: *but* the noise of *them that*
sing do I hear.
19 And it came to pass, as soon as he
came nigh unto the camp, that he saw
the calf, and the dancing: and Moses'
anger waxed hot, and he cast the tables
out of his hands, and brake them
beneath the mount.
20 And he took the calf which they
had made, and burnt *it* in the fire, and
ground *it* to powder, and strawed *it*
upon the water, and made the children
of Israel drink *of it*.
21 And Moses said unto Aaron, What
did this people unto thee, that thou
hast brought so great a sin upon them?
22 And Aaron said, Let not the anger
of my lord wax hot: thou knowest the
people, that they *are set* on mischief.
23 For they said unto me, Make us
gods, which shall go before us: for *as for*
this Moses, the man that brought us up
out of the land of Egypt, we wot not
what is become of him.
24 And I said unto them, Whosoever
hath any gold, let them break *it* off. So
they gave *it* me: then I cast it into the
fire, and there came out this calf.
25 And when Moses saw that the
people *were* naked; (for Aaron had
made them naked unto *their* shame
among their enemies:)
26 Then Moses stood in the gate of
the camp, and said, Who *is* on the

LORD's side? *let him come* unto me. And all the sons of Levi gathered themselves together unto him.

27 And he said unto them, Thus saith the LORD God of Israel, Put every man his sword by his side, *and* go in and out from gate to gate throughout the camp, and slay every man his brother, and every man his companion, and every man his neighbour.

28 And the children of Levi did according to the word of Moses: and there fell of the people that day about three thousand men.

29 For Moses had said, Consecrate yourselves to day to the LORD, even every man upon his son, and upon his brother; that he may bestow upon you a blessing this day.

30 And it came to pass on the morrow, that Moses said unto the people, Ye have sinned a great sin: and now I will go up unto the LORD; peradventure I shall make an atonement for your sin.

31 And Moses returned unto the LORD, and said, Oh, this people have sinned a great sin, and have made them gods of gold.

32 Yet now, if thou wilt forgive their sin—; and if not, blot me, I pray thee, out of thy book which thou hast written.

33 And the LORD said unto Moses, Whosoever hath sinned against me, him will I blot out of my book.

34 Therefore now go, lead the people unto *the place* of which I have spoken unto thee: behold, mine Angel shall go before thee: nevertheless in the day when I visit I will visit their sin upon them.

35 And the LORD plagued the people, because they made the calf, which Aaron made.

33 And the LORD said unto Moses, Depart, *and* go up hence, thou and the people which thou hast brought up out of the land of Egypt, unto the land which I sware unto Abraham, to Isaac, and to Jacob, saying, Unto thy seed will I give it:

2 And I will send an angel before thee; and I will drive out the Canaanite, the Amorite, and the Hittite, and the Perizzite, the Hivite, and the Jebusite:

3 Unto a land flowing with milk and honey: for I will not go up in the midst of thee; for thou *art* a stiffnecked people: lest I consume thee in the way.

4 And when the people heard these evil tidings, they mourned: and no man did put on him his ornaments.

5 For the LORD had said unto Moses, Say unto the children of Israel, Ye *are* a stiffnecked people: I will come up into the midst of thee in a moment, and consume thee: therefore now put off thy ornaments from thee, that I may know what to do unto thee.

6 And the children of Israel stripped themselves of their ornaments by the mount Horeb.

7 And Moses took the tabernacle, and pitched it without the camp, afar off from the camp, and called it the Tabernacle of the congregation. And it came to pass, *that* every one which sought the LORD went out unto the tabernacle of the congregation, which *was* without the camp.

8 And it came to pass, when Moses went out unto the tabernacle, *that* all the people rose up, and stood every man *at* his tent door, and looked after Moses, until he was gone into the tabernacle.

9 And it came to pass, as Moses entered into the tabernacle, the cloudy

pillar descended, and stood *at* the door
of the tabernacle, and *the* Lord talked
with Moses.
10 And all the people saw the cloudy
pillar stand *at* the tabernacle door: and
all the people rose up and worshipped,
every man *in* his tent door.
11 And the Lord spake unto Moses
face to face, as a man speaketh unto his
friend. And he turned again into the
camp: but his servant Joshua, the son of
Nun, a young man, departed not out of
the tabernacle.
12 And Moses said unto the Lord,
See, thou sayest unto me, Bring up this
people: and thou hast not let me know
whom thou wilt send with me. Yet thou
hast said, I know thee by name, and
thou hast also found grace in my sight.
13 Now therefore, I pray thee, if I have
found grace in thy sight, shew me now
thy way, that I may know thee, that I
may find grace in thy sight: and consider that this nation *is* thy people.
14 And he said, My presence shall go
with thee, and I will give thee rest.
15 And he said unto him, If thy presence go not *with me*, carry us not up
hence.
16 For wherein shall it be known here
that I and thy people have found grace
in thy sight? *is it* not in that thou goest
with us? so shall we be separated, I and
thy people, from all the people that *are*
upon the face of the earth.
17 And the Lord said unto Moses, I
will do this thing also that thou hast
spoken: for thou hast found grace in my
sight, and I know thee by name.
18 And he said, I beseech thee, shew
me thy glory.
19 And he said, I will make all my
goodness pass before thee, and I will
proclaim the name of the Lord before
thee; and will be gracious to whom I
will be gracious, and will shew mercy
on whom I will shew mercy.
20 And he said, Thou canst not see my
face: for there shall no man see me, and
live.
21 And the Lord said, Behold, *there is*
a place by me, and thou shalt stand
upon a rock:
22 And it shall come to pass, while my
glory passeth by, that I will put thee in
a clift of the rock, and will cover thee
with my hand while I pass by:
23 And I will take away mine hand,
and thou shalt see my back parts: but
my face shall not be seen.

34 And the Lord said unto Moses,
Hew thee two tables of stone like
unto the first: and I will write upon
these tables the words that were in the
first tables, which thou brakest.
2 And be ready in the morning, and
come up in the morning unto mount
Sinai, and present thyself there to me
in the top of the mount.
3 And no man shall come up with
thee, neither let any man be seen
throughout all the mount; neither let
the flocks nor herds feed before that
mount.
4 And he hewed two tables of stone
like unto the first; and Moses rose up
early in the morning, and went up unto
mount Sinai, as the Lord had commanded him, and took in his hand the
two tables of stone.
5 And the Lord descended in the
cloud, and stood with him there, and
proclaimed the name of the Lord.
6 And the Lord passed by before him,
and proclaimed, The Lord, The Lord
God, merciful and gracious, longsuffering, and abundant in goodness and
truth,

7 Keeping mercy for thousands, forgiving iniquity and transgression and
sin, and that will by no means clear *the
guilty*; visiting the iniquity of the
fathers upon the children, and upon the
children's children, unto the third and
to the fourth *generation*.
8 And Moses made haste, and bowed
his head toward the earth, and worshipped.
9 And he said, If now I have found
grace in thy sight, O Lord, let my Lord,
I pray thee, go among us; for it *is* a
stiffnecked people; and pardon our
iniquity and our sin, and take us for
thine inheritance.
10 And he said, Behold, I make a covenant: before all thy people I will do
marvels, such as have not been done in
all the earth, nor in any nation: and all
the people among which thou *art* shall
see the work of the Lord: for it *is* a terrible thing that I will do with thee.
11 Observe thou that which I command thee this day: behold, I drive out
before thee the Amorite, and the
Canaanite, and the Hittite, and the
Perizzite, and the Hivite, and the
Jebusite.
12 Take heed to thyself, lest thou
make a covenant with the inhabitants
of the land whither thou goest, lest it be
for a snare in the midst of thee:
13 But ye shall destroy their altars,
break their images, and cut down their
groves:
14 For thou shalt worship no other
god: for the Lord, whose name *is*
Jealous, *is* a jealous God:
15 Lest thou make a covenant with
the inhabitants of the land, and they go
a whoring after their gods, and do sacrifice unto their gods, and *one* call thee,
and thou eat of his sacrifice;
16 And thou take of their daughters
unto thy sons, and their daughters go a
whoring after their gods, and make thy
sons go a whoring after their gods.
17 Thou shalt make thee no molten
gods.
18 The feast of unleavened bread
shalt thou keep. Seven days thou shalt
eat unleavened bread, as I commanded
thee, in the time of the month Abib: for
in the month Abib thou camest out
from Egypt.
19 All that openeth the matrix *is*
mine; and every firstling among thy
cattle, *whether* ox or sheep, *that is
male*.
20 But the firstling of an ass thou
shalt redeem with a lamb: and if thou
redeem *him* not, then shalt thou break
his neck. All the firstborn of thy sons
thou shalt redeem. And none shall
appear before me empty.
21 Six days thou shalt work, but on
the seventh day thou shalt rest: in earing time and in harvest thou shalt rest.
22 And thou shalt observe the feast of
weeks, of the firstfruits of wheat harvest, and the feast of ingathering at the
year's end.
23 Thrice in the year shall all your
men children appear before the Lord
God, the God of Israel.
24 For I will cast out the nations
before thee, and enlarge thy borders:
neither shall any man desire thy land,
when thou shalt go up to appear before
the Lord thy God thrice in the year.
25 Thou shalt not offer the blood of
my sacrifice with leaven; neither shall
the sacrifice of the feast of the passover
be left unto the morning.
26 The first of the firstfruits of thy
land thou shalt bring unto the house of

the LORD thy God. Thou shalt not seethe a kid in his mother's milk.

27 And the LORD said unto Moses, Write thou these words: for after the tenor of these words I have made a covenant with thee and with Israel.

28 And he was there with the LORD forty days and forty nights; he did neither eat bread, nor drink water. And he wrote upon the tables the words of the covenant, the ten commandments.

29 And it came to pass, when Moses came down from mount Sinai with the two tables of testimony in Moses' hand, when he came down from the mount, that Moses wist not that the skin of his face shone while he talked with him.

30 And when Aaron and all the children of Israel saw Moses, behold, the skin of his face shone; and they were afraid to come nigh him.

31 And Moses called unto them; and Aaron and all the rulers of the congregation returned unto him: and Moses talked with them.

32 And afterward all the children of Israel came nigh: and he gave them in commandment all that the LORD had spoken with him in mount Sinai.

33 And *till* Moses had done speaking with them, he put a vail on his face.

34 But when Moses went in before the LORD to speak with him, he took the vail off, until he came out. And he came out, and spake unto the children of Israel *that* which he was commanded.

35 And the children of Israel saw the face of Moses, that the skin of Moses' face shone: and Moses put the vail upon his face again, until he went in to speak with him.

35 And Moses gathered all the congregation of the children of Israel together, and said unto them, These *are* the words which the LORD hath commanded, that *ye* should do them.

2 Six days shall work be done, but on the seventh day there shall be to you an holy day, a sabbath of rest to the LORD: whosoever doeth work therein shall be put to death.

3 Ye shall kindle no fire throughout your habitations upon the sabbath day.

4 And Moses spake unto all the congregation of the children of Israel, saying, This *is* the thing which the LORD commanded, saying,

5 Take ye from among you an offering unto the LORD: whosoever *is* of a willing heart, let him bring it, an offering of the LORD; gold, and silver, and brass,

6 And blue, and purple, and scarlet, and fine linen, and goats' *hair*,

7 And rams' skins dyed red, and badgers' skins, and shittim wood,

8 And oil for the light, and spices for anointing oil, and for the sweet incense,

9 And onyx stones, and stones to be set for the ephod, and for the breastplate.

10 And every wise hearted among you shall come, and make all that the LORD hath commanded;

11 The tabernacle, his tent, and his covering, his taches, and his boards, his bars, his pillars, and his sockets,

12 The ark, and the staves thereof, *with* the mercy seat, and the vail of the covering,

13 The table, and his staves, and all his vessels, and the shewbread,

14 The candlestick also for the light, and his furniture, and his lamps, with the oil for the light,

15 And the incense altar, and his staves, and the anointing oil, and the sweet incense, and the hanging for the

door at the entering in of the tabernacle,

16 The altar of burnt offering, with his brasen grate, his staves, and all his vessels, the laver and his foot,

17 The hangings of the court, his pillars, and their sockets, and the hanging for the door of the court,

18 The pins of the tabernacle, and the pins of the court, and their cords,

19 The cloths of service, to do service in the holy *place*, the holy garments for Aaron the priest, and the garments of his sons, to minister in the priest's office.

20 And all the congregation of the children of Israel departed from the presence of Moses.

21 And they came, every one whose heart stirred him up, and every one whom his spirit made willing, *and* they brought the LORD's offering to the work of the tabernacle of the congregation, and for all his service, and for the holy garments.

22 And they came, both men and women, as many as were willing hearted, *and* brought bracelets, and earrings, and rings, and tablets, all jewels of gold: and every man that offered *offered* an offering of gold unto the LORD.

23 And every man, with whom was found blue, and purple, and scarlet, and fine linen, and goats' *hair*, and red skins of rams, and badgers' skins, brought *them*.

24 Every one that did offer an offering of silver and brass brought the LORD's offering: and every man, with whom was found shittim wood for any work of the service, brought *it*.

25 And all the women that were wise hearted did spin with their hands, and brought that which they had spun, *both* of blue, and of purple, *and* of scarlet, and of fine linen.

26 And all the women whose heart stirred them up in wisdom spun goats' *hair*.

27 And the rulers brought onyx stones, and stones to be set, for the ephod, and for the breastplate;

28 And spice, and oil for the light, and for the anointing oil, and for the sweet incense.

29 The children of Israel brought a willing offering unto the LORD, every man and woman, whose heart made them willing to bring for all manner of work, which the LORD had commanded to be made by the hand of Moses.

30 And Moses said unto the children of Israel, See, the LORD hath called by name Bezaleel the son of Uri, the son of Hur, of the tribe of Judah;

31 And he hath filled him with the spirit of God, in wisdom, in understanding, and in knowledge, and in all manner of workmanship;

32 And to devise curious works, to work in gold, and in silver, and in brass,

33 And in the cutting of stones, to set *them*, and in carving of wood, to make any manner of cunning work.

34 And he hath put in his heart that he may teach, *both* he, and Aholiab, the son of Ahisamach, of the tribe of Dan.

35 Them hath he filled with wisdom of heart, to work all manner of work, of the engraver, and of the cunning workman, and of the embroiderer, in blue, and in purple, in scarlet, and in fine linen, and of the weaver, *even* of them that do any work, and of those that devise cunning work.

36 Then wrought Bezaleel and Aholiab, and every wise hearted

man, in whom the LORD put wisdom
and understanding to know how to
work all manner of work for the service
of the sanctuary, according to all that
the LORD had commanded.
2 And Moses called Bezaleel and
Aholiab, and every wise hearted man,
in whose heart the LORD had put wisdom, *even* every one whose heart
stirred him up to come unto the work to
do it:
3 And they received of Moses all the
offering, which the children of Israel
had brought for the work of the service
of the sanctuary, to make it *withal*. And
they brought yet unto him free offerings every morning.
4 And all the wise men, that wrought
all the work of the sanctuary, came
every man from his work which they
made;
5 And they spake unto Moses, saying,
The people bring much more than
enough for the service of the work,
which the LORD commanded to make.
6 And Moses gave commandment,
and they caused it to be proclaimed
throughout the camp, saying, Let neither man nor woman make any more
work for the offering of the sanctuary.
So the people were restrained from
bringing.
7 For the stuff they had was sufficient
for all the work to make it, and too
much.
8 And every wise hearted man among
them that wrought the work of the
tabernacle made ten curtains *of* fine
twined linen, and blue, and purple, and
scarlet: *with* cherubims of cunning
work made he them.
9 The length of one curtain *was* twenty and eight cubits, and the breadth of
one curtain four cubits: the curtains
were all of one size.
10 And he coupled the five curtains
one unto another: and *the other* five
curtains he coupled one unto another.
11 And he made loops of blue on the
edge of one curtain from the selvedge
in the coupling: likewise he made in
the uttermost side of *another* curtain,
in the coupling of the second.
12 Fifty loops made he in one curtain,
and fifty loops made he in the edge of
the curtain which *was* in the coupling
of the second: the loops held one *curtain* to another.
13 And he made fifty taches of gold,
and coupled the curtains one unto
another with the taches: so it became
one tabernacle.
14 And he made curtains *of* goats'
hair for the tent over the tabernacle:
eleven curtains he made them.
15 The length of one curtain *was*
thirty cubits, and four cubits *was* the
breadth of one curtain: the eleven curtains *were* of one size.
16 And he coupled five curtains by
themselves, and six curtains by themselves.
17 And he made fifty loops upon the
uttermost edge of the curtain in the
coupling, and fifty loops made he upon
the edge of the curtain which coupleth
the second.
18 And he made fifty taches *of* brass
to couple the tent together, that it
might be one.
19 And he made a covering for the
tent *of* rams' skins dyed red, and a covering *of* badgers' skins above *that*.
20 And he made boards for the tabernacle *of* shittim wood, standing up.

21 The length of a board *was* ten cubits, and the breadth of a board one cubit and a half.

22 One board had two tenons, equally distant one from another: thus did he make for all the boards of the tabernacle.

23 And he made boards for the tabernacle; twenty boards for the south side southward:

24 And forty sockets of silver he made under the twenty boards; two sockets under one board for his two tenons, and two sockets under another board for his two tenons.

25 And for the other side of the tabernacle, *which is* toward the north corner, he made twenty boards,

26 And their forty sockets of silver; two sockets under one board, and two sockets under another board.

27 And for the sides of the tabernacle westward he made six boards.

28 And two boards made he for the corners of the tabernacle in the two sides.

29 And they were coupled beneath, and coupled together at the head thereof, to one ring: thus he did to both of them in both the corners.

30 And there were eight boards; and their sockets *were* sixteen sockets of silver, under every board two sockets.

31 And he made bars of shittim wood; five for the boards of the one side of the tabernacle,

32 And five bars for the boards of the other side of the tabernacle, and five bars for the boards of the tabernacle for the sides westward.

33 And he made the middle bar to shoot through the boards from the one end to the other.

34 And he overlaid the boards with gold, and made their rings *of* gold *to be* places for the bars, and overlaid the bars with gold.

35 And he made a vail *of* blue, and purple, and scarlet, and fine twined linen: *with* cherubims made he it of cunning work.

36 And he made thereunto four pillars *of* shittim *wood*, and overlaid them with gold: their hooks *were of* gold; and he cast for them four sockets of silver.

37 And he made an hanging for the tabernacle door *of* blue, and purple, and scarlet, and fine twined linen, of needlework;

38 And the five pillars of it with their hooks: and he overlaid their chapiters and their fillets with gold: but their five sockets *were of* brass.

37 And Bezaleel made the ark *of* shittim wood: two cubits and a half *was* the length of it, and a cubit and a half the breadth of it, and a cubit and a half the height of it:

2 And he overlaid it with pure gold within and without, and made a crown of gold to it round about.

3 And he cast for it four rings of gold, *to be set* by the four corners of it; even two rings upon the one side of it, and two rings upon the other side of it.

4 And he made staves *of* shittim wood, and overlaid them with gold.

5 And he put the staves into the rings by the sides of the ark, to bear the ark.

6 And he made the mercy seat *of* pure gold: two cubits and a half *was* the length thereof, and one cubit and a half the breadth thereof.

7 And he made two cherubims *of* gold, beaten out of one piece made he them, on the two ends of the mercy seat;

8 One cherub on the end on this side,
and another cherub on the *other* end
on that side: out of the mercy seat
made he the cherubims on the two
ends thereof.
9 And the cherubims spread out *their*
wings on high, *and* covered with their
wings over the mercy seat, with their
faces one to another; *even* to the mercy
seatward were the faces of the cherubims.
10 And he made the table *of* shittim
wood: two cubits *was* the length thereof, and a cubit the breadth thereof, and
a cubit and a half the height thereof:
11 And he overlaid it with pure gold,
and made thereunto a crown of gold
round about.
12 Also he made thereunto a border
of an handbreadth round about; and
made a crown of gold for the border
thereof round about.
13 And he cast for it four rings of
gold, and put the rings upon the four
corners that *were* in the four feet thereof.
14 Over against the border were the
rings, the places for the staves to bear
the table.
15 And he made the staves *of* shittim
wood, and overlaid them with gold, to
bear the table.
16 And he made the vessels which
were upon the table, his dishes, and his
spoons, and his bowls, and his covers to
cover withal, *of* pure gold.
17 And he made the candlestick *of*
pure gold: *of* beaten work made he the
candlestick; his shaft, and his branch,
his bowls, his knops, and his flowers,
were of the same:
18 And six branches going out of the
sides thereof; three branches of the
candlestick out of the one side thereof,
and three branches of the candlestick
out of the other side thereof:
19 Three bowls made after the fashion of almonds in one branch, a knop
and a flower; and three bowls made
like almonds in another branch, a knop
and a flower: so throughout the six
branches going out of the candlestick.
20 And in the candlestick *were* four
bowls made like almonds, his knops,
and his flowers:
21 And a knop under two branches of
the same, and a knop under two
branches of the same, and a knop
under two branches of the same,
according to the six branches going out
of it.
22 Their knops and their branches
were of the same: all of it *was* one
beaten work *of* pure gold.
23 And he made his seven lamps, and
his snuffers, and his snuffdishes, *of*
pure gold.
24 *Of* a talent of pure gold made he it,
and all the vessels thereof.
25 And he made the incense altar *of*
shittim wood: the length of it *was* a
cubit, and the breadth of it a cubit; *it*
was foursquare; and two cubits *was* the
height of it; the horns thereof were of
the same.
26 And he overlaid it with pure gold,
both the top of it, and the sides thereof
round about, and the horns of it: also he
made unto it a crown of gold round
about.
27 And he made two rings of gold for
it under the crown thereof, by the two
corners of it, upon the two sides thereof, to be places for the staves to bear it
withal.
28 And he made the staves *of* shittim
wood, and overlaid them with gold.

29 And he made the holy anointing oil, and the pure incense of sweet spices, according to the work of the apothecary.

38 And he made the altar of burnt offering *of* shittim wood: five cubits *was* the length thereof, and five cubits the breadth thereof; *it was* foursquare; and three cubits the height thereof.

2 And he made the horns thereof on the four corners of it; the horns thereof were of the same: and he overlaid it with brass.

3 And he made all the vessels of the altar, the pots, and the shovels, and the basons, *and* the fleshhooks, and the firepans: all the vessels thereof made he *of* brass.

4 And he made for the altar a brasen grate of network under the compass thereof beneath unto the midst of it.

5 And he cast four rings for the four ends of the grate of brass, *to be* places for the staves.

6 And he made the staves *of* shittim wood, and overlaid them with brass.

7 And he put the staves into the rings on the sides of the altar, to bear it withal; he made the altar hollow with boards.

8 And he made the laver *of* brass, and the foot of it *of* brass, of the lookingglasses of *the women* assembling, which assembled *at* the door of the tabernacle of the congregation.

9 And he made the court: on the south side southward the hangings of the court *were of* fine twined linen, an hundred cubits:

10 Their pillars *were* twenty, and their brasen sockets twenty; the hooks of the pillars and their fillets *were of* silver.

11 And for the north side *the hangings were* an hundred cubits, their pillars *were* twenty, and their sockets of brass twenty; the hooks of the pillars and their fillets *of* silver.

12 And for the west side *were* hangings of fifty cubits, their pillars ten, and their sockets ten; the hooks of the pillars and their fillets *of* silver.

13 And for the east side eastward fifty cubits.

14 The hangings of the one side *of the gate were* fifteen cubits; their pillars three, and their sockets three.

15 And for the other side of the court gate, on this hand and that hand, *were* hangings of fifteen cubits; their pillars three, and their sockets three.

16 All the hangings of the court round about *were* of fine twined linen.

17 And the sockets for the pillars *were of* brass; the hooks of the pillars and their fillets *of* silver; and the overlaying of their chapiters *of* silver; and all the pillars of the court *were* filleted with silver.

18 And the hanging for the gate of the court *was* needlework, *of* blue, and purple, and scarlet, and fine twined linen: and twenty cubits *was* the length, and the height in the breadth *was* five cubits, answerable to the hangings of the court.

19 And their pillars *were* four, and their sockets *of* brass four; their hooks *of* silver, and the overlaying of their chapiters and their fillets *of* silver.

20 And all the pins of the tabernacle, and of the court round about, *were of* brass.

21 This is the sum of the tabernacle, *even* of the tabernacle of testimony, as it was counted, according to the commandment of Moses, *for* the service of the Levites, by the hand of Ithamar, son to Aaron the priest.

22 And Bezaleel the son of Uri, the
son of Hur, of the tribe of Judah, made
all that the LORD commanded Moses.
23 And with him *was* Aholiab, son of
Ahisamach, of the tribe of Dan, an
engraver, and a cunning workman, and
an embroiderer in blue, and in purple,
and in scarlet, and fine linen.
24 All the gold that was occupied for
the work in all the work of the holy
place, even the gold of the offering, was
twenty and nine talents, and seven
hundred and thirty shekels, after the
shekel of the sanctuary.
25 And the silver of them that were
numbered of the congregation *was* an
hundred talents, and a thousand seven
hundred and threescore and fifteen
shekels, after the shekel of the sanctuary:
26 A bekah for every man, *that is*,
half a shekel, after the shekel of the
sanctuary, for every one that went to be
numbered, from twenty years old and
upward, for six hundred thousand and
three thousand and five hundred and
fifty *men*.
27 And of the hundred talents of
silver were cast the sockets of the sanctuary, and the sockets of the vail; an
hundred sockets of the hundred talents,
a talent for a socket.
28 And of the thousand seven hundred seventy and five shekels he made
hooks for the pillars, and overlaid their
chapiters, and filleted them.
29 And the brass of the offering *was*
seventy talents, and two thousand and
four hundred shekels.
30 And therewith he made the sockets to the door of the tabernacle of the
congregation, and the brasen altar, and
the brasen grate for it, and all the vessels of the altar,
31 And the sockets of the court round
about, and the sockets of the court gate,
and all the pins of the tabernacle, and
all the pins of the court round about.

39 And of the blue, and purple, and
scarlet, they made cloths of service, to do service in the holy *place*, and
made the holy garments for Aaron; as
the LORD commanded Moses.
2 And he made the ephod *of* gold,
blue, and purple, and scarlet, and fine
twined linen.
3 And they did beat the gold into thin
plates, and cut *it into* wires, to work *it*
in the blue, and in the purple, and in
the scarlet, and in the fine linen, *with*
cunning work.
4 They made shoulderpieces for it, to
couple *it* together: by the two edges
was it coupled together.
5 And the curious girdle of his ephod,
that *was* upon it, *was* of the same,
according to the work thereof; *of* gold,
blue, and purple, and scarlet, and fine
twined linen; as the LORD commanded
Moses.
6 And they wrought onyx stones
inclosed in ouches of gold, graven, as
signets are graven, with the names of
the children of Israel.
7 And he put them on the shoulders
of the ephod, *that they should be*
stones for a memorial to the children of
Israel; as the LORD commanded Moses.
8 And he made the breastplate *of*
cunning work, like the work of the
ephod; *of* gold, blue, and purple, and
scarlet, and fine twined linen.
9 It was foursquare; they made the
breastplate double: a span *was* the
length thereof, and a span the breadth
thereof, *being* doubled.
10 And they set in it four rows of
stones: *the first* row *was* a sardius, a

topaz, and a carbuncle: this *was* the
first row.
11 And the second row, an emerald, a
sapphire, and a diamond.
12 And the third row, a ligure, an
agate, and an amethyst.
13 And the fourth row, a beryl, an
onyx, and a jasper: *they were* inclosed
in ouches of gold in their inclosings.
14 And the stones *were* according to
the names of the children of Israel,
twelve, according to their names, *like*
the engravings of a signet, every one
with his name, according to the twelve
tribes.
15 And they made upon the breastplate chains at the ends, *of* wreathen
work *of* pure gold.
16 And they made two ouches *of* gold,
and two gold rings; and put the two
rings in the two ends of the breastplate.
17 And they put the two wreathen
chains of gold in the two rings on the
ends of the breastplate.
18 And the two ends of the two wreathen chains they fastened in the two
ouches, and put them on the shoulderpieces of the ephod, before it.
19 And they made two rings of gold,
and put *them* on the two ends of the
breastplate, upon the border of it,
which *was* on the side of the ephod
inward.
20 And they made two *other* golden
rings, and put them on the two sides of
the ephod underneath, toward the forepart of it, over against the *other* coupling thereof, above the curious girdle
of the ephod.
21 And they did bind the breastplate
by his rings unto the rings of the ephod
with a lace of blue, that it might be
above the curious girdle of the ephod,
and that the breastplate might not be
loosed from the ephod; as the LORD
commanded Moses.
22 And he made the robe of the
ephod *of* woven work, all *of* blue.
23 And *there was* an hole in the midst
of the robe, as the hole of an habergeon, *with* a band round about the
hole, that it should not rend.
24 And they made upon the hems of
the robe pomegranates *of* blue, and
purple, and scarlet, *and* twined *linen*.
25 And they made bells *of* pure gold,
and put the bells between the pomegranates upon the hem of the robe,
round about between the pomegranates;
26 A bell and a pomegranate, a bell
and a pomegranate, round about the
hem of the robe to minister *in*; as the
LORD commanded Moses.
27 And they made coats *of* fine linen
of woven work for Aaron, and for his
sons,
28 And a mitre *of* fine linen, and
goodly bonnets *of* fine linen, and linen
breeches *of* fine twined linen,
29 And a girdle *of* fine twined linen,
and blue, and purple, and scarlet, *of*
needlework; as the LORD commanded
Moses.
30 And they made the plate of the
holy crown *of* pure gold, and wrote
upon it a writing, *like to* the engravings
of a signet, HOLINESS TO THE LORD.
31 And they tied unto it a lace of blue,
to fasten *it* on high upon the mitre; as
the LORD commanded Moses.
32 Thus was all the work of the tabernacle of the tent of the congregation
finished: and the children of Israel did
according to all that the LORD commanded Moses, so did they.
33 And they brought the tabernacle
unto Moses, the tent, and all his furni-

ture, his taches, his boards, his bars,
and his pillars, and his sockets,
34 And the covering of rams' skins
dyed red, and the covering of badgers'
skins, and the vail of the covering,
35 The ark of the testimony, and the
staves thereof, and the mercy seat,
36 The table, *and* all the vessels
thereof, and the shewbread,
37 The pure candlestick, *with* the
lamps thereof, *even with* the lamps to
be set in order, and all the vessels
thereof, and the oil for light,
38 And the golden altar, and the
anointing oil, and the sweet incense,
and the hanging for the tabernacle
door,
39 The brasen altar, and his grate of
brass, his staves, and all his vessels, the
laver and his foot,
40 The hangings of the court, his pillars, and his sockets, and the hanging
for the court gate, his cords, and his
pins, and all the vessels of the service
of the tabernacle, for the tent of the
congregation,
41 The cloths of service to do service
in the holy *place*, and the holy garments for Aaron the priest, and his
sons' garments, to minister in the
priest's office.
42 According to all that the LORD
commanded Moses, so the children of
Israel made all the work.
43 And Moses did look upon all the
work, and, behold, they had done it as
the LORD had commanded, even so had
they done it: and Moses blessed them.

40 And the LORD spake unto Moses,
saying,
2 On the first day of the first month
shalt thou set up the tabernacle of the
tent of the congregation.
3 And thou shalt put therein the ark
of the testimony, and cover the ark with
the vail.
4 And thou shalt bring in the table,
and set in order the things that are to
be set in order upon it; and thou shalt
bring in the candlestick, and light the
lamps thereof.
5 And thou shalt set the altar of gold
for the incense before the ark of the
testimony, and put the hanging of the
door to the tabernacle.
6 And thou shalt set the altar of the
burnt offering before the door of the
tabernacle of the tent of the congregation.
7 And thou shalt set the laver
between the tent of the congregation
and the altar, and shalt put water
therein.
8 And thou shalt set up the court
round about, and hang up the hanging
at the court gate.
9 And thou shalt take the anointing
oil, and anoint the tabernacle, and all
that *is* therein, and shalt hallow it, and
all the vessels thereof: and it shall be
holy.
10 And thou shalt anoint the altar of
the burnt offering, and all his vessels,
and sanctify the altar: and it shall be an
altar most holy.
11 And thou shalt anoint the laver
and his foot, and sanctify it.
12 And thou shalt bring Aaron and
his sons unto the door of the tabernacle
of the congregation, and wash them
with water.
13 And thou shalt put upon Aaron the
holy garments, and anoint him, and
sanctify him; that he may minister unto
me in the priest's office.
14 And thou shalt bring his sons, and
clothe them with coats:

15 And thou shalt anoint them, as
thou didst anoint their father, that they
may minister unto me in the priest's
office: for their anointing shall surely
be an everlasting priesthood throughout their generations.
16 Thus did Moses: according to all
that the LORD commanded him, so did
he.
17 And it came to pass in the first
month in the second year, on the first
day of the month, *that* the tabernacle
was reared up.
18 And Moses reared up the tabernacle, and fastened his sockets, and set up
the boards thereof, and put in the bars
thereof, and reared up his pillars.
19 And he spread abroad the tent
over the tabernacle, and put the covering of the tent above upon it; as the
LORD commanded Moses.
20 And he took and put the testimony
into the ark, and set the staves on the
ark, and put the mercy seat above upon
the ark:
21 And he brought the ark into the
tabernacle, and set up the vail of the
covering, and covered the ark of the
testimony; as the LORD commanded
Moses.
22 And he put the table in the tent of
the congregation, upon the side of the
tabernacle northward, without the vail.
23 And he set the bread in order upon
it before the LORD; as the LORD had
commanded Moses.
24 And he put the candlestick in the
tent of the congregation, over against
the table, on the side of the tabernacle
southward.
25 And he lighted the lamps before
the LORD; as the LORD commanded
Moses.
26 And he put the golden altar in the
tent of the congregation before the vail:
27 And he burnt sweet incense thereon; as the LORD commanded Moses.
28 And he set up the hanging *at* the
door of the tabernacle.
29 And he put the altar of burnt offering *by* the door of the tabernacle of the
tent of the congregation, and offered
upon it the burnt offering and the meat
offering; as the LORD commanded
Moses.
30 And he set the laver between the
tent of the congregation and the altar,
and put water there, to wash *withal*.
31 And Moses and Aaron and his sons
washed their hands and their feet
thereat:
32 When they went into the tent of
the congregation, and when they came
near unto the altar, they washed; as the
LORD commanded Moses.
33 And he reared up the court round
about the tabernacle and the altar, and
set up the hanging of the court gate. So
Moses finished the work.
34 Then a cloud covered the tent of
the congregation, and the glory of the
LORD filled the tabernacle.
35 And Moses was not able to enter
into the tent of the congregation,
because the cloud abode thereon, and
the glory of the LORD filled the tabernacle.
36 And when the cloud was taken up
from over the tabernacle, the children
of Israel went onward in all their journeys:
37 But if the cloud were not taken up,
then they journeyed not till the day
that it was taken up.
38 For the cloud of the LORD *was*
upon the tabernacle by day, and fire
was on it by night, in the sight of all the
house of Israel, throughout all their
journeys.

THE THIRD BOOK OF MOSES

CALLED

LEVITICUS

1 And the LORD called unto Moses, and spake unto him out of the tabernacle of the congregation, saying,

2 Speak unto the children of Israel, and say unto them, If any man of you bring an offering unto the LORD, ye shall bring your offering of the cattle, *even* of the herd, and of the flock.

3 If his offering *be* a burnt sacrifice of the herd, let him offer a male without blemish: he shall offer it of his own voluntary will at the door of the tabernacle of the congregation before the LORD.

4 And he shall put his hand upon the head of the burnt offering; and it shall be accepted for him to make atonement for him.

5 And he shall kill the bullock before the LORD: and the priests, Aaron's sons, shall bring the blood, and sprinkle the blood round about upon the altar that *is by* the door of the tabernacle of the congregation.

6 And he shall flay the burnt offering, and cut it into his pieces.

7 And the sons of Aaron the priest shall put fire upon the altar, and lay the wood in order upon the fire:

8 And the priests, Aaron's sons, shall lay the parts, the head, and the fat, in order upon the wood that *is* on the fire which *is* upon the altar:

9 But his inwards and his legs shall he wash in water: and the priest shall burn all on the altar, *to be* a burnt sacrifice, an offering made by fire, of a sweet savour unto the LORD.

10 And if his offering *be* of the flocks, *namely*, of the sheep, or of the goats, for a burnt sacrifice; he shall bring it a male without blemish.

11 And he shall kill it on the side of the altar northward before the LORD: and the priests, Aaron's sons, shall sprinkle his blood round about upon the altar.

12 And he shall cut it into his pieces, with his head and his fat: and the priest shall lay them in order on the wood that *is* on the fire which *is* upon the altar:

13 But he shall wash the inwards and the legs with water: and the priest shall bring *it* all, and burn *it* upon the altar: it *is* a burnt sacrifice, an offering made by fire, of a sweet savour unto the LORD.

14 And if the burnt sacrifice for his offering to the LORD *be* of fowls, then he shall bring his offering of turtledoves, or of young pigeons.

15 And the priest shall bring it unto the altar, and wring off his head, and burn *it* on the altar; and the blood thereof shall be wrung out at the side of the altar:

16 And he shall pluck away his crop with his feathers, and cast it beside the altar on the east part, by the place of the ashes:

17 And he shall cleave it with the wings thereof, *but* shall not divide *it* asunder: and the priest shall burn it upon the altar, upon the wood that *is* upon the fire: it *is* a burnt sacrifice, an offering made by fire, of a sweet savour unto the LORD.

2 And when any will offer a meat offering unto the LORD, his offering shall be *of* fine flour; and he shall pour

oil upon it, and put frankincense thereon:

2 And he shall bring it to Aaron's sons the priests: and he shall take thereout his handful of the flour thereof, and of the oil thereof, with all the frankincense thereof; and the priest shall burn the memorial of it upon the altar, *to be* an offering made by fire, of a sweet savour unto the LORD:

3 And the remnant of the meat offering *shall be* Aaron's and his sons': *it is* a thing most holy of the offerings of the LORD made by fire.

4 And if thou bring an oblation of a meat offering baken in the oven, *it shall be* unleavened cakes of fine flour mingled with oil, or unleavened wafers anointed with oil.

5 And if thy oblation *be* a meat offering *baken* in a pan, it shall be *of* fine flour unleavened, mingled with oil.

6 Thou shalt part it in pieces, and pour oil thereon: it *is* a meat offering.

7 And if thy oblation *be* a meat offering *baken* in the fryingpan, it shall be made *of* fine flour with oil.

8 And thou shalt bring the meat offering that is made of these things unto the LORD: and when it is presented unto the priest, he shall bring it unto the altar.

9 And the priest shall take from the meat offering a memorial thereof, and shall burn *it* upon the altar: *it is* an offering made by fire, of a sweet savour unto the LORD.

10 And that which is left of the meat offering *shall be* Aaron's and his sons': *it is* a thing most holy of the offerings of the LORD made by fire.

11 No meat offering, which ye shall bring unto the LORD, shall be made with leaven: for ye shall burn no leaven, nor any honey, in any offering of the LORD made by fire.

12 As for the oblation of the firstfruits, ye shall offer them unto the LORD: but they shall not be burnt on the altar for a sweet savour.

13 And every oblation of thy meat offering shalt thou season with salt; neither shalt thou suffer the salt of the covenant of thy God to be lacking from thy meat offering: with all thine offerings thou shalt offer salt.

14 And if thou offer a meat offering of thy firstfruits unto the LORD, thou shalt offer for the meat offering of thy firstfruits green ears of corn dried by the fire, *even* corn beaten out of full ears.

15 And thou shalt put oil upon it, and lay frankincense thereon: it *is* a meat offering.

16 And the priest shall burn the memorial of it, *part* of the beaten corn thereof, and *part* of the oil thereof, with all the frankincense thereof: *it is* an offering made by fire unto the LORD.

3 And if his oblation *be* a sacrifice of peace offering, if he offer *it* of the herd; whether *it be* a male or female, he shall offer it without blemish before the LORD.

2 And he shall lay his hand upon the head of his offering, and kill it *at* the door of the tabernacle of the congregation: and Aaron's sons the priests shall sprinkle the blood upon the altar round about.

3 And he shall offer of the sacrifice of the peace offering an offering made by fire unto the LORD; the fat that covereth the inwards, and all the fat that *is* upon the inwards,

4 And the two kidneys, and the fat that *is* on them, which *is* by the flanks,

and the caul above the liver, with the
kidneys, it shall he take away.
5 And Aaron's sons shall burn it on
the altar upon the burnt sacrifice,
which *is* upon the wood that *is* on the
fire: *it is* an offering made by fire, of a
sweet savour unto the LORD.
6 And if his offering for a sacrifice of
peace offering unto the LORD *be* of the
flock; male or female, he shall offer it
without blemish.
7 If he offer a lamb for his offering,
then shall he offer it before the LORD.
8 And he shall lay his hand upon the
head of his offering, and kill it before
the tabernacle of the congregation: and
Aaron's sons shall sprinkle the blood
thereof round about upon the altar.
9 And he shall offer of the sacrifice of
the peace offering an offering made by
fire unto the LORD; the fat thereof, *and*
the whole rump, it shall he take off
hard by the backbone; and the fat that
covereth the inwards, and all the fat
that *is* upon the inwards,
10 And the two kidneys, and the fat
that *is* upon them, which *is* by the
flanks, and the caul above the liver,
with the kidneys, it shall he take away.
11 And the priest shall burn it upon
the altar: *it is* the food of the offering
made by fire unto the LORD.
12 And if his offering *be* a goat, then
he shall offer it before the LORD.
13 And he shall lay his hand upon the
head of it, and kill it before the tabernacle of the congregation: and the sons
of Aaron shall sprinkle the blood thereof upon the altar round about.
14 And he shall offer thereof his
offering, *even* an offering made by fire
unto the LORD; the fat that covereth the
inwards, and all the fat that *is* upon the
inwards,
15 And the two kidneys, and the fat
that *is* upon them, which *is* by the
flanks, and the caul above the liver,
with the kidneys, it shall he take away.
16 And the priest shall burn them
upon the altar: *it is* the food of the
offering made by fire for a sweet
savour: all the fat *is* the LORD's.
17 *It shall be* a perpetual statute for
your generations throughout all your
dwellings, that ye eat neither fat nor
blood.

4 And the LORD spake unto Moses,
saying,
2 Speak unto the children of Israel,
saying, If a soul shall sin through ignorance against any of the commandments of the LORD *concerning things*
which ought not to be done, and shall
do against any of them:
3 If the priest that is anointed do sin
according to the sin of the people; then
let him bring for his sin, which he hath
sinned, a young bullock without blemish unto the LORD for a sin offering.
4 And he shall bring the bullock unto
the door of the tabernacle of the congregation before the LORD; and shall
lay his hand upon the bullock's head,
and kill the bullock before the LORD.
5 And the priest that is anointed shall
take of the bullock's blood, and bring it
to the tabernacle of the congregation:
6 And the priest shall dip his finger in
the blood, and sprinkle of the blood
seven times before the LORD, before the
vail of the sanctuary.
7 And the priest shall put *some* of the
blood upon the horns of the altar of
sweet incense before the LORD, which *is*
in the tabernacle of the congregation;
and shall pour all the blood of the bullock at the bottom of the altar of the

burnt offering, which *is at* the door of
the tabernacle of the congregation.
8 And he shall take off from it all the
fat of the bullock for the sin offering;
the fat that covereth the inwards, and
all the fat that *is* upon the inwards,
9 And the two kidneys, and the fat
that *is* upon them, which *is* by the
flanks, and the caul above the liver,
with the kidneys, it shall he take away,
10 As it was taken off from the bullock of the sacrifice of peace offerings:
and the priest shall burn them upon
the altar of the burnt offering.
11 And the skin of the bullock, and all
his flesh, with his head, and with his
legs, and his inwards, and his dung,
12 Even the whole bullock shall he
carry forth without the camp unto a
clean place, where the ashes are poured
out, and burn him on the wood with
fire: where the ashes are poured out
shall he be burnt.
13 And if the whole congregation of
Israel sin through ignorance, and the
thing be hid from the eyes of the assembly, and they have done *somewhat*
against any of the commandments of
the LORD *concerning things* which
should not be done, and are guilty;
14 When the sin, which they have
sinned against it, is known, then the
congregation shall offer a young bullock for the sin, and bring him before
the tabernacle of the congregation.
15 And the elders of the congregation
shall lay their hands upon the head of
the bullock before the LORD: and the
bullock shall be killed before the LORD.
16 And the priest that is anointed
shall bring of the bullock's blood to the
tabernacle of the congregation:
17 And the priest shall dip his finger
in some of the blood, and sprinkle *it*
seven times before the LORD, *even*
before the vail.
18 And he shall put *some* of the blood
upon the horns of the altar which *is*
before the LORD, that *is* in the tabernacle of the congregation, and shall pour
out all the blood at the bottom of the
altar of the burnt offering, which *is at*
the door of the tabernacle of the congregation.
19 And he shall take all his fat from
him, and burn *it* upon the altar.
20 And he shall do with the bullock as
he did with the bullock for a sin offering, so shall he do with this: and the
priest shall make an atonement for
them, and it shall be forgiven them.
21 And he shall carry forth the bullock without the camp, and burn him as
he burned the first bullock: it *is* a sin
offering for the congregation.
22 When a ruler hath sinned, and
done *somewhat* through ignorance
against any of the commandments of
the LORD his God *concerning things*
which should not be done, and is guilty;
23 Or if his sin, wherein he hath
sinned, come to his knowledge; he shall
bring his offering, a kid of the goats, a
male without blemish:
24 And he shall lay his hand upon the
head of the goat, and kill it in the place
where they kill the burnt offering
before the LORD: it *is* a sin offering.
25 And the priest shall take of the
blood of the sin offering with his finger,
and put *it* upon the horns of the altar of
burnt offering, and shall pour out his
blood at the bottom of the altar of
burnt offering.
26 And he shall burn all his fat upon
the altar, as the fat of the sacrifice of
peace offerings: and the priest shall

make an atonement for him as concerning his sin, and it shall be forgiven him.
27 And if any one of the common
people sin through ignorance, while he
doeth *somewhat against* any of the
commandments of the LORD *concerning things* which ought not to be done,
and be guilty;
28 Or if his sin, which he hath sinned,
come to his knowledge: then he shall
bring his offering, a kid of the goats, a
female without blemish, for his sin
which he hath sinned.
29 And he shall lay his hand upon the
head of the sin offering, and slay the
sin offering in the place of the burnt
offering.
30 And the priest shall take of the
blood thereof with his finger, and put *it*
upon the horns of the altar of burnt
offering, and shall pour out all the
blood thereof at the bottom of the altar.
31 And he shall take away all the fat
thereof, as the fat is taken away from
off the sacrifice of peace offerings; and
the priest shall burn *it* upon the altar
for a sweet savour unto the LORD; and
the priest shall make an atonement for
him, and it shall be forgiven him.
32 And if he bring a lamb for a sin
offering, he shall bring it a female without blemish.
33 And he shall lay his hand upon the
head of the sin offering, and slay it for
a sin offering in the place where they
kill the burnt offering.
34 And the priest shall take of the
blood of the sin offering with his finger,
and put *it* upon the horns of the altar of
burnt offering, and shall pour out all
the blood thereof at the bottom of the
altar:
35 And he shall take away all the fat
thereof, as the fat of the lamb is taken
away from the sacrifice of the peace
offerings; and the priest shall burn
them upon the altar, according to the
offerings made by fire unto the LORD:
and the priest shall make an atonement for his sin that he hath committed, and it shall be forgiven him.

5 And if a soul sin, and hear the voice
of swearing, and *is* a witness,
whether he hath seen or known *of it*; if
he do not utter *it*, then he shall bear his
iniquity.
2 Or if a soul touch any unclean thing,
whether *it be* a carcase of an unclean
beast, or a carcase of unclean cattle, or
the carcase of unclean creeping things,
and *if* it be hidden from him; he also
shall be unclean, and guilty.
3 Or if he touch the uncleanness of
man, whatsoever uncleanness *it be* that
a man shall be defiled withal, and it be
hid from him; when he knoweth *of it*,
then he shall be guilty.
4 Or if a soul swear, pronouncing with
his lips to do evil, or to do good, whatsoever *it be* that a man shall pronounce
with an oath, and it be hid from him;
when he knoweth *of it*, then he shall be
guilty in one of these.
5 And it shall be, when he shall be
guilty in one of these *things*, that he
shall confess that he hath sinned in
that *thing*:
6 And he shall bring his trespass
offering unto the LORD for his sin which
he hath sinned, a female from the flock,
a lamb or a kid of the goats, for a sin
offering; and the priest shall make an
atonement for him concerning his sin.
7 And if he be not able to bring a
lamb, then he shall bring for his trespass, which he hath committed, two
turtledoves, or two young pigeons, unto

the LORD; one for a sin offering, and the other for a burnt offering.

8 And he shall bring them unto the priest, who shall offer *that* which *is* for the sin offering first, and wring off his head from his neck, but shall not divide *it* asunder:

9 And he shall sprinkle of the blood of the sin offering upon the side of the altar; and the rest of the blood shall be wrung out at the bottom of the altar: it *is* a sin offering.

10 And he shall offer the second *for* a burnt offering, according to the manner: and the priest shall make an atonement for him for his sin which he hath sinned, and it shall be forgiven him.

11 But if he be not able to bring two turtledoves, or two young pigeons, then he that sinned shall bring for his offering the tenth part of an ephah of fine flour for a sin offering; he shall put no oil upon it, neither shall he put *any* frankincense thereon: for it *is* a sin offering.

12 Then shall he bring it to the priest, and the priest shall take his handful of it, *even* a memorial thereof, and burn *it* on the altar, according to the offerings made by fire unto the LORD: it *is* a sin offering.

13 And the priest shall make an atonement for him as touching his sin that he hath sinned in one of these, and it shall be forgiven him: and *the remnant* shall be the priest's, as a meat offering.

14 And the LORD spake unto Moses, saying,

15 If a soul commit a trespass, and sin through ignorance, in the holy things of the LORD; then he shall bring for his trespass unto the LORD a ram without blemish out of the flocks, with thy estimation by shekels of silver, after the shekel of the sanctuary, for a trespass offering:

16 And he shall make amends for the harm that he hath done in the holy thing, and shall add the fifth part thereto, and give it unto the priest: and the priest shall make an atonement for him with the ram of the trespass offering, and it shall be forgiven him.

17 And if a soul sin, and commit any of these things which are forbidden to be done by the commandments of the LORD; though he wist *it* not, yet is he guilty, and shall bear his iniquity.

18 And he shall bring a ram without blemish out of the flock, with thy estimation, for a trespass offering, unto the priest: and the priest shall make an atonement for him concerning his ignorance wherein he erred and wist *it* not, and it shall be forgiven him.

19 It *is* a trespass offering: he hath certainly trespassed against the LORD.

6 And the LORD spake unto Moses, saying,

2 If a soul sin, and commit a trespass against the LORD, and lie unto his neighbour in that which was delivered him to keep, or in fellowship, or in a thing taken away by violence, or hath deceived his neighbour;

3 Or have found that which was lost, and lieth concerning it, and sweareth falsely; in any of all these that a man doeth, sinning therein:

4 Then it shall be, because he hath sinned, and is guilty, that he shall restore that which he took violently away, or the thing which he hath deceitfully gotten, or that which was delivered him to keep, or the lost thing which he found,

5 Or all that about which he hath sworn falsely; he shall even restore it in the principal, and shall add the fifth part more thereto, *and* give it unto him to whom it appertaineth, in the day of his trespass offering.

6 And he shall bring his trespass offering unto the LORD, a ram without blemish out of the flock, with thy estimation, for a trespass offering, unto the priest:

7 And the priest shall make an atonement for him before the LORD: and it shall be forgiven him for any thing of all that he hath done in trespassing therein.

8 And the LORD spake unto Moses, saying,

9 Command Aaron and his sons, saying, This *is* the law of the burnt offering: It *is* the burnt offering, because of the burning upon the altar all night unto the morning, and the fire of the altar shall be burning in it.

10 And the priest shall put on his linen garment, and his linen breeches shall he put upon his flesh, and take up the ashes which the fire hath consumed with the burnt offering on the altar, and he shall put them beside the altar.

11 And he shall put off his garments, and put on other garments, and carry forth the ashes without the camp unto a clean place.

12 And the fire upon the altar shall be burning in it; it shall not be put out: and the priest shall burn wood on it every morning, and lay the burnt offering in order upon it; and he shall burn thereon the fat of the peace offerings.

13 The fire shall ever be burning upon the altar; it shall never go out.

14 And this *is* the law of the meat offering: the sons of Aaron shall offer it before the LORD, before the altar.

15 And he shall take of it his handful, of the flour of the meat offering, and of the oil thereof, and all the frankincense which *is* upon the meat offering, and shall burn *it* upon the altar *for* a sweet savour, *even* the memorial of it, unto the LORD.

16 And the remainder thereof shall Aaron and his sons eat: with unleavened bread shall it be eaten in the holy place; in the court of the tabernacle of the congregation they shall eat it.

17 It shall not be baken with leaven. I have given it *unto them for* their portion of my offerings made by fire; it *is* most holy, as *is* the sin offering, and as the trespass offering.

18 All the males among the children of Aaron shall eat of it. *It shall be* a statute for ever in your generations concerning the offerings of the LORD made by fire: every one that toucheth them shall be holy.

19 And the LORD spake unto Moses, saying,

20 This *is* the offering of Aaron and of his sons, which they shall offer unto the LORD in the day when he is anointed; the tenth part of an ephah of fine flour for a meat offering perpetual, half of it in the morning, and half thereof at night.

21 In a pan it shall be made with oil; *and when it is* baken, thou shalt bring it in: *and* the baken pieces of the meat offering shalt thou offer *for* a sweet savour unto the LORD.

22 And the priest of his sons that is anointed in his stead shall offer it: *it is* a statute for ever unto the LORD; it shall be wholly burnt.

23 For every meat offering for the priest shall be wholly burnt: it shall not be eaten.

24 And the LORD spake unto Moses, saying,

25 Speak unto Aaron and to his sons, saying, This *is* the law of the sin offering: In the place where the burnt offering is killed shall the sin offering be killed before the LORD: it *is* most holy.

26 The priest that offereth it for sin shall eat it: in the holy place shall it be eaten, in the court of the tabernacle of the congregation.

27 Whatsoever shall touch the flesh thereof shall be holy: and when there is sprinkled of the blood thereof upon any garment, thou shalt wash that whereon it was sprinkled in the holy place.

28 But the earthen vessel wherein it is sodden shall be broken: and if it be sodden in a brasen pot, it shall be both scoured, and rinsed in water.

29 All the males among the priests shall eat thereof: it *is* most holy.

30 And no sin offering, whereof *any* of the blood is brought into the tabernacle of the congregation to reconcile *withal* in the holy *place*, shall be eaten: it shall be burnt in the fire.

7 Likewise this *is* the law of the trespass offering: it *is* most holy.

2 In the place where they kill the burnt offering shall they kill the trespass offering: and the blood thereof shall he sprinkle round about upon the altar.

3 And he shall offer of it all the fat thereof; the rump, and the fat that covereth the inwards,

4 And the two kidneys, and the fat that *is* on them, which *is* by the flanks, and the caul *that is* above the liver, with the kidneys, it shall he take away:

5 And the priest shall burn them upon the altar *for* an offering made by fire unto the LORD: it *is* a trespass offering.

6 Every male among the priests shall eat thereof: it shall be eaten in the holy place: it *is* most holy.

7 As the sin offering *is*, so *is* the trespass offering: *there is* one law for them: the priest that maketh atonement therewith shall have *it*.

8 And the priest that offereth any man's burnt offering, *even* the priest shall have to himself the skin of the burnt offering which he hath offered.

9 And all the meat offering that is baken in the oven, and all that is dressed in the fryingpan, and in the pan, shall be the priest's that offereth it.

10 And every meat offering, mingled with oil, and dry, shall all the sons of Aaron have, one *as much* as another.

11 And this *is* the law of the sacrifice of peace offerings, which he shall offer unto the LORD.

12 If he offer it for a thanksgiving, then he shall offer with the sacrifice of thanksgiving unleavened cakes mingled with oil, and unleavened wafers anointed with oil, and cakes mingled with oil, of fine flour, fried.

13 Besides the cakes, he shall offer *for* his offering leavened bread with the sacrifice of thanksgiving of his peace offerings.

14 And of it he shall offer one out of the whole oblation *for* an heave offering unto the LORD, *and* it shall be the priest's that sprinkleth the blood of the peace offerings.

15 And the flesh of the sacrifice of his peace offerings for thanksgiving shall be eaten the same day that it is offered; he shall not leave any of it until the morning.

16 But if the sacrifice of his offering *be* a vow, or a voluntary offering, it shall be eaten the same day that he offereth his sacrifice: and on the morrow also the remainder of it shall be eaten:

17 But the remainder of the flesh of the sacrifice on the third day shall be burnt with fire.

18 And if *any* of the flesh of the sacrifice of his peace offerings be eaten at all on the third day, it shall not be accepted, neither shall it be imputed unto him that offereth it: it shall be an abomination, and the soul that eateth of it shall bear his iniquity.

19 And the flesh that toucheth any unclean *thing* shall not be eaten; it shall be burnt with fire: and as for the flesh, all that be clean shall eat thereof.

20 But the soul that eateth *of* the flesh of the sacrifice of peace offerings, that *pertain* unto the LORD, having his uncleanness upon him, even that soul shall be cut off from his people.

21 Moreover the soul that shall touch any unclean *thing, as* the uncleanness of man, or *any* unclean beast, or any abominable unclean *thing*, and eat of the flesh of the sacrifice of peace offerings, which *pertain* unto the LORD, even that soul shall be cut off from his people.

22 And the LORD spake unto Moses, saying,

23 Speak unto the children of Israel, saying, Ye shall eat no manner of fat, of ox, or of sheep, or of goat.

24 And the fat of the beast that dieth of itself, and the fat of that which is torn with beasts, may be used in any other use: but ye shall in no wise eat of it.

25 For whosoever eateth the fat of the beast, of which men offer an offering made by fire unto the LORD, even the soul that eateth *it* shall be cut off from his people.

26 Moreover ye shall eat no manner of blood, *whether it be* of fowl or of beast, in any of your dwellings.

27 Whatsoever soul *it be* that eateth any manner of blood, even that soul shall be cut off from his people.

28 And the LORD spake unto Moses, saying,

29 Speak unto the children of Israel, saying, He that offereth the sacrifice of his peace offerings unto the LORD shall bring his oblation unto the LORD of the sacrifice of his peace offerings.

30 His own hands shall bring the offerings of the LORD made by fire, the fat with the breast, it shall he bring, that the breast may be waved *for* a wave offering before the LORD.

31 And the priest shall burn the fat upon the altar: but the breast shall be Aaron's and his sons'.

32 And the right shoulder shall ye give unto the priest *for* an heave offering of the sacrifices of your peace offerings.

33 He among the sons of Aaron, that offereth the blood of the peace offerings, and the fat, shall have the right shoulder for *his* part.

34 For the wave breast and the heave shoulder have I taken of the children of Israel from off the sacrifices of their peace offerings, and have given them unto Aaron the priest and unto his sons by a statute for ever from among the children of Israel.

35 This *is the portion* of the anointing of Aaron, and of the anointing of his sons, out of the offerings of the LORD made by fire, in the day *when* he presented them to minister unto the LORD in the priest's office;
36 Which the LORD commanded to be given them of the children of Israel, in the day that he anointed them, *by* a statute for ever throughout their generations.
37 This *is* the law of the burnt offering, of the meat offering, and of the sin offering, and of the trespass offering, and of the consecrations, and of the sacrifice of the peace offerings;
38 Which the LORD commanded Moses in mount Sinai, in the day that he commanded the children of Israel to offer their oblations unto the LORD, in the wilderness of Sinai.

8 And the LORD spake unto Moses, saying,
2 Take Aaron and his sons with him, and the garments, and the anointing oil, and a bullock for the sin offering, and two rams, and a basket of unleavened bread;
3 And gather thou all the congregation together unto the door of the tabernacle of the congregation.
4 And Moses did as the LORD commanded him; and the assembly was gathered together unto the door of the tabernacle of the congregation.
5 And Moses said unto the congregation, This *is* the thing which the LORD commanded to be done.
6 And Moses brought Aaron and his sons, and washed them with water.
7 And he put upon him the coat, and girded him with the girdle, and clothed him with the robe, and put the ephod upon him, and he girded him with the curious girdle of the ephod, and bound *it* unto him therewith.
8 And he put the breastplate upon him: also he put in the breastplate the Urim and the Thummim.
9 And he put the mitre upon his head; also upon the mitre, *even* upon his forefront, did he put the golden plate, the holy crown; as the LORD commanded Moses.
10 And Moses took the anointing oil, and anointed the tabernacle and all that *was* therein, and sanctified them.
11 And he sprinkled thereof upon the altar seven times, and anointed the altar and all his vessels, both the laver and his foot, to sanctify them.
12 And he poured of the anointing oil upon Aaron's head, and anointed him, to sanctify him.
13 And Moses brought Aaron's sons, and put coats upon them, and girded them with girdles, and put bonnets upon them; as the LORD commanded Moses.
14 And he brought the bullock for the sin offering: and Aaron and his sons laid their hands upon the head of the bullock for the sin offering.
15 And he slew *it*; and Moses took the blood, and put *it* upon the horns of the altar round about with his finger, and purified the altar, and poured the blood at the bottom of the altar, and sanctified it, to make reconciliation upon it.
16 And he took all the fat that *was* upon the inwards, and the caul *above* the liver, and the two kidneys, and their fat, and Moses burned *it* upon the altar.
17 But the bullock, and his hide, his flesh, and his dung, he burnt with fire without the camp; as the LORD commanded Moses.

18 And he brought the ram for the burnt offering: and Aaron and his sons laid their hands upon the head of the ram.

19 And he killed *it*; and Moses sprinkled the blood upon the altar round about.

20 And he cut the ram into pieces; and Moses burnt the head, and the pieces, and the fat.

21 And he washed the inwards and the legs in water; and Moses burnt the whole ram upon the altar: it *was* a burnt sacrifice for a sweet savour, *and* an offering made by fire unto the LORD; as the LORD commanded Moses.

22 And he brought the other ram, the ram of consecration: and Aaron and his sons laid their hands upon the head of the ram.

23 And he slew *it*; and Moses took of the blood of it, and put *it* upon the tip of Aaron's right ear, and upon the thumb of his right hand, and upon the great toe of his right foot.

24 And he brought Aaron's sons, and Moses put of the blood upon the tip of their right ear, and upon the thumbs of their right hands, and upon the great toes of their right feet: and Moses sprinkled the blood upon the altar round about.

25 And he took the fat, and the rump, and all the fat that *was* upon the inwards, and the caul *above* the liver, and the two kidneys, and their fat, and the right shoulder:

26 And out of the basket of unleavened bread, that *was* before the LORD, he took one unleavened cake, and a cake of oiled bread, and one wafer, and put *them* on the fat, and upon the right shoulder:

27 And he put all upon Aaron's hands, and upon his sons' hands, and waved them *for* a wave offering before the LORD.

28 And Moses took them from off their hands, and burnt *them* on the altar upon the burnt offering: they *were* consecrations for a sweet savour: it *is* an offering made by fire unto the LORD.

29 And Moses took the breast, and waved it *for* a wave offering before the LORD: *for* of the ram of consecration it was Moses' part; as the LORD commanded Moses.

30 And Moses took of the anointing oil, and of the blood which *was* upon the altar, and sprinkled *it* upon Aaron, *and* upon his garments, and upon his sons, and upon his sons' garments with him; and sanctified Aaron, *and* his garments, and his sons, and his sons' garments with him.

31 And Moses said unto Aaron and to his sons, Boil the flesh *at* the door of the tabernacle of the congregation: and there eat it with the bread that *is* in the basket of consecrations, as I commanded, saying, Aaron and his sons shall eat it.

32 And that which remaineth of the flesh and of the bread shall ye burn with fire.

33 And ye shall not go out of the door of the tabernacle of the congregation *in* seven days, until the days of your consecration be at an end: for seven days shall he consecrate you.

34 As he hath done this day, *so* the LORD hath commanded to do, to make an atonement for you.

35 Therefore shall ye abide *at* the door of the tabernacle of the congregation day and night seven days, and keep the charge of the LORD, that ye die not: for so I am commanded.

36 So Aaron and his sons did all things which the LORD commanded by the hand of Moses.

9 And it came to pass on the eighth day, *that* Moses called Aaron and his sons, and the elders of Israel;

2 And he said unto Aaron, Take thee a young calf for a sin offering, and a ram for a burnt offering, without blemish, and offer *them* before the LORD.

3 And unto the children of Israel thou shalt speak, saying, Take ye a kid of the goats for a sin offering; and a calf and a lamb, *both* of the first year, without blemish, for a burnt offering;

4 Also a bullock and a ram for peace offerings, to sacrifice before the LORD; and a meat offering mingled with oil: for to day the LORD will appear unto you.

5 And they brought *that* which Moses commanded before the tabernacle of the congregation: and all the congregation drew near and stood before the LORD.

6 And Moses said, This *is* the thing which the LORD commanded that ye should do: and the glory of the LORD shall appear unto you.

7 And Moses said unto Aaron, Go unto the altar, and offer thy sin offering, and thy burnt offering, and make an atonement for thyself, and for the people: and offer the offering of the people, and make an atonement for them; as the LORD commanded.

8 Aaron therefore went unto the altar, and slew the calf of the sin offering, which *was* for himself.

9 And the sons of Aaron brought the blood unto him: and he dipped his finger in the blood, and put *it* upon the horns of the altar, and poured out the blood at the bottom of the altar:

10 But the fat, and the kidneys, and the caul above the liver of the sin offering, he burnt upon the altar; as the LORD commanded Moses.

11 And the flesh and the hide he burnt with fire without the camp.

12 And he slew the burnt offering; and Aaron's sons presented unto him the blood, which he sprinkled round about upon the altar.

13 And they presented the burnt offering unto him, with the pieces thereof, and the head: and he burnt *them* upon the altar.

14 And he did wash the inwards and the legs, and burnt *them* upon the burnt offering on the altar.

15 And he brought the people's offering, and took the goat, which *was* the sin offering for the people, and slew it, and offered it for sin, as the first.

16 And he brought the burnt offering, and offered it according to the manner.

17 And he brought the meat offering, and took an handful thereof, and burnt *it* upon the altar, beside the burnt sacrifice of the morning.

18 He slew also the bullock and the ram *for* a sacrifice of peace offerings, which *was* for the people: and Aaron's sons presented unto him the blood, which he sprinkled upon the altar round about,

19 And the fat of the bullock and of the ram, the rump, and that which covereth *the inwards*, and the kidneys, and the caul *above* the liver:

20 And they put the fat upon the breasts, and he burnt the fat upon the altar:

21 And the breasts and the right shoulder Aaron waved *for* a wave offering before the LORD; as Moses commanded.

22 And Aaron lifted up his hand toward the people, and blessed them, and came down from offering of the sin offering, and the burnt offering, and peace offerings.

23 And Moses and Aaron went into the tabernacle of the congregation, and came out, and blessed the people: and the glory of the LORD appeared unto all the people.

24 And there came a fire out from before the LORD, and consumed upon the altar the burnt offering and the fat: *which* when all the people saw, they shouted, and fell on their faces.

10 And Nadab and Abihu, the sons of Aaron, took either of them his censer, and put fire therein, and put incense thereon, and offered strange fire before the LORD, which he commanded them not.

2 And there went out fire from the LORD, and devoured them, and they died before the LORD.

3 Then Moses said unto Aaron, This *is it* that the LORD spake, saying, I will be sanctified in them that come nigh me, and before all the people I will be glorified. And Aaron held his peace.

4 And Moses called Mishael and Elzaphan, the sons of Uzziel the uncle of Aaron, and said unto them, Come near, carry your brethren from before the sanctuary out of the camp.

5 So they went near, and carried them in their coats out of the camp; as Moses had said.

6 And Moses said unto Aaron, and unto Eleazar and unto Ithamar, his sons, Uncover not your heads, neither rend your clothes; lest ye die, and lest wrath come upon all the people: but let your brethren, the whole house of Israel, bewail the burning which the LORD hath kindled.

7 And ye shall not go out from the door of the tabernacle of the congregation, lest ye die: for the anointing oil of the LORD *is* upon you. And they did according to the word of Moses.

8 And the LORD spake unto Aaron, saying,

9 Do not drink wine nor strong drink, thou, nor thy sons with thee, when ye go into the tabernacle of the congregation, lest ye die: *it shall be* a statute for ever throughout your generations:

10 And that ye may put difference between holy and unholy, and between unclean and clean;

11 And that ye may teach the children of Israel all the statutes which the LORD hath spoken unto them by the hand of Moses.

12 And Moses spake unto Aaron, and unto Eleazar and unto Ithamar, his sons that were left, Take the meat offering that remaineth of the offerings of the LORD made by fire, and eat it without leaven beside the altar: for it *is* most holy:

13 And ye shall eat it in the holy place, because it *is* thy due, and thy sons' due, of the sacrifices of the LORD made by fire: for so I am commanded.

14 And the wave breast and heave shoulder shall ye eat in a clean place; thou, and thy sons, and thy daughters with thee: for *they be* thy due, and thy sons' due, *which* are given out of the sacrifices of peace offerings of the children of Israel.

15 The heave shoulder and the wave breast shall they bring with the offer-

ings made by fire of the fat, to wave *it*
for a wave offering before the LORD;
and it shall be thine, and thy sons' with
thee, by a statute for ever; as the LORD
hath commanded.
16 And Moses diligently sought the
goat of the sin offering, and, behold, it
was burnt: and he was angry with
Eleazar and Ithamar, the sons of Aaron
which were left *alive*, saying,
17 Wherefore have ye not eaten the
sin offering in the holy place, seeing it
is most holy, and *God* hath given it you
to bear the iniquity of the congregation, to make atonement for them
before the LORD?
18 Behold, the blood of it was not
brought in within the holy *place*: ye
should indeed have eaten it in the holy
place, as I commanded.
19 And Aaron said unto Moses,
Behold, this day have they offered their
sin offering and their burnt offering
before the LORD; and such things have
befallen me: and *if* I had eaten the sin
offering to day, should it have been
accepted in the sight of the LORD?
20 And when Moses heard *that*, he
was content.

11 And the LORD spake unto Moses
and to Aaron, saying unto them,
2 Speak unto the children of Israel,
saying, These *are* the beasts which ye
shall eat among all the beasts that *are*
on the earth.
3 Whatsoever parteth the hoof, and is
clovenfooted, *and* cheweth the cud,
among the beasts, that shall ye eat.
4 Nevertheless these shall ye not eat
of them that chew the cud, or of them
that divide the hoof: *as* the camel,
because he cheweth the cud, but divideth not the hoof; he *is* unclean unto
you.
5 And the coney, because he cheweth
the cud, but divideth not the hoof; he *is*
unclean unto you.
6 And the hare, because he cheweth
the cud, but divideth not the hoof; he *is*
unclean unto you.
7 And the swine, though he divide the
hoof, and be clovenfooted, yet he cheweth not the cud; he *is* unclean to you.
8 Of their flesh shall ye not eat, and
their carcase shall ye not touch; they
are unclean to you.
9 These shall ye eat of all that *are* in
the waters: whatsoever hath fins and
scales in the waters, in the seas, and in
the rivers, them shall ye eat.
10 And all that have not fins and
scales in the seas, and in the rivers, of
all that move in the waters, and of any
living thing which *is* in the waters, they
shall be an abomination unto you:
11 They shall be even an abomination
unto you; ye shall not eat of their flesh,
but ye shall have their carcases in
abomination.
12 Whatsoever hath no fins nor scales
in the waters, that *shall be* an abomination unto you.
13 And these *are they which* ye shall
have in abomination among the fowls;
they shall not be eaten, they *are* an
abomination: the eagle, and the ossi-
frage, and the ospray,
14 And the vulture, and the kite after
his kind;
15 Every raven after his kind;
16 And the owl, and the night hawk,
and the cuckow, and the hawk after his
kind,
17 And the little owl, and the cormorant, and the great owl,
18 And the swan, and the pelican, and
the gier eagle,

19 And the stork, the heron after her
kind, and the lapwing, and the bat.
20 All fowls that creep, going upon *all*
four, *shall be* an abomination unto you.
21 Yet these may ye eat of every flying creeping thing that goeth upon *all*
four, which have legs above their feet,
to leap withal upon the earth;
22 *Even* these of them ye may eat; the
locust after his kind, and the bald
locust after his kind, and the beetle
after his kind, and the grasshopper
after his kind.
23 But all *other* flying creeping
things, which have four feet, *shall be* an
abomination unto you.
24 And for these ye shall be unclean:
whosoever toucheth the carcase of
them shall be unclean until the even.
25 And whosoever beareth *ought* of
the carcase of them shall wash his
clothes, and be unclean until the even.
26 *The carcases* of every beast which
divideth the hoof, and *is* not clovenfooted, nor cheweth the cud, *are*
unclean unto you: every one that
toucheth them shall be unclean.
27 And whatsoever goeth upon his
paws, among all manner of beasts that
go on *all* four, those *are* unclean unto
you: whoso toucheth their carcase shall
be unclean until the even.
28 And he that beareth the carcase of
them shall wash his clothes, and be
unclean until the even: they *are*
unclean unto you.
29 These also *shall be* unclean unto
you among the creeping things that
creep upon the earth; the weasel, and
the mouse, and the tortoise after his
kind,
30 And the ferret, and the chameleon,
and the lizard, and the snail, and the
mole.
31 These *are* unclean to you among
all that creep: whosoever doth touch
them, when they be dead, shall be
unclean until the even.
32 And upon whatsoever *any* of them,
when they are dead, doth fall, it shall
be unclean; whether *it be* any vessel of
wood, or raiment, or skin, or sack, whatsoever vessel *it be*, wherein *any* work is
done, it must be put into water, and it
shall be unclean until the even; so it
shall be cleansed.
33 And every earthen vessel, whereinto *any* of them falleth, whatsoever *is*
in it shall be unclean; and ye shall
break it.
34 Of all meat which may be eaten,
that on which *such* water cometh shall
be unclean: and all drink that may be
drunk in every *such* vessel shall be
unclean.
35 And every *thing* whereupon *any*
part of their carcase falleth shall be
unclean; *whether it be* oven, or ranges
for pots, they shall be broken down: *for*
they *are* unclean, and shall be unclean
unto you.
36 Nevertheless a fountain or pit,
wherein there is plenty of water, shall
be clean: but that which toucheth their
carcase shall be unclean.
37 And if *any part* of their carcase
fall upon any sowing seed which is to
be sown, it *shall be* clean.
38 But if *any* water be put upon the
seed, and *any part* of their carcase fall
thereon, it *shall be* unclean unto you.
39 And if any beast, of which ye may
eat, die; he that toucheth the carcase
thereof shall be unclean until the even.
40 And he that eateth of the carcase
of it shall wash his clothes, and be
unclean until the even: he also that

beareth the carcase of it shall wash his clothes, and be unclean until the even.

41 And every creeping thing that creepeth upon the earth *shall be* an abomination; it shall not be eaten.

42 Whatsoever goeth upon the belly, and whatsoever goeth upon *all* four, or whatsoever hath more feet among all creeping things that creep upon the earth, them ye shall not eat; for they *are* an abomination.

43 Ye shall not make yourselves abominable with any creeping thing that creepeth, neither shall ye make yourselves unclean with them, that ye should be defiled thereby.

44 For I *am* the LORD your God: ye shall therefore sanctify yourselves, and ye shall be holy; for I *am* holy: neither shall ye defile yourselves with any manner of creeping thing that creepeth upon the earth.

45 For I *am* the LORD that bringeth you up out of the land of Egypt, to be your God: ye shall therefore be holy, for I *am* holy.

46 This *is* the law of the beasts, and of the fowl, and of every living creature that moveth in the waters, and of every creature that creepeth upon the earth:

47 To make a difference between the unclean and the clean, and between the beast that may be eaten and the beast that may not be eaten.

12 And the LORD spake unto Moses, saying,

2 Speak unto the children of Israel, saying, If a woman have conceived seed, and born a man child: then she shall be unclean seven days; according to the days of the separation for her infirmity shall she be unclean.

3 And in the eighth day the flesh of his foreskin shall be circumcised.

4 And she shall then continue in the blood of her purifying three and thirty days; she shall touch no hallowed thing, nor come into the sanctuary, until the days of her purifying be fulfilled.

5 But if she bear a maid child, then she shall be unclean two weeks, as in her separation: and she shall continue in the blood of her purifying threescore and six days.

6 And when the days of her purifying are fulfilled, for a son, or for a daughter, she shall bring a lamb of the first year for a burnt offering, and a young pigeon, or a turtledove, for a sin offering, unto the door of the tabernacle of the congregation, unto the priest:

7 Who shall offer it before the LORD, and make an atonement for her; and she shall be cleansed from the issue of her blood. This *is* the law for her that hath born a male or a female.

8 And if she be not able to bring a lamb, then she shall bring two turtles, or two young pigeons; the one for the burnt offering, and the other for a sin offering: and the priest shall make an atonement for her, and she shall be clean.

13 And the LORD spake unto Moses and Aaron, saying,

2 When a man shall have in the skin of his flesh a rising, a scab, or bright spot, and it be in the skin of his flesh *like* the plague of leprosy; then he shall be brought unto Aaron the priest, or unto one of his sons the priests:

3 And the priest shall look on the plague in the skin of the flesh: and *when* the hair in the plague is turned white, and the plague in sight *be* deeper than the skin of his flesh, it *is* a plague of leprosy: and the priest shall

look on him, and pronounce him
unclean.
4 If the bright spot *be* white in the
skin of his flesh, and in sight *be* not
deeper than the skin, and the hair
thereof be not turned white; then the
priest shall shut up *him that hath* the
plague seven days:
5 And the priest shall look on him the
seventh day: and, behold, *if* the plague
in his sight be at a stay, *and* the plague
spread not in the skin; then the priest
shall shut him up seven days more:
6 And the priest shall look on him
again the seventh day: and, behold, *if*
the plague *be* somewhat dark, *and* the
plague spread not in the skin, the priest
shall pronounce him clean: it *is but* a
scab: and he shall wash his clothes, and
be clean.
7 But if the scab spread much abroad
in the skin, after that he hath been
seen of the priest for his cleansing, he
shall be seen of the priest again:
8 And *if* the priest see that, behold,
the scab spreadeth in the skin, then the
priest shall pronounce him unclean: it
is a leprosy.
9 When the plague of leprosy is in a
man, then he shall be brought unto the
priest;
10 And the priest shall see *him*: and,
behold, *if* the rising *be* white in the
skin, and it have turned the hair white,
and *there be* quick raw flesh in the rising;
11 It *is* an old leprosy in the skin of
his flesh, and the priest shall pronounce him unclean, and shall not shut
him up: for he *is* unclean.
12 And if a leprosy break out abroad
in the skin, and the leprosy cover all
the skin of *him that hath* the plague
from his head even to his foot, wheresoever the priest looketh;
13 Then the priest shall consider:
and, behold, *if* the leprosy have covered
all his flesh, he shall pronounce *him*
clean *that hath* the plague: it is all
turned white: he *is* clean.
14 But when raw flesh appeareth in
him, he shall be unclean.
15 And the priest shall see the raw
flesh, and pronounce him to be unclean:
for the raw flesh *is* unclean: it *is* a leprosy.
16 Or if the raw flesh turn again, and
be changed unto white, he shall come
unto the priest;
17 And the priest shall see him: and,
behold, *if* the plague be turned into
white; then the priest shall pronounce
him clean *that hath* the plague: he *is*
clean.
18 The flesh also, in which, *even* in
the skin thereof, was a boil, and is
healed,
19 And in the place of the boil there
be a white rising, or a bright spot,
white, and somewhat reddish, and it be
shewed to the priest;
20 And if, when the priest seeth it,
behold, it *be* in sight lower than the
skin, and the hair thereof be turned
white; the priest shall pronounce him
unclean: it *is* a plague of leprosy broken out of the boil.
21 But if the priest look on it, and,
behold, *there be* no white hairs therein,
and *if* it *be* not lower than the skin, but
be somewhat dark; then the priest shall
shut him up seven days:
22 And if it spread much abroad in
the skin, then the priest shall pronounce him unclean: it *is* a plague.
23 But if the bright spot stay in his
place, *and* spread not, it *is* a burning

boil; and the priest shall pronounce
him clean.
24 Or if there be *any* flesh, in the skin
whereof *there is* a hot burning, and the
quick *flesh* that burneth have a white
bright spot, somewhat reddish, or
white;
25 Then the priest shall look upon it:
and, behold, *if* the hair in the bright
spot be turned white, and it *be in* sight
deeper than the skin; it *is* a leprosy
broken out of the burning: wherefore
the priest shall pronounce him unclean:
it *is* the plague of leprosy.
26 But if the priest look on it, and,
behold, *there be* no white hair in the
bright spot, and it *be* no lower than the
other skin, but *be* somewhat dark; then
the priest shall shut him up seven days:
27 And the priest shall look upon him
the seventh day: *and* if it be spread
much abroad in the skin, then the
priest shall pronounce him unclean: it
is the plague of leprosy.
28 And if the bright spot stay in his
place, *and* spread not in the skin, but it
be somewhat dark; it *is* a rising of the
burning, and the priest shall pronounce
him clean: for it *is* an inflammation of
the burning.
29 If a man or woman have a plague
upon the head or the beard;
30 Then the priest shall see the
plague: and, behold, if it *be* in sight
deeper than the skin; *and there be* in it
a yellow thin hair; then the priest shall
pronounce him unclean: it *is* a dry scall,
even a leprosy upon the head or beard.
31 And if the priest look on the
plague of the scall, and, behold, it *be*
not in sight deeper than the skin, and
that there is no black hair in it; then
the priest shall shut up *him that hath*
the plague of the scall seven days:
32 And in the seventh day the priest
shall look on the plague: and, behold, *if*
the scall spread not, and there be in it
no yellow hair, and the scall *be* not in
sight deeper than the skin;
33 He shall be shaven, but the scall
shall he not shave; and the priest shall
shut up *him that hath* the scall seven
days more:
34 And in the seventh day the priest
shall look on the scall: and, behold, *if*
the scall be not spread in the skin, nor
be in sight deeper than the skin; then
the priest shall pronounce him clean:
and he shall wash his clothes, and be
clean.
35 But if the scall spread much in the
skin after his cleansing;
36 Then the priest shall look on him:
and, behold, if the scall be spread in the
skin, the priest shall not seek for yellow
hair; he *is* unclean.
37 But if the scall be in his sight at a
stay, and *that* there is black hair grown
up therein; the scall is healed, he *is*
clean: and the priest shall pronounce
him clean.
38 If a man also or a woman have in
the skin of their flesh bright spots, *even*
white bright spots;
39 Then the priest shall look: and,
behold, *if* the bright spots in the skin of
their flesh *be* darkish white; it *is* a
freckled spot *that* groweth in the skin;
he *is* clean.
40 And the man whose hair is fallen
off his head, he *is* bald; *yet is* he clean.
41 And he that hath his hair fallen off
from the part of his head toward his
face, he *is* forehead bald: *yet is* he
clean.
42 And if there be in the bald head, or
bald forehead, a white reddish sore; it

is a leprosy sprung up in his bald head,
or his bald forehead.
43 Then the priest shall look upon it:
and, behold, *if* the rising of the sore *be*
white reddish in his bald head, or in his
bald forehead, as the leprosy appeareth
in the skin of the flesh;
44 He is a leprous man, he *is* unclean:
the priest shall pronounce him utterly
unclean; his plague *is* in his head.
45 And the leper in whom the plague
is, his clothes shall be rent, and his
head bare, and he shall put a covering
upon his upper lip, and shall cry,
Unclean, unclean.
46 All the days wherein the plague
shall be in him he shall be defiled; he *is*
unclean: he shall dwell alone; without
the camp *shall* his habitation *be*.
47 The garment also that the plague
of leprosy is in, *whether it be* a woollen
garment, or a linen garment;
48 Whether *it be* in the warp, or woof;
of linen, or of woollen; whether in a
skin, or in any thing made of skin;
49 And if the plague be greenish or
reddish in the garment, or in the skin,
either in the warp, or in the woof, or in
any thing of skin; it *is* a plague of leprosy, and shall be shewed unto the
priest:
50 And the priest shall look upon the
plague, and shut up *it that hath* the
plague seven days:
51 And he shall look on the plague on
the seventh day: if the plague be spread
in the garment, either in the warp, or in
the woof, or in a skin, *or* in any work
that is made of skin; the plague *is* a
fretting leprosy; it *is* unclean.
52 He shall therefore burn that garment, whether warp or woof, in woollen
or in linen, or any thing of skin, wherein the plague is: for it *is* a fretting leprosy; it shall be burnt in the fire.
53 And if the priest shall look, and,
behold, the plague be not spread in the
garment, either in the warp, or in the
woof, or in any thing of skin;
54 Then the priest shall command
that they wash *the thing* wherein the
plague *is*, and he shall shut it up seven
days more:
55 And the priest shall look on the
plague, after that it is washed: and,
behold, *if* the plague have not changed
his colour, and the plague be not
spread; it *is* unclean; thou shalt burn it
in the fire; it *is* fret inward, *whether* it
be bare within or without.
56 And if the priest look, and, behold,
the plague *be* somewhat dark after the
washing of it; then he shall rend it out
of the garment, or out of the skin, or out
of the warp, or out of the woof:
57 And if it appear still in the garment, either in the warp, or in the woof,
or in any thing of skin; it *is* a spreading
plague: thou shalt burn that wherein
the plague *is* with fire.
58 And the garment, either warp, or
woof, or whatsoever thing of skin *it be*,
which thou shalt wash, if the plague be
departed from them, then it shall be
washed the second time, and shall be
clean.
59 This *is* the law of the plague of
leprosy in a garment of woollen or
linen, either in the warp, or woof, or any
thing of skins, to pronounce it clean, or
to pronounce it unclean.

14 And the LORD spake unto Moses,
saying,
2 This shall be the law of the leper in
the day of his cleansing: He shall be
brought unto the priest:

3 And the priest shall go forth out of
the camp; and the priest shall look,
and, behold, *if* the plague of leprosy be
healed in the leper;
4 Then shall the priest command to
take for him that is to be cleansed two
birds alive *and* clean, and cedar wood,
and scarlet, and hyssop:
5 And the priest shall command that
one of the birds be killed in an earthen
vessel over running water:
6 As for the living bird, he shall take
it, and the cedar wood, and the scarlet,
and the hyssop, and shall dip them and
the living bird in the blood of the bird
that was killed over the running water:
7 And he shall sprinkle upon him that
is to be cleansed from the leprosy seven
times, and shall pronounce him clean,
and shall let the living bird loose into
the open field.
8 And he that is to be cleansed shall
wash his clothes, and shave off all his
hair, and wash himself in water, that he
may be clean: and after that he shall
come into the camp, and shall tarry
abroad out of his tent seven days.
9 But it shall be on the seventh day,
that he shall shave all his hair off his
head and his beard and his eyebrows,
even all his hair he shall shave off: and
he shall wash his clothes, also he shall
wash his flesh in water, and he shall be
clean.
10 And on the eighth day he shall
take two he lambs without blemish,
and one ewe lamb of the first year without blemish, and three tenth deals of
fine flour *for* a meat offering, mingled
with oil, and one log of oil.
11 And the priest that maketh *him*
clean shall present the man that is to
be made clean, and those things, before
the LORD, *at* the door of the tabernacle
of the congregation:
12 And the priest shall take one he
lamb, and offer him for a trespass offering, and the log of oil, and wave them
for a wave offering before the LORD:
13 And he shall slay the lamb in the
place where he shall kill the sin offering and the burnt offering, in the holy
place: for as the sin offering *is* the
priest's, *so is* the trespass offering: it *is*
most holy:
14 And the priest shall take *some* of
the blood of the trespass offering, and
the priest shall put *it* upon the tip of
the right ear of him that is to be
cleansed, and upon the thumb of his
right hand, and upon the great toe of
his right foot:
15 And the priest shall take *some* of
the log of oil, and pour *it* into the palm
of his own left hand:
16 And the priest shall dip his right
finger in the oil that *is* in his left hand,
and shall sprinkle of the oil with his
finger seven times before the LORD:
17 And of the rest of the oil that *is* in
his hand shall the priest put upon the
tip of the right ear of him that is to be
cleansed, and upon the thumb of his
right hand, and upon the great toe of
his right foot, upon the blood of the
trespass offering:
18 And the remnant of the oil that *is*
in the priest's hand he shall pour upon
the head of him that is to be cleansed:
and the priest shall make an atonement for him before the LORD.
19 And the priest shall offer the sin
offering, and make an atonement for
him that is to be cleansed from his
uncleanness; and afterward he shall
kill the burnt offering:

20 And the priest shall offer the burnt offering and the meat offering upon the altar: and the priest shall make an atonement for him, and he shall be clean.

21 And if he *be* poor, and cannot get so much; then he shall take one lamb *for* a trespass offering to be waved, to make an atonement for him, and one tenth deal of fine flour mingled with oil for a meat offering, and a log of oil;

22 And two turtledoves, or two young pigeons, such as he is able to get; and the one shall be a sin offering, and the other a burnt offering.

23 And he shall bring them on the eighth day for his cleansing unto the priest, unto the door of the tabernacle of the congregation, before the LORD.

24 And the priest shall take the lamb of the trespass offering, and the log of oil, and the priest shall wave them *for* a wave offering before the LORD:

25 And he shall kill the lamb of the trespass offering, and the priest shall take *some* of the blood of the trespass offering, and put *it* upon the tip of the right ear of him that is to be cleansed, and upon the thumb of his right hand, and upon the great toe of his right foot:

26 And the priest shall pour of the oil into the palm of his own left hand:

27 And the priest shall sprinkle with his right finger *some* of the oil that *is* in his left hand seven times before the LORD:

28 And the priest shall put of the oil that *is* in his hand upon the tip of the right ear of him that is to be cleansed, and upon the thumb of his right hand, and upon the great toe of his right foot, upon the place of the blood of the trespass offering:

29 And the rest of the oil that *is* in the priest's hand he shall put upon the head of him that is to be cleansed, to make an atonement for him before the LORD.

30 And he shall offer the one of the turtledoves, or of the young pigeons, such as he can get;

31 *Even* such as he is able to get, the one *for* a sin offering, and the other *for* a burnt offering, with the meat offering: and the priest shall make an atonement for him that is to be cleansed before the LORD.

32 This *is* the law *of him* in whom *is* the plague of leprosy, whose hand is not able to get *that which pertaineth* to his cleansing.

33 And the LORD spake unto Moses and unto Aaron, saying,

34 When ye be come into the land of Canaan, which I give to you for a possession, and I put the plague of leprosy in a house of the land of your possession;

35 And he that owneth the house shall come and tell the priest, saying, It seemeth to me *there is* as it were a plague in the house:

36 Then the priest shall command that they empty the house, before the priest go *into it* to see the plague, that all that *is* in the house be not made unclean: and afterward the priest shall go in to see the house:

37 And he shall look on the plague, and, behold, *if* the plague *be* in the walls of the house with hollow strakes, greenish or reddish, which in sight *are* lower than the wall;

38 Then the priest shall go out of the house to the door of the house, and shut up the house seven days:

39 And the priest shall come again the seventh day, and shall look: and, behold, *if* the plague be spread in the walls of the house;

40 Then the priest shall command that they take away the stones in which the plague *is*, and they shall cast them into an unclean place without the city:

41 And he shall cause the house to be scraped within round about, and they shall pour out the dust that they scrape off without the city into an unclean place:

42 And they shall take other stones, and put *them* in the place of those stones; and he shall take other morter, and shall plaister the house.

43 And if the plague come again, and break out in the house, after that he hath taken away the stones, and after he hath scraped the house, and after it is plaistered;

44 Then the priest shall come and look, and, behold, *if* the plague be spread in the house, it *is* a fretting leprosy in the house: it *is* unclean.

45 And he shall break down the house, the stones of it, and the timber thereof, and all the morter of the house; and he shall carry *them* forth out of the city into an unclean place.

46 Moreover he that goeth into the house all the while that it is shut up shall be unclean until the even.

47 And he that lieth in the house shall wash his clothes; and he that eateth in the house shall wash his clothes.

48 And if the priest shall come in, and look *upon it*, and, behold, the plague hath not spread in the house, after the house was plaistered: then the priest shall pronounce the house clean, because the plague is healed.

49 And he shall take to cleanse the house two birds, and cedar wood, and scarlet, and hyssop:

50 And he shall kill the one of the birds in an earthen vessel over running water:

51 And he shall take the cedar wood, and the hyssop, and the scarlet, and the living bird, and dip them in the blood of the slain bird, and in the running water, and sprinkle the house seven times:

52 And he shall cleanse the house with the blood of the bird, and with the running water, and with the living bird, and with the cedar wood, and with the hyssop, and with the scarlet:

53 But he shall let go the living bird out of the city into the open fields, and make an atonement for the house: and it shall be clean.

54 This *is* the law for all manner of plague of leprosy, and scall,

55 And for the leprosy of a garment, and of a house,

56 And for a rising, and for a scab, and for a bright spot:

57 To teach when *it is* unclean, and when *it is* clean: this *is* the law of leprosy.

15 And the LORD spake unto Moses and to Aaron, saying,

2 Speak unto the children of Israel, and say unto them, When any man hath a running issue out of his flesh, *because of* his issue he *is* unclean.

3 And this shall be his uncleanness in his issue: whether his flesh run with his issue, or his flesh be stopped from his issue, it *is* his uncleanness.

4 Every bed, whereon he lieth that hath the issue, is unclean: and every thing, whereon he sitteth, shall be unclean.

5 And whosoever toucheth his bed shall wash his clothes, and bathe *himself* in water, and be unclean until the even.

6 And he that sitteth on *any* thing whereon he sat that hath the issue shall wash his clothes, and bathe *himself* in water, and be unclean until the even.

7 And he that toucheth the flesh of him that hath the issue shall wash his clothes, and bathe *himself* in water, and be unclean until the even.

8 And if he that hath the issue spit upon him that is clean; then he shall wash his clothes, and bathe *himself* in water, and be unclean until the even.

9 And what saddle soever he rideth upon that hath the issue shall be unclean.

10 And whosoever toucheth any thing that was under him shall be unclean until the even: and he that beareth *any of* those things shall wash his clothes, and bathe *himself* in water, and be unclean until the even.

11 And whomsoever he toucheth that hath the issue, and hath not rinsed his hands in water, he shall wash his clothes, and bathe *himself* in water, and be unclean until the even.

12 And the vessel of earth, that he toucheth which hath the issue, shall be broken: and every vessel of wood shall be rinsed in water.

13 And when he that hath an issue is cleansed of his issue; then he shall number to himself seven days for his cleansing, and wash his clothes, and bathe his flesh in running water, and shall be clean.

14 And on the eighth day he shall take to him two turtledoves, or two young pigeons, and come before the LORD unto the door of the tabernacle of the congregation, and give them unto the priest:

15 And the priest shall offer them, the one *for* a sin offering, and the other *for* a burnt offering; and the priest shall make an atonement for him before the LORD for his issue.

16 And if any man's seed of copulation go out from him, then he shall wash all his flesh in water, and be unclean until the even.

17 And every garment, and every skin, whereon is the seed of copulation, shall be washed with water, and be unclean until the even.

18 The woman also with whom man shall lie *with* seed of copulation, they shall *both* bathe *themselves* in water, and be unclean until the even.

19 And if a woman have an issue, *and* her issue in her flesh be blood, she shall be put apart seven days: and whosoever toucheth her shall be unclean until the even.

20 And every thing that she lieth upon in her separation shall be unclean: every thing also that she sitteth upon shall be unclean.

21 And whosoever toucheth her bed shall wash his clothes, and bathe *himself* in water, and be unclean until the even.

22 And whosoever toucheth any thing that she sat upon shall wash his clothes, and bathe *himself* in water, and be unclean until the even.

23 And if it *be* on *her* bed, or on any thing whereon she sitteth, when he toucheth it, he shall be unclean until the even.

24 And if any man lie with her at all, and her flowers be upon him, he shall be unclean seven days; and all the bed whereon he lieth shall be unclean.

25 And if a woman have an issue of her blood many days out of the time of her separation, or if it run beyond the time of her separation; all the days of the issue of her uncleanness shall be as the days of her separation: she *shall be* unclean.

26 Every bed whereon she lieth all the days of her issue shall be unto her as the bed of her separation: and whatsoever she sitteth upon shall be unclean, as the uncleanness of her separation.

27 And whosoever toucheth those things shall be unclean, and shall wash his clothes, and bathe *himself* in water, and be unclean until the even.

28 But if she be cleansed of her issue, then she shall number to herself seven days, and after that she shall be clean.

29 And on the eighth day she shall take unto her two turtles, or two young pigeons, and bring them unto the priest, to the door of the tabernacle of the congregation.

30 And the priest shall offer the one *for* a sin offering, and the other *for* a burnt offering; and the priest shall make an atonement for her before the LORD for the issue of her uncleanness.

31 Thus shall ye separate the children of Israel from their uncleanness; that they die not in their uncleanness, when they defile my tabernacle that *is* among them.

32 This *is* the law of him that hath an issue, and *of him* whose seed goeth from him, and is defiled therewith;

33 And of her that is sick of her flowers, and of him that hath an issue, of the man, and of the woman, and of him that lieth with her that is unclean.

16 And the LORD spake unto Moses after the death of the two sons of Aaron, when they offered before the LORD, and died;

2 And the LORD said unto Moses, Speak unto Aaron thy brother, that he come not at all times into the holy *place* within the vail before the mercy seat, which *is* upon the ark; that he die not: for I will appear in the cloud upon the mercy seat.

3 Thus shall Aaron come into the holy *place*: with a young bullock for a sin offering, and a ram for a burnt offering.

4 He shall put on the holy linen coat, and he shall have the linen breeches upon his flesh, and shall be girded with a linen girdle, and with the linen mitre shall he be attired: these *are* holy garments; therefore shall he wash his flesh in water, and *so* put them on.

5 And he shall take of the congregation of the children of Israel two kids of the goats for a sin offering, and one ram for a burnt offering.

6 And Aaron shall offer his bullock of the sin offering, which *is* for himself, and make an atonement for himself, and for his house.

7 And he shall take the two goats, and present them before the LORD *at* the door of the tabernacle of the congregation.

8 And Aaron shall cast lots upon the two goats; one lot for the LORD, and the other lot for the scapegoat.

9 And Aaron shall bring the goat upon which the LORD's lot fell, and offer him *for* a sin offering.

10 But the goat, on which the lot fell to be the scapegoat, shall be presented alive before the LORD, to make an atonement with him, *and* to let him go for a scapegoat into the wilderness.

11 And Aaron shall bring the bullock of the sin offering, which *is* for himself,

and shall make an atonement for himself, and for his house, and shall kill the
bullock of the sin offering which *is* for
himself:
12 And he shall take a censer full of
burning coals of fire from off the altar
before the LORD, and his hands full of
sweet incense beaten small, and bring
it within the vail:
13 And he shall put the incense upon
the fire before the LORD, that the cloud
of the incense may cover the mercy
seat that *is* upon the testimony, that he
die not:
14 And he shall take of the blood of
the bullock, and sprinkle *it* with his
finger upon the mercy seat eastward;
and before the mercy seat shall he
sprinkle of the blood with his finger
seven times.
15 Then shall he kill the goat of the
sin offering, that *is* for the people, and
bring his blood within the vail, and do
with that blood as he did with the blood
of the bullock, and sprinkle it upon the
mercy seat, and before the mercy seat:
16 And he shall make an atonement
for the holy *place*, because of the
uncleanness of the children of Israel,
and because of their transgressions in
all their sins: and so shall he do for the
tabernacle of the congregation, that
remaineth among them in the midst of
their uncleanness.
17 And there shall be no man in the
tabernacle of the congregation when
he goeth in to make an atonement in
the holy *place*, until he come out, and
have made an atonement for himself,
and for his household, and for all the
congregation of Israel.
18 And he shall go out unto the altar
that *is* before the LORD, and make an
atonement for it; and shall take of the
blood of the bullock, and of the blood
of the goat, and put *it* upon the horns of
the altar round about.
19 And he shall sprinkle of the blood
upon it with his finger seven times, and
cleanse it, and hallow it from the
uncleanness of the children of Israel.
20 And when he hath made an end of
reconciling the holy *place*, and the tabernacle of the congregation, and the
altar, he shall bring the live goat:
21 And Aaron shall lay both his hands
upon the head of the live goat, and
confess over him all the iniquities of
the children of Israel, and all their
transgressions in all their sins, putting
them upon the head of the goat, and
shall send *him* away by the hand of a fit
man into the wilderness:
22 And the goat shall bear upon him
all their iniquities unto a land not
inhabited: and he shall let go the goat
in the wilderness.
23 And Aaron shall come into the
tabernacle of the congregation, and
shall put off the linen garments, which
he put on when he went into the holy
place, and shall leave them there:
24 And he shall wash his flesh with
water in the holy place, and put on his
garments, and come forth, and offer his
burnt offering, and the burnt offering
of the people, and make an atonement
for himself, and for the people.
25 And the fat of the sin offering shall
he burn upon the altar.
26 And he that let go the goat for the
scapegoat shall wash his clothes, and
bathe his flesh in water, and afterward
come into the camp.
27 And the bullock *for* the sin offering, and the goat *for* the sin offering,
whose blood was brought in to make
atonement in the holy *place*, shall *one*

carry forth without the camp; and they shall burn in the fire their skins, and their flesh, and their dung.

28 And he that burneth them shall wash his clothes, and bathe his flesh in water, and afterward he shall come into the camp.

29 And *this* shall be a statute for ever unto you: *that* in the seventh month, on the tenth *day* of the month, ye shall afflict your souls, and do no work at all, *whether it be* one of your own country, or a stranger that sojourneth among you:

30 For on that day shall *the priest* make an atonement for you, to cleanse you, *that* ye may be clean from all your sins before the LORD.

31 It *shall be* a sabbath of rest unto you, and ye shall afflict your souls, by a statute for ever.

32 And the priest, whom he shall anoint, and whom he shall consecrate to minister in the priest's office in his father's stead, shall make the atonement, and shall put on the linen clothes, *even* the holy garments:

33 And he shall make an atonement for the holy sanctuary, and he shall make an atonement for the tabernacle of the congregation, and for the altar, and he shall make an atonement for the priests, and for all the people of the congregation.

34 And this shall be an everlasting statute unto you, to make an atonement for the children of Israel for all their sins once a year. And he did as the LORD commanded Moses.

17 And the LORD spake unto Moses, saying,

2 Speak unto Aaron, and unto his sons, and unto all the children of Israel, and say unto them; This *is* the thing which the LORD hath commanded, saying,

3 What man soever *there be* of the house of Israel, that killeth an ox, or lamb, or goat, in the camp, or that killeth *it* out of the camp,

4 And bringeth it not unto the door of the tabernacle of the congregation, to offer an offering unto the LORD before the tabernacle of the LORD; blood shall be imputed unto that man; he hath shed blood; and that man shall be cut off from among his people:

5 To the end that the children of Israel may bring their sacrifices, which they offer in the open field, even that they may bring them unto the LORD, unto the door of the tabernacle of the congregation, unto the priest, and offer them *for* peace offerings unto the LORD.

6 And the priest shall sprinkle the blood upon the altar of the LORD *at* the door of the tabernacle of the congregation, and burn the fat for a sweet savour unto the LORD.

7 And they shall no more offer their sacrifices unto devils, after whom they have gone a whoring. This shall be a statute for ever unto them throughout their generations.

8 And thou shalt say unto them, Whatsoever man *there be* of the house of Israel, or of the strangers which sojourn among you, that offereth a burnt offering or sacrifice,

9 And bringeth it not unto the door of the tabernacle of the congregation, to offer it unto the LORD; even that man shall be cut off from among his people.

10 And whatsoever man *there be* of the house of Israel, or of the strangers that sojourn among you, that eateth any manner of blood; I will even set my face against that soul that eateth blood, and will cut him off from among his people.

11 For the life of the flesh *is* in the blood: and I have given it to you upon the altar to make an atonement for your souls: for it *is* the blood *that* maketh an atonement for the soul.

12 Therefore I said unto the children of Israel, No soul of you shall eat blood, neither shall any stranger that sojourneth among you eat blood.

13 And whatsoever man *there be* of the children of Israel, or of the strangers that sojourn among you, which hunteth and catcheth any beast or fowl that may be eaten; he shall even pour out the blood thereof, and cover it with dust.

14 For *it is* the life of all flesh; the blood of it *is* for the life thereof: therefore I said unto the children of Israel, Ye shall eat the blood of no manner of flesh: for the life of all flesh *is* the blood thereof: whosoever eateth it shall be cut off.

15 And every soul that eateth that which died *of itself*, or that which was torn *with beasts, whether it be* one of your own country, or a stranger, he shall both wash his clothes, and bathe *himself* in water, and be unclean until the even: then shall he be clean.

16 But if he wash *them* not, nor bathe his flesh; then he shall bear his iniquity.

18 And the LORD spake unto Moses, saying,

2 Speak unto the children of Israel, and say unto them, I am the LORD your God.

3 After the doings of the land of Egypt, wherein ye dwelt, shall ye not do: and after the doings of the land of Canaan, whither I bring you, shall ye not do: neither shall ye walk in their ordinances.

4 Ye shall do my judgments, and keep mine ordinances, to walk therein: I *am* the LORD your God.

5 Ye shall therefore keep my statutes, and my judgments: which if a man do, he shall live in them: I *am* the LORD.

6 None of you shall approach to any that is near of kin to him, to uncover *their* nakedness: I *am* the LORD.

7 The nakedness of thy father, or the nakedness of thy mother, shalt thou not uncover: she *is* thy mother; thou shalt not uncover her nakedness.

8 The nakedness of thy father's wife shalt thou not uncover: it *is* thy father's nakedness.

9 The nakedness of thy sister, the daughter of thy father, or daughter of thy mother, *whether she be* born at home, or born abroad, *even* their nakedness thou shalt not uncover.

10 The nakedness of thy son's daughter, or of thy daughter's daughter, *even* their nakedness thou shalt not uncover: for theirs *is* thine own nakedness.

11 The nakedness of thy father's wife's daughter, begotten of thy father, she *is* thy sister, thou shalt not uncover her nakedness.

12 Thou shalt not uncover the nakedness of thy father's sister: she *is* thy father's near kinswoman.

13 Thou shalt not uncover the nakedness of thy mother's sister: for she *is* thy mother's near kinswoman.

14 Thou shalt not uncover the nakedness of thy father's brother, thou shalt not approach to his wife: she *is* thine aunt.

15 Thou shalt not uncover the nakedness of thy daughter in law: she *is* thy

son's wife; thou shalt not uncover her
nakedness.
16 Thou shalt not uncover the nakedness of thy brother's wife: it *is* thy
brother's nakedness.
17 Thou shalt not uncover the nakedness of a woman and her daughter,
neither shalt thou take her son's daughter, or her daughter's daughter, to
uncover her nakedness; *for* they *are* her
near kinswomen: it *is* wickedness.
18 Neither shalt thou take a wife to
her sister, to vex *her*, to uncover her
nakedness, beside the other in her life
time.
19 Also thou shalt not approach unto
a woman to uncover her nakedness, as
long as she is put apart for her uncleanness.
20 Moreover thou shalt not lie carnally with thy neighbour's wife, to
defile thyself with her.
21 And thou shalt not let any of thy
seed pass through *the fire* to Molech,
neither shalt thou profane the name of
thy God: I *am* the LORD.
22 Thou shalt not lie with mankind, as
with womankind: it *is* abomination.
23 Neither shalt thou lie with any
beast to defile thyself therewith: neither shall any woman stand before a
beast to lie down thereto: it *is* confusion.
24 Defile not ye yourselves in any of
these things: for in all these the nations
are defiled which I cast out before you:
25 And the land is defiled: therefore I
do visit the iniquity thereof upon it,
and the land itself vomiteth out her
inhabitants.
26 Ye shall therefore keep my statutes and my judgments, and shall not
commit *any* of these abominations;
neither any of your own nation, nor any
stranger that sojourneth among you:
27 (For all these abominations have
the men of the land done, which *were*
before you, and the land is defiled;)
28 That the land spue not you out
also, when ye defile it, as it spued out
the nations that *were* before you.
29 For whosoever shall commit any of
these abominations, even the souls that
commit *them* shall be cut off from
among their people.
30 Therefore shall ye keep mine ordinance, that *ye* commit not *any one* of
these abominable customs, which were
committed before you, and that ye
defile not yourselves therein: I *am* the
LORD your God.

19 And the LORD spake unto Moses,
saying,
2 Speak unto all the congregation of
the children of Israel, and say unto
them, Ye shall be holy: for I the LORD
your God *am* holy.
3 Ye shall fear every man his mother,
and his father, and keep my sabbaths: I
am the LORD your God.
4 Turn ye not unto idols, nor make to
yourselves molten gods: I *am* the LORD
your God.
5 And if ye offer a sacrifice of peace
offerings unto the LORD, ye shall offer it
at your own will.
6 It shall be eaten the same day ye
offer it, and on the morrow: and if
ought remain until the third day, it
shall be burnt in the fire.
7 And if it be eaten at all on the third
day, it *is* abominable; it shall not be
accepted.
8 Therefore *every one* that eateth it
shall bear his iniquity, because he hath
profaned the hallowed thing of the

LORD: and that soul shall be cut off
from among his people.
9 And when ye reap the harvest of
your land, thou shalt not wholly reap
the corners of thy field, neither shalt
thou gather the gleanings of thy harvest.
10 And thou shalt not glean thy vineyard,
neither shalt thou gather *every*
grape of thy vineyard; thou shalt leave
them for the poor and stranger: I *am*
the LORD your God.
11 Ye shall not steal, neither deal
falsely, neither lie one to another.
12 And ye shall not swear by my
name falsely, neither shalt thou profane
the name of thy God: I *am* the
LORD.
13 Thou shalt not defraud thy neighbour,
neither rob *him*: the wages of him
that is hired shall not abide with thee
all night until the morning.
14 Thou shalt not curse the deaf, nor
put a stumblingblock before the blind,
but shalt fear thy God: I *am* the LORD.
15 Ye shall do no unrighteousness in
judgment: thou shalt not respect the
person of the poor, nor honour the person
of the mighty: *but* in righteousness
shalt thou judge thy neighbour.
16 Thou shalt not go up and down *as*
a talebearer among thy people: neither
shalt thou stand against the blood of
thy neighbour: I *am* the LORD.
17 Thou shalt not hate thy brother in
thine heart: thou shalt in any wise
rebuke thy neighbour, and not suffer
sin upon him.
18 Thou shalt not avenge, nor bear
any grudge against the children of thy
people, but thou shalt love thy neighbour
as thyself: I *am* the LORD.
19 Ye shall keep my statutes. Thou
shalt not let thy cattle gender with a
diverse kind: thou shalt not sow thy
field with mingled seed: neither shall a
garment mingled of linen and woollen
come upon thee.
20 And whosoever lieth carnally with
a woman, that *is* a bondmaid, betrothed
to an husband, and not at all redeemed,
nor freedom given her; she shall be
scourged; they shall not be put to
death, because she was not free.
21 And he shall bring his trespass
offering unto the LORD, unto the door
of the tabernacle of the congregation,
even a ram for a trespass offering.
22 And the priest shall make an
atonement for him with the ram of the
trespass offering before the LORD for
his sin which he hath done: and the sin
which he hath done shall be forgiven
him.
23 And when ye shall come into the
land, and shall have planted all manner
of trees for food, then ye shall count the
fruit thereof as uncircumcised: three
years shall it be as uncircumcised unto
you: it shall not be eaten of.
24 But in the fourth year all the fruit
thereof shall be holy to praise the LORD
withal.
25 And in the fifth year shall ye eat of
the fruit thereof, that it may yield unto
you the increase thereof: I *am* the LORD
your God.
26 Ye shall not eat *any thing* with the
blood: neither shall ye use enchantment,
nor observe times.
27 Ye shall not round the corners of
your heads, neither shalt thou mar the
corners of thy beard.
28 Ye shall not make any cuttings in
your flesh for the dead, nor print any
marks upon you: I *am* the LORD.
29 Do not prostitute thy daughter, to
cause her to be a whore; lest the land

fall to whoredom, and the land become
full of wickedness.
30 Ye shall keep my sabbaths, and
reverence my sanctuary: I *am* the LORD.
31 Regard not them that have familiar spirits, neither seek after wizards, to
be defiled by them: I *am* the LORD your
God.
32 Thou shalt rise up before the hoary
head, and honour the face of the old
man, and fear thy God: I *am* the LORD.
33 And if a stranger sojourn with thee
in your land, ye shall not vex him.
34 *But* the stranger that dwelleth
with you shall be unto you as one born
among you, and thou shalt love him as
thyself; for ye were strangers in the
land of Egypt: I *am* the LORD your God.
35 Ye shall do no unrighteousness in
judgment, in meteyard, in weight, or in
measure.
36 Just balances, just weights, a just
ephah, and a just hin, shall ye have: I
am the LORD your God, which brought
you out of the land of Egypt.
37 Therefore shall ye observe all my
statutes, and all my judgments, and do
them: I *am* the LORD.

20 And the LORD spake unto Moses,
saying,
2 Again, thou shalt say to the children
of Israel, Whosoever *he be* of the children of Israel, or of the strangers that
sojourn in Israel, that giveth *any* of his
seed unto Molech; he shall surely be
put to death: the people of the land
shall stone him with stones.
3 And I will set my face against that
man, and will cut him off from among
his people; because he hath given of his
seed unto Molech, to defile my sanctuary, and to profane my holy name.
4 And if the people of the land do any
ways hide their eyes from the man,
when he giveth of his seed unto Molech,
and kill him not:
5 Then I will set my face against that
man, and against his family, and will
cut him off, and all that go a whoring
after him, to commit whoredom with
Molech, from among their people.
6 And the soul that turneth after such
as have familiar spirits, and after wizards, to go a whoring after them, I will
even set my face against that soul, and
will cut him off from among his people.
7 Sanctify yourselves therefore, and
be ye holy: for I *am* the LORD your God.
8 And ye shall keep my statutes, and
do them: I *am* the LORD which sanctify
you.
9 For every one that curseth his father
or his mother shall be surely put to
death: he hath cursed his father or his
mother; his blood *shall be* upon him.
10 And the man that committeth
adultery with *another* man's wife, *even*
he that committeth adultery with his
neighbour's wife, the adulterer and the
adulteress shall surely be put to death.
11 And the man that lieth with his
father's wife hath uncovered his
father's nakedness: both of them shall
surely be put to death; their blood *shall*
be upon them.
12 And if a man lie with his daughter
in law, both of them shall surely be put
to death: they have wrought confusion;
their blood *shall be* upon them.
13 If a man also lie with mankind, as
he lieth with a woman, both of them
have committed an abomination: they
shall surely be put to death; their blood
shall be upon them.
14 And if a man take a wife and her
mother, it *is* wickedness: they shall be
burnt with fire, both he and they; that
there be no wickedness among you.

15 And if a man lie with a beast, he shall surely be put to death: and ye shall slay the beast.

16 And if a woman approach unto any beast, and lie down thereto, thou shalt kill the woman, and the beast: they shall surely be put to death; their blood *shall be* upon them.

17 And if a man shall take his sister, his father's daughter, or his mother's daughter, and see her nakedness, and she see his nakedness; it *is* a wicked thing; and they shall be cut off in the sight of their people: he hath uncovered his sister's nakedness; he shall bear his iniquity.

18 And if a man shall lie with a woman having her sickness, and shall uncover her nakedness; he hath discovered her fountain, and she hath uncovered the fountain of her blood: and both of them shall be cut off from among their people.

19 And thou shalt not uncover the nakedness of thy mother's sister, nor of thy father's sister: for he uncovereth his near kin: they shall bear their iniquity.

20 And if a man shall lie with his uncle's wife, he hath uncovered his uncle's nakedness: they shall bear their sin; they shall die childless.

21 And if a man shall take his brother's wife, it *is* an unclean thing: he hath uncovered his brother's nakedness; they shall be childless.

22 Ye shall therefore keep all my statutes, and all my judgments, and do them: that the land, whither I bring you to dwell therein, spue you not out.

23 And ye shall not walk in the manners of the nation, which I cast out before you: for they committed all these things, and therefore I abhorred them.

24 But I have said unto you, Ye shall inherit their land, and I will give it unto you to possess it, a land that floweth with milk and honey: I *am* the LORD your God, which have separated you from *other* people.

25 Ye shall therefore put difference between clean beasts and unclean, and between unclean fowls and clean: and ye shall not make your souls abominable by beast, or by fowl, or by any manner of living thing that creepeth on the ground, which I have separated from you as unclean.

26 And ye shall be holy unto me: for I the LORD *am* holy, and have severed you from *other* people, that ye should be mine.

27 A man also or woman that hath a familiar spirit, or that is a wizard, shall surely be put to death: they shall stone them with stones: their blood *shall be* upon them.

21

And the LORD said unto Moses, Speak unto the priests the sons of Aaron, and say unto them, There shall none be defiled for the dead among his people:

2 But for his kin, that is near unto him, *that is*, for his mother, and for his father, and for his son, and for his daughter, and for his brother,

3 And for his sister a virgin, that is nigh unto him, which hath had no husband; for her may he be defiled.

4 *But* he shall not defile himself, *being* a chief man among his people, to profane himself.

5 They shall not make baldness upon their head, neither shall they shave off the corner of their beard, nor make any cuttings in their flesh.

6 They shall be holy unto their God, and not profane the name of their God:

for the offerings of the LORD made by fire, *and* the bread of their God, they do offer: therefore they shall be holy.

7 They shall not take a wife *that is* a whore, or profane; neither shall they take a woman put away from her husband: for he *is* holy unto his God.

8 Thou shalt sanctify him therefore; for he offereth the bread of thy God: he shall be holy unto thee: for I the LORD, which sanctify you, *am* holy.

9 And the daughter of any priest, if she profane herself by playing the whore, she profaneth her father: she shall be burnt with fire.

10 And *he that is* the high priest among his brethren, upon whose head the anointing oil was poured, and that is consecrated to put on the garments, shall not uncover his head, nor rend his clothes;

11 Neither shall he go in to any dead body, nor defile himself for his father, or for his mother;

12 Neither shall he go out of the sanctuary, nor profane the sanctuary of his God; for the crown of the anointing oil of his God *is* upon him: I *am* the LORD.

13 And he shall take a wife in her virginity.

14 A widow, or a divorced woman, or profane, *or* an harlot, these shall he not take: but he shall take a virgin of his own people to wife.

15 Neither shall he profane his seed among his people: for I the LORD do sanctify him.

16 And the LORD spake unto Moses, saying,

17 Speak unto Aaron, saying, Whosoever *he be* of thy seed in their generations that hath *any* blemish, let him not approach to offer the bread of his God.

18 For whatsoever man *he be* that hath a blemish, he shall not approach: a blind man, or a lame, or he that hath a flat nose, or any thing superfluous,

19 Or a man that is brokenfooted, or brokenhanded,

20 Or crookbackt, or a dwarf, or that hath a blemish in his eye, or be scurvy, or scabbed, or hath his stones broken;

21 No man that hath a blemish of the seed of Aaron the priest shall come nigh to offer the offerings of the LORD made by fire: he hath a blemish; he shall not come nigh to offer the bread of his God.

22 He shall eat the bread of his God, *both* of the most holy, and of the holy.

23 Only he shall not go in unto the vail, nor come nigh unto the altar, because he hath a blemish; that he profane not my sanctuaries: for I the LORD do sanctify them.

24 And Moses told *it* unto Aaron, and to his sons, and unto all the children of Israel.

22 And the LORD spake unto Moses, saying,

2 Speak unto Aaron and to his sons, that they separate themselves from the holy things of the children of Israel, and that they profane not my holy name *in those things* which they hallow unto me: I *am* the LORD.

3 Say unto them, Whosoever *he be* of all your seed among your generations, that goeth unto the holy things, which the children of Israel hallow unto the LORD, having his uncleanness upon him, that soul shall be cut off from my presence: I *am* the LORD.

4 What man soever of the seed of Aaron *is* a leper, or hath a running issue; he shall not eat of the holy things, until he be clean. And whoso toucheth

any thing *that is* unclean *by* the dead,
or a man whose seed goeth from him;
5 Or whosoever toucheth any creeping thing, whereby he may be made
unclean, or a man of whom he may take
uncleanness, whatsoever uncleanness
he hath;
6 The soul which hath touched any
such shall be unclean until even, and
shall not eat of the holy things, unless
he wash his flesh with water.
7 And when the sun is down, he shall
be clean, and shall afterward eat of the
holy things; because it *is* his food.
8 That which dieth of itself, or is torn
with beasts, he shall not eat to defile
himself therewith: I *am* the LORD.
9 They shall therefore keep mine
ordinance, lest they bear sin for it, and
die therefore, if they profane it: I the
LORD do sanctify them.
10 There shall no stranger eat *of* the
holy thing: a sojourner of the priest, or
an hired servant, shall not eat *of* the
holy thing.
11 But if the priest buy *any* soul with
his money, he shall eat of it, and he that
is born in his house: they shall eat of his
meat.
12 If the priest's daughter also be
married unto a stranger, she may not
eat of an offering of the holy things.
13 But if the priest's daughter be a
widow, or divorced, and have no child,
and is returned unto her father's house,
as in her youth, she shall eat of her
father's meat: but there shall no stranger eat thereof.
14 And if a man eat *of* the holy thing
unwittingly, then he shall put the fifth
part thereof unto it, and shall give *it*
unto the priest with the holy thing.
15 And they shall not profane the
holy things of the children of Israel,
which they offer unto the LORD;
16 Or suffer them to bear the iniquity
of trespass, when they eat their holy
things: for I the LORD do sanctify them.
17 And the LORD spake unto Moses,
saying,
18 Speak unto Aaron, and to his sons,
and unto all the children of Israel, and
say unto them, Whatsoever *he be* of the
house of Israel, or of the strangers in
Israel, that will offer his oblation for all
his vows, and for all his freewill offerings, which they will offer unto the
LORD for a burnt offering;
19 *Ye shall offer* at your own will a
male without blemish, of the beeves, of
the sheep, or of the goats.
20 *But* whatsoever hath a blemish,
that shall ye not offer: for it shall not be
acceptable for you.
21 And whosoever offereth a sacrifice
of peace offerings unto the LORD to
accomplish *his* vow, or a freewill offering in beeves or sheep, it shall be perfect to be accepted; there shall be no
blemish therein.
22 Blind, or broken, or maimed, or
having a wen, or scurvy, or scabbed, ye
shall not offer these unto the LORD, nor
make an offering by fire of them upon
the altar unto the LORD.
23 Either a bullock or a lamb that
hath any thing superfluous or lacking
in his parts, that mayest thou offer *for* a
freewill offering; but for a vow it shall
not be accepted.
24 Ye shall not offer unto the LORD
that which is bruised, or crushed, or
broken, or cut; neither shall ye make
any offering thereof in your land.
25 Neither from a stranger's hand
shall ye offer the bread of your God of

any of these; because their corruption
is in them, *and* blemishes *be* in them:
they shall not be accepted for you.
26 And the LORD spake unto Moses,
saying,
27 When a bullock, or a sheep, or a
goat, is brought forth, then it shall be
seven days under the dam; and from
the eighth day and thenceforth it shall
be accepted for an offering made by
fire unto the LORD.
28 And *whether it be* cow or ewe, ye
shall not kill it and her young both in
one day.
29 And when ye will offer a sacrifice
of thanksgiving unto the LORD, offer *it*
at your own will.
30 On the same day it shall be eaten
up; ye shall leave none of it until the
morrow: I *am* the LORD.
31 Therefore shall ye keep my commandments, and do them: I *am* the
LORD.
32 Neither shall ye profane my holy
name; but I will be hallowed among the
children of Israel: I *am* the LORD which
hallow you,
33 That brought you out of the land of
Egypt, to be your God: I *am* the LORD.

23 And the LORD spake unto Moses,
saying,
2 Speak unto the children of Israel,
and say unto them, *Concerning* the
feasts of the LORD, which ye shall proclaim *to be* holy convocations, *even*
these *are* my feasts.
3 Six days shall work be done: but the
seventh day *is* the sabbath of rest, an
holy convocation; ye shall do no work
therein: it *is* the sabbath of the LORD in
all your dwellings.
4 These *are* the feasts of the LORD,
even holy convocations, which ye shall
proclaim in their seasons.
5 In the fourteenth *day* of the first
month at even *is* the LORD's passover.
6 And on the fifteenth day of the
same month *is* the feast of unleavened
bread unto the LORD: seven days ye
must eat unleavened bread.
7 In the first day ye shall have an holy
convocation: ye shall do no servile work
therein.
8 But ye shall offer an offering made
by fire unto the LORD seven days: in the
seventh day *is* an holy convocation: ye
shall do no servile work *therein*.
9 And the LORD spake unto Moses,
saying,
10 Speak unto the children of Israel,
and say unto them, When ye be come
into the land which I give unto you, and
shall reap the harvest thereof, then ye
shall bring a sheaf of the firstfruits of
your harvest unto the priest:
11 And he shall wave the sheaf before
the LORD, to be accepted for you: on the
morrow after the sabbath the priest
shall wave it.
12 And ye shall offer that day when
ye wave the sheaf an he lamb without
blemish of the first year for a burnt
offering unto the LORD.
13 And the meat offering thereof
shall be two tenth deals of fine flour
mingled with oil, an offering made by
fire unto the LORD *for* a sweet savour:
and the drink offering thereof *shall be*
of wine, the fourth *part* of an hin.
14 And ye shall eat neither bread, nor
parched corn, nor green ears, until the
selfsame day that ye have brought an
offering unto your God: *it shall be* a
statute for ever throughout your generations in all your dwellings.
15 And ye shall count unto you from
the morrow after the sabbath, from the
day that ye brought the sheaf of the

wave offering; seven sabbaths shall be
complete:
16 Even unto the morrow after the
seventh sabbath shall ye number fifty
days; and ye shall offer a new meat
offering unto the LORD.
17 Ye shall bring out of your habitations two wave loaves of two tenth
deals: they shall be of fine flour; they
shall be baken with leaven; *they are*
the firstfruits unto the LORD.
18 And ye shall offer with the bread
seven lambs without blemish of the
first year, and one young bullock, and
two rams: they shall be *for* a burnt
offering unto the LORD, with their meat
offering, and their drink offerings, *even*
an offering made by fire, of sweet
savour unto the LORD.
19 Then ye shall sacrifice one kid of
the goats for a sin offering, and two
lambs of the first year for a sacrifice of
peace offerings.
20 And the priest shall wave them
with the bread of the firstfruits *for* a
wave offering before the LORD, with the
two lambs: they shall be holy to the
LORD for the priest.
21 And ye shall proclaim on the selfsame day, *that* it may be an holy convocation unto you: ye shall do no servile
work *therein: it shall be* a statute for
ever in all your dwellings throughout
your generations.
22 And when ye reap the harvest of
your land, thou shalt not make clean
riddance of the corners of thy field
when thou reapest, neither shalt thou
gather any gleaning of thy harvest:
thou shalt leave them unto the poor,
and to the stranger: I *am* the LORD your
God.
23 And the LORD spake unto Moses,
saying,
24 Speak unto the children of Israel,
saying, In the seventh month, in the
first *day* of the month, shall ye have a
sabbath, a memorial of blowing of
trumpets, an holy convocation.
25 Ye shall do no servile work *therein*:
but ye shall offer an offering made by
fire unto the LORD.
26 And the LORD spake unto Moses,
saying,
27 Also on the tenth *day* of this seventh month *there shall be* a day of
atonement: it shall be an holy convocation unto you; and ye shall afflict your
souls, and offer an offering made by
fire unto the LORD.
28 And ye shall do no work in that
same day: for it *is* a day of atonement,
to make an atonement for you before
the LORD your God.
29 For whatsoever soul *it be* that shall
not be afflicted in that same day, he
shall be cut off from among his people.
30 And whatsoever soul *it be* that
doeth any work in that same day, the
same soul will I destroy from among his
people.
31 Ye shall do no manner of work: *it
shall be* a statute for ever throughout
your generations in all your dwellings.
32 It *shall be* unto you a sabbath of
rest, and ye shall afflict your souls: in
the ninth *day* of the month at even,
from even unto even, shall ye celebrate
your sabbath.
33 And the LORD spake unto Moses,
saying,
34 Speak unto the children of Israel,
saying, The fifteenth day of this seventh month *shall be* the feast of tabernacles *for* seven days unto the LORD.
35 On the first day *shall be* an holy
convocation: ye shall do no servile work
therein.

36 Seven days ye shall offer an offering made by fire unto the LORD: on the eighth day shall be an holy convocation unto you; and ye shall offer an offering made by fire unto the LORD: it *is* a solemn assembly; *and* ye shall do no servile work *therein*.

37 These *are* the feasts of the LORD, which ye shall proclaim *to be* holy convocations, to offer an offering made by fire unto the LORD, a burnt offering, and a meat offering, a sacrifice, and drink offerings, every thing upon his day:

38 Beside the sabbaths of the LORD, and beside your gifts, and beside all your vows, and beside all your freewill offerings, which ye give unto the LORD.

39 Also in the fifteenth day of the seventh month, when ye have gathered in the fruit of the land, ye shall keep a feast unto the LORD seven days: on the first day *shall be* a sabbath, and on the eighth day *shall be* a sabbath.

40 And ye shall take you on the first day the boughs of goodly trees, branches of palm trees, and the boughs of thick trees, and willows of the brook; and ye shall rejoice before the LORD your God seven days.

41 And ye shall keep it a feast unto the LORD seven days in the year. *It shall be* a statute for ever in your generations: ye shall celebrate it in the seventh month.

42 Ye shall dwell in booths seven days; all that are Israelites born shall dwell in booths:

43 That your generations may know that I made the children of Israel to dwell in booths, when I brought them out of the land of Egypt: I *am* the LORD your God.

44 And Moses declared unto the children of Israel the feasts of the LORD.

24

And the LORD spake unto Moses, saying,

2 Command the children of Israel, that they bring unto thee pure oil olive beaten for the light, to cause the lamps to burn continually.

3 Without the vail of the testimony, in the tabernacle of the congregation, shall Aaron order it from the evening unto the morning before the LORD continually: *it shall be* a statute for ever in your generations.

4 He shall order the lamps upon the pure candlestick before the LORD continually.

5 And thou shalt take fine flour, and bake twelve cakes thereof: two tenth deals shall be in one cake.

6 And thou shalt set them in two rows, six on a row, upon the pure table before the LORD.

7 And thou shalt put pure frankincense upon *each* row, that it may be on the bread for a memorial, *even* an offering made by fire unto the LORD.

8 Every sabbath he shall set it in order before the LORD continually, *being taken* from the children of Israel by an everlasting covenant.

9 And it shall be Aaron's and his sons'; and they shall eat it in the holy place: for it *is* most holy unto him of the offerings of the LORD made by fire by a perpetual statute.

10 And the son of an Israelitish woman, whose father *was* an Egyptian, went out among the children of Israel: and this son of the Israelitish *woman* and a man of Israel strove together in the camp;

11 And the Israelitish woman's son blasphemed the name *of the LORD*, and cursed. And they brought him unto Moses: (and his mother's name *was* Shelomith, the daughter of Dibri, of the tribe of Dan:)

12 And they put him in ward, that the mind of the LORD might be shewed them.

13 And the LORD spake unto Moses, saying,

14 Bring forth him that hath cursed without the camp; and let all that heard *him* lay their hands upon his head, and let all the congregation stone him.

15 And thou shalt speak unto the children of Israel, saying, Whosoever curseth his God shall bear his sin.

16 And he that blasphemeth the name of the LORD, he shall surely be put to death, *and* all the congregation shall certainly stone him: as well the stranger, as he that is born in the land, when he blasphemeth the name *of the LORD*, shall be put to death.

17 And he that killeth any man shall surely be put to death.

18 And he that killeth a beast shall make it good; beast for beast.

19 And if a man cause a blemish in his neighbour; as he hath done, so shall it be done to him;

20 Breach for breach, eye for eye, tooth for tooth: as he hath caused a blemish in a man, so shall it be done to him *again*.

21 And he that killeth a beast, he shall restore it: and he that killeth a man, he shall be put to death.

22 Ye shall have one manner of law, as well for the stranger, as for one of your own country: for I *am* the LORD your God.

23 And Moses spake to the children of Israel, that they should bring forth him that had cursed out of the camp, and stone him with stones. And the children of Israel did as the LORD commanded Moses.

25 And the LORD spake unto Moses in mount Sinai, saying,

2 Speak unto the children of Israel, and say unto them, When ye come into the land which I give you, then shall the land keep a sabbath unto the LORD.

3 Six years thou shalt sow thy field, and six years thou shalt prune thy vineyard, and gather in the fruit thereof;

4 But in the seventh year shall be a sabbath of rest unto the land, a sabbath for the LORD: thou shalt neither sow thy field, nor prune thy vineyard.

5 That which groweth of its own accord of thy harvest thou shalt not reap, neither gather the grapes of thy vine undressed: *for* it is a year of rest unto the land.

6 And the sabbath of the land shall be meat for you; for thee, and for thy servant, and for thy maid, and for thy hired servant, and for thy stranger that sojourneth with thee,

7 And for thy cattle, and for the beast that *are* in thy land, shall all the increase thereof be meat.

8 And thou shalt number seven sabbaths of years unto thee, seven times seven years; and the space of the seven sabbaths of years shall be unto thee forty and nine years.

9 Then shalt thou cause the trumpet of the jubile to sound on the tenth *day* of the seventh month, in the day of atonement shall ye make the trumpet sound throughout all your land.

10 And ye shall hallow the fiftieth year, and proclaim liberty throughout *all* the land unto all the inhabitants thereof: it shall be a jubile unto you; and ye shall return every man unto his

possession, and ye shall return every man unto his family.
11 A jubile shall that fiftieth year be unto you: ye shall not sow, neither reap that which groweth of itself in it, nor gather *the grapes* in it of thy vine undressed.
12 For it *is* the jubile; it shall be holy unto you: ye shall eat the increase thereof out of the field.
13 In the year of this jubile ye shall return every man unto his possession.
14 And if thou sell ought unto thy neighbour, or buyest *ought* of thy neighbour's hand, ye shall not oppress one another:
15 According to the number of years after the jubile thou shalt buy of thy neighbour, *and* according unto the number of years of the fruits he shall sell unto thee:
16 According to the multitude of years thou shalt increase the price thereof, and according to the fewness of years thou shalt diminish the price of it: for *according* to the number *of the years* of the fruits doth he sell unto thee.
17 Ye shall not therefore oppress one another; but thou shalt fear thy God: for I *am* the LORD your God.
18 Wherefore ye shall do my statutes, and keep my judgments, and do them; and ye shall dwell in the land in safety.
19 And the land shall yield her fruit, and ye shall eat your fill, and dwell therein in safety.
20 And if ye shall say, What shall we eat the seventh year? behold, we shall not sow, nor gather in our increase:
21 Then I will command my blessing upon you in the sixth year, and it shall bring forth fruit for three years.
22 And ye shall sow the eighth year, and eat *yet* of old fruit until the ninth year; until her fruits come in ye shall eat *of* the old *store*.
23 The land shall not be sold for ever: for the land *is* mine; for ye *are* strangers and sojourners with me.
24 And in all the land of your possession ye shall grant a redemption for the land.
25 If thy brother be waxen poor, and hath sold away *some* of his possession, and if any of his kin come to redeem it, then shall he redeem that which his brother sold.
26 And if the man have none to redeem it, and himself be able to redeem it;
27 Then let him count the years of the sale thereof, and restore the overplus unto the man to whom he sold it; that he may return unto his possession.
28 But if he be not able to restore *it* to him, then that which is sold shall remain in the hand of him that hath bought it until the year of jubile: and in the jubile it shall go out, and he shall return unto his possession.
29 And if a man sell a dwelling house in a walled city, then he may redeem it within a whole year after it is sold; *within* a full year may he redeem it.
30 And if it be not redeemed within the space of a full year, then the house that *is* in the walled city shall be established for ever to him that bought it throughout his generations: it shall not go out in the jubile.
31 But the houses of the villages which have no wall round about them shall be counted as the fields of the country: they may be redeemed, and they shall go out in the jubile.

32 Notwithstanding the cities of the Levites, *and* the houses of the cities of their possession, may the Levites redeem at any time.

33 And if a man purchase of the Levites, then the house that was sold, and the city of his possession, shall go out in *the year of* jubile: for the houses of the cities of the Levites *are* their possession among the children of Israel.

34 But the field of the suburbs of their cities may not be sold; for it *is* their perpetual possession.

35 And if thy brother be waxen poor, and fallen in decay with thee; then thou shalt relieve him: *yea, though he be* a stranger, or a sojourner; that he may live with thee.

36 Take thou no usury of him, or increase: but fear thy God; that thy brother may live with thee.

37 Thou shalt not give him thy money upon usury, nor lend him thy victuals for increase.

38 I *am* the LORD your God, which brought you forth out of the land of Egypt, to give you the land of Canaan, *and* to be your God.

39 And if thy brother *that dwelleth* by thee be waxen poor, and be sold unto thee; thou shalt not compel him to serve as a bondservant:

40 *But* as an hired servant, *and* as a sojourner, he shall be with thee, *and* shall serve thee unto the year of jubile:

41 And *then* shall he depart from thee, *both* he and his children with him, and shall return unto his own family, and unto the possession of his fathers shall he return.

42 For they *are* my servants, which I brought forth out of the land of Egypt: they shall not be sold as bondmen.

43 Thou shalt not rule over him with rigour; but shalt fear thy God.

44 Both thy bondmen, and thy bondmaids, which thou shalt have, *shall be* of the heathen that are round about you; of them shall ye buy bondmen and bondmaids.

45 Moreover of the children of the strangers that do sojourn among you, of them shall ye buy, and of their families that *are* with you, which they begat in your land: and they shall be your possession.

46 And ye shall take them as an inheritance for your children after you, to inherit *them for* a possession; they shall be your bondmen for ever: but over your brethren the children of Israel, ye shall not rule one over another with rigour.

47 And if a sojourner or stranger wax rich by thee, and thy brother *that dwelleth* by him wax poor, and sell himself unto the stranger *or* sojourner by thee, or to the stock of the stranger's family:

48 After that he is sold he may be redeemed again; one of his brethren may redeem him:

49 Either his uncle, or his uncle's son, may redeem him, or *any* that is nigh of kin unto him of his family may redeem him; or if he be able, he may redeem himself.

50 And he shall reckon with him that bought him from the year that he was sold to him unto the year of jubile: and the price of his sale shall be according unto the number of years, according to the time of an hired servant shall it be with him.

51 If *there be* yet many years *behind*, according unto them he shall give

again the price of his redemption out of
the money that he was bought for.
52 And if there remain but few years
unto the year of jubile, then he shall
count with him, *and* according unto his
years shall he give him again the price
of his redemption.
53 *And* as a yearly hired servant shall
he be with him: *and the other* shall not
rule with rigour over him in thy sight.
54 And if he be not redeemed in
these *years*, then he shall go out in the
year of jubile, *both* he, and his children
with him.
55 For unto me the children of Israel
are servants; they *are* my servants
whom I brought forth out of the land of
Egypt: I *am* the LORD your God.

26 Ye shall make you no idols nor
graven image, neither rear you
up a standing image, neither shall ye
set up *any* image of stone in your land,
to bow down unto it: for I *am* the LORD
your God.
2 Ye shall keep my sabbaths, and reverence my sanctuary: I *am* the LORD.
3 If ye walk in my statutes, and keep
my commandments, and do them;
4 Then I will give you rain in due season, and the land shall yield her
increase, and the trees of the field shall
yield their fruit.
5 And your threshing shall reach unto
the vintage, and the vintage shall reach
unto the sowing time: and ye shall eat
your bread to the full, and dwell in your
land safely.
6 And I will give peace in the land,
and ye shall lie down, and none shall
make *you* afraid: and I will rid evil
beasts out of the land, neither shall the
sword go through your land.
7 And ye shall chase your enemies,
and they shall fall before you by the
sword.
8 And five of you shall chase an hundred, and an hundred of you shall put
ten thousand to flight: and your enemies shall fall before you by the sword.
9 For I will have respect unto you, and
make you fruitful, and multiply you,
and establish my covenant with you.
10 And ye shall eat old store, and
bring forth the old because of the new.
11 And I will set my tabernacle
among you: and my soul shall not abhor
you.
12 And I will walk among you, and
will be your God, and ye shall be my
people.
13 I *am* the LORD your God, which
brought you forth out of the land of
Egypt, that ye should not be their bondmen; and I have broken the bands of
your yoke, and made you go upright.
14 But if ye will not hearken unto me,
and will not do all these commandments;
15 And if ye shall despise my statutes,
or if your soul abhor my judgments, so
that ye will not do all my commandments, *but* that ye break my covenant:
16 I also will do this unto you; I will
even appoint over you terror, consumption, and the burning ague, that shall
consume the eyes, and cause sorrow of
heart: and ye shall sow your seed in
vain, for your enemies shall eat it.
17 And I will set my face against you,
and ye shall be slain before your enemies: they that hate you shall reign
over you; and ye shall flee when none
pursueth you.
18 And if ye will not yet for all this
hearken unto me, then I will punish you
seven times more for your sins.

19 And I will break the pride of your
power; and I will make your heaven as
iron, and your earth as brass:
20 And your strength shall be spent in
vain: for your land shall not yield her
increase, neither shall the trees of the
land yield their fruits.
21 And if ye walk contrary unto me,
and will not hearken unto me; I will
bring seven times more plagues upon
you according to your sins.
22 I will also send wild beasts among
you, which shall rob you of your children, and destroy your cattle, and make
you few in number; and your *high* ways
shall be desolate.
23 And if ye will not be reformed by
me by these things, but will walk contrary unto me;
24 Then will I also walk contrary unto
you, and will punish you yet seven
times for your sins.
25 And I will bring a sword upon you,
that shall avenge the quarrel of *my*
covenant: and when ye are gathered
together within your cities, I will send
the pestilence among you; and ye shall
be delivered into the hand of the
enemy.
26 *And* when I have broken the staff
of your bread, ten women shall bake
your bread in one oven, and they shall
deliver *you* your bread again by weight:
and ye shall eat, and not be satisfied.
27 And if ye will not for all this heark-
en unto me, but walk contrary unto me;
28 Then I will walk contrary unto you
also in fury; and I, even I, will chastise
you seven times for your sins.
29 And ye shall eat the flesh of your
sons, and the flesh of your daughters
shall ye eat.
30 And I will destroy your high places, and cut down your images, and cast
your carcases upon the carcases of your
idols, and my soul shall abhor you.
31 And I will make your cities waste,
and bring your sanctuaries unto desolation, and I will not smell the savour of
your sweet odours.
32 And I will bring the land into desolation: and your enemies which dwell
therein shall be astonished at it.
33 And I will scatter you among the
heathen, and will draw out a sword
after you: and your land shall be desolate, and your cities waste.
34 Then shall the land enjoy her sabbaths, as long as it lieth desolate, and
ye *be* in your enemies' land; *even* then
shall the land rest, and enjoy her sabbaths.
35 As long as it lieth desolate it shall
rest; because it did not rest in your sabbaths, when ye dwelt upon it.
36 And upon them that are left *alive*
of you I will send a faintness into their
hearts in the lands of their enemies;
and the sound of a shaken leaf shall
chase them; and they shall flee, as fleeing from a sword; and they shall fall
when none pursueth.
37 And they shall fall one upon another, as it were before a sword, when none
pursueth: and ye shall have no power to
stand before your enemies.
38 And ye shall perish among the
heathen, and the land of your enemies
shall eat you up.
39 And they that are left of you shall
pine away in their iniquity in your
enemies' lands; and also in the iniquities of their fathers shall they pine
away with them.
40 If they shall confess their iniquity,
and the iniquity of their fathers, with

their trespass which they trespassed against me, and that also they have walked contrary unto me;

41 And *that* I also have walked contrary unto them, and have brought them into the land of their enemies; if then their uncircumcised hearts be humbled, and they then accept of the punishment of their iniquity:

42 Then will I remember my covenant with Jacob, and also my covenant with Isaac, and also my covenant with Abraham will I remember; and I will remember the land.

43 The land also shall be left of them, and shall enjoy her sabbaths, while she lieth desolate without them: and they shall accept of the punishment of their iniquity: because, even because they despised my judgments, and because their soul abhorred my statutes.

44 And yet for all that, when they be in the land of their enemies, I will not cast them away, neither will I abhor them, to destroy them utterly, and to break my covenant with them: for I *am* the LORD their God.

45 But I will for their sakes remember the covenant of their ancestors, whom I brought forth out of the land of Egypt in the sight of the heathen, that I might be their God: I *am* the LORD.

46 These *are* the statutes and judgments and laws, which the LORD made between him and the children of Israel in mount Sinai by the hand of Moses.

27 And the LORD spake unto Moses, saying,

2 Speak unto the children of Israel, and say unto them, When a man shall make a singular vow, the persons *shall be* for the LORD by thy estimation.

3 And thy estimation shall be of the male from twenty years old even unto sixty years old, even thy estimation shall be fifty shekels of silver, after the shekel of the sanctuary.

4 And if it *be* a female, then thy estimation shall be thirty shekels.

5 And if *it be* from five years old even unto twenty years old, then thy estimation shall be of the male twenty shekels, and for the female ten shekels.

6 And if *it be* from a month old even unto five years old, then thy estimation shall be of the male five shekels of silver, and for the female thy estimation *shall be* three shekels of silver.

7 And if *it be* from sixty years old and above; if *it be* a male, then thy estimation shall be fifteen shekels, and for the female ten shekels.

8 But if he be poorer than thy estimation, then he shall present himself before the priest, and the priest shall value him; according to his ability that vowed shall the priest value him.

9 And if *it be* a beast, whereof men bring an offering unto the LORD, all that *any man* giveth of such unto the LORD shall be holy.

10 He shall not alter it, nor change it, a good for a bad, or a bad for a good: and if he shall at all change beast for beast, then it and the exchange thereof shall be holy.

11 And if *it be* any unclean beast, of which they do not offer a sacrifice unto the LORD, then he shall present the beast before the priest:

12 And the priest shall value it, whether it be good or bad: as thou valuest it, *who art* the priest, so shall it be.

13 But if he will at all redeem it, then he shall add a fifth *part* thereof unto thy estimation.

14 And when a man shall sanctify his house *to be* holy unto the LORD, then the priest shall estimate it, whether it be good or bad: as the priest shall estimate it, so shall it stand.

15 And if he that sanctified it will redeem his house, then he shall add the fifth *part* of the money of thy estimation unto it, and it shall be his.

16 And if a man shall sanctify unto the LORD *some part* of a field of his possession, then thy estimation shall be according to the seed thereof: an homer of barley seed *shall be valued* at fifty shekels of silver.

17 If he sanctify his field from the year of jubile, according to thy estimation it shall stand.

18 But if he sanctify his field after the jubile, then the priest shall reckon unto him the money according to the years that remain, even unto the year of the jubile, and it shall be abated from thy estimation.

19 And if he that sanctified the field will in any wise redeem it, then he shall add the fifth *part* of the money of thy estimation unto it, and it shall be assured to him.

20 And if he will not redeem the field, or if he have sold the field to another man, it shall not be redeemed any more.

21 But the field, when it goeth out in the jubile, shall be holy unto the LORD, as a field devoted; the possession thereof shall be the priest's.

22 And if *a man* sanctify unto the LORD a field which he hath bought, which *is* not of the fields of his possession;

23 Then the priest shall reckon unto him the worth of thy estimation, *even* unto the year of the jubile: and he shall give thine estimation in that day, *as* a holy thing unto the LORD.

24 In the year of the jubile the field shall return unto him of whom it was bought, *even* to him to whom the possession of the land *did belong*.

25 And all thy estimations shall be according to the shekel of the sanctuary: twenty gerahs shall be the shekel.

26 Only the firstling of the beasts, which should be the LORD's firstling, no man shall sanctify it; whether *it be* ox, or sheep: it *is* the LORD's.

27 And if *it be* of an unclean beast, then he shall redeem *it* according to thine estimation, and shall add a fifth *part* of it thereto: or if it be not redeemed, then it shall be sold according to thy estimation.

28 Notwithstanding no devoted thing, that a man shall devote unto the LORD of all that he hath, *both* of man and beast, and of the field of his possession, shall be sold or redeemed: every devoted thing *is* most holy unto the LORD.

29 None devoted, which shall be devoted of men, shall be redeemed; *but* shall surely be put to death.

30 And all the tithe of the land, *whether* of the seed of the land, *or* of the fruit of the tree, *is* the LORD's: *it is* holy unto the LORD.

31 And if a man will at all redeem *ought* of his tithes, he shall add thereto the fifth *part* thereof.

32 And concerning the tithe of the herd, or of the flock, *even* of whatsoever passeth under the rod, the tenth shall be holy unto the LORD.

33 He shall not search whether it be good or bad, neither shall he change it: and if he change it at all, then both it and the change thereof shall be holy; it shall not be redeemed.

34 These *are* the commandments, which the LORD commanded Moses for the children of Israel in mount Sinai.

THE FOURTH BOOK OF MOSES
CALLED

NUMBERS

1 And the LORD spake unto Moses in the wilderness of Sinai, in the tabernacle of the congregation, on the first *day* of the second month, in the second year after they were come out of the land of Egypt, saying,

2 Take ye the sum of all the congregation of the children of Israel, after their families, by the house of their fathers, with the number of *their* names, every male by their polls;

3 From twenty years old and upward, all that are able to go forth to war in Israel: thou and Aaron shall number them by their armies.

4 And with you there shall be a man of every tribe; every one head of the house of his fathers.

5 And these *are* the names of the men that shall stand with you: of *the tribe of* Reuben; Elizur the son of Shedeur.

6 Of Simeon; Shelumiel the son of Zurishaddai.

7 Of Judah; Nahshon the son of Amminadab.

8 Of Issachar; Nethaneel the son of Zuar.

9 Of Zebulun; Eliab the son of Helon.

10 Of the children of Joseph: of Ephraim; Elishama the son of Ammihud: of Manasseh; Gamaliel the son of Pedahzur.

11 Of Benjamin; Abidan the son of Gideoni.

12 Of Dan; Ahiezer the son of Ammishaddai.

13 Of Asher; Pagiel the son of Ocran.

14 Of Gad; Eliasaph the son of Deuel.

15 Of Naphtali; Ahira the son of Enan.

16 These *were* the renowned of the congregation, princes of the tribes of their fathers, heads of thousands in Israel.

17 And Moses and Aaron took these men which are expressed by *their* names:

18 And they assembled all the congregation together on the first *day* of the second month, and they declared their pedigrees after their families, by the house of their fathers, according to the number of the names, from twenty years old and upward, by their polls.

19 As the LORD commanded Moses, so he numbered them in the wilderness of Sinai.

20 And the children of Reuben, Israel's eldest son, by their generations, after their families, by the house of their fathers, according to the number of the names, by their polls, every male from twenty years old and upward, all that were able to go forth to war;

21 Those that were numbered of them, *even* of the tribe of Reuben, *were* forty and six thousand and five hundred.

22 Of the children of Simeon, by their generations, after their families, by the house of their fathers, those that were numbered of them, according to the number of the names, by their polls, every male from twenty years old and upward, all that were able to go forth to war;

23 Those that were numbered of them, *even* of the tribe of Simeon, *were* fifty and nine thousand and three hundred.

24 Of the children of Gad, by their
generations, after their families, by the
house of their fathers, according to the
number of the names, from twenty
years old and upward, all that were
able to go forth to war;
25 Those that were numbered of
them, *even* of the tribe of Gad, *were*
forty and five thousand six hundred
and fifty.
26 Of the children of Judah, by their
generations, after their families, by the
house of their fathers, according to the
number of the names, from twenty
years old and upward, all that were
able to go forth to war;
27 Those that were numbered of
them, *even* of the tribe of Judah, *were*
threescore and fourteen thousand and
six hundred.
28 Of the children of Issachar, by their
generations, after their families, by the
house of their fathers, according to the
number of the names, from twenty
years old and upward, all that were
able to go forth to war;
29 Those that were numbered of
them, *even* of the tribe of Issachar, *were*
fifty and four thousand and four hundred.
30 Of the children of Zebulun, by
their generations, after their families,
by the house of their fathers, according
to the number of the names, from
twenty years old and upward, all that
were able to go forth to war;
31 Those that were numbered of
them, *even* of the tribe of Zebulun,
were fifty and seven thousand and four
hundred.
32 Of the children of Joseph, *namely*,
of the children of Ephraim, by their
generations, after their families, by the
house of their fathers, according to the
number of the names, from twenty
years old and upward, all that were
able to go forth to war;
33 Those that were numbered of
them, *even* of the tribe of Ephraim,
were forty thousand and five hundred.
34 Of the children of Manasseh, by
their generations, after their families,
by the house of their fathers, according
to the number of the names, from
twenty years old and upward, all that
were able to go forth to war;
35 Those that were numbered of
them, *even* of the tribe of Manasseh,
were thirty and two thousand and two
hundred.
36 Of the children of Benjamin, by
their generations, after their families,
by the house of their fathers, according
to the number of the names, from
twenty years old and upward, all that
were able to go forth to war;
37 Those that were numbered of
them, *even* of the tribe of Benjamin,
were thirty and five thousand and four
hundred.
38 Of the children of Dan, by their
generations, after their families, by the
house of their fathers, according to the
number of the names, from twenty
years old and upward, all that were
able to go forth to war;
39 Those that were numbered of
them, *even* of the tribe of Dan, *were*
threescore and two thousand and seven
hundred.
40 Of the children of Asher, by their
generations, after their families, by the
house of their fathers, according to the
number of the names, from twenty
years old and upward, all that were
able to go forth to war;

41 Those that were numbered of them, *even* of the tribe of Asher, *were* forty and one thousand and five hundred.

42 Of the children of Naphtali, throughout their generations, after their families, by the house of their fathers, according to the number of the names, from twenty years old and upward, all that were able to go forth to war;

43 Those that were numbered of them, *even* of the tribe of Naphtali, *were* fifty and three thousand and four hundred.

44 These *are* those that were numbered, which Moses and Aaron numbered, and the princes of Israel, *being* twelve men: each one was for the house of his fathers.

45 So were all those that were numbered of the children of Israel, by the house of their fathers, from twenty years old and upward, all that were able to go forth to war in Israel;

46 Even all they that were numbered were six hundred thousand and three thousand and five hundred and fifty.

47 But the Levites after the tribe of their fathers were not numbered among them.

48 For the LORD had spoken unto Moses, saying,

49 Only thou shalt not number the tribe of Levi, neither take the sum of them among the children of Israel:

50 But thou shalt appoint the Levites over the tabernacle of testimony, and over all the vessels thereof, and over all things that *belong* to it: they shall bear the tabernacle, and all the vessels thereof; and they shall minister unto it, and shall encamp round about the tabernacle.

51 And when the tabernacle setteth forward, the Levites shall take it down: and when the tabernacle is to be pitched, the Levites shall set it up: and the stranger that cometh nigh shall be put to death.

52 And the children of Israel shall pitch their tents, every man by his own camp, and every man by his own standard, throughout their hosts.

53 But the Levites shall pitch round about the tabernacle of testimony, that there be no wrath upon the congregation of the children of Israel: and the Levites shall keep the charge of the tabernacle of testimony.

54 And the children of Israel did according to all that the LORD commanded Moses, so did they.

2 And the LORD spake unto Moses and unto Aaron, saying,

2 Every man of the children of Israel shall pitch by his own standard, with the ensign of their father's house: far off about the tabernacle of the congregation shall they pitch.

3 And on the east side toward the rising of the sun shall they of the standard of the camp of Judah pitch throughout their armies: and Nahshon the son of Amminadab *shall be* captain of the children of Judah.

4 And his host, and those that were numbered of them, *were* threescore and fourteen thousand and six hundred.

5 And those that do pitch next unto him *shall be* the tribe of Issachar: and Nethaneel the son of Zuar *shall be* captain of the children of Issachar.

6 And his host, and those that were numbered thereof, *were* fifty and four thousand and four hundred.

7 *Then* the tribe of Zebulun: and
Eliab the son of Helon *shall be* captain
of the children of Zebulun.
8 And his host, and those that were
numbered thereof, *were* fifty and seven
thousand and four hundred.
9 All that were numbered in the camp
of Judah *were* an hundred thousand
and fourscore thousand and six thousand and four hundred, throughout
their armies. These shall first set forth.
10 On the south side *shall be* the standard of the camp of Reuben according
to their armies: and the captain of the
children of Reuben *shall be* Elizur the
son of Shedeur.
11 And his host, and those that were
numbered thereof, *were* forty and six
thousand and five hundred.
12 And those which pitch by him
shall be the tribe of Simeon: and the
captain of the children of Simeon *shall
be* Shelumiel the son of Zurishaddai.
13 And his host, and those that were
numbered of them, *were* fifty and nine
thousand and three hundred.
14 Then the tribe of Gad: and the
captain of the sons of Gad *shall be*
Eliasaph the son of Reuel.
15 And his host, and those that were
numbered of them, *were* forty and five
thousand and six hundred and fifty.
16 All that were numbered in the
camp of Reuben *were* an hundred thousand and fifty and one thousand and
four hundred and fifty, throughout
their armies. And they shall set forth in
the second rank.
17 Then the tabernacle of the congregation shall set forward with the camp
of the Levites in the midst of the camp:
as they encamp, so shall they set forward, every man in his place by their
standards.

18 On the west side *shall be* the standard of the camp of Ephraim according
to their armies: and the captain of the
sons of Ephraim *shall be* Elishama the
son of Ammihud.
19 And his host, and those that were
numbered of them, *were* forty thousand
and five hundred.
20 And by him *shall be* the tribe of
Manasseh: and the captain of the children of Manasseh *shall be* Gamaliel the
son of Pedahzur.
21 And his host, and those that were
numbered of them, *were* thirty and two
thousand and two hundred.
22 Then the tribe of Benjamin: and
the captain of the sons of Benjamin
shall be Abidan the son of Gideoni.
23 And his host, and those that were
numbered of them, *were* thirty and five
thousand and four hundred.
24 All that were numbered of the
camp of Ephraim *were* an hundred
thousand and eight thousand and an
hundred, throughout their armies. And
they shall go forward in the third rank.
25 The standard of the camp of Dan
shall be on the north side by their
armies: and the captain of the children
of Dan *shall be* Ahiezer the son of
Ammishaddai.
26 And his host, and those that were
numbered of them, *were* threescore
and two thousand and seven hundred.
27 And those that encamp by him
shall be the tribe of Asher: and the
captain of the children of Asher *shall
be* Pagiel the son of Ocran.
28 And his host, and those that were
numbered of them, *were* forty and one
thousand and five hundred.
29 Then the tribe of Naphtali: and the
captain of the children of Naphtali
shall be Ahira the son of Enan.

30 And his host, and those that were numbered of them, *were* fifty and three thousand and four hundred.

31 All they that were numbered in the camp of Dan *were* an hundred thousand and fifty and seven thousand and six hundred. They shall go hindmost with their standards.

32 These *are* those which were numbered of the children of Israel by the house of their fathers: all those that were numbered of the camps throughout their hosts *were* six hundred thousand and three thousand and five hundred and fifty.

33 But the Levites were not numbered among the children of Israel; as the LORD commanded Moses.

34 And the children of Israel did according to all that the LORD commanded Moses: so they pitched by their standards, and so they set forward, every one after their families, according to the house of their fathers.

3 These also *are* the generations of Aaron and Moses in the day *that* the LORD spake with Moses in mount Sinai.

2 And these *are* the names of the sons of Aaron; Nadab the firstborn, and Abihu, Eleazar, and Ithamar.

3 These *are* the names of the sons of Aaron, the priests which were anointed, whom he consecrated to minister in the priest's office.

4 And Nadab and Abihu died before the LORD, when they offered strange fire before the LORD, in the wilderness of Sinai, and they had no children: and Eleazar and Ithamar ministered in the priest's office in the sight of Aaron their father.

5 And the LORD spake unto Moses, saying,

6 Bring the tribe of Levi near, and present them before Aaron the priest, that they may minister unto him.

7 And they shall keep his charge, and the charge of the whole congregation before the tabernacle of the congregation, to do the service of the tabernacle.

8 And they shall keep all the instruments of the tabernacle of the congregation, and the charge of the children of Israel, to do the service of the tabernacle.

9 And thou shalt give the Levites unto Aaron and to his sons: they *are* wholly given unto him out of the children of Israel.

10 And thou shalt appoint Aaron and his sons, and they shall wait on their priest's office: and the stranger that cometh nigh shall be put to death.

11 And the LORD spake unto Moses, saying,

12 And I, behold, I have taken the Levites from among the children of Israel instead of all the firstborn that openeth the matrix among the children of Israel: therefore the Levites shall be mine;

13 Because all the firstborn *are* mine; *for* on the day that I smote all the firstborn in the land of Egypt I hallowed unto me all the firstborn in Israel, both man and beast: mine shall they be: I *am* the LORD.

14 And the LORD spake unto Moses in the wilderness of Sinai, saying,

15 Number the children of Levi after the house of their fathers, by their families: every male from a month old and upward shalt thou number them.

16 And Moses numbered them according to the word of the LORD, as he was commanded.

17 And these were the sons of Levi by
their names; Gershon, and Kohath, and
Merari.
18 And these *are* the names of the
sons of Gershon by their families;
Libni, and Shimei.
19 And the sons of Kohath by their
families; Amram, and Izehar, Hebron,
and Uzziel.
20 And the sons of Merari by their
families; Mahli, and Mushi. These *are*
the families of the Levites according to
the house of their fathers.
21 Of Gershon *was* the family of the
Libnites, and the family of the Shimites:
these *are* the families of the Gershonites.
22 Those that were numbered of
them, according to the number of all
the males, from a month old and
upward, *even* those that were numbered of them *were* seven thousand
and five hundred.
23 The families of the Gershonites
shall pitch behind the tabernacle westward.
24 And the chief of the house of the
father of the Gershonites *shall be*
Eliasaph the son of Lael.
25 And the charge of the sons of
Gershon in the tabernacle of the congregation *shall be* the tabernacle, and
the tent, the covering thereof, and the
hanging for the door of the tabernacle
of the congregation,
26 And the hangings of the court, and
the curtain for the door of the court,
which *is* by the tabernacle, and by the
altar round about, and the cords of it
for all the service thereof.
27 And of Kohath *was* the family of
the Amramites, and the family of the
Izeharites, and the family of the
Hebronites, and the family of the
Uzzielites: these *are* the families of the
Kohathites.
28 In the number of all the males,
from a month old and upward, *were*
eight thousand and six hundred, keeping the charge of the sanctuary.
29 The families of the sons of Kohath
shall pitch on the side of the tabernacle
southward.
30 And the chief of the house of the
father of the families of the Kohathites
shall be Elizaphan the son of Uzziel.
31 And their charge *shall be* the ark,
and the table, and the candlestick, and
the altars, and the vessels of the sanctuary wherewith they minister, and the
hanging, and all the service thereof.
32 And Eleazar the son of Aaron the
priest *shall be* chief over the chief of
the Levites, *and have* the oversight of
them that keep the charge of the sanctuary.
33 Of Merari *was* the family of the
Mahlites, and the family of the
Mushites: these *are* the families of
Merari.
34 And those that were numbered of
them, according to the number of all
the males, from a month old and
upward, *were* six thousand and two
hundred.
35 And the chief of the house of the
father of the families of Merari *was*
Zuriel the son of Abihail: *these* shall
pitch on the side of the tabernacle
northward.
36 And *under* the custody and charge
of the sons of Merari *shall be* the
boards of the tabernacle, and the bars
thereof, and the pillars thereof, and the
sockets thereof, and all the vessels
thereof, and all that serveth thereto,

37 And the pillars of the court round
about, and their sockets, and their pins,
and their cords.
38 But those that encamp before the
tabernacle toward the east, *even* before
the tabernacle of the congregation
eastward, *shall be* Moses, and Aaron
and his sons, keeping the charge of the
sanctuary for the charge of the children
of Israel; and the stranger that cometh
nigh shall be put to death.
39 All that were numbered of the
Levites, which Moses and Aaron numbered at the commandment of the
LORD, throughout their families, all the
males from a month old and upward,
were twenty and two thousand.
40 And the LORD said unto Moses,
Number all the firstborn of the males
of the children of Israel from a month
old and upward, and take the number
of their names.
41 And thou shalt take the Levites for
me (I *am* the LORD) instead of all the
firstborn among the children of Israel;
and the cattle of the Levites instead of
all the firstlings among the cattle of the
children of Israel.
42 And Moses numbered, as the LORD
commanded him, all the firstborn
among the children of Israel.
43 And all the firstborn males by the
number of names, from a month old
and upward, of those that were numbered of them, were twenty and two
thousand two hundred and threescore
and thirteen.
44 And the LORD spake unto Moses,
saying,
45 Take the Levites instead of all the
firstborn among the children of Israel,
and the cattle of the Levites instead of
their cattle; and the Levites shall be
mine: I *am* the LORD.
46 And for those that are to be
redeemed of the two hundred and
threescore and thirteen of the firstborn
of the children of Israel, which are
more than the Levites;
47 Thou shalt even take five shekels
apiece by the poll, after the shekel of
the sanctuary shalt thou take *them*:
(the shekel *is* twenty gerahs:)
48 And thou shalt give the money,
wherewith the odd number of them is
to be redeemed, unto Aaron and to his
sons.
49 And Moses took the redemption
money of them that were over and
above them that were redeemed by the
Levites:
50 Of the firstborn of the children of
Israel took he the money; a thousand
three hundred and threescore and five
shekels, after the shekel of the sanctuary:
51 And Moses gave the money of
them that were redeemed unto Aaron
and to his sons, according to the word
of the LORD, as the LORD commanded
Moses.

4 And the LORD spake unto Moses
and unto Aaron, saying,
2 Take the sum of the sons of Kohath
from among the sons of Levi, after their
families, by the house of their fathers,
3 From thirty years old and upward
even until fifty years old, all that enter
into the host, to do the work in the
tabernacle of the congregation.
4 This *shall be* the service of the sons
of Kohath in the tabernacle of the congregation, *about* the most holy things:
5 And when the camp setteth forward, Aaron shall come, and his sons,
and they shall take down the covering
vail, and cover the ark of testimony
with it:

6 And shall put thereon the covering
of badgers' skins, and shall spread over
it a cloth wholly of blue, and shall put
in the staves thereof.
7 And upon the table of shewbread
they shall spread a cloth of blue, and
put thereon the dishes, and the spoons,
and the bowls, and covers to cover
withal: and the continual bread shall
be thereon:
8 And they shall spread upon them a
cloth of scarlet, and cover the same
with a covering of badgers' skins, and
shall put in the staves thereof.
9 And they shall take a cloth of blue,
and cover the candlestick of the light,
and his lamps, and his tongs, and his
snuffdishes, and all the oil vessels
thereof, wherewith they minister unto
it:
10 And they shall put it and all the
vessels thereof within a covering of
badgers' skins, and shall put *it* upon a
bar.
11 And upon the golden altar they
shall spread a cloth of blue, and cover it
with a covering of badgers' skins, and
shall put to the staves thereof:
12 And they shall take all the instruments of ministry, wherewith they minister in the sanctuary, and put *them* in
a cloth of blue, and cover them with a
covering of badgers' skins, and shall
put *them* on a bar:
13 And they shall take away the ashes
from the altar, and spread a purple
cloth thereon:
14 And they shall put upon it all the
vessels thereof, wherewith they minister about it, *even* the censers, the fleshhooks, and the shovels, and the basons,
all the vessels of the altar; and they
shall spread upon it a covering of badgers' skins, and put to the staves of it.
15 And when Aaron and his sons have
made an end of covering the sanctuary,
and all the vessels of the sanctuary, as
the camp is to set forward; after that,
the sons of Kohath shall come to bear
it: but they shall not touch *any* holy
thing, lest they die. These *things are*
the burden of the sons of Kohath in the
tabernacle of the congregation.
16 And to the office of Eleazar the
son of Aaron the priest *pertaineth* the
oil for the light, and the sweet incense,
and the daily meat offering, and the
anointing oil, *and* the oversight of all
the tabernacle, and of all that therein
is, in the sanctuary, and in the vessels
thereof.
17 And the LORD spake unto Moses
and unto Aaron, saying,
18 Cut ye not off the tribe of the
families of the Kohathites from among
the Levites:
19 But thus do unto them, that they
may live, and not die, when they
approach unto the most holy things:
Aaron and his sons shall go in, and
appoint them every one to his service
and to his burden:
20 But they shall not go in to see
when the holy things are covered, lest
they die.
21 And the LORD spake unto Moses,
saying,
22 Take also the sum of the sons of
Gershon, throughout the houses of
their fathers, by their families;
23 From thirty years old and upward
until fifty years old shalt thou number
them; all that enter in to perform the
service, to do the work in the tabernacle of the congregation.
24 This *is* the service of the families
of the Gershonites, to serve, and for
burdens:

25 And they shall bear the curtains of
the tabernacle, and the tabernacle of
the congregation, his covering, and the
covering of the badgers' skins that *is*
above upon it, and the hanging for the
door of the tabernacle of the congregation,
26 And the hangings of the court, and
the hanging for the door of the gate of
the court, which *is* by the tabernacle
and by the altar round about, and their
cords, and all the instruments of their
service, and all that is made for them:
so shall they serve.
27 At the appointment of Aaron and
his sons shall be all the service of the
sons of the Gershonites, in all their
burdens, and in all their service: and ye
shall appoint unto them in charge all
their burdens.
28 This *is* the service of the families
of the sons of Gershon in the tabernacle of the congregation: and their
charge *shall be* under the hand of
Ithamar the son of Aaron the priest.
29 As for the sons of Merari, thou
shalt number them after their families,
by the house of their fathers;
30 From thirty years old and upward
even unto fifty years old shalt thou
number them, every one that entereth
into the service, to do the work of the
tabernacle of the congregation.
31 And this *is* the charge of their burden, according to all their service in the
tabernacle of the congregation; the
boards of the tabernacle, and the bars
thereof, and the pillars thereof, and
sockets thereof,
32 And the pillars of the court round
about, and their sockets, and their pins,
and their cords, with all their instruments, and with all their service: and
by name ye shall reckon the instruments of the charge of their burden.
33 This *is* the service of the families
of the sons of Merari, according to all
their service, in the tabernacle of the
congregation, under the hand of
Ithamar the son of Aaron the priest.
34 And Moses and Aaron and the
chief of the congregation numbered
the sons of the Kohathites after their
families, and after the house of their
fathers,
35 From thirty years old and upward
even unto fifty years old, every one that
entereth into the service, for the work
in the tabernacle of the congregation:
36 And those that were numbered of
them by their families were two thousand seven hundred and fifty.
37 These *were* they that were numbered of the families of the Kohathites,
all that might do service in the tabernacle of the congregation, which Moses
and Aaron did number according to the
commandment of the LORD by the hand
of Moses.
38 And those that were numbered of
the sons of Gershon, throughout their
families, and by the house of their
fathers,
39 From thirty years old and upward
even unto fifty years old, every one that
entereth into the service, for the work
in the tabernacle of the congregation,
40 Even those that were numbered of
them, throughout their families, by the
house of their fathers, were two thousand and six hundred and thirty.
41 These *are* they that were numbered of the families of the sons of
Gershon, of all that might do service in
the tabernacle of the congregation,
whom Moses and Aaron did number

according to the commandment of the LORD.

42 And those that were numbered of the families of the sons of Merari, throughout their families, by the house of their fathers,

43 From thirty years old and upward even unto fifty years old, every one that entereth into the service, for the work in the tabernacle of the congregation,

44 Even those that were numbered of them after their families, were three thousand and two hundred.

45 These *be* those that were numbered of the families of the sons of Merari, whom Moses and Aaron numbered according to the word of the LORD by the hand of Moses.

46 All those that were numbered of the Levites, whom Moses and Aaron and the chief of Israel numbered, after their families, and after the house of their fathers,

47 From thirty years old and upward even unto fifty years old, every one that came to do the service of the ministry, and the service of the burden in the tabernacle of the congregation,

48 Even those that were numbered of them, were eight thousand and five hundred and fourscore.

49 According to the commandment of the LORD they were numbered by the hand of Moses, every one according to his service, and according to his burden: thus were they numbered of him, as the LORD commanded Moses.

5 And the LORD spake unto Moses, saying,

2 Command the children of Israel, that they put out of the camp every leper, and every one that hath an issue, and whosoever is defiled by the dead:

3 Both male and female shall ye put out, without the camp shall ye put them; that they defile not their camps, in the midst whereof I dwell.

4 And the children of Israel did so, and put them out without the camp: as the LORD spake unto Moses, so did the children of Israel.

5 And the LORD spake unto Moses, saying,

6 Speak unto the children of Israel, When a man or woman shall commit any sin that men commit, to do a trespass against the LORD, and that person be guilty;

7 Then they shall confess their sin which they have done: and he shall recompense his trespass with the principal thereof, and add unto it the fifth *part* thereof, and give *it* unto *him* against whom he hath trespassed.

8 But if the man have no kinsman to recompense the trespass unto, let the trespass be recompensed unto the LORD, *even* to the priest; beside the ram of the atonement, whereby an atonement shall be made for him.

9 And every offering of all the holy things of the children of Israel, which they bring unto the priest, shall be his.

10 And every man's hallowed things shall be his: whatsoever any man giveth the priest, it shall be his.

11 And the LORD spake unto Moses, saying,

12 Speak unto the children of Israel, and say unto them, If any man's wife go aside, and commit a trespass against him,

13 And a man lie with her carnally, and it be hid from the eyes of her husband, and be kept close, and she be defiled, and *there be* no witness against

her, neither she be taken *with the manner*;

14 And the spirit of jealousy come upon him, and he be jealous of his wife, and she be defiled: or if the spirit of jealousy come upon him, and he be jealous of his wife, and she be not defiled:

15 Then shall the man bring his wife unto the priest, and he shall bring her offering for her, the tenth *part* of an ephah of barley meal; he shall pour no oil upon it, nor put frankincense thereon; for it *is* an offering of jealousy, an offering of memorial, bringing iniquity to remembrance.

16 And the priest shall bring her near, and set her before the LORD:

17 And the priest shall take holy water in an earthen vessel; and of the dust that is in the floor of the tabernacle the priest shall take, and put *it* into the water:

18 And the priest shall set the woman before the LORD, and uncover the woman's head, and put the offering of memorial in her hands, which *is* the jealousy offering: and the priest shall have in his hand the bitter water that causeth the curse:

19 And the priest shall charge her by an oath, and say unto the woman, If no man have lain with thee, and if thou hast not gone aside to uncleanness *with another* instead of thy husband, be thou free from this bitter water that causeth the curse:

20 But if thou hast gone aside *to another* instead of thy husband, and if thou be defiled, and some man have lain with thee beside thine husband:

21 Then the priest shall charge the woman with an oath of cursing, and the priest shall say unto the woman, The LORD make thee a curse and an oath among thy people, when the LORD doth make thy thigh to rot, and thy belly to swell;

22 And this water that causeth the curse shall go into thy bowels, to make *thy* belly to swell, and *thy* thigh to rot: And the woman shall say, Amen, amen.

23 And the priest shall write these curses in a book, and he shall blot *them* out with the bitter water:

24 And he shall cause the woman to drink the bitter water that causeth the curse: and the water that causeth the curse shall enter into her, *and become* bitter.

25 Then the priest shall take the jealousy offering out of the woman's hand, and shall wave the offering before the LORD, and offer it upon the altar:

26 And the priest shall take an handful of the offering, *even* the memorial thereof, and burn *it* upon the altar, and afterward shall cause the woman to drink the water.

27 And when he hath made her to drink the water, then it shall come to pass, *that*, if she be defiled, and have done trespass against her husband, that the water that causeth the curse shall enter into her, *and become* bitter, and her belly shall swell, and her thigh shall rot: and the woman shall be a curse among her people.

28 And if the woman be not defiled, but be clean; then she shall be free, and shall conceive seed.

29 This *is* the law of jealousies, when a wife goeth aside *to another* instead of her husband, and is defiled;

30 Or when the spirit of jealousy cometh upon him, and he be jealous over his wife, and shall set the woman

before the LORD, and the priest shall
execute upon her all this law.
31 Then shall the man be guiltless
from iniquity, and this woman shall
bear her iniquity.

6 And the LORD spake unto Moses,
saying,
2 Speak unto the children of Israel,
and say unto them, When either man or
woman shall separate *themselves* to
vow a vow of a Nazarite, to separate
themselves unto the LORD:
3 He shall separate *himself* from
wine and strong drink, and shall drink
no vinegar of wine, or vinegar of strong
drink, neither shall he drink any liquor
of grapes, nor eat moist grapes, or
dried.
4 All the days of his separation shall
he eat nothing that is made of the vine
tree, from the kernels even to the husk.
5 All the days of the vow of his separation there shall no razor come upon his
head: until the days be fulfilled, in the
which he separateth *himself* unto the
LORD, he shall be holy, *and* shall let the
locks of the hair of his head grow.
6 All the days that he separateth *himself* unto the LORD he shall come at no
dead body.
7 He shall not make himself unclean
for his father, or for his mother, for his
brother, or for his sister, when they die:
because the consecration of his God *is*
upon his head.
8 All the days of his separation he *is*
holy unto the LORD.
9 And if any man die very suddenly
by him, and he hath defiled the head of
his consecration; then he shall shave
his head in the day of his cleansing, on
the seventh day shall he shave it.
10 And on the eighth day he shall
bring two turtles, or two young pigeons,
to the priest, to the door of the tabernacle of the congregation:
11 And the priest shall offer the one
for a sin offering, and the other for a
burnt offering, and make an atonement
for him, for that he sinned by the dead,
and shall hallow his head that same
day.
12 And he shall consecrate unto the
LORD the days of his separation, and
shall bring a lamb of the first year for a
trespass offering: but the days that
were before shall be lost, because his
separation was defiled.
13 And this *is* the law of the Nazarite,
when the days of his separation are
fulfilled: he shall be brought unto the
door of the tabernacle of the congregation:
14 And he shall offer his offering
unto the LORD, one he lamb of the first
year without blemish for a burnt offering, and one ewe lamb of the first year
without blemish for a sin offering, and
one ram without blemish for peace
offerings,
15 And a basket of unleavened bread,
cakes of fine flour mingled with oil, and
wafers of unleavened bread anointed
with oil, and their meat offering, and
their drink offerings.
16 And the priest shall bring *them*
before the LORD, and shall offer his sin
offering, and his burnt offering:
17 And he shall offer the ram *for* a
sacrifice of peace offerings unto the
LORD, with the basket of unleavened
bread: the priest shall offer also his
meat offering, and his drink offering.
18 And the Nazarite shall shave the
head of his separation *at* the door of
the tabernacle of the congregation, and
shall take the hair of the head of his
separation, and put *it* in the fire which

is under the sacrifice of the peace offerings.

19 And the priest shall take the sodden shoulder of the ram, and one unleavened cake out of the basket, and one unleavened wafer, and shall put *them* upon the hands of the Nazarite, after *the hair of* his separation is shaven:

20 And the priest shall wave them *for* a wave offering before the LORD: this *is* holy for the priest, with the wave breast and heave shoulder: and after that the Nazarite may drink wine.

21 This *is* the law of the Nazarite who hath vowed, *and of* his offering unto the LORD for his separation, beside *that* that his hand shall get: according to the vow which he vowed, so he must do after the law of his separation.

22 And the LORD spake unto Moses, saying,

23 Speak unto Aaron and unto his sons, saying, On this wise ye shall bless the children of Israel, saying unto them,

24 The LORD bless thee, and keep thee:

25 The LORD make his face shine upon thee, and be gracious unto thee:

26 The LORD lift up his countenance upon thee, and give thee peace.

27 And they shall put my name upon the children of Israel; and I will bless them.

7 And it came to pass on the day that Moses had fully set up the tabernacle, and had anointed it, and sanctified it, and all the instruments thereof, both the altar and all the vessels thereof, and had anointed them, and sanctified them;

2 That the princes of Israel, heads of the house of their fathers, who *were* the princes of the tribes, and were over them that were numbered, offered:

3 And they brought their offering before the LORD, six covered wagons, and twelve oxen; a wagon for two of the princes, and for each one an ox: and they brought them before the tabernacle.

4 And the LORD spake unto Moses, saying,

5 Take *it* of them, that they may be to do the service of the tabernacle of the congregation; and thou shalt give them unto the Levites, to every man according to his service.

6 And Moses took the wagons and the oxen, and gave them unto the Levites.

7 Two wagons and four oxen he gave unto the sons of Gershon, according to their service:

8 And four wagons and eight oxen he gave unto the sons of Merari, according unto their service, under the hand of Ithamar the son of Aaron the priest.

9 But unto the sons of Kohath he gave none: because the service of the sanctuary belonging unto them *was that* they should bear upon their shoulders.

10 And the princes offered for dedicating of the altar in the day that it was anointed, even the princes offered their offering before the altar.

11 And the LORD said unto Moses, They shall offer their offering, each prince on his day, for the dedicating of the altar.

12 And he that offered his offering the first day was Nahshon the son of Amminadab, of the tribe of Judah:

13 And his offering *was* one silver charger, the weight thereof *was* an hundred and thirty *shekels*, one silver bowl of seventy shekels, after the shekel of the sanctuary; both of them *were* full of

fine flour mingled with oil for a meat
offering:
14 One spoon of ten *shekels* of gold,
full of incense:
15 One young bullock, one ram, one
lamb of the first year, for a burnt offering:
16 One kid of the goats for a sin offering:
17 And for a sacrifice of peace offerings, two oxen, five rams, five he goats,
five lambs of the first year: this *was* the
offering of Nahshon the son of Amminadab.
18 On the second day Nethaneel the
son of Zuar, prince of Issachar, did
offer:
19 He offered *for* his offering one silver charger, the weight whereof *was* an
hundred and thirty *shekels*, one silver
bowl of seventy shekels, after the shekel of the sanctuary; both of them full of
fine flour mingled with oil for a meat
offering:
20 One spoon of gold of ten *shekels*,
full of incense:
21 One young bullock, one ram, one
lamb of the first year, for a burnt offering:
22 One kid of the goats for a sin offering:
23 And for a sacrifice of peace offerings, two oxen, five rams, five he goats,
five lambs of the first year: this *was* the
offering of Nethaneel the son of Zuar.
24 On the third day Eliab the son of
Helon, prince of the children of
Zebulun, *did offer*:
25 His offering *was* one silver charger, the weight whereof *was* an hundred and thirty *shekels*, one silver bowl
of seventy shekels, after the shekel of
the sanctuary; both of them full of fine
flour mingled with oil for a meat offering:
26 One golden spoon of ten *shekels*,
full of incense:
27 One young bullock, one ram, one
lamb of the first year, for a burnt offering:
28 One kid of the goats for a sin offering:
29 And for a sacrifice of peace offerings, two oxen, five rams, five he goats,
five lambs of the first year: this *was* the
offering of Eliab the son of Helon.
30 On the fourth day Elizur the son of
Shedeur, prince of the children of
Reuben, *did offer*:
31 His offering *was* one silver charger
of the weight of an hundred and thirty
shekels, one silver bowl of seventy shekels, after the shekel of the sanctuary;
both of them full of fine flour mingled
with oil for a meat offering:
32 One golden spoon of ten *shekels*,
full of incense:
33 One young bullock, one ram, one
lamb of the first year, for a burnt
offering:
34 One kid of the goats for a sin offering:
35 And for a sacrifice of peace offerings, two oxen, five rams, five he goats,
five lambs of the first year: this *was* the
offering of Elizur the son of Shedeur.
36 On the fifth day Shelumiel the son
of Zurishaddai, prince of the children
of Simeon, *did offer*:
37 His offering *was* one silver charger, the weight whereof *was* an hundred and thirty *shekels*, one silver bowl
of seventy shekels, after the shekel of
the sanctuary; both of them full of fine
flour mingled with oil for a meat offering:

38 One golden spoon of ten *shekels*,
full of incense:
39 One young bullock, one ram, one
lamb of the first year, for a burnt offering:
40 One kid of the goats for a sin offering:
41 And for a sacrifice of peace offerings, two oxen, five rams, five he goats,
five lambs of the first year: this *was* the
offering of Shelumiel the son of
Zurishaddai.
42 On the sixth day Eliasaph the son
of Deuel, prince of the children of Gad,
offered:
43 His offering *was* one silver charger
of the weight of an hundred and thirty
shekels, a silver bowl of seventy shekels, after the shekel of the sanctuary;
both of them full of fine flour mingled
with oil for a meat offering:
44 One golden spoon of ten *shekels*,
full of incense:
45 One young bullock, one ram, one
lamb of the first year, for a burnt offering:
46 One kid of the goats for a sin offering:
47 And for a sacrifice of peace offerings, two oxen, five rams, five he goats,
five lambs of the first year: this *was* the
offering of Eliasaph the son of Deuel.
48 On the seventh day Elishama the
son of Ammihud, prince of the children
of Ephraim, *offered*:
49 His offering *was* one silver charger, the weight whereof *was* an hundred and thirty *shekels*, one silver bowl
of seventy shekels, after the shekel of
the sanctuary; both of them full of fine
flour mingled with oil for a meat offering:
50 One golden spoon of ten *shekels*,
full of incense:
51 One young bullock, one ram, one
lamb of the first year, for a burnt offering:
52 One kid of the goats for a sin offering:
53 And for a sacrifice of peace offerings, two oxen, five rams, five he goats,
five lambs of the first year: this *was* the
offering of Elishama the son of
Ammihud.
54 On the eighth day *offered* Gamaliel
the son of Pedahzur, prince of the children of Manasseh:
55 His offering *was* one silver charger
of the weight of an hundred and thirty
shekels, one silver bowl of seventy shekels, after the shekel of the sanctuary;
both of them full of fine flour mingled
with oil for a meat offering:
56 One golden spoon of ten *shekels*,
full of incense:
57 One young bullock, one ram, one
lamb of the first year, for a burnt offering:
58 One kid of the goats for a sin offering:
59 And for a sacrifice of peace offerings, two oxen, five rams, five he goats,
five lambs of the first year: this *was* the
offering of Gamaliel the son of Pedahzur.
60 On the ninth day Abidan the son of
Gideoni, prince of the children of
Benjamin, *offered*:
61 His offering *was* one silver charger, the weight whereof *was* an hundred and thirty *shekels*, one silver bowl
of seventy shekels, after the shekel of
the sanctuary; both of them full of fine
flour mingled with oil for a meat offering:
62 One golden spoon of ten *shekels*,
full of incense:

63 One young bullock, one ram, one
lamb of the first year, for a burnt offering:
64 One kid of the goats for a sin offering:
65 And for a sacrifice of peace offerings, two oxen, five rams, five he goats,
five lambs of the first year: this *was* the
offering of Abidan the son of Gideoni.
66 On the tenth day Ahiezer the son
of Ammishaddai, prince of the children
of Dan, *offered*:
67 His offering *was* one silver charger, the weight whereof *was* an hundred and thirty *shekels*, one silver bowl
of seventy shekels, after the shekel of
the sanctuary; both of them full of fine
flour mingled with oil for a meat offering:
68 One golden spoon of ten *shekels*,
full of incense:
69 One young bullock, one ram, one
lamb of the first year, for a burnt offering:
70 One kid of the goats for a sin offering:
71 And for a sacrifice of peace offerings, two oxen, five rams, five he goats,
five lambs of the first year: this *was* the
offering of Ahiezer the son of Ammishaddai.
72 On the eleventh day Pagiel the son
of Ocran, prince of the children of
Asher, *offered*:
73 His offering *was* one silver charger, the weight whereof *was* an hundred and thirty *shekels*, one silver bowl
of seventy shekels, after the shekel of
the sanctuary; both of them full of fine
flour mingled with oil for a meat offering:
74 One golden spoon of ten *shekels*,
full of incense:
75 One young bullock, one ram, one
lamb of the first year, for a burnt offering:
76 One kid of the goats for a sin offering:
77 And for a sacrifice of peace offerings, two oxen, five rams, five he goats,
five lambs of the first year: this *was* the
offering of Pagiel the son of Ocran.
78 On the twelfth day Ahira the son of
Enan, prince of the children of Naphtali, *offered*:
79 His offering *was* one silver charger, the weight whereof *was* an hundred and thirty *shekels*, one silver bowl
of seventy shekels, after the shekel of
the sanctuary; both of them full of fine
flour mingled with oil for a meat offering:
80 One golden spoon of ten *shekels*,
full of incense:
81 One young bullock, one ram, one
lamb of the first year, for a burnt offering:
82 One kid of the goats for a sin offering:
83 And for a sacrifice of peace offerings, two oxen, five rams, five he goats,
five lambs of the first year: this *was* the
offering of Ahira the son of Enan.
84 This *was* the dedication of the
altar, in the day when it was anointed,
by the princes of Israel: twelve chargers
of silver, twelve silver bowls, twelve
spoons of gold:
85 Each charger of silver *weighing* an
hundred and thirty *shekels*, each bowl
seventy: all the silver vessels *weighed*
two thousand and four hundred *shekels*, after the shekel of the sanctuary:
86 The golden spoons *were* twelve,
full of incense, *weighing* ten *shekels*
apiece, after the shekel of the sanctu-

ary: all the gold of the spoons *was* an hundred and twenty *shekels*.

87 All the oxen for the burnt offering *were* twelve bullocks, the rams twelve, the lambs of the first year twelve, with their meat offering: and the kids of the goats for sin offering twelve.

88 And all the oxen for the sacrifice of the peace offerings *were* twenty and four bullocks, the rams sixty, the he goats sixty, the lambs of the first year sixty. This *was* the dedication of the altar, after that it was anointed.

89 And when Moses was gone into the tabernacle of the congregation to speak with him, then he heard the voice of one speaking unto him from off the mercy seat that *was* upon the ark of testimony, from between the two cherubims: and he spake unto him.

8 And the LORD spake unto Moses, saying,

2 Speak unto Aaron, and say unto him, When thou lightest the lamps, the seven lamps shall give light over against the candlestick.

3 And Aaron did so; he lighted the lamps thereof over against the candlestick, as the LORD commanded Moses.

4 And this work of the candlestick *was of* beaten gold, unto the shaft thereof, unto the flowers thereof, *was* beaten work: according unto the pattern which the LORD had shewed Moses, so he made the candlestick.

5 And the LORD spake unto Moses, saying,

6 Take the Levites from among the children of Israel, and cleanse them.

7 And thus shalt thou do unto them, to cleanse them: Sprinkle water of purifying upon them, and let them shave all their flesh, and let them wash their clothes, and *so* make themselves clean.

8 Then let them take a young bullock with his meat offering, *even* fine flour mingled with oil, and another young bullock shalt thou take for a sin offering.

9 And thou shalt bring the Levites before the tabernacle of the congregation: and thou shalt gather the whole assembly of the children of Israel together:

10 And thou shalt bring the Levites before the LORD: and the children of Israel shall put their hands upon the Levites:

11 And Aaron shall offer the Levites before the LORD *for* an offering of the children of Israel, that they may execute the service of the LORD.

12 And the Levites shall lay their hands upon the heads of the bullocks: and thou shalt offer the one *for* a sin offering, and the other *for* a burnt offering, unto the LORD, to make an atonement for the Levites.

13 And thou shalt set the Levites before Aaron, and before his sons, and offer them *for* an offering unto the LORD.

14 Thus shalt thou separate the Levites from among the children of Israel: and the Levites shall be mine.

15 And after that shall the Levites go in to do the service of the tabernacle of the congregation: and thou shalt cleanse them, and offer them *for* an offering.

16 For they *are* wholly given unto me from among the children of Israel; instead of such as open every womb, *even instead of* the firstborn of all the children of Israel, have I taken them unto me.

17 For all the firstborn of the children of Israel *are* mine, *both* man and beast:

on the day that I smote every firstborn
in the land of Egypt I sanctified them
for myself.
18 And I have taken the Levites for
all the firstborn of the children of
Israel.
19 And I have given the Levites *as* a
gift to Aaron and to his sons from
among the children of Israel, to do the
service of the children of Israel in the
tabernacle of the congregation, and to
make an atonement for the children of
Israel: that there be no plague among
the children of Israel, when the children of Israel come nigh unto the sanctuary.
20 And Moses, and Aaron, and all the
congregation of the children of Israel,
did to the Levites according unto all
that the LORD commanded Moses concerning the Levites, so did the children
of Israel unto them.
21 And the Levites were purified, and
they washed their clothes; and Aaron
offered them *as* an offering before the
LORD; and Aaron made an atonement
for them to cleanse them.
22 And after that went the Levites in
to do their service in the tabernacle of
the congregation before Aaron, and
before his sons: as the LORD had commanded Moses concerning the Levites,
so did they unto them.
23 And the LORD spake unto Moses,
saying,
24 This *is it* that *belongeth* unto the
Levites: from twenty and five years old
and upward they shall go in to wait
upon the service of the tabernacle of
the congregation:
25 And from the age of fifty years
they shall cease waiting upon the service *thereof*, and shall serve no more:
26 But shall minister with their brethren in the tabernacle of the congregation, to keep the charge, and shall do no
service. Thus shalt thou do unto the
Levites touching their charge.

9 And the LORD spake unto Moses in
the wilderness of Sinai, in the first
month of the second year after they
were come out of the land of Egypt,
saying,
2 Let the children of Israel also keep
the passover at his appointed season.
3 In the fourteenth day of this month,
at even, ye shall keep it in his appointed season: according to all the rites of
it, and according to all the ceremonies
thereof, shall ye keep it.
4 And Moses spake unto the children
of Israel, that they should keep the
passover.
5 And they kept the passover on the
fourteenth day of the first month at
even in the wilderness of Sinai: according to all that the LORD commanded
Moses, so did the children of Israel.
6 And there were certain men, who
were defiled by the dead body of a
man, that they could not keep the passover on that day: and they came before
Moses and before Aaron on that day:
7 And those men said unto him, We
are defiled by the dead body of a man:
wherefore are we kept back, that we
may not offer an offering of the LORD in
his appointed season among the children of Israel?
8 And Moses said unto them, Stand
still, and I will hear what the LORD will
command concerning you.
9 And the LORD spake unto Moses,
saying,
10 Speak unto the children of Israel,
saying, If any man of you or of your
posterity shall be unclean by reason of

a dead body, or *be* in a journey afar off,
yet he shall keep the passover unto the
LORD.
11 The fourteenth day of the second
month at even they shall keep it, *and*
eat it with unleavened bread and bitter
herbs.
12 They shall leave none of it unto the
morning, nor break any bone of it:
according to all the ordinances of the
passover they shall keep it.
13 But the man that *is* clean, and is
not in a journey, and forbeareth to keep
the passover, even the same soul shall
be cut off from among his people:
because he brought not the offering of
the LORD in his appointed season, that
man shall bear his sin.
14 And if a stranger shall sojourn
among you, and will keep the passover
unto the LORD; according to the ordinance of the passover, and according to
the manner thereof, so shall he do: ye
shall have one ordinance, both for the
stranger, and for him that was born in
the land.
15 And on the day that the tabernacle
was reared up the cloud covered the
tabernacle, *namely*, the tent of the testimony: and at even there was upon the
tabernacle as it were the appearance of
fire, until the morning.
16 So it was alway: the cloud covered
it *by day*, and the appearance of fire by
night.
17 And when the cloud was taken up
from the tabernacle, then after that the
children of Israel journeyed: and in the
place where the cloud abode, there the
children of Israel pitched their tents.
18 At the commandment of the LORD
the children of Israel journeyed, and at
the commandment of the LORD they
pitched: as long as the cloud abode
upon the tabernacle they rested in
their tents.
19 And when the cloud tarried long
upon the tabernacle many days, then
the children of Israel kept the charge of
the LORD, and journeyed not.
20 And *so* it was, when the cloud was
a few days upon the tabernacle; according to the commandment of the LORD
they abode in their tents, and according to the commandment of the LORD
they journeyed.
21 And *so* it was, when the cloud
abode from even unto the morning, and
that the cloud was taken up in the
morning, then they journeyed: whether
it was by day or by night that the cloud
was taken up, they journeyed.
22 Or *whether it were* two days, or a
month, or a year, that the cloud tarried
upon the tabernacle, remaining thereon, the children of Israel abode in their
tents, and journeyed not: but when it
was taken up, they journeyed.
23 At the commandment of the LORD
they rested in the tents, and at the commandment of the LORD they journeyed:
they kept the charge of the LORD, at the
commandment of the LORD by the hand
of Moses.

10 And the LORD spake unto Moses,
saying,
2 Make thee two trumpets of silver; of
a whole piece shalt thou make them:
that thou mayest use them for the calling of the assembly, and for the journeying of the camps.
3 And when they shall blow with
them, all the assembly shall assemble
themselves to thee at the door of the
tabernacle of the congregation.
4 And if they blow *but* with one *trumpet*, then the princes, *which are* heads

of the thousands of Israel, shall gather
themselves unto thee.
5 When ye blow an alarm, then the
camps that lie on the east parts shall go
forward.
6 When ye blow an alarm the second
time, then the camps that lie on the
south side shall take their journey:
they shall blow an alarm for their journeys.
7 But when the congregation is to be
gathered together, ye shall blow, but ye
shall not sound an alarm.
8 And the sons of Aaron, the priests,
shall blow with the trumpets; and they
shall be to you for an ordinance for ever
throughout your generations.
9 And if ye go to war in your land
against the enemy that oppresseth you,
then ye shall blow an alarm with the
trumpets; and ye shall be remembered
before the LORD your God, and ye shall
be saved from your enemies.
10 Also in the day of your gladness,
and in your solemn days, and in the
beginnings of your months, ye shall
blow with the trumpets over your burnt
offerings, and over the sacrifices of
your peace offerings; that they may be
to you for a memorial before your God:
I *am* the LORD your God.
11 And it came to pass on the twentieth *day* of the second month, in the
second year, that the cloud was taken
up from off the tabernacle of the testimony.
12 And the children of Israel took
their journeys out of the wilderness of
Sinai; and the cloud rested in the wilderness of Paran.
13 And they first took their journey
according to the commandment of the
LORD by the hand of Moses.
14 In the first *place* went the standard
of the camp of the children of Judah
according to their armies: and over his
host *was* Nahshon the son of Amminadab.
15 And over the host of the tribe of
the children of Issachar *was* Nethaneel
the son of Zuar.
16 And over the host of the tribe of
the children of Zebulun *was* Eliab the
son of Helon.
17 And the tabernacle was taken
down; and the sons of Gershon and the
sons of Merari set forward, bearing the
tabernacle.
18 And the standard of the camp of
Reuben set forward according to their
armies: and over his host *was* Elizur the
son of Shedeur.
19 And over the host of the tribe of
the children of Simeon *was* Shelumiel
the son of Zurishaddai.
20 And over the host of the tribe of
the children of Gad *was* Eliasaph the
son of Deuel.
21 And the Kohathites set forward,
bearing the sanctuary: and *the other*
did set up the tabernacle against they
came.
22 And the standard of the camp of
the children of Ephraim set forward
according to their armies: and over his
host *was* Elishama the son of Ammihud.
23 And over the host of the tribe of
the children of Manasseh *was* Gamaliel
the son of Pedahzur.
24 And over the host of the tribe of
the children of Benjamin *was* Abidan
the son of Gideoni.
25 And the standard of the camp of
the children of Dan set forward, *which*
was the rereward of all the camps
throughout their hosts: and over his

host *was* Ahiezer the son of Ammishaddai.
26 And over the host of the tribe of
the children of Asher *was* Pagiel the
son of Ocran.
27 And over the host of the tribe of
the children of Naphtali *was* Ahira the
son of Enan.
28 Thus *were* the journeyings of the
children of Israel according to their
armies, when they set forward.
29 And Moses said unto Hobab, the
son of Raguel the Midianite, Moses'
father in law, We are journeying unto
the place of which the LORD said, I will
give it you: come thou with us, and we
will do thee good: for the LORD hath
spoken good concerning Israel.
30 And he said unto him, I will not go;
but I will depart to mine own land, and
to my kindred.
31 And he said, Leave us not, I pray
thee; forasmuch as thou knowest how
we are to encamp in the wilderness,
and thou mayest be to us instead of
eyes.
32 And it shall be, if thou go with us,
yea, it shall be, that what goodness the
LORD shall do unto us, the same will we
do unto thee.
33 And they departed from the mount
of the LORD three days' journey: and
the ark of the covenant of the LORD
went before them in the three days'
journey, to search out a resting place
for them.
34 And the cloud of the LORD *was*
upon them by day, when they went out
of the camp.
35 And it came to pass, when the ark
set forward, that Moses said, Rise up,
LORD, and let thine enemies be scattered; and let them that hate thee flee
before thee.
36 And when it rested, he said,
Return, O LORD, unto the many thousands of Israel.

11 And *when* the people complained, it displeased the LORD:
and the LORD heard *it*; and his anger
was kindled; and the fire of the LORD
burnt among them, and consumed
them that were in the uttermost parts
of the camp.
2 And the people cried unto Moses;
and when Moses prayed unto the LORD,
the fire was quenched.
3 And he called the name of the place
Taberah: because the fire of the LORD
burnt among them.
4 And the mixt multitude that *was*
among them fell a lusting: and the children of Israel also wept again, and said,
Who shall give us flesh to eat?
5 We remember the fish, which we
did eat in Egypt freely; the cucumbers,
and the melons, and the leeks, and the
onions, and the garlick:
6 But now our soul *is* dried away:
there is nothing at all, beside this
manna, *before* our eyes.
7 And the manna *was* as coriander
seed, and the colour thereof as the
colour of bdellium.
8 *And* the people went about, and
gathered *it*, and ground *it* in mills, or
beat *it* in a mortar, and baked *it* in
pans, and made cakes of it: and the
taste of it was as the taste of fresh oil.
9 And when the dew fell upon the
camp in the night, the manna fell upon
it.
10 Then Moses heard the people
weep throughout their families, every
man in the door of his tent: and the
anger of the LORD was kindled greatly;
Moses also was displeased.

11 And Moses said unto the Lord,
Wherefore hast thou afflicted thy servant? and wherefore have I not found
favour in thy sight, that thou layest the
burden of all this people upon me?
12 Have I conceived all this people?
have I begotten them, that thou shouldest say unto me, Carry them in thy
bosom, as a nursing father beareth the
sucking child, unto the land which thou
swarest unto their fathers?
13 Whence should I have flesh to give
unto all this people? for they weep unto
me, saying, Give us flesh, that we may
eat.
14 I am not able to bear all this people alone, because *it is* too heavy for
me.
15 And if thou deal thus with me, kill
me, I pray thee, out of hand, if I have
found favour in thy sight; and let me
not see my wretchedness.
16 And the Lord said unto Moses,
Gather unto me seventy men of the
elders of Israel, whom thou knowest to
be the elders of the people, and officers
over them; and bring them unto the
tabernacle of the congregation, that
they may stand there with thee.
17 And I will come down and talk
with thee there: and I will take of the
spirit which *is* upon thee, and will put
it upon them; and they shall bear the
burden of the people with thee, that
thou bear *it* not thyself alone.
18 And say thou unto the people,
Sanctify yourselves against to morrow,
and ye shall eat flesh: for ye have wept
in the ears of the Lord, saying, Who
shall give us flesh to eat? for *it was* well
with us in Egypt: therefore the Lord
will give you flesh, and ye shall eat.
19 Ye shall not eat one day, nor two
days, nor five days, neither ten days,
nor twenty days;
20 *But* even a whole month, until it
come out at your nostrils, and it be
loathsome unto you: because that ye
have despised the Lord which *is* among
you, and have wept before him, saying,
Why came we forth out of Egypt?
21 And Moses said, The people,
among whom I *am*, *are* six hundred
thousand footmen; and thou hast said, I
will give them flesh, that they may eat
a whole month.
22 Shall the flocks and the herds be
slain for them, to suffice them? or shall
all the fish of the sea be gathered
together for them, to suffice them?
23 And the Lord said unto Moses, Is
the Lord's hand waxed short? thou
shalt see now whether my word shall
come to pass unto thee or not.
24 And Moses went out, and told the
people the words of the Lord, and gathered the seventy men of the elders of
the people, and set them round about
the tabernacle.
25 And the Lord came down in a
cloud, and spake unto him, and took of
the spirit that *was* upon him, and gave
it unto the seventy elders: and it came
to pass, *that*, when the spirit rested
upon them, they prophesied, and did
not cease.
26 But there remained two *of the* men
in the camp, the name of the one *was*
Eldad, and the name of the other
Medad: and the spirit rested upon
them; and they *were* of them that were
written, but went not out unto the tabernacle: and they prophesied in the
camp.

27 And there ran a young man, and told Moses, and said, Eldad and Medad do prophesy in the camp.

28 And Joshua the son of Nun, the servant of Moses, *one* of his young men, answered and said, My lord Moses, forbid them.

29 And Moses said unto him, Enviest thou for my sake? would God that all the LORD's people were prophets, *and* that the LORD would put his spirit upon them!

30 And Moses gat him into the camp, he and the elders of Israel.

31 And there went forth a wind from the LORD, and brought quails from the sea, and let *them* fall by the camp, as it were a day's journey on this side, and as it were a day's journey on the other side, round about the camp, and as it were two cubits *high* upon the face of the earth.

32 And the people stood up all that day, and all *that* night, and all the next day, and they gathered the quails: he that gathered least gathered ten homers: and they spread *them* all abroad for themselves round about the camp.

33 And while the flesh *was* yet between their teeth, ere it was chewed, the wrath of the LORD was kindled against the people, and the LORD smote the people with a very great plague.

34 And he called the name of that place Kibroth-hattaavah: because there they buried the people that lusted.

35 *And* the people journeyed from Kibroth-hattaavah unto Hazeroth; and abode at Hazeroth.

12 And Miriam and Aaron spake against Moses because of the Ethiopian woman whom he had married: for he had married an Ethiopian woman.

2 And they said, Hath the LORD indeed spoken only by Moses? hath he not spoken also by us? And the LORD heard *it*.

3 (Now the man Moses *was* very meek, above all the men which *were* upon the face of the earth.)

4 And the LORD spake suddenly unto Moses, and unto Aaron, and unto Miriam, Come out ye three unto the tabernacle of the congregation. And they three came out.

5 And the LORD came down in the pillar of the cloud, and stood *in* the door of the tabernacle, and called Aaron and Miriam: and they both came forth.

6 And he said, Hear now my words: If there be a prophet among you, *I* the LORD will make myself known unto him in a vision, *and* will speak unto him in a dream.

7 My servant Moses *is* not so, who *is* faithful in all mine house.

8 With him will I speak mouth to mouth, even apparently, and not in dark speeches; and the similitude of the LORD shall he behold: wherefore then were ye not afraid to speak against my servant Moses?

9 And the anger of the LORD was kindled against them; and he departed.

10 And the cloud departed from off the tabernacle; and, behold, Miriam *became* leprous, *white* as snow: and Aaron looked upon Miriam, and, behold, *she was* leprous.

11 And Aaron said unto Moses, Alas, my lord, I beseech thee, lay not the sin upon us, wherein we have done foolishly, and wherein we have sinned.

12 Let her not be as one dead, of whom the flesh is half consumed when he cometh out of his mother's womb.

13 And Moses cried unto the LORD, saying, Heal her now, O God, I beseech thee.

14 And the LORD said unto Moses, If her father had but spit in her face, should she not be ashamed seven days? let her be shut out from the camp seven days, and after that let her be received in *again*.

15 And Miriam was shut out from the camp seven days: and the people journeyed not till Miriam was brought in *again*.

16 And afterward the people removed from Hazeroth, and pitched in the wilderness of Paran.

13 And the LORD spake unto Moses, saying,

2 Send thou men, that they may search the land of Canaan, which I give unto the children of Israel: of every tribe of their fathers shall ye send a man, every one a ruler among them.

3 And Moses by the commandment of the LORD sent them from the wilderness of Paran: all those men *were* heads of the children of Israel.

4 And these *were* their names: of the tribe of Reuben, Shammua the son of Zaccur.

5 Of the tribe of Simeon, Shaphat the son of Hori.

6 Of the tribe of Judah, Caleb the son of Jephunneh.

7 Of the tribe of Issachar, Igal the son of Joseph.

8 Of the tribe of Ephraim, Oshea the son of Nun.

9 Of the tribe of Benjamin, Palti the son of Raphu.

10 Of the tribe of Zebulun, Gaddiel the son of Sodi.

11 Of the tribe of Joseph, *namely*, of the tribe of Manasseh, Gaddi the son of Susi.

12 Of the tribe of Dan, Ammiel the son of Gemalli.

13 Of the tribe of Asher, Sethur the son of Michael.

14 Of the tribe of Naphtali, Nahbi the son of Vophsi.

15 Of the tribe of Gad, Geuel the son of Machi.

16 These *are* the names of the men which Moses sent to spy out the land. And Moses called Oshea the son of Nun Jehoshua.

17 And Moses sent them to spy out the land of Canaan, and said unto them, Get you up this *way* southward, and go up into the mountain:

18 And see the land, what it *is*; and the people that dwelleth therein, whether they *be* strong or weak, few or many;

19 And what the land *is* that they dwell in, whether it *be* good or bad; and what cities *they be* that they dwell in, whether in tents, or in strong holds;

20 And what the land *is*, whether it *be* fat or lean, whether there be wood therein, or not. And be ye of good courage, and bring of the fruit of the land. Now the time *was* the time of the firstripe grapes.

21 So they went up, and searched the land from the wilderness of Zin unto Rehob, as men come to Hamath.

22 And they ascended by the south, and came unto Hebron; where Ahiman, Sheshai, and Talmai, the children of Anak, *were*. (Now Hebron was built seven years before Zoan in Egypt.)

23 And they came unto the brook of Eshcol, and cut down from thence a branch with one cluster of grapes, and they bare it between two upon a staff; and *they brought* of the pomegranates, and of the figs.

24 The place was called the brook Eshcol, because of the cluster of grapes which the children of Israel cut down from thence.

25 And they returned from searching of the land after forty days.

26 And they went and came to Moses, and to Aaron, and to all the congregation of the children of Israel, unto the wilderness of Paran, to Kadesh; and brought back word unto them, and unto all the congregation, and shewed them the fruit of the land.

27 And they told him, and said, We came unto the land whither thou sentest us, and surely it floweth with milk and honey; and this *is* the fruit of it.

28 Nevertheless the people *be* strong that dwell in the land, and the cities *are* walled, *and* very great: and moreover we saw the children of Anak there.

29 The Amalekites dwell in the land of the south: and the Hittites, and the Jebusites, and the Amorites, dwell in the mountains: and the Canaanites dwell by the sea, and by the coast of Jordan.

30 And Caleb stilled the people before Moses, and said, Let us go up at once, and possess it; for we are well able to overcome it.

31 But the men that went up with him said, We be not able to go up against the people; for they *are* stronger than we.

32 And they brought up an evil report of the land which they had searched unto the children of Israel, saying, The land, through which we have gone to search it, *is* a land that eateth up the inhabitants thereof; and all the people that we saw in it *are* men of a great stature.

33 And there we saw the giants, the sons of Anak, *which come* of the giants: and we were in our own sight as grasshoppers, and so we were in their sight.

14 And all the congregation lifted up their voice, and cried; and the people wept that night.

2 And all the children of Israel murmured against Moses and against Aaron: and the whole congregation said unto them, Would God that we had died in the land of Egypt! or would God we had died in this wilderness!

3 And wherefore hath the LORD brought us unto this land, to fall by the sword, that our wives and our children should be a prey? were it not better for us to return into Egypt?

4 And they said one to another, Let us make a captain, and let us return into Egypt.

5 Then Moses and Aaron fell on their faces before all the assembly of the congregation of the children of Israel.

6 And Joshua the son of Nun, and Caleb the son of Jephunneh, *which were* of them that searched the land, rent their clothes:

7 And they spake unto all the company of the children of Israel, saying, The land, which we passed through to search it, *is* an exceeding good land.

8 If the LORD delight in us, then he will bring us into this land, and give it us; a land which floweth with milk and honey.

9 Only rebel not ye against the LORD, neither fear ye the people of the land; for they *are* bread for us: their defence is departed from them, and the LORD *is* with us: fear them not.

10 But all the congregation bade stone them with stones. And the glory of the LORD appeared in the tabernacle of the congregation before all the children of Israel.

11 And the LORD said unto Moses, How long will this people provoke me? and how long will it be ere they believe me, for all the signs which I have shewed among them?

12 I will smite them with the pestilence, and disinherit them, and will make of thee a greater nation and mightier than they.

13 And Moses said unto the LORD, Then the Egyptians shall hear *it*, (for thou broughtest up this people in thy might from among them;)

14 And they will tell *it* to the inhabitants of this land: *for* they have heard that thou LORD *art* among this people, that thou LORD art seen face to face, and *that* thy cloud standeth over them, and *that* thou goest before them, by day time in a pillar of a cloud, and in a pillar of fire by night.

15 Now *if* thou shalt kill *all* this people as one man, then the nations which have heard the fame of thee will speak, saying,

16 Because the LORD was not able to bring this people into the land which he sware unto them, therefore he hath slain them in the wilderness.

17 And now, I beseech thee, let the power of my Lord be great, according as thou hast spoken, saying,

18 The LORD *is* longsuffering, and of great mercy, forgiving iniquity and transgression, and by no means clearing *the guilty*, visiting the iniquity of the fathers upon the children unto the third and fourth *generation*.

19 Pardon, I beseech thee, the iniquity of this people according unto the greatness of thy mercy, and as thou hast forgiven this people, from Egypt even until now.

20 And the LORD said, I have pardoned according to thy word:

21 But *as* truly *as* I live, all the earth shall be filled with the glory of the LORD.

22 Because all those men which have seen my glory, and my miracles, which I did in Egypt and in the wilderness, and have tempted me now these ten times, and have not hearkened to my voice;

23 Surely they shall not see the land which I sware unto their fathers, neither shall any of them that provoked me see it:

24 But my servant Caleb, because he had another spirit with him, and hath followed me fully, him will I bring into the land whereinto he went; and his seed shall possess it.

25 (Now the Amalekites and the Canaanites dwelt in the valley.) To morrow turn you, and get you into the wilderness by the way of the Red sea.

26 And the LORD spake unto Moses and unto Aaron, saying,

27 How long *shall I bear with* this evil congregation, which murmur against me? I have heard the murmurings of the children of Israel, which they murmur against me.

28 Say unto them, *As truly as* I live, saith the LORD, as ye have spoken in mine ears, so will I do to you:

29 Your carcases shall fall in this wilderness; and all that were numbered of you, according to your whole number, from twenty years old and upward, which have murmured against me,

30 Doubtless ye shall not come into the land, *concerning* which I sware to make you dwell therein, save Caleb the son of Jephunneh, and Joshua the son of Nun.

31 But your little ones, which ye said should be a prey, them will I bring in, and they shall know the land which ye have despised.

32 But *as for* you, your carcases, they shall fall in this wilderness.

33 And your children shall wander in the wilderness forty years, and bear your whoredoms, until your carcases be wasted in the wilderness.

34 After the number of the days in which ye searched the land, *even* forty days, each day for a year, shall ye bear your iniquities, *even* forty years, and ye shall know my breach of promise.

35 I the LORD have said, I will surely do it unto all this evil congregation, that are gathered together against me: in this wilderness they shall be consumed, and there they shall die.

36 And the men, which Moses sent to search the land, who returned, and made all the congregation to murmur against him, by bringing up a slander upon the land,

37 Even those men that did bring up the evil report upon the land, died by the plague before the LORD.

38 But Joshua the son of Nun, and Caleb the son of Jephunneh, *which were* of the men that went to search the land, lived *still*.

39 And Moses told these sayings unto all the children of Israel: and the people mourned greatly.

40 And they rose up early in the morning, and gat them up into the top of the mountain, saying, Lo, we *be here*, and will go up unto the place which the LORD hath promised: for we have sinned.

41 And Moses said, Wherefore now do ye transgress the commandment of the LORD? but it shall not prosper.

42 Go not up, for the LORD *is* not among you; that ye be not smitten before your enemies.

43 For the Amalekites and the Canaanites *are* there before you, and ye shall fall by the sword: because ye are turned away from the LORD, therefore the LORD will not be with you.

44 But they presumed to go up unto the hill top: nevertheless the ark of the covenant of the LORD, and Moses, departed not out of the camp.

45 Then the Amalekites came down, and the Canaanites which dwelt in that hill, and smote them, and discomfited them, *even* unto Hormah.

15

And the LORD spake unto Moses, saying,

2 Speak unto the children of Israel, and say unto them, When ye be come into the land of your habitations, which I give unto you,

3 And will make an offering by fire unto the LORD, a burnt offering, or a sacrifice in performing a vow, or in a freewill offering, or in your solemn feasts, to make a sweet savour unto the LORD, of the herd, or of the flock:

4 Then shall he that offereth his offering unto the LORD bring a meat offering of a tenth deal of flour mingled with the fourth *part* of an hin of oil.

5 And the fourth *part* of an hin of wine for a drink offering shalt thou prepare with the burnt offering or sacrifice, for one lamb.

6 Or for a ram, thou shalt prepare *for* a meat offering two tenth deals of flour mingled with the third *part* of an hin of oil.

7 And for a drink offering thou shalt offer the third *part* of an hin of wine, *for* a sweet savour unto the LORD.

8 And when thou preparest a bullock *for* a burnt offering, or *for* a sacrifice in performing a vow, or peace offerings unto the LORD:

9 Then shall he bring with a bullock a meat offering of three tenth deals of flour mingled with half an hin of oil.

10 And thou shalt bring for a drink offering half an hin of wine, *for* an offering made by fire, of a sweet savour unto the LORD.

11 Thus shall it be done for one bullock, or for one ram, or for a lamb, or a kid.

12 According to the number that ye shall prepare, so shall ye do to every one according to their number.

13 All that are born of the country shall do these things after this manner, in offering an offering made by fire, of a sweet savour unto the LORD.

14 And if a stranger sojourn with you, or whosoever *be* among you in your generations, and will offer an offering made by fire, of a sweet savour unto the LORD; as ye do, so he shall do.

15 One ordinance *shall be both* for you of the congregation, and also for the stranger that sojourneth *with you*, an ordinance for ever in your generations: as ye *are*, so shall the stranger be before the LORD.

16 One law and one manner shall be for you, and for the stranger that sojourneth with you.

17 And the LORD spake unto Moses, saying,

18 Speak unto the children of Israel, and say unto them, When ye come into the land whither I bring you,

19 Then it shall be, that, when ye eat of the bread of the land, ye shall offer up an heave offering unto the LORD.

20 Ye shall offer up a cake of the first of your dough *for* an heave offering: as *ye do* the heave offering of the threshingfloor, so shall ye heave it.

21 Of the first of your dough ye shall give unto the LORD an heave offering in your generations.

22 And if ye have erred, and not observed all these commandments, which the LORD hath spoken unto Moses,

23 *Even* all that the LORD hath commanded you by the hand of Moses, from the day that the LORD commanded *Moses*, and henceforward among your generations;

24 Then it shall be, if *ought* be committed by ignorance without the knowledge of the congregation, that all the congregation shall offer one young bullock for a burnt offering, for a sweet savour unto the LORD, with his meat offering, and his drink offering, according to the manner, and one kid of the goats for a sin offering.

25 And the priest shall make an atonement for all the congregation of the children of Israel, and it shall be forgiven them; for it *is* ignorance: and they shall bring their offering, a sacrifice made by fire unto the LORD, and their sin offering before the LORD, for their ignorance:

26 And it shall be forgiven all the congregation of the children of Israel, and the stranger that sojourneth among them; seeing all the people *were* in ignorance.

27 And if any soul sin through ignorance, then he shall bring a she goat of
the first year for a sin offering.
28 And the priest shall make an
atonement for the soul that sinneth
ignorantly, when he sinneth by ignorance before the LORD, to make an
atonement for him; and it shall be forgiven him.
29 Ye shall have one law for him that
sinneth through ignorance, *both for*
him that is born among the children of
Israel, and for the stranger that sojourneth among them.
30 But the soul that doeth *ought* presumptuously, *whether he be* born in the
land, or a stranger, the same reproacheth the LORD; and that soul shall
be cut off from among his people.
31 Because he hath despised the word
of the LORD, and hath broken his commandment, that soul shall utterly be
cut off; his iniquity *shall be* upon him.
32 And while the children of Israel
were in the wilderness, they found a
man that gathered sticks upon the sabbath day.
33 And they that found him gathering
sticks brought him unto Moses and
Aaron, and unto all the congregation.
34 And they put him in ward, because
it was not declared what should be
done to him.
35 And the LORD said unto Moses, The
man shall be surely put to death: all the
congregation shall stone him with
stones without the camp.
36 And all the congregation brought
him without the camp, and stoned him
with stones, and he died; as the LORD
commanded Moses.
37 And the LORD spake unto Moses,
saying,
38 Speak unto the children of Israel,
and bid them that they make them
fringes in the borders of their garments
throughout their generations, and that
they put upon the fringe of the borders
a ribband of blue:
39 And it shall be unto you for a
fringe, that ye may look upon it, and
remember all the commandments of
the LORD, and do them; and that ye
seek not after your own heart and your
own eyes, after which ye use to go a
whoring:
40 That ye may remember, and do all
my commandments, and be holy unto
your God.
41 I *am* the LORD your God, which
brought you out of the land of Egypt, to
be your God: I *am* the LORD your God.

16 Now Korah, the son of Izhar, the
son of Kohath, the son of Levi,
and Dathan and Abiram, the sons of
Eliab, and On, the son of Peleth, sons of
Reuben, took *men*:
2 And they rose up before Moses,
with certain of the children of Israel,
two hundred and fifty princes of the
assembly, famous in the congregation,
men of renown:
3 And they gathered themselves
together against Moses and against
Aaron, and said unto them, *Ye take* too
much upon you, seeing all the congregation *are* holy, every one of them, and
the LORD *is* among them: wherefore
then lift ye up yourselves above the
congregation of the LORD?
4 And when Moses heard *it*, he fell
upon his face:
5 And he spake unto Korah and unto
all his company, saying, Even to morrow the LORD will shew who *are* his, and
who is holy; and will cause *him* to come
near unto him: even *him* whom he hath

chosen will he cause to come near unto
him.
6 This do; Take you censers, Korah,
and all his company;
7 And put fire therein, and put
incense in them before the LORD to
morrow: and it shall be *that* the man
whom the LORD doth choose, he *shall*
be holy: *ye take* too much upon you, ye
sons of Levi.
8 And Moses said unto Korah, Hear, I
pray you, ye sons of Levi:
9 *Seemeth it but* a small thing unto
you, that the God of Israel hath separated
you from the congregation of
Israel, to bring you near to himself to
do the service of the tabernacle of the
LORD, and to stand before the congregation
to minister unto them?
10 And he hath brought thee near *to*
him, and all thy brethren the sons of
Levi with thee: and seek ye the priesthood
also?
11 For which cause *both* thou and all
thy company *are* gathered together
against the LORD: and what *is* Aaron,
that ye murmur against him?
12 And Moses sent to call Dathan and
Abiram, the sons of Eliab: which said,
We will not come up:
13 *Is it* a small thing that thou hast
brought us up out of a land that floweth
with milk and honey, to kill us in the
wilderness, except thou make thyself
altogether a prince over us?
14 Moreover thou hast not brought us
into a land that floweth with milk and
honey, or given us inheritance of fields
and vineyards: wilt thou put out the
eyes of these men? we will not come up.
15 And Moses was very wroth, and
said unto the LORD, Respect not thou
their offering: I have not taken one ass
from them, neither have I hurt one of
them.
16 And Moses said unto Korah, Be
thou and all thy company before the
LORD, thou, and they, and Aaron, to
morrow:
17 And take every man his censer,
and put incense in them, and bring ye
before the LORD every man his censer,
two hundred and fifty censers; thou
also, and Aaron, each *of you* his censer.
18 And they took every man his censer,
and put fire in them, and laid
incense thereon, and stood in the door
of the tabernacle of the congregation
with Moses and Aaron.
19 And Korah gathered all the congregation
against them unto the door
of the tabernacle of the congregation:
and the glory of the LORD appeared
unto all the congregation.
20 And the LORD spake unto Moses
and unto Aaron, saying,
21 Separate yourselves from among
this congregation, that I may consume
them in a moment.
22 And they fell upon their faces, and
said, O God, the God of the spirits of all
flesh, shall one man sin, and wilt thou
be wroth with all the congregation?
23 And the LORD spake unto Moses,
saying,
24 Speak unto the congregation, saying,
Get you up from about the tabernacle
of Korah, Dathan, and Abiram.
25 And Moses rose up and went unto
Dathan and Abiram; and the elders of
Israel followed him.
26 And he spake unto the congregation,
saying, Depart, I pray you, from
the tents of these wicked men, and
touch nothing of theirs, lest ye be consumed
in all their sins.

27 So they gat up from the tabernacle
of Korah, Dathan, and Abiram, on every
side: and Dathan and Abiram came out,
and stood in the door of their tents, and
their wives, and their sons, and their
little children.
28 And Moses said, Hereby ye shall
know that the LORD hath sent me to do
all these works; for *I have* not *done*
them of mine own mind.
29 If these men die the common
death of all men, or if they be visited
after the visitation of all men; *then* the
LORD hath not sent me.
30 But if the LORD make a new thing,
and the earth open her mouth, and
swallow them up, with all that *apper-*
tain unto them, and they go down
quick into the pit; then ye shall understand that these men have provoked
the LORD.
31 And it came to pass, as he had
made an end of speaking all these
words, that the ground clave asunder
that *was* under them:
32 And the earth opened her mouth,
and swallowed them up, and their houses, and all the men that *appertained*
unto Korah, and all *their* goods.
33 They, and all that *appertained* to
them, went down alive into the pit, and
the earth closed upon them: and they
perished from among the congregation.
34 And all Israel that *were* round
about them fled at the cry of them: for
they said, Lest the earth swallow us up
also.
35 And there came out a fire from the
LORD, and consumed the two hundred
and fifty men that offered incense.
36 And the LORD spake unto Moses,
saying,
37 Speak unto Eleazar the son of
Aaron the priest, that he take up the
censers out of the burning, and scatter
thou the fire yonder; for they are hallowed.
38 The censers of these sinners
against their own souls, let them make
them broad plates *for* a covering of the
altar: for they offered them before the
LORD, therefore they are hallowed: and
they shall be a sign unto the children of
Israel.
39 And Eleazar the priest took the
brasen censers, wherewith they that
were burnt had offered; and they were
made broad *plates for* a covering of the
altar:
40 *To be* a memorial unto the children
of Israel, that no stranger, which *is* not
of the seed of Aaron, come near to offer
incense before the LORD; that he be not
as Korah, and as his company: as the
LORD said to him by the hand of Moses.
41 But on the morrow all the congregation of the children of Israel murmured against Moses and against
Aaron, saying, Ye have killed the people of the LORD.
42 And it came to pass, when the
congregation was gathered against
Moses and against Aaron, that they
looked toward the tabernacle of the
congregation: and, behold, the cloud
covered it, and the glory of the LORD
appeared.
43 And Moses and Aaron came before
the tabernacle of the congregation.
44 And the LORD spake unto Moses,
saying,
45 Get you up from among this congregation, that I may consume them as
in a moment. And they fell upon their
faces.
46 And Moses said unto Aaron, Take a
censer, and put fire therein from off the
altar, and put on incense, and go quick-

ly unto the congregation, and make an atonement for them: for there is wrath gone out from the LORD; the plague is begun.

47 And Aaron took as Moses commanded, and ran into the midst of the congregation; and, behold, the plague was begun among the people: and he put on incense, and made an atonement for the people.

48 And he stood between the dead and the living; and the plague was stayed.

49 Now they that died in the plague were fourteen thousand and seven hundred, beside them that died about the matter of Korah.

50 And Aaron returned unto Moses unto the door of the tabernacle of the congregation: and the plague was stayed.

17 And the LORD spake unto Moses, saying,

2 Speak unto the children of Israel, and take of every one of them a rod according to the house of *their* fathers, of all their princes according to the house of their fathers twelve rods: write thou every man's name upon his rod.

3 And thou shalt write Aaron's name upon the rod of Levi: for one rod *shall be* for the head of the house of their fathers.

4 And thou shalt lay them up in the tabernacle of the congregation before the testimony, where I will meet with you.

5 And it shall come to pass, *that* the man's rod, whom I shall choose, shall blossom: and I will make to cease from me the murmurings of the children of Israel, whereby they murmur against you.

6 And Moses spake unto the children of Israel, and every one of their princes gave him a rod apiece, for each prince one, according to their fathers' houses, *even* twelve rods: and the rod of Aaron *was* among their rods.

7 And Moses laid up the rods before the LORD in the tabernacle of witness.

8 And it came to pass, that on the morrow Moses went into the tabernacle of witness; and, behold, the rod of Aaron for the house of Levi was budded, and brought forth buds, and bloomed blossoms, and yielded almonds.

9 And Moses brought out all the rods from before the LORD unto all the children of Israel: and they looked, and took every man his rod.

10 And the LORD said unto Moses, Bring Aaron's rod again before the testimony, to be kept for a token against the rebels; and thou shalt quite take away their murmurings from me, that they die not.

11 And Moses did *so*: as the LORD commanded him, so did he.

12 And the children of Israel spake unto Moses, saying, Behold, we die, we perish, we all perish.

13 Whosoever cometh any thing near unto the tabernacle of the LORD shall die: shall we be consumed with dying?

18 And the LORD said unto Aaron, Thou and thy sons and thy father's house with thee shall bear the iniquity of the sanctuary: and thou and thy sons with thee shall bear the iniquity of your priesthood.

2 And thy brethren also of the tribe of Levi, the tribe of thy father, bring thou with thee, that they may be joined unto thee, and minister unto thee: but thou

and thy sons with thee *shall minister* before the tabernacle of witness.

3 And they shall keep thy charge, and the charge of all the tabernacle: only they shall not come nigh the vessels of the sanctuary and the altar, that neither they, nor ye also, die.

4 And they shall be joined unto thee, and keep the charge of the tabernacle of the congregation, for all the service of the tabernacle: and a stranger shall not come nigh unto you.

5 And ye shall keep the charge of the sanctuary, and the charge of the altar: that there be no wrath any more upon the children of Israel.

6 And I, behold, I have taken your brethren the Levites from among the children of Israel: to you *they are* given *as* a gift for the LORD, to do the service of the tabernacle of the congregation.

7 Therefore thou and thy sons with thee shall keep your priest's office for every thing of the altar, and within the vail; and ye shall serve: I have given your priest's office *unto you* as a service of gift: and the stranger that cometh nigh shall be put to death.

8 And the LORD spake unto Aaron, Behold, I also have given thee the charge of mine heave offerings of all the hallowed things of the children of Israel; unto thee have I given them by reason of the anointing, and to thy sons, by an ordinance for ever.

9 This shall be thine of the most holy things, *reserved* from the fire: every oblation of theirs, every meat offering of theirs, and every sin offering of theirs, and every trespass offering of theirs, which they shall render unto me, *shall be* most holy for thee and for thy sons.

10 In the most holy *place* shalt thou eat it; every male shall eat it: it shall be holy unto thee.

11 And this *is* thine; the heave offering of their gift, with all the wave offerings of the children of Israel: I have given them unto thee, and to thy sons and to thy daughters with thee, by a statute for ever: every one that is clean in thy house shall eat of it.

12 All the best of the oil, and all the best of the wine, and of the wheat, the firstfruits of them which they shall offer unto the LORD, them have I given thee.

13 *And* whatsoever is first ripe in the land, which they shall bring unto the LORD, shall be thine; every one that is clean in thine house shall eat *of* it.

14 Every thing devoted in Israel shall be thine.

15 Every thing that openeth the matrix in all flesh, which they bring unto the LORD, *whether it be* of men or beasts, shall be thine: nevertheless the firstborn of man shalt thou surely redeem, and the firstling of unclean beasts shalt thou redeem.

16 And those that are to be redeemed from a month old shalt thou redeem, according to thine estimation, for the money of five shekels, after the shekel of the sanctuary, which *is* twenty gerahs.

17 But the firstling of a cow, or the firstling of a sheep, or the firstling of a goat, thou shalt not redeem; they *are* holy: thou shalt sprinkle their blood upon the altar, and shalt burn their fat *for* an offering made by fire, for a sweet savour unto the LORD.

18 And the flesh of them shall be thine, as the wave breast and as the right shoulder are thine.

19 All the heave offerings of the holy things, which the children of Israel offer unto the LORD, have I given thee, and thy sons and thy daughters with thee, by a statute for ever: it *is* a covenant of salt for ever before the LORD unto thee and to thy seed with thee.

20 And the LORD spake unto Aaron, Thou shalt have no inheritance in their land, neither shalt thou have any part among them: I *am* thy part and thine inheritance among the children of Israel.

21 And, behold, I have given the children of Levi all the tenth in Israel for an inheritance, for their service which they serve, *even* the service of the tabernacle of the congregation.

22 Neither must the children of Israel henceforth come nigh the tabernacle of the congregation, lest they bear sin, and die.

23 But the Levites shall do the service of the tabernacle of the congregation, and they shall bear their iniquity: *it shall be* a statute for ever throughout your generations, that among the children of Israel they have no inheritance.

24 But the tithes of the children of Israel, which they offer *as* an heave offering unto the LORD, I have given to the Levites to inherit: therefore I have said unto them, Among the children of Israel they shall have no inheritance.

25 And the LORD spake unto Moses, saying,

26 Thus speak unto the Levites, and say unto them, When ye take of the children of Israel the tithes which I have given you from them for your inheritance, then ye shall offer up an heave offering of it for the LORD, *even* a tenth *part* of the tithe.

27 And *this* your heave offering shall be reckoned unto you, as though *it were* the corn of the threshingfloor, and as the fulness of the winepress.

28 Thus ye also shall offer an heave offering unto the LORD of all your tithes, which ye receive of the children of Israel; and ye shall give thereof the LORD's heave offering to Aaron the priest.

29 Out of all your gifts ye shall offer every heave offering of the LORD, of all the best thereof, *even* the hallowed part thereof out of it.

30 Therefore thou shalt say unto them, When ye have heaved the best thereof from it, then it shall be counted unto the Levites as the increase of the threshingfloor, and as the increase of the winepress.

31 And ye shall eat it in every place, ye and your households: for it *is* your reward for your service in the tabernacle of the congregation.

32 And ye shall bear no sin by reason of it, when ye have heaved from it the best of it: neither shall ye pollute the holy things of the children of Israel, lest ye die.

19 And the LORD spake unto Moses and unto Aaron, saying,

2 This *is* the ordinance of the law which the LORD hath commanded, saying, Speak unto the children of Israel, that they bring thee a red heifer without spot, wherein *is* no blemish, *and* upon which never came yoke:

3 And ye shall give her unto Eleazar the priest, that he may bring her forth without the camp, and *one* shall slay her before his face:

4 And Eleazar the priest shall take of her blood with his finger, and sprinkle

of her blood directly before the tabernacle of the congregation seven times:
5 And *one* shall burn the heifer in his
sight; her skin, and her flesh, and her
blood, with her dung, shall he burn:
6 And the priest shall take cedar
wood, and hyssop, and scarlet, and cast
it into the midst of the burning of the
heifer.
7 Then the priest shall wash his
clothes, and he shall bathe his flesh in
water, and afterward he shall come into
the camp, and the priest shall be
unclean until the even.
8 And he that burneth her shall wash
his clothes in water, and bathe his flesh
in water, and shall be unclean until the
even.
9 And a man *that is* clean shall gather up the ashes of the heifer, and lay
them up without the camp in a clean
place, and it shall be kept for the congregation of the children of Israel for a
water of separation: it *is* a purification
for sin.
10 And he that gathereth the ashes of
the heifer shall wash his clothes, and be
unclean until the even: and it shall be
unto the children of Israel, and unto the
stranger that sojourneth among them,
for a statute for ever.
11 He that toucheth the dead body of
any man shall be unclean seven days.
12 He shall purify himself with it on
the third day, and on the seventh day he
shall be clean: but if he purify not himself the third day, then the seventh day
he shall not be clean.
13 Whosoever toucheth the dead
body of any man that is dead, and purifieth not himself, defileth the tabernacle of the LORD; and that soul shall be
cut off from Israel: because the water
of separation was not sprinkled upon
him, he shall be unclean; his uncleanness *is* yet upon him.
14 This *is* the law, when a man dieth
in a tent: all that come into the tent,
and all that *is* in the tent, shall be
unclean seven days.
15 And every open vessel, which hath
no covering bound upon it, *is* unclean.
16 And whosoever toucheth one that
is slain with a sword in the open fields,
or a dead body, or a bone of a man, or a
grave, shall be unclean seven days.
17 And for an unclean *person* they
shall take of the ashes of the burnt
heifer of purification for sin, and running water shall be put thereto in a
vessel:
18 And a clean person shall take hyssop, and dip *it* in the water, and sprinkle *it* upon the tent, and upon all the
vessels, and upon the persons that were
there, and upon him that touched a
bone, or one slain, or one dead, or a
grave:
19 And the clean *person* shall sprinkle upon the unclean on the third day,
and on the seventh day: and on the
seventh day he shall purify himself,
and wash his clothes, and bathe himself
in water, and shall be clean at even.
20 But the man that shall be unclean,
and shall not purify himself, that soul
shall be cut off from among the congregation, because he hath defiled the
sanctuary of the LORD: the water of
separation hath not been sprinkled
upon him; he *is* unclean.
21 And it shall be a perpetual statute
unto them, that he that sprinkleth the
water of separation shall wash his
clothes; and he that toucheth the water
of separation shall be unclean until
even.

22 And whatsoever the unclean *person* toucheth shall be unclean; and the
soul that toucheth *it* shall be unclean
until even.

20 Then came the children of Israel,
even the whole congregation,
into the desert of Zin in the first month:
and the people abode in Kadesh; and
Miriam died there, and was buried
there.
2 And there was no water for the congregation: and they gathered themselves together against Moses and
against Aaron.
3 And the people chode with Moses,
and spake, saying, Would God that we
had died when our brethren died
before the LORD!
4 And why have ye brought up the
congregation of the LORD into this wilderness, that we and our cattle should
die there?
5 And wherefore have ye made us to
come up out of Egypt, to bring us in
unto this evil place? it *is* no place of
seed, or of figs, or of vines, or of pomegranates; neither *is* there any water to
drink.
6 And Moses and Aaron went from
the presence of the assembly unto the
door of the tabernacle of the congregation, and they fell upon their faces: and
the glory of the LORD appeared unto
them.
7 And the LORD spake unto Moses,
saying,
8 Take the rod, and gather thou the
assembly together, thou, and Aaron thy
brother, and speak ye unto the rock
before their eyes; and it shall give forth
his water, and thou shalt bring forth to
them water out of the rock: so thou
shalt give the congregation and their
beasts drink.
9 And Moses took the rod from before
the LORD, as he commanded him.
10 And Moses and Aaron gathered
the congregation together before the
rock, and he said unto them, Hear now,
ye rebels; must we fetch you water out
of this rock?
11 And Moses lifted up his hand, and
with his rod he smote the rock twice:
and the water came out abundantly,
and the congregation drank, and their
beasts *also*.
12 And the LORD spake unto Moses
and Aaron, Because ye believed me not,
to sanctify me in the eyes of the children of Israel, therefore ye shall not
bring this congregation into the land
which I have given them.
13 This *is* the water of Meribah;
because the children of Israel strove
with the LORD, and he was sanctified in
them.
14 And Moses sent messengers from
Kadesh unto the king of Edom, Thus
saith thy brother Israel, Thou knowest
all the travail that hath befallen us:
15 How our fathers went down into
Egypt, and we have dwelt in Egypt a
long time; and the Egyptians vexed us,
and our fathers:
16 And when we cried unto the LORD,
he heard our voice, and sent an angel,
and hath brought us forth out of Egypt:
and, behold, we *are* in Kadesh, a city in
the uttermost of thy border:
17 Let us pass, I pray thee, through
thy country: we will not pass through
the fields, or through the vineyards,
neither will we drink *of* the water of
the wells: we will go by the king's *high*
way, we will not turn to the right hand
nor to the left, until we have passed thy
borders.

18 And Edom said unto him, Thou
shalt not pass by me, lest I come out
against thee with the sword.
19 And the children of Israel said
unto him, We will go by the high way:
and if I and my cattle drink of thy
water, then I will pay for it: I will only,
without *doing* any thing *else*, go through
on my feet.
20 And he said, Thou shalt not go
through. And Edom came out against
him with much people, and with a
strong hand.
21 Thus Edom refused to give Israel
passage through his border: wherefore
Israel turned away from him.
22 And the children of Israel, *even* the
whole congregation, journeyed from
Kadesh, and came unto mount Hor.
23 And the LORD spake unto Moses
and Aaron in mount Hor, by the coast of
the land of Edom, saying,
24 Aaron shall be gathered unto his
people: for he shall not enter into the
land which I have given unto the children of Israel, because ye rebelled
against my word at the water of Meribah.
25 Take Aaron and Eleazar his son,
and bring them up unto mount Hor:
26 And strip Aaron of his garments,
and put them upon Eleazar his son: and
Aaron shall be gathered *unto his people*, and shall die there.
27 And Moses did as the LORD commanded: and they went up into mount
Hor in the sight of all the congregation.
28 And Moses stripped Aaron of his
garments, and put them upon Eleazar
his son; and Aaron died there in the top
of the mount: and Moses and Eleazar
came down from the mount.
29 And when all the congregation saw
that Aaron was dead, they mourned for
Aaron thirty days, *even* all the house of
Israel.

21 And *when* king Arad the
Canaanite, which dwelt in the
south, heard tell that Israel came by the
way of the spies; then he fought against
Israel, and took *some* of them prisoners.
2 And Israel vowed a vow unto the
LORD, and said, If thou wilt indeed
deliver this people into my hand, then I
will utterly destroy their cities.
3 And the LORD hearkened to the
voice of Israel, and delivered up the
Canaanites; and they utterly destroyed
them and their cities: and he called the
name of the place Hormah.
4 And they journeyed from mount
Hor by the way of the Red sea, to compass the land of Edom: and the soul of
the people was much discouraged
because of the way.
5 And the people spake against God,
and against Moses, Wherefore have ye
brought us up out of Egypt to die in the
wilderness? for *there is* no bread, neither *is there any* water; and our soul
loatheth this light bread.
6 And the LORD sent fiery serpents
among the people, and they bit the
people; and much people of Israel died.
7 Therefore the people came to
Moses, and said, We have sinned, for we
have spoken against the LORD, and
against thee; pray unto the LORD, that
he take away the serpents from us. And
Moses prayed for the people.
8 And the LORD said unto Moses,
Make thee a fiery serpent, and set it
upon a pole: and it shall come to pass,
that every one that is bitten, when he
looketh upon it, shall live.
9 And Moses made a serpent of brass,
and put it upon a pole, and it came to
pass, that if a serpent had bitten any

man, when he beheld the serpent of brass, he lived.

10 And the children of Israel set forward, and pitched in Oboth.

11 And they journeyed from Oboth, and pitched at Ijeabarim, in the wilderness which *is* before Moab, toward the sunrising.

12 From thence they removed, and pitched in the valley of Zared.

13 From thence they removed, and pitched on the other side of Arnon, which *is* in the wilderness that cometh out of the coasts of the Amorites: for Arnon *is* the border of Moab, between Moab and the Amorites.

14 Wherefore it is said in the book of the wars of the LORD, What he did in the Red sea, and in the brooks of Arnon,

15 And at the stream of the brooks that goeth down to the dwelling of Ar, and lieth upon the border of Moab.

16 And from thence *they went* to Beer: that *is* the well whereof the LORD spake unto Moses, Gather the people together, and I will give them water.

17 Then Israel sang this song, Spring up, O well; sing ye unto it:

18 The princes digged the well, the nobles of the people digged it, by *the direction of* the lawgiver, with their staves. And from the wilderness *they went* to Mattanah:

19 And from Mattanah to Nahaliel: and from Nahaliel to Bamoth:

20 And from Bamoth *in* the valley, that *is* in the country of Moab, to the top of Pisgah, which looketh toward Jeshimon.

21 And Israel sent messengers unto Sihon king of the Amorites, saying,

22 Let me pass through thy land: we will not turn into the fields, or into the vineyards; we will not drink *of* the waters of the well: *but* we will go along by the king's *high* way, until we be past thy borders.

23 And Sihon would not suffer Israel to pass through his border: but Sihon gathered all his people together, and went out against Israel into the wilderness: and he came to Jahaz, and fought against Israel.

24 And Israel smote him with the edge of the sword, and possessed his land from Arnon unto Jabbok, even unto the children of Ammon: for the border of the children of Ammon *was* strong.

25 And Israel took all these cities: and Israel dwelt in all the cities of the Amorites, in Heshbon, and in all the villages thereof.

26 For Heshbon *was* the city of Sihon the king of the Amorites, who had fought against the former king of Moab, and taken all his land out of his hand, even unto Arnon.

27 Wherefore they that speak in proverbs say, Come into Heshbon, let the city of Sihon be built and prepared:

28 For there is a fire gone out of Heshbon, a flame from the city of Sihon: it hath consumed Ar of Moab, *and* the lords of the high places of Arnon.

29 Woe to thee, Moab! thou art undone, O people of Chemosh: he hath given his sons that escaped, and his daughters, into captivity unto Sihon king of the Amorites.

30 We have shot at them; Heshbon is perished even unto Dibon, and we have laid them waste even unto Nophah, which *reacheth* unto Medeba.

31 Thus Israel dwelt in the land of the Amorites.

32 And Moses sent to spy out Jaazer, and they took the villages thereof, and drove out the Amorites that *were* there.

33 And they turned and went up by the way of Bashan: and Og the king of Bashan went out against them, he, and all his people, to the battle at Edrei.

34 And the LORD said unto Moses, Fear him not: for I have delivered him into thy hand, and all his people, and his land; and thou shalt do to him as thou didst unto Sihon king of the Amorites, which dwelt at Heshbon.

35 So they smote him, and his sons, and all his people, until there was none left him alive: and they possessed his land.

22 And the children of Israel set forward, and pitched in the plains of Moab on this side Jordan *by* Jericho.

2 And Balak the son of Zippor saw all that Israel had done to the Amorites.

3 And Moab was sore afraid of the people, because they *were* many: and Moab was distressed because of the children of Israel.

4 And Moab said unto the elders of Midian, Now shall this company lick up all *that are* round about us, as the ox licketh up the grass of the field. And Balak the son of Zippor *was* king of the Moabites at that time.

5 He sent messengers therefore unto Balaam the son of Beor to Pethor, which *is* by the river of the land of the children of his people, to call him, saying, Behold, there is a people come out from Egypt: behold, they cover the face of the earth, and they abide over against me:

6 Come now therefore, I pray thee, curse me this people; for they *are* too mighty for me: peradventure I shall prevail, *that* we may smite them, and *that* I may drive them out of the land: for I wot that he whom thou blessest *is* blessed, and he whom thou cursest is cursed.

7 And the elders of Moab and the elders of Midian departed with the rewards of divination in their hand; and they came unto Balaam, and spake unto him the words of Balak.

8 And he said unto them, Lodge here this night, and I will bring you word again, as the LORD shall speak unto me: and the princes of Moab abode with Balaam.

9 And God came unto Balaam, and said, What men *are* these with thee?

10 And Balaam said unto God, Balak the son of Zippor, king of Moab, hath sent unto me, *saying*,

11 Behold, *there is* a people come out of Egypt, which covereth the face of the earth: come now, curse me them; peradventure I shall be able to overcome them, and drive them out.

12 And God said unto Balaam, Thou shalt not go with them; thou shalt not curse the people: for they *are* blessed.

13 And Balaam rose up in the morning, and said unto the princes of Balak, Get you into your land: for the LORD refuseth to give me leave to go with you.

14 And the princes of Moab rose up, and they went unto Balak, and said, Balaam refuseth to come with us.

15 And Balak sent yet again princes, more, and more honourable than they.

16 And they came to Balaam, and said to him, Thus saith Balak the son of Zippor, Let nothing, I pray thee, hinder thee from coming unto me:

17 For I will promote thee unto very great honour, and I will do whatsoever

thou sayest unto me: come therefore, I
pray thee, curse me this people.
18 And Balaam answered and said
unto the servants of Balak, If Balak
would give me his house full of silver
and gold, I cannot go beyond the word
of the LORD my God, to do less or more.
19 Now therefore, I pray you, tarry ye
also here this night, that I may know
what the LORD will say unto me more.
20 And God came unto Balaam at
night, and said unto him, If the men
come to call thee, rise up, *and* go with
them; but yet the word which I shall say
unto thee, that shalt thou do.
21 And Balaam rose up in the morning, and saddled his ass, and went with
the princes of Moab.
22 And God's anger was kindled
because he went: and the angel of the
LORD stood in the way for an adversary
against him. Now he was riding upon
his ass, and his two servants *were* with
him.
23 And the ass saw the angel of the
LORD standing in the way, and his sword
drawn in his hand: and the ass turned
aside out of the way, and went into the
field: and Balaam smote the ass, to turn
her into the way.
24 But the angel of the LORD stood in
a path of the vineyards, a wall *being* on
this side, and a wall on that side.
25 And when the ass saw the angel of
the LORD, she thrust herself unto the
wall, and crushed Balaam's foot against
the wall: and he smote her again.
26 And the angel of the LORD went
further, and stood in a narrow place,
where *was* no way to turn either to the
right hand or to the left.
27 And when the ass saw the angel of
the LORD, she fell down under Balaam:
and Balaam's anger was kindled, and
he smote the ass with a staff.
28 And the LORD opened the mouth
of the ass, and she said unto Balaam,
What have I done unto thee, that thou
hast smitten me these three times?
29 And Balaam said unto the ass,
Because thou hast mocked me: I would
there were a sword in mine hand, for
now would I kill thee.
30 And the ass said unto Balaam, *Am*
not I thine ass, upon which thou hast
ridden ever since *I was* thine unto this
day? was I ever wont to do so unto
thee? And he said, Nay.
31 Then the LORD opened the eyes of
Balaam, and he saw the angel of the
LORD standing in the way, and his sword
drawn in his hand: and he bowed down
his head, and fell flat on his face.
32 And the angel of the LORD said
unto him, Wherefore hast thou smitten
thine ass these three times? behold, I
went out to withstand thee, because
thy way is perverse before me:
33 And the ass saw me, and turned
from me these three times: unless she
had turned from me, surely now also I
had slain thee, and saved her alive.
34 And Balaam said unto the angel of
the LORD, I have sinned; for I knew not
that thou stoodest in the way against
me: now therefore, if it displease thee, I
will get me back again.
35 And the angel of the LORD said
unto Balaam, Go with the men: but only
the word that I shall speak unto thee,
that thou shalt speak. So Balaam went
with the princes of Balak.
36 And when Balak heard that
Balaam was come, he went out to meet
him unto a city of Moab, which *is* in the
border of Arnon, which *is* in the utmost
coast.

37 And Balak said unto Balaam, Did I not earnestly send unto thee to call thee? wherefore camest thou not unto me? am I not able indeed to promote thee to honour?

38 And Balaam said unto Balak, Lo, I am come unto thee: have I now any power at all to say any thing? the word that God putteth in my mouth, that shall I speak.

39 And Balaam went with Balak, and they came unto Kirjath-huzoth.

40 And Balak offered oxen and sheep, and sent to Balaam, and to the princes that *were* with him.

41 And it came to pass on the morrow, that Balak took Balaam, and brought him up into the high places of Baal, that thence he might see the utmost *part* of the people.

23 And Balaam said unto Balak, Build me here seven altars, and prepare me here seven oxen and seven rams.

2 And Balak did as Balaam had spoken; and Balak and Balaam offered on *every* altar a bullock and a ram.

3 And Balaam said unto Balak, Stand by thy burnt offering, and I will go: peradventure the LORD will come to meet me: and whatsoever he sheweth me I will tell thee. And he went to an high place.

4 And God met Balaam: and he said unto him, I have prepared seven altars, and I have offered upon *every* altar a bullock and a ram.

5 And the LORD put a word in Balaam's mouth, and said, Return unto Balak, and thus thou shalt speak.

6 And he returned unto him, and, lo, he stood by his burnt sacrifice, he, and all the princes of Moab.

7 And he took up his parable, and said, Balak the king of Moab hath brought me from Aram, out of the mountains of the east, *saying*, Come, curse me Jacob, and come, defy Israel.

8 How shall I curse, whom God hath not cursed? or how shall I defy, *whom* the LORD hath not defied?

9 For from the top of the rocks I see him, and from the hills I behold him: lo, the people shall dwell alone, and shall not be reckoned among the nations.

10 Who can count the dust of Jacob, and the number of the fourth *part* of Israel? Let me die the death of the righteous, and let my last end be like his!

11 And Balak said unto Balaam, What hast thou done unto me? I took thee to curse mine enemies, and, behold, thou hast blessed *them* altogether.

12 And he answered and said, Must I not take heed to speak that which the LORD hath put in my mouth?

13 And Balak said unto him, Come, I pray thee, with me unto another place, from whence thou mayest see them: thou shalt see but the utmost part of them, and shalt not see them all: and curse me them from thence.

14 And he brought him into the field of Zophim, to the top of Pisgah, and built seven altars, and offered a bullock and a ram on *every* altar.

15 And he said unto Balak, Stand here by thy burnt offering, while I meet *the LORD* yonder.

16 And the LORD met Balaam, and put a word in his mouth, and said, Go again unto Balak, and say thus.

17 And when he came to him, behold, he stood by his burnt offering, and the princes of Moab with him. And Balak

said unto him, What hath the LORD spoken?

18 And he took up his parable, and said, Rise up, Balak, and hear; hearken unto me, thou son of Zippor:

19 God *is* not a man, that he should lie; neither the son of man, that he should repent: hath he said, and shall he not do *it*? or hath he spoken, and shall he not make it good?

20 Behold, I have received *commandment* to bless: and he hath blessed; and I cannot reverse it.

21 He hath not beheld iniquity in Jacob, neither hath he seen perverseness in Israel: the LORD his God *is* with him, and the shout of a king *is* among them.

22 God brought them out of Egypt; he hath as it were the strength of an unicorn.

23 Surely *there is* no enchantment against Jacob, neither *is there* any divination against Israel: according to this time it shall be said of Jacob and of Israel, What hath God wrought!

24 Behold, the people shall rise up as a great lion, and lift up himself as a young lion: he shall not lie down until he eat *of* the prey, and drink the blood of the slain.

25 And Balak said unto Balaam, Neither curse them at all, nor bless them at all.

26 But Balaam answered and said unto Balak, Told not I thee, saying, All that the LORD speaketh, that I must do?

27 And Balak said unto Balaam, Come, I pray thee, I will bring thee unto another place; peradventure it will please God that thou mayest curse me them from thence.

28 And Balak brought Balaam unto the top of Peor, that looketh toward Jeshimon.

29 And Balaam said unto Balak, Build me here seven altars, and prepare me here seven bullocks and seven rams.

30 And Balak did as Balaam had said, and offered a bullock and a ram on *every* altar.

24 And when Balaam saw that it pleased the LORD to bless Israel, he went not, as at other times, to seek for enchantments, but he set his face toward the wilderness.

2 And Balaam lifted up his eyes, and he saw Israel abiding *in his tents* according to their tribes; and the spirit of God came upon him.

3 And he took up his parable, and said, Balaam the son of Beor hath said, and the man whose eyes are open hath said:

4 He hath said, which heard the words of God, which saw the vision of the Almighty, falling *into a trance*, but having his eyes open:

5 How goodly are thy tents, O Jacob, *and* thy tabernacles, O Israel!

6 As the valleys are they spread forth, as gardens by the river's side, as the trees of lign aloes which the LORD hath planted, *and* as cedar trees beside the waters.

7 He shall pour the water out of his buckets, and his seed *shall be* in many waters, and his king shall be higher than Agag, and his kingdom shall be exalted.

8 God brought him forth out of Egypt; he hath as it were the strength of an unicorn: he shall eat up the nations his enemies, and shall break their bones, and pierce *them* through with his arrows.

9 He couched, he lay down as a lion,
and as a great lion: who shall stir him
up? Blessed *is* he that blesseth thee,
and cursed *is* he that curseth thee.
10 And Balak's anger was kindled
against Balaam, and he smote his
hands together: and Balak said unto
Balaam, I called thee to curse mine
enemies, and, behold, thou hast altogether blessed *them* these three times.
11 Therefore now flee thou to thy
place: I thought to promote thee unto
great honour; but, lo, the LORD hath
kept thee back from honour.
12 And Balaam said unto Balak,
Spake I not also to thy messengers
which thou sentest unto me, saying,
13 If Balak would give me his house
full of silver and gold, I cannot go
beyond the commandment of the LORD,
to do *either* good or bad of mine own
mind; *but* what the LORD saith, that will
I speak?
14 And now, behold, I go unto my
people: come *therefore, and* I will
advertise thee what this people shall
do to thy people in the latter days.
15 And he took up his parable, and
said, Balaam the son of Beor hath said,
and the man whose eyes are open hath
said:
16 He hath said, which heard the
words of God, and knew the knowledge
of the most High, *which* saw the vision
of the Almighty, falling *into a trance*,
but having his eyes open:
17 I shall see him, but not now: I shall
behold him, but not nigh: there shall
come a Star out of Jacob, and a Sceptre
shall rise out of Israel, and shall smite
the corners of Moab, and destroy all the
children of Sheth.
18 And Edom shall be a possession,
Seir also shall be a possession for his
enemies; and Israel shall do valiantly.
19 Out of Jacob shall come he that
shall have dominion, and shall destroy
him that remaineth of the city.
20 And when he looked on Amalek,
he took up his parable, and said,
Amalek *was* the first of the nations; but
his latter end *shall be* that he perish for
ever.
21 And he looked on the Kenites, and
took up his parable, and said, Strong is
thy dwellingplace, and thou puttest thy
nest in a rock.
22 Nevertheless the Kenite shall be
wasted, until Asshur shall carry thee
away captive.
23 And he took up his parable, and
said, Alas, who shall live when God
doeth this!
24 And ships *shall come* from the
coast of Chittim, and shall afflict
Asshur, and shall afflict Eber, and he
also shall perish for ever.
25 And Balaam rose up, and went and
returned to his place: and Balak also
went his way.

25 And Israel abode in Shittim, and
the people began to commit
whoredom with the daughters of Moab.
2 And they called the people unto the
sacrifices of their gods: and the people
did eat, and bowed down to their gods.
3 And Israel joined himself unto Baal-
peor: and the anger of the LORD was
kindled against Israel.
4 And the LORD said unto Moses, Take
all the heads of the people, and hang
them up before the LORD against the
sun, that the fierce anger of the LORD
may be turned away from Israel.

5 And Moses said unto the judges of Israel, Slay ye every one his men that were joined unto Baal-peor.

6 And, behold, one of the children of Israel came and brought unto his brethren a Midianitish woman in the sight of Moses, and in the sight of all the congregation of the children of Israel, who *were* weeping *before* the door of the tabernacle of the congregation.

7 And when Phinehas, the son of Eleazar, the son of Aaron the priest, saw *it*, he rose up from among the congregation, and took a javelin in his hand;

8 And he went after the man of Israel into the tent, and thrust both of them through, the man of Israel, and the woman through her belly. So the plague was stayed from the children of Israel.

9 And those that died in the plague were twenty and four thousand.

10 And the LORD spake unto Moses, saying,

11 Phinehas, the son of Eleazar, the son of Aaron the priest, hath turned my wrath away from the children of Israel, while he was zealous for my sake among them, that I consumed not the children of Israel in my jealousy.

12 Wherefore say, Behold, I give unto him my covenant of peace:

13 And he shall have it, and his seed after him, *even* the covenant of an everlasting priesthood; because he was zealous for his God, and made an atonement for the children of Israel.

14 Now the name of the Israelite that was slain, *even* that was slain with the Midianitish woman, *was* Zimri, the son of Salu, a prince of a chief house among the Simeonites.

15 And the name of the Midianitish woman that was slain *was* Cozbi, the daughter of Zur; he *was* head over a people, *and* of a chief house in Midian.

16 And the LORD spake unto Moses, saying,

17 Vex the Midianites, and smite them:

18 For they vex you with their wiles, wherewith they have beguiled you in the matter of Peor, and in the matter of Cozbi, the daughter of a prince of Midian, their sister, which was slain in the day of the plague for Peor's sake.

26 And it came to pass after the plague, that the LORD spake unto Moses and unto Eleazar the son of Aaron the priest, saying,

2 Take the sum of all the congregation of the children of Israel, from twenty years old and upward, throughout their fathers' house, all that are able to go to war in Israel.

3 And Moses and Eleazar the priest spake with them in the plains of Moab by Jordan *near* Jericho, saying,

4 *Take the sum of the people*, from twenty years old and upward; as the LORD commanded Moses and the children of Israel, which went forth out of the land of Egypt.

5 Reuben, the eldest son of Israel: the children of Reuben; Hanoch, *of whom cometh* the family of the Hanochites: of Pallu, the family of the Palluites:

6 Of Hezron, the family of the Hezronites: of Carmi, the family of the Carmites.

7 These *are* the families of the Reubenites: and they that were numbered of them were forty and three thousand and seven hundred and thirty.

8 And the sons of Pallu; Eliab.

9 And the sons of Eliab; Nemuel, and Dathan, and Abiram. This *is that*

Dathan and Abiram, *which were*
famous in the congregation, who strove
against Moses and against Aaron in the
company of Korah, when they strove
against the LORD:
10 And the earth opened her mouth,
and swallowed them up together with
Korah, when that company died, what
time the fire devoured two hundred
and fifty men: and they became a sign.
11 Notwithstanding the children of
Korah died not.
12 The sons of Simeon after their
families: of Nemuel, the family of the
Nemuelites: of Jamin, the family of the
Jaminites: of Jachin, the family of the
Jachinites:
13 Of Zerah, the family of the
Zarhites: of Shaul, the family of the
Shaulites.
14 These *are* the families of the
Simeonites, twenty and two thousand
and two hundred.
15 The children of Gad after their
families: of Zephon, the family of the
Zephonites: of Haggi, the family of the
Haggites: of Shuni, the family of the
Shunites:
16 Of Ozni, the family of the Oznites:
of Eri, the family of the Erites:
17 Of Arod, the family of the Arodites:
of Areli, the family of the Arelites.
18 These *are* the families of the children of Gad according to those that
were numbered of them, forty thousand and five hundred.
19 The sons of Judah *were* Er and
Onan: and Er and Onan died in the
land of Canaan.
20 And the sons of Judah after their
families were; of Shelah, the family of
the Shelanites: of Pharez, the family of
the Pharzites: of Zerah, the family of
the Zarhites.
21 And the sons of Pharez were; of
Hezron, the family of the Hezronites: of
Hamul, the family of the Hamulites.
22 These *are* the families of Judah
according to those that were numbered
of them, threescore and sixteen thousand and five hundred.
23 *Of* the sons of Issachar after their
families: *of* Tola, the family of the
Tolaites: of Pua, the family of the
Punites:
24 Of Jashub, the family of the
Jashubites: of Shimron, the family of
the Shimronites.
25 These *are* the families of Issachar
according to those that were numbered
of them, threescore and four thousand
and three hundred.
26 *Of* the sons of Zebulun after their
families: of Sered, the family of the
Sardites: of Elon, the family of the
Elonites: of Jahleel, the family of the
Jahleelites.
27 These *are* the families of the
Zebulunites according to those that
were numbered of them, threescore
thousand and five hundred.
28 The sons of Joseph after their
families *were* Manasseh and Ephraim.
29 Of the sons of Manasseh: of Machir,
the family of the Machirites: and
Machir begat Gilead: of Gilead *come*
the family of the Gileadites.
30 These *are* the sons of Gilead: *of*
Jeezer, the family of the Jeezerites: of
Helek, the family of the Helekites:
31 And *of* Asriel, the family of the
Asrielites: and *of* Shechem, the family
of the Shechemites:
32 And *of* Shemida, the family of the
Shemidaites: and *of* Hepher, the family
of the Hepherites.
33 And Zelophehad the son of
Hepher had no sons, but daughters:

and the names of the daughters of
Zelophehad *were* Mahlah, and Noah,
Hoglah, Milcah, and Tirzah.
34 These *are* the families of Manasseh,
and those that were numbered of them,
fifty and two thousand and seven hundred.
35 These *are* the sons of Ephraim
after their families: of Shuthelah, the
family of the Shuthalhites: of Becher,
the family of the Bachrites: of Tahan,
the family of the Tahanites.
36 And these *are* the sons of
Shuthelah: of Eran, the family of the
Eranites.
37 These *are* the families of the sons
of Ephraim according to those that
were numbered of them, thirty and two
thousand and five hundred. These *are*
the sons of Joseph after their families.
38 The sons of Benjamin after their
families: of Bela, the family of the
Belaites: of Ashbel, the family of the
Ashbelites: of Ahiram, the family of the
Ahiramites:
39 Of Shupham, the family of the
Shuphamites: of Hupham, the family of
the Huphamites.
40 And the sons of Bela were Ard and
Naaman: *of Ard*, the family of the
Ardites: *and* of Naaman, the family of
the Naamites.
41 These *are* the sons of Benjamin
after their families: and they that were
numbered of them *were* forty and five
thousand and six hundred.
42 These *are* the sons of Dan after
their families: of Shuham, the family of
the Shuhamites. These *are* the families
of Dan after their families.
43 All the families of the Shuhamites,
according to those that were numbered
of them, *were* threescore and four thousand and four hundred.
44 *Of* the children of Asher after their
families: of Jimna, the family of the
Jimnites: of Jesui, the family of the
Jesuites: of Beriah, the family of the
Beriites.
45 Of the sons of Beriah: of Heber, the
family of the Heberites: of Malchiel,
the family of the Malchielites.
46 And the name of the daughter of
Asher *was* Sarah.
47 These *are* the families of the sons
of Asher according to those that were
numbered of them; *who were* fifty and
three thousand and four hundred.
48 *Of* the sons of Naphtali after their
families: of Jahzeel, the family of the
Jahzeelites: of Guni, the family of the
Gunites:
49 Of Jezer, the family of the
Jezerites: of Shillem, the family of the
Shillemites.
50 These *are* the families of Naphtali
according to their families: and they
that were numbered of them *were* forty
and five thousand and four hundred.
51 These *were* the numbered of the
children of Israel, six hundred thousand and a thousand seven hundred
and thirty.
52 And the LORD spake unto Moses,
saying,
53 Unto these the land shall be divided for an inheritance according to the
number of names.
54 To many thou shalt give the more
inheritance, and to few thou shalt give
the less inheritance: to every one shall
his inheritance be given according to
those that were numbered of him.
55 Notwithstanding the land shall be
divided by lot: according to the names
of the tribes of their fathers they shall
inherit.

56 According to the lot shall the possession thereof be divided between many and few.

57 And these *are* they that were numbered of the Levites after their families: of Gershon, the family of the Gershonites: of Kohath, the family of the Kohathites: of Merari, the family of the Merarites.

58 These *are* the families of the Levites: the family of the Libnites, the family of the Hebronites, the family of the Mahlites, the family of the Mushites, the family of the Korathites. And Kohath begat Amram.

59 And the name of Amram's wife *was* Jochebed, the daughter of Levi, whom *her mother* bare to Levi in Egypt: and she bare unto Amram Aaron and Moses, and Miriam their sister.

60 And unto Aaron was born Nadab, and Abihu, Eleazar, and Ithamar.

61 And Nadab and Abihu died, when they offered strange fire before the LORD.

62 And those that were numbered of them were twenty and three thousand, all males from a month old and upward: for they were not numbered among the children of Israel, because there was no inheritance given them among the children of Israel.

63 These *are* they that were numbered by Moses and Eleazar the priest, who numbered the children of Israel in the plains of Moab by Jordan *near* Jericho.

64 But among these there was not a man of them whom Moses and Aaron the priest numbered, when they numbered the children of Israel in the wilderness of Sinai.

65 For the LORD had said of them, They shall surely die in the wilderness. And there was not left a man of them, save Caleb the son of Jephunneh, and Joshua the son of Nun.

27 Then came the daughters of Zelophehad, the son of Hepher, the son of Gilead, the son of Machir, the son of Manasseh, of the families of Manasseh the son of Joseph: and these *are* the names of his daughters; Mahlah, Noah, and Hoglah, and Milcah, and Tirzah.

2 And they stood before Moses, and before Eleazar the priest, and before the princes and all the congregation, *by* the door of the tabernacle of the congregation, saying,

3 Our father died in the wilderness, and he was not in the company of them that gathered themselves together against the LORD in the company of Korah; but died in his own sin, and had no sons.

4 Why should the name of our father be done away from among his family, because he hath no son? Give unto us *therefore* a possession among the brethren of our father.

5 And Moses brought their cause before the LORD.

6 And the LORD spake unto Moses, saying,

7 The daughters of Zelophehad speak right: thou shalt surely give them a possession of an inheritance among their father's brethren; and thou shalt cause the inheritance of their father to pass unto them.

8 And thou shalt speak unto the children of Israel, saying, If a man die, and have no son, then ye shall cause his inheritance to pass unto his daughter.

9 And if he have no daughter, then ye shall give his inheritance unto his brethren.

10 And if he have no brethren, then ye shall give his inheritance unto his father's brethren.

11 And if his father have no brethren, then ye shall give his inheritance unto his kinsman that is next to him of his family, and he shall possess it: and it shall be unto the children of Israel a statute of judgment, as the LORD commanded Moses.

12 And the LORD said unto Moses, Get thee up into this mount Abarim, and see the land which I have given unto the children of Israel.

13 And when thou hast seen it, thou also shalt be gathered unto thy people, as Aaron thy brother was gathered.

14 For ye rebelled against my commandment in the desert of Zin, in the strife of the congregation, to sanctify me at the water before their eyes: that *is* the water of Meribah in Kadesh in the wilderness of Zin.

15 And Moses spake unto the LORD, saying,

16 Let the LORD, the God of the spirits of all flesh, set a man over the congregation,

17 Which may go out before them, and which may go in before them, and which may lead them out, and which may bring them in; that the congregation of the LORD be not as sheep which have no shepherd.

18 And the LORD said unto Moses, Take thee Joshua the son of Nun, a man in whom *is* the spirit, and lay thine hand upon him;

19 And set him before Eleazar the priest, and before all the congregation; and give him a charge in their sight.

20 And thou shalt put *some* of thine honour upon him, that all the congregation of the children of Israel may be obedient.

21 And he shall stand before Eleazar the priest, who shall ask *counsel* for him after the judgment of Urim before the LORD: at his word shall they go out, and at his word they shall come in, *both* he, and all the children of Israel with him, even all the congregation.

22 And Moses did as the LORD commanded him: and he took Joshua, and set him before Eleazar the priest, and before all the congregation:

23 And he laid his hands upon him, and gave him a charge, as the LORD commanded by the hand of Moses.

28 And the LORD spake unto Moses, saying,

2 Command the children of Israel, and say unto them, My offering, *and* my bread for my sacrifices made by fire, *for* a sweet savour unto me, shall ye observe to offer unto me in their due season.

3 And thou shalt say unto them, This *is* the offering made by fire which ye shall offer unto the LORD; two lambs of the first year without spot day by day, *for* a continual burnt offering.

4 The one lamb shalt thou offer in the morning, and the other lamb shalt thou offer at even;

5 And a tenth *part* of an ephah of flour for a meat offering, mingled with the fourth *part* of an hin of beaten oil.

6 *It is* a continual burnt offering, which was ordained in mount Sinai for a sweet savour, a sacrifice made by fire unto the LORD.

7 And the drink offering thereof *shall be* the fourth *part* of an hin for the one lamb: in the holy *place* shalt thou cause

the strong wine to be poured unto the
LORD *for* a drink offering.
8 And the other lamb shalt thou offer
at even: as the meat offering of the
morning, and as the drink offering
thereof, thou shalt offer *it*, a sacrifice
made by fire, of a sweet savour unto the
LORD.
9 And on the sabbath day two lambs
of the first year without spot, and two
tenth deals of flour *for* a meat offering,
mingled with oil, and the drink offering
thereof:
10 *This is* the burnt offering of every
sabbath, beside the continual burnt
offering, and his drink offering.
11 And in the beginnings of your
months ye shall offer a burnt offering
unto the LORD; two young bullocks, and
one ram, seven lambs of the first year
without spot;
12 And three tenth deals of flour *for* a
meat offering, mingled with oil, for one
bullock; and two tenth deals of flour *for*
a meat offering, mingled with oil, for
one ram;
13 And a several tenth deal of flour
mingled with oil *for* a meat offering
unto one lamb; *for* a burnt offering of a
sweet savour, a sacrifice made by fire
unto the LORD.
14 And their drink offerings shall be
half an hin of wine unto a bullock, and
the third *part* of an hin unto a ram, and
a fourth *part* of an hin unto a lamb: this
is the burnt offering of every month
throughout the months of the year.
15 And one kid of the goats for a sin
offering unto the LORD shall be offered,
beside the continual burnt offering,
and his drink offering.
16 And in the fourteenth day of the
first month *is* the passover of the LORD.
17 And in the fifteenth day of this
month *is* the feast: seven days shall
unleavened bread be eaten.
18 In the first day *shall be* an holy
convocation; ye shall do no manner of
servile work *therein*:
19 But ye shall offer a sacrifice made
by fire *for* a burnt offering unto the
LORD; two young bullocks, and one ram,
and seven lambs of the first year: they
shall be unto you without blemish:
20 And their meat offering *shall be of*
flour mingled with oil: three tenth
deals shall ye offer for a bullock, and
two tenth deals for a ram;
21 A several tenth deal shalt thou
offer for every lamb, throughout the
seven lambs:
22 And one goat *for* a sin offering, to
make an atonement for you.
23 Ye shall offer these beside the
burnt offering in the morning, which *is*
for a continual burnt offering.
24 After this manner ye shall offer
daily, throughout the seven days, the
meat of the sacrifice made by fire, of a
sweet savour unto the LORD: it shall be
offered beside the continual burnt
offering, and his drink offering.
25 And on the seventh day ye shall
have an holy convocation; ye shall do
no servile work.
26 Also in the day of the firstfruits,
when ye bring a new meat offering
unto the LORD, after your weeks *be out*,
ye shall have an holy convocation; ye
shall do no servile work:
27 But ye shall offer the burnt offering for a sweet savour unto the LORD;
two young bullocks, one ram, seven
lambs of the first year;

28 And their meat offering of flour
mingled with oil, three tenth deals unto
one bullock, two tenth deals unto one
ram,
29 A several tenth deal unto one
lamb, throughout the seven lambs;
30 *And* one kid of the goats, to make
an atonement for you.
31 Ye shall offer *them* beside the
continual burnt offering, and his meat
offering, (they shall be unto you without blemish) and their drink offerings.

29 And in the seventh month, on the
first *day* of the month, ye shall
have an holy convocation; ye shall do
no servile work: it is a day of blowing
the trumpets unto you.
2 And ye shall offer a burnt offering
for a sweet savour unto the LORD; one
young bullock, one ram, *and* seven
lambs of the first year without blemish:
3 And their meat offering *shall be of*
flour mingled with oil, three tenth
deals for a bullock, *and* two tenth deals
for a ram,
4 And one tenth deal for one lamb,
throughout the seven lambs:
5 And one kid of the goats *for* a sin
offering, to make an atonement for you:
6 Beside the burnt offering of the
month, and his meat offering, and the
daily burnt offering, and his meat offering, and their drink offerings, according unto their manner, for a sweet
savour, a sacrifice made by fire unto the
LORD.
7 And ye shall have on the tenth *day*
of this seventh month an holy convocation; and ye shall afflict your souls: ye
shall not do any work *therein*:
8 But ye shall offer a burnt offering
unto the LORD *for* a sweet savour; one
young bullock, one ram, *and* seven
lambs of the first year; they shall be
unto you without blemish:
9 And their meat offering *shall be of*
flour mingled with oil, three tenth
deals to a bullock, *and* two tenth deals
to one ram,
10 A several tenth deal for one lamb,
throughout the seven lambs:
11 One kid of the goats *for* a sin offering; beside the sin offering of atonement, and the continual burnt offering,
and the meat offering of it, and their
drink offerings.
12 And on the fifteenth day of the
seventh month ye shall have an holy
convocation; ye shall do no servile
work, and ye shall keep a feast unto the
LORD seven days:
13 And ye shall offer a burnt offering,
a sacrifice made by fire, of a sweet
savour unto the LORD; thirteen young
bullocks, two rams, *and* fourteen lambs
of the first year; they shall be without
blemish:
14 And their meat offering *shall be of*
flour mingled with oil, three tenth
deals unto every bullock of the thirteen
bullocks, two tenth deals to each ram of
the two rams,
15 And a several tenth deal to each
lamb of the fourteen lambs:
16 And one kid of the goats *for* a sin
offering; beside the continual burnt
offering, his meat offering, and his
drink offering.
17 And on the second day *ye shall*
offer twelve young bullocks, two rams,
fourteen lambs of the first year without
spot:
18 And their meat offering and their
drink offerings for the bullocks, for the
rams, and for the lambs, *shall be*
according to their number, after the
manner:

19 And one kid of the goats *for* a sin
offering; beside the continual burnt
offering, and the meat offering thereof,
and their drink offerings.
20 And on the third day eleven bullocks, two rams, fourteen lambs of the
first year without blemish;
21 And their meat offering and their
drink offerings for the bullocks, for the
rams, and for the lambs, *shall be*
according to their number, after the
manner:
22 And one goat *for* a sin offering;
beside the continual burnt offering,
and his meat offering, and his drink
offering.
23 And on the fourth day ten bullocks, two rams, *and* fourteen lambs of
the first year without blemish:
24 Their meat offering and their
drink offerings for the bullocks, for the
rams, and for the lambs, *shall be*
according to their number, after the
manner:
25 And one kid of the goats *for* a sin
offering; beside the continual burnt
offering, his meat offering, and his
drink offering.
26 And on the fifth day nine bullocks,
two rams, *and* fourteen lambs of the
first year without spot:
27 And their meat offering and their
drink offerings for the bullocks, for the
rams, and for the lambs, *shall be*
according to their number, after the
manner:
28 And one goat *for* a sin offering;
beside the continual burnt offering,
and his meat offering, and his drink
offering.
29 And on the sixth day eight bullocks, two rams, *and* fourteen lambs of
the first year without blemish:
30 And their meat offering and their
drink offerings for the bullocks, for the
rams, and for the lambs, *shall be*
according to their number, after the
manner:
31 And one goat *for* a sin offering;
beside the continual burnt offering, his
meat offering, and his drink offering.
32 And on the seventh day seven bullocks, two rams, *and* fourteen lambs of
the first year without blemish:
33 And their meat offering and their
drink offerings for the bullocks, for the
rams, and for the lambs, *shall be*
according to their number, after the
manner:
34 And one goat *for* a sin offering;
beside the continual burnt offering, his
meat offering, and his drink offering.
35 On the eighth day ye shall have a
solemn assembly: ye shall do no servile
work *therein*:
36 But ye shall offer a burnt offering,
a sacrifice made by fire, of a sweet
savour unto the LORD: one bullock, one
ram, seven lambs of the first year without blemish:
37 Their meat offering and their
drink offerings for the bullock, for the
ram, and for the lambs, *shall be* according to their number, after the manner:
38 And one goat *for* a sin offering;
beside the continual burnt offering,
and his meat offering, and his drink
offering.
39 These *things* ye shall do unto the
LORD in your set feasts, beside your
vows, and your freewill offerings, for
your burnt offerings, and for your meat
offerings, and for your drink offerings,
and for your peace offerings.
40 And Moses told the children of
Israel according to all that the LORD
commanded Moses.

30 And Moses spake unto the heads
of the tribes concerning the children of Israel, saying, This *is* the thing
which the LORD hath commanded.
2 If a man vow a vow unto the LORD,
or swear an oath to bind his soul with a
bond; he shall not break his word, he
shall do according to all that proceedeth out of his mouth.
3 If a woman also vow a vow unto the
LORD, and bind herself by a bond, *being*
in her father's house in her youth;
4 And her father hear her vow, and
her bond wherewith she hath bound
her soul, and her father shall hold his
peace at her: then all her vows shall
stand, and every bond wherewith she
hath bound her soul shall stand.
5 But if her father disallow her in the
day that he heareth; not any of her
vows, or of her bonds wherewith she
hath bound her soul, shall stand: and
the LORD shall forgive her, because her
father disallowed her.
6 And if she had at all an husband,
when she vowed, or uttered ought out
of her lips, wherewith she bound her
soul;
7 And her husband heard *it*, and held
his peace at her in the day that he
heard *it*: then her vows shall stand, and
her bonds wherewith she bound her
soul shall stand.
8 But if her husband disallowed her
on the day that he heard *it*; then he
shall make her vow which she vowed,
and that which she uttered with her
lips, wherewith she bound her soul, of
none effect: and the LORD shall forgive
her.
9 But every vow of a widow, and of her
that is divorced, wherewith they have
bound their souls, shall stand against
her.
10 And if she vowed in her husband's
house, or bound her soul by a bond
with an oath;
11 And her husband heard *it*, and
held his peace at her, *and* disallowed
her not: then all her vows shall stand,
and every bond wherewith she bound
her soul shall stand.
12 But if her husband hath utterly
made them void on the day he heard
them; then whatsoever proceeded out
of her lips concerning her vows, or concerning the bond of her soul, shall not
stand: her husband hath made them
void; and the LORD shall forgive her.
13 Every vow, and every binding oath
to afflict the soul, her husband may
establish it, or her husband may make
it void.
14 But if her husband altogether hold
his peace at her from day to day; then
he establisheth all her vows, or all her
bonds, which *are* upon her: he confirmeth them, because he held his peace
at her in the day that he heard *them*.
15 But if he shall any ways make them
void after that he hath heard *them*;
then he shall bear her iniquity.
16 These *are* the statutes, which the
LORD commanded Moses, between a
man and his wife, between the father
and his daughter, *being yet* in her youth
in her father's house.

31 And the LORD spake unto Moses,
saying,
2 Avenge the children of Israel of the
Midianites: afterward shalt thou be
gathered unto thy people.
3 And Moses spake unto the people,
saying, Arm some of yourselves unto
the war, and let them go against the
Midianites, and avenge the LORD of
Midian.

4 Of every tribe a thousand, throughout all the tribes of Israel, shall ye send to the war.

5 So there were delivered out of the thousands of Israel, a thousand of *every* tribe, twelve thousand armed for war.

6 And Moses sent them to the war, a thousand of *every* tribe, them and Phinehas the son of Eleazar the priest, to the war, with the holy instruments, and the trumpets to blow in his hand.

7 And they warred against the Midianites, as the LORD commanded Moses; and they slew all the males.

8 And they slew the kings of Midian, beside the rest of them that were slain; *namely*, Evi, and Rekem, and Zur, and Hur, and Reba, five kings of Midian: Balaam also the son of Beor they slew with the sword.

9 And the children of Israel took *all* the women of Midian captives, and their little ones, and took the spoil of all their cattle, and all their flocks, and all their goods.

10 And they burnt all their cities wherein they dwelt, and all their goodly castles, with fire.

11 And they took all the spoil, and all the prey, *both* of men and of beasts.

12 And they brought the captives, and the prey, and the spoil, unto Moses, and Eleazar the priest, and unto the congregation of the children of Israel, unto the camp at the plains of Moab, which *are* by Jordan *near* Jericho.

13 And Moses, and Eleazar the priest, and all the princes of the congregation, went forth to meet them without the camp.

14 And Moses was wroth with the officers of the host, *with* the captains over thousands, and captains over hundreds, which came from the battle.

15 And Moses said unto them, Have ye saved all the women alive?

16 Behold, these caused the children of Israel, through the counsel of Balaam, to commit trespass against the LORD in the matter of Peor, and there was a plague among the congregation of the LORD.

17 Now therefore kill every male among the little ones, and kill every woman that hath known man by lying with him.

18 But all the women children, that have not known a man by lying with him, keep alive for yourselves.

19 And do ye abide without the camp seven days: whosoever hath killed any person, and whosoever hath touched any slain, purify *both* yourselves and your captives on the third day, and on the seventh day.

20 And purify all *your* raiment, and all that is made of skins, and all work of goats' *hair*, and all things made of wood.

21 And Eleazar the priest said unto the men of war which went to the battle, This *is* the ordinance of the law which the LORD commanded Moses;

22 Only the gold, and the silver, the brass, the iron, the tin, and the lead,

23 Every thing that may abide the fire, ye shall make *it* go through the fire, and it shall be clean: nevertheless it shall be purified with the water of separation: and all that abideth not the fire ye shall make go through the water.

24 And ye shall wash your clothes on the seventh day, and ye shall be clean, and afterward ye shall come into the camp.

25 And the LORD spake unto Moses, saying,

26 Take the sum of the prey that was taken, *both* of man and of beast, thou, and Eleazar the priest, and the chief fathers of the congregation:

27 And divide the prey into two parts; between them that took the war upon them, who went out to battle, and between all the congregation:

28 And levy a tribute unto the LORD of the men of war which went out to battle: one soul of five hundred, *both* of the persons, and of the beeves, and of the asses, and of the sheep:

29 Take *it* of their half, and give it unto Eleazar the priest, *for* an heave offering of the LORD.

30 And of the children of Israel's half, thou shalt take one portion of fifty, of the persons, of the beeves, of the asses, and of the flocks, of all manner of beasts, and give them unto the Levites, which keep the charge of the tabernacle of the LORD.

31 And Moses and Eleazar the priest did as the LORD commanded Moses.

32 And the booty, *being* the rest of the prey which the men of war had caught, was six hundred thousand and seventy thousand and five thousand sheep,

33 And threescore and twelve thousand beeves,

34 And threescore and one thousand asses,

35 And thirty and two thousand persons in all, of women that had not known man by lying with him.

36 And the half, *which was* the portion of them that went out to war, was in number three hundred thousand and seven and thirty thousand and five hundred sheep:

37 And the LORD's tribute of the sheep was six hundred and threescore and fifteen.

38 And the beeves *were* thirty and six thousand; of which the LORD's tribute *was* threescore and twelve.

39 And the asses *were* thirty thousand and five hundred; of which the LORD's tribute *was* threescore and one.

40 And the persons *were* sixteen thousand; of which the LORD's tribute *was* thirty and two persons.

41 And Moses gave the tribute, *which was* the LORD's heave offering, unto Eleazar the priest, as the LORD commanded Moses.

42 And of the children of Israel's half, which Moses divided from the men that warred,

43 (Now the half *that pertained unto* the congregation was three hundred thousand and thirty thousand *and* seven thousand and five hundred sheep,

44 And thirty and six thousand beeves,

45 And thirty thousand asses and five hundred,

46 And sixteen thousand persons;)

47 Even of the children of Israel's half, Moses took one portion of fifty, *both* of man and of beast, and gave them unto the Levites, which kept the charge of the tabernacle of the LORD; as the LORD commanded Moses.

48 And the officers which *were* over thousands of the host, the captains of thousands, and captains of hundreds, came near unto Moses:

49 And they said unto Moses, Thy servants have taken the sum of the men of war which *are* under our charge, and there lacketh not one man of us.

50 We have therefore brought an oblation for the LORD, what every man hath gotten, of jewels of gold, chains, and bracelets, rings, earrings, and tab-

lets, to make an atonement for our
souls before the LORD.
51 And Moses and Eleazar the priest
took the gold of them, *even* all wrought
jewels.
52 And all the gold of the offering
that they offered up to the LORD, of the
captains of thousands, and of the captains of hundreds, was sixteen thousand seven hundred and fifty shekels.
53 (*For* the men of war had taken
spoil, every man for himself.)
54 And Moses and Eleazar the priest
took the gold of the captains of thousands and of hundreds, and brought it
into the tabernacle of the congregation,
for a memorial for the children of Israel
before the LORD.

32 Now the children of Reuben and
the children of Gad had a very
great multitude of cattle: and when
they saw the land of Jazer, and the land
of Gilead, that, behold, the place *was* a
place for cattle;
2 The children of Gad and the children of Reuben came and spake unto
Moses, and to Eleazar the priest, and
unto the princes of the congregation,
saying,
3 Ataroth, and Dibon, and Jazer, and
Nimrah, and Heshbon, and Elealeh,
and Shebam, and Nebo, and Beon,
4 *Even* the country which the LORD
smote before the congregation of Israel,
is a land for cattle, and thy servants
have cattle:
5 Wherefore, said they, if we have
found grace in thy sight, let this land be
given unto thy servants for a possession, *and* bring us not over Jordan.
6 And Moses said unto the children of
Gad and to the children of Reuben,
Shall your brethren go to war, and shall
ye sit here?
7 And wherefore discourage ye the
heart of the children of Israel from
going over into the land which the LORD
hath given them?
8 Thus did your fathers, when I sent
them from Kadesh-barnea to see the
land.
9 For when they went up unto the valley of Eshcol, and saw the land, they
discouraged the heart of the children of
Israel, that they should not go into the
land which the LORD had given them.
10 And the LORD's anger was kindled
the same time, and he sware, saying,
11 Surely none of the men that came
up out of Egypt, from twenty years old
and upward, shall see the land which I
sware unto Abraham, unto Isaac, and
unto Jacob; because they have not
wholly followed me:
12 Save Caleb the son of Jephunneh
the Kenezite, and Joshua the son of
Nun: for they have wholly followed the
LORD.
13 And the LORD's anger was kindled
against Israel, and he made them wander in the wilderness forty years, until
all the generation, that had done evil in
the sight of the LORD, was consumed.
14 And, behold, ye are risen up in
your fathers' stead, an increase of sinful men, to augment yet the fierce
anger of the LORD toward Israel.
15 For if ye turn away from after him,
he will yet again leave them in the wilderness; and ye shall destroy all this
people.
16 And they came near unto him, and
said, We will build sheepfolds here for
our cattle, and cities for our little ones:
17 But we ourselves will go ready
armed before the children of Israel,
until we have brought them unto their
place: and our little ones shall dwell in

the fenced cities because of the inhabitants of the land.
18 We will not return unto our houses, until the children of Israel have inherited every man his inheritance.
19 For we will not inherit with them on yonder side Jordan, or forward; because our inheritance is fallen to us on this side Jordan eastward.
20 And Moses said unto them, If ye will do this thing, if ye will go armed before the LORD to war,
21 And will go all of you armed over Jordan before the LORD, until he hath driven out his enemies from before him,
22 And the land be subdued before the LORD: then afterward ye shall return, and be guiltless before the LORD, and before Israel; and this land shall be your possession before the LORD.
23 But if ye will not do so, behold, ye have sinned against the LORD: and be sure your sin will find you out.
24 Build you cities for your little ones, and folds for your sheep; and do that which hath proceeded out of your mouth.
25 And the children of Gad and the children of Reuben spake unto Moses, saying, Thy servants will do as my lord commandeth.
26 Our little ones, our wives, our flocks, and all our cattle, shall be there in the cities of Gilead:
27 But thy servants will pass over, every man armed for war, before the LORD to battle, as my lord saith.
28 So concerning them Moses commanded Eleazar the priest, and Joshua the son of Nun, and the chief fathers of the tribes of the children of Israel:
29 And Moses said unto them, If the children of Gad and the children of Reuben will pass with you over Jordan, every man armed to battle, before the LORD, and the land shall be subdued before you; then ye shall give them the land of Gilead for a possession:
30 But if they will not pass over with you armed, they shall have possessions among you in the land of Canaan.
31 And the children of Gad and the children of Reuben answered, saying, As the LORD hath said unto thy servants, so will we do.
32 We will pass over armed before the LORD into the land of Canaan, that the possession of our inheritance on this side Jordan *may be* ours.
33 And Moses gave unto them, *even* to the children of Gad, and to the children of Reuben, and unto half the tribe of Manasseh the son of Joseph, the kingdom of Sihon king of the Amorites, and the kingdom of Og king of Bashan, the land, with the cities thereof in the coasts, *even* the cities of the country round about.
34 And the children of Gad built Dibon, and Ataroth, and Aroer,
35 And Atroth, Shophan, and Jaazer, and Jogbehah,
36 And Beth-nimrah, and Beth-haran, fenced cities: and folds for sheep.
37 And the children of Reuben built Heshbon, and Elealeh, and Kirjathaim,
38 And Nebo, and Baal-meon, (their names being changed,) and Shibmah: and gave other names unto the cities which they builded.
39 And the children of Machir the son of Manasseh went to Gilead, and took it, and dispossessed the Amorite which *was* in it.

40 And Moses gave Gilead unto Machir the son of Manasseh; and he dwelt therein.

41 And Jair the son of Manasseh went and took the small towns thereof, and called them Havoth-jair.

42 And Nobah went and took Kenath, and the villages thereof, and called it Nobah, after his own name.

33 These *are* the journeys of the children of Israel, which went forth out of the land of Egypt with their armies under the hand of Moses and Aaron.

2 And Moses wrote their goings out according to their journeys by the commandment of the LORD: and these *are* their journeys according to their goings out.

3 And they departed from Rameses in the first month, on the fifteenth day of the first month; on the morrow after the passover the children of Israel went out with an high hand in the sight of all the Egyptians.

4 For the Egyptians buried all *their* firstborn, which the LORD had smitten among them: upon their gods also the LORD executed judgments.

5 And the children of Israel removed from Rameses, and pitched in Succoth.

6 And they departed from Succoth, and pitched in Etham, which *is* in the edge of the wilderness.

7 And they removed from Etham, and turned again unto Pi-hahiroth, which *is* before Baal-zephon: and they pitched before Migdol.

8 And they departed from before Pi-hahiroth, and passed through the midst of the sea into the wilderness, and went three days' journey in the wilderness of Etham, and pitched in Marah.

9 And they removed from Marah, and came unto Elim: and in Elim *were* twelve fountains of water, and threescore and ten palm trees; and they pitched there.

10 And they removed from Elim, and encamped by the Red sea.

11 And they removed from the Red sea, and encamped in the wilderness of Sin.

12 And they took their journey out of the wilderness of Sin, and encamped in Dophkah.

13 And they departed from Dophkah, and encamped in Alush.

14 And they removed from Alush, and encamped at Rephidim, where was no water for the people to drink.

15 And they departed from Rephidim, and pitched in the wilderness of Sinai.

16 And they removed from the desert of Sinai, and pitched at Kibrothhattaavah.

17 And they departed from Kibroth-hattaavah, and encamped at Hazeroth.

18 And they departed from Hazeroth, and pitched in Rithmah.

19 And they departed from Rithmah, and pitched at Rimmon-parez.

20 And they departed from Rimmon-parez, and pitched in Libnah.

21 And they removed from Libnah, and pitched at Rissah.

22 And they journeyed from Rissah, and pitched in Kehelathah.

23 And they went from Kehelathah, and pitched in mount Shapher.

24 And they removed from mount Shapher, and encamped in Haradah.

25 And they removed from Haradah, and pitched in Makheloth.

26 And they removed from Makheloth, and encamped at Tahath.

27 And they departed from Tahath,
and pitched at Tarah.
28 And they removed from Tarah, and
pitched in Mithcah.
29 And they went from Mithcah, and
pitched in Hashmonah.
30 And they departed from Hashmonah, and encamped at Moseroth.
31 And they departed from Moseroth,
and pitched in Bene-jaakan.
32 And they removed from Bene-
jaakan, and encamped at Hor-hagidgad.
33 And they went from Hor-hagidgad,
and pitched in Jotbathah.
34 And they removed from Jotbathah,
and encamped at Ebronah.
35 And they departed from Ebronah,
and encamped at Ezion-gaber.
36 And they removed from Ezion-
gaber, and pitched in the wilderness of
Zin, which *is* Kadesh.
37 And they removed from Kadesh,
and pitched in mount Hor, in the edge
of the land of Edom.
38 And Aaron the priest went up into
mount Hor at the commandment of the
LORD, and died there, in the fortieth
year after the children of Israel were
come out of the land of Egypt, in the
first *day* of the fifth month.
39 And Aaron *was* an hundred and
twenty and three years old when he
died in mount Hor.
40 And king Arad the Canaanite,
which dwelt in the south in the land of
Canaan, heard of the coming of the
children of Israel.
41 And they departed from mount
Hor, and pitched in Zalmonah.
42 And they departed from Zalmonah,
and pitched in Punon.
43 And they departed from Punon,
and pitched in Oboth.
44 And they departed from Oboth,
and pitched in Ijeabarim, in the border
of Moab.
45 And they departed from Iim, and
pitched in Dibon-gad.
46 And they removed from Dibongad,
and encamped in Almondiblathaim.
47 And they removed from Almondiblathaim, and pitched in the mountains
of Abarim, before Nebo.
48 And they departed from the mountains of Abarim, and pitched in the
plains of Moab by Jordan *near* Jericho.
49 And they pitched by Jordan, from
Beth-jesimoth *even* unto Abel-shittim
in the plains of Moab.
50 And the LORD spake unto Moses in
the plains of Moab by Jordan *near*
Jericho, saying,
51 Speak unto the children of Israel,
and say unto them, When ye are passed
over Jordan into the land of Canaan;
52 Then ye shall drive out all the
inhabitants of the land from before
you, and destroy all their pictures, and
destroy all their molten images, and
quite pluck down all their high places:
53 And ye shall dispossess *the inhabitants* of the land, and dwell therein:
for I have given you the land to possess
it.
54 And ye shall divide the land by lot
for an inheritance among your families:
and to the more ye shall give the more
inheritance, and to the fewer ye shall
give the less inheritance: every man's
inheritance shall be in the place where
his lot falleth; according to the tribes of
your fathers ye shall inherit.
55 But if ye will not drive out the
inhabitants of the land from before
you; then it shall come to pass, that
those which ye let remain of them *shall
be* pricks in your eyes, and thorns in

your sides, and shall vex you in the land wherein ye dwell.

56 Moreover it shall come to pass, *that* I shall do unto you, as I thought to do unto them.

34 And the LORD spake unto Moses, saying,

2 Command the children of Israel, and say unto them, When ye come into the land of Canaan; (this *is* the land that shall fall unto you for an inheritance, *even* the land of Canaan with the coasts thereof:)

3 Then your south quarter shall be from the wilderness of Zin along by the coast of Edom, and your south border shall be the outmost coast of the salt sea eastward:

4 And your border shall turn from the south to the ascent of Akrabbim, and pass on to Zin: and the going forth thereof shall be from the south to Kadesh-barnea, and shall go on to Hazar-addar, and pass on to Azmon:

5 And the border shall fetch a compass from Azmon unto the river of Egypt, and the goings out of it shall be at the sea.

6 And *as for* the western border, ye shall even have the great sea for a border: this shall be your west border.

7 And this shall be your north border: from the great sea ye shall point out for you mount Hor:

8 From mount Hor ye shall point out *your border* unto the entrance of Hamath; and the goings forth of the border shall be to Zedad:

9 And the border shall go on to Ziphron, and the goings out of it shall be at Hazar-enan: this shall be your north border.

10 And ye shall point out your east border from Hazar-enan to Shepham:

11 And the coast shall go down from Shepham to Riblah, on the east side of Ain; and the border shall descend, and shall reach unto the side of the sea of Chinnereth eastward:

12 And the border shall go down to Jordan, and the goings out of it shall be at the salt sea: this shall be your land with the coasts thereof round about.

13 And Moses commanded the children of Israel, saying, This *is* the land which ye shall inherit by lot, which the LORD commanded to give unto the nine tribes, and to the half tribe:

14 For the tribe of the children of Reuben according to the house of their fathers, and the tribe of the children of Gad according to the house of their fathers, have received *their inheritance*; and half the tribe of Manasseh have received their inheritance:

15 The two tribes and the half tribe have received their inheritance on this side Jordan *near* Jericho eastward, toward the sunrising.

16 And the LORD spake unto Moses, saying,

17 These *are* the names of the men which shall divide the land unto you: Eleazar the priest, and Joshua the son of Nun.

18 And ye shall take one prince of every tribe, to divide the land by inheritance.

19 And the names of the men *are* these: Of the tribe of Judah, Caleb the son of Jephunneh.

20 And of the tribe of the children of Simeon, Shemuel the son of Ammihud.

21 Of the tribe of Benjamin, Elidad the son of Chislon.

22 And the prince of the tribe of the children of Dan, Bukki the son of Jogli.

23 The prince of the children of
Joseph, for the tribe of the children of
Manasseh, Hanniel the son of Ephod.
24 And the prince of the tribe of the
children of Ephraim, Kemuel the son of
Shiphtan.
25 And the prince of the tribe of the
children of Zebulun, Elizaphan the son
of Parnach.
26 And the prince of the tribe of the
children of Issachar, Paltiel the son of
Azzan.
27 And the prince of the tribe of the
children of Asher, Ahihud the son of
Shelomi.
28 And the prince of the tribe of the
children of Naphtali, Pedahel the son of
Ammihud.
29 These *are they* whom the LORD
commanded to divide the inheritance
unto the children of Israel in the land of
Canaan.

35 And the LORD spake unto Moses
in the plains of Moab by Jordan
near Jericho, saying,
2 Command the children of Israel,
that they give unto the Levites of the
inheritance of their possession cities to
dwell in; and ye shall give *also* unto the
Levites suburbs for the cities round
about them.
3 And the cities shall they have to
dwell in; and the suburbs of them shall
be for their cattle, and for their goods,
and for all their beasts.
4 And the suburbs of the cities, which
ye shall give unto the Levites, *shall
reach* from the wall of the city and outward a thousand cubits round about.
5 And ye shall measure from without
the city on the east side two thousand
cubits, and on the south side two thousand cubits, and on the west side two
thousand cubits, and on the north side
two thousand cubits; and the city *shall
be* in the midst: this shall be to them
the suburbs of the cities.
6 And among the cities which ye shall
give unto the Levites *there shall be* six
cities for refuge, which ye shall appoint
for the manslayer, that he may flee
thither: and to them ye shall add forty
and two cities.
7 *So* all the cities which ye shall give
to the Levites *shall be* forty and eight
cities: them *shall ye give* with their
suburbs.
8 And the cities which ye shall give
shall be of the possession of the children of Israel: from *them that have*
many ye shall give many; but from
them that have few ye shall give few:
every one shall give of his cities unto
the Levites according to his inheritance
which he inheriteth.
9 And the LORD spake unto Moses,
saying,
10 Speak unto the children of Israel,
and say unto them, When ye be come
over Jordan into the land of Canaan;
11 Then ye shall appoint you cities to
be cities of refuge for you; that the
slayer may flee thither, which killeth
any person at unawares.
12 And they shall be unto you cities
for refuge from the avenger; that the
manslayer die not, until he stand before
the congregation in judgment.
13 And of these cities which ye shall
give six cities shall ye have for refuge.
14 Ye shall give three cities on this
side Jordan, and three cities shall ye
give in the land of Canaan, *which* shall
be cities of refuge.

15 These six cities shall be a refuge, *both* for the children of Israel, and for the stranger, and for the sojourner among them: that every one that killeth any person unawares may flee thither.

16 And if he smite him with an instrument of iron, so that he die, he *is* a murderer: the murderer shall surely be put to death.

17 And if he smite him with throwing a stone, wherewith he may die, and he die, he *is* a murderer: the murderer shall surely be put to death.

18 Or *if* he smite him with an hand weapon of wood, wherewith he may die, and he die, he *is* a murderer: the murderer shall surely be put to death.

19 The revenger of blood himself shall slay the murderer: when he meeteth him, he shall slay him.

20 But if he thrust him of hatred, or hurl at him by laying of wait, that he die;

21 Or in enmity smite him with his hand, that he die: he that smote *him* shall surely be put to death; *for* he *is* a murderer: the revenger of blood shall slay the murderer, when he meeteth him.

22 But if he thrust him suddenly without enmity, or have cast upon him any thing without laying of wait,

23 Or with any stone, wherewith a man may die, seeing *him* not, and cast *it* upon him, that he die, and *was* not his enemy, neither sought his harm:

24 Then the congregation shall judge between the slayer and the revenger of blood according to these judgments:

25 And the congregation shall deliver the slayer out of the hand of the revenger of blood, and the congregation shall restore him to the city of his refuge, whither he was fled: and he shall abide in it unto the death of the high priest, which was anointed with the holy oil.

26 But if the slayer shall at any time come without the border of the city of his refuge, whither he was fled;

27 And the revenger of blood find him without the borders of the city of his refuge, and the revenger of blood kill the slayer; he shall not be guilty of blood:

28 Because he should have remained in the city of his refuge until the death of the high priest: but after the death of the high priest the slayer shall return into the land of his possession.

29 So these *things* shall be for a statute of judgment unto you throughout your generations in all your dwellings.

30 Whoso killeth any person, the murderer shall be put to death by the mouth of witnesses: but one witness shall not testify against any person *to cause him* to die.

31 Moreover ye shall take no satisfaction for the life of a murderer, which *is* guilty of death: but he shall be surely put to death.

32 And ye shall take no satisfaction for him that is fled to the city of his refuge, that he should come again to dwell in the land, until the death of the priest.

33 So ye shall not pollute the land wherein ye *are*: for blood it defileth the land: and the land cannot be cleansed of the blood that is shed therein, but by the blood of him that shed it.

34 Defile not therefore the land which ye shall inhabit, wherein I dwell: for I the LORD dwell among the children of Israel.

36 And the chief fathers of the
families of the children of Gilead,
the son of Machir, the son of Manasseh,
of the families of the sons of Joseph,
came near, and spake before Moses,
and before the princes, the chief
fathers of the children of Israel:
2 And they said, The LORD commanded my lord to give the land for an
inheritance by lot to the children of
Israel: and my lord was commanded by
the LORD to give the inheritance of
Zelophehad our brother unto his
daughters.
3 And if they be married to any of the
sons of the *other* tribes of the children
of Israel, then shall their inheritance be
taken from the inheritance of our
fathers, and shall be put to the inheritance of the tribe whereunto they are
received: so shall it be taken from the
lot of our inheritance.
4 And when the jubile of the children
of Israel shall be, then shall their
inheritance be put unto the inheritance of the tribe whereunto they are
received: so shall their inheritance be
taken away from the inheritance of the
tribe of our fathers.
5 And Moses commanded the children of Israel according to the word of
the LORD, saying, The tribe of the sons
of Joseph hath said well.
6 This *is* the thing which the LORD
doth command concerning the daughters of Zelophehad, saying, Let them
marry to whom they think best; only to
the family of the tribe of their father
shall they marry.
7 So shall not the inheritance of the
children of Israel remove from tribe to
tribe: for every one of the children of
Israel shall keep himself to the inheritance of the tribe of his fathers.
8 And every daughter, that possesseth
an inheritance in any tribe of the children of Israel, shall be wife unto one of
the family of the tribe of her father,
that the children of Israel may enjoy
every man the inheritance of his
fathers.
9 Neither shall the inheritance remove from *one* tribe to another tribe;
but every one of the tribes of the children of Israel shall keep himself to his
own inheritance.
10 Even as the LORD commanded
Moses, so did the daughters of Zelophehad:
11 For Mahlah, Tirzah, and Hoglah,
and Milcah, and Noah, the daughters of
Zelophehad, were married unto their
father's brothers' sons:
12 *And* they were married into the
families of the sons of Manasseh the
son of Joseph, and their inheritance
remained in the tribe of the family of
their father.
13 These *are* the commandments and
the judgments, which the LORD commanded by the hand of Moses unto the
children of Israel in the plains of Moab
by Jordan *near* Jericho.

THE FIFTH BOOK OF MOSES
CALLED

DEUTERONOMY

1 These *be* the words which Moses
spake unto all Israel on this side
Jordan in the wilderness, in the plain
over against the Red *sea*, between
Paran, and Tophel, and Laban, and
Hazeroth, and Dizahab.
2 (*There are* eleven days' *journey*
from Horeb by the way of mount Seir
unto Kadesh-barnea.)
3 And it came to pass in the fortieth
year, in the eleventh month, on the first
day of the month, *that* Moses spake
unto the children of Israel, according
unto all that the LORD had given him in
commandment unto them;
4 After he had slain Sihon the king of
the Amorites, which dwelt in Heshbon,
and Og the king of Bashan, which dwelt
at Astaroth in Edrei:
5 On this side Jordan, in the land of
Moab, began Moses to declare this law,
saying,
6 The LORD our God spake unto us in
Horeb, saying, Ye have dwelt long
enough in this mount:
7 Turn you, and take your journey,
and go to the mount of the Amorites,
and unto all *the places* nigh thereunto,
in the plain, in the hills, and in the vale,
and in the south, and by the sea side, to
the land of the Canaanites, and unto
Lebanon, unto the great river, the river
Euphrates.
8 Behold, I have set the land before
you: go in and possess the land which
the LORD sware unto your fathers,
Abraham, Isaac, and Jacob, to give unto
them and to their seed after them.
9 And I spake unto you at that time,
saying, I am not able to bear you myself
alone:
10 The LORD your God hath multiplied you, and, behold, ye *are* this day
as the stars of heaven for multitude.
11 (The LORD God of your fathers
make you a thousand times so many
more as ye *are*, and bless you, as he
hath promised you!)
12 How can I myself alone bear your
cumbrance, and your burden, and your
strife?
13 Take you wise men, and understanding, and known among your
tribes, and I will make them rulers over
you.
14 And ye answered me, and said, The
thing which thou hast spoken *is* good
for us to do.
15 So I took the chief of your tribes,
wise men, and known, and made them
heads over you, captains over thousands, and captains over hundreds, and
captains over fifties, and captains over
tens, and officers among your tribes.
16 And I charged your judges at that
time, saying, Hear *the causes* between
your brethren, and judge righteously
between *every* man and his brother,
and the stranger *that is* with him.
17 Ye shall not respect persons in
judgment; *but* ye shall hear the small
as well as the great; ye shall not be
afraid of the face of man; for the judgment *is* God's: and the cause that is too
hard for you, bring *it* unto me, and I
will hear it.
18 And I commanded you at that time
all the things which ye should do.

19 And when we departed from Horeb, we went through all that great and terrible wilderness, which ye saw by the way of the mountain of the Amorites, as the LORD our God commanded us; and we came to Kadesh-barnea.

20 And I said unto you, Ye are come unto the mountain of the Amorites, which the LORD our God doth give unto us.

21 Behold, the LORD thy God hath set the land before thee: go up *and* possess *it*, as the LORD God of thy fathers hath said unto thee; fear not, neither be discouraged.

22 And ye came near unto me every one of you, and said, We will send men before us, and they shall search us out the land, and bring us word again by what way we must go up, and into what cities we shall come.

23 And the saying pleased me well: and I took twelve men of you, one of a tribe:

24 And they turned and went up into the mountain, and came unto the valley of Eshcol, and searched it out.

25 And they took of the fruit of the land in their hands, and brought *it* down unto us, and brought us word again, and said, *It is* a good land which the LORD our God doth give us.

26 Notwithstanding ye would not go up, but rebelled against the commandment of the LORD your God:

27 And ye murmured in your tents, and said, Because the LORD hated us, he hath brought us forth out of the land of Egypt, to deliver us into the hand of the Amorites, to destroy us.

28 Whither shall we go up? our brethren have discouraged our heart, saying, The people *is* greater and taller than we; the cities *are* great and walled up to heaven; and moreover we have seen the sons of the Anakims there.

29 Then I said unto you, Dread not, neither be afraid of them.

30 The LORD your God which goeth before you, he shall fight for you, according to all that he did for you in Egypt before your eyes;

31 And in the wilderness, where thou hast seen how that the LORD thy God bare thee, as a man doth bear his son, in all the way that ye went, until ye came into this place.

32 Yet in this thing ye did not believe the LORD your God,

33 Who went in the way before you, to search you out a place to pitch your tents *in*, in fire by night, to shew you by what way ye should go, and in a cloud by day.

34 And the LORD heard the voice of your words, and was wroth, and sware, saying,

35 Surely there shall not one of these men of this evil generation see that good land, which I sware to give unto your fathers,

36 Save Caleb the son of Jephunneh; he shall see it, and to him will I give the land that he hath trodden upon, and to his children, because he hath wholly followed the LORD.

37 Also the LORD was angry with me for your sakes, saying, Thou also shalt not go in thither.

38 *But* Joshua the son of Nun, which standeth before thee, he shall go in thither: encourage him: for he shall cause Israel to inherit it.

39 Moreover your little ones, which ye said should be a prey, and your children, which in that day had no knowledge between good and evil, they shall go in thither, and unto them will I give it, and they shall possess it.

40 But *as for* you, turn you, and take your journey into the wilderness by the way of the Red sea.

41 Then ye answered and said unto me, We have sinned against the LORD, we will go up and fight, according to all that the LORD our God commanded us. And when ye had girded on every man his weapons of war, ye were ready to go up into the hill.

42 And the LORD said unto me, Say unto them, Go not up, neither fight; for I *am* not among you; lest ye be smitten before your enemies.

43 So I spake unto you; and ye would not hear, but rebelled against the commandment of the LORD, and went presumptuously up into the hill.

44 And the Amorites, which dwelt in that mountain, came out against you, and chased you, as bees do, and destroyed you in Seir, *even* unto Hormah.

45 And ye returned and wept before the LORD; but the LORD would not hearken to your voice, nor give ear unto you.

46 So ye abode in Kadesh many days, according unto the days that ye abode *there*.

2 Then we turned, and took our journey into the wilderness by the way of the Red sea, as the LORD spake unto me: and we compassed mount Seir many days.

2 And the LORD spake unto me, saying,

3 Ye have compassed this mountain long enough: turn you northward.

4 And command thou the people, saying, Ye *are* to pass through the coast of your brethren the children of Esau, which dwell in Seir; and they shall be afraid of you: take ye good heed unto yourselves therefore:

5 Meddle not with them; for I will not give you of their land, no, not so much as a foot breadth; because I have given mount Seir unto Esau *for* a possession.

6 Ye shall buy meat of them for money, that ye may eat; and ye shall also buy water of them for money, that ye may drink.

7 For the LORD thy God hath blessed thee in all the works of thy hand: he knoweth thy walking through this great wilderness: these forty years the LORD thy God *hath been* with thee; thou hast lacked nothing.

8 And when we passed by from our brethren the children of Esau, which dwelt in Seir, through the way of the plain from Elath, and from Ezion-gaber, we turned and passed by the way of the wilderness of Moab.

9 And the LORD said unto me, Distress not the Moabites, neither contend with them in battle: for I will not give thee of their land *for* a possession; because I have given Ar unto the children of Lot *for* a possession.

10 The Emims dwelt therein in times past, a people great, and many, and tall, as the Anakims;

11 Which also were accounted giants, as the Anakims; but the Moabites call them Emims.

12 The Horims also dwelt in Seir beforetime; but the children of Esau succeeded them, when they had destroyed them from before them, and dwelt in their stead; as Israel did unto the land of his possession, which the LORD gave unto them.

13 Now rise up, *said I*, and get you over the brook Zered. And we went over the brook Zered.

14 And the space in which we came from Kadesh-barnea, until we were come over the brook Zered, *was* thirty and eight years; until all the generation of the men of war were wasted out from among the host, as the LORD sware unto them.

15 For indeed the hand of the LORD was against them, to destroy them from among the host, until they were consumed.

16 So it came to pass, when all the men of war were consumed and dead from among the people,

17 That the LORD spake unto me, saying,

18 Thou art to pass over through Ar, the coast of Moab, this day:

19 And *when* thou comest nigh over against the children of Ammon, distress them not, nor meddle with them: for I will not give thee of the land of the children of Ammon *any* possession; because I have given it unto the children of Lot *for* a possession.

20 (That also was accounted a land of giants: giants dwelt therein in old time; and the Ammonites call them Zamzummims;

21 A people great, and many, and tall, as the Anakims; but the LORD destroyed them before them; and they succeeded them, and dwelt in their stead:

22 As he did to the children of Esau, which dwelt in Seir, when he destroyed the Horims from before them; and they succeeded them, and dwelt in their stead even unto this day:

23 And the Avims which dwelt in Hazerim, *even* unto Azzah, the Caphtorims, which came forth out of Caphtor, destroyed them, and dwelt in their stead.)

24 Rise ye up, take your journey, and pass over the river Arnon: behold, I have given into thine hand Sihon the Amorite, king of Heshbon, and his land: begin to possess *it*, and contend with him in battle.

25 This day will I begin to put the dread of thee and the fear of thee upon the nations *that are* under the whole heaven, who shall hear report of thee, and shall tremble, and be in anguish because of thee.

26 And I sent messengers out of the wilderness of Kedemoth unto Sihon king of Heshbon with words of peace, saying,

27 Let me pass through thy land: I will go along by the high way, I will neither turn unto the right hand nor to the left.

28 Thou shalt sell me meat for money, that I may eat; and give me water for money, that I may drink: only I will pass through on my feet;

29 (As the children of Esau which dwell in Seir, and the Moabites which dwell in Ar, did unto me;) until I shall pass over Jordan into the land which the LORD our God giveth us.

30 But Sihon king of Heshbon would not let us pass by him: for the LORD thy God hardened his spirit, and made his heart obstinate, that he might deliver him into thy hand, as *appeareth* this day.

31 And the LORD said unto me, Behold, I have begun to give Sihon and his land before thee: begin to possess, that thou mayest inherit his land.

32 Then Sihon came out against us, he and all his people, to fight at Jahaz.

33 And the LORD our God delivered him before us; and we smote him, and his sons, and all his people.

34 And we took all his cities at that
time, and utterly destroyed the men,
and the women, and the little ones, of
every city, we left none to remain:
35 Only the cattle we took for a prey
unto ourselves, and the spoil of the cities which we took.
36 From Aroer, which *is* by the brink
of the river of Arnon, and *from* the city
that *is* by the river, even unto Gilead,
there was not one city too strong for us:
the LORD our God delivered all unto us:
37 Only unto the land of the children
of Ammon thou camest not, *nor* unto
any place of the river Jabbok, nor unto
the cities in the mountains, nor unto
whatsoever the LORD our God forbad
us.

3 Then we turned, and went up the
way to Bashan: and Og the king of
Bashan came out against us, he and all
his people, to battle at Edrei.
2 And the LORD said unto me, Fear
him not: for I will deliver him, and all
his people, and his land, into thy hand;
and thou shalt do unto him as thou
didst unto Sihon king of the Amorites,
which dwelt at Heshbon.
3 So the LORD our God delivered into
our hands Og also, the king of Bashan,
and all his people: and we smote him
until none was left to him remaining.
4 And we took all his cities at that
time, there was not a city which we
took not from them, threescore cities,
all the region of Argob, the kingdom of
Og in Bashan.
5 All these cities *were* fenced with
high walls, gates, and bars; beside
unwalled towns a great many.
6 And we utterly destroyed them, as
we did unto Sihon king of Heshbon,
utterly destroying the men, women,
and children, of every city.
7 But all the cattle, and the spoil of
the cities, we took for a prey to ourselves.
8 And we took at that time out of the
hand of the two kings of the Amorites
the land that *was* on this side Jordan,
from the river of Arnon unto mount
Hermon;
9 (*Which* Hermon the Sidonians call
Sirion; and the Amorites call it Shenir;)
10 All the cities of the plain, and all
Gilead, and all Bashan, unto Salchah
and Edrei, cities of the kingdom of Og
in Bashan.
11 For only Og king of Bashan
remained of the remnant of giants;
behold, his bedstead *was* a bedstead of
iron; *is* it not in Rabbath of the children
of Ammon? nine cubits *was* the length
thereof, and four cubits the breadth of
it, after the cubit of a man.
12 And this land, *which* we possessed
at that time, from Aroer, which *is* by the
river Arnon, and half mount Gilead,
and the cities thereof, gave I unto the
Reubenites and to the Gadites.
13 And the rest of Gilead, and all
Bashan, *being* the kingdom of Og, gave
I unto the half tribe of Manasseh; all
the region of Argob, with all Bashan,
which was called the land of giants.
14 Jair the son of Manasseh took all
the country of Argob unto the coasts of
Geshuri and Maachathi; and called
them after his own name, Bashan-
havoth-jair, unto this day.
15 And I gave Gilead unto Machir.
16 And unto the Reubenites and unto
the Gadites I gave from Gilead even
unto the river Arnon half the valley,
and the border even unto the river
Jabbok, *which is* the border of the children of Ammon;

17 The plain also, and Jordan, and the
coast *thereof*, from Chinnereth even
unto the sea of the plain, *even* the salt
sea, under Ashdoth-pisgah eastward.
18 And I commanded you at that
time, saying, The LORD your God hath
given you this land to possess it: ye
shall pass over armed before your
brethren the children of Israel, all *that*
are meet for the war.
19 But your wives, and your little
ones, and your cattle, (*for* I know that
ye have much cattle,) shall abide in
your cities which I have given you;
20 Until the LORD have given rest
unto your brethren, as well as unto you,
and *until* they also possess the land
which the LORD your God hath given
them beyond Jordan: and *then* shall ye
return every man unto his possession,
which I have given you.
21 And I commanded Joshua at that
time, saying, Thine eyes have seen all
that the LORD your God hath done unto
these two kings: so shall the LORD do
unto all the kingdoms whither thou
passest.
22 Ye shall not fear them: for the
LORD your God he shall fight for you.
23 And I besought the LORD at that
time, saying,
24 O Lord GOD, thou hast begun to
shew thy servant thy greatness, and thy
mighty hand: for what God *is there* in
heaven or in earth, that can do according to thy works, and according to thy
might?
25 I pray thee, let me go over, and see
the good land that *is* beyond Jordan,
that goodly mountain, and Lebanon.
26 But the LORD was wroth with me
for your sakes, and would not hear me:
and the LORD said unto me, Let it suffice thee; speak no more unto me of
this matter.
27 Get thee up into the top of Pisgah,
and lift up thine eyes westward, and
northward, and southward, and eastward, and behold *it* with thine eyes: for
thou shalt not go over this Jordan.
28 But charge Joshua, and encourage
him, and strengthen him: for he shall go
over before this people, and he shall
cause them to inherit the land which
thou shalt see.
29 So we abode in the valley over
against Beth-peor.

4 Now therefore hearken, O Israel,
unto the statutes and unto the
judgments, which I teach you, for to do
them, that ye may live, and go in and
possess the land which the LORD God of
your fathers giveth you.
2 Ye shall not add unto the word
which I command you, neither shall ye
diminish *ought* from it, that ye may
keep the commandments of the LORD
your God which I command you.
3 Your eyes have seen what the LORD
did because of Baal-peor: for all the
men that followed Baal-peor, the LORD
thy God hath destroyed them from
among you.
4 But ye that did cleave unto the LORD
your God *are* alive every one of you this
day.
5 Behold, I have taught you statutes
and judgments, even as the LORD my
God commanded me, that ye should do
so in the land whither ye go to possess
it.
6 Keep therefore and do *them*; for
this *is* your wisdom and your understanding in the sight of the nations,
which shall hear all these statutes, and
say, Surely this great nation *is* a wise
and understanding people.

7 For what nation *is there so* great,
who *hath* God *so* nigh unto them, as the
LORD our God *is* in all *things that* we
call upon him *for*?
8 And what nation *is there so* great,
that hath statutes and judgments *so*
righteous as all this law, which I set
before you this day?
9 Only take heed to thyself, and keep
thy soul diligently, lest thou forget the
things which thine eyes have seen, and
lest they depart from thy heart all the
days of thy life: but teach them thy
sons, and thy sons' sons;
10 *Specially* the day that thou stoodest before the LORD thy God in Horeb,
when the LORD said unto me, Gather
me the people together, and I will make
them hear my words, that they may
learn to fear me all the days that they
shall live upon the earth, and *that* they
may teach their children.
11 And ye came near and stood under
the mountain; and the mountain
burned with fire unto the midst of
heaven, with darkness, clouds, and
thick darkness.
12 And the LORD spake unto you out
of the midst of the fire: ye heard the
voice of the words, but saw no similitude; only *ye heard* a voice.
13 And he declared unto you his covenant, which he commanded you to
perform, *even* ten commandments; and
he wrote them upon two tables of
stone.
14 And the LORD commanded me at
that time to teach you statutes and
judgments, that ye might do them in
the land whither ye go over to possess
it.
15 Take ye therefore good heed unto
yourselves; for ye saw no manner of
similitude on the day *that* the LORD
spake unto you in Horeb out of the
midst of the fire:
16 Lest ye corrupt *yourselves*, and
make you a graven image, the similitude of any figure, the likeness of male
or female,
17 The likeness of any beast that *is* on
the earth, the likeness of any winged
fowl that flieth in the air,
18 The likeness of any thing that
creepeth on the ground, the likeness of
any fish that *is* in the waters beneath
the earth:
19 And lest thou lift up thine eyes
unto heaven, and when thou seest the
sun, and the moon, and the stars, *even*
all the host of heaven, shouldest be
driven to worship them, and serve
them, which the LORD thy God hath
divided unto all nations under the
whole heaven.
20 But the LORD hath taken you, and
brought you forth out of the iron furnace, *even* out of Egypt, to be unto him
a people of inheritance, as *ye are* this
day.
21 Furthermore the LORD was angry
with me for your sakes, and sware that
I should not go over Jordan, and that I
should not go in unto that good land,
which the LORD thy God giveth thee *for*
an inheritance:
22 But I must die in this land, I must
not go over Jordan: but ye shall go over,
and possess that good land.
23 Take heed unto yourselves, lest ye
forget the covenant of the LORD your
God, which he made with you, and
make you a graven image, *or* the likeness of any *thing*, which the LORD thy
God hath forbidden thee.
24 For the LORD thy God *is* a consuming fire, *even* a jealous God.

25 When thou shalt beget children,
and children's children, and ye shall
have remained long in the land, and
shall corrupt *yourselves*, and make a
graven image, *or* the likeness of any
thing, and shall do evil in the sight of
the LORD thy God, to provoke him to
anger:
26 I call heaven and earth to witness
against you this day, that ye shall soon
utterly perish from off the land whereunto ye go over Jordan to possess it; ye
shall not prolong *your* days upon it, but
shall utterly be destroyed.
27 And the LORD shall scatter you
among the nations, and ye shall be left
few in number among the heathen,
whither the LORD shall lead you.
28 And there ye shall serve gods, the
work of men's hands, wood and stone,
which neither see, nor hear, nor eat, nor
smell.
29 But if from thence thou shalt seek
the LORD thy God, thou shalt find *him*,
if thou seek him with all thy heart and
with all thy soul.
30 When thou art in tribulation, and
all these things are come upon thee,
even in the latter days, if thou turn to
the LORD thy God, and shalt be obedient unto his voice;
31 (For the LORD thy God *is* a merciful
God;) he will not forsake thee, neither
destroy thee, nor forget the covenant of
thy fathers which he sware unto them.
32 For ask now of the days that are
past, which were before thee, since the
day that God created man upon the
earth, and *ask* from the one side of
heaven unto the other, whether there
hath been *any such thing* as this great
thing *is*, or hath been heard like it?
33 Did *ever* people hear the voice of
God speaking out of the midst of the
fire, as thou hast heard, and live?
34 Or hath God assayed to go *and*
take him a nation from the midst of
another nation, by temptations, by
signs, and by wonders, and by war, and
by a mighty hand, and by a stretched
out arm, and by great terrors, according
to all that the LORD your God did for
you in Egypt before your eyes?
35 Unto thee it was shewed, that thou
mightest know that the LORD he *is* God;
there is none else beside him.
36 Out of heaven he made thee to
hear his voice, that he might instruct
thee: and upon earth he shewed thee
his great fire; and thou heardest his
words out of the midst of the fire.
37 And because he loved thy fathers,
therefore he chose their seed after
them, and brought thee out in his sight
with his mighty power out of Egypt;
38 To drive out nations from before
thee greater and mightier than thou
art, to bring thee in, to give thee their
land *for* an inheritance, as *it is* this day.
39 Know therefore this day, and consider *it* in thine heart, that the LORD he
is God in heaven above, and upon the
earth beneath: *there is* none else.
40 Thou shalt keep therefore his statutes, and his commandments, which I
command thee this day, that it may go
well with thee, and with thy children
after thee, and that thou mayest prolong *thy* days upon the earth, which the
LORD thy God giveth thee, for ever.
41 Then Moses severed three cities on
this side Jordan toward the sunrising;
42 That the slayer might flee thither,
which should kill his neighbour unawares, and hated him not in times

past; and that fleeing unto one of these
cities he might live:
43 *Namely*, Bezer in the wilderness,
in the plain country, of the Reubenites;
and Ramoth in Gilead, of the Gadites;
and Golan in Bashan, of the Manassites.
44 And this *is* the law which Moses
set before the children of Israel:
45 These *are* the testimonies, and the
statutes, and the judgments, which
Moses spake unto the children of Israel,
after they came forth out of Egypt,
46 On this side Jordan, in the valley
over against Beth-peor, in the land of
Sihon king of the Amorites, who dwelt
at Heshbon, whom Moses and the children of Israel smote, after they were
come forth out of Egypt:
47 And they possessed his land, and
the land of Og king of Bashan, two
kings of the Amorites, which *were* on
this side Jordan toward the sunrising;
48 From Aroer, which *is* by the bank
of the river Arnon, even unto mount
Sion, which *is* Hermon,
49 And all the plain on this side
Jordan eastward, even unto the sea of
the plain, under the springs of Pisgah.

5 And Moses called all Israel, and
said unto them, Hear, O Israel, the
statutes and judgments which I speak
in your ears this day, that ye may learn
them, and keep, and do them.
2 The LORD our God made a covenant
with us in Horeb.
3 The LORD made not this covenant
with our fathers, but with us, *even* us,
who *are* all of us here alive this day.
4 The LORD talked with you face to
face in the mount out of the midst of
the fire,
5 (I stood between the LORD and you
at that time, to shew you the word of
the LORD: for ye were afraid by reason
of the fire, and went not up into the
mount;) saying,
6 I *am* the LORD thy God, which
brought thee out of the land of Egypt,
from the house of bondage.
7 Thou shalt have none other gods
before me.
8 Thou shalt not make thee *any* grav-
en image, *or* any likeness *of any thing*
that *is* in heaven above, or that *is* in the
earth beneath, or that *is* in the waters
beneath the earth:
9 Thou shalt not bow down thyself
unto them, nor serve them: for I the
LORD thy God *am* a jealous God, visiting the iniquity of the fathers upon the
children unto the third and fourth *generation* of them that hate me,
10 And shewing mercy unto thousands of them that love me and keep
my commandments.
11 Thou shalt not take the name of
the LORD thy God in vain: for the LORD
will not hold *him* guiltless that taketh
his name in vain.
12 Keep the sabbath day to sanctify
it, as the LORD thy God hath commanded thee.
13 Six days thou shalt labour, and do
all thy work:
14 But the seventh day *is* the sabbath
of the LORD thy God: *in it* thou shalt not
do any work, thou, nor thy son, nor thy
daughter, nor thy manservant, nor thy
maidservant, nor thine ox, nor thine
ass, nor any of thy cattle, nor thy
stranger that *is* within thy gates; that
thy manservant and thy maidservant
may rest as well as thou.
15 And remember that thou wast a
servant in the land of Egypt, and *that*
the LORD thy God brought thee out
thence through a mighty hand and by a
stretched out arm: therefore the LORD

thy God commanded thee to keep the sabbath day.

16 Honour thy father and thy mother, as the LORD thy God hath commanded thee; that thy days may be prolonged, and that it may go well with thee, in the land which the LORD thy God giveth thee.

17 Thou shalt not kill.

18 Neither shalt thou commit adultery.

19 Neither shalt thou steal.

20 Neither shalt thou bear false witness against thy neighbour.

21 Neither shalt thou desire thy neighbour's wife, neither shalt thou covet thy neighbour's house, his field, or his manservant, or his maidservant, his ox, or his ass, or any *thing* that *is* thy neighbour's.

22 These words the LORD spake unto all your assembly in the mount out of the midst of the fire, of the cloud, and of the thick darkness, with a great voice: and he added no more. And he wrote them in two tables of stone, and delivered them unto me.

23 And it came to pass, when ye heard the voice out of the midst of the darkness, (for the mountain did burn with fire,) that ye came near unto me, *even* all the heads of your tribes, and your elders;

24 And ye said, Behold, the LORD our God hath shewed us his glory and his greatness, and we have heard his voice out of the midst of the fire: we have seen this day that God doth talk with man, and he liveth.

25 Now therefore why should we die? for this great fire will consume us: if we hear the voice of the LORD our God any more, then we shall die.

26 For who *is there of* all flesh, that hath heard the voice of the living God speaking out of the midst of the fire, as we *have*, and lived?

27 Go thou near, and hear all that the LORD our God shall say: and speak thou unto us all that the LORD our God shall speak unto thee; and we will hear *it*, and do *it*.

28 And the LORD heard the voice of your words, when ye spake unto me; and the LORD said unto me, I have heard the voice of the words of this people, which they have spoken unto thee: they have well said all that they have spoken.

29 O that there were such an heart in them, that they would fear me, and keep all my commandments always, that it might be well with them, and with their children for ever!

30 Go say to them, Get you into your tents again.

31 But as for thee, stand thou here by me, and I will speak unto thee all the commandments, and the statutes, and the judgments, which thou shalt teach them, that they may do *them* in the land which I give them to possess it.

32 Ye shall observe to do therefore as the LORD your God hath commanded you: ye shall not turn aside to the right hand or to the left.

33 Ye shall walk in all the ways which the LORD your God hath commanded you, that ye may live, and *that it may be* well with you, and *that* ye may prolong *your* days in the land which ye shall possess.

6 Now these *are* the commandments, the statutes, and the judgments, which the LORD your God commanded to teach you, that ye might do *them* in the land whither ye go to possess it:

2 That thou mightest fear the LORD thy God, to keep all his statutes and his commandments, which I command thee, thou, and thy son, and thy son's son, all the days of thy life; and that thy days may be prolonged.

3 Hear therefore, O Israel, and observe to do *it*; that it may be well with thee, and that ye may increase mightily, as the LORD God of thy fathers hath promised thee, in the land that floweth with milk and honey.

4 Hear, O Israel: The LORD our God *is* one LORD:

5 And thou shalt love the LORD thy God with all thine heart, and with all thy soul, and with all thy might.

6 And these words, which I command thee this day, shall be in thine heart:

7 And thou shalt teach them diligently unto thy children, and shalt talk of them when thou sittest in thine house, and when thou walkest by the way, and when thou liest down, and when thou risest up.

8 And thou shalt bind them for a sign upon thine hand, and they shall be as frontlets between thine eyes.

9 And thou shalt write them upon the posts of thy house, and on thy gates.

10 And it shall be, when the LORD thy God shall have brought thee into the land which he sware unto thy fathers, to Abraham, to Isaac, and to Jacob, to give thee great and goodly cities, which thou buildedst not,

11 And houses full of all good *things*, which thou filledst not, and wells digged, which thou diggedst not, vineyards and olive trees, which thou plantedst not; when thou shalt have eaten and be full;

12 *Then* beware lest thou forget the LORD, which brought thee forth out of the land of Egypt, from the house of bondage.

13 Thou shalt fear the LORD thy God, and serve him, and shalt swear by his name.

14 Ye shall not go after other gods, of the gods of the people which *are* round about you;

15 (For the LORD thy God *is* a jealous God among you) lest the anger of the LORD thy God be kindled against thee, and destroy thee from off the face of the earth.

16 Ye shall not tempt the LORD your God, as ye tempted *him* in Massah.

17 Ye shall diligently keep the commandments of the LORD your God, and his testimonies, and his statutes, which he hath commanded thee.

18 And thou shalt do *that which is* right and good in the sight of the LORD: that it may be well with thee, and that thou mayest go in and possess the good land which the LORD sware unto thy fathers,

19 To cast out all thine enemies from before thee, as the LORD hath spoken.

20 *And* when thy son asketh thee in time to come, saying, What *mean* the testimonies, and the statutes, and the judgments, which the LORD our God hath commanded you?

21 Then thou shalt say unto thy son, We were Pharaoh's bondmen in Egypt; and the LORD brought us out of Egypt with a mighty hand:

22 And the LORD shewed signs and wonders, great and sore, upon Egypt, upon Pharaoh, and upon all his household, before our eyes:

23 And he brought us out from thence, that he might bring us in, to give us the land which he sware unto our fathers.

24 And the LORD commanded us to do
all these statutes, to fear the LORD our
God, for our good always, that he might
preserve us alive, as *it is* at this day.
25 And it shall be our righteousness,
if we observe to do all these commandments before the LORD our God, as he
hath commanded us.

7 When the LORD thy God shall bring
thee into the land whither thou
goest to possess it, and hath cast out
many nations before thee, the Hittites,
and the Girgashites, and the Amorites,
and the Canaanites, and the Perizzites,
and the Hivites, and the Jebusites,
seven nations greater and mightier
than thou;
2 And when the LORD thy God shall
deliver them before thee; thou shalt
smite them, *and* utterly destroy them;
thou shalt make no covenant with
them, nor shew mercy unto them:
3 Neither shalt thou make marriages
with them; thy daughter thou shalt not
give unto his son, nor his daughter shalt
thou take unto thy son.
4 For they will turn away thy son from
following me, that they may serve other
gods: so will the anger of the LORD be
kindled against you, and destroy thee
suddenly.
5 But thus shall ye deal with them; ye
shall destroy their altars, and break
down their images, and cut down their
groves, and burn their graven images
with fire.
6 For thou *art* an holy people unto the
LORD thy God: the LORD thy God hath
chosen thee to be a special people unto
himself, above all people that *are* upon
the face of the earth.
7 The LORD did not set his love upon
you, nor choose you, because ye were
more in number than any people; for ye
were the fewest of all people:
8 But because the LORD loved you,
and because he would keep the oath
which he had sworn unto your fathers,
hath the LORD brought you out with a
mighty hand, and redeemed you out of
the house of bondmen, from the hand
of Pharaoh king of Egypt.
9 Know therefore that the LORD thy
God, he *is* God, the faithful God, which
keepeth covenant and mercy with them
that love him and keep his commandments to a thousand generations;
10 And repayeth them that hate him
to their face, to destroy them: he will
not be slack to him that hateth him, he
will repay him to his face.
11 Thou shalt therefore keep the commandments, and the statutes, and the
judgments, which I command thee this
day, to do them.
12 Wherefore it shall come to pass, if
ye hearken to these judgments, and
keep, and do them, that the LORD thy
God shall keep unto thee the covenant
and the mercy which he sware unto thy
fathers:
13 And he will love thee, and bless
thee, and multiply thee: he will also
bless the fruit of thy womb, and the
fruit of thy land, thy corn, and thy wine,
and thine oil, the increase of thy kine,
and the flocks of thy sheep, in the land
which he sware unto thy fathers to give
thee.
14 Thou shalt be blessed above all
people: there shall not be male or
female barren among you, or among
your cattle.
15 And the LORD will take away from
thee all sickness, and will put none of
the evil diseases of Egypt, which thou

knowest, upon thee; but will lay them upon all *them* that hate thee.

16 And thou shalt consume all the people which the LORD thy God shall deliver thee; thine eye shall have no pity upon them: neither shalt thou serve their gods; for that *will be* a snare unto thee.

17 If thou shalt say in thine heart, These nations *are* more than I; how can I dispossess them?

18 Thou shalt not be afraid of them: *but* shalt well remember what the LORD thy God did unto Pharaoh, and unto all Egypt;

19 The great temptations which thine eyes saw, and the signs, and the wonders, and the mighty hand, and the stretched out arm, whereby the LORD thy God brought thee out: so shall the LORD thy God do unto all the people of whom thou art afraid.

20 Moreover the LORD thy God will send the hornet among them, until they that are left, and hide themselves from thee, be destroyed.

21 Thou shalt not be affrighted at them: for the LORD thy God *is* among you, a mighty God and terrible.

22 And the LORD thy God will put out those nations before thee by little and little: thou mayest not consume them at once, lest the beasts of the field increase upon thee.

23 But the LORD thy God shall deliver them unto thee, and shall destroy them with a mighty destruction, until they be destroyed.

24 And he shall deliver their kings into thine hand, and thou shalt destroy their name from under heaven: there shall no man be able to stand before thee, until thou have destroyed them.

25 The graven images of their gods shall ye burn with fire: thou shalt not desire the silver or gold *that is* on them, nor take *it* unto thee, lest thou be snared therein: for it *is* an abomination to the LORD thy God.

26 Neither shalt thou bring an abomination into thine house, lest thou be a cursed thing like it: *but* thou shalt utterly detest it, and thou shalt utterly abhor it; for it *is* a cursed thing.

8 All the commandments which I command thee this day shall ye observe to do, that ye may live, and multiply, and go in and possess the land which the LORD sware unto your fathers.

2 And thou shalt remember all the way which the LORD thy God led thee these forty years in the wilderness, to humble thee, *and* to prove thee, to know what *was* in thine heart, whether thou wouldest keep his commandments, or no.

3 And he humbled thee, and suffered thee to hunger, and fed thee with manna, which thou knewest not, neither did thy fathers know; that he might make thee know that man doth not live by bread only, but by every *word* that proceedeth out of the mouth of the LORD doth man live.

4 Thy raiment waxed not old upon thee, neither did thy foot swell, these forty years.

5 Thou shalt also consider in thine heart, that, as a man chasteneth his son, *so* the LORD thy God chasteneth thee.

6 Therefore thou shalt keep the commandments of the LORD thy God, to walk in his ways, and to fear him.

7 For the LORD thy God bringeth thee into a good land, a land of brooks of

water, of fountains and depths that
spring out of valleys and hills;
8 A land of wheat, and barley, and
vines, and fig trees, and pomegranates;
a land of oil olive, and honey;
9 A land wherein thou shalt eat bread
without scarceness, thou shalt not lack
any *thing* in it; a land whose stones *are*
iron, and out of whose hills thou mayest
dig brass.
10 When thou hast eaten and art full,
then thou shalt bless the LORD thy God
for the good land which he hath given
thee.
11 Beware that thou forget not the
LORD thy God, in not keeping his commandments, and his judgments, and
his statutes, which I command thee this
day:
12 Lest *when* thou hast eaten and art
full, and hast built goodly houses, and
dwelt *therein*;
13 And *when* thy herds and thy flocks
multiply, and thy silver and thy gold is
multiplied, and all that thou hast is
multiplied;
14 Then thine heart be lifted up, and
thou forget the LORD thy God, which
brought thee forth out of the land of
Egypt, from the house of bondage;
15 Who led thee through that great
and terrible wilderness, *wherein were*
fiery serpents, and scorpions, and
drought, where *there was* no water;
who brought thee forth water out of the
rock of flint;
16 Who fed thee in the wilderness
with manna, which thy fathers knew
not, that he might humble thee, and
that he might prove thee, to do thee
good at thy latter end;
17 And thou say in thine heart, My
power and the might of *mine* hand
hath gotten me this wealth.
18 But thou shalt remember the LORD
thy God: for *it is* he that giveth thee
power to get wealth, that he may establish his covenant which he sware unto
thy fathers, as *it is* this day.
19 And it shall be, if thou do at all
forget the LORD thy God, and walk after
other gods, and serve them, and worship them, I testify against you this day
that ye shall surely perish.
20 As the nations which the LORD
destroyeth before your face, so shall ye
perish; because ye would not be obedient unto the voice of the LORD your
God.

9 Hear, O Israel: Thou *art* to pass over
Jordan this day, to go in to possess
nations greater and mightier than
thyself, cities great and fenced up to
heaven,
2 A people great and tall, the children
of the Anakims, whom thou knowest,
and *of whom* thou hast heard *say*, Who
can stand before the children of Anak!
3 Understand therefore this day, that
the LORD thy God *is* he which goeth
over before thee; *as* a consuming fire
he shall destroy them, and he shall
bring them down before thy face: so
shalt thou drive them out, and destroy
them quickly, as the LORD hath said
unto thee.
4 Speak not thou in thine heart, after
that the LORD thy God hath cast them
out from before thee, saying, For my
righteousness the LORD hath brought
me in to possess this land: but for the
wickedness of these nations the LORD
doth drive them out from before thee.
5 Not for thy righteousness, or for the
uprightness of thine heart, dost thou go
to possess their land: but for the wickedness of these nations the LORD thy
God doth drive them out from before

thee, and that he may perform the word
which the LORD sware unto thy fathers,
Abraham, Isaac, and Jacob.
6 Understand therefore, that the
LORD thy God giveth thee not this good
land to possess it for thy righteousness;
for thou *art* a stiffnecked people.
7 Remember, *and* forget not, how
thou provokedst the LORD thy God to
wrath in the wilderness: from the day
that thou didst depart out of the land of
Egypt, until ye came unto this place, ye
have been rebellious against the LORD.
8 Also in Horeb ye provoked the LORD
to wrath, so that the LORD was angry
with you to have destroyed you.
9 When I was gone up into the mount
to receive the tables of stone, *even* the
tables of the covenant which the LORD
made with you, then I abode in the
mount forty days and forty nights, I
neither did eat bread nor drink water:
10 And the LORD delivered unto me
two tables of stone written with the
finger of God; and on them *was written*
according to all the words, which the
LORD spake with you in the mount out
of the midst of the fire in the day of the
assembly.
11 And it came to pass at the end of
forty days and forty nights, *that* the
LORD gave me the two tables of stone,
even the tables of the covenant.
12 And the LORD said unto me, Arise,
get thee down quickly from hence; for
thy people which thou hast brought
forth out of Egypt have corrupted
themselves; they are quickly turned
aside out of the way which I commanded them; they have made them a molten image.
13 Furthermore the LORD spake unto
me, saying, I have seen this people, and,
behold, it *is* a stiffnecked people:
14 Let me alone, that I may destroy
them, and blot out their name from
under heaven: and I will make of thee
a nation mightier and greater than
they.
15 So I turned and came down from
the mount, and the mount burned with
fire: and the two tables of the covenant
were in my two hands.
16 And I looked, and, behold, ye had
sinned against the LORD your God, *and*
had made you a molten calf: ye had
turned aside quickly out of the way
which the LORD had commanded you.
17 And I took the two tables, and cast
them out of my two hands, and brake
them before your eyes.
18 And I fell down before the LORD, as
at the first, forty days and forty nights:
I did neither eat bread, nor drink water,
because of all your sins which ye
sinned, in doing wickedly in the sight of
the LORD, to provoke him to anger.
19 For I was afraid of the anger and
hot displeasure, wherewith the LORD
was wroth against you to destroy you.
But the LORD hearkened unto me at
that time also.
20 And the LORD was very angry with
Aaron to have destroyed him: and I
prayed for Aaron also the same time.
21 And I took your sin, the calf which
ye had made, and burnt it with fire, and
stamped it, *and* ground *it* very small,
even until it was as small as dust: and I
cast the dust thereof into the brook
that descended out of the mount.
22 And at Taberah, and at Massah,
and at Kibroth-hattaavah, ye provoked
the LORD to wrath.
23 Likewise when the LORD sent you
from Kadesh-barnea, saying, Go up and
possess the land which I have given
you; then ye rebelled against the com-

mandment of the LORD your God, and
ye believed him not, nor hearkened to
his voice.
24 Ye have been rebellious against
the LORD from the day that I knew you.
25 Thus I fell down before the LORD
forty days and forty nights, as I fell
down *at the first*; because the LORD
had said he would destroy you.
26 I prayed therefore unto the LORD,
and said, O Lord GOD, destroy not thy
people and thine inheritance, which
thou hast redeemed through thy greatness, which thou hast brought forth out
of Egypt with a mighty hand.
27 Remember thy servants, Abraham,
Isaac, and Jacob; look not unto the
stubbornness of this people, nor to
their wickedness, nor to their sin:
28 Lest the land whence thou broughtest us out say, Because the LORD was
not able to bring them into the land
which he promised them, and because
he hated them, he hath brought them
out to slay them in the wilderness.
29 Yet they *are* thy people and thine
inheritance, which thou broughtest out
by thy mighty power and by thy
stretched out arm.

10 At that time the LORD said unto
me, Hew thee two tables of stone
like unto the first, and come up unto
me into the mount, and make thee an
ark of wood.
2 And I will write on the tables the
words that were in the first tables
which thou brakest, and thou shalt put
them in the ark.
3 And I made an ark *of* shittim wood,
and hewed two tables of stone like unto
the first, and went up into the mount,
having the two tables in mine hand.
4 And he wrote on the tables, according to the first writing, the ten commandments, which the LORD spake
unto you in the mount out of the midst
of the fire in the day of the assembly:
and the LORD gave them unto me.
5 And I turned myself and came
down from the mount, and put the
tables in the ark which I had made; and
there they be, as the LORD commanded
me.
6 And the children of Israel took their
journey from Beeroth of the children of
Jaakan to Mosera: there Aaron died,
and there he was buried; and Eleazar
his son ministered in the priest's office
in his stead.
7 From thence they journeyed unto
Gudgodah; and from Gudgodah to
Jotbath, a land of rivers of waters.
8 At that time the LORD separated the
tribe of Levi, to bear the ark of the
covenant of the LORD, to stand before
the LORD to minister unto him, and to
bless in his name, unto this day.
9 Wherefore Levi hath no part nor
inheritance with his brethren; the LORD
is his inheritance, according as the
LORD thy God promised him.
10 And I stayed in the mount, according to the first time, forty days and
forty nights; and the LORD hearkened
unto me at that time also, *and* the LORD
would not destroy thee.
11 And the LORD said unto me, Arise,
take *thy* journey before the people,
that they may go in and possess the
land, which I sware unto their fathers to
give unto them.
12 And now, Israel, what doth the
LORD thy God require of thee, but to
fear the LORD thy God, to walk in all his
ways, and to love him, and to serve the
LORD thy God with all thy heart and
with all thy soul,

13 To keep the commandments of the LORD, and his statutes, which I command thee this day for thy good?

14 Behold, the heaven and the heaven of heavens *is* the LORD's thy God, the earth *also*, with all that therein *is*.

15 Only the LORD had a delight in thy fathers to love them, and he chose their seed after them, *even* you above all people, as *it is* this day.

16 Circumcise therefore the foreskin of your heart, and be no more stiffnecked.

17 For the LORD your God *is* God of gods, and Lord of lords, a great God, a mighty, and a terrible, which regardeth not persons, nor taketh reward:

18 He doth execute the judgment of the fatherless and widow, and loveth the stranger, in giving him food and raiment.

19 Love ye therefore the stranger: for ye were strangers in the land of Egypt.

20 Thou shalt fear the LORD thy God; him shalt thou serve, and to him shalt thou cleave, and swear by his name.

21 He *is* thy praise, and he *is* thy God, that hath done for thee these great and terrible things, which thine eyes have seen.

22 Thy fathers went down into Egypt with threescore and ten persons; and now the LORD thy God hath made thee as the stars of heaven for multitude.

11 Therefore thou shalt love the LORD thy God, and keep his charge, and his statutes, and his judgments, and his commandments, alway.

2 And know ye this day: for *I speak* not with your children which have not known, and which have not seen the chastisement of the LORD your God, his greatness, his mighty hand, and his stretched out arm,

3 And his miracles, and his acts, which he did in the midst of Egypt unto Pharaoh the king of Egypt, and unto all his land;

4 And what he did unto the army of Egypt, unto their horses, and to their chariots; how he made the water of the Red sea to overflow them as they pursued after you, and *how* the LORD hath destroyed them unto this day;

5 And what he did unto you in the wilderness, until ye came into this place;

6 And what he did unto Dathan and Abiram, the sons of Eliab, the son of Reuben: how the earth opened her mouth, and swallowed them up, and their households, and their tents, and all the substance that *was* in their possession, in the midst of all Israel:

7 But your eyes have seen all the great acts of the LORD which he did.

8 Therefore shall ye keep all the commandments which I command you this day, that ye may be strong, and go in and possess the land, whither ye go to possess it;

9 And that ye may prolong *your* days in the land, which the LORD sware unto your fathers to give unto them and to their seed, a land that floweth with milk and honey.

10 For the land, whither thou goest in to possess it, *is* not as the land of Egypt, from whence ye came out, where thou sowedst thy seed, and wateredst *it* with thy foot, as a garden of herbs:

11 But the land, whither ye go to possess it, *is* a land of hills and valleys, *and* drinketh water of the rain of heaven:

12 A land which the LORD thy God careth for: the eyes of the LORD thy God *are* always upon it, from the beginning

of the year even unto the end of the
year.
13 And it shall come to pass, if ye
shall hearken diligently unto my commandments which I command you this
day, to love the LORD your God, and to
serve him with all your heart and with
all your soul,
14 That I will give *you* the rain of your
land in his due season, the first rain and
the latter rain, that thou mayest gather
in thy corn, and thy wine, and thine oil.
15 And I will send grass in thy fields
for thy cattle, that thou mayest eat and
be full.
16 Take heed to yourselves, that your
heart be not deceived, and ye turn
aside, and serve other gods, and worship them;
17 And *then* the LORD's wrath be kindled against you, and he shut up the
heaven, that there be no rain, and that
the land yield not her fruit; and *lest* ye
perish quickly from off the good land
which the LORD giveth you.
18 Therefore shall ye lay up these my
words in your heart and in your soul,
and bind them for a sign upon your
hand, that they may be as frontlets
between your eyes.
19 And ye shall teach them your children, speaking of them when thou sittest in thine house, and when thou
walkest by the way, when thou liest
down, and when thou risest up.
20 And thou shalt write them upon
the door posts of thine house, and upon
thy gates:
21 That your days may be multiplied,
and the days of your children, in the
land which the LORD sware unto your
fathers to give them, as the days of
heaven upon the earth.
22 For if ye shall diligently keep all
these commandments which I command you, to do them, to love the LORD
your God, to walk in all his ways, and to
cleave unto him;
23 Then will the LORD drive out all
these nations from before you, and ye
shall possess greater nations and
mightier than yourselves.
24 Every place whereon the soles of
your feet shall tread shall be yours:
from the wilderness and Lebanon, from
the river, the river Euphrates, even
unto the uttermost sea shall your coast
be.
25 There shall no man be able to
stand before you: *for* the LORD your
God shall lay the fear of you and the
dread of you upon all the land that ye
shall tread upon, as he hath said unto
you.
26 Behold, I set before you this day a
blessing and a curse;
27 A blessing, if ye obey the commandments of the LORD your God,
which I command you this day:
28 And a curse, if ye will not obey the
commandments of the LORD your God,
but turn aside out of the way which I
command you this day, to go after other
gods, which ye have not known.
29 And it shall come to pass, when the
LORD thy God hath brought thee in
unto the land whither thou goest to
possess it, that thou shalt put the blessing upon mount Gerizim, and the curse
upon mount Ebal.
30 *Are* they not on the other side
Jordan, by the way where the sun goeth
down, in the land of the Canaanites,
which dwell in the champaign over
against Gilgal, beside the plains of
Moreh?

31 For ye shall pass over Jordan to go
in to possess the land which the LORD
your God giveth you, and ye shall possess it, and dwell therein.
32 And ye shall observe to do all the
statutes and judgments which I set
before you this day.

12 These *are* the statutes and judgments, which ye shall observe to
do in the land, which the LORD God of
thy fathers giveth thee to possess it, all
the days that ye live upon the earth.
2 Ye shall utterly destroy all the places, wherein the nations which ye shall
possess served their gods, upon the
high mountains, and upon the hills, and
under every green tree:
3 And ye shall overthrow their altars,
and break their pillars, and burn their
groves with fire; and ye shall hew down
the graven images of their gods, and
destroy the names of them out of that
place.
4 Ye shall not do so unto the LORD
your God.
5 But unto the place which the LORD
your God shall choose out of all your
tribes to put his name there, *even* unto
his habitation shall ye seek, and thither
thou shalt come:
6 And thither ye shall bring your
burnt offerings, and your sacrifices,
and your tithes, and heave offerings of
your hand, and your vows, and your
freewill offerings, and the firstlings of
your herds and of your flocks:
7 And there ye shall eat before the
LORD your God, and ye shall rejoice in
all that ye put your hand unto, ye and
your households, wherein the LORD thy
God hath blessed thee.
8 Ye shall not do after all *the things*
that we do here this day, every man
whatsoever *is* right in his own eyes.
9 For ye are not as yet come to the
rest and to the inheritance, which the
LORD your God giveth you.
10 But *when* ye go over Jordan, and
dwell in the land which the LORD your
God giveth you to inherit, and *when* he
giveth you rest from all your enemies
round about, so that ye dwell in safety;
11 Then there shall be a place which
the LORD your God shall choose to
cause his name to dwell there; thither
shall ye bring all that I command you;
your burnt offerings, and your sacrifices, your tithes, and the heave offering
of your hand, and all your choice vows
which ye vow unto the LORD:
12 And ye shall rejoice before the
LORD your God, ye, and your sons, and
your daughters, and your menservants,
and your maidservants, and the Levite
that *is* within your gates; forasmuch as
he hath no part nor inheritance with
you.
13 Take heed to thyself that thou
offer not thy burnt offerings in every
place that thou seest:
14 But in the place which the LORD
shall choose in one of thy tribes, there
thou shalt offer thy burnt offerings,
and there thou shalt do all that I command thee.
15 Notwithstanding thou mayest kill
and eat flesh in all thy gates, whatsoever thy soul lusteth after, according to
the blessing of the LORD thy God which
he hath given thee: the unclean and the
clean may eat thereof, as of the roebuck, and as of the hart.
16 Only ye shall not eat the blood; ye
shall pour it upon the earth as water.
17 Thou mayest not eat within thy
gates the tithe of thy corn, or of thy
wine, or of thy oil, or the firstlings of
thy herds or of thy flock, nor any of thy

vows which thou vowest, nor thy freewill offerings, or heave offering of
thine hand:
18 But thou must eat them before the
LORD thy God in the place which the
LORD thy God shall choose, thou, and
thy son, and thy daughter, and thy manservant, and thy maidservant, and the
Levite that *is* within thy gates: and
thou shalt rejoice before the LORD thy
God in all that thou puttest thine hands
unto.
19 Take heed to thyself that thou forsake not the Levite as long as thou livest upon the earth.
20 When the LORD thy God shall
enlarge thy border, as he hath promised
thee, and thou shalt say, I will eat flesh,
because thy soul longeth to eat flesh;
thou mayest eat flesh, whatsoever thy
soul lusteth after.
21 If the place which the LORD thy
God hath chosen to put his name there
be too far from thee, then thou shalt
kill of thy herd and of thy flock, which
the LORD hath given thee, as I have
commanded thee, and thou shalt eat in
thy gates whatsoever thy soul lusteth
after.
22 Even as the roebuck and the hart
is eaten, so thou shalt eat them: the
unclean and the clean shall eat *of* them
alike.
23 Only be sure that thou eat not the
blood: for the blood *is* the life; and thou
mayest not eat the life with the flesh.
24 Thou shalt not eat it; thou shalt
pour it upon the earth as water.
25 Thou shalt not eat it; that it may go
well with thee, and with thy children
after thee, when thou shalt do *that
which is* right in the sight of the LORD.
26 Only thy holy things which thou
hast, and thy vows, thou shalt take, and
go unto the place which the LORD shall
choose:
27 And thou shalt offer thy burnt
offerings, the flesh and the blood, upon
the altar of the LORD thy God: and the
blood of thy sacrifices shall be poured
out upon the altar of the LORD thy God,
and thou shalt eat the flesh.
28 Observe and hear all these words
which I command thee, that it may go
well with thee, and with thy children
after thee for ever, when thou doest
that which is good and right in the
sight of the LORD thy God.
29 When the LORD thy God shall cut
off the nations from before thee, whither thou goest to possess them, and thou
succeedest them, and dwellest in their
land;
30 Take heed to thyself that thou be
not snared by following them, after that
they be destroyed from before thee;
and that thou enquire not after their
gods, saying, How did these nations
serve their gods? even so will I do likewise.
31 Thou shalt not do so unto the LORD
thy God: for every abomination to the
LORD, which he hateth, have they done
unto their gods; for even their sons and
their daughters they have burnt in the
fire to their gods.
32 What thing soever I command you,
observe to do it: thou shalt not add
thereto, nor diminish from it.

13 If there arise among you a prophet, or a dreamer of dreams, and
giveth thee a sign or a wonder,
2 And the sign or the wonder come to
pass, whereof he spake unto thee, saying, Let us go after other gods, which
thou hast not known, and let us serve
them;

3 Thou shalt not hearken unto the
words of that prophet, or that dreamer
of dreams: for the LORD your God
proveth you, to know whether ye love
the LORD your God with all your heart
and with all your soul.
4 Ye shall walk after the LORD your
God, and fear him, and keep his commandments, and obey his voice, and ye
shall serve him, and cleave unto him.
5 And that prophet, or that dreamer
of dreams, shall be put to death;
because he hath spoken to turn *you*
away from the LORD your God, which
brought you out of the land of Egypt,
and redeemed you out of the house of
bondage, to thrust thee out of the way
which the LORD thy God commanded
thee to walk in. So shalt thou put the
evil away from the midst of thee.
6 If thy brother, the son of thy mother,
or thy son, or thy daughter, or the wife
of thy bosom, or thy friend, which *is* as
thine own soul, entice thee secretly,
saying, Let us go and serve other gods,
which thou hast not known, thou, nor
thy fathers;
7 *Namely*, of the gods of the people
which *are* round about you, nigh unto
thee, or far off from thee, from the *one*
end of the earth even unto the *other*
end of the earth;
8 Thou shalt not consent unto him,
nor hearken unto him; neither shall
thine eye pity him, neither shalt thou
spare, neither shalt thou conceal him:
9 But thou shalt surely kill him; thine
hand shall be first upon him to put him
to death, and afterwards the hand of all
the people.
10 And thou shalt stone him with
stones, that he die; because he hath
sought to thrust thee away from the
LORD thy God, which brought thee out
of the land of Egypt, from the house of
bondage.
11 And all Israel shall hear, and fear,
and shall do no more any such wickedness as this is among you.
12 If thou shalt hear *say* in one of thy
cities, which the LORD thy God hath
given thee to dwell there, saying,
13 *Certain* men, the children of Belial,
are gone out from among you, and have
withdrawn the inhabitants of their city,
saying, Let us go and serve other gods,
which ye have not known;
14 Then shalt thou enquire, and make
search, and ask diligently; and, behold,
if it be truth, *and* the thing certain,
that such abomination is wrought
among you;
15 Thou shalt surely smite the inhabitants of that city with the edge of the
sword, destroying it utterly, and all that
is therein, and the cattle thereof, with
the edge of the sword.
16 And thou shalt gather all the spoil
of it into the midst of the street thereof,
and shalt burn with fire the city, and all
the spoil thereof every whit, for the
LORD thy God: and it shall be an heap
for ever; it shall not be built again.
17 And there shall cleave nought of
the cursed thing to thine hand: that the
LORD may turn from the fierceness of
his anger, and shew thee mercy, and
have compassion upon thee, and multiply thee, as he hath sworn unto thy
fathers;
18 When thou shalt hearken to the
voice of the LORD thy God, to keep all
his commandments which I command
thee this day, to do *that which is* right
in the eyes of the LORD thy God.

14 Ye *are* the children of the LORD
your God: ye shall not cut yourselves, nor make any baldness between
your eyes for the dead.
2 For thou *art* an holy people unto the
LORD thy God, and the LORD hath chosen thee to be a peculiar people unto
himself, above all the nations that *are*
upon the earth.
3 Thou shalt not eat any abominable
thing.
4 These *are* the beasts which ye shall
eat: the ox, the sheep, and the goat,
5 The hart, and the roebuck, and the
fallow deer, and the wild goat, and the
pygarg, and the wild ox, and the cham-
ois.
6 And every beast that parteth the
hoof, and cleaveth the cleft into two
claws, *and* cheweth the cud among the
beasts, that ye shall eat.
7 Nevertheless these ye shall not eat
of them that chew the cud, or of them
that divide the cloven hoof; *as* the
camel, and the hare, and the coney: for
they chew the cud, but divide not the
hoof; *therefore* they *are* unclean unto
you.
8 And the swine, because it divideth
the hoof, yet cheweth not the cud, it *is*
unclean unto you: ye shall not eat of
their flesh, nor touch their dead carcase.
9 These ye shall eat of all that *are* in
the waters: all that have fins and scales
shall ye eat:
10 And whatsoever hath not fins and
scales ye may not eat; it *is* unclean unto
you.
11 *Of* all clean birds ye shall eat.
12 But these *are they* of which ye
shall not eat: the eagle, and the ossi-
frage, and the ospray,
13 And the glede, and the kite, and
the vulture after his kind,
14 And every raven after his kind,
15 And the owl, and the night hawk,
and the cuckow, and the hawk after his
kind,
16 The little owl, and the great owl,
and the swan,
17 And the pelican, and the gier
eagle, and the cormorant,
18 And the stork, and the heron after
her kind, and the lapwing, and the bat.
19 And every creeping thing that
flieth *is* unclean unto you: they shall
not be eaten.
20 *But of* all clean fowls ye may eat.
21 Ye shall not eat *of* any thing that
dieth of itself: thou shalt give it unto
the stranger that *is* in thy gates, that he
may eat it; or thou mayest sell it unto
an alien: for thou *art* an holy people
unto the LORD thy God. Thou shalt not
seethe a kid in his mother's milk.
22 Thou shalt truly tithe all the increase of thy seed, that the field
bringeth forth year by year.
23 And thou shalt eat before the LORD
thy God, in the place which he shall
choose to place his name there, the
tithe of thy corn, of thy wine, and of
thine oil, and the firstlings of thy herds
and of thy flocks; that thou mayest
learn to fear the LORD thy God always.
24 And if the way be too long for thee,
so that thou art not able to carry it; *or* if
the place be too far from thee, which
the LORD thy God shall choose to set his
name there, when the LORD thy God
hath blessed thee:
25 Then shalt thou turn *it* into money,
and bind up the money in thine hand,
and shalt go unto the place which the
LORD thy God shall choose:

26 And thou shalt bestow that money for whatsoever thy soul lusteth after, for oxen, or for sheep, or for wine, or for strong drink, or for whatsoever thy soul desireth: and thou shalt eat there before the LORD thy God, and thou shalt rejoice, thou, and thine household,

27 And the Levite that *is* within thy gates; thou shalt not forsake him; for he hath no part nor inheritance with thee.

28 At the end of three years thou shalt bring forth all the tithe of thine increase the same year, and shalt lay *it* up within thy gates:

29 And the Levite, (because he hath no part nor inheritance with thee,) and the stranger, and the fatherless, and the widow, which *are* within thy gates, shall come, and shall eat and be satisfied; that the LORD thy God may bless thee in all the work of thine hand which thou doest.

15 At the end of *every* seven years thou shalt make a release.

2 And this *is* the manner of the release: Every creditor that lendeth *ought* unto his neighbour shall release *it*; he shall not exact *it* of his neighbour, or of his brother; because it is called the LORD's release.

3 Of a foreigner thou mayest exact *it again*: but *that* which is thine with thy brother thine hand shall release;

4 Save when there shall be no poor among you; for the LORD shall greatly bless thee in the land which the LORD thy God giveth thee *for* an inheritance to possess it:

5 Only if thou carefully hearken unto the voice of the LORD thy God, to observe to do all these commandments which I command thee this day.

6 For the LORD thy God blesseth thee, as he promised thee: and thou shalt lend unto many nations, but thou shalt not borrow; and thou shalt reign over many nations, but they shall not reign over thee.

7 If there be among you a poor man of one of thy brethren within any of thy gates in thy land which the LORD thy God giveth thee, thou shalt not harden thine heart, nor shut thine hand from thy poor brother:

8 But thou shalt open thine hand wide unto him, and shalt surely lend him sufficient for his need, *in that* which he wanteth.

9 Beware that there be not a thought in thy wicked heart, saying, The seventh year, the year of release, is at hand; and thine eye be evil against thy poor brother, and thou givest him nought; and he cry unto the LORD against thee, and it be sin unto thee.

10 Thou shalt surely give him, and thine heart shall not be grieved when thou givest unto him: because that for this thing the LORD thy God shall bless thee in all thy works, and in all that thou puttest thine hand unto.

11 For the poor shall never cease out of the land: therefore I command thee, saying, Thou shalt open thine hand wide unto thy brother, to thy poor, and to thy needy, in thy land.

12 *And* if thy brother, an Hebrew man, or an Hebrew woman, be sold unto thee, and serve thee six years; then in the seventh year thou shalt let him go free from thee.

13 And when thou sendest him out free from thee, thou shalt not let him go away empty:

14 Thou shalt furnish him liberally out of thy flock, and out of thy floor, and

out of thy winepress: *of that* wherewith
the LORD thy God hath blessed thee
thou shalt give unto him.
15 And thou shalt remember that
thou wast a bondman in the land of
Egypt, and the LORD thy God redeemed
thee: therefore I command thee this
thing to day.
16 And it shall be, if he say unto thee,
I will not go away from thee; because
he loveth thee and thine house, because
he is well with thee;
17 Then thou shalt take an aul, and
thrust *it* through his ear unto the door,
and he shall be thy servant for ever.
And also unto thy maidservant thou
shalt do likewise.
18 It shall not seem hard unto thee,
when thou sendest him away free from
thee; for he hath been worth a double
hired servant *to thee*, in serving thee
six years: and the LORD thy God shall
bless thee in all that thou doest.
19 All the firstling males that come of
thy herd and of thy flock thou shalt
sanctify unto the LORD thy God: thou
shalt do no work with the firstling of
thy bullock, nor shear the firstling of
thy sheep.
20 Thou shalt eat *it* before the LORD
thy God year by year in the place which
the LORD shall choose, thou and thy
household.
21 And if there be *any* blemish therein, *as if it be* lame, or blind, *or have* any
ill blemish, thou shalt not sacrifice it
unto the LORD thy God.
22 Thou shalt eat it within thy gates:
the unclean and the clean *person shall*
eat it alike, as the roebuck, and as the
hart.
23 Only thou shalt not eat the blood
thereof; thou shalt pour it upon the
ground as water.

16 Observe the month of Abib, and
keep the passover unto the LORD
thy God: for in the month of Abib the
LORD thy God brought thee forth out of
Egypt by night.
2 Thou shalt therefore sacrifice the
passover unto the LORD thy God, of the
flock and the herd, in the place which
the LORD shall choose to place his name
there.
3 Thou shalt eat no leavened bread
with it; seven days shalt thou eat
unleavened bread therewith, *even* the
bread of affliction; for thou camest
forth out of the land of Egypt in haste:
that thou mayest remember the day
when thou camest forth out of the land
of Egypt all the days of thy life.
4 And there shall be no leavened
bread seen with thee in all thy coast
seven days; neither shall there *any*
thing of the flesh, which thou sacri-
ficedst the first day at even, remain all
night until the morning.
5 Thou mayest not sacrifice the passover within any of thy gates, which the
LORD thy God giveth thee:
6 But at the place which the LORD thy
God shall choose to place his name in,
there thou shalt sacrifice the passover
at even, at the going down of the sun, at
the season that thou camest forth out
of Egypt.
7 And thou shalt roast and eat *it* in
the place which the LORD thy God shall
choose: and thou shalt turn in the
morning, and go unto thy tents.
8 Six days thou shalt eat unleavened
bread: and on the seventh day *shall be*
a solemn assembly to the LORD thy God:
thou shalt do no work *therein*.
9 Seven weeks shalt thou number
unto thee: begin to number the seven

weeks from *such time as* thou beginnest *to put* the sickle to the corn.
10 And thou shalt keep the feast of
weeks unto the LORD thy God with a
tribute of a freewill offering of thine
hand, which thou shalt give *unto the*
LORD thy God, according as the LORD
thy God hath blessed thee:
11 And thou shalt rejoice before the
LORD thy God, thou, and thy son, and
thy daughter, and thy manservant, and
thy maidservant, and the Levite that *is*
within thy gates, and the stranger, and
the fatherless, and the widow, that *are*
among you, in the place which the LORD
thy God hath chosen to place his name
there.
12 And thou shalt remember that
thou wast a bondman in Egypt: and
thou shalt observe and do these statutes.
13 Thou shalt observe the feast of
tabernacles seven days, after that thou
hast gathered in thy corn and thy wine:
14 And thou shalt rejoice in thy feast,
thou, and thy son, and thy daughter,
and thy manservant, and thy maidservant, and the Levite, the stranger, and
the fatherless, and the widow, that *are*
within thy gates.
15 Seven days shalt thou keep a solemn feast unto the LORD thy God in the
place which the LORD shall choose:
because the LORD thy God shall bless
thee in all thine increase, and in all the
works of thine hands, therefore thou
shalt surely rejoice.
16 Three times in a year shall all thy
males appear before the LORD thy God
in the place which he shall choose; in
the feast of unleavened bread, and in
the feast of weeks, and in the feast of
tabernacles: and they shall not appear
before the LORD empty:
17 Every man *shall give* as he is able,
according to the blessing of the LORD
thy God which he hath given thee.
18 Judges and officers shalt thou
make thee in all thy gates, which the
LORD thy God giveth thee, throughout
thy tribes: and they shall judge the
people with just judgment.
19 Thou shalt not wrest judgment;
thou shalt not respect persons, neither
take a gift: for a gift doth blind the eyes
of the wise, and pervert the words of
the righteous.
20 That which is altogether just shalt
thou follow, that thou mayest live, and
inherit the land which the LORD thy
God giveth thee.
21 Thou shalt not plant thee a grove
of any trees near unto the altar of the
LORD thy God, which thou shalt make
thee.
22 Neither shalt thou set thee up *any*
image; which the LORD thy God hateth.

17 Thou shalt not sacrifice unto the
LORD thy God *any* bullock, or
sheep, wherein is blemish, *or* any evilfavouredness: for that *is* an abomination
unto the LORD thy God.
2 If there be found among you, within
any of thy gates which the LORD thy
God giveth thee, man or woman, that
hath wrought wickedness in the sight
of the LORD thy God, in transgressing
his covenant,
3 And hath gone and served other
gods, and worshipped them, either the
sun, or moon, or any of the host of
heaven, which I have not commanded;
4 And it be told thee, and thou hast
heard *of it*, and enquired diligently,
and, behold, *it be* true, *and* the thing
certain, *that* such abomination is
wrought in Israel:

5 Then shalt thou bring forth that
man or that woman, which have committed that wicked thing, unto thy
gates, *even* that man or that woman,
and shalt stone them with stones, till
they die.
6 At the mouth of two witnesses, or
three witnesses, shall he that is worthy
of death be put to death; *but* at the
mouth of one witness he shall not be
put to death.
7 The hands of the witnesses shall be
first upon him to put him to death, and
afterward the hands of all the people.
So thou shalt put the evil away from
among you.
8 If there arise a matter too hard for
thee in judgment, between blood and
blood, between plea and plea, and
between stroke and stroke, *being* matters of controversy within thy gates:
then shalt thou arise, and get thee up
into the place which the LORD thy God
shall choose;
9 And thou shalt come unto the
priests the Levites, and unto the judge
that shall be in those days, and enquire;
and they shall shew thee the sentence
of judgment:
10 And thou shalt do according to the
sentence, which they of that place
which the LORD shall choose shall shew
thee; and thou shalt observe to do
according to all that they inform thee:
11 According to the sentence of the
law which they shall teach thee, and
according to the judgment which they
shall tell thee, thou shalt do: thou shalt
not decline from the sentence which
they shall shew thee, *to* the right hand,
nor *to* the left.
12 And the man that will do presumptuously, and will not hearken unto the
priest that standeth to minister there
before the LORD thy God, or unto the
judge, even that man shall die: and
thou shalt put away the evil from Israel.
13 And all the people shall hear, and
fear, and do no more presumptuously.
14 When thou art come unto the land
which the LORD thy God giveth thee,
and shalt possess it, and shalt dwell
therein, and shalt say, I will set a king
over me, like as all the nations that *are*
about me;
15 Thou shalt in any wise set *him*
king over thee, whom the LORD thy God
shall choose: *one* from among thy brethren shalt thou set king over thee: thou
mayest not set a stranger over thee,
which *is* not thy brother.
16 But he shall not multiply horses to
himself, nor cause the people to return
to Egypt, to the end that he should
multiply horses: forasmuch as the LORD
hath said unto you, Ye shall henceforth
return no more that way.
17 Neither shall he multiply wives to
himself, that his heart turn not away:
neither shall he greatly multiply to
himself silver and gold.
18 And it shall be, when he sitteth
upon the throne of his kingdom, that he
shall write him a copy of this law in a
book out of *that which is* before the
priests the Levites:
19 And it shall be with him, and he
shall read therein all the days of his
life: that he may learn to fear the LORD
his God, to keep all the words of this
law and these statutes, to do them:
20 That his heart be not lifted up
above his brethren, and that he turn
not aside from the commandment, *to*
the right hand, or *to* the left: to the end
that he may prolong *his* days in his
kingdom, he, and his children, in the
midst of Israel.

18 The priests the Levites, *and* all
the tribe of Levi, shall have no
part nor inheritance with Israel: they
shall eat the offerings of the LORD
made by fire, and his inheritance.
2 Therefore shall they have no inheritance among their brethren: the LORD
is their inheritance, as he hath said
unto them.
3 And this shall be the priest's due
from the people, from them that offer a
sacrifice, whether *it be* ox or sheep;
and they shall give unto the priest the
shoulder, and the two cheeks, and the
maw.
4 The firstfruit *also* of thy corn, of thy
wine, and of thine oil, and the first of
the fleece of thy sheep, shalt thou give
him.
5 For the LORD thy God hath chosen
him out of all thy tribes, to stand to
minister in the name of the LORD, him
and his sons for ever.
6 And if a Levite come from any of
thy gates out of all Israel, where he
sojourned, and come with all the desire
of his mind unto the place which the
LORD shall choose;
7 Then he shall minister in the name
of the LORD his God, as all his brethren
the Levites *do*, which stand there
before the LORD.
8 They shall have like portions to eat,
beside that which cometh of the sale of
his patrimony.
9 When thou art come into the land
which the LORD thy God giveth thee,
thou shalt not learn to do after the
abominations of those nations.
10 There shall not be found among
you *any one* that maketh his son or his
daughter to pass through the fire, *or*
that useth divination, *or* an observer of
times, or an enchanter, or a witch,
11 Or a charmer, or a consulter with
familiar spirits, or a wizard, or a necro-
mancer.
12 For all that do these things *are* an
abomination unto the LORD: and
because of these abominations the
LORD thy God doth drive them out from
before thee.
13 Thou shalt be perfect with the
LORD thy God.
14 For these nations, which thou shalt
possess, hearkened unto observers of
times, and unto diviners: but as for
thee, the LORD thy God hath not suffered thee so *to do*.
15 The LORD thy God will raise up
unto thee a Prophet from the midst of
thee, of thy brethren, like unto me;
unto him ye shall hearken;
16 According to all that thou desiredst
of the LORD thy God in Horeb in the day
of the assembly, saying, Let me not
hear again the voice of the LORD my
God, neither let me see this great fire
any more, that I die not.
17 And the LORD said unto me, They
have well *spoken that* which they have
spoken.
18 I will raise them up a Prophet from
among their brethren, like unto thee,
and will put my words in his mouth;
and he shall speak unto them all that I
shall command him.
19 And it shall come to pass, *that*
whosoever will not hearken unto my
words which he shall speak in my
name, I will require *it* of him.
20 But the prophet, which shall presume to speak a word in my name,
which I have not commanded him to
speak, or that shall speak in the name
of other gods, even that prophet shall
die.

21 And if thou say in thine heart, How shall we know the word which the LORD hath not spoken?

22 When a prophet speaketh in the name of the LORD, if the thing follow not, nor come to pass, that *is* the thing which the LORD hath not spoken, *but* the prophet hath spoken it presumptuously: thou shalt not be afraid of him.

19 When the LORD thy God hath cut off the nations, whose land the LORD thy God giveth thee, and thou succeedest them, and dwellest in their cities, and in their houses;

2 Thou shalt separate three cities for thee in the midst of thy land, which the LORD thy God giveth thee to possess it.

3 Thou shalt prepare thee a way, and divide the coasts of thy land, which the LORD thy God giveth thee to inherit, into three parts, that every slayer may flee thither.

4 And this *is* the case of the slayer, which shall flee thither, that he may live: Whoso killeth his neighbour ignorantly, whom he hated not in time past;

5 As when a man goeth into the wood with his neighbour to hew wood, and his hand fetcheth a stroke with the axe to cut down the tree, and the head slippeth from the helve, and lighteth upon his neighbour, that he die; he shall flee unto one of those cities, and live:

6 Lest the avenger of the blood pursue the slayer, while his heart is hot, and overtake him, because the way is long, and slay him; whereas he *was* not worthy of death, inasmuch as he hated him not in time past.

7 Wherefore I command thee, saying, Thou shalt separate three cities for thee.

8 And if the LORD thy God enlarge thy coast, as he hath sworn unto thy fathers, and give thee all the land which he promised to give unto thy fathers;

9 If thou shalt keep all these commandments to do them, which I command thee this day, to love the LORD thy God, and to walk ever in his ways; then shalt thou add three cities more for thee, beside these three:

10 That innocent blood be not shed in thy land, which the LORD thy God giveth thee *for* an inheritance, and *so* blood be upon thee.

11 But if any man hate his neighbour, and lie in wait for him, and rise up against him, and smite him mortally that he die, and fleeth into one of these cities:

12 Then the elders of his city shall send and fetch him thence, and deliver him into the hand of the avenger of blood, that he may die.

13 Thine eye shall not pity him, but thou shalt put away *the guilt of* innocent blood from Israel, that it may go well with thee.

14 Thou shalt not remove thy neighbour's landmark, which they of old time have set in thine inheritance, which thou shalt inherit in the land that the LORD thy God giveth thee to possess it.

15 One witness shall not rise up against a man for any iniquity, or for any sin, in any sin that he sinneth: at the mouth of two witnesses, or at the mouth of three witnesses, shall the matter be established.

16 If a false witness rise up against any man to testify against him *that which is* wrong;

17 Then both the men, between whom the controversy *is*, shall stand before the LORD, before the priests and the judges, which shall be in those days;

18 And the judges shall make diligent
inquisition: and, behold, *if* the witness
be a false witness, *and* hath testified
falsely against his brother;
19 Then shall ye do unto him, as he
had thought to have done unto his
brother: so shalt thou put the evil away
from among you.
20 And those which remain shall hear,
and fear, and shall henceforth commit
no more any such evil among you.
21 And thine eye shall not pity; *but*
life *shall go* for life, eye for eye, tooth
for tooth, hand for hand, foot for foot.

20 When thou goest out to battle
against thine enemies, and seest
horses, and chariots, *and* a people more
than thou, be not afraid of them: for the
LORD thy God *is* with thee, which
brought thee up out of the land of
Egypt.
2 And it shall be, when ye are come
nigh unto the battle, that the priest
shall approach and speak unto the
people,
3 And shall say unto them, Hear, O
Israel, ye approach this day unto battle
against your enemies: let not your
hearts faint, fear not, and do not tremble, neither be ye terrified because of
them;
4 For the LORD your God *is* he that
goeth with you, to fight for you against
your enemies, to save you.
5 And the officers shall speak unto
the people, saying, What man *is there*
that hath built a new house, and hath
not dedicated it? let him go and return
to his house, lest he die in the battle,
and another man dedicate it.
6 And what man *is he* that hath
planted a vineyard, and hath not *yet*
eaten of it? let him *also* go and return
unto his house, lest he die in the battle,
and another man eat of it.
7 And what man *is there* that hath
betrothed a wife, and hath not taken
her? let him go and return unto his
house, lest he die in the battle, and
another man take her.
8 And the officers shall speak further
unto the people, and they shall say,
What man *is there that is* fearful and
fainthearted? let him go and return
unto his house, lest his brethren's heart
faint as well as his heart.
9 And it shall be, when the officers
have made an end of speaking unto the
people, that they shall make captains
of the armies to lead the people.
10 When thou comest nigh unto a city
to fight against it, then proclaim peace
unto it.
11 And it shall be, if it make thee
answer of peace, and open unto thee,
then it shall be, *that* all the people *that*
is found therein shall be tributaries
unto thee, and they shall serve thee.
12 And if it will make no peace with
thee, but will make war against thee,
then thou shalt besiege it:
13 And when the LORD thy God hath
delivered it into thine hands, thou shalt
smite every male thereof with the edge
of the sword:
14 But the women, and the little ones,
and the cattle, and all that is in the city,
even all the spoil thereof, shalt thou
take unto thyself; and thou shalt eat
the spoil of thine enemies, which the
LORD thy God hath given thee.
15 Thus shalt thou do unto all the cities *which are* very far off from thee,
which *are* not of the cities of these
nations.
16 But of the cities of these people,
which the LORD thy God doth give thee

for an inheritance, thou shalt save alive nothing that breatheth:

17 But thou shalt utterly destroy them; *namely*, the Hittites, and the Amorites, the Canaanites, and the Perizzites, the Hivites, and the Jebusites; as the LORD thy God hath commanded thee:

18 That they teach you not to do after all their abominations, which they have done unto their gods; so should ye sin against the LORD your God.

19 When thou shalt besiege a city a long time, in making war against it to take it, thou shalt not destroy the trees thereof by forcing an axe against them: for thou mayest eat of them, and thou shalt not cut them down (for the tree of the field *is* man's *life*) to employ *them* in the siege:

20 Only the trees which thou knowest that they *be* not trees for meat, thou shalt destroy and cut them down; and thou shalt build bulwarks against the city that maketh war with thee, until it be subdued.

21 If *one* be found slain in the land which the LORD thy God giveth thee to possess it, lying in the field, *and* it be not known who hath slain him:

2 Then thy elders and thy judges shall come forth, and they shall measure unto the cities which *are* round about him that is slain:

3 And it shall be, *that* the city *which is* next unto the slain man, even the elders of that city shall take an heifer, which hath not been wrought with, *and* which hath not drawn in the yoke;

4 And the elders of that city shall bring down the heifer unto a rough valley, which is neither eared nor sown, and shall strike off the heifer's neck there in the valley:

5 And the priests the sons of Levi shall come near; for them the LORD thy God hath chosen to minister unto him, and to bless in the name of the LORD; and by their word shall every controversy and every stroke be *tried*:

6 And all the elders of that city, *that are* next unto the slain *man*, shall wash their hands over the heifer that is beheaded in the valley:

7 And they shall answer and say, Our hands have not shed this blood, neither have our eyes seen *it*.

8 Be merciful, O LORD, unto thy people Israel, whom thou hast redeemed, and lay not innocent blood unto thy people of Israel's charge. And the blood shall be forgiven them.

9 So shalt thou put away the *guilt of* innocent blood from among you, when thou shalt do *that which is* right in the sight of the LORD.

10 When thou goest forth to war against thine enemies, and the LORD thy God hath delivered them into thine hands, and thou hast taken them captive,

11 And seest among the captives a beautiful woman, and hast a desire unto her, that thou wouldest have her to thy wife;

12 Then thou shalt bring her home to thine house; and she shall shave her head, and pare her nails;

13 And she shall put the raiment of her captivity from off her, and shall remain in thine house, and bewail her father and her mother a full month: and after that thou shalt go in unto her, and be her husband, and she shall be thy wife.

14 And it shall be, if thou have no delight in her, then thou shalt let her go whither she will; but thou shalt not sell

her at all for money, thou shalt not
make merchandise of her, because thou
hast humbled her.
15 If a man have two wives, one
beloved, and another hated, and they
have born him children, *both* the
beloved and the hated; and *if* the firstborn son be hers that was hated:
16 Then it shall be, when he maketh
his sons to inherit *that* which he hath,
that he may not make the son of the
beloved firstborn before the son of the
hated, *which is indeed* the firstborn:
17 But he shall acknowledge the son
of the hated *for* the firstborn, by giving
him a double portion of all that he
hath: for he *is* the beginning of his
strength; the right of the firstborn *is*
his.
18 If a man have a stubborn and
rebellious son, which will not obey the
voice of his father, or the voice of his
mother, and *that*, when they have chastened him, will not hearken unto them:
19 Then shall his father and his mother lay hold on him, and bring him out
unto the elders of his city, and unto the
gate of his place;
20 And they shall say unto the elders
of his city, This our son *is* stubborn and
rebellious, he will not obey our voice;
he is a glutton, and a drunkard.
21 And all the men of his city shall
stone him with stones, that he die: so
shalt thou put evil away from among
you; and all Israel shall hear, and fear.
22 And if a man have committed a sin
worthy of death, and he be to be put to
death, and thou hang him on a tree:
23 His body shall not remain all night
upon the tree, but thou shalt in any
wise bury him that day; (for he that is
hanged *is* accursed of God;) that thy
land be not defiled, which the LORD thy
God giveth thee *for* an inheritance.

22 Thou shalt not see thy brother's
ox or his sheep go astray, and
hide thyself from them: thou shalt in
any case bring them again unto thy
brother.
2 And if thy brother *be* not nigh unto
thee, or if thou know him not, then thou
shalt bring it unto thine own house, and
it shall be with thee until thy brother
seek after it, and thou shalt restore it to
him again.
3 In like manner shalt thou do with
his ass; and so shalt thou do with his
raiment; and with all lost thing of thy
brother's, which he hath lost, and thou
hast found, shalt thou do likewise: thou
mayest not hide thyself.
4 Thou shalt not see thy brother's ass
or his ox fall down by the way, and hide
thyself from them: thou shalt surely
help him to lift *them* up again.
5 The woman shall not wear that
which pertaineth unto a man, neither
shall a man put on a woman's garment:
for all that do so *are* abomination unto
the LORD thy God.
6 If a bird's nest chance to be before
thee in the way in any tree, or on the
ground, *whether they be* young ones, or
eggs, and the dam sitting upon the
young, or upon the eggs, thou shalt not
take the dam with the young:
7 *But* thou shalt in any wise let the
dam go, and take the young to thee;
that it may be well with thee, and *that*
thou mayest prolong *thy* days.
8 When thou buildest a new house,
then thou shalt make a battlement for
thy roof, that thou bring not blood upon
thine house, if any man fall from
thence.

9 Thou shalt not sow thy vineyard with divers seeds: lest the fruit of thy seed which thou hast sown, and the fruit of thy vineyard, be defiled.

10 Thou shalt not plow with an ox and an ass together.

11 Thou shalt not wear a garment of divers sorts, *as* of woollen and linen together.

12 Thou shalt make thee fringes upon the four quarters of thy vesture, wherewith thou coverest *thyself*.

13 If any man take a wife, and go in unto her, and hate her,

14 And give occasions of speech against her, and bring up an evil name upon her, and say, I took this woman, and when I came to her, I found her not a maid:

15 Then shall the father of the damsel, and her mother, take and bring forth *the tokens of* the damsel's virginity unto the elders of the city in the gate:

16 And the damsel's father shall say unto the elders, I gave my daughter unto this man to wife, and he hateth her;

17 And, lo, he hath given occasions of speech *against her*, saying, I found not thy daughter a maid; and yet these *are the tokens of* my daughter's virginity. And they shall spread the cloth before the elders of the city.

18 And the elders of that city shall take that man and chastise him;

19 And they shall amerce him in an hundred *shekels* of silver, and give *them* unto the father of the damsel, because he hath brought up an evil name upon a virgin of Israel: and she shall be his wife; he may not put her away all his days.

20 But if this thing be true, *and the tokens of* virginity be not found for the damsel:

21 Then they shall bring out the damsel to the door of her father's house, and the men of her city shall stone her with stones that she die: because she hath wrought folly in Israel, to play the whore in her father's house: so shalt thou put evil away from among you.

22 If a man be found lying with a woman married to an husband, then they shall both of them die, *both* the man that lay with the woman, and the woman: so shalt thou put away evil from Israel.

23 If a damsel *that is* a virgin be betrothed unto an husband, and a man find her in the city, and lie with her;

24 Then ye shall bring them both out unto the gate of that city, and ye shall stone them with stones that they die; the damsel, because she cried not, *being* in the city; and the man, because he hath humbled his neighbour's wife: so thou shalt put away evil from among you.

25 But if a man find a betrothed damsel in the field, and the man force her, and lie with her: then the man only that lay with her shall die:

26 But unto the damsel thou shalt do nothing; *there is* in the damsel no sin *worthy* of death: for as when a man riseth against his neighbour, and slayeth him, even so *is* this matter:

27 For he found her in the field, *and* the betrothed damsel cried, and *there was* none to save her.

28 If a man find a damsel *that is* a virgin, which is not betrothed, and lay hold on her, and lie with her, and they be found;

29 Then the man that lay with her shall give unto the damsel's father fifty *shekels* of silver, and she shall be his wife; because he hath humbled her, he may not put her away all his days.

30 A man shall not take his father's wife, nor discover his father's skirt.

23 He that is wounded in the stones, or hath his privy member cut off, shall not enter into the congregation of the LORD.

2 A bastard shall not enter into the congregation of the LORD; even to his tenth generation shall he not enter into the congregation of the LORD.

3 An Ammonite or Moabite shall not enter into the congregation of the LORD; even to their tenth generation shall they not enter into the congregation of the LORD for ever:

4 Because they met you not with bread and with water in the way, when ye came forth out of Egypt; and because they hired against thee Balaam the son of Beor of Pethor of Mesopotamia, to curse thee.

5 Nevertheless the LORD thy God would not hearken unto Balaam; but the LORD thy God turned the curse into a blessing unto thee, because the LORD thy God loved thee.

6 Thou shalt not seek their peace nor their prosperity all thy days for ever.

7 Thou shalt not abhor an Edomite; for he *is* thy brother: thou shalt not abhor an Egyptian; because thou wast a stranger in his land.

8 The children that are begotten of them shall enter into the congregation of the LORD in their third generation.

9 When the host goeth forth against thine enemies, then keep thee from every wicked thing.

10 If there be among you any man, that is not clean by reason of uncleanness that chanceth him by night, then shall he go abroad out of the camp, he shall not come within the camp:

11 But it shall be, when evening cometh on, he shall wash *himself* with water: and when the sun is down, he shall come into the camp *again*.

12 Thou shalt have a place also without the camp, whither thou shalt go forth abroad:

13 And thou shalt have a paddle upon thy weapon; and it shall be, when thou wilt ease thyself abroad, thou shalt dig therewith, and shalt turn back and cover that which cometh from thee:

14 For the LORD thy God walketh in the midst of thy camp, to deliver thee, and to give up thine enemies before thee; therefore shall thy camp be holy: that he see no unclean thing in thee, and turn away from thee.

15 Thou shalt not deliver unto his master the servant which is escaped from his master unto thee:

16 He shall dwell with thee, *even* among you, in that place which he shall choose in one of thy gates, where it liketh him best: thou shalt not oppress him.

17 There shall be no whore of the daughters of Israel, nor a sodomite of the sons of Israel.

18 Thou shalt not bring the hire of a whore, or the price of a dog, into the house of the LORD thy God for any vow: for even both these *are* abomination unto the LORD thy God.

19 Thou shalt not lend upon usury to thy brother; usury of money, usury of victuals, usury of any thing that is lent upon usury:

20 Unto a stranger thou mayest lend upon usury; but unto thy brother thou shalt not lend upon usury: that the LORD thy God may bless thee in all that thou settest thine hand to in the land whither thou goest to possess it.

21 When thou shalt vow a vow unto the LORD thy God, thou shalt not slack to pay it: for the LORD thy God will surely require it of thee; and it would be sin in thee.

22 But if thou shalt forbear to vow, it shall be no sin in thee.

23 That which is gone out of thy lips thou shalt keep and perform; *even* a freewill offering, according as thou hast vowed unto the LORD thy God, which thou hast promised with thy mouth.

24 When thou comest into thy neighbour's vineyard, then thou mayest eat grapes thy fill at thine own pleasure; but thou shalt not put *any* in thy vessel.

25 When thou comest into the standing corn of thy neighbour, then thou mayest pluck the ears with thine hand; but thou shalt not move a sickle unto thy neighbour's standing corn.

24 When a man hath taken a wife, and married her, and it come to pass that she find no favour in his eyes, because he hath found some uncleanness in her: then let him write her a bill of divorcement, and give *it* in her hand, and send her out of his house.

2 And when she is departed out of his house, she may go and be another man's *wife*.

3 And *if* the latter husband hate her, and write her a bill of divorcement, and giveth *it* in her hand, and sendeth her out of his house; or if the latter husband die, which took her *to be* his wife;

4 Her former husband, which sent her away, may not take her again to be his wife, after that she is defiled; for that *is* abomination before the LORD: and thou shalt not cause the land to sin, which the LORD thy God giveth thee *for* an inheritance.

5 When a man hath taken a new wife, he shall not go out to war, neither shall he be charged with any business: *but* he shall be free at home one year, and shall cheer up his wife which he hath taken.

6 No man shall take the nether or the upper millstone to pledge: for he taketh *a man's* life to pledge.

7 If a man be found stealing any of his brethren of the children of Israel, and maketh merchandise of him, or selleth him; then that thief shall die; and thou shalt put evil away from among you.

8 Take heed in the plague of leprosy, that thou observe diligently, and do according to all that the priests the Levites shall teach you: as I commanded them, *so* ye shall observe to do.

9 Remember what the LORD thy God did unto Miriam by the way, after that ye were come forth out of Egypt.

10 When thou dost lend thy brother any thing, thou shalt not go into his house to fetch his pledge.

11 Thou shalt stand abroad, and the man to whom thou dost lend shall bring out the pledge abroad unto thee.

12 And if the man *be* poor, thou shalt not sleep with his pledge:

13 In any case thou shalt deliver him the pledge again when the sun goeth down, that he may sleep in his own raiment, and bless thee: and it shall be righteousness unto thee before the LORD thy God.

14 Thou shalt not oppress an hired
servant *that is* poor and needy, *whether*
he be of thy brethren, or of thy strangers that *are* in thy land within thy gates:
15 At his day thou shalt give *him* his
hire, neither shall the sun go down
upon it; for he *is* poor, and setteth his
heart upon it: lest he cry against thee
unto the LORD, and it be sin unto thee.
16 The fathers shall not be put to
death for the children, neither shall the
children be put to death for the fathers:
every man shall be put to death for his
own sin.
17 Thou shalt not pervert the judgment of the stranger, *nor* of the fatherless; nor take a widow's raiment to
pledge:
18 But thou shalt remember that thou
wast a bondman in Egypt, and the LORD
thy God redeemed thee thence: therefore I command thee to do this thing.
19 When thou cuttest down thine
harvest in thy field, and hast forgot a
sheaf in the field, thou shalt not go
again to fetch it: it shall be for the
stranger, for the fatherless, and for the
widow: that the LORD thy God may
bless thee in all the work of thine
hands.
20 When thou beatest thine olive
tree, thou shalt not go over the boughs
again: it shall be for the stranger, for
the fatherless, and for the widow.
21 When thou gatherest the grapes of
thy vineyard, thou shalt not glean *it*
afterward: it shall be for the stranger,
for the fatherless, and for the widow.
22 And thou shalt remember that
thou wast a bondman in the land of
Egypt: therefore I command thee to do
this thing.

25 If there be a controversy between
men, and they come unto judgment, that *the judges* may judge them;
then they shall justify the righteous,
and condemn the wicked.
2 And it shall be, if the wicked man *be*
worthy to be beaten, that the judge
shall cause him to lie down, and to be
beaten before his face, according to his
fault, by a certain number.
3 Forty stripes he may give him, *and*
not exceed: lest, *if* he should exceed,
and beat him above these with many
stripes, then thy brother should seem
vile unto thee.
4 Thou shalt not muzzle the ox when
he treadeth out *the corn*.
5 If brethren dwell together, and one
of them die, and have no child, the wife
of the dead shall not marry without
unto a stranger: her husband's brother
shall go in unto her, and take her to him
to wife, and perform the duty of an
husband's brother unto her.
6 And it shall be, *that* the firstborn
which she beareth shall succeed in the
name of his brother *which is* dead, that
his name be not put out of Israel.
7 And if the man like not to take his
brother's wife, then let his brother's
wife go up to the gate unto the elders,
and say, My husband's brother refuseth
to raise up unto his brother a name in
Israel, he will not perform the duty of
my husband's brother.
8 Then the elders of his city shall call
him, and speak unto him: and *if* he
stand *to it*, and say, I like not to take
her;
9 Then shall his brother's wife come
unto him in the presence of the elders,
and loose his shoe from off his foot, and
spit in his face, and shall answer and
say, So shall it be done unto that man
that will not build up his brother's
house.

10 And his name shall be called in Israel, The house of him that hath his shoe loosed.

11 When men strive together one with another, and the wife of the one draweth near for to deliver her husband out of the hand of him that smiteth him, and putteth forth her hand, and taketh him by the secrets:

12 Then thou shalt cut off her hand, thine eye shall not pity *her*.

13 Thou shalt not have in thy bag divers weights, a great and a small.

14 Thou shalt not have in thine house divers measures, a great and a small.

15 *But* thou shalt have a perfect and just weight, a perfect and just measure shalt thou have: that thy days may be lengthened in the land which the LORD thy God giveth thee.

16 For all that do such things, *and* all that do unrighteously, *are* an abomination unto the LORD thy God.

17 Remember what Amalek did unto thee by the way, when ye were come forth out of Egypt;

18 How he met thee by the way, and smote the hindmost of thee, *even* all *that were* feeble behind thee, when thou *wast* faint and weary; and he feared not God.

19 Therefore it shall be, when the LORD thy God hath given thee rest from all thine enemies round about, in the land which the LORD thy God giveth thee *for* an inheritance to possess it, *that* thou shalt blot out the remembrance of Amalek from under heaven; thou shalt not forget *it*.

26 And it shall be, when thou *art* come in unto the land which the LORD thy God giveth thee *for* an inheritance, and possessest it, and dwellest therein;

2 That thou shalt take of the first of all the fruit of the earth, which thou shalt bring of thy land that the LORD thy God giveth thee, and shalt put *it* in a basket, and shalt go unto the place which the LORD thy God shall choose to place his name there.

3 And thou shalt go unto the priest that shall be in those days, and say unto him, I profess this day unto the LORD thy God, that I am come unto the country which the LORD sware unto our fathers for to give us.

4 And the priest shall take the basket out of thine hand, and set it down before the altar of the LORD thy God.

5 And thou shalt speak and say before the LORD thy God, A Syrian ready to perish *was* my father, and he went down into Egypt, and sojourned there with a few, and became there a nation, great, mighty, and populous:

6 And the Egyptians evil entreated us, and afflicted us, and laid upon us hard bondage:

7 And when we cried unto the LORD God of our fathers, the LORD heard our voice, and looked on our affliction, and our labour, and our oppression:

8 And the LORD brought us forth out of Egypt with a mighty hand, and with an outstretched arm, and with great terribleness, and with signs, and with wonders:

9 And he hath brought us into this place, and hath given us this land, *even* a land that floweth with milk and honey.

10 And now, behold, I have brought the firstfruits of the land, which thou, O LORD, hast given me. And thou shalt set it before the LORD thy God, and worship before the LORD thy God:

11 And thou shalt rejoice in every good *thing* which the LORD thy God hath given unto thee, and unto thine house, thou, and the Levite, and the stranger that *is* among you.

12 When thou hast made an end of tithing all the tithes of thine increase the third year, *which is* the year of tithing, and hast given *it* unto the Levite, the stranger, the fatherless, and the widow, that they may eat within thy gates, and be filled;

13 Then thou shalt say before the LORD thy God, I have brought away the hallowed things out of *mine* house, and also have given them unto the Levite, and unto the stranger, to the fatherless, and to the widow, according to all thy commandments which thou hast commanded me: I have not transgressed thy commandments, neither have I forgotten *them*:

14 I have not eaten thereof in my mourning, neither have I taken away *ought* thereof for *any* unclean *use*, nor given *ought* thereof for the dead: *but* I have hearkened to the voice of the LORD my God, *and* have done according to all that thou hast commanded me.

15 Look down from thy holy habitation, from heaven, and bless thy people Israel, and the land which thou hast given us, as thou swarest unto our fathers, a land that floweth with milk and honey.

16 This day the LORD thy God hath commanded thee to do these statutes and judgments: thou shalt therefore keep and do them with all thine heart, and with all thy soul.

17 Thou hast avouched the LORD this day to be thy God, and to walk in his ways, and to keep his statutes, and his commandments, and his judgments, and to hearken unto his voice:

18 And the LORD hath avouched thee this day to be his peculiar people, as he hath promised thee, and that *thou* shouldest keep all his commandments;

19 And to make thee high above all nations which he hath made, in praise, and in name, and in honour; and that thou mayest be an holy people unto the LORD thy God, as he hath spoken.

27 And Moses with the elders of Israel commanded the people, saying, Keep all the commandments which I command you this day.

2 And it shall be on the day when ye shall pass over Jordan unto the land which the LORD thy God giveth thee, that thou shalt set thee up great stones, and plaister them with plaister:

3 And thou shalt write upon them all the words of this law, when thou art passed over, that thou mayest go in unto the land which the LORD thy God giveth thee, a land that floweth with milk and honey; as the LORD God of thy fathers hath promised thee.

4 Therefore it shall be when ye be gone over Jordan, *that* ye shall set up these stones, which I command you this day, in mount Ebal, and thou shalt plaister them with plaister.

5 And there shalt thou build an altar unto the LORD thy God, an altar of stones: thou shalt not lift up *any* iron *tool* upon them.

6 Thou shalt build the altar of the LORD thy God of whole stones: and thou shalt offer burnt offerings thereon unto the LORD thy God:

7 And thou shalt offer peace offerings, and shalt eat there, and rejoice before the LORD thy God.

8 And thou shalt write upon the stones all the words of this law very plainly.

9 And Moses and the priests the Levites spake unto all Israel, saying, Take heed, and hearken, O Israel; this day thou art become the people of the LORD thy God.

10 Thou shalt therefore obey the voice of the LORD thy God, and do his commandments and his statutes, which I command thee this day.

11 And Moses charged the people the same day, saying,

12 These shall stand upon mount Gerizim to bless the people, when ye are come over Jordan; Simeon, and Levi, and Judah, and Issachar, and Joseph, and Benjamin:

13 And these shall stand upon mount Ebal to curse; Reuben, Gad, and Asher, and Zebulun, Dan, and Naphtali.

14 And the Levites shall speak, and say unto all the men of Israel with a loud voice,

15 Cursed *be* the man that maketh *any* graven or molten image, an abomination unto the LORD, the work of the hands of the craftsman, and putteth *it* in *a* secret *place*. And all the people shall answer and say, Amen.

16 Cursed *be* he that setteth light by his father or his mother. And all the people shall say, Amen.

17 Cursed *be* he that removeth his neighbour's landmark. And all the people shall say, Amen.

18 Cursed *be* he that maketh the blind to wander out of the way. And all the people shall say, Amen.

19 Cursed *be* he that perverteth the judgment of the stranger, fatherless, and widow. And all the people shall say, Amen.

20 Cursed *be* he that lieth with his father's wife; because he uncovereth his father's skirt. And all the people shall say, Amen.

21 Cursed *be* he that lieth with any manner of beast. And all the people shall say, Amen.

22 Cursed *be* he that lieth with his sister, the daughter of his father, or the daughter of his mother. And all the people shall say, Amen.

23 Cursed *be* he that lieth with his mother in law. And all the people shall say, Amen.

24 Cursed *be* he that smiteth his neighbour secretly. And all the people shall say, Amen.

25 Cursed *be* he that taketh reward to slay an innocent person. And all the people shall say, Amen.

26 Cursed *be* he that confirmeth not *all* the words of this law to do them. And all the people shall say, Amen.

28

And it shall come to pass, if thou shalt hearken diligently unto the voice of the LORD thy God, to observe *and* to do all his commandments which I command thee this day, that the LORD thy God will set thee on high above all nations of the earth:

2 And all these blessings shall come on thee, and overtake thee, if thou shalt hearken unto the voice of the LORD thy God.

3 Blessed *shalt* thou *be* in the city, and blessed *shalt* thou *be* in the field.

4 Blessed *shall be* the fruit of thy body, and the fruit of thy ground, and the fruit of thy cattle, the increase of thy kine, and the flocks of thy sheep.

5 Blessed *shall be* thy basket and thy store.

6 Blessed *shalt* thou *be* when thou
comest in, and blessed *shalt* thou *be*
when thou goest out.
7 The LORD shall cause thine enemies
that rise up against thee to be smitten
before thy face: they shall come out
against thee one way, and flee before
thee seven ways.
8 The LORD shall command the blessing upon thee in thy storehouses, and in
all that thou settest thine hand unto;
and he shall bless thee in the land
which the LORD thy God giveth thee.
9 The LORD shall establish thee an
holy people unto himself, as he hath
sworn unto thee, if thou shalt keep the
commandments of the LORD thy God,
and walk in his ways.
10 And all people of the earth shall
see that thou art called by the name of
the LORD; and they shall be afraid of
thee.
11 And the LORD shall make thee
plenteous in goods, in the fruit of thy
body, and in the fruit of thy cattle, and
in the fruit of thy ground, in the land
which the LORD sware unto thy fathers
to give thee.
12 The LORD shall open unto thee his
good treasure, the heaven to give the
rain unto thy land in his season, and to
bless all the work of thine hand: and
thou shalt lend unto many nations, and
thou shalt not borrow.
13 And the LORD shall make thee the
head, and not the tail; and thou shalt be
above only, and thou shalt not be
beneath; if that thou hearken unto the
commandments of the LORD thy God,
which I command thee this day, to
observe and to do *them*:
14 And thou shalt not go aside from
any of the words which I command thee
this day, *to* the right hand, or *to* the left,
to go after other gods to serve them.
15 But it shall come to pass, if thou
wilt not hearken unto the voice of the
LORD thy God, to observe to do all his
commandments and his statutes which
I command thee this day; that all these
curses shall come upon thee, and overtake thee:
16 Cursed *shalt* thou *be* in the city,
and cursed *shalt* thou *be* in the field.
17 Cursed *shall be* thy basket and thy
store.
18 Cursed *shall be* the fruit of thy
body, and the fruit of thy land, the
increase of thy kine, and the flocks of
thy sheep.
19 Cursed *shalt* thou *be* when thou
comest in, and cursed *shalt* thou *be*
when thou goest out.
20 The LORD shall send upon thee
cursing, vexation, and rebuke, in all
that thou settest thine hand unto for to
do, until thou be destroyed, and until
thou perish quickly; because of the
wickedness of thy doings, whereby thou
hast forsaken me.
21 The LORD shall make the pestilence cleave unto thee, until he have
consumed thee from off the land,
whither thou goest to possess it.
22 The LORD shall smite thee with a
consumption, and with a fever, and
with an inflammation, and with an
extreme burning, and with the sword,
and with blasting, and with mildew;
and they shall pursue thee until thou
perish.
23 And thy heaven that *is* over thy
head shall be brass, and the earth that
is under thee *shall be* iron.
24 The LORD shall make the rain of
thy land powder and dust: from heaven

shall it come down upon thee, until
thou be destroyed.
25 The LORD shall cause thee to be
smitten before thine enemies: thou
shalt go out one way against them, and
flee seven ways before them: and shalt
be removed into all the kingdoms of
the earth.
26 And thy carcase shall be meat unto
all fowls of the air, and unto the beasts
of the earth, and no man shall fray
them away.
27 The LORD will smite thee with the
botch of Egypt, and with the emerods,
and with the scab, and with the itch,
whereof thou canst not be healed.
28 The LORD shall smite thee with
madness, and blindness, and astonishment of heart:
29 And thou shalt grope at noonday,
as the blind gropeth in darkness, and
thou shalt not prosper in thy ways: and
thou shalt be only oppressed and
spoiled evermore, and no man shall
save *thee*.
30 Thou shalt betroth a wife, and
another man shall lie with her: thou
shalt build an house, and thou shalt not
dwell therein: thou shalt plant a vineyard, and shalt not gather the grapes
thereof.
31 Thine ox *shall be* slain before
thine eyes, and thou shalt not eat
thereof: thine ass *shall be* violently
taken away from before thy face, and
shall not be restored to thee: thy sheep
shall be given unto thine enemies, and
thou shalt have none to rescue *them*.
32 Thy sons and thy daughters *shall
be* given unto another people, and
thine eyes shall look, and fail *with
longing* for them all the day long: and
there shall be no might in thine hand.
33 The fruit of thy land, and all thy
labours, shall a nation which thou
knowest not eat up; and thou shalt be
only oppressed and crushed alway:
34 So that thou shalt be mad for the
sight of thine eyes which thou shalt see.
35 The LORD shall smite thee in the
knees, and in the legs, with a sore botch
that cannot be healed, from the sole of
thy foot unto the top of thy head.
36 The LORD shall bring thee, and thy
king which thou shalt set over thee,
unto a nation which neither thou nor
thy fathers have known; and there shalt
thou serve other gods, wood and stone.
37 And thou shalt become an astonishment, a proverb, and a byword,
among all nations whither the LORD
shall lead thee.
38 Thou shalt carry much seed out
into the field, and shalt gather *but* little
in; for the locust shall consume it.
39 Thou shalt plant vineyards, and
dress *them*, but shalt neither drink *of*
the wine, nor gather *the grapes*; for the
worms shall eat them.
40 Thou shalt have olive trees
throughout all thy coasts, but thou shalt
not anoint *thyself* with the oil; for thine
olive shall cast *his fruit*.
41 Thou shalt beget sons and daughters, but thou shalt not enjoy them; for
they shall go into captivity.
42 All thy trees and fruit of thy land
shall the locust consume.
43 The stranger that *is* within thee
shall get up above thee very high; and
thou shalt come down very low.
44 He shall lend to thee, and thou
shalt not lend to him: he shall be the
head, and thou shalt be the tail.
45 Moreover all these curses shall
come upon thee, and shall pursue thee,
and overtake thee, till thou be

destroyed; because thou hearkenedst not unto the voice of the LORD thy God, to keep his commandments and his statutes which he commanded thee:

46 And they shall be upon thee for a sign and for a wonder, and upon thy seed for ever.

47 Because thou servedst not the LORD thy God with joyfulness, and with gladness of heart, for the abundance of all *things*;

48 Therefore shalt thou serve thine enemies which the LORD shall send against thee, in hunger, and in thirst, and in nakedness, and in want of all *things*: and he shall put a yoke of iron upon thy neck, until he have destroyed thee.

49 The LORD shall bring a nation against thee from far, from the end of the earth, *as swift* as the eagle flieth; a nation whose tongue thou shalt not understand;

50 A nation of fierce countenance, which shall not regard the person of the old, nor shew favour to the young:

51 And he shall eat the fruit of thy cattle, and the fruit of thy land, until thou be destroyed: which *also* shall not leave thee *either* corn, wine, or oil, *or* the increase of thy kine, or flocks of thy sheep, until he have destroyed thee.

52 And he shall besiege thee in all thy gates, until thy high and fenced walls come down, wherein thou trustedst, throughout all thy land: and he shall besiege thee in all thy gates throughout all thy land, which the LORD thy God hath given thee.

53 And thou shalt eat the fruit of thine own body, the flesh of thy sons and of thy daughters, which the LORD thy God hath given thee, in the siege, and in the straitness, wherewith thine enemies shall distress thee:

54 *So that* the man *that is* tender among you, and very delicate, his eye shall be evil toward his brother, and toward the wife of his bosom, and toward the remnant of his children which he shall leave:

55 So that he will not give to any of them of the flesh of his children whom he shall eat: because he hath nothing left him in the siege, and in the straitness, wherewith thine enemies shall distress thee in all thy gates.

56 The tender and delicate woman among you, which would not adventure to set the sole of her foot upon the ground for delicateness and tenderness, her eye shall be evil toward the husband of her bosom, and toward her son, and toward her daughter,

57 And toward her young one that cometh out from between her feet, and toward her children which she shall bear: for she shall eat them for want of all *things* secretly in the siege and straitness, wherewith thine enemy shall distress thee in thy gates.

58 If thou wilt not observe to do all the words of this law that are written in this book, that thou mayest fear this glorious and fearful name, THE LORD THY GOD;

59 Then the LORD will make thy plagues wonderful, and the plagues of thy seed, *even* great plagues, and of long continuance, and sore sicknesses, and of long continuance.

60 Moreover he will bring upon thee all the diseases of Egypt, which thou wast afraid of; and they shall cleave unto thee.

61 Also every sickness, and every plague, which *is* not written in the book of this law, them will the LORD bring upon thee, until thou be destroyed.

62 And ye shall be left few in number, whereas ye were as the stars of heaven for multitude; because thou wouldest not obey the voice of the LORD thy God.

63 And it shall come to pass, *that* as the LORD rejoiced over you to do you good, and to multiply you; so the LORD will rejoice over you to destroy you, and to bring you to nought; and ye shall be plucked from off the land whither thou goest to possess it.

64 And the LORD shall scatter thee among all people, from the one end of the earth even unto the other; and there thou shalt serve other gods, which neither thou nor thy fathers have known, *even* wood and stone.

65 And among these nations shalt thou find no ease, neither shall the sole of thy foot have rest: but the LORD shall give thee there a trembling heart, and failing of eyes, and sorrow of mind:

66 And thy life shall hang in doubt before thee; and thou shalt fear day and night, and shalt have none assurance of thy life:

67 In the morning thou shalt say, Would God it were even! and at even thou shalt say, Would God it were morning! for the fear of thine heart wherewith thou shalt fear, and for the sight of thine eyes which thou shalt see.

68 And the LORD shall bring thee into Egypt again with ships, by the way whereof I spake unto thee, Thou shalt see it no more again: and there ye shall be sold unto your enemies for bondmen and bondwomen, and no man shall buy *you*.

29

These *are* the words of the covenant, which the LORD commanded Moses to make with the children of Israel in the land of Moab, beside the covenant which he made with them in Horeb.

2 And Moses called unto all Israel, and said unto them, Ye have seen all that the LORD did before your eyes in the land of Egypt unto Pharaoh, and unto all his servants, and unto all his land;

3 The great temptations which thine eyes have seen, the signs, and those great miracles:

4 Yet the LORD hath not given you an heart to perceive, and eyes to see, and ears to hear, unto this day.

5 And I have led you forty years in the wilderness: your clothes are not waxen old upon you, and thy shoe is not waxen old upon thy foot.

6 Ye have not eaten bread, neither have ye drunk wine or strong drink: that ye might know that I *am* the LORD your God.

7 And when ye came unto this place, Sihon the king of Heshbon, and Og the king of Bashan, came out against us unto battle, and we smote them:

8 And we took their land, and gave it for an inheritance unto the Reubenites, and to the Gadites, and to the half tribe of Manasseh.

9 Keep therefore the words of this covenant, and do them, that ye may prosper in all that ye do.

10 Ye stand this day all of you before the LORD your God; your captains of your tribes, your elders, and your officers, *with* all the men of Israel,

11 Your little ones, your wives, and thy stranger that *is* in thy camp, from

the hewer of thy wood unto the drawer
of thy water:
12 That thou shouldest enter into
covenant with the LORD thy God, and
into his oath, which the LORD thy God
maketh with thee this day:
13 That he may establish thee to day
for a people unto himself, and *that* he
may be unto thee a God, as he hath said
unto thee, and as he hath sworn unto
thy fathers, to Abraham, to Isaac, and to
Jacob.
14 Neither with you only do I make
this covenant and this oath;
15 But with *him* that standeth here
with us this day before the LORD our
God, and also with *him* that *is* not here
with us this day:
16 (For ye know how we have dwelt in
the land of Egypt; and how we came
through the nations which ye passed
by;
17 And ye have seen their abominations, and their idols, wood and stone,
silver and gold, which *were* among
them:)
18 Lest there should be among you
man, or woman, or family, or tribe,
whose heart turneth away this day from
the LORD our God, to go *and* serve the
gods of these nations; lest there should
be among you a root that beareth gall
and wormwood;
19 And it come to pass, when he
heareth the words of this curse, that he
bless himself in his heart, saying, I shall
have peace, though I walk in the imagination of mine heart, to add drunkenness to thirst:
20 The LORD will not spare him, but
then the anger of the LORD and his
jealousy shall smoke against that man,
and all the curses that are written in
this book shall lie upon him, and the
LORD shall blot out his name from
under heaven.
21 And the LORD shall separate him
unto evil out of all the tribes of Israel,
according to all the curses of the covenant that are written in this book of the
law:
22 So that the generation to come of
your children that shall rise up after
you, and the stranger that shall come
from a far land, shall say, when they see
the plagues of that land, and the sicknesses which the LORD hath laid upon
it;
23 *And that* the whole land thereof *is*
brimstone, and salt, *and* burning, *that*
it is not sown, nor beareth, nor any
grass groweth therein, like the overthrow of Sodom, and Gomorrah,
Admah, and Zeboim, which the LORD
overthrew in his anger, and in his
wrath:
24 Even all nations shall say,
Wherefore hath the LORD done thus
unto this land? what *meaneth* the heat
of this great anger?
25 Then men shall say, Because they
have forsaken the covenant of the LORD
God of their fathers, which he made
with them when he brought them forth
out of the land of Egypt:
26 For they went and served other
gods, and worshipped them, gods whom
they knew not, and *whom* he had not
given unto them:
27 And the anger of the LORD was
kindled against this land, to bring upon
it all the curses that are written in this
book:
28 And the LORD rooted them out of
their land in anger, and in wrath, and in
great indignation, and cast them into
another land, as *it is* this day.

29 The secret *things belong* unto the
LORD our God: but those *things which*
are revealed *belong* unto us and to our
children for ever, that *we* may do all the
words of this law.

30 And it shall come to pass, when
all these things are come upon
thee, the blessing and the curse, which
I have set before thee, and thou shalt
call *them* to mind among all the
nations, whither the LORD thy God hath
driven thee,
2 And shalt return unto the LORD thy
God, and shalt obey his voice according
to all that I command thee this day,
thou and thy children, with all thine
heart, and with all thy soul;
3 That then the LORD thy God will
turn thy captivity, and have compassion
upon thee, and will return and gather
thee from all the nations, whither the
LORD thy God hath scattered thee.
4 If *any* of thine be driven out unto
the outmost *parts* of heaven, from
thence will the LORD thy God gather
thee, and from thence will he fetch
thee:
5 And the LORD thy God will bring
thee into the land which thy fathers
possessed, and thou shalt possess it;
and he will do thee good, and multiply
thee above thy fathers.
6 And the LORD thy God will circumcise thine heart, and the heart of thy
seed, to love the LORD thy God with all
thine heart, and with all thy soul, that
thou mayest live.
7 And the LORD thy God will put all
these curses upon thine enemies, and
on them that hate thee, which persecuted thee.
8 And thou shalt return and obey the
voice of the LORD, and do all his commandments which I command thee this
day.
9 And the LORD thy God will make
thee plenteous in every work of thine
hand, in the fruit of thy body, and in the
fruit of thy cattle, and in the fruit of thy
land, for good: for the LORD will again
rejoice over thee for good, as he
rejoiced over thy fathers:
10 If thou shalt hearken unto the
voice of the LORD thy God, to keep his
commandments and his statutes which
are written in this book of the law, *and*
if thou turn unto the LORD thy God with
all thine heart, and with all thy soul.
11 For this commandment which I
command thee this day, it *is* not hidden
from thee, neither *is* it far off.
12 It *is* not in heaven, that thou shouldest say, Who shall go up for us to
heaven, and bring it unto us, that we
may hear it, and do it?
13 Neither *is* it beyond the sea, that
thou shouldest say, Who shall go over
the sea for us, and bring it unto us, that
we may hear it, and do it?
14 But the word *is* very nigh unto
thee, in thy mouth, and in thy heart,
that thou mayest do it.
15 See, I have set before thee this day
life and good, and death and evil;
16 In that I command thee this day to
love the LORD thy God, to walk in his
ways, and to keep his commandments
and his statutes and his judgments,
that thou mayest live and multiply: and
the LORD thy God shall bless thee in the
land whither thou goest to possess it.
17 But if thine heart turn away, so
that thou wilt not hear, but shalt be
drawn away, and worship other gods,
and serve them;
18 I denounce unto you this day, that
ye shall surely perish, *and that* ye shall

not prolong *your* days upon the land,
whither thou passest over Jordan to go
to possess it.
19 I call heaven and earth to record
this day against you, *that* I have set
before you life and death, blessing and
cursing: therefore choose life, that both
thou and thy seed may live:
20 That thou mayest love the LORD
thy God, *and* that thou mayest obey his
voice, and that thou mayest cleave unto
him: for he *is* thy life, and the length of
thy days: that thou mayest dwell in the
land which the LORD sware unto thy
fathers, to Abraham, to Isaac, and to
Jacob, to give them.

31 And Moses went and spake these
words unto all Israel.
2 And he said unto them, I *am* an
hundred and twenty years old this day;
I can no more go out and come in: also
the LORD hath said unto me, Thou shalt
not go over this Jordan.
3 The LORD thy God, he will go over
before thee, *and* he will destroy these
nations from before thee, and thou
shalt possess them: *and* Joshua, he
shall go over before thee, as the LORD
hath said.
4 And the LORD shall do unto them as
he did to Sihon and to Og, kings of the
Amorites, and unto the land of them,
whom he destroyed.
5 And the LORD shall give them up
before your face, that ye may do unto
them according unto all the commandments which I have commanded you.
6 Be strong and of a good courage,
fear not, nor be afraid of them: for the
LORD thy God, he *it is* that doth go with
thee; he will not fail thee, nor forsake
thee.
7 And Moses called unto Joshua, and
said unto him in the sight of all Israel,
Be strong and of a good courage: for
thou must go with this people unto the
land which the LORD hath sworn unto
their fathers to give them; and thou
shalt cause them to inherit it.
8 And the LORD, he *it is* that doth go
before thee; he will be with thee, he
will not fail thee, neither forsake thee:
fear not, neither be dismayed.
9 And Moses wrote this law, and delivered it unto the priests the sons of Levi,
which bare the ark of the covenant of
the LORD, and unto all the elders of
Israel.
10 And Moses commanded them, saying, At the end of *every* seven years, in
the solemnity of the year of release, in
the feast of tabernacles,
11 When all Israel is come to appear
before the LORD thy God in the place
which he shall choose, thou shalt read
this law before all Israel in their hearing.
12 Gather the people together, men,
and women, and children, and thy
stranger that *is* within thy gates, that
they may hear, and that they may learn,
and fear the LORD your God, and
observe to do all the words of this law:
13 And *that* their children, which
have not known *any thing*, may hear,
and learn to fear the LORD your God, as
long as ye live in the land whither ye go
over Jordan to possess it.
14 And the LORD said unto Moses,
Behold, thy days approach that thou
must die: call Joshua, and present yourselves in the tabernacle of the congregation, that I may give him a charge.
And Moses and Joshua went, and presented themselves in the tabernacle of
the congregation.
15 And the LORD appeared in the
tabernacle in a pillar of a cloud: and

the pillar of the cloud stood over the
door of the tabernacle.
16 And the LORD said unto Moses,
Behold, thou shalt sleep with thy
fathers; and this people will rise up,
and go a whoring after the gods of the
strangers of the land, whither they go
to be among them, and will forsake me,
and break my covenant which I have
made with them.
17 Then my anger shall be kindled
against them in that day, and I will forsake them, and I will hide my face from
them, and they shall be devoured, and
many evils and troubles shall befall
them; so that they will say in that day,
Are not these evils come upon us,
because our God *is* not among us?
18 And I will surely hide my face in
that day for all the evils which they
shall have wrought, in that they are
turned unto other gods.
19 Now therefore write ye this song
for you, and teach it the children of
Israel: put it in their mouths, that this
song may be a witness for me against
the children of Israel.
20 For when I shall have brought
them into the land which I sware unto
their fathers, that floweth with milk
and honey; and they shall have eaten
and filled themselves, and waxen fat;
then will they turn unto other gods, and
serve them, and provoke me, and break
my covenant.
21 And it shall come to pass, when
many evils and troubles are befallen
them, that this song shall testify against
them as a witness; for it shall not be
forgotten out of the mouths of their
seed: for I know their imagination
which they go about, even now, before I
have brought them into the land which
I sware.
22 Moses therefore wrote this song
the same day, and taught it the children
of Israel.
23 And he gave Joshua the son of Nun
a charge, and said, Be strong and of a
good courage: for thou shalt bring the
children of Israel into the land which I
sware unto them: and I will be with
thee.
24 And it came to pass, when Moses
had made an end of writing the words
of this law in a book, until they were
finished,
25 That Moses commanded the
Levites, which bare the ark of the covenant of the LORD, saying,
26 Take this book of the law, and put
it in the side of the ark of the covenant
of the LORD your God, that it may be
there for a witness against thee.
27 For I know thy rebellion, and thy
stiff neck: behold, while I am yet alive
with you this day, ye have been rebellious against the LORD; and how much
more after my death?
28 Gather unto me all the elders of
your tribes, and your officers, that I
may speak these words in their ears,
and call heaven and earth to record
against them.
29 For I know that after my death ye
will utterly corrupt *yourselves*, and
turn aside from the way which I have
commanded you; and evil will befall
you in the latter days; because ye will
do evil in the sight of the LORD, to provoke him to anger through the work of
your hands.
30 And Moses spake in the ears of all
the congregation of Israel the words of
this song, until they were ended.

32 Give ear, O ye heavens, and I will
speak; and hear, O earth, the
words of my mouth.

2 My doctrine shall drop as the rain,
my speech shall distil as the dew, as the
small rain upon the tender herb, and as
the showers upon the grass:
3 Because I will publish the name of
the LORD: ascribe ye greatness unto our
God.
4 *He is* the Rock, his work *is* perfect:
for all his ways *are* judgment: a God of
truth and without iniquity, just and
right *is* he.
5 They have corrupted themselves,
their spot *is* not *the spot* of his children:
they are a perverse and crooked generation.
6 Do ye thus requite the LORD, O foolish people and unwise? *is* not he thy
father *that* hath bought thee? hath he
not made thee, and established thee?
7 Remember the days of old, consider
the years of many generations: ask thy
father, and he will shew thee; thy
elders, and they will tell thee.
8 When the most High divided to the
nations their inheritance, when he separated the sons of Adam, he set the
bounds of the people according to the
number of the children of Israel.
9 For the LORD's portion *is* his people;
Jacob *is* the lot of his inheritance.
10 He found him in a desert land, and
in the waste howling wilderness; he led
him about, he instructed him, he kept
him as the apple of his eye.
11 As an eagle stirreth up her nest,
fluttereth over her young, spreadeth
abroad her wings, taketh them, beareth
them on her wings:
12 *So* the LORD alone did lead him,
and *there was* no strange god with him.
13 He made him ride on the high
places of the earth, that he might eat
the increase of the fields; and he made
him to suck honey out of the rock, and
oil out of the flinty rock;
14 Butter of kine, and milk of sheep,
with fat of lambs, and rams of the breed
of Bashan, and goats, with the fat of
kidneys of wheat; and thou didst drink
the pure blood of the grape.
15 But Jeshurun waxed fat, and
kicked: thou art waxen fat, thou art
grown thick, thou art covered *with fatness*; then he forsook God *which* made
him, and lightly esteemed the Rock of
his salvation.
16 They provoked him to jealousy
with strange *gods*, with abominations
provoked they him to anger.
17 They sacrificed unto devils, not to
God; to gods whom they knew not, to
new *gods that* came newly up, whom
your fathers feared not.
18 Of the Rock *that* begat thee thou
art unmindful, and hast forgotten God
that formed thee.
19 And when the LORD saw *it*, he
abhorred *them*, because of the provoking of his sons, and of his daughters.
20 And he said, I will hide my face
from them, I will see what their end
shall be: for they *are* a very froward
generation, children in whom *is* no
faith.
21 They have moved me to jealousy
with *that which is* not God; they have
provoked me to anger with their vanities: and I will move them to jealousy
with *those which are* not a people; I
will provoke them to anger with a foolish nation.
22 For a fire is kindled in mine anger,
and shall burn unto the lowest hell, and
shall consume the earth with her
increase, and set on fire the foundations of the mountains.

23 I will heap mischiefs upon them; I
will spend mine arrows upon them.
24 *They shall be* burnt with hunger,
and devoured with burning heat, and
with bitter destruction: I will also send
the teeth of beasts upon them, with the
poison of serpents of the dust.
25 The sword without, and terror
within, shall destroy both the young
man and the virgin, the suckling *also*
with the man of gray hairs.
26 I said, I would scatter them into
corners, I would make the remembrance of them to cease from among
men:
27 Were it not that I feared the wrath
of the enemy, lest their adversaries
should behave themselves strangely,
and lest they should say, Our hand *is*
high, and the LORD hath not done all
this.
28 For they *are* a nation void of counsel, neither *is there any* understanding
in them.
29 O that they were wise, *that* they
understood this, *that* they would consider their latter end!
30 How should one chase a thousand,
and two put ten thousand to flight,
except their Rock had sold them, and
the LORD had shut them up?
31 For their rock *is* not as our Rock,
even our enemies themselves *being*
judges.
32 For their vine *is* of the vine of
Sodom, and of the fields of Gomorrah:
their grapes *are* grapes of gall, their
clusters *are* bitter:
33 Their wine *is* the poison of dragons, and the cruel venom of asps.
34 *Is* not this laid up in store with me,
and sealed up among my treasures?
35 To me *belongeth* vengeance, and
recompence; their foot shall slide in
due time: for the day of their calamity
is at hand, and the things that shall
come upon them make haste.
36 For the LORD shall judge his people, and repent himself for his servants,
when he seeth that *their* power is gone,
and *there is* none shut up, or left.
37 And he shall say, Where *are* their
gods, *their* rock in whom they trusted,
38 Which did eat the fat of their sacrifices, *and* drank the wine of their drink
offerings? let them rise up and help
you, *and* be your protection.
39 See now that I, *even* I, *am* he, and
there is no god with me: I kill, and I
make alive; I wound, and I heal: neither
is there any that can deliver out of my
hand.
40 For I lift up my hand to heaven,
and say, I live for ever.
41 If I whet my glittering sword, and
mine hand take hold on judgment; I
will render vengeance to mine enemies, and will reward them that hate
me.
42 I will make mine arrows drunk
with blood, and my sword shall devour
flesh; *and that* with the blood of the
slain and of the captives, from the
beginning of revenges upon the enemy.
43 Rejoice, O ye nations, *with* his
people: for he will avenge the blood of
his servants, and will render vengeance
to his adversaries, and will be merciful
unto his land, *and* to his people.
44 And Moses came and spake all the
words of this song in the ears of the
people, he, and Hoshea the son of Nun.
45 And Moses made an end of speaking all these words to all Israel:
46 And he said unto them, Set your
hearts unto all the words which I testify
among you this day, which ye shall

command your children to observe to
do, all the words of this law.
47 For it *is* not a vain thing for you;
because it *is* your life: and through this
thing ye shall prolong *your* days in the
land, whither ye go over Jordan to possess it.
48 And the LORD spake unto Moses
that selfsame day, saying,
49 Get thee up into this mountain
Abarim, *unto* mount Nebo, which *is* in
the land of Moab, that *is* over against
Jericho; and behold the land of Canaan,
which I give unto the children of Israel
for a possession:
50 And die in the mount whither thou
goest up, and be gathered unto thy
people; as Aaron thy brother died in
mount Hor, and was gathered unto his
people:
51 Because ye trespassed against me
among the children of Israel at the
waters of Meribah-Kadesh, in the wilderness of Zin; because ye sanctified
me not in the midst of the children of
Israel.
52 Yet thou shalt see the land before
thee; but thou shalt not go thither unto
the land which I give the children of
Israel.

33 And this *is* the blessing, wherewith Moses the man of God
blessed the children of Israel before his
death.
2 And he said, The LORD came from
Sinai, and rose up from Seir unto them;
he shined forth from mount Paran, and
he came with ten thousands of saints:
from his right hand *went* a fiery law for
them.
3 Yea, he loved the people; all his
saints *are* in thy hand: and they sat
down at thy feet; *every one* shall receive
of thy words.
4 Moses commanded us a law, *even*
the inheritance of the congregation of
Jacob.
5 And he was king in Jeshurun, when
the heads of the people *and* the tribes
of Israel were gathered together.
6 Let Reuben live, and not die; and
let *not* his men be few.
7 And this *is the blessing* of Judah:
and he said, Hear, LORD, the voice of
Judah, and bring him unto his people:
let his hands be sufficient for him; and
be thou an help *to him* from his enemies.
8 And of Levi he said, *Let* thy
Thummim and thy Urim *be* with thy
holy one, whom thou didst prove at
Massah, *and with* whom thou didst
strive at the waters of Meribah;
9 Who said unto his father and to his
mother, I have not seen him; neither
did he acknowledge his brethren, nor
knew his own children: for they have
observed thy word, and kept thy covenant.
10 They shall teach Jacob thy judgments, and Israel thy law: they shall put
incense before thee, and whole burnt
sacrifice upon thine altar.
11 Bless, LORD, his substance, and
accept the work of his hands: smite
through the loins of them that rise
against him, and of them that hate him,
that they rise not again.
12 *And* of Benjamin he said, The
beloved of the LORD shall dwell in
safety by him; *and the LORD* shall cover
him all the day long, and he shall dwell
between his shoulders.
13 And of Joseph he said, Blessed of
the LORD *be* his land, for the precious
things of heaven, for the dew, and for
the deep that coucheth beneath,

14 And for the precious fruits *brought forth* by the sun, and for the precious things put forth by the moon,

15 And for the chief things of the ancient mountains, and for the precious things of the lasting hills,

16 And for the precious things of the earth and fulness thereof, and *for* the good will of him that dwelt in the bush: let *the blessing* come upon the head of Joseph, and upon the top of the head of him *that was* separated from his brethren.

17 His glory *is like* the firstling of his bullock, and his horns *are like* the horns of unicorns: with them he shall push the people together to the ends of the earth: and they *are* the ten thousands of Ephraim, and they *are* the thousands of Manasseh.

18 And of Zebulun he said, Rejoice, Zebulun, in thy going out; and, Issachar, in thy tents.

19 They shall call the people unto the mountain; there they shall offer sacrifices of righteousness: for they shall suck *of* the abundance of the seas, and *of* treasures hid in the sand.

20 And of Gad he said, Blessed *be* he that enlargeth Gad: he dwelleth as a lion, and teareth the arm with the crown of the head.

21 And he provided the first part for himself, because there, *in* a portion of the lawgiver, *was he* seated; and he came with the heads of the people, he executed the justice of the LORD, and his judgments with Israel.

22 And of Dan he said, Dan *is* a lion's whelp: he shall leap from Bashan.

23 And of Naphtali he said, O Naphtali, satisfied with favour, and full with the blessing of the LORD: possess thou the west and the south.

24 And of Asher he said, *Let* Asher *be* blessed with children; let him be acceptable to his brethren, and let him dip his foot in oil.

25 Thy shoes *shall be* iron and brass; and as thy days, *so shall* thy strength *be*.

26 *There is* none like unto the God of Jeshurun, *who* rideth upon the heaven in thy help, and in his excellency on the sky.

27 The eternal God *is thy* refuge, and underneath *are* the everlasting arms: and he shall thrust out the enemy from before thee; and shall say, Destroy *them*.

28 Israel then shall dwell in safety alone: the fountain of Jacob *shall be* upon a land of corn and wine; also his heavens shall drop down dew.

29 Happy *art* thou, O Israel: who *is* like unto thee, O people saved by the LORD, the shield of thy help, and who *is* the sword of thy excellency! and thine enemies shall be found liars unto thee; and thou shalt tread upon their high places.

34 And Moses went up from the plains of Moab unto the mountain of Nebo, to the top of Pisgah, that *is* over against Jericho. And the LORD shewed him all the land of Gilead, unto Dan,

2 And all Naphtali, and the land of Ephraim, and Manasseh, and all the land of Judah, unto the utmost sea,

3 And the south, and the plain of the valley of Jericho, the city of palm trees, unto Zoar.

4 And the LORD said unto him, This *is* the land which I sware unto Abraham, unto Isaac, and unto Jacob, saying, I will give it unto thy seed: I have caused thee to see *it* with thine eyes, but thou shalt not go over thither.

5 So Moses the servant of the LORD died there in the land of Moab, according to the word of the LORD.

6 And he buried him in a valley in the land of Moab, over against Beth-peor: but no man knoweth of his sepulchre unto this day.

7 And Moses *was* an hundred and twenty years old when he died: his eye was not dim, nor his natural force abated.

8 And the children of Israel wept for Moses in the plains of Moab thirty days: so the days of weeping *and* mourning for Moses were ended.

9 And Joshua the son of Nun was full of the spirit of wisdom; for Moses had laid his hands upon him: and the children of Israel hearkened unto him, and did as the LORD commanded Moses.

10 And there arose not a prophet since in Israel like unto Moses, whom the LORD knew face to face,

11 In all the signs and the wonders, which the LORD sent him to do in the land of Egypt to Pharaoh, and to all his servants, and to all his land,

12 And in all that mighty hand, and in all the great terror which Moses shewed in the sight of all Israel.

THE BOOK OF JOSHUA

1 Now after the death of Moses the servant of the LORD it came to pass, that the LORD spake unto Joshua the son of Nun, Moses' minister, saying,

2 Moses my servant is dead; now therefore arise, go over this Jordan, thou, and all this people, unto the land which I do give to them, *even* to the children of Israel.

3 Every place that the sole of your foot shall tread upon, that have I given unto you, as I said unto Moses.

4 From the wilderness and this Lebanon even unto the great river, the river Euphrates, all the land of the Hittites, and unto the great sea toward the going down of the sun, shall be your coast.

5 There shall not any man be able to stand before thee all the days of thy life: as I was with Moses, *so* I will be with thee: I will not fail thee, nor forsake thee.

6 Be strong and of a good courage: for unto this people shalt thou divide for an inheritance the land, which I sware unto their fathers to give them.

7 Only be thou strong and very courageous, that thou mayest observe to do according to all the law, which Moses my servant commanded thee: turn not from it *to* the right hand or *to* the left, that thou mayest prosper whithersoever thou goest.

8 This book of the law shall not depart out of thy mouth; but thou shalt meditate therein day and night, that thou mayest observe to do according to all that is written therein: for then thou shalt make thy way prosperous, and then thou shalt have good success.

9 Have not I commanded thee? Be strong and of a good courage; be not afraid, neither be thou dismayed: for the LORD thy God *is* with thee whithersoever thou goest.

10 Then Joshua commanded the officers of the people, saying,
11 Pass through the host, and command the people, saying, Prepare you victuals; for within three days ye shall pass over this Jordan, to go in to possess the land, which the LORD your God giveth you to possess it.
12 And to the Reubenites, and to the Gadites, and to half the tribe of Manasseh, spake Joshua, saying,
13 Remember the word which Moses the servant of the LORD commanded you, saying, The LORD your God hath given you rest, and hath given you this land.
14 Your wives, your little ones, and your cattle, shall remain in the land which Moses gave you on this side Jordan; but ye shall pass before your brethren armed, all the mighty men of valour, and help them;
15 Until the LORD have given your brethren rest, as *he hath given* you, and they also have possessed the land which the LORD your God giveth them: then ye shall return unto the land of your possession, and enjoy it, which Moses the LORD's servant gave you on this side Jordan toward the sunrising.
16 And they answered Joshua, saying, All that thou commandest us we will do, and whithersoever thou sendest us, we will go.
17 According as we hearkened unto Moses in all things, so will we hearken unto thee: only the LORD thy God be with thee, as he was with Moses.
18 Whosoever *he be* that doth rebel against thy commandment, and will not hearken unto thy words in all that thou commandest him, he shall be put to death: only be strong and of a good courage.

2 And Joshua the son of Nun sent out of Shittim two men to spy secretly, saying, Go view the land, even Jericho. And they went, and came into an harlot's house, named Rahab, and lodged there.
2 And it was told the king of Jericho, saying, Behold, there came men in hither to night of the children of Israel to search out the country.
3 And the king of Jericho sent unto Rahab, saying, Bring forth the men that are come to thee, which are entered into thine house: for they be come to search out all the country.
4 And the woman took the two men, and hid them, and said thus, There came men unto me, but I wist not whence they *were*:
5 And it came to pass *about the time* of shutting of the gate, when it was dark, that the men went out: whither the men went I wot not: pursue after them quickly; for ye shall overtake them.
6 But she had brought them up to the roof of the house, and hid them with the stalks of flax, which she had laid in order upon the roof.
7 And the men pursued after them the way to Jordan unto the fords: and as soon as they which pursued after them were gone out, they shut the gate.
8 And before they were laid down, she came up unto them upon the roof;
9 And she said unto the men, I know that the LORD hath given you the land, and that your terror is fallen upon us, and that all the inhabitants of the land faint because of you.
10 For we have heard how the LORD dried up the water of the Red sea for you, when ye came out of Egypt; and what ye did unto the two kings of the

Amorites, that *were* on the other side Jordan, Sihon and Og, whom ye utterly destroyed.

11 And as soon as we had heard *these things*, our hearts did melt, neither did there remain any more courage in any man, because of you: for the LORD your God, he *is* God in heaven above, and in earth beneath.

12 Now therefore, I pray you, swear unto me by the LORD, since I have shewed you kindness, that ye will also shew kindness unto my father's house, and give me a true token:

13 And *that* ye will save alive my father, and my mother, and my brethren, and my sisters, and all that they have, and deliver our lives from death.

14 And the men answered her, Our life for yours, if ye utter not this our business. And it shall be, when the LORD hath given us the land, that we will deal kindly and truly with thee.

15 Then she let them down by a cord through the window: for her house *was* upon the town wall, and she dwelt upon the wall.

16 And she said unto them, Get you to the mountain, lest the pursuers meet you; and hide yourselves there three days, until the pursuers be returned: and afterward may ye go your way.

17 And the men said unto her, We *will be* blameless of this thine oath which thou hast made us swear.

18 Behold, *when* we come into the land, thou shalt bind this line of scarlet thread in the window which thou didst let us down by: and thou shalt bring thy father, and thy mother, and thy brethren, and all thy father's household, home unto thee.

19 And it shall be, *that* whosoever shall go out of the doors of thy house into the street, his blood *shall be* upon his head, and we *will be* guiltless: and whosoever shall be with thee in the house, his blood *shall be* on our head, if *any* hand be upon him.

20 And if thou utter this our business, then we will be quit of thine oath which thou hast made us to swear.

21 And she said, According unto your words, so *be* it. And she sent them away, and they departed: and she bound the scarlet line in the window.

22 And they went, and came unto the mountain, and abode there three days, until the pursuers were returned: and the pursuers sought *them* throughout all the way, but found *them* not.

23 So the two men returned, and descended from the mountain, and passed over, and came to Joshua the son of Nun, and told him all *things* that befell them:

24 And they said unto Joshua, Truly the LORD hath delivered into our hands all the land; for even all the inhabitants of the country do faint because of us.

3 And Joshua rose early in the morning; and they removed from Shittim, and came to Jordan, he and all the children of Israel, and lodged there before they passed over.

2 And it came to pass after three days, that the officers went through the host;

3 And they commanded the people, saying, When ye see the ark of the covenant of the LORD your God, and the priests the Levites bearing it, then ye shall remove from your place, and go after it.

4 Yet there shall be a space between you and it, about two thousand cubits by measure: come not near unto it, that ye may know the way by which ye must

go: for ye have not passed *this* way heretofore.

5 And Joshua said unto the people, Sanctify yourselves: for to morrow the LORD will do wonders among you.

6 And Joshua spake unto the priests, saying, Take up the ark of the covenant, and pass over before the people. And they took up the ark of the covenant, and went before the people.

7 And the LORD said unto Joshua, This day will I begin to magnify thee in the sight of all Israel, that they may know that, as I was with Moses, *so* I will be with thee.

8 And thou shalt command the priests that bear the ark of the covenant, saying, When ye are come to the brink of the water of Jordan, ye shall stand still in Jordan.

9 And Joshua said unto the children of Israel, Come hither, and hear the words of the LORD your God.

10 And Joshua said, Hereby ye shall know that the living God *is* among you, and *that* he will without fail drive out from before you the Canaanites, and the Hittites, and the Hivites, and the Perizzites, and the Girgashites, and the Amorites, and the Jebusites.

11 Behold, the ark of the covenant of the Lord of all the earth passeth over before you into Jordan.

12 Now therefore take you twelve men out of the tribes of Israel, out of every tribe a man.

13 And it shall come to pass, as soon as the soles of the feet of the priests that bear the ark of the LORD, the Lord of all the earth, shall rest in the waters of Jordan, *that* the waters of Jordan shall be cut off *from* the waters that come down from above; and they shall stand upon an heap.

14 And it came to pass, when the people removed from their tents, to pass over Jordan, and the priests bearing the ark of the covenant before the people;

15 And as they that bare the ark were come unto Jordan, and the feet of the priests that bare the ark were dipped in the brim of the water, (for Jordan overfloweth all his banks all the time of harvest,)

16 That the waters which came down from above stood *and* rose up upon an heap very far from the city Adam, that *is* beside Zaretan: and those that came down toward the sea of the plain, *even* the salt sea, failed, *and* were cut off: and the people passed over right against Jericho.

17 And the priests that bare the ark of the covenant of the LORD stood firm on dry ground in the midst of Jordan, and all the Israelites passed over on dry ground, until all the people were passed clean over Jordan.

4 And it came to pass, when all the people were clean passed over Jordan, that the LORD spake unto Joshua, saying,

2 Take you twelve men out of the people, out of every tribe a man,

3 And command ye them, saying, Take you hence out of the midst of Jordan, out of the place where the priests' feet stood firm, twelve stones, and ye shall carry them over with you, and leave them in the lodging place, where ye shall lodge this night.

4 Then Joshua called the twelve men, whom he had prepared of the children of Israel, out of every tribe a man:

5 And Joshua said unto them, Pass over before the ark of the LORD your God into the midst of Jordan, and take ye up every man of you a stone upon his shoulder, according unto the number of the tribes of the children of Israel:

6 That this may be a sign among you, *that* when your children ask *their fathers* in time to come, saying, What *mean* ye by these stones?

7 Then ye shall answer them, That the waters of Jordan were cut off before the ark of the covenant of the LORD; when it passed over Jordan, the waters of Jordan were cut off: and these stones shall be for a memorial unto the children of Israel for ever.

8 And the children of Israel did so as Joshua commanded, and took up twelve stones out of the midst of Jordan, as the LORD spake unto Joshua, according to the number of the tribes of the children of Israel, and carried them over with them unto the place where they lodged, and laid them down there.

9 And Joshua set up twelve stones in the midst of Jordan, in the place where the feet of the priests which bare the ark of the covenant stood: and they are there unto this day.

10 For the priests which bare the ark stood in the midst of Jordan, until every thing was finished that the LORD commanded Joshua to speak unto the people, according to all that Moses commanded Joshua: and the people hasted and passed over.

11 And it came to pass, when all the people were clean passed over, that the ark of the LORD passed over, and the priests, in the presence of the people.

12 And the children of Reuben, and the children of Gad, and half the tribe of Manasseh, passed over armed before the children of Israel, as Moses spake unto them:

13 About forty thousand prepared for war passed over before the LORD unto battle, to the plains of Jericho.

14 On that day the LORD magnified Joshua in the sight of all Israel; and they feared him, as they feared Moses, all the days of his life.

15 And the LORD spake unto Joshua, saying,

16 Command the priests that bear the ark of the testimony, that they come up out of Jordan.

17 Joshua therefore commanded the priests, saying, Come ye up out of Jordan.

18 And it came to pass, when the priests that bare the ark of the covenant of the LORD were come up out of the midst of Jordan, *and* the soles of the priests' feet were lifted up unto the dry land, that the waters of Jordan returned unto their place, and flowed over all his banks, as *they did* before.

19 And the people came up out of Jordan on the tenth *day* of the first month, and encamped in Gilgal, in the east border of Jericho.

20 And those twelve stones, which they took out of Jordan, did Joshua pitch in Gilgal.

21 And he spake unto the children of Israel, saying, When your children shall ask their fathers in time to come, saying, What *mean* these stones?

22 Then ye shall let your children know, saying, Israel came over this Jordan on dry land.

23 For the LORD your God dried up the waters of Jordan from before you, until ye were passed over, as the LORD your God did to the Red sea, which he dried up from before us, until we were gone over:

24 That all the people of the earth
might know the hand of the LORD, that
it *is* mighty: that ye might fear the LORD
your God for ever.

5 And it came to pass, when all the
kings of the Amorites, which *were*
on the side of Jordan westward, and all
the kings of the Canaanites, which *were*
by the sea, heard that the LORD had
dried up the waters of Jordan from
before the children of Israel, until we
were passed over, that their heart
melted, neither was there spirit in
them any more, because of the children
of Israel.
2 At that time the LORD said unto
Joshua, Make thee sharp knives, and
circumcise again the children of Israel
the second time.
3 And Joshua made him sharp knives,
and circumcised the children of Israel
at the hill of the foreskins.
4 And this *is* the cause why Joshua
did circumcise: All the people that
came out of Egypt, *that were* males,
even all the men of war, died in the
wilderness by the way, after they came
out of Egypt.
5 Now all the people that came out
were circumcised: but all the people
that were born in the wilderness by the
way as they came forth out of Egypt,
them they had not circumcised.
6 For the children of Israel walked
forty years in the wilderness, till all the
people *that were* men of war, which
came out of Egypt, were consumed,
because they obeyed not the voice of
the LORD: unto whom the LORD sware
that he would not shew them the land,
which the LORD sware unto their fathers
that he would give us, a land that
floweth with milk and honey.
7 And their children, *whom* he raised
up in their stead, them Joshua circumcised: for they were uncircumcised,
because they had not circumcised them
by the way.
8 And it came to pass, when they had
done circumcising all the people, that
they abode in their places in the camp,
till they were whole.
9 And the LORD said unto Joshua, This
day have I rolled away the reproach of
Egypt from off you. Wherefore the
name of the place is called Gilgal unto
this day.
10 And the children of Israel encamped in Gilgal, and kept the passover on
the fourteenth day of the month at
even in the plains of Jericho.
11 And they did eat of the old corn of
the land on the morrow after the passover, unleavened cakes, and parched
corn in the selfsame day.
12 And the manna ceased on the morrow after they had eaten of the old corn
of the land; neither had the children of
Israel manna any more; but they did
eat of the fruit of the land of Canaan
that year.
13 And it came to pass, when Joshua
was by Jericho, that he lifted up his
eyes and looked, and, behold, there
stood a man over against him with his
sword drawn in his hand: and Joshua
went unto him, and said unto him, *Art*
thou for us, or for our adversaries?
14 And he said, Nay; but *as* captain of
the host of the LORD am I now come.
And Joshua fell on his face to the earth,
and did worship, and said unto him,
What saith my lord unto his servant?
15 And the captain of the LORD's host
said unto Joshua, Loose thy shoe from
off thy foot; for the place whereon thou
standest *is* holy. And Joshua did so.

6 Now Jericho was straitly shut up because of the children of Israel: none went out, and none came in.

2 And the LORD said unto Joshua, See, I have given into thine hand Jericho, and the king thereof, *and* the mighty men of valour.

3 And ye shall compass the city, all *ye* men of war, *and* go round about the city once. Thus shalt thou do six days.

4 And seven priests shall bear before the ark seven trumpets of rams' horns: and the seventh day ye shall compass the city seven times, and the priests shall blow with the trumpets.

5 And it shall come to pass, that when they make a long *blast* with the ram's horn, *and* when ye hear the sound of the trumpet, all the people shall shout with a great shout; and the wall of the city shall fall down flat, and the people shall ascend up every man straight before him.

6 And Joshua the son of Nun called the priests, and said unto them, Take up the ark of the covenant, and let seven priests bear seven trumpets of rams' horns before the ark of the LORD.

7 And he said unto the people, Pass on, and compass the city, and let him that is armed pass on before the ark of the LORD.

8 And it came to pass, when Joshua had spoken unto the people, that the seven priests bearing the seven trumpets of rams' horns passed on before the LORD, and blew with the trumpets: and the ark of the covenant of the LORD followed them.

9 And the armed men went before the priests that blew with the trumpets, and the rereward came after the ark, *the priests* going on, and blowing with the trumpets.

10 And Joshua had commanded the people, saying, Ye shall not shout, nor make any noise with your voice, neither shall *any* word proceed out of your mouth, until the day I bid you shout; then shall ye shout.

11 So the ark of the LORD compassed the city, going about *it* once: and they came into the camp, and lodged in the camp.

12 And Joshua rose early in the morning, and the priests took up the ark of the LORD.

13 And seven priests bearing seven trumpets of rams' horns before the ark of the LORD went on continually, and blew with the trumpets: and the armed men went before them; but the rereward came after the ark of the LORD, *the priests* going on, and blowing with the trumpets.

14 And the second day they compassed the city once, and returned into the camp: so they did six days.

15 And it came to pass on the seventh day, that they rose early about the dawning of the day, and compassed the city after the same manner seven times: only on that day they compassed the city seven times.

16 And it came to pass at the seventh time, when the priests blew with the trumpets, Joshua said unto the people, Shout; for the LORD hath given you the city.

17 And the city shall be accursed, *even* it, and all that *are* therein, to the LORD: only Rahab the harlot shall live, she and all that *are* with her in the house, because she hid the messengers that we sent.

18 And ye, in any wise keep *yourselves* from the accursed thing, lest ye make *yourselves* accursed, when ye

take of the accursed thing, and make the camp of Israel a curse, and trouble it.

19 But all the silver, and gold, and vessels of brass and iron, *are* consecrated unto the Lord: they shall come into the treasury of the Lord.

20 So the people shouted when *the priests* blew with the trumpets: and it came to pass, when the people heard the sound of the trumpet, and the people shouted with a great shout, that the wall fell down flat, so that the people went up into the city, every man straight before him, and they took the city.

21 And they utterly destroyed all that *was* in the city, both man and woman, young and old, and ox, and sheep, and ass, with the edge of the sword.

22 But Joshua had said unto the two men that had spied out the country, Go into the harlot's house, and bring out thence the woman, and all that she hath, as ye sware unto her.

23 And the young men that were spies went in, and brought out Rahab, and her father, and her mother, and her brethren, and all that she had; and they brought out all her kindred, and left them without the camp of Israel.

24 And they burnt the city with fire, and all that *was* therein: only the silver, and the gold, and the vessels of brass and of iron, they put into the treasury of the house of the Lord.

25 And Joshua saved Rahab the harlot alive, and her father's household, and all that she had; and she dwelleth in Israel *even* unto this day; because she hid the messengers, which Joshua sent to spy out Jericho.

26 And Joshua adjured *them* at that time, saying, Cursed *be* the man before the Lord, that riseth up and buildeth this city Jericho: he shall lay the foundation thereof in his firstborn, and in his youngest *son* shall he set up the gates of it.

27 So the Lord was with Joshua; and his fame was *noised* throughout all the country.

7 But the children of Israel committed a trespass in the accursed thing: for Achan, the son of Carmi, the son of Zabdi, the son of Zerah, of the tribe of Judah, took of the accursed thing: and the anger of the Lord was kindled against the children of Israel.

2 And Joshua sent men from Jericho to Ai, which *is* beside Beth-aven, on the east side of Beth-el, and spake unto them, saying, Go up and view the country. And the men went up and viewed Ai.

3 And they returned to Joshua, and said unto him, Let not all the people go up; but let about two or three thousand men go up and smite Ai; *and* make not all the people to labour thither; for they *are but* few.

4 So there went up thither of the people about three thousand men: and they fled before the men of Ai.

5 And the men of Ai smote of them about thirty and six men: for they chased them *from* before the gate *even* unto Shebarim, and smote them in the going down: wherefore the hearts of the people melted, and became as water.

6 And Joshua rent his clothes, and fell to the earth upon his face before the ark of the Lord until the eventide, he and the elders of Israel, and put dust upon their heads.

7 And Joshua said, Alas, O Lord GOD, wherefore hast thou at all brought this people over Jordan, to deliver us into the hand of the Amorites, to destroy us? would to God we had been content, and dwelt on the other side Jordan!

8 O Lord, what shall I say, when Israel turneth their backs before their enemies!

9 For the Canaanites and all the inhabitants of the land shall hear *of it*, and shall environ us round, and cut off our name from the earth: and what wilt thou do unto thy great name?

10 And the LORD said unto Joshua, Get thee up; wherefore liest thou thus upon thy face?

11 Israel hath sinned, and they have also transgressed my covenant which I commanded them: for they have even taken of the accursed thing, and have also stolen, and dissembled also, and they have put *it* even among their own stuff.

12 Therefore the children of Israel could not stand before their enemies, *but* turned *their* backs before their enemies, because they were accursed: neither will I be with you any more, except ye destroy the accursed from among you.

13 Up, sanctify the people, and say, Sanctify yourselves against to morrow: for thus saith the LORD God of Israel, *There is* an accursed thing in the midst of thee, O Israel: thou canst not stand before thine enemies, until ye take away the accursed thing from among you.

14 In the morning therefore ye shall be brought according to your tribes: and it shall be, *that* the tribe which the LORD taketh shall come according to the families *thereof*; and the family which the LORD shall take shall come by households; and the household which the LORD shall take shall come man by man.

15 And it shall be, *that* he that is taken with the accursed thing shall be burnt with fire, he and all that he hath: because he hath transgressed the covenant of the LORD, and because he hath wrought folly in Israel.

16 So Joshua rose up early in the morning, and brought Israel by their tribes; and the tribe of Judah was taken:

17 And he brought the family of Judah; and he took the family of the Zarhites: and he brought the family of the Zarhites man by man; and Zabdi was taken:

18 And he brought his household man by man; and Achan, the son of Carmi, the son of Zabdi, the son of Zerah, of the tribe of Judah, was taken.

19 And Joshua said unto Achan, My son, give, I pray thee, glory to the LORD God of Israel, and make confession unto him; and tell me now what thou hast done; hide *it* not from me.

20 And Achan answered Joshua, and said, Indeed I have sinned against the LORD God of Israel, and thus and thus have I done:

21 When I saw among the spoils a goodly Babylonish garment, and two hundred shekels of silver, and a wedge of gold of fifty shekels weight, then I coveted them, and took them; and, behold, they *are* hid in the earth in the midst of my tent, and the silver under it.

22 So Joshua sent messengers, and they ran unto the tent; and, behold, *it was* hid in his tent, and the silver under it.

23 And they took them out of the
midst of the tent, and brought them
unto Joshua, and unto all the children
of Israel, and laid them out before the
LORD.
24 And Joshua, and all Israel with
him, took Achan the son of Zerah, and
the silver, and the garment, and the
wedge of gold, and his sons, and his
daughters, and his oxen, and his asses,
and his sheep, and his tent, and all that
he had: and they brought them unto
the valley of Achor.
25 And Joshua said, Why hast thou
troubled us? the LORD shall trouble
thee this day. And all Israel stoned him
with stones, and burned them with fire,
after they had stoned them with stones.
26 And they raised over him a great
heap of stones unto this day. So the
LORD turned from the fierceness of his
anger. Wherefore the name of that
place was called, The valley of Achor,
unto this day.

8 And the LORD said unto Joshua,
Fear not, neither be thou dismayed:
take all the people of war with thee,
and arise, go up to Ai: see, I have given
into thy hand the king of Ai, and his
people, and his city, and his land:
2 And thou shalt do to Ai and her
king as thou didst unto Jericho and her
king: only the spoil thereof, and the
cattle thereof, shall ye take for a prey
unto yourselves: lay thee an ambush for
the city behind it.
3 So Joshua arose, and all the people
of war, to go up against Ai: and Joshua
chose out thirty thousand mighty men
of valour, and sent them away by night.
4 And he commanded them, saying,
Behold, ye shall lie in wait against the
city, *even* behind the city: go not very
far from the city, but be ye all ready:
5 And I, and all the people that *are*
with me, will approach unto the city:
and it shall come to pass, when they
come out against us, as at the first, that
we will flee before them,
6 (For they will come out after us) till
we have drawn them from the city; for
they will say, They flee before us, as at
the first: therefore we will flee before
them.
7 Then ye shall rise up from the
ambush, and seize upon the city: for the
LORD your God will deliver it into your
hand.
8 And it shall be, when ye have taken
the city, *that* ye shall set the city on
fire: according to the commandment of
the LORD shall ye do. See, I have commanded you.
9 Joshua therefore sent them forth:
and they went to lie in ambush, and
abode between Beth-el and Ai, on the
west side of Ai: but Joshua lodged that
night among the people.
10 And Joshua rose up early in the
morning, and numbered the people,
and went up, he and the elders of Israel,
before the people to Ai.
11 And all the people, *even the people*
of war that *were* with him, went up, and
drew nigh, and came before the city,
and pitched on the north side of Ai:
now *there was* a valley between them
and Ai.
12 And he took about five thousand
men, and set them to lie in ambush
between Beth-el and Ai, on the west
side of the city.
13 And when they had set the people,
even all the host that *was* on the north
of the city, and their liers in wait on the
west of the city, Joshua went that night
into the midst of the valley.

14 And it came to pass, when the king of Ai saw *it*, that they hasted and rose up early, and the men of the city went out against Israel to battle, he and all his people, at a time appointed, before the plain; but he wist not that *there were* liers in ambush against him behind the city.

15 And Joshua and all Israel made as if they were beaten before them, and fled by the way of the wilderness.

16 And all the people that *were* in Ai were called together to pursue after them: and they pursued after Joshua, and were drawn away from the city.

17 And there was not a man left in Ai or Beth-el, that went not out after Israel: and they left the city open, and pursued after Israel.

18 And the LORD said unto Joshua, Stretch out the spear that *is* in thy hand toward Ai; for I will give it into thine hand. And Joshua stretched out the spear that *he had* in his hand toward the city.

19 And the ambush arose quickly out of their place, and they ran as soon as he had stretched out his hand: and they entered into the city, and took it, and hasted and set the city on fire.

20 And when the men of Ai looked behind them, they saw, and, behold, the smoke of the city ascended up to heaven, and they had no power to flee this way or that way: and the people that fled to the wilderness turned back upon the pursuers.

21 And when Joshua and all Israel saw that the ambush had taken the city, and that the smoke of the city ascended, then they turned again, and slew the men of Ai.

22 And the other issued out of the city against them; so they were in the midst of Israel, some on this side, and some on that side: and they smote them, so that they let none of them remain or escape.

23 And the king of Ai they took alive, and brought him to Joshua.

24 And it came to pass, when Israel had made an end of slaying all the inhabitants of Ai in the field, in the wilderness wherein they chased them, and when they were all fallen on the edge of the sword, until they were consumed, that all the Israelites returned unto Ai, and smote it with the edge of the sword.

25 And *so* it was, *that* all that fell that day, both of men and women, *were* twelve thousand, *even* all the men of Ai.

26 For Joshua drew not his hand back, wherewith he stretched out the spear, until he had utterly destroyed all the inhabitants of Ai.

27 Only the cattle and the spoil of that city Israel took for a prey unto themselves, according unto the word of the LORD which he commanded Joshua.

28 And Joshua burnt Ai, and made it an heap for ever, *even* a desolation unto this day.

29 And the king of Ai he hanged on a tree until eventide: and as soon as the sun was down, Joshua commanded that they should take his carcase down from the tree, and cast it at the entering of the gate of the city, and raise thereon a great heap of stones, *that remaineth* unto this day.

30 Then Joshua built an altar unto the LORD God of Israel in mount Ebal,

31 As Moses the servant of the LORD commanded the children of Israel, as it is written in the book of the law of Moses, an altar of whole stones, over which no man hath lift up *any* iron: and they offered thereon burnt offerings unto the LORD, and sacrificed peace offerings.

32 And he wrote there upon the stones a copy of the law of Moses, which he wrote in the presence of the children of Israel.

33 And all Israel, and their elders, and officers, and their judges, stood on this side the ark and on that side before the priests the Levites, which bare the ark of the covenant of the LORD, as well the stranger, as he that was born among them; half of them over against mount Gerizim, and half of them over against mount Ebal; as Moses the servant of the LORD had commanded before, that they should bless the people of Israel.

34 And afterward he read all the words of the law, the blessings and cursings, according to all that is written in the book of the law.

35 There was not a word of all that Moses commanded, which Joshua read not before all the congregation of Israel, with the women, and the little ones, and the strangers that were conversant among them.

9 And it came to pass, when all the kings which *were* on this side Jordan, in the hills, and in the valleys, and in all the coasts of the great sea over against Lebanon, the Hittite, and the Amorite, the Canaanite, the Perizzite, the Hivite, and the Jebusite, heard *thereof*;

2 That they gathered themselves together, to fight with Joshua and with Israel, with one accord.

3 And when the inhabitants of Gibeon heard what Joshua had done unto Jericho and to Ai,

4 They did work wilily, and went and made as if they had been ambassadors, and took old sacks upon their asses, and wine bottles, old, and rent, and bound up;

5 And old shoes and clouted upon their feet, and old garments upon them; and all the bread of their provision was dry *and* mouldy.

6 And they went to Joshua unto the camp at Gilgal, and said unto him, and to the men of Israel, We be come from a far country: now therefore make ye a league with us.

7 And the men of Israel said unto the Hivites, Peradventure ye dwell among us; and how shall we make a league with you?

8 And they said unto Joshua, We *are* thy servants. And Joshua said unto them, Who *are* ye? and from whence come ye?

9 And they said unto him, From a very far country thy servants are come because of the name of the LORD thy God: for we have heard the fame of him, and all that he did in Egypt,

10 And all that he did to the two kings of the Amorites, that *were* beyond Jordan, to Sihon king of Heshbon, and to Og king of Bashan, which *was* at Ashtaroth.

11 Wherefore our elders and all the inhabitants of our country spake to us, saying, Take victuals with you for the journey, and go to meet them, and say unto them, We *are* your servants: therefore now make ye a league with us.

12 This our bread we took hot *for* our provision out of our houses on the day we came forth to go unto you; but now, behold, it is dry, and it is mouldy:

13 And these bottles of wine, which we filled, *were* new; and, behold, they be rent: and these our garments and our shoes are become old by reason of the very long journey.

14 And the men took of their victuals, and asked not *counsel* at the mouth of the LORD.

15 And Joshua made peace with them, and made a league with them, to let them live: and the princes of the congregation sware unto them.

16 And it came to pass at the end of three days after they had made a league with them, that they heard that they *were* their neighbours, and *that* they dwelt among them.

17 And the children of Israel journeyed, and came unto their cities on the third day. Now their cities *were* Gibeon, and Chephirah, and Beeroth, and Kirjath-jearim.

18 And the children of Israel smote them not, because the princes of the congregation had sworn unto them by the LORD God of Israel. And all the congregation murmured against the princes.

19 But all the princes said unto all the congregation, We have sworn unto them by the LORD God of Israel: now therefore we may not touch them.

20 This we will do to them; we will even let them live, lest wrath be upon us, because of the oath which we sware unto them.

21 And the princes said unto them, Let them live; but let them be hewers of wood and drawers of water unto all the congregation; as the princes had promised them.

22 And Joshua called for them, and he spake unto them, saying, Wherefore have ye beguiled us, saying, We *are* very far from you; when ye dwell among us?

23 Now therefore ye *are* cursed, and there shall none of you be freed from being bondmen, and hewers of wood and drawers of water for the house of my God.

24 And they answered Joshua, and said, Because it was certainly told thy servants, how that the LORD thy God commanded his servant Moses to give you all the land, and to destroy all the inhabitants of the land from before you, therefore we were sore afraid of our lives because of you, and have done this thing.

25 And now, behold, we *are* in thine hand: as it seemeth good and right unto thee to do unto us, do.

26 And so did he unto them, and delivered them out of the hand of the children of Israel, that they slew them not.

27 And Joshua made them that day hewers of wood and drawers of water for the congregation, and for the altar of the LORD, even unto this day, in the place which he should choose.

10 Now it came to pass, when Adoni-zedek king of Jerusalem had heard how Joshua had taken Ai, and had utterly destroyed it; as he had done to Jericho and her king, so he had done to Ai and her king; and how the inhabitants of Gibeon had made peace with Israel, and were among them;

2 That they feared greatly, because Gibeon *was* a great city, as one of the royal cities, and because it *was* greater than Ai, and all the men thereof *were* mighty.

3 Wherefore Adoni-zedek king of Jerusalem sent unto Hoham king of Hebron, and unto Piram king of Jarmuth, and unto Japhia king of

Lachish, and unto Debir king of Eglon,
saying,
4 Come up unto me, and help me, that
we may smite Gibeon: for it hath made
peace with Joshua and with the children of Israel.
5 Therefore the five kings of the
Amorites, the king of Jerusalem, the
king of Hebron, the king of Jarmuth,
the king of Lachish, the king of Eglon,
gathered themselves together, and
went up, they and all their hosts, and
encamped before Gibeon, and made
war against it.
6 And the men of Gibeon sent unto
Joshua to the camp to Gilgal, saying,
Slack not thy hand from thy servants;
come up to us quickly, and save us, and
help us: for all the kings of the Amorites
that dwell in the mountains are gathered together against us.
7 So Joshua ascended from Gilgal, he,
and all the people of war with him, and
all the mighty men of valour.
8 And the LORD said unto Joshua,
Fear them not: for I have delivered
them into thine hand; there shall not a
man of them stand before thee.
9 Joshua therefore came unto them
suddenly, *and* went up from Gilgal all
night.
10 And the LORD discomfited them
before Israel, and slew them with a
great slaughter at Gibeon, and chased
them along the way that goeth up to
Beth-horon, and smote them to Azekah,
and unto Makkedah.
11 And it came to pass, as they fled
from before Israel, *and* were in the
going down to Beth-horon, that the
LORD cast down great stones from heav-
en upon them unto Azekah, and they
died: *they were* more which died with
hailstones than *they* whom the children of Israel slew with the sword.
12 Then spake Joshua to the LORD in
the day when the LORD delivered up
the Amorites before the children of
Israel, and he said in the sight of Israel,
Sun, stand thou still upon Gibeon; and
thou, Moon, in the valley of Ajalon.
13 And the sun stood still, and the
moon stayed, until the people had
avenged themselves upon their enemies. *Is* not this written in the book of
Jasher? So the sun stood still in the
midst of heaven, and hasted not to go
down about a whole day.
14 And there was no day like that
before it or after it, that the LORD
hearkened unto the voice of a man: for
the LORD fought for Israel.
15 And Joshua returned, and all
Israel with him, unto the camp to
Gilgal.
16 But these five kings fled, and hid
themselves in a cave at Makkedah.
17 And it was told Joshua, saying, The
five kings are found hid in a cave at
Makkedah.
18 And Joshua said, Roll great stones
upon the mouth of the cave, and set
men by it for to keep them:
19 And stay ye not, *but* pursue after
your enemies, and smite the hindmost
of them; suffer them not to enter into
their cities: for the LORD your God hath
delivered them into your hand.
20 And it came to pass, when Joshua
and the children of Israel had made an
end of slaying them with a very great
slaughter, till they were consumed, that
the rest *which* remained of them
entered into fenced cities.
21 And all the people returned to the
camp to Joshua at Makkedah in peace:

none moved his tongue against any of
the children of Israel.
22 Then said Joshua, Open the mouth
of the cave, and bring out those five
kings unto me out of the cave.
23 And they did so, and brought forth
those five kings unto him out of the
cave, the king of Jerusalem, the king of
Hebron, the king of Jarmuth, the king
of Lachish, *and* the king of Eglon.
24 And it came to pass, when they
brought out those kings unto Joshua,
that Joshua called for all the men of
Israel, and said unto the captains of the
men of war which went with him, Come
near, put your feet upon the necks of
these kings. And they came near, and
put their feet upon the necks of them.
25 And Joshua said unto them, Fear
not, nor be dismayed, be strong and of
good courage: for thus shall the LORD
do to all your enemies against whom ye
fight.
26 And afterward Joshua smote them,
and slew them, and hanged them on
five trees: and they were hanging upon
the trees until the evening.
27 And it came to pass at the time of
the going down of the sun, *that* Joshua
commanded, and they took them down
off the trees, and cast them into the
cave wherein they had been hid, and
laid great stones in the cave's mouth,
which remain until this very day.
28 And that day Joshua took
Makkedah, and smote it with the edge
of the sword, and the king thereof he
utterly destroyed, them, and all the
souls that *were* therein; he let none
remain: and he did to the king of
Makkedah as he did unto the king of
Jericho.
29 Then Joshua passed from Makkedah, and all Israel with him, unto
Libnah, and fought against Libnah:
30 And the LORD delivered it also, and
the king thereof, into the hand of
Israel; and he smote it with the edge of
the sword, and all the souls that *were*
therein; he let none remain in it; but
did unto the king thereof as he did unto
the king of Jericho.
31 And Joshua passed from Libnah,
and all Israel with him, unto Lachish,
and encamped against it, and fought
against it:
32 And the LORD delivered Lachish
into the hand of Israel, which took it on
the second day, and smote it with the
edge of the sword, and all the souls that
were therein, according to all that he
had done to Libnah.
33 Then Horam king of Gezer came
up to help Lachish; and Joshua smote
him and his people, until he had left
him none remaining.
34 And from Lachish Joshua passed
unto Eglon, and all Israel with him; and
they encamped against it, and fought
against it:
35 And they took it on that day, and
smote it with the edge of the sword, and
all the souls that *were* therein he utterly destroyed that day, according to all
that he had done to Lachish.
36 And Joshua went up from Eglon,
and all Israel with him, unto Hebron;
and they fought against it:
37 And they took it, and smote it with
the edge of the sword, and the king
thereof, and all the cities thereof, and
all the souls that *were* therein; he left
none remaining, according to all that
he had done to Eglon; but destroyed it
utterly, and all the souls that *were*
therein.

38 And Joshua returned, and all Israel with him, to Debir; and fought against it:

39 And he took it, and the king thereof, and all the cities thereof; and they smote them with the edge of the sword, and utterly destroyed all the souls that *were* therein; he left none remaining: as he had done to Hebron, so he did to Debir, and to the king thereof; as he had done also to Libnah, and to her king.

40 So Joshua smote all the country of the hills, and of the south, and of the vale, and of the springs, and all their kings: he left none remaining, but utterly destroyed all that breathed, as the Lord God of Israel commanded.

41 And Joshua smote them from Kadesh-barnea even unto Gaza, and all the country of Goshen, even unto Gibeon.

42 And all these kings and their land did Joshua take at one time, because the Lord God of Israel fought for Israel.

43 And Joshua returned, and all Israel with him, unto the camp to Gilgal.

11 And it came to pass, when Jabin king of Hazor had heard *those things*, that he sent to Jobab king of Madon, and to the king of Shimron, and to the king of Achshaph,

2 And to the kings that *were* on the north of the mountains, and of the plains south of Chinneroth, and in the valley, and in the borders of Dor on the west,

3 *And to* the Canaanite on the east and on the west, and *to* the Amorite, and the Hittite, and the Perizzite, and the Jebusite in the mountains, and *to* the Hivite under Hermon in the land of Mizpeh.

4 And they went out, they and all their hosts with them, much people, even as the sand that *is* upon the sea shore in multitude, with horses and chariots very many.

5 And when all these kings were met together, they came and pitched together at the waters of Merom, to fight against Israel.

6 And the Lord said unto Joshua, Be not afraid because of them: for to morrow about this time will I deliver them up all slain before Israel: thou shalt hough their horses, and burn their chariots with fire.

7 So Joshua came, and all the people of war with him, against them by the waters of Merom suddenly; and they fell upon them.

8 And the Lord delivered them into the hand of Israel, who smote them, and chased them unto great Zidon, and unto Misrephoth-maim, and unto the valley of Mizpeh eastward; and they smote them, until they left them none remaining.

9 And Joshua did unto them as the Lord bade him: he houghed their horses, and burnt their chariots with fire.

10 And Joshua at that time turned back, and took Hazor, and smote the king thereof with the sword: for Hazor beforetime was the head of all those kingdoms.

11 And they smote all the souls that *were* therein with the edge of the sword, utterly destroying *them*: there was not any left to breathe: and he burnt Hazor with fire.

12 And all the cities of those kings, and all the kings of them, did Joshua take, and smote them with the edge of the sword, *and* he utterly destroyed them, as Moses the servant of the LORD commanded.

13 But *as for* the cities that stood still in their strength, Israel burned none of them, save Hazor only; *that* did Joshua burn.

14 And all the spoil of these cities, and the cattle, the children of Israel took for a prey unto themselves; but every man they smote with the edge of the sword, until they had destroyed them, neither left they any to breathe.

15 As the LORD commanded Moses his servant, so did Moses command Joshua, and so did Joshua; he left nothing undone of all that the LORD commanded Moses.

16 So Joshua took all that land, the hills, and all the south country, and all the land of Goshen, and the valley, and the plain, and the mountain of Israel, and the valley of the same;

17 *Even* from the mount Halak, that goeth up to Seir, even unto Baal-gad in the valley of Lebanon under mount Hermon: and all their kings he took, and smote them, and slew them.

18 Joshua made war a long time with all those kings.

19 There was not a city that made peace with the children of Israel, save the Hivites the inhabitants of Gibeon: all *other* they took in battle.

20 For it was of the LORD to harden their hearts, that they should come against Israel in battle, that he might destroy them utterly, *and* that they might have no favour, but that he might destroy them, as the LORD commanded Moses.

21 And at that time came Joshua, and cut off the Anakims from the mountains, from Hebron, from Debir, from Anab, and from all the mountains of Judah, and from all the mountains of Israel: Joshua destroyed them utterly with their cities.

22 There was none of the Anakims left in the land of the children of Israel: only in Gaza, in Gath, and in Ashdod, there remained.

23 So Joshua took the whole land, according to all that the LORD said unto Moses; and Joshua gave it for an inheritance unto Israel according to their divisions by their tribes. And the land rested from war.

12 Now these *are* the kings of the land, which the children of Israel smote, and possessed their land on the other side Jordan toward the rising of the sun, from the river Arnon unto mount Hermon, and all the plain on the east:

2 Sihon king of the Amorites, who dwelt in Heshbon, *and* ruled from Aroer, which *is* upon the bank of the river Arnon, and from the middle of the river, and from half Gilead, even unto the river Jabbok, *which is* the border of the children of Ammon;

3 And from the plain to the sea of Chinneroth on the east, and unto the sea of the plain, *even* the salt sea on the east, the way to Beth-jeshimoth; and from the south, under Ashdoth-pisgah:

4 And the coast of Og king of Bashan, *which was* of the remnant of the giants, that dwelt at Ashtaroth and at Edrei,

5 And reigned in mount Hermon, and in Salcah, and in all Bashan, unto the border of the Geshurites and the Maachathites, and half Gilead, the border of Sihon king of Heshbon.

6 Them did Moses the servant of the LORD and the children of Israel smite: and Moses the servant of the LORD gave it *for* a possession unto the Reubenites,

and the Gadites, and the half tribe of Manasseh.

7 And these *are* the kings of the country which Joshua and the children of Israel smote on this side Jordan on the west, from Baal-gad in the valley of Lebanon even unto the mount Halak, that goeth up to Seir; which Joshua gave unto the tribes of Israel *for* a possession according to their divisions;

8 In the mountains, and in the valleys, and in the plains, and in the springs, and in the wilderness, and in the south country; the Hittites, the Amorites, and the Canaanites, the Perizzites, the Hivites, and the Jebusites:

9 The king of Jericho, one; the king of Ai, which *is* beside Beth-el, one;

10 The king of Jerusalem, one; the king of Hebron, one;

11 The king of Jarmuth, one; the king of Lachish, one;

12 The king of Eglon, one; the king of Gezer, one;

13 The king of Debir, one; the king of Geder, one;

14 The king of Hormah, one; the king of Arad, one;

15 The king of Libnah, one; the king of Adullam, one;

16 The king of Makkedah, one; the king of Beth-el, one;

17 The king of Tappuah, one; the king of Hepher, one;

18 The king of Aphek, one; the king of Lasharon, one;

19 The king of Madon, one; the king of Hazor, one;

20 The king of Shimron-meron, one; the king of Achshaph, one;

21 The king of Taanach, one; the king of Megiddo, one;

22 The king of Kedesh, one; the king of Jokneam of Carmel, one;

23 The king of Dor in the coast of Dor, one; the king of the nations of Gilgal, one;

24 The king of Tirzah, one: all the kings thirty and one.

13 Now Joshua was old *and* stricken in years; and the LORD said unto him, Thou art old *and* stricken in years, and there remaineth yet very much land to be possessed.

2 This *is* the land that yet remaineth: all the borders of the Philistines, and all Geshuri,

3 From Sihor, which *is* before Egypt, even unto the borders of Ekron northward, *which* is counted to the Canaanite: five lords of the Philistines; the Gazathites, and the Ashdothites, the Eshkalonites, the Gittites, and the Ekronites; also the Avites:

4 From the south, all the land of the Canaanites, and Mearah that *is* beside the Sidonians, unto Aphek, to the borders of the Amorites:

5 And the land of the Giblites, and all Lebanon, toward the sunrising, from Baal-gad under mount Hermon unto the entering into Hamath.

6 All the inhabitants of the hill country from Lebanon unto Misrephoth-maim, *and* all the Sidonians, them will I drive out from before the children of Israel: only divide thou it by lot unto the Israelites for an inheritance, as I have commanded thee.

7 Now therefore divide this land for an inheritance unto the nine tribes, and the half tribe of Manasseh,

8 With whom the Reubenites and the Gadites have received their inheritance, which Moses gave them, beyond Jordan eastward, *even* as Moses the servant of the LORD gave them;

9 From Aroer, that *is* upon the bank of
the river Arnon, and the city that *is* in
the midst of the river, and all the plain
of Medeba unto Dibon;
10 And all the cities of Sihon king of
the Amorites, which reigned in Heshbon, unto the border of the children of
Ammon;
11 And Gilead, and the border of the
Geshurites and Maachathites, and all
mount Hermon, and all Bashan unto
Salcah;
12 All the kingdom of Og in Bashan,
which reigned in Ashtaroth and in
Edrei, who remained of the remnant of
the giants: for these did Moses smite,
and cast them out.
13 Nevertheless the children of Israel
expelled not the Geshurites, nor the
Maachathites: but the Geshurites and
the Maachathites dwell among the
Israelites until this day.
14 Only unto the tribe of Levi he gave
none inheritance; the sacrifices of the
LORD God of Israel made by fire *are*
their inheritance, as he said unto them.
15 And Moses gave unto the tribe of
the children of Reuben *inheritance*
according to their families.
16 And their coast was from Aroer,
that *is* on the bank of the river Arnon,
and the city that *is* in the midst of the
river, and all the plain by Medeba;
17 Heshbon, and all her cities that *are*
in the plain; Dibon, and Bamoth-baal,
and Beth-baal-meon,
18 And Jahazah, and Kedemoth, and
Mephaath,
19 And Kirjathaim, and Sibmah, and
Zarethshahar in the mount of the valley,
20 And Beth-peor, and Ashdothpis-
gah, and Beth-jeshimoth,
21 And all the cities of the plain, and
all the kingdom of Sihon king of the
Amorites, which reigned in Heshbon,
whom Moses smote with the princes of
Midian, Evi, and Rekem, and Zur, and
Hur, and Reba, *which were* dukes of
Sihon, dwelling in the country.
22 Balaam also the son of Beor, the
soothsayer, did the children of Israel
slay with the sword among them that
were slain by them.
23 And the border of the children of
Reuben was Jordan, and the border
thereof. This *was* the inheritance of the
children of Reuben after their families,
the cities and the villages thereof.
24 And Moses gave *inheritance* unto
the tribe of Gad, *even* unto the children
of Gad according to their families.
25 And their coast was Jazer, and all
the cities of Gilead, and half the land of
the children of Ammon, unto Aroer that
is before Rabbah;
26 And from Heshbon unto Ramath-
mizpeh, and Betonim; and from Mahanaim unto the border of Debir;
27 And in the valley, Beth-aram, and
Beth-nimrah, and Succoth, and Zaphon,
the rest of the kingdom of Sihon king of
Heshbon, Jordan and *his* border, *even*
unto the edge of the sea of Chinnereth
on the other side Jordan eastward.
28 This *is* the inheritance of the children of Gad after their families, the
cities, and their villages.
29 And Moses gave *inheritance* unto
the half tribe of Manasseh: and *this*
was *the possession* of the half tribe of
the children of Manasseh by their families.
30 And their coast was from
Mahanaim, all Bashan, all the kingdom
of Og king of Bashan, and all the towns

of Jair, which *are* in Bashan, threescore cities:

31 And half Gilead, and Ashtaroth, and Edrei, cities of the kingdom of Og in Bashan, *were pertaining* unto the children of Machir the son of Manasseh, *even* to the one half of the children of Machir by their families.

32 These *are the countries* which Moses did distribute for inheritance in the plains of Moab, on the other side Jordan, by Jericho, eastward.

33 But unto the tribe of Levi Moses gave not *any* inheritance: the LORD God of Israel *was* their inheritance, as he said unto them.

14 And these *are the countries* which the children of Israel inherited in the land of Canaan, which Eleazar the priest, and Joshua the son of Nun, and the heads of the fathers of the tribes of the children of Israel, distributed for inheritance to them.

2 By lot *was* their inheritance, as the LORD commanded by the hand of Moses, for the nine tribes, and *for* the half tribe.

3 For Moses had given the inheritance of two tribes and an half tribe on the other side Jordan: but unto the Levites he gave none inheritance among them.

4 For the children of Joseph were two tribes, Manasseh and Ephraim: therefore they gave no part unto the Levites in the land, save cities to dwell *in*, with their suburbs for their cattle and for their substance.

5 As the LORD commanded Moses, so the children of Israel did, and they divided the land.

6 Then the children of Judah came unto Joshua in Gilgal: and Caleb the son of Jephunneh the Kenezite said unto him, Thou knowest the thing that the LORD said unto Moses the man of God concerning me and thee in Kadesh-barnea.

7 Forty years old *was* I when Moses the servant of the LORD sent me from Kadesh-barnea to espy out the land; and I brought him word again as *it was* in mine heart.

8 Nevertheless my brethren that went up with me made the heart of the people melt: but I wholly followed the LORD my God.

9 And Moses sware on that day, saying, Surely the land whereon thy feet have trodden shall be thine inheritance, and thy children's for ever, because thou hast wholly followed the LORD my God.

10 And now, behold, the LORD hath kept me alive, as he said, these forty and five years, even since the LORD spake this word unto Moses, while *the children of* Israel wandered in the wilderness: and now, lo, I *am* this day fourscore and five years old.

11 As yet I *am as* strong this day as *I was* in the day that Moses sent me: as my strength *was* then, even so *is* my strength now, for war, both to go out, and to come in.

12 Now therefore give me this mountain, whereof the LORD spake in that day; for thou heardest in that day how the Anakims *were* there, and *that* the cities *were* great *and* fenced: if so be the LORD *will be* with me, then I shall be able to drive them out, as the LORD said.

13 And Joshua blessed him, and gave unto Caleb the son of Jephunneh Hebron for an inheritance.

14 Hebron therefore became the inheritance of Caleb the son of

Jephunneh the Kenezite unto this day, because that he wholly followed the LORD God of Israel.

15 And the name of Hebron before *was* Kirjath-arba; *which Arba was* a great man among the Anakims. And the land had rest from war.

15 *This* then was the lot of the tribe of the children of Judah by their families; *even* to the border of Edom the wilderness of Zin southward *was* the uttermost part of the south coast.

2 And their south border was from the shore of the salt sea, from the bay that looketh southward:

3 And it went out to the south side to Maaleh-acrabbim, and passed along to Zin, and ascended up on the south side unto Kadesh-barnea, and passed along to Hezron, and went up to Adar, and fetched a compass to Karkaa:

4 *From thence* it passed toward Azmon, and went out unto the river of Egypt; and the goings out of that coast were at the sea: this shall be your south coast.

5 And the east border *was* the salt sea, *even* unto the end of Jordan. And *their* border in the north quarter *was* from the bay of the sea at the uttermost part of Jordan:

6 And the border went up to Beth-hogla, and passed along by the north of Beth-arabah; and the border went up to the stone of Bohan the son of Reuben:

7 And the border went up toward Debir from the valley of Achor, and so northward, looking toward Gilgal, that *is* before the going up to Adummim, which *is* on the south side of the river: and the border passed toward the waters of En-shemesh, and the goings out thereof were at En-rogel:

8 And the border went up by the valley of the son of Hinnom unto the south side of the Jebusite; the same *is* Jerusalem: and the border went up to the top of the mountain that *lieth* before the valley of Hinnom westward, which *is* at the end of the valley of the giants northward:

9 And the border was drawn from the top of the hill unto the fountain of the water of Nephtoah, and went out to the cities of mount Ephron; and the border was drawn to Baalah, which *is* Kirjath-jearim:

10 And the border compassed from Baalah westward unto mount Seir, and passed along unto the side of mount Jearim, which *is* Chesalon, on the north side, and went down to Beth-shemesh, and passed on to Timnah:

11 And the border went out unto the side of Ekron northward: and the border was drawn to Shicron, and passed along to mount Baalah, and went out unto Jabneel; and the goings out of the border were at the sea.

12 And the west border *was* to the great sea, and the coast *thereof*. This *is* the coast of the children of Judah round about according to their families.

13 And unto Caleb the son of Jephunneh he gave a part among the children of Judah, according to the commandment of the LORD to Joshua, *even* the city of Arba the father of Anak, which *city is* Hebron.

14 And Caleb drove thence the three sons of Anak, Sheshai, and Ahiman, and Talmai, the children of Anak.

15 And he went up thence to the inhabitants of Debir: and the name of Debir before *was* Kirjath-sepher.

16 And Caleb said, He that smiteth
Kirjath-sepher, and taketh it, to him
will I give Achsah my daughter to wife.
17 And Othniel the son of Kenaz, the
brother of Caleb, took it: and he gave
him Achsah his daughter to wife.
18 And it came to pass, as she came
unto him, that she moved him to ask of
her father a field: and she lighted off
her ass; and Caleb said unto her, What
wouldest thou?
19 Who answered, Give me a blessing;
for thou hast given me a south land;
give me also springs of water. And he
gave her the upper springs, and the
nether springs.
20 This *is* the inheritance of the tribe
of the children of Judah according to
their families.
21 And the uttermost cities of the
tribe of the children of Judah toward
the coast of Edom southward were
Kabzeel, and Eder, and Jagur,
22 And Kinah, and Dimonah, and
Adadah,
23 And Kedesh, and Hazor, and Ithnan,
24 Ziph, and Telem, and Bealoth,
25 And Hazor, Hadattah, and Kerioth,
and Hezron, which *is* Hazor,
26 Amam, and Shema, and Moladah,
27 And Hazar-gaddah, and Heshmon,
and Beth-palet,
28 And Hazar-shual, and Beer-sheba,
and Bizjothjah,
29 Baalah, and Iim, and Azem,
30 And Eltolad, and Chesil, and
Hormah,
31 And Ziklag, and Madmannah, and
Sansannah,
32 And Lebaoth, and Shilhim, and
Ain, and Rimmon: all the cities *are*
twenty and nine, with their villages:
33 *And* in the valley, Eshtaol, and
Zoreah, and Ashnah,
34 And Zanoah, and En-gannim,
Tappuah, and Enam,
35 Jarmuth, and Adullam, Socoh, and
Azekah,
36 And Sharaim, and Adithaim, and
Gederah, and Gederothaim; fourteen
cities with their villages:
37 Zenan, and Hadashah, and Migdal-gad,
38 And Dilean, and Mizpeh, and
Joktheel,
39 Lachish, and Bozkath, and Eglon,
40 And Cabbon, and Lahmam, and
Kithlish,
41 And Gederoth, Beth-dagon, and
Naamah, and Makkedah; sixteen cities
with their villages:
42 Libnah, and Ether, and Ashan,
43 And Jiphtah, and Ashnah, and
Nezib,
44 And Keilah, and Achzib, and
Mareshah; nine cities with their villages:
45 Ekron, with her towns and her villages:
46 From Ekron even unto the sea, all
that *lay* near Ashdod, with their
villages:
47 Ashdod with her towns and her
villages, Gaza with her towns and her
villages, unto the river of Egypt, and
the great sea, and the border *thereof*:
48 And in the mountains, Shamir, and
Jattir, and Socoh,
49 And Dannah, and Kirjath-sannah,
which *is* Debir,
50 And Anab, and Eshtemoh, and
Anim,
51 And Goshen, and Holon, and
Giloh; eleven cities with their villages:
52 Arab, and Dumah, and Eshean,

53 And Janum, and Beth-tappuah, and Aphekah,

54 And Humtah, and Kirjath-arba, which *is* Hebron, and Zior; nine cities with their villages:

55 Maon, Carmel, and Ziph, and Juttah,

56 And Jezreel, and Jokdeam, and Zanoah,

57 Cain, Gibeah, and Timnah; ten cities with their villages:

58 Halhul, Beth-zur, and Gedor,

59 And Maarath, and Beth-anoth, and Eltekon; six cities with their villages:

60 Kirjath-baal, which *is* Kirjath-jearim, and Rabbah; two cities with their villages:

61 In the wilderness, Beth-arabah, Middin, and Secacah,

62 And Nibshan, and the city of Salt, and En-gedi; six cities with their villages.

63 As for the Jebusites the inhabitants of Jerusalem, the children of Judah could not drive them out: but the Jebusites dwell with the children of Judah at Jerusalem unto this day.

16 And the lot of the children of Joseph fell from Jordan by Jericho, unto the water of Jericho on the east, to the wilderness that goeth up from Jericho throughout mount Beth-el,

2 And goeth out from Beth-el to Luz, and passeth along unto the borders of Archi to Ataroth,

3 And goeth down westward to the coast of Japhleti, unto the coast of Beth-horon the nether, and to Gezer: and the goings out thereof are at the sea.

4 So the children of Joseph, Manasseh and Ephraim, took their inheritance.

5 And the border of the children of Ephraim according to their families was *thus*: even the border of their inheritance on the east side was Ataroth-addar, unto Beth-horon the upper;

6 And the border went out toward the sea to Michmethah on the north side; and the border went about eastward unto Taanathshiloh, and passed by it on the east to Janohah;

7 And it went down from Janohah to Ataroth, and to Naarath, and came to Jericho, and went out at Jordan.

8 The border went out from Tappuah westward unto the river Kanah; and the goings out thereof were at the sea. This *is* the inheritance of the tribe of the children of Ephraim by their families.

9 And the separate cities for the children of Ephraim *were* among the inheritance of the children of Manasseh, all the cities with their villages.

10 And they drave not out the Canaanites that dwelt in Gezer: but the Canaanites dwell among the Ephraimites unto this day, and serve under tribute.

17 There was also a lot for the tribe of Manasseh; for he *was* the firstborn of Joseph; *to wit*, for Machir the firstborn of Manasseh, the father of Gilead: because he was a man of war, therefore he had Gilead and Bashan.

2 There was also *a lot* for the rest of the children of Manasseh by their families; for the children of Abiezer, and for the children of Helek, and for the children of Asriel, and for the children of Shechem, and for the children of Hepher, and for the children of Shemida: these *were* the male children of Manasseh the son of Joseph by their families.

3 But Zelophehad, the son of Hepher, the son of Gilead, the son of Machir, the son of Manasseh, had no sons, but daughters: and these *are* the names of his daughters, Mahlah, and Noah, Hoglah, Milcah, and Tirzah.

4 And they came near before Eleazar the priest, and before Joshua the son of Nun, and before the princes, saying, The LORD commanded Moses to give us an inheritance among our brethren. Therefore according to the commandment of the LORD he gave them an inheritance among the brethren of their father.

5 And there fell ten portions to Manasseh, beside the land of Gilead and Bashan, which *were* on the other side Jordan;

6 Because the daughters of Manasseh had an inheritance among his sons: and the rest of Manasseh's sons had the land of Gilead.

7 And the coast of Manasseh was from Asher to Michmethah, that *lieth* before Shechem; and the border went along on the right hand unto the inhabitants of En-tappuah.

8 *Now* Manasseh had the land of Tappuah: but Tappuah on the border of Manasseh *belonged* to the children of Ephraim;

9 And the coast descended unto the river Kanah, southward of the river: these cities of Ephraim *are* among the cities of Manasseh: the coast of Manasseh also *was* on the north side of the river, and the outgoings of it were at the sea:

10 Southward *it was* Ephraim's, and northward *it was* Manasseh's, and the sea is his border; and they met together in Asher on the north, and in Issachar on the east.

11 And Manasseh had in Issachar and in Asher Beth-shean and her towns, and Ibleam and her towns, and the inhabitants of Dor and her towns, and the inhabitants of Endor and her towns, and the inhabitants of Taanach and her towns, and the inhabitants of Megiddo and her towns, *even* three countries.

12 Yet the children of Manasseh could not drive out *the inhabitants of* those cities; but the Canaanites would dwell in that land.

13 Yet it came to pass, when the children of Israel were waxen strong, that they put the Canaanites to tribute; but did not utterly drive them out.

14 And the children of Joseph spake unto Joshua, saying, Why hast thou given me *but* one lot and one portion to inherit, seeing I *am* a great people, forasmuch as the LORD hath blessed me hitherto?

15 And Joshua answered them, If thou *be* a great people, *then* get thee up to the wood *country*, and cut down for thyself there in the land of the Perizzites and of the giants, if mount Ephraim be too narrow for thee.

16 And the children of Joseph said, The hill is not enough for us: and all the Canaanites that dwell in the land of the valley have chariots of iron, *both they* who *are* of Beth-shean and her towns, and *they* who *are* of the valley of Jezreel.

17 And Joshua spake unto the house of Joseph, *even* to Ephraim and to Manasseh, saying, Thou *art* a great people, and hast great power: thou shalt not have one lot *only*:

18 But the mountain shall be thine; for it *is* a wood, and thou shalt cut it down: and the outgoings of it shall be thine: for thou shalt drive out the

Canaanites, though they have iron
chariots, *and* though they *be* strong.

18 And the whole congregation of
the children of Israel assembled
together at Shiloh, and set up the tabernacle of the congregation there. And
the land was subdued before them.
2 And there remained among the
children of Israel seven tribes, which
had not yet received their inheritance.
3 And Joshua said unto the children
of Israel, How long *are* ye slack to go to
possess the land, which the LORD God
of your fathers hath given you?
4 Give out from among you three men
for *each* tribe: and I will send them, and
they shall rise, and go through the land,
and describe it according to the inheritance of them; and they shall come
again to me.
5 And they shall divide it into seven
parts: Judah shall abide in their coast
on the south, and the house of Joseph
shall abide in their coasts on the north.
6 Ye shall therefore describe the land
into seven parts, and bring *the descrip-
tion* hither to me, that I may cast lots
for you here before the LORD our God.
7 But the Levites have no part among
you; for the priesthood of the LORD *is*
their inheritance: and Gad, and
Reuben, and half the tribe of Manasseh,
have received their inheritance beyond
Jordan on the east, which Moses the
servant of the LORD gave them.
8 And the men arose, and went away:
and Joshua charged them that went to
describe the land, saying, Go and walk
through the land, and describe it, and
come again to me, that I may here cast
lots for you before the LORD in Shiloh.
9 And the men went and passed
through the land, and described it by
cities into seven parts in a book, and
came *again* to Joshua to the host at
Shiloh.
10 And Joshua cast lots for them in
Shiloh before the LORD: and there
Joshua divided the land unto the children of Israel according to their divisions.
11 And the lot of the tribe of the children of Benjamin came up according to
their families: and the coast of their lot
came forth between the children of
Judah and the children of Joseph.
12 And their border on the north side
was from Jordan; and the border went
up to the side of Jericho on the north
side, and went up through the mountains westward; and the goings out
thereof were at the wilderness of Beth-
aven.
13 And the border went over from
thence toward Luz, to the side of Luz,
which *is* Beth-el, southward; and the
border descended to Ataroth-adar, near
the hill that *lieth* on the south side of
the nether Beth-horon.
14 And the border was drawn *thence*,
and compassed the corner of the sea
southward, from the hill that *lieth*
before Beth-horon southward; and the
goings out thereof were at Kirjath-baal,
which *is* Kirjath-jearim, a city of the
children of Judah: this *was* the west
quarter.
15 And the south quarter *was* from
the end of Kirjath-jearim, and the border went out on the west, and went out
to the well of waters of Nephtoah:
16 And the border came down to the
end of the mountain that *lieth* before
the valley of the son of Hinnom, *and*
which *is* in the valley of the giants on
the north, and descended to the valley
of Hinnom, to the side of Jebusi on the
south, and descended to En-rogel,

17 And was drawn from the north,
and went forth to En-shemesh, and
went forth toward Geliloth, which *is*
over against the going up of Adummim,
and descended to the stone of Bohan
the son of Reuben,
18 And passed along toward the side
over against Arabah northward, and
went down unto Arabah:
19 And the border passed along to
the side of Beth-hoglah northward: and
the outgoings of the border were at the
north bay of the salt sea at the south
end of Jordan: this *was* the south coast.
20 And Jordan was the border of it on
the east side. This *was* the inheritance
of the children of Benjamin, by the
coasts thereof round about, according
to their families.
21 Now the cities of the tribe of the
children of Benjamin according to their
families were Jericho, and Beth-hoglah,
and the valley of Keziz,
22 And Beth-arabah, and Zemaraim,
and Beth-el,
23 And Avim, and Parah, and Ophrah,
24 And Chephar-haammonai, and
Ophni, and Gaba; twelve cities with
their villages:
25 Gibeon, and Ramah, and Beeroth,
26 And Mizpeh, and Chephirah, and
Mozah,
27 And Rekem, and Irpeel, and
Taralah,
28 And Zelah, Eleph, and Jebusi,
which *is* Jerusalem, Gibeath, *and*
Kirjath; fourteen cities with their villages. This *is* the inheritance of the
children of Benjamin according to their
families.

19 And the second lot came forth to
Simeon, *even* for the tribe of the
children of Simeon according to their
families: and their inheritance was
within the inheritance of the children
of Judah.
2 And they had in their inheritance
Beer-sheba, or Sheba, and Moladah,
3 And Hazar-shual, and Balah, and
Azem,
4 And Eltolad, and Bethul, and
Hormah,
5 And Ziklag, and Beth-marcaboth,
and Hazar-susah,
6 And Beth-lebaoth, and Sharuhen;
thirteen cities and their villages:
7 Ain, Remmon, and Ether, and
Ashan; four cities and their villages:
8 And all the villages that *were* round
about these cities to Baalath-beer,
Ramath of the south. This *is* the inheritance of the tribe of the children of
Simeon according to their families.
9 Out of the portion of the children of
Judah *was* the inheritance of the children of Simeon: for the part of the
children of Judah was too much for
them: therefore the children of Simeon
had their inheritance within the inheritance of them.
10 And the third lot came up for the
children of Zebulun according to their
families: and the border of their inheritance was unto Sarid:
11 And their border went up toward
the sea, and Maralah, and reached to
Dabbasheth, and reached to the river
that *is* before Jokneam;
12 And turned from Sarid eastward
toward the sunrising unto the border of
Chislothtabor, and then goeth out to
Daberath, and goeth up to Japhia,
13 And from thence passeth on along
on the east to Gittah-hepher, to Ittah-
kazin, and goeth out to Remmon-
methoar to Neah;
14 And the border compasseth it on
the north side to Hannathon: and the

outgoings thereof are in the valley of
Jiphthah-el:
15 And Kattath, and Nahallal, and
Shimron, and Idalah, and Beth-lehem:
twelve cities with their villages.
16 This *is* the inheritance of the children of Zebulun according to their
families, these cities with their villages.
17 *And* the fourth lot came out to
Issachar, for the children of Issachar
according to their families.
18 And their border was toward
Jezreel, and Chesulloth, and Shunem,
19 And Hapharaim, and Shion, and
Anaharath,
20 And Rabbith, and Kishion, and
Abez,
21 And Remeth, and En-gannim, and
En-haddah, and Beth-pazzez;
22 And the coast reacheth to Tabor,
and Shahazimah, and Beth-shemesh;
and the outgoings of their border were
at Jordan: sixteen cities with their villages.
23 This *is* the inheritance of the tribe
of the children of Issachar according to
their families, the cities and their villages.
24 And the fifth lot came out for the
tribe of the children of Asher according
to their families.
25 And their border was Helkath, and
Hali, and Beten, and Achshaph,
26 And Alammelech, and Amad, and
Misheal; and reacheth to Carmel westward, and to Shihor-libnath;
27 And turneth toward the sunrising
to Beth-dagon, and reacheth to Zebulun, and to the valley of Jiphthah-el
toward the north side of Beth-emek,
and Neiel, and goeth out to Cabul on
the left hand,
28 And Hebron, and Rehob, and
Hammon, and Kanah, *even* unto great
Zidon;
29 And *then* the coast turneth to
Ramah, and to the strong city Tyre; and
the coast turneth to Hosah; and the
outgoings thereof are at the sea from
the coast to Achzib:
30 Ummah also, and Aphek, and
Rehob: twenty and two cities with their
villages.
31 This *is* the inheritance of the tribe
of the children of Asher according to
their families, these cities with their
villages.
32 The sixth lot came out to the children of Naphtali, *even* for the children
of Naphtali according to their families.
33 And their coast was from Heleph,
from Allon to Zaanannim, and Adami,
Nekeb, and Jabneel, unto Lakum; and
the outgoings thereof were at Jordan:
34 And *then* the coast turneth westward to Aznoth-tabor, and goeth out
from thence to Hukkok, and reacheth
to Zebulun on the south side, and
reacheth to Asher on the west side, and
to Judah upon Jordan toward the sunrising.
35 And the fenced cities *are* Ziddim,
Zer, and Hammath, Rakkath, and
Chinnereth,
36 And Adamah, and Ramah, and
Hazor,
37 And Kedesh, and Edrei, and En-hazor,
38 And Iron, and Migdalel, Horem,
and Beth-anath, and Beth-shemesh;
nineteen cities with their villages.
39 This *is* the inheritance of the tribe
of the children of Naphtali according to
their families, the cities and their villages.

40 *And* the seventh lot came out for the tribe of the children of Dan according to their families.

41 And the coast of their inheritance was Zorah, and Eshtaol, and Ir-shemesh,

42 And Shaalabbin, and Ajalon, and Jethlah,

43 And Elon, and Thimnathah, and Ekron,

44 And Eltekeh, and Gibbethon, and Baalath,

45 And Jehud, and Bene-berak, and Gath-rimmon,

46 And Me-jarkon, and Rakkon, with the border before Japho.

47 And the coast of the children of Dan went out *too little* for them: therefore the children of Dan went up to fight against Leshem, and took it, and smote it with the edge of the sword, and possessed it, and dwelt therein, and called Leshem, Dan, after the name of Dan their father.

48 This *is* the inheritance of the tribe of the children of Dan according to their families, these cities with their villages.

49 When they had made an end of dividing the land for inheritance by their coasts, the children of Israel gave an inheritance to Joshua the son of Nun among them:

50 According to the word of the LORD they gave him the city which he asked, *even* Timnath-serah in mount Ephraim: and he built the city, and dwelt therein.

51 These *are* the inheritances, which Eleazar the priest, and Joshua the son of Nun, and the heads of the fathers of the tribes of the children of Israel, divided for an inheritance by lot in Shiloh before the LORD, at the door of the tabernacle of the congregation. So they made an end of dividing the country.

20 The LORD also spake unto Joshua, saying,

2 Speak to the children of Israel, saying, Appoint out for you cities of refuge, whereof I spake unto you by the hand of Moses:

3 That the slayer that killeth *any* person unawares *and* unwittingly may flee thither: and they shall be your refuge from the avenger of blood.

4 And when he that doth flee unto one of those cities shall stand at the entering of the gate of the city, and shall declare his cause in the ears of the elders of that city, they shall take him into the city unto them, and give him a place, that he may dwell among them.

5 And if the avenger of blood pursue after him, then they shall not deliver the slayer up into his hand; because he smote his neighbour unwittingly, and hated him not beforetime.

6 And he shall dwell in that city, until he stand before the congregation for judgment, *and* until the death of the high priest that shall be in those days: then shall the slayer return, and come unto his own city, and unto his own house, unto the city from whence he fled.

7 And they appointed Kedesh in Galilee in mount Naphtali, and Shechem in mount Ephraim, and Kirjath-arba, which *is* Hebron, in the mountain of Judah.

8 And on the other side Jordan by Jericho eastward, they assigned Bezer in the wilderness upon the plain out of the tribe of Reuben, and Ramoth in Gilead out of the tribe of Gad, and Golan in Bashan out of the tribe of Manasseh.

9 These were the cities appointed for all the children of Israel, and for the stranger that sojourneth among them, that whosoever killeth *any* person at unawares might flee thither, and not die by the hand of the avenger of blood, until he stood before the congregation.

21 Then came near the heads of the fathers of the Levites unto Eleazar the priest, and unto Joshua the son of Nun, and unto the heads of the fathers of the tribes of the children of Israel;

2 And they spake unto them at Shiloh in the land of Canaan, saying, The LORD commanded by the hand of Moses to give us cities to dwell in, with the suburbs thereof for our cattle.

3 And the children of Israel gave unto the Levites out of their inheritance, at the commandment of the LORD, these cities and their suburbs.

4 And the lot came out for the families of the Kohathites: and the children of Aaron the priest, *which were* of the Levites, had by lot out of the tribe of Judah, and out of the tribe of Simeon, and out of the tribe of Benjamin, thirteen cities.

5 And the rest of the children of Kohath *had* by lot out of the families of the tribe of Ephraim, and out of the tribe of Dan, and out of the half tribe of Manasseh, ten cities.

6 And the children of Gershon *had* by lot out of the families of the tribe of Issachar, and out of the tribe of Asher, and out of the tribe of Naphtali, and out of the half tribe of Manasseh in Bashan, thirteen cities.

7 The children of Merari by their families *had* out of the tribe of Reuben, and out of the tribe of Gad, and out of the tribe of Zebulun, twelve cities.

8 And the children of Israel gave by lot unto the Levites these cities with their suburbs, as the LORD commanded by the hand of Moses.

9 And they gave out of the tribe of the children of Judah, and out of the tribe of the children of Simeon, these cities which are *here* mentioned by name,

10 Which the children of Aaron, *being* of the families of the Kohathites, *who were* of the children of Levi, had: for theirs was the first lot.

11 And they gave them the city of Arba the father of Anak, which *city is* Hebron, in the hill *country* of Judah, with the suburbs thereof round about it.

12 But the fields of the city, and the villages thereof, gave they to Caleb the son of Jephunneh for his possession.

13 Thus they gave to the children of Aaron the priest Hebron with her suburbs, *to be* a city of refuge for the slayer; and Libnah with her suburbs,

14 And Jattir with her suburbs, and Eshtemoa with her suburbs,

15 And Holon with her suburbs, and Debir with her suburbs,

16 And Ain with her suburbs, and Juttah with her suburbs, *and* Beth-shemesh with her suburbs; nine cities out of those two tribes.

17 And out of the tribe of Benjamin, Gibeon with her suburbs, Geba with her suburbs,

18 Anathoth with her suburbs, and Almon with her suburbs; four cities.

19 All the cities of the children of Aaron, the priests, *were* thirteen cities with their suburbs.

20 And the families of the children of Kohath, the Levites which remained of the children of Kohath, even they had

the cities of their lot out of the tribe of Ephraim.

21 For they gave them Shechem with her suburbs in mount Ephraim, *to be* a city of refuge for the slayer; and Gezer with her suburbs,

22 And Kibzaim with her suburbs, and Beth-horon with her suburbs; four cities.

23 And out of the tribe of Dan, Eltekeh with her suburbs, Gibbethon with her suburbs,

24 Aijalon with her suburbs, Gath-rimmon with her suburbs; four cities.

25 And out of the half tribe of Manasseh, Tanach with her suburbs, and Gath-rimmon with her suburbs; two cities.

26 All the cities *were* ten with their suburbs for the families of the children of Kohath that remained.

27 And unto the children of Gershon, of the families of the Levites, out of the *other* half tribe of Manasseh *they gave* Golan in Bashan with her suburbs, *to be* a city of refuge for the slayer; and Beeshterah with her suburbs; two cities.

28 And out of the tribe of Issachar, Kishon with her suburbs, Dabareh with her suburbs,

29 Jarmuth with her suburbs, En-gannim with her suburbs; four cities.

30 And out of the tribe of Asher, Mishal with her suburbs, Abdon with her suburbs,

31 Helkath with her suburbs, and Rehob with her suburbs; four cities.

32 And out of the tribe of Naphtali, Kedesh in Galilee with her suburbs, *to be* a city of refuge for the slayer; and Hammoth-dor with her suburbs, and Kartan with her suburbs; three cities.

33 All the cities of the Gershonites according to their families *were* thirteen cities with their suburbs.

34 And unto the families of the children of Merari, the rest of the Levites, out of the tribe of Zebulun, Jokneam with her suburbs, and Kartah with her suburbs,

35 Dimnah with her suburbs, Nahalal with her suburbs; four cities.

36 And out of the tribe of Reuben, Bezer with her suburbs, and Jahazah with her suburbs,

37 Kedemoth with her suburbs, and Mephaath with her suburbs; four cities.

38 And out of the tribe of Gad, Ramoth in Gilead with her suburbs, *to be* a city of refuge for the slayer; and Mahanaim with her suburbs,

39 Heshbon with her suburbs, Jazer with her suburbs; four cities in all.

40 So all the cities for the children of Merari by their families, which were remaining of the families of the Levites, were *by* their lot twelve cities.

41 All the cities of the Levites within the possession of the children of Israel *were* forty and eight cities with their suburbs.

42 These cities were every one with their suburbs round about them: thus *were* all these cities.

43 And the LORD gave unto Israel all the land which he sware to give unto their fathers; and they possessed it, and dwelt therein.

44 And the LORD gave them rest round about, according to all that he sware unto their fathers: and there stood not a man of all their enemies before them; the LORD delivered all their enemies into their hand.

45 There failed not ought of any good thing which the LORD had spoken unto the house of Israel; all came to pass.

22 Then Joshua called the Reubenites, and the Gadites, and the half tribe of Manasseh,

2 And said unto them, Ye have kept all that Moses the servant of the LORD commanded you, and have obeyed my voice in all that I commanded you:

3 Ye have not left your brethren these many days unto this day, but have kept the charge of the commandment of the LORD your God.

4 And now the LORD your God hath given rest unto your brethren, as he promised them: therefore now return ye, and get you unto your tents, *and* unto the land of your possession, which Moses the servant of the LORD gave you on the other side Jordan.

5 But take diligent heed to do the commandment and the law, which Moses the servant of the LORD charged you, to love the LORD your God, and to walk in all his ways, and to keep his commandments, and to cleave unto him, and to serve him with all your heart and with all your soul.

6 So Joshua blessed them, and sent them away: and they went unto their tents.

7 Now to the *one* half of the tribe of Manasseh Moses had given *possession* in Bashan: but unto the *other* half thereof gave Joshua among their brethren on this side Jordan westward. And when Joshua sent them away also unto their tents, then he blessed them,

8 And he spake unto them, saying, Return with much riches unto your tents, and with very much cattle, with silver, and with gold, and with brass, and with iron, and with very much raiment: divide the spoil of your enemies with your brethren.

9 And the children of Reuben and the children of Gad and the half tribe of Manasseh returned, and departed from the children of Israel out of Shiloh, which *is* in the land of Canaan, to go unto the country of Gilead, to the land of their possession, whereof they were possessed, according to the word of the LORD by the hand of Moses.

10 And when they came unto the borders of Jordan, that *are* in the land of Canaan, the children of Reuben and the children of Gad and the half tribe of Manasseh built there an altar by Jordan, a great altar to see to.

11 And the children of Israel heard say, Behold, the children of Reuben and the children of Gad and the half tribe of Manasseh have built an altar over against the land of Canaan, in the borders of Jordan, at the passage of the children of Israel.

12 And when the children of Israel heard *of it*, the whole congregation of the children of Israel gathered themselves together at Shiloh, to go up to war against them.

13 And the children of Israel sent unto the children of Reuben, and to the children of Gad, and to the half tribe of Manasseh, into the land of Gilead, Phinehas the son of Eleazar the priest,

14 And with him ten princes, of each chief house a prince throughout all the tribes of Israel; and each one *was* an head of the house of their fathers among the thousands of Israel.

15 And they came unto the children of Reuben, and to the children of Gad, and to the half tribe of Manasseh, unto the land of Gilead, and they spake with them, saying,

16 Thus saith the whole congregation of the LORD, What trespass *is* this that ye have committed against the God of Israel, to turn away this day from following the LORD, in that ye have builded you an altar, that ye might rebel this day against the LORD?

17 *Is* the iniquity of Peor too little for us, from which we are not cleansed until this day, although there was a plague in the congregation of the LORD,

18 But that ye must turn away this day from following the LORD? and it will be, *seeing* ye rebel to day against the LORD, that to morrow he will be wroth with the whole congregation of Israel.

19 Notwithstanding, if the land of your possession *be* unclean, *then* pass ye over unto the land of the possession of the LORD, wherein the LORD's tabernacle dwelleth, and take possession among us: but rebel not against the LORD, nor rebel against us, in building you an altar beside the altar of the LORD our God.

20 Did not Achan the son of Zerah commit a trespass in the accursed thing, and wrath fell on all the congregation of Israel? and that man perished not alone in his iniquity.

21 Then the children of Reuben and the children of Gad and the half tribe of Manasseh answered, and said unto the heads of the thousands of Israel,

22 The LORD God of gods, the LORD God of gods, he knoweth, and Israel he shall know; if *it be* in rebellion, or if in transgression against the LORD, (save us not this day,)

23 That we have built us an altar to turn from following the LORD, or if to offer thereon burnt offering or meat offering, or if to offer peace offerings thereon, let the LORD himself require *it*;

24 And if we have not *rather* done it for fear of *this* thing, saying, In time to come your children might speak unto our children, saying, What have ye to do with the LORD God of Israel?

25 For the LORD hath made Jordan a border between us and you, ye children of Reuben and children of Gad; ye have no part in the LORD: so shall your children make our children cease from fearing the LORD.

26 Therefore we said, Let us now prepare to build us an altar, not for burnt offering, nor for sacrifice:

27 But *that* it *may be* a witness between us, and you, and our generations after us, that we might do the service of the LORD before him with our burnt offerings, and with our sacrifices, and with our peace offerings; that your children may not say to our children in time to come, Ye have no part in the LORD.

28 Therefore said we, that it shall be, when they should *so* say to us or to our generations in time to come, that we may say *again*, Behold the pattern of the altar of the LORD, which our fathers made, not for burnt offerings, nor for sacrifices; but it *is* a witness between us and you.

29 God forbid that we should rebel against the LORD, and turn this day from following the LORD, to build an altar for burnt offerings, for meat offerings, or for sacrifices, beside the altar of the LORD our God that *is* before his tabernacle.

30 And when Phinehas the priest, and the princes of the congregation and heads of the thousands of Israel which *were* with him, heard the words

that the children of Reuben and the
children of Gad and the children of
Manasseh spake, it pleased them.
31 And Phinehas the son of Eleazar
the priest said unto the children of
Reuben, and to the children of Gad,
and to the children of Manasseh, This
day we perceive that the LORD *is* among
us, because ye have not committed this
trespass against the LORD: now ye have
delivered the children of Israel out of
the hand of the LORD.
32 And Phinehas the son of Eleazar
the priest, and the princes, returned
from the children of Reuben, and from
the children of Gad, out of the land of
Gilead, unto the land of Canaan, to the
children of Israel, and brought them
word again.
33 And the thing pleased the children
of Israel; and the children of Israel
blessed God, and did not intend to go
up against them in battle, to destroy
the land wherein the children of
Reuben and Gad dwelt.
34 And the children of Reuben and
the children of Gad called the altar *Ed*:
for it *shall be* a witness between us that
the LORD *is* God.

23 And it came to pass a long time
after that the LORD had given
rest unto Israel from all their enemies
round about, that Joshua waxed old
and stricken in age.
2 And Joshua called for all Israel, *and*
for their elders, and for their heads,
and for their judges, and for their officers, and said unto them, I am old *and*
stricken in age:
3 And ye have seen all that the LORD
your God hath done unto all these
nations because of you; for the LORD
your God *is* he that hath fought for you.
4 Behold, I have divided unto you by
lot these nations that remain, to be an
inheritance for your tribes, from
Jordan, with all the nations that I have
cut off, even unto the great sea westward.
5 And the LORD your God, he shall
expel them from before you, and drive
them from out of your sight; and ye
shall possess their land, as the LORD
your God hath promised unto you.
6 Be ye therefore very courageous to
keep and to do all that is written in the
book of the law of Moses, that ye turn
not aside therefrom *to* the right hand
or *to* the left;
7 That ye come not among these
nations, these that remain among you;
neither make mention of the name of
their gods, nor cause to swear *by them*,
neither serve them, nor bow yourselves
unto them:
8 But cleave unto the LORD your God,
as ye have done unto this day.
9 For the LORD hath driven out from
before you great nations and strong:
but *as for* you, no man hath been able
to stand before you unto this day.
10 One man of you shall chase a thousand: for the LORD your God, he *it is*
that fighteth for you, as he hath promised you.
11 Take good heed therefore unto
yourselves, that ye love the LORD your
God.
12 Else if ye do in any wise go back,
and cleave unto the remnant of these
nations, *even* these that remain among
you, and shall make marriages with
them, and go in unto them, and they to
you:
13 Know for a certainty that the LORD
your God will no more drive out *any of*
these nations from before you; but they

shall be snares and traps unto you, and scourges in your sides, and thorns in your eyes, until ye perish from off this good land which the LORD your God hath given you.

14 And, behold, this day I *am* going the way of all the earth: and ye know in all your hearts and in all your souls, that not one thing hath failed of all the good things which the LORD your God spake concerning you; all are come to pass unto you, *and* not one thing hath failed thereof.

15 Therefore it shall come to pass, *that* as all good things are come upon you, which the LORD your God promised you; so shall the LORD bring upon you all evil things, until he have destroyed you from off this good land which the LORD your God hath given you.

16 When ye have transgressed the covenant of the LORD your God, which he commanded you, and have gone and served other gods, and bowed yourselves to them; then shall the anger of the LORD be kindled against you, and ye shall perish quickly from off the good land which he hath given unto you.

24

And Joshua gathered all the tribes of Israel to Shechem, and called for the elders of Israel, and for their heads, and for their judges, and for their officers; and they presented themselves before God.

2 And Joshua said unto all the people, Thus saith the LORD God of Israel, Your fathers dwelt on the other side of the flood in old time, *even* Terah, the father of Abraham, and the father of Nachor: and they served other gods.

3 And I took your father Abraham from the other side of the flood, and led him throughout all the land of Canaan, and multiplied his seed, and gave him Isaac.

4 And I gave unto Isaac Jacob and Esau: and I gave unto Esau mount Seir, to possess it; but Jacob and his children went down into Egypt.

5 I sent Moses also and Aaron, and I plagued Egypt, according to that which I did among them: and afterward I brought you out.

6 And I brought your fathers out of Egypt: and ye came unto the sea; and the Egyptians pursued after your fathers with chariots and horsemen unto the Red sea.

7 And when they cried unto the LORD, he put darkness between you and the Egyptians, and brought the sea upon them, and covered them; and your eyes have seen what I have done in Egypt: and ye dwelt in the wilderness a long season.

8 And I brought you into the land of the Amorites, which dwelt on the other side Jordan; and they fought with you: and I gave them into your hand, that ye might possess their land; and I destroyed them from before you.

9 Then Balak the son of Zippor, king of Moab, arose and warred against Israel, and sent and called Balaam the son of Beor to curse you:

10 But I would not hearken unto Balaam; therefore he blessed you still: so I delivered you out of his hand.

11 And ye went over Jordan, and came unto Jericho: and the men of Jericho fought against you, the Amorites, and the Perizzites, and the Canaanites, and the Hittites, and the Girgashites, the Hivites, and the Jebusites; and I delivered them into your hand.

12 And I sent the hornet before you,
which drave them out from before you,
even the two kings of the Amorites; *but*
not with thy sword, nor with thy bow.
13 And I have given you a land for
which ye did not labour, and cities
which ye built not, and ye dwell in
them; of the vineyards and oliveyards
which ye planted not do ye eat.
14 Now therefore fear the LORD, and
serve him in sincerity and in truth: and
put away the gods which your fathers
served on the other side of the flood,
and in Egypt; and serve ye the LORD.
15 And if it seem evil unto you to
serve the LORD, choose you this day
whom ye will serve; whether the gods
which your fathers served that *were* on
the other side of the flood, or the gods
of the Amorites, in whose land ye dwell:
but as for me and my house, we will
serve the LORD.
16 And the people answered and said,
God forbid that we should forsake the
LORD, to serve other gods;
17 For the LORD our God, he *it is* that
brought us up and our fathers out of
the land of Egypt, from the house of
bondage, and which did those great
signs in our sight, and preserved us in
all the way wherein we went, and
among all the people through whom we
passed:
18 And the LORD drave out from
before us all the people, even the
Amorites which dwelt in the land:
therefore will we also serve the LORD;
for he *is* our God.
19 And Joshua said unto the people,
Ye cannot serve the LORD: for he *is* an
holy God; he *is* a jealous God; he will
not forgive your transgressions nor
your sins.
20 If ye forsake the LORD, and serve
strange gods, then he will turn and do
you hurt, and consume you, after that
he hath done you good.
21 And the people said unto Joshua,
Nay; but we will serve the LORD.
22 And Joshua said unto the people,
Ye *are* witnesses against yourselves
that ye have chosen you the LORD, to
serve him. And they said, *We are* witnesses.
23 Now therefore put away, *said he*,
the strange gods which *are* among you,
and incline your heart unto the LORD
God of Israel.
24 And the people said unto Joshua,
The LORD our God will we serve, and
his voice will we obey.
25 So Joshua made a covenant with
the people that day, and set them a
statute and an ordinance in Shechem.
26 And Joshua wrote these words in
the book of the law of God, and took a
great stone, and set it up there under
an oak, that *was* by the sanctuary of the
LORD.
27 And Joshua said unto all the people, Behold, this stone shall be a witness unto us; for it hath heard all the
words of the LORD which he spake unto
us: it shall be therefore a witness unto
you, lest ye deny your God.
28 So Joshua let the people depart,
every man unto his inheritance.
29 And it came to pass after these
things, that Joshua the son of Nun, the
servant of the LORD, died, *being* an
hundred and ten years old.
30 And they buried him in the border
of his inheritance in Timnath-serah,
which *is* in mount Ephraim, on the
north side of the hill of Gaash.
31 And Israel served the LORD all the
days of Joshua, and all the days of the

elders that overlived Joshua, and which
had known all the works of the LORD,
that he had done for Israel.
32 And the bones of Joseph, which
the children of Israel brought up out of
Egypt, buried they in Shechem, in a
parcel of ground which Jacob bought of
the sons of Hamor the father of
Shechem for an hundred pieces of silver: and it became the inheritance of
the children of Joseph.
33 And Eleazar the son of Aaron died;
and they buried him in a hill *that pertained to* Phinehas his son, which was
given him in mount Ephraim.

THE BOOK OF JUDGES

1 Now after the death of Joshua it
came to pass, that the children of
Israel asked the LORD, saying, Who shall
go up for us against the Canaanites
first, to fight against them?
2 And the LORD said, Judah shall go
up: behold, I have delivered the land
into his hand.
3 And Judah said unto Simeon his
brother, Come up with me into my lot,
that we may fight against the Canaanites; and I likewise will go with
thee into thy lot. So Simeon went with
him.
4 And Judah went up; and the LORD
delivered the Canaanites and the
Perizzites into their hand: and they
slew of them in Bezek ten thousand
men.
5 And they found Adonibezek in
Bezek: and they fought against him,
and they slew the Canaanites and the
Perizzites.
6 But Adonibezek fled; and they pursued after him, and caught him, and cut
off his thumbs and his great toes.
7 And Adonibezek said, Threescore
and ten kings, having their thumbs and
their great toes cut off, gathered *their
meat* under my table: as I have done, so
God hath requited me. And they
brought him to Jerusalem, and there he
died.
8 Now the children of Judah had
fought against Jerusalem, and had
taken it, and smitten it with the edge of
the sword, and set the city on fire.
9 And afterward the children of
Judah went down to fight against the
Canaanites, that dwelt in the mountain,
and in the south, and in the valley.
10 And Judah went against the
Canaanites that dwelt in Hebron: (now
the name of Hebron before *was*
Kirjatharba:) and they slew Sheshai,
and Ahiman, and Talmai.
11 And from thence he went against
the inhabitants of Debir: and the name
of Debir before *was* Kirjath-sepher:
12 And Caleb said, He that smiteth
Kirjath-sepher, and taketh it, to him
will I give Achsah my daughter to wife.
13 And Othniel the son of Kenaz,
Caleb's younger brother, took it: and he
gave him Achsah his daughter to wife.

14 And it came to pass, when she came *to him*, that she moved him to ask of her father a field: and she lighted from off *her* ass; and Caleb said unto her, What wilt thou?

15 And she said unto him, Give me a blessing: for thou hast given me a south land; give me also springs of water. And Caleb gave her the upper springs and the nether springs.

16 And the children of the Kenite, Moses' father in law, went up out of the city of palm trees with the children of Judah into the wilderness of Judah, which *lieth* in the south of Arad; and they went and dwelt among the people.

17 And Judah went with Simeon his brother, and they slew the Canaanites that inhabited Zephath, and utterly destroyed it. And the name of the city was called Hormah.

18 Also Judah took Gaza with the coast thereof, and Askelon with the coast thereof, and Ekron with the coast thereof.

19 And the LORD was with Judah; and he drave out *the inhabitants of* the mountain; but could not drive out the inhabitants of the valley, because they had chariots of iron.

20 And they gave Hebron unto Caleb, as Moses said: and he expelled thence the three sons of Anak.

21 And the children of Benjamin did not drive out the Jebusites that inhabited Jerusalem; but the Jebusites dwell with the children of Benjamin in Jerusalem unto this day.

22 And the house of Joseph, they also went up against Beth-el: and the LORD *was* with them.

23 And the house of Joseph sent to descry Beth-el. (Now the name of the city before *was* Luz.)

24 And the spies saw a man come forth out of the city, and they said unto him, Shew us, we pray thee, the entrance into the city, and we will shew thee mercy.

25 And when he shewed them the entrance into the city, they smote the city with the edge of the sword; but they let go the man and all his family.

26 And the man went into the land of the Hittites, and built a city, and called the name thereof Luz: which *is* the name thereof unto this day.

27 Neither did Manasseh drive out *the inhabitants of* Beth-shean and her towns, nor Taanach and her towns, nor the inhabitants of Dor and her towns, nor the inhabitants of Ibleam and her towns, nor the inhabitants of Megiddo and her towns: but the Canaanites would dwell in that land.

28 And it came to pass, when Israel was strong, that they put the Canaanites to tribute, and did not utterly drive them out.

29 Neither did Ephraim drive out the Canaanites that dwelt in Gezer; but the Canaanites dwelt in Gezer among them.

30 Neither did Zebulun drive out the inhabitants of Kitron, nor the inhabitants of Nahalol; but the Canaanites dwelt among them, and became tributaries.

31 Neither did Asher drive out the inhabitants of Accho, nor the inhabitants of Zidon, nor of Ahlab, nor of Achzib, nor of Helbah, nor of Aphik, nor of Rehob:

32 But the Asherites dwelt among the Canaanites, the inhabitants of the land: for they did not drive them out.

33 Neither did Naphtali drive out the inhabitants of Beth-shemesh, nor the

inhabitants of Beth-anath; but he dwelt among the Canaanites, the inhabitants of the land: nevertheless the inhabitants of Beth-shemesh and of Beth-anath became tributaries unto them.

34 And the Amorites forced the children of Dan into the mountain: for they would not suffer them to come down to the valley:

35 But the Amorites would dwell in mount Heres in Aijalon, and in Shaalbim: yet the hand of the house of Joseph prevailed, so that they became tributaries.

36 And the coast of the Amorites *was* from the going up to Akrabbim, from the rock, and upward.

2 And an angel of the LORD came up from Gilgal to Bochim, and said, I made you to go up out of Egypt, and have brought you unto the land which I sware unto your fathers; and I said, I will never break my covenant with you.

2 And ye shall make no league with the inhabitants of this land; ye shall throw down their altars: but ye have not obeyed my voice: why have ye done this?

3 Wherefore I also said, I will not drive them out from before you; but they shall be *as thorns* in your sides, and their gods shall be a snare unto you.

4 And it came to pass, when the angel of the LORD spake these words unto all the children of Israel, that the people lifted up their voice, and wept.

5 And they called the name of that place Bochim: and they sacrificed there unto the LORD.

6 And when Joshua had let the people go, the children of Israel went every man unto his inheritance to possess the land.

7 And the people served the LORD all the days of Joshua, and all the days of the elders that outlived Joshua, who had seen all the great works of the LORD, that he did for Israel.

8 And Joshua the son of Nun, the servant of the LORD, died, *being* an hundred and ten years old.

9 And they buried him in the border of his inheritance in Timnath-heres, in the mount of Ephraim, on the north side of the hill Gaash.

10 And also all that generation were gathered unto their fathers: and there arose another generation after them, which knew not the LORD, nor yet the works which he had done for Israel.

11 And the children of Israel did evil in the sight of the LORD, and served Baalim:

12 And they forsook the LORD God of their fathers, which brought them out of the land of Egypt, and followed other gods, of the gods of the people that *were* round about them, and bowed themselves unto them, and provoked the LORD to anger.

13 And they forsook the LORD, and served Baal and Ashtaroth.

14 And the anger of the LORD was hot against Israel, and he delivered them into the hands of spoilers that spoiled them, and he sold them into the hands of their enemies round about, so that they could not any longer stand before their enemies.

15 Whithersoever they went out, the hand of the LORD was against them for evil, as the LORD had said, and as the LORD had sworn unto them: and they were greatly distressed.

16 Nevertheless the LORD raised up judges, which delivered them out of the hand of those that spoiled them.

17 And yet they would not hearken unto their judges, but they went a whoring after other gods, and bowed themselves unto them: they turned quickly out of the way which their fathers walked in, obeying the commandments of the LORD; *but* they did not so.

18 And when the LORD raised them up judges, then the LORD was with the judge, and delivered them out of the hand of their enemies all the days of the judge: for it repented the LORD because of their groanings by reason of them that oppressed them and vexed them.

19 And it came to pass, when the judge was dead, *that* they returned, and corrupted *themselves* more than their fathers, in following other gods to serve them, and to bow down unto them; they ceased not from their own doings, nor from their stubborn way.

20 And the anger of the LORD was hot against Israel; and he said, Because that this people hath transgressed my covenant which I commanded their fathers, and have not hearkened unto my voice;

21 I also will not henceforth drive out any from before them of the nations which Joshua left when he died:

22 That through them I may prove Israel, whether they will keep the way of the LORD to walk therein, as their fathers did keep *it*, or not.

23 Therefore the LORD left those nations, without driving them out hastily; neither delivered he them into the hand of Joshua.

3 Now these *are* the nations which the LORD left, to prove Israel by them, *even* as many *of Israel* as had not known all the wars of Canaan;

2 Only that the generations of the children of Israel might know, to teach them war, at the least such as before knew nothing thereof;

3 *Namely*, five lords of the Philistines, and all the Canaanites, and the Sidonians, and the Hivites that dwelt in mount Lebanon, from mount Baalhermon unto the entering in of Hamath.

4 And they were to prove Israel by them, to know whether they would hearken unto the commandments of the LORD, which he commanded their fathers by the hand of Moses.

5 And the children of Israel dwelt among the Canaanites, Hittites, and Amorites, and Perizzites, and Hivites, and Jebusites:

6 And they took their daughters to be their wives, and gave their daughters to their sons, and served their gods.

7 And the children of Israel did evil in the sight of the LORD, and forgat the LORD their God, and served Baalim and the groves.

8 Therefore the anger of the LORD was hot against Israel, and he sold them into the hand of Chushan-rishathaim king of Mesopotamia: and the children of Israel served Chushan-rishathaim eight years.

9 And when the children of Israel cried unto the LORD, the LORD raised up a deliverer to the children of Israel, who delivered them, *even* Othniel the son of Kenaz, Caleb's younger brother.

10 And the Spirit of the LORD came upon him, and he judged Israel, and went out to war: and the LORD delivered Chushan-rishathaim king of Mesopotamia into his hand; and his hand prevailed against Chushan-rishathaim.

11 And the land had rest forty years.
And Othniel the son of Kenaz died.
12 And the children of Israel did evil
again in the sight of the LORD: and the
LORD strengthened Eglon the king of
Moab against Israel, because they had
done evil in the sight of the LORD.
13 And he gathered unto him the
children of Ammon and Amalek, and
went and smote Israel, and possessed
the city of palm trees.
14 So the children of Israel served
Eglon the king of Moab eighteen years.
15 But when the children of Israel
cried unto the LORD, the LORD raised
them up a deliverer, Ehud the son of
Gera, a Benjamite, a man lefthanded:
and by him the children of Israel sent a
present unto Eglon the king of Moab.
16 But Ehud made him a dagger
which had two edges, of a cubit length;
and he did gird it under his raiment
upon his right thigh.
17 And he brought the present unto
Eglon king of Moab: and Eglon *was* a
very fat man.
18 And when he had made an end to
offer the present, he sent away the
people that bare the present.
19 But he himself turned again from
the quarries that *were* by Gilgal, and
said, I have a secret errand unto thee, O
king: who said, Keep silence. And all
that stood by him went out from him.
20 And Ehud came unto him; and he
was sitting in a summer parlour, which
he had for himself alone. And Ehud
said, I have a message from God unto
thee. And he arose out of *his* seat.
21 And Ehud put forth his left hand,
and took the dagger from his right
thigh, and thrust it into his belly:
22 And the haft also went in after the
blade; and the fat closed upon the
blade, so that he could not draw the
dagger out of his belly; and the dirt
came out.
23 Then Ehud went forth through the
porch, and shut the doors of the parlour
upon him, and locked them.
24 When he was gone out, his servants came; and when they saw that,
behold, the doors of the parlour *were*
locked, they said, Surely he covereth
his feet in his summer chamber.
25 And they tarried till they were
ashamed: and, behold, he opened not
the doors of the parlour; therefore they
took a key, and opened *them*: and,
behold, their lord *was* fallen down dead
on the earth.
26 And Ehud escaped while they tarried, and passed beyond the quarries,
and escaped unto Seirath.
27 And it came to pass, when he was
come, that he blew a trumpet in the
mountain of Ephraim, and the children
of Israel went down with him from the
mount, and he before them.
28 And he said unto them, Follow
after me: for the LORD hath delivered
your enemies the Moabites into your
hand. And they went down after him,
and took the fords of Jordan toward
Moab, and suffered not a man to pass
over.
29 And they slew of Moab at that time
about ten thousand men, all lusty, and
all men of valour; and there escaped
not a man.
30 So Moab was subdued that day
under the hand of Israel. And the land
had rest fourscore years.
31 And after him was Shamgar the
son of Anath, which slew of the
Philistines six hundred men with an ox
goad: and he also delivered Israel.

4 And the children of Israel again did evil in the sight of the LORD, when Ehud was dead.

2 And the LORD sold them into the hand of Jabin king of Canaan, that reigned in Hazor; the captain of whose host *was* Sisera, which dwelt in Harosheth of the Gentiles.

3 And the children of Israel cried unto the LORD: for he had nine hundred chariots of iron; and twenty years he mightily oppressed the children of Israel.

4 And Deborah, a prophetess, the wife of Lapidoth, she judged Israel at that time.

5 And she dwelt under the palm tree of Deborah between Ramah and Beth-el in mount Ephraim: and the children of Israel came up to her for judgment.

6 And she sent and called Barak the son of Abinoam out of Kedesh-naphtali, and said unto him, Hath not the LORD God of Israel commanded, *saying*, Go and draw toward mount Tabor, and take with thee ten thousand men of the children of Naphtali and of the children of Zebulun?

7 And I will draw unto thee to the river Kishon Sisera, the captain of Jabin's army, with his chariots and his multitude; and I will deliver him into thine hand.

8 And Barak said unto her, If thou wilt go with me, then I will go: but if thou wilt not go with me, *then* I will not go.

9 And she said, I will surely go with thee: notwithstanding the journey that thou takest shall not be for thine honour; for the LORD shall sell Sisera into the hand of a woman. And Deborah arose, and went with Barak to Kedesh.

10 And Barak called Zebulun and Naphtali to Kedesh; and he went up with ten thousand men at his feet: and Deborah went up with him.

11 Now Heber the Kenite, *which was* of the children of Hobab the father in law of Moses, had severed himself from the Kenites, and pitched his tent unto the plain of Zaanaim, which *is* by Kedesh.

12 And they shewed Sisera that Barak the son of Abinoam was gone up to mount Tabor.

13 And Sisera gathered together all his chariots, *even* nine hundred chariots of iron, and all the people that *were* with him, from Harosheth of the Gentiles unto the river of Kishon.

14 And Deborah said unto Barak, Up; for this *is* the day in which the LORD hath delivered Sisera into thine hand: is not the LORD gone out before thee? So Barak went down from mount Tabor, and ten thousand men after him.

15 And the LORD discomfited Sisera, and all *his* chariots, and all *his* host, with the edge of the sword before Barak; so that Sisera lighted down off *his* chariot, and fled away on his feet.

16 But Barak pursued after the chariots, and after the host, unto Harosheth of the Gentiles: and all the host of Sisera fell upon the edge of the sword; *and* there was not a man left.

17 Howbeit Sisera fled away on his feet to the tent of Jael the wife of Heber the Kenite: for *there was* peace between Jabin the king of Hazor and the house of Heber the Kenite.

18 And Jael went out to meet Sisera, and said unto him, Turn in, my lord, turn in to me; fear not. And when he had turned in unto her into the tent, she covered him with a mantle.

19 And he said unto her, Give me, I
pray thee, a little water to drink; for I
am thirsty. And she opened a bottle of
milk, and gave him drink, and covered
him.
20 Again he said unto her, Stand in
the door of the tent, and it shall be,
when any man doth come and enquire
of thee, and say, Is there any man here?
that thou shalt say, No.
21 Then Jael Heber's wife took a nail
of the tent, and took an hammer in her
hand, and went softly unto him, and
smote the nail into his temples, and
fastened it into the ground: for he was
fast asleep and weary. So he died.
22 And, behold, as Barak pursued
Sisera, Jael came out to meet him, and
said unto him, Come, and I will shew
thee the man whom thou seekest. And
when he came into her *tent*, behold,
Sisera lay dead, and the nail *was* in his
temples.
23 So God subdued on that day Jabin
the king of Canaan before the children
of Israel.
24 And the hand of the children of
Israel prospered, and prevailed against
Jabin the king of Canaan, until they
had destroyed Jabin king of Canaan.

5 Then sang Deborah and Barak the
son of Abinoam on that day, saying,
2 Praise ye the LORD for the avenging
of Israel, when the people willingly
offered themselves.
3 Hear, O ye kings; give ear, O ye
princes; I, *even* I, will sing unto the
LORD; I will sing *praise* to the LORD God
of Israel.
4 LORD, when thou wentest out of
Seir, when thou marchedst out of the
field of Edom, the earth trembled, and
the heavens dropped, the clouds also
dropped water.
5 The mountains melted from before
the LORD, *even* that Sinai from before
the LORD God of Israel.
6 In the days of Shamgar the son of
Anath, in the days of Jael, the highways
were unoccupied, and the travellers
walked through byways.
7 *The inhabitants of* the villages
ceased, they ceased in Israel, until that
I Deborah arose, that I arose a mother
in Israel.
8 They chose new gods; then *was* war
in the gates: was there a shield or spear
seen among forty thousand in Israel?
9 My heart *is* toward the governors of
Israel, that offered themselves willingly among the people. Bless ye the LORD.
10 Speak, ye that ride on white asses,
ye that sit in judgment, and walk by the
way.
11 *They that are delivered* from the
noise of archers in the places of drawing water, there shall they rehearse the
righteous acts of the LORD, *even* the
righteous acts *toward the inhabitants*
of his villages in Israel: then shall the
people of the LORD go down to the
gates.
12 Awake, awake, Deborah: awake,
awake, utter a song: arise, Barak, and
lead thy captivity captive, thou son of
Abinoam.
13 Then he made him that remaineth
have dominion over the nobles among
the people: the LORD made me have
dominion over the mighty.
14 Out of Ephraim *was there* a root of
them against Amalek; after thee,
Benjamin, among thy people; out of
Machir came down governors, and out
of Zebulun they that handle the pen of
the writer.
15 And the princes of Issachar *were*
with Deborah; even Issachar, and also

Barak: he was sent on foot into the valley. For the divisions of Reuben *there*
were great thoughts of heart.
16 Why abodest thou among the
sheepfolds, to hear the bleatings of the
flocks? For the divisions of Reuben
there were great searchings of heart.
17 Gilead abode beyond Jordan: and
why did Dan remain in ships? Asher
continued on the sea shore, and abode
in his breaches.
18 Zebulun and Naphtali *were* a people *that* jeoparded their lives unto the
death in the high places of the field.
19 The kings came *and* fought, then
fought the kings of Canaan in Taanach
by the waters of Megiddo; they took no
gain of money.
20 They fought from heaven; the stars
in their courses fought against Sisera.
21 The river of Kishon swept them
away, that ancient river, the river
Kishon. O my soul, thou hast trodden
down strength.
22 Then were the horsehoofs broken
by the means of the pransings, the
pransings of their mighty ones.
23 Curse ye Meroz, said the angel of
the LORD, curse ye bitterly the inhabitants thereof; because they came not to
the help of the LORD, to the help of the
LORD against the mighty.
24 Blessed above women shall Jael
the wife of Heber the Kenite be,
blessed shall she be above women in
the tent.
25 He asked water, *and* she gave *him*
milk; she brought forth butter in a
lordly dish.
26 She put her hand to the nail, and
her right hand to the workmen's hammer; and with the hammer she smote
Sisera, she smote off his head, when
she had pierced and stricken through
his temples.
27 At her feet he bowed, he fell, he
lay down: at her feet he bowed, he fell:
where he bowed, there he fell down
dead.
28 The mother of Sisera looked out at
a window, and cried through the lattice,
Why is his chariot *so* long in coming?
why tarry the wheels of his chariots?
29 Her wise ladies answered her, yea,
she returned answer to herself,
30 Have they not sped? have they *not*
divided the prey; to every man a damsel *or* two; to Sisera a prey of divers
colours, a prey of divers colours of needlework, of divers colours of needlework on both sides, *meet* for the necks
of *them that take* the spoil?
31 So let all thine enemies perish, O
LORD: but *let* them that love him *be* as
the sun when he goeth forth in his
might. And the land had rest forty
years.

6 And the children of Israel did evil
in the sight of the LORD: and the
LORD delivered them into the hand of
Midian seven years.
2 And the hand of Midian prevailed
against Israel: *and* because of the
Midianites the children of Israel made
them the dens which *are* in the mountains, and caves, and strong holds.
3 And *so* it was, when Israel had sown,
that the Midianites came up, and the
Amalekites, and the children of the
east, even they came up against them;
4 And they encamped against them,
and destroyed the increase of the earth,
till thou come unto Gaza, and left no
sustenance for Israel, neither sheep,
nor ox, nor ass.
5 For they came up with their cattle
and their tents, and they came as grass-

hoppers for multitude; *for* both they and their camels were without number: and they entered into the land to destroy it.

6 And Israel was greatly impoverished because of the Midianites; and the children of Israel cried unto the LORD.

7 And it came to pass, when the children of Israel cried unto the LORD because of the Midianites,

8 That the LORD sent a prophet unto the children of Israel, which said unto them, Thus saith the LORD God of Israel, I brought you up from Egypt, and brought you forth out of the house of bondage;

9 And I delivered you out of the hand of the Egyptians, and out of the hand of all that oppressed you, and drave them out from before you, and gave you their land;

10 And I said unto you, I *am* the LORD your God; fear not the gods of the Amorites, in whose land ye dwell: but ye have not obeyed my voice.

11 And there came an angel of the LORD, and sat under an oak which *was* in Ophrah, that *pertained* unto Joash the Abiezrite: and his son Gideon threshed wheat by the winepress, to hide *it* from the Midianites.

12 And the angel of the LORD appeared unto him, and said unto him, The LORD *is* with thee, thou mighty man of valour.

13 And Gideon said unto him, Oh my Lord, if the LORD be with us, why then is all this befallen us? and where *be* all his miracles which our fathers told us of, saying, Did not the LORD bring us up from Egypt? but now the LORD hath forsaken us, and delivered us into the hands of the Midianites.

14 And the LORD looked upon him, and said, Go in this thy might, and thou shalt save Israel from the hand of the Midianites: have not I sent thee?

15 And he said unto him, Oh my Lord, wherewith shall I save Israel? behold, my family *is* poor in Manasseh, and I *am* the least in my father's house.

16 And the LORD said unto him, Surely I will be with thee, and thou shalt smite the Midianites as one man.

17 And he said unto him, If now I have found grace in thy sight, then shew me a sign that thou talkest with me.

18 Depart not hence, I pray thee, until I come unto thee, and bring forth my present, and set *it* before thee. And he said, I will tarry until thou come again.

19 And Gideon went in, and made ready a kid, and unleavened cakes of an ephah of flour: the flesh he put in a basket, and he put the broth in a pot, and brought *it* out unto him under the oak, and presented *it*.

20 And the angel of God said unto him, Take the flesh and the unleavened cakes, and lay *them* upon this rock, and pour out the broth. And he did so.

21 Then the angel of the LORD put forth the end of the staff that *was* in his hand, and touched the flesh and the unleavened cakes; and there rose up fire out of the rock, and consumed the flesh and the unleavened cakes. Then the angel of the LORD departed out of his sight.

22 And when Gideon perceived that he *was* an angel of the LORD, Gideon said, Alas, O Lord GOD! for because I have seen an angel of the LORD face to face.

23 And the LORD said unto him, Peace *be* unto thee; fear not: thou shalt not die.

24 Then Gideon built an altar there unto the LORD, and called it Jehovah-shalom: unto this day it *is* yet in Ophrah of the Abiezrites.

25 And it came to pass the same night, that the LORD said unto him, Take thy father's young bullock, even the second bullock of seven years old, and throw down the altar of Baal that thy father hath, and cut down the grove that *is* by it:

26 And build an altar unto the LORD thy God upon the top of this rock, in the ordered place, and take the second bullock, and offer a burnt sacrifice with the wood of the grove which thou shalt cut down.

27 Then Gideon took ten men of his servants, and did as the LORD had said unto him: and *so* it was, because he feared his father's household, and the men of the city, that he could not do *it* by day, that he did *it* by night.

28 And when the men of the city arose early in the morning, behold, the altar of Baal was cast down, and the grove was cut down that *was* by it, and the second bullock was offered upon the altar *that was* built.

29 And they said one to another, Who hath done this thing? And when they enquired and asked, they said, Gideon the son of Joash hath done this thing.

30 Then the men of the city said unto Joash, Bring out thy son, that he may die: because he hath cast down the altar of Baal, and because he hath cut down the grove that *was* by it.

31 And Joash said unto all that stood against him, Will ye plead for Baal? will ye save him? he that will plead for him, let him be put to death whilst *it is yet* morning: if he *be* a god, let him plead for himself, because *one* hath cast down his altar.

32 Therefore on that day he called him Jerubbaal, saying, Let Baal plead against him, because he hath thrown down his altar.

33 Then all the Midianites and the Amalekites and the children of the east were gathered together, and went over, and pitched in the valley of Jezreel.

34 But the Spirit of the LORD came upon Gideon, and he blew a trumpet; and Abiezer was gathered after him.

35 And he sent messengers throughout all Manasseh; who also was gathered after him: and he sent messengers unto Asher, and unto Zebulun, and unto Naphtali; and they came up to meet them.

36 And Gideon said unto God, If thou wilt save Israel by mine hand, as thou hast said,

37 Behold, I will put a fleece of wool in the floor; *and* if the dew be on the fleece only, and *it be* dry upon all the earth *beside*, then shall I know that thou wilt save Israel by mine hand, as thou hast said.

38 And it was so: for he rose up early on the morrow, and thrust the fleece together, and wringed the dew out of the fleece, a bowl full of water.

39 And Gideon said unto God, Let not thine anger be hot against me, and I will speak but this once: let me prove, I pray thee, but this once with the fleece; let it now be dry only upon the fleece, and upon all the ground let there be dew.

40 And God did so that night: for it was dry upon the fleece only, and there was dew on all the ground.

7 Then Jerubbaal, who *is* Gideon, and
all the people that *were* with him,
rose up early, and pitched beside the
well of Harod: so that the host of the
Midianites were on the north side of
them, by the hill of Moreh, in the valley.
2 And the LORD said unto Gideon, The
people that *are* with thee *are* too many
for me to give the Midianites into their
hands, lest Israel vaunt themselves
against me, saying, Mine own hand
hath saved me.
3 Now therefore go to, proclaim in the
ears of the people, saying, Whosoever *is*
fearful and afraid, let him return and
depart early from mount Gilead. And
there returned of the people twenty
and two thousand; and there remained
ten thousand.
4 And the LORD said unto Gideon, The
people *are* yet *too* many; bring them
down unto the water, and I will try
them for thee there: and it shall be,
that of whom I say unto thee, This shall
go with thee, the same shall go with
thee; and of whomsoever I say unto
thee, This shall not go with thee, the
same shall not go.
5 So he brought down the people unto
the water: and the LORD said unto
Gideon, Every one that lappeth of the
water with his tongue, as a dog lappeth,
him shalt thou set by himself; likewise
every one that boweth down upon his
knees to drink.
6 And the number of them that
lapped, *putting* their hand to their
mouth, were three hundred men: but
all the rest of the people bowed down
upon their knees to drink water.
7 And the LORD said unto Gideon, By
the three hundred men that lapped will
I save you, and deliver the Midianites
into thine hand: and let all the *other*
people go every man unto his place.
8 So the people took victuals in their
hand, and their trumpets: and he sent
all *the rest of* Israel every man unto his
tent, and retained those three hundred
men: and the host of Midian was
beneath him in the valley.
9 And it came to pass the same night,
that the LORD said unto him, Arise, get
thee down unto the host; for I have
delivered it into thine hand.
10 But if thou fear to go down, go thou
with Phurah thy servant down to the
host:
11 And thou shalt hear what they say;
and afterward shall thine hands be
strengthened to go down unto the host.
Then went he down with Phurah his
servant unto the outside of the armed
men that *were* in the host.
12 And the Midianites and the
Amalekites and all the children of the
east lay along in the valley like grasshoppers for multitude; and their camels *were* without number, as the sand by
the sea side for multitude.
13 And when Gideon was come,
behold, *there was* a man that told a
dream unto his fellow, and said, Behold,
I dreamed a dream, and, lo, a cake of
barley bread tumbled into the host of
Midian, and came unto a tent, and
smote it that it fell, and overturned it,
that the tent lay along.
14 And his fellow answered and said,
This *is* nothing else save the sword of
Gideon the son of Joash, a man of
Israel: *for* into his hand hath God delivered Midian, and all the host.
15 And it was *so*, when Gideon heard
the telling of the dream, and the interpretation thereof, that he worshipped,
and returned into the host of Israel,

and said, Arise; for the LORD hath delivered into your hand the host of Midian.
16 And he divided the three hundred men *into* three companies, and he put a trumpet in every man's hand, with empty pitchers, and lamps within the pitchers.
17 And he said unto them, Look on me, and do likewise: and, behold, when I come to the outside of the camp, it shall be *that*, as I do, so shall ye do.
18 When I blow with a trumpet, I and all that *are* with me, then blow ye the trumpets also on every side of all the camp, and say, *The sword* of the LORD, and of Gideon.
19 So Gideon, and the hundred men that *were* with him, came unto the outside of the camp in the beginning of the middle watch; and they had but newly set the watch: and they blew the trumpets, and brake the pitchers that *were* in their hands.
20 And the three companies blew the trumpets, and brake the pitchers, and held the lamps in their left hands, and the trumpets in their right hands to blow *withal*: and they cried, The sword of the LORD, and of Gideon.
21 And they stood every man in his place round about the camp: and all the host ran, and cried, and fled.
22 And the three hundred blew the trumpets, and the LORD set every man's sword against his fellow, even throughout all the host: and the host fled to Beth-shittah in Zererath, *and* to the border of Abel-meholah, unto Tabbath.
23 And the men of Israel gathered themselves together out of Naphtali, and out of Asher, and out of all Manasseh, and pursued after the Midianites.
24 And Gideon sent messengers throughout all mount Ephraim, saying, Come down against the Midianites, and take before them the waters unto Beth-barah and Jordan. Then all the men of Ephraim gathered themselves together, and took the waters unto Beth-barah and Jordan.
25 And they took two princes of the Midianites, Oreb and Zeeb; and they slew Oreb upon the rock Oreb, and Zeeb they slew at the winepress of Zeeb, and pursued Midian, and brought the heads of Oreb and Zeeb to Gideon on the other side Jordan.

8 And the men of Ephraim said unto him, Why hast thou served us thus, that thou calledst us not, when thou wentest to fight with the Midianites? And they did chide with him sharply.
2 And he said unto them, What have I done now in comparison of you? *Is* not the gleaning of the grapes of Ephraim better than the vintage of Abiezer?
3 God hath delivered into your hands the princes of Midian, Oreb and Zeeb: and what was I able to do in comparison of you? Then their anger was abated toward him, when he had said that.
4 And Gideon came to Jordan, *and* passed over, he, and the three hundred men that *were* with him, faint, yet pursuing *them*.
5 And he said unto the men of Succoth, Give, I pray you, loaves of bread unto the people that follow me; for they *be* faint, and I am pursuing after Zebah and Zalmunna, kings of Midian.
6 And the princes of Succoth said, *Are* the hands of Zebah and Zalmunna now in thine hand, that we should give bread unto thine army?

7 And Gideon said, Therefore when the LORD hath delivered Zebah and Zalmunna into mine hand, then I will tear your flesh with the thorns of the wilderness and with briers.

8 And he went up thence to Penuel, and spake unto them likewise: and the men of Penuel answered him as the men of Succoth had answered *him*.

9 And he spake also unto the men of Penuel, saying, When I come again in peace, I will break down this tower.

10 Now Zebah and Zalmunna *were* in Karkor, and their hosts with them, about fifteen thousand *men*, all that were left of all the hosts of the children of the east: for there fell an hundred and twenty thousand men that drew sword.

11 And Gideon went up by the way of them that dwelt in tents on the east of Nobah and Jogbehah, and smote the host: for the host was secure.

12 And when Zebah and Zalmunna fled, he pursued after them, and took the two kings of Midian, Zebah and Zalmunna, and discomfited all the host.

13 And Gideon the son of Joash returned from battle before the sun *was up*,

14 And caught a young man of the men of Succoth, and enquired of him: and he described unto him the princes of Succoth, and the elders thereof, *even* threescore and seventeen men.

15 And he came unto the men of Succoth, and said, Behold Zebah and Zalmunna, with whom ye did upbraid me, saying, *Are* the hands of Zebah and Zalmunna now in thine hand, that we should give bread unto thy men *that are* weary?

16 And he took the elders of the city, and thorns of the wilderness and briers, and with them he taught the men of Succoth.

17 And he beat down the tower of Penuel, and slew the men of the city.

18 Then said he unto Zebah and Zalmunna, What manner of men *were they* whom ye slew at Tabor? And they answered, As thou *art*, so *were* they; each one resembled the children of a king.

19 And he said, They *were* my brethren, *even* the sons of my mother: *as* the LORD liveth, if ye had saved them alive, I would not slay you.

20 And he said unto Jether his firstborn, Up, *and* slay them. But the youth drew not his sword: for he feared, because he *was* yet a youth.

21 Then Zebah and Zalmunna said, Rise thou, and fall upon us: for as the man *is, so is* his strength. And Gideon arose, and slew Zebah and Zalmunna, and took away the ornaments that *were* on their camels' necks.

22 Then the men of Israel said unto Gideon, Rule thou over us, both thou, and thy son, and thy son's son also: for thou hast delivered us from the hand of Midian.

23 And Gideon said unto them, I will not rule over you, neither shall my son rule over you: the LORD shall rule over you.

24 And Gideon said unto them, I would desire a request of you, that ye would give me every man the earrings of his prey. (For they had golden earrings, because they *were* Ishmaelites.)

25 And they answered, We will willingly give *them*. And they spread a garment, and did cast therein every man the earrings of his prey.

26 And the weight of the golden earrings that he requested was a thousand

and seven hundred *shekels* of gold;
beside ornaments, and collars, and purple raiment that *was* on the kings of
Midian, and beside the chains that *were*
about their camels' necks.
27 And Gideon made an ephod thereof, and put it in his city, *even* in Ophrah:
and all Israel went thither a whoring
after it: which thing became a snare
unto Gideon, and to his house.
28 Thus was Midian subdued before
the children of Israel, so that they lifted
up their heads no more. And the country was in quietness forty years in the
days of Gideon.
29 And Jerubbaal the son of Joash
went and dwelt in his own house.
30 And Gideon had threescore and
ten sons of his body begotten: for he
had many wives.
31 And his concubine that *was* in
Shechem, she also bare him a son,
whose name he called Abimelech.
32 And Gideon the son of Joash died
in a good old age, and was buried in the
sepulchre of Joash his father, in Ophrah
of the Abiezrites.
33 And it came to pass, as soon as
Gideon was dead, that the children of
Israel turned again, and went a whoring after Baalim, and made Baal-berith
their god.
34 And the children of Israel remembered not the LORD their God, who had
delivered them out of the hands of all
their enemies on every side:
35 Neither shewed they kindness to
the house of Jerubbaal, *namely*, Gideon, according to all the goodness
which he had shewed unto Israel.

9 And Abimelech the son of Jerubbaal went to Shechem unto his
mother's brethren, and communed with
them, and with all the family of the
house of his mother's father, saying,
2 Speak, I pray you, in the ears of all
the men of Shechem, Whether *is* better
for you, either that all the sons of
Jerubbaal, *which are* threescore and
ten persons, reign over you, or that one
reign over you? remember also that I
am your bone and your flesh.
3 And his mother's brethren spake of
him in the ears of all the men of
Shechem all these words: and their
hearts inclined to follow Abimelech; for
they said, He *is* our brother.
4 And they gave him threescore and
ten *pieces* of silver out of the house of
Baal-berith, wherewith Abimelech
hired vain and light persons, which followed him.
5 And he went unto his father's house
at Ophrah, and slew his brethren the
sons of Jerubbaal, *being* threescore and
ten persons, upon one stone: notwithstanding yet Jotham the youngest son
of Jerubbaal was left; for he hid himself.
6 And all the men of Shechem gathered together, and all the house of
Millo, and went, and made Abimelech
king, by the plain of the pillar that *was*
in Shechem.
7 And when they told *it* to Jotham, he
went and stood in the top of mount
Gerizim, and lifted up his voice, and
cried, and said unto them, Hearken
unto me, ye men of Shechem, that God
may hearken unto you.
8 The trees went forth *on a time* to
anoint a king over them; and they said
unto the olive tree, Reign thou over us.
9 But the olive tree said unto them,
Should I leave my fatness, wherewith
by me they honour God and man, and
go to be promoted over the trees?

10 And the trees said to the fig tree,
Come thou, *and* reign over us.
11 But the fig tree said unto them,
Should I forsake my sweetness, and my
good fruit, and go to be promoted over
the trees?
12 Then said the trees unto the vine,
Come thou, *and* reign over us.
13 And the vine said unto them,
Should I leave my wine, which cheereth
God and man, and go to be promoted
over the trees?
14 Then said all the trees unto the
bramble, Come thou, *and* reign over us.
15 And the bramble said unto the
trees, If in truth ye anoint me king over
you, *then* come *and* put your trust in
my shadow: and if not, let fire come out
of the bramble, and devour the cedars
of Lebanon.
16 Now therefore, if ye have done
truly and sincerely, in that ye have
made Abimelech king, and if ye have
dealt well with Jerubbaal and his
house, and have done unto him according to the deserving of his hands;
17 (For my father fought for you, and
adventured his life far, and delivered
you out of the hand of Midian:
18 And ye are risen up against my
father's house this day, and have slain
his sons, threescore and ten persons,
upon one stone, and have made
Abimelech, the son of his maidservant,
king over the men of Shechem, because
he *is* your brother;)
19 If ye then have dealt truly and
sincerely with Jerubbaal and with his
house this day, *then* rejoice ye in
Abimelech, and let him also rejoice in
you:
20 But if not, let fire come out from
Abimelech, and devour the men of
Shechem, and the house of Millo; and
let fire come out from the men of
Shechem, and from the house of Millo,
and devour Abimelech.
21 And Jotham ran away, and fled,
and went to Beer, and dwelt there, for
fear of Abimelech his brother.
22 When Abimelech had reigned
three years over Israel,
23 Then God sent an evil spirit
between Abimelech and the men of
Shechem; and the men of Shechem
dealt treacherously with Abimelech:
24 That the cruelty *done* to the threescore and ten sons of Jerubbaal might
come, and their blood be laid upon
Abimelech their brother, which slew
them; and upon the men of Shechem,
which aided him in the killing of his
brethren.
25 And the men of Shechem set liers
in wait for him in the top of the mountains, and they robbed all that came
along that way by them: and it was told
Abimelech.
26 And Gaal the son of Ebed came
with his brethren, and went over to
Shechem: and the men of Shechem put
their confidence in him.
27 And they went out into the fields,
and gathered their vineyards, and
trode *the grapes*, and made merry, and
went into the house of their god, and
did eat and drink, and cursed Abimelech.
28 And Gaal the son of Ebed said,
Who *is* Abimelech, and who *is* Shechem,
that we should serve him? *is* not *he* the
son of Jerubbaal? and Zebul his officer? serve the men of Hamor the father
of Shechem: for why should we serve
him?
29 And would to God this people were
under my hand! then would I remove

Abimelech. And he said to Abimelech,
Increase thine army, and come out.
30 And when Zebul the ruler of the
city heard the words of Gaal the son of
Ebed, his anger was kindled.
31 And he sent messengers unto
Abimelech privily, saying, Behold, Gaal
the son of Ebed and his brethren be
come to Shechem; and, behold, they
fortify the city against thee.
32 Now therefore up by night, thou
and the people that *is* with thee, and lie
in wait in the field:
33 And it shall be, *that* in the morning, as soon as the sun is up, thou shalt
rise early, and set upon the city: and,
behold, *when* he and the people that *is*
with him come out against thee, then
mayest thou do to them as thou shalt
find occasion.
34 And Abimelech rose up, and all
the people that *were* with him, by night,
and they laid wait against Shechem in
four companies.
35 And Gaal the son of Ebed went
out, and stood in the entering of the
gate of the city: and Abimelech rose up,
and the people that *were* with him,
from lying in wait.
36 And when Gaal saw the people, he
said to Zebul, Behold, there come people down from the top of the mountains. And Zebul said unto him, Thou
seest the shadow of the mountains as *if*
they were men.
37 And Gaal spake again and said,
See there come people down by the
middle of the land, and another company come along by the plain of
Meonenim.
38 Then said Zebul unto him, Where
is now thy mouth, wherewith thou
saidst, Who *is* Abimelech, that we
should serve him? *is* not this the people
that thou hast despised? go out, I pray
now, and fight with them.
39 And Gaal went out before the men
of Shechem, and fought with Abimelech.
40 And Abimelech chased him, and
he fled before him, and many were
overthrown *and* wounded, *even* unto
the entering of the gate.
41 And Abimelech dwelt at Arumah:
and Zebul thrust out Gaal and his
brethren, that they should not dwell in
Shechem.
42 And it came to pass on the morrow,
that the people went out into the field;
and they told Abimelech.
43 And he took the people, and divided them into three companies, and laid
wait in the field, and looked, and,
behold, the people *were* come forth out
of the city; and he rose up against
them, and smote them.
44 And Abimelech, and the company
that *was* with him, rushed forward, and
stood in the entering of the gate of the
city: and the two *other* companies ran
upon all *the people* that *were* in the
fields, and slew them.
45 And Abimelech fought against the
city all that day; and he took the city,
and slew the people that *was* therein,
and beat down the city, and sowed it
with salt.
46 And when all the men of the tower
of Shechem heard *that*, they entered
into an hold of the house of the god
Berith.
47 And it was told Abimelech, that all
the men of the tower of Shechem were
gathered together.
48 And Abimelech gat him up to
mount Zalmon, he and all the people
that *were* with him; and Abimelech
took an axe in his hand, and cut down a

bough from the trees, and took it, and laid *it* on his shoulder, and said unto the people that *were* with him, What ye have seen me do, make haste, *and* do as I *have done.*

49 And all the people likewise cut down every man his bough, and followed Abimelech, and put *them* to the hold, and set the hold on fire upon them; so that all the men of the tower of Shechem died also, about a thousand men and women.

50 Then went Abimelech to Thebez, and encamped against Thebez, and took it.

51 But there was a strong tower within the city, and thither fled all the men and women, and all they of the city, and shut *it* to them, and gat them up to the top of the tower.

52 And Abimelech came unto the tower, and fought against it, and went hard unto the door of the tower to burn it with fire.

53 And a certain woman cast a piece of a millstone upon Abimelech's head, and all to brake his skull.

54 Then he called hastily unto the young man his armourbearer, and said unto him, Draw thy sword, and slay me, that men say not of me, A woman slew him. And his young man thrust him through, and he died.

55 And when the men of Israel saw that Abimelech was dead, they departed every man unto his place.

56 Thus God rendered the wickedness of Abimelech, which he did unto his father, in slaying his seventy brethren:

57 And all the evil of the men of Shechem did God render upon their heads: and upon them came the curse of Jotham the son of Jerubbaal.

10 And after Abimelech there arose to defend Israel Tola the son of Puah, the son of Dodo, a man of Issachar; and he dwelt in Shamir in mount Ephraim.

2 And he judged Israel twenty and three years, and died, and was buried in Shamir.

3 And after him arose Jair, a Gileadite, and judged Israel twenty and two years.

4 And he had thirty sons that rode on thirty ass colts, and they had thirty cities, which are called Havoth-jair unto this day, which *are* in the land of Gilead.

5 And Jair died, and was buried in Camon.

6 And the children of Israel did evil again in the sight of the LORD, and served Baalim, and Ashtaroth, and the gods of Syria, and the gods of Zidon, and the gods of Moab, and the gods of the children of Ammon, and the gods of the Philistines, and forsook the LORD, and served not him.

7 And the anger of the LORD was hot against Israel, and he sold them into the hands of the Philistines, and into the hands of the children of Ammon.

8 And that year they vexed and oppressed the children of Israel: eighteen years, all the children of Israel that *were* on the other side Jordan in the land of the Amorites, which *is* in Gilead.

9 Moreover the children of Ammon passed over Jordan to fight also against Judah, and against Benjamin, and against the house of Ephraim; so that Israel was sore distressed.

10 And the children of Israel cried unto the LORD, saying, We have sinned against thee, both because we have

forsaken our God, and also served
Baalim.
11 And the LORD said unto the children of Israel, *Did* not *I deliver you*
from the Egyptians, and from the
Amorites, from the children of Ammon,
and from the Philistines?
12 The Zidonians also, and the
Amalekites, and the Maonites, did
oppress you; and ye cried to me, and I
delivered you out of their hand.
13 Yet ye have forsaken me, and
served other gods: wherefore I will
deliver you no more.
14 Go and cry unto the gods which ye
have chosen; let them deliver you in the
time of your tribulation.
15 And the children of Israel said
unto the LORD, We have sinned: do thou
unto us whatsoever seemeth good unto
thee; deliver us only, we pray thee, this
day.
16 And they put away the strange
gods from among them, and served the
LORD: and his soul was grieved for the
misery of Israel.
17 Then the children of Ammon were
gathered together, and encamped in
Gilead. And the children of Israel
assembled themselves together, and
encamped in Mizpeh.
18 And the people *and* princes of
Gilead said one to another, What man *is*
he that will begin to fight against the
children of Ammon? he shall be head
over all the inhabitants of Gilead.

11 Now Jephthah the Gileadite was
a mighty man of valour, and he
was the son of an harlot: and Gilead
begat Jephthah.
2 And Gilead's wife bare him sons;
and his wife's sons grew up, and they
thrust out Jephthah, and said unto him,
Thou shalt not inherit in our father's
house; for thou *art* the son of a strange
woman.
3 Then Jephthah fled from his brethren, and dwelt in the land of Tob: and
there were gathered vain men to
Jephthah, and went out with him.
4 And it came to pass in process of
time, that the children of Ammon made
war against Israel.
5 And it was so, that when the children of Ammon made war against
Israel, the elders of Gilead went to
fetch Jephthah out of the land of Tob:
6 And they said unto Jephthah, Come,
and be our captain, that we may fight
with the children of Ammon.
7 And Jephthah said unto the elders
of Gilead, Did not ye hate me, and
expel me out of my father's house? and
why are ye come unto me now when ye
are in distress?
8 And the elders of Gilead said unto
Jephthah, Therefore we turn again to
thee now, that thou mayest go with us,
and fight against the children of
Ammon, and be our head over all the
inhabitants of Gilead.
9 And Jephthah said unto the elders
of Gilead, If ye bring me home again to
fight against the children of Ammon,
and the LORD deliver them before me,
shall I be your head?
10 And the elders of Gilead said unto
Jephthah, The LORD be witness between us, if we do not so according to
thy words.
11 Then Jephthah went with the
elders of Gilead, and the people made
him head and captain over them: and
Jephthah uttered all his words before
the LORD in Mizpeh.
12 And Jephthah sent messengers
unto the king of the children of Ammon,
saying, What hast thou to do with me,

that thou art come against me to fight
in my land?
13 And the king of the children of
Ammon answered unto the messengers
of Jephthah, Because Israel took away
my land, when they came up out of
Egypt, from Arnon even unto Jabbok,
and unto Jordan: now therefore restore
those *lands* again peaceably.
14 And Jephthah sent messengers
again unto the king of the children of
Ammon:
15 And said unto him, Thus saith
Jephthah, Israel took not away the land
of Moab, nor the land of the children of
Ammon:
16 But when Israel came up from
Egypt, and walked through the wilderness unto the Red sea, and came to
Kadesh;
17 Then Israel sent messengers unto
the king of Edom, saying, Let me, I pray
thee, pass through thy land: but the
king of Edom would not hearken *thereto*. And in like manner they sent unto
the king of Moab: but he would not
consent: and Israel abode in Kadesh.
18 Then they went along through the
wilderness, and compassed the land of
Edom, and the land of Moab, and came
by the east side of the land of Moab,
and pitched on the other side of Arnon,
but came not within the border of
Moab: for Arnon *was* the border of
Moab.
19 And Israel sent messengers unto
Sihon king of the Amorites, the king of
Heshbon; and Israel said unto him, Let
us pass, we pray thee, through thy land
into my place.
20 But Sihon trusted not Israel to pass
through his coast: but Sihon gathered
all his people together, and pitched in
Jahaz, and fought against Israel.
21 And the LORD God of Israel delivered Sihon and all his people into the
hand of Israel, and they smote them: so
Israel possessed all the land of the
Amorites, the inhabitants of that country.
22 And they possessed all the coasts
of the Amorites, from Arnon even unto
Jabbok, and from the wilderness even
unto Jordan.
23 So now the LORD God of Israel hath
dispossessed the Amorites from before
his people Israel, and shouldest thou
possess it?
24 Wilt not thou possess that which
Chemosh thy god giveth thee to possess? So whomsoever the LORD our God
shall drive out from before us, them
will we possess.
25 And now *art* thou any thing better
than Balak the son of Zippor, king of
Moab? did he ever strive against Israel,
or did he ever fight against them,
26 While Israel dwelt in Heshbon and
her towns, and in Aroer and her towns,
and in all the cities that *be* along by the
coasts of Arnon, three hundred years?
why therefore did ye not recover *them*
within that time?
27 Wherefore I have not sinned
against thee, but thou doest me wrong
to war against me: the LORD the Judge
be judge this day between the children
of Israel and the children of Ammon.
28 Howbeit the king of the children of
Ammon hearkened not unto the words
of Jephthah which he sent him.
29 Then the Spirit of the LORD came
upon Jephthah, and he passed over
Gilead, and Manasseh, and passed over
Mizpeh of Gilead, and from Mizpeh of
Gilead he passed over *unto* the children of Ammon.

30 And Jephthah vowed a vow unto
the LORD, and said, If thou shalt without fail deliver the children of Ammon
into mine hands,
31 Then it shall be, that whatsoever
cometh forth of the doors of my house
to meet me, when I return in peace
from the children of Ammon, shall
surely be the LORD's, and I will offer it
up for a burnt offering.
32 So Jephthah passed over unto the
children of Ammon to fight against
them; and the LORD delivered them
into his hands.
33 And he smote them from Aroer,
even till thou come to Minnith, *even*
twenty cities, and unto the plain of the
vineyards, with a very great slaughter.
Thus the children of Ammon were subdued before the children of Israel.
34 And Jephthah came to Mizpeh
unto his house, and, behold, his daughter came out to meet him with timbrels
and with dances: and she *was his* only
child; beside her he had neither son nor
daughter.
35 And it came to pass, when he saw
her, that he rent his clothes, and said,
Alas, my daughter! thou hast brought
me very low, and thou art one of them
that trouble me: for I have opened my
mouth unto the LORD, and I cannot go
back.
36 And she said unto him, My father,
if thou hast opened thy mouth unto the
LORD, do to me according to that which
hath proceeded out of thy mouth; forasmuch as the LORD hath taken vengeance for thee of thine enemies, *even*
of the children of Ammon.
37 And she said unto her father, Let
this thing be done for me: let me alone
two months, that I may go up and down
upon the mountains, and bewail my
virginity, I and my fellows.
38 And he said, Go. And he sent her
away *for* two months: and she went
with her companions, and bewailed her
virginity upon the mountains.
39 And it came to pass at the end of
two months, that she returned unto her
father, who did with her *according* to
his vow which he had vowed: and she
knew no man. And it was a custom in
Israel,
40 *That* the daughters of Israel went
yearly to lament the daughter of
Jephthah the Gileadite four days in a
year.

12

And the men of Ephraim gathered themselves together, and
went northward, and said unto Jephthah, Wherefore passedst thou over to
fight against the children of Ammon,
and didst not call us to go with thee? we
will burn thine house upon thee with
fire.
2 And Jephthah said unto them, I and
my people were at great strife with the
children of Ammon; and when I called
you, ye delivered me not out of their
hands.
3 And when I saw that ye delivered
me not, I put my life in my hands, and
passed over against the children of
Ammon, and the LORD delivered them
into my hand: wherefore then are ye
come up unto me this day, to fight
against me?
4 Then Jephthah gathered together
all the men of Gilead, and fought with
Ephraim: and the men of Gilead smote
Ephraim, because they said, Ye
Gileadites *are* fugitives of Ephraim
among the Ephraimites, *and* among
the Manassites.

5 And the Gileadites took the passages of Jordan before the Ephraimites: and it was *so*, that when those Ephraimites which were escaped said, Let me go over; that the men of Gilead said unto him, *Art* thou an Ephraimite? If he said, Nay;

6 Then said they unto him, Say now Shibboleth: and he said Sibboleth: for he could not frame to pronounce *it* right. Then they took him, and slew him at the passages of Jordan: and there fell at that time of the Ephraimites forty and two thousand.

7 And Jephthah judged Israel six years. Then died Jephthah the Gileadite, and was buried in *one of* the cities of Gilead.

8 And after him Ibzan of Beth-lehem judged Israel.

9 And he had thirty sons, and thirty daughters, *whom* he sent abroad, and took in thirty daughters from abroad for his sons. And he judged Israel seven years.

10 Then died Ibzan, and was buried at Beth-lehem.

11 And after him Elon, a Zebulonite, judged Israel; and he judged Israel ten years.

12 And Elon the Zebulonite died, and was buried in Aijalon in the country of Zebulun.

13 And after him Abdon the son of Hillel, a Pirathonite, judged Israel.

14 And he had forty sons and thirty nephews, that rode on threescore and ten ass colts: and he judged Israel eight years.

15 And Abdon the son of Hillel the Pirathonite died, and was buried in Pirathon in the land of Ephraim, in the mount of the Amalekites.

13 And the children of Israel did evil again in the sight of the LORD; and the LORD delivered them into the hand of the Philistines forty years.

2 And there was a certain man of Zorah, of the family of the Danites, whose name *was* Manoah; and his wife *was* barren, and bare not.

3 And the angel of the LORD appeared unto the woman, and said unto her, Behold now, thou *art* barren, and bearest not: but thou shalt conceive, and bear a son.

4 Now therefore beware, I pray thee, and drink not wine nor strong drink, and eat not any unclean *thing*:

5 For, lo, thou shalt conceive, and bear a son; and no razor shall come on his head: for the child shall be a Nazarite unto God from the womb: and he shall begin to deliver Israel out of the hand of the Philistines.

6 Then the woman came and told her husband, saying, A man of God came unto me, and his countenance *was* like the countenance of an angel of God, very terrible: but I asked him not whence he *was*, neither told he me his name:

7 But he said unto me, Behold, thou shalt conceive, and bear a son; and now drink no wine nor strong drink, neither eat any unclean *thing*: for the child shall be a Nazarite to God from the womb to the day of his death.

8 Then Manoah intreated the LORD, and said, O my Lord, let the man of God which thou didst send come again unto us, and teach us what we shall do unto the child that shall be born.

9 And God hearkened to the voice of Manoah; and the angel of God came again unto the woman as she sat in the

field: but Manoah her husband *was* not with her.

10 And the woman made haste, and ran, and shewed her husband, and said unto him, Behold, the man hath appeared unto me, that came unto me the *other* day.

11 And Manoah arose, and went after his wife, and came to the man, and said unto him, *Art* thou the man that spakest unto the woman? And he said, I *am*.

12 And Manoah said, Now let thy words come to pass. How shall we order the child, and *how* shall we do unto him?

13 And the angel of the LORD said unto Manoah, Of all that I said unto the woman let her beware.

14 She may not eat of any *thing* that cometh of the vine, neither let her drink wine or strong drink, nor eat any unclean *thing*: all that I commanded her let her observe.

15 And Manoah said unto the angel of the LORD, I pray thee, let us detain thee, until we shall have made ready a kid for thee.

16 And the angel of the LORD said unto Manoah, Though thou detain me, I will not eat of thy bread: and if thou wilt offer a burnt offering, thou must offer it unto the LORD. For Manoah knew not that he *was* an angel of the LORD.

17 And Manoah said unto the angel of the LORD, What *is* thy name, that when thy sayings come to pass we may do thee honour?

18 And the angel of the LORD said unto him, Why askest thou thus after my name, seeing it *is* secret?

19 So Manoah took a kid with a meat offering, and offered *it* upon a rock unto the LORD: and *the angel* did wondrously; and Manoah and his wife looked on.

20 For it came to pass, when the flame went up toward heaven from off the altar, that the angel of the LORD ascended in the flame of the altar. And Manoah and his wife looked on *it*, and fell on their faces to the ground.

21 But the angel of the LORD did no more appear to Manoah and to his wife. Then Manoah knew that he *was* an angel of the LORD.

22 And Manoah said unto his wife, We shall surely die, because we have seen God.

23 But his wife said unto him, If the LORD were pleased to kill us, he would not have received a burnt offering and a meat offering at our hands, neither would he have shewed us all these *things*, nor would as at this time have told us *such things* as these.

24 And the woman bare a son, and called his name Samson: and the child grew, and the LORD blessed him.

25 And the Spirit of the LORD began to move him at times in the camp of Dan between Zorah and Eshtaol.

14

And Samson went down to Timnath, and saw a woman in Timnath of the daughters of the Philistines.

2 And he came up, and told his father and his mother, and said, I have seen a woman in Timnath of the daughters of the Philistines: now therefore get her for me to wife.

3 Then his father and his mother said unto him, *Is there* never a woman among the daughters of thy brethren, or among all my people, that thou goest to take a wife of the uncircumcised Philistines? And Samson said unto his

father, Get her for me; for she pleaseth
me well.
4 But his father and his mother knew
not that it *was* of the LORD, that he
sought an occasion against the
Philistines: for at that time the
Philistines had dominion over Israel.
5 Then went Samson down, and his
father and his mother, to Timnath, and
came to the vineyards of Timnath: and,
behold, a young lion roared against
him.
6 And the Spirit of the LORD came
mightily upon him, and he rent him as
he would have rent a kid, and *he had*
nothing in his hand: but he told not his
father or his mother what he had done.
7 And he went down, and talked with
the woman; and she pleased Samson
well.
8 And after a time he returned to
take her, and he turned aside to see the
carcase of the lion: and, behold, *there*
was a swarm of bees and honey in the
carcase of the lion.
9 And he took thereof in his hands,
and went on eating, and came to his
father and mother, and he gave them,
and they did eat: but he told not them
that he had taken the honey out of the
carcase of the lion.
10 So his father went down unto the
woman: and Samson made there a
feast; for so used the young men to do.
11 And it came to pass, when they
saw him, that they brought thirty companions to be with him.
12 And Samson said unto them, I will
now put forth a riddle unto you: if ye
can certainly declare it me within the
seven days of the feast, and find *it* out,
then I will give you thirty sheets and
thirty change of garments:
13 But if ye cannot declare *it* me, then
shall ye give me thirty sheets and thirty
change of garments. And they said unto
him, Put forth thy riddle, that we may
hear it.
14 And he said unto them, Out of the
eater came forth meat, and out of the
strong came forth sweetness. And they
could not in three days expound the
riddle.
15 And it came to pass on the seventh
day, that they said unto Samson's wife,
Entice thy husband, that he may
declare unto us the riddle, lest we burn
thee and thy father's house with fire:
have ye called us to take that we have?
is it not *so*?
16 And Samson's wife wept before
him, and said, Thou dost but hate me,
and lovest me not: thou hast put forth a
riddle unto the children of my people,
and hast not told *it* me. And he said
unto her, Behold, I have not told *it* my
father nor my mother, and shall I tell *it*
thee?
17 And she wept before him the seven
days, while their feast lasted: and it
came to pass on the seventh day, that
he told her, because she lay sore upon
him: and she told the riddle to the children of her people.
18 And the men of the city said unto
him on the seventh day before the sun
went down, What *is* sweeter than
honey? and what *is* stronger than a
lion? And he said unto them, If ye had
not plowed with my heifer, ye had not
found out my riddle.
19 And the Spirit of the LORD came
upon him, and he went down to
Ashkelon, and slew thirty men of them,
and took their spoil, and gave change of
garments unto them which expounded

the riddle. And his anger was kindled,
and he went up to his father's house.
20 But Samson's wife was *given* to his
companion, whom he had used as his
friend.

15 But it came to pass within a
while after, in the time of wheat
harvest, that Samson visited his wife
with a kid; and he said, I will go in to
my wife into the chamber. But her
father would not suffer him to go in.
2 And her father said, I verily thought
that thou hadst utterly hated her;
therefore I gave her to thy companion:
is not her younger sister fairer than
she? take her, I pray thee, instead of
her.
3 And Samson said concerning them,
Now shall I be more blameless than the
Philistines, though I do them a displeasure.
4 And Samson went and caught three
hundred foxes, and took firebrands,
and turned tail to tail, and put a firebrand in the midst between two tails.
5 And when he had set the brands on
fire, he let *them* go into the standing
corn of the Philistines, and burnt up
both the shocks, and also the standing
corn, with the vineyards *and* olives.
6 Then the Philistines said, Who hath
done this? And they answered, Samson,
the son in law of the Timnite, because
he had taken his wife, and given her to
his companion. And the Philistines
came up, and burnt her and her father
with fire.
7 And Samson said unto them,
Though ye have done this, yet will I be
avenged of you, and after that I will
cease.
8 And he smote them hip and thigh
with a great slaughter: and he went
down and dwelt in the top of the rock
Etam.
9 Then the Philistines went up, and
pitched in Judah, and spread themselves in Lehi.
10 And the men of Judah said, Why
are ye come up against us? And they
answered, To bind Samson are we come
up, to do to him as he hath done to us.
11 Then three thousand men of Judah
went to the top of the rock Etam, and
said to Samson, Knowest thou not that
the Philistines *are* rulers over us? what
is this *that* thou hast done unto us?
And he said unto them, As they did
unto me, so have I done unto them.
12 And they said unto him, We are
come down to bind thee, that we may
deliver thee into the hand of the
Philistines. And Samson said unto
them, Swear unto me, that ye will not
fall upon me yourselves.
13 And they spake unto him, saying,
No; but we will bind thee fast, and
deliver thee into their hand: but surely
we will not kill thee. And they bound
him with two new cords, and brought
him up from the rock.
14 *And* when he came unto Lehi, the
Philistines shouted against him: and
the Spirit of the Lord came mightily
upon him, and the cords that *were* upon
his arms became as flax that was burnt
with fire, and his bands loosed from off
his hands.
15 And he found a new jawbone of an
ass, and put forth his hand, and took it,
and slew a thousand men therewith.
16 And Samson said, With the jawbone of an ass, heaps upon heaps, with
the jaw of an ass have I slain a thousand men.

17 And it came to pass, when he had made an end of speaking, that he cast away the jawbone out of his hand, and called that place Ramath-lehi.

18 And he was sore athirst, and called on the LORD, and said, Thou hast given this great deliverance into the hand of thy servant: and now shall I die for thirst, and fall into the hand of the uncircumcised?

19 But God clave an hollow place that *was* in the jaw, and there came water thereout; and when he had drunk, his spirit came again, and he revived: wherefore he called the name thereof En-hakkore, which *is* in Lehi unto this day.

20 And he judged Israel in the days of the Philistines twenty years.

16 Then went Samson to Gaza, and saw there an harlot, and went in unto her.

2 *And it was told* the Gazites, saying, Samson is come hither. And they compassed *him* in, and laid wait for him all night in the gate of the city, and were quiet all the night, saying, In the morning, when it is day, we shall kill him.

3 And Samson lay till midnight, and arose at midnight, and took the doors of the gate of the city, and the two posts, and went away with them, bar and all, and put *them* upon his shoulders, and carried them up to the top of an hill that *is* before Hebron.

4 And it came to pass afterward, that he loved a woman in the valley of Sorek, whose name *was* Delilah.

5 And the lords of the Philistines came up unto her, and said unto her, Entice him, and see wherein his great strength *lieth*, and by what *means* we may prevail against him, that we may bind him to afflict him: and we will give thee every one of us eleven hundred *pieces* of silver.

6 And Delilah said to Samson, Tell me, I pray thee, wherein thy great strength *lieth*, and wherewith thou mightest be bound to afflict thee.

7 And Samson said unto her, If they bind me with seven green withs that were never dried, then shall I be weak, and be as another man.

8 Then the lords of the Philistines brought up to her seven green withs which had not been dried, and she bound him with them.

9 Now *there were* men lying in wait, abiding with her in the chamber. And she said unto him, The Philistines *be* upon thee, Samson. And he brake the withs, as a thread of tow is broken when it toucheth the fire. So his strength was not known.

10 And Delilah said unto Samson, Behold, thou hast mocked me, and told me lies: now tell me, I pray thee, wherewith thou mightest be bound.

11 And he said unto her, If they bind me fast with new ropes that never were occupied, then shall I be weak, and be as another man.

12 Delilah therefore took new ropes, and bound him therewith, and said unto him, The Philistines *be* upon thee, Samson. And *there were* liers in wait abiding in the chamber. And he brake them from off his arms like a thread.

13 And Delilah said unto Samson, Hitherto thou hast mocked me, and told me lies: tell me wherewith thou mightest be bound. And he said unto her, If thou weavest the seven locks of my head with the web.

14 And she fastened *it* with the pin, and said unto him, The Philistines *be* upon thee, Samson. And he awaked out

of his sleep, and went away with the pin
of the beam, and with the web.
15 And she said unto him, How canst
thou say, I love thee, when thine heart
is not with me? thou hast mocked me
these three times, and hast not told me
wherein thy great strength *lieth*.
16 And it came to pass, when she
pressed him daily with her words, and
urged him, *so* that his soul was vexed
unto death;
17 That he told her all his heart, and
said unto her, There hath not come a
razor upon mine head; for I *have been* a
Nazarite unto God from my mother's
womb: if I be shaven, then my strength
will go from me, and I shall become
weak, and be like any *other* man.
18 And when Delilah saw that he had
told her all his heart, she sent and
called for the lords of the Philistines,
saying, Come up this once, for he hath
shewed me all his heart. Then the lords
of the Philistines came up unto her, and
brought money in their hand.
19 And she made him sleep upon her
knees; and she called for a man, and
she caused him to shave off the seven
locks of his head; and she began to
afflict him, and his strength went from
him.
20 And she said, The Philistines *be*
upon thee, Samson. And he awoke out
of his sleep, and said, I will go out as at
other times before, and shake myself.
And he wist not that the LORD was
departed from him.
21 But the Philistines took him, and
put out his eyes, and brought him down
to Gaza, and bound him with fetters of
brass; and he did grind in the prison
house.
22 Howbeit the hair of his head began
to grow again after he was shaven.
23 Then the lords of the Philistines
gathered them together for to offer a
great sacrifice unto Dagon their god,
and to rejoice: for they said, Our god
hath delivered Samson our enemy into
our hand.
24 And when the people saw him,
they praised their god: for they said,
Our god hath delivered into our hands
our enemy, and the destroyer of our
country, which slew many of us.
25 And it came to pass, when their
hearts were merry, that they said, Call
for Samson, that he may make us sport.
And they called for Samson out of the
prison house; and he made them sport:
and they set him between the pillars.
26 And Samson said unto the lad that
held him by the hand, Suffer me that I
may feel the pillars whereupon the
house standeth, that I may lean upon
them.
27 Now the house was full of men and
women; and all the lords of the
Philistines *were* there; and *there were*
upon the roof about three thousand
men and women, that beheld while
Samson made sport.
28 And Samson called unto the LORD,
and said, O Lord GOD, remember me, I
pray thee, and strengthen me, I pray
thee, only this once, O God, that I may
be at once avenged of the Philistines
for my two eyes.
29 And Samson took hold of the two
middle pillars upon which the house
stood, and on which it was borne up, of
the one with his right hand, and of the
other with his left.
30 And Samson said, Let me die with
the Philistines. And he bowed himself
with *all his* might; and the house fell
upon the lords, and upon all the people
that *were* therein. So the dead which he

slew at his death were more than *they*
which he slew in his life.
31 Then his brethren and all the
house of his father came down, and
took him, and brought *him* up, and
buried him between Zorah and Eshtaol
in the buryingplace of Manoah his
father. And he judged Israel twenty
years.

17 And there was a man of mount
Ephraim, whose name *was*
Micah.
2 And he said unto his mother, The
eleven hundred *shekels* of silver that
were taken from thee, about which
thou cursedst, and spakest of also in
mine ears, behold, the silver *is* with me;
I took it. And his mother said, Blessed
be thou of the LORD, my son.
3 And when he had restored the elev-
en hundred *shekels* of silver to his
mother, his mother said, I had wholly
dedicated the silver unto the LORD
from my hand for my son, to make a
graven image and a molten image: now
therefore I will restore it unto thee.
4 Yet he restored the money unto his
mother; and his mother took two hundred *shekels* of silver, and gave them to
the founder, who made thereof a grav-
en image and a molten image: and they
were in the house of Micah.
5 And the man Micah had an house of
gods, and made an ephod, and teraphim, and consecrated one of his sons,
who became his priest.
6 In those days *there was* no king in
Israel, *but* every man did *that which*
was right in his own eyes.
7 And there was a young man out of
Beth-lehem-judah of the family of
Judah, who *was* a Levite, and he
sojourned there.
8 And the man departed out of the
city from Beth-lehem-judah to sojourn
where he could find *a place*: and he
came to mount Ephraim to the house of
Micah, as he journeyed.
9 And Micah said unto him, Whence
comest thou? And he said unto him, I
am a Levite of Beth-lehem-judah, and I
go to sojourn where I may find *a place*.
10 And Micah said unto him, Dwell
with me, and be unto me a father and a
priest, and I will give thee ten *shekels*
of silver by the year, and a suit of
apparel, and thy victuals. So the Levite
went in.
11 And the Levite was content to
dwell with the man; and the young man
was unto him as one of his sons.
12 And Micah consecrated the Levite;
and the young man became his priest,
and was in the house of Micah.
13 Then said Micah, Now know I that
the LORD will do me good, seeing I have
a Levite to *my* priest.

18 In those days *there was* no king
in Israel: and in those days the
tribe of the Danites sought them an
inheritance to dwell in; for unto that
day *all their* inheritance had not fallen
unto them among the tribes of Israel.
2 And the children of Dan sent of
their family five men from their coasts,
men of valour, from Zorah, and from
Eshtaol, to spy out the land, and to
search it; and they said unto them, Go,
search the land: who when they came
to mount Ephraim, to the house of
Micah, they lodged there.
3 When they *were* by the house of
Micah, they knew the voice of the
young man the Levite: and they turned
in thither, and said unto him, Who
brought thee hither? and what makest

thou in this *place*? and what hast thou
here?
4 And he said unto them, Thus and
thus dealeth Micah with me, and hath
hired me, and I am his priest.
5 And they said unto him, Ask counsel, we pray thee, of God, that we may
know whether our way which we go
shall be prosperous.
6 And the priest said unto them, Go
in peace: before the LORD *is* your way
wherein ye go.
7 Then the five men departed, and
came to Laish, and saw the people that
were therein, how they dwelt careless,
after the manner of the Zidonians,
quiet and secure; and *there was* no
magistrate in the land, that might put
them to shame in *any* thing; and they
were far from the Zidonians, and had
no business with *any* man.
8 And they came unto their brethren
to Zorah and Eshtaol: and their brethren said unto them, What *say* ye?
9 And they said, Arise, that we may go
up against them: for we have seen the
land, and, behold, it *is* very good: and
are ye still? be not slothful to go, *and* to
enter to possess the land.
10 When ye go, ye shall come unto a
people secure, and to a large land: for
God hath given it into your hands; a
place where *there is* no want of any
thing that *is* in the earth.
11 And there went from thence of the
family of the Danites, out of Zorah and
out of Eshtaol, six hundred men
appointed with weapons of war.
12 And they went up, and pitched in
Kirjath-jearim, in Judah: wherefore
they called that place Mahaneh-dan
unto this day: behold, *it is* behind
Kirjath-jearim.
13 And they passed thence unto
mount Ephraim, and came unto the
house of Micah.
14 Then answered the five men that
went to spy out the country of Laish,
and said unto their brethren, Do ye
know that there is in these houses an
ephod, and teraphim, and a graven
image, and a molten image? now therefore consider what ye have to do.
15 And they turned thitherward, and
came to the house of the young man
the Levite, *even* unto the house of
Micah, and saluted him.
16 And the six hundred men appointed with their weapons of war, which
were of the children of Dan, stood by
the entering of the gate.
17 And the five men that went to spy
out the land went up, *and* came in
thither, *and* took the graven image, and
the ephod, and the teraphim, and the
molten image: and the priest stood in
the entering of the gate with the six
hundred men *that were* appointed with
weapons of war.
18 And these went into Micah's
house, and fetched the carved image,
the ephod, and the teraphim, and the
molten image. Then said the priest
unto them, What do ye?
19 And they said unto him, Hold thy
peace, lay thine hand upon thy mouth,
and go with us, and be to us a father
and a priest: *is it* better for thee to be a
priest unto the house of one man, or
that thou be a priest unto a tribe and a
family in Israel?
20 And the priest's heart was glad,
and he took the ephod, and the teraphim, and the graven image, and went
in the midst of the people.

21 So they turned and departed, and put the little ones and the cattle and the carriage before them.

22 *And* when they were a good way from the house of Micah, the men that *were* in the houses near to Micah's house were gathered together, and overtook the children of Dan.

23 And they cried unto the children of Dan. And they turned their faces, and said unto Micah, What aileth thee, that thou comest with such a company?

24 And he said, Ye have taken away my gods which I made, and the priest, and ye are gone away: and what have I more? and what *is* this *that* ye say unto me, What aileth thee?

25 And the children of Dan said unto him, Let not thy voice be heard among us, lest angry fellows run upon thee, and thou lose thy life, with the lives of thy household.

26 And the children of Dan went their way: and when Micah saw that they *were* too strong for him, he turned and went back unto his house.

27 And they took *the things* which Micah had made, and the priest which he had, and came unto Laish, unto a people *that were* at quiet and secure: and they smote them with the edge of the sword, and burnt the city with fire.

28 And *there was* no deliverer, because it *was* far from Zidon, and they had no business with *any* man; and it was in the valley that *lieth* by Beth-rehob. And they built a city, and dwelt therein.

29 And they called the name of the city Dan, after the name of Dan their father, who was born unto Israel: howbeit the name of the city *was* Laish at the first.

30 And the children of Dan set up the graven image: and Jonathan, the son of Gershom, the son of Manasseh, he and his sons were priests to the tribe of Dan until the day of the captivity of the land.

31 And they set them up Micah's graven image, which he made, all the time that the house of God was in Shiloh.

19 And it came to pass in those days, when *there was* no king in Israel, that there was a certain Levite sojourning on the side of mount Ephraim, who took to him a concubine out of Beth-lehem-judah.

2 And his concubine played the whore against him, and went away from him unto her father's house to Beth-lehem-judah, and was there four whole months.

3 And her husband arose, and went after her, to speak friendly unto her, *and* to bring her again, having his servant with him, and a couple of asses: and she brought him into her father's house: and when the father of the damsel saw him, he rejoiced to meet him.

4 And his father in law, the damsel's father, retained him; and he abode with him three days: so they did eat and drink, and lodged there.

5 And it came to pass on the fourth day, when they arose early in the morning, that he rose up to depart: and the damsel's father said unto his son in law, Comfort thine heart with a morsel of bread, and afterward go your way.

6 And they sat down, and did eat and drink both of them together: for the damsel's father had said unto the man, Be content, I pray thee, and tarry all night, and let thine heart be merry.

7 And when the man rose up to
depart, his father in law urged him:
therefore he lodged there again.
8 And he arose early in the morning
on the fifth day to depart: and the damsel's father said, Comfort thine heart, I
pray thee. And they tarried until after-
noon, and they did eat both of them.
9 And when the man rose up to
depart, he, and his concubine, and his
servant, his father in law, the damsel's
father, said unto him, Behold, now the
day draweth toward evening, I pray you
tarry all night: behold, the day groweth
to an end, lodge here, that thine heart
may be merry; and to morrow get you
early on your way, that thou mayest go
home.
10 But the man would not tarry that
night, but he rose up and departed, and
came over against Jebus, which *is*
Jerusalem; and *there were* with him
two asses saddled, his concubine also
was with him.
11 *And* when they *were* by Jebus, the
day was far spent; and the servant said
unto his master, Come, I pray thee, and
let us turn in into this city of the
Jebusites, and lodge in it.
12 And his master said unto him, We
will not turn aside hither into the city
of a stranger, that *is* not of the children
of Israel; we will pass over to Gibeah.
13 And he said unto his servant,
Come, and let us draw near to one of
these places to lodge all night, in
Gibeah, or in Ramah.
14 And they passed on and went their
way; and the sun went down upon them
when they were by Gibeah, which
belongeth to Benjamin.
15 And they turned aside thither, to
go in *and* to lodge in Gibeah: and when
he went in, he sat him down in a street
of the city: for *there was* no man that
took them into his house to lodging.
16 And, behold, there came an old
man from his work out of the field at
even, which *was* also of mount Ephraim;
and he sojourned in Gibeah: but the
men of the place *were* Benjamites.
17 And when he had lifted up his
eyes, he saw a wayfaring man in the
street of the city: and the old man said,
Whither goest thou? and whence
comest thou?
18 And he said unto him, We *are* passing from Beth-lehem-judah toward the
side of mount Ephraim; from thence
am I: and I went to Beth-lehem-judah,
but I *am now* going to the house of the
LORD; and there *is* no man that
receiveth me to house.
19 Yet there is both straw and provender for our asses; and there is bread
and wine also for me, and for thy handmaid, and for the young man *which is*
with thy servants: *there is* no want of
any thing.
20 And the old man said, Peace *be*
with thee; howsoever *let* all thy wants
lie upon me; only lodge not in the
street.
21 So he brought him into his house,
and gave provender unto the asses: and
they washed their feet, and did eat and
drink.
22 *Now* as they were making their
hearts merry, behold, the men of the
city, certain sons of Belial, beset the
house round about, *and* beat at the
door, and spake to the master of the
house, the old man, saying, Bring forth
the man that came into thine house,
that we may know him.
23 And the man, the master of the
house, went out unto them, and said
unto them, Nay, my brethren, *nay*, I

pray you, do not *so* wickedly; seeing
that this man is come into mine house,
do not this folly.
24 Behold, *here is* my daughter a
maiden, and his concubine; them I will
bring out now, and humble ye them,
and do with them what seemeth good
unto you: but unto this man do not so
vile a thing.
25 But the men would not hearken to
him: so the man took his concubine,
and brought her forth unto them; and
they knew her, and abused her all the
night until the morning: and when the
day began to spring, they let her go.
26 Then came the woman in the
dawning of the day, and fell down at the
door of the man's house where her lord
was, till it was light.
27 And her lord rose up in the morning, and opened the doors of the house,
and went out to go his way: and, behold,
the woman his concubine was fallen
down *at* the door of the house, and her
hands *were* upon the threshold.
28 And he said unto her, Up, and let
us be going. But none answered. Then
the man took her *up* upon an ass, and
the man rose up, and gat him unto his
place.
29 And when he was come into his
house, he took a knife, and laid hold on
his concubine, and divided her, *together* with her bones, into twelve pieces,
and sent her into all the coasts of Israel.
30 And it was so, that all that saw it
said, There was no such deed done nor
seen from the day that the children of
Israel came up out of the land of Egypt
unto this day: consider of it, take
advice, and speak *your minds*.

20 Then all the children of Israel
went out, and the congregation
was gathered together as one man,
from Dan even to Beer-sheba, with the
land of Gilead, unto the LORD in
Mizpeh.
2 And the chief of all the people, *even*
of all the tribes of Israel, presented
themselves in the assembly of the people of God, four hundred thousand
footmen that drew sword.
3 (Now the children of Benjamin
heard that the children of Israel were
gone up to Mizpeh.) Then said the children of Israel, Tell *us*, how was this
wickedness?
4 And the Levite, the husband of the
woman that was slain, answered and
said, I came into Gibeah that *belongeth*
to Benjamin, I and my concubine, to
lodge.
5 And the men of Gibeah rose against
me, and beset the house round about
upon me by night, *and* thought to have
slain me: and my concubine have they
forced, that she is dead.
6 And I took my concubine, and cut
her in pieces, and sent her throughout
all the country of the inheritance of
Israel: for they have committed lewdness and folly in Israel.
7 Behold, ye *are* all children of Israel;
give here your advice and counsel.
8 And all the people arose as one
man, saying, We will not any *of us* go to
his tent, neither will we any *of us* turn
into his house.
9 But now this *shall be* the thing
which we will do to Gibeah; *we will go
up* by lot against it;
10 And we will take ten men of an
hundred throughout all the tribes of
Israel, and an hundred of a thousand,
and a thousand out of ten thousand, to
fetch victual for the people, that they
may do, when they come to Gibeah of

Benjamin, according to all the folly that
they have wrought in Israel.
11 So all the men of Israel were gathered against the city, knit together as
one man.
12 And the tribes of Israel sent men
through all the tribe of Benjamin, saying, What wickedness *is* this that is
done among you?
13 Now therefore deliver *us* the men,
the children of Belial, which *are* in
Gibeah, that we may put them to death,
and put away evil from Israel. But the
children of Benjamin would not heark-
en to the voice of their brethren the
children of Israel:
14 But the children of Benjamin gathered themselves together out of the
cities unto Gibeah, to go out to battle
against the children of Israel.
15 And the children of Benjamin
were numbered at that time out of the
cities twenty and six thousand men
that drew sword, beside the inhabitants
of Gibeah, which were numbered seven
hundred chosen men.
16 Among all this people *there were*
seven hundred chosen men lefthanded;
every one could sling stones at an hair
breadth, and not miss.
17 And the men of Israel, beside
Benjamin, were numbered four hundred thousand men that drew sword: all
these *were* men of war.
18 And the children of Israel arose,
and went up to the house of God, and
asked counsel of God, and said, Which
of us shall go up first to the battle
against the children of Benjamin? And
the LORD said, Judah *shall go up* first.
19 And the children of Israel rose up
in the morning, and encamped against
Gibeah.
20 And the men of Israel went out to
battle against Benjamin; and the men
of Israel put themselves in array to
fight against them at Gibeah.
21 And the children of Benjamin
came forth out of Gibeah, and destroyed
down to the ground of the Israelites
that day twenty and two thousand men.
22 And the people the men of Israel
encouraged themselves, and set their
battle again in array in the place where
they put themselves in array the first
day.
23 (And the children of Israel went up
and wept before the LORD until even,
and asked counsel of the LORD, saying,
Shall I go up again to battle against the
children of Benjamin my brother? And
the LORD said, Go up against him.)
24 And the children of Israel came
near against the children of Benjamin
the second day.
25 And Benjamin went forth against
them out of Gibeah the second day, and
destroyed down to the ground of the
children of Israel again eighteen thousand men; all these drew the sword.
26 Then all the children of Israel, and
all the people, went up, and came unto
the house of God, and wept, and sat
there before the LORD, and fasted that
day until even, and offered burnt offerings and peace offerings before the
LORD.
27 And the children of Israel enquired
of the LORD, (for the ark of the covenant of God *was* there in those days,
28 And Phinehas, the son of Eleazar,
the son of Aaron, stood before it in
those days,) saying, Shall I yet again go
out to battle against the children of
Benjamin my brother, or shall I cease?
And the LORD said, Go up; for to morrow I will deliver them into thine hand.

29 And Israel set liers in wait round
about Gibeah.
30 And the children of Israel went up
against the children of Benjamin on the
third day, and put themselves in array
against Gibeah, as at other times.
31 And the children of Benjamin
went out against the people, *and* were
drawn away from the city; and they
began to smite of the people, *and* kill,
as at other times, in the highways, of
which one goeth up to the house of
God, and the other to Gibeah in the
field, about thirty men of Israel.
32 And the children of Benjamin said,
They *are* smitten down before us, as at
the first. But the children of Israel said,
Let us flee, and draw them from the
city unto the highways.
33 And all the men of Israel rose up
out of their place, and put themselves
in array at Baal-tamar: and the liers in
wait of Israel came forth out of their
places, *even* out of the meadows of
Gibeah.
34 And there came against Gibeah
ten thousand chosen men out of all
Israel, and the battle was sore: but they
knew not that evil *was* near them.
35 And the LORD smote Benjamin
before Israel: and the children of Israel
destroyed of the Benjamites that day
twenty and five thousand and an hundred men: all these drew the sword.
36 So the children of Benjamin saw
that they were smitten: for the men of
Israel gave place to the Benjamites,
because they trusted unto the liers in
wait which they had set beside Gibeah.
37 And the liers in wait hasted, and
rushed upon Gibeah; and the liers in
wait drew *themselves* along, and smote
all the city with the edge of the sword.
38 Now there was an appointed sign
between the men of Israel and the liers
in wait, that they should make a great
flame with smoke rise up out of the
city.
39 And when the men of Israel retired
in the battle, Benjamin began to smite
and kill of the men of Israel about
thirty persons: for they said, Surely
they are smitten down before us, as *in*
the first battle.
40 But when the flame began to arise
up out of the city with a pillar of smoke,
the Benjamites looked behind them,
and, behold, the flame of the city
ascended up to heaven.
41 And when the men of Israel turned
again, the men of Benjamin were
amazed: for they saw that evil was
come upon them.
42 Therefore they turned *their backs*
before the men of Israel unto the way
of the wilderness; but the battle overtook them; and them which *came* out of
the cities they destroyed in the midst of
them.
43 *Thus* they inclosed the Benjamites
round about, *and* chased them, *and*
trode them down with ease over against
Gibeah toward the sunrising.
44 And there fell of Benjamin eighteen thousand men; all these *were* men
of valour.
45 And they turned and fled toward
the wilderness unto the rock of
Rimmon: and they gleaned of them in
the highways five thousand men; and
pursued hard after them unto Gidom,
and slew two thousand men of them.
46 So that all which fell that day of
Benjamin were twenty and five thousand men that drew the sword; all these
were men of valour.

47 But six hundred men turned and fled to the wilderness unto the rock Rimmon, and abode in the rock Rimmon four months.

48 And the men of Israel turned again upon the children of Benjamin, and smote them with the edge of the sword, as well the men of *every* city, as the beast, and all that came to hand: also they set on fire all the cities that they came to.

21 Now the men of Israel had sworn in Mizpeh, saying, There shall not any of us give his daughter unto Benjamin to wife.

2 And the people came to the house of God, and abode there till even before God, and lifted up their voices, and wept sore;

3 And said, O LORD God of Israel, why is this come to pass in Israel, that there should be to day one tribe lacking in Israel?

4 And it came to pass on the morrow, that the people rose early, and built there an altar, and offered burnt offerings and peace offerings.

5 And the children of Israel said, Who *is there* among all the tribes of Israel that came not up with the congregation unto the LORD? For they had made a great oath concerning him that came not up to the LORD to Mizpeh, saying, He shall surely be put to death.

6 And the children of Israel repented them for Benjamin their brother, and said, There is one tribe cut off from Israel this day.

7 How shall we do for wives for them that remain, seeing we have sworn by the LORD that we will not give them of our daughters to wives?

8 And they said, What one *is there* of the tribes of Israel that came not up to Mizpeh to the LORD? And, behold, there came none to the camp from Jabesh-gilead to the assembly.

9 For the people were numbered, and, behold, *there were* none of the inhabitants of Jabesh-gilead there.

10 And the congregation sent thither twelve thousand men of the valiantest, and commanded them, saying, Go and smite the inhabitants of Jabesh-gilead with the edge of the sword, with the women and the children.

11 And this *is* the thing that ye shall do, Ye shall utterly destroy every male, and every woman that hath lain by man.

12 And they found among the inhabitants of Jabesh-gilead four hundred young virgins, that had known no man by lying with any male: and they brought them unto the camp to Shiloh, which *is* in the land of Canaan.

13 And the whole congregation sent *some* to speak to the children of Benjamin that *were* in the rock Rimmon, and to call peaceably unto them.

14 And Benjamin came again at that time; and they gave them wives which they had saved alive of the women of Jabesh-gilead: and yet so they sufficed them not.

15 And the people repented them for Benjamin, because that the LORD had made a breach in the tribes of Israel.

16 Then the elders of the congregation said, How shall we do for wives for them that remain, seeing the women are destroyed out of Benjamin?

17 And they said, *There must be* an inheritance for them that be escaped of Benjamin, that a tribe be not destroyed out of Israel.

18 Howbeit we may not give them wives of our daughters: for the children of Israel have sworn, saying, Cursed *be* he that giveth a wife to Benjamin.

19 Then they said, Behold, *there is* a feast of the LORD in Shiloh yearly *in a place* which *is* on the north side of Beth-el, on the east side of the highway that goeth up from Beth-el to Shechem, and on the south of Lebonah.

20 Therefore they commanded the children of Benjamin, saying, Go and lie in wait in the vineyards;

21 And see, and, behold, if the daughters of Shiloh come out to dance in dances, then come ye out of the vineyards, and catch you every man his wife of the daughters of Shiloh, and go to the land of Benjamin.

22 And it shall be, when their fathers or their brethren come unto us to complain, that we will say unto them, Be favourable unto them for our sakes: because we reserved not to each man his wife in the war: for ye did not give unto them at this time, *that* ye should be guilty.

23 And the children of Benjamin did so, and took *them* wives, according to their number, of them that danced, whom they caught: and they went and returned unto their inheritance, and repaired the cities, and dwelt in them.

24 And the children of Israel departed thence at that time, every man to his tribe and to his family, and they went out from thence every man to his inheritance.

25 In those days *there was* no king in Israel: every man did *that which was* right in his own eyes.

THE BOOK OF RUTH

1 Now it came to pass in the days when the judges ruled, that there was a famine in the land. And a certain man of Beth-lehem-judah went to sojourn in the country of Moab, he, and his wife, and his two sons.

2 And the name of the man *was* Elimelech, and the name of his wife Naomi, and the name of his two sons Mahlon and Chilion, Ephrathites of Beth-lehem-judah. And they came into the country of Moab, and continued there.

3 And Elimelech Naomi's husband died; and she was left, and her two sons.

4 And they took them wives of the women of Moab; the name of the one *was* Orpah, and the name of the other Ruth: and they dwelled there about ten years.

5 And Mahlon and Chilion died also both of them; and the woman was left of her two sons and her husband.

6 Then she arose with her daughters in law, that she might return from the country of Moab: for she had heard in the country of Moab how that the LORD had visited his people in giving them bread.

7 Wherefore she went forth out of the place where she was, and her two daughters in law with her; and they went on the way to return unto the land of Judah.

8 And Naomi said unto her two daughters in law, Go, return each to her mother's house: the LORD deal kindly with you, as ye have dealt with the dead, and with me.

9 The LORD grant you that ye may find rest, each *of you* in the house of her husband. Then she kissed them; and they lifted up their voice, and wept.

10 And they said unto her, Surely we will return with thee unto thy people.

11 And Naomi said, Turn again, my daughters: why will ye go with me? *are* there yet *any more* sons in my womb, that they may be your husbands?

12 Turn again, my daughters, go *your way*; for I am too old to have an husband. If I should say, I have hope, *if* I should have an husband also to night, and should also bear sons;

13 Would ye tarry for them till they were grown? would ye stay for them from having husbands? nay, my daughters; for it grieveth me much for your sakes that the hand of the LORD is gone out against me.

14 And they lifted up their voice, and wept again: and Orpah kissed her mother in law; but Ruth clave unto her.

15 And she said, Behold, thy sister in law is gone back unto her people, and unto her gods: return thou after thy sister in law.

16 And Ruth said, Intreat me not to leave thee, *or* to return from following after thee: for whither thou goest, I will go; and where thou lodgest, I will lodge: thy people *shall be* my people, and thy God my God:

17 Where thou diest, will I die, and there will I be buried: the LORD do so to me, and more also, *if ought* but death part thee and me.

18 When she saw that she was stedfastly minded to go with her, then she left speaking unto her.

19 So they two went until they came to Beth-lehem. And it came to pass, when they were come to Beth-lehem, that all the city was moved about them, and they said, *Is* this Naomi?

20 And she said unto them, Call me not Naomi, call me Mara: for the Almighty hath dealt very bitterly with me.

21 I went out full, and the LORD hath brought me home again empty: why *then* call ye me Naomi, seeing the LORD hath testified against me, and the Almighty hath afflicted me?

22 So Naomi returned, and Ruth the Moabitess, her daughter in law, with her, which returned out of the country of Moab: and they came to Beth-lehem in the beginning of barley harvest.

2 And Naomi had a kinsman of her husband's, a mighty man of wealth, of the family of Elimelech; and his name *was* Boaz.

2 And Ruth the Moabitess said unto Naomi, Let me now go to the field, and glean ears of corn after *him* in whose sight I shall find grace. And she said unto her, Go, my daughter.

3 And she went, and came, and gleaned in the field after the reapers: and her hap was to light on a part of the field *belonging* unto Boaz, who *was* of the kindred of Elimelech.

4 And, behold, Boaz came from Beth-lehem, and said unto the reapers, The LORD *be* with you. And they answered him, The LORD bless thee.

5 Then said Boaz unto his servant that was set over the reapers, Whose damsel *is* this?

6 And the servant that was set over the reapers answered and said, It *is* the Moabitish damsel that came back with Naomi out of the country of Moab:

7 And she said, I pray you, let me glean and gather after the reapers among the sheaves: so she came, and hath continued even from the morning until now, that she tarried a little in the house.

8 Then said Boaz unto Ruth, Hearest thou not, my daughter? Go not to glean in another field, neither go from hence, but abide here fast by my maidens:

9 *Let* thine eyes *be* on the field that they do reap, and go thou after them: have I not charged the young men that they shall not touch thee? and when thou art athirst, go unto the vessels, and drink of *that* which the young men have drawn.

10 Then she fell on her face, and bowed herself to the ground, and said unto him, Why have I found grace in thine eyes, that thou shouldest take knowledge of me, seeing I *am* a stranger?

11 And Boaz answered and said unto her, It hath fully been shewed me, all that thou hast done unto thy mother in law since the death of thine husband: and *how* thou hast left thy father and thy mother, and the land of thy nativity, and art come unto a people which thou knewest not heretofore.

12 The LORD recompense thy work, and a full reward be given thee of the LORD God of Israel, under whose wings thou art come to trust.

13 Then she said, Let me find favour in thy sight, my lord; for that thou hast comforted me, and for that thou hast spoken friendly unto thine handmaid, though I be not like unto one of thine handmaidens.

14 And Boaz said unto her, At mealtime come thou hither, and eat of the bread, and dip thy morsel in the vinegar. And she sat beside the reapers: and he reached her parched *corn*, and she did eat, and was sufficed, and left.

15 And when she was risen up to glean, Boaz commanded his young men, saying, Let her glean even among the sheaves, and reproach her not:

16 And let fall also *some* of the handfuls of purpose for her, and leave *them*, that she may glean *them*, and rebuke her not.

17 So she gleaned in the field until even, and beat out that she had gleaned: and it was about an ephah of barley.

18 And she took *it* up, and went into the city: and her mother in law saw what she had gleaned: and she brought forth, and gave to her that she had reserved after she was sufficed.

19 And her mother in law said unto her, Where hast thou gleaned to day? and where wroughtest thou? blessed be he that did take knowledge of thee. And she shewed her mother in law with whom she had wrought, and said, The man's name with whom I wrought to day *is* Boaz.

20 And Naomi said unto her daughter in law, Blessed *be* he of the LORD, who hath not left off his kindness to the living and to the dead. And Naomi said unto her, The man *is* near of kin unto us, one of our next kinsmen.

21 And Ruth the Moabitess said, He
said unto me also, Thou shalt keep fast
by my young men, until they have
ended all my harvest.
22 And Naomi said unto Ruth her
daughter in law, *It is* good, my daughter, that thou go out with his maidens,
that they meet thee not in any other
field.
23 So she kept fast by the maidens of
Boaz to glean unto the end of barley
harvest and of wheat harvest; and
dwelt with her mother in law.

3

Then Naomi her mother in law said
unto her, My daughter, shall I not
seek rest for thee, that it may be well
with thee?
2 And now *is* not Boaz of our kindred,
with whose maidens thou wast? Behold,
he winnoweth barley to night in the
threshingfloor.
3 Wash thyself therefore, and anoint
thee, and put thy raiment upon thee,
and get thee down to the floor: *but*
make not thyself known unto the man,
until he shall have done eating and
drinking.
4 And it shall be, when he lieth down,
that thou shalt mark the place where
he shall lie, and thou shalt go in, and
uncover his feet, and lay thee down;
and he will tell thee what thou shalt do.
5 And she said unto her, All that thou
sayest unto me I will do.
6 And she went down unto the floor,
and did according to all that her mother in law bade her.
7 And when Boaz had eaten and
drunk, and his heart was merry, he
went to lie down at the end of the heap
of corn: and she came softly, and uncovered his feet, and laid her down.
8 And it came to pass at midnight,
that the man was afraid, and turned
himself: and, behold, a woman lay at his
feet.
9 And he said, Who *art* thou? And she
answered, I *am* Ruth thine handmaid:
spread therefore thy skirt over thine
handmaid; for thou *art* a near kinsman.
10 And he said, Blessed *be* thou of the
LORD, my daughter: *for* thou hast
shewed more kindness in the latter end
than at the beginning, inasmuch as
thou followedst not young men, whether poor or rich.
11 And now, my daughter, fear not; I
will do to thee all that thou requirest:
for all the city of my people doth know
that thou *art* a virtuous woman.
12 And now it is true that I *am thy*
near kinsman: howbeit there is a kinsman nearer than I.
13 Tarry this night, and it shall be in
the morning, *that* if he will perform
unto thee the part of a kinsman, well;
let him do the kinsman's part: but if he
will not do the part of a kinsman to
thee, then will I do the part of a kinsman to thee, *as* the LORD liveth: lie
down until the morning.
14 And she lay at his feet until the
morning: and she rose up before one
could know another. And he said, Let it
not be known that a woman came into
the floor.
15 Also he said, Bring the vail that
thou hast upon thee, and hold it. And
when she held it, he measured six *measures* of barley, and laid *it* on her: and
she went into the city.
16 And when she came to her mother
in law, she said, Who *art* thou, my
daughter? And she told her all that the
man had done to her.
17 And she said, These six *measures*
of barley gave he me; for he said to me,
Go not empty unto thy mother in law.

18 Then said she, Sit still, my daughter, until thou know how the matter will
fall: for the man will not be in rest, until
he have finished the thing this day.

4 Then went Boaz up to the gate, and
sat him down there: and, behold,
the kinsman of whom Boaz spake came
by; unto whom he said, Ho, such a one!
turn aside, sit down here. And he
turned aside, and sat down.
2 And he took ten men of the elders
of the city, and said, Sit ye down here.
And they sat down.
3 And he said unto the kinsman,
Naomi, that is come again out of the
country of Moab, selleth a parcel of
land, which *was* our brother Elimelech's:
4 And I thought to advertise thee, saying, Buy *it* before the inhabitants, and
before the elders of my people. If thou
wilt redeem *it*, redeem *it*: but if thou
wilt not redeem *it*, *then* tell me, that I
may know: for *there is* none to redeem
it beside thee; and I *am* after thee. And
he said, I will redeem *it*.
5 Then said Boaz, What day thou buyest the field of the hand of Naomi, thou
must buy *it* also of Ruth the Moabitess,
the wife of the dead, to raise up the
name of the dead upon his inheritance.
6 And the kinsman said, I cannot
redeem *it* for myself, lest I mar mine
own inheritance: redeem thou my right
to thyself; for I cannot redeem *it*.
7 Now this *was the manner* in former
time in Israel concerning redeeming
and concerning changing, for to confirm all things; a man plucked off his
shoe, and gave *it* to his neighbour: and
this *was* a testimony in Israel.
8 Therefore the kinsman said unto
Boaz, Buy *it* for thee. So he drew off his
shoe.
9 And Boaz said unto the elders, and
unto all the people, Ye *are* witnesses
this day, that I have bought all that *was*
Elimelech's, and all that *was* Chilion's
and Mahlon's, of the hand of Naomi.
10 Moreover Ruth the Moabitess, the
wife of Mahlon, have I purchased to be
my wife, to raise up the name of the
dead upon his inheritance, that the
name of the dead be not cut off from
among his brethren, and from the gate
of his place: ye *are* witnesses this day.
11 And all the people that *were* in the
gate, and the elders, said, *We are* witnesses. The LORD make the woman that
is come into thine house like Rachel
and like Leah, which two did build the
house of Israel: and do thou worthily in
Ephratah, and be famous in Beth-
lehem:
12 And let thy house be like the
house of Pharez, whom Tamar bare
unto Judah, of the seed which the LORD
shall give thee of this young woman.
13 So Boaz took Ruth, and she was his
wife: and when he went in unto her, the
LORD gave her conception, and she bare
a son.
14 And the women said unto Naomi,
Blessed *be* the LORD, which hath not
left thee this day without a kinsman,
that his name may be famous in Israel.
15 And he shall be unto thee a restorer of *thy* life, and a nourisher of thine
old age: for thy daughter in law, which
loveth thee, which is better to thee than
seven sons, hath born him.
16 And Naomi took the child, and laid
it in her bosom, and became nurse unto
it.
17 And the women her neighbours
gave it a name, saying, There is a son
born to Naomi; and they called his

name Obed: he *is* the father of Jesse,
the father of David.
18 Now these *are* the generations of
Pharez: Pharez begat Hezron,
19 And Hezron begat Ram, and Ram
begat Amminadab,
20 And Amminadab begat Nahshon,
and Nahshon begat Salmon,
21 And Salmon begat Boaz, and Boaz
begat Obed,
22 And Obed begat Jesse, and Jesse
begat David.

THE FIRST BOOK OF SAMUEL

1 Now there was a certain man of
Ramathaim-zophim, of mount
Ephraim, and his name *was* Elkanah,
the son of Jeroham, the son of Elihu,
the son of Tohu, the son of Zuph, an
Ephrathite:
2 And he had two wives; the name of
the one *was* Hannah, and the name of
the other Peninnah: and Peninnah had
children, but Hannah had no children.
3 And this man went up out of his city
yearly to worship and to sacrifice unto
the LORD of hosts in Shiloh. And the
two sons of Eli, Hophni and Phinehas,
the priests of the LORD, *were* there.
4 And when the time was that
Elkanah offered, he gave to Peninnah
his wife, and to all her sons and her
daughters, portions:
5 But unto Hannah he gave a worthy
portion; for he loved Hannah: but the
LORD had shut up her womb.
6 And her adversary also provoked
her sore, for to make her fret, because
the LORD had shut up her womb.
7 And *as* he did so year by year, when
she went up to the house of the LORD,
so she provoked her; therefore she
wept, and did not eat.
8 Then said Elkanah her husband to
her, Hannah, why weepest thou? and
why eatest thou not? and why is thy
heart grieved? *am* not I better to thee
than ten sons?
9 So Hannah rose up after they had
eaten in Shiloh, and after they had
drunk. Now Eli the priest sat upon a
seat by a post of the temple of the
LORD.
10 And she *was* in bitterness of soul,
and prayed unto the LORD, and wept
sore.
11 And she vowed a vow, and said, O
LORD of hosts, if thou wilt indeed look
on the affliction of thine handmaid,
and remember me, and not forget thine
handmaid, but wilt give unto thine
handmaid a man child, then I will give
him unto the LORD all the days of his
life, and there shall no razor come upon
his head.
12 And it came to pass, as she continued praying before the LORD, that Eli
marked her mouth.
13 Now Hannah, she spake in her
heart; only her lips moved, but her
voice was not heard: therefore Eli
thought she had been drunken.

14 And Eli said unto her, How long
wilt thou be drunken? put away thy
wine from thee.
15 And Hannah answered and said,
No, my lord, I *am* a woman of a sorrowful spirit: I have drunk neither wine nor
strong drink, but have poured out my
soul before the LORD.
16 Count not thine handmaid for a
daughter of Belial: for out of the abundance of my complaint and grief have I
spoken hitherto.
17 Then Eli answered and said, Go in
peace: and the God of Israel grant *thee*
thy petition that thou hast asked of
him.
18 And she said, Let thine handmaid
find grace in thy sight. So the woman
went her way, and did eat, and her
countenance was no more *sad*.
19 And they rose up in the morning
early, and worshipped before the LORD,
and returned, and came to their house
to Ramah: and Elkanah knew Hannah
his wife; and the LORD remembered
her.
20 Wherefore it came to pass, when
the time was come about after Hannah
had conceived, that she bare a son, and
called his name Samuel, *saying*,
Because I have asked him of the LORD.
21 And the man Elkanah, and all his
house, went up to offer unto the LORD
the yearly sacrifice, and his vow.
22 But Hannah went not up; for she
said unto her husband, *I will not go up*
until the child be weaned, and *then* I
will bring him, that he may appear
before the LORD, and there abide for
ever.
23 And Elkanah her husband said
unto her, Do what seemeth thee good;
tarry until thou have weaned him; only
the LORD establish his word. So the
woman abode, and gave her son suck
until she weaned him.
24 And when she had weaned him,
she took him up with her, with three
bullocks, and one ephah of flour, and a
bottle of wine, and brought him unto
the house of the LORD in Shiloh: and
the child *was* young.
25 And they slew a bullock, and
brought the child to Eli.
26 And she said, Oh my lord, *as* thy
soul liveth, my lord, I *am* the woman
that stood by thee here, praying unto
the LORD.
27 For this child I prayed; and the
LORD hath given me my petition which
I asked of him:
28 Therefore also I have lent him to
the LORD; as long as he liveth he shall
be lent to the LORD. And he worshipped
the LORD there.

2 And Hannah prayed, and said, My
heart rejoiceth in the LORD, mine
horn is exalted in the LORD: my mouth
is enlarged over mine enemies; because
I rejoice in thy salvation.
2 *There is* none holy as the LORD: for
there is none beside thee: neither *is*
there any rock like our God.
3 Talk no more so exceeding proudly;
let *not* arrogancy come out of your
mouth: for the LORD *is* a God of knowledge, and by him actions are weighed.
4 The bows of the mighty men *are*
broken, and they that stumbled are
girded with strength.
5 *They that were* full have hired out
themselves for bread; and *they that*
were hungry ceased: so that the barren
hath born seven; and she that hath
many children is waxed feeble.
6 The LORD killeth, and maketh alive:
he bringeth down to the grave, and
bringeth up.

7 The LORD maketh poor, and maketh rich: he bringeth low, and lifteth up.

8 He raiseth up the poor out of the dust, *and* lifteth up the beggar from the dunghill, to set *them* among princes, and to make them inherit the throne of glory: for the pillars of the earth *are* the LORD's, and he hath set the world upon them.

9 He will keep the feet of his saints, and the wicked shall be silent in darkness; for by strength shall no man prevail.

10 The adversaries of the LORD shall be broken to pieces; out of heaven shall he thunder upon them: the LORD shall judge the ends of the earth; and he shall give strength unto his king, and exalt the horn of his anointed.

11 And Elkanah went to Ramah to his house. And the child did minister unto the LORD before Eli the priest.

12 Now the sons of Eli *were* sons of Belial; they knew not the LORD.

13 And the priests' custom with the people *was, that*, when any man offered sacrifice, the priest's servant came, while the flesh was in seething, with a fleshhook of three teeth in his hand;

14 And he struck *it* into the pan, or kettle, or caldron, or pot; all that the fleshhook brought up the priest took for himself. So they did in Shiloh unto all the Israelites that came thither.

15 Also before they burnt the fat, the priest's servant came, and said to the man that sacrificed, Give flesh to roast for the priest; for he will not have sodden flesh of thee, but raw.

16 And *if* any man said unto him, Let them not fail to burn the fat presently, and *then* take *as much* as thy soul desireth; then he would answer him, *Nay*; but thou shalt give *it me* now: and if not, I will take *it* by force.

17 Wherefore the sin of the young men was very great before the LORD: for men abhorred the offering of the LORD.

18 But Samuel ministered before the LORD, *being* a child, girded with a linen ephod.

19 Moreover his mother made him a little coat, and brought *it* to him from year to year, when she came up with her husband to offer the yearly sacrifice.

20 And Eli blessed Elkanah and his wife, and said, The LORD give thee seed of this woman for the loan which is lent to the LORD. And they went unto their own home.

21 And the LORD visited Hannah, so that she conceived, and bare three sons and two daughters. And the child Samuel grew before the LORD.

22 Now Eli was very old, and heard all that his sons did unto all Israel; and how they lay with the women that assembled *at* the door of the tabernacle of the congregation.

23 And he said unto them, Why do ye such things? for I hear of your evil dealings by all this people.

24 Nay, my sons; for *it is* no good report that I hear: ye make the LORD's people to transgress.

25 If one man sin against another, the judge shall judge him: but if a man sin against the LORD, who shall intreat for him? Notwithstanding they hearkened not unto the voice of their father, because the LORD would slay them.

26 And the child Samuel grew on, and was in favour both with the LORD, and also with men.

27 And there came a man of God unto
Eli, and said unto him, Thus saith the
LORD, Did I plainly appear unto the
house of thy father, when they were in
Egypt in Pharaoh's house?
28 And did I choose him out of all the
tribes of Israel *to be* my priest, to offer
upon mine altar, to burn incense, to
wear an ephod before me? and did I
give unto the house of thy father all the
offerings made by fire of the children
of Israel?
29 Wherefore kick ye at my sacrifice
and at mine offering, which I have commanded *in my* habitation; and honour-
est thy sons above me, to make yourselves fat with the chiefest of all the
offerings of Israel my people?
30 Wherefore the LORD God of Israel
saith, I said indeed *that* thy house, and
the house of thy father, should walk
before me for ever: but now the LORD
saith, Be it far from me; for them that
honour me I will honour, and they that
despise me shall be lightly esteemed.
31 Behold, the days come, that I will
cut off thine arm, and the arm of thy
father's house, that there shall not be
an old man in thine house.
32 And thou shalt see an enemy *in
my* habitation, in all *the wealth* which
God shall give Israel: and there shall
not be an old man in thine house for
ever.
33 And the man of thine, *whom* I
shall not cut off from mine altar, *shall
be* to consume thine eyes, and to grieve
thine heart: and all the increase of
thine house shall die in the flower of
their age.
34 And this *shall be* a sign unto thee,
that shall come upon thy two sons, on
Hophni and Phinehas; in one day they
shall die both of them.
35 And I will raise me up a faithful
priest, *that* shall do according to *that*
which *is* in mine heart and in my mind:
and I will build him a sure house; and
he shall walk before mine anointed for
ever.
36 And it shall come to pass, *that*
every one that is left in thine house
shall come *and* crouch to him for a
piece of silver and a morsel of bread,
and shall say, Put me, I pray thee, into
one of the priests' offices, that I may
eat a piece of bread.

3 And the child Samuel ministered
unto the LORD before Eli. And the
word of the LORD was precious in those
days; *there was* no open vision.
2 And it came to pass at that time,
when Eli *was* laid down in his place,
and his eyes began to wax dim, *that* he
could not see;
3 And ere the lamp of God went out
in the temple of the LORD, where the
ark of God *was*, and Samuel was laid
down *to sleep*;
4 That the LORD called Samuel: and
he answered, Here *am* I.
5 And he ran unto Eli, and said, Here
am I; for thou calledst me. And he said,
I called not; lie down again. And he
went and lay down.
6 And the LORD called yet again,
Samuel. And Samuel arose and went to
Eli, and said, Here *am* I; for thou didst
call me. And he answered, I called not,
my son; lie down again.
7 Now Samuel did not yet know the
LORD, neither was the word of the LORD
yet revealed unto him.
8 And the LORD called Samuel again
the third time. And he arose and went
to Eli, and said, Here *am* I; for thou
didst call me. And Eli perceived that
the LORD had called the child.

9 Therefore Eli said unto Samuel, Go, lie down: and it shall be, if he call thee, that thou shalt say, Speak, LORD; for thy servant heareth. So Samuel went and lay down in his place.

10 And the LORD came, and stood, and called as at other times, Samuel, Samuel. Then Samuel answered, Speak; for thy servant heareth.

11 And the LORD said to Samuel, Behold, I will do a thing in Israel, at which both the ears of every one that heareth it shall tingle.

12 In that day I will perform against Eli all *things* which I have spoken concerning his house: when I begin, I will also make an end.

13 For I have told him that I will judge his house for ever for the iniquity which he knoweth; because his sons made themselves vile, and he restrained them not.

14 And therefore I have sworn unto the house of Eli, that the iniquity of Eli's house shall not be purged with sacrifice nor offering for ever.

15 And Samuel lay until the morning, and opened the doors of the house of the LORD. And Samuel feared to shew Eli the vision.

16 Then Eli called Samuel, and said, Samuel, my son. And he answered, Here *am* I.

17 And he said, What *is* the thing that *the* LORD hath said unto thee? I pray thee hide *it* not from me: God do so to thee, and more also, if thou hide *any* thing from me of all the things that he said unto thee.

18 And Samuel told him every whit, and hid nothing from him. And he said, It *is* the LORD: let him do what seemeth him good.

19 And Samuel grew, and the LORD was with him, and did let none of his words fall to the ground.

20 And all Israel from Dan even to Beer-sheba knew that Samuel *was* established *to be* a prophet of the LORD.

21 And the LORD appeared again in Shiloh: for the LORD revealed himself to Samuel in Shiloh by the word of the LORD.

4 And the word of Samuel came to all Israel. Now Israel went out against the Philistines to battle, and pitched beside Eben-ezer: and the Philistines pitched in Aphek.

2 And the Philistines put themselves in array against Israel: and when they joined battle, Israel was smitten before the Philistines: and they slew of the army in the field about four thousand men.

3 And when the people were come into the camp, the elders of Israel said, Wherefore hath the LORD smitten us to day before the Philistines? Let us fetch the ark of the covenant of the LORD out of Shiloh unto us, that, when it cometh among us, it may save us out of the hand of our enemies.

4 So the people sent to Shiloh, that they might bring from thence the ark of the covenant of the LORD of hosts, which dwelleth *between* the cherubims: and the two sons of Eli, Hophni and Phinehas, *were* there with the ark of the covenant of God.

5 And when the ark of the covenant of the LORD came into the camp, all Israel shouted with a great shout, so that the earth rang again.

6 And when the Philistines heard the noise of the shout, they said, What *meaneth* the noise of this great shout in the camp of the Hebrews? And they

understood that the ark of the LORD
was come into the camp.
7 And the Philistines were afraid, for
they said, God is come into the camp.
And they said, Woe unto us! for there
hath not been such a thing heretofore.
8 Woe unto us! who shall deliver us
out of the hand of these mighty Gods?
these *are* the Gods that smote the
Egyptians with all the plagues in the
wilderness.
9 Be strong, and quit yourselves like
men, O ye Philistines, that ye be not
servants unto the Hebrews, as they
have been to you: quit yourselves like
men, and fight.
10 And the Philistines fought, and
Israel was smitten, and they fled every
man into his tent: and there was a very
great slaughter; for there fell of Israel
thirty thousand footmen.
11 And the ark of God was taken; and
the two sons of Eli, Hophni and
Phinehas, were slain.
12 And there ran a man of Benjamin
out of the army, and came to Shiloh the
same day with his clothes rent, and
with earth upon his head.
13 And when he came, lo, Eli sat upon
a seat by the wayside watching: for his
heart trembled for the ark of God. And
when the man came into the city, and
told *it*, all the city cried out.
14 And when Eli heard the noise of
the crying, he said, What *meaneth* the
noise of this tumult? And the man
came in hastily, and told Eli.
15 Now Eli was ninety and eight years
old; and his eyes were dim, that he
could not see.
16 And the man said unto Eli, I *am* he
that came out of the army, and I fled to
day out of the army. And he said, What
is there done, my son?
17 And the messenger answered and
said, Israel is fled before the Philistines,
and there hath been also a great
slaughter among the people, and thy
two sons also, Hophni and Phinehas,
are dead, and the ark of God is taken.
18 And it came to pass, when he made
mention of the ark of God, that he fell
from off the seat backward by the side
of the gate, and his neck brake, and he
died: for he was an old man, and heavy.
And he had judged Israel forty years.
19 And his daughter in law, Phinehas'
wife, was with child, *near* to be delivered: and when she heard the tidings
that the ark of God was taken, and that
her father in law and her husband were
dead, she bowed herself and travailed;
for her pains came upon her.
20 And about the time of her death
the women that stood by her said unto
her, Fear not; for thou hast born a son.
But she answered not, neither did she
regard *it*.
21 And she named the child Ichabod,
saying, The glory is departed from
Israel: because the ark of God was
taken, and because of her father in law
and her husband.
22 And she said, The glory is departed
from Israel: for the ark of God is taken.

5 And the Philistines took the ark of
God, and brought it from Eben-ezer
unto Ashdod.
2 When the Philistines took the ark of
God, they brought it into the house of
Dagon, and set it by Dagon.
3 And when they of Ashdod arose
early on the morrow, behold, Dagon
was fallen upon his face to the earth
before the ark of the LORD. And they
took Dagon, and set him in his place
again.

4 And when they arose early on the morrow morning, behold, Dagon *was* fallen upon his face to the ground before the ark of the LORD; and the head of Dagon and both the palms of his hands *were* cut off upon the threshold; only *the stump of* Dagon was left to him.

5 Therefore neither the priests of Dagon, nor any that come into Dagon's house, tread on the threshold of Dagon in Ashdod unto this day.

6 But the hand of the LORD was heavy upon them of Ashdod, and he destroyed them, and smote them with emerods, *even* Ashdod and the coasts thereof.

7 And when the men of Ashdod saw that *it was* so, they said, The ark of the God of Israel shall not abide with us: for his hand is sore upon us, and upon Dagon our god.

8 They sent therefore and gathered all the lords of the Philistines unto them, and said, What shall we do with the ark of the God of Israel? And they answered, Let the ark of the God of Israel be carried about unto Gath. And they carried the ark of the God of Israel about *thither*.

9 And it was *so*, that, after they had carried it about, the hand of the LORD was against the city with a very great destruction: and he smote the men of the city, both small and great, and they had emerods in their secret parts.

10 Therefore they sent the ark of God to Ekron. And it came to pass, as the ark of God came to Ekron, that the Ekronites cried out, saying, They have brought about the ark of the God of Israel to us, to slay us and our people.

11 So they sent and gathered together all the lords of the Philistines, and said, Send away the ark of the God of Israel, and let it go again to his own place, that it slay us not, and our people: for there was a deadly destruction throughout all the city; the hand of God was very heavy there.

12 And the men that died not were smitten with the emerods: and the cry of the city went up to heaven.

6 And the ark of the LORD was in the country of the Philistines seven months.

2 And the Philistines called for the priests and the diviners, saying, What shall we do to the ark of the LORD? tell us wherewith we shall send it to his place.

3 And they said, If ye send away the ark of the God of Israel, send it not empty; but in any wise return him a trespass offering: then ye shall be healed, and it shall be known to you why his hand is not removed from you.

4 Then said they, What *shall be* the trespass offering which we shall return to him? They answered, Five golden emerods, and five golden mice, *according to* the number of the lords of the Philistines: for one plague *was* on you all, and on your lords.

5 Wherefore ye shall make images of your emerods, and images of your mice that mar the land; and ye shall give glory unto the God of Israel: peradventure he will lighten his hand from off you, and from off your gods, and from off your land.

6 Wherefore then do ye harden your hearts, as the Egyptians and Pharaoh hardened their hearts? when he had wrought wonderfully among them, did they not let the people go, and they departed?

7 Now therefore make a new cart, and take two milch kine, on which there hath come no yoke, and tie the kine to the cart, and bring their calves home from them:

8 And take the ark of the LORD, and lay it upon the cart; and put the jewels of gold, which ye return him *for* a trespass offering, in a coffer by the side thereof; and send it away, that it may go.

9 And see, if it goeth up by the way of his own coast to Beth-shemesh, *then* he hath done us this great evil: but if not, then we shall know that *it is* not his hand *that* smote us: it *was* a chance *that* happened to us.

10 And the men did so; and took two milch kine, and tied them to the cart, and shut up their calves at home:

11 And they laid the ark of the LORD upon the cart, and the coffer with the mice of gold and the images of their emerods.

12 And the kine took the straight way to the way of Beth-shemesh, *and* went along the highway, lowing as they went, and turned not aside *to* the right hand or *to* the left; and the lords of the Philistines went after them unto the border of Beth-shemesh.

13 And *they of* Beth-shemesh *were* reaping their wheat harvest in the valley: and they lifted up their eyes, and saw the ark, and rejoiced to see *it*.

14 And the cart came into the field of Joshua, a Beth-shemite, and stood there, where *there was* a great stone: and they clave the wood of the cart, and offered the kine a burnt offering unto the LORD.

15 And the Levites took down the ark of the LORD, and the coffer that *was* with it, wherein the jewels of gold *were*, and put *them* on the great stone: and the men of Beth-shemesh offered burnt offerings and sacrificed sacrifices the same day unto the LORD.

16 And when the five lords of the Philistines had seen *it*, they returned to Ekron the same day.

17 And these *are* the golden emerods which the Philistines returned *for* a trespass offering unto the LORD; for Ashdod one, for Gaza one, for Askelon one, for Gath one, for Ekron one;

18 And the golden mice, *according to* the number of all the cities of the Philistines *belonging* to the five lords, *both* of fenced cities, and of country villages, even unto the great *stone of* Abel, whereon they set down the ark of the LORD: *which stone remaineth* unto this day in the field of Joshua, the Beth-shemite.

19 And he smote the men of Beth-shemesh, because they had looked into the ark of the LORD, even he smote of the people fifty thousand and threescore and ten men: and the people lamented, because the LORD had smitten *many* of the people with a great slaughter.

20 And the men of Beth-shemesh said, Who is able to stand before this holy LORD God? and to whom shall he go up from us?

21 And they sent messengers to the inhabitants of Kirjath-jearim, saying, The Philistines have brought again the ark of the LORD; come ye down, *and* fetch it up to you.

7 And the men of Kirjath-jearim came, and fetched up the ark of the LORD, and brought it into the house of Abinadab in the hill, and sanctified Eleazar his son to keep the ark of the LORD.

2 And it came to pass, while the ark
abode in Kirjath-jearim, that the time
was long; for it was twenty years: and
all the house of Israel lamented after
the LORD.
3 And Samuel spake unto all the
house of Israel, saying, If ye do return
unto the LORD with all your hearts, *then*
put away the strange gods and
Ashtaroth from among you, and prepare your hearts unto the LORD, and
serve him only: and he will deliver you
out of the hand of the Philistines.
4 Then the children of Israel did put
away Baalim and Ashtaroth, and served
the LORD only.
5 And Samuel said, Gather all Israel
to Mizpeh, and I will pray for you unto
the LORD.
6 And they gathered together to
Mizpeh, and drew water, and poured *it*
out before the LORD, and fasted on that
day, and said there, We have sinned
against the LORD. And Samuel judged
the children of Israel in Mizpeh.
7 And when the Philistines heard
that the children of Israel were gathered together to Mizpeh, the lords of
the Philistines went up against Israel.
And when the children of Israel heard
it, they were afraid of the Philistines.
8 And the children of Israel said to
Samuel, Cease not to cry unto the LORD
our God for us, that he will save us out
of the hand of the Philistines.
9 And Samuel took a sucking lamb,
and offered *it for* a burnt offering
wholly unto the LORD: and Samuel
cried unto the LORD for Israel; and the
LORD heard him.
10 And as Samuel was offering up the
burnt offering, the Philistines drew
near to battle against Israel: but the
LORD thundered with a great thunder
on that day upon the Philistines, and
discomfited them; and they were smitten before Israel.
11 And the men of Israel went out of
Mizpeh, and pursued the Philistines,
and smote them, until *they came* under
Beth-car.
12 Then Samuel took a stone, and set
it between Mizpeh and Shen, and
called the name of it Eben-ezer, saying,
Hitherto hath the LORD helped us.
13 So the Philistines were subdued,
and they came no more into the coast
of Israel: and the hand of the LORD was
against the Philistines all the days of
Samuel.
14 And the cities which the Philistines
had taken from Israel were restored to
Israel, from Ekron even unto Gath; and
the coasts thereof did Israel deliver out
of the hands of the Philistines. And
there was peace between Israel and the
Amorites.
15 And Samuel judged Israel all the
days of his life.
16 And he went from year to year in
circuit to Beth-el, and Gilgal, and
Mizpeh, and judged Israel in all those
places.
17 And his return *was* to Ramah; for
there *was* his house; and there he
judged Israel; and there he built an
altar unto the LORD.

8 And it came to pass, when Samuel
was old, that he made his sons
judges over Israel.
2 Now the name of his firstborn was
Joel; and the name of his second,
Abiah: *they were* judges in Beer-sheba.
3 And his sons walked not in his ways,
but turned aside after lucre, and took
bribes, and perverted judgment.

4 Then all the elders of Israel gathered themselves together, and came to
Samuel unto Ramah,
5 And said unto him, Behold, thou art
old, and thy sons walk not in thy ways:
now make us a king to judge us like all
the nations.
6 But the thing displeased Samuel,
when they said, Give us a king to judge
us. And Samuel prayed unto the LORD.
7 And the LORD said unto Samuel,
Hearken unto the voice of the people in
all that they say unto thee: for they
have not rejected thee, but they have
rejected me, that I should not reign
over them.
8 According to all the works which
they have done since the day that I
brought them up out of Egypt even
unto this day, wherewith they have forsaken me, and served other gods, so do
they also unto thee.
9 Now therefore hearken unto their
voice: howbeit yet protest solemnly
unto them, and shew them the manner
of the king that shall reign over them.
10 And Samuel told all the words of
the LORD unto the people that asked of
him a king.
11 And he said, This will be the manner of the king that shall reign over
you: He will take your sons, and appoint
them for himself, for his chariots, and
to be his horsemen; and *some* shall run
before his chariots.
12 And he will appoint him captains
over thousands, and captains over fifties; and *will set them* to ear his
ground, and to reap his harvest, and to
make his instruments of war, and
instruments of his chariots.
13 And he will take your daughters *to
be* confectionaries, and *to be* cooks, and
to be bakers.
14 And he will take your fields, and
your vineyards, and your oliveyards,
even the best *of them*, and give *them* to
his servants.
15 And he will take the tenth of your
seed, and of your vineyards, and give to
his officers, and to his servants.
16 And he will take your menservants, and your maidservants, and your
goodliest young men, and your asses,
and put *them* to his work.
17 He will take the tenth of your
sheep: and ye shall be his servants.
18 And ye shall cry out in that day
because of your king which ye shall
have chosen you; and the LORD will not
hear you in that day.
19 Nevertheless the people refused to
obey the voice of Samuel; and they
said, Nay; but we will have a king over
us;
20 That we also may be like all the
nations; and that our king may judge
us, and go out before us, and fight our
battles.
21 And Samuel heard all the words of
the people, and he rehearsed them in
the ears of the LORD.
22 And the LORD said to Samuel,
Hearken unto their voice, and make
them a king. And Samuel said unto the
men of Israel, Go ye every man unto his
city.

9 Now there was a man of Benjamin,
whose name *was* Kish, the son of
Abiel, the son of Zeror, the son of
Bechorath, the son of Aphiah, a Benjamite, a mighty man of power.
2 And he had a son, whose name *was*
Saul, a choice young man, and a goodly:
and *there was* not among the children
of Israel a goodlier person than he:
from his shoulders and upward *he was*
higher than any of the people.

3 And the asses of Kish Saul's father
were lost. And Kish said to Saul his son,
Take now one of the servants with thee,
and arise, go seek the asses.
4 And he passed through mount
Ephraim, and passed through the land
of Shalisha, but they found *them* not:
then they passed through the land of
Shalim, and *there they were* not: and
he passed through the land of the
Benjamites, but they found *them* not.
5 *And* when they were come to the
land of Zuph, Saul said to his servant
that *was* with him, Come, and let us
return; lest my father leave *caring* for
the asses, and take thought for us.
6 And he said unto him, Behold now,
there is in this city a man of God, and
he is an honourable man; all that he
saith cometh surely to pass: now let us
go thither; peradventure he can shew
us our way that we should go.
7 Then said Saul to his servant, But,
behold, *if* we go, what shall we bring
the man? for the bread is spent in our
vessels, and *there is* not a present to
bring to the man of God: what have we?
8 And the servant answered Saul
again, and said, Behold, I have here at
hand the fourth part of a shekel of silver: *that* will I give to the man of God,
to tell us our way.
9 (Beforetime in Israel, when a man
went to enquire of God, thus he spake,
Come, and let us go to the seer: for *he
that is* now *called* a Prophet was
beforetime called a Seer.)
10 Then said Saul to his servant, Well
said; come, let us go. So they went unto
the city where the man of God *was*.
11 *And* as they went up the hill to the
city, they found young maidens going
out to draw water, and said unto them,
Is the seer here?
12 And they answered them, and said,
He is; behold, *he is* before you: make
haste now, for he came to day to the
city; for *there is* a sacrifice of the people to day in the high place:
13 As soon as ye be come into the city,
ye shall straightway find him, before he
go up to the high place to eat: for the
people will not eat until he come,
because he doth bless the sacrifice; *and*
afterwards they eat that be bidden.
Now therefore get you up; for about
this time ye shall find him.
14 And they went up into the city:
and when they were come into the city,
behold, Samuel came out against them,
for to go up to the high place.
15 Now the LORD had told Samuel in
his ear a day before Saul came, saying,
16 To morrow about this time I will
send thee a man out of the land of
Benjamin, and thou shalt anoint him *to
be* captain over my people Israel, that
he may save my people out of the hand
of the Philistines: for I have looked
upon my people, because their cry is
come unto me.
17 And when Samuel saw Saul, the
LORD said unto him, Behold the man
whom I spake to thee of! this same
shall reign over my people.
18 Then Saul drew near to Samuel in
the gate, and said, Tell me, I pray thee,
where the seer's house *is*.
19 And Samuel answered Saul, and
said, I *am* the seer: go up before me
unto the high place; for ye shall eat
with me to day, and to morrow I will let
thee go, and will tell thee all that *is* in
thine heart.
20 And as for thine asses that were
lost three days ago, set not thy mind on
them; for they are found. And on whom

is all the desire of Israel? *Is it* not on thee, and on all thy father's house?

21 And Saul answered and said, *Am* not I a Benjamite, of the smallest of the tribes of Israel? and my family the least of all the families of the tribe of Benjamin? wherefore then speakest thou so to me?

22 And Samuel took Saul and his servant, and brought them into the parlour, and made them sit in the chiefest place among them that were bidden, which *were* about thirty persons.

23 And Samuel said unto the cook, Bring the portion which I gave thee, of which I said unto thee, Set it by thee.

24 And the cook took up the shoulder, and *that* which *was* upon it, and set *it* before Saul. And *Samuel* said, Behold that which is left! set *it* before thee, *and* eat: for unto this time hath it been kept for thee since I said, I have invited the people. So Saul did eat with Samuel that day.

25 And when they were come down from the high place into the city, *Samuel* communed with Saul upon the top of the house.

26 And they arose early: and it came to pass about the spring of the day, that Samuel called Saul to the top of the house, saying, Up, that I may send thee away. And Saul arose, and they went out both of them, he and Samuel, abroad.

27 *And* as they were going down to the end of the city, Samuel said to Saul, Bid the servant pass on before us, (and he passed on,) but stand thou still a while, that I may shew thee the word of God.

10 Then Samuel took a vial of oil, and poured *it* upon his head, and kissed him, and said, *Is it* not because the LORD hath anointed thee *to be* captain over his inheritance?

2 When thou art departed from me to day, then thou shalt find two men by Rachel's sepulchre in the border of Benjamin at Zelzah; and they will say unto thee, The asses which thou wentest to seek are found: and, lo, thy father hath left the care of the asses, and sorroweth for you, saying, What shall I do for my son?

3 Then shalt thou go on forward from thence, and thou shalt come to the plain of Tabor, and there shall meet thee three men going up to God to Beth-el, one carrying three kids, and another carrying three loaves of bread, and another carrying a bottle of wine:

4 And they will salute thee, and give thee two *loaves* of bread; which thou shalt receive of their hands.

5 After that thou shalt come to the hill of God, where *is* the garrison of the Philistines: and it shall come to pass, when thou art come thither to the city, that thou shalt meet a company of prophets coming down from the high place with a psaltery, and a tabret, and a pipe, and a harp, before them; and they shall prophesy:

6 And the Spirit of the LORD will come upon thee, and thou shalt prophesy with them, and shalt be turned into another man.

7 And let it be, when these signs are come unto thee, *that* thou do as occasion serve thee; for God *is* with thee.

8 And thou shalt go down before me to Gilgal; and, behold, I will come down unto thee, to offer burnt offerings, *and* to sacrifice sacrifices of peace offerings: seven days shalt thou tarry, till I come to thee, and shew thee what thou shalt do.

9 And it was *so*, that when he had
turned his back to go from Samuel, God
gave him another heart: and all those
signs came to pass that day.
10 And when they came thither to the
hill, behold, a company of prophets met
him; and the Spirit of God came upon
him, and he prophesied among them.
11 And it came to pass, when all that
knew him beforetime saw that, behold,
he prophesied among the prophets,
then the people said one to another,
What *is* this *that* is come unto the son
of Kish? *Is* Saul also among the prophets?
12 And one of the same place
answered and said, But who *is* their
father? Therefore it became a proverb,
Is Saul also among the prophets?
13 And when he had made an end of
prophesying, he came to the high place.
14 And Saul's uncle said unto him
and to his servant, Whither went ye?
And he said, To seek the asses: and
when we saw that *they were* no where,
we came to Samuel.
15 And Saul's uncle said, Tell me, I
pray thee, what Samuel said unto you.
16 And Saul said unto his uncle, He
told us plainly that the asses were
found. But of the matter of the kingdom, whereof Samuel spake, he told
him not.
17 And Samuel called the people
together unto the LORD to Mizpeh;
18 And said unto the children of
Israel, Thus saith the LORD God of
Israel, I brought up Israel out of Egypt,
and delivered you out of the hand of
the Egyptians, and out of the hand of
all kingdoms, *and* of them that
oppressed you:
19 And ye have this day rejected your
God, who himself saved you out of all
your adversities and your tribulations;
and ye have said unto him, *Nay*, but set
a king over us. Now therefore present
yourselves before the LORD by your
tribes, and by your thousands.
20 And when Samuel had caused all
the tribes of Israel to come near, the
tribe of Benjamin was taken.
21 When he had caused the tribe of
Benjamin to come near by their families, the family of Matri was taken, and
Saul the son of Kish was taken: and
when they sought him, he could not be
found.
22 Therefore they enquired of the
LORD further, if the man should yet
come thither. And the LORD answered,
Behold, he hath hid himself among the
stuff.
23 And they ran and fetched him
thence: and when he stood among the
people, he was higher than any of the
people from his shoulders and upward.
24 And Samuel said to all the people,
See ye him whom the LORD hath chosen, that *there is* none like him among
all the people? And all the people
shouted, and said, God save the king.
25 Then Samuel told the people the
manner of the kingdom, and wrote *it* in
a book, and laid *it* up before the LORD.
And Samuel sent all the people away,
every man to his house.
26 And Saul also went home to
Gibeah; and there went with him a
band of men, whose hearts God had
touched.
27 But the children of Belial said,
How shall this man save us? And they
despised him, and brought him no presents. But he held his peace.

11 Then Nahash the Ammonite
came up, and encamped against
Jabesh-gilead: and all the men of
Jabesh said unto Nahash, Make a covenant with us, and we will serve thee.
2 And Nahash the Ammonite answered them, On this *condition* will I
make *a covenant* with you, that I may
thrust out all your right eyes, and lay it
for a reproach upon all Israel.
3 And the elders of Jabesh said unto
him, Give us seven days' respite, that
we may send messengers unto all the
coasts of Israel: and then, if *there be* no
man to save us, we will come out to
thee.
4 Then came the messengers to
Gibeah of Saul, and told the tidings in
the ears of the people: and all the people lifted up their voices, and wept.
5 And, behold, Saul came after the
herd out of the field; and Saul said,
What *aileth* the people that they weep?
And they told him the tidings of the
men of Jabesh.
6 And the Spirit of God came upon
Saul when he heard those tidings, and
his anger was kindled greatly.
7 And he took a yoke of oxen, and
hewed them in pieces, and sent *them*
throughout all the coasts of Israel by
the hands of messengers, saying,
Whosoever cometh not forth after Saul
and after Samuel, so shall it be done
unto his oxen. And the fear of the LORD
fell on the people, and they came out
with one consent.
8 And when he numbered them in
Bezek, the children of Israel were three
hundred thousand, and the men of
Judah thirty thousand.
9 And they said unto the messengers
that came, Thus shall ye say unto the
men of Jabesh-gilead, To morrow, by
that time the sun be hot, ye shall have
help. And the messengers came and
shewed *it* to the men of Jabesh; and
they were glad.
10 Therefore the men of Jabesh said,
To morrow we will come out unto you,
and ye shall do with us all that seemeth
good unto you.
11 And it was *so* on the morrow, that
Saul put the people in three companies; and they came into the midst of
the host in the morning watch, and slew
the Ammonites until the heat of the
day: and it came to pass, that they
which remained were scattered, so that
two of them were not left together.
12 And the people said unto Samuel,
Who *is* he that said, Shall Saul reign
over us? bring the men, that we may
put them to death.
13 And Saul said, There shall not a
man be put to death this day: for to day
the LORD hath wrought salvation in
Israel.
14 Then said Samuel to the people,
Come, and let us go to Gilgal, and
renew the kingdom there.
15 And all the people went to Gilgal;
and there they made Saul king before
the LORD in Gilgal; and there they sacrificed sacrifices of peace offerings
before the LORD; and there Saul and all
the men of Israel rejoiced greatly.

12 And Samuel said unto all Israel,
Behold, I have hearkened unto
your voice in all that ye said unto me,
and have made a king over you.
2 And now, behold, the king walketh
before you: and I am old and grayheaded; and, behold, my sons *are* with
you: and I have walked before you from
my childhood unto this day.
3 Behold, here I *am*: witness against
me before the LORD, and before his

anointed: whose ox have I taken? or
whose ass have I taken? or whom have
I defrauded? whom have I oppressed?
or of whose hand have I received *any*
bribe to blind mine eyes therewith?
and I will restore it you.
4 And they said, Thou hast not
defrauded us, nor oppressed us, neither
hast thou taken ought of any man's
hand.
5 And he said unto them, The LORD *is*
witness against you, and his anointed *is*
witness this day, that ye have not found
ought in my hand. And they answered,
He is witness.
6 And Samuel said unto the people, *It*
is the LORD that advanced Moses and
Aaron, and that brought your fathers
up out of the land of Egypt.
7 Now therefore stand still, that I may
reason with you before the LORD of all
the righteous acts of the LORD, which
he did to you and to your fathers.
8 When Jacob was come into Egypt,
and your fathers cried unto the LORD,
then the LORD sent Moses and Aaron,
which brought forth your fathers out of
Egypt, and made them dwell in this
place.
9 And when they forgat the LORD
their God, he sold them into the hand
of Sisera, captain of the host of Hazor,
and into the hand of the Philistines,
and into the hand of the king of Moab,
and they fought against them.
10 And they cried unto the LORD, and
said, We have sinned, because we have
forsaken the LORD, and have served
Baalim and Ashtaroth: but now deliver
us out of the hand of our enemies, and
we will serve thee.
11 And the LORD sent Jerubbaal, and
Bedan, and Jephthah, and Samuel, and
delivered you out of the hand of your
enemies on every side, and ye dwelled
safe.
12 And when ye saw that Nahash the
king of the children of Ammon came
against you, ye said unto me, Nay; but a
king shall reign over us: when the LORD
your God *was* your king.
13 Now therefore behold the king
whom ye have chosen, *and* whom ye
have desired! and, behold, the LORD
hath set a king over you.
14 If ye will fear the LORD, and serve
him, and obey his voice, and not rebel
against the commandment of the LORD,
then shall both ye and also the king
that reigneth over you continue following the LORD your God:
15 But if ye will not obey the voice of
the LORD, but rebel against the commandment of the LORD, then shall the
hand of the LORD be against you, as *it*
was against your fathers.
16 Now therefore stand and see this
great thing, which the LORD will do
before your eyes.
17 *Is it* not wheat harvest to day? I
will call unto the LORD, and he shall
send thunder and rain; that ye may
perceive and see that your wickedness
is great, which ye have done in the sight
of the LORD, in asking you a king.
18 So Samuel called unto the LORD;
and the LORD sent thunder and rain
that day: and all the people greatly
feared the LORD and Samuel.
19 And all the people said unto
Samuel, Pray for thy servants unto the
LORD thy God, that we die not: for we
have added unto all our sins *this* evil, to
ask us a king.
20 And Samuel said unto the people,
Fear not: ye have done all this wickedness: yet turn not aside from following

the LORD, but serve the LORD with all your heart;

21 And turn ye not aside: for *then should ye go* after vain *things*, which cannot profit nor deliver; for they *are* vain.

22 For the LORD will not forsake his people for his great name's sake: because it hath pleased the LORD to make you his people.

23 Moreover as for me, God forbid that I should sin against the LORD in ceasing to pray for you: but I will teach you the good and the right way:

24 Only fear the LORD, and serve him in truth with all your heart: for consider how great *things* he hath done for you.

25 But if ye shall still do wickedly, ye shall be consumed, both ye and your king.

13 Saul reigned one year; and when he had reigned two years over Israel,

2 Saul chose him three thousand *men* of Israel; *whereof* two thousand were with Saul in Michmash and in mount Beth-el, and a thousand were with Jonathan in Gibeah of Benjamin: and the rest of the people he sent every man to his tent.

3 And Jonathan smote the garrison of the Philistines that *was* in Geba, and the Philistines heard *of it*. And Saul blew the trumpet throughout all the land, saying, Let the Hebrews hear.

4 And all Israel heard say *that* Saul had smitten a garrison of the Philistines, and *that* Israel also was had in abomination with the Philistines. And the people were called together after Saul to Gilgal.

5 And the Philistines gathered themselves together to fight with Israel, thirty thousand chariots, and six thousand horsemen, and people as the sand which *is* on the sea shore in multitude: and they came up, and pitched in Michmash, eastward from Beth-aven.

6 When the men of Israel saw that they were in a strait, (for the people were distressed,) then the people did hide themselves in caves, and in thickets, and in rocks, and in high places, and in pits.

7 And *some of* the Hebrews went over Jordan to the land of Gad and Gilead. As for Saul, he *was* yet in Gilgal, and all the people followed him trembling.

8 And he tarried seven days, according to the set time that Samuel *had appointed*: but Samuel came not to Gilgal; and the people were scattered from him.

9 And Saul said, Bring hither a burnt offering to me, and peace offerings. And he offered the burnt offering.

10 And it came to pass, that as soon as he had made an end of offering the burnt offering, behold, Samuel came; and Saul went out to meet him, that he might salute him.

11 And Samuel said, What hast thou done? And Saul said, Because I saw that the people were scattered from me, and *that* thou camest not within the days appointed, and *that* the Philistines gathered themselves together at Michmash;

12 Therefore said I, The Philistines will come down now upon me to Gilgal, and I have not made supplication unto the LORD: I forced myself therefore, and offered a burnt offering.

13 And Samuel said to Saul, Thou hast done foolishly: thou hast not kept the commandment of the LORD thy God, which he commanded thee: for

now would the LORD have established
thy kingdom upon Israel for ever.
14 But now thy kingdom shall not
continue: the LORD hath sought him a
man after his own heart, and the LORD
hath commanded him *to be* captain
over his people, because thou hast not
kept *that* which the LORD commanded
thee.
15 And Samuel arose, and gat him up
from Gilgal unto Gibeah of Benjamin.
And Saul numbered the people *that*
were present with him, about six hundred men.
16 And Saul, and Jonathan his son,
and the people *that were* present with
them, abode in Gibeah of Benjamin:
but the Philistines encamped in Michmash.
17 And the spoilers came out of the
camp of the Philistines in three companies: one company turned unto the way
that leadeth to Ophrah, unto the land
of Shual:
18 And another company turned the
way *to* Beth-horon: and another company turned *to* the way of the border
that looketh to the valley of Zeboim
toward the wilderness.
19 Now there was no smith found
throughout all the land of Israel: for the
Philistines said, Lest the Hebrews
make *them* swords or spears:
20 But all the Israelites went down to
the Philistines, to sharpen every man
his share, and his coulter, and his axe,
and his mattock.
21 Yet they had a file for the mat-
tocks, and for the coulters, and for the
forks, and for the axes, and to sharpen
the goads.
22 So it came to pass in the day of
battle, that there was neither sword nor
spear found in the hand of any of the
people that *were* with Saul and
Jonathan: but with Saul and with
Jonathan his son was there found.
23 And the garrison of the Philistines
went out to the passage of Michmash.

14 Now it came to pass upon a day,
that Jonathan the son of Saul
said unto the young man that bare his
armour, Come, and let us go over to the
Philistines' garrison, that *is* on the
other side. But he told not his father.
2 And Saul tarried in the uttermost
part of Gibeah under a pomegranate
tree which *is* in Migron: and the people
that *were* with him *were* about six hundred men;
3 And Ahiah, the son of Ahitub,
Ichabod's brother, the son of Phinehas,
the son of Eli, the LORD's priest in
Shiloh, wearing an ephod. And the
people knew not that Jonathan was
gone.
4 And between the passages, by
which Jonathan sought to go over unto
the Philistines' garrison, *there was* a
sharp rock on the one side, and a sharp
rock on the other side: and the name of
the one *was* Bozez, and the name of the
other Seneh.
5 The forefront of the one *was* situate
northward over against Michmash, and
the other southward over against
Gibeah.
6 And Jonathan said to the young
man that bare his armour, Come, and
let us go over unto the garrison of these
uncircumcised: it may be that the LORD
will work for us: for *there is* no restraint
to the LORD to save by many or by few.
7 And his armourbearer said unto
him, Do all that *is* in thine heart: turn
thee; behold, I *am* with thee according
to thy heart.

8 Then said Jonathan, Behold, we will
pass over unto *these* men, and we will
discover ourselves unto them.
9 If they say thus unto us, Tarry until
we come to you; then we will stand still
in our place, and will not go up unto
them.
10 But if they say thus, Come up unto
us; then we will go up: for the LORD
hath delivered them into our hand: and
this *shall be* a sign unto us.
11 And both of them discovered
themselves unto the garrison of the
Philistines: and the Philistines said,
Behold, the Hebrews come forth out of
the holes where they had hid themselves.
12 And the men of the garrison
answered Jonathan and his armourbearer, and said, Come up to us, and we
will shew you a thing. And Jonathan
said unto his armourbearer, Come up
after me: for the LORD hath delivered
them into the hand of Israel.
13 And Jonathan climbed up upon his
hands and upon his feet, and his
armourbearer after him: and they fell
before Jonathan; and his armourbearer
slew after him.
14 And that first slaughter, which
Jonathan and his armourbearer made,
was about twenty men, within as it
were an half acre of land, *which* a yoke
of oxen might plow.
15 And there was trembling in the
host, in the field, and among all the
people: the garrison, and the spoilers,
they also trembled, and the earth
quaked: so it was a very great trembling.
16 And the watchmen of Saul in
Gibeah of Benjamin looked; and,
behold, the multitude melted away,
and they went on beating down *one
another*.
17 Then said Saul unto the people
that *were* with him, Number now, and
see who is gone from us. And when they
had numbered, behold, Jonathan and
his armourbearer *were* not *there*.
18 And Saul said unto Ahiah, Bring
hither the ark of God. For the ark of
God was at that time with the children
of Israel.
19 And it came to pass, while Saul
talked unto the priest, that the noise
that *was* in the host of the Philistines
went on and increased: and Saul said
unto the priest, Withdraw thine hand.
20 And Saul and all the people that
were with him assembled themselves,
and they came to the battle: and,
behold, every man's sword was against
his fellow, *and there was* a very great
discomfiture.
21 Moreover the Hebrews *that* were
with the Philistines before that time,
which went up with them into the camp
from the country round about, even
they also *turned* to be with the
Israelites that *were* with Saul and
Jonathan.
22 Likewise all the men of Israel
which had hid themselves in mount
Ephraim, *when* they heard that the
Philistines fled, even they also followed
hard after them in the battle.
23 So the LORD saved Israel that day:
and the battle passed over unto Beth-
aven.
24 And the men of Israel were distressed that day: for Saul had adjured
the people, saying, Cursed *be* the man
that eateth *any* food until evening, that
I may be avenged on mine enemies. So
none of the people tasted *any* food.

25 And all *they of* the land came to a
wood; and there was honey upon the
ground.
26 And when the people were come
into the wood, behold, the honey
dropped; but no man put his hand to
his mouth: for the people feared the
oath.
27 But Jonathan heard not when his
father charged the people with the
oath: wherefore he put forth the end of
the rod that *was* in his hand, and
dipped it in an honeycomb, and put his
hand to his mouth; and his eyes were
enlightened.
28 Then answered one of the people,
and said, Thy father straitly charged
the people with an oath, saying, Cursed
be the man that eateth *any* food this
day. And the people were faint.
29 Then said Jonathan, My father
hath troubled the land: see, I pray you,
how mine eyes have been enlightened,
because I tasted a little of this honey.
30 How much more, if haply the people had eaten freely to day of the spoil
of their enemies which they found? for
had there not been now a much greater
slaughter among the Philistines?
31 And they smote the Philistines
that day from Michmash to Aijalon:
and the people were very faint.
32 And the people flew upon the
spoil, and took sheep, and oxen, and
calves, and slew *them* on the ground:
and the people did eat *them* with the
blood.
33 Then they told Saul, saying,
Behold, the people sin against the
LORD, in that they eat with the blood.
And he said, Ye have transgressed: roll
a great stone unto me this day.
34 And Saul said, Disperse yourselves
among the people, and say unto them,
Bring me hither every man his ox, and
every man his sheep, and slay *them*
here, and eat; and sin not against the
LORD in eating with the blood. And all
the people brought every man his ox
with him that night, and slew *them*
there.
35 And Saul built an altar unto the
LORD: the same was the first altar that
he built unto the LORD.
36 And Saul said, Let us go down
after the Philistines by night, and spoil
them until the morning light, and let us
not leave a man of them. And they said,
Do whatsoever seemeth good unto
thee. Then said the priest, Let us draw
near hither unto God.
37 And Saul asked counsel of God,
Shall I go down after the Philistines?
wilt thou deliver them into the hand of
Israel? But he answered him not that
day.
38 And Saul said, Draw ye near hither, all the chief of the people: and know
and see wherein this sin hath been this
day.
39 For, *as* the LORD liveth, which
saveth Israel, though it be in Jonathan
my son, he shall surely die. But *there*
was not a man among all the people
that answered him.
40 Then said he unto all Israel, Be ye
on one side, and I and Jonathan my son
will be on the other side. And the people said unto Saul, Do what seemeth
good unto thee.
41 Therefore Saul said unto the LORD
God of Israel, Give a perfect *lot*. And
Saul and Jonathan were taken: but the
people escaped.
42 And Saul said, Cast *lots* between
me and Jonathan my son. And Jonathan
was taken.

43 Then Saul said to Jonathan, Tell
me what thou hast done. And Jonathan
told him, and said, I did but taste a little honey with the end of the rod that
was in mine hand, *and*, lo, I must die.
44 And Saul answered, God do so and
more also: for thou shalt surely die, Jonathan.
45 And the people said unto Saul,
Shall Jonathan die, who hath wrought
this great salvation in Israel? God forbid: *as* the LORD liveth, there shall not
one hair of his head fall to the ground;
for he hath wrought with God this day.
So the people rescued Jonathan, that
he died not.
46 Then Saul went up from following
the Philistines: and the Philistines
went to their own place.
47 So Saul took the kingdom over
Israel, and fought against all his enemies on every side, against Moab, and
against the children of Ammon, and
against Edom, and against the kings of
Zobah, and against the Philistines: and
whithersoever he turned himself, he
vexed *them*.
48 And he gathered an host, and
smote the Amalekites, and delivered
Israel out of the hands of them that
spoiled them.
49 Now the sons of Saul were
Jonathan, and Ishui, and Melchishua:
and the names of his two daughters
were these; the name of the firstborn
Merab, and the name of the younger
Michal:
50 And the name of Saul's wife *was*
Ahinoam, the daughter of Ahimaaz:
and the name of the captain of his host
was Abner, the son of Ner, Saul's uncle.
51 And Kish *was* the father of Saul;
and Ner the father of Abner *was* the
son of Abiel.
52 And there was sore war against the
Philistines all the days of Saul: and
when Saul saw any strong man, or any
valiant man, he took him unto him.

15 Samuel also said unto Saul, The
LORD sent me to anoint thee *to be*
king over his people, over Israel: now
therefore hearken thou unto the voice
of the words of the LORD.
2 Thus saith the LORD of hosts, I
remember *that* which Amalek did to
Israel, how he laid *wait* for him in the
way, when he came up from Egypt.
3 Now go and smite Amalek, and
utterly destroy all that they have, and
spare them not; but slay both man and
woman, infant and suckling, ox and
sheep, camel and ass.
4 And Saul gathered the people
together, and numbered them in
Telaim, two hundred thousand footmen, and ten thousand men of Judah.
5 And Saul came to a city of Amalek,
and laid wait in the valley.
6 And Saul said unto the Kenites, Go,
depart, get you down from among the
Amalekites, lest I destroy you with
them: for ye shewed kindness to all the
children of Israel, when they came up
out of Egypt. So the Kenites departed
from among the Amalekites.
7 And Saul smote the Amalekites
from Havilah *until* thou comest to
Shur, that *is* over against Egypt.
8 And he took Agag the king of the
Amalekites alive, and utterly destroyed
all the people with the edge of the
sword.
9 But Saul and the people spared
Agag, and the best of the sheep, and of
the oxen, and of the fatlings, and the
lambs, and all *that was* good, and
would not utterly destroy them: but

every thing *that was* vile and refuse,
that they destroyed utterly.
10 Then came the word of the LORD
unto Samuel, saying,
11 It repenteth me that I have set up
Saul *to be* king: for he is turned back
from following me, and hath not performed my commandments. And it
grieved Samuel; and he cried unto the
LORD all night.
12 And when Samuel rose early to
meet Saul in the morning, it was told
Samuel, saying, Saul came to Carmel,
and, behold, he set him up a place, and
is gone about, and passed on, and gone
down to Gilgal.
13 And Samuel came to Saul: and
Saul said unto him, Blessed *be* thou of
the LORD: I have performed the commandment of the LORD.
14 And Samuel said, What *meaneth*
then this bleating of the sheep in mine
ears, and the lowing of the oxen which
I hear?
15 And Saul said, They have brought
them from the Amalekites: for the
people spared the best of the sheep
and of the oxen, to sacrifice unto the
LORD thy God; and the rest we have
utterly destroyed.
16 Then Samuel said unto Saul, Stay,
and I will tell thee what the LORD hath
said to me this night. And he said unto
him, Say on.
17 And Samuel said, When thou *wast*
little in thine own sight, *wast* thou not
made the head of the tribes of Israel,
and the LORD anointed thee king over
Israel?
18 And the LORD sent thee on a journey, and said, Go and utterly destroy
the sinners the Amalekites, and fight
against them until they be consumed.
19 Wherefore then didst thou not
obey the voice of the LORD, but didst fly
upon the spoil, and didst evil in the
sight of the LORD?
20 And Saul said unto Samuel, Yea, I
have obeyed the voice of the LORD, and
have gone the way which the LORD sent
me, and have brought Agag the king of
Amalek, and have utterly destroyed the
Amalekites.
21 But the people took of the spoil,
sheep and oxen, the chief of the things
which should have been utterly
destroyed, to sacrifice unto the LORD
thy God in Gilgal.
22 And Samuel said, Hath the LORD
as great delight in burnt offerings and
sacrifices, as in obeying the voice of the
LORD? Behold, to obey *is* better than
sacrifice, *and* to hearken than the fat of
rams.
23 For rebellion *is as* the sin of witchcraft, and stubbornness *is as* iniquity
and idolatry. Because thou hast rejected the word of the LORD, he hath also
rejected thee from *being* king.
24 And Saul said unto Samuel, I have
sinned: for I have transgressed the commandment of the LORD, and thy words:
because I feared the people, and
obeyed their voice.
25 Now therefore, I pray thee, pardon
my sin, and turn again with me, that I
may worship the LORD.
26 And Samuel said unto Saul, I will
not return with thee: for thou hast
rejected the word of the LORD, and the
LORD hath rejected thee from being
king over Israel.
27 And as Samuel turned about to go
away, he laid hold upon the skirt of his
mantle, and it rent.
28 And Samuel said unto him, The
LORD hath rent the kingdom of Israel

from thee this day, and hath given it to
a neighbour of thine, *that is* better
than thou.
29 And also the Strength of Israel will
not lie nor repent: for he *is* not a man,
that he should repent.
30 Then he said, I have sinned: *yet*
honour me now, I pray thee, before the
elders of my people, and before Israel,
and turn again with me, that I may worship the LORD thy God.
31 So Samuel turned again after Saul;
and Saul worshipped the LORD.
32 Then said Samuel, Bring ye hither
to me Agag the king of the Amalekites.
And Agag came unto him delicately.
And Agag said, Surely the bitterness of
death is past.
33 And Samuel said, As thy sword
hath made women childless, so shall
thy mother be childless among women.
And Samuel hewed Agag in pieces
before the LORD in Gilgal.
34 Then Samuel went to Ramah; and
Saul went up to his house to Gibeah of
Saul.
35 And Samuel came no more to see
Saul until the day of his death: nevertheless Samuel mourned for Saul: and
the LORD repented that he had made
Saul king over Israel.

16 And the LORD said unto Samuel,
How long wilt thou mourn for
Saul, seeing I have rejected him from
reigning over Israel? fill thine horn
with oil, and go, I will send thee to Jesse
the Beth-lehemite: for I have provided
me a king among his sons.
2 And Samuel said, How can I go? if
Saul hear *it*, he will kill me. And the
LORD said, Take an heifer with thee,
and say, I am come to sacrifice to the
LORD.
3 And call Jesse to the sacrifice, and I
will shew thee what thou shalt do: and
thou shalt anoint unto me *him* whom I
name unto thee.
4 And Samuel did that which the
LORD spake, and came to Beth-lehem.
And the elders of the town trembled at
his coming, and said, Comest thou
peaceably?
5 And he said, Peaceably: I am come
to sacrifice unto the LORD: sanctify
yourselves, and come with me to the
sacrifice. And he sanctified Jesse and
his sons, and called them to the sacrifice.
6 And it came to pass, when they
were come, that he looked on Eliab,
and said, Surely the LORD's anointed *is*
before him.
7 But the LORD said unto Samuel,
Look not on his countenance, or on the
height of his stature; because I have
refused him: for *the LORD seeth* not as
man seeth; for man looketh on the outward appearance, but the LORD looketh
on the heart.
8 Then Jesse called Abinadab, and
made him pass before Samuel. And he
said, Neither hath the LORD chosen this.
9 Then Jesse made Shammah to pass
by. And he said, Neither hath the LORD
chosen this.
10 Again, Jesse made seven of his
sons to pass before Samuel. And
Samuel said unto Jesse, The LORD hath
not chosen these.
11 And Samuel said unto Jesse, Are
here all *thy* children? And he said,
There remaineth yet the youngest, and,
behold, he keepeth the sheep. And
Samuel said unto Jesse, Send and fetch
him: for we will not sit down till he
come hither.

12 And he sent, and brought him in.
Now he *was* ruddy, *and* withal of a
beautiful countenance, and goodly to
look to. And the LORD said, Arise,
anoint him: for this *is* he.
13 Then Samuel took the horn of oil,
and anointed him in the midst of his
brethren: and the Spirit of the LORD
came upon David from that day forward. So Samuel rose up, and went to
Ramah.
14 But the Spirit of the LORD departed from Saul, and an evil spirit from
the LORD troubled him.
15 And Saul's servants said unto him,
Behold now, an evil spirit from God
troubleth thee.
16 Let our lord now command thy
servants, *which are* before thee, to seek
out a man, *who is* a cunning player on
an harp: and it shall come to pass, when
the evil spirit from God is upon thee,
that he shall play with his hand, and
thou shalt be well.
17 And Saul said unto his servants,
Provide me now a man that can play
well, and bring *him* to me.
18 Then answered one of the servants,
and said, Behold, I have seen a son of
Jesse the Beth-lehemite, *that is* cunning in playing, and a mighty valiant
man, and a man of war, and prudent in
matters, and a comely person, and the
LORD *is* with him.
19 Wherefore Saul sent messengers
unto Jesse, and said, Send me David
thy son, which *is* with the sheep.
20 And Jesse took an ass *laden* with
bread, and a bottle of wine, and a kid,
and sent *them* by David his son unto
Saul.
21 And David came to Saul, and stood
before him: and he loved him greatly;
and he became his armourbearer.
22 And Saul sent to Jesse, saying, Let
David, I pray thee, stand before me; for
he hath found favour in my sight.
23 And it came to pass, when the *evil*
spirit from God was upon Saul, that
David took an harp, and played with his
hand: so Saul was refreshed, and was
well, and the evil spirit departed from
him.

17 Now the Philistines gathered
together their armies to battle,
and were gathered together at Shochoh,
which *belongeth* to Judah, and pitched
between Shochoh and Azekah, in
Ephes-dammim.
2 And Saul and the men of Israel
were gathered together, and pitched by
the valley of Elah, and set the battle in
array against the Philistines.
3 And the Philistines stood on a
mountain on the one side, and Israel
stood on a mountain on the other side:
and *there was* a valley between them.
4 And there went out a champion out
of the camp of the Philistines, named
Goliath, of Gath, whose height *was* six
cubits and a span.
5 And *he had* an helmet of brass upon
his head, and he *was* armed with a coat
of mail; and the weight of the coat *was*
five thousand shekels of brass.
6 And *he had* greaves of brass upon
his legs, and a target of brass between
his shoulders.
7 And the staff of his spear *was* like a
weaver's beam; and his spear's head
weighed six hundred shekels of iron:
and one bearing a shield went before
him.
8 And he stood and cried unto the
armies of Israel, and said unto them,
Why are ye come out to set *your* battle
in array? *am* not I a Philistine, and ye

servants to Saul? choose you a man for
you, and let him come down to me.
9 If he be able to fight with me, and to
kill me, then will we be your servants:
but if I prevail against him, and kill
him, then shall ye be our servants, and
serve us.
10 And the Philistine said, I defy the
armies of Israel this day; give me a
man, that we may fight together.
11 When Saul and all Israel heard
those words of the Philistine, they were
dismayed, and greatly afraid.
12 Now David *was* the son of that
Ephrathite of Beth-lehem-judah, whose
name *was* Jesse; and he had eight sons:
and the man went among men *for* an
old man in the days of Saul.
13 And the three eldest sons of Jesse
went *and* followed Saul to the battle:
and the names of his three sons that
went to the battle *were* Eliab the firstborn, and next unto him Abinadab, and
the third Shammah.
14 And David *was* the youngest: and
the three eldest followed Saul.
15 But David went and returned from
Saul to feed his father's sheep at Beth-
lehem.
16 And the Philistine drew near
morning and evening, and presented
himself forty days.
17 And Jesse said unto David his son,
Take now for thy brethren an ephah of
this parched *corn*, and these ten loaves,
and run to the camp to thy brethren;
18 And carry these ten cheeses unto
the captain of *their* thousand, and look
how thy brethren fare, and take their
pledge.
19 Now Saul, and they, and all the
men of Israel, *were* in the valley of
Elah, fighting with the Philistines.
20 And David rose up early in the
morning, and left the sheep with a
keeper, and took, and went, as Jesse
had commanded him; and he came to
the trench, as the host was going forth
to the fight, and shouted for the battle.
21 For Israel and the Philistines had
put the battle in array, army against
army.
22 And David left his carriage in the
hand of the keeper of the carriage, and
ran into the army, and came and saluted his brethren.
23 And as he talked with them,
behold, there came up the champion,
the Philistine of Gath, Goliath by name,
out of the armies of the Philistines, and
spake according to the same words: and
David heard *them*.
24 And all the men of Israel, when
they saw the man, fled from him, and
were sore afraid.
25 And the men of Israel said, Have
ye seen this man that is come up?
surely to defy Israel is he come up: and
it shall be, *that* the man who killeth
him, the king will enrich him with great
riches, and will give him his daughter,
and make his father's house free in
Israel.
26 And David spake to the men that
stood by him, saying, What shall be
done to the man that killeth this
Philistine, and taketh away the
reproach from Israel? for who *is* this
uncircumcised Philistine, that he
should defy the armies of the living
God?
27 And the people answered him
after this manner, saying, So shall it be
done to the man that killeth him.
28 And Eliab his eldest brother heard
when he spake unto the men; and
Eliab's anger was kindled against

David, and he said, Why camest thou
down hither? and with whom hast thou
left those few sheep in the wilderness?
I know thy pride, and the naughtiness
of thine heart; for thou art come down
that thou mightest see the battle.
29 And David said, What have I now
done? *Is there* not a cause?
30 And he turned from him toward
another, and spake after the same manner: and the people answered him
again after the former manner.
31 And when the words were heard
which David spake, they rehearsed
them before Saul: and he sent for him.
32 And David said to Saul, Let no
man's heart fail because of him; thy
servant will go and fight with this
Philistine.
33 And Saul said to David, Thou art
not able to go against this Philistine to
fight with him: for thou *art but* a youth,
and he a man of war from his youth.
34 And David said unto Saul, Thy
servant kept his father's sheep, and
there came a lion, and a bear, and took
a lamb out of the flock:
35 And I went out after him, and
smote him, and delivered *it* out of his
mouth: and when he arose against me,
I caught *him* by his beard, and smote
him, and slew him.
36 Thy servant slew both the lion and
the bear: and this uncircumcised
Philistine shall be as one of them, seeing he hath defied the armies of the
living God.
37 David said moreover, The LORD
that delivered me out of the paw of the
lion, and out of the paw of the bear, he
will deliver me out of the hand of this
Philistine. And Saul said unto David,
Go, and the LORD be with thee.
38 And Saul armed David with his
armour, and he put an helmet of brass
upon his head; also he armed him with
a coat of mail.
39 And David girded his sword upon
his armour, and he assayed to go; for he
had not proved *it*. And David said unto
Saul, I cannot go with these; for I have
not proved *them*. And David put them
off him.
40 And he took his staff in his hand,
and chose him five smooth stones out of
the brook, and put them in a shepherd's
bag which he had, even in a scrip; and
his sling *was* in his hand: and he drew
near to the Philistine.
41 And the Philistine came on and
drew near unto David; and the man
that bare the shield *went* before him.
42 And when the Philistine looked
about, and saw David, he disdained
him: for he was *but* a youth, and ruddy,
and of a fair countenance.
43 And the Philistine said unto David,
Am I a dog, that thou comest to me with
staves? And the Philistine cursed David
by his gods.
44 And the Philistine said to David,
Come to me, and I will give thy flesh
unto the fowls of the air, and to the
beasts of the field.
45 Then said David to the Philistine,
Thou comest to me with a sword, and
with a spear, and with a shield: but I
come to thee in the name of the LORD
of hosts, the God of the armies of Israel,
whom thou hast defied.
46 This day will the LORD deliver thee
into mine hand; and I will smite thee,
and take thine head from thee; and I
will give the carcases of the host of the
Philistines this day unto the fowls of
the air, and to the wild beasts of the

earth; that all the earth may know that there is a God in Israel.

47 And all this assembly shall know that the LORD saveth not with sword and spear: for the battle *is* the LORD's, and he will give you into our hands.

48 And it came to pass, when the Philistine arose, and came and drew nigh to meet David, that David hasted, and ran toward the army to meet the Philistine.

49 And David put his hand in his bag, and took thence a stone, and slang *it*, and smote the Philistine in his forehead, that the stone sunk into his forehead; and he fell upon his face to the earth.

50 So David prevailed over the Philistine with a sling and with a stone, and smote the Philistine, and slew him; but *there was* no sword in the hand of David.

51 Therefore David ran, and stood upon the Philistine, and took his sword, and drew it out of the sheath thereof, and slew him, and cut off his head therewith. And when the Philistines saw their champion was dead, they fled.

52 And the men of Israel and of Judah arose, and shouted, and pursued the Philistines, until thou come to the valley, and to the gates of Ekron. And the wounded of the Philistines fell down by the way to Shaaraim, even unto Gath, and unto Ekron.

53 And the children of Israel returned from chasing after the Philistines, and they spoiled their tents.

54 And David took the head of the Philistine, and brought it to Jerusalem; but he put his armour in his tent.

55 And when Saul saw David go forth against the Philistine, he said unto Abner, the captain of the host, Abner, whose son *is* this youth? And Abner said, *As* thy soul liveth, O king, I cannot tell.

56 And the king said, Enquire thou whose son the stripling *is*.

57 And as David returned from the slaughter of the Philistine, Abner took him, and brought him before Saul with the head of the Philistine in his hand.

58 And Saul said to him, Whose son *art* thou, *thou* young man? And David answered, I *am* the son of thy servant Jesse the Beth-lehemite.

18 And it came to pass, when he had made an end of speaking unto Saul, that the soul of Jonathan was knit with the soul of David, and Jonathan loved him as his own soul.

2 And Saul took him that day, and would let him go no more home to his father's house.

3 Then Jonathan and David made a covenant, because he loved him as his own soul.

4 And Jonathan stripped himself of the robe that *was* upon him, and gave it to David, and his garments, even to his sword, and to his bow, and to his girdle.

5 And David went out whithersoever Saul sent him, *and* behaved himself wisely: and Saul set him over the men of war, and he was accepted in the sight of all the people, and also in the sight of Saul's servants.

6 And it came to pass as they came, when David was returned from the slaughter of the Philistine, that the women came out of all cities of Israel, singing and dancing, to meet king Saul, with tabrets, with joy, and with instruments of musick.

7 And the women answered *one another* as they played, and said, Saul

hath slain his thousands, and David his
ten thousands.
8 And Saul was very wroth, and the
saying displeased him; and he said,
They have ascribed unto David ten
thousands, and to me they have
ascribed *but* thousands: and *what* can
he have more but the kingdom?
9 And Saul eyed David from that day
and forward.
10 And it came to pass on the morrow,
that the evil spirit from God came upon
Saul, and he prophesied in the midst of
the house: and David played with his
hand, as at other times: and *there was*
a javelin in Saul's hand.
11 And Saul cast the javelin; for he
said, I will smite David even to the wall
with it. And David avoided out of his
presence twice.
12 And Saul was afraid of David,
because the LORD was with him, and
was departed from Saul.
13 Therefore Saul removed him from
him, and made him his captain over a
thousand; and he went out and came in
before the people.
14 And David behaved himself wisely
in all his ways; and the LORD *was* with
him.
15 Wherefore when Saul saw that he
behaved himself very wisely, he was
afraid of him.
16 But all Israel and Judah loved
David, because he went out and came
in before them.
17 And Saul said to David, Behold my
elder daughter Merab, her will I give
thee to wife: only be thou valiant for
me, and fight the LORD's battles. For
Saul said, Let not mine hand be upon
him, but let the hand of the Philistines
be upon him.
18 And David said unto Saul, Who *am*
I? and what *is* my life, *or* my father's
family in Israel, that I should be son in
law to the king?
19 But it came to pass at the time
when Merab Saul's daughter should
have been given to David, that she was
given unto Adriel the Meholathite to
wife.
20 And Michal Saul's daughter loved
David: and they told Saul, and the thing
pleased him.
21 And Saul said, I will give him her,
that she may be a snare to him, and
that the hand of the Philistines may be
against him. Wherefore Saul said to
David, Thou shalt this day be my son in
law in *the one of* the twain.
22 And Saul commanded his servants,
saying, Commune with David secretly,
and say, Behold, the king hath delight
in thee, and all his servants love thee:
now therefore be the king's son in law.
23 And Saul's servants spake those
words in the ears of David. And David
said, Seemeth it to you *a* light *thing* to
be a king's son in law, seeing that I *am*
a poor man, and lightly esteemed?
24 And the servants of Saul told him,
saying, On this manner spake David.
25 And Saul said, Thus shall ye say to
David, The king desireth not any dowry,
but an hundred foreskins of the
Philistines, to be avenged of the king's
enemies. But Saul thought to make
David fall by the hand of the Philistines.
26 And when his servants told David
these words, it pleased David well to be
the king's son in law: and the days were
not expired.
27 Wherefore David arose and went,
he and his men, and slew of the
Philistines two hundred men; and
David brought their foreskins, and they

gave them in full tale to the king, that he might be the king's son in law. And Saul gave him Michal his daughter to wife.

28 And Saul saw and knew that the LORD *was* with David, and *that* Michal Saul's daughter loved him.

29 And Saul was yet the more afraid of David; and Saul became David's enemy continually.

30 Then the princes of the Philistines went forth: and it came to pass, after they went forth, *that* David behaved himself more wisely than all the servants of Saul; so that his name was much set by.

19 And Saul spake to Jonathan his son, and to all his servants, that they should kill David.

2 But Jonathan Saul's son delighted much in David: and Jonathan told David, saying, Saul my father seeketh to kill thee: now therefore, I pray thee, take heed to thyself until the morning, and abide in a secret *place*, and hide thyself:

3 And I will go out and stand beside my father in the field where thou *art*, and I will commune with my father of thee; and what I see, that I will tell thee.

4 And Jonathan spake good of David unto Saul his father, and said unto him, Let not the king sin against his servant, against David; because he hath not sinned against thee, and because his works *have been* to thee-ward very good:

5 For he did put his life in his hand, and slew the Philistine, and the LORD wrought a great salvation for all Israel: thou sawest *it*, and didst rejoice: wherefore then wilt thou sin against innocent blood, to slay David without a cause?

6 And Saul hearkened unto the voice of Jonathan: and Saul sware, *As* the LORD liveth, he shall not be slain.

7 And Jonathan called David, and Jonathan shewed him all those things. And Jonathan brought David to Saul, and he was in his presence, as in times past.

8 And there was war again: and David went out, and fought with the Philistines, and slew them with a great slaughter; and they fled from him.

9 And the evil spirit from the LORD was upon Saul, as he sat in his house with his javelin in his hand: and David played with *his* hand.

10 And Saul sought to smite David even to the wall with the javelin; but he slipped away out of Saul's presence, and he smote the javelin into the wall: and David fled, and escaped that night.

11 Saul also sent messengers unto David's house, to watch him, and to slay him in the morning: and Michal David's wife told him, saying, If thou save not thy life to night, to morrow thou shalt be slain.

12 So Michal let David down through a window: and he went, and fled, and escaped.

13 And Michal took an image, and laid *it* in the bed, and put a pillow of goats' *hair* for his bolster, and covered *it* with a cloth.

14 And when Saul sent messengers to take David, she said, He *is* sick.

15 And Saul sent the messengers *again* to see David, saying, Bring him up to me in the bed, that I may slay him.

16 And when the messengers were come in, behold, *there was* an image in the bed, with a pillow of goats' *hair* for his bolster.

17 And Saul said unto Michal, Why
hast thou deceived me so, and sent
away mine enemy, that he is escaped?
And Michal answered Saul, He said
unto me, Let me go; why should I kill
thee?
18 So David fled, and escaped, and
came to Samuel to Ramah, and told
him all that Saul had done to him. And
he and Samuel went and dwelt in
Naioth.
19 And it was told Saul, saying,
Behold, David *is* at Naioth in Ramah.
20 And Saul sent messengers to take
David: and when they saw the company
of the prophets prophesying, and
Samuel standing *as* appointed over
them, the Spirit of God was upon the
messengers of Saul, and they also
prophesied.
21 And when it was told Saul, he sent
other messengers, and they prophesied
likewise. And Saul sent messengers
again the third time, and they prophesied also.
22 Then went he also to Ramah, and
came to a great well that *is* in Sechu:
and he asked and said, Where *are*
Samuel and David? And *one* said,
Behold, *they be* at Naioth in Ramah.
23 And he went thither to Naioth in
Ramah: and the Spirit of God was upon
him also, and he went on, and prophesied, until he came to Naioth in Ramah.
24 And he stripped off his clothes
also, and prophesied before Samuel in
like manner, and lay down naked all
that day and all that night. Wherefore
they say, *Is* Saul also among the prophets?

20 And David fled from Naioth in
Ramah, and came and said
before Jonathan, What have I done?
what *is* mine iniquity? and what *is* my
sin before thy father, that he seeketh
my life?
2 And he said unto him, God forbid;
thou shalt not die: behold, my father
will do nothing either great or small,
but that he will shew it me: and why
should my father hide this thing from
me? it *is* not *so*.
3 And David sware moreover, and
said, Thy father certainly knoweth that
I have found grace in thine eyes; and he
saith, Let not Jonathan know this, lest
he be grieved: but truly *as* the LORD
liveth, and *as* thy soul liveth, *there is*
but a step between me and death.
4 Then said Jonathan unto David,
Whatsoever thy soul desireth, I will
even do *it* for thee.
5 And David said unto Jonathan,
Behold, to morrow *is* the new moon,
and I should not fail to sit with the king
at meat: but let me go, that I may hide
myself in the field unto the third *day* at
even.
6 If thy father at all miss me, then say,
David earnestly asked *leave* of me that
he might run to Beth-lehem his city: for
there is a yearly sacrifice there for all
the family.
7 If he say thus, *It is* well; thy servant
shall have peace: but if he be very
wroth, *then* be sure that evil is determined by him.
8 Therefore thou shalt deal kindly
with thy servant; for thou hast brought
thy servant into a covenant of the LORD
with thee: notwithstanding, if there be
in me iniquity, slay me thyself; for why
shouldest thou bring me to thy father?
9 And Jonathan said, Far be it from
thee: for if I knew certainly that evil
were determined by my father to come
upon thee, then would not I tell it thee?

10 Then said David to Jonathan, Who shall tell me? or what *if* thy father answer thee roughly?

11 And Jonathan said unto David, Come, and let us go out into the field. And they went out both of them into the field.

12 And Jonathan said unto David, O LORD God of Israel, when I have sounded my father about to morrow any time, *or* the third *day*, and, behold, *if there be* good toward David, and I then send not unto thee, and shew it thee;

13 The LORD do so and much more to Jonathan: but if it please my father *to do* thee evil, then I will shew it thee, and send thee away, that thou mayest go in peace: and the LORD be with thee, as he hath been with my father.

14 And thou shalt not only while yet I live shew me the kindness of the LORD, that I die not:

15 But *also* thou shalt not cut off thy kindness from my house for ever: no, not when the LORD hath cut off the enemies of David every one from the face of the earth.

16 So Jonathan made *a covenant* with the house of David, *saying*, Let the LORD even require *it* at the hand of David's enemies.

17 And Jonathan caused David to swear again, because he loved him: for he loved him as he loved his own soul.

18 Then Jonathan said to David, To morrow *is* the new moon: and thou shalt be missed, because thy seat will be empty.

19 And *when* thou hast stayed three days, *then* thou shalt go down quickly, and come to the place where thou didst hide thyself when the business was *in hand*, and shalt remain by the stone Ezel.

20 And I will shoot three arrows on the side *thereof*, as though I shot at a mark.

21 And, behold, I will send a lad, *saying*, Go, find out the arrows. If I expressly say unto the lad, Behold, the arrows *are* on this side of thee, take them; then come thou: for *there is* peace to thee, and no hurt; *as* the LORD liveth.

22 But if I say thus unto the young man, Behold, the arrows *are* beyond thee; go thy way: for the LORD hath sent thee away.

23 And *as touching* the matter which thou and I have spoken of, behold, the LORD *be* between thee and me for ever.

24 So David hid himself in the field: and when the new moon was come, the king sat him down to eat meat.

25 And the king sat upon his seat, as at other times, *even* upon a seat by the wall: and Jonathan arose, and Abner sat by Saul's side, and David's place was empty.

26 Nevertheless Saul spake not any thing that day: for he thought, Something hath befallen him, he *is* not clean; surely he *is* not clean.

27 And it came to pass on the morrow, *which was* the second *day* of the month, that David's place was empty: and Saul said unto Jonathan his son, Wherefore cometh not the son of Jesse to meat, neither yesterday, nor to day?

28 And Jonathan answered Saul, David earnestly asked *leave* of me *to go* to Beth-lehem:

29 And he said, Let me go, I pray thee; for our family hath a sacrifice in the city; and my brother, he hath commanded me *to be there*: and now, if I have found favour in thine eyes, let me get away, I pray thee, and see my breth-

ren. Therefore he cometh not unto the
king's table.
30 Then Saul's anger was kindled
against Jonathan, and he said unto him,
Thou son of the perverse rebellious
woman, do not I know that thou hast
chosen the son of Jesse to thine own
confusion, and unto the confusion of
thy mother's nakedness?
31 For as long as the son of Jesse
liveth upon the ground, thou shalt not
be established, nor thy kingdom.
Wherefore now send and fetch him
unto me, for he shall surely die.
32 And Jonathan answered Saul his
father, and said unto him, Wherefore
shall he be slain? what hath he done?
33 And Saul cast a javelin at him to
smite him: whereby Jonathan knew
that it was determined of his father to
slay David.
34 So Jonathan arose from the table
in fierce anger, and did eat no meat the
second day of the month: for he was
grieved for David, because his father
had done him shame.
35 And it came to pass in the morning, that Jonathan went out into the
field at the time appointed with David,
and a little lad with him.
36 And he said unto his lad, Run, find
out now the arrows which I shoot. *And*
as the lad ran, he shot an arrow beyond
him.
37 And when the lad was come to the
place of the arrow which Jonathan had
shot, Jonathan cried after the lad, and
said, *Is* not the arrow beyond thee?
38 And Jonathan cried after the lad,
Make speed, haste, stay not. And
Jonathan's lad gathered up the arrows,
and came to his master.
39 But the lad knew not any thing:
only Jonathan and David knew the
matter.
40 And Jonathan gave his artillery
unto his lad, and said unto him, Go,
carry *them* to the city.
41 *And* as soon as the lad was gone,
David arose out of *a place* toward the
south, and fell on his face to the ground,
and bowed himself three times: and
they kissed one another, and wept one
with another, until David exceeded.
42 And Jonathan said to David, Go in
peace, forasmuch as we have sworn
both of us in the name of the LORD, saying, The LORD be between me and thee,
and between my seed and thy seed for
ever. And he arose and departed: and
Jonathan went into the city.

21 Then came David to Nob to
Ahimelech the priest: and
Ahimelech was afraid at the meeting of
David, and said unto him, Why *art* thou
alone, and no man with thee?
2 And David said unto Ahimelech the
priest, The king hath commanded me a
business, and hath said unto me, Let no
man know any thing of the business
whereabout I send thee, and what I
have commanded thee: and I have
appointed *my* servants to such and
such a place.
3 Now therefore what is under thine
hand? give *me* five *loaves of* bread in
mine hand, or what there is present.
4 And the priest answered David, and
said, *There is* no common bread under
mine hand, but there is hallowed bread;
if the young men have kept themselves
at least from women.
5 And David answered the priest, and
said unto him, Of a truth women *have
been* kept from us about these three
days, since I came out, and the vessels

of the young men are holy, and *the*
bread is in a manner common, yea,
though it were sanctified this day in the
vessel.
6 So the priest gave him hallowed
bread: for there was no bread there but
the shewbread, that was taken from
before the LORD, to put hot bread in the
day when it was taken away.
7 Now a certain man of the servants
of Saul *was* there that day, detained
before the LORD; and his name *was*
Doeg, an Edomite, the chiefest of the
herdmen that *belonged* to Saul.
8 And David said unto Ahimelech,
And is there not here under thine hand
spear or sword? for I have neither
brought my sword nor my weapons
with me, because the king's business
required haste.
9 And the priest said, The sword of
Goliath the Philistine, whom thou slew-
est in the valley of Elah, behold, it *is*
here wrapped in a cloth behind the
ephod: if thou wilt take that, take *it*: for
there is no other save that here. And
David said, *There is* none like that; give
it me.
10 And David arose, and fled that day
for fear of Saul, and went to Achish the
king of Gath.
11 And the servants of Achish said
unto him, *Is* not this David the king of
the land? did they not sing one to
another of him in dances, saying, Saul
hath slain his thousands, and David his
ten thousands?
12 And David laid up these words in
his heart, and was sore afraid of Achish
the king of Gath.
13 And he changed his behaviour
before them, and feigned himself mad
in their hands, and scrabbled on the
doors of the gate, and let his spittle fall
down upon his beard.
14 Then said Achish unto his servants,
Lo, ye see the man is mad: wherefore
then have ye brought him to me?
15 Have I need of mad men, that ye
have brought this *fellow* to play the
mad man in my presence? shall this
fellow come into my house?

22 David therefore departed thence,
and escaped to the cave Adullam:
and when his brethren and all his
father's house heard *it*, they went down
thither to him.
2 And every one *that was* in distress,
and every one that *was* in debt, and
every one *that was* discontented, gathered themselves unto him; and he
became a captain over them: and there
were with him about four hundred
men.
3 And David went thence to Mizpeh
of Moab: and he said unto the king of
Moab, Let my father and my mother, I
pray thee, come forth, *and be* with you,
till I know what God will do for me.
4 And he brought them before the
king of Moab: and they dwelt with him
all the while that David was in the hold.
5 And the prophet Gad said unto
David, Abide not in the hold; depart,
and get thee into the land of Judah.
Then David departed, and came into
the forest of Hareth.
6 When Saul heard that David was
discovered, and the men that *were* with
him, (now Saul abode in Gibeah under
a tree in Ramah, having his spear in his
hand, and all his servants *were* standing about him;)
7 Then Saul said unto his servants
that stood about him, Hear now, ye
Benjamites; will the son of Jesse give
every one of you fields and vineyards,

and make you all captains of thousands, and captains of hundreds;
8 That all of you have conspired
against me, and *there is* none that
sheweth me that my son hath made a
league with the son of Jesse, and *there*
is none of you that is sorry for me, or
sheweth unto me that my son hath
stirred up my servant against me, to lie
in wait, as at this day?
9 Then answered Doeg the Edomite,
which was set over the servants of Saul,
and said, I saw the son of Jesse coming
to Nob, to Ahimelech the son of Ahitub.
10 And he enquired of the LORD for
him, and gave him victuals, and gave
him the sword of Goliath the Philistine.
11 Then the king sent to call
Ahimelech the priest, the son of Ahitub,
and all his father's house, the priests
that *were* in Nob: and they came all of
them to the king.
12 And Saul said, Hear now, thou son
of Ahitub. And he answered, Here I *am*,
my lord.
13 And Saul said unto him, Why have
ye conspired against me, thou and the
son of Jesse, in that thou hast given him
bread, and a sword, and hast enquired
of God for him, that he should rise
against me, to lie in wait, as at this day?
14 Then Ahimelech answered the
king, and said, And who *is so* faithful
among all thy servants as David, which
is the king's son in law, and goeth at thy
bidding, and is honourable in thine
house?
15 Did I then begin to enquire of God
for him? be it far from me: let not the
king impute *any* thing unto his servant,
nor to all the house of my father: for thy
servant knew nothing of all this, less or
more.
16 And the king said, Thou shalt surely die, Ahimelech, thou, and all thy
father's house.
17 And the king said unto the footmen that stood about him, Turn, and
slay the priests of the LORD; because
their hand also *is* with David, and
because they knew when he fled, and
did not shew it to me. But the servants
of the king would not put forth their
hand to fall upon the priests of the
LORD.
18 And the king said to Doeg, Turn
thou, and fall upon the priests. And
Doeg the Edomite turned, and he fell
upon the priests, and slew on that day
fourscore and five persons that did
wear a linen ephod.
19 And Nob, the city of the priests,
smote he with the edge of the sword,
both men and women, children and
sucklings, and oxen, and asses, and
sheep, with the edge of the sword.
20 And one of the sons of Ahimelech
the son of Ahitub, named Abiathar,
escaped, and fled after David.
21 And Abiathar shewed David that
Saul had slain the LORD's priests.
22 And David said unto Abiathar, I
knew *it* that day, when Doeg the
Edomite *was* there, that he would surely tell Saul: I have occasioned *the death*
of all the persons of thy father's house.
23 Abide thou with me, fear not: for
he that seeketh my life seeketh thy life:
but with me thou *shalt be* in safeguard.

23 Then they told David, saying,
Behold, the Philistines fight
against Keilah, and they rob the threshingfloors.
2 Therefore David enquired of the
LORD, saying, Shall I go and smite these
Philistines? And the LORD said unto

David, Go, and smite the Philistines, and save Keilah.

3 And David's men said unto him, Behold, we be afraid here in Judah: how much more then if we come to Keilah against the armies of the Philistines?

4 Then David enquired of the LORD yet again. And the LORD answered him and said, Arise, go down to Keilah; for I will deliver the Philistines into thine hand.

5 So David and his men went to Keilah, and fought with the Philistines, and brought away their cattle, and smote them with a great slaughter. So David saved the inhabitants of Keilah.

6 And it came to pass, when Abiathar the son of Ahimelech fled to David to Keilah, *that* he came down *with* an ephod in his hand.

7 And it was told Saul that David was come to Keilah. And Saul said, God hath delivered him into mine hand; for he is shut in, by entering into a town that hath gates and bars.

8 And Saul called all the people together to war, to go down to Keilah, to besiege David and his men.

9 And David knew that Saul secretly practised mischief against him; and he said to Abiathar the priest, Bring hither the ephod.

10 Then said David, O LORD God of Israel, thy servant hath certainly heard that Saul seeketh to come to Keilah, to destroy the city for my sake.

11 Will the men of Keilah deliver me up into his hand? will Saul come down, as thy servant hath heard? O LORD God of Israel, I beseech thee, tell thy servant. And the LORD said, He will come down.

12 Then said David, Will the men of Keilah deliver me and my men into the hand of Saul? And the LORD said, They will deliver *thee* up.

13 Then David and his men, *which were* about six hundred, arose and departed out of Keilah, and went whithersoever they could go. And it was told Saul that David was escaped from Keilah; and he forbare to go forth.

14 And David abode in the wilderness in strong holds, and remained in a mountain in the wilderness of Ziph. And Saul sought him every day, but God delivered him not into his hand.

15 And David saw that Saul was come out to seek his life: and David *was* in the wilderness of Ziph in a wood.

16 And Jonathan Saul's son arose, and went to David into the wood, and strengthened his hand in God.

17 And he said unto him, Fear not: for the hand of Saul my father shall not find thee; and thou shalt be king over Israel, and I shall be next unto thee; and that also Saul my father knoweth.

18 And they two made a covenant before the LORD: and David abode in the wood, and Jonathan went to his house.

19 Then came up the Ziphites to Saul to Gibeah, saying, Doth not David hide himself with us in strong holds in the wood, in the hill of Hachilah, which *is* on the south of Jeshimon?

20 Now therefore, O king, come down according to all the desire of thy soul to come down; and our part *shall be* to deliver him into the king's hand.

21 And Saul said, Blessed *be* ye of the LORD; for ye have compassion on me.

22 Go, I pray you, prepare yet, and
know and see his place where his haunt
is, *and* who hath seen him there: for it
is told me *that* he dealeth very subtilly.
23 See therefore, and take knowledge
of all the lurking places where he
hideth himself, and come ye again to
me with the certainty, and I will go with
you: and it shall come to pass, if he be
in the land, that I will search him out
throughout all the thousands of Judah.
24 And they arose, and went to Ziph
before Saul: but David and his men
were in the wilderness of Maon, in the
plain on the south of Jeshimon.
25 Saul also and his men went to seek
him. And they told David: wherefore he
came down into a rock, and abode in
the wilderness of Maon. And when Saul
heard *that*, he pursued after David in
the wilderness of Maon.
26 And Saul went on this side of the
mountain, and David and his men on
that side of the mountain: and David
made haste to get away for fear of Saul;
for Saul and his men compassed David
and his men round about to take them.
27 But there came a messenger unto
Saul, saying, Haste thee, and come; for
the Philistines have invaded the land.
28 Wherefore Saul returned from pursuing after David, and went against the
Philistines: therefore they called that
place Selaham-mahlekoth.
29 And David went up from thence,
and dwelt in strong holds at En-gedi.

24 And it came to pass, when Saul
was returned from following the
Philistines, that it was told him, saying,
Behold, David *is* in the wilderness of
En-gedi.
2 Then Saul took three thousand chosen men out of all Israel, and went to
seek David and his men upon the rocks
of the wild goats.
3 And he came to the sheepcotes by
the way, where *was* a cave; and Saul
went in to cover his feet: and David and
his men remained in the sides of the
cave.
4 And the men of David said unto
him, Behold the day of which the LORD
said unto thee, Behold, I will deliver
thine enemy into thine hand, that thou
mayest do to him as it shall seem good
unto thee. Then David arose, and cut
off the skirt of Saul's robe privily.
5 And it came to pass afterward, that
David's heart smote him, because he
had cut off Saul's skirt.
6 And he said unto his men, The LORD
forbid that I should do this thing unto
my master, the LORD's anointed, to
stretch forth mine hand against him,
seeing he *is* the anointed of the LORD.
7 So David stayed his servants with
these words, and suffered them not to
rise against Saul. But Saul rose up out
of the cave, and went on *his* way.
8 David also arose afterward, and
went out of the cave, and cried after
Saul, saying, My lord the king. And
when Saul looked behind him, David
stooped with his face to the earth, and
bowed himself.
9 And David said to Saul, Wherefore
hearest thou men's words, saying,
Behold, David seeketh thy hurt?
10 Behold, this day thine eyes have
seen how that the LORD had delivered
thee to day into mine hand in the cave:
and *some* bade *me* kill thee: but *mine*
eye spared thee; and I said, I will not
put forth mine hand against my lord;
for he *is* the LORD's anointed.

11 Moreover, my father, see, yea, see
the skirt of thy robe in my hand: for in
that I cut off the skirt of thy robe, and
killed thee not, know thou and see that
there is neither evil nor transgression
in mine hand, and I have not sinned
against thee; yet thou huntest my soul
to take it.
12 The LORD judge between me and
thee, and the LORD avenge me of thee:
but mine hand shall not be upon thee.
13 As saith the proverb of the
ancients, Wickedness proceedeth from
the wicked: but mine hand shall not be
upon thee.
14 After whom is the king of Israel
come out? after whom dost thou pursue? after a dead dog, after a flea.
15 The LORD therefore be judge, and
judge between me and thee, and see,
and plead my cause, and deliver me out
of thine hand.
16 And it came to pass, when David
had made an end of speaking these
words unto Saul, that Saul said, *Is* this
thy voice, my son David? And Saul lifted up his voice, and wept.
17 And he said to David, Thou *art*
more righteous than I: for thou hast
rewarded me good, whereas I have
rewarded thee evil.
18 And thou hast shewed this day
how that thou hast dealt well with me:
forasmuch as when the LORD had delivered me into thine hand, thou killedst
me not.
19 For if a man find his enemy, will he
let him go well away? wherefore the
LORD reward thee good for that thou
hast done unto me this day.
20 And now, behold, I know well that
thou shalt surely be king, and that the
kingdom of Israel shall be established
in thine hand.
21 Swear now therefore unto me by
the LORD, that thou wilt not cut off my
seed after me, and that thou wilt not
destroy my name out of my father's
house.
22 And David sware unto Saul. And
Saul went home; but David and his
men gat them up unto the hold.

25 And Samuel died; and all the
Israelites were gathered together, and lamented him, and buried him
in his house at Ramah. And David
arose, and went down to the wilderness
of Paran.
2 And *there was* a man in Maon,
whose possessions *were* in Carmel; and
the man *was* very great, and he had
three thousand sheep, and a thousand
goats: and he was shearing his sheep in
Carmel.
3 Now the name of the man *was*
Nabal; and the name of his wife Abigail:
and *she was* a woman of good understanding, and of a beautiful countenance: but the man *was* churlish and
evil in his doings; and he *was* of the
house of Caleb.
4 And David heard in the wilderness
that Nabal did shear his sheep.
5 And David sent out ten young men,
and David said unto the young men,
Get you up to Carmel, and go to Nabal,
and greet him in my name:
6 And thus shall ye say to him that
liveth *in prosperity*, Peace *be* both to
thee, and peace *be* to thine house, and
peace *be* unto all that thou hast.
7 And now I have heard that thou
hast shearers: now thy shepherds which
were with us, we hurt them not, neither
was there ought missing unto them, all
the while they were in Carmel.
8 Ask thy young men, and they will
shew thee. Wherefore let the young

men find favour in thine eyes: for we come in a good day: give, I pray thee, whatsoever cometh to thine hand unto thy servants, and to thy son David.
9 And when David's young men came, they spake to Nabal according to all those words in the name of David, and ceased.
10 And Nabal answered David's servants, and said, Who *is* David? and who *is* the son of Jesse? there be many servants now a days that break away every man from his master.
11 Shall I then take my bread, and my water, and my flesh that I have killed for my shearers, and give *it* unto men, whom I know not whence they *be*?
12 So David's young men turned their way, and went again, and came and told him all those sayings.
13 And David said unto his men, Gird ye on every man his sword. And they girded on every man his sword; and David also girded on his sword: and there went up after David about four hundred men; and two hundred abode by the stuff.
14 But one of the young men told Abigail, Nabal's wife, saying, Behold, David sent messengers out of the wilderness to salute our master; and he railed on them.
15 But the men *were* very good unto us, and we were not hurt, neither missed we any thing, as long as we were conversant with them, when we were in the fields:
16 They were a wall unto us both by night and day, all the while we were with them keeping the sheep.
17 Now therefore know and consider what thou wilt do; for evil is determined against our master, and against all his household: for he *is such* a son of Belial, that *a man* cannot speak to him.
18 Then Abigail made haste, and took two hundred loaves, and two bottles of wine, and five sheep ready dressed, and five measures of parched *corn*, and an hundred clusters of raisins, and two hundred cakes of figs, and laid *them* on asses.
19 And she said unto her servants, Go on before me; behold, I come after you. But she told not her husband Nabal.
20 And it was *so, as* she rode on the ass, that she came down by the covert of the hill, and, behold, David and his men came down against her; and she met them.
21 Now David had said, Surely in vain have I kept all that this *fellow* hath in the wilderness, so that nothing was missed of all that *pertained* unto him: and he hath requited me evil for good.
22 So and more also do God unto the enemies of David, if I leave of all that *pertain* to him by the morning light any that pisseth against the wall.
23 And when Abigail saw David, she hasted, and lighted off the ass, and fell before David on her face, and bowed herself to the ground,
24 And fell at his feet, and said, Upon me, my lord, *upon* me *let this* iniquity *be*: and let thine handmaid, I pray thee, speak in thine audience, and hear the words of thine handmaid.
25 Let not my lord, I pray thee, regard this man of Belial, *even* Nabal: for as his name *is*, so *is* he; Nabal *is* his name, and folly *is* with him: but I thine handmaid saw not the young men of my lord, whom thou didst send.
26 Now therefore, my lord, *as* the LORD liveth, and *as* thy soul liveth, seeing the LORD hath withholden thee

from coming to *shed* blood, and from
avenging thyself with thine own hand,
now let thine enemies, and they that
seek evil to my lord, be as Nabal.
27 And now this blessing which thine
handmaid hath brought unto my lord,
let it even be given unto the young men
that follow my lord.
28 I pray thee, forgive the trespass of
thine handmaid: for the LORD will certainly make my lord a sure house;
because my lord fighteth the battles of
the LORD, and evil hath not been found
in thee *all* thy days.
29 Yet a man is risen to pursue thee,
and to seek thy soul: but the soul of my
lord shall be bound in the bundle of life
with the LORD thy God; and the souls of
thine enemies, them shall he sling out,
as out of the middle of a sling.
30 And it shall come to pass, when the
LORD shall have done to my lord according to all the good that he hath spoken
concerning thee, and shall have
appointed thee ruler over Israel;
31 That this shall be no grief unto
thee, nor offence of heart unto my lord,
either that thou hast shed blood causeless, or that my lord hath avenged himself: but when the LORD shall have
dealt well with my lord, then remember
thine handmaid.
32 And David said to Abigail, Blessed
be the LORD God of Israel, which sent
thee this day to meet me:
33 And blessed *be* thy advice, and
blessed *be* thou, which hast kept me
this day from coming to *shed* blood, and
from avenging myself with mine own
hand.
34 For in very deed, *as* the LORD God
of Israel liveth, which hath kept me
back from hurting thee, except thou
hadst hasted and come to meet me,
surely there had not been left unto
Nabal by the morning light any that
pisseth against the wall.
35 So David received of her hand *that*
which she had brought him, and said
unto her, Go up in peace to thine house;
see, I have hearkened to thy voice, and
have accepted thy person.
36 And Abigail came to Nabal; and,
behold, he held a feast in his house, like
the feast of a king; and Nabal's heart
was merry within him, for he *was* very
drunken: wherefore she told him nothing, less or more, until the morning
light.
37 But it came to pass in the morning,
when the wine was gone out of Nabal,
and his wife had told him these things,
that his heart died within him, and he
became *as* a stone.
38 And it came to pass about ten days
after, that the LORD smote Nabal, that
he died.
39 And when David heard that Nabal
was dead, he said, Blessed *be* the LORD,
that hath pleaded the cause of my
reproach from the hand of Nabal, and
hath kept his servant from evil: for the
LORD hath returned the wickedness of
Nabal upon his own head. And David
sent and communed with Abigail, to
take her to him to wife.
40 And when the servants of David
were come to Abigail to Carmel, they
spake unto her, saying, David sent us
unto thee, to take thee to him to wife.
41 And she arose, and bowed herself
on *her* face to the earth, and said,
Behold, *let* thine handmaid *be* a servant to wash the feet of the servants of
my lord.

42 And Abigail hasted, and arose, and
rode upon an ass, with five damsels of
hers that went after her; and she went
after the messengers of David, and
became his wife.
43 David also took Ahinoam of
Jezreel; and they were also both of
them his wives.
44 But Saul had given Michal his
daughter, David's wife, to Phalti the son
of Laish, which *was* of Gallim.

26 And the Ziphites came unto Saul
to Gibeah, saying, Doth not
David hide himself in the hill of
Hachilah, *which is* before Jeshimon?
2 Then Saul arose, and went down to
the wilderness of Ziph, having three
thousand chosen men of Israel with
him, to seek David in the wilderness of
Ziph.
3 And Saul pitched in the hill of
Hachilah, which *is* before Jeshimon, by
the way. But David abode in the wilderness, and he saw that Saul came after
him into the wilderness.
4 David therefore sent out spies, and
understood that Saul was come in very
deed.
5 And David arose, and came to the
place where Saul had pitched: and
David beheld the place where Saul lay,
and Abner the son of Ner, the captain
of his host: and Saul lay in the trench,
and the people pitched round about
him.
6 Then answered David and said to
Ahimelech the Hittite, and to Abishai
the son of Zeruiah, brother to Joab, saying, Who will go down with me to Saul
to the camp? And Abishai said, I will go
down with thee.
7 So David and Abishai came to the
people by night: and, behold, Saul lay
sleeping within the trench, and his
spear stuck in the ground at his bolster:
but Abner and the people lay round
about him.
8 Then said Abishai to David, God
hath delivered thine enemy into thine
hand this day: now therefore let me
smite him, I pray thee, with the spear
even to the earth at once, and I will not
smite him the second time.
9 And David said to Abishai, Destroy
him not: for who can stretch forth his
hand against the LORD's anointed, and
be guiltless?
10 David said furthermore, *As* the
LORD liveth, the LORD shall smite him;
or his day shall come to die; or he shall
descend into battle, and perish.
11 The LORD forbid that I should
stretch forth mine hand against the
LORD's anointed: but, I pray thee, take
thou now the spear that *is* at his bolster,
and the cruse of water, and let us go.
12 So David took the spear and the
cruse of water from Saul's bolster; and
they gat them away, and no man saw *it*,
nor knew *it*, neither awaked: for they
were all asleep; because a deep sleep
from the LORD was fallen upon them.
13 Then David went over to the other
side, and stood on the top of an hill afar
off; a great space *being* between them:
14 And David cried to the people, and
to Abner the son of Ner, saying,
Answerest thou not, Abner? Then
Abner answered and said, Who *art*
thou *that* criest to the king?
15 And David said to Abner, *Art* not
thou a *valiant* man? and who *is* like to
thee in Israel? wherefore then hast
thou not kept thy lord the king? for
there came one of the people in to
destroy the king thy lord.

16 This thing *is* not good that thou
hast done. *As* the LORD liveth, ye *are*
worthy to die, because ye have not kept
your master, the LORD's anointed. And
now see where the king's spear *is*, and
the cruse of water that *was* at his
bolster.
17 And Saul knew David's voice, and
said, *Is* this thy voice, my son David?
And David said, *It is* my voice, my lord,
O king.
18 And he said, Wherefore doth my
lord thus pursue after his servant? for
what have I done? or what evil *is* in
mine hand?
19 Now therefore, I pray thee, let my
lord the king hear the words of his servant. If the LORD have stirred thee up
against me, let him accept an offering:
but if *they be* the children of men,
cursed *be* they before the LORD; for
they have driven me out this day from
abiding in the inheritance of the LORD,
saying, Go, serve other gods.
20 Now therefore, let not my blood
fall to the earth before the face of the
LORD: for the king of Israel is come out
to seek a flea, as when one doth hunt a
partridge in the mountains.
21 Then said Saul, I have sinned:
return, my son David: for I will no more
do thee harm, because my soul was precious in thine eyes this day: behold, I
have played the fool, and have erred
exceedingly.
22 And David answered and said,
Behold the king's spear! and let one of
the young men come over and fetch it.
23 The LORD render to every man his
righteousness and his faithfulness: for
the LORD delivered thee into *my* hand
to day, but I would not stretch forth
mine hand against the LORD's anointed.
24 And, behold, as thy life was much
set by this day in mine eyes, so let my
life be much set by in the eyes of the
LORD, and let him deliver me out of all
tribulation.
25 Then Saul said to David, Blessed
be thou, my son David: thou shalt both
do great *things*, and also shalt still prevail. So David went on his way, and Saul
returned to his place.

27 And David said in his heart, I
shall now perish one day by the
hand of Saul: *there is* nothing better for
me than that I should speedily escape
into the land of the Philistines; and
Saul shall despair of me, to seek me
any more in any coast of Israel: so shall
I escape out of his hand.
2 And David arose, and he passed
over with the six hundred men that
were with him unto Achish, the son of
Maoch, king of Gath.
3 And David dwelt with Achish at
Gath, he and his men, every man with
his household, *even* David with his two
wives, Ahinoam the Jezreelitess, and
Abigail the Carmelitess, Nabal's wife.
4 And it was told Saul that David was
fled to Gath: and he sought no more
again for him.
5 And David said unto Achish, If I
have now found grace in thine eyes, let
them give me a place in some town in
the country, that I may dwell there: for
why should thy servant dwell in the
royal city with thee?
6 Then Achish gave him Ziklag that
day: wherefore Ziklag pertaineth unto
the kings of Judah unto this day.
7 And the time that David dwelt in
the country of the Philistines was a full
year and four months.

8 And David and his men went up, and invaded the Geshurites, and the Gezrites, and the Amalekites: for those *nations were* of old the inhabitants of the land, as thou goest to Shur, even unto the land of Egypt.

9 And David smote the land, and left neither man nor woman alive, and took away the sheep, and the oxen, and the asses, and the camels, and the apparel, and returned, and came to Achish.

10 And Achish said, Whither have ye made a road to day? And David said, Against the south of Judah, and against the south of the Jerahmeelites, and against the south of the Kenites.

11 And David saved neither man nor woman alive, to bring *tidings* to Gath, saying, Lest they should tell on us, saying, So did David, and so *will be* his manner all the while he dwelleth in the country of the Philistines.

12 And Achish believed David, saying, He hath made his people Israel utterly to abhor him; therefore he shall be my servant for ever.

28 And it came to pass in those days, that the Philistines gathered their armies together for warfare, to fight with Israel. And Achish said unto David, Know thou assuredly, that thou shalt go out with me to battle, thou and thy men.

2 And David said to Achish, Surely thou shalt know what thy servant can do. And Achish said to David, Therefore will I make thee keeper of mine head for ever.

3 Now Samuel was dead, and all Israel had lamented him, and buried him in Ramah, even in his own city. And Saul had put away those that had familiar spirits, and the wizards, out of the land.

4 And the Philistines gathered themselves together, and came and pitched in Shunem: and Saul gathered all Israel together, and they pitched in Gilboa.

5 And when Saul saw the host of the Philistines, he was afraid, and his heart greatly trembled.

6 And when Saul enquired of the LORD, the LORD answered him not, neither by dreams, nor by Urim, nor by prophets.

7 Then said Saul unto his servants, Seek me a woman that hath a familiar spirit, that I may go to her, and enquire of her. And his servants said to him, Behold, *there is* a woman that hath a familiar spirit at En-dor.

8 And Saul disguised himself, and put on other raiment, and he went, and two men with him, and they came to the woman by night: and he said, I pray thee, divine unto me by the familiar spirit, and bring me *him* up, whom I shall name unto thee.

9 And the woman said unto him, Behold, thou knowest what Saul hath done, how he hath cut off those that have familiar spirits, and the wizards, out of the land: wherefore then layest thou a snare for my life, to cause me to die?

10 And Saul sware to her by the LORD, saying, *As* the LORD liveth, there shall no punishment happen to thee for this thing.

11 Then said the woman, Whom shall I bring up unto thee? And he said, Bring me up Samuel.

12 And when the woman saw Samuel, she cried with a loud voice: and the woman spake to Saul, saying, Why hast thou deceived me? for thou *art* Saul.

13 And the king said unto her, Be not afraid: for what sawest thou? And the woman said unto Saul, I saw gods ascending out of the earth.

14 And he said unto her, What form *is* he of? And she said, An old man cometh up; and he *is* covered with a mantle. And Saul perceived that it *was* Samuel, and he stooped with *his* face to the ground, and bowed himself.

15 And Samuel said to Saul, Why hast thou disquieted me, to bring me up? And Saul answered, I am sore distressed; for the Philistines make war against me, and God is departed from me, and answereth me no more, neither by prophets, nor by dreams: therefore I have called thee, that thou mayest make known unto me what I shall do.

16 Then said Samuel, Wherefore then dost thou ask of me, seeing the LORD is departed from thee, and is become thine enemy?

17 And the LORD hath done to him, as he spake by me: for the LORD hath rent the kingdom out of thine hand, and given it to thy neighbour, *even* to David:

18 Because thou obeyedst not the voice of the LORD, nor executedst his fierce wrath upon Amalek, therefore hath the LORD done this thing unto thee this day.

19 Moreover the LORD will also deliver Israel with thee into the hand of the Philistines: and to morrow *shalt* thou and thy sons *be* with me: the LORD also shall deliver the host of Israel into the hand of the Philistines.

20 Then Saul fell straightway all along on the earth, and was sore afraid, because of the words of Samuel: and there was no strength in him; for he had eaten no bread all the day, nor all the night.

21 And the woman came unto Saul, and saw that he was sore troubled, and said unto him, Behold, thine handmaid hath obeyed thy voice, and I have put my life in my hand, and have hearkened unto thy words which thou spakest unto me.

22 Now therefore, I pray thee, hearken thou also unto the voice of thine handmaid, and let me set a morsel of bread before thee; and eat, that thou mayest have strength, when thou goest on thy way.

23 But he refused, and said, I will not eat. But his servants, together with the woman, compelled him; and he hearkened unto their voice. So he arose from the earth, and sat upon the bed.

24 And the woman had a fat calf in the house; and she hasted, and killed it, and took flour, and kneaded *it*, and did bake unleavened bread thereof:

25 And she brought *it* before Saul, and before his servants; and they did eat. Then they rose up, and went away that night.

29 Now the Philistines gathered together all their armies to Aphek: and the Israelites pitched by a fountain which *is* in Jezreel.

2 And the lords of the Philistines passed on by hundreds, and by thousands: but David and his men passed on in the rereward with Achish.

3 Then said the princes of the Philistines, What *do* these Hebrews *here*? And Achish said unto the princes of the Philistines, *Is* not this David, the servant of Saul the king of Israel, which hath been with me these days, or these years, and I have found no fault in him since he fell *unto me* unto this day?

4 And the princes of the Philistines were wroth with him; and the princes

of the Philistines said unto him, Make
this fellow return, that he may go again
to his place which thou hast appointed
him, and let him not go down with us to
battle, lest in the battle he be an adversary to us: for wherewith should he
reconcile himself unto his master?
should it not *be* with the heads of these
men?
5 *Is* not this David, of whom they sang
one to another in dances, saying, Saul
slew his thousands, and David his ten
thousands?
6 Then Achish called David, and said
unto him, Surely, *as* the LORD liveth,
thou hast been upright, and thy going
out and thy coming in with me in the
host *is* good in my sight: for I have not
found evil in thee since the day of thy
coming unto me unto this day: nevertheless the lords favour thee not.
7 Wherefore now return, and go in
peace, that thou displease not the lords
of the Philistines.
8 And David said unto Achish, But
what have I done? and what hast thou
found in thy servant so long as I have
been with thee unto this day, that I may
not go fight against the enemies of my
lord the king?
9 And Achish answered and said to
David, I know that thou *art* good in my
sight, as an angel of God: notwithstanding the princes of the Philistines have
said, He shall not go up with us to the
battle.
10 Wherefore now rise up early in the
morning with thy master's servants that
are come with thee: and as soon as ye
be up early in the morning, and have
light, depart.
11 So David and his men rose up early
to depart in the morning, to return into
the land of the Philistines. And the
Philistines went up to Jezreel.

30 And it came to pass, when David
and his men were come to Ziklag
on the third day, that the Amalekites
had invaded the south, and Ziklag, and
smitten Ziklag, and burned it with fire;
2 And had taken the women captives,
that *were* therein: they slew not any,
either great or small, but carried *them*
away, and went on their way.
3 So David and his men came to the
city, and, behold, *it was* burned with
fire; and their wives, and their sons,
and their daughters, were taken captives.
4 Then David and the people that
were with him lifted up their voice and
wept, until they had no more power to
weep.
5 And David's two wives were taken
captives, Ahinoam the Jezreelitess, and
Abigail the wife of Nabal the Carmelite.
6 And David was greatly distressed;
for the people spake of stoning him,
because the soul of all the people was
grieved, every man for his sons and for
his daughters: but David encouraged
himself in the LORD his God.
7 And David said to Abiathar the
priest, Ahimelech's son, I pray thee,
bring me hither the ephod. And
Abiathar brought thither the ephod to
David.
8 And David enquired at the LORD,
saying, Shall I pursue after this troop?
shall I overtake them? And he answered
him, Pursue: for thou shalt surely overtake *them*, and without fail recover *all*.
9 So David went, he and the six hundred men that *were* with him, and came
to the brook Besor, where those that
were left behind stayed.

10 But David pursued, he and four
hundred men: for two hundred abode
behind, which were so faint that they
could not go over the brook Besor.
11 And they found an Egyptian in the
field, and brought him to David, and
gave him bread, and he did eat; and
they made him drink water;
12 And they gave him a piece of a
cake of figs, and two clusters of raisins:
and when he had eaten, his spirit came
again to him: for he had eaten no
bread, nor drunk *any* water, three days
and three nights.
13 And David said unto him, To whom
belongest thou? and whence *art* thou?
And he said, I *am* a young man of
Egypt, servant to an Amalekite; and my
master left me, because three days
agone I fell sick.
14 We made an invasion *upon* the
south of the Cherethites, and upon *the
coast* which *belongeth* to Judah, and
upon the south of Caleb; and we burned
Ziklag with fire.
15 And David said to him, Canst thou
bring me down to this company? And
he said, Swear unto me by God, that
thou wilt neither kill me, nor deliver
me into the hands of my master, and I
will bring thee down to this company.
16 And when he had brought him
down, behold, *they were* spread abroad
upon all the earth, eating and drinking,
and dancing, because of all the great
spoil that they had taken out of the
land of the Philistines, and out of the
land of Judah.
17 And David smote them from the
twilight even unto the evening of the
next day: and there escaped not a man
of them, save four hundred young men,
which rode upon camels, and fled.
18 And David recovered all that the
Amalekites had carried away: and
David rescued his two wives.
19 And there was nothing lacking to
them, neither small nor great, neither
sons nor daughters, neither spoil, nor
any *thing* that they had taken to them:
David recovered all.
20 And David took all the flocks and
the herds, *which* they drave before
those *other* cattle, and said, This *is*
David's spoil.
21 And David came to the two hundred men, which were so faint that they
could not follow David, whom they had
made also to abide at the brook Besor:
and they went forth to meet David, and
to meet the people that *were* with him:
and when David came near to the people, he saluted them.
22 Then answered all the wicked men
and *men* of Belial, of those that went
with David, and said, Because they
went not with us, we will not give them
ought of the spoil that we have recovered, save to every man his wife and his
children, that they may lead *them* away,
and depart.
23 Then said David, Ye shall not do so,
my brethren, with that which the LORD
hath given us, who hath preserved us,
and delivered the company that came
against us into our hand.
24 For who will hearken unto you in
this matter? but as his part *is* that
goeth down to the battle, so *shall* his
part *be* that tarrieth by the stuff: they
shall part alike.
25 And it was *so* from that day forward, that he made it a statute and an
ordinance for Israel unto this day.
26 And when David came to Ziklag,
he sent of the spoil unto the elders of
Judah, *even* to his friends, saying,

Behold a present for you of the spoil of
the enemies of the LORD;
27 To *them* which *were* in Beth-el, and
to *them* which *were* in south Ramoth,
and to *them* which *were* in Jattir,
28 And to *them* which *were* in Aroer,
and to *them* which *were* in Siphmoth,
and to *them* which *were* in Eshtemoa,
29 And to *them* which *were* in Rachal,
and to *them* which *were* in the cities of
the Jerahmeelites, and to *them* which
were in the cities of the Kenites,
30 And to *them* which *were* in
Hormah, and to *them* which *were* in
Chorashan, and to *them* which *were* in
Athach,
31 And to *them* which *were* in
Hebron, and to all the places where
David himself and his men were wont
to haunt.

31 Now the Philistines fought
against Israel: and the men of
Israel fled from before the Philistines,
and fell down slain in mount Gilboa.
2 And the Philistines followed hard
upon Saul and upon his sons; and the
Philistines slew Jonathan, and Abinadab, and Malchishua, Saul's sons.
3 And the battle went sore against
Saul, and the archers hit him; and he
was sore wounded of the archers.
4 Then said Saul unto his armourbearer, Draw thy sword, and thrust me
through therewith; lest these uncircumcised come and thrust me through, and
abuse me. But his armourbearer would
not; for he was sore afraid. Therefore
Saul took a sword, and fell upon it.
5 And when his armourbearer saw
that Saul was dead, he fell likewise
upon his sword, and died with him.
6 So Saul died, and his three sons, and
his armourbearer, and all his men, that
same day together.
7 And when the men of Israel that
were on the other side of the valley, and
they that *were* on the other side Jordan,
saw that the men of Israel fled, and that
Saul and his sons were dead, they forsook the cities, and fled; and the
Philistines came and dwelt in them.
8 And it came to pass on the morrow,
when the Philistines came to strip the
slain, that they found Saul and his
three sons fallen in mount Gilboa.
9 And they cut off his head, and
stripped off his armour, and sent into
the land of the Philistines round about,
to publish *it in* the house of their idols,
and among the people.
10 And they put his armour in the
house of Ashtaroth: and they fastened
his body to the wall of Beth-shan.
11 And when the inhabitants of
Jabesh-gilead heard of that which the
Philistines had done to Saul;
12 All the valiant men arose, and
went all night, and took the body of
Saul and the bodies of his sons from the
wall of Beth-shan, and came to Jabesh,
and burnt them there.
13 And they took their bones, and
buried *them* under a tree at Jabesh,
and fasted seven days.

THE SECOND BOOK OF
SAMUEL

1 Now it came to pass after the death
of Saul, when David was returned
from the slaughter of the Amalekites,
and David had abode two days in
Ziklag;
2 It came even to pass on the third
day, that, behold, a man came out of the
camp from Saul with his clothes rent,
and earth upon his head: and *so* it was,
when he came to David, that he fell to
the earth, and did obeisance.
3 And David said unto him, From
whence comest thou? And he said unto
him, Out of the camp of Israel am I
escaped.
4 And David said unto him, How went
the matter? I pray thee, tell me. And he
answered, That the people are fled
from the battle, and many of the people
also are fallen and dead; and Saul and
Jonathan his son are dead also.
5 And David said unto the young man
that told him, How knowest thou that
Saul and Jonathan his son be dead?
6 And the young man that told him
said, As I happened by chance upon
mount Gilboa, behold, Saul leaned
upon his spear; and, lo, the chariots and
horsemen followed hard after him.
7 And when he looked behind him, he
saw me, and called unto me. And I
answered, Here *am* I.
8 And he said unto me, Who *art* thou?
And I answered him, I *am* an Amalekite.
9 He said unto me again, Stand, I pray
thee, upon me, and slay me: for anguish
is come upon me, because my life *is* yet
whole in me.
10 So I stood upon him, and slew him,
because I was sure that he could not
live after that he was fallen: and I took
the crown that *was* upon his head, and
the bracelet that *was* on his arm, and
have brought them hither unto my lord.
11 Then David took hold on his
clothes, and rent them; and likewise all
the men that *were* with him:
12 And they mourned, and wept, and
fasted until even, for Saul, and for
Jonathan his son, and for the people of
the LORD, and for the house of Israel;
because they were fallen by the sword.
13 And David said unto the young
man that told him, Whence *art* thou?
And he answered, I *am* the son of a
stranger, an Amalekite.
14 And David said unto him, How
wast thou not afraid to stretch forth
thine hand to destroy the LORD's
anointed?
15 And David called one of the young
men, and said, Go near, *and* fall upon
him. And he smote him that he died.
16 And David said unto him, Thy
blood *be* upon thy head; for thy mouth
hath testified against thee, saying, I
have slain the LORD's anointed.
17 And David lamented with this lamentation over Saul and over Jonathan
his son:
18 (Also he bade them teach the children of Judah *the use of* the bow:
behold, *it is* written in the book of
Jasher.)
19 The beauty of Israel is slain upon
thy high places: how are the mighty
fallen!
20 Tell *it* not in Gath, publish *it* not in
the streets of Askelon; lest the
daughters of the Philistines rejoice,

lest the daughters of the uncircumcised triumph.

21 Ye mountains of Gilboa, *let there be* no dew, neither *let there be* rain, upon you, nor fields of offerings: for there the shield of the mighty is vilely cast away, the shield of Saul, *as though he had* not *been* anointed with oil.

22 From the blood of the slain, from the fat of the mighty, the bow of Jonathan turned not back, and the sword of Saul returned not empty.

23 Saul and Jonathan *were* lovely and pleasant in their lives, and in their death they were not divided: they were swifter than eagles, they were stronger than lions.

24 Ye daughters of Israel, weep over Saul, who clothed you in scarlet, with *other* delights, who put on ornaments of gold upon your apparel.

25 How are the mighty fallen in the midst of the battle! O Jonathan, *thou wast* slain in thine high places.

26 I am distressed for thee, my brother Jonathan: very pleasant hast thou been unto me: thy love to me was wonderful, passing the love of women.

27 How are the mighty fallen, and the weapons of war perished!

2 And it came to pass after this, that David enquired of the LORD, saying, Shall I go up into any of the cities of Judah? And the LORD said unto him, Go up. And David said, Whither shall I go up? And he said, Unto Hebron.

2 So David went up thither, and his two wives also, Ahinoam the Jezreelitess, and Abigail Nabal's wife the Carmelite.

3 And his men that *were* with him did David bring up, every man with his household: and they dwelt in the cities of Hebron.

4 And the men of Judah came, and there they anointed David king over the house of Judah. And they told David, saying, *That* the men of Jabesh-gilead *were they* that buried Saul.

5 And David sent messengers unto the men of Jabesh-gilead, and said unto them, Blessed *be* ye of the LORD, that ye have shewed this kindness unto your lord, *even* unto Saul, and have buried him.

6 And now the LORD shew kindness and truth unto you: and I also will requite you this kindness, because ye have done this thing.

7 Therefore now let your hands be strengthened, and be ye valiant: for your master Saul is dead, and also the house of Judah have anointed me king over them.

8 But Abner the son of Ner, captain of Saul's host, took Ish-bosheth the son of Saul, and brought him over to Mahanaim;

9 And made him king over Gilead, and over the Ashurites, and over Jezreel, and over Ephraim, and over Benjamin, and over all Israel.

10 Ish-bosheth Saul's son *was* forty years old when he began to reign over Israel, and reigned two years. But the house of Judah followed David.

11 And the time that David was king in Hebron over the house of Judah was seven years and six months.

12 And Abner the son of Ner, and the servants of Ish-bosheth the son of Saul, went out from Mahanaim to Gibeon.

13 And Joab the son of Zeruiah, and the servants of David, went out, and met together by the pool of Gibeon: and they sat down, the one on the one side of the pool, and the other on the other side of the pool.

14 And Abner said to Joab, Let the young men now arise, and play before us. And Joab said, Let them arise.

15 Then there arose and went over by number twelve of Benjamin, which *pertained* to Ish-bosheth the son of Saul, and twelve of the servants of David.

16 And they caught every one his fellow by the head, and *thrust* his sword in his fellow's side; so they fell down together: wherefore that place was called Helkath-hazzurim, which *is* in Gibeon.

17 And there was a very sore battle that day; and Abner was beaten, and the men of Israel, before the servants of David.

18 And there were three sons of Zeruiah there, Joab, and Abishai, and Asahel: and Asahel *was as* light of foot as a wild roe.

19 And Asahel pursued after Abner; and in going he turned not to the right hand nor to the left from following Abner.

20 Then Abner looked behind him, and said, *Art* thou Asahel? And he answered, I *am*.

21 And Abner said to him, Turn thee aside to thy right hand or to thy left, and lay thee hold on one of the young men, and take thee his armour. But Asahel would not turn aside from following of him.

22 And Abner said again to Asahel, Turn thee aside from following me: wherefore should I smite thee to the ground? how then should I hold up my face to Joab thy brother?

23 Howbeit he refused to turn aside: wherefore Abner with the hinder end of the spear smote him under the fifth *rib*, that the spear came out behind him; and he fell down there, and died in the same place: and it came to pass, *that* as many as came to the place where Asahel fell down and died stood still.

24 Joab also and Abishai pursued after Abner: and the sun went down when they were come to the hill of Ammah, that *lieth* before Giah by the way of the wilderness of Gibeon.

25 And the children of Benjamin gathered themselves together after Abner, and became one troop, and stood on the top of an hill.

26 Then Abner called to Joab, and said, Shall the sword devour for ever? knowest thou not that it will be bitterness in the latter end? how long shall it be then, ere thou bid the people return from following their brethren?

27 And Joab said, *As* God liveth, unless thou hadst spoken, surely then in the morning the people had gone up every one from following his brother.

28 So Joab blew a trumpet, and all the people stood still, and pursued after Israel no more, neither fought they any more.

29 And Abner and his men walked all that night through the plain, and passed over Jordan, and went through all Bithron, and they came to Mahanaim.

30 And Joab returned from following Abner: and when he had gathered all the people together, there lacked of David's servants nineteen men and Asahel.

31 But the servants of David had smitten of Benjamin, and of Abner's men, *so that* three hundred and threescore men died.

32 And they took up Asahel, and buried him in the sepulchre of his father, which *was in* Beth-lehem. And Joab and his men went all night, and they came to Hebron at break of day.

3 Now there was long war between the house of Saul and the house of David: but David waxed stronger and stronger, and the house of Saul waxed weaker and weaker.

2 And unto David were sons born in Hebron: and his firstborn was Amnon, of Ahinoam the Jezreelitess;

3 And his second, Chileab, of Abigail the wife of Nabal the Carmelite; and the third, Absalom the son of Maacah the daughter of Talmai king of Geshur;

4 And the fourth, Adonijah the son of Haggith; and the fifth, Shephatiah the son of Abital;

5 And the sixth, Ithream, by Eglah David's wife. These were born to David in Hebron.

6 And it came to pass, while there was war between the house of Saul and the house of David, that Abner made himself strong for the house of Saul.

7 And Saul had a concubine, whose name *was* Rizpah, the daughter of Aiah: and *Ish-bosheth* said to Abner, Wherefore hast thou gone in unto my father's concubine?

8 Then was Abner very wroth for the words of Ish-bosheth, and said, *Am* I a dog's head, which against Judah do shew kindness this day unto the house of Saul thy father, to his brethren, and to his friends, and have not delivered thee into the hand of David, that thou chargest me to day with a fault concerning this woman?

9 So do God to Abner, and more also, except, as the LORD hath sworn to David, even so I do to him;

10 To translate the kingdom from the house of Saul, and to set up the throne of David over Israel and over Judah, from Dan even to Beer-sheba.

11 And he could not answer Abner a word again, because he feared him.

12 And Abner sent messengers to David on his behalf, saying, Whose *is* the land? saying *also*, Make thy league with me, and, behold, my hand *shall be* with thee, to bring about all Israel unto thee.

13 And he said, Well; I will make a league with thee: but one thing I require of thee, that is, Thou shalt not see my face, except thou first bring Michal Saul's daughter, when thou comest to see my face.

14 And David sent messengers to Ish-bosheth Saul's son, saying, Deliver *me* my wife Michal, which I espoused to me for an hundred foreskins of the Philistines.

15 And Ish-bosheth sent, and took her from *her* husband, *even* from Phaltiel the son of Laish.

16 And her husband went with her along weeping behind her to Bahurim. Then said Abner unto him, Go, return. And he returned.

17 And Abner had communication with the elders of Israel, saying, Ye sought for David in times past *to be* king over you:

18 Now then do *it*: for the LORD hath spoken of David, saying, By the hand of my servant David I will save my people Israel out of the hand of the Philistines, and out of the hand of all their enemies.

19 And Abner also spake in the ears of Benjamin: and Abner went also to speak in the ears of David in Hebron all that seemed good to Israel, and that

seemed good to the whole house of
Benjamin.
20 So Abner came to David to Hebron,
and twenty men with him. And David
made Abner and the men that *were*
with him a feast.
21 And Abner said unto David, I will
arise and go, and will gather all Israel
unto my lord the king, that they may
make a league with thee, and that thou
mayest reign over all that thine heart
desireth. And David sent Abner away;
and he went in peace.
22 And, behold, the servants of David
and Joab came from *pursuing* a troop,
and brought in a great spoil with them:
but Abner *was* not with David in
Hebron; for he had sent him away, and
he was gone in peace.
23 When Joab and all the host that
was with him were come, they told
Joab, saying, Abner the son of Ner
came to the king, and he hath sent him
away, and he is gone in peace.
24 Then Joab came to the king, and
said, What hast thou done? behold,
Abner came unto thee; why *is* it *that*
thou hast sent him away, and he is quite
gone?
25 Thou knowest Abner the son of
Ner, that he came to deceive thee, and
to know thy going out and thy coming
in, and to know all that thou doest.
26 And when Joab was come out from
David, he sent messengers after Abner,
which brought him again from the well
of Sirah: but David knew *it* not.
27 And when Abner was returned to
Hebron, Joab took him aside in the
gate to speak with him quietly, and
smote him there under the fifth *rib*,
that he died, for the blood of Asahel his
brother.
28 And afterward when David heard
it, he said, I and my kingdom *are* guiltless before the LORD for ever from the
blood of Abner the son of Ner:
29 Let it rest on the head of Joab, and
on all his father's house; and let there
not fail from the house of Joab one that
hath an issue, or that is a leper, or that
leaneth on a staff, or that falleth on the
sword, or that lacketh bread.
30 So Joab and Abishai his brother
slew Abner, because he had slain their
brother Asahel at Gibeon in the battle.
31 And David said to Joab, and to all
the people that *were* with him, Rend
your clothes, and gird you with sackcloth, and mourn before Abner. And
king David *himself* followed the bier.
32 And they buried Abner in Hebron:
and the king lifted up his voice, and
wept at the grave of Abner; and all the
people wept.
33 And the king lamented over Abner,
and said, Died Abner as a fool dieth?
34 Thy hands *were* not bound, nor thy
feet put into fetters: as a man falleth
before wicked men, *so* fellest thou. And
all the people wept again over him.
35 And when all the people came to
cause David to eat meat while it was
yet day, David sware, saying, So do God
to me, and more also, if I taste bread, or
ought else, till the sun be down.
36 And all the people took notice *of*
it, and it pleased them: as whatsoever
the king did pleased all the people.
37 For all the people and all Israel
understood that day that it was not of
the king to slay Abner the son of Ner.
38 And the king said unto his servants, Know ye not that there is a
prince and a great man fallen this day
in Israel?

39 And I *am* this day weak, though
anointed king; and these men the sons
of Zeruiah *be* too hard for me: the LORD
shall reward the doer of evil according
to his wickedness.

4 And when Saul's son heard that
Abner was dead in Hebron, his
hands were feeble, and all the Israelites
were troubled.
2 And Saul's son had two men *that*
were captains of bands: the name of the
one *was* Baanah, and the name of the
other Rechab, the sons of Rimmon a
Beerothite, of the children of Benjamin:
(for Beeroth also was reckoned to
Benjamin:
3 And the Beerothites fled to Gittaim,
and were sojourners there until this
day.)
4 And Jonathan, Saul's son, had a son
that was lame of *his* feet. He was five
years old when the tidings came of Saul
and Jonathan out of Jezreel, and his
nurse took him up, and fled: and it
came to pass, as she made haste to flee,
that he fell, and became lame. And his
name *was* Mephibosheth.
5 And the sons of Rimmon the
Beerothite, Rechab and Baanah, went,
and came about the heat of the day to
the house of Ish-bosheth, who lay on a
bed at noon.
6 And they came thither into the
midst of the house, *as though* they
would have fetched wheat; and they
smote him under the fifth *rib*: and
Rechab and Baanah his brother
escaped.
7 For when they came into the house,
he lay on his bed in his bedchamber,
and they smote him, and slew him, and
beheaded him, and took his head, and
gat them away through the plain all
night.
8 And they brought the head of Ish-
bosheth unto David to Hebron, and
said to the king, Behold the head of
Ish-bosheth the son of Saul thine
enemy, which sought thy life; and the
LORD hath avenged my lord the king
this day of Saul, and of his seed.
9 And David answered Rechab and
Baanah his brother, the sons of Rimmon
the Beerothite, and said unto them, *As*
the LORD liveth, who hath redeemed
my soul out of all adversity,
10 When one told me, saying, Behold,
Saul is dead, thinking to have brought
good tidings, I took hold of him, and
slew him in Ziklag, who *thought* that I
would have given him a reward for his
tidings:
11 How much more, when wicked
men have slain a righteous person in
his own house upon his bed? shall I not
therefore now require his blood of your
hand, and take you away from the
earth?
12 And David commanded his young
men, and they slew them, and cut off
their hands and their feet, and hanged
them up over the pool in Hebron. But
they took the head of Ish-bosheth, and
buried *it* in the sepulchre of Abner in
Hebron.

5 Then came all the tribes of Israel to
David unto Hebron, and spake,
saying, Behold, we *are* thy bone and thy
flesh.
2 Also in time past, when Saul was
king over us, thou wast he that leddest
out and broughtest in Israel: and the
LORD said to thee, Thou shalt feed my
people Israel, and thou shalt be a captain over Israel.
3 So all the elders of Israel came to
the king to Hebron; and king David
made a league with them in Hebron

before the LORD: and they anointed David king over Israel.

4 David *was* thirty years old when he began to reign, *and* he reigned forty years.

5 In Hebron he reigned over Judah seven years and six months: and in Jerusalem he reigned thirty and three years over all Israel and Judah.

6 And the king and his men went to Jerusalem unto the Jebusites, the inhabitants of the land: which spake unto David, saying, Except thou take away the blind and the lame, thou shalt not come in hither: thinking, David cannot come in hither.

7 Nevertheless David took the strong hold of Zion: the same *is* the city of David.

8 And David said on that day, Whosoever getteth up to the gutter, and smiteth the Jebusites, and the lame and the blind, *that are* hated of David's soul, *he shall be chief and captain*. Wherefore they said, The blind and the lame shall not come into the house.

9 So David dwelt in the fort, and called it the city of David. And David built round about from Millo and inward.

10 And David went on, and grew great, and the LORD God of hosts *was* with him.

11 And Hiram king of Tyre sent messengers to David, and cedar trees, and carpenters, and masons: and they built David an house.

12 And David perceived that the LORD had established him king over Israel, and that he had exalted his kingdom for his people Israel's sake.

13 And David took *him* more concubines and wives out of Jerusalem, after he was come from Hebron: and there were yet sons and daughters born to David.

14 And these *be* the names of those that were born unto him in Jerusalem; Shammua, and Shobab, and Nathan, and Solomon,

15 Ibhar also, and Elishua, and Nepheg, and Japhia,

16 And Elishama, and Eliada, and Eliphalet.

17 But when the Philistines heard that they had anointed David king over Israel, all the Philistines came up to seek David; and David heard *of it*, and went down to the hold.

18 The Philistines also came and spread themselves in the valley of Rephaim.

19 And David enquired of the LORD, saying, Shall I go up to the Philistines? wilt thou deliver them into mine hand? And the LORD said unto David, Go up: for I will doubtless deliver the Philistines into thine hand.

20 And David came to Baal-perazim, and David smote them there, and said, The LORD hath broken forth upon mine enemies before me, as the breach of waters. Therefore he called the name of that place Baal-perazim.

21 And there they left their images, and David and his men burned them.

22 And the Philistines came up yet again, and spread themselves in the valley of Rephaim.

23 And when David enquired of the LORD, he said, Thou shalt not go up; *but* fetch a compass behind them, and come upon them over against the mulberry trees.

24 And let it be, when thou hearest the sound of a going in the tops of the mulberry trees, that then thou shalt

bestir thyself: for then shall the LORD
go out before thee, to smite the host of
the Philistines.
25 And David did so, as the LORD had
commanded him; and smote the
Philistines from Geba until thou come
to Gazer.

6 Again, David gathered together all
the chosen *men* of Israel, thirty
thousand.
2 And David arose, and went with all
the people that *were* with him from
Baale of Judah, to bring up from thence
the ark of God, whose name is called by
the name of the LORD of hosts that
dwelleth *between* the cherubims.
3 And they set the ark of God upon a
new cart, and brought it out of the
house of Abinadab that *was* in Gibeah:
and Uzzah and Ahio, the sons of
Abinadab, drave the new cart.
4 And they brought it out of the house
of Abinadab which *was* at Gibeah,
accompanying the ark of God: and Ahio
went before the ark.
5 And David and all the house of
Israel played before the LORD on all
manner of *instruments made of* fir
wood, even on harps, and on psalteries,
and on timbrels, and on cornets, and on
cymbals.
6 And when they came to Nachon's
threshingfloor, Uzzah put forth *his
hand* to the ark of God, and took hold
of it; for the oxen shook *it*.
7 And the anger of the LORD was kindled against Uzzah; and God smote him
there for *his* error; and there he died by
the ark of God.
8 And David was displeased, because
the LORD had made a breach upon
Uzzah: and he called the name of the
place Perez-uzzah to this day.
9 And David was afraid of the LORD
that day, and said, How shall the ark of
the LORD come to me?
10 So David would not remove the ark
of the LORD unto him into the city of
David: but David carried it aside into
the house of Obed-edom the Gittite.
11 And the ark of the LORD continued
in the house of Obed-edom the Gittite
three months: and the LORD blessed
Obed-edom, and all his household.
12 And it was told king David, saying,
The LORD hath blessed the house of
Obed-edom, and all that *pertaineth*
unto him, because of the ark of God. So
David went and brought up the ark of
God from the house of Obed-edom into
the city of David with gladness.
13 And it was *so*, that when they that
bare the ark of the LORD had gone six
paces, he sacrificed oxen and fatlings.
14 And David danced before the LORD
with all *his* might; and David *was* girded with a linen ephod.
15 So David and all the house of
Israel brought up the ark of the LORD
with shouting, and with the sound of
the trumpet.
16 And as the ark of the LORD came
into the city of David, Michal Saul's
daughter looked through a window, and
saw king David leaping and dancing
before the LORD; and she despised him
in her heart.
17 And they brought in the ark of the
LORD, and set it in his place, in the
midst of the tabernacle that David had
pitched for it: and David offered burnt
offerings and peace offerings before
the LORD.
18 And as soon as David had made an
end of offering burnt offerings and
peace offerings, he blessed the people
in the name of the LORD of hosts.

19 And he dealt among all the people,
even among the whole multitude of
Israel, as well to the women as men, to
every one a cake of bread, and a good
piece *of flesh*, and a flagon *of wine*. So
all the people departed every one to his
house.
20 Then David returned to bless his
household. And Michal the daughter of
Saul came out to meet David, and said,
How glorious was the king of Israel to
day, who uncovered himself to day in
the eyes of the handmaids of his servants, as one of the vain fellows shame-
lessly uncovereth himself!
21 And David said unto Michal, *It was*
before the LORD, which chose me before
thy father, and before all his house, to
appoint me ruler over the people of the
LORD, over Israel: therefore will I play
before the LORD.
22 And I will yet be more vile than
thus, and will be base in mine own
sight: and of the maidservants which
thou hast spoken of, of them shall I be
had in honour.
23 Therefore Michal the daughter of
Saul had no child unto the day of her
death.

7

And it came to pass, when the king
sat in his house, and the LORD had
given him rest round about from all his
enemies;
2 That the king said unto Nathan the
prophet, See now, I dwell in an house of
cedar, but the ark of God dwelleth
within curtains.
3 And Nathan said to the king, Go, do
all that *is* in thine heart; for the LORD *is*
with thee.
4 And it came to pass that night, that
the word of the LORD came unto
Nathan, saying,
5 Go and tell my servant David, Thus
saith the LORD, Shalt thou build me an
house for me to dwell in?
6 Whereas I have not dwelt in *any*
house since the time that I brought up
the children of Israel out of Egypt, even
to this day, but have walked in a tent
and in a tabernacle.
7 In all *the places* wherein I have
walked with all the children of Israel
spake I a word with any of the tribes of
Israel, whom I commanded to feed my
people Israel, saying, Why build ye not
me an house of cedar?
8 Now therefore so shalt thou say
unto my servant David, Thus saith the
LORD of hosts, I took thee from the
sheepcote, from following the sheep, to
be ruler over my people, over Israel:
9 And I was with thee whithersoever
thou wentest, and have cut off all thine
enemies out of thy sight, and have
made thee a great name, like unto the
name of the great *men* that *are* in the
earth.
10 Moreover I will appoint a place for
my people Israel, and will plant them,
that they may dwell in a place of their
own, and move no more; neither shall
the children of wickedness afflict them
any more, as beforetime,
11 And as since the time that I commanded judges *to be* over my people
Israel, and have caused thee to rest
from all thine enemies. Also the LORD
telleth thee that he will make thee an
house.
12 And when thy days be fulfilled,
and thou shalt sleep with thy fathers, I
will set up thy seed after thee, which
shall proceed out of thy bowels, and I
will establish his kingdom.

13 He shall build an house for my name, and I will stablish the throne of his kingdom for ever.

14 I will be his father, and he shall be my son. If he commit iniquity, I will chasten him with the rod of men, and with the stripes of the children of men:

15 But my mercy shall not depart away from him, as I took *it* from Saul, whom I put away before thee.

16 And thine house and thy kingdom shall be established for ever before thee: thy throne shall be established for ever.

17 According to all these words, and according to all this vision, so did Nathan speak unto David.

18 Then went king David in, and sat before the LORD, and he said, Who *am* I, O Lord GOD? and what *is* my house, that thou hast brought me hitherto?

19 And this was yet a small thing in thy sight, O Lord GOD; but thou hast spoken also of thy servant's house for a great while to come. And *is* this the manner of man, O Lord GOD?

20 And what can David say more unto thee? for thou, Lord GOD, knowest thy servant.

21 For thy word's sake, and according to thine own heart, hast thou done all these great things, to make thy servant know *them*.

22 Wherefore thou art great, O LORD God: for *there is* none like thee, neither *is there any* God beside thee, according to all that we have heard with our ears.

23 And what one nation in the earth *is* like thy people, *even* like Israel, whom God went to redeem for a people to himself, and to make him a name, and to do for you great things and terrible, for thy land, before thy people, which thou redeemedst to thee from Egypt, *from* the nations and their gods?

24 For thou hast confirmed to thyself thy people Israel *to be* a people unto thee for ever: and thou, LORD, art become their God.

25 And now, O LORD God, the word that thou hast spoken concerning thy servant, and concerning his house, establish *it* for ever, and do as thou hast said.

26 And let thy name be magnified for ever, saying, The LORD of hosts *is* the God over Israel: and let the house of thy servant David be established before thee.

27 For thou, O LORD of hosts, God of Israel, hast revealed to thy servant, saying, I will build thee an house: therefore hath thy servant found in his heart to pray this prayer unto thee.

28 And now, O Lord GOD, thou *art* that God, and thy words be true, and thou hast promised this goodness unto thy servant:

29 Therefore now let it please thee to bless the house of thy servant, that it may continue for ever before thee: for thou, O Lord GOD, hast spoken *it*: and with thy blessing let the house of thy servant be blessed for ever.

8 And after this it came to pass, that David smote the Philistines, and subdued them: and David took Metheg-ammah out of the hand of the Philistines.

2 And he smote Moab, and measured them with a line, casting them down to the ground; even with two lines measured he to put to death, and with one full line to keep alive. And *so* the Moabites became David's servants, *and* brought gifts.

3 David smote also Hadadezer, the son of Rehob, king of Zobah, as he went to recover his border at the river Euphrates.

4 And David took from him a thousand *chariots*, and seven hundred horsemen, and twenty thousand footmen: and David houghed all the chariot *horses*, but reserved of them *for* an hundred chariots.

5 And when the Syrians of Damascus came to succour Hadadezer king of Zobah, David slew of the Syrians two and twenty thousand men.

6 Then David put garrisons in Syria of Damascus: and the Syrians became servants to David, *and* brought gifts. And the LORD preserved David whithersoever he went.

7 And David took the shields of gold that were on the servants of Hadadezer, and brought them to Jerusalem.

8 And from Betah, and from Berothai, cities of Hadadezer, king David took exceeding much brass.

9 When Toi king of Hamath heard that David had smitten all the host of Hadadezer,

10 Then Toi sent Joram his son unto king David, to salute him, and to bless him, because he had fought against Hadadezer, and smitten him: for Hadadezer had wars with Toi. And *Joram* brought with him vessels of silver, and vessels of gold, and vessels of brass:

11 Which also king David did dedicate unto the LORD, with the silver and gold that he had dedicated of all nations which he subdued;

12 Of Syria, and of Moab, and of the children of Ammon, and of the Philistines, and of Amalek, and of the spoil of Hadadezer, son of Rehob, king of Zobah.

13 And David gat *him* a name when he returned from smiting of the Syrians in the valley of salt, *being* eighteen thousand *men*.

14 And he put garrisons in Edom; throughout all Edom put he garrisons, and all they of Edom became David's servants. And the LORD preserved David whithersoever he went.

15 And David reigned over all Israel; and David executed judgment and justice unto all his people.

16 And Joab the son of Zeruiah *was* over the host; and Jehoshaphat the son of Ahilud *was* recorder;

17 And Zadok the son of Ahitub, and Ahimelech the son of Abiathar, *were* the priests; and Seraiah *was* the scribe;

18 And Benaiah the son of Jehoiada *was over* both the Cherethites and the Pelethites; and David's sons were chief rulers.

9 And David said, Is there yet any that is left of the house of Saul, that I may shew him kindness for Jonathan's sake?

2 And *there was* of the house of Saul a servant whose name *was* Ziba. And when they had called him unto David, the king said unto him, *Art* thou Ziba? And he said, Thy servant *is he*.

3 And the king said, *Is* there not yet any of the house of Saul, that I may shew the kindness of God unto him? And Ziba said unto the king, Jonathan hath yet a son, *which is* lame on *his* feet.

4 And the king said unto him, Where *is* he? And Ziba said unto the king, Behold, he *is* in the house of Machir, the son of Ammiel, in Lo-debar.

5 Then king David sent, and fetched
him out of the house of Machir, the son
of Ammiel, from Lo-debar.
6 Now when Mephibosheth, the son
of Jonathan, the son of Saul, was come
unto David, he fell on his face, and did
reverence. And David said, Mephibosheth. And he answered, Behold thy
servant!
7 And David said unto him, Fear not:
for I will surely shew thee kindness for
Jonathan thy father's sake, and will
restore thee all the land of Saul thy
father; and thou shalt eat bread at my
table continually.
8 And he bowed himself, and said,
What *is* thy servant, that thou shouldest
look upon such a dead dog as I *am*?
9 Then the king called to Ziba, Saul's
servant, and said unto him, I have given
unto thy master's son all that pertained
to Saul and to all his house.
10 Thou therefore, and thy sons, and
thy servants, shall till the land for him,
and thou shalt bring in *the fruits*, that
thy master's son may have food to eat:
but Mephibosheth thy master's son
shall eat bread alway at my table. Now
Ziba had fifteen sons and twenty servants.
11 Then said Ziba unto the king,
According to all that my lord the king
hath commanded his servant, so shall
thy servant do. As for Mephibosheth,
said the king, he shall eat at my table,
as one of the king's sons.
12 And Mephibosheth had a young
son, whose name *was* Micha. And all
that dwelt in the house of Ziba *were*
servants unto Mephibosheth.
13 So Mephibosheth dwelt in Jerusalem: for he did eat continually at the
king's table; and was lame on both his
feet.

10 And it came to pass after this,
that the king of the children of
Ammon died, and Hanun his son
reigned in his stead.
2 Then said David, I will shew kindness unto Hanun the son of Nahash, as
his father shewed kindness unto me.
And David sent to comfort him by the
hand of his servants for his father. And
David's servants came into the land of
the children of Ammon.
3 And the princes of the children of
Ammon said unto Hanun their lord,
Thinkest thou that David doth honour
thy father, that he hath sent comforters
unto thee? hath not David *rather* sent
his servants unto thee, to search the
city, and to spy it out, and to overthrow
it?
4 Wherefore Hanun took David's servants, and shaved off the one half of
their beards, and cut off their garments
in the middle, *even* to their buttocks,
and sent them away.
5 When they told *it* unto David, he
sent to meet them, because the men
were greatly ashamed: and the king
said, Tarry at Jericho until your beards
be grown, and *then* return.
6 And when the children of Ammon
saw that they stank before David, the
children of Ammon sent and hired the
Syrians of Beth-rehob, and the Syrians
of Zoba, twenty thousand footmen, and
of king Maacah a thousand men, and of
Ish-tob twelve thousand men.
7 And when David heard of *it*, he sent
Joab, and all the host of the mighty
men.
8 And the children of Ammon came
out, and put the battle in array at the
entering in of the gate: and the Syrians
of Zoba, and of Rehob, and Ish-tob, and

Maacah, *were* by themselves in the field.

9 When Joab saw that the front of the battle was against him before and behind, he chose of all the choice *men* of Israel, and put *them* in array against the Syrians:

10 And the rest of the people he delivered into the hand of Abishai his brother, that he might put *them* in array against the children of Ammon.

11 And he said, If the Syrians be too strong for me, then thou shalt help me: but if the children of Ammon be too strong for thee, then I will come and help thee.

12 Be of good courage, and let us play the men for our people, and for the cities of our God: and the LORD do that which seemeth him good.

13 And Joab drew nigh, and the people that *were* with him, unto the battle against the Syrians: and they fled before him.

14 And when the children of Ammon saw that the Syrians were fled, then fled they also before Abishai, and entered into the city. So Joab returned from the children of Ammon, and came to Jerusalem.

15 And when the Syrians saw that they were smitten before Israel, they gathered themselves together.

16 And Hadarezer sent, and brought out the Syrians that *were* beyond the river: and they came to Helam; and Shobach the captain of the host of Hadarezer *went* before them.

17 And when it was told David, he gathered all Israel together, and passed over Jordan, and came to Helam. And the Syrians set themselves in array against David, and fought with him.

18 And the Syrians fled before Israel; and David slew *the men of* seven hundred chariots of the Syrians, and forty thousand horsemen, and smote Shobach the captain of their host, who died there.

19 And when all the kings *that were* servants to Hadarezer saw that they were smitten before Israel, they made peace with Israel, and served them. So the Syrians feared to help the children of Ammon any more.

11 And it came to pass, after the year was expired, at the time when kings go forth *to battle*, that David sent Joab, and his servants with him, and all Israel; and they destroyed the children of Ammon, and besieged Rabbah. But David tarried still at Jerusalem.

2 And it came to pass in an eveningtide, that David arose from off his bed, and walked upon the roof of the king's house: and from the roof he saw a woman washing herself; and the woman *was* very beautiful to look upon.

3 And David sent and enquired after the woman. And *one* said, *Is* not this Bath-sheba, the daughter of Eliam, the wife of Uriah the Hittite?

4 And David sent messengers, and took her; and she came in unto him, and he lay with her; for she was purified from her uncleanness: and she returned unto her house.

5 And the woman conceived, and sent and told David, and said, I *am* with child.

6 And David sent to Joab, *saying*, Send me Uriah the Hittite. And Joab sent Uriah to David.

7 And when Uriah was come unto him, David demanded *of him* how Joab did, and how the people did, and how the war prospered.

8 And David said to Uriah, Go down to thy house, and wash thy feet. And Uriah departed out of the king's house, and there followed him a mess *of meat* from the king.

9 But Uriah slept at the door of the king's house with all the servants of his lord, and went not down to his house.

10 And when they had told David, saying, Uriah went not down unto his house, David said unto Uriah, Camest thou not from *thy* journey? why *then* didst thou not go down unto thine house?

11 And Uriah said unto David, The ark, and Israel, and Judah, abide in tents; and my lord Joab, and the servants of my lord, are encamped in the open fields; shall I then go into mine house, to eat and to drink, and to lie with my wife? *as* thou livest, and *as* thy soul liveth, I will not do this thing.

12 And David said to Uriah, Tarry here to day also, and to morrow I will let thee depart. So Uriah abode in Jerusalem that day, and the morrow.

13 And when David had called him, he did eat and drink before him; and he made him drunk: and at even he went out to lie on his bed with the servants of his lord, but went not down to his house.

14 And it came to pass in the morning, that David wrote a letter to Joab, and sent *it* by the hand of Uriah.

15 And he wrote in the letter, saying, Set ye Uriah in the forefront of the hottest battle, and retire ye from him, that he may be smitten, and die.

16 And it came to pass, when Joab observed the city, that he assigned Uriah unto a place where he knew that valiant men *were*.

17 And the men of the city went out, and fought with Joab: and there fell *some* of the people of the servants of David; and Uriah the Hittite died also.

18 Then Joab sent and told David all the things concerning the war;

19 And charged the messenger, saying, When thou hast made an end of telling the matters of the war unto the king,

20 And if so be that the king's wrath arise, and he say unto thee, Wherefore approached ye so nigh unto the city when ye did fight? knew ye not that they would shoot from the wall?

21 Who smote Abimelech the son of Jerubbesheth? did not a woman cast a piece of a millstone upon him from the wall, that he died in Thebez? why went ye nigh the wall? then say thou, Thy servant Uriah the Hittite is dead also.

22 So the messenger went, and came and shewed David all that Joab had sent him for.

23 And the messenger said unto David, Surely the men prevailed against us, and came out unto us into the field, and we were upon them even unto the entering of the gate.

24 And the shooters shot from off the wall upon thy servants; and *some* of the king's servants be dead, and thy servant Uriah the Hittite is dead also.

25 Then David said unto the messenger, Thus shalt thou say unto Joab, Let not this thing displease thee, for the sword devoureth one as well as another: make thy battle more strong against the city, and overthrow it: and encourage thou him.

26 And when the wife of Uriah heard
that Uriah her husband was dead, she
mourned for her husband.
27 And when the mourning was past,
David sent and fetched her to his
house, and she became his wife, and
bare him a son. But the thing that
David had done displeased the LORD.

12 And the LORD sent Nathan unto
David. And he came unto him,
and said unto him, There were two men
in one city; the one rich, and the other
poor.
2 The rich *man* had exceeding many
flocks and herds:
3 But the poor *man* had nothing, save
one little ewe lamb, which he had
bought and nourished up: and it grew
up together with him, and with his children; it did eat of his own meat, and
drank of his own cup, and lay in his
bosom, and was unto him as a daughter.
4 And there came a traveller unto the
rich man, and he spared to take of his
own flock and of his own herd, to dress
for the wayfaring man that was come
unto him; but took the poor man's
lamb, and dressed it for the man that
was come to him.
5 And David's anger was greatly kindled against the man; and he said to
Nathan, *As* the LORD liveth, the man
that hath done this *thing* shall surely
die:
6 And he shall restore the lamb fourfold, because he did this thing, and
because he had no pity.
7 And Nathan said to David, Thou *art*
the man. Thus saith the LORD God of
Israel, I anointed thee king over Israel,
and I delivered thee out of the hand of
Saul;
8 And I gave thee thy master's house,
and thy master's wives into thy bosom,
and gave thee the house of Israel and of
Judah; and if *that had been* too little, I
would moreover have given unto thee
such and such things.
9 Wherefore hast thou despised the
commandment of the LORD, to do evil
in his sight? thou hast killed Uriah the
Hittite with the sword, and hast taken
his wife *to be* thy wife, and hast slain
him with the sword of the children of
Ammon.
10 Now therefore the sword shall
never depart from thine house; because
thou hast despised me, and hast taken
the wife of Uriah the Hittite to be thy
wife.
11 Thus saith the LORD, Behold, I will
raise up evil against thee out of thine
own house, and I will take thy wives
before thine eyes, and give *them* unto
thy neighbour, and he shall lie with thy
wives in the sight of this sun.
12 For thou didst *it* secretly: but I will
do this thing before all Israel, and
before the sun.
13 And David said unto Nathan, I
have sinned against the LORD. And
Nathan said unto David, The LORD also
hath put away thy sin; thou shalt not
die.
14 Howbeit, because by this deed
thou hast given great occasion to the
enemies of the LORD to blaspheme, the
child also *that is* born unto thee shall
surely die.
15 And Nathan departed unto his
house. And the LORD struck the child
that Uriah's wife bare unto David, and
it was very sick.
16 David therefore besought God for
the child; and David fasted, and went
in, and lay all night upon the earth.

17 And the elders of his house arose,
and went to him, to raise him up from
the earth: but he would not, neither did
he eat bread with them.
18 And it came to pass on the seventh
day, that the child died. And the servants of David feared to tell him that
the child was dead: for they said,
Behold, while the child was yet alive,
we spake unto him, and he would not
hearken unto our voice: how will he
then vex himself, if we tell him that the
child is dead?
19 But when David saw that his servants whispered, David perceived that
the child was dead: therefore David
said unto his servants, Is the child
dead? And they said, He is dead.
20 Then David arose from the earth,
and washed, and anointed *himself*, and
changed his apparel, and came into the
house of the LORD, and worshipped:
then he came to his own house; and
when he required, they set bread
before him, and he did eat.
21 Then said his servants unto him,
What thing *is* this that thou hast done?
thou didst fast and weep for the child,
while it was alive; but when the child
was dead, thou didst rise and eat bread.
22 And he said, While the child was
yet alive, I fasted and wept: for I said,
Who can tell *whether* GOD will be gracious to me, that the child may live?
23 But now he is dead, wherefore
should I fast? can I bring him back
again? I shall go to him, but he shall not
return to me.
24 And David comforted Bath-sheba
his wife, and went in unto her, and lay
with her: and she bare a son, and he
called his name Solomon: and the LORD
loved him.
25 And he sent by the hand of Nathan
the prophet; and he called his name
Jedidiah, because of the LORD.
26 And Joab fought against Rabbah
of the children of Ammon, and took the
royal city.
27 And Joab sent messengers to
David, and said, I have fought against
Rabbah, and have taken the city of
waters.
28 Now therefore gather the rest of
the people together, and encamp
against the city, and take it: lest I take
the city, and it be called after my name.
29 And David gathered all the people
together, and went to Rabbah, and
fought against it, and took it.
30 And he took their king's crown
from off his head, the weight whereof
was a talent of gold with the precious
stones: and it was *set* on David's head.
And he brought forth the spoil of the
city in great abundance.
31 And he brought forth the people
that *were* therein, and put *them* under
saws, and under harrows of iron, and
under axes of iron, and made them pass
through the brickkiln: and thus did he
unto all the cities of the children of
Ammon. So David and all the people
returned unto Jerusalem.

13 And it came to pass after this,
that Absalom the son of David
had a fair sister, whose name *was*
Tamar; and Amnon the son of David
loved her.
2 And Amnon was so vexed, that he
fell sick for his sister Tamar; for she *was*
a virgin; and Amnon thought it hard for
him to do any thing to her.
3 But Amnon had a friend, whose
name *was* Jonadab, the son of Shimeah
David's brother: and Jonadab *was* a
very subtil man.

4 And he said unto him, Why *art* thou, *being* the king's son, lean from day to day? wilt thou not tell me? And Amnon said unto him, I love Tamar, my brother Absalom's sister.

5 And Jonadab said unto him, Lay thee down on thy bed, and make thyself sick: and when thy father cometh to see thee, say unto him, I pray thee, let my sister Tamar come, and give me meat, and dress the meat in my sight, that I may see *it*, and eat *it* at her hand.

6 So Amnon lay down, and made himself sick: and when the king was come to see him, Amnon said unto the king, I pray thee, let Tamar my sister come, and make me a couple of cakes in my sight, that I may eat at her hand.

7 Then David sent home to Tamar, saying, Go now to thy brother Amnon's house, and dress him meat.

8 So Tamar went to her brother Amnon's house; and he was laid down. And she took flour, and kneaded *it*, and made cakes in his sight, and did bake the cakes.

9 And she took a pan, and poured *them* out before him; but he refused to eat. And Amnon said, Have out all men from me. And they went out every man from him.

10 And Amnon said unto Tamar, Bring the meat into the chamber, that I may eat of thine hand. And Tamar took the cakes which she had made, and brought *them* into the chamber to Amnon her brother.

11 And when she had brought *them* unto him to eat, he took hold of her, and said unto her, Come lie with me, my sister.

12 And she answered him, Nay, my brother, do not force me; for no such thing ought to be done in Israel: do not thou this folly.

13 And I, whither shall I cause my shame to go? and as for thee, thou shalt be as one of the fools in Israel. Now therefore, I pray thee, speak unto the king; for he will not withhold me from thee.

14 Howbeit he would not hearken unto her voice: but, being stronger than she, forced her, and lay with her.

15 Then Amnon hated her exceedingly; so that the hatred wherewith he hated her *was* greater than the love wherewith he had loved her. And Amnon said unto her, Arise, be gone.

16 And she said unto him, *There is* no cause: this evil in sending me away *is* greater than the other that thou didst unto me. But he would not hearken unto her.

17 Then he called his servant that ministered unto him, and said, Put now this *woman* out from me, and bolt the door after her.

18 And *she had* a garment of divers colours upon her: for with such robes were the king's daughters *that were* virgins apparelled. Then his servant brought her out, and bolted the door after her.

19 And Tamar put ashes on her head, and rent her garment of divers colours that *was* on her, and laid her hand on her head, and went on crying.

20 And Absalom her brother said unto her, Hath Amnon thy brother been with thee? but hold now thy peace, my sister: he *is* thy brother; regard not this thing. So Tamar remained desolate in her brother Absalom's house.

21 But when king David heard of all
these things, he was very wroth.
22 And Absalom spake unto his
brother Amnon neither good nor bad:
for Absalom hated Amnon, because he
had forced his sister Tamar.
23 And it came to pass after two full
years, that Absalom had sheepshearers
in Baalhazor, which *is* beside Ephraim:
and Absalom invited all the king's sons.
24 And Absalom came to the king,
and said, Behold now, thy servant hath
sheepshearers; let the king, I beseech
thee, and his servants go with thy servant.
25 And the king said to Absalom, Nay,
my son, let us not all now go, lest we be
chargeable unto thee. And he pressed
him: howbeit he would not go, but
blessed him.
26 Then said Absalom, If not, I pray
thee, let my brother Amnon go with us.
And the king said unto him, Why
should he go with thee?
27 But Absalom pressed him, that he
let Amnon and all the king's sons go
with him.
28 Now Absalom had commanded his
servants, saying, Mark ye now when
Amnon's heart is merry with wine, and
when I say unto you, Smite Amnon;
then kill him, fear not: have not I commanded
you? be courageous, and be
valiant.
29 And the servants of Absalom did
unto Amnon as Absalom had commanded.
Then all the king's sons arose,
and every man gat him up upon his
mule, and fled.
30 And it came to pass, while they
were in the way, that tidings came to
David, saying, Absalom hath slain all
the king's sons, and there is not one of
them left.
31 Then the king arose, and tare his
garments, and lay on the earth; and all
his servants stood by with their clothes
rent.
32 And Jonadab, the son of Shimeah
David's brother, answered and said, Let
not my lord suppose *that* they have
slain all the young men the king's sons;
for Amnon only is dead: for by the
appointment of Absalom this hath
been determined from the day that he
forced his sister Tamar.
33 Now therefore let not my lord the
king take the thing to his heart, to
think that all the king's sons are dead:
for Amnon only is dead.
34 But Absalom fled. And the young
man that kept the watch lifted up his
eyes, and looked, and, behold, there
came much people by the way of the
hill side behind him.
35 And Jonadab said unto the king,
Behold, the king's sons come: as thy
servant said, so it is.
36 And it came to pass, as soon as he
had made an end of speaking, that,
behold, the king's sons came, and lifted
up their voice and wept: and the king
also and all his servants wept very sore.
37 But Absalom fled, and went to
Talmai, the son of Ammihud, king of
Geshur. And *David* mourned for his son
every day.
38 So Absalom fled, and went to
Geshur, and was there three years.
39 And *the soul of* king David longed
to go forth unto Absalom: for he was
comforted concerning Amnon, seeing
he was dead.

14 Now Joab the son of Zeruiah
perceived that the king's heart
was toward Absalom.
2 And Joab sent to Tekoah, and
fetched thence a wise woman, and said

unto her, I pray thee, feign thyself to be
a mourner, and put on now mourning
apparel, and anoint not thyself with oil,
but be as a woman that had a long time
mourned for the dead:
3 And come to the king, and speak on
this manner unto him. So Joab put the
words in her mouth.
4 And when the woman of Tekoah
spake to the king, she fell on her face to
the ground, and did obeisance, and
said, Help, O king.
5 And the king said unto her, What
aileth thee? And she answered, I *am*
indeed a widow woman, and mine husband is dead.
6 And thy handmaid had two sons,
and they two strove together in the
field, and *there was* none to part them,
but the one smote the other, and slew
him.
7 And, behold, the whole family is
risen against thine handmaid, and they
said, Deliver him that smote his brother, that we may kill him, for the life of
his brother whom he slew; and we will
destroy the heir also: and so they shall
quench my coal which is left, and shall
not leave to my husband *neither* name
nor remainder upon the earth.
8 And the king said unto the woman,
Go to thine house, and I will give
charge concerning thee.
9 And the woman of Tekoah said unto
the king, My lord, O king, the iniquity
be on me, and on my father's house: and
the king and his throne *be* guiltless.
10 And the king said, Whosoever
saith *ought* unto thee, bring him to me,
and he shall not touch thee any more.
11 Then said she, I pray thee, let the
king remember the LORD thy God, that
thou wouldest not suffer the revengers
of blood to destroy any more, lest they
destroy my son. And he said, *As* the
LORD liveth, there shall not one hair of
thy son fall to the earth.
12 Then the woman said, Let thine
handmaid, I pray thee, speak *one* word
unto my lord the king. And he said, Say
on.
13 And the woman said, Wherefore
then hast thou thought such a thing
against the people of God? for the king
doth speak this thing as one which is
faulty, in that the king doth not fetch
home again his banished.
14 For we must needs die, and *are* as
water spilt on the ground, which cannot
be gathered up again; neither doth God
respect *any* person: yet doth he devise
means, that his banished be not
expelled from him.
15 Now therefore that I am come to
speak of this thing unto my lord the
king, *it is* because the people have
made me afraid: and thy handmaid
said, I will now speak unto the king; it
may be that the king will perform the
request of his handmaid.
16 For the king will hear, to deliver
his handmaid out of the hand of the
man *that would* destroy me and my son
together out of the inheritance of God.
17 Then thine handmaid said, The
word of my lord the king shall now be
comfortable: for as an angel of God, so
is my lord the king to discern good and
bad: therefore the LORD thy God will be
with thee.
18 Then the king answered and said
unto the woman, Hide not from me, I
pray thee, the thing that I shall ask
thee. And the woman said, Let my lord
the king now speak.
19 And the king said, *Is not* the hand
of Joab with thee in all this? And the
woman answered and said, *As* thy soul

liveth, my lord the king, none can turn
to the right hand or to the left from
ought that my lord the king hath spoken: for thy servant Joab, he bade me,
and he put all these words in the mouth
of thine handmaid:
20 To fetch about this form of speech
hath thy servant Joab done this thing:
and my lord *is* wise, according to the
wisdom of an angel of God, to know all
things that *are* in the earth.
21 And the king said unto Joab,
Behold now, I have done this thing: go
therefore, bring the young man
Absalom again.
22 And Joab fell to the ground on his
face, and bowed himself, and thanked
the king: and Joab said, To day thy servant knoweth that I have found grace in
thy sight, my lord, O king, in that the
king hath fulfilled the request of his
servant.
23 So Joab arose and went to Geshur,
and brought Absalom to Jerusalem.
24 And the king said, Let him turn to
his own house, and let him not see my
face. So Absalom returned to his own
house, and saw not the king's face.
25 But in all Israel there was none to
be so much praised as Absalom for his
beauty: from the sole of his foot even to
the crown of his head there was no
blemish in him.
26 And when he polled his head, (for
it was at every year's end that he polled
it: because *the hair* was heavy on him,
therefore he polled it:) he weighed the
hair of his head at two hundred shekels
after the king's weight.
27 And unto Absalom there were
born three sons, and one daughter,
whose name *was* Tamar: she was a
woman of a fair countenance.
28 So Absalom dwelt two full years in
Jerusalem, and saw not the king's face.
29 Therefore Absalom sent for Joab,
to have sent him to the king; but he
would not come to him: and when he
sent again the second time, he would
not come.
30 Therefore he said unto his servants, See, Joab's field is near mine,
and he hath barley there; go and set it
on fire. And Absalom's servants set the
field on fire.
31 Then Joab arose, and came to
Absalom unto *his* house, and said unto
him, Wherefore have thy servants set
my field on fire?
32 And Absalom answered Joab,
Behold, I sent unto thee, saying, Come
hither, that I may send thee to the king,
to say, Wherefore am I come from
Geshur? *it had been* good for me *to
have been* there still: now therefore let
me see the king's face; and if there be
any iniquity in me, let him kill me.
33 So Joab came to the king, and told
him: and when he had called for
Absalom, he came to the king, and
bowed himself on his face to the ground
before the king: and the king kissed
Absalom.

15 And it came to pass after this,
that Absalom prepared him chariots and horses, and fifty men to run
before him.
2 And Absalom rose up early, and
stood beside the way of the gate: and it
was *so*, that when any man that had a
controversy came to the king for judgment, then Absalom called unto him,
and said, Of what city *art* thou? And he
said, Thy servant *is* of one of the tribes
of Israel.

3 And Absalom said unto him, See, thy matters *are* good and right; but *there is* no man *deputed* of the king to hear thee.

4 Absalom said moreover, Oh that I were made judge in the land, that every man which hath any suit or cause might come unto me, and I would do him justice!

5 And it was *so*, that when any man came nigh *to him* to do him obeisance, he put forth his hand, and took him, and kissed him.

6 And on this manner did Absalom to all Israel that came to the king for judgment: so Absalom stole the hearts of the men of Israel.

7 And it came to pass after forty years, that Absalom said unto the king, I pray thee, let me go and pay my vow, which I have vowed unto the LORD, in Hebron.

8 For thy servant vowed a vow while I abode at Geshur in Syria, saying, If the LORD shall bring me again indeed to Jerusalem, then I will serve the LORD.

9 And the king said unto him, Go in peace. So he arose, and went to Hebron.

10 But Absalom sent spies throughout all the tribes of Israel, saying, As soon as ye hear the sound of the trumpet, then ye shall say, Absalom reigneth in Hebron.

11 And with Absalom went two hundred men out of Jerusalem, *that were* called; and they went in their simplicity, and they knew not any thing.

12 And Absalom sent for Ahithophel the Gilonite, David's counsellor, from his city, *even* from Giloh, while he offered sacrifices. And the conspiracy was strong; for the people increased continually with Absalom.

13 And there came a messenger to David, saying, The hearts of the men of Israel are after Absalom.

14 And David said unto all his servants that *were* with him at Jerusalem, Arise, and let us flee; for we shall not *else* escape from Absalom: make speed to depart, lest he overtake us suddenly, and bring evil upon us, and smite the city with the edge of the sword.

15 And the king's servants said unto the king, Behold, thy servants *are ready to do* whatsoever my lord the king shall appoint.

16 And the king went forth, and all his household after him. And the king left ten women, *which were* concubines, to keep the house.

17 And the king went forth, and all the people after him, and tarried in a place that was far off.

18 And all his servants passed on beside him; and all the Cherethites, and all the Pelethites, and all the Gittites, six hundred men which came after him from Gath, passed on before the king.

19 Then said the king to Ittai the Gittite, Wherefore goest thou also with us? return to thy place, and abide with the king: for thou *art* a stranger, and also an exile.

20 Whereas thou camest *but* yesterday, should I this day make thee go up and down with us? seeing I go whither I may, return thou, and take back thy brethren: mercy and truth *be* with thee.

21 And Ittai answered the king, and said, *As* the LORD liveth, and *as* my lord the king liveth, surely in what place my lord the king shall be, whether in death or life, even there also will thy servant be.

22 And David said to Ittai, Go and pass over. And Ittai the Gittite passed over, and all his men, and all the little ones that *were* with him.

23 And all the country wept with a loud voice, and all the people passed over: the king also himself passed over the brook Kidron, and all the people passed over, toward the way of the wilderness.

24 And lo Zadok also, and all the Levites *were* with him, bearing the ark of the covenant of God: and they set down the ark of God; and Abiathar went up, until all the people had done passing out of the city.

25 And the king said unto Zadok, Carry back the ark of God into the city: if I shall find favour in the eyes of the LORD, he will bring me again, and shew me *both* it, and his habitation:

26 But if he thus say, I have no delight in thee; behold, *here am* I, let him do to me as seemeth good unto him.

27 The king said also unto Zadok the priest, *Art not* thou a seer? return into the city in peace, and your two sons with you, Ahimaaz thy son, and Jonathan the son of Abiathar.

28 See, I will tarry in the plain of the wilderness, until there come word from you to certify me.

29 Zadok therefore and Abiathar carried the ark of God again to Jerusalem: and they tarried there.

30 And David went up by the ascent of *mount* Olivet, and wept as he went up, and had his head covered, and he went barefoot: and all the people that *was* with him covered every man his head, and they went up, weeping as they went up.

31 And *one* told David, saying, Ahithophel *is* among the conspirators with Absalom. And David said, O LORD, I pray thee, turn the counsel of Ahithophel into foolishness.

32 And it came to pass, that *when* David was come to the top *of the mount*, where he worshipped God, behold, Hushai the Archite came to meet him with his coat rent, and earth upon his head:

33 Unto whom David said, If thou passest on with me, then thou shalt be a burden unto me:

34 But if thou return to the city, and say unto Absalom, I will be thy servant, O king; *as* I *have been* thy father's servant hitherto, so *will* I now also *be* thy servant: then mayest thou for me defeat the counsel of Ahithophel.

35 And *hast thou* not there with thee Zadok and Abiathar the priests? therefore it shall be, *that* what thing soever thou shalt hear out of the king's house, thou shalt tell *it* to Zadok and Abiathar the priests.

36 Behold, *they have* there with them their two sons, Ahimaaz Zadok's *son*, and Jonathan Abiathar's *son*; and by them ye shall send unto me every thing that ye can hear.

37 So Hushai David's friend came into the city, and Absalom came into Jerusalem.

16 And when David was a little past the top *of the hill*, behold, Ziba the servant of Mephibosheth met him, with a couple of asses saddled, and upon them two hundred *loaves* of bread, and an hundred bunches of raisins, and an hundred of summer fruits, and a bottle of wine.

2 And the king said unto Ziba, What
meanest thou by these? And Ziba said,
The asses *be* for the king's household to
ride on; and the bread and summer
fruit for the young men to eat; and the
wine, that such as be faint in the wilderness may drink.
3 And the king said, And where *is* thy
master's son? And Ziba said unto the
king, Behold, he abideth at Jerusalem:
for he said, To day shall the house of
Israel restore me the kingdom of my
father.
4 Then said the king to Ziba, Behold,
thine *are* all that *pertained* unto
Mephibosheth. And Ziba said, I humbly
beseech thee *that* I may find grace in
thy sight, my lord, O king.
5 And when king David came to
Bahurim, behold, thence came out a
man of the family of the house of Saul,
whose name *was* Shimei, the son of
Gera: he came forth, and cursed still as
he came.
6 And he cast stones at David, and at
all the servants of king David: and all
the people and all the mighty men *were*
on his right hand and on his left.
7 And thus said Shimei when he
cursed, Come out, come out, thou
bloody man, and thou man of Belial:
8 The LORD hath returned upon thee
all the blood of the house of Saul, in
whose stead thou hast reigned; and the
LORD hath delivered the kingdom into
the hand of Absalom thy son: and,
behold, thou *art taken* in thy mischief,
because thou *art* a bloody man.
9 Then said Abishai the son of
Zeruiah unto the king, Why should this
dead dog curse my lord the king? let
me go over, I pray thee, and take off his
head.
10 And the king said, What have I to
do with you, ye sons of Zeruiah? so let
him curse, because the LORD hath said
unto him, Curse David. Who shall then
say, Wherefore hast thou done so?
11 And David said to Abishai, and to
all his servants, Behold, my son, which
came forth of my bowels, seeketh my
life: how much more now *may this*
Benjamite *do it*? let him alone, and let
him curse; for the LORD hath bidden
him.
12 It may be that the LORD will look
on mine affliction, and that the LORD
will requite me good for his cursing this
day.
13 And as David and his men went by
the way, Shimei went along on the hill's
side over against him, and cursed as he
went, and threw stones at him, and cast
dust.
14 And the king, and all the people
that *were* with him, came weary, and
refreshed themselves there.
15 And Absalom, and all the people
the men of Israel, came to Jerusalem,
and Ahithophel with him.
16 And it came to pass, when Hushai
the Archite, David's friend, was come
unto Absalom, that Hushai said unto
Absalom, God save the king, God save
the king.
17 And Absalom said to Hushai, *Is*
this thy kindness to thy friend? why
wentest thou not with thy friend?
18 And Hushai said unto Absalom,
Nay; but whom the LORD, and this people, and all the men of Israel, choose,
his will I be, and with him will I abide.
19 And again, whom should I serve?
should I not *serve* in the presence of his
son? as I have served in thy father's
presence, so will I be in thy presence.

20 Then said Absalom to Ahithophel,
Give counsel among you what we shall
do.
21 And Ahithophel said unto Absalom, Go in unto thy father's concubines,
which he hath left to keep the house;
and all Israel shall hear that thou art
abhorred of thy father: then shall the
hands of all that *are* with thee be
strong.
22 So they spread Absalom a tent
upon the top of the house; and Absalom
went in unto his father's concubines in
the sight of all Israel.
23 And the counsel of Ahithophel,
which he counselled in those days, *was*
as if a man had enquired at the oracle
of God: so *was* all the counsel of
Ahithophel both with David and with
Absalom.

17 Moreover Ahithophel said unto
Absalom, Let me now choose out
twelve thousand men, and I will arise
and pursue after David this night:
2 And I will come upon him while he
is weary and weak handed, and will
make him afraid: and all the people
that *are* with him shall flee; and I will
smite the king only:
3 And I will bring back all the people
unto thee: the man whom thou seekest
is as if all returned: *so* all the people
shall be in peace.
4 And the saying pleased Absalom
well, and all the elders of Israel.
5 Then said Absalom, Call now
Hushai the Archite also, and let us hear
likewise what he saith.
6 And when Hushai was come to
Absalom, Absalom spake unto him, saying, Ahithophel hath spoken after this
manner: shall we do *after* his saying? if
not; speak thou.
7 And Hushai said unto Absalom, The
counsel that Ahithophel hath given *is*
not good at this time.
8 For, said Hushai, thou knowest thy
father and his men, that they *be* mighty
men, and they *be* chafed in their minds,
as a bear robbed of her whelps in the
field: and thy father *is* a man of war,
and will not lodge with the people.
9 Behold, he is hid now in some pit, or
in some *other* place: and it will come to
pass, when some of them be overthrown at the first, that whosoever
heareth it will say, There is a slaughter
among the people that follow Absalom.
10 And he also *that is* valiant, whose
heart *is* as the heart of a lion, shall
utterly melt: for all Israel knoweth that
thy father *is* a mighty man, and *they*
which *be* with him *are* valiant men.
11 Therefore I counsel that all Israel
be generally gathered unto thee, from
Dan even to Beer-sheba, as the sand
that *is* by the sea for multitude; and
that thou go to battle in thine own person.
12 So shall we come upon him in
some place where he shall be found,
and we will light upon him as the dew
falleth on the ground: and of him and
of all the men that *are* with him there
shall not be left so much as one.
13 Moreover, if he be gotten into a
city, then shall all Israel bring ropes to
that city, and we will draw it into the
river, until there be not one small stone
found there.
14 And Absalom and all the men of
Israel said, The counsel of Hushai the
Archite *is* better than the counsel of
Ahithophel. For the LORD had appointed to defeat the good counsel of
Ahithophel, to the intent that the LORD
might bring evil upon Absalom.

15 Then said Hushai unto Zadok and to Abiathar the priests, Thus and thus did Ahithophel counsel Absalom and the elders of Israel; and thus and thus have I counselled.

16 Now therefore send quickly, and tell David, saying, Lodge not this night in the plains of the wilderness, but speedily pass over; lest the king be swallowed up, and all the people that *are* with him.

17 Now Jonathan and Ahimaaz stayed by En-rogel; for they might not be seen to come into the city: and a wench went and told them; and they went and told king David.

18 Nevertheless a lad saw them, and told Absalom: but they went both of them away quickly, and came to a man's house in Bahurim, which had a well in his court; whither they went down.

19 And the woman took and spread a covering over the well's mouth, and spread ground corn thereon; and the thing was not known.

20 And when Absalom's servants came to the woman to the house, they said, Where *is* Ahimaaz and Jonathan? And the woman said unto them, They be gone over the brook of water. And when they had sought and could not find *them*, they returned to Jerusalem.

21 And it came to pass, after they were departed, that they came up out of the well, and went and told king David, and said unto David, Arise, and pass quickly over the water: for thus hath Ahithophel counselled against you.

22 Then David arose, and all the people that *were* with him, and they passed over Jordan: by the morning light there lacked not one of them that was not gone over Jordan.

23 And when Ahithophel saw that his counsel was not followed, he saddled *his* ass, and arose, and gat him home to his house, to his city, and put his household in order, and hanged himself, and died, and was buried in the sepulchre of his father.

24 Then David came to Mahanaim. And Absalom passed over Jordan, he and all the men of Israel with him.

25 And Absalom made Amasa captain of the host instead of Joab: which Amasa *was* a man's son, whose name *was* Ithra an Israelite, that went in to Abigail the daughter of Nahash, sister to Zeruiah Joab's mother.

26 So Israel and Absalom pitched in the land of Gilead.

27 And it came to pass, when David was come to Mahanaim, that Shobi the son of Nahash of Rabbah of the children of Ammon, and Machir the son of Ammiel of Lo-debar, and Barzillai the Gileadite of Rogelim,

28 Brought beds, and basons, and earthen vessels, and wheat, and barley, and flour, and parched *corn*, and beans, and lentiles, and parched *pulse*,

29 And honey, and butter, and sheep, and cheese of kine, for David, and for the people that *were* with him, to eat: for they said, The people *is* hungry, and weary, and thirsty, in the wilderness.

18 And David numbered the people that *were* with him, and set captains of thousands and captains of hundreds over them.

2 And David sent forth a third part of the people under the hand of Joab, and a third part under the hand of Abishai the son of Zeruiah, Joab's brother, and a third part under the hand of Ittai the Gittite. And the king said unto the people, I will surely go forth with you myself also.

3 But the people answered, Thou shalt not go forth: for if we flee away, they will not care for us; neither if half of us die, will they care for us: but now *thou art* worth ten thousand of us: therefore now *it is* better that thou succour us out of the city.

4 And the king said unto them, What seemeth you best I will do. And the king stood by the gate side, and all the people came out by hundreds and by thousands.

5 And the king commanded Joab and Abishai and Ittai, saying, *Deal* gently for my sake with the young man, *even* with Absalom. And all the people heard when the king gave all the captains charge concerning Absalom.

6 So the people went out into the field against Israel: and the battle was in the wood of Ephraim;

7 Where the people of Israel were slain before the servants of David, and there was there a great slaughter that day of twenty thousand *men*.

8 For the battle was there scattered over the face of all the country: and the wood devoured more people that day than the sword devoured.

9 And Absalom met the servants of David. And Absalom rode upon a mule, and the mule went under the thick boughs of a great oak, and his head caught hold of the oak, and he was taken up between the heaven and the earth; and the mule that *was* under him went away.

10 And a certain man saw *it*, and told Joab, and said, Behold, I saw Absalom hanged in an oak.

11 And Joab said unto the man that told him, And, behold, thou sawest *him*, and why didst thou not smite him there to the ground? and I would have given thee ten *shekels* of silver, and a girdle.

12 And the man said unto Joab, Though I should receive a thousand *shekels* of silver in mine hand, *yet* would I not put forth mine hand against the king's son: for in our hearing the king charged thee and Abishai and Ittai, saying, Beware that none *touch* the young man Absalom.

13 Otherwise I should have wrought falsehood against mine own life: for there is no matter hid from the king, and thou thyself wouldest have set thyself against *me*.

14 Then said Joab, I may not tarry thus with thee. And he took three darts in his hand, and thrust them through the heart of Absalom, while he *was* yet alive in the midst of the oak.

15 And ten young men that bare Joab's armour compassed about and smote Absalom, and slew him.

16 And Joab blew the trumpet, and the people returned from pursuing after Israel: for Joab held back the people.

17 And they took Absalom, and cast him into a great pit in the wood, and laid a very great heap of stones upon him: and all Israel fled every one to his tent.

18 Now Absalom in his lifetime had taken and reared up for himself a pillar, which *is* in the king's dale: for he said, I have no son to keep my name in remembrance: and he called the pillar after his own name: and it is called unto this day, Absalom's place.

19 Then said Ahimaaz the son of Zadok, Let me now run, and bear the king tidings, how that the LORD hath avenged him of his enemies.

20 And Joab said unto him, Thou
shalt not bear tidings this day, but thou
shalt bear tidings another day: but this
day thou shalt bear no tidings, because
the king's son is dead.
21 Then said Joab to Cushi, Go tell
the king what thou hast seen. And
Cushi bowed himself unto Joab, and
ran.
22 Then said Ahimaaz the son of
Zadok yet again to Joab, But howsoever, let me, I pray thee, also run after
Cushi. And Joab said, Wherefore wilt
thou run, my son, seeing that thou hast
no tidings ready?
23 But howsoever, *said he*, let me run.
And he said unto him, Run. Then
Ahimaaz ran by the way of the plain,
and overran Cushi.
24 And David sat between the two
gates: and the watchman went up to
the roof over the gate unto the wall,
and lifted up his eyes, and looked, and
behold a man running alone.
25 And the watchman cried, and told
the king. And the king said, If he *be*
alone, *there is* tidings in his mouth. And
he came apace, and drew near.
26 And the watchman saw another
man running: and the watchman called
unto the porter, and said, Behold
another man running alone. And the
king said, He also bringeth tidings.
27 And the watchman said, Me thinketh the running of the foremost is like
the running of Ahimaaz the son of
Zadok. And the king said, He *is* a good
man, and cometh with good tidings.
28 And Ahimaaz called, and said unto
the king, All is well. And he fell down to
the earth upon his face before the king,
and said, Blessed *be* the LORD thy God,
which hath delivered up the men that
lifted up their hand against my lord the
king.
29 And the king said, Is the young
man Absalom safe? And Ahimaaz
answered, When Joab sent the king's
servant, and *me* thy servant, I saw a
great tumult, but I knew not what *it*
was.
30 And the king said *unto him*, Turn
aside, *and* stand here. And he turned
aside, and stood still.
31 And, behold, Cushi came; and
Cushi said, Tidings, my lord the king:
for the LORD hath avenged thee this
day of all them that rose up against
thee.
32 And the king said unto Cushi, Is
the young man Absalom safe? And
Cushi answered, The enemies of my
lord the king, and all that rise against
thee to do *thee* hurt, be as *that* young
man *is*.
33 And the king was much moved,
and went up to the chamber over the
gate, and wept: and as he went, thus he
said, O my son Absalom, my son, my son
Absalom! would God I had died for
thee, O Absalom, my son, my son!

19 And it was told Joab, Behold, the
king weepeth and mourneth for
Absalom.
2 And the victory that day was *turned*
into mourning unto all the people: for
the people heard say that day how the
king was grieved for his son.
3 And the people gat them by stealth
that day into the city, as people being
ashamed steal away when they flee in
battle.
4 But the king covered his face, and
the king cried with a loud voice, O my
son Absalom, O Absalom, my son, my
son!

5 And Joab came into the house to
the king, and said, Thou hast shamed
this day the faces of all thy servants,
which this day have saved thy life, and
the lives of thy sons and of thy daughters, and the lives of thy wives, and the
lives of thy concubines;
6 In that thou lovest thine enemies,
and hatest thy friends. For thou hast
declared this day, that thou regardest
neither princes nor servants: for this
day I perceive, that if Absalom had
lived, and all we had died this day, then
it had pleased thee well.
7 Now therefore arise, go forth, and
speak comfortably unto thy servants:
for I swear by the LORD, if thou go not
forth, there will not tarry one with thee
this night: and that will be worse unto
thee than all the evil that befell thee
from thy youth until now.
8 Then the king arose, and sat in the
gate. And they told unto all the people,
saying, Behold, the king doth sit in the
gate. And all the people came before
the king: for Israel had fled every man
to his tent.
9 And all the people were at strife
throughout all the tribes of Israel, saying, The king saved us out of the hand
of our enemies, and he delivered us out
of the hand of the Philistines; and now
he is fled out of the land for Absalom.
10 And Absalom, whom we anointed
over us, is dead in battle. Now therefore
why speak ye not a word of bringing
the king back?
11 And king David sent to Zadok and
to Abiathar the priests, saying, Speak
unto the elders of Judah, saying, Why
are ye the last to bring the king back to
his house? seeing the speech of all
Israel is come to the king, *even* to his
house.
12 Ye *are* my brethren, ye *are* my
bones and my flesh: wherefore then are
ye the last to bring back the king?
13 And say ye to Amasa, *Art* thou not
of my bone, and of my flesh? God do so
to me, and more also, if thou be not
captain of the host before me continually in the room of Joab.
14 And he bowed the heart of all the
men of Judah, even as *the heart of* one
man; so that they sent *this word* unto
the king, Return thou, and all thy servants.
15 So the king returned, and came to
Jordan. And Judah came to Gilgal, to
go to meet the king, to conduct the king
over Jordan.
16 And Shimei the son of Gera, a
Benjamite, which *was* of Bahurim, hasted and came down with the men of
Judah to meet king David.
17 And *there were* a thousand men of
Benjamin with him, and Ziba the servant of the house of Saul, and his fifteen sons and his twenty servants with
him; and they went over Jordan before
the king.
18 And there went over a ferry boat to
carry over the king's household, and to
do what he thought good. And Shimei
the son of Gera fell down before the
king, as he was come over Jordan;
19 And said unto the king, Let not my
lord impute iniquity unto me, neither
do thou remember that which thy servant did perversely the day that my
lord the king went out of Jerusalem,
that the king should take it to his heart.
20 For thy servant doth know that I
have sinned: therefore, behold, I am
come the first this day of all the house
of Joseph to go down to meet my lord
the king.

21 But Abishai the son of Zeruiah
answered and said, Shall not Shimei be
put to death for this, because he cursed
the LORD's anointed?
22 And David said, What have I to do
with you, ye sons of Zeruiah, that ye
should this day be adversaries unto
me? shall there any man be put to
death this day in Israel? for do not I
know that I *am* this day king over
Israel?
23 Therefore the king said unto
Shimei, Thou shalt not die. And the
king sware unto him.
24 And Mephibosheth the son of Saul
came down to meet the king, and had
neither dressed his feet, nor trimmed
his beard, nor washed his clothes, from
the day the king departed until the day
he came *again* in peace.
25 And it came to pass, when he was
come to Jerusalem to meet the king,
that the king said unto him, Wherefore
wentest not thou with me, Mephibosheth?
26 And he answered, My lord, O king,
my servant deceived me: for thy servant said, I will saddle me an ass, that I
may ride thereon, and go to the king;
because thy servant *is* lame.
27 And he hath slandered thy servant
unto my lord the king; but my lord the
king *is* as an angel of God: do therefore
what is good in thine eyes.
28 For all *of* my father's house were
but dead men before my lord the king:
yet didst thou set thy servant among
them that did eat at thine own table.
What right therefore have I yet to cry
any more unto the king?
29 And the king said unto him, Why
speakest thou any more of thy matters?
I have said, Thou and Ziba divide the
land.
30 And Mephibosheth said unto the
king, Yea, let him take all, forasmuch as
my lord the king is come again in peace
unto his own house.
31 And Barzillai the Gileadite came
down from Rogelim, and went over
Jordan with the king, to conduct him
over Jordan.
32 Now Barzillai was a very aged man,
even fourscore years old: and he had
provided the king of sustenance while
he lay at Mahanaim; for he *was* a very
great man.
33 And the king said unto Barzillai,
Come thou over with me, and I will
feed thee with me in Jerusalem.
34 And Barzillai said unto the king,
How long have I to live, that I should go
up with the king unto Jerusalem?
35 I *am* this day fourscore years old:
and can I discern between good and
evil? can thy servant taste what I eat or
what I drink? can I hear any more the
voice of singing men and singing
women? wherefore then should thy
servant be yet a burden unto my lord
the king?
36 Thy servant will go a little way over
Jordan with the king: and why should
the king recompense it me with such a
reward?
37 Let thy servant, I pray thee, turn
back again, that I may die in mine own
city, *and be buried* by the grave of my
father and of my mother. But behold
thy servant Chimham; let him go over
with my lord the king; and do to him
what shall seem good unto thee.
38 And the king answered, Chimham
shall go over with me, and I will do to
him that which shall seem good unto
thee: and whatsoever thou shalt require
of me, *that* will I do for thee.

39 And all the people went over Jordan. And when the king was come over, the king kissed Barzillai, and blessed him; and he returned unto his own place.

40 Then the king went on to Gilgal, and Chimham went on with him: and all the people of Judah conducted the king, and also half the people of Israel.

41 And, behold, all the men of Israel came to the king, and said unto the king, Why have our brethren the men of Judah stolen thee away, and have brought the king, and his household, and all David's men with him, over Jordan?

42 And all the men of Judah answered the men of Israel, Because the king *is* near of kin to us: wherefore then be ye angry for this matter? have we eaten at all of the king's *cost*? or hath he given us any gift?

43 And the men of Israel answered the men of Judah, and said, We have ten parts in the king, and we have also more *right* in David than ye: why then did ye despise us, that our advice should not be first had in bringing back our king? And the words of the men of Judah were fiercer than the words of the men of Israel.

20 And there happened to be there a man of Belial, whose name *was* Sheba, the son of Bichri, a Benjamite: and he blew a trumpet, and said, We have no part in David, neither have we inheritance in the son of Jesse: every man to his tents, O Israel.

2 So every man of Israel went up from after David, *and* followed Sheba the son of Bichri: but the men of Judah clave unto their king, from Jordan even to Jerusalem.

3 And David came to his house at Jerusalem; and the king took the ten women *his* concubines, whom he had left to keep the house, and put them in ward, and fed them, but went not in unto them. So they were shut up unto the day of their death, living in widowhood.

4 Then said the king to Amasa, Assemble me the men of Judah within three days, and be thou here present.

5 So Amasa went to assemble *the men of* Judah: but he tarried longer than the set time which he had appointed him.

6 And David said to Abishai, Now shall Sheba the son of Bichri do us more harm than *did* Absalom: take thou thy lord's servants, and pursue after him, lest he get him fenced cities, and escape us.

7 And there went out after him Joab's men, and the Cherethites, and the Pelethites, and all the mighty men: and they went out of Jerusalem, to pursue after Sheba the son of Bichri.

8 When they *were* at the great stone which *is* in Gibeon, Amasa went before them. And Joab's garment that he had put on was girded unto him, and upon it a girdle *with* a sword fastened upon his loins in the sheath thereof; and as he went forth it fell out.

9 And Joab said to Amasa, *Art* thou in health, my brother? And Joab took Amasa by the beard with the right hand to kiss him.

10 But Amasa took no heed to the sword that *was* in Joab's hand: so he smote him therewith in the fifth *rib*, and shed out his bowels to the ground, and struck him not again; and he died. So Joab and Abishai his brother pursued after Sheba the son of Bichri.

11 And one of Joab's men stood by
him, and said, He that favoureth Joab,
and he that *is* for David, *let him go*
after Joab.
12 And Amasa wallowed in blood in
the midst of the highway. And when the
man saw that all the people stood still,
he removed Amasa out of the highway
into the field, and cast a cloth upon
him, when he saw that every one that
came by him stood still.
13 When he was removed out of the
highway, all the people went on after
Joab, to pursue after Sheba the son of
Bichri.
14 And he went through all the tribes
of Israel unto Abel, and to Beth-
maachah, and all the Berites: and they
were gathered together, and went also
after him.
15 And they came and besieged him
in Abel of Beth-maachah, and they cast
up a bank against the city, and it stood
in the trench: and all the people that
were with Joab battered the wall, to
throw it down.
16 Then cried a wise woman out of
the city, Hear, hear; say, I pray you, unto
Joab, Come near hither, that I may
speak with thee.
17 And when he was come near unto
her, the woman said, *Art* thou Joab?
And he answered, I *am he*. Then she
said unto him, Hear the words of thine
handmaid. And he answered, I do hear.
18 Then she spake, saying, They were
wont to speak in old time, saying, They
shall surely ask *counsel* at Abel: and so
they ended *the matter*.
19 I *am one of them that are* peaceable *and* faithful in Israel: thou seekest
to destroy a city and a mother in Israel:
why wilt thou swallow up the inheritance of the LORD?
20 And Joab answered and said, Far
be it, far be it from me, that I should
swallow up or destroy.
21 The matter *is* not so: but a man of
mount Ephraim, Sheba the son of
Bichri by name, hath lifted up his hand
against the king, *even* against David:
deliver him only, and I will depart from
the city. And the woman said unto Joab,
Behold, his head shall be thrown to
thee over the wall.
22 Then the woman went unto all the
people in her wisdom. And they cut off
the head of Sheba the son of Bichri, and
cast *it* out to Joab. And he blew a trumpet, and they retired from the city,
every man to his tent. And Joab
returned to Jerusalem unto the king.
23 Now Joab *was* over all the host of
Israel: and Benaiah the son of Jehoiada
was over the Cherethites and over the
Pelethites:
24 And Adoram *was* over the tribute:
and Jehoshaphat the son of Ahilud *was*
recorder:
25 And Sheva *was* scribe: and Zadok
and Abiathar *were* the priests:
26 And Ira also the Jairite was a chief
ruler about David.

21 Then there was a famine in the
days of David three years, year
after year; and David enquired of the
LORD. And the LORD answered, *It is* for
Saul, and for *his* bloody house, because
he slew the Gibeonites.
2 And the king called the Gibeonites,
and said unto them; (now the
Gibeonites *were* not of the children of
Israel, but of the remnant of the
Amorites; and the children of Israel
had sworn unto them: and Saul sought
to slay them in his zeal to the children
of Israel and Judah.)

3 Wherefore David said unto the Gibeonites, What shall I do for you? and wherewith shall I make the atonement, that ye may bless the inheritance of the LORD?

4 And the Gibeonites said unto him, We will have no silver nor gold of Saul, nor of his house; neither for us shalt thou kill any man in Israel. And he said, What ye shall say, *that* will I do for you.

5 And they answered the king, The man that consumed us, and that devised against us *that* we should be destroyed from remaining in any of the coasts of Israel,

6 Let seven men of his sons be delivered unto us, and we will hang them up unto the LORD in Gibeah of Saul, *whom* the LORD did choose. And the king said, I will give *them*.

7 But the king spared Mephibosheth, the son of Jonathan the son of Saul, because of the LORD's oath that *was* between them, between David and Jonathan the son of Saul.

8 But the king took the two sons of Rizpah the daughter of Aiah, whom she bare unto Saul, Armoni and Mephibosheth; and the five sons of Michal the daughter of Saul, whom she brought up for Adriel the son of Barzillai the Meholathite:

9 And he delivered them into the hands of the Gibeonites, and they hanged them in the hill before the LORD: and they fell *all* seven together, and were put to death in the days of harvest, in the first *days*, in the beginning of barley harvest.

10 And Rizpah the daughter of Aiah took sackcloth, and spread it for her upon the rock, from the beginning of harvest until water dropped upon them out of heaven, and suffered neither the birds of the air to rest on them by day, nor the beasts of the field by night.

11 And it was told David what Rizpah the daughter of Aiah, the concubine of Saul, had done.

12 And David went and took the bones of Saul and the bones of Jonathan his son from the men of Jabesh-gilead, which had stolen them from the street of Beth-shan, where the Philistines had hanged them, when the Philistines had slain Saul in Gilboa:

13 And he brought up from thence the bones of Saul and the bones of Jonathan his son; and they gathered the bones of them that were hanged.

14 And the bones of Saul and Jonathan his son buried they in the country of Benjamin in Zelah, in the sepulchre of Kish his father: and they performed all that the king commanded. And after that God was intreated for the land.

15 Moreover the Philistines had yet war again with Israel; and David went down, and his servants with him, and fought against the Philistines: and David waxed faint.

16 And Ishbi-benob, which *was* of the sons of the giant, the weight of whose spear *weighed* three hundred *shekels* of brass in weight, he being girded with a new *sword*, thought to have slain David.

17 But Abishai the son of Zeruiah succoured him, and smote the Philistine, and killed him. Then the men of David sware unto him, saying, Thou shalt go no more out with us to battle, that thou quench not the light of Israel.

18 And it came to pass after this, that there was again a battle with the Philistines at Gob: then Sibbechai the Hushathite slew Saph, which *was* of the sons of the giant.

19 And there was again a battle in
Gob with the Philistines, where
Elhanan the son of Jaareoregim, a
Beth-lehemite, slew *the brother of*
Goliath the Gittite, the staff of whose
spear *was* like a weaver's beam.
20 And there was yet a battle in Gath,
where was a man of *great* stature, that
had on every hand six fingers, and on
every foot six toes, four and twenty in
number; and he also was born to the
giant.
21 And when he defied Israel, Jonathan the son of Shimea the brother of
David slew him.
22 These four were born to the giant
in Gath, and fell by the hand of David,
and by the hand of his servants.

22 And David spake unto the LORD
the words of this song in the day
that the LORD had delivered him out of
the hand of all his enemies, and out of
the hand of Saul:
2 And he said, The LORD *is* my rock,
and my fortress, and my deliverer;
3 The God of my rock; in him will I
trust: *he is* my shield, and the horn of
my salvation, my high tower, and my
refuge, my saviour; thou savest me
from violence.
4 I will call on the LORD, *who is* worthy to be praised: so shall I be saved
from mine enemies.
5 When the waves of death compassed me, the floods of ungodly men
made me afraid;
6 The sorrows of hell compassed me
about; the snares of death prevented
me;
7 In my distress I called upon the
LORD, and cried to my God: and he did
hear my voice out of his temple, and my
cry *did enter* into his ears.
8 Then the earth shook and trembled;
the foundations of heaven moved and
shook, because he was wroth.
9 There went up a smoke out of his
nostrils, and fire out of his mouth
devoured: coals were kindled by it.
10 He bowed the heavens also, and
came down; and darkness *was* under
his feet.
11 And he rode upon a cherub, and
did fly: and he was seen upon the wings
of the wind.
12 And he made darkness pavilions
round about him, dark waters, *and*
thick clouds of the skies.
13 Through the brightness before him
were coals of fire kindled.
14 The LORD thundered from heaven,
and the most High uttered his voice.
15 And he sent out arrows, and scattered them; lightning, and discomfited
them.
16 And the channels of the sea
appeared, the foundations of the world
were discovered, at the rebuking of the
LORD, at the blast of the breath of his
nostrils.
17 He sent from above, he took me; he
drew me out of many waters;
18 He delivered me from my strong
enemy, *and* from them that hated me:
for they were too strong for me.
19 They prevented me in the day of
my calamity: but the LORD was my stay.
20 He brought me forth also into a
large place: he delivered me, because
he delighted in me.
21 The LORD rewarded me according
to my righteousness: according to the
cleanness of my hands hath he recompensed me.
22 For I have kept the ways of the
LORD, and have not wickedly departed
from my God.

23 For all his judgments *were* before me: and *as for* his statutes, I did not depart from them.

24 I was also upright before him, and have kept myself from mine iniquity.

25 Therefore the LORD hath recompensed me according to my righteousness; according to my cleanness in his eye sight.

26 With the merciful thou wilt shew thyself merciful, *and* with the upright man thou wilt shew thyself upright.

27 With the pure thou wilt shew thyself pure; and with the froward thou wilt shew thyself unsavoury.

28 And the afflicted people thou wilt save: but thine eyes *are* upon the haughty, *that* thou mayest bring *them* down.

29 For thou *art* my lamp, O LORD: and the LORD will lighten my darkness.

30 For by thee I have run through a troop: by my God have I leaped over a wall.

31 *As for* God, his way *is* perfect; the word of the LORD *is* tried: he *is* a buckler to all them that trust in him.

32 For who *is* God, save the LORD? and who *is* a rock, save our God?

33 God *is* my strength *and* power: and he maketh my way perfect.

34 He maketh my feet like hinds' *feet*: and setteth me upon my high places.

35 He teacheth my hands to war; so that a bow of steel is broken by mine arms.

36 Thou hast also given me the shield of thy salvation: and thy gentleness hath made me great.

37 Thou hast enlarged my steps under me; so that my feet did not slip.

38 I have pursued mine enemies, and destroyed them; and turned not again until I had consumed them.

39 And I have consumed them, and wounded them, that they could not arise: yea, they are fallen under my feet.

40 For thou hast girded me with strength to battle: them that rose up against me hast thou subdued under me.

41 Thou hast also given me the necks of mine enemies, that I might destroy them that hate me.

42 They looked, but *there was* none to save; *even* unto the LORD, but he answered them not.

43 Then did I beat them as small as the dust of the earth, I did stamp them as the mire of the street, *and* did spread them abroad.

44 Thou also hast delivered me from the strivings of my people, thou hast kept me *to be* head of the heathen: a people *which* I knew not shall serve me.

45 Strangers shall submit themselves unto me: as soon as they hear, they shall be obedient unto me.

46 Strangers shall fade away, and they shall be afraid out of their close places.

47 The LORD liveth; and blessed *be* my rock; and exalted be the God of the rock of my salvation.

48 It *is* God that avengeth me, and that bringeth down the people under me,

49 And that bringeth me forth from mine enemies: thou also hast lifted me up on high above them that rose up against me: thou hast delivered me from the violent man.

50 Therefore I will give thanks unto thee, O LORD, among the heathen, and I will sing praises unto thy name.

51 *He is* the tower of salvation for his king: and sheweth mercy to his anointed, unto David, and to his seed for evermore.

23 Now these *be* the last words of David. David the son of Jesse said, and the man *who was* raised up on high, the anointed of the God of Jacob, and the sweet psalmist of Israel, said,

2 The Spirit of the LORD spake by me, and his word *was* in my tongue.

3 The God of Israel said, the Rock of Israel spake to me, He that ruleth over men *must be* just, ruling in the fear of God.

4 And *he shall be* as the light of the morning, *when* the sun riseth, *even* a morning without clouds; *as* the tender grass *springing* out of the earth by clear shining after rain.

5 Although my house *be* not so with God; yet he hath made with me an everlasting covenant, ordered in all *things*, and sure: for *this is* all my salvation, and all *my* desire, although he make *it* not to grow.

6 But *the sons* of Belial *shall be* all of them as thorns thrust away, because they cannot be taken with hands:

7 But the man *that* shall touch them must be fenced with iron and the staff of a spear; and they shall be utterly burned with fire in the *same* place.

8 These *be* the names of the mighty men whom David had: The Tachmonite that sat in the seat, chief among the captains; the same *was* Adino the Eznite: *he lift up his spear* against eight hundred, whom he slew at one time.

9 And after him *was* Eleazar the son of Dodo the Ahohite, *one* of the three mighty men with David, when they defied the Philistines *that* were there gathered together to battle, and the men of Israel were gone away:

10 He arose, and smote the Philistines until his hand was weary, and his hand clave unto the sword: and the LORD wrought a great victory that day; and the people returned after him only to spoil.

11 And after him *was* Shammah the son of Agee the Hararite. And the Philistines were gathered together into a troop, where was a piece of ground full of lentiles: and the people fled from the Philistines.

12 But he stood in the midst of the ground, and defended it, and slew the Philistines: and the LORD wrought a great victory.

13 And three of the thirty chief went down, and came to David in the harvest time unto the cave of Adullam: and the troop of the Philistines pitched in the valley of Rephaim.

14 And David *was* then in an hold, and the garrison of the Philistines *was* then *in* Beth-lehem.

15 And David longed, and said, Oh that one would give me drink of the water of the well of Beth-lehem, which *is* by the gate!

16 And the three mighty men brake through the host of the Philistines, and drew water out of the well of Beth-lehem, that *was* by the gate, and took *it*, and brought *it* to David: nevertheless he would not drink thereof, but poured it out unto the LORD.

17 And he said, Be it far from me, O LORD, that I should do this: *is not this* the blood of the men that went in jeopardy of their lives? therefore he would not drink it. These things did these three mighty men.

18 And Abishai, the brother of Joab,
the son of Zeruiah, was chief among
three. And he lifted up his spear
against three hundred, *and* slew *them*,
and had the name among three.
19 Was he not most honourable of
three? therefore he was their captain:
howbeit he attained not unto the *first*
three.
20 And Benaiah the son of Jehoiada,
the son of a valiant man, of Kabzeel,
who had done many acts, he slew two
lionlike men of Moab: he went down
also and slew a lion in the midst of a pit
in time of snow:
21 And he slew an Egyptian, a goodly
man: and the Egyptian had a spear in
his hand; but he went down to him with
a staff, and plucked the spear out of the
Egyptian's hand, and slew him with his
own spear.
22 These *things* did Benaiah the son
of Jehoiada, and had the name among
three mighty men.
23 He was more honourable than the
thirty, but he attained not to the *first*
three. And David set him over his
guard.
24 Asahel the brother of Joab *was*
one of the thirty; Elhanan the son of
Dodo of Beth-lehem,
25 Shammah the Harodite, Elika the
Harodite,
26 Helez the Paltite, Ira the son of
Ikkesh the Tekoite,
27 Abiezer the Anethothite, Mebu-
nnai the Hushathite,
28 Zalmon the Ahohite, Maharai the
Netophathite,
29 Heleb the son of Baanah, a
Netophathite, Ittai the son of Ribai out
of Gibeah of the children of Benjamin,
30 Benaiah the Pirathonite, Hiddai of
the brooks of Gaash,
31 Abialbon the Arbathite, Azmaveth
the Barhu-mite,
32 Eliahba the Shaalbonite, of the
sons of Jashen, Jonathan,
33 Shammah the Hararite, Ahiam the
son of Sharar the Hararite,
34 Eliphelet the son of Ahasbai, the
son of the Maachathite, Eliam the son
of Ahithophel the Gilonite,
35 Hezrai the Carmelite, Paarai the
Arbite,
36 Igal the son of Nathan of Zobah,
Bani the Gadite,
37 Zelek the Ammonite, Naharai the
Beerothite, armourbearer to Joab the
son of Zeruiah,
38 Ira an Ithrite, Gareb an Ithrite,
39 Uriah the Hittite: thirty and seven
in all.

24 And again the anger of the LORD
was kindled against Israel, and
he moved David against them to say,
Go, number Israel and Judah.
2 For the king said to Joab the captain of the host, which *was* with him,
Go now through all the tribes of Israel,
from Dan even to Beer-sheba, and number ye the people, that I may know the
number of the people.
3 And Joab said unto the king, Now
the LORD thy God add unto the people,
how many soever they be, an hundredfold, and that the eyes of my lord the
king may see *it*: but why doth my lord
the king delight in this thing?
4 Notwithstanding the king's word
prevailed against Joab, and against the
captains of the host. And Joab and the
captains of the host went out from the
presence of the king, to number the
people of Israel.

5 And they passed over Jordan, and pitched in Aroer, on the right side of the city that *lieth* in the midst of the river of Gad, and toward Jazer:

6 Then they came to Gilead, and to the land of Tahtim-hodshi; and they came to Dan-jaan, and about to Zidon,

7 And came to the strong hold of Tyre, and to all the cities of the Hivites, and of the Canaanites: and they went out to the south of Judah, *even* to Beer-sheba.

8 So when they had gone through all the land, they came to Jerusalem at the end of nine months and twenty days.

9 And Joab gave up the sum of the number of the people unto the king: and there were in Israel eight hundred thousand valiant men that drew the sword; and the men of Judah *were* five hundred thousand men.

10 And David's heart smote him after that he had numbered the people. And David said unto the LORD, I have sinned greatly in that I have done: and now, I beseech thee, O LORD, take away the iniquity of thy servant; for I have done very foolishly.

11 For when David was up in the morning, the word of the LORD came unto the prophet Gad, David's seer, saying,

12 Go and say unto David, Thus saith the LORD, I offer thee three *things*; choose thee one of them, that I may *do it* unto thee.

13 So Gad came to David, and told him, and said unto him, Shall seven years of famine come unto thee in thy land? or wilt thou flee three months before thine enemies, while they pursue thee? or that there be three days' pestilence in thy land? now advise, and see what answer I shall return to him that sent me.

14 And David said unto Gad, I am in a great strait: let us fall now into the hand of the LORD; for his mercies *are* great: and let me not fall into the hand of man.

15 So the LORD sent a pestilence upon Israel from the morning even to the time appointed: and there died of the people from Dan even to Beer-sheba seventy thousand men.

16 And when the angel stretched out his hand upon Jerusalem to destroy it, the LORD repented him of the evil, and said to the angel that destroyed the people, It is enough: stay now thine hand. And the angel of the LORD was by the threshingplace of Araunah the Jebusite.

17 And David spake unto the LORD when he saw the angel that smote the people, and said, Lo, I have sinned, and I have done wickedly: but these sheep, what have they done? let thine hand, I pray thee, be against me, and against my father's house.

18 And Gad came that day to David, and said unto him, Go up, rear an altar unto the LORD in the threshingfloor of Araunah the Jebusite.

19 And David, according to the saying of Gad, went up as the LORD commanded.

20 And Araunah looked, and saw the king and his servants coming on toward him: and Araunah went out, and bowed himself before the king on his face upon the ground.

21 And Araunah said, Wherefore is my lord the king come to his servant? And David said, To buy the threshingfloor of thee, to build an altar unto the LORD, that the plague may be stayed from the people.

22 And Araunah said unto David, Let my lord the king take and offer up what *seemeth* good unto him: behold, *here be* oxen for burnt sacrifice, and threshing instruments and *other* instruments of the oxen for wood.

23 All these *things* did Araunah, *as* a king, give unto the king. And Araunah said unto the king, The LORD thy God accept thee.

24 And the king said unto Araunah, Nay; but I will surely buy *it* of thee at a price: neither will I offer burnt offerings unto the LORD my God of that which doth cost me nothing. So David bought the threshingfloor and the oxen for fifty shekels of silver.

25 And David built there an altar unto the LORD, and offered burnt offerings and peace offerings. So the LORD was intreated for the land, and the plague was stayed from Israel.

THE FIRST BOOK OF KINGS

1 Now king David was old *and* stricken in years; and they covered him with clothes, but he gat no heat.

2 Wherefore his servants said unto him, Let there be sought for my lord the king a young virgin: and let her stand before the king, and let her cherish him, and let her lie in thy bosom, that my lord the king may get heat.

3 So they sought for a fair damsel throughout all the coasts of Israel, and found Abishag a Shunammite, and brought her to the king.

4 And the damsel *was* very fair, and cherished the king, and ministered to him: but the king knew her not.

5 Then Adonijah the son of Haggith exalted himself, saying, I will be king: and he prepared him chariots and horsemen, and fifty men to run before him.

6 And his father had not displeased him at any time in saying, Why hast thou done so? and he also *was a* very goodly *man*; and *his mother* bare him after Absalom.

7 And he conferred with Joab the son of Zeruiah, and with Abiathar the priest: and they following Adonijah helped *him*.

8 But Zadok the priest, and Benaiah the son of Jehoiada, and Nathan the prophet, and Shimei, and Rei, and the mighty men which *belonged* to David, were not with Adonijah.

9 And Adonijah slew sheep and oxen and fat cattle by the stone of Zoheleth, which *is* by En-rogel, and called all his brethren the king's sons, and all the men of Judah the king's servants:

10 But Nathan the prophet, and Benaiah, and the mighty men, and Solomon his brother, he called not.

11 Wherefore Nathan spake unto Bath-sheba the mother of Solomon, saying, Hast thou not heard that Adonijah the son of Haggith doth reign, and David our lord knoweth *it* not?

12 Now therefore come, let me, I pray thee, give thee counsel, that thou mayest save thine own life, and the life of thy son Solomon.

13 Go and get thee in unto king David, and say unto him, Didst not thou, my lord, O king, swear unto thine handmaid, saying, Assuredly Solomon thy son shall reign after me, and he shall sit upon my throne? why then doth Adonijah reign?

14 Behold, while thou yet talkest there with the king, I also will come in after thee, and confirm thy words.

15 And Bath-sheba went in unto the king into the chamber: and the king was very old; and Abishag the Shunammite ministered unto the king.

16 And Bath-sheba bowed, and did obeisance unto the king. And the king said, What wouldest thou?

17 And she said unto him, My lord, thou swarest by the LORD thy God unto thine handmaid, *saying*, Assuredly Solomon thy son shall reign after me, and he shall sit upon my throne.

18 And now, behold, Adonijah reigneth; and now, my lord the king, thou knowest *it* not:

19 And he hath slain oxen and fat cattle and sheep in abundance, and hath called all the sons of the king, and Abiathar the priest, and Joab the captain of the host: but Solomon thy servant hath he not called.

20 And thou, my lord, O king, the eyes of all Israel *are* upon thee, that thou shouldest tell them who shall sit on the throne of my lord the king after him.

21 Otherwise it shall come to pass, when my lord the king shall sleep with his fathers, that I and my son Solomon shall be counted offenders.

22 And, lo, while she yet talked with the king, Nathan the prophet also came in.

23 And they told the king, saying, Behold Nathan the prophet. And when he was come in before the king, he bowed himself before the king with his face to the ground.

24 And Nathan said, My lord, O king, hast thou said, Adonijah shall reign after me, and he shall sit upon my throne?

25 For he is gone down this day, and hath slain oxen and fat cattle and sheep in abundance, and hath called all the king's sons, and the captains of the host, and Abiathar the priest; and, behold, they eat and drink before him, and say, God save king Adonijah.

26 But me, *even* me thy servant, and Zadok the priest, and Benaiah the son of Jehoiada, and thy servant Solomon, hath he not called.

27 Is this thing done by my lord the king, and thou hast not shewed *it* unto thy servant, who should sit on the throne of my lord the king after him?

28 Then king David answered and said, Call me Bath-sheba. And she came into the king's presence, and stood before the king.

29 And the king sware, and said, *As* the LORD liveth, that hath redeemed my soul out of all distress,

30 Even as I sware unto thee by the LORD God of Israel, saying, Assuredly Solomon thy son shall reign after me, and he shall sit upon my throne in my stead; even so will I certainly do this day.

31 Then Bath-sheba bowed with *her* face to the earth, and did reverence to the king, and said, Let my lord king David live for ever.

32 And king David said, Call me Zadok the priest, and Nathan the prophet, and Benaiah the son of Jehoiada. And they came before the king.

33 The king also said unto them, Take with you the servants of your lord, and cause Solomon my son to ride upon mine own mule, and bring him down to Gihon:

34 And let Zadok the priest and Nathan the prophet anoint him there king over Israel: and blow ye with the trumpet, and say, God save king Solomon.

35 Then ye shall come up after him, that he may come and sit upon my throne; for he shall be king in my stead: and I have appointed him to be ruler over Israel and over Judah.

36 And Benaiah the son of Jehoiada answered the king, and said, Amen: the LORD God of my lord the king say so *too*.

37 As the LORD hath been with my lord the king, even so be he with Solomon, and make his throne greater than the throne of my lord king David.

38 So Zadok the priest, and Nathan the prophet, and Benaiah the son of Jehoiada, and the Cherethites, and the Pelethites, went down, and caused Solomon to ride upon king David's mule, and brought him to Gihon.

39 And Zadok the priest took an horn of oil out of the tabernacle, and anointed Solomon. And they blew the trumpet; and all the people said, God save king Solomon.

40 And all the people came up after him, and the people piped with pipes, and rejoiced with great joy, so that the earth rent with the sound of them.

41 And Adonijah and all the guests that *were* with him heard *it* as they had made an end of eating. And when Joab heard the sound of the trumpet, he said, Wherefore *is this* noise of the city being in an uproar?

42 And while he yet spake, behold, Jonathan the son of Abiathar the priest came: and Adonijah said unto him, Come in; for thou *art* a valiant man, and bringest good tidings.

43 And Jonathan answered and said to Adonijah, Verily our lord king David hath made Solomon king.

44 And the king hath sent with him Zadok the priest, and Nathan the prophet, and Benaiah the son of Jehoiada, and the Cherethites, and the Pelethites, and they have caused him to ride upon the king's mule:

45 And Zadok the priest and Nathan the prophet have anointed him king in Gihon: and they are come up from thence rejoicing, so that the city rang again. This *is* the noise that ye have heard.

46 And also Solomon sitteth on the throne of the kingdom.

47 And moreover the king's servants came to bless our lord king David, saying, God make the name of Solomon better than thy name, and make his throne greater than thy throne. And the king bowed himself upon the bed.

48 And also thus said the king, Blessed *be* the LORD God of Israel, which hath given *one* to sit on my throne this day, mine eyes even seeing *it*.

49 And all the guests that *were* with Adonijah were afraid, and rose up, and went every man his way.

50 And Adonijah feared because of Solomon, and arose, and went, and caught hold on the horns of the altar.

51 And it was told Solomon, saying, Behold, Adonijah feareth king Solomon: for, lo, he hath caught hold on the horns of the altar, saying, Let king Solomon swear unto me to day that he will not slay his servant with the sword.

52 And Solomon said, If he will shew himself a worthy man, there shall not an hair of him fall to the earth: but if wickedness shall be found in him, he shall die.

53 So king Solomon sent, and they brought him down from the altar. And he came and bowed himself to king Solomon: and Solomon said unto him, Go to thine house.

2 Now the days of David drew nigh that he should die; and he charged Solomon his son, saying,

2 I go the way of all the earth: be thou strong therefore, and shew thyself a man;

3 And keep the charge of the LORD thy God, to walk in his ways, to keep his statutes, and his commandments, and his judgments, and his testimonies, as it is written in the law of Moses, that thou mayest prosper in all that thou doest, and whithersoever thou turnest thyself:

4 That the LORD may continue his word which he spake concerning me, saying, If thy children take heed to their way, to walk before me in truth with all their heart and with all their soul, there shall not fail thee (said he) a man on the throne of Israel.

5 Moreover thou knowest also what Joab the son of Zeruiah did to me, *and* what he did to the two captains of the hosts of Israel, unto Abner the son of Ner, and unto Amasa the son of Jether, whom he slew, and shed the blood of war in peace, and put the blood of war upon his girdle that *was* about his loins, and in his shoes that *were* on his feet.

6 Do therefore according to thy wisdom, and let not his hoar head go down to the grave in peace.

7 But shew kindness unto the sons of Barzillai the Gileadite, and let them be of those that eat at thy table: for so they came to me when I fled because of Absalom thy brother.

8 And, behold, *thou hast* with thee Shimei the son of Gera, a Benjamite of Bahurim, which cursed me with a grievous curse in the day when I went to Mahanaim: but he came down to meet me at Jordan, and I sware to him by the LORD, saying, I will not put thee to death with the sword.

9 Now therefore hold him not guiltless: for thou *art* a wise man, and knowest what thou oughtest to do unto him; but his hoar head bring thou down to the grave with blood.

10 So David slept with his fathers, and was buried in the city of David.

11 And the days that David reigned over Israel *were* forty years: seven years reigned he in Hebron, and thirty and three years reigned he in Jerusalem.

12 Then sat Solomon upon the throne of David his father; and his kingdom was established greatly.

13 And Adonijah the son of Haggith came to Bath-sheba the mother of Solomon. And she said, Comest thou peaceably? And he said, Peaceably.

14 He said moreover, I have somewhat to say unto thee. And she said, Say on.

15 And he said, Thou knowest that the kingdom was mine, and *that* all Israel set their faces on me, that I should reign: howbeit the kingdom is turned about, and is become my brother's: for it was his from the LORD.

16 And now I ask one petition of thee, deny me not. And she said unto him, Say on.

17 And he said, Speak, I pray thee, unto Solomon the king, (for he will not say thee nay,) that he give me Abishag the Shunammite to wife.

18 And Bath-sheba said, Well; I will speak for thee unto the king.

19 Bath-sheba therefore went unto king Solomon, to speak unto him for Adonijah. And the king rose up to meet her, and bowed himself unto her, and sat down on his throne, and caused a seat to be set for the king's mother; and she sat on his right hand.

20 Then she said, I desire one small petition of thee; *I pray thee*, say me not nay. And the king said unto her, Ask on, my mother: for I will not say thee nay.

21 And she said, Let Abishag the Shunammite be given to Adonijah thy brother to wife.

22 And king Solomon answered and said unto his mother, And why dost thou ask Abishag the Shunammite for Adonijah? ask for him the kingdom also; for he *is* mine elder brother; even for him, and for Abiathar the priest, and for Joab the son of Zeruiah.

23 Then king Solomon sware by the LORD, saying, God do so to me, and more also, if Adonijah have not spoken this word against his own life.

24 Now therefore, *as* the LORD liveth, which hath established me, and set me on the throne of David my father, and who hath made me an house, as he promised, Adonijah shall be put to death this day.

25 And king Solomon sent by the hand of Benaiah the son of Jehoiada; and he fell upon him that he died.

26 And unto Abiathar the priest said the king, Get thee to Anathoth, unto thine own fields; for thou *art* worthy of death: but I will not at this time put thee to death, because thou barest the ark of the Lord GOD before David my father, and because thou hast been afflicted in all wherein my father was afflicted.

27 So Solomon thrust out Abiathar from being priest unto the LORD; that he might fulfil the word of the LORD, which he spake concerning the house of Eli in Shiloh.

28 Then tidings came to Joab: for Joab had turned after Adonijah, though he turned not after Absalom. And Joab fled unto the tabernacle of the LORD, and caught hold on the horns of the altar.

29 And it was told king Solomon that Joab was fled unto the tabernacle of the LORD; and, behold, *he is* by the altar. Then Solomon sent Benaiah the son of Jehoiada, saying, Go, fall upon him.

30 And Benaiah came to the tabernacle of the LORD, and said unto him, Thus saith the king, Come forth. And he said, Nay; but I will die here. And Benaiah brought the king word again, saying, Thus said Joab, and thus he answered me.

31 And the king said unto him, Do as he hath said, and fall upon him, and bury him; that thou mayest take away the innocent blood, which Joab shed, from me, and from the house of my father.

32 And the LORD shall return his blood upon his own head, who fell upon two men more righteous and better than he, and slew them with the sword, my father David not knowing *thereof, to wit*, Abner the son of Ner, captain of the host of Israel, and Amasa the son of Jether, captain of the host of Judah.

33 Their blood shall therefore return upon the head of Joab, and upon the head of his seed for ever: but upon David, and upon his seed, and upon his house, and upon his throne, shall there be peace for ever from the LORD.

34 So Benaiah the son of Jehoiada went up, and fell upon him, and slew him: and he was buried in his own house in the wilderness.

35 And the king put Benaiah the son of Jehoiada in his room over the host: and Zadok the priest did the king put in the room of Abiathar.

36 And the king sent and called for Shimei, and said unto him, Build thee an house in Jerusalem, and dwell there, and go not forth thence any whither.

37 For it shall be, *that* on the day thou goest out, and passest over the brook Kidron, thou shalt know for certain that thou shalt surely die: thy blood shall be upon thine own head.

38 And Shimei said unto the king, The saying *is* good: as my lord the king hath said, so will thy servant do. And Shimei dwelt in Jerusalem many days.

39 And it came to pass at the end of three years, that two of the servants of Shimei ran away unto Achish son of Maachah king of Gath. And they told Shimei, saying, Behold, thy servants *be* in Gath.

40 And Shimei arose, and saddled his ass, and went to Gath to Achish to seek his servants: and Shimei went, and brought his servants from Gath.

41 And it was told Solomon that Shimei had gone from Jerusalem to Gath, and was come again.

42 And the king sent and called for Shimei, and said unto him, Did I not make thee to swear by the LORD, and protested unto thee, saying, Know for a certain, on the day thou goest out, and walkest abroad any whither, that thou shalt surely die? and thou saidst unto me, The word *that* I have heard *is* good.

43 Why then hast thou not kept the oath of the LORD, and the commandment that I have charged thee with?

44 The king said moreover to Shimei, Thou knowest all the wickedness which thine heart is privy to, that thou didst to David my father: therefore the LORD shall return thy wickedness upon thine own head;

45 And king Solomon *shall be* blessed, and the throne of David shall be established before the LORD for ever.

46 So the king commanded Benaiah the son of Jehoiada; which went out, and fell upon him, that he died. And the kingdom was established in the hand of Solomon.

3 And Solomon made affinity with Pharaoh king of Egypt, and took Pharaoh's daughter, and brought her into the city of David, until he had made an end of building his own house, and the house of the LORD, and the wall of Jerusalem round about.

2 Only the people sacrificed in high places, because there was no house built unto the name of the LORD, until those days.

3 And Solomon loved the LORD, walking in the statutes of David his father: only he sacrificed and burnt incense in high places.

4 And the king went to Gibeon to sacrifice there; for that *was* the great high place: a thousand burnt offerings did Solomon offer upon that altar.

5 In Gibeon the LORD appeared to Solomon in a dream by night: and God said, Ask what I shall give thee.

6 And Solomon said, Thou hast shewed unto thy servant David my father great mercy, according as he walked before thee in truth, and in righteousness, and in uprightness of heart with thee; and thou hast kept for him this great kindness, that thou hast given him a son to sit on his throne, as *it is* this day.

7 And now, O LORD my God, thou hast made thy servant king instead of David my father: and I *am but* a little child: I know not *how* to go out or come in.

8 And thy servant *is* in the midst of thy people which thou hast chosen, a great people, that cannot be numbered nor counted for multitude.

9 Give therefore thy servant an understanding heart to judge thy people, that I may discern between good and bad: for who is able to judge this thy so great a people?

10 And the speech pleased the Lord, that Solomon had asked this thing.

11 And God said unto him, Because thou hast asked this thing, and hast not asked for thyself long life; neither hast asked riches for thyself, nor hast asked the life of thine enemies; but hast asked for thyself understanding to discern judgment;

12 Behold, I have done according to thy words: lo, I have given thee a wise and an understanding heart; so that there was none like thee before thee, neither after thee shall any arise like unto thee.

13 And I have also given thee that which thou hast not asked, both riches, and honour: so that there shall not be any among the kings like unto thee all thy days.

14 And if thou wilt walk in my ways, to keep my statutes and my commandments, as thy father David did walk, then I will lengthen thy days.

15 And Solomon awoke; and, behold, *it was* a dream. And he came to Jerusalem, and stood before the ark of the covenant of the LORD, and offered up burnt offerings, and offered peace offerings, and made a feast to all his servants.

16 Then came there two women, *that were* harlots, unto the king, and stood before him.

17 And the one woman said, O my lord, I and this woman dwell in one house; and I was delivered of a child with her in the house.

18 And it came to pass the third day after that I was delivered, that this woman was delivered also: and we *were* together; *there was* no stranger with us in the house, save we two in the house.

19 And this woman's child died in the night; because she overlaid it.

20 And she arose at midnight, and took my son from beside me, while thine handmaid slept, and laid it in her bosom, and laid her dead child in my bosom.

21 And when I rose in the morning to give my child suck, behold, it was dead: but when I had considered it in the morning, behold, it was not my son, which I did bear.

22 And the other woman said, Nay; but the living *is* my son, and the dead *is* thy son. And this said, No; but the dead *is* thy son, and the living *is* my son. Thus they spake before the king.

23 Then said the king, The one saith, This *is* my son that liveth, and thy son *is* the dead: and the other saith, Nay; but thy son *is* the dead, and my son *is* the living.

24 And the king said, Bring me a sword. And they brought a sword before the king.

25 And the king said, Divide the living child in two, and give half to the one, and half to the other.

26 Then spake the woman whose the living child *was* unto the king, for her bowels yearned upon her son, and she said, O my lord, give her the living child, and in no wise slay it. But the other said, Let it be neither mine nor thine, *but* divide *it*.

27 Then the king answered and said, Give her the living child, and in no wise slay it: she *is* the mother thereof.

28 And all Israel heard of the judgment which the king had judged; and they feared the king: for they saw that the wisdom of God *was* in him, to do judgment.

4 So king Solomon was king over all Israel.

2 And these *were* the princes which he had; Azariah the son of Zadok the priest,

3 Elihoreph and Ahiah, the sons of Shisha, scribes; Jehoshaphat the son of Ahilud, the recorder.

4 And Benaiah the son of Jehoiada *was* over the host: and Zadok and Abiathar *were* the priests:

5 And Azariah the son of Nathan *was* over the officers: and Zabud the son of Nathan *was* principal officer, *and* the king's friend:

6 And Ahishar *was* over the household: and Adoniram the son of Abda *was* over the tribute.

7 And Solomon had twelve officers over all Israel, which provided victuals for the king and his household: each man his month in a year made provision.

8 And these *are* their names: The son of Hur, in mount Ephraim:

9 The son of Dekar, in Makaz, and in Shaalbim, and Beth-shemesh, and Elon-beth-hanan:

10 The son of Hesed, in Aruboth; to him *pertained* Sochoh, and all the land of Hepher:

11 The son of Abinadab, in all the region of Dor; which had Taphath the daughter of Solomon to wife:

12 Baana the son of Ahilud; *to him pertained* Taanach and Megiddo, and all Beth-shean, which *is* by Zartanah beneath Jezreel, from Beth-shean to Abel-meholah, *even* unto *the place that is* beyond Jokneam:

13 The son of Geber, in Ramoth-gilead; to him *pertained* the towns of Jair the son of Manasseh, which *are* in Gilead; to him *also pertained* the region of Argob, which *is* in Bashan, threescore great cities with walls and brasen bars:

14 Ahinadab the son of Iddo *had* Mahanaim:

15 Ahimaaz *was* in Naphtali; he also took Basmath the daughter of Solomon to wife:

16 Baanah the son of Hushai *was* in Asher and in Aloth:

17 Jehoshaphat the son of Paruah, in Issachar:

18 Shimei the son of Elah, in Benjamin:

19 Geber the son of Uri *was* in the country of Gilead, *in* the country of Sihon king of the Amorites, and of Og king of Bashan; and *he was* the only officer which *was* in the land.

20 Judah and Israel *were* many, as the sand which *is* by the sea in multitude, eating and drinking, and making merry.

21 And Solomon reigned over all kingdoms from the river unto the land of the Philistines, and unto the border of Egypt: they brought presents, and served Solomon all the days of his life.

22 And Solomon's provision for one day was thirty measures of fine flour, and threescore measures of meal,

23 Ten fat oxen, and twenty oxen out of the pastures, and an hundred sheep, beside harts, and roebucks, and fallowdeer, and fatted fowl.

24 For he had dominion over all *the region* on this side the river, from Tiphsah even to Azzah, over all the kings on this side the river: and he had peace on all sides round about him.

25 And Judah and Israel dwelt safely, every man under his vine and under his fig tree, from Dan even to Beer-sheba, all the days of Solomon.

26 And Solomon had forty thousand stalls of horses for his chariots, and twelve thousand horsemen.

27 And those officers provided victual for king Solomon, and for all that came unto king Solomon's table, every man in his month: they lacked nothing.

28 Barley also and straw for the horses and dromedaries brought they unto the place where *the officers* were, every man according to his charge.

29 And God gave Solomon wisdom and understanding exceeding much, and largeness of heart, even as the sand that *is* on the sea shore.

30 And Solomon's wisdom excelled the wisdom of all the children of the east country, and all the wisdom of Egypt.

31 For he was wiser than all men; than Ethan the Ezrahite, and Heman, and Chalcol, and Darda, the sons of Mahol: and his fame was in all nations round about.

32 And he spake three thousand proverbs: and his songs were a thousand and five.

33 And he spake of trees, from the cedar tree that *is* in Lebanon even unto the hyssop that springeth out of the wall: he spake also of beasts, and of fowl, and of creeping things, and of fishes.

34 And there came of all people to hear the wisdom of Solomon, from all kings of the earth, which had heard of his wisdom.

5 And Hiram king of Tyre sent his servants unto Solomon; for he had heard that they had anointed him king in the room of his father: for Hiram was ever a lover of David.

2 And Solomon sent to Hiram, saying,

3 Thou knowest how that David my father could not build an house unto the name of the LORD his God for the wars which were about him on every side, until the LORD put them under the soles of his feet.

4 But now the LORD my God hath given me rest on every side, *so that there is* neither adversary nor evil occurrent.

5 And, behold, I purpose to build an
house unto the name of the LORD my
God, as the LORD spake unto David my
father, saying, Thy son, whom I will set
upon thy throne in thy room, he shall
build an house unto my name.
6 Now therefore command thou that
they hew me cedar trees out of
Lebanon; and my servants shall be with
thy servants: and unto thee will I give
hire for thy servants according to all
that thou shalt appoint: for thou knowest that *there is* not among us any that
can skill to hew timber like unto the
Sidonians.
7 And it came to pass, when Hiram
heard the words of Solomon, that he
rejoiced greatly, and said, Blessed *be*
the LORD this day, which hath given
unto David a wise son over this great
people.
8 And Hiram sent to Solomon, saying,
I have considered the things which
thou sentest to me for: *and* I will do all
thy desire concerning timber of cedar,
and concerning timber of fir.
9 My servants shall bring *them* down
from Lebanon unto the sea: and I will
convey them by sea in floats unto the
place that thou shalt appoint me, and
will cause them to be discharged there,
and thou shalt receive *them*: and thou
shalt accomplish my desire, in giving
food for my household.
10 So Hiram gave Solomon cedar
trees and fir trees *according to* all his
desire.
11 And Solomon gave Hiram twenty
thousand measures of wheat *for* food to
his household, and twenty measures of
pure oil: thus gave Solomon to Hiram
year by year.
12 And the LORD gave Solomon wisdom, as he promised him: and there
was peace between Hiram and
Solomon; and they two made a league
together.
13 And king Solomon raised a levy
out of all Israel; and the levy was thirty
thousand men.
14 And he sent them to Lebanon, ten
thousand a month by courses: a month
they were in Lebanon, *and* two months
at home: and Adoniram *was* over the
levy.
15 And Solomon had threescore and
ten thousand that bare burdens, and
fourscore thousand hewers in the
mountains;
16 Beside the chief of Solomon's officers which *were* over the work, three
thousand and three hundred, which
ruled over the people that wrought in
the work.
17 And the king commanded, and
they brought great stones, costly stones,
and hewed stones, to lay the foundation of the house.
18 And Solomon's builders and
Hiram's builders did hew *them*, and the
stonesquarers: so they prepared timber
and stones to build the house.

6 And it came to pass in the four
hundred and eightieth year after
the children of Israel were come out of
the land of Egypt, in the fourth year of
Solomon's reign over Israel, in the
month Zif, which *is* the second month,
that he began to build the house of the
LORD.
2 And the house which king Solomon
built for the LORD, the length thereof
was threescore cubits, and the breadth
thereof twenty *cubits*, and the height
thereof thirty cubits.

3 And the porch before the temple of the house, twenty cubits *was* the length thereof, according to the breadth of the house; *and* ten cubits *was* the breadth thereof before the house.

4 And for the house he made windows of narrow lights.

5 And against the wall of the house he built chambers round about, *against* the walls of the house round about, *both* of the temple and of the oracle: and he made chambers round about:

6 The nethermost chamber *was* five cubits broad, and the middle *was* six cubits broad, and the third *was* seven cubits broad: for without *in the wall* of the house he made narrowed rests round about, that *the beams* should not be fastened in the walls of the house.

7 And the house, when it was in building, was built of stone made ready before it was brought thither: so that there was neither hammer nor axe *nor* any tool of iron heard in the house, while it was in building.

8 The door for the middle chamber *was* in the right side of the house: and they went up with winding stairs into the middle *chamber*, and out of the middle into the third.

9 So he built the house, and finished it; and covered the house with beams and boards of cedar.

10 And *then* he built chambers against all the house, five cubits high: and they rested on the house with timber of cedar.

11 And the word of the LORD came to Solomon, saying,

12 *Concerning* this house which thou art in building, if thou wilt walk in my statutes, and execute my judgments, and keep all my commandments to walk in them; then will I perform my word with thee, which I spake unto David thy father:

13 And I will dwell among the children of Israel, and will not forsake my people Israel.

14 So Solomon built the house, and finished it.

15 And he built the walls of the house within with boards of cedar, both the floor of the house, and the walls of the cieling: *and* he covered *them* on the inside with wood, and covered the floor of the house with planks of fir.

16 And he built twenty cubits on the sides of the house, both the floor and the walls with boards of cedar: he even built *them* for it within, *even* for the oracle, *even* for the most holy *place*.

17 And the house, that *is*, the temple before it, was forty cubits *long*.

18 And the cedar of the house within *was* carved with knops and open flowers: all *was* cedar; there was no stone seen.

19 And the oracle he prepared in the house within, to set there the ark of the covenant of the LORD.

20 And the oracle in the forepart *was* twenty cubits in length, and twenty cubits in breadth, and twenty cubits in the height thereof: and he overlaid it with pure gold; and *so* covered the altar *which was of* cedar.

21 So Solomon overlaid the house within with pure gold: and he made a partition by the chains of gold before the oracle; and he overlaid it with gold.

22 And the whole house he overlaid with gold, until he had finished all the house: also the whole altar that *was* by the oracle he overlaid with gold.

23 And within the oracle he made two cherubims *of* olive tree, *each* ten cubits high.

24 And five cubits *was* the one wing
of the cherub, and five cubits the other
wing of the cherub: from the uttermost
part of the one wing unto the uttermost
part of the other *were* ten cubits.
25 And the other cherub *was* ten
cubits: both the cherubims *were* of one
measure and one size.
26 The height of the one cherub *was*
ten cubits, and so *was it* of the other
cherub.
27 And he set the cherubims within
the inner house: and they stretched
forth the wings of the cherubims, so
that the wing of the one touched the
one wall, and the wing of the other
cherub touched the other wall; and
their wings touched one another in the
midst of the house.
28 And he overlaid the cherubims
with gold.
29 And he carved all the walls of the
house round about with carved figures
of cherubims and palm trees and open
flowers, within and without.
30 And the floor of the house he overlaid with gold, within and without.
31 And for the entering of the oracle
he made doors *of* olive tree: the lintel
and side posts *were* a fifth part *of the
wall.*
32 The two doors also *were of* olive
tree; and he carved upon them carvings
of cherubims and palm trees and open
flowers, and overlaid *them* with gold,
and spread gold upon the cherubims,
and upon the palm trees.
33 So also made he for the door of the
temple posts *of* olive tree, a fourth part
of the wall.
34 And the two doors *were of* fir tree:
the two leaves of the one door *were*
folding, and the two leaves of the other
door *were* folding.
35 And he carved *thereon* cherubims
and palm trees and open flowers: and
covered *them* with gold fitted upon the
carved work.
36 And he built the inner court with
three rows of hewed stone, and a row of
cedar beams.
37 In the fourth year was the foundation of the house of the LORD laid, in
the month Zif:
38 And in the eleventh year, in the
month Bul, which *is* the eighth month,
was the house finished throughout all
the parts thereof, and according to all
the fashion of it. So was he seven years
in building it.

7 But Solomon was building his own
house thirteen years, and he
finished all his house.
2 He built also the house of the forest
of Lebanon; the length thereof *was* an
hundred cubits, and the breadth thereof fifty cubits, and the height thereof
thirty cubits, upon four rows of cedar
pillars, with cedar beams upon the pillars.
3 And *it was* covered with cedar
above upon the beams, that *lay* on forty
five pillars, fifteen *in* a row.
4 And *there were* windows *in* three
rows, and light *was* against light *in*
three ranks.
5 And all the doors and posts *were*
square, with the windows: and light
was against light *in* three ranks.
6 And he made a porch of pillars; the
length thereof *was* fifty cubits, and the
breadth thereof thirty cubits: and the
porch *was* before them: and the *other*
pillars and the thick beam *were* before
them.
7 Then he made a porch for the
throne where he might judge, *even* the
porch of judgment: and *it was* covered

with cedar from one side of the floor to
the other.
8 And his house where he dwelt *had*
another court within the porch, *which*
was of the like work. Solomon made
also an house for Pharaoh's daughter,
whom he had taken *to wife*, like unto
this porch.
9 All these *were of* costly stones,
according to the measures of hewed
stones, sawed with saws, within and
without, even from the foundation unto
the coping, and *so* on the outside
toward the great court.
10 And the foundation *was of* costly
stones, even great stones, stones of ten
cubits, and stones of eight cubits.
11 And above *were* costly stones, after
the measures of hewed stones, and
cedars.
12 And the great court round about
was with three rows of hewed stones,
and a row of cedar beams, both for the
inner court of the house of the LORD,
and for the porch of the house.
13 And king Solomon sent and
fetched Hiram out of Tyre.
14 He *was* a widow's son of the tribe
of Naphtali, and his father *was* a man
of Tyre, a worker in brass: and he was
filled with wisdom, and understanding,
and cunning to work all works in brass.
And he came to king Solomon, and
wrought all his work.
15 For he cast two pillars of brass, of
eighteen cubits high apiece: and a line
of twelve cubits did compass either of
them about.
16 And he made two chapiters *of* molten brass, to set upon the tops of the
pillars: the height of the one chapiter
was five cubits, and the height of the
other chapiter *was* five cubits:
17 *And* nets of checker work, and
wreaths of chain work, for the chapiters
which *were* upon the top of the pillars;
seven for the one chapiter, and seven
for the other chapiter.
18 And he made the pillars, and two
rows round about upon the one network, to cover the chapiters that *were*
upon the top, with pomegranates: and
so did he for the other chapiter.
19 And the chapiters that *were* upon
the top of the pillars *were* of lily work
in the porch, four cubits.
20 And the chapiters upon the two
pillars *had pomegranates* also above,
over against the belly which *was* by the
network: and the pomegranates *were*
two hundred in rows round about upon
the other chapiter.
21 And he set up the pillars in the
porch of the temple: and he set up the
right pillar, and called the name thereof Jachin: and he set up the left pillar,
and called the name thereof Boaz.
22 And upon the top of the pillars *was*
lily work: so was the work of the pillars
finished.
23 And he made a molten sea, ten
cubits from the one brim to the other:
it was round all about, and his height
was five cubits: and a line of thirty
cubits did compass it round about.
24 And under the brim of it round
about *there were* knops compassing it,
ten in a cubit, compassing the sea
round about: the knops *were* cast in two
rows, when it was cast.
25 It stood upon twelve oxen, three
looking toward the north, and three
looking toward the west, and three
looking toward the south, and three
looking toward the east: and the sea
was set above upon them, and all their
hinder parts *were* inward.

26 And it *was* an hand breadth thick,
and the brim thereof was wrought like
the brim of a cup, with flowers of lilies:
it contained two thousand baths.
27 And he made ten bases of brass;
four cubits *was* the length of one base,
and four cubits the breadth thereof,
and three cubits the height of it.
28 And the work of the bases *was* on
this *manner*: they had borders, and the
borders *were* between the ledges:
29 And on the borders that *were*
between the ledges *were* lions, oxen,
and cherubims: and upon the ledges
there was a base above: and beneath
the lions and oxen *were* certain additions made of thin work.
30 And every base had four brasen
wheels, and plates of brass: and the
four corners thereof had undersetters:
under the laver *were* undersetters molten, at the side of every addition.
31 And the mouth of it within the
chapiter and above *was* a cubit: but the
mouth thereof *was* round *after* the
work of the base, a cubit and an half:
and also upon the mouth of it *were*
gravings with their borders, foursquare,
not round.
32 And under the borders *were* four
wheels; and the axletrees of the wheels
were joined to the base: and the height
of a wheel *was* a cubit and half a cubit.
33 And the work of the wheels *was*
like the work of a chariot wheel: their
axletrees, and their naves, and their
felloes, and their spokes, *were* all molten.
34 And *there were* four undersetters
to the four corners of one base: *and* the
undersetters *were* of the very base
itself.
35 And in the top of the base *was*
there a round compass of half a cubit
high: and on the top of the base the
ledges thereof and the borders thereof
were of the same.
36 For on the plates of the ledges
thereof, and on the borders thereof, he
graved cherubims, lions, and palm
trees, according to the proportion of
every one, and additions round about.
37 After this *manner* he made the ten
bases: all of them had one casting, one
measure, *and* one size.
38 Then made he ten lavers of brass:
one laver contained forty baths: *and*
every laver was four cubits: *and* upon
every one of the ten bases one laver.
39 And he put five bases on the right
side of the house, and five on the left
side of the house: and he set the sea on
the right side of the house eastward
over against the south.
40 And Hiram made the lavers, and
the shovels, and the basons. So Hiram
made an end of doing all the work that
he made king Solomon for the house of
the LORD:
41 The two pillars, and the *two* bowls
of the chapiters that *were* on the top of
the two pillars; and the two networks,
to cover the two bowls of the chapiters
which *were* upon the top of the pillars;
42 And four hundred pomegranates
for the two networks, *even* two rows of
pomegranates for one network, to cover
the two bowls of the chapiters that *were*
upon the pillars;
43 And the ten bases, and ten lavers
on the bases;
44 And one sea, and twelve oxen
under the sea;

45 And the pots, and the shovels, and the basons: and all these vessels, which Hiram made to king Solomon for the house of the LORD, *were of* bright brass.

46 In the plain of Jordan did the king cast them, in the clay ground between Succoth and Zarthan.

47 And Solomon left all the vessels *unweighed*, because they were exceeding many: neither was the weight of the brass found out.

48 And Solomon made all the vessels that *pertained* unto the house of the LORD: the altar of gold, and the table of gold, whereupon the shewbread *was*,

49 And the candlesticks of pure gold, five on the right *side*, and five on the left, before the oracle, with the flowers, and the lamps, and the tongs *of* gold,

50 And the bowls, and the snuffers, and the basons, and the spoons, and the censers *of* pure gold; and the hinges *of* gold, *both* for the doors of the inner house, the most holy *place, and* for the doors of the house, *to wit*, of the temple.

51 So was ended all the work that king Solomon made for the house of the LORD. And Solomon brought in the things which David his father had dedicated; *even* the silver, and the gold, and the vessels, did he put among the treasures of the house of the LORD.

8 Then Solomon assembled the elders of Israel, and all the heads of the tribes, the chief of the fathers of the children of Israel, unto king Solomon in Jerusalem, that they might bring up the ark of the covenant of the LORD out of the city of David, which *is* Zion.

2 And all the men of Israel assembled themselves unto king Solomon at the feast in the month Ethanim, which *is* the seventh month.

3 And all the elders of Israel came, and the priests took up the ark.

4 And they brought up the ark of the LORD, and the tabernacle of the congregation, and all the holy vessels that *were* in the tabernacle, even those did the priests and the Levites bring up.

5 And king Solomon, and all the congregation of Israel, that were assembled unto him, *were* with him before the ark, sacrificing sheep and oxen, that could not be told nor numbered for multitude.

6 And the priests brought in the ark of the covenant of the LORD unto his place, into the oracle of the house, to the most holy *place, even* under the wings of the cherubims.

7 For the cherubims spread forth *their* two wings over the place of the ark, and the cherubims covered the ark and the staves thereof above.

8 And they drew out the staves, that the ends of the staves were seen out in the holy *place* before the oracle, and they were not seen without: and there they are unto this day.

9 *There was* nothing in the ark save the two tables of stone, which Moses put there at Horeb, when the LORD made *a covenant* with the children of Israel, when they came out of the land of Egypt.

10 And it came to pass, when the priests were come out of the holy *place*, that the cloud filled the house of the LORD,

11 So that the priests could not stand to minister because of the cloud: for the glory of the LORD had filled the house of the LORD.

12 Then spake Solomon, The LORD said that he would dwell in the thick darkness.

13 I have surely built thee an house to dwell in, a settled place for thee to abide in for ever.

14 And the king turned his face about, and blessed all the congregation of Israel: (and all the congregation of Israel stood;)

15 And he said, Blessed *be* the LORD God of Israel, which spake with his mouth unto David my father, and hath with his hand fulfilled *it*, saying,

16 Since the day that I brought forth my people Israel out of Egypt, I chose no city out of all the tribes of Israel to build an house, that my name might be therein; but I chose David to be over my people Israel.

17 And it was in the heart of David my father to build an house for the name of the LORD God of Israel.

18 And the LORD said unto David my father, Whereas it was in thine heart to build an house unto my name, thou didst well that it was in thine heart.

19 Nevertheless thou shalt not build the house; but thy son that shall come forth out of thy loins, he shall build the house unto my name.

20 And the LORD hath performed his word that he spake, and I am risen up in the room of David my father, and sit on the throne of Israel, as the LORD promised, and have built an house for the name of the LORD God of Israel.

21 And I have set there a place for the ark, wherein *is* the covenant of the LORD, which he made with our fathers, when he brought them out of the land of Egypt.

22 And Solomon stood before the altar of the LORD in the presence of all the congregation of Israel, and spread forth his hands toward heaven:

23 And he said, LORD God of Israel, *there is* no God like thee, in heaven above, or on earth beneath, who keepest covenant and mercy with thy servants that walk before thee with all their heart:

24 Who hast kept with thy servant David my father that thou promisedst him: thou spakest also with thy mouth, and hast fulfilled *it* with thine hand, as *it is* this day.

25 Therefore now, LORD God of Israel, keep with thy servant David my father that thou promisedst him, saying, There shall not fail thee a man in my sight to sit on the throne of Israel; so that thy children take heed to their way, that they walk before me as thou hast walked before me.

26 And now, O God of Israel, let thy word, I pray thee, be verified, which thou spakest unto thy servant David my father.

27 But will God indeed dwell on the earth? behold, the heaven and heaven of heavens cannot contain thee; how much less this house that I have builded?

28 Yet have thou respect unto the prayer of thy servant, and to his supplication, O LORD my God, to hearken unto the cry and to the prayer, which thy servant prayeth before thee to day:

29 That thine eyes may be open toward this house night and day, *even* toward the place of which thou hast said, My name shall be there: that thou mayest hearken unto the prayer which thy servant shall make toward this place.

30 And hearken thou to the supplication of thy servant, and of thy people Israel, when they shall pray toward this place: and hear thou in heaven thy

dwelling place: and when thou hearest,
forgive.
31 If any man trespass against his
neighbour, and an oath be laid upon
him to cause him to swear, and the oath
come before thine altar in this house:
32 Then hear thou in heaven, and do,
and judge thy servants, condemning
the wicked, to bring his way upon his
head; and justifying the righteous, to
give him according to his righteousness.
33 When thy people Israel be smitten
down before the enemy, because they
have sinned against thee, and shall
turn again to thee, and confess thy
name, and pray, and make supplication
unto thee in this house:
34 Then hear thou in heaven, and
forgive the sin of thy people Israel, and
bring them again unto the land which
thou gavest unto their fathers.
35 When heaven is shut up, and there
is no rain, because they have sinned
against thee; if they pray toward this
place, and confess thy name, and turn
from their sin, when thou afflictest
them:
36 Then hear thou in heaven, and
forgive the sin of thy servants, and of
thy people Israel, that thou teach them
the good way wherein they should
walk, and give rain upon thy land,
which thou hast given to thy people for
an inheritance.
37 If there be in the land famine, if
there be pestilence, blasting, mildew,
locust, *or* if there be caterpiller; if their
enemy besiege them in the land of
their cities; whatsoever plague, whatsoever
sickness *there be*;
38 What prayer and supplication
soever be *made* by any man, *or* by all
thy people Israel, which shall know
every man the plague of his own heart,
and spread forth his hands toward this
house:
39 Then hear thou in heaven thy
dwelling place, and forgive, and do, and
give to every man according to his ways,
whose heart thou knowest; (for thou,
even thou only, knowest the hearts of
all the children of men;)
40 That they may fear thee all the
days that they live in the land which
thou gavest unto our fathers.
41 Moreover concerning a stranger,
that *is* not of thy people Israel, but
cometh out of a far country for thy
name's sake;
42 (For they shall hear of thy great
name, and of thy strong hand, and of
thy stretched out arm;) when he shall
come and pray toward this house;
43 Hear thou in heaven thy dwelling
place, and do according to all that the
stranger calleth to thee for: that all
people of the earth may know thy
name, to fear thee, as *do* thy people
Israel; and that they may know that this
house, which I have builded, is called
by thy name.
44 If thy people go out to battle
against their enemy, whithersoever
thou shalt send them, and shall pray
unto the LORD toward the city which
thou hast chosen, and *toward* the house
that I have built for thy name:
45 Then hear thou in heaven their
prayer and their supplication, and
maintain their cause.
46 If they sin against thee, (for *there*
is no man that sinneth not,) and thou
be angry with them, and deliver them
to the enemy, so that they carry them
away captives unto the land of the
enemy, far or near;

47 *Yet* if they shall bethink themselves in the land whither they were
carried captives, and repent, and make
supplication unto thee in the land of
them that carried them captives, saying, We have sinned, and have done
perversely, we have committed wickedness;
48 And *so* return unto thee with all
their heart, and with all their soul, in
the land of their enemies, which led
them away captive, and pray unto thee
toward their land, which thou gavest
unto their fathers, the city which thou
hast chosen, and the house which I
have built for thy name:
49 Then hear thou their prayer and
their supplication in heaven thy dwelling place, and maintain their cause,
50 And forgive thy people that have
sinned against thee, and all their
transgressions wherein they have
transgressed against thee, and give
them compassion before them who
carried them captive, that they may
have compassion on them:
51 For they *be* thy people, and thine
inheritance, which thou broughtest
forth out of Egypt, from the midst of
the furnace of iron:
52 That thine eyes may be open unto
the supplication of thy servant, and
unto the supplication of thy people
Israel, to hearken unto them in all that
they call for unto thee.
53 For thou didst separate them from
among all the people of the earth, *to be*
thine inheritance, as thou spakest by
the hand of Moses thy servant, when
thou broughtest our fathers out of
Egypt, O Lord GOD.
54 And it was *so*, that when Solomon
had made an end of praying all this
prayer and supplication unto the LORD,
he arose from before the altar of the
LORD, from kneeling on his knees with
his hands spread up to heaven.
55 And he stood, and blessed all the
congregation of Israel with a loud
voice, saying,
56 Blessed *be* the LORD, that hath
given rest unto his people Israel,
according to all that he promised: there
hath not failed one word of all his good
promise, which he promised by the
hand of Moses his servant.
57 The LORD our God be with us, as he
was with our fathers: let him not leave
us, nor forsake us:
58 That he may incline our hearts
unto him, to walk in all his ways, and to
keep his commandments, and his statutes, and his judgments, which he commanded our fathers.
59 And let these my words, wherewith
I have made supplication before the
LORD, be nigh unto the LORD our God
day and night, that he maintain the
cause of his servant, and the cause of
his people Israel at all times, as the
matter shall require:
60 That all the people of the earth
may know that the LORD *is* God, *and
that there is* none else.
61 Let your heart therefore be perfect
with the LORD our God, to walk in his
statutes, and to keep his commandments, as at this day.
62 And the king, and all Israel with
him, offered sacrifice before the LORD.
63 And Solomon offered a sacrifice of
peace offerings, which he offered unto
the LORD, two and twenty thousand
oxen, and an hundred and twenty thousand sheep. So the king and all the
children of Israel dedicated the house
of the LORD.

64 The same day did the king hallow
the middle of the court that *was* before
the house of the LORD: for there he
offered burnt offerings, and meat offerings, and the fat of the peace offerings:
because the brasen altar that *was*
before the LORD *was* too little to receive
the burnt offerings, and meat offerings,
and the fat of the peace offerings.
65 And at that time Solomon held a
feast, and all Israel with him, a great
congregation, from the entering in of
Hamath unto the river of Egypt, before
the LORD our God, seven days and
seven days, *even* fourteen days.
66 On the eighth day he sent the
people away: and they blessed the king,
and went unto their tents joyful and
glad of heart for all the goodness that
the LORD had done for David his servant, and for Israel his people.

9 And it came to pass, when Solomon
had finished the building of the
house of the LORD, and the king's
house, and all Solomon's desire which
he was pleased to do,
2 That the LORD appeared to Solomon
the second time, as he had appeared
unto him at Gibeon.
3 And the LORD said unto him, I have
heard thy prayer and thy supplication,
that thou hast made before me: I have
hallowed this house, which thou hast
built, to put my name there for ever;
and mine eyes and mine heart shall be
there perpetually.
4 And if thou wilt walk before me, as
David thy father walked, in integrity of
heart, and in uprightness, to do according to all that I have commanded thee,
and wilt keep my statutes and my judgments:
5 Then I will establish the throne of
thy kingdom upon Israel for ever, as I
promised to David thy father, saying,
There shall not fail thee a man upon
the throne of Israel.
6 *But* if ye shall at all turn from following me, ye or your children, and will
not keep my commandments *and* my
statutes which I have set before you,
but go and serve other gods, and worship them:
7 Then will I cut off Israel out of the
land which I have given them; and this
house, which I have hallowed for my
name, will I cast out of my sight; and
Israel shall be a proverb and a byword
among all people:
8 And at this house, *which* is high,
every one that passeth by it shall be
astonished, and shall hiss; and they
shall say, Why hath the LORD done thus
unto this land, and to this house?
9 And they shall answer, Because they
forsook the LORD their God, who
brought forth their fathers out of the
land of Egypt, and have taken hold
upon other gods, and have worshipped
them, and served them: therefore hath
the LORD brought upon them all this
evil.
10 And it came to pass at the end of
twenty years, when Solomon had built
the two houses, the house of the LORD,
and the king's house,
11 (*Now* Hiram the king of Tyre had
furnished Solomon with cedar trees
and fir trees, and with gold, according
to all his desire,) that then king
Solomon gave Hiram twenty cities in
the land of Galilee.
12 And Hiram came out from Tyre to
see the cities which Solomon had given
him; and they pleased him not.

13 And he said, What cities *are* these which thou hast given me, my brother? And he called them the land of Cabul unto this day.

14 And Hiram sent to the king sixscore talents of gold.

15 And this *is* the reason of the levy which king Solomon raised; for to build the house of the LORD, and his own house, and Millo, and the wall of Jerusalem, and Hazor, and Megiddo, and Gezer.

16 *For* Pharaoh king of Egypt had gone up, and taken Gezer, and burnt it with fire, and slain the Canaanites that dwelt in the city, and given it *for* a present unto his daughter, Solomon's wife.

17 And Solomon built Gezer, and Beth-horon the nether,

18 And Baalath, and Tadmor in the wilderness, in the land,

19 And all the cities of store that Solomon had, and cities for his chariots, and cities for his horsemen, and that which Solomon desired to build in Jerusalem, and in Lebanon, and in all the land of his dominion.

20 *And* all the people *that were* left of the Amorites, Hittites, Perizzites, Hivites, and Jebusites, which *were* not of the children of Israel,

21 Their children that were left after them in the land, whom the children of Israel also were not able utterly to destroy, upon those did Solomon levy a tribute of bondservice unto this day.

22 But of the children of Israel did Solomon make no bondmen: but they *were* men of war, and his servants, and his princes, and his captains, and rulers of his chariots, and his horsemen.

23 These *were* the chief of the officers that *were* over Solomon's work, five hundred and fifty, which bare rule over the people that wrought in the work.

24 But Pharaoh's daughter came up out of the city of David unto her house which *Solomon* had built for her: then did he build Millo.

25 And three times in a year did Solomon offer burnt offerings and peace offerings upon the altar which he built unto the LORD, and he burnt incense upon the altar that *was* before the LORD. So he finished the house.

26 And king Solomon made a navy of ships in Ezion-geber, which *is* beside Eloth, on the shore of the Red sea, in the land of Edom.

27 And Hiram sent in the navy his servants, shipmen that had knowledge of the sea, with the servants of Solomon.

28 And they came to Ophir, and fetched from thence gold, four hundred and twenty talents, and brought *it* to king Solomon.

10 And when the queen of Sheba heard of the fame of Solomon concerning the name of the LORD, she came to prove him with hard questions.

2 And she came to Jerusalem with a very great train, with camels that bare spices, and very much gold, and precious stones: and when she was come to Solomon, she communed with him of all that was in her heart.

3 And Solomon told her all her questions: there was not *any* thing hid from the king, which he told her not.

4 And when the queen of Sheba had seen all Solomon's wisdom, and the house that he had built,

5 And the meat of his table, and the sitting of his servants, and the attendance of his ministers, and their apparel, and his cupbearers, and his ascent by which he went up unto the house of the LORD; there was no more spirit in her.

6 And she said to the king, It was a true report that I heard in mine own land of thy acts and of thy wisdom.

7 Howbeit I believed not the words, until I came, and mine eyes had seen *it*: and, behold, the half was not told me: thy wisdom and prosperity exceedeth the fame which I heard.

8 Happy *are* thy men, happy *are* these thy servants, which stand continually before thee, *and* that hear thy wisdom.

9 Blessed be the LORD thy God, which delighted in thee, to set thee on the throne of Israel: because the LORD loved Israel for ever, therefore made he thee king, to do judgment and justice.

10 And she gave the king an hundred and twenty talents of gold, and of spices very great store, and precious stones: there came no more such abundance of spices as these which the queen of Sheba gave to king Solomon.

11 And the navy also of Hiram, that brought gold from Ophir, brought in from Ophir great plenty of almug trees, and precious stones.

12 And the king made of the almug trees pillars for the house of the LORD, and for the king's house, harps also and psalteries for singers: there came no such almug trees, nor were seen unto this day.

13 And king Solomon gave unto the queen of Sheba all her desire, whatsoever she asked, beside *that* which Solomon gave her of his royal bounty. So she turned and went to her own country, she and her servants.

14 Now the weight of gold that came to Solomon in one year was six hundred threescore and six talents of gold,

15 Beside *that he had* of the merchantmen, and of the traffick of the spice merchants, and of all the kings of Arabia, and of the governors of the country.

16 And king Solomon made two hundred targets *of* beaten gold: six hundred *shekels* of gold went to one target.

17 And *he made* three hundred shields *of* beaten gold; three pound of gold went to one shield: and the king put them in the house of the forest of Lebanon.

18 Moreover the king made a great throne of ivory, and overlaid it with the best gold.

19 The throne had six steps, and the top of the throne *was* round behind: and *there were* stays on either side on the place of the seat, and two lions stood beside the stays.

20 And twelve lions stood there on the one side and on the other upon the six steps: there was not the like made in any kingdom.

21 And all king Solomon's drinking vessels *were of* gold, and all the vessels of the house of the forest of Lebanon *were of* pure gold; none *were of* silver: it was nothing accounted of in the days of Solomon.

22 For the king had at sea a navy of Tharshish with the navy of Hiram: once in three years came the navy of Tharshish, bringing gold, and silver, ivory, and apes, and peacocks.

23 So king Solomon exceeded all the kings of the earth for riches and for wisdom.

24 And all the earth sought to Solomon, to hear his wisdom, which God had put in his heart.

25 And they brought every man his present, vessels of silver, and vessels of gold, and garments, and armour, and spices, horses, and mules, a rate year by year.

26 And Solomon gathered together chariots and horsemen: and he had a thousand and four hundred chariots, and twelve thousand horsemen, whom he bestowed in the cities for chariots, and with the king at Jerusalem.

27 And the king made silver *to be* in Jerusalem as stones, and cedars made he *to be* as the sycomore trees that *are* in the vale, for abundance.

28 And Solomon had horses brought out of Egypt, and linen yarn: the king's merchants received the linen yarn at a price.

29 And a chariot came up and went out of Egypt for six hundred *shekels* of silver, and an horse for an hundred and fifty: and so for all the kings of the Hittites, and for the kings of Syria, did they bring *them* out by their means.

11 But king Solomon loved many strange women, together with the daughter of Pharaoh, women of the Moabites, Ammonites, Edomites, Zidonians, *and* Hittites;

2 Of the nations *concerning* which the LORD said unto the children of Israel, Ye shall not go in to them, neither shall they come in unto you: *for* surely they will turn away your heart after their gods: Solomon clave unto these in love.

3 And he had seven hundred wives, princesses, and three hundred concubines: and his wives turned away his heart.

4 For it came to pass, when Solomon was old, *that* his wives turned away his heart after other gods: and his heart was not perfect with the LORD his God, as *was* the heart of David his father.

5 For Solomon went after Ashtoreth the goddess of the Zidonians, and after Milcom the abomination of the Ammonites.

6 And Solomon did evil in the sight of the LORD, and went not fully after the LORD, as *did* David his father.

7 Then did Solomon build an high place for Chemosh, the abomination of Moab, in the hill that *is* before Jerusalem, and for Molech, the abomination of the children of Ammon.

8 And likewise did he for all his strange wives, which burnt incense and sacrificed unto their gods.

9 And the LORD was angry with Solomon, because his heart was turned from the LORD God of Israel, which had appeared unto him twice,

10 And had commanded him concerning this thing, that he should not go after other gods: but he kept not that which the LORD commanded.

11 Wherefore the LORD said unto Solomon, Forasmuch as this is done of thee, and thou hast not kept my covenant and my statutes, which I have commanded thee, I will surely rend the kingdom from thee, and will give it to thy servant.

12 Notwithstanding in thy days I will not do it for David thy father's sake: *but* I will rend it out of the hand of thy son.

13 Howbeit I will not rend away all the kingdom; *but* will give one tribe to thy son for David my servant's sake, and for Jerusalem's sake which I have chosen.

14 And the LORD stirred up an adversary unto Solomon, Hadad the Edomite:
he *was* of the king's seed in Edom.
15 For it came to pass, when David
was in Edom, and Joab the captain of
the host was gone up to bury the slain,
after he had smitten every male in
Edom;
16 (For six months did Joab remain
there with all Israel, until he had cut off
every male in Edom:)
17 That Hadad fled, he and certain
Edomites of his father's servants with
him, to go into Egypt; Hadad *being* yet
a little child.
18 And they arose out of Midian, and
came to Paran: and they took men with
them out of Paran, and they came to
Egypt, unto Pharaoh king of Egypt;
which gave him an house, and appointed him victuals, and gave him land.
19 And Hadad found great favour in
the sight of Pharaoh, so that he gave
him to wife the sister of his own wife,
the sister of Tahpenes the queen.
20 And the sister of Tahpenes bare
him Genubath his son, whom Tahpenes
weaned in Pharaoh's house: and
Genubath was in Pharaoh's household
among the sons of Pharaoh.
21 And when Hadad heard in Egypt
that David slept with his fathers, and
that Joab the captain of the host was
dead, Hadad said to Pharaoh, Let me
depart, that I may go to mine own country.
22 Then Pharaoh said unto him, But
what hast thou lacked with me, that,
behold, thou seekest to go to thine own
country? And he answered, Nothing:
howbeit let me go in any wise.
23 And God stirred him up *another*
adversary, Rezon the son of Eliadah,
which fled from his lord Hadadezer
king of Zobah:
24 And he gathered men unto him,
and became captain over a band, when
David slew them *of Zobah*: and they
went to Damascus, and dwelt therein,
and reigned in Damascus.
25 And he was an adversary to Israel
all the days of Solomon, beside the
mischief that Hadad *did*: and he
abhorred Israel, and reigned over Syria.
26 And Jeroboam the son of Nebat,
an Ephrathite of Zereda, Solomon's
servant, whose mother's name *was*
Zeruah, a widow woman, even he lifted
up *his* hand against the king.
27 And this *was* the cause that he
lifted up *his* hand against the king:
Solomon built Millo, *and* repaired the
breaches of the city of David his father.
28 And the man Jeroboam *was* a
mighty man of valour: and Solomon
seeing the young man that he was
industrious, he made him ruler over all
the charge of the house of Joseph.
29 And it came to pass at that time
when Jeroboam went out of Jerusalem,
that the prophet Ahijah the Shilonite
found him in the way; and he had clad
himself with a new garment; and they
two *were* alone in the field:
30 And Ahijah caught the new garment that *was* on him, and rent it *in*
twelve pieces:
31 And he said to Jeroboam, Take
thee ten pieces: for thus saith the LORD,
the God of Israel, Behold, I will rend
the kingdom out of the hand of
Solomon, and will give ten tribes to
thee:
32 (But he shall have one tribe for my
servant David's sake, and for Jerusalem's sake, the city which I have chosen
out of all the tribes of Israel:)

33 Because that they have forsaken me, and have worshipped Ashtoreth the goddess of the Zidonians, Chemosh the god of the Moabites, and Milcom the god of the children of Ammon, and have not walked in my ways, to do *that which is* right in mine eyes, and *to keep* my statutes and my judgments, as *did* David his father.

34 Howbeit I will not take the whole kingdom out of his hand: but I will make him prince all the days of his life for David my servant's sake, whom I chose, because he kept my commandments and my statutes:

35 But I will take the kingdom out of his son's hand, and will give it unto thee, *even* ten tribes.

36 And unto his son will I give one tribe, that David my servant may have a light alway before me in Jerusalem, the city which I have chosen me to put my name there.

37 And I will take thee, and thou shalt reign according to all that thy soul desireth, and shalt be king over Israel.

38 And it shall be, if thou wilt hearken unto all that I command thee, and wilt walk in my ways, and do *that is* right in my sight, to keep my statutes and my commandments, as David my servant did; that I will be with thee, and build thee a sure house, as I built for David, and will give Israel unto thee.

39 And I will for this afflict the seed of David, but not for ever.

40 Solomon sought therefore to kill Jeroboam. And Jeroboam arose, and fled into Egypt, unto Shishak king of Egypt, and was in Egypt until the death of Solomon.

41 And the rest of the acts of Solomon, and all that he did, and his wisdom, *are* they not written in the book of the acts of Solomon?

42 And the time that Solomon reigned in Jerusalem over all Israel *was* forty years.

43 And Solomon slept with his fathers, and was buried in the city of David his father: and Rehoboam his son reigned in his stead.

12 And Rehoboam went to Shechem: for all Israel were come to Shechem to make him king.

2 And it came to pass, when Jeroboam the son of Nebat, who was yet in Egypt, heard *of it*, (for he was fled from the presence of king Solomon, and Jeroboam dwelt in Egypt;)

3 That they sent and called him. And Jeroboam and all the congregation of Israel came, and spake unto Rehoboam, saying,

4 Thy father made our yoke grievous: now therefore make thou the grievous service of thy father, and his heavy yoke which he put upon us, lighter, and we will serve thee.

5 And he said unto them, Depart yet *for* three days, then come again to me. And the people departed.

6 And king Rehoboam consulted with the old men, that stood before Solomon his father while he yet lived, and said, How do ye advise that I may answer this people?

7 And they spake unto him, saying, If thou wilt be a servant unto this people this day, and wilt serve them, and answer them, and speak good words to them, then they will be thy servants for ever.

8 But he forsook the counsel of the old men, which they had given him, and consulted with the young men that were grown up with him, *and* which stood before him:

9 And he said unto them, What counsel give ye that we may answer this people, who have spoken to me, saying, Make the yoke which thy father did put upon us lighter?

10 And the young men that were grown up with him spake unto him, saying, Thus shalt thou speak unto this people that spake unto thee, saying, Thy father made our yoke heavy, but make thou *it* lighter unto us; thus shalt thou say unto them, My little *finger* shall be thicker than my father's loins.

11 And now whereas my father did lade you with a heavy yoke, I will add to your yoke: my father hath chastised you with whips, but I will chastise you with scorpions.

12 So Jeroboam and all the people came to Rehoboam the third day, as the king had appointed, saying, Come to me again the third day.

13 And the king answered the people roughly, and forsook the old men's counsel that they gave him;

14 And spake to them after the counsel of the young men, saying, My father made your yoke heavy, and I will add to your yoke: my father *also* chastised you with whips, but I will chastise you with scorpions.

15 Wherefore the king hearkened not unto the people; for the cause was from the LORD, that he might perform his saying, which the LORD spake by Ahijah the Shilonite unto Jeroboam the son of Nebat.

16 So when all Israel saw that the king hearkened not unto them, the people answered the king, saying, What portion have we in David? neither *have we* inheritance in the son of Jesse: to your tents, O Israel: now see to thine own house, David. So Israel departed unto their tents.

17 But *as for* the children of Israel which dwelt in the cities of Judah, Rehoboam reigned over them.

18 Then king Rehoboam sent Adoram, who *was* over the tribute; and all Israel stoned him with stones, that he died. Therefore king Rehoboam made speed to get him up to his chariot, to flee to Jerusalem.

19 So Israel rebelled against the house of David unto this day.

20 And it came to pass, when all Israel heard that Jeroboam was come again, that they sent and called him unto the congregation, and made him king over all Israel: there was none that followed the house of David, but the tribe of Judah only.

21 And when Rehoboam was come to Jerusalem, he assembled all the house of Judah, with the tribe of Benjamin, an hundred and fourscore thousand chosen men, which were warriors, to fight against the house of Israel, to bring the kingdom again to Rehoboam the son of Solomon.

22 But the word of God came unto Shemaiah the man of God, saying,

23 Speak unto Rehoboam, the son of Solomon, king of Judah, and unto all the house of Judah and Benjamin, and to the remnant of the people, saying,

24 Thus saith the LORD, Ye shall not go up, nor fight against your brethren the children of Israel: return every man to his house; for this thing is from me.

They hearkened therefore to the word of the LORD, and returned to depart, according to the word of the LORD.

25 Then Jeroboam built Shechem in mount Ephraim, and dwelt therein; and went out from thence, and built Penuel.

26 And Jeroboam said in his heart, Now shall the kingdom return to the house of David:

27 If this people go up to do sacrifice in the house of the LORD at Jerusalem, then shall the heart of this people turn again unto their lord, *even* unto Rehoboam king of Judah, and they shall kill me, and go again to Rehoboam king of Judah.

28 Whereupon the king took counsel, and made two calves *of* gold, and said unto them, It is too much for you to go up to Jerusalem: behold thy gods, O Israel, which brought thee up out of the land of Egypt.

29 And he set the one in Beth-el, and the other put he in Dan.

30 And this thing became a sin: for the people went *to worship* before the one, *even* unto Dan.

31 And he made an house of high places, and made priests of the lowest of the people, which were not of the sons of Levi.

32 And Jeroboam ordained a feast in the eighth month, on the fifteenth day of the month, like unto the feast that *is* in Judah, and he offered upon the altar. So did he in Beth-el, sacrificing unto the calves that he had made: and he placed in Beth-el the priests of the high places which he had made.

33 So he offered upon the altar which he had made in Beth-el the fifteenth day of the eighth month, *even* in the month which he had devised of his own heart; and ordained a feast unto the children of Israel: and he offered upon the altar, and burnt incense.

13 And, behold, there came a man of God out of Judah by the word of the LORD unto Beth-el: and Jeroboam stood by the altar to burn incense.

2 And he cried against the altar in the word of the LORD, and said, O altar, altar, thus saith the LORD; Behold, a child shall be born unto the house of David, Josiah by name; and upon thee shall he offer the priests of the high places that burn incense upon thee, and men's bones shall be burnt upon thee.

3 And he gave a sign the same day, saying, This *is* the sign which the LORD hath spoken; Behold, the altar shall be rent, and the ashes that *are* upon it shall be poured out.

4 And it came to pass, when king Jeroboam heard the saying of the man of God, which had cried against the altar in Beth-el, that he put forth his hand from the altar, saying, Lay hold on him. And his hand, which he put forth against him, dried up, so that he could not pull it in again to him.

5 The altar also was rent, and the ashes poured out from the altar, according to the sign which the man of God had given by the word of the LORD.

6 And the king answered and said unto the man of God, Intreat now the face of the LORD thy God, and pray for me, that my hand may be restored me again. And the man of God besought the LORD, and the king's hand was restored him again, and became as *it was* before.

7 And the king said unto the man of God, Come home with me, and refresh thyself, and I will give thee a reward.

8 And the man of God said unto the
king, If thou wilt give me half thine
house, I will not go in with thee, neither
will I eat bread nor drink water in this
place:
9 For so was it charged me by the
word of the LORD, saying, Eat no bread,
nor drink water, nor turn again by the
same way that thou camest.
10 So he went another way, and
returned not by the way that he came
to Beth-el.
11 Now there dwelt an old prophet in
Beth-el; and his sons came and told him
all the works that the man of God had
done that day in Beth-el: the words
which he had spoken unto the king,
them they told also to their father.
12 And their father said unto them,
What way went he? For his sons had
seen what way the man of God went,
which came from Judah.
13 And he said unto his sons, Saddle
me the ass. So they saddled him the ass:
and he rode thereon,
14 And went after the man of God,
and found him sitting under an oak:
and he said unto him, *Art* thou the man
of God that camest from Judah? And he
said, I *am*.
15 Then he said unto him, Come
home with me, and eat bread.
16 And he said, I may not return with
thee, nor go in with thee: neither will I
eat bread nor drink water with thee in
this place:
17 For it was said to me by the word of
the LORD, Thou shalt eat no bread nor
drink water there, nor turn again to go
by the way that thou camest.
18 He said unto him, I *am* a prophet
also as thou *art*; and an angel spake
unto me by the word of the LORD, saying, Bring him back with thee into
thine house, that he may eat bread and
drink water. *But* he lied unto him.
19 So he went back with him, and did
eat bread in his house, and drank water.
20 And it came to pass, as they sat at
the table, that the word of the LORD
came unto the prophet that brought
him back:
21 And he cried unto the man of God
that came from Judah, saying, Thus
saith the LORD, Forasmuch as thou hast
disobeyed the mouth of the LORD, and
hast not kept the commandment which
the LORD thy God commanded thee,
22 But camest back, and hast eaten
bread and drunk water in the place, of
the which *the LORD* did say to thee, Eat
no bread, and drink no water; thy carcase shall not come unto the sepulchre
of thy fathers.
23 And it came to pass, after he had
eaten bread, and after he had drunk,
that he saddled for him the ass, *to wit*,
for the prophet whom he had brought
back.
24 And when he was gone, a lion met
him by the way, and slew him: and his
carcase was cast in the way, and the ass
stood by it, the lion also stood by the
carcase.
25 And, behold, men passed by, and
saw the carcase cast in the way, and the
lion standing by the carcase: and they
came and told *it* in the city where the
old prophet dwelt.
26 And when the prophet that
brought him back from the way heard
thereof, he said, It *is* the man of God,
who was disobedient unto the word of
the LORD: therefore the LORD hath
delivered him unto the lion, which hath
torn him, and slain him, according to
the word of the LORD, which he spake
unto him.

27 And he spake to his sons, saying,
Saddle me the ass. And they saddled
him.
28 And he went and found his carcase
cast in the way, and the ass and the lion
standing by the carcase: the lion had
not eaten the carcase, nor torn the ass.
29 And the prophet took up the carcase of the man of God, and laid it upon
the ass, and brought it back: and the
old prophet came to the city, to mourn
and to bury him.
30 And he laid his carcase in his own
grave; and they mourned over him, *saying*, Alas, my brother!
31 And it came to pass, after he had
buried him, that he spake to his sons,
saying, When I am dead, then bury me
in the sepulchre wherein the man of
God *is* buried; lay my bones beside his
bones:
32 For the saying which he cried by
the word of the LORD against the altar
in Beth-el, and against all the houses of
the high places which *are* in the cities
of Samaria, shall surely come to pass.
33 After this thing Jeroboam returned
not from his evil way, but made again of
the lowest of the people priests of the
high places: whosoever would, he consecrated him, and he became *one* of the
priests of the high places.
34 And this thing became sin unto the
house of Jeroboam, even to cut *it* off,
and to destroy *it* from off the face of
the earth.

14 At that time Abijah the son of
Jeroboam fell sick.
2 And Jeroboam said to his wife,
Arise, I pray thee, and disguise thyself,
that thou be not known to be the wife
of Jeroboam; and get thee to Shiloh:
behold, there *is* Ahijah the prophet,
which told me that *I should be* king
over this people.
3 And take with thee ten loaves, and
cracknels, and a cruse of honey, and go
to him: he shall tell thee what shall
become of the child.
4 And Jeroboam's wife did so, and
arose, and went to Shiloh, and came to
the house of Ahijah. But Ahijah could
not see; for his eyes were set by reason
of his age.
5 And the LORD said unto Ahijah,
Behold, the wife of Jeroboam cometh
to ask a thing of thee for her son; for he
is sick: thus and thus shalt thou say
unto her: for it shall be, when she
cometh in, that she shall feign herself
to be another *woman*.
6 And it was *so*, when Ahijah heard
the sound of her feet, as she came in at
the door, that he said, Come in, thou
wife of Jeroboam; why feignest thou
thyself *to be* another? for I *am* sent to
thee *with* heavy *tidings*.
7 Go, tell Jeroboam, Thus saith the
LORD God of Israel, Forasmuch as I
exalted thee from among the people,
and made thee prince over my people
Israel,
8 And rent the kingdom away from
the house of David, and gave it thee:
and *yet* thou hast not been as my servant David, who kept my commandments, and who followed me with all
his heart, to do *that* only *which was*
right in mine eyes;
9 But hast done evil above all that
were before thee: for thou hast gone
and made thee other gods, and molten
images, to provoke me to anger, and
hast cast me behind thy back:
10 Therefore, behold, I will bring evil
upon the house of Jeroboam, and will
cut off from Jeroboam him that pisseth

against the wall, *and* him that is shut
up and left in Israel, and will take away
the remnant of the house of Jeroboam,
as a man taketh away dung, till it be all
gone.
11 Him that dieth of Jeroboam in the
city shall the dogs eat; and him that
dieth in the field shall the fowls of the
air eat: for the LORD hath spoken *it*.
12 Arise thou therefore, get thee to
thine own house: *and* when thy feet
enter into the city, the child shall die.
13 And all Israel shall mourn for him,
and bury him: for he only of Jeroboam
shall come to the grave, because in him
there is found *some* good thing toward
the LORD God of Israel in the house of
Jeroboam.
14 Moreover the LORD shall raise him
up a king over Israel, who shall cut off
the house of Jeroboam that day: but
what? even now.
15 For the LORD shall smite Israel, as
a reed is shaken in the water, and he
shall root up Israel out of this good
land, which he gave to their fathers,
and shall scatter them beyond the river,
because they have made their groves,
provoking the LORD to anger.
16 And he shall give Israel up because
of the sins of Jeroboam, who did sin,
and who made Israel to sin.
17 And Jeroboam's wife arose, and
departed, and came to Tirzah: *and*
when she came to the threshold of the
door, the child died;
18 And they buried him; and all Israel
mourned for him, according to the word
of the LORD, which he spake by the
hand of his servant Ahijah the prophet.
19 And the rest of the acts of
Jeroboam, how he warred, and how he
reigned, behold, they *are* written in the
book of the chronicles of the kings of
Israel.
20 And the days which Jeroboam
reigned *were* two and twenty years: and
he slept with his fathers, and Nadab his
son reigned in his stead.
21 And Rehoboam the son of Solomon
reigned in Judah. Rehoboam *was* forty
and one years old when he began to
reign, and he reigned seventeen years
in Jerusalem, the city which the LORD
did choose out of all the tribes of Israel,
to put his name there. And his mother's
name *was* Naamah an Ammonitess.
22 And Judah did evil in the sight of
the LORD, and they provoked him to
jealousy with their sins which they had
committed, above all that their fathers
had done.
23 For they also built them high places, and images, and groves, on every
high hill, and under every green tree.
24 And there were also sodomites in
the land: *and* they did according to all
the abominations of the nations which
the LORD cast out before the children of
Israel.
25 And it came to pass in the fifth
year of king Rehoboam, *that* Shishak
king of Egypt came up against Jerusalem:
26 And he took away the treasures of
the house of the LORD, and the treasures of the king's house; he even took
away all: and he took away all the
shields of gold which Solomon had
made.
27 And king Rehoboam made in their
stead brasen shields, and committed
them unto the hands of the chief of the
guard, which kept the door of the king's
house.

28 And it was *so*, when the king went into the house of the LORD, that the guard bare them, and brought them back into the guard chamber.

29 Now the rest of the acts of Rehoboam, and all that he did, *are* they not written in the book of the chronicles of the kings of Judah?

30 And there was war between Rehoboam and Jeroboam all *their* days.

31 And Rehoboam slept with his fathers, and was buried with his fathers in the city of David. And his mother's name *was* Naamah an Ammonitess. And Abijam his son reigned in his stead.

15 Now in the eighteenth year of king Jeroboam the son of Nebat reigned Abijam over Judah.

2 Three years reigned he in Jerusalem. And his mother's name *was* Maachah, the daughter of Abishalom.

3 And he walked in all the sins of his father, which he had done before him: and his heart was not perfect with the LORD his God, as the heart of David his father.

4 Nevertheless for David's sake did the LORD his God give him a lamp in Jerusalem, to set up his son after him, and to establish Jerusalem:

5 Because David did *that which was* right in the eyes of the LORD, and turned not aside from any *thing* that he commanded him all the days of his life, save only in the matter of Uriah the Hittite.

6 And there was war between Rehoboam and Jeroboam all the days of his life.

7 Now the rest of the acts of Abijam, and all that he did, *are* they not written in the book of the chronicles of the kings of Judah? And there was war between Abijam and Jeroboam.

8 And Abijam slept with his fathers; and they buried him in the city of David: and Asa his son reigned in his stead.

9 And in the twentieth year of Jeroboam king of Israel reigned Asa over Judah.

10 And forty and one years reigned he in Jerusalem. And his mother's name *was* Maachah, the daughter of Abishalom.

11 And Asa did *that which was* right in the eyes of the LORD, as *did* David his father.

12 And he took away the sodomites out of the land, and removed all the idols that his fathers had made.

13 And also Maachah his mother, even her he removed from *being* queen, because she had made an idol in a grove; and Asa destroyed her idol, and burnt *it* by the brook Kidron.

14 But the high places were not removed: nevertheless Asa's heart was perfect with the LORD all his days.

15 And he brought in the things which his father had dedicated, and the things which himself had dedicated, into the house of the LORD, silver, and gold, and vessels.

16 And there was war between Asa and Baasha king of Israel all their days.

17 And Baasha king of Israel went up against Judah, and built Ramah, that he might not suffer any to go out or come in to Asa king of Judah.

18 Then Asa took all the silver and the gold *that were* left in the treasures of the house of the LORD, and the treasures of the king's house, and delivered them into the hand of his servants: and king Asa sent them to Ben-hadad, the

son of Tabrimon, the son of Hezion,
king of Syria, that dwelt at Damascus,
saying,
19 *There is* a league between me and
thee, *and* between my father and thy
father: behold, I have sent unto thee a
present of silver and gold; come and
break thy league with Baasha king of
Israel, that he may depart from me.
20 So Ben-hadad hearkened unto
king Asa, and sent the captains of the
hosts which he had against the cities of
Israel, and smote Ijon, and Dan, and
Abel-beth-maachah, and all Cinneroth,
with all the land of Naphtali.
21 And it came to pass, when Baasha
heard *thereof*, that he left off building
of Ramah, and dwelt in Tirzah.
22 Then king Asa made a proclamation throughout all Judah; none *was*
exempted: and they took away the
stones of Ramah, and the timber thereof, wherewith Baasha had builded; and
king Asa built with them Geba of
Benjamin, and Mizpah.
23 The rest of all the acts of Asa, and
all his might, and all that he did, and
the cities which he built, *are* they not
written in the book of the chronicles of
the kings of Judah? Nevertheless in the
time of his old age he was diseased in
his feet.
24 And Asa slept with his fathers, and
was buried with his fathers in the city
of David his father: and Jehoshaphat
his son reigned in his stead.
25 And Nadab the son of Jeroboam
began to reign over Israel in the second
year of Asa king of Judah, and reigned
over Israel two years.
26 And he did evil in the sight of the
LORD, and walked in the way of his
father, and in his sin wherewith he
made Israel to sin.
27 And Baasha the son of Ahijah, of
the house of Issachar, conspired against
him; and Baasha smote him at
Gibbethon, which *belonged* to the
Philistines; for Nadab and all Israel laid
siege to Gibbethon.
28 Even in the third year of Asa king
of Judah did Baasha slay him, and
reigned in his stead.
29 And it came to pass, when he
reigned, *that* he smote all the house of
Jeroboam; he left not to Jeroboam any
that breathed, until he had destroyed
him, according unto the saying of the
LORD, which he spake by his servant
Ahijah the Shilonite:
30 Because of the sins of Jeroboam
which he sinned, and which he made
Israel sin, by his provocation wherewith
he provoked the LORD God of Israel to
anger.
31 Now the rest of the acts of Nadab,
and all that he did, *are* they not written
in the book of the chronicles of the
kings of Israel?
32 And there was war between Asa
and Baasha king of Israel all their days.
33 In the third year of Asa king of
Judah began Baasha the son of Ahijah
to reign over all Israel in Tirzah, twenty
and four years.
34 And he did evil in the sight of the
LORD, and walked in the way of
Jeroboam, and in his sin wherewith he
made Israel to sin.

16 Then the word of the LORD came
to Jehu the son of Hanani against
Baasha, saying,
2 Forasmuch as I exalted thee out of
the dust, and made thee prince over my
people Israel; and thou hast walked in
the way of Jeroboam, and hast made
my people Israel to sin, to provoke me
to anger with their sins;

3 Behold, I will take away the posterity of Baasha, and the posterity of his house; and will make thy house like the house of Jeroboam the son of Nebat.
4 Him that dieth of Baasha in the city shall the dogs eat; and him that dieth of his in the fields shall the fowls of the air eat.
5 Now the rest of the acts of Baasha, and what he did, and his might, *are* they not written in the book of the chronicles of the kings of Israel?
6 So Baasha slept with his fathers, and was buried in Tirzah: and Elah his son reigned in his stead.
7 And also by the hand of the prophet Jehu the son of Hanani came the word of the LORD against Baasha, and against his house, even for all the evil that he did in the sight of the LORD, in provoking him to anger with the work of his hands, in being like the house of Jeroboam; and because he killed him.
8 In the twenty and sixth year of Asa king of Judah began Elah the son of Baasha to reign over Israel in Tirzah, two years.
9 And his servant Zimri, captain of half *his* chariots, conspired against him, as he was in Tirzah, drinking himself drunk in the house of Arza steward of *his* house in Tirzah.
10 And Zimri went in and smote him, and killed him, in the twenty and seventh year of Asa king of Judah, and reigned in his stead.
11 And it came to pass, when he began to reign, as soon as he sat on his throne, *that* he slew all the house of Baasha: he left him not one that pisseth against a wall, neither of his kinsfolks, nor of his friends.
12 Thus did Zimri destroy all the house of Baasha, according to the word of the LORD, which he spake against Baasha by Jehu the prophet,
13 For all the sins of Baasha, and the sins of Elah his son, by which they sinned, and by which they made Israel to sin, in provoking the LORD God of Israel to anger with their vanities.
14 Now the rest of the acts of Elah, and all that he did, *are* they not written in the book of the chronicles of the kings of Israel?
15 In the twenty and seventh year of Asa king of Judah did Zimri reign seven days in Tirzah. And the people *were* encamped against Gibbethon, which *belonged* to the Philistines.
16 And the people *that were* encamped heard say, Zimri hath conspired, and hath also slain the king: wherefore all Israel made Omri, the captain of the host, king over Israel that day in the camp.
17 And Omri went up from Gibbethon, and all Israel with him, and they besieged Tirzah.
18 And it came to pass, when Zimri saw that the city was taken, that he went into the palace of the king's house, and burnt the king's house over him with fire, and died,
19 For his sins which he sinned in doing evil in the sight of the LORD, in walking in the way of Jeroboam, and in his sin which he did, to make Israel to sin.
20 Now the rest of the acts of Zimri, and his treason that he wrought, *are* they not written in the book of the chronicles of the kings of Israel?
21 Then were the people of Israel divided into two parts: half of the peo-

ple followed Tibni the son of Ginath, to
make him king; and half followed Omri.
22 But the people that followed Omri
prevailed against the people that followed Tibni the son of Ginath: so Tibni
died, and Omri reigned.
23 In the thirty and first year of Asa
king of Judah began Omri to reign over
Israel, twelve years: six years reigned
he in Tirzah.
24 And he bought the hill Samaria of
Shemer for two talents of silver, and
built on the hill, and called the name of
the city which he built, after the name
of Shemer, owner of the hill, Samaria.
25 But Omri wrought evil in the eyes
of the LORD, and did worse than all that
were before him.
26 For he walked in all the way of
Jeroboam the son of Nebat, and in his
sin wherewith he made Israel to sin, to
provoke the LORD God of Israel to anger
with their vanities.
27 Now the rest of the acts of Omri
which he did, and his might that he
shewed, *are* they not written in the
book of the chronicles of the kings of
Israel?
28 So Omri slept with his fathers, and
was buried in Samaria: and Ahab his
son reigned in his stead.
29 And in the thirty and eighth year
of Asa king of Judah began Ahab the
son of Omri to reign over Israel: and
Ahab the son of Omri reigned over
Israel in Samaria twenty and two years.
30 And Ahab the son of Omri did evil
in the sight of the LORD above all that
were before him.
31 And it came to pass, as if it had
been a light thing for him to walk in the
sins of Jeroboam the son of Nebat, that
he took to wife Jezebel the daughter of
Ethbaal king of the Zidonians, and
went and served Baal, and worshipped
him.
32 And he reared up an altar for Baal
in the house of Baal, which he had built
in Samaria.
33 And Ahab made a grove; and Ahab
did more to provoke the LORD God of
Israel to anger than all the kings of
Israel that were before him.
34 In his days did Hiel the Bethelite
build Jericho: he laid the foundation
thereof in Abiram his firstborn, and set
up the gates thereof in his youngest *son*
Segub, according to the word of the
LORD, which he spake by Joshua the
son of Nun.

17 And Elijah the Tishbite, *who was*
of the inhabitants of Gilead, said
unto Ahab, *As* the LORD God of Israel
liveth, before whom I stand, there shall
not be dew nor rain these years, but
according to my word.
2 And the word of the LORD came
unto him, saying,
3 Get thee hence, and turn thee eastward, and hide thyself by the brook
Cherith, that *is* before Jordan.
4 And it shall be, *that* thou shalt
drink of the brook; and I have commanded the ravens to feed thee there.
5 So he went and did according unto
the word of the LORD: for he went and
dwelt by the brook Cherith, that *is*
before Jordan.
6 And the ravens brought him bread
and flesh in the morning, and bread
and flesh in the evening; and he drank
of the brook.
7 And it came to pass after a while,
that the brook dried up, because there
had been no rain in the land.

8 And the word of the LORD came
unto him, saying,
9 Arise, get thee to Zarephath, which
belongeth to Zidon, and dwell there:
behold, I have commanded a widow
woman there to sustain thee.
10 So he arose and went to Zarephath.
And when he came to the gate of the
city, behold, the widow woman *was*
there gathering of sticks: and he called
to her, and said, Fetch me, I pray thee, a
little water in a vessel, that I may drink.
11 And as she was going to fetch *it*, he
called to her, and said, Bring me, I pray
thee, a morsel of bread in thine hand.
12 And she said, *As* the LORD thy God
liveth, I have not a cake, but an handful
of meal in a barrel, and a little oil in a
cruse: and, behold, I *am* gathering two
sticks, that I may go in and dress it for
me and my son, that we may eat it, and
die.
13 And Elijah said unto her, Fear not;
go *and* do as thou hast said: but make
me thereof a little cake first, and bring
it unto me, and after make for thee and
for thy son.
14 For thus saith the LORD God of
Israel, The barrel of meal shall not
waste, neither shall the cruse of oil fail,
until the day *that* the LORD sendeth
rain upon the earth.
15 And she went and did according to
the saying of Elijah: and she, and he,
and her house, did eat *many* days.
16 *And* the barrel of meal wasted not,
neither did the cruse of oil fail, according to the word of the LORD, which he
spake by Elijah.
17 And it came to pass after these
things, *that* the son of the woman, the
mistress of the house, fell sick; and his
sickness was so sore, that there was no
breath left in him.
18 And she said unto Elijah, What
have I to do with thee, O thou man of
God? art thou come unto me to call my
sin to remembrance, and to slay my
son?
19 And he said unto her, Give me thy
son. And he took him out of her bosom,
and carried him up into a loft, where he
abode, and laid him upon his own bed.
20 And he cried unto the LORD, and
said, O LORD my God, hast thou also
brought evil upon the widow with
whom I sojourn, by slaying her son?
21 And he stretched himself upon the
child three times, and cried unto the
LORD, and said, O LORD my God, I pray
thee, let this child's soul come into him
again.
22 And the LORD heard the voice of
Elijah; and the soul of the child came
into him again, and he revived.
23 And Elijah took the child, and
brought him down out of the chamber
into the house, and delivered him unto
his mother: and Elijah said, See, thy
son liveth.
24 And the woman said to Elijah,
Now by this I know that thou *art* a man
of God, *and* that the word of the LORD
in thy mouth *is* truth.

18 And it came to pass *after* many
days, that the word of the LORD
came to Elijah in the third year, saying,
Go, shew thyself unto Ahab; and I will
send rain upon the earth.
2 And Elijah went to shew himself
unto Ahab. And *there was* a sore famine in Samaria.
3 And Ahab called Obadiah, which
was the governor of *his* house. (Now
Obadiah feared the LORD greatly:
4 For it was *so*, when Jezebel cut off
the prophets of the LORD, that Obadiah
took an hundred prophets, and hid

them by fifty in a cave, and fed them
with bread and water.)
5 And Ahab said unto Obadiah, Go
into the land, unto all fountains of
water, and unto all brooks: peradventure we may find grass to save the
horses and mules alive, that we lose not
all the beasts.
6 So they divided the land between
them to pass throughout it: Ahab went
one way by himself, and Obadiah went
another way by himself.
7 And as Obadiah was in the way,
behold, Elijah met him: and he knew
him, and fell on his face, and said, *Art*
thou that my lord Elijah?
8 And he answered him, I *am*: go, tell
thy lord, Behold, Elijah *is here.*
9 And he said, What have I sinned,
that thou wouldest deliver thy servant
into the hand of Ahab, to slay me?
10 *As* the LORD thy God liveth, there is
no nation or kingdom, whither my lord
hath not sent to seek thee: and when
they said, *He is* not *there*; he took an
oath of the kingdom and nation, that
they found thee not.
11 And now thou sayest, Go, tell thy
lord, Behold, Elijah *is here.*
12 And it shall come to pass, *as soon*
as I am gone from thee, that the Spirit
of the LORD shall carry thee whither I
know not; and *so* when I come and tell
Ahab, and he cannot find thee, he shall
slay me: but I thy servant fear the LORD
from my youth.
13 Was it not told my lord what I did
when Jezebel slew the prophets of the
LORD, how I hid an hundred men of the
LORD's prophets by fifty in a cave, and
fed them with bread and water?
14 And now thou sayest, Go, tell thy
lord, Behold, Elijah *is here*: and he shall
slay me.
15 And Elijah said, *As* the LORD of
hosts liveth, before whom I stand, I will
surely shew myself unto him to day.
16 So Obadiah went to meet Ahab,
and told him: and Ahab went to meet
Elijah.
17 And it came to pass, when Ahab
saw Elijah, that Ahab said unto him,
Art thou he that troubleth Israel?
18 And he answered, I have not troubled Israel; but thou, and thy father's
house, in that ye have forsaken the
commandments of the LORD, and thou
hast followed Baalim.
19 Now therefore send, *and* gather to
me all Israel unto mount Carmel, and
the prophets of Baal four hundred and
fifty, and the prophets of the groves
four hundred, which eat at Jezebel's
table.
20 So Ahab sent unto all the children
of Israel, and gathered the prophets
together unto mount Carmel.
21 And Elijah came unto all the people, and said, How long halt ye between
two opinions? if the LORD *be* God, follow him: but if Baal, *then* follow him.
And the people answered him not a
word.
22 Then said Elijah unto the people, I,
even I only, remain a prophet of the
LORD; but Baal's prophets *are* four hundred and fifty men.
23 Let them therefore give us two
bullocks; and let them choose one bullock for themselves, and cut it in pieces,
and lay *it* on wood, and put no fire
under: and I will dress the other bullock, and lay *it* on wood, and put no fire
under:
24 And call ye on the name of your
gods, and I will call on the name of the
LORD: and the God that answereth by

fire, let him be God. And all the people answered and said, It is well spoken.

25 And Elijah said unto the prophets of Baal, Choose you one bullock for yourselves, and dress *it* first; for ye *are* many; and call on the name of your gods, but put no fire *under*.

26 And they took the bullock which was given them, and they dressed *it*, and called on the name of Baal from morning even until noon, saying, O Baal, hear us. But *there was* no voice, nor any that answered. And they leaped upon the altar which was made.

27 And it came to pass at noon, that Elijah mocked them, and said, Cry aloud: for he *is* a god; either he is talking, or he is pursuing, or he is in a journey, *or* peradventure he sleepeth, and must be awaked.

28 And they cried aloud, and cut themselves after their manner with knives and lancets, till the blood gushed out upon them.

29 And it came to pass, when midday was past, and they prophesied until the *time* of the offering of the *evening* sacrifice, that *there was* neither voice, nor any to answer, nor any that regarded.

30 And Elijah said unto all the people, Come near unto me. And all the people came near unto him. And he repaired the altar of the LORD *that was* broken down.

31 And Elijah took twelve stones, according to the number of the tribes of the sons of Jacob, unto whom the word of the LORD came, saying, Israel shall be thy name:

32 And with the stones he built an altar in the name of the LORD: and he made a trench about the altar, as great as would contain two measures of seed.

33 And he put the wood in order, and cut the bullock in pieces, and laid *him* on the wood, and said, Fill four barrels with water, and pour *it* on the burnt sacrifice, and on the wood.

34 And he said, Do *it* the second time. And they did *it* the second time. And he said, Do *it* the third time. And they did *it* the third time.

35 And the water ran round about the altar; and he filled the trench also with water.

36 And it came to pass at *the time of* the offering of the *evening* sacrifice, that Elijah the prophet came near, and said, LORD God of Abraham, Isaac, and of Israel, let it be known this day that thou *art* God in Israel, and *that* I *am* thy servant, and *that* I have done all these things at thy word.

37 Hear me, O LORD, hear me, that this people may know that thou *art* the LORD God, and *that* thou hast turned their heart back again.

38 Then the fire of the LORD fell, and consumed the burnt sacrifice, and the wood, and the stones, and the dust, and licked up the water that *was* in the trench.

39 And when all the people saw *it*, they fell on their faces: and they said, The LORD, he *is* the God; the LORD, he *is* the God.

40 And Elijah said unto them, Take the prophets of Baal; let not one of them escape. And they took them: and Elijah brought them down to the brook Kishon, and slew them there.

41 And Elijah said unto Ahab, Get thee up, eat and drink; for *there is* a sound of abundance of rain.

42 So Ahab went up to eat and to drink. And Elijah went up to the top of Carmel; and he cast himself down upon

the earth, and put his face between his
knees,
43 And said to his servant, Go up now,
look toward the sea. And he went up,
and looked, and said, *There is* nothing.
And he said, Go again seven times.
44 And it came to pass at the seventh
time, that he said, Behold, there ariseth
a little cloud out of the sea, like a man's
hand. And he said, Go up, say unto
Ahab, Prepare *thy chariot*, and get
thee down, that the rain stop thee not.
45 And it came to pass in the mean
while, that the heaven was black with
clouds and wind, and there was a great
rain. And Ahab rode, and went to
Jezreel.
46 And the hand of the LORD was on
Elijah; and he girded up his loins, and
ran before Ahab to the entrance of
Jezreel.

19 And Ahab told Jezebel all that
Elijah had done, and withal how
he had slain all the prophets with the
sword.
2 Then Jezebel sent a messenger unto
Elijah, saying, So let the gods do *to me*,
and more also, if I make not thy life as
the life of one of them by to morrow
about this time.
3 And when he saw *that*, he arose,
and went for his life, and came to Beer-
sheba, which *belongeth* to Judah, and
left his servant there.
4 But he himself went a day's journey
into the wilderness, and came and sat
down under a juniper tree: and he
requested for himself that he might
die; and said, It is enough; now, O LORD,
take away my life; for I *am* not better
than my fathers.
5 And as he lay and slept under a
juniper tree, behold, then an angel
touched him, and said unto him, Arise
and eat.
6 And he looked, and, behold, *there*
was a cake baken on the coals, and a
cruse of water at his head. And he did
eat and drink, and laid him down again.
7 And the angel of the LORD came
again the second time, and touched
him, and said, Arise *and* eat; because
the journey *is* too great for thee.
8 And he arose, and did eat and drink,
and went in the strength of that meat
forty days and forty nights unto Horeb
the mount of God.
9 And he came thither unto a cave,
and lodged there; and, behold, the word
of the LORD *came* to him, and he said
unto him, What doest thou here, Elijah?
10 And he said, I have been very jealous for the LORD God of hosts: for the
children of Israel have forsaken thy
covenant, thrown down thine altars,
and slain thy prophets with the sword;
and I, *even* I only, am left; and they seek
my life, to take it away.
11 And he said, Go forth, and stand
upon the mount before the LORD. And,
behold, the LORD passed by, and a great
and strong wind rent the mountains,
and brake in pieces the rocks before
the LORD; *but* the LORD *was* not in the
wind: and after the wind an earthquake; *but* the LORD *was* not in the
earthquake:
12 And after the earthquake a fire;
but the LORD *was* not in the fire: and
after the fire a still small voice.
13 And it was *so*, when Elijah heard
it, that he wrapped his face in his
mantle, and went out, and stood in the
entering in of the cave. And, behold,
there came a voice unto him, and said,
What doest thou here, Elijah?

14 And he said, I have been very jealous for the LORD God of hosts: because
the children of Israel have forsaken thy
covenant, thrown down thine altars,
and slain thy prophets with the sword;
and I, *even* I only, am left; and they seek
my life, to take it away.
15 And the LORD said unto him, Go,
return on thy way to the wilderness of
Damascus: and when thou comest,
anoint Hazael *to be* king over Syria:
16 And Jehu the son of Nimshi shalt
thou anoint *to be* king over Israel: and
Elisha the son of Shaphat of Abel-
meholah shalt thou anoint *to be* prophet in thy room.
17 And it shall come to pass, *that* him
that escapeth the sword of Hazael shall
Jehu slay: and him that escapeth from
the sword of Jehu shall Elisha slay.
18 Yet I have left *me* seven thousand
in Israel, all the knees which have not
bowed unto Baal, and every mouth
which hath not kissed him.
19 So he departed thence, and found
Elisha the son of Shaphat, who *was*
plowing *with* twelve yoke *of oxen*
before him, and he with the twelfth:
and Elijah passed by him, and cast his
mantle upon him.
20 And he left the oxen, and ran after
Elijah, and said, Let me, I pray thee,
kiss my father and my mother, and *then*
I will follow thee. And he said unto him,
Go back again: for what have I done to
thee?
21 And he returned back from him,
and took a yoke of oxen, and slew them,
and boiled their flesh with the instruments of the oxen, and gave unto the
people, and they did eat. Then he arose,
and went after Elijah, and ministered
unto him.

20 And Ben-hadad the king of Syria
gathered all his host together:
and *there were* thirty and two kings
with him, and horses, and chariots: and
he went up and besieged Samaria, and
warred against it.
2 And he sent messengers to Ahab
king of Israel into the city, and said
unto him, Thus saith Ben-hadad,
3 Thy silver and thy gold *is* mine; thy
wives also and thy children, *even* the
goodliest, *are* mine.
4 And the king of Israel answered and
said, My lord, O king, according to thy
saying, I *am* thine, and all that I have.
5 And the messengers came again,
and said, Thus speaketh Ben-hadad,
saying, Although I have sent unto thee,
saying, Thou shalt deliver me thy silver,
and thy gold, and thy wives, and thy
children;
6 Yet I will send my servants unto
thee to morrow about this time, and
they shall search thine house, and the
houses of thy servants; and it shall be,
that whatsoever is pleasant in thine
eyes, they shall put *it* in their hand, and
take *it* away.
7 Then the king of Israel called all the
elders of the land, and said, Mark, I
pray you, and see how this *man* seeketh
mischief: for he sent unto me for my
wives, and for my children, and for my
silver, and for my gold; and I denied
him not.
8 And all the elders and all the people said unto him, Hearken not *unto
him*, nor consent.
9 Wherefore he said unto the messengers of Ben-hadad, Tell my lord the
king, All that thou didst send for to thy
servant at the first I will do: but this
thing I may not do. And the messengers
departed, and brought him word again.

10 And Ben-hadad sent unto him, and said, The gods do so unto me, and more also, if the dust of Samaria shall suffice for handfuls for all the people that follow me.

11 And the king of Israel answered and said, Tell *him*, Let not him that girdeth on *his harness* boast himself as he that putteth it off.

12 And it came to pass, when *Ben-hadad* heard this message, as he *was* drinking, he and the kings in the pavilions, that he said unto his servants, Set *yourselves in array*. And they set *themselves in array* against the city.

13 And, behold, there came a prophet unto Ahab king of Israel, saying, Thus saith the LORD, Hast thou seen all this great multitude? behold, I will deliver it into thine hand this day; and thou shalt know that I *am* the LORD.

14 And Ahab said, By whom? And he said, Thus saith the LORD, *Even* by the young men of the princes of the provinces. Then he said, Who shall order the battle? And he answered, Thou.

15 Then he numbered the young men of the princes of the provinces, and they were two hundred and thirty two: and after them he numbered all the people, *even* all the children of Israel, *being* seven thousand.

16 And they went out at noon. But Ben-hadad *was* drinking himself drunk in the pavilions, he and the kings, the thirty and two kings that helped him.

17 And the young men of the princes of the provinces went out first; and Ben-hadad sent out, and they told him, saying, There are men come out of Samaria.

18 And he said, Whether they be come out for peace, take them alive; or whether they be come out for war, take them alive.

19 So these young men of the princes of the provinces came out of the city, and the army which followed them.

20 And they slew every one his man: and the Syrians fled; and Israel pursued them: and Ben-hadad the king of Syria escaped on an horse with the horsemen.

21 And the king of Israel went out, and smote the horses and chariots, and slew the Syrians with a great slaughter.

22 And the prophet came to the king of Israel, and said unto him, Go, strengthen thyself, and mark, and see what thou doest: for at the return of the year the king of Syria will come up against thee.

23 And the servants of the king of Syria said unto him, Their gods *are* gods of the hills; therefore they were stronger than we; but let us fight against them in the plain, and surely we shall be stronger than they.

24 And do this thing, Take the kings away, every man out of his place, and put captains in their rooms:

25 And number thee an army, like the army that thou hast lost, horse for horse, and chariot for chariot: and we will fight against them in the plain, *and* surely we shall be stronger than they. And he hearkened unto their voice, and did so.

26 And it came to pass at the return of the year, that Ben-hadad numbered the Syrians, and went up to Aphek, to fight against Israel.

27 And the children of Israel were numbered, and were all present, and went against them: and the children of Israel pitched before them like two

little flocks of kids; but the Syrians
filled the country.
28 And there came a man of God, and
spake unto the king of Israel, and said,
Thus saith the LORD, Because the
Syrians have said, The LORD *is* God of
the hills, but he *is* not God of the valleys, therefore will I deliver all this
great multitude into thine hand, and ye
shall know that I *am* the LORD.
29 And they pitched one over against
the other seven days. And *so* it was, that
in the seventh day the battle was
joined: and the children of Israel slew
of the Syrians an hundred thousand
footmen in one day.
30 But the rest fled to Aphek, into the
city; and *there* a wall fell upon twenty
and seven thousand of the men *that*
were left. And Ben-hadad fled, and
came into the city, into an inner chamber.
31 And his servants said unto him,
Behold now, we have heard that the
kings of the house of Israel *are* merciful
kings: let us, I pray thee, put sackcloth
on our loins, and ropes upon our heads,
and go out to the king of Israel: peradventure he will save thy life.
32 So they girded sackcloth on their
loins, and *put* ropes on their heads, and
came to the king of Israel, and said, Thy
servant Ben-hadad saith, I pray thee, let
me live. And he said, *Is* he yet alive? he
is my brother.
33 Now the men did diligently
observe whether *any thing would*
come from him, and did hastily catch *it*:
and they said, Thy brother Ben-hadad.
Then he said, Go ye, bring him. Then
Ben-hadad came forth to him; and he
caused him to come up into the chariot.

34 And *Ben-hadad* said unto him, The
cities, which my father took from thy
father, I will restore; and thou shalt
make streets for thee in Damascus, as
my father made in Samaria. Then *said*
Ahab, I will send thee away with this
covenant. So he made a covenant with
him, and sent him away.
35 And a certain man of the sons of
the prophets said unto his neighbour in
the word of the LORD, Smite me, I pray
thee. And the man refused to smite
him.
36 Then said he unto him, Because
thou hast not obeyed the voice of the
LORD, behold, as soon as thou art
departed from me, a lion shall slay
thee. And as soon as he was departed
from him, a lion found him, and slew
him.
37 Then he found another man, and
said, Smite me, I pray thee. And the
man smote him, so that in smiting he
wounded *him*.
38 So the prophet departed, and waited for the king by the way, and disguised himself with ashes upon his
face.
39 And as the king passed by, he cried
unto the king: and he said, Thy servant
went out into the midst of the battle;
and, behold, a man turned aside, and
brought a man unto me, and said, Keep
this man: if by any means he be missing, then shall thy life be for his life, or
else thou shalt pay a talent of silver.
40 And as thy servant was busy here
and there, he was gone. And the king of
Israel said unto him, So *shall* thy judgment *be*; thyself hast decided *it*.
41 And he hasted, and took the ashes
away from his face; and the king of
Israel discerned him that he *was* of the
prophets.

42 And he said unto him, Thus saith
the LORD, Because thou hast let go out
of *thy* hand a man whom I appointed to
utter destruction, therefore thy life
shall go for his life, and thy people for
his people.
43 And the king of Israel went to his
house heavy and displeased, and came
to Samaria.

21 And it came to pass after these
things, *that* Naboth the Jezreelite
had a vineyard, which *was* in Jezreel,
hard by the palace of Ahab king of
Samaria.
2 And Ahab spake unto Naboth, saying, Give me thy vineyard, that I may
have it for a garden of herbs, because it
is near unto my house: and I will give
thee for it a better vineyard than it; *or*,
if it seem good to thee, I will give thee
the worth of it in money.
3 And Naboth said to Ahab, The LORD
forbid it me, that I should give the
inheritance of my fathers unto thee.
4 And Ahab came into his house
heavy and displeased because of the
word which Naboth the Jezreelite had
spoken to him: for he had said, I will
not give thee the inheritance of my
fathers. And he laid him down upon his
bed, and turned away his face, and
would eat no bread.
5 But Jezebel his wife came to him,
and said unto him, Why is thy spirit so
sad, that thou eatest no bread?
6 And he said unto her, Because I
spake unto Naboth the Jezreelite, and
said unto him, Give me thy vineyard for
money; or else, if it please thee, I will
give thee *another* vineyard for it: and
he answered, I will not give thee my
vineyard.
7 And Jezebel his wife said unto him,
Dost thou now govern the kingdom of
Israel? arise, *and* eat bread, and let
thine heart be merry: I will give thee
the vineyard of Naboth the Jezreelite.
8 So she wrote letters in Ahab's name,
and sealed *them* with his seal, and sent
the letters unto the elders and to the
nobles that *were* in his city, dwelling
with Naboth.
9 And she wrote in the letters, saying,
Proclaim a fast, and set Naboth on high
among the people:
10 And set two men, sons of Belial,
before him, to bear witness against
him, saying, Thou didst blaspheme God
and the king. And *then* carry him out,
and stone him, that he may die.
11 And the men of his city, *even* the
elders and the nobles who were the
inhabitants in his city, did as Jezebel
had sent unto them, *and* as it *was* written in the letters which she had sent
unto them.
12 They proclaimed a fast, and set
Naboth on high among the people.
13 And there came in two men, children of Belial, and sat before him: and
the men of Belial witnessed against
him, *even* against Naboth, in the presence of the people, saying, Naboth did
blaspheme God and the king. Then
they carried him forth out of the city,
and stoned him with stones, that he
died.
14 Then they sent to Jezebel, saying,
Naboth is stoned, and is dead.
15 And it came to pass, when Jezebel
heard that Naboth was stoned, and was
dead, that Jezebel said to Ahab, Arise,
take possession of the vineyard of
Naboth the Jezreelite, which he refused
to give thee for money: for Naboth is
not alive, but dead.

16 And it came to pass, when Ahab heard that Naboth was dead, that Ahab rose up to go down to the vineyard of Naboth the Jezreelite, to take possession of it.

17 And the word of the LORD came to Elijah the Tishbite, saying,

18 Arise, go down to meet Ahab king of Israel, which *is* in Samaria: behold, *he is* in the vineyard of Naboth, whither he is gone down to possess it.

19 And thou shalt speak unto him, saying, Thus saith the LORD, Hast thou killed, and also taken possession? And thou shalt speak unto him, saying, Thus saith the LORD, In the place where dogs licked the blood of Naboth shall dogs lick thy blood, even thine.

20 And Ahab said to Elijah, Hast thou found me, O mine enemy? And he answered, I have found *thee*: because thou hast sold thyself to work evil in the sight of the LORD.

21 Behold, I will bring evil upon thee, and will take away thy posterity, and will cut off from Ahab him that pisseth against the wall, and him that is shut up and left in Israel,

22 And will make thine house like the house of Jeroboam the son of Nebat, and like the house of Baasha the son of Ahijah, for the provocation wherewith thou hast provoked *me* to anger, and made Israel to sin.

23 And of Jezebel also spake the LORD, saying, The dogs shall eat Jezebel by the wall of Jezreel.

24 Him that dieth of Ahab in the city the dogs shall eat; and him that dieth in the field shall the fowls of the air eat.

25 But there was none like unto Ahab, which did sell himself to work wickedness in the sight of the LORD, whom Jezebel his wife stirred up.

26 And he did very abominably in following idols, according to all *things* as did the Amorites, whom the LORD cast out before the children of Israel.

27 And it came to pass, when Ahab heard those words, that he rent his clothes, and put sackcloth upon his flesh, and fasted, and lay in sackcloth, and went softly.

28 And the word of the LORD came to Elijah the Tishbite, saying,

29 Seest thou how Ahab humbleth himself before me? because he humbleth himself before me, I will not bring the evil in his days: *but* in his son's days will I bring the evil upon his house.

22

And they continued three years without war between Syria and Israel.

2 And it came to pass in the third year, that Jehoshaphat the king of Judah came down to the king of Israel.

3 And the king of Israel said unto his servants, Know ye that Ramoth in Gilead *is* ours, and we *be* still, *and* take it not out of the hand of the king of Syria?

4 And he said unto Jehoshaphat, Wilt thou go with me to battle to Ramoth-gilead? And Jehoshaphat said to the king of Israel, I *am* as thou *art*, my people as thy people, my horses as thy horses.

5 And Jehoshaphat said unto the king of Israel, Enquire, I pray thee, at the word of the LORD to day.

6 Then the king of Israel gathered the prophets together, about four hundred men, and said unto them, Shall I go against Ramoth-gilead to battle, or shall I forbear? And they said, Go up; for the Lord shall deliver *it* into the hand of the king.

7 And Jehoshaphat said, *Is there* not here a prophet of the LORD besides, that we might enquire of him?

8 And the king of Israel said unto Jehoshaphat, *There is* yet one man, Micaiah the son of Imlah, by whom we may enquire of the LORD: but I hate him; for he doth not prophesy good concerning me, but evil. And Jehoshaphat said, Let not the king say so.

9 Then the king of Israel called an officer, and said, Hasten *hither* Micaiah the son of Imlah.

10 And the king of Israel and Jehoshaphat the king of Judah sat each on his throne, having put on their robes, in a void place in the entrance of the gate of Samaria; and all the prophets prophesied before them.

11 And Zedekiah the son of Chenaanah made him horns of iron: and he said, Thus saith the LORD, With these shalt thou push the Syrians, until thou have consumed them.

12 And all the prophets prophesied so, saying, Go up to Ramoth-gilead, and prosper: for the LORD shall deliver *it* into the king's hand.

13 And the messenger that was gone to call Micaiah spake unto him, saying, Behold now, the words of the prophets *declare* good unto the king with one mouth: let thy word, I pray thee, be like the word of one of them, and speak *that which is* good.

14 And Micaiah said, *As* the LORD liveth, what the LORD saith unto me, that will I speak.

15 So he came to the king. And the king said unto him, Micaiah, shall we go against Ramoth-gilead to battle, or shall we forbear? And he answered him, Go, and prosper: for the LORD shall deliver *it* into the hand of the king.

16 And the king said unto him, How many times shall I adjure thee that thou tell me nothing but *that which is* true in the name of the LORD?

17 And he said, I saw all Israel scattered upon the hills, as sheep that have not a shepherd: and the LORD said, These have no master: let them return every man to his house in peace.

18 And the king of Israel said unto Jehoshaphat, Did I not tell thee that he would prophesy no good concerning me, but evil?

19 And he said, Hear thou therefore the word of the LORD: I saw the LORD sitting on his throne, and all the host of heaven standing by him on his right hand and on his left.

20 And the LORD said, Who shall persuade Ahab, that he may go up and fall at Ramoth-gilead? And one said on this manner, and another said on that manner.

21 And there came forth a spirit, and stood before the LORD, and said, I will persuade him.

22 And the LORD said unto him, Wherewith? And he said, I will go forth, and I will be a lying spirit in the mouth of all his prophets. And he said, Thou shalt persuade *him*, and prevail also: go forth, and do so.

23 Now therefore, behold, the LORD hath put a lying spirit in the mouth of all these thy prophets, and the LORD hath spoken evil concerning thee.

24 But Zedekiah the son of Chenaanah went near, and smote Micaiah on the cheek, and said, Which way went the Spirit of the LORD from me to speak unto thee?

25 And Micaiah said, Behold, thou shalt see in that day, when thou shalt go into an inner chamber to hide thyself.

26 And the king of Israel said, Take Micaiah, and carry him back unto Amon the governor of the city, and to Joash the king's son;

27 And say, Thus saith the king, Put this *fellow* in the prison, and feed him with bread of affliction and with water of affliction, until I come in peace.

28 And Micaiah said, If thou return at all in peace, the LORD hath not spoken by me. And he said, Hearken, O people, every one of you.

29 So the king of Israel and Jehoshaphat the king of Judah went up to Ramoth-gilead.

30 And the king of Israel said unto Jehoshaphat, I will disguise myself, and enter into the battle; but put thou on thy robes. And the king of Israel disguised himself, and went into the battle.

31 But the king of Syria commanded his thirty and two captains that had rule over his chariots, saying, Fight neither with small nor great, save only with the king of Israel.

32 And it came to pass, when the captains of the chariots saw Jehoshaphat, that they said, Surely it *is* the king of Israel. And they turned aside to fight against him: and Jehoshaphat cried out.

33 And it came to pass, when the captains of the chariots perceived that it *was* not the king of Israel, that they turned back from pursuing him.

34 And a *certain* man drew a bow at a venture, and smote the king of Israel between the joints of the harness: wherefore he said unto the driver of his chariot, Turn thine hand, and carry me out of the host; for I am wounded.

35 And the battle increased that day: and the king was stayed up in his chariot against the Syrians, and died at even: and the blood ran out of the wound into the midst of the chariot.

36 And there went a proclamation throughout the host about the going down of the sun, saying, Every man to his city, and every man to his own country.

37 So the king died, and was brought to Samaria; and they buried the king in Samaria.

38 And *one* washed the chariot in the pool of Samaria; and the dogs licked up his blood; and they washed his armour; according unto the word of the LORD which he spake.

39 Now the rest of the acts of Ahab, and all that he did, and the ivory house which he made, and all the cities that he built, *are* they not written in the book of the chronicles of the kings of Israel?

40 So Ahab slept with his fathers; and Ahaziah his son reigned in his stead.

41 And Jehoshaphat the son of Asa began to reign over Judah in the fourth year of Ahab king of Israel.

42 Jehoshaphat *was* thirty and five years old when he began to reign; and he reigned twenty and five years in Jerusalem. And his mother's name *was* Azubah the daughter of Shilhi.

43 And he walked in all the ways of Asa his father; he turned not aside from it, doing *that which was* right in the eyes of the LORD: nevertheless the high places were not taken away; *for* the people offered and burnt incense yet in the high places.

44 And Jehoshaphat made peace with the king of Israel.

45 Now the rest of the acts of Jehoshaphat, and his might that he shewed, and how he warred, *are* they not written in the book of the chronicles of the kings of Judah?

46 And the remnant of the sodomites, which remained in the days of his father Asa, he took out of the land.

47 *There was* then no king in Edom: a deputy *was* king.

48 Jehoshaphat made ships of Tharshish to go to Ophir for gold: but they went not; for the ships were broken at Ezion-geber.

49 Then said Ahaziah the son of Ahab unto Jehoshaphat, Let my servants go with thy servants in the ships. But Jehoshaphat would not.

50 And Jehoshaphat slept with his fathers, and was buried with his fathers in the city of David his father: and Jehoram his son reigned in his stead.

51 Ahaziah the son of Ahab began to reign over Israel in Samaria the seventeenth year of Jehoshaphat king of Judah, and reigned two years over Israel.

52 And he did evil in the sight of the LORD, and walked in the way of his father, and in the way of his mother, and in the way of Jeroboam the son of Nebat, who made Israel to sin:

53 For he served Baal, and worshipped him, and provoked to anger the LORD God of Israel, according to all that his father had done.

THE SECOND BOOK OF KINGS

1 Then Moab rebelled against Israel after the death of Ahab.

2 And Ahaziah fell down through a lattice in his upper chamber that *was* in Samaria, and was sick: and he sent messengers, and said unto them, Go, enquire of Baal-zebub the god of Ekron whether I shall recover of this disease.

3 But the angel of the LORD said to Elijah the Tishbite, Arise, go up to meet the messengers of the king of Samaria, and say unto them, *Is it* not because *there is* not a God in Israel, *that* ye go to enquire of Baal-zebub the god of Ekron?

4 Now therefore thus saith the LORD, Thou shalt not come down from that bed on which thou art gone up, but shalt surely die. And Elijah departed.

5 And when the messengers turned back unto him, he said unto them, Why are ye now turned back?

6 And they said unto him, There came a man up to meet us, and said unto us, Go, turn again unto the king that sent you, and say unto him, Thus saith the LORD, *Is it* not because *there is* not a God in Israel, *that* thou sendest to enquire of Baal-zebub the god of Ekron? therefore thou shalt not come

down from that bed on which thou art gone up, but shalt surely die.

7 And he said unto them, What manner of man *was he* which came up to meet you, and told you these words?

8 And they answered him, *He was* an hairy man, and girt with a girdle of leather about his loins. And he said, It *is* Elijah the Tishbite.

9 Then the king sent unto him a captain of fifty with his fifty. And he went up to him: and, behold, he sat on the top of an hill. And he spake unto him, Thou man of God, the king hath said, Come down.

10 And Elijah answered and said to the captain of fifty, If I *be* a man of God, then let fire come down from heaven, and consume thee and thy fifty. And there came down fire from heaven, and consumed him and his fifty.

11 Again also he sent unto him another captain of fifty with his fifty. And he answered and said unto him, O man of God, thus hath the king said, Come down quickly.

12 And Elijah answered and said unto them, If I *be* a man of God, let fire come down from heaven, and consume thee and thy fifty. And the fire of God came down from heaven, and consumed him and his fifty.

13 And he sent again a captain of the third fifty with his fifty. And the third captain of fifty went up, and came and fell on his knees before Elijah, and besought him, and said unto him, O man of God, I pray thee, let my life, and the life of these fifty thy servants, be precious in thy sight.

14 Behold, there came fire down from heaven, and burnt up the two captains of the former fifties with their fifties: therefore let my life now be precious in thy sight.

15 And the angel of the LORD said unto Elijah, Go down with him: be not afraid of him. And he arose, and went down with him unto the king.

16 And he said unto him, Thus saith the LORD, Forasmuch as thou hast sent messengers to enquire of Baal-zebub the god of Ekron, *is it* not because *there is* no God in Israel to enquire of his word? therefore thou shalt not come down off that bed on which thou art gone up, but shalt surely die.

17 So he died according to the word of the LORD which Elijah had spoken. And Jehoram reigned in his stead in the second year of Jehoram the son of Jehoshaphat king of Judah; because he had no son.

18 Now the rest of the acts of Ahaziah which he did, *are* they not written in the book of the chronicles of the kings of Israel?

2 And it came to pass, when the LORD would take up Elijah into heaven by a whirlwind, that Elijah went with Elisha from Gilgal.

2 And Elijah said unto Elisha, Tarry here, I pray thee; for the LORD hath sent me to Beth-el. And Elisha said *unto him, As* the LORD liveth, and *as* thy soul liveth, I will not leave thee. So they went down to Beth-el.

3 And the sons of the prophets that *were* at Beth-el came forth to Elisha, and said unto him, Knowest thou that the LORD will take away thy master from thy head to day? And he said, Yea, I know *it*; hold ye your peace.

4 And Elijah said unto him, Elisha, tarry here, I pray thee; for the LORD hath sent me to Jericho. And he said, *As* the LORD liveth, and *as* thy soul liveth, I will not leave thee. So they came to Jericho.

5 And the sons of the prophets that *were* at Jericho came to Elisha, and said unto him, Knowest thou that the LORD will take away thy master from thy head to day? And he answered, Yea, I know *it*; hold ye your peace.

6 And Elijah said unto him, Tarry, I pray thee, here; for the LORD hath sent me to Jordan. And he said, *As* the LORD liveth, and *as* thy soul liveth, I will not leave thee. And they two went on.

7 And fifty men of the sons of the prophets went, and stood to view afar off: and they two stood by Jordan.

8 And Elijah took his mantle, and wrapped *it* together, and smote the waters, and they were divided hither and thither, so that they two went over on dry ground.

9 And it came to pass, when they were gone over, that Elijah said unto Elisha, Ask what I shall do for thee, before I be taken away from thee. And Elisha said, I pray thee, let a double portion of thy spirit be upon me.

10 And he said, Thou hast asked a hard thing: *nevertheless*, if thou see me *when I am* taken from thee, it shall be so unto thee; but if not, it shall not be *so*.

11 And it came to pass, as they still went on, and talked, that, behold, *there appeared* a chariot of fire, and horses of fire, and parted them both asunder; and Elijah went up by a whirlwind into heaven.

12 And Elisha saw *it*, and he cried, My father, my father, the chariot of Israel, and the horsemen thereof. And he saw him no more: and he took hold of his own clothes, and rent them in two pieces.

13 He took up also the mantle of Elijah that fell from him, and went back, and stood by the bank of Jordan;

14 And he took the mantle of Elijah that fell from him, and smote the waters, and said, Where *is* the LORD God of Elijah? and when he also had smitten the waters, they parted hither and thither: and Elisha went over.

15 And when the sons of the prophets which *were* to view at Jericho saw him, they said, The spirit of Elijah doth rest on Elisha. And they came to meet him, and bowed themselves to the ground before him.

16 And they said unto him, Behold now, there be with thy servants fifty strong men; let them go, we pray thee, and seek thy master: lest peradventure the Spirit of the LORD hath taken him up, and cast him upon some mountain, or into some valley. And he said, Ye shall not send.

17 And when they urged him till he was ashamed, he said, Send. They sent therefore fifty men; and they sought three days, but found him not.

18 And when they came again to him, (for he tarried at Jericho,) he said unto them, Did I not say unto you, Go not?

19 And the men of the city said unto Elisha, Behold, I pray thee, the situation of this city *is* pleasant, as my lord seeth: but the water *is* naught, and the ground barren.

20 And he said, Bring me a new cruse, and put salt therein. And they brought *it* to him.

21 And he went forth unto the spring of the waters, and cast the salt in there, and said, Thus saith the LORD, I have healed these waters; there shall not be from thence any more death or barren *land*.

22 So the waters were healed unto
this day, according to the saying of
Elisha which he spake.
23 And he went up from thence unto
Beth-el: and as he was going up by the
way, there came forth little children out
of the city, and mocked him, and said
unto him, Go up, thou bald head; go up,
thou bald head.
24 And he turned back, and looked on
them, and cursed them in the name of
the LORD. And there came forth two she
bears out of the wood, and tare forty
and two children of them.
25 And he went from thence to mount
Carmel, and from thence he returned
to Samaria.

3 Now Jehoram the son of Ahab
began to reign over Israel in
Samaria the eighteenth year of
Jehoshaphat king of Judah, and
reigned twelve years.
2 And he wrought evil in the sight of
the LORD; but not like his father, and
like his mother: for he put away the
image of Baal that his father had made.
3 Nevertheless he cleaved unto the
sins of Jeroboam the son of Nebat,
which made Israel to sin; he departed
not therefrom.
4 And Mesha king of Moab was a
sheepmaster, and rendered unto the
king of Israel an hundred thousand
lambs, and an hundred thousand rams,
with the wool.
5 But it came to pass, when Ahab was
dead, that the king of Moab rebelled
against the king of Israel.
6 And king Jehoram went out of
Samaria the same time, and numbered
all Israel.
7 And he went and sent to Jehoshaphat the king of Judah, saying, The
king of Moab hath rebelled against me:
wilt thou go with me against Moab to
battle? And he said, I will go up: I *am*
as thou *art*, my people as thy people,
and my horses as thy horses.
8 And he said, Which way shall we go
up? And he answered, The way through
the wilderness of Edom.
9 So the king of Israel went, and the
king of Judah, and the king of Edom:
and they fetched a compass of seven
days' journey: and there was no water
for the host, and for the cattle that followed them.
10 And the king of Israel said, Alas!
that the LORD hath called these three
kings together, to deliver them into the
hand of Moab!
11 But Jehoshaphat said, *Is there* not
here a prophet of the LORD, that we
may enquire of the LORD by him? And
one of the king of Israel's servants
answered and said, Here *is* Elisha the
son of Shaphat, which poured water on
the hands of Elijah.
12 And Jehoshaphat said, The word of
the LORD is with him. So the king of
Israel and Jehoshaphat and the king of
Edom went down to him.
13 And Elisha said unto the king of
Israel, What have I to do with thee? get
thee to the prophets of thy father, and
to the prophets of thy mother. And the
king of Israel said unto him, Nay: for
the LORD hath called these three kings
together, to deliver them into the hand
of Moab.
14 And Elisha said, *As* the LORD of
hosts liveth, before whom I stand, surely, were it not that I regard the presence
of Jehoshaphat the king of Judah, I
would not look toward thee, nor see
thee.

15 But now bring me a minstrel. And it came to pass, when the minstrel played, that the hand of the LORD came upon him.

16 And he said, Thus saith the LORD, Make this valley full of ditches.

17 For thus saith the LORD, Ye shall not see wind, neither shall ye see rain; yet that valley shall be filled with water, that ye may drink, both ye, and your cattle, and your beasts.

18 And this is *but* a light thing in the sight of the LORD: he will deliver the Moabites also into your hand.

19 And ye shall smite every fenced city, and every choice city, and shall fell every good tree, and stop all wells of water, and mar every good piece of land with stones.

20 And it came to pass in the morning, when the meat offering was offered, that, behold, there came water by the way of Edom, and the country was filled with water.

21 And when all the Moabites heard that the kings were come up to fight against them, they gathered all that were able to put on armour, and upward, and stood in the border.

22 And they rose up early in the morning, and the sun shone upon the water, and the Moabites saw the water on the other side *as* red as blood:

23 And they said, This *is* blood: the kings are surely slain, and they have smitten one another: now therefore, Moab, to the spoil.

24 And when they came to the camp of Israel, the Israelites rose up and smote the Moabites, so that they fled before them: but they went forward smiting the Moabites, even in *their* country.

25 And they beat down the cities, and on every good piece of land cast every man his stone, and filled it; and they stopped all the wells of water, and felled all the good trees: only in Kir-haraseth left they the stones thereof; howbeit the slingers went about *it*, and smote it.

26 And when the king of Moab saw that the battle was too sore for him, he took with him seven hundred men that drew swords, to break through *even* unto the king of Edom: but they could not.

27 Then he took his eldest son that should have reigned in his stead, and offered him *for* a burnt offering upon the wall. And there was great indignation against Israel: and they departed from him, and returned to *their own* land.

4 Now there cried a certain woman of the wives of the sons of the prophets unto Elisha, saying, Thy servant my husband is dead; and thou knowest that thy servant did fear the LORD: and the creditor is come to take unto him my two sons to be bondmen.

2 And Elisha said unto her, What shall I do for thee? tell me, what hast thou in the house? And she said, Thine handmaid hath not any thing in the house, save a pot of oil.

3 Then he said, Go, borrow thee vessels abroad of all thy neighbours, *even* empty vessels; borrow not a few.

4 And when thou art come in, thou shalt shut the door upon thee and upon thy sons, and shalt pour out into all those vessels, and thou shalt set aside that which is full.

5 So she went from him, and shut the
door upon her and upon her sons, who
brought *the vessels* to her; and she
poured out.
6 And it came to pass, when the vessels were full, that she said unto her
son, Bring me yet a vessel. And he said
unto her, *There is* not a vessel more.
And the oil stayed.
7 Then she came and told the man of
God. And he said, Go, sell the oil, and
pay thy debt, and live thou and thy
children of the rest.
8 And it fell on a day, that Elisha
passed to Shunem, where *was* a great
woman; and she constrained him to eat
bread. And *so* it was, *that* as oft as he
passed by, he turned in thither to eat
bread.
9 And she said unto her husband,
Behold now, I perceive that this *is* an
holy man of God, which passeth by us
continually.
10 Let us make a little chamber, I
pray thee, on the wall; and let us set for
him there a bed, and a table, and a
stool, and a candlestick: and it shall be,
when he cometh to us, that he shall
turn in thither.
11 And it fell on a day, that he came
thither, and he turned into the chamber, and lay there.
12 And he said to Gehazi his servant,
Call this Shunammite. And when he
had called her, she stood before him.
13 And he said unto him, Say now
unto her, Behold, thou hast been careful for us with all this care; what *is* to be
done for thee? wouldest thou be spoken for to the king, or to the captain of
the host? And she answered, I dwell
among mine own people.
14 And he said, What then *is* to be
done for her? And Gehazi answered,
Verily she hath no child, and her husband is old.
15 And he said, Call her. And when he
had called her, she stood in the door.
16 And he said, About this season,
according to the time of life, thou shalt
embrace a son. And she said, Nay, my
lord, *thou* man of God, do not lie unto
thine handmaid.
17 And the woman conceived, and
bare a son at that season that Elisha
had said unto her, according to the time
of life.
18 And when the child was grown, it
fell on a day, that he went out to his
father to the reapers.
19 And he said unto his father, My
head, my head. And he said to a lad,
Carry him to his mother.
20 And when he had taken him, and
brought him to his mother, he sat on
her knees till noon, and *then* died.
21 And she went up, and laid him on
the bed of the man of God, and shut *the
door* upon him, and went out.
22 And she called unto her husband,
and said, Send me, I pray thee, one of
the young men, and one of the asses,
that I may run to the man of God, and
come again.
23 And he said, Wherefore wilt thou
go to him to day? *it is* neither new
moon, nor sabbath. And she said, *It
shall be* well.
24 Then she saddled an ass, and said
to her servant, Drive, and go forward;
slack not *thy* riding for me, except I bid
thee.
25 So she went and came unto the
man of God to mount Carmel. And it
came to pass, when the man of God saw
her afar off, that he said to Gehazi his
servant, Behold, *yonder is* that
Shunammite:

26 Run now, I pray thee, to meet her,
and say unto her, *Is it* well with thee? *is*
it well with thy husband? *is it* well with
the child? And she answered, *It is* well.
27 And when she came to the man of
God to the hill, she caught him by the
feet: but Gehazi came near to thrust
her away. And the man of God said, Let
her alone; for her soul *is* vexed within
her: and the LORD hath hid *it* from me,
and hath not told me.
28 Then she said, Did I desire a son of
my lord? did I not say, Do not deceive
me?
29 Then he said to Gehazi, Gird up
thy loins, and take my staff in thine
hand, and go thy way: if thou meet any
man, salute him not; and if any salute
thee, answer him not again: and lay my
staff upon the face of the child.
30 And the mother of the child said,
As the LORD liveth, and *as* thy soul
liveth, I will not leave thee. And he
arose, and followed her.
31 And Gehazi passed on before
them, and laid the staff upon the face
of the child; but *there was* neither
voice, nor hearing. Wherefore he went
again to meet him, and told him, saying,
The child is not awaked.
32 And when Elisha was come into
the house, behold, the child was dead,
and laid upon his bed.
33 He went in therefore, and shut the
door upon them twain, and prayed unto
the LORD.
34 And he went up, and lay upon the
child, and put his mouth upon his
mouth, and his eyes upon his eyes, and
his hands upon his hands: and he
stretched himself upon the child; and
the flesh of the child waxed warm.
35 Then he returned, and walked in
the house to and fro; and went up, and
stretched himself upon him: and the
child sneezed seven times, and the
child opened his eyes.
36 And he called Gehazi, and said,
Call this Shunammite. So he called her.
And when she was come in unto him,
he said, Take up thy son.
37 Then she went in, and fell at his
feet, and bowed herself to the ground,
and took up her son, and went out.
38 And Elisha came again to Gilgal:
and *there was* a dearth in the land; and
the sons of the prophets *were* sitting
before him: and he said unto his servant, Set on the great pot, and seethe
pottage for the sons of the prophets.
39 And one went out into the field to
gather herbs, and found a wild vine,
and gathered thereof wild gourds his
lap full, and came and shred *them* into
the pot of pottage: for they knew *them*
not.
40 So they poured out for the men to
eat. And it came to pass, as they were
eating of the pottage, that they cried
out, and said, O *thou* man of God, *there*
is death in the pot. And they could not
eat *thereof*.
41 But he said, Then bring meal. And
he cast *it* into the pot; and he said, Pour
out for the people, that they may eat.
And there was no harm in the pot.
42 And there came a man from Baal-
shalisha, and brought the man of God
bread of the firstfruits, twenty loaves of
barley, and full ears of corn in the husk
thereof. And he said, Give unto the
people, that they may eat.
43 And his servitor said, What, should
I set this before an hundred men? He
said again, Give the people, that they
may eat: for thus saith the LORD, They
shall eat, and shall leave *thereof*.

44 So he set *it* before them, and they did eat, and left *thereof*, according to the word of the LORD.

5 Now Naaman, captain of the host of the king of Syria, was a great man with his master, and honourable, because by him the LORD had given deliverance unto Syria: he was also a mighty man in valour, *but he was* a leper.

2 And the Syrians had gone out by companies, and had brought away captive out of the land of Israel a little maid; and she waited on Naaman's wife.

3 And she said unto her mistress, Would God my lord *were* with the prophet that *is* in Samaria! for he would recover him of his leprosy.

4 And *one* went in, and told his lord, saying, Thus and thus said the maid that *is* of the land of Israel.

5 And the king of Syria said, Go to, go, and I will send a letter unto the king of Israel. And he departed, and took with him ten talents of silver, and six thousand *pieces* of gold, and ten changes of raiment.

6 And he brought the letter to the king of Israel, saying, Now when this letter is come unto thee, behold, I have *therewith* sent Naaman my servant to thee, that thou mayest recover him of his leprosy.

7 And it came to pass, when the king of Israel had read the letter, that he rent his clothes, and said, *Am* I God, to kill and to make alive, that this man doth send unto me to recover a man of his leprosy? wherefore consider, I pray you, and see how he seeketh a quarrel against me.

8 And it was *so*, when Elisha the man of God had heard that the king of Israel had rent his clothes, that he sent to the king, saying, Wherefore hast thou rent thy clothes? let him come now to me, and he shall know that there is a prophet in Israel.

9 So Naaman came with his horses and with his chariot, and stood at the door of the house of Elisha.

10 And Elisha sent a messenger unto him, saying, Go and wash in Jordan seven times, and thy flesh shall come again to thee, and thou shalt be clean.

11 But Naaman was wroth, and went away, and said, Behold, I thought, He will surely come out to me, and stand, and call on the name of the LORD his God, and strike his hand over the place, and recover the leper.

12 *Are* not Abana and Pharpar, rivers of Damascus, better than all the waters of Israel? may I not wash in them, and be clean? So he turned and went away in a rage.

13 And his servants came near, and spake unto him, and said, My father, *if* the prophet had bid thee *do some* great thing, wouldest thou not have done *it*? how much rather then, when he saith to thee, Wash, and be clean?

14 Then went he down, and dipped himself seven times in Jordan, according to the saying of the man of God: and his flesh came again like unto the flesh of a little child, and he was clean.

15 And he returned to the man of God, he and all his company, and came, and stood before him: and he said, Behold, now I know that *there is* no God in all the earth, but in Israel: now therefore, I pray thee, take a blessing of thy servant.

16 But he said, *As* the LORD liveth,
before whom I stand, I will receive
none. And he urged him to take *it*; but
he refused.
17 And Naaman said, Shall there not
then, I pray thee, be given to thy servant two mules' burden of earth? for
thy servant will henceforth offer neither burnt offering nor sacrifice unto
other gods, but unto the LORD.
18 In this thing the LORD pardon thy
servant, *that* when my master goeth
into the house of Rimmon to worship
there, and he leaneth on my hand, and
I bow myself in the house of Rimmon:
when I bow down myself in the house
of Rimmon, the LORD pardon thy servant in this thing.
19 And he said unto him, Go in peace.
So he departed from him a little way.
20 But Gehazi, the servant of Elisha
the man of God, said, Behold, my master hath spared Naaman this Syrian, in
not receiving at his hands that which he
brought: but, *as* the LORD liveth, I will
run after him, and take somewhat of
him.
21 So Gehazi followed after Naaman.
And when Naaman saw *him* running
after him, he lighted down from the
chariot to meet him, and said, *Is* all
well?
22 And he said, All *is* well. My master
hath sent me, saying, Behold, even now
there be come to me from mount
Ephraim two young men of the sons of
the prophets: give them, I pray thee, a
talent of silver, and two changes of garments.
23 And Naaman said, Be content,
take two talents. And he urged him,
and bound two talents of silver in two
bags, with two changes of garments,
and laid *them* upon two of his servants;
and they bare *them* before him.
24 And when he came to the tower, he
took *them* from their hand, and
bestowed *them* in the house: and he let
the men go, and they departed.
25 But he went in, and stood before
his master. And Elisha said unto him,
Whence *comest thou*, Gehazi? And he
said, Thy servant went no whither.
26 And he said unto him, Went not
mine heart *with thee*, when the man
turned again from his chariot to meet
thee? *Is it* a time to receive money, and
to receive garments, and oliveyards,
and vineyards, and sheep, and oxen,
and menservants, and maidservants?
27 The leprosy therefore of Naaman
shall cleave unto thee, and unto thy
seed for ever. And he went out from his
presence a leper *as white* as snow.

6 And the sons of the prophets said
unto Elisha, Behold now, the place
where we dwell with thee is too strait
for us.
2 Let us go, we pray thee, unto Jordan,
and take thence every man a beam, and
let us make us a place there, where we
may dwell. And he answered, Go ye.
3 And one said, Be content, I pray
thee, and go with thy servants. And he
answered, I will go.
4 So he went with them. And when
they came to Jordan, they cut down
wood.
5 But as one was felling a beam, the
axe head fell into the water: and he
cried, and said, Alas, master! for it was
borrowed.
6 And the man of God said, Where fell
it? And he shewed him the place. And
he cut down a stick, and cast *it* in
thither; and the iron did swim.

7 Therefore said he, Take *it* up to thee. And he put out his hand, and took it.

8 Then the king of Syria warred against Israel, and took counsel with his servants, saying, In such and such a place *shall be* my camp.

9 And the man of God sent unto the king of Israel, saying, Beware that thou pass not such a place; for thither the Syrians are come down.

10 And the king of Israel sent to the place which the man of God told him and warned him of, and saved himself there, not once nor twice.

11 Therefore the heart of the king of Syria was sore troubled for this thing; and he called his servants, and said unto them, Will ye not shew me which of us *is* for the king of Israel?

12 And one of his servants said, None, my lord, O king: but Elisha, the prophet that *is* in Israel, telleth the king of Israel the words that thou speakest in thy bedchamber.

13 And he said, Go and spy where he *is*, that I may send and fetch him. And it was told him, saying, Behold, *he is* in Dothan.

14 Therefore sent he thither horses, and chariots, and a great host: and they came by night, and compassed the city about.

15 And when the servant of the man of God was risen early, and gone forth, behold, an host compassed the city both with horses and chariots. And his servant said unto him, Alas, my master! how shall we do?

16 And he answered, Fear not: for they that *be* with us *are* more than they that *be* with them.

17 And Elisha prayed, and said, LORD, I pray thee, open his eyes, that he may see. And the LORD opened the eyes of the young man; and he saw: and, behold, the mountain *was* full of horses and chariots of fire round about Elisha.

18 And when they came down to him, Elisha prayed unto the LORD, and said, Smite this people, I pray thee, with blindness. And he smote them with blindness according to the word of Elisha.

19 And Elisha said unto them, This *is* not the way, neither *is* this the city: follow me, and I will bring you to the man whom ye seek. But he led them to Samaria.

20 And it came to pass, when they were come into Samaria, that Elisha said, LORD, open the eyes of these *men*, that they may see. And the LORD opened their eyes, and they saw; and, behold, *they were* in the midst of Samaria.

21 And the king of Israel said unto Elisha, when he saw them, My father, shall I smite *them*? shall I smite *them*?

22 And he answered, Thou shalt not smite *them*: wouldest thou smite those whom thou hast taken captive with thy sword and with thy bow? set bread and water before them, that they may eat and drink, and go to their master.

23 And he prepared great provision for them: and when they had eaten and drunk, he sent them away, and they went to their master. So the bands of Syria came no more into the land of Israel.

24 And it came to pass after this, that Ben-hadad king of Syria gathered all his host, and went up, and besieged Samaria.

25 And there was a great famine in
Samaria: and, behold, they besieged it,
until an ass's head was *sold* for fourscore *pieces* of silver, and the fourth
part of a cab of dove's dung for five
pieces of silver.
26 And as the king of Israel was passing by upon the wall, there cried a
woman unto him, saying, Help, my lord,
O king.
27 And he said, If the LORD do not
help thee, whence shall I help thee? out
of the barnfloor, or out of the winepress?
28 And the king said unto her, What
aileth thee? And she answered, This
woman said unto me, Give thy son, that
we may eat him to day, and we will eat
my son to morrow.
29 So we boiled my son, and did eat
him: and I said unto her on the next
day, Give thy son, that we may eat him:
and she hath hid her son.
30 And it came to pass, when the king
heard the words of the woman, that he
rent his clothes; and he passed by upon
the wall, and the people looked, and,
behold, *he had* sackcloth within upon
his flesh.
31 Then he said, God do so and more
also to me, if the head of Elisha the son
of Shaphat shall stand on him this day.
32 But Elisha sat in his house, and the
elders sat with him; and *the king* sent a
man from before him: but ere the messenger came to him, he said to the
elders, See ye how this son of a murderer hath sent to take away mine
head? look, when the messenger
cometh, shut the door, and hold him
fast at the door: *is* not the sound of his
master's feet behind him?
33 And while he yet talked with them,
behold, the messenger came down unto
him: and he said, Behold, this evil *is* of
the LORD; what should I wait for the
LORD any longer?

7 Then Elisha said, Hear ye the word
of the LORD; Thus saith the LORD, To
morrow about this time *shall* a measure
of fine flour *be sold* for a shekel, and
two measures of barley for a shekel, in
the gate of Samaria.
2 Then a lord on whose hand the king
leaned answered the man of God, and
said, Behold, *if* the LORD would make
windows in heaven, might this thing
be? And he said, Behold, thou shalt see
it with thine eyes, but shalt not eat
thereof.
3 And there were four leprous men at
the entering in of the gate: and they
said one to another, Why sit we here
until we die?
4 If we say, We will enter into the city,
then the famine *is* in the city, and we
shall die there: and if we sit still here,
we die also. Now therefore come, and
let us fall unto the host of the Syrians:
if they save us alive, we shall live; and if
they kill us, we shall but die.
5 And they rose up in the twilight, to
go unto the camp of the Syrians: and
when they were come to the uttermost
part of the camp of Syria, behold, *there
was* no man there.
6 For the Lord had made the host of
the Syrians to hear a noise of chariots,
and a noise of horses, *even* the noise of
a great host: and they said one to
another, Lo, the king of Israel hath
hired against us the kings of the
Hittites, and the kings of the Egyptians,
to come upon us.
7 Wherefore they arose and fled in
the twilight, and left their tents, and
their horses, and their asses, even the
camp as it *was*, and fled for their life.

8 And when these lepers came to the
uttermost part of the camp, they went
into one tent, and did eat and drink,
and carried thence silver, and gold, and
raiment, and went and hid *it*; and came
again, and entered into another tent,
and carried thence *also*, and went and
hid *it*.
9 Then they said one to another, We
do not well: this day *is* a day of good
tidings, and we hold our peace: if we
tarry till the morning light, some mischief will come upon us: now therefore
come, that we may go and tell the king's
household.
10 So they came and called unto the
porter of the city: and they told them,
saying, We came to the camp of the
Syrians, and, behold, *there was* no man
there, neither voice of man, but horses
tied, and asses tied, and the tents as
they *were*.
11 And he called the porters; and
they told *it* to the king's house within.
12 And the king arose in the night,
and said unto his servants, I will now
shew you what the Syrians have done
to us. They know that we *be* hungry;
therefore are they gone out of the camp
to hide themselves in the field, saying,
When they come out of the city, we
shall catch them alive, and get into the
city.
13 And one of his servants answered
and said, Let *some* take, I pray thee,
five of the horses that remain, which
are left in the city, (behold, they *are* as
all the multitude of Israel that are left
in it: behold, *I say*, they *are* even as all
the multitude of the Israelites that are
consumed:) and let us send and see.
14 They took therefore two chariot
horses; and the king sent after the host
of the Syrians, saying, Go and see.
15 And they went after them unto
Jordan: and, lo, all the way *was* full of
garments and vessels, which the
Syrians had cast away in their haste.
And the messengers returned, and told
the king.
16 And the people went out, and
spoiled the tents of the Syrians. So a
measure of fine flour was *sold* for a
shekel, and two measures of barley for
a shekel, according to the word of the
LORD.
17 And the king appointed the lord
on whose hand he leaned to have the
charge of the gate: and the people
trode upon him in the gate, and he
died, as the man of God had said, who
spake when the king came down to
him.
18 And it came to pass as the man of
God had spoken to the king, saying,
Two measures of barley for a shekel,
and a measure of fine flour for a shekel,
shall be to morrow about this time in
the gate of Samaria:
19 And that lord answered the man of
God, and said, Now, behold, *if* the LORD
should make windows in heaven, might
such a thing be? And he said, Behold,
thou shalt see it with thine eyes, but
shalt not eat thereof.
20 And so it fell out unto him: for the
people trode upon him in the gate, and
he died.

8 Then spake Elisha unto the woman,
whose son he had restored to life,
saying, Arise, and go thou and thine
household, and sojourn wheresoever
thou canst sojourn: for the LORD hath
called for a famine; and it shall also
come upon the land seven years.
2 And the woman arose, and did after
the saying of the man of God: and she
went with her household, and

sojourned in the land of the Philistines
seven years.
3 And it came to pass at the seven
years' end, that the woman returned
out of the land of the Philistines: and
she went forth to cry unto the king for
her house and for her land.
4 And the king talked with Gehazi
the servant of the man of God, saying,
Tell me, I pray thee, all the great things
that Elisha hath done.
5 And it came to pass, as he was telling the king how he had restored a
dead body to life, that, behold, the
woman, whose son he had restored to
life, cried to the king for her house and
for her land. And Gehazi said, My lord,
O king, this *is* the woman, and this *is*
her son, whom Elisha restored to life.
6 And when the king asked the
woman, she told him. So the king
appointed unto her a certain officer,
saying, Restore all that *was* hers, and
all the fruits of the field since the day
that she left the land, even until now.
7 And Elisha came to Damascus; and
Ben-hadad the king of Syria was sick;
and it was told him, saying, The man of
God is come hither.
8 And the king said unto Hazael, Take
a present in thine hand, and go, meet
the man of God, and enquire of the
LORD by him, saying, Shall I recover of
this disease?
9 So Hazael went to meet him, and
took a present with him, even of every
good thing of Damascus, forty camels'
burden, and came and stood before
him, and said, Thy son Ben-hadad king
of Syria hath sent me to thee, saying,
Shall I recover of this disease?
10 And Elisha said unto him, Go, say
unto him, Thou mayest certainly recover: howbeit the LORD hath shewed me
that he shall surely die.
11 And he settled his countenance
stedfastly, until he was ashamed: and
the man of God wept.
12 And Hazael said, Why weepeth my
lord? And he answered, Because I know
the evil that thou wilt do unto the children of Israel: their strong holds wilt
thou set on fire, and their young men
wilt thou slay with the sword, and wilt
dash their children, and rip up their
women with child.
13 And Hazael said, But what, *is* thy
servant a dog, that he should do this
great thing? And Elisha answered, The
LORD hath shewed me that thou *shalt*
be king over Syria.
14 So he departed from Elisha, and
came to his master; who said to him,
What said Elisha to thee? And he
answered, He told me *that* thou shouldest surely recover.
15 And it came to pass on the morrow,
that he took a thick cloth, and dipped *it*
in water, and spread *it* on his face, so
that he died: and Hazael reigned in his
stead.
16 And in the fifth year of Joram the
son of Ahab king of Israel, Jehoshaphat
being then king of Judah, Jehoram the
son of Jehoshaphat king of Judah
began to reign.
17 Thirty and two years old was he
when he began to reign; and he reigned
eight years in Jerusalem.
18 And he walked in the way of the
kings of Israel, as did the house of
Ahab: for the daughter of Ahab was his
wife: and he did evil in the sight of the
LORD.

19 Yet the LORD would not destroy
Judah for David his servant's sake, as
he promised him to give him alway a
light, *and* to his children.
20 In his days Edom revolted from
under the hand of Judah, and made a
king over themselves.
21 So Joram went over to Zair, and all
the chariots with him: and he rose by
night, and smote the Edomites which
compassed him about, and the captains
of the chariots: and the people fled into
their tents.
22 Yet Edom revolted from under the
hand of Judah unto this day. Then
Libnah revolted at the same time.
23 And the rest of the acts of Joram,
and all that he did, *are* they not written
in the book of the chronicles of the
kings of Judah?
24 And Joram slept with his fathers,
and was buried with his fathers in the
city of David: and Ahaziah his son
reigned in his stead.
25 In the twelfth year of Joram the
son of Ahab king of Israel did Ahaziah
the son of Jehoram king of Judah begin
to reign.
26 Two and twenty years old *was*
Ahaziah when he began to reign; and
he reigned one year in Jerusalem. And
his mother's name *was* Athaliah, the
daughter of Omri king of Israel.
27 And he walked in the way of the
house of Ahab, and did evil in the sight
of the LORD, as *did* the house of Ahab:
for he *was* the son in law of the house
of Ahab.
28 And he went with Joram the son of
Ahab to the war against Hazael king of
Syria in Ramoth-gilead; and the
Syrians wounded Joram.
29 And king Joram went back to be
healed in Jezreel of the wounds which
the Syrians had given him at Ramah,
when he fought against Hazael king of
Syria. And Ahaziah the son of Jehoram
king of Judah went down to see Joram
the son of Ahab in Jezreel, because he
was sick.

9 And Elisha the prophet called one
of the children of the prophets, and
said unto him, Gird up thy loins, and
take this box of oil in thine hand, and
go to Ramoth-gilead:
2 And when thou comest thither, look
out there Jehu the son of Jehoshaphat
the son of Nimshi, and go in, and make
him arise up from among his brethren,
and carry him to an inner chamber;
3 Then take the box of oil, and pour *it*
on his head, and say, Thus saith the
LORD, I have anointed thee king over
Israel. Then open the door, and flee,
and tarry not.
4 So the young man, *even* the young
man the prophet, went to Ramoth-
gilead.
5 And when he came, behold, the
captains of the host *were* sitting; and he
said, I have an errand to thee, O captain. And Jehu said, Unto which of all
us? And he said, To thee, O captain.
6 And he arose, and went into the
house; and he poured the oil on his
head, and said unto him, Thus saith the
LORD God of Israel, I have anointed
thee king over the people of the LORD,
even over Israel.
7 And thou shalt smite the house of
Ahab thy master, that I may avenge the
blood of my servants the prophets, and
the blood of all the servants of the
LORD, at the hand of Jezebel.
8 For the whole house of Ahab shall
perish: and I will cut off from Ahab him
that pisseth against the wall, and him
that is shut up and left in Israel:

9 And I will make the house of Ahab
like the house of Jeroboam the son of
Nebat, and like the house of Baasha the
son of Ahijah:
10 And the dogs shall eat Jezebel in
the portion of Jezreel, and *there shall
be* none to bury *her*. And he opened the
door, and fled.
11 Then Jehu came forth to the servants of his lord: and *one* said unto him,
Is all well? wherefore came this mad
fellow to thee? And he said unto them,
Ye know the man, and his communication.
12 And they said, *It is* false; tell us
now. And he said, Thus and thus spake
he to me, saying, Thus saith the LORD, I
have anointed thee king over Israel.
13 Then they hasted, and took every
man his garment, and put *it* under him
on the top of the stairs, and blew with
trumpets, saying, Jehu is king.
14 So Jehu the son of Jehoshaphat
the son of Nimshi conspired against
Joram. (Now Joram had kept Ramoth-
gilead, he and all Israel, because of
Hazael king of Syria.
15 But king Joram was returned to be
healed in Jezreel of the wounds which
the Syrians had given him, when he
fought with Hazael king of Syria.) And
Jehu said, If it be your minds, *then* let
none go forth *nor* escape out of the city
to go to tell *it* in Jezreel.
16 So Jehu rode in a chariot, and went
to Jezreel; for Joram lay there. And
Ahaziah king of Judah was come down
to see Joram.
17 And there stood a watchman on
the tower in Jezreel, and he spied the
company of Jehu as he came, and said,
I see a company. And Joram said, Take
an horseman, and send to meet them,
and let him say, *Is it* peace?
18 So there went one on horseback to
meet him, and said, Thus saith the king,
Is it peace? And Jehu said, What hast
thou to do with peace? turn thee
behind me. And the watchman told,
saying, The messenger came to them,
but he cometh not again.
19 Then he sent out a second on
horseback, which came to them, and
said, Thus saith the king, *Is it* peace?
And Jehu answered, What hast thou to
do with peace? turn thee behind me.
20 And the watchman told, saying, He
came even unto them, and cometh not
again: and the driving *is* like the driving of Jehu the son of Nimshi; for he
driveth furiously.
21 And Joram said, Make ready. And
his chariot was made ready. And Joram
king of Israel and Ahaziah king of
Judah went out, each in his chariot, and
they went out against Jehu, and met
him in the portion of Naboth the
Jezreelite.
22 And it came to pass, when Joram
saw Jehu, that he said, *Is it* peace,
Jehu? And he answered, What peace, so
long as the whoredoms of thy mother
Jezebel and her witchcrafts *are so*
many?
23 And Joram turned his hands, and
fled, and said to Ahaziah, *There is*
treachery, O Ahaziah.
24 And Jehu drew a bow with his full
strength, and smote Jehoram between
his arms, and the arrow went out at his
heart, and he sunk down in his chariot.
25 Then said *Jehu* to Bidkar his captain, Take up, *and* cast him in the portion of the field of Naboth the
Jezreelite: for remember how that,
when I and thou rode together after
Ahab his father, the LORD laid this burden upon him;

26 Surely I have seen yesterday the
blood of Naboth, and the blood of his
sons, saith the LORD; and I will requite
thee in this plat, saith the LORD. Now
therefore take *and* cast him into the
plat *of ground*, according to the word of
the LORD.
27 But when Ahaziah the king of
Judah saw *this*, he fled by the way of
the garden house. And Jehu followed
after him, and said, Smite him also in
the chariot. *And they did so* at the
going up to Gur, which *is* by Ibleam.
And he fled to Megiddo, and died
there.
28 And his servants carried him in a
chariot to Jerusalem, and buried him in
his sepulchre with his fathers in the
city of David.
29 And in the eleventh year of Joram
the son of Ahab began Ahaziah to reign
over Judah.
30 And when Jehu was come to
Jezreel, Jezebel heard *of it*; and she
painted her face, and tired her head,
and looked out at a window.
31 And as Jehu entered in at the gate,
she said, *Had* Zimri peace, who slew his
master?
32 And he lifted up his face to the
window, and said, Who *is* on my side?
who? And there looked out to him two
or three eunuchs.
33 And he said, Throw her down. So
they threw her down: and *some* of her
blood was sprinkled on the wall, and on
the horses: and he trode her under foot.
34 And when he was come in, he did
eat and drink, and said, Go, see now
this cursed *woman*, and bury her: for
she *is* a king's daughter.
35 And they went to bury her: but
they found no more of her than the
skull, and the feet, and the palms of *her*
hands.
36 Wherefore they came again, and
told him. And he said, This *is* the word
of the LORD, which he spake by his servant Elijah the Tishbite, saying, In the
portion of Jezreel shall dogs eat the
flesh of Jezebel:
37 And the carcase of Jezebel shall be
as dung upon the face of the field in the
portion of Jezreel; *so* that they shall not
say, This *is* Jezebel.

10 And Ahab had seventy sons in
Samaria. And Jehu wrote letters,
and sent to Samaria, unto the rulers of
Jezreel, to the elders, and to them that
brought up Ahab's *children*, saying,
2 Now as soon as this letter cometh to
you, seeing your master's sons *are* with
you, and *there are* with you chariots
and horses, a fenced city also, and
armour;
3 Look even out the best and meetest
of your master's sons, and set *him* on
his father's throne, and fight for your
master's house.
4 But they were exceedingly afraid,
and said, Behold, two kings stood not
before him: how then shall we stand?
5 And he that *was* over the house, and
he that *was* over the city, the elders
also, and the bringers up *of the children*, sent to Jehu, saying, We *are* thy
servants, and will do all that thou shalt
bid us; we will not make any king: do
thou *that which is* good in thine eyes.
6 Then he wrote a letter the second
time to them, saying, If ye *be* mine, and
if ye will hearken unto my voice, take
ye the heads of the men your master's
sons, and come to me to Jezreel by to
morrow this time. Now the king's sons,
being seventy persons, *were* with the

great men of the city, which brought
them up.
7 And it came to pass, when the letter
came to them, that they took the king's
sons, and slew seventy persons, and put
their heads in baskets, and sent him
them to Jezreel.
8 And there came a messenger, and
told him, saying, They have brought the
heads of the king's sons. And he said,
Lay ye them in two heaps at the entering in of the gate until the morning.
9 And it came to pass in the morning,
that he went out, and stood, and said to
all the people, Ye *be* righteous: behold,
I conspired against my master, and slew
him: but who slew all these?
10 Know now that there shall fall
unto the earth nothing of the word of
the LORD, which the LORD spake concerning the house of Ahab: for the LORD
hath done *that* which he spake by his
servant Elijah.
11 So Jehu slew all that remained of
the house of Ahab in Jezreel, and all his
great men, and his kinsfolks, and his
priests, until he left him none remaining.
12 And he arose and departed, and
came to Samaria. *And* as he *was* at the
shearing house in the way,
13 Jehu met with the brethren of
Ahaziah king of Judah, and said, Who
are ye? And they answered, We *are* the
brethren of Ahaziah; and we go down to
salute the children of the king and the
children of the queen.
14 And he said, Take them alive. And
they took them alive, and slew them at
the pit of the shearing house, *even* two
and forty men; neither left he any of
them.
15 And when he was departed thence,
he lighted on Jehonadab the son of
Rechab *coming* to meet him: and he
saluted him, and said to him, Is thine
heart right, as my heart *is* with thy
heart? And Jehonadab answered, It is.
If it be, give *me* thine hand. And he
gave *him* his hand; and he took him up
to him into the chariot.
16 And he said, Come with me, and
see my zeal for the LORD. So they made
him ride in his chariot.
17 And when he came to Samaria, he
slew all that remained unto Ahab in
Samaria, till he had destroyed him,
according to the saying of the LORD,
which he spake to Elijah.
18 And Jehu gathered all the people
together, and said unto them, Ahab
served Baal a little; *but* Jehu shall
serve him much.
19 Now therefore call unto me all the
prophets of Baal, all his servants, and
all his priests; let none be wanting: for
I have a great sacrifice *to do* to Baal;
whosoever shall be wanting, he shall
not live. But Jehu did *it* in subtilty, to
the intent that he might destroy the
worshippers of Baal.
20 And Jehu said, Proclaim a solemn
assembly for Baal. And they proclaimed
it.
21 And Jehu sent through all Israel:
and all the worshippers of Baal came,
so that there was not a man left that
came not. And they came into the
house of Baal; and the house of Baal
was full from one end to another.
22 And he said unto him that *was*
over the vestry, Bring forth vestments
for all the worshippers of Baal. And he
brought them forth vestments.

23 And Jehu went, and Jehonadab
the son of Rechab, into the house of
Baal, and said unto the worshippers of
Baal, Search, and look that there be
here with you none of the servants of
the LORD, but the worshippers of Baal
only.
24 And when they went in to offer
sacrifices and burnt offerings, Jehu
appointed fourscore men without, and
said, *If* any of the men whom I have
brought into your hands escape, *he
that letteth him go*, his life *shall be* for
the life of him.
25 And it came to pass, as soon as he
had made an end of offering the burnt
offering, that Jehu said to the guard
and to the captains, Go in, *and* slay
them; let none come forth. And they
smote them with the edge of the sword;
and the guard and the captains cast
them out, and went to the city of the
house of Baal.
26 And they brought forth the images
out of the house of Baal, and burned
them.
27 And they brake down the image of
Baal, and brake down the house of
Baal, and made it a draught house unto
this day.
28 Thus Jehu destroyed Baal out of
Israel.
29 Howbeit *from* the sins of Jeroboam
the son of Nebat, who made Israel to
sin, Jehu departed not from after them,
to wit, the golden calves that *were* in
Beth-el, and that *were* in Dan.
30 And the LORD said unto Jehu,
Because thou hast done well in executing *that which is* right in mine eyes,
and hast done unto the house of Ahab
according to all that *was* in mine heart,
thy children of the fourth *generation*
shall sit on the throne of Israel.
31 But Jehu took no heed to walk in
the law of the LORD God of Israel with
all his heart: for he departed not from
the sins of Jeroboam, which made
Israel to sin.
32 In those days the LORD began to
cut Israel short: and Hazael smote
them in all the coasts of Israel;
33 From Jordan eastward, all the land
of Gilead, the Gadites, and the
Reubenites, and the Manassites, from
Aroer, which *is* by the river Arnon, even
Gilead and Bashan.
34 Now the rest of the acts of Jehu,
and all that he did, and all his might,
are they not written in the book of the
chronicles of the kings of Israel?
35 And Jehu slept with his fathers:
and they buried him in Samaria. And
Jehoahaz his son reigned in his stead.
36 And the time that Jehu reigned
over Israel in Samaria *was* twenty and
eight years.

11 And when Athaliah the mother
of Ahaziah saw that her son was
dead, she arose and destroyed all the
seed royal.
2 But Jehosheba, the daughter of
king Joram, sister of Ahaziah, took
Joash the son of Ahaziah, and stole him
from among the king's sons *which were*
slain; and they hid him, *even* him and
his nurse, in the bedchamber from
Athaliah, so that he was not slain.
3 And he was with her hid in the
house of the LORD six years. And
Athaliah did reign over the land.
4 And the seventh year Jehoiada sent
and fetched the rulers over hundreds,
with the captains and the guard, and
brought them to him into the house of
the LORD, and made a covenant with
them, and took an oath of them in the

house of the LORD, and shewed them
the king's son.
5 And he commanded them, saying,
This *is* the thing that ye shall do; A
third part of you that enter in on the
sabbath shall even be keepers of the
watch of the king's house;
6 And a third part *shall be* at the gate
of Sur; and a third part at the gate
behind the guard: so shall ye keep the
watch of the house, that it be not broken down.
7 And two parts of all you that go
forth on the sabbath, even they shall
keep the watch of the house of the
LORD about the king.
8 And ye shall compass the king
round about, every man with his weapons in his hand: and he that cometh
within the ranges, let him be slain: and
be ye with the king as he goeth out and
as he cometh in.
9 And the captains over the hundreds
did according to all *things* that
Jehoiada the priest commanded: and
they took every man his men that were
to come in on the sabbath, with them
that should go out on the sabbath, and
came to Jehoiada the priest.
10 And to the captains over hundreds
did the priest give king David's spears
and shields, that *were* in the temple of
the LORD.
11 And the guard stood, every man
with his weapons in his hand, round
about the king, from the right corner of
the temple to the left corner of the
temple, *along* by the altar and the
temple.
12 And he brought forth the king's
son, and put the crown upon him, and
gave him the testimony; and they made
him king, and anointed him; and they
clapped their hands, and said, God save
the king.
13 And when Athaliah heard the
noise of the guard *and* of the people,
she came to the people into the temple
of the LORD.
14 And when she looked, behold, the
king stood by a pillar, as the manner
was, and the princes and the trumpeters by the king, and all the people of
the land rejoiced, and blew with trumpets: and Athaliah rent her clothes, and
cried, Treason, Treason.
15 But Jehoiada the priest commanded the captains of the hundreds, the
officers of the host, and said unto them,
Have her forth without the ranges: and
him that followeth her kill with the
sword. For the priest had said, Let her
not be slain in the house of the LORD.
16 And they laid hands on her; and
she went by the way by the which the
horses came into the king's house: and
there was she slain.
17 And Jehoiada made a covenant
between the LORD and the king and the
people, that they should be the LORD's
people; between the king also and the
people.
18 And all the people of the land
went into the house of Baal, and brake
it down; his altars and his images brake
they in pieces thoroughly, and slew
Mattan the priest of Baal before the
altars. And the priest appointed officers over the house of the LORD.
19 And he took the rulers over hundreds, and the captains, and the guard,
and all the people of the land; and they
brought down the king from the house
of the LORD, and came by the way of the
gate of the guard to the king's house.
And he sat on the throne of the kings.

20 And all the people of the land rejoiced, and the city was in quiet: and they slew Athaliah with the sword *beside* the king's house.

21 Seven years old *was* Jehoash when he began to reign.

12 In the seventh year of Jehu Jehoash began to reign; and forty years reigned he in Jerusalem. And his mother's name *was* Zibiah of Beer-sheba.

2 And Jehoash did *that which was* right in the sight of the LORD all his days wherein Jehoiada the priest instructed him.

3 But the high places were not taken away: the people still sacrificed and burnt incense in the high places.

4 And Jehoash said to the priests, All the money of the dedicated things that is brought into the house of the LORD, *even* the money of every one that passeth *the account*, the money that every man is set at, *and* all the money that cometh into any man's heart to bring into the house of the LORD,

5 Let the priests take *it* to them, every man of his acquaintance: and let them repair the breaches of the house, wheresoever any breach shall be found.

6 But it was *so, that* in the three and twentieth year of king Jehoash the priests had not repaired the breaches of the house.

7 Then king Jehoash called for Jehoiada the priest, and the *other* priests, and said unto them, Why repair ye not the breaches of the house? now therefore receive no *more* money of your acquaintance, but deliver it for the breaches of the house.

8 And the priests consented to receive no *more* money of the people, neither to repair the breaches of the house.

9 But Jehoiada the priest took a chest, and bored a hole in the lid of it, and set it beside the altar, on the right side as one cometh into the house of the LORD: and the priests that kept the door put therein all the money *that was* brought into the house of the LORD.

10 And it was *so*, when they saw that *there was* much money in the chest, that the king's scribe and the high priest came up, and they put up in bags, and told the money that was found in the house of the LORD.

11 And they gave the money, being told, into the hands of them that did the work, that had the oversight of the house of the LORD: and they laid it out to the carpenters and builders, that wrought upon the house of the LORD,

12 And to masons, and hewers of stone, and to buy timber and hewed stone to repair the breaches of the house of the LORD, and for all that was laid out for the house to repair *it*.

13 Howbeit there were not made for the house of the LORD bowls of silver, snuffers, basons, trumpets, any vessels of gold, or vessels of silver, of the money *that was* brought into the house of the LORD:

14 But they gave that to the workmen, and repaired therewith the house of the LORD.

15 Moreover they reckoned not with the men, into whose hand they delivered the money to be bestowed on workmen: for they dealt faithfully.

16 The trespass money and sin money was not brought into the house of the LORD: it was the priests'.

17 Then Hazael king of Syria went up, and fought against Gath, and took it: and Hazael set his face to go up to Jerusalem.

18 And Jehoash king of Judah took all the hallowed things that Jehoshaphat, and Jehoram, and Ahaziah, his fathers, kings of Judah, had dedicated, and his own hallowed things, and all the gold *that was* found in the treasures of the house of the LORD, and in the king's house, and sent *it* to Hazael king of Syria: and he went away from Jerusalem.

19 And the rest of the acts of Joash, and all that he did, *are* they not written in the book of the chronicles of the kings of Judah?

20 And his servants arose, and made a conspiracy, and slew Joash in the house of Millo, which goeth down to Silla.

21 For Jozachar the son of Shimeath, and Jehozabad the son of Shomer, his servants, smote him, and he died; and they buried him with his fathers in the city of David: and Amaziah his son reigned in his stead.

13 In the three and twentieth year of Joash the son of Ahaziah king of Judah Jehoahaz the son of Jehu began to reign over Israel in Samaria, *and reigned* seventeen years.

2 And he did *that which was* evil in the sight of the LORD, and followed the sins of Jeroboam the son of Nebat, which made Israel to sin; he departed not therefrom.

3 And the anger of the LORD was kindled against Israel, and he delivered them into the hand of Hazael king of Syria, and into the hand of Ben-hadad the son of Hazael, all *their* days.

4 And Jehoahaz besought the LORD, and the LORD hearkened unto him: for he saw the oppression of Israel, because the king of Syria oppressed them.

5 (And the LORD gave Israel a saviour, so that they went out from under the hand of the Syrians: and the children of Israel dwelt in their tents, as beforetime.

6 Nevertheless they departed not from the sins of the house of Jeroboam, who made Israel sin, *but* walked therein: and there remained the grove also in Samaria.)

7 Neither did he leave of the people to Jehoahaz but fifty horsemen, and ten chariots, and ten thousand footmen; for the king of Syria had destroyed them, and had made them like the dust by threshing.

8 Now the rest of the acts of Jehoahaz, and all that he did, and his might, *are* they not written in the book of the chronicles of the kings of Israel?

9 And Jehoahaz slept with his fathers; and they buried him in Samaria: and Joash his son reigned in his stead.

10 In the thirty and seventh year of Joash king of Judah began Jehoash the son of Jehoahaz to reign over Israel in Samaria, *and reigned* sixteen years.

11 And he did *that which was* evil in the sight of the LORD; he departed not from all the sins of Jeroboam the son of Nebat, who made Israel sin: *but* he walked therein.

12 And the rest of the acts of Joash, and all that he did, and his might wherewith he fought against Amaziah king of Judah, *are* they not written in the book of the chronicles of the kings of Israel?

13 And Joash slept with his fathers; and Jeroboam sat upon his throne: and Joash was buried in Samaria with the kings of Israel.

14 Now Elisha was fallen sick of his sickness whereof he died. And Joash the king of Israel came down unto him, and wept over his face, and said, O my father, my father, the chariot of Israel, and the horsemen thereof.

15 And Elisha said unto him, Take bow and arrows. And he took unto him bow and arrows.

16 And he said to the king of Israel, Put thine hand upon the bow. And he put his hand *upon it*: and Elisha put his hands upon the king's hands.

17 And he said, Open the window eastward. And he opened *it*. Then Elisha said, Shoot. And he shot. And he said, The arrow of the LORD's deliverance, and the arrow of deliverance from Syria: for thou shalt smite the Syrians in Aphek, till thou have consumed *them*.

18 And he said, Take the arrows. And he took *them*. And he said unto the king of Israel, Smite upon the ground. And he smote thrice, and stayed.

19 And the man of God was wroth with him, and said, Thou shouldest have smitten five or six times; then hadst thou smitten Syria till thou hadst consumed *it*: whereas now thou shalt smite Syria *but* thrice.

20 And Elisha died, and they buried him. And the bands of the Moabites invaded the land at the coming in of the year.

21 And it came to pass, as they were burying a man, that, behold, they spied a band *of men*; and they cast the man into the sepulchre of Elisha: and when the man was let down, and touched the bones of Elisha, he revived, and stood up on his feet.

22 But Hazael king of Syria oppressed Israel all the days of Jehoahaz.

23 And the LORD was gracious unto them, and had compassion on them, and had respect unto them, because of his covenant with Abraham, Isaac, and Jacob, and would not destroy them, neither cast he them from his presence as yet.

24 So Hazael king of Syria died; and Ben-hadad his son reigned in his stead.

25 And Jehoash the son of Jehoahaz took again out of the hand of Ben-hadad the son of Hazael the cities, which he had taken out of the hand of Jehoahaz his father by war. Three times did Joash beat him, and recovered the cities of Israel.

14 In the second year of Joash son of Jehoahaz king of Israel reigned Amaziah the son of Joash king of Judah.

2 He was twenty and five years old when he began to reign, and reigned twenty and nine years in Jerusalem. And his mother's name *was* Jehoaddan of Jerusalem.

3 And he did *that which was* right in the sight of the LORD, yet not like David his father: he did according to all things as Joash his father did.

4 Howbeit the high places were not taken away: as yet the people did sacrifice and burnt incense on the high places.

5 And it came to pass, as soon as the kingdom was confirmed in his hand, that he slew his servants which had slain the king his father.

6 But the children of the murderers he slew not: according unto that which is written in the book of the law of Moses, wherein the LORD commanded, saying, The fathers shall not be put to death for the children, nor the children be put to death for the fathers; but

every man shall be put to death for his
own sin.
7 He slew of Edom in the valley of salt
ten thousand, and took Selah by war,
and called the name of it Joktheel unto
this day.
8 Then Amaziah sent messengers to
Jehoash, the son of Jehoahaz son of
Jehu, king of Israel, saying, Come, let us
look one another in the face.
9 And Jehoash the king of Israel sent
to Amaziah king of Judah, saying, The
thistle that *was* in Lebanon sent to the
cedar that *was* in Lebanon, saying, Give
thy daughter to my son to wife: and
there passed by a wild beast that *was* in
Lebanon, and trode down the thistle.
10 Thou hast indeed smitten Edom,
and thine heart hath lifted thee up:
glory *of this*, and tarry at home: for why
shouldest thou meddle to *thy* hurt, that
thou shouldest fall, *even* thou, and
Judah with thee?
11 But Amaziah would not hear.
Therefore Jehoash king of Israel went
up; and he and Amaziah king of Judah
looked one another in the face at Beth-
shemesh, which *belongeth* to Judah.
12 And Judah was put to the worse
before Israel; and they fled every man
to their tents.
13 And Jehoash king of Israel took
Amaziah king of Judah, the son of
Jehoash the son of Ahaziah, at Beth-
shemesh, and came to Jerusalem, and
brake down the wall of Jerusalem from
the gate of Ephraim unto the corner
gate, four hundred cubits.
14 And he took all the gold and silver,
and all the vessels that were found in
the house of the LORD, and in the treasures of the king's house, and hostages,
and returned to Samaria.
15 Now the rest of the acts of Jehoash
which he did, and his might, and how
he fought with Amaziah king of Judah,
are they not written in the book of the
chronicles of the kings of Israel?
16 And Jehoash slept with his fathers,
and was buried in Samaria with the
kings of Israel; and Jeroboam his son
reigned in his stead.
17 And Amaziah the son of Joash king
of Judah lived after the death of
Jehoash son of Jehoahaz king of Israel
fifteen years.
18 And the rest of the acts of Amaziah,
are they not written in the book of the
chronicles of the kings of Judah?
19 Now they made a conspiracy
against him in Jerusalem: and he fled
to Lachish; but they sent after him to
Lachish, and slew him there.
20 And they brought him on horses:
and he was buried at Jerusalem with
his fathers in the city of David.
21 And all the people of Judah took
Azariah, which *was* sixteen years old,
and made him king instead of his
father Amaziah.
22 He built Elath, and restored it to
Judah, after that the king slept with his
fathers.
23 In the fifteenth year of Amaziah
the son of Joash king of Judah
Jeroboam the son of Joash king of
Israel began to reign in Samaria, *and*
reigned forty and one years.
24 And he did *that which was* evil in
the sight of the LORD: he departed not
from all the sins of Jeroboam the son of
Nebat, who made Israel to sin.
25 He restored the coast of Israel
from the entering of Hamath unto the
sea of the plain, according to the word
of the LORD God of Israel, which he
spake by the hand of his servant Jonah,

the son of Amittai, the prophet, which
was of Gath-hepher.
26 For the LORD saw the affliction of
Israel, *that it was* very bitter: for *there*
was not any shut up, nor any left, nor
any helper for Israel.
27 And the LORD said not that he
would blot out the name of Israel from
under heaven: but he saved them by
the hand of Jeroboam the son of Joash.
28 Now the rest of the acts of
Jeroboam, and all that he did, and his
might, how he warred, and how he
recovered Damascus, and Hamath,
which belonged to Judah, for Israel, are
they not written in the book of the
chronicles of the kings of Israel?
29 And Jeroboam slept with his
fathers, *even* with the kings of Israel;
and Zachariah his son reigned in his
stead.

15 In the twenty and seventh year
of Jeroboam king of Israel began
Azariah son of Amaziah king of Judah
to reign.
2 Sixteen years old was he when he
began to reign, and he reigned two and
fifty years in Jerusalem. And his mother's name *was* Jecholiah of Jerusalem.
3 And he did *that which was* right in
the sight of the LORD, according to all
that his father Amaziah had done;
4 Save that the high places were not
removed: the people sacrificed and
burnt incense still on the high places.
5 And the LORD smote the king, so
that he was a leper unto the day of his
death, and dwelt in a several house.
And Jotham the king's son *was* over the
house, judging the people of the land.
6 And the rest of the acts of Azariah,
and all that he did, *are* they not written
in the book of the chronicles of the
kings of Judah?
7 So Azariah slept with his fathers;
and they buried him with his fathers in
the city of David: and Jotham his son
reigned in his stead.
8 In the thirty and eighth year of
Azariah king of Judah did Zachariah
the son of Jeroboam reign over Israel in
Samaria six months.
9 And he did *that which was* evil in
the sight of the LORD, as his fathers had
done: he departed not from the sins of
Jeroboam the son of Nebat, who made
Israel to sin.
10 And Shallum the son of Jabesh
conspired against him, and smote him
before the people, and slew him, and
reigned in his stead.
11 And the rest of the acts of
Zachariah, behold, they *are* written in
the book of the chronicles of the kings
of Israel.
12 This *was* the word of the LORD
which he spake unto Jehu, saying, Thy
sons shall sit on the throne of Israel
unto the fourth *generation*. And so it
came to pass.
13 Shallum the son of Jabesh began
to reign in the nine and thirtieth year
of Uzziah king of Judah; and he reigned
a full month in Samaria.
14 For Menahem the son of Gadi went
up from Tirzah, and came to Samaria,
and smote Shallum the son of Jabesh in
Samaria, and slew him, and reigned in
his stead.
15 And the rest of the acts of Shallum,
and his conspiracy which he made,
behold, they *are* written in the book of
the chronicles of the kings of Israel.
16 Then Menahem smote Tiphsah,
and all that *were* therein, and the
coasts thereof from Tirzah: because
they opened not *to him*, therefore he

smote *it;* *and* all the women therein that were with child he ripped up.

17 In the nine and thirtieth year of Azariah king of Judah began Menahem the son of Gadi to reign over Israel, *and reigned* ten years in Samaria.

18 And he did *that which was* evil in the sight of the LORD: he departed not all his days from the sins of Jeroboam the son of Nebat, who made Israel to sin.

19 *And* Pul the king of Assyria came against the land: and Menahem gave Pul a thousand talents of silver, that his hand might be with him to confirm the kingdom in his hand.

20 And Menahem exacted the money of Israel, *even* of all the mighty men of wealth, of each man fifty shekels of silver, to give to the king of Assyria. So the king of Assyria turned back, and stayed not there in the land.

21 And the rest of the acts of Menahem, and all that he did, *are* they not written in the book of the chronicles of the kings of Israel?

22 And Menahem slept with his fathers; and Pekahiah his son reigned in his stead.

23 In the fiftieth year of Azariah king of Judah Pekahiah the son of Menahem began to reign over Israel in Samaria, *and reigned* two years.

24 And he did *that which was* evil in the sight of the LORD: he departed not from the sins of Jeroboam the son of Nebat, who made Israel to sin.

25 But Pekah the son of Remaliah, a captain of his, conspired against him, and smote him in Samaria, in the palace of the king's house, with Argob and Arieh, and with him fifty men of the Gileadites: and he killed him, and reigned in his room.

26 And the rest of the acts of Pekahiah, and all that he did, behold, they *are* written in the book of the chronicles of the kings of Israel.

27 In the two and fiftieth year of Azariah king of Judah Pekah the son of Remaliah began to reign over Israel in Samaria, *and reigned* twenty years.

28 And he did *that which was* evil in the sight of the LORD: he departed not from the sins of Jeroboam the son of Nebat, who made Israel to sin.

29 In the days of Pekah king of Israel came Tiglath-pileser king of Assyria, and took Ijon, and Abel-beth-maachah, and Janoah, and Kedesh, and Hazor, and Gilead, and Galilee, all the land of Naphtali, and carried them captive to Assyria.

30 And Hoshea the son of Elah made a conspiracy against Pekah the son of Remaliah, and smote him, and slew him, and reigned in his stead, in the twentieth year of Jotham the son of Uzziah.

31 And the rest of the acts of Pekah, and all that he did, behold, they *are* written in the book of the chronicles of the kings of Israel.

32 In the second year of Pekah the son of Remaliah king of Israel began Jotham the son of Uzziah king of Judah to reign.

33 Five and twenty years old was he when he began to reign, and he reigned sixteen years in Jerusalem. And his mother's name *was* Jerusha, the daughter of Zadok.

34 And he did *that which was* right in the sight of the LORD: he did according to all that his father Uzziah had done.

35 Howbeit the high places were not removed: the people sacrificed and burned incense still in the high places. He built the higher gate of the house of the LORD.

36 Now the rest of the acts of Jotham, and all that he did, *are* they not written in the book of the chronicles of the kings of Judah?

37 In those days the LORD began to send against Judah Rezin the king of Syria, and Pekah the son of Remaliah.

38 And Jotham slept with his fathers, and was buried with his fathers in the city of David his father: and Ahaz his son reigned in his stead.

16 In the seventeenth year of Pekah the son of Remaliah Ahaz the son of Jotham king of Judah began to reign.

2 Twenty years old *was* Ahaz when he began to reign, and reigned sixteen years in Jerusalem, and did not *that which was* right in the sight of the LORD his God, like David his father.

3 But he walked in the way of the kings of Israel, yea, and made his son to pass through the fire, according to the abominations of the heathen, whom the LORD cast out from before the children of Israel.

4 And he sacrificed and burnt incense in the high places, and on the hills, and under every green tree.

5 Then Rezin king of Syria and Pekah son of Remaliah king of Israel came up to Jerusalem to war: and they besieged Ahaz, but could not overcome *him*.

6 At that time Rezin king of Syria recovered Elath to Syria, and drave the Jews from Elath: and the Syrians came to Elath, and dwelt there unto this day.

7 So Ahaz sent messengers to Tiglath-pileser king of Assyria, saying, I *am* thy servant and thy son: come up, and save me out of the hand of the king of Syria, and out of the hand of the king of Israel, which rise up against me.

8 And Ahaz took the silver and gold that was found in the house of the LORD, and in the treasures of the king's house, and sent *it for* a present to the king of Assyria.

9 And the king of Assyria hearkened unto him: for the king of Assyria went up against Damascus, and took it, and carried *the people of* it captive to Kir, and slew Rezin.

10 And king Ahaz went to Damascus to meet Tiglath-pileser king of Assyria, and saw an altar that *was* at Damascus: and king Ahaz sent to Urijah the priest the fashion of the altar, and the pattern of it, according to all the workmanship thereof.

11 And Urijah the priest built an altar according to all that king Ahaz had sent from Damascus: so Urijah the priest made *it* against king Ahaz came from Damascus.

12 And when the king was come from Damascus, the king saw the altar: and the king approached to the altar, and offered thereon.

13 And he burnt his burnt offering and his meat offering, and poured his drink offering, and sprinkled the blood of his peace offerings, upon the altar.

14 And he brought also the brasen altar, which *was* before the LORD, from the forefront of the house, from between the altar and the house of the LORD, and put it on the north side of the altar.

15 And king Ahaz commanded Urijah the priest, saying, Upon the great altar burn the morning burnt offering, and the evening meat offering, and the king's burnt sacrifice, and his meat offering, with the burnt offering of all the people of the land, and their meat offering, and their drink offerings; and sprinkle upon it all the blood of the burnt offering, and all the blood of the sacrifice: and the brasen altar shall be for me to enquire *by*.

16 Thus did Urijah the priest, according to all that king Ahaz commanded.

17 And king Ahaz cut off the borders of the bases, and removed the laver from off them; and took down the sea from off the brasen oxen that *were* under it, and put it upon a pavement of stones.

18 And the covert for the sabbath that they had built in the house, and the king's entry without, turned he from the house of the LORD for the king of Assyria.

19 Now the rest of the acts of Ahaz which he did, *are* they not written in the book of the chronicles of the kings of Judah?

20 And Ahaz slept with his fathers, and was buried with his fathers in the city of David: and Hezekiah his son reigned in his stead.

17 In the twelfth year of Ahaz king of Judah began Hoshea the son of Elah to reign in Samaria over Israel nine years.

2 And he did *that which was* evil in the sight of the LORD, but not as the kings of Israel that were before him.

3 Against him came up Shalmaneser king of Assyria; and Hoshea became his servant, and gave him presents.

4 And the king of Assyria found conspiracy in Hoshea: for he had sent messengers to So king of Egypt, and brought no present to the king of Assyria, as *he had done* year by year: therefore the king of Assyria shut him up, and bound him in prison.

5 Then the king of Assyria came up throughout all the land, and went up to Samaria, and besieged it three years.

6 In the ninth year of Hoshea the king of Assyria took Samaria, and carried Israel away into Assyria, and placed them in Halah and in Habor *by* the river of Gozan, and in the cities of the Medes.

7 For *so* it was, that the children of Israel had sinned against the LORD their God, which had brought them up out of the land of Egypt, from under the hand of Pharaoh king of Egypt, and had feared other gods,

8 And walked in the statutes of the heathen, whom the LORD cast out from before the children of Israel, and of the kings of Israel, which they had made.

9 And the children of Israel did secretly *those* things that *were* not right against the LORD their God, and they built them high places in all their cities, from the tower of the watchmen to the fenced city.

10 And they set them up images and groves in every high hill, and under every green tree:

11 And there they burnt incense in all the high places, as *did* the heathen whom the LORD carried away before them; and wrought wicked things to provoke the LORD to anger:

12 For they served idols, whereof the LORD had said unto them, Ye shall not do this thing.

13 Yet the LORD testified against Israel, and against Judah, by all the prophets, *and by* all the seers, saying, Turn ye from your evil ways, and keep my commandments *and* my statutes, according to all the law which I

commanded your fathers, and which I sent to you by my servants the prophets.
14 Notwithstanding they would not hear, but hardened their necks, like to the neck of their fathers, that did not believe in the LORD their God.
15 And they rejected his statutes, and his covenant that he made with their fathers, and his testimonies which he testified against them; and they followed vanity, and became vain, and went after the heathen that *were* round about them, *concerning* whom the LORD had charged them, that they should not do like them.
16 And they left all the commandments of the LORD their God, and made them molten images, *even* two calves, and made a grove, and worshipped all the host of heaven, and served Baal.
17 And they caused their sons and their daughters to pass through the fire, and used divination and enchantments, and sold themselves to do evil in the sight of the LORD, to provoke him to anger.
18 Therefore the LORD was very angry with Israel, and removed them out of his sight: there was none left but the tribe of Judah only.
19 Also Judah kept not the commandments of the LORD their God, but walked in the statutes of Israel which they made.
20 And the LORD rejected all the seed of Israel, and afflicted them, and delivered them into the hand of spoilers, until he had cast them out of his sight.
21 For he rent Israel from the house of David; and they made Jeroboam the son of Nebat king: and Jeroboam drave Israel from following the LORD, and made them sin a great sin.
22 For the children of Israel walked in all the sins of Jeroboam which he did; they departed not from them;
23 Until the LORD removed Israel out of his sight, as he had said by all his servants the prophets. So was Israel carried away out of their own land to Assyria unto this day.
24 And the king of Assyria brought *men* from Babylon, and from Cuthah, and from Ava, and from Hamath, and from Sepharvaim, and placed *them* in the cities of Samaria instead of the children of Israel: and they possessed Samaria, and dwelt in the cities thereof.
25 And *so* it was at the beginning of their dwelling there, *that* they feared not the LORD: therefore the LORD sent lions among them, which slew *some* of them.
26 Wherefore they spake to the king of Assyria, saying, The nations which thou hast removed, and placed in the cities of Samaria, know not the manner of the God of the land: therefore he hath sent lions among them, and, behold, they slay them, because they know not the manner of the God of the land.
27 Then the king of Assyria commanded, saying, Carry thither one of the priests whom ye brought from thence; and let them go and dwell there, and let him teach them the manner of the God of the land.
28 Then one of the priests whom they had carried away from Samaria came and dwelt in Bethel, and taught them how they should fear the LORD.
29 Howbeit every nation made gods of their own, and put *them* in the houses of the high places which the

Samaritans had made, every nation in their cities wherein they dwelt.

30 And the men of Babylon made Succoth-benoth, and the men of Cuth made Nergal, and the men of Hamath made Ashima,

31 And the Avites made Nibhaz and Tartak, and the Sepharvites burnt their children in fire to Adrammelech and Anammelech, the gods of Sepharvaim.

32 So they feared the LORD, and made unto themselves of the lowest of them priests of the high places, which sacrificed for them in the houses of the high places.

33 They feared the LORD, and served their own gods, after the manner of the nations whom they carried away from thence.

34 Unto this day they do after the former manners: they fear not the LORD, neither do they after their statutes, or after their ordinances, or after the law and commandment which the LORD commanded the children of Jacob, whom he named Israel;

35 With whom the LORD had made a covenant, and charged them, saying, Ye shall not fear other gods, nor bow yourselves to them, nor serve them, nor sacrifice to them:

36 But the LORD, who brought you up out of the land of Egypt with great power and a stretched out arm, him shall ye fear, and him shall ye worship, and to him shall ye do sacrifice.

37 And the statutes, and the ordinances, and the law, and the commandment, which he wrote for you, ye shall observe to do for evermore; and ye shall not fear other gods.

38 And the covenant that I have made with you ye shall not forget; neither shall ye fear other gods.

39 But the LORD your God ye shall fear; and he shall deliver you out of the hand of all your enemies.

40 Howbeit they did not hearken, but they did after their former manner.

41 So these nations feared the LORD, and served their graven images, both their children, and their children's children: as did their fathers, so do they unto this day.

18 Now it came to pass in the third year of Hoshea son of Elah king of Israel, *that* Hezekiah the son of Ahaz king of Judah began to reign.

2 Twenty and five years old was he when he began to reign; and he reigned twenty and nine years in Jerusalem. His mother's name also *was* Abi, the daughter of Zachariah.

3 And he did *that which was* right in the sight of the LORD, according to all that David his father did.

4 He removed the high places, and brake the images, and cut down the groves, and brake in pieces the brasen serpent that Moses had made: for unto those days the children of Israel did burn incense to it: and he called it Nehushtan.

5 He trusted in the LORD God of Israel; so that after him was none like him among all the kings of Judah, nor *any* that were before him.

6 For he clave to the LORD, *and* departed not from following him, but kept his commandments, which the LORD commanded Moses.

7 And the LORD was with him; *and* he prospered whithersoever he went forth: and he rebelled against the king of Assyria, and served him not.

8 He smote the Philistines, *even* unto Gaza, and the borders thereof, from the tower of the watchmen to the fenced city.

9 And it came to pass in the fourth year of king Hezekiah, which *was* the seventh year of Hoshea son of Elah king of Israel, *that* Shalmaneser king of Assyria came up against Samaria, and besieged it.

10 And at the end of three years they took it: *even* in the sixth year of Hezekiah, that *is* the ninth year of Hoshea king of Israel, Samaria was taken.

11 And the king of Assyria did carry away Israel unto Assyria, and put them in Halah and in Habor *by* the river of Gozan, and in the cities of the Medes:

12 Because they obeyed not the voice of the LORD their God, but transgressed his covenant, *and* all that Moses the servant of the LORD commanded, and would not hear *them*, nor do *them*.

13 Now in the fourteenth year of king Hezekiah did Sennacherib king of Assyria come up against all the fenced cities of Judah, and took them.

14 And Hezekiah king of Judah sent to the king of Assyria to Lachish, saying, I have offended; return from me: that which thou puttest on me will I bear. And the king of Assyria appointed unto Hezekiah king of Judah three hundred talents of silver and thirty talents of gold.

15 And Hezekiah gave *him* all the silver that was found in the house of the LORD, and in the treasures of the king's house.

16 At that time did Hezekiah cut off *the gold from* the doors of the temple of the LORD, and *from* the pillars which Hezekiah king of Judah had overlaid, and gave it to the king of Assyria.

17 And the king of Assyria sent Tartan and Rab-saris and Rab-shakeh from Lachish to king Hezekiah with a great host against Jerusalem. And they went up and came to Jerusalem. And when they were come up, they came and stood by the conduit of the upper pool, which *is* in the highway of the fuller's field.

18 And when they had called to the king, there came out to them Eliakim the son of Hilkiah, which *was* over the household, and Shebna the scribe, and Joah the son of Asaph the recorder.

19 And Rab-shakeh said unto them, Speak ye now to Hezekiah, Thus saith the great king, the king of Assyria, What confidence *is* this wherein thou trustest?

20 Thou sayest, (but *they are but* vain words,) *I have* counsel and strength for the war. Now on whom dost thou trust, that thou rebellest against me?

21 Now, behold, thou trustest upon the staff of this bruised reed, *even* upon Egypt, on which if a man lean, it will go into his hand, and pierce it: so *is* Pharaoh king of Egypt unto all that trust on him.

22 But if ye say unto me, We trust in the LORD our God: *is* not that he, whose high places and whose altars Hezekiah hath taken away, and hath said to Judah and Jerusalem, Ye shall worship before this altar in Jerusalem?

23 Now therefore, I pray thee, give pledges to my lord the king of Assyria, and I will deliver thee two thousand horses, if thou be able on thy part to set riders upon them.

24 How then wilt thou turn away the face of one captain of the least of my master's servants, and put thy trust on Egypt for chariots and for horsemen?

25 Am I now come up without the LORD against this place to destroy it? The LORD said to me, Go up against this land, and destroy it.

26 Then said Eliakim the son of Hilkiah, and Shebna, and Joah, unto Rab-shakeh, Speak, I pray thee, to thy servants in the Syrian language; for we understand *it*: and talk not with us in the Jews' language in the ears of the people that *are* on the wall.

27 But Rab-shakeh said unto them, Hath my master sent me to thy master, and to thee, to speak these words? *hath he* not *sent me* to the men which sit on the wall, that they may eat their own dung, and drink their own piss with you?

28 Then Rab-shakeh stood and cried with a loud voice in the Jews' language, and spake, saying, Hear the word of the great king, the king of Assyria:

29 Thus saith the king, Let not Hezekiah deceive you: for he shall not be able to deliver you out of his hand:

30 Neither let Hezekiah make you trust in the LORD, saying, The LORD will surely deliver us, and this city shall not be delivered into the hand of the king of Assyria.

31 Hearken not to Hezekiah: for thus saith the king of Assyria, Make *an agreement* with me by a present, and come out to me, and *then* eat ye every man of his own vine, and every one of his fig tree, and drink ye every one the waters of his cistern:

32 Until I come and take you away to a land like your own land, a land of corn and wine, a land of bread and vineyards, a land of oil olive and of honey, that ye may live, and not die: and hearken not unto Hezekiah, when he persuadeth you, saying, The LORD will deliver us.

33 Hath any of the gods of the nations delivered at all his land out of the hand of the king of Assyria?

34 Where *are* the gods of Hamath, and of Arpad? where *are* the gods of Sepharvaim, Hena, and Ivah? have they delivered Samaria out of mine hand?

35 Who *are* they among all the gods of the countries, that have delivered their country out of mine hand, that the LORD should deliver Jerusalem out of mine hand?

36 But the people held their peace, and answered him not a word: for the king's commandment was, saying, Answer him not.

37 Then came Eliakim the son of Hilkiah, which *was* over the household, and Shebna the scribe, and Joah the son of Asaph the recorder, to Hezekiah with *their* clothes rent, and told him the words of Rab-shakeh.

19 And it came to pass, when king Hezekiah heard *it*, that he rent his clothes, and covered himself with sackcloth, and went into the house of the LORD.

2 And he sent Eliakim, which *was* over the household, and Shebna the scribe, and the elders of the priests, covered with sackcloth, to Isaiah the prophet the son of Amoz.

3 And they said unto him, Thus saith Hezekiah, This day *is* a day of trouble, and of rebuke, and blasphemy: for the children are come to the birth, and *there is* not strength to bring forth.

4 It may be the LORD thy God will
hear all the words of Rab-shakeh,
whom the king of Assyria his master
hath sent to reproach the living God;
and will reprove the words which the
LORD thy God hath heard: wherefore
lift up *thy* prayer for the remnant that
are left.
5 So the servants of king Hezekiah
came to Isaiah.
6 And Isaiah said unto them, Thus
shall ye say to your master, Thus saith
the LORD, Be not afraid of the words
which thou hast heard, with which the
servants of the king of Assyria have
blasphemed me.
7 Behold, I will send a blast upon him,
and he shall hear a rumour, and shall
return to his own land; and I will cause
him to fall by the sword in his own land.
8 So Rab-shakeh returned, and found
the king of Assyria warring against
Libnah: for he had heard that he was
departed from Lachish.
9 And when he heard say of Tirhakah
king of Ethiopia, Behold, he is come out
to fight against thee: he sent messengers again unto Hezekiah, saying,
10 Thus shall ye speak to Hezekiah
king of Judah, saying, Let not thy God
in whom thou trustest deceive thee,
saying, Jerusalem shall not be delivered into the hand of the king of
Assyria.
11 Behold, thou hast heard what the
kings of Assyria have done to all lands,
by destroying them utterly: and shalt
thou be delivered?
12 Have the gods of the nations delivered them which my fathers have
destroyed; *as* Gozan, and Haran, and
Rezeph, and the children of Eden
which *were* in Thelasar?
13 Where *is* the king of Hamath, and
the king of Arpad, and the king of the
city of Sepharvaim, of Hena, and Ivah?
14 And Hezekiah received the letter
of the hand of the messengers, and
read it: and Hezekiah went up into the
house of the LORD, and spread it before
the LORD.
15 And Hezekiah prayed before the
LORD, and said, O LORD God of Israel,
which dwellest *between* the cherubims,
thou art the God, *even* thou alone, of all
the kingdoms of the earth; thou hast
made heaven and earth.
16 LORD, bow down thine ear, and
hear: open, LORD, thine eyes, and see:
and hear the words of Sennacherib,
which hath sent him to reproach the
living God.
17 Of a truth, LORD, the kings of
Assyria have destroyed the nations and
their lands,
18 And have cast their gods into the
fire: for they *were* no gods, but the work
of men's hands, wood and stone: therefore they have destroyed them.
19 Now therefore, O LORD our God, I
beseech thee, save thou us out of his
hand, that all the kingdoms of the earth
may know that thou *art* the LORD God,
even thou only.
20 Then Isaiah the son of Amoz sent
to Hezekiah, saying, Thus saith the
LORD God of Israel, *That* which thou
hast prayed to me against Sennacherib
king of Assyria I have heard.
21 This *is* the word that the LORD hath
spoken concerning him; The virgin the
daughter of Zion hath despised thee,
and laughed thee to scorn; the daughter of Jerusalem hath shaken her head
at thee.
22 Whom hast thou reproached and
blasphemed? and against whom hast

thou exalted *thy* voice, and lifted up
thine eyes on high? *even* against the
Holy *One* of Israel.
23 By thy messengers thou hast
reproached the Lord, and hast said,
With the multitude of my chariots I am
come up to the height of the mountains, to the sides of Lebanon, and will
cut down the tall cedar trees thereof,
and the choice fir trees thereof: and I
will enter into the lodgings of his borders, *and into* the forest of his Carmel.
24 I have digged and drunk strange
waters, and with the sole of my feet
have I dried up all the rivers of besieged
places.
25 Hast thou not heard long ago *how*
I have done it, *and* of ancient times that
I have formed it? now have I brought it
to pass, that thou shouldest be to lay
waste fenced cities *into* ruinous heaps.
26 Therefore their inhabitants were
of small power, they were dismayed and
confounded; they were *as* the grass of
the field, and *as* the green herb, *as* the
grass on the housetops, and *as corn*
blasted before it be grown up.
27 But I know thy abode, and thy
going out, and thy coming in, and thy
rage against me.
28 Because thy rage against me and
thy tumult is come up into mine ears,
therefore I will put my hook in thy
nose, and my bridle in thy lips, and I
will turn thee back by the way by which
thou camest.
29 And this *shall be* a sign unto thee,
Ye shall eat this year such things as
grow of themselves, and in the second
year that which springeth of the same;
and in the third year sow ye, and reap,
and plant vineyards, and eat the fruits
thereof.
30 And the remnant that is escaped
of the house of Judah shall yet again
take root downward, and bear fruit
upward.
31 For out of Jerusalem shall go forth
a remnant, and they that escape out of
mount Zion: the zeal of the LORD *of
hosts* shall do this.
32 Therefore thus saith the LORD concerning the king of Assyria, He shall
not come into this city, nor shoot an
arrow there, nor come before it with
shield, nor cast a bank against it.
33 By the way that he came, by the
same shall he return, and shall not
come into this city, saith the LORD.
34 For I will defend this city, to save it,
for mine own sake, and for my servant
David's sake.
35 And it came to pass that night, that
the angel of the LORD went out, and
smote in the camp of the Assyrians an
hundred fourscore and five thousand:
and when they arose early in the morning, behold, they *were* all dead corpses.
36 So Sennacherib king of Assyria
departed, and went and returned, and
dwelt at Nineveh.
37 And it came to pass, as he was
worshipping in the house of Nisroch his
god, that Adram-melech and Sharezer
his sons smote him with the sword: and
they escaped into the land of Armenia.
And Esar-haddon his son reigned in his
stead.

20 In those days was Hezekiah sick
unto death. And the prophet
Isaiah the son of Amoz came to him,
and said unto him, Thus saith the LORD,
Set thine house in order; for thou shalt
die, and not live.
2 Then he turned his face to the wall,
and prayed unto the LORD, saying,

3 I beseech thee, O LORD, remember
now how I have walked before thee in
truth and with a perfect heart, and
have done *that which is* good in thy
sight. And Hezekiah wept sore.
4 And it came to pass, afore Isaiah
was gone out into the middle court, that
the word of the LORD came to him, saying,
5 Turn again, and tell Hezekiah the
captain of my people, Thus saith the
LORD, the God of David thy father, I
have heard thy prayer, I have seen thy
tears: behold, I will heal thee: on the
third day thou shalt go up unto the
house of the LORD.
6 And I will add unto thy days fifteen
years; and I will deliver thee and this
city out of the hand of the king of
Assyria; and I will defend this city for
mine own sake, and for my servant
David's sake.
7 And Isaiah said, Take a lump of figs.
And they took and laid *it* on the boil,
and he recovered.
8 And Hezekiah said unto Isaiah,
What *shall be* the sign that the LORD
will heal me, and that I shall go up into
the house of the LORD the third day?
9 And Isaiah said, This sign shalt thou
have of the LORD, that the LORD will do
the thing that he hath spoken: shall the
shadow go forward ten degrees, or go
back ten degrees?
10 And Hezekiah answered, It is a
light thing for the shadow to go down
ten degrees: nay, but let the shadow
return backward ten degrees.
11 And Isaiah the prophet cried unto
the LORD: and he brought the shadow
ten degrees backward, by which it had
gone down in the dial of Ahaz.
12 At that time Berodach-baladan,
the son of Baladan, king of Babylon,
sent letters and a present unto
Hezekiah: for he had heard that
Hezekiah had been sick.
13 And Hezekiah hearkened unto
them, and shewed them all the house of
his precious things, the silver, and the
gold, and the spices, and the precious
ointment, and *all* the house of his
armour, and all that was found in his
treasures: there was nothing in his
house, nor in all his dominion, that
Hezekiah shewed them not.
14 Then came Isaiah the prophet
unto king Hezekiah, and said unto him,
What said these men? and from whence
came they unto thee? And Hezekiah
said, They are come from a far country,
even from Babylon.
15 And he said, What have they seen
in thine house? And Hezekiah
answered, All *the things* that *are* in
mine house have they seen: there is
nothing among my treasures that I have
not shewed them.
16 And Isaiah said unto Hezekiah,
Hear the word of the LORD.
17 Behold, the days come, that all that
is in thine house, and that which thy
fathers have laid up in store unto this
day, shall be carried into Babylon: nothing shall be left, saith the LORD.
18 And of thy sons that shall issue
from thee, which thou shalt beget, shall
they take away; and they shall be
eunuchs in the palace of the king of
Babylon.
19 Then said Hezekiah unto Isaiah,
Good *is* the word of the LORD which
thou hast spoken. And he said, *Is it* not
good, if peace and truth be in my days?
20 And the rest of the acts of
Hezekiah, and all his might, and how
he made a pool, and a conduit, and
brought water into the city, *are* they not

written in the book of the chronicles of the kings of Judah?

21 And Hezekiah slept with his fathers: and Manasseh his son reigned in his stead.

21 Manasseh *was* twelve years old when he began to reign, and reigned fifty and five years in Jerusalem. And his mother's name *was* Hephzi-bah.

2 And he did *that which was* evil in the sight of the LORD, after the abominations of the heathen, whom the LORD cast out before the children of Israel.

3 For he built up again the high places which Hezekiah his father had destroyed; and he reared up altars for Baal, and made a grove, as did Ahab king of Israel; and worshipped all the host of heaven, and served them.

4 And he built altars in the house of the LORD, of which the LORD said, In Jerusalem will I put my name.

5 And he built altars for all the host of heaven in the two courts of the house of the LORD.

6 And he made his son pass through the fire, and observed times, and used enchantments, and dealt with familiar spirits and wizards: he wrought much wickedness in the sight of the LORD, to provoke *him* to anger.

7 And he set a graven image of the grove that he had made in the house, of which the LORD said to David, and to Solomon his son, In this house, and in Jerusalem, which I have chosen out of all tribes of Israel, will I put my name for ever:

8 Neither will I make the feet of Israel move any more out of the land which I gave their fathers; only if they will observe to do according to all that I have commanded them, and according to all the law that my servant Moses commanded them.

9 But they hearkened not: and Manasseh seduced them to do more evil than did the nations whom the LORD destroyed before the children of Israel.

10 And the LORD spake by his servants the prophets, saying,

11 Because Manasseh king of Judah hath done these abominations, *and* hath done wickedly above all that the Amorites did, which *were* before him, and hath made Judah also to sin with his idols:

12 Therefore thus saith the LORD God of Israel, Behold, I *am* bringing *such* evil upon Jerusalem and Judah, that whosoever heareth of it, both his ears shall tingle.

13 And I will stretch over Jerusalem the line of Samaria, and the plummet of the house of Ahab: and I will wipe Jerusalem as *a man* wipeth a dish, wiping *it*, and turning *it* upside down.

14 And I will forsake the remnant of mine inheritance, and deliver them into the hand of their enemies; and they shall become a prey and a spoil to all their enemies;

15 Because they have done *that which was* evil in my sight, and have provoked me to anger, since the day their fathers came forth out of Egypt, even unto this day.

16 Moreover Manasseh shed innocent blood very much, till he had filled Jerusalem from one end to another; beside his sin wherewith he made Judah to sin, in doing *that which was* evil in the sight of the LORD.

17 Now the rest of the acts of Manasseh, and all that he did, and his sin that he sinned, *are* they not written

in the book of the chronicles of the
kings of Judah?
18 And Manasseh slept with his
fathers, and was buried in the garden
of his own house, in the garden of Uzza:
and Amon his son reigned in his stead.
19 Amon *was* twenty and two years
old when he began to reign, and he
reigned two years in Jerusalem. And
his mother's name *was* Meshullemeth,
the daughter of Haruz of Jotbah.
20 And he did *that which was* evil in
the sight of the LORD, as his father
Manasseh did.
21 And he walked in all the way that
his father walked in, and served the
idols that his father served, and worshipped them:
22 And he forsook the LORD God of
his fathers, and walked not in the way
of the LORD.
23 And the servants of Amon conspired against him, and slew the king in
his own house.
24 And the people of the land slew all
them that had conspired against king
Amon; and the people of the land made
Josiah his son king in his stead.
25 Now the rest of the acts of Amon
which he did, *are* they not written in
the book of the chronicles of the kings
of Judah?
26 And he was buried in his sepulchre
in the garden of Uzza: and Josiah his
son reigned in his stead.

22 Josiah *was* eight years old when
he began to reign, and he reigned
thirty and one years in Jerusalem. And
his mother's name *was* Jedidah, the
daughter of Adaiah of Boscath.
2 And he did *that which was* right in
the sight of the LORD, and walked in all
the way of David his father, and turned
not aside to the right hand or to the
left.
3 And it came to pass in the eighteenth year of king Josiah, *that* the
king sent Shaphan the son of Azaliah,
the son of Meshullam, the scribe, to the
house of the LORD, saying,
4 Go up to Hilkiah the high priest,
that he may sum the silver which is
brought into the house of the LORD,
which the keepers of the door have
gathered of the people:
5 And let them deliver it into the
hand of the doers of the work, that have
the oversight of the house of the LORD:
and let them give it to the doers of the
work which *is* in the house of the LORD,
to repair the breaches of the house,
6 Unto carpenters, and builders, and
masons, and to buy timber and hewn
stone to repair the house.
7 Howbeit there was no reckoning
made with them of the money that was
delivered into their hand, because they
dealt faithfully.
8 And Hilkiah the high priest said
unto Shaphan the scribe, I have found
the book of the law in the house of the
LORD. And Hilkiah gave the book to
Shaphan, and he read it.
9 And Shaphan the scribe came to
the king, and brought the king word
again, and said, Thy servants have gathered the money that was found in the
house, and have delivered it into the
hand of them that do the work, that
have the oversight of the house of the
LORD.
10 And Shaphan the scribe shewed
the king, saying, Hilkiah the priest hath
delivered me a book. And Shaphan
read it before the king.

11 And it came to pass, when the king
had heard the words of the book of the
law, that he rent his clothes.
12 And the king commanded Hilkiah
the priest, and Ahikam the son of
Shaphan, and Achbor the son of
Michaiah, and Shaphan the scribe, and
Asahiah a servant of the king's, saying,
13 Go ye, enquire of the LORD for me,
and for the people, and for all Judah,
concerning the words of this book that
is found: for great *is* the wrath of the
LORD that is kindled against us, because
our fathers have not hearkened unto
the words of this book, to do according
unto all that which is written concerning us.
14 So Hilkiah the priest, and Ahikam,
and Achbor, and Shaphan, and Asahiah,
went unto Huldah the prophetess, the
wife of Shallum the son of Tikvah, the
son of Harhas, keeper of the wardrobe;
(now she dwelt in Jerusalem in the college;) and they communed with her.
15 And she said unto them, Thus saith
the LORD God of Israel, Tell the man
that sent you to me,
16 Thus saith the LORD, Behold, I will
bring evil upon this place, and upon the
inhabitants thereof, *even* all the words
of the book which the king of Judah
hath read:
17 Because they have forsaken me,
and have burned incense unto other
gods, that they might provoke me to
anger with all the works of their hands;
therefore my wrath shall be kindled
against this place, and shall not be
quenched.
18 But to the king of Judah which
sent you to enquire of the LORD, thus
shall ye say to him, Thus saith the LORD
God of Israel, *As touching* the words
which thou hast heard;
19 Because thine heart was tender,
and thou hast humbled thyself before
the LORD, when thou heardest what I
spake against this place, and against
the inhabitants thereof, that they
should become a desolation and a
curse, and hast rent thy clothes, and
wept before me; I also have heard *thee*,
saith the LORD.
20 Behold therefore, I will gather
thee unto thy fathers, and thou shalt be
gathered into thy grave in peace; and
thine eyes shall not see all the evil
which I will bring upon this place. And
they brought the king word again.

23

And the king sent, and they gathered unto him all the elders of
Judah and of Jerusalem.
2 And the king went up into the
house of the LORD, and all the men of
Judah and all the inhabitants of
Jerusalem with him, and the priests,
and the prophets, and all the people,
both small and great: and he read in
their ears all the words of the book of
the covenant which was found in the
house of the LORD.
3 And the king stood by a pillar, and
made a covenant before the LORD, to
walk after the LORD, and to keep his
commandments and his testimonies
and his statutes with all *their* heart and
all *their* soul, to perform the words of
this covenant that were written in this
book. And all the people stood to the
covenant.
4 And the king commanded Hilkiah
the high priest, and the priests of the
second order, and the keepers of the
door, to bring forth out of the temple of
the LORD all the vessels that were made
for Baal, and for the grove, and for all
the host of heaven: and he burned
them without Jerusalem in the fields of

Kidron, and carried the ashes of them
unto Beth-el.
5 And he put down the idolatrous
priests, whom the kings of Judah had
ordained to burn incense in the high
places in the cities of Judah, and in the
places round about Jerusalem; them
also that burned incense unto Baal, to
the sun, and to the moon, and to the
planets, and to all the host of heaven.
6 And he brought out the grove from
the house of the LORD, without
Jerusalem, unto the brook Kidron, and
burned it at the brook Kidron, and
stamped *it* small to powder, and cast
the powder thereof upon the graves of
the children of the people.
7 And he brake down the houses of
the sodomites, that *were* by the house
of the LORD, where the women wove
hangings for the grove.
8 And he brought all the priests out of
the cities of Judah, and defiled the high
places where the priests had burned
incense, from Geba to Beer-sheba, and
brake down the high places of the gates
that *were* in the entering in of the gate
of Joshua the governor of the city,
which *were* on a man's left hand at the
gate of the city.
9 Nevertheless the priests of the high
places came not up to the altar of the
LORD in Jerusalem, but they did eat of
the unleavened bread among their
brethren.
10 And he defiled Topheth, which *is*
in the valley of the children of Hinnom,
that no man might make his son or his
daughter to pass through the fire to
Molech.
11 And he took away the horses that
the kings of Judah had given to the sun,
at the entering in of the house of the
LORD, by the chamber of Nathan-
melech the chamberlain, which *was* in
the suburbs, and burned the chariots of
the sun with fire.
12 And the altars that *were* on the top
of the upper chamber of Ahaz, which
the kings of Judah had made, and the
altars which Manasseh had made in the
two courts of the house of the LORD, did
the king beat down, and brake *them*
down from thence, and cast the dust of
them into the brook Kidron.
13 And the high places that *were*
before Jerusalem, which *were* on the
right hand of the mount of corruption,
which Solomon the king of Israel had
builded for Ashtoreth the abomination
of the Zidonians, and for Chemosh the
abomination of the Moabites, and for
Milcom the abomination of the children of Ammon, did the king defile.
14 And he brake in pieces the images,
and cut down the groves, and filled
their places with the bones of men.
15 Moreover the altar that *was* at
Beth-el, *and* the high place which
Jeroboam the son of Nebat, who made
Israel to sin, had made, both that altar
and the high place he brake down, and
burned the high place, *and* stamped *it*
small to powder, and burned the grove.
16 And as Josiah turned himself, he
spied the sepulchres that *were* there in
the mount, and sent, and took the
bones out of the sepulchres, and
burned *them* upon the altar, and polluted it, according to the word of the
LORD which the man of God proclaimed,
who proclaimed these words.
17 Then he said, What title *is* that
that I see? And the men of the city told
him, *It is* the sepulchre of the man of
God, which came from Judah, and proclaimed these things that thou hast
done against the altar of Beth-el.

18 And he said, Let him alone; let no
man move his bones. So they let his
bones alone, with the bones of the
prophet that came out of Samaria.
19 And all the houses also of the high
places that *were* in the cities of
Samaria, which the kings of Israel had
made to provoke *the* LORD to anger,
Josiah took away, and did to them
according to all the acts that he had
done in Beth-el.
20 And he slew all the priests of the
high places that *were* there upon the
altars, and burned men's bones upon
them, and returned to Jerusalem.
21 And the king commanded all the
people, saying, Keep the passover unto
the LORD your God, as *it is* written in
the book of this covenant.
22 Surely there was not holden such a
passover from the days of the judges
that judged Israel, nor in all the days of
the kings of Israel, nor of the kings of
Judah;
23 But in the eighteenth year of king
Josiah, *wherein* this passover was hold-
en to the LORD in Jerusalem.
24 Moreover the *workers with* familiar spirits, and the wizards, and the
images, and the idols, and all the abominations that were spied in the land of
Judah and in Jerusalem, did Josiah put
away, that he might perform the words
of the law which were written in the
book that Hilkiah the priest found in
the house of the LORD.
25 And like unto him was there no
king before him, that turned to the
LORD with all his heart, and with all his
soul, and with all his might, according
to all the law of Moses; neither after
him arose there *any* like him.
26 Notwithstanding the LORD turned
not from the fierceness of his great
wrath, wherewith his anger was kindled against Judah, because of all the
provocations that Manasseh had provoked him withal.
27 And the LORD said, I will remove
Judah also out of my sight, as I have
removed Israel, and will cast off this
city Jerusalem which I have chosen,
and the house of which I said, My name
shall be there.
28 Now the rest of the acts of Josiah,
and all that he did, *are* they not written
in the book of the chronicles of the
kings of Judah?
29 In his days Pharaoh-nechoh king of
Egypt went up against the king of
Assyria to the river Euphrates: and
king Josiah went against him; and he
slew him at Megiddo, when he had seen
him.
30 And his servants carried him in a
chariot dead from Megiddo, and
brought him to Jerusalem, and buried
him in his own sepulchre. And the people of the land took Jehoahaz the son of
Josiah, and anointed him, and made
him king in his father's stead.
31 Jehoahaz *was* twenty and three
years old when he began to reign; and
he reigned three months in Jerusalem.
And his mother's name *was* Hamutal,
the daughter of Jeremiah of Libnah.
32 And he did *that which was* evil in
the sight of the LORD, according to all
that his fathers had done.
33 And Pharaoh-nechoh put him in
bands at Riblah in the land of Hamath,
that he might not reign in Jerusalem;
and put the land to a tribute of an hundred talents of silver, and a talent of
gold.
34 And Pharaoh-nechoh made Eliakim the son of Josiah king in the room
of Josiah his father, and turned his

name to Jehoiakim, and took Jehoahaz away: and he came to Egypt, and died there.

35 And Jehoiakim gave the silver and the gold to Pharaoh; but he taxed the land to give the money according to the commandment of Pharaoh: he exacted the silver and the gold of the people of the land, of every one according to his taxation, to give *it* unto Pharaoh-nechoh.

36 Jehoiakim *was* twenty and five years old when he began to reign; and he reigned eleven years in Jerusalem. And his mother's name *was* Zebudah, the daughter of Pedaiah of Rumah.

37 And he did *that which was* evil in the sight of the LORD, according to all that his fathers had done.

24 In his days Nebuchadnezzar king of Babylon came up, and Jehoiakim became his servant three years: then he turned and rebelled against him.

2 And the LORD sent against him bands of the Chaldees, and bands of the Syrians, and bands of the Moabites, and bands of the children of Ammon, and sent them against Judah to destroy it, according to the word of the LORD, which he spake by his servants the prophets.

3 Surely at the commandment of the LORD came *this* upon Judah, to remove *them* out of his sight, for the sins of Manasseh, according to all that he did;

4 And also for the innocent blood that he shed: for he filled Jerusalem with innocent blood; which the LORD would not pardon.

5 Now the rest of the acts of Jehoiakim, and all that he did, *are* they not written in the book of the chronicles of the kings of Judah?

6 So Jehoiakim slept with his fathers: and Jehoiachin his son reigned in his stead.

7 And the king of Egypt came not again any more out of his land: for the king of Babylon had taken from the river of Egypt unto the river Euphrates all that pertained to the king of Egypt.

8 Jehoiachin *was* eighteen years old when he began to reign, and he reigned in Jerusalem three months. And his mother's name *was* Nehushta, the daughter of Elnathan of Jerusalem.

9 And he did *that which was* evil in the sight of the LORD, according to all that his father had done.

10 At that time the servants of Nebuchadnezzar king of Babylon came up against Jerusalem, and the city was besieged.

11 And Nebuchadnezzar king of Babylon came against the city, and his servants did besiege it.

12 And Jehoiachin the king of Judah went out to the king of Babylon, he, and his mother, and his servants, and his princes, and his officers: and the king of Babylon took him in the eighth year of his reign.

13 And he carried out thence all the treasures of the house of the LORD, and the treasures of the king's house, and cut in pieces all the vessels of gold which Solomon king of Israel had made in the temple of the LORD, as the LORD had said.

14 And he carried away all Jerusalem, and all the princes, and all the mighty men of valour, *even* ten thousand captives, and all the craftsmen and smiths: none remained, save the poorest sort of the people of the land.

15 And he carried away Jehoiachin to Babylon, and the king's mother, and the

king's wives, and his officers, and the
mighty of the land, *those* carried he
into captivity from Jerusalem to
Babylon.
16 And all the men of might, *even*
seven thousand, and craftsmen and
smiths a thousand, all *that were* strong
and apt for war, even them the king of
Babylon brought captive to Babylon.
17 And the king of Babylon made
Mattaniah his father's brother king in
his stead, and changed his name to
Zedekiah.
18 Zedekiah *was* twenty and one
years old when he began to reign, and
he reigned eleven years in Jerusalem.
And his mother's name *was* Hamutal,
the daughter of Jeremiah of Libnah.
19 And he did *that which was* evil in
the sight of the LORD, according to all
that Jehoiakim had done.
20 For through the anger of the LORD
it came to pass in Jerusalem and Judah,
until he had cast them out from his
presence, that Zedekiah rebelled
against the king of Babylon.

25 And it came to pass in the ninth
year of his reign, in the tenth
month, in the tenth *day* of the month,
that Nebuchadnezzar king of Babylon
came, he, and all his host, against
Jerusalem, and pitched against it; and
they built forts against it round about.
2 And the city was besieged unto the
eleventh year of king Zedekiah.
3 And on the ninth *day* of the *fourth*
month the famine prevailed in the city,
and there was no bread for the people
of the land.
4 And the city was broken up, and all
the men of war *fled* by night by the way
of the gate between two walls, which *is*
by the king's garden: (now the Chaldees
were against the city round about:) and
the king went the way toward the plain.
5 And the army of the Chaldees pursued after the king, and overtook him
in the plains of Jericho: and all his
army were scattered from him.
6 So they took the king, and brought
him up to the king of Babylon to
Riblah; and they gave judgment upon
him.
7 And they slew the sons of Zedekiah
before his eyes, and put out the eyes of
Zedekiah, and bound him with fetters
of brass, and carried him to Babylon.
8 And in the fifth month, on the seventh *day* of the month, which *is* the
nineteenth year of king Nebuchadnezzar king of Babylon, came
Nebuzar-adan, captain of the guard, a
servant of the king of Babylon, unto
Jerusalem:
9 And he burnt the house of the LORD,
and the king's house, and all the houses
of Jerusalem, and every great *man's*
house burnt he with fire.
10 And all the army of the Chaldees,
that *were with* the captain of the
guard, brake down the walls of
Jerusalem round about.
11 Now the rest of the people *that*
were left in the city, and the fugitives
that fell away to the king of Babylon,
with the remnant of the multitude, did
Nebuzar-adan the captain of the guard
carry away.
12 But the captain of the guard left of
the poor of the land *to be* vinedressers
and husbandmen.
13 And the pillars of brass that *were*
in the house of the LORD, and the bases,
and the brasen sea that *was* in the
house of the LORD, did the Chaldees
break in pieces, and carried the brass
of them to Babylon.

14 And the pots, and the shovels, and
the snuffers, and the spoons, and all the
vessels of brass wherewith they ministered, took they away.
15 And the firepans, and the bowls,
and such things as *were* of gold, *in* gold,
and of silver, *in* silver, the captain of the
guard took away.
16 The two pillars, one sea, and the
bases which Solomon had made for the
house of the LORD; the brass of all these
vessels was without weight.
17 The height of the one pillar *was*
eighteen cubits, and the chapiter upon
it *was* brass: and the height of the
chapiter three cubits; and the wreathen
work, and pomegranates upon the
chapiter round about, all of brass: and
like unto these had the second pillar
with wreathen work.
18 And the captain of the guard took
Seraiah the chief priest, and Zephaniah
the second priest, and the three keepers of the door:
19 And out of the city he took an officer that was set over the men of war,
and five men of them that were in the
king's presence, which were found in
the city, and the principal scribe of the
host, which mustered the people of the
land, and threescore men of the people
of the land *that were* found in the city:
20 And Nebuzar-adan captain of the
guard took these, and brought them to
the king of Babylon to Riblah:
21 And the king of Babylon smote
them, and slew them at Riblah in the
land of Hamath. So Judah was carried
away out of their land.
22 And *as for* the people that
remained in the land of Judah, whom
Nebuchadnezzar king of Babylon had
left, even over them he made Gedaliah
the son of Ahikam, the son of Shaphan,
ruler.
23 And when all the captains of the
armies, they and their men, heard that
the king of Babylon had made Gedaliah
governor, there came to Gedaliah to
Mizpah, even Ishmael the son of
Nethaniah, and Johanan the son of
Careah, and Seraiah the son of
Tanhumeth the Netophathite, and
Jaazaniah the son of a Maachathite,
they and their men.
24 And Gedaliah sware to them, and
to their men, and said unto them, Fear
not to be the servants of the Chaldees:
dwell in the land, and serve the king of
Babylon; and it shall be well with you.
25 But it came to pass in the seventh
month, that Ishmael the son of
Nethaniah, the son of Elishama, of the
seed royal, came, and ten men with
him, and smote Gedaliah, that he died,
and the Jews and the Chaldees that
were with him at Mizpah.
26 And all the people, both small and
great, and the captains of the armies,
arose, and came to Egypt: for they were
afraid of the Chaldees.
27 And it came to pass in the seven
and thirtieth year of the captivity of
Jehoiachin king of Judah, in the twelfth
month, on the seven and twentieth *day*
of the month, *that* Evil-merodach king
of Babylon in the year that he began to
reign did lift up the head of Jehoiachin
king of Judah out of prison;
28 And he spake kindly to him, and
set his throne above the throne of the
kings that *were* with him in Babylon;
29 And changed his prison garments:
and he did eat bread continually before
him all the days of his life.
30 And his allowance *was* a continual
allowance given him of the king, a daily
rate for every day, all the days of his
life.

THE FIRST BOOK OF
CHRONICLES

1 Adam, Sheth, Enosh,
2 Kenan, Mahalaleel, Jered,
3 Henoch, Methuselah, Lamech,
4 Noah, Shem, Ham, and Japheth.
5 The sons of Japheth; Gomer, and Magog, and Madai, and Javan, and Tubal, and Meshech, and Tiras.
6 And the sons of Gomer; Ashchenaz, and Riphath, and Togarmah.
7 And the sons of Javan; Elishah, and Tarshish, Kittim, and Dodanim.
8 The sons of Ham; Cush, and Mizraim, Put, and Canaan.
9 And the sons of Cush; Seba, and Havilah, and Sabta, and Raamah, and Sabtecha. And the sons of Raamah; Sheba, and Dedan.
10 And Cush begat Nimrod: he began to be mighty upon the earth.
11 And Mizraim begat Ludim, and Anamim, and Lehabim, and Naphtuhim,
12 And Pathrusim, and Casluhim, (of whom came the Philistines,) and Caphthorim.
13 And Canaan begat Zidon his firstborn, and Heth,
14 The Jebusite also, and the Amorite, and the Girgashite,
15 And the Hivite, and the Arkite, and the Sinite,
16 And the Arvadite, and the Zemarite, and the Hamathite.
17 The sons of Shem; Elam, and Asshur, and Arphaxad, and Lud, and Aram, and Uz, and Hul, and Gether, and Meshech.
18 And Arphaxad begat Shelah, and Shelah begat Eber.
19 And unto Eber were born two sons: the name of the one *was* Peleg; because in his days the earth was divided: and his brother's name *was* Joktan.
20 And Joktan begat Almodad, and Sheleph, and Hazar-maveth, and Jerah,
21 Hadoram also, and Uzal, and Diklah,
22 And Ebal, and Abimael, and Sheba,
23 And Ophir, and Havilah, and Jobab. All these *were* the sons of Joktan.
24 Shem, Arphaxad, Shelah,
25 Eber, Peleg, Reu,
26 Serug, Nahor, Terah,
27 Abram; the same *is* Abraham.
28 The sons of Abraham; Isaac, and Ishmael.
29 These *are* their generations: The firstborn of Ishmael, Nebaioth; then Kedar, and Adbeel, and Mibsam,
30 Mishma, and Dumah, Massa, Hadad, and Tema,
31 Jetur, Naphish, and Kedemah. These are the sons of Ishmael.
32 Now the sons of Keturah, Abraham's concubine: she bare Zimran, and Jokshan, and Medan, and Midian, and Ishbak, and Shuah. And the sons of Jokshan; Sheba, and Dedan.
33 And the sons of Midian; Ephah, and Epher, and Henoch, and Abida, and Eldaah. All these *are* the sons of Keturah.
34 And Abraham begat Isaac. The sons of Isaac; Esau and Israel.
35 The sons of Esau; Eliphaz, Reuel, and Jeush, and Jaalam, and Korah.

36 The sons of Eliphaz; Teman, and Omar, Zephi, and Gatam, Kenaz, and Timna, and Amalek.

37 The sons of Reuel; Nahath, Zerah, Shammah, and Mizzah.

38 And the sons of Seir; Lotan, and Shobal, and Zibeon, and Anah, and Dishon, and Ezer, and Dishan.

39 And the sons of Lotan; Hori, and Homam: and Timna *was* Lotan's sister.

40 The sons of Shobal; Alian, and Manahath, and Ebal, Shephi, and Onam. And the sons of Zibeon; Aiah, and Anah.

41 The sons of Anah; Dishon. And the sons of Dishon; Amram, and Eshban, and Ithran, and Cheran.

42 The sons of Ezer; Bilhan, and Zavan, *and* Jakan. The sons of Dishan; Uz, and Aran.

43 Now these *are* the kings that reigned in the land of Edom before *any* king reigned over the children of Israel; Bela the son of Beor: and the name of his city *was* Dinhabah.

44 And when Bela was dead, Jobab the son of Zerah of Bozrah reigned in his stead.

45 And when Jobab was dead, Husham of the land of the Temanites reigned in his stead.

46 And when Husham was dead, Hadad the son of Bedad, which smote Midian in the field of Moab, reigned in his stead: and the name of his city *was* Avith.

47 And when Hadad was dead, Samlah of Masrekah reigned in his stead.

48 And when Samlah was dead, Shaul of Rehoboth by the river reigned in his stead.

49 And when Shaul was dead, Baal-hanan the son of Achbor reigned in his stead.

50 And when Baal-hanan was dead, Hadad reigned in his stead: and the name of his city *was* Pai; and his wife's name *was* Mehetabel, the daughter of Matred, the daughter of Mezahab.

51 Hadad died also. And the dukes of Edom were; duke Timnah, duke Aliah, duke Jetheth,

52 Duke Aholibamah, duke Elah, duke Pinon,

53 Duke Kenaz, duke Teman, duke Mibzar,

54 Duke Magdiel, duke Iram. These *are* the dukes of Edom.

2 These *are* the sons of Israel; Reuben, Simeon, Levi, and Judah, Issachar, and Zebulun,

2 Dan, Joseph, and Benjamin, Naphtali, Gad, and Asher.

3 The sons of Judah; Er, and Onan, and Shelah: *which* three were born unto him of the daughter of Shua the Canaanitess. And Er, the firstborn of Judah, was evil in the sight of the LORD; and he slew him.

4 And Tamar his daughter in law bare him Pharez and Zerah. All the sons of Judah *were* five.

5 The sons of Pharez; Hezron, and Hamul.

6 And the sons of Zerah; Zimri, and Ethan, and Heman, and Calcol, and Dara: five of them in all.

7 And the sons of Carmi; Achar, the troubler of Israel, who transgressed in the thing accursed.

8 And the sons of Ethan; Azariah.

9 The sons also of Hezron, that were born unto him; Jerahmeel, and Ram, and Chelubai.

10 And Ram begat Amminadab; and Amminadab begat Nahshon, prince of the children of Judah;

11 And Nahshon begat Salma, and Salma begat Boaz,

12 And Boaz begat Obed, and Obed begat Jesse,

13 And Jesse begat his firstborn Eliab, and Abinadab the second, and Shimma the third,

14 Nethaneel the fourth, Raddai the fifth,

15 Ozem the sixth, David the seventh:

16 Whose sisters *were* Zeruiah, and Abigail. And the sons of Zeruiah; Abishai, and Joab, and Asahel, three.

17 And Abigail bare Amasa: and the father of Amasa *was* Jether the Ishmeelite.

18 And Caleb the son of Hezron begat *children* of Azubah *his* wife, and of Jerioth: her sons *are* these; Jesher, and Shobab, and Ardon.

19 And when Azubah was dead, Caleb took unto him Ephrath, which bare him Hur.

20 And Hur begat Uri, and Uri begat Bezaleel.

21 And afterward Hezron went in to the daughter of Machir the father of Gilead, whom he married when he *was* threescore years old; and she bare him Segub.

22 And Segub begat Jair, who had three and twenty cities in the land of Gilead.

23 And he took Geshur, and Aram, with the towns of Jair, from them, with Kenath, and the towns thereof, *even* threescore cities. All these *belonged to* the sons of Machir the father of Gilead.

24 And after that Hezron was dead in Caleb-ephratah, then Abiah Hezron's wife bare him Ashur the father of Tekoa.

25 And the sons of Jerahmeel the firstborn of Hezron were, Ram the firstborn, and Bunah, and Oren, and Ozem, *and* Ahijah.

26 Jerahmeel had also another wife, whose name *was* Atarah; she *was* the mother of Onam.

27 And the sons of Ram the firstborn of Jerahmeel were, Maaz, and Jamin, and Eker.

28 And the sons of Onam were, Shammai, and Jada. And the sons of Shammai; Nadab, and Abishur.

29 And the name of the wife of Abishur *was* Abihail, and she bare him Ahban, and Molid.

30 And the sons of Nadab; Seled, and Appaim: but Seled died without children.

31 And the sons of Appaim; Ishi. And the sons of Ishi; Sheshan. And the children of Sheshan; Ahlai.

32 And the sons of Jada the brother of Shammai; Jether, and Jonathan: and Jether died without children.

33 And the sons of Jonathan; Peleth, and Zaza. These were the sons of Jerahmeel.

34 Now Sheshan had no sons, but daughters. And Sheshan had a servant, an Egyptian, whose name *was* Jarha.

35 And Sheshan gave his daughter to Jarha his servant to wife; and she bare him Attai.

36 And Attai begat Nathan, and Nathan begat Zabad,

37 And Zabad begat Ephlal, and Ephlal begat Obed,

38 And Obed begat Jehu, and Jehu begat Azariah,

39 And Azariah begat Helez, and Helez begat Eleasah,

40 And Eleasah begat Sisamai, and
Sisamai begat Shallum,
41 And Shallum begat Jekamiah, and
Jekamiah begat Elishama.
42 Now the sons of Caleb the brother
of Jerahmeel *were*, Mesha his firstborn,
which was the father of Ziph; and the
sons of Mareshah the father of Hebron.
43 And the sons of Hebron; Korah,
and Tappuah, and Rekem, and Shema.
44 And Shema begat Raham, the
father of Jorkoam: and Rekem begat
Shammai.
45 And the son of Shammai *was*
Maon: and Maon *was* the father of
Beth-zur.
46 And Ephah, Caleb's concubine,
bare Haran, and Moza, and Gazez: and
Haran begat Gazez.
47 And the sons of Jahdai; Regem,
and Jotham, and Geshan, and Pelet,
and Ephah, and Shaaph.
48 Maachah, Caleb's concubine, bare
Sheber, and Tirhanah.
49 She bare also Shaaph the father of
Madmannah, Sheva the father of
Machbenah, and the father of Gibea:
and the daughter of Caleb *was* Achsah.
50 These were the sons of Caleb the
son of Hur, the firstborn of Ephratah;
Shobal the father of Kirjath-jearim,
51 Salma the father of Beth-lehem,
Hareph the father of Beth-gader.
52 And Shobal the father of Kirjath-
jearim had sons; Haroeh, *and* half of
the Manahethites.
53 And the families of Kirjath-jearim;
the Ithrites, and the Puhites, and the
Shumathites, and the Mishraites; of
them came the Zareathites, and the
Eshtaulites.
54 The sons of Salma; Beth-lehem,
and the Netophathites, Ataroth, the
house of Joab, and half of the
Manahethites, the Zorites.
55 And the families of the scribes
which dwelt at Jabez; the Tirathites, the
Shimeathites, *and* Suchathites. These
are the Kenites that came of Hemath,
the father of the house of Rechab.

3 Now these were the sons of David,
which were born unto him in
Hebron; the firstborn Amnon, of
Ahinoam the Jezreelitess; the second
Daniel, of Abigail the Carmelitess:
2 The third, Absalom the son of
Maachah the daughter of Talmai king
of Geshur: the fourth, Adonijah the son
of Haggith:
3 The fifth, Shephatiah of Abital: the
sixth, Ithream by Eglah his wife.
4 *These* six were born unto him in
Hebron; and there he reigned seven
years and six months: and in Jerusalem
he reigned thirty and three years.
5 And these were born unto him in
Jerusalem; Shimea, and Shobab, and
Nathan, and Solomon, four, of Bath-
shua the daughter of Ammiel:
6 Ibhar also, and Elishama, and
Eliphelet,
7 And Nogah, and Nepheg, and
Japhia,
8 And Elishama, and Eliada, and
Eliphelet, nine.
9 *These were* all the sons of David,
beside the sons of the concubines, and
Tamar their sister.
10 And Solomon's son *was* Rehoboam,
Abia his son, Asa his son, Jehoshaphat
his son,
11 Joram his son, Ahaziah his son,
Joash his son,
12 Amaziah his son, Azariah his son,
Jotham his son,
13 Ahaz his son, Hezekiah his son,
Manasseh his son,

14 Amon his son, Josiah his son.
15 And the sons of Josiah *were*, the
firstborn Johanan, the second Jehoiakim, the third Zedekiah, the fourth
Shallum.
16 And the sons of Jehoiakim:
Jeconiah his son, Zedekiah his son.
17 And the sons of Jeconiah; Assir,
Salathiel his son,
18 Malchiram also, and Pedaiah, and
Shenazar, Jecamiah, Hoshama, and
Nedabiah.
19 And the sons of Pedaiah *were*,
Zerubbabel, and Shimei: and the sons
of Zerubbabel; Meshullam, and
Hananiah, and Shelomith their sister:
20 And Hashubah, and Ohel, and
Berechiah, and Hasadiah, Jushab-
hesed, five.
21 And the sons of Hananiah;
Pelatiah, and Jesaiah: the sons of
Rephaiah, the sons of Arnan, the sons
of Obadiah, the sons of Shechaniah.
22 And the sons of Shechaniah;
Shemaiah: and the sons of Shemaiah;
Hattush, and Igeal, and Bariah, and
Neariah, and Shaphat, six.
23 And the sons of Neariah; Elioenai,
and Hezekiah, and Azrikam, three.
24 And the sons of Elioenai *were*,
Hodaiah, and Eliashib, and Pelaiah,
and Akkub, and Johanan, and Dalaiah,
and Anani, seven.

4 The sons of Judah; Pharez, Hezron,
and Carmi, and Hur, and Shobal.
2 And Reaiah the son of Shobal begat
Jahath; and Jahath begat Ahumai, and
Lahad. These *are* the families of the
Zorathites.
3 And these *were of* the father of
Etam; Jezreel, and Ishma, and Idbash:
and the name of their sister *was*
Hazelelponi:
4 And Penuel the father of Gedor, and
Ezer the father of Hushah. These *are*
the sons of Hur, the firstborn of
Ephratah, the father of Beth-lehem.
5 And Ashur the father of Tekoa had
two wives, Helah and Naarah.
6 And Naarah bare him Ahuzam, and
Hepher, and Temeni, and Haahashtari.
These *were* the sons of Naarah.
7 And the sons of Helah *were*, Zereth,
and Jezoar, and Ethnan.
8 And Coz begat Anub, and Zobebah,
and the families of Aharhel the son of
Harum.
9 And Jabez was more honourable
than his brethren: and his mother
called his name Jabez, saying, Because
I bare him with sorrow.
10 And Jabez called on the God of
Israel, saying, Oh that thou wouldest
bless me indeed, and enlarge my coast,
and that thine hand might be with me,
and that thou wouldest keep *me* from
evil, that it may not grieve me! And
God granted him that which he
requested.
11 And Chelub the brother of Shuah
begat Mehir, which *was* the father of
Eshton.
12 And Eshton begat Beth-rapha, and
Paseah, and Tehinnah the father of
Ir-nahash. These *are* the men of Rechah.
13 And the sons of Kenaz; Othniel,
and Seraiah: and the sons of Othniel;
Hathath.
14 And Meonothai begat Ophrah: and
Seraiah begat Joab, the father of the
valley of Charashim; for they were
craftsmen.
15 And the sons of Caleb the son of
Jephunneh; Iru, Elah, and Naam: and
the sons of Elah, even Kenaz.
16 And the sons of Jehaleleel; Ziph,
and Ziphah, Tiria, and Asareel.

17 And the sons of Ezra *were*, Jether, and Mered, and Epher, and Jalon: and she bare Miriam, and Shammai, and Ishbah the father of Eshtemoa.

18 And his wife Jehudijah bare Jered the father of Gedor, and Heber the father of Socho, and Jekuthiel the father of Zanoah. And these *are* the sons of Bithiah the daughter of Pharaoh, which Mered took.

19 And the sons of *his* wife Hodiah the sister of Naham, the father of Keilah the Garmite, and Eshtemoa the Maachathite.

20 And the sons of Shimon *were*, Amnon, and Rinnah, Ben-hanan, and Tilon. And the sons of Ishi *were*, Zoheth, and Ben-zoheth.

21 The sons of Shelah the son of Judah *were*, Er the father of Lecah, and Laadah the father of Mareshah, and the families of the house of them that wrought fine linen, of the house of Ashbea,

22 And Jokim, and the men of Chozeba, and Joash, and Saraph, who had the dominion in Moab, and Jashubi-lehem. And *these are* ancient things.

23 These *were* the potters, and those that dwelt among plants and hedges: there they dwelt with the king for his work.

24 The sons of Simeon *were*, Nemuel, and Jamin, Jarib, Zerah, *and* Shaul:

25 Shallum his son, Mibsam his son, Mishma his son.

26 And the sons of Mishma; Hamuel his son, Zacchur his son, Shimei his son.

27 And Shimei had sixteen sons and six daughters; but his brethren had not many children, neither did all their family multiply, like to the children of Judah.

28 And they dwelt at Beer-sheba, and Moladah, and Hazar-shual,

29 And at Bilhah, and at Ezem, and at Tolad,

30 And at Bethuel, and at Hormah, and at Ziklag,

31 And at Beth-marcaboth, and Hazar-susim, and at Beth-birei, and at Shaaraim. These *were* their cities unto the reign of David.

32 And their villages *were*, Etam, and Ain, Rimmon, and Tochen, and Ashan, five cities:

33 And all their villages that *were* round about the same cities, unto Baal. These *were* their habitations, and their genealogy.

34 And Meshobab, and Jamlech, and Joshah the son of Amaziah,

35 And Joel, and Jehu the son of Josibiah, the son of Seraiah, the son of Asiel,

36 And Elioenai, and Jaakobah, and Jeshohaiah, and Asaiah, and Adiel, and Jesimiel, and Benaiah,

37 And Ziza the son of Shiphi, the son of Allon, the son of Jedaiah, the son of Shimri, the son of Shemaiah;

38 These mentioned by *their* names *were* princes in their families: and the house of their fathers increased greatly.

39 And they went to the entrance of Gedor, *even* unto the east side of the valley, to seek pasture for their flocks.

40 And they found fat pasture and good, and the land *was* wide, and quiet, and peaceable; for *they* of Ham had dwelt there of old.

41 And these written by name came in the days of Hezekiah king of Judah, and smote their tents, and the habitations that were found there, and destroyed them utterly unto this day, and dwelt in their rooms: because *there* *was* pasture there for their flocks.

42 And *some* of them, *even* of the sons of Simeon, five hundred men, went to mount Seir, having for their captains Pelatiah, and Neariah, and Rephaiah, and Uzziel, the sons of Ishi.

43 And they smote the rest of the Amalekites that were escaped, and dwelt there unto this day.

5 Now the sons of Reuben the firstborn of Israel, (for he *was* the firstborn; but, forasmuch as he defiled his father's bed, his birthright was given unto the sons of Joseph the son of Israel: and the genealogy is not to be reckoned after the birthright.

2 For Judah prevailed above his brethren, and of him *came* the chief ruler; but the birthright *was* Joseph's:)

3 The sons, *I say*, of Reuben the firstborn of Israel *were*, Hanoch, and Pallu, Hezron, and Carmi.

4 The sons of Joel; Shemaiah his son, Gog his son, Shimei his son,

5 Micah his son, Reaia his son, Baal his son,

6 Beerah his son, whom Tilgath-pilneser king of Assyria carried away *captive*: he *was* prince of the Reubenites.

7 And his brethren by their families, when the genealogy of their generations was reckoned, *were* the chief, Jeiel, and Zechariah,

8 And Bela the son of Azaz, the son of Shema, the son of Joel, who dwelt in Aroer, even unto Nebo and Baal-meon:

9 And eastward he inhabited unto the entering in of the wilderness from the river Euphrates: because their cattle were multiplied in the land of Gilead.

10 And in the days of Saul they made war with the Hagarites, who fell by their hand: and they dwelt in their tents throughout all the east *land* of Gilead.

11 And the children of Gad dwelt over against them, in the land of Bashan unto Salchah:

12 Joel the chief, and Shapham the next, and Jaanai, and Shaphat in Bashan.

13 And their brethren of the house of their fathers *were*, Michael, and Meshullam, and Sheba, and Jorai, and Jachan, and Zia, and Heber, seven.

14 These *are* the children of Abihail the son of Huri, the son of Jaroah, the son of Gilead, the son of Michael, the son of Jeshishai, the son of Jahdo, the son of Buz;

15 Ahi the son of Abdiel, the son of Guni, chief of the house of their fathers.

16 And they dwelt in Gilead in Bashan, and in her towns, and in all the suburbs of Sharon, upon their borders.

17 All these were reckoned by genealogies in the days of Jotham king of Judah, and in the days of Jeroboam king of Israel.

18 The sons of Reuben, and the Gadites, and half the tribe of Manasseh, of valiant men, men able to bear buckler and sword, and to shoot with bow, and skilful in war, *were* four and forty thousand seven hundred and threescore, that went out to the war.

19 And they made war with the Hagarites, with Jetur, and Nephish, and Nodab.

20 And they were helped against them, and the Hagarites were delivered into their hand, and all that *were* with them: for they cried to God in the battle, and he was intreated of them; because they put their trust in him.

21 And they took away their cattle; of
their camels fifty thousand, and of
sheep two hundred and fifty thousand,
and of asses two thousand, and of men
an hundred thousand.
22 For there fell down many slain,
because the war *was* of God. And they
dwelt in their steads until the captivity.
23 And the children of the half tribe
of Manasseh dwelt in the land: they
increased from Bashan unto Baalhermon and Senir, and unto mount
Hermon.
24 And these *were* the heads of the
house of their fathers, even Epher, and
Ishi, and Eliel, and Azriel, and
Jeremiah, and Hodaviah, and Jahdiel,
mighty men of valour, famous men, *and*
heads of the house of their fathers.
25 And they transgressed against the
God of their fathers, and went a whoring after the gods of the people of the
land, whom God destroyed before
them.
26 And the God of Israel stirred up
the spirit of Pul king of Assyria, and the
spirit of Tilgath-pilneser king of
Assyria, and he carried them away,
even the Reubenites, and the Gadites,
and the half tribe of Manasseh, and
brought them unto Halah, and Habor,
and Hara, and to the river Gozan, unto
this day.

6 The sons of Levi; Gershon, Kohath,
and Merari.
2 And the sons of Kohath; Amram,
Izhar, and Hebron, and Uzziel.
3 And the children of Amram; Aaron,
and Moses, and Miriam. The sons also
of Aaron; Nadab, and Abihu, Eleazar,
and Ithamar.
4 Eleazar begat Phinehas, Phinehas
begat Abishua,
5 And Abishua begat Bukki, and
Bukki begat Uzzi,
6 And Uzzi begat Zerahiah, and
Zerahiah begat Meraioth,
7 Meraioth begat Amariah, and
Amariah begat Ahitub,
8 And Ahitub begat Zadok, and
Zadok begat Ahimaaz,
9 And Ahimaaz begat Azariah, and
Azariah begat Johanan,
10 And Johanan begat Azariah, (he *it*
is that executed the priest's office in
the temple that Solomon built in
Jerusalem:)
11 And Azariah begat Amariah, and
Amariah begat Ahitub,
12 And Ahitub begat Zadok, and
Zadok begat Shallum,
13 And Shallum begat Hilkiah, and
Hilkiah begat Azariah,
14 And Azariah begat Seraiah, and
Seraiah begat Jehozadak,
15 And Jehozadak went *into captivi-*
ty, when the LORD carried away Judah
and Jerusalem by the hand of Nebuchadnezzar.
16 The sons of Levi; Gershom, Kohath,
and Merari.
17 And these *be* the names of the sons
of Gershom; Libni, and Shimei.
18 And the sons of Kohath *were*,
Amram, and Izhar, and Hebron, and
Uzziel.
19 The sons of Merari; Mahli, and
Mushi. And these *are* the families of
the Levites according to their fathers.
20 Of Gershom; Libni his son, Jahath
his son, Zimmah his son,
21 Joah his son, Iddo his son, Zerah
his son, Jeaterai his son.
22 The sons of Kohath; Amminadab
his son, Korah his son, Assir his son,
23 Elkanah his son, and Ebiasaph his
son, and Assir his son,

24 Tahath his son, Uriel his son, Uzziah his son, and Shaul his son.

25 And the sons of Elkanah; Amasai, and Ahimoth.

26 *As for* Elkanah: the sons of Elkanah; Zophai his son, and Nahath his son,

27 Eliab his son, Jeroham his son, Elkanah his son.

28 And the sons of Samuel; the first-born Vashni, and Abiah.

29 The sons of Merari; Mahli, Libni his son, Shimei his son, Uzza his son,

30 Shimea his son, Haggiah his son, Asaiah his son.

31 And these *are they* whom David set over the service of song in the house of the LORD, after that the ark had rest.

32 And they ministered before the dwelling place of the tabernacle of the congregation with singing, until Solomon had built the house of the LORD in Jerusalem: and *then* they waited on their office according to their order.

33 And these *are* they that waited with their children. Of the sons of the Kohathites: Heman a singer, the son of Joel, the son of Shemuel,

34 The son of Elkanah, the son of Jeroham, the son of Eliel, the son of Toah,

35 The son of Zuph, the son of Elkanah, the son of Mahath, the son of Amasai,

36 The son of Elkanah, the son of Joel, the son of Azariah, the son of Zephaniah,

37 The son of Tahath, the son of Assir, the son of Ebiasaph, the son of Korah,

38 The son of Izhar, the son of Kohath, the son of Levi, the son of Israel.

39 And his brother Asaph, who stood on his right hand, *even* Asaph the son of Berachiah, the son of Shimea,

40 The son of Michael, the son of Baaseiah, the son of Malchiah,

41 The son of Ethni, the son of Zerah, the son of Adaiah,

42 The son of Ethan, the son of Zimmah, the son of Shimei,

43 The son of Jahath, the son of Gershom, the son of Levi.

44 And their brethren the sons of Merari *stood* on the left hand: Ethan the son of Kishi, the son of Abdi, the son of Malluch,

45 The son of Hashabiah, the son of Amaziah, the son of Hilkiah,

46 The son of Amzi, the son of Bani, the son of Shamer,

47 The son of Mahli, the son of Mushi, the son of Merari, the son of Levi.

48 Their brethren also the Levites *were* appointed unto all manner of service of the tabernacle of the house of God.

49 But Aaron and his sons offered upon the altar of the burnt offering, and on the altar of incense, *and were appointed* for all the work of the *place* most holy, and to make an atonement for Israel, according to all that Moses the servant of God had commanded.

50 And these *are* the sons of Aaron; Eleazar his son, Phinehas his son, Abishua his son,

51 Bukki his son, Uzzi his son, Zerahiah his son,

52 Meraioth his son, Amariah his son, Ahitub his son,

53 Zadok his son, Ahimaaz his son.

54 Now these *are* their dwelling places throughout their castles in their coasts, of the sons of Aaron, of the

families of the Kohathites: for theirs
was the lot.
55 And they gave them Hebron in the
land of Judah, and the suburbs thereof
round about it.
56 But the fields of the city, and the
villages thereof, they gave to Caleb the
son of Jephunneh.
57 And to the sons of Aaron they gave
the cities of Judah, *namely*, Hebron,
the city of refuge, and Libnah with her
suburbs, and Jattir, and Eshtemoa, with
their suburbs,
58 And Hilen with her suburbs, Debir
with her suburbs,
59 And Ashan with her suburbs, and
Beth-shemesh with her suburbs:
60 And out of the tribe of Benjamin;
Geba with her suburbs, and Alemeth
with her suburbs, and Anathoth with
her suburbs. All their cities throughout
their families *were* thirteen cities.
61 And unto the sons of Kohath,
which were left of the family of that
tribe, *were cities given* out of the half
tribe, *namely, out of* the half *tribe* of
Manasseh, by lot, ten cities.
62 And to the sons of Gershom
throughout their families out of the
tribe of Issachar, and out of the tribe of
Asher, and out of the tribe of Naphtali,
and out of the tribe of Manasseh in
Bashan, thirteen cities.
63 Unto the sons of Merari *were given*
by lot, throughout their families, out of
the tribe of Reuben, and out of the
tribe of Gad, and out of the tribe of
Zebulun, twelve cities.
64 And the children of Israel gave to
the Levites *these* cities with their suburbs.
65 And they gave by lot out of the
tribe of the children of Judah, and out
of the tribe of the children of Simeon,
and out of the tribe of the children of
Benjamin, these cities, which are called
by *their* names.
66 And *the residue* of the families of
the sons of Kohath had cities of their
coasts out of the tribe of Ephraim.
67 And they gave unto them, *of* the
cities of refuge, Shechem in mount
Ephraim with her suburbs; *they gave*
also Gezer with her suburbs,
68 And Jokmeam with her suburbs,
and Beth-horon with her suburbs,
69 And Aijalon with her suburbs, and
Gath-rimmon with her suburbs:
70 And out of the half tribe of
Manasseh; Aner with her suburbs, and
Bileam with her suburbs, for the family
of the remnant of the sons of Kohath.
71 Unto the sons of Gershom *were
given* out of the family of the half tribe
of Manasseh, Golan in Bashan with her
suburbs, and Ashtaroth with her suburbs:
72 And out of the tribe of Issachar;
Kedesh with her suburbs, Daberath
with her suburbs,
73 And Ramoth with her suburbs,
and Anem with her suburbs:
74 And out of the tribe of Asher;
Mashal with her suburbs, and Abdon
with her suburbs,
75 And Hukok with her suburbs, and
Rehob with her suburbs:
76 And out of the tribe of Naphtali;
Kedesh in Galilee with her suburbs,
and Hammon with her suburbs, and
Kirjathaim with her suburbs.
77 Unto the rest of the children of
Merari *were given* out of the tribe of
Zebulun, Rimmon with her suburbs,
Tabor with her suburbs:
78 And on the other side Jordan by
Jericho, on the east side of Jordan, *were
given them* out of the tribe of Reuben,

Bezer in the wilderness with her suburbs, and Jahzah with her suburbs,

79 Kedemoth also with her suburbs,
and Mephaath with her suburbs:

80 And out of the tribe of Gad;
Ramoth in Gilead with her suburbs,
and Mahanaim with her suburbs,

81 And Heshbon with her suburbs,
and Jazer with her suburbs.

7 Now the sons of Issachar *were*, Tola,
and Puah, Jashub, and Shimron,
four.

2 And the sons of Tola; Uzzi, and
Rephaiah, and Jeriel, and Jahmai, and
Jibsam, and Shemuel, heads of their
father's house, *to wit*, of Tola: *they were*
valiant men of might in their generations; whose number *was* in the days of
David two and twenty thousand and six
hundred.

3 And the sons of Uzzi; Izrahiah: and
the sons of Izrahiah; Michael, and
Obadiah, and Joel, Ishiah, five: all of
them chief men.

4 And with them, by their generations, after the house of their fathers,
were bands of soldiers for war, six and
thirty thousand *men*: for they had
many wives and sons.

5 And their brethren among all the
families of Issachar *were* valiant men of
might, reckoned in all by their genealogies fourscore and seven thousand.

6 *The sons* of Benjamin; Bela, and
Becher, and Jediael, three.

7 And the sons of Bela; Ezbon, and
Uzzi, and Uzziel, and Jerimoth, and Iri,
five; heads of the house of *their* fathers,
mighty men of valour; and were reckoned by their genealogies twenty and
two thousand and thirty and four.

8 And the sons of Becher; Zemira, and
Joash, and Eliezer, and Elioenai, and
Omri, and Jerimoth, and Abiah, and
Anathoth, and Alameth. All these *are*
the sons of Becher.

9 And the number of them, after their
genealogy by their generations, heads
of the house of their fathers, mighty
men of valour, *was* twenty thousand
and two hundred.

10 The sons also of Jediael; Bilhan:
and the sons of Bilhan; Jeush, and
Benjamin, and Ehud, and Chenaanah,
and Zethan, and Tharshish, and
Ahishahar.

11 All these the sons of Jediael, by
the heads of their fathers, mighty men
of valour, *were* seventeen thousand and
two hundred *soldiers*, fit to go out for
war *and* battle.

12 Shuppim also, and Huppim, the
children of Ir, *and* Hushim, the sons of
Aher.

13 The sons of Naphtali; Jahziel, and
Guni, and Jezer, and Shallum, the sons
of Bilhah.

14 The sons of Manasseh; Ashriel,
whom she bare: (*but* his concubine the
Aramitess bare Machir the father of
Gilead:

15 And Machir took to wife *the sister*
of Huppim and Shuppim, whose sister's
name *was* Maachah;) and the name of
the second *was* Zelophehad: and
Zelophehad had daughters.

16 And Maachah the wife of Machir
bare a son, and she called his name
Peresh; and the name of his brother
was Sheresh; and his sons *were* Ulam
and Rakem.

17 And the sons of Ulam; Bedan.
These *were* the sons of Gilead, the son
of Machir, the son of Manasseh.

18 And his sister Hammoleketh bare
Ishod, and Abiezer, and Mahalah.

19 And the sons of Shemida were,
Ahian, and Shechem, and Likhi, and
Aniam.
20 And the sons of Ephraim;
Shuthelah, and Bered his son, and
Tahath his son, and Eladah his son, and
Tahath his son,
21 And Zabad his son, and Shuthelah
his son, and Ezer, and Elead, whom the
men of Gath *that were* born in *that*
land slew, because they came down to
take away their cattle.
22 And Ephraim their father mourned many days, and his brethren came to
comfort him.
23 And when he went in to his wife,
she conceived, and bare a son, and he
called his name Beriah, because it went
evil with his house.
24 (And his daughter *was* Sherah,
who built Beth-horon the nether, and
the upper, and Uzzen-sherah.)
25 And Rephah *was* his son, also
Resheph, and Telah his son, and Tahan
his son,
26 Laadan his son, Ammihud his son,
Elishama his son,
27 Non his son, Jehoshua his son.
28 And their possessions and habitations *were*, Beth-el and the towns thereof, and eastward Naaran, and westward
Gezer, with the towns thereof; Shechem
also and the towns thereof, unto Gaza
and the towns thereof:
29 And by the borders of the children
of Manasseh, Beth-shean and her
towns, Taanach and her towns, Megiddo
and her towns, Dor and her towns. In
these dwelt the children of Joseph the
son of Israel.
30 The sons of Asher; Imnah, and
Isuah, and Ishuai, and Beriah, and
Serah their sister.
31 And the sons of Beriah; Heber, and
Malchiel, who *is* the father of Birzavith.
32 And Heber begat Japhlet, and
Shomer, and Hotham, and Shua their
sister.
33 And the sons of Japhlet; Pasach,
and Bimhal, and Ashvath. These *are* the
children of Japhlet.
34 And the sons of Shamer; Ahi, and
Rohgah, Jehubbah, and Aram.
35 And the sons of his brother Helem;
Zophah, and Imna, and Shelesh, and
Amal.
36 The sons of Zophah; Suah, and
Harnepher, and Shual, and Beri, and
Imrah,
37 Bezer, and Hod, and Shamma, and
Shilshah, and Ithran, and Beera.
38 And the sons of Jether; Jephunneh,
and Pispah, and Ara.
39 And the sons of Ulla; Arah, and
Haniel, and Rezia.
40 All these *were* the children of
Asher, heads of *their* father's house,
choice *and* mighty men of valour, chief
of the princes. And the number
throughout the genealogy of them that
were apt to the war *and* to battle *was*
twenty and six thousand men.

8 Now Benjamin begat Bela his
firstborn, Ashbel the second, and
Aharah the third,
2 Nohah the fourth, and Rapha the
fifth.
3 And the sons of Bela were, Addar,
and Gera, and Abihud,
4 And Abishua, and Naaman, and
Ahoah,
5 And Gera, and Shephuphan, and
Huram.
6 And these *are* the sons of Ehud:
these are the heads of the fathers of the
inhabitants of Geba, and they removed
them to Manahath:

7 And Naaman, and Ahiah, and Gera, he removed them, and begat Uzza, and Ahihud.

8 And Shaharaim begat *children* in the country of Moab, after he had sent them away; Hushim and Baara *were* his wives.

9 And he begat of Hodesh his wife, Jobab, and Zibia, and Mesha, and Malcham,

10 And Jeuz, and Shachia, and Mirma. These *were* his sons, heads of the fathers.

11 And of Hushim he begat Abitub, and Elpaal.

12 The sons of Elpaal; Eber, and Misham, and Shamed, who built Ono, and Lod, with the towns thereof:

13 Beriah also, and Shema, who *were* heads of the fathers of the inhabitants of Aijalon, who drove away the inhabitants of Gath:

14 And Ahio, Shashak, and Jeremoth,

15 And Zebadiah, and Arad, and Ader,

16 And Michael, and Ispah, and Joha, the sons of Beriah;

17 And Zebadiah, and Meshullam, and Hezeki, and Heber,

18 Ishmerai also, and Jezliah, and Jobab, the sons of Elpaal;

19 And Jakim, and Zichri, and Zabdi,

20 And Elienai, and Zilthai, and Eliel,

21 And Adaiah, and Beraiah, and Shimrath, the sons of Shimhi;

22 And Ishpan, and Heber, and Eliel,

23 And Abdon, and Zichri, and Hanan,

24 And Hananiah, and Elam, and Antothijah,

25 And Iphedeiah, and Penuel, the sons of Shashak;

26 And Shamsherai, and Shehariah, and Athaliah,

27 And Jaresiah, and Eliah, and Zichri, the sons of Jeroham.

28 These *were* heads of the fathers, by their generations, chief *men*. These dwelt in Jerusalem.

29 And at Gibeon dwelt the father of Gibeon; whose wife's name *was* Maachah:

30 And his firstborn son Abdon, and Zur, and Kish, and Baal, and Nadab,

31 And Gedor, and Ahio, and Zacher.

32 And Mikloth begat Shimeah. And these also dwelt with their brethren in Jerusalem, over against them.

33 And Ner begat Kish, and Kish begat Saul, and Saul begat Jonathan, and Malchi-shua, and Abinadab, and Esh-baal.

34 And the son of Jonathan *was* Merib-baal; and Merib-baal begat Micah.

35 And the sons of Micah *were*, Pithon, and Melech, and Tarea, and Ahaz.

36 And Ahaz begat Jehoadah; and Jehoadah begat Alemeth, and Azmaveth, and Zimri; and Zimri begat Moza,

37 And Moza begat Binea: Rapha *was* his son, Eleasah his son, Azel his son:

38 And Azel had six sons, whose names *are* these, Azrikam, Bocheru, and Ishmael, and Sheariah, and Obadiah, and Hanan. All these *were* the sons of Azel.

39 And the sons of Eshek his brother *were*, Ulam his firstborn, Jehush the second, and Eliphelet the third.

40 And the sons of Ulam were mighty men of valour, archers, and had many sons, and sons' sons, an hundred and fifty. All these *are* of the sons of Benjamin.

9 So all Israel were reckoned by
genealogies; and, behold, they *were*
written in the book of the kings of
Israel and Judah, *who* were carried
away to Babylon for their transgression.
2 Now the first inhabitants that *dwelt*
in their possessions in their cities *were*,
the Israelites, the priests, Levites, and
the Nethinims.
3 And in Jerusalem dwelt of the children of Judah, and of the children of
Benjamin, and of the children of
Ephraim, and Manasseh;
4 Uthai the son of Ammihud, the son
of Omri, the son of Imri, the son of Bani,
of the children of Pharez the son of
Judah.
5 And of the Shilonites; Asaiah the
firstborn, and his sons.
6 And of the sons of Zerah; Jeuel, and
their brethren, six hundred and ninety.
7 And of the sons of Benjamin; Sallu
the son of Meshullam, the son of
Hodaviah, the son of Hasenuah,
8 And Ibneiah the son of Jeroham,
and Elah the son of Uzzi, the son of
Michri, and Meshullam the son of
Shephathiah, the son of Reuel, the son
of Ibnijah;
9 And their brethren, according to
their generations, nine hundred and
fifty and six. All these men *were* chief
of the fathers in the house of their
fathers.
10 And of the priests; Jedaiah, and
Jehoiarib, and Jachin,
11 And Azariah the son of Hilkiah,
the son of Meshullam, the son of Zadok,
the son of Meraioth, the son of Ahitub,
the ruler of the house of God;
12 And Adaiah the son of Jeroham,
the son of Pashur, the son of Malchijah,
and Maasiai the son of Adiel, the son of
Jahzerah, the son of Meshullam, the
son of Meshillemith, the son of Immer;
13 And their brethren, heads of the
house of their fathers, a thousand and
seven hundred and threescore; very
able men for the work of the service of
the house of God.
14 And of the Levites; Shemaiah the
son of Hasshub, the son of Azrikam, the
son of Hashabiah, of the sons of Merari;
15 And Bakbakkar, Heresh, and
Galal, and Mattaniah the son of Micah,
the son of Zichri, the son of Asaph;
16 And Obadiah the son of Shemaiah,
the son of Galal, the son of Jeduthun,
and Berechiah the son of Asa, the son of
Elkanah, that dwelt in the villages of
the Netophathites.
17 And the porters *were*, Shallum,
and Akkub, and Talmon, and Ahiman,
and their brethren: Shallum *was* the
chief;
18 Who hitherto *waited* in the king's
gate eastward: they *were* porters in the
companies of the children of Levi.
19 And Shallum the son of Kore, the
son of Ebiasaph, the son of Korah, and
his brethren, of the house of his father,
the Korahites, *were* over the work of
the service, keepers of the gates of the
tabernacle: and their fathers, *being*
over the host of the LORD, *were* keepers
of the entry.
20 And Phinehas the son of Eleazar
was the ruler over them in time past,
and the LORD *was* with him.
21 *And* Zechariah the son of Meshelemiah *was* porter of the door of the
tabernacle of the congregation.
22 All these *which were* chosen to be
porters in the gates *were* two hundred
and twelve. These were reckoned by
their genealogy in their villages, whom

David and Samuel the seer did ordain
in their set office.
23 So they and their children *had* the
oversight of the gates of the house of
the LORD, *namely*, the house of the
tabernacle, by wards.
24 In four quarters were the porters,
toward the east, west, north, and south.
25 And their brethren, *which were* in
their villages, *were* to come after seven
days from time to time with them.
26 For these Levites, the four chief
porters, were in *their* set office, and
were over the chambers and treasuries
of the house of God.
27 And they lodged round about the
house of God, because the charge *was*
upon them, and the opening thereof
every morning *pertained* to them.
28 And *certain* of them had the
charge of the ministering vessels, that
they should bring them in and out by
tale.
29 *Some* of them also *were* appointed
to oversee the vessels, and all the
instruments of the sanctuary, and the
fine flour, and the wine, and the oil, and
the frankincense, and the spices.
30 And *some* of the sons of the priests
made the ointment of the spices.
31 And Mattithiah, *one* of the Levites,
who *was* the firstborn of Shallum the
Korahite, had the set office over the
things that were made in the pans.
32 And *other* of their brethren, of the
sons of the Kohathites, *were* over the
shewbread, to prepare *it* every sabbath.
33 And these *are* the singers, chief of
the fathers of the Levites, *who remaining* in the chambers *were* free: for they
were employed in *that* work day and
night.
34 These chief fathers of the Levites
were chief throughout their generations; these dwelt at Jerusalem.
35 And in Gibeon dwelt the father of
Gibeon, Jehiel, whose wife's name *was*
Maachah:
36 And his firstborn son Abdon, then
Zur, and Kish, and Baal, and Ner, and
Nadab,
37 And Gedor, and Ahio, and
Zechariah, and Mikloth.
38 And Mikloth begat Shimeam. And
they also dwelt with their brethren at
Jerusalem, over against their brethren.
39 And Ner begat Kish; and Kish
begat Saul; and Saul begat Jonathan,
and Malchi-shua, and Abinadab, and
Esh-baal.
40 And the son of Jonathan *was*
Merib-baal: and Merib-baal begat
Micah.
41 And the sons of Micah *were*,
Pithon, and Melech, and Tahrea, *and
Ahaz*.
42 And Ahaz begat Jarah; and Jarah
begat Alemeth, and Azmaveth, and
Zimri; and Zimri begat Moza;
43 And Moza begat Binea; and
Rephaiah his son, Eleasah his son, Azel
his son.
44 And Azel had six sons, whose
names *are* these, Azrikam, Bocheru,
and Ishmael, and Sheariah, and
Obadiah, and Hanan: these *were* the
sons of Azel.

10 Now the Philistines fought
against Israel; and the men of
Israel fled from before the Philistines,
and fell down slain in mount Gilboa.
2 And the Philistines followed hard
after Saul, and after his sons; and the
Philistines slew Jonathan, and Abinadab, and Malchi-shua, the sons of
Saul.

3 And the battle went sore against
Saul, and the archers hit him, and he
was wounded of the archers.
4 Then said Saul to his armourbearer,
Draw thy sword, and thrust me through
therewith; lest these uncircumcised
come and abuse me. But his armourbearer would not; for he was sore
afraid. So Saul took a sword, and fell
upon it.
5 And when his armourbearer saw
that Saul was dead, he fell likewise on
the sword, and died.
6 So Saul died, and his three sons, and
all his house died together.
7 And when all the men of Israel that
were in the valley saw that they fled,
and that Saul and his sons were dead,
then they forsook their cities, and fled:
and the Philistines came and dwelt in
them.
8 And it came to pass on the morrow,
when the Philistines came to strip the
slain, that they found Saul and his sons
fallen in mount Gilboa.
9 And when they had stripped him,
they took his head, and his armour, and
sent into the land of the Philistines
round about, to carry tidings unto their
idols, and to the people.
10 And they put his armour in the
house of their gods, and fastened his
head in the temple of Dagon.
11 And when all Jabesh-gilead heard
all that the Philistines had done to
Saul,
12 They arose, all the valiant men,
and took away the body of Saul, and the
bodies of his sons, and brought them to
Jabesh, and buried their bones under
the oak in Jabesh, and fasted seven
days.
13 So Saul died for his transgression
which he committed against the LORD,
even against the word of the LORD,
which he kept not, and also for asking
counsel of *one that had* a familiar
spirit, to enquire *of it*;
14 And enquired not of the LORD:
therefore he slew him, and turned the
kingdom unto David the son of Jesse.

11

Then all Israel gathered themselves to David unto Hebron,
saying, Behold, we *are* thy bone and thy
flesh.
2 And moreover in time past, even
when Saul was king, thou *wast* he that
leddest out and broughtest in Israel:
and the LORD thy God said unto thee,
Thou shalt feed my people Israel, and
thou shalt be ruler over my people
Israel.
3 Therefore came all the elders of
Israel to the king to Hebron; and David
made a covenant with them in Hebron
before the LORD; and they anointed
David king over Israel, according to the
word of the LORD by Samuel.
4 And David and all Israel went to
Jerusalem, which *is* Jebus; where the
Jebusites *were*, the inhabitants of the
land.
5 And the inhabitants of Jebus said to
David, Thou shalt not come hither.
Nevertheless David took the castle of
Zion, which *is* the city of David.
6 And David said, Whosoever smiteth
the Jebusites first shall be chief and
captain. So Joab the son of Zeruiah
went first up, and was chief.
7 And David dwelt in the castle;
therefore they called it the city of
David.
8 And he built the city round about,
even from Millo round about: and Joab
repaired the rest of the city.
9 So David waxed greater and greater: for the LORD of hosts *was* with him.

10 These also *are* the chief of the mighty men whom David had, who strengthened themselves with him in his kingdom, *and* with all Israel, to make him king, according to the word of the LORD concerning Israel.

11 And this *is* the number of the mighty men whom David had; Jashobeam, an Hachmonite, the chief of the captains: he lifted up his spear against three hundred slain *by him* at one time.

12 And after him *was* Eleazar the son of Dodo, the Ahohite, who *was one* of the three mighties.

13 He was with David at Pas-dammim, and there the Philistines were gathered together to battle, where was a parcel of ground full of barley; and the people fled from before the Philistines.

14 And they set themselves in the midst of *that* parcel, and delivered it, and slew the Philistines; and the LORD saved *them* by a great deliverance.

15 Now three of the thirty captains went down to the rock to David, into the cave of Adullam; and the host of the Philistines encamped in the valley of Rephaim.

16 And David *was* then in the hold, and the Philistines' garrison *was* then at Beth-lehem.

17 And David longed, and said, Oh that one would give me drink of the water of the well of Beth-lehem, that *is* at the gate!

18 And the three brake through the host of the Philistines, and drew water out of the well of Beth-lehem, that *was* by the gate, and took *it*, and brought *it* to David: but David would not drink *of* it, but poured it out to the LORD,

19 And said, My God forbid it me, that I should do this thing: shall I drink the blood of these men that have put their lives in jeopardy? for with *the jeopardy of* their lives they brought it. Therefore he would not drink it. These things did these three mightiest.

20 And Abishai the brother of Joab, he was chief of the three: for lifting up his spear against three hundred, he slew *them*, and had a name among the three.

21 Of the three, he was more honourable than the two; for he was their captain: howbeit he attained not to the *first* three.

22 Benaiah the son of Jehoiada, the son of a valiant man of Kabzeel, who had done many acts; he slew two lionlike men of Moab: also he went down and slew a lion in a pit in a snowy day.

23 And he slew an Egyptian, a man of *great* stature, five cubits high; and in the Egyptian's hand *was* a spear like a weaver's beam; and he went down to him with a staff, and plucked the spear out of the Egyptian's hand, and slew him with his own spear.

24 These *things* did Benaiah the son of Jehoiada, and had the name among the three mighties.

25 Behold, he was honourable among the thirty, but attained not to the *first* three: and David set him over his guard.

26 Also the valiant men of the armies *were*, Asahel the brother of Joab, Elhanan the son of Dodo of Beth-lehem,

27 Shammoth the Harorite, Helez the Pelonite,

28 Ira the son of Ikkesh the Tekoite, Abi-ezer the Antothite,

29 Sibbecai the Hushathite, Ilai the Ahohite,

30 Maharai the Netophathite, Heled
the son of Baanah the Netophathite,
31 Ithai the son of Ribai of Gibeah,
that pertained to the children of
Benjamin, Benaiah the Pirathonite,
32 Hurai of the brooks of Gaash,
Abiel the Arbathite,
33 Azmaveth the Baharumite, Eliahba the Shaalbonite,
34 The sons of Hashem the Gizonite,
Jonathan the son of Shage the Hararite,
35 Ahiam the son of Sacar the
Hararite, Eliphal the son of Ur,
36 Hepher the Mecherathite, Ahijah
the Pelonite,
37 Hezro the Carmelite, Naarai the
son of Ezbai,
38 Joel the brother of Nathan, Mibhar
the son of Haggeri,
39 Zelek the Ammonite, Naharai the
Berothite, the armourbearer of Joab
the son of Zeruiah,
40 Ira the Ithrite, Gareb the Ithrite,
41 Uriah the Hittite, Zabad the son of
Ahlai,
42 Adina the son of Shiza the
Reubenite, a captain of the Reubenites,
and thirty with him,
43 Hanan the son of Maachah, and
Joshaphat the Mithnite,
44 Uzzia the Ashterathite, Shama and
Jehiel the sons of Hothan the Aroerite,
45 Jediael the son of Shimri, and Joha
his brother, the Tizite,
46 Eliel the Mahavite, and Jeribai,
and Joshaviah, the sons of Elnaam, and
Ithmah the Moabite,
47 Eliel, and Obed, and Jasiel the
Mesobaite.

12 Now these *are* they that came to
David to Ziklag, while he yet
kept himself close because of Saul the
son of Kish: and they *were* among the
mighty men, helpers of the war.
2 *They were* armed with bows, and
could use both the right hand and the
left in *hurling* stones and *shooting*
arrows out of a bow, *even* of Saul's
brethren of Benjamin.
3 The chief *was* Ahiezer, then Joash,
the sons of Shemaah the Gibeathite;
and Jeziel, and Pelet, the sons of
Azmaveth; and Berachah, and Jehu the
Antothite,
4 And Ismaiah the Gibeonite, a
mighty man among the thirty, and over
the thirty; and Jeremiah, and Jahaziel,
and Johanan, and Josabad the Geder-
athite,
5 Eluzai, and Jerimoth, and Bealiah,
and Shemariah, and Shephatiah the
Haruphite,
6 Elkanah, and Jesiah, and Azareel,
and Joezer, and Jashobeam, the Korhites,
7 And Joelah, and Zebadiah, the sons
of Jeroham of Gedor.
8 And of the Gadites there separated
themselves unto David into the hold to
the wilderness men of might, *and* men
of war *fit* for the battle, that could
handle shield and buckler, whose faces
were like the faces of lions, and *were* as
swift as the roes upon the mountains;
9 Ezer the first, Obadiah the second,
Eliab the third,
10 Mishmannah the fourth, Jeremiah
the fifth,
11 Attai the sixth, Eliel the seventh,
12 Johanan the eighth, Elzabad the
ninth,
13 Jeremiah the tenth, Machbanai
the eleventh.
14 These *were* of the sons of Gad,
captains of the host: one of the least
was over an hundred, and the greatest
over a thousand.
15 These *are* they that went over
Jordan in the first month, when it had

overflown all his banks; and they put to
flight all *them* of the valleys, *both*
toward the east, and toward the west.
16 And there came of the children of
Benjamin and Judah to the hold unto
David.
17 And David went out to meet them,
and answered and said unto them, If ye
be come peaceably unto me to help me,
mine heart shall be knit unto you: but
if *ye be come* to betray me to mine
enemies, seeing *there is* no wrong in
mine hands, the God of our fathers look
thereon, and rebuke *it*.
18 Then the spirit came upon Amasai,
who was chief of the captains, *and he*
said, Thine *are we*, David, and on thy
side, thou son of Jesse: peace, peace *be*
unto thee, and peace *be* to thine helpers; for thy God helpeth thee. Then
David received them, and made them
captains of the band.
19 And there fell *some* of Manasseh
to David, when he came with the
Philistines against Saul to battle: but
they helped them not: for the lords of
the Philistines upon advisement sent
him away, saying, He will fall to his
master Saul to *the jeopardy of* our
heads.
20 As he went to Ziklag, there fell to
him of Manasseh, Adnah, and Jozabad,
and Jediael, and Michael, and Jozabad,
and Elihu, and Zilthai, captains of the
thousands that *were* of Manasseh.
21 And they helped David against the
band *of the rovers*: for they *were* all
mighty men of valour, and were captains in the host.
22 For at *that* time day by day there
came to David to help him, until *it was*
a great host, like the host of God.
23 And these *are* the numbers of the
bands *that were* ready armed to the
war, *and* came to David to Hebron, to
turn the kingdom of Saul to him,
according to the word of the LORD.
24 The children of Judah that bare
shield and spear *were* six thousand and
eight hundred, ready armed to the war.
25 Of the children of Simeon, mighty
men of valour for the war, seven thousand and one hundred.
26 Of the children of Levi four thousand and six hundred.
27 And Jehoiada *was* the leader of
the Aaronites, and with him *were* three
thousand and seven hundred;
28 And Zadok, a young man mighty of
valour, and of his father's house twenty
and two captains.
29 And of the children of Benjamin,
the kindred of Saul, three thousand: for
hitherto the greatest part of them had
kept the ward of the house of Saul.
30 And of the children of Ephraim
twenty thousand and eight hundred,
mighty men of valour, famous throughout the house of their fathers.
31 And of the half tribe of Manasseh
eighteen thousand, which were
expressed by name, to come and make
David king.
32 And of the children of Issachar,
which were men that had understanding of the times, to know what Israel
ought to do; the heads of them *were* two
hundred; and all their brethren *were* at
their commandment.
33 Of Zebulun, such as went forth to
battle, expert in war, with all instruments of war, fifty thousand, which
could keep rank: *they were* not of double heart.
34 And of Naphtali a thousand captains, and with them with shield and
spear thirty and seven thousand.
35 And of the Danites expert in war
twenty and eight thousand and six hundred.

36 And of Asher, such as went forth to
battle, expert in war, forty thousand.
37 And on the other side of Jordan, of
the Reubenites, and the Gadites, and of
the half tribe of Manasseh, with all
manner of instruments of war for the
battle, an hundred and twenty thousand.
38 All these men of war, that could
keep rank, came with a perfect heart to
Hebron, to make David king over all
Israel: and all the rest also of Israel
were of one heart to make David king.
39 And there they were with David
three days, eating and drinking: for
their brethren had prepared for them.
40 Moreover they that were nigh
them, *even* unto Issachar and Zebulun
and Naphtali, brought bread on asses,
and on camels, and on mules, and on
oxen, *and* meat, meal, cakes of figs, and
bunches of raisins, and wine, and oil,
and oxen, and sheep abundantly: for
there was joy in Israel.

13 And David consulted with the
captains of thousands and hundreds, *and* with every leader.
2 And David said unto all the congregation of Israel, If *it seem* good unto
you, and *that it be* of the LORD our God,
let us send abroad unto our brethren
every where, *that are* left in all the
land of Israel, and with them *also* to the
priests and Levites *which are* in their
cities *and* suburbs, that they may gather themselves unto us:
3 And let us bring again the ark of our
God to us: for we enquired not at it in
the days of Saul.
4 And all the congregation said that
they would do so: for the thing was
right in the eyes of all the people.
5 So David gathered all Israel together, from Shihor of Egypt even unto the
entering of Hemath, to bring the ark of
God from Kirjath-jearim.
6 And David went up, and all Israel, to
Baalah, *that is*, to Kirjath-jearim,
which *belonged* to Judah, to bring up
thence the ark of God the LORD, that
dwelleth *between* the cherubims,
whose name is called *on it*.
7 And they carried the ark of God in
a new cart out of the house of Abinadab:
and Uzza and Ahio drave the cart.
8 And David and all Israel played
before God with all *their* might, and
with singing, and with harps, and with
psalteries, and with timbrels, and with
cymbals, and with trumpets.
9 And when they came unto the
threshingfloor of Chidon, Uzza put
forth his hand to hold the ark; for the
oxen stumbled.
10 And the anger of the LORD was
kindled against Uzza, and he smote
him, because he put his hand to the
ark: and there he died before God.
11 And David was displeased,
because the LORD had made a breach
upon Uzza: wherefore that place is
called Perez-uzza to this day.
12 And David was afraid of God that
day, saying, How shall I bring the ark of
God *home* to me?
13 So David brought not the ark *home*
to himself to the city of David, but carried it aside into the house of Obed-
edom the Gittite.
14 And the ark of God remained with
the family of Obed-edom in his house
three months. And the LORD blessed
the house of Obed-edom, and all that
he had.

14 Now Hiram king of Tyre sent
messengers to David, and timber
of cedars, with masons and carpenters,
to build him an house.

2 And David perceived that the LORD
had confirmed him king over Israel, for
his kingdom was lifted up on high,
because of his people Israel.
3 And David took more wives at
Jerusalem: and David begat more sons
and daughters.
4 Now these *are* the names of *his*
children which he had in Jerusalem;
Shammua, and Shobab, Nathan, and
Solomon,
5 And Ibhar, and Elishua, and Elpalet,
6 And Nogah, and Nepheg, and
Japhia,
7 And Elishama, and Beeliada, and
Eliphalet.
8 And when the Philistines heard
that David was anointed king over all
Israel, all the Philistines went up to
seek David. And David heard *of it*, and
went out against them.
9 And the Philistines came and
spread themselves in the valley of
Rephaim.
10 And David enquired of God, saying, Shall I go up against the Philistines?
and wilt thou deliver them into mine
hand? And the LORD said unto him, Go
up; for I will deliver them into thine
hand.
11 So they came up to Baal-perazim;
and David smote them there. Then
David said, God hath broken in upon
mine enemies by mine hand like the
breaking forth of waters: therefore they
called the name of that place Baal-
perazim.
12 And when they had left their gods
there, David gave a commandment, and
they were burned with fire.
13 And the Philistines yet again
spread themselves abroad in the valley.
14 Therefore David enquired again of
God; and God said unto him, Go not up
after them; turn away from them, and
come upon them over against the mulberry trees.
15 And it shall be, when thou shalt
hear a sound of going in the tops of the
mulberry trees, *that* then thou shalt go
out to battle: for God is gone forth
before thee to smite the host of the
Philistines.
16 David therefore did as God commanded him: and they smote the host
of the Philistines from Gibeon even to
Gazer.
17 And the fame of David went out
into all lands; and the LORD brought the
fear of him upon all nations.

15 And *David* made him houses in
the city of David, and prepared a
place for the ark of God, and pitched
for it a tent.
2 Then David said, None ought to
carry the ark of God but the Levites: for
them hath the LORD chosen to carry the
ark of God, and to minister unto him
for ever.
3 And David gathered all Israel
together to Jerusalem, to bring up the
ark of the LORD unto his place, which
he had prepared for it.
4 And David assembled the children
of Aaron, and the Levites:
5 Of the sons of Kohath; Uriel the
chief, and his brethren an hundred and
twenty:
6 Of the sons of Merari; Asaiah the
chief, and his brethren two hundred
and twenty:
7 Of the sons of Gershom; Joel the
chief, and his brethren an hundred and
thirty:
8 Of the sons of Elizaphan; Shemaiah
the chief, and his brethren two hundred:

9 Of the sons of Hebron; Eliel the
chief, and his brethren fourscore:
10 Of the sons of Uzziel; Amminadab
the chief, and his brethren an hundred
and twelve.
11 And David called for Zadok and
Abiathar the priests, and for the
Levites, for Uriel, Asaiah, and Joel,
Shemaiah, and Eliel, and Amminadab,
12 And said unto them, Ye *are* the
chief of the fathers of the Levites: sanctify yourselves, *both* ye and your brethren, that ye may bring up the ark of the
LORD God of Israel unto *the place that*
I have prepared for it.
13 For because ye *did it* not at the
first, the LORD our God made a breach
upon us, for that we sought him not
after the due order.
14 So the priests and the Levites
sanctified themselves to bring up the
ark of the LORD God of Israel.
15 And the children of the Levites
bare the ark of God upon their shoulders with the staves thereon, as Moses
commanded according to the word of
the LORD.
16 And David spake to the chief of
the Levites to appoint their brethren *to
be* the singers with instruments of
musick, psalteries and harps and cymbals, sounding, by lifting up the voice
with joy.
17 So the Levites appointed Heman
the son of Joel; and of his brethren,
Asaph the son of Berechiah; and of the
sons of Merari their brethren, Ethan
the son of Kushaiah;
18 And with them their brethren of
the second *degree*, Zechariah, Ben, and
Jaaziel, and Shemiramoth, and Jehiel,
and Unni, Eliab, and Benaiah, and
Maaseiah, and Mattithiah, and Elipheleh, and Mikneiah, and Obed-edom,
and Jeiel, the porters.
19 So the singers, Heman, Asaph, and
Ethan, *were appointed* to sound with
cymbals of brass;
20 And Zechariah, and Aziel, and
Shemiramoth, and Jehiel, and Unni,
and Eliab, and Maaseiah, and Benaiah,
with psalteries on Alamoth;
21 And Mattithiah, and Elipheleh,
and Mikneiah, and Obed-edom, and
Jeiel, and Azaziah, with harps on the
Sheminith to excel.
22 And Chenaniah, chief of the
Levites, *was* for song: he instructed
about the song, because he *was* skilful.
23 And Berechiah and Elkanah *were*
doorkeepers for the ark.
24 And Shebaniah, and Jehoshaphat,
and Nethaneel, and Amasai, and
Zechariah, and Benaiah, and Eliezer,
the priests, did blow with the trumpets
before the ark of God: and Obed-edom
and Jehiah *were* doorkeepers for the
ark.
25 So David, and the elders of Israel,
and the captains over thousands, went
to bring up the ark of the covenant of
the LORD out of the house of Obed-
edom with joy.
26 And it came to pass, when God
helped the Levites that bare the ark of
the covenant of the LORD, that they
offered seven bullocks and seven rams.
27 And David *was* clothed with a robe
of fine linen, and all the Levites that
bare the ark, and the singers, and
Chenaniah the master of the song with
the singers: David also *had* upon him
an ephod of linen.
28 Thus all Israel brought up the ark
of the covenant of the LORD with shouting, and with sound of the cornet, and

with trumpets, and with cymbals, making a noise with psalteries and harps.
29 And it came to pass, *as* the ark of
the covenant of the LORD came to the
city of David, that Michal the daughter
of Saul looking out at a window saw
king David dancing and playing: and
she despised him in her heart.

16 So they brought the ark of God,
and set it in the midst of the tent
that David had pitched for it: and they
offered burnt sacrifices and peace
offerings before God.
2 And when David had made an end
of offering the burnt offerings and the
peace offerings, he blessed the people
in the name of the LORD.
3 And he dealt to every one of Israel,
both man and woman, to every one a
loaf of bread, and a good piece of flesh,
and a flagon *of wine*.
4 And he appointed *certain* of the
Levites to minister before the ark of
the LORD, and to record, and to thank
and praise the LORD God of Israel:
5 Asaph the chief, and next to him
Zechariah, Jeiel, and Shemiramoth,
and Jehiel, and Mattithiah, and Eliab,
and Benaiah, and Obed-edom: and
Jeiel with psalteries and with harps;
but Asaph made a sound with cymbals;
6 Benaiah also and Jahaziel the
priests with trumpets continually
before the ark of the covenant of God.
7 Then on that day David delivered
first *this psalm* to thank the LORD into
the hand of Asaph and his brethren.
8 Give thanks unto the LORD, call
upon his name, make known his deeds
among the people.
9 Sing unto him, sing psalms unto
him, talk ye of all his wondrous works.
10 Glory ye in his holy name: let the
heart of them rejoice that seek the
LORD.
11 Seek the LORD and his strength,
seek his face continually.
12 Remember his marvellous works
that he hath done, his wonders, and the
judgments of his mouth;
13 O ye seed of Israel his servant, ye
children of Jacob, his chosen ones.
14 He *is* the LORD our God; his judgments *are* in all the earth.
15 Be ye mindful always of his covenant; the word *which* he commanded to
a thousand generations;
16 *Even of the covenant* which he
made with Abraham, and of his oath
unto Isaac;
17 And hath confirmed the same to
Jacob for a law, *and* to Israel *for* an
everlasting covenant,
18 Saying, Unto thee will I give the
land of Canaan, the lot of your inheritance;
19 When ye were but few, even a few,
and strangers in it.
20 And *when* they went from nation
to nation, and from *one* kingdom to
another people;
21 He suffered no man to do them
wrong: yea, he reproved kings for their
sakes,
22 *Saying*, Touch not mine anointed,
and do my prophets no harm.
23 Sing unto the LORD, all the earth;
shew forth from day to day his salvation.
24 Declare his glory among the heathen; his marvellous works among all
nations.
25 For great *is* the LORD, and greatly
to be praised: he also *is* to be feared
above all gods.

26 For all the gods of the people *are* idols: but the LORD made the heavens.

27 Glory and honour *are* in his presence; strength and gladness *are* in his place.

28 Give unto the LORD, ye kindreds of the people, give unto the LORD glory and strength.

29 Give unto the LORD the glory *due* unto his name: bring an offering, and come before him: worship the LORD in the beauty of holiness.

30 Fear before him, all the earth: the world also shall be stable, that it be not moved.

31 Let the heavens be glad, and let the earth rejoice: and let *men* say among the nations, The LORD reigneth.

32 Let the sea roar, and the fulness thereof: let the fields rejoice, and all that *is* therein.

33 Then shall the trees of the wood sing out at the presence of the LORD, because he cometh to judge the earth.

34 O give thanks unto the LORD; for *he is* good; for his mercy *endureth* for ever.

35 And say ye, Save us, O God of our salvation, and gather us together, and deliver us from the heathen, that we may give thanks to thy holy name, *and* glory in thy praise.

36 Blessed *be* the LORD God of Israel for ever and ever. And all the people said, Amen, and praised the LORD.

37 So he left there before the ark of the covenant of the LORD Asaph and his brethren, to minister before the ark continually, as every day's work required:

38 And Obed-edom with their brethren, threescore and eight; Obed-edom also the son of Jeduthun and Hosah *to be* porters:

39 And Zadok the priest, and his brethren the priests, before the tabernacle of the LORD in the high place that *was* at Gibeon,

40 To offer burnt offerings unto the LORD upon the altar of the burnt offering continually morning and evening, and *to do* according to all that is written in the law of the LORD, which he commanded Israel;

41 And with them Heman and Jeduthun, and the rest that were chosen, who were expressed by name, to give thanks to the LORD, because his mercy *endureth* for ever;

42 And with them Heman and Jeduthun with trumpets and cymbals for those that should make a sound, and with musical instruments of God. And the sons of Jeduthun *were* porters.

43 And all the people departed every man to his house: and David returned to bless his house.

17

Now it came to pass, as David sat in his house, that David said to Nathan the prophet, Lo, I dwell in an house of cedars, but the ark of the covenant of the LORD *remaineth* under curtains.

2 Then Nathan said unto David, Do all that *is* in thine heart; for God *is* with thee.

3 And it came to pass the same night, that the word of God came to Nathan, saying,

4 Go and tell David my servant, Thus saith the LORD, Thou shalt not build me an house to dwell in:

5 For I have not dwelt in an house since the day that I brought up Israel unto this day; but have gone from tent to tent, and from *one* tabernacle *to another*.

6 Wheresoever I have walked with all
Israel, spake I a word to any of the
judges of Israel, whom I commanded to
feed my people, saying, Why have ye
not built me an house of cedars?
7 Now therefore thus shalt thou say
unto my servant David, Thus saith the
LORD of hosts, I took thee from the
sheepcote, *even* from following the
sheep, that thou shouldest be ruler over
my people Israel:
8 And I have been with thee whithersoever thou hast walked, and have cut
off all thine enemies from before thee,
and have made thee a name like the
name of the great men that *are* in the
earth.
9 Also I will ordain a place for my
people Israel, and will plant them, and
they shall dwell in their place, and shall
be moved no more; neither shall the
children of wickedness waste them any
more, as at the beginning,
10 And since the time that I commanded judges *to be* over my people
Israel. Moreover I will subdue all thine
enemies. Furthermore I tell thee that
the LORD will build thee an house.
11 And it shall come to pass, when thy
days be expired that thou must go *to be*
with thy fathers, that I will raise up thy
seed after thee, which shall be of thy
sons; and I will establish his kingdom.
12 He shall build me an house, and I
will stablish his throne for ever.
13 I will be his father, and he shall be
my son: and I will not take my mercy
away from him, as I took *it* from *him*
that was before thee:
14 But I will settle him in mine house
and in my kingdom for ever: and his
throne shall be established for evermore.
15 According to all these words, and
according to all this vision, so did
Nathan speak unto David.
16 And David the king came and sat
before the LORD, and said, Who *am* I, O
LORD God, and what *is* mine house, that
thou hast brought me hitherto?
17 And *yet* this was a small thing in
thine eyes, O God; for thou hast *also*
spoken of thy servant's house for a
great while to come, and hast regarded
me according to the estate of a man of
high degree, O LORD God.
18 What can David *speak* more to
thee for the honour of thy servant? for
thou knowest thy servant.
19 O LORD, for thy servant's sake, and
according to thine own heart, hast thou
done all this greatness, in making
known all *these* great things.
20 O LORD, *there is* none like thee,
neither *is there any* God beside thee,
according to all that we have heard
with our ears.
21 And what one nation in the earth
is like thy people Israel, whom God
went to redeem *to be* his own people, to
make thee a name of greatness and terribleness, by driving out nations from
before thy people, whom thou hast
redeemed out of Egypt?
22 For thy people Israel didst thou
make thine own people for ever; and
thou, LORD, becamest their God.
23 Therefore now, LORD, let the thing
that thou hast spoken concerning thy
servant and concerning his house be
established for ever, and do as thou
hast said.
24 Let it even be established, that thy
name may be magnified for ever, saying, The LORD of hosts *is* the God of
Israel, *even* a God to Israel: and *let* the

house of David thy servant *be* established before thee.
25 For thou, O my God, hast told thy
servant that thou wilt build him an
house: therefore thy servant hath found
in his heart to pray before thee.
26 And now, LORD, thou art God, and
hast promised this goodness unto thy
servant:
27 Now therefore let it please thee to
bless the house of thy servant, that it
may be before thee for ever: for thou
blessest, O LORD, and *it shall be* blessed
for ever.

18 Now after this it came to pass,
that David smote the Philistines,
and subdued them, and took Gath and
her towns out of the hand of the
Philistines.
2 And he smote Moab; and the
Moabites became David's servants, *and*
brought gifts.
3 And David smote Hadarezer king of
Zobah unto Hamath, as he went to stablish his dominion by the river
Euphrates.
4 And David took from him a thousand chariots, and seven thousand
horsemen, and twenty thousand footmen: David also houghed all the chariot *horses*, but reserved of them an hundred chariots.
5 And when the Syrians of Damascus
came to help Hadarezer king of Zobah,
David slew of the Syrians two and
twenty thousand men.
6 Then David put *garrisons* in Syria-
damascus; and the Syrians became
David's servants, *and* brought gifts.
Thus the LORD preserved David whithersoever he went.
7 And David took the shields of gold
that were on the servants of Hadarezer,
and brought them to Jerusalem.
8 Likewise from Tibhath, and from
Chun, cities of Hadarezer, brought
David very much brass, wherewith
Solomon made the brasen sea, and the
pillars, and the vessels of brass.
9 Now when Tou king of Hamath
heard how David had smitten all the
host of Hadarezer king of Zobah;
10 He sent Hadoram his son to king
David, to enquire of his welfare, and to
congratulate him, because he had
fought against Hadarezer, and smitten
him; (for Hadarezer had war with Tou;)
and *with him* all manner of vessels of
gold and silver and brass.
11 Them also king David dedicated
unto the LORD, with the silver and the
gold that he brought from all *these*
nations; from Edom, and from Moab,
and from the children of Ammon, and
from the Philistines, and from Amalek.
12 Moreover Abishai the son of
Zeruiah slew of the Edomites in the
valley of salt eighteen thousand.
13 And he put garrisons in Edom; and
all the Edomites became David's servants. Thus the LORD preserved David
whithersoever he went.
14 So David reigned over all Israel,
and executed judgment and justice
among all his people.
15 And Joab the son of Zeruiah *was*
over the host; and Jehoshaphat the son
of Ahilud, recorder.
16 And Zadok the son of Ahitub, and
Abimelech the son of Abiathar, *were*
the priests; and Shavsha was scribe;
17 And Benaiah the son of Jehoiada
was over the Cherethites and the
Pelethites; and the sons of David *were*
chief about the king.

19 Now it came to pass after this, that Nahash the king of the children of Ammon died, and his son reigned in his stead.
2 And David said, I will shew kindness unto Hanun the son of Nahash, because his father shewed kindness to me. And David sent messengers to comfort him concerning his father. So the servants of David came into the land of the children of Ammon to Hanun, to comfort him.
3 But the princes of the children of Ammon said to Hanun, Thinkest thou that David doth honour thy father, that he hath sent comforters unto thee? are not his servants come unto thee for to search, and to overthrow, and to spy out the land?
4 Wherefore Hanun took David's servants, and shaved them, and cut off their garments in the midst hard by their buttocks, and sent them away.
5 Then there went *certain*, and told David how the men were served. And he sent to meet them: for the men were greatly ashamed. And the king said, Tarry at Jericho until your beards be grown, and *then* return.
6 And when the children of Ammon saw that they had made themselves odious to David, Hanun and the children of Ammon sent a thousand talents of silver to hire them chariots and horsemen out of Mesopotamia, and out of Syria-maachah, and out of Zobah.
7 So they hired thirty and two thousand chariots, and the king of Maachah and his people; who came and pitched before Medeba. And the children of Ammon gathered themselves together from their cities, and came to battle.
8 And when David heard *of it*, he sent Joab, and all the host of the mighty men.
9 And the children of Ammon came out, and put the battle in array before the gate of the city: and the kings that were come *were* by themselves in the field.
10 Now when Joab saw that the battle was set against him before and behind, he chose out of all the choice of Israel, and put *them* in array against the Syrians.
11 And the rest of the people he delivered unto the hand of Abishai his brother, and they set *themselves* in array against the children of Ammon.
12 And he said, If the Syrians be too strong for me, then thou shalt help me: but if the children of Ammon be too strong for thee, then I will help thee.
13 Be of good courage, and let us behave ourselves valiantly for our people, and for the cities of our God: and let the LORD do *that which is* good in his sight.
14 So Joab and the people that *were* with him drew nigh before the Syrians unto the battle; and they fled before him.
15 And when the children of Ammon saw that the Syrians were fled, they likewise fled before Abishai his brother, and entered into the city. Then Joab came to Jerusalem.
16 And when the Syrians saw that they were put to the worse before Israel, they sent messengers, and drew forth the Syrians that *were* beyond the river: and Shophach the captain of the host of Hadarezer *went* before them.
17 And it was told David; and he gathered all Israel, and passed over Jordan, and came upon them, and set *the battle*

in array against them. So when David had put the battle in array against the Syrians, they fought with him.

18 But the Syrians fled before Israel; and David slew of the Syrians seven thousand *men which fought in* chariots, and forty thousand footmen, and killed Shophach the captain of the host.

19 And when the servants of Hadarezer saw that they were put to the worse before Israel, they made peace with David, and became his servants: neither would the Syrians help the children of Ammon any more.

20

And it came to pass, that after the year was expired, at the time that kings go out *to battle*, Joab led forth the power of the army, and wasted the country of the children of Ammon, and came and besieged Rabbah. But David tarried at Jerusalem. And Joab smote Rabbah, and destroyed it.

2 And David took the crown of their king from off his head, and found it to weigh a talent of gold, and *there were* precious stones in it; and it was set upon David's head: and he brought also exceeding much spoil out of the city.

3 And he brought out the people that *were* in it, and cut *them* with saws, and with harrows of iron, and with axes. Even so dealt David with all the cities of the children of Ammon. And David and all the people returned to Jerusalem.

4 And it came to pass after this, that there arose war at Gezer with the Philistines; at which time Sibbechai the Hushathite slew Sippai, *that was* of the children of the giant: and they were subdued.

5 And there was war again with the Philistines; and Elhanan the son of Jair slew Lahmi the brother of Goliath the Gittite, whose spear staff *was* like a weaver's beam.

6 And yet again there was war at Gath, where was a man of *great* stature, whose fingers and toes *were* four and twenty, six *on each hand*, and six *on each foot*: and he also was the son of the giant.

7 But when he defied Israel, Jonathan the son of Shimea David's brother slew him.

8 These were born unto the giant in Gath; and they fell by the hand of David, and by the hand of his servants.

21

And Satan stood up against Israel, and provoked David to number Israel.

2 And David said to Joab and to the rulers of the people, Go, number Israel from Beer-sheba even to Dan; and bring the number of them to me, that I may know *it*.

3 And Joab answered, The LORD make his people an hundred times so many more as they *be*: but, my lord the king, *are* they not all my lord's servants? why then doth my lord require this thing? why will he be a cause of trespass to Israel?

4 Nevertheless the king's word prevailed against Joab. Wherefore Joab departed, and went throughout all Israel, and came to Jerusalem.

5 And Joab gave the sum of the number of the people unto David. And all *they of* Israel were a thousand thousand and an hundred thousand men that drew sword: and Judah *was* four hundred threescore and ten thousand men that drew sword.

6 But Levi and Benjamin counted he not among them: for the king's word was abominable to Joab.

7 And God was displeased with this thing; therefore he smote Israel.

8 And David said unto God, I have sinned greatly, because I have done this thing: but now, I beseech thee, do away the iniquity of thy servant; for I have done very foolishly.

9 And the LORD spake unto Gad, David's seer, saying,

10 Go and tell David, saying, Thus saith the LORD, I offer thee three *things*: choose thee one of them, that I may do *it* unto thee.

11 So Gad came to David, and said unto him, Thus saith the LORD, Choose thee

12 Either three years' famine; or three months to be destroyed before thy foes, while that the sword of thine enemies overtaketh *thee*; or else three days the sword of the LORD, even the pestilence, in the land, and the angel of the LORD destroying throughout all the coasts of Israel. Now therefore advise thyself what word I shall bring again to him that sent me.

13 And David said unto Gad, I am in a great strait: let me fall now into the hand of the LORD; for very great *are* his mercies: but let me not fall into the hand of man.

14 So the LORD sent pestilence upon Israel: and there fell of Israel seventy thousand men.

15 And God sent an angel unto Jerusalem to destroy it: and as he was destroying, the LORD beheld, and he repented him of the evil, and said to the angel that destroyed, It is enough, stay now thine hand. And the angel of the LORD stood by the threshingfloor of Ornan the Jebusite.

16 And David lifted up his eyes, and saw the angel of the LORD stand between the earth and the heaven, having a drawn sword in his hand stretched out over Jerusalem. Then David and the elders *of Israel, who were* clothed in sackcloth, fell upon their faces.

17 And David said unto God, *Is it* not I *that* commanded the people to be numbered? even I it is that have sinned and done evil indeed; but *as for* these sheep, what have they done? let thine hand, I pray thee, O LORD my God, be on me, and on my father's house; but not on thy people, that they should be plagued.

18 Then the angel of the LORD commanded Gad to say to David, that David should go up, and set up an altar unto the LORD in the threshingfloor of Ornan the Jebusite.

19 And David went up at the saying of Gad, which he spake in the name of the LORD.

20 And Ornan turned back, and saw the angel; and his four sons with him hid themselves. Now Ornan was threshing wheat.

21 And as David came to Ornan, Ornan looked and saw David, and went out of the threshingfloor, and bowed himself to David with *his* face to the ground.

22 Then David said to Ornan, Grant me the place of *this* threshingfloor, that I may build an altar therein unto the LORD: thou shalt grant it me for the full price: that the plague may be stayed from the people.

23 And Ornan said unto David, Take *it* to thee, and let my lord the king do *that which is* good in his eyes: lo, I give

thee the oxen *also* for burnt offerings, and the threshing instruments for wood, and the wheat for the meat offering; I give it all.

24 And king David said to Ornan, Nay; but I will verily buy it for the full price: for I will not take *that* which *is* thine for the LORD, nor offer burnt offerings without cost.

25 So David gave to Ornan for the place six hundred shekels of gold by weight.

26 And David built there an altar unto the LORD, and offered burnt offerings and peace offerings, and called upon the LORD; and he answered him from heaven by fire upon the altar of burnt offering.

27 And the LORD commanded the angel; and he put up his sword again into the sheath thereof.

28 At that time when David saw that the LORD had answered him in the threshingfloor of Ornan the Jebusite, then he sacrificed there.

29 For the tabernacle of the LORD, which Moses made in the wilderness, and the altar of the burnt offering, *were* at that season in the high place at Gibeon.

30 But David could not go before it to enquire of God: for he was afraid because of the sword of the angel of the LORD.

22 Then David said, This *is* the house of the LORD God, and this *is* the altar of the burnt offering for Israel.

2 And David commanded to gather together the strangers that *were* in the land of Israel; and he set masons to hew wrought stones to build the house of God.

3 And David prepared iron in abundance for the nails for the doors of the gates, and for the joinings; and brass in abundance without weight;

4 Also cedar trees in abundance: for the Zidonians and they of Tyre brought much cedar wood to David.

5 And David said, Solomon my son *is* young and tender, and the house *that is* to be builded for the LORD *must be* exceeding magnifical, of fame and of glory throughout all countries: I will *therefore* now make preparation for it. So David prepared abundantly before his death.

6 Then he called for Solomon his son, and charged him to build an house for the LORD God of Israel.

7 And David said to Solomon, My son, as for me, it was in my mind to build an house unto the name of the LORD my God:

8 But the word of the LORD came to me, saying, Thou hast shed blood abundantly, and hast made great wars: thou shalt not build an house unto my name, because thou hast shed much blood upon the earth in my sight.

9 Behold, a son shall be born to thee, who shall be a man of rest; and I will give him rest from all his enemies round about: for his name shall be Solomon, and I will give peace and quietness unto Israel in his days.

10 He shall build an house for my name; and he shall be my son, and I *will be* his father; and I will establish the throne of his kingdom over Israel for ever.

11 Now, my son, the LORD be with thee; and prosper thou, and build the house of the LORD thy God, as he hath said of thee.

12 Only the LORD give thee wisdom and understanding, and give thee charge concerning Israel, that thou mayest keep the law of the LORD thy God.

13 Then shalt thou prosper, if thou takest heed to fulfil the statutes and judgments which the LORD charged Moses with concerning Israel: be strong, and of good courage; dread not, nor be dismayed.

14 Now, behold, in my trouble I have prepared for the house of the LORD an hundred thousand talents of gold, and a thousand thousand talents of silver; and of brass and iron without weight; for it is in abundance: timber also and stone have I prepared; and thou mayest add thereto.

15 Moreover *there are* workmen with thee in abundance, hewers and workers of stone and timber, and all manner of cunning men for every manner of work.

16 Of the gold, the silver, and the brass, and the iron, *there is* no number. Arise *therefore*, and be doing, and the LORD be with thee.

17 David also commanded all the princes of Israel to help Solomon his son, *saying*,

18 *Is* not the LORD your God with you? and hath he *not* given you rest on every side? for he hath given the inhabitants of the land into mine hand; and the land is subdued before the LORD, and before his people.

19 Now set your heart and your soul to seek the LORD your God; arise therefore, and build ye the sanctuary of the LORD God, to bring the ark of the covenant of the LORD, and the holy vessels of God, into the house that is to be built to the name of the LORD.

23

So when David was old and full of days, he made Solomon his son king over Israel.

2 And he gathered together all the princes of Israel, with the priests and the Levites.

3 Now the Levites were numbered from the age of thirty years and upward: and their number by their polls, man by man, was thirty and eight thousand.

4 Of which, twenty and four thousand *were* to set forward the work of the house of the LORD; and six thousand *were* officers and judges:

5 Moreover four thousand *were* porters; and four thousand praised the LORD with the instruments which I made, *said David*, to praise *therewith*.

6 And David divided them into courses among the sons of Levi, *namely*, Gershon, Kohath, and Merari.

7 Of the Gershonites *were*, Laadan, and Shimei.

8 The sons of Laadan; the chief *was* Jehiel, and Zetham, and Joel, three.

9 The sons of Shimei; Shelomith, and Haziel, and Haran, three. These *were* the chief of the fathers of Laadan.

10 And the sons of Shimei *were*, Jahath, Zina, and Jeush, and Beriah. These four *were* the sons of Shimei.

11 And Jahath was the chief, and Zizah the second: but Jeush and Beriah had not many sons; therefore they were in one reckoning, according to *their* father's house.

12 The sons of Kohath; Amram, Izhar, Hebron, and Uzziel, four.

13 The sons of Amram; Aaron and Moses: and Aaron was separated, that he should sanctify the most holy things, he and his sons for ever, to burn incense

before the LORD, to minister unto him,
and to bless in his name for ever.
14 Now *concerning* Moses the man of
God, his sons were named of the tribe
of Levi.
15 The sons of Moses *were*, Gershom,
and Eliezer.
16 Of the sons of Gershom, Shebuel
was the chief.
17 And the sons of Eliezer *were*,
Rehabiah the chief. And Eliezer had
none other sons; but the sons of
Rehabiah were very many.
18 Of the sons of Izhar; Shelomith the
chief.
19 Of the sons of Hebron; Jeriah the
first, Amariah the second, Jahaziel the
third, and Jekameam the fourth.
20 Of the sons of Uzziel; Michah the
first, and Jesiah the second.
21 The sons of Merari; Mahli, and
Mushi. The sons of Mahli; Eleazar, and
Kish.
22 And Eleazar died, and had no sons,
but daughters: and their brethren the
sons of Kish took them.
23 The sons of Mushi; Mahli, and
Eder, and Jeremoth, three.
24 These *were* the sons of Levi after
the house of their fathers; *even* the
chief of the fathers, as they were counted by number of names by their polls,
that did the work for the service of the
house of the LORD, from the age of
twenty years and upward.
25 For David said, The LORD God of
Israel hath given rest unto his people,
that they may dwell in Jerusalem for
ever:
26 And also unto the Levites; they
shall no *more* carry the tabernacle, nor
any vessels of it for the service thereof.
27 For by the last words of David the
Levites *were* numbered from twenty
years old and above:
28 Because their office *was* to wait on
the sons of Aaron for the service of the
house of the LORD, in the courts, and in
the chambers, and in the purifying of
all holy things, and the work of the
service of the house of God;
29 Both for the shewbread, and for
the fine flour for meat offering, and for
the unleavened cakes, and for *that
which is baked in* the pan, and for that
which is fried, and for all manner of
measure and size;
30 And to stand every morning to
thank and praise the LORD, and likewise at even;
31 And to offer all burnt sacrifices
unto the LORD in the sabbaths, in the
new moons, and on the set feasts, by
number, according to the order commanded unto them, continually before
the LORD:
32 And that they should keep the
charge of the tabernacle of the congregation, and the charge of the holy *place*,
and the charge of the sons of Aaron
their brethren, in the service of the
house of the LORD.

24 Now *these are* the divisions of
the sons of Aaron. The sons of
Aaron; Nadab, and Abihu, Eleazar, and
Ithamar.
2 But Nadab and Abihu died before
their father, and had no children: therefore Eleazar and Ithamar executed the
priest's office.
3 And David distributed them, both
Zadok of the sons of Eleazar, and
Ahimelech of the sons of Ithamar,
according to their offices in their service.

4 And there were more chief men
found of the sons of Eleazar than of the
sons of Ithamar; and *thus* were they
divided. Among the sons of Eleazar
there were sixteen chief men of the
house of *their* fathers, and eight among
the sons of Ithamar according to the
house of their fathers.
5 Thus were they divided by lot, one
sort with another; for the governors of
the sanctuary, and governors *of the
house* of God, were of the sons of
Eleazar, and of the sons of Ithamar.
6 And Shemaiah the son of Nethaneel
the scribe, *one* of the Levites, wrote
them before the king, and the princes,
and Zadok the priest, and Ahimelech
the son of Abiathar, and *before* the
chief of the fathers of the priests and
Levites: one principal household being
taken for Eleazar, and *one* taken for
Ithamar.
7 Now the first lot came forth to
Jehoiarib, the second to Jedaiah,
8 The third to Harim, the fourth to
Seorim,
9 The fifth to Malchijah, the sixth to
Mijamin,
10 The seventh to Hakkoz, the eighth
to Abijah,
11 The ninth to Jeshua, the tenth to
Shecaniah,
12 The eleventh to Eliashib, the
twelfth to Jakim,
13 The thirteenth to Huppah, the
fourteenth to Jeshebeab,
14 The fifteenth to Bilgah, the sixteenth to Immer,
15 The seventeenth to Hezir, the eighteenth to Aphses,
16 The nineteenth to Pethahiah, the
twentieth to Jehezekel,
17 The one and twentieth to Jachin,
the two and twentieth to Gamul,
18 The three and twentieth to
Delaiah, the four and twentieth to
Maaziah.
19 These *were* the orderings of them
in their service to come into the house
of the LORD, according to their manner,
under Aaron their father, as the LORD
God of Israel had commanded him.
20 And the rest of the sons of Levi
were these: Of the sons of Amram;
Shubael: of the sons of Shubael;
Jehdeiah.
21 Concerning Rehabiah: of the sons
of Rehabiah, the first *was* Isshiah.
22 Of the Izharites; Shelomoth: of the
sons of Shelomoth; Jahath.
23 And the sons *of Hebron*; Jeriah *the
first*, Amariah the second, Jahaziel the
third, Jekameam the fourth.
24 *Of* the sons of Uzziel; Michah: of
the sons of Michah; Shamir.
25 The brother of Michah *was* Isshiah:
of the sons of Isshiah; Zechariah.
26 The sons of Merari *were* Mahli and
Mushi: the sons of Jaaziah; Beno.
27 The sons of Merari by Jaaziah;
Beno, and Shoham, and Zaccur, and
Ibri.
28 Of Mahli *came* Eleazar, who had
no sons.
29 Concerning Kish: the son of Kish
was Jerahmeel.
30 The sons also of Mushi; Mahli, and
Eder, and Jerimoth. These *were* the
sons of the Levites after the house of
their fathers.
31 These likewise cast lots over
against their brethren the sons of
Aaron in the presence of David the
king, and Zadok, and Ahimelech, and
the chief of the fathers of the priests
and Levites, even the principal fathers
over against their younger brethren.

25 Moreover David and the captains of the host separated to the service of the sons of Asaph, and of Heman, and of Jeduthun, who should prophesy with harps, with psalteries, and with cymbals: and the number of the workmen according to their service was:

2 Of the sons of Asaph; Zaccur, and Joseph, and Nethaniah, and Asarelah, the sons of Asaph under the hands of Asaph, which prophesied according to the order of the king.

3 Of Jeduthun: the sons of Jeduthun; Gedaliah, and Zeri, and Jeshaiah, Hashabiah, and Mattithiah, six, under the hands of their father Jeduthun, who prophesied with a harp, to give thanks and to praise the LORD.

4 Of Heman: the sons of Heman; Bukkiah, Mattaniah, Uzziel, Shebuel, and Jerimoth, Hananiah, Hanani, Eliathah, Giddalti, and Romamti-ezer, Joshbekashah, Mallothi, Hothir, *and* Mahazioth:

5 All these *were* the sons of Heman the king's seer in the words of God, to lift up the horn. And God gave to Heman fourteen sons and three daughters.

6 All these *were* under the hands of their father for song *in* the house of the LORD, with cymbals, psalteries, and harps, for the service of the house of God, according to the king's order to Asaph, Jeduthun, and Heman.

7 So the number of them, with their brethren that were instructed in the songs of the LORD, *even* all that were cunning, was two hundred fourscore and eight.

8 And they cast lots, ward against *ward*, as well the small as the great, the teacher as the scholar.

9 Now the first lot came forth for Asaph to Joseph: the second to Gedaliah, who with his brethren and sons *were* twelve:

10 The third to Zaccur, *he*, his sons, and his brethren, *were* twelve:

11 The fourth to Izri, *he*, his sons, and his brethren, *were* twelve:

12 The fifth to Nethaniah, *he*, his sons, and his brethren, *were* twelve:

13 The sixth to Bukkiah, *he*, his sons, and his brethren, *were* twelve:

14 The seventh to Jesharelah, *he*, his sons, and his brethren, *were* twelve:

15 The eighth to Jeshaiah, *he*, his sons, and his brethren, *were* twelve:

16 The ninth to Mattaniah, *he*, his sons, and his brethren, *were* twelve:

17 The tenth to Shimei, *he*, his sons, and his brethren, *were* twelve:

18 The eleventh to Azareel, *he*, his sons, and his brethren, *were* twelve:

19 The twelfth to Hashabiah, *he*, his sons, and his brethren, *were* twelve:

20 The thirteenth to Shubael, *he*, his sons, and his brethren, *were* twelve:

21 The fourteenth to Mattithiah, *he*, his sons, and his brethren, *were* twelve:

22 The fifteenth to Jeremoth, *he*, his sons, and his brethren, *were* twelve:

23 The sixteenth to Hananiah, *he*, his sons, and his brethren, *were* twelve:

24 The seventeenth to Joshbekashah, *he*, his sons, and his brethren, *were* twelve:

25 The eighteenth to Hanani, *he*, his sons, and his brethren, *were* twelve:

26 The nineteenth to Mallothi, *he*, his sons, and his brethren, *were* twelve:

27 The twentieth to Eliathah, *he*, his sons, and his brethren, *were* twelve:

28 The one and twentieth to Hothir, *he*, his sons, and his brethren, *were* twelve:

29 The two and twentieth to Giddalti,
he, his sons, and his brethren, *were*
twelve:
30 The three and twentieth to
Mahazioth, *he*, his sons, and his brethren, *were* twelve:
31 The four and twentieth to
Romamti-ezer, *he*, his sons, and his
brethren, *were* twelve.

26 Concerning the divisions of the
porters: Of the Korhites *was*
Meshelemiah the son of Kore, of the
sons of Asaph.
2 And the sons of Meshelemiah *were*,
Zechariah the firstborn, Jediael the
second, Zebadiah the third, Jathniel
the fourth,
3 Elam the fifth, Jehohanan the sixth,
Elioenai the seventh.
4 Moreover the sons of Obed-edom
were, Shemaiah the firstborn, Jehozabad the second, Joah the third, and
Sacar the fourth, and Nethaneel the
fifth,
5 Ammiel the sixth, Issachar the seventh, Peulthai the eighth: for God
blessed him.
6 Also unto Shemaiah his son were
sons born, that ruled throughout the
house of their father: for they *were*
mighty men of valour.
7 The sons of Shemaiah; Othni, and
Rephael, and Obed, Elzabad, whose
brethren *were* strong men, Elihu, and
Semachiah.
8 All these of the sons of Obed-edom:
they and their sons and their brethren,
able men for strength for the service,
were threescore and two of Obed-edom.
9 And Meshelemiah had sons and
brethren, strong men, eighteen.
10 Also Hosah, of the children of
Merari, had sons; Simri the chief, (for
though he was not the firstborn, yet his
father made him the chief;)
11 Hilkiah the second, Tebaliah the
third, Zechariah the fourth: all the sons
and brethren of Hosah *were* thirteen.
12 Among these *were* the divisions of
the porters, *even* among the chief men,
having wards one against another, to
minister in the house of the LORD.
13 And they cast lots, as well the
small as the great, according to the
house of their fathers, for every gate.
14 And the lot eastward fell to
Shelemiah. Then for Zechariah his son,
a wise counsellor, they cast lots; and his
lot came out northward.
15 To Obed-edom southward; and to
his sons the house of Asuppim.
16 To Shuppim and Hosah *the lot*
came forth westward, with the gate
Shallecheth, by the causeway of the
going up, ward against ward.
17 Eastward *were* six Levites, northward four a day, southward four a day,
and toward Asuppim two *and* two.
18 At Parbar westward, four at the
causeway, *and* two at Parbar.
19 These *are* the divisions of the porters among the sons of Kore, and among
the sons of Merari.
20 And of the Levites, Ahijah *was*
over the treasures of the house of God,
and over the treasures of the dedicated
things.
21 *As concerning* the sons of Laadan;
the sons of the Gershonite Laadan,
chief fathers, *even* of Laadan the
Gershonite, *were* Jehieli.
22 The sons of Jehieli; Zetham, and
Joel his brother, *which were* over the
treasures of the house of the LORD.
23 Of the Amramites, *and* the
Izharites, the Hebronites, *and* the
Uzzielites:

24 And Shebuel the son of Gershom,
the son of Moses, *was* ruler of the treasures.
25 And his brethren by Eliezer;
Rehabiah his son, and Jeshaiah his son,
and Joram his son, and Zichri his son,
and Shelomith his son.
26 Which Shelomith and his brethren
were over all the treasures of the dedicated things, which David the king, and
the chief fathers, the captains over
thousands and hundreds, and the captains of the host, had dedicated.
27 Out of the spoils won in battles did
they dedicate to maintain the house of
the LORD.
28 And all that Samuel the seer, and
Saul the son of Kish, and Abner the son
of Ner, and Joab the son of Zeruiah, had
dedicated; *and* whosoever had dedicated *any thing, it was* under the hand
of Shelomith, and of his brethren.
29 Of the Izharites, Chenaniah and
his sons *were* for the outward business
over Israel, for officers and judges.
30 *And* of the Hebronites, Hashabiah
and his brethren, men of valour, a thousand and seven hundred, *were* officers
among them of Israel on this side
Jordan westward in all the business of
the LORD, and in the service of the king.
31 Among the Hebronites *was* Jerijah
the chief, *even* among the Hebronites,
according to the generations of his
fathers. In the fortieth year of the reign
of David they were sought for, and
there were found among them mighty
men of valour at Jazer of Gilead.
32 And his brethren, men of valour,
were two thousand and seven hundred
chief fathers, whom king David made
rulers over the Reubenites, the Gadites,
and the half tribe of Manasseh, for
every matter pertaining to God, and
affairs of the king.

27 Now the children of Israel after
their number, *to wit*, the chief
fathers and captains of thousands and
hundreds, and their officers that served
the king in any matter of the courses,
which came in and went out month by
month throughout all the months of the
year, of every course *were* twenty and
four thousand.
2 Over the first course for the first
month *was* Jashobeam the son of
Zabdiel: and in his course *were* twenty
and four thousand.
3 Of the children of Perez *was* the
chief of all the captains of the host for
the first month.
4 And over the course of the second
month *was* Dodai an Ahohite, and of
his course *was* Mikloth also the ruler:
in his course likewise *were* twenty and
four thousand.
5 The third captain of the host for the
third month *was* Benaiah the son of
Jehoiada, a chief priest: and in his
course *were* twenty and four thousand.
6 This *is that* Benaiah, *who was*
mighty *among* the thirty, and above the
thirty: and in his course *was* Am-
mizabad his son.
7 The fourth *captain* for the fourth
month *was* Asahel the brother of Joab,
and Zebadiah his son after him: and in
his course *were* twenty and four thousand.
8 The fifth captain for the fifth month
was Shamhuth the Izrahite: and in his
course *were* twenty and four thousand.
9 The sixth *captain* for the sixth
month *was* Ira the son of Ikkesh the
Tekoite: and in his course *were* twenty
and four thousand.
10 The seventh *captain* for the seventh month *was* Helez the Pelonite, of

the children of Ephraim: and in his
course *were* twenty and four thousand.
11 The eighth *captain* for the eighth
month *was* Sibbecai the Hushathite, of
the Zarhites: and in his course *were*
twenty and four thousand.
12 The ninth *captain* for the ninth
month *was* Abi-ezer the Anetothite, of
the Benjamites: and in his course *were*
twenty and four thousand.
13 The tenth *captain* for the tenth
month *was* Maharai the Netophathite,
of the Zarhites: and in his course *were*
twenty and four thousand.
14 The eleventh *captain* for the eleventh month *was* Benaiah the
Pirathonite, of the children of Ephraim:
and in his course *were* twenty and four
thousand.
15 The twelfth *captain* for the twelfth
month *was* Heldai the Netophathite, of
Othniel: and in his course *were* twenty
and four thousand.
16 Furthermore over the tribes of
Israel: the ruler of the Reubenites *was*
Eliezer the son of Zichri: of the
Simeonites, Shephatiah the son of
Maachah:
17 Of the Levites, Hashabiah the son
of Kemuel: of the Aaronites, Zadok:
18 Of Judah, Elihu, *one* of the brethren of David: of Issachar, Omri the son
of Michael:
19 Of Zebulun, Ishmaiah the son of
Obadiah: of Naphtali, Jerimoth the son
of Azriel:
20 Of the children of Ephraim,
Hoshea the son of Azaziah: of the half
tribe of Manasseh, Joel the son of
Pedaiah:
21 Of the half *tribe* of Manasseh in
Gilead, Iddo the son of Zechariah: of
Benjamin, Jaasiel the son of Abner:
22 Of Dan, Azareel the son of
Jeroham. These *were* the princes of the
tribes of Israel.
23 But David took not the number of
them from twenty years old and under:
because the LORD had said he would
increase Israel like to the stars of the
heavens.
24 Joab the son of Zeruiah began to
number, but he finished not, because
there fell wrath for it against Israel;
neither was the number put in the
account of the chronicles of king David.
25 And over the king's treasures *was*
Azmaveth the son of Adiel: and over
the storehouses in the fields, in the cities, and in the villages, and in the castles, *was* Jehonathan the son of Uzziah:
26 And over them that did the work
of the field for tillage of the ground *was*
Ezri the son of Chelub:
27 And over the vineyards *was* Shimei
the Ramathite: over the increase of the
vineyards for the wine cellars *was*
Zabdi the Shiphmite:
28 And over the olive trees and the
sycomore trees that *were* in the low
plains *was* Baal-hanan the Gederite:
and over the cellars of oil *was* Joash:
29 And over the herds that fed in
Sharon *was* Shitrai the Sharonite: and
over the herds *that were* in the valleys
was Shaphat the son of Adlai:
30 Over the camels also *was* Obil the
Ishmaelite: and over the asses *was*
Jehdeiah the Meronothite:
31 And over the flocks *was* Jaziz the
Hagerite. All these *were* the rulers of
the substance which *was* king David's.
32 Also Jonathan David's uncle was a
counsellor, a wise man, and a scribe:
and Jehiel the son of Hachmoni *was*
with the king's sons:

33 And Ahithophel *was* the king's
counsellor: and Hushai the Archite *was*
the king's companion:
34 And after Ahithophel *was* Jehoiada the son of Benaiah, and Abiathar:
and the general of the king's army *was*
Joab.

28 And David assembled all the
princes of Israel, the princes of
the tribes, and the captains of the companies that ministered to the king by
course, and the captains over the thousands, and captains over the hundreds,
and the stewards over all the substance
and possession of the king, and of his
sons, with the officers, and with the
mighty men, and with all the valiant
men, unto Jerusalem.
2 Then David the king stood up upon
his feet, and said, Hear me, my brethren, and my people: *As for me*, I *had* in
mine heart to build an house of rest for
the ark of the covenant of the LORD,
and for the footstool of our God, and
had made ready for the building:
3 But God said unto me, Thou shalt
not build an house for my name,
because thou *hast been* a man of war,
and hast shed blood.
4 Howbeit the LORD God of Israel
chose me before all the house of my
father to be king over Israel for ever:
for he hath chosen Judah *to be* the
ruler; and of the house of Judah, the
house of my father; and among the sons
of my father he liked me to make *me*
king over all Israel:
5 And of all my sons, (for the LORD
hath given me many sons,) he hath
chosen Solomon my son to sit upon the
throne of the kingdom of the LORD over
Israel.
6 And he said unto me, Solomon thy
son, he shall build my house and my
courts: for I have chosen him *to be* my
son, and I will be his father.
7 Moreover I will establish his kingdom for ever, if he be constant to do my
commandments and my judgments, as
at this day.
8 Now therefore in the sight of all
Israel the congregation of the LORD,
and in the audience of our God, keep
and seek for all the commandments of
the LORD your God: that ye may possess
this good land, and leave *it* for an
inheritance for your children after you
for ever.
9 And thou, Solomon my son, know
thou the God of thy father, and serve
him with a perfect heart and with a
willing mind: for the LORD searcheth all
hearts, and understandeth all the imaginations of the thoughts: if thou seek
him, he will be found of thee; but if
thou forsake him, he will cast thee off
for ever.
10 Take heed now; for the LORD hath
chosen thee to build an house for the
sanctuary: be strong, and do *it*.
11 Then David gave to Solomon his
son the pattern of the porch, and of the
houses thereof, and of the treasuries
thereof, and of the upper chambers
thereof, and of the inner parlours thereof, and of the place of the mercy seat,
12 And the pattern of all that he had
by the spirit, of the courts of the house
of the LORD, and of all the chambers
round about, of the treasuries of the
house of God, and of the treasuries of
the dedicated things:
13 Also for the courses of the priests
and the Levites, and for all the work of
the service of the house of the LORD,
and for all the vessels of service in the
house of the LORD.

14 *He gave* of gold by weight for
things of gold, for all instruments of all
manner of service; *silver also* for all
instruments of silver by weight, for all
instruments of every kind of service:
15 Even the weight for the candlesticks of gold, and for their lamps of
gold, by weight for every candlestick,
and for the lamps thereof: and for the
candlesticks of silver by weight, *both*
for the candlestick, and *also* for the
lamps thereof, according to the use of
every candlestick.
16 And by weight *he gave* gold for the
tables of shewbread, for every table;
and *likewise* silver for the tables of silver:
17 Also pure gold for the fleshhooks,
and the bowls, and the cups: and for the
golden basons *he gave gold* by weight
for every bason; and *likewise silver* by
weight for every bason of silver:
18 And for the altar of incense refined
gold by weight; and gold for the pattern
of the chariot of the cherubims, that
spread out *their wings*, and covered the
ark of the covenant of the LORD.
19 All *this, said David*, the LORD
made me understand in writing by *his*
hand upon me, *even* all the works of
this pattern.
20 And David said to Solomon his son,
Be strong and of good courage, and do
it: fear not, nor be dismayed: for the
LORD God, *even* my God, *will be* with
thee; he will not fail thee, nor forsake
thee, until thou hast finished all the
work for the service of the house of the
LORD.
21 And, behold, the courses of the
priests and the Levites, *even they shall
be with thee* for all the service of the
house of God: and *there shall be* with
thee for all manner of workmanship
every willing skilful man, for any manner of service: also the princes and all
the people *will be* wholly at thy commandment.

29 Furthermore David the king said
unto all the congregation,
Solomon my son, whom alone God hath
chosen, *is yet* young and tender, and
the work *is* great: for the palace *is* not
for man, but for the LORD God.
2 Now I have prepared with all my
might for the house of my God the gold
for *things to be made* of gold, and the
silver for *things* of silver, and the brass
for *things* of brass, the iron for *things*
of iron, and wood for *things* of wood;
onyx stones, and *stones* to be set, glistering stones, and of divers colours, and
all manner of precious stones, and
marble stones in abundance.
3 Moreover, because I have set my
affection to the house of my God, I have
of mine own proper good, of gold and
silver, *which* I have given to the house
of my God, over and above all that I
have prepared for the holy house,
4 *Even* three thousand talents of gold,
of the gold of Ophir, and seven thousand talents of refined silver, to overlay
the walls of the houses *withal*:
5 The gold for *things* of gold, and the
silver for *things* of silver, and for all
manner of work *to be made* by the
hands of artificers. And who *then* is
willing to consecrate his service this
day unto the LORD?
6 Then the chief of the fathers and
princes of the tribes of Israel, and the
captains of thousands and of hundreds,
with the rulers of the king's work,
offered willingly,
7 And gave for the service of the
house of God of gold five thousand talents and ten thousand drams, and of

silver ten thousand talents, and of brass
eighteen thousand talents, and one
hundred thousand talents of iron.
8 And they with whom *precious*
stones were found gave *them* to the
treasure of the house of the LORD, by
the hand of Jehiel the Gershonite.
9 Then the people rejoiced, for that
they offered willingly, because with
perfect heart they offered willingly to
the LORD: and David the king also
rejoiced with great joy.
10 Wherefore David blessed the LORD
before all the congregation: and David
said, Blessed *be* thou, LORD God of
Israel our father, for ever and ever.
11 Thine, O LORD, *is* the greatness,
and the power, and the glory, and the
victory, and the majesty: for all *that is*
in the heaven and in the earth *is thine*;
thine *is* the kingdom, O LORD, and thou
art exalted as head above all.
12 Both riches and honour *come* of
thee, and thou reignest over all; and in
thine hand *is* power and might; and in
thine hand *it is* to make great, and to
give strength unto all.
13 Now therefore, our God, we thank
thee, and praise thy glorious name.
14 But who *am* I, and what *is* my
people, that we should be able to offer
so willingly after this sort? for all things
come of thee, and of thine own have we
given thee.
15 For we *are* strangers before thee,
and sojourners, as *were* all our fathers:
our days on the earth *are* as a shadow,
and *there is* none abiding.
16 O LORD our God, all this store that
we have prepared to build thee an
house for thine holy name *cometh* of
thine hand, and *is* all thine own.
17 I know also, my God, that thou triest the heart, and hast pleasure in
uprightness. As for me, in the uprightness of mine heart I have willingly
offered all these things: and now have I
seen with joy thy people, which are
present here, to offer willingly unto
thee.
18 O LORD God of Abraham, Isaac,
and of Israel, our fathers, keep this for
ever in the imagination of the thoughts
of the heart of thy people, and prepare
their heart unto thee:
19 And give unto Solomon my son a
perfect heart, to keep thy commandments, thy testimonies, and thy statutes, and to do all *these things*, and to
build the palace, *for* the which I have
made provision.
20 And David said to all the congregation, Now bless the LORD your God. And
all the congregation blessed the LORD
God of their fathers, and bowed down
their heads, and worshipped the LORD,
and the king.
21 And they sacrificed sacrifices unto
the LORD, and offered burnt offerings
unto the LORD, on the morrow after that
day, *even* a thousand bullocks, a thousand rams, *and* a thousand lambs, with
their drink offerings, and sacrifices in
abundance for all Israel:
22 And did eat and drink before the
LORD on that day with great gladness.
And they made Solomon the son of
David king the second time, and
anointed *him* unto the LORD *to be* the
chief governor, and Zadok *to be* priest.
23 Then Solomon sat on the throne of
the LORD as king instead of David his
father, and prospered; and all Israel
obeyed him.
24 And all the princes, and the mighty
men, and all the sons likewise of king
David, submitted themselves unto
Solomon the king.

25 And the LORD magnified Solomon exceedingly in the sight of all Israel, and bestowed upon him *such* royal majesty as had not been on any king before him in Israel.

26 Thus David the son of Jesse reigned over all Israel.

27 And the time that he reigned over Israel *was* forty years; seven years reigned he in Hebron, and thirty and three *years* reigned he in Jerusalem.

28 And he died in a good old age, full of days, riches, and honour: and Solomon his son reigned in his stead.

29 Now the acts of David the king, first and last, behold, they *are* written in the book of Samuel the seer, and in the book of Nathan the prophet, and in the book of Gad the seer,

30 With all his reign and his might, and the times that went over him, and over Israel, and over all the kingdoms of the countries.

THE SECOND BOOK OF CHRONICLES

1 And Solomon the son of David was strengthened in his kingdom, and the LORD his God *was* with him, and magnified him exceedingly.

2 Then Solomon spake unto all Israel, to the captains of thousands and of hundreds, and to the judges, and to every governor in all Israel, the chief of the fathers.

3 So Solomon, and all the congregation with him, went to the high place that *was* at Gibeon; for there was the tabernacle of the congregation of God, which Moses the servant of the LORD had made in the wilderness.

4 But the ark of God had David brought up from Kirjath-jearim to *the place which* David had prepared for it: for he had pitched a tent for it at Jerusalem.

5 Moreover the brasen altar, that Bezaleel the son of Uri, the son of Hur, had made, he put before the tabernacle of the LORD: and Solomon and the congregation sought unto it.

6 And Solomon went up thither to the brasen altar before the LORD, which *was* at the tabernacle of the congregation, and offered a thousand burnt offerings upon it.

7 In that night did God appear unto Solomon, and said unto him, Ask what I shall give thee.

8 And Solomon said unto God, Thou hast shewed great mercy unto David my father, and hast made me to reign in his stead.

9 Now, O LORD God, let thy promise unto David my father be established: for thou hast made me king over a people like the dust of the earth in multitude.

10 Give me now wisdom and knowledge, that I may go out and come in before this people: for who can judge this thy people, *that is so* great?

11 And God said to Solomon, Because this was in thine heart, and thou hast not asked riches, wealth, or honour, nor the life of thine enemies, neither yet hast asked long life; but hast asked

wisdom and knowledge for thyself, that thou mayest judge my people, over whom I have made thee king:

12 Wisdom and knowledge *is* granted unto thee; and I will give thee riches, and wealth, and honour, such as none of the kings have had that *have been* before thee, neither shall there any after thee have the like.

13 Then Solomon came *from his journey* to the high place that *was* at Gibeon to Jerusalem, from before the tabernacle of the congregation, and reigned over Israel.

14 And Solomon gathered chariots and horsemen: and he had a thousand and four hundred chariots, and twelve thousand horsemen, which he placed in the chariot cities, and with the king at Jerusalem.

15 And the king made silver and gold at Jerusalem *as plenteous* as stones, and cedar trees made he as the sycomore trees that *are* in the vale for abundance.

16 And Solomon had horses brought out of Egypt, and linen yarn: the king's merchants received the linen yarn at a price.

17 And they fetched up, and brought forth out of Egypt a chariot for six hundred *shekels* of silver, and an horse for an hundred and fifty: and so brought they out *horses* for all the kings of the Hittites, and for the kings of Syria, by their means.

2 And Solomon determined to build an house for the name of the LORD, and an house for his kingdom.

2 And Solomon told out threescore and ten thousand men to bear burdens, and fourscore thousand to hew in the mountain, and three thousand and six hundred to oversee them.

3 And Solomon sent to Huram the king of Tyre, saying, As thou didst deal with David my father, and didst send him cedars to build him an house to dwell therein, *even so deal with me*.

4 Behold, I build an house to the name of the LORD my God, to dedicate *it* to him, *and* to burn before him sweet incense, and for the continual shewbread, and for the burnt offerings morning and evening, on the sabbaths, and on the new moons, and on the solemn feasts of the LORD our God. This *is an ordinance* for ever to Israel.

5 And the house which I build *is* great: for great *is* our God above all gods.

6 But who is able to build him an house, seeing the heaven and heaven of heavens cannot contain him? who *am* I then, that I should build him an house, save only to burn sacrifice before him?

7 Send me now therefore a man cunning to work in gold, and in silver, and in brass, and in iron, and in purple, and crimson, and blue, and that can skill to grave with the cunning men that *are* with me in Judah and in Jerusalem, whom David my father did provide.

8 Send me also cedar trees, fir trees, and algum trees, out of Lebanon: for I know that thy servants can skill to cut timber in Lebanon; and, behold, my servants *shall be* with thy servants,

9 Even to prepare me timber in abundance: for the house which I am about to build *shall be* wonderful great.

10 And, behold, I will give to thy servants, the hewers that cut timber, twenty thousand measures of beaten wheat, and twenty thousand measures of barley, and twenty thousand baths of wine, and twenty thousand baths of oil.

11 Then Huram the king of Tyre
answered in writing, which he sent to
Solomon, Because the LORD hath loved
his people, he hath made thee king
over them.
12 Huram said moreover, Blessed *be*
the LORD God of Israel, that made
heaven and earth, who hath given to
David the king a wise son, endued with
prudence and understanding, that
might build an house for the LORD, and
an house for his kingdom.
13 And now I have sent a cunning
man, endued with understanding, of
Huram my father's,
14 The son of a woman of the daughters of Dan, and his father *was* a man of
Tyre, skilful to work in gold, and in silver, in brass, in iron, in stone, and in
timber, in purple, in blue, and in fine
linen, and in crimson; also to grave any
manner of graving, and to find out
every device which shall be put to him,
with thy cunning men, and with the
cunning men of my lord David thy
father.
15 Now therefore the wheat, and the
barley, the oil, and the wine, which my
lord hath spoken of, let him send unto
his servants:
16 And we will cut wood out of
Lebanon, as much as thou shalt need:
and we will bring it to thee in floats by
sea to Joppa; and thou shalt carry it up
to Jerusalem.
17 And Solomon numbered all the
strangers that *were* in the land of Israel,
after the numbering wherewith David
his father had numbered them; and
they were found an hundred and fifty
thousand and three thousand and six
hundred.
18 And he set threescore and ten
thousand of them *to be* bearers of burdens, and fourscore thousand *to be*
hewers in the mountain, and three
thousand and six hundred overseers to
set the people a work.

3 Then Solomon began to build the
house of the LORD at Jerusalem in
mount Moriah, where *the* LORD
appeared unto David his father, in the
place that David had prepared in the
threshingfloor of Ornan the Jebusite.
2 And he began to build in the second
day of the second month, in the fourth
year of his reign.
3 Now these *are the things wherein*
Solomon was instructed for the building of the house of God. The length by
cubits after the first measure *was*
threescore cubits, and the breadth
twenty cubits.
4 And the porch that *was* in the front
of the house, the length *of it was*
according to the breadth of the house,
twenty cubits, and the height *was* an
hundred and twenty: and he overlaid it
within with pure gold.
5 And the greater house he cieled
with fir tree, which he overlaid with
fine gold, and set thereon palm trees
and chains.
6 And he garnished the house with
precious stones for beauty: and the
gold *was* gold of Parvaim.
7 He overlaid also the house, the
beams, the posts, and the walls thereof,
and the doors thereof, with gold; and
graved cherubims on the walls.
8 And he made the most holy house,
the length whereof *was* according to
the breadth of the house, twenty cubits,
and the breadth thereof twenty cubits:
and he overlaid it with fine gold,
amounting to six hundred talents.

9 And the weight of the nails *was* fifty shekels of gold. And he overlaid the upper chambers with gold.

10 And in the most holy house he made two cherubims of image work, and overlaid them with gold.

11 And the wings of the cherubims *were* twenty cubits long: one wing *of the one cherub was* five cubits, reaching to the wall of the house: and the other wing *was likewise* five cubits, reaching to the wing of the other cherub.

12 And *one* wing of the other cherub *was* five cubits, reaching to the wall of the house: and the other wing *was* five cubits *also*, joining to the wing of the other cherub.

13 The wings of these cherubims spread themselves forth twenty cubits: and they stood on their feet, and their faces *were* inward.

14 And he made the vail *of* blue, and purple, and crimson, and fine linen, and wrought cherubims thereon.

15 Also he made before the house two pillars of thirty and five cubits high, and the chapiter that *was* on the top of each of them *was* five cubits.

16 And he made chains, *as* in the oracle, and put *them* on the heads of the pillars; and made an hundred pomegranates, and put *them* on the chains.

17 And he reared up the pillars before the temple, one on the right hand, and the other on the left; and called the name of that on the right hand Jachin, and the name of that on the left Boaz.

4 Moreover he made an altar of brass, twenty cubits the length thereof, and twenty cubits the breadth thereof, and ten cubits the height thereof.

2 Also he made a molten sea of ten cubits from brim to brim, round in compass, and five cubits the height thereof; and a line of thirty cubits did compass it round about.

3 And under it *was* the similitude of oxen, which did compass it round about: ten in a cubit, compassing the sea round about. Two rows of oxen *were* cast, when it was cast.

4 It stood upon twelve oxen, three looking toward the north, and three looking toward the west, and three looking toward the south, and three looking toward the east: and the sea *was set* above upon them, and all their hinder parts *were* inward.

5 And the thickness of it *was* an handbreadth, and the brim of it like the work of the brim of a cup, with flowers of lilies; *and* it received and held three thousand baths.

6 He made also ten lavers, and put five on the right hand, and five on the left, to wash in them: such things as they offered for the burnt offering they washed in them; but the sea *was* for the priests to wash in.

7 And he made ten candlesticks of gold according to their form, and set *them* in the temple, five on the right hand, and five on the left.

8 He made also ten tables, and placed *them* in the temple, five on the right side, and five on the left. And he made an hundred basons of gold.

9 Furthermore he made the court of the priests, and the great court, and doors for the court, and overlaid the doors of them with brass.

10 And he set the sea on the right side of the east end, over against the south.

11 And Huram made the pots, and
the shovels, and the basons. And
Huram finished the work that he was to
make for king Solomon for the house of
God;
12 *To wit*, the two pillars, and the
pommels, and the chapiters *which were*
on the top of the two pillars, and the
two wreaths to cover the two pommels
of the chapiters which *were* on the top
of the pillars;
13 And four hundred pomegranates
on the two wreaths; two rows of pomegranates on each wreath, to cover the
two pommels of the chapiters which
were upon the pillars.
14 He made also bases, and lavers
made he upon the bases;
15 One sea, and twelve oxen under it.
16 The pots also, and the shovels, and
the fleshhooks, and all their instruments, did Huram his father make to
king Solomon for the house of the LORD
of bright brass.
17 In the plain of Jordan did the king
cast them, in the clay ground between
Succoth and Zeredathah.
18 Thus Solomon made all these vessels in great abundance: for the weight
of the brass could not be found out.
19 And Solomon made all the vessels
that *were for* the house of God, the
golden altar also, and the tables whereon the shewbread *was set*;
20 Moreover the candlesticks with
their lamps, that they should burn after
the manner before the oracle, of pure
gold;
21 And the flowers, and the lamps,
and the tongs, *made he of* gold, *and*
that perfect gold;
22 And the snuffers, and the basons,
and the spoons, and the censers, *of* pure
gold: and the entry of the house, the
inner doors thereof for the most holy
place, and the doors of the house of the
temple, *were of* gold.

5

Thus all the work that Solomon
made for the house of the LORD was
finished: and Solomon brought in *all*
the things that David his father had
dedicated; and the silver, and the gold,
and all the instruments, put he among
the treasures of the house of God.
2 Then Solomon assembled the elders
of Israel, and all the heads of the tribes,
the chief of the fathers of the children
of Israel, unto Jerusalem, to bring up
the ark of the covenant of the LORD out
of the city of David, which *is* Zion.
3 Wherefore all the men of Israel
assembled themselves unto the king in
the feast which *was* in the seventh
month.
4 And all the elders of Israel came;
and the Levites took up the ark.
5 And they brought up the ark, and
the tabernacle of the congregation, and
all the holy vessels that *were* in the
tabernacle, these did the priests *and*
the Levites bring up.
6 Also king Solomon, and all the congregation of Israel that were assembled
unto him before the ark, sacrificed
sheep and oxen, which could not be
told nor numbered for multitude.
7 And the priests brought in the ark
of the covenant of the LORD unto his
place, to the oracle of the house, into
the most holy *place*, *even* under the
wings of the cherubims:
8 For the cherubims spread forth
their wings over the place of the ark,
and the cherubims covered the ark and
the staves thereof above.
9 And they drew out the staves *of the*
ark, that the ends of the staves were
seen from the ark before the oracle; but

they were not seen without. And there it is unto this day.

10 *There was* nothing in the ark save the two tables which Moses put *therein* at Horeb, when the LORD made *a covenant* with the children of Israel, when they came out of Egypt.

11 And it came to pass, when the priests were come out of the holy *place*: (for all the priests *that were* present were sanctified, *and* did not *then* wait by course:

12 Also the Levites *which were* the singers, all of them of Asaph, of Heman, of Jeduthun, with their sons and their brethren, *being* arrayed in white linen, having cymbals and psalteries and harps, stood at the east end of the altar, and with them an hundred and twenty priests sounding with trumpets:)

13 It came even to pass, as the trumpeters and singers *were* as one, to make one sound to be heard in praising and thanking the LORD; and when they lifted up *their* voice with the trumpets and cymbals and instruments of musick, and praised the LORD, *saying*, For *he is* good; for his mercy *endureth* for ever: that *then* the house was filled with a cloud, *even* the house of the LORD;

14 So that the priests could not stand to minister by reason of the cloud: for the glory of the LORD had filled the house of God.

6 Then said Solomon, The LORD hath said that he would dwell in the thick darkness.

2 But I have built an house of habitation for thee, and a place for thy dwelling for ever.

3 And the king turned his face, and blessed the whole congregation of Israel: and all the congregation of Israel stood.

4 And he said, Blessed *be* the LORD God of Israel, who hath with his hands fulfilled *that* which he spake with his mouth to my father David, saying,

5 Since the day that I brought forth my people out of the land of Egypt I chose no city among all the tribes of Israel to build an house in, that my name might be there; neither chose I any man to be a ruler over my people Israel:

6 But I have chosen Jerusalem, that my name might be there; and have chosen David to be over my people Israel.

7 Now it was in the heart of David my father to build an house for the name of the LORD God of Israel.

8 But the LORD said to David my father, Forasmuch as it was in thine heart to build an house for my name, thou didst well in that it was in thine heart:

9 Notwithstanding thou shalt not build the house; but thy son which shall come forth out of thy loins, he shall build the house for my name.

10 The LORD therefore hath performed his word that he hath spoken: for I am risen up in the room of David my father, and am set on the throne of Israel, as the LORD promised, and have built the house for the name of the LORD God of Israel.

11 And in it have I put the ark, wherein *is* the covenant of the LORD, that he made with the children of Israel.

12 And he stood before the altar of the LORD in the presence of all the congregation of Israel, and spread forth his hands:

13 For Solomon had made a brasen scaffold, of five cubits long, and five cubits broad, and three cubits high, and had set it in the midst of the court: and upon it he stood, and kneeled down upon his knees before all the congregation of Israel, and spread forth his hands toward heaven,

14 And said, O LORD God of Israel, *there is* no God like thee in the heaven, nor in the earth; which keepest covenant, and *shewest* mercy unto thy servants, that walk before thee with all their hearts:

15 Thou which hast kept with thy servant David my father that which thou hast promised him; and spakest with thy mouth, and hast fulfilled *it* with thine hand, as *it is* this day.

16 Now therefore, O LORD God of Israel, keep with thy servant David my father that which thou hast promised him, saying, There shall not fail thee a man in my sight to sit upon the throne of Israel; yet so that thy children take heed to their way to walk in my law, as thou hast walked before me.

17 Now then, O LORD God of Israel, let thy word be verified, which thou hast spoken unto thy servant David.

18 But will God in very deed dwell with men on the earth? behold, heaven and the heaven of heavens cannot contain thee; how much less this house which I have built!

19 Have respect therefore to the prayer of thy servant, and to his supplication, O LORD my God, to hearken unto the cry and the prayer which thy servant prayeth before thee:

20 That thine eyes may be open upon this house day and night, upon the place whereof thou hast said that thou wouldest put thy name there; to hearken unto the prayer which thy servant prayeth toward this place.

21 Hearken therefore unto the supplications of thy servant, and of thy people Israel, which they shall make toward this place: hear thou from thy dwelling place, *even* from heaven; and when thou hearest, forgive.

22 If a man sin against his neighbour, and an oath be laid upon him to make him swear, and the oath come before thine altar in this house;

23 Then hear thou from heaven, and do, and judge thy servants, by requiting the wicked, by recompensing his way upon his own head; and by justifying the righteous, by giving him according to his righteousness.

24 And if thy people Israel be put to the worse before the enemy, because they have sinned against thee; and shall return and confess thy name, and pray and make supplication before thee in this house;

25 Then hear thou from the heavens, and forgive the sin of thy people Israel, and bring them again unto the land which thou gavest to them and to their fathers.

26 When the heaven is shut up, and there is no rain, because they have sinned against thee; *yet* if they pray toward this place, and confess thy name, and turn from their sin, when thou dost afflict them;

27 Then hear thou from heaven, and forgive the sin of thy servants, and of thy people Israel, when thou hast taught them the good way, wherein they should walk; and send rain upon thy land, which thou hast given unto thy people for an inheritance.

28 If there be dearth in the land, if there be pestilence, if there be blasting, or mildew, locusts, or caterpillers; if their enemies besiege them in the cities of their land; whatsoever sore or whatsoever sickness *there be*:

29 *Then* what prayer *or* what supplication soever shall be made of any man, or of all thy people Israel, when every one shall know his own sore and his own grief, and shall spread forth his hands in this house:

30 Then hear thou from heaven thy dwelling place, and forgive, and render unto every man according unto all his ways, whose heart thou knowest; (for thou only knowest the hearts of the children of men:)

31 That they may fear thee, to walk in thy ways, so long as they live in the land which thou gavest unto our fathers.

32 Moreover concerning the stranger, which is not of thy people Israel, but is come from a far country for thy great name's sake, and thy mighty hand, and thy stretched out arm; if they come and pray in this house;

33 Then hear thou from the heavens, *even* from thy dwelling place, and do according to all that the stranger calleth to thee for; that all people of the earth may know thy name, and fear thee, as *doth* thy people Israel, and may know that this house which I have built is called by thy name.

34 If thy people go out to war against their enemies by the way that thou shalt send them, and they pray unto thee toward this city which thou hast chosen, and the house which I have built for thy name;

35 Then hear thou from the heavens their prayer and their supplication, and maintain their cause.

36 If they sin against thee, (for *there is* no man which sinneth not,) and thou be angry with them, and deliver them over before *their* enemies, and they carry them away captives unto a land far off or near;

37 Yet *if* they bethink themselves in the land whither they are carried captive, and turn and pray unto thee in the land of their captivity, saying, We have sinned, we have done amiss, and have dealt wickedly;

38 If they return to thee with all their heart and with all their soul in the land of their captivity, whither they have carried them captives, and pray toward their land, which thou gavest unto their fathers, and *toward* the city which thou hast chosen, and toward the house which I have built for thy name:

39 Then hear thou from the heavens, *even* from thy dwelling place, their prayer and their supplications, and maintain their cause, and forgive thy people which have sinned against thee.

40 Now, my God, let, I beseech thee, thine eyes be open, and *let* thine ears *be* attent unto the prayer *that is made* in this place.

41 Now therefore arise, O LORD God, into thy resting place, thou, and the ark of thy strength: let thy priests, O LORD God, be clothed with salvation, and let thy saints rejoice in goodness.

42 O LORD God, turn not away the face of thine anointed: remember the mercies of David thy servant.

7 Now when Solomon had made an end of praying, the fire came down from heaven, and consumed the burnt offering and the sacrifices; and the glory of the LORD filled the house.

2 And the priests could not enter into
the house of the LORD, because the
glory of the LORD had filled the LORD's
house.
3 And when all the children of Israel
saw how the fire came down, and the
glory of the LORD upon the house, they
bowed themselves with their faces to
the ground upon the pavement, and
worshipped, and praised the LORD, *saying*, For *he is* good; for his mercy
endureth for ever.
4 Then the king and all the people
offered sacrifices before the LORD.
5 And king Solomon offered a sacrifice of twenty and two thousand oxen,
and an hundred and twenty thousand
sheep: so the king and all the people
dedicated the house of God.
6 And the priests waited on their
offices: the Levites also with instruments of musick of the LORD, which
David the king had made to praise the
LORD, because his mercy *endureth* for
ever, when David praised by their ministry; and the priests sounded trumpets
before them, and all Israel stood.
7 Moreover Solomon hallowed the
middle of the court that *was* before the
house of the LORD: for there he offered
burnt offerings, and the fat of the
peace offerings, because the brasen
altar which Solomon had made was not
able to receive the burnt offerings, and
the meat offerings, and the fat.
8 Also at the same time Solomon kept
the feast seven days, and all Israel with
him, a very great congregation, from
the entering in of Hamath unto the
river of Egypt.
9 And in the eighth day they made a
solemn assembly: for they kept the
dedication of the altar seven days, and
the feast seven days.
10 And on the three and twentieth
day of the seventh month he sent the
people away into their tents, glad and
merry in heart for the goodness that
the LORD had shewed unto David, and
to Solomon, and to Israel his people.
11 Thus Solomon finished the house
of the LORD, and the king's house: and
all that came into Solomon's heart to
make in the house of the LORD, and in
his own house, he prosperously effect-
ed.
12 And the LORD appeared to
Solomon by night, and said unto him, I
have heard thy prayer, and have chosen
this place to myself for an house of
sacrifice.
13 If I shut up heaven that there be no
rain, or if I command the locusts to
devour the land, or if I send pestilence
among my people;
14 If my people, which are called by
my name, shall humble themselves,
and pray, and seek my face, and turn
from their wicked ways; then will I hear
from heaven, and will forgive their sin,
and will heal their land.
15 Now mine eyes shall be open, and
mine ears attent unto the prayer *that is
made* in this place.
16 For now have I chosen and sanctified this house, that my name may be
there for ever: and mine eyes and mine
heart shall be there perpetually.
17 And as for thee, if thou wilt walk
before me, as David thy father walked,
and do according to all that I have commanded thee, and shalt observe my
statutes and my judgments;
18 Then will I stablish the throne of
thy kingdom, according as I have covenanted with David thy father, saying,
There shall not fail thee a man *to be*
ruler in Israel.

19 But if ye turn away, and forsake my
statutes and my commandments, which
I have set before you, and shall go and
serve other gods, and worship them;
20 Then will I pluck them up by the
roots out of my land which I have given
them; and this house, which I have
sanctified for my name, will I cast out
of my sight, and will make it *to be* a
proverb and a byword among all
nations.
21 And this house, which is high, shall
be an astonishment to every one that
passeth by it; so that he shall say, Why
hath the LORD done thus unto this land,
and unto this house?
22 And it shall be answered, Because
they forsook the LORD God of their
fathers, which brought them forth out
of the land of Egypt, and laid hold on
other gods, and worshipped them, and
served them: therefore hath he brought
all this evil upon them.

8 And it came to pass at the end of
twenty years, wherein Solomon had
built the house of the LORD, and his
own house,
2 That the cities which Huram had
restored to Solomon, Solomon built
them, and caused the children of Israel
to dwell there.
3 And Solomon went to Hamath-
zobah, and prevailed against it.
4 And he built Tadmor in the wilderness, and all the store cities, which he
built in Hamath.
5 Also he built Beth-horon the upper,
and Beth-horon the nether, fenced cities, with walls, gates, and bars;
6 And Baalath, and all the store cities
that Solomon had, and all the chariot
cities, and the cities of the horsemen,
and all that Solomon desired to build in
Jerusalem, and in Lebanon, and
throughout all the land of his dominion.
7 *As for* all the people *that were* left
of the Hittites, and the Amorites, and
the Perizzites, and the Hivites, and the
Jebusites, which *were* not of Israel,
8 *But* of their children, who were left
after them in the land, whom the children of Israel consumed not, them did
Solomon make to pay tribute until this
day.
9 But of the children of Israel did
Solomon make no servants for his work;
but they *were* men of war, and chief of
his captains, and captains of his chariots and horsemen.
10 And these *were* the chief of king
Solomon's officers, *even* two hundred
and fifty, that bare rule over the people.
11 And Solomon brought up the
daughter of Pharaoh out of the city of
David unto the house that he had built
for her: for he said, My wife shall not
dwell in the house of David king of
Israel, because *the places are* holy,
whereunto the ark of the LORD hath
come.
12 Then Solomon offered burnt offerings unto the LORD on the altar of the
LORD, which he had built before the
porch,
13 Even after a certain rate every day,
offering according to the commandment of Moses, on the sabbaths, and on
the new moons, and on the solemn
feasts, three times in the year, *even* in
the feast of unleavened bread, and in
the feast of weeks, and in the feast of
tabernacles.
14 And he appointed, according to
the order of David his father, the courses of the priests to their service, and
the Levites to their charges, to praise
and minister before the priests, as the

duty of every day required: the porters also by their courses at every gate: for so had David the man of God commanded.

15 And they departed not from the commandment of the king unto the priests and Levites concerning any matter, or concerning the treasures.

16 Now all the work of Solomon was prepared unto the day of the foundation of the house of the LORD, and until it was finished. *So* the house of the LORD was perfected.

17 Then went Solomon to Eziongeber, and to Eloth, at the sea side in the land of Edom.

18 And Huram sent him by the hands of his servants ships, and servants that had knowledge of the sea; and they went with the servants of Solomon to Ophir, and took thence four hundred and fifty talents of gold, and brought *them* to king Solomon.

9 And when the queen of Sheba heard of the fame of Solomon, she came to prove Solomon with hard questions at Jerusalem, with a very great company, and camels that bare spices, and gold in abundance, and precious stones: and when she was come to Solomon, she communed with him of all that was in her heart.

2 And Solomon told her all her questions: and there was nothing hid from Solomon which he told her not.

3 And when the queen of Sheba had seen the wisdom of Solomon, and the house that he had built,

4 And the meat of his table, and the sitting of his servants, and the attendance of his ministers, and their apparel; his cupbearers also, and their apparel; and his ascent by which he went up into the house of the LORD; there was no more spirit in her.

5 And she said to the king, *It was* a true report which I heard in mine own land of thine acts, and of thy wisdom:

6 Howbeit I believed not their words, until I came, and mine eyes had seen *it*: and, behold, the one half of the greatness of thy wisdom was not told me: *for* thou exceedest the fame that I heard.

7 Happy *are* thy men, and happy *are* these thy servants, which stand continually before thee, and hear thy wisdom.

8 Blessed be the LORD thy God, which delighted in thee to set thee on his throne, *to be* king for the LORD thy God: because thy God loved Israel, to establish them for ever, therefore made he thee king over them, to do judgment and justice.

9 And she gave the king an hundred and twenty talents of gold, and of spices great abundance, and precious stones: neither was there any such spice as the queen of Sheba gave king Solomon.

10 And the servants also of Huram, and the servants of Solomon, which brought gold from Ophir, brought algum trees and precious stones.

11 And the king made *of* the algum trees terraces to the house of the LORD, and to the king's palace, and harps and psalteries for singers: and there were none such seen before in the land of Judah.

12 And king Solomon gave to the queen of Sheba all her desire, whatsoever she asked, beside *that* which she had brought unto the king. So she turned, and went away to her own land, she and her servants.

13 Now the weight of gold that came to Solomon in one year was six hundred and threescore and six talents of gold;

14 Beside *that which* chapmen and merchants brought. And all the kings of Arabia and governors of the country brought gold and silver to Solomon.

15 And king Solomon made two hundred targets *of* beaten gold: six hundred *shekels* of beaten gold went to one target.

16 And three hundred shields *made he of* beaten gold: three hundred *shekels* of gold went to one shield. And the king put them in the house of the forest of Lebanon.

17 Moreover the king made a great throne of ivory, and overlaid it with pure gold.

18 And *there were* six steps to the throne, with a footstool of gold, *which were* fastened to the throne, and stays on each side of the sitting place, and two lions standing by the stays:

19 And twelve lions stood there on the one side and on the other upon the six steps. There was not the like made in any kingdom.

20 And all the drinking vessels of king Solomon *were of* gold, and all the vessels of the house of the forest of Lebanon *were of* pure gold: none *were of* silver; it was *not* any thing accounted of in the days of Solomon.

21 For the king's ships went to Tarshish with the servants of Huram: every three years once came the ships of Tarshish bringing gold, and silver, ivory, and apes, and peacocks.

22 And king Solomon passed all the kings of the earth in riches and wisdom.

23 And all the kings of the earth sought the presence of Solomon, to hear his wisdom, that God had put in his heart.

24 And they brought every man his present, vessels of silver, and vessels of gold, and raiment, harness, and spices, horses, and mules, a rate year by year.

25 And Solomon had four thousand stalls for horses and chariots, and twelve thousand horsemen; whom he bestowed in the chariot cities, and with the king at Jerusalem.

26 And he reigned over all the kings from the river even unto the land of the Philistines, and to the border of Egypt.

27 And the king made silver in Jerusalem as stones, and cedar trees made he as the sycomore trees that *are* in the low plains in abundance.

28 And they brought unto Solomon horses out of Egypt, and out of all lands.

29 Now the rest of the acts of Solomon, first and last, *are* they not written in the book of Nathan the prophet, and in the prophecy of Ahijah the Shilonite, and in the visions of Iddo the seer against Jeroboam the son of Nebat?

30 And Solomon reigned in Jerusalem over all Israel forty years.

31 And Solomon slept with his fathers, and he was buried in the city of David his father: and Rehoboam his son reigned in his stead.

10 And Rehoboam went to Shechem: for to Shechem were all Israel come to make him king.

2 And it came to pass, when Jeroboam the son of Nebat, who *was* in Egypt, whither he had fled from the presence of Solomon the king, heard *it*, that Jeroboam returned out of Egypt.

3 And they sent and called him. So Jeroboam and all Israel came and spake to Rehoboam, saying,

4 Thy father made our yoke grievous: now therefore ease thou somewhat the grievous servitude of thy father, and his heavy yoke that he put upon us, and we will serve thee.

5 And he said unto them, Come again unto me after three days. And the people departed.

6 And king Rehoboam took counsel with the old men that had stood before Solomon his father while he yet lived, saying, What counsel give ye *me* to return answer to this people?

7 And they spake unto him, saying, If thou be kind to this people, and please them, and speak good words to them, they will be thy servants for ever.

8 But he forsook the counsel which the old men gave him, and took counsel with the young men that were brought up with him, that stood before him.

9 And he said unto them, What advice give ye that we may return answer to this people, which have spoken to me, saying, Ease somewhat the yoke that thy father did put upon us?

10 And the young men that were brought up with him spake unto him, saying, Thus shalt thou answer the people that spake unto thee, saying, Thy father made our yoke heavy, but make thou *it* somewhat lighter for us; thus shalt thou say unto them, My little *finger* shall be thicker than my father's loins.

11 For whereas my father put a heavy yoke upon you, I will put more to your yoke: my father chastised you with whips, but I *will chastise you* with scorpions.

12 So Jeroboam and all the people came to Rehoboam on the third day, as the king bade, saying, Come again to me on the third day.

13 And the king answered them roughly; and king Rehoboam forsook the counsel of the old men,

14 And answered them after the advice of the young men, saying, My father made your yoke heavy, but I will add thereto: my father chastised you with whips, but I *will chastise you* with scorpions.

15 So the king hearkened not unto the people: for the cause was of God, that the LORD might perform his word, which he spake by the hand of Ahijah the Shilonite to Jeroboam the son of Nebat.

16 And when all Israel *saw* that the king would not hearken unto them, the people answered the king, saying, What portion have we in David? and *we have* none inheritance in the son of Jesse: every man to your tents, O Israel: *and* now, David, see to thine own house. So all Israel went to their tents.

17 But *as for* the children of Israel that dwelt in the cities of Judah, Rehoboam reigned over them.

18 Then king Rehoboam sent Hadoram that *was* over the tribute; and the children of Israel stoned him with stones, that he died. But king Rehoboam made speed to get him up to *his* chariot, to flee to Jerusalem.

19 And Israel rebelled against the house of David unto this day.

11 And when Rehoboam was come to Jerusalem, he gathered of the house of Judah and Benjamin an hundred and fourscore thousand chosen *men*, which were warriors, to fight

against Israel, that he might bring the
kingdom again to Rehoboam.
2 But the word of the LORD came to
Shemaiah the man of God, saying,
3 Speak unto Rehoboam the son of
Solomon, king of Judah, and to all
Israel in Judah and Benjamin, saying,
4 Thus saith the LORD, Ye shall not go
up, nor fight against your brethren:
return every man to his house: for this
thing is done of me. And they obeyed
the words of the LORD, and returned
from going against Jeroboam.
5 And Rehoboam dwelt in Jerusalem,
and built cities for defence in Judah.
6 He built even Beth-lehem, and
Etam, and Tekoa,
7 And Beth-zur, and Shoco, and
Adullam,
8 And Gath, and Mareshah, and Ziph,
9 And Adoraim, and Lachish, and
Azekah,
10 And Zorah, and Aijalon, and
Hebron, which *are* in Judah and in
Benjamin fenced cities.
11 And he fortified the strong holds,
and put captains in them, and store of
victual, and of oil and wine.
12 And in every several city *he put*
shields and spears, and made them
exceeding strong, having Judah and
Benjamin on his side.
13 And the priests and the Levites
that *were* in all Israel resorted to him
out of all their coasts.
14 For the Levites left their suburbs
and their possession, and came to
Judah and Jerusalem: for Jeroboam
and his sons had cast them off from
executing the priest's office unto the
LORD:
15 And he ordained him priests for
the high places, and for the devils, and
for the calves which he had made.
16 And after them out of all the tribes
of Israel such as set their hearts to seek
the LORD God of Israel came to Jerusalem, to sacrifice unto the LORD God
of their fathers.
17 So they strengthened the kingdom
of Judah, and made Rehoboam the son
of Solomon strong, three years: for
three years they walked in the way of
David and Solomon.
18 And Rehoboam took him Mahalath
the daughter of Jerimoth the son of
David to wife, *and* Abihail the daughter of Eliab the son of Jesse;
19 Which bare him children; Jeush,
and Shamariah, and Zaham.
20 And after her he took Maachah
the daughter of Absalom; which bare
him Abijah, and Attai, and Ziza, and
Shelomith.
21 And Rehoboam loved Maachah
the daughter of Absalom above all his
wives and his concubines: (for he took
eighteen wives, and threescore concubines; and begat twenty and eight sons,
and threescore daughters.)
22 And Rehoboam made Abijah the
son of Maachah the chief, *to be* ruler
among his brethren: for *he thought* to
make him king.
23 And he dealt wisely, and dispersed
of all his children throughout all the
countries of Judah and Benjamin, unto
every fenced city: and he gave them
victual in abundance. And he desired
many wives.

12 And it came to pass, when
Rehoboam had established the
kingdom, and had strengthened himself, he forsook the law of the LORD, and
all Israel with him.
2 And it came to pass, *that* in the fifth
year of king Rehoboam Shishak king of
Egypt came up against Jerusalem,

because they had transgressed against
the LORD,
3 With twelve hundred chariots, and
threescore thousand horsemen: and the
people *were* without number that came
with him out of Egypt; the Lubims, the
Sukkiims, and the Ethiopians.
4 And he took the fenced cities which
pertained to Judah, and came to Jerusalem.
5 Then came Shemaiah the prophet
to Rehoboam, and *to* the princes of
Judah, that were gathered together to
Jerusalem because of Shishak, and said
unto them, Thus saith the LORD, Ye have
forsaken me, and therefore have I also
left you in the hand of Shishak.
6 Whereupon the princes of Israel
and the king humbled themselves; and
they said, The LORD *is* righteous.
7 And when the LORD saw that they
humbled themselves, the word of the
LORD came to Shemaiah, saying, They
have humbled themselves; *therefore* I
will not destroy them, but I will grant
them some deliverance; and my wrath
shall not be poured out upon Jerusalem
by the hand of Shishak.
8 Nevertheless they shall be his servants;
that they may know my service,
and the service of the kingdoms of the
countries.
9 So Shishak king of Egypt came up
against Jerusalem, and took away the
treasures of the house of the LORD, and
the treasures of the king's house; he
took all: he carried away also the
shields of gold which Solomon had
made.
10 Instead of which king Rehoboam
made shields of brass, and committed
them to the hands of the chief of the
guard, that kept the entrance of the
king's house.
11 And when the king entered into
the house of the LORD, the guard came
and fetched them, and brought them
again into the guard chamber.
12 And when he humbled himself,
the wrath of the LORD turned from him,
that he would not destroy *him* altogether:
and also in Judah things went
well.
13 So king Rehoboam strengthened
himself in Jerusalem, and reigned: for
Rehoboam *was* one and forty years old
when he began to reign, and he reigned
seventeen years in Jerusalem, the city
which the LORD had chosen out of all
the tribes of Israel, to put his name
there. And his mother's name *was*
Naamah an Ammonitess.
14 And he did evil, because he prepared
not his heart to seek the LORD.
15 Now the acts of Rehoboam, first
and last, *are* they not written in the
book of Shemaiah the prophet, and of
Iddo the seer concerning genealogies?
And *there were* wars between Rehoboam
and Jeroboam continually.
16 And Rehoboam slept with his
fathers, and was buried in the city of
David: and Abijah his son reigned in
his stead.

13 Now in the eighteenth year of
king Jeroboam began Abijah to
reign over Judah.
2 He reigned three years in Jerusalem.
His mother's name also *was* Michaiah
the daughter of Uriel of Gibeah. And
there was war between Abijah and
Jeroboam.
3 And Abijah set the battle in array
with an army of valiant men of war,
even four hundred thousand chosen
men: Jeroboam also set the battle in
array against him with eight hundred

thousand chosen men, *being* mighty men of valour.

4 And Abijah stood up upon mount Zemaraim, which *is* in mount Ephraim, and said, Hear me, thou Jeroboam, and all Israel;

5 Ought ye not to know that the LORD God of Israel gave the kingdom over Israel to David for ever, *even* to him and to his sons by a covenant of salt?

6 Yet Jeroboam the son of Nebat, the servant of Solomon the son of David, is risen up, and hath rebelled against his lord.

7 And there are gathered unto him vain men, the children of Belial, and have strengthened themselves against Rehoboam the son of Solomon, when Rehoboam was young and tenderhearted, and could not withstand them.

8 And now ye think to withstand the kingdom of the LORD in the hand of the sons of David; and ye *be* a great multitude, and *there are* with you golden calves, which Jeroboam made you for gods.

9 Have ye not cast out the priests of the LORD, the sons of Aaron, and the Levites, and have made you priests after the manner of the nations of *other* lands? so that whosoever cometh to consecrate himself with a young bullock and seven rams, *the same* may be a priest of *them that are* no gods.

10 But as for us, the LORD *is* our God, and we have not forsaken him; and the priests, which minister unto the LORD, *are* the sons of Aaron, and the Levites *wait* upon *their* business:

11 And they burn unto the LORD every morning and every evening burnt sacrifices and sweet incense: the shewbread also *set they in order* upon the pure table; and the candlestick of gold with the lamps thereof, to burn every evening: for we keep the charge of the LORD our God; but ye have forsaken him.

12 And, behold, God himself *is* with us for *our* captain, and his priests with sounding trumpets to cry alarm against you. O children of Israel, fight ye not against the LORD God of your fathers; for ye shall not prosper.

13 But Jeroboam caused an ambushment to come about behind them: so they were before Judah, and the ambushment *was* behind them.

14 And when Judah looked back, behold, the battle *was* before and behind: and they cried unto the LORD, and the priests sounded with the trumpets.

15 Then the men of Judah gave a shout: and as the men of Judah shouted, it came to pass, that God smote Jeroboam and all Israel before Abijah and Judah.

16 And the children of Israel fled before Judah: and God delivered them into their hand.

17 And Abijah and his people slew them with a great slaughter: so there fell down slain of Israel five hundred thousand chosen men.

18 Thus the children of Israel were brought under at that time, and the children of Judah prevailed, because they relied upon the LORD God of their fathers.

19 And Abijah pursued after Jeroboam, and took cities from him, Beth-el with the towns thereof, and Jeshanah with the towns thereof, and Ephrain with the towns thereof.

20 Neither did Jeroboam recover strength again in the days of Abijah: and the LORD struck him, and he died.

21 But Abijah waxed mighty, and married fourteen wives, and begat twenty and two sons, and sixteen daughters.

22 And the rest of the acts of Abijah, and his ways, and his sayings, *are* written in the story of the prophet Iddo.

14 So Abijah slept with his fathers, and they buried him in the city of David: and Asa his son reigned in his stead. In his days the land was quiet ten years.

2 And Asa did *that which was* good and right in the eyes of the LORD his God:

3 For he took away the altars of the strange *gods*, and the high places, and brake down the images, and cut down the groves:

4 And commanded Judah to seek the LORD God of their fathers, and to do the law and the commandment.

5 Also he took away out of all the cities of Judah the high places and the images: and the kingdom was quiet before him.

6 And he built fenced cities in Judah: for the land had rest, and he had no war in those years; because the LORD had given him rest.

7 Therefore he said unto Judah, Let us build these cities, and make about *them* walls, and towers, gates, and bars, *while* the land *is* yet before us; because we have sought the LORD our God, we have sought *him*, and he hath given us rest on every side. So they built and prospered.

8 And Asa had an army *of men* that bare targets and spears, out of Judah three hundred thousand; and out of Benjamin, that bare shields and drew bows, two hundred and fourscore thousand: all these *were* mighty men of valour.

9 And there came out against them Zerah the Ethiopian with an host of a thousand thousand, and three hundred chariots; and came unto Mareshah.

10 Then Asa went out against him, and they set the battle in array in the valley of Zephathah at Mareshah.

11 And Asa cried unto the LORD his God, and said, LORD, *it is* nothing with thee to help, whether with many, or with them that have no power: help us, O LORD our God; for we rest on thee, and in thy name we go against this multitude. O LORD, thou *art* our God; let not man prevail against thee.

12 So the LORD smote the Ethiopians before Asa, and before Judah; and the Ethiopians fled.

13 And Asa and the people that *were* with him pursued them unto Gerar: and the Ethiopians were overthrown, that they could not recover themselves; for they were destroyed before the LORD, and before his host; and they carried away very much spoil.

14 And they smote all the cities round about Gerar; for the fear of the LORD came upon them: and they spoiled all the cities; for there was exceeding much spoil in them.

15 They smote also the tents of cattle, and carried away sheep and camels in abundance, and returned to Jerusalem.

15 And the Spirit of God came upon Azariah the son of Oded:

2 And he went out to meet Asa, and said unto him, Hear ye me, Asa, and all Judah and Benjamin; The LORD *is* with you, while ye be with him; and if ye seek him, he will be found of you; but if ye forsake him, he will forsake you.

3 Now for a long season Israel *hath*
been without the true God, and without
a teaching priest, and without law.
4 But when they in their trouble did
turn unto the LORD God of Israel, and
sought him, he was found of them.
5 And in those times *there was* no
peace to him that went out, nor to him
that came in, but great vexations *were*
upon all the inhabitants of the countries.
6 And nation was destroyed of nation,
and city of city: for God did vex them
with all adversity.
7 Be ye strong therefore, and let not
your hands be weak: for your work
shall be rewarded.
8 And when Asa heard these words,
and the prophecy of Oded the prophet,
he took courage, and put away the
abominable idols out of all the land of
Judah and Benjamin, and out of the
cities which he had taken from mount
Ephraim, and renewed the altar of the
LORD, that *was* before the porch of the
LORD.
9 And he gathered all Judah and
Benjamin, and the strangers with them
out of Ephraim and Manasseh, and out
of Simeon: for they fell to him out of
Israel in abundance, when they saw
that the LORD his God *was* with him.
10 So they gathered themselves
together at Jerusalem in the third
month, in the fifteenth year of the
reign of Asa.
11 And they offered unto the LORD
the same time, of the spoil *which* they
had brought, seven hundred oxen and
seven thousand sheep.
12 And they entered into a covenant
to seek the LORD God of their fathers
with all their heart and with all their
soul;
13 That whosoever would not seek
the LORD God of Israel should be put to
death, whether small or great, whether
man or woman.
14 And they sware unto the LORD with
a loud voice, and with shouting, and
with trumpets, and with cornets.
15 And all Judah rejoiced at the oath:
for they had sworn with all their heart,
and sought him with their whole desire;
and he was found of them: and the
LORD gave them rest round about.
16 And also *concerning* Maachah the
mother of Asa the king, he removed her
from *being* queen, because she had
made an idol in a grove: and Asa cut
down her idol, and stamped *it*, and
burnt *it* at the brook Kidron.
17 But the high places were not taken
away out of Israel: nevertheless the
heart of Asa was perfect all his days.
18 And he brought into the house of
God the things that his father had
dedicated, and that he himself had
dedicated, silver, and gold, and vessels.
19 And there was no *more* war unto
the five and thirtieth year of the reign
of Asa.

16 In the six and thirtieth year of
the reign of Asa Baasha king of
Israel came up against Judah, and built
Ramah, to the intent that he might let
none go out or come in to Asa king of
Judah.
2 Then Asa brought out silver and
gold out of the treasures of the house of
the LORD and of the king's house, and
sent to Ben-hadad king of Syria, that
dwelt at Damascus, saying,
3 *There is* a league between me and
thee, as *there was* between my father
and thy father: behold, I have sent thee
silver and gold; go, break thy league

with Baasha king of Israel, that he may depart from me.

4 And Ben-hadad hearkened unto king Asa, and sent the captains of his armies against the cities of Israel; and they smote Ijon, and Dan, and Abel-maim, and all the store cities of Naphtali.

5 And it came to pass, when Baasha heard *it*, that he left off building of Ramah, and let his work cease.

6 Then Asa the king took all Judah; and they carried away the stones of Ramah, and the timber thereof, wherewith Baasha was building; and he built therewith Geba and Mizpah.

7 And at that time Hanani the seer came to Asa king of Judah, and said unto him, Because thou hast relied on the king of Syria, and not relied on the LORD thy God, therefore is the host of the king of Syria escaped out of thine hand.

8 Were not the Ethiopians and the Lubims a huge host, with very many chariots and horsemen? yet, because thou didst rely on the LORD, he delivered them into thine hand.

9 For the eyes of the LORD run to and fro throughout the whole earth, to shew himself strong in the behalf of *them* whose heart *is* perfect toward him. Herein thou hast done foolishly: therefore from henceforth thou shalt have wars.

10 Then Asa was wroth with the seer, and put him in a prison house; for *he was* in a rage with him because of this *thing*. And Asa oppressed *some* of the people the same time.

11 And, behold, the acts of Asa, first and last, lo, they *are* written in the book of the kings of Judah and Israel.

12 And Asa in the thirty and ninth year of his reign was diseased in his feet, until his disease *was* exceeding *great*: yet in his disease he sought not to the LORD, but to the physicians.

13 And Asa slept with his fathers, and died in the one and fortieth year of his reign.

14 And they buried him in his own sepulchres, which he had made for himself in the city of David, and laid him in the bed which was filled with sweet odours and divers kinds *of spices* prepared by the apothecaries' art: and they made a very great burning for him.

17 And Jehoshaphat his son reigned in his stead, and strengthened himself against Israel.

2 And he placed forces in all the fenced cities of Judah, and set garrisons in the land of Judah, and in the cities of Ephraim, which Asa his father had taken.

3 And the LORD was with Jehoshaphat, because he walked in the first ways of his father David, and sought not unto Baalim;

4 But sought to the *LORD* God of his father, and walked in his commandments, and not after the doings of Israel.

5 Therefore the LORD stablished the kingdom in his hand; and all Judah brought to Jehoshaphat presents; and he had riches and honour in abundance.

6 And his heart was lifted up in the ways of the LORD: moreover he took away the high places and groves out of Judah.

7 Also in the third year of his reign he sent to his princes, *even* to Ben-hail, and to Obadiah, and to Zechariah, and

to Nethaneel, and to Michaiah, to teach
in the cities of Judah.
8 And with them *he sent* Levites, *even*
Shemaiah, and Nethaniah, and Zebadiah, and Asahel, and Shemiramoth,
and Jehonathan, and Adonijah, and
Tobijah, and Tob-adonijah, Levites; and
with them Elishama and Jehoram,
priests.
9 And they taught in Judah, and *had*
the book of the law of the LORD with
them, and went about throughout all
the cities of Judah, and taught the
people.
10 And the fear of the LORD fell upon
all the kingdoms of the lands that *were*
round about Judah, so that they made
no war against Jehoshaphat.
11 Also *some* of the Philistines
brought Jehoshaphat presents, and
tribute silver; and the Arabians brought
him flocks, seven thousand and seven
hundred rams, and seven thousand and
seven hundred he goats.
12 And Jehoshaphat waxed great
exceedingly; and he built in Judah castles, and cities of store.
13 And he had much business in the
cities of Judah: and the men of war,
mighty men of valour, *were* in
Jerusalem.
14 And these *are* the numbers of
them according to the house of their
fathers: Of Judah, the captains of thousands; Adnah the chief, and with him
mighty men of valour three hundred
thousand.
15 And next to him *was* Jehohanan
the captain, and with him two hundred
and fourscore thousand.
16 And next him *was* Amasiah the
son of Zichri, who willingly offered
himself unto the LORD; and with him
two hundred thousand mighty men of
valour.
17 And of Benjamin; Eliada a mighty
man of valour, and with him armed
men with bow and shield two hundred
thousand.
18 And next him *was* Jehozabad, and
with him an hundred and fourscore
thousand ready prepared for the war.
19 These waited on the king, beside
those whom the king put in the fenced
cities throughout all Judah.

18 Now Jehoshaphat had riches and
honour in abundance, and joined
affinity with Ahab.
2 And after *certain* years he went
down to Ahab to Samaria. And Ahab
killed sheep and oxen for him in abundance, and for the people that *he had*
with him, and persuaded him to go up
with him to Ramoth-gilead.
3 And Ahab king of Israel said unto
Jehoshaphat king of Judah, Wilt thou
go with me to Ramoth-gilead? And he
answered him, I *am* as thou *art*, and my
people as thy people; and *we will be*
with thee in the war.
4 And Jehoshaphat said unto the king
of Israel, Enquire, I pray thee, at the
word of the LORD to day.
5 Therefore the king of Israel gathered together of prophets four hundred
men, and said unto them, Shall we go to
Ramoth-gilead to battle, or shall I forbear? And they said, Go up; for God
will deliver *it* into the king's hand.
6 But Jehoshaphat said, *Is there* not
here a prophet of the LORD besides,
that we might enquire of him?
7 And the king of Israel said unto
Jehoshaphat, *There is* yet one man, by
whom we may enquire of the LORD: but
I hate him; for he never prophesied
good unto me, but always evil: the same

is Micaiah the son of Imla. And
Jehoshaphat said, Let not the king say
so.
8 And the king of Israel called for one
of his officers, and said, Fetch quickly
Micaiah the son of Imla.
9 And the king of Israel and
Jehoshaphat king of Judah sat either of
them on his throne, clothed in *their*
robes, and they sat in a void place at
the entering in of the gate of Samaria;
and all the prophets prophesied before
them.
10 And Zedekiah the son of Chenaanah had made him horns of iron,
and said, Thus saith the LORD, With
these thou shalt push Syria until they
be consumed.
11 And all the prophets prophesied
so, saying, Go up to Ramoth-gilead, and
prosper: for the LORD shall deliver *it*
into the hand of the king.
12 And the messenger that went to
call Micaiah spake to him, saying,
Behold, the words of the prophets
declare good to the king with one
assent; let thy word therefore, I pray
thee, be like one of theirs, and speak
thou good.
13 And Micaiah said, *As* the LORD
liveth, even what my God saith, that
will I speak.
14 And when he was come to the
king, the king said unto him, Micaiah,
shall we go to Ramoth-gilead to battle,
or shall I forbear? And he said, Go ye
up, and prosper, and they shall be delivered into your hand.
15 And the king said to him, How
many times shall I adjure thee that
thou say nothing but the truth to me in
the name of the LORD?
16 Then he said, I did see all Israel
scattered upon the mountains, as sheep
that have no shepherd: and the LORD
said, These have no master; let them
return *therefore* every man to his house
in peace.
17 And the king of Israel said to
Jehoshaphat, Did I not tell thee *that* he
would not prophesy good unto me, but
evil?
18 Again he said, Therefore hear the
word of the LORD; I saw the LORD sitting
upon his throne, and all the host of
heaven standing on his right hand and
on his left.
19 And the LORD said, Who shall
entice Ahab king of Israel, that he may
go up and fall at Ramoth-gilead? And
one spake saying after this manner, and
another saying after that manner.
20 Then there came out a spirit, and
stood before the LORD, and said, I will
entice him. And the LORD said unto
him, Wherewith?
21 And he said, I will go out, and be a
lying spirit in the mouth of all his
prophets. And *the LORD* said, Thou shalt
entice *him*, and thou shalt also prevail:
go out, and do *even* so.
22 Now therefore, behold, the LORD
hath put a lying spirit in the mouth of
these thy prophets, and the LORD hath
spoken evil against thee.
23 Then Zedekiah the son of
Chenaanah came near, and smote
Micaiah upon the cheek, and said,
Which way went the Spirit of the LORD
from me to speak unto thee?
24 And Micaiah said, Behold, thou
shalt see on that day when thou shalt
go into an inner chamber to hide thyself.
25 Then the king of Israel said, Take
ye Micaiah, and carry him back to
Amon the governor of the city, and to
Joash the king's son;

26 And say, Thus saith the king, Put
this *fellow* in the prison, and feed him
with bread of affliction and with water
of affliction, until I return in peace.
27 And Micaiah said, If thou certainly
return in peace, *then* hath not the LORD
spoken by me. And he said, Hearken,
all ye people.
28 So the king of Israel and
Jehoshaphat the king of Judah went up
to Ramoth-gilead.
29 And the king of Israel said unto
Jehoshaphat, I will disguise myself, and
will go to the battle; but put thou on thy
robes. So the king of Israel disguised
himself; and they went to the battle.
30 Now the king of Syria had commanded the captains of the chariots
that *were* with him, saying, Fight ye not
with small or great, save only with the
king of Israel.
31 And it came to pass, when the
captains of the chariots saw
Jehoshaphat, that they said, It *is* the
king of Israel. Therefore they compassed about him to fight: but
Jehoshaphat cried out, and the LORD
helped him; and God moved them *to*
depart from him.
32 For it came to pass, that, when the
captains of the chariots perceived that
it was not the king of Israel, they
turned back again from pursuing him.
33 And a *certain* man drew a bow at a
venture, and smote the king of Israel
between the joints of the harness:
therefore he said to his chariot man,
Turn thine hand, that thou mayest
carry me out of the host; for I am
wounded.
34 And the battle increased that day:
howbeit the king of Israel stayed *him-*
self up in *his* chariot against the Syrians
until the even: and about the time of
the sun going down he died.

19 And Jehoshaphat the king of
Judah returned to his house in
peace to Jerusalem.
2 And Jehu the son of Hanani the
seer went out to meet him, and said to
king Jehoshaphat, Shouldest thou help
the ungodly, and love them that hate
the LORD? therefore *is* wrath upon thee
from before the LORD.
3 Nevertheless there are good things
found in thee, in that thou hast taken
away the groves out of the land, and
hast prepared thine heart to seek God.
4 And Jehoshaphat dwelt at Jerusalem: and he went out again through
the people from Beer-sheba to mount
Ephraim, and brought them back unto
the LORD God of their fathers.
5 And he set judges in the land
throughout all the fenced cities of
Judah, city by city,
6 And said to the judges, Take heed
what ye do: for ye judge not for man,
but for the LORD, who *is* with you in the
judgment.
7 Wherefore now let the fear of the
LORD be upon you; take heed and do *it*:
for *there is* no iniquity with the LORD
our God, nor respect of persons, nor
taking of gifts.
8 Moreover in Jerusalem did Jehoshaphat set of the Levites, and *of* the
priests, and of the chief of the fathers
of Israel, for the judgment of the LORD,
and for controversies, when they
returned to Jerusalem.
9 And he charged them, saying, Thus
shall ye do in the fear of the LORD,
faithfully, and with a perfect heart.
10 And what cause soever shall come
to you of your brethren that dwell in
their cities, between blood and blood,

between law and commandment, statutes and judgments, ye shall even warn
them that they trespass not against the
LORD, and *so* wrath come upon you, and
upon your brethren: this do, and ye
shall not trespass.
11 And, behold, Amariah the chief
priest *is* over you in all matters of the
LORD; and Zebadiah the son of Ishmael,
the ruler of the house of Judah, for all
the king's matters: also the Levites
shall be officers before you. Deal coura-
geously, and the LORD shall be with the
good.

20 It came to pass after this also,
that the children of Moab, and
the children of Ammon, and with them
other beside the Ammonites, came
against Jehoshaphat to battle.
2 Then there came some that told
Jehoshaphat, saying, There cometh a
great multitude against thee from
beyond the sea on this side Syria; and,
behold, they *be* in Hazazon-tamar,
which *is* En-gedi.
3 And Jehoshaphat feared, and set
himself to seek the LORD, and proclaimed a fast throughout all Judah.
4 And Judah gathered themselves
together, to ask *help* of the LORD: even
out of all the cities of Judah they came
to seek the LORD.
5 And Jehoshaphat stood in the congregation of Judah and Jerusalem, in
the house of the LORD, before the new
court,
6 And said, O LORD God of our fathers,
art not thou God in heaven? and rulest
not thou over all the kingdoms of the
heathen? and in thine hand *is there not*
power and might, so that none is able to
withstand thee?
7 *Art* not thou our God, *who* didst
drive out the inhabitants of this land
before thy people Israel, and gavest it
to the seed of Abraham thy friend for
ever?
8 And they dwelt therein, and have
built thee a sanctuary therein for thy
name, saying,
9 If, *when* evil cometh upon us, *as* the
sword, judgment, or pestilence, or famine, we stand before this house, and in
thy presence, (for thy name *is* in this
house,) and cry unto thee in our affliction, then thou wilt hear and help.
10 And now, behold, the children of
Ammon and Moab and mount Seir,
whom thou wouldest not let Israel
invade, when they came out of the land
of Egypt, but they turned from them,
and destroyed them not;
11 Behold, *I say, how* they reward us,
to come to cast us out of thy possession,
which thou hast given us to inherit.
12 O our God, wilt thou not judge
them? for we have no might against this
great company that cometh against us;
neither know we what to do: but our
eyes *are* upon thee.
13 And all Judah stood before the
LORD, with their little ones, their wives,
and their children.
14 Then upon Jahaziel the son of
Zechariah, the son of Benaiah, the son
of Jeiel, the son of Mattaniah, a Levite
of the sons of Asaph, came the Spirit of
the LORD in the midst of the congregation;
15 And he said, Hearken ye, all Judah,
and ye inhabitants of Jerusalem, and
thou king Jehoshaphat, Thus saith the
LORD unto you, Be not afraid nor dismayed by reason of this great multitude; for the battle *is* not yours, but
God's.
16 To morrow go ye down against
them: behold, they come up by the cliff

of Ziz; and ye shall find them at the end of the brook, before the wilderness of Jeruel.

17 Ye shall not *need* to fight in this *battle*: set yourselves, stand ye *still*, and see the salvation of the LORD with you, O Judah and Jerusalem: fear not, nor be dismayed; to morrow go out against them: for the LORD *will be* with you.

18 And Jehoshaphat bowed his head with *his* face to the ground: and all Judah and the inhabitants of Jerusalem fell before the LORD, worshipping the LORD.

19 And the Levites, of the children of the Kohathites, and of the children of the Korhites, stood up to praise the LORD God of Israel with a loud voice on high.

20 And they rose early in the morning, and went forth into the wilderness of Tekoa: and as they went forth, Jehoshaphat stood and said, Hear me, O Judah, and ye inhabitants of Jerusalem; Believe in the LORD your God, so shall ye be established; believe his prophets, so shall ye prosper.

21 And when he had consulted with the people, he appointed singers unto the LORD, and that should praise the beauty of holiness, as they went out before the army, and to say, Praise the LORD; for his mercy *endureth* for ever.

22 And when they began to sing and to praise, the LORD set ambushments against the children of Ammon, Moab, and mount Seir, which were come against Judah; and they were smitten.

23 For the children of Ammon and Moab stood up against the inhabitants of mount Seir, utterly to slay and destroy *them*: and when they had made an end of the inhabitants of Seir, every one helped to destroy another.

24 And when Judah came toward the watch tower in the wilderness, they looked unto the multitude, and, behold, they *were* dead bodies fallen to the earth, and none escaped.

25 And when Jehoshaphat and his people came to take away the spoil of them, they found among them in abundance both riches with the dead bodies, and precious jewels, which they stripped off for themselves, more than they could carry away: and they were three days in gathering of the spoil, it was so much.

26 And on the fourth day they assembled themselves in the valley of Berachah; for there they blessed the LORD: therefore the name of the same place was called, The valley of Berachah, unto this day.

27 Then they returned, every man of Judah and Jerusalem, and Jehoshaphat in the forefront of them, to go again to Jerusalem with joy; for the LORD had made them to rejoice over their enemies.

28 And they came to Jerusalem with psalteries and harps and trumpets unto the house of the LORD.

29 And the fear of God was on all the kingdoms of *those* countries, when they had heard that the LORD fought against the enemies of Israel.

30 So the realm of Jehoshaphat was quiet: for his God gave him rest round about.

31 And Jehoshaphat reigned over Judah: *he was* thirty and five years old when he began to reign, and he reigned twenty and five years in Jerusalem. And his mother's name *was* Azubah the daughter of Shilhi.

32 And he walked in the way of Asa his father, and departed not from it,

doing *that which was* right in the sight of the LORD.

33 Howbeit the high places were not taken away: for as yet the people had not prepared their hearts unto the God of their fathers.

34 Now the rest of the acts of Jehoshaphat, first and last, behold, they *are* written in the book of Jehu the son of Hanani, who *is* mentioned in the book of the kings of Israel.

35 And after this did Jehoshaphat king of Judah join himself with Ahaziah king of Israel, who did very wickedly:

36 And he joined himself with him to make ships to go to Tarshish: and they made the ships in Ezion-geber.

37 Then Eliezer the son of Dodavah of Mareshah prophesied against Jehoshaphat, saying, Because thou hast joined thyself with Ahaziah, the LORD hath broken thy works. And the ships were broken, that they were not able to go to Tarshish.

21 Now Jehoshaphat slept with his fathers, and was buried with his fathers in the city of David. And Jehoram his son reigned in his stead.

2 And he had brethren the sons of Jehoshaphat, Azariah, and Jehiel, and Zechariah, and Azariah, and Michael, and Shephatiah: all these *were* the sons of Jehoshaphat king of Israel.

3 And their father gave them great gifts of silver, and of gold, and of precious things, with fenced cities in Judah: but the kingdom gave he to Jehoram; because he *was* the firstborn.

4 Now when Jehoram was risen up to the kingdom of his father, he strengthened himself, and slew all his brethren with the sword, and *divers* also of the princes of Israel.

5 Jehoram *was* thirty and two years old when he began to reign, and he reigned eight years in Jerusalem.

6 And he walked in the way of the kings of Israel, like as did the house of Ahab: for he had the daughter of Ahab to wife: and he wrought *that which was* evil in the eyes of the LORD.

7 Howbeit the LORD would not destroy the house of David, because of the covenant that he had made with David, and as he promised to give a light to him and to his sons for ever.

8 In his days the Edomites revolted from under the dominion of Judah, and made themselves a king.

9 Then Jehoram went forth with his princes, and all his chariots with him: and he rose up by night, and smote the Edomites which compassed him in, and the captains of the chariots.

10 So the Edomites revolted from under the hand of Judah unto this day. The same time *also* did Libnah revolt from under his hand; because he had forsaken the LORD God of his fathers.

11 Moreover he made high places in the mountains of Judah, and caused the inhabitants of Jerusalem to commit fornication, and compelled Judah *thereto*.

12 And there came a writing to him from Elijah the prophet, saying, Thus saith the LORD God of David thy father, Because thou hast not walked in the ways of Jehoshaphat thy father, nor in the ways of Asa king of Judah,

13 But hast walked in the way of the kings of Israel, and hast made Judah and the inhabitants of Jerusalem to go a whoring, like to the whoredoms of the house of Ahab, and also hast slain thy brethren of thy father's house, *which were* better than thyself:

14 Behold, with a great plague will the LORD smite thy people, and thy children, and thy wives, and all thy goods:

15 And thou *shalt have* great sickness by disease of thy bowels, until thy bowels fall out by reason of the sickness day by day.

16 Moreover the LORD stirred up against Jehoram the spirit of the Philistines, and of the Arabians, that *were* near the Ethiopians:

17 And they came up into Judah, and brake into it, and carried away all the substance that was found in the king's house, and his sons also, and his wives; so that there was never a son left him, save Jehoahaz, the youngest of his sons.

18 And after all this the LORD smote him in his bowels with an incurable disease.

19 And it came to pass, that in process of time, after the end of two years, his bowels fell out by reason of his sickness: so he died of sore diseases. And his people made no burning for him, like the burning of his fathers.

20 Thirty and two years old was he when he began to reign, and he reigned in Jerusalem eight years, and departed without being desired. Howbeit they buried him in the city of David, but not in the sepulchres of the kings.

22 And the inhabitants of Jerusalem made Ahaziah his youngest son king in his stead: for the band of men that came with the Arabians to the camp had slain all the eldest. So Ahaziah the son of Jehoram king of Judah reigned.

2 Forty and two years old *was* Ahaziah when he began to reign, and he reigned one year in Jerusalem. His mother's name also *was* Athaliah the daughter of Omri.

3 He also walked in the ways of the house of Ahab: for his mother was his counsellor to do wickedly.

4 Wherefore he did evil in the sight of the LORD like the house of Ahab: for they were his counsellors after the death of his father to his destruction.

5 He walked also after their counsel, and went with Jehoram the son of Ahab king of Israel to war against Hazael king of Syria at Ramoth-gilead: and the Syrians smote Joram.

6 And he returned to be healed in Jezreel because of the wounds which were given him at Ramah, when he fought with Hazael king of Syria. And Azariah the son of Jehoram king of Judah went down to see Jehoram the son of Ahab at Jezreel, because he was sick.

7 And the destruction of Ahaziah was of God by coming to Joram: for when he was come, he went out with Jehoram against Jehu the son of Nimshi, whom the LORD had anointed to cut off the house of Ahab.

8 And it came to pass, that, when Jehu was executing judgment upon the house of Ahab, and found the princes of Judah, and the sons of the brethren of Ahaziah, that ministered to Ahaziah, he slew them.

9 And he sought Ahaziah: and they caught him, (for he was hid in Samaria,) and brought him to Jehu: and when they had slain him, they buried him: Because, said they, he *is* the son of Jehoshaphat, who sought the LORD with all his heart. So the house of Ahaziah had no power to keep still the kingdom.

10 But when Athaliah the mother of Ahaziah saw that her son was dead, she arose and destroyed all the seed royal of the house of Judah.

11 But Jehoshabeath, the daughter of the king, took Joash the son of Ahaziah, and stole him from among the king's sons that were slain, and put him and his nurse in a bedchamber. So Jehoshabeath, the daughter of king Jehoram, the wife of Jehoiada the priest, (for she was the sister of Ahaziah,) hid him from Athaliah, so that she slew him not.

12 And he was with them hid in the house of God six years: and Athaliah reigned over the land.

23 And in the seventh year Jehoiada strengthened himself, and took the captains of hundreds, Azariah the son of Jeroham, and Ishmael the son of Jehohanan, and Azariah the son of Obed, and Maaseiah the son of Adaiah, and Elishaphat the son of Zichri, into covenant with him.

2 And they went about in Judah, and gathered the Levites out of all the cities of Judah, and the chief of the fathers of Israel, and they came to Jerusalem.

3 And all the congregation made a covenant with the king in the house of God. And he said unto them, Behold, the king's son shall reign, as the LORD hath said of the sons of David.

4 This *is* the thing that ye shall do; A third part of you entering on the sabbath, of the priests and of the Levites, *shall be* porters of the doors;

5 And a third part *shall be* at the king's house; and a third part at the gate of the foundation: and all the people *shall be* in the courts of the house of the LORD.

6 But let none come into the house of the LORD, save the priests, and they that minister of the Levites; they shall go in, for they *are* holy: but all the people shall keep the watch of the LORD.

7 And the Levites shall compass the king round about, every man with his weapons in his hand; and whosoever *else* cometh into the house, he shall be put to death: but be ye with the king when he cometh in, and when he goeth out.

8 So the Levites and all Judah did according to all things that Jehoiada the priest had commanded, and took every man his men that were to come in on the sabbath, with them that were to go *out* on the sabbath: for Jehoiada the priest dismissed not the courses.

9 Moreover Jehoiada the priest delivered to the captains of hundreds spears, and bucklers, and shields, that *had been* king David's, which *were* in the house of God.

10 And he set all the people, every man having his weapon in his hand, from the right side of the temple to the left side of the temple, along by the altar and the temple, by the king round about.

11 Then they brought out the king's son, and put upon him the crown, and *gave him* the testimony, and made him king. And Jehoiada and his sons anointed him, and said, God save the king.

12 Now when Athaliah heard the noise of the people running and praising the king, she came to the people into the house of the LORD:

13 And she looked, and, behold, the king stood at his pillar at the entering in, and the princes and the trumpets by the king: and all the people of the land rejoiced, and sounded with trumpets, also the singers with instruments of musick, and such as taught to sing praise. Then Athaliah rent her clothes, and said, Treason, Treason.

14 Then Jehoiada the priest brought out the captains of hundreds that were set over the host, and said unto them, Have her forth of the ranges: and whoso followeth her, let him be slain with the sword. For the priest said, Slay her not in the house of the LORD.

15 So they laid hands on her; and when she was come to the entering of the horse gate by the king's house, they slew her there.

16 And Jehoiada made a covenant between him, and between all the people, and between the king, that they should be the LORD's people.

17 Then all the people went to the house of Baal, and brake it down, and brake his altars and his images in pieces, and slew Mattan the priest of Baal before the altars.

18 Also Jehoiada appointed the offices of the house of the LORD by the hand of the priests the Levites, whom David had distributed in the house of the LORD, to offer the burnt offerings of the LORD, as *it is* written in the law of Moses, with rejoicing and with singing, *as it was ordained* by David.

19 And he set the porters at the gates of the house of the LORD, that none *which was* unclean in any thing should enter in.

20 And he took the captains of hundreds, and the nobles, and the governors of the people, and all the people of the land, and brought down the king from the house of the LORD: and they came through the high gate into the king's house, and set the king upon the throne of the kingdom.

21 And all the people of the land rejoiced: and the city was quiet, after that they had slain Athaliah with the sword.

24 Joash *was* seven years old when he began to reign, and he reigned forty years in Jerusalem. His mother's name also *was* Zibiah of Beer-sheba.

2 And Joash did *that which was* right in the sight of the LORD all the days of Jehoiada the priest.

3 And Jehoiada took for him two wives; and he begat sons and daughters.

4 And it came to pass after this, *that* Joash was minded to repair the house of the LORD.

5 And he gathered together the priests and the Levites, and said to them, Go out unto the cities of Judah, and gather of all Israel money to repair the house of your God from year to year, and see that ye hasten the matter. Howbeit the Levites hastened *it* not.

6 And the king called for Jehoiada the chief, and said unto him, Why hast thou not required of the Levites to bring in out of Judah and out of Jerusalem the collection, *according to the commandment* of Moses the servant of the LORD, and of the congregation of Israel, for the tabernacle of witness?

7 For the sons of Athaliah, that wicked woman, had broken up the house of God; and also all the dedicated things of the house of the LORD did they bestow upon Baalim.

8 And at the king's commandment they made a chest, and set it without at the gate of the house of the LORD.

9 And they made a proclamation through Judah and Jerusalem, to bring in to the LORD the collection *that*

Moses the servant of God *laid* upon Israel in the wilderness.

10 And all the princes and all the people rejoiced, and brought in, and cast into the chest, until they had made an end.

11 Now it came to pass, that at what time the chest was brought unto the king's office by the hand of the Levites, and when they saw that *there was* much money, the king's scribe and the high priest's officer came and emptied the chest, and took it, and carried it to his place again. Thus they did day by day, and gathered money in abundance.

12 And the king and Jehoiada gave it to such as did the work of the service of the house of the LORD, and hired masons and carpenters to repair the house of the LORD, and also such as wrought iron and brass to mend the house of the LORD.

13 So the workmen wrought, and the work was perfected by them, and they set the house of God in his state, and strengthened it.

14 And when they had finished *it*, they brought the rest of the money before the king and Jehoiada, whereof were made vessels for the house of the LORD, *even* vessels to minister, and to offer *withal*, and spoons, and vessels of gold and silver. And they offered burnt offerings in the house of the LORD continually all the days of Jehoiada.

15 But Jehoiada waxed old, and was full of days when he died; an hundred and thirty years old *was he* when he died.

16 And they buried him in the city of David among the kings, because he had done good in Israel, both toward God, and toward his house.

17 Now after the death of Jehoiada came the princes of Judah, and made obeisance to the king. Then the king hearkened unto them.

18 And they left the house of the LORD God of their fathers, and served groves and idols: and wrath came upon Judah and Jerusalem for this their trespass.

19 Yet he sent prophets to them, to bring them again unto the LORD; and they testified against them: but they would not give ear.

20 And the Spirit of God came upon Zechariah the son of Jehoiada the priest, which stood above the people, and said unto them, Thus saith God, Why transgress ye the commandments of the LORD, that ye cannot prosper? because ye have forsaken the LORD, he hath also forsaken you.

21 And they conspired against him, and stoned him with stones at the commandment of the king in the court of the house of the LORD.

22 Thus Joash the king remembered not the kindness which Jehoiada his father had done to him, but slew his son. And when he died, he said, The LORD look upon *it*, and require *it*.

23 And it came to pass at the end of the year, *that* the host of Syria came up against him: and they came to Judah and Jerusalem, and destroyed all the princes of the people from among the people, and sent all the spoil of them unto the king of Damascus.

24 For the army of the Syrians came with a small company of men, and the LORD delivered a very great host into their hand, because they had forsaken the LORD God of their fathers. So they executed judgment against Joash.

25 And when they were departed from him, (for they left him in great diseases,) his own servants conspired against him for the blood of the sons of Jehoiada the priest, and slew him on his bed, and he died: and they buried him in the city of David, but they buried him not in the sepulchres of the kings.

26 And these are they that conspired against him; Zabad the son of Shimeath an Ammonitess, and Jehozabad the son of Shimrith a Moabitess.

27 Now *concerning* his sons, and the greatness of the burdens *laid* upon him, and the repairing of the house of God, behold, they *are* written in the story of the book of the kings. And Amaziah his son reigned in his stead.

25 Amaziah *was* twenty and five years old *when* he began to reign, and he reigned twenty and nine years in Jerusalem. And his mother's name *was* Jehoaddan of Jerusalem.

2 And he did *that which was* right in the sight of the LORD, but not with a perfect heart.

3 Now it came to pass, when the kingdom was established to him, that he slew his servants that had killed the king his father.

4 But he slew not their children, but *did* as *it is* written in the law in the book of Moses, where the LORD commanded, saying, The fathers shall not die for the children, neither shall the children die for the fathers, but every man shall die for his own sin.

5 Moreover Amaziah gathered Judah together, and made them captains over thousands, and captains over hundreds, according to the houses of *their* fathers, throughout all Judah and Benjamin: and he numbered them from twenty years old and above, and found them three hundred thousand choice *men, able* to go forth to war, that could handle spear and shield.

6 He hired also an hundred thousand mighty men of valour out of Israel for an hundred talents of silver.

7 But there came a man of God to him, saying, O king, let not the army of Israel go with thee; for the LORD *is* not with Israel, *to wit, with* all the children of Ephraim.

8 But if thou wilt go, do *it*, be strong for the battle: God shall make thee fall before the enemy: for God hath power to help, and to cast down.

9 And Amaziah said to the man of God, But what shall we do for the hundred talents which I have given to the army of Israel? And the man of God answered, The LORD is able to give thee much more than this.

10 Then Amaziah separated them, *to wit*, the army that was come to him out of Ephraim, to go home again: wherefore their anger was greatly kindled against Judah, and they returned home in great anger.

11 And Amaziah strengthened himself, and led forth his people, and went to the valley of salt, and smote of the children of Seir ten thousand.

12 And *other* ten thousand *left* alive did the children of Judah carry away captive, and brought them unto the top of the rock, and cast them down from the top of the rock, that they all were broken in pieces.

13 But the soldiers of the army which Amaziah sent back, that they should not go with him to battle, fell upon the cities of Judah, from Samaria even unto Beth-horon, and smote three thousand of them, and took much spoil.

14 Now it came to pass, after that
Amaziah was come from the slaughter
of the Edomites, that he brought the
gods of the children of Seir, and set
them up *to be* his gods, and bowed
down himself before them, and burned
incense unto them.
15 Wherefore the anger of the LORD
was kindled against Amaziah, and he
sent unto him a prophet, which said
unto him, Why hast thou sought after
the gods of the people, which could not
deliver their own people out of thine
hand?
16 And it came to pass, as he talked
with him, that *the king* said unto him,
Art thou made of the king's counsel?
forbear; why shouldest thou be smitten? Then the prophet forbare, and
said, I know that God hath determined
to destroy thee, because thou hast done
this, and hast not hearkened unto my
counsel.
17 Then Amaziah king of Judah took
advice, and sent to Joash, the son of
Jehoahaz, the son of Jehu, king of
Israel, saying, Come, let us see one
another in the face.
18 And Joash king of Israel sent to
Amaziah king of Judah, saying, The
thistle that *was* in Lebanon sent to the
cedar that *was* in Lebanon, saying, Give
thy daughter to my son to wife: and
there passed by a wild beast that *was* in
Lebanon, and trode down the thistle.
19 Thou sayest, Lo, thou hast smitten
the Edomites; and thine heart lifteth
thee up to boast: abide now at home;
why shouldest thou meddle to *thine*
hurt, that thou shouldest fall, *even*
thou, and Judah with thee?
20 But Amaziah would not hear; for it
came of God, that he might deliver
them into the hand *of their enemies*,
because they sought after the gods of
Edom.
21 So Joash the king of Israel went
up; and they saw one another in the
face, *both* he and Amaziah king of
Judah, at Beth-shemesh, which *belongeth* to Judah.
22 And Judah was put to the worse
before Israel, and they fled every man
to his tent.
23 And Joash the king of Israel took
Amaziah king of Judah, the son of
Joash, the son of Jehoahaz, at Beth-
shemesh, and brought him to
Jerusalem, and brake down the wall of
Jerusalem from the gate of Ephraim to
the corner gate, four hundred cubits.
24 And *he took* all the gold and the
silver, and all the vessels that were
found in the house of God with Obed-
edom, and the treasures of the king's
house, the hostages also, and returned
to Samaria.
25 And Amaziah the son of Joash king
of Judah lived after the death of Joash
son of Jehoahaz king of Israel fifteen
years.
26 Now the rest of the acts of Amaziah,
first and last, behold, *are* they not written in the book of the kings of Judah
and Israel?
27 Now after the time that Amaziah
did turn away from following the LORD
they made a conspiracy against him in
Jerusalem; and he fled to Lachish: but
they sent to Lachish after him, and slew
him there.
28 And they brought him upon horses, and buried him with his fathers in
the city of Judah.

26 Then all the people of Judah
took Uzziah, who *was* sixteen
years old, and made him king in the
room of his father Amaziah.

2 He built Eloth, and restored it to
Judah, after that the king slept with his
fathers.
3 Sixteen years old *was* Uzziah when
he began to reign, and he reigned fifty
and two years in Jerusalem. His
mother's name also *was* Jecoliah of
Jerusalem.
4 And he did *that which was* right in
the sight of the LORD, according to all
that his father Amaziah did.
5 And he sought God in the days of
Zechariah, who had understanding in
the visions of God: and as long as he
sought the LORD, God made him to
prosper.
6 And he went forth and warred
against the Philistines, and brake down
the wall of Gath, and the wall of
Jabneh, and the wall of Ashdod, and
built cities about Ashdod, and among
the Philistines.
7 And God helped him against the
Philistines, and against the Arabians
that dwelt in Gur-baal, and the Me-
hunims.
8 And the Ammonites gave gifts to
Uzziah: and his name spread abroad
even to the entering in of Egypt; for he
strengthened *himself* exceedingly.
9 Moreover Uzziah built towers in
Jerusalem at the corner gate, and at
the valley gate, and at the turning *of
the wall*, and fortified them.
10 Also he built towers in the desert,
and digged many wells: for he had
much cattle, both in the low country,
and in the plains: husbandmen *also*,
and vine dressers in the mountains, and
in Carmel: for he loved husbandry.
11 Moreover Uzziah had an host of
fighting men, that went out to war by
bands, according to the number of their
account by the hand of Jeiel the scribe
and Maaseiah the ruler, under the hand
of Hananiah, *one* of the king's captains.
12 The whole number of the chief of
the fathers of the mighty men of valour
were two thousand and six hundred.
13 And under their hand *was* an
army, three hundred thousand and
seven thousand and five hundred, that
made war with mighty power, to help
the king against the enemy.
14 And Uzziah prepared for them
throughout all the host shields, and
spears, and helmets, and habergeons,
and bows, and slings *to cast* stones.
15 And he made in Jerusalem
engines, invented by cunning men, to
be on the towers and upon the bulwarks, to shoot arrows and great stones
withal. And his name spread far abroad;
for he was marvellously helped, till he
was strong.
16 But when he was strong, his heart
was lifted up to *his* destruction: for he
transgressed against the LORD his God,
and went into the temple of the LORD to
burn incense upon the altar of incense.
17 And Azariah the priest went in
after him, and with him fourscore
priests of the LORD, *that were* valiant
men:
18 And they withstood Uzziah the
king, and said unto him, *It appertaineth* not unto thee, Uzziah, to burn
incense unto the LORD, but to the
priests the sons of Aaron, that are consecrated to burn incense: go out of the
sanctuary; for thou hast trespassed;
neither *shall it be* for thine honour
from the LORD God.
19 Then Uzziah was wroth, and *had* a
censer in his hand to burn incense: and
while he was wroth with the priests, the
leprosy even rose up in his forehead

before the priests in the house of the
LORD, from beside the incense altar.
20 And Azariah the chief priest, and
all the priests, looked upon him, and,
behold, he *was* leprous in his forehead,
and they thrust him out from thence;
yea, himself hasted also to go out,
because the LORD had smitten him.
21 And Uzziah the king was a leper
unto the day of his death, and dwelt in
a several house, *being* a leper; for he
was cut off from the house of the LORD:
and Jotham his son *was* over the king's
house, judging the people of the land.
22 Now the rest of the acts of Uzziah,
first and last, did Isaiah the prophet,
the son of Amoz, write.
23 So Uzziah slept with his fathers,
and they buried him with his fathers in
the field of the burial which *belonged*
to the kings; for they said, He *is* a leper:
and Jotham his son reigned in his
stead.

27 Jotham *was* twenty and five
years old when he began to reign,
and he reigned sixteen years in Jerusalem. His mother's name also *was*
Jerushah, the daughter of Zadok.
2 And he did *that which was* right in
the sight of the LORD, according to all
that his father Uzziah did: howbeit he
entered not into the temple of the
LORD. And the people did yet corruptly.
3 He built the high gate of the house
of the LORD, and on the wall of Ophel
he built much.
4 Moreover he built cities in the
mountains of Judah, and in the forests
he built castles and towers.
5 He fought also with the king of the
Ammonites, and prevailed against
them. And the children of Ammon gave
him the same year an hundred talents
of silver, and ten thousand measures of
wheat, and ten thousand of barley. So
much did the children of Ammon pay
unto him, both the second year, and the
third.
6 So Jotham became mighty, because
he prepared his ways before the LORD
his God.
7 Now the rest of the acts of Jotham,
and all his wars, and his ways, lo, they
are written in the book of the kings of
Israel and Judah.
8 He was five and twenty years old
when he began to reign, and reigned
sixteen years in Jerusalem.
9 And Jotham slept with his fathers,
and they buried him in the city of
David: and Ahaz his son reigned in his
stead.

28 Ahaz *was* twenty years old when
he began to reign, and he reigned
sixteen years in Jerusalem: but he did
not *that which was* right in the sight of
the LORD, like David his father:
2 For he walked in the ways of the
kings of Israel, and made also molten
images for Baalim.
3 Moreover he burnt incense in the
valley of the son of Hinnom, and burnt
his children in the fire, after the abominations of the heathen whom the LORD
had cast out before the children of
Israel.
4 He sacrificed also and burnt incense
in the high places, and on the hills, and
under every green tree.
5 Wherefore the LORD his God delivered him into the hand of the king of
Syria; and they smote him, and carried
away a great multitude of them captives, and brought *them* to Damascus.
And he was also delivered into the
hand of the king of Israel, who smote
him with a great slaughter.

6 For Pekah the son of Remaliah slew
in Judah an hundred and twenty thousand in one day, *which were* all valiant
men; because they had forsaken the
LORD God of their fathers.
7 And Zichri, a mighty man of Ephraim, slew Maaseiah the king's son, and
Azrikam the governor of the house, and
Elkanah *that was* next to the king.
8 And the children of Israel carried
away captive of their brethren two hundred thousand, women, sons, and
daughters, and took also away much
spoil from them, and brought the spoil
to Samaria.
9 But a prophet of the LORD was there,
whose name *was* Oded: and he went
out before the host that came to
Samaria, and said unto them, Behold,
because the LORD God of your fathers
was wroth with Judah, he hath delivered them into your hand, and ye have
slain them in a rage *that* reacheth up
unto heaven.
10 And now ye purpose to keep under
the children of Judah and Jerusalem
for bondmen and bondwomen unto
you: *but are there* not with you, even
with you, sins against the LORD your
God?
11 Now hear me therefore, and deliver the captives again, which ye have
taken captive of your brethren: for the
fierce wrath of the LORD *is* upon you.
12 Then certain of the heads of the
children of Ephraim, Azariah the son of
Johanan, Berechiah the son of
Meshillemoth, and Jehizkiah the son of
Shallum, and Amasa the son of Hadlai,
stood up against them that came from
the war,
13 And said unto them, Ye shall not
bring in the captives hither: for whereas we have offended against the LORD
already, ye intend to add *more* to our
sins and to our trespass: for our trespass is great, and *there is* fierce wrath
against Israel.
14 So the armed men left the captives
and the spoil before the princes and all
the congregation.
15 And the men which were expressed
by name rose up, and took the captives,
and with the spoil clothed all that were
naked among them, and arrayed them,
and shod them, and gave them to eat
and to drink, and anointed them, and
carried all the feeble of them upon
asses, and brought them to Jericho, the
city of palm trees, to their brethren:
then they returned to Samaria.
16 At that time did king Ahaz send
unto the kings of Assyria to help him.
17 For again the Edomites had come
and smitten Judah, and carried away
captives.
18 The Philistines also had invaded
the cities of the low country, and of the
south of Judah, and had taken Beth-
shemesh, and Ajalon, and Gederoth,
and Shocho with the villages thereof,
and Timnah with the villages thereof,
Gimzo also and the villages thereof:
and they dwelt there.
19 For the LORD brought Judah low
because of Ahaz king of Israel; for he
made Judah naked, and transgressed
sore against the LORD.
20 And Tilgath-pilneser king of
Assyria came unto him, and distressed
him, but strengthened him not.
21 For Ahaz took away a portion *out*
of the house of the LORD, and *out* of the
house of the king, and of the princes,
and gave *it* unto the king of Assyria:
but he helped him not.

22 And in the time of his distress did
he trespass yet more against the LORD:
this *is that* king Ahaz.
23 For he sacrificed unto the gods of
Damascus, which smote him: and he
said, Because the gods of the kings of
Syria help them, *therefore* will I sacrifice to them, that they may help me.
But they were the ruin of him, and of all
Israel.
24 And Ahaz gathered together the
vessels of the house of God, and cut in
pieces the vessels of the house of God,
and shut up the doors of the house of
the LORD, and he made him altars in
every corner of Jerusalem.
25 And in every several city of Judah
he made high places to burn incense
unto other gods, and provoked to anger
the LORD God of his fathers.
26 Now the rest of his acts and of all
his ways, first and last, behold, they *are*
written in the book of the kings of
Judah and Israel.
27 And Ahaz slept with his fathers,
and they buried him in the city, *even* in
Jerusalem: but they brought him not
into the sepulchres of the kings of
Israel: and Hezekiah his son reigned in
his stead.

29 Hezekiah began to reign *when*
he was five and twenty years old,
and he reigned nine and twenty years
in Jerusalem. And his mother's name
was Abijah, the daughter of Zechariah.
2 And he did *that which was* right in
the sight of the LORD, according to all
that David his father had done.
3 He in the first year of his reign, in
the first month, opened the doors of the
house of the LORD, and repaired them.
4 And he brought in the priests and
the Levites, and gathered them together into the east street,
5 And said unto them, Hear me, ye
Levites, sanctify now yourselves, and
sanctify the house of the LORD God of
your fathers, and carry forth the filthiness out of the holy *place*.
6 For our fathers have trespassed, and
done *that which was* evil in the eyes of
the LORD our God, and have forsaken
him, and have turned away their faces
from the habitation of the LORD, and
turned *their* backs.
7 Also they have shut up the doors of
the porch, and put out the lamps, and
have not burned incense nor offered
burnt offerings in the holy *place* unto
the God of Israel.
8 Wherefore the wrath of the LORD
was upon Judah and Jerusalem, and he
hath delivered them to trouble, to
astonishment, and to hissing, as ye see
with your eyes.
9 For, lo, our fathers have fallen by the
sword, and our sons and our daughters
and our wives *are* in captivity for this.
10 Now *it is* in mine heart to make a
covenant with the LORD God of Israel,
that his fierce wrath may turn away
from us.
11 My sons, be not now negligent: for
the LORD hath chosen you to stand
before him, to serve him, and that ye
should minister unto him, and burn
incense.
12 Then the Levites arose, Mahath
the son of Amasai, and Joel the son of
Azariah, of the sons of the Kohathites:
and of the sons of Merari, Kish the son
of Abdi, and Azariah the son of
Jehalelel: and of the Gershonites; Joah
the son of Zimmah, and Eden the son of
Joah:
13 And of the sons of Elizaphan;
Shimri, and Jeiel: and of the sons of
Asaph; Zechariah, and Mattaniah:

14 And of the sons of Heman; Jehiel, and Shimei: and of the sons of Jeduthun; Shemaiah, and Uzziel.

15 And they gathered their brethren, and sanctified themselves, and came, according to the commandment of the king, by the words of the LORD, to cleanse the house of the LORD.

16 And the priests went into the inner part of the house of the LORD, to cleanse *it*, and brought out all the uncleanness that they found in the temple of the LORD into the court of the house of the LORD. And the Levites took *it*, to carry *it* out abroad into the brook Kidron.

17 Now they began on the first *day* of the first month to sanctify, and on the eighth day of the month came they to the porch of the LORD: so they sanctified the house of the LORD in eight days; and in the sixteenth day of the first month they made an end.

18 Then they went in to Hezekiah the king, and said, We have cleansed all the house of the LORD, and the altar of burnt offering, with all the vessels thereof, and the shewbread table, with all the vessels thereof.

19 Moreover all the vessels, which king Ahaz in his reign did cast away in his transgression, have we prepared and sanctified, and, behold, they *are* before the altar of the LORD.

20 Then Hezekiah the king rose early, and gathered the rulers of the city, and went up to the house of the LORD.

21 And they brought seven bullocks, and seven rams, and seven lambs, and seven he goats, for a sin offering for the kingdom, and for the sanctuary, and for Judah. And he commanded the priests the sons of Aaron to offer *them* on the altar of the LORD.

22 So they killed the bullocks, and the priests received the blood, and sprinkled *it* on the altar: likewise, when they had killed the rams, they sprinkled the blood upon the altar: they killed also the lambs, and they sprinkled the blood upon the altar.

23 And they brought forth the he goats *for* the sin offering before the king and the congregation; and they laid their hands upon them:

24 And the priests killed them, and they made reconciliation with their blood upon the altar, to make an atonement for all Israel: for the king commanded *that* the burnt offering and the sin offering *should be made* for all Israel.

25 And he set the Levites in the house of the LORD with cymbals, with psalteries, and with harps, according to the commandment of David, and of Gad the king's seer, and Nathan the prophet: for *so was* the commandment of the LORD by his prophets.

26 And the Levites stood with the instruments of David, and the priests with the trumpets.

27 And Hezekiah commanded to offer the burnt offering upon the altar. And when the burnt offering began, the song of the LORD began *also* with the trumpets, and with the instruments *ordained* by David king of Israel.

28 And all the congregation worshipped, and the singers sang, and the trumpeters sounded: *and* all *this continued* until the burnt offering was finished.

29 And when they had made an end of offering, the king and all that were present with him bowed themselves, and worshipped.

30 Moreover Hezekiah the king and the princes commanded the Levites to sing praise unto the LORD with the words of David, and of Asaph the seer. And they sang praises with gladness, and they bowed their heads and worshipped.

31 Then Hezekiah answered and said, Now ye have consecrated yourselves unto the LORD, come near and bring sacrifices and thank offerings into the house of the LORD. And the congregation brought in sacrifices and thank offerings; and as many as were of a free heart burnt offerings.

32 And the number of the burnt offerings, which the congregation brought, was threescore and ten bullocks, an hundred rams, *and* two hundred lambs: all these *were* for a burnt offering to the LORD.

33 And the consecrated things *were* six hundred oxen and three thousand sheep.

34 But the priests were too few, so that they could not flay all the burnt offerings: wherefore their brethren the Levites did help them, till the work was ended, and until the *other* priests had sanctified themselves: for the Levites *were* more upright in heart to sanctify themselves than the priests.

35 And also the burnt offerings *were* in abundance, with the fat of the peace offerings, and the drink offerings for *every* burnt offering. So the service of the house of the LORD was set in order.

36 And Hezekiah rejoiced, and all the people, that God had prepared the people: for the thing was *done* suddenly.

30 And Hezekiah sent to all Israel and Judah, and wrote letters also to Ephraim and Manasseh, that they should come to the house of the LORD at Jerusalem, to keep the passover unto the LORD God of Israel.

2 For the king had taken counsel, and his princes, and all the congregation in Jerusalem, to keep the passover in the second month.

3 For they could not keep it at that time, because the priests had not sanctified themselves sufficiently, neither had the people gathered themselves together to Jerusalem.

4 And the thing pleased the king and all the congregation.

5 So they established a decree to make proclamation throughout all Israel, from Beer-sheba even to Dan, that they should come to keep the passover unto the LORD God of Israel at Jerusalem: for they had not done *it* of a long *time in such sort* as it was written.

6 So the posts went with the letters from the king and his princes throughout all Israel and Judah, and according to the commandment of the king, saying, Ye children of Israel, turn again unto the LORD God of Abraham, Isaac, and Israel, and he will return to the remnant of you, that are escaped out of the hand of the kings of Assyria.

7 And be not ye like your fathers, and like your brethren, which trespassed against the LORD God of their fathers, *who* therefore gave them up to desolation, as ye see.

8 Now be ye not stiffnecked, as your fathers *were, but* yield yourselves unto the LORD, and enter into his sanctuary, which he hath sanctified for ever: and serve the LORD your God, that the fierceness of his wrath may turn away from you.

9 For if ye turn again unto the LORD, your brethren and your children *shall*

find compassion before them that lead
them captive, so that they shall come
again into this land: for the LORD your
God *is* gracious and merciful, and will
not turn away *his* face from you, if ye
return unto him.
10 So the posts passed from city to
city through the country of Ephraim
and Manasseh even unto Zebulun: but
they laughed them to scorn, and
mocked them.
11 Nevertheless divers of Asher and
Manasseh and of Zebulun humbled
themselves, and came to Jerusalem.
12 Also in Judah the hand of God was
to give them one heart to do the commandment of the king and of the
princes, by the word of the LORD.
13 And there assembled at Jerusalem
much people to keep the feast of
unleavened bread in the second month,
a very great congregation.
14 And they arose and took away the
altars that *were* in Jerusalem, and all
the altars for incense took they away,
and cast *them* into the brook Kidron.
15 Then they killed the passover on
the fourteenth *day* of the second
month: and the priests and the Levites
were ashamed, and sanctified themselves, and brought in the burnt offerings into the house of the LORD.
16 And they stood in their place after
their manner, according to the law of
Moses the man of God: the priests
sprinkled the blood, *which they
received* of the hand of the Levites.
17 For *there were* many in the congregation that were not sanctified: therefore the Levites had the charge of the
killing of the passovers for every one
that was not clean, to sanctify *them*
unto the LORD.
18 For a multitude of the people, *even*
many of Ephraim, and Manasseh,
Issachar, and Zebulun, had not cleansed
themselves, yet did they eat the passover otherwise than it was written. But
Hezekiah prayed for them, saying, The
good LORD pardon every one
19 *That* prepareth his heart to seek
God, the LORD God of his fathers,
though *he be* not *cleansed* according to
the purification of the sanctuary.
20 And the LORD hearkened to
Hezekiah, and healed the people.
21 And the children of Israel that
were present at Jerusalem kept the
feast of unleavened bread seven days
with great gladness: and the Levites
and the priests praised the LORD day by
day, *singing* with loud instruments unto
the LORD.
22 And Hezekiah spake comfortably
unto all the Levites that taught the
good knowledge of the LORD: and they
did eat throughout the feast seven
days, offering peace offerings, and
making confession to the LORD God of
their fathers.
23 And the whole assembly took
counsel to keep other seven days: and
they kept *other* seven days with gladness.
24 For Hezekiah king of Judah did
give to the congregation a thousand
bullocks and seven thousand sheep;
and the princes gave to the congregation a thousand bullocks and ten thousand sheep: and a great number of
priests sanctified themselves.
25 And all the congregation of Judah,
with the priests and the Levites, and all
the congregation that came out of
Israel, and the strangers that came out
of the land of Israel, and that dwelt in
Judah, rejoiced.

26 So there was great joy in Jerusalem: for since the time of Solomon
the son of David king of Israel *there*
was not the like in Jerusalem.
27 Then the priests the Levites arose
and blessed the people: and their voice
was heard, and their prayer came *up* to
his holy dwelling place, *even* unto
heaven.

31 Now when all this was finished,
all Israel that were present went
out to the cities of Judah, and brake the
images in pieces, and cut down the
groves, and threw down the high places
and the altars out of all Judah and
Benjamin, in Ephraim also and Manasseh, until they had utterly destroyed
them all. Then all the children of Israel
returned, every man to his possession,
into their own cities.
2 And Hezekiah appointed the courses of the priests and the Levites after
their courses, every man according to
his service, the priests and Levites for
burnt offerings and for peace offerings,
to minister, and to give thanks, and to
praise in the gates of the tents of the
LORD.
3 *He appointed* also the king's portion
of his substance for the burnt offerings,
to wit, for the morning and evening
burnt offerings, and the burnt offerings
for the sabbaths, and for the new
moons, and for the set feasts, as *it is*
written in the law of the LORD.
4 Moreover he commanded the people that dwelt in Jerusalem to give the
portion of the priests and the Levites,
that they might be encouraged in the
law of the LORD.
5 And as soon as the commandment
came abroad, the children of Israel
brought in abundance the firstfruits of
corn, wine, and oil, and honey, and of all
the increase of the field; and the tithe
of all *things* brought they in abundantly.
6 And *concerning* the children of
Israel and Judah, that dwelt in the cities of Judah, they also brought in the
tithe of oxen and sheep, and the tithe of
holy things which were consecrated
unto the LORD their God, and laid *them*
by heaps.
7 In the third month they began to lay
the foundation of the heaps, and finished *them* in the seventh month.
8 And when Hezekiah and the princes came and saw the heaps, they
blessed the LORD, and his people Israel.
9 Then Hezekiah questioned with the
priests and the Levites concerning the
heaps.
10 And Azariah the chief priest of the
house of Zadok answered him, and
said, Since *the people* began to bring
the offerings into the house of the
LORD, we have had enough to eat, and
have left plenty: for the LORD hath
blessed his people; and that which is
left *is* this great store.
11 Then Hezekiah commanded to
prepare chambers in the house of the
LORD; and they prepared *them*,
12 And brought in the offerings and
the tithes and the dedicated *things*
faithfully: over which Cononiah the
Levite *was* ruler, and Shimei his brother *was* the next.
13 And Jehiel, and Azaziah, and
Nahath, and Asahel, and Jerimoth, and
Jozabad, and Eliel, and Ismachiah, and
Mahath, and Benaiah, *were* overseers
under the hand of Cononiah and
Shimei his brother, at the commandment of Hezekiah the king, and Azariah
the ruler of the house of God.
14 And Kore the son of Imnah the
Levite, the porter toward the east, *was*

over the freewill offerings of God, to
distribute the oblations of the LORD,
and the most holy things.
15 And next him *were* Eden, and
Miniamin, and Jeshua, and Shemaiah,
Amariah, and Shecaniah, in the cities
of the priests, in *their* set office, to give
to their brethren by courses, as well to
the great as to the small:
16 Beside their genealogy of males,
from three years old and upward, *even*
unto every one that entereth into the
house of the LORD, his daily portion for
their service in their charges according
to their courses;
17 Both to the genealogy of the
priests by the house of their fathers,
and the Levites from twenty years old
and upward, in their charges by their
courses;
18 And to the genealogy of all their
little ones, their wives, and their sons,
and their daughters, through all the
congregation: for in their set office they
sanctified themselves in holiness:
19 Also of the sons of Aaron the
priests, *which were* in the fields of the
suburbs of their cities, in every several
city, the men that were expressed by
name, to give portions to all the males
among the priests, and to all that were
reckoned by genealogies among the
Levites.
20 And thus did Hezekiah throughout
all Judah, and wrought *that which was*
good and right and truth before the
LORD his God.
21 And in every work that he began in
the service of the house of God, and in
the law, and in the commandments, to
seek his God, he did *it* with all his
heart, and prospered.

32 After these things, and the estab-
lishment thereof, Sennacherib
king of Assyria came, and entered into
Judah, and encamped against the
fenced cities, and thought to win them
for himself.
2 And when Hezekiah saw that
Sennacherib was come, and that he was
purposed to fight against Jerusalem,
3 He took counsel with his princes
and his mighty men to stop the waters
of the fountains which *were* without
the city: and they did help him.
4 So there was gathered much people
together, who stopped all the fountains,
and the brook that ran through the
midst of the land, saying, Why should
the kings of Assyria come, and find
much water?
5 Also he strengthened himself, and
built up all the wall that was broken,
and raised *it* up to the towers, and
another wall without, and repaired
Millo *in* the city of David, and made
darts and shields in abundance.
6 And he set captains of war over the
people, and gathered them together to
him in the street of the gate of the city,
and spake comfortably to them, saying,
7 Be strong and courageous, be not
afraid nor dismayed for the king of
Assyria, nor for all the multitude that *is*
with him: for *there be* more with us
than with him:
8 With him *is* an arm of flesh; but
with us *is* the LORD our God to help us,
and to fight our battles. And the people
rested themselves upon the words of
Hezekiah king of Judah.
9 After this did Sennacherib king of
Assyria send his servants to Jerusalem,
(but he *himself laid siege* against
Lachish, and all his power with him,)
unto Hezekiah king of Judah, and unto
all Judah that *were* at Jerusalem,
saying,

10 Thus saith Sennacherib king of Assyria, Whereon do ye trust, that ye abide in the siege in Jerusalem?

11 Doth not Hezekiah persuade you to give over yourselves to die by famine and by thirst, saying, The LORD our God shall deliver us out of the hand of the king of Assyria?

12 Hath not the same Hezekiah taken away his high places and his altars, and commanded Judah and Jerusalem, saying, Ye shall worship before one altar, and burn incense upon it?

13 Know ye not what I and my fathers have done unto all the people of *other* lands? were the gods of the nations of those lands any ways able to deliver their lands out of mine hand?

14 Who *was there* among all the gods of those nations that my fathers utterly destroyed, that could deliver his people out of mine hand, that your God should be able to deliver you out of mine hand?

15 Now therefore let not Hezekiah deceive you, nor persuade you on this manner, neither yet believe him: for no god of any nation or kingdom was able to deliver his people out of mine hand, and out of the hand of my fathers: how much less shall your God deliver you out of mine hand?

16 And his servants spake yet *more* against the LORD God, and against his servant Hezekiah.

17 He wrote also letters to rail on the LORD God of Israel, and to speak against him, saying, As the gods of the nations of *other* lands have not delivered their people out of mine hand, so shall not the God of Hezekiah deliver his people out of mine hand.

18 Then they cried with a loud voice in the Jews' speech unto the people of Jerusalem that *were* on the wall, to affright them, and to trouble them; that they might take the city.

19 And they spake against the God of Jerusalem, as against the gods of the people of the earth, *which were* the work of the hands of man.

20 And for this *cause* Hezekiah the king, and the prophet Isaiah the son of Amoz, prayed and cried to heaven.

21 And the LORD sent an angel, which cut off all the mighty men of valour, and the leaders and captains in the camp of the king of Assyria. So he returned with shame of face to his own land. And when he was come into the house of his god, they that came forth of his own bowels slew him there with the sword.

22 Thus the LORD saved Hezekiah and the inhabitants of Jerusalem from the hand of Sennacherib the king of Assyria, and from the hand of all *other*, and guided them on every side.

23 And many brought gifts unto the LORD to Jerusalem, and presents to Hezekiah king of Judah: so that he was magnified in the sight of all nations from thenceforth.

24 In those days Hezekiah was sick to the death, and prayed unto the LORD: and he spake unto him, and he gave him a sign.

25 But Hezekiah rendered not again according to the benefit *done* unto him; for his heart was lifted up: therefore there was wrath upon him, and upon Judah and Jerusalem.

26 Notwithstanding Hezekiah humbled himself for the pride of his heart, *both* he and the inhabitants of Jerusalem, so that the wrath of the LORD came not upon them in the days of Hezekiah.

27 And Hezekiah had exceeding much riches and honour: and he made himself treasuries for silver, and for gold, and for precious stones, and for spices, and for shields, and for all manner of pleasant jewels;

28 Storehouses also for the increase of corn, and wine, and oil; and stalls for all manner of beasts, and cotes for flocks.

29 Moreover he provided him cities, and possessions of flocks and herds in abundance: for God had given him substance very much.

30 This same Hezekiah also stopped the upper watercourse of Gihon, and brought it straight down to the west side of the city of David. And Hezekiah prospered in all his works.

31 Howbeit in *the business of* the ambassadors of the princes of Babylon, who sent unto him to enquire of the wonder that was *done* in the land, God left him, to try him, that he might know all *that was* in his heart.

32 Now the rest of the acts of Hezekiah, and his goodness, behold, they *are* written in the vision of Isaiah the prophet, the son of Amoz, *and* in the book of the kings of Judah and Israel.

33 And Hezekiah slept with his fathers, and they buried him in the chiefest of the sepulchres of the sons of David: and all Judah and the inhabitants of Jerusalem did him honour at his death. And Manasseh his son reigned in his stead.

33 Manasseh *was* twelve years old when he began to reign, and he reigned fifty and five years in Jerusalem:

2 But did *that which was* evil in the sight of the LORD, like unto the abominations of the heathen, whom the LORD had cast out before the children of Israel.

3 For he built again the high places which Hezekiah his father had broken down, and he reared up altars for Baalim, and made groves, and worshipped all the host of heaven, and served them.

4 Also he built altars in the house of the LORD, whereof the LORD had said, In Jerusalem shall my name be for ever.

5 And he built altars for all the host of heaven in the two courts of the house of the LORD.

6 And he caused his children to pass through the fire in the valley of the son of Hinnom: also he observed times, and used enchantments, and used witchcraft, and dealt with a familiar spirit, and with wizards: he wrought much evil in the sight of the LORD, to provoke him to anger.

7 And he set a carved image, the idol which he had made, in the house of God, of which God had said to David and to Solomon his son, In this house, and in Jerusalem, which I have chosen before all the tribes of Israel, will I put my name for ever:

8 Neither will I any more remove the foot of Israel from out of the land which I have appointed for your fathers; so that they will take heed to do all that I have commanded them, according to the whole law and the statutes and the ordinances by the hand of Moses.

9 So Manasseh made Judah and the inhabitants of Jerusalem to err, *and* to do worse than the heathen, whom the LORD had destroyed before the children of Israel.

10 And the LORD spake to Manasseh, and to his people: but they would not hearken.

11 Wherefore the LORD brought upon them the captains of the host of the king of Assyria, which took Manasseh among the thorns, and bound him with fetters, and carried him to Babylon.

12 And when he was in affliction, he besought the LORD his God, and humbled himself greatly before the God of his fathers,

13 And prayed unto him: and he was intreated of him, and heard his supplication, and brought him again to Jerusalem into his kingdom. Then Manasseh knew that the LORD he *was* God.

14 Now after this he built a wall without the city of David, on the west side of Gihon, in the valley, even to the entering in at the fish gate, and compassed about Ophel, and raised it up a very great height, and put captains of war in all the fenced cities of Judah.

15 And he took away the strange gods, and the idol out of the house of the LORD, and all the altars that he had built in the mount of the house of the LORD, and in Jerusalem, and cast *them* out of the city.

16 And he repaired the altar of the LORD, and sacrificed thereon peace offerings and thank offerings, and commanded Judah to serve the LORD God of Israel.

17 Nevertheless the people did sacrifice still in the high places, *yet* unto the LORD their God only.

18 Now the rest of the acts of Manasseh, and his prayer unto his God, and the words of the seers that spake to him in the name of the LORD God of Israel, behold, they *are written* in the book of the kings of Israel.

19 His prayer also, and *how God* was intreated of him, and all his sin, and his trespass, and the places wherein he built high places, and set up groves and graven images, before he was humbled: behold, they *are* written among the sayings of the seers.

20 So Manasseh slept with his fathers, and they buried him in his own house: and Amon his son reigned in his stead.

21 Amon *was* two and twenty years old when he began to reign, and reigned two years in Jerusalem.

22 But he did *that which was* evil in the sight of the LORD, as did Manasseh his father: for Amon sacrificed unto all the carved images which Manasseh his father had made, and served them;

23 And humbled not himself before the LORD, as Manasseh his father had humbled himself; but Amon trespassed more and more.

24 And his servants conspired against him, and slew him in his own house.

25 But the people of the land slew all them that had conspired against king Amon; and the people of the land made Josiah his son king in his stead.

34 Josiah *was* eight years old when he began to reign, and he reigned in Jerusalem one and thirty years.

2 And he did *that which was* right in the sight of the LORD, and walked in the ways of David his father, and declined *neither* to the right hand, nor to the left.

3 For in the eighth year of his reign, while he was yet young, he began to seek after the God of David his father: and in the twelfth year he began to purge Judah and Jerusalem from the

high places, and the groves, and the
carved images, and the molten images.
4 And they brake down the altars of
Baalim in his presence; and the images,
that *were* on high above them, he cut
down; and the groves, and the carved
images, and the molten images, he
brake in pieces, and made dust *of*
them, and strowed *it* upon the graves of
them that had sacrificed unto them.
5 And he burnt the bones of the
priests upon their altars, and cleansed
Judah and Jerusalem.
6 And *so did he* in the cities of
Manasseh, and Ephraim, and Simeon,
even unto Naphtali, with their mat-
tocks round about.
7 And when he had broken down the
altars and the groves, and had beaten
the graven images into powder, and cut
down all the idols throughout all the
land of Israel, he returned to Jerusalem.
8 Now in the eighteenth year of his
reign, when he had purged the land,
and the house, he sent Shaphan the son
of Azaliah, and Maaseiah the governor
of the city, and Joah the son of Joahaz
the recorder, to repair the house of the
LORD his God.
9 And when they came to Hilkiah the
high priest, they delivered the money
that was brought into the house of God,
which the Levites that kept the doors
had gathered of the hand of Manasseh
and Ephraim, and of all the remnant of
Israel, and of all Judah and Benjamin;
and they returned to Jerusalem.
10 And they put *it* in the hand of the
workmen that had the oversight of the
house of the LORD, and they gave it to
the workmen that wrought in the house
of the LORD, to repair and amend the
house:
11 Even to the artificers and builders
gave they *it*, to buy hewn stone, and
timber for couplings, and to floor the
houses which the kings of Judah had
destroyed.
12 And the men did the work faithfully: and the overseers of them *were*
Jahath and Obadiah, the Levites, of the
sons of Merari; and Zechariah and
Meshullam, of the sons of the
Kohathites, to set *it* forward; and *other*
of the Levites, all that could skill of
instruments of musick.
13 Also *they were* over the bearers of
burdens, and *were* overseers of all that
wrought the work in any manner of
service: and of the Levites *there were*
scribes, and officers, and porters.
14 And when they brought out the
money that was brought into the house
of the LORD, Hilkiah the priest found a
book of the law of the LORD *given* by
Moses.
15 And Hilkiah answered and said to
Shaphan the scribe, I have found the
book of the law in the house of the
LORD. And Hilkiah delivered the book
to Shaphan.
16 And Shaphan carried the book to
the king, and brought the king word
back again, saying, All that was committed to thy servants, they do *it*.
17 And they have gathered together
the money that was found in the house
of the LORD, and have delivered it into
the hand of the overseers, and to the
hand of the workmen.
18 Then Shaphan the scribe told the
king, saying, Hilkiah the priest hath
given me a book. And Shaphan read it
before the king.
19 And it came to pass, when the king
had heard the words of the law, that he
rent his clothes.

20 And the king commanded Hilkiah,
and Ahikam the son of Shaphan, and
Abdon the son of Micah, and Shaphan
the scribe, and Asaiah a servant of the
king's, saying,
21 Go, enquire of the LORD for me,
and for them that are left in Israel and
in Judah, concerning the words of the
book that is found: for great *is* the
wrath of the LORD that is poured out
upon us, because our fathers have not
kept the word of the LORD, to do after
all that is written in this book.
22 And Hilkiah, and *they* that the
king *had appointed*, went to Huldah
the prophetess, the wife of Shallum the
son of Tikvath, the son of Hasrah,
keeper of the wardrobe; (now she dwelt
in Jerusalem in the college:) and they
spake to her to that *effect*.
23 And she answered them, Thus
saith the LORD God of Israel, Tell ye the
man that sent you to me,
24 Thus saith the LORD, Behold, I will
bring evil upon this place, and upon the
inhabitants thereof, *even* all the curses
that are written in the book which they
have read before the king of Judah:
25 Because they have forsaken me,
and have burned incense unto other
gods, that they might provoke me to
anger with all the works of their hands;
therefore my wrath shall be poured out
upon this place, and shall not be
quenched.
26 And as for the king of Judah, who
sent you to enquire of the LORD, so shall
ye say unto him, Thus saith the LORD
God of Israel *concerning* the words
which thou hast heard;
27 Because thine heart was tender,
and thou didst humble thyself before
God, when thou heardest his words
against this place, and against the
inhabitants thereof, and humbledst
thyself before me, and didst rend thy
clothes, and weep before me; I have
even heard *thee* also, saith the LORD.
28 Behold, I will gather thee to thy
fathers, and thou shalt be gathered to
thy grave in peace, neither shall thine
eyes see all the evil that I will bring
upon this place, and upon the inhabitants of the same. So they brought the
king word again.
29 Then the king sent and gathered
together all the elders of Judah and
Jerusalem.
30 And the king went up into the
house of the LORD, and all the men of
Judah, and the inhabitants of
Jerusalem, and the priests, and the
Levites, and all the people, great and
small: and he read in their ears all the
words of the book of the covenant that
was found in the house of the LORD.
31 And the king stood in his place,
and made a covenant before the LORD,
to walk after the LORD, and to keep his
commandments, and his testimonies,
and his statutes, with all his heart, and
with all his soul, to perform the words
of the covenant which are written in
this book.
32 And he caused all that were present in Jerusalem and Benjamin to
stand *to it*. And the inhabitants of
Jerusalem did according to the covenant of God, the God of their fathers.
33 And Josiah took away all the
abominations out of all the countries
that *pertained* to the children of Israel,
and made all that were present in
Israel to serve, *even* to serve the LORD
their God. *And* all his days they departed not from following the LORD, the
God of their fathers.

35 Moreover Josiah kept a passover
unto the LORD in Jerusalem: and
they killed the passover on the fourteenth *day* of the first month.
2 And he set the priests in their
charges, and encouraged them to the
service of the house of the LORD,
3 And said unto the Levites that
taught all Israel, which were holy unto
the LORD, Put the holy ark in the house
which Solomon the son of David king of
Israel did build; *it shall* not *be* a burden
upon *your* shoulders: serve now the
LORD your God, and his people Israel,
4 And prepare *yourselves* by the
houses of your fathers, after your courses, according to the writing of David
king of Israel, and according to the
writing of Solomon his son.
5 And stand in the holy *place* according to the divisions of the families of
the fathers of your brethren the people,
and *after* the division of the families of
the Levites.
6 So kill the passover, and sanctify
yourselves, and prepare your brethren,
that *they* may do according to the word
of the LORD by the hand of Moses.
7 And Josiah gave to the people, of
the flock, lambs and kids, all for the
passover offerings, for all that were
present, to the number of thirty thousand, and three thousand bullocks:
these *were* of the king's substance.
8 And his princes gave willingly unto
the people, to the priests, and to the
Levites: Hilkiah and Zechariah and
Jehiel, rulers of the house of God, gave
unto the priests for the passover offerings two thousand and six hundred
small cattle, and three hundred oxen.
9 Conaniah also, and Shemaiah and
Nethaneel, his brethren, and Hashabiah
and Jeiel and Jozabad, chief of the
Levites, gave unto the Levites for passover offerings five thousand *small cattle*, and five hundred oxen.
10 So the service was prepared, and
the priests stood in their place, and the
Levites in their courses, according to
the king's commandment.
11 And they killed the passover, and
the priests sprinkled *the blood* from
their hands, and the Levites flayed
them.
12 And they removed the burnt offerings, that they might give according to
the divisions of the families of the people, to offer unto the LORD, as *it is* written in the book of Moses. And so *did
they* with the oxen.
13 And they roasted the passover
with fire according to the ordinance:
but the *other* holy *offerings* sod they in
pots, and in caldrons, and in pans, and
divided *them* speedily among all the
people.
14 And afterward they made ready
for themselves, and for the priests:
because the priests the sons of Aaron
were busied in offering of burnt offerings and the fat until night; therefore
the Levites prepared for themselves,
and for the priests the sons of Aaron.
15 And the singers the sons of Asaph
were in their place, according to the
commandment of David, and Asaph,
and Heman, and Jeduthun the king's
seer; and the porters *waited* at every
gate; they might not depart from their
service; for their brethren the Levites
prepared for them.
16 So all the service of the LORD was
prepared the same day, to keep the
passover, and to offer burnt offerings
upon the altar of the LORD, according to
the commandment of king Josiah.

17 And the children of Israel that
were present kept the passover at that
time, and the feast of unleavened
bread seven days.
18 And there was no passover like to
that kept in Israel from the days of
Samuel the prophet; neither did all the
kings of Israel keep such a passover as
Josiah kept, and the priests, and the
Levites, and all Judah and Israel that
were present, and the inhabitants of
Jerusalem.
19 In the eighteenth year of the reign
of Josiah was this passover kept.
20 After all this, when Josiah had
prepared the temple, Necho king of
Egypt came up to fight against
Carchemish by Euphrates: and Josiah
went out against him.
21 But he sent ambassadors to him,
saying, What have I to do with thee,
thou king of Judah? *I come* not against
thee this day, but against the house
wherewith I have war: for God commanded me to make haste: forbear
thee from *meddling with* God, who *is*
with me, that he destroy thee not.
22 Nevertheless Josiah would not
turn his face from him, but disguised
himself, that he might fight with him,
and hearkened not unto the words of
Necho from the mouth of God, and
came to fight in the valley of Megiddo.
23 And the archers shot at king
Josiah; and the king said to his servants, Have me away; for I am sore
wounded.
24 His servants therefore took him
out of that chariot, and put him in the
second chariot that he had; and they
brought him to Jerusalem, and he died,
and was buried in *one of* the sepulchres
of his fathers. And all Judah and
Jerusalem mourned for Josiah.
25 And Jeremiah lamented for
Josiah: and all the singing men and the
singing women spake of Josiah in their
lamentations to this day, and made
them an ordinance in Israel: and,
behold, they *are* written in the lamentations.
26 Now the rest of the acts of Josiah,
and his goodness, according to *that
which was* written in the law of the
LORD,
27 And his deeds, first and last,
behold, they *are* written in the book of
the kings of Israel and Judah.

36 Then the people of the land took
Jehoahaz the son of Josiah, and
made him king in his father's stead in
Jerusalem.
2 Jehoahaz *was* twenty and three
years old when he began to reign, and
he reigned three months in Jerusalem.
3 And the king of Egypt put him
down at Jerusalem, and condemned
the land in an hundred talents of silver
and a talent of gold.
4 And the king of Egypt made
Eliakim his brother king over Judah
and Jerusalem, and turned his name to
Jehoiakim. And Necho took Jehoahaz
his brother, and carried him to Egypt.
5 Jehoiakim *was* twenty and five
years old when he began to reign, and
he reigned eleven years in Jerusalem:
and he did *that which was* evil in the
sight of the LORD his God.
6 Against him came up Nebuchadnezzar king of Babylon, and bound him
in fetters, to carry him to Babylon.
7 Nebuchadnezzar also carried of the
vessels of the house of the LORD to
Babylon, and put them in his temple at
Babylon.

8 Now the rest of the acts of Jehoiakim, and his abominations which he did, and that which was found in him, behold, they *are* written in the book of the kings of Israel and Judah: and Jehoiachin his son reigned in his stead.

9 Jehoiachin *was* eight years old when he began to reign, and he reigned three months and ten days in Jerusalem: and he did *that which was* evil in the sight of the LORD.

10 And when the year was expired, king Nebuchadnezzar sent, and brought him to Babylon, with the goodly vessels of the house of the LORD, and made Zedekiah his brother king over Judah and Jerusalem.

11 Zedekiah *was* one and twenty years old when he began to reign, and reigned eleven years in Jerusalem.

12 And he did *that which was* evil in the sight of the LORD his God, *and* humbled not himself before Jeremiah the prophet *speaking* from the mouth of the LORD.

13 And he also rebelled against king Nebuchadnezzar, who had made him swear by God: but he stiffened his neck, and hardened his heart from turning unto the LORD God of Israel.

14 Moreover all the chief of the priests, and the people, transgressed very much after all the abominations of the heathen; and polluted the house of the LORD which he had hallowed in Jerusalem.

15 And the LORD God of their fathers sent to them by his messengers, rising up betimes, and sending; because he had compassion on his people, and on his dwelling place:

16 But they mocked the messengers of God, and despised his words, and misused his prophets, until the wrath of the LORD arose against his people, till *there was* no remedy.

17 Therefore he brought upon them the king of the Chaldees, who slew their young men with the sword in the house of their sanctuary, and had no compassion upon young man or maiden, old man, or him that stooped for age: he gave *them* all into his hand.

18 And all the vessels of the house of God, great and small, and the treasures of the house of the LORD, and the treasures of the king, and of his princes; all *these* he brought to Babylon.

19 And they burnt the house of God, and brake down the wall of Jerusalem, and burnt all the palaces thereof with fire, and destroyed all the goodly vessels thereof.

20 And them that had escaped from the sword carried he away to Babylon; where they were servants to him and his sons until the reign of the kingdom of Persia:

21 To fulfil the word of the LORD by the mouth of Jeremiah, until the land had enjoyed her sabbaths: *for* as long as she lay desolate she kept sabbath, to fulfil threescore and ten years.

22 Now in the first year of Cyrus king of Persia, that the word of the LORD *spoken* by the mouth of Jeremiah might be accomplished, the LORD stirred up the spirit of Cyrus king of Persia, that he made a proclamation throughout all his kingdom, and *put it* also in writing, saying,

23 Thus saith Cyrus king of Persia, All the kingdoms of the earth hath the LORD God of heaven given me; and he hath charged me to build him an house in Jerusalem, which *is* in Judah. Who *is there* among you of all his people? The LORD his God *be* with him, and let him go up.

THE BOOK OF

EZRA

1 Now in the first year of Cyrus king of Persia, that the word of the LORD by the mouth of Jeremiah might be fulfilled, the LORD stirred up the spirit of Cyrus king of Persia, that he made a proclamation throughout all his kingdom, and *put it* also in writing, saying,

2 Thus saith Cyrus king of Persia, The LORD God of heaven hath given me all the kingdoms of the earth; and he hath charged me to build him an house at Jerusalem, which *is* in Judah.

3 Who *is there* among you of all his people? his God be with him, and let him go up to Jerusalem, which *is* in Judah, and build the house of the LORD God of Israel, (he *is* the God,) which *is* in Jerusalem.

4 And whosoever remaineth in any place where he sojourneth, let the men of his place help him with silver, and with gold, and with goods, and with beasts, beside the freewill offering for the house of God that *is* in Jerusalem.

5 Then rose up the chief of the fathers of Judah and Benjamin, and the priests, and the Levites, with all *them* whose spirit God had raised, to go up to build the house of the LORD which *is* in Jerusalem.

6 And all they that *were* about them strengthened their hands with vessels of silver, with gold, with goods, and with beasts, and with precious things, beside all *that* was willingly offered.

7 Also Cyrus the king brought forth the vessels of the house of the LORD, which Nebuchadnezzar had brought forth out of Jerusalem, and had put them in the house of his gods;

8 Even those did Cyrus king of Persia bring forth by the hand of Mithredath the treasurer, and numbered them unto Sheshbazzar, the prince of Judah.

9 And this *is* the number of them: thirty chargers of gold, a thousand chargers of silver, nine and twenty knives,

10 Thirty basons of gold, silver basons of a second *sort* four hundred and ten, *and* other vessels a thousand.

11 All the vessels of gold and of silver *were* five thousand and four hundred. All *these* did Sheshbazzar bring up with *them of* the captivity that were brought up from Babylon unto Jerusalem.

2 Now these *are* the children of the province that went up out of the captivity, of those which had been carried away, whom Nebuchadnezzar the king of Babylon had carried away unto Babylon, and came again unto Jerusalem and Judah, every one unto his city;

2 Which came with Zerubbabel: Jeshua, Nehemiah, Seraiah, Reelaiah, Mordecai, Bilshan, Mispar, Bigvai, Rehum, Baanah. The number of the men of the people of Israel:

3 The children of Parosh, two thousand an hundred seventy and two.

4 The children of Shephatiah, three hundred seventy and two.

5 The children of Arah, seven hundred seventy and five.

6 The children of Pahath-moab, of the children of Jeshua *and* Joab, two thousand eight hundred and twelve.

7 The children of Elam, a thousand two hundred fifty and four.

8 The children of Zattu, nine hundred forty and five.
9 The children of Zaccai, seven hundred and threescore.
10 The children of Bani, six hundred forty and two.
11 The children of Bebai, six hundred twenty and three.
12 The children of Azgad, a thousand two hundred twenty and two.
13 The children of Adonikam, six hundred sixty and six.
14 The children of Bigvai, two thousand fifty and six.
15 The children of Adin, four hundred fifty and four.
16 The children of Ater of Hezekiah, ninety and eight.
17 The children of Bezai, three hundred twenty and three.
18 The children of Jorah, an hundred and twelve.
19 The children of Hashum, two hundred twenty and three.
20 The children of Gibbar, ninety and five.
21 The children of Beth-lehem, an hundred twenty and three.
22 The men of Netophah, fifty and six.
23 The men of Anathoth, an hundred twenty and eight.
24 The children of Azmaveth, forty and two.
25 The children of Kirjath-arim, Chephirah, and Beeroth, seven hundred and forty and three.
26 The children of Ramah and Gaba, six hundred twenty and one.
27 The men of Michmas, an hundred twenty and two.
28 The men of Bethel and Ai, two hundred twenty and three.
29 The children of Nebo, fifty and two.
30 The children of Magbish, an hundred fifty and six.
31 The children of the other Elam, a thousand two hundred fifty and four.
32 The children of Harim, three hundred and twenty.
33 The children of Lod, Hadid, and Ono, seven hundred twenty and five.
34 The children of Jericho, three hundred forty and five.
35 The children of Senaah, three thousand and six hundred and thirty.
36 The priests: the children of Jedaiah, of the house of Jeshua, nine hundred seventy and three.
37 The children of Immer, a thousand fifty and two.
38 The children of Pashur, a thousand two hundred forty and seven.
39 The children of Harim, a thousand and seventeen.
40 The Levites: the children of Jeshua and Kadmiel, of the children of Hodaviah, seventy and four.
41 The singers: the children of Asaph, an hundred twenty and eight.
42 The children of the porters: the children of Shallum, the children of Ater, the children of Talmon, the children of Akkub, the children of Hatita, the children of Shobai, *in* all an hundred thirty and nine.
43 The Nethinims: the children of Ziha, the children of Hasupha, the children of Tabbaoth,
44 The children of Keros, the children of Siaha, the children of Padon,
45 The children of Lebanah, the children of Hagabah, the children of Akkub,
46 The children of Hagab, the children of Shalmai, the children of Hanan,

47 The children of Giddel, the children of Gahar, the children of Reaiah,

48 The children of Rezin, the children of Nekoda, the children of Gazzam,

49 The children of Uzza, the children of Paseah, the children of Besai,

50 The children of Asnah, the children of Mehunim, the children of Nephusim,

51 The children of Bakbuk, the children of Hakupha, the children of Harhur,

52 The children of Bazluth, the children of Mehida, the children of Harsha,

53 The children of Barkos, the children of Sisera, the children of Thamah,

54 The children of Neziah, the children of Hatipha.

55 The children of Solomon's servants: the children of Sotai, the children of Sophereth, the children of Peruda,

56 The children of Jaalah, the children of Darkon, the children of Giddel,

57 The children of Shephatiah, the children of Hattil, the children of Pochereth of Zebaim, the children of Ami.

58 All the Nethinims, and the children of Solomon's servants, *were* three hundred ninety and two.

59 And these *were* they which went up from Tel-melah, Tel-harsa, Cherub, Addan, *and* Immer: but they could not shew their father's house, and their seed, whether they *were* of Israel:

60 The children of Delaiah, the children of Tobiah, the children of Nekoda, six hundred fifty and two.

61 And of the children of the priests: the children of Habaiah, the children of Koz, the children of Barzillai; which took a wife of the daughters of Barzillai the Gileadite, and was called a their name:

62 These sought their register *among* those that were reckoned by genealogy, but they were not found: therefore were they, as polluted, put from the priesthood.

63 And the Tirshatha said unto them, that they should not eat of the most holy things, till there stood up a priest with Urim and with Thummim.

64 The whole congregation together *was* forty and two thousand three hundred *and* threescore,

65 Beside their servants and their maids, of whom *there were* seven thousand three hundred thirty and seven: and *there were* among them two hundred singing men and singing women.

66 Their horses *were* seven hundred thirty and six; their mules, two hundred forty and five;

67 Their camels, four hundred thirty and five; *their* asses, six thousand seven hundred and twenty.

68 And *some* of the chief of the fathers, when they came to the house of the LORD which *is* at Jerusalem, offered freely for the house of God to set it up in his place:

69 They gave after their ability unto the treasure of the work threescore and one thousand drams of gold, and five thousand pound of silver, and one hundred priests' garments.

70 So the priests, and the Levites, and *some* of the people, and the singers, and the porters, and the Nethinims, dwelt in their cities, and all Israel in their cities.

3 And when the seventh month was come, and the children of Israel *were* in the cities, the people gathered

themselves together as one man to
Jerusalem.
2 Then stood up Jeshua the son of
Jozadak, and his brethren the priests,
and Zerubbabel the son of Shealtiel,
and his brethren, and builded the altar
of the God of Israel, to offer burnt offerings thereon, as *it is* written in the law
of Moses the man of God.
3 And they set the altar upon his
bases; for fear *was* upon them because
of the people of those countries: and
they offered burnt offerings thereon
unto the LORD, *even* burnt offerings
morning and evening.
4 They kept also the feast of tabernacles, as *it is* written, and *offered* the
daily burnt offerings by number,
according to the custom, as the duty of
every day required;
5 And afterward *offered* the continual
burnt offering, both of the new moons,
and of all the set feasts of the LORD that
were consecrated, and of every one that
willingly offered a freewill offering
unto the LORD.
6 From the first day of the seventh
month began they to offer burnt offerings unto the LORD. But the foundation
of the temple of the LORD was not *yet*
laid.
7 They gave money also unto the
masons, and to the carpenters; and
meat, and drink, and oil, unto them of
Zidon, and to them of Tyre, to bring
cedar trees from Lebanon to the sea of
Joppa, according to the grant that they
had of Cyrus king of Persia.
8 Now in the second year of their
coming unto the house of God at
Jerusalem, in the second month, began
Zerubbabel the son of Shealtiel, and
Jeshua the son of Jozadak, and the
remnant of their brethren the priests
and the Levites, and all they that were
come out of the captivity unto Jerusalem; and appointed the Levites, from
twenty years old and upward, to set
forward the work of the house of the
LORD.
9 Then stood Jeshua *with* his sons
and his brethren, Kadmiel and his sons,
the sons of Judah, together, to set forward the workmen in the house of God:
the sons of Henadad, *with* their sons
and their brethren the Levites.
10 And when the builders laid the
foundation of the temple of the LORD,
they set the priests in their apparel
with trumpets, and the Levites the sons
of Asaph with cymbals, to praise the
LORD, after the ordinance of David king
of Israel.
11 And they sang together by course
in praising and giving thanks unto the
LORD; because *he is* good, for his mercy
endureth for ever toward Israel. And all
the people shouted with a great shout,
when they praised the LORD, because
the foundation of the house of the LORD
was laid.
12 But many of the priests and
Levites and chief of the fathers, *who
were* ancient men, that had seen the
first house, when the foundation of this
house was laid before their eyes, wept
with a loud voice; and many shouted
aloud for joy:
13 So that the people could not discern the noise of the shout of joy from
the noise of the weeping of the people:
for the people shouted with a loud
shout, and the noise was heard afar off.

4 Now when the adversaries of Judah
and Benjamin heard that the
children of the captivity builded the
temple unto the LORD God of Israel;

2 Then they came to Zerubbabel, and
to the chief of the fathers, and said unto
them, Let us build with you: for we seek
your God, as ye *do*; and we do sacrifice
unto him since the days of Esar-haddon
king of Assur, which brought us up
hither.
3 But Zerubbabel, and Jeshua, and
the rest of the chief of the fathers of
Israel, said unto them, Ye have nothing
to do with us to build an house unto our
God; but we ourselves together will
build unto the LORD God of Israel, as
king Cyrus the king of Persia hath commanded us.
4 Then the people of the land weakened the hands of the people of Judah,
and troubled them in building,
5 And hired counsellors against them,
to frustrate their purpose, all the days
of Cyrus king of Persia, even until the
reign of Darius king of Persia.
6 And in the reign of Ahasuerus, in
the beginning of his reign, wrote they
unto him an accusation against the
inhabitants of Judah and Jerusalem.
7 And in the days of Artaxerxes wrote
Bishlam, Mithredath, Tabeel, and the
rest of their companions, unto Artaxerxes king of Persia; and the writing
of the letter *was* written in the Syrian
tongue, and interpreted in the Syrian
tongue.
8 Rehum the chancellor and Shimshai
the scribe wrote a letter against
Jerusalem to Artaxerxes the king in
this sort:
9 Then *wrote* Rehum the chancellor,
and Shimshai the scribe, and the rest of
their companions; the Dinaites, the
Apharsathchites, the Tarpelites, the
Apharsites, the Archevites, the Babylonians, the Susanchites, the Dehavites,
and the Elamites,
10 And the rest of the nations whom
the great and noble Asnappar brought
over, and set in the cities of Samaria,
and the rest *that are* on this side the
river, and at such a time.
11 This *is* the copy of the letter that
they sent unto him, *even* unto Artaxerxes the king; Thy servants the men
on this side the river, and at such a
time.
12 Be it known unto the king, that the
Jews which came up from thee to us are
come unto Jerusalem, building the
rebellious and the bad city, and have
set up the walls *thereof*, and joined the
foundations.
13 Be it known now unto the king,
that, if this city be builded, and the
walls set up *again, then* will they not
pay toll, tribute, and custom, and *so*
thou shalt endamage the revenue of
the kings.
14 Now because we have maintenance from *the king's* palace, and it
was not meet for us to see the king's
dishonour, therefore have we sent and
certified the king;
15 That search may be made in the
book of the records of thy fathers: so
shalt thou find in the book of the
records, and know that this city *is* a
rebellious city, and hurtful unto kings
and provinces, and that they have
moved sedition within the same of old
time: for which cause was this city
destroyed.
16 We certify the king that, if this city
be builded *again*, and the walls thereof
set up, by this means thou shalt have no
portion on this side the river.
17 *Then* sent the king an answer unto
Rehum the chancellor, and *to* Shimshai
the scribe, and *to* the rest of their companions that dwell in Samaria, and

unto the rest beyond the river, Peace,
and at such a time.
18 The letter which ye sent unto us
hath been plainly read before me.
19 And I commanded, and search
hath been made, and it is found that
this city of old time hath made insurrection against kings, and *that* rebellion and sedition have been made
therein.
20 There have been mighty kings also
over Jerusalem, which have ruled over
all *countries* beyond the river; and toll,
tribute, and custom, was paid unto
them.
21 Give ye now commandment to
cause these men to cease, and that this
city be not builded, until *another* commandment shall be given from me.
22 Take heed now that ye fail not to
do this: why should damage grow to the
hurt of the kings?
23 Now when the copy of king
Artaxerxes' letter *was* read before
Rehum, and Shimshai the scribe, and
their companions, they went up in
haste to Jerusalem unto the Jews, and
made them to cease by force and power.
24 Then ceased the work of the house
of God which *is* at Jerusalem. So it
ceased unto the second year of the
reign of Darius king of Persia.

5 Then the prophets, Haggai the
prophet, and Zechariah the son of
Iddo, prophesied unto the Jews that
were in Judah and Jerusalem in the
name of the God of Israel, *even* unto
them.
2 Then rose up Zerubbabel the son of
Shealtiel, and Jeshua the son of
Jozadak, and began to build the house
of God which *is* at Jerusalem: and with
them *were* the prophets of God helping
them.
3 At the same time came to them
Tatnai, governor on this side the river,
and Shethar-boznai, and their companions, and said thus unto them, Who
hath commanded you to build this
house, and to make up this wall?
4 Then said we unto them after this
manner, What are the names of the
men that make this building?
5 But the eye of their God was upon
the elders of the Jews, that they could
not cause them to cease, till the matter
came to Darius: and then they returned
answer by letter concerning this *matter*.
6 The copy of the letter that Tatnai,
governor on this side the river, and
Shethar-boznai, and his companions
the Apharsachites, which *were* on this
side the river, sent unto Darius the
king:
7 They sent a letter unto him, wherein was written thus; Unto Darius the
king, all peace.
8 Be it known unto the king, that we
went into the province of Judea, to the
house of the great God, which is builded with great stones, and timber is laid
in the walls, and this work goeth fast
on, and prospereth in their hands.
9 Then asked we those elders, *and*
said unto them thus, Who commanded
you to build this house, and to make up
these walls?
10 We asked their names also, to certify thee, that we might write the
names of the men that *were* the chief of
them.
11 And thus they returned us answer,
saying, We are the servants of the God
of heaven and earth, and build the
house that was builded these many
years ago, which a great king of Israel
builded and set up.

12 But after that our fathers had provoked the God of heaven unto wrath,
he gave them into the hand of
Nebuchadnezzar the king of Babylon,
the Chaldean, who destroyed this
house, and carried the people away
into Babylon.
13 But in the first year of Cyrus the
king of Babylon *the same* king Cyrus
made a decree to build this house of
God.
14 And the vessels also of gold and
silver of the house of God, which
Nebuchadnezzar took out of the temple
that *was* in Jerusalem, and brought
them into the temple of Babylon, those
did Cyrus the king take out of the
temple of Babylon, and they were delivered unto *one*, whose name *was*
Sheshbazzar, whom he had made governor;
15 And said unto him, Take these vessels, go, carry them into the temple that
is in Jerusalem, and let the house of
God be builded in his place.
16 Then came the same Sheshbazzar,
and laid the foundation of the house of
God which *is* in Jerusalem: and since
that time even until now hath it been in
building, and *yet* it is not finished.
17 Now therefore, if *it seem* good to
the king, let there be search made in
the king's treasure house, which *is*
there at Babylon, whether it be *so*, that
a decree was made of Cyrus the king to
build this house of God at Jerusalem,
and let the king send his pleasure to us
concerning this matter.

6 Then Darius the king made a
decree, and search was made in the
house of the rolls, where the treasures
were laid up in Babylon.
2 And there was found at Achmetha,
in the palace that *is* in the province of
the Medes, a roll, and therein *was* a
record thus written:
3 In the first year of Cyrus the king
the same Cyrus the king made a decree
concerning the house of God at
Jerusalem, Let the house be builded,
the place where they offered sacrifices,
and let the foundations thereof be
strongly laid; the height thereof threescore cubits, *and* the breadth thereof
threescore cubits;
4 *With* three rows of great stones, and
a row of new timber: and let the
expenses be given out of the king's
house:
5 And also let the golden and silver
vessels of the house of God, which
Nebuchadnezzar took forth out of the
temple which *is* at Jerusalem, and
brought unto Babylon, be restored, and
brought again unto the temple which *is*
at Jerusalem, *every one* to his place,
and place *them* in the house of God.
6 Now *therefore*, Tatnai, governor
beyond the river, Shethar-boznai, and
your companions the Apharsachites,
which *are* beyond the river, be ye far
from thence:
7 Let the work of this house of God
alone; let the governor of the Jews and
the elders of the Jews build this house
of God in his place.
8 Moreover I make a decree what ye
shall do to the elders of these Jews for
the building of this house of God: that
of the king's goods, *even* of the tribute
beyond the river, forthwith expenses be
given unto these men, that they be not
hindered.
9 And that which they have need of,
both young bullocks, and rams, and
lambs, for the burnt offerings of the

God of heaven, wheat, salt, wine, and oil, according to the appointment of the priests which *are* at Jerusalem, let it be given them day by day without fail:

10 That they may offer sacrifices of sweet savours unto the God of heaven, and pray for the life of the king, and of his sons.

11 Also I have made a decree, that whosoever shall alter this word, let timber be pulled down from his house, and being set up, let him be hanged thereon; and let his house be made a dunghill for this.

12 And the God that hath caused his name to dwell there destroy all kings and people, that shall put to their hand to alter *and* to destroy this house of God which *is* at Jerusalem. I Darius have made a decree; let it be done with speed.

13 Then Tatnai, governor on this side the river, Shethar-boznai, and their companions, according to that which Darius the king had sent, so they did speedily.

14 And the elders of the Jews builded, and they prospered through the prophesying of Haggai the prophet and Zechariah the son of Iddo. And they builded, and finished *it*, according to the commandment of the God of Israel, and according to the commandment of Cyrus, and Darius, and Artaxerxes king of Persia.

15 And this house was finished on the third day of the month Adar, which was in the sixth year of the reign of Darius the king.

16 And the children of Israel, the priests, and the Levites, and the rest of the children of the captivity, kept the dedication of this house of God with joy,

17 And offered at the dedication of this house of God an hundred bullocks, two hundred rams, four hundred lambs; and for a sin offering for all Israel, twelve he goats, according to the number of the tribes of Israel.

18 And they set the priests in their divisions, and the Levites in their courses, for the service of God, which *is* at Jerusalem; as it is written in the book of Moses.

19 And the children of the captivity kept the passover upon the fourteenth *day* of the first month.

20 For the priests and the Levites were purified together, all of them *were* pure, and killed the passover for all the children of the captivity, and for their brethren the priests, and for themselves.

21 And the children of Israel, which were come again out of captivity, and all such as had separated themselves unto them from the filthiness of the heathen of the land, to seek the LORD God of Israel, did eat,

22 And kept the feast of unleavened bread seven days with joy: for the LORD had made them joyful, and turned the heart of the king of Assyria unto them, to strengthen their hands in the work of the house of God, the God of Israel.

7 Now after these things, in the reign of Artaxerxes king of Persia, Ezra the son of Seraiah, the son of Azariah, the son of Hilkiah,

2 The son of Shallum, the son of Zadok, the son of Ahitub,

3 The son of Amariah, the son of Azariah, the son of Meraioth,

4 The son of Zerahiah, the son of Uzzi, the son of Bukki,

5 The son of Abishua, the son of
Phinehas, the son of Eleazar, the son of
Aaron the chief priest:
6 This Ezra went up from Babylon;
and he *was* a ready scribe in the law of
Moses, which the LORD God of Israel
had given: and the king granted him all
his request, according to the hand of
the LORD his God upon him.
7 And there went up *some* of the children of Israel, and of the priests, and
the Levites, and the singers, and the
porters, and the Nethinims, unto
Jerusalem, in the seventh year of
Artaxerxes the king.
8 And he came to Jerusalem in the
fifth month, which *was* in the seventh
year of the king.
9 For upon the first *day* of the first
month began he to go up from Babylon,
and on the first *day* of the fifth month
came he to Jerusalem, according to the
good hand of his God upon him.
10 For Ezra had prepared his heart to
seek the law of the LORD, and to do *it*,
and to teach in Israel statutes and judgments.
11 Now this *is* the copy of the letter
that the king Artaxerxes gave unto
Ezra the priest, the scribe, *even* a scribe
of the words of the commandments of
the LORD, and of his statutes to Israel.
12 Artaxerxes, king of kings, unto
Ezra the priest, a scribe of the law of
the God of heaven, perfect *peace*, and
at such a time.
13 I make a decree, that all they of
the people of Israel, and *of* his priests
and Levites, in my realm, which are
minded of their own freewill to go up to
Jerusalem, go with thee.
14 Forasmuch as thou art sent of the
king, and of his seven counsellors, to
enquire concerning Judah and Jerusalem, according to the law of thy God
which *is* in thine hand;
15 And to carry the silver and gold,
which the king and his counsellors have
freely offered unto the God of Israel,
whose habitation *is* in Jerusalem,
16 And all the silver and gold that
thou canst find in all the province of
Babylon, with the freewill offering of
the people, and of the priests, offering
willingly for the house of their God
which *is* in Jerusalem:
17 That thou mayest buy speedily
with this money bullocks, rams, lambs,
with their meat offerings and their
drink offerings, and offer them upon
the altar of the house of your God
which *is* in Jerusalem.
18 And whatsoever shall seem good
to thee, and to thy brethren, to do with
the rest of the silver and the gold, that
do after the will of your God.
19 The vessels also that are given
thee for the service of the house of thy
God, *those* deliver thou before the God
of Jerusalem.
20 And whatsoever more shall be
needful for the house of thy God, which
thou shalt have occasion to bestow,
bestow *it* out of the king's treasure
house.
21 And I, *even* I Artaxerxes the king,
do make a decree to all the treasurers
which *are* beyond the river, that whatsoever Ezra the priest, the scribe of the
law of the God of heaven, shall require
of you, it be done speedily,
22 Unto an hundred talents of silver,
and to an hundred measures of wheat,
and to an hundred baths of wine, and to
an hundred baths of oil, and salt without prescribing *how much*.

23 Whatsoever is commanded by the God of heaven, let it be diligently done for the house of the God of heaven: for why should there be wrath against the realm of the king and his sons?

24 Also we certify you, that touching any of the priests and Levites, singers, porters, Nethinims, or ministers of this house of God, it shall not be lawful to impose toll, tribute, or custom, upon them.

25 And thou, Ezra, after the wisdom of thy God, that *is* in thine hand, set magistrates and judges, which may judge all the people that *are* beyond the river, all such as know the laws of thy God; and teach ye them that know *them* not.

26 And whosoever will not do the law of thy God, and the law of the king, let judgment be executed speedily upon him, whether *it be* unto death, or to banishment, or to confiscation of goods, or to imprisonment.

27 Blessed *be* the LORD God of our fathers, which hath put *such a thing* as this in the king's heart, to beautify the house of the LORD which *is* in Jerusalem:

28 And hath extended mercy unto me before the king, and his counsellors, and before all the king's mighty princes. And I was strengthened as the hand of the LORD my God *was* upon me, and I gathered together out of Israel chief men to go up with me.

8 These *are* now the chief of their fathers, and *this is* the genealogy of them that went up with me from Babylon, in the reign of Artaxerxes the king.

2 Of the sons of Phinehas; Gershom: of the sons of Ithamar; Daniel: of the sons of David; Hattush.

3 Of the sons of Shechaniah, of the sons of Pharosh; Zechariah: and with him were reckoned by genealogy of the males an hundred and fifty.

4 Of the sons of Pahath-moab; Elihoenai the son of Zerahiah, and with him two hundred males.

5 Of the sons of Shechaniah; the son of Jahaziel, and with him three hundred males.

6 Of the sons also of Adin; Ebed the son of Jonathan, and with him fifty males.

7 And of the sons of Elam; Jeshaiah the son of Athaliah, and with him seventy males.

8 And of the sons of Shephatiah; Zebadiah the son of Michael, and with him fourscore males.

9 Of the sons of Joab; Obadiah the son of Jehiel, and with him two hundred and eighteen males.

10 And of the sons of Shelomith; the son of Josiphiah, and with him an hundred and threescore males.

11 And of the sons of Bebai; Zechariah the son of Bebai, and with him twenty and eight males.

12 And of the sons of Azgad; Johanan the son of Hakkatan, and with him an hundred and ten males.

13 And of the last sons of Adonikam, whose names *are* these, Eliphelet, Jeiel, and Shemaiah, and with them threescore males.

14 Of the sons also of Bigvai; Uthai, and Zabbud, and with them seventy males.

15 And I gathered them together to the river that runneth to Ahava; and there abode we in tents three days: and I viewed the people, and the priests, and found there none of the sons of Levi.

16 Then sent I for Eliezer, for Ariel,
for Shemaiah, and for Elnathan, and
for Jarib, and for Elnathan, and for
Nathan, and for Zechariah, and for
Meshullam, chief men; also for Joiarib,
and for Elnathan, men of understanding.
17 And I sent them with commandment unto Iddo the chief at the place
Casiphia, and I told them what they
should say unto Iddo, *and* to his brethren the Nethinims, at the place
Casiphia, that they should bring unto
us ministers for the house of our God.
18 And by the good hand of our God
upon us they brought us a man of
understanding, of the sons of Mahli, the
son of Levi, the son of Israel; and
Sherebiah, with his sons and his brethren, eighteen;
19 And Hashabiah, and with him
Jeshaiah of the sons of Merari, his
brethren and their sons, twenty;
20 Also of the Nethinims, whom
David and the princes had appointed
for the service of the Levites, two hundred and twenty Nethinims: all of them
were expressed by name.
21 Then I proclaimed a fast there, at
the river of Ahava, that we might afflict
ourselves before our God, to seek of
him a right way for us, and for our little
ones, and for all our substance.
22 For I was ashamed to require of
the king a band of soldiers and horsemen to help us against the enemy in
the way: because we had spoken unto
the king, saying, The hand of our God *is*
upon all them for good that seek him;
but his power and his wrath *is* against
all them that forsake him.
23 So we fasted and besought our
God for this: and he was intreated of us.
24 Then I separated twelve of the
chief of the priests, Sherebiah, Hashabiah, and ten of their brethren with
them,
25 And weighed unto them the silver,
and the gold, and the vessels, *even* the
offering of the house of our God, which
the king, and his counsellors, and his
lords, and all Israel *there* present, had
offered:
26 I even weighed unto their hand six
hundred and fifty talents of silver, and
silver vessels an hundred talents, *and*
of gold an hundred talents;
27 Also twenty basons of gold, of a
thousand drams; and two vessels of fine
copper, precious as gold.
28 And I said unto them, Ye *are* holy
unto the LORD; the vessels *are* holy also;
and the silver and the gold *are* a freewill offering unto the LORD God of your
fathers.
29 Watch ye, and keep *them*, until ye
weigh *them* before the chief of the
priests and the Levites, and chief of the
fathers of Israel, at Jerusalem, in the
chambers of the house of the LORD.
30 So took the priests and the Levites
the weight of the silver, and the gold,
and the vessels, to bring *them* to
Jerusalem unto the house of our God.
31 Then we departed from the river
of Ahava on the twelfth *day* of the first
month, to go unto Jerusalem: and the
hand of our God was upon us, and he
delivered us from the hand of the
enemy, and of such as lay in wait by the
way.
32 And we came to Jerusalem, and
abode there three days.
33 Now on the fourth day was the silver and the gold and the vessels

weighed in the house of our God by the
hand of Meremoth the son of Uriah the
priest; and with him *was* Eleazar the
son of Phinehas; and with them *was*
Jozabad the son of Jeshua, and Noadiah
the son of Binnui, Levites;
34 By number *and* by weight of every
one: and all the weight was written at
that time.
35 *Also* the children of those that had
been carried away, which were come
out of the captivity, offered burnt offerings unto the God of Israel, twelve
bullocks for all Israel, ninety and six
rams, seventy and seven lambs, twelve
he goats *for* a sin offering: all *this was*
a burnt offering unto the LORD.
36 And they delivered the king's com-
missions unto the king's lieutenants,
and to the governors on this side the
river: and they furthered the people,
and the house of God.

9 Now when these things were done,
the princes came to me, saying, The
people of Israel, and the priests, and
the Levites, have not separated themselves from the people of the lands,
doing according to their abominations,
even of the Canaanites, the Hittites, the
Perizzites, the Jebusites, the Ammonites, the Moabites, the Egyptians, and
the Amorites.
2 For they have taken of their daughters for themselves, and for their sons:
so that the holy seed have mingled
themselves with the people of *those*
lands: yea, the hand of the princes and
rulers hath been chief in this trespass.
3 And when I heard this thing, I rent
my garment and my mantle, and
plucked off the hair of my head and of
my beard, and sat down astonied.
4 Then were assembled unto me
every one that trembled at the words of
the God of Israel, because of the transgression of those that had been carried
away; and I sat astonied until the evening sacrifice.
5 And at the evening sacrifice I arose
up from my heaviness; and having rent
my garment and my mantle, I fell upon
my knees, and spread out my hands
unto the LORD my God,
6 And said, O my God, I am ashamed
and blush to lift up my face to thee, my
God: for our iniquities are increased
over *our* head, and our trespass is
grown up unto the heavens.
7 Since the days of our fathers *have*
we *been* in a great trespass unto this
day; and for our iniquities have we, our
kings, *and* our priests, been delivered
into the hand of the kings of the lands,
to the sword, to captivity, and to a spoil,
and to confusion of face, as *it is* this
day.
8 And now for a little space grace
hath been *shewed* from the LORD our
God, to leave us a remnant to escape,
and to give us a nail in his holy place,
that our God may lighten our eyes, and
give us a little reviving in our bondage.
9 For we *were* bondmen; yet our God
hath not forsaken us in our bondage,
but hath extended mercy unto us in the
sight of the kings of Persia, to give us a
reviving, to set up the house of our God,
and to repair the desolations thereof,
and to give us a wall in Judah and in
Jerusalem.
10 And now, O our God, what shall we
say after this? for we have forsaken thy
commandments,
11 Which thou hast commanded by
thy servants the prophets, saying, The
land, unto which ye go to possess it, is

an unclean land with the filthiness of the people of the lands, with their abominations, which have filled it from one end to another with their uncleanness.

12 Now therefore give not your daughters unto their sons, neither take their daughters unto your sons, nor seek their peace or their wealth for ever: that ye may be strong, and eat the good of the land, and leave *it* for an inheritance to your children for ever.

13 And after all that is come upon us for our evil deeds, and for our great trespass, seeing that thou our God hast punished us less than our iniquities *deserve*, and hast given us *such* deliverance as this;

14 Should we again break thy commandments, and join in affinity with the people of these abominations? wouldest not thou be angry with us till thou hadst consumed *us*, so that *there should be* no remnant nor escaping?

15 O LORD God of Israel, thou *art* righteous: for we remain yet escaped, as *it is* this day: behold, we *are* before thee in our trespasses: for we cannot stand before thee because of this.

10 Now when Ezra had prayed, and when he had confessed, weeping and casting himself down before the house of God, there assembled unto him out of Israel a very great congregation of men and women and children: for the people wept very sore.

2 And Shechaniah the son of Jehiel, *one* of the sons of Elam, answered and said unto Ezra, We have trespassed against our God, and have taken strange wives of the people of the land: yet now there is hope in Israel concerning this thing.

3 Now therefore let us make a covenant with our God to put away all the wives, and such as are born of them, according to the counsel of my lord, and of those that tremble at the commandment of our God; and let it be done according to the law.

4 Arise; for *this* matter *belongeth* unto thee: we also *will be* with thee: be of good courage, and do *it*.

5 Then arose Ezra, and made the chief priests, the Levites, and all Israel, to swear that they should do according to this word. And they sware.

6 Then Ezra rose up from before the house of God, and went into the chamber of Johanan the son of Eliashib: and *when* he came thither, he did eat no bread, nor drink water: for he mourned because of the transgression of them that had been carried away.

7 And they made proclamation throughout Judah and Jerusalem unto all the children of the captivity, that they should gather themselves together unto Jerusalem;

8 And that whosoever would not come within three days, according to the counsel of the princes and the elders, all his substance should be forfeited, and himself separated from the congregation of those that had been carried away.

9 Then all the men of Judah and Benjamin gathered themselves together unto Jerusalem within three days. It *was* the ninth month, on the twentieth *day* of the month; and all the people sat in the street of the house of God, trembling because of *this* matter, and for the great rain.

10 And Ezra the priest stood up, and said unto them, Ye have transgressed, and have taken strange wives, to increase the trespass of Israel.

11 Now therefore make confession unto the LORD God of your fathers, and do his pleasure: and separate yourselves from the people of the land, and from the strange wives.

12 Then all the congregation answered and said with a loud voice, As thou hast said, so must we do.

13 But the people *are* many, and *it is* a time of much rain, and we are not able to stand without, neither *is this* a work of one day or two: for we are many that have transgressed in this thing.

14 Let now our rulers of all the congregation stand, and let all them which have taken strange wives in our cities come at appointed times, and with them the elders of every city, and the judges thereof, until the fierce wrath of our God for this matter be turned from us.

15 Only Jonathan the son of Asahel and Jahaziah the son of Tikvah were employed about this *matter*: and Meshullam and Shabbethai the Levite helped them.

16 And the children of the captivity did so. And Ezra the priest, *with* certain chief of the fathers, after the house of their fathers, and all of them by *their* names, were separated, and sat down in the first day of the tenth month to examine the matter.

17 And they made an end with all the men that had taken strange wives by the first day of the first month.

18 And among the sons of the priests there were found that had taken strange wives: *namely*, of the sons of Jeshua the son of Jozadak, and his brethren; Maaseiah, and Eliezer, and Jarib, and Gedaliah.

19 And they gave their hands that they would put away their wives; and *being* guilty, *they offered* a ram of the flock for their trespass.

20 And of the sons of Immer; Hanani, and Zebadiah.

21 And of the sons of Harim; Maaseiah, and Elijah, and Shemaiah, and Jehiel, and Uzziah.

22 And of the sons of Pashur; Elioenai, Maaseiah, Ishmael, Nethaneel, Jozabad, and Elasah.

23 Also of the Levites; Jozabad, and Shimei, and Kelaiah, (the same *is* Kelita,) Pethahiah, Judah, and Eliezer.

24 Of the singers also; Eliashib: and of the porters; Shallum, and Telem, and Uri.

25 Moreover of Israel: of the sons of Parosh; Ramiah, and Jeziah, and Malchiah, and Miamin, and Eleazar, and Malchijah, and Benaiah.

26 And of the sons of Elam; Mattaniah, Zechariah, and Jehiel, and Abdi, and Jeremoth, and Eliah.

27 And of the sons of Zattu; Elioenai, Eliashib, Mattaniah, and Jeremoth, and Zabad, and Aziza.

28 Of the sons also of Bebai; Jehohanan, Hananiah, Zabbai, *and* Athlai.

29 And of the sons of Bani; Meshullam, Malluch, and Adaiah, Jashub, and Sheal, and Ramoth.

30 And of the sons of Pahath-moab; Adna, and Chelal, Benaiah, Maaseiah, Mattaniah, Bezaleel, and Binnui, and Manasseh.

31 And *of* the sons of Harim; Eliezer, Ishijah, Malchiah, Shemaiah, Shimeon,

32 Benjamin, Malluch, *and* Shemariah.

33 Of the sons of Hashum; Mattenai, Mattathah, Zabad, Eliphelet, Jeremai, Manasseh, *and* Shimei.

34 Of the sons of Bani; Maadai,
Amram, and Uel,
35 Benaiah, Bedeiah, Chelluh,
36 Vaniah, Meremoth, Eliashib,
37 Mattaniah, Mattenai, and Jaasau,
38 And Bani, and Binnui, Shimei,
39 And Shelemiah, and Nathan, and
Adaiah,
40 Machnadebai, Shashai, Sharai,
41 Azareel, and Shelemiah, Shemariah,
42 Shallum, Amariah, *and* Joseph.
43 Of the sons of Nebo; Jeiel, Mattithiah, Zabad, Zebina, Jadau, and Joel,
Benaiah.
44 All these had taken strange wives:
and *some* of them had wives by whom
they had children.

THE BOOK OF NEHEMIAH

1 The words of Nehemiah the son of
Hachaliah. And it came to pass in
the month Chisleu, in the twentieth
year, as I was in Shushan the palace,
2 That Hanani, one of my brethren,
came, he and *certain* men of Judah;
and I asked them concerning the Jews
that had escaped, which were left of
the captivity, and concerning Jerusalem.
3 And they said unto me, The remnant that are left of the captivity there
in the province *are* in great affliction
and reproach: the wall of Jerusalem
also *is* broken down, and the gates
thereof are burned with fire.
4 And it came to pass, when I heard
these words, that I sat down and wept,
and mourned *certain* days, and fasted,
and prayed before the God of heaven,
5 And said, I beseech thee, O LORD
God of heaven, the great and terrible
God, that keepeth covenant and mercy
for them that love him and observe his
commandments:
6 Let thine ear now be attentive, and
thine eyes open, that thou mayest hear
the prayer of thy servant, which I pray
before thee now, day and night, for the
children of Israel thy servants, and confess the sins of the children of Israel,
which we have sinned against thee:
both I and my father's house have
sinned.
7 We have dealt very corruptly
against thee, and have not kept the
commandments, nor the statutes, nor
the judgments, which thou commandedst thy servant Moses.
8 Remember, I beseech thee, the
word that thou commandedst thy servant Moses, saying, *If* ye transgress, I
will scatter you abroad among the
nations:
9 But *if* ye turn unto me, and keep my
commandments, and do them; though
there were of you cast out unto the
uttermost part of the heaven, *yet* will I
gather them from thence, and will
bring them unto the place that I have
chosen to set my name there.
10 Now these *are* thy servants and thy
people, whom thou hast redeemed by
thy great power, and by thy strong
hand.

11 O Lord, I beseech thee, let now thine ear be attentive to the prayer of thy servant, and to the prayer of thy servants, who desire to fear thy name: and prosper, I pray thee, thy servant this day, and grant him mercy in the sight of this man. For I was the king's cupbearer.

2 And it came to pass in the month Nisan, in the twentieth year of Artaxerxes the king, *that* wine *was* before him: and I took up the wine, and gave *it* unto the king. Now I had not been *beforetime* sad in his presence.

2 Wherefore the king said unto me, Why *is* thy countenance sad, seeing thou *art* not sick? this *is* nothing *else* but sorrow of heart. Then I was very sore afraid,

3 And said unto the king, Let the king live for ever: why should not my countenance be sad, when the city, the place of my fathers' sepulchres, *lieth* waste, and the gates thereof are consumed with fire?

4 Then the king said unto me, For what dost thou make request? So I prayed to the God of heaven.

5 And I said unto the king, If it please the king, and if thy servant have found favour in thy sight, that thou wouldest send me unto Judah, unto the city of my fathers' sepulchres, that I may build it.

6 And the king said unto me, (the queen also sitting by him,) For how long shall thy journey be? and when wilt thou return? So it pleased the king to send me; and I set him a time.

7 Moreover I said unto the king, If it please the king, let letters be given me to the governors beyond the river, that they may convey me over till I come into Judah;

8 And a letter unto Asaph the keeper of the king's forest, that he may give me timber to make beams for the gates of the palace which *appertained* to the house, and for the wall of the city, and for the house that I shall enter into. And the king granted me, according to the good hand of my God upon me.

9 Then I came to the governors beyond the river, and gave them the king's letters. Now the king had sent captains of the army and horsemen with me.

10 When Sanballat the Horonite, and Tobiah the servant, the Ammonite, heard *of it*, it grieved them exceedingly that there was come a man to seek the welfare of the children of Israel.

11 So I came to Jerusalem, and was there three days.

12 And I arose in the night, I and some few men with me; neither told I *any* man what my God had put in my heart to do at Jerusalem: neither *was there any* beast with me, save the beast that I rode upon.

13 And I went out by night by the gate of the valley, even before the dragon well, and to the dung port, and viewed the walls of Jerusalem, which were broken down, and the gates thereof were consumed with fire.

14 Then I went on to the gate of the fountain, and to the king's pool: but *there was* no place for the beast *that was* under me to pass.

15 Then went I up in the night by the brook, and viewed the wall, and turned back, and entered by the gate of the valley, and *so* returned.

16 And the rulers knew not whither I went, or what I did; neither had I as yet told *it* to the Jews, nor to the priests,

nor to the nobles, nor to the rulers, nor to the rest that did the work.

17 Then said I unto them, Ye see the distress that we *are* in, how Jerusalem *lieth* waste, and the gates thereof are burned with fire: come, and let us build up the wall of Jerusalem, that we be no more a reproach.

18 Then I told them of the hand of my God which was good upon me; as also the king's words that he had spoken unto me. And they said, Let us rise up and build. So they strengthened their hands for *this* good *work*.

19 But when Sanballat the Horonite, and Tobiah the servant, the Ammonite, and Geshem the Arabian, heard *it*, they laughed us to scorn, and despised us, and said, What *is* this thing that ye do? will ye rebel against the king?

20 Then answered I them, and said unto them, The God of heaven, he will prosper us; therefore we his servants will arise and build: but ye have no portion, nor right, nor memorial, in Jerusalem.

3 Then Eliashib the high priest rose up with his brethren the priests, and they builded the sheep gate; they sanctified it, and set up the doors of it; even unto the tower of Meah they sanctified it, unto the tower of Hananeel.

2 And next unto him builded the men of Jericho. And next to them builded Zaccur the son of Imri.

3 But the fish gate did the sons of Hassenaah build, who *also* laid the beams thereof, and set up the doors thereof, the locks thereof, and the bars thereof.

4 And next unto them repaired Meremoth the son of Urijah, the son of Koz. And next unto them repaired Meshullam the son of Berechiah, the son of Meshezabeel. And next unto them repaired Zadok the son of Baana.

5 And next unto them the Tekoites repaired; but their nobles put not their necks to the work of their Lord.

6 Moreover the old gate repaired Jehoiada the son of Paseah, and Meshullam the son of Besodeiah; they laid the beams thereof, and set up the doors thereof, and the locks thereof, and the bars thereof.

7 And next unto them repaired Melatiah the Gibeonite, and Jadon the Meronothite, the men of Gibeon, and of Mizpah, unto the throne of the governor on this side the river.

8 Next unto him repaired Uzziel the son of Harhaiah, of the goldsmiths. Next unto him also repaired Hananiah the son of *one of* the apothecaries, and they fortified Jerusalem unto the broad wall.

9 And next unto them repaired Rephaiah the son of Hur, the ruler of the half part of Jerusalem.

10 And next unto them repaired Jedaiah the son of Harumaph, even over against his house. And next unto him repaired Hattush the son of Hashabniah.

11 Malchijah the son of Harim, and Hashub the son of Pahath-moab, repaired the other piece, and the tower of the furnaces.

12 And next unto him repaired Shallum the son of Halohesh, the ruler of the half part of Jerusalem, he and his daughters.

13 The valley gate repaired Hanun, and the inhabitants of Zanoah; they built it, and set up the doors thereof, the locks thereof, and the bars thereof,

and a thousand cubits on the wall unto
the dung gate.
14 But the dung gate repaired
Malchiah the son of Rechab, the ruler
of part of Beth-haccerem; he built it,
and set up the doors thereof, the locks
thereof, and the bars thereof.
15 But the gate of the fountain
repaired Shallun the son of Colhozeh,
the ruler of part of Mizpah; he built it,
and covered it, and set up the doors
thereof, the locks thereof, and the bars
thereof, and the wall of the pool of
Siloah by the king's garden, and unto
the stairs that go down from the city of
David.
16 After him repaired Nehemiah the
son of Azbuk, the ruler of the half part
of Beth-zur, unto *the place* over against
the sepulchres of David, and to the pool
that was made, and unto the house of
the mighty.
17 After him repaired the Levites,
Rehum the son of Bani. Next unto him
repaired Hashabiah, the ruler of the
half part of Keilah, in his part.
18 After him repaired their brethren,
Bavai the son of Henadad, the ruler of
the half part of Keilah.
19 And next to him repaired Ezer the
son of Jeshua, the ruler of Mizpah,
another piece over against the going up
to the armoury at the turning *of the
wall*.
20 After him Baruch the son of Zabbai
earnestly repaired the other piece,
from the turning *of the wall* unto the
door of the house of Eliashib the high
priest.
21 After him repaired Meremoth the
son of Urijah the son of Koz another
piece, from the door of the house of
Eliashib even to the end of the house of
Eliashib.
22 And after him repaired the priests,
the men of the plain.
23 After him repaired Benjamin and
Hashub over against their house. After
him repaired Azariah the son of
Maaseiah the son of Ananiah by his
house.
24 After him repaired Binnui the son
of Henadad another piece, from the
house of Azariah unto the turning *of
the wall*, even unto the corner.
25 Palal the son of Uzai, over against
the turning *of the wall*, and the tower
which lieth out from the king's high
house, that *was* by the court of the
prison. After him Pedaiah the son of
Parosh.
26 Moreover the Nethinims dwelt in
Ophel, unto *the place* over against the
water gate toward the east, and the
tower that lieth out.
27 After them the Tekoites repaired
another piece, over against the great
tower that lieth out, even unto the wall
of Ophel.
28 From above the horse gate
repaired the priests, every one over
against his house.
29 After them repaired Zadok the son
of Immer over against his house. After
him repaired also Shemaiah the son of
Shechaniah, the keeper of the east
gate.
30 After him repaired Hananiah the
son of Shelemiah, and Hanun the sixth
son of Zalaph, another piece. After him
repaired Meshullam the son of
Berechiah over against his chamber.
31 After him repaired Malchiah the
goldsmith's son unto the place of the
Nethinims, and of the merchants, over
against the gate Miphkad, and to the
going up of the corner.

32 And between the going up of the
corner unto the sheep gate repaired
the goldsmiths and the merchants.

4 But it came to pass, that when
Sanballat heard that we builded
the wall, he was wroth, and took great
indignation, and mocked the Jews.
2 And he spake before his brethren
and the army of Samaria, and said,
What do these feeble Jews? will they
fortify themselves? will they sacrifice?
will they make an end in a day? will
they revive the stones out of the heaps
of the rubbish which are burned?
3 Now Tobiah the Ammonite *was* by
him, and he said, Even that which they
build, if a fox go up, he shall even break
down their stone wall.
4 Hear, O our God; for we are
despised: and turn their reproach upon
their own head, and give them for a
prey in the land of captivity:
5 And cover not their iniquity, and let
not their sin be blotted out from before
thee: for they have provoked *thee* to
anger before the builders.
6 So built we the wall; and all the wall
was joined together unto the half thereof: for the people had a mind to work.
7 But it came to pass, *that* when
Sanballat, and Tobiah, and the
Arabians, and the Ammonites, and the
Ashdodites, heard that the walls of
Jerusalem were made up, *and* that the
breaches began to be stopped, then
they were very wroth,
8 And conspired all of them together
to come *and* to fight against Jerusalem,
and to hinder it.
9 Nevertheless we made our prayer
unto our God, and set a watch against
them day and night, because of them.
10 And Judah said, The strength of
the bearers of burdens is decayed, and
there is much rubbish; so that we are
not able to build the wall.
11 And our adversaries said, They
shall not know, neither see, till we come
in the midst among them, and slay
them, and cause the work to cease.
12 And it came to pass, that when the
Jews which dwelt by them came, they
said unto us ten times, From all places
whence ye shall return unto us *they
will be upon you.*
13 Therefore set I in the lower places
behind the wall, *and* on the higher
places, I even set the people after their
families with their swords, their spears,
and their bows.
14 And I looked, and rose up, and said
unto the nobles, and to the rulers, and
to the rest of the people, Be not ye
afraid of them: remember the Lord,
which is great and terrible, and fight
for your brethren, your sons, and your
daughters, your wives, and your houses.
15 And it came to pass, when our
enemies heard that it was known unto
us, and God had brought their counsel
to nought, that we returned all of us to
the wall, every one unto his work.
16 And it came to pass from that time
forth, *that* the half of my servants
wrought in the work, and the other half
of them held both the spears, the
shields, and the bows, and the habergeons; and the rulers *were* behind all
the house of Judah.
17 They which builded on the wall,
and they that bare burdens, with those
that laded, *every one* with one of his
hands wrought in the work, and with
the other *hand* held a weapon.
18 For the builders, every one had his
sword girded by his side, and *so* builded. And he that sounded the trumpet
was by me.

19 And I said unto the nobles, and to
the rulers, and to the rest of the people,
The work *is* great and large, and we are
separated upon the wall, one far from
another.
20 In what place *therefore* ye hear the
sound of the trumpet, resort ye thither
unto us: our God shall fight for us.
21 So we laboured in the work: and
half of them held the spears from the
rising of the morning till the stars
appeared.
22 Likewise at the same time said I
unto the people, Let every one with his
servant lodge within Jerusalem, that in
the night they may be a guard to us,
and labour on the day.
23 So neither I, nor my brethren, nor
my servants, nor the men of the guard
which followed me, none of us put off
our clothes, *saving that* every one put
them off for washing.

5 And there was a great cry of the
people and of their wives against
their brethren the Jews.
2 For there were that said, We, our
sons, and our daughters, *are* many:
therefore we take up corn *for them*,
that we may eat, and live.
3 *Some* also there were that said, We
have mortgaged our lands, vineyards,
and houses, that we might buy corn,
because of the dearth.
4 There were also that said, We have
borrowed money for the king's tribute,
and that upon our lands and vineyards.
5 Yet now our flesh *is* as the flesh of
our brethren, our children as their children: and, lo, we bring into bondage our
sons and our daughters to be servants,
and *some* of our daughters are brought
unto bondage *already*: neither *is it* in
our power *to redeem them*; for other
men have our lands and vineyards.
6 And I was very angry when I heard
their cry and these words.
7 Then I consulted with myself, and I
rebuked the nobles, and the rulers, and
said unto them, Ye exact usury, every
one of his brother. And I set a great
assembly against them.
8 And I said unto them, We after our
ability have redeemed our brethren the
Jews, which were sold unto the heathen; and will ye even sell your brethren? or shall they be sold unto us? Then
held they their peace, and found nothing *to answer*.
9 Also I said, It *is* not good that ye do:
ought ye not to walk in the fear of our
God because of the reproach of the
heathen our enemies?
10 I likewise, *and* my brethren, and
my servants, might exact of them
money and corn: I pray you, let us leave
off this usury.
11 Restore, I pray you, to them, even
this day, their lands, their vineyards,
their oliveyards, and their houses, also
the hundredth *part* of the money, and
of the corn, the wine, and the oil, that
ye exact of them.
12 Then said they, We will restore
them, and will require nothing of them;
so will we do as thou sayest. Then I
called the priests, and took an oath of
them, that they should do according to
this promise.
13 Also I shook my lap, and said, So
God shake out every man from his
house, and from his labour, that performeth not this promise, even thus be he
shaken out, and emptied. And all the
congregation said, Amen, and praised
the LORD. And the people did according
to this promise.

14 Moreover from the time that I was appointed to be their governor in the land of Judah, from the twentieth year even unto the two and thirtieth year of Artaxerxes the king, *that is*, twelve years, I and my brethren have not eaten the bread of the governor.

15 But the former governors that *had been* before me were chargeable unto the people, and had taken of them bread and wine, beside forty shekels of silver; yea, even their servants bare rule over the people: but so did not I, because of the fear of God.

16 Yea, also I continued in the work of this wall, neither bought we any land: and all my servants *were* gathered thither unto the work.

17 Moreover *there were* at my table an hundred and fifty of the Jews and rulers, beside those that came unto us from among the heathen that *are* about us.

18 Now *that* which was prepared *for me* daily *was* one ox *and* six choice sheep; also fowls were prepared for me, and once in ten days store of all sorts of wine: yet for all this required not I the bread of the governor, because the bondage was heavy upon this people.

19 Think upon me, my God, for good, *according* to all that I have done for this people.

6 Now it came to pass, when Sanballat, and Tobiah, and Geshem the Arabian, and the rest of our enemies, heard that I had builded the wall, and *that* there was no breach left therein; (though at that time I had not set up the doors upon the gates;)

2 That Sanballat and Geshem sent unto me, saying, Come, let us meet together in *some one of* the villages in the plain of Ono. But they thought to do me mischief.

3 And I sent messengers unto them, saying, I *am* doing a great work, so that I cannot come down: why should the work cease, whilst I leave it, and come down to you?

4 Yet they sent unto me four times after this sort; and I answered them after the same manner.

5 Then sent Sanballat his servant unto me in like manner the fifth time with an open letter in his hand;

6 Wherein *was* written, It is reported among the heathen, and Gashmu saith *it, that* thou and the Jews think to rebel: for which cause thou buildest the wall, that thou mayest be their king, according to these words.

7 And thou hast also appointed prophets to preach of thee at Jerusalem, saying, *There is* a king in Judah: and now shall it be reported to the king according to these words. Come now therefore, and let us take counsel together.

8 Then I sent unto him, saying, There are no such things done as thou sayest, but thou feignest them out of thine own heart.

9 For they all made us afraid, saying, Their hands shall be weakened from the work, that it be not done. Now therefore, *O God*, strengthen my hands.

10 Afterward I came unto the house of Shemaiah the son of Delaiah the son of Mehetabeel, who *was* shut up; and he said, Let us meet together in the house of God, within the temple, and let us shut the doors of the temple: for they will come to slay thee; yea, in the night will they come to slay thee.

11 And I said, Should such a man as I flee? and who *is there*, that, *being* as I *am*, would go into the temple to save his life? I will not go in.

12 And, lo, I perceived that God had not sent him; but that he pronounced this prophecy against me: for Tobiah and Sanballat had hired him.

13 Therefore *was* he hired, that I should be afraid, and do so, and sin, and *that* they might have *matter* for an evil report, that they might reproach me.

14 My God, think thou upon Tobiah and Sanballat according to these their works, and on the prophetess Noadiah, and the rest of the prophets, that would have put me in fear.

15 So the wall was finished in the twenty and fifth *day* of *the month* Elul, in fifty and two days.

16 And it came to pass, that when all our enemies heard *thereof*, and all the heathen that *were* about us saw *these things*, they were much cast down in their own eyes: for they perceived that this work was wrought of our God.

17 Moreover in those days the nobles of Judah sent many letters unto Tobiah, and *the letters* of Tobiah came unto them.

18 For *there were* many in Judah sworn unto him, because he *was* the son in law of Shechaniah the son of Arah; and his son Johanan had taken the daughter of Meshullam the son of Berechiah.

19 Also they reported his good deeds before me, and uttered my words to him. *And* Tobiah sent letters to put me in fear.

7 Now it came to pass, when the wall was built, and I had set up the doors, and the porters and the singers and the Levites were appointed,

2 That I gave my brother Hanani, and Hananiah the ruler of the palace, charge over Jerusalem: for he *was* a faithful man, and feared God above many.

3 And I said unto them, Let not the gates of Jerusalem be opened until the sun be hot; and while they stand by, let them shut the doors, and bar *them*: and appoint watches of the inhabitants of Jerusalem, every one in his watch, and every one *to be* over against his house.

4 Now the city *was* large and great: but the people *were* few therein, and the houses *were* not builded.

5 And my God put into mine heart to gather together the nobles, and the rulers, and the people, that they might be reckoned by genealogy. And I found a register of the genealogy of them which came up at the first, and found written therein,

6 These *are* the children of the province, that went up out of the captivity, of those that had been carried away, whom Nebuchadnezzar the king of Babylon had carried away, and came again to Jerusalem and to Judah, every one unto his city;

7 Who came with Zerubbabel, Jeshua, Nehemiah, Azariah, Raamiah, Nahamani, Mordecai, Bilshan, Mispereth, Bigvai, Nehum, Baanah. The number, *I say*, of the men of the people of Israel *was this*;

8 The children of Parosh, two thousand an hundred seventy and two.

9 The children of Shephatiah, three hundred seventy and two.

10 The children of Arah, six hundred fifty and two.

11 The children of Pahath-moab, of
the children of Jeshua and Joab, two
thousand and eight hundred *and* eighteen.
12 The children of Elam, a thousand
two hundred fifty and four.
13 The children of Zattu, eight hundred forty and five.
14 The children of Zaccai, seven hundred and threescore.
15 The children of Binnui, six hundred forty and eight.
16 The children of Bebai, six hundred
twenty and eight.
17 The children of Azgad, two thousand three hundred twenty and two.
18 The children of Adonikam, six hundred threescore and seven.
19 The children of Bigvai, two thousand threescore and seven.
20 The children of Adin, six hundred
fifty and five.
21 The children of Ater of Hezekiah,
ninety and eight.
22 The children of Hashum, three
hundred twenty and eight.
23 The children of Bezai, three hundred twenty and four.
24 The children of Hariph, an hundred and twelve.
25 The children of Gibeon, ninety and
five.
26 The men of Beth-lehem and Netophah, an hundred fourscore and eight.
27 The men of Anathoth, an hundred
twenty and eight.
28 The men of Beth-azmaveth, forty
and two.
29 The men of Kirjath-jearim, Chephirah, and Beeroth, seven hundred
forty and three.
30 The men of Ramah and Geba, six
hundred twenty and one.
31 The men of Michmas, an hundred
and twenty and two.
32 The men of Beth-el and Ai, an hundred twenty and three.
33 The men of the other Nebo, fifty
and two.
34 The children of the other Elam, a
thousand two hundred fifty and four.
35 The children of Harim, three hundred and twenty.
36 The children of Jericho, three hundred forty and five.
37 The children of Lod, Hadid, and
Ono, seven hundred twenty and one.
38 The children of Senaah, three
thousand nine hundred and thirty.
39 The priests: the children of
Jedaiah, of the house of Jeshua, nine
hundred seventy and three.
40 The children of Immer, a thousand
fifty and two.
41 The children of Pashur, a thousand
two hundred forty and seven.
42 The children of Harim, a thousand
and seventeen.
43 The Levites: the children of Jeshua, of Kadmiel, *and* of the children of
Hodevah, seventy and four.
44 The singers: the children of Asaph,
an hundred forty and eight.
45 The porters: the children of Shallum, the children of Ater, the children
of Talmon, the children of Akkub, the
children of Hatita, the children of
Shobai, an hundred thirty and eight.
46 The Nethinims: the children of
Ziha, the children of Hashupha, the
children of Tabbaoth,
47 The children of Keros, the children
of Sia, the children of Padon,
48 The children of Lebana, the children of Hagaba, the children of Shalmai,

49 The children of Hanan, the children of Giddel, the children of Gahar,
50 The children of Reaiah, the children of Rezin, the children of Nekoda,
51 The children of Gazzam, the children of Uzza, the children of Phaseah,
52 The children of Besai, the children of Meunim, the children of Nephishesim,
53 The children of Bakbuk, the children of Hakupha, the children of Harhur,
54 The children of Bazlith, the children of Mehida, the children of Harsha,
55 The children of Barkos, the children of Sisera, the children of Tamah,
56 The children of Neziah, the children of Hatipha.
57 The children of Solomon's servants: the children of Sotai, the children of Sophereth, the children of Perida,
58 The children of Jaala, the children of Darkon, the children of Giddel,
59 The children of Shephatiah, the children of Hattil, the children of Pochereth of Zebaim, the children of Amon.
60 All the Nethinims, and the children of Solomon's servants, *were* three hundred ninety and two.
61 And these *were* they which went up *also* from Tel-melah, Tel-haresha, Cherub, Addon, and Immer: but they could not shew their father's house, nor their seed, whether they *were* of Israel.
62 The children of Delaiah, the children of Tobiah, the children of Nekoda, six hundred forty and two.
63 And of the priests: the children of Habaiah, the children of Koz, the children of Barzillai, which took *one* of the daughters of Barzillai the Gileadite to wife, and was called after their name.
64 These sought their register *among* those that were reckoned by genealogy, but it was not found: therefore were they, as polluted, put from the priesthood.
65 And the Tirshatha said unto them, that they should not eat of the most holy things, till there stood *up* a priest with Urim and Thummim.
66 The whole congregation together *was* forty and two thousand three hundred and threescore,
67 Beside their manservants and their maidservants, of whom *there were* seven thousand three hundred thirty and seven: and they had two hundred forty and five singing men and singing women.
68 Their horses, seven hundred thirty and six: their mules, two hundred forty and five:
69 *Their* camels, four hundred thirty and five: six thousand seven hundred and twenty asses.
70 And some of the chief of the fathers gave unto the work. The Tirshatha gave to the treasure a thousand drams of gold, fifty basons, five hundred and thirty priests' garments.
71 And *some* of the chief of the fathers gave to the treasure of the work twenty thousand drams of gold, and two thousand and two hundred pound of silver.
72 And *that* which the rest of the people gave *was* twenty thousand drams of gold, and two thousand pound of silver, and threescore and seven priests' garments.
73 So the priests, and the Levites, and the porters, and the singers, and *some* of the people, and the Nethinims, and all Israel, dwelt in their cities; and

when the seventh month came, the
children of Israel *were* in their cities.

8 And all the people gathered
themselves together as one man
into the street that *was* before the
water gate; and they spake unto Ezra
the scribe to bring the book of the law
of Moses, which the LORD had commanded to Israel.
2 And Ezra the priest brought the law
before the congregation both of men
and women, and all that could hear
with understanding, upon the first day
of the seventh month.
3 And he read therein before the
street that *was* before the water gate
from the morning until midday, before
the men and the women, and those that
could understand; and the ears of all
the people *were attentive* unto the
book of the law.
4 And Ezra the scribe stood upon a
pulpit of wood, which they had made
for the purpose; and beside him stood
Mattithiah, and Shema, and Anaiah,
and Urijah, and Hilkiah, and Maaseiah,
on his right hand; and on his left hand,
Pedaiah, and Mishael, and Malchiah,
and Hashum, and Hashbadana,
Zechariah, *and* Meshullam.
5 And Ezra opened the book in the
sight of all the people; (for he was
above all the people;) and when he
opened it, all the people stood up:
6 And Ezra blessed the LORD, the
great God. And all the people answered,
Amen, Amen, with lifting up their
hands: and they bowed their heads, and
worshipped the LORD with *their* faces
to the ground.
7 Also Jeshua, and Bani, and
Sherebiah, Jamin, Akkub, Shabbethai,
Hodijah, Maaseiah, Kelita, Azariah,
Jozabad, Hanan, Pelaiah, and the
Levites, caused the people to understand the law: and the people *stood* in
their place.
8 So they read in the book in the law
of God distinctly, and gave the sense,
and caused *them* to understand the
reading.
9 And Nehemiah, which *is* the
Tirshatha, and Ezra the priest the
scribe, and the Levites that taught the
people, said unto all the people, This
day *is* holy unto the LORD your God;
mourn not, nor weep. For all the people
wept, when they heard the words of the
law.
10 Then he said unto them, Go your
way, eat the fat, and drink the sweet,
and send portions unto them for whom
nothing is prepared: for *this* day *is* holy
unto our Lord: neither be ye sorry; for
the joy of the LORD is your strength.
11 So the Levites stilled all the people, saying, Hold your peace, for the
day *is* holy; neither be ye grieved.
12 And all the people went their way
to eat, and to drink, and to send portions, and to make great mirth, because
they had understood the words that
were declared unto them.
13 And on the second day were gathered together the chief of the fathers of
all the people, the priests, and the
Levites, unto Ezra the scribe, even to
understand the words of the law.
14 And they found written in the law
which the LORD had commanded by
Moses, that the children of Israel
should dwell in booths in the feast of
the seventh month:
15 And that they should publish and
proclaim in all their cities, and in
Jerusalem, saying, Go forth unto the
mount, and fetch olive branches, and
pine branches, and myrtle branches,

and palm branches, and branches of thick trees, to make booths, as *it is* written.

16 So the people went forth, and brought *them*, and made themselves booths, every one upon the roof of his house, and in their courts, and in the courts of the house of God, and in the street of the water gate, and in the street of the gate of Ephraim.

17 And all the congregation of them that were come again out of the captivity made booths, and sat under the booths: for since the days of Jeshua the son of Nun unto that day had not the children of Israel done so. And there was very great gladness.

18 Also day by day, from the first day unto the last day, he read in the book of the law of God. And they kept the feast seven days; and on the eighth day *was* a solemn assembly, according unto the manner.

9 Now in the twenty and fourth day of this month the children of Israel were assembled with fasting, and with sackclothes, and earth upon them.

2 And the seed of Israel separated themselves from all strangers, and stood and confessed their sins, and the iniquities of their fathers.

3 And they stood up in their place, and read in the book of the law of the LORD their God *one* fourth part of the day; and *another* fourth part they confessed, and worshipped the LORD their God.

4 Then stood up upon the stairs, of the Levites, Jeshua, and Bani, Kadmiel, Shebaniah, Bunni, Sherebiah, Bani, *and* Chenani, and cried with a loud voice unto the LORD their God.

5 Then the Levites, Jeshua, and Kadmiel, Bani, Hashabniah, Sherebiah, Hodijah, Shebaniah, *and* Pethahiah, said, Stand up *and* bless the LORD your God for ever and ever: and blessed be thy glorious name, which is exalted above all blessing and praise.

6 Thou, *even* thou, *art* LORD alone; thou hast made heaven, the heaven of heavens, with all their host, the earth, and all *things* that *are* therein, the seas, and all that *is* therein, and thou preservest them all; and the host of heaven worshippeth thee.

7 Thou *art* the LORD the God, who didst choose Abram, and broughtest him forth out of Ur of the Chaldees, and gavest him the name of Abraham;

8 And foundest his heart faithful before thee, and madest a covenant with him to give the land of the Canaanites, the Hittites, the Amorites, and the Perizzites, and the Jebusites, and the Girgashites, to give *it*, *I say*, to his seed, and hast performed thy words; for thou *art* righteous:

9 And didst see the affliction of our fathers in Egypt, and heardest their cry by the Red sea;

10 And shewedst signs and wonders upon Pharaoh, and on all his servants, and on all the people of his land: for thou knewest that they dealt proudly against them. So didst thou get thee a name, as *it is* this day.

11 And thou didst divide the sea before them, so that they went through the midst of the sea on the dry land; and their persecutors thou threwest into the deeps, as a stone into the mighty waters.

12 Moreover thou leddest them in the day by a cloudy pillar; and in the night by a pillar of fire, to give them light in the way wherein they should go.

13 Thou camest down also upon
mount Sinai, and spakest with them
from heaven, and gavest them right
judgments, and true laws, good statutes
and commandments:
14 And madest known unto them thy
holy sabbath, and commandedst them
precepts, statutes, and laws, by the
hand of Moses thy servant:
15 And gavest them bread from heav-
en for their hunger, and broughtest
forth water for them out of the rock for
their thirst, and promisedst them that
they should go in to possess the land
which thou hadst sworn to give them.
16 But they and our fathers dealt
proudly, and hardened their necks, and
hearkened not to thy commandments,
17 And refused to obey, neither were
mindful of thy wonders that thou didst
among them; but hardened their necks,
and in their rebellion appointed a captain to return to their bondage: but
thou *art* a God ready to pardon, gracious and merciful, slow to anger, and
of great kindness, and forsookest them
not.
18 Yea, when they had made them a
molten calf, and said, This *is* thy God
that brought thee up out of Egypt, and
had wrought great provocations;
19 Yet thou in thy manifold mercies
forsookest them not in the wilderness:
the pillar of the cloud departed not
from them by day, to lead them in the
way; neither the pillar of fire by night,
to shew them light, and the way wherein they should go.
20 Thou gavest also thy good spirit to
instruct them, and withheldest not thy
manna from their mouth, and gavest
them water for their thirst.
21 Yea, forty years didst thou sustain
them in the wilderness, *so that* they
lacked nothing; their clothes waxed not
old, and their feet swelled not.
22 Moreover thou gavest them kingdoms and nations, and didst divide
them into corners: so they possessed
the land of Sihon, and the land of the
king of Heshbon, and the land of Og
king of Bashan.
23 Their children also multipliedst
thou as the stars of heaven, and broughtest them into the land, concerning
which thou hadst promised to their
fathers, that they should go in to possess *it*.
24 So the children went in and possessed the land, and thou subduedst
before them the inhabitants of the
land, the Canaanites, and gavest them
into their hands, with their kings, and
the people of the land, that they might
do with them as they would.
25 And they took strong cities, and a
fat land, and possessed houses full of
all goods, wells digged, vineyards, and
oliveyards, and fruit trees in abundance: so they did eat, and were filled,
and became fat, and delighted themselves in thy great goodness.
26 Nevertheless they were disobedient, and rebelled against thee, and cast
thy law behind their backs, and slew
thy prophets which testified against
them to turn them to thee, and they
wrought great provocations.
27 Therefore thou deliveredst them
into the hand of their enemies, who
vexed them: and in the time of their
trouble, when they cried unto thee,
thou heardest *them* from heaven; and
according to thy manifold mercies thou
gavest them saviours, who saved them
out of the hand of their enemies.

28 But after they had rest, they did
evil again before thee: therefore leftest
thou them in the hand of their enemies,
so that they had the dominion over
them: yet when they returned, and
cried unto thee, thou heardest *them*
from heaven; and many times didst
thou deliver them according to thy mercies;

29 And testifiedst against them, that
thou mightest bring them again unto
thy law: yet they dealt proudly, and
hearkened not unto thy commandments,
but sinned against thy judgments,
(which if a man do, he shall live
in them;) and withdrew the shoulder,
and hardened their neck, and would
not hear.

30 Yet many years didst thou forbear
them, and testifiedst against them by
thy spirit in thy prophets: yet would
they not give ear: therefore gavest thou
them into the hand of the people of the
lands.

31 Nevertheless for thy great mercies'
sake thou didst not utterly consume
them, nor forsake them; for thou *art* a
gracious and merciful God.

32 Now therefore, our God, the great,
the mighty, and the terrible God, who
keepest covenant and mercy, let not all
the trouble seem little before thee, that
hath come upon us, on our kings, on our
princes, and on our priests, and on our
prophets, and on our fathers, and on all
thy people, since the time of the kings
of Assyria unto this day.

33 Howbeit thou *art* just in all that is
brought upon us; for thou hast done
right, but we have done wickedly:

34 Neither have our kings, our princes,
our priests, nor our fathers, kept thy
law, nor hearkened unto thy commandments
and thy testimonies, wherewith
thou didst testify against them.

35 For they have not served thee in
their kingdom, and in thy great goodness
that thou gavest them, and in the
large and fat land which thou gavest
before them, neither turned they from
their wicked works.

36 Behold, we *are* servants this day,
and *for* the land that thou gavest unto
our fathers to eat the fruit thereof and
the good thereof, behold, we *are* servants
in it:

37 And it yieldeth much increase
unto the kings whom thou hast set over
us because of our sins: also they have
dominion over our bodies, and over our
cattle, at their pleasure, and we *are* in
great distress.

38 And because of all this we make a
sure *covenant*, and write *it*; and our
princes, Levites, *and* priests, seal *unto
it*.

10 Now those that sealed *were*,
Nehemiah, the Tirshatha, the son
of Hachaliah, and Zidkijah,

2 Seraiah, Azariah, Jeremiah,

3 Pashur, Amariah, Malchijah,

4 Hattush, Shebaniah, Malluch,

5 Harim, Meremoth, Obadiah,

6 Daniel, Ginnethon, Baruch,

7 Meshullam, Abijah, Mijamin,

8 Maaziah, Bilgai, Shemaiah: these
were the priests.

9 And the Levites: both Jeshua the
son of Azaniah, Binnui of the sons of
Henadad, Kadmiel;

10 And their brethren, Shebaniah,
Hodijah, Kelita, Pelaiah, Hanan,

11 Micha, Rehob, Hashabiah,

12 Zaccur, Sherebiah, Shebaniah,

13 Hodijah, Bani, Beninu.

14 The chief of the people; Parosh,
Pahathmoab, Elam, Zatthu, Bani,
15 Bunni, Azgad, Bebai,
16 Adonijah, Bigvai, Adin,
17 Ater, Hizkijah, Azzur,
18 Hodijah, Hashum, Bezai,
19 Hariph, Anathoth, Nebai,
20 Magpiash, Meshullam, Hezir,
21 Meshezabeel, Zadok, Jaddua,
22 Pelatiah, Hanan, Anaiah,
23 Hoshea, Hananiah, Hashub,
24 Hallohesh, Pileha, Shobek,
25 Rehum, Hashabnah, Maaseiah,
26 And Ahijah, Hanan, Anan,
27 Malluch, Harim, Baanah.
28 And the rest of the people, the
priests, the Levites, the porters, the
singers, the Nethinims, and all they
that had separated themselves from
the people of the lands unto the law of
God, their wives, their sons, and their
daughters, every one having knowledge, and having understanding;
29 They clave to their brethren, their
nobles, and entered into a curse, and
into an oath, to walk in God's law, which
was given by Moses the servant of God,
and to observe and do all the commandments of the LORD our Lord, and
his judgments and his statutes;
30 And that we would not give our
daughters unto the people of the land,
nor take their daughters for our sons:
31 And *if* the people of the land bring
ware or any victuals on the sabbath day
to sell, *that* we would not buy it of them
on the sabbath, or on the holy day: and
that we would leave the seventh year,
and the exaction of every debt.
32 Also we made ordinances for us, to
charge ourselves yearly with the third
part of a shekel for the service of the
house of our God;
33 For the shewbread, and for the
continual meat offering, and for the
continual burnt offering, of the sabbaths, of the new moons, for the set
feasts, and for the holy *things*, and for
the sin offerings to make an atonement
for Israel, and *for* all the work of the
house of our God.
34 And we cast the lots among the
priests, the Levites, and the people, for
the wood offering, to bring *it* into the
house of our God, after the houses of
our fathers, at times appointed year by
year, to burn upon the altar of the LORD
our God, as *it is* written in the law:
35 And to bring the firstfruits of our
ground, and the firstfruits of all fruit of
all trees, year by year, unto the house of
the LORD:
36 Also the firstborn of our sons, and
of our cattle, as *it is* written in the law,
and the firstlings of our herds and of
our flocks, to bring to the house of our
God, unto the priests that minister in
the house of our God:
37 And *that* we should bring the firstfruits of our dough, and our offerings,
and the fruit of all manner of trees, of
wine and of oil, unto the priests, to the
chambers of the house of our God; and
the tithes of our ground unto the
Levites, that the same Levites might
have the tithes in all the cities of our
tillage.
38 And the priest the son of Aaron
shall be with the Levites, when the
Levites take tithes: and the Levites
shall bring up the tithe of the tithes
unto the house of our God, to the chambers, into the treasure house.
39 For the children of Israel and the
children of Levi shall bring the offering
of the corn, of the new wine, and the oil,
unto the chambers, where *are* the

vessels of the sanctuary, and the priests
that minister, and the porters, and the
singers: and we will not forsake the
house of our God.

11

And the rulers of the people
dwelt at Jerusalem: the rest of
the people also cast lots, to bring one of
ten to dwell in Jerusalem the holy city,
and nine parts *to dwell* in *other* cities.
2 And the people blessed all the men,
that willingly offered themselves to
dwell at Jerusalem.
3 Now these *are* the chief of the province that dwelt in Jerusalem: but in the
cities of Judah dwelt every one in his
possession in their cities, *to wit*, Israel,
the priests, and the Levites, and the
Nethinims, and the children of Solomon's servants.
4 And at Jerusalem dwelt *certain* of
the children of Judah, and of the children of Benjamin. Of the children of
Judah; Athaiah the son of Uzziah, the
son of Zechariah, the son of Amariah,
the son of Shephatiah, the son of
Mahalaleel, of the children of Perez;
5 And Maaseiah the son of Baruch,
the son of Col-hozeh, the son of
Hazaiah, the son of Adaiah, the son of
Joiarib, the son of Zechariah, the son of
Shiloni.
6 All the sons of Perez that dwelt at
Jerusalem *were* four hundred threescore and eight valiant men.
7 And these *are* the sons of Benjamin;
Sallu the son of Meshullam, the son of
Joed, the son of Pedaiah, the son of
Kolaiah, the son of Maaseiah, the son of
Ithiel, the son of Jesaiah.
8 And after him Gabbai, Sallai, nine
hundred twenty and eight.
9 And Joel the son of Zichri *was* their
overseer: and Judah the son of Senuah
was second over the city.
10 Of the priests: Jedaiah the son of
Joiarib, Jachin.
11 Seraiah the son of Hilkiah, the son
of Meshullam, the son of Zadok, the son
of Meraioth, the son of Ahitub, *was* the
ruler of the house of God.
12 And their brethren that did the
work of the house *were* eight hundred
twenty and two: and Adaiah the son of
Jeroham, the son of Pelaliah, the son of
Amzi, the son of Zechariah, the son of
Pashur, the son of Malchiah,
13 And his brethren, chief of the
fathers, two hundred forty and two: and
Amashai the son of Azareel, the son of
Ahasai, the son of Meshillemoth, the
son of Immer,
14 And their brethren, mighty men of
valour, an hundred twenty and eight:
and their overseer *was* Zabdiel, the son
of *one of* the great men.
15 Also of the Levites: Shemaiah the
son of Hashub, the son of Azrikam, the
son of Hashabiah, the son of Bunni;
16 And Shabbethai and Jozabad, of
the chief of the Levites, *had* the oversight of the outward business of the
house of God.
17 And Mattaniah the son of Micha,
the son of Zabdi, the son of Asaph, *was*
the principal to begin the thanksgiving
in prayer: and Bakbukiah the second
among his brethren, and Abda the son
of Shammua, the son of Galal, the son
of Jeduthun.
18 All the Levites in the holy city
were two hundred fourscore and four.
19 Moreover the porters, Akkub,
Talmon, and their brethren that kept
the gates, *were* an hundred seventy and
two.

20 And the residue of Israel, of the priests, *and* the Levites, *were* in all the cities of Judah, every one in his inheritance.

21 But the Nethinims dwelt in Ophel: and Ziha and Gispa *were* over the Nethinims.

22 The overseer also of the Levites at Jerusalem *was* Uzzi the son of Bani, the son of Hashabiah, the son of Mattaniah, the son of Micha. Of the sons of Asaph, the singers *were* over the business of the house of God.

23 For *it was* the king's commandment concerning them, that a certain portion should be for the singers, due for every day.

24 And Pethahiah the son of Meshezabeel, of the children of Zerah the son of Judah, *was* at the king's hand in all matters concerning the people.

25 And for the villages, with their fields, *some* of the children of Judah dwelt at Kirjath-arba, and *in* the villages thereof, and at Dibon, and *in* the villages thereof, and at Jekabzeel, and *in* the villages thereof,

26 And at Jeshua, and at Moladah, and at Beth-phelet,

27 And at Hazar-shual, and at Beersheba, and *in* the villages thereof,

28 And at Ziklag, and at Mekonah, and in the villages thereof,

29 And at En-rimmon, and at Zareah, and at Jarmuth,

30 Zanoah, Adullam, and *in* their villages, at Lachish, and the fields thereof, at Azekah, and *in* the villages thereof. And they dwelt from Beer-sheba unto the valley of Hinnom.

31 The children also of Benjamin from Geba *dwelt* at Michmash, and Aija, and Beth-el, and *in* their villages,

32 *And* at Anathoth, Nob, Ananiah,

33 Hazor, Ramah, Gittaim,

34 Hadid, Zeboim, Neballat,

35 Lod, and Ono, the valley of craftsmen.

36 And of the Levites *were* divisions *in* Judah, *and* in Benjamin.

12 Now these *are* the priests and the Levites that went up with Zerubbabel the son of Shealtiel, and Jeshua: Seraiah, Jeremiah, Ezra,

2 Amariah, Malluch, Hattush,

3 Shechaniah, Rehum, Meremoth,

4 Iddo, Ginnetho, Abijah,

5 Miamin, Maadiah, Bilgah,

6 Shemaiah, and Joiarib, Jedaiah,

7 Sallu, Amok, Hilkiah, Jedaiah. These *were* the chief of the priests and of their brethren in the days of Jeshua.

8 Moreover the Levites: Jeshua, Binnui, Kadmiel, Sherebiah, Judah, *and* Mattaniah, *which was* over the thanksgiving, he and his brethren.

9 Also Bakbukiah and Unni, their brethren, *were* over against them in the watches.

10 And Jeshua begat Joiakim, Joiakim also begat Eliashib, and Eliashib begat Joiada,

11 And Joiada begat Jonathan, and Jonathan begat Jaddua.

12 And in the days of Joiakim were priests, the chief of the fathers: of Seraiah, Meraiah; of Jeremiah, Hananiah;

13 Of Ezra, Meshullam; of Amariah, Jehohanan;

14 Of Melicu, Jonathan; of Shebaniah, Joseph;

15 Of Harim, Adna; of Meraioth, Helkai;

16 Of Iddo, Zechariah; of Ginnethon, Meshullam;

17 Of Abijah, Zichri; of Miniamin, of Moadiah, Piltai;

18 Of Bilgah, Shammua; of Shemaiah, Jehonathan;

19 And of Joiarib, Mattenai; of Jedaiah, Uzzi;

20 Of Sallai, Kallai; of Amok, Eber;

21 Of Hilkiah, Hashabiah; of Jedaiah, Nethaneel.

22 The Levites in the days of Eliashib, Joiada, and Johanan, and Jaddua, *were* recorded chief of the fathers: also the priests, to the reign of Darius the Persian.

23 The sons of Levi, the chief of the fathers, *were* written in the book of the chronicles, even until the days of Johanan the son of Eliashib.

24 And the chief of the Levites: Hashabiah, Sherebiah, and Jeshua the son of Kadmiel, with their brethren over against them, to praise *and* to give thanks, according to the commandment of David the man of God, ward over against ward.

25 Mattaniah, and Bakbukiah, Obadiah, Meshullam, Talmon, Akkub, *were* porters keeping the ward at the thresholds of the gates.

26 These *were* in the days of Joiakim the son of Jeshua, the son of Jozadak, and in the days of Nehemiah the governor, and of Ezra the priest, the scribe.

27 And at the dedication of the wall of Jerusalem they sought the Levites out of all their places, to bring them to Jerusalem, to keep the dedication with gladness, both with thanksgivings, and with singing, *with* cymbals, psalteries, and with harps.

28 And the sons of the singers gathered themselves together, both out of the plain country round about Jerusalem, and from the villages of Netophathi;

29 Also from the house of Gilgal, and out of the fields of Geba and Azmaveth: for the singers had builded them villages round about Jerusalem.

30 And the priests and the Levites purified themselves, and purified the people, and the gates, and the wall.

31 Then I brought up the princes of Judah upon the wall, and appointed two great *companies of them that gave* thanks, *whereof one* went on the right hand upon the wall toward the dung gate:

32 And after them went Hoshaiah, and half of the princes of Judah,

33 And Azariah, Ezra, and Meshullam,

34 Judah, and Benjamin, and Shemaiah, and Jeremiah,

35 And *certain* of the priests' sons with trumpets; *namely*, Zechariah the son of Jonathan, the son of Shemaiah, the son of Mattaniah, the son of Michaiah, the son of Zaccur, the son of Asaph:

36 And his brethren, Shemaiah, and Azarael, Milalai, Gilalai, Maai, Nethaneel, and Judah, Hanani, with the musical instruments of David the man of God, and Ezra the scribe before them.

37 And at the fountain gate, which was over against them, they went up by the stairs of the city of David, at the going up of the wall, above the house of David, even unto the water gate eastward.

38 And the other *company of them that gave* thanks went over against *them*, and I after them, and the half of the people upon the wall, from beyond the tower of the furnaces even unto the broad wall;

39 And from above the gate of Ephraim, and above the old gate, and above the fish gate, and the tower of Hananeel, and the tower of Meah, even unto the sheep gate: and they stood still in the prison gate.

40 So stood the two *companies of them that gave* thanks in the house of God, and I, and the half of the rulers with me:

41 And the priests; Eliakim, Maaseiah, Miniamin, Michaiah, Elioenai, Zechariah, *and* Hananiah, with trumpets;

42 And Maaseiah, and Shemaiah, and Eleazar, and Uzzi, and Jehohanan, and Malchijah, and Elam, and Ezer. And the singers sang loud, with Jezrahiah *their* overseer.

43 Also that day they offered great sacrifices, and rejoiced: for God had made them rejoice with great joy: the wives also and the children rejoiced: so that the joy of Jerusalem was heard even afar off.

44 And at that time were some appointed over the chambers for the treasures, for the offerings, for the firstfruits, and for the tithes, to gather into them out of the fields of the cities the portions of the law for the priests and Levites: for Judah rejoiced for the priests and for the Levites that waited.

45 And both the singers and the porters kept the ward of their God, and the ward of the purification, according to the commandment of David, *and* of Solomon his son.

46 For in the days of David and Asaph of old *there were* chief of the singers, and songs of praise and thanksgiving unto God.

47 And all Israel in the days of Zerubbabel, and in the days of Nehemiah, gave the portions of the singers and the porters, every day his portion: and they sanctified *holy things* unto the Levites; and the Levites sanctified *them* unto the children of Aaron.

13 On that day they read in the book of Moses in the audience of the people; and therein was found written, that the Ammonite and the Moabite should not come into the congregation of God for ever;

2 Because they met not the children of Israel with bread and with water, but hired Balaam against them, that he should curse them: howbeit our God turned the curse into a blessing.

3 Now it came to pass, when they had heard the law, that they separated from Israel all the mixed multitude.

4 And before this, Eliashib the priest, having the oversight of the chamber of the house of our God, *was* allied unto Tobiah:

5 And he had prepared for him a great chamber, where aforetime they laid the meat offerings, the frankincense, and the vessels, and the tithes of the corn, the new wine, and the oil, which was commanded *to be given* to the Levites, and the singers, and the porters; and the offerings of the priests.

6 But in all this *time* was not I at Jerusalem: for in the two and thirtieth year of Artaxerxes king of Babylon came I unto the king, and after certain days obtained I leave of the king:

7 And I came to Jerusalem, and understood of the evil that Eliashib did for Tobiah, in preparing him a chamber in the courts of the house of God.

8 And it grieved me sore: therefore I cast forth all the household stuff of Tobiah out of the chamber.

9 Then I commanded, and they cleansed the chambers: and thither brought I again the vessels of the house of God, with the meat offering and the frankincense.

10 And I perceived that the portions of the Levites had not been given *them*: for the Levites and the singers, that did the work, were fled every one to his field.

11 Then contended I with the rulers, and said, Why is the house of God forsaken? And I gathered them together, and set them in their place.

12 Then brought all Judah the tithe of the corn and the new wine and the oil unto the treasuries.

13 And I made treasurers over the treasuries, Shelemiah the priest, and Zadok the scribe, and of the Levites, Pedaiah: and next to them *was* Hanan the son of Zaccur, the son of Mattaniah: for they were counted faithful, and their office *was* to distribute unto their brethren.

14 Remember me, O my God, concerning this, and wipe not out my good deeds that I have done for the house of my God, and for the offices thereof.

15 In those days saw I in Judah *some* treading wine presses on the sabbath, and bringing in sheaves, and lading asses; as also wine, grapes, and figs, and all *manner of* burdens, which they brought into Jerusalem on the sabbath day: and I testified *against them* in the day wherein they sold victuals.

16 There dwelt men of Tyre also therein, which brought fish, and all manner of ware, and sold on the sabbath unto the children of Judah, and in Jerusalem.

17 Then I contended with the nobles of Judah, and said unto them, What evil thing *is* this that ye do, and profane the sabbath day?

18 Did not your fathers thus, and did not our God bring all this evil upon us, and upon this city? yet ye bring more wrath upon Israel by profaning the sabbath.

19 And it came to pass, that when the gates of Jerusalem began to be dark before the sabbath, I commanded that the gates should be shut, and charged that they should not be opened till after the sabbath: and *some* of my servants set I at the gates, *that* there should no burden be brought in on the sabbath day.

20 So the merchants and sellers of all kind of ware lodged without Jerusalem once or twice.

21 Then I testified against them, and said unto them, Why lodge ye about the wall? if ye do *so* again, I will lay hands on you. From that time forth came they no *more* on the sabbath.

22 And I commanded the Levites that they should cleanse themselves, and *that* they should come *and* keep the gates, to sanctify the sabbath day. Remember me, O my God, *concerning* this also, and spare me according to the greatness of thy mercy.

23 In those days also saw I Jews *that* had married wives of Ashdod, of Ammon, *and* of Moab:

24 And their children spake half in the speech of Ashdod, and could not speak in the Jews' language, but according to the language of each people.

25 And I contended with them, and cursed them, and smote certain of them, and plucked off their hair, and made them swear by God, *saying*, Ye shall not give your daughters unto their

sons, nor take their daughters unto
your sons, or for yourselves.
26 Did not Solomon king of Israel sin
by these things? yet among many
nations was there no king like him, who
was beloved of his God, and God made
him king over all Israel: nevertheless
even him did outlandish women cause
to sin.
27 Shall we then hearken unto you to
do all this great evil, to transgress
against our God in marrying strange
wives?
28 And *one* of the sons of Joiada, the
son of Eliashib the high priest, *was* son
in law to Sanballat the Horonite: therefore I chased him from me.
29 Remember them, O my God,
because they have defiled the priesthood, and the covenant of the priesthood, and of the Levites.
30 Thus cleansed I them from all
strangers, and appointed the wards of
the priests and the Levites, every one
in his business;
31 And for the wood offering, at times
appointed, and for the firstfruits.
Remember me, O my God, for good.

THE BOOK OF ESTHER

1 Now it came to pass in the days of
Ahasuerus, (this *is* Ahasuerus
which reigned, from India even unto
Ethiopia, *over* an hundred and seven
and twenty provinces:)
2 *That* in those days, when the king
Ahasuerus sat on the throne of his kingdom, which *was* in Shushan the palace,
3 In the third year of his reign, he
made a feast unto all his princes and
his servants; the power of Persia and
Media, the nobles and princes of the
provinces, *being* before him:
4 When he shewed the riches of his
glorious kingdom and the honour of his
excellent majesty many days, *even* an
hundred and fourscore days.
5 And when these days were expired,
the king made a feast unto all the people that were present in Shushan the
palace, both unto great and small,
seven days, in the court of the garden of
the king's palace;
6 *Where were* white, green, and blue,
hangings, fastened with cords of fine
linen and purple to silver rings and pillars of marble: the beds *were of* gold
and silver, upon a pavement of red, and
blue, and white, and black, marble.
7 And they gave *them* drink in vessels
of gold, (the vessels being diverse one
from another,) and royal wine in abundance, according to the state of the
king.
8 And the drinking *was* according to
the law; none did compel: for so the
king had appointed to all the officers of
his house, that they should do according to every man's pleasure.
9 Also Vashti the queen made a feast
for the women *in* the royal house which
belonged to king Ahasuerus.

10 On the seventh day, when the heart of the king was merry with wine, he commanded Mehuman, Biztha, Harbona, Bigtha, and Abagtha, Zethar, and Carcas, the seven chamberlains that served in the presence of Ahasuerus the king,

11 To bring Vashti the queen before the king with the crown royal, to shew the people and the princes her beauty: for she *was* fair to look on.

12 But the queen Vashti refused to come at the king's commandment by *his* chamberlains: therefore was the king very wroth, and his anger burned in him.

13 Then the king said to the wise men, which knew the times, (for so *was* the king's manner toward all that knew law and judgment:

14 And the next unto him *was* Carshena, Shethar, Admatha, Tarshish, Meres, Marsena, *and* Memucan, the seven princes of Persia and Media, which saw the king's face, *and* which sat the first in the kingdom;)

15 What shall we do unto the queen Vashti according to law, because she hath not performed the commandment of the king Ahasuerus by the chamberlains?

16 And Memucan answered before the king and the princes, Vashti the queen hath not done wrong to the king only, but also to all the princes, and to all the people that *are* in all the provinces of the king Ahasuerus.

17 For *this* deed of the queen shall come abroad unto all women, so that they shall despise their husbands in their eyes, when it shall be reported, The king Ahasuerus commanded Vashti the queen to be brought in before him, but she came not.

18 *Likewise* shall the ladies of Persia and Media say this day unto all the king's princes, which have heard of the deed of the queen. Thus *shall there arise* too much contempt and wrath.

19 If it please the king, let there go a royal commandment from him, and let it be written among the laws of the Persians and the Medes, that it be not altered, That Vashti come no more before king Ahasuerus; and let the king give her royal estate unto another that is better than she.

20 And when the king's decree which he shall make shall be published throughout all his empire, (for it is great,) all the wives shall give to their husbands honour, both to great and small.

21 And the saying pleased the king and the princes; and the king did according to the word of Memucan:

22 For he sent letters into all the king's provinces, into every province according to the writing thereof, and to every people after their language, that every man should bear rule in his own house, and that *it* should be published according to the language of every people.

2 After these things, when the wrath of king Ahasuerus was appeased, he remembered Vashti, and what she had done, and what was decreed against her.

2 Then said the king's servants that ministered unto him, Let there be fair young virgins sought for the king:

3 And let the king appoint officers in all the provinces of his kingdom, that they may gather together all the fair young virgins unto Shushan the palace, to the house of the women, unto the custody of Hege the king's chamber-

lain, keeper of the women; and let their things for purification be given *them*:

4 And let the maiden which pleaseth the king be queen instead of Vashti. And the thing pleased the king; and he did so.

5 *Now* in Shushan the palace there was a certain Jew, whose name *was* Mordecai, the son of Jair, the son of Shimei, the son of Kish, a Benjamite;

6 Who had been carried away from Jerusalem with the captivity which had been carried away with Jeconiah king of Judah, whom Nebuchadnezzar the king of Babylon had carried away.

7 And he brought up Hadassah, that *is*, Esther, his uncle's daughter: for she had neither father nor mother, and the maid *was* fair and beautiful; whom Mordecai, when her father and mother were dead, took for his own daughter.

8 So it came to pass, when the king's commandment and his decree was heard, and when many maidens were gathered together unto Shushan the palace, to the custody of Hegai, that Esther was brought also unto the king's house, to the custody of Hegai, keeper of the women.

9 And the maiden pleased him, and she obtained kindness of him; and he speedily gave her her things for purification, with such things as belonged to her, and seven maidens, *which were* meet to be given her, out of the king's house: and he preferred her and her maids unto the best *place* of the house of the women.

10 Esther had not shewed her people nor her kindred: for Mordecai had charged her that she should not shew *it*.

11 And Mordecai walked every day before the court of the women's house, to know how Esther did, and what should become of her.

12 Now when every maid's turn was come to go in to king Ahasuerus, after that she had been twelve months, according to the manner of the women, (for so were the days of their purifications accomplished, *to wit*, six months with oil of myrrh, and six months with sweet odours, and with *other* things for the purifying of the women;)

13 Then thus came *every* maiden unto the king; whatsoever she desired was given her to go with her out of the house of the women unto the king's house.

14 In the evening she went, and on the morrow she returned into the second house of the women, to the custody of Shaashgaz, the king's chamberlain, which kept the concubines: she came in unto the king no more, except the king delighted in her, and that she were called by name.

15 Now when the turn of Esther, the daughter of Abihail the uncle of Mordecai, who had taken her for his daughter, was come to go in unto the king, she required nothing but what Hegai the king's chamberlain, the keeper of the women, appointed. And Esther obtained favour in the sight of all them that looked upon her.

16 So Esther was taken unto king Ahasuerus into his house royal in the tenth month, which *is* the month Tebeth, in the seventh year of his reign.

17 And the king loved Esther above all the women, and she obtained grace and favour in his sight more than all the virgins; so that he set the royal crown upon her head, and made her queen instead of Vashti.

18 Then the king made a great feast unto all his princes and his servants, *even* Esther's feast; and he made a release to the provinces, and gave gifts, according to the state of the king.

19 And when the virgins were gathered together the second time, then Mordecai sat in the king's gate.

20 Esther had not *yet* shewed her kindred nor her people; as Mordecai had charged her: for Esther did the commandment of Mordecai, like as when she was brought up with him.

21 In those days, while Mordecai sat in the king's gate, two of the king's chamberlains, Bigthan and Teresh, of those which kept the door, were wroth, and sought to lay hand on the king Ahasuerus.

22 And the thing was known to Mordecai, who told *it* unto Esther the queen; and Esther certified the king *thereof* in Mordecai's name.

23 And when inquisition was made of the matter, it was found out; therefore they were both hanged on a tree: and it was written in the book of the chronicles before the king.

3 After these things did king Ahasuerus promote Haman the son of Hammedatha the Agagite, and advanced him, and set his seat above all the princes that *were* with him.

2 And all the king's servants, that *were* in the king's gate, bowed, and reverenced Haman: for the king had so commanded concerning him. But Mordecai bowed not, nor did *him* reverence.

3 Then the king's servants, which *were* in the king's gate, said unto Mordecai, Why transgressest thou the king's commandment?

4 Now it came to pass, when they spake daily unto him, and he hearkened not unto them, that they told Haman, to see whether Mordecai's matters would stand: for he had told them that he *was* a Jew.

5 And when Haman saw that Mordecai bowed not, nor did him reverence, then was Haman full of wrath.

6 And he thought scorn to lay hands on Mordecai alone; for they had shewed him the people of Mordecai: wherefore Haman sought to destroy all the Jews that *were* throughout the whole kingdom of Ahasuerus, *even* the people of Mordecai.

7 In the first month, that *is*, the month Nisan, in the twelfth year of king Ahasuerus, they cast Pur, that *is*, the lot, before Haman from day to day, and from month to month, *to* the twelfth *month*, that *is*, the month Adar.

8 And Haman said unto king Ahasuerus, There is a certain people scattered abroad and dispersed among the people in all the provinces of thy kingdom; and their laws *are* diverse from all people; neither keep they the king's laws: therefore it *is* not for the king's profit to suffer them.

9 If it please the king, let it be written that they may be destroyed: and I will pay ten thousand talents of silver to the hands of those that have the charge of the business, to bring *it* into the king's treasuries.

10 And the king took his ring from his hand, and gave it unto Haman the son of Hammedatha the Agagite, the Jews' enemy.

11 And the king said unto Haman, The silver *is* given to thee, the people also, to do with them as it seemeth good to thee.

12 Then were the king's scribes called
on the thirteenth day of the first month,
and there was written according to all
that Haman had commanded unto the
king's lieutenants, and to the governors
that *were* over every province, and to
the rulers of every people of every province according to the writing thereof,
and *to* every people after their language; in the name of king Ahasuerus
was it written, and sealed with the
king's ring.
13 And the letters were sent by posts
into all the king's provinces, to destroy,
to kill, and to cause to perish, all Jews,
both young and old, little children and
women, in one day, *even* upon the thirteenth *day* of the twelfth month, which
is the month Adar, and *to take* the spoil
of them for a prey.
14 The copy of the writing for a commandment to be given in every province was published unto all people, that
they should be ready against that day.
15 The posts went out, being hastened by the king's commandment, and
the decree was given in Shushan the
palace. And the king and Haman sat
down to drink; but the city Shushan
was perplexed.

4 When Mordecai perceived all that
was done, Mordecai rent his clothes,
and put on sackcloth with ashes, and
went out into the midst of the city, and
cried with a loud and a bitter cry;
2 And came even before the king's
gate: for none *might* enter into the
king's gate clothed with sackcloth.
3 And in every province, whithersoever the king's commandment and his
decree came, *there was* great mourning
among the Jews, and fasting, and weeping, and wailing; and many lay in sackcloth and ashes.
4 So Esther's maids and her chamberlains came and told *it* her. Then was the
queen exceedingly grieved; and she
sent raiment to clothe Mordecai, and to
take away his sackcloth from him: but
he received *it* not.
5 Then called Esther for Hatach, *one*
of the king's chamberlains, whom he
had appointed to attend upon her, and
gave him a commandment to Mordecai,
to know what it *was*, and why it *was*.
6 So Hatach went forth to Mordecai
unto the street of the city, which *was*
before the king's gate.
7 And Mordecai told him of all that
had happened unto him, and of the
sum of the money that Haman had
promised to pay to the king's treasuries
for the Jews, to destroy them.
8 Also he gave him the copy of the
writing of the decree that was given at
Shushan to destroy them, to shew *it*
unto Esther, and to declare *it* unto her,
and to charge her that she should go in
unto the king, to make supplication
unto him, and to make request before
him for her people.
9 And Hatach came and told Esther
the words of Mordecai.
10 Again Esther spake unto Hatach,
and gave him commandment unto
Mordecai;
11 All the king's servants, and the
people of the king's provinces, do know,
that whosoever, whether man or
woman, shall come unto the king into
the inner court, who is not called, *there
is* one law of his to put *him* to death,
except such to whom the king shall
hold out the golden sceptre, that he
may live: but I have not been called to
come in unto the king these thirty days.
12 And they told to Mordecai Esther's
words.

13 Then Mordecai commanded to answer Esther, Think not with thyself that thou shalt escape in the king's house, more than all the Jews.

14 For if thou altogether holdest thy peace at this time, *then* shall there enlargement and deliverance arise to the Jews from another place; but thou and thy father's house shall be destroyed: and who knoweth whether thou art come to the kingdom for *such* a time as this?

15 Then Esther bade *them* return Mordecai *this answer*,

16 Go, gather together all the Jews that are present in Shushan, and fast ye for me, and neither eat nor drink three days, night or day: I also and my maidens will fast likewise; and so will I go in unto the king, which *is* not according to the law: and if I perish, I perish.

17 So Mordecai went his way, and did according to all that Esther had commanded him.

5 Now it came to pass on the third day, that Esther put on *her* royal *apparel*, and stood in the inner court of the king's house, over against the king's house: and the king sat upon his royal throne in the royal house, over against the gate of the house.

2 And it was so, when the king saw Esther the queen standing in the court, *that* she obtained favour in his sight: and the king held out to Esther the golden sceptre that *was* in his hand. So Esther drew near, and touched the top of the sceptre.

3 Then said the king unto her, What wilt thou, queen Esther? and what *is* thy request? it shall be even given thee to the half of the kingdom.

4 And Esther answered, If *it seem* good unto the king, let the king and Haman come this day unto the banquet that I have prepared for him.

5 Then the king said, Cause Haman to make haste, that he may do as Esther hath said. So the king and Haman came to the banquet that Esther had prepared.

6 And the king said unto Esther at the banquet of wine, What *is* thy petition? and it shall be granted thee: and what *is* thy request? even to the half of the kingdom it shall be performed.

7 Then answered Esther, and said, My petition and my request *is*;

8 If I have found favour in the sight of the king, and if it please the king to grant my petition, and to perform my request, let the king and Haman come to the banquet that I shall prepare for them, and I will do to morrow as the king hath said.

9 Then went Haman forth that day joyful and with a glad heart: but when Haman saw Mordecai in the king's gate, that he stood not up, nor moved for him, he was full of indignation against Mordecai.

10 Nevertheless Haman refrained himself: and when he came home, he sent and called for his friends, and Zeresh his wife.

11 And Haman told them of the glory of his riches, and the multitude of his children, and all *the things* wherein the king had promoted him, and how he had advanced him above the princes and servants of the king.

12 Haman said moreover, Yea, Esther the queen did let no man come in with the king unto the banquet that she had prepared but myself; and to morrow am I invited unto her also with the king.

13 Yet all this availeth me nothing, so
long as I see Mordecai the Jew sitting
at the king's gate.
14 Then said Zeresh his wife and all
his friends unto him, Let a gallows be
made of fifty cubits high, and to morrow speak thou unto the king that
Mordecai may be hanged thereon: then
go thou in merrily with the king unto
the banquet. And the thing pleased
Haman; and he caused the gallows to
be made.

6 On that night could not the king
sleep, and he commanded to bring
the book of records of the chronicles;
and they were read before the king.
2 And it was found written, that
Mordecai had told of Bigthana and
Teresh, two of the king's chamberlains,
the keepers of the door, who sought to
lay hand on the king Ahasuerus.
3 And the king said, What honour and
dignity hath been done to Mordecai for
this? Then said the king's servants that
ministered unto him, There is nothing
done for him.
4 And the king said, Who *is* in the
court? Now Haman was come into the
outward court of the king's house, to
speak unto the king to hang Mordecai
on the gallows that he had prepared for
him.
5 And the king's servants said unto
him, Behold, Haman standeth in the
court. And the king said, Let him come
in.
6 So Haman came in. And the king
said unto him, What shall be done unto
the man whom the king delighteth to
honour? Now Haman thought in his
heart, To whom would the king delight
to do honour more than to myself?
7 And Haman answered the king, For
the man whom the king delighteth to
honour,
8 Let the royal apparel be brought
which the king *useth* to wear, and the
horse that the king rideth upon, and
the crown royal which is set upon his
head:
9 And let this apparel and horse be
delivered to the hand of one of the
king's most noble princes, that they
may array the man *withal* whom the
king delighteth to honour, and bring
him on horseback through the street of
the city, and proclaim before him, Thus
shall it be done to the man whom the
king delighteth to honour.
10 Then the king said to Haman,
Make haste, *and* take the apparel and
the horse, as thou hast said, and do
even so to Mordecai the Jew, that
sitteth at the king's gate: let nothing
fail of all that thou hast spoken.
11 Then took Haman the apparel and
the horse, and arrayed Mordecai, and
brought him on horseback through the
street of the city, and proclaimed
before him, Thus shall it be done unto
the man whom the king delighteth to
honour.
12 And Mordecai came again to the
king's gate. But Haman hasted to his
house mourning, and having his head
covered.
13 And Haman told Zeresh his wife
and all his friends every *thing* that had
befallen him. Then said his wise men
and Zeresh his wife unto him, If
Mordecai *be* of the seed of the Jews,
before whom thou hast begun to fall,
thou shalt not prevail against him, but
shalt surely fall before him.

14 And while they *were* yet talking with him, came the king's chamberlains, and hasted to bring Haman unto the banquet that Esther had prepared.

7 So the king and Haman came to banquet with Esther the queen.

2 And the king said again unto Esther on the second day at the banquet of wine, What *is* thy petition, queen Esther? and it shall be granted thee: and what *is* thy request? and it shall be performed, *even* to the half of the kingdom.

3 Then Esther the queen answered and said, If I have found favour in thy sight, O king, and if it please the king, let my life be given me at my petition, and my people at my request:

4 For we are sold, I and my people, to be destroyed, to be slain, and to perish. But if we had been sold for bondmen and bondwomen, I had held my tongue, although the enemy could not countervail the king's damage.

5 Then the king Ahasuerus answered and said unto Esther the queen, Who is he, and where is he, that durst presume in his heart to do so?

6 And Esther said, The adversary and enemy *is* this wicked Haman. Then Haman was afraid before the king and the queen.

7 And the king arising from the banquet of wine in his wrath *went* into the palace garden: and Haman stood up to make request for his life to Esther the queen; for he saw that there was evil determined against him by the king.

8 Then the king returned out of the palace garden into the place of the banquet of wine; and Haman was fallen upon the bed whereon Esther *was*. Then said the king, Will he force the queen also before me in the house? As the word went out of the king's mouth, they covered Haman's face.

9 And Harbonah, one of the chamberlains, said before the king, Behold also, the gallows fifty cubits high, which Haman had made for Mordecai, who had spoken good for the king, standeth in the house of Haman. Then the king said, Hang him thereon.

10 So they hanged Haman on the gallows that he had prepared for Mordecai. Then was the king's wrath pacified.

8 On that day did the king Ahasuerus give the house of Haman the Jews' enemy unto Esther the queen. And Mordecai came before the king; for Esther had told what he *was* unto her.

2 And the king took off his ring, which he had taken from Haman, and gave it unto Mordecai. And Esther set Mordecai over the house of Haman.

3 And Esther spake yet again before the king, and fell down at his feet, and besought him with tears to put away the mischief of Haman the Agagite, and his device that he had devised against the Jews.

4 Then the king held out the golden sceptre toward Esther. So Esther arose, and stood before the king,

5 And said, If it please the king, and if I have found favour in his sight, and the thing *seem* right before the king, and I *be* pleasing in his eyes, let it be written to reverse the letters devised by Haman the son of Hammedatha the Agagite, which he wrote to destroy the Jews which *are* in all the king's provinces:

6 For how can I endure to see the evil that shall come unto my people? or how can I endure to see the destruction of my kindred?

7 Then the king Ahasuerus said unto Esther the queen and to Mordecai the Jew, Behold, I have given Esther the house of Haman, and him they have hanged upon the gallows, because he laid his hand upon the Jews.

8 Write ye also for the Jews, as it liketh you, in the king's name, and seal *it* with the king's ring: for the writing which is written in the king's name, and sealed with the king's ring, may no man reverse.

9 Then were the king's scribes called at that time in the third month, that *is*, the month Sivan, on the three and twentieth *day* thereof; and it was written according to all that Mordecai commanded unto the Jews, and to the lieutenants, and the deputies and rulers of the provinces which *are* from India unto Ethiopia, an hundred twenty and seven provinces, unto every province according to the writing thereof, and unto every people after their language, and to the Jews according to their writing, and according to their language.

10 And he wrote in the king Ahasuerus' name, and sealed *it* with the king's ring, and sent letters by posts on horseback, *and* riders on mules, camels, *and* young dromedaries:

11 Wherein the king granted the Jews which *were* in every city to gather themselves together, and to stand for their life, to destroy, to slay, and to cause to perish, all the power of the people and province that would assault them, *both* little ones and women, and *to take* the spoil of them for a prey,

12 Upon one day in all the provinces of king Ahasuerus, *namely*, upon the thirteenth *day* of the twelfth month, which *is* the month Adar.

13 The copy of the writing for a commandment to be given in every province *was* published unto all people, and that the Jews should be ready against that day to avenge themselves on their enemies.

14 *So* the posts that rode upon mules *and* camels went out, being hastened and pressed on by the king's commandment. And the decree was given at Shushan the palace.

15 And Mordecai went out from the presence of the king in royal apparel of blue and white, and with a great crown of gold, and with a garment of fine linen and purple: and the city of Shushan rejoiced and was glad.

16 The Jews had light, and gladness, and joy, and honour.

17 And in every province, and in every city, whithersoever the king's commandment and his decree came, the Jews had joy and gladness, a feast and a good day. And many of the people of the land became Jews; for the fear of the Jews fell upon them.

9 Now in the twelfth month, that *is*, the month Adar, on the thirteenth day of the same, when the king's commandment and his decree drew near to be put in execution, in the day that the enemies of the Jews hoped to have power over them, (though it was turned to the contrary, that the Jews had rule over them that hated them;)

2 The Jews gathered themselves together in their cities throughout all the provinces of the king Ahasuerus, to lay hand on such as sought their hurt: and no man could withstand them; for the fear of them fell upon all people.

3 And all the rulers of the provinces, and the lieutenants, and the deputies, and officers of the king, helped the

Jews; because the fear of Mordecai fell
upon them.
4 For Mordecai *was* great in the king's
house, and his fame went out throughout all the provinces: for this man
Mordecai waxed greater and greater.
5 Thus the Jews smote all their enemies with the stroke of the sword, and
slaughter, and destruction, and did
what they would unto those that hated
them.
6 And in Shushan the palace the Jews
slew and destroyed five hundred men.
7 And Parshandatha, and Dalphon,
and Aspatha,
8 And Poratha, and Adalia, and Ari-
datha,
9 And Parmashta, and Arisai, and
Aridai, and Vajezatha,
10 The ten sons of Haman the son of
Hammedatha, the enemy of the Jews,
slew they; but on the spoil laid they not
their hand.
11 On that day the number of those
that were slain in Shushan the palace
was brought before the king.
12 And the king said unto Esther the
queen, The Jews have slain and
destroyed five hundred men in Shushan
the palace, and the ten sons of Haman;
what have they done in the rest of the
king's provinces? now what *is* thy petition? and it shall be granted thee: or
what *is* thy request further? and it shall
be done.
13 Then said Esther, If it please the
king, let it be granted to the Jews which
are in Shushan to do to morrow also
according unto this day's decree, and
let Haman's ten sons be hanged upon
the gallows.
14 And the king commanded it so to
be done: and the decree was given at
Shushan; and they hanged Haman's ten
sons.
15 For the Jews that *were* in Shushan
gathered themselves together on the
fourteenth day also of the month Adar,
and slew three hundred men at
Shushan; but on the prey they laid not
their hand.
16 But the other Jews that *were* in the
king's provinces gathered themselves
together, and stood for their lives, and
had rest from their enemies, and slew
of their foes seventy and five thousand,
but they laid not their hands on the
prey,
17 On the thirteenth day of the month
Adar; and on the fourteenth day of the
same rested they, and made it a day of
feasting and gladness.
18 But the Jews that *were* at Shushan
assembled together on the thirteenth
day thereof, and on the fourteenth
thereof; and on the fifteenth *day* of the
same they rested, and made it a day of
feasting and gladness.
19 Therefore the Jews of the villages,
that dwelt in the unwalled towns, made
the fourteenth day of the month Adar *a*
day of gladness and feasting, and a
good day, and of sending portions one
to another.
20 And Mordecai wrote these things,
and sent letters unto all the Jews that
were in all the provinces of the king
Ahasuerus, *both* nigh and far,
21 To stablish *this* among them, that
they should keep the fourteenth day of
the month Adar, and the fifteenth day
of the same, yearly,
22 As the days wherein the Jews
rested from their enemies, and the
month which was turned unto them
from sorrow to joy, and from mourning
into a good day: that they should make

them days of feasting and joy, and of
sending portions one to another, and
gifts to the poor.
23 And the Jews undertook to do as
they had begun, and as Mordecai had
written unto them;
24 Because Haman the son of
Hammedatha, the Agagite, the enemy
of all the Jews, had devised against the
Jews to destroy them, and had cast Pur,
that *is*, the lot, to consume them, and to
destroy them;
25 But when *Esther* came before the
king, he commanded by letters that his
wicked device, which he devised
against the Jews, should return upon
his own head, and that he and his sons
should be hanged on the gallows.
26 Wherefore they called these days
Purim after the name of Pur. Therefore
for all the words of this letter, and *of
that* which they had seen concerning
this matter, and which had come unto
them,
27 The Jews ordained, and took upon
them, and upon their seed, and upon all
such as joined themselves unto them,
so as it should not fail, that they would
keep these two days according to their
writing, and according to their *appointed* time every year;
28 And *that* these days *should be*
remembered and kept throughout
every generation, every family, every
province, and every city; and *that* these
days of Purim should not fail from
among the Jews, nor the memorial of
them perish from their seed.
29 Then Esther the queen, the daughter of Abihail, and Mordecai the Jew,
wrote with all authority, to confirm this
second letter of Purim.
30 And he sent the letters unto all the
Jews, to the hundred twenty and seven
provinces of the kingdom of Ahasuerus,
with words of peace and truth,
31 To confirm these days of Purim in
their times *appointed*, according as
Mordecai the Jew and Esther the
queen had enjoined them, and as they
had decreed for themselves and for
their seed, the matters of the fastings
and their cry.
32 And the decree of Esther confirmed these matters of Purim; and it
was written in the book.

10 And the king Ahasuerus laid a
tribute upon the land, and *upon*
the isles of the sea.
2 And all the acts of his power and of
his might, and the declaration of the
greatness of Mordecai, whereunto the
king advanced him, *are* they not written in the book of the chronicles of the
kings of Media and Persia?
3 For Mordecai the Jew *was* next unto
king Ahasuerus, and great among the
Jews, and accepted of the multitude of
his brethren, seeking the wealth of his
people, and speaking peace to all his
seed.

THE BOOK OF
JOB

1 There was a man in the land of Uz,
whose name *was* Job; and that man
was perfect and upright, and one that
feared God, and eschewed evil.
2 And there were born unto him
seven sons and three daughters.
3 His substance also was seven thousand sheep, and three thousand camels,
and five hundred yoke of oxen, and five
hundred she asses, and a very great
household; so that this man was the
greatest of all the men of the east.
4 And his sons went and feasted *in
their* houses, every one his day; and
sent and called for their three sisters to
eat and to drink with them.
5 And it was so, when the days of
their feasting were gone about, that
Job sent and sanctified them, and rose
up early in the morning, and offered
burnt offerings *according* to the number of them all: for Job said, It may be
that my sons have sinned, and cursed
God in their hearts. Thus did Job continually.
6 Now there was a day when the sons
of God came to present themselves
before the LORD, and Satan came also
among them.
7 And the LORD said unto Satan,
Whence comest thou? Then Satan
answered the LORD, and said, From
going to and fro in the earth, and from
walking up and down in it.
8 And the LORD said unto Satan, Hast
thou considered my servant Job, that
there is none like him in the earth, a
perfect and an upright man, one that
feareth God, and escheweth evil?
9 Then Satan answered the LORD, and
said, Doth Job fear God for nought?
10 Hast not thou made an hedge
about him, and about his house, and
about all that he hath on every side?
thou hast blessed the work of his hands,
and his substance is increased in the
land.
11 But put forth thine hand now, and
touch all that he hath, and he will curse
thee to thy face.
12 And the LORD said unto Satan,
Behold, all that he hath *is* in thy power;
only upon himself put not forth thine
hand. So Satan went forth from the
presence of the LORD.
13 And there was a day when his sons
and his daughters *were* eating and
drinking wine in their eldest brother's
house:
14 And there came a messenger unto
Job, and said, The oxen were plowing,
and the asses feeding beside them:
15 And the Sabeans fell *upon them*,
and took them away; yea, they have
slain the servants with the edge of the
sword; and I only am escaped alone to
tell thee.
16 While he *was* yet speaking, there
came also another, and said, The fire of
God is fallen from heaven, and hath
burned up the sheep, and the servants,
and consumed them; and I only am
escaped alone to tell thee.
17 While he *was* yet speaking, there
came also another, and said, The
Chaldeans made out three bands, and
fell upon the camels, and have carried
them away, yea, and slain the servants

with the edge of the sword; and I only
am escaped alone to tell thee.
18 While he *was* yet speaking, there
came also another, and said, Thy sons
and thy daughters *were* eating and
drinking wine in their eldest brother's
house:
19 And, behold, there came a great
wind from the wilderness, and smote
the four corners of the house, and it fell
upon the young men, and they are
dead; and I only am escaped alone to
tell thee.
20 Then Job arose, and rent his mantle,
and shaved his head, and fell down
upon the ground, and worshipped,
21 And said, Naked came I out of my
mother's womb, and naked shall I
return thither: the LORD gave, and the
LORD hath taken away; blessed be the
name of the LORD.
22 In all this Job sinned not, nor
charged God foolishly.

2 Again there was a day when the
sons of God came to present
themselves before the LORD, and Satan
came also among them to present
himself before the LORD.
2 And the LORD said unto Satan, From
whence comest thou? And Satan
answered the LORD, and said, From
going to and fro in the earth, and from
walking up and down in it.
3 And the LORD said unto Satan, Hast
thou considered my servant Job, that
there is none like him in the earth, a
perfect and an upright man, one that
feareth God, and escheweth evil? and
still he holdeth fast his integrity,
although thou movedst me against him,
to destroy him without cause.
4 And Satan answered the LORD, and
said, Skin for skin, yea, all that a man
hath will he give for his life.
5 But put forth thine hand now, and
touch his bone and his flesh, and he will
curse thee to thy face.
6 And the LORD said unto Satan,
Behold, he *is* in thine hand; but save his
life.
7 So went Satan forth from the presence
of the LORD, and smote Job with
sore boils from the sole of his foot unto
his crown.
8 And he took him a potsherd to
scrape himself withal; and he sat down
among the ashes.
9 Then said his wife unto him, Dost
thou still retain thine integrity? curse
God, and die.
10 But he said unto her, Thou speakest
as one of the foolish women speaketh.
What? shall we receive good at the
hand of God, and shall we not receive
evil? In all this did not Job sin with his
lips.
11 Now when Job's three friends
heard of all this evil that was come
upon him, they came every one from
his own place; Eliphaz the Temanite,
and Bildad the Shuhite, and Zophar the
Naamathite: for they had made an
appointment together to come to
mourn with him and to comfort him.
12 And when they lifted up their eyes
afar off, and knew him not, they lifted
up their voice, and wept; and they rent
every one his mantle, and sprinkled
dust upon their heads toward heaven.
13 So they sat down with him upon
the ground seven days and seven
nights, and none spake a word unto
him: for they saw that *his* grief was very
great.

3 After this opened Job his mouth,
and cursed his day.
2 And Job spake, and said,

3 Let the day perish wherein I was born, and the night *in which* it was said, There is a man child conceived.

4 Let that day be darkness; let not God regard it from above, neither let the light shine upon it.

5 Let darkness and the shadow of death stain it; let a cloud dwell upon it; let the blackness of the day terrify it.

6 *As for* that night, let darkness seize upon it; let it not be joined unto the days of the year, let it not come into the number of the months.

7 Lo, let that night be solitary, let no joyful voice come therein.

8 Let them curse it that curse the day, who are ready to raise up their mourning.

9 Let the stars of the twilight thereof be dark; let it look for light, but *have* none; neither let it see the dawning of the day:

10 Because it shut not up the doors of my *mother's* womb, nor hid sorrow from mine eyes.

11 Why died I not from the womb? *why* did I *not* give up the ghost when I came out of the belly?

12 Why did the knees prevent me? or why the breasts that I should suck?

13 For now should I have lain still and been quiet, I should have slept: then had I been at rest,

14 With kings and counsellors of the earth, which built desolate places for themselves;

15 Or with princes that had gold, who filled their houses with silver:

16 Or as an hidden untimely birth I had not been; as infants *which* never saw light.

17 There the wicked cease *from* troubling; and there the weary be at rest.

18 *There* the prisoners rest together; they hear not the voice of the oppressor.

19 The small and great are there; and the servant *is* free from his master.

20 Wherefore is light given to him that is in misery, and life unto the bitter *in* soul;

21 Which long for death, but it *cometh* not; and dig for it more than for hid treasures;

22 Which rejoice exceedingly, *and* are glad, when they can find the grave?

23 *Why is light given* to a man whose way is hid, and whom God hath hedged in?

24 For my sighing cometh before I eat, and my roarings are poured out like the waters.

25 For the thing which I greatly feared is come upon me, and that which I was afraid of is come unto me.

26 I was not in safety, neither had I rest, neither was I quiet; yet trouble came.

4 Then Eliphaz the Temanite answered and said,

2 *If* we assay to commune with thee, wilt thou be grieved? but who can withhold himself from speaking?

3 Behold, thou hast instructed many, and thou hast strengthened the weak hands.

4 Thy words have upholden him that was falling, and thou hast strengthened the feeble knees.

5 But now it is come upon thee, and thou faintest; it toucheth thee, and thou art troubled.

6 *Is* not *this* thy fear, thy confidence, thy hope, and the uprightness of thy ways?

7 Remember, I pray thee, who *ever* perished, being innocent? or where were the righteous cut off?

8 Even as I have seen, they that plow iniquity, and sow wickedness, reap the same.

9 By the blast of God they perish, and by the breath of his nostrils are they consumed.

10 The roaring of the lion, and the voice of the fierce lion, and the teeth of the young lions, are broken.

11 The old lion perisheth for lack of prey, and the stout lion's whelps are scattered abroad.

12 Now a thing was secretly brought to me, and mine ear received a little thereof.

13 In thoughts from the visions of the night, when deep sleep falleth on men,

14 Fear came upon me, and trembling, which made all my bones to shake.

15 Then a spirit passed before my face; the hair of my flesh stood up:

16 It stood still, but I could not discern the form thereof: an image *was* before mine eyes, *there was* silence, and I heard a voice, *saying*,

17 Shall mortal man be more just than God? shall a man be more pure than his maker?

18 Behold, he put no trust in his servants; and his angels he charged with folly:

19 How much less *in* them that dwell in houses of clay, whose foundation *is* in the dust, *which* are crushed before the moth?

20 They are destroyed from morning to evening: they perish for ever without any regarding *it*.

21 Doth not their excellency *which is* in them go away? they die, even without wisdom.

5 Call now, if there be any that will answer thee; and to which of the saints wilt thou turn?

2 For wrath killeth the foolish man, and envy slayeth the silly one.

3 I have seen the foolish taking root: but suddenly I cursed his habitation.

4 His children are far from safety, and they are crushed in the gate, neither *is there* any to deliver *them*.

5 Whose harvest the hungry eateth up, and taketh it even out of the thorns, and the robber swalloweth up their substance.

6 Although affliction cometh not forth of the dust, neither doth trouble spring out of the ground;

7 Yet man is born unto trouble, as the sparks fly upward.

8 I would seek unto God, and unto God would I commit my cause:

9 Which doeth great things and unsearchable; marvellous things without number:

10 Who giveth rain upon the earth, and sendeth waters upon the fields:

11 To set up on high those that be low; that those which mourn may be exalted to safety.

12 He disappointeth the devices of the crafty, so that their hands cannot perform *their* enterprise.

13 He taketh the wise in their own craftiness: and the counsel of the froward is carried headlong.

14 They meet with darkness in the daytime, and grope in the noonday as in the night.

15 But he saveth the poor from the sword, from their mouth, and from the hand of the mighty.

16 So the poor hath hope, and iniquity stoppeth her mouth.
17 Behold, happy *is* the man whom
God correcteth: therefore despise not
thou the chastening of the Almighty:
18 For he maketh sore, and bindeth
up: he woundeth, and his hands make
whole.
19 He shall deliver thee in six troubles: yea, in seven there shall no evil
touch thee.
20 In famine he shall redeem thee
from death: and in war from the power
of the sword.
21 Thou shalt be hid from the scourge
of the tongue: neither shalt thou be
afraid of destruction when it cometh.
22 At destruction and famine thou
shalt laugh: neither shalt thou be afraid
of the beasts of the earth.
23 For thou shalt be in league with
the stones of the field: and the beasts of
the field shall be at peace with thee.
24 And thou shalt know that thy tabernacle *shall be* in peace; and thou
shalt visit thy habitation, and shalt not
sin.
25 Thou shalt know also that thy seed
shall be great, and thine offspring as
the grass of the earth.
26 Thou shalt come to *thy* grave in a
full age, like as a shock of corn cometh
in in his season.
27 Lo this, we have searched it, so it
is; hear it, and know thou *it* for thy
good.

6 But Job answered and said,
2 Oh that my grief were throughly
weighed, and my calamity laid in the
balances together!
3 For now it would be heavier than
the sand of the sea: therefore my words
are swallowed up.
4 For the arrows of the Almighty *are*
within me, the poison whereof drinketh
up my spirit: the terrors of God do set
themselves in array against me.
5 Doth the wild ass bray when he hath
grass? or loweth the ox over his fodder?
6 Can that which is unsavoury be
eaten without salt? or is there *any* taste
in the white of an egg?
7 The things *that* my soul refused to
touch *are* as my sorrowful meat.
8 Oh that I might have my request;
and that God would grant *me* the thing
that I long for!
9 Even that it would please God to
destroy me; that he would let loose his
hand, and cut me off!
10 Then should I yet have comfort;
yea, I would harden myself in sorrow:
let him not spare; for I have not concealed the words of the Holy One.
11 What *is* my strength, that I should
hope? and what *is* mine end, that I
should prolong my life?
12 *Is* my strength the strength of
stones? or *is* my flesh of brass?
13 *Is* not my help in me? and is wisdom driven quite from me?
14 To him that is afflicted pity *should
be shewed* from his friend; but he forsaketh the fear of the Almighty.
15 My brethren have dealt deceitfully
as a brook, *and* as the stream of brooks
they pass away;
16 Which are blackish by reason of
the ice, *and* wherein the snow is hid:
17 What time they wax warm, they
vanish: when it is hot, they are consumed out of their place.
18 The paths of their way are turned
aside; they go to nothing, and perish.
19 The troops of Tema looked, the
companies of Sheba waited for them.

20 They were confounded because they had hoped; they came thither, and were ashamed.

21 For now ye are nothing; ye see *my* casting down, and are afraid.

22 Did I say, Bring unto me? or, Give a reward for me of your substance?

23 Or, Deliver me from the enemy's hand? or, Redeem me from the hand of the mighty?

24 Teach me, and I will hold my tongue: and cause me to understand wherein I have erred.

25 How forcible are right words! but what doth your arguing reprove?

26 Do ye imagine to reprove words, and the speeches of one that is desperate, *which are* as wind?

27 Yea, ye overwhelm the fatherless, and ye dig *a pit* for your friend.

28 Now therefore be content, look upon me; for *it is* evident unto you if I lie.

29 Return, I pray you, let it not be iniquity; yea, return again, my righteousness *is* in it.

30 Is there iniquity in my tongue? cannot my taste discern perverse things?

7 *Is there* not an appointed time to man upon earth? *are not* his days also like the days of an hireling?

2 As a servant earnestly desireth the shadow, and as an hireling looketh for *the reward of* his work:

3 So am I made to possess months of vanity, and wearisome nights are appointed to me.

4 When I lie down, I say, When shall I arise, and the night be gone? and I am full of tossings to and fro unto the dawning of the day.

5 My flesh is clothed with worms and clods of dust; my skin is broken, and become loathsome.

6 My days are swifter than a weaver's shuttle, and are spent without hope.

7 O remember that my life *is* wind: mine eye shall no more see good.

8 The eye of him that hath seen me shall see me no *more*: thine eyes *are* upon me, and I *am* not.

9 *As* the cloud is consumed and vanisheth away: so he that goeth down to the grave shall come up no *more*.

10 He shall return no more to his house, neither shall his place know him any more.

11 Therefore I will not refrain my mouth; I will speak in the anguish of my spirit; I will complain in the bitterness of my soul.

12 *Am* I a sea, or a whale, that thou settest a watch over me?

13 When I say, My bed shall comfort me, my couch shall ease my complaint;

14 Then thou scarest me with dreams, and terrifiest me through visions:

15 So that my soul chooseth strangling, *and* death rather than my life.

16 I loathe *it*; I would not live alway: let me alone; for my days *are* vanity.

17 What *is* man, that thou shouldest magnify him? and that thou shouldest set thine heart upon him?

18 And *that* thou shouldest visit him every morning, *and* try him every moment?

19 How long wilt thou not depart from me, nor let me alone till I swallow down my spittle?

20 I have sinned; what shall I do unto thee, O thou preserver of men? why hast thou set me as a mark against thee, so that I am a burden to myself?

21 And why dost thou not pardon my transgression, and take away mine iniquity? for now shall I sleep in the dust; and thou shalt seek me in the morning, but I *shall* not *be*.

8 Then answered Bildad the Shuhite, and said,

2 How long wilt thou speak these *things*? and *how long shall* the words of thy mouth *be like* a strong wind?

3 Doth God pervert judgment? or doth the Almighty pervert justice?

4 If thy children have sinned against him, and he have cast them away for their transgression;

5 If thou wouldest seek unto God betimes, and make thy supplication to the Almighty;

6 If thou *wert* pure and upright; surely now he would awake for thee, and make the habitation of thy righteousness prosperous.

7 Though thy beginning was small, yet thy latter end should greatly increase.

8 For enquire, I pray thee, of the former age, and prepare thyself to the search of their fathers:

9 (For we *are but of* yesterday, and know nothing, because our days upon earth *are* a shadow:)

10 Shall not they teach thee, *and* tell thee, and utter words out of their heart?

11 Can the rush grow up without mire? can the flag grow without water?

12 Whilst it *is* yet in his greenness, *and* not cut down, it withereth before any *other* herb.

13 So *are* the paths of all that forget God; and the hypocrite's hope shall perish:

14 Whose hope shall be cut off, and whose trust *shall be* a spider's web.

15 He shall lean upon his house, but it shall not stand: he shall hold it fast, but it shall not endure.

16 He *is* green before the sun, and his branch shooteth forth in his garden.

17 His roots are wrapped about the heap, *and* seeth the place of stones.

18 If he destroy him from his place, then *it* shall deny him, *saying*, I have not seen thee.

19 Behold, this *is* the joy of his way, and out of the earth shall others grow.

20 Behold, God will not cast away a perfect *man*, neither will he help the evil doers:

21 Till he fill thy mouth with laughing, and thy lips with rejoicing.

22 They that hate thee shall be clothed with shame; and the dwelling place of the wicked shall come to nought.

9 Then Job answered and said,

2 I know *it is* so of a truth: but how should man be just with God?

3 If he will contend with him, he cannot answer him one of a thousand.

4 *He is* wise in heart, and mighty in strength: who hath hardened *himself* against him, and hath prospered?

5 Which removeth the mountains, and they know not: which overturneth them in his anger.

6 Which shaketh the earth out of her place, and the pillars thereof tremble.

7 Which commandeth the sun, and it riseth not; and sealeth up the stars.

8 Which alone spreadeth out the heavens, and treadeth upon the waves of the sea.

9 Which maketh Arcturus, Orion, and Pleiades, and the chambers of the south.

10 Which doeth great things past finding out; yea, and wonders without number.

11 Lo, he goeth by me, and I see *him* not: he passeth on also, but I perceive him not.

12 Behold, he taketh away, who can hinder him? who will say unto him, What doest thou?

13 *If* God will not withdraw his anger, the proud helpers do stoop under him.

14 How much less shall I answer him, *and* choose out my words *to reason* with him?

15 Whom, though I were righteous, *yet* would I not answer, *but* I would make supplication to my judge.

16 If I had called, and he had answered me; *yet* would I not believe that he had hearkened unto my voice.

17 For he breaketh me with a tempest, and multiplieth my wounds without cause.

18 He will not suffer me to take my breath, but filleth me with bitterness.

19 If *I speak* of strength, lo, *he is* strong: and if of judgment, who shall set me a time *to plead*?

20 If I justify myself, mine own mouth shall condemn me: *if I say*, I *am* perfect, it shall also prove me perverse.

21 *Though* I *were* perfect, *yet* would I not know my soul: I would despise my life.

22 This *is* one *thing*, therefore I said *it*, He destroyeth the perfect and the wicked.

23 If the scourge slay suddenly, he will laugh at the trial of the innocent.

24 The earth is given into the hand of the wicked: he covereth the faces of the judges thereof; if not, where, *and* who *is* he?

25 Now my days are swifter than a post: they flee away, they see no good.

26 They are passed away as the swift ships: as the eagle *that* hasteth to the prey.

27 If I say, I will forget my complaint, I will leave off my heaviness, and comfort *myself*:

28 I am afraid of all my sorrows, I know that thou wilt not hold me innocent.

29 *If* I be wicked, why then labour I in vain?

30 If I wash myself with snow water, and make my hands never so clean;

31 Yet shalt thou plunge me in the ditch, and mine own clothes shall abhor me.

32 For *he is* not a man, as I *am, that* I should answer him, *and* we should come together in judgment.

33 Neither is there any daysman betwixt us, *that* might lay his hand upon us both.

34 Let him take his rod away from me, and let not his fear terrify me:

35 *Then* would I speak, and not fear him; but *it is* not so with me.

10 My soul is weary of my life; I will leave my complaint upon myself; I will speak in the bitterness of my soul.

2 I will say unto God, Do not condemn me; shew me wherefore thou contendest with me.

3 *Is it* good unto thee that thou shouldest oppress, that thou shouldest despise the work of thine hands, and shine upon the counsel of the wicked?

4 Hast thou eyes of flesh? or seest thou as man seeth?

5 *Are* thy days as the days of man? *are* thy years as man's days,

6 That thou enquirest after mine iniquity, and searchest after my sin?

7 Thou knowest that I am not wicked; and *there is* none that can deliver out of thine hand.

8 Thine hands have made me and fashioned me together round about; yet thou dost destroy me.

9 Remember, I beseech thee, that thou hast made me as the clay; and wilt thou bring me into dust again?

10 Hast thou not poured me out as milk, and curdled me like cheese?

11 Thou hast clothed me with skin and flesh, and hast fenced me with bones and sinews.

12 Thou hast granted me life and favour, and thy visitation hath preserved my spirit.

13 And these *things* hast thou hid in thine heart: I know that this *is* with thee.

14 If I sin, then thou markest me, and thou wilt not acquit me from mine iniquity.

15 If I be wicked, woe unto me; and *if* I be righteous, *yet* will I not lift up my head. *I am* full of confusion; therefore see thou mine affliction;

16 For it increaseth. Thou huntest me as a fierce lion: and again thou shewest thyself marvellous upon me.

17 Thou renewest thy witnesses against me, and increasest thine indignation upon me; changes and war *are* against me.

18 Wherefore then hast thou brought me forth out of the womb? Oh that I had given up the ghost, and no eye had seen me!

19 I should have been as though I had not been; I should have been carried from the womb to the grave.

20 *Are* not my days few? cease *then, and* let me alone, that I may take comfort a little,

21 Before I go *whence* I shall not return, *even* to the land of darkness and the shadow of death;

22 A land of darkness, as darkness *itself; and* of the shadow of death, without any order, and *where* the light *is* as darkness.

11 Then answered Zophar the Naamathite, and said,

2 Should not the multitude of words be answered? and should a man full of talk be justified?

3 Should thy lies make men hold their peace? and when thou mockest, shall no man make thee ashamed?

4 For thou hast said, My doctrine *is* pure, and I am clean in thine eyes.

5 But oh that God would speak, and open his lips against thee;

6 And that he would shew thee the secrets of wisdom, that *they are* double to that which is! Know therefore that God exacteth of thee *less* than thine iniquity *deserveth*.

7 Canst thou by searching find out God? canst thou find out the Almighty unto perfection?

8 *It is* as high as heaven; what canst thou do? deeper than hell; what canst thou know?

9 The measure thereof *is* longer than the earth, and broader than the sea.

10 If he cut off, and shut up, or gather together, then who can hinder him?

11 For he knoweth vain men: he seeth wickedness also; will he not then consider *it*?

12 For vain man would be wise, though man be born *like* a wild ass's colt.

13 If thou prepare thine heart, and stretch out thine hands toward him;

14 If iniquity *be* in thine hand, put it
far away, and let not wickedness dwell
in thy tabernacles.
15 For then shalt thou lift up thy face
without spot; yea, thou shalt be stedfast, and shalt not fear:
16 Because thou shalt forget *thy* misery, *and* remember *it* as waters *that*
pass away:
17 And *thine* age shall be clearer
than the noonday; thou shalt shine
forth, thou shalt be as the morning.
18 And thou shalt be secure, because
there is hope; yea, thou shalt dig *about*
thee, and thou shalt take thy rest in
safety.
19 Also thou shalt lie down, and none
shall make *thee* afraid; yea, many shall
make suit unto thee.
20 But the eyes of the wicked shall
fail, and they shall not escape, and
their hope *shall be as* the giving up of
the ghost.

12

And Job answered and said,
2 No doubt but ye *are* the people, and wisdom shall die with you.
3 But I have understanding as well as
you; I *am* not inferior to you: yea, who
knoweth not such things as these?
4 I am *as* one mocked of his neighbour, who calleth upon God, and he
answereth him: the just upright *man is*
laughed to scorn.
5 He that is ready to slip with *his* feet
is as a lamp despised in the thought of
him that is at ease.
6 The tabernacles of robbers prosper,
and they that provoke God are secure;
into whose hand God bringeth *abun-*
dantly.
7 But ask now the beasts, and they
shall teach thee; and the fowls of the
air, and they shall tell thee:
8 Or speak to the earth, and it shall
teach thee: and the fishes of the sea
shall declare unto thee.
9 Who knoweth not in all these that
the hand of the LORD hath wrought
this?
10 In whose hand *is* the soul of every
living thing, and the breath of all mankind.
11 Doth not the ear try words? and
the mouth taste his meat?
12 With the ancient *is* wisdom; and in
length of days understanding.
13 With him *is* wisdom and strength,
he hath counsel and understanding.
14 Behold, he breaketh down, and it
cannot be built again: he shutteth up a
man, and there can be no opening.
15 Behold, he withholdeth the waters,
and they dry up: also he sendeth them
out, and they overturn the earth.
16 With him *is* strength and wisdom:
the deceived and the deceiver *are* his.
17 He leadeth counsellors away
spoiled, and maketh the judges fools.
18 He looseth the bond of kings, and
girdeth their loins with a girdle.
19 He leadeth princes away spoiled,
and overthroweth the mighty.
20 He removeth away the speech of
the trusty, and taketh away the understanding of the aged.
21 He poureth contempt upon princes, and weakeneth the strength of the
mighty.
22 He discovereth deep things out of
darkness, and bringeth out to light the
shadow of death.
23 He increaseth the nations, and
destroyeth them: he enlargeth the
nations, and straiteneth them *again*.

24 He taketh away the heart of the
chief of the people of the earth, and
causeth them to wander in a wilderness
where there is no way.
25 They grope in the dark without
light, and he maketh them to stagger
like *a* drunken *man*.

13 Lo, mine eye hath seen all *this*,
mine ear hath heard and understood it.
2 What ye know, *the same* do I know
also: I *am* not inferior unto you.
3 Surely I would speak to the Almighty, and I desire to reason with God.
4 But ye *are* forgers of lies, ye *are* all
physicians of no value.
5 O that ye would altogether hold
your peace! and it should be your wisdom.
6 Hear now my reasoning, and heark-
en to the pleadings of my lips.
7 Will ye speak wickedly for God?
and talk deceitfully for him?
8 Will ye accept his person? will ye
contend for God?
9 Is it good that he should search you
out? or as one man mocketh another, do
ye *so* mock him?
10 He will surely reprove you, if ye do
secretly accept persons.
11 Shall not his excellency make you
afraid? and his dread fall upon you?
12 Your remembrances *are* like unto
ashes, your bodies to bodies of clay.
13 Hold your peace, let me alone, that
I may speak, and let come on me what
will.
14 Wherefore do I take my flesh in my
teeth, and put my life in mine hand?
15 Though he slay me, yet will I trust
in him: but I will maintain mine own
ways before him.
16 He also *shall be* my salvation: for
an hypocrite shall not come before him.
17 Hear diligently my speech, and my
declaration with your ears.
18 Behold now, I have ordered *my*
cause; I know that I shall be justified.
19 Who *is* he *that* will plead with me?
for now, if I hold my tongue, I shall give
up the ghost.
20 Only do not two *things* unto me:
then will I not hide myself from thee.
21 Withdraw thine hand far from me:
and let not thy dread make me afraid.
22 Then call thou, and I will answer:
or let me speak, and answer thou me.
23 How many *are* mine iniquities and
sins? make me to know my transgression and my sin.
24 Wherefore hidest thou thy face,
and holdest me for thine enemy?
25 Wilt thou break a leaf driven to
and fro? and wilt thou pursue the dry
stubble?
26 For thou writest bitter things
against me, and makest me to possess
the iniquities of my youth.
27 Thou puttest my feet also in the
stocks, and lookest narrowly unto all
my paths; thou settest a print upon the
heels of my feet.
28 And he, as a rotten thing, consumeth, as a garment that is moth
eaten.

14 Man *that is* born of a woman *is*
of few days, and full of trouble.
2 He cometh forth like a flower, and is
cut down: he fleeth also as a shadow,
and continueth not.
3 And dost thou open thine eyes upon
such an one, and bringest me into judgment with thee?
4 Who can bring a clean *thing* out of
an unclean? not one.
5 Seeing his days *are* determined, the
number of his months *are* with thee,

thou hast appointed his bounds that he
cannot pass;
6 Turn from him, that he may rest, till
he shall accomplish, as an hireling, his
day.
7 For there is hope of a tree, if it be
cut down, that it will sprout again, and
that the tender branch thereof will not
cease.
8 Though the root thereof wax old in
the earth, and the stock thereof die in
the ground;
9 *Yet* through the scent of water it
will bud, and bring forth boughs like a
plant.
10 But man dieth, and wasteth away:
yea, man giveth up the ghost, and
where *is* he?
11 *As* the waters fail from the sea, and
the flood decayeth and drieth up:
12 So man lieth down, and riseth not:
till the heavens *be* no more, they shall
not awake, nor be raised out of their
sleep.
13 O that thou wouldest hide me in
the grave, that thou wouldest keep me
secret, until thy wrath be past, that
thou wouldest appoint me a set time,
and remember me!
14 If a man die, shall he live *again*?
all the days of my appointed time will I
wait, till my change come.
15 Thou shalt call, and I will answer
thee: thou wilt have a desire to the
work of thine hands.
16 For now thou numberest my steps:
dost thou not watch over my sin?
17 My transgression *is* sealed up in a
bag, and thou sewest up mine iniquity.
18 And surely the mountain falling
cometh to nought, and the rock is
removed out of his place.
19 The waters wear the stones: thou
washest away the things which grow
out of the dust of the earth; and thou
destroyest the hope of man.
20 Thou prevailest for ever against
him, and he passeth: thou changest his
countenance, and sendest him away.
21 His sons come to honour, and he
knoweth *it* not; and they are brought
low, but he perceiveth *it* not of them.
22 But his flesh upon him shall have
pain, and his soul within him shall
mourn.

15 Then answered Eliphaz the Temanite, and said,
2 Should a wise man utter vain knowledge, and fill his belly with the east
wind?
3 Should he reason with unprofitable
talk? or with speeches wherewith he
can do no good?
4 Yea, thou castest off fear, and
restrainest prayer before God.
5 For thy mouth uttereth thine iniquity, and thou choosest the tongue of
the crafty.
6 Thine own mouth condemneth thee,
and not I: yea, thine own lips testify
against thee.
7 *Art* thou the first man *that* was
born? or wast thou made before the
hills?
8 Hast thou heard the secret of God?
and dost thou restrain wisdom to thyself?
9 What knowest thou, that we know
not? *what* understandest thou, which *is*
not in us?
10 With us *are* both the grayheaded
and very aged men, much elder than
thy father.
11 *Are* the consolations of God small
with thee? is there any secret thing
with thee?
12 Why doth thine heart carry thee
away? and what do thy eyes wink at,

13 That thou turnest thy spirit against God, and lettest *such* words go out of thy mouth?

14 What *is* man, that he should be clean? and *he which is* born of a woman, that he should be righteous?

15 Behold, he putteth no trust in his saints; yea, the heavens are not clean in his sight.

16 How much more abominable and filthy *is* man, which drinketh iniquity like water?

17 I will shew thee, hear me; and that *which* I have seen I will declare;

18 Which wise men have told from their fathers, and have not hid *it*:

19 Unto whom alone the earth was given, and no stranger passed among them.

20 The wicked man travaileth with pain all *his* days, and the number of years is hidden to the oppressor.

21 A dreadful sound *is* in his ears: in prosperity the destroyer shall come upon him.

22 He believeth not that he shall return out of darkness, and he is waited for of the sword.

23 He wandereth abroad for bread, *saying*, Where *is it*? he knoweth that the day of darkness is ready at his hand.

24 Trouble and anguish shall make him afraid; they shall prevail against him, as a king ready to the battle.

25 For he stretcheth out his hand against God, and strengtheneth himself against the Almighty.

26 He runneth upon him, *even* on *his* neck, upon the thick bosses of his bucklers:

27 Because he covereth his face with his fatness, and maketh collops of fat on *his* flanks.

28 And he dwelleth in desolate cities, *and* in houses which no man inhabiteth, which are ready to become heaps.

29 He shall not be rich, neither shall his substance continue, neither shall he prolong the perfection thereof upon the earth.

30 He shall not depart out of darkness; the flame shall dry up his branches, and by the breath of his mouth shall he go away.

31 Let not him that is deceived trust in vanity: for vanity shall be his recompence.

32 It shall be accomplished before his time, and his branch shall not be green.

33 He shall shake off his unripe grape as the vine, and shall cast off his flower as the olive.

34 For the congregation of hypocrites *shall be* desolate, and fire shall consume the tabernacles of bribery.

35 They conceive mischief, and bring forth vanity, and their belly prepareth deceit.

16

Then Job answered and said,

2 I have heard many such things: miserable comforters *are* ye all.

3 Shall vain words have an end? or what emboldeneth thee that thou answerest?

4 I also could speak as ye *do*: if your soul were in my soul's stead, I could heap up words against you, and shake mine head at you.

5 *But* I would strengthen you with my mouth, and the moving of my lips should asswage *your grief*.

6 Though I speak, my grief is not asswaged: and *though* I forbear, what am I eased?

7 But now he hath made me weary: thou hast made desolate all my company.

8 And thou hast filled me with wrinkles, *which* is a witness *against me*: and my leanness rising up in me beareth witness to my face.

9 He teareth *me* in his wrath, who hateth me: he gnasheth upon me with his teeth; mine enemy sharpeneth his eyes upon me.

10 They have gaped upon me with their mouth; they have smitten me upon the cheek reproachfully; they have gathered themselves together against me.

11 God hath delivered me to the ungodly, and turned me over into the hands of the wicked.

12 I was at ease, but he hath broken me asunder: he hath also taken *me* by my neck, and shaken me to pieces, and set me up for his mark.

13 His archers compass me round about, he cleaveth my reins asunder, and doth not spare; he poureth out my gall upon the ground.

14 He breaketh me with breach upon breach, he runneth upon me like a giant.

15 I have sewed sackcloth upon my skin, and defiled my horn in the dust.

16 My face is foul with weeping, and on my eyelids *is* the shadow of death;

17 Not for *any* injustice in mine hands: also my prayer *is* pure.

18 O earth, cover not thou my blood, and let my cry have no place.

19 Also now, behold, my witness *is* in heaven, and my record *is* on high.

20 My friends scorn me: *but* mine eye poureth out *tears* unto God.

21 O that one might plead for a man with God, as a man *pleadeth* for his neighbour!

22 When a few years are come, then I shall go the way *whence* I shall not return.

17 My breath is corrupt, my days are extinct, the graves *are ready* for me.

2 *Are there* not mockers with me? and doth not mine eye continue in their provocation?

3 Lay down now, put me in a surety with thee; who *is* he *that* will strike hands with me?

4 For thou hast hid their heart from understanding: therefore shalt thou not exalt *them*.

5 He that speaketh flattery to *his* friends, even the eyes of his children shall fail.

6 He hath made me also a byword of the people; and aforetime I was as a tabret.

7 Mine eye also is dim by reason of sorrow, and all my members *are* as a shadow.

8 Upright *men* shall be astonied at this, and the innocent shall stir up himself against the hypocrite.

9 The righteous also shall hold on his way, and he that hath clean hands shall be stronger and stronger.

10 But as for you all, do ye return, and come now: for I cannot find *one* wise *man* among you.

11 My days are past, my purposes are broken off, *even* the thoughts of my heart.

12 They change the night into day: the light *is* short because of darkness.

13 If I wait, the grave *is* mine house: I have made my bed in the darkness.

14 I have said to corruption, Thou *art* my father: to the worm, *Thou art* my mother, and my sister.

15 And where *is* now my hope? as for my hope, who shall see it?

16 They shall go down to the bars of the pit, when *our* rest together *is* in the dust.

18 Then answered Bildad the Shuhite, and said,

2 How long *will it be ere* ye make an end of words? mark, and afterwards we will speak.

3 Wherefore are we counted as beasts, *and* reputed vile in your sight?

4 He teareth himself in his anger: shall the earth be forsaken for thee? and shall the rock be removed out of his place?

5 Yea, the light of the wicked shall be put out, and the spark of his fire shall not shine.

6 The light shall be dark in his tabernacle, and his candle shall be put out with him.

7 The steps of his strength shall be straitened, and his own counsel shall cast him down.

8 For he is cast into a net by his own feet, and he walketh upon a snare.

9 The gin shall take *him* by the heel, *and* the robber shall prevail against him.

10 The snare *is* laid for him in the ground, and a trap for him in the way.

11 Terrors shall make him afraid on every side, and shall drive him to his feet.

12 His strength shall be hungerbitten, and destruction *shall be* ready at his side.

13 It shall devour the strength of his skin: *even* the firstborn of death shall devour his strength.

14 His confidence shall be rooted out of his tabernacle, and it shall bring him to the king of terrors.

15 It shall dwell in his tabernacle, because *it is* none of his: brimstone shall be scattered upon his habitation.

16 His roots shall be dried up beneath, and above shall his branch be cut off.

17 His remembrance shall perish from the earth, and he shall have no name in the street.

18 He shall be driven from light into darkness, and chased out of the world.

19 He shall neither have son nor nephew among his people, nor any remaining in his dwellings.

20 They that come after *him* shall be astonied at his day, as they that went before were affrighted.

21 Surely such *are* the dwellings of the wicked, and this *is* the place *of him that* knoweth not God.

19 Then Job answered and said,
2 How long will ye vex my soul, and break me in pieces with words?

3 These ten times have ye reproached me: ye are not ashamed *that* ye make yourselves strange to me.

4 And be it indeed *that* I have erred, mine error remaineth with myself.

5 If indeed ye will magnify *yourselves* against me, and plead against me my reproach:

6 Know now that God hath overthrown me, and hath compassed me with his net.

7 Behold, I cry out of wrong, but I am not heard: I cry aloud, but *there is* no judgment.

8 He hath fenced up my way that I cannot pass, and he hath set darkness in my paths.

9 He hath stripped me of my glory, and taken the crown *from* my head.

10 He hath destroyed me on every side, and I am gone: and mine hope hath he removed like a tree.

11 He hath also kindled his wrath
against me, and he counteth me unto
him as *one of* his enemies.
12 His troops come together, and
raise up their way against me, and
encamp round about my tabernacle.
13 He hath put my brethren far from
me, and mine acquaintance are verily
estranged from me.
14 My kinsfolk have failed, and my
familiar friends have forgotten me.
15 They that dwell in mine house, and
my maids, count me for a stranger: I am
an alien in their sight.
16 I called my servant, and he gave
me no answer; I intreated him with my
mouth.
17 My breath is strange to my wife,
though I intreated for the children's
sake of mine own body.
18 Yea, young children despised me; I
arose, and they spake against me.
19 All my inward friends abhorred
me: and they whom I loved are turned
against me.
20 My bone cleaveth to my skin and
to my flesh, and I am escaped with the
skin of my teeth.
21 Have pity upon me, have pity upon
me, O ye my friends; for the hand of
God hath touched me.
22 Why do ye persecute me as God,
and are not satisfied with my flesh?
23 Oh that my words were now written! oh that they were printed in a
book!
24 That they were graven with an iron
pen and lead in the rock for ever!
25 For I know *that* my redeemer
liveth, and *that* he shall stand at the
latter *day* upon the earth:
26 And *though* after my skin *worms*
destroy this *body*, yet in my flesh shall
I see God:
27 Whom I shall see for myself, and
mine eyes shall behold, and not another; *though* my reins be consumed within me.
28 But ye should say, Why persecute
we him, seeing the root of the matter is
found in me?
29 Be ye afraid of the sword: for wrath
bringeth the punishments of the sword,
that ye may know *there is* a judgment.

20 Then answered Zophar the
Naamathite, and said,
2 Therefore do my thoughts cause me
to answer, and for *this* I make haste.
3 I have heard the check of my
reproach, and the spirit of my understanding causeth me to answer.
4 Knowest thou *not* this of old, since
man was placed upon earth,
5 That the triumphing of the wicked
is short, and the joy of the hypocrite
but for a moment?
6 Though his excellency mount up to
the heavens, and his head reach unto
the clouds;
7 *Yet* he shall perish for ever like his
own dung: they which have seen him
shall say, Where *is* he?
8 He shall fly away as a dream, and
shall not be found: yea, he shall be
chased away as a vision of the night.
9 The eye also *which* saw him shall
see him no more; neither shall his place
any more behold him.
10 His children shall seek to please
the poor, and his hands shall restore
their goods.
11 His bones are full *of the sin* of his
youth, which shall lie down with him in
the dust.
12 Though wickedness be sweet in his
mouth, *though* he hide it under his
tongue;

13 *Though* he spare it, and forsake it not; but keep it still within his mouth:

14 *Yet* his meat in his bowels is turned, *it is* the gall of asps within him.

15 He hath swallowed down riches, and he shall vomit them up again: God shall cast them out of his belly.

16 He shall suck the poison of asps: the viper's tongue shall slay him.

17 He shall not see the rivers, the floods, the brooks of honey and butter.

18 That which he laboured for shall he restore, and shall not swallow *it* down: according to *his* substance *shall* the restitution *be*, and he shall not rejoice *therein*.

19 Because he hath oppressed *and* hath forsaken the poor; *because* he hath violently taken away an house which he builded not;

20 Surely he shall not feel quietness in his belly, he shall not save of that which he desired.

21 There shall none of his meat be left; therefore shall no man look for his goods.

22 In the fulness of his sufficiency he shall be in straits: every hand of the wicked shall come upon him.

23 *When* he is about to fill his belly, *God* shall cast the fury of his wrath upon him, and shall rain *it* upon him while he is eating.

24 He shall flee from the iron weapon, *and* the bow of steel shall strike him through.

25 It is drawn, and cometh out of the body; yea, the glittering sword cometh out of his gall: terrors *are* upon him.

26 All darkness *shall be* hid in his secret places: a fire not blown shall consume him; it shall go ill with him that is left in his tabernacle.

27 The heaven shall reveal his iniquity; and the earth shall rise up against him.

28 The increase of his house shall depart, *and his goods* shall flow away in the day of his wrath.

29 This *is* the portion of a wicked man from God, and the heritage appointed unto him by God.

21 But Job answered and said,
2 Hear diligently my speech, and
let this be your consolations.

3 Suffer me that I may speak; and after that I have spoken, mock on.

4 As for me, *is* my complaint to man? and if *it were so*, why should not my spirit be troubled?

5 Mark me, and be astonished, and lay *your* hand upon *your* mouth.

6 Even when I remember I am afraid, and trembling taketh hold on my flesh.

7 Wherefore do the wicked live, become old, yea, are mighty in power?

8 Their seed is established in their sight with them, and their offspring before their eyes.

9 Their houses *are* safe from fear, neither *is* the rod of God upon them.

10 Their bull gendereth, and faileth not; their cow calveth, and casteth not her calf.

11 They send forth their little ones like a flock, and their children dance.

12 They take the timbrel and harp, and rejoice at the sound of the organ.

13 They spend their days in wealth, and in a moment go down to the grave.

14 Therefore they say unto God, Depart from us; for we desire not the knowledge of thy ways.

15 What *is* the Almighty, that we should serve him? and what profit should we have, if we pray unto him?

16 Lo, their good *is* not in their hand:
the counsel of the wicked is far from
me.
17 How oft is the candle of the wicked
put out! and *how oft* cometh their
destruction upon them! *God* distribu-
teth sorrows in his anger.
18 They are as stubble before the
wind, and as chaff that the storm carrieth away.
19 God layeth up his iniquity for his
children: he rewardeth him, and he
shall know *it*.
20 His eyes shall see his destruction,
and he shall drink of the wrath of the
Almighty.
21 For what pleasure *hath* he in his
house after him, when the number of
his months is cut off in the midst?
22 Shall *any* teach God knowledge?
seeing he judgeth those that are high.
23 One dieth in his full strength,
being wholly at ease and quiet.
24 His breasts are full of milk, and his
bones are moistened with marrow.
25 And another dieth in the bitterness of his soul, and never eateth with
pleasure.
26 They shall lie down alike in the
dust, and the worms shall cover them.
27 Behold, I know your thoughts, and
the devices *which* ye wrongfully imagine against me.
28 For ye say, Where *is* the house of
the prince? and where *are* the dwelling
places of the wicked?
29 Have ye not asked them that go by
the way? and do ye not know their
tokens,
30 That the wicked is reserved to the
day of destruction? they shall be
brought forth to the day of wrath.
31 Who shall declare his way to his
face? and who shall repay him *what* he
hath done?
32 Yet shall he be brought to the
grave, and shall remain in the tomb.
33 The clods of the valley shall be
sweet unto him, and every man shall
draw after him, as *there are* innumerable before him.
34 How then comfort ye me in vain,
seeing in your answers there remaineth
falsehood?

22 Then Eliphaz the Temanite answered and said,
2 Can a man be profitable unto God,
as he that is wise may be profitable
unto himself?
3 *Is it* any pleasure to the Almighty,
that thou art righteous? or *is it* gain *to*
him, that thou makest thy ways perfect?
4 Will he reprove thee for fear of
thee? will he enter with thee into judgment?
5 *Is* not thy wickedness great? and
thine iniquities infinite?
6 For thou hast taken a pledge from
thy brother for nought, and stripped
the naked of their clothing.
7 Thou hast not given water to the
weary to drink, and thou hast withholden bread from the hungry.
8 But *as for* the mighty man, he had
the earth; and the honourable man
dwelt in it.
9 Thou hast sent widows away empty,
and the arms of the fatherless have
been broken.

10 Therefore snares *are* round about thee, and sudden fear troubleth thee;

11 Or darkness, *that* thou canst not see; and abundance of waters cover thee.

12 *Is* not God in the height of heaven? and behold the height of the stars, how high they are!

13 And thou sayest, How doth God know? can he judge through the dark cloud?

14 Thick clouds *are* a covering to him, that he seeth not; and he walketh in the circuit of heaven.

15 Hast thou marked the old way which wicked men have trodden?

16 Which were cut down out of time, whose foundation was overflown with a flood:

17 Which said unto God, Depart from us: and what can the Almighty do for them?

18 Yet he filled their houses with good *things*: but the counsel of the wicked is far from me.

19 The righteous see *it*, and are glad: and the innocent laugh them to scorn.

20 Whereas our substance is not cut down, but the remnant of them the fire consumeth.

21 Acquaint now thyself with him, and be at peace: thereby good shall come unto thee.

22 Receive, I pray thee, the law from his mouth, and lay up his words in thine heart.

23 If thou return to the Almighty, thou shalt be built up, thou shalt put away iniquity far from thy tabernacles.

24 Then shalt thou lay up gold as dust, and the *gold* of Ophir as the stones of the brooks.

25 Yea, the Almighty shall be thy defence, and thou shalt have plenty of silver.

26 For then shalt thou have thy delight in the Almighty, and shalt lift up thy face unto God.

27 Thou shalt make thy prayer unto him, and he shall hear thee, and thou shalt pay thy vows.

28 Thou shalt also decree a thing, and it shall be established unto thee: and the light shall shine upon thy ways.

29 When *men* are cast down, then thou shalt say, *There is* lifting up; and he shall save the humble person.

30 He shall deliver the island of the innocent: and it is delivered by the pureness of thine hands.

23

Then Job answered and said,

2 Even to day *is* my complaint bitter: my stroke is heavier than my groaning.

3 Oh that I knew where I might find him! *that* I might come *even* to his seat!

4 I would order *my* cause before him, and fill my mouth with arguments.

5 I would know the words *which* he would answer me, and understand what he would say unto me.

6 Will he plead against me with *his* great power? No; but he would put *strength* in me.

7 There the righteous might dispute with him; so should I be delivered for ever from my judge.

8 Behold, I go forward, but he *is* not *there*; and backward, but I cannot perceive him:

9 On the left hand, where he doth work, but I cannot behold *him*: he hideth himself on the right hand, that I cannot see *him*:

10 But he knoweth the way that I
take: *when* he hath tried me, I shall
come forth as gold.
11 My foot hath held his steps, his
way have I kept, and not declined.
12 Neither have I gone back from the
commandment of his lips; I have
esteemed the words of his mouth more
than my necessary *food*.
13 But he *is* in one *mind*, and who can
turn him? and *what* his soul desireth,
even *that* he doeth.
14 For he performeth *the thing that*
is appointed for me: and many such
things are with him.
15 Therefore am I troubled at his
presence: when I consider, I am afraid
of him.
16 For God maketh my heart soft, and
the Almighty troubleth me:
17 Because I was not cut off before
the darkness, *neither* hath he covered
the darkness from my face.

24 Why, seeing times are not hidden
from the Almighty, do they that
know him not see his days?
2 *Some* remove the landmarks; they
violently take away flocks, and feed
thereof.
3 They drive away the ass of the
fatherless, they take the widow's ox for
a pledge.
4 They turn the needy out of the way:
the poor of the earth hide themselves
together.
5 Behold, *as* wild asses in the desert,
go they forth to their work; rising
betimes for a prey: the wilderness *yiel-*
deth food for them *and* for *their* children.
6 They reap *every one* his corn in the
field: and they gather the vintage of
the wicked.
7 They cause the naked to lodge without clothing, that *they have* no covering in the cold.
8 They are wet with the showers of
the mountains, and embrace the rock
for want of a shelter.
9 They pluck the fatherless from the
breast, and take a pledge of the poor.
10 They cause *him* to go naked without clothing, and they take away the
sheaf *from* the hungry;
11 *Which* make oil within their walls,
and tread *their* winepresses, and suffer
thirst.
12 Men groan from out of the city, and
the soul of the wounded crieth out: yet
God layeth not folly *to them*.
13 They are of those that rebel against
the light; they know not the ways
thereof, nor abide in the paths thereof.
14 The murderer rising with the light
killeth the poor and needy, and in the
night is as a thief.
15 The eye also of the adulterer waiteth for the twilight, saying, No eye shall
see me: and disguiseth *his* face.
16 In the dark they dig through houses, *which* they had marked for themselves in the daytime: they know not
the light.
17 For the morning *is* to them even as
the shadow of death: if *one* know *them*,
they are in the terrors of the shadow of
death.
18 He *is* swift as the waters; their portion is cursed in the earth: he beholdeth not the way of the vineyards.
19 Drought and heat consume the
snow waters: *so doth* the grave *those*
which have sinned.
20 The womb shall forget him; the
worm shall feed sweetly on him; he
shall be no more remembered; and
wickedness shall be broken as a tree.

21 He evil entreateth the barren *that* beareth not: and doeth not good to the widow.

22 He draweth also the mighty with his power: he riseth up, and no *man* is sure of life.

23 *Though* it be given him *to be* in safety, whereon he resteth; yet his eyes *are* upon their ways.

24 They are exalted for a little while, but are gone and brought low; they are taken out of the way as all *other*, and cut off as the tops of the ears of corn.

25 And if *it be* not *so* now, who will make me a liar, and make my speech nothing worth?

25 Then answered Bildad the Shuhite, and said,

2 Dominion and fear *are* with him, he maketh peace in his high places.

3 Is there any number of his armies? and upon whom doth not his light arise?

4 How then can man be justified with God? or how can he be clean *that is* born of a woman?

5 Behold even to the moon, and it shineth not; yea, the stars are not pure in his sight.

6 How much less man, *that is* a worm? and the son of man, *which is* a worm?

26 But Job answered and said,

2 How hast thou helped *him that is* without power? *how* savest thou the arm *that hath* no strength?

3 How hast thou counselled *him that hath* no wisdom? and *how* hast thou plentifully declared the thing as it is?

4 To whom hast thou uttered words? and whose spirit came from thee?

5 Dead *things* are formed from under the waters, and the inhabitants thereof.

6 Hell *is* naked before him, and destruction hath no covering.

7 He stretcheth out the north over the empty place, *and* hangeth the earth upon nothing.

8 He bindeth up the waters in his thick clouds; and the cloud is not rent under them.

9 He holdeth back the face of his throne, *and* spreadeth his cloud upon it.

10 He hath compassed the waters with bounds, until the day and night come to an end.

11 The pillars of heaven tremble and are astonished at his reproof.

12 He divideth the sea with his power, and by his understanding he smiteth through the proud.

13 By his spirit he hath garnished the heavens; his hand hath formed the crooked serpent.

14 Lo, these *are* parts of his ways: but how little a portion is heard of him? but the thunder of his power who can understand?

27 Moreover Job continued his parable, and said,

2 *As* God liveth, *who* hath taken away my judgment; and the Almighty, *who* hath vexed my soul;

3 All the while my breath *is* in me, and the spirit of God *is* in my nostrils;

4 My lips shall not speak wickedness, nor my tongue utter deceit.

5 God forbid that I should justify you: till I die I will not remove mine integrity from me.

6 My righteousness I hold fast, and will not let it go: my heart shall not reproach *me* so long as I live.

7 Let mine enemy be as the wicked, and he that riseth up against me as the unrighteous.

8 For what *is* the hope of the hypocrite, though he hath gained, when God
taketh away his soul?
9 Will God hear his cry when trouble
cometh upon him?
10 Will he delight himself in the
Almighty? will he always call upon
God?
11 I will teach you by the hand of
God: *that* which *is* with the Almighty
will I not conceal.
12 Behold, all ye yourselves have seen
it; why then are ye thus altogether
vain?
13 This *is* the portion of a wicked man
with God, and the heritage of oppressors, *which* they shall receive of the
Almighty.
14 If his children be multiplied, *it is*
for the sword: and his offspring shall
not be satisfied with bread.
15 Those that remain of him shall be
buried in death: and his widows shall
not weep.
16 Though he heap up silver as the
dust, and prepare raiment as the clay;
17 He may prepare *it*, but the just
shall put *it* on, and the innocent shall
divide the silver.
18 He buildeth his house as a moth,
and as a booth *that* the keeper maketh.
19 The rich man shall lie down, but he
shall not be gathered: he openeth his
eyes, and he *is* not.
20 Terrors take hold on him as waters,
a tempest stealeth him away in the
night.
21 The east wind carrieth him away,
and he departeth: and as a storm hur-
leth him out of his place.
22 For *God* shall cast upon him, and
not spare: he would fain flee out of his
hand.
23 *Men* shall clap their hands at him,
and shall hiss him out of his place.

28 Surely there is a vein for the silver, and a place for gold *where*
they fine *it*.
2 Iron is taken out of the earth, and
brass *is* molten *out of* the stone.
3 He setteth an end to darkness, and
searcheth out all perfection: the stones
of darkness, and the shadow of death.
4 The flood breaketh out from the
inhabitant; *even the waters* forgotten
of the foot: they are dried up, they are
gone away from men.
5 *As for* the earth, out of it cometh
bread: and under it is turned up as it
were fire.
6 The stones of it *are* the place of sapphires: and it hath dust of gold.
7 *There is* a path which no fowl
knoweth, and which the vulture's eye
hath not seen:
8 The lion's whelps have not trodden
it, nor the fierce lion passed by it.
9 He putteth forth his hand upon the
rock; he overturneth the mountains by
the roots.
10 He cutteth out rivers among the
rocks; and his eye seeth every precious
thing.
11 He bindeth the floods from overflowing; and *the thing that is* hid bringeth he forth to light.
12 But where shall wisdom be found?
and where *is* the place of understanding?
13 Man knoweth not the price thereof; neither is it found in the land of the
living.
14 The depth saith, It *is* not in me:
and the sea saith, *It is* not with me.
15 It cannot be gotten for gold, neither shall silver be weighed *for* the
price thereof.

16 It cannot be valued with the gold of Ophir, with the precious onyx, or the sapphire.

17 The gold and the crystal cannot equal it: and the exchange of it *shall not be for* jewels of fine gold.

18 No mention shall be made of coral, or of pearls: for the price of wisdom *is* above rubies.

19 The topaz of Ethiopia shall not equal it, neither shall it be valued with pure gold.

20 Whence then cometh wisdom? and where *is* the place of understanding?

21 Seeing it is hid from the eyes of all living, and kept close from the fowls of the air.

22 Destruction and death say, We have heard the fame thereof with our ears.

23 God understandeth the way thereof, and he knoweth the place thereof.

24 For he looketh to the ends of the earth, *and* seeth under the whole heaven;

25 To make the weight for the winds; and he weigheth the waters by measure.

26 When he made a decree for the rain, and a way for the lightning of the thunder:

27 Then did he see it, and declare it; he prepared it, yea, and searched it out.

28 And unto man he said, Behold, the fear of the Lord, that *is* wisdom; and to depart from evil *is* understanding.

29

Moreover Job continued his parable, and said,

2 Oh that I were as *in* months past, as *in* the days *when* God preserved me;

3 When his candle shined upon my head, *and when* by his light I walked *through* darkness;

4 As I was in the days of my youth, when the secret of God *was* upon my tabernacle;

5 When the Almighty *was* yet with me, *when* my children *were* about me;

6 When I washed my steps with butter, and the rock poured me out rivers of oil;

7 When I went out to the gate through the city, *when* I prepared my seat in the street!

8 The young men saw me, and hid themselves: and the aged arose, *and* stood up.

9 The princes refrained talking, and laid *their* hand on their mouth.

10 The nobles held their peace, and their tongue cleaved to the roof of their mouth.

11 When the ear heard *me*, then it blessed me; and when the eye saw *me*, it gave witness to me:

12 Because I delivered the poor that cried, and the fatherless, and *him that had* none to help him.

13 The blessing of him that was ready to perish came upon me: and I caused the widow's heart to sing for joy.

14 I put on righteousness, and it clothed me: my judgment *was* as a robe and a diadem.

15 I was eyes to the blind, and feet *was* I to the lame.

16 I *was* a father to the poor: and the cause *which* I knew not I searched out.

17 And I brake the jaws of the wicked, and plucked the spoil out of his teeth.

18 Then I said, I shall die in my nest, and I shall multiply *my* days as the sand.

19 My root *was* spread out by the waters, and the dew lay all night upon my branch.

20 My glory *was* fresh in me, and my bow was renewed in my hand.

21 Unto me *men* gave ear, and waited, and kept silence at my counsel.

22 After my words they spake not again; and my speech dropped upon them.

23 And they waited for me as for the rain; and they opened their mouth wide *as* for the latter rain.

24 *If* I laughed on them, they believed *it* not; and the light of my countenance they cast not down.

25 I chose out their way, and sat chief, and dwelt as a king in the army, as one *that* comforteth the mourners.

30 But now *they that are* younger than I have me in derision, whose fathers I would have disdained to have set with the dogs of my flock.

2 Yea, whereto *might* the strength of their hands *profit* me, in whom old age was perished?

3 For want and famine *they were* solitary; fleeing into the wilderness in former time desolate and waste.

4 Who cut up mallows by the bushes, and juniper roots *for* their meat.

5 They were driven forth from among *men*, (they cried after them as *after* a thief;)

6 To dwell in the clifts of the valleys, *in* caves of the earth, and *in* the rocks.

7 Among the bushes they brayed; under the nettles they were gathered together.

8 *They were* children of fools, yea, children of base men: they were viler than the earth.

9 And now am I their song, yea, I am their byword.

10 They abhor me, they flee far from me, and spare not to spit in my face.

11 Because he hath loosed my cord, and afflicted me, they have also let loose the bridle before me.

12 Upon *my* right *hand* rise the youth; they push away my feet, and they raise up against me the ways of their destruction.

13 They mar my path, they set forward my calamity, they have no helper.

14 They came *upon me* as a wide breaking in *of waters*: in the desolation they rolled themselves *upon me*.

15 Terrors are turned upon me: they pursue my soul as the wind: and my welfare passeth away as a cloud.

16 And now my soul is poured out upon me; the days of affliction have taken hold upon me.

17 My bones are pierced in me in the night season: and my sinews take no rest.

18 By the great force *of my disease* is my garment changed: it bindeth me about as the collar of my coat.

19 He hath cast me into the mire, and I am become like dust and ashes.

20 I cry unto thee, and thou dost not hear me: I stand up, and thou regardest me *not*.

21 Thou art become cruel to me: with thy strong hand thou opposest thyself against me.

22 Thou liftest me up to the wind; thou causest me to ride *upon it*, and dissolvest my substance.

23 For I know *that* thou wilt bring me *to* death, and *to* the house appointed for all living.

24 Howbeit he will not stretch out *his* hand to the grave, though they cry in his destruction.

25 Did not I weep for him that was in trouble? was *not* my soul grieved for the poor?

26 When I looked for good, then evil came *unto me*: and when I waited for light, there came darkness.

27 My bowels boiled, and rested not: the days of affliction prevented me.

28 I went mourning without the sun: I stood up, *and* I cried in the congregation.

29 I am a brother to dragons, and a companion to owls.

30 My skin is black upon me, and my bones are burned with heat.

31 My harp also is *turned* to mourning, and my organ into the voice of them that weep.

31

I made a covenant with mine eyes; why then should I think upon a maid?

2 For what portion of God *is there* from above? and *what* inheritance of the Almighty from on high?

3 *Is* not destruction to the wicked? and a strange *punishment* to the workers of iniquity?

4 Doth not he see my ways, and count all my steps?

5 If I have walked with vanity, or if my foot hath hasted to deceit;

6 Let me be weighed in an even balance, that God may know mine integrity.

7 If my step hath turned out of the way, and mine heart walked after mine eyes, and if any blot hath cleaved to mine hands;

8 *Then* let me sow, and let another eat; yea, let my offspring be rooted out.

9 If mine heart have been deceived by a woman, or *if* I have laid wait at my neighbour's door;

10 *Then* let my wife grind unto another, and let others bow down upon her.

11 For this *is* an heinous crime; yea, it *is* an iniquity *to be punished by* the judges.

12 For it *is* a fire *that* consumeth to destruction, and would root out all mine increase.

13 If I did despise the cause of my manservant or of my maidservant, when they contended with me;

14 What then shall I do when God riseth up? and when he visiteth, what shall I answer him?

15 Did not he that made me in the womb make him? and did not one fashion us in the womb?

16 If I have withheld the poor from *their* desire, or have caused the eyes of the widow to fail;

17 Or have eaten my morsel myself alone, and the fatherless hath not eaten thereof;

18 (For from my youth he was brought up with me, as *with* a father, and I have guided her from my mother's womb;)

19 If I have seen any perish for want of clothing, or any poor without covering;

20 If his loins have not blessed me, and *if* he were *not* warmed with the fleece of my sheep;

21 If I have lifted up my hand against the fatherless, when I saw my help in the gate:

22 *Then* let mine arm fall from my shoulder blade, and mine arm be broken from the bone.

23 For destruction *from* God *was* a terror to me, and by reason of his highness I could not endure.

24 If I have made gold my hope, or have said to the fine gold, *Thou art* my confidence;

25 If I rejoiced because my wealth
was great, and because mine hand had
gotten much;
26 If I beheld the sun when it shined,
or the moon walking *in* brightness;
27 And my heart hath been secretly
enticed, or my mouth hath kissed my
hand:
28 This also *were* an iniquity *to be
punished by* the judge: for I should
have denied the God *that is* above.
29 If I rejoiced at the destruction of
him that hated me, or lifted up myself
when evil found him:
30 Neither have I suffered my mouth
to sin by wishing a curse to his soul.
31 If the men of my tabernacle said
not, Oh that we had of his flesh! we cannot be satisfied.
32 The stranger did not lodge in the
street: *but* I opened my doors to the
traveller.
33 If I covered my transgressions as
Adam, by hiding mine iniquity in my
bosom:
34 Did I fear a great multitude, or did
the contempt of families terrify me,
that I kept silence, *and* went not out of
the door?
35 Oh that one would hear me!
behold, my desire *is, that* the Almighty
would answer me, and *that* mine adversary had written a book.
36 Surely I would take it upon my
shoulder, *and* bind it *as* a crown to me.
37 I would declare unto him the number of my steps; as a prince would I go
near unto him.
38 If my land cry against me, or that
the furrows likewise thereof complain;
39 If I have eaten the fruits thereof
without money, or have caused the
owners thereof to lose their life:
40 Let thistles grow instead of wheat,
and cockle instead of barley. The words
of Job are ended.

32 So these three men ceased to
answer Job, because he *was* righteous in his own eyes.
2 Then was kindled the wrath of
Elihu the son of Barachel the Buzite, of
the kindred of Ram: against Job was
his wrath kindled, because he justified
himself rather than God.
3 Also against his three friends was
his wrath kindled, because they had
found no answer, and *yet* had condemned Job.
4 Now Elihu had waited till Job had
spoken, because they *were* elder than
he.
5 When Elihu saw that *there was* no
answer in the mouth of *these* three
men, then his wrath was kindled.
6 And Elihu the son of Barachel the
Buzite answered and said, I *am* young,
and ye *are* very old; wherefore I was
afraid, and durst not shew you mine
opinion.
7 I said, Days should speak, and multitude of years should teach wisdom.
8 But *there is* a spirit in man: and the
inspiration of the Almighty giveth
them understanding.
9 Great men are not *always* wise:
neither do the aged understand judgment.
10 Therefore I said, Hearken to me; I
also will shew mine opinion.
11 Behold, I waited for your words; I
gave ear to your reasons, whilst ye
searched out what to say.
12 Yea, I attended unto you, and,
behold, *there was* none of you that
convinced Job, *or* that answered his
words:

13 Lest ye should say, We have found
out wisdom: God thrusteth him down,
not man.
14 Now he hath not directed *his*
words against me: neither will I answer
him with your speeches.
15 They were amazed, they answered
no more: they left off speaking.
16 When I had waited, (for they spake
not, but stood still, *and* answered no
more;)
17 *I said*, I will answer also my part, I
also will shew mine opinion.
18 For I am full of matter, the spirit
within me constraineth me.
19 Behold, my belly *is* as wine *which*
hath no vent; it is ready to burst like
new bottles.
20 I will speak, that I may be
refreshed: I will open my lips and
answer.
21 Let me not, I pray you, accept any
man's person, neither let me give flattering titles unto man.
22 For I know not to give flattering
titles; *in so doing* my maker would soon
take me away.

33 Wherefore, Job, I pray thee, hear
my speeches, and hearken to all
my words.
2 Behold, now I have opened my
mouth, my tongue hath spoken in my
mouth.
3 My words *shall be of* the uprightness of my heart: and my lips shall
utter knowledge clearly.
4 The Spirit of God hath made me,
and the breath of the Almighty hath
given me life.
5 If thou canst answer me, set *thy
words* in order before me, stand up.
6 Behold, I *am* according to thy wish
in God's stead: I also am formed out of
the clay.
7 Behold, my terror shall not make
thee afraid, neither shall my hand be
heavy upon thee.
8 Surely thou hast spoken in mine
hearing, and I have heard the voice of
thy words, *saying*,
9 I am clean without transgression, I
am innocent; neither *is there* iniquity
in me.
10 Behold, he findeth occasions
against me, he counteth me for his
enemy,
11 He putteth my feet in the stocks,
he marketh all my paths.
12 Behold, *in* this thou art not just: I
will answer thee, that God is greater
than man.
13 Why dost thou strive against him?
for he giveth not account of any of his
matters.
14 For God speaketh once, yea twice,
yet man perceiveth it not.
15 In a dream, in a vision of the night,
when deep sleep falleth upon men, in
slumberings upon the bed;
16 Then he openeth the ears of men,
and sealeth their instruction,
17 That he may withdraw man *from
his* purpose, and hide pride from man.
18 He keepeth back his soul from the
pit, and his life from perishing by the
sword.
19 He is chastened also with pain
upon his bed, and the multitude of his
bones with strong *pain*:
20 So that his life abhorreth bread,
and his soul dainty meat.
21 His flesh is consumed away, that it
cannot be seen; and his bones *that*
were not seen stick out.

22 Yea, his soul draweth near unto the grave, and his life to the destroyers.

23 If there be a messenger with him, an interpreter, one among a thousand, to shew unto man his uprightness:

24 Then he is gracious unto him, and saith, Deliver him from going down to the pit: I have found a ransom.

25 His flesh shall be fresher than a child's: he shall return to the days of his youth:

26 He shall pray unto God, and he will be favourable unto him: and he shall see his face with joy: for he will render unto man his righteousness.

27 He looketh upon men, and *if any* say, I have sinned, and perverted *that which was* right, and it profited me not;

28 He will deliver his soul from going into the pit, and his life shall see the light.

29 Lo, all these *things* worketh God oftentimes with man,

30 To bring back his soul from the pit, to be enlightened with the light of the living.

31 Mark well, O Job, hearken unto me: hold thy peace, and I will speak.

32 If thou hast any thing to say, answer me: speak, for I desire to justify thee.

33 If not, hearken unto me: hold thy peace, and I shall teach thee wisdom.

34 Furthermore Elihu answered and said,

2 Hear my words, O ye wise *men*; and give ear unto me, ye that have knowledge.

3 For the ear trieth words, as the mouth tasteth meat.

4 Let us choose to us judgment: let us know among ourselves what *is* good.

5 For Job hath said, I am righteous: and God hath taken away my judgment.

6 Should I lie against my right? my wound *is* incurable without transgression.

7 What man *is* like Job, *who* drinketh up scorning like water?

8 Which goeth in company with the workers of iniquity, and walketh with wicked men.

9 For he hath said, It profiteth a man nothing that he should delight himself with God.

10 Therefore hearken unto me, ye men of understanding: far be it from God, *that he should do* wickedness; and *from* the Almighty, *that he should commit* iniquity.

11 For the work of a man shall he render unto him, and cause every man to find according to *his* ways.

12 Yea, surely God will not do wickedly, neither will the Almighty pervert judgment.

13 Who hath given him a charge over the earth? or who hath disposed the whole world?

14 If he set his heart upon man, *if* he gather unto himself his spirit and his breath;

15 All flesh shall perish together, and man shall turn again unto dust.

16 If now *thou hast* understanding, hear this: hearken to the voice of my words.

17 Shall even he that hateth right govern? and wilt thou condemn him that is most just?

18 *Is it fit* to say to a king, *Thou art* wicked? *and* to princes, *Ye are* ungodly?

19 *How much less to him* that accepteth not the persons of princes, nor regardeth the rich more than the poor? for they all *are* the work of his hands.

20 In a moment shall they die, and the people shall be troubled at midnight, and pass away: and the mighty shall be taken away without hand.

21 For his eyes *are* upon the ways of man, and he seeth all his goings.

22 *There is* no darkness, nor shadow of death, where the workers of iniquity may hide themselves.

23 For he will not lay upon man more *than right*; that he should enter into judgment with God.

24 He shall break in pieces mighty men without number, and set others in their stead.

25 Therefore he knoweth their works, and he overturneth *them* in the night, so that they are destroyed.

26 He striketh them as wicked men in the open sight of others;

27 Because they turned back from him, and would not consider any of his ways:

28 So that they cause the cry of the poor to come unto him, and he heareth the cry of the afflicted.

29 When he giveth quietness, who then can make trouble? and when he hideth *his* face, who then can behold him? whether *it be done* against a nation, or against a man only:

30 That the hypocrite reign not, lest the people be ensnared.

31 Surely it is meet to be said unto God, I have borne *chastisement*, I will not offend *any more*:

32 *That which* I see not teach thou me: if I have done iniquity, I will do no more.

33 *Should it be* according to thy mind? he will recompense it, whether thou refuse, or whether thou choose; and not I: therefore speak what thou knowest.

34 Let men of understanding tell me, and let a wise man hearken unto me.

35 Job hath spoken without knowledge, and his words *were* without wisdom.

36 My desire *is that* Job may be tried unto the end because of *his* answers for wicked men.

37 For he addeth rebellion unto his sin, he clappeth *his hands* among us, and multiplieth his words against God.

35

Elihu spake moreover, and said,

2 Thinkest thou this to be right, *that* thou saidst, My righteousness *is* more than God's?

3 For thou saidst, What advantage will it be unto thee? *and*, What profit shall I have, *if I be cleansed* from my sin?

4 I will answer thee, and thy companions with thee.

5 Look unto the heavens, and see; and behold the clouds *which* are higher than thou.

6 If thou sinnest, what doest thou against him? or *if* thy transgressions be multiplied, what doest thou unto him?

7 If thou be righteous, what givest thou him? or what receiveth he of thine hand?

8 Thy wickedness *may hurt* a man as thou *art*; and thy righteousness *may profit* the son of man.

9 By reason of the multitude of oppressions they make *the oppressed* to cry: they cry out by reason of the arm of the mighty.

10 But none saith, Where *is* God my maker, who giveth songs in the night;

11 Who teacheth us more than the beasts of the earth, and maketh us wiser than the fowls of heaven?

12 There they cry, but none giveth
answer, because of the pride of evil
men.
13 Surely God will not hear vanity,
neither will the Almighty regard it.
14 Although thou sayest thou shalt
not see him, *yet* judgment *is* before
him; therefore trust thou in him.
15 But now, because *it is* not *so*, he
hath visited in his anger; yet he
knoweth *it* not in great extremity:
16 Therefore doth Job open his mouth
in vain; he multiplieth words without
knowledge.

36 Elihu also proceeded, and said,
2 Suffer me a little, and I will
shew thee that *I have* yet to speak on
God's behalf.
3 I will fetch my knowledge from afar,
and will ascribe righteousness to my
Maker.
4 For truly my words *shall* not *be*
false: he that is perfect in knowledge *is*
with thee.
5 Behold, God *is* mighty, and despiseth not *any: he is* mighty in strength
and wisdom.
6 He preserveth not the life of the
wicked: but giveth right to the poor.
7 He withdraweth not his eyes from
the righteous: but with kings *are they*
on the throne; yea, he doth establish
them for ever, and they are exalted.
8 And if *they be* bound in fetters, *and*
be holden in cords of affliction;
9 Then he sheweth them their work,
and their transgressions that they have
exceeded.
10 He openeth also their ear to disci-
pline, and commandeth that they
return from iniquity.
11 If they obey and serve *him*, they
shall spend their days in prosperity,
and their years in pleasures.
12 But if they obey not, they shall perish by the sword, and they shall die
without knowledge.
13 But the hypocrites in heart heap
up wrath: they cry not when he bindeth
them.
14 They die in youth, and their life *is*
among the unclean.
15 He delivereth the poor in his affliction, and openeth their ears in oppression.
16 Even so would he have removed
thee out of the strait *into* a broad place,
where *there is* no straitness; and that
which should be set on thy table *should*
be full of fatness.
17 But thou hast fulfilled the judgment of the wicked: judgment and justice take hold *on thee.*
18 Because *there is* wrath, *beware* lest
he take thee away with *his* stroke: then
a great ransom cannot deliver thee.
19 Will he esteem thy riches? *no*, not
gold, nor all the forces of strength.
20 Desire not the night, when people
are cut off in their place.
21 Take heed, regard not iniquity: for
this hast thou chosen rather than affliction.
22 Behold, God exalteth by his power:
who teacheth like him?
23 Who hath enjoined him his way?
or who can say, Thou hast wrought iniquity?
24 Remember that thou magnify his
work, which men behold.
25 Every man may see it; man may
behold *it* afar off.
26 Behold, God *is* great, and we know
him not, neither can the number of his
years be searched out.
27 For he maketh small the drops of
water: they pour down rain according
to the vapour thereof:

28 Which the clouds do drop *and* distil upon man abundantly.

29 Also can *any* understand the spreadings of the clouds, *or* the noise of his tabernacle?

30 Behold, he spreadeth his light upon it, and covereth the bottom of the sea.

31 For by them judgeth he the people; he giveth meat in abundance.

32 With clouds he covereth the light; and commandeth it *not to shine* by *the cloud* that cometh betwixt.

33 The noise thereof sheweth concerning it, the cattle also concerning the vapour.

37 At this also my heart trembleth, and is moved out of his place.

2 Hear attentively the noise of his voice, and the sound *that* goeth out of his mouth.

3 He directeth it under the whole heaven, and his lightning unto the ends of the earth.

4 After it a voice roareth: he thundereth with the voice of his excellency; and he will not stay them when his voice is heard.

5 God thundereth marvellously with his voice; great things doeth he, which we cannot comprehend.

6 For he saith to the snow, Be thou *on* the earth; likewise to the small rain, and to the great rain of his strength.

7 He sealeth up the hand of every man; that all men may know his work.

8 Then the beasts go into dens, and remain in their places.

9 Out of the south cometh the whirlwind: and cold out of the north.

10 By the breath of God frost is given: and the breadth of the waters is straitened.

11 Also by watering he wearieth the thick cloud: he scattereth his bright cloud:

12 And it is turned round about by his counsels: that they may do whatsoever he commandeth them upon the face of the world in the earth.

13 He causeth it to come, whether for correction, or for his land, or for mercy.

14 Hearken unto this, O Job: stand still, and consider the wondrous works of God.

15 Dost thou know when God disposed them, and caused the light of his cloud to shine?

16 Dost thou know the balancings of the clouds, the wondrous works of him which is perfect in knowledge?

17 How thy garments *are* warm, when he quieteth the earth by the south *wind*?

18 Hast thou with him spread out the sky, *which is* strong, *and* as a molten looking glass?

19 Teach us what we shall say unto him; *for* we cannot order *our speech* by reason of darkness.

20 Shall it be told him that I speak? if a man speak, surely he shall be swallowed up.

21 And now *men* see not the bright light which *is* in the clouds: but the wind passeth, and cleanseth them.

22 Fair weather cometh out of the north: with God *is* terrible majesty.

23 *Touching* the Almighty, we cannot find him out: *he is* excellent in power, and in judgment, and in plenty of justice: he will not afflict.

24 Men do therefore fear him: he respecteth not any *that are* wise of heart.

38 Then the LORD answered Job out of the whirlwind, and said,

2 Who *is* this that darkeneth counsel by words without knowledge?

3 Gird up now thy loins like a man; for I will demand of thee, and answer thou me.

4 Where wast thou when I laid the foundations of the earth? declare, if thou hast understanding.

5 Who hath laid the measures thereof, if thou knowest? or who hath stretched the line upon it?

6 Whereupon are the foundations thereof fastened? or who laid the corner stone thereof;

7 When the morning stars sang together, and all the sons of God shouted for joy?

8 Or *who* shut up the sea with doors, when it brake forth, *as if* it had issued out of the womb?

9 When I made the cloud the garment thereof, and thick darkness a swaddlingband for it,

10 And brake up for it my decreed *place*, and set bars and doors,

11 And said, Hitherto shalt thou come, but no further: and here shall thy proud waves be stayed?

12 Hast thou commanded the morning since thy days; *and* caused the dayspring to know his place;

13 That it might take hold of the ends of the earth, that the wicked might be shaken out of it?

14 It is turned as clay *to* the seal; and they stand as a garment.

15 And from the wicked their light is withholden, and the high arm shall be broken.

16 Hast thou entered into the springs of the sea? or hast thou walked in the search of the depth?

17 Have the gates of death been opened unto thee? or hast thou seen the doors of the shadow of death?

18 Hast thou perceived the breadth of the earth? declare if thou knowest it all.

19 Where *is* the way *where* light dwelleth? and *as for* darkness, where *is* the place thereof,

20 That thou shouldest take it to the bound thereof, and that thou shouldest know the paths *to* the house thereof?

21 Knowest thou *it*, because thou wast then born? or *because* the number of thy days *is* great?

22 Hast thou entered into the treasures of the snow? or hast thou seen the treasures of the hail,

23 Which I have reserved against the time of trouble, against the day of battle and war?

24 By what way is the light parted, *which* scattereth the east wind upon the earth?

25 Who hath divided a watercourse for the overflowing of waters, or a way for the lightning of thunder;

26 To cause it to rain on the earth, *where* no man *is; on* the wilderness, wherein *there is* no man;

27 To satisfy the desolate and waste *ground*; and to cause the bud of the tender herb to spring forth?

28 Hath the rain a father? or who hath begotten the drops of dew?

29 Out of whose womb came the ice? and the hoary frost of heaven, who hath gendered it?

30 The waters are hid as *with* a stone, and the face of the deep is frozen.

31 Canst thou bind the sweet influences of Pleiades, or loose the bands of Orion?

32 Canst thou bring forth Mazzaroth in his season? or canst thou guide Arcturus with his sons?

33 Knowest thou the ordinances of heaven? canst thou set the dominion thereof in the earth?

34 Canst thou lift up thy voice to the clouds, that abundance of waters may cover thee?

35 Canst thou send lightnings, that they may go, and say unto thee, Here we *are*?

36 Who hath put wisdom in the inward parts? or who hath given understanding to the heart?

37 Who can number the clouds in wisdom? or who can stay the bottles of heaven,

38 When the dust groweth into hardness, and the clods cleave fast together?

39 Wilt thou hunt the prey for the lion? or fill the appetite of the young lions,

40 When they couch in *their* dens, *and* abide in the covert to lie in wait?

41 Who provideth for the raven his food? when his young ones cry unto God, they wander for lack of meat.

39 Knowest thou the time when the wild goats of the rock bring forth? *or* canst thou mark when the hinds do calve?

2 Canst thou number the months *that* they fulfil? or knowest thou the time when they bring forth?

3 They bow themselves, they bring forth their young ones, they cast out their sorrows.

4 Their young ones are in good liking, they grow up with corn; they go forth, and return not unto them.

5 Who hath sent out the wild ass free? or who hath loosed the bands of the wild ass?

6 Whose house I have made the wilderness, and the barren land his dwellings.

7 He scorneth the multitude of the city, neither regardeth he the crying of the driver.

8 The range of the mountains *is* his pasture, and he searcheth after every green thing.

9 Will the unicorn be willing to serve thee, or abide by thy crib?

10 Canst thou bind the unicorn with his band in the furrow? or will he harrow the valleys after thee?

11 Wilt thou trust him, because his strength *is* great? or wilt thou leave thy labour to him?

12 Wilt thou believe him, that he will bring home thy seed, and gather *it into* thy barn?

13 *Gavest thou* the goodly wings unto the peacocks? or wings and feathers unto the ostrich?

14 Which leaveth her eggs in the earth, and warmeth them in dust,

15 And forgetteth that the foot may crush them, or that the wild beast may break them.

16 She is hardened against her young ones, as though *they were* not hers: her labour is in vain without fear;

17 Because God hath deprived her of wisdom, neither hath he imparted to her understanding.

18 What time she lifteth up herself on high, she scorneth the horse and his rider.

19 Hast thou given the horse strength? hast thou clothed his neck with thunder?

20 Canst thou make him afraid as a
grasshopper? the glory of his nostrils *is*
terrible.
21 He paweth in the valley, and rejoiceth in *his* strength: he goeth on to
meet the armed men.
22 He mocketh at fear, and is not
affrighted; neither turneth he back
from the sword.
23 The quiver rattleth against him,
the glittering spear and the shield.
24 He swalloweth the ground with
fierceness and rage: neither believeth
he that *it is* the sound of the trumpet.
25 He saith among the trumpets, Ha,
ha; and he smelleth the battle afar off,
the thunder of the captains, and the
shouting.
26 Doth the hawk fly by thy wisdom,
and stretch her wings toward the
south?
27 Doth the eagle mount up at thy
command, and make her nest on high?
28 She dwelleth and abideth on the
rock, upon the crag of the rock, and the
strong place.
29 From thence she seeketh the prey,
and her eyes behold afar off.
30 Her young ones also suck up blood:
and where the slain *are*, there *is* she.

40

Moreover the LORD answered
Job, and said,
2 Shall he that contendeth with the
Almighty instruct *him*? he that
reproveth God, let him answer it.
3 Then Job answered the LORD, and
said,
4 Behold, I am vile; what shall I
answer thee? I will lay mine hand upon
my mouth.
5 Once have I spoken; but I will not
answer: yea, twice; but I will proceed
no further.
6 Then answered the LORD unto Job
out of the whirlwind, and said,
7 Gird up thy loins now like a man: I
will demand of thee, and declare thou
unto me.
8 Wilt thou also disannul my judgment? wilt thou condemn me, that thou
mayest be righteous?
9 Hast thou an arm like God? or canst
thou thunder with a voice like him?
10 Deck thyself now *with* majesty
and excellency; and array thyself with
glory and beauty.
11 Cast abroad the rage of thy wrath:
and behold every one *that is* proud,
and abase him.
12 Look on every one *that is* proud,
and bring him low; and tread down the
wicked in their place.
13 Hide them in the dust together;
and bind their faces in secret.
14 Then will I also confess unto thee
that thine own right hand can save
thee.
15 Behold now behemoth, which I
made with thee; he eateth grass as an
ox.
16 Lo now, his strength *is* in his loins,
and his force *is* in the navel of his belly.
17 He moveth his tail like a cedar: the
sinews of his stones are wrapped
together.
18 His bones *are as* strong pieces of
brass; his bones *are* like bars of iron.
19 He *is* the chief of the ways of God:
he that made him can make his sword
to approach *unto him*.
20 Surely the mountains bring him
forth food, where all the beasts of the
field play.
21 He lieth under the shady trees, in
the covert of the reed, and fens.

22 The shady trees cover him *with* their shadow; the willows of the brook compass him about.

23 Behold, he drinketh up a river, *and* hasteth not: he trusteth that he can draw up Jordan into his mouth.

24 He taketh it with his eyes: *his* nose pierceth through snares.

41 Canst thou draw out leviathan with an hook? or his tongue with a cord *which* thou lettest down?

2 Canst thou put an hook into his nose? or bore his jaw through with a thorn?

3 Will he make many supplications unto thee? will he speak soft *words* unto thee?

4 Will he make a covenant with thee? wilt thou take him for a servant for ever?

5 Wilt thou play with him as *with* a bird? or wilt thou bind him for thy maidens?

6 Shall the companions make a banquet of him? shall they part him among the merchants?

7 Canst thou fill his skin with barbed irons? or his head with fish spears?

8 Lay thine hand upon him, remember the battle, do no more.

9 Behold, the hope of him is in vain: shall not *one* be cast down even at the sight of him?

10 None *is so* fierce that dare stir him up: who then is able to stand before me?

11 Who hath prevented me, that I should repay *him? whatsoever is* under the whole heaven is mine.

12 I will not conceal his parts, nor his power, nor his comely proportion.

13 Who can discover the face of his garment? *or* who can come *to him* with his double bridle?

14 Who can open the doors of his face? his teeth *are* terrible round about.

15 *His* scales *are his* pride, shut up together *as with* a close seal.

16 One is so near to another, that no air can come between them.

17 They are joined one to another, they stick together, that they cannot be sundered.

18 By his neesings a light doth shine, and his eyes *are* like the eyelids of the morning.

19 Out of his mouth go burning lamps, *and* sparks of fire leap out.

20 Out of his nostrils goeth smoke, as *out* of a seething pot or caldron.

21 His breath kindleth coals, and a flame goeth out of his mouth.

22 In his neck remaineth strength, and sorrow is turned into joy before him.

23 The flakes of his flesh are joined together: they are firm in themselves; they cannot be moved.

24 His heart is as firm as a stone; yea, as hard as a piece of the nether *millstone.*

25 When he raiseth up himself, the mighty are afraid: by reason of breakings they purify themselves.

26 The sword of him that layeth at him cannot hold: the spear, the dart, nor the habergeon.

27 He esteemeth iron as straw, *and* brass as rotten wood.

28 The arrow cannot make him flee: slingstones are turned with him into stubble.

29 Darts are counted as stubble: he laugheth at the shaking of a spear.

30 Sharp stones *are* under him: he spreadeth sharp pointed things upon the mire.

31 He maketh the deep to boil like a pot: he maketh the sea like a pot of ointment.

32 He maketh a path to shine after him; *one* would think the deep *to be* hoary.

33 Upon earth there is not his like, who is made without fear.

34 He beholdeth all high *things*: he *is* a king over all the children of pride.

42 Then Job answered the LORD, and said,

2 I know that thou canst do every *thing*, and *that* no thought can be withholden from thee.

3 Who *is* he that hideth counsel without knowledge? therefore have I uttered that I understood not; things too wonderful for me, which I knew not.

4 Hear, I beseech thee, and I will speak: I will demand of thee, and declare thou unto me.

5 I have heard of thee by the hearing of the ear: but now mine eye seeth thee.

6 Wherefore I abhor *myself*, and repent in dust and ashes.

7 And it was *so*, that after the LORD had spoken these words unto Job, the LORD said to Eliphaz the Temanite, My wrath is kindled against thee, and against thy two friends: for ye have not spoken of me *the thing that is* right, as my servant Job *hath*.

8 Therefore take unto you now seven bullocks and seven rams, and go to my servant Job, and offer up for yourselves a burnt offering; and my servant Job shall pray for you: for him will I accept: lest I deal with you *after your* folly, in that ye have not spoken of me *the thing which is* right, like my servant Job.

9 So Eliphaz the Temanite and Bildad the Shuhite *and* Zophar the Naamathite went, and did according as the LORD commanded them: the LORD also accepted Job.

10 And the LORD turned the captivity of Job, when he prayed for his friends: also the LORD gave Job twice as much as he had before.

11 Then came there unto him all his brethren, and all his sisters, and all they that had been of his acquaintance before, and did eat bread with him in his house: and they bemoaned him, and comforted him over all the evil that the LORD had brought upon him: every man also gave him a piece of money, and every one an earring of gold.

12 So the LORD blessed the latter end of Job more than his beginning: for he had fourteen thousand sheep, and six thousand camels, and a thousand yoke of oxen, and a thousand she asses.

13 He had also seven sons and three daughters.

14 And he called the name of the first, Jemima; and the name of the second, Kezia; and the name of the third, Keren-happuch.

15 And in all the land were no women found *so* fair as the daughters of Job: and their father gave them inheritance among their brethren.

16 After this lived Job an hundred and forty years, and saw his sons, and his sons' sons, *even* four generations.

17 So Job died, *being* old and full of days.

THE BOOK OF
PSALMS

PSALM 1

Blessed *is* the man that walketh not in the counsel of the ungodly, nor standeth in the way of sinners, nor sitteth in the seat of the scornful.

2 But his delight *is* in the law of the LORD; and in his law doth he meditate day and night.

3 And he shall be like a tree planted by the rivers of water, that bringeth forth his fruit in his season; his leaf also shall not wither; and whatsoever he doeth shall prosper.

4 The ungodly *are* not so: but *are* like the chaff which the wind driveth away.

5 Therefore the ungodly shall not stand in the judgment, nor sinners in the congregation of the righteous.

6 For the LORD knoweth the way of the righteous: but the way of the ungodly shall perish.

PSALM 2

Why do the heathen rage, and the people imagine a vain thing?

2 The kings of the earth set themselves, and the rulers take counsel together, against the LORD, and against his anointed, *saying*,

3 Let us break their bands asunder, and cast away their cords from us.

4 He that sitteth in the heavens shall laugh: the Lord shall have them in derision.

5 Then shall he speak unto them in his wrath, and vex them in his sore displeasure.

6 Yet have I set my king upon my holy hill of Zion.

7 I will declare the decree: the LORD hath said unto me, Thou *art* my Son; this day have I begotten thee.

8 Ask of me, and I shall give *thee* the heathen *for* thine inheritance, and the uttermost parts of the earth *for* thy possession.

9 Thou shalt break them with a rod of iron; thou shalt dash them in pieces like a potter's vessel.

10 Be wise now therefore, O ye kings: be instructed, ye judges of the earth.

11 Serve the LORD with fear, and rejoice with trembling.

12 Kiss the Son, lest he be angry, and ye perish *from* the way, when his wrath is kindled but a little. Blessed *are* all they that put their trust in him.

PSALM 3

A Psalm of David, when he fled from Absalom his son.

LORD, how are they increased that trouble me! many *are* they that rise up against me.

2 Many *there be* which say of my soul, *There is* no help for him in God. Selah.

3 But thou, O LORD, *art* a shield for me; my glory, and the lifter up of mine head.

4 I cried unto the LORD with my voice, and he heard me out of his holy hill. Selah.

5 I laid me down and slept; I awaked; for the LORD sustained me.

6 I will not be afraid of ten thousands of people, that have set *themselves* against me round about.

7 Arise, O LORD; save me, O my God: for thou hast smitten all mine enemies *upon* the cheek bone; thou hast broken the teeth of the ungodly.

8 Salvation *belongeth* unto the LORD: thy blessing *is* upon thy people. Selah.

PSALM 4

To the chief Musician on Neginoth, A Psalm of David.

Hear me when I call, O God of my righteousness: thou hast enlarged me *when I was* in distress; have mercy upon me, and hear my prayer.

2 O ye sons of men, how long *will ye turn* my glory into shame? *how long* will ye love vanity, *and* seek after leasing? Selah.

3 But know that the LORD hath set apart him that is godly for himself: the LORD will hear when I call unto him.

4 Stand in awe, and sin not: commune with your own heart upon your bed, and be still. Selah.

5 Offer the sacrifices of righteousness, and put your trust in the LORD.

6 *There be* many that say, Who will shew us *any* good? LORD, lift thou up the light of thy countenance upon us.

7 Thou hast put gladness in my heart, more than in the time *that* their corn and their wine increased.

8 I will both lay me down in peace, and sleep: for thou, LORD, only makest me dwell in safety.

PSALM 5

To the chief Musician upon Nehiloth, A Psalm of David.

Give ear to my words, O LORD, consider my meditation.

2 Hearken unto the voice of my cry, my King, and my God: for unto thee will I pray.

3 My voice shalt thou hear in the morning, O LORD; in the morning will I direct *my prayer* unto thee, and will look up.

4 For thou *art* not a God that hath pleasure in wickedness: neither shall evil dwell with thee.

5 The foolish shall not stand in thy sight: thou hatest all workers of iniquity.

6 Thou shalt destroy them that speak leasing: the LORD will abhor the bloody and deceitful man.

7 But as for me, I will come *into* thy house in the multitude of thy mercy: *and* in thy fear will I worship toward thy holy temple.

8 Lead me, O LORD, in thy righteousness because of mine enemies; make thy way straight before my face.

9 For *there is* no faithfulness in their mouth; their inward part *is* very wickedness; their throat *is* an open sepulchre; they flatter with their tongue.

10 Destroy thou them, O God; let them fall by their own counsels; cast them out in the multitude of their transgressions; for they have rebelled against thee.

11 But let all those that put their trust in thee rejoice: let them ever shout for joy, because thou defendest them: let them also that love thy name be joyful in thee.

12 For thou, LORD, wilt bless the righteous; with favour wilt thou compass him as *with* a shield.

PSALM 6

To the chief Musician on Neginoth upon Sheminith, A Psalm of David.

O LORD, rebuke me not in thine anger, neither chasten me in thy hot displeasure.

2 Have mercy upon me, O LORD; for I
am weak: O LORD, heal me; for my
bones are vexed.
3 My soul is also sore vexed: but thou,
O LORD, how long?
4 Return, O LORD, deliver my soul: oh
save me for thy mercies' sake.
5 For in death *there is* no remembrance of thee: in the grave who shall
give thee thanks?
6 I am weary with my groaning; all
the night make I my bed to swim; I
water my couch with my tears.
7 Mine eye is consumed because of
grief; it waxeth old because of all mine
enemies.
8 Depart from me, all ye workers of
iniquity; for the LORD hath heard the
voice of my weeping.
9 The LORD hath heard my supplication; the LORD will receive my prayer.
10 Let all mine enemies be ashamed
and sore vexed: let them return *and* be
ashamed suddenly.

PSALM 7

Shiggaion of David, which he sang unto the LORD, concerning the words of Cush the Benjamite.

O LORD my God, in thee do I put my
trust: save me from all them that
persecute me, and deliver me:
2 Lest he tear my soul like a lion,
rending *it* in pieces, while *there is* none
to deliver.
3 O LORD my God, if I have done this;
if there be iniquity in my hands;
4 If I have rewarded evil unto him
that was at peace with me; (yea, I have
delivered him that without cause is
mine enemy:)
5 Let the enemy persecute my soul,
and take *it*; yea, let him tread down my
life upon the earth, and lay mine honour in the dust. Selah.
6 Arise, O LORD, in thine anger, lift up
thyself because of the rage of mine
enemies: and awake for me *to* the judgment *that* thou hast commanded.
7 So shall the congregation of the
people compass thee about: for their
sakes therefore return thou on high.
8 The LORD shall judge the people:
judge me, O LORD, according to my
righteousness, and according to mine
integrity *that is* in me.
9 Oh let the wickedness of the wicked
come to an end; but establish the just:
for the righteous God trieth the hearts
and reins.
10 My defence *is* of God, which saveth
the upright in heart.
11 God judgeth the righteous, and
God is angry *with the wicked* every
day.
12 If he turn not, he will whet his
sword; he hath bent his bow, and made
it ready.
13 He hath also prepared for him the
instruments of death; he ordaineth his
arrows against the persecutors.
14 Behold, he travaileth with iniquity,
and hath conceived mischief, and
brought forth falsehood.
15 He made a pit, and digged it, and
is fallen into the ditch *which* he made.
16 His mischief shall return upon his
own head, and his violent dealing shall
come down upon his own pate.
17 I will praise the LORD according to
his righteousness: and will sing praise
to the name of the LORD most high.

PSALM 8

To the chief Musician upon Gittith, A Psalm of David.

O LORD our Lord, how excellent *is* thy name in all the earth! who hast set thy glory above the heavens.

2 Out of the mouth of babes and sucklings hast thou ordained strength because of thine enemies, that thou mightest still the enemy and the avenger.

3 When I consider thy heavens, the work of thy fingers, the moon and the stars, which thou hast ordained;

4 What is man, that thou art mindful of him? and the son of man, that thou visitest him?

5 For thou hast made him a little lower than the angels, and hast crowned him with glory and honour.

6 Thou madest him to have dominion over the works of thy hands; thou hast put all *things* under his feet:

7 All sheep and oxen, yea, and the beasts of the field;

8 The fowl of the air, and the fish of the sea, *and whatsoever* passeth through the paths of the seas.

9 O LORD our Lord, how excellent *is* thy name in all the earth!

PSALM 9

To the chief Musician upon Muthlabben, A Psalm of David.

I will praise *thee*, O LORD, with my whole heart; I will shew forth all thy marvellous works.

2 I will be glad and rejoice in thee: I will sing praise to thy name, O thou most High.

3 When mine enemies are turned back, they shall fall and perish at thy presence.

4 For thou hast maintained my right and my cause; thou satest in the throne judging right.

5 Thou hast rebuked the heathen, thou hast destroyed the wicked, thou hast put out their name for ever and ever.

6 O thou enemy, destructions are come to a perpetual end: and thou hast destroyed cities; their memorial is perished with them.

7 But the LORD shall endure for ever: he hath prepared his throne for judgment.

8 And he shall judge the world in righteousness, he shall minister judgment to the people in uprightness.

9 The LORD also will be a refuge for the oppressed, a refuge in times of trouble.

10 And they that know thy name will put their trust in thee: for thou, LORD, hast not forsaken them that seek thee.

11 Sing praises to the LORD, which dwelleth in Zion: declare among the people his doings.

12 When he maketh inquisition for blood, he remembereth them: he forgetteth not the cry of the humble.

13 Have mercy upon me, O LORD; consider my trouble *which I suffer* of them that hate me, thou that liftest me up from the gates of death:

14 That I may shew forth all thy praise in the gates of the daughter of Zion: I will rejoice in thy salvation.

15 The heathen are sunk down in the pit *that* they made: in the net which they hid is their own foot taken.

16 The LORD is known *by* the judgment *which* he executeth: the wicked is snared in the work of his own hands. Higgaion. Selah.

17 The wicked shall be turned into hell, *and* all the nations that forget God.

18 For the needy shall not alway be forgotten: the expectation of the poor shall *not* perish for ever.

19 Arise, O LORD; let not man prevail: let the heathen be judged in thy sight.

20 Put them in fear, O LORD: *that* the nations may know themselves *to be but* men. Selah.

PSALM 10

Why standest thou afar off, O LORD? *why* hidest thou *thyself* in times of trouble?

2 The wicked in *his* pride doth persecute the poor: let them be taken in the devices that they have imagined.

3 For the wicked boasteth of his heart's desire, and blesseth the covetous, *whom* the LORD abhorreth.

4 The wicked, through the pride of his countenance, will not seek *after God*: God *is* not in all his thoughts.

5 His ways are always grievous; thy judgments *are* far above out of his sight: *as for* all his enemies, he puffeth at them.

6 He hath said in his heart, I shall not be moved: for *I shall* never *be* in adversity.

7 His mouth is full of cursing and deceit and fraud: under his tongue *is* mischief and vanity.

8 He sitteth in the lurking places of the villages: in the secret places doth he murder the innocent: his eyes are privily set against the poor.

9 He lieth in wait secretly as a lion in his den: he lieth in wait to catch the poor: he doth catch the poor, when he draweth him into his net.

10 He croucheth, *and* humbleth himself, that the poor may fall by his strong ones.

11 He hath said in his heart, God hath forgotten: he hideth his face; he will never see *it*.

12 Arise, O LORD; O God, lift up thine hand: forget not the humble.

13 Wherefore doth the wicked contemn God? he hath said in his heart, Thou wilt not require *it*.

14 Thou hast seen *it*; for thou beholdest mischief and spite, to requite *it* with thy hand: the poor committeth himself unto thee; thou art the helper of the fatherless.

15 Break thou the arm of the wicked and the evil *man*: seek out his wickedness *till* thou find none.

16 The LORD *is* King for ever and ever: the heathen are perished out of his land.

17 LORD, thou hast heard the desire of the humble: thou wilt prepare their heart, thou wilt cause thine ear to hear:

18 To judge the fatherless and the oppressed, that the man of the earth may no more oppress.

PSALM 11

To the chief Musician, A Psalm of David.

In the LORD put I my trust: how say ye to my soul, Flee *as* a bird to your mountain?

2 For, lo, the wicked bend *their* bow, they make ready their arrow upon the string, that they may privily shoot at the upright in heart.

3 If the foundations be destroyed, what can the righteous do?

4 The LORD *is* in his holy temple, the LORD's throne *is* in heaven: his eyes behold, his eyelids try, the children of men.

5 The LORD trieth the righteous: but
the wicked and him that loveth violence his soul hateth.
6 Upon the wicked he shall rain
snares, fire and brimstone, and an horrible tempest: *this shall be* the portion
of their cup.
7 For the righteous LORD loveth righteousness; his countenance doth behold the upright.

PSALM 12

To the chief Musician upon Sheminith, A Psalm of David.

Help, LORD; for the godly man
ceaseth; for the faithful fail from
among the children of men.
2 They speak vanity every one with
his neighbour: *with* flattering lips *and*
with a double heart do they speak.
3 The LORD shall cut off all flattering
lips, *and* the tongue that speaketh
proud things:
4 Who have said, With our tongue will
we prevail; our lips *are* our own: who *is*
lord over us?
5 For the oppression of the poor, for
the sighing of the needy, now will I
arise, saith the LORD; I will set *him* in
safety *from him that* puffeth at him.
6 The words of the LORD *are* pure
words: *as* silver tried in a furnace of
earth, purified seven times.
7 Thou shalt keep them, O LORD, thou
shalt preserve them from this generation for ever.
8 The wicked walk on every side,
when the vilest men are exalted.

PSALM 13

To the chief Musician, A Psalm of David.

How long wilt thou forget me, O
LORD? for ever? how long wilt thou
hide thy face from me?
2 How long shall I take counsel in my
soul, *having* sorrow in my heart daily?
how long shall mine enemy be exalted
over me?
3 Consider *and* hear me, O LORD my
God: lighten mine eyes, lest I sleep the
sleep of death;
4 Lest mine enemy say, I have prevailed against him; *and* those that
trouble me rejoice when I am moved.
5 But I have trusted in thy mercy; my
heart shall rejoice in thy salvation.
6 I will sing unto the LORD, because
he hath dealt bountifully with me.

PSALM 14

To the chief Musician, *A Psalm* of David.

The fool hath said in his heart, *There
is* no God. They are corrupt, they
have done abominable works, *there is*
none that doeth good.
2 The LORD looked down from heaven
upon the children of men, to see if
there were any that did understand,
and seek God.
3 They are all gone aside, they are *all*
together become filthy: *there is* none
that doeth good, no, not one.
4 Have all the workers of iniquity no
knowledge? who eat up my people *as*
they eat bread, and call not upon the
LORD.
5 There were they in great fear: for
God *is* in the generation of the righteous.
6 Ye have shamed the counsel of the
poor, because the LORD *is* his refuge.
7 Oh that the salvation of Israel *were
come* out of Zion! when the LORD bringeth back the captivity of his people,
Jacob shall rejoice, *and* Israel shall be
glad.

PSALM 15

A Psalm of David.

LORD, who shall abide in thy
tabernacle? who shall dwell in thy
holy hill?
2 He that walketh uprightly, and worketh righteousness, and speaketh the
truth in his heart.
3 *He that* backbiteth not with his
tongue, nor doeth evil to his neighbour,
nor taketh up a reproach against his
neighbour.
4 In whose eyes a vile person is contemned; but he honoureth them that
fear the LORD. *He that* sweareth to *his
own* hurt, and changeth not.
5 *He that* putteth not out his money
to usury, nor taketh reward against the
innocent. He that doeth these *things*
shall never be moved.

PSALM 16

Michtam of David.

Preserve me, O God: for in thee do I
put my trust.
2 *O my soul*, thou hast said unto the
LORD, Thou *art* my Lord: my goodness
extendeth not to thee;
3 *But* to the saints that *are* in the
earth, and *to* the excellent, in whom *is*
all my delight.
4 Their sorrows shall be multiplied
that hasten *after* another *god*: their
drink offerings of blood will I not offer,
nor take up their names into my lips.
5 The LORD *is* the portion of mine
inheritance and of my cup: thou main-
tainest my lot.
6 The lines are fallen unto me in
pleasant *places*; yea, I have a goodly
heritage.
7 I will bless the LORD, who hath given
me counsel: my reins also instruct me
in the night seasons.
8 I have set the LORD always before
me: because *he is* at my right hand, I
shall not be moved.
9 Therefore my heart is glad, and my
glory rejoiceth: my flesh also shall rest
in hope.
10 For thou wilt not leave my soul in
hell; neither wilt thou suffer thine Holy
One to see corruption.
11 Thou wilt shew me the path of life:
in thy presence *is* fulness of joy; at thy
right hand *there are* pleasures for evermore.

PSALM 17

A Prayer of David.

Hear the right, O LORD, attend unto
my cry, give ear unto my prayer,
that goeth not out of feigned lips.
2 Let my sentence come forth from
thy presence; let thine eyes behold the
things that are equal.
3 Thou hast proved mine heart; thou
hast visited *me* in the night; thou hast
tried me, *and* shalt find nothing; I am
purposed *that* my mouth shall not
transgress.
4 Concerning the works of men, by
the word of thy lips I have kept *me from*
the paths of the destroyer.
5 Hold up my goings in thy paths, *that*
my footsteps slip not.
6 I have called upon thee, for thou
wilt hear me, O God: incline thine ear
unto me, *and hear* my speech.
7 Shew thy marvellous lovingkindness, O thou that savest by thy right
hand them which put their trust *in thee*
from those that rise up *against them*.
8 Keep me as the apple of the eye,
hide me under the shadow of thy wings,
9 From the wicked that oppress me,
from my deadly enemies, *who* compass
me about.

10 They are inclosed in their own fat: with their mouth they speak proudly.

11 They have now compassed us in our steps: they have set their eyes bowing down to the earth;

12 Like as a lion *that* is greedy of his prey, and as it were a young lion lurking in secret places.

13 Arise, O LORD, disappoint him, cast him down: deliver my soul from the wicked, *which is* thy sword:

14 From men *which are* thy hand, O LORD, from men of the world, *which have* their portion in *this* life, and whose belly thou fillest with thy hid *treasure*: they are full of children, and leave the rest of their *substance* to their babes.

15 As for me, I will behold thy face in righteousness: I shall be satisfied, when I awake, with thy likeness.

PSALM 18

To the chief Musician, *A Psalm* of David, the servant of the LORD, who spake unto the LORD the words of this song in the day *that* the LORD delivered him from the hand of all his enemies, and from the hand of Saul: And he said,

I will love thee, O LORD, my strength.

2 The LORD *is* my rock, and my fortress, and my deliverer; my God, my strength, in whom I will trust; my buckler, and the horn of my salvation, *and* my high tower.

3 I will call upon the LORD, *who is worthy* to be praised: so shall I be saved from mine enemies.

4 The sorrows of death compassed me, and the floods of ungodly men made me afraid.

5 The sorrows of hell compassed me about: the snares of death prevented me.

6 In my distress I called upon the LORD, and cried unto my God: he heard my voice out of his temple, and my cry came before him, *even* into his ears.

7 Then the earth shook and trembled; the foundations also of the hills moved and were shaken, because he was wroth.

8 There went up a smoke out of his nostrils, and fire out of his mouth devoured: coals were kindled by it.

9 He bowed the heavens also, and came down: and darkness *was* under his feet.

10 And he rode upon a cherub, and did fly: yea, he did fly upon the wings of the wind.

11 He made darkness his secret place; his pavilion round about him *were* dark waters *and* thick clouds of the skies.

12 At the brightness *that was* before him his thick clouds passed, hail *stones* and coals of fire.

13 The LORD also thundered in the heavens, and the Highest gave his voice; hail *stones* and coals of fire.

14 Yea, he sent out his arrows, and scattered them; and he shot out lightnings, and discomfited them.

15 Then the channels of waters were seen, and the foundations of the world were discovered at thy rebuke, O LORD, at the blast of the breath of thy nostrils.

16 He sent from above, he took me, he drew me out of many waters.

17 He delivered me from my strong enemy, and from them which hated me: for they were too strong for me.

18 They prevented me in the day of my calamity: but the LORD was my stay.

19 He brought me forth also into a large place; he delivered me, because he delighted in me.

20 The Lord rewarded me according to my righteousness; according to the cleanness of my hands hath he recompensed me.

21 For I have kept the ways of the Lord, and have not wickedly departed from my God.

22 For all his judgments *were* before me, and I did not put away his statutes from me.

23 I was also upright before him, and I kept myself from mine iniquity.

24 Therefore hath the Lord recompensed me according to my righteousness, according to the cleanness of my hands in his eyesight.

25 With the merciful thou wilt shew thyself merciful; with an upright man thou wilt shew thyself upright;

26 With the pure thou wilt shew thyself pure; and with the froward thou wilt shew thyself froward.

27 For thou wilt save the afflicted people; but wilt bring down high looks.

28 For thou wilt light my candle: the Lord my God will enlighten my darkness.

29 For by thee I have run through a troop; and by my God have I leaped over a wall.

30 *As for* God, his way *is* perfect: the word of the Lord is tried: he *is* a buckler to all those that trust in him.

31 For who *is* God save the Lord? or who *is* a rock save our God?

32 *It is* God that girdeth me with strength, and maketh my way perfect.

33 He maketh my feet like hinds' *feet*, and setteth me upon my high places.

34 He teacheth my hands to war, so that a bow of steel is broken by mine arms.

35 Thou hast also given me the shield of thy salvation: and thy right hand hath holden me up, and thy gentleness hath made me great.

36 Thou hast enlarged my steps under me, that my feet did not slip.

37 I have pursued mine enemies, and overtaken them: neither did I turn again till they were consumed.

38 I have wounded them that they were not able to rise: they are fallen under my feet.

39 For thou hast girded me with strength unto the battle: thou hast subdued under me those that rose up against me.

40 Thou hast also given me the necks of mine enemies; that I might destroy them that hate me.

41 They cried, but *there was* none to save *them: even* unto the Lord, but he answered them not.

42 Then did I beat them small as the dust before the wind: I did cast them out as the dirt in the streets.

43 Thou hast delivered me from the strivings of the people; *and* thou hast made me the head of the heathen: a people *whom* I have not known shall serve me.

44 As soon as they hear of me, they shall obey me: the strangers shall submit themselves unto me.

45 The strangers shall fade away, and be afraid out of their close places.

46 The Lord liveth; and blessed *be* my rock; and let the God of my salvation be exalted.

47 *It is* God that avengeth me, and subdueth the people under me.

48 He delivereth me from mine enemies: yea, thou liftest me up above those that rise up against me: thou hast delivered me from the violent man.

49 Therefore will I give thanks unto
thee, O LORD, among the heathen, and
sing praises unto thy name.
50 Great deliverance giveth he to his
king; and sheweth mercy to his anointed, to David, and to his seed for evermore.

PSALM 19

To the chief Musician, A Psalm of David.

The heavens declare the glory of God;
and the firmament sheweth his
handywork.
2 Day unto day uttereth speech, and
night unto night sheweth knowledge.
3 *There is* no speech nor language,
where their voice is not heard.
4 Their line is gone out through all
the earth, and their words to the end of
the world. In them hath he set a tabernacle for the sun,
5 Which *is* as a bridegroom coming
out of his chamber, *and* rejoiceth as a
strong man to run a race.
6 His going forth *is* from the end of
the heaven, and his circuit unto the
ends of it: and there is nothing hid from
the heat thereof.
7 The law of the LORD *is* perfect, con-
verting the soul: the testimony of the
LORD *is* sure, making wise the simple.
8 The statutes of the LORD *are* right,
rejoicing the heart: the commandment
of the LORD *is* pure, enlightening the
eyes.
9 The fear of the LORD *is* clean, enduring for ever: the judgments of the LORD
are true *and* righteous altogether.
10 More to be desired *are they* than
gold, yea, than much fine gold: sweeter
also than honey and the honeycomb.
11 Moreover by them is thy servant
warned: *and* in keeping of them *there*
is great reward.
12 Who can understand *his* errors?
cleanse thou me from secret *faults*.
13 Keep back thy servant also from
presumptuous *sins*; let them not have
dominion over me: then shall I be
upright, and I shall be innocent from
the great transgression.
14 Let the words of my mouth, and
the meditation of my heart, be acceptable in thy sight, O LORD, my strength,
and my redeemer.

PSALM 20

To the chief Musician, A Psalm of David.

The LORD hear thee in the day of
trouble; the name of the God of
Jacob defend thee;
2 Send thee help from the sanctuary,
and strengthen thee out of Zion;
3 Remember all thy offerings, and
accept thy burnt sacrifice; Selah.
4 Grant thee according to thine own
heart, and fulfil all thy counsel.
5 We will rejoice in thy salvation, and
in the name of our God we will set up
our banners: the LORD fulfil all thy petitions.
6 Now know I that the LORD saveth his
anointed; he will hear him from his
holy heaven with the saving strength of
his right hand.
7 Some *trust* in chariots, and some in
horses: but we will remember the name
of the LORD our God.
8 They are brought down and fallen:
but we are risen, and stand upright.
9 Save, LORD: let the king hear us
when we call.

PSALM 21

To the chief Musician, A Psalm of David.

The king shall joy in thy strength, O
LORD; and in thy salvation how
greatly shall he rejoice!

2 Thou hast given him his heart's desire, and hast not withholden the request of his lips. Selah.

3 For thou preventest him with the blessings of goodness: thou settest a crown of pure gold on his head.

4 He asked life of thee, *and* thou gavest *it* him, *even* length of days for ever and ever.

5 His glory *is* great in thy salvation: honour and majesty hast thou laid upon him.

6 For thou hast made him most blessed for ever: thou hast made him exceeding glad with thy countenance.

7 For the king trusteth in the LORD, and through the mercy of the most High he shall not be moved.

8 Thine hand shall find out all thine enemies: thy right hand shall find out those that hate thee.

9 Thou shalt make them as a fiery oven in the time of thine anger: the LORD shall swallow them up in his wrath, and the fire shall devour them.

10 Their fruit shalt thou destroy from the earth, and their seed from among the children of men.

11 For they intended evil against thee: they imagined a mischievous device, *which* they are not able *to perform*.

12 Therefore shalt thou make them turn their back, *when* thou shalt make ready *thine arrows* upon thy strings against the face of them.

13 Be thou exalted, LORD, in thine own strength: *so* will we sing and praise thy power.

PSALM 22

To the chief Musician upon Aijeleth Shahar, A Psalm of David.

My God, my God, why hast thou forsaken me? *why art thou so* far from helping me, *and from* the words of my roaring?

2 O my God, I cry in the daytime, but thou hearest not; and in the night season, and am not silent.

3 But thou *art* holy, *O thou* that inhabitest the praises of Israel.

4 Our fathers trusted in thee: they trusted, and thou didst deliver them.

5 They cried unto thee, and were delivered: they trusted in thee, and were not confounded.

6 But I *am* a worm, and no man; a reproach of men, and despised of the people.

7 All they that see me laugh me to scorn: they shoot out the lip, they shake the head, *saying*,

8 He trusted on the LORD *that* he would deliver him: let him deliver him, seeing he delighted in him.

9 But thou *art* he that took me out of the womb: thou didst make me hope *when I was* upon my mother's breasts.

10 I was cast upon thee from the womb: thou *art* my God from my mother's belly.

11 Be not far from me; for trouble *is* near; for *there is* none to help.

12 Many bulls have compassed me: strong *bulls* of Bashan have beset me round.

13 They gaped upon me *with* their mouths, *as* a ravening and a roaring lion.

14 I am poured out like water, and all my bones are out of joint: my heart is like wax; it is melted in the midst of my bowels.

15 My strength is dried up like a potsherd; and my tongue cleaveth to my jaws; and thou hast brought me into the dust of death.
16 For dogs have compassed me: the assembly of the wicked have inclosed me: they pierced my hands and my feet.
17 I may tell all my bones: they look *and* stare upon me.
18 They part my garments among them, and cast lots upon my vesture.
19 But be not thou far from me, O LORD: O my strength, haste thee to help me.
20 Deliver my soul from the sword; my darling from the power of the dog.
21 Save me from the lion's mouth: for thou hast heard me from the horns of the unicorns.
22 I will declare thy name unto my brethren: in the midst of the congregation will I praise thee.
23 Ye that fear the LORD, praise him; all ye the seed of Jacob, glorify him; and fear him, all ye the seed of Israel.
24 For he hath not despised nor abhorred the affliction of the afflicted; neither hath he hid his face from him; but when he cried unto him, he heard.
25 My praise *shall be* of thee in the great congregation: I will pay my vows before them that fear him.
26 The meek shall eat and be satisfied: they shall praise the LORD that seek him: your heart shall live for ever.
27 All the ends of the world shall remember and turn unto the LORD: and all the kindreds of the nations shall worship before thee.
28 For the kingdom *is* the LORD's: and he *is* the governor among the nations.
29 All *they that be* fat upon earth shall eat and worship: all they that go down to the dust shall bow before him: and none can keep alive his own soul.
30 A seed shall serve him; it shall be accounted to the Lord for a generation.
31 They shall come, and shall declare his righteousness unto a people that shall be born, that he hath done *this*.

PSALM 23

A Psalm of David.

The LORD *is* my shepherd; I shall not want.
2 He maketh me to lie down in green pastures: he leadeth me beside the still waters.
3 He restoreth my soul: he leadeth me in the paths of righteousness for his name's sake.
4 Yea, though I walk through the valley of the shadow of death, I will fear no evil: for thou *art* with me; thy rod and thy staff they comfort me.
5 Thou preparest a table before me in the presence of mine enemies: thou anointest my head with oil; my cup runneth over.
6 Surely goodness and mercy shall follow me all the days of my life: and I will dwell in the house of the LORD for ever.

PSALM 24

A Psalm of David.

The earth *is* the LORD's, and the fulness thereof; the world, and they that dwell therein.
2 For he hath founded it upon the seas, and established it upon the floods.
3 Who shall ascend into the hill of the LORD? or who shall stand in his holy place?
4 He that hath clean hands, and a pure heart; who hath not lifted up his soul unto vanity, nor sworn deceitfully.

5 He shall receive the blessing from
the LORD, and righteousness from the
God of his salvation.
6 This *is* the generation of them that
seek him, that seek thy face, O Jacob.
Selah.
7 Lift up your heads, O ye gates; and
be ye lift up, ye everlasting doors; and
the King of glory shall come in.
8 Who *is* this King of glory? The LORD
strong and mighty, the LORD mighty in
battle.
9 Lift up your heads, O ye gates; even
lift *them* up, ye everlasting doors; and
the King of glory shall come in.
10 Who is this King of glory? The
LORD of hosts, he *is* the King of glory.
Selah.

PSALM 25

A Psalm of David.

Unto thee, O LORD, do I lift up my
soul.
2 O my God, I trust in thee: let me not
be ashamed, let not mine enemies triumph over me.
3 Yea, let none that wait on thee be
ashamed: let them be ashamed which
transgress without cause.
4 Shew me thy ways, O LORD; teach
me thy paths.
5 Lead me in thy truth, and teach me:
for thou *art* the God of my salvation; on
thee do I wait all the day.
6 Remember, O LORD, thy tender mercies and thy lovingkindnesses; for they
have been ever of old.
7 Remember not the sins of my youth,
nor my transgressions: according to thy
mercy remember thou me for thy goodness' sake, O LORD.
8 Good and upright *is* the LORD:
therefore will he teach sinners in the
way.
9 The meek will he guide in judgment: and the meek will he teach his
way.
10 All the paths of the LORD *are*
mercy and truth unto such as keep his
covenant and his testimonies.
11 For thy name's sake, O LORD, pardon mine iniquity; for it *is* great.
12 What man *is* he that feareth the
LORD? him shall he teach in the way
that he shall choose.
13 His soul shall dwell at ease; and his
seed shall inherit the earth.
14 The secret of the LORD *is* with
them that fear him; and he will shew
them his covenant.
15 Mine eyes *are* ever toward the
LORD; for he shall pluck my feet out of
the net.
16 Turn thee unto me, and have
mercy upon me; for I *am* desolate and
afflicted.
17 The troubles of my heart are
enlarged: *O* bring thou me out of my
distresses.
18 Look upon mine affliction and my
pain; and forgive all my sins.
19 Consider mine enemies; for they
are many; and they hate me with cruel
hatred.
20 O keep my soul, and deliver me: let
me not be ashamed; for I put my trust
in thee.
21 Let integrity and uprightness preserve me; for I wait on thee.
22 Redeem Israel, O God, out of all
his troubles.

PSALM 26

A Psalm of David.

Judge me, O LORD; for I have walked in
mine integrity: I have trusted also in
the LORD; *therefore* I shall not slide.

2 Examine me, O LORD, and prove me; try my reins and my heart.

3 For thy lovingkindness *is* before mine eyes: and I have walked in thy truth.

4 I have not sat with vain persons, neither will I go in with dissemblers.

5 I have hated the congregation of evil doers; and will not sit with the wicked.

6 I will wash mine hands in innocency: so will I compass thine altar, O LORD:

7 That I may publish with the voice of thanksgiving, and tell of all thy wondrous works.

8 LORD, I have loved the habitation of thy house, and the place where thine honour dwelleth.

9 Gather not my soul with sinners, nor my life with bloody men:

10 In whose hands *is* mischief, and their right hand is full of bribes.

11 But as for me, I will walk in mine integrity: redeem me, and be merciful unto me.

12 My foot standeth in an even place: in the congregations will I bless the LORD.

PSALM 27

A Psalm of David.

The LORD *is* my light and my salvation; whom shall I fear? the LORD *is* the strength of my life; of whom shall I be afraid?

2 When the wicked, *even* mine enemies and my foes, came upon me to eat up my flesh, they stumbled and fell.

3 Though an host should encamp against me, my heart shall not fear: though war should rise against me, in this *will* I *be* confident.

4 One *thing* have I desired of the LORD, that will I seek after; that I may dwell in the house of the LORD all the days of my life, to behold the beauty of the LORD, and to enquire in his temple.

5 For in the time of trouble he shall hide me in his pavilion: in the secret of his tabernacle shall he hide me; he shall set me up upon a rock.

6 And now shall mine head be lifted up above mine enemies round about me: therefore will I offer in his tabernacle sacrifices of joy; I will sing, yea, I will sing praises unto the LORD.

7 Hear, O LORD, *when* I cry with my voice: have mercy also upon me, and answer me.

8 *When thou saidst*, Seek ye my face; my heart said unto thee, Thy face, LORD, will I seek.

9 Hide not thy face *far* from me; put not thy servant away in anger: thou hast been my help; leave me not, neither forsake me, O God of my salvation.

10 When my father and my mother forsake me, then the LORD will take me up.

11 Teach me thy way, O LORD, and lead me in a plain path, because of mine enemies.

12 Deliver me not over unto the will of mine enemies: for false witnesses are risen up against me, and such as breathe out cruelty.

13 *I had fainted*, unless I had believed to see the goodness of the LORD in the land of the living.

14 Wait on the LORD: be of good courage, and he shall strengthen thine heart: wait, I say, on the LORD.

PSALM 28

A Psalm of David.

Unto thee will I cry, O LORD my rock; be not silent to me: lest, *if* thou be

silent to me, I become like them that go
down into the pit.
2 Hear the voice of my supplications,
when I cry unto thee, when I lift up my
hands toward thy holy oracle.
3 Draw me not away with the wicked,
and with the workers of iniquity, which
speak peace to their neighbours, but
mischief *is* in their hearts.
4 Give them according to their deeds,
and according to the wickedness of
their endeavours: give them after the
work of their hands; render to them
their desert.
5 Because they regard not the works
of the LORD, nor the operation of his
hands, he shall destroy them, and not
build them up.
6 Blessed *be* the LORD, because he
hath heard the voice of my supplications.
7 The LORD *is* my strength and my
shield; my heart trusted in him, and I
am helped: therefore my heart greatly
rejoiceth; and with my song will I
praise him.
8 The LORD *is* their strength, and he *is*
the saving strength of his anointed.
9 Save thy people, and bless thine
inheritance: feed them also, and lift
them up for ever.

PSALM 29

A Psalm of David.

Give unto the LORD, O ye mighty, give
unto the LORD glory and strength.
2 Give unto the LORD the glory due
unto his name; worship the LORD in the
beauty of holiness.
3 The voice of the LORD *is* upon the
waters: the God of glory thundereth:
the LORD *is* upon many waters.
4 The voice of the LORD *is* powerful;
the voice of the LORD *is* full of majesty.
5 The voice of the LORD breaketh the
cedars; yea, the LORD breaketh the
cedars of Lebanon.
6 He maketh them also to skip like a
calf; Lebanon and Sirion like a young
unicorn.
7 The voice of the LORD divideth the
flames of fire.
8 The voice of the LORD shaketh the
wilderness; the LORD shaketh the wilderness of Kadesh.
9 The voice of the LORD maketh the
hinds to calve, and discovereth the forests: and in his temple doth every one
speak of *his* glory.
10 The LORD sitteth upon the flood;
yea, the LORD sitteth King for ever.
11 The LORD will give strength unto
his people; the LORD will bless his people with peace.

PSALM 30

A Psalm *and* Song *at* the dedication of the house of David.

I will extol thee, O LORD; for thou hast
lifted me up, and hast not made my
foes to rejoice over me.
2 O LORD my God, I cried unto thee,
and thou hast healed me.
3 O LORD, thou hast brought up my
soul from the grave: thou hast kept me
alive, that I should not go down to the
pit.
4 Sing unto the LORD, O ye saints of
his, and give thanks at the remembrance of his holiness.
5 For his anger *endureth but* a
moment; in his favour *is* life: weeping
may endure for a night, but joy *cometh*
in the morning.
6 And in my prosperity I said, I shall
never be moved.

7 LORD, by thy favour thou hast made my mountain to stand strong: thou didst hide thy face, *and* I was troubled.

8 I cried to thee, O LORD; and unto the LORD I made supplication.

9 What profit *is there* in my blood, when I go down to the pit? Shall the dust praise thee? shall it declare thy truth?

10 Hear, O LORD, and have mercy upon me: LORD, be thou my helper.

11 Thou hast turned for me my mourning into dancing: thou hast put off my sackcloth, and girded me with gladness;

12 To the end that *my* glory may sing praise to thee, and not be silent. O LORD my God, I will give thanks unto thee for ever.

PSALM 31

To the chief Musician, A Psalm of David.

In thee, O LORD, do I put my trust; let me never be ashamed: deliver me in thy righteousness.

2 Bow down thine ear to me; deliver me speedily: be thou my strong rock, for an house of defence to save me.

3 For thou *art* my rock and my fortress; therefore for thy name's sake lead me, and guide me.

4 Pull me out of the net that they have laid privily for me: for thou *art* my strength.

5 Into thine hand I commit my spirit: thou hast redeemed me, O LORD God of truth.

6 I have hated them that regard lying vanities: but I trust in the LORD.

7 I will be glad and rejoice in thy mercy: for thou hast considered my trouble; thou hast known my soul in adversities;

8 And hast not shut me up into the hand of the enemy: thou hast set my feet in a large room.

9 Have mercy upon me, O LORD, for I am in trouble: mine eye is consumed with grief, *yea*, my soul and my belly.

10 For my life is spent with grief, and my years with sighing: my strength faileth because of mine iniquity, and my bones are consumed.

11 I was a reproach among all mine enemies, but especially among my neighbours, and a fear to mine acquaintance: they that did see me without fled from me.

12 I am forgotten as a dead man out of mind: I am like a broken vessel.

13 For I have heard the slander of many: fear *was* on every side: while they took counsel together against me, they devised to take away my life.

14 But I trusted in thee, O LORD: I said, Thou *art* my God.

15 My times *are* in thy hand: deliver me from the hand of mine enemies, and from them that persecute me.

16 Make thy face to shine upon thy servant: save me for thy mercies' sake.

17 Let me not be ashamed, O LORD; for I have called upon thee: let the wicked be ashamed, *and* let them be silent in the grave.

18 Let the lying lips be put to silence; which speak grievous things proudly and contemptuously against the righteous.

19 *Oh* how great *is* thy goodness, which thou hast laid up for them that fear thee; *which* thou hast wrought for them that trust in thee before the sons of men!

20 Thou shalt hide them in the secret of thy presence from the pride of man:

thou shalt keep them secretly in a pavilion from the strife of tongues.

21 Blessed *be* the LORD: for he hath shewed me his marvellous kindness in a strong city.

22 For I said in my haste, I am cut off from before thine eyes: nevertheless thou heardest the voice of my supplications when I cried unto thee.

23 O love the LORD, all ye his saints: *for* the LORD preserveth the faithful, and plentifully rewardeth the proud doer.

24 Be of good courage, and he shall strengthen your heart, all ye that hope in the LORD.

PSALM 32

A Psalm of David, Maschil.

Blessed *is he whose* transgression *is* forgiven, *whose* sin *is* covered.

2 Blessed *is* the man unto whom the LORD imputeth not iniquity, and in whose spirit *there is* no guile.

3 When I kept silence, my bones waxed old through my roaring all the day long.

4 For day and night thy hand was heavy upon me: my moisture is turned into the drought of summer. Selah.

5 I acknowledged my sin unto thee, and mine iniquity have I not hid. I said, I will confess my transgressions unto the LORD; and thou forgavest the iniquity of my sin. Selah.

6 For this shall every one that is godly pray unto thee in a time when thou mayest be found: surely in the floods of great waters they shall not come nigh unto him.

7 Thou *art* my hiding place; thou shalt preserve me from trouble; thou shalt compass me about with songs of deliverance. Selah.

8 I will instruct thee and teach thee in the way which thou shalt go: I will guide thee with mine eye.

9 Be ye not as the horse, *or* as the mule, *which* have no understanding: whose mouth must be held in with bit and bridle, lest they come near unto thee.

10 Many sorrows *shall be* to the wicked: but he that trusteth in the LORD, mercy shall compass him about.

11 Be glad in the LORD, and rejoice, ye righteous: and shout for joy, all *ye that are* upright in heart.

PSALM 33

Rejoice in the LORD, O ye righteous: *for* praise is comely for the upright.

2 Praise the LORD with harp: sing unto him with the psaltery *and* an instrument of ten strings.

3 Sing unto him a new song; play skilfully with a loud noise.

4 For the word of the LORD *is* right; and all his works *are done* in truth.

5 He loveth righteousness and judgment: the earth is full of the goodness of the LORD.

6 By the word of the LORD were the heavens made; and all the host of them by the breath of his mouth.

7 He gathereth the waters of the sea together as an heap: he layeth up the depth in storehouses.

8 Let all the earth fear the LORD: let all the inhabitants of the world stand in awe of him.

9 For he spake, and it was *done*; he commanded, and it stood fast.

10 The LORD bringeth the counsel of the heathen to nought: he maketh the devices of the people of none effect.

11 The counsel of the Lord standeth
for ever, the thoughts of his heart to all
generations.
12 Blessed *is* the nation whose God *is*
the Lord; *and* the people *whom* he
hath chosen for his own inheritance.
13 The Lord looketh from heaven; he
beholdeth all the sons of men.
14 From the place of his habitation he
looketh upon all the inhabitants of the
earth.
15 He fashioneth their hearts alike;
he considereth all their works.
16 There is no king saved by the multitude of an host: a mighty man is not
delivered by much strength.
17 An horse *is* a vain thing for safety:
neither shall he deliver *any* by his
great strength.
18 Behold, the eye of the Lord *is* upon
them that fear him, upon them that
hope in his mercy;
19 To deliver their soul from death,
and to keep them alive in famine.
20 Our soul waiteth for the Lord: he *is*
our help and our shield.
21 For our heart shall rejoice in him,
because we have trusted in his holy
name.
22 Let thy mercy, O Lord, be upon us,
according as we hope in thee.

PSALM 34

***A Psalm* of David, when he changed his behaviour before Abimelech; who drove him away, and he departed.**

I will bless the Lord at all times: his
praise *shall* continually *be* in my
mouth.
2 My soul shall make her boast in the
Lord: the humble shall hear *thereof*,
and be glad.
3 O magnify the Lord with me, and
let us exalt his name together.
4 I sought the Lord, and he heard me,
and delivered me from all my fears.
5 They looked unto him, and were
lightened: and their faces were not
ashamed.
6 This poor man cried, and the Lord
heard *him*, and saved him out of all his
troubles.
7 The angel of the Lord encampeth
round about them that fear him, and
delivereth them.
8 O taste and see that the Lord *is*
good: blessed *is* the man *that* trusteth
in him.
9 O fear the Lord, ye his saints: for
there is no want to them that fear him.
10 The young lions do lack, and suffer
hunger: but they that seek the Lord
shall not want any good *thing*.
11 Come, ye children, hearken unto
me: I will teach you the fear of the
Lord.
12 What man *is he that* desireth life,
and loveth *many* days, that he may see
good?
13 Keep thy tongue from evil, and thy
lips from speaking guile.
14 Depart from evil, and do good;
seek peace, and pursue it.
15 The eyes of the Lord *are* upon the
righteous, and his ears *are open* unto
their cry.
16 The face of the Lord *is* against
them that do evil, to cut off the remembrance of them from the earth.
17 *The righteous* cry, and the Lord
heareth, and delivereth them out of all
their troubles.
18 The Lord *is* nigh unto them that
are of a broken heart; and saveth such
as be of a contrite spirit.
19 Many *are* the afflictions of the
righteous: but the Lord delivereth him
out of them all.

20 He keepeth all his bones: not one of them is broken.

21 Evil shall slay the wicked: and they that hate the righteous shall be desolate.

22 The LORD redeemeth the soul of his servants: and none of them that trust in him shall be desolate.

PSALM 35

A Psalm of David.

Plead *my cause*, O LORD, with them that strive with me: fight against them that fight against me.

2 Take hold of shield and buckler, and stand up for mine help.

3 Draw out also the spear, and stop *the way* against them that persecute me: say unto my soul, I *am* thy salvation.

4 Let them be confounded and put to shame that seek after my soul: let them be turned back and brought to confusion that devise my hurt.

5 Let them be as chaff before the wind: and let the angel of the LORD chase *them*.

6 Let their way be dark and slippery: and let the angel of the LORD persecute them.

7 For without cause have they hid for me their net *in* a pit, *which* without cause they have digged for my soul.

8 Let destruction come upon him at unawares; and let his net that he hath hid catch himself: into that very destruction let him fall.

9 And my soul shall be joyful in the LORD: it shall rejoice in his salvation.

10 All my bones shall say, LORD, who *is* like unto thee, which deliverest the poor from him that is too strong for him, yea, the poor and the needy from him that spoileth him?

11 False witnesses did rise up; they laid to my charge *things* that I knew not.

12 They rewarded me evil for good *to* the spoiling of my soul.

13 But as for me, when they were sick, my clothing *was* sackcloth: I humbled my soul with fasting; and my prayer returned into mine own bosom.

14 I behaved myself as though *he had been* my friend *or* brother: I bowed down heavily, as one that mourneth *for his* mother.

15 But in mine adversity they rejoiced, and gathered themselves together: *yea*, the abjects gathered themselves together against me, and I knew *it* not; they did tear *me*, and ceased not:

16 With hypocritical mockers in feasts, they gnashed upon me with their teeth.

17 Lord, how long wilt thou look on? rescue my soul from their destructions, my darling from the lions.

18 I will give thee thanks in the great congregation: I will praise thee among much people.

19 Let not them that are mine enemies wrongfully rejoice over me: *neither* let them wink with the eye that hate me without a cause.

20 For they speak not peace: but they devise deceitful matters against *them that are* quiet in the land.

21 Yea, they opened their mouth wide against me, *and* said, Aha, aha, our eye hath seen *it*.

22 *This* thou hast seen, O LORD: keep not silence: O Lord, be not far from me.

23 Stir up thyself, and awake to my judgment, *even* unto my cause, my God and my Lord.

24 Judge me, O LORD my God, according to thy righteousness; and let them not rejoice over me.

25 Let them not say in their hearts, Ah, so would we have it: let them not say, We have swallowed him up.

26 Let them be ashamed and brought to confusion together that rejoice at mine hurt: let them be clothed with shame and dishonour that magnify *themselves* against me.

27 Let them shout for joy, and be glad, that favour my righteous cause: yea, let them say continually, Let the LORD be magnified, which hath pleasure in the prosperity of his servant.

28 And my tongue shall speak of thy righteousness *and* of thy praise all the day long.

PSALM 36

To the chief Musician, *A Psalm* of David the servant of the LORD.

The transgression of the wicked saith within my heart, *that there is* no fear of God before his eyes.

2 For he flattereth himself in his own eyes, until his iniquity be found to be hateful.

3 The words of his mouth *are* iniquity and deceit: he hath left off to be wise, *and* to do good.

4 He deviseth mischief upon his bed; he setteth himself in a way *that is* not good; he abhorreth not evil.

5 Thy mercy, O LORD, *is* in the heavens; *and* thy faithfulness *reacheth* unto the clouds.

6 Thy righteousness *is* like the great mountains; thy judgments *are* a great deep: O LORD, thou preservest man and beast.

7 How excellent *is* thy lovingkindness, O God! therefore the children of men put their trust under the shadow of thy wings.

8 They shall be abundantly satisfied with the fatness of thy house; and thou shalt make them drink of the river of thy pleasures.

9 For with thee *is* the fountain of life: in thy light shall we see light.

10 O continue thy lovingkindness unto them that know thee; and thy righteousness to the upright in heart.

11 Let not the foot of pride come against me, and let not the hand of the wicked remove me.

12 There are the workers of iniquity fallen: they are cast down, and shall not be able to rise.

PSALM 37

***A Psalm* of David.**

Fret not thyself because of evildoers, neither be thou envious against the workers of iniquity.

2 For they shall soon be cut down like the grass, and wither as the green herb.

3 Trust in the LORD, and do good; *so* shalt thou dwell in the land, and verily thou shalt be fed.

4 Delight thyself also in the LORD; and he shall give thee the desires of thine heart.

5 Commit thy way unto the LORD; trust also in him; and he shall bring *it* to pass.

6 And he shall bring forth thy righteousness as the light, and thy judgment as the noonday.

7 Rest in the LORD, and wait patiently for him: fret not thyself because of him who prospereth in his way, because of the man who bringeth wicked devices to pass.

8 Cease from anger, and forsake wrath: fret not thyself in any wise to do evil.

9 For evildoers shall be cut off: but those that wait upon the LORD, they shall inherit the earth.

10 For yet a little while, and the wicked *shall* not *be*: yea, thou shalt diligently consider his place, and it *shall* not *be*.

11 But the meek shall inherit the earth; and shall delight themselves in the abundance of peace.

12 The wicked plotteth against the just, and gnasheth upon him with his teeth.

13 The Lord shall laugh at him: for he seeth that his day is coming.

14 The wicked have drawn out the sword, and have bent their bow, to cast down the poor and needy, *and* to slay such as be of upright conversation.

15 Their sword shall enter into their own heart, and their bows shall be broken.

16 A little that a righteous man hath *is* better than the riches of many wicked.

17 For the arms of the wicked shall be broken: but the LORD upholdeth the righteous.

18 The LORD knoweth the days of the upright: and their inheritance shall be for ever.

19 They shall not be ashamed in the evil time: and in the days of famine they shall be satisfied.

20 But the wicked shall perish, and the enemies of the LORD *shall be* as the fat of lambs: they shall consume; into smoke shall they consume away.

21 The wicked borroweth, and payeth not again: but the righteous sheweth mercy, and giveth.

22 For *such as be* blessed of him shall inherit the earth; and *they that be* cursed of him shall be cut off.

23 The steps of a *good* man are ordered by the LORD: and he delighteth in his way.

24 Though he fall, he shall not be utterly cast down: for the LORD upholdeth *him with* his hand.

25 I have been young, and *now* am old; yet have I not seen the righteous forsaken, nor his seed begging bread.

26 *He is* ever merciful, and lendeth; and his seed *is* blessed.

27 Depart from evil, and do good; and dwell for evermore.

28 For the LORD loveth judgment, and forsaketh not his saints; they are preserved for ever: but the seed of the wicked shall be cut off.

29 The righteous shall inherit the land, and dwell therein for ever.

30 The mouth of the righteous speaketh wisdom, and his tongue talketh of judgment.

31 The law of his God *is* in his heart; none of his steps shall slide.

32 The wicked watcheth the righteous, and seeketh to slay him.

33 The LORD will not leave him in his hand, nor condemn him when he is judged.

34 Wait on the LORD, and keep his way, and he shall exalt thee to inherit the land: when the wicked are cut off, thou shalt see *it*.

35 I have seen the wicked in great power, and spreading himself like a green bay tree.

36 Yet he passed away, and, lo, he *was* not: yea, I sought him, but he could not be found.

37 Mark the perfect *man*, and behold the upright: for the end of *that* man *is* peace.

38 But the transgressors shall be destroyed together: the end of the wicked shall be cut off.

39 But the salvation of the righteous *is* of the LORD: *he is* their strength in the time of trouble.

40 And the LORD shall help them, and deliver them: he shall deliver them from the wicked, and save them, because they trust in him.

PSALM 38

A Psalm of David, to bring to remembrance.

O LORD, rebuke me not in thy wrath: neither chasten me in thy hot displeasure.

2 For thine arrows stick fast in me, and thy hand presseth me sore.

3 *There is* no soundness in my flesh because of thine anger; neither *is there any* rest in my bones because of my sin.

4 For mine iniquities are gone over mine head: as an heavy burden they are too heavy for me.

5 My wounds stink *and* are corrupt because of my foolishness.

6 I am troubled; I am bowed down greatly; I go mourning all the day long.

7 For my loins are filled with a loathsome *disease*: and *there is* no soundness in my flesh.

8 I am feeble and sore broken: I have roared by reason of the disquietness of my heart.

9 Lord, all my desire *is* before thee; and my groaning is not hid from thee.

10 My heart panteth, my strength faileth me: as for the light of mine eyes, it also is gone from me.

11 My lovers and my friends stand aloof from my sore; and my kinsmen stand afar off.

12 They also that seek after my life lay snares *for me*: and they that seek my hurt speak mischievous things, and imagine deceits all the day long.

13 But I, as a deaf *man*, heard not; and *I was* as a dumb man *that* openeth not his mouth.

14 Thus I was as a man that heareth not, and in whose mouth *are* no reproofs.

15 For in thee, O LORD, do I hope: thou wilt hear, O Lord my God.

16 For I said, *Hear me*, lest *otherwise* they should rejoice over me: when my foot slippeth, they magnify *themselves* against me.

17 For I *am* ready to halt, and my sorrow *is* continually before me.

18 For I will declare mine iniquity; I will be sorry for my sin.

19 But mine enemies *are* lively, *and* they are strong: and they that hate me wrongfully are multiplied.

20 They also that render evil for good are mine adversaries; because I follow *the thing that* good *is*.

21 Forsake me not, O LORD: O my God, be not far from me.

22 Make haste to help me, O Lord my salvation.

PSALM 39

To the chief Musician, *even* to Jeduthun, A Psalm of David.

I said, I will take heed to my ways, that I sin not with my tongue: I will keep my mouth with a bridle, while the wicked is before me.

2 I was dumb with silence, I held my peace, *even* from good; and my sorrow was stirred.

3 My heart was hot within me, while I was musing the fire burned: *then* spake I with my tongue,

4 LORD, make me to know mine end, and the measure of my days, what it *is*; *that* I may know how frail I *am*.

5 Behold, thou hast made my days *as* an handbreadth; and mine age *is* as nothing before thee: verily every man at his best state *is* altogether vanity. Selah.

6 Surely every man walketh in a vain shew: surely they are disquieted in vain: he heapeth up *riches*, and knoweth not who shall gather them.

7 And now, Lord, what wait I for? my hope *is* in thee.

8 Deliver me from all my transgressions: make me not the reproach of the foolish.

9 I was dumb, I opened not my mouth; because thou didst *it*.

10 Remove thy stroke away from me: I am consumed by the blow of thine hand.

11 When thou with rebukes dost correct man for iniquity, thou makest his beauty to consume away like a moth: surely every man *is* vanity. Selah.

12 Hear my prayer, O LORD, and give ear unto my cry; hold not thy peace at my tears: for I *am* a stranger with thee, *and* a sojourner, as all my fathers *were*.

13 O spare me, that I may recover strength, before I go hence, and be no more.

PSALM 40

To the chief Musician, A Psalm of David.

I waited patiently for the LORD; and he inclined unto me, and heard my cry.

2 He brought me up also out of an horrible pit, out of the miry clay, and set my feet upon a rock, *and* established my goings.

3 And he hath put a new song in my mouth, *even* praise unto our God: many shall see *it*, and fear, and shall trust in the LORD.

4 Blessed *is* that man that maketh the LORD his trust, and respecteth not the proud, nor such as turn aside to lies.

5 Many, O LORD my God, *are* thy wonderful works *which* thou hast done, and thy thoughts *which are* to us-ward: they cannot be reckoned up in order unto thee: *if* I would declare and speak *of them*, they are more than can be numbered.

6 Sacrifice and offering thou didst not desire; mine ears hast thou opened: burnt offering and sin offering hast thou not required.

7 Then said I, Lo, I come: in the volume of the book *it is* written of me,

8 I delight to do thy will, O my God: yea, thy law *is* within my heart.

9 I have preached righteousness in the great congregation: lo, I have not refrained my lips, O LORD, thou knowest.

10 I have not hid thy righteousness within my heart; I have declared thy faithfulness and thy salvation: I have not concealed thy lovingkindness and thy truth from the great congregation.

11 Withhold not thou thy tender mercies from me, O LORD: let thy lovingkindness and thy truth continually preserve me.

12 For innumerable evils have compassed me about: mine iniquities have taken hold upon me, so that I am not able to look up; they are more than the hairs of mine head: therefore my heart faileth me.

13 Be pleased, O LORD, to deliver me:
O LORD, make haste to help me.
14 Let them be ashamed and confounded together that seek after my
soul to destroy it; let them be driven
backward and put to shame that wish
me evil.
15 Let them be desolate for a reward
of their shame that say unto me, Aha,
aha.
16 Let all those that seek thee rejoice
and be glad in thee: let such as love thy
salvation say continually, The LORD be
magnified.
17 But I *am* poor and needy; *yet* the
Lord thinketh upon me: thou *art* my
help and my deliverer; make no tarrying, O my God.

PSALM 41

To the chief Musician, A Psalm of David.

Blessed *is* he that considereth the
poor: the LORD will deliver him in
time of trouble.
2 The LORD will preserve him, and
keep him alive; *and* he shall be blessed
upon the earth: and thou wilt not
deliver him unto the will of his enemies.
3 The LORD will strengthen him upon
the bed of languishing: thou wilt make
all his bed in his sickness.
4 I said, LORD, be merciful unto me:
heal my soul; for I have sinned against
thee.
5 Mine enemies speak evil of me,
When shall he die, and his name perish?
6 And if he come to see *me*, he speaketh vanity: his heart gathereth iniquity to itself; *when* he goeth abroad, he
telleth *it*.
7 All that hate me whisper together
against me: against me do they devise
my hurt.
8 An evil disease, *say they*, cleaveth
fast unto him: and *now* that he lieth he
shall rise up no more.
9 Yea, mine own familiar friend, in
whom I trusted, which did eat of my
bread, hath lifted up *his* heel against
me.
10 But thou, O LORD, be merciful unto
me, and raise me up, that I may requite
them.
11 By this I know that thou favourest
me, because mine enemy doth not triumph over me.
12 And as for me, thou upholdest me
in mine integrity, and settest me before
thy face for ever.
13 Blessed *be* the LORD God of Israel
from everlasting, and to everlasting.
Amen, and Amen.

PSALM 42

To the chief Musician, Maschil, for the sons of Korah.

As the hart panteth after the water
brooks, so panteth my soul after
thee, O God.
2 My soul thirsteth for God, for the
living God: when shall I come and
appear before God?
3 My tears have been my meat day
and night, while they continually say
unto me, Where *is* thy God?
4 When I remember these *things*, I
pour out my soul in me: for I had gone
with the multitude, I went with them to
the house of God, with the voice of joy
and praise, with a multitude that kept
holyday.
5 Why art thou cast down, O my soul?
and *why* art thou disquieted in me?

hope thou in God: for I shall yet praise him *for* the help of his countenance.

6 O my God, my soul is cast down within me: therefore will I remember thee from the land of Jordan, and of the Hermonites, from the hill Mizar.

7 Deep calleth unto deep at the noise of thy waterspouts: all thy waves and thy billows are gone over me.

8 *Yet* the LORD will command his lovingkindness in the daytime, and in the night his song *shall be* with me, *and* my prayer unto the God of my life.

9 I will say unto God my rock, Why hast thou forgotten me? why go I mourning because of the oppression of the enemy?

10 *As* with a sword in my bones, mine enemies reproach me; while they say daily unto me, Where *is* thy God?

11 Why art thou cast down, O my soul? and why art thou disquieted within me? hope thou in God: for I shall yet praise him, *who is* the health of my countenance, and my God.

PSALM 43

Judge me, O God, and plead my cause against an ungodly nation: O deliver me from the deceitful and unjust man.

2 For thou *art* the God of my strength: why dost thou cast me off? why go I mourning because of the oppression of the enemy?

3 O send out thy light and thy truth: let them lead me; let them bring me unto thy holy hill, and to thy tabernacles.

4 Then will I go unto the altar of God, unto God my exceeding joy: yea, upon the harp will I praise thee, O God my God.

5 Why art thou cast down, O my soul? and why art thou disquieted within me? hope in God: for I shall yet praise him, *who is* the health of my countenance, and my God.

PSALM 44

To the chief Musician for the sons of Korah, Maschil.

We have heard with our ears, O God, our fathers have told us, *what* work thou didst in their days, in the times of old.

2 *How* thou didst drive out the heathen with thy hand, and plantedst them; *how* thou didst afflict the people, and cast them out.

3 For they got not the land in possession by their own sword, neither did their own arm save them: but thy right hand, and thine arm, and the light of thy countenance, because thou hadst a favour unto them.

4 Thou art my King, O God: command deliverances for Jacob.

5 Through thee will we push down our enemies: through thy name will we tread them under that rise up against us.

6 For I will not trust in my bow, neither shall my sword save me.

7 But thou hast saved us from our enemies, and hast put them to shame that hated us.

8 In God we boast all the day long, and praise thy name for ever. Selah.

9 But thou hast cast off, and put us to shame; and goest not forth with our armies.

10 Thou makest us to turn back from the enemy: and they which hate us spoil for themselves.

11 Thou hast given us like sheep *appointed* for meat; and hast scattered us among the heathen.

12 Thou sellest thy people for nought, and dost not increase *thy wealth* by their price.

13 Thou makest us a reproach to our neighbours, a scorn and a derision to them that are round about us.

14 Thou makest us a byword among the heathen, a shaking of the head among the people.

15 My confusion *is* continually before me, and the shame of my face hath covered me,

16 For the voice of him that reproacheth and blasphemeth; by reason of the enemy and avenger.

17 All this is come upon us; yet have we not forgotten thee, neither have we dealt falsely in thy covenant.

18 Our heart is not turned back, neither have our steps declined from thy way;

19 Though thou hast sore broken us in the place of dragons, and covered us with the shadow of death.

20 If we have forgotten the name of our God, or stretched out our hands to a strange god;

21 Shall not God search this out? for he knoweth the secrets of the heart.

22 Yea, for thy sake are we killed all the day long; we are counted as sheep for the slaughter.

23 Awake, why sleepest thou, O Lord? arise, cast *us* not off for ever.

24 Wherefore hidest thou thy face, *and* forgettest our affliction and our oppression?

25 For our soul is bowed down to the dust: our belly cleaveth unto the earth.

26 Arise for our help, and redeem us for thy mercies' sake.

PSALM 45

To the chief Musician upon Shoshannim, for the sons of Korah, Maschil, A Song of loves.

My heart is inditing a good matter: I speak of the things which I have made touching the king: my tongue *is* the pen of a ready writer.

2 Thou art fairer than the children of men: grace is poured into thy lips: therefore God hath blessed thee for ever.

3 Gird thy sword upon *thy* thigh, O *most* mighty, with thy glory and thy majesty.

4 And in thy majesty ride prosperously because of truth and meekness *and* righteousness; and thy right hand shall teach thee terrible things.

5 Thine arrows *are* sharp in the heart of the king's enemies; *whereby* the people fall under thee.

6 Thy throne, O God, *is* for ever and ever: the sceptre of thy kingdom *is* a right sceptre.

7 Thou lovest righteousness, and hatest wickedness: therefore God, thy God, hath anointed thee with the oil of gladness above thy fellows.

8 All thy garments *smell* of myrrh, and aloes, *and* cassia, out of the ivory palaces, whereby they have made thee glad.

9 Kings' daughters *were* among thy honourable women: upon thy right hand did stand the queen in gold of Ophir.

10 Hearken, O daughter, and consider, and incline thine ear; forget also thine own people, and thy father's house;

11 So shall the king greatly desire thy beauty: for he *is* thy Lord; and worship thou him.

12 And the daughter of Tyre *shall be there* with a gift; *even* the rich among the people shall intreat thy favour.

13 The king's daughter *is* all glorious within: her clothing *is* of wrought gold.

14 She shall be brought unto the king in raiment of needlework: the virgins her companions that follow her shall be brought unto thee.

15 With gladness and rejoicing shall they be brought: they shall enter into the king's palace.

16 Instead of thy fathers shall be thy children, whom thou mayest make princes in all the earth.

17 I will make thy name to be remembered in all generations: therefore shall the people praise thee for ever and ever.

PSALM 46

To the chief Musician for the sons of Korah, A Song upon Alamoth.

God *is* our refuge and strength, a very present help in trouble.

2 Therefore will not we fear, though the earth be removed, and though the mountains be carried into the midst of the sea;

3 *Though* the waters thereof roar *and* be troubled, *though* the mountains shake with the swelling thereof. Selah.

4 *There is* a river, the streams whereof shall make glad the city of God, the holy *place* of the tabernacles of the most High.

5 God *is* in the midst of her; she shall not be moved: God shall help her, *and that* right early.

6 The heathen raged, the kingdoms were moved: he uttered his voice, the earth melted.

7 The LORD of hosts *is* with us; the God of Jacob *is* our refuge. Selah.

8 Come, behold the works of the LORD, what desolations he hath made in the earth.

9 He maketh wars to cease unto the end of the earth; he breaketh the bow, and cutteth the spear in sunder; he burneth the chariot in the fire.

10 Be still, and know that I *am* God: I will be exalted among the heathen, I will be exalted in the earth.

11 The LORD of hosts *is* with us; the God of Jacob *is* our refuge. Selah.

PSALM 47

To the chief Musician, A Psalm for the sons of Korah.

O clap your hands, all ye people; shout unto God with the voice of triumph.

2 For the LORD most high *is* terrible; *he is* a great King over all the earth.

3 He shall subdue the people under us, and the nations under our feet.

4 He shall choose our inheritance for us, the excellency of Jacob whom he loved. Selah.

5 God is gone up with a shout, the LORD with the sound of a trumpet.

6 Sing praises to God, sing praises: sing praises unto our King, sing praises.

7 For God *is* the King of all the earth: sing ye praises with understanding.

8 God reigneth over the heathen: God sitteth upon the throne of his holiness.

9 The princes of the people are gathered together, *even* the people of the God of Abraham: for the shields of the earth *belong* unto God: he is greatly exalted.

PSALM 48

A Song *and* Psalm for the sons of Korah.

Great *is* the LORD, and greatly to be praised in the city of our God, *in* the mountain of his holiness.

2 Beautiful for situation, the joy of the whole earth, *is* mount Zion, *on* the sides of the north, the city of the great King.

3 God is known in her palaces for a refuge.

4 For, lo, the kings were assembled, they passed by together.

5 They saw *it, and* so they marvelled; they were troubled, *and* hasted away.

6 Fear took hold upon them there, *and* pain, as of a woman in travail.

7 Thou breakest the ships of Tarshish with an east wind.

8 As we have heard, so have we seen in the city of the LORD of hosts, in the city of our God: God will establish it for ever. Selah.

9 We have thought of thy lovingkindness, O God, in the midst of thy temple.

10 According to thy name, O God, so *is* thy praise unto the ends of the earth: thy right hand is full of righteousness.

11 Let mount Zion rejoice, let the daughters of Judah be glad, because of thy judgments.

12 Walk about Zion, and go round about her: tell the towers thereof.

13 Mark ye well her bulwarks, consider her palaces; that ye may tell *it* to the generation following.

14 For this God *is* our God for ever and ever: he will be our guide *even* unto death.

PSALM 49

To the chief Musician,
A Psalm for the sons of Korah.

Hear this, all *ye* people; give ear, all *ye* inhabitants of the world:

2 Both low and high, rich and poor, together.

3 My mouth shall speak of wisdom; and the meditation of my heart *shall be* of understanding.

4 I will incline mine ear to a parable: I will open my dark saying upon the harp.

5 Wherefore should I fear in the days of evil, *when* the iniquity of my heels shall compass me about?

6 They that trust in their wealth, and boast themselves in the multitude of their riches;

7 None *of them* can by any means redeem his brother, nor give to God a ransom for him:

8 (For the redemption of their soul *is* precious, and it ceaseth for ever:)

9 That he should still live for ever, *and* not see corruption.

10 For he seeth *that* wise men die, likewise the fool and the brutish person perish, and leave their wealth to others.

11 Their inward thought *is, that* their houses *shall continue* for ever, *and* their dwelling places to all generations; they call *their* lands after their own names.

12 Nevertheless man *being* in honour abideth not: he is like the beasts *that* perish.

13 This their way *is* their folly: yet their posterity approve their sayings. Selah.

14 Like sheep they are laid in the grave; death shall feed on them; and the upright shall have dominion over them in the morning; and their beauty

shall consume in the grave from their
dwelling.
15 But God will redeem my soul from
the power of the grave: for he shall
receive me. Selah.
16 Be not thou afraid when one is
made rich, when the glory of his house
is increased;
17 For when he dieth he shall carry
nothing away: his glory shall not
descend after him.
18 Though while he lived he blessed
his soul: and *men* will praise thee,
when thou doest well to thyself.
19 He shall go to the generation of his
fathers; they shall never see light.
20 Man *that is* in honour, and understandeth not, is like the beasts *that*
perish.

PSALM 50

A Psalm of Asaph.

The mighty God, *even* the LORD, hath
spoken, and called the earth from
the rising of the sun unto the going
down thereof.
2 Out of Zion, the perfection of beauty, God hath shined.
3 Our God shall come, and shall not
keep silence: a fire shall devour before
him, and it shall be very tempestuous
round about him.
4 He shall call to the heavens from
above, and to the earth, that he may
judge his people.
5 Gather my saints together unto me;
those that have made a covenant with
me by sacrifice.
6 And the heavens shall declare his
righteousness: for God *is* judge himself.
Selah.
7 Hear, O my people, and I will speak;
O Israel, and I will testify against thee:
I *am* God, *even* thy God.
8 I will not reprove thee for thy sacrifices or thy burnt offerings, *to have
been* continually before me.
9 I will take no bullock out of thy
house, *nor* he goats out of thy folds.
10 For every beast of the forest *is*
mine, *and* the cattle upon a thousand
hills.
11 I know all the fowls of the mountains: and the wild beasts of the field
are mine.
12 If I were hungry, I would not tell
thee: for the world *is* mine, and the fulness thereof.
13 Will I eat the flesh of bulls, or
drink the blood of goats?
14 Offer unto God thanksgiving; and
pay thy vows unto the most High:
15 And call upon me in the day of
trouble: I will deliver thee, and thou
shalt glorify me.
16 But unto the wicked God saith,
What hast thou to do to declare my
statutes, or *that* thou shouldest take
my covenant in thy mouth?
17 Seeing thou hatest instruction, and
castest my words behind thee.
18 When thou sawest a thief, then
thou consentedst with him, and hast
been partaker with adulterers.
19 Thou givest thy mouth to evil, and
thy tongue frameth deceit.
20 Thou sittest *and* speakest against
thy brother; thou slanderest thine own
mother's son.
21 These *things* hast thou done, and I
kept silence; thou thoughtest that I was
altogether *such an one* as thyself: *but* I
will reprove thee, and set *them* in order
before thine eyes.

22 Now consider this, ye that forget God, lest I tear *you* in pieces, and *there be* none to deliver.

23 Whoso offereth praise glorifieth me: and to him that ordereth *his* conversation *aright* will I shew the salvation of God.

PSALM 51

To the chief Musician, A Psalm of David, when Nathan the prophet came unto him, after he had gone in to Bath-sheba.

Have mercy upon me, O God, according to thy lovingkindness: according unto the multitude of thy tender mercies blot out my transgressions.

2 Wash me throughly from mine iniquity, and cleanse me from my sin.

3 For I acknowledge my transgressions: and my sin *is* ever before me.

4 Against thee, thee only, have I sinned, and done *this* evil in thy sight: that thou mightest be justified when thou speakest, *and* be clear when thou judgest.

5 Behold, I was shapen in iniquity; and in sin did my mother conceive me.

6 Behold, thou desirest truth in the inward parts: and in the hidden *part* thou shalt make me to know wisdom.

7 Purge me with hyssop, and I shall be clean: wash me, and I shall be whiter than snow.

8 Make me to hear joy and gladness; *that* the bones *which* thou hast broken may rejoice.

9 Hide thy face from my sins, and blot out all mine iniquities.

10 Create in me a clean heart, O God; and renew a right spirit within me.

11 Cast me not away from thy presence; and take not thy holy spirit from me.

12 Restore unto me the joy of thy salvation; and uphold me *with thy* free spirit.

13 *Then* will I teach transgressors thy ways; and sinners shall be converted unto thee.

14 Deliver me from bloodguiltiness, O God, thou God of my salvation: *and* my tongue shall sing aloud of thy righteousness.

15 O Lord, open thou my lips; and my mouth shall shew forth thy praise.

16 For thou desirest not sacrifice; else would I give *it*: thou delightest not in burnt offering.

17 The sacrifices of God *are* a broken spirit: a broken and a contrite heart, O God, thou wilt not despise.

18 Do good in thy good pleasure unto Zion: build thou the walls of Jerusalem.

19 Then shalt thou be pleased with the sacrifices of righteousness, with burnt offering and whole burnt offering: then shall they offer bullocks upon thine altar.

PSALM 52

To the chief Musician, Maschil, *A Psalm* of David, when Doeg the Edomite came and told Saul, and said unto him, David is come to the house of Ahimelech.

Why boastest thou thyself in mischief, O mighty man? the goodness of God *endureth* continually.

2 Thy tongue deviseth mischiefs; like a sharp razor, working deceitfully.

3 Thou lovest evil more than good; *and* lying rather than to speak righteousness. Selah.

4 Thou lovest all devouring words, O *thou* deceitful tongue.

5 God shall likewise destroy thee for ever, he shall take thee away, and pluck thee out of *thy* dwelling place, and root thee out of the land of the living. Selah.

6 The righteous also shall see, and fear, and shall laugh at him:

7 Lo, *this is* the man *that* made not God his strength; but trusted in the abundance of his riches, *and* strengthened himself in his wickedness.

8 But I *am* like a green olive tree in the house of God: I trust in the mercy of God for ever and ever.

9 I will praise thee for ever, because thou hast done *it*: and I will wait on thy name; for *it is* good before thy saints.

PSALM 53

To the chief Musician upon Mahalath, Maschil, *A Psalm* of David.

The fool hath said in his heart, *There is* no God. Corrupt are they, and have done abominable iniquity: *there is* none that doeth good.

2 God looked down from heaven upon the children of men, to see if there were *any* that did understand, that did seek God.

3 Every one of them is gone back: they are altogether become filthy; *there is* none that doeth good, no, not one.

4 Have the workers of iniquity no knowledge? who eat up my people *as* they eat bread: they have not called upon God.

5 There were they in great fear, *where* no fear was: for God hath scattered the bones of him that encampeth *against* thee: thou hast put *them* to shame, because God hath despised them.

6 Oh that the salvation of Israel *were come* out of Zion! When God bringeth back the captivity of his people, Jacob shall rejoice, *and* Israel shall be glad.

PSALM 54

To the chief Musician on Neginoth, Maschil, *A Psalm* of David, when the Ziphims came and said to Saul, Doth not David hide himself with us?

Save me, O God, by thy name, and judge me by thy strength.

2 Hear my prayer, O God; give ear to the words of my mouth.

3 For strangers are risen up against me, and oppressors seek after my soul: they have not set God before them. Selah.

4 Behold, God *is* mine helper: the Lord *is* with them that uphold my soul.

5 He shall reward evil unto mine enemies: cut them off in thy truth.

6 I will freely sacrifice unto thee: I will praise thy name, O LORD; for *it is* good.

7 For he hath delivered me out of all trouble: and mine eye hath seen *his desire* upon mine enemies.

PSALM 55

To the chief Musician on Neginoth, Maschil, *A Psalm* of David.

Give ear to my prayer, O God; and hide not thyself from my supplication.

2 Attend unto me, and hear me: I mourn in my complaint, and make a noise;

3 Because of the voice of the enemy, because of the oppression of the wicked: for they cast iniquity upon me, and in wrath they hate me.

4 My heart is sore pained within me: and the terrors of death are fallen upon me.

5 Fearfulness and trembling are come
upon me, and horror hath overwhelmed
me.
6 And I said, Oh that I had wings like
a dove! *for then* would I fly away, and
be at rest.
7 Lo, *then* would I wander far off, *and*
remain in the wilderness. Selah.
8 I would hasten my escape from the
windy storm *and* tempest.
9 Destroy, O Lord, *and* divide their
tongues: for I have seen violence and
strife in the city.
10 Day and night they go about it
upon the walls thereof: mischief also
and sorrow *are* in the midst of it.
11 Wickedness *is* in the midst thereof:
deceit and guile depart not from her
streets.
12 For *it was* not an enemy *that*
reproached me; then I could have
borne *it*: neither *was it* he that hated
me *that* did magnify *himself* against
me; then I would have hid myself from
him:
13 But *it was* thou, a man mine equal,
my guide, and mine acquaintance.
14 We took sweet counsel together,
and walked unto the house of God in
company.
15 Let death seize upon them, *and* let
them go down quick into hell: for wickedness *is* in their dwellings, *and* among
them.
16 As for me, I will call upon God; and
the LORD shall save me.
17 Evening, and morning, and at
noon, will I pray, and cry aloud: and he
shall hear my voice.
18 He hath delivered my soul in
peace from the battle *that was* against
me: for there were many with me.
19 God shall hear, and afflict them,
even he that abideth of old. Selah.
Because they have no changes, therefore they fear not God.
20 He hath put forth his hands against
such as be at peace with him: he hath
broken his covenant.
21 *The words* of his mouth were
smoother than butter, but war *was* in
his heart: his words were softer than oil,
yet *were* they drawn swords.
22 Cast thy burden upon the LORD,
and he shall sustain thee: he shall
never suffer the righteous to be moved.
23 But thou, O God, shalt bring them
down into the pit of destruction: bloody
and deceitful men shall not live out
half their days; but I will trust in thee.

PSALM 56

To the chief Musician upon Jonathelem-rechokim, Michtam of David, when the Philistines took him in Gath.

Be merciful unto me, O God: for man
would swallow me up; he fighting
daily oppresseth me.
2 Mine enemies would daily swallow
me up: for *they be* many that fight
against me, O thou most High.
3 What time I am afraid, I will trust in
thee.
4 In God I will praise his word, in God
I have put my trust; I will not fear what
flesh can do unto me.
5 Every day they wrest my words: all
their thoughts *are* against me for evil.
6 They gather themselves together,
they hide themselves, they mark my
steps, when they wait for my soul.
7 Shall they escape by iniquity? in
thine anger cast down the people, O
God.
8 Thou tellest my wanderings: put
thou my tears into thy bottle: *are they*
not in thy book?

9 When I cry *unto thee*, then shall mine enemies turn back: this I know; for God *is* for me.

10 In God will I praise *his* word: in the LORD will I praise *his* word.

11 In God have I put my trust: I will not be afraid what man can do unto me.

12 Thy vows *are* upon me, O God: I will render praises unto thee.

13 For thou hast delivered my soul from death: *wilt* not *thou deliver* my feet from falling, that I may walk before God in the light of the living?

PSALM 57

To the chief Musician, Al-taschith, Michtam of David, when he fled from Saul in the cave.

Be merciful unto me, O God, be merciful unto me: for my soul trusteth in thee: yea, in the shadow of thy wings will I make my refuge, until *these* calamities be overpast.

2 I will cry unto God most high; unto God that performeth *all things* for me.

3 He shall send from heaven, and save me *from* the reproach of him that would swallow me up. Selah. God shall send forth his mercy and his truth.

4 My soul *is* among lions: *and* I lie *even among* them that are set on fire, *even* the sons of men, whose teeth *are* spears and arrows, and their tongue a sharp sword.

5 Be thou exalted, O God, above the heavens; *let* thy glory *be* above all the earth.

6 They have prepared a net for my steps; my soul is bowed down: they have digged a pit before me, into the midst whereof they are fallen *themselves*. Selah.

7 My heart is fixed, O God, my heart is fixed: I will sing and give praise.

8 Awake up, my glory; awake, psaltery and harp: I *myself* will awake early.

9 I will praise thee, O Lord, among the people: I will sing unto thee among the nations.

10 For thy mercy *is* great unto the heavens, and thy truth unto the clouds.

11 Be thou exalted, O God, above the heavens: *let* thy glory *be* above all the earth.

PSALM 58

To the chief Musician, Altaschith, Michtam of David.

Do ye indeed speak righteousness, O congregation? do ye judge uprightly, O ye sons of men?

2 Yea, in heart ye work wickedness; ye weigh the violence of your hands in the earth.

3 The wicked are estranged from the womb: they go astray as soon as they be born, speaking lies.

4 Their poison *is* like the poison of a serpent: *they are* like the deaf adder *that* stoppeth her ear;

5 Which will not hearken to the voice of charmers, charming never so wisely.

6 Break their teeth, O God, in their mouth: break out the great teeth of the young lions, O LORD.

7 Let them melt away as waters *which* run continually: *when* he bendeth *his bow to shoot* his arrows, let them be as cut in pieces.

8 As a snail *which* melteth, let *every one of them* pass away: *like* the untimely birth of a woman, *that* they may not see the sun.

9 Before your pots can feel the thorns, he shall take them away as with a whirlwind, both living, and in *his* wrath.

10 The righteous shall rejoice when
he seeth the vengeance: he shall wash
his feet in the blood of the wicked.
11 So that a man shall say, Verily *there*
is a reward for the righteous: verily he
is a God that judgeth in the earth.

PSALM 59

To the chief Musician, Al-taschith, Michtam of David; when Saul sent, and they watched the house to kill him.

Deliver me from mine enemies, O my
God: defend me from them that rise
up against me.
2 Deliver me from the workers of
iniquity, and save me from bloody men.
3 For, lo, they lie in wait for my soul:
the mighty are gathered against me;
not *for* my transgression, nor *for* my sin,
O LORD.
4 They run and prepare themselves
without *my* fault: awake to help me,
and behold.
5 Thou therefore, O LORD God of
hosts, the God of Israel, awake to visit
all the heathen: be not merciful to any
wicked transgressors. Selah.
6 They return at evening: they make a
noise like a dog, and go round about the
city.
7 Behold, they belch out with their
mouth: swords *are* in their lips: for who,
say they, doth hear?
8 But thou, O LORD, shalt laugh at
them; thou shalt have all the heathen
in derision.
9 *Because of* his strength will I wait
upon thee: for God *is* my defence.
10 The God of my mercy shall prevent
me: God shall let me see *my desire*
upon mine enemies.
11 Slay them not, lest my people forget: scatter them by thy power; and
bring them down, O Lord our shield.
12 *For* the sin of their mouth *and* the
words of their lips let them even be
taken in their pride: and for cursing
and lying *which* they speak.
13 Consume *them* in wrath, consume
them, that they *may* not *be*: and let
them know that God ruleth in Jacob
unto the ends of the earth. Selah.
14 And at evening let them return;
and let them make a noise like a dog,
and go round about the city.
15 Let them wander up and down for
meat, and grudge if they be not satisfied.
16 But I will sing of thy power; yea, I
will sing aloud of thy mercy in the
morning: for thou hast been my defence
and refuge in the day of my trouble.
17 Unto thee, O my strength, will I
sing: for God *is* my defence, *and* the
God of my mercy.

PSALM 60

To the chief Musician upon Shushan-eduth, Michtam of David, to teach; when he strove with Aram-naharaim and with Aram-zobah, when Joab returned, and smote of Edom in the valley of salt twelve thousand.

O God, thou hast cast us off, thou hast
scattered us, thou hast been displeased; O turn thyself to us again.
2 Thou hast made the earth to tremble; thou hast broken it: heal the
breaches thereof; for it shaketh.
3 Thou hast shewed thy people hard
things: thou hast made us to drink the
wine of astonishment.
4 Thou hast given a banner to them
that fear thee, that it may be displayed
because of the truth. Selah.
5 That thy beloved may be delivered;
save *with* thy right hand, and hear me.

6 God hath spoken in his holiness; I
will rejoice, I will divide Shechem, and
mete out the valley of Succoth.
7 Gilead *is* mine, and Manasseh *is*
mine; Ephraim also *is* the strength of
mine head; Judah *is* my lawgiver;
8 Moab *is* my washpot; over Edom
will I cast out my shoe: Philistia, triumph thou because of me.
9 Who will bring me *into* the strong
city? who will lead me into Edom?
10 *Wilt* not thou, O God, *which* hadst
cast us off? and *thou*, O God, *which*
didst not go out with our armies?
11 Give us help from trouble: for vain
is the help of man.
12 Through God we shall do valiantly:
for he *it is that* shall tread down our
enemies.

PSALM 61

To the chief Musician upon Neginah, *A Psalm* of David.

Hear my cry, O God; attend unto my
prayer.
2 From the end of the earth will I cry
unto thee, when my heart is overwhelmed: lead me to the rock *that* is
higher than I.
3 For thou hast been a shelter for me,
and a strong tower from the enemy.
4 I will abide in thy tabernacle for
ever: I will trust in the covert of thy
wings. Selah.
5 For thou, O God, hast heard my
vows: thou hast given *me* the heritage
of those that fear thy name.
6 Thou wilt prolong the king's life:
and his years as many generations.
7 He shall abide before God for ever:
O prepare mercy and truth, *which* may
preserve him.
8 So will I sing praise unto thy name
for ever, that I may daily perform my
vows.

PSALM 62

To the chief Musician, to Jeduthun, A Psalm of David.

Truly my soul waiteth upon God: from
him *cometh* my salvation.
2 He only *is* my rock and my salvation; *he is* my defence; I shall not be
greatly moved.
3 How long will ye imagine mischief
against a man? ye shall be slain all of
you: as a bowing wall *shall ye be, and*
as a tottering fence.
4 They only consult to cast *him* down
from his excellency: they delight in lies:
they bless with their mouth, but they
curse inwardly. Selah.
5 My soul, wait thou only upon God;
for my expectation *is* from him.
6 He only *is* my rock and my salvation: *he is* my defence; I shall not be
moved.
7 In God *is* my salvation and my glory:
the rock of my strength, *and* my refuge,
is in God.
8 Trust in him at all times; *ye* people,
pour out your heart before him: God *is*
a refuge for us. Selah.
9 Surely men of low degree *are* vanity,
and men of high degree *are* a lie: to be
laid in the balance, they *are* altogether
lighter than vanity.
10 Trust not in oppression, and
become not vain in robbery: if riches
increase, set not your heart *upon them*.
11 God hath spoken once; twice have
I heard this; that power *belongeth* unto
God.
12 Also unto thee, O Lord, *belongeth*
mercy: for thou renderest to every man
according to his work.

PSALM 63

A Psalm of David, when he was in the wilderness of Judah.

O God, thou *art* my God; early will I seek thee: my soul thirsteth for thee, my flesh longeth for thee in a dry and thirsty land, where no water is;

2 To see thy power and thy glory, so *as* I have seen thee in the sanctuary.

3 Because thy lovingkindness *is* better than life, my lips shall praise thee.

4 Thus will I bless thee while I live: I will lift up my hands in thy name.

5 My soul shall be satisfied as *with* marrow and fatness; and my mouth shall praise *thee* with joyful lips:

6 When I remember thee upon my bed, *and* meditate on thee in the *night* watches.

7 Because thou hast been my help, therefore in the shadow of thy wings will I rejoice.

8 My soul followeth hard after thee: thy right hand upholdeth me.

9 But those *that* seek my soul, to destroy *it*, shall go into the lower parts of the earth.

10 They shall fall by the sword: they shall be a portion for foxes.

11 But the king shall rejoice in God; every one that sweareth by him shall glory: but the mouth of them that speak lies shall be stopped.

PSALM 64

To the chief Musician, A Psalm of David.

Hear my voice, O God, in my prayer: preserve my life from fear of the enemy.

2 Hide me from the secret counsel of the wicked; from the insurrection of the workers of iniquity:

3 Who whet their tongue like a sword, *and* bend *their bows to shoot* their arrows, *even* bitter words:

4 That they may shoot in secret at the perfect: suddenly do they shoot at him, and fear not.

5 They encourage themselves *in* an evil matter: they commune of laying snares privily; they say, Who shall see them?

6 They search out iniquities; they accomplish a diligent search: both the inward *thought* of every one *of them*, and the heart, *is* deep.

7 But God shall shoot at them *with* an arrow; suddenly shall they be wounded.

8 So they shall make their own tongue to fall upon themselves: all that see them shall flee away.

9 And all men shall fear, and shall declare the work of God; for they shall wisely consider of his doing.

10 The righteous shall be glad in the LORD, and shall trust in him; and all the upright in heart shall glory.

PSALM 65

To the chief Musician, A Psalm *and* Song of David.

Praise waiteth for thee, O God, in Sion: and unto thee shall the vow be performed.

2 O thou that hearest prayer, unto thee shall all flesh come.

3 Iniquities prevail against me: *as for* our transgressions, thou shalt purge them away.

4 Blessed *is the man whom* thou choosest, and causest to approach *unto thee, that* he may dwell in thy courts: we shall be satisfied with the goodness of thy house, *even* of thy holy temple.

5 *By* terrible things in righteousness wilt thou answer us, O God of our salva-

tion; *who art* the confidence of all the
ends of the earth, and of them that are
afar off *upon* the sea:
6 Which by his strength setteth fast
the mountains; *being* girded with
power:
7 Which stilleth the noise of the seas,
the noise of their waves, and the tumult
of the people.
8 They also that dwell in the uttermost parts are afraid at thy tokens:
thou makest the outgoings of the morning and evening to rejoice.
9 Thou visitest the earth, and waterest it: thou greatly enrichest it with the
river of God, *which* is full of water: thou
preparest them corn, when thou hast so
provided for it.
10 Thou waterest the ridges thereof
abundantly: thou settlest the furrows
thereof: thou makest it soft with showers: thou blessest the springing thereof.
11 Thou crownest the year with thy
goodness; and thy paths drop fatness.
12 They drop *upon* the pastures of the
wilderness: and the little hills rejoice
on every side.
13 The pastures are clothed with
flocks; the valleys also are covered over
with corn; they shout for joy, they also
sing.

PSALM 66

To the chief Musician, A Song *or* Psalm.

Make a joyful noise unto God, all ye
lands:
2 Sing forth the honour of his name:
make his praise glorious.
3 Say unto God, How terrible *art thou*
in thy works! through the greatness of
thy power shall thine enemies submit
themselves unto thee.
4 All the earth shall worship thee,
and shall sing unto thee; they shall sing
to thy name. Selah.
5 Come and see the works of God: *he*
is terrible *in his* doing toward the children of men.
6 He turned the sea into dry *land*:
they went through the flood on foot:
there did we rejoice in him.
7 He ruleth by his power for ever; his
eyes behold the nations: let not the
rebellious exalt themselves. Selah.
8 O bless our God, ye people, and
make the voice of his praise to be
heard:
9 Which holdeth our soul in life, and
suffereth not our feet to be moved.
10 For thou, O God, hast proved us:
thou hast tried us, as silver is tried.
11 Thou broughtest us into the net;
thou laidst affliction upon our loins.
12 Thou hast caused men to ride over
our heads; we went through fire and
through water: but thou broughtest us
out into a wealthy *place*.
13 I will go into thy house with burnt
offerings: I will pay thee my vows,
14 Which my lips have uttered, and
my mouth hath spoken, when I was in
trouble.
15 I will offer unto thee burnt sacrifices of fatlings, with the incense of
rams; I will offer bullocks with goats.
Selah.
16 Come *and* hear, all ye that fear
God, and I will declare what he hath
done for my soul.
17 I cried unto him with my mouth,
and he was extolled with my tongue.
18 If I regard iniquity in my heart, the
Lord will not hear *me*:
19 *But* verily God hath heard *me*; he
hath attended to the voice of my prayer.

20 Blessed *be* God, which hath not
turned away my prayer, nor his mercy
from me.

PSALM 67

**To the chief Musician on Neginoth,
A Psalm *or* Song.**

God be merciful unto us, and bless us;
and cause his face to shine upon us;
Selah.
2 That thy way may be known upon
earth, thy saving health among all
nations.
3 Let the people praise thee, O God;
let all the people praise thee.
4 O let the nations be glad and sing
for joy: for thou shalt judge the people
righteously, and govern the nations
upon earth. Selah.
5 Let the people praise thee, O God;
let all the people praise thee.
6 *Then* shall the earth yield her
increase; *and* God, *even* our own God,
shall bless us.
7 God shall bless us; and all the ends
of the earth shall fear him.

PSALM 68

**To the chief Musician, A Psalm *or* Song
of David.**

Let God arise, let his enemies be
scattered: let them also that hate
him flee before him.
2 As smoke is driven away, *so* drive
them away: as wax melteth before the
fire, *so* let the wicked perish at the presence of God.
3 But let the righteous be glad; let
them rejoice before God: yea, let them
exceedingly rejoice.
4 Sing unto God, sing praises to his
name: extol him that rideth upon the
heavens by his name JAH, and rejoice
before him.
5 A father of the fatherless, and a
judge of the widows, *is* God in his holy
habitation.
6 God setteth the solitary in families:
he bringeth out those which are bound
with chains: but the rebellious dwell in
a dry *land*.
7 O God, when thou wentest forth
before thy people, when thou didst
march through the wilderness; Selah:
8 The earth shook, the heavens also
dropped at the presence of God: *even*
Sinai itself *was moved* at the presence
of God, the God of Israel.
9 Thou, O God, didst send a plentiful
rain, whereby thou didst confirm thine
inheritance, when it was weary.
10 Thy congregation hath dwelt
therein: thou, O God, hast prepared of
thy goodness for the poor.
11 The Lord gave the word: great *was*
the company of those that published *it*.
12 Kings of armies did flee apace:
and she that tarried at home divided
the spoil.
13 Though ye have lien among the
pots, *yet shall ye be as* the wings of a
dove covered with silver, and her feathers with yellow gold.
14 When the Almighty scattered
kings in it, it was *white* as snow in
Salmon.
15 The hill of God *is as* the hill of
Bashan; an high hill *as* the hill of
Bashan.
16 Why leap ye, ye high hills? *this is*
the hill *which* God desireth to dwell in;
yea, the LORD will dwell *in it* for ever.
17 The chariots of God *are* twenty
thousand, *even* thousands of angels:
the Lord *is* among them, *as in* Sinai, in
the holy *place*.
18 Thou hast ascended on high, thou
hast led captivity captive: thou hast

received gifts for men; yea, *for* the
rebellious also, that the LORD God
might dwell *among them.*
19 Blessed *be* the Lord, *who* daily
loadeth us *with benefits, even* the God
of our salvation. Selah.
20 *He that is* our God *is* the God of
salvation; and unto GOD the Lord
belong the issues from death.
21 But God shall wound the head of
his enemies, *and* the hairy scalp of such
an one as goeth on still in his trespasses.
22 The Lord said, I will bring again
from Bashan, I will bring *my people*
again from the depths of the sea:
23 That thy foot may be dipped in the
blood of *thine* enemies, *and* the tongue
of thy dogs in the same.
24 They have seen thy goings, O God;
even the goings of my God, my King, in
the sanctuary.
25 The singers went before, the players on instruments *followed* after;
among *them were* the damsels playing
with timbrels.
26 Bless ye God in the congregations,
even the Lord, from the fountain of
Israel.
27 There *is* little Benjamin *with* their
ruler, the princes of Judah *and* their
council, the princes of Zebulun, *and*
the princes of Naphtali.
28 Thy God hath commanded thy
strength: strengthen, O God, that which
thou hast wrought for us.
29 Because of thy temple at Jerusalem
shall kings bring presents unto thee.
30 Rebuke the company of spearmen,
the multitude of the bulls, with the
calves of the people, *till every one* submit himself with pieces of silver: scatter thou the people *that* delight in war.
31 Princes shall come out of Egypt;
Ethiopia shall soon stretch out her
hands unto God.
32 Sing unto God, ye kingdoms of the
earth; O sing praises unto the Lord;
Selah:
33 To him that rideth upon the heavens of heavens, *which were* of old; lo, he
doth send out his voice, *and that* a
mighty voice.
34 Ascribe ye strength unto God: his
excellency *is* over Israel, and his
strength *is* in the clouds.
35 O God, *thou art* terrible out of thy
holy places: the God of Israel *is* he that
giveth strength and power unto *his*
people. Blessed *be* God.

PSALM 69

To the chief Musician upon Shoshannim, *A Psalm* of David.

Save me, O God; for the waters are
come in unto *my* soul.
2 I sink in deep mire, where *there is*
no standing: I am come into deep
waters, where the floods overflow me.
3 I am weary of my crying: my throat
is dried: mine eyes fail while I wait for
my God.
4 They that hate me without a cause
are more than the hairs of mine head:
they that would destroy me, *being* mine
enemies wrongfully, are mighty: then I
restored *that* which I took not away.
5 O God, thou knowest my foolishness; and my sins are not hid from thee.
6 Let not them that wait on thee, O
Lord GOD of hosts, be ashamed for my
sake: let not those that seek thee be
confounded for my sake, O God of
Israel.
7 Because for thy sake I have borne
reproach; shame hath covered my face.

8 I am become a stranger unto my
brethren, and an alien unto my mother's children.
9 For the zeal of thine house hath
eaten me up; and the reproaches of
them that reproached thee are fallen
upon me.
10 When I wept, *and chastened* my
soul with fasting, that was to my
reproach.
11 I made sackcloth also my garment;
and I became a proverb to them.
12 They that sit in the gate speak
against me; and I *was* the song of the
drunkards.
13 But as for me, my prayer *is* unto
thee, O LORD, *in* an acceptable time: O
God, in the multitude of thy mercy hear
me, in the truth of thy salvation.
14 Deliver me out of the mire, and let
me not sink: let me be delivered from
them that hate me, and out of the deep
waters.
15 Let not the waterflood overflow
me, neither let the deep swallow me up,
and let not the pit shut her mouth upon
me.
16 Hear me, O LORD; for thy lovingkindness *is* good: turn unto me according to the multitude of thy tender mercies.
17 And hide not thy face from thy
servant; for I am in trouble: hear me
speedily.
18 Draw nigh unto my soul, *and*
redeem it: deliver me because of mine
enemies.
19 Thou hast known my reproach, and
my shame, and my dishonour: mine
adversaries *are* all before thee.
20 Reproach hath broken my heart;
and I am full of heaviness: and I looked
for some to take pity, but *there was*
none; and for comforters, but I found
none.
21 They gave me also gall for my
meat; and in my thirst they gave me
vinegar to drink.
22 Let their table become a snare
before them: and *that which should
have been* for *their* welfare, *let it
become* a trap.
23 Let their eyes be darkened, that
they see not; and make their loins continually to shake.
24 Pour out thine indignation upon
them, and let thy wrathful anger take
hold of them.
25 Let their habitation be desolate;
and let none dwell in their tents.
26 For they persecute *him* whom
thou hast smitten; and they talk to the
grief of those whom thou hast wounded.
27 Add iniquity unto their iniquity:
and let them not come into thy righteousness.
28 Let them be blotted out of the
book of the living, and not be written
with the righteous.
29 But I *am* poor and sorrowful: let
thy salvation, O God, set me up on high.
30 I will praise the name of God with
a song, and will magnify him with
thanksgiving.
31 *This* also shall please the LORD better than an ox *or* bullock that hath
horns and hoofs.
32 The humble shall see *this, and* be
glad: and your heart shall live that seek
God.
33 For the LORD heareth the poor, and
despiseth not his prisoners.
34 Let the heaven and earth praise
him, the seas, and every thing that
moveth therein.

35 For God will save Zion, and will build the cities of Judah: that they may dwell there, and have it in possession.

36 The seed also of his servants shall inherit it: and they that love his name shall dwell therein.

PSALM 70

To the chief Musician, *A Psalm* of David, to bring to remembrance.

M*ake haste*, O God, to deliver me; make haste to help me, O LORD.

2 Let them be ashamed and confounded that seek after my soul: let them be turned backward, and put to confusion, that desire my hurt.

3 Let them be turned back for a reward of their shame that say, Aha, aha.

4 Let all those that seek thee rejoice and be glad in thee: and let such as love thy salvation say continually, Let God be magnified.

5 But I *am* poor and needy: make haste unto me, O God: thou *art* my help and my deliverer; O LORD, make no tarrying.

PSALM 71

In thee, O LORD, do I put my trust: let me never be put to confusion.

2 Deliver me in thy righteousness, and cause me to escape: incline thine ear unto me, and save me.

3 Be thou my strong habitation, whereunto I may continually resort: thou hast given commandment to save me; for thou *art* my rock and my fortress.

4 Deliver me, O my God, out of the hand of the wicked, out of the hand of the unrighteous and cruel man.

5 For thou *art* my hope, O Lord GOD: *thou art* my trust from my youth.

6 By thee have I been holden up from the womb: thou art he that took me out of my mother's bowels: my praise *shall be* continually of thee.

7 I am as a wonder unto many; but thou *art* my strong refuge.

8 Let my mouth be filled *with* thy praise *and with* thy honour all the day.

9 Cast me not off in the time of old age; forsake me not when my strength faileth.

10 For mine enemies speak against me; and they that lay wait for my soul take counsel together,

11 Saying, God hath forsaken him: persecute and take him; for *there is* none to deliver *him*.

12 O God, be not far from me: O my God, make haste for my help.

13 Let them be confounded *and* consumed that are adversaries to my soul; let them be covered *with* reproach and dishonour that seek my hurt.

14 But I will hope continually, and will yet praise thee more and more.

15 My mouth shall shew forth thy righteousness *and* thy salvation all the day; for I know not the numbers *thereof*.

16 I will go in the strength of the Lord GOD: I will make mention of thy righteousness, *even* of thine only.

17 O God, thou hast taught me from my youth: and hitherto have I declared thy wondrous works.

18 Now also when I am old and grayheaded, O God, forsake me not; until I have shewed thy strength unto *this* generation, *and* thy power to every one *that* is to come.

19 Thy righteousness also, O God, *is*
very high, who hast done great things:
O God, who *is* like unto thee!
20 *Thou*, which hast shewed me great
and sore troubles, shalt quicken me
again, and shalt bring me up again
from the depths of the earth.
21 Thou shalt increase my greatness,
and comfort me on every side.
22 I will also praise thee with the
psaltery, *even* thy truth, O my God: unto
thee will I sing with the harp, O thou
Holy One of Israel.
23 My lips shall greatly rejoice when
I sing unto thee; and my soul, which
thou hast redeemed.
24 My tongue also shall talk of thy
righteousness all the day long: for they
are confounded, for they are brought
unto shame, that seek my hurt.

PSALM 72

A Psalm for Solomon.

Give the king thy judgments, O God,
and thy righteousness unto the
king's son.
2 He shall judge thy people with righteousness, and thy poor with judgment.
3 The mountains shall bring peace to
the people, and the little hills, by righteousness.
4 He shall judge the poor of the people, he shall save the children of the
needy, and shall break in pieces the
oppressor.
5 They shall fear thee as long as the
sun and moon endure, throughout all
generations.
6 He shall come down like rain upon
the mown grass: as showers *that* water
the earth.
7 In his days shall the righteous flourish; and abundance of peace so long as
the moon endureth.
8 He shall have dominion also from
sea to sea, and from the river unto the
ends of the earth.
9 They that dwell in the wilderness
shall bow before him; and his enemies
shall lick the dust.
10 The kings of Tarshish and of the
isles shall bring presents: the kings of
Sheba and Seba shall offer gifts.
11 Yea, all kings shall fall down
before him: all nations shall serve him.
12 For he shall deliver the needy
when he crieth; the poor also, and *him*
that hath no helper.
13 He shall spare the poor and needy,
and shall save the souls of the needy.
14 He shall redeem their soul from
deceit and violence: and precious shall
their blood be in his sight.
15 And he shall live, and to him shall
be given of the gold of Sheba: prayer
also shall be made for him continually;
and daily shall he be praised.
16 There shall be an handful of corn
in the earth upon the top of the mountains; the fruit thereof shall shake like
Lebanon: and *they* of the city shall
flourish like grass of the earth.
17 His name shall endure for ever: his
name shall be continued as long as the
sun: and *men* shall be blessed in him:
all nations shall call him blessed.
18 Blessed *be* the LORD God, the God
of Israel, who only doeth wondrous
things.
19 And blessed *be* his glorious name
for ever: and let the whole earth be
filled *with* his glory; Amen, and Amen.
20 The prayers of David the son of
Jesse are ended.

PSALM 73

A Psalm of Asaph.

Truly God *is* good to Israel, *even* to such as are of a clean heart.

2 But as for me, my feet were almost gone; my steps had well nigh slipped.

3 For I was envious at the foolish, *when* I saw the prosperity of the wicked.

4 For *there are* no bands in their death: but their strength *is* firm.

5 They *are* not in trouble *as other* men; neither are they plagued like *other* men.

6 Therefore pride compasseth them about as a chain; violence covereth them *as* a garment.

7 Their eyes stand out with fatness: they have more than heart could wish.

8 They are corrupt, and speak wickedly *concerning* oppression: they speak loftily.

9 They set their mouth against the heavens, and their tongue walketh through the earth.

10 Therefore his people return hither: and waters of a full *cup* are wrung out to them.

11 And they say, How doth God know? and is there knowledge in the most High?

12 Behold, these *are* the ungodly, who prosper in the world; they increase *in* riches.

13 Verily I have cleansed my heart *in* vain, and washed my hands in innocency.

14 For all the day long have I been plagued, and chastened every morning.

15 If I say, I will speak thus; behold, I should offend *against* the generation of thy children.

16 When I thought to know this, it *was* too painful for me;

17 Until I went into the sanctuary of God; *then* understood I their end.

18 Surely thou didst set them in slippery places: thou castedst them down into destruction.

19 How are they *brought* into desolation, as in a moment! they are utterly consumed with terrors.

20 As a dream when *one* awaketh; *so,* O Lord, when thou awakest, thou shalt despise their image.

21 Thus my heart was grieved, and I was pricked in my reins.

22 So foolish *was* I, and ignorant: I was *as* a beast before thee.

23 Nevertheless I *am* continually with thee: thou hast holden *me* by my right hand.

24 Thou shalt guide me with thy counsel, and afterward receive me *to* glory.

25 Whom have I in heaven *but thee*? and *there is* none upon earth *that* I desire beside thee.

26 My flesh and my heart faileth: *but* God *is* the strength of my heart, and my portion for ever.

27 For, lo, they that are far from thee shall perish: thou hast destroyed all them that go a whoring from thee.

28 But *it is* good for me to draw near to God: I have put my trust in the Lord GOD, that I may declare all thy works.

PSALM 74

Maschil of Asaph.

O God, why hast thou cast *us* off for ever? *why* doth thine anger smoke against the sheep of thy pasture?

2 Remember thy congregation, *which* thou hast purchased of old; the rod of thine inheritance, *which* thou hast redeemed; this mount Zion, wherein thou hast dwelt.

3 Lift up thy feet unto the perpetual desolations; *even* all *that* the enemy hath done wickedly in the sanctuary.

4 Thine enemies roar in the midst of thy congregations; they set up their ensigns *for* signs.

5 *A man* was famous according as he had lifted up axes upon the thick trees.

6 But now they break down the carved work thereof at once with axes and hammers.

7 They have cast fire into thy sanctuary, they have defiled *by casting down* the dwelling place of thy name to the ground.

8 They said in their hearts, Let us destroy them together: they have burned up all the synagogues of God in the land.

9 We see not our signs: *there is* no more any prophet: neither *is there* among us any that knoweth how long.

10 O God, how long shall the adversary reproach? shall the enemy blaspheme thy name for ever?

11 Why withdrawest thou thy hand, even thy right hand? pluck *it* out of thy bosom.

12 For God *is* my King of old, working salvation in the midst of the earth.

13 Thou didst divide the sea by thy strength: thou brakest the heads of the dragons in the waters.

14 Thou brakest the heads of leviathan in pieces, *and* gavest him *to be* meat to the people inhabiting the wilderness.

15 Thou didst cleave the fountain and the flood: thou driedst up mighty rivers.

16 The day *is* thine, the night also *is* thine: thou hast prepared the light and the sun.

17 Thou hast set all the borders of the earth: thou hast made summer and winter.

18 Remember this, *that* the enemy hath reproached, O LORD, and *that* the foolish people have blasphemed thy name.

19 O deliver not the soul of thy turtledove unto the multitude *of the wicked*: forget not the congregation of thy poor for ever.

20 Have respect unto the covenant: for the dark places of the earth are full of the habitations of cruelty.

21 O let not the oppressed return ashamed: let the poor and needy praise thy name.

22 Arise, O God, plead thine own cause: remember how the foolish man reproacheth thee daily.

23 Forget not the voice of thine enemies: the tumult of those that rise up against thee increaseth continually.

PSALM 75

To the chief Musician, Al-taschith, A Psalm *or* Song of Asaph.

Unto thee, O God, do we give thanks, *unto thee* do we give thanks: for *that* thy name is near thy wondrous works declare.

2 When I shall receive the congregation I will judge uprightly.

3 The earth and all the inhabitants thereof are dissolved: I bear up the pillars of it. Selah.

4 I said unto the fools, Deal not foolishly: and to the wicked, Lift not up the horn:

5 Lift not up your horn on high: speak *not with* a stiff neck.

6 For promotion *cometh* neither from the east, nor from the west, nor from the south.

7 But God *is* the judge: he putteth
down one, and setteth up another.
8 For in the hand of the LORD *there is*
a cup, and the wine is red; it is full of
mixture; and he poureth out of the
same: but the dregs thereof, all the
wicked of the earth shall wring *them*
out, *and* drink *them*.
9 But I will declare for ever; I will sing
praises to the God of Jacob.
10 All the horns of the wicked also
will I cut off; *but* the horns of the righteous shall be exalted.

PSALM 76

To the chief Musician on Neginoth, A Psalm *or* Song of Asaph.

In Judah *is* God known: his name *is*
great in Israel.
2 In Salem also is his tabernacle, and
his dwelling place in Zion.
3 There brake he the arrows of the
bow, the shield, and the sword, and the
battle. Selah.
4 Thou *art* more glorious *and* excellent than the mountains of prey.
5 The stouthearted are spoiled, they
have slept their sleep: and none of the
men of might have found their hands.
6 At thy rebuke, O God of Jacob, both
the chariot and horse are cast into a
dead sleep.
7 Thou, *even* thou, *art* to be feared:
and who may stand in thy sight when
once thou art angry?
8 Thou didst cause judgment to be
heard from heaven; the earth feared,
and was still,
9 When God arose to judgment, to
save all the meek of the earth. Selah.
10 Surely the wrath of man shall
praise thee: the remainder of wrath
shalt thou restrain.
11 Vow, and pay unto the LORD your
God: let all that be round about him
bring presents unto him that ought to
be feared.
12 He shall cut off the spirit of princes: *he is* terrible to the kings of the
earth.

PSALM 77

To the chief Musician, to Jeduthun, A Psalm of Asaph.

I cried unto God with my voice, *even*
unto God with my voice; and he gave
ear unto me.
2 In the day of my trouble I sought the
Lord: my sore ran in the night, and
ceased not: my soul refused to be comforted.
3 I remembered God, and was troubled: I complained, and my spirit was
overwhelmed. Selah.
4 Thou holdest mine eyes waking: I
am so troubled that I cannot speak.
5 I have considered the days of old,
the years of ancient times.
6 I call to remembrance my song in
the night: I commune with mine own
heart: and my spirit made diligent
search.
7 Will the Lord cast off for ever? and
will he be favourable no more?
8 Is his mercy clean gone for ever?
doth *his* promise fail for evermore?
9 Hath God forgotten to be gracious?
hath he in anger shut up his tender
mercies? Selah.
10 And I said, This *is* my infirmity: *but*
I will remember the years of the right
hand of the most High.
11 I will remember the works of the
LORD: surely I will remember thy wonders of old.
12 I will meditate also of all thy work,
and talk of thy doings.

13 Thy way, O God, *is* in the sanctuary: who *is so* great a God as *our* God?

14 Thou *art* the God that doest wonders: thou hast declared thy strength among the people.

15 Thou hast with *thine* arm redeemed thy people, the sons of Jacob and Joseph. Selah.

16 The waters saw thee, O God, the waters saw thee; they were afraid: the depths also were troubled.

17 The clouds poured out water: the skies sent out a sound: thine arrows also went abroad.

18 The voice of thy thunder *was* in the heaven: the lightnings lightened the world: the earth trembled and shook.

19 Thy way *is* in the sea, and thy path in the great waters, and thy footsteps are not known.

20 Thou leddest thy people like a flock by the hand of Moses and Aaron.

PSALM 78

Maschil of Asaph.

Give ear, O my people, *to* my law: incline your ears to the words of my mouth.

2 I will open my mouth in a parable: I will utter dark sayings of old:

3 Which we have heard and known, and our fathers have told us.

4 We will not hide *them* from their children, shewing to the generation to come the praises of the LORD, and his strength, and his wonderful works that he hath done.

5 For he established a testimony in Jacob, and appointed a law in Israel, which he commanded our fathers, that they should make them known to their children:

6 That the generation to come might know *them, even* the children *which* should be born; *who* should arise and declare *them* to their children:

7 That they might set their hope in God, and not forget the works of God, but keep his commandments:

8 And might not be as their fathers, a stubborn and rebellious generation; a generation *that* set not their heart aright, and whose spirit was not stedfast with God.

9 The children of Ephraim, *being* armed, *and* carrying bows, turned back in the day of battle.

10 They kept not the covenant of God, and refused to walk in his law;

11 And forgat his works, and his wonders that he had shewed them.

12 Marvellous things did he in the sight of their fathers, in the land of Egypt, *in* the field of Zoan.

13 He divided the sea, and caused them to pass through; and he made the waters to stand as an heap.

14 In the daytime also he led them with a cloud, and all the night with a light of fire.

15 He clave the rocks in the wilderness, and gave *them* drink as *out of* the great depths.

16 He brought streams also out of the rock, and caused waters to run down like rivers.

17 And they sinned yet more against him by provoking the most High in the wilderness.

18 And they tempted God in their heart by asking meat for their lust.

19 Yea, they spake against God; they said, Can God furnish a table in the wilderness?

20 Behold, he smote the rock, that the waters gushed out, and the streams overflowed; can he give bread also? can he provide flesh for his people?

21 Therefore the LORD heard *this*, and was wroth: so a fire was kindled against Jacob, and anger also came up against Israel;

22 Because they believed not in God, and trusted not in his salvation:

23 Though he had commanded the clouds from above, and opened the doors of heaven,

24 And had rained down manna upon them to eat, and had given them of the corn of heaven.

25 Man did eat angels' food: he sent them meat to the full.

26 He caused an east wind to blow in the heaven: and by his power he brought in the south wind.

27 He rained flesh also upon them as dust, and feathered fowls like as the sand of the sea:

28 And he let *it* fall in the midst of their camp, round about their habitations.

29 So they did eat, and were well filled: for he gave them their own desire;

30 They were not estranged from their lust. But while their meat *was* yet in their mouths,

31 The wrath of God came upon them, and slew the fattest of them, and smote down the chosen *men* of Israel.

32 For all this they sinned still, and believed not for his wondrous works.

33 Therefore their days did he consume in vanity, and their years in trouble.

34 When he slew them, then they sought him: and they returned and enquired early after God.

35 And they remembered that God *was* their rock, and the high God their redeemer.

36 Nevertheless they did flatter him with their mouth, and they lied unto him with their tongues.

37 For their heart was not right with him, neither were they stedfast in his covenant.

38 But he, *being* full of compassion, forgave *their* iniquity, and destroyed *them* not: yea, many a time turned he his anger away, and did not stir up all his wrath.

39 For he remembered that they *were but* flesh; a wind that passeth away, and cometh not again.

40 How oft did they provoke him in the wilderness, *and* grieve him in the desert!

41 Yea, they turned back and tempted God, and limited the Holy One of Israel.

42 They remembered not his hand, *nor* the day when he delivered them from the enemy.

43 How he had wrought his signs in Egypt, and his wonders in the field of Zoan:

44 And had turned their rivers into blood; and their floods, that they could not drink.

45 He sent divers sorts of flies among them, which devoured them; and frogs, which destroyed them.

46 He gave also their increase unto the caterpiller, and their labour unto the locust.

47 He destroyed their vines with hail, and their sycomore trees with frost.

48 He gave up their cattle also to the hail, and their flocks to hot thunderbolts.

49 He cast upon them the fierceness of his anger, wrath, and indignation, and trouble, by sending evil angels *among them*.

50 He made a way to his anger; he spared not their soul from death, but gave their life over to the pestilence;

51 And smote all the firstborn in Egypt; the chief of *their* strength in the tabernacles of Ham:

52 But made his own people to go forth like sheep, and guided them in the wilderness like a flock.

53 And he led them on safely, so that they feared not: but the sea overwhelmed their enemies.

54 And he brought them to the border of his sanctuary, *even to* this mountain, *which* his right hand had purchased.

55 He cast out the heathen also before them, and divided them an inheritance by line, and made the tribes of Israel to dwell in their tents.

56 Yet they tempted and provoked the most high God, and kept not his testimonies:

57 But turned back, and dealt unfaithfully like their fathers: they were turned aside like a deceitful bow.

58 For they provoked him to anger with their high places, and moved him to jealousy with their graven images.

59 When God heard *this*, he was wroth, and greatly abhorred Israel:

60 So that he forsook the tabernacle of Shiloh, the tent *which* he placed among men;

61 And delivered his strength into captivity, and his glory into the enemy's hand.

62 He gave his people over also unto the sword; and was wroth with his inheritance.

63 The fire consumed their young men; and their maidens were not given to marriage.

64 Their priests fell by the sword; and their widows made no lamentation.

65 Then the Lord awaked as one out of sleep, *and* like a mighty man that shouteth by reason of wine.

66 And he smote his enemies in the hinder parts: he put them to a perpetual reproach.

67 Moreover he refused the tabernacle of Joseph, and chose not the tribe of Ephraim:

68 But chose the tribe of Judah, the mount Zion which he loved.

69 And he built his sanctuary like high *palaces*, like the earth which he hath established for ever.

70 He chose David also his servant, and took him from the sheepfolds:

71 From following the ewes great with young he brought him to feed Jacob his people, and Israel his inheritance.

72 So he fed them according to the integrity of his heart; and guided them by the skilfulness of his hands.

PSALM 79

A Psalm of Asaph.

O God, the heathen are come into thine inheritance; thy holy temple have they defiled; they have laid Jerusalem on heaps.

2 The dead bodies of thy servants have they given *to be* meat unto the fowls of the heaven, the flesh of thy saints unto the beasts of the earth.

3 Their blood have they shed like water round about Jerusalem; and *there was* none to bury *them*.

4 We are become a reproach to our neighbours, a scorn and derision to them that are round about us.

5 How long, LORD? wilt thou be angry
for ever? shall thy jealousy burn like
fire?
6 Pour out thy wrath upon the heathen that have not known thee, and
upon the kingdoms that have not called
upon thy name.
7 For they have devoured Jacob, and
laid waste his dwelling place.
8 O remember not against us former
iniquities: let thy tender mercies speedily prevent us: for we are brought very
low.
9 Help us, O God of our salvation, for
the glory of thy name: and deliver us,
and purge away our sins, for thy name's
sake.
10 Wherefore should the heathen say,
Where *is* their God? let him be known
among the heathen in our sight *by* the
revenging of the blood of thy servants
which is shed.
11 Let the sighing of the prisoner
come before thee; according to the
greatness of thy power preserve thou
those that are appointed to die;
12 And render unto our neighbours
sevenfold into their bosom their
reproach, wherewith they have
reproached thee, O Lord.
13 So we thy people and sheep of thy
pasture will give thee thanks for ever:
we will shew forth thy praise to all generations.

PSALM 80

To the chief Musician upon Shoshannim-Eduth, A Psalm of Asaph.

Give ear, O Shepherd of Israel, thou
that leadest Joseph like a flock;
thou that dwellest *between* the cherubims, shine forth.
2 Before Ephraim and Benjamin and
Manasseh stir up thy strength, and
come *and* save us.
3 Turn us again, O God, and cause thy
face to shine; and we shall be saved.
4 O LORD God of hosts, how long wilt
thou be angry against the prayer of thy
people?
5 Thou feedest them with the bread
of tears; and givest them tears to drink
in great measure.
6 Thou makest us a strife unto our
neighbours: and our enemies laugh
among themselves.
7 Turn us again, O God of hosts, and
cause thy face to shine; and we shall be
saved.
8 Thou hast brought a vine out of
Egypt: thou hast cast out the heathen,
and planted it.
9 Thou preparedst *room* before it,
and didst cause it to take deep root,
and it filled the land.
10 The hills were covered with the
shadow of it, and the boughs thereof
were like the goodly cedars.
11 She sent out her boughs unto the
sea, and her branches unto the river.
12 Why hast thou *then* broken down
her hedges, so that all they which pass
by the way do pluck her?
13 The boar out of the wood doth
waste it, and the wild beast of the field
doth devour it.
14 Return, we beseech thee, O God of
hosts: look down from heaven, and
behold, and visit this vine;
15 And the vineyard which thy right
hand hath planted, and the branch *that*
thou madest strong for thyself.
16 *It is* burned with fire, *it is* cut
down: they perish at the rebuke of thy
countenance.

17 Let thy hand be upon the man of thy right hand, upon the son of man *whom* thou madest strong for thyself.

18 So will not we go back from thee: quicken us, and we will call upon thy name.

19 Turn us again, O LORD God of hosts, cause thy face to shine; and we shall be saved.

PSALM 81

To the chief Musician upon Gittith, *A Psalm* of Asaph.

Sing aloud unto God our strength: make a joyful noise unto the God of Jacob.

2 Take a psalm, and bring hither the timbrel, the pleasant harp with the psaltery.

3 Blow up the trumpet in the new moon, in the time appointed, on our solemn feast day.

4 For this *was* a statute for Israel, *and* a law of the God of Jacob.

5 This he ordained in Joseph *for* a testimony, when he went out through the land of Egypt: *where* I heard a language *that* I understood not.

6 I removed his shoulder from the burden: his hands were delivered from the pots.

7 Thou calledst in trouble, and I delivered thee; I answered thee in the secret place of thunder: I proved thee at the waters of Meribah. Selah.

8 Hear, O my people, and I will testify unto thee: O Israel, if thou wilt hearken unto me;

9 There shall no strange god be in thee; neither shalt thou worship any strange god.

10 I *am* the LORD thy God, which brought thee out of the land of Egypt: open thy mouth wide, and I will fill it.

11 But my people would not hearken to my voice; and Israel would none of me.

12 So I gave them up unto their own hearts' lust: *and* they walked in their own counsels.

13 Oh that my people had hearkened unto me, *and* Israel had walked in my ways!

14 I should soon have subdued their enemies, and turned my hand against their adversaries.

15 The haters of the LORD should have submitted themselves unto him: but their time should have endured for ever.

16 He should have fed them also with the finest of the wheat: and with honey out of the rock should I have satisfied thee.

PSALM 82

A Psalm of Asaph.

God standeth in the congregation of the mighty; he judgeth among the gods.

2 How long will ye judge unjustly, and accept the persons of the wicked? Selah.

3 Defend the poor and fatherless: do justice to the afflicted and needy.

4 Deliver the poor and needy: rid *them* out of the hand of the wicked.

5 They know not, neither will they understand; they walk on in darkness: all the foundations of the earth are out of course.

6 I have said, Ye *are* gods; and all of you *are* children of the most High.

7 But ye shall die like men, and fall like one of the princes.

8 Arise, O God, judge the earth: for thou shalt inherit all nations.

PSALM 83

A Song *or* Psalm of Asaph.

Keep not thou silence, O God: hold not thy peace, and be not still, O God.

2 For, lo, thine enemies make a tumult: and they that hate thee have lifted up the head.

3 They have taken crafty counsel against thy people, and consulted against thy hidden ones.

4 They have said, Come, and let us cut them off from *being* a nation; that the name of Israel may be no more in remembrance.

5 For they have consulted together with one consent: they are confederate against thee:

6 The tabernacles of Edom, and the Ishmaelites; of Moab, and the Hagarenes;

7 Gebal, and Ammon, and Amalek; the Philistines with the inhabitants of Tyre;

8 Assur also is joined with them: they have holpen the children of Lot. Selah.

9 Do unto them as *unto* the Midianites; as *to* Sisera, as *to* Jabin, at the brook of Kison:

10 *Which* perished at En-dor: they became *as* dung for the earth.

11 Make their nobles like Oreb, and like Zeeb: yea, all their princes as Zebah, and as Zalmunna:

12 Who said, Let us take to ourselves the houses of God in possession.

13 O my God, make them like a wheel; as the stubble before the wind.

14 As the fire burneth a wood, and as the flame setteth the mountains on fire;

15 So persecute them with thy tempest, and make them afraid with thy storm.

16 Fill their faces with shame; that they may seek thy name, O LORD.

17 Let them be confounded and troubled for ever; yea, let them be put to shame, and perish:

18 That *men* may know that thou, whose name alone *is* JEHOVAH, *art* the most high over all the earth.

PSALM 84

To the chief Musician upon Gittith, A Psalm for the sons of Korah.

How amiable *are* thy tabernacles, O LORD of hosts!

2 My soul longeth, yea, even fainteth for the courts of the LORD: my heart and my flesh crieth out for the living God.

3 Yea, the sparrow hath found an house, and the swallow a nest for herself, where she may lay her young, *even* thine altars, O LORD of hosts, my King, and my God.

4 Blessed *are* they that dwell in thy house: they will be still praising thee. Selah.

5 Blessed *is* the man whose strength *is* in thee; in whose heart *are* the ways *of them.*

6 *Who* passing through the valley of Baca make it a well; the rain also filleth the pools.

7 They go from strength to strength, *every one of them* in Zion appeareth before God.

8 O LORD God of hosts, hear my prayer: give ear, O God of Jacob. Selah.

9 Behold, O God our shield, and look upon the face of thine anointed.

10 For a day in thy courts *is* better than a thousand. I had rather be a doorkeeper in the house of my God, than to dwell in the tents of wickedness.

11 For the LORD God *is* a sun and shield: the LORD will give grace and glory: no good *thing* will he withhold from them that walk uprightly.
12 O LORD of hosts, blessed *is* the man that trusteth in thee.

PSALM 85

**To the chief Musician,
A Psalm for the sons of Korah.**

LORD, thou hast been favourable unto thy land: thou hast brought back the captivity of Jacob.
2 Thou hast forgiven the iniquity of thy people, thou hast covered all their sin. Selah.
3 Thou hast taken away all thy wrath: thou hast turned *thyself* from the fierceness of thine anger.
4 Turn us, O God of our salvation, and cause thine anger toward us to cease.
5 Wilt thou be angry with us for ever? wilt thou draw out thine anger to all generations?
6 Wilt thou not revive us again: that thy people may rejoice in thee?
7 Shew us thy mercy, O LORD, and grant us thy salvation.
8 I will hear what God the LORD will speak: for he will speak peace unto his people, and to his saints: but let them not turn again to folly.
9 Surely his salvation *is* nigh them that fear him; that glory may dwell in our land.
10 Mercy and truth are met together; righteousness and peace have kissed *each other*.
11 Truth shall spring out of the earth; and righteousness shall look down from heaven.
12 Yea, the LORD shall give *that which is* good; and our land shall yield her increase.
13 Righteousness shall go before him; and shall set *us* in the way of his steps.

PSALM 86

A Prayer of David.

Bow down thine ear, O LORD, hear me: for I *am* poor and needy.
2 Preserve my soul; for I *am* holy: O thou my God, save thy servant that trusteth in thee.
3 Be merciful unto me, O Lord: for I cry unto thee daily.
4 Rejoice the soul of thy servant: for unto thee, O Lord, do I lift up my soul.
5 For thou, Lord, *art* good, and ready to forgive; and plenteous in mercy unto all them that call upon thee.
6 Give ear, O LORD, unto my prayer; and attend to the voice of my supplications.
7 In the day of my trouble I will call upon thee: for thou wilt answer me.
8 Among the gods *there is* none like unto thee, O Lord; neither *are there any works* like unto thy works.
9 All nations whom thou hast made shall come and worship before thee, O Lord; and shall glorify thy name.
10 For thou *art* great, and doest wondrous things: thou *art* God alone.
11 Teach me thy way, O LORD; I will walk in thy truth: unite my heart to fear thy name.
12 I will praise thee, O Lord my God, with all my heart: and I will glorify thy name for evermore.
13 For great *is* thy mercy toward me: and thou hast delivered my soul from the lowest hell.
14 O God, the proud are risen against me, and the assemblies of violent *men* have sought after my soul; and have not set thee before them.

15 But thou, O Lord, *art* a God full of compassion, and gracious, longsuffering, and plenteous in mercy and truth.

16 O turn unto me, and have mercy upon me; give thy strength unto thy servant, and save the son of thine handmaid.

17 Shew me a token for good; that they which hate me may see *it*, and be ashamed: because thou, LORD, hast holpen me, and comforted me.

PSALM 87

A Psalm *or* Song for the sons of Korah.

His foundation *is* in the holy mountains.

2 The LORD loveth the gates of Zion more than all the dwellings of Jacob.

3 Glorious things are spoken of thee, O city of God. Selah.

4 I will make mention of Rahab and Babylon to them that know me: behold Philistia, and Tyre, with Ethiopia; this *man* was born there.

5 And of Zion it shall be said, This and that man was born in her: and the highest himself shall establish her.

6 The LORD shall count, when he writeth up the people, *that* this *man* was born there. Selah.

7 As well the singers as the players on instruments *shall be there*: all my springs *are* in thee.

PSALM 88

A Song *or* Psalm for the sons of Korah, to the chief Musician upon Mahalath Leannoth, Maschil of Heman the Ezrahite.

O LORD God of my salvation, I have cried day *and* night before thee:

2 Let my prayer come before thee: incline thine ear unto my cry;

3 For my soul is full of troubles: and my life draweth nigh unto the grave.

4 I am counted with them that go down into the pit: I am as a man *that hath* no strength:

5 Free among the dead, like the slain that lie in the grave, whom thou rememberest no more: and they are cut off from thy hand.

6 Thou hast laid me in the lowest pit, in darkness, in the deeps.

7 Thy wrath lieth hard upon me, and thou hast afflicted *me* with all thy waves. Selah.

8 Thou hast put away mine acquaintance far from me; thou hast made me an abomination unto them: *I am* shut up, and I cannot come forth.

9 Mine eye mourneth by reason of affliction: LORD, I have called daily upon thee, I have stretched out my hands unto thee.

10 Wilt thou shew wonders to the dead? shall the dead arise *and* praise thee? Selah.

11 Shall thy lovingkindness be declared in the grave? *or* thy faithfulness in destruction?

12 Shall thy wonders be known in the dark? and thy righteousness in the land of forgetfulness?

13 But unto thee have I cried, O LORD; and in the morning shall my prayer prevent thee.

14 LORD, why castest thou off my soul? *why* hidest thou thy face from me?

15 I *am* afflicted and ready to die from *my* youth up: *while* I suffer thy terrors I am distracted.

16 Thy fierce wrath goeth over me; thy terrors have cut me off.

17 They came round about me daily
like water; they compassed me about
together.
18 Lover and friend hast thou put far
from me, *and* mine acquaintance into
darkness.

PSALM 89

Maschil of Ethan the Ezrahite.

I will sing of the mercies of the LORD
for ever: with my mouth will I make
known thy faithfulness to all generations.
2 For I have said, Mercy shall be built
up for ever: thy faithfulness shalt thou
establish in the very heavens.
3 I have made a covenant with my
chosen, I have sworn unto David my
servant,
4 Thy seed will I establish for ever,
and build up thy throne to all generations. Selah.
5 And the heavens shall praise thy
wonders, O LORD: thy faithfulness also
in the congregation of the saints.
6 For who in the heaven can be compared unto the LORD? *who* among the
sons of the mighty can be likened unto
the LORD?
7 God is greatly to be feared in the
assembly of the saints, and to be had in
reverence of all *them that are* about
him.
8 O LORD God of hosts, who *is* a strong
LORD like unto thee? or to thy faithfulness round about thee?
9 Thou rulest the raging of the sea:
when the waves thereof arise, thou still-
est them.
10 Thou hast broken Rahab in pieces,
as one that is slain; thou hast scattered
thine enemies with thy strong arm.
11 The heavens *are* thine, the earth
also *is* thine: *as for* the world and the
fulness thereof, thou hast founded
them.
12 The north and the south thou hast
created them: Tabor and Hermon shall
rejoice in thy name.
13 Thou hast a mighty arm: strong is
thy hand, *and* high is thy right hand.
14 Justice and judgment *are* the habitation of thy throne: mercy and truth
shall go before thy face.
15 Blessed *is* the people that know
the joyful sound: they shall walk, O
LORD, in the light of thy countenance.
16 In thy name shall they rejoice all
the day: and in thy righteousness shall
they be exalted.
17 For thou *art* the glory of their
strength: and in thy favour our horn
shall be exalted.
18 For the LORD *is* our defence; and
the Holy One of Israel *is* our king.
19 Then thou spakest in vision to thy
holy one, and saidst, I have laid help
upon *one that is* mighty; I have exalted
one chosen out of the people.
20 I have found David my servant;
with my holy oil have I anointed him:
21 With whom my hand shall be
established: mine arm also shall
strengthen him.
22 The enemy shall not exact upon
him; nor the son of wickedness afflict
him.
23 And I will beat down his foes
before his face, and plague them that
hate him.
24 But my faithfulness and my mercy
shall be with him: and in my name shall
his horn be exalted.
25 I will set his hand also in the sea,
and his right hand in the rivers.
26 He shall cry unto me, Thou *art* my
father, my God, and the rock of my salvation.

27 Also I will make him *my* firstborn, higher than the kings of the earth.

28 My mercy will I keep for him for evermore, and my covenant shall stand fast with him.

29 His seed also will I make *to endure* for ever, and his throne as the days of heaven.

30 If his children forsake my law, and walk not in my judgments;

31 If they break my statutes, and keep not my commandments;

32 Then will I visit their transgression with the rod, and their iniquity with stripes.

33 Nevertheless my lovingkindness will I not utterly take from him, nor suffer my faithfulness to fail.

34 My covenant will I not break, nor alter the thing that is gone out of my lips.

35 Once have I sworn by my holiness that I will not lie unto David.

36 His seed shall endure for ever, and his throne as the sun before me.

37 It shall be established for ever as the moon, and *as* a faithful witness in heaven. Selah.

38 But thou hast cast off and abhorred, thou hast been wroth with thine anointed.

39 Thou hast made void the covenant of thy servant: thou hast profaned his crown *by casting it* to the ground.

40 Thou hast broken down all his hedges; thou hast brought his strong holds to ruin.

41 All that pass by the way spoil him: he is a reproach to his neighbours.

42 Thou hast set up the right hand of his adversaries; thou hast made all his enemies to rejoice.

43 Thou hast also turned the edge of his sword, and hast not made him to stand in the battle.

44 Thou hast made his glory to cease, and cast his throne down to the ground.

45 The days of his youth hast thou shortened: thou hast covered him with shame. Selah.

46 How long, LORD? wilt thou hide thyself for ever? shall thy wrath burn like fire?

47 Remember how short my time is: wherefore hast thou made all men in vain?

48 What man *is he that* liveth, and shall not see death? shall he deliver his soul from the hand of the grave? Selah.

49 Lord, where *are* thy former lovingkindnesses, *which* thou swarest unto David in thy truth?

50 Remember, Lord, the reproach of thy servants; *how* I do bear in my bosom *the reproach of* all the mighty people;

51 Wherewith thine enemies have reproached, O LORD; wherewith they have reproached the footsteps of thine anointed.

52 Blessed *be* the LORD for evermore. Amen, and Amen.

PSALM 90

A Prayer of Moses the man of God.

Lord, thou hast been our dwelling place in all generations.

2 Before the mountains were brought forth, or ever thou hadst formed the earth and the world, even from everlasting to everlasting, thou *art* God.

3 Thou turnest man to destruction; and sayest, Return, ye children of men.

4 For a thousand years in thy sight *are but* as yesterday when it is past, and *as* a watch in the night.

5 Thou carriest them away as with a
flood; they are *as* a sleep: in the morning *they are* like grass *which* groweth
up.
6 In the morning it flourisheth, and
groweth up; in the evening it is cut
down, and withereth.
7 For we are consumed by thine
anger, and by thy wrath are we troubled.
8 Thou hast set our iniquities before
thee, our secret *sins* in the light of thy
countenance.
9 For all our days are passed away in
thy wrath: we spend our years as a tale
that is told.
10 The days of our years *are* threescore years and ten; and if by reason of
strength *they be* fourscore years, yet *is*
their strength labour and sorrow; for it
is soon cut off, and we fly away.
11 Who knoweth the power of thine
anger? even according to thy fear, *so is*
thy wrath.
12 So teach *us* to number our days,
that we may apply *our* hearts unto wisdom.
13 Return, O LORD, how long? and let
it repent thee concerning thy servants.
14 O satisfy us early with thy mercy;
that we may rejoice and be glad all our
days.
15 Make us glad according to the days
wherein thou hast afflicted us, *and* the
years *wherein* we have seen evil.
16 Let thy work appear unto thy servants, and thy glory unto their children.
17 And let the beauty of the LORD our
God be upon us: and establish thou the
work of our hands upon us; yea, the
work of our hands establish thou it.

PSALM 91

He that dwelleth in the secret place
of the most High shall abide under
the shadow of the Almighty.
2 I will say of the LORD, *He is* my refuge and my fortress: my God; in him
will I trust.
3 Surely he shall deliver thee from
the snare of the fowler, *and* from the
noisome pestilence.
4 He shall cover thee with his feathers, and under his wings shalt thou
trust: his truth *shall be thy* shield and
buckler.
5 Thou shalt not be afraid for the terror by night; *nor* for the arrow *that*
flieth by day;
6 *Nor* for the pestilence *that* walketh
in darkness; *nor* for the destruction
that wasteth at noonday.
7 A thousand shall fall at thy side,
and ten thousand at thy right hand; *but*
it shall not come nigh thee.
8 Only with thine eyes shalt thou
behold and see the reward of the wicked.
9 Because thou hast made the LORD,
which is my refuge, *even* the most
High, thy habitation;
10 There shall no evil befall thee,
neither shall any plague come nigh thy
dwelling.
11 For he shall give his angels charge
over thee, to keep thee in all thy ways.
12 They shall bear thee up in *their*
hands, lest thou dash thy foot against a
stone.
13 Thou shalt tread upon the lion and
adder: the young lion and the dragon
shalt thou trample under feet.
14 Because he hath set his love upon
me, therefore will I deliver him: I will
set him on high, because he hath
known my name.

15 He shall call upon me, and I will answer him: I *will be* with him in trouble; I will deliver him, and honour him.

16 With long life will I satisfy him, and shew him my salvation.

PSALM 92

A Psalm *or* Song for the sabbath day.

I*t is a* good *thing* to give thanks unto the LORD, and to sing praises unto thy name, O most High:

2 To shew forth thy lovingkindness in the morning, and thy faithfulness every night,

3 Upon an instrument of ten strings, and upon the psaltery; upon the harp with a solemn sound.

4 For thou, LORD, hast made me glad through thy work: I will triumph in the works of thy hands.

5 O LORD, how great are thy works! *and* thy thoughts are very deep.

6 A brutish man knoweth not; neither doth a fool understand this.

7 When the wicked spring as the grass, and when all the workers of iniquity do flourish; *it is* that they shall be destroyed for ever:

8 But thou, LORD, *art most* high for evermore.

9 For, lo, thine enemies, O LORD, for, lo, thine enemies shall perish; all the workers of iniquity shall be scattered.

10 But my horn shalt thou exalt like *the horn of* an unicorn: I shall be anointed with fresh oil.

11 Mine eye also shall see *my desire* on mine enemies, *and* mine ears shall hear *my desire* of the wicked that rise up against me.

12 The righteous shall flourish like the palm tree: he shall grow like a cedar in Lebanon.

13 Those that be planted in the house of the LORD shall flourish in the courts of our God.

14 They shall still bring forth fruit in old age; they shall be fat and flourishing;

15 To shew that the LORD *is* upright: *he is* my rock, and *there is* no unrighteousness in him.

PSALM 93

The LORD reigneth, he is clothed with majesty; the LORD is clothed with strength, *wherewith* he hath girded himself: the world also is stablished, that it cannot be moved.

2 Thy throne *is* established of old: thou *art* from everlasting.

3 The floods have lifted up, O LORD, the floods have lifted up their voice; the floods lift up their waves.

4 The LORD on high *is* mightier than the noise of many waters, *yea, than* the mighty waves of the sea.

5 Thy testimonies are very sure: holiness becometh thine house, O LORD, for ever.

PSALM 94

O LORD God, to whom vengeance belongeth; O God, to whom vengeance belongeth, shew thyself.

2 Lift up thyself, thou judge of the earth: render a reward to the proud.

3 LORD, how long shall the wicked, how long shall the wicked triumph?

4 *How long* shall they utter *and* speak hard things? *and* all the workers of iniquity boast themselves?

5 They break in pieces thy people, O LORD, and afflict thine heritage.

6 They slay the widow and the stranger, and murder the fatherless.

7 Yet they say, The LORD shall not see,
neither shall the God of Jacob regard
it.
8 Understand, ye brutish among the
people: and *ye* fools, when will ye be
wise?
9 He that planted the ear, shall he not
hear? he that formed the eye, shall he
not see?
10 He that chastiseth the heathen,
shall not he correct? he that teacheth
man knowledge, *shall not he know*?
11 The LORD knoweth the thoughts of
man, that they *are* vanity.
12 Blessed *is* the man whom thou
chastenest, O LORD, and teachest him
out of thy law;
13 That thou mayest give him rest
from the days of adversity, until the pit
be digged for the wicked.
14 For the LORD will not cast off his
people, neither will he forsake his
inheritance.
15 But judgment shall return unto
righteousness: and all the upright in
heart shall follow it.
16 Who will rise up for me against the
evildoers? *or* who will stand up for me
against the workers of iniquity?
17 Unless the LORD *had been* my help,
my soul had almost dwelt in silence.
18 When I said, My foot slippeth; thy
mercy, O LORD, held me up.
19 In the multitude of my thoughts
within me thy comforts delight my soul.
20 Shall the throne of iniquity have
fellowship with thee, which frameth
mischief by a law?
21 They gather themselves together
against the soul of the righteous, and
condemn the innocent blood.
22 But the LORD is my defence; and
my God *is* the rock of my refuge.
23 And he shall bring upon them
their own iniquity, and shall cut them
off in their own wickedness; *yea*, the
LORD our God shall cut them off.

PSALM 95

O come, let us sing unto the LORD: let
us make a joyful noise to the rock
of our salvation.
2 Let us come before his presence
with thanksgiving, and make a joyful
noise unto him with psalms.
3 For the LORD *is* a great God, and a
great King above all gods.
4 In his hand *are* the deep places of
the earth: the strength of the hills *is* his
also.
5 The sea *is* his, and he made it: and
his hands formed the dry *land*.
6 O come, let us worship and bow
down: let us kneel before the LORD our
maker.
7 For he *is* our God; and we *are* the
people of his pasture, and the sheep of
his hand. To day if ye will hear his voice,
8 Harden not your heart, as in the
provocation, *and* as *in* the day of temptation in the wilderness:
9 When your fathers tempted me,
proved me, and saw my work.
10 Forty years long was I grieved with
this generation, and said, It *is* a people
that do err in their heart, and they have
not known my ways:
11 Unto whom I sware in my wrath
that they should not enter into my rest.

PSALM 96

O sing unto the LORD a new song: sing
unto the LORD, all the earth.
2 Sing unto the LORD, bless his name;
shew forth his salvation from day to
day.

3 Declare his glory among the heathen, his wonders among all people.
4 For the LORD *is* great, and greatly to be praised: he *is* to be feared above all gods.
5 For all the gods of the nations *are* idols: but the LORD made the heavens.
6 Honour and majesty *are* before him: strength and beauty *are* in his sanctuary.
7 Give unto the LORD, O ye kindreds of the people, give unto the LORD glory and strength.
8 Give unto the LORD the glory *due unto* his name: bring an offering, and come into his courts.
9 O worship the LORD in the beauty of holiness: fear before him, all the earth.
10 Say among the heathen *that* the LORD reigneth: the world also shall be established that it shall not be moved: he shall judge the people righteously.
11 Let the heavens rejoice, and let the earth be glad; let the sea roar, and the fulness thereof.
12 Let the field be joyful, and all that *is* therein: then shall all the trees of the wood rejoice
13 Before the LORD: for he cometh, for he cometh to judge the earth: he shall judge the world with righteousness, and the people with his truth.

PSALM 97

The LORD reigneth; let the earth rejoice; let the multitude of isles be glad *thereof*.
2 Clouds and darkness *are* round about him: righteousness and judgment *are* the habitation of his throne.
3 A fire goeth before him, and burneth up his enemies round about.
4 His lightnings enlightened the world: the earth saw, and trembled.
5 The hills melted like wax at the presence of the LORD, at the presence of the Lord of the whole earth.
6 The heavens declare his righteousness, and all the people see his glory.
7 Confounded be all they that serve graven images, that boast themselves of idols: worship him, all *ye* gods.
8 Zion heard, and was glad; and the daughters of Judah rejoiced because of thy judgments, O LORD.
9 For thou, LORD, *art* high above all the earth: thou art exalted far above all gods.
10 Ye that love the LORD, hate evil: he preserveth the souls of his saints; he delivereth them out of the hand of the wicked.
11 Light is sown for the righteous, and gladness for the upright in heart.
12 Rejoice in the LORD, ye righteous; and give thanks at the remembrance of his holiness.

PSALM 98

A Psalm.

O sing unto the LORD a new song; for he hath done marvellous things: his right hand, and his holy arm, hath gotten him the victory.
2 The LORD hath made known his salvation: his righteousness hath he openly shewed in the sight of the heathen.
3 He hath remembered his mercy and his truth toward the house of Israel: all the ends of the earth have seen the salvation of our God.
4 Make a joyful noise unto the LORD, all the earth: make a loud noise, and rejoice, and sing praise.
5 Sing unto the LORD with the harp; with the harp, and the voice of a psalm.

6 With trumpets and sound of cornet make a joyful noise before the LORD, the King.

7 Let the sea roar, and the fulness thereof; the world, and they that dwell therein.

8 Let the floods clap *their* hands: let the hills be joyful together

9 Before the LORD; for he cometh to judge the earth: with righteousness shall he judge the world, and the people with equity.

PSALM 99

The LORD reigneth; let the people tremble: he sitteth *between* the cherubims; let the earth be moved.

2 The LORD *is* great in Zion; and he *is* high above all the people.

3 Let them praise thy great and terrible name; *for* it *is* holy.

4 The king's strength also loveth judgment; thou dost establish equity, thou executest judgment and righteousness in Jacob.

5 Exalt ye the LORD our God, and worship at his footstool; *for* he *is* holy.

6 Moses and Aaron among his priests, and Samuel among them that call upon his name; they called upon the LORD, and he answered them.

7 He spake unto them in the cloudy pillar: they kept his testimonies, and the ordinance *that* he gave them.

8 Thou answeredst them, O LORD our God: thou wast a God that forgavest them, though thou tookest vengeance of their inventions.

9 Exalt the LORD our God, and worship at his holy hill; for the LORD our God *is* holy.

PSALM 100

A Psalm of praise.

Make a joyful noise unto the LORD, all ye lands.

2 Serve the LORD with gladness: come before his presence with singing.

3 Know ye that the LORD he *is* God: *it is* he *that* hath made us, and not we ourselves; *we are* his people, and the sheep of his pasture.

4 Enter into his gates with thanksgiving, *and* into his courts with praise: be thankful unto him, *and* bless his name.

5 For the LORD *is* good; his mercy *is* everlasting; and his truth *endureth* to all generations.

PSALM 101

A Psalm of David.

I will sing of mercy and judgment: unto thee, O LORD, will I sing.

2 I will behave myself wisely in a perfect way. O when wilt thou come unto me? I will walk within my house with a perfect heart.

3 I will set no wicked thing before mine eyes: I hate the work of them that turn aside; *it* shall not cleave to me.

4 A froward heart shall depart from me: I will not know a wicked *person*.

5 Whoso privily slandereth his neighbour, him will I cut off: him that hath an high look and a proud heart will not I suffer.

6 Mine eyes *shall be* upon the faithful of the land, that they may dwell with me: he that walketh in a perfect way, he shall serve me.

7 He that worketh deceit shall not dwell within my house: he that telleth lies shall not tarry in my sight.

8 I will early destroy all the wicked of the land; that I may cut off all wicked doers from the city of the LORD.

PSALM 102

A Prayer of the afflicted, when he is overwhelmed, and poureth out his complaint before the LORD.

Hear my prayer, O LORD, and let my cry come unto thee.

2 Hide not thy face from me in the day *when* I am in trouble; incline thine ear unto me: in the day *when* I call answer me speedily.

3 For my days are consumed like smoke, and my bones are burned as an hearth.

4 My heart is smitten, and withered like grass; so that I forget to eat my bread.

5 By reason of the voice of my groaning my bones cleave to my skin.

6 I am like a pelican of the wilderness: I am like an owl of the desert.

7 I watch, and am as a sparrow alone upon the house top.

8 Mine enemies reproach me all the day; *and* they that are mad against me are sworn against me.

9 For I have eaten ashes like bread, and mingled my drink with weeping,

10 Because of thine indignation and thy wrath: for thou hast lifted me up, and cast me down.

11 My days *are* like a shadow that declineth; and I am withered like grass.

12 But thou, O LORD, shalt endure for ever; and thy remembrance unto all generations.

13 Thou shalt arise, *and* have mercy upon Zion: for the time to favour her, yea, the set time, is come.

14 For thy servants take pleasure in her stones, and favour the dust thereof.

15 So the heathen shall fear the name of the LORD, and all the kings of the earth thy glory.

16 When the LORD shall build up Zion, he shall appear in his glory.

17 He will regard the prayer of the destitute, and not despise their prayer.

18 This shall be written for the generation to come: and the people which shall be created shall praise the LORD.

19 For he hath looked down from the height of his sanctuary; from heaven did the LORD behold the earth;

20 To hear the groaning of the prisoner; to loose those that are appointed to death;

21 To declare the name of the LORD in Zion, and his praise in Jerusalem;

22 When the people are gathered together, and the kingdoms, to serve the LORD.

23 He weakened my strength in the way; he shortened my days.

24 I said, O my God, take me not away in the midst of my days: thy years *are* throughout all generations.

25 Of old hast thou laid the foundation of the earth: and the heavens *are* the work of thy hands.

26 They shall perish, but thou shalt endure: yea, all of them shall wax old like a garment; as a vesture shalt thou change them, and they shall be changed:

27 But thou *art* the same, and thy years shall have no end.

28 The children of thy servants shall continue, and their seed shall be established before thee.

PSALM 103

A *Psalm* of David.

Bless the LORD, O my soul: and all that is within me, *bless* his holy name.

2 Bless the LORD, O my soul, and forget not all his benefits:

3 Who forgiveth all thine iniquities;
who healeth all thy diseases;
4 Who redeemeth thy life from
destruction; who crowneth thee with
lovingkindness and tender mercies;
5 Who satisfieth thy mouth with good
things; so that thy youth is renewed
like the eagle's.
6 The LORD executeth righteousness
and judgment for all that are oppressed.
7 He made known his ways unto
Moses, his acts unto the children of
Israel.
8 The LORD *is* merciful and gracious,
slow to anger, and plenteous in mercy.
9 He will not always chide: neither
will he keep *his anger* for ever.
10 He hath not dealt with us after our
sins; nor rewarded us according to our
iniquities.
11 For as the heaven is high above the
earth, *so* great is his mercy toward them
that fear him.
12 As far as the east is from the west,
so far hath he removed our transgressions from us.
13 Like as a father pitieth *his* children, *so* the LORD pitieth them that fear
him.
14 For he knoweth our frame; he
remembereth that we *are* dust.
15 *As for* man, his days *are* as grass: as
a flower of the field, so he flourisheth.
16 For the wind passeth over it, and it
is gone; and the place thereof shall
know it no more.
17 But the mercy of the LORD *is* from
everlasting to everlasting upon them
that fear him, and his righteousness
unto children's children;
18 To such as keep his covenant, and
to those that remember his commandments to do them.
19 The LORD hath prepared his throne
in the heavens; and his kingdom ruleth
over all.
20 Bless the LORD, ye his angels, that
excel in strength, that do his commandments, hearkening unto the voice of his
word.
21 Bless ye the LORD, all *ye* his hosts;
ye ministers of his, that do his pleasure.
22 Bless the LORD, all his works in all
places of his dominion: bless the LORD,
O my soul.

PSALM 104

Bless the LORD, O my soul. O LORD my
God, thou art very great; thou art
clothed with honour and majesty.
2 Who coverest *thyself* with light as
with a garment: who stretchest out the
heavens like a curtain:
3 Who layeth the beams of his chambers in the waters: who maketh the
clouds his chariot: who walketh upon
the wings of the wind:
4 Who maketh his angels spirits; his
ministers a flaming fire:
5 *Who* laid the foundations of the
earth, *that* it should not be removed for
ever.
6 Thou coveredst it with the deep as
with a garment: the waters stood above
the mountains.
7 At thy rebuke they fled; at the voice
of thy thunder they hasted away.
8 They go up by the mountains; they
go down by the valleys unto the place
which thou hast founded for them.
9 Thou hast set a bound that they may
not pass over; that they turn not again
to cover the earth.
10 He sendeth the springs into the
valleys, *which* run among the hills.

11 They give drink to every beast of the field: the wild asses quench their thirst.

12 By them shall the fowls of the heaven have their habitation, *which* sing among the branches.

13 He watereth the hills from his chambers: the earth is satisfied with the fruit of thy works.

14 He causeth the grass to grow for the cattle, and herb for the service of man: that he may bring forth food out of the earth;

15 And wine *that* maketh glad the heart of man, *and* oil to make *his* face to shine, and bread *which* strengtheneth man's heart.

16 The trees of the LORD are full *of sap*; the cedars of Lebanon, which he hath planted;

17 Where the birds make their nests: *as for* the stork, the fir trees *are* her house.

18 The high hills *are* a refuge for the wild goats; *and* the rocks for the conies.

19 He appointed the moon for seasons: the sun knoweth his going down.

20 Thou makest darkness, and it is night: wherein all the beasts of the forest do creep *forth*.

21 The young lions roar after their prey, and seek their meat from God.

22 The sun ariseth, they gather themselves together, and lay them down in their dens.

23 Man goeth forth unto his work and to his labour until the evening.

24 O LORD, how manifold are thy works! in wisdom hast thou made them all: the earth is full of thy riches.

25 *So is* this great and wide sea, wherein *are* things creeping innumerable, both small and great beasts.

26 There go the ships: *there is* that leviathan, *whom* thou hast made to play therein.

27 These wait all upon thee; that thou mayest give *them* their meat in due season.

28 *That* thou givest them they gather: thou openest thine hand, they are filled with good.

29 Thou hidest thy face, they are troubled: thou takest away their breath, they die, and return to their dust.

30 Thou sendest forth thy spirit, they are created: and thou renewest the face of the earth.

31 The glory of the LORD shall endure for ever: the LORD shall rejoice in his works.

32 He looketh on the earth, and it trembleth: he toucheth the hills, and they smoke.

33 I will sing unto the LORD as long as I live: I will sing praise to my God while I have my being.

34 My meditation of him shall be sweet: I will be glad in the LORD.

35 Let the sinners be consumed out of the earth, and let the wicked be no more. Bless thou the LORD, O my soul. Praise ye the LORD.

PSALM 105

O give thanks unto the LORD; call upon his name: make known his deeds among the people.

2 Sing unto him, sing psalms unto him: talk ye of all his wondrous works.

3 Glory ye in his holy name: let the heart of them rejoice that seek the LORD.

4 Seek the LORD, and his strength: seek his face evermore.

5 Remember his marvellous works
that he hath done; his wonders, and the
judgments of his mouth;
6 O ye seed of Abraham his servant,
ye children of Jacob his chosen.
7 He *is* the LORD our God: his judgments *are* in all the earth.
8 He hath remembered his covenant
for ever, the word *which* he commanded to a thousand generations.
9 Which *covenant* he made with
Abraham, and his oath unto Isaac;
10 And confirmed the same unto
Jacob for a law, *and* to Israel *for* an
everlasting covenant:
11 Saying, Unto thee will I give the
land of Canaan, the lot of your inheritance:
12 When they were *but* a few men in
number; yea, very few, and strangers in
it.
13 When they went from one nation
to another, from *one* kingdom to another people;
14 He suffered no man to do them
wrong: yea, he reproved kings for their
sakes;
15 *Saying*, Touch not mine anointed,
and do my prophets no harm.
16 Moreover he called for a famine
upon the land: he brake the whole staff
of bread.
17 He sent a man before them, *even*
Joseph, *who* was sold for a servant:
18 Whose feet they hurt with fetters:
he was laid in iron:
19 Until the time that his word came:
the word of the LORD tried him.
20 The king sent and loosed him; *even*
the ruler of the people, and let him go
free.
21 He made him lord of his house,
and ruler of all his substance:
22 To bind his princes at his pleasure;
and teach his senators wisdom.
23 Israel also came into Egypt; and
Jacob sojourned in the land of Ham.
24 And he increased his people greatly; and made them stronger than their
enemies.
25 He turned their heart to hate his
people, to deal subtilly with his servants.
26 He sent Moses his servant; *and*
Aaron whom he had chosen.
27 They shewed his signs among
them, and wonders in the land of Ham.
28 He sent darkness, and made it
dark; and they rebelled not against his
word.
29 He turned their waters into blood,
and slew their fish.
30 Their land brought forth frogs in
abundance, in the chambers of their
kings.
31 He spake, and there came divers
sorts of flies, *and* lice in all their coasts.
32 He gave them hail for rain, *and*
flaming fire in their land.
33 He smote their vines also and their
fig trees; and brake the trees of their
coasts.
34 He spake, and the locusts came,
and caterpillers, and that without number,
35 And did eat up all the herbs in
their land, and devoured the fruit of
their ground.
36 He smote also all the firstborn in
their land, the chief of all their strength.
37 He brought them forth also with
silver and gold: and *there was* not one
feeble *person* among their tribes.
38 Egypt was glad when they departed: for the fear of them fell upon them.
39 He spread a cloud for a covering;
and fire to give light in the night.

40 *The people* asked, and he brought quails, and satisfied them with the bread of heaven.

41 He opened the rock, and the waters gushed out; they ran in the dry places *like* a river.

42 For he remembered his holy promise, *and* Abraham his servant.

43 And he brought forth his people with joy, *and* his chosen with gladness:

44 And gave them the lands of the heathen: and they inherited the labour of the people;

45 That they might observe his statutes, and keep his laws. Praise ye the LORD.

PSALM 106

Praise ye the LORD. O give thanks unto the LORD; for *he is* good: for his mercy *endureth* for ever.

2 Who can utter the mighty acts of the LORD? *who* can shew forth all his praise?

3 Blessed *are* they that keep judgment, *and* he that doeth righteousness at all times.

4 Remember me, O LORD, with the favour *that thou bearest unto* thy people: O visit me with thy salvation;

5 That I may see the good of thy chosen, that I may rejoice in the gladness of thy nation, that I may glory with thine inheritance.

6 We have sinned with our fathers, we have committed iniquity, we have done wickedly.

7 Our fathers understood not thy wonders in Egypt; they remembered not the multitude of thy mercies; but provoked *him* at the sea, *even* at the Red sea.

8 Nevertheless he saved them for his name's sake, that he might make his mighty power to be known.

9 He rebuked the Red sea also, and it was dried up: so he led them through the depths, as through the wilderness.

10 And he saved them from the hand of him that hated *them*, and redeemed them from the hand of the enemy.

11 And the waters covered their enemies: there was not one of them left.

12 Then believed they his words; they sang his praise.

13 They soon forgat his works; they waited not for his counsel:

14 But lusted exceedingly in the wilderness, and tempted God in the desert.

15 And he gave them their request; but sent leanness into their soul.

16 They envied Moses also in the camp, *and* Aaron the saint of the LORD.

17 The earth opened and swallowed up Dathan, and covered the company of Abiram.

18 And a fire was kindled in their company; the flame burned up the wicked.

19 They made a calf in Horeb, and worshipped the molten image.

20 Thus they changed their glory into the similitude of an ox that eateth grass.

21 They forgat God their saviour, which had done great things in Egypt;

22 Wondrous works in the land of Ham, *and* terrible things by the Red sea.

23 Therefore he said that he would destroy them, had not Moses his chosen stood before him in the breach, to turn away his wrath, lest he should destroy *them*.

24 Yea, they despised the pleasant
land, they believed not his word:
25 But murmured in their tents, *and*
hearkened not unto the voice of the
LORD.
26 Therefore he lifted up his hand
against them, to overthrow them in the
wilderness:
27 To overthrow their seed also
among the nations, and to scatter them
in the lands.
28 They joined themselves also unto
Baal-peor, and ate the sacrifices of the
dead.
29 Thus they provoked *him* to anger
with their inventions: and the plague
brake in upon them.
30 Then stood up Phinehas, and executed judgment: and *so* the plague was
stayed.
31 And that was counted unto him for
righteousness unto all generations for
evermore.
32 They angered *him* also at the
waters of strife, so that it went ill with
Moses for their sakes:
33 Because they provoked his spirit,
so that he spake unadvisedly with his
lips.
34 They did not destroy the nations,
concerning whom the LORD commanded them:
35 But were mingled among the heathen, and learned their works.
36 And they served their idols: which
were a snare unto them.
37 Yea, they sacrificed their sons and
their daughters unto devils,
38 And shed innocent blood, *even* the
blood of their sons and of their daughters, whom they sacrificed unto the
idols of Canaan: and the land was polluted with blood.
39 Thus were they defiled with their
own works, and went a whoring with
their own inventions.
40 Therefore was the wrath of the
LORD kindled against his people, insomuch that he abhorred his own inheritance.
41 And he gave them into the hand of
the heathen; and they that hated them
ruled over them.
42 Their enemies also oppressed
them, and they were brought into subjection under their hand.
43 Many times did he deliver them;
but they provoked *him* with their counsel, and were brought low for their
iniquity.
44 Nevertheless he regarded their
affliction, when he heard their cry:
45 And he remembered for them his
covenant, and repented according to
the multitude of his mercies.
46 He made them also to be pitied of
all those that carried them captives.
47 Save us, O LORD our God, and
gather us from among the heathen, to
give thanks unto thy holy name, *and* to
triumph in thy praise.
48 Blessed *be* the LORD God of Israel
from everlasting to everlasting: and let
all the people say, Amen. Praise ye the
LORD.

PSALM 107

O give thanks unto the LORD, for *he is*
good: for his mercy *endureth* for
ever.
2 Let the redeemed of the LORD say
so, whom he hath redeemed from the
hand of the enemy;
3 And gathered them out of the lands,
from the east, and from the west, from
the north, and from the south.

4 They wandered in the wilderness in
a solitary way; they found no city to
dwell in.
5 Hungry and thirsty, their soul fainted in them.
6 Then they cried unto the LORD in
their trouble, *and* he delivered them
out of their distresses.
7 And he led them forth by the right
way, that they might go to a city of
habitation.
8 Oh that *men* would praise the LORD
for his goodness, and *for* his wonderful
works to the children of men!
9 For he satisfieth the longing soul,
and filleth the hungry soul with goodness.
10 Such as sit in darkness and in the
shadow of death, *being* bound in affliction and iron;
11 Because they rebelled against the
words of God, and contemned the counsel of the most High:
12 Therefore he brought down their
heart with labour; they fell down, and
there was none to help.
13 Then they cried unto the LORD in
their trouble, *and* he saved them out of
their distresses.
14 He brought them out of darkness
and the shadow of death, and brake
their bands in sunder.
15 Oh that *men* would praise the
LORD *for* his goodness, and *for* his wonderful works to the children of men!
16 For he hath broken the gates of
brass, and cut the bars of iron in sunder.
17 Fools because of their transgression, and because of their iniquities,
are afflicted.
18 Their soul abhorreth all manner of
meat; and they draw near unto the
gates of death.
19 Then they cry unto the LORD in
their trouble, *and* he saveth them out
of their distresses.
20 He sent his word, and healed them,
and delivered *them* from their destructions.
21 Oh that *men* would praise the
LORD *for* his goodness, and *for* his wonderful works to the children of men!
22 And let them sacrifice the sacrifices of thanksgiving, and declare his
works with rejoicing.
23 They that go down to the sea in
ships, that do business in great waters;
24 These see the works of the LORD,
and his wonders in the deep.
25 For he commandeth, and raiseth
the stormy wind, which lifteth up the
waves thereof.
26 They mount up to the heaven, they
go down again to the depths: their soul
is melted because of trouble.
27 They reel to and fro, and stagger
like a drunken man, and are at their
wits' end.
28 Then they cry unto the LORD in
their trouble, and he bringeth them out
of their distresses.
29 He maketh the storm a calm, so
that the waves thereof are still.
30 Then are they glad because they
be quiet; so he bringeth them unto
their desired haven.
31 Oh that *men* would praise the
LORD *for* his goodness, and *for* his wonderful works to the children of men!
32 Let them exalt him also in the
congregation of the people, and praise
him in the assembly of the elders.
33 He turneth rivers into a wilderness, and the watersprings into dry
ground;

34 A fruitful land into barrenness, for the wickedness of them that dwell therein.

35 He turneth the wilderness into a standing water, and dry ground into watersprings.

36 And there he maketh the hungry to dwell, that they may prepare a city for habitation;

37 And sow the fields, and plant vineyards, which may yield fruits of increase.

38 He blesseth them also, so that they are multiplied greatly; and suffereth not their cattle to decrease.

39 Again, they are minished and brought low through oppression, affliction, and sorrow.

40 He poureth contempt upon princes, and causeth them to wander in the wilderness, *where there is* no way.

41 Yet setteth he the poor on high from affliction, and maketh *him* families like a flock.

42 The righteous shall see *it*, and rejoice: and all iniquity shall stop her mouth.

43 Whoso *is* wise, and will observe these *things*, even they shall understand the lovingkindness of the LORD.

PSALM 108

A Song *or* Psalm of David.

O God, my heart is fixed; I will sing and give praise, even with my glory.

2 Awake, psaltery and harp: I *myself* will awake early.

3 I will praise thee, O LORD, among the people: and I will sing praises unto thee among the nations.

4 For thy mercy *is* great above the heavens: and thy truth *reacheth* unto the clouds.

5 Be thou exalted, O God, above the heavens: and thy glory above all the earth;

6 That thy beloved may be delivered: save *with* thy right hand, and answer me.

7 God hath spoken in his holiness; I will rejoice, I will divide Shechem, and mete out the valley of Succoth.

8 Gilead *is* mine; Manasseh *is* mine; Ephraim also *is* the strength of mine head; Judah *is* my lawgiver;

9 Moab *is* my washpot; over Edom will I cast out my shoe; over Philistia will I triumph.

10 Who will bring me into the strong city? who will lead me into Edom?

11 *Wilt* not *thou*, O God, *who* hast cast us off? and wilt not thou, O God, go forth with our hosts?

12 Give us help from trouble: for vain *is* the help of man.

13 Through God we shall do valiantly: for he *it is that* shall tread down our enemies.

PSALM 109

To the chief Musician, A Psalm of David.

Hold not thy peace, O God of my praise;

2 For the mouth of the wicked and the mouth of the deceitful are opened against me: they have spoken against me with a lying tongue.

3 They compassed me about also with words of hatred; and fought against me without a cause.

4 For my love they are my adversaries: but I *give myself unto* prayer.

5 And they have rewarded me evil for good, and hatred for my love.

6 Set thou a wicked man over him: and let Satan stand at his right hand.

7 When he shall be judged, let him be condemned: and let his prayer become sin.

8 Let his days be few; *and* let another take his office.

9 Let his children be fatherless, and his wife a widow.

10 Let his children be continually vagabonds, and beg: let them seek *their bread* also out of their desolate places.

11 Let the extortioner catch all that he hath; and let the strangers spoil his labour.

12 Let there be none to extend mercy unto him: neither let there be any to favour his fatherless children.

13 Let his posterity be cut off; *and* in the generation following let their name be blotted out.

14 Let the iniquity of his fathers be remembered with the LORD; and let not the sin of his mother be blotted out.

15 Let them be before the LORD continually, that he may cut off the memory of them from the earth.

16 Because that he remembered not to shew mercy, but persecuted the poor and needy man, that he might even slay the broken in heart.

17 As he loved cursing, so let it come unto him: as he delighted not in blessing, so let it be far from him.

18 As he clothed himself with cursing like as with his garment, so let it come into his bowels like water, and like oil into his bones.

19 Let it be unto him as the garment *which* covereth him, and for a girdle wherewith he is girded continually.

20 *Let* this *be* the reward of mine adversaries from the LORD, and of them that speak evil against my soul.

21 But do thou for me, O GOD the Lord, for thy name's sake: because thy mercy *is* good, deliver thou me.

22 For I *am* poor and needy, and my heart is wounded within me.

23 I am gone like the shadow when it declineth: I am tossed up and down as the locust.

24 My knees are weak through fasting; and my flesh faileth of fatness.

25 I became also a reproach unto them: *when* they looked upon me they shaked their heads.

26 Help me, O LORD my God: O save me according to thy mercy:

27 That they may know that this *is* thy hand; *that* thou, LORD, hast done it.

28 Let them curse, but bless thou: when they arise, let them be ashamed; but let thy servant rejoice.

29 Let mine adversaries be clothed with shame, and let them cover themselves with their own confusion, as with a mantle.

30 I will greatly praise the LORD with my mouth; yea, I will praise him among the multitude.

31 For he shall stand at the right hand of the poor, to save *him* from those that condemn his soul.

PSALM 110

A Psalm of David.

The LORD said unto my Lord, Sit thou at my right hand, until I make thine enemies thy footstool.

2 The LORD shall send the rod of thy strength out of Zion: rule thou in the midst of thine enemies.

3 Thy people *shall be* willing in the day of thy power, in the beauties of holiness from the womb of the morning: thou hast the dew of thy youth.

4 The LORD hath sworn, and will not
repent, Thou *art* a priest for ever after
the order of Melchizedek.
5 The Lord at thy right hand shall
strike through kings in the day of his
wrath.
6 He shall judge among the heathen,
he shall fill *the places* with the dead
bodies; he shall wound the heads over
many countries.
7 He shall drink of the brook in the
way: therefore shall he lift up the head.

PSALM 111

Praise ye the LORD. I will praise the
LORD with *my* whole heart, in the
assembly of the upright, and *in* the
congregation.
2 The works of the LORD *are* great,
sought out of all them that have pleasure therein.
3 His work *is* honourable and glorious: and his righteousness endureth for
ever.
4 He hath made his wonderful works
to be remembered: the LORD *is* gracious
and full of compassion.
5 He hath given meat unto them that
fear him: he will ever be mindful of his
covenant.
6 He hath shewed his people the
power of his works, that he may give
them the heritage of the heathen.
7 The works of his hands *are* verity
and judgment; all his commandments
are sure.
8 They stand fast for ever and ever,
and are done in truth and uprightness.
9 He sent redemption unto his people: he hath commanded his covenant
for ever: holy and reverend *is* his name.
10 The fear of the LORD *is* the beginning of wisdom: a good understanding
have all they that do *his commandments*: his praise endureth for ever.

PSALM 112

Praise ye the LORD. Blessed *is* the
man *that* feareth the LORD, *that*
delighteth greatly in his commandments.
2 His seed shall be mighty upon
earth: the generation of the upright
shall be blessed.
3 Wealth and riches *shall be* in his
house: and his righteousness endureth
for ever.
4 Unto the upright there ariseth light
in the darkness: *he is* gracious, and full
of compassion, and righteous.
5 A good man sheweth favour, and
lendeth: he will guide his affairs with
discretion.
6 Surely he shall not be moved for
ever: the righteous shall be in everlasting remembrance.
7 He shall not be afraid of evil tidings:
his heart is fixed, trusting in the LORD.
8 His heart *is* established, he shall not
be afraid, until he see *his desire* upon
his enemies.
9 He hath dispersed, he hath given to
the poor; his righteousness endureth
for ever; his horn shall be exalted with
honour.
10 The wicked shall see *it*, and be
grieved; he shall gnash with his teeth,
and melt away: the desire of the wicked
shall perish.

PSALM 113

Praise ye the LORD. Praise, O ye
servants of the LORD, praise the
name of the LORD.
2 Blessed be the name of the LORD
from this time forth and for evermore.

3 From the rising of the sun unto the going down of the same the LORD's name *is* to be praised.

4 The LORD *is* high above all nations, *and* his glory above the heavens.

5 Who *is* like unto the LORD our God, who dwelleth on high,

6 Who humbleth *himself* to behold *the things that are* in heaven, and in the earth!

7 He raiseth up the poor out of the dust, *and* lifteth the needy out of the dunghill;

8 That he may set *him* with princes, *even* with the princes of his people.

9 He maketh the barren woman to keep house, *and to be* a joyful mother of children. Praise ye the LORD.

PSALM 114

When Israel went out of Egypt, the house of Jacob from a people of strange language;

2 Judah was his sanctuary, *and* Israel his dominion.

3 The sea saw *it*, and fled: Jordan was driven back.

4 The mountains skipped like rams, *and* the little hills like lambs.

5 What *ailed* thee, O thou sea, that thou fleddest? thou Jordan, *that* thou wast driven back?

6 Ye mountains, *that* ye skipped like rams; *and* ye little hills, like lambs?

7 Tremble, thou earth, at the presence of the Lord, at the presence of the God of Jacob;

8 Which turned the rock *into* a standing water, the flint into a fountain of waters.

PSALM 115

Not unto us, O LORD, not unto us, but unto thy name give glory, for thy mercy, *and* for thy truth's sake.

2 Wherefore should the heathen say, Where *is* now their God?

3 But our God *is* in the heavens: he hath done whatsoever he hath pleased.

4 Their idols *are* silver and gold, the work of men's hands.

5 They have mouths, but they speak not: eyes have they, but they see not:

6 They have ears, but they hear not: noses have they, but they smell not:

7 They have hands, but they handle not: feet have they, but they walk not: neither speak they through their throat.

8 They that make them are like unto them; *so is* every one that trusteth in them.

9 O Israel, trust thou in the LORD: he *is* their help and their shield.

10 O house of Aaron, trust in the LORD: he *is* their help and their shield.

11 Ye that fear the LORD, trust in the LORD: he *is* their help and their shield.

12 The LORD hath been mindful of us: he will bless *us*; he will bless the house of Israel; he will bless the house of Aaron.

13 He will bless them that fear the LORD, *both* small and great.

14 The LORD shall increase you more and more, you and your children.

15 Ye *are* blessed of the LORD which made heaven and earth.

16 The heaven, *even* the heavens, *are* the LORD's: but the earth hath he given to the children of men.

17 The dead praise not the LORD, neither any that go down into silence.

18 But we will bless the LORD from
this time forth and for evermore. Praise
the LORD.

PSALM 116

I love the LORD, because he hath
heard my voice *and* my supplications.
2 Because he hath inclined his ear
unto me, therefore will I call upon *him*
as long as I live.
3 The sorrows of death compassed
me, and the pains of hell gat hold upon
me: I found trouble and sorrow.
4 Then called I upon the name of the
LORD; O LORD, I beseech thee, deliver
my soul.
5 Gracious *is* the LORD, and righteous;
yea, our God *is* merciful.
6 The LORD preserveth the simple: I
was brought low, and he helped me.
7 Return unto thy rest, O my soul; for
the LORD hath dealt bountifully with
thee.
8 For thou hast delivered my soul
from death, mine eyes from tears, *and*
my feet from falling.
9 I will walk before the LORD in the
land of the living.
10 I believed, therefore have I spoken:
I was greatly afflicted:
11 I said in my haste, All men *are*
liars.
12 What shall I render unto the LORD
for all his benefits toward me?
13 I will take the cup of salvation, and
call upon the name of the LORD.
14 I will pay my vows unto the LORD
now in the presence of all his people.
15 Precious in the sight of the LORD *is*
the death of his saints.
16 O LORD, truly I *am* thy servant; I
am thy servant, *and* the son of thine
handmaid: thou hast loosed my bonds.
17 I will offer to thee the sacrifice of
thanksgiving, and will call upon the
name of the LORD.
18 I will pay my vows unto the LORD
now in the presence of all his people,
19 In the courts of the LORD's house,
in the midst of thee, O Jerusalem.
Praise ye the LORD.

PSALM 117

O praise the LORD, all ye nations:
praise him, all ye people.
2 For his merciful kindness is great
toward us: and the truth of the LORD
endureth for ever. Praise ye the LORD.

PSALM 118

O give thanks unto the LORD; for *he is*
good: because his mercy *endureth*
for ever.
2 Let Israel now say, that his mercy
endureth for ever.
3 Let the house of Aaron now say, that
his mercy *endureth* for ever.
4 Let them now that fear the LORD
say, that his mercy *endureth* for ever.
5 I called upon the LORD in distress:
the LORD answered me, *and set me* in a
large place.
6 The LORD *is* on my side; I will not
fear: what can man do unto me?
7 The LORD taketh my part with them
that help me: therefore shall I see *my*
desire upon them that hate me.
8 *It is* better to trust in the LORD than
to put confidence in man.
9 *It is* better to trust in the LORD than
to put confidence in princes.
10 All nations compassed me about:
but in the name of the LORD will I
destroy them.
11 They compassed me about; yea,
they compassed me about: but in the
name of the LORD I will destroy them.

12 They compassed me about like
bees; they are quenched as the fire of
thorns: for in the name of the LORD I
will destroy them.
13 Thou hast thrust sore at me that I
might fall: but the LORD helped me.
14 The LORD *is* my strength and song,
and is become my salvation.
15 The voice of rejoicing and salvation *is* in the tabernacles of the righteous: the right hand of the LORD doeth
valiantly.
16 The right hand of the LORD is
exalted: the right hand of the LORD
doeth valiantly.
17 I shall not die, but live, and declare
the works of the LORD.
18 The LORD hath chastened me sore:
but he hath not given me over unto
death.
19 Open to me the gates of righteousness: I will go into them, *and* I will
praise the LORD:
20 This gate of the LORD, into which
the righteous shall enter.
21 I will praise thee: for thou hast
heard me, and art become my salvation.
22 The stone *which* the builders
refused is become the head *stone* of the
corner.
23 This is the LORD's doing; it *is* marvellous in our eyes.
24 This *is* the day *which* the LORD
hath made; we will rejoice and be glad
in it.
25 Save now, I beseech thee, O LORD:
O LORD, I beseech thee, send now prosperity.
26 Blessed *be* he that cometh in the
name of the LORD: we have blessed you
out of the house of the LORD.
27 God *is* the LORD, which hath
shewed us light: bind the sacrifice with
cords, *even* unto the horns of the altar.
28 Thou *art* my God, and I will praise
thee: *thou art* my God, I will exalt thee.
29 O give thanks unto the LORD; for *he*
is good: for his mercy *endureth* for ever.

PSALM 119

ALEPH

Blessed *are* the undefiled in the way,
who walk in the law of the LORD.
2 Blessed *are* they that keep his testimonies, *and that* seek him with the
whole heart.
3 They also do no iniquity: they walk
in his ways.
4 Thou hast commanded *us* to keep
thy precepts diligently.
5 O that my ways were directed to
keep thy statutes!
6 Then shall I not be ashamed, when I
have respect unto all thy commandments.
7 I will praise thee with uprightness
of heart, when I shall have learned thy
righteous judgments.
8 I will keep thy statutes: O forsake
me not utterly.

BETH

9 Wherewithal shall a young man
cleanse his way? by taking heed *thereto*
according to thy word.
10 With my whole heart have I sought
thee: O let me not wander from thy
commandments.
11 Thy word have I hid in mine heart,
that I might not sin against thee.
12 Blessed *art* thou, O LORD: teach me
thy statutes.
13 With my lips have I declared all
the judgments of thy mouth.

14 I have rejoiced in the way of thy testimonies, as *much as* in all riches.

15 I will meditate in thy precepts, and have respect unto thy ways.

16 I will delight myself in thy statutes: I will not forget thy word.

GIMEL

17 Deal bountifully with thy servant, *that* I may live, and keep thy word.

18 Open thou mine eyes, that I may behold wondrous things out of thy law.

19 I *am* a stranger in the earth: hide not thy commandments from me.

20 My soul breaketh for the longing *that it hath* unto thy judgments at all times.

21 Thou hast rebuked the proud *that are* cursed, which do err from thy commandments.

22 Remove from me reproach and contempt; for I have kept thy testimonies.

23 Princes also did sit *and* speak against me: *but* thy servant did meditate in thy statutes.

24 Thy testimonies also *are* my delight *and* my counsellors.

DALETH

25 My soul cleaveth unto the dust: quicken thou me according to thy word.

26 I have declared my ways, and thou heardest me: teach me thy statutes.

27 Make me to understand the way of thy precepts: so shall I talk of thy wondrous works.

28 My soul melteth for heaviness: strengthen thou me according unto thy word.

29 Remove from me the way of lying: and grant me thy law graciously.

30 I have chosen the way of truth: thy judgments have I laid *before me.*

31 I have stuck unto thy testimonies: O LORD, put me not to shame.

32 I will run the way of thy commandments, when thou shalt enlarge my heart.

HE

33 Teach me, O LORD, the way of thy statutes; and I shall keep it *unto* the end.

34 Give me understanding, and I shall keep thy law; yea, I shall observe it with *my* whole heart.

35 Make me to go in the path of thy commandments; for therein do I delight.

36 Incline my heart unto thy testimonies, and not to covetousness.

37 Turn away mine eyes from beholding vanity; *and* quicken thou me in thy way.

38 Stablish thy word unto thy servant, who *is devoted* to thy fear.

39 Turn away my reproach which I fear: for thy judgments *are* good.

40 Behold, I have longed after thy precepts: quicken me in thy righteousness.

VAU

41 Let thy mercies come also unto me, O LORD, *even* thy salvation, according to thy word.

42 So shall I have wherewith to answer him that reproacheth me: for I trust in thy word.

43 And take not the word of truth utterly out of my mouth; for I have hoped in thy judgments.

44 So shall I keep thy law continually for ever and ever.

45 And I will walk at liberty: for I seek thy precepts.

46 I will speak of thy testimonies also before kings, and will not be ashamed.

47 And I will delight myself in thy commandments, which I have loved.

48 My hands also will I lift up unto thy commandments, which I have loved; and I will meditate in thy statutes.

ZAIN

49 Remember the word unto thy servant, upon which thou hast caused me to hope.

50 This *is* my comfort in my affliction: for thy word hath quickened me.

51 The proud have had me greatly in derision: *yet* have I not declined from thy law.

52 I remembered thy judgments of old, O LORD; and have comforted myself.

53 Horror hath taken hold upon me because of the wicked that forsake thy law.

54 Thy statutes have been my songs in the house of my pilgrimage.

55 I have remembered thy name, O LORD, in the night, and have kept thy law.

56 This I had, because I kept thy precepts.

CHETH

57 *Thou art* my portion, O LORD: I have said that I would keep thy words.

58 I intreated thy favour with *my* whole heart: be merciful unto me according to thy word.

59 I thought on my ways, and turned my feet unto thy testimonies.

60 I made haste, and delayed not to keep thy commandments.

61 The bands of the wicked have robbed me: *but* I have not forgotten thy law.

62 At midnight I will rise to give thanks unto thee because of thy righteous judgments.

63 I *am* a companion of all *them* that fear thee, and of them that keep thy precepts.

64 The earth, O LORD, is full of thy mercy: teach me thy statutes.

TETH

65 Thou hast dealt well with thy servant, O LORD, according unto thy word.

66 Teach me good judgment and knowledge: for I have believed thy commandments.

67 Before I was afflicted I went astray: but now have I kept thy word.

68 Thou *art* good, and doest good; teach me thy statutes.

69 The proud have forged a lie against me: *but* I will keep thy precepts with *my* whole heart.

70 Their heart is as fat as grease; *but* I delight in thy law.

71 *It is* good for me that I have been afflicted; that I might learn thy statutes.

72 The law of thy mouth *is* better unto me than thousands of gold and silver.

JOD

73 Thy hands have made me and fashioned me: give me understanding, that I may learn thy commandments.

74 They that fear thee will be glad when they see me; because I have hoped in thy word.

75 I know, O LORD, that thy judgments *are* right, and *that* thou in faithfulness hast afflicted me.

76 Let, I pray thee, thy merciful kindness be for my comfort, according to thy word unto thy servant.

77 Let thy tender mercies come unto me, that I may live: for thy law *is* my delight.

78 Let the proud be ashamed; for they dealt perversely with me without a cause: *but* I will meditate in thy precepts.

79 Let those that fear thee turn unto me, and those that have known thy testimonies.

80 Let my heart be sound in thy statutes; that I be not ashamed.

CAPH

81 My soul fainteth for thy salvation: *but* I hope in thy word.

82 Mine eyes fail for thy word, saying, When wilt thou comfort me?

83 For I am become like a bottle in the smoke; *yet* do I not forget thy statutes.

84 How many *are* the days of thy servant? when wilt thou execute judgment on them that persecute me?

85 The proud have digged pits for me, which *are* not after thy law.

86 All thy commandments *are* faithful: they persecute me wrongfully; help thou me.

87 They had almost consumed me upon earth; but I forsook not thy precepts.

88 Quicken me after thy lovingkindness; so shall I keep the testimony of thy mouth.

LAMED

89 For ever, O LORD, thy word is settled in heaven.

90 Thy faithfulness *is* unto all generations: thou hast established the earth, and it abideth.

91 They continue this day according to thine ordinances: for all *are* thy servants.

92 Unless thy law *had been* my delights, I should then have perished in mine affliction.

93 I will never forget thy precepts: for with them thou hast quickened me.

94 I *am* thine, save me; for I have sought thy precepts.

95 The wicked have waited for me to destroy me: *but* I will consider thy testimonies.

96 I have seen an end of all perfection: *but* thy commandment *is* exceeding broad.

MEM

97 O how love I thy law! it *is* my meditation all the day.

98 Thou through thy commandments hast made me wiser than mine enemies: for they *are* ever with me.

99 I have more understanding than all my teachers: for thy testimonies *are* my meditation.

100 I understand more than the ancients, because I keep thy precepts.

101 I have refrained my feet from every evil way, that I might keep thy word.

102 I have not departed from thy judgments: for thou hast taught me.

103 How sweet are thy words unto my taste! *yea, sweeter* than honey to my mouth!

104 Through thy precepts I get understanding: therefore I hate every false way.

NUN

105 Thy word *is* a lamp unto my feet, and a light unto my path.

106 I have sworn, and I will perform *it*, that I will keep thy righteous judgments.

107 I am afflicted very much: quicken me, O LORD, according unto thy word.

108 Accept, I beseech thee, the freewill offerings of my mouth, O LORD, and teach me thy judgments.

109 My soul *is* continually in my hand: yet do I not forget thy law.

110 The wicked have laid a snare for me: yet I erred not from thy precepts.

111 Thy testimonies have I taken as an heritage for ever: for they *are* the rejoicing of my heart.

112 I have inclined mine heart to perform thy statutes alway, *even unto* the end.

SAMECH

113 I hate *vain* thoughts: but thy law do I love.

114 Thou *art* my hiding place and my shield: I hope in thy word.

115 Depart from me, ye evildoers: for I will keep the commandments of my God.

116 Uphold me according unto thy word, that I may live: and let me not be ashamed of my hope.

117 Hold thou me up, and I shall be safe: and I will have respect unto thy statutes continually.

118 Thou hast trodden down all them that err from thy statutes: for their deceit *is* falsehood.

119 Thou puttest away all the wicked of the earth *like* dross: therefore I love thy testimonies.

120 My flesh trembleth for fear of thee; and I am afraid of thy judgments.

AIN

121 I have done judgment and justice: leave me not to mine oppressors.

122 Be surety for thy servant for good: let not the proud oppress me.

123 Mine eyes fail for thy salvation, and for the word of thy righteousness.

124 Deal with thy servant according unto thy mercy, and teach me thy statutes.

125 I *am* thy servant; give me understanding, that I may know thy testimonies.

126 *It is* time for *thee*, LORD, to work: *for* they have made void thy law.

127 Therefore I love thy commandments above gold; yea, above fine gold.

128 Therefore I esteem all *thy* precepts *concerning* all *things to be* right; *and* I hate every false way.

PE

129 Thy testimonies *are* wonderful: therefore doth my soul keep them.

130 The entrance of thy words giveth light; it giveth understanding unto the simple.

131 I opened my mouth, and panted: for I longed for thy commandments.

132 Look thou upon me, and be merciful unto me, as thou usest to do unto those that love thy name.

133 Order my steps in thy word: and let not any iniquity have dominion over me.

134 Deliver me from the oppression of man: so will I keep thy precepts.

135 Make thy face to shine upon thy servant; and teach me thy statutes.

136 Rivers of waters run down mine eyes, because they keep not thy law.

TZADDI

137 Righteous *art* thou, O LORD, and upright *are* thy judgments.

138 Thy testimonies *that* thou hast commanded *are* righteous and very faithful.

139 My zeal hath consumed me, because mine enemies have forgotten thy words.

140 Thy word *is* very pure: therefore thy servant loveth it.

141 I *am* small and despised: *yet* do not I forget thy precepts.

142 Thy righteousness *is* an everlasting righteousness, and thy law *is* the truth.

143 Trouble and anguish have taken hold on me: *yet* thy commandments *are* my delights.

144 The righteousness of thy testimonies *is* everlasting: give me understanding, and I shall live.

KOPH

145 I cried with *my* whole heart; hear me, O LORD: I will keep thy statutes.

146 I cried unto thee; save me, and I shall keep thy testimonies.

147 I prevented the dawning of the morning, and cried: I hoped in thy word.

148 Mine eyes prevent the *night* watches, that I might meditate in thy word.

149 Hear my voice according unto thy lovingkindness: O LORD, quicken me according to thy judgment.

150 They draw nigh that follow after mischief: they are far from thy law.

151 Thou *art* near, O LORD; and all thy commandments *are* truth.

152 Concerning thy testimonies, I have known of old that thou hast founded them for ever.

RESH

153 Consider mine affliction, and deliver me: for I do not forget thy law.

154 Plead my cause, and deliver me: quicken me according to thy word.

155 Salvation *is* far from the wicked: for they seek not thy statutes.

156 Great *are* thy tender mercies, O LORD: quicken me according to thy judgments.

157 Many *are* my persecutors and mine enemies; *yet* do I not decline from thy testimonies.

158 I beheld the transgressors, and was grieved; because they kept not thy word.

159 Consider how I love thy precepts: quicken me, O LORD, according to thy lovingkindness.

160 Thy word *is* true *from* the beginning: and every one of thy righteous judgments *endureth* for ever.

SCHIN

161 Princes have persecuted me without a cause: but my heart standeth in awe of thy word.

162 I rejoice at thy word, as one that findeth great spoil.

163 I hate and abhor lying: *but* thy law do I love.

164 Seven times a day do I praise thee because of thy righteous judgments.

165 Great peace have they which love thy law: and nothing shall offend them.

166 LORD, I have hoped for thy salvation, and done thy commandments.

167 My soul hath kept thy testimonies; and I love them exceedingly.

168 I have kept thy precepts and thy testimonies: for all my ways *are* before thee.

TAU

169 Let my cry come near before thee, O LORD: give me understanding according to thy word.

170 Let my supplication come before thee: deliver me according to thy word.

171 My lips shall utter praise, when thou hast taught me thy statutes.

172 My tongue shall speak of thy word: for all thy commandments *are* righteousness.
173 Let thine hand help me; for I have chosen thy precepts.
174 I have longed for thy salvation, O LORD; and thy law *is* my delight.
175 Let my soul live, and it shall praise thee; and let thy judgments help me.
176 I have gone astray like a lost sheep; seek thy servant; for I do not forget thy commandments.

PSALM 120

A Song of degrees.

In my distress I cried unto the LORD, and he heard me.
2 Deliver my soul, O LORD, from lying lips, *and* from a deceitful tongue.
3 What shall be given unto thee? or what shall be done unto thee, thou false tongue?
4 Sharp arrows of the mighty, with coals of juniper.
5 Woe is me, that I sojourn in Mesech, *that* I dwell in the tents of Kedar!
6 My soul hath long dwelt with him that hateth peace.
7 I *am for* peace: but when I speak, they *are* for war.

PSALM 121

A Song of degrees.

I will lift up mine eyes unto the hills, from whence cometh my help.
2 My help *cometh* from the LORD, which made heaven and earth.
3 He will not suffer thy foot to be moved: he that keepeth thee will not slumber.
4 Behold, he that keepeth Israel shall neither slumber nor sleep.
5 The LORD *is* thy keeper: the LORD *is* thy shade upon thy right hand.
6 The sun shall not smite thee by day, nor the moon by night.
7 The LORD shall preserve thee from all evil: he shall preserve thy soul.
8 The LORD shall preserve thy going out and thy coming in from this time forth, and even for evermore.

PSALM 122

A Song of degrees of David.

I was glad when they said unto me, Let us go into the house of the LORD.
2 Our feet shall stand within thy gates, O Jerusalem.
3 Jerusalem is builded as a city that is compact together:
4 Whither the tribes go up, the tribes of the LORD, unto the testimony of Israel, to give thanks unto the name of the LORD.
5 For there are set thrones of judgment, the thrones of the house of David.
6 Pray for the peace of Jerusalem: they shall prosper that love thee.
7 Peace be within thy walls, *and* prosperity within thy palaces.
8 For my brethren and companions' sakes, I will now say, Peace *be* within thee.
9 Because of the house of the LORD our God I will seek thy good.

PSALM 123

A Song of degrees.

Unto thee lift I up mine eyes, O thou that dwellest in the heavens.
2 Behold, as the eyes of servants *look* unto the hand of their masters, *and* as the eyes of a maiden unto the hand of her mistress; so our eyes *wait* upon the

LORD our God, until that he have mercy
upon us.
3 Have mercy upon us, O LORD, have
mercy upon us: for we are exceedingly
filled with contempt.
4 Our soul is exceedingly filled with
the scorning of those that are at ease,
and with the contempt of the proud.

PSALM 124

A Song of degrees of David.

If *it had not been* the LORD who was
on our side, now may Israel say;
2 If *it had not been* the LORD who was
on our side, when men rose up against
us:
3 Then they had swallowed us up
quick, when their wrath was kindled
against us:
4 Then the waters had overwhelmed
us, the stream had gone over our soul:
5 Then the proud waters had gone
over our soul.
6 Blessed *be* the LORD, who hath not
given us *as* a prey to their teeth.
7 Our soul is escaped as a bird out of
the snare of the fowlers: the snare is
broken, and we are escaped.
8 Our help *is* in the name of the LORD,
who made heaven and earth.

PSALM 125

A Song of degrees.

They that trust in the LORD *shall be* as
mount Zion, *which* cannot be
removed, *but* abideth for ever.
2 As the mountains *are* round about
Jerusalem, so the LORD *is* round about
his people from henceforth even for
ever.
3 For the rod of the wicked shall not
rest upon the lot of the righteous; lest
the righteous put forth their hands
unto iniquity.
4 Do good, O LORD, unto *those that be*
good, and *to them that are* upright in
their hearts.
5 As for such as turn aside unto their
crooked ways, the LORD shall lead them
forth with the workers of iniquity: *but*
peace *shall be* upon Israel.

PSALM 126

A Song of degrees.

When the LORD turned again the
captivity of Zion, we were like
them that dream.
2 Then was our mouth filled with
laughter, and our tongue with singing:
then said they among the heathen, The
LORD hath done great things for them.
3 The LORD hath done great things for
us; *whereof* we are glad.
4 Turn again our captivity, O LORD, as
the streams in the south.
5 They that sow in tears shall reap in
joy.
6 He that goeth forth and weepeth,
bearing precious seed, shall doubtless
come again with rejoicing, bringing his
sheaves *with him*.

PSALM 127

A Song of degrees for Solomon.

Except the LORD build the house, they
labour in vain that build it: except
the LORD keep the city, the watchman
waketh *but* in vain.
2 *It is* vain for you to rise up early, to
sit up late, to eat the bread of sorrows:
for so he giveth his beloved sleep.
3 Lo, children *are* an heritage of the
LORD: *and* the fruit of the womb *is his*
reward.
4 As arrows *are* in the hand of a
mighty man; so *are* children of the
youth.

5 Happy *is* the man that hath his quiver full of them: they shall not be ashamed, but they shall speak with the enemies in the gate.

PSALM 128

A Song of degrees.

Blessed *is* every one that feareth the LORD; that walketh in his ways.

2 For thou shalt eat the labour of thine hands: happy *shalt* thou *be*, and *it shall be* well with thee.

3 Thy wife *shall be* as a fruitful vine by the sides of thine house: thy children like olive plants round about thy table.

4 Behold, that thus shall the man be blessed that feareth the LORD.

5 The LORD shall bless thee out of Zion: and thou shalt see the good of Jerusalem all the days of thy life.

6 Yea, thou shalt see thy children's children, *and* peace upon Israel.

PSALM 129

A Song of degrees.

Many a time have they afflicted me from my youth, may Israel now say:

2 Many a time have they afflicted me from my youth: yet they have not prevailed against me.

3 The plowers plowed upon my back: they made long their furrows.

4 The LORD *is* righteous: he hath cut asunder the cords of the wicked.

5 Let them all be confounded and turned back that hate Zion.

6 Let them be as the grass *upon* the housetops, which withereth afore it groweth up:

7 Wherewith the mower filleth not his hand; nor he that bindeth sheaves his bosom.

8 Neither do they which go by say, The blessing of the LORD *be* upon you: we bless you in the name of the LORD.

PSALM 130

A Song of degrees.

Out of the depths have I cried unto thee, O LORD.

2 Lord, hear my voice: let thine ears be attentive to the voice of my supplications.

3 If thou, LORD, shouldest mark iniquities, O Lord, who shall stand?

4 But *there is* forgiveness with thee, that thou mayest be feared.

5 I wait for the LORD, my soul doth wait, and in his word do I hope.

6 My soul *waiteth* for the Lord more than they that watch for the morning: *I say, more than* they that watch for the morning.

7 Let Israel hope in the LORD: for with the LORD *there is* mercy, and with him *is* plenteous redemption.

8 And he shall redeem Israel from all his iniquities.

PSALM 131

A Song of degrees of David.

LORD, my heart is not haughty, nor mine eyes lofty: neither do I exercise myself in great matters, or in things too high for me.

2 Surely I have behaved and quieted myself, as a child that is weaned of his mother: my soul *is* even as a weaned child.

3 Let Israel hope in the LORD from henceforth and for ever.

PSALM 132

A Song of degrees.

LORD, remember David, *and* all his afflictions:

2 How he sware unto the LORD, *and*
vowed unto the mighty *God* of Jacob;
3 Surely I will not come into the tabernacle of my house, nor go up into my
bed;
4 I will not give sleep to mine eyes, *or*
slumber to mine eyelids,
5 Until I find out a place for the LORD,
an habitation for the mighty *God* of
Jacob.
6 Lo, we heard of it at Ephratah: we
found it in the fields of the wood.
7 We will go into his tabernacles: we
will worship at his footstool.
8 Arise, O LORD, into thy rest; thou,
and the ark of thy strength.
9 Let thy priests be clothed with righteousness; and let thy saints shout for
joy.
10 For thy servant David's sake turn
not away the face of thine anointed.
11 The LORD hath sworn *in* truth unto
David; he will not turn from it; Of the
fruit of thy body will I set upon thy
throne.
12 If thy children will keep my covenant and my testimony that I shall
teach them, their children shall also sit
upon thy throne for evermore.
13 For the LORD hath chosen Zion; he
hath desired *it* for his habitation.
14 This *is* my rest for ever: here will I
dwell; for I have desired it.
15 I will abundantly bless her provision: I will satisfy her poor with bread.
16 I will also clothe her priests with
salvation: and her saints shall shout
aloud for joy.
17 There will I make the horn of
David to bud: I have ordained a lamp
for mine anointed.
18 His enemies will I clothe with
shame: but upon himself shall his
crown flourish.

PSALM 133

A Song of degrees of David.

Behold, how good and how pleasant *it*
is for brethren to dwell together in
unity!
2 *It is* like the precious ointment
upon the head, that ran down upon the
beard, *even* Aaron's beard: that went
down to the skirts of his garments;
3 As the dew of Hermon, *and as the*
dew that descended upon the mountains of Zion: for there the LORD commanded the blessing, *even* life for evermore.

PSALM 134

A Song of degrees.

Behold, bless ye the LORD, all *ye*
servants of the LORD, which by night
stand in the house of the LORD.
2 Lift up your hands *in* the sanctuary,
and bless the LORD.
3 The LORD that made heaven and
earth bless thee out of Zion.

PSALM 135

Praise ye the LORD. Praise ye the
name of the LORD; praise *him*, O ye
servants of the LORD.
2 Ye that stand in the house of the
LORD, in the courts of the house of our
God,
3 Praise the LORD; for the LORD *is*
good: sing praises unto his name; for *it*
is pleasant.
4 For the LORD hath chosen Jacob
unto himself, *and* Israel for his peculiar
treasure.
5 For I know that the LORD *is* great,
and *that* our Lord *is* above all gods.
6 Whatsoever the LORD pleased, *that*
did he in heaven, and in earth, in the
seas, and all deep places.

7 He causeth the vapours to ascend from the ends of the earth; he maketh lightnings for the rain; he bringeth the wind out of his treasuries.

8 Who smote the firstborn of Egypt, both of man and beast.

9 *Who* sent tokens and wonders into the midst of thee, O Egypt, upon Pharaoh, and upon all his servants.

10 Who smote great nations, and slew mighty kings;

11 Sihon king of the Amorites, and Og king of Bashan, and all the kingdoms of Canaan:

12 And gave their land *for* an heritage, an heritage unto Israel his people.

13 Thy name, O LORD, *endureth* for ever; *and* thy memorial, O LORD, throughout all generations.

14 For the LORD will judge his people, and he will repent himself concerning his servants.

15 The idols of the heathen *are* silver and gold, the work of men's hands.

16 They have mouths, but they speak not; eyes have they, but they see not;

17 They have ears, but they hear not; neither is there *any* breath in their mouths.

18 They that make them are like unto them: *so is* every one that trusteth in them.

19 Bless the LORD, O house of Israel: bless the LORD, O house of Aaron:

20 Bless the LORD, O house of Levi: ye that fear the LORD, bless the LORD.

21 Blessed be the LORD out of Zion, which dwelleth at Jerusalem. Praise ye the LORD.

PSALM 136

O give thanks unto the LORD; for *he is* good: for his mercy *endureth* for ever.

2 O give thanks unto the God of gods: for his mercy *endureth* for ever.

3 O give thanks to the Lord of lords: for his mercy *endureth* for ever.

4 To him who alone doeth great wonders: for his mercy *endureth* for ever.

5 To him that by wisdom made the heavens: for his mercy *endureth* for ever.

6 To him that stretched out the earth above the waters: for his mercy *endureth* for ever.

7 To him that made great lights: for his mercy *endureth* for ever:

8 The sun to rule by day: for his mercy *endureth* for ever:

9 The moon and stars to rule by night: for his mercy *endureth* for ever.

10 To him that smote Egypt in their firstborn: for his mercy *endureth* for ever:

11 And brought out Israel from among them: for his mercy *endureth* for ever:

12 With a strong hand, and with a stretched out arm: for his mercy *endureth* for ever.

13 To him which divided the Red sea into parts: for his mercy *endureth* for ever:

14 And made Israel to pass through the midst of it: for his mercy *endureth* for ever:

15 But overthrew Pharaoh and his host in the Red sea: for his mercy *endureth* for ever.

16 To him which led his people through the wilderness: for his mercy *endureth* for ever.

17 To him which smote great kings: for his mercy *endureth* for ever:

18 And slew famous kings: for his mercy *endureth* for ever:

19 Sihon king of the Amorites: for his mercy *endureth* for ever:

20 And Og the king of Bashan: for his mercy *endureth* for ever:

21 And gave their land for an heritage: for his mercy *endureth* for ever:

22 *Even* an heritage unto Israel his servant: for his mercy *endureth* for ever.

23 Who remembered us in our low estate: for his mercy *endureth* for ever:

24 And hath redeemed us from our enemies: for his mercy *endureth* for ever.

25 Who giveth food to all flesh: for his mercy *endureth* for ever.

26 O give thanks unto the God of heaven: for his mercy *endureth* for ever.

PSALM 137

By the rivers of Babylon, there we sat down, yea, we wept, when we remembered Zion.

2 We hanged our harps upon the willows in the midst thereof.

3 For there they that carried us away captive required of us a song; and they that wasted us *required of us* mirth, *saying*, Sing us *one* of the songs of Zion.

4 How shall we sing the Lord's song in a strange land?

5 If I forget thee, O Jerusalem, let my right hand forget *her cunning*.

6 If I do not remember thee, let my tongue cleave to the roof of my mouth; if I prefer not Jerusalem above my chief joy.

7 Remember, O Lord, the children of Edom in the day of Jerusalem; who said, Rase *it*, rase *it*, *even* to the foundation thereof.

8 O daughter of Babylon, who art to be destroyed; happy *shall he be*, that rewardeth thee as thou hast served us.

9 Happy *shall he be*, that taketh and dasheth thy little ones against the stones.

PSALM 138

A Psalm **of David.**

I will praise thee with my whole heart: before the gods will I sing praise unto thee.

2 I will worship toward thy holy temple, and praise thy name for thy lovingkindness and for thy truth: for thou hast magnified thy word above all thy name.

3 In the day when I cried thou answeredst me, *and* strengthenedst me *with* strength in my soul.

4 All the kings of the earth shall praise thee, O Lord, when they hear the words of thy mouth.

5 Yea, they shall sing in the ways of the Lord: for great *is* the glory of the Lord.

6 Though the Lord *be* high, yet hath he respect unto the lowly: but the proud he knoweth afar off.

7 Though I walk in the midst of trouble, thou wilt revive me: thou shalt stretch forth thine hand against the wrath of mine enemies, and thy right hand shall save me.

8 The Lord will perfect *that which* concerneth me: thy mercy, O Lord, *endureth* for ever: forsake not the works of thine own hands.

PSALM 139

To the chief Musician, A Psalm of David.

O Lord, thou hast searched me, and known *me*.

2 Thou knowest my downsitting and mine uprising, thou understandest my thought afar off.

3 Thou compassest my path and my lying down, and art acquainted *with* all my ways.

4 For *there is* not a word in my tongue, *but*, lo, O LORD, thou knowest it altogether.

5 Thou hast beset me behind and before, and laid thine hand upon me.

6 *Such* knowledge *is* too wonderful for me; it is high, I cannot *attain* unto it.

7 Whither shall I go from thy spirit? or whither shall I flee from thy presence?

8 If I ascend up into heaven, thou *art* there: if I make my bed in hell, behold, thou *art there.*

9 *If* I take the wings of the morning, *and* dwell in the uttermost parts of the sea;

10 Even there shall thy hand lead me, and thy right hand shall hold me.

11 If I say, Surely the darkness shall cover me; even the night shall be light about me.

12 Yea, the darkness hideth not from thee; but the night shineth as the day: the darkness and the light *are* both alike *to thee.*

13 For thou hast possessed my reins: thou hast covered me in my mother's womb.

14 I will praise thee; for I am fearfully *and* wonderfully made: marvellous *are* thy works; and *that* my soul knoweth right well.

15 My substance was not hid from thee, when I was made in secret, *and* curiously wrought in the lowest parts of the earth.

16 Thine eyes did see my substance, yet being unperfect; and in thy book all *my members* were written, *which* in continuance were fashioned, when *as yet there was* none of them.

17 How precious also are thy thoughts unto me, O God! how great is the sum of them!

18 *If* I should count them, they are more in number than the sand: when I awake, I am still with thee.

19 Surely thou wilt slay the wicked, O God: depart from me therefore, ye bloody men.

20 For they speak against thee wickedly, *and* thine enemies take *thy name* in vain.

21 Do not I hate them, O LORD, that hate thee? and am not I grieved with those that rise up against thee?

22 I hate them with perfect hatred: I count them mine enemies.

23 Search me, O God, and know my heart: try me, and know my thoughts:

24 And see if *there be any* wicked way in me, and lead me in the way everlasting.

PSALM 140

To the chief Musician, A Psalm of David.

Deliver me, O LORD, from the evil man: preserve me from the violent man;

2 Which imagine mischiefs in *their* heart; continually are they gathered together *for* war.

3 They have sharpened their tongues like a serpent; adders' poison *is* under their lips. Selah.

4 Keep me, O LORD, from the hands of the wicked; preserve me from the violent man; who have purposed to overthrow my goings.

5 The proud have hid a snare for me, and cords; they have spread a net by the wayside; they have set gins for me. Selah.

6 I said unto the LORD, Thou *art* my
God: hear the voice of my supplications, O LORD.
7 O GOD the Lord, the strength of my
salvation, thou hast covered my head in
the day of battle.
8 Grant not, O LORD, the desires of the
wicked: further not his wicked device;
lest they exalt themselves. Selah.
9 *As for* the head of those that compass me about, let the mischief of their
own lips cover them.
10 Let burning coals fall upon them:
let them be cast into the fire; into deep
pits, that they rise not up again.
11 Let not an evil speaker be established in the earth: evil shall hunt the
violent man to overthrow *him*.
12 I know that the LORD will maintain
the cause of the afflicted, *and* the right
of the poor.
13 Surely the righteous shall give
thanks unto thy name: the upright shall
dwell in thy presence.

PSALM 141

A Psalm of David.

LORD, I cry unto thee: make haste unto
me; give ear unto my voice, when I
cry unto thee.
2 Let my prayer be set forth before
thee *as* incense; *and* the lifting up of
my hands *as* the evening sacrifice.
3 Set a watch, O LORD, before my
mouth; keep the door of my lips.
4 Incline not my heart to *any* evil
thing, to practise wicked works with
men that work iniquity: and let me not
eat of their dainties.
5 Let the righteous smite me; *it shall*
be a kindness: and let him reprove me;
it shall be an excellent oil, *which* shall
not break my head: for yet my prayer
also *shall be* in their calamities.
6 When their judges are overthrown
in stony places, they shall hear my
words; for they are sweet.
7 Our bones are scattered at the
grave's mouth, as when one cutteth and
cleaveth *wood* upon the earth.
8 But mine eyes *are* unto thee, O GOD
the Lord: in thee is my trust; leave not
my soul destitute.
9 Keep me from the snares *which*
they have laid for me, and the gins of
the workers of iniquity.
10 Let the wicked fall into their own
nets, whilst that I withal escape.

PSALM 142

Maschil of David;
A Prayer when he was in the cave.

I cried unto the LORD with my voice;
with my voice unto the LORD did I
make my supplication.
2 I poured out my complaint before
him; I shewed before him my trouble.
3 When my spirit was overwhelmed
within me, then thou knewest my path.
In the way wherein I walked have they
privily laid a snare for me.
4 I looked on *my* right hand, and
beheld, but *there was* no man that
would know me: refuge failed me; no
man cared for my soul.
5 I cried unto thee, O LORD: I said,
Thou *art* my refuge *and* my portion in
the land of the living.
6 Attend unto my cry; for I am
brought very low: deliver me from my
persecutors; for they are stronger than
I.
7 Bring my soul out of prison, that I
may praise thy name: the righteous
shall compass me about; for thou shalt
deal bountifully with me.

PSALM 143

A Psalm of David.

Hear my prayer, O LORD, give ear to my supplications: in thy faithfulness answer me, *and* in thy righteousness.

2 And enter not into judgment with thy servant: for in thy sight shall no man living be justified.

3 For the enemy hath persecuted my soul; he hath smitten my life down to the ground; he hath made me to dwell in darkness, as those that have been long dead.

4 Therefore is my spirit overwhelmed within me; my heart within me is desolate.

5 I remember the days of old; I meditate on all thy works; I muse on the work of thy hands.

6 I stretch forth my hands unto thee: my soul *thirsteth* after thee, as a thirsty land. Selah.

7 Hear me speedily, O LORD: my spirit faileth: hide not thy face from me, lest I be like unto them that go down into the pit.

8 Cause me to hear thy lovingkindness in the morning; for in thee do I trust: cause me to know the way wherein I should walk; for I lift up my soul unto thee.

9 Deliver me, O LORD, from mine enemies: I flee unto thee to hide me.

10 Teach me to do thy will; for thou *art* my God: thy spirit *is* good; lead me into the land of uprightness.

11 Quicken me, O LORD, for thy name's sake: for thy righteousness' sake bring my soul out of trouble.

12 And of thy mercy cut off mine enemies, and destroy all them that afflict my soul: for I *am* thy servant.

PSALM 144

A Psalm of David.

Blessed *be* the LORD my strength, which teacheth my hands to war, *and* my fingers to fight:

2 My goodness, and my fortress; my high tower, and my deliverer; my shield, and *he* in whom I trust; who subdueth my people under me.

3 LORD, what *is* man, that thou takest knowledge of him! *or* the son of man, that thou makest account of him!

4 Man is like to vanity: his days *are* as a shadow that passeth away.

5 Bow thy heavens, O LORD, and come down: touch the mountains, and they shall smoke.

6 Cast forth lightning, and scatter them: shoot out thine arrows, and destroy them.

7 Send thine hand from above; rid me, and deliver me out of great waters, from the hand of strange children;

8 Whose mouth speaketh vanity, and their right hand *is* a right hand of falsehood.

9 I will sing a new song unto thee, O God: upon a psaltery *and* an instrument of ten strings will I sing praises unto thee.

10 *It is he* that giveth salvation unto kings: who delivereth David his servant from the hurtful sword.

11 Rid me, and deliver me from the hand of strange children, whose mouth speaketh vanity, and their right hand *is* a right hand of falsehood:

12 That our sons *may be* as plants grown up in their youth; *that* our daughters *may be* as corner stones, polished *after* the similitude of a palace:

13 *That* our garners *may be* full, affording all manner of store: *that* our sheep may bring forth thousands and ten thousands in our streets:

14 *That* our oxen *may be* strong to labour; *that there be* no breaking in, nor going out; that *there be* no complaining in our streets.

15 Happy *is that* people, that is in such a case: *yea*, happy *is that* people, whose God *is* the LORD.

PSALM 145

David's *Psalm* of praise.

I will extol thee, my God, O king; and I will bless thy name for ever and ever.

2 Every day will I bless thee; and I will praise thy name for ever and ever.

3 Great *is* the LORD, and greatly to be praised; and his greatness *is* unsearchable.

4 One generation shall praise thy works to another, and shall declare thy mighty acts.

5 I will speak of the glorious honour of thy majesty, and of thy wondrous works.

6 And *men* shall speak of the might of thy terrible acts: and I will declare thy greatness.

7 They shall abundantly utter the memory of thy great goodness, and shall sing of thy righteousness.

8 The LORD *is* gracious, and full of compassion; slow to anger, and of great mercy.

9 The LORD *is* good to all: and his tender mercies *are* over all his works.

10 All thy works shall praise thee, O LORD; and thy saints shall bless thee.

11 They shall speak of the glory of thy kingdom, and talk of thy power;

12 To make known to the sons of men his mighty acts, and the glorious majesty of his kingdom.

13 Thy kingdom *is* an everlasting kingdom, and thy dominion *endureth* throughout all generations.

14 The LORD upholdeth all that fall, and raiseth up all *those that be* bowed down.

15 The eyes of all wait upon thee; and thou givest them their meat in due season.

16 Thou openest thine hand, and satisfiest the desire of every living thing.

17 The LORD *is* righteous in all his ways, and holy in all his works.

18 The LORD *is* nigh unto all them that call upon him, to all that call upon him in truth.

19 He will fulfil the desire of them that fear him: he also will hear their cry, and will save them.

20 The LORD preserveth all them that love him: but all the wicked will he destroy.

21 My mouth shall speak the praise of the LORD: and let all flesh bless his holy name for ever and ever.

PSALM 146

Praise ye the LORD. Praise the LORD, O my soul.

2 While I live will I praise the LORD: I will sing praises unto my God while I have any being.

3 Put not your trust in princes, *nor* in the son of man, in whom *there is* no help.

4 His breath goeth forth, he returneth to his earth; in that very day his thoughts perish.

5 Happy *is he* that *hath* the God of Jacob for his help, whose hope *is* in the LORD his God:

6 Which made heaven, and earth, the sea, and all that therein *is*: which keepeth truth for ever:

7 Which executeth judgment for the oppressed: which giveth food to the hungry. The LORD looseth the prisoners:

8 The LORD openeth *the eyes of* the blind: the LORD raiseth them that are bowed down: the LORD loveth the righteous:

9 The LORD preserveth the strangers; he relieveth the fatherless and widow: but the way of the wicked he turneth upside down.

10 The LORD shall reign for ever, *even* thy God, O Zion, unto all generations. Praise ye the LORD.

PSALM 147

Praise ye the LORD: for *it is* good to sing praises unto our God; for *it is* pleasant; *and* praise is comely.

2 The LORD doth build up Jerusalem: he gathereth together the outcasts of Israel.

3 He healeth the broken in heart, and bindeth up their wounds.

4 He telleth the number of the stars; he calleth them all by *their* names.

5 Great *is* our Lord, and of great power: his understanding *is* infinite.

6 The LORD lifteth up the meek: he casteth the wicked down to the ground.

7 Sing unto the LORD with thanksgiving; sing praise upon the harp unto our God:

8 Who covereth the heaven with clouds, who prepareth rain for the earth, who maketh grass to grow upon the mountains.

9 He giveth to the beast his food, *and* to the young ravens which cry.

10 He delighteth not in the strength of the horse: he taketh not pleasure in the legs of a man.

11 The LORD taketh pleasure in them that fear him, in those that hope in his mercy.

12 Praise the LORD, O Jerusalem; praise thy God, O Zion.

13 For he hath strengthened the bars of thy gates; he hath blessed thy children within thee.

14 He maketh peace *in* thy borders, *and* filleth thee with the finest of the wheat.

15 He sendeth forth his commandment *upon* earth: his word runneth very swiftly.

16 He giveth snow like wool: he scattereth the hoarfrost like ashes.

17 He casteth forth his ice like morsels: who can stand before his cold?

18 He sendeth out his word, and melteth them: he causeth his wind to blow, *and* the waters flow.

19 He sheweth his word unto Jacob, his statutes and his judgments unto Israel.

20 He hath not dealt so with any nation: and *as for his* judgments, they have not known them. Praise ye the LORD.

PSALM 148

Praise ye the LORD. Praise ye the LORD from the heavens: praise him in the heights.

2 Praise ye him, all his angels: praise ye him, all his hosts.

3 Praise ye him, sun and moon: praise him, all ye stars of light.

4 Praise him, ye heavens of heavens, and ye waters that *be* above the heavens.

5 Let them praise the name of the LORD: for he commanded, and they were created.

6 He hath also stablished them for
ever and ever: he hath made a decree
which shall not pass.
7 Praise the LORD from the earth, ye
dragons, and all deeps:
8 Fire, and hail; snow, and vapour;
stormy wind fulfilling his word:
9 Mountains, and all hills; fruitful
trees, and all cedars:
10 Beasts, and all cattle; creeping
things, and flying fowl:
11 Kings of the earth, and all people;
princes, and all judges of the earth:
12 Both young men, and maidens; old
men, and children:
13 Let them praise the name of the
LORD: for his name alone is excellent;
his glory *is* above the earth and heaven.
14 He also exalteth the horn of his
people, the praise of all his saints; *even*
of the children of Israel, a people near
unto him. Praise ye the LORD.

PSALM 149

Praise ye the LORD. Sing unto the
LORD a new song, *and* his praise in
the congregation of saints.
2 Let Israel rejoice in him that made
him: let the children of Zion be joyful
in their King.
3 Let them praise his name in the
dance: let them sing praises unto him
with the timbrel and harp.
4 For the LORD taketh pleasure in his
people: he will beautify the meek with
salvation.
5 Let the saints be joyful in glory: let
them sing aloud upon their beds.
6 *Let* the high *praises* of God *be* in
their mouth, and a twoedged sword in
their hand;
7 To execute vengeance upon the
heathen, *and* punishments upon the
people;
8 To bind their kings with chains, and
their nobles with fetters of iron;
9 To execute upon them the judgment written: this honour have all his
saints. Praise ye the LORD.

PSALM 150

Praise ye the LORD. Praise God in his
sanctuary: praise him in the firmament of his power.
2 Praise him for his mighty acts:
praise him according to his excellent
greatness.
3 Praise him with the sound of the
trumpet: praise him with the psaltery
and harp.
4 Praise him with the timbrel and
dance: praise him with stringed instruments and organs.
5 Praise him upon the loud cymbals:
praise him upon the high sounding
cymbals.
6 Let every thing that hath breath
praise the LORD. Praise ye the LORD.

THE PROVERBS

1

1 The proverbs of Solomon the son of David, king of Israel;

2 To know wisdom and instruction; to perceive the words of understanding;

3 To receive the instruction of wisdom, justice, and judgment, and equity;

4 To give subtilty to the simple, to the young man knowledge and discretion.

5 A wise *man* will hear, and will increase learning; and a man of understanding shall attain unto wise counsels:

6 To understand a proverb, and the interpretation; the words of the wise, and their dark sayings.

7 The fear of the LORD *is* the beginning of knowledge: *but* fools despise wisdom and instruction.

8 My son, hear the instruction of thy father, and forsake not the law of thy mother:

9 For they *shall be* an ornament of grace unto thy head, and chains about thy neck.

10 My son, if sinners entice thee, consent thou not.

11 If they say, Come with us, let us lay wait for blood, let us lurk privily for the innocent without cause:

12 Let us swallow them up alive as the grave; and whole, as those that go down into the pit:

13 We shall find all precious substance, we shall fill our houses with spoil:

14 Cast in thy lot among us; let us all have one purse:

15 My son, walk not thou in the way with them; refrain thy foot from their path:

16 For their feet run to evil, and make haste to shed blood.

17 Surely in vain the net is spread in the sight of any bird.

18 And they lay wait for their *own* blood; they lurk privily for their *own* lives.

19 So *are* the ways of every one that is greedy of gain; *which* taketh away the life of the owners thereof.

20 Wisdom crieth without; she uttereth her voice in the streets:

21 She crieth in the chief place of concourse, in the openings of the gates: in the city she uttereth her words, *saying*,

22 How long, ye simple ones, will ye love simplicity? and the scorners delight in their scorning, and fools hate knowledge?

23 Turn you at my reproof: behold, I will pour out my spirit unto you, I will make known my words unto you.

24 Because I have called, and ye refused; I have stretched out my hand, and no man regarded;

25 But ye have set at nought all my counsel, and would none of my reproof:

26 I also will laugh at your calamity; I will mock when your fear cometh;

27 When your fear cometh as desolation, and your destruction cometh as a whirlwind; when distress and anguish cometh upon you.

28 Then shall they call upon me, but I will not answer; they shall seek me early, but they shall not find me:

29 For that they hated knowledge, and did not choose the fear of the LORD:

30 They would none of my counsel: they despised all my reproof.

31 Therefore shall they eat of the fruit of their own way, and be filled with their own devices.

32 For the turning away of the simple shall slay them, and the prosperity of fools shall destroy them.

33 But whoso hearkeneth unto me shall dwell safely, and shall be quiet from fear of evil.

2 My son, if thou wilt receive my words, and hide my commandments with thee;

2 So that thou incline thine ear unto wisdom, *and* apply thine heart to understanding;

3 Yea, if thou criest after knowledge, *and* liftest up thy voice for understanding;

4 If thou seekest her as silver, and searchest for her as *for* hid treasures;

5 Then shalt thou understand the fear of the LORD, and find the knowledge of God.

6 For the LORD giveth wisdom: out of his mouth *cometh* knowledge and understanding.

7 He layeth up sound wisdom for the righteous: *he is* a buckler to them that walk uprightly.

8 He keepeth the paths of judgment, and preserveth the way of his saints.

9 Then shalt thou understand righteousness, and judgment, and equity; *yea*, every good path.

10 When wisdom entereth into thine heart, and knowledge is pleasant unto thy soul;

11 Discretion shall preserve thee, understanding shall keep thee:

12 To deliver thee from the way of the evil *man*, from the man that speaketh froward things;

13 Who leave the paths of uprightness, to walk in the ways of darkness;

14 Who rejoice to do evil, *and* delight in the frowardness of the wicked;

15 Whose ways *are* crooked, and *they* froward in their paths:

16 To deliver thee from the strange woman, *even* from the stranger *which* flattereth with her words;

17 Which forsaketh the guide of her youth, and forgetteth the covenant of her God.

18 For her house inclineth unto death, and her paths unto the dead.

19 None that go unto her return again, neither take they hold of the paths of life.

20 That thou mayest walk in the way of good *men*, and keep the paths of the righteous.

21 For the upright shall dwell in the land, and the perfect shall remain in it.

22 But the wicked shall be cut off from the earth, and the transgressors shall be rooted out of it.

3 My son, forget not my law; but let thine heart keep my commandments:

2 For length of days, and long life, and peace, shall they add to thee.

3 Let not mercy and truth forsake thee: bind them about thy neck; write them upon the table of thine heart:

4 So shalt thou find favour and good understanding in the sight of God and man.

5 Trust in the LORD with all thine heart; and lean not unto thine own understanding.

6 In all thy ways acknowledge him, and he shall direct thy paths.

7 Be not wise in thine own eyes: fear the LORD, and depart from evil.

8 It shall be health to thy navel, and marrow to thy bones.

9 Honour the LORD with thy substance, and with the firstfruits of all thine increase:

10 So shall thy barns be filled with plenty, and thy presses shall burst out with new wine.

11 My son, despise not the chastening of the LORD; neither be weary of his correction:

12 For whom the LORD loveth he correcteth; even as a father the son *in whom* he delighteth.

13 Happy *is* the man *that* findeth wisdom, and the man *that* getteth understanding.

14 For the merchandise of it *is* better than the merchandise of silver, and the gain thereof than fine gold.

15 She *is* more precious than rubies: and all the things thou canst desire are not to be compared unto her.

16 Length of days *is* in her right hand; *and* in her left hand riches and honour.

17 Her ways *are* ways of pleasantness, and all her paths *are* peace.

18 She *is* a tree of life to them that lay hold upon her: and happy *is every one* that retaineth her.

19 The LORD by wisdom hath founded the earth; by understanding hath he established the heavens.

20 By his knowledge the depths are broken up, and the clouds drop down the dew.

21 My son, let not them depart from thine eyes: keep sound wisdom and discretion:

22 So shall they be life unto thy soul, and grace to thy neck.

23 Then shalt thou walk in thy way safely, and thy foot shall not stumble.

24 When thou liest down, thou shalt not be afraid: yea, thou shalt lie down, and thy sleep shall be sweet.

25 Be not afraid of sudden fear, neither of the desolation of the wicked, when it cometh.

26 For the LORD shall be thy confidence, and shall keep thy foot from being taken.

27 Withhold not good from them to whom it is due, when it is in the power of thine hand to do *it*.

28 Say not unto thy neighbour, Go, and come again, and to morrow I will give; when thou hast it by thee.

29 Devise not evil against thy neighbour, seeing he dwelleth securely by thee.

30 Strive not with a man without cause, if he have done thee no harm.

31 Envy thou not the oppressor, and choose none of his ways.

32 For the froward *is* abomination to the LORD: but his secret *is* with the righteous.

33 The curse of the LORD *is* in the house of the wicked: but he blesseth the habitation of the just.

34 Surely he scorneth the scorners: but he giveth grace unto the lowly.

35 The wise shall inherit glory: but shame shall be the promotion of fools.

4 Hear, ye children, the instruction of a father, and attend to know understanding.

2 For I give you good doctrine, forsake ye not my law.

3 For I was my father's son, tender and only *beloved* in the sight of my mother.

4 He taught me also, and said unto me, Let thine heart retain my words: keep my commandments, and live.

5 Get wisdom, get understanding: forget *it* not; neither decline from the words of my mouth.

6 Forsake her not, and she shall preserve thee: love her, and she shall keep thee.

7 Wisdom *is* the principal thing; *therefore* get wisdom: and with all thy getting get understanding.

8 Exalt her, and she shall promote thee: she shall bring thee to honour, when thou dost embrace her.

9 She shall give to thine head an ornament of grace: a crown of glory shall she deliver to thee.

10 Hear, O my son, and receive my sayings; and the years of thy life shall be many.

11 I have taught thee in the way of wisdom; I have led thee in right paths.

12 When thou goest, thy steps shall not be straitened; and when thou runnest, thou shalt not stumble.

13 Take fast hold of instruction; let *her* not go: keep her; for she *is* thy life.

14 Enter not into the path of the wicked, and go not in the way of evil *men*.

15 Avoid it, pass not by it, turn from it, and pass away.

16 For they sleep not, except they have done mischief; and their sleep is taken away, unless they cause *some* to fall.

17 For they eat the bread of wickedness, and drink the wine of violence.

18 But the path of the just *is* as the shining light, that shineth more and more unto the perfect day.

19 The way of the wicked *is* as darkness: they know not at what they stumble.

20 My son, attend to my words; incline thine ear unto my sayings.

21 Let them not depart from thine eyes; keep them in the midst of thine heart.

22 For they *are* life unto those that find them, and health to all their flesh.

23 Keep thy heart with all diligence; for out of it *are* the issues of life.

24 Put away from thee a froward mouth, and perverse lips put far from thee.

25 Let thine eyes look right on, and let thine eyelids look straight before thee.

26 Ponder the path of thy feet, and let all thy ways be established.

27 Turn not to the right hand nor to the left: remove thy foot from evil.

5

My son, attend unto my wisdom, *and* bow thine ear to my understanding:

2 That thou mayest regard discretion, and *that* thy lips may keep knowledge.

3 For the lips of a strange woman drop *as* an honeycomb, and her mouth *is* smoother than oil:

4 But her end is bitter as wormwood, sharp as a twoedged sword.

5 Her feet go down to death; her steps take hold on hell.

6 Lest thou shouldest ponder the path of life, her ways are moveable, *that* thou canst not know *them*.

7 Hear me now therefore, O ye children, and depart not from the words of my mouth.

8 Remove thy way far from her, and come not nigh the door of her house:

9 Lest thou give thine honour unto others, and thy years unto the cruel:

10 Lest strangers be filled with thy wealth; and thy labours *be* in the house of a stranger;

11 And thou mourn at the last, when thy flesh and thy body are consumed,

12 And say, How have I hated instruction, and my heart despised reproof;

13 And have not obeyed the voice of my teachers, nor inclined mine ear to them that instructed me!

14 I was almost in all evil in the midst of the congregation and assembly.

15 Drink waters out of thine own cistern, and running waters out of thine own well.

16 Let thy fountains be dispersed abroad, *and* rivers of waters in the streets.

17 Let them be only thine own, and not strangers' with thee.

18 Let thy fountain be blessed: and rejoice with the wife of thy youth.

19 *Let her be as* the loving hind and pleasant roe; let her breasts satisfy thee at all times; and be thou ravished always with her love.

20 And why wilt thou, my son, be ravished with a strange woman, and embrace the bosom of a stranger?

21 For the ways of man *are* before the eyes of the LORD, and he pondereth all his goings.

22 His own iniquities shall take the wicked himself, and he shall be holden with the cords of his sins.

23 He shall die without instruction; and in the greatness of his folly he shall go astray.

6 My son, if thou be surety for thy friend, *if* thou hast stricken thy hand with a stranger,

2 Thou art snared with the words of thy mouth, thou art taken with the words of thy mouth.

3 Do this now, my son, and deliver thyself, when thou art come into the hand of thy friend; go, humble thyself, and make sure thy friend.

4 Give not sleep to thine eyes, nor slumber to thine eyelids.

5 Deliver thyself as a roe from the hand *of the hunter*, and as a bird from the hand of the fowler.

6 Go to the ant, thou sluggard; consider her ways, and be wise:

7 Which having no guide, overseer, or ruler,

8 Provideth her meat in the summer, *and* gathereth her food in the harvest.

9 How long wilt thou sleep, O sluggard? when wilt thou arise out of thy sleep?

10 *Yet* a little sleep, a little slumber, a little folding of the hands to sleep:

11 So shall thy poverty come as one that travelleth, and thy want as an armed man.

12 A naughty person, a wicked man, walketh with a froward mouth.

13 He winketh with his eyes, he speaketh with his feet, he teacheth with his fingers;

14 Frowardness *is* in his heart, he deviseth mischief continually; he soweth discord.

15 Therefore shall his calamity come suddenly; suddenly shall he be broken without remedy.

16 These six *things* doth the LORD hate: yea, seven *are* an abomination unto him:

17 A proud look, a lying tongue, and hands that shed innocent blood,

18 An heart that deviseth wicked
imaginations, feet that be swift in running to mischief,
19 A false witness *that* speaketh lies,
and he that soweth discord among
brethren.
20 My son, keep thy father's commandment, and forsake not the law of
thy mother:
21 Bind them continually upon thine
heart, *and* tie them about thy neck.
22 When thou goest, it shall lead thee;
when thou sleepest, it shall keep thee;
and *when* thou awakest, it shall talk
with thee.
23 For the commandment *is* a lamp;
and the law *is* light; and reproofs of
instruction *are* the way of life:
24 To keep thee from the evil woman,
from the flattery of the tongue of a
strange woman.
25 Lust not after her beauty in thine
heart; neither let her take thee with
her eyelids.
26 For by means of a whorish woman
a man is brought to a piece of bread:
and the adulteress will hunt for the precious life.
27 Can a man take fire in his bosom,
and his clothes not be burned?
28 Can one go upon hot coals, and his
feet not be burned?
29 So he that goeth in to his neighbour's wife; whosoever toucheth her
shall not be innocent.
30 *Men* do not despise a thief, if he
steal to satisfy his soul when he is hungry;
31 But *if* he be found, he shall restore
sevenfold; he shall give all the substance of his house.
32 *But* whoso committeth adultery
with a woman lacketh understanding:
he *that* doeth it destroyeth his own
soul.
33 A wound and dishonour shall he
get; and his reproach shall not be wiped
away.
34 For jealousy *is* the rage of a man:
therefore he will not spare in the day of
vengeance.
35 He will not regard any ransom;
neither will he rest content, though
thou givest many gifts.

7 My son, keep my words, and lay up
my commandments with thee.
2 Keep my commandments, and live;
and my law as the apple of thine eye.
3 Bind them upon thy fingers, write
them upon the table of thine heart.
4 Say unto wisdom, Thou *art* my
sister; and call understanding *thy*
kinswoman:
5 That they may keep thee from the
strange woman, from the stranger
which flattereth with her words.
6 For at the window of my house I
looked through my casement,
7 And beheld among the simple ones,
I discerned among the youths, a young
man void of understanding,
8 Passing through the street near her
corner; and he went the way to her
house,
9 In the twilight, in the evening, in the
black and dark night:
10 And, behold, there met him a
woman *with* the attire of an harlot, and
subtil of heart.
11 (She *is* loud and stubborn; her feet
abide not in her house:
12 Now *is she* without, now in the
streets, and lieth in wait at every
corner.)

13 So she caught him, and kissed him, *and* with an impudent face said unto him,

14 *I have* peace offerings with me; this day have I payed my vows.

15 Therefore came I forth to meet thee, diligently to seek thy face, and I have found thee.

16 I have decked my bed with coverings of tapestry, with carved *works*, with fine linen of Egypt.

17 I have perfumed my bed with myrrh, aloes, and cinnamon.

18 Come, let us take our fill of love until the morning: let us solace ourselves with loves.

19 For the goodman *is* not at home, he is gone a long journey:

20 He hath taken a bag of money with him, *and* will come home at the day appointed.

21 With her much fair speech she caused him to yield, with the flattering of her lips she forced him.

22 He goeth after her straightway, as an ox goeth to the slaughter, or as a fool to the correction of the stocks;

23 Till a dart strike through his liver; as a bird hasteth to the snare, and knoweth not that it *is* for his life.

24 Hearken unto me now therefore, O ye children, and attend to the words of my mouth.

25 Let not thine heart decline to her ways, go not astray in her paths.

26 For she hath cast down many wounded: yea, many strong *men* have been slain by her.

27 Her house *is* the way to hell, going down to the chambers of death.

8 Doth not wisdom cry? and understanding put forth her voice?

2 She standeth in the top of high places, by the way in the places of the paths.

3 She crieth at the gates, at the entry of the city, at the coming in at the doors.

4 Unto you, O men, I call; and my voice *is* to the sons of man.

5 O ye simple, understand wisdom: and, ye fools, be ye of an understanding heart.

6 Hear; for I will speak of excellent things; and the opening of my lips *shall be* right things.

7 For my mouth shall speak truth; and wickedness *is* an abomination to my lips.

8 All the words of my mouth *are* in righteousness; *there is* nothing froward or perverse in them.

9 They *are* all plain to him that understandeth, and right to them that find knowledge.

10 Receive my instruction, and not silver; and knowledge rather than choice gold.

11 For wisdom *is* better than rubies; and all the things that may be desired are not to be compared to it.

12 I wisdom dwell with prudence, and find out knowledge of witty inventions.

13 The fear of the LORD *is* to hate evil: pride, and arrogancy, and the evil way, and the froward mouth, do I hate.

14 Counsel *is* mine, and sound wisdom: I *am* understanding; I have strength.

15 By me kings reign, and princes decree justice.

16 By me princes rule, and nobles, *even* all the judges of the earth.

17 I love them that love me; and those that seek me early shall find me.

18 Riches and honour *are* with me; *yea*, durable riches and righteousness.

19 My fruit *is* better than gold, yea, than fine gold; and my revenue than choice silver.

20 I lead in the way of righteousness, in the midst of the paths of judgment:

21 That I may cause those that love me to inherit substance; and I will fill their treasures.

22 The LORD possessed me in the beginning of his way, before his works of old.

23 I was set up from everlasting, from the beginning, or ever the earth was.

24 When *there were* no depths, I was brought forth; when *there were* no fountains abounding with water.

25 Before the mountains were settled, before the hills was I brought forth:

26 While as yet he had not made the earth, nor the fields, nor the highest part of the dust of the world.

27 When he prepared the heavens, I *was* there: when he set a compass upon the face of the depth:

28 When he established the clouds above: when he strengthened the fountains of the deep:

29 When he gave to the sea his decree, that the waters should not pass his commandment: when he appointed the foundations of the earth:

30 Then I was by him, *as* one brought up *with him*: and I was daily *his* delight, rejoicing always before him;

31 Rejoicing in the habitable part of his earth; and my delights *were* with the sons of men.

32 Now therefore hearken unto me, O ye children: for blessed *are they that* keep my ways.

33 Hear instruction, and be wise, and refuse it not.

34 Blessed *is* the man that heareth me, watching daily at my gates, waiting at the posts of my doors.

35 For whoso findeth me findeth life, and shall obtain favour of the LORD.

36 But he that sinneth against me wrongeth his own soul: all they that hate me love death.

9 Wisdom hath builded her house, she hath hewn out her seven pillars:

2 She hath killed her beasts; she hath mingled her wine; she hath also furnished her table.

3 She hath sent forth her maidens: she crieth upon the highest places of the city,

4 Whoso *is* simple, let him turn in hither: *as for* him that wanteth understanding, she saith to him,

5 Come, eat of my bread, and drink of the wine *which* I have mingled.

6 Forsake the foolish, and live; and go in the way of understanding.

7 He that reproveth a scorner getteth to himself shame: and he that rebuketh a wicked *man getteth* himself a blot.

8 Reprove not a scorner, lest he hate thee: rebuke a wise man, and he will love thee.

9 Give *instruction* to a wise *man*, and he will be yet wiser: teach a just *man*, and he will increase in learning.

10 The fear of the LORD *is* the beginning of wisdom: and the knowledge of the holy *is* understanding.

11 For by me thy days shall be multiplied, and the years of thy life shall be increased.

12 If thou be wise, thou shalt be wise for thyself: but *if* thou scornest, thou alone shalt bear *it*.

13 A foolish woman *is* clamorous: *she is* simple, and knoweth nothing.

14 For she sitteth at the door of her house, on a seat in the high places of the city,

15 To call passengers who go right on their ways:

16 Whoso *is* simple, let him turn in hither: and *as for* him that wanteth understanding, she saith to him,

17 Stolen waters are sweet, and bread *eaten* in secret is pleasant.

18 But he knoweth not that the dead *are* there; *and that* her guests *are* in the depths of hell.

10 The proverbs of Solomon. A wise son maketh a glad father: but a foolish son *is* the heaviness of his mother.

2 Treasures of wickedness profit nothing: but righteousness delivereth from death.

3 The LORD will not suffer the soul of the righteous to famish: but he casteth away the substance of the wicked.

4 He becometh poor that dealeth *with* a slack hand: but the hand of the diligent maketh rich.

5 He that gathereth in summer *is* a wise son: *but* he that sleepeth in harvest *is* a son that causeth shame.

6 Blessings *are* upon the head of the just: but violence covereth the mouth of the wicked.

7 The memory of the just *is* blessed: but the name of the wicked shall rot.

8 The wise in heart will receive commandments: but a prating fool shall fall.

9 He that walketh uprightly walketh surely: but he that perverteth his ways shall be known.

10 He that winketh with the eye causeth sorrow: but a prating fool shall fall.

11 The mouth of a righteous *man is* a well of life: but violence covereth the mouth of the wicked.

12 Hatred stirreth up strifes: but love covereth all sins.

13 In the lips of him that hath understanding wisdom is found: but a rod *is* for the back of him that is void of understanding.

14 Wise *men* lay up knowledge: but the mouth of the foolish *is* near destruction.

15 The rich man's wealth *is* his strong city: the destruction of the poor *is* their poverty.

16 The labour of the righteous *tendeth* to life: the fruit of the wicked to sin.

17 He *is in* the way of life that keepeth instruction: but he that refuseth reproof erreth.

18 He that hideth hatred *with* lying lips, and he that uttereth a slander, *is* a fool.

19 In the multitude of words there wanteth not sin: but he that refraineth his lips *is* wise.

20 The tongue of the just *is as* choice silver: the heart of the wicked *is* little worth.

21 The lips of the righteous feed many: but fools die for want of wisdom.

22 The blessing of the LORD, it maketh rich, and he addeth no sorrow with it.

23 *It is* as sport to a fool to do mischief: but a man of understanding hath wisdom.

24 The fear of the wicked, it shall come upon him: but the desire of the righteous shall be granted.

25 As the whirlwind passeth, so *is* the wicked no *more*: but the righteous *is* an everlasting foundation.

26 As vinegar to the teeth, and as
smoke to the eyes, so *is* the sluggard to
them that send him.
27 The fear of the LORD prolongeth
days: but the years of the wicked shall
be shortened.
28 The hope of the righteous *shall be*
gladness: but the expectation of the
wicked shall perish.
29 The way of the LORD *is* strength to
the upright: but destruction *shall be* to
the workers of iniquity.
30 The righteous shall never be
removed: but the wicked shall not
inhabit the earth.
31 The mouth of the just bringeth
forth wisdom: but the froward tongue
shall be cut out.
32 The lips of the righteous know
what is acceptable: but the mouth of
the wicked *speaketh* frowardness.

11 A false balance *is* abomination to
the LORD: but a just weight *is* his
delight.
2 *When* pride cometh, then cometh
shame: but with the lowly *is* wisdom.
3 The integrity of the upright shall
guide them: but the perverseness of
transgressors shall destroy them.
4 Riches profit not in the day of
wrath: but righteousness delivereth
from death.
5 The righteousness of the perfect
shall direct his way: but the wicked
shall fall by his own wickedness.
6 The righteousness of the upright
shall deliver them: but transgressors
shall be taken in *their own* naughtiness.
7 When a wicked man dieth, *his*
expectation shall perish: and the hope
of unjust *men* perisheth.
8 The righteous is delivered out of
trouble, and the wicked cometh in his
stead.
9 An hypocrite with *his* mouth
destroyeth his neighbour: but through
knowledge shall the just be delivered.
10 When it goeth well with the righteous, the city rejoiceth: and when the
wicked perish, *there is* shouting.
11 By the blessing of the upright the
city is exalted: but it is overthrown by
the mouth of the wicked.
12 He that is void of wisdom despiseth his neighbour: but a man of understanding holdeth his peace.
13 A talebearer revealeth secrets: but
he that is of a faithful spirit concealeth
the matter.
14 Where no counsel *is*, the people
fall: but in the multitude of counsellors
there is safety.
15 He that is surety for a stranger
shall smart *for it*: and he that hateth
suretiship is sure.
16 A gracious woman retaineth honour: and strong *men* retain riches.
17 The merciful man doeth good to
his own soul: but *he that is* cruel troubleth his own flesh.
18 The wicked worketh a deceitful
work: but to him that soweth righteousness *shall be* a sure reward.
19 As righteousness *tendeth* to life: so
he that pursueth evil *pursueth it* to his
own death.
20 They that are of a froward heart
are abomination to the LORD: but *such*
as are upright in *their* way *are* his
delight.
21 *Though* hand *join* in hand, the
wicked shall not be unpunished: but
the seed of the righteous shall be delivered.

22 *As* a jewel of gold in a swine's snout, *so is* a fair woman which is without discretion.

23 The desire of the righteous *is* only good: *but* the expectation of the wicked *is* wrath.

24 There is that scattereth, and yet increaseth; and *there is* that withholdeth more than is meet, but *it tendeth* to poverty.

25 The liberal soul shall be made fat: and he that watereth shall be watered also himself.

26 He that withholdeth corn, the people shall curse him: but blessing *shall be* upon the head of him that selleth *it*.

27 He that diligently seeketh good procureth favour: but he that seeketh mischief, it shall come unto him.

28 He that trusteth in his riches shall fall: but the righteous shall flourish as a branch.

29 He that troubleth his own house shall inherit the wind: and the fool *shall be* servant to the wise of heart.

30 The fruit of the righteous *is* a tree of life; and he that winneth souls *is* wise.

31 Behold, the righteous shall be recompensed in the earth: much more the wicked and the sinner.

12 Whoso loveth instruction loveth knowledge: but he that hateth reproof *is* brutish.

2 A good *man* obtaineth favour of the LORD: but a man of wicked devices will he condemn.

3 A man shall not be established by wickedness: but the root of the righteous shall not be moved.

4 A virtuous woman *is* a crown to her husband: but she that maketh ashamed *is* as rottenness in his bones.

5 The thoughts of the righteous *are* right: *but* the counsels of the wicked *are* deceit.

6 The words of the wicked *are* to lie in wait for blood: but the mouth of the upright shall deliver them.

7 The wicked are overthrown, and *are* not: but the house of the righteous shall stand.

8 A man shall be commended according to his wisdom: but he that is of a perverse heart shall be despised.

9 *He that is* despised, and hath a servant, *is* better than he that honoureth himself, and lacketh bread.

10 A righteous *man* regardeth the life of his beast: but the tender mercies of the wicked *are* cruel.

11 He that tilleth his land shall be satisfied with bread: but he that followeth vain *persons is* void of understanding.

12 The wicked desireth the net of evil *men*: but the root of the righteous yieldeth *fruit*.

13 The wicked is snared by the transgression of *his* lips: but the just shall come out of trouble.

14 A man shall be satisfied with good by the fruit of *his* mouth: and the recompence of a man's hands shall be rendered unto him.

15 The way of a fool *is* right in his own eyes: but he that hearkeneth unto counsel *is* wise.

16 A fool's wrath is presently known: but a prudent *man* covereth shame.

17 *He that* speaketh truth sheweth forth righteousness: but a false witness deceit.

18 There is that speaketh like the piercings of a sword: but the tongue of the wise *is* health.

19 The lip of truth shall be established for ever: but a lying tongue *is* but for a moment.

20 Deceit *is* in the heart of them that imagine evil: but to the counsellors of peace *is* joy.

21 There shall no evil happen to the just: but the wicked shall be filled with mischief.

22 Lying lips *are* abomination to the LORD: but they that deal truly *are* his delight.

23 A prudent man concealeth knowledge: but the heart of fools proclaimeth foolishness.

24 The hand of the diligent shall bear rule: but the slothful shall be under tribute.

25 Heaviness in the heart of man maketh it stoop: but a good word maketh it glad.

26 The righteous *is* more excellent than his neighbour: but the way of the wicked seduceth them.

27 The slothful *man* roasteth not that which he took in hunting: but the substance of a diligent man *is* precious.

28 In the way of righteousness *is* life; and *in* the pathway *thereof there is* no death.

13

13 A wise son *heareth* his father's instruction: but a scorner heareth not rebuke.

2 A man shall eat good by the fruit of *his* mouth: but the soul of the transgressors *shall eat* violence.

3 He that keepeth his mouth keepeth his life: *but* he that openeth wide his lips shall have destruction.

4 The soul of the sluggard desireth, and *hath* nothing: but the soul of the diligent shall be made fat.

5 A righteous *man* hateth lying: but a wicked *man* is loathsome, and cometh to shame.

6 Righteousness keepeth *him that is* upright in the way: but wickedness overthroweth the sinner.

7 There is that maketh himself rich, yet *hath* nothing: *there is* that maketh himself poor, yet *hath* great riches.

8 The ransom of a man's life *are* his riches: but the poor heareth not rebuke.

9 The light of the righteous rejoiceth: but the lamp of the wicked shall be put out.

10 Only by pride cometh contention: but with the well advised *is* wisdom.

11 Wealth *gotten* by vanity shall be diminished: but he that gathereth by labour shall increase.

12 Hope deferred maketh the heart sick: but *when* the desire cometh, *it is* a tree of life.

13 Whoso despiseth the word shall be destroyed: but he that feareth the commandment shall be rewarded.

14 The law of the wise *is* a fountain of life, to depart from the snares of death.

15 Good understanding giveth favour: but the way of transgressors *is* hard.

16 Every prudent *man* dealeth with knowledge: but a fool layeth open *his* folly.

17 A wicked messenger falleth into mischief: but a faithful ambassador *is* health.

18 Poverty and shame *shall be to* him that refuseth instruction: but he that regardeth reproof shall be honoured.

19 The desire accomplished is sweet to the soul: but *it is* abomination to fools to depart from evil.

20 He that walketh with wise *men* shall be wise: but a companion of fools shall be destroyed.

21 Evil pursueth sinners: but to the righteous good shall be repayed.

22 A good *man* leaveth an inheritance to his children's children: and the wealth of the sinner *is* laid up for the just.

23 Much food *is in* the tillage of the poor: but there is *that is* destroyed for want of judgment.

24 He that spareth his rod hateth his son: but he that loveth him chasteneth him betimes.

25 The righteous eateth to the satisfying of his soul: but the belly of the wicked shall want.

14 Every wise woman buildeth her house: but the foolish plucketh it down with her hands.

2 He that walketh in his uprightness feareth the LORD: but *he that is* perverse in his ways despiseth him.

3 In the mouth of the foolish *is* a rod of pride: but the lips of the wise shall preserve them.

4 Where no oxen *are*, the crib *is* clean: but much increase *is* by the strength of the ox.

5 A faithful witness will not lie: but a false witness will utter lies.

6 A scorner seeketh wisdom, and *findeth it* not: but knowledge *is* easy unto him that understandeth.

7 Go from the presence of a foolish man, when thou perceivest not *in him* the lips of knowledge.

8 The wisdom of the prudent *is* to understand his way: but the folly of fools *is* deceit.

9 Fools make a mock at sin: but among the righteous *there is* favour.

10 The heart knoweth his own bitterness; and a stranger doth not intermeddle with his joy.

11 The house of the wicked shall be overthrown: but the tabernacle of the upright shall flourish.

12 There is a way which seemeth right unto a man, but the end thereof *are* the ways of death.

13 Even in laughter the heart is sorrowful; and the end of that mirth *is* heaviness.

14 The backslider in heart shall be filled with his own ways: and a good man *shall be satisfied* from himself.

15 The simple believeth every word: but the prudent *man* looketh well to his going.

16 A wise *man* feareth, and departeth from evil: but the fool rageth, and is confident.

17 *He that is* soon angry dealeth foolishly: and a man of wicked devices is hated.

18 The simple inherit folly: but the prudent are crowned with knowledge.

19 The evil bow before the good; and the wicked at the gates of the righteous.

20 The poor is hated even of his own neighbour: but the rich *hath* many friends.

21 He that despiseth his neighbour sinneth: but he that hath mercy on the poor, happy *is* he.

22 Do they not err that devise evil? but mercy and truth *shall be* to them that devise good.

23 In all labour there is profit: but the talk of the lips *tendeth* only to penury.

24 The crown of the wise *is* their riches: *but* the foolishness of fools *is* folly.

25 A true witness delivereth souls: but a deceitful *witness* speaketh lies.

26 In the fear of the LORD *is* strong confidence: and his children shall have a place of refuge.
27 The fear of the LORD *is* a fountain of life, to depart from the snares of death.
28 In the multitude of people *is* the king's honour: but in the want of people *is* the destruction of the prince.
29 *He that is* slow to wrath *is* of great understanding: but *he that is* hasty of spirit exalteth folly.
30 A sound heart *is* the life of the flesh: but envy the rottenness of the bones.
31 He that oppresseth the poor reproacheth his Maker: but he that honoureth him hath mercy on the poor.
32 The wicked is driven away in his wickedness: but the righteous hath hope in his death.
33 Wisdom resteth in the heart of him that hath understanding: but *that which is* in the midst of fools is made known.
34 Righteousness exalteth a nation: but sin *is* a reproach to any people.
35 The king's favour *is* toward a wise servant: but his wrath is *against* him that causeth shame.

15 A soft answer turneth away wrath: but grievous words stir up anger.
2 The tongue of the wise useth knowledge aright: but the mouth of fools poureth out foolishness.
3 The eyes of the LORD *are* in every place, beholding the evil and the good.
4 A wholesome tongue *is* a tree of life: but perverseness therein *is* a breach in the spirit.
5 A fool despiseth his father's instruction: but he that regardeth reproof is prudent.
6 In the house of the righteous *is* much treasure: but in the revenues of the wicked is trouble.
7 The lips of the wise disperse knowledge: but the heart of the foolish *doeth* not so.
8 The sacrifice of the wicked *is* an abomination to the LORD: but the prayer of the upright *is* his delight.
9 The way of the wicked *is* an abomination unto the LORD: but he loveth him that followeth after righteousness.
10 Correction *is* grievous unto him that forsaketh the way: *and* he that hateth reproof shall die.
11 Hell and destruction *are* before the LORD: how much more then the hearts of the children of men?
12 A scorner loveth not one that reproveth him: neither will he go unto the wise.
13 A merry heart maketh a cheerful countenance: but by sorrow of the heart the spirit is broken.
14 The heart of him that hath understanding seeketh knowledge: but the mouth of fools feedeth on foolishness.
15 All the days of the afflicted *are* evil: but he that is of a merry heart *hath* a continual feast.
16 Better *is* little with the fear of the LORD than great treasure and trouble therewith.
17 Better *is* a dinner of herbs where love is, than a stalled ox and hatred therewith.
18 A wrathful man stirreth up strife: but *he that is* slow to anger appeaseth strife.
19 The way of the slothful *man is* as an hedge of thorns: but the way of the righteous *is* made plain.
20 A wise son maketh a glad father: but a foolish man despiseth his mother.

21 Folly *is* joy to *him that is* destitute of wisdom: but a man of understanding walketh uprightly.

22 Without counsel purposes are disappointed: but in the multitude of counsellors they are established.

23 A man hath joy by the answer of his mouth: and a word *spoken* in due season, how good *is it*!

24 The way of life *is* above to the wise, that he may depart from hell beneath.

25 The LORD will destroy the house of the proud: but he will establish the border of the widow.

26 The thoughts of the wicked *are* an abomination to the LORD: but *the words* of the pure *are* pleasant words.

27 He that is greedy of gain troubleth his own house; but he that hateth gifts shall live.

28 The heart of the righteous studieth to answer: but the mouth of the wicked poureth out evil things.

29 The LORD *is* far from the wicked: but he heareth the prayer of the righteous.

30 The light of the eyes rejoiceth the heart: *and* a good report maketh the bones fat.

31 The ear that heareth the reproof of life abideth among the wise.

32 He that refuseth instruction despiseth his own soul: but he that heareth reproof getteth understanding.

33 The fear of the LORD *is* the instruction of wisdom; and before honour *is* humility.

16 The preparations of the heart in man, and the answer of the tongue, *is* from the LORD.

2 All the ways of a man *are* clean in his own eyes; but the LORD weigheth the spirits.

3 Commit thy works unto the LORD, and thy thoughts shall be established.

4 The LORD hath made all *things* for himself: yea, even the wicked for the day of evil.

5 Every one *that is* proud in heart *is* an abomination to the LORD: *though* hand *join* in hand, he shall not be unpunished.

6 By mercy and truth iniquity is purged: and by the fear of the LORD *men* depart from evil.

7 When a man's ways please the LORD, he maketh even his enemies to be at peace with him.

8 Better *is* a little with righteousness than great revenues without right.

9 A man's heart deviseth his way: but the LORD directeth his steps.

10 A divine sentence *is* in the lips of the king: his mouth transgresseth not in judgment.

11 A just weight and balance *are* the LORD's: all the weights of the bag *are* his work.

12 *It is* an abomination to kings to commit wickedness: for the throne is established by righteousness.

13 Righteous lips *are* the delight of kings; and they love him that speaketh right.

14 The wrath of a king *is as* messengers of death: but a wise man will pacify it.

15 In the light of the king's countenance *is* life; and his favour *is* as a cloud of the latter rain.

16 How much better *is it* to get wisdom than gold! and to get understanding rather to be chosen than silver!

17 The highway of the upright *is* to depart from evil: he that keepeth his way preserveth his soul.

18 Pride *goeth* before destruction, and an haughty spirit before a fall.

19 Better *it is to be* of an humble spirit with the lowly, than to divide the spoil with the proud.

20 He that handleth a matter wisely shall find good: and whoso trusteth in the LORD, happy *is* he.

21 The wise in heart shall be called prudent: and the sweetness of the lips increaseth learning.

22 Understanding *is* a wellspring of life unto him that hath it: but the instruction of fools *is* folly.

23 The heart of the wise teacheth his mouth, and addeth learning to his lips.

24 Pleasant words *are as* an honeycomb, sweet to the soul, and health to the bones.

25 There is a way that seemeth right unto a man, but the end thereof *are* the ways of death.

26 He that laboureth laboureth for himself; for his mouth craveth it of him.

27 An ungodly man diggeth up evil: and in his lips *there is* as a burning fire.

28 A froward man soweth strife: and a whisperer separateth chief friends.

29 A violent man enticeth his neighbour, and leadeth him into the way *that is* not good.

30 He shutteth his eyes to devise froward things: moving his lips he bringeth evil to pass.

31 The hoary head *is* a crown of glory, *if* it be found in the way of righteousness.

32 *He that is* slow to anger *is* better than the mighty; and he that ruleth his spirit than he that taketh a city.

33 The lot is cast into the lap; but the whole disposing thereof *is* of the LORD.

17 Better *is* a dry morsel, and quietness therewith, than an house full of sacrifices *with* strife.

2 A wise servant shall have rule over a son that causeth shame, and shall have part of the inheritance among the brethren.

3 The fining pot *is* for silver, and the furnace for gold: but the LORD trieth the hearts.

4 A wicked doer giveth heed to false lips; *and* a liar giveth ear to a naughty tongue.

5 Whoso mocketh the poor reproacheth his Maker: *and* he that is glad at calamities shall not be unpunished.

6 Children's children *are* the crown of old men; and the glory of children *are* their fathers.

7 Excellent speech becometh not a fool: much less do lying lips a prince.

8 A gift *is as* a precious stone in the eyes of him that hath it: whithersoever it turneth, it prospereth.

9 He that covereth a transgression seeketh love; but he that repeateth a matter separateth *very* friends.

10 A reproof entereth more into a wise man than an hundred stripes into a fool.

11 An evil *man* seeketh only rebellion: therefore a cruel messenger shall be sent against him.

12 Let a bear robbed of her whelps meet a man, rather than a fool in his folly.

13 Whoso rewardeth evil for good, evil shall not depart from his house.

14 The beginning of strife *is as* when one letteth out water: therefore leave off contention, before it be meddled with.

15 He that justifieth the wicked, and he that condemneth the just, even they both *are* abomination to the LORD.

16 Wherefore *is there* a price in the hand of a fool to get wisdom, seeing *he hath* no heart *to it*?

17 A friend loveth at all times, and a brother is born for adversity.

18 A man void of understanding striketh hands, *and* becometh surety in the presence of his friend.

19 He loveth transgression that loveth strife: *and* he that exalteth his gate seeketh destruction.

20 He that hath a froward heart findeth no good: and he that hath a perverse tongue falleth into mischief.

21 He that begetteth a fool *doeth it* to his sorrow: and the father of a fool hath no joy.

22 A merry heart doeth good *like* a medicine: but a broken spirit drieth the bones.

23 A wicked *man* taketh a gift out of the bosom to pervert the ways of judgment.

24 Wisdom *is* before him that hath understanding; but the eyes of a fool *are* in the ends of the earth.

25 A foolish son *is* a grief to his father, and bitterness to her that bare him.

26 Also to punish the just *is* not good, *nor* to strike princes for equity.

27 He that hath knowledge spareth his words: *and* a man of understanding is of an excellent spirit.

28 Even a fool, when he holdeth his peace, is counted wise: *and* he that shutteth his lips *is esteemed* a man of understanding.

18 Through desire a man, having separated himself, seeketh *and* intermeddleth with all wisdom.

2 A fool hath no delight in understanding, but that his heart may discover itself.

3 When the wicked cometh, *then* cometh also contempt, and with ignominy reproach.

4 The words of a man's mouth *are as* deep waters, *and* the wellspring of wisdom *as* a flowing brook.

5 *It is* not good to accept the person of the wicked, to overthrow the righteous in judgment.

6 A fool's lips enter into contention, and his mouth calleth for strokes.

7 A fool's mouth *is* his destruction, and his lips *are* the snare of his soul.

8 The words of a talebearer *are* as wounds, and they go down into the innermost parts of the belly.

9 He also that is slothful in his work is brother to him that is a great waster.

10 The name of the LORD *is* a strong tower: the righteous runneth into it, and is safe.

11 The rich man's wealth *is* his strong city, and as an high wall in his own conceit.

12 Before destruction the heart of man is haughty, and before honour *is* humility.

13 He that answereth a matter before he heareth *it*, it *is* folly and shame unto him.

14 The spirit of a man will sustain his infirmity; but a wounded spirit who can bear?

15 The heart of the prudent getteth knowledge; and the ear of the wise seeketh knowledge.

16 A man's gift maketh room for him, and bringeth him before great men.

17 *He that is* first in his own cause
seemeth just; but his neighbour cometh
and searcheth him.
18 The lot causeth contentions to
cease, and parteth between the mighty.
19 A brother offended *is harder to be*
won than a strong city: and *their* contentions *are* like the bars of a castle.
20 A man's belly shall be satisfied
with the fruit of his mouth; *and* with
the increase of his lips shall he be
filled.
21 Death and life *are* in the power of
the tongue: and they that love it shall
eat the fruit thereof.
22 *Whoso* findeth a wife findeth a
good *thing*, and obtaineth favour of the
LORD.
23 The poor useth intreaties; but the
rich answereth roughly.
24 A man *that hath* friends must
shew himself friendly: and there is a
friend *that* sticketh closer than a
brother.

19 Better *is* the poor that walketh in
his integrity, than *he that is* perverse in his lips, and is a fool.
2 Also, *that* the soul *be* without
knowledge, *it is* not good; and he that
hasteth with *his* feet sinneth.
3 The foolishness of man perverteth
his way: and his heart fretteth against
the LORD.
4 Wealth maketh many friends; but
the poor is separated from his neighbour.
5 A false witness shall not be unpunished, and *he that* speaketh lies shall
not escape.
6 Many will intreat the favour of the
prince: and every man *is* a friend to
him that giveth gifts.
7 All the brethren of the poor do hate
him: how much more do his friends go
far from him? he pursueth *them with*
words, *yet* they *are* wanting *to him*.
8 He that getteth wisdom loveth his
own soul: he that keepeth understanding shall find good.
9 A false witness shall not be unpunished, and *he that* speaketh lies shall
perish.
10 Delight is not seemly for a fool;
much less for a servant to have rule
over princes.
11 The discretion of a man deferreth
his anger; and *it is* his glory to pass over
a transgression.
12 The king's wrath *is* as the roaring
of a lion; but his favour *is* as dew upon
the grass.
13 A foolish son *is* the calamity of his
father: and the contentions of a wife
are a continual dropping.
14 House and riches *are* the inheritance of fathers: and a prudent wife *is*
from the LORD.
15 Slothfulness casteth into a deep
sleep; and an idle soul shall suffer hunger.
16 He that keepeth the commandment keepeth his own soul; *but* he that
despiseth his ways shall die.
17 He that hath pity upon the poor
lendeth unto the LORD; and that which
he hath given will he pay him again.
18 Chasten thy son while there is
hope, and let not thy soul spare for his
crying.
19 A man of great wrath shall suffer
punishment: for if thou deliver *him*, yet
thou must do it again.
20 Hear counsel, and receive instruction, that thou mayest be wise in thy
latter end.
21 *There are* many devices in a man's
heart; nevertheless the counsel of the
LORD, that shall stand.

22 The desire of a man *is* his kindness: and a poor man *is* better than a liar.

23 The fear of the LORD *tendeth* to life: and *he that hath it* shall abide satisfied; he shall not be visited with evil.

24 A slothful *man* hideth his hand in *his* bosom, and will not so much as bring it to his mouth again.

25 Smite a scorner, and the simple will beware: and reprove one that hath understanding, *and* he will understand knowledge.

26 He that wasteth *his* father, *and* chaseth away *his* mother, *is* a son that causeth shame, and bringeth reproach.

27 Cease, my son, to hear the instruction *that causeth* to err from the words of knowledge.

28 An ungodly witness scorneth judgment: and the mouth of the wicked devoureth iniquity.

29 Judgments are prepared for scorners, and stripes for the back of fools.

20 Wine *is* a mocker, strong drink *is* raging: and whosoever is deceived thereby is not wise.

2 The fear of a king *is* as the roaring of a lion: *whoso* provoketh him to anger sinneth *against* his own soul.

3 *It is* an honour for a man to cease from strife: but every fool will be meddling.

4 The sluggard will not plow by reason of the cold; *therefore* shall he beg in harvest, and *have* nothing.

5 Counsel in the heart of man *is like* deep water; but a man of understanding will draw it out.

6 Most men will proclaim every one his own goodness: but a faithful man who can find?

7 The just *man* walketh in his integrity: his children *are* blessed after him.

8 A king that sitteth in the throne of judgment scattereth away all evil with his eyes.

9 Who can say, I have made my heart clean, I am pure from my sin?

10 Divers weights, *and* divers measures, both of them *are* alike abomination to the LORD.

11 Even a child is known by his doings, whether his work *be* pure, and whether *it be* right.

12 The hearing ear, and the seeing eye, the LORD hath made even both of them.

13 Love not sleep, lest thou come to poverty; open thine eyes, *and* thou shalt be satisfied with bread.

14 *It is* naught, *it is* naught, saith the buyer: but when he is gone his way, then he boasteth.

15 There is gold, and a multitude of rubies: but the lips of knowledge *are* a precious jewel.

16 Take his garment that is surety *for* a stranger: and take a pledge of him for a strange woman.

17 Bread of deceit *is* sweet to a man; but afterwards his mouth shall be filled with gravel.

18 *Every* purpose is established by counsel: and with good advice make war.

19 He that goeth about *as* a talebearer revealeth secrets: therefore meddle not with him that flattereth with his lips.

20 Whoso curseth his father or his mother, his lamp shall be put out in obscure darkness.

21 An inheritance *may be* gotten hastily at the beginning; but the end thereof shall not be blessed.

22 Say not thou, I will recompense evil; *but* wait on the LORD, and he shall save thee.

23 Divers weights *are* an abomination unto the LORD; and a false balance *is* not good.

24 Man's goings *are* of the LORD; how can a man then understand his own way?

25 *It is* a snare to the man *who* devoureth *that which is* holy, and after vows to make enquiry.

26 A wise king scattereth the wicked, and bringeth the wheel over them.

27 The spirit of man *is* the candle of the LORD, searching all the inward parts of the belly.

28 Mercy and truth preserve the king: and his throne is upholden by mercy.

29 The glory of young men *is* their strength: and the beauty of old men *is* the gray head.

30 The blueness of a wound cleanseth away evil: so *do* stripes the inward parts of the belly.

21 The king's heart *is* in the hand of the LORD, *as* the rivers of water: he turneth it whithersoever he will.

2 Every way of a man *is* right in his own eyes: but the LORD pondereth the hearts.

3 To do justice and judgment *is* more acceptable to the LORD than sacrifice.

4 An high look, and a proud heart, *and* the plowing of the wicked, *is* sin.

5 The thoughts of the diligent *tend* only to plenteousness; but of every one *that is* hasty only to want.

6 The getting of treasures by a lying tongue *is* a vanity tossed to and fro of them that seek death.

7 The robbery of the wicked shall destroy them; because they refuse to do judgment.

8 The way of man *is* froward and strange: but *as for* the pure, his work *is* right.

9 *It is* better to dwell in a corner of the housetop, than with a brawling woman in a wide house.

10 The soul of the wicked desireth evil: his neighbour findeth no favour in his eyes.

11 When the scorner is punished, the simple is made wise: and when the wise is instructed, he receiveth knowledge.

12 The righteous *man* wisely considereth the house of the wicked: *but God* overthroweth the wicked for *their* wickedness.

13 Whoso stoppeth his ears at the cry of the poor, he also shall cry himself, but shall not be heard.

14 A gift in secret pacifieth anger: and a reward in the bosom strong wrath.

15 *It is* joy to the just to do judgment: but destruction *shall be* to the workers of iniquity.

16 The man that wandereth out of the way of understanding shall remain in the congregation of the dead.

17 He that loveth pleasure *shall be* a poor man: he that loveth wine and oil shall not be rich.

18 The wicked *shall be* a ransom for the righteous, and the transgressor for the upright.

19 *It is* better to dwell in the wilderness, than with a contentious and an angry woman.

20 *There is* treasure to be desired and oil in the dwelling of the wise; but a foolish man spendeth it up.

21 He that followeth after righteousness and mercy findeth life, righteousness, and honour.

22 A wise *man* scaleth the city of the mighty, and casteth down the strength of the confidence thereof.

23 Whoso keepeth his mouth and his tongue keepeth his soul from troubles.

24 Proud *and* haughty scorner *is* his name, who dealeth in proud wrath.

25 The desire of the slothful killeth him; for his hands refuse to labour.

26 He coveteth greedily all the day long: but the righteous giveth and spareth not.

27 The sacrifice of the wicked *is* abomination: how much more, *when* he bringeth it with a wicked mind?

28 A false witness shall perish: but the man that heareth speaketh constantly.

29 A wicked man hardeneth his face: but *as for* the upright, he directeth his way.

30 *There is* no wisdom nor understanding nor counsel against the LORD.

31 The horse *is* prepared against the day of battle: but safety *is* of the LORD.

22 A *good* name *is* rather to be chosen than great riches, *and* loving favour rather than silver and gold.

2 The rich and poor meet together: the LORD *is* the maker of them all.

3 A prudent *man* foreseeth the evil, and hideth himself: but the simple pass on, and are punished.

4 By humility *and* the fear of the LORD *are* riches, and honour, and life.

5 Thorns *and* snares *are* in the way of the froward: he that doth keep his soul shall be far from them.

6 Train up a child in the way he should go: and when he is old, he will not depart from it.

7 The rich ruleth over the poor, and the borrower *is* servant to the lender.

8 He that soweth iniquity shall reap vanity: and the rod of his anger shall fail.

9 He that hath a bountiful eye shall be blessed; for he giveth of his bread to the poor.

10 Cast out the scorner, and contention shall go out; yea, strife and reproach shall cease.

11 He that loveth pureness of heart, *for* the grace of his lips the king *shall be* his friend.

12 The eyes of the LORD preserve knowledge, and he overthroweth the words of the transgressor.

13 The slothful *man* saith, *There is* a lion without, I shall be slain in the streets.

14 The mouth of strange women *is* a deep pit: he that is abhorred of the LORD shall fall therein.

15 Foolishness *is* bound in the heart of a child; *but* the rod of correction shall drive it far from him.

16 He that oppresseth the poor to increase his *riches, and* he that giveth to the rich, *shall* surely *come* to want.

17 Bow down thine ear, and hear the words of the wise, and apply thine heart unto my knowledge.

18 For *it is* a pleasant thing if thou keep them within thee; they shall withal be fitted in thy lips.

19 That thy trust may be in the LORD, I have made known to thee this day, even to thee.

20 Have not I written to thee excellent things in counsels and knowledge,

21 That I might make thee know the certainty of the words of truth; that thou mightest answer the words of truth to them that send unto thee?

22 Rob not the poor, because he *is* poor: neither oppress the afflicted in the gate:

23 For the LORD will plead their cause, and spoil the soul of those that spoiled them.

24 Make no friendship with an angry man; and with a furious man thou shalt not go:

25 Lest thou learn his ways, and get a snare to thy soul.

26 Be not thou *one* of them that strike hands, *or* of them that are sureties for debts.

27 If thou hast nothing to pay, why should he take away thy bed from under thee?

28 Remove not the ancient landmark, which thy fathers have set.

29 Seest thou a man diligent in his business? he shall stand before kings; he shall not stand before mean *men*.

23 When thou sittest to eat with a ruler, consider diligently what *is* before thee:

2 And put a knife to thy throat, if thou *be* a man given to appetite.

3 Be not desirous of his dainties: for they *are* deceitful meat.

4 Labour not to be rich: cease from thine own wisdom.

5 Wilt thou set thine eyes upon that which is not? for *riches* certainly make themselves wings; they fly away as an eagle toward heaven.

6 Eat thou not the bread of *him that hath* an evil eye, neither desire thou his dainty meats:

7 For as he thinketh in his heart, so *is* he: Eat and drink, saith he to thee; but his heart *is* not with thee.

8 The morsel *which* thou hast eaten shalt thou vomit up, and lose thy sweet words.

9 Speak not in the ears of a fool: for he will despise the wisdom of thy words.

10 Remove not the old landmark; and enter not into the fields of the fatherless:

11 For their redeemer *is* mighty; he shall plead their cause with thee.

12 Apply thine heart unto instruction, and thine ears to the words of knowledge.

13 Withhold not correction from the child: for *if* thou beatest him with the rod, he shall not die.

14 Thou shalt beat him with the rod, and shalt deliver his soul from hell.

15 My son, if thine heart be wise, my heart shall rejoice, even mine.

16 Yea, my reins shall rejoice, when thy lips speak right things.

17 Let not thine heart envy sinners: but *be thou* in the fear of the LORD all the day long.

18 For surely there is an end; and thine expectation shall not be cut off.

19 Hear thou, my son, and be wise, and guide thine heart in the way.

20 Be not among winebibbers; among riotous eaters of flesh:

21 For the drunkard and the glutton shall come to poverty: and drowsiness shall clothe *a man* with rags.

22 Hearken unto thy father that begat thee, and despise not thy mother when she is old.

23 Buy the truth, and sell *it* not; *also* wisdom, and instruction, and understanding.

24 The father of the righteous shall greatly rejoice: and he that begetteth a wise *child* shall have joy of him.

25 Thy father and thy mother shall be glad, and she that bare thee shall rejoice.

26 My son, give me thine heart, and
let thine eyes observe my ways.
27 For a whore *is* a deep ditch; and a
strange woman *is* a narrow pit.
28 She also lieth in wait as *for* a prey,
and increaseth the transgressors among
men.
29 Who hath woe? who hath sorrow?
who hath contentions? who hath bab-
bling? who hath wounds without cause?
who hath redness of eyes?
30 They that tarry long at the wine;
they that go to seek mixed wine.
31 Look not thou upon the wine when
it is red, when it giveth his colour in the
cup, *when* it moveth itself aright.
32 At the last it biteth like a serpent,
and stingeth like an adder.
33 Thine eyes shall behold strange
women, and thine heart shall utter
perverse things.
34 Yea, thou shalt be as he that lieth
down in the midst of the sea, or as he
that lieth upon the top of a mast.
35 They have stricken me, *shalt thou
say, and* I was not sick; they have beat-
en me, *and* I felt *it* not: when shall I
awake? I will seek it yet again.

24 Be not thou envious against evil
men, neither desire to be with
them.
2 For their heart studieth destruction,
and their lips talk of mischief.
3 Through wisdom is an house builded; and by understanding it is established:
4 And by knowledge shall the chambers be filled with all precious and
pleasant riches.
5 A wise man *is* strong; yea, a man of
knowledge increaseth strength.
6 For by wise counsel thou shalt make
thy war: and in multitude of counsellors *there is* safety.
7 Wisdom *is* too high for a fool: he
openeth not his mouth in the gate.
8 He that deviseth to do evil shall be
called a mischievous person.
9 The thought of foolishness *is* sin:
and the scorner *is* an abomination to
men.
10 *If* thou faint in the day of adversity,
thy strength *is* small.
11 If thou forbear to deliver *them
that are* drawn unto death, and *those
that are* ready to be slain;
12 If thou sayest, Behold, we knew it
not; doth not he that pondereth the
heart consider *it*? and he that keepeth
thy soul, doth *not* he know *it*? and shall
not he render to *every* man according
to his works?
13 My son, eat thou honey, because *it
is* good; and the honeycomb, *which is*
sweet to thy taste:
14 So *shall* the knowledge of wisdom
be unto thy soul: when thou hast found
it, then there shall be a reward, and thy
expectation shall not be cut off.
15 Lay not wait, O wicked *man*,
against the dwelling of the righteous;
spoil not his resting place:
16 For a just *man* falleth seven times,
and riseth up again: but the wicked
shall fall into mischief.
17 Rejoice not when thine enemy
falleth, and let not thine heart be glad
when he stumbleth:
18 Lest the LORD see *it*, and it displease him, and he turn away his wrath
from him.
19 Fret not thyself because of evil
men, neither be thou envious at the
wicked;
20 For there shall be no reward to the
evil *man*; the candle of the wicked
shall be put out.

21 My son, fear thou the LORD and the
king: *and* meddle not with them that
are given to change:
22 For their calamity shall rise suddenly; and who knoweth the ruin of
them both?
23 These *things* also *belong* to the
wise. *It is* not good to have respect of
persons in judgment.
24 He that saith unto the wicked,
Thou *art* righteous; him shall the people curse, nations shall abhor him:
25 But to them that rebuke *him* shall
be delight, and a good blessing shall
come upon them.
26 *Every man* shall kiss *his* lips that
giveth a right answer.
27 Prepare thy work without, and
make it fit for thyself in the field; and
afterwards build thine house.
28 Be not a witness against thy neighbour without cause; and deceive *not*
with thy lips.
29 Say not, I will do so to him as he
hath done to me: I will render to the
man according to his work.
30 I went by the field of the slothful,
and by the vineyard of the man void of
understanding;
31 And, lo, it was all grown over with
thorns, *and* nettles had covered the
face thereof, and the stone wall thereof
was broken down.
32 Then I saw, *and* considered *it* well:
I looked upon *it, and* received instruction.
33 *Yet* a little sleep, a little slumber, a
little folding of the hands to sleep:
34 So shall thy poverty come *as* one
that travelleth; and thy want as an
armed man.

25 These *are* also proverbs of Solomon, which the men of Heze-
kiah king of Judah copied out.
2 *It is* the glory of God to conceal a
thing: but the honour of kings *is* to
search out a matter.
3 The heaven for height, and the
earth for depth, and the heart of kings
is unsearchable.
4 Take away the dross from the silver,
and there shall come forth a vessel for
the finer.
5 Take away the wicked *from* before
the king, and his throne shall be established in righteousness.
6 Put not forth thyself in the presence
of the king, and stand not in the place
of great *men*:
7 For better *it is* that it be said unto
thee, Come up hither; than that thou
shouldest be put lower in the presence
of the prince whom thine eyes have
seen.
8 Go not forth hastily to strive, lest
thou know not what to do in the end
thereof, when thy neighbour hath put
thee to shame.
9 Debate thy cause with thy neighbour *himself*; and discover not a secret
to another:
10 Lest he that heareth *it* put thee to
shame, and thine infamy turn not away.
11 A word fitly spoken *is like* apples
of gold in pictures of silver.
12 *As* an earring of gold, and an ornament of fine gold, *so is* a wise reprover
upon an obedient ear.
13 As the cold of snow in the time of
harvest, *so is* a faithful messenger to
them that send him: for he refresheth
the soul of his masters.
14 Whoso boasteth himself of a false
gift *is like* clouds and wind without
rain.
15 By long forbearing is a prince persuaded, and a soft tongue breaketh the
bone.

16 Hast thou found honey? eat so much as is sufficient for thee, lest thou be filled therewith, and vomit it.

17 Withdraw thy foot from thy neighbour's house; lest he be weary of thee, and *so* hate thee.

18 A man that beareth false witness against his neighbour *is* a maul, and a sword, and a sharp arrow.

19 Confidence in an unfaithful man in time of trouble *is like* a broken tooth, and a foot out of joint.

20 *As* he that taketh away a garment in cold weather, *and as* vinegar upon nitre, so *is* he that singeth songs to an heavy heart.

21 If thine enemy be hungry, give him bread to eat; and if he be thirsty, give him water to drink:

22 For thou shalt heap coals of fire upon his head, and the LORD shall reward thee.

23 The north wind driveth away rain: so *doth* an angry countenance a backbiting tongue.

24 *It is* better to dwell in the corner of the housetop, than with a brawling woman and in a wide house.

25 *As* cold waters to a thirsty soul, so *is* good news from a far country.

26 A righteous man falling down before the wicked *is as* a troubled fountain, and a corrupt spring.

27 *It is* not good to eat much honey: so *for men* to search their own glory *is not* glory.

28 He that *hath* no rule over his own spirit *is like* a city *that is* broken down, *and* without walls.

26 As snow in summer, and as rain in harvest, so honour is not seemly for a fool.

2 As the bird by wandering, as the swallow by flying, so the curse causeless shall not come.

3 A whip for the horse, a bridle for the ass, and a rod for the fool's back.

4 Answer not a fool according to his folly, lest thou also be like unto him.

5 Answer a fool according to his folly, lest he be wise in his own conceit.

6 He that sendeth a message by the hand of a fool cutteth off the feet, *and* drinketh damage.

7 The legs of the lame are not equal: so *is* a parable in the mouth of fools.

8 As he that bindeth a stone in a sling, so *is* he that giveth honour to a fool.

9 *As* a thorn goeth up into the hand of a drunkard, so *is* a parable in the mouth of fools.

10 The great *God* that formed all *things* both rewardeth the fool, and rewardeth transgressors.

11 As a dog returneth to his vomit, *so* a fool returneth to his folly.

12 Seest thou a man wise in his own conceit? *there is* more hope of a fool than of him.

13 The slothful *man* saith, *There is* a lion in the way; a lion *is* in the streets.

14 *As* the door turneth upon his hinges, so *doth* the slothful upon his bed.

15 The slothful hideth his hand in *his* bosom; it grieveth him to bring it again to his mouth.

16 The sluggard *is* wiser in his own conceit than seven men that can render a reason.

17 He that passeth by, *and* meddleth with strife *belonging* not to him, *is like* one that taketh a dog by the ears.

18 As a mad *man* who casteth firebrands, arrows, and death,

19 So *is* the man *that* deceiveth his neighbour, and saith, Am not I in sport?

20 Where no wood is, *there* the fire goeth out: so where *there is* no talebearer, the strife ceaseth.

21 *As* coals *are* to burning coals, and wood to fire; so *is* a contentious man to kindle strife.

22 The words of a talebearer *are* as wounds, and they go down into the innermost parts of the belly.

23 Burning lips and a wicked heart *are like* a potsherd covered with silver dross.

24 He that hateth dissembleth with his lips, and layeth up deceit within him;

25 When he speaketh fair, believe him not: for *there are* seven abominations in his heart.

26 *Whose* hatred is covered by deceit, his wickedness shall be shewed before the *whole* congregation.

27 Whoso diggeth a pit shall fall therein: and he that rolleth a stone, it will return upon him.

28 A lying tongue hateth *those that are* afflicted by it; and a flattering mouth worketh ruin.

27 Boast not thyself of to morrow; for thou knowest not what a day may bring forth.

2 Let another man praise thee, and not thine own mouth; a stranger, and not thine own lips.

3 A stone *is* heavy, and the sand weighty; but a fool's wrath *is* heavier than them both.

4 Wrath *is* cruel, and anger *is* outrageous; but who *is* able to stand before envy?

5 Open rebuke *is* better than secret love.

6 Faithful *are* the wounds of a friend; but the kisses of an enemy *are* deceitful.

7 The full soul loatheth an honeycomb; but to the hungry soul every bitter thing is sweet.

8 As a bird that wandereth from her nest, so *is* a man that wandereth from his place.

9 Ointment and perfume rejoice the heart: so *doth* the sweetness of a man's friend by hearty counsel.

10 Thine own friend, and thy father's friend, forsake not; neither go into thy brother's house in the day of thy calamity: *for* better *is* a neighbour *that is* near than a brother far off.

11 My son, be wise, and make my heart glad, that I may answer him that reproacheth me.

12 A prudent *man* foreseeth the evil, *and* hideth himself; *but* the simple pass on, *and* are punished.

13 Take his garment that is surety for a stranger, and take a pledge of him for a strange woman.

14 He that blesseth his friend with a loud voice, rising early in the morning, it shall be counted a curse to him.

15 A continual dropping in a very rainy day and a contentious woman are alike.

16 Whosoever hideth her hideth the wind, and the ointment of his right hand, *which* bewrayeth *itself*.

17 Iron sharpeneth iron; so a man sharpeneth the countenance of his friend.

18 Whoso keepeth the fig tree shall eat the fruit thereof: so he that waiteth on his master shall be honoured.

19 As in water face *answereth* to face, so the heart of man to man.

20 Hell and destruction are never full; so the eyes of man are never satisfied.

21 *As* the fining pot for silver, and the
furnace for gold; so *is* a man to his
praise.
22 Though thou shouldest bray a fool
in a mortar among wheat with a pestle,
yet will not his foolishness depart from
him.
23 Be thou diligent to know the state
of thy flocks, *and* look well to thy herds.
24 For riches *are* not for ever: and
doth the crown *endure* to every generation?
25 The hay appeareth, and the tender
grass sheweth itself, and herbs of the
mountains are gathered.
26 The lambs *are* for thy clothing, and
the goats *are* the price of the field.
27 And *thou shalt have* goats' milk
enough for thy food, for the food of thy
household, and *for* the maintenance for
thy maidens.

28 The wicked flee when no man
pursueth: but the righteous are
bold as a lion.
2 For the transgression of a land
many *are* the princes thereof: but by a
man of understanding *and* knowledge
the state *thereof* shall be prolonged.
3 A poor man that oppresseth the
poor *is like* a sweeping rain which leaveth no food.
4 They that forsake the law praise the
wicked: but such as keep the law contend with them.
5 Evil men understand not judgment:
but they that seek the LORD understand
all *things*.
6 Better *is* the poor that walketh in
his uprightness, than *he that is* perverse *in his* ways, though he *be* rich.
7 Whoso keepeth the law *is* a wise
son: but he that is a companion of riotous *men* shameth his father.
8 He that by usury and unjust gain
increaseth his substance, he shall gather it for him that will pity the poor.
9 He that turneth away his ear from
hearing the law, even his prayer *shall
be* abomination.
10 Whoso causeth the righteous to go
astray in an evil way, he shall fall himself into his own pit: but the upright
shall have good *things* in possession.
11 The rich man *is* wise in his own
conceit; but the poor that hath understanding searcheth him out.
12 When righteous *men* do rejoice,
there is great glory: but when the
wicked rise, a man is hidden.
13 He that covereth his sins shall not
prosper: but whoso confesseth and forsaketh *them* shall have mercy.
14 Happy *is* the man that feareth
alway: but he that hardeneth his heart
shall fall into mischief.
15 *As* a roaring lion, and a ranging
bear; *so is* a wicked ruler over the poor
people.
16 The prince that wanteth understanding *is* also a great oppressor: *but*
he that hateth covetousness shall prolong *his* days.
17 A man that doeth violence to the
blood of *any* person shall flee to the pit;
let no man stay him.
18 Whoso walketh uprightly shall be
saved: but *he that is* perverse *in his*
ways shall fall at once.
19 He that tilleth his land shall have
plenty of bread: but he that followeth
after vain *persons* shall have poverty
enough.
20 A faithful man shall abound with
blessings: but he that maketh haste to
be rich shall not be innocent.

21 To have respect of persons *is* not good: for for a piece of bread *that* man will transgress.

22 He that hasteth to be rich *hath* an evil eye, and considereth not that poverty shall come upon him.

23 He that rebuketh a man afterwards shall find more favour than he that flattereth with the tongue.

24 Whoso robbeth his father or his mother, and saith, *It is* no transgression; the same *is* the companion of a destroyer.

25 He that is of a proud heart stirreth up strife: but he that putteth his trust in the LORD shall be made fat.

26 He that trusteth in his own heart is a fool: but whoso walketh wisely, he shall be delivered.

27 He that giveth unto the poor shall not lack: but he that hideth his eyes shall have many a curse.

28 When the wicked rise, men hide themselves: but when they perish, the righteous increase.

29 He, that being often reproved hardeneth *his* neck, shall suddenly be destroyed, and that without remedy.

2 When the righteous are in authority, the people rejoice: but when the wicked beareth rule, the people mourn.

3 Whoso loveth wisdom rejoiceth his father: but he that keepeth company with harlots spendeth *his* substance.

4 The king by judgment establisheth the land: but he that receiveth gifts overthroweth it.

5 A man that flattereth his neighbour spreadeth a net for his feet.

6 In the transgression of an evil man *there is* a snare: but the righteous doth sing and rejoice.

7 The righteous considereth the cause of the poor: *but* the wicked regardeth not to know *it*.

8 Scornful men bring a city into a snare: but wise *men* turn away wrath.

9 *If* a wise man contendeth with a foolish man, whether he rage or laugh, *there is* no rest.

10 The bloodthirsty hate the upright: but the just seek his soul.

11 A fool uttereth all his mind: but a wise *man* keepeth it in till afterwards.

12 If a ruler hearken to lies, all his servants *are* wicked.

13 The poor and the deceitful man meet together: the LORD lighteneth both their eyes.

14 The king that faithfully judgeth the poor, his throne shall be established for ever.

15 The rod and reproof give wisdom: but a child left *to himself* bringeth his mother to shame.

16 When the wicked are multiplied, transgression increaseth: but the righteous shall see their fall.

17 Correct thy son, and he shall give thee rest; yea, he shall give delight unto thy soul.

18 Where *there is* no vision, the people perish: but he that keepeth the law, happy *is* he.

19 A servant will not be corrected by words: for though he understand he will not answer.

20 Seest thou a man *that is* hasty in his words? *there is* more hope of a fool than of him.

21 He that delicately bringeth up his servant from a child shall have him become *his* son at the length.

22 An angry man stirreth up strife, and a furious man aboundeth in transgression.

23 A man's pride shall bring him low:
but honour shall uphold the humble in
spirit.
24 Whoso is partner with a thief
hateth his own soul: he heareth cursing,
and bewrayeth *it* not.
25 The fear of man bringeth a snare:
but whoso putteth his trust in the LORD
shall be safe.
26 Many seek the ruler's favour; but
every man's judgment *cometh* from the
LORD.
27 An unjust man *is* an abomination
to the just: and *he that is* upright in the
way *is* abomination to the wicked.

30 The words of Agur the son of
Jakeh, *even* the prophecy: the
man spake unto Ithiel, even unto Ithiel
and Ucal,
2 Surely I *am* more brutish than *any*
man, and have not the understanding
of a man.
3 I neither learned wisdom, nor have
the knowledge of the holy.
4 Who hath ascended up into heaven,
or descended? who hath gathered the
wind in his fists? who hath bound the
waters in a garment? who hath established all the ends of the earth? what *is*
his name, and what *is* his son's name, if
thou canst tell?
5 Every word of God *is* pure: he *is* a
shield unto them that put their trust in
him.
6 Add thou not unto his words, lest he
reprove thee, and thou be found a liar.
7 Two *things* have I required of thee;
deny me *them* not before I die:
8 Remove far from me vanity and lies:
give me neither poverty nor riches;
feed me with food convenient for me:
9 Lest I be full, and deny *thee*, and
say, Who *is* the LORD? or lest I be poor,
and steal, and take the name of my God
in vain.
10 Accuse not a servant unto his master, lest he curse thee, and thou be
found guilty.
11 *There is* a generation *that* curseth
their father, and doth not bless their
mother.
12 *There is* a generation *that are* pure
in their own eyes, and *yet* is not washed
from their filthiness.
13 *There is* a generation, O how lofty
are their eyes! and their eyelids are
lifted up.
14 *There is* a generation, whose teeth
are as swords, and their jaw teeth *as*
knives, to devour the poor from off the
earth, and the needy from *among* men.
15 The horseleach hath two daughters, *crying*, Give, give. There are three
things that are never satisfied, *yea*,
four *things* say not, *It is* enough:
16 The grave; and the barren womb;
the earth *that* is not filled with water;
and the fire *that* saith not, *It is* enough.
17 The eye *that* mocketh at *his* father,
and despiseth to obey *his* mother, the
ravens of the valley shall pick it out,
and the young eagles shall eat it.
18 There be three *things which* are
too wonderful for me, yea, four which I
know not:
19 The way of an eagle in the air; the
way of a serpent upon a rock; the way
of a ship in the midst of the sea; and the
way of a man with a maid.
20 Such *is* the way of an adulterous
woman; she eateth, and wipeth her
mouth, and saith, I have done no wickedness.
21 For three *things* the earth is disquieted, and for four *which* it cannot
bear:

22 For a servant when he reigneth;
and a fool when he is filled with meat;
23 For an odious *woman* when she is
married; and an handmaid that is heir
to her mistress.
24 There be four *things which are*
little upon the earth, but they *are*
exceeding wise:
25 The ants *are* a people not strong,
yet they prepare their meat in the summer;
26 The conies *are but* a feeble folk,
yet make they their houses in the rocks;
27 The locusts have no king, yet go
they forth all of them by bands;
28 The spider taketh hold with her
hands, and is in kings' palaces.
29 There be three *things* which go
well, yea, four are comely in going:
30 A lion *which is* strongest among
beasts, and turneth not away for any;
31 A greyhound; an he goat also; and
a king, against whom *there is* no rising
up.
32 If thou hast done foolishly in lifting up thyself, or if thou hast thought
evil, *lay* thine hand upon thy mouth.
33 Surely the churning of milk bringeth forth butter, and the wringing of
the nose bringeth forth blood: so the
forcing of wrath bringeth forth strife.

31 The words of king Lemuel, the
prophecy that his mother taught
him.
2 What, my son? and what, the son of
my womb? and what, the son of my
vows?
3 Give not thy strength unto women,
nor thy ways to that which destroyeth
kings.
4 *It is* not for kings, O Lemuel, *it is*
not for kings to drink wine; nor for
princes strong drink:
5 Lest they drink, and forget the law,
and pervert the judgment of any of the
afflicted.
6 Give strong drink unto him that is
ready to perish, and wine unto those
that be of heavy hearts.
7 Let him drink, and forget his poverty, and remember his misery no more.
8 Open thy mouth for the dumb in the
cause of all such as are appointed to
destruction.
9 Open thy mouth, judge righteously,
and plead the cause of the poor and
needy.
10 Who can find a virtuous woman?
for her price *is* far above rubies.
11 The heart of her husband doth
safely trust in her, so that he shall have
no need of spoil.
12 She will do him good and not evil
all the days of her life.
13 She seeketh wool, and flax, and
worketh willingly with her hands.
14 She is like the merchants' ships;
she bringeth her food from afar.
15 She riseth also while it is yet night,
and giveth meat to her household, and
a portion to her maidens.
16 She considereth a field, and buyeth it: with the fruit of her hands she
planteth a vineyard.
17 She girdeth her loins with strength,
and strengtheneth her arms.
18 She perceiveth that her merchandise *is* good: her candle goeth not out
by night.
19 She layeth her hands to the spin-
dle, and her hands hold the distaff.
20 She stretcheth out her hand to the
poor; yea, she reacheth forth her hands
to the needy.
21 She is not afraid of the snow for
her household: for all her household
are clothed with scarlet.

22 She maketh herself coverings of tapestry; her clothing *is* silk and purple.

23 Her husband is known in the gates, when he sitteth among the elders of the land.

24 She maketh fine linen, and selleth *it*; and delivereth girdles unto the merchant.

25 Strength and honour *are* her clothing; and she shall rejoice in time to come.

26 She openeth her mouth with wisdom; and in her tongue *is* the law of kindness.

27 She looketh well to the ways of her household, and eateth not the bread of idleness.

28 Her children arise up, and call her blessed; her husband *also*, and he praiseth her.

29 Many daughters have done virtuously, but thou excellest them all.

30 Favour *is* deceitful, and beauty *is* vain: *but* a woman *that* feareth the LORD, she shall be praised.

31 Give her of the fruit of her hands; and let her own works praise her in the gates.

ECCLESIASTES

1 The words of the Preacher, the son of David, king in Jerusalem.

2 Vanity of vanities, saith the Preacher, vanity of vanities; all *is* vanity.

3 What profit hath a man of all his labour which he taketh under the sun?

4 *One* generation passeth away, and *another* generation cometh: but the earth abideth for ever.

5 The sun also ariseth, and the sun goeth down, and hasteth to his place where he arose.

6 The wind goeth toward the south, and turneth about unto the north; it whirleth about continually, and the wind returneth again according to his circuits.

7 All the rivers run into the sea; yet the sea *is* not full; unto the place from whence the rivers come, thither they return again.

8 All things *are* full of labour; man cannot utter *it*: the eye is not satisfied with seeing, nor the ear filled with hearing.

9 The thing that hath been, it *is that* which shall be; and that which is done *is* that which shall be done: and *there is* no new *thing* under the sun.

10 Is there *any* thing whereof it may be said, See, this *is* new? it hath been already of old time, which was before us.

11 *There is* no remembrance of former *things*; neither shall there be *any* remembrance of *things* that are to come with *those* that shall come after.

12 I the Preacher was king over Israel in Jerusalem.

13 And I gave my heart to seek and search out by wisdom concerning all *things* that are done under heaven: this sore travail hath God given to the sons of man to be exercised therewith.

14 I have seen all the works that are
done under the sun; and, behold, all *is*
vanity and vexation of spirit.
15 *That which is* crooked cannot be
made straight: and that which is wanting cannot be numbered.
16 I communed with mine own heart,
saying, Lo, I am come to great estate,
and have gotten more wisdom than all
they that have been before me in
Jerusalem: yea, my heart had great
experience of wisdom and knowledge.
17 And I gave my heart to know wisdom, and to know madness and folly: I
perceived that this also is vexation of
spirit.
18 For in much wisdom *is* much grief:
and he that increaseth knowledge
increaseth sorrow.

2 I said in mine heart, Go to now, I
will prove thee with mirth, therefore
enjoy pleasure: and, behold, this also *is*
vanity.
2 I said of laughter, *It is* mad: and of
mirth, What doeth it?
3 I sought in mine heart to give myself
unto wine, yet acquainting mine heart
with wisdom; and to lay hold on folly,
till I might see what *was* that good for
the sons of men, which they should do
under the heaven all the days of their
life.
4 I made me great works; I builded
me houses; I planted me vineyards:
5 I made me gardens and orchards,
and I planted trees in them of all *kind*
of fruits:
6 I made me pools of water, to water
therewith the wood that bringeth forth
trees:
7 I got *me* servants and maidens, and
had servants born in my house; also I
had great possessions of great and
small cattle above all that were in
Jerusalem before me:
8 I gathered me also silver and gold,
and the peculiar treasure of kings and
of the provinces: I gat me men singers
and women singers, and the delights of
the sons of men, *as* musical instruments, and that of all sorts.
9 So I was great, and increased more
than all that were before me in
Jerusalem: also my wisdom remained
with me.
10 And whatsoever mine eyes desired
I kept not from them, I withheld not my
heart from any joy; for my heart
rejoiced in all my labour: and this was
my portion of all my labour.
11 Then I looked on all the works that
my hands had wrought, and on the
labour that I had laboured to do: and,
behold, all *was* vanity and vexation of
spirit, and *there was* no profit under
the sun.
12 And I turned myself to behold
wisdom, and madness, and folly: for
what *can* the man *do* that cometh after
the king? *even* that which hath been
already done.
13 Then I saw that wisdom excelleth
folly, as far as light excelleth darkness.
14 The wise man's eyes *are* in his
head; but the fool walketh in darkness:
and I myself perceived also that one
event happeneth to them all.
15 Then said I in my heart, As it happeneth to the fool, so it happeneth even
to me; and why was I then more wise?
Then I said in my heart, that this also *is*
vanity.
16 For *there is* no remembrance of
the wise more than of the fool for ever;
seeing that which now *is* in the days to
come shall all be forgotten. And how
dieth the wise *man*? as the fool.

17 Therefore I hated life; because the
work that is wrought under the sun *is*
grievous unto me: for all *is* vanity and
vexation of spirit.
18 Yea, I hated all my labour which I
had taken under the sun: because I
should leave it unto the man that shall
be after me.
19 And who knoweth whether he
shall be a wise *man* or a fool? yet shall
he have rule over all my labour wherein
I have laboured, and wherein I have
shewed myself wise under the sun. This
is also vanity.
20 Therefore I went about to cause
my heart to despair of all the labour
which I took under the sun.
21 For there is a man whose labour *is*
in wisdom, and in knowledge, and in
equity; yet to a man that hath not
laboured therein shall he leave it *for*
his portion. This also *is* vanity and a
great evil.
22 For what hath man of all his labour,
and of the vexation of his heart, wherein he hath laboured under the sun?
23 For all his days *are* sorrows, and his
travail grief; yea, his heart taketh not
rest in the night. This is also vanity.
24 *There is* nothing better for a man,
than that he should eat and drink, and
that he should make his soul enjoy
good in his labour. This also I saw, that
it *was* from the hand of God.
25 For who can eat, or who else can
hasten *hereunto*, more than I?
26 For *God* giveth to a man that *is*
good in his sight wisdom, and knowledge, and joy: but to the sinner he
giveth travail, to gather and to heap up,
that he may give to *him that is* good
before God. This also *is* vanity and vexation of spirit.

3 To every *thing there is* a season,
and a time to every purpose under
the heaven:
2 A time to be born, and a time to die;
a time to plant, and a time to pluck up
that which is planted;
3 A time to kill, and a time to heal; a
time to break down, and a time to build
up;
4 A time to weep, and a time to laugh;
a time to mourn, and a time to dance;
5 A time to cast away stones, and a
time to gather stones together; a time
to embrace, and a time to refrain from
embracing;
6 A time to get, and a time to lose; a
time to keep, and a time to cast away;
7 A time to rend, and a time to sew; a
time to keep silence, and a time to
speak;
8 A time to love, and a time to hate; a
time of war, and a time of peace.
9 What profit hath he that worketh in
that wherein he laboureth?
10 I have seen the travail, which God
hath given to the sons of men to be
exercised in it.
11 He hath made every *thing* beautiful in his time: also he hath set the
world in their heart, so that no man can
find out the work that God maketh
from the beginning to the end.
12 I know that *there is* no good in
them, but for *a man* to rejoice, and to
do good in his life.
13 And also that every man should
eat and drink, and enjoy the good of all
his labour, it *is* the gift of God.
14 I know that, whatsoever God
doeth, it shall be for ever: nothing can
be put to it, nor any thing taken from it:
and God doeth *it*, that *men* should fear
before him.

15 That which hath been is now; and
that which is to be hath already been;
and God requireth that which is past.
16 And moreover I saw under the sun
the place of judgment, *that* wickedness
was there; and the place of righteousness, *that* iniquity *was* there.
17 I said in mine heart, God shall
judge the righteous and the wicked: for
there is a time there for every purpose
and for every work.
18 I said in mine heart concerning the
estate of the sons of men, that God
might manifest them, and that they
might see that they themselves are
beasts.
19 For that which befalleth the sons
of men befalleth beasts; even one thing
befalleth them: as the one dieth, so
dieth the other; yea, they have all one
breath; so that a man hath no preeminence above a beast: for all *is* vanity.
20 All go unto one place; all are of the
dust, and all turn to dust again.
21 Who knoweth the spirit of man
that goeth upward, and the spirit of the
beast that goeth downward to the
earth?
22 Wherefore I perceive that *there is*
nothing better, than that a man should
rejoice in his own works; for that *is* his
portion: for who shall bring him to see
what shall be after him?

4 So I returned, and considered all
the oppressions that are done
under the sun: and behold the tears of
such as were oppressed, and they had
no comforter; and on the side of their
oppressors *there was* power; but they
had no comforter.
2 Wherefore I praised the dead which
are already dead more than the living
which are yet alive.
3 Yea, better *is he* than both they,
which hath not yet been, who hath not
seen the evil work that is done under
the sun.
4 Again, I considered all travail, and
every right work, that for this a man is
envied of his neighbour. This *is* also
vanity and vexation of spirit.
5 The fool foldeth his hands together,
and eateth his own flesh.
6 Better *is* an handful *with* quietness,
than both the hands full *with* travail
and vexation of spirit.
7 Then I returned, and I saw vanity
under the sun.
8 There is one *alone*, and *there is* not
a second; yea, he hath neither child nor
brother: yet *is there* no end of all his
labour; neither is his eye satisfied with
riches; neither *saith he*, For whom do I
labour, and bereave my soul of good?
This *is* also vanity, yea, it *is* a sore travail.
9 Two *are* better than one; because
they have a good reward for their
labour.
10 For if they fall, the one will lift up
his fellow: but woe to him *that is* alone
when he falleth; for *he hath* not another to help him up.
11 Again, if two lie together, then they
have heat: but how can one be warm
alone?
12 And if one prevail against him, two
shall withstand him; and a threefold
cord is not quickly broken.
13 Better *is* a poor and a wise child
than an old and foolish king, who will
no more be admonished.
14 For out of prison he cometh to
reign; whereas also *he that is* born in
his kingdom becometh poor.

15 I considered all the living which walk under the sun, with the second child that shall stand up in his stead.

16 *There is* no end of all the people, *even* of all that have been before them: they also that come after shall not rejoice in him. Surely this also *is* vanity and vexation of spirit.

5 Keep thy foot when thou goest to the house of God, and be more ready to hear, than to give the sacrifice of fools: for they consider not that they do evil.

2 Be not rash with thy mouth, and let not thine heart be hasty to utter *any* thing before God: for God *is* in heaven, and thou upon earth: therefore let thy words be few.

3 For a dream cometh through the multitude of business; and a fool's voice *is known* by multitude of words.

4 When thou vowest a vow unto God, defer not to pay it; for *he hath* no pleasure in fools: pay that which thou hast vowed.

5 Better *is it* that thou shouldest not vow, than that thou shouldest vow and not pay.

6 Suffer not thy mouth to cause thy flesh to sin; neither say thou before the angel, that it *was* an error: wherefore should God be angry at thy voice, and destroy the work of thine hands?

7 For in the multitude of dreams and many words *there are* also *divers* vanities: but fear thou God.

8 If thou seest the oppression of the poor, and violent perverting of judgment and justice in a province, marvel not at the matter: for *he that is* higher than the highest regardeth; and *there be* higher than they.

9 Moreover the profit of the earth is for all: the king *himself* is served by the field.

10 He that loveth silver shall not be satisfied with silver; nor he that loveth abundance with increase: this *is* also vanity.

11 When goods increase, they are increased that eat them: and what good *is there* to the owners thereof, saving the beholding *of them* with their eyes?

12 The sleep of a labouring man *is* sweet, whether he eat little or much: but the abundance of the rich will not suffer him to sleep.

13 There is a sore evil *which* I have seen under the sun, *namely*, riches kept for the owners thereof to their hurt.

14 But those riches perish by evil travail: and he begetteth a son, and *there is* nothing in his hand.

15 As he came forth of his mother's womb, naked shall he return to go as he came, and shall take nothing of his labour, which he may carry away in his hand.

16 And this also *is* a sore evil, *that* in all points as he came, so shall he go: and what profit hath he that hath laboured for the wind?

17 All his days also he eateth in darkness, and *he hath* much sorrow and wrath with his sickness.

18 Behold *that* which I have seen: *it is* good and comely *for one* to eat and to drink, and to enjoy the good of all his labour that he taketh under the sun all the days of his life, which God giveth him: for it *is* his portion.

19 Every man also to whom God hath given riches and wealth, and hath given him power to eat thereof, and to take

his portion, and to rejoice in his labour;
this *is* the gift of God.
20 For he shall not much remember
the days of his life; because God
answereth *him* in the joy of his heart.

6 There is an evil which I have seen
under the sun, and it *is* common
among men:
2 A man to whom God hath given
riches, wealth, and honour, so that he
wanteth nothing for his soul of all that
he desireth, yet God giveth him not
power to eat thereof, but a stranger
eateth it: this *is* vanity, and it *is* an evil
disease.
3 If a man beget an hundred *children*,
and live many years, so that the days of
his years be many, and his soul be not
filled with good, and also *that* he have
no burial; I say, *that* an untimely birth
is better than he.
4 For he cometh in with vanity, and
departeth in darkness, and his name
shall be covered with darkness.
5 Moreover he hath not seen the sun,
nor known *any thing*: this hath more
rest than the other.
6 Yea, though he live a thousand
years twice *told*, yet hath he seen no
good: do not all go to one place?
7 All the labour of man *is* for his
mouth, and yet the appetite is not
filled.
8 For what hath the wise more than
the fool? what hath the poor, that
knoweth to walk before the living?
9 Better *is* the sight of the eyes than
the wandering of the desire: this *is* also
vanity and vexation of spirit.
10 That which hath been is named
already, and it is known that it *is* man:
neither may he contend with him that
is mightier than he.
11 Seeing there be many things that
increase vanity, what *is* man the better?
12 For who knoweth what *is* good for
man in *this* life, all the days of his vain
life which he spendeth as a shadow? for
who can tell a man what shall be after
him under the sun?

7 A good name *is* better than precious
ointment; and the day of death than
the day of one's birth.
2 *It is* better to go to the house of
mourning, than to go to the house of
feasting: for that *is* the end of all men;
and the living will lay *it* to his heart.
3 Sorrow *is* better than laughter: for
by the sadness of the countenance the
heart is made better.
4 The heart of the wise *is* in the house
of mourning; but the heart of fools *is* in
the house of mirth.
5 *It is* better to hear the rebuke of the
wise, than for a man to hear the song of
fools.
6 For as the crackling of thorns under
a pot, so *is* the laughter of the fool: this
also *is* vanity.
7 Surely oppression maketh a wise
man mad; and a gift destroyeth the
heart.
8 Better *is* the end of a thing than the
beginning thereof: *and* the patient in
spirit *is* better than the proud in spirit.
9 Be not hasty in thy spirit to be
angry: for anger resteth in the bosom of
fools.
10 Say not thou, What is *the cause*
that the former days were better than
these? for thou dost not enquire wisely
concerning this.
11 Wisdom *is* good with an inheritance: and *by it there is* profit to them
that see the sun.

12 For wisdom *is* a defence, *and* money *is* a defence: but the excellency of knowledge *is, that* wisdom giveth life to them that have it.

13 Consider the work of God: for who can make *that* straight, which he hath made crooked?

14 In the day of prosperity be joyful, but in the day of adversity consider: God also hath set the one over against the other, to the end that man should find nothing after him.

15 All *things* have I seen in the days of my vanity: there is a just *man* that perisheth in his righteousness, and there is a wicked *man* that prolongeth *his life* in his wickedness.

16 Be not righteous over much; neither make thyself over wise: why shouldest thou destroy thyself?

17 Be not over much wicked, neither be thou foolish: why shouldest thou die before thy time?

18 *It is* good that thou shouldest take hold of this; yea, also from this withdraw not thine hand: for he that feareth God shall come forth of them all.

19 Wisdom strengtheneth the wise more than ten mighty *men* which are in the city.

20 For *there is* not a just man upon earth, that doeth good, and sinneth not.

21 Also take no heed unto all words that are spoken; lest thou hear thy servant curse thee:

22 For oftentimes also thine own heart knoweth that thou thyself likewise hast cursed others.

23 All this have I proved by wisdom: I said, I will be wise; but it *was* far from me.

24 That which is far off, and exceeding deep, who can find it out?

25 I applied mine heart to know, and to search, and to seek out wisdom, and the reason *of things*, and to know the wickedness of folly, even of foolishness *and* madness:

26 And I find more bitter than death the woman, whose heart *is* snares and nets, *and* her hands *as* bands: whoso pleaseth God shall escape from her; but the sinner shall be taken by her.

27 Behold, this have I found, saith the preacher, *counting* one by one, to find out the account:

28 Which yet my soul seeketh, but I find not: one man among a thousand have I found; but a woman among all those have I not found.

29 Lo, this only have I found, that God hath made man upright; but they have sought out many inventions.

8 Who *is* as the wise *man*? and who knoweth the interpretation of a thing? a man's wisdom maketh his face to shine, and the boldness of his face shall be changed.

2 I *counsel thee* to keep the king's commandment, and *that* in regard of the oath of God.

3 Be not hasty to go out of his sight: stand not in an evil thing; for he doeth whatsoever pleaseth him.

4 Where the word of a king *is, there is* power: and who may say unto him, What doest thou?

5 Whoso keepeth the commandment shall feel no evil thing: and a wise man's heart discerneth both time and judgment.

6 Because to every purpose there is time and judgment, therefore the misery of man *is* great upon him.

7 For he knoweth not that which shall be: for who can tell him when it shall be?

8 *There is* no man that hath power over the spirit to retain the spirit; neither *hath he* power in the day of death: and *there is* no discharge in *that* war; neither shall wickedness deliver those that are given to it.

9 All this have I seen, and applied my heart unto every work that is done under the sun: *there is* a time wherein one man ruleth over another to his own hurt.

10 And so I saw the wicked buried, who had come and gone from the place of the holy, and they were forgotten in the city where they had so done: this *is* also vanity.

11 Because sentence against an evil work is not executed speedily, therefore the heart of the sons of men is fully set in them to do evil.

12 Though a sinner do evil an hundred times, and his *days* be prolonged, yet surely I know that it shall be well with them that fear God, which fear before him:

13 But it shall not be well with the wicked, neither shall he prolong *his* days, *which are* as a shadow; because he feareth not before God.

14 There is a vanity which is done upon the earth; that there be just *men*, unto whom it happeneth according to the work of the wicked; again, there be wicked *men*, to whom it happeneth according to the work of the righteous: I said that this also *is* vanity.

15 Then I commended mirth, because a man hath no better thing under the sun, than to eat, and to drink, and to be merry: for that shall abide with him of his labour the days of his life, which God giveth him under the sun.

16 When I applied mine heart to know wisdom, and to see the business that is done upon the earth: (for also *there is that* neither day nor night seeth sleep with his eyes:)

17 Then I beheld all the work of God, that a man cannot find out the work that is done under the sun: because though a man labour to seek *it* out, yet he shall not find *it*; yea further; though a wise *man* think to know *it*, yet shall he not be able to find *it*.

9 For all this I considered in my heart even to declare all this, that the righteous, and the wise, and their works, *are* in the hand of God: no man knoweth either love or hatred *by* all *that is* before them.

2 All *things come* alike to all: *there is* one event to the righteous, and to the wicked; to the good and to the clean, and to the unclean; to him that sacrificeth, and to him that sacrificeth not: as *is* the good, so *is* the sinner; *and* he that sweareth, as *he* that feareth an oath.

3 This *is* an evil among all *things* that are done under the sun, that *there is* one event unto all: yea, also the heart of the sons of men is full of evil, and madness *is* in their heart while they live, and after that *they go* to the dead.

4 For to him that is joined to all the living there is hope: for a living dog is better than a dead lion.

5 For the living know that they shall die: but the dead know not any thing, neither have they any more a reward; for the memory of them is forgotten.

6 Also their love, and their hatred, and their envy, is now perished; neither have they any more a portion for ever in any *thing* that is done under the sun.

7 Go thy way, eat thy bread with joy, and drink thy wine with a merry heart; for God now accepteth thy works.

8 Let thy garments be always white;
and let thy head lack no ointment.
9 Live joyfully with the wife whom
thou lovest all the days of the life of thy
vanity, which he hath given thee under
the sun, all the days of thy vanity: for
that *is* thy portion in *this* life, and in thy
labour which thou takest under the
sun.
10 Whatsoever thy hand findeth to
do, do *it* with thy might; for *there is* no
work, nor device, nor knowledge, nor
wisdom, in the grave, whither thou
goest.
11 I returned, and saw under the sun,
that the race *is* not to the swift, nor the
battle to the strong, neither yet bread
to the wise, nor yet riches to men of
understanding, nor yet favour to men of
skill; but time and chance happeneth
to them all.
12 For man also knoweth not his time:
as the fishes that are taken in an evil
net, and as the birds that are caught in
the snare; so *are* the sons of men snared
in an evil time, when it falleth suddenly
upon them.
13 This wisdom have I seen also
under the sun, and it *seemed* great unto
me:
14 *There was* a little city, and few men
within it; and there came a great king
against it, and besieged it, and built
great bulwarks against it:
15 Now there was found in it a poor
wise man, and he by his wisdom delivered the city; yet no man remembered
that same poor man.
16 Then said I, Wisdom *is* better than
strength: nevertheless the poor man's
wisdom *is* despised, and his words are
not heard.
17 The words of wise *men are* heard
in quiet more than the cry of him that
ruleth among fools.
18 Wisdom *is* better than weapons of
war: but one sinner destroyeth much
good.

10 Dead flies cause the ointment of
the apothecary to send forth a
stinking savour: *so doth* a little folly
him that is in reputation for wisdom
and honour.
2 A wise man's heart *is* at his right
hand; but a fool's heart at his left.
3 Yea also, when he that is a fool
walketh by the way, his wisdom faileth
him, and he saith to every one *that* he
is a fool.
4 If the spirit of the ruler rise up
against thee, leave not thy place; for
yielding pacifieth great offences.
5 There is an evil *which* I have seen
under the sun, as an error *which* proceedeth from the ruler:
6 Folly is set in great dignity, and the
rich sit in low place.
7 I have seen servants upon horses,
and princes walking as servants upon
the earth.
8 He that diggeth a pit shall fall into
it; and whoso breaketh an hedge, a
serpent shall bite him.
9 Whoso removeth stones shall be
hurt therewith; *and* he that cleaveth
wood shall be endangered thereby.
10 If the iron be blunt, and he do not
whet the edge, then must he put to
more strength: but wisdom *is* profitable
to direct.
11 Surely the serpent will bite without enchantment; and a babbler is no
better.
12 The words of a wise man's mouth
are gracious; but the lips of a fool will
swallow up himself.

13 The beginning of the words of his mouth *is* foolishness: and the end of his talk *is* mischievous madness.

14 A fool also is full of words: a man cannot tell what shall be; and what shall be after him, who can tell him?

15 The labour of the foolish wearieth every one of them, because he knoweth not how to go to the city.

16 Woe to thee, O land, when thy king *is* a child, and thy princes eat in the morning!

17 Blessed *art* thou, O land, when thy king *is* the son of nobles, and thy princes eat in due season, for strength, and not for drunkenness!

18 By much slothfulness the building decayeth; and through idleness of the hands the house droppeth through.

19 A feast is made for laughter, and wine maketh merry: but money answereth all *things*.

20 Curse not the king, no not in thy thought; and curse not the rich in thy bedchamber: for a bird of the air shall carry the voice, and that which hath wings shall tell the matter.

11 Cast thy bread upon the waters: for thou shalt find it after many days.

2 Give a portion to seven, and also to eight; for thou knowest not what evil shall be upon the earth.

3 If the clouds be full of rain, they empty *themselves* upon the earth: and if the tree fall toward the south, or toward the north, in the place where the tree falleth, there it shall be.

4 He that observeth the wind shall not sow; and he that regardeth the clouds shall not reap.

5 As thou knowest not what *is* the way of the spirit, *nor* how the bones *do grow* in the womb of her that is with child: even so thou knowest not the works of God who maketh all.

6 In the morning sow thy seed, and in the evening withhold not thine hand: for thou knowest not whether shall prosper, either this or that, or whether they both *shall be* alike good.

7 Truly the light *is* sweet, and a pleasant *thing it is* for the eyes to behold the sun:

8 But if a man live many years, *and* rejoice in them all; yet let him remember the days of darkness; for they shall be many. All that cometh *is* vanity.

9 Rejoice, O young man, in thy youth; and let thy heart cheer thee in the days of thy youth, and walk in the ways of thine heart, and in the sight of thine eyes: but know thou, that for all these *things* God will bring thee into judgment.

10 Therefore remove sorrow from thy heart, and put away evil from thy flesh: for childhood and youth *are* vanity.

12 Remember now thy Creator in the days of thy youth, while the evil days come not, nor the years draw nigh, when thou shalt say, I have no pleasure in them;

2 While the sun, or the light, or the moon, or the stars, be not darkened, nor the clouds return after the rain:

3 In the day when the keepers of the house shall tremble, and the strong men shall bow themselves, and the grinders cease because they are few, and those that look out of the windows be darkened,

4 And the doors shall be shut in the streets, when the sound of the grinding is low, and he shall rise up at the voice of the bird, and all the daughters of musick shall be brought low;

5 Also *when* they shall be afraid of *that which is* high, and fears *shall be* in the way, and the almond tree shall flourish, and the grasshopper shall be a burden, and desire shall fail: because man goeth to his long home, and the mourners go about the streets:

6 Or ever the silver cord be loosed, or the golden bowl be broken, or the pitcher be broken at the fountain, or the wheel broken at the cistern.

7 Then shall the dust return to the earth as it was: and the spirit shall return unto God who gave it.

8 Vanity of vanities, saith the preacher; all *is* vanity.

9 And moreover, because the preacher was wise, he still taught the people knowledge; yea, he gave good heed, and sought out, *and* set in order many proverbs.

10 The preacher sought to find out acceptable words: and *that which was* written *was* upright, *even* words of truth.

11 The words of the wise *are* as goads, and as nails fastened *by* the masters of assemblies, *which* are given from one shepherd.

12 And further, by these, my son, be admonished: of making many books *there is* no end; and much study *is* a weariness of the flesh.

13 Let us hear the conclusion of the whole matter: Fear God, and keep his commandments: for this *is* the whole *duty* of man.

14 For God shall bring every work into judgment, with every secret thing, whether *it be* good, or whether *it be* evil.

THE SONG OF SOLOMON

1 The song of songs, which *is* Solomon's.

2 Let him kiss me with the kisses of his mouth: for thy love *is* better than wine.

3 Because of the savour of thy good ointments thy name *is as* ointment poured forth, therefore do the virgins love thee.

4 Draw me, we will run after thee: the king hath brought me into his chambers: we will be glad and rejoice in thee, we will remember thy love more than wine: the upright love thee.

5 I *am* black, but comely, O ye daughters of Jerusalem, as the tents of Kedar, as the curtains of Solomon.

6 Look not upon me, because I *am* black, because the sun hath looked upon me: my mother's children were angry with me; they made me the keeper of the vineyards; *but* mine own vineyard have I not kept.

7 Tell me, O thou whom my soul loveth, where thou feedest, where thou makest *thy flock* to rest at noon: for why should I be as one that turneth aside by the flocks of thy companions?

8 If thou know not, O thou fairest among women, go thy way forth by the footsteps of the flock, and feed thy kids beside the shepherds' tents.

9 I have compared thee, O my love, to a company of horses in Pharaoh's chariots.

10 Thy cheeks are comely with rows *of jewels*, thy neck with chains *of gold*.

11 We will make thee borders of gold with studs of silver.

12 While the king *sitteth* at his table, my spikenard sendeth forth the smell thereof.

13 A bundle of myrrh *is* my wellbeloved unto me; he shall lie all night betwixt my breasts.

14 My beloved *is* unto me *as* a cluster of camphire in the vineyards of En-gedi.

15 Behold, thou *art* fair, my love; behold, thou *art* fair; thou *hast* doves' eyes.

16 Behold, thou *art* fair, my beloved, yea, pleasant: also our bed *is* green.

17 The beams of our house *are* cedar, *and* our rafters of fir.

2 I *am* the rose of Sharon, *and* the lily of the valleys.

2 As the lily among thorns, so *is* my love among the daughters.

3 As the apple tree among the trees of the wood, so *is* my beloved among the sons. I sat down under his shadow with great delight, and his fruit *was* sweet to my taste.

4 He brought me to the banqueting house, and his banner over me *was* love.

5 Stay me with flagons, comfort me with apples: for I *am* sick of love.

6 His left hand *is* under my head, and his right hand doth embrace me.

7 I charge you, O ye daughters of Jerusalem, by the roes, and by the hinds of the field, that ye stir not up, nor awake *my* love, till he please.

8 The voice of my beloved! behold, he cometh leaping upon the mountains, skipping upon the hills.

9 My beloved is like a roe or a young hart: behold, he standeth behind our wall, he looketh forth at the windows, shewing himself through the lattice.

10 My beloved spake, and said unto me, Rise up, my love, my fair one, and come away.

11 For, lo, the winter is past, the rain is over *and* gone;

12 The flowers appear on the earth; the time of the singing *of birds* is come, and the voice of the turtle is heard in our land;

13 The fig tree putteth forth her green figs, and the vines *with* the tender grape give a *good* smell. Arise, my love, my fair one, and come away.

14 O my dove, *that art* in the clefts of the rock, in the secret *places* of the stairs, let me see thy countenance, let me hear thy voice; for sweet *is* thy voice, and thy countenance *is* comely.

15 Take us the foxes, the little foxes, that spoil the vines: for our vines *have* tender grapes.

16 My beloved *is* mine, and I *am* his: he feedeth among the lilies.

17 Until the day break, and the shadows flee away, turn, my beloved, and be thou like a roe or a young hart upon the mountains of Bether.

3 By night on my bed I sought him whom my soul loveth: I sought him, but I found him not.

2 I will rise now, and go about the city
in the streets, and in the broad ways I
will seek him whom my soul loveth: I
sought him, but I found him not.
3 The watchmen that go about the
city found me: *to whom I said*, Saw ye
him whom my soul loveth?
4 *It was* but a little that I passed from
them, but I found him whom my soul
loveth: I held him, and would not let
him go, until I had brought him into my
mother's house, and into the chamber
of her that conceived me.
5 I charge you, O ye daughters of
Jerusalem, by the roes, and by the
hinds of the field, that ye stir not up,
nor awake *my* love, till he please.
6 Who *is* this that cometh out of the
wilderness like pillars of smoke, perfumed with myrrh and frankincense,
with all powders of the merchant?
7 Behold his bed, which *is* Solomon's;
threescore valiant men *are* about it, of
the valiant of Israel.
8 They all hold swords, *being* expert
in war: every man *hath* his sword upon
his thigh because of fear in the night.
9 King Solomon made himself a chariot of the wood of Lebanon.
10 He made the pillars thereof *of* silver, the bottom thereof *of* gold, the
covering of it *of* purple, the midst
thereof being paved *with* love, for the
daughters of Jerusalem.
11 Go forth, O ye daughters of Zion,
and behold king Solomon with the
crown wherewith his mother crowned
him in the day of his espousals, and in
the day of the gladness of his heart.

4 Behold, thou *art* fair, my love;
behold, thou *art* fair; thou *hast*
doves' eyes within thy locks: thy hair *is*
as a flock of goats, that appear from
mount Gilead.
2 Thy teeth *are* like a flock *of sheep*
that are even shorn, which came up
from the washing; whereof every one
bear twins, and none *is* barren among
them.
3 Thy lips *are* like a thread of scarlet,
and thy speech *is* comely: thy temples
are like a piece of a pomegranate
within thy locks.
4 Thy neck *is* like the tower of David
builded for an armoury, whereon there
hang a thousand bucklers, all shields of
mighty men.
5 Thy two breasts *are* like two young
roes that are twins, which feed among
the lilies.
6 Until the day break, and the shadows flee away, I will get me to the
mountain of myrrh, and to the hill of
frankincense.
7 Thou *art* all fair, my love; *there is* no
spot in thee.
8 Come with me from Lebanon, *my*
spouse, with me from Lebanon: look
from the top of Amana, from the top of
Shenir and Hermon, from the lions'
dens, from the mountains of the leopards.
9 Thou hast ravished my heart, my
sister, *my* spouse; thou hast ravished
my heart with one of thine eyes, with
one chain of thy neck.
10 How fair is thy love, my sister, *my*
spouse! how much better is thy love
than wine! and the smell of thine ointments than all spices!
11 Thy lips, O *my* spouse, drop *as* the
honeycomb: honey and milk *are* under
thy tongue; and the smell of thy garments *is* like the smell of Lebanon.
12 A garden inclosed *is* my sister, *my*
spouse; a spring shut up, a fountain
sealed.

13 Thy plants *are* an orchard of pomegranates, with pleasant fruits; camphire, with spikenard,

14 Spikenard and saffron; calamus and cinnamon, with all trees of frankincense; myrrh and aloes, with all the chief spices:

15 A fountain of gardens, a well of living waters, and streams from Lebanon.

16 Awake, O north wind; and come, thou south; blow upon my garden, *that* the spices thereof may flow out. Let my beloved come into his garden, and eat his pleasant fruits.

5 I am come into my garden, my sister, *my* spouse: I have gathered my myrrh with my spice; I have eaten my honeycomb with my honey; I have drunk my wine with my milk: eat, O friends; drink, yea, drink abundantly, O beloved.

2 I sleep, but my heart waketh: *it is* the voice of my beloved that knocketh, *saying*, Open to me, my sister, my love, my dove, my undefiled: for my head is filled with dew, *and* my locks with the drops of the night.

3 I have put off my coat; how shall I put it on? I have washed my feet; how shall I defile them?

4 My beloved put in his hand by the hole *of the door*, and my bowels were moved for him.

5 I rose up to open to my beloved; and my hands dropped *with* myrrh, and my fingers *with* sweet smelling myrrh, upon the handles of the lock.

6 I opened to my beloved; but my beloved had withdrawn himself, *and* was gone: my soul failed when he spake: I sought him, but I could not find him; I called him, but he gave me no answer.

7 The watchmen that went about the city found me, they smote me, they wounded me; the keepers of the walls took away my veil from me.

8 I charge you, O daughters of Jerusalem, if ye find my beloved, that ye tell him, that I *am* sick of love.

9 What *is* thy beloved more than *another* beloved, O thou fairest among women? what *is* thy beloved more than *another* beloved, that thou dost so charge us?

10 My beloved *is* white and ruddy, the chiefest among ten thousand.

11 His head *is as* the most fine gold, his locks *are* bushy, *and* black as a raven.

12 His eyes *are* as *the eyes* of doves by the rivers of waters, washed with milk, *and* fitly set.

13 His cheeks *are* as a bed of spices, *as* sweet flowers: his lips *like* lilies, dropping sweet smelling myrrh.

14 His hands *are as* gold rings set with the beryl: his belly *is as* bright ivory overlaid *with* sapphires.

15 His legs *are as* pillars of marble, set upon sockets of fine gold: his countenance *is* as Lebanon, excellent as the cedars.

16 His mouth *is* most sweet: yea, he *is* altogether lovely. This *is* my beloved, and this *is* my friend, O daughters of Jerusalem.

6 Whither is thy beloved gone, O thou fairest among women? whither is thy beloved turned aside? that we may seek him with thee.

2 My beloved is gone down into his garden, to the beds of spices, to feed in the gardens, and to gather lilies.

3 I *am* my beloved's, and my beloved *is* mine: he feedeth among the lilies.

4 Thou *art* beautiful, O my love, as Tirzah, comely as Jerusalem, terrible as *an army* with banners.

5 Turn away thine eyes from me, for they have overcome me: thy hair *is* as a flock of goats that appear from Gilead.

6 Thy teeth *are* as a flock of sheep which go up from the washing, whereof every one beareth twins, and *there is* not one barren among them.

7 As a piece of a pomegranate *are* thy temples within thy locks.

8 There are threescore queens, and fourscore concubines, and virgins without number.

9 My dove, my undefiled is *but* one; she *is* the *only* one of her mother, she *is* the choice *one* of her that bare her. The daughters saw her, and blessed her; *yea*, the queens and the concubines, and they praised her.

10 Who *is* she *that* looketh forth as the morning, fair as the moon, clear as the sun, *and* terrible as *an army* with banners?

11 I went down into the garden of nuts to see the fruits of the valley, *and* to see whether the vine flourished, *and* the pomegranates budded.

12 Or ever I was aware, my soul made me *like* the chariots of Amminadib.

13 Return, return, O Shulamite; return, return, that we may look upon thee. What will ye see in the Shulamite? As it were the company of two armies.

7 How beautiful are thy feet with shoes, O prince's daughter! the joints of thy thighs *are* like jewels, the work of the hands of a cunning workman.

2 Thy navel *is like* a round goblet, *which* wanteth not liquor: thy belly *is like* an heap of wheat set about with lilies.

3 Thy two breasts *are* like two young roes *that are* twins.

4 Thy neck *is* as a tower of ivory; thine eyes *like* the fishpools in Heshbon, by the gate of Bath-rabbim: thy nose *is* as the tower of Lebanon which looketh toward Damascus.

5 Thine head upon thee *is* like Carmel, and the hair of thine head like purple; the king *is* held in the galleries.

6 How fair and how pleasant art thou, O love, for delights!

7 This thy stature is like to a palm tree, and thy breasts to clusters *of grapes*.

8 I said, I will go up to the palm tree, I will take hold of the boughs thereof: now also thy breasts shall be as clusters of the vine, and the smell of thy nose like apples;

9 And the roof of thy mouth like the best wine for my beloved, that goeth *down* sweetly, causing the lips of those that are asleep to speak.

10 I *am* my beloved's, and his desire *is* toward me.

11 Come, my beloved, let us go forth into the field; let us lodge in the villages.

12 Let us get up early to the vineyards; let us see if the vine flourish, *whether* the tender grape appear, *and* the pomegranates bud forth: there will I give thee my loves.

13 The mandrakes give a smell, and at our gates *are* all manner of pleasant *fruits*, new and old, *which* I have laid up for thee, O my beloved.

8 O that thou *wert* as my brother, that
sucked the breasts of my mother!
when I should find thee without, I
would kiss thee; yea, I should not be
despised.
2 I would lead thee, *and* bring thee
into my mother's house, *who* would
instruct me: I would cause thee to drink
of spiced wine of the juice of my pomegranate.
3 His left hand *should be* under my
head, and his right hand should
embrace me.
4 I charge you, O daughters of
Jerusalem, that ye stir not up, nor
awake *my* love, until he please.
5 Who *is* this that cometh up from the
wilderness, leaning upon her beloved?
I raised thee up under the apple tree:
there thy mother brought thee forth:
there she brought thee forth *that* bare
thee.
6 Set me as a seal upon thine heart, as
a seal upon thine arm: for love *is* strong
as death; jealousy *is* cruel as the grave:
the coals thereof *are* coals of fire, *which
hath a* most vehement flame.
7 Many waters cannot quench love,
neither can the floods drown it: if *a*
man would give all the substance of his
house for love, it would utterly be contemned.
8 We have a little sister, and she hath
no breasts: what shall we do for our
sister in the day when she shall be spoken for?
9 If she *be* a wall, we will build upon
her a palace of silver: and if she *be* a
door, we will inclose her with boards of
cedar.
10 I *am* a wall, and my breasts like
towers: then was I in his eyes as one
that found favour.
11 Solomon had a vineyard at Baal-
hamon; he let out the vineyard unto
keepers; every one for the fruit thereof
was to bring a thousand *pieces* of silver.
12 My vineyard, which *is* mine, *is*
before me: thou, O Solomon, *must have*
a thousand, and those that keep the
fruit thereof two hundred.
13 Thou that dwellest in the gardens,
the companions hearken to thy voice:
cause me to hear *it*.
14 Make haste, my beloved, and be
thou like to a roe or to a young hart
upon the mountains of spices.

THE BOOK OF THE PROPHET
ISAIAH

1 The vision of Isaiah the son of Amoz, which he saw concerning Judah and Jerusalem in the days of Uzziah, Jotham, Ahaz, *and* Hezekiah, kings of Judah.

2 Hear, O heavens, and give ear, O earth: for the LORD hath spoken, I have nourished and brought up children, and they have rebelled against me.

3 The ox knoweth his owner, and the ass his master's crib: *but* Israel doth not know, my people doth not consider.

4 Ah sinful nation, a people laden with iniquity, a seed of evildoers, children that are corrupters: they have forsaken the LORD, they have provoked the Holy One of Israel unto anger, they are gone away backward.

5 Why should ye be stricken any more? ye will revolt more and more: the whole head is sick, and the whole heart faint.

6 From the sole of the foot even unto the head *there is* no soundness in it; *but* wounds, and bruises, and putrifying sores: they have not been closed, neither bound up, neither mollified with ointment.

7 Your country *is* desolate, your cities *are* burned with fire: your land, strangers devour it in your presence, and *it is* desolate, as overthrown by strangers.

8 And the daughter of Zion is left as a cottage in a vineyard, as a lodge in a garden of cucumbers, as a besieged city.

9 Except the LORD of hosts had left unto us a very small remnant, we should have been as Sodom, *and* we should have been like unto Gomorrah.

10 Hear the word of the LORD, ye rulers of Sodom; give ear unto the law of our God, ye people of Gomorrah.

11 To what purpose *is* the multitude of your sacrifices unto me? saith the LORD: I am full of the burnt offerings of rams, and the fat of fed beasts; and I delight not in the blood of bullocks, or of lambs, or of he goats.

12 When ye come to appear before me, who hath required this at your hand, to tread my courts?

13 Bring no more vain oblations; incense is an abomination unto me; the new moons and sabbaths, the calling of assemblies, I cannot away with; *it is* iniquity, even the solemn meeting.

14 Your new moons and your appointed feasts my soul hateth: they are a trouble unto me; I am weary to bear *them*.

15 And when ye spread forth your hands, I will hide mine eyes from you: yea, when ye make many prayers, I will not hear: your hands are full of blood.

16 Wash you, make you clean; put away the evil of your doings from before mine eyes; cease to do evil;

17 Learn to do well; seek judgment, relieve the oppressed, judge the fatherless, plead for the widow.

18 Come now, and let us reason together, saith the LORD: though your sins be as scarlet, they shall be as white as snow; though they be red like crimson, they shall be as wool.

19 If ye be willing and obedient, ye shall eat the good of the land:

20 But if ye refuse and rebel, ye shall be devoured with the sword: for the mouth of the LORD hath spoken *it*.

21 How is the faithful city become an harlot! it was full of judgment; righteousness lodged in it; but now murderers.

22 Thy silver is become dross, thy wine mixed with water:

23 Thy princes *are* rebellious, and companions of thieves: every one loveth gifts, and followeth after rewards: they judge not the fatherless, neither doth the cause of the widow come unto them.

24 Therefore saith the Lord, the LORD of hosts, the mighty One of Israel, Ah, I will ease me of mine adversaries, and avenge me of mine enemies:

25 And I will turn my hand upon thee, and purely purge away thy dross, and take away all thy tin:

26 And I will restore thy judges as at the first, and thy counsellors as at the beginning: afterward thou shalt be called, The city of righteousness, the faithful city.

27 Zion shall be redeemed with judgment, and her converts with righteousness.

28 And the destruction of the transgressors and of the sinners *shall be* together, and they that forsake the LORD shall be consumed.

29 For they shall be ashamed of the oaks which ye have desired, and ye shall be confounded for the gardens that ye have chosen.

30 For ye shall be as an oak whose leaf fadeth, and as a garden that hath no water.

31 And the strong shall be as tow, and the maker of it as a spark, and they shall both burn together, and none shall quench *them*.

2 The word that Isaiah the son of Amoz saw concerning Judah and Jerusalem.

2 And it shall come to pass in the last days, *that* the mountain of the LORD's house shall be established in the top of the mountains, and shall be exalted above the hills; and all nations shall flow unto it.

3 And many people shall go and say, Come ye, and let us go up to the mountain of the LORD, to the house of the God of Jacob; and he will teach us of his ways, and we will walk in his paths: for out of Zion shall go forth the law, and the word of the LORD from Jerusalem.

4 And he shall judge among the nations, and shall rebuke many people: and they shall beat their swords into plowshares, and their spears into pruninghooks: nation shall not lift up sword against nation, neither shall they learn war any more.

5 O house of Jacob, come ye, and let us walk in the light of the LORD.

6 Therefore thou hast forsaken thy people the house of Jacob, because they be replenished from the east, and *are* soothsayers like the Philistines, and they please themselves in the children of strangers.

7 Their land also is full of silver and gold, neither *is there any* end of their treasures; their land is also full of horses, neither *is there any* end of their chariots:

8 Their land also is full of idols; they
worship the work of their own hands,
that which their own fingers have
made:
9 And the mean man boweth down,
and the great man humbleth himself:
therefore forgive them not.
10 Enter into the rock, and hide thee
in the dust, for fear of the LORD, and for
the glory of his majesty.
11 The lofty looks of man shall be
humbled, and the haughtiness of men
shall be bowed down, and the LORD
alone shall be exalted in that day.
12 For the day of the LORD of hosts
shall be upon every *one that is* proud
and lofty, and upon every *one that is*
lifted up; and he shall be brought low:
13 And upon all the cedars of
Lebanon, *that are* high and lifted up,
and upon all the oaks of Bashan,
14 And upon all the high mountains,
and upon all the hills *that are* lifted up,
15 And upon every high tower, and
upon every fenced wall,
16 And upon all the ships of Tarshish,
and upon all pleasant pictures.
17 And the loftiness of man shall be
bowed down, and the haughtiness of
men shall be made low: and the LORD
alone shall be exalted in that day.
18 And the idols he shall utterly abol-
ish.
19 And they shall go into the holes of
the rocks, and into the caves of the
earth, for fear of the LORD, and for the
glory of his majesty, when he ariseth to
shake terribly the earth.
20 In that day a man shall cast his
idols of silver, and his idols of gold,
which they made *each one* for himself
to worship, to the moles and to the bats;
21 To go into the clefts of the rocks,
and into the tops of the ragged rocks,
for fear of the LORD, and for the glory of
his majesty, when he ariseth to shake
terribly the earth.
22 Cease ye from man, whose breath
is in his nostrils: for wherein is he to be
accounted of?

3 For, behold, the Lord, the LORD of
hosts, doth take away from
Jerusalem and from Judah the stay and
the staff, the whole stay of bread, and
the whole stay of water,
2 The mighty man, and the man of
war, the judge, and the prophet, and
the prudent, and the ancient,
3 The captain of fifty, and the honourable man, and the counsellor, and the
cunning artificer, and the eloquent orator.
4 And I will give children *to be* their
princes, and babes shall rule over them.
5 And the people shall be oppressed,
every one by another, and every one by
his neighbour: the child shall behave
himself proudly against the ancient,
and the base against the honourable.
6 When a man shall take hold of his
brother of the house of his father, *saying*, Thou hast clothing, be thou our
ruler, and *let* this ruin *be* under thy
hand:
7 In that day shall he swear, saying, I
will not be an healer; for in my house *is*
neither bread nor clothing: make me
not a ruler of the people.
8 For Jerusalem is ruined, and Judah
is fallen: because their tongue and
their doings *are* against the LORD, to
provoke the eyes of his glory.
9 The shew of their countenance doth
witness against them; and they declare
their sin as Sodom, they hide *it* not.
Woe unto their soul! for they have
rewarded evil unto themselves.

10 Say ye to the righteous, that *it shall be* well *with him*: for they shall eat the fruit of their doings.

11 Woe unto the wicked! *it shall be* ill *with him*: for the reward of his hands shall be given him.

12 *As for* my people, children *are* their oppressors, and women rule over them. O my people, they which lead thee cause *thee* to err, and destroy the way of thy paths.

13 The LORD standeth up to plead, and standeth to judge the people.

14 The LORD will enter into judgment with the ancients of his people, and the princes thereof: for ye have eaten up the vineyard; the spoil of the poor *is* in your houses.

15 What mean ye *that* ye beat my people to pieces, and grind the faces of the poor? saith the Lord GOD of hosts.

16 Moreover the LORD saith, Because the daughters of Zion are haughty, and walk with stretched forth necks and wanton eyes, walking and mincing *as* they go, and making a tinkling with their feet:

17 Therefore the Lord will smite with a scab the crown of the head of the daughters of Zion, and the LORD will discover their secret parts.

18 In that day the Lord will take away the bravery of *their* tinkling ornaments *about their feet*, and *their* cauls, and *their* round tires like the moon,

19 The chains, and the bracelets, and the mufflers,

20 The bonnets, and the ornaments of the legs, and the headbands, and the tablets, and the earrings,

21 The rings, and nose jewels,

22 The changeable suits of apparel, and the mantles, and the wimples, and the crisping pins,

23 The glasses, and the fine linen, and the hoods, and the vails.

24 And it shall come to pass, *that* instead of sweet smell there shall be stink; and instead of a girdle a rent; and instead of well set hair baldness; and instead of a stomacher a girding of sackcloth; *and* burning instead of beauty.

25 Thy men shall fall by the sword, and thy mighty in the war.

26 And her gates shall lament and mourn; and she *being* desolate shall sit upon the ground.

4 And in that day seven women shall take hold of one man, saying, We will eat our own bread, and wear our own apparel: only let us be called by thy name, to take away our reproach.

2 In that day shall the branch of the LORD be beautiful and glorious, and the fruit of the earth *shall be* excellent and comely for them that are escaped of Israel.

3 And it shall come to pass, *that he that is* left in Zion, and *he that* remaineth in Jerusalem, shall be called holy, *even* every one that is written among the living in Jerusalem:

4 When the Lord shall have washed away the filth of the daughters of Zion, and shall have purged the blood of Jerusalem from the midst thereof by the spirit of judgment, and by the spirit of burning.

5 And the LORD will create upon every dwelling place of mount Zion, and upon her assemblies, a cloud and smoke by day, and the shining of a flaming fire by night: for upon all the glory *shall be* a defence.

6 And there shall be a tabernacle for a shadow in the daytime from the heat, and for a place of refuge, and for a covert from storm and from rain.

5 Now will I sing to my wellbeloved a song of my beloved touching his vineyard. My wellbeloved hath a vineyard in a very fruitful hill:

2 And he fenced it, and gathered out the stones thereof, and planted it with the choicest vine, and built a tower in the midst of it, and also made a winepress therein: and he looked that it should bring forth grapes, and it brought forth wild grapes.

3 And now, O inhabitants of Jerusalem, and men of Judah, judge, I pray you, betwixt me and my vineyard.

4 What could have been done more to my vineyard, that I have not done in it? wherefore, when I looked that it should bring forth grapes, brought it forth wild grapes?

5 And now go to; I will tell you what I will do to my vineyard: I will take away the hedge thereof, and it shall be eaten up; *and* break down the wall thereof, and it shall be trodden down:

6 And I will lay it waste: it shall not be pruned, nor digged; but there shall come up briers and thorns: I will also command the clouds that they rain no rain upon it.

7 For the vineyard of the LORD of hosts *is* the house of Israel, and the men of Judah his pleasant plant: and he looked for judgment, but behold oppression; for righteousness, but behold a cry.

8 Woe unto them that join house to house, *that* lay field to field, till *there be* no place, that they may be placed alone in the midst of the earth!

9 In mine ears *said* the LORD of hosts, Of a truth many houses shall be desolate, *even* great and fair, without inhabitant.

10 Yea, ten acres of vineyard shall yield one bath, and the seed of an homer shall yield an ephah.

11 Woe unto them that rise up early in the morning, *that* they may follow strong drink; that continue until night, *till* wine inflame them!

12 And the harp, and the viol, the tabret, and pipe, and wine, are in their feasts: but they regard not the work of the LORD, neither consider the operation of his hands.

13 Therefore my people are gone into captivity, because *they have* no knowledge: and their honourable men *are* famished, and their multitude dried up with thirst.

14 Therefore hell hath enlarged herself, and opened her mouth without measure: and their glory, and their multitude, and their pomp, and he that rejoiceth, shall descend into it.

15 And the mean man shall be brought down, and the mighty man shall be humbled, and the eyes of the lofty shall be humbled:

16 But the LORD of hosts shall be exalted in judgment, and God that is holy shall be sanctified in righteousness.

17 Then shall the lambs feed after their manner, and the waste places of the fat ones shall strangers eat.

18 Woe unto them that draw iniquity with cords of vanity, and sin as it were with a cart rope:

19 That say, Let him make speed, *and* hasten his work, that we may see *it*: and let the counsel of the Holy One of Israel draw nigh and come, that we may know *it*!

20 Woe unto them that call evil good, and good evil; that put darkness for light, and light for darkness; that put bitter for sweet, and sweet for bitter!

21 Woe unto *them that are* wise in their own eyes, and prudent in their own sight!

22 Woe unto *them that are* mighty to drink wine, and men of strength to mingle strong drink:

23 Which justify the wicked for reward, and take away the righteousness of the righteous from him!

24 Therefore as the fire devoureth the stubble, and the flame consumeth the chaff, *so* their root shall be as rottenness, and their blossom shall go up as dust: because they have cast away the law of the LORD of hosts, and despised the word of the Holy One of Israel.

25 Therefore is the anger of the LORD kindled against his people, and he hath stretched forth his hand against them, and hath smitten them: and the hills did tremble, and their carcases *were* torn in the midst of the streets. For all this his anger is not turned away, but his hand *is* stretched out still.

26 And he will lift up an ensign to the nations from far, and will hiss unto them from the end of the earth: and, behold, they shall come with speed swiftly:

27 None shall be weary nor stumble among them; none shall slumber nor sleep; neither shall the girdle of their loins be loosed, nor the latchet of their shoes be broken:

28 Whose arrows *are* sharp, and all their bows bent, their horses' hoofs shall be counted like flint, and their wheels like a whirlwind:

29 Their roaring *shall be* like a lion, they shall roar like young lions: yea, they shall roar, and lay hold of the prey, and shall carry *it* away safe, and none shall deliver *it*.

30 And in that day they shall roar against them like the roaring of the sea: and if *one* look unto the land, behold darkness *and* sorrow, and the light is darkened in the heavens thereof.

6 In the year that king Uzziah died I saw also the Lord sitting upon a throne, high and lifted up, and his train filled the temple.

2 Above it stood the seraphims: each one had six wings; with twain he covered his face, and with twain he covered his feet, and with twain he did fly.

3 And one cried unto another, and said, Holy, holy, holy, *is* the LORD of hosts: the whole earth *is* full of his glory.

4 And the posts of the door moved at the voice of him that cried, and the house was filled with smoke.

5 Then said I, Woe *is* me! for I am undone; because I *am* a man of unclean lips, and I dwell in the midst of a people of unclean lips: for mine eyes have seen the King, the LORD of hosts.

6 Then flew one of the seraphims unto me, having a live coal in his hand, *which* he had taken with the tongs from off the altar:

7 And he laid *it* upon my mouth, and said, Lo, this hath touched thy lips; and thine iniquity is taken away, and thy sin purged.

8 Also I heard the voice of the Lord, saying, Whom shall I send, and who will go for us? Then said I, Here *am* I; send me.

9 And he said, Go, and tell this people, Hear ye indeed, but understand not; and see ye indeed, but perceive not.

10 Make the heart of this people fat, and make their ears heavy, and shut their eyes; lest they see with their eyes, and hear with their ears, and understand with their heart, and convert, and be healed.

11 Then said I, Lord, how long? And he answered, Until the cities be wasted without inhabitant, and the houses without man, and the land be utterly desolate,

12 And the LORD have removed men far away, and *there be* a great forsaking in the midst of the land.

13 But yet in it *shall be* a tenth, and *it* shall return, and shall be eaten: as a teil tree, and as an oak, whose substance *is* in them, when they cast *their leaves: so* the holy seed *shall be* the substance thereof.

7 And it came to pass in the days of Ahaz the son of Jotham, the son of Uzziah, king of Judah, *that* Rezin the king of Syria, and Pekah the son of Remaliah, king of Israel, went up toward Jerusalem to war against it, but could not prevail against it.

2 And it was told the house of David, saying, Syria is confederate with Ephraim. And his heart was moved, and the heart of his people, as the trees of the wood are moved with the wind.

3 Then said the LORD unto Isaiah, Go forth now to meet Ahaz, thou, and Shear-jashub thy son, at the end of the conduit of the upper pool in the highway of the fuller's field;

4 And say unto him, Take heed, and be quiet; fear not, neither be fainthearted for the two tails of these smoking firebrands, for the fierce anger of Rezin with Syria, and of the son of Remaliah.

5 Because Syria, Ephraim, and the son of Remaliah, have taken evil counsel against thee, saying,

6 Let us go up against Judah, and vex it, and let us make a breach therein for us, and set a king in the midst of it, *even* the son of Tabeal:

7 Thus saith the Lord GOD, It shall not stand, neither shall it come to pass.

8 For the head of Syria *is* Damascus, and the head of Damascus *is* Rezin; and within threescore and five years shall Ephraim be broken, that it be not a people.

9 And the head of Ephraim *is* Samaria, and the head of Samaria *is* Remaliah's son. If ye will not believe, surely ye shall not be established.

10 Moreover the LORD spake again unto Ahaz, saying,

11 Ask thee a sign of the LORD thy God; ask it either in the depth, or in the height above.

12 But Ahaz said, I will not ask, neither will I tempt the LORD.

13 And he said, Hear ye now, O house of David; *Is it* a small thing for you to weary men, but will ye weary my God also?

14 Therefore the Lord himself shall give you a sign; Behold, a virgin shall conceive, and bear a son, and shall call his name Immanuel.

15 Butter and honey shall he eat, that he may know to refuse the evil, and choose the good.

16 For before the child shall know to refuse the evil, and choose the good, the land that thou abhorrest shall be forsaken of both her kings.

17 The LORD shall bring upon thee, and upon thy people, and upon thy father's house, days that have not come, from the day that Ephraim departed from Judah; *even* the king of Assyria.

18 And it shall come to pass in that day, *that* the LORD shall hiss for the fly that *is* in the uttermost part of the rivers of Egypt, and for the bee that *is* in the land of Assyria.

19 And they shall come, and shall rest all of them in the desolate valleys, and in the holes of the rocks, and upon all thorns, and upon all bushes.

20 In the same day shall the Lord shave with a razor that is hired, *namely*, by them beyond the river, by the king of Assyria, the head, and the hair of the feet: and it shall also consume the beard.

21 And it shall come to pass in that day, *that* a man shall nourish a young cow, and two sheep;

22 And it shall come to pass, for the abundance of milk *that* they shall give he shall eat butter: for butter and honey shall every one eat that is left in the land.

23 And it shall come to pass in that day, *that* every place shall be, where there were a thousand vines at a thousand silverlings, it shall *even* be for briers and thorns.

24 With arrows and with bows shall *men* come thither; because all the land shall become briers and thorns.

25 And *on* all hills that shall be digged with the mattock, there shall not come thither the fear of briers and thorns: but it shall be for the sending forth of oxen, and for the treading of lesser cattle.

8 Moreover the LORD said unto me, Take thee a great roll, and write in it with a man's pen concerning Maher-shalal-hashbaz.

2 And I took unto me faithful witnesses to record, Uriah the priest, and Zechariah the son of Jeberechiah.

3 And I went unto the prophetess; and she conceived, and bare a son. Then said the LORD to me, Call his name Maher-shalal-hashbaz.

4 For before the child shall have knowledge to cry, My father, and my mother, the riches of Damascus and the spoil of Samaria shall be taken away before the king of Assyria.

5 The LORD spake also unto me again, saying,

6 Forasmuch as this people refuseth the waters of Shiloah that go softly, and rejoice in Rezin and Remaliah's son;

7 Now therefore, behold, the Lord bringeth up upon them the waters of the river, strong and many, *even* the king of Assyria, and all his glory: and he shall come up over all his channels, and go over all his banks:

8 And he shall pass through Judah; he shall overflow and go over, he shall reach *even* to the neck; and the stretching out of his wings shall fill the breadth of thy land, O Immanuel.

9 Associate yourselves, O ye people, and ye shall be broken in pieces; and give ear, all ye of far countries: gird yourselves, and ye shall be broken in pieces; gird yourselves, and ye shall be broken in pieces.

10 Take counsel together, and it shall come to nought; speak the word, and it shall not stand: for God *is* with us.

11 For the LORD spake thus to me with a strong hand, and instructed me that I should not walk in the way of this people, saying,

12 Say ye not, A confederacy, to all *them to* whom this people shall say, A confederacy; neither fear ye their fear, nor be afraid.

13 Sanctify the LORD of hosts himself; and *let* him *be* your fear, and *let* him *be* your dread.

14 And he shall be for a sanctuary; but for a stone of stumbling and for a rock of offence to both the houses of Israel, for a gin and for a snare to the inhabitants of Jerusalem.

15 And many among them shall stumble, and fall, and be broken, and be snared, and be taken.

16 Bind up the testimony, seal the law among my disciples.

17 And I will wait upon the LORD, that hideth his face from the house of Jacob, and I will look for him.

18 Behold, I and the children whom the LORD hath given me *are* for signs and for wonders in Israel from the LORD of hosts, which dwelleth in mount Zion.

19 And when they shall say unto you, Seek unto them that have familiar spirits, and unto wizards that peep, and that mutter: should not a people seek unto their God? for the living to the dead?

20 To the law and to the testimony: if they speak not according to this word, *it is* because *there is* no light in them.

21 And they shall pass through it, hardly bestead and hungry: and it shall come to pass, that when they shall be hungry, they shall fret themselves, and curse their king and their God, and look upward.

22 And they shall look unto the earth; and behold trouble and darkness, dimness of anguish; and *they shall be* driven to darkness.

9 Nevertheless the dimness *shall* not *be* such as *was* in her vexation, when at the first he lightly afflicted the land of Zebulun and the land of Naphtali, and afterward did more grievously afflict *her by* the way of the sea, beyond Jordan, in Galilee of the nations.

2 The people that walked in darkness have seen a great light: they that dwell in the land of the shadow of death, upon them hath the light shined.

3 Thou hast multiplied the nation, *and* not increased the joy: they joy before thee according to the joy in harvest, *and* as *men* rejoice when they divide the spoil.

4 For thou hast broken the yoke of his burden, and the staff of his shoulder, the rod of his oppressor, as in the day of Midian.

5 For every battle of the warrior *is* with confused noise, and garments rolled in blood; but *this* shall be with burning *and* fuel of fire.

6 For unto us a child is born, unto us a son is given: and the government shall be upon his shoulder: and his name shall be called Wonderful, Counsellor, The mighty God, The everlasting Father, The Prince of Peace.

7 Of the increase of *his* government and peace *there shall be* no end, upon the throne of David, and upon his kingdom, to order it, and to establish it with judgment and with justice from henceforth even for ever. The zeal of the LORD of hosts will perform this.

8 The Lord sent a word into Jacob, and it hath lighted upon Israel.

9 And all the people shall know, *even* Ephraim and the inhabitant of Samaria, that say in the pride and stoutness of heart,

10 The bricks are fallen down, but we will build with hewn stones: the sycomores are cut down, but we will change *them into* cedars.

11 Therefore the LORD shall set up the adversaries of Rezin against him, and join his enemies together;

12 The Syrians before, and the Philistines behind; and they shall devour Israel with open mouth. For all this his anger is not turned away, but his hand *is* stretched out still.

13 For the people turneth not unto him that smiteth them, neither do they seek the LORD of hosts.

14 Therefore the LORD will cut off from Israel head and tail, branch and rush, in one day.

15 The ancient and honourable, he *is* the head; and the prophet that teacheth lies, he *is* the tail.

16 For the leaders of this people cause *them* to err; and *they that are* led of them *are* destroyed.

17 Therefore the Lord shall have no joy in their young men, neither shall have mercy on their fatherless and widows: for every one *is* an hypocrite and an evildoer, and every mouth speaketh folly. For all this his anger is not turned away, but his hand *is* stretched out still.

18 For wickedness burneth as the fire: it shall devour the briers and thorns, and shall kindle in the thickets of the forest, and they shall mount up *like* the lifting up of smoke.

19 Through the wrath of the LORD of hosts is the land darkened, and the people shall be as the fuel of the fire: no man shall spare his brother.

20 And he shall snatch on the right hand, and be hungry; and he shall eat on the left hand, and they shall not be satisfied: they shall eat every man the flesh of his own arm:

21 Manasseh, Ephraim; and Ephraim, Manasseh: *and* they together *shall be* against Judah. For all this his anger is not turned away, but his hand *is* stretched out still.

10 Woe unto them that decree unrighteous decrees, and that write grievousness *which* they have prescribed;

2 To turn aside the needy from judgment, and to take away the right from the poor of my people, that widows may be their prey, and *that* they may rob the fatherless!

3 And what will ye do in the day of visitation, and in the desolation *which* shall come from far? to whom will ye flee for help? and where will ye leave your glory?

4 Without me they shall bow down under the prisoners, and they shall fall under the slain. For all this his anger is not turned away, but his hand *is* stretched out still.

5 O Assyrian, the rod of mine anger, and the staff in their hand is mine indignation.

6 I will send him against an hypocritical nation, and against the people of my wrath will I give him a charge, to take the spoil, and to take the prey, and to tread them down like the mire of the streets.

7 Howbeit he meaneth not so, neither doth his heart think so; but *it is* in his heart to destroy and cut off nations not a few.

8 For he saith, *Are* not my princes altogether kings?

9 *Is* not Calno as Carchemish? *is* not Hamath as Arpad? *is* not Samaria as Damascus?

10 As my hand hath found the kingdoms of the idols, and whose graven images did excel them of Jerusalem and of Samaria;

11 Shall I not, as I have done unto Samaria and her idols, so do to Jerusalem and her idols?

12 Wherefore it shall come to pass, *that* when the Lord hath performed his whole work upon mount Zion and on Jerusalem, I will punish the fruit of the stout heart of the king of Assyria, and the glory of his high looks.

13 For he saith, By the strength of my hand I have done *it*, and by my wisdom; for I am prudent: and I have removed the bounds of the people, and have robbed their treasures, and I have put down the inhabitants like a valiant *man*:

14 And my hand hath found as a nest the riches of the people: and as one gathereth eggs *that are* left, have I gathered all the earth; and there was none that moved the wing, or opened the mouth, or peeped.

15 Shall the axe boast itself against him that heweth therewith? *or* shall the saw magnify itself against him that shaketh it? as if the rod should shake *itself* against them that lift it up, *or* as if the staff should lift up *itself, as if it were* no wood.

16 Therefore shall the Lord, the Lord of hosts, send among his fat ones leanness; and under his glory he shall kindle a burning like the burning of a fire.

17 And the light of Israel shall be for a fire, and his Holy One for a flame: and it shall burn and devour his thorns and his briers in one day;

18 And shall consume the glory of his forest, and of his fruitful field, both soul and body: and they shall be as when a standardbearer fainteth.

19 And the rest of the trees of his forest shall be few, that a child may write them.

20 And it shall come to pass in that day, *that* the remnant of Israel, and such as are escaped of the house of Jacob, shall no more again stay upon him that smote them; but shall stay upon the LORD, the Holy One of Israel, in truth.

21 The remnant shall return, *even* the remnant of Jacob, unto the mighty God.

22 For though thy people Israel be as the sand of the sea, *yet* a remnant of them shall return: the consumption decreed shall overflow with righteousness.

23 For the Lord GOD of hosts shall make a consumption, even determined, in the midst of all the land.

24 Therefore thus saith the Lord GOD of hosts, O my people that dwellest in Zion, be not afraid of the Assyrian: he shall smite thee with a rod, and shall lift up his staff against thee, after the manner of Egypt.

25 For yet a very little while, and the indignation shall cease, and mine anger in their destruction.

26 And the LORD of hosts shall stir up a scourge for him according to the slaughter of Midian at the rock of Oreb: and *as* his rod *was* upon the sea, so shall he lift it up after the manner of Egypt.

27 And it shall come to pass in that day, *that* his burden shall be taken away from off thy shoulder, and his yoke from off thy neck, and the yoke shall be destroyed because of the anointing.

28 He is come to Aiath, he is passed to Migron; at Michmash he hath laid up his carriages:

29 They are gone over the passage: they have taken up their lodging at Geba; Ramah is afraid; Gibeah of Saul is fled.

30 Lift up thy voice, O daughter of Gallim: cause it to be heard unto Laish, O poor Anathoth.

31 Madmenah is removed; the inhabitants of Gebim gather themselves to flee.

32 As yet shall he remain at Nob that day: he shall shake his hand *against* the mount of the daughter of Zion, the hill of Jerusalem.

33 Behold, the Lord, the LORD of hosts, shall lop the bough with terror: and the high ones of stature *shall be* hewn down, and the haughty shall be humbled.

34 And he shall cut down the thickets of the forest with iron, and Lebanon shall fall by a mighty one.

11 And there shall come forth a rod out of the stem of Jesse, and a Branch shall grow out of his roots:

2 And the spirit of the LORD shall rest upon him, the spirit of wisdom and understanding, the spirit of counsel and might, the spirit of knowledge and of the fear of the LORD;

3 And shall make him of quick understanding in the fear of the LORD: and he shall not judge after the sight of his eyes, neither reprove after the hearing of his ears:

4 But with righteousness shall he judge the poor, and reprove with equity for the meek of the earth: and he shall smite the earth with the rod of his mouth, and with the breath of his lips shall he slay the wicked.

5 And righteousness shall be the girdle of his loins, and faithfulness the girdle of his reins.

6 The wolf also shall dwell with the lamb, and the leopard shall lie down with the kid; and the calf and the young lion and the fatling together; and a little child shall lead them.

7 And the cow and the bear shall feed; their young ones shall lie down together: and the lion shall eat straw like the ox.

8 And the sucking child shall play on the hole of the asp, and the weaned child shall put his hand on the cockatrice' den.

9 They shall not hurt nor destroy in all my holy mountain: for the earth shall be full of the knowledge of the LORD, as the waters cover the sea.

10 And in that day there shall be a root of Jesse, which shall stand for an ensign of the people; to it shall the Gentiles seek: and his rest shall be glorious.

11 And it shall come to pass in that day, *that* the Lord shall set his hand again the second time to recover the remnant of his people, which shall be left, from Assyria, and from Egypt, and from Pathros, and from Cush, and from Elam, and from Shinar, and from Hamath, and from the islands of the sea.

12 And he shall set up an ensign for the nations, and shall assemble the outcasts of Israel, and gather together the dispersed of Judah from the four corners of the earth.

13 The envy also of Ephraim shall depart, and the adversaries of Judah shall be cut off: Ephraim shall not envy Judah, and Judah shall not vex Ephraim.

14 But they shall fly upon the shoulders of the Philistines toward the west; they shall spoil them of the east together: they shall lay their hand upon Edom and Moab; and the children of Ammon shall obey them.

15 And the LORD shall utterly destroy the tongue of the Egyptian sea; and with his mighty wind shall he shake his hand over the river, and shall smite it in the seven streams, and make *men* go over dryshod.

16 And there shall be an highway for the remnant of his people, which shall be left, from Assyria; like as it was to Israel in the day that he came up out of the land of Egypt.

12 And in that day thou shalt say, O LORD, I will praise thee: though thou wast angry with me, thine anger is turned away, and thou comfortedst me.

2 Behold, God *is* my salvation; I will trust, and not be afraid: for the LORD JEHOVAH *is* my strength and *my* song; he also is become my salvation.

3 Therefore with joy shall ye draw water out of the wells of salvation.

4 And in that day shall ye say, Praise the LORD, call upon his name, declare his doings among the people, make mention that his name is exalted.

5 Sing unto the LORD; for he hath done excellent things: this *is* known in all the earth.

6 Cry out and shout, thou inhabitant of Zion: for great *is* the Holy One of Israel in the midst of thee.

13 The burden of Babylon, which Isaiah the son of Amoz did see.

2 Lift ye up a banner upon the high mountain, exalt the voice unto them, shake the hand, that they may go into the gates of the nobles.

3 I have commanded my sanctified ones, I have also called my mighty ones for mine anger, *even* them that rejoice in my highness.

4 The noise of a multitude in the mountains, like as of a great people; a tumultuous noise of the kingdoms of nations gathered together: the LORD of hosts mustereth the host of the battle.

5 They come from a far country, from the end of heaven, *even* the LORD, and the weapons of his indignation, to destroy the whole land.

6 Howl ye; for the day of the LORD *is* at hand; it shall come as a destruction from the Almighty.

7 Therefore shall all hands be faint, and every man's heart shall melt:

8 And they shall be afraid: pangs and sorrows shall take hold of them; they shall be in pain as a woman that travaileth: they shall be amazed one at another; their faces *shall be as* flames.

9 Behold, the day of the LORD cometh, cruel both with wrath and fierce anger, to lay the land desolate: and he shall destroy the sinners thereof out of it.

10 For the stars of heaven and the constellations thereof shall not give their light: the sun shall be darkened in his going forth, and the moon shall not cause her light to shine.

11 And I will punish the world for *their* evil, and the wicked for their iniquity; and I will cause the arrogancy of the proud to cease, and will lay low the haughtiness of the terrible.

12 I will make a man more precious than fine gold; even a man than the golden wedge of Ophir.

13 Therefore I will shake the heavens, and the earth shall remove out of her place, in the wrath of the LORD of hosts, and in the day of his fierce anger.

14 And it shall be as the chased roe, and as a sheep that no man taketh up: they shall every man turn to his own people, and flee every one into his own land.

15 Every one that is found shall be thrust through; and every one that is joined *unto them* shall fall by the sword.

16 Their children also shall be dashed to pieces before their eyes; their houses shall be spoiled, and their wives ravished.

17 Behold, I will stir up the Medes against them, which shall not regard silver; and *as for* gold, they shall not delight in it.

18 *Their* bows also shall dash the young men to pieces; and they shall have no pity on the fruit of the womb; their eye shall not spare children.

19 And Babylon, the glory of kingdoms, the beauty of the Chaldees' excellency, shall be as when God overthrew Sodom and Gomorrah.

20 It shall never be inhabited, neither shall it be dwelt in from generation to generation: neither shall the Arabian pitch tent there; neither shall the shepherds make their fold there.

21 But wild beasts of the desert shall lie there; and their houses shall be full of doleful creatures; and owls shall dwell there, and satyrs shall dance there.

22 And the wild beasts of the islands shall cry in their desolate houses, and dragons in *their* pleasant palaces: and her time *is* near to come, and her days shall not be prolonged.

14 For the LORD will have mercy on Jacob, and will yet choose Israel, and set them in their own land: and the strangers shall be joined with them, and they shall cleave to the house of Jacob.

2 And the people shall take them, and bring them to their place: and the house of Israel shall possess them in the land of the LORD for servants and handmaids: and they shall take them captives, whose captives they were; and they shall rule over their oppressors.

3 And it shall come to pass in the day that the LORD shall give thee rest from thy sorrow, and from thy fear, and from the hard bondage wherein thou wast made to serve,

4 That thou shalt take up this proverb against the king of Babylon, and say, How hath the oppressor ceased! the golden city ceased!

5 The LORD hath broken the staff of the wicked, *and* the sceptre of the rulers.

6 He who smote the people in wrath with a continual stroke, he that ruled the nations in anger, is persecuted, *and* none hindereth.

7 The whole earth is at rest, *and* is quiet: they break forth into singing.

8 Yea, the fir trees rejoice at thee, *and* the cedars of Lebanon, *saying*, Since thou art laid down, no feller is come up against us.

9 Hell from beneath is moved for thee to meet *thee* at thy coming: it stirreth up the dead for thee, *even* all the chief ones of the earth; it hath raised up from their thrones all the kings of the nations.

10 All they shall speak and say unto thee, Art thou also become weak as we? art thou become like unto us?

11 Thy pomp is brought down to the grave, *and* the noise of thy viols: the worm is spread under thee, and the worms cover thee.

12 How art thou fallen from heaven, O Lucifer, son of the morning! *how* art thou cut down to the ground, which didst weaken the nations!

13 For thou hast said in thine heart, I will ascend into heaven, I will exalt my throne above the stars of God: I will sit also upon the mount of the congregation, in the sides of the north:

14 I will ascend above the heights of the clouds; I will be like the most High.

15 Yet thou shalt be brought down to hell, to the sides of the pit.

16 They that see thee shall narrowly look upon thee, *and* consider thee, *saying, Is* this the man that made the earth to tremble, that did shake kingdoms;

17 *That* made the world as a wilderness, and destroyed the cities thereof; *that* opened not the house of his prisoners?

18 All the kings of the nations, *even* all of them, lie in glory, every one in his own house.

19 But thou art cast out of thy grave like an abominable branch, *and as* the raiment of those that are slain, thrust through with a sword, that go down to the stones of the pit; as a carcase trodden under feet.

20 Thou shalt not be joined with them in burial, because thou hast destroyed thy land, *and* slain thy people: the seed of evildoers shall never be renowned.

21 Prepare slaughter for his children for the iniquity of their fathers; that they do not rise, nor possess the land, nor fill the face of the world with cities.

22 For I will rise up against them, saith the LORD of hosts, and cut off from Babylon the name, and remnant, and son, and nephew, saith the LORD.

23 I will also make it a possession for the bittern, and pools of water: and I will sweep it with the besom of destruction, saith the LORD of hosts.

24 The LORD of hosts hath sworn, saying, Surely as I have thought, so shall it come to pass; and as I have purposed, *so* shall it stand:

25 That I will break the Assyrian in my land, and upon my mountains tread him under foot: then shall his yoke depart from off them, and his burden depart from off their shoulders.

26 This *is* the purpose that is purposed upon the whole earth: and this *is* the hand that is stretched out upon all the nations.

27 For the LORD of hosts hath purposed, and who shall disannul *it*? and his hand *is* stretched out, and who shall turn it back?

28 In the year that king Ahaz died was this burden.

29 Rejoice not thou, whole Palestina, because the rod of him that smote thee is broken: for out of the serpent's root shall come forth a cockatrice, and his fruit *shall be* a fiery flying serpent.

30 And the firstborn of the poor shall feed, and the needy shall lie down in safety: and I will kill thy root with famine, and he shall slay thy remnant.

31 Howl, O gate; cry, O city; thou, whole Palestina, *art* dissolved: for there shall come from the north a smoke, and none *shall be* alone in his appointed times.

32 What shall *one* then answer the messengers of the nation? That the LORD hath founded Zion, and the poor of his people shall trust in it.

15 The burden of Moab. Because in the night Ar of Moab is laid waste, *and* brought to silence; because in the night Kir of Moab is laid waste, *and* brought to silence;

2 He is gone up to Bajith, and to Dibon, the high places, to weep: Moab shall howl over Nebo, and over Medeba: on all their heads *shall be* baldness, *and* every beard cut off.

3 In their streets they shall gird themselves with sackcloth: on the tops of their houses, and in their streets, every one shall howl, weeping abundantly.

4 And Heshbon shall cry, and Elealeh: their voice shall be heard *even* unto Jahaz: therefore the armed soldiers of Moab shall cry out; his life shall be grievous unto him.

5 My heart shall cry out for Moab; his fugitives *shall flee* unto Zoar, an heifer of three years old: for by the mounting up of Luhith with weeping shall they go it up; for in the way of Horonaim they shall raise up a cry of destruction.

6 For the waters of Nimrim shall be desolate: for the hay is withered away, the grass faileth, there is no green thing.

7 Therefore the abundance they have gotten, and that which they have laid up, shall they carry away to the brook of the willows.

8 For the cry is gone round about the borders of Moab; the howling thereof unto Eglaim, and the howling thereof unto Beer-elim.

9 For the waters of Dimon shall be full of blood: for I will bring more upon Dimon, lions upon him that escapeth of Moab, and upon the remnant of the land.

16 Send ye the lamb to the ruler of the land from Sela to the wilderness, unto the mount of the daughter of Zion.

2 For it shall be, *that*, as a wandering bird cast out of the nest, *so* the daughters of Moab shall be at the fords of Arnon.

3 Take counsel, execute judgment; make thy shadow as the night in the midst of the noonday; hide the outcasts; bewray not him that wandereth.

4 Let mine outcasts dwell with thee, Moab; be thou a covert to them from the face of the spoiler: for the extortioner is at an end, the spoiler ceaseth, the oppressors are consumed out of the land.

5 And in mercy shall the throne be established: and he shall sit upon it in truth in the tabernacle of David, judging, and seeking judgment, and hasting righteousness.

6 We have heard of the pride of Moab; *he is* very proud: *even* of his haughtiness, and his pride, and his wrath: *but* his lies *shall* not *be* so.

7 Therefore shall Moab howl for Moab, every one shall howl: for the foundations of Kir-hareseth shall ye mourn; surely *they are* stricken.

8 For the fields of Heshbon languish, *and* the vine of Sibmah: the lords of the heathen have broken down the principal plants thereof, they are come *even* unto Jazer, they wandered *through* the

wilderness: her branches are stretched out, they are gone over the sea.

9 Therefore I will bewail with the weeping of Jazer the vine of Sibmah: I will water thee with my tears, O Heshbon, and Elealeh: for the shouting for thy summer fruits and for thy harvest is fallen.

10 And gladness is taken away, and joy out of the plentiful field; and in the vineyards there shall be no singing, neither shall there be shouting: the treaders shall tread out no wine in *their* presses; I have made *their vintage* shouting to cease.

11 Wherefore my bowels shall sound like an harp for Moab, and mine inward parts for Kir-haresh.

12 And it shall come to pass, when it is seen that Moab is weary on the high place, that he shall come to his sanctuary to pray; but he shall not prevail.

13 This *is* the word that the LORD hath spoken concerning Moab since that time.

14 But now the LORD hath spoken, saying, Within three years, as the years of an hireling, and the glory of Moab shall be contemned, with all that great multitude; and the remnant *shall be* very small *and* feeble.

17 The burden of Damascus. Behold, Damascus is taken away from *being* a city, and it shall be a ruinous heap.

2 The cities of Aroer *are* forsaken: they shall be for flocks, which shall lie down, and none shall make *them* afraid.

3 The fortress also shall cease from Ephraim, and the kingdom from Damascus, and the remnant of Syria: they shall be as the glory of the children of Israel, saith the LORD of hosts.

4 And in that day it shall come to pass, *that* the glory of Jacob shall be made thin, and the fatness of his flesh shall wax lean.

5 And it shall be as when the harvestman gathereth the corn, and reapeth the ears with his arm; and it shall be as he that gathereth ears in the valley of Rephaim.

6 Yet gleaning grapes shall be left in it, as the shaking of an olive tree, two *or* three berries in the top of the uppermost bough, four *or* five in the outmost fruitful branches thereof, saith the LORD God of Israel.

7 At that day shall a man look to his Maker, and his eyes shall have respect to the Holy One of Israel.

8 And he shall not look to the altars, the work of his hands, neither shall respect *that* which his fingers have made, either the groves, or the images.

9 In that day shall his strong cities be as a forsaken bough, and an uppermost branch, which they left because of the children of Israel: and there shall be desolation.

10 Because thou hast forgotten the God of thy salvation, and hast not been mindful of the rock of thy strength, therefore shalt thou plant pleasant plants, and shalt set it with strange slips:

11 In the day shalt thou make thy plant to grow, and in the morning shalt thou make thy seed to flourish: *but* the harvest *shall be* a heap in the day of grief and of desperate sorrow.

12 Woe to the multitude of many people, *which* make a noise like the noise of the seas; and to the rushing of nations, *that* make a rushing like the rushing of mighty waters!

13 The nations shall rush like the rushing of many waters: but *God* shall rebuke them, and they shall flee far off, and shall be chased as the chaff of the mountains before the wind, and like a rolling thing before the whirlwind.

14 And behold at eveningtide trouble; *and* before the morning he *is* not. This *is* the portion of them that spoil us, and the lot of them that rob us.

18 Woe to the land shadowing with wings, which *is* beyond the rivers of Ethiopia:

2 That sendeth ambassadors by the sea, even in vessels of bulrushes upon the waters, *saying*, Go, ye swift messengers, to a nation scattered and peeled, to a people terrible from their beginning hitherto; a nation meted out and trodden down, whose land the rivers have spoiled!

3 All ye inhabitants of the world, and dwellers on the earth, see ye, when he lifteth up an ensign on the mountains; and when he bloweth a trumpet, hear ye.

4 For so the LORD said unto me, I will take my rest, and I will consider in my dwelling place like a clear heat upon herbs, *and* like a cloud of dew in the heat of harvest.

5 For afore the harvest, when the bud is perfect, and the sour grape is ripening in the flower, he shall both cut off the sprigs with pruning hooks, and take away *and* cut down the branches.

6 They shall be left together unto the fowls of the mountains, and to the beasts of the earth: and the fowls shall summer upon them, and all the beasts of the earth shall winter upon them.

7 In that time shall the present be brought unto the LORD of hosts of a people scattered and peeled, and from a people terrible from their beginning hitherto; a nation meted out and trodden under foot, whose land the rivers have spoiled, to the place of the name of the LORD of hosts, the mount Zion.

19 The burden of Egypt. Behold, the LORD rideth upon a swift cloud, and shall come into Egypt: and the idols of Egypt shall be moved at his presence, and the heart of Egypt shall melt in the midst of it.

2 And I will set the Egyptians against the Egyptians: and they shall fight every one against his brother, and every one against his neighbour; city against city, *and* kingdom against kingdom.

3 And the spirit of Egypt shall fail in the midst thereof; and I will destroy the counsel thereof: and they shall seek to the idols, and to the charmers, and to them that have familiar spirits, and to the wizards.

4 And the Egyptians will I give over into the hand of a cruel lord; and a fierce king shall rule over them, saith the Lord, the LORD of hosts.

5 And the waters shall fail from the sea, and the river shall be wasted and dried up.

6 And they shall turn the rivers far away; *and* the brooks of defence shall be emptied and dried up: the reeds and flags shall wither.

7 The paper reeds by the brooks, by the mouth of the brooks, and every thing sown by the brooks, shall wither, be driven away, and be no *more*.

8 The fishers also shall mourn, and all they that cast angle into the brooks shall lament, and they that spread nets upon the waters shall languish.

9 Moreover they that work in fine flax, and they that weave networks, shall be confounded.

10 And they shall be broken in the purposes thereof, all that make sluices *and* ponds for fish.

11 Surely the princes of Zoan *are* fools, the counsel of the wise counsellors of Pharaoh is become brutish: how say ye unto Pharaoh, I *am* the son of the wise, the son of ancient kings?

12 Where *are* they? where *are* thy wise *men*? and let them tell thee now, and let them know what the LORD of hosts hath purposed upon Egypt.

13 The princes of Zoan are become fools, the princes of Noph are deceived; they have also seduced Egypt, *even they that are* the stay of the tribes thereof.

14 The LORD hath mingled a perverse spirit in the midst thereof: and they have caused Egypt to err in every work thereof, as a drunken *man* staggereth in his vomit.

15 Neither shall there be *any* work for Egypt, which the head or tail, branch or rush, may do.

16 In that day shall Egypt be like unto women: and it shall be afraid and fear because of the shaking of the hand of the LORD of hosts, which he shaketh over it.

17 And the land of Judah shall be a terror unto Egypt, every one that maketh mention thereof shall be afraid in himself, because of the counsel of the LORD of hosts, which he hath determined against it.

18 In that day shall five cities in the land of Egypt speak the language of Canaan, and swear to the LORD of hosts; one shall be called, The city of destruction.

19 In that day shall there be an altar to the LORD in the midst of the land of Egypt, and a pillar at the border thereof to the LORD.

20 And it shall be for a sign and for a witness unto the LORD of hosts in the land of Egypt: for they shall cry unto the LORD because of the oppressors, and he shall send them a saviour, and a great one, and he shall deliver them.

21 And the LORD shall be known to Egypt, and the Egyptians shall know the LORD in that day, and shall do sacrifice and oblation; yea, they shall vow a vow unto the LORD, and perform *it*.

22 And the LORD shall smite Egypt: he shall smite and heal *it*: and they shall return *even* to the LORD, and he shall be intreated of them, and shall heal them.

23 In that day shall there be a highway out of Egypt to Assyria, and the Assyrian shall come into Egypt, and the Egyptian into Assyria, and the Egyptians shall serve with the Assyrians.

24 In that day shall Israel be the third with Egypt and with Assyria, *even* a blessing in the midst of the land:

25 Whom the LORD of hosts shall bless, saying, Blessed *be* Egypt my people, and Assyria the work of my hands, and Israel mine inheritance.

20

In the year that Tartan came unto Ashdod, (when Sargon the king of Assyria sent him,) and fought against Ashdod, and took it;

2 At the same time spake the LORD by Isaiah the son of Amoz, saying, Go and loose the sackcloth from off thy loins, and put off thy shoe from thy foot. And he did so, walking naked and barefoot.

3 And the LORD said, Like as my servant Isaiah hath walked naked and

barefoot three years *for* a sign and wonder upon Egypt and upon Ethiopia;

4 So shall the king of Assyria lead away the Egyptians prisoners, and the Ethiopians captives, young and old, naked and barefoot, even with *their* buttocks uncovered, to the shame of Egypt.

5 And they shall be afraid and ashamed of Ethiopia their expectation, and of Egypt their glory.

6 And the inhabitant of this isle shall say in that day, Behold, such *is* our expectation, whither we flee for help to be delivered from the king of Assyria: and how shall we escape?

21 The burden of the desert of the sea. As whirlwinds in the south pass through; *so* it cometh from the desert, from a terrible land.

2 A grievous vision is declared unto me; the treacherous dealer dealeth treacherously, and the spoiler spoileth. Go up, O Elam: besiege, O Media; all the sighing thereof have I made to cease.

3 Therefore are my loins filled with pain: pangs have taken hold upon me, as the pangs of a woman that travaileth: I was bowed down at the hearing *of it*; I was dismayed at the seeing *of it*.

4 My heart panted, fearfulness affrighted me: the night of my pleasure hath he turned into fear unto me.

5 Prepare the table, watch in the watchtower, eat, drink: arise, ye princes, *and* anoint the shield.

6 For thus hath the Lord said unto me, Go, set a watchman, let him declare what he seeth.

7 And he saw a chariot *with* a couple of horsemen, a chariot of asses, *and* a chariot of camels; and he hearkened diligently with much heed:

8 And he cried, A lion: My lord, I stand continually upon the watchtower in the daytime, and I am set in my ward whole nights:

9 And, behold, here cometh a chariot of men, *with* a couple of horsemen. And he answered and said, Babylon is fallen, is fallen; and all the graven images of her gods he hath broken unto the ground.

10 O my threshing, and the corn of my floor: that which I have heard of the LORD of hosts, the God of Israel, have I declared unto you.

11 The burden of Dumah. He calleth to me out of Seir, Watchman, what of the night? Watchman, what of the night?

12 The watchman said, The morning cometh, and also the night: if ye will enquire, enquire ye: return, come.

13 The burden upon Arabia. In the forest in Arabia shall ye lodge, O ye travelling companies of Dedanim.

14 The inhabitants of the land of Tema brought water to him that was thirsty, they prevented with their bread him that fled.

15 For they fled from the swords, from the drawn sword, and from the bent bow, and from the grievousness of war.

16 For thus hath the Lord said unto me, Within a year, according to the years of an hireling, and all the glory of Kedar shall fail:

17 And the residue of the number of archers, the mighty men of the children of Kedar, shall be diminished: for the LORD God of Israel hath spoken *it*.

22 The burden of the valley of vision. What aileth thee now, that thou art wholly gone up to the housetops?

2 Thou that art full of stirs, a tumultuous city, a joyous city: thy slain *men are* not slain with the sword, nor dead in battle.

3 All thy rulers are fled together, they are bound by the archers: all that are found in thee are bound together, *which* have fled from far.

4 Therefore said I, Look away from me; I will weep bitterly, labour not to comfort me, because of the spoiling of the daughter of my people.

5 For *it is* a day of trouble, and of treading down, and of perplexity by the Lord GOD of hosts in the valley of vision, breaking down the walls, and of crying to the mountains.

6 And Elam bare the quiver with chariots of men *and* horsemen, and Kir uncovered the shield.

7 And it shall come to pass, *that* thy choicest valleys shall be full of chariots, and the horsemen shall set themselves in array at the gate.

8 And he discovered the covering of Judah, and thou didst look in that day to the armour of the house of the forest.

9 Ye have seen also the breaches of the city of David, that they are many: and ye gathered together the waters of the lower pool.

10 And ye have numbered the houses of Jerusalem, and the houses have ye broken down to fortify the wall.

11 Ye made also a ditch between the two walls for the water of the old pool: but ye have not looked unto the maker thereof, neither had respect unto him that fashioned it long ago.

12 And in that day did the Lord GOD of hosts call to weeping, and to mourning, and to baldness, and to girding with sackcloth:

13 And behold joy and gladness, slaying oxen, and killing sheep, eating flesh, and drinking wine: let us eat and drink; for to morrow we shall die.

14 And it was revealed in mine ears by the LORD of hosts, Surely this iniquity shall not be purged from you till ye die, saith the Lord GOD of hosts.

15 Thus saith the Lord GOD of hosts, Go, get thee unto this treasurer, *even* unto Shebna, which *is* over the house, *and say*,

16 What hast thou here? and whom hast thou here, that thou hast hewed thee out a sepulchre here, *as* he that heweth him out a sepulchre on high, *and* that graveth an habitation for himself in a rock?

17 Behold, the LORD will carry thee away with a mighty captivity, and will surely cover thee.

18 He will surely violently turn and toss thee *like* a ball into a large country: there shalt thou die, and there the chariots of thy glory *shall be* the shame of thy lord's house.

19 And I will drive thee from thy station, and from thy state shall he pull thee down.

20 And it shall come to pass in that day, that I will call my servant Eliakim the son of Hilkiah:

21 And I will clothe him with thy robe, and strengthen him with thy girdle, and I will commit thy government into his hand: and he shall be a father to the inhabitants of Jerusalem, and to the house of Judah.

22 And the key of the house of David will I lay upon his shoulder; so he shall open, and none shall shut; and he shall shut, and none shall open.

23 And I will fasten him *as* a nail in a sure place; and he shall be for a glorious throne to his father's house.

24 And they shall hang upon him all the glory of his father's house, the offspring and the issue, all vessels of small quantity, from the vessels of cups, even to all the vessels of flagons.

25 In that day, saith the LORD of hosts, shall the nail that is fastened in the sure place be removed, and be cut down, and fall; and the burden that *was* upon it shall be cut off: for the LORD hath spoken *it*.

23 The burden of Tyre. Howl, ye ships of Tarshish; for it is laid waste, so that there is no house, no entering in: from the land of Chittim it is revealed to them.

2 Be still, ye inhabitants of the isle; thou whom the merchants of Zidon, that pass over the sea, have replenished.

3 And by great waters the seed of Sihor, the harvest of the river, *is* her revenue; and she is a mart of nations.

4 Be thou ashamed, O Zidon: for the sea hath spoken, *even* the strength of the sea, saying, I travail not, nor bring forth children, neither do I nourish up young men, *nor* bring up virgins.

5 As at the report concerning Egypt, *so* shall they be sorely pained at the report of Tyre.

6 Pass ye over to Tarshish; howl, ye inhabitants of the isle.

7 *Is* this your joyous *city*, whose antiquity *is* of ancient days? her own feet shall carry her afar off to sojourn.

8 Who hath taken this counsel against Tyre, the crowning *city*, whose merchants *are* princes, whose traffickers *are* the honourable of the earth?

9 The LORD of hosts hath purposed it, to stain the pride of all glory, *and* to bring into contempt all the honourable of the earth.

10 Pass through thy land as a river, O daughter of Tarshish: *there is* no more strength.

11 He stretched out his hand over the sea, he shook the kingdoms: the LORD hath given a commandment against the merchant *city*, to destroy the strong holds thereof.

12 And he said, Thou shalt no more rejoice, O thou oppressed virgin, daughter of Zidon: arise, pass over to Chittim; there also shalt thou have no rest.

13 Behold the land of the Chaldeans; this people was not, *till* the Assyrian founded it for them that dwell in the wilderness: they set up the towers thereof, they raised up the palaces thereof; *and* he brought it to ruin.

14 Howl, ye ships of Tarshish: for your strength is laid waste.

15 And it shall come to pass in that day, that Tyre shall be forgotten seventy years, according to the days of one king: after the end of seventy years shall Tyre sing as an harlot.

16 Take an harp, go about the city, thou harlot that hast been forgotten; make sweet melody, sing many songs, that thou mayest be remembered.

17 And it shall come to pass after the end of seventy years, that the LORD will visit Tyre, and she shall turn to her hire, and shall commit fornication with all the kingdoms of the world upon the face of the earth.

18 And her merchandise and her hire shall be holiness to the LORD: it shall not be treasured nor laid up; for her merchandise shall be for them that

dwell before the LORD, to eat sufficiently, and for durable clothing.

24 Behold, the LORD maketh the
earth empty, and maketh it
waste, and turneth it upside down, and
scattereth abroad the inhabitants
thereof.
2 And it shall be, as with the people,
so with the priest; as with the servant,
so with his master; as with the maid, so
with her mistress; as with the buyer, so
with the seller; as with the lender, so
with the borrower; as with the taker of
usury, so with the giver of usury to him.
3 The land shall be utterly emptied,
and utterly spoiled: for the LORD hath
spoken this word.
4 The earth mourneth *and* fadeth
away, the world languisheth *and* fadeth
away, the haughty people of the earth
do languish.
5 The earth also is defiled under the
inhabitants thereof; because they have
transgressed the laws, changed the
ordinance, broken the everlasting covenant.
6 Therefore hath the curse devoured
the earth, and they that dwell therein
are desolate: therefore the inhabitants
of the earth are burned, and few men
left.
7 The new wine mourneth, the vine
languisheth, all the merryhearted do
sigh.
8 The mirth of tabrets ceaseth, the
noise of them that rejoice endeth, the
joy of the harp ceaseth.
9 They shall not drink wine with a
song; strong drink shall be bitter to
them that drink it.
10 The city of confusion is broken
down: every house is shut up, that no
man may come in.
11 *There is* a crying for wine in the
streets; all joy is darkened, the mirth of
the land is gone.
12 In the city is left desolation, and
the gate is smitten with destruction.
13 When thus it shall be in the midst
of the land among the people, *there
shall be* as the shaking of an olive tree,
and as the gleaning grapes when the
vintage is done.
14 They shall lift up their voice, they
shall sing for the majesty of the LORD,
they shall cry aloud from the sea.
15 Wherefore glorify ye the LORD in
the fires, *even* the name of the LORD
God of Israel in the isles of the sea.
16 From the uttermost part of the
earth have we heard songs, *even* glory
to the righteous. But I said, My leanness, my leanness, woe unto me! the
treacherous dealers have dealt treacherously; yea, the treacherous dealers
have dealt very treacherously.
17 Fear, and the pit, and the snare, *are*
upon thee, O inhabitant of the earth.
18 And it shall come to pass, *that* he
who fleeth from the noise of the fear
shall fall into the pit; and he that
cometh up out of the midst of the pit
shall be taken in the snare: for the windows from on high are open, and the
foundations of the earth do shake.
19 The earth is utterly broken down,
the earth is clean dissolved, the earth is
moved exceedingly.
20 The earth shall reel to and fro like
a drunkard, and shall be removed like a
cottage; and the transgression thereof
shall be heavy upon it; and it shall fall,
and not rise again.
21 And it shall come to pass in that
day, *that* the LORD shall punish the host
of the high ones *that are* on high, and
the kings of the earth upon the earth.

22 And they shall be gathered together, *as* prisoners are gathered in the pit, and shall be shut up in the prison, and after many days shall they be visited.

23 Then the moon shall be confounded, and the sun ashamed, when the LORD of hosts shall reign in mount Zion, and in Jerusalem, and before his ancients gloriously.

25 O LORD, thou *art* my God; I will exalt thee, I will praise thy name; for thou hast done wonderful *things; thy* counsels of old *are* faithfulness *and* truth.

2 For thou hast made of a city an heap; *of* a defenced city a ruin: a palace of strangers to be no city; it shall never be built.

3 Therefore shall the strong people glorify thee, the city of the terrible nations shall fear thee.

4 For thou hast been a strength to the poor, a strength to the needy in his distress, a refuge from the storm, a shadow from the heat, when the blast of the terrible ones *is* as a storm *against* the wall.

5 Thou shalt bring down the noise of strangers, as the heat in a dry place; *even* the heat with the shadow of a cloud: the branch of the terrible ones shall be brought low.

6 And in this mountain shall the LORD of hosts make unto all people a feast of fat things, a feast of wines on the lees, of fat things full of marrow, of wines on the lees well refined.

7 And he will destroy in this mountain the face of the covering cast over all people, and the vail that is spread over all nations.

8 He will swallow up death in victory; and the Lord GOD will wipe away tears from off all faces; and the rebuke of his people shall he take away from off all the earth: for the LORD hath spoken *it*.

9 And it shall be said in that day, Lo, this *is* our God; we have waited for him, and he will save us: this *is* the LORD; we have waited for him, we will be glad and rejoice in his salvation.

10 For in this mountain shall the hand of the LORD rest, and Moab shall be trodden down under him, even as straw is trodden down for the dunghill.

11 And he shall spread forth his hands in the midst of them, as he that swimmeth spreadeth forth *his hands* to swim: and he shall bring down their pride together with the spoils of their hands.

12 And the fortress of the high fort of thy walls shall he bring down, lay low, *and* bring to the ground, *even* to the dust.

26 In that day shall this song be sung in the land of Judah; We have a strong city; salvation will *God* appoint *for* walls and bulwarks.

2 Open ye the gates, that the righteous nation which keepeth the truth may enter in.

3 Thou wilt keep *him* in perfect peace, *whose* mind *is* stayed *on thee*: because he trusteth in thee.

4 Trust ye in the LORD for ever: for in the LORD JEHOVAH *is* everlasting strength:

5 For he bringeth down them that dwell on high; the lofty city, he layeth it low; he layeth it low, *even* to the ground; he bringeth it *even* to the dust.

6 The foot shall tread it down, *even* the feet of the poor, *and* the steps of the needy.

7 The way of the just *is* uprightness: thou, most upright, dost weigh the path of the just.

8 Yea, in the way of thy judgments, O LORD, have we waited for thee; the desire of *our* soul *is* to thy name, and to the remembrance of thee.

9 With my soul have I desired thee in the night; yea, with my spirit within me will I seek thee early: for when thy judgments *are* in the earth, the inhabitants of the world will learn righteousness.

10 Let favour be shewed to the wicked, *yet* will he not learn righteousness: in the land of uprightness will he deal unjustly, and will not behold the majesty of the LORD.

11 LORD, *when* thy hand is lifted up, they will not see: *but* they shall see, and be ashamed for *their* envy at the people; yea, the fire of thine enemies shall devour them.

12 LORD, thou wilt ordain peace for us: for thou also hast wrought all our works in us.

13 O LORD our God, *other* lords beside thee have had dominion over us: *but* by thee only will we make mention of thy name.

14 *They are* dead, they shall not live; *they are* deceased, they shall not rise: therefore hast thou visited and destroyed them, and made all their memory to perish.

15 Thou hast increased the nation, O LORD, thou hast increased the nation: thou art glorified: thou hadst removed *it* far *unto* all the ends of the earth.

16 LORD, in trouble have they visited thee, they poured out a prayer *when* thy chastening *was* upon them.

17 Like as a woman with child, *that* draweth near the time of her delivery, is in pain, *and* crieth out in her pangs; so have we been in thy sight, O LORD.

18 We have been with child, we have been in pain, we have as it were brought forth wind; we have not wrought any deliverance in the earth; neither have the inhabitants of the world fallen.

19 Thy dead *men* shall live, *together with* my dead body shall they arise. Awake and sing, ye that dwell in dust: for thy dew *is as* the dew of herbs, and the earth shall cast out the dead.

20 Come, my people, enter thou into thy chambers, and shut thy doors about thee: hide thyself as it were for a little moment, until the indignation be overpast.

21 For, behold, the LORD cometh out of his place to punish the inhabitants of the earth for their iniquity: the earth also shall disclose her blood, and shall no more cover her slain.

27 In that day the LORD with his sore and great and strong sword shall punish leviathan the piercing serpent, even leviathan that crooked serpent; and he shall slay the dragon that *is* in the sea.

2 In that day sing ye unto her, A vineyard of red wine.

3 I the LORD do keep it; I will water it every moment: lest *any* hurt it, I will keep it night and day.

4 Fury *is* not in me: who would set the briers *and* thorns against me in battle? I would go through them, I would burn them together.

5 Or let him take hold of my strength, *that* he may make peace with me; *and* he shall make peace with me.

6 He shall cause them that come of Jacob to take root: Israel shall blossom and bud, and fill the face of the world with fruit.

7 Hath he smitten him, as he smote those that smote him? *or* is he slain

according to the slaughter of them that
are slain by him?
8 In measure, when it shooteth forth,
thou wilt debate with it: he stayeth his
rough wind in the day of the east wind.
9 By this therefore shall the iniquity
of Jacob be purged; and this *is* all the
fruit to take away his sin; when he
maketh all the stones of the altar as
chalkstones that are beaten in sunder,
the groves and images shall not stand
up.
10 Yet the defenced city *shall be* desolate,
and the habitation forsaken, and
left like a wilderness: there shall the
calf feed, and there shall he lie down,
and consume the branches thereof.
11 When the boughs thereof are withered,
they shall be broken off: the
women come, *and* set them on fire: for
it *is* a people of no understanding:
therefore he that made them will not
have mercy on them, and he that
formed them will shew them no favour.
12 And it shall come to pass in that
day, *that* the LORD shall beat off from
the channel of the river unto the stream
of Egypt, and ye shall be gathered one
by one, O ye children of Israel.
13 And it shall come to pass in that
day, *that* the great trumpet shall be
blown, and they shall come which were
ready to perish in the land of Assyria,
and the outcasts in the land of Egypt,
and shall worship the LORD in the holy
mount at Jerusalem.

28 Woe to the crown of pride, to the
drunkards of Ephraim, whose
glorious beauty *is* a fading flower,
which *are* on the head of the fat valleys
of them that are overcome with wine!
2 Behold, the Lord hath a mighty and
strong one, *which* as a tempest of hail
and a destroying storm, as a flood of
mighty waters overflowing, shall cast
down to the earth with the hand.
3 The crown of pride, the drunkards
of Ephraim, shall be trodden under
feet:
4 And the glorious beauty, which *is* on
the head of the fat valley, shall be a
fading flower, *and* as the hasty fruit
before the summer; which *when* he
that looketh upon it seeth, while it is
yet in his hand he eateth it up.
5 In that day shall the LORD of hosts
be for a crown of glory, and for a diadem
of beauty, unto the residue of his
people,
6 And for a spirit of judgment to him
that sitteth in judgment, and for
strength to them that turn the battle to
the gate.
7 But they also have erred through
wine, and through strong drink are out
of the way; the priest and the prophet
have erred through strong drink, they
are swallowed up of wine, they are out
of the way through strong drink; they
err in vision, they stumble *in* judgment.
8 For all tables are full of vomit *and*
filthiness, *so that there is* no place
clean.
9 Whom shall he teach knowledge?
and whom shall he make to understand
doctrine? *them that are* weaned from
the milk, *and* drawn from the breasts.
10 For precept *must be* upon precept,
precept upon precept; line upon line,
line upon line; here a little, *and* there a
little:
11 For with stammering lips and
another tongue will he speak to this
people.
12 To whom he said, This *is* the rest
wherewith ye may cause the weary to
rest; and this *is* the refreshing: yet they
would not hear.

13 But the word of the LORD was unto them precept upon precept, precept upon precept; line upon line, line upon line; here a little, *and* there a little; that they might go, and fall backward, and be broken, and snared, and taken.

14 Wherefore hear the word of the LORD, ye scornful men, that rule this people which *is* in Jerusalem.

15 Because ye have said, We have made a covenant with death, and with hell are we at agreement; when the overflowing scourge shall pass through, it shall not come unto us: for we have made lies our refuge, and under falsehood have we hid ourselves:

16 Therefore thus saith the Lord GOD, Behold, I lay in Zion for a foundation a stone, a tried stone, a precious corner *stone*, a sure foundation: he that believeth shall not make haste.

17 Judgment also will I lay to the line, and righteousness to the plummet: and the hail shall sweep away the refuge of lies, and the waters shall overflow the hiding place.

18 And your covenant with death shall be disannulled, and your agreement with hell shall not stand; when the overflowing scourge shall pass through, then ye shall be trodden down by it.

19 From the time that it goeth forth it shall take you: for morning by morning shall it pass over, by day and by night: and it shall be a vexation only *to* understand the report.

20 For the bed is shorter than that *a man* can stretch himself *on it*: and the covering narrower than that he can wrap himself *in it*.

21 For the LORD shall rise up as *in* mount Perazim, he shall be wroth as *in* the valley of Gibeon, that he may do his work, his strange work; and bring to pass his act, his strange act.

22 Now therefore be ye not mockers, lest your bands be made strong: for I have heard from the Lord GOD of hosts a consumption, even determined upon the whole earth.

23 Give ye ear, and hear my voice; hearken, and hear my speech.

24 Doth the plowman plow all day to sow? doth he open and break the clods of his ground?

25 When he hath made plain the face thereof, doth he not cast abroad the fitches, and scatter the cummin, and cast in the principal wheat and the appointed barley and the rie in their place?

26 For his God doth instruct him to discretion, *and* doth teach him.

27 For the fitches are not threshed with a threshing instrument, neither is a cart wheel turned about upon the cummin; but the fitches are beaten out with a staff, and the cummin with a rod.

28 Bread *corn* is bruised; because he will not ever be threshing it, nor break *it with* the wheel of his cart, nor bruise it *with* his horsemen.

29 This also cometh forth from the LORD of hosts, *which* is wonderful in counsel, *and* excellent in working.

29 Woe to Ariel, to Ariel, the city *where* David dwelt! add ye year to year; let them kill sacrifices.

2 Yet I will distress Ariel, and there shall be heaviness and sorrow: and it shall be unto me as Ariel.

3 And I will camp against thee round about, and will lay siege against thee with a mount, and I will raise forts against thee.

4 And thou shalt be brought down, *and* shalt speak out of the ground, and

thy speech shall be low out of the dust, and thy voice shall be, as of one that hath a familiar spirit, out of the ground, and thy speech shall whisper out of the dust.
5 Moreover the multitude of thy strangers shall be like small dust, and the multitude of the terrible ones *shall be* as chaff that passeth away: yea, it shall be at an instant suddenly.
6 Thou shalt be visited of the LORD of hosts with thunder, and with earthquake, and great noise, with storm and tempest, and the flame of devouring fire.
7 And the multitude of all the nations that fight against Ariel, even all that fight against her and her munition, and that distress her, shall be as a dream of a night vision.
8 It shall even be as when an hungry *man* dreameth, and, behold, he eateth; but he awaketh, and his soul is empty: or as when a thirsty man dreameth, and, behold, he drinketh; but he awaketh, and, behold, *he is* faint, and his soul hath appetite: so shall the multitude of all the nations be, that fight against mount Zion.
9 Stay yourselves, and wonder; cry ye out, and cry: they are drunken, but not with wine; they stagger, but not with strong drink.
10 For the LORD hath poured out upon you the spirit of deep sleep, and hath closed your eyes: the prophets and your rulers, the seers hath he covered.
11 And the vision of all is become unto you as the words of a book that is sealed, which *men* deliver to one that is learned, saying, Read this, I pray thee: and he saith, I cannot; for it *is* sealed:
12 And the book is delivered to him that is not learned, saying, Read this, I pray thee: and he saith, I am not learned.
13 Wherefore the Lord said, Forasmuch as this people draw near *me* with their mouth, and with their lips do honour me, but have removed their heart far from me, and their fear toward me is taught by the precept of men:
14 Therefore, behold, I will proceed to do a marvellous work among this people, *even* a marvellous work and a wonder: for the wisdom of their wise *men* shall perish, and the understanding of their prudent *men* shall be hid.
15 Woe unto them that seek deep to hide their counsel from the LORD, and their works are in the dark, and they say, Who seeth us? and who knoweth us?
16 Surely your turning of things upside down shall be esteemed as the potter's clay: for shall the work say of him that made it, He made me not? or shall the thing framed say of him that framed it, He had no understanding?
17 *Is* it not yet a very little while, and Lebanon shall be turned into a fruitful field, and the fruitful field shall be esteemed as a forest?
18 And in that day shall the deaf hear the words of the book, and the eyes of the blind shall see out of obscurity, and out of darkness.
19 The meek also shall increase *their* joy in the LORD, and the poor among men shall rejoice in the Holy One of Israel.
20 For the terrible one is brought to nought, and the scorner is consumed, and all that watch for iniquity are cut off:

21 That make a man an offender for a word, and lay a snare for him that reproveth in the gate, and turn aside the just for a thing of nought.

22 Therefore thus saith the LORD, who redeemed Abraham, concerning the house of Jacob, Jacob shall not now be ashamed, neither shall his face now wax pale.

23 But when he seeth his children, the work of mine hands, in the midst of him, they shall sanctify my name, and sanctify the Holy One of Jacob, and shall fear the God of Israel.

24 They also that erred in spirit shall come to understanding, and they that murmured shall learn doctrine.

30 Woe to the rebellious children, saith the LORD, that take counsel, but not of me; and that cover with a covering, but not of my spirit, that they may add sin to sin:

2 That walk to go down into Egypt, and have not asked at my mouth; to strengthen themselves in the strength of Pharaoh, and to trust in the shadow of Egypt!

3 Therefore shall the strength of Pharaoh be your shame, and the trust in the shadow of Egypt *your* confusion.

4 For his princes were at Zoan, and his ambassadors came to Hanes.

5 They were all ashamed of a people *that* could not profit them, nor be an help nor profit, but a shame, and also a reproach.

6 The burden of the beasts of the south: into the land of trouble and anguish, from whence *come* the young and old lion, the viper and fiery flying serpent, they will carry their riches upon the shoulders of young asses, and their treasures upon the bunches of camels, to a people *that* shall not profit *them*.

7 For the Egyptians shall help in vain, and to no purpose: therefore have I cried concerning this, Their strength *is* to sit still.

8 Now go, write it before them in a table, and note it in a book, that it may be for the time to come for ever and ever:

9 That this *is* a rebellious people, lying children, children *that* will not hear the law of the LORD:

10 Which say to the seers, See not; and to the prophets, Prophesy not unto us right things, speak unto us smooth things, prophesy deceits:

11 Get you out of the way, turn aside out of the path, cause the Holy One of Israel to cease from before us.

12 Wherefore thus saith the Holy One of Israel, Because ye despise this word, and trust in oppression and perverseness, and stay thereon:

13 Therefore this iniquity shall be to you as a breach ready to fall, swelling out in a high wall, whose breaking cometh suddenly at an instant.

14 And he shall break it as the breaking of the potters' vessel that is broken in pieces; he shall not spare: so that there shall not be found in the bursting of it a sherd to take fire from the hearth, or to take water *withal* out of the pit.

15 For thus saith the Lord GOD, the Holy One of Israel; In returning and rest shall ye be saved; in quietness and in confidence shall be your strength: and ye would not.

16 But ye said, No; for we will flee upon horses; therefore shall ye flee: and, We will ride upon the swift; therefore shall they that pursue you be swift.

17 One thousand *shall flee* at the rebuke of one; at the rebuke of five shall ye flee: till ye be left as a beacon upon the top of a mountain, and as an ensign on an hill.

18 And therefore will the LORD wait, that he may be gracious unto you, and therefore will he be exalted, that he may have mercy upon you: for the LORD *is* a God of judgment: blessed *are* all they that wait for him.

19 For the people shall dwell in Zion at Jerusalem: thou shalt weep no more: he will be very gracious unto thee at the voice of thy cry; when he shall hear it, he will answer thee.

20 And *though* the Lord give you the bread of adversity, and the water of affliction, yet shall not thy teachers be removed into a corner any more, but thine eyes shall see thy teachers:

21 And thine ears shall hear a word behind thee, saying, This *is* the way, walk ye in it, when ye turn to the right hand, and when ye turn to the left.

22 Ye shall defile also the covering of thy graven images of silver, and the ornament of thy molten images of gold: thou shalt cast them away as a menstruous cloth; thou shalt say unto it, Get thee hence.

23 Then shall he give the rain of thy seed, that thou shalt sow the ground withal; and bread of the increase of the earth, and it shall be fat and plenteous: in that day shall thy cattle feed in large pastures.

24 The oxen likewise and the young asses that ear the ground shall eat clean provender, which hath been winnowed with the shovel and with the fan.

25 And there shall be upon every high mountain, and upon every high hill, rivers *and* streams of waters in the day of the great slaughter, when the towers fall.

26 Moreover the light of the moon shall be as the light of the sun, and the light of the sun shall be sevenfold, as the light of seven days, in the day that the LORD bindeth up the breach of his people, and healeth the stroke of their wound.

27 Behold, the name of the LORD cometh from far, burning *with* his anger, and the burden *thereof is* heavy: his lips are full of indignation, and his tongue as a devouring fire:

28 And his breath, as an overflowing stream, shall reach to the midst of the neck, to sift the nations with the sieve of vanity: and *there shall be* a bridle in the jaws of the people, causing *them* to err.

29 Ye shall have a song, as in the night *when* a holy solemnity is kept; and gladness of heart, as when one goeth with a pipe to come into the mountain of the LORD, to the mighty One of Israel.

30 And the LORD shall cause his glorious voice to be heard, and shall shew the lighting down of his arm, with the indignation of *his* anger, and *with* the flame of a devouring fire, *with* scattering, and tempest, and hailstones.

31 For through the voice of the LORD shall the Assyrian be beaten down, *which* smote with a rod.

32 And *in* every place where the grounded staff shall pass, which the LORD shall lay upon him, *it* shall be with tabrets and harps: and in battles of shaking will he fight with it.

33 For Tophet *is* ordained of old; yea, for the king it is prepared; he hath made *it* deep *and* large: the pile thereof *is* fire and much wood; the breath of the LORD, like a stream of brimstone, doth kindle it.

31 Woe to them that go down to
Egypt for help; and stay on horses, and trust in chariots, because *they*
are many; and in horsemen, because
they are very strong; but they look not
unto the Holy One of Israel, neither
seek the LORD!
2 Yet he also *is* wise, and will bring
evil, and will not call back his words:
but will arise against the house of the
evildoers, and against the help of them
that work iniquity.
3 Now the Egyptians *are* men, and not
God; and their horses flesh, and not
spirit. When the LORD shall stretch out
his hand, both he that helpeth shall fall,
and he that is holpen shall fall down,
and they all shall fail together.
4 For thus hath the LORD spoken unto
me, Like as the lion and the young lion
roaring on his prey, when a multitude
of shepherds is called forth against
him, *he* will not be afraid of their voice,
nor abase himself for the noise of them:
so shall the LORD of hosts come down to
fight for mount Zion, and for the hill
thereof.
5 As birds flying, so will the LORD of
hosts defend Jerusalem; defending
also he will deliver *it; and* passing over
he will preserve it.
6 Turn ye unto *him from* whom the
children of Israel have deeply revolted.
7 For in that day every man shall cast
away his idols of silver, and his idols of
gold, which your own hands have made
unto you *for* a sin.
8 Then shall the Assyrian fall with the
sword, not of a mighty man; and the
sword, not of a mean man, shall devour
him: but he shall flee from the sword,
and his young men shall be discomfited.
9 And he shall pass over to his strong
hold for fear, and his princes shall be
afraid of the ensign, saith the LORD,
whose fire *is* in Zion, and his furnace in
Jerusalem.

32 Behold, a king shall reign in righteousness, and princes shall rule
in judgment.
2 And a man shall be as an hiding
place from the wind, and a covert from
the tempest; as rivers of water in a dry
place, as the shadow of a great rock in
a weary land.
3 And the eyes of them that see shall
not be dim, and the ears of them that
hear shall hearken.
4 The heart also of the rash shall
understand knowledge, and the tongue
of the stammerers shall be ready to
speak plainly.
5 The vile person shall be no more
called liberal, nor the churl said *to be*
bountiful.
6 For the vile person will speak villany, and his heart will work iniquity, to
practise hypocrisy, and to utter error
against the LORD, to make empty the
soul of the hungry, and he will cause
the drink of the thirsty to fail.
7 The instruments also of the churl
are evil: he deviseth wicked devices to
destroy the poor with lying words, even
when the needy speaketh right.
8 But the liberal deviseth liberal
things; and by liberal things shall he
stand.
9 Rise up, ye women that are at ease;
hear my voice, ye careless daughters;
give ear unto my speech.
10 Many days and years shall ye be
troubled, ye careless women: for the
vintage shall fail, the gathering shall
not come.

11 Tremble, ye women that are at ease; be troubled, ye careless ones: strip you, and make you bare, and gird *sackcloth* upon *your* loins.

12 They shall lament for the teats, for the pleasant fields, for the fruitful vine.

13 Upon the land of my people shall come up thorns *and* briers; yea, upon all the houses of joy *in* the joyous city:

14 Because the palaces shall be forsaken; the multitude of the city shall be left; the forts and towers shall be for dens for ever, a joy of wild asses, a pasture of flocks;

15 Until the spirit be poured upon us from on high, and the wilderness be a fruitful field, and the fruitful field be counted for a forest.

16 Then judgment shall dwell in the wilderness, and righteousness remain in the fruitful field.

17 And the work of righteousness shall be peace; and the effect of righteousness quietness and assurance for ever.

18 And my people shall dwell in a peaceable habitation, and in sure dwellings, and in quiet resting places;

19 When it shall hail, coming down on the forest; and the city shall be low in a low place.

20 Blessed *are* ye that sow beside all waters, that send forth *thither* the feet of the ox and the ass.

33

Woe to thee that spoilest, and thou *wast* not spoiled; and dealest treacherously, and they dealt not treacherously with thee! when thou shalt cease to spoil, thou shalt be spoiled; *and* when thou shalt make an end to deal treacherously, they shall deal treacherously with thee.

2 O Lord, be gracious unto us; we have waited for thee: be thou their arm every morning, our salvation also in the time of trouble.

3 At the noise of the tumult the people fled; at the lifting up of thyself the nations were scattered.

4 And your spoil shall be gathered *like* the gathering of the caterpiller: as the running to and fro of locusts shall he run upon them.

5 The Lord is exalted; for he dwelleth on high: he hath filled Zion with judgment and righteousness.

6 And wisdom and knowledge shall be the stability of thy times, *and* strength of salvation: the fear of the Lord *is* his treasure.

7 Behold, their valiant ones shall cry without: the ambassadors of peace shall weep bitterly.

8 The highways lie waste, the wayfaring man ceaseth: he hath broken the covenant, he hath despised the cities, he regardeth no man.

9 The earth mourneth *and* languisheth: Lebanon is ashamed *and* hewn down: Sharon is like a wilderness; and Bashan and Carmel shake off *their* *fruits*.

10 Now will I rise, saith the Lord; now will I be exalted; now will I lift up myself.

11 Ye shall conceive chaff, ye shall bring forth stubble: your breath, *as* fire, shall devour you.

12 And the people shall be *as* the burnings of lime: *as* thorns cut up shall they be burned in the fire.

13 Hear, ye *that are* far off, what I have done; and, ye *that are* near, acknowledge my might.

14 The sinners in Zion are afraid;
fearfulness hath surprised the hypocrites. Who among us shall dwell with
the devouring fire? who among us shall
dwell with everlasting burnings?
15 He that walketh righteously, and
speaketh uprightly; he that despiseth
the gain of oppressions, that shaketh
his hands from holding of bribes, that
stoppeth his ears from hearing of
blood, and shutteth his eyes from seeing evil;
16 He shall dwell on high: his place of
defence *shall be* the munitions of rocks:
bread shall be given him; his waters
shall be sure.
17 Thine eyes shall see the king in his
beauty: they shall behold the land that
is very far off.
18 Thine heart shall meditate terror.
Where *is* the scribe? where *is* the
receiver? where *is* he that counted the
towers?
19 Thou shalt not see a fierce people,
a people of a deeper speech than thou
canst perceive; of a stammering tongue,
that thou canst not understand.
20 Look upon Zion, the city of our
solemnities: thine eyes shall see
Jerusalem a quiet habitation, a tabernacle *that* shall not be taken down; not
one of the stakes thereof shall ever be
removed, neither shall any of the cords
thereof be broken.
21 But there the glorious LORD *will be*
unto us a place of broad rivers *and*
streams; wherein shall go no galley
with oars, neither shall gallant ship
pass thereby.
22 For the LORD *is* our judge, the
LORD *is* our lawgiver, the LORD *is* our
king; he will save us.
23 Thy tacklings are loosed; they
could not well strengthen their mast,
they could not spread the sail: then is
the prey of a great spoil divided; the
lame take the prey.
24 And the inhabitant shall not say, I
am sick: the people that dwell therein
shall be forgiven *their* iniquity.

34 Come near, ye nations, to hear;
and hearken, ye people: let the
earth hear, and all that is therein; the
world, and all things that come forth of
it.
2 For the indignation of the LORD *is*
upon all nations, and *his* fury upon all
their armies: he hath utterly destroyed
them, he hath delivered them to the
slaughter.
3 Their slain also shall be cast out,
and their stink shall come up out of
their carcases, and the mountains shall
be melted with their blood.
4 And all the host of heaven shall be
dissolved, and the heavens shall be
rolled together as a scroll: and all their
host shall fall down, as the leaf falleth
off from the vine, and as a falling *fig*
from the fig tree.
5 For my sword shall be bathed in
heaven: behold, it shall come down
upon Idumea, and upon the people of
my curse, to judgment.
6 The sword of the LORD is filled with
blood, it is made fat with fatness, *and*
with the blood of lambs and goats, with
the fat of the kidneys of rams: for the
LORD hath a sacrifice in Bozrah, and a
great slaughter in the land of Idumea.
7 And the unicorns shall come down
with them, and the bullocks with the
bulls; and their land shall be soaked
with blood, and their dust made fat
with fatness.
8 For *it is* the day of the LORD's vengeance, *and* the year of recompences
for the controversy of Zion.

9 And the streams thereof shall be turned into pitch, and the dust thereof into brimstone, and the land thereof shall become burning pitch.

10 It shall not be quenched night nor day; the smoke thereof shall go up for ever: from generation to generation it shall lie waste; none shall pass through it for ever and ever.

11 But the cormorant and the bittern shall possess it; the owl also and the raven shall dwell in it: and he shall stretch out upon it the line of confusion, and the stones of emptiness.

12 They shall call the nobles thereof to the kingdom, but none *shall be* there, and all her princes shall be nothing.

13 And thorns shall come up in her palaces, nettles and brambles in the fortresses thereof: and it shall be an habitation of dragons, *and* a court for owls.

14 The wild beasts of the desert shall also meet with the wild beasts of the island, and the satyr shall cry to his fellow; the screech owl also shall rest there, and find for herself a place of rest.

15 There shall the great owl make her nest, and lay, and hatch, and gather under her shadow: there shall the vultures also be gathered, every one with her mate.

16 Seek ye out of the book of the LORD, and read: no one of these shall fail, none shall want her mate: for my mouth it hath commanded, and his spirit it hath gathered them.

17 And he hath cast the lot for them, and his hand hath divided it unto them by line: they shall possess it for ever, from generation to generation shall they dwell therein.

35

The wilderness and the solitary place shall be glad for them; and the desert shall rejoice, and blossom as the rose.

2 It shall blossom abundantly, and rejoice even with joy and singing: the glory of Lebanon shall be given unto it, the excellency of Carmel and Sharon, they shall see the glory of the LORD, *and* the excellency of our God.

3 Strengthen ye the weak hands, and confirm the feeble knees.

4 Say to them *that are* of a fearful heart, Be strong, fear not: behold, your God will come *with* vengeance, *even* God *with* a recompence; he will come and save you.

5 Then the eyes of the blind shall be opened, and the ears of the deaf shall be unstopped.

6 Then shall the lame *man* leap as an hart, and the tongue of the dumb sing: for in the wilderness shall waters break out, and streams in the desert.

7 And the parched ground shall become a pool, and the thirsty land springs of water: in the habitation of dragons, where each lay, *shall be* grass with reeds and rushes.

8 And an highway shall be there, and a way, and it shall be called The way of holiness; the unclean shall not pass over it; but it *shall be* for those: the wayfaring men, though fools, shall not err *therein*.

9 No lion shall be there, nor *any* ravenous beast shall go up thereon, it shall not be found there; but the redeemed shall walk *there*:

10 And the ransomed of the LORD shall return, and come to Zion with songs and everlasting joy upon their heads: they shall obtain joy and gladness, and sorrow and sighing shall flee away.

36 Now it came to pass in the fourteenth year of king Hezekiah, *that* Sennacherib king of Assyria came up against all the defenced cities of Judah, and took them.

2 And the king of Assyria sent Rabshakeh from Lachish to Jerusalem unto king Hezekiah with a great army. And he stood by the conduit of the upper pool in the highway of the fuller's field.

3 Then came forth unto him Eliakim, Hilkiah's son, which was over the house, and Shebna the scribe, and Joah, Asaph's son, the recorder.

4 And Rabshakeh said unto them, Say ye now to Hezekiah, Thus saith the great king, the king of Assyria, What confidence *is* this wherein thou trustest?

5 I say, *sayest thou*, (but *they are but* vain words) *I have* counsel and strength for war: now on whom dost thou trust, that thou rebellest against me?

6 Lo, thou trustest in the staff of this broken reed, on Egypt; whereon if a man lean, it will go into his hand, and pierce it: so *is* Pharaoh king of Egypt to all that trust in him.

7 But if thou say to me, We trust in the LORD our God: *is it* not he, whose high places and whose altars Hezekiah hath taken away, and said to Judah and to Jerusalem, Ye shall worship before this altar?

8 Now therefore give pledges, I pray thee, to my master the king of Assyria, and I will give thee two thousand horses, if thou be able on thy part to set riders upon them.

9 How then wilt thou turn away the face of one captain of the least of my master's servants, and put thy trust on Egypt for chariots and for horsemen?

10 And am I now come up without the LORD against this land to destroy it? the LORD said unto me, Go up against this land, and destroy it.

11 Then said Eliakim and Shebna and Joah unto Rabshakeh, Speak, I pray thee, unto thy servants in the Syrian language; for we understand *it*: and speak not to us in the Jews' language, in the ears of the people that *are* on the wall.

12 But Rabshakeh said, Hath my master sent me to thy master and to thee to speak these words? *hath he* not *sent me* to the men that sit upon the wall, that they may eat their own dung, and drink their own piss with you?

13 Then Rabshakeh stood, and cried with a loud voice in the Jews' language, and said, Hear ye the words of the great king, the king of Assyria.

14 Thus saith the king, Let not Hezekiah deceive you: for he shall not be able to deliver you.

15 Neither let Hezekiah make you trust in the LORD, saying, The LORD will surely deliver us: this city shall not be delivered into the hand of the king of Assyria.

16 Hearken not to Hezekiah: for thus saith the king of Assyria, Make *an agreement* with me *by* a present, and come out to me: and eat ye every one of his vine, and every one of his fig tree, and drink ye every one the waters of his own cistern;

17 Until I come and take you away to a land like your own land, a land of corn and wine, a land of bread and vineyards.

18 *Beware* lest Hezekiah persuade you, saying, The LORD will deliver us. Hath any of the gods of the nations

delivered his land out of the hand of
the king of Assyria?
19 Where *are* the gods of Hamath and
Arphad? where *are* the gods of
Sepharvaim? and have they delivered
Samaria out of my hand?
20 Who *are they* among all the gods
of these lands, that have delivered their
land out of my hand, that the LORD
should deliver Jerusalem out of my
hand?
21 But they held their peace, and
answered him not a word: for the king's
commandment was, saying, Answer
him not.
22 Then came Eliakim, the son of
Hilkiah, that *was* over the household,
and Shebna the scribe, and Joah, the
son of Asaph, the recorder, to Hezekiah
with *their* clothes rent, and told him
the words of Rabshakeh.

37 And it came to pass, when king
Hezekiah heard *it*, that he rent
his clothes, and covered himself with
sackcloth, and went into the house of
the LORD.
2 And he sent Eliakim, who *was* over
the household, and Shebna the scribe,
and the elders of the priests covered
with sackcloth, unto Isaiah the prophet
the son of Amoz.
3 And they said unto him, Thus saith
Hezekiah, This day *is* a day of trouble,
and of rebuke, and of blasphemy: for
the children are come to the birth, and
there is not strength to bring forth.
4 It may be the LORD thy God will
hear the words of Rabshakeh, whom
the king of Assyria his master hath sent
to reproach the living God, and will
reprove the words which the LORD thy
God hath heard: wherefore lift up *thy*
prayer for the remnant that is left.
5 So the servants of king Hezekiah
came to Isaiah.
6 And Isaiah said unto them, Thus
shall ye say unto your master, Thus
saith the LORD, Be not afraid of the
words that thou hast heard, wherewith
the servants of the king of Assyria have
blasphemed me.
7 Behold, I will send a blast upon him,
and he shall hear a rumour, and return
to his own land; and I will cause him to
fall by the sword in his own land.
8 So Rabshakeh returned, and found
the king of Assyria warring against
Libnah: for he had heard that he was
departed from Lachish.
9 And he heard say concerning
Tirhakah king of Ethiopia, He is come
forth to make war with thee. And when
he heard *it*, he sent messengers to
Hezekiah, saying,
10 Thus shall ye speak to Hezekiah
king of Judah, saying, Let not thy God,
in whom thou trustest, deceive thee,
saying, Jerusalem shall not be given
into the hand of the king of Assyria.
11 Behold, thou hast heard what the
kings of Assyria have done to all lands
by destroying them utterly; and shalt
thou be delivered?
12 Have the gods of the nations delivered them which my fathers have
destroyed, *as* Gozan, and Haran, and
Rezeph, and the children of Eden
which *were* in Telassar?
13 Where *is* the king of Hamath, and
the king of Arphad, and the king of the
city of Sepharvaim, Hena, and Ivah?
14 And Hezekiah received the letter
from the hand of the messengers, and
read it: and Hezekiah went up unto the
house of the LORD, and spread it before
the LORD.

15 And Hezekiah prayed unto the LORD, saying,

16 O LORD of hosts, God of Israel, that dwellest *between* the cherubims, thou *art* the God, *even* thou alone, of all the kingdoms of the earth: thou hast made heaven and earth.

17 Incline thine ear, O LORD, and hear; open thine eyes, O LORD, and see: and hear all the words of Sennacherib, which hath sent to reproach the living God.

18 Of a truth, LORD, the kings of Assyria have laid waste all the nations, and their countries,

19 And have cast their gods into the fire: for they *were* no gods, but the work of men's hands, wood and stone: therefore they have destroyed them.

20 Now therefore, O LORD our God, save us from his hand, that all the kingdoms of the earth may know that thou *art* the LORD, *even* thou only.

21 Then Isaiah the son of Amoz sent unto Hezekiah, saying, Thus saith the LORD God of Israel, Whereas thou hast prayed to me against Sennacherib king of Assyria:

22 This *is* the word which the LORD hath spoken concerning him; The virgin, the daughter of Zion, hath despised thee, *and* laughed thee to scorn; the daughter of Jerusalem hath shaken her head at thee.

23 Whom hast thou reproached and blasphemed? and against whom hast thou exalted *thy* voice, and lifted up thine eyes on high? *even* against the Holy One of Israel.

24 By thy servants hast thou reproached the Lord, and hast said, By the multitude of my chariots am I come up to the height of the mountains, to the sides of Lebanon; and I will cut down the tall cedars thereof, *and* the choice fir trees thereof: and I will enter into the height of his border, *and* the forest of his Carmel.

25 I have digged, and drunk water; and with the sole of my feet have I dried up all the rivers of the besieged places.

26 Hast thou not heard long ago, *how* I have done it; *and* of ancient times, that I have formed it? now have I brought it to pass, that thou shouldest be to lay waste defenced cities *into* ruinous heaps.

27 Therefore their inhabitants *were* of small power, they were dismayed and confounded: they were *as* the grass of the field, and *as* the green herb, *as* the grass on the housetops, and *as corn* blasted before it be grown up.

28 But I know thy abode, and thy going out, and thy coming in, and thy rage against me.

29 Because thy rage against me, and thy tumult, is come up into mine ears, therefore will I put my hook in thy nose, and my bridle in thy lips, and I will turn thee back by the way by which thou camest.

30 And this *shall be* a sign unto thee, Ye shall eat *this* year such as groweth of itself; and the second year that which springeth of the same: and in the third year sow ye, and reap, and plant vineyards, and eat the fruit thereof.

31 And the remnant that is escaped of the house of Judah shall again take root downward, and bear fruit upward:

32 For out of Jerusalem shall go forth a remnant, and they that escape out of mount Zion: the zeal of the LORD of hosts shall do this.

33 Therefore thus saith the LORD concerning the king of Assyria, He shall
not come into this city, nor shoot an
arrow there, nor come before it with
shields, nor cast a bank against it.
34 By the way that he came, by the
same shall he return, and shall not
come into this city, saith the LORD.
35 For I will defend this city to save it
for mine own sake, and for my servant
David's sake.
36 Then the angel of the LORD went
forth, and smote in the camp of the
Assyrians a hundred and fourscore and
five thousand: and when they arose
early in the morning, behold, they *were*
all dead corpses.
37 So Sennacherib king of Assyria
departed, and went and returned, and
dwelt at Nineveh.
38 And it came to pass, as he was
worshipping in the house of Nisroch his
god, that Adrammelech and Sharezer
his sons smote him with the sword; and
they escaped into the land of Armenia:
and Esar-haddon his son reigned in his
stead.

38 In those days was Hezekiah sick
unto death. And Isaiah the
prophet the son of Amoz came unto
him, and said unto him, Thus saith the
LORD, Set thine house in order: for thou
shalt die, and not live.
2 Then Hezekiah turned his face
toward the wall, and prayed unto the
LORD,
3 And said, Remember now, O LORD, I
beseech thee, how I have walked before
thee in truth and with a perfect heart,
and have done *that which is* good in
thy sight. And Hezekiah wept sore.
4 Then came the word of the LORD to
Isaiah, saying,
5 Go, and say to Hezekiah, Thus saith
the LORD, the God of David thy father, I
have heard thy prayer, I have seen thy
tears: behold, I will add unto thy days
fifteen years.
6 And I will deliver thee and this city
out of the hand of the king of Assyria:
and I will defend this city.
7 And this *shall be* a sign unto thee
from the LORD, that the LORD will do
this thing that he hath spoken;
8 Behold, I will bring again the shadow of the degrees, which is gone down
in the sun dial of Ahaz, ten degrees
backward. So the sun returned ten
degrees, by which degrees it was gone
down.
9 The writing of Hezekiah king of
Judah, when he had been sick, and was
recovered of his sickness:
10 I said in the cutting off of my days,
I shall go to the gates of the grave: I am
deprived of the residue of my years.
11 I said, I shall not see the LORD, *even*
the LORD, in the land of the living: I
shall behold man no more with the
inhabitants of the world.
12 Mine age is departed, and is
removed from me as a shepherd's tent:
I have cut off like a weaver my life: he
will cut me off with pining sickness:
from day *even* to night wilt thou make
an end of me.
13 I reckoned till morning, *that*, as a
lion, so will he break all my bones: from
day *even* to night wilt thou make an
end of me.
14 Like a crane *or* a swallow, so did I
chatter: I did mourn as a dove: mine
eyes fail *with looking* upward: O LORD,
I am oppressed; undertake for me.

15 What shall I say? he hath both spoken unto me, and himself hath done *it*: I shall go softly all my years in the bitterness of my soul.

16 O Lord, by these *things men* live, and in all these *things is* the life of my spirit: so wilt thou recover me, and make me to live.

17 Behold, for peace I had great bitterness: but thou hast in love to my soul *delivered it* from the pit of corruption: for thou hast cast all my sins behind thy back.

18 For the grave cannot praise thee, death can *not* celebrate thee: they that go down into the pit cannot hope for thy truth.

19 The living, the living, he shall praise thee, as I *do* this day: the father to the children shall make known thy truth.

20 The LORD *was ready* to save me: therefore we will sing my songs to the stringed instruments all the days of our life in the house of the LORD.

21 For Isaiah had said, Let them take a lump of figs, and lay *it* for a plaister upon the boil, and he shall recover.

22 Hezekiah also had said, What *is* the sign that I shall go up to the house of the LORD?

39 At that time Merodach-baladan, the son of Baladan, king of Babylon, sent letters and a present to Hezekiah: for he had heard that he had been sick, and was recovered.

2 And Hezekiah was glad of them, and shewed them the house of his precious things, the silver, and the gold, and the spices, and the precious ointment, and all the house of his armour, and all that was found in his treasures: there was nothing in his house, nor in all his dominion, that Hezekiah shewed them not.

3 Then came Isaiah the prophet unto king Hezekiah, and said unto him, What said these men? and from whence came they unto thee? And Hezekiah said, They are come from a far country unto me, *even* from Babylon.

4 Then said he, What have they seen in thine house? And Hezekiah answered, All that *is* in mine house have they seen: there is nothing among my treasures that I have not shewed them.

5 Then said Isaiah to Hezekiah, Hear the word of the LORD of hosts:

6 Behold, the days come, that all that *is* in thine house, and *that* which thy fathers have laid up in store until this day, shall be carried to Babylon: nothing shall be left, saith the LORD.

7 And of thy sons that shall issue from thee, which thou shalt beget, shall they take away; and they shall be eunuchs in the palace of the king of Babylon.

8 Then said Hezekiah to Isaiah, Good *is* the word of the LORD which thou hast spoken. He said moreover, For there shall be peace and truth in my days.

40 Comfort ye, comfort ye my people, saith your God.

2 Speak ye comfortably to Jerusalem, and cry unto her, that her warfare is accomplished, that her iniquity is pardoned: for she hath received of the LORD's hand double for all her sins.

3 The voice of him that crieth in the wilderness, Prepare ye the way of the LORD, make straight in the desert a highway for our God.

4 Every valley shall be exalted, and every mountain and hill shall be made low: and the crooked shall be made straight, and the rough places plain:

5 And the glory of the LORD shall be
revealed, and all flesh shall see *it*
together: for the mouth of the LORD
hath spoken *it*.
6 The voice said, Cry. And he said,
What shall I cry? All flesh *is* grass, and
all the goodliness thereof *is* as the
flower of the field:
7 The grass withereth, the flower
fadeth: because the spirit of the LORD
bloweth upon it: surely the people *is*
grass.
8 The grass withereth, the flower
fadeth: but the word of our God shall
stand for ever.
9 O Zion, that bringest good tidings,
get thee up into the high mountain; O
Jerusalem, that bringest good tidings,
lift up thy voice with strength; lift *it* up,
be not afraid; say unto the cities of
Judah, Behold your God!
10 Behold, the Lord GOD will come
with strong *hand*, and his arm shall
rule for him: behold, his reward *is* with
him, and his work before him.
11 He shall feed his flock like a shepherd: he shall gather the lambs with his
arm, and carry *them* in his bosom, *and*
shall gently lead those that are with
young.
12 Who hath measured the waters in
the hollow of his hand, and meted out
heaven with the span, and comprehended the dust of the earth in a measure, and weighed the mountains in
scales, and the hills in a balance?
13 Who hath directed the Spirit of the
LORD, or *being* his counsellor hath
taught him?
14 With whom took he counsel, and
who instructed him, and taught him in
the path of judgment, and taught him
knowledge, and shewed to him the way
of understanding?
15 Behold, the nations *are* as a drop of
a bucket, and are counted as the small
dust of the balance: behold, he taketh
up the isles as a very little thing.
16 And Lebanon *is* not sufficient to
burn, nor the beasts thereof sufficient
for a burnt offering.
17 All nations before him *are* as nothing; and they are counted to him less
than nothing, and vanity.
18 To whom then will ye liken God?
or what likeness will ye compare unto
him?
19 The workman melteth a graven
image, and the goldsmith spreadeth it
over with gold, and casteth silver
chains.
20 He that *is* so impoverished that he
hath no oblation chooseth a tree *that*
will not rot; he seeketh unto him a cunning workman to prepare a graven
image, *that* shall not be moved.
21 Have ye not known? have ye not
heard? hath it not been told you from
the beginning? have ye not understood
from the foundations of the earth?
22 *It is* he that sitteth upon the circle
of the earth, and the inhabitants thereof *are* as grasshoppers; that stretcheth
out the heavens as a curtain, and
spreadeth them out as a tent to dwell
in:
23 That bringeth the princes to nothing; he maketh the judges of the earth
as vanity.
24 Yea, they shall not be planted; yea,
they shall not be sown: yea, their stock
shall not take root in the earth: and he
shall also blow upon them, and they
shall wither, and the whirlwind shall
take them away as stubble.
25 To whom then will ye liken me, or
shall I be equal? saith the Holy One.

26 Lift up your eyes on high, and behold who hath created these *things*, that bringeth out their host by number: he calleth them all by names by the greatness of his might, for that *he is* strong in power; not one faileth.

27 Why sayest thou, O Jacob, and speakest, O Israel, My way is hid from the LORD, and my judgment is passed over from my God?

28 Hast thou not known? hast thou not heard, *that* the everlasting God, the LORD, the Creator of the ends of the earth, fainteth not, neither is weary? *there is* no searching of his understanding.

29 He giveth power to the faint; and to *them that have* no might he increaseth strength.

30 Even the youths shall faint and be weary, and the young men shall utterly fall:

31 But they that wait upon the LORD shall renew *their* strength; they shall mount up with wings as eagles; they shall run, and not be weary; *and* they shall walk, and not faint.

41

Keep silence before me, O islands; and let the people renew *their* strength: let them come near; then let them speak: let us come near together to judgment.

2 Who raised up the righteous *man* from the east, called him to his foot, gave the nations before him, and made *him* rule over kings? he gave *them* as the dust to his sword, *and* as driven stubble to his bow.

3 He pursued them, *and* passed safely; *even* by the way *that* he had not gone with his feet.

4 Who hath wrought and done *it*, calling the generations from the beginning? I the LORD, the first, and with the last; I *am* he.

5 The isles saw *it*, and feared; the ends of the earth were afraid, drew near, and came.

6 They helped every one his neighbour; and *every one* said to his brother, Be of good courage.

7 So the carpenter encouraged the goldsmith, *and* he that smootheth *with* the hammer him that smote the anvil, saying, It *is* ready for the sodering: and he fastened it with nails, *that* it should not be moved.

8 But thou, Israel, *art* my servant, Jacob whom I have chosen, the seed of Abraham my friend.

9 *Thou* whom I have taken from the ends of the earth, and called thee from the chief men thereof, and said unto thee, Thou *art* my servant; I have chosen thee, and not cast thee away.

10 Fear thou not; for I *am* with thee: be not dismayed; for I *am* thy God: I will strengthen thee; yea, I will help thee; yea, I will uphold thee with the right hand of my righteousness.

11 Behold, all they that were incensed against thee shall be ashamed and confounded: they shall be as nothing; and they that strive with thee shall perish.

12 Thou shalt seek them, and shalt not find them, *even* them that contended with thee: they that war against thee shall be as nothing, and as a thing of nought.

13 For I the LORD thy God will hold thy right hand, saying unto thee, Fear not; I will help thee.

14 Fear not, thou worm Jacob, *and* ye men of Israel; I will help thee, saith the LORD, and thy redeemer, the Holy One of Israel.

15 Behold, I will make thee a new
sharp threshing instrument having
teeth: thou shalt thresh the mountains,
and beat *them* small, and shalt make
the hills as chaff.
16 Thou shalt fan them, and the wind
shall carry them away, and the whirlwind shall scatter them: and thou shalt
rejoice in the LORD, *and* shalt glory in
the Holy One of Israel.
17 *When* the poor and needy seek
water, and *there is* none, *and* their
tongue faileth for thirst, I the LORD will
hear them, *I* the God of Israel will not
forsake them.
18 I will open rivers in high places,
and fountains in the midst of the valleys: I will make the wilderness a pool
of water, and the dry land springs of
water.
19 I will plant in the wilderness the
cedar, the shittah tree, and the myrtle,
and the oil tree; I will set in the desert
the fir tree, *and* the pine, and the box
tree together:
20 That they may see, and know, and
consider, and understand together, that
the hand of the LORD hath done this,
and the Holy One of Israel hath created
it.
21 Produce your cause, saith the
LORD; bring forth your strong *reasons*,
saith the King of Jacob.
22 Let them bring *them* forth, and
shew us what shall happen: let them
shew the former things, what they *be*,
that we may consider them, and know
the latter end of them; or declare us
things for to come.
23 Shew the things that are to come
hereafter, that we may know that ye *are*
gods: yea, do good, or do evil, that we
may be dismayed, and behold *it*
together.
24 Behold, ye *are* of nothing, and your
work of nought: an abomination *is he*
that chooseth you.
25 I have raised up *one* from the
north, and he shall come: from the rising of the sun shall he call upon my
name: and he shall come upon princes
as *upon* morter, and as the potter
treadeth clay.
26 Who hath declared from the beginning, that we may know? and beforetime, that we may say, *He is* righteous?
yea, *there is* none that sheweth, yea,
there is none that declareth, yea, *there*
is none that heareth your words.
27 The first *shall say* to Zion, Behold,
behold them: and I will give to
Jerusalem one that bringeth good tidings.
28 For I beheld, and *there was* no
man; even among them, and *there was*
no counsellor, that, when I asked of
them, could answer a word.
29 Behold, they *are* all vanity; their
works *are* nothing: their molten images
are wind and confusion.

42 Behold my servant, whom I
uphold; mine elect, *in whom* my
soul delighteth; I have put my spirit
upon him: he shall bring forth judgment to the Gentiles.
2 He shall not cry, nor lift up, nor
cause his voice to be heard in the
street.
3 A bruised reed shall he not break,
and the smoking flax shall he not
quench: he shall bring forth judgment
unto truth.
4 He shall not fail nor be discouraged,
till he have set judgment in the earth:
and the isles shall wait for his law.
5 Thus saith God the LORD, he that
created the heavens, and stretched
them out; he that spread forth the

earth, and that which cometh out of it; he that giveth breath unto the people upon it, and spirit to them that walk therein:

6 I the LORD have called thee in righteousness, and will hold thine hand, and will keep thee, and give thee for a covenant of the people, for a light of the Gentiles;

7 To open the blind eyes, to bring out the prisoners from the prison, *and* them that sit in darkness out of the prison house.

8 I *am* the LORD: that *is* my name: and my glory will I not give to another, neither my praise to graven images.

9 Behold, the former things are come to pass, and new things do I declare: before they spring forth I tell you of them.

10 Sing unto the LORD a new song, *and* his praise from the end of the earth, ye that go down to the sea, and all that is therein; the isles, and the inhabitants thereof.

11 Let the wilderness and the cities thereof lift up *their voice*, the villages *that* Kedar doth inhabit: let the inhabitants of the rock sing, let them shout from the top of the mountains.

12 Let them give glory unto the LORD, and declare his praise in the islands.

13 The LORD shall go forth as a mighty man, he shall stir up jealousy like a man of war: he shall cry, yea, roar; he shall prevail against his enemies.

14 I have long time holden my peace; I have been still, *and* refrained myself: *now* will I cry like a travailing woman; I will destroy and devour at once.

15 I will make waste mountains and hills, and dry up all their herbs; and I will make the rivers islands, and I will dry up the pools.

16 And I will bring the blind by a way *that* they knew not; I will lead them in paths *that* they have not known: I will make darkness light before them, and crooked things straight. These things will I do unto them, and not forsake them.

17 They shall be turned back, they shall be greatly ashamed, that trust in graven images, that say to the molten images, Ye *are* our gods.

18 Hear, ye deaf; and look, ye blind, that ye may see.

19 Who *is* blind, but my servant? or deaf, as my messenger *that* I sent? who *is* blind as *he that is* perfect, and blind as the LORD's servant?

20 Seeing many things, but thou observest not; opening the ears, but he heareth not.

21 The LORD is well pleased for his righteousness' sake; he will magnify the law, and make *it* honourable.

22 But this *is* a people robbed and spoiled; *they are* all of them snared in holes, and they are hid in prison houses: they are for a prey, and none delivereth; for a spoil, and none saith, Restore.

23 Who among you will give ear to this? *who* will hearken and hear for the time to come?

24 Who gave Jacob for a spoil, and Israel to the robbers? did not the LORD, he against whom we have sinned? for they would not walk in his ways, neither were they obedient unto his law.

25 Therefore he hath poured upon him the fury of his anger, and the strength of battle: and it hath set him on fire round about, yet he knew not; and it burned him, yet he laid *it* not to heart.

43 But now thus saith the LORD that
created thee, O Jacob, and he
that formed thee, O Israel, Fear not: for
I have redeemed thee, I have called
thee by thy name; thou *art* mine.
2 When thou passest through the
waters, I *will be* with thee; and through
the rivers, they shall not overflow thee:
when thou walkest through the fire,
thou shalt not be burned; neither shall
the flame kindle upon thee.
3 For I *am* the LORD thy God, the Holy
One of Israel, thy Saviour: I gave Egypt
for thy ransom, Ethiopia and Seba for
thee.
4 Since thou wast precious in my
sight, thou hast been honourable, and I
have loved thee: therefore will I give
men for thee, and people for thy life.
5 Fear not: for I *am* with thee: I will
bring thy seed from the east, and gather thee from the west;
6 I will say to the north, Give up; and
to the south, Keep not back: bring my
sons from far, and my daughters from
the ends of the earth;
7 *Even* every one that is called by my
name: for I have created him for my
glory, I have formed him; yea, I have
made him.
8 Bring forth the blind people that
have eyes, and the deaf that have ears.
9 Let all the nations be gathered
together, and let the people be assembled: who among them can declare this,
and shew us former things? let them
bring forth their witnesses, that they
may be justified: or let them hear, and
say, *It is* truth.
10 Ye *are* my witnesses, saith the
LORD, and my servant whom I have
chosen: that ye may know and believe
me, and understand that I *am* he:
before me there was no God formed,
neither shall there be after me.
11 I, *even* I, *am* the LORD; and beside
me *there is* no saviour.
12 I have declared, and have saved,
and I have shewed, when *there was* no
strange *god* among you: therefore ye
are my witnesses, saith the LORD, that I
am God.
13 Yea, before the day *was* I *am* he;
and *there is* none that can deliver out
of my hand: I will work, and who shall
let it?
14 Thus saith the LORD, your redeemer, the Holy One of Israel; For your sake
I have sent to Babylon, and have
brought down all their nobles, and the
Chaldeans, whose cry *is* in the ships.
15 I *am* the LORD, your Holy One, the
creator of Israel, your King.
16 Thus saith the LORD, which maketh
a way in the sea, and a path in the
mighty waters;
17 Which bringeth forth the chariot
and horse, the army and the power;
they shall lie down together, they shall
not rise: they are extinct, they are
quenched as tow.
18 Remember ye not the former
things, neither consider the things of
old.
19 Behold, I will do a new thing; now
it shall spring forth; shall ye not know
it? I will even make a way in the wilderness, *and* rivers in the desert.
20 The beast of the field shall honour
me, the dragons and the owls: because
I give waters in the wilderness, *and* rivers in the desert, to give drink to my
people, my chosen.
21 This people have I formed for
myself; they shall shew forth my praise.

22 But thou hast not called upon me,
O Jacob; but thou hast been weary of
me, O Israel.
23 Thou hast not brought me the
small cattle of thy burnt offerings; neither hast thou honoured me with thy
sacrifices. I have not caused thee to
serve with an offering, nor wearied
thee with incense.
24 Thou hast bought me no sweet
cane with money, neither hast thou
filled me with the fat of thy sacrifices:
but thou hast made me to serve with
thy sins, thou hast wearied me with
thine iniquities.
25 I, *even* I, *am* he that blotteth out
thy transgressions for mine own sake,
and will not remember thy sins.
26 Put me in remembrance: let us
plead together: declare thou, that thou
mayest be justified.
27 Thy first father hath sinned, and
thy teachers have transgressed against
me.
28 Therefore I have profaned the
princes of the sanctuary, and have
given Jacob to the curse, and Israel to
reproaches.

44 Yet now hear, O Jacob my servant; and Israel, whom I have
chosen:
2 Thus saith the LORD that made thee,
and formed thee from the womb, *which*
will help thee; Fear not, O Jacob, my
servant; and thou, Jesurun, whom I
have chosen.
3 For I will pour water upon him that
is thirsty, and floods upon the dry
ground: I will pour my spirit upon thy
seed, and my blessing upon thine offspring:
4 And they shall spring up *as* among
the grass, as willows by the water
courses.
5 One shall say, I *am* the LORD's; and
another shall call *himself* by the name
of Jacob; and another shall subscribe
with his hand unto the LORD, and surname *himself* by the name of Israel.
6 Thus saith the LORD the King of
Israel, and his redeemer the LORD of
hosts; I *am* the first, and I *am* the last;
and beside me *there is* no God.
7 And who, as I, shall call, and shall
declare it, and set it in order for me,
since I appointed the ancient people?
and the things that are coming, and
shall come, let them shew unto them.
8 Fear ye not, neither be afraid: have
not I told thee from that time, and have
declared *it*? ye *are* even my witnesses.
Is there a God beside me? yea, *there is*
no God; I know not *any*.
9 They that make a graven image *are*
all of them vanity; and their delectable
things shall not profit; and they *are*
their own witnesses; they see not, nor
know; that they may be ashamed.
10 Who hath formed a god, or molten
a graven image *that* is profitable for
nothing?
11 Behold, all his fellows shall be
ashamed: and the workmen, they *are* of
men: let them all be gathered together,
let them stand up; *yet* they shall fear,
and they shall be ashamed together.
12 The smith with the tongs both worketh in the coals, and fashioneth it with
hammers, and worketh it with the
strength of his arms: yea, he is hungry,
and his strength faileth: he drinketh no
water, and is faint.
13 The carpenter stretcheth out *his*
rule; he marketh it out with a line; he
fitteth it with planes, and he marketh it
out with the compass, and maketh it
after the figure of a man, according to

the beauty of a man; that it may remain in the house.

14 He heweth him down cedars, and taketh the cypress and the oak, which he strengtheneth for himself among the trees of the forest: he planteth an ash, and the rain doth nourish *it*.

15 Then shall it be for a man to burn: for he will take thereof, and warm himself; yea, he kindleth *it*, and baketh bread; yea, he maketh a god, and worshippeth *it*; he maketh it a graven image, and falleth down thereto.

16 He burneth part thereof in the fire; with part thereof he eateth flesh; he roasteth roast, and is satisfied: yea, he warmeth *himself*, and saith, Aha, I am warm, I have seen the fire:

17 And the residue thereof he maketh a god, *even* his graven image: he falleth down unto it, and worshippeth *it*, and prayeth unto it, and saith, Deliver me; for thou *art* my god.

18 They have not known nor understood: for he hath shut their eyes, that they cannot see; *and* their hearts, that they cannot understand.

19 And none considereth in his heart, neither *is there* knowledge nor understanding to say, I have burned part of it in the fire; yea, also I have baked bread upon the coals thereof; I have roasted flesh, and eaten *it*: and shall I make the residue thereof an abomination? shall I fall down to the stock of a tree?

20 He feedeth on ashes: a deceived heart hath turned him aside, that he cannot deliver his soul, nor say, *Is there* not a lie in my right hand?

21 Remember these, O Jacob and Israel; for thou *art* my servant: I have formed thee; thou *art* my servant: O Israel, thou shalt not be forgotten of me.

22 I have blotted out, as a thick cloud, thy transgressions, and, as a cloud, thy sins: return unto me; for I have redeemed thee.

23 Sing, O ye heavens; for the LORD hath done *it*: shout, ye lower parts of the earth: break forth into singing, ye mountains, O forest, and every tree therein: for the LORD hath redeemed Jacob, and glorified himself in Israel.

24 Thus saith the LORD, thy redeemer, and he that formed thee from the womb, I *am* the LORD that maketh all *things*; that stretcheth forth the heavens alone; that spreadeth abroad the earth by myself;

25 That frustrateth the tokens of the liars, and maketh diviners mad; that turneth wise *men* backward, and maketh their knowledge foolish;

26 That confirmeth the word of his servant, and performeth the counsel of his messengers; that saith to Jerusalem, Thou shalt be inhabited; and to the cities of Judah, Ye shall be built, and I will raise up the decayed places thereof:

27 That saith to the deep, Be dry, and I will dry up thy rivers:

28 That saith of Cyrus, *He is* my shepherd, and shall perform all my pleasure: even saying to Jerusalem, Thou shalt be built; and to the temple, Thy foundation shall be laid.

45 Thus saith the LORD to his anointed, to Cyrus, whose right hand I have holden, to subdue nations before him; and I will loose the loins of kings, to open before him the two leaved gates; and the gates shall not be shut;

2 I will go before thee, and make the crooked places straight: I will break in pieces the gates of brass, and cut in sunder the bars of iron:

3 And I will give thee the treasures of darkness, and hidden riches of secret places, that thou mayest know that I, the LORD, which call *thee* by thy name, *am* the God of Israel.

4 For Jacob my servant's sake, and Israel mine elect, I have even called thee by thy name: I have surnamed thee, though thou hast not known me.

5 I *am* the LORD, and *there is* none else, *there is* no God beside me: I girded thee, though thou hast not known me:

6 That they may know from the rising of the sun, and from the west, that *there is* none beside me. I *am* the LORD, and *there is* none else.

7 I form the light, and create darkness: I make peace, and create evil: I the LORD do all these *things*.

8 Drop down, ye heavens, from above, and let the skies pour down righteousness: let the earth open, and let them bring forth salvation, and let righteousness spring up together; I the LORD have created it.

9 Woe unto him that striveth with his Maker! *Let* the potsherd *strive* with the potsherds of the earth. Shall the clay say to him that fashioneth it, What makest thou? or thy work, He hath no hands?

10 Woe unto him that saith unto *his* father, What begettest thou? or to the woman, What hast thou brought forth?

11 Thus saith the LORD, the Holy One of Israel, and his Maker, Ask me of things to come concerning my sons, and concerning the work of my hands command ye me.

12 I have made the earth, and created man upon it: I, *even* my hands, have stretched out the heavens, and all their host have I commanded.

13 I have raised him up in righteousness, and I will direct all his ways: he shall build my city, and he shall let go my captives, not for price nor reward, saith the LORD of hosts.

14 Thus saith the LORD, The labour of Egypt, and merchandise of Ethiopia and of the Sabeans, men of stature, shall come over unto thee, and they shall be thine: they shall come after thee; in chains they shall come over, and they shall fall down unto thee, they shall make supplication unto thee, *saying*, Surely God *is* in thee; and *there is* none else, *there is* no God.

15 Verily thou *art* a God that hidest thyself, O God of Israel, the Saviour.

16 They shall be ashamed, and also confounded, all of them: they shall go to confusion together *that are* makers of idols.

17 *But* Israel shall be saved in the LORD with an everlasting salvation: ye shall not be ashamed nor confounded world without end.

18 For thus saith the LORD that created the heavens; God himself that formed the earth and made it; he hath established it, he created it not in vain, he formed it to be inhabited: I *am* the LORD; and *there is* none else.

19 I have not spoken in secret, in a dark place of the earth: I said not unto the seed of Jacob, Seek ye me in vain: I the LORD speak righteousness, I declare things that are right.

20 Assemble yourselves and come; draw near together, ye *that are* escaped of the nations: they have no knowledge that set up the wood of their graven image, and pray unto a god *that* cannot save.

21 Tell ye, and bring *them* near; yea, let them take counsel together: who hath declared this from ancient time? *who* hath told it from that time? *have* not I the LORD? and *there is* no God else beside me; a just God and a Saviour; *there is* none beside me.

22 Look unto me, and be ye saved, all the ends of the earth: for I *am* God, and *there is* none else.

23 I have sworn by myself, the word is gone out of my mouth *in* righteousness, and shall not return, That unto me every knee shall bow, every tongue shall swear.

24 Surely, shall *one* say, in the LORD have I righteousness and strength: *even* to him shall *men* come; and all that are incensed against him shall be ashamed.

25 In the LORD shall all the seed of Israel be justified, and shall glory.

46 Bel boweth down, Nebo stoopeth, their idols were upon the beasts, and upon the cattle: your carriages *were* heavy loaden; *they are* a burden to the weary *beast*.

2 They stoop, they bow down together; they could not deliver the burden, but themselves are gone into captivity.

3 Hearken unto me, O house of Jacob, and all the remnant of the house of Israel, which are borne *by me* from the belly, which are carried from the womb:

4 And *even* to *your* old age I *am* he; and *even* to hoar hairs will I carry *you*: I have made, and I will bear; even I will carry, and will deliver *you*.

5 To whom will ye liken me, and make *me* equal, and compare me, that we may be like?

6 They lavish gold out of the bag, and weigh silver in the balance, *and* hire a goldsmith; and he maketh it a god: they fall down, yea, they worship.

7 They bear him upon the shoulder, they carry him, and set him in his place, and he standeth; from his place shall he not remove: yea, *one* shall cry unto him, yet can he not answer, nor save him out of his trouble.

8 Remember this, and shew yourselves men: bring *it* again to mind, O ye transgressors.

9 Remember the former things of old: for I *am* God, and *there is* none else; *I am* God, and *there is* none like me,

10 Declaring the end from the beginning, and from ancient times *the things* that are not *yet* done, saying, My counsel shall stand, and I will do all my pleasure:

11 Calling a ravenous bird from the east, the man that executeth my counsel from a far country: yea, I have spoken *it*, I will also bring it to pass; I have purposed *it*, I will also do it.

12 Hearken unto me, ye stouthearted, that *are* far from righteousness:

13 I bring near my righteousness; it shall not be far off, and my salvation shall not tarry: and I will place salvation in Zion for Israel my glory.

47 Come down, and sit in the dust, O virgin daughter of Babylon, sit on the ground: *there is* no throne, O daughter of the Chaldeans: for thou shalt no more be called tender and delicate.

2 Take the millstones, and grind meal: uncover thy locks, make bare the leg, uncover the thigh, pass over the rivers.

3 Thy nakedness shall be uncovered, yea, thy shame shall be seen: I will take vengeance, and I will not meet *thee as* a man.

4 *As for* our redeemer, the LORD of hosts *is* his name, the Holy One of Israel.

5 Sit thou silent, and get thee into darkness, O daughter of the Chaldeans: for thou shalt no more be called, The lady of kingdoms.

6 I was wroth with my people, I have polluted mine inheritance, and given them into thine hand: thou didst shew them no mercy; upon the ancient hast thou very heavily laid thy yoke.

7 And thou saidst, I shall be a lady for ever: *so* that thou didst not lay these *things* to thy heart, neither didst remember the latter end of it.

8 Therefore hear now this, *thou that art* given to pleasures, that dwellest carelessly, that sayest in thine heart, I *am*, and none else beside me; I shall not sit *as* a widow, neither shall I know the loss of children:

9 But these two *things* shall come to thee in a moment in one day, the loss of children, and widowhood: they shall come upon thee in their perfection for the multitude of thy sorceries, *and* for the great abundance of thine enchantments.

10 For thou hast trusted in thy wickedness: thou hast said, None seeth me. Thy wisdom and thy knowledge, it hath perverted thee; and thou hast said in thine heart, I *am*, and none else beside me.

11 Therefore shall evil come upon thee; thou shalt not know from whence it riseth: and mischief shall fall upon thee; thou shalt not be able to put it off: and desolation shall come upon thee suddenly, *which* thou shalt not know.

12 Stand now with thine enchantments, and with the multitude of thy sorceries, wherein thou hast laboured from thy youth; if so be thou shalt be able to profit, if so be thou mayest prevail.

13 Thou art wearied in the multitude of thy counsels. Let now the astrologers, the stargazers, the monthly prognosticators, stand up, and save thee from *these things* that shall come upon thee.

14 Behold, they shall be as stubble; the fire shall burn them; they shall not deliver themselves from the power of the flame: *there shall* not *be* a coal to warm at, *nor* fire to sit before it.

15 Thus shall they be unto thee with whom thou hast laboured, *even* thy merchants, from thy youth: they shall wander every one to his quarter; none shall save thee.

48 Hear ye this, O house of Jacob, which are called by the name of Israel, and are come forth out of the waters of Judah, which swear by the name of the LORD, and make mention of the God of Israel, *but* not in truth, nor in righteousness.

2 For they call themselves of the holy city, and stay themselves upon the God of Israel; The LORD of hosts *is* his name.

3 I have declared the former things from the beginning; and they went forth out of my mouth, and I shewed them; I did *them* suddenly, and they came to pass.

4 Because I knew that thou *art* obstinate, and thy neck *is* an iron sinew, and thy brow brass;

5 I have even from the beginning declared *it* to thee; before it came to pass I shewed *it* thee: lest thou shouldest say, Mine idol hath done them, and my graven image, and my molten image, hath commanded them.

6 Thou hast heard, see all this; and will not ye declare *it*? I have shewed thee new things from this time, even

hidden things, and thou didst not know
them.
7 They are created now, and not from
the beginning; even before the day
when thou heardest them not; lest thou
shouldest say, Behold, I knew them.
8 Yea, thou heardest not; yea, thou
knewest not; yea, from that time *that*
thine ear was not opened: for I knew
that thou wouldest deal very treacherously, and wast called a transgressor
from the womb.
9 For my name's sake will I defer
mine anger, and for my praise will I
refrain for thee, that I cut thee not off.
10 Behold, I have refined thee, but
not with silver; I have chosen thee in
the furnace of affliction.
11 For mine own sake, *even* for mine
own sake, will I do *it*: for how should
my name be polluted? and I will not
give my glory unto another.
12 Hearken unto me, O Jacob and
Israel, my called; I *am* he; I *am* the first,
I also *am* the last.
13 Mine hand also hath laid the foundation of the earth, and my right hand
hath spanned the heavens: *when* I call
unto them, they stand up together.
14 All ye, assemble yourselves, and
hear; which among them hath declared
these *things*? The LORD hath loved him:
he will do his pleasure on Babylon, and
his arm *shall be on* the Chaldeans.
15 I, *even* I, have spoken; yea, I have
called him: I have brought him, and he
shall make his way prosperous.
16 Come ye near unto me, hear ye
this; I have not spoken in secret from
the beginning; from the time that it
was, there *am* I: and now the Lord GOD,
and his Spirit, hath sent me.
17 Thus saith the LORD, thy Redeemer,
the Holy One of Israel; I *am* the LORD
thy God which teacheth thee to profit,
which leadeth thee by the way *that*
thou shouldest go.
18 O that thou hadst hearkened to my
commandments! then had thy peace
been as a river, and thy righteousness
as the waves of the sea:
19 Thy seed also had been as the
sand, and the offspring of thy bowels
like the gravel thereof; his name should
not have been cut off nor destroyed
from before me.
20 Go ye forth of Babylon, flee ye
from the Chaldeans, with a voice of
singing declare ye, tell this, utter it
even to the end of the earth; say ye, The
LORD hath redeemed his servant Jacob.
21 And they thirsted not *when* he led
them through the deserts: he caused
the waters to flow out of the rock for
them: he clave the rock also, and the
waters gushed out.
22 *There is* no peace, saith the LORD,
unto the wicked.

49 Listen, O isles, unto me; and
hearken, ye people, from far; The
LORD hath called me from the womb;
from the bowels of my mother hath he
made mention of my name.
2 And he hath made my mouth like a
sharp sword; in the shadow of his hand
hath he hid me, and made me a polished shaft; in his quiver hath he hid
me;
3 And said unto me, Thou *art* my servant, O Israel, in whom I will be glorified.
4 Then I said, I have laboured in vain,
I have spent my strength for nought,
and in vain: *yet* surely my judgment *is*
with the LORD, and my work with my
God.

5 And now, saith the LORD that
formed me from the womb *to be* his
servant, to bring Jacob again to him,
Though Israel be not gathered, yet shall
I be glorious in the eyes of the LORD,
and my God shall be my strength.
6 And he said, It is a light thing that
thou shouldest be my servant to raise
up the tribes of Jacob, and to restore
the preserved of Israel: I will also give
thee for a light to the Gentiles, that
thou mayest be my salvation unto the
end of the earth.
7 Thus saith the LORD, the Redeemer
of Israel, *and* his Holy One, to him
whom man despiseth, to him whom the
nation abhorreth, to a servant of rulers,
Kings shall see and arise, princes also
shall worship, because of the LORD that
is faithful, *and* the Holy One of Israel,
and he shall choose thee.
8 Thus saith the LORD, In an acceptable time have I heard thee, and in a
day of salvation have I helped thee: and
I will preserve thee, and give thee for a
covenant of the people, to establish the
earth, to cause to inherit the desolate
heritages;
9 That thou mayest say to the prisoners, Go forth; to them that *are* in darkness, Shew yourselves. They shall feed
in the ways, and their pastures *shall be*
in all high places.
10 They shall not hunger nor thirst;
neither shall the heat nor sun smite
them: for he that hath mercy on them
shall lead them, even by the springs of
water shall he guide them.
11 And I will make all my mountains
a way, and my highways shall be
exalted.
12 Behold, these shall come from far:
and, lo, these from the north and from
the west; and these from the land of
Sinim.
13 Sing, O heavens; and be joyful, O
earth; and break forth into singing, O
mountains: for the LORD hath comforted his people, and will have mercy
upon his afflicted.
14 But Zion said, The LORD hath forsaken me, and my Lord hath forgotten
me.
15 Can a woman forget her sucking
child, that she should not have compassion on the son of her womb? yea, they
may forget, yet will I not forget thee.
16 Behold, I have graven thee upon
the palms of *my* hands; thy walls *are*
continually before me.
17 Thy children shall make haste; thy
destroyers and they that made thee
waste shall go forth of thee.
18 Lift up thine eyes round about, and
behold: all these gather themselves
together, *and* come to thee. *As* I live,
saith the LORD, thou shalt surely clothe
thee with them all, as with an ornament, and bind them *on thee*, as a bride
doeth.
19 For thy waste and thy desolate
places, and the land of thy destruction,
shall even now be too narrow by reason
of the inhabitants, and they that swallowed thee up shall be far away.
20 The children which thou shalt
have, after thou hast lost the other,
shall say again in thine ears, The place
is too strait for me: give place to me
that I may dwell.
21 Then shalt thou say in thine heart,
Who hath begotten me these, seeing I
have lost my children, and am desolate,
a captive, and removing to and fro? and
who hath brought up these? Behold, I
was left alone; these, where *had* they
been?

22 Thus saith the Lord GOD, Behold, I will lift up mine hand to the Gentiles, and set up my standard to the people: and they shall bring thy sons in *their* arms, and thy daughters shall be carried upon *their* shoulders.
23 And kings shall be thy nursing fathers, and their queens thy nursing mothers: they shall bow down to thee with *their* face toward the earth, and lick up the dust of thy feet; and thou shalt know that I *am* the LORD: for they shall not be ashamed that wait for me.
24 Shall the prey be taken from the mighty, or the lawful captive delivered?
25 But thus saith the LORD, Even the captives of the mighty shall be taken away, and the prey of the terrible shall be delivered: for I will contend with him that contendeth with thee, and I will save thy children.
26 And I will feed them that oppress thee with their own flesh; and they shall be drunken with their own blood, as with sweet wine: and all flesh shall know that I the LORD *am* thy Saviour and thy Redeemer, the mighty One of Jacob.

50 Thus saith the LORD, Where *is* the bill of your mother's divorcement, whom I have put away? or which of my creditors *is it* to whom I have sold you? Behold, for your iniquities have ye sold yourselves, and for your transgressions is your mother put away.
2 Wherefore, when I came, *was there* no man? when I called, *was there* none to answer? Is my hand shortened at all, that it cannot redeem? or have I no power to deliver? behold, at my rebuke I dry up the sea, I make the rivers a wilderness: their fish stinketh, because *there is* no water, and dieth for thirst.
3 I clothe the heavens with blackness, and I make sackcloth their covering.
4 The Lord GOD hath given me the tongue of the learned, that I should know how to speak a word in season to *him that is* weary: he wakeneth morning by morning, he wakeneth mine ear to hear as the learned.
5 The Lord GOD hath opened mine ear, and I was not rebellious, neither turned away back.
6 I gave my back to the smiters, and my cheeks to them that plucked off the hair: I hid not my face from shame and spitting.
7 For the Lord GOD will help me; therefore shall I not be confounded: therefore have I set my face like a flint, and I know that I shall not be ashamed.
8 *He is* near that justifieth me; who will contend with me? let us stand together: who *is* mine adversary? let him come near to me.
9 Behold, the Lord GOD will help me; who *is* he *that* shall condemn me? lo, they all shall wax old as a garment; the moth shall eat them up.
10 Who *is* among you that feareth the LORD, that obeyeth the voice of his servant, that walketh *in* darkness, and hath no light? let him trust in the name of the LORD, and stay upon his God.
11 Behold, all ye that kindle a fire, that compass *yourselves* about with sparks: walk in the light of your fire, and in the sparks *that* ye have kindled. This shall ye have of mine hand; ye shall lie down in sorrow.

51 Hearken to me, ye that follow after righteousness, ye that seek the LORD: look unto the rock *whence* ye are hewn, and to the hole of the pit *whence* ye are digged.

2 Look unto Abraham your father, and unto Sarah *that* bare you: for I called him alone, and blessed him, and increased him.

3 For the LORD shall comfort Zion: he will comfort all her waste places; and he will make her wilderness like Eden, and her desert like the garden of the LORD; joy and gladness shall be found therein, thanksgiving, and the voice of melody.

4 Hearken unto me, my people; and give ear unto me, O my nation: for a law shall proceed from me, and I will make my judgment to rest for a light of the people.

5 My righteousness *is* near; my salvation is gone forth, and mine arms shall judge the people; the isles shall wait upon me, and on mine arm shall they trust.

6 Lift up your eyes to the heavens, and look upon the earth beneath: for the heavens shall vanish away like smoke, and the earth shall wax old like a garment, and they that dwell therein shall die in like manner: but my salvation shall be for ever, and my righteousness shall not be abolished.

7 Hearken unto me, ye that know righteousness, the people in whose heart *is* my law; fear ye not the reproach of men, neither be ye afraid of their revilings.

8 For the moth shall eat them up like a garment, and the worm shall eat them like wool: but my righteousness shall be for ever, and my salvation from generation to generation.

9 Awake, awake, put on strength, O arm of the LORD; awake, as in the ancient days, in the generations of old. *Art* thou not it that hath cut Rahab, *and* wounded the dragon?

10 *Art* thou not it which hath dried the sea, the waters of the great deep; that hath made the depths of the sea a way for the ransomed to pass over?

11 Therefore the redeemed of the LORD shall return, and come with singing unto Zion; and everlasting joy *shall be* upon their head: they shall obtain gladness and joy; *and* sorrow and mourning shall flee away.

12 I, *even* I, *am* he that comforteth you: who *art* thou, that thou shouldest be afraid of a man *that* shall die, and of the son of man *which* shall be made *as* grass;

13 And forgettest the LORD thy maker, that hath stretched forth the heavens, and laid the foundations of the earth; and hast feared continually every day because of the fury of the oppressor, as if he were ready to destroy? and where *is* the fury of the oppressor?

14 The captive exile hasteneth that he may be loosed, and that he should not die in the pit, nor that his bread should fail.

15 But I *am* the LORD thy God, that divided the sea, whose waves roared: The LORD of hosts *is* his name.

16 And I have put my words in thy mouth, and I have covered thee in the shadow of mine hand, that I may plant the heavens, and lay the foundations of the earth, and say unto Zion, Thou *art* my people.

17 Awake, awake, stand up, O Jerusalem, which hast drunk at the hand of the LORD the cup of his fury; thou hast drunken the dregs of the cup of trembling, *and* wrung *them* out.

18 *There is* none to guide her among all the sons *whom* she hath brought forth; neither *is there any* that taketh her by the hand of all the sons *that* she hath brought up.

19 These two *things* are come unto thee; who shall be sorry for thee? desolation, and destruction, and the famine, and the sword: by whom shall I comfort thee?

20 Thy sons have fainted, they lie at the head of all the streets, as a wild bull in a net: they are full of the fury of the LORD, the rebuke of thy God.

21 Therefore hear now this, thou afflicted, and drunken, but not with wine:

22 Thus saith thy Lord the LORD, and thy God *that* pleadeth the cause of his people, Behold, I have taken out of thine hand the cup of trembling, *even* the dregs of the cup of my fury; thou shalt no more drink it again:

23 But I will put it into the hand of them that afflict thee; which have said to thy soul, Bow down, that we may go over: and thou hast laid thy body as the ground, and as the street, to them that went over.

52 Awake, awake; put on thy strength, O Zion; put on thy beautiful garments, O Jerusalem, the holy city: for henceforth there shall no more come into thee the uncircumcised and the unclean.

2 Shake thyself from the dust; arise, *and* sit down, O Jerusalem: loose thyself from the bands of thy neck, O captive daughter of Zion.

3 For thus saith the LORD, Ye have sold yourselves for nought; and ye shall be redeemed without money.

4 For thus saith the Lord GOD, My people went down aforetime into Egypt to sojourn there; and the Assyrian oppressed them without cause.

5 Now therefore, what have I here, saith the LORD, that my people is taken away for nought? they that rule over them make them to howl, saith the LORD; and my name continually every day *is* blasphemed.

6 Therefore my people shall know my name: therefore *they shall know* in that day that I *am* he that doth speak: behold, *it is* I.

7 How beautiful upon the mountains are the feet of him that bringeth good tidings, that publisheth peace; that bringeth good tidings of good, that publisheth salvation; that saith unto Zion, Thy God reigneth!

8 Thy watchmen shall lift up the voice; with the voice together shall they sing: for they shall see eye to eye, when the LORD shall bring again Zion.

9 Break forth into joy, sing together, ye waste places of Jerusalem: for the LORD hath comforted his people, he hath redeemed Jerusalem.

10 The LORD hath made bare his holy arm in the eyes of all the nations; and all the ends of the earth shall see the salvation of our God.

11 Depart ye, depart ye, go ye out from thence, touch no unclean *thing*; go ye out of the midst of her; be ye clean, that bear the vessels of the LORD.

12 For ye shall not go out with haste, nor go by flight: for the LORD will go before you; and the God of Israel *will be* your rereward.

13 Behold, my servant shall deal prudently, he shall be exalted and extolled, and be very high.

14 As many were astonied at thee; his visage was so marred more than any man, and his form more than the sons of men:

15 So shall he sprinkle many nations;
the kings shall shut their mouths at
him: for *that* which had not been told
them shall they see; and *that* which
they had not heard shall they consider.

53 Who hath believed our report?
and to whom is the arm of the
LORD revealed?
2 For he shall grow up before him as a
tender plant, and as a root out of a dry
ground: he hath no form nor comeliness; and when we shall see him, *there*
is no beauty that we should desire him.
3 He is despised and rejected of men;
a man of sorrows, and acquainted with
grief: and we hid as it were *our* faces
from him; he was despised, and we
esteemed him not.
4 Surely he hath borne our griefs, and
carried our sorrows: yet we did esteem
him stricken, smitten of God, and
afflicted.
5 But he *was* wounded for our transgressions, *he was* bruised for our iniquities: the chastisement of our peace *was*
upon him; and with his stripes we are
healed.
6 All we like sheep have gone astray;
we have turned every one to his own
way; and the LORD hath laid on him the
iniquity of us all.
7 He was oppressed, and he was
afflicted, yet he opened not his mouth:
he is brought as a lamb to the slaughter,
and as a sheep before her shearers is
dumb, so he openeth not his mouth.
8 He was taken from prison and from
judgment: and who shall declare his
generation? for he was cut off out of the
land of the living: for the transgression
of my people was he stricken.
9 And he made his grave with the
wicked, and with the rich in his death;
because he had done no violence, neither *was any* deceit in his mouth.
10 Yet it pleased the LORD to bruise
him; he hath put *him* to grief: when
thou shalt make his soul an offering for
sin, he shall see *his* seed, he shall prolong *his* days, and the pleasure of the
LORD shall prosper in his hand.
11 He shall see of the travail of his
soul, *and* shall be satisfied: by his
knowledge shall my righteous servant
justify many; for he shall bear their
iniquities.
12 Therefore will I divide him *a por-*
tion with the great, and he shall divide
the spoil with the strong; because he
hath poured out his soul unto death:
and he was numbered with the transgressors; and he bare the sin of many,
and made intercession for the transgressors.

54 Sing, O barren, thou *that* didst
not bear; break forth into singing, and cry aloud, thou *that* didst not
travail with child: for more *are* the
children of the desolate than the children of the married wife, saith the
LORD.
2 Enlarge the place of thy tent, and
let them stretch forth the curtains of
thine habitations: spare not, lengthen
thy cords, and strengthen thy stakes;
3 For thou shalt break forth on the
right hand and on the left; and thy seed
shall inherit the Gentiles, and make the
desolate cities to be inhabited.
4 Fear not; for thou shalt not be
ashamed: neither be thou confounded;
for thou shalt not be put to shame: for
thou shalt forget the shame of thy
youth, and shalt not remember the
reproach of thy widowhood any more.
5 For thy Maker *is* thine husband; the
LORD of hosts *is* his name; and thy

Redeemer the Holy One of Israel; The God of the whole earth shall he be called.

6 For the LORD hath called thee as a woman forsaken and grieved in spirit, and a wife of youth, when thou wast refused, saith thy God.

7 For a small moment have I forsaken thee; but with great mercies will I gather thee.

8 In a little wrath I hid my face from thee for a moment; but with everlasting kindness will I have mercy on thee, saith the LORD thy Redeemer.

9 For this *is as* the waters of Noah unto me: for *as* I have sworn that the waters of Noah should no more go over the earth; so have I sworn that I would not be wroth with thee, nor rebuke thee.

10 For the mountains shall depart, and the hills be removed; but my kindness shall not depart from thee, neither shall the covenant of my peace be removed, saith the LORD that hath mercy on thee.

11 O thou afflicted, tossed with tempest, *and* not comforted, behold, I will lay thy stones with fair colours, and lay thy foundations with sapphires.

12 And I will make thy windows of agates, and thy gates of carbuncles, and all thy borders of pleasant stones.

13 And all thy children *shall be* taught of the LORD; and great *shall be* the peace of thy children.

14 In righteousness shalt thou be established: thou shalt be far from oppression; for thou shalt not fear: and from terror; for it shall not come near thee.

15 Behold, they shall surely gather together, *but* not by me: whosoever shall gather together against thee shall fall for thy sake.

16 Behold, I have created the smith that bloweth the coals in the fire, and that bringeth forth an instrument for his work; and I have created the waster to destroy.

17 No weapon that is formed against thee shall prosper; and every tongue *that* shall rise against thee in judgment thou shalt condemn. This *is* the heritage of the servants of the LORD, and their righteousness *is* of me, saith the LORD.

55 Ho, every one that thirsteth, come ye to the waters, and he that hath no money; come ye, buy, and eat; yea, come, buy wine and milk without money and without price.

2 Wherefore do ye spend money for *that which is* not bread? and your labour for *that which* satisfieth not? hearken diligently unto me, and eat ye *that which is* good, and let your soul delight itself in fatness.

3 Incline your ear, and come unto me: hear, and your soul shall live; and I will make an everlasting covenant with you, *even* the sure mercies of David.

4 Behold, I have given him *for* a witness to the people, a leader and commander to the people.

5 Behold, thou shalt call a nation *that* thou knowest not, and nations *that* knew not thee shall run unto thee because of the LORD thy God, and for the Holy One of Israel; for he hath glorified thee.

6 Seek ye the LORD while he may be found, call ye upon him while he is near:

7 Let the wicked forsake his way, and the unrighteous man his thoughts: and let him return unto the LORD, and he will have mercy upon him; and to our God, for he will abundantly pardon.

8 For my thoughts *are* not your thoughts, neither *are* your ways my ways, saith the LORD.

9 For *as* the heavens are higher than the earth, so are my ways higher than your ways, and my thoughts than your thoughts.

10 For as the rain cometh down, and the snow from heaven, and returneth not thither, but watereth the earth, and maketh it bring forth and bud, that it may give seed to the sower, and bread to the eater:

11 So shall my word be that goeth forth out of my mouth: it shall not return unto me void, but it shall accomplish that which I please, and it shall prosper *in the thing* whereto I sent it.

12 For ye shall go out with joy, and be led forth with peace: the mountains and the hills shall break forth before you into singing, and all the trees of the field shall clap *their* hands.

13 Instead of the thorn shall come up the fir tree, and instead of the brier shall come up the myrtle tree: and it shall be to the LORD for a name, for an everlasting sign *that* shall not be cut off.

56 Thus saith the LORD, Keep ye judgment, and do justice: for my salvation *is* near to come, and my righteousness to be revealed.

2 Blessed *is* the man *that* doeth this, and the son of man *that* layeth hold on it; that keepeth the sabbath from polluting it, and keepeth his hand from doing any evil.

3 Neither let the son of the stranger, that hath joined himself to the LORD, speak, saying, The LORD hath utterly separated me from his people: neither let the eunuch say, Behold, I *am* a dry tree.

4 For thus saith the LORD unto the eunuchs that keep my sabbaths, and choose *the things* that please me, and take hold of my covenant;

5 Even unto them will I give in mine house and within my walls a place and a name better than of sons and of daughters: I will give them an everlasting name, that shall not be cut off.

6 Also the sons of the stranger, that join themselves to the LORD, to serve him, and to love the name of the LORD, to be his servants, every one that keepeth the sabbath from polluting it, and taketh hold of my covenant;

7 Even them will I bring to my holy mountain, and make them joyful in my house of prayer: their burnt offerings and their sacrifices *shall be* accepted upon mine altar; for mine house shall be called an house of prayer for all people.

8 The Lord GOD which gathereth the outcasts of Israel saith, Yet will I gather *others* to him, beside those that are gathered unto him.

9 All ye beasts of the field, come to devour, *yea*, all ye beasts in the forest.

10 His watchmen *are* blind: they are all ignorant, they *are* all dumb dogs, they cannot bark; sleeping, lying down, loving to slumber.

11 Yea, *they are* greedy dogs *which* can never have enough, and they *are* shepherds *that* cannot understand: they all look to their own way, every one for his gain, from his quarter.

12 Come ye, *say they*, I will fetch wine, and we will fill ourselves with strong drink; and to morrow shall be as this day, *and* much more abundant.

57 The righteous perisheth, and no man layeth *it* to heart: and merciful men *are* taken away, none considering that the righteous is taken away from the evil *to come*.

2 He shall enter into peace: they shall rest in their beds, *each one* walking *in* his uprightness.

3 But draw near hither, ye sons of the sorceress, the seed of the adulterer and the whore.

4 Against whom do ye sport yourselves? against whom make ye a wide mouth, *and* draw out the tongue? *are* ye not children of transgression, a seed of falsehood,

5 Enflaming yourselves with idols under every green tree, slaying the children in the valleys under the clifts of the rocks?

6 Among the smooth *stones* of the stream *is* thy portion; they, they *are* thy lot: even to them hast thou poured a drink offering, thou hast offered a meat offering. Should I receive comfort in these?

7 Upon a lofty and high mountain hast thou set thy bed: even thither wentest thou up to offer sacrifice.

8 Behind the doors also and the posts hast thou set up thy remembrance: for thou hast discovered *thyself to another* than me, and art gone up; thou hast enlarged thy bed, and made thee *a covenant* with them; thou lovedst their bed where thou sawest *it*.

9 And thou wentest to the king with ointment, and didst increase thy perfumes, and didst send thy messengers far off, and didst debase *thyself even* unto hell.

10 Thou art wearied in the greatness of thy way; *yet* saidst thou not, There is no hope: thou hast found the life of thine hand; therefore thou wast not grieved.

11 And of whom hast thou been afraid or feared, that thou hast lied, and hast not remembered me, nor laid *it* to thy heart? have not I held my peace even of old, and thou fearest me not?

12 I will declare thy righteousness, and thy works; for they shall not profit thee.

13 When thou criest, let thy companies deliver thee; but the wind shall carry them all away; vanity shall take *them*: but he that putteth his trust in me shall possess the land, and shall inherit my holy mountain;

14 And shall say, Cast ye up, cast ye up, prepare the way, take up the stumblingblock out of the way of my people.

15 For thus saith the high and lofty One that inhabiteth eternity, whose name *is* Holy; I dwell in the high and holy *place*, with him also *that is* of a contrite and humble spirit, to revive the spirit of the humble, and to revive the heart of the contrite ones.

16 For I will not contend for ever, neither will I be always wroth: for the spirit should fail before me, and the souls *which* I have made.

17 For the iniquity of his covetousness was I wroth, and smote him: I hid me, and was wroth, and he went on frowardly in the way of his heart.

18 I have seen his ways, and will heal him: I will lead him also, and restore comforts unto him and to his mourners.

19 I create the fruit of the lips; Peace, peace to *him that is* far off, and to *him that is* near, saith the Lord; and I will heal him.

20 But the wicked *are* like the troubled sea, when it cannot rest, whose waters cast up mire and dirt.

21 *There is* no peace, saith my God, to the wicked.

58 Cry aloud, spare not, lift up thy voice like a trumpet, and shew my people their transgression, and the house of Jacob their sins.

2 Yet they seek me daily, and delight to know my ways, as a nation that did righteousness, and forsook not the ordinance of their God: they ask of me the ordinances of justice; they take delight in approaching to God.

3 Wherefore have we fasted, *say they*, and thou seest not? *wherefore* have we afflicted our soul, and thou takest no knowledge? Behold, in the day of your fast ye find pleasure, and exact all your labours.

4 Behold, ye fast for strife and debate, and to smite with the fist of wickedness: ye shall not fast as *ye do this* day, to make your voice to be heard on high.

5 Is it such a fast that I have chosen? a day for a man to afflict his soul? *is it* to bow down his head as a bulrush, and to spread sackcloth and ashes *under him*? wilt thou call this a fast, and an acceptable day to the LORD?

6 *Is* not this the fast that I have chosen? to loose the bands of wickedness, to undo the heavy burdens, and to let the oppressed go free, and that ye break every yoke?

7 *Is it* not to deal thy bread to the hungry, and that thou bring the poor that are cast out to thy house? when thou seest the naked, that thou cover him; and that thou hide not thyself from thine own flesh?

8 Then shall thy light break forth as the morning, and thine health shall spring forth speedily: and thy righteousness shall go before thee; the glory of the LORD shall be thy rereward.

9 Then shalt thou call, and the LORD shall answer; thou shalt cry, and he shall say, Here I *am*. If thou take away from the midst of thee the yoke, the putting forth of the finger, and speaking vanity;

10 And *if* thou draw out thy soul to the hungry, and satisfy the afflicted soul; then shall thy light rise in obscurity, and thy darkness *be* as the noonday:

11 And the LORD shall guide thee continually, and satisfy thy soul in drought, and make fat thy bones: and thou shalt be like a watered garden, and like a spring of water, whose waters fail not.

12 And *they that shall be* of thee shall build the old waste places: thou shalt raise up the foundations of many generations; and thou shalt be called, The repairer of the breach, The restorer of paths to dwell in.

13 If thou turn away thy foot from the sabbath, *from* doing thy pleasure on my holy day; and call the sabbath a delight, the holy of the LORD, honourable; and shalt honour him, not doing thine own ways, nor finding thine own pleasure, nor speaking *thine own* words:

14 Then shalt thou delight thyself in the LORD; and I will cause thee to ride upon the high places of the earth, and feed thee with the heritage of Jacob thy father: for the mouth of the LORD hath spoken *it*.

59 Behold, the LORD's hand is not shortened, that it cannot save; neither his ear heavy, that it cannot hear:

2 But your iniquities have separated between you and your God, and your sins have hid *his* face from you, that he will not hear.

3 For your hands are defiled with blood, and your fingers with iniquity; your lips have spoken lies, your tongue hath muttered perverseness.

4 None calleth for justice, nor *any* pleadeth for truth: they trust in vanity, and speak lies; they conceive mischief, and bring forth iniquity.

5 They hatch cockatrice' eggs, and weave the spider's web: he that eateth of their eggs dieth, and that which is crushed breaketh out into a viper.

6 Their webs shall not become garments, neither shall they cover themselves with their works: their works *are* works of iniquity, and the act of violence *is* in their hands.

7 Their feet run to evil, and they make haste to shed innocent blood: their thoughts *are* thoughts of iniquity; wasting and destruction *are* in their paths.

8 The way of peace they know not; and *there is* no judgment in their goings: they have made them crooked paths: whosoever goeth therein shall not know peace.

9 Therefore is judgment far from us, neither doth justice overtake us: we wait for light, but behold obscurity; for brightness, *but* we walk in darkness.

10 We grope for the wall like the blind, and we grope as if *we had* no eyes: we stumble at noonday as in the night; *we are* in desolate places as dead *men*.

11 We roar all like bears, and mourn sore like doves: we look for judgment, but *there is* none; for salvation, *but* it is far off from us.

12 For our transgressions are multiplied before thee, and our sins testify against us: for our transgressions *are* with us; and *as for* our iniquities, we know them;

13 In transgressing and lying against the LORD, and departing away from our God, speaking oppression and revolt, conceiving and uttering from the heart words of falsehood.

14 And judgment is turned away backward, and justice standeth afar off: for truth is fallen in the street, and equity cannot enter.

15 Yea, truth faileth; and he *that* departeth from evil maketh himself a prey: and the LORD saw *it*, and it displeased him that *there was* no judgment.

16 And he saw that *there was* no man, and wondered that *there was* no intercessor: therefore his arm brought salvation unto him; and his righteousness, it sustained him.

17 For he put on righteousness as a breastplate, and an helmet of salvation upon his head; and he put on the garments of vengeance *for* clothing, and was clad with zeal as a cloke.

18 According to *their* deeds, accordingly he will repay, fury to his adversaries, recompence to his enemies; to the islands he will repay recompence.

19 So shall they fear the name of the LORD from the west, and his glory from the rising of the sun. When the enemy shall come in like a flood, the Spirit of the LORD shall lift up a standard against him.

20 And the Redeemer shall come to Zion, and unto them that turn from transgression in Jacob, saith the LORD.

21 As for me, this *is* my covenant with them, saith the LORD; My spirit that *is*

upon thee, and my words which I have
put in thy mouth, shall not depart out
of thy mouth, nor out of the mouth of
thy seed, nor out of the mouth of thy
seed's seed, saith the LORD, from henceforth and for ever.

60 Arise, shine; for thy light is come,
and the glory of the LORD is risen
upon thee.
2 For, behold, the darkness shall cover
the earth, and gross darkness the people: but the LORD shall arise upon thee,
and his glory shall be seen upon thee.
3 And the Gentiles shall come to thy
light, and kings to the brightness of thy
rising.
4 Lift up thine eyes round about, and
see: all they gather themselves together, they come to thee: thy sons shall
come from far, and thy daughters shall
be nursed at *thy* side.
5 Then thou shalt see, and flow
together, and thine heart shall fear, and
be enlarged; because the abundance of
the sea shall be converted unto thee,
the forces of the Gentiles shall come
unto thee.
6 The multitude of camels shall cover
thee, the dromedaries of Midian and
Ephah; all they from Sheba shall come:
they shall bring gold and incense; and
they shall shew forth the praises of the
LORD.
7 All the flocks of Kedar shall be
gathered together unto thee, the rams
of Nebaioth shall minister unto thee:
they shall come up with acceptance on
mine altar, and I will glorify the house
of my glory.
8 Who *are* these *that* fly as a cloud,
and as the doves to their windows?
9 Surely the isles shall wait for me,
and the ships of Tarshish first, to bring
thy sons from far, their silver and their
gold with them, unto the name of the
LORD thy God, and to the Holy One of
Israel, because he hath glorified thee.
10 And the sons of strangers shall
build up thy walls, and their kings shall
minister unto thee: for in my wrath I
smote thee, but in my favour have I had
mercy on thee.
11 Therefore thy gates shall be open
continually; they shall not be shut day
nor night; that *men* may bring unto
thee the forces of the Gentiles, and *that*
their kings *may be* brought.
12 For the nation and kingdom that
will not serve thee shall perish; yea,
those nations shall be utterly wasted.
13 The glory of Lebanon shall come
unto thee, the fir tree, the pine tree,
and the box together, to beautify the
place of my sanctuary; and I will make
the place of my feet glorious.
14 The sons also of them that afflicted thee shall come bending unto thee;
and all they that despised thee shall
bow themselves down at the soles of
thy feet; and they shall call thee, The
city of the LORD, The Zion of the Holy
One of Israel.
15 Whereas thou hast been forsaken
and hated, so that no man went through
thee, I will make thee an eternal excellency, a joy of many generations.
16 Thou shalt also suck the milk of
the Gentiles, and shalt suck the breast
of kings: and thou shalt know that I the
LORD *am* thy Saviour and thy Redeemer,
the mighty One of Jacob.
17 For brass I will bring gold, and for
iron I will bring silver, and for wood
brass, and for stones iron: I will also
make thy officers peace, and thine
exactors righteousness.
18 Violence shall no more be heard in
thy land, wasting nor destruction with-

in thy borders; but thou shalt call thy
walls Salvation, and thy gates Praise.
19 The sun shall be no more thy light
by day; neither for brightness shall the
moon give light unto thee: but the LORD
shall be unto thee an everlasting light,
and thy God thy glory.
20 Thy sun shall no more go down;
neither shall thy moon withdraw itself:
for the LORD shall be thine everlasting
light, and the days of thy mourning
shall be ended.
21 Thy people also *shall be* all righteous: they shall inherit the land for
ever, the branch of my planting, the
work of my hands, that I may be glorified.
22 A little one shall become a thousand, and a small one a strong nation: I
the LORD will hasten it in his time.

61 The Spirit of the Lord GOD *is*
upon me; because the LORD hath
anointed me to preach good tidings
unto the meek; he hath sent me to bind
up the brokenhearted, to proclaim liberty to the captives, and the opening of
the prison to *them that are* bound;
2 To proclaim the acceptable year of
the LORD, and the day of vengeance of
our God; to comfort all that mourn;
3 To appoint unto them that mourn in
Zion, to give unto them beauty for
ashes, the oil of joy for mourning, the
garment of praise for the spirit of
heaviness; that they might be called
trees of righteousness, the planting of
the LORD, that he might be glorified.
4 And they shall build the old wastes,
they shall raise up the former desolations, and they shall repair the waste
cities, the desolations of many generations.
5 And strangers shall stand and feed
your flocks, and the sons of the alien
shall be your plowmen and your vinedressers.
6 But ye shall be named the Priests of
the LORD: *men* shall call you the
Ministers of our God: ye shall eat the
riches of the Gentiles, and in their glory
shall ye boast yourselves.
7 For your shame *ye shall have* double; and *for* confusion they shall rejoice
in their portion: therefore in their land
they shall possess the double: everlasting joy shall be unto them.
8 For I the LORD love judgment, I hate
robbery for burnt offering; and I will
direct their work in truth, and I will
make an everlasting covenant with
them.
9 And their seed shall be known
among the Gentiles, and their offspring
among the people: all that see them
shall acknowledge them, that they *are*
the seed *which* the LORD hath blessed.
10 I will greatly rejoice in the LORD,
my soul shall be joyful in my God; for
he hath clothed me with the garments
of salvation, he hath covered me with
the robe of righteousness, as a bridegroom decketh *himself* with ornaments, and as a bride adorneth *herself*
with her jewels.
11 For as the earth bringeth forth her
bud, and as the garden causeth the
things that are sown in it to spring
forth; so the Lord GOD will cause righteousness and praise to spring forth
before all the nations.

62 For Zion's sake will I not hold my
peace, and for Jerusalem's sake I
will not rest, until the righteousness
thereof go forth as brightness, and the
salvation thereof as a lamp *that* burneth.

2 And the Gentiles shall see thy righteousness, and all kings thy glory: and thou shalt be called by a new name, which the mouth of the LORD shall name.

3 Thou shalt also be a crown of glory in the hand of the LORD, and a royal diadem in the hand of thy God.

4 Thou shalt no more be termed Forsaken; neither shall thy land any more be termed Desolate: but thou shalt be called Hephzi-bah, and thy land Beulah: for the LORD delighteth in thee, and thy land shall be married.

5 For *as* a young man marrieth a virgin, *so* shall thy sons marry thee: and *as* the bridegroom rejoiceth over the bride, *so* shall thy God rejoice over thee.

6 I have set watchmen upon thy walls, O Jerusalem, *which* shall never hold their peace day nor night: ye that make mention of the LORD, keep not silence,

7 And give him no rest, till he establish, and till he make Jerusalem a praise in the earth.

8 The LORD hath sworn by his right hand, and by the arm of his strength, Surely I will no more give thy corn *to be* meat for thine enemies; and the sons of the stranger shall not drink thy wine, for the which thou hast laboured:

9 But they that have gathered it shall eat it, and praise the LORD; and they that have brought it together shall drink it in the courts of my holiness.

10 Go through, go through the gates; prepare ye the way of the people; cast up, cast up the highway; gather out the stones; lift up a standard for the people.

11 Behold, the LORD hath proclaimed unto the end of the world, Say ye to the daughter of Zion, Behold, thy salvation cometh; behold, his reward *is* with him, and his work before him.

12 And they shall call them, The holy people, The redeemed of the LORD: and thou shalt be called, Sought out, A city not forsaken.

63 Who *is* this that cometh from Edom, with dyed garments from Bozrah? this *that is* glorious in his apparel, travelling in the greatness of his strength? I that speak in righteousness, mighty to save.

2 Wherefore *art thou* red in thine apparel, and thy garments like him that treadeth in the winefat?

3 I have trodden the winepress alone; and of the people *there was* none with me: for I will tread them in mine anger, and trample them in my fury; and their blood shall be sprinkled upon my garments, and I will stain all my raiment.

4 For the day of vengeance *is* in mine heart, and the year of my redeemed is come.

5 And I looked, and *there was* none to help; and I wondered that *there was* none to uphold: therefore mine own arm brought salvation unto me; and my fury, it upheld me.

6 And I will tread down the people in mine anger, and make them drunk in my fury, and I will bring down their strength to the earth.

7 I will mention the lovingkindnesses of the LORD, *and* the praises of the LORD, according to all that the LORD hath bestowed on us, and the great goodness toward the house of Israel, which he hath bestowed on them according to his mercies, and according to the multitude of his lovingkindnesses.

8 For he said, Surely they *are* my people, children *that* will not lie: so he was their Saviour.

9 In all their affliction he was afflicted, and the angel of his presence saved them: in his love and in his pity he redeemed them; and he bare them, and carried them all the days of old.

10 But they rebelled, and vexed his holy Spirit: therefore he was turned to be their enemy, *and* he fought against them.

11 Then he remembered the days of old, Moses, *and* his people, *saying*, Where *is* he that brought them up out of the sea with the shepherd of his flock? where *is* he that put his holy Spirit within him?

12 That led *them* by the right hand of Moses with his glorious arm, dividing the water before them, to make himself an everlasting name?

13 That led them through the deep, as an horse in the wilderness, *that* they should not stumble?

14 As a beast goeth down into the valley, the Spirit of the LORD caused him to rest: so didst thou lead thy people, to make thyself a glorious name.

15 Look down from heaven, and behold from the habitation of thy holiness and of thy glory: where *is* thy zeal and thy strength, the sounding of thy bowels and of thy mercies toward me? are they restrained?

16 Doubtless thou *art* our father, though Abraham be ignorant of us, and Israel acknowledge us not: thou, O LORD, *art* our father, our redeemer; thy name *is* from everlasting.

17 O LORD, why hast thou made us to err from thy ways, *and* hardened our heart from thy fear? Return for thy servants' sake, the tribes of thine inheritance.

18 The people of thy holiness have possessed *it* but a little while: our adversaries have trodden down thy sanctuary.

19 We are *thine*: thou never barest rule over them; they were not called by thy name.

64 Oh that thou wouldest rend the heavens, that thou wouldest come down, that the mountains might flow down at thy presence,

2 As *when* the melting fire burneth, the fire causeth the waters to boil, to make thy name known to thine adversaries, *that* the nations may tremble at thy presence!

3 When thou didst terrible things *which* we looked not for, thou camest down, the mountains flowed down at thy presence.

4 For since the beginning of the world *men* have not heard, nor perceived by the ear, neither hath the eye seen, O God, beside thee, *what* he hath prepared for him that waiteth for him.

5 Thou meetest him that rejoiceth and worketh righteousness, *those that* remember thee in thy ways: behold, thou art wroth; for we have sinned: in those is continuance, and we shall be saved.

6 But we are all as an unclean *thing*, and all our righteousnesses *are* as filthy rags; and we all do fade as a leaf; and our iniquities, like the wind, have taken us away.

7 And *there is* none that calleth upon thy name, that stirreth up himself to take hold of thee: for thou hast hid thy face from us, and hast consumed us, because of our iniquities.

8 But now, O LORD, thou *art* our father; we *are* the clay, and thou our potter; and we all *are* the work of thy hand.

9 Be not wroth very sore, O LORD, neither remember iniquity for ever: behold, see, we beseech thee, we *are* all thy people.

10 Thy holy cities are a wilderness, Zion is a wilderness, Jerusalem a desolation.

11 Our holy and our beautiful house, where our fathers praised thee, is burned up with fire: and all our pleasant things are laid waste.

12 Wilt thou refrain thyself for these *things*, O LORD? wilt thou hold thy peace, and afflict us very sore?

65 I am sought of *them that* asked not *for me*; I am found of *them that* sought me not: I said, Behold me, behold me, unto a nation *that* was not called by my name.

2 I have spread out my hands all the day unto a rebellious people, which walketh in a way *that was* not good, after their own thoughts;

3 A people that provoketh me to anger continually to my face; that sacrificeth in gardens, and burneth incense upon altars of brick;

4 Which remain among the graves, and lodge in the monuments, which eat swine's flesh, and broth of abominable *things is in* their vessels;

5 Which say, Stand by thyself, come not near to me; for I am holier than thou. These *are* a smoke in my nose, a fire that burneth all the day.

6 Behold, *it is* written before me: I will not keep silence, but will recompense, even recompense into their bosom,

7 Your iniquities, and the iniquities of your fathers together, saith the LORD, which have burned incense upon the mountains, and blasphemed me upon the hills: therefore will I measure their former work into their bosom.

8 Thus saith the LORD, As the new wine is found in the cluster, and *one* saith, Destroy it not; for a blessing *is* in it: so will I do for my servants' sakes, that I may not destroy them all.

9 And I will bring forth a seed out of Jacob, and out of Judah an inheritor of my mountains: and mine elect shall inherit it, and my servants shall dwell there.

10 And Sharon shall be a fold of flocks, and the valley of Achor a place for the herds to lie down in, for my people that have sought me.

11 But ye *are* they that forsake the LORD, that forget my holy mountain, that prepare a table for that troop, and that furnish the drink offering unto that number.

12 Therefore will I number you to the sword, and ye shall all bow down to the slaughter: because when I called, ye did not answer; when I spake, ye did not hear; but did evil before mine eyes, and did choose *that* wherein I delighted not.

13 Therefore thus saith the Lord GOD, Behold, my servants shall eat, but ye shall be hungry: behold, my servants shall drink, but ye shall be thirsty: behold, my servants shall rejoice, but ye shall be ashamed:

14 Behold, my servants shall sing for joy of heart, but ye shall cry for sorrow of heart, and shall howl for vexation of spirit.

15 And ye shall leave your name for a
curse unto my chosen: for the Lord GOD
shall slay thee, and call his servants by
another name:
16 That he who blesseth himself in
the earth shall bless himself in the God
of truth; and he that sweareth in the
earth shall swear by the God of truth;
because the former troubles are forgotten, and because they are hid from
mine eyes.
17 For, behold, I create new heavens
and a new earth: and the former shall
not be remembered, nor come into
mind.
18 But be ye glad and rejoice for ever
in that which I create: for, behold, I create Jerusalem a rejoicing, and her
people a joy.
19 And I will rejoice in Jerusalem,
and joy in my people: and the voice of
weeping shall be no more heard in her,
nor the voice of crying.
20 There shall be no more thence an
infant of days, nor an old man that hath
not filled his days: for the child shall
die an hundred years old; but the sinner *being* an hundred years old shall be
accursed.
21 And they shall build houses, and
inhabit *them*; and they shall plant vineyards, and eat the fruit of them.
22 They shall not build, and another
inhabit; they shall not plant, and another eat: for as the days of a tree *are* the
days of my people, and mine elect shall
long enjoy the work of their hands.
23 They shall not labour in vain, nor
bring forth for trouble; for they *are* the
seed of the blessed of the LORD, and
their offspring with them.
24 And it shall come to pass, that
before they call, I will answer; and
while they are yet speaking, I will hear.
25 The wolf and the lamb shall feed
together, and the lion shall eat straw
like the bullock: and dust *shall be* the
serpent's meat. They shall not hurt nor
destroy in all my holy mountain, saith
the LORD.

66 Thus saith the LORD, The heaven
is my throne, and the earth *is* my
footstool: where *is* the house that ye
build unto me? and where *is* the place
of my rest?
2 For all those *things* hath mine hand
made, and all those *things* have been,
saith the LORD: but to this *man* will I
look, *even* to *him that is* poor and of a
contrite spirit, and trembleth at my
word.
3 He that killeth an ox *is as if* he slew
a man; he that sacrificeth a lamb, *as if*
he cut off a dog's neck; he that offereth
an oblation, *as if he offered* swine's
blood; he that burneth incense, *as if* he
blessed an idol. Yea, they have chosen
their own ways, and their soul delighteth in their abominations.
4 I also will choose their delusions,
and will bring their fears upon them;
because when I called, none did
answer; when I spake, they did not
hear: but they did evil before mine
eyes, and chose *that* in which I delighted not.
5 Hear the word of the LORD, ye that
tremble at his word; Your brethren that
hated you, that cast you out for my
name's sake, said, Let the LORD be glorified: but he shall appear to your joy,
and they shall be ashamed.
6 A voice of noise from the city, a
voice from the temple, a voice of the
LORD that rendereth recompence to his
enemies.

7 Before she travailed, she brought
forth; before her pain came, she was
delivered of a man child.
8 Who hath heard such a thing? who
hath seen such things? Shall the earth
be made to bring forth in one day? *or*
shall a nation be born at once? for as
soon as Zion travailed, she brought
forth her children.
9 Shall I bring to the birth, and not
cause to bring forth? saith the LORD:
shall I cause to bring forth, and shut *the*
womb? saith thy God.
10 Rejoice ye with Jerusalem, and be
glad with her, all ye that love her:
rejoice for joy with her, all ye that
mourn for her:
11 That ye may suck, and be satisfied
with the breasts of her consolations;
that ye may milk out, and be delighted
with the abundance of her glory.
12 For thus saith the LORD, Behold, I
will extend peace to her like a river,
and the glory of the Gentiles like a
flowing stream: then shall ye suck, ye
shall be borne upon *her* sides, and be
dandled upon *her* knees.
13 As one whom his mother comforteth, so will I comfort you; and ye shall
be comforted in Jerusalem.
14 And when ye see *this*, your heart
shall rejoice, and your bones shall
flourish like an herb: and the hand of
the LORD shall be known toward his
servants, and *his* indignation toward
his enemies.
15 For, behold, the LORD will come
with fire, and with his chariots like a
whirlwind, to render his anger with
fury, and his rebuke with flames of fire.
16 For by fire and by his sword will
the LORD plead with all flesh: and the
slain of the LORD shall be many.
17 They that sanctify themselves, and
purify themselves in the gardens
behind one *tree* in the midst, eating
swine's flesh, and the abomination, and
the mouse, shall be consumed together,
saith the LORD.
18 For I *know* their works and their
thoughts: it shall come, that I will
gather all nations and tongues; and
they shall come, and see my glory.
19 And I will set a sign among them,
and I will send those that escape of
them unto the nations, *to* Tarshish, Pul,
and Lud, that draw the bow, *to* Tubal,
and Javan, *to* the isles afar off, that
have not heard my fame, neither have
seen my glory; and they shall declare
my glory among the Gentiles.
20 And they shall bring all your brethren *for* an offering unto the LORD out of
all nations upon horses, and in chariots,
and in litters, and upon mules, and
upon swift beasts, to my holy mountain
Jerusalem, saith the LORD, as the children of Israel bring an offering in a
clean vessel into the house of the LORD.
21 And I will also take of them for
priests *and* for Levites, saith the LORD.
22 For as the new heavens and the
new earth, which I will make, shall
remain before me, saith the LORD, so
shall your seed and your name remain.
23 And it shall come to pass, *that*
from one new moon to another, and
from one sabbath to another, shall all
flesh come to worship before me, saith
the LORD.
24 And they shall go forth, and look
upon the carcases of the men that have
transgressed against me: for their
worm shall not die, neither shall their
fire be quenched; and they shall be an
abhorring unto all flesh.

THE BOOK OF THE PROPHET
JEREMIAH

1 The words of Jeremiah the son of
Hilkiah, of the priests that *were* in
Anathoth in the land of Benjamin:
2 To whom the word of the LORD came
in the days of Josiah the son of Amon
king of Judah, in the thirteenth year of
his reign.
3 It came also in the days of Jehoiakim
the son of Josiah king of Judah, unto
the end of the eleventh year of
Zedekiah the son of Josiah king of
Judah, unto the carrying away of
Jerusalem captive in the fifth month.
4 Then the word of the LORD came
unto me, saying,
5 Before I formed thee in the belly I
knew thee; and before thou camest
forth out of the womb I sanctified thee,
and I ordained thee a prophet unto the
nations.
6 Then said I, Ah, Lord GOD! behold, I
cannot speak: for I *am* a child.
7 But the LORD said unto me, Say not,
I *am* a child: for thou shalt go to all that
I shall send thee, and whatsoever I command thee thou shalt speak.
8 Be not afraid of their faces: for I *am*
with thee to deliver thee, saith the
LORD.
9 Then the LORD put forth his hand,
and touched my mouth. And the LORD
said unto me, Behold, I have put my
words in thy mouth.
10 See, I have this day set thee over
the nations and over the kingdoms, to
root out, and to pull down, and to
destroy, and to throw down, to build,
and to plant.
11 Moreover the word of the LORD
came unto me, saying, Jeremiah, what
seest thou? And I said, I see a rod of an
almond tree.
12 Then said the LORD unto me, Thou
hast well seen: for I will hasten my
word to perform it.
13 And the word of the LORD came
unto me the second time, saying, What
seest thou? And I said, I see a seething
pot; and the face thereof *is* toward the
north.
14 Then the LORD said unto me, Out
of the north an evil shall break forth
upon all the inhabitants of the land.
15 For, lo, I will call all the families of
the kingdoms of the north, saith the
LORD; and they shall come, and they
shall set every one his throne at the
entering of the gates of Jerusalem, and
against all the walls thereof round
about, and against all the cities of
Judah.
16 And I will utter my judgments
against them touching all their wickedness, who have forsaken me, and have
burned incense unto other gods, and
worshipped the works of their own
hands.
17 Thou therefore gird up thy loins,
and arise, and speak unto them all that
I command thee: be not dismayed at
their faces, lest I confound thee before
them.
18 For, behold, I have made thee this
day a defenced city, and an iron pillar,
and brasen walls against the whole
land, against the kings of Judah,
against the princes thereof, against the
priests thereof, and against the people
of the land.

19 And they shall fight against thee; but they shall not prevail against thee; for I *am* with thee, saith the LORD, to deliver thee.

2 Moreover the word of the LORD came to me, saying,

2 Go and cry in the ears of Jerusalem, saying, Thus saith the LORD; I remember thee, the kindness of thy youth, the love of thine espousals, when thou wentest after me in the wilderness, in a land *that was* not sown.

3 Israel *was* holiness unto the LORD, *and* the firstfruits of his increase: all that devour him shall offend; evil shall come upon them, saith the LORD.

4 Hear ye the word of the LORD, O house of Jacob, and all the families of the house of Israel:

5 Thus saith the LORD, What iniquity have your fathers found in me, that they are gone far from me, and have walked after vanity, and are become vain?

6 Neither said they, Where *is* the LORD that brought us up out of the land of Egypt, that led us through the wilderness, through a land of deserts and of pits, through a land of drought, and of the shadow of death, through a land that no man passed through, and where no man dwelt?

7 And I brought you into a plentiful country, to eat the fruit thereof and the goodness thereof; but when ye entered, ye defiled my land, and made mine heritage an abomination.

8 The priests said not, Where *is* the LORD? and they that handle the law knew me not: the pastors also transgressed against me, and the prophets prophesied by Baal, and walked after *things that* do not profit.

9 Wherefore I will yet plead with you, saith the LORD, and with your children's children will I plead.

10 For pass over the isles of Chittim, and see; and send unto Kedar, and consider diligently, and see if there be such a thing.

11 Hath a nation changed *their* gods, which *are* yet no gods? but my people have changed their glory for *that which* doth not profit.

12 Be astonished, O ye heavens, at this, and be horribly afraid, be ye very desolate, saith the LORD.

13 For my people have committed two evils; they have forsaken me the fountain of living waters, *and* hewed them out cisterns, broken cisterns, that can hold no water.

14 *Is* Israel a servant? *is* he a homeborn *slave*? why is he spoiled?

15 The young lions roared upon him, *and* yelled, and they made his land waste: his cities are burned without inhabitant.

16 Also the children of Noph and Tahapanes have broken the crown of thy head.

17 Hast thou not procured this unto thyself, in that thou hast forsaken the LORD thy God, when he led thee by the way?

18 And now what hast thou to do in the way of Egypt, to drink the waters of Sihor? or what hast thou to do in the way of Assyria, to drink the waters of the river?

19 Thine own wickedness shall correct thee, and thy backslidings shall reprove thee: know therefore and see that *it is* an evil *thing* and bitter, that thou hast forsaken the LORD thy God, and that my fear *is* not in thee, saith the Lord GOD of hosts.

20 For of old time I have broken thy
yoke, *and* burst thy bands; and thou
saidst, I will not transgress; when upon
every high hill and under every green
tree thou wanderest, playing the harlot.
21 Yet I had planted thee a noble
vine, wholly a right seed: how then art
thou turned into the degenerate plant
of a strange vine unto me?
22 For though thou wash thee with
nitre, and take thee much soap, *yet*
thine iniquity is marked before me,
saith the Lord GOD.
23 How canst thou say, I am not polluted, I have not gone after Baalim? see
thy way in the valley, know what thou
hast done: *thou art* a swift dromedary
traversing her ways;
24 A wild ass used to the wilderness,
that snuffeth up the wind at her pleasure; in her occasion who can turn her
away? all they that seek her will not
weary themselves; in her month they
shall find her.
25 Withhold thy foot from being
unshod, and thy throat from thirst: but
thou saidst, There is no hope: no; for I
have loved strangers, and after them
will I go.
26 As the thief is ashamed when he is
found, so is the house of Israel ashamed;
they, their kings, their princes, and
their priests, and their prophets,
27 Saying to a stock, Thou *art* my
father; and to a stone, Thou hast
brought me forth: for they have turned
their back unto me, and not *their* face:
but in the time of their trouble they
will say, Arise, and save us.
28 But where *are* thy gods that thou
hast made thee? let them arise, if they
can save thee in the time of thy trouble:
for *according to* the number of thy cities are thy gods, O Judah.
29 Wherefore will ye plead with me?
ye all have transgressed against me,
saith the LORD.
30 In vain have I smitten your children; they received no correction: your
own sword hath devoured your prophets, like a destroying lion.
31 O generation, see ye the word of
the LORD. Have I been a wilderness
unto Israel? a land of darkness? wherefore say my people, We are lords; we
will come no more unto thee?
32 Can a maid forget her ornaments,
or a bride her attire? yet my people
have forgotten me days without number.
33 Why trimmest thou thy way to
seek love? therefore hast thou also
taught the wicked ones thy ways.
34 Also in thy skirts is found the
blood of the souls of the poor innocents: I have not found it by secret
search, but upon all these.
35 Yet thou sayest, Because I am innocent, surely his anger shall turn from
me. Behold, I will plead with thee,
because thou sayest, I have not sinned.
36 Why gaddest thou about so much
to change thy way? thou also shalt be
ashamed of Egypt, as thou wast
ashamed of Assyria.
37 Yea, thou shalt go forth from him,
and thine hands upon thine head: for
the LORD hath rejected thy confidenc-
es, and thou shalt not prosper in them.

3 They say, If a man put away his wife,
and she go from him, and become
another man's, shall he return unto her
again? shall not that land be greatly
polluted? but thou hast played the
harlot with many lovers; yet return
again to me, saith the LORD.

2 Lift up thine eyes unto the high places, and see where thou hast not been lien with. In the ways hast thou sat for them, as the Arabian in the wilderness; and thou hast polluted the land with thy whoredoms and with thy wickedness.

3 Therefore the showers have been withholden, and there hath been no latter rain; and thou hadst a whore's forehead, thou refusedst to be ashamed.

4 Wilt thou not from this time cry unto me, My father, thou *art* the guide of my youth?

5 Will he reserve *his anger* for ever? will he keep *it* to the end? Behold, thou hast spoken and done evil things as thou couldest.

6 The LORD said also unto me in the days of Josiah the king, Hast thou seen *that* which backsliding Israel hath done? she is gone up upon every high mountain and under every green tree, and there hath played the harlot.

7 And I said after she had done all these *things*, Turn thou unto me. But she returned not. And her treacherous sister Judah saw *it*.

8 And I saw, when for all the causes whereby backsliding Israel committed adultery I had put her away, and given her a bill of divorce; yet her treacherous sister Judah feared not, but went and played the harlot also.

9 And it came to pass through the lightness of her whoredom, that she defiled the land, and committed adultery with stones and with stocks.

10 And yet for all this her treacherous sister Judah hath not turned unto me with her whole heart, but feignedly, saith the LORD.

11 And the LORD said unto me, The backsliding Israel hath justified herself more than treacherous Judah.

12 Go and proclaim these words toward the north, and say, Return, thou backsliding Israel, saith the LORD; *and* I will not cause mine anger to fall upon you: for I *am* merciful, saith the LORD, *and* I will not keep *anger* for ever.

13 Only acknowledge thine iniquity, that thou hast transgressed against the LORD thy God, and hast scattered thy ways to the strangers under every green tree, and ye have not obeyed my voice, saith the LORD.

14 Turn, O backsliding children, saith the LORD; for I am married unto you: and I will take you one of a city, and two of a family, and I will bring you to Zion:

15 And I will give you pastors according to mine heart, which shall feed you with knowledge and understanding.

16 And it shall come to pass, when ye be multiplied and increased in the land, in those days, saith the LORD, they shall say no more, The ark of the covenant of the LORD: neither shall it come to mind: neither shall they remember it; neither shall they visit *it*; neither shall *that* be done any more.

17 At that time they shall call Jerusalem the throne of the LORD; and all the nations shall be gathered unto it, to the name of the LORD, to Jerusalem: neither shall they walk any more after the imagination of their evil heart.

18 In those days the house of Judah shall walk with the house of Israel, and they shall come together out of the land of the north to the land that I have given for an inheritance unto your fathers.

19 But I said, How shall I put thee
among the children, and give thee a
pleasant land, a goodly heritage of the
hosts of nations? and I said, Thou shalt
call me, My father; and shalt not turn
away from me.
20 Surely *as* a wife treacherously
departeth from her husband, so have ye
dealt treacherously with me, O house of
Israel, saith the LORD.
21 A voice was heard upon the high
places, weeping *and* supplications of
the children of Israel: for they have
perverted their way, *and* they have forgotten the LORD their God.
22 Return, ye backsliding children,
and I will heal your backslidings.
Behold, we come unto thee; for thou *art*
the LORD our God.
23 Truly in vain *is salvation hoped for*
from the hills, *and from* the multitude
of mountains: truly in the LORD our God
is the salvation of Israel.
24 For shame hath devoured the
labour of our fathers from our youth;
their flocks and their herds, their sons
and their daughters.
25 We lie down in our shame, and our
confusion covereth us: for we have
sinned against the LORD our God, we
and our fathers, from our youth even
unto this day, and have not obeyed the
voice of the LORD our God.

4 If thou wilt return, O Israel, saith
the LORD, return unto me: and if
thou wilt put away thine abominations
out of my sight, then shalt thou not
remove.
2 And thou shalt swear, The LORD
liveth, in truth, in judgment, and in
righteousness; and the nations shall
bless themselves in him, and in him
shall they glory.
3 For thus saith the LORD to the men
of Judah and Jerusalem, Break up your
fallow ground, and sow not among
thorns.
4 Circumcise yourselves to the LORD,
and take away the foreskins of your
heart, ye men of Judah and inhabitants
of Jerusalem: lest my fury come forth
like fire, and burn that none can
quench *it*, because of the evil of your
doings.
5 Declare ye in Judah, and publish in
Jerusalem; and say, Blow ye the trumpet in the land: cry, gather together,
and say, Assemble yourselves, and let
us go into the defenced cities.
6 Set up the standard toward Zion:
retire, stay not: for I will bring evil from
the north, and a great destruction.
7 The lion is come up from his thicket,
and the destroyer of the Gentiles is on
his way; he is gone forth from his place
to make thy land desolate; *and* thy cities shall be laid waste, without an
inhabitant.
8 For this gird you with sackcloth,
lament and howl: for the fierce anger of
the LORD is not turned back from us.
9 And it shall come to pass at that day,
saith the LORD, *that* the heart of the
king shall perish, and the heart of the
princes; and the priests shall be astonished, and the prophets shall wonder.
10 Then said I, Ah, Lord GOD! surely
thou hast greatly deceived this people
and Jerusalem, saying, Ye shall have
peace; whereas the sword reacheth
unto the soul.
11 At that time shall it be said to this
people and to Jerusalem, A dry wind of
the high places in the wilderness
toward the daughter of my people, not
to fan, nor to cleanse,

12 *Even* a full wind from those *places* shall come unto me: now also will I give sentence against them.

13 Behold, he shall come up as clouds, and his chariots *shall be* as a whirlwind: his horses are swifter than eagles. Woe unto us! for we are spoiled.

14 O Jerusalem, wash thine heart from wickedness, that thou mayest be saved. How long shall thy vain thoughts lodge within thee?

15 For a voice declareth from Dan, and publisheth affliction from mount Ephraim.

16 Make ye mention to the nations; behold, publish against Jerusalem, *that* watchers come from a far country, and give out their voice against the cities of Judah.

17 As keepers of a field, are they against her round about; because she hath been rebellious against me, saith the LORD.

18 Thy way and thy doings have procured these *things* unto thee; this *is* thy wickedness, because it is bitter, because it reacheth unto thine heart.

19 My bowels, my bowels! I am pained at my very heart; my heart maketh a noise in me; I cannot hold my peace, because thou hast heard, O my soul, the sound of the trumpet, the alarm of war.

20 Destruction upon destruction is cried; for the whole land is spoiled: suddenly are my tents spoiled, *and* my curtains in a moment.

21 How long shall I see the standard, *and* hear the sound of the trumpet?

22 For my people *is* foolish, they have not known me; they *are* sottish children, and they have none understanding: they *are* wise to do evil, but to do good they have no knowledge.

23 I beheld the earth, and, lo, *it was* without form, and void; and the heavens, and they *had* no light.

24 I beheld the mountains, and, lo, they trembled, and all the hills moved lightly.

25 I beheld, and, lo, *there was* no man, and all the birds of the heavens were fled.

26 I beheld, and, lo, the fruitful place *was* a wilderness, and all the cities thereof were broken down at the presence of the LORD, *and* by his fierce anger.

27 For thus hath the LORD said, The whole land shall be desolate; yet will I not make a full end.

28 For this shall the earth mourn, and the heavens above be black: because I have spoken *it*, I have purposed *it*, and will not repent, neither will I turn back from it.

29 The whole city shall flee for the noise of the horsemen and bowmen; they shall go into thickets, and climb up upon the rocks: every city *shall be* forsaken, and not a man dwell therein.

30 And *when* thou *art* spoiled, what wilt thou do? Though thou clothest thyself with crimson, though thou deckest thee with ornaments of gold, though thou rentest thy face with painting, in vain shalt thou make thyself fair; *thy* lovers will despise thee, they will seek thy life.

31 For I have heard a voice as of a woman in travail, *and* the anguish as of her that bringeth forth her first child, the voice of the daughter of Zion, *that* bewaileth herself, *that* spreadeth her hands, *saying*, Woe *is* me now! for my soul is wearied because of murderers.

5 Run ye to and fro through the
streets of Jerusalem, and see now,
and know, and seek in the broad places
thereof, if ye can find a man, if there be
any that executeth judgment, that
seeketh the truth; and I will pardon it.
2 And though they say, The LORD
liveth; surely they swear falsely.
3 O LORD, *are* not thine eyes upon the
truth? thou hast stricken them, but
they have not grieved; thou hast consumed them, *but* they have refused to
receive correction: they have made
their faces harder than a rock; they
have refused to return.
4 Therefore I said, Surely these *are*
poor; they are foolish: for they know
not the way of the LORD, *nor* the judgment of their God.
5 I will get me unto the great men,
and will speak unto them; for they have
known the way of the LORD, *and* the
judgment of their God: but these have
altogether broken the yoke, *and* burst
the bonds.
6 Wherefore a lion out of the forest
shall slay them, *and* a wolf of the eve-
nings shall spoil them, a leopard shall
watch over their cities: every one that
goeth out thence shall be torn in pieces: because their transgressions are
many, *and* their backslidings are
increased.
7 How shall I pardon thee for this?
thy children have forsaken me, and
sworn by *them that are* no gods: when
I had fed them to the full, they then
committed adultery, and assembled
themselves by troops in the harlots'
houses.
8 They were *as* fed horses in the
morning: every one neighed after his
neighbour's wife.
9 Shall I not visit for these *things*?
saith the LORD: and shall not my soul be
avenged on such a nation as this?
10 Go ye up upon her walls, and
destroy; but make not a full end: take
away her battlements; for they *are* not
the LORD'S.
11 For the house of Israel and the
house of Judah have dealt very treacherously against me, saith the LORD.
12 They have belied the LORD, and
said, *It is* not he; neither shall evil come
upon us; neither shall we see sword nor
famine:
13 And the prophets shall become
wind, and the word *is* not in them: thus
shall it be done unto them.
14 Wherefore thus saith the LORD
God of hosts, Because ye speak this
word, behold, I will make my words in
thy mouth fire, and this people wood,
and it shall devour them.
15 Lo, I will bring a nation upon you
from far, O house of Israel, saith the
LORD: it *is* a mighty nation, it *is* an
ancient nation, a nation whose language thou knowest not, neither understandest what they say.
16 Their quiver *is* as an open sepulchre, they *are* all mighty men.
17 And they shall eat up thine harvest, and thy bread, *which* thy sons and
thy daughters should eat: they shall eat
up thy flocks and thine herds: they
shall eat up thy vines and thy fig trees:
they shall impoverish thy fenced cities,
wherein thou trustedst, with the sword.
18 Nevertheless in those days, saith
the LORD, I will not make a full end
with you.
19 And it shall come to pass, when ye
shall say, Wherefore doeth the LORD our
God all these *things* unto us? then shalt
thou answer them, Like as ye have

forsaken me, and served strange gods
in your land, so shall ye serve strangers
in a land *that is* not yours.
20 Declare this in the house of Jacob,
and publish it in Judah, saying,
21 Hear now this, O foolish people,
and without understanding; which
have eyes, and see not; which have ears,
and hear not:
22 Fear ye not me? saith the LORD:
will ye not tremble at my presence,
which have placed the sand *for* the
bound of the sea by a perpetual decree,
that it cannot pass it: and though the
waves thereof toss themselves, yet can
they not prevail; though they roar, yet
can they not pass over it?
23 But this people hath a revolting
and a rebellious heart; they are revolted and gone.
24 Neither say they in their heart, Let
us now fear the LORD our God, that
giveth rain, both the former and the
latter, in his season: he reserveth unto
us the appointed weeks of the harvest.
25 Your iniquities have turned away
these *things*, and your sins have withholden good *things* from you.
26 For among my people are found
wicked *men*: they lay wait, as he that
setteth snares; they set a trap, they
catch men.
27 As a cage is full of birds, so *are*
their houses full of deceit: therefore
they are become great, and waxen rich.
28 They are waxen fat, they shine:
yea, they overpass the deeds of the
wicked: they judge not the cause, the
cause of the fatherless, yet they prosper; and the right of the needy do they
not judge.
29 Shall I not visit for these *things*?
saith the LORD: shall not my soul be
avenged on such a nation as this?
30 A wonderful and horrible thing is
committed in the land;
31 The prophets prophesy falsely, and
the priests bear rule by their means;
and my people love *to have it* so: and
what will ye do in the end thereof?

6 O ye children of Benjamin, gather
yourselves to flee out of the midst
of Jerusalem, and blow the trumpet in
Tekoa, and set up a sign of fire in Beth-
haccerem: for evil appeareth out of the
north, and great destruction.
2 I have likened the daughter of Zion
to a comely and delicate *woman*.
3 The shepherds with their flocks
shall come unto her; they shall pitch
their tents against her round about;
they shall feed every one in his place.
4 Prepare ye war against her; arise,
and let us go up at noon. Woe unto us!
for the day goeth away, for the shadows
of the evening are stretched out.
5 Arise, and let us go by night, and let
us destroy her palaces.
6 For thus hath the LORD of hosts said,
Hew ye down trees, and cast a mount
against Jerusalem: this *is* the city to be
visited; she *is* wholly oppression in the
midst of her.
7 As a fountain casteth out her
waters, so she casteth out her wickedness: violence and spoil is heard in her;
before me continually *is* grief and
wounds.
8 Be thou instructed, O Jerusalem,
lest my soul depart from thee; lest I
make thee desolate, a land not inhabited.
9 Thus saith the LORD of hosts, They
shall throughly glean the remnant of
Israel as a vine: turn back thine hand as
a grapegatherer into the baskets.
10 To whom shall I speak, and give
warning, that they may hear? behold,

their ear *is* uncircumcised, and they
cannot hearken: behold, the word of
the LORD is unto them a reproach; they
have no delight in it.
11 Therefore I am full of the fury of
the LORD; I am weary with holding in: I
will pour it out upon the children
abroad, and upon the assembly of
young men together: for even the husband with the wife shall be taken, the
aged with *him that is* full of days.
12 And their houses shall be turned
unto others, *with their* fields and wives
together: for I will stretch out my hand
upon the inhabitants of the land, saith
the LORD.
13 For from the least of them even
unto the greatest of them every one *is*
given to covetousness; and from the
prophet even unto the priest every one
dealeth falsely.
14 They have healed also the hurt *of*
the daughter of my people slightly, saying, Peace, peace; when *there is* no
peace.
15 Were they ashamed when they had
committed abomination? nay, they
were not at all ashamed, neither could
they blush: therefore they shall fall
among them that fall: at the time *that* I
visit them they shall be cast down, saith
the LORD.
16 Thus saith the LORD, Stand ye in
the ways, and see, and ask for the old
paths, where *is* the good way, and walk
therein, and ye shall find rest for your
souls. But they said, We will not walk
therein.
17 Also I set watchmen over you, *say-*
ing, Hearken to the sound of the trumpet. But they said, We will not hearken.
18 Therefore hear, ye nations, and
know, O congregation, what *is* among
them.
19 Hear, O earth: behold, I will bring
evil upon this people, *even* the fruit of
their thoughts, because they have not
hearkened unto my words, nor to my
law, but rejected it.
20 To what purpose cometh there to
me incense from Sheba, and the sweet
cane from a far country? your burnt
offerings *are* not acceptable, nor your
sacrifices sweet unto me.
21 Therefore thus saith the LORD,
Behold, I will lay stumblingblocks
before this people, and the fathers and
the sons together shall fall upon them;
the neighbour and his friend shall perish.
22 Thus saith the LORD, Behold, a
people cometh from the north country,
and a great nation shall be raised from
the sides of the earth.
23 They shall lay hold on bow and
spear; they *are* cruel, and have no
mercy; their voice roareth like the sea;
and they ride upon horses, set in array
as men for war against thee, O daughter of Zion.
24 We have heard the fame thereof:
our hands wax feeble: anguish hath
taken hold of us, *and* pain, as of a
woman in travail.
25 Go not forth into the field, nor
walk by the way; for the sword of the
enemy *and* fear *is* on every side.
26 O daughter of my people, gird *thee*
with sackcloth, and wallow thyself in
ashes: make thee mourning, *as for* an
only son, most bitter lamentation: for
the spoiler shall suddenly come upon
us.
27 I have set thee *for* a tower *and* a
fortress among my people, that thou
mayest know and try their way.

28 They *are* all grievous revolters, walking with slanders: *they are* brass and iron; they *are* all corrupters.

29 The bellows are burned, the lead is consumed of the fire; the founder melteth in vain: for the wicked are not plucked away.

30 Reprobate silver shall *men* call them, because the LORD hath rejected them.

7 The word that came to Jeremiah from the LORD, saying,

2 Stand in the gate of the LORD's house, and proclaim there this word, and say, Hear the word of the LORD, all *ye of* Judah, that enter in at these gates to worship the LORD.

3 Thus saith the LORD of hosts, the God of Israel, Amend your ways and your doings, and I will cause you to dwell in this place.

4 Trust ye not in lying words, saying, The temple of the LORD, The temple of the LORD, The temple of the LORD, *are* these.

5 For if ye throughly amend your ways and your doings; if ye throughly execute judgment between a man and his neighbour;

6 *If* ye oppress not the stranger, the fatherless, and the widow, and shed not innocent blood in this place, neither walk after other gods to your hurt:

7 Then will I cause you to dwell in this place, in the land that I gave to your fathers, for ever and ever.

8 Behold, ye trust in lying words, that cannot profit.

9 Will ye steal, murder, and commit adultery, and swear falsely, and burn incense unto Baal, and walk after other gods whom ye know not;

10 And come and stand before me in this house, which is called by my name, and say, We are delivered to do all these abominations?

11 Is this house, which is called by my name, become a den of robbers in your eyes? Behold, even I have seen *it*, saith the LORD.

12 But go ye now unto my place which *was* in Shiloh, where I set my name at the first, and see what I did to it for the wickedness of my people Israel.

13 And now, because ye have done all these works, saith the LORD, and I spake unto you, rising up early and speaking, but ye heard not; and I called you, but ye answered not;

14 Therefore will I do unto *this* house, which is called by my name, wherein ye trust, and unto the place which I gave to you and to your fathers, as I have done to Shiloh.

15 And I will cast you out of my sight, as I have cast out all your brethren, *even* the whole seed of Ephraim.

16 Therefore pray not thou for this people, neither lift up cry nor prayer for them, neither make intercession to me: for I will not hear thee.

17 Seest thou not what they do in the cities of Judah and in the streets of Jerusalem?

18 The children gather wood, and the fathers kindle the fire, and the women knead *their* dough, to make cakes to the queen of heaven, and to pour out drink offerings unto other gods, that they may provoke me to anger.

19 Do they provoke me to anger? saith the LORD: *do they* not *provoke* themselves to the confusion of their own faces?

20 Therefore thus saith the Lord GOD; Behold, mine anger and my fury shall be poured out upon this place, upon man, and upon beast, and upon the

trees of the field, and upon the fruit of
the ground; and it shall burn, and shall
not be quenched.
21 Thus saith the LORD of hosts, the
God of Israel; Put your burnt offerings
unto your sacrifices, and eat flesh.
22 For I spake not unto your fathers,
nor commanded them in the day that I
brought them out of the land of Egypt,
concerning burnt offerings or sacrifices:
23 But this thing commanded I them,
saying, Obey my voice, and I will be
your God, and ye shall be my people:
and walk ye in all the ways that I have
commanded you, that it may be well
unto you.
24 But they hearkened not, nor
inclined their ear, but walked in the
counsels *and* in the imagination of
their evil heart, and went backward,
and not forward.
25 Since the day that your fathers
came forth out of the land of Egypt
unto this day I have even sent unto you
all my servants the prophets, daily rising up early and sending *them*:
26 Yet they hearkened not unto me,
nor inclined their ear, but hardened
their neck: they did worse than their
fathers.
27 Therefore thou shalt speak all
these words unto them; but they will
not hearken to thee: thou shalt also call
unto them; but they will not answer
thee.
28 But thou shalt say unto them, This
is a nation that obeyeth not the voice of
the LORD their God, nor receiveth correction: truth is perished, and is cut off
from their mouth.
29 Cut off thine hair, *O Jerusalem*,
and cast *it* away, and take up a lamentation on high places; for the LORD hath
rejected and forsaken the generation
of his wrath.
30 For the children of Judah have
done evil in my sight, saith the LORD:
they have set their abominations in the
house which is called by my name, to
pollute it.
31 And they have built the high places of Tophet, which *is* in the valley of
the son of Hinnom, to burn their sons
and their daughters in the fire; which I
commanded *them* not, neither came it
into my heart.
32 Therefore, behold, the days come,
saith the LORD, that it shall no more be
called Tophet, nor the valley of the son
of Hinnom, but the valley of slaughter:
for they shall bury in Tophet, till there
be no place.
33 And the carcases of this people
shall be meat for the fowls of the heav-
en, and for the beasts of the earth; and
none shall fray *them* away.
34 Then will I cause to cease from the
cities of Judah, and from the streets of
Jerusalem, the voice of mirth, and the
voice of gladness, the voice of the
bridegroom, and the voice of the bride:
for the land shall be desolate.

8 At that time, saith the LORD, they
shall bring out the bones of the
kings of Judah, and the bones of his
princes, and the bones of the priests,
and the bones of the prophets, and the
bones of the inhabitants of Jerusalem,
out of their graves:
2 And they shall spread them before
the sun, and the moon, and all the host
of heaven, whom they have loved, and
whom they have served, and after
whom they have walked, and whom
they have sought, and whom they have
worshipped: they shall not be gathered,

nor be buried; they shall be for dung
upon the face of the earth.
3 And death shall be chosen rather
than life by all the residue of them that
remain of this evil family, which remain
in all the places whither I have driven
them, saith the LORD of hosts.
4 Moreover thou shalt say unto them,
Thus saith the LORD; Shall they fall, and
not arise? shall he turn away, and not
return?
5 Why *then* is this people of Jerusalem
slidden back by a perpetual backsliding?
they hold fast deceit, they refuse
to return.
6 I hearkened and heard, *but* they
spake not aright: no man repented him
of his wickedness, saying, What have I
done? every one turned to his course, as
the horse rusheth into the battle.
7 Yea, the stork in the heaven
knoweth her appointed times; and the
turtle and the crane and the swallow
observe the time of their coming; but
my people know not the judgment of
the LORD.
8 How do ye say, We *are* wise, and the
law of the LORD *is* with us? Lo, certainly
in vain made he *it*; the pen of the
scribes *is* in vain.
9 The wise *men* are ashamed, they
are dismayed and taken: lo, they have
rejected the word of the LORD; and
what wisdom *is* in them?
10 Therefore will I give their wives
unto others, *and* their fields to them
that shall inherit *them*: for every one
from the least even unto the greatest is
given to covetousness, from the prophet
even unto the priest every one dealeth
falsely.
11 For they have healed the hurt of
the daughter of my people slightly, saying,
Peace, peace; when *there is* no
peace.
12 Were they ashamed when they had
committed abomination? nay, they
were not at all ashamed, neither could
they blush: therefore shall they fall
among them that fall: in the time of
their visitation they shall be cast down,
saith the LORD.
13 I will surely consume them, saith
the LORD: *there shall be* no grapes on
the vine, nor figs on the fig tree, and
the leaf shall fade; and *the things that*
I have given them shall pass away from
them.
14 Why do we sit still? assemble yourselves,
and let us enter into the
defenced cities, and let us be silent
there: for the LORD our God hath put us
to silence, and given us water of gall to
drink, because we have sinned against
the LORD.
15 We looked for peace, but no good
came; and for a time of health, and
behold trouble!
16 The snorting of his horses was
heard from Dan: the whole land trembled
at the sound of the neighing of his
strong ones; for they are come, and
have devoured the land, and all that is
in it; the city, and those that dwell
therein.
17 For, behold, I will send serpents,
cockatrices, among you, which *will* not
be charmed, and they shall bite you,
saith the LORD.
18 *When* I would comfort myself
against sorrow, my heart *is* faint in me.
19 Behold the voice of the cry of the
daughter of my people because of them
that dwell in a far country: *Is* not the
LORD in Zion? *is* not her king in her?
Why have they provoked me to anger

with their graven images, *and* with
strange vanities?
20 The harvest is past, the summer is
ended, and we are not saved.
21 For the hurt of the daughter of my
people am I hurt; I am black; astonishment hath taken hold on me.
22 *Is there* no balm in Gilead; *is there*
no physician there? why then is not the
health of the daughter of my people
recovered?

9 Oh that my head were waters, and
mine eyes a fountain of tears, that I
might weep day and night for the slain
of the daughter of my people!
2 Oh that I had in the wilderness a
lodging place of wayfaring men; that I
might leave my people, and go from
them! for they *be* all adulterers, an
assembly of treacherous men.
3 And they bend their tongues *like*
their bow *for* lies: but they are not valiant for the truth upon the earth; for
they proceed from evil to evil, and they
know not me, saith the LORD.
4 Take ye heed every one of his neighbour, and trust ye not in any brother:
for every brother will utterly supplant,
and every neighbour will walk with
slanders.
5 And they will deceive every one his
neighbour, and will not speak the truth:
they have taught their tongue to speak
lies, *and* weary themselves to commit
iniquity.
6 Thine habitation *is* in the midst of
deceit; through deceit they refuse to
know me, saith the LORD.
7 Therefore thus saith the LORD of
hosts, Behold, I will melt them, and try
them; for how shall I do for the daughter of my people?
8 Their tongue *is as* an arrow shot
out; it speaketh deceit: *one* speaketh
peaceably to his neighbour with his
mouth, but in heart he layeth his wait.
9 Shall I not visit them for these
things? saith the LORD: shall not my
soul be avenged on such a nation as
this?
10 For the mountains will I take up a
weeping and wailing, and for the habitations of the wilderness a lamentation,
because they are burned up, so that
none can pass through *them*; neither
can *men* hear the voice of the cattle;
both the fowl of the heavens and the
beast are fled; they are gone.
11 And I will make Jerusalem heaps,
and a den of dragons; and I will make
the cities of Judah desolate, without an
inhabitant.
12 Who *is* the wise man, that may
understand this? and *who is he* to
whom the mouth of the LORD hath spoken, that he may declare it, for what the
land perisheth *and* is burned up like a
wilderness, that none passeth through?
13 And the LORD saith, Because they
have forsaken my law which I set
before them, and have not obeyed my
voice, neither walked therein;
14 But have walked after the imagination of their own heart, and after
Baalim, which their fathers taught
them:
15 Therefore thus saith the LORD of
hosts, the God of Israel; Behold, I will
feed them, *even* this people, with
wormwood, and give them water of gall
to drink.
16 I will scatter them also among the
heathen, whom neither they nor their
fathers have known: and I will send a
sword after them, till I have consumed
them.

17 Thus saith the LORD of hosts,
Consider ye, and call for the mourning
women, that they may come; and send
for cunning *women*, that they may
come:
18 And let them make haste, and take
up a wailing for us, that our eyes may
run down with tears, and our eyelids
gush out with waters.
19 For a voice of wailing is heard out
of Zion, How are we spoiled! we are
greatly confounded, because we have
forsaken the land, because our dwellings have cast *us* out.
20 Yet hear the word of the LORD, O
ye women, and let your ear receive the
word of his mouth, and teach your
daughters wailing, and every one her
neighbour lamentation.
21 For death is come up into our windows, *and* is entered into our palaces,
to cut off the children from without,
and the young men from the streets.
22 Speak, Thus saith the LORD, Even
the carcases of men shall fall as dung
upon the open field, and as the handful
after the harvestman, and none shall
gather *them*.
23 Thus saith the LORD, Let not the
wise *man* glory in his wisdom, neither
let the mighty *man* glory in his might,
let not the rich *man* glory in his riches:
24 But let him that glorieth glory in
this, that he understandeth and
knoweth me, that I *am* the LORD which
exercise lovingkindness, judgment, and
righteousness, in the earth: for in these
things I delight, saith the LORD.
25 Behold, the days come, saith the
LORD, that I will punish all *them which*
are circumcised with the uncircumcised;
26 Egypt, and Judah, and Edom, and
the children of Ammon, and Moab, and
all *that are* in the utmost corners, that
dwell in the wilderness: for all *these*
nations *are* uncircumcised, and all the
house of Israel *are* uncircumcised in
the heart.

10 Hear ye the word which the LORD
speaketh unto you, O house of
Israel:
2 Thus saith the LORD, Learn not the
way of the heathen, and be not dismayed at the signs of heaven; for the
heathen are dismayed at them.
3 For the customs of the people *are*
vain: for *one* cutteth a tree out of the
forest, the work of the hands of the
workman, with the axe.
4 They deck it with silver and with
gold; they fasten it with nails and with
hammers, that it move not.
5 They *are* upright as the palm tree,
but speak not: they must needs be
borne, because they cannot go. Be not
afraid of them; for they cannot do evil,
neither also *is it* in them to do good.
6 Forasmuch as *there is* none like
unto thee, O LORD; thou *art* great, and
thy name *is* great in might.
7 Who would not fear thee, O King of
nations? for to thee doth it appertain:
forasmuch as among all the wise *men*
of the nations, and in all their kingdoms, *there is* none like unto thee.
8 But they are altogether brutish and
foolish: the stock *is* a doctrine of vanities.
9 Silver spread into plates is brought
from Tarshish, and gold from Uphaz,
the work of the workman, and of the
hands of the founder: blue and purple
is their clothing: they *are* all the work
of cunning *men*.
10 But the LORD *is* the true God, he *is*
the living God, and an everlasting king:
at his wrath the earth shall tremble,

and the nations shall not be able to abide his indignation.

11 Thus shall ye say unto them, The gods that have not made the heavens and the earth, *even* they shall perish from the earth, and from under these heavens.

12 He hath made the earth by his power, he hath established the world by his wisdom, and hath stretched out the heavens by his discretion.

13 When he uttereth his voice, *there is* a multitude of waters in the heavens, and he causeth the vapours to ascend from the ends of the earth; he maketh lightnings with rain, and bringeth forth the wind out of his treasures.

14 Every man is brutish in *his* knowledge: every founder is confounded by the graven image: for his molten image *is* falsehood, and *there is* no breath in them.

15 They *are* vanity, *and* the work of errors: in the time of their visitation they shall perish.

16 The portion of Jacob *is* not like them: for he *is* the former of all *things*; and Israel *is* the rod of his inheritance: The LORD of hosts *is* his name.

17 Gather up thy wares out of the land, O inhabitant of the fortress.

18 For thus saith the LORD, Behold, I will sling out the inhabitants of the land at this once, and will distress them, that they may find *it so*.

19 Woe is me for my hurt! my wound is grievous: but I said, Truly this *is* a grief, and I must bear it.

20 My tabernacle is spoiled, and all my cords are broken: my children are gone forth of me, and they *are* not: *there is* none to stretch forth my tent any more, and to set up my curtains.

21 For the pastors are become brutish, and have not sought the LORD: therefore they shall not prosper, and all their flocks shall be scattered.

22 Behold, the noise of the bruit is come, and a great commotion out of the north country, to make the cities of Judah desolate, *and* a den of dragons.

23 O LORD, I know that the way of man *is* not in himself: *it is* not in man that walketh to direct his steps.

24 O LORD, correct me, but with judgment; not in thine anger, lest thou bring me to nothing.

25 Pour out thy fury upon the heathen that know thee not, and upon the families that call not on thy name: for they have eaten up Jacob, and devoured him, and consumed him, and have made his habitation desolate.

11 The word that came to Jeremiah from the LORD, saying,

2 Hear ye the words of this covenant, and speak unto the men of Judah, and to the inhabitants of Jerusalem;

3 And say thou unto them, Thus saith the LORD God of Israel; Cursed *be* the man that obeyeth not the words of this covenant,

4 Which I commanded your fathers in the day *that* I brought them forth out of the land of Egypt, from the iron furnace, saying, Obey my voice, and do them, according to all which I command you: so shall ye be my people, and I will be your God:

5 That I may perform the oath which I have sworn unto your fathers, to give them a land flowing with milk and honey, as *it is* this day. Then answered I, and said, So be it, O LORD.

6 Then the LORD said unto me, Proclaim all these words in the cities of Judah, and in the streets of Jerusalem, saying, Hear ye the words of this covenant, and do them.

7 For I earnestly protested unto your fathers in the day *that* I brought them up out of the land of Egypt, *even* unto this day, rising early and protesting, saying, Obey my voice.

8 Yet they obeyed not, nor inclined their ear, but walked every one in the imagination of their evil heart: therefore I will bring upon them all the words of this covenant, which I commanded *them* to do; but they did *them* not.

9 And the LORD said unto me, A conspiracy is found among the men of Judah, and among the inhabitants of Jerusalem.

10 They are turned back to the iniquities of their forefathers, which refused to hear my words; and they went after other gods to serve them: the house of Israel and the house of Judah have broken my covenant which I made with their fathers.

11 Therefore thus saith the LORD, Behold, I will bring evil upon them, which they shall not be able to escape; and though they shall cry unto me, I will not hearken unto them.

12 Then shall the cities of Judah and inhabitants of Jerusalem go, and cry unto the gods unto whom they offer incense: but they shall not save them at all in the time of their trouble.

13 For *according to* the number of thy cities were thy gods, O Judah; and *according to* the number of the streets of Jerusalem have ye set up altars to *that* shameful thing, *even* altars to burn incense unto Baal.

14 Therefore pray not thou for this people, neither lift up a cry or prayer for them: for I will not hear *them* in the time that they cry unto me for their trouble.

15 What hath my beloved to do in mine house, *seeing* she hath wrought lewdness with many, and the holy flesh is passed from thee? when thou doest evil, then thou rejoicest.

16 The LORD called thy name, A green olive tree, fair, *and* of goodly fruit: with the noise of a great tumult he hath kindled fire upon it, and the branches of it are broken.

17 For the LORD of hosts, that planted thee, hath pronounced evil against thee, for the evil of the house of Israel and of the house of Judah, which they have done against themselves to provoke me to anger in offering incense unto Baal.

18 And the LORD hath given me knowledge *of it*, and I know *it*: then thou shewedst me their doings.

19 But I *was* like a lamb *or* an ox *that* is brought to the slaughter; and I knew not that they had devised devices against me, *saying*, Let us destroy the tree with the fruit thereof, and let us cut him off from the land of the living, that his name may be no more remembered.

20 But, O LORD of hosts, that judgest righteously, that triest the reins and the heart, let me see thy vengeance on them: for unto thee have I revealed my cause.

21 Therefore thus saith the LORD of the men of Anathoth, that seek thy life, saying, Prophesy not in the name of the LORD, that thou die not by our hand:

22 Therefore thus saith the LORD of hosts, Behold, I will punish them: the young men shall die by the sword; their sons and their daughters shall die by famine:

23 And there shall be no remnant of
them: for I will bring evil upon the men
of Anathoth, *even* the year of their visitation.

12 Righteous *art* thou, O LORD,
when I plead with thee: yet let
me talk with thee of *thy* judgments:
Wherefore doth the way of the wicked
prosper? *wherefore* are all they happy
that deal very treacherously?
2 Thou hast planted them, yea, they
have taken root: they grow, yea, they
bring forth fruit: thou *art* near in their
mouth, and far from their reins.
3 But thou, O LORD, knowest me: thou
hast seen me, and tried mine heart
toward thee: pull them out like sheep
for the slaughter, and prepare them for
the day of slaughter.
4 How long shall the land mourn, and
the herbs of every field wither, for the
wickedness of them that dwell therein?
the beasts are consumed, and the birds;
because they said, He shall not see our
last end.
5 If thou hast run with the footmen,
and they have wearied thee, then how
canst thou contend with horses? and *if*
in the land of peace, *wherein* thou
trustedst, *they wearied thee*, then how
wilt thou do in the swelling of Jordan?
6 For even thy brethren, and the
house of thy father, even they have
dealt treacherously with thee; yea, they
have called a multitude after thee:
believe them not, though they speak
fair words unto thee.
7 I have forsaken mine house, I have
left mine heritage; I have given the
dearly beloved of my soul into the hand
of her enemies.
8 Mine heritage is unto me as a lion in
the forest; it crieth out against me:
therefore have I hated it.
9 Mine heritage *is* unto me *as* a
speckled bird, the birds round about
are against her; come ye, assemble all
the beasts of the field, come to devour.
10 Many pastors have destroyed my
vineyard, they have trodden my portion
under foot, they have made my pleasant portion a desolate wilderness.
11 They have made it desolate, *and*
being desolate it mourneth unto me;
the whole land is made desolate,
because no man layeth *it* to heart.
12 The spoilers are come upon all
high places through the wilderness: for
the sword of the LORD shall devour
from the *one* end of the land even to
the *other* end of the land: no flesh shall
have peace.
13 They have sown wheat, but shall
reap thorns: they have put themselves
to pain, *but* shall not profit: and they
shall be ashamed of your revenues
because of the fierce anger of the LORD.
14 Thus saith the LORD against all
mine evil neighbours, that touch the
inheritance which I have caused my
people Israel to inherit; Behold, I will
pluck them out of their land, and pluck
out the house of Judah from among
them.
15 And it shall come to pass, after
that I have plucked them out I will
return, and have compassion on them,
and will bring them again, every man to
his heritage, and every man to his land.
16 And it shall come to pass, if they
will diligently learn the ways of my
people, to swear by my name, The LORD
liveth; as they taught my people to
swear by Baal; then shall they be built
in the midst of my people.
17 But if they will not obey, I will
utterly pluck up and destroy that
nation, saith the LORD.

13 Thus saith the LORD unto me, Go and get thee a linen girdle, and put it upon thy loins, and put it not in water.

2 So I got a girdle according to the word of the LORD, and put *it* on my loins.

3 And the word of the LORD came unto me the second time, saying,

4 Take the girdle that thou hast got, which *is* upon thy loins, and arise, go to Euphrates, and hide it there in a hole of the rock.

5 So I went, and hid it by Euphrates, as the LORD commanded me.

6 And it came to pass after many days, that the LORD said unto me, Arise, go to Euphrates, and take the girdle from thence, which I commanded thee to hide there.

7 Then I went to Euphrates, and digged, and took the girdle from the place where I had hid it: and, behold, the girdle was marred, it was profitable for nothing.

8 Then the word of the LORD came unto me, saying,

9 Thus saith the LORD, After this manner will I mar the pride of Judah, and the great pride of Jerusalem.

10 This evil people, which refuse to hear my words, which walk in the imagination of their heart, and walk after other gods, to serve them, and to worship them, shall even be as this girdle, which is good for nothing.

11 For as the girdle cleaveth to the loins of a man, so have I caused to cleave unto me the whole house of Israel and the whole house of Judah, saith the LORD; that they might be unto me for a people, and for a name, and for a praise, and for a glory: but they would not hear.

12 Therefore thou shalt speak unto them this word; Thus saith the LORD God of Israel, Every bottle shall be filled with wine: and they shall say unto thee, Do we not certainly know that every bottle shall be filled with wine?

13 Then shalt thou say unto them, Thus saith the LORD, Behold, I will fill all the inhabitants of this land, even the kings that sit upon David's throne, and the priests, and the prophets, and all the inhabitants of Jerusalem, with drunkenness.

14 And I will dash them one against another, even the fathers and the sons together, saith the LORD: I will not pity, nor spare, nor have mercy, but destroy them.

15 Hear ye, and give ear; be not proud: for the LORD hath spoken.

16 Give glory to the LORD your God, before he cause darkness, and before your feet stumble upon the dark mountains, and, while ye look for light, he turn it into the shadow of death, *and* make *it* gross darkness.

17 But if ye will not hear it, my soul shall weep in secret places for *your* pride; and mine eye shall weep sore, and run down with tears, because the LORD's flock is carried away captive.

18 Say unto the king and to the queen, Humble yourselves, sit down: for your principalities shall come down, *even* the crown of your glory.

19 The cities of the south shall be shut up, and none shall open *them*: Judah shall be carried away captive all of it, it shall be wholly carried away captive.

20 Lift up your eyes, and behold them that come from the north: where *is* the flock *that* was given thee, thy beautiful flock?

21 What wilt thou say when he shall punish thee? for thou hast taught them *to be* captains, *and* as chief over thee: shall not sorrows take thee, as a woman in travail?

22 And if thou say in thine heart, Wherefore come these things upon me? For the greatness of thine iniquity are thy skirts discovered, *and* thy heels made bare.

23 Can the Ethiopian change his skin, or the leopard his spots? *then* may ye also do good, that are accustomed to do evil.

24 Therefore will I scatter them as the stubble that passeth away by the wind of the wilderness.

25 This *is* thy lot, the portion of thy measures from me, saith the LORD; because thou hast forgotten me, and trusted in falsehood.

26 Therefore will I discover thy skirts upon thy face, that thy shame may appear.

27 I have seen thine adulteries, and thy neighings, the lewdness of thy whoredom, *and* thine abominations on the hills in the fields. Woe unto thee, O Jerusalem! wilt thou not be made clean? when *shall it* once *be*?

14 The word of the LORD that came to Jeremiah concerning the dearth.

2 Judah mourneth, and the gates thereof languish; they are black unto the ground; and the cry of Jerusalem is gone up.

3 And their nobles have sent their little ones to the waters: they came to the pits, *and* found no water; they returned with their vessels empty; they were ashamed and confounded, and covered their heads.

4 Because the ground is chapt, for there was no rain in the earth, the plowmen were ashamed, they covered their heads.

5 Yea, the hind also calved in the field, and forsook *it*, because there was no grass.

6 And the wild asses did stand in the high places, they snuffed up the wind like dragons; their eyes did fail, because *there was* no grass.

7 O LORD, though our iniquities testify against us, do thou *it* for thy name's sake: for our backslidings are many; we have sinned against thee.

8 O the hope of Israel, the saviour thereof in time of trouble, why shouldest thou be as a stranger in the land, and as a wayfaring man *that* turneth aside to tarry for a night?

9 Why shouldest thou be as a man astonied, as a mighty man *that* cannot save? yet thou, O LORD, *art* in the midst of us, and we are called by thy name; leave us not.

10 Thus saith the LORD unto this people, Thus have they loved to wander, they have not refrained their feet, therefore the LORD doth not accept them; he will now remember their iniquity, and visit their sins.

11 Then said the LORD unto me, Pray not for this people for *their* good.

12 When they fast, I will not hear their cry; and when they offer burnt offering and an oblation, I will not accept them: but I will consume them by the sword, and by the famine, and by the pestilence.

13 Then said I, Ah, Lord GOD! behold, the prophets say unto them, Ye shall not see the sword, neither shall ye have famine; but I will give you assured peace in this place.

14 Then the LORD said unto me, The prophets prophesy lies in my name: I sent them not, neither have I commanded them, neither spake unto them: they prophesy unto you a false vision and divination, and a thing of nought, and the deceit of their heart.

15 Therefore thus saith the LORD concerning the prophets that prophesy in my name, and I sent them not, yet they say, Sword and famine shall not be in this land; By sword and famine shall those prophets be consumed.

16 And the people to whom they prophesy shall be cast out in the streets of Jerusalem because of the famine and the sword; and they shall have none to bury them, them, their wives, nor their sons, nor their daughters: for I will pour their wickedness upon them.

17 Therefore thou shalt say this word unto them; Let mine eyes run down with tears night and day, and let them not cease: for the virgin daughter of my people is broken with a great breach, with a very grievous blow.

18 If I go forth into the field, then behold the slain with the sword! and if I enter into the city, then behold them that are sick with famine! yea, both the prophet and the priest go about into a land that they know not.

19 Hast thou utterly rejected Judah? hath thy soul lothed Zion? why hast thou smitten us, and *there is* no healing for us? we looked for peace, and *there is* no good; and for the time of healing, and behold trouble!

20 We acknowledge, O LORD, our wickedness, *and* the iniquity of our fathers: for we have sinned against thee.

21 Do not abhor *us*, for thy name's sake, do not disgrace the throne of thy glory: remember, break not thy covenant with us.

22 Are there *any* among the vanities of the Gentiles that can cause rain? or can the heavens give showers? *art* not thou he, O LORD our God? therefore we will wait upon thee: for thou hast made all these *things*.

15 Then said the LORD unto me, Though Moses and Samuel stood before me, *yet* my mind *could* not *be* toward this people: cast *them* out of my sight, and let them go forth.

2 And it shall come to pass, if they say unto thee, Whither shall we go forth? then thou shalt tell them, Thus saith the LORD; Such as *are* for death, to death; and such as *are* for the sword, to the sword; and such as *are* for the famine, to the famine; and such as *are* for the captivity, to the captivity.

3 And I will appoint over them four kinds, saith the LORD: the sword to slay, and the dogs to tear, and the fowls of the heaven, and the beasts of the earth, to devour and destroy.

4 And I will cause them to be removed into all kingdoms of the earth, because of Manasseh the son of Hezekiah king of Judah, for *that* which he did in Jerusalem.

5 For who shall have pity upon thee, O Jerusalem? or who shall bemoan thee? or who shall go aside to ask how thou doest?

6 Thou hast forsaken me, saith the LORD, thou art gone backward: therefore will I stretch out my hand against thee, and destroy thee; I am weary with repenting.

7 And I will fan them with a fan in the gates of the land; I will bereave *them* of children, I will destroy my people, *since* they return not from their ways.

8 Their widows are increased to me above the sand of the seas: I have brought upon them against the mother of the young men a spoiler at noonday: I have caused *him* to fall upon it suddenly, and terrors upon the city.

9 She that hath borne seven languisheth: she hath given up the ghost; her sun is gone down while *it was* yet day: she hath been ashamed and confounded: and the residue of them will I deliver to the sword before their enemies, saith the LORD.

10 Woe is me, my mother, that thou hast borne me a man of strife and a man of contention to the whole earth! I have neither lent on usury, nor men have lent to me on usury; *yet* every one of them doth curse me.

11 The LORD said, Verily it shall be well with thy remnant; verily I will cause the enemy to entreat thee *well* in the time of evil and in the time of affliction.

12 Shall iron break the northern iron and the steel?

13 Thy substance and thy treasures will I give to the spoil without price, and *that* for all thy sins, even in all thy borders.

14 And I will make *thee* to pass with thine enemies into a land *which* thou knowest not: for a fire is kindled in mine anger, *which* shall burn upon you.

15 O LORD, thou knowest: remember me, and visit me, and revenge me of my persecutors; take me not away in thy longsuffering: know that for thy sake I have suffered rebuke.

16 Thy words were found, and I did eat them; and thy word was unto me the joy and rejoicing of mine heart: for I am called by thy name, O LORD God of hosts.

17 I sat not in the assembly of the mockers, nor rejoiced; I sat alone because of thy hand: for thou hast filled me with indignation.

18 Why is my pain perpetual, and my wound incurable, *which* refuseth to be healed? wilt thou be altogether unto me as a liar, *and as* waters *that* fail?

19 Therefore thus saith the LORD, If thou return, then will I bring thee again, *and* thou shalt stand before me: and if thou take forth the precious from the vile, thou shalt be as my mouth: let them return unto thee; but return not thou unto them.

20 And I will make thee unto this people a fenced brasen wall: and they shall fight against thee, but they shall not prevail against thee: for I *am* with thee to save thee and to deliver thee, saith the LORD.

21 And I will deliver thee out of the hand of the wicked, and I will redeem thee out of the hand of the terrible.

16 The word of the LORD came also unto me, saying,

2 Thou shalt not take thee a wife, neither shalt thou have sons or daughters in this place.

3 For thus saith the LORD concerning the sons and concerning the daughters that are born in this place, and concerning their mothers that bare them, and concerning their fathers that begat them in this land;

4 They shall die of grievous deaths; they shall not be lamented; neither shall they be buried; *but* they shall be as dung upon the face of the earth: and they shall be consumed by the sword, and by famine; and their carcases shall be meat for the fowls of heaven, and for the beasts of the earth.

5 For thus saith the LORD, Enter not into the house of mourning, neither go to lament nor bemoan them: for I have taken away my peace from this people, saith the LORD, *even* lovingkindness and mercies.

6 Both the great and the small shall die in this land: they shall not be buried, neither shall *men* lament for them, nor cut themselves, nor make themselves bald for them:

7 Neither shall *men* tear *themselves* for them in mourning, to comfort them for the dead; neither shall *men* give them the cup of consolation to drink for their father or for their mother.

8 Thou shalt not also go into the house of feasting, to sit with them to eat and to drink.

9 For thus saith the LORD of hosts, the God of Israel; Behold, I will cause to cease out of this place in your eyes, and in your days, the voice of mirth, and the voice of gladness, the voice of the bridegroom, and the voice of the bride.

10 And it shall come to pass, when thou shalt shew this people all these words, and they shall say unto thee, Wherefore hath the LORD pronounced all this great evil against us? or what *is* our iniquity? or what *is* our sin that we have committed against the LORD our God?

11 Then shalt thou say unto them, Because your fathers have forsaken me, saith the LORD, and have walked after other gods, and have served them, and have worshipped them, and have forsaken me, and have not kept my law;

12 And ye have done worse than your fathers; for, behold, ye walk every one after the imagination of his evil heart, that they may not hearken unto me:

13 Therefore will I cast you out of this land into a land that ye know not, *neither* ye nor your fathers; and there shall ye serve other gods day and night; where I will not shew you favour.

14 Therefore, behold, the days come, saith the LORD, that it shall no more be said, The LORD liveth, that brought up the children of Israel out of the land of Egypt;

15 But, The LORD liveth, that brought up the children of Israel from the land of the north, and from all the lands whither he had driven them: and I will bring them again into their land that I gave unto their fathers.

16 Behold, I will send for many fishers, saith the LORD, and they shall fish them; and after will I send for many hunters, and they shall hunt them from every mountain, and from every hill, and out of the holes of the rocks.

17 For mine eyes *are* upon all their ways: they are not hid from my face, neither is their iniquity hid from mine eyes.

18 And first I will recompense their iniquity and their sin double; because they have defiled my land, they have filled mine inheritance with the carcases of their detestable and abominable things.

19 O LORD, my strength, and my fortress, and my refuge in the day of affliction, the Gentiles shall come unto thee from the ends of the earth, and shall say, Surely our fathers have inherited lies, vanity, and *things* wherein *there is* no profit.

20 Shall a man make gods unto himself, and they *are* no gods?

21 Therefore, behold, I will this once cause them to know, I will cause them to know mine hand and my might; and they shall know that my name *is* The LORD.

17 The sin of Judah *is* written with a pen of iron, *and* with the point of a diamond: *it is* graven upon the table of their heart, and upon the horns of your altars;

2 Whilst their children remember their altars and their groves by the green trees upon the high hills.

3 O my mountain in the field, I will give thy substance *and* all thy treasures to the spoil, *and* thy high places for sin, throughout all thy borders.

4 And thou, even thyself, shalt discontinue from thine heritage that I gave thee; and I will cause thee to serve thine enemies in the land which thou knowest not: for ye have kindled a fire in mine anger, *which* shall burn for ever.

5 Thus saith the LORD; Cursed *be* the man that trusteth in man, and maketh flesh his arm, and whose heart departeth from the LORD.

6 For he shall be like the heath in the desert, and shall not see when good cometh; but shall inhabit the parched places in the wilderness, *in* a salt land and not inhabited.

7 Blessed *is* the man that trusteth in the LORD, and whose hope the LORD is.

8 For he shall be as a tree planted by the waters, and *that* spreadeth out her roots by the river, and shall not see when heat cometh, but her leaf shall be green; and shall not be careful in the year of drought, neither shall cease from yielding fruit.

9 The heart *is* deceitful above all *things*, and desperately wicked: who can know it?

10 I the LORD search the heart, *I* try the reins, even to give every man according to his ways, *and* according to the fruit of his doings.

11 *As* the partridge sitteth *on eggs*, and hatcheth *them* not; *so* he that getteth riches, and not by right, shall leave them in the midst of his days, and at his end shall be a fool.

12 A glorious high throne from the beginning *is* the place of our sanctuary.

13 O LORD, the hope of Israel, all that forsake thee shall be ashamed, *and* they that depart from me shall be written in the earth, because they have forsaken the LORD, the fountain of living waters.

14 Heal me, O LORD, and I shall be healed; save me, and I shall be saved: for thou *art* my praise.

15 Behold, they say unto me, Where *is* the word of the LORD? let it come now.

16 As for me, I have not hastened from *being* a pastor to follow thee: neither have I desired the woeful day; thou knowest: that which came out of my lips was *right* before thee.

17 Be not a terror unto me: thou *art* my hope in the day of evil.

18 Let them be confounded that persecute me, but let not me be confounded: let them be dismayed, but let not me be dismayed: bring upon them the day of evil, and destroy them with double destruction.

19 Thus said the LORD unto me; Go and stand in the gate of the children of the people, whereby the kings of Judah come in, and by the which they go out, and in all the gates of Jerusalem;

20 And say unto them, Hear ye the word of the LORD, ye kings of Judah, and all Judah, and all the inhabitants of Jerusalem, that enter in by these gates:

21 Thus saith the LORD; Take heed to yourselves, and bear no burden on the sabbath day, nor bring *it* in by the gates of Jerusalem;

22 Neither carry forth a burden out of
your houses on the sabbath day, neither
do ye any work, but hallow ye the sabbath day, as I commanded your fathers.
23 But they obeyed not, neither
inclined their ear, but made their neck
stiff, that they might not hear, nor
receive instruction.
24 And it shall come to pass, if ye diligently hearken unto me, saith the
LORD, to bring in no burden through the
gates of this city on the sabbath day,
but hallow the sabbath day, to do no
work therein;
25 Then shall there enter into the
gates of this city kings and princes sitting upon the throne of David, riding in
chariots and on horses, they, and their
princes, the men of Judah, and the
inhabitants of Jerusalem: and this city
shall remain for ever.
26 And they shall come from the cities of Judah, and from the places about
Jerusalem, and from the land of
Benjamin, and from the plain, and from
the mountains, and from the south,
bringing burnt offerings, and sacrifices,
and meat offerings, and incense, and
bringing sacrifices of praise, unto the
house of the LORD.
27 But if ye will not hearken unto me
to hallow the sabbath day, and not to
bear a burden, even entering in at the
gates of Jerusalem on the sabbath day;
then will I kindle a fire in the gates
thereof, and it shall devour the palaces
of Jerusalem, and it shall not be
quenched.

18 The word which came to
Jeremiah from the LORD, saying,
2 Arise, and go down to the potter's
house, and there I will cause thee to
hear my words.
3 Then I went down to the potter's
house, and, behold, he wrought a work
on the wheels.
4 And the vessel that he made of clay
was marred in the hand of the potter:
so he made it again another vessel, as
seemed good to the potter to make *it*.
5 Then the word of the LORD came to
me, saying,
6 O house of Israel, cannot I do with
you as this potter? saith the LORD.
Behold, as the clay *is* in the potter's
hand, so *are* ye in mine hand, O house
of Israel.
7 *At what* instant I shall speak concerning a nation, and concerning a
kingdom, to pluck up, and to pull down,
and to destroy *it*;
8 If that nation, against whom I have
pronounced, turn from their evil, I will
repent of the evil that I thought to do
unto them.
9 And *at what* instant I shall speak
concerning a nation, and concerning a
kingdom, to build and to plant *it*;
10 If it do evil in my sight, that it obey
not my voice, then I will repent of the
good, wherewith I said I would benefit
them.
11 Now therefore go to, speak to the
men of Judah, and to the inhabitants of
Jerusalem, saying, Thus saith the LORD;
Behold, I frame evil against you, and
devise a device against you: return ye
now every one from his evil way, and
make your ways and your doings good.
12 And they said, There is no hope:
but we will walk after our own devices,
and we will every one do the imagination of his evil heart.
13 Therefore thus saith the LORD; Ask
ye now among the heathen, who hath
heard such things: the virgin of Israel
hath done a very horrible thing.

14 Will *a man* leave the snow of
Lebanon *which cometh* from the rock
of the field? *or* shall the cold flowing
waters that come from another place
be forsaken?
15 Because my people hath forgotten
me, they have burned incense to vanity,
and they have caused them to stumble
in their ways *from* the ancient paths, to
walk in paths, *in* a way not cast up;
16 To make their land desolate, *and* a
perpetual hissing; every one that passeth thereby shall be astonished, and
wag his head.
17 I will scatter them as with an east
wind before the enemy; I will shew
them the back, and not the face, in the
day of their calamity.
18 Then said they, Come, and let us
devise devices against Jeremiah; for
the law shall not perish from the priest,
nor counsel from the wise, nor the word
from the prophet. Come, and let us
smite him with the tongue, and let us
not give heed to any of his words.
19 Give heed to me, O LORD, and
hearken to the voice of them that
contend with me.
20 Shall evil be recompensed for
good? for they have digged a pit for my
soul. Remember that I stood before
thee to speak good for them, *and* to
turn away thy wrath from them.
21 Therefore deliver up their children
to the famine, and pour out their *blood*
by the force of the sword; and let their
wives be bereaved of their children,
and *be* widows; and let their men be
put to death; *let* their young men *be*
slain by the sword in battle.
22 Let a cry be heard from their
houses, when thou shalt bring a troop
suddenly upon them: for they have
digged a pit to take me, and hid snares
for my feet.
23 Yet, LORD, thou knowest all their
counsel against me to slay *me*: forgive
not their iniquity, neither blot out their
sin from thy sight, but let them be overthrown before thee; deal *thus* with
them in the time of thine anger.

19 Thus saith the LORD, Go and get
a potter's earthen bottle, and
take of the ancients of the people, and
of the ancients of the priests;
2 And go forth unto the valley of the
son of Hinnom, which *is* by the entry of
the east gate, and proclaim there the
words that I shall tell thee,
3 And say, Hear ye the word of the
LORD, O kings of Judah, and inhabitants of Jerusalem; Thus saith the LORD
of hosts, the God of Israel; Behold, I will
bring evil upon this place, the which
whosoever heareth, his ears shall tingle.
4 Because they have forsaken me, and
have estranged this place, and have
burned incense in it unto other gods,
whom neither they nor their fathers
have known, nor the kings of Judah,
and have filled this place with the
blood of innocents;
5 They have built also the high places
of Baal, to burn their sons with fire *for*
burnt offerings unto Baal, which I commanded not, nor spake *it*, neither came
it into my mind:
6 Therefore, behold, the days come,
saith the LORD, that this place shall no
more be called Tophet, nor The valley
of the son of Hinnom, but The valley of
slaughter.
7 And I will make void the counsel of
Judah and Jerusalem in this place; and
I will cause them to fall by the sword
before their enemies, and by the hands
of them that seek their lives: and their
carcases will I give to be meat for the

fowls of the heaven, and for the beasts
of the earth.
8 And I will make this city desolate,
and an hissing; every one that passeth
thereby shall be astonished and hiss
because of all the plagues thereof.
9 And I will cause them to eat the
flesh of their sons and the flesh of their
daughters, and they shall eat every one
the flesh of his friend in the siege and
straitness, wherewith their enemies,
and they that seek their lives, shall
straiten them.
10 Then shalt thou break the bottle in
the sight of the men that go with thee,
11 And shalt say unto them, Thus
saith the LORD of hosts; Even so will I
break this people and this city, as *one*
breaketh a potter's vessel, that cannot
be made whole again: and they shall
bury *them* in Tophet, till *there be* no
place to bury.
12 Thus will I do unto this place, saith
the LORD, and to the inhabitants thereof, and *even* make this city as Tophet:
13 And the houses of Jerusalem, and
the houses of the kings of Judah, shall
be defiled as the place of Tophet,
because of all the houses upon whose
roofs they have burned incense unto all
the host of heaven, and have poured
out drink offerings unto other gods.
14 Then came Jeremiah from Tophet,
whither the LORD had sent him to
prophesy; and he stood in the court of
the LORD's house; and said to all the
people,
15 Thus saith the LORD of hosts, the
God of Israel; Behold, I will bring upon
this city and upon all her towns all the
evil that I have pronounced against it,
because they have hardened their
necks, that they might not hear my
words.

20 Now Pashur the son of Immer the
priest, who *was* also chief governor in the house of the LORD, heard that
Jeremiah prophesied these things.
2 Then Pashur smote Jeremiah the
prophet, and put him in the stocks that
were in the high gate of Benjamin,
which *was* by the house of the LORD.
3 And it came to pass on the morrow,
that Pashur brought forth Jeremiah out
of the stocks. Then said Jeremiah unto
him, The LORD hath not called thy
name Pashur, but Magor-missabib.
4 For thus saith the LORD, Behold, I
will make thee a terror to thyself, and
to all thy friends: and they shall fall by
the sword of their enemies, and thine
eyes shall behold *it*: and I will give all
Judah into the hand of the king of
Babylon, and he shall carry them captive into Babylon, and shall slay them
with the sword.
5 Moreover I will deliver all the
strength of this city, and all the labours
thereof, and all the precious things
thereof, and all the treasures of the
kings of Judah will I give into the hand
of their enemies, which shall spoil
them, and take them, and carry them to
Babylon.
6 And thou, Pashur, and all that dwell
in thine house shall go into captivity:
and thou shalt come to Babylon, and
there thou shalt die, and shalt be buried there, thou, and all thy friends, to
whom thou hast prophesied lies.
7 O LORD, thou hast deceived me, and
I was deceived: thou art stronger than I,
and hast prevailed: I am in derision
daily, every one mocketh me.
8 For since I spake, I cried out, I cried
violence and spoil; because the word of
the LORD was made a reproach unto me,
and a derision, daily.

9 Then I said, I will not make mention of him, nor speak any more in his name. But *his word* was in mine heart as a burning fire shut up in my bones, and I was weary with forbearing, and I could not *stay*.

10 For I heard the defaming of many, fear on every side. Report, *say they*, and we will report it. All my familiars watched for my halting, *saying*, Peradventure he will be enticed, and we shall prevail against him, and we shall take our revenge on him.

11 But the LORD *is* with me as a mighty terrible one: therefore my persecutors shall stumble, and they shall not prevail: they shall be greatly ashamed; for they shall not prosper: *their* everlasting confusion shall never be forgotten.

12 But, O LORD of hosts, that triest the righteous, *and* seest the reins and the heart, let me see thy vengeance on them: for unto thee have I opened my cause.

13 Sing unto the LORD, praise ye the LORD: for he hath delivered the soul of the poor from the hand of evildoers.

14 Cursed *be* the day wherein I was born: let not the day wherein my mother bare me be blessed.

15 Cursed *be* the man who brought tidings to my father, saying, A man child is born unto thee; making him very glad.

16 And let that man be as the cities which the LORD overthrew, and repented not: and let him hear the cry in the morning, and the shouting at noontide;

17 Because he slew me not from the womb; or that my mother might have been my grave, and her womb *to be* always great *with me*.

18 Wherefore came I forth out of the womb to see labour and sorrow, that my days should be consumed with shame?

21 The word which came unto Jeremiah from the LORD, when king Zedekiah sent unto him Pashur the son of Melchiah, and Zephaniah the son of Maaseiah the priest, saying,

2 Enquire, I pray thee, of the LORD for us; for Nebuchadrezzar king of Babylon maketh war against us; if so be that the LORD will deal with us according to all his wondrous works, that he may go up from us.

3 Then said Jeremiah unto them, Thus shall ye say to Zedekiah:

4 Thus saith the LORD God of Israel; Behold, I will turn back the weapons of war that *are* in your hands, wherewith ye fight against the king of Babylon, and *against* the Chaldeans, which besiege you without the walls, and I will assemble them into the midst of this city.

5 And I myself will fight against you with an outstretched hand and with a strong arm, even in anger, and in fury, and in great wrath.

6 And I will smite the inhabitants of this city, both man and beast: they shall die of a great pestilence.

7 And afterward, saith the LORD, I will deliver Zedekiah king of Judah, and his servants, and the people, and such as are left in this city from the pestilence, from the sword, and from the famine, into the hand of Nebuchadrezzar king of Babylon, and into the hand of their enemies, and into the hand of those that seek their life: and he shall smite them with the edge of the sword; he shall not spare them, neither have pity, nor have mercy.

8 And unto this people thou shalt say, Thus saith the LORD; Behold, I set before you the way of life, and the way of death.

9 He that abideth in this city shall die by the sword, and by the famine, and by the pestilence: but he that goeth out, and falleth to the Chaldeans that besiege you, he shall live, and his life shall be unto him for a prey.

10 For I have set my face against this city for evil, and not for good, saith the LORD: it shall be given into the hand of the king of Babylon, and he shall burn it with fire.

11 And touching the house of the king of Judah, *say*, Hear ye the word of the LORD;

12 O house of David, thus saith the LORD; Execute judgment in the morning, and deliver *him that is* spoiled out of the hand of the oppressor, lest my fury go out like fire, and burn that none can quench *it*, because of the evil of your doings.

13 Behold, I *am* against thee, O inhabitant of the valley, *and* rock of the plain, saith the LORD; which say, Who shall come down against us? or who shall enter into our habitations?

14 But I will punish you according to the fruit of your doings, saith the LORD: and I will kindle a fire in the forest thereof, and it shall devour all things round about it.

22 Thus saith the LORD; Go down to the house of the king of Judah, and speak there this word,

2 And say, Hear the word of the LORD, O king of Judah, that sittest upon the throne of David, thou, and thy servants, and thy people that enter in by these gates:

3 Thus saith the LORD; Execute ye judgment and righteousness, and deliver the spoiled out of the hand of the oppressor: and do no wrong, do no violence to the stranger, the fatherless, nor the widow, neither shed innocent blood in this place.

4 For if ye do this thing indeed, then shall there enter in by the gates of this house kings sitting upon the throne of David, riding in chariots and on horses, he, and his servants, and his people.

5 But if ye will not hear these words, I swear by myself, saith the LORD, that this house shall become a desolation.

6 For thus saith the LORD unto the king's house of Judah; Thou *art* Gilead unto me, *and* the head of Lebanon: *yet* surely I will make thee a wilderness, *and* cities *which* are not inhabited.

7 And I will prepare destroyers against thee, every one with his weapons: and they shall cut down thy choice cedars, and cast *them* into the fire.

8 And many nations shall pass by this city, and they shall say every man to his neighbour, Wherefore hath the LORD done thus unto this great city?

9 Then they shall answer, Because they have forsaken the covenant of the LORD their God, and worshipped other gods, and served them.

10 Weep ye not for the dead, neither bemoan him: *but* weep sore for him that goeth away: for he shall return no more, nor see his native country.

11 For thus saith the LORD touching Shallum the son of Josiah king of Judah, which reigned instead of Josiah his father, which went forth out of this place; He shall not return thither any more:

12 But he shall die in the place whither they have led him captive, and shall
see this land no more.
13 Woe unto him that buildeth his
house by unrighteousness, and his
chambers by wrong; *that* useth his
neighbour's service without wages, and
giveth him not for his work;
14 That saith, I will build me a wide
house and large chambers, and cutteth
him out windows; and *it is* cieled with
cedar, and painted with vermilion.
15 Shalt thou reign, because thou
closest *thyself* in cedar? did not thy
father eat and drink, and do judgment
and justice, *and* then *it was* well with
him?
16 He judged the cause of the poor
and needy; then *it was* well *with him:*
was not this to know me? saith the
LORD.
17 But thine eyes and thine heart *are*
not but for thy covetousness, and for to
shed innocent blood, and for oppression, and for violence, to do *it*.
18 Therefore thus saith the LORD concerning Jehoiakim the son of Josiah
king of Judah; They shall not lament for
him, *saying*, Ah my brother! or, Ah sister! they shall not lament for him, *saying*, Ah lord! or, Ah his glory!
19 He shall be buried with the burial
of an ass, drawn and cast forth beyond
the gates of Jerusalem.
20 Go up to Lebanon, and cry; and lift
up thy voice in Bashan, and cry from
the passages: for all thy lovers are
destroyed.
21 I spake unto thee in thy prosperity;
but thou saidst, I will not hear. This
hath been thy manner from thy youth,
that thou obeyedst not my voice.
22 The wind shall eat up all thy
pastors, and thy lovers shall go into
captivity: surely then shalt thou be
ashamed and confounded for all thy
wickedness.
23 O inhabitant of Lebanon, that
makest thy nest in the cedars, how gracious shalt thou be when pangs come
upon thee, the pain as of a woman in
travail!
24 *As* I live, saith the LORD, though
Coniah the son of Jehoiakim king of
Judah were the signet upon my right
hand, yet would I pluck thee thence;
25 And I will give thee into the hand
of them that seek thy life, and into the
hand *of them* whose face thou fearest,
even into the hand of Nebuchadrezzar
king of Babylon, and into the hand of
the Chaldeans.
26 And I will cast thee out, and thy
mother that bare thee, into another
country, where ye were not born; and
there shall ye die.
27 But to the land whereunto they
desire to return, thither shall they not
return.
28 *Is* this man Coniah a despised broken idol? *is he* a vessel wherein *is* no
pleasure? wherefore are they cast out,
he and his seed, and are cast into a land
which they know not?
29 O earth, earth, earth, hear the
word of the LORD.
30 Thus saith the LORD, Write ye this
man childless, a man *that* shall not
prosper in his days: for no man of his
seed shall prosper, sitting upon the
throne of David, and ruling any more in
Judah.

23 Woe be unto the pastors that
destroy and scatter the sheep of
my pasture! saith the LORD.
2 Therefore thus saith the LORD God
of Israel against the pastors that feed
my people; Ye have scattered my flock,

and driven them away, and have not
visited them: behold, I will visit upon
you the evil of your doings, saith the
LORD.
3 And I will gather the remnant of my
flock out of all countries whither I have
driven them, and will bring them again
to their folds; and they shall be fruitful
and increase.
4 And I will set up shepherds over
them which shall feed them: and they
shall fear no more, nor be dismayed,
neither shall they be lacking, saith the
LORD.
5 Behold, the days come, saith the
LORD, that I will raise unto David a
righteous Branch, and a King shall
reign and prosper, and shall execute
judgment and justice in the earth.
6 In his days Judah shall be saved,
and Israel shall dwell safely: and this *is*
his name whereby he shall be called,
THE LORD OUR RIGHTEOUSNESS.
7 Therefore, behold, the days come,
saith the LORD, that they shall no more
say, The LORD liveth, which brought up
the children of Israel out of the land of
Egypt;
8 But, The LORD liveth, which brought
up and which led the seed of the house
of Israel out of the north country, and
from all countries whither I had driven
them; and they shall dwell in their own
land.
9 Mine heart within me is broken
because of the prophets; all my bones
shake; I am like a drunken man, and
like a man whom wine hath overcome,
because of the LORD, and because of
the words of his holiness.
10 For the land is full of adulterers;
for because of swearing the land mourneth; the pleasant places of the wilderness are dried up, and their course is
evil, and their force *is* not right.
11 For both prophet and priest are
profane; yea, in my house have I found
their wickedness, saith the LORD.
12 Wherefore their way shall be unto
them as slippery *ways* in the darkness:
they shall be driven on, and fall therein: for I will bring evil upon them, *even*
the year of their visitation, saith the
LORD.
13 And I have seen folly in the prophets of Samaria; they prophesied in Baal,
and caused my people Israel to err.
14 I have seen also in the prophets of
Jerusalem an horrible thing: they commit adultery, and walk in lies: they
strengthen also the hands of evildoers,
that none doth return from his wickedness: they are all of them unto me as
Sodom, and the inhabitants thereof as
Gomorrah.
15 Therefore thus saith the LORD of
hosts concerning the prophets; Behold,
I will feed them with wormwood, and
make them drink the water of gall: for
from the prophets of Jerusalem is pro-
faneness gone forth into all the land.
16 Thus saith the LORD of hosts,
Hearken not unto the words of the
prophets that prophesy unto you: they
make you vain: they speak a vision of
their own heart, *and* not out of the
mouth of the LORD.
17 They say still unto them that
despise me, The LORD hath said, Ye
shall have peace; and they say unto
every one that walketh after the imagination of his own heart, No evil shall
come upon you.
18 For who hath stood in the counsel
of the LORD, and hath perceived and
heard his word? who hath marked his
word, and heard *it*?

19 Behold, a whirlwind of the LORD is gone forth in fury, even a grievous whirlwind: it shall fall grievously upon the head of the wicked.

20 The anger of the LORD shall not return, until he have executed, and till he have performed the thoughts of his heart: in the latter days ye shall consider it perfectly.

21 I have not sent these prophets, yet they ran: I have not spoken to them, yet they prophesied.

22 But if they had stood in my counsel, and had caused my people to hear my words, then they should have turned them from their evil way, and from the evil of their doings.

23 *Am* I a God at hand, saith the LORD, and not a God afar off?

24 Can any hide himself in secret places that I shall not see him? saith the LORD. Do not I fill heaven and earth? saith the LORD.

25 I have heard what the prophets said, that prophesy lies in my name, saying, I have dreamed, I have dreamed.

26 How long shall *this* be in the heart of the prophets that prophesy lies? yea, *they are* prophets of the deceit of their own heart;

27 Which think to cause my people to forget my name by their dreams which they tell every man to his neighbour, as their fathers have forgotten my name for Baal.

28 The prophet that hath a dream, let him tell a dream; and he that hath my word, let him speak my word faithfully. What *is* the chaff to the wheat? saith the LORD.

29 *Is* not my word like as a fire? saith the LORD; and like a hammer *that* breaketh the rock in pieces?

30 Therefore, behold, I *am* against the prophets, saith the LORD, that steal my words every one from his neighbour.

31 Behold, I *am* against the prophets, saith the LORD, that use their tongues, and say, He saith.

32 Behold, I *am* against them that prophesy false dreams, saith the LORD, and do tell them, and cause my people to err by their lies, and by their lightness; yet I sent them not, nor commanded them: therefore they shall not profit this people at all, saith the LORD.

33 And when this people, or the prophet, or a priest, shall ask thee, saying, What *is* the burden of the LORD? thou shalt then say unto them, What burden? I will even forsake you, saith the LORD.

34 And *as for* the prophet, and the priest, and the people, that shall say, The burden of the LORD, I will even punish that man and his house.

35 Thus shall ye say every one to his neighbour, and every one to his brother, What hath the LORD answered? and, What hath the LORD spoken?

36 And the burden of the LORD shall ye mention no more: for every man's word shall be his burden; for ye have perverted the words of the living God, of the LORD of hosts our God.

37 Thus shalt thou say to the prophet, What hath the LORD answered thee? and, What hath the LORD spoken?

38 But since ye say, The burden of the LORD; therefore thus saith the LORD; Because ye say this word, The burden of the LORD, and I have sent unto you, saying, Ye shall not say, The burden of the LORD;

39 Therefore, behold, I, even I, will utterly forget you, and I will forsake you, and the city that I gave you and

your fathers, *and cast you* out of my
presence:
40 And I will bring an everlasting
reproach upon you, and a perpetual
shame, which shall not be forgotten.

24 The LORD shewed me, and,
behold, two baskets of figs *were*
set before the temple of the LORD, after
that Nebuchadrezzar king of Babylon
had carried away captive Jeconiah the
son of Jehoiakim king of Judah, and
the princes of Judah, with the carpenters and smiths, from Jerusalem, and
had brought them to Babylon.
2 One basket *had* very good figs, *even*
like the figs *that are* first ripe: and the
other basket *had* very naughty figs,
which could not be eaten, they were so
bad.
3 Then said the LORD unto me, What
seest thou, Jeremiah? And I said, Figs;
the good figs, very good; and the evil,
very evil, that cannot be eaten, they are
so evil.
4 Again the word of the LORD came
unto me, saying,
5 Thus saith the LORD, the God of
Israel; Like these good figs, so will I
acknowledge them that are carried
away captive of Judah, whom I have
sent out of this place into the land of
the Chaldeans for *their* good.
6 For I will set mine eyes upon them
for good, and I will bring them again to
this land: and I will build them, and not
pull *them* down; and I will plant them,
and not pluck *them* up.
7 And I will give them an heart to
know me, that I *am* the LORD: and they
shall be my people, and I will be their
God: for they shall return unto me with
their whole heart.
8 And as the evil figs, which cannot
be eaten, they are so evil; surely thus
saith the LORD, So will I give Zedekiah
the king of Judah, and his princes, and
the residue of Jerusalem, that remain
in this land, and them that dwell in the
land of Egypt:
9 And I will deliver them to be
removed into all the kingdoms of the
earth for *their* hurt, *to be* a reproach
and a proverb, a taunt and a curse, in
all places whither I shall drive them.
10 And I will send the sword, the famine, and the pestilence, among them,
till they be consumed from off the land
that I gave unto them and to their
fathers.

25 The word that came to Jeremiah
concerning all the people of
Judah in the fourth year of Jehoiakim
the son of Josiah king of Judah, that
was the first year of Nebuchadrezzar
king of Babylon;
2 The which Jeremiah the prophet
spake unto all the people of Judah, and
to all the inhabitants of Jerusalem, saying,
3 From the thirteenth year of Josiah
the son of Amon king of Judah, even
unto this day, that *is* the three and
twentieth year, the word of the LORD
hath come unto me, and I have spoken
unto you, rising early and speaking; but
ye have not hearkened.
4 And the LORD hath sent unto you all
his servants the prophets, rising early
and sending *them*; but ye have not
hearkened, nor inclined your ear to
hear.
5 They said, Turn ye again now every
one from his evil way, and from the evil
of your doings, and dwell in the land
that the LORD hath given unto you and
to your fathers for ever and ever:
6 And go not after other gods to serve
them, and to worship them, and pro-

voke me not to anger with the works of
your hands; and I will do you no hurt.
7 Yet ye have not hearkened unto me,
saith the LORD; that ye might provoke
me to anger with the works of your
hands to your own hurt.
8 Therefore thus saith the LORD of
hosts; Because ye have not heard my
words,
9 Behold, I will send and take all the
families of the north, saith the LORD,
and Nebuchadrezzar the king of
Babylon, my servant, and will bring
them against this land, and against the
inhabitants thereof, and against all
these nations round about, and will
utterly destroy them, and make them
an astonishment, and an hissing, and
perpetual desolations.
10 Moreover I will take from them the
voice of mirth, and the voice of gladness, the voice of the bridegroom, and
the voice of the bride, the sound of the
millstones, and the light of the candle.
11 And this whole land shall be a
desolation, *and* an astonishment; and
these nations shall serve the king of
Babylon seventy years.
12 And it shall come to pass, when
seventy years are accomplished, *that* I
will punish the king of Babylon, and
that nation, saith the LORD, for their
iniquity, and the land of the Chaldeans,
and will make it perpetual desolations.
13 And I will bring upon that land all
my words which I have pronounced
against it, *even* all that is written in this
book, which Jeremiah hath prophesied
against all the nations.
14 For many nations and great kings
shall serve themselves of them also:
and I will recompense them according
to their deeds, and according to the
works of their own hands.

15 For thus saith the LORD God of
Israel unto me; Take the wine cup of
this fury at my hand, and cause all the
nations, to whom I send thee, to drink
it.
16 And they shall drink, and be
moved, and be mad, because of the
sword that I will send among them.
17 Then took I the cup at the LORD's
hand, and made all the nations to
drink, unto whom the LORD had sent
me:
18 *To wit*, Jerusalem, and the cities of
Judah, and the kings thereof, and the
princes thereof, to make them a desolation, an astonishment, an hissing, and a
curse; as *it is* this day;
19 Pharaoh king of Egypt, and his
servants, and his princes, and all his
people;
20 And all the mingled people, and
all the kings of the land of Uz, and all
the kings of the land of the Philistines,
and Ashkelon, and Azzah, and Ekron,
and the remnant of Ashdod,
21 Edom, and Moab, and the children
of Ammon,
22 And all the kings of Tyrus, and all
the kings of Zidon, and the kings of the
isles which *are* beyond the sea,
23 Dedan, and Tema, and Buz, and all
that are in the utmost corners,
24 And all the kings of Arabia, and all
the kings of the mingled people that
dwell in the desert,
25 And all the kings of Zimri, and all
the kings of Elam, and all the kings of
the Medes,
26 And all the kings of the north, far
and near, one with another, and all the
kingdoms of the world, which *are* upon
the face of the earth: and the king of
Sheshach shall drink after them.

27 Therefore thou shalt say unto
them, Thus saith the LORD of hosts, the
God of Israel; Drink ye, and be drunk-
en, and spue, and fall, and rise no more,
because of the sword which I will send
among you.
28 And it shall be, if they refuse to
take the cup at thine hand to drink,
then shalt thou say unto them, Thus
saith the LORD of hosts; Ye shall certainly drink.
29 For, lo, I begin to bring evil on the
city which is called by my name, and
should ye be utterly unpunished? Ye
shall not be unpunished: for I will call
for a sword upon all the inhabitants of
the earth, saith the LORD of hosts.
30 Therefore prophesy thou against
them all these words, and say unto
them, The LORD shall roar from on high,
and utter his voice from his holy habitation; he shall mightily roar upon his
habitation; he shall give a shout, as they
that tread *the grapes*, against all the
inhabitants of the earth.
31 A noise shall come *even* to the
ends of the earth; for the LORD hath a
controversy with the nations, he will
plead with all flesh; he will give them
that are wicked to the sword, saith the
LORD.
32 Thus saith the LORD of hosts,
Behold, evil shall go forth from nation
to nation, and a great whirlwind shall
be raised up from the coasts of the
earth.
33 And the slain of the LORD shall be
at that day from *one* end of the earth
even unto the *other* end of the earth:
they shall not be lamented, neither
gathered, nor buried; they shall be
dung upon the ground.
34 Howl, ye shepherds, and cry; and
wallow yourselves *in the ashes*, ye principal of the flock: for the days of your
slaughter and of your dispersions are
accomplished; and ye shall fall like a
pleasant vessel.
35 And the shepherds shall have no
way to flee, nor the principal of the
flock to escape.
36 A voice of the cry of the shepherds,
and an howling of the principal of the
flock, *shall be heard*: for the LORD hath
spoiled their pasture.
37 And the peaceable habitations are
cut down because of the fierce anger of
the LORD.
38 He hath forsaken his covert, as the
lion: for their land is desolate because
of the fierceness of the oppressor, and
because of his fierce anger.

26

In the beginning of the reign of
Jehoiakim the son of Josiah king
of Judah came this word from the LORD,
saying,
2 Thus saith the LORD; Stand in the
court of the LORD's house, and speak
unto all the cities of Judah, which come
to worship in the LORD's house, all the
words that I command thee to speak
unto them; diminish not a word:
3 If so be they will hearken, and turn
every man from his evil way, that I may
repent me of the evil, which I purpose
to do unto them because of the evil of
their doings.
4 And thou shalt say unto them, Thus
saith the LORD; If ye will not hearken to
me, to walk in my law, which I have set
before you,
5 To hearken to the words of my servants the prophets, whom I sent unto
you, both rising up early, and sending
them, but ye have not hearkened;
6 Then will I make this house like
Shiloh, and will make this city a curse
to all the nations of the earth.

7 So the priests and the prophets and
all the people heard Jeremiah speaking these words in the house of the
LORD.
8 Now it came to pass, when Jeremiah
had made an end of speaking all that
the LORD had commanded *him* to
speak unto all the people, that the
priests and the prophets and all the
people took him, saying, Thou shalt
surely die.
9 Why hast thou prophesied in the
name of the LORD, saying, This house
shall be like Shiloh, and this city shall
be desolate without an inhabitant? And
all the people were gathered against
Jeremiah in the house of the LORD.
10 When the princes of Judah heard
these things, then they came up from
the king's house unto the house of the
LORD, and sat down in the entry of the
new gate of the LORD's *house*.
11 Then spake the priests and the
prophets unto the princes and to all the
people, saying, This man *is* worthy to
die; for he hath prophesied against this
city, as ye have heard with your ears.
12 Then spake Jeremiah unto all the
princes and to all the people, saying,
The LORD sent me to prophesy against
this house and against this city all the
words that ye have heard.
13 Therefore now amend your ways
and your doings, and obey the voice of
the LORD your God; and the LORD will
repent him of the evil that he hath
pronounced against you.
14 As for me, behold, I *am* in your
hand: do with me as seemeth good and
meet unto you.
15 But know ye for certain, that if ye
put me to death, ye shall surely bring
innocent blood upon yourselves, and
upon this city, and upon the inhabitants
thereof: for of a truth the LORD hath
sent me unto you to speak all these
words in your ears.
16 Then said the princes and all the
people unto the priests and to the
prophets; This man *is* not worthy to die:
for he hath spoken to us in the name of
the LORD our God.
17 Then rose up certain of the elders
of the land, and spake to all the assembly of the people, saying,
18 Micah the Morasthite prophesied
in the days of Hezekiah king of Judah,
and spake to all the people of Judah,
saying, Thus saith the LORD of hosts;
Zion shall be plowed *like* a field, and
Jerusalem shall become heaps, and the
mountain of the house as the high
places of a forest.
19 Did Hezekiah king of Judah and
all Judah put him at all to death? did
he not fear the LORD, and besought the
LORD, and the LORD repented him of
the evil which he had pronounced
against them? Thus might we procure
great evil against our souls.
20 And there was also a man that
prophesied in the name of the LORD,
Urijah the son of Shemaiah of Kirjath-
jearim, who prophesied against this
city and against this land according to
all the words of Jeremiah:
21 And when Jehoiakim the king,
with all his mighty men, and all the
princes, heard his words, the king
sought to put him to death: but when
Urijah heard it, he was afraid, and fled,
and went into Egypt;
22 And Jehoiakim the king sent men
into Egypt, *namely*, Elnathan the son
of Achbor, and *certain* men with him
into Egypt.

23 And they fetched forth Urijah out of Egypt, and brought him unto Jehoiakim the king; who slew him with the sword, and cast his dead body into the graves of the common people.
24 Nevertheless the hand of Ahikam the son of Shaphan was with Jeremiah, that they should not give him into the hand of the people to put him to death.

27 In the beginning of the reign of Jehoiakim the son of Josiah king of Judah came this word unto Jeremiah from the LORD, saying,
2 Thus saith the LORD to me; Make thee bonds and yokes, and put them upon thy neck,
3 And send them to the king of Edom, and to the king of Moab, and to the king of the Ammonites, and to the king of Tyrus, and to the king of Zidon, by the hand of the messengers which come to Jerusalem unto Zedekiah king of Judah;
4 And command them to say unto their masters, Thus saith the LORD of hosts, the God of Israel; Thus shall ye say unto your masters;
5 I have made the earth, the man and the beast that *are* upon the ground, by my great power and by my outstretched arm, and have given it unto whom it seemed meet unto me.
6 And now have I given all these lands into the hand of Nebuchadnezzar the king of Babylon, my servant; and the beasts of the field have I given him also to serve him.
7 And all nations shall serve him, and his son, and his son's son, until the very time of his land come: and then many nations and great kings shall serve themselves of him.
8 And it shall come to pass, *that* the nation and kingdom which will not serve the same Nebuchadnezzar the king of Babylon, and that will not put their neck under the yoke of the king of Babylon, that nation will I punish, saith the LORD, with the sword, and with the famine, and with the pestilence, until I have consumed them by his hand.
9 Therefore hearken not ye to your prophets, nor to your diviners, nor to your dreamers, nor to your enchanters, nor to your sorcerers, which speak unto you, saying, Ye shall not serve the king of Babylon:
10 For they prophesy a lie unto you, to remove you far from your land; and that I should drive you out, and ye should perish.
11 But the nations that bring their neck under the yoke of the king of Babylon, and serve him, those will I let remain still in their own land, saith the LORD; and they shall till it, and dwell therein.
12 I spake also to Zedekiah king of Judah according to all these words, saying, Bring your necks under the yoke of the king of Babylon, and serve him and his people, and live.
13 Why will ye die, thou and thy people, by the sword, by the famine, and by the pestilence, as the LORD hath spoken against the nation that will not serve the king of Babylon?
14 Therefore hearken not unto the words of the prophets that speak unto you, saying, Ye shall not serve the king of Babylon: for they prophesy a lie unto you.
15 For I have not sent them, saith the LORD, yet they prophesy a lie in my name; that I might drive you out, and that ye might perish, ye, and the prophets that prophesy unto you.

16 Also I spake to the priests and to
all this people, saying, Thus saith the
LORD; Hearken not to the words of your
prophets that prophesy unto you, saying,
Behold, the vessels of the LORD's
house shall now shortly be brought
again from Babylon: for they prophesy
a lie unto you.
17 Hearken not unto them; serve the
king of Babylon, and live: wherefore
should this city be laid waste?
18 But if they *be* prophets, and if the
word of the LORD be with them, let
them now make intercession to the
LORD of hosts, that the vessels which
are left in the house of the LORD, and *in*
the house of the king of Judah, and at
Jerusalem, go not to Babylon.
19 For thus saith the LORD of hosts
concerning the pillars, and concerning
the sea, and concerning the bases, and
concerning the residue of the vessels
that remain in this city,
20 Which Nebuchadnezzar king of
Babylon took not, when he carried
away captive Jeconiah the son of
Jehoiakim king of Judah from
Jerusalem to Babylon, and all the
nobles of Judah and Jerusalem;
21 Yea, thus saith the LORD of hosts,
the God of Israel, concerning the vessels
that remain *in* the house of the
LORD, and *in* the house of the king of
Judah and of Jerusalem;
22 They shall be carried to Babylon,
and there shall they be until the day
that I visit them, saith the LORD; then
will I bring them up, and restore them
to this place.

28 And it came to pass the same
year, in the beginning of the
reign of Zedekiah king of Judah, in the
fourth year, *and* in the fifth month, *that*
Hananiah the son of Azur the prophet,
which *was* of Gibeon, spake unto me in
the house of the LORD, in the presence
of the priests and of all the people, saying,
2 Thus speaketh the LORD of hosts,
the God of Israel, saying, I have broken
the yoke of the king of Babylon.
3 Within two full years will I bring
again into this place all the vessels of
the LORD's house, that Nebuchadnezzar
king of Babylon took away from this
place, and carried them to Babylon:
4 And I will bring again to this place
Jeconiah the son of Jehoiakim king of
Judah, with all the captives of Judah,
that went into Babylon, saith the LORD:
for I will break the yoke of the king of
Babylon.
5 Then the prophet Jeremiah said
unto the prophet Hananiah in the presence
of the priests, and in the presence
of all the people that stood in the house
of the LORD,
6 Even the prophet Jeremiah said,
Amen: the LORD do so: the LORD perform
thy words which thou hast prophesied,
to bring again the vessels of the
LORD's house, and all that is carried
away captive, from Babylon into this
place.
7 Nevertheless hear thou now this
word that I speak in thine ears, and in
the ears of all the people;
8 The prophets that have been before
me and before thee of old prophesied
both against many countries, and
against great kingdoms, of war, and of
evil, and of pestilence.
9 The prophet which prophesieth of
peace, when the word of the prophet
shall come to pass, *then* shall the
prophet be known, that the LORD hath
truly sent him.

10 Then Hananiah the prophet took the yoke from off the prophet Jeremiah's neck, and brake it.

11 And Hananiah spake in the presence of all the people, saying, Thus saith the LORD; Even so will I break the yoke of Nebuchadnezzar king of Babylon from the neck of all nations within the space of two full years. And the prophet Jeremiah went his way.

12 Then the word of the LORD came unto Jeremiah *the prophet*, after that Hananiah the prophet had broken the yoke from off the neck of the prophet Jeremiah, saying,

13 Go and tell Hananiah, saying, Thus saith the LORD; Thou hast broken the yokes of wood; but thou shalt make for them yokes of iron.

14 For thus saith the LORD of hosts, the God of Israel; I have put a yoke of iron upon the neck of all these nations, that they may serve Nebuchadnezzar king of Babylon; and they shall serve him: and I have given him the beasts of the field also.

15 Then said the prophet Jeremiah unto Hananiah the prophet, Hear now, Hananiah; The LORD hath not sent thee; but thou makest this people to trust in a lie.

16 Therefore thus saith the LORD; Behold, I will cast thee from off the face of the earth: this year thou shalt die, because thou hast taught rebellion against the LORD.

17 So Hananiah the prophet died the same year in the seventh month.

29 Now these *are* the words of the letter that Jeremiah the prophet sent from Jerusalem unto the residue of the elders which were carried away captives, and to the priests, and to the prophets, and to all the people whom Nebuchadnezzar had carried away captive from Jerusalem to Babylon;

2 (After that Jeconiah the king, and the queen, and the eunuchs, the princes of Judah and Jerusalem, and the carpenters, and the smiths, were departed from Jerusalem;)

3 By the hand of Elasah the son of Shaphan, and Gemariah the son of Hilkiah, (whom Zedekiah king of Judah sent unto Babylon to Nebuchadnezzar king of Babylon) saying,

4 Thus saith the LORD of hosts, the God of Israel, unto all that are carried away captives, whom I have caused to be carried away from Jerusalem unto Babylon;

5 Build ye houses, and dwell *in them*; and plant gardens, and eat the fruit of them;

6 Take ye wives, and beget sons and daughters; and take wives for your sons, and give your daughters to husbands, that they may bear sons and daughters; that ye may be increased there, and not diminished.

7 And seek the peace of the city whither I have caused you to be carried away captives, and pray unto the LORD for it: for in the peace thereof shall ye have peace.

8 For thus saith the LORD of hosts, the God of Israel; Let not your prophets and your diviners, that *be* in the midst of you, deceive you, neither hearken to your dreams which ye cause to be dreamed.

9 For they prophesy falsely unto you in my name: I have not sent them, saith the LORD.

10 For thus saith the LORD, That after seventy years be accomplished at Babylon I will visit you, and perform my good word toward you, in causing you to return to this place.

11 For I know the thoughts that I think toward you, saith the LORD, thoughts of peace, and not of evil, to give you an expected end.

12 Then shall ye call upon me, and ye shall go and pray unto me, and I will hearken unto you.

13 And ye shall seek me, and find *me*, when ye shall search for me with all your heart.

14 And I will be found of you, saith the LORD: and I will turn away your captivity, and I will gather you from all the nations, and from all the places whither I have driven you, saith the LORD; and I will bring you again into the place whence I caused you to be carried away captive.

15 Because ye have said, The LORD hath raised us up prophets in Babylon;

16 *Know* that thus saith the LORD of the king that sitteth upon the throne of David, and of all the people that dwelleth in this city, *and* of your brethren that are not gone forth with you into captivity;

17 Thus saith the LORD of hosts; Behold, I will send upon them the sword, the famine, and the pestilence, and will make them like vile figs, that cannot be eaten, they are so evil.

18 And I will persecute them with the sword, with the famine, and with the pestilence, and will deliver them to be removed to all the kingdoms of the earth, to be a curse, and an astonishment, and an hissing, and a reproach, among all the nations whither I have driven them:

19 Because they have not hearkened to my words, saith the LORD, which I sent unto them by my servants the prophets, rising up early and sending *them*; but ye would not hear, saith the LORD.

20 Hear ye therefore the word of the LORD, all ye of the captivity, whom I have sent from Jerusalem to Babylon:

21 Thus saith the LORD of hosts, the God of Israel, of Ahab the son of Kolaiah, and of Zedekiah the son of Maaseiah, which prophesy a lie unto you in my name; Behold, I will deliver them into the hand of Nebuchadrezzar king of Babylon; and he shall slay them before your eyes;

22 And of them shall be taken up a curse by all the captivity of Judah which *are* in Babylon, saying, The LORD make thee like Zedekiah and like Ahab, whom the king of Babylon roasted in the fire;

23 Because they have committed villany in Israel, and have committed adultery with their neighbours' wives, and have spoken lying words in my name, which I have not commanded them; even I know, and *am* a witness, saith the LORD.

24 *Thus* shalt thou also speak to Shemaiah the Nehelamite, saying,

25 Thus speaketh the LORD of hosts, the God of Israel, saying, Because thou hast sent letters in thy name unto all the people that *are* at Jerusalem, and to Zephaniah the son of Maaseiah the priest, and to all the priests, saying,

26 The LORD hath made thee priest in the stead of Jehoiada the priest, that ye should be officers in the house of the LORD, for every man *that is* mad, and maketh himself a prophet, that thou shouldest put him in prison, and in the stocks.

27 Now therefore why hast thou not
reproved Jeremiah of Anathoth, which
maketh himself a prophet to you?
28 For therefore he sent unto us *in*
Babylon, saying, This *captivity is* long:
build ye houses, and dwell *in them*; and
plant gardens, and eat the fruit of
them.
29 And Zephaniah the priest read
this letter in the ears of Jeremiah the
prophet.
30 Then came the word of the LORD
unto Jeremiah, saying,
31 Send to all them of the captivity,
saying, Thus saith the LORD concerning
Shemaiah the Nehelamite; Because
that Shemaiah hath prophesied unto
you, and I sent him not, and he caused
you to trust in a lie:
32 Therefore thus saith the LORD;
Behold, I will punish Shemaiah the
Nehelamite, and his seed: he shall not
have a man to dwell among this people;
neither shall he behold the good that I
will do for my people, saith the LORD;
because he hath taught rebellion
against the LORD.

30 The word that came to Jeremiah
from the LORD, saying,
2 Thus speaketh the LORD God of
Israel, saying, Write thee all the words
that I have spoken unto thee in a book.
3 For, lo, the days come, saith the
LORD, that I will bring again the captivity of my people Israel and Judah, saith
the LORD: and I will cause them to
return to the land that I gave to their
fathers, and they shall possess it.
4 And these *are* the words that the
LORD spake concerning Israel and concerning Judah.
5 For thus saith the LORD; We have
heard a voice of trembling, of fear, and
not of peace.
6 Ask ye now, and see whether a man
doth travail with child? wherefore do I
see every man with his hands on his
loins, as a woman in travail, and all
faces are turned into paleness?
7 Alas! for that day *is* great, so that
none *is* like it: it *is* even the time of
Jacob's trouble; but he shall be saved
out of it.
8 For it shall come to pass in that day,
saith the LORD of hosts, *that* I will
break his yoke from off thy neck, and
will burst thy bonds, and strangers shall
no more serve themselves of him:
9 But they shall serve the LORD their
God, and David their king, whom I will
raise up unto them.
10 Therefore fear thou not, O my servant Jacob, saith the LORD; neither be
dismayed, O Israel: for, lo, I will save
thee from afar, and thy seed from the
land of their captivity; and Jacob shall
return, and shall be in rest, and be
quiet, and none shall make *him* afraid.
11 For I *am* with thee, saith the LORD,
to save thee: though I make a full end
of all nations whither I have scattered
thee, yet will I not make a full end of
thee: but I will correct thee in measure,
and will not leave thee altogether
unpunished.
12 For thus saith the LORD, Thy bruise
is incurable, *and* thy wound *is* grievous.
13 *There is* none to plead thy cause,
that thou mayest be bound up: thou
hast no healing medicines.
14 All thy lovers have forgotten thee;
they seek thee not; for I have wounded
thee with the wound of an enemy, with
the chastisement of a cruel one, for the
multitude of thine iniquity; *because* thy
sins were increased.
15 Why criest thou for thine affliction? thy sorrow *is* incurable for the

multitude of thine iniquity: *because* thy sins were increased, I have done these things unto thee.

16 Therefore all they that devour thee shall be devoured; and all thine adversaries, every one of them, shall go into captivity; and they that spoil thee shall be a spoil, and all that prey upon thee will I give for a prey.

17 For I will restore health unto thee, and I will heal thee of thy wounds, saith the LORD; because they called thee an Outcast, *saying*, This *is* Zion, whom no man seeketh after.

18 Thus saith the LORD; Behold, I will bring again the captivity of Jacob's tents, and have mercy on his dwellingplaces; and the city shall be builded upon her own heap, and the palace shall remain after the manner thereof.

19 And out of them shall proceed thanksgiving and the voice of them that make merry: and I will multiply them, and they shall not be few; I will also glorify them, and they shall not be small.

20 Their children also shall be as aforetime, and their congregation shall be established before me, and I will punish all that oppress them.

21 And their nobles shall be of themselves, and their governor shall proceed from the midst of them; and I will cause him to draw near, and he shall approach unto me: for who *is* this that engaged his heart to approach unto me? saith the LORD.

22 And ye shall be my people, and I will be your God.

23 Behold, the whirlwind of the LORD goeth forth with fury, a continuing whirlwind: it shall fall with pain upon the head of the wicked.

24 The fierce anger of the LORD shall not return, until he have done *it*, and until he have performed the intents of his heart: in the latter days ye shall consider it.

31 At the same time, saith the LORD, will I be the God of all the families of Israel, and they shall be my people.

2 Thus saith the LORD, The people *which were* left of the sword found grace in the wilderness; *even* Israel, when I went to cause him to rest.

3 The LORD hath appeared of old unto me, *saying*, Yea, I have loved thee with an everlasting love: therefore with lovingkindness have I drawn thee.

4 Again I will build thee, and thou shalt be built, O virgin of Israel: thou shalt again be adorned with thy tabrets, and shalt go forth in the dances of them that make merry.

5 Thou shalt yet plant vines upon the mountains of Samaria: the planters shall plant, and shall eat *them* as common things.

6 For there shall be a day, *that* the watchmen upon the mount Ephraim shall cry, Arise ye, and let us go up to Zion unto the LORD our God.

7 For thus saith the LORD; Sing with gladness for Jacob, and shout among the chief of the nations: publish ye, praise ye, and say, O LORD, save thy people, the remnant of Israel.

8 Behold, I will bring them from the north country, and gather them from the coasts of the earth, *and* with them the blind and the lame, the woman with child and her that travaileth with child together: a great company shall return thither.

9 They shall come with weeping, and with supplications will I lead them: I

will cause them to walk by the rivers of waters in a straight way, wherein they shall not stumble: for I am a father to Israel, and Ephraim *is* my firstborn.

10 Hear the word of the LORD, O ye nations, and declare *it* in the isles afar off, and say, He that scattered Israel will gather him, and keep him, as a shepherd *doth* his flock.

11 For the LORD hath redeemed Jacob, and ransomed him from the hand of *him that was* stronger than he.

12 Therefore they shall come and sing in the height of Zion, and shall flow together to the goodness of the LORD, for wheat, and for wine, and for oil, and for the young of the flock and of the herd: and their soul shall be as a watered garden; and they shall not sorrow any more at all.

13 Then shall the virgin rejoice in the dance, both young men and old together: for I will turn their mourning into joy, and will comfort them, and make them rejoice from their sorrow.

14 And I will satiate the soul of the priests with fatness, and my people shall be satisfied with my goodness, saith the LORD.

15 Thus saith the LORD; A voice was heard in Ramah, lamentation, *and* bitter weeping; Rahel weeping for her children refused to be comforted for her children, because they *were* not.

16 Thus saith the LORD; Refrain thy voice from weeping, and thine eyes from tears: for thy work shall be rewarded, saith the LORD; and they shall come again from the land of the enemy.

17 And there is hope in thine end, saith the LORD, that thy children shall come again to their own border.

18 I have surely heard Ephraim bemoaning himself *thus*; Thou hast chastised me, and I was chastised, as a bullock unaccustomed *to the yoke*: turn thou me, and I shall be turned; for thou *art* the LORD my God.

19 Surely after that I was turned, I repented; and after that I was instructed, I smote upon *my* thigh: I was ashamed, yea, even confounded, because I did bear the reproach of my youth.

20 *Is* Ephraim my dear son? *is he* a pleasant child? for since I spake against him, I do earnestly remember him still: therefore my bowels are troubled for him; I will surely have mercy upon him, saith the LORD.

21 Set thee up waymarks, make thee high heaps: set thine heart toward the highway, *even* the way *which* thou wentest: turn again, O virgin of Israel, turn again to these thy cities.

22 How long wilt thou go about, O thou backsliding daughter? for the LORD hath created a new thing in the earth, A woman shall compass a man.

23 Thus saith the LORD of hosts, the God of Israel; As yet they shall use this speech in the land of Judah and in the cities thereof, when I shall bring again their captivity; The LORD bless thee, O habitation of justice, *and* mountain of holiness.

24 And there shall dwell in Judah itself, and in all the cities thereof together, husbandmen, and they *that* go forth with flocks.

25 For I have satiated the weary soul, and I have replenished every sorrowful soul.

26 Upon this I awaked, and beheld; and my sleep was sweet unto me.

27 Behold, the days come, saith the
LORD, that I will sow the house of Israel
and the house of Judah with the seed of
man, and with the seed of beast.
28 And it shall come to pass, *that* like
as I have watched over them, to pluck
up, and to break down, and to throw
down, and to destroy, and to afflict; so
will I watch over them, to build, and to
plant, saith the LORD.
29 In those days they shall say no
more, The fathers have eaten a sour
grape, and the children's teeth are set
on edge.
30 But every one shall die for his own
iniquity: every man that eateth the
sour grape, his teeth shall be set on
edge.
31 Behold, the days come, saith the
LORD, that I will make a new covenant
with the house of Israel, and with the
house of Judah:
32 Not according to the covenant that
I made with their fathers in the day
that I took them by the hand to bring
them out of the land of Egypt; which
my covenant they brake, although I was
an husband unto them, saith the LORD:
33 But this *shall be* the covenant that
I will make with the house of Israel;
After those days, saith the LORD, I will
put my law in their inward parts, and
write it in their hearts; and will be their
God, and they shall be my people.
34 And they shall teach no more
every man his neighbour, and every
man his brother, saying, Know the
LORD: for they shall all know me, from
the least of them unto the greatest of
them, saith the LORD: for I will forgive
their iniquity, and I will remember
their sin no more.
35 Thus saith the LORD, which giveth
the sun for a light by day, *and* the ordinances of the moon and of the stars for
a light by night, which divideth the sea
when the waves thereof roar; The LORD
of hosts *is* his name:
36 If those ordinances depart from
before me, saith the LORD, *then* the
seed of Israel also shall cease from
being a nation before me for ever.
37 Thus saith the LORD; If heaven
above can be measured, and the foundations of the earth searched out
beneath, I will also cast off all the seed
of Israel for all that they have done,
saith the LORD.
38 Behold, the days come, saith the
LORD, that the city shall be built to the
LORD from the tower of Hananeel unto
the gate of the corner.
39 And the measuring line shall yet
go forth over against it upon the hill
Gareb, and shall compass about to
Goath.
40 And the whole valley of the dead
bodies, and of the ashes, and all the
fields unto the brook of Kidron, unto
the corner of the horse gate toward the
east, *shall be* holy unto the LORD; it
shall not be plucked up, nor thrown
down any more for ever.

32 The word that came to Jeremiah
from the LORD in the tenth year
of Zedekiah king of Judah, which *was*
the eighteenth year of Nebuchadrezzar.
2 For then the king of Babylon's army
besieged Jerusalem: and Jeremiah the
prophet was shut up in the court of the
prison, which *was* in the king of Judah's
house.
3 For Zedekiah king of Judah had
shut him up, saying, Wherefore dost
thou prophesy, and say, Thus saith the
LORD, Behold, I will give this city into

the hand of the king of Babylon, and he shall take it;

4 And Zedekiah king of Judah shall not escape out of the hand of the Chaldeans, but shall surely be delivered into the hand of the king of Babylon, and shall speak with him mouth to mouth, and his eyes shall behold his eyes;

5 And he shall lead Zedekiah to Babylon, and there shall he be until I visit him, saith the LORD: though ye fight with the Chaldeans, ye shall not prosper.

6 And Jeremiah said, The word of the LORD came unto me, saying,

7 Behold, Hanameel the son of Shallum thine uncle shall come unto thee, saying, Buy thee my field that *is* in Anathoth: for the right of redemption *is* thine to buy *it*.

8 So Hanameel mine uncle's son came to me in the court of the prison according to the word of the LORD, and said unto me, Buy my field, I pray thee, that *is* in Anathoth, which *is* in the country of Benjamin: for the right of inheritance *is* thine, and the redemption *is* thine; buy *it* for thyself. Then I knew that this *was* the word of the LORD.

9 And I bought the field of Hanameel my uncle's son, that *was* in Anathoth, and weighed him the money, *even* seventeen shekels of silver.

10 And I subscribed the evidence, and sealed *it*, and took witnesses, and weighed *him* the money in the balances.

11 So I took the evidence of the purchase, *both* that which was sealed *according* to the law and custom, and that which was open:

12 And I gave the evidence of the purchase unto Baruch the son of Neriah, the son of Maaseiah, in the sight of Hanameel mine uncle's *son*, and in the presence of the witnesses that subscribed the book of the purchase, before all the Jews that sat in the court of the prison.

13 And I charged Baruch before them, saying,

14 Thus saith the LORD of hosts, the God of Israel; Take these evidences, this evidence of the purchase, both which is sealed, and this evidence which is open; and put them in an earthen vessel, that they may continue many days.

15 For thus saith the LORD of hosts, the God of Israel; Houses and fields and vineyards shall be possessed again in this land.

16 Now when I had delivered the evidence of the purchase unto Baruch the son of Neriah, I prayed unto the LORD, saying,

17 Ah Lord GOD! behold, thou hast made the heaven and the earth by thy great power and stretched out arm, *and* there is nothing too hard for thee:

18 Thou shewest lovingkindness unto thousands, and recompensest the iniquity of the fathers into the bosom of their children after them: the Great, the Mighty God, the LORD of hosts, *is* his name,

19 Great in counsel, and mighty in work: for thine eyes *are* open upon all the ways of the sons of men: to give every one according to his ways, and according to the fruit of his doings:

20 Which hast set signs and wonders in the land of Egypt, *even* unto this day, and in Israel, and among *other* men;

and hast made thee a name, as at this
day;
21 And hast brought forth thy people
Israel out of the land of Egypt with
signs, and with wonders, and with a
strong hand, and with a stretched out
arm, and with great terror;
22 And hast given them this land,
which thou didst swear to their fathers
to give them, a land flowing with milk
and honey;
23 And they came in, and possessed
it; but they obeyed not thy voice, neither walked in thy law; they have done
nothing of all that thou commandedst
them to do: therefore thou hast caused
all this evil to come upon them:
24 Behold the mounts, they are come
unto the city to take it; and the city is
given into the hand of the Chaldeans,
that fight against it, because of the
sword, and of the famine, and of the
pestilence: and what thou hast spoken
is come to pass; and, behold, thou seest
it.
25 And thou hast said unto me, O
Lord GOD, Buy thee the field for money,
and take witnesses; for the city is given
into the hand of the Chaldeans.
26 Then came the word of the LORD
unto Jeremiah, saying,
27 Behold, I *am* the LORD, the God of
all flesh: is there any thing too hard for
me?
28 Therefore thus saith the LORD;
Behold, I will give this city into the
hand of the Chaldeans, and into the
hand of Nebuchadrezzar king of Babylon, and he shall take it:
29 And the Chaldeans, that fight
against this city, shall come and set fire
on this city, and burn it with the houses,
upon whose roofs they have offered
incense unto Baal, and poured out
drink offerings unto other gods, to provoke me to anger.
30 For the children of Israel and the
children of Judah have only done evil
before me from their youth: for the
children of Israel have only provoked
me to anger with the work of their
hands, saith the LORD.
31 For this city hath been to me *as* a
provocation of mine anger and of my
fury from the day that they built it even
unto this day; that I should remove it
from before my face,
32 Because of all the evil of the children of Israel and of the children of
Judah, which they have done to provoke me to anger, they, their kings,
their princes, their priests, and their
prophets, and the men of Judah, and
the inhabitants of Jerusalem.
33 And they have turned unto me the
back, and not the face: though I taught
them, rising up early and teaching
them, yet they have not hearkened to
receive instruction.
34 But they set their abominations in
the house, which is called by my name,
to defile it.
35 And they built the high places of
Baal, which *are* in the valley of the son
of Hinnom, to cause their sons and
their daughters to pass through *the fire*
unto Molech; which I commanded them
not, neither came it into my mind, that
they should do this abomination, to
cause Judah to sin.
36 And now therefore thus saith the
LORD, the God of Israel, concerning this
city, whereof ye say, It shall be delivered into the hand of the king of
Babylon by the sword, and by the famine, and by the pestilence;
37 Behold, I will gather them out of
all countries, whither I have driven

them in mine anger, and in my fury, and
in great wrath; and I will bring them
again unto this place, and I will cause
them to dwell safely:
38 And they shall be my people, and I
will be their God:
39 And I will give them one heart, and
one way, that they may fear me for ever,
for the good of them, and of their children after them:
40 And I will make an everlasting
covenant with them, that I will not turn
away from them, to do them good; but I
will put my fear in their hearts, that
they shall not depart from me.
41 Yea, I will rejoice over them to do
them good, and I will plant them in this
land assuredly with my whole heart
and with my whole soul.
42 For thus saith the LORD; Like as I
have brought all this great evil upon
this people, so will I bring upon them
all the good that I have promised them.
43 And fields shall be bought in this
land, whereof ye say, *It is* desolate without man or beast; it is given into the
hand of the Chaldeans.
44 Men shall buy fields for money,
and subscribe evidences, and seal
them, and take witnesses in the land of
Benjamin, and in the places about
Jerusalem, and in the cities of Judah,
and in the cities of the mountains, and
in the cities of the valley, and in the
cities of the south: for I will cause their
captivity to return, saith the LORD.

33 Moreover the word of the LORD
came unto Jeremiah the second
time, while he was yet shut up in the
court of the prison, saying,
2 Thus saith the LORD the maker
thereof, the LORD that formed it, to
establish it; the LORD *is* his name;
3 Call unto me, and I will answer thee,
and shew thee great and mighty things,
which thou knowest not.
4 For thus saith the LORD, the God of
Israel, concerning the houses of this
city, and concerning the houses of the
kings of Judah, which are thrown down
by the mounts, and by the sword;
5 They come to fight with the
Chaldeans, but *it is* to fill them with
the dead bodies of men, whom I have
slain in mine anger and in my fury, and
for all whose wickedness I have hid my
face from this city.
6 Behold, I will bring it health and
cure, and I will cure them, and will
reveal unto them the abundance of
peace and truth.
7 And I will cause the captivity of
Judah and the captivity of Israel to
return, and will build them, as at the
first.
8 And I will cleanse them from all
their iniquity, whereby they have
sinned against me; and I will pardon all
their iniquities, whereby they have
sinned, and whereby they have transgressed against me.
9 And it shall be to me a name of joy,
a praise and an honour before all the
nations of the earth, which shall hear
all the good that I do unto them: and
they shall fear and tremble for all the
goodness and for all the prosperity that
I procure unto it.
10 Thus saith the LORD; Again there
shall be heard in this place, which ye
say *shall be* desolate without man and
without beast, *even* in the cities of
Judah, and in the streets of Jerusalem,
that are desolate, without man, and
without inhabitant, and without beast,
11 The voice of joy, and the voice of
gladness, the voice of the bridegroom,

and the voice of the bride, the voice of
them that shall say, Praise the LORD of
hosts: for the LORD *is* good; for his
mercy *endureth* for ever: *and* of them
that shall bring the sacrifice of praise
into the house of the LORD. For I will
cause to return the captivity of the
land, as at the first, saith the LORD.
12 Thus saith the LORD of hosts; Again
in this place, which is desolate without
man and without beast, and in all the
cities thereof, shall be an habitation of
shepherds causing *their* flocks to lie
down.
13 In the cities of the mountains, in
the cities of the vale, and in the cities of
the south, and in the land of Benjamin,
and in the places about Jerusalem, and
in the cities of Judah, shall the flocks
pass again under the hands of him that
telleth *them*, saith the LORD.
14 Behold, the days come, saith the
LORD, that I will perform that good
thing which I have promised unto the
house of Israel and to the house of
Judah.
15 In those days, and at that time, will
I cause the Branch of righteousness to
grow up unto David; and he shall execute judgment and righteousness in
the land.
16 In those days shall Judah be saved,
and Jerusalem shall dwell safely: and
this *is the name* wherewith she shall be
called, The LORD our righteousness.
17 For thus saith the LORD; David
shall never want a man to sit upon the
throne of the house of Israel;
18 Neither shall the priests the
Levites want a man before me to offer
burnt offerings, and to kindle meat
offerings, and to do sacrifice continually.
19 And the word of the LORD came
unto Jeremiah, saying,
20 Thus saith the LORD; If ye can
break my covenant of the day, and my
covenant of the night, and that there
should not be day and night in their
season;
21 *Then* may also my covenant be
broken with David my servant, that he
should not have a son to reign upon his
throne; and with the Levites the priests,
my ministers.
22 As the host of heaven cannot be
numbered, neither the sand of the sea
measured: so will I multiply the seed of
David my servant, and the Levites that
minister unto me.
23 Moreover the word of the LORD
came to Jeremiah, saying,
24 Considerest thou not what this
people have spoken, saying, The two
families which the LORD hath chosen,
he hath even cast them off? thus they
have despised my people, that they
should be no more a nation before
them.
25 Thus saith the LORD; If my covenant *be* not with day and night, *and if* I
have not appointed the ordinances of
heaven and earth;
26 Then will I cast away the seed of
Jacob, and David my servant, *so* that I
will not take *any* of his seed *to be* rulers
over the seed of Abraham, Isaac, and
Jacob: for I will cause their captivity to
return, and have mercy on them.

34 The word which came unto
Jeremiah from the LORD, when
Nebuchadnezzar king of Babylon, and
all his army, and all the kingdoms of
the earth of his dominion, and all the
people, fought against Jerusalem, and
against all the cities thereof, saying,

2 Thus saith the LORD, the God of Israel; Go and speak to Zedekiah king of Judah, and tell him, Thus saith the LORD; Behold, I will give this city into the hand of the king of Babylon, and he shall burn it with fire:

3 And thou shalt not escape out of his hand, but shalt surely be taken, and delivered into his hand; and thine eyes shall behold the eyes of the king of Babylon, and he shall speak with thee mouth to mouth, and thou shalt go to Babylon.

4 Yet hear the word of the LORD, O Zedekiah king of Judah; Thus saith the LORD of thee, Thou shalt not die by the sword:

5 *But* thou shalt die in peace: and with the burnings of thy fathers, the former kings which were before thee, so shall they burn *odours* for thee; and they will lament thee, *saying*, Ah lord! for I have pronounced the word, saith the LORD.

6 Then Jeremiah the prophet spake all these words unto Zedekiah king of Judah in Jerusalem,

7 When the king of Babylon's army fought against Jerusalem, and against all the cities of Judah that were left, against Lachish, and against Azekah: for these defenced cities remained of the cities of Judah.

8 *This is* the word that came unto Jeremiah from the LORD, after that the king Zedekiah had made a covenant with all the people which *were* at Jerusalem, to proclaim liberty unto them;

9 That every man should let his manservant, and every man his maidservant, *being* an Hebrew or an Hebrewess, go free; that none should serve himself of them, *to wit*, of a Jew his brother.

10 Now when all the princes, and all the people, which had entered into the covenant, heard that every one should let his manservant, and every one his maidservant, go free, that none should serve themselves of them any more, then they obeyed, and let *them* go.

11 But afterward they turned, and caused the servants and the handmaids, whom they had let go free, to return, and brought them into subjection for servants and for handmaids.

12 Therefore the word of the LORD came to Jeremiah from the LORD, saying,

13 Thus saith the LORD, the God of Israel; I made a covenant with your fathers in the day that I brought them forth out of the land of Egypt, out of the house of bondmen, saying,

14 At the end of seven years let ye go every man his brother an Hebrew, which hath been sold unto thee; and when he hath served thee six years, thou shalt let him go free from thee: but your fathers hearkened not unto me, neither inclined their ear.

15 And ye were now turned, and had done right in my sight, in proclaiming liberty every man to his neighbour; and ye had made a covenant before me in the house which is called by my name:

16 But ye turned and polluted my name, and caused every man his servant, and every man his handmaid, whom ye had set at liberty at their pleasure, to return, and brought them into subjection, to be unto you for servants and for handmaids.

17 Therefore thus saith the LORD; Ye have not hearkened unto me, in proclaiming liberty, every one to his brother, and every man to his neighbour: behold, I proclaim a liberty for you,

saith the LORD, to the sword, to the
pestilence, and to the famine; and I will
make you to be removed into all the
kingdoms of the earth.
18 And I will give the men that have
transgressed my covenant, which have
not performed the words of the covenant which they had made before me,
when they cut the calf in twain, and
passed between the parts thereof,
19 The princes of Judah, and the
princes of Jerusalem, the eunuchs, and
the priests, and all the people of the
land, which passed between the parts
of the calf;
20 I will even give them into the hand
of their enemies, and into the hand of
them that seek their life: and their
dead bodies shall be for meat unto the
fowls of the heaven, and to the beasts of
the earth.
21 And Zedekiah king of Judah and
his princes will I give into the hand of
their enemies, and into the hand of
them that seek their life, and into the
hand of the king of Babylon's army,
which are gone up from you.
22 Behold, I will command, saith the
LORD, and cause them to return to this
city; and they shall fight against it, and
take it, and burn it with fire: and I will
make the cities of Judah a desolation
without an inhabitant.

35 The word which came unto
Jeremiah from the LORD in the
days of Jehoiakim the son of Josiah
king of Judah, saying,
2 Go unto the house of the Rechabites,
and speak unto them, and bring them
into the house of the LORD, into one of
the chambers, and give them wine to
drink.
3 Then I took Jaazaniah the son of
Jeremiah, the son of Habaziniah, and
his brethren, and all his sons, and the
whole house of the Rechabites;
4 And I brought them into the house
of the LORD, into the chamber of the
sons of Hanan, the son of Igdaliah, a
man of God, which *was* by the chamber
of the princes, which *was* above the
chamber of Maaseiah the son of
Shallum, the keeper of the door:
5 And I set before the sons of the
house of the Rechabites pots full of
wine, and cups, and I said unto them,
Drink ye wine.
6 But they said, We will drink no
wine: for Jonadab the son of Rechab
our father commanded us, saying, Ye
shall drink no wine, *neither ye*, nor
your sons for ever:
7 Neither shall ye build house, nor
sow seed, nor plant vineyard, nor have
any: but all your days ye shall dwell in
tents; that ye may live many days in the
land where ye *be* strangers.
8 Thus have we obeyed the voice of
Jonadab the son of Rechab our father
in all that he hath charged us, to drink
no wine all our days, we, our wives, our
sons, nor our daughters;
9 Nor to build houses for us to dwell
in: neither have we vineyard, nor field,
nor seed:
10 But we have dwelt in tents, and
have obeyed, and done according to all
that Jonadab our father commanded
us.
11 But it came to pass, when Nebuchadrezzar king of Babylon came up
into the land, that we said, Come, and
let us go to Jerusalem for fear of the
army of the Chaldeans, and for fear of
the army of the Syrians: so we dwell at
Jerusalem.

12 Then came the word of the LORD
unto Jeremiah, saying,
13 Thus saith the LORD of hosts, the
God of Israel; Go and tell the men of
Judah and the inhabitants of Jerusalem,
Will ye not receive instruction to heark-
en to my words? saith the LORD.
14 The words of Jonadab the son of
Rechab, that he commanded his sons
not to drink wine, are performed; for
unto this day they drink none, but obey
their father's commandment: notwithstanding I have spoken unto you, rising
early and speaking; but ye hearkened
not unto me.
15 I have sent also unto you all my
servants the prophets, rising up early
and sending *them*, saying, Return ye
now every man from his evil way, and
amend your doings, and go not after
other gods to serve them, and ye shall
dwell in the land which I have given to
you and to your fathers: but ye have not
inclined your ear, nor hearkened unto
me.
16 Because the sons of Jonadab the
son of Rechab have performed the commandment of their father, which he
commanded them; but this people hath
not hearkened unto me:
17 Therefore thus saith the LORD God
of hosts, the God of Israel; Behold, I will
bring upon Judah and upon all the
inhabitants of Jerusalem all the evil
that I have pronounced against them:
because I have spoken unto them, but
they have not heard; and I have called
unto them, but they have not answered.
18 And Jeremiah said unto the house
of the Rechabites, Thus saith the LORD
of hosts, the God of Israel; Because ye
have obeyed the commandment of
Jonadab your father, and kept all his
precepts, and done according unto all
that he hath commanded you:
19 Therefore thus saith the LORD of
hosts, the God of Israel; Jonadab the
son of Rechab shall not want a man to
stand before me for ever.

36

And it came to pass in the fourth
year of Jehoiakim the son of
Josiah king of Judah, *that* this word
came unto Jeremiah from the LORD,
saying,
2 Take thee a roll of a book, and write
therein all the words that I have spoken
unto thee against Israel, and against
Judah, and against all the nations, from
the day I spake unto thee, from the
days of Josiah, even unto this day.
3 It may be that the house of Judah
will hear all the evil which I purpose to
do unto them; that they may return
every man from his evil way; that I may
forgive their iniquity and their sin.
4 Then Jeremiah called Baruch the
son of Neriah: and Baruch wrote from
the mouth of Jeremiah all the words of
the LORD, which he had spoken unto
him, upon a roll of a book.
5 And Jeremiah commanded Baruch,
saying, I *am* shut up; I cannot go into
the house of the LORD:
6 Therefore go thou, and read in the
roll, which thou hast written from my
mouth, the words of the LORD in the
ears of the people in the LORD's house
upon the fasting day: and also thou
shalt read them in the ears of all Judah
that come out of their cities.
7 It may be they will present their
supplication before the LORD, and will
return every one from his evil way: for
great *is* the anger and the fury that the
LORD hath pronounced against this
people.

8 And Baruch the son of Neriah did according to all that Jeremiah the prophet commanded him, reading in the book the words of the LORD in the LORD's house.

9 And it came to pass in the fifth year of Jehoiakim the son of Josiah king of Judah, in the ninth month, *that* they proclaimed a fast before the LORD to all the people in Jerusalem, and to all the people that came from the cities of Judah unto Jerusalem.

10 Then read Baruch in the book the words of Jeremiah in the house of the LORD, in the chamber of Gemariah the son of Shaphan the scribe, in the higher court, at the entry of the new gate of the LORD's house, in the ears of all the people.

11 When Michaiah the son of Gemariah, the son of Shaphan, had heard out of the book all the words of the LORD,

12 Then he went down into the king's house, into the scribe's chamber: and, lo, all the princes sat there, *even* Elishama the scribe, and Delaiah the son of Shemaiah, and Elnathan the son of Achbor, and Gemariah the son of Shaphan, and Zedekiah the son of Hananiah, and all the princes.

13 Then Michaiah declared unto them all the words that he had heard, when Baruch read the book in the ears of the people.

14 Therefore all the princes sent Jehudi the son of Nethaniah, the son of Shelemiah, the son of Cushi, unto Baruch, saying, Take in thine hand the roll wherein thou hast read in the ears of the people, and come. So Baruch the son of Neriah took the roll in his hand, and came unto them.

15 And they said unto him, Sit down now, and read it in our ears. So Baruch read *it* in their ears.

16 Now it came to pass, when they had heard all the words, they were afraid both one and other, and said unto Baruch, We will surely tell the king of all these words.

17 And they asked Baruch, saying, Tell us now, How didst thou write all these words at his mouth?

18 Then Baruch answered them, He pronounced all these words unto me with his mouth, and I wrote *them* with ink in the book.

19 Then said the princes unto Baruch, Go, hide thee, thou and Jeremiah; and let no man know where ye be.

20 And they went in to the king into the court, but they laid up the roll in the chamber of Elishama the scribe, and told all the words in the ears of the king.

21 So the king sent Jehudi to fetch the roll: and he took it out of Elishama the scribe's chamber. And Jehudi read it in the ears of the king, and in the ears of all the princes which stood beside the king.

22 Now the king sat in the winterhouse in the ninth month: and *there was a fire* on the hearth burning before him.

23 And it came to pass, *that* when Jehudi had read three or four leaves, he cut it with the penknife, and cast *it* into the fire that *was* on the hearth, until all the roll was consumed in the fire that *was* on the hearth.

24 Yet they were not afraid, nor rent their garments, *neither* the king, nor any of his servants that heard all these words.

25 Nevertheless Elnathan and
Delaiah and Gemariah had made intercession to the king that he would not
burn the roll: but he would not hear
them.
26 But the king commanded Jerahmeel the son of Hammelech, and
Seraiah the son of Azriel, and Shelemiah the son of Abdeel, to take
Baruch the scribe and Jeremiah the
prophet: but the LORD hid them.
27 Then the word of the LORD came to
Jeremiah, after that the king had
burned the roll, and the words which
Baruch wrote at the mouth of Jeremiah,
saying,
28 Take thee again another roll, and
write in it all the former words that
were in the first roll, which Jehoiakim
the king of Judah hath burned.
29 And thou shalt say to Jehoiakim
king of Judah, Thus saith the LORD;
Thou hast burned this roll, saying, Why
hast thou written therein, saying, The
king of Babylon shall certainly come
and destroy this land, and shall cause
to cease from thence man and beast?
30 Therefore thus saith the LORD of
Jehoiakim king of Judah; He shall have
none to sit upon the throne of David:
and his dead body shall be cast out in
the day to the heat, and in the night to
the frost.
31 And I will punish him and his seed
and his servants for their iniquity; and
I will bring upon them, and upon the
inhabitants of Jerusalem, and upon the
men of Judah, all the evil that I have
pronounced against them; but they
hearkened not.
32 Then took Jeremiah another roll,
and gave it to Baruch the scribe, the
son of Neriah; who wrote therein from
the mouth of Jeremiah all the words of
the book which Jehoiakim king of
Judah had burned in the fire: and there
were added besides unto them many
like words.

37 And king Zedekiah the son of
Josiah reigned instead of Coniah
the son of Jehoiakim, whom Nebuchadrezzar king of Babylon made king
in the land of Judah.
2 But neither he, nor his servants, nor
the people of the land, did hearken
unto the words of the LORD, which he
spake by the prophet Jeremiah.
3 And Zedekiah the king sent Jehucal
the son of Shelemiah and Zephaniah
the son of Maaseiah the priest to the
prophet Jeremiah, saying, Pray now
unto the LORD our God for us.
4 Now Jeremiah came in and went
out among the people: for they had not
put him into prison.
5 Then Pharaoh's army was come
forth out of Egypt: and when the
Chaldeans that besieged Jerusalem
heard tidings of them, they departed
from Jerusalem.
6 Then came the word of the LORD
unto the prophet Jeremiah, saying,
7 Thus saith the LORD, the God of
Israel; Thus shall ye say to the king of
Judah, that sent you unto me to enquire
of me; Behold, Pharaoh's army, which is
come forth to help you, shall return to
Egypt into their own land.
8 And the Chaldeans shall come
again, and fight against this city, and
take it, and burn it with fire.
9 Thus saith the LORD; Deceive not
yourselves, saying, The Chaldeans shall
surely depart from us: for they shall not
depart.
10 For though ye had smitten the
whole army of the Chaldeans that fight
against you, and there remained *but*

wounded men among them, *yet* should they rise up every man in his tent, and burn this city with fire.

11 And it came to pass, that when the army of the Chaldeans was broken up from Jerusalem for fear of Pharaoh's army,

12 Then Jeremiah went forth out of Jerusalem to go into the land of Benjamin, to separate himself thence in the midst of the people.

13 And when he was in the gate of Benjamin, a captain of the ward *was* there, whose name *was* Irijah, the son of Shelemiah, the son of Hananiah; and he took Jeremiah the prophet, saying, Thou fallest away to the Chaldeans.

14 Then said Jeremiah, *It is* false; I fall not away to the Chaldeans. But he hearkened not to him: so Irijah took Jeremiah, and brought him to the princes.

15 Wherefore the princes were wroth with Jeremiah, and smote him, and put him in prison in the house of Jonathan the scribe: for they had made that the prison.

16 When Jeremiah was entered into the dungeon, and into the cabins, and Jeremiah had remained there many days;

17 Then Zedekiah the king sent, and took him out: and the king asked him secretly in his house, and said, Is there *any* word from the Lord? And Jeremiah said, There is: for, said he, thou shalt be delivered into the hand of the king of Babylon.

18 Moreover Jeremiah said unto king Zedekiah, What have I offended against thee, or against thy servants, or against this people, that ye have put me in prison?

19 Where *are* now your prophets which prophesied unto you, saying, The king of Babylon shall not come against you, nor against this land?

20 Therefore hear now, I pray thee, O my lord the king: let my supplication, I pray thee, be accepted before thee; that thou cause me not to return to the house of Jonathan the scribe, lest I die there.

21 Then Zedekiah the king commanded that they should commit Jeremiah into the court of the prison, and that they should give him daily a piece of bread out of the bakers' street, until all the bread in the city were spent. Thus Jeremiah remained in the court of the prison.

38 Then Shephatiah the son of Mattan, and Gedaliah the son of Pashur, and Jucal the son of Shelemiah, and Pashur the son of Malchiah, heard the words that Jeremiah had spoken unto all the people, saying,

2 Thus saith the Lord, He that remaineth in this city shall die by the sword, by the famine, and by the pestilence: but he that goeth forth to the Chaldeans shall live; for he shall have his life for a prey, and shall live.

3 Thus saith the Lord, This city shall surely be given into the hand of the king of Babylon's army, which shall take it.

4 Therefore the princes said unto the king, We beseech thee, let this man be put to death: for thus he weakeneth the hands of the men of war that remain in this city, and the hands of all the people, in speaking such words unto them: for this man seeketh not the welfare of this people, but the hurt.

5 Then Zedekiah the king said,
Behold, he *is* in your hand: for the king
is not *he that* can do *any* thing against
you.
6 Then took they Jeremiah, and cast
him into the dungeon of Malchiah the
son of Hammelech, that *was* in the
court of the prison: and they let down
Jeremiah with cords. And in the dungeon *there was* no water, but mire: so
Jeremiah sunk in the mire.
7 Now when Ebed-melech the
Ethiopian, one of the eunuchs which
was in the king's house, heard that they
had put Jeremiah in the dungeon; the
king then sitting in the gate of
Benjamin;
8 Ebed-melech went forth out of the
king's house, and spake to the king, saying,
9 My lord the king, these men have
done evil in all that they have done to
Jeremiah the prophet, whom they have
cast into the dungeon; and he is like to
die for hunger in the place where he is:
for *there is* no more bread in the city.
10 Then the king commanded Ebed-
melech the Ethiopian, saying, Take
from hence thirty men with thee, and
take up Jeremiah the prophet out of
the dungeon, before he die.
11 So Ebed-melech took the men with
him, and went into the house of the
king under the treasury, and took
thence old cast clouts and old rotten
rags, and let them down by cords into
the dungeon to Jeremiah.
12 And Ebed-melech the Ethiopian
said unto Jeremiah, Put now *these* old
cast clouts and rotten rags under thine
armholes under the cords. And
Jeremiah did so.
13 So they drew up Jeremiah with
cords, and took him up out of the dungeon: and Jeremiah remained in the
court of the prison.
14 Then Zedekiah the king sent, and
took Jeremiah the prophet unto him
into the third entry that *is* in the house
of the LORD: and the king said unto
Jeremiah, I will ask thee a thing; hide
nothing from me.
15 Then Jeremiah said unto Zedekiah,
If I declare *it* unto thee, wilt thou not
surely put me to death? and if I give
thee counsel, wilt thou not hearken
unto me?
16 So Zedekiah the king sware secretly unto Jeremiah, saying, *As* the LORD
liveth, that made us this soul, I will not
put thee to death, neither will I give
thee into the hand of these men that
seek thy life.
17 Then said Jeremiah unto Zedekiah,
Thus saith the LORD, the God of hosts,
the God of Israel; If thou wilt assuredly
go forth unto the king of Babylon's
princes, then thy soul shall live, and
this city shall not be burned with fire;
and thou shalt live, and thine house:
18 But if thou wilt not go forth to the
king of Babylon's princes, then shall
this city be given into the hand of the
Chaldeans, and they shall burn it with
fire, and thou shalt not escape out of
their hand.
19 And Zedekiah the king said unto
Jeremiah, I am afraid of the Jews that
are fallen to the Chaldeans, lest they
deliver me into their hand, and they
mock me.
20 But Jeremiah said, They shall not
deliver *thee*. Obey, I beseech thee, the
voice of the LORD, which I speak unto
thee: so it shall be well unto thee, and
thy soul shall live.

21 But if thou refuse to go forth, this *is* the word that the LORD hath shewed me:

22 And, behold, all the women that are left in the king of Judah's house *shall be* brought forth to the king of Babylon's princes, and those *women* shall say, Thy friends have set thee on, and have prevailed against thee: thy feet are sunk in the mire, *and* they are turned away back.

23 So they shall bring out all thy wives and thy children to the Chaldeans: and thou shalt not escape out of their hand, but shalt be taken by the hand of the king of Babylon: and thou shalt cause this city to be burned with fire.

24 Then said Zedekiah unto Jeremiah, Let no man know of these words, and thou shalt not die.

25 But if the princes hear that I have talked with thee, and they come unto thee, and say unto thee, Declare unto us now what thou hast said unto the king, hide it not from us, and we will not put thee to death; also what the king said unto thee:

26 Then thou shalt say unto them, I presented my supplication before the king, that he would not cause me to return to Jonathan's house, to die there.

27 Then came all the princes unto Jeremiah, and asked him: and he told them according to all these words that the king had commanded. So they left off speaking with him; for the matter was not perceived.

28 So Jeremiah abode in the court of the prison until the day that Jerusalem was taken: and he was *there* when Jerusalem was taken.

39 In the ninth year of Zedekiah king of Judah, in the tenth month, came Nebuchadrezzar king of Babylon and all his army against Jerusalem, and they besieged it.

2 *And* in the eleventh year of Zedekiah, in the fourth month, the ninth *day* of the month, the city was broken up.

3 And all the princes of the king of Babylon came in, and sat in the middle gate, *even* Nergal-sharezer, Samgar-nebo, Sarsechim, Rab-saris, Nergal-sharezer, Rab-mag, with all the residue of the princes of the king of Babylon.

4 And it came to pass, *that* when Zedekiah the king of Judah saw them, and all the men of war, then they fled, and went forth out of the city by night, by the way of the king's garden, by the gate betwixt the two walls: and he went out the way of the plain.

5 But the Chaldeans' army pursued after them, and overtook Zedekiah in the plains of Jericho: and when they had taken him, they brought him up to Nebuchadnezzar king of Babylon to Riblah in the land of Hamath, where he gave judgment upon him.

6 Then the king of Babylon slew the sons of Zedekiah in Riblah before his eyes: also the king of Babylon slew all the nobles of Judah.

7 Moreover he put out Zedekiah's eyes, and bound him with chains, to carry him to Babylon.

8 And the Chaldeans burned the king's house, and the houses of the people, with fire, and brake down the walls of Jerusalem.

9 Then Nebuzar-adan the captain of the guard carried away captive into Babylon the remnant of the people that remained in the city, and those that fell away, that fell to him, with the rest of the people that remained.

10 But Nebuzar-adan the captain of the guard left of the poor of the people, which had nothing, in the land of Judah, and gave them vineyards and fields at the same time.

11 Now Nebuchadrezzar king of Babylon gave charge concerning Jeremiah to Nebuzar-adan the captain of the guard, saying,

12 Take him, and look well to him, and do him no harm; but do unto him even as he shall say unto thee.

13 So Nebuzar-adan the captain of the guard sent, and Nebushasban, Rabsaris, and Nergal-sharezer, Rab-mag, and all the king of Babylon's princes;

14 Even they sent, and took Jeremiah out of the court of the prison, and committed him unto Gedaliah the son of Ahikam the son of Shaphan, that he should carry him home: so he dwelt among the people.

15 Now the word of the LORD came unto Jeremiah, while he was shut up in the court of the prison, saying,

16 Go and speak to Ebed-melech the Ethiopian, saying, Thus saith the LORD of hosts, the God of Israel; Behold, I will bring my words upon this city for evil, and not for good; and they shall be *accomplished* in that day before thee.

17 But I will deliver thee in that day, saith the LORD: and thou shalt not be given into the hand of the men of whom thou *art* afraid.

18 For I will surely deliver thee, and thou shalt not fall by the sword, but thy life shall be for a prey unto thee: because thou hast put thy trust in me, saith the LORD.

40 The word that came to Jeremiah from the LORD, after that Nebuzar-adan the captain of the guard had let him go from Ramah, when he had taken him being bound in chains among all that were carried away captive of Jerusalem and Judah, which were carried away captive unto Babylon.

2 And the captain of the guard took Jeremiah, and said unto him, The LORD thy God hath pronounced this evil upon this place.

3 Now the LORD hath brought *it*, and done according as he hath said: because ye have sinned against the LORD, and have not obeyed his voice, therefore this thing is come upon you.

4 And now, behold, I loose thee this day from the chains which *were* upon thine hand. If it seem good unto thee to come with me into Babylon, come; and I will look well unto thee: but if it seem ill unto thee to come with me into Babylon, forbear: behold, all the land *is* before thee: whither it seemeth good and convenient for thee to go, thither go.

5 Now while he was not yet gone back, *he said*, Go back also to Gedaliah the son of Ahikam the son of Shaphan, whom the king of Babylon hath made governor over the cities of Judah, and dwell with him among the people: or go wheresoever it seemeth convenient unto thee to go. So the captain of the guard gave him victuals and a reward, and let him go.

6 Then went Jeremiah unto Gedaliah the son of Ahikam to Mizpah; and dwelt with him among the people that were left in the land.

7 Now when all the captains of the forces which *were* in the fields, *even*

they and their men, heard that the king
of Babylon had made Gedaliah the son
of Ahikam governor in the land, and
had committed unto him men, and
women, and children, and of the poor of
the land, of them that were not carried
away captive to Babylon;
8 Then they came to Gedaliah to
Mizpah, even Ishmael the son of
Nethaniah, and Johanan and Jonathan
the sons of Kareah, and Seraiah the son
of Tanhumeth, and the sons of Ephai
the Netophathite, and Jezaniah the son
of a Maachathite, they and their men.
9 And Gedaliah the son of Ahikam
the son of Shaphan sware unto them
and to their men, saying, Fear not to
serve the Chaldeans: dwell in the land,
and serve the king of Babylon, and it
shall be well with you.
10 As for me, behold, I will dwell at
Mizpah to serve the Chaldeans, which
will come unto us: but ye, gather ye
wine, and summer fruits, and oil, and
put *them* in your vessels, and dwell in
your cities that ye have taken.
11 Likewise when all the Jews that
were in Moab, and among the
Ammonites, and in Edom, and that
were in all the countries, heard that the
king of Babylon had left a remnant of
Judah, and that he had set over them
Gedaliah the son of Ahikam the son of
Shaphan;
12 Even all the Jews returned out of
all places whither they were driven,
and came to the land of Judah, to
Gedaliah, unto Mizpah, and gathered
wine and summer fruits very much.
13 Moreover Johanan the son of
Kareah, and all the captains of the
forces that *were* in the fields, came to
Gedaliah to Mizpah,
14 And said unto him, Dost thou certainly know that Baalis the king of the
Ammonites hath sent Ishmael the son
of Nethaniah to slay thee? But Gedaliah
the son of Ahikam believed them not.
15 Then Johanan the son of Kareah
spake to Gedaliah in Mizpah secretly,
saying, Let me go, I pray thee, and I will
slay Ishmael the son of Nethaniah, and
no man shall know *it*: wherefore should
he slay thee, that all the Jews which are
gathered unto thee should be scattered, and the remnant in Judah perish?
16 But Gedaliah the son of Ahikam
said unto Johanan the son of Kareah,
Thou shalt not do this thing: for thou
speakest falsely of Ishmael.

41 Now it came to pass in the seventh month, *that* Ishmael the son
of Nethaniah the son of Elishama, of
the seed royal, and the princes of the
king, even ten men with him, came
unto Gedaliah the son of Ahikam to
Mizpah; and there they did eat bread
together in Mizpah.
2 Then arose Ishmael the son of
Nethaniah, and the ten men that were
with him, and smote Gedaliah the son
of Ahikam the son of Shaphan with the
sword, and slew him, whom the king of
Babylon had made governor over the
land.
3 Ishmael also slew all the Jews that
were with him, *even* with Gedaliah, at
Mizpah, and the Chaldeans that were
found there, *and* the men of war.
4 And it came to pass the second day
after he had slain Gedaliah, and no
man knew *it*,
5 That there came certain from
Shechem, from Shiloh, and from
Samaria, *even* fourscore men, having
their beards shaven, and their clothes

rent, and having cut themselves, with
offerings and incense in their hand, to
bring *them* to the house of the LORD.
6 And Ishmael the son of Nethaniah
went forth from Mizpah to meet them,
weeping all along as he went: and it
came to pass, as he met them, he said
unto them, Come to Gedaliah the son of
Ahikam.
7 And it was *so*, when they came into
the midst of the city, that Ishmael the
son of Nethaniah slew them, *and cast
them* into the midst of the pit, he, and
the men that *were* with him.
8 But ten men were found among
them that said unto Ishmael, Slay us
not: for we have treasures in the field,
of wheat, and of barley, and of oil, and
of honey. So he forbare, and slew them
not among their brethren.
9 Now the pit wherein Ishmael had
cast all the dead bodies of the men,
whom he had slain because of Gedaliah,
was it which Asa the king had made for
fear of Baasha king of Israel: *and*
Ishmael the son of Nethaniah filled it
with *them that were* slain.
10 Then Ishmael carried away captive
all the residue of the people that *were*
in Mizpah, *even* the king's daughters,
and all the people that remained in
Mizpah, whom Nebuzar-adan the captain of the guard had committed to
Gedaliah the son of Ahikam: and
Ishmael the son of Nethaniah carried
them away captive, and departed to go
over to the Ammonites.
11 But when Johanan the son of
Kareah, and all the captains of the
forces that *were* with him, heard of all
the evil that Ishmael the son of
Nethaniah had done,
12 Then they took all the men, and
went to fight with Ishmael the son of
Nethaniah, and found him by the great
waters that *are* in Gibeon.
13 Now it came to pass, *that* when all
the people which *were* with Ishmael
saw Johanan the son of Kareah, and all
the captains of the forces that *were*
with him, then they were glad.
14 So all the people that Ishmael had
carried away captive from Mizpah cast
about and returned, and went unto
Johanan the son of Kareah.
15 But Ishmael the son of Nethaniah
escaped from Johanan with eight men,
and went to the Ammonites.
16 Then took Johanan the son of
Kareah, and all the captains of the
forces that *were* with him, all the remnant of the people whom he had recovered from Ishmael the son of Nethaniah,
from Mizpah, after *that* he had slain
Gedaliah the son of Ahikam, *even*
mighty men of war, and the women, and
the children, and the eunuchs, whom
he had brought again from Gibeon:
17 And they departed, and dwelt in
the habitation of Chimham, which is by
Beth-lehem, to go to enter into Egypt,
18 Because of the Chaldeans: for they
were afraid of them, because Ishmael
the son of Nethaniah had slain
Gedaliah the son of Ahikam, whom the
king of Babylon made governor in the
land.

42 Then all the captains of the forces, and Johanan the son of
Kareah, and Jezaniah the son of
Hoshaiah, and all the people from the
least even unto the greatest, came near,
2 And said unto Jeremiah the prophet, Let, we beseech thee, our supplication be accepted before thee, and pray
for us unto the LORD thy God, *even* for
all this remnant; (for we are left *but* a

few of many, as thine eyes do behold
us:)
3 That the LORD thy God may shew us
the way wherein we may walk, and the
thing that we may do.
4 Then Jeremiah the prophet said
unto them, I have heard *you*; behold, I
will pray unto the LORD your God
according to your words; and it shall
come to pass, *that* whatsoever thing
the LORD shall answer you, I will
declare *it* unto you; I will keep nothing
back from you.
5 Then they said to Jeremiah, The
LORD be a true and faithful witness
between us, if we do not even according
to all things for the which the LORD thy
God shall send thee to us.
6 Whether *it be* good, or whether *it be*
evil, we will obey the voice of the LORD
our God, to whom we send thee; that it
may be well with us, when we obey the
voice of the LORD our God.
7 And it came to pass after ten days,
that the word of the LORD came unto
Jeremiah.
8 Then called he Johanan the son of
Kareah, and all the captains of the
forces which *were* with him, and all the
people from the least even to the greatest,
9 And said unto them, Thus saith the
LORD, the God of Israel, unto whom ye
sent me to present your supplication
before him;
10 If ye will still abide in this land,
then will I build you, and not pull *you*
down, and I will plant you, and not
pluck *you* up: for I repent me of the evil
that I have done unto you.
11 Be not afraid of the king of
Babylon, of whom ye are afraid; be not
afraid of him, saith the LORD: for I *am*
with you to save you, and to deliver you
from his hand.
12 And I will shew mercies unto you,
that he may have mercy upon you, and
cause you to return to your own land.
13 But if ye say, We will not dwell in
this land, neither obey the voice of the
LORD your God,
14 Saying, No; but we will go into the
land of Egypt, where we shall see no
war, nor hear the sound of the trumpet,
nor have hunger of bread; and there
will we dwell:
15 And now therefore hear the word
of the LORD, ye remnant of Judah; Thus
saith the LORD of hosts, the God of
Israel; If ye wholly set your faces to
enter into Egypt, and go to sojourn
there;
16 Then it shall come to pass, *that* the
sword, which ye feared, shall overtake
you there in the land of Egypt, and the
famine, whereof ye were afraid, shall
follow close after you there in Egypt;
and there ye shall die.
17 So shall it be with all the men that
set their faces to go into Egypt to
sojourn there; they shall die by the
sword, by the famine, and by the pestilence: and none of them shall remain or
escape from the evil that I will bring
upon them.
18 For thus saith the LORD of hosts,
the God of Israel; As mine anger and
my fury hath been poured forth upon
the inhabitants of Jerusalem; so shall
my fury be poured forth upon you,
when ye shall enter into Egypt: and ye
shall be an execration, and an astonishment, and a curse, and a reproach; and
ye shall see this place no more.
19 The LORD hath said concerning
you, O ye remnant of Judah; Go ye not

into Egypt: know certainly that I have
admonished you this day.
20 For ye dissembled in your hearts,
when ye sent me unto the LORD your
God, saying, Pray for us unto the LORD
our God; and according unto all that
the LORD our God shall say, so declare
unto us, and we will do *it*.
21 And *now* I have this day declared
it to you; but ye have not obeyed the
voice of the LORD your God, nor any
thing for the which he hath sent me
unto you.
22 Now therefore know certainly that
ye shall die by the sword, by the famine,
and by the pestilence, in the place
whither ye desire to go *and* to sojourn.

43 And it came to pass, *that* when
Jeremiah had made an end of
speaking unto all the people all the
words of the LORD their God, for which
the LORD their God had sent him to
them, *even* all these words,
2 Then spake Azariah the son of
Hoshaiah, and Johanan the son of
Kareah, and all the proud men, saying
unto Jeremiah, Thou speakest falsely:
the LORD our God hath not sent thee to
say, Go not into Egypt to sojourn there:
3 But Baruch the son of Neriah
setteth thee on against us, for to deliver
us into the hand of the Chaldeans, that
they might put us to death, and carry us
away captives into Babylon.
4 So Johanan the son of Kareah, and
all the captains of the forces, and all
the people, obeyed not the voice of the
LORD, to dwell in the land of Judah.
5 But Johanan the son of Kareah, and
all the captains of the forces, took all
the remnant of Judah, that were
returned from all nations, whither they
had been driven, to dwell in the land of
Judah;
6 *Even* men, and women, and children, and the king's daughters, and
every person that Nebuzar-adan the
captain of the guard had left with
Gedaliah the son of Ahikam the son of
Shaphan, and Jeremiah the prophet,
and Baruch the son of Neriah.
7 So they came into the land of Egypt:
for they obeyed not the voice of the
LORD: thus came they *even* to Tahpanhes.
8 Then came the word of the LORD
unto Jeremiah in Tahpanhes, saying,
9 Take great stones in thine hand, and
hide them in the clay in the brickkiln,
which *is* at the entry of Pharaoh's house
in Tahpanhes, in the sight of the men of
Judah;
10 And say unto them, Thus saith the
LORD of hosts, the God of Israel; Behold,
I will send and take Nebuchadrezzar
the king of Babylon, my servant, and
will set his throne upon these stones
that I have hid; and he shall spread his
royal pavilion over them.
11 And when he cometh, he shall
smite the land of Egypt, *and deliver*
such *as are* for death to death; and such
as are for captivity to captivity; and
such *as are* for the sword to the sword.
12 And I will kindle a fire in the
houses of the gods of Egypt; and he
shall burn them, and carry them away
captives: and he shall array himself
with the land of Egypt, as a shepherd
putteth on his garment; and he shall go
forth from thence in peace.
13 He shall break also the images of
Beth-shemesh, that *is* in the land of
Egypt; and the houses of the gods of
the Egyptians shall he burn with fire.

44 The word that came to Jeremiah
concerning all the Jews which
dwell in the land of Egypt, which dwell
at Migdol, and at Tahpanhes, and at
Noph, and in the country of Pathros,
saying,
2 Thus saith the LORD of hosts, the
God of Israel; Ye have seen all the evil
that I have brought upon Jerusalem,
and upon all the cities of Judah; and,
behold, this day they *are* a desolation,
and no man dwelleth therein,
3 Because of their wickedness which
they have committed to provoke me to
anger, in that they went to burn incense,
and to serve other gods, whom they
knew not, *neither* they, ye, nor your
fathers.
4 Howbeit I sent unto you all my servants the prophets, rising early and
sending *them*, saying, Oh, do not this
abominable thing that I hate.
5 But they hearkened not, nor
inclined their ear to turn from their
wickedness, to burn no incense unto
other gods.
6 Wherefore my fury and mine anger
was poured forth, and was kindled in
the cities of Judah and in the streets of
Jerusalem; and they are wasted *and*
desolate, as at this day.
7 Therefore now thus saith the LORD,
the God of hosts, the God of Israel;
Wherefore commit ye *this* great evil
against your souls, to cut off from you
man and woman, child and suckling,
out of Judah, to leave you none to
remain;
8 In that ye provoke me unto wrath
with the works of your hands, burning
incense unto other gods in the land of
Egypt, whither ye be gone to dwell, that
ye might cut yourselves off, and that ye
might be a curse and a reproach among
all the nations of the earth?
9 Have ye forgotten the wickedness of
your fathers, and the wickedness of the
kings of Judah, and the wickedness of
their wives, and your own wickedness,
and the wickedness of your wives,
which they have committed in the land
of Judah, and in the streets of
Jerusalem?
10 They are not humbled *even* unto
this day, neither have they feared, nor
walked in my law, nor in my statutes,
that I set before you and before your
fathers.
11 Therefore thus saith the LORD of
hosts, the God of Israel; Behold, I will
set my face against you for evil, and to
cut off all Judah.
12 And I will take the remnant of
Judah, that have set their faces to go
into the land of Egypt to sojourn there,
and they shall all be consumed, *and* fall
in the land of Egypt; they shall *even* be
consumed by the sword *and* by the
famine: they shall die, from the least
even unto the greatest, by the sword
and by the famine: and they shall be an
execration, *and* an astonishment, and a
curse, and a reproach.
13 For I will punish them that dwell in
the land of Egypt, as I have punished
Jerusalem, by the sword, by the famine,
and by the pestilence:
14 So that none of the remnant of
Judah, which are gone into the land of
Egypt to sojourn there, shall escape or
remain, that they should return into the
land of Judah, to the which they have a
desire to return to dwell there: for none
shall return but such as shall escape.
15 Then all the men which knew that
their wives had burned incense unto
other gods, and all the women that

stood by, a great multitude, even all the
people that dwelt in the land of Egypt,
in Pathros, answered Jeremiah, saying,
16 *As for* the word that thou hast spoken unto us in the name of the LORD,
we will not hearken unto thee.
17 But we will certainly do whatsoever thing goeth forth out of our own
mouth, to burn incense unto the queen
of heaven, and to pour out drink offerings unto her, as we have done, we, and
our fathers, our kings, and our princes,
in the cities of Judah, and in the streets
of Jerusalem: for *then* had we plenty of
victuals, and were well, and saw no evil.
18 But since we left off to burn
incense to the queen of heaven, and to
pour out drink offerings unto her, we
have wanted all *things*, and have been
consumed by the sword and by the
famine.
19 And when we burned incense to
the queen of heaven, and poured out
drink offerings unto her, did we make
her cakes to worship her, and pour out
drink offerings unto her, without our
men?
20 Then Jeremiah said unto all the
people, to the men, and to the women,
and to all the people which had given
him *that* answer, saying,
21 The incense that ye burned in the
cities of Judah, and in the streets of
Jerusalem, ye, and your fathers, your
kings, and your princes, and the people
of the land, did not the LORD remember
them, and came it *not* into his mind?
22 So that the LORD could no longer
bear, because of the evil of your doings,
and because of the abominations which
ye have committed; therefore is your
land a desolation, and an astonishment,
and a curse, without an inhabitant, as
at this day.
23 Because ye have burned incense,
and because ye have sinned against the
LORD, and have not obeyed the voice of
the LORD, nor walked in his law, nor in
his statutes, nor in his testimonies;
therefore this evil is happened unto
you, as at this day.
24 Moreover Jeremiah said unto all
the people, and to all the women, Hear
the word of the LORD, all Judah that *are*
in the land of Egypt:
25 Thus saith the LORD of hosts, the
God of Israel, saying; Ye and your wives
have both spoken with your mouths,
and fulfilled with your hand, saying, We
will surely perform our vows that we
have vowed, to burn incense to the
queen of heaven, and to pour out drink
offerings unto her: ye will surely
accomplish your vows, and surely perform your vows.
26 Therefore hear ye the word of the
LORD, all Judah that dwell in the land
of Egypt; Behold, I have sworn by my
great name, saith the LORD, that my
name shall no more be named in the
mouth of any man of Judah in all the
land of Egypt, saying, The Lord GOD
liveth.
27 Behold, I will watch over them for
evil, and not for good: and all the men
of Judah that *are* in the land of Egypt
shall be consumed by the sword and by
the famine, until there be an end of
them.
28 Yet a small number that escape
the sword shall return out of the land of
Egypt into the land of Judah, and all
the remnant of Judah, that are gone
into the land of Egypt to sojourn there,
shall know whose words shall stand,
mine, or theirs.
29 And this *shall be* a sign unto you,
saith the LORD, that I will punish you in

this place, that ye may know that my words shall surely stand against you for evil:

30 Thus saith the LORD; Behold, I will give Pharaoh-hophra king of Egypt into the hand of his enemies, and into the hand of them that seek his life; as I gave Zedekiah king of Judah into the hand of Nebuchadrezzar king of Babylon, his enemy, and that sought his life.

45 The word that Jeremiah the prophet spake unto Baruch the son of Neriah, when he had written these words in a book at the mouth of Jeremiah, in the fourth year of Jehoiakim the son of Josiah king of Judah, saying,

2 Thus saith the LORD, the God of Israel, unto thee, O Baruch;

3 Thou didst say, Woe is me now! for the LORD hath added grief to my sorrow; I fainted in my sighing, and I find no rest.

4 Thus shalt thou say unto him, The LORD saith thus; Behold, *that* which I have built will I break down, and that which I have planted I will pluck up, even this whole land.

5 And seekest thou great things for thyself? seek *them* not: for, behold, I will bring evil upon all flesh, saith the LORD: but thy life will I give unto thee for a prey in all places whither thou goest.

46 The word of the LORD which came to Jeremiah the prophet against the Gentiles;

2 Against Egypt, against the army of Pharaoh-necho king of Egypt, which was by the river Euphrates in Carchemish, which Nebuchadrezzar king of Babylon smote in the fourth year of Jehoiakim the son of Josiah king of Judah.

3 Order ye the buckler and shield, and draw near to battle.

4 Harness the horses; and get up, ye horsemen, and stand forth with *your* helmets; furbish the spears, *and* put on the brigandines.

5 Wherefore have I seen them dismayed *and* turned away back? and their mighty ones are beaten down, and are fled apace, and look not back: *for* fear *was* round about, saith the LORD.

6 Let not the swift flee away, nor the mighty man escape; they shall stumble, and fall toward the north by the river Euphrates.

7 Who *is* this *that* cometh up as a flood, whose waters are moved as the rivers?

8 Egypt riseth up like a flood, and *his* waters are moved like the rivers; and he saith, I will go up, *and* will cover the earth; I will destroy the city and the inhabitants thereof.

9 Come up, ye horses; and rage, ye chariots; and let the mighty men come forth; the Ethiopians and the Libyans, that handle the shield; and the Lydians, that handle *and* bend the bow.

10 For this *is* the day of the Lord GOD of hosts, a day of vengeance, that he may avenge him of his adversaries: and the sword shall devour, and it shall be satiate and made drunk with their blood: for the Lord GOD of hosts hath a sacrifice in the north country by the river Euphrates.

11 Go up into Gilead, and take balm, O virgin, the daughter of Egypt: in vain shalt thou use many medicines; *for* thou shalt not be cured.

12 The nations have heard of thy shame, and thy cry hath filled the land:

for the mighty man hath stumbled against the mighty, *and* they are fallen both together.

13 The word that the LORD spake to Jeremiah the prophet, how Nebuchadrezzar king of Babylon should come *and* smite the land of Egypt.

14 Declare ye in Egypt, and publish in Migdol, and publish in Noph and in Tahpanhes: say ye, Stand fast, and prepare thee; for the sword shall devour round about thee.

15 Why are thy valiant *men* swept away? they stood not, because the LORD did drive them.

16 He made many to fall, yea, one fell upon another: and they said, Arise, and let us go again to our own people, and to the land of our nativity, from the oppressing sword.

17 They did cry there, Pharaoh king of Egypt *is but* a noise; he hath passed the time appointed.

18 *As* I live, saith the King, whose name *is* the LORD of hosts, Surely as Tabor *is* among the mountains, and as Carmel by the sea, *so* shall he come.

19 O thou daughter dwelling in Egypt, furnish thyself to go into captivity: for Noph shall be waste and desolate without an inhabitant.

20 Egypt *is like* a very fair heifer, *but* destruction cometh; it cometh out of the north.

21 Also her hired men *are* in the midst of her like fatted bullocks; for they also are turned back, *and* are fled away together: they did not stand, because the day of their calamity was come upon them, *and* the time of their visitation.

22 The voice thereof shall go like a serpent; for they shall march with an army, and come against her with axes, as hewers of wood.

23 They shall cut down her forest, saith the LORD, though it cannot be searched; because they are more than the grasshoppers, and *are* innumerable.

24 The daughter of Egypt shall be confounded; she shall be delivered into the hand of the people of the north.

25 The LORD of hosts, the God of Israel, saith; Behold, I will punish the multitude of No, and Pharaoh, and Egypt, with their gods, and their kings; even Pharaoh, and *all* them that trust in him:

26 And I will deliver them into the hand of those that seek their lives, and into the hand of Nebuchadrezzar king of Babylon, and into the hand of his servants: and afterward it shall be inhabited, as in the days of old, saith the LORD.

27 But fear not thou, O my servant Jacob, and be not dismayed, O Israel: for, behold, I will save thee from afar off, and thy seed from the land of their captivity; and Jacob shall return, and be in rest and at ease, and none shall make *him* afraid.

28 Fear thou not, O Jacob my servant, saith the LORD: for I *am* with thee; for I will make a full end of all the nations whither I have driven thee: but I will not make a full end of thee, but correct thee in measure; yet will I not leave thee wholly unpunished.

47

The word of the LORD that came to Jeremiah the prophet against the Philistines, before that Pharaoh smote Gaza.

2 Thus saith the LORD; Behold, waters rise up out of the north, and shall be an overflowing flood, and shall overflow the land, and all that is therein; the city,

and them that dwell therein: then the
men shall cry, and all the inhabitants of
the land shall howl.
3 At the noise of the stamping of the
hoofs of his strong *horses*, at the rushing of his chariots, *and at* the rumbling
of his wheels, the fathers shall not look
back to *their* children for feebleness of
hands;
4 Because of the day that cometh to
spoil all the Philistines, *and* to cut off
from Tyrus and Zidon every helper that
remaineth: for the LORD will spoil the
Philistines, the remnant of the country
of Caphtor.
5 Baldness is come upon Gaza; Ashkelon is cut off *with* the remnant of
their valley: how long wilt thou cut
thyself?
6 O thou sword of the LORD, how long
will it be ere thou be quiet? put up
thyself into thy scabbard, rest, and be
still.
7 How can it be quiet, seeing the
LORD hath given it a charge against
Ashkelon, and against the sea shore?
there hath he appointed it.

48 Against Moab thus saith the
LORD of hosts, the God of Israel;
Woe unto Nebo! for it is spoiled:
Kiriathaim is confounded *and* taken:
Misgab is confounded and dismayed.
2 *There shall be* no more praise of
Moab: in Heshbon they have devised
evil against it; come, and let us cut it off
from *being* a nation. Also thou shalt be
cut down, O Madmen; the sword shall
pursue thee.
3 A voice of crying *shall be* from
Horonaim, spoiling and great destruction.
4 Moab is destroyed; her little ones
have caused a cry to be heard.
5 For in the going up of Luhith continual weeping shall go up; for in the
going down of Horonaim the enemies
have heard a cry of destruction.
6 Flee, save your lives, and be like the
heath in the wilderness.
7 For because thou hast trusted in thy
works and in thy treasures, thou shalt
also be taken: and Chemosh shall go
forth into captivity *with* his priests and
his princes together.
8 And the spoiler shall come upon
every city, and no city shall escape: the
valley also shall perish, and the plain
shall be destroyed, as the LORD hath
spoken.
9 Give wings unto Moab, that it may
flee and get away: for the cities thereof
shall be desolate, without any to dwell
therein.
10 Cursed *be* he that doeth the work
of the LORD deceitfully, and cursed *be*
he that keepeth back his sword from
blood.
11 Moab hath been at ease from his
youth, and he hath settled on his lees,
and hath not been emptied from vessel
to vessel, neither hath he gone into
captivity: therefore his taste remained
in him, and his scent is not changed.
12 Therefore, behold, the days come,
saith the LORD, that I will send unto
him wanderers, that shall cause him to
wander, and shall empty his vessels,
and break their bottles.
13 And Moab shall be ashamed of
Chemosh, as the house of Israel was
ashamed of Beth-el their confidence.
14 How say ye, We *are* mighty and
strong men for the war?

15 Moab is spoiled, and gone up *out of* her cities, and his chosen young men are gone down to the slaughter, saith the King, whose name *is* the LORD of hosts.

16 The calamity of Moab *is* near to come, and his affliction hasteth fast.

17 All ye that are about him, bemoan him; and all ye that know his name, say, How is the strong staff broken, *and* the beautiful rod!

18 Thou daughter that dost inhabit Dibon, come down from *thy* glory, and sit in thirst; for the spoiler of Moab shall come upon thee, *and* he shall destroy thy strong holds.

19 O inhabitant of Aroer, stand by the way, and espy; ask him that fleeth, and her that escapeth, *and* say, What is done?

20 Moab is confounded; for it is broken down: howl and cry; tell ye it in Arnon, that Moab is spoiled,

21 And judgment is come upon the plain country; upon Holon, and upon Jahazah, and upon Mephaath,

22 And upon Dibon, and upon Nebo, and upon Beth-diblathaim,

23 And upon Kiriathaim, and upon Beth-gamul, and upon Beth-meon,

24 And upon Kerioth, and upon Bozrah, and upon all the cities of the land of Moab, far or near.

25 The horn of Moab is cut off, and his arm is broken, saith the LORD.

26 Make ye him drunken: for he magnified *himself* against the LORD: Moab also shall wallow in his vomit, and he also shall be in derision.

27 For was not Israel a derision unto thee? was he found among thieves? for since thou spakest of him, thou skippedst for joy.

28 O ye that dwell in Moab, leave the cities, and dwell in the rock, and be like the dove *that* maketh her nest in the sides of the hole's mouth.

29 We have heard the pride of Moab, (he is exceeding proud) his loftiness, and his arrogancy, and his pride, and the haughtiness of his heart.

30 I know his wrath, saith the LORD; but *it shall* not *be* so; his lies shall not so effect *it*.

31 Therefore will I howl for Moab, and I will cry out for all Moab; *mine heart* shall mourn for the men of Kir-heres.

32 O vine of Sibmah, I will weep for thee with the weeping of Jazer: thy plants are gone over the sea, they reach *even* to the sea of Jazer: the spoiler is fallen upon thy summer fruits and upon thy vintage.

33 And joy and gladness is taken from the plentiful field, and from the land of Moab; and I have caused wine to fail from the winepresses: none shall tread with shouting; *their* shouting *shall be* no shouting.

34 From the cry of Heshbon *even* unto Elealeh, *and even* unto Jahaz, have they uttered their voice, from Zoar *even* unto Horonaim, *as* an heifer of three years old: for the waters also of Nimrim shall be desolate.

35 Moreover I will cause to cease in Moab, saith the LORD, him that offereth in the high places, and him that burneth incense to his gods.

36 Therefore mine heart shall sound for Moab like pipes, and mine heart shall sound like pipes for the men of Kir-heres: because the riches *that* he hath gotten are perished.

37 For every head *shall be* bald, and every beard clipped: upon all the hands

shall be cuttings, and upon the loins sackcloth.

38 *There shall be* lamentation generally upon all the housetops of Moab, and in the streets thereof: for I have broken Moab like a vessel wherein *is* no pleasure, saith the LORD.

39 They shall howl, *saying*, How is it broken down! how hath Moab turned the back with shame! so shall Moab be a derision and a dismaying to all them about him.

40 For thus saith the LORD; Behold, he shall fly as an eagle, and shall spread his wings over Moab.

41 Kerioth is taken, and the strong holds are surprised, and the mighty men's hearts in Moab at that day shall be as the heart of a woman in her pangs.

42 And Moab shall be destroyed from *being* a people, because he hath magnified *himself* against the LORD.

43 Fear, and the pit, and the snare, *shall be* upon thee, O inhabitant of Moab, saith the LORD.

44 He that fleeth from the fear shall fall into the pit; and he that getteth up out of the pit shall be taken in the snare: for I will bring upon it, *even* upon Moab, the year of their visitation, saith the LORD.

45 They that fled stood under the shadow of Heshbon because of the force: but a fire shall come forth out of Heshbon, and a flame from the midst of Sihon, and shall devour the corner of Moab, and the crown of the head of the tumultuous ones.

46 Woe be unto thee, O Moab! the people of Chemosh perisheth: for thy sons are taken captives, and thy daughters captives.

47 Yet will I bring again the captivity of Moab in the latter days, saith the LORD. Thus far *is* the judgment of Moab.

49 Concerning the Ammonites, thus saith the LORD; Hath Israel no sons? hath he no heir? why *then* doth their king inherit Gad, and his people dwell in his cities?

2 Therefore, behold, the days come, saith the LORD, that I will cause an alarm of war to be heard in Rabbah of the Ammonites; and it shall be a desolate heap, and her daughters shall be burned with fire: then shall Israel be heir unto them that were his heirs, saith the LORD.

3 Howl, O Heshbon, for Ai is spoiled: cry, ye daughters of Rabbah, gird you with sackcloth; lament, and run to and fro by the hedges; for their king shall go into captivity, *and* his priests and his princes together.

4 Wherefore gloriest thou in the valleys, thy flowing valley, O backsliding daughter? that trusted in her treasures, *saying*, Who shall come unto me?

5 Behold, I will bring a fear upon thee, saith the Lord GOD of hosts, from all those that be about thee; and ye shall be driven out every man right forth; and none shall gather up him that wandereth.

6 And afterward I will bring again the captivity of the children of Ammon, saith the LORD.

7 Concerning Edom, thus saith the LORD of hosts; *Is* wisdom no more in Teman? is counsel perished from the prudent? is their wisdom vanished?

8 Flee ye, turn back, dwell deep, O inhabitants of Dedan; for I will bring the calamity of Esau upon him, the time *that* I will visit him.

9 If grapegatherers come to thee, would they not leave *some* gleaning grapes? if thieves by night, they will destroy till they have enough.

10 But I have made Esau bare, I have uncovered his secret places, and he shall not be able to hide himself: his seed is spoiled, and his brethren, and his neighbours, and he *is* not.

11 Leave thy fatherless children, I will preserve *them* alive; and let thy widows trust in me.

12 For thus saith the LORD; Behold, they whose judgment *was* not to drink of the cup have assuredly drunken; and *art* thou he *that* shall altogether go unpunished? thou shalt not go unpunished, but thou shalt surely drink *of it*.

13 For I have sworn by myself, saith the LORD, that Bozrah shall become a desolation, a reproach, a waste, and a curse; and all the cities thereof shall be perpetual wastes.

14 I have heard a rumour from the LORD, and an ambassador is sent unto the heathen, *saying*, Gather ye together, and come against her, and rise up to the battle.

15 For, lo, I will make thee small among the heathen, *and* despised among men.

16 Thy terribleness hath deceived thee, *and* the pride of thine heart, O thou that dwellest in the clefts of the rock, that holdest the height of the hill: though thou shouldest make thy nest as high as the eagle, I will bring thee down from thence, saith the LORD.

17 Also Edom shall be a desolation: every one that goeth by it shall be astonished, and shall hiss at all the plagues thereof.

18 As in the overthrow of Sodom and Gomorrah and the neighbour *cities* thereof, saith the LORD, no man shall abide there, neither shall a son of man dwell in it.

19 Behold, he shall come up like a lion from the swelling of Jordan against the habitation of the strong: but I will suddenly make him run away from her: and who *is* a chosen *man, that* I may appoint over her? for who *is* like me? and who will appoint me the time? and who *is* that shepherd that will stand before me?

20 Therefore hear the counsel of the LORD, that he hath taken against Edom; and his purposes, that he hath purposed against the inhabitants of Teman: Surely the least of the flock shall draw them out: surely he shall make their habitations desolate with them.

21 The earth is moved at the noise of their fall, at the cry the noise thereof was heard in the Red sea.

22 Behold, he shall come up and fly as the eagle, and spread his wings over Bozrah: and at that day shall the heart of the mighty men of Edom be as the heart of a woman in her pangs.

23 Concerning Damascus. Hamath is confounded, and Arpad: for they have heard evil tidings: they are fainthearted; *there is* sorrow on the sea; it cannot be quiet.

24 Damascus is waxed feeble, *and* turneth herself to flee, and fear hath seized on *her*: anguish and sorrows have taken her, as a woman in travail.

25 How is the city of praise not left, the city of my joy!

26 Therefore her young men shall fall in her streets, and all the men of war shall be cut off in that day, saith the LORD of hosts.

27 And I will kindle a fire in the wall
of Damascus, and it shall consume the
palaces of Ben-hadad.
28 Concerning Kedar, and concerning
the kingdoms of Hazor, which Nebuchadrezzar king of Babylon shall smite,
thus saith the LORD; Arise ye, go up to
Kedar, and spoil the men of the east.
29 Their tents and their flocks shall
they take away: they shall take to themselves their curtains, and all their vessels, and their camels; and they shall
cry unto them, Fear *is* on every side.
30 Flee, get you far off, dwell deep, O
ye inhabitants of Hazor, saith the LORD;
for Nebuchadrezzar king of Babylon
hath taken counsel against you, and
hath conceived a purpose against you.
31 Arise, get you up unto the wealthy
nation, that dwelleth without care,
saith the LORD, which have neither
gates nor bars, *which* dwell alone.
32 And their camels shall be a booty,
and the multitude of their cattle a
spoil: and I will scatter into all winds
them *that are* in the utmost corners;
and I will bring their calamity from all
sides thereof, saith the LORD.
33 And Hazor shall be a dwelling for
dragons, *and* a desolation for ever:
there shall no man abide there, nor *any*
son of man dwell in it.
34 The word of the LORD that came to
Jeremiah the prophet against Elam in
the beginning of the reign of Zedekiah
king of Judah, saying,
35 Thus saith the LORD of hosts;
Behold, I will break the bow of Elam,
the chief of their might.
36 And upon Elam will I bring the
four winds from the four quarters of
heaven, and will scatter them toward
all those winds; and there shall be no
nation whither the outcasts of Elam
shall not come.
37 For I will cause Elam to be dismayed before their enemies, and
before them that seek their life: and I
will bring evil upon them, *even* my
fierce anger, saith the LORD; and I will
send the sword after them, till I have
consumed them:
38 And I will set my throne in Elam,
and will destroy from thence the king
and the princes, saith the LORD.
39 But it shall come to pass in the latter days, *that* I will bring again the
captivity of Elam, saith the LORD.

50 The word that the LORD spake
against Babylon *and* against the
land of the Chaldeans by Jeremiah the
prophet.
2 Declare ye among the nations, and
publish, and set up a standard; publish,
and conceal not: say, Babylon is taken,
Bel is confounded, Merodach is broken
in pieces; her idols are confounded, her
images are broken in pieces.
3 For out of the north there cometh
up a nation against her, which shall
make her land desolate, and none shall
dwell therein: they shall remove, they
shall depart, both man and beast.
4 In those days, and in that time, saith
the LORD, the children of Israel shall
come, they and the children of Judah
together, going and weeping: they shall
go, and seek the LORD their God.
5 They shall ask the way to Zion with
their faces thitherward, *saying*, Come,
and let us join ourselves to the LORD in
a perpetual covenant *that* shall not be
forgotten.
6 My people hath been lost sheep:
their shepherds have caused them to go
astray, they have turned them away *on*
the mountains: they have gone from

mountain to hill, they have forgotten their restingplace.

7 All that found them have devoured them: and their adversaries said, We offend not, because they have sinned against the LORD, the habitation of justice, even the LORD, the hope of their fathers.

8 Remove out of the midst of Babylon, and go forth out of the land of the Chaldeans, and be as the he goats before the flocks.

9 For, lo, I will raise and cause to come up against Babylon an assembly of great nations from the north country: and they shall set themselves in array against her; from thence she shall be taken: their arrows *shall be* as of a mighty expert man; none shall return in vain.

10 And Chaldea shall be a spoil: all that spoil her shall be satisfied, saith the LORD.

11 Because ye were glad, because ye rejoiced, O ye destroyers of mine heritage, because ye are grown fat as the heifer at grass, and bellow as bulls;

12 Your mother shall be sore confounded; she that bare you shall be ashamed: behold, the hindermost of the nations *shall be* a wilderness, a dry land, and a desert.

13 Because of the wrath of the LORD it shall not be inhabited, but it shall be wholly desolate: every one that goeth by Babylon shall be astonished, and hiss at all her plagues.

14 Put yourselves in array against Babylon round about: all ye that bend the bow, shoot at her, spare no arrows: for she hath sinned against the LORD.

15 Shout against her round about: she hath given her hand: her foundations are fallen, her walls are thrown down: for it *is* the vengeance of the LORD: take vengeance upon her; as she hath done, do unto her.

16 Cut off the sower from Babylon, and him that handleth the sickle in the time of harvest: for fear of the oppressing sword they shall turn every one to his people, and they shall flee every one to his own land.

17 Israel *is* a scattered sheep; the lions have driven *him* away: first the king of Assyria hath devoured him; and last this Nebuchadrezzar king of Babylon hath broken his bones.

18 Therefore thus saith the LORD of hosts, the God of Israel; Behold, I will punish the king of Babylon and his land, as I have punished the king of Assyria.

19 And I will bring Israel again to his habitation, and he shall feed on Carmel and Bashan, and his soul shall be satisfied upon mount Ephraim and Gilead.

20 In those days, and in that time, saith the LORD, the iniquity of Israel shall be sought for, and *there shall be* none; and the sins of Judah, and they shall not be found: for I will pardon them whom I reserve.

21 Go up against the land of Merathaim, *even* against it, and against the inhabitants of Pekod: waste and utterly destroy after them, saith the LORD, and do according to all that I have commanded thee.

22 A sound of battle *is* in the land, and of great destruction.

23 How is the hammer of the whole earth cut asunder and broken! how is Babylon become a desolation among the nations!

24 I have laid a snare for thee, and thou art also taken, O Babylon, and thou wast not aware: thou art found, and also caught, because thou hast striven against the LORD.

25 The LORD hath opened his armoury, and hath brought forth the weapons of his indignation: for this *is* the work of the Lord GOD of hosts in the land of the Chaldeans.

26 Come against her from the utmost border, open her storehouses: cast her up as heaps, and destroy her utterly: let nothing of her be left.

27 Slay all her bullocks; let them go down to the slaughter: woe unto them! for their day is come, the time of their visitation.

28 The voice of them that flee and escape out of the land of Babylon, to declare in Zion the vengeance of the LORD our God, the vengeance of his temple.

29 Call together the archers against Babylon: all ye that bend the bow, camp against it round about; let none thereof escape: recompense her according to her work; according to all that she hath done, do unto her: for she hath been proud against the LORD, against the Holy One of Israel.

30 Therefore shall her young men fall in the streets, and all her men of war shall be cut off in that day, saith the LORD.

31 Behold, I *am* against thee, *O thou* most proud, saith the Lord GOD of hosts: for thy day is come, the time *that* I will visit thee.

32 And the most proud shall stumble and fall, and none shall raise him up: and I will kindle a fire in his cities, and it shall devour all round about him.

33 Thus saith the LORD of hosts; The children of Israel and the children of Judah *were* oppressed together: and all that took them captives held them fast; they refused to let them go.

34 Their Redeemer *is* strong; the LORD of hosts *is* his name: he shall throughly plead their cause, that he may give rest to the land, and disquiet the inhabitants of Babylon.

35 A sword *is* upon the Chaldeans, saith the LORD, and upon the inhabitants of Babylon, and upon her princes, and upon her wise *men*.

36 A sword *is* upon the liars; and they shall dote: a sword *is* upon her mighty men; and they shall be dismayed.

37 A sword *is* upon their horses, and upon their chariots, and upon all the mingled people that *are* in the midst of her; and they shall become as women: a sword *is* upon her treasures; and they shall be robbed.

38 A drought *is* upon her waters; and they shall be dried up: for it *is* the land of graven images, and they are mad upon *their* idols.

39 Therefore the wild beasts of the desert with the wild beasts of the islands shall dwell *there*, and the owls shall dwell therein: and it shall be no more inhabited for ever; neither shall it be dwelt in from generation to generation.

40 As God overthrew Sodom and Gomorrah and the neighbour *cities* thereof, saith the LORD; *so* shall no man abide there, neither shall any son of man dwell therein.

41 Behold, a people shall come from the north, and a great nation, and many kings shall be raised up from the coasts of the earth.

42 They shall hold the bow and the lance: they *are* cruel, and will not shew mercy: their voice shall roar like the sea, and they shall ride upon horses, *every one* put in array, like a man to the battle, against thee, O daughter of Babylon.

43 The king of Babylon hath heard the report of them, and his hands waxed feeble: anguish took hold of him, *and* pangs as of a woman in travail.

44 Behold, he shall come up like a lion from the swelling of Jordan unto the habitation of the strong: but I will make them suddenly run away from her: and who *is* a chosen *man, that* I may appoint over her? for who *is* like me? and who will appoint me the time? and who *is* that shepherd that will stand before me?

45 Therefore hear ye the counsel of the LORD, that he hath taken against Babylon; and his purposes, that he hath purposed against the land of the Chaldeans: Surely the least of the flock shall draw them out: surely he shall make *their* habitation desolate with them.

46 At the noise of the taking of Babylon the earth is moved, and the cry is heard among the nations.

51 Thus saith the LORD; Behold, I will raise up against Babylon, and against them that dwell in the midst of them that rise up against me, a destroying wind;

2 And will send unto Babylon fanners, that shall fan her, and shall empty her land: for in the day of trouble they shall be against her round about.

3 Against *him that* bendeth let the archer bend his bow, and against *him that* lifteth himself up in his brigandine: and spare ye not her young men; destroy ye utterly all her host.

4 Thus the slain shall fall in the land of the Chaldeans, and *they that are* thrust through in her streets.

5 For Israel *hath* not *been* forsaken, nor Judah of his God, of the LORD of hosts; though their land was filled with sin against the Holy One of Israel.

6 Flee out of the midst of Babylon, and deliver every man his soul: be not cut off in her iniquity; for this *is* the time of the LORD's vengeance; he will render unto her a recompence.

7 Babylon *hath been* a golden cup in the LORD's hand, that made all the earth drunken: the nations have drunken of her wine; therefore the nations are mad.

8 Babylon is suddenly fallen and destroyed: howl for her; take balm for her pain, if so be she may be healed.

9 We would have healed Babylon, but she is not healed: forsake her, and let us go every one into his own country: for her judgment reacheth unto heaven, and is lifted up *even* to the skies.

10 The LORD hath brought forth our righteousness: come, and let us declare in Zion the work of the LORD our God.

11 Make bright the arrows; gather the shields: the LORD hath raised up the spirit of the kings of the Medes: for his device *is* against Babylon, to destroy it; because it *is* the vengeance of the LORD, the vengeance of his temple.

12 Set up the standard upon the walls of Babylon, make the watch strong, set up the watchmen, prepare the ambushes: for the LORD hath both devised and done that which he spake against the inhabitants of Babylon.

13 O thou that dwellest upon many waters, abundant in treasures, thine end is come, *and* the measure of thy covetousness.

14 The LORD of hosts hath sworn by
himself, *saying*, Surely I will fill thee
with men, as with caterpillers; and they
shall lift up a shout against thee.
15 He hath made the earth by his
power, he hath established the world by
his wisdom, and hath stretched out the
heaven by his understanding.
16 When he uttereth *his* voice, *there*
is a multitude of waters in the heavens;
and he causeth the vapours to ascend
from the ends of the earth: he maketh
lightnings with rain, and bringeth forth
the wind out of his treasures.
17 Every man is brutish by *his* knowledge; every founder is confounded by
the graven image: for his molten image
is falsehood, and *there is* no breath in
them.
18 They *are* vanity, the work of errors:
in the time of their visitation they shall
perish.
19 The portion of Jacob *is* not like
them; for he *is* the former of all things:
and *Israel is* the rod of his inheritance:
the LORD of hosts *is* his name.
20 Thou *art* my battle axe *and* weapons of war: for with thee will I break in
pieces the nations, and with thee will I
destroy kingdoms;
21 And with thee will I break in pieces the horse and his rider; and with
thee will I break in pieces the chariot
and his rider;
22 With thee also will I break in
pieces man and woman; and with thee
will I break in pieces old and young;
and with thee will I break in pieces the
young man and the maid;
23 I will also break in pieces with
thee the shepherd and his flock; and
with thee will I break in pieces the
husbandman and his yoke of oxen; and
with thee will I break in pieces captains and rulers.
24 And I will render unto Babylon
and to all the inhabitants of Chaldea all
their evil that they have done in Zion in
your sight, saith the LORD.
25 Behold, I *am* against thee, O
destroying mountain, saith the LORD,
which destroyest all the earth: and I
will stretch out mine hand upon thee,
and roll thee down from the rocks, and
will make thee a burnt mountain.
26 And they shall not take of thee a
stone for a corner, nor a stone for foundations; but thou shalt be desolate for
ever, saith the LORD.
27 Set ye up a standard in the land,
blow the trumpet among the nations,
prepare the nations against her, call
together against her the kingdoms of
Ararat, Minni, and Ashchenaz; appoint
a captain against her; cause the horses
to come up as the rough caterpillers.
28 Prepare against her the nations
with the kings of the Medes, the captains thereof, and all the rulers thereof,
and all the land of his dominion.
29 And the land shall tremble and
sorrow: for every purpose of the LORD
shall be performed against Babylon, to
make the land of Babylon a desolation
without an inhabitant.
30 The mighty men of Babylon have
forborn to fight, they have remained in
their holds: their might hath failed;
they became as women: they have
burned her dwellingplaces; her bars
are broken.
31 One post shall run to meet another,
and one messenger to meet another, to
shew the king of Babylon that his city is
taken at *one* end,

32 And that the passages are stopped,
and the reeds they have burned with
fire, and the men of war are affrighted.
33 For thus saith the LORD of hosts,
the God of Israel; The daughter of
Babylon *is* like a threshingfloor, *it is*
time to thresh her: yet a little while,
and the time of her harvest shall come.
34 Nebuchadrezzar the king of
Babylon hath devoured me, he hath
crushed me, he hath made me an
empty vessel, he hath swallowed me up
like a dragon, he hath filled his belly
with my delicates, he hath cast me out.
35 The violence done to me and to my
flesh *be* upon Babylon, shall the inhabitant of Zion say; and my blood upon
the inhabitants of Chaldea, shall Jerusalem say.
36 Therefore thus saith the LORD;
Behold, I will plead thy cause, and take
vengeance for thee; and I will dry up
her sea, and make her springs dry.
37 And Babylon shall become heaps,
a dwellingplace for dragons, an astonishment, and an hissing, without an
inhabitant.
38 They shall roar together like lions:
they shall yell as lions' whelps.
39 In their heat I will make their
feasts, and I will make them drunken,
that they may rejoice, and sleep a perpetual sleep, and not wake, saith the
LORD.
40 I will bring them down like lambs
to the slaughter, like rams with he
goats.
41 How is Sheshach taken! and how is
the praise of the whole earth surprised!
how is Babylon become an astonishment among the nations!
42 The sea is come up upon Babylon:
she is covered with the multitude of the
waves thereof.
43 Her cities are a desolation, a dry
land, and a wilderness, a land wherein
no man dwelleth, neither doth *any* son
of man pass thereby.
44 And I will punish Bel in Babylon,
and I will bring forth out of his mouth
that which he hath swallowed up: and
the nations shall not flow together any
more unto him: yea, the wall of Babylon
shall fall.
45 My people, go ye out of the midst
of her, and deliver ye every man his
soul from the fierce anger of the LORD.
46 And lest your heart faint, and ye
fear for the rumour that shall be heard
in the land; a rumour shall both come
one year, and after that in *another* year
shall come a rumour, and violence in
the land, ruler against ruler.
47 Therefore, behold, the days come,
that I will do judgment upon the grav-
en images of Babylon: and her whole
land shall be confounded, and all her
slain shall fall in the midst of her.
48 Then the heaven and the earth,
and all that *is* therein, shall sing for
Babylon: for the spoilers shall come
unto her from the north, saith the LORD.
49 As Babylon *hath caused* the slain
of Israel to fall, so at Babylon shall fall
the slain of all the earth.
50 Ye that have escaped the sword, go
away, stand not still: remember the
LORD afar off, and let Jerusalem come
into your mind.
51 We are confounded, because we
have heard reproach: shame hath covered our faces: for strangers are come
into the sanctuaries of the LORD's
house.
52 Wherefore, behold, the days come,
saith the LORD, that I will do judgment
upon her graven images: and through
all her land the wounded shall groan.

53 Though Babylon should mount up to heaven, and though she should fortify the height of her strength, *yet* from me shall spoilers come unto her, saith the LORD.

54 A sound of a cry *cometh* from Babylon, and great destruction from the land of the Chaldeans:

55 Because the LORD hath spoiled Babylon, and destroyed out of her the great voice; when her waves do roar like great waters, a noise of their voice is uttered:

56 Because the spoiler is come upon her, *even* upon Babylon, and her mighty men are taken, every one of their bows is broken: for the LORD God of recompences shall surely requite.

57 And I will make drunk her princes, and her wise *men*, her captains, and her rulers, and her mighty men: and they shall sleep a perpetual sleep, and not wake, saith the King, whose name *is* the LORD of hosts.

58 Thus saith the LORD of hosts; The broad walls of Babylon shall be utterly broken, and her high gates shall be burned with fire; and the people shall labour in vain, and the folk in the fire, and they shall be weary.

59 The word which Jeremiah the prophet commanded Seraiah the son of Neriah, the son of Maaseiah, when he went with Zedekiah the king of Judah into Babylon in the fourth year of his reign. And *this* Seraiah *was* a quiet prince.

60 So Jeremiah wrote in a book all the evil that should come upon Babylon, *even* all these words that are written against Babylon.

61 And Jeremiah said to Seraiah, When thou comest to Babylon, and shalt see, and shalt read all these words;

62 Then shalt thou say, O LORD, thou hast spoken against this place, to cut it off, that none shall remain in it, neither man nor beast, but that it shall be desolate for ever.

63 And it shall be, when thou hast made an end of reading this book, *that* thou shalt bind a stone to it, and cast it into the midst of Euphrates:

64 And thou shalt say, Thus shall Babylon sink, and shall not rise from the evil that I will bring upon her: and they shall be weary. Thus far *are* the words of Jeremiah.

52 Zedekiah *was* one and twenty years old when he began to reign, and he reigned eleven years in Jerusalem. And his mother's name *was* Hamutal the daughter of Jeremiah of Libnah.

2 And he did *that which was* evil in the eyes of the LORD, according to all that Jehoiakim had done.

3 For through the anger of the LORD it came to pass in Jerusalem and Judah, till he had cast them out from his presence, that Zedekiah rebelled against the king of Babylon.

4 And it came to pass in the ninth year of his reign, in the tenth month, in the tenth *day* of the month, *that* Nebuchadrezzar king of Babylon came, he and all his army, against Jerusalem, and pitched against it, and built forts against it round about.

5 So the city was besieged unto the eleventh year of king Zedekiah.

6 And in the fourth month, in the ninth *day* of the month, the famine was sore in the city, so that there was no bread for the people of the land.

7 Then the city was broken up, and all the men of war fled, and went forth out of the city by night by the way of the gate between the two walls, which *was* by the king's garden; (now the Chaldeans *were* by the city round about:) and they went by the way of the plain.

8 But the army of the Chaldeans pursued after the king, and overtook Zedekiah in the plains of Jericho; and all his army was scattered from him.

9 Then they took the king, and carried him up unto the king of Babylon to Riblah in the land of Hamath; where he gave judgment upon him.

10 And the king of Babylon slew the sons of Zedekiah before his eyes: he slew also all the princes of Judah in Riblah.

11 Then he put out the eyes of Zedekiah; and the king of Babylon bound him in chains, and carried him to Babylon, and put him in prison till the day of his death.

12 Now in the fifth month, in the tenth *day* of the month, which *was* the nineteenth year of Nebuchadrezzar king of Babylon, came Nebuzar-adan, captain of the guard, *which* served the king of Babylon, into Jerusalem,

13 And burned the house of the LORD, and the king's house; and all the houses of Jerusalem, and all the houses of the great *men*, burned he with fire:

14 And all the army of the Chaldeans, that *were* with the captain of the guard, brake down all the walls of Jerusalem round about.

15 Then Nebuzar-adan the captain of the guard carried away captive *certain* of the poor of the people, and the residue of the people that remained in the city, and those that fell away, that fell to the king of Babylon, and the rest of the multitude.

16 But Nebuzar-adan the captain of the guard left *certain* of the poor of the land for vinedressers and for husbandmen.

17 Also the pillars of brass that *were* in the house of the LORD, and the bases, and the brasen sea that *was* in the house of the LORD, the Chaldeans brake, and carried all the brass of them to Babylon.

18 The caldrons also, and the shovels, and the snuffers, and the bowls, and the spoons, and all the vessels of brass wherewith they ministered, took they away.

19 And the basons, and the firepans, and the bowls, and the caldrons, and the candlesticks, and the spoons, and the cups; *that* which *was* of gold *in* gold, and *that* which *was* of silver *in* silver, took the captain of the guard away.

20 The two pillars, one sea, and twelve brasen bulls that *were* under the bases, which king Solomon had made in the house of the LORD: the brass of all these vessels was without weight.

21 And *concerning* the pillars, the height of one pillar *was* eighteen cubits; and a fillet of twelve cubits did compass it; and the thickness thereof *was* four fingers: *it was* hollow.

22 And a chapiter of brass *was* upon it; and the height of one chapiter *was* five cubits, with network and pomegranates upon the chapiters round about, all *of* brass. The second pillar

also and the pomegranates *were* like
unto these.
23 And there were ninety and six
pomegranates on a side; *and* all the
pomegranates upon the network *were*
an hundred round about.
24 And the captain of the guard took
Seraiah the chief priest, and Zephaniah
the second priest, and the three keepers of the door:
25 He took also out of the city an
eunuch, which had the charge of the
men of war; and seven men of them
that were near the king's person, which
were found in the city; and the principal scribe of the host, who mustered
the people of the land; and threescore
men of the people of the land, that
were found in the midst of the city.
26 So Nebuzar-adan the captain of
the guard took them, and brought them
to the king of Babylon to Riblah.
27 And the king of Babylon smote
them, and put them to death in Riblah
in the land of Hamath. Thus Judah was
carried away captive out of his own
land.
28 This *is* the people whom
Nebuchadrezzar carried away captive:
in the seventh year three thousand
Jews and three and twenty:
29 In the eighteenth year of Nebuchadrezzar he carried away captive
from Jerusalem eight hundred thirty
and two persons:
30 In the three and twentieth year of
Nebuchadrezzar Nebuzar-adan the captain of the guard carried away captive
of the Jews seven hundred forty and
five persons: all the persons *were* four
thousand and six hundred.
31 And it came to pass in the seven
and thirtieth year of the captivity of
Jehoiachin king of Judah, in the twelfth
month, in the five and twentieth *day* of
the month, *that* Evil-merodach king of
Babylon in the *first* year of his reign
lifted up the head of Jehoiachin king of
Judah, and brought him forth out of
prison,
32 And spake kindly unto him, and
set his throne above the throne of the
kings that *were* with him in Babylon,
33 And changed his prison garments:
and he did continually eat bread before
him all the days of his life.
34 And *for* his diet, there was a continual diet given him of the king of
Babylon, every day a portion until the
day of his death, all the days of his life.

THE

LAMENTATIONS

OF JEREMIAH

1 How doth the city sit solitary, *that was* full of people! *how* is she become as a widow! she *that was* great among the nations, *and* princess among the provinces, *how* is she become tributary!

2 She weepeth sore in the night, and her tears *are* on her cheeks: among all her lovers she hath none to comfort *her*: all her friends have dealt treacherously with her, they are become her enemies.

3 Judah is gone into captivity because of affliction, and because of great servitude: she dwelleth among the heathen, she findeth no rest: all her persecutors overtook her between the straits.

4 The ways of Zion do mourn, because none come to the solemn feasts: all her gates are desolate: her priests sigh, her virgins are afflicted, and she *is* in bitterness.

5 Her adversaries are the chief, her enemies prosper; for the LORD hath afflicted her for the multitude of her transgressions: her children are gone into captivity before the enemy.

6 And from the daughter of Zion all her beauty is departed: her princes are become like harts *that* find no pasture, and they are gone without strength before the pursuer.

7 Jerusalem remembered in the days of her affliction and of her miseries all her pleasant things that she had in the days of old, when her people fell into the hand of the enemy, and none did help her: the adversaries saw her, *and* did mock at her sabbaths.

8 Jerusalem hath grievously sinned; therefore she is removed: all that honoured her despise her, because they have seen her nakedness: yea, she sigheth, and turneth backward.

9 Her filthiness *is* in her skirts; she remembereth not her last end; therefore she came down wonderfully: she had no comforter. O LORD, behold my affliction: for the enemy hath magnified *himself*.

10 The adversary hath spread out his hand upon all her pleasant things: for she hath seen *that* the heathen entered into her sanctuary, whom thou didst command *that* they should not enter into thy congregation.

11 All her people sigh, they seek bread; they have given their pleasant things for meat to relieve the soul: see, O LORD, and consider; for I am become vile.

12 *Is it* nothing to you, all ye that pass by? behold, and see if there be any sorrow like unto my sorrow, which is done unto me, wherewith the LORD hath afflicted *me* in the day of his fierce anger.

13 From above hath he sent fire into my bones, and it prevaileth against them: he hath spread a net for my feet, he hath turned me back: he hath made me desolate *and* faint all the day.

14 The yoke of my transgressions is bound by his hand: they are wreathed, *and* come up upon my neck: he hath made my strength to fall, the Lord hath delivered me into *their* hands, *from whom* I am not able to rise up.

15 The Lord hath trodden under foot all my mighty *men* in the midst of me: he hath called an assembly against me to crush my young men: the Lord hath trodden the virgin, the daughter of Judah, *as* in a winepress.

16 For these *things* I weep; mine eye, mine eye runneth down with water, because the comforter that should relieve my soul is far from me: my children are desolate, because the enemy prevailed.

17 Zion spreadeth forth her hands, *and there is* none to comfort her: the LORD hath commanded concerning Jacob, *that* his adversaries *should be* round about him: Jerusalem is as a menstruous woman among them.

18 The LORD is righteous; for I have rebelled against his commandment: hear, I pray you, all people, and behold my sorrow: my virgins and my young men are gone into captivity.

19 I called for my lovers, *but* they deceived me: my priests and mine elders gave up the ghost in the city, while they sought their meat to relieve their souls.

20 Behold, O LORD; for I *am* in distress: my bowels are troubled; mine heart is turned within me; for I have grievously rebelled: abroad the sword bereaveth, at home *there is* as death.

21 They have heard that I sigh: *there is* none to comfort me: all mine enemies have heard of my trouble; they are glad that thou hast done *it*: thou wilt bring the day *that* thou hast called, and they shall be like unto me.

22 Let all their wickedness come before thee; and do unto them, as thou hast done unto me for all my transgressions: for my sighs *are* many, and my heart *is* faint.

2 How hath the Lord covered the daughter of Zion with a cloud in his anger, *and* cast down from heaven unto the earth the beauty of Israel, and remembered not his footstool in the day of his anger!

2 The Lord hath swallowed up all the habitations of Jacob, and hath not pitied: he hath thrown down in his wrath the strong holds of the daughter of Judah; he hath brought *them* down to the ground: he hath polluted the kingdom and the princes thereof.

3 He hath cut off in *his* fierce anger all the horn of Israel: he hath drawn back his right hand from before the enemy, and he burned against Jacob like a flaming fire, *which* devoureth round about.

4 He hath bent his bow like an enemy: he stood with his right hand as an adversary, and slew all *that were* pleasant to the eye in the tabernacle of the daughter of Zion: he poured out his fury like fire.

5 The Lord was as an enemy: he hath swallowed up Israel, he hath swallowed up all her palaces: he hath destroyed his strong holds, and hath increased in the daughter of Judah mourning and lamentation.

6 And he hath violently taken away his tabernacle, as *if it were of* a garden: he hath destroyed his places of the assembly: the LORD hath caused the solemn feasts and sabbaths to be forgotten in Zion, and hath despised in the indignation of his anger the king and the priest.

7 The Lord hath cast off his altar, he hath abhorred his sanctuary, he hath given up into the hand of the enemy the walls of her palaces; they have

made a noise in the house of the LORD, as in the day of a solemn feast.

8 The LORD hath purposed to destroy the wall of the daughter of Zion: he hath stretched out a line, he hath not withdrawn his hand from destroying: therefore he made the rampart and the wall to lament; they languished together.

9 Her gates are sunk into the ground; he hath destroyed and broken her bars: her king and her princes *are* among the Gentiles: the law *is* no *more*; her prophets also find no vision from the LORD.

10 The elders of the daughter of Zion sit upon the ground, *and* keep silence: they have cast up dust upon their heads; they have girded themselves with sackcloth: the virgins of Jerusalem hang down their heads to the ground.

11 Mine eyes do fail with tears, my bowels are troubled, my liver is poured upon the earth, for the destruction of the daughter of my people; because the children and the sucklings swoon in the streets of the city.

12 They say to their mothers, Where *is* corn and wine? when they swooned as the wounded in the streets of the city, when their soul was poured out into their mothers' bosom.

13 What thing shall I take to witness for thee? what thing shall I liken to thee, O daughter of Jerusalem? what shall I equal to thee, that I may comfort thee, O virgin daughter of Zion? for thy breach *is* great like the sea: who can heal thee?

14 Thy prophets have seen vain and foolish things for thee: and they have not discovered thine iniquity, to turn away thy captivity; but have seen for thee false burdens and causes of banishment.

15 All that pass by clap *their* hands at thee; they hiss and wag their head at the daughter of Jerusalem, *saying, Is* this the city that *men* call The perfection of beauty, The joy of the whole earth?

16 All thine enemies have opened their mouth against thee: they hiss and gnash the teeth: they say, We have swallowed *her* up: certainly this *is* the day that we looked for; we have found, we have seen *it*.

17 The LORD hath done *that* which he had devised; he hath fulfilled his word that he had commanded in the days of old: he hath thrown down, and hath not pitied: and he hath caused *thine* enemy to rejoice over thee, he hath set up the horn of thine adversaries.

18 Their heart cried unto the Lord, O wall of the daughter of Zion, let tears run down like a river day and night: give thyself no rest; let not the apple of thine eye cease.

19 Arise, cry out in the night: in the beginning of the watches pour out thine heart like water before the face of the Lord: lift up thy hands toward him for the life of thy young children, that faint for hunger in the top of every street.

20 Behold, O LORD, and consider to whom thou hast done this. Shall the women eat their fruit, *and* children of a span long? shall the priest and the prophet be slain in the sanctuary of the Lord?

21 The young and the old lie on the ground in the streets: my virgins and my young men are fallen by the sword; thou hast slain *them* in the day of thine anger; thou hast killed, *and* not pitied.

22 Thou hast called as in a solemn day my terrors round about, so that in

the day of the LORD's anger none
escaped nor remained: those that I
have swaddled and brought up hath
mine enemy consumed.

3 I *am* the man *that* hath seen
affliction by the rod of his wrath.
2 He hath led me, and brought *me*
into darkness, but not *into* light.
3 Surely against me is he turned; he
turneth his hand *against me* all the
day.
4 My flesh and my skin hath he made
old; he hath broken my bones.
5 He hath builded against me, and
compassed *me* with gall and travail.
6 He hath set me in dark places, as
they that be dead of old.
7 He hath hedged me about, that I
cannot get out: he hath made my chain
heavy.
8 Also when I cry and shout, he
shutteth out my prayer.
9 He hath inclosed my ways with
hewn stone, he hath made my paths
crooked.
10 He *was* unto me *as* a bear lying in
wait, *and as* a lion in secret places.
11 He hath turned aside my ways, and
pulled me in pieces: he hath made me
desolate.
12 He hath bent his bow, and set me
as a mark for the arrow.
13 He hath caused the arrows of his
quiver to enter into my reins.
14 I was a derision to all my people;
and their song all the day.
15 He hath filled me with bitterness,
he hath made me drunken with wormwood.
16 He hath also broken my teeth with
gravel stones, he hath covered me with
ashes.
17 And thou hast removed my soul far
off from peace: I forgat prosperity.
18 And I said, My strength and my
hope is perished from the LORD:
19 Remembering mine affliction and
my misery, the wormwood and the gall.
20 My soul hath *them* still in remembrance, and is humbled in me.
21 This I recall to my mind, therefore
have I hope.
22 *It is of* the LORD's mercies that we
are not consumed, because his compassions fail not.
23 *They are* new every morning: great
is thy faithfulness.
24 The LORD *is* my portion, saith my
soul; therefore will I hope in him.
25 The LORD *is* good unto them that
wait for him, to the soul *that* seeketh
him.
26 *It is* good that *a man* should both
hope and quietly wait for the salvation
of the LORD.
27 *It is* good for a man that he bear
the yoke in his youth.
28 He sitteth alone and keepeth
silence, because he hath borne *it* upon
him.
29 He putteth his mouth in the dust;
if so be there may be hope.
30 He giveth *his* cheek to him that
smiteth him: he is filled full with
reproach.
31 For the Lord will not cast off for
ever:
32 But though he cause grief, yet will
he have compassion according to the
multitude of his mercies.
33 For he doth not afflict willingly nor
grieve the children of men.
34 To crush under his feet all the
prisoners of the earth,
35 To turn aside the right of a man
before the face of the most High,
36 To subvert a man in his cause, the
Lord approveth not.

37 Who *is* he *that* saith, and it cometh to pass, *when* the Lord commandeth *it* not?

38 Out of the mouth of the most High proceedeth not evil and good?

39 Wherefore doth a living man complain, a man for the punishment of his sins?

40 Let us search and try our ways, and turn again to the LORD.

41 Let us lift up our heart with *our* hands unto God in the heavens.

42 We have transgressed and have rebelled: thou hast not pardoned.

43 Thou hast covered with anger, and persecuted us: thou hast slain, thou hast not pitied.

44 Thou hast covered thyself with a cloud, that *our* prayer should not pass through.

45 Thou hast made us *as* the offscouring and refuse in the midst of the people.

46 All our enemies have opened their mouths against us.

47 Fear and a snare is come upon us, desolation and destruction.

48 Mine eye runneth down with rivers of water for the destruction of the daughter of my people.

49 Mine eye trickleth down, and ceaseth not, without any intermission,

50 Till the LORD look down, and behold from heaven.

51 Mine eye affecteth mine heart because of all the daughters of my city.

52 Mine enemies chased me sore, like a bird, without cause.

53 They have cut off my life in the dungeon, and cast a stone upon me.

54 Waters flowed over mine head; *then* I said, I am cut off.

55 I called upon thy name, O LORD, out of the low dungeon.

56 Thou hast heard my voice: hide not thine ear at my breathing, at my cry.

57 Thou drewest near in the day *that* I called upon thee: thou saidst, Fear not.

58 O Lord, thou hast pleaded the causes of my soul; thou hast redeemed my life.

59 O LORD, thou hast seen my wrong: judge thou my cause.

60 Thou hast seen all their vengeance *and* all their imaginations against me.

61 Thou hast heard their reproach, O LORD, *and* all their imaginations against me;

62 The lips of those that rose up against me, and their device against me all the day.

63 Behold their sitting down, and their rising up; I *am* their musick.

64 Render unto them a recompence, O LORD, according to the work of their hands.

65 Give them sorrow of heart, thy curse unto them.

66 Persecute and destroy them in anger from under the heavens of the LORD.

4 How is the gold become dim! *how* is the most fine gold changed! the stones of the sanctuary are poured out in the top of every street.

2 The precious sons of Zion, comparable to fine gold, how are they esteemed as earthen pitchers, the work of the hands of the potter!

3 Even the sea monsters draw out the breast, they give suck to their young ones: the daughter of my people *is become* cruel, like the ostriches in the wilderness.

4 The tongue of the sucking child cleaveth to the roof of his mouth for

thirst: the young children ask bread,
and no man breaketh *it* unto them.
5 They that did feed delicately are
desolate in the streets: they that were
brought up in scarlet embrace dung-
hills.
6 For the punishment of the iniquity
of the daughter of my people is greater
than the punishment of the sin of
Sodom, that was overthrown as in a
moment, and no hands stayed on her.
7 Her Nazarites were purer than
snow, they were whiter than milk, they
were more ruddy in body than rubies,
their polishing *was* of sapphire:
8 Their visage is blacker than a coal;
they are not known in the streets: their
skin cleaveth to their bones; it is withered, it is become like a stick.
9 *They that be* slain with the sword
are better than *they that be* slain with
hunger: for these pine away, stricken
through for *want of* the fruits of the
field.
10 The hands of the pitiful women
have sodden their own children: they
were their meat in the destruction of
the daughter of my people.
11 The LORD hath accomplished his
fury; he hath poured out his fierce
anger, and hath kindled a fire in Zion,
and it hath devoured the foundations
thereof.
12 The kings of the earth, and all the
inhabitants of the world, would not
have believed that the adversary and
the enemy should have entered into
the gates of Jerusalem.
13 For the sins of her prophets, *and*
the iniquities of her priests, that have
shed the blood of the just in the midst
of her,
14 They have wandered *as* blind *men*
in the streets, they have polluted themselves with blood, so that men could
not touch their garments.
15 They cried unto them, Depart ye; *it*
is unclean; depart, depart, touch not:
when they fled away and wandered,
they said among the heathen, They
shall no more sojourn *there*.
16 The anger of the LORD hath divided them; he will no more regard them:
they respected not the persons of the
priests, they favoured not the elders.
17 As for us, our eyes as yet failed for
our vain help: in our watching we have
watched for a nation *that* could not
save *us*.
18 They hunt our steps, that we cannot go in our streets: our end is near,
our days are fulfilled; for our end is
come.
19 Our persecutors are swifter than
the eagles of the heaven: they pursued
us upon the mountains, they laid wait
for us in the wilderness.
20 The breath of our nostrils, the
anointed of the LORD, was taken in
their pits, of whom we said, Under his
shadow we shall live among the heathen.
21 Rejoice and be glad, O daughter of
Edom, that dwellest in the land of Uz;
the cup also shall pass through unto
thee: thou shalt be drunken, and shalt
make thyself naked.
22 The punishment of thine iniquity
is accomplished, O daughter of Zion; he
will no more carry thee away into captivity: he will visit thine iniquity, O
daughter of Edom; he will discover thy
sins.

5 Remember, O LORD, what is come upon us: consider, and behold our reproach.

2 Our inheritance is turned to strangers, our houses to aliens.

3 We are orphans and fatherless, our mothers *are* as widows.

4 We have drunken our water for money; our wood is sold unto us.

5 Our necks *are* under persecution: we labour, *and* have no rest.

6 We have given the hand *to* the Egyptians, *and to* the Assyrians, to be satisfied with bread.

7 Our fathers have sinned, *and are* not; and we have borne their iniquities.

8 Servants have ruled over us: *there is* none that doth deliver *us* out of their hand.

9 We gat our bread with *the peril of* our lives because of the sword of the wilderness.

10 Our skin was black like an oven because of the terrible famine.

11 They ravished the women in Zion, *and* the maids in the cities of Judah.

12 Princes are hanged up by their hand: the faces of elders were not honoured.

13 They took the young men to grind, and the children fell under the wood.

14 The elders have ceased from the gate, the young men from their musick.

15 The joy of our heart is ceased; our dance is turned into mourning.

16 The crown is fallen *from* our head: woe unto us, that we have sinned!

17 For this our heart is faint; for these *things* our eyes are dim.

18 Because of the mountain of Zion, which is desolate, the foxes walk upon it.

19 Thou, O LORD, remainest for ever; thy throne from generation to generation.

20 Wherefore dost thou forget us for ever, *and* forsake us so long time?

21 Turn thou us unto thee, O LORD, and we shall be turned; renew our days as of old.

22 But thou hast utterly rejected us; thou art very wroth against us.

THE BOOK OF THE PROPHET

EZEKIEL

1 Now it came to pass in the thirtieth year, in the fourth *month*, in the fifth *day* of the month, as I *was* among the captives by the river of Chebar, *that* the heavens were opened, and I saw visions of God.

2 In the fifth *day* of the month, which *was* the fifth year of king Jehoiachin's captivity,

3 The word of the LORD came expressly unto Ezekiel the priest, the son of Buzi, in the land of the Chaldeans by the river Chebar; and the hand of the LORD was there upon him.

4 And I looked, and, behold, a whirlwind came out of the north, a great cloud, and a fire infolding itself, and a brightness *was* about it, and out of the

midst thereof as the colour of amber, out of the midst of the fire.

5 Also out of the midst thereof *came* the likeness of four living creatures. And this *was* their appearance; they had the likeness of a man.

6 And every one had four faces, and every one had four wings.

7 And their feet *were* straight feet; and the sole of their feet *was* like the sole of a calf's foot: and they sparkled like the colour of burnished brass.

8 And *they had* the hands of a man under their wings on their four sides; and they four had their faces and their wings.

9 Their wings *were* joined one to another; they turned not when they went; they went every one straight forward.

10 As for the likeness of their faces, they four had the face of a man, and the face of a lion, on the right side: and they four had the face of an ox on the left side; they four also had the face of an eagle.

11 Thus *were* their faces: and their wings *were* stretched upward; two *wings* of every one *were* joined one to another, and two covered their bodies.

12 And they went every one straight forward: whither the spirit was to go, they went; *and* they turned not when they went.

13 As for the likeness of the living creatures, their appearance *was* like burning coals of fire, *and* like the appearance of lamps: it went up and down among the living creatures; and the fire was bright, and out of the fire went forth lightning.

14 And the living creatures ran and returned as the appearance of a flash of lightning.

15 Now as I beheld the living creatures, behold one wheel upon the earth by the living creatures, with his four faces.

16 The appearance of the wheels and their work *was* like unto the colour of a beryl: and they four had one likeness: and their appearance and their work *was* as it were a wheel in the middle of a wheel.

17 When they went, they went upon their four sides: *and* they turned not when they went.

18 As for their rings, they were so high that they were dreadful; and their rings *were* full of eyes round about them four.

19 And when the living creatures went, the wheels went by them: and when the living creatures were lifted up from the earth, the wheels were lifted up.

20 Whithersoever the spirit was to go, they went, thither *was their* spirit to go; and the wheels were lifted up over against them: for the spirit of the living creature *was* in the wheels.

21 When those went, *these* went; and when those stood, *these* stood; and when those were lifted up from the earth, the wheels were lifted up over against them: for the spirit of the living creature *was* in the wheels.

22 And the likeness of the firmament upon the heads of the living creature *was* as the colour of the terrible crystal, stretched forth over their heads above.

23 And under the firmament *were* their wings straight, the one toward the other: every one had two, which covered on this side, and every one had two, which covered on that side, their bodies.

24 And when they went, I heard the noise of their wings, like the noise of great waters, as the voice of the Almighty, the voice of speech, as the noise of an host: when they stood, they let down their wings.

25 And there was a voice from the firmament that *was* over their heads, when they stood, *and* had let down their wings.

26 And above the firmament that *was* over their heads *was* the likeness of a throne, as the appearance of a sapphire stone: and upon the likeness of the throne *was* the likeness as the appearance of a man above upon it.

27 And I saw as the colour of amber, as the appearance of fire round about within it, from the appearance of his loins even upward, and from the appearance of his loins even downward, I saw as it were the appearance of fire, and it had brightness round about.

28 As the appearance of the bow that is in the cloud in the day of rain, so *was* the appearance of the brightness round about. This *was* the appearance of the likeness of the glory of the LORD. And when I saw *it*, I fell upon my face, and I heard a voice of one that spake.

2 And he said unto me, Son of man, stand upon thy feet, and I will speak unto thee.

2 And the spirit entered into me when he spake unto me, and set me upon my feet, that I heard him that spake unto me.

3 And he said unto me, Son of man, I send thee to the children of Israel, to a rebellious nation that hath rebelled against me: they and their fathers have transgressed against me, *even* unto this very day.

4 For *they are* impudent children and stiffhearted. I do send thee unto them; and thou shalt say unto them, Thus saith the Lord GOD.

5 And they, whether they will hear, or whether they will forbear, (for they *are* a rebellious house,) yet shall know that there hath been a prophet among them.

6 And thou, son of man, be not afraid of them, neither be afraid of their words, though briers and thorns *be* with thee, and thou dost dwell among scorpions: be not afraid of their words, nor be dismayed at their looks, though they *be* a rebellious house.

7 And thou shalt speak my words unto them, whether they will hear, or whether they will forbear: for they *are* most rebellious.

8 But thou, son of man, hear what I say unto thee; Be not thou rebellious like that rebellious house: open thy mouth, and eat that I give thee.

9 And when I looked, behold, an hand *was* sent unto me; and, lo, a roll of a book *was* therein;

10 And he spread it before me; and it *was* written within and without: and *there was* written therein lamentations, and mourning, and woe.

3 Moreover he said unto me, Son of man, eat that thou findest; eat this roll, and go speak unto the house of Israel.

2 So I opened my mouth, and he caused me to eat that roll.

3 And he said unto me, Son of man, cause thy belly to eat, and fill thy bowels with this roll that I give thee. Then did I eat *it*; and it was in my mouth as honey for sweetness.

4 And he said unto me, Son of man,
go, get thee unto the house of Israel,
and speak with my words unto them.
5 For thou *art* not sent to a people of
a strange speech and of an hard language, *but* to the house of Israel;
6 Not to many people of a strange
speech and of an hard language, whose
words thou canst not understand.
Surely, had I sent thee to them, they
would have hearkened unto thee.
7 But the house of Israel will not hearken unto thee; for they will not hearken
unto me: for all the house of Israel *are*
impudent and hardhearted.
8 Behold, I have made thy face strong
against their faces, and thy forehead
strong against their foreheads.
9 As an adamant harder than flint
have I made thy forehead: fear them
not, neither be dismayed at their looks,
though they *be* a rebellious house.
10 Moreover he said unto me, Son of
man, all my words that I shall speak
unto thee receive in thine heart, and
hear with thine ears.
11 And go, get thee to them of the
captivity, unto the children of thy people, and speak unto them, and tell
them, Thus saith the Lord GOD; whether they will hear, or whether they will
forbear.
12 Then the spirit took me up, and I
heard behind me a voice of a great
rushing, *saying*, Blessed *be* the glory of
the LORD from his place.
13 *I heard* also the noise of the wings
of the living creatures that touched one
another, and the noise of the wheels
over against them, and a noise of a
great rushing.
14 So the spirit lifted me up, and took
me away, and I went in bitterness, in
the heat of my spirit; but the hand of
the LORD was strong upon me.
15 Then I came to them of the captivity at Tel-abib, that dwelt by the river of
Chebar, and I sat where they sat, and
remained there astonished among
them seven days.
16 And it came to pass at the end of
seven days, that the word of the LORD
came unto me, saying,
17 Son of man, I have made thee a
watchman unto the house of Israel:
therefore hear the word at my mouth,
and give them warning from me.
18 When I say unto the wicked, Thou
shalt surely die; and thou givest him
not warning, nor speakest to warn the
wicked from his wicked way, to save his
life; the same wicked *man* shall die in
his iniquity; but his blood will I require
at thine hand.
19 Yet if thou warn the wicked, and
he turn not from his wickedness, nor
from his wicked way, he shall die in his
iniquity; but thou hast delivered thy
soul.
20 Again, When a righteous *man* doth
turn from his righteousness, and commit iniquity, and I lay a stumblingblock
before him, he shall die: because thou
hast not given him warning, he shall die
in his sin, and his righteousness which
he hath done shall not be remembered;
but his blood will I require at thine
hand.
21 Nevertheless if thou warn the righteous *man*, that the righteous sin not,
and he doth not sin, he shall surely live,
because he is warned; also thou hast
delivered thy soul.
22 And the hand of the LORD was
there upon me; and he said unto me,
Arise, go forth into the plain, and I will
there talk with thee.

23 Then I arose, and went forth into
the plain: and, behold, the glory of the
LORD stood there, as the glory which I
saw by the river of Chebar: and I fell on
my face.
24 Then the spirit entered into me,
and set me upon my feet, and spake
with me, and said unto me, Go, shut
thyself within thine house.
25 But thou, O son of man, behold,
they shall put bands upon thee, and
shall bind thee with them, and thou
shalt not go out among them:
26 And I will make thy tongue cleave
to the roof of thy mouth, that thou shalt
be dumb, and shalt not be to them a
reprover: for they *are* a rebellious
house.
27 But when I speak with thee, I will
open thy mouth, and thou shalt say
unto them, Thus saith the Lord GOD; He
that heareth, let him hear; and he that
forbeareth, let him forbear: for they *are*
a rebellious house.

4 Thou also, son of man, take thee a
tile, and lay it before thee, and
pourtray upon it the city, *even* Jerusalem:
2 And lay siege against it, and build a
fort against it, and cast a mount against
it; set the camp also against it, and set
battering rams against it round about.
3 Moreover take thou unto thee an
iron pan, and set it *for* a wall of iron
between thee and the city: and set thy
face against it, and it shall be besieged,
and thou shalt lay siege against it. This
shall be a sign to the house of Israel.
4 Lie thou also upon thy left side, and
lay the iniquity of the house of Israel
upon it: *according* to the number of the
days that thou shalt lie upon it thou
shalt bear their iniquity.
5 For I have laid upon thee the years
of their iniquity, according to the number of the days, three hundred and
ninety days: so shalt thou bear the
iniquity of the house of Israel.
6 And when thou hast accomplished
them, lie again on thy right side, and
thou shalt bear the iniquity of the
house of Judah forty days: I have
appointed thee each day for a year.
7 Therefore thou shalt set thy face
toward the siege of Jerusalem, and
thine arm *shall be* uncovered, and thou
shalt prophesy against it.
8 And, behold, I will lay bands upon
thee, and thou shalt not turn thee from
one side to another, till thou hast ended
the days of thy siege.
9 Take thou also unto thee wheat, and
barley, and beans, and lentiles, and mil-
let, and fitches, and put them in one
vessel, and make thee bread thereof,
according to the number of the days
that thou shalt lie upon thy side, three
hundred and ninety days shalt thou eat
thereof.
10 And thy meat which thou shalt eat
shall be by weight, twenty shekels a
day: from time to time shalt thou eat it.
11 Thou shalt drink also water by
measure, the sixth part of an hin: from
time to time shalt thou drink.
12 And thou shalt eat it *as* barley
cakes, and thou shalt bake it with dung
that cometh out of man, in their sight.
13 And the LORD said, Even thus shall
the children of Israel eat their defiled
bread among the Gentiles, whither I
will drive them.
14 Then said I, Ah Lord GOD! behold,
my soul hath not been polluted: for
from my youth up even till now have I
not eaten of that which dieth of itself,

or is torn in pieces; neither came there
abominable flesh into my mouth.
15 Then he said unto me, Lo, I have
given thee cow's dung for man's dung,
and thou shalt prepare thy bread therewith.
16 Moreover he said unto me, Son of
man, behold, I will break the staff of
bread in Jerusalem: and they shall eat
bread by weight, and with care; and
they shall drink water by measure, and
with astonishment:
17 That they may want bread and
water, and be astonied one with another, and consume away for their iniquity.

5 And thou, son of man, take thee a
sharp knife, take thee a barber's
razor, and cause *it* to pass upon thine
head and upon thy beard: then take
thee balances to weigh, and divide the
hair.
2 Thou shalt burn with fire a third
part in the midst of the city, when the
days of the siege are fulfilled: and thou
shalt take a third part, *and* smite about
it with a knife: and a third part thou
shalt scatter in the wind; and I will
draw out a sword after them.
3 Thou shalt also take thereof a few in
number, and bind them in thy skirts.
4 Then take of them again, and cast
them into the midst of the fire, and
burn them in the fire; *for* thereof shall
a fire come forth into all the house of
Israel.
5 Thus saith the Lord GOD; This *is*
Jerusalem: I have set it in the midst of
the nations and countries *that are*
round about her.
6 And she hath changed my judgments into wickedness more than the
nations, and my statutes more than the
countries that *are* round about her: for
they have refused my judgments and
my statutes, they have not walked in
them.
7 Therefore thus saith the Lord GOD;
Because ye multiplied more than the
nations that *are* round about you, *and*
have not walked in my statutes, neither
have kept my judgments, neither have
done according to the judgments of the
nations that *are* round about you;
8 Therefore thus saith the Lord GOD;
Behold, I, even I, *am* against thee, and
will execute judgments in the midst of
thee in the sight of the nations.
9 And I will do in thee that which I
have not done, and whereunto I will not
do any more the like, because of all
thine abominations.
10 Therefore the fathers shall eat the
sons in the midst of thee, and the sons
shall eat their fathers; and I will execute judgments in thee, and the whole
remnant of thee will I scatter into all
the winds.
11 Wherefore, *as* I live, saith the Lord
GOD; Surely, because thou hast defiled
my sanctuary with all thy detestable
things, and with all thine abominations,
therefore will I also diminish *thee*; neither shall mine eye spare, neither will I
have any pity.
12 A third part of thee shall die with
the pestilence, and with famine shall
they be consumed in the midst of thee:
and a third part shall fall by the sword
round about thee; and I will scatter a
third part into all the winds, and I will
draw out a sword after them.
13 Thus shall mine anger be accomplished, and I will cause my fury to rest
upon them, and I will be comforted:
and they shall know that I the LORD
have spoken *it* in my zeal, when I have
accomplished my fury in them.

14 Moreover I will make thee waste,
and a reproach among the nations that
are round about thee, in the sight of all
that pass by.
15 So it shall be a reproach and a
taunt, an instruction and an astonishment unto the nations that *are* round
about thee, when I shall execute judgments in thee in anger and in fury and
in furious rebukes. I the LORD have
spoken *it*.
16 When I shall send upon them the
evil arrows of famine, which shall be for
their destruction, *and* which I will send
to destroy you: and I will increase the
famine upon you, and will break your
staff of bread:
17 So will I send upon you famine and
evil beasts, and they shall bereave thee;
and pestilence and blood shall pass
through thee; and I will bring the sword
upon thee. I the LORD have spoken *it*.

6 And the word of the LORD came
unto me, saying,
2 Son of man, set thy face toward the
mountains of Israel, and prophesy
against them,
3 And say, Ye mountains of Israel,
hear the word of the Lord GOD; Thus
saith the Lord GOD to the mountains,
and to the hills, to the rivers, and to the
valleys; Behold, I, *even* I, will bring a
sword upon you, and I will destroy your
high places.
4 And your altars shall be desolate,
and your images shall be broken: and I
will cast down your slain *men* before
your idols.
5 And I will lay the dead carcases of
the children of Israel before their idols;
and I will scatter your bones round
about your altars.
6 In all your dwellingplaces the cities
shall be laid waste, and the high places
shall be desolate; that your altars may
be laid waste and made desolate, and
your idols may be broken and cease,
and your images may be cut down, and
your works may be abolished.
7 And the slain shall fall in the midst
of you, and ye shall know that I *am* the
LORD.
8 Yet will I leave a remnant, that ye
may have *some* that shall escape the
sword among the nations, when ye shall
be scattered through the countries.
9 And they that escape of you shall
remember me among the nations
whither they shall be carried captives,
because I am broken with their whorish heart, which hath departed from
me, and with their eyes, which go a
whoring after their idols: and they shall
lothe themselves for the evils which
they have committed in all their abominations.
10 And they shall know that I *am* the
LORD, *and that* I have not said in vain
that I would do this evil unto them.
11 Thus saith the Lord GOD; Smite
with thine hand, and stamp with thy
foot, and say, Alas for all the evil abominations of the house of Israel! for they
shall fall by the sword, by the famine,
and by the pestilence.
12 He that is far off shall die of the
pestilence; and he that is near shall fall
by the sword; and he that remaineth
and is besieged shall die by the famine:
thus will I accomplish my fury upon
them.
13 Then shall ye know that I *am* the
LORD, when their slain *men* shall be
among their idols round about their
altars, upon every high hill, in all the
tops of the mountains, and under every
green tree, and under every thick oak,

the place where they did offer sweet
savour to all their idols.
14 So will I stretch out my hand upon
them, and make the land desolate, yea,
more desolate than the wilderness
toward Diblath, in all their habitations:
and they shall know that I *am* the
LORD.

7 Moreover the word of the LORD
came unto me, saying,
2 Also, thou son of man, thus saith the
Lord GOD unto the land of Israel; An
end, the end is come upon the four
corners of the land.
3 Now *is* the end *come* upon thee, and
I will send mine anger upon thee, and
will judge thee according to thy ways,
and will recompense upon thee all
thine abominations.
4 And mine eye shall not spare thee,
neither will I have pity: but I will recompense thy ways upon thee, and thine
abominations shall be in the midst of
thee: and ye shall know that I *am* the
LORD.
5 Thus saith the Lord GOD; An evil, an
only evil, behold, is come.
6 An end is come, the end is come: it
watcheth for thee; behold, it is come.
7 The morning is come unto thee, O
thou that dwellest in the land: the time
is come, the day of trouble *is* near, and
not the sounding again of the mountains.
8 Now will I shortly pour out my fury
upon thee, and accomplish mine anger
upon thee: and I will judge thee according to thy ways, and will recompense
thee for all thine abominations.
9 And mine eye shall not spare, neither will I have pity: I will recompense
thee according to thy ways and thine
abominations *that* are in the midst of
thee; and ye shall know that I *am* the
LORD that smiteth.
10 Behold the day, behold, it is come:
the morning is gone forth; the rod hath
blossomed, pride hath budded.
11 Violence is risen up into a rod of
wickedness: none of them *shall remain*,
nor of their multitude, nor of any of
theirs: neither *shall there be* wailing
for them.
12 The time is come, the day draweth
near: let not the buyer rejoice, nor the
seller mourn: for wrath *is* upon all the
multitude thereof.
13 For the seller shall not return to
that which is sold, although they were
yet alive: for the vision *is* touching the
whole multitude thereof, *which* shall
not return; neither shall any strengthen
himself in the iniquity of his life.
14 They have blown the trumpet,
even to make all ready; but none goeth
to the battle: for my wrath *is* upon all
the multitude thereof.
15 The sword *is* without, and the pestilence and the famine within: he that
is in the field shall die with the sword;
and he that *is* in the city, famine and
pestilence shall devour him.
16 But they that escape of them shall
escape, and shall be on the mountains
like doves of the valleys, all of them
mourning, every one for his iniquity.
17 All hands shall be feeble, and all
knees shall be weak *as* water.
18 They shall also gird *themselves*
with sackcloth, and horror shall cover
them; and shame *shall be* upon all
faces, and baldness upon all their
heads.
19 They shall cast their silver in the
streets, and their gold shall be removed:
their silver and their gold shall not be
able to deliver them in the day of the

wrath of the LORD: they shall not satisfy
their souls, neither fill their bowels:
because it is the stumblingblock of
their iniquity.
20 As for the beauty of his ornament,
he set it in majesty: but they made the
images of their abominations *and* of
their detestable things therein: therefore have I set it far from them.
21 And I will give it into the hands of
the strangers for a prey, and to the
wicked of the earth for a spoil; and they
shall pollute it.
22 My face will I turn also from them,
and they shall pollute my secret *place*:
for the robbers shall enter into it, and
defile it.
23 Make a chain: for the land is full of
bloody crimes, and the city is full of
violence.
24 Wherefore I will bring the worst of
the heathen, and they shall possess
their houses: I will also make the pomp
of the strong to cease; and their holy
places shall be defiled.
25 Destruction cometh; and they shall
seek peace, and *there shall be* none.
26 Mischief shall come upon mischief,
and rumour shall be upon rumour; then
shall they seek a vision of the prophet;
but the law shall perish from the priest,
and counsel from the ancients.
27 The king shall mourn, and the
prince shall be clothed with desolation,
and the hands of the people of the land
shall be troubled: I will do unto them
after their way, and according to their
deserts will I judge them; and they
shall know that I *am* the LORD.

8 And it came to pass in the sixth
year, in the sixth *month*, in the fifth
day of the month, *as* I sat in mine
house, and the elders of Judah sat
before me, that the hand of the Lord
GOD fell there upon me.
2 Then I beheld, and lo a likeness as
the appearance of fire: from the
appearance of his loins even downward, fire; and from his loins even
upward, as the appearance of brightness, as the colour of amber.
3 And he put forth the form of an
hand, and took me by a lock of mine
head; and the spirit lifted me up
between the earth and the heaven, and
brought me in the visions of God to
Jerusalem, to the door of the inner gate
that looketh toward the north; where
was the seat of the image of jealousy,
which provoketh to jealousy.
4 And, behold, the glory of the God of
Israel *was* there, according to the vision
that I saw in the plain.
5 Then said he unto me, Son of man,
lift up thine eyes now the way toward
the north. So I lifted up mine eyes the
way toward the north, and behold
northward at the gate of the altar this
image of jealousy in the entry.
6 He said furthermore unto me, Son
of man, seest thou what they do? *even*
the great abominations that the house
of Israel committeth here, that I should
go far off from my sanctuary? but turn
thee yet again, *and* thou shalt see
greater abominations.
7 And he brought me to the door of
the court; and when I looked, behold a
hole in the wall.
8 Then said he unto me, Son of man,
dig now in the wall: and when I had
digged in the wall, behold a door.
9 And he said unto me, Go in, and
behold the wicked abominations that
they do here.
10 So I went in and saw; and behold
every form of creeping things, and

abominable beasts, and all the idols of the house of Israel, pourtrayed upon the wall round about.

11 And there stood before them seventy men of the ancients of the house of Israel, and in the midst of them stood Jaazaniah the son of Shaphan, with every man his censer in his hand; and a thick cloud of incense went up.

12 Then said he unto me, Son of man, hast thou seen what the ancients of the house of Israel do in the dark, every man in the chambers of his imagery? for they say, The LORD seeth us not; the LORD hath forsaken the earth.

13 He said also unto me, Turn thee yet again, *and* thou shalt see greater abominations that they do.

14 Then he brought me to the door of the gate of the LORD's house which *was* toward the north; and, behold, there sat women weeping for Tammuz.

15 Then said he unto me, Hast thou seen *this*, O son of man? turn thee yet again, *and* thou shalt see greater abominations than these.

16 And he brought me into the inner court of the LORD's house, and, behold, at the door of the temple of the LORD, between the porch and the altar, *were* about five and twenty men, with their backs toward the temple of the LORD, and their faces toward the east; and they worshipped the sun toward the east.

17 Then he said unto me, Hast thou seen *this*, O son of man? Is it a light thing to the house of Judah that they commit the abominations which they commit here? for they have filled the land with violence, and have returned to provoke me to anger: and, lo, they put the branch to their nose.

18 Therefore will I also deal in fury: mine eye shall not spare, neither will I have pity: and though they cry in mine ears with a loud voice, *yet* will I not hear them.

9 He cried also in mine ears with a loud voice, saying, Cause them that have charge over the city to draw near, even every man *with* his destroying weapon in his hand.

2 And, behold, six men came from the way of the higher gate, which lieth toward the north, and every man a slaughter weapon in his hand; and one man among them *was* clothed with linen, with a writer's inkhorn by his side: and they went in, and stood beside the brasen altar.

3 And the glory of the God of Israel was gone up from the cherub, whereupon he was, to the threshold of the house. And he called to the man clothed with linen, which *had* the writer's inkhorn by his side;

4 And the LORD said unto him, Go through the midst of the city, through the midst of Jerusalem, and set a mark upon the foreheads of the men that sigh and that cry for all the abominations that be done in the midst thereof.

5 And to the others he said in mine hearing, Go ye after him through the city, and smite: let not your eye spare, neither have ye pity:

6 Slay utterly old *and* young, both maids, and little children, and women: but come not near any man upon whom *is* the mark; and begin at my sanctuary. Then they began at the ancient men which *were* before the house.

7 And he said unto them, Defile the house, and fill the courts with the slain: go ye forth. And they went forth, and slew in the city.

8 And it came to pass, while they were slaying them, and I was left, that I fell upon my face, and cried, and said, Ah Lord God! wilt thou destroy all the residue of Israel in thy pouring out of thy fury upon Jerusalem?

9 Then said he unto me, The iniquity of the house of Israel and Judah *is* exceeding great, and the land is full of blood, and the city full of perverseness: for they say, The Lord hath forsaken the earth, and the Lord seeth not.

10 And as for me also, mine eye shall not spare, neither will I have pity, *but* I will recompense their way upon their head.

11 And, behold, the man clothed with linen, which *had* the inkhorn by his side, reported the matter, saying, I have done as thou hast commanded me.

10 Then I looked, and, behold, in the firmament that was above the head of the cherubims there appeared over them as it were a sapphire stone, as the appearance of the likeness of a throne.

2 And he spake unto the man clothed with linen, and said, Go in between the wheels, *even* under the cherub, and fill thine hand with coals of fire from between the cherubims, and scatter *them* over the city. And he went in in my sight.

3 Now the cherubims stood on the right side of the house, when the man went in; and the cloud filled the inner court.

4 Then the glory of the Lord went up from the cherub, *and stood* over the threshold of the house; and the house was filled with the cloud, and the court was full of the brightness of the Lord's glory.

5 And the sound of the cherubims' wings was heard *even* to the outer court, as the voice of the Almighty God when he speaketh.

6 And it came to pass, *that* when he had commanded the man clothed with linen, saying, Take fire from between the wheels, from between the cherubims; then he went in, and stood beside the wheels.

7 And *one* cherub stretched forth his hand from between the cherubims unto the fire that *was* between the cherubims, and took *thereof*, and put *it* into the hands of *him that was* clothed with linen: who took *it*, and went out.

8 And there appeared in the cherubims the form of a man's hand under their wings.

9 And when I looked, behold the four wheels by the cherubims, one wheel by one cherub, and another wheel by another cherub: and the appearance of the wheels *was* as the colour of a beryl stone.

10 And *as for* their appearances, they four had one likeness, as if a wheel had been in the midst of a wheel.

11 When they went, they went upon their four sides; they turned not as they went, but to the place whither the head looked they followed it; they turned not as they went.

12 And their whole body, and their backs, and their hands, and their wings, and the wheels, *were* full of eyes round about, *even* the wheels that they four had.

13 As for the wheels, it was cried unto them in my hearing, O wheel.

14 And every one had four faces: the first face *was* the face of a cherub, and the second face *was* the face of a man,

and the third the face of a lion, and the
fourth the face of an eagle.
15 And the cherubims were lifted up.
This *is* the living creature that I saw by
the river of Chebar.
16 And when the cherubims went, the
wheels went by them: and when the
cherubims lifted up their wings to
mount up from the earth, the same
wheels also turned not from beside
them.
17 When they stood, *these* stood; and
when they were lifted up, *these* lifted
up themselves *also*: for the spirit of the
living creature *was* in them.
18 Then the glory of the LORD departed from off the threshold of the house,
and stood over the cherubims.
19 And the cherubims lifted up their
wings, and mounted up from the earth
in my sight: when they went out, the
wheels also *were* beside them, and
every one stood at the door of the east
gate of the LORD's house; and the glory
of the God of Israel *was* over them
above.
20 This *is* the living creature that I
saw under the God of Israel by the river
of Chebar; and I knew that they *were*
the cherubims.
21 Every one had four faces apiece,
and every one four wings; and the likeness of the hands of a man *was* under
their wings.
22 And the likeness of their faces *was*
the same faces which I saw by the river
of Chebar, their appearances and themselves: they went every one straight
forward.

11 Moreover the spirit lifted me up,
and brought me unto the east
gate of the LORD's house, which looketh
eastward: and behold at the door of the
gate five and twenty men; among
whom I saw Jaazaniah the son of Azur,
and Pelatiah the son of Benaiah, princes of the people.
2 Then said he unto me, Son of man,
these *are* the men that devise mischief,
and give wicked counsel in this city:
3 Which say, *It is* not near; let us build
houses: this *city is* the caldron, and we
be the flesh.
4 Therefore prophesy against them,
prophesy, O son of man.
5 And the Spirit of the LORD fell upon
me, and said unto me, Speak; Thus
saith the LORD; Thus have ye said, O
house of Israel: for I know the things
that come into your mind, *every one of*
them.
6 Ye have multiplied your slain in this
city, and ye have filled the streets
thereof with the slain.
7 Therefore thus saith the Lord GOD;
Your slain whom ye have laid in the
midst of it, they *are* the flesh, and this
city is the caldron: but I will bring you
forth out of the midst of it.
8 Ye have feared the sword; and I will
bring a sword upon you, saith the Lord
GOD.
9 And I will bring you out of the midst
thereof, and deliver you into the hands
of strangers, and will execute judgments among you.
10 Ye shall fall by the sword; I will
judge you in the border of Israel; and
ye shall know that I *am* the LORD.
11 This *city* shall not be your caldron,
neither shall ye be the flesh in the
midst thereof; *but* I will judge you in
the border of Israel:
12 And ye shall know that I *am* the
LORD: for ye have not walked in my
statutes, neither executed my judgments, but have done after the manners

of the heathen that *are* round about
you.
13 And it came to pass, when I prophesied, that Pelatiah the son of Benaiah
died. Then fell I down upon my face,
and cried with a loud voice, and said,
Ah Lord GOD! wilt thou make a full end
of the remnant of Israel?
14 Again the word of the LORD came
unto me, saying,
15 Son of man, thy brethren, *even* thy
brethren, the men of thy kindred, and
all the house of Israel wholly, *are* they
unto whom the inhabitants of
Jerusalem have said, Get you far from
the LORD: unto us is this land given in
possession.
16 Therefore say, Thus saith the Lord
GOD; Although I have cast them far off
among the heathen, and although I
have scattered them among the countries, yet will I be to them as a little
sanctuary in the countries where they
shall come.
17 Therefore say, Thus saith the Lord
GOD; I will even gather you from the
people, and assemble you out of the
countries where ye have been scattered, and I will give you the land of
Israel.
18 And they shall come thither, and
they shall take away all the detestable
things thereof and all the abominations
thereof from thence.
19 And I will give them one heart, and
I will put a new spirit within you; and I
will take the stony heart out of their
flesh, and will give them an heart of
flesh:
20 That they may walk in my statutes,
and keep mine ordinances, and do
them: and they shall be my people, and
I will be their God.
21 But *as for them* whose heart
walketh after the heart of their detestable things and their abominations, I
will recompense their way upon their
own heads, saith the Lord GOD.
22 Then did the cherubims lift up
their wings, and the wheels beside
them; and the glory of the God of Israel
was over them above.
23 And the glory of the LORD went up
from the midst of the city, and stood
upon the mountain which *is* on the east
side of the city.
24 Afterwards the spirit took me up,
and brought me in a vision by the Spirit
of God into Chaldea, to them of the
captivity. So the vision that I had seen
went up from me.
25 Then I spake unto them of the
captivity all the things that the LORD
had shewed me.

12 The word of the LORD also came
unto me, saying,
2 Son of man, thou dwellest in the
midst of a rebellious house, which have
eyes to see, and see not; they have ears
to hear, and hear not: for they *are* a
rebellious house.
3 Therefore, thou son of man, prepare
thee stuff for removing, and remove by
day in their sight; and thou shalt
remove from thy place to another place
in their sight: it may be they will consider, though they *be* a rebellious house.
4 Then shalt thou bring forth thy stuff
by day in their sight, as stuff for removing: and thou shalt go forth at even in
their sight, as they that go forth into
captivity.
5 Dig thou through the wall in their
sight, and carry out thereby.
6 In their sight shalt thou bear *it*
upon *thy* shoulders, *and* carry *it* forth
in the twilight: thou shalt cover thy

face, that thou see not the ground: for I
have set thee *for* a sign unto the house
of Israel.
7 And I did so as I was commanded: I
brought forth my stuff by day, as stuff
for captivity, and in the even I digged
through the wall with mine hand; I
brought *it* forth in the twilight, *and* I
bare *it* upon *my* shoulder in their sight.
8 And in the morning came the word
of the LORD unto me, saying,
9 Son of man, hath not the house of
Israel, the rebellious house, said unto
thee, What doest thou?
10 Say thou unto them, Thus saith the
Lord GOD; This burden *concerneth* the
prince in Jerusalem, and all the house
of Israel that *are* among them.
11 Say, I *am* your sign: like as I have
done, so shall it be done unto them:
they shall remove *and* go into captivity.
12 And the prince that *is* among them
shall bear upon *his* shoulder in the
twilight, and shall go forth: they shall
dig through the wall to carry out thereby: he shall cover his face, that he see
not the ground with *his* eyes.
13 My net also will I spread upon him,
and he shall be taken in my snare: and
I will bring him to Babylon *to* the land
of the Chaldeans; yet shall he not see it,
though he shall die there.
14 And I will scatter toward every
wind all that *are* about him to help him,
and all his bands; and I will draw out
the sword after them.
15 And they shall know that I *am* the
LORD, when I shall scatter them among
the nations, and disperse them in the
countries.
16 But I will leave a few men of them
from the sword, from the famine, and
from the pestilence; that they may
declare all their abominations among
the heathen whither they come; and
they shall know that I *am* the LORD.
17 Moreover the word of the LORD
came to me, saying,
18 Son of man, eat thy bread with
quaking, and drink thy water with
trembling and with carefulness;
19 And say unto the people of the
land, Thus saith the Lord GOD of the
inhabitants of Jerusalem, *and* of the
land of Israel; They shall eat their
bread with carefulness, and drink their
water with astonishment, that her land
may be desolate from all that is therein,
because of the violence of all them that
dwell therein.
20 And the cities that are inhabited
shall be laid waste, and the land shall
be desolate; and ye shall know that I
am the LORD.
21 And the word of the LORD came
unto me, saying,
22 Son of man, what *is* that proverb
that ye have in the land of Israel, saying, The days are prolonged, and every
vision faileth?
23 Tell them therefore, Thus saith the
Lord GOD; I will make this proverb to
cease, and they shall no more use it as
a proverb in Israel; but say unto them,
The days are at hand, and the effect of
every vision.
24 For there shall be no more any vain
vision nor flattering divination within
the house of Israel.
25 For I *am* the LORD: I will speak,
and the word that I shall speak shall
come to pass; it shall be no more prolonged: for in your days, O rebellious
house, will I say the word, and will perform it, saith the Lord GOD.
26 Again the word of the LORD came
to me, saying,

27 Son of man, behold, *they of* the
house of Israel say, The vision that he
seeth *is* for many days *to come*, and he
prophesieth of the times *that are* far
off.
28 Therefore say unto them, Thus
saith the Lord GOD; There shall none of
my words be prolonged any more, but
the word which I have spoken shall be
done, saith the Lord GOD.

13 And the word of the LORD came
unto me, saying,
2 Son of man, prophesy against the
prophets of Israel that prophesy, and
say thou unto them that prophesy out
of their own hearts, Hear ye the word of
the LORD;
3 Thus saith the Lord GOD; Woe unto
the foolish prophets, that follow their
own spirit, and have seen nothing!
4 O Israel, thy prophets are like the
foxes in the deserts.
5 Ye have not gone up into the gaps,
neither made up the hedge for the
house of Israel to stand in the battle in
the day of the LORD.
6 They have seen vanity and lying
divination, saying, The LORD saith: and
the LORD hath not sent them: and they
have made *others* to hope that they
would confirm the word.
7 Have ye not seen a vain vision, and
have ye not spoken a lying divination,
whereas ye say, The LORD saith *it*; albeit
I have not spoken?
8 Therefore thus saith the Lord GOD;
Because ye have spoken vanity, and
seen lies, therefore, behold, I *am*
against you, saith the Lord GOD.
9 And mine hand shall be upon the
prophets that see vanity, and that
divine lies: they shall not be in the
assembly of my people, neither shall
they be written in the writing of the
house of Israel, neither shall they enter
into the land of Israel; and ye shall
know that I *am* the Lord GOD.
10 Because, even because they have
seduced my people, saying, Peace; and
there was no peace; and one built up a
wall, and, lo, others daubed it with
untempered *morter*:
11 Say unto them which daub *it* with
untempered *morter*, that it shall fall:
there shall be an overflowing shower;
and ye, O great hailstones, shall fall;
and a stormy wind shall rend *it*.
12 Lo, when the wall is fallen, shall it
not be said unto you, Where *is* the
daubing wherewith ye have daubed *it*?
13 Therefore thus saith the Lord GOD;
I will even rend *it* with a stormy wind
in my fury; and there shall be an overflowing shower in mine anger, and
great hailstones in *my* fury to consume
it.
14 So will I break down the wall that
ye have daubed with untempered
morter, and bring it down to the
ground, so that the foundation thereof
shall be discovered, and it shall fall,
and ye shall be consumed in the midst
thereof: and ye shall know that I *am*
the LORD.
15 Thus will I accomplish my wrath
upon the wall, and upon them that have
daubed it with untempered *morter*,
and will say unto you, The wall *is* no
more, neither they that daubed it;
16 *To wit*, the prophets of Israel which
prophesy concerning Jerusalem, and
which see visions of peace for her, and
there is no peace, saith the Lord GOD.
17 Likewise, thou son of man, set thy
face against the daughters of thy people, which prophesy out of their own
heart; and prophesy thou against them,

18 And say, Thus saith the Lord GOD; Woe to the *women* that sew pillows to all armholes, and make kerchiefs upon the head of every stature to hunt souls! Will ye hunt the souls of my people, and will ye save the souls alive *that come* unto you?

19 And will ye pollute me among my people for handfuls of barley and for pieces of bread, to slay the souls that should not die, and to save the souls alive that should not live, by your lying to my people that hear *your* lies?

20 Wherefore thus saith the Lord GOD; Behold, I *am* against your pillows, wherewith ye there hunt the souls to make *them* fly, and I will tear them from your arms, and will let the souls go, *even* the souls that ye hunt to make *them* fly.

21 Your kerchiefs also will I tear, and deliver my people out of your hand, and they shall be no more in your hand to be hunted; and ye shall know that I *am* the LORD.

22 Because with lies ye have made the heart of the righteous sad, whom I have not made sad; and strengthened the hands of the wicked, that he should not return from his wicked way, by promising him life:

23 Therefore ye shall see no more vanity, nor divine divinations: for I will deliver my people out of your hand: and ye shall know that I *am* the LORD.

14 Then came certain of the elders of Israel unto me, and sat before me.

2 And the word of the LORD came unto me, saying,

3 Son of man, these men have set up their idols in their heart, and put the stumblingblock of their iniquity before their face: should I be enquired of at all by them?

4 Therefore speak unto them, and say unto them, Thus saith the Lord GOD; Every man of the house of Israel that setteth up his idols in his heart, and putteth the stumblingblock of his iniquity before his face, and cometh to the prophet; I the LORD will answer him that cometh according to the multitude of his idols;

5 That I may take the house of Israel in their own heart, because they are all estranged from me through their idols.

6 Therefore say unto the house of Israel, Thus saith the Lord GOD; Repent, and turn *yourselves* from your idols; and turn away your faces from all your abominations.

7 For every one of the house of Israel, or of the stranger that sojourneth in Israel, which separateth himself from me, and setteth up his idols in his heart, and putteth the stumblingblock of his iniquity before his face, and cometh to a prophet to enquire of him concerning me; I the LORD will answer him by myself:

8 And I will set my face against that man, and will make him a sign and a proverb, and I will cut him off from the midst of my people; and ye shall know that I *am* the LORD.

9 And if the prophet be deceived when he hath spoken a thing, I the LORD have deceived that prophet, and I will stretch out my hand upon him, and will destroy him from the midst of my people Israel.

10 And they shall bear the punishment of their iniquity: the punishment of the prophet shall be even as the punishment of him that seeketh *unto him*;

11 That the house of Israel may go no
more astray from me, neither be polluted any more with all their transgressions; but that they may be my people,
and I may be their God, saith the Lord
GOD.
12 The word of the LORD came again
to me, saying,
13 Son of man, when the land sinneth
against me by trespassing grievously,
then will I stretch out mine hand upon
it, and will break the staff of the bread
thereof, and will send famine upon it,
and will cut off man and beast from it:
14 Though these three men, Noah,
Daniel, and Job, were in it, they should
deliver *but* their own souls by their
righteousness, saith the Lord GOD.
15 If I cause noisome beasts to pass
through the land, and they spoil it, so
that it be desolate, that no man may
pass through because of the beasts:
16 *Though* these three men *were* in it,
as I live, saith the Lord GOD, they shall
deliver neither sons nor daughters;
they only shall be delivered, but the
land shall be desolate.
17 Or *if* I bring a sword upon that
land, and say, Sword, go through the
land; so that I cut off man and beast
from it:
18 Though these three men *were* in it,
as I live, saith the Lord GOD, they shall
deliver neither sons nor daughters, but
they only shall be delivered themselves.
19 Or *if* I send a pestilence into that
land, and pour out my fury upon it in
blood, to cut off from it man and beast:
20 Though Noah, Daniel, and Job,
were in it, *as* I live, saith the Lord GOD,
they shall deliver neither son nor
daughter; they shall *but* deliver their
own souls by their righteousness.
21 For thus saith the Lord GOD; How
much more when I send my four sore
judgments upon Jerusalem, the sword,
and the famine, and the noisome beast,
and the pestilence, to cut off from it
man and beast?
22 Yet, behold, therein shall be left a
remnant that shall be brought forth,
both sons and daughters: behold, they
shall come forth unto you, and ye shall
see their way and their doings: and ye
shall be comforted concerning the evil
that I have brought upon Jerusalem,
even concerning all that I have brought
upon it.
23 And they shall comfort you, when
ye see their ways and their doings: and
ye shall know that I have not done without cause all that I have done in it, saith
the Lord GOD.

15

And the word of the LORD came
unto me, saying,
2 Son of man, What is the vine tree
more than any tree, *or than* a branch
which is among the trees of the forest?
3 Shall wood be taken thereof to do
any work? or will *men* take a pin of it to
hang any vessel thereon?
4 Behold, it is cast into the fire for
fuel; the fire devoureth both the ends
of it, and the midst of it is burned. Is it
meet for *any* work?
5 Behold, when it was whole, it was
meet for no work: how much less shall
it be meet yet for *any* work, when the
fire hath devoured it, and it is burned?
6 Therefore thus saith the Lord GOD;
As the vine tree among the trees of the
forest, which I have given to the fire for
fuel, so will I give the inhabitants of
Jerusalem.
7 And I will set my face against them;
they shall go out from *one* fire, and
another fire shall devour them; and ye

shall know that I *am* the LORD, when I
set my face against them.
8 And I will make the land desolate,
because they have committed a trespass, saith the Lord GOD.

16 Again the word of the LORD came
unto me, saying,
2 Son of man, cause Jerusalem to
know her abominations,
3 And say, Thus saith the Lord GOD
unto Jerusalem; Thy birth and thy
nativity *is* of the land of Canaan; thy
father *was* an Amorite, and thy mother
an Hittite.
4 And *as for* thy nativity, in the day
thou wast born thy navel was not cut,
neither wast thou washed in water to
supple *thee*; thou wast not salted at all,
nor swaddled at all.
5 None eye pitied thee, to do any of
these unto thee, to have compassion
upon thee; but thou wast cast out in the
open field, to the lothing of thy person,
in the day that thou wast born.
6 And when I passed by thee, and saw
thee polluted in thine own blood, I said
unto thee *when thou wast* in thy blood,
Live; yea, I said unto thee *when thou
wast* in thy blood, Live.
7 I have caused thee to multiply as
the bud of the field, and thou hast
increased and waxen great, and thou
art come to excellent ornaments: *thy*
breasts are fashioned, and thine hair is
grown, whereas thou *wast* naked and
bare.
8 Now when I passed by thee, and
looked upon thee, behold, thy time *was*
the time of love; and I spread my skirt
over thee, and covered thy nakedness:
yea, I sware unto thee, and entered into
a covenant with thee, saith the Lord
GOD, and thou becamest mine.
9 Then washed I thee with water; yea,
I throughly washed away thy blood
from thee, and I anointed thee with oil.
10 I clothed thee also with broidered
work, and shod thee with badgers' skin,
and I girded thee about with fine linen,
and I covered thee with silk.
11 I decked thee also with ornaments,
and I put bracelets upon thy hands, and
a chain on thy neck.
12 And I put a jewel on thy forehead,
and earrings in thine ears, and a beautiful crown upon thine head.
13 Thus wast thou decked with gold
and silver; and thy raiment *was of* fine
linen, and silk, and broidered work;
thou didst eat fine flour, and honey, and
oil: and thou wast exceeding beautiful,
and thou didst prosper into a kingdom.
14 And thy renown went forth among
the heathen for thy beauty: for it *was*
perfect through my comeliness, which I
had put upon thee, saith the Lord GOD.
15 But thou didst trust in thine own
beauty, and playedst the harlot because
of thy renown, and pouredst out thy
fornications on every one that passed
by; his it was.
16 And of thy garments thou didst
take, and deckedst thy high places with
divers colours, and playedst the harlot
thereupon: *the like things* shall not
come, neither shall it be *so*.
17 Thou hast also taken thy fair jewels of my gold and of my silver, which I
had given thee, and madest to thyself
images of men, and didst commit
whoredom with them,
18 And tookest thy broidered garments, and coveredst them: and thou
hast set mine oil and mine incense
before them.
19 My meat also which I gave thee,
fine flour, and oil, and honey, *where-*

with I fed thee, thou hast even set it before them for a sweet savour: and *thus* it was, saith the Lord GOD.

20 Moreover thou hast taken thy sons and thy daughters, whom thou hast borne unto me, and these hast thou sacrificed unto them to be devoured. *Is this* of thy whoredoms a small matter,

21 That thou hast slain my children, and delivered them to cause them to pass through *the fire* for them?

22 And in all thine abominations and thy whoredoms thou hast not remembered the days of thy youth, when thou wast naked and bare, *and* wast polluted in thy blood.

23 And it came to pass after all thy wickedness, (woe, woe unto thee! saith the Lord GOD;)

24 *That* thou hast also built unto thee an eminent place, and hast made thee an high place in every street.

25 Thou hast built thy high place at every head of the way, and hast made thy beauty to be abhorred, and hast opened thy feet to every one that passed by, and multiplied thy whoredoms.

26 Thou hast also committed fornication with the Egyptians thy neighbours, great of flesh; and hast increased thy whoredoms, to provoke me to anger.

27 Behold, therefore I have stretched out my hand over thee, and have diminished thine ordinary *food*, and delivered thee unto the will of them that hate thee, the daughters of the Philistines, which are ashamed of thy lewd way.

28 Thou hast played the whore also with the Assyrians, because thou wast unsatiable; yea, thou hast played the harlot with them, and yet couldest not be satisfied.

29 Thou hast moreover multiplied thy fornication in the land of Canaan unto Chaldea; and yet thou wast not satisfied herewith.

30 How weak is thine heart, saith the Lord GOD, seeing thou doest all these *things*, the work of an imperious whorish woman;

31 In that thou buildest thine eminent place in the head of every way, and makest thine high place in every street; and hast not been as an harlot, in that thou scornest hire;

32 *But as* a wife that committeth adultery, *which* taketh strangers instead of her husband!

33 They give gifts to all whores: but thou givest thy gifts to all thy lovers, and hirest them, that they may come unto thee on every side for thy whoredom.

34 And the contrary is in thee from *other* women in thy whoredoms, whereas none followeth thee to commit whoredoms: and in that thou givest a reward, and no reward is given unto thee, therefore thou art contrary.

35 Wherefore, O harlot, hear the word of the LORD:

36 Thus saith the Lord GOD; Because thy filthiness was poured out, and thy nakedness discovered through thy whoredoms with thy lovers, and with all the idols of thy abominations, and by the blood of thy children, which thou didst give unto them;

37 Behold, therefore I will gather all thy lovers, with whom thou hast taken pleasure, and all *them* that thou hast loved, with all *them* that thou hast hated; I will even gather them round about against thee, and will discover thy nakedness unto them, that they may see all thy nakedness.

38 And I will judge thee, as women
that break wedlock and shed blood are
judged; and I will give thee blood in
fury and jealousy.
39 And I will also give thee into their
hand, and they shall throw down thine
eminent place, and shall break down
thy high places: they shall strip thee
also of thy clothes, and shall take thy
fair jewels, and leave thee naked and
bare.
40 They shall also bring up a company against thee, and they shall stone
thee with stones, and thrust thee
through with their swords.
41 And they shall burn thine houses
with fire, and execute judgments upon
thee in the sight of many women: and I
will cause thee to cease from playing
the harlot, and thou also shalt give no
hire any more.
42 So will I make my fury toward thee
to rest, and my jealousy shall depart
from thee, and I will be quiet, and will
be no more angry.
43 Because thou hast not remembered the days of thy youth, but hast
fretted me in all these *things*; behold,
therefore I also will recompense thy
way upon *thine* head, saith the Lord
GOD: and thou shalt not commit this
lewdness above all thine abominations.
44 Behold, every one that useth proverbs shall use *this* proverb against
thee, saying, As *is* the mother, *so is* her
daughter.
45 Thou *art* thy mother's daughter,
that lotheth her husband and her children; and thou *art* the sister of thy sisters, which lothed their husbands and
their children: your mother *was* an
Hittite, and your father an Amorite.
46 And thine elder sister *is* Samaria,
she and her daughters that dwell at thy
left hand: and thy younger sister, that
dwelleth at thy right hand, *is* Sodom
and her daughters.
47 Yet hast thou not walked after
their ways, nor done after their abominations: but, as *if that were* a very little
thing, thou wast corrupted more than
they in all thy ways.
48 *As* I live, saith the Lord GOD,
Sodom thy sister hath not done, she nor
her daughters, as thou hast done, thou
and thy daughters.
49 Behold, this was the iniquity of thy
sister Sodom, pride, fulness of bread,
and abundance of idleness was in her
and in her daughters, neither did she
strengthen the hand of the poor and
needy.
50 And they were haughty, and committed abomination before me: therefore I took them away as I saw *good*.
51 Neither hath Samaria committed
half of thy sins; but thou hast multiplied thine abominations more than
they, and hast justified thy sisters in all
thine abominations which thou hast
done.
52 Thou also, which hast judged thy
sisters, bear thine own shame for thy
sins that thou hast committed more
abominable than they: they are more
righteous than thou: yea, be thou confounded also, and bear thy shame, in
that thou hast justified thy sisters.
53 When I shall bring again their
captivity, the captivity of Sodom and
her daughters, and the captivity of
Samaria and her daughters, then *will I*
bring again the captivity of thy captives in the midst of them:

54 That thou mayest bear thine own shame, and mayest be confounded in all that thou hast done, in that thou art a comfort unto them.

55 When thy sisters, Sodom and her daughters, shall return to their former estate, and Samaria and her daughters shall return to their former estate, then thou and thy daughters shall return to your former estate.

56 For thy sister Sodom was not mentioned by thy mouth in the day of thy pride,

57 Before thy wickedness was discovered, as at the time of *thy* reproach of the daughters of Syria, and all *that are* round about her, the daughters of the Philistines, which despise thee round about.

58 Thou hast borne thy lewdness and thine abominations, saith the LORD.

59 For thus saith the Lord GOD; I will even deal with thee as thou hast done, which hast despised the oath in breaking the covenant.

60 Nevertheless I will remember my covenant with thee in the days of thy youth, and I will establish unto thee an everlasting covenant.

61 Then thou shalt remember thy ways, and be ashamed, when thou shalt receive thy sisters, thine elder and thy younger: and I will give them unto thee for daughters, but not by thy covenant.

62 And I will establish my covenant with thee; and thou shalt know that I *am* the LORD:

63 That thou mayest remember, and be confounded, and never open thy mouth any more because of thy shame, when I am pacified toward thee for all that thou hast done, saith the Lord GOD.

17

And the word of the LORD came unto me, saying,

2 Son of man, put forth a riddle, and speak a parable unto the house of Israel;

3 And say, Thus saith the Lord GOD; A great eagle with great wings, longwinged, full of feathers, which had divers colours, came unto Lebanon, and took the highest branch of the cedar:

4 He cropped off the top of his young twigs, and carried it into a land of traffick; he set it in a city of merchants.

5 He took also of the seed of the land, and planted it in a fruitful field; he placed *it* by great waters, *and* set it *as* a willow tree.

6 And it grew, and became a spreading vine of low stature, whose branches turned toward him, and the roots thereof were under him: so it became a vine, and brought forth branches, and shot forth sprigs.

7 There was also another great eagle with great wings and many feathers: and, behold, this vine did bend her roots toward him, and shot forth her branches toward him, that he might water it by the furrows of her plantation.

8 It was planted in a good soil by great waters, that it might bring forth branches, and that it might bear fruit, that it might be a goodly vine.

9 Say thou, Thus saith the Lord GOD; Shall it prosper? shall he not pull up the roots thereof, and cut off the fruit thereof, that it wither? it shall wither in all the leaves of her spring, even without great power or many people to pluck it up by the roots thereof.

10 Yea, behold, *being* planted, shall it
prosper? shall it not utterly wither,
when the east wind toucheth it? it shall
wither in the furrows where it grew.
11 Moreover the word of the LORD
came unto me, saying,
12 Say now to the rebellious house,
Know ye not what these *things mean*?
tell *them*, Behold, the king of Babylon
is come to Jerusalem, and hath taken
the king thereof, and the princes thereof, and led them with him to Babylon;
13 And hath taken of the king's seed,
and made a covenant with him, and
hath taken an oath of him: he hath also
taken the mighty of the land:
14 That the kingdom might be base,
that it might not lift itself up, *but* that
by keeping of his covenant it might
stand.
15 But he rebelled against him in
sending his ambassadors into Egypt,
that they might give him horses and
much people. Shall he prosper? shall he
escape that doeth such *things*? or shall
he break the covenant, and be delivered?
16 *As* I live, saith the Lord GOD, surely
in the place *where* the king *dwelleth*
that made him king, whose oath he
despised, and whose covenant he
brake, *even* with him in the midst of
Babylon he shall die.
17 Neither shall Pharaoh with *his*
mighty army and great company make
for him in the war, by casting up
mounts, and building forts, to cut off
many persons:
18 Seeing he despised the oath by
breaking the covenant, when, lo, he had
given his hand, and hath done all these
things, he shall not escape.
19 Therefore thus saith the Lord GOD;
As I live, surely mine oath that he hath
despised, and my covenant that he hath
broken, even it will I recompense upon
his own head.
20 And I will spread my net upon him,
and he shall be taken in my snare, and
I will bring him to Babylon, and will
plead with him there for his trespass
that he hath trespassed against me.
21 And all his fugitives with all his
bands shall fall by the sword, and they
that remain shall be scattered toward
all winds: and ye shall know that I the
LORD have spoken *it*.
22 Thus saith the Lord GOD; I will also
take of the highest branch of the high
cedar, and will set *it*; I will crop off from
the top of his young twigs a tender one,
and will plant *it* upon an high mountain and eminent:
23 In the mountain of the height of
Israel will I plant it: and it shall bring
forth boughs, and bear fruit, and be a
goodly cedar: and under it shall dwell
all fowl of every wing; in the shadow of
the branches thereof shall they dwell.
24 And all the trees of the field shall
know that I the LORD have brought
down the high tree, have exalted the
low tree, have dried up the green tree,
and have made the dry tree to flourish:
I the LORD have spoken and have done
it.

18 The word of the LORD came unto
me again, saying,
2 What mean ye, that ye use this proverb concerning the land of Israel, saying, The fathers have eaten sour grapes,
and the children's teeth are set on
edge?
3 *As* I live, saith the Lord GOD, ye shall
not have *occasion* any more to use this
proverb in Israel.
4 Behold, all souls are mine; as the
soul of the father, so also the soul of the

son is mine: the soul that sinneth, it
shall die.
5 But if a man be just, and do that
which is lawful and right,
6 *And* hath not eaten upon the
mountains, neither hath lifted up his
eyes to the idols of the house of Israel,
neither hath defiled his neighbour's
wife, neither hath come near to a
menstruous woman,
7 And hath not oppressed any, *but*
hath restored to the debtor his pledge,
hath spoiled none by violence, hath
given his bread to the hungry, and hath
covered the naked with a garment;
8 He *that* hath not given forth upon
usury, neither hath taken any increase,
that hath withdrawn his hand from
iniquity, hath executed true judgment
between man and man,
9 Hath walked in my statutes, and
hath kept my judgments, to deal truly;
he *is* just, he shall surely live, saith the
Lord GOD.
10 If he beget a son *that is* a robber, a
shedder of blood, and *that* doeth the
like to *any* one of these *things*,
11 And that doeth not any of those
duties, but even hath eaten upon the
mountains, and defiled his neighbour's
wife,
12 Hath oppressed the poor and
needy, hath spoiled by violence, hath
not restored the pledge, and hath lifted
up his eyes to the idols, hath committed
abomination,
13 Hath given forth upon usury, and
hath taken increase: shall he then live?
he shall not live: he hath done all these
abominations; he shall surely die; his
blood shall be upon him.
14 Now, lo, *if* he beget a son, that
seeth all his father's sins which he hath
done, and considereth, and doeth not
such like,
15 *That* hath not eaten upon the
mountains, neither hath lifted up his
eyes to the idols of the house of Israel,
hath not defiled his neighbour's wife,
16 Neither hath oppressed any, hath
not withholden the pledge, neither
hath spoiled by violence, *but* hath
given his bread to the hungry, and hath
covered the naked with a garment,
17 *That* hath taken off his hand from
the poor, *that* hath not received usury
nor increase, hath executed my judgments, hath walked in my statutes; he
shall not die for the iniquity of his
father, he shall surely live.
18 *As for* his father, because he cruel-
ly oppressed, spoiled his brother by
violence, and did *that* which *is* not
good among his people, lo, even he
shall die in his iniquity.
19 Yet say ye, Why? doth not the son
bear the iniquity of the father? When
the son hath done that which is lawful
and right, *and* hath kept all my statutes, and hath done them, he shall
surely live.
20 The soul that sinneth, it shall die.
The son shall not bear the iniquity of
the father, neither shall the father bear
the iniquity of the son: the righteousness of the righteous shall be upon him,
and the wickedness of the wicked shall
be upon him.
21 But if the wicked will turn from all
his sins that he hath committed, and
keep all my statutes, and do that which
is lawful and right, he shall surely live,
he shall not die.

22 All his transgressions that he hath committed, they shall not be mentioned unto him: in his righteousness that he hath done he shall live.

23 Have I any pleasure at all that the wicked should die? saith the Lord God: *and* not that he should return from his ways, and live?

24 But when the righteous turneth away from his righteousness, and committeth iniquity, *and* doeth according to all the abominations that the wicked *man* doeth, shall he live? All his righteousness that he hath done shall not be mentioned: in his trespass that he hath trespassed, and in his sin that he hath sinned, in them shall he die.

25 Yet ye say, The way of the Lord is not equal. Hear now, O house of Israel; Is not my way equal? are not your ways unequal?

26 When a righteous *man* turneth away from his righteousness, and committeth iniquity, and dieth in them; for his iniquity that he hath done shall he die.

27 Again, when the wicked *man* turneth away from his wickedness that he hath committed, and doeth that which is lawful and right, he shall save his soul alive.

28 Because he considereth, and turneth away from all his transgressions that he hath committed, he shall surely live, he shall not die.

29 Yet saith the house of Israel, The way of the Lord is not equal. O house of Israel, are not my ways equal? are not your ways unequal?

30 Therefore I will judge you, O house of Israel, every one according to his ways, saith the Lord God. Repent, and turn *yourselves* from all your transgressions; so iniquity shall not be your ruin.

31 Cast away from you all your transgressions, whereby ye have transgressed; and make you a new heart and a new spirit: for why will ye die, O house of Israel?

32 For I have no pleasure in the death of him that dieth, saith the Lord God: wherefore turn *yourselves*, and live ye.

19 Moreover take thou up a lamentation for the princes of Israel,

2 And say, What *is* thy mother? A lioness: she lay down among lions, she nourished her whelps among young lions.

3 And she brought up one of her whelps: it became a young lion, and it learned to catch the prey; it devoured men.

4 The nations also heard of him; he was taken in their pit, and they brought him with chains unto the land of Egypt.

5 Now when she saw that she had waited, *and* her hope was lost, then she took another of her whelps, *and* made him a young lion.

6 And he went up and down among the lions, he became a young lion, and learned to catch the prey, *and* devoured men.

7 And he knew their desolate palaces, and he laid waste their cities; and the land was desolate, and the fulness thereof, by the noise of his roaring.

8 Then the nations set against him on every side from the provinces, and spread their net over him: he was taken in their pit.

9 And they put him in ward in chains, and brought him to the king of Babylon: they brought him into holds, that his voice should no more be heard upon the mountains of Israel.

10 Thy mother *is* like a vine in thy
blood, planted by the waters: she was
fruitful and full of branches by reason
of many waters.
11 And she had strong rods for the
sceptres of them that bare rule, and her
stature was exalted among the thick
branches, and she appeared in her
height with the multitude of her
branches.
12 But she was plucked up in fury, she
was cast down to the ground, and the
east wind dried up her fruit: her strong
rods were broken and withered; the fire
consumed them.
13 And now she *is* planted in the wilderness, in a dry and thirsty ground.
14 And fire is gone out of a rod of her
branches, *which* hath devoured her
fruit, so that she hath no strong rod *to
be* a sceptre to rule. This *is* a lamentation, and shall be for a lamentation.

20 And it came to pass in the seventh year, in the fifth *month*, the
tenth *day* of the month, *that* certain of
the elders of Israel came to enquire of
the LORD, and sat before me.
2 Then came the word of the LORD
unto me, saying,
3 Son of man, speak unto the elders of
Israel, and say unto them, Thus saith
the Lord GOD; Are ye come to enquire
of me? *As* I live, saith the Lord GOD, I
will not be enquired of by you.
4 Wilt thou judge them, son of man,
wilt thou judge *them*? cause them to
know the abominations of their fathers:
5 And say unto them, Thus saith the
Lord GOD; In the day when I chose
Israel, and lifted up mine hand unto
the seed of the house of Jacob, and
made myself known unto them in the
land of Egypt, when I lifted up mine
hand unto them, saying, I *am* the LORD
your God;
6 In the day *that* I lifted up mine
hand unto them, to bring them forth of
the land of Egypt into a land that I had
espied for them, flowing with milk and
honey, which *is* the glory of all lands:
7 Then said I unto them, Cast ye away
every man the abominations of his
eyes, and defile not yourselves with the
idols of Egypt: I *am* the LORD your God.
8 But they rebelled against me, and
would not hearken unto me: they did
not every man cast away the abominations of their eyes, neither did they
forsake the idols of Egypt: then I said, I
will pour out my fury upon them, to
accomplish my anger against them in
the midst of the land of Egypt.
9 But I wrought for my name's sake,
that it should not be polluted before
the heathen, among whom they *were*,
in whose sight I made myself known
unto them, in bringing them forth out
of the land of Egypt.
10 Wherefore I caused them to go
forth out of the land of Egypt, and
brought them into the wilderness.
11 And I gave them my statutes, and
shewed them my judgments, which *if* a
man do, he shall even live in them.
12 Moreover also I gave them my sabbaths, to be a sign between me and
them, that they might know that I *am*
the LORD that sanctify them.
13 But the house of Israel rebelled
against me in the wilderness: they
walked not in my statutes, and they
despised my judgments, which *if* a man
do, he shall even live in them; and my
sabbaths they greatly polluted: then I
said, I would pour out my fury upon
them in the wilderness, to consume
them.

14 But I wrought for my name's sake, that it should not be polluted before the heathen, in whose sight I brought them out.

15 Yet also I lifted up my hand unto them in the wilderness, that I would not bring them into the land which I had given *them*, flowing with milk and honey, which *is* the glory of all lands;

16 Because they despised my judgments, and walked not in my statutes, but polluted my sabbaths: for their heart went after their idols.

17 Nevertheless mine eye spared them from destroying them, neither did I make an end of them in the wilderness.

18 But I said unto their children in the wilderness, Walk ye not in the statutes of your fathers, neither observe their judgments, nor defile yourselves with their idols:

19 I *am* the LORD your God; walk in my statutes, and keep my judgments, and do them;

20 And hallow my sabbaths; and they shall be a sign between me and you, that ye may know that I *am* the LORD your God.

21 Notwithstanding the children rebelled against me: they walked not in my statutes, neither kept my judgments to do them, which *if* a man do, he shall even live in them; they polluted my sabbaths: then I said, I would pour out my fury upon them, to accomplish my anger against them in the wilderness.

22 Nevertheless I withdrew mine hand, and wrought for my name's sake, that it should not be polluted in the sight of the heathen, in whose sight I brought them forth.

23 I lifted up mine hand unto them also in the wilderness, that I would scatter them among the heathen, and disperse them through the countries;

24 Because they had not executed my judgments, but had despised my statutes, and had polluted my sabbaths, and their eyes were after their fathers' idols.

25 Wherefore I gave them also statutes *that were* not good, and judgments whereby they should not live;

26 And I polluted them in their own gifts, in that they caused to pass through *the fire* all that openeth the womb, that I might make them desolate, to the end that they might know that I *am* the LORD.

27 Therefore, son of man, speak unto the house of Israel, and say unto them, Thus saith the Lord GOD; Yet in this your fathers have blasphemed me, in that they have committed a trespass against me.

28 *For* when I had brought them into the land, *for* the which I lifted up mine hand to give it to them, then they saw every high hill, and all the thick trees, and they offered there their sacrifices, and there they presented the provocation of their offering: there also they made their sweet savour, and poured out there their drink offerings.

29 Then I said unto them, What *is* the high place whereunto ye go? And the name thereof is called Bamah unto this day.

30 Wherefore say unto the house of Israel, Thus saith the Lord GOD; Are ye polluted after the manner of your fathers? and commit ye whoredom after their abominations?

31 For when ye offer your gifts, when ye make your sons to pass through the

fire, ye pollute yourselves with all your
idols, even unto this day: and shall I be
enquired of by you, O house of Israel?
As I live, saith the Lord GOD, I will not
be enquired of by you.
32 And that which cometh into your
mind shall not be at all, that ye say, We
will be as the heathen, as the families
of the countries, to serve wood and
stone.
33 *As* I live, saith the Lord GOD, surely
with a mighty hand, and with a
stretched out arm, and with fury
poured out, will I rule over you:
34 And I will bring you out from the
people, and will gather you out of the
countries wherein ye are scattered,
with a mighty hand, and with a
stretched out arm, and with fury
poured out.
35 And I will bring you into the wilderness of the people, and there will I
plead with you face to face.
36 Like as I pleaded with your fathers
in the wilderness of the land of Egypt,
so will I plead with you, saith the Lord
GOD.
37 And I will cause you to pass under
the rod, and I will bring you into the
bond of the covenant:
38 And I will purge out from among
you the rebels, and them that transgress against me: I will bring them
forth out of the country where they
sojourn, and they shall not enter into
the land of Israel: and ye shall know
that I *am* the LORD.
39 As for you, O house of Israel, thus
saith the Lord GOD; Go ye, serve ye
every one his idols, and hereafter *also*,
if ye will not hearken unto me: but pollute ye my holy name no more with
your gifts, and with your idols.
40 For in mine holy mountain, in the
mountain of the height of Israel, saith
the Lord GOD, there shall all the house
of Israel, all of them in the land, serve
me: there will I accept them, and there
will I require your offerings, and the
firstfruits of your oblations, with all
your holy things.
41 I will accept you with your sweet
savour, when I bring you out from the
people, and gather you out of the countries wherein ye have been scattered;
and I will be sanctified in you before
the heathen.
42 And ye shall know that I *am* the
LORD, when I shall bring you into the
land of Israel, into the country *for* the
which I lifted up mine hand to give it to
your fathers.
43 And there shall ye remember your
ways, and all your doings, wherein ye
have been defiled; and ye shall lothe
yourselves in your own sight for all your
evils that ye have committed.
44 And ye shall know that I *am* the
LORD, when I have wrought with you for
my name's sake, not according to your
wicked ways, nor according to your corrupt doings, O ye house of Israel, saith
the Lord GOD.
45 Moreover the word of the LORD
came unto me, saying,
46 Son of man, set thy face toward the
south, and drop *thy word* toward the
south, and prophesy against the forest
of the south field;
47 And say to the forest of the south,
Hear the word of the LORD; Thus saith
the Lord GOD; Behold, I will kindle a
fire in thee, and it shall devour every
green tree in thee, and every dry tree:
the flaming flame shall not be
quenched, and all faces from the south
to the north shall be burned therein.

48 And all flesh shall see that I the LORD have kindled it: it shall not be quenched.

49 Then said I, Ah Lord GOD! they say of me, Doth he not speak parables?

21

And the word of the LORD came unto me, saying,

2 Son of man, set thy face toward Jerusalem, and drop *thy word* toward the holy places, and prophesy against the land of Israel,

3 And say to the land of Israel, Thus saith the LORD; Behold, I *am* against thee, and will draw forth my sword out of his sheath, and will cut off from thee the righteous and the wicked.

4 Seeing then that I will cut off from thee the righteous and the wicked, therefore shall my sword go forth out of his sheath against all flesh from the south to the north:

5 That all flesh may know that I the LORD have drawn forth my sword out of his sheath: it shall not return any more.

6 Sigh therefore, thou son of man, with the breaking of *thy* loins; and with bitterness sigh before their eyes.

7 And it shall be, when they say unto thee, Wherefore sighest thou? that thou shalt answer, For the tidings; because it cometh: and every heart shall melt, and all hands shall be feeble, and every spirit shall faint, and all knees shall be weak *as* water: behold, it cometh, and shall be brought to pass, saith the Lord GOD.

8 Again the word of the LORD came unto me, saying,

9 Son of man, prophesy, and say, Thus saith the LORD; Say, A sword, a sword is sharpened, and also furbished:

10 It is sharpened to make a sore slaughter; it is furbished that it may glitter: should we then make mirth? it contemneth the rod of my son, *as* every tree.

11 And he hath given it to be furbished, that it may be handled: this sword is sharpened, and it is furbished, to give it into the hand of the slayer.

12 Cry and howl, son of man: for it shall be upon my people, it *shall be* upon all the princes of Israel: terrors by reason of the sword shall be upon my people: smite therefore upon *thy* thigh.

13 Because *it is* a trial, and what if *the sword* contemn even the rod? it shall be no *more*, saith the Lord GOD.

14 Thou therefore, son of man, prophesy, and smite *thine* hands together, and let the sword be doubled the third time, the sword of the slain: it *is* the sword of the great *men that are* slain, which entereth into their privy chambers.

15 I have set the point of the sword against all their gates, that *their* heart may faint, and *their* ruins be multiplied: ah! *it is* made bright, *it is* wrapped up for the slaughter.

16 Go thee one way or other, *either* on the right hand, *or* on the left, whithersoever thy face *is* set.

17 I will also smite mine hands together, and I will cause my fury to rest: I the LORD have said *it*.

18 The word of the LORD came unto me again, saying,

19 Also, thou son of man, appoint thee two ways, that the sword of the king of Babylon may come: both twain shall come forth out of one land: and choose thou a place, choose *it* at the head of the way to the city.

20 Appoint a way, that the sword may come to Rabbath of the Ammonites, and to Judah in Jerusalem the defenced.

21 For the king of Babylon stood at
the parting of the way, at the head of
the two ways, to use divination: he
made *his* arrows bright, he consulted
with images, he looked in the liver.
22 At his right hand was the divination for Jerusalem, to appoint captains,
to open the mouth in the slaughter, to
lift up the voice with shouting, to
appoint *battering* rams against the
gates, to cast a mount, *and* to build a
fort.
23 And it shall be unto them as a false
divination in their sight, to them that
have sworn oaths: but he will call to
remembrance the iniquity, that they
may be taken.
24 Therefore thus saith the Lord GOD;
Because ye have made your iniquity to
be remembered, in that your transgressions are discovered, so that in all your
doings your sins do appear; because, *I*
say, that ye are come to remembrance,
ye shall be taken with the hand.
25 And thou, profane wicked prince
of Israel, whose day is come, when iniquity *shall have* an end,
26 Thus saith the Lord GOD; Remove
the diadem, and take off the crown: this
shall not *be* the same: exalt *him that is*
low, and abase *him that is* high.
27 I will overturn, overturn, overturn,
it: and it shall be no *more*, until he
come whose right it is; and I will give it
him.
28 And thou, son of man, prophesy
and say, Thus saith the Lord GOD concerning the Ammonites, and concerning their reproach; even say thou, The
sword, the sword *is* drawn: for the
slaughter *it is* furbished, to consume
because of the glittering:
29 Whiles they see vanity unto thee,
whiles they divine a lie unto thee, to
bring thee upon the necks of *them that*
are slain, of the wicked, whose day is
come, when their iniquity *shall have*
an end.
30 Shall I cause *it* to return into his
sheath? I will judge thee in the place
where thou wast created, in the land of
thy nativity.
31 And I will pour out mine indignation upon thee, I will blow against thee
in the fire of my wrath, and deliver thee
into the hand of brutish men, *and* skilful to destroy.
32 Thou shalt be for fuel to the fire;
thy blood shall be in the midst of the
land; thou shalt be no *more* remembered: for I the LORD have spoken *it*.

22 Moreover the word of the LORD
came unto me, saying,
2 Now, thou son of man, wilt thou
judge, wilt thou judge the bloody city?
yea, thou shalt shew her all her abominations.
3 Then say thou, Thus saith the Lord
GOD, The city sheddeth blood in the
midst of it, that her time may come, and
maketh idols against herself to defile
herself.
4 Thou art become guilty in thy blood
that thou hast shed; and hast defiled
thyself in thine idols which thou hast
made; and thou hast caused thy days to
draw near, and art come *even* unto thy
years: therefore have I made thee a
reproach unto the heathen, and a mocking to all countries.
5 *Those that be* near, and *those that*
be far from thee, shall mock thee,
which art infamous *and* much vexed.
6 Behold, the princes of Israel, every
one were in thee to their power to shed
blood.
7 In thee have they set light by father
and mother: in the midst of thee have

they dealt by oppression with the stranger: in thee have they vexed the fatherless and the widow.

8 Thou hast despised mine holy things, and hast profaned my sabbaths.

9 In thee are men that carry tales to shed blood: and in thee they eat upon the mountains: in the midst of thee they commit lewdness.

10 In thee have they discovered their fathers' nakedness: in thee have they humbled her that was set apart for pollution.

11 And one hath committed abomination with his neighbour's wife; and another hath lewdly defiled his daughter in law; and another in thee hath humbled his sister, his father's daughter.

12 In thee have they taken gifts to shed blood; thou hast taken usury and increase, and thou hast greedily gained of thy neighbours by extortion, and hast forgotten me, saith the Lord GOD.

13 Behold, therefore I have smitten mine hand at thy dishonest gain which thou hast made, and at thy blood which hath been in the midst of thee.

14 Can thine heart endure, or can thine hands be strong, in the days that I shall deal with thee? I the LORD have spoken *it*, and will do *it*.

15 And I will scatter thee among the heathen, and disperse thee in the countries, and will consume thy filthiness out of thee.

16 And thou shalt take thine inheritance in thyself in the sight of the heathen, and thou shalt know that I *am* the LORD.

17 And the word of the LORD came unto me, saying,

18 Son of man, the house of Israel is to me become dross: all they *are* brass, and tin, and iron, and lead, in the midst of the furnace; they are *even* the dross of silver.

19 Therefore thus saith the Lord GOD; Because ye are all become dross, behold, therefore I will gather you into the midst of Jerusalem.

20 *As* they gather silver, and brass, and iron, and lead, and tin, into the midst of the furnace, to blow the fire upon it, to melt *it*; so will I gather *you* in mine anger and in my fury, and I will leave *you there*, and melt you.

21 Yea, I will gather you, and blow upon you in the fire of my wrath, and ye shall be melted in the midst thereof.

22 As silver is melted in the midst of the furnace, so shall ye be melted in the midst thereof; and ye shall know that I the LORD have poured out my fury upon you.

23 And the word of the LORD came unto me, saying,

24 Son of man, say unto her, Thou *art* the land that is not cleansed, nor rained upon in the day of indignation.

25 *There is* a conspiracy of her prophets in the midst thereof, like a roaring lion ravening the prey; they have devoured souls; they have taken the treasure and precious things; they have made her many widows in the midst thereof.

26 Her priests have violated my law, and have profaned mine holy things: they have put no difference between the holy and profane, neither have they shewed *difference* between the unclean and the clean, and have hid their eyes from my sabbaths, and I am profaned among them.

27 Her princes in the midst thereof
are like wolves ravening the prey, to
shed blood, *and* to destroy souls, to get
dishonest gain.
28 And her prophets have daubed
them with untempered *morter*, seeing
vanity, and divining lies unto them, saying,
Thus saith the Lord GOD, when the
LORD hath not spoken.
29 The people of the land have used
oppression, and exercised robbery, and
have vexed the poor and needy: yea,
they have oppressed the stranger
wrongfully.
30 And I sought for a man among
them, that should make up the hedge,
and stand in the gap before me for the
land, that I should not destroy it: but I
found none.
31 Therefore have I poured out mine
indignation upon them; I have consumed
them with the fire of my wrath:
their own way have I recompensed
upon their heads, saith the Lord GOD.

23 The word of the LORD came again
unto me, saying,
2 Son of man, there were two women,
the daughters of one mother:
3 And they committed whoredoms in
Egypt; they committed whoredoms in
their youth: there were their breasts
pressed, and there they bruised the
teats of their virginity.
4 And the names of them *were* Aholah
the elder, and Aholibah her sister: and
they were mine, and they bare sons and
daughters. Thus *were* their names;
Samaria *is* Aholah, and Jerusalem
Aholibah.
5 And Aholah played the harlot when
she was mine; and she doted on her
lovers, on the Assyrians *her* neighbours,
6 *Which were* clothed with blue,
captains and rulers, all of them
desirable young men, horsemen riding
upon horses.
7 Thus she committed her whoredoms
with them, with all them *that*
were the chosen men of Assyria, and
with all on whom she doted: with all
their idols she defiled herself.
8 Neither left she her whoredoms
brought from Egypt: for in her youth
they lay with her, and they bruised the
breasts of her virginity, and poured
their whoredom upon her.
9 Wherefore I have delivered her into
the hand of her lovers, into the hand of
the Assyrians, upon whom she doted.
10 These discovered her nakedness:
they took her sons and her daughters,
and slew her with the sword: and she
became famous among women; for
they had executed judgment upon her.
11 And when her sister Aholibah saw
this, she was more corrupt in her inordinate
love than she, and in her whoredoms
more than her sister in *her*
whoredoms.
12 She doted upon the Assyrians *her*
neighbours, captains and rulers clothed
most gorgeously, horsemen riding upon
horses, all of them desirable young
men.
13 Then I saw that she was defiled,
that they *took* both one way,
14 And *that* she increased her whoredoms:
for when she saw men pourtrayed
upon the wall, the images of the
Chaldeans pourtrayed with vermilion,
15 Girded with girdles upon their
loins, exceeding in dyed attire upon
their heads, all of them princes to look
to, after the manner of the Babylonians
of Chaldea, the land of their nativity:

16 And as soon as she saw them with
her eyes, she doted upon them, and
sent messengers unto them into
Chaldea.
17 And the Babylonians came to her
into the bed of love, and they defiled
her with their whoredom, and she was
polluted with them, and her mind was
alienated from them.
18 So she discovered her whoredoms,
and discovered her nakedness: then my
mind was alienated from her, like as my
mind was alienated from her sister.
19 Yet she multiplied her whoredoms,
in calling to remembrance the days of
her youth, wherein she had played the
harlot in the land of Egypt.
20 For she doted upon their para-
mours, whose flesh *is as* the flesh of
asses, and whose issue *is like* the issue
of horses.
21 Thus thou calledst to remembrance the lewdness of thy youth, in
bruising thy teats by the Egyptians for
the paps of thy youth.
22 Therefore, O Aholibah, thus saith
the Lord GOD; Behold, I will raise up thy
lovers against thee, from whom thy
mind is alienated, and I will bring them
against thee on every side;
23 The Babylonians, and all the
Chaldeans, Pekod, and Shoa, and Koa,
and all the Assyrians with them: all of
them desirable young men, captains
and rulers, great lords and renowned,
all of them riding upon horses.
24 And they shall come against thee
with chariots, wagons, and wheels, and
with an assembly of people, *which* shall
set against thee buckler and shield and
helmet round about: and I will set judgment before them, and they shall judge
thee according to their judgments.
25 And I will set my jealousy against
thee, and they shall deal furiously with
thee: they shall take away thy nose and
thine ears; and thy remnant shall fall
by the sword: they shall take thy sons
and thy daughters; and thy residue
shall be devoured by the fire.
26 They shall also strip thee out of thy
clothes, and take away thy fair jewels.
27 Thus will I make thy lewdness to
cease from thee, and thy whoredom
brought from the land of Egypt: so that
thou shalt not lift up thine eyes unto
them, nor remember Egypt any more.
28 For thus saith the Lord GOD;
Behold, I will deliver thee into the hand
of them whom thou hatest, into the
hand *of them* from whom thy mind is
alienated:
29 And they shall deal with thee hate-
fully, and shall take away all thy labour,
and shall leave thee naked and bare:
and the nakedness of thy whoredoms
shall be discovered, both thy lewdness
and thy whoredoms.
30 I will do these *things* unto thee,
because thou hast gone a whoring after
the heathen, *and* because thou art polluted with their idols.
31 Thou hast walked in the way of thy
sister; therefore will I give her cup into
thine hand.
32 Thus saith the Lord GOD; Thou
shalt drink of thy sister's cup deep and
large: thou shalt be laughed to scorn
and had in derision; it containeth
much.
33 Thou shalt be filled with drunkenness and sorrow, with the cup of astonishment and desolation, with the cup of
thy sister Samaria.
34 Thou shalt even drink it and suck
it out, and thou shalt break the sherds
thereof, and pluck off thine own

breasts: for I have spoken *it*, saith the Lord GOD.

35 Therefore thus saith the Lord GOD; Because thou hast forgotten me, and cast me behind thy back, therefore bear thou also thy lewdness and thy whoredoms.

36 The LORD said moreover unto me; Son of man, wilt thou judge Aholah and Aholibah? yea, declare unto them their abominations;

37 That they have committed adultery, and blood *is* in their hands, and with their idols have they committed adultery, and have also caused their sons, whom they bare unto me, to pass for them through *the fire*, to devour *them*.

38 Moreover this they have done unto me: they have defiled my sanctuary in the same day, and have profaned my sabbaths.

39 For when they had slain their children to their idols, then they came the same day into my sanctuary to profane it; and, lo, thus have they done in the midst of mine house.

40 And furthermore, that ye have sent for men to come from far, unto whom a messenger *was* sent; and, lo, they came: for whom thou didst wash thyself, paintedst thy eyes, and deckedst thyself with ornaments,

41 And satest upon a stately bed, and a table prepared before it, whereupon thou hast set mine incense and mine oil.

42 And a voice of a multitude being at ease *was* with her: and with the men of the common sort *were* brought Sabeans from the wilderness, which put bracelets upon their hands, and beautiful crowns upon their heads.

43 Then said I unto *her that was* old in adulteries, Will they now commit whoredoms with her, and she *with them*?

44 Yet they went in unto her, as they go in unto a woman that playeth the harlot: so went they in unto Aholah and unto Aholibah, the lewd women.

45 And the righteous men, they shall judge them after the manner of adulteresses, and after the manner of women that shed blood; because they *are* adulteresses, and blood *is* in their hands.

46 For thus saith the Lord GOD; I will bring up a company upon them, and will give them to be removed and spoiled.

47 And the company shall stone them with stones, and dispatch them with their swords; they shall slay their sons and their daughters, and burn up their houses with fire.

48 Thus will I cause lewdness to cease out of the land, that all women may be taught not to do after your lewdness.

49 And they shall recompense your lewdness upon you, and ye shall bear the sins of your idols: and ye shall know that I *am* the Lord GOD.

24 Again in the ninth year, in the tenth month, in the tenth *day* of the month, the word of the LORD came unto me, saying,

2 Son of man, write thee the name of the day, *even* of this same day: the king of Babylon set himself against Jerusalem this same day.

3 And utter a parable unto the rebellious house, and say unto them, Thus saith the Lord GOD; Set on a pot, set *it* on, and also pour water into it:

4 Gather the pieces thereof into it, *even* every good piece, the thigh, and

the shoulder; fill *it* with the choice
bones.
5 Take the choice of the flock, and
burn also the bones under it, *and* make
it boil well, and let them seethe the
bones of it therein.
6 Wherefore thus saith the Lord GOD;
Woe to the bloody city, to the pot whose
scum *is* therein, and whose scum is not
gone out of it! bring it out piece by
piece; let no lot fall upon it.
7 For her blood is in the midst of her;
she set it upon the top of a rock; she
poured it not upon the ground, to cover
it with dust;
8 That it might cause fury to come up
to take vengeance; I have set her blood
upon the top of a rock, that it should
not be covered.
9 Therefore thus saith the Lord GOD;
Woe to the bloody city! I will even
make the pile for fire great.
10 Heap on wood, kindle the fire,
consume the flesh, and spice it well,
and let the bones be burned.
11 Then set it empty upon the coals
thereof, that the brass of it may be hot,
and may burn, and *that* the filthiness
of it may be molten in it, *that* the scum
of it may be consumed.
12 She hath wearied *herself* with lies,
and her great scum went not forth out
of her: her scum *shall be* in the fire.
13 In thy filthiness *is* lewdness:
because I have purged thee, and thou
wast not purged, thou shalt not be
purged from thy filthiness any more,
till I have caused my fury to rest upon
thee.
14 I the LORD have spoken *it*: it shall
come to pass, and I will do *it*; I will not
go back, neither will I spare, neither
will I repent; according to thy ways, and
according to thy doings, shall they
judge thee, saith the Lord GOD.
15 Also the word of the LORD came
unto me, saying,
16 Son of man, behold, I take away
from thee the desire of thine eyes with
a stroke: yet neither shalt thou mourn
nor weep, neither shall thy tears run
down.
17 Forbear to cry, make no mourning
for the dead, bind the tire of thine head
upon thee, and put on thy shoes upon
thy feet, and cover not *thy* lips, and eat
not the bread of men.
18 So I spake unto the people in the
morning: and at even my wife died; and
I did in the morning as I was commanded.
19 And the people said unto me, Wilt
thou not tell us what these *things are* to
us, that thou doest *so*?
20 Then I answered them, The word of
the LORD came unto me, saying,
21 Speak unto the house of Israel,
Thus saith the Lord GOD; Behold, I will
profane my sanctuary, the excellency of
your strength, the desire of your eyes,
and that which your soul pitieth; and
your sons and your daughters whom ye
have left shall fall by the sword.
22 And ye shall do as I have done: ye
shall not cover *your* lips, nor eat the
bread of men.
23 And your tires *shall be* upon your
heads, and your shoes upon your feet:
ye shall not mourn nor weep; but ye
shall pine away for your iniquities, and
mourn one toward another.
24 Thus Ezekiel is unto you a sign:
according to all that he hath done shall
ye do: and when this cometh, ye shall
know that I *am* the Lord GOD.

25 Also, thou son of man, *shall it* not
be in the day when I take from them
their strength, the joy of their glory, the
desire of their eyes, and that whereupon they set their minds, their sons and
their daughters,
26 *That* he that escapeth in that day
shall come unto thee, to cause *thee* to
hear *it* with *thine* ears?
27 In that day shall thy mouth be
opened to him which is escaped, and
thou shalt speak, and be no more
dumb: and thou shalt be a sign unto
them; and they shall know that I *am*
the LORD.

25 The word of the LORD came again
unto me, saying,
2 Son of man, set thy face against the
Ammonites, and prophesy against
them;
3 And say unto the Ammonites, Hear
the word of the Lord GOD; Thus saith
the Lord GOD; Because thou saidst,
Aha, against my sanctuary, when it was
profaned; and against the land of
Israel, when it was desolate; and
against the house of Judah, when they
went into captivity;
4 Behold, therefore I will deliver thee
to the men of the east for a possession,
and they shall set their palaces in thee,
and make their dwellings in thee: they
shall eat thy fruit, and they shall drink
thy milk.
5 And I will make Rabbah a stable for
camels, and the Ammonites a couching-
place for flocks: and ye shall know that
I *am* the LORD.
6 For thus saith the Lord GOD; Because thou hast clapped *thine* hands,
and stamped with the feet, and rejoiced
in heart with all thy despite against the
land of Israel;
7 Behold, therefore I will stretch out
mine hand upon thee, and will deliver
thee for a spoil to the heathen; and I
will cut thee off from the people, and I
will cause thee to perish out of the
countries: I will destroy thee; and thou
shalt know that I *am* the LORD.
8 Thus saith the Lord GOD; Because
that Moab and Seir do say, Behold, the
house of Judah *is* like unto all the heathen;
9 Therefore, behold, I will open the
side of Moab from the cities, from his
cities *which are* on his frontiers, the
glory of the country, Beth-jeshimoth,
Baal-meon, and Kiriathaim,
10 Unto the men of the east with the
Ammonites, and will give them in possession, that the Ammonites may not
be remembered among the nations.
11 And I will execute judgments
upon Moab; and they shall know that I
am the LORD.
12 Thus saith the Lord GOD; Because
that Edom hath dealt against the house
of Judah by taking vengeance, and
hath greatly offended, and revenged
himself upon them;
13 Therefore thus saith the Lord GOD;
I will also stretch out mine hand upon
Edom, and will cut off man and beast
from it; and I will make it desolate from
Teman; and they of Dedan shall fall by
the sword.
14 And I will lay my vengeance upon
Edom by the hand of my people Israel:
and they shall do in Edom according to
mine anger and according to my fury;
and they shall know my vengeance,
saith the Lord GOD.
15 Thus saith the Lord GOD; Because
the Philistines have dealt by revenge,
and have taken vengeance with a

despiteful heart, to destroy *it* for the old hatred;

16 Therefore thus saith the Lord GOD; Behold, I will stretch out mine hand upon the Philistines, and I will cut off the Cherethims, and destroy the remnant of the sea coast.

17 And I will execute great vengeance upon them with furious rebukes; and they shall know that I *am* the LORD, when I shall lay my vengeance upon them.

26 And it came to pass in the eleventh year, in the first *day* of the month, *that* the word of the LORD came unto me, saying,

2 Son of man, because that Tyrus hath said against Jerusalem, Aha, she is broken *that was* the gates of the people: she is turned unto me: I shall be replenished, *now* she is laid waste:

3 Therefore thus saith the Lord GOD; Behold, I *am* against thee, O Tyrus, and will cause many nations to come up against thee, as the sea causeth his waves to come up.

4 And they shall destroy the walls of Tyrus, and break down her towers: I will also scrape her dust from her, and make her like the top of a rock.

5 It shall be *a place for* the spreading of nets in the midst of the sea: for I have spoken *it*, saith the Lord GOD: and it shall become a spoil to the nations.

6 And her daughters which *are* in the field shall be slain by the sword; and they shall know that I *am* the LORD.

7 For thus saith the Lord GOD; Behold, I will bring upon Tyrus Nebuchadrezzar king of Babylon, a king of kings, from the north, with horses, and with chariots, and with horsemen, and companies, and much people.

8 He shall slay with the sword thy daughters in the field: and he shall make a fort against thee, and cast a mount against thee, and lift up the buckler against thee.

9 And he shall set engines of war against thy walls, and with his axes he shall break down thy towers.

10 By reason of the abundance of his horses their dust shall cover thee: thy walls shall shake at the noise of the horsemen, and of the wheels, and of the chariots, when he shall enter into thy gates, as men enter into a city wherein is made a breach.

11 With the hoofs of his horses shall he tread down all thy streets: he shall slay thy people by the sword, and thy strong garrisons shall go down to the ground.

12 And they shall make a spoil of thy riches, and make a prey of thy merchandise: and they shall break down thy walls, and destroy thy pleasant houses: and they shall lay thy stones and thy timber and thy dust in the midst of the water.

13 And I will cause the noise of thy songs to cease; and the sound of thy harps shall be no more heard.

14 And I will make thee like the top of a rock: thou shalt be *a place* to spread nets upon; thou shalt be built no more: for I the LORD have spoken *it*, saith the Lord GOD.

15 Thus saith the Lord GOD to Tyrus; Shall not the isles shake at the sound of thy fall, when the wounded cry, when the slaughter is made in the midst of thee?

16 Then all the princes of the sea shall come down from their thrones, and lay away their robes, and put off their broidered garments: they shall

clothe themselves with trembling; they
shall sit upon the ground, and shall
tremble at *every* moment, and be astonished at thee.
17 And they shall take up a lamentation for thee, and say to thee, How art
thou destroyed, *that wast* inhabited of
seafaring men, the renowned city,
which wast strong in the sea, she and
her inhabitants, which cause their terror *to be* on all that haunt it!
18 Now shall the isles tremble in the
day of thy fall; yea, the isles that *are* in
the sea shall be troubled at thy departure.
19 For thus saith the Lord GOD; When
I shall make thee a desolate city, like
the cities that are not inhabited; when
I shall bring up the deep upon thee,
and great waters shall cover thee;
20 When I shall bring thee down with
them that descend into the pit, with the
people of old time, and shall set thee in
the low parts of the earth, in places
desolate of old, with them that go down
to the pit, that thou be not inhabited;
and I shall set glory in the land of the
living;
21 I will make thee a terror, and thou
shalt be no *more*: though thou be
sought for, yet shalt thou never be
found again, saith the Lord GOD.

27 The word of the LORD came again
unto me, saying,
2 Now, thou son of man, take up a
lamentation for Tyrus;
3 And say unto Tyrus, O thou that art
situate at the entry of the sea, *which
art* a merchant of the people for many
isles, Thus saith the Lord GOD; O Tyrus,
thou hast said, I *am* of perfect beauty.
4 Thy borders *are* in the midst of the
seas, thy builders have perfected thy
beauty.
5 They have made all thy *ship* boards
of fir trees of Senir: they have taken
cedars from Lebanon to make masts for
thee.
6 *Of* the oaks of Bashan have they
made thine oars; the company of the
Ashurites have made thy benches *of*
ivory, *brought* out of the isles of
Chittim.
7 Fine linen with broidered work
from Egypt was that which thou spread-
est forth to be thy sail; blue and purple
from the isles of Elishah was that which
covered thee.
8 The inhabitants of Zidon and Arvad
were thy mariners: thy wise *men*, O
Tyrus, *that* were in thee, were thy
pilots.
9 The ancients of Gebal and the wise
men thereof were in thee thy calkers:
all the ships of the sea with their mariners were in thee to occupy thy merchandise.
10 They of Persia and of Lud and of
Phut were in thine army, thy men of
war: they hanged the shield and helmet
in thee; they set forth thy comeliness.
11 The men of Arvad with thine army
were upon thy walls round about, and
the Gammadims were in thy towers:
they hanged their shields upon thy
walls round about; they have made thy
beauty perfect.
12 Tarshish *was* thy merchant by reason of the multitude of all *kind of*
riches; with silver, iron, tin, and lead,
they traded in thy fairs.
13 Javan, Tubal, and Meshech, they
were thy merchants: they traded the
persons of men and vessels of brass in
thy market.
14 They of the house of Togarmah
traded in thy fairs with horses and
horsemen and mules.

15 The men of Dedan *were* thy merchants; many isles *were* the merchandise of thine hand: they brought thee *for* a present horns of ivory and ebony.
16 Syria *was* thy merchant by reason of the multitude of the wares of thy making: they occupied in thy fairs with emeralds, purple, and broidered work, and fine linen, and coral, and agate.
17 Judah, and the land of Israel, they *were* thy merchants: they traded in thy market wheat of Minnith, and Pannag, and honey, and oil, and balm.
18 Damascus *was* thy merchant in the multitude of the wares of thy making, for the multitude of all riches; in the wine of Helbon, and white wool.
19 Dan also and Javan going to and fro occupied in thy fairs: bright iron, cassia, and calamus, were in thy market.
20 Dedan *was* thy merchant in precious clothes for chariots.
21 Arabia, and all the princes of Kedar, they occupied with thee in lambs, and rams, and goats: in these *were they* thy merchants.
22 The merchants of Sheba and Raamah, they *were* thy merchants: they occupied in thy fairs with chief of all spices, and with all precious stones, and gold.
23 Haran, and Canneh, and Eden, the merchants of Sheba, Asshur, *and* Chilmad, *were* thy merchants.
24 These *were* thy merchants in all sorts *of things*, in blue clothes, and broidered work, and in chests of rich apparel, bound with cords, and made of cedar, among thy merchandise.
25 The ships of Tarshish did sing of thee in thy market: and thou wast replenished, and made very glorious in the midst of the seas.
26 Thy rowers have brought thee into great waters: the east wind hath broken thee in the midst of the seas.
27 Thy riches, and thy fairs, thy merchandise, thy mariners, and thy pilots, thy calkers, and the occupiers of thy merchandise, and all thy men of war, that *are* in thee, and in all thy company which *is* in the midst of thee, shall fall into the midst of the seas in the day of thy ruin.
28 The suburbs shall shake at the sound of the cry of thy pilots.
29 And all that handle the oar, the mariners, *and* all the pilots of the sea, shall come down from their ships, they shall stand upon the land;
30 And shall cause their voice to be heard against thee, and shall cry bitterly, and shall cast up dust upon their heads, they shall wallow themselves in the ashes:
31 And they shall make themselves utterly bald for thee, and gird them with sackcloth, and they shall weep for thee with bitterness of heart *and* bitter wailing.
32 And in their wailing they shall take up a lamentation for thee, and lament over thee, *saying*, What *city is* like Tyrus, like the destroyed in the midst of the sea?
33 When thy wares went forth out of the seas, thou filledst many people; thou didst enrich the kings of the earth with the multitude of thy riches and of thy merchandise.
34 In the time *when* thou shalt be broken by the seas in the depths of the waters thy merchandise and all thy company in the midst of thee shall fall.
35 All the inhabitants of the isles shall be astonished at thee, and their

kings shall be sore afraid, they shall be troubled in *their* countenance.

36 The merchants among the people shall hiss at thee; thou shalt be a terror, and never *shalt be* any more.

28 The word of the LORD came again unto me, saying,

2 Son of man, say unto the prince of Tyrus, Thus saith the Lord GOD; Because thine heart *is* lifted up, and thou hast said, I *am* a God, I sit *in* the seat of God, in the midst of the seas; yet thou *art* a man, and not God, though thou set thine heart as the heart of God:

3 Behold, thou *art* wiser than Daniel; there is no secret that they can hide from thee:

4 With thy wisdom and with thine understanding thou hast gotten thee riches, and hast gotten gold and silver into thy treasures:

5 By thy great wisdom *and* by thy traffick hast thou increased thy riches, and thine heart is lifted up because of thy riches:

6 Therefore thus saith the Lord GOD; Because thou hast set thine heart as the heart of God;

7 Behold, therefore I will bring strangers upon thee, the terrible of the nations: and they shall draw their swords against the beauty of thy wisdom, and they shall defile thy brightness.

8 They shall bring thee down to the pit, and thou shalt die the deaths of *them that are* slain in the midst of the seas.

9 Wilt thou yet say before him that slayeth thee, I *am* God? but thou *shalt be* a man, and no God, in the hand of him that slayeth thee.

10 Thou shalt die the deaths of the uncircumcised by the hand of strangers: for I have spoken *it*, saith the Lord GOD.

11 Moreover the word of the LORD came unto me, saying,

12 Son of man, take up a lamentation upon the king of Tyrus, and say unto him, Thus saith the Lord GOD; Thou sealest up the sum, full of wisdom, and perfect in beauty.

13 Thou hast been in Eden the garden of God; every precious stone *was* thy covering, the sardius, topaz, and the diamond, the beryl, the onyx, and the jasper, the sapphire, the emerald, and the carbuncle, and gold: the workmanship of thy tabrets and of thy pipes was prepared in thee in the day that thou wast created.

14 Thou *art* the anointed cherub that covereth; and I have set thee *so*: thou wast upon the holy mountain of God; thou hast walked up and down in the midst of the stones of fire.

15 Thou *wast* perfect in thy ways from the day that thou wast created, till iniquity was found in thee.

16 By the multitude of thy merchandise they have filled the midst of thee with violence, and thou hast sinned: therefore I will cast thee as profane out of the mountain of God: and I will destroy thee, O covering cherub, from the midst of the stones of fire.

17 Thine heart was lifted up because of thy beauty, thou hast corrupted thy wisdom by reason of thy brightness: I will cast thee to the ground, I will lay thee before kings, that they may behold thee.

18 Thou hast defiled thy sanctuaries by the multitude of thine iniquities, by the iniquity of thy traffick; therefore will I bring forth a fire from the midst of thee, it shall devour thee, and I will bring thee to ashes upon the earth in the sight of all them that behold thee.

19 All they that know thee among the people shall be astonished at thee: thou shalt be a terror, and never *shalt* thou *be* any more.

20 Again the word of the LORD came unto me, saying,

21 Son of man, set thy face against Zidon, and prophesy against it,

22 And say, Thus saith the Lord GOD; Behold, I *am* against thee, O Zidon; and I will be glorified in the midst of thee: and they shall know that I *am* the LORD, when I shall have executed judgments in her, and shall be sanctified in her.

23 For I will send into her pestilence, and blood into her streets; and the wounded shall be judged in the midst of her by the sword upon her on every side; and they shall know that I *am* the LORD.

24 And there shall be no more a pricking brier unto the house of Israel, nor *any* grieving thorn of all *that are* round about them, that despised them; and they shall know that I *am* the Lord GOD.

25 Thus saith the Lord GOD; When I shall have gathered the house of Israel from the people among whom they are scattered, and shall be sanctified in them in the sight of the heathen, then shall they dwell in their land that I have given to my servant Jacob.

26 And they shall dwell safely therein, and shall build houses, and plant vineyards; yea, they shall dwell with confidence, when I have executed judgments upon all those that despise them round about them; and they shall know that I *am* the LORD their God.

29 In the tenth year, in the tenth *month*, in the twelfth *day* of the month, the word of the LORD came unto me, saying,

2 Son of man, set thy face against Pharaoh king of Egypt, and prophesy against him, and against all Egypt:

3 Speak, and say, Thus saith the Lord GOD; Behold, I *am* against thee, Pharaoh king of Egypt, the great dragon that lieth in the midst of his rivers, which hath said, My river *is* mine own, and I have made *it* for myself.

4 But I will put hooks in thy jaws, and I will cause the fish of thy rivers to stick unto thy scales, and I will bring thee up out of the midst of thy rivers, and all the fish of thy rivers shall stick unto thy scales.

5 And I will leave thee *thrown* into the wilderness, thee and all the fish of thy rivers: thou shalt fall upon the open fields; thou shalt not be brought together, nor gathered: I have given thee for meat to the beasts of the field and to the fowls of the heaven.

6 And all the inhabitants of Egypt shall know that I *am* the LORD, because they have been a staff of reed to the house of Israel.

7 When they took hold of thee by thy hand, thou didst break, and rend all their shoulder: and when they leaned upon thee, thou brakest, and madest all their loins to be at a stand.

8 Therefore thus saith the Lord GOD; Behold, I will bring a sword upon thee, and cut off man and beast out of thee.

9 And the land of Egypt shall be desolate and waste; and they shall know that I *am* the LORD: because he hath said, The river *is* mine, and I have made *it*.

10 Behold, therefore I *am* against thee, and against thy rivers, and I will make the land of Egypt utterly waste *and* desolate, from the tower of Syene even unto the border of Ethiopia.

11 No foot of man shall pass through it, nor foot of beast shall pass through it, neither shall it be inhabited forty years.

12 And I will make the land of Egypt desolate in the midst of the countries *that are* desolate, and her cities among the cities *that are* laid waste shall be desolate forty years: and I will scatter the Egyptians among the nations, and will disperse them through the countries.

13 Yet thus saith the Lord GOD; At the end of forty years will I gather the Egyptians from the people whither they were scattered:

14 And I will bring again the captivity of Egypt, and will cause them to return *into* the land of Pathros, into the land of their habitation; and they shall be there a base kingdom.

15 It shall be the basest of the kingdoms; neither shall it exalt itself any more above the nations: for I will diminish them, that they shall no more rule over the nations.

16 And it shall be no more the confidence of the house of Israel, which bringeth *their* iniquity to remembrance, when they shall look after them: but they shall know that I *am* the Lord GOD.

17 And it came to pass in the seven and twentieth year, in the first *month*, in the first *day* of the month, the word of the LORD came unto me, saying,

18 Son of man, Nebuchadrezzar king of Babylon caused his army to serve a great service against Tyrus: every head *was* made bald, and every shoulder *was* peeled: yet had he no wages, nor his army, for Tyrus, for the service that he had served against it:

19 Therefore thus saith the Lord GOD; Behold, I will give the land of Egypt unto Nebuchadrezzar king of Babylon; and he shall take her multitude, and take her spoil, and take her prey; and it shall be the wages for his army.

20 I have given him the land of Egypt *for* his labour wherewith he served against it, because they wrought for me, saith the Lord GOD.

21 In that day will I cause the horn of the house of Israel to bud forth, and I will give thee the opening of the mouth in the midst of them; and they shall know that I *am* the LORD.

30 The word of the LORD came again unto me, saying,

2 Son of man, prophesy and say, Thus saith the Lord GOD; Howl ye, Woe worth the day!

3 For the day *is* near, even the day of the LORD *is* near, a cloudy day; it shall be the time of the heathen.

4 And the sword shall come upon Egypt, and great pain shall be in Ethiopia, when the slain shall fall in Egypt, and they shall take away her multitude, and her foundations shall be broken down.

5 Ethiopia, and Libya, and Lydia, and all the mingled people, and Chub, and the men of the land that is in league, shall fall with them by the sword.

6 Thus saith the LORD; They also that uphold Egypt shall fall; and the pride of her power shall come down: from the tower of Syene shall they fall in it by the sword, saith the Lord GOD.

7 And they shall be desolate in the midst of the countries *that are* deso-

late, and her cities shall be in the midst
of the cities *that are* wasted.
8 And they shall know that I *am* the
LORD, when I have set a fire in Egypt,
and *when* all her helpers shall be
destroyed.
9 In that day shall messengers go
forth from me in ships to make the
careless Ethiopians afraid, and great
pain shall come upon them, as in the
day of Egypt: for, lo, it cometh.
10 Thus saith the Lord GOD; I will also
make the multitude of Egypt to cease
by the hand of Nebuchadrezzar king of
Babylon.
11 He and his people with him, the
terrible of the nations, shall be brought
to destroy the land: and they shall draw
their swords against Egypt, and fill the
land with the slain.
12 And I will make the rivers dry, and
sell the land into the hand of the wicked: and I will make the land waste, and
all that is therein, by the hand of
strangers: I the LORD have spoken *it*.
13 Thus saith the Lord GOD; I will also
destroy the idols, and I will cause *their*
images to cease out of Noph; and there
shall be no more a prince of the land of
Egypt: and I will put a fear in the land
of Egypt.
14 And I will make Pathros desolate,
and will set fire in Zoan, and will execute judgments in No.
15 And I will pour my fury upon Sin,
the strength of Egypt; and I will cut off
the multitude of No.
16 And I will set fire in Egypt: Sin
shall have great pain, and No shall be
rent asunder, and Noph *shall have* distresses daily.
17 The young men of Aven and of
Pi-beseth shall fall by the sword: and
these *cities* shall go into captivity.
18 At Tehaphnehes also the day shall
be darkened, when I shall break there
the yokes of Egypt: and the pomp of
her strength shall cease in her: as for
her, a cloud shall cover her, and her
daughters shall go into captivity.
19 Thus will I execute judgments in
Egypt: and they shall know that I *am*
the LORD.
20 And it came to pass in the eleventh
year, in the first *month*, in the seventh
day of the month, *that* the word of the
LORD came unto me, saying,
21 Son of man, I have broken the arm
of Pharaoh king of Egypt; and, lo, it
shall not be bound up to be healed, to
put a roller to bind it, to make it strong
to hold the sword.
22 Therefore thus saith the Lord GOD;
Behold, I *am* against Pharaoh king of
Egypt, and will break his arms, the
strong, and that which was broken; and
I will cause the sword to fall out of his
hand.
23 And I will scatter the Egyptians
among the nations, and will disperse
them through the countries.
24 And I will strengthen the arms of
the king of Babylon, and put my sword
in his hand: but I will break Pharaoh's
arms, and he shall groan before him
with the groanings of a deadly wounded *man*.
25 But I will strengthen the arms of
the king of Babylon, and the arms of
Pharaoh shall fall down; and they shall
know that I *am* the LORD, when I shall
put my sword into the hand of the king
of Babylon, and he shall stretch it out
upon the land of Egypt.
26 And I will scatter the Egyptians
among the nations, and disperse them
among the countries; and they shall
know that I *am* the LORD.

31 And it came to pass in the eleventh year, in the third *month*, in
the first *day* of the month, *that* the
word of the LORD came unto me, saying,
2 Son of man, speak unto Pharaoh
king of Egypt, and to his multitude;
Whom art thou like in thy greatness?
3 Behold, the Assyrian *was* a cedar in
Lebanon with fair branches, and with a
shadowing shroud, and of an high stature; and his top was among the thick
boughs.
4 The waters made him great, the
deep set him up on high with her rivers
running round about his plants, and
sent out her little rivers unto all the
trees of the field.
5 Therefore his height was exalted
above all the trees of the field, and his
boughs were multiplied, and his
branches became long because of the
multitude of waters, when he shot
forth.
6 All the fowls of heaven made their
nests in his boughs, and under his branches did all the beasts of the field bring
forth their young, and under his shadow dwelt all great nations.
7 Thus was he fair in his greatness, in
the length of his branches: for his root
was by great waters.
8 The cedars in the garden of God
could not hide him: the fir trees were
not like his boughs, and the chesnut
trees were not like his branches; nor
any tree in the garden of God was like
unto him in his beauty.
9 I have made him fair by the multitude of his branches: so that all the
trees of Eden, that *were* in the garden
of God, envied him.
10 Therefore thus saith the Lord GOD;
Because thou hast lifted up thyself in
height, and he hath shot up his top
among the thick boughs, and his heart
is lifted up in his height;
11 I have therefore delivered him into
the hand of the mighty one of the heathen; he shall surely deal with him: I
have driven him out for his wickedness.
12 And strangers, the terrible of the
nations, have cut him off, and have left
him: upon the mountains and in all the
valleys his branches are fallen, and his
boughs are broken by all the rivers of
the land; and all the people of the earth
are gone down from his shadow, and
have left him.
13 Upon his ruin shall all the fowls of
the heaven remain, and all the beasts
of the field shall be upon his branches:
14 To the end that none of all the
trees by the waters exalt themselves for
their height, neither shoot up their top
among the thick boughs, neither their
trees stand up in their height, all that
drink water: for they are all delivered
unto death, to the nether parts of the
earth, in the midst of the children of
men, with them that go down to the pit.
15 Thus saith the Lord GOD; In the
day when he went down to the grave I
caused a mourning: I covered the deep
for him, and I restrained the floods
thereof, and the great waters were
stayed: and I caused Lebanon to mourn
for him, and all the trees of the field
fainted for him.
16 I made the nations to shake at the
sound of his fall, when I cast him down
to hell with them that descend into the
pit: and all the trees of Eden, the choice
and best of Lebanon, all that drink
water, shall be comforted in the nether
parts of the earth.
17 They also went down into hell with
him unto *them that be* slain with the
sword; and *they that were* his arm, *that*

dwelt under his shadow in the midst of
the heathen.
18 To whom art thou thus like in glory
and in greatness among the trees of
Eden? yet shalt thou be brought down
with the trees of Eden unto the nether
parts of the earth: thou shalt lie in the
midst of the uncircumcised with *them*
that be slain by the sword. This *is*
Pharaoh and all his multitude, saith the
Lord GOD.

32 And it came to pass in the twelfth
year, in the twelfth month, in the
first *day* of the month, *that* the word of
the LORD came unto me, saying,
2 Son of man, take up a lamentation
for Pharaoh king of Egypt, and say unto
him, Thou art like a young lion of the
nations, and thou *art* as a whale in the
seas: and thou camest forth with thy
rivers, and troubledst the waters with
thy feet, and fouledst their rivers.
3 Thus saith the Lord GOD; I will
therefore spread out my net over thee
with a company of many people; and
they shall bring thee up in my net.
4 Then will I leave thee upon the
land, I will cast thee forth upon the
open field, and will cause all the fowls
of the heaven to remain upon thee, and
I will fill the beasts of the whole earth
with thee.
5 And I will lay thy flesh upon the
mountains, and fill the valleys with thy
height.
6 I will also water with thy blood the
land wherein thou swimmest, *even* to
the mountains; and the rivers shall be
full of thee.
7 And when I shall put thee out, I will
cover the heaven, and make the stars
thereof dark; I will cover the sun with a
cloud, and the moon shall not give her
light.
8 All the bright lights of heaven will I
make dark over thee, and set darkness
upon thy land, saith the Lord GOD.
9 I will also vex the hearts of many
people, when I shall bring thy destruction among the nations, into the countries which thou hast not known.
10 Yea, I will make many people
amazed at thee, and their kings shall
be horribly afraid for thee, when I shall
brandish my sword before them; and
they shall tremble at *every* moment,
every man for his own life, in the day of
thy fall.
11 For thus saith the Lord GOD; The
sword of the king of Babylon shall come
upon thee.
12 By the swords of the mighty will I
cause thy multitude to fall, the terrible
of the nations, all of them: and they
shall spoil the pomp of Egypt, and all
the multitude thereof shall be destroyed.
13 I will destroy also all the beasts
thereof from beside the great waters;
neither shall the foot of man trouble
them any more, nor the hoofs of beasts
trouble them.
14 Then will I make their waters
deep, and cause their rivers to run like
oil, saith the Lord GOD.
15 When I shall make the land of
Egypt desolate, and the country shall
be destitute of that whereof it was full,
when I shall smite all them that dwell
therein, then shall they know that I *am*
the LORD.
16 This *is* the lamentation wherewith
they shall lament her: the daughters of
the nations shall lament her: they shall
lament for her, *even* for Egypt, and for
all her multitude, saith the Lord GOD.

17 It came to pass also in the twelfth
year, in the fifteenth *day* of the month,
that the word of the LORD came unto
me, saying,
18 Son of man, wail for the multitude
of Egypt, and cast them down, *even* her,
and the daughters of the famous
nations, unto the nether parts of the
earth, with them that go down into the
pit.
19 Whom dost thou pass in beauty?
go down, and be thou laid with the
uncircumcised.
20 They shall fall in the midst of *them
that are* slain by the sword: she is delivered to the sword: draw her and all her
multitudes.
21 The strong among the mighty shall
speak to him out of the midst of hell
with them that help him: they are gone
down, they lie uncircumcised, slain by
the sword.
22 Asshur *is* there and all her company: his graves *are* about him: all of them
slain, fallen by the sword:
23 Whose graves are set in the sides
of the pit, and her company is round
about her grave: all of them slain, fallen
by the sword, which caused terror in
the land of the living.
24 There *is* Elam and all her multitude round about her grave, all of them
slain, fallen by the sword, which are
gone down uncircumcised into the
nether parts of the earth, which caused
their terror in the land of the living; yet
have they borne their shame with them
that go down to the pit.
25 They have set her a bed in the
midst of the slain with all her multitude: her graves *are* round about him:
all of them uncircumcised, slain by the
sword: though their terror was caused
in the land of the living, yet have they
borne their shame with them that go
down to the pit: he is put in the midst
of *them that be* slain.
26 There *is* Meshech, Tubal, and all
her multitude: her graves *are* round
about him: all of them uncircumcised,
slain by the sword, though they caused
their terror in the land of the living.
27 And they shall not lie with the
mighty *that are* fallen of the uncircumcised, which are gone down to hell with
their weapons of war: and they have
laid their swords under their heads, but
their iniquities shall be upon their
bones, though *they were* the terror of
the mighty in the land of the living.
28 Yea, thou shalt be broken in the
midst of the uncircumcised, and shalt
lie with *them that are* slain with the
sword.
29 There *is* Edom, her kings, and all
her princes, which with their might are
laid by *them that were* slain by the
sword: they shall lie with the uncircumcised, and with them that go down to
the pit.
30 There *be* the princes of the north,
all of them, and all the Zidonians,
which are gone down with the slain;
with their terror they are ashamed of
their might; and they lie uncircumcised
with *them that be* slain by the sword,
and bear their shame with them that go
down to the pit.
31 Pharaoh shall see them, and shall
be comforted over all his multitude,
even Pharaoh and all his army slain by
the sword, saith the Lord GOD.
32 For I have caused my terror in the
land of the living: and he shall be laid
in the midst of the uncircumcised with
them that are slain with the sword,
even Pharaoh and all his multitude,
saith the Lord GOD.

33 Again the word of the LORD came
unto me, saying,
2 Son of man, speak to the children of
thy people, and say unto them, When I
bring the sword upon a land, if the
people of the land take a man of their
coasts, and set him for their watchman:
3 If when he seeth the sword come
upon the land, he blow the trumpet,
and warn the people;
4 Then whosoever heareth the sound
of the trumpet, and taketh not warning;
if the sword come, and take him away,
his blood shall be upon his own head.
5 He heard the sound of the trumpet,
and took not warning; his blood shall
be upon him. But he that taketh warning shall deliver his soul.
6 But if the watchman see the sword
come, and blow not the trumpet, and
the people be not warned; if the sword
come, and take *any* person from among
them, he is taken away in his iniquity;
but his blood will I require at the
watchman's hand.
7 So thou, O son of man, I have set
thee a watchman unto the house of
Israel; therefore thou shalt hear the
word at my mouth, and warn them from
me.
8 When I say unto the wicked, O
wicked *man*, thou shalt surely die; if
thou dost not speak to warn the wicked
from his way, that wicked *man* shall die
in his iniquity; but his blood will I
require at thine hand.
9 Nevertheless, if thou warn the wicked of his way to turn from it; if he do
not turn from his way, he shall die in his
iniquity; but thou hast delivered thy
soul.
10 Therefore, O thou son of man,
speak unto the house of Israel; Thus ye
speak, saying, If our transgressions and
our sins *be* upon us, and we pine away
in them, how should we then live?
11 Say unto them, *As* I live, saith the
Lord GOD, I have no pleasure in the
death of the wicked; but that the wicked turn from his way and live: turn ye,
turn ye from your evil ways; for why
will ye die, O house of Israel?
12 Therefore, thou son of man, say
unto the children of thy people, The
righteousness of the righteous shall not
deliver him in the day of his transgression: as for the wickedness of the wicked, he shall not fall thereby in the day
that he turneth from his wickedness;
neither shall the righteous be able to
live for his *righteousness* in the day
that he sinneth.
13 When I shall say to the righteous,
that he shall surely live; if he trust to
his own righteousness, and commit
iniquity, all his righteousnesses shall
not be remembered; but for his iniquity
that he hath committed, he shall die for
it.
14 Again, when I say unto the wicked,
Thou shalt surely die; if he turn from
his sin, and do that which is lawful and
right;
15 *If* the wicked restore the pledge,
give again that he had robbed, walk in
the statutes of life, without committing
iniquity; he shall surely live, he shall
not die.
16 None of his sins that he hath committed shall be mentioned unto him: he
hath done that which is lawful and
right; he shall surely live.
17 Yet the children of thy people say,
The way of the Lord is not equal: but as
for them, their way is not equal.
18 When the righteous turneth from
his righteousness, and committeth iniquity, he shall even die thereby.

19 But if the wicked turn from his wickedness, and do that which is lawful and right, he shall live thereby.

20 Yet ye say, The way of the Lord is not equal. O ye house of Israel, I will judge you every one after his ways.

21 And it came to pass in the twelfth year of our captivity, in the tenth *month*, in the fifth *day* of the month, *that* one that had escaped out of Jerusalem came unto me, saying, The city is smitten.

22 Now the hand of the LORD was upon me in the evening, afore he that was escaped came; and had opened my mouth, until he came to me in the morning; and my mouth was opened, and I was no more dumb.

23 Then the word of the LORD came unto me, saying,

24 Son of man, they that inhabit those wastes of the land of Israel speak, saying, Abraham was one, and he inherited the land: but we *are* many; the land is given us for inheritance.

25 Wherefore say unto them, Thus saith the Lord GOD; Ye eat with the blood, and lift up your eyes toward your idols, and shed blood: and shall ye possess the land?

26 Ye stand upon your sword, ye work abomination, and ye defile every one his neighbour's wife: and shall ye possess the land?

27 Say thou thus unto them, Thus saith the Lord GOD; *As* I live, surely they that *are* in the wastes shall fall by the sword, and him that *is* in the open field will I give to the beasts to be devoured, and they that *be* in the forts and in the caves shall die of the pestilence.

28 For I will lay the land most desolate, and the pomp of her strength shall cease; and the mountains of Israel shall be desolate, that none shall pass through.

29 Then shall they know that I *am* the LORD, when I have laid the land most desolate because of all their abominations which they have committed.

30 Also, thou son of man, the children of thy people still are talking against thee by the walls and in the doors of the houses, and speak one to another, every one to his brother, saying, Come, I pray you, and hear what is the word that cometh forth from the LORD.

31 And they come unto thee as the people cometh, and they sit before thee *as* my people, and they hear thy words, but they will not do them: for with their mouth they shew much love, *but* their heart goeth after their covetousness.

32 And, lo, thou *art* unto them as a very lovely song of one that hath a pleasant voice, and can play well on an instrument: for they hear thy words, but they do them not.

33 And when this cometh to pass, (lo, it will come,) then shall they know that a prophet hath been among them.

34

And the word of the LORD came unto me, saying,

2 Son of man, prophesy against the shepherds of Israel, prophesy, and say unto them, Thus saith the Lord GOD unto the shepherds; Woe *be* to the shepherds of Israel that do feed themselves! should not the shepherds feed the flocks?

3 Ye eat the fat, and ye clothe you with the wool, ye kill them that are fed: *but* ye feed not the flock.

4 The diseased have ye not strengthened, neither have ye healed that which was sick, neither have ye bound up *that which was* broken, neither have ye brought again that which was

driven away, neither have ye sought
that which was lost; but with force and
with cruelty have ye ruled them.
5 And they were scattered, because
there is no shepherd: and they became
meat to all the beasts of the field, when
they were scattered.
6 My sheep wandered through all the
mountains, and upon every high hill:
yea, my flock was scattered upon all the
face of the earth, and none did search
or seek *after them*.
7 Therefore, ye shepherds, hear the
word of the LORD;
8 *As* I live, saith the Lord GOD, surely
because my flock became a prey, and
my flock became meat to every beast of
the field, because *there was* no shepherd, neither did my shepherds search
for my flock, but the shepherds fed
themselves, and fed not my flock;
9 Therefore, O ye shepherds, hear the
word of the LORD;
10 Thus saith the Lord GOD; Behold, I
am against the shepherds; and I will
require my flock at their hand, and
cause them to cease from feeding the
flock; neither shall the shepherds feed
themselves any more; for I will deliver
my flock from their mouth, that they
may not be meat for them.
11 For thus saith the Lord GOD;
Behold, I, *even* I, will both search my
sheep, and seek them out.
12 As a shepherd seeketh out his
flock in the day that he is among his
sheep *that are* scattered; so will I seek
out my sheep, and will deliver them out
of all places where they have been scattered in the cloudy and dark day.
13 And I will bring them out from the
people, and gather them from the countries, and will bring them to their own
land, and feed them upon the mountains of Israel by the rivers, and in all
the inhabited places of the country.
14 I will feed them in a good pasture,
and upon the high mountains of Israel
shall their fold be: there shall they lie
in a good fold, and *in* a fat pasture shall
they feed upon the mountains of Israel.
15 I will feed my flock, and I will
cause them to lie down, saith the Lord
GOD.
16 I will seek that which was lost, and
bring again that which was driven away,
and will bind up *that which was* broken, and will strengthen that which was
sick: but I will destroy the fat and the
strong; I will feed them with judgment.
17 And *as for* you, O my flock, thus
saith the Lord GOD; Behold, I judge
between cattle and cattle, between the
rams and the he goats.
18 *Seemeth it* a small thing unto you
to have eaten up the good pasture, but
ye must tread down with your feet the
residue of your pastures? and to have
drunk of the deep waters, but ye must
foul the residue with your feet?
19 And *as for* my flock, they eat that
which ye have trodden with your feet;
and they drink that which ye have
fouled with your feet.
20 Therefore thus saith the Lord GOD
unto them; Behold, I, *even* I, will judge
between the fat cattle and between the
lean cattle.
21 Because ye have thrust with side
and with shoulder, and pushed all the
diseased with your horns, till ye have
scattered them abroad;
22 Therefore will I save my flock, and
they shall no more be a prey; and I will
judge between cattle and cattle.
23 And I will set up one shepherd
over them, and he shall feed them, *even*

my servant David; he shall feed them, and he shall be their shepherd.

24 And I the LORD will be their God, and my servant David a prince among them; I the LORD have spoken *it*.

25 And I will make with them a covenant of peace, and will cause the evil beasts to cease out of the land: and they shall dwell safely in the wilderness, and sleep in the woods.

26 And I will make them and the places round about my hill a blessing; and I will cause the shower to come down in his season; there shall be showers of blessing.

27 And the tree of the field shall yield her fruit, and the earth shall yield her increase, and they shall be safe in their land, and shall know that I *am* the LORD, when I have broken the bands of their yoke, and delivered them out of the hand of those that served themselves of them.

28 And they shall no more be a prey to the heathen, neither shall the beast of the land devour them; but they shall dwell safely, and none shall make *them* afraid.

29 And I will raise up for them a plant of renown, and they shall be no more consumed with hunger in the land, neither bear the shame of the heathen any more.

30 Thus shall they know that I the LORD their God *am* with them, and *that* they, *even* the house of Israel, *are* my people, saith the Lord GOD.

31 And ye my flock, the flock of my pasture, *are* men, *and* I *am* your God, saith the Lord GOD.

35 Moreover the word of the LORD came unto me, saying,

2 Son of man, set thy face against mount Seir, and prophesy against it,

3 And say unto it, Thus saith the Lord GOD; Behold, O mount Seir, I *am* against thee, and I will stretch out mine hand against thee, and I will make thee most desolate.

4 I will lay thy cities waste, and thou shalt be desolate, and thou shalt know that I *am* the LORD.

5 Because thou hast had a perpetual hatred, and hast shed *the blood of* the children of Israel by the force of the sword in the time of their calamity, in the time *that their* iniquity *had* an end:

6 Therefore, *as* I live, saith the Lord GOD, I will prepare thee unto blood, and blood shall pursue thee: sith thou hast not hated blood, even blood shall pursue thee.

7 Thus will I make mount Seir most desolate, and cut off from it him that passeth out and him that returneth.

8 And I will fill his mountains with his slain *men*: in thy hills, and in thy valleys, and in all thy rivers, shall they fall that are slain with the sword.

9 I will make thee perpetual desolations, and thy cities shall not return: and ye shall know that I *am* the LORD.

10 Because thou hast said, These two nations and these two countries shall be mine, and we will possess it; whereas the LORD was there:

11 Therefore, *as* I live, saith the Lord GOD, I will even do according to thine anger, and according to thine envy which thou hast used out of thy hatred against them; and I will make myself known among them, when I have judged thee.

12 And thou shalt know that I *am* the LORD, *and that* I have heard all thy blasphemies which thou hast spoken against the mountains of Israel, saying,

They are laid desolate, they are given us to consume.

13 Thus with your mouth ye have boasted against me, and have multiplied your words against me: I have heard *them*.

14 Thus saith the Lord GOD; When the whole earth rejoiceth, I will make thee desolate.

15 As thou didst rejoice at the inheritance of the house of Israel, because it was desolate, so will I do unto thee: thou shalt be desolate, O mount Seir, and all Idumea, *even* all of it: and they shall know that I *am* the LORD.

36 Also, thou son of man, prophesy unto the mountains of Israel, and say, Ye mountains of Israel, hear the word of the LORD:

2 Thus saith the Lord GOD; Because the enemy hath said against you, Aha, even the ancient high places are ours in possession:

3 Therefore prophesy and say, Thus saith the Lord GOD; Because they have made *you* desolate, and swallowed you up on every side, that ye might be a possession unto the residue of the heathen, and ye are taken up in the lips of talkers, and *are* an infamy of the people:

4 Therefore, ye mountains of Israel, hear the word of the Lord GOD; Thus saith the Lord GOD to the mountains, and to the hills, to the rivers, and to the valleys, to the desolate wastes, and to the cities that are forsaken, which became a prey and derision to the residue of the heathen that *are* round about;

5 Therefore thus saith the Lord GOD; Surely in the fire of my jealousy have I spoken against the residue of the heathen, and against all Idumea, which have appointed my land into their possession with the joy of all *their* heart, with despiteful minds, to cast it out for a prey.

6 Prophesy therefore concerning the land of Israel, and say unto the mountains, and to the hills, to the rivers, and to the valleys, Thus saith the Lord GOD; Behold, I have spoken in my jealousy and in my fury, because ye have borne the shame of the heathen:

7 Therefore thus saith the Lord GOD; I have lifted up mine hand, Surely the heathen that *are* about you, they shall bear their shame.

8 But ye, O mountains of Israel, ye shall shoot forth your branches, and yield your fruit to my people of Israel; for they are at hand to come.

9 For, behold, I *am* for you, and I will turn unto you, and ye shall be tilled and sown:

10 And I will multiply men upon you, all the house of Israel, *even* all of it: and the cities shall be inhabited, and the wastes shall be builded:

11 And I will multiply upon you man and beast; and they shall increase and bring fruit: and I will settle you after your old estates, and will do better *unto you* than at your beginnings: and ye shall know that I *am* the LORD.

12 Yea, I will cause men to walk upon you, *even* my people Israel; and they shall possess thee, and thou shalt be their inheritance, and thou shalt no more henceforth bereave them *of men*.

13 Thus saith the Lord GOD; Because they say unto you, Thou *land* devourest up men, and hast bereaved thy nations;

14 Therefore thou shalt devour men no more, neither bereave thy nations any more, saith the Lord GOD.

15 Neither will I cause *men* to hear in thee the shame of the heathen any more, neither shalt thou bear the reproach of the people any more, neither shalt thou cause thy nations to fall any more, saith the Lord GOD.

16 Moreover the word of the LORD came unto me, saying,

17 Son of man, when the house of Israel dwelt in their own land, they defiled it by their own way and by their doings: their way was before me as the uncleanness of a removed woman.

18 Wherefore I poured my fury upon them for the blood that they had shed upon the land, and for their idols *wherewith* they had polluted it:

19 And I scattered them among the heathen, and they were dispersed through the countries: according to their way and according to their doings I judged them.

20 And when they entered unto the heathen, whither they went, they profaned my holy name, when they said to them, These *are* the people of the LORD, and are gone forth out of his land.

21 But I had pity for mine holy name, which the house of Israel had profaned among the heathen, whither they went.

22 Therefore say unto the house of Israel, Thus saith the Lord GOD; I do not *this* for your sakes, O house of Israel, but for mine holy name's sake, which ye have profaned among the heathen, whither ye went.

23 And I will sanctify my great name, which was profaned among the heathen, which ye have profaned in the midst of them; and the heathen shall know that I *am* the LORD, saith the Lord GOD, when I shall be sanctified in you before their eyes.

24 For I will take you from among the heathen, and gather you out of all countries, and will bring you into your own land.

25 Then will I sprinkle clean water upon you, and ye shall be clean: from all your filthiness, and from all your idols, will I cleanse you.

26 A new heart also will I give you, and a new spirit will I put within you: and I will take away the stony heart out of your flesh, and I will give you an heart of flesh.

27 And I will put my spirit within you, and cause you to walk in my statutes, and ye shall keep my judgments, and do *them*.

28 And ye shall dwell in the land that I gave to your fathers; and ye shall be my people, and I will be your God.

29 I will also save you from all your uncleannesses: and I will call for the corn, and will increase it, and lay no famine upon you.

30 And I will multiply the fruit of the tree, and the increase of the field, that ye shall receive no more reproach of famine among the heathen.

31 Then shall ye remember your own evil ways, and your doings that *were* not good, and shall lothe yourselves in your own sight for your iniquities and for your abominations.

32 Not for your sakes do I *this*, saith the Lord GOD, be it known unto you: be ashamed and confounded for your own ways, O house of Israel.

33 Thus saith the Lord GOD; In the day that I shall have cleansed you from all your iniquities I will also cause *you* to dwell in the cities, and the wastes shall be builded.

34 And the desolate land shall be tilled, whereas it lay desolate in the sight of all that passed by.

35 And they shall say, This land that was desolate is become like the garden of Eden; and the waste and desolate and ruined cities *are become* fenced, *and* are inhabited.

36 Then the heathen that are left round about you shall know that I the LORD build the ruined *places, and* plant that that was desolate: I the LORD have spoken *it*, and I will do *it*.

37 Thus saith the Lord GOD; I will yet *for* this be enquired of by the house of Israel, to do *it* for them; I will increase them with men like a flock.

38 As the holy flock, as the flock of Jerusalem in her solemn feasts; so shall the waste cities be filled with flocks of men: and they shall know that I *am* the LORD.

37

The hand of the LORD was upon me, and carried me out in the spirit of the LORD, and set me down in the midst of the valley which *was* full of bones,

2 And caused me to pass by them round about: and, behold, *there were* very many in the open valley; and, lo, *they were* very dry.

3 And he said unto me, Son of man, can these bones live? And I answered, O Lord GOD, thou knowest.

4 Again he said unto me, Prophesy upon these bones, and say unto them, O ye dry bones, hear the word of the LORD.

5 Thus saith the Lord GOD unto these bones; Behold, I will cause breath to enter into you, and ye shall live:

6 And I will lay sinews upon you, and will bring up flesh upon you, and cover you with skin, and put breath in you, and ye shall live; and ye shall know that I *am* the LORD.

7 So I prophesied as I was commanded: and as I prophesied, there was a noise, and behold a shaking, and the bones came together, bone to his bone.

8 And when I beheld, lo, the sinews and the flesh came up upon them, and the skin covered them above: but *there was* no breath in them.

9 Then said he unto me, Prophesy unto the wind, prophesy, son of man, and say to the wind, Thus saith the Lord GOD; Come from the four winds, O breath, and breathe upon these slain, that they may live.

10 So I prophesied as he commanded me, and the breath came into them, and they lived, and stood up upon their feet, an exceeding great army.

11 Then he said unto me, Son of man, these bones are the whole house of Israel: behold, they say, Our bones are dried, and our hope is lost: we are cut off for our parts.

12 Therefore prophesy and say unto them, Thus saith the Lord GOD; Behold, O my people, I will open your graves, and cause you to come up out of your graves, and bring you into the land of Israel.

13 And ye shall know that I *am* the LORD, when I have opened your graves, O my people, and brought you up out of your graves,

14 And shall put my spirit in you, and ye shall live, and I shall place you in your own land: then shall ye know that I the LORD have spoken *it*, and performed *it*, saith the LORD.

15 The word of the LORD came again unto me, saying,

16 Moreover, thou son of man, take thee one stick, and write upon it, For

Judah, and for the children of Israel his
companions: then take another stick,
and write upon it, For Joseph, the stick
of Ephraim, and *for* all the house of
Israel his companions:
17 And join them one to another into
one stick; and they shall become one in
thine hand.
18 And when the children of thy people
shall speak unto thee, saying, Wilt
thou not shew us what thou *meanest* by
these?
19 Say unto them, Thus saith the Lord
GOD; Behold, I will take the stick of
Joseph, which *is* in the hand of
Ephraim, and the tribes of Israel his
fellows, and will put them with him,
even with the stick of Judah, and make
them one stick, and they shall be one in
mine hand.
20 And the sticks whereon thou writest
shall be in thine hand before their
eyes.
21 And say unto them, Thus saith the
Lord GOD; Behold, I will take the children
of Israel from among the heathen,
whither they be gone, and will gather
them on every side, and bring them
into their own land:
22 And I will make them one nation
in the land upon the mountains of
Israel; and one king shall be king to
them all: and they shall be no more two
nations, neither shall they be divided
into two kingdoms any more at all:
23 Neither shall they defile themselves
any more with their idols, nor
with their detestable things, nor with
any of their transgressions: but I will
save them out of all their dwelling-places,
wherein they have sinned, and
will cleanse them: so shall they be my
people, and I will be their God.
24 And David my servant *shall be*
king over them; and they all shall have
one shepherd: they shall also walk in
my judgments, and observe my statutes,
and do them.
25 And they shall dwell in the land
that I have given unto Jacob my servant,
wherein your fathers have dwelt;
and they shall dwell therein, *even* they,
and their children, and their children's
children for ever: and my servant David
shall be their prince for ever.
26 Moreover I will make a covenant of
peace with them; it shall be an everlasting
covenant with them: and I will
place them, and multiply them, and
will set my sanctuary in the midst of
them for evermore.
27 My tabernacle also shall be with
them: yea, I will be their God, and they
shall be my people.
28 And the heathen shall know that I
the LORD do sanctify Israel, when my
sanctuary shall be in the midst of them
for evermore.

38 And the word of the LORD came
unto me, saying,
2 Son of man, set thy face against
Gog, the land of Magog, the chief
prince of Meshech and Tubal, and prophesy
against him,
3 And say, Thus saith the Lord GOD;
Behold, I *am* against thee, O Gog, the
chief prince of Meshech and Tubal:
4 And I will turn thee back, and put
hooks into thy jaws, and I will bring
thee forth, and all thine army, horses
and horsemen, all of them clothed with
all sorts *of armour*, *even* a great company
with bucklers and shields, all of
them handling swords:
5 Persia, Ethiopia, and Libya with
them; all of them with shield and helmet:

6 Gomer, and all his bands; the house
of Togarmah of the north quarters, and
all his bands: *and* many people with
thee.
7 Be thou prepared, and prepare for
thyself, thou, and all thy company that
are assembled unto thee, and be thou a
guard unto them.
8 After many days thou shalt be visited: in the latter years thou shalt come
into the land *that is* brought back from
the sword, *and is* gathered out of many
people, against the mountains of Israel,
which have been always waste: but it is
brought forth out of the nations, and
they shall dwell safely all of them.
9 Thou shalt ascend and come like a
storm, thou shalt be like a cloud to
cover the land, thou, and all thy bands,
and many people with thee.
10 Thus saith the Lord God; It shall
also come to pass, *that* at the same
time shall things come into thy mind,
and thou shalt think an evil thought:
11 And thou shalt say, I will go up to
the land of unwalled villages; I will go
to them that are at rest, that dwell
safely, all of them dwelling without
walls, and having neither bars nor
gates,
12 To take a spoil, and to take a prey;
to turn thine hand upon the desolate
places *that are now* inhabited, and
upon the people *that are* gathered out
of the nations, which have gotten cattle
and goods, that dwell in the midst of
the land.
13 Sheba, and Dedan, and the merchants of Tarshish, with all the young
lions thereof, shall say unto thee, Art
thou come to take a spoil? hast thou
gathered thy company to take a prey?
to carry away silver and gold, to take
away cattle and goods, to take a great
spoil?
14 Therefore, son of man, prophesy
and say unto Gog, Thus saith the Lord
God; In that day when my people of
Israel dwelleth safely, shalt thou not
know *it*?
15 And thou shalt come from thy
place out of the north parts, thou, and
many people with thee, all of them riding upon horses, a great company, and
a mighty army:
16 And thou shalt come up against
my people of Israel, as a cloud to cover
the land; it shall be in the latter days,
and I will bring thee against my land,
that the heathen may know me, when I
shall be sanctified in thee, O Gog,
before their eyes.
17 Thus saith the Lord God; *Art* thou
he of whom I have spoken in old time
by my servants the prophets of Israel,
which prophesied in those days *many*
years that I would bring thee against
them?
18 And it shall come to pass at the
same time when Gog shall come against
the land of Israel, saith the Lord God,
that my fury shall come up in my face.
19 For in my jealousy *and* in the fire
of my wrath have I spoken, Surely in
that day there shall be a great shaking
in the land of Israel;
20 So that the fishes of the sea, and
the fowls of the heaven, and the beasts
of the field, and all creeping things that
creep upon the earth, and all the men
that *are* upon the face of the earth,
shall shake at my presence, and the
mountains shall be thrown down, and
the steep places shall fall, and every
wall shall fall to the ground.
21 And I will call for a sword against
him throughout all my mountains, saith

the Lord GOD: every man's sword shall
be against his brother.
22 And I will plead against him with
pestilence and with blood; and I will
rain upon him, and upon his bands, and
upon the many people that *are* with
him, an overflowing rain, and great
hailstones, fire, and brimstone.
23 Thus will I magnify myself, and
sanctify myself; and I will be known in
the eyes of many nations, and they shall
know that I *am* the LORD.

39 Therefore, thou son of man,
prophesy against Gog, and say,
Thus saith the Lord GOD; Behold, I *am*
against thee, O Gog, the chief prince of
Meshech and Tubal:
2 And I will turn thee back, and leave
but the sixth part of thee, and will
cause thee to come up from the north
parts, and will bring thee upon the
mountains of Israel:
3 And I will smite thy bow out of thy
left hand, and will cause thine arrows
to fall out of thy right hand.
4 Thou shalt fall upon the mountains
of Israel, thou, and all thy bands, and
the people that *is* with thee: I will give
thee unto the ravenous birds of every
sort, and *to* the beasts of the field to be
devoured.
5 Thou shalt fall upon the open field:
for I have spoken *it*, saith the Lord GOD.
6 And I will send a fire on Magog, and
among them that dwell carelessly in
the isles: and they shall know that I *am*
the LORD.
7 So will I make my holy name known
in the midst of my people Israel; and I
will not *let them* pollute my holy name
any more: and the heathen shall know
that I *am* the LORD, the Holy One in
Israel.
8 Behold, it is come, and it is done,
saith the Lord GOD; this *is* the day
whereof I have spoken.
9 And they that dwell in the cities of
Israel shall go forth, and shall set on
fire and burn the weapons, both the
shields and the bucklers, the bows and
the arrows, and the handstaves, and the
spears, and they shall burn them with
fire seven years:
10 So that they shall take no wood out
of the field, neither cut down *any* out of
the forests; for they shall burn the
weapons with fire: and they shall spoil
those that spoiled them, and rob those
that robbed them, saith the Lord GOD.
11 And it shall come to pass in that
day, *that* I will give unto Gog a place
there of graves in Israel, the valley of
the passengers on the east of the sea:
and it shall stop the *noses* of the passengers: and there shall they bury Gog
and all his multitude: and they shall
call *it* The valley of Hamon-gog.
12 And seven months shall the house
of Israel be burying of them, that they
may cleanse the land.
13 Yea, all the people of the land shall
bury *them*; and it shall be to them a
renown the day that I shall be glorified,
saith the Lord GOD.
14 And they shall sever out men of
continual employment, passing through
the land to bury with the passengers
those that remain upon the face of the
earth, to cleanse it: after the end of
seven months shall they search.
15 And the passengers *that* pass
through the land, when *any* seeth a
man's bone, then shall he set up a sign
by it, till the buriers have buried it in
the valley of Hamon-gog.

16 And also the name of the city *shall*
be Hamonah. Thus shall they cleanse
the land.
17 And, thou son of man, thus saith
the Lord GOD; Speak unto every feathered fowl, and to every beast of the
field, Assemble yourselves, and come;
gather yourselves on every side to my
sacrifice that I do sacrifice for you, *even*
a great sacrifice upon the mountains of
Israel, that ye may eat flesh, and drink
blood.
18 Ye shall eat the flesh of the mighty,
and drink the blood of the princes of
the earth, of rams, of lambs, and of
goats, of bullocks, all of them fatlings of
Bashan.
19 And ye shall eat fat till ye be full,
and drink blood till ye be drunken, of
my sacrifice which I have sacrificed for
you.
20 Thus ye shall be filled at my table
with horses and chariots, with mighty
men, and with all men of war, saith the
Lord GOD.
21 And I will set my glory among the
heathen, and all the heathen shall see
my judgment that I have executed, and
my hand that I have laid upon them.
22 So the house of Israel shall know
that I *am* the LORD their God from that
day and forward.
23 And the heathen shall know that
the house of Israel went into captivity
for their iniquity: because they trespassed against me, therefore hid I my
face from them, and gave them into the
hand of their enemies: so fell they all
by the sword.
24 According to their uncleanness
and according to their transgressions
have I done unto them, and hid my face
from them.
25 Therefore thus saith the Lord GOD;
Now will I bring again the captivity of
Jacob, and have mercy upon the whole
house of Israel, and will be jealous for
my holy name;
26 After that they have borne their
shame, and all their trespasses whereby they have trespassed against me,
when they dwelt safely in their land,
and none made *them* afraid.
27 When I have brought them again
from the people, and gathered them
out of their enemies' lands, and am
sanctified in them in the sight of many
nations;
28 Then shall they know that I *am* the
LORD their God, which caused them to
be led into captivity among the heathen: but I have gathered them unto
their own land, and have left none of
them any more there.
29 Neither will I hide my face any
more from them: for I have poured out
my spirit upon the house of Israel, saith
the Lord GOD.

40 In the five and twentieth year of
our captivity, in the beginning of
the year, in the tenth *day* of the month,
in the fourteenth year after that the
city was smitten, in the selfsame day
the hand of the LORD was upon me, and
brought me thither.
2 In the visions of God brought he me
into the land of Israel, and set me upon
a very high mountain, by which *was* as
the frame of a city on the south.
3 And he brought me thither, and,
behold, *there was* a man, whose appearance *was* like the appearance of brass,
with a line of flax in his hand, and a
measuring reed; and he stood in the
gate.

4 And the man said unto me, Son of man, behold with thine eyes, and hear with thine ears, and set thine heart upon all that I shall shew thee; for to the intent that I might shew *them* unto thee *art* thou brought hither: declare all that thou seest to the house of Israel.

5 And behold a wall on the outside of the house round about, and in the man's hand a measuring reed of six cubits *long* by the cubit and an hand breadth: so he measured the breadth of the building, one reed; and the height, one reed.

6 Then came he unto the gate which looketh toward the east, and went up the stairs thereof, and measured the threshold of the gate, *which was* one reed broad; and the other threshold *of the gate, which was* one reed broad.

7 And *every* little chamber *was* one reed long, and one reed broad; and between the little chambers *were* five cubits; and the threshold of the gate by the porch of the gate within *was* one reed.

8 He measured also the porch of the gate within, one reed.

9 Then measured he the porch of the gate, eight cubits; and the posts thereof, two cubits; and the porch of the gate *was* inward.

10 And the little chambers of the gate eastward *were* three on this side, and three on that side; they three *were* of one measure: and the posts had one measure on this side and on that side.

11 And he measured the breadth of the entry of the gate, ten cubits; *and* the length of the gate, thirteen cubits.

12 The space also before the little chambers *was* one cubit *on this side*, and the space *was* one cubit on that side: and the little chambers *were* six cubits on this side, and six cubits on that side.

13 He measured then the gate from the roof of *one* little chamber to the roof of another: the breadth *was* five and twenty cubits, door against door.

14 He made also posts of threescore cubits, even unto the post of the court round about the gate.

15 And from the face of the gate of the entrance unto the face of the porch of the inner gate *were* fifty cubits.

16 And *there were* narrow windows to the little chambers, and to their posts within the gate round about, and likewise to the arches: and windows *were* round about inward: and upon *each* post *were* palm trees.

17 Then brought he me into the outward court, and, lo, *there were* chambers, and a pavement made for the court round about: thirty chambers *were* upon the pavement.

18 And the pavement by the side of the gates over against the length of the gates *was* the lower pavement.

19 Then he measured the breadth from the forefront of the lower gate unto the forefront of the inner court without, an hundred cubits eastward and northward.

20 And the gate of the outward court that looked toward the north, he measured the length thereof, and the breadth thereof.

21 And the little chambers thereof *were* three on this side and three on that side; and the posts thereof and the arches thereof were after the measure of the first gate: the length thereof *was* fifty cubits, and the breadth five and twenty cubits.

22 And their windows, and their arches, and their palm trees, *were* after the
measure of the gate that looketh toward the east; and they went up unto it
by seven steps; and the arches thereof
were before them.
23 And the gate of the inner court
was over against the gate toward the
north, and toward the east; and he measured from gate to gate an hundred
cubits.
24 After that he brought me toward
the south, and behold a gate toward the
south: and he measured the posts
thereof and the arches thereof according to these measures.
25 And *there were* windows in it and
in the arches thereof round about, like
those windows: the length *was* fifty
cubits, and the breadth five and twenty
cubits.
26 And *there were* seven steps to go
up to it, and the arches thereof *were*
before them: and it had palm trees, one
on this side, and another on that side,
upon the posts thereof.
27 And *there was* a gate in the inner
court toward the south: and he measured from gate to gate toward the
south an hundred cubits.
28 And he brought me to the inner
court by the south gate: and he measured the south gate according to these
measures;
29 And the little chambers thereof,
and the posts thereof, and the arches
thereof, according to these measures:
and *there were* windows in it and in the
arches thereof round about: *it was* fifty
cubits long, and five and twenty cubits
broad.
30 And the arches round about *were*
five and twenty cubits long, and five
cubits broad.
31 And the arches thereof *were* toward the utter court; and palm trees
were upon the posts thereof: and the
going up to it *had* eight steps.
32 And he brought me into the inner
court toward the east: and he measured
the gate according to these measures.
33 And the little chambers thereof,
and the posts thereof, and the arches
thereof, *were* according to these measures: and *there were* windows therein
and in the arches thereof round about:
it was fifty cubits long, and five and
twenty cubits broad.
34 And the arches thereof *were*
toward the outward court; and palm
trees *were* upon the posts thereof, on
this side, and on that side: and the
going up to it *had* eight steps.
35 And he brought me to the north
gate, and measured *it* according to
these measures;
36 The little chambers thereof, the
posts thereof, and the arches thereof,
and the windows to it round about: the
length *was* fifty cubits, and the breadth
five and twenty cubits.
37 And the posts thereof *were* toward
the utter court; and palm trees *were*
upon the posts thereof, on this side, and
on that side: and the going up to it *had*
eight steps.
38 And the chambers and the entries
thereof *were* by the posts of the gates,
where they washed the burnt offering.
39 And in the porch of the gate *were*
two tables on this side, and two tables
on that side, to slay thereon the burnt
offering and the sin offering and the
trespass offering.
40 And at the side without, as one
goeth up to the entry of the north gate,
were two tables; and on the other side,

which *was* at the porch of the gate, *were* two tables.

41 Four tables *were* on this side, and four tables on that side, by the side of the gate; eight tables, whereupon they slew *their sacrifices*.

42 And the four tables *were* of hewn stone for the burnt offering, of a cubit and an half long, and a cubit and an half broad, and one cubit high: whereupon also they laid the instruments wherewith they slew the burnt offering and the sacrifice.

43 And within *were* hooks, an hand broad, fastened round about: and upon the tables *was* the flesh of the offering.

44 And without the inner gate *were* the chambers of the singers in the inner court, which *was* at the side of the north gate; and their prospect *was* toward the south: one at the side of the east gate *having* the prospect toward the north.

45 And he said unto me, This chamber, whose prospect *is* toward the south, *is* for the priests, the keepers of the charge of the house.

46 And the chamber whose prospect *is* toward the north *is* for the priests, the keepers of the charge of the altar: these *are* the sons of Zadok among the sons of Levi, which come near to the LORD to minister unto him.

47 So he measured the court, an hundred cubits long, and an hundred cubits broad, foursquare; and the altar *that was* before the house.

48 And he brought me to the porch of the house, and measured *each* post of the porch, five cubits on this side, and five cubits on that side: and the breadth of the gate *was* three cubits on this side, and three cubits on that side.

49 The length of the porch *was* twenty cubits, and the breadth eleven cubits; and *he brought me* by the steps whereby they went up to it: and *there were* pillars by the posts, one on this side, and another on that side.

41 Afterward he brought me to the temple, and measured the posts, six cubits broad on the one side, and six cubits broad on the other side, *which was* the breadth of the tabernacle.

2 And the breadth of the door *was* ten cubits; and the sides of the door *were* five cubits on the one side, and five cubits on the other side: and he measured the length thereof, forty cubits: and the breadth, twenty cubits.

3 Then went he inward, and measured the post of the door, two cubits; and the door, six cubits; and the breadth of the door, seven cubits.

4 So he measured the length thereof, twenty cubits; and the breadth, twenty cubits, before the temple: and he said unto me, This *is* the most holy *place*.

5 After he measured the wall of the house, six cubits; and the breadth of *every* side chamber, four cubits, round about the house on every side.

6 And the side chambers *were* three, one over another, and thirty in order; and they entered into the wall which *was* of the house for the side chambers round about, that they might have hold, but they had not hold in the wall of the house.

7 And *there was* an enlarging, and a winding about still upward to the side chambers: for the winding about of the house went still upward round about the house: therefore the breadth of the house *was still* upward, and so increased *from* the lowest *chamber* to the highest by the midst.

8 I saw also the height of the house
round about: the foundations of the
side chambers *were* a full reed of six
great cubits.
9 The thickness of the wall, which *was*
for the side chamber without, *was* five
cubits: and *that* which *was* left *was* the
place of the side chambers that *were*
within.
10 And between the chambers *was*
the wideness of twenty cubits round
about the house on every side.
11 And the doors of the side chambers *were* toward *the place that was*
left, one door toward the north, and
another door toward the south: and the
breadth of the place that was left *was*
five cubits round about.
12 Now the building that *was* before
the separate place at the end toward
the west *was* seventy cubits broad; and
the wall of the building *was* five cubits
thick round about, and the length
thereof ninety cubits.
13 So he measured the house, an hundred cubits long; and the separate
place, and the building, with the walls
thereof, an hundred cubits long;
14 Also the breadth of the face of the
house, and of the separate place toward
the east, an hundred cubits.
15 And he measured the length of the
building over against the separate
place which *was* behind it, and the galleries thereof on the one side and on
the other side, an hundred cubits, with
the inner temple, and the porches of
the court;
16 The door posts, and the narrow
windows, and the galleries round about
on their three stories, over against the
door, cieled with wood round about,
and from the ground up to the windows, and the windows *were* covered;
17 To that above the door, even unto
the inner house, and without, and by all
the wall round about within and without, by measure.
18 And *it was* made with cherubims
and palm trees, so that a palm tree *was*
between a cherub and a cherub; and
every cherub had two faces;
19 So that the face of a man *was*
toward the palm tree on the one side,
and the face of a young lion toward the
palm tree on the other side: *it was*
made through all the house round
about.
20 From the ground unto above the
door *were* cherubims and palm trees
made, and *on* the wall of the temple.
21 The posts of the temple *were*
squared, *and* the face of the sanctuary;
the appearance *of the one* as the
appearance *of the other*.
22 The altar of wood *was* three cubits
high, and the length thereof two cubits;
and the corners thereof, and the length
thereof, and the walls thereof, *were* of
wood: and he said unto me, This *is* the
table that *is* before the LORD.
23 And the temple and the sanctuary
had two doors.
24 And the doors had two leaves
apiece, two turning leaves; two *leaves*
for the one door, and two leaves for the
other *door*.
25 And *there were* made on them, on
the doors of the temple, cherubims and
palm trees, like as *were* made upon the
walls; and *there were* thick planks upon
the face of the porch without.
26 And *there were* narrow windows
and palm trees on the one side and on
the other side, on the sides of the porch,
and *upon* the side chambers of the
house, and thick planks.

42 Then he brought me forth into
the utter court, the way toward
the north: and he brought me into the
chamber that *was* over against the
separate place, and which *was* before
the building toward the north.
2 Before the length of an hundred
cubits *was* the north door, and the
breadth *was* fifty cubits.
3 Over against the twenty *cubits*
which *were* for the inner court, and
over against the pavement which *was*
for the utter court, *was* gallery against
gallery in three *stories*.
4 And before the chambers *was* a
walk of ten cubits breadth inward, a
way of one cubit; and their doors
toward the north.
5 Now the upper chambers *were*
shorter: for the galleries were higher
than these, than the lower, and than the
middlemost of the building.
6 For they *were* in three *stories*, but
had not pillars as the pillars of the
courts: therefore *the building* was
straitened more than the lowest and
the middlemost from the ground.
7 And the wall that *was* without over
against the chambers, toward the utter
court on the forepart of the chambers,
the length thereof *was* fifty cubits.
8 For the length of the chambers that
were in the utter court *was* fifty cubits:
and, lo, before the temple *were* an hundred cubits.
9 And from under these chambers
was the entry on the east side, as one
goeth into them from the utter court.
10 The chambers *were* in the thickness of the wall of the court toward the
east, over against the separate place,
and over against the building.
11 And the way before them *was* like
the appearance of the chambers which
were toward the north, as long as they,
and as broad as they: and all their
goings out *were* both according to their
fashions, and according to their doors.
12 And according to the doors of the
chambers that *were* toward the south
was a door in the head of the way, *even*
the way directly before the wall toward
the east, as one entereth into them.
13 Then said he unto me, The north
chambers *and* the south chambers,
which *are* before the separate place,
they *be* holy chambers, where the
priests that approach unto the LORD
shall eat the most holy things: there
shall they lay the most holy things, and
the meat offering, and the sin offering,
and the trespass offering; for the place
is holy.
14 When the priests enter therein,
then shall they not go out of the holy
place into the utter court, but there
they shall lay their garments wherein
they minister; for they *are* holy; and
shall put on other garments, and shall
approach to *those things* which *are* for
the people.
15 Now when he had made an end of
measuring the inner house, he brought
me forth toward the gate whose prospect *is* toward the east, and measured it
round about.
16 He measured the east side with
the measuring reed, five hundred
reeds, with the measuring reed round
about.
17 He measured the north side, five
hundred reeds, with the measuring
reed round about.
18 He measured the south side, five
hundred reeds, with the measuring
reed.

19 He turned about to the west side, *and* measured five hundred reeds with the measuring reed.

20 He measured it by the four sides: it had a wall round about, five hundred *reeds* long, and five hundred broad, to make a separation between the sanctuary and the profane place.

43 Afterward he brought me to the gate, *even* the gate that looketh toward the east:

2 And, behold, the glory of the God of Israel came from the way of the east: and his voice *was* like a noise of many waters: and the earth shined with his glory.

3 And *it was* according to the appearance of the vision which I saw, *even* according to the vision that I saw when I came to destroy the city: and the visions *were* like the vision that I saw by the river Chebar; and I fell upon my face.

4 And the glory of the LORD came into the house by the way of the gate whose prospect *is* toward the east.

5 So the spirit took me up, and brought me into the inner court; and, behold, the glory of the LORD filled the house.

6 And I heard *him* speaking unto me out of the house; and the man stood by me.

7 And he said unto me, Son of man, the place of my throne, and the place of the soles of my feet, where I will dwell in the midst of the children of Israel for ever, and my holy name, shall the house of Israel no more defile, *neither* they, nor their kings, by their whoredom, nor by the carcases of their kings in their high places.

8 In their setting of their threshold by my thresholds, and their post by my posts, and the wall between me and them, they have even defiled my holy name by their abominations that they have committed: wherefore I have consumed them in mine anger.

9 Now let them put away their whoredom, and the carcases of their kings, far from me, and I will dwell in the midst of them for ever.

10 Thou son of man, shew the house to the house of Israel, that they may be ashamed of their iniquities: and let them measure the pattern.

11 And if they be ashamed of all that they have done, shew them the form of the house, and the fashion thereof, and the goings out thereof, and the comings in thereof, and all the forms thereof, and all the ordinances thereof, and all the forms thereof, and all the laws thereof: and write *it* in their sight, that they may keep the whole form thereof, and all the ordinances thereof, and do them.

12 This *is* the law of the house; Upon the top of the mountain the whole limit thereof round about *shall be* most holy. Behold, this *is* the law of the house.

13 And these *are* the measures of the altar after the cubits: The cubit *is* a cubit and an hand breadth; even the bottom *shall be* a cubit, and the breadth a cubit, and the border thereof by the edge thereof round about *shall be* a span: and this *shall be* the higher place of the altar.

14 And from the bottom *upon* the ground *even* to the lower settle *shall be* two cubits, and the breadth one cubit; and from the lesser settle *even* to the greater settle *shall be* four cubits, and the breadth *one* cubit.

15 So the altar *shall be* four cubits; and from the altar and upward *shall be* four horns.

16 And the altar *shall be* twelve *cubits* long, twelve broad, square in the four squares thereof.

17 And the settle *shall be* fourteen *cubits* long and fourteen broad in the four squares thereof; and the border about it *shall be* half a cubit; and the bottom thereof *shall be* a cubit about; and his stairs shall look toward the east.

18 And he said unto me, Son of man, thus saith the Lord GOD; These *are* the ordinances of the altar in the day when they shall make it, to offer burnt offerings thereon, and to sprinkle blood thereon.

19 And thou shalt give to the priests the Levites that be of the seed of Zadok, which approach unto me, to minister unto me, saith the Lord GOD, a young bullock for a sin offering.

20 And thou shalt take of the blood thereof, and put *it* on the four horns of it, and on the four corners of the settle, and upon the border round about: thus shalt thou cleanse and purge it.

21 Thou shalt take the bullock also of the sin offering, and he shall burn it in the appointed place of the house, without the sanctuary.

22 And on the second day thou shalt offer a kid of the goats without blemish for a sin offering; and they shall cleanse the altar, as they did cleanse *it* with the bullock.

23 When thou hast made an end of cleansing *it*, thou shalt offer a young bullock without blemish, and a ram out of the flock without blemish.

24 And thou shalt offer them before the LORD, and the priests shall cast salt upon them, and they shall offer them up *for* a burnt offering unto the LORD.

25 Seven days shalt thou prepare every day a goat *for* a sin offering: they shall also prepare a young bullock, and a ram out of the flock, without blemish.

26 Seven days shall they purge the altar and purify it; and they shall consecrate themselves.

27 And when these days are expired, it shall be, *that* upon the eighth day, and *so* forward, the priests shall make your burnt offerings upon the altar, and your peace offerings; and I will accept you, saith the Lord GOD.

44

Then he brought me back the way of the gate of the outward sanctuary which looketh toward the east; and it *was* shut.

2 Then said the LORD unto me; This gate shall be shut, it shall not be opened, and no man shall enter in by it; because the LORD, the God of Israel, hath entered in by it, therefore it shall be shut.

3 *It is* for the prince; the prince, he shall sit in it to eat bread before the LORD; he shall enter by the way of the porch of *that* gate, and shall go out by the way of the same.

4 Then brought he me the way of the north gate before the house: and I looked, and, behold, the glory of the LORD filled the house of the LORD: and I fell upon my face.

5 And the LORD said unto me, Son of man, mark well, and behold with thine eyes, and hear with thine ears all that I say unto thee concerning all the ordinances of the house of the LORD, and all the laws thereof; and mark well the entering in of the house, with every going forth of the sanctuary.

6 And thou shalt say to the rebellious,
even to the house of Israel, Thus saith
the Lord GOD; O ye house of Israel, let
it suffice you of all your abominations,
7 In that ye have brought *into my*
sanctuary strangers, uncircumcised in
heart, and uncircumcised in flesh, to be
in my sanctuary, to pollute it, *even* my
house, when ye offer my bread, the fat
and the blood, and they have broken
my covenant because of all your abominations.
8 And ye have not kept the charge of
mine holy things: but ye have set keepers of my charge in my sanctuary for
yourselves.
9 Thus saith the Lord GOD; No stranger, uncircumcised in heart, nor uncircumcised in flesh, shall enter into my
sanctuary, of any stranger that *is* among
the children of Israel.
10 And the Levites that are gone
away far from me, when Israel went
astray, which went astray away from me
after their idols; they shall even bear
their iniquity.
11 Yet they shall be ministers in my
sanctuary, *having* charge at the gates of
the house, and ministering to the
house: they shall slay the burnt offering and the sacrifice for the people, and
they shall stand before them to minister unto them.
12 Because they ministered unto
them before their idols, and caused the
house of Israel to fall into iniquity;
therefore have I lifted up mine hand
against them, saith the Lord GOD, and
they shall bear their iniquity.
13 And they shall not come near unto
me, to do the office of a priest unto me,
nor to come near to any of my holy
things, in the most holy *place*: but they
shall bear their shame, and their abominations which they have committed.
14 But I will make them keepers of
the charge of the house, for all the service thereof, and for all that shall be
done therein.
15 But the priests the Levites, the
sons of Zadok, that kept the charge of
my sanctuary when the children of
Israel went astray from me, they shall
come near to me to minister unto me,
and they shall stand before me to offer
unto me the fat and the blood, saith the
Lord GOD:
16 They shall enter into my sanctuary,
and they shall come near to my table, to
minister unto me, and they shall keep
my charge.
17 And it shall come to pass, *that*
when they enter in at the gates of the
inner court, they shall be clothed with
linen garments; and no wool shall come
upon them, whiles they minister in the
gates of the inner court, and within.
18 They shall have linen bonnets
upon their heads, and shall have linen
breeches upon their loins; they shall
not gird *themselves* with any thing that
causeth sweat.
19 And when they go forth into the
utter court, *even* into the utter court to
the people, they shall put off their garments wherein they ministered, and lay
them in the holy chambers, and they
shall put on other garments; and they
shall not sanctify the people with their
garments.
20 Neither shall they shave their
heads, nor suffer their locks to grow
long; they shall only poll their heads.
21 Neither shall any priest drink
wine, when they enter into the inner
court.

22 Neither shall they take for their
wives a widow, nor her that is put away:
but they shall take maidens of the seed
of the house of Israel, or a widow that
had a priest before.
23 And they shall teach my people
the difference between the holy and
profane, and cause them to discern
between the unclean and the clean.
24 And in controversy they shall
stand in judgment; *and* they shall
judge it according to my judgments:
and they shall keep my laws and my
statutes in all mine assemblies; and
they shall hallow my sabbaths.
25 And they shall come at no dead
person to defile themselves: but for
father, or for mother, or for son, or for
daughter, for brother, or for sister that
hath had no husband, they may defile
themselves.
26 And after he is cleansed, they shall
reckon unto him seven days.
27 And in the day that he goeth into
the sanctuary, unto the inner court, to
minister in the sanctuary, he shall offer
his sin offering, saith the Lord GOD.
28 And it shall be unto them for an
inheritance: I *am* their inheritance:
and ye shall give them no possession in
Israel: I *am* their possession.
29 They shall eat the meat offering,
and the sin offering, and the trespass
offering; and every dedicated thing in
Israel shall be theirs.
30 And the first of all the firstfruits of
all *things*, and every oblation of all, of
every *sort* of your oblations, shall be
the priest's: ye shall also give unto the
priest the first of your dough, that he
may cause the blessing to rest in thine
house.
31 The priests shall not eat of any
thing that is dead of itself, or torn,
whether it be fowl or beast.

45 Moreover, when ye shall divide
by lot the land for inheritance, ye
shall offer an oblation unto the LORD,
an holy portion of the land: the length
shall be the length of five and twenty
thousand *reeds*, and the breadth *shall*
be ten thousand. This *shall be* holy in
all the borders thereof round about.
2 Of this there shall be for the sanctuary five hundred *in length*, with five
hundred *in breadth*, square round
about; and fifty cubits round about for
the suburbs thereof.
3 And of this measure shalt thou measure the length of five and twenty
thousand, and the breadth of ten thousand: and in it shall be the sanctuary
and the most holy *place*.
4 The holy *portion* of the land shall
be for the priests the ministers of the
sanctuary, which shall come near to
minister unto the LORD: and it shall be
a place for their houses, and an holy
place for the sanctuary.
5 And the five and twenty thousand
of length, and the ten thousand of
breadth, shall also the Levites, the ministers of the house, have for themselves,
for a possession for twenty chambers.
6 And ye shall appoint the possession
of the city five thousand broad, and five
and twenty thousand long, over against
the oblation of the holy *portion*: it shall
be for the whole house of Israel.
7 And a *portion shall be* for the
prince on the one side and on the other
side of the oblation of the holy *portion*,
and of the possession of the city, before
the oblation of the holy *portion*, and
before the possession of the city, from
the west side westward, and from the

east side eastward: and the length *shall be* over against one of the portions, from the west border unto the east border.

8 In the land shall be his possession in Israel: and my princes shall no more oppress my people; and *the rest of* the land shall they give to the house of Israel according to their tribes.

9 Thus saith the Lord GOD; Let it suffice you, O princes of Israel: remove violence and spoil, and execute judgment and justice, take away your exactions from my people, saith the Lord GOD.

10 Ye shall have just balances, and a just ephah, and a just bath.

11 The ephah and the bath shall be of one measure, that the bath may contain the tenth part of an homer, and the ephah the tenth part of an homer: the measure thereof shall be after the homer.

12 And the shekel *shall be* twenty gerahs: twenty shekels, five and twenty shekels, fifteen shekels, shall be your maneh.

13 This *is* the oblation that ye shall offer; the sixth part of an ephah of an homer of wheat, and ye shall give the sixth part of an ephah of an homer of barley:

14 Concerning the ordinance of oil, the bath of oil, *ye shall offer* the tenth part of a bath out of the cor, *which is* an homer of ten baths; for ten baths *are* an homer:

15 And one lamb out of the flock, out of two hundred, out of the fat pastures of Israel; for a meat offering, and for a burnt offering, and for peace offerings, to make reconciliation for them, saith the Lord GOD.

16 All the people of the land shall give this oblation for the prince in Israel.

17 And it shall be the prince's part *to give* burnt offerings, and meat offerings, and drink offerings, in the feasts, and in the new moons, and in the sabbaths, in all solemnities of the house of Israel: he shall prepare the sin offering, and the meat offering, and the burnt offering, and the peace offerings, to make reconciliation for the house of Israel.

18 Thus saith the Lord GOD; In the first *month*, in the first *day* of the month, thou shalt take a young bullock without blemish, and cleanse the sanctuary:

19 And the priest shall take of the blood of the sin offering, and put *it* upon the posts of the house, and upon the four corners of the settle of the altar, and upon the posts of the gate of the inner court.

20 And so thou shalt do the seventh *day* of the month for every one that erreth, and for *him that is* simple: so shall ye reconcile the house.

21 In the first *month*, in the fourteenth day of the month, ye shall have the passover, a feast of seven days; unleavened bread shall be eaten.

22 And upon that day shall the prince prepare for himself and for all the people of the land a bullock *for* a sin offering.

23 And seven days of the feast he shall prepare a burnt offering to the LORD, seven bullocks and seven rams without blemish daily the seven days; and a kid of the goats daily *for* a sin offering.

24 And he shall prepare a meat offering of an ephah for a bullock, and an ephah for a ram, and an hin of oil for an ephah.

25 In the seventh *month*, in the fifteenth day of the month, shall he do the like in the feast of the seven days, according to the sin offering, according to the burnt offering, and according to the meat offering, and according to the oil.

46 Thus saith the Lord GOD; The gate of the inner court that looketh toward the east shall be shut the six working days; but on the sabbath it shall be opened, and in the day of the new moon it shall be opened.

2 And the prince shall enter by the way of the porch of *that* gate without, and shall stand by the post of the gate, and the priests shall prepare his burnt offering and his peace offerings, and he shall worship at the threshold of the gate: then he shall go forth; but the gate shall not be shut until the evening.

3 Likewise the people of the land shall worship at the door of this gate before the LORD in the sabbaths and in the new moons.

4 And the burnt offering that the prince shall offer unto the LORD in the sabbath day *shall be* six lambs without blemish, and a ram without blemish.

5 And the meat offering *shall be* an ephah for a ram, and the meat offering for the lambs as he shall be able to give, and an hin of oil to an ephah.

6 And in the day of the new moon *it shall be* a young bullock without blemish, and six lambs, and a ram: they shall be without blemish.

7 And he shall prepare a meat offering, an ephah for a bullock, and an ephah for a ram, and for the lambs according as his hand shall attain unto, and an hin of oil to an ephah.

8 And when the prince shall enter, he shall go in by the way of the porch of *that* gate, and he shall go forth by the way thereof.

9 But when the people of the land shall come before the LORD in the solemn feasts, he that entereth in by the way of the north gate to worship shall go out by the way of the south gate; and he that entereth by the way of the south gate shall go forth by the way of the north gate: he shall not return by the way of the gate whereby he came in, but shall go forth over against it.

10 And the prince in the midst of them, when they go in, shall go in; and when they go forth, shall go forth.

11 And in the feasts and in the solemnities the meat offering shall be an ephah to a bullock, and an ephah to a ram, and to the lambs as he is able to give, and an hin of oil to an ephah.

12 Now when the prince shall prepare a voluntary burnt offering or peace offerings voluntarily unto the LORD, *one* shall then open him the gate that looketh toward the east, and he shall prepare his burnt offering and his peace offerings, as he did on the sabbath day: then he shall go forth; and after his going forth *one* shall shut the gate.

13 Thou shalt daily prepare a burnt offering unto the LORD *of* a lamb of the first year without blemish: thou shalt prepare it every morning.

14 And thou shalt prepare a meat offering for it every morning, the sixth part of an ephah, and the third part of an hin of oil, to temper with the fine flour; a meat offering continually by a perpetual ordinance unto the LORD.

15 Thus shall they prepare the lamb, and the meat offering, and the oil, every morning *for* a continual burnt offering.

16 Thus saith the Lord GOD; If the prince give a gift unto any of his sons, the inheritance thereof shall be his sons'; it *shall be* their possession by inheritance.

17 But if he give a gift of his inheritance to one of his servants, then it shall be his to the year of liberty; after it shall return to the prince: but his inheritance shall be his sons' for them.

18 Moreover the prince shall not take of the people's inheritance by oppression, to thrust them out of their possession; *but* he shall give his sons inheritance out of his own possession: that my people be not scattered every man from his possession.

19 After he brought me through the entry, which *was* at the side of the gate, into the holy chambers of the priests, which looked toward the north: and, behold, there *was* a place on the two sides westward.

20 Then said he unto me, This *is* the place where the priests shall boil the trespass offering and the sin offering, where they shall bake the meat offering; that they bear *them* not out into the utter court, to sanctify the people.

21 Then he brought me forth into the utter court, and caused me to pass by the four corners of the court; and, behold, in every corner of the court *there was* a court.

22 In the four corners of the court *there were* courts joined of forty *cubits* long and thirty broad: these four corners *were* of one measure.

23 And *there was* a row *of building* round about in them, round about them four, and *it was* made with boiling places under the rows round about.

24 Then said he unto me, These *are* the places of them that boil, where the ministers of the house shall boil the sacrifice of the people.

47 Afterward he brought me again unto the door of the house; and, behold, waters issued out from under the threshold of the house eastward: for the forefront of the house *stood toward* the east, and the waters came down from under from the right side of the house, at the south *side* of the altar.

2 Then brought he me out of the way of the gate northward, and led me about the way without unto the utter gate by the way that looketh eastward; and, behold, there ran out waters on the right side.

3 And when the man that had the line in his hand went forth eastward, he measured a thousand cubits, and he brought me through the waters; the waters *were* to the ankles.

4 Again he measured a thousand, and brought me through the waters; the waters *were* to the knees. Again he measured a thousand, and brought me through; the waters *were* to the loins.

5 Afterward he measured a thousand; *and it was* a river that I could not pass over: for the waters were risen, waters to swim in, a river that could not be passed over.

6 And he said unto me, Son of man, hast thou seen *this*? Then he brought me, and caused me to return to the brink of the river.

7 Now when I had returned, behold, at the bank of the river *were* very many trees on the one side and on the other.

8 Then said he unto me, These waters
issue out toward the east country, and
go down into the desert, and go into the
sea: *which being* brought forth into the
sea, the waters shall be healed.
9 And it shall come to pass, *that* every
thing that liveth, which moveth, whithersoever the rivers shall come, shall
live: and there shall be a very great
multitude of fish, because these waters
shall come thither: for they shall be
healed; and every thing shall live
whither the river cometh.
10 And it shall come to pass, *that* the
fishers shall stand upon it from En-gedi
even unto En-eglaim; they shall be a
place to spread forth nets; their fish
shall be according to their kinds, as the
fish of the great sea, exceeding many.
11 But the miry places thereof and
the marishes thereof shall not be
healed; they shall be given to salt.
12 And by the river upon the bank
thereof, on this side and on that side,
shall grow all trees for meat, whose leaf
shall not fade, neither shall the fruit
thereof be consumed: it shall bring
forth new fruit according to his months,
because their waters they issued out of
the sanctuary: and the fruit thereof
shall be for meat, and the leaf thereof
for medicine.
13 Thus saith the Lord GOD; This *shall
be* the border, whereby ye shall inherit
the land according to the twelve tribes
of Israel: Joseph *shall have two* portions.
14 And ye shall inherit it, one as well
as another: *concerning* the which I lifted up mine hand to give it unto your
fathers: and this land shall fall unto you
for inheritance.
15 And this *shall be* the border of the
land toward the north side, from the
great sea, the way of Hethlon, as men
go to Zedad;
16 Hamath, Berothah, Sibraim, which
is between the border of Damascus and
the border of Hamath; Hazar-hatticon,
which *is* by the coast of Hauran.
17 And the border from the sea shall
be Hazar-enan, the border of Damascus,
and the north northward, and the border of Hamath. And *this is* the north
side.
18 And the east side ye shall measure
from Hauran, and from Damascus, and
from Gilead, and from the land of Israel
by Jordan, from the border unto the
east sea. And *this is* the east side.
19 And the south side southward,
from Tamar *even* to the waters of strife
in Kadesh, the river to the great sea.
And *this is* the south side southward.
20 The west side also *shall be* the
great sea from the border, till a man
come over against Hamath. This *is* the
west side.
21 So shall ye divide this land unto
you according to the tribes of Israel.
22 And it shall come to pass, *that* ye
shall divide it by lot for an inheritance
unto you, and to the strangers that
sojourn among you, which shall beget
children among you: and they shall be
unto you as born in the country among
the children of Israel; they shall have
inheritance with you among the tribes
of Israel.
23 And it shall come to pass, *that* in
what tribe the stranger sojourneth,
there shall ye give *him* his inheritance,
saith the Lord GOD.

48 Now these *are* the names of the
tribes. From the north end to the
coast of the way of Hethlon, as one
goeth to Hamath, Hazar-enan, the border of Damascus northward, to the

coast of Hamath; for these are his sides
east *and* west; a *portion for* Dan.
2 And by the border of Dan, from the
east side unto the west side, a *portion*
for Asher.
3 And by the border of Asher, from
the east side even unto the west side, a
portion for Naphtali.
4 And by the border of Naphtali, from
the east side unto the west side, a *por-*
tion for Manasseh.
5 And by the border of Manasseh,
from the east side unto the west side, a
portion for Ephraim.
6 And by the border of Ephraim, from
the east side even unto the west side, a
portion for Reuben.
7 And by the border of Reuben, from
the east side unto the west side, a *por-*
tion for Judah.
8 And by the border of Judah, from
the east side unto the west side, shall
be the offering which ye shall offer of
five and twenty thousand *reeds in*
breadth, and *in* length as one of the
other parts, from the east side unto the
west side: and the sanctuary shall be in
the midst of it.
9 The oblation that ye shall offer unto
the LORD *shall be* of five and twenty
thousand in length, and of ten thousand in breadth.
10 And for them, *even* for the priests,
shall be *this* holy oblation; toward the
north five and twenty thousand *in*
length, and toward the west ten thousand in breadth, and toward the east
ten thousand in breadth, and toward
the south five and twenty thousand in
length: and the sanctuary of the LORD
shall be in the midst thereof.
11 *It shall be* for the priests that are
sanctified of the sons of Zadok; which
have kept my charge, which went not
astray when the children of Israel went
astray, as the Levites went astray.
12 And *this* oblation of the land that
is offered shall be unto them a thing
most holy by the border of the Levites.
13 And over against the border of the
priests the Levites *shall have* five and
twenty thousand in length, and ten
thousand in breadth: all the length
shall be five and twenty thousand, and
the breadth ten thousand.
14 And they shall not sell of it, neither exchange, nor alienate the firstfruits of the land: for *it is* holy unto the
LORD.
15 And the five thousand, that are left
in the breadth over against the five and
twenty thousand, shall be a profane
place for the city, for dwelling, and for
suburbs: and the city shall be in the
midst thereof.
16 And these *shall be* the measures
thereof; the north side four thousand
and five hundred, and the south side
four thousand and five hundred, and on
the east side four thousand and five
hundred, and the west side four thousand and five hundred.
17 And the suburbs of the city shall
be toward the north two hundred and
fifty, and toward the south two hundred
and fifty, and toward the east two hundred and fifty, and toward the west two
hundred and fifty.
18 And the residue in length over
against the oblation of the holy *portion*
shall be ten thousand eastward, and
ten thousand westward: and it shall be
over against the oblation of the holy
portion; and the increase thereof shall
be for food unto them that serve the
city.
19 And they that serve the city shall
serve it out of all the tribes of Israel.

20 All the oblation *shall be* five and
twenty thousand by five and twenty
thousand: ye shall offer the holy oblation foursquare, with the possession of
the city.

21 And the residue *shall be* for the
prince, on the one side and on the other
of the holy oblation, and of the possession of the city, over against the five
and twenty thousand of the oblation
toward the east border, and westward
over against the five and twenty thousand toward the west border, over
against the portions for the prince: and
it shall be the holy oblation; and the
sanctuary of the house *shall be* in the
midst thereof.

22 Moreover from the possession of
the Levites, and from the possession of
the city, *being* in the midst *of that*
which is the prince's, between the border of Judah and the border of
Benjamin, shall be for the prince.

23 As for the rest of the tribes, from
the east side unto the west side,
Benjamin *shall have* a *portion*.

24 And by the border of Benjamin,
from the east side unto the west side,
Simeon *shall have* a *portion*.

25 And by the border of Simeon, from
the east side unto the west side,
Issachar a *portion*.

26 And by the border of Issachar,
from the east side unto the west side,
Zebulun a *portion*.

27 And by the border of Zebulun,
from the east side unto the west side,
Gad a *portion*.

28 And by the border of Gad, at the
south side southward, the border shall
be even from Tamar *unto* the waters of
strife *in* Kadesh, *and* to the river
toward the great sea.

29 This *is* the land which ye shall
divide by lot unto the tribes of Israel
for inheritance, and these *are* their portions, saith the Lord GOD.

30 And these *are* the goings out of the
city on the north side, four thousand
and five hundred measures.

31 And the gates of the city *shall be*
after the names of the tribes of Israel:
three gates northward; one gate of
Reuben, one gate of Judah, one gate of
Levi.

32 And at the east side four thousand
and five hundred: and three gates; and
one gate of Joseph, one gate of
Benjamin, one gate of Dan.

33 And at the south side four thousand and five hundred measures: and
three gates; one gate of Simeon, one
gate of Issachar, one gate of Zebulun.

34 At the west side four thousand and
five hundred, *with* their three gates;
one gate of Gad, one gate of Asher, one
gate of Naphtali.

35 *It was* round about eighteen thousand *measures*: and the name of the
city from *that* day *shall be*, The LORD *is*
there.

THE BOOK OF

DANIEL

1 In the third year of the reign of
Jehoiakim king of Judah came
Nebuchadnezzar king of Babylon unto
Jerusalem, and besieged it.
2 And the Lord gave Jehoiakim king
of Judah into his hand, with part of the
vessels of the house of God: which he
carried into the land of Shinar to the
house of his god; and he brought the
vessels into the treasure house of his
god.
3 And the king spake unto Ashpenaz
the master of his eunuchs, that he
should bring *certain* of the children of
Israel, and of the king's seed, and of the
princes;
4 Children in whom *was* no blemish,
but well favoured, and skilful in all
wisdom, and cunning in knowledge,
and understanding science, and such as
had ability in them to stand in the
king's palace, and whom they might
teach the learning and the tongue of
the Chaldeans.
5 And the king appointed them a
daily provision of the king's meat, and
of the wine which he drank: so nourish-
ing them three years, that at the end
thereof they might stand before the
king.
6 Now among these were of the children of Judah, Daniel, Hananiah, Mishael, and Azariah:
7 Unto whom the prince of the
eunuchs gave names: for he gave unto
Daniel *the name* of Belteshazzar; and
to Hananiah, of Shadrach; and to
Mishael, of Meshach; and to Azariah, of
Abed-nego.
8 But Daniel purposed in his heart
that he would not defile himself with
the portion of the king's meat, nor with
the wine which he drank: therefore he
requested of the prince of the eunuchs
that he might not defile himself.
9 Now God had brought Daniel into
favour and tender love with the prince
of the eunuchs.
10 And the prince of the eunuchs said
unto Daniel, I fear my lord the king,
who hath appointed your meat and
your drink: for why should he see your
faces worse liking than the children
which *are* of your sort? then shall ye
make *me* endanger my head to the
king.
11 Then said Daniel to Melzar, whom
the prince of the eunuchs had set over
Daniel, Hananiah, Mishael, and Azariah,
12 Prove thy servants, I beseech thee,
ten days; and let them give us pulse to
eat, and water to drink.
13 Then let our countenances be
looked upon before thee, and the countenance of the children that eat of the
portion of the king's meat: and as thou
seest, deal with thy servants.
14 So he consented to them in this
matter, and proved them ten days.
15 And at the end of ten days their
countenances appeared fairer and fat-
ter in flesh than all the children which
did eat the portion of the king's meat.
16 Thus Melzar took away the portion
of their meat, and the wine that they
should drink; and gave them pulse.
17 As for these four children, God
gave them knowledge and skill in all

learning and wisdom: and Daniel had understanding in all visions and dreams.
18 Now at the end of the days that the king had said he should bring them in, then the prince of the eunuchs brought them in before Nebuchadnezzar.
19 And the king communed with them; and among them all was found none like Daniel, Hananiah, Mishael, and Azariah: therefore stood they before the king.
20 And in all matters of wisdom *and* understanding, that the king enquired of them, he found them ten times better than all the magicians *and* astrologers that *were* in all his realm.
21 And Daniel continued *even* unto the first year of king Cyrus.

2 And in the second year of the reign of Nebuchadnezzar Nebuchadnezzar dreamed dreams, wherewith his spirit was troubled, and his sleep brake from him.
2 Then the king commanded to call the magicians, and the astrologers, and the sorcerers, and the Chaldeans, for to shew the king his dreams. So they came and stood before the king.
3 And the king said unto them, I have dreamed a dream, and my spirit was troubled to know the dream.
4 Then spake the Chaldeans to the king in Syriack, O king, live for ever: tell thy servants the dream, and we will shew the interpretation.
5 The king answered and said to the Chaldeans, The thing is gone from me: if ye will not make known unto me the dream, with the interpretation thereof, ye shall be cut in pieces, and your houses shall be made a dunghill.
6 But if ye shew the dream, and the interpretation thereof, ye shall receive of me gifts and rewards and great honour: therefore shew me the dream, and the interpretation thereof.
7 They answered again and said, Let the king tell his servants the dream, and we will shew the interpretation of it.
8 The king answered and said, I know of certainty that ye would gain the time, because ye see the thing is gone from me.
9 But if ye will not make known unto me the dream, *there is but* one decree for you: for ye have prepared lying and corrupt words to speak before me, till the time be changed: therefore tell me the dream, and I shall know that ye can shew me the interpretation thereof.
10 The Chaldeans answered before the king, and said, There is not a man upon the earth that can shew the king's matter: therefore *there is* no king, lord, nor ruler, *that* asked such things at any magician, or astrologer, or Chaldean.
11 And *it is* a rare thing that the king requireth, and there is none other that can shew it before the king, except the gods, whose dwelling is not with flesh.
12 For this cause the king was angry and very furious, and commanded to destroy all the wise *men* of Babylon.
13 And the decree went forth that the wise *men* should be slain; and they sought Daniel and his fellows to be slain.
14 Then Daniel answered with counsel and wisdom to Arioch the captain of the king's guard, which was gone forth to slay the wise *men* of Babylon:
15 He answered and said to Arioch the king's captain, Why *is* the decree *so* hasty from the king? Then Arioch made the thing known to Daniel.

16 Then Daniel went in, and desired of the king that he would give him time, and that he would shew the king the interpretation.

17 Then Daniel went to his house, and made the thing known to Hananiah, Mishael, and Azariah, his companions:

18 That they would desire mercies of the God of heaven concerning this secret; that Daniel and his fellows should not perish with the rest of the wise *men* of Babylon.

19 Then was the secret revealed unto Daniel in a night vision. Then Daniel blessed the God of heaven.

20 Daniel answered and said, Blessed be the name of God for ever and ever: for wisdom and might are his:

21 And he changeth the times and the seasons: he removeth kings, and setteth up kings: he giveth wisdom unto the wise, and knowledge to them that know understanding:

22 He revealeth the deep and secret things: he knoweth what *is* in the darkness, and the light dwelleth with him.

23 I thank thee, and praise thee, O thou God of my fathers, who hast given me wisdom and might, and hast made known unto me now what we desired of thee: for thou hast *now* made known unto us the king's matter.

24 Therefore Daniel went in unto Arioch, whom the king had ordained to destroy the wise *men* of Babylon: he went and said thus unto him; Destroy not the wise *men* of Babylon: bring me in before the king, and I will shew unto the king the interpretation.

25 Then Arioch brought in Daniel before the king in haste, and said thus unto him, I have found a man of the captives of Judah, that will make known unto the king the interpretation.

26 The king answered and said to Daniel, whose name *was* Belteshazzar, Art thou able to make known unto me the dream which I have seen, and the interpretation thereof?

27 Daniel answered in the presence of the king, and said, The secret which the king hath demanded cannot the wise *men*, the astrologers, the magicians, the soothsayers, shew unto the king;

28 But there is a God in heaven that revealeth secrets, and maketh known to the king Nebuchadnezzar what shall be in the latter days. Thy dream, and the visions of thy head upon thy bed, are these;

29 As for thee, O king, thy thoughts came *into thy mind* upon thy bed, what should come to pass hereafter: and he that revealeth secrets maketh known to thee what shall come to pass.

30 But as for me, this secret is not revealed to me for *any* wisdom that I have more than any living, but for *their* sakes that shall make known the interpretation to the king, and that thou mightest know the thoughts of thy heart.

31 Thou, O king, sawest, and behold a great image. This great image, whose brightness *was* excellent, stood before thee; and the form thereof *was* terrible.

32 This image's head *was* of fine gold, his breast and his arms of silver, his belly and his thighs of brass,

33 His legs of iron, his feet part of iron and part of clay.

34 Thou sawest till that a stone was cut out without hands, which smote the image upon his feet *that were* of iron and clay, and brake them to pieces.

35 Then was the iron, the clay, the brass, the silver, and the gold, broken to pieces together, and became like the chaff of the summer threshingfloors; and the wind carried them away, that no place was found for them: and the stone that smote the image became a great mountain, and filled the whole earth.

36 This *is* the dream; and we will tell the interpretation thereof before the king.

37 Thou, O king, *art* a king of kings: for the God of heaven hath given thee a kingdom, power, and strength, and glory.

38 And wheresoever the children of men dwell, the beasts of the field and the fowls of the heaven hath he given into thine hand, and hath made thee ruler over them all. Thou *art* this head of gold.

39 And after thee shall arise another kingdom inferior to thee, and another third kingdom of brass, which shall bear rule over all the earth.

40 And the fourth kingdom shall be strong as iron: forasmuch as iron breaketh in pieces and subdueth all *things*: and as iron that breaketh all these, shall it break in pieces and bruise.

41 And whereas thou sawest the feet and toes, part of potters' clay, and part of iron, the kingdom shall be divided; but there shall be in it of the strength of the iron, forasmuch as thou sawest the iron mixed with miry clay.

42 And *as* the toes of the feet *were* part of iron, and part of clay, *so* the kingdom shall be partly strong, and partly broken.

43 And whereas thou sawest iron mixed with miry clay, they shall mingle themselves with the seed of men: but they shall not cleave one to another, even as iron is not mixed with clay.

44 And in the days of these kings shall the God of heaven set up a kingdom, which shall never be destroyed: and the kingdom shall not be left to other people, *but* it shall break in pieces and consume all these kingdoms, and it shall stand for ever.

45 Forasmuch as thou sawest that the stone was cut out of the mountain without hands, and that it brake in pieces the iron, the brass, the clay, the silver, and the gold; the great God hath made known to the king what shall come to pass hereafter: and the dream *is* certain, and the interpretation thereof sure.

46 Then the king Nebuchadnezzar fell upon his face, and worshipped Daniel, and commanded that they should offer an oblation and sweet odours unto him.

47 The king answered unto Daniel, and said, Of a truth *it is*, that your God *is* a God of gods, and a Lord of kings, and a revealer of secrets, seeing thou couldest reveal this secret.

48 Then the king made Daniel a great man, and gave him many great gifts, and made him ruler over the whole province of Babylon, and chief of the governors over all the wise *men* of Babylon.

49 Then Daniel requested of the king, and he set Shadrach, Meshach, and Abed-nego, over the affairs of the province of Babylon: but Daniel *sat* in the gate of the king.

3 Nebuchadnezzar the king made an image of gold, whose height *was* threescore cubits, *and* the breadth thereof six cubits: he set it up in the plain of Dura, in the province of Babylon.

2 Then Nebuchadnezzar the king sent to gather together the princes, the governors, and the captains, the judges, the treasurers, the counsellors, the sheriffs, and all the rulers of the provinces, to come to the dedication of the image which Nebuchadnezzar the king had set up.

3 Then the princes, the governors, and captains, the judges, the treasurers, the counsellors, the sheriffs, and all the rulers of the provinces, were gathered together unto the dedication of the image that Nebuchadnezzar the king had set up; and they stood before the image that Nebuchadnezzar had set up.

4 Then an herald cried aloud, To you it is commanded, O people, nations, and languages,

5 *That* at what time ye hear the sound of the cornet, flute, harp, sackbut, psaltery, dulcimer, and all kinds of musick, ye fall down and worship the golden image that Nebuchadnezzar the king hath set up:

6 And whoso falleth not down and worshippeth shall the same hour be cast into the midst of a burning fiery furnace.

7 Therefore at that time, when all the people heard the sound of the cornet, flute, harp, sackbut, psaltery, and all kinds of musick, all the people, the nations, and the languages, fell down *and* worshipped the golden image that Nebuchadnezzar the king had set up.

8 Wherefore at that time certain Chaldeans came near, and accused the Jews.

9 They spake and said to the king Nebuchadnezzar, O king, live for ever.

10 Thou, O king, hast made a decree, that every man that shall hear the sound of the cornet, flute, harp, sackbut, psaltery, and dulcimer, and all kinds of musick, shall fall down and worship the golden image:

11 And whoso falleth not down and worshippeth, *that* he should be cast into the midst of a burning fiery furnace.

12 There are certain Jews whom thou hast set over the affairs of the province of Babylon, Shadrach, Meshach, and Abed-nego; these men, O king, have not regarded thee: they serve not thy gods, nor worship the golden image which thou hast set up.

13 Then Nebuchadnezzar in *his* rage and fury commanded to bring Shadrach, Meshach, and Abed-nego. Then they brought these men before the king.

14 Nebuchadnezzar spake and said unto them, *Is it* true, O Shadrach, Meshach, and Abed-nego, do not ye serve my gods, nor worship the golden image which I have set up?

15 Now if ye be ready that at what time ye hear the sound of the cornet, flute, harp, sackbut, psaltery, and dulcimer, and all kinds of musick, ye fall down and worship the image which I have made; *well*: but if ye worship not, ye shall be cast the same hour into the midst of a burning fiery furnace; and who *is* that God that shall deliver you out of my hands?

16 Shadrach, Meshach, and Abed-nego, answered and said to the king, O Nebuchadnezzar, we *are* not careful to answer thee in this matter.

17 If it be *so*, our God whom we serve is able to deliver us from the burning fiery furnace, and he will deliver *us* out of thine hand, O king.

18 But if not, be it known unto thee, O king, that we will not serve thy gods, nor worship the golden image which thou hast set up.

19 Then was Nebuchadnezzar full of fury, and the form of his visage was changed against Shadrach, Meshach, and Abed-nego: *therefore* he spake, and commanded that they should heat the furnace one seven times more than it was wont to be heated.

20 And he commanded the most mighty men that *were* in his army to bind Shadrach, Meshach, and Abed-nego, *and* to cast *them* into the burning fiery furnace.

21 Then these men were bound in their coats, their hosen, and their hats, and their *other* garments, and were cast into the midst of the burning fiery furnace.

22 Therefore because the king's commandment was urgent, and the furnace exceeding hot, the flame of the fire slew those men that took up Shadrach, Meshach, and Abed-nego.

23 And these three men, Shadrach, Meshach, and Abed-nego, fell down bound into the midst of the burning fiery furnace.

24 Then Nebuchadnezzar the king was astonied, and rose up in haste, *and* spake, and said unto his counsellors, Did not we cast three men bound into the midst of the fire? They answered and said unto the king, True, O king.

25 He answered and said, Lo, I see four men loose, walking in the midst of the fire, and they have no hurt; and the form of the fourth is like the Son of God.

26 Then Nebuchadnezzar came near to the mouth of the burning fiery furnace, *and* spake, and said, Shadrach, Meshach, and Abed-nego, ye servants of the most high God, come forth, and come *hither*. Then Shadrach, Meshach, and Abed-nego, came forth of the midst of the fire.

27 And the princes, governors, and captains, and the king's counsellors, being gathered together, saw these men, upon whose bodies the fire had no power, nor was an hair of their head singed, neither were their coats changed, nor the smell of fire had passed on them.

28 *Then* Nebuchadnezzar spake, and said, Blessed *be* the God of Shadrach, Meshach, and Abed-nego, who hath sent his angel, and delivered his servants that trusted in him, and have changed the king's word, and yielded their bodies, that they might not serve nor worship any god, except their own God.

29 Therefore I make a decree, That every people, nation, and language, which speak any thing amiss against the God of Shadrach, Meshach, and Abed-nego, shall be cut in pieces, and their houses shall be made a dunghill: because there is no other God that can deliver after this sort.

30 Then the king promoted Shadrach, Meshach, and Abed-nego, in the province of Babylon.

4 Nebuchadnezzar the king, unto all people, nations, and languages, that dwell in all the earth; Peace be multiplied unto you.

2 I thought it good to shew the signs and wonders that the high God hath wrought toward me.

3 How great *are* his signs! and how
mighty *are* his wonders! his kingdom *is*
an everlasting kingdom, and his dominion *is* from generation to generation.
4 I Nebuchadnezzar was at rest in
mine house, and flourishing in my palace:
5 I saw a dream which made me
afraid, and the thoughts upon my bed
and the visions of my head troubled
me.
6 Therefore made I a decree to bring
in all the wise *men* of Babylon before
me, that they might make known unto
me the interpretation of the dream.
7 Then came in the magicians, the
astrologers, the Chaldeans, and the
soothsayers: and I told the dream
before them; but they did not make
known unto me the interpretation
thereof.
8 But at the last Daniel came in
before me, whose name *was* Belteshazzar, according to the name of my
god, and in whom *is* the spirit of the
holy gods: and before him I told the
dream, *saying*,
9 O Belteshazzar, master of the magicians, because I know that the spirit of
the holy gods *is* in thee, and no secret
troubleth thee, tell me the visions of
my dream that I have seen, and the
interpretation thereof.
10 Thus *were* the visions of mine head
in my bed; I saw, and behold a tree in
the midst of the earth, and the height
thereof *was* great.
11 The tree grew, and was strong, and
the height thereof reached unto heav-
en, and the sight thereof to the end of
all the earth:
12 The leaves thereof *were* fair, and
the fruit thereof much, and in it *was*
meat for all: the beasts of the field had
shadow under it, and the fowls of the
heaven dwelt in the boughs thereof,
and all flesh was fed of it.
13 I saw in the visions of my head
upon my bed, and, behold, a watcher
and an holy one came down from
heaven;
14 He cried aloud, and said thus, Hew
down the tree, and cut off his branches,
shake off his leaves, and scatter his
fruit: let the beasts get away from
under it, and the fowls from his branches:
15 Nevertheless leave the stump of
his roots in the earth, even with a band
of iron and brass, in the tender grass of
the field; and let it be wet with the dew
of heaven, and *let* his portion *be* with
the beasts in the grass of the earth:
16 Let his heart be changed from
man's, and let a beast's heart be given
unto him; and let seven times pass over
him.
17 This matter *is* by the decree of the
watchers, and the demand by the word
of the holy ones: to the intent that the
living may know that the most High
ruleth in the kingdom of men, and
giveth it to whomsoever he will, and
setteth up over it the basest of men.
18 This dream I king Nebuchadnezzar
have seen. Now thou, O Belteshazzar,
declare the interpretation thereof, forasmuch as all the wise *men* of my kingdom are not able to make known unto
me the interpretation: but thou *art*
able; for the spirit of the holy gods *is* in
thee.
19 Then Daniel, whose name *was*
Belteshazzar, was astonied for one hour,
and his thoughts troubled him. The
king spake, and said, Belteshazzar, let
not the dream, or the interpretation
thereof, trouble thee. Belteshazzar

answered and said, My lord, the dream *be* to them that hate thee, and the interpretation thereof to thine enemies.

20 The tree that thou sawest, which grew, and was strong, whose height reached unto the heaven, and the sight thereof to all the earth;

21 Whose leaves *were* fair, and the fruit thereof much, and in it *was* meat for all; under which the beasts of the field dwelt, and upon whose branches the fowls of the heaven had their habitation:

22 It *is* thou, O king, that art grown and become strong: for thy greatness is grown, and reacheth unto heaven, and thy dominion to the end of the earth.

23 And whereas the king saw a watcher and an holy one coming down from heaven, and saying, Hew the tree down, and destroy it; yet leave the stump of the roots thereof in the earth, even with a band of iron and brass, in the tender grass of the field; and let it be wet with the dew of heaven, and *let* his portion *be* with the beasts of the field, till seven times pass over him;

24 This *is* the interpretation, O king, and this *is* the decree of the most High, which is come upon my lord the king:

25 That they shall drive thee from men, and thy dwelling shall be with the beasts of the field, and they shall make thee to eat grass as oxen, and they shall wet thee with the dew of heaven, and seven times shall pass over thee, till thou know that the most High ruleth in the kingdom of men, and giveth it to whomsoever he will.

26 And whereas they commanded to leave the stump of the tree roots; thy kingdom shall be sure unto thee, after that thou shalt have known that the heavens do rule.

27 Wherefore, O king, let my counsel be acceptable unto thee, and break off thy sins by righteousness, and thine iniquities by shewing mercy to the poor; if it may be a lengthening of thy tranquillity.

28 All this came upon the king Nebuchadnezzar.

29 At the end of twelve months he walked in the palace of the kingdom of Babylon.

30 The king spake, and said, Is not this great Babylon, that I have built for the house of the kingdom by the might of my power, and for the honour of my majesty?

31 While the word *was* in the king's mouth, there fell a voice from heaven, *saying*, O king Nebuchadnezzar, to thee it is spoken; The kingdom is departed from thee.

32 And they shall drive thee from men, and thy dwelling *shall be* with the beasts of the field: they shall make thee to eat grass as oxen, and seven times shall pass over thee, until thou know that the most High ruleth in the kingdom of men, and giveth it to whomsoever he will.

33 The same hour was the thing fulfilled upon Nebuchadnezzar: and he was driven from men, and did eat grass as oxen, and his body was wet with the dew of heaven, till his hairs were grown like eagles' *feathers*, and his nails like birds' *claws*.

34 And at the end of the days I Nebuchadnezzar lifted up mine eyes unto heaven, and mine understanding returned unto me, and I blessed the most High, and I praised and honoured him that liveth for ever, whose dominion *is* an everlasting dominion, and his kingdom *is* from generation to generation:

35 And all the inhabitants of the earth *are* reputed as nothing: and he doeth according to his will in the army of heaven, and *among* the inhabitants of the earth: and none can stay his hand, or say unto him, What doest thou?

36 At the same time my reason returned unto me; and for the glory of my kingdom, mine honour and brightness returned unto me; and my counsellors and my lords sought unto me; and I was established in my kingdom, and excellent majesty was added unto me.

37 Now I Nebuchadnezzar praise and extol and honour the King of heaven, all whose works *are* truth, and his ways judgment: and those that walk in pride he is able to abase.

5 Belshazzar the king made a great feast to a thousand of his lords, and drank wine before the thousand.

2 Belshazzar, whiles he tasted the wine, commanded to bring the golden and silver vessels which his father Nebuchadnezzar had taken out of the temple which *was* in Jerusalem; that the king, and his princes, his wives, and his concubines, might drink therein.

3 Then they brought the golden vessels that were taken out of the temple of the house of God which *was* at Jerusalem; and the king, and his princes, his wives, and his concubines, drank in them.

4 They drank wine, and praised the gods of gold, and of silver, of brass, of iron, of wood, and of stone.

5 In the same hour came forth fingers of a man's hand, and wrote over against the candlestick upon the plaister of the wall of the king's palace: and the king saw the part of the hand that wrote.

6 Then the king's countenance was changed, and his thoughts troubled him, so that the joints of his loins were loosed, and his knees smote one against another.

7 The king cried aloud to bring in the astrologers, the Chaldeans, and the soothsayers. *And* the king spake, and said to the wise *men* of Babylon, Whosoever shall read this writing, and shew me the interpretation thereof, shall be clothed with scarlet, and *have* a chain of gold about his neck, and shall be the third ruler in the kingdom.

8 Then came in all the king's wise *men*: but they could not read the writing, nor make known to the king the interpretation thereof.

9 Then was king Belshazzar greatly troubled, and his countenance was changed in him, and his lords were astonied.

10 *Now* the queen, by reason of the words of the king and his lords, came into the banquet house: *and* the queen spake and said, O king, live for ever: let not thy thoughts trouble thee, nor let thy countenance be changed:

11 There is a man in thy kingdom, in whom *is* the spirit of the holy gods; and in the days of thy father light and understanding and wisdom, like the wisdom of the gods, was found in him; whom the king Nebuchadnezzar thy father, the king, *I say*, thy father, made master of the magicians, astrologers, Chaldeans, *and* soothsayers;

12 Forasmuch as an excellent spirit, and knowledge, and understanding, interpreting of dreams, and shewing of hard sentences, and dissolving of doubts, were found in the same Daniel,

whom the king named Belteshazzar:
now let Daniel be called, and he will
shew the interpretation.
13 Then was Daniel brought in before
the king. *And* the king spake and said
unto Daniel, *Art* thou that Daniel,
which *art* of the children of the captivity of Judah, whom the king my father
brought out of Jewry?
14 I have even heard of thee, that the
spirit of the gods *is* in thee, and *that*
light and understanding and excellent
wisdom is found in thee.
15 And now the wise *men*, the astrologers, have been brought in before me,
that they should read this writing, and
make known unto me the interpretation thereof: but they could not shew
the interpretation of the thing:
16 And I have heard of thee, that thou
canst make interpretations, and dis-
solve doubts: now if thou canst read the
writing, and make known to me the
interpretation thereof, thou shalt be
clothed with scarlet, and *have* a chain
of gold about thy neck, and shalt be the
third ruler in the kingdom.
17 Then Daniel answered and said
before the king, Let thy gifts be to thyself, and give thy rewards to another;
yet I will read the writing unto the king,
and make known to him the interpretation.
18 O thou king, the most high God
gave Nebuchadnezzar thy father a kingdom, and majesty, and glory, and honour:
19 And for the majesty that he gave
him, all people, nations, and languages,
trembled and feared before him: whom
he would he slew; and whom he would
he kept alive; and whom he would he
set up; and whom he would he put
down.
20 But when his heart was lifted up,
and his mind hardened in pride, he was
deposed from his kingly throne, and
they took his glory from him:
21 And he was driven from the sons of
men; and his heart was made like the
beasts, and his dwelling *was* with the
wild asses: they fed him with grass like
oxen, and his body was wet with the
dew of heaven; till he knew that the
most high God ruled in the kingdom of
men, and *that* he appointeth over it
whomsoever he will.
22 And thou his son, O Belshazzar,
hast not humbled thine heart, though
thou knewest all this;
23 But hast lifted up thyself against
the Lord of heaven; and they have
brought the vessels of his house before
thee, and thou, and thy lords, thy wives,
and thy concubines, have drunk wine
in them; and thou hast praised the gods
of silver, and gold, of brass, iron, wood,
and stone, which see not, nor hear, nor
know: and the God in whose hand thy
breath *is*, and whose *are* all thy ways,
hast thou not glorified:
24 Then was the part of the hand sent
from him; and this writing was written.
25 And this *is* the writing that was
written, MENE, MENE, TEKEL,
UPHARSIN.
26 This *is* the interpretation of the
thing: MENE; God hath numbered thy
kingdom, and finished it.
27 TEKEL; Thou art weighed in the
balances, and art found wanting.
28 PERES; Thy kingdom is divided,
and given to the Medes and Persians.
29 Then commanded Belshazzar, and
they clothed Daniel with scarlet, and
put a chain of gold about his neck, and
made a proclamation concerning him,

that he should be the third ruler in the
kingdom.
30 In that night was Belshazzar the
king of the Chaldeans slain.
31 And Darius the Median took the
kingdom, *being* about threescore and
two years old.

6 It pleased Darius to set over the
kingdom an hundred and twenty
princes, which should be over the
whole kingdom;
2 And over these three presidents; of
whom Daniel *was* first: that the princes
might give accounts unto them, and the
king should have no damage.
3 Then this Daniel was preferred
above the presidents and princes, because an excellent spirit *was* in him;
and the king thought to set him over
the whole realm.
4 Then the presidents and princes
sought to find occasion against Daniel
concerning the kingdom; but they
could find none occasion nor fault; forasmuch as he *was* faithful, neither was
there any error or fault found in him.
5 Then said these men, We shall not
find any occasion against this Daniel,
except we find *it* against him concerning the law of his God.
6 Then these presidents and princes
assembled together to the king, and
said thus unto him, King Darius, live for
ever.
7 All the presidents of the kingdom,
the governors, and the princes, the
counsellors, and the captains, have
consulted together to establish a royal
statute, and to make a firm decree, that
whosoever shall ask a petition of any
God or man for thirty days, save of thee,
O king, he shall be cast into the den of
lions.
8 Now, O king, establish the decree,
and sign the writing, that it be not
changed, according to the law of the
Medes and Persians, which altereth
not.
9 Wherefore king Darius signed the
writing and the decree.
10 Now when Daniel knew that the
writing was signed, he went into his
house; and his windows being open in
his chamber toward Jerusalem, he
kneeled upon his knees three times a
day, and prayed, and gave thanks
before his God, as he did aforetime.
11 Then these men assembled, and
found Daniel praying and making supplication before his God.
12 Then they came near, and spake
before the king concerning the king's
decree; Hast thou not signed a decree,
that every man that shall ask *a petition*
of any God or man within thirty days,
save of thee, O king, shall be cast into
the den of lions? The king answered
and said, The thing *is* true, according to
the law of the Medes and Persians,
which altereth not.
13 Then answered they and said
before the king, That Daniel, which *is* of
the children of the captivity of Judah,
regardeth not thee, O king, nor the
decree that thou hast signed, but
maketh his petition three times a day.
14 Then the king, when he heard
these words, was sore displeased with
himself, and set *his* heart on Daniel to
deliver him: and he laboured till the
going down of the sun to deliver him.
15 Then these men assembled unto
the king, and said unto the king, Know,
O king, that the law of the Medes and
Persians *is*, That no decree nor statute
which the king establisheth may be
changed.

16 Then the king commanded, and they brought Daniel, and cast *him* into the den of lions. *Now* the king spake and said unto Daniel, Thy God whom thou servest continually, he will deliver thee.

17 And a stone was brought, and laid upon the mouth of the den; and the king sealed it with his own signet, and with the signet of his lords; that the purpose might not be changed concerning Daniel.

18 Then the king went to his palace, and passed the night fasting: neither were instruments of musick brought before him: and his sleep went from him.

19 Then the king arose very early in the morning, and went in haste unto the den of lions.

20 And when he came to the den, he cried with a lamentable voice unto Daniel: *and* the king spake and said to Daniel, O Daniel, servant of the living God, is thy God, whom thou servest continually, able to deliver thee from the lions?

21 Then said Daniel unto the king, O king, live for ever.

22 My God hath sent his angel, and hath shut the lions' mouths, that they have not hurt me: forasmuch as before him innocency was found in me; and also before thee, O king, have I done no hurt.

23 Then was the king exceeding glad for him, and commanded that they should take Daniel up out of the den. So Daniel was taken up out of the den, and no manner of hurt was found upon him, because he believed in his God.

24 And the king commanded, and they brought those men which had accused Daniel, and they cast *them* into the den of lions, them, their children, and their wives; and the lions had the mastery of them, and brake all their bones in pieces or ever they came at the bottom of the den.

25 Then king Darius wrote unto all people, nations, and languages, that dwell in all the earth; Peace be multiplied unto you.

26 I make a decree, That in every dominion of my kingdom men tremble and fear before the God of Daniel: for he *is* the living God, and stedfast for ever, and his kingdom *that* which shall not be destroyed, and his dominion *shall be even* unto the end.

27 He delivereth and rescueth, and he worketh signs and wonders in heaven and in earth, who hath delivered Daniel from the power of the lions.

28 So this Daniel prospered in the reign of Darius, and in the reign of Cyrus the Persian.

7 In the first year of Belshazzar king of Babylon Daniel had a dream and visions of his head upon his bed: then he wrote the dream, *and* told the sum of the matters.

2 Daniel spake and said, I saw in my vision by night, and, behold, the four winds of the heaven strove upon the great sea.

3 And four great beasts came up from the sea, diverse one from another.

4 The first *was* like a lion, and had eagle's wings: I beheld till the wings thereof were plucked, and it was lifted up from the earth, and made stand upon the feet as a man, and a man's heart was given to it.

5 And behold another beast, a second, like to a bear, and it raised up itself on one side, and *it had* three ribs in the mouth of it between the teeth of

it: and they said thus unto it, Arise,
devour much flesh.
6 After this I beheld, and lo another,
like a leopard, which had upon the
back of it four wings of a fowl; the beast
had also four heads; and dominion was
given to it.
7 After this I saw in the night visions,
and behold a fourth beast, dreadful
and terrible, and strong exceedingly;
and it had great iron teeth: it devoured
and brake in pieces, and stamped the
residue with the feet of it: and it *was*
diverse from all the beasts that *were*
before it; and it had ten horns.
8 I considered the horns, and, behold,
there came up among them another
little horn, before whom there were
three of the first horns plucked up by
the roots: and, behold, in this horn *were*
eyes like the eyes of man, and a mouth
speaking great things.
9 I beheld till the thrones were cast
down, and the Ancient of days did sit,
whose garment *was* white as snow, and
the hair of his head like the pure wool:
his throne *was like* the fiery flame, *and*
his wheels *as* burning fire.
10 A fiery stream issued and came
forth from before him: thousand thousands ministered unto him, and ten
thousand times ten thousand stood
before him: the judgment was set, and
the books were opened.
11 I beheld then because of the voice
of the great words which the horn
spake: I beheld *even* till the beast was
slain, and his body destroyed, and given
to the burning flame.
12 As concerning the rest of the
beasts, they had their dominion taken
away: yet their lives were prolonged for
a season and time.
13 I saw in the night visions, and,
behold, *one* like the Son of man came
with the clouds of heaven, and came to
the Ancient of days, and they brought
him near before him.
14 And there was given him dominion, and glory, and a kingdom, that all
people, nations, and languages, should
serve him: his dominion *is* an everlasting dominion, which shall not pass
away, and his kingdom *that* which shall
not be destroyed.
15 I Daniel was grieved in my spirit in
the midst of *my* body, and the visions of
my head troubled me.
16 I came near unto one of them that
stood by, and asked him the truth of all
this. So he told me, and made me know
the interpretation of the things.
17 These great beasts, which are four,
are four kings, *which* shall arise out of
the earth.
18 But the saints of the most High
shall take the kingdom, and possess the
kingdom for ever, even for ever and
ever.
19 Then I would know the truth of the
fourth beast, which was diverse from all
the others, exceeding dreadful, whose
teeth *were of* iron, and his nails *of*
brass; *which* devoured, brake in pieces,
and stamped the residue with his feet;
20 And of the ten horns that *were* in
his head, and *of* the other which came
up, and before whom three fell; even *of*
that horn that had eyes, and a mouth
that spake very great things, whose
look *was* more stout than his fellows.
21 I beheld, and the same horn made
war with the saints, and prevailed
against them;

22 Until the Ancient of days came,
and judgment was given to the saints of
the most High; and the time came that
the saints possessed the kingdom.
23 Thus he said, The fourth beast
shall be the fourth kingdom upon
earth, which shall be diverse from all
kingdoms, and shall devour the whole
earth, and shall tread it down, and
break it in pieces.
24 And the ten horns out of this kingdom *are* ten kings *that* shall arise: and
another shall rise after them; and he
shall be diverse from the first, and he
shall subdue three kings.
25 And he shall speak *great* words
against the most High, and shall wear
out the saints of the most High, and
think to change times and laws: and
they shall be given into his hand until a
time and times and the dividing of
time.
26 But the judgment shall sit, and
they shall take away his dominion, to
consume and to destroy *it* unto the end.
27 And the kingdom and dominion,
and the greatness of the kingdom
under the whole heaven, shall be given
to the people of the saints of the most
High, whose kingdom *is* an everlasting
kingdom, and all dominions shall serve
and obey him.
28 Hitherto *is* the end of the matter.
As for me Daniel, my cogitations much
troubled me, and my countenance
changed in me: but I kept the matter in
my heart.

8 In the third year of the reign of king
Belshazzar a vision appeared unto
me, *even unto* me Daniel, after that
which appeared unto me at the first.
2 And I saw in a vision; and it came to
pass, when I saw, that I *was* at Shushan
in the palace, which *is* in the province
of Elam; and I saw in a vision, and I was
by the river of Ulai.
3 Then I lifted up mine eyes, and saw,
and, behold, there stood before the
river a ram which had *two* horns: and
the *two* horns *were* high; but one *was*
higher than the other, and the higher
came up last.
4 I saw the ram pushing westward,
and northward, and southward; so that
no beasts might stand before him, neither *was there any* that could deliver
out of his hand; but he did according to
his will, and became great.
5 And as I was considering, behold, an
he goat came from the west on the face
of the whole earth, and touched not the
ground: and the goat *had* a notable
horn between his eyes.
6 And he came to the ram that had
two horns, which I had seen standing
before the river, and ran unto him in
the fury of his power.
7 And I saw him come close unto the
ram, and he was moved with choler
against him, and smote the ram, and
brake his two horns: and there was no
power in the ram to stand before him,
but he cast him down to the ground,
and stamped upon him: and there was
none that could deliver the ram out of
his hand.
8 Therefore the he goat waxed very
great: and when he was strong, the
great horn was broken; and for it came
up four notable ones toward the four
winds of heaven.
9 And out of one of them came forth
a little horn, which waxed exceeding
great, toward the south, and toward the
east, and toward the pleasant *land*.
10 And it waxed great, *even* to the
host of heaven; and it cast down *some*

of the host and of the stars to the ground, and stamped upon them.

11 Yea, he magnified *himself* even to the prince of the host, and by him the daily *sacrifice* was taken away, and the place of his sanctuary was cast down.

12 And an host was given *him* against the daily *sacrifice* by reason of transgression, and it cast down the truth to the ground; and it practised, and prospered.

13 Then I heard one saint speaking, and another saint said unto that certain *saint* which spake, How long *shall be* the vision *concerning* the daily *sacrifice*, and the transgression of desolation, to give both the sanctuary and the host to be trodden under foot?

14 And he said unto me, Unto two thousand and three hundred days; then shall the sanctuary be cleansed.

15 And it came to pass, when I, *even* I Daniel, had seen the vision, and sought for the meaning, then, behold, there stood before me as the appearance of a man.

16 And I heard a man's voice between *the banks of* Ulai, which called, and said, Gabriel, make this *man* to understand the vision.

17 So he came near where I stood: and when he came, I was afraid, and fell upon my face: but he said unto me, Understand, O son of man: for at the time of the end *shall be* the vision.

18 Now as he was speaking with me, I was in a deep sleep on my face toward the ground: but he touched me, and set me upright.

19 And he said, Behold, I will make thee know what shall be in the last end of the indignation: for at the time appointed the end *shall be.*

20 The ram which thou sawest having *two* horns *are* the kings of Media and Persia.

21 And the rough goat *is* the king of Grecia: and the great horn that *is* between his eyes *is* the first king.

22 Now that being broken, whereas four stood up for it, four kingdoms shall stand up out of the nation, but not in his power.

23 And in the latter time of their kingdom, when the transgressors are come to the full, a king of fierce countenance, and understanding dark sentences, shall stand up.

24 And his power shall be mighty, but not by his own power: and he shall destroy wonderfully, and shall prosper, and practise, and shall destroy the mighty and the holy people.

25 And through his policy also he shall cause craft to prosper in his hand; and he shall magnify *himself* in his heart, and by peace shall destroy many: he shall also stand up against the Prince of princes; but he shall be broken without hand.

26 And the vision of the evening and the morning which was told *is* true: wherefore shut thou up the vision; for it *shall be* for many days.

27 And I Daniel fainted, and was sick *certain* days; afterward I rose up, and did the king's business; and I was astonished at the vision, but none understood *it*.

9 In the first year of Darius the son of Ahasuerus, of the seed of the Medes, which was made king over the realm of the Chaldeans;

2 In the first year of his reign I Daniel understood by books the number of the years, whereof the word of the LORD came to Jeremiah the prophet, that he would accomplish seventy years in the desolations of Jerusalem.

3 And I set my face unto the Lord God, to seek by prayer and supplications, with fasting, and sackcloth, and ashes:

4 And I prayed unto the LORD my God, and made my confession, and said, O Lord, the great and dreadful God, keeping the covenant and mercy to them that love him, and to them that keep his commandments;

5 We have sinned, and have committed iniquity, and have done wickedly, and have rebelled, even by departing from thy precepts and from thy judgments:

6 Neither have we hearkened unto thy servants the prophets, which spake in thy name to our kings, our princes, and our fathers, and to all the people of the land.

7 O Lord, righteousness *belongeth* unto thee, but unto us confusion of faces, as at this day; to the men of Judah, and to the inhabitants of Jerusalem, and unto all Israel, *that are* near, and *that are* far off, through all the countries whither thou hast driven them, because of their trespass that they have trespassed against thee.

8 O Lord, to us *belongeth* confusion of face, to our kings, to our princes, and to our fathers, because we have sinned against thee.

9 To the Lord our God *belong* mercies and forgivenesses, though we have rebelled against him;

10 Neither have we obeyed the voice of the LORD our God, to walk in his laws, which he set before us by his servants the prophets.

11 Yea, all Israel have transgressed thy law, even by departing, that they might not obey thy voice; therefore the curse is poured upon us, and the oath that *is* written in the law of Moses the servant of God, because we have sinned against him.

12 And he hath confirmed his words, which he spake against us, and against our judges that judged us, by bringing upon us a great evil: for under the whole heaven hath not been done as hath been done upon Jerusalem.

13 As *it is* written in the law of Moses, all this evil is come upon us: yet made we not our prayer before the LORD our God, that we might turn from our iniquities, and understand thy truth.

14 Therefore hath the LORD watched upon the evil, and brought it upon us: for the LORD our God *is* righteous in all his works which he doeth: for we obeyed not his voice.

15 And now, O Lord our God, that hast brought thy people forth out of the land of Egypt with a mighty hand, and hast gotten thee renown, as at this day; we have sinned, we have done wickedly.

16 O Lord, according to all thy righteousness, I beseech thee, let thine anger and thy fury be turned away from thy city Jerusalem, thy holy mountain: because for our sins, and for the iniquities of our fathers, Jerusalem and thy people *are become* a reproach to all *that are* about us.

17 Now therefore, O our God, hear the prayer of thy servant, and his supplications, and cause thy face to shine upon thy sanctuary that is desolate, for the Lord's sake.

18 O my God, incline thine ear, and hear; open thine eyes, and behold our desolations, and the city which is called by thy name: for we do not present our

supplications before thee for our righteousnesses, but for thy great mercies.
19 O Lord, hear; O Lord, forgive; O
Lord, hearken and do; defer not, for
thine own sake, O my God: for thy city
and thy people are called by thy name.
20 And whiles I *was* speaking, and
praying, and confessing my sin and the
sin of my people Israel, and presenting
my supplication before the LORD my
God for the holy mountain of my God;
21 Yea, whiles I *was* speaking in
prayer, even the man Gabriel, whom I
had seen in the vision at the beginning,
being caused to fly swiftly, touched me
about the time of the evening oblation.
22 And he informed *me*, and talked
with me, and said, O Daniel, I am now
come forth to give thee skill and understanding.
23 At the beginning of thy supplications the commandment came forth,
and I am come to shew *thee*; for thou
art greatly beloved: therefore understand the matter, and consider the
vision.
24 Seventy weeks are determined
upon thy people and upon thy holy city,
to finish the transgression, and to make
an end of sins, and to make reconciliation for iniquity, and to bring in everlasting righteousness, and to seal up
the vision and prophecy, and to anoint
the most Holy.
25 Know therefore and understand,
that from the going forth of the commandment to restore and to build
Jerusalem unto the Messiah the Prince
shall be seven weeks, and threescore
and two weeks: the street shall be built
again, and the wall, even in troublous
times.
26 And after threescore and two
weeks shall Messiah be cut off, but not
for himself: and the people of the
prince that shall come shall destroy the
city and the sanctuary; and the end
thereof *shall be* with a flood, and unto
the end of the war desolations are
determined.
27 And he shall confirm the covenant
with many for one week: and in the
midst of the week he shall cause the
sacrifice and the oblation to cease, and
for the overspreading of abominations
he shall make *it* desolate, even until
the consummation, and that determined shall be poured upon the desolate.

10 In the third year of Cyrus king of
Persia a thing was revealed unto
Daniel, whose name was called Belteshazzar; and the thing *was* true, but the
time appointed *was* long: and he understood the thing, and had understanding
of the vision.
2 In those days I Daniel was mourning
three full weeks.
3 I ate no pleasant bread, neither
came flesh nor wine in my mouth, neither did I anoint myself at all, till three
whole weeks were fulfilled.
4 And in the four and twentieth day
of the first month, as I was by the side
of the great river, which *is* Hiddekel;
5 Then I lifted up mine eyes, and
looked, and behold a certain man
clothed in linen, whose loins *were* girded with fine gold of Uphaz:
6 His body also *was* like the beryl,
and his face as the appearance of lightning, and his eyes as lamps of fire, and
his arms and his feet like in colour to
polished brass, and the voice of his
words like the voice of a multitude.
7 And I Daniel alone saw the vision:
for the men that were with me saw not
the vision; but a great quaking fell

upon them, so that they fled to hide themselves.

8 Therefore I was left alone, and saw this great vision, and there remained no strength in me: for my comeliness was turned in me into corruption, and I retained no strength.

9 Yet heard I the voice of his words: and when I heard the voice of his words, then was I in a deep sleep on my face, and my face toward the ground.

10 And, behold, an hand touched me, which set me upon my knees and *upon* the palms of my hands.

11 And he said unto me, O Daniel, a man greatly beloved, understand the words that I speak unto thee, and stand upright: for unto thee am I now sent. And when he had spoken this word unto me, I stood trembling.

12 Then said he unto me, Fear not, Daniel: for from the first day that thou didst set thine heart to understand, and to chasten thyself before thy God, thy words were heard, and I am come for thy words.

13 But the prince of the kingdom of Persia withstood me one and twenty days: but, lo, Michael, one of the chief princes, came to help me; and I remained there with the kings of Persia.

14 Now I am come to make thee understand what shall befall thy people in the latter days: for yet the vision *is* for *many* days.

15 And when he had spoken such words unto me, I set my face toward the ground, and I became dumb.

16 And, behold, *one* like the similitude of the sons of men touched my lips: then I opened my mouth, and spake, and said unto him that stood before me, O my lord, by the vision my sorrows are turned upon me, and I have retained no strength.

17 For how can the servant of this my lord talk with this my lord? for as for me, straightway there remained no strength in me, neither is there breath left in me.

18 Then there came again and touched me *one* like the appearance of a man, and he strengthened me,

19 And said, O man greatly beloved, fear not: peace *be* unto thee, be strong, yea, be strong. And when he had spoken unto me, I was strengthened, and said, Let my lord speak; for thou hast strengthened me.

20 Then said he, Knowest thou wherefore I come unto thee? and now will I return to fight with the prince of Persia: and when I am gone forth, lo, the prince of Grecia shall come.

21 But I will shew thee that which is noted in the scripture of truth: and *there is* none that holdeth with me in these things, but Michael your prince.

11 Also I in the first year of Darius the Mede, *even* I, stood to confirm and to strengthen him.

2 And now will I shew thee the truth. Behold, there shall stand up yet three kings in Persia; and the fourth shall be far richer than *they* all: and by his strength through his riches he shall stir up all against the realm of Grecia.

3 And a mighty king shall stand up, that shall rule with great dominion, and do according to his will.

4 And when he shall stand up, his kingdom shall be broken, and shall be divided toward the four winds of heaven; and not to his posterity, nor according to his dominion which he ruled: for his kingdom shall be plucked up, even for others beside those.

5 And the king of the south shall be
strong, and *one* of his princes; and he
shall be strong above him, and have
dominion; his dominion *shall be* a great
dominion.
6 And in the end of years they shall
join themselves together; for the king's
daughter of the south shall come to the
king of the north to make an agreement: but she shall not retain the
power of the arm; neither shall he
stand, nor his arm: but she shall be
given up, and they that brought her,
and he that begat her, and he that
strengthened her in *these* times.
7 But out of a branch of her roots shall
one stand up in his estate, which shall
come with an army, and shall enter into
the fortress of the king of the north,
and shall deal against them, and shall
prevail:
8 And shall also carry captives into
Egypt their gods, with their princes,
and with their precious vessels of silver
and of gold; and he shall continue *more*
years than the king of the north.
9 So the king of the south shall come
into *his* kingdom, and shall return into
his own land.
10 But his sons shall be stirred up,
and shall assemble a multitude of great
forces: and *one* shall certainly come,
and overflow, and pass through: then
shall he return, and be stirred up, *even*
to his fortress.
11 And the king of the south shall be
moved with choler, and shall come
forth and fight with him, *even* with the
king of the north: and he shall set forth
a great multitude; but the multitude
shall be given into his hand.
12 *And* when he hath taken away the
multitude, his heart shall be lifted up;
and he shall cast down *many* ten thousands: but he shall not be strengthened
by it.
13 For the king of the north shall
return, and shall set forth a multitude
greater than the former, and shall certainly come after certain years with a
great army and with much riches.
14 And in those times there shall
many stand up against the king of the
south: also the robbers of thy people
shall exalt themselves to establish the
vision; but they shall fall.
15 So the king of the north shall
come, and cast up a mount, and take
the most fenced cities: and the arms of
the south shall not withstand, neither
his chosen people, neither *shall there
be any* strength to withstand.
16 But he that cometh against him
shall do according to his own will, and
none shall stand before him: and he
shall stand in the glorious land, which
by his hand shall be consumed.
17 He shall also set his face to enter
with the strength of his whole kingdom,
and upright ones with him; thus shall
he do: and he shall give him the daughter of women, corrupting her: but she
shall not stand *on his side*, neither be
for him.
18 After this shall he turn his face
unto the isles, and shall take many: but
a prince for his own behalf shall cause
the reproach offered by him to cease;
without his own reproach he shall
cause *it* to turn upon him.
19 Then he shall turn his face toward
the fort of his own land: but he shall
stumble and fall, and not be found.
20 Then shall stand up in his estate a
raiser of taxes *in* the glory of the
kingdom: but within few days he shall
be destroyed, neither in anger, nor in
battle.

21 And in his estate shall stand up a vile person, to whom they shall not give the honour of the kingdom: but he shall come in peaceably, and obtain the kingdom by flatteries.

22 And with the arms of a flood shall they be overflown from before him, and shall be broken; yea, also the prince of the covenant.

23 And after the league *made* with him he shall work deceitfully: for he shall come up, and shall become strong with a small people.

24 He shall enter peaceably even upon the fattest places of the province; and he shall do *that* which his fathers have not done, nor his fathers' fathers; he shall scatter among them the prey, and spoil, and riches: *yea*, and he shall forecast his devices against the strong holds, even for a time.

25 And he shall stir up his power and his courage against the king of the south with a great army; and the king of the south shall be stirred up to battle with a very great and mighty army; but he shall not stand: for they shall forecast devices against him.

26 Yea, they that feed of the portion of his meat shall destroy him, and his army shall overflow: and many shall fall down slain.

27 And both these kings' hearts *shall be* to do mischief, and they shall speak lies at one table; but it shall not prosper: for yet the end *shall be* at the time appointed.

28 Then shall he return into his land with great riches; and his heart *shall be* against the holy covenant; and he shall do *exploits*, and return to his own land.

29 At the time appointed he shall return, and come toward the south; but it shall not be as the former, or as the latter.

30 For the ships of Chittim shall come against him: therefore he shall be grieved, and return, and have indignation against the holy covenant: so shall he do; he shall even return, and have intelligence with them that forsake the holy covenant.

31 And arms shall stand on his part, and they shall pollute the sanctuary of strength, and shall take away the daily *sacrifice*, and they shall place the abomination that maketh desolate.

32 And such as do wickedly against the covenant shall he corrupt by flatteries: but the people that do know their God shall be strong, and do *exploits*.

33 And they that understand among the people shall instruct many: yet they shall fall by the sword, and by flame, by captivity, and by spoil, *many* days.

34 Now when they shall fall, they shall be holpen with a little help: but many shall cleave to them with flatteries.

35 And *some* of them of understanding shall fall, to try them, and to purge, and to make *them* white, *even* to the time of the end: because *it is* yet for a time appointed.

36 And the king shall do according to his will; and he shall exalt himself, and magnify himself above every god, and shall speak marvellous things against the God of gods, and shall prosper till the indignation be accomplished: for that that is determined shall be done.

37 Neither shall he regard the God of his fathers, nor the desire of women, nor regard any god: for he shall magnify himself above all.

38 But in his estate shall he honour the God of forces: and a god whom his fathers knew not shall he honour with gold, and silver, and with precious stones, and pleasant things.

39 Thus shall he do in the most strong holds with a strange god, whom he shall acknowledge *and* increase with glory: and he shall cause them to rule over many, and shall divide the land for gain.

40 And at the time of the end shall the king of the south push at him: and the king of the north shall come against him like a whirlwind, with chariots, and with horsemen, and with many ships; and he shall enter into the countries, and shall overflow and pass over.

41 He shall enter also into the glorious land, and many *countries* shall be overthrown: but these shall escape out of his hand, *even* Edom, and Moab, and the chief of the children of Ammon.

42 He shall stretch forth his hand also upon the countries: and the land of Egypt shall not escape.

43 But he shall have power over the treasures of gold and of silver, and over all the precious things of Egypt: and the Libyans and the Ethiopians *shall be* at his steps.

44 But tidings out of the east and out of the north shall trouble him: therefore he shall go forth with great fury to destroy, and utterly to make away many.

45 And he shall plant the tabernacles of his palace between the seas in the glorious holy mountain; yet he shall come to his end, and none shall help him.

12 And at that time shall Michael stand up, the great prince which standeth for the children of thy people: and there shall be a time of trouble, such as never was since there was a nation *even* to that same time: and at that time thy people shall be delivered, every one that shall be found written in the book.

2 And many of them that sleep in the dust of the earth shall awake, some to everlasting life, and some to shame *and* everlasting contempt.

3 And they that be wise shall shine as the brightness of the firmament; and they that turn many to righteousness as the stars for ever and ever.

4 But thou, O Daniel, shut up the words, and seal the book, *even* to the time of the end: many shall run to and fro, and knowledge shall be increased.

5 Then I Daniel looked, and, behold, there stood other two, the one on this side of the bank of the river, and the other on that side of the bank of the river.

6 And *one* said to the man clothed in linen, which *was* upon the waters of the river, How long *shall it be to* the end of these wonders?

7 And I heard the man clothed in linen, which *was* upon the waters of the river, when he held up his right hand and his left hand unto heaven, and sware by him that liveth for ever that *it shall be* for a time, times, and an half; and when he shall have accomplished to scatter the power of the holy people, all these *things* shall be finished.

8 And I heard, but I understood not: then said I, O my Lord, what *shall be* the end of these *things*?

9 And he said, Go thy way, Daniel: for
the words *are* closed up and sealed till
the time of the end.
10 Many shall be purified, and made
white, and tried; but the wicked shall
do wickedly: and none of the wicked
shall understand; but the wise shall
understand.
11 And from the time *that* the daily
sacrifice shall be taken away, and the
abomination that maketh desolate set
up, *there shall be* a thousand two hundred and ninety days.
12 Blessed *is* he that waiteth, and
cometh to the thousand three hundred
and five and thirty days.
13 But go thou thy way till the end *be*:
for thou shalt rest, and stand in thy lot
at the end of the days.

THE BOOK OF HOSEA

1 The word of the LORD that came
unto Hosea, the son of Beeri, in the
days of Uzziah, Jotham, Ahaz, *and*
Hezekiah, kings of Judah, and in the
days of Jeroboam the son of Joash, king
of Israel.
2 The beginning of the word of the
LORD by Hosea. And the LORD said to
Hosea, Go, take unto thee a wife of
whoredoms and children of whoredoms: for the land hath committed
great whoredom, *departing* from the
LORD.
3 So he went and took Gomer the
daughter of Diblaim; which conceived,
and bare him a son.
4 And the LORD said unto him, Call
his name Jezreel; for yet a little *while*,
and I will avenge the blood of Jezreel
upon the house of Jehu, and will cause
to cease the kingdom of the house of
Israel.
5 And it shall come to pass at that day,
that I will break the bow of Israel in the
valley of Jezreel.
6 And she conceived again, and bare
a daughter. And *God* said unto him,
Call her name Lo-ruhamah: for I will no
more have mercy upon the house of
Israel; but I will utterly take them away.
7 But I will have mercy upon the
house of Judah, and will save them by
the LORD their God, and will not save
them by bow, nor by sword, nor by battle, by horses, nor by horsemen.
8 Now when she had weaned Lo-
ruhamah, she conceived, and bare a
son.
9 Then said *God*, Call his name Lo-
ammi: for ye *are* not my people, and I
will not be your *God*.
10 Yet the number of the children of
Israel shall be as the sand of the sea,
which cannot be measured nor numbered; and it shall come to pass, *that* in
the place where it was said unto them,
Ye *are* not my people, *there* it shall be
said unto them, *Ye are* the sons of the
living God.
11 Then shall the children of Judah
and the children of Israel be gathered

together, and appoint themselves one head, and they shall come up out of the land: for great *shall be* the day of Jezreel.

2 Say ye unto your brethren, Ammi; and to your sisters, Ruhamah.

2 Plead with your mother, plead: for she *is* not my wife, neither *am* I her husband: let her therefore put away her whoredoms out of her sight, and her adulteries from between her breasts;

3 Lest I strip her naked, and set her as in the day that she was born, and make her as a wilderness, and set her like a dry land, and slay her with thirst.

4 And I will not have mercy upon her children; for they *be* the children of whoredoms.

5 For their mother hath played the harlot: she that conceived them hath done shamefully: for she said, I will go after my lovers, that give *me* my bread and my water, my wool and my flax, mine oil and my drink.

6 Therefore, behold, I will hedge up thy way with thorns, and make a wall, that she shall not find her paths.

7 And she shall follow after her lovers, but she shall not overtake them; and she shall seek them, but shall not find *them*: then shall she say, I will go and return to my first husband; for then *was it* better with me than now.

8 For she did not know that I gave her corn, and wine, and oil, and multiplied her silver and gold, *which* they prepared for Baal.

9 Therefore will I return, and take away my corn in the time thereof, and my wine in the season thereof, and will recover my wool and my flax *given* to cover her nakedness.

10 And now will I discover her lewdness in the sight of her lovers, and none shall deliver her out of mine hand.

11 I will also cause all her mirth to cease, her feast days, her new moons, and her sabbaths, and all her solemn feasts.

12 And I will destroy her vines and her fig trees, whereof she hath said, These *are* my rewards that my lovers have given me: and I will make them a forest, and the beasts of the field shall eat them.

13 And I will visit upon her the days of Baalim, wherein she burned incense to them, and she decked herself with her earrings and her jewels, and she went after her lovers, and forgat me, saith the LORD.

14 Therefore, behold, I will allure her, and bring her into the wilderness, and speak comfortably unto her.

15 And I will give her her vineyards from thence, and the valley of Achor for a door of hope: and she shall sing there, as in the days of her youth, and as in the day when she came up out of the land of Egypt.

16 And it shall be at that day, saith the LORD, *that* thou shalt call me Ishi; and shalt call me no more Baali.

17 For I will take away the names of Baalim out of her mouth, and they shall no more be remembered by their name.

18 And in that day will I make a covenant for them with the beasts of the field, and with the fowls of heaven, and *with* the creeping things of the ground: and I will break the bow and the sword and the battle out of the earth, and will make them to lie down safely.

19 And I will betroth thee unto me for
ever; yea, I will betroth thee unto me in
righteousness, and in judgment, and in
lovingkindness, and in mercies.
20 I will even betroth thee unto me in
faithfulness: and thou shalt know the
LORD.
21 And it shall come to pass in that
day, I will hear, saith the LORD, I will
hear the heavens, and they shall hear
the earth;
22 And the earth shall hear the corn,
and the wine, and the oil; and they shall
hear Jezreel.
23 And I will sow her unto me in the
earth; and I will have mercy upon her
that had not obtained mercy; and I will
say to *them which were* not my people,
Thou *art* my people; and they shall say,
Thou art my God.

3 Then said the LORD unto me, Go yet,
love a woman beloved of *her* friend,
yet an adulteress, according to the love
of the LORD toward the children of
Israel, who look to other gods, and love
flagons of wine.
2 So I bought her to me for fifteen
pieces of silver, and *for* an homer of
barley, and an half homer of barley:
3 And I said unto her, Thou shalt
abide for me many days; thou shalt not
play the harlot, and thou shalt not be
for *another* man: so *will* I also *be* for
thee.
4 For the children of Israel shall abide
many days without a king, and without
a prince, and without a sacrifice, and
without an image, and without an
ephod, and *without* teraphim:
5 Afterward shall the children of
Israel return, and seek the LORD their
God, and David their king; and shall
fear the LORD and his goodness in the
latter days.

4 Hear the word of the LORD, ye
children of Israel: for the LORD hath
a controversy with the inhabitants of
the land, because *there is* no truth, nor
mercy, nor knowledge of God in the
land.
2 By swearing, and lying, and killing,
and stealing, and committing adultery,
they break out, and blood toucheth
blood.
3 Therefore shall the land mourn, and
every one that dwelleth therein shall
languish, with the beasts of the field,
and with the fowls of heaven; yea, the
fishes of the sea also shall be taken
away.
4 Yet let no man strive, nor reprove
another: for thy people *are* as they that
strive with the priest.
5 Therefore shalt thou fall in the day,
and the prophet also shall fall with
thee in the night, and I will destroy thy
mother.
6 My people are destroyed for lack of
knowledge: because thou hast rejected
knowledge, I will also reject thee, that
thou shalt be no priest to me: seeing
thou hast forgotten the law of thy God,
I will also forget thy children.
7 As they were increased, so they
sinned against me: *therefore* will I
change their glory into shame.
8 They eat up the sin of my people,
and they set their heart on their iniquity.
9 And there shall be, like people, like
priest: and I will punish them for their
ways, and reward them their doings.
10 For they shall eat, and not have
enough: they shall commit whoredom,
and shall not increase: because they
have left off to take heed to the LORD.
11 Whoredom and wine and new
wine take away the heart.

12 My people ask counsel at their
stocks, and their staff declareth unto
them: for the spirit of whoredoms hath
caused *them* to err, and they have gone
a whoring from under their God.
13 They sacrifice upon the tops of the
mountains, and burn incense upon the
hills, under oaks and poplars and elms,
because the shadow thereof *is* good:
therefore your daughters shall commit
whoredom, and your spouses shall commit adultery.
14 I will not punish your daughters
when they commit whoredom, nor your
spouses when they commit adultery:
for themselves are separated with
whores, and they sacrifice with harlots:
therefore the people *that* doth not
understand shall fall.
15 Though thou, Israel, play the harlot, *yet* let not Judah offend; and come
not ye unto Gilgal, neither go ye up to
Beth-aven, nor swear, The LORD liveth.
16 For Israel slideth back as a backsliding heifer: now the LORD will feed
them as a lamb in a large place.
17 Ephraim *is* joined to idols: let him
alone.
18 Their drink is sour: they have committed whoredom continually: her rulers *with* shame do love, Give ye.
19 The wind hath bound her up in her
wings, and they shall be ashamed
because of their sacrifices.

5 Hear ye this, O priests; and hearken,
ye house of Israel; and give ye ear,
O house of the king; for judgment *is*
toward you, because ye have been a
snare on Mizpah, and a net spread upon
Tabor.
2 And the revolters are profound to
make slaughter, though I *have been* a
rebuker of them all.
3 I know Ephraim, and Israel is not
hid from me: for now, O Ephraim, thou
committest whoredom, *and* Israel is
defiled.
4 They will not frame their doings to
turn unto their God: for the spirit of
whoredoms *is* in the midst of them, and
they have not known the LORD.
5 And the pride of Israel doth testify
to his face: therefore shall Israel and
Ephraim fall in their iniquity; Judah
also shall fall with them.
6 They shall go with their flocks and
with their herds to seek the LORD; but
they shall not find *him*; he hath withdrawn himself from them.
7 They have dealt treacherously
against the LORD: for they have begotten strange children: now shall a month
devour them with their portions.
8 Blow ye the cornet in Gibeah, *and*
the trumpet in Ramah: cry aloud *at*
Beth-aven, after thee, O Benjamin.
9 Ephraim shall be desolate in the
day of rebuke: among the tribes of
Israel have I made known that which
shall surely be.
10 The princes of Judah were like
them that remove the bound: *therefore*
I will pour out my wrath upon them like
water.
11 Ephraim *is* oppressed *and* broken
in judgment, because he willingly
walked after the commandment.
12 Therefore *will* I *be* unto Ephraim
as a moth, and to the house of Judah as
rottenness.
13 When Ephraim saw his sickness,
and Judah *saw* his wound, then went
Ephraim to the Assyrian, and sent to
king Jareb: yet could he not heal you,
nor cure you of your wound.
14 For I *will be* unto Ephraim as a
lion, and as a young lion to the house of

Judah: I, *even* I, will tear and go away; I
will take away, and none shall rescue
him.
15 I will go *and* return to my place, till
they acknowledge their offence, and
seek my face: in their affliction they
will seek me early.

6 Come, and let us return unto the
LORD: for he hath torn, and he will
heal us; he hath smitten, and he will
bind us up.
2 After two days will he revive us: in
the third day he will raise us up, and we
shall live in his sight.
3 Then shall we know, *if* we follow on
to know the LORD: his going forth is
prepared as the morning; and he shall
come unto us as the rain, as the latter
and former rain unto the earth.
4 O Ephraim, what shall I do unto
thee? O Judah, what shall I do unto
thee? for your goodness *is* as a morning
cloud, and as the early dew it goeth
away.
5 Therefore have I hewed *them* by the
prophets; I have slain them by the
words of my mouth: and thy judgments
are as the light *that* goeth forth.
6 For I desired mercy, and not sacrifice;
and the knowledge of God more
than burnt offerings.
7 But they like men have transgressed
the covenant: there have they dealt
treacherously against me.
8 Gilead *is* a city of them that work
iniquity, *and is* polluted with blood.
9 And as troops of robbers wait for a
man, *so* the company of priests murder
in the way by consent: for they commit
lewdness.
10 I have seen an horrible thing in the
house of Israel: there *is* the whoredom
of Ephraim, Israel is defiled.
11 Also, O Judah, he hath set an harvest
for thee, when I returned the captivity
of my people.

7 When I would have healed Israel,
then the iniquity of Ephraim was
discovered, and the wickedness of Samaria:
for they commit falsehood; and
the thief cometh in, *and* the troop of
robbers spoileth without.
2 And they consider not in their
hearts *that* I remember all their wickedness:
now their own doings have
beset them about; they are before my
face.
3 They make the king glad with their
wickedness, and the princes with their
lies.
4 They *are* all adulterers, as an oven
heated by the baker, *who* ceaseth from
raising after he hath kneaded the
dough, until it be leavened.
5 In the day of our king the princes
have made *him* sick with bottles of
wine; he stretched out his hand with
scorners.
6 For they have made ready their
heart like an oven, whiles they lie in
wait: their baker sleepeth all the night;
in the morning it burneth as a flaming
fire.
7 They are all hot as an oven, and
have devoured their judges; all their
kings are fallen: *there is* none among
them that calleth unto me.
8 Ephraim, he hath mixed himself
among the people; Ephraim is a cake
not turned.
9 Strangers have devoured his strength,
and he knoweth *it* not: yea, gray
hairs are here and there upon him, yet
he knoweth not.
10 And the pride of Israel testifieth to
his face: and they do not return to the

LORD their God, nor seek him for all this.

11 Ephraim also is like a silly dove without heart: they call to Egypt, they go to Assyria.

12 When they shall go, I will spread my net upon them; I will bring them down as the fowls of the heaven; I will chastise them, as their congregation hath heard.

13 Woe unto them! for they have fled from me: destruction unto them! because they have transgressed against me: though I have redeemed them, yet they have spoken lies against me.

14 And they have not cried unto me with their heart, when they howled upon their beds: they assemble themselves for corn and wine, *and* they rebel against me.

15 Though I have bound *and* strengthened their arms, yet do they imagine mischief against me.

16 They return, *but* not to the most High: they are like a deceitful bow: their princes shall fall by the sword for the rage of their tongue: this *shall be* their derision in the land of Egypt.

8 *Set* the trumpet to thy mouth. *He shall come* as an eagle against the house of the LORD, because they have transgressed my covenant, and trespassed against my law.

2 Israel shall cry unto me, My God, we know thee.

3 Israel hath cast off *the thing that is* good: the enemy shall pursue him.

4 They have set up kings, but not by me: they have made princes, and I knew *it* not: of their silver and their gold have they made them idols, that they may be cut off.

5 Thy calf, O Samaria, hath cast *thee* off; mine anger is kindled against them: how long *will it be* ere they attain to innocency?

6 For from Israel *was* it also: the workman made it; therefore it *is* not God: but the calf of Samaria shall be broken in pieces.

7 For they have sown the wind, and they shall reap the whirlwind: it hath no stalk: the bud shall yield no meal: if so be it yield, the strangers shall swallow it up.

8 Israel is swallowed up: now shall they be among the Gentiles as a vessel wherein *is* no pleasure.

9 For they are gone up to Assyria, a wild ass alone by himself: Ephraim hath hired lovers.

10 Yea, though they have hired among the nations, now will I gather them, and they shall sorrow a little for the burden of the king of princes.

11 Because Ephraim hath made many altars to sin, altars shall be unto him to sin.

12 I have written to him the great things of my law, *but* they were counted as a strange thing.

13 They sacrifice flesh *for* the sacrifices of mine offerings, and eat *it; but* the LORD accepteth them not; now will he remember their iniquity, and visit their sins: they shall return to Egypt.

14 For Israel hath forgotten his Maker, and buildeth temples; and Judah hath multiplied fenced cities: but I will send a fire upon his cities, and it shall devour the palaces thereof.

9 Rejoice not, O Israel, for joy, as *other* people: for thou hast gone a whoring from thy God, thou hast loved a reward upon every cornfloor.

2 The floor and the winepress shall not feed them, and the new wine shall fail in her.

3 They shall not dwell in the LORD's land; but Ephraim shall return to Egypt, and they shall eat unclean *things* in Assyria.

4 They shall not offer wine *offerings* to the LORD, neither shall they be pleasing unto him: their sacrifices *shall be* unto them as the bread of mourners; all that eat thereof shall be polluted: for their bread for their soul shall not come into the house of the LORD.

5 What will ye do in the solemn day, and in the day of the feast of the LORD?

6 For, lo, they are gone because of destruction: Egypt shall gather them up, Memphis shall bury them: the pleasant *places* for their silver, nettles shall possess them: thorns *shall be* in their tabernacles.

7 The days of visitation are come, the days of recompence are come; Israel shall know *it*: the prophet *is* a fool, the spiritual man *is* mad, for the multitude of thine iniquity, and the great hatred.

8 The watchman of Ephraim *was* with my God: *but* the prophet *is* a snare of a fowler in all his ways, *and* hatred in the house of his God.

9 They have deeply corrupted *themselves*, as in the days of Gibeah: *therefore* he will remember their iniquity, he will visit their sins.

10 I found Israel like grapes in the wilderness; I saw your fathers as the firstripe in the fig tree at her first time: *but* they went to Baal-peor, and separated themselves unto *that* shame; and *their* abominations were according as they loved.

11 *As for* Ephraim, their glory shall fly away like a bird, from the birth, and from the womb, and from the conception.

12 Though they bring up their children, yet will I bereave them, *that there shall* not *be* a man *left*: yea, woe also to them when I depart from them!

13 Ephraim, as I saw Tyrus, *is* planted in a pleasant place: but Ephraim shall bring forth his children to the murderer.

14 Give them, O LORD: what wilt thou give? give them a miscarrying womb and dry breasts.

15 All their wickedness *is* in Gilgal: for there I hated them: for the wickedness of their doings I will drive them out of mine house, I will love them no more: all their princes *are* revolters.

16 Ephraim is smitten, their root is dried up, they shall bear no fruit: yea, though they bring forth, yet will I slay *even* the beloved *fruit* of their womb.

17 My God will cast them away, because they did not hearken unto him: and they shall be wanderers among the nations.

10 Israel *is* an empty vine, he bringeth forth fruit unto himself: according to the multitude of his fruit he hath increased the altars; according to the goodness of his land they have made goodly images.

2 Their heart is divided; now shall they be found faulty: he shall break down their altars, he shall spoil their images.

3 For now they shall say, We have no king, because we feared not the LORD; what then should a king do to us?

4 They have spoken words, swearing
falsely in making a covenant: thus judgment springeth up as hemlock in the
furrows of the field.
5 The inhabitants of Samaria shall
fear because of the calves of Beth-aven:
for the people thereof shall mourn over
it, and the priests thereof *that* rejoiced
on it, for the glory thereof, because it is
departed from it.
6 It shall be also carried unto Assyria
for a present to king Jareb: Ephraim
shall receive shame, and Israel shall be
ashamed of his own counsel.
7 *As for* Samaria, her king is cut off as
the foam upon the water.
8 The high places also of Aven, the sin
of Israel, shall be destroyed: the thorn
and the thistle shall come up on their
altars; and they shall say to the mountains, Cover us; and to the hills, Fall on
us.
9 O Israel, thou hast sinned from the
days of Gibeah: there they stood: the
battle in Gibeah against the children of
iniquity did not overtake them.
10 *It is* in my desire that I should
chastise them; and the people shall be
gathered against them, when they shall
bind themselves in their two furrows.
11 And Ephraim *is as* an heifer *that*
is taught, *and* loveth to tread out *the*
corn; but I passed over upon her fair
neck: I will make Ephraim to ride;
Judah shall plow, *and* Jacob shall break
his clods.
12 Sow to yourselves in righteousness,
reap in mercy; break up your fallow
ground: for *it is* time to seek the LORD,
till he come and rain righteousness
upon you.
13 Ye have plowed wickedness, ye
have reaped iniquity; ye have eaten the
fruit of lies: because thou didst trust in
thy way, in the multitude of thy mighty
men.
14 Therefore shall a tumult arise
among thy people, and all thy fortresses shall be spoiled, as Shalman spoiled
Beth-arbel in the day of battle: the
mother was dashed in pieces upon *her*
children.
15 So shall Beth-el do unto you
because of your great wickedness: in a
morning shall the king of Israel utterly
be cut off.

11 When Israel *was* a child, then I
loved him, and called my son out
of Egypt.
2 *As* they called them, so they went
from them: they sacrificed unto Baalim,
and burned incense to graven images.
3 I taught Ephraim also to go, taking
them by their arms; but they knew not
that I healed them.
4 I drew them with cords of a man,
with bands of love: and I was to them as
they that take off the yoke on their
jaws, and I laid meat unto them.
5 He shall not return into the land of
Egypt, but the Assyrian shall be his
king, because they refused to return.
6 And the sword shall abide on his
cities, and shall consume his branches,
and devour *them*, because of their own
counsels.
7 And my people are bent to backsliding from me: though they called them
to the most High, none at all would
exalt *him*.
8 How shall I give thee up, Ephraim?
how shall I deliver thee, Israel? how
shall I make thee as Admah? *how* shall
I set thee as Zeboim? mine heart is
turned within me, my repentings are
kindled together.

9 I will not execute the fierceness of
mine anger, I will not return to destroy
Ephraim: for I *am* God, and not man;
the Holy One in the midst of thee: and
I will not enter into the city.
10 They shall walk after the LORD: he
shall roar like a lion: when he shall roar,
then the children shall tremble from
the west.
11 They shall tremble as a bird out of
Egypt, and as a dove out of the land of
Assyria: and I will place them in their
houses, saith the LORD.
12 Ephraim compasseth me about
with lies, and the house of Israel with
deceit: but Judah yet ruleth with God,
and is faithful with the saints.

12 Ephraim feedeth on wind, and
followeth after the east wind: he
daily increaseth lies and desolation;
and they do make a covenant with the
Assyrians, and oil is carried into Egypt.
2 The LORD hath also a controversy
with Judah, and will punish Jacob
according to his ways; according to his
doings will he recompense him.
3 He took his brother by the heel in
the womb, and by his strength he had
power with God:
4 Yea, he had power over the angel,
and prevailed: he wept, and made supplication unto him: he found him *in*
Beth-el, and there he spake with us;
5 Even the LORD God of hosts; the
LORD *is* his memorial.
6 Therefore turn thou to thy God:
keep mercy and judgment, and wait on
thy God continually.
7 *He is* a merchant, the balances of
deceit *are* in his hand: he loveth to
oppress.
8 And Ephraim said, Yet I am become
rich, I have found me out substance: *in*
all my labours they shall find none
iniquity in me that *were* sin.
9 And I *that am* the LORD thy God
from the land of Egypt will yet make
thee to dwell in tabernacles, as in the
days of the solemn feast.
10 I have also spoken by the prophets,
and I have multiplied visions, and used
similitudes, by the ministry of the
prophets.
11 *Is there* iniquity *in* Gilead? surely
they are vanity: they sacrifice bullocks
in Gilgal; yea, their altars *are* as heaps
in the furrows of the fields.
12 And Jacob fled into the country of
Syria, and Israel served for a wife, and
for a wife he kept *sheep*.
13 And by a prophet the LORD brought
Israel out of Egypt, and by a prophet
was he preserved.
14 Ephraim provoked *him* to anger
most bitterly: therefore shall he leave
his blood upon him, and his reproach
shall his Lord return unto him.

13 When Ephraim spake trembling,
he exalted himself in Israel; but
when he offended in Baal, he died.
2 And now they sin more and more,
and have made them molten images of
their silver, *and* idols according to their
own understanding, all of it the work of
the craftsmen: they say of them, Let the
men that sacrifice kiss the calves.
3 Therefore they shall be as the morning cloud, and as the early dew that
passeth away, as the chaff *that* is driven
with the whirlwind out of the floor, and
as the smoke out of the chimney.
4 Yet I *am* the LORD thy God from the
land of Egypt, and thou shalt know no
god but me: for *there is* no saviour
beside me.
5 I did know thee in the wilderness, in
the land of great drought.

6 According to their pasture, so were
they filled; they were filled, and their
heart was exalted; therefore have they
forgotten me.
7 Therefore I will be unto them as a
lion: as a leopard by the way will I
observe *them*:
8 I will meet them as a bear *that is*
bereaved *of her whelps*, and will rend
the caul of their heart, and there will I
devour them like a lion: the wild beast
shall tear them.
9 O Israel, thou hast destroyed thyself; but in me *is* thine help.
10 I will be thy king: where *is any*
other that may save thee in all thy cities? and thy judges of whom thou
saidst, Give me a king and princes?
11 I gave thee a king in mine anger,
and took *him* away in my wrath.
12 The iniquity of Ephraim *is* bound
up; his sin *is* hid.
13 The sorrows of a travailing woman
shall come upon him: he *is* an unwise
son; for he should not stay long in *the*
place of the breaking forth of children.
14 I will ransom them from the power
of the grave; I will redeem them from
death: O death, I will be thy plagues; O
grave, I will be thy destruction: repentance shall be hid from mine eyes.
15 Though he be fruitful among *his*
brethren, an east wind shall come, the
wind of the LORD shall come up from
the wilderness, and his spring shall
become dry, and his fountain shall be
dried up: he shall spoil the treasure of
all pleasant vessels.
16 Samaria shall become desolate; for
she hath rebelled against her God: they
shall fall by the sword: their infants
shall be dashed in pieces, and their
women with child shall be ripped up.

14 O Israel, return unto the LORD
thy God; for thou hast fallen by
thine iniquity.
2 Take with you words, and turn to
the LORD: say unto him, Take away all
iniquity, and receive *us* graciously: so
will we render the calves of our lips.
3 Asshur shall not save us; we will not
ride upon horses: neither will we say
any more to the work of our hands, *Ye*
are our gods: for in thee the fatherless
findeth mercy.
4 I will heal their backsliding, I will
love them freely: for mine anger is
turned away from him.
5 I will be as the dew unto Israel: he
shall grow as the lily, and cast forth his
roots as Lebanon.
6 His branches shall spread, and his
beauty shall be as the olive tree, and
his smell as Lebanon.
7 They that dwell under his shadow
shall return; they shall revive *as* the
corn, and grow as the vine: the scent
thereof *shall be* as the wine of Lebanon.
8 Ephraim *shall say*, What have I to
do any more with idols? I have heard
him, and observed him: I *am* like a
green fir tree. From me is thy fruit
found.
9 Who *is* wise, and he shall understand these *things*? prudent, and he
shall know them? for the ways of the
LORD *are* right, and the just shall walk
in them: but the transgressors shall fall
therein.

THE BOOK OF
JOEL

1 The word of the LORD that came to
Joel the son of Pethuel.
2 Hear this, ye old men, and give ear,
all ye inhabitants of the land. Hath this
been in your days, or even in the days
of your fathers?
3 Tell ye your children of it, and *let*
your children *tell* their children, and
their children another generation.
4 That which the palmerworm hath
left hath the locust eaten; and that
which the locust hath left hath the cankerworm eaten; and that which the
cankerworm hath left hath the caterpiller eaten.
5 Awake, ye drunkards, and weep;
and howl, all ye drinkers of wine,
because of the new wine; for it is cut off
from your mouth.
6 For a nation is come up upon my
land, strong, and without number,
whose teeth *are* the teeth of a lion, and
he hath the cheek teeth of a great lion.
7 He hath laid my vine waste, and
barked my fig tree: he hath made it
clean bare, and cast *it* away; the
branches thereof are made white.
8 Lament like a virgin girded with
sackcloth for the husband of her youth.
9 The meat offering and the drink
offering is cut off from the house of the
LORD; the priests, the LORD's ministers,
mourn.
10 The field is wasted, the land mourneth; for the corn is wasted: the new
wine is dried up, the oil languisheth.
11 Be ye ashamed, O ye husbandmen;
howl, O ye vinedressers, for the wheat
and for the barley; because the harvest
of the field is perished.
12 The vine is dried up, and the fig
tree languisheth; the pomegranate
tree, the palm tree also, and the apple
tree, *even* all the trees of the field, are
withered: because joy is withered away
from the sons of men.
13 Gird yourselves, and lament, ye
priests: howl, ye ministers of the altar:
come, lie all night in sackcloth, ye ministers of my God: for the meat offering
and the drink offering is withholden
from the house of your God.
14 Sanctify ye a fast, call a solemn
assembly, gather the elders *and* all the
inhabitants of the land *into* the house
of the LORD your God, and cry unto the
LORD,
15 Alas for the day! for the day of the
LORD *is* at hand, and as a destruction
from the Almighty shall it come.
16 Is not the meat cut off before our
eyes, *yea*, joy and gladness from the
house of our God?
17 The seed is rotten under their
clods, the garners are laid desolate, the
barns are broken down; for the corn is
withered.
18 How do the beasts groan! the
herds of cattle are perplexed, because
they have no pasture; yea, the flocks of
sheep are made desolate.
19 O LORD, to thee will I cry: for the
fire hath devoured the pastures of the
wilderness, and the flame hath burned
all the trees of the field.
20 The beasts of the field cry also
unto thee: for the rivers of waters are
dried up, and the fire hath devoured
the pastures of the wilderness.

2 Blow ye the trumpet in Zion, and sound an alarm in my holy mountain: let all the inhabitants of the land tremble: for the day of the LORD cometh, for *it is* nigh at hand;

2 A day of darkness and of gloominess, a day of clouds and of thick darkness, as the morning spread upon the mountains: a great people and a strong; there hath not been ever the like, neither shall be any more after it, *even* to the years of many generations.

3 A fire devoureth before them; and behind them a flame burneth: the land *is* as the garden of Eden before them, and behind them a desolate wilderness; yea, and nothing shall escape them.

4 The appearance of them *is* as the appearance of horses; and as horsemen, so shall they run.

5 Like the noise of chariots on the tops of mountains shall they leap, like the noise of a flame of fire that devoureth the stubble, as a strong people set in battle array.

6 Before their face the people shall be much pained: all faces shall gather blackness.

7 They shall run like mighty men; they shall climb the wall like men of war; and they shall march every one on his ways, and they shall not break their ranks:

8 Neither shall one thrust another; they shall walk every one in his path: and *when* they fall upon the sword, they shall not be wounded.

9 They shall run to and fro in the city; they shall run upon the wall, they shall climb up upon the houses; they shall enter in at the windows like a thief.

10 The earth shall quake before them; the heavens shall tremble: the sun and the moon shall be dark, and the stars shall withdraw their shining:

11 And the LORD shall utter his voice before his army: for his camp *is* very great: for *he is* strong that executeth his word: for the day of the LORD *is* great and very terrible; and who can abide it?

12 Therefore also now, saith the LORD, turn ye *even* to me with all your heart, and with fasting, and with weeping, and with mourning:

13 And rend your heart, and not your garments, and turn unto the LORD your God: for he *is* gracious and merciful, slow to anger, and of great kindness, and repenteth him of the evil.

14 Who knoweth *if* he will return and repent, and leave a blessing behind him; *even* a meat offering and a drink offering unto the LORD your God?

15 Blow the trumpet in Zion, sanctify a fast, call a solemn assembly:

16 Gather the people, sanctify the congregation, assemble the elders, gather the children, and those that suck the breasts: let the bridegroom go forth of his chamber, and the bride out of her closet.

17 Let the priests, the ministers of the LORD, weep between the porch and the altar, and let them say, Spare thy people, O LORD, and give not thine heritage to reproach, that the heathen should rule over them: wherefore should they say among the people, Where *is* their God?

18 Then will the LORD be jealous for his land, and pity his people.

19 Yea, the LORD will answer and say unto his people, Behold, I will send you corn, and wine, and oil, and ye shall be satisfied therewith: and I will no more make you a reproach among the heathen:

20 But I will remove far off from you the northern *army*, and will drive him into a land barren and desolate, with his face toward the east sea, and his hinder part toward the utmost sea, and his stink shall come up, and his ill savour shall come up, because he hath done great things.

21 Fear not, O land; be glad and rejoice: for the LORD will do great things.

22 Be not afraid, ye beasts of the field: for the pastures of the wilderness do spring, for the tree beareth her fruit, the fig tree and the vine do yield their strength.

23 Be glad then, ye children of Zion, and rejoice in the LORD your God: for he hath given you the former rain moderately, and he will cause to come down for you the rain, the former rain, and the latter rain in the first *month*.

24 And the floors shall be full of wheat, and the fats shall overflow with wine and oil.

25 And I will restore to you the years that the locust hath eaten, the cankerworm, and the caterpiller, and the palmerworm, my great army which I sent among you.

26 And ye shall eat in plenty, and be satisfied, and praise the name of the LORD your God, that hath dealt wondrously with you: and my people shall never be ashamed.

27 And ye shall know that I *am* in the midst of Israel, and *that* I *am* the LORD your God, and none else: and my people shall never be ashamed.

28 And it shall come to pass afterward, *that* I will pour out my spirit upon all flesh; and your sons and your daughters shall prophesy, your old men shall dream dreams, your young men shall see visions:

29 And also upon the servants and upon the handmaids in those days will I pour out my spirit.

30 And I will shew wonders in the heavens and in the earth, blood, and fire, and pillars of smoke.

31 The sun shall be turned into darkness, and the moon into blood, before the great and the terrible day of the LORD come.

32 And it shall come to pass, *that* whosoever shall call on the name of the LORD shall be delivered: for in mount Zion and in Jerusalem shall be deliverance, as the LORD hath said, and in the remnant whom the LORD shall call.

3 For, behold, in those days, and in that time, when I shall bring again the captivity of Judah and Jerusalem,

2 I will also gather all nations, and will bring them down into the valley of Jehoshaphat, and will plead with them there for my people and *for* my heritage Israel, whom they have scattered among the nations, and parted my land.

3 And they have cast lots for my people; and have given a boy for an harlot, and sold a girl for wine, that they might drink.

4 Yea, and what have ye to do with me, O Tyre, and Zidon, and all the coasts of Palestine? will ye render me a recompence? and if ye recompense me, swiftly *and* speedily will I return your recompence upon your own head;

5 Because ye have taken my silver and my gold, and have carried into your temples my goodly pleasant things:

6 The children also of Judah and the children of Jerusalem have ye sold unto the Grecians, that ye might remove them far from their border.

7 Behold, I will raise them out of the place whither ye have sold them, and will return your recompence upon your own head:

8 And I will sell your sons and your daughters into the hand of the children of Judah, and they shall sell them to the Sabeans, to a people far off: for the LORD hath spoken *it*.

9 Proclaim ye this among the Gentiles; Prepare war, wake up the mighty men, let all the men of war draw near; let them come up:

10 Beat your plowshares into swords, and your pruninghooks into spears: let the weak say, I *am* strong.

11 Assemble yourselves, and come, all ye heathen, and gather yourselves together round about: thither cause thy mighty ones to come down, O LORD.

12 Let the heathen be wakened, and come up to the valley of Jehoshaphat: for there will I sit to judge all the heathen round about.

13 Put ye in the sickle, for the harvest is ripe: come, get you down; for the press is full, the fats overflow; for their wickedness *is* great.

14 Multitudes, multitudes in the valley of decision: for the day of the LORD *is* near in the valley of decision.

15 The sun and the moon shall be darkened, and the stars shall withdraw their shining.

16 The LORD also shall roar out of Zion, and utter his voice from Jerusalem; and the heavens and the earth shall shake: but the LORD *will be* the hope of his people, and the strength of the children of Israel.

17 So shall ye know that I *am* the LORD your God dwelling in Zion, my holy mountain: then shall Jerusalem be holy, and there shall no strangers pass through her any more.

18 And it shall come to pass in that day, *that* the mountains shall drop down new wine, and the hills shall flow with milk, and all the rivers of Judah shall flow with waters, and a fountain shall come forth of the house of the LORD, and shall water the valley of Shittim.

19 Egypt shall be a desolation, and Edom shall be a desolate wilderness, for the violence *against* the children of Judah, because they have shed innocent blood in their land.

20 But Judah shall dwell for ever, and Jerusalem from generation to generation.

21 For I will cleanse their blood *that* I have not cleansed: for the LORD dwelleth in Zion.

THE BOOK OF
AMOS

1 The words of Amos, who was among
the herdmen of Tekoa, which he
saw concerning Israel in the days of
Uzziah king of Judah, and in the days of
Jeroboam the son of Joash king of
Israel, two years before the earthquake.
2 And he said, The LORD will roar
from Zion, and utter his voice from
Jerusalem; and the habitations of the
shepherds shall mourn, and the top of
Carmel shall wither.
3 Thus saith the LORD; For three
transgressions of Damascus, and for
four, I will not turn away *the punishment* thereof; because they have
threshed Gilead with threshing instruments of iron:
4 But I will send a fire into the house
of Hazael, which shall devour the palaces of Ben-hadad.
5 I will break also the bar of
Damascus, and cut off the inhabitant
from the plain of Aven, and him that
holdeth the sceptre from the house of
Eden: and the people of Syria shall go
into captivity unto Kir, saith the LORD.
6 Thus saith the LORD; For three
transgressions of Gaza, and for four, I
will not turn away *the punishment*
thereof; because they carried away captive the whole captivity, to deliver *them*
up to Edom:
7 But I will send a fire on the wall of
Gaza, which shall devour the palaces
thereof:
8 And I will cut off the inhabitant
from Ashdod, and him that holdeth the
sceptre from Ashkelon, and I will turn
mine hand against Ekron: and the remnant of the Philistines shall perish,
saith the Lord GOD.
9 Thus saith the LORD; For three
transgressions of Tyrus, and for four, I
will not turn away *the punishment*
thereof; because they delivered up the
whole captivity to Edom, and remembered not the brotherly covenant:
10 But I will send a fire on the wall of
Tyrus, which shall devour the palaces
thereof.
11 Thus saith the LORD; For three
transgressions of Edom, and for four, I
will not turn away *the punishment*
thereof; because he did pursue his
brother with the sword, and did cast off
all pity, and his anger did tear perpetually, and he kept his wrath for ever:
12 But I will send a fire upon Teman,
which shall devour the palaces of
Bozrah.
13 Thus saith the LORD; For three
transgressions of the children of
Ammon, and for four, I will not turn
away *the punishment* thereof; because
they have ripped up the women with
child of Gilead, that they might enlarge
their border:
14 But I will kindle a fire in the wall
of Rabbah, and it shall devour the palaces thereof, with shouting in the day
of battle, with a tempest in the day of
the whirlwind:
15 And their king shall go into captivity, he and his princes together, saith
the LORD.

2 Thus saith the LORD; For three transgressions of Moab, and for four, I will not turn away *the punishment* thereof; because he burned the bones of the king of Edom into lime:

2 But I will send a fire upon Moab, and it shall devour the palaces of Kerioth: and Moab shall die with tumult, with shouting, *and* with the sound of the trumpet:

3 And I will cut off the judge from the midst thereof, and will slay all the princes thereof with him, saith the LORD.

4 Thus saith the LORD; For three transgressions of Judah, and for four, I will not turn away *the punishment* thereof; because they have despised the law of the LORD, and have not kept his commandments, and their lies caused them to err, after the which their fathers have walked:

5 But I will send a fire upon Judah, and it shall devour the palaces of Jerusalem.

6 Thus saith the LORD; For three transgressions of Israel, and for four, I will not turn away *the punishment* thereof; because they sold the righteous for silver, and the poor for a pair of shoes;

7 That pant after the dust of the earth on the head of the poor, and turn aside the way of the meek: and a man and his father will go in unto the *same* maid, to profane my holy name:

8 And they lay *themselves* down upon clothes laid to pledge by every altar, and they drink the wine of the condemned *in* the house of their god.

9 Yet destroyed I the Amorite before them, whose height *was* like the height of the cedars, and he *was* strong as the oaks; yet I destroyed his fruit from above, and his roots from beneath.

10 Also I brought you up from the land of Egypt, and led you forty years through the wilderness, to possess the land of the Amorite.

11 And I raised up of your sons for prophets, and of your young men for Nazarites. *Is it* not even thus, O ye children of Israel? saith the LORD.

12 But ye gave the Nazarites wine to drink; and commanded the prophets, saying, Prophesy not.

13 Behold, I am pressed under you, as a cart is pressed *that is* full of sheaves.

14 Therefore the flight shall perish from the swift, and the strong shall not strengthen his force, neither shall the mighty deliver himself:

15 Neither shall he stand that handleth the bow; and *he that is* swift of foot shall not deliver *himself*: neither shall he that rideth the horse deliver himself.

16 And *he that is* courageous among the mighty shall flee away naked in that day, saith the LORD.

3 Hear this word that the LORD hath spoken against you, O children of Israel, against the whole family which I brought up from the land of Egypt, saying,

2 You only have I known of all the families of the earth: therefore I will punish you for all your iniquities.

3 Can two walk together, except they be agreed?

4 Will a lion roar in the forest, when he hath no prey? will a young lion cry out of his den, if he have taken nothing?

5 Can a bird fall in a snare upon the
earth, where no gin *is* for him? shall *one*
take up a snare from the earth, and
have taken nothing at all?
6 Shall a trumpet be blown in the city,
and the people not be afraid? shall
there be evil in a city, and the LORD
hath not done *it*?
7 Surely the Lord GOD will do nothing, but he revealeth his secret unto his
servants the prophets.
8 The lion hath roared, who will not
fear? the Lord GOD hath spoken, who
can but prophesy?
9 Publish in the palaces at Ashdod,
and in the palaces in the land of Egypt,
and say, Assemble yourselves upon the
mountains of Samaria, and behold the
great tumults in the midst thereof, and
the oppressed in the midst thereof.
10 For they know not to do right, saith
the LORD, who store up violence and
robbery in their palaces.
11 Therefore thus saith the Lord GOD;
An adversary *there shall be* even round
about the land; and he shall bring down
thy strength from thee, and thy palaces
shall be spoiled.
12 Thus saith the LORD; As the shepherd taketh out of the mouth of the lion
two legs, or a piece of an ear; so shall
the children of Israel be taken out that
dwell in Samaria in the corner of a bed,
and in Damascus *in* a couch.
13 Hear ye, and testify in the house of
Jacob, saith the Lord GOD, the God of
hosts,
14 That in the day that I shall visit the
transgressions of Israel upon him I will
also visit the altars of Beth-el: and the
horns of the altar shall be cut off, and
fall to the ground.
15 And I will smite the winter house
with the summer house; and the houses
of ivory shall perish, and the great
houses shall have an end, saith the
LORD.

4 Hear this word, ye kine of Bashan,
that *are* in the mountain of Samaria,
which oppress the poor, which crush
the needy, which say to their masters,
Bring, and let us drink.
2 The Lord GOD hath sworn by his
holiness, that, lo, the days shall come
upon you, that he will take you away
with hooks, and your posterity with
fishhooks.
3 And ye shall go out at the breaches,
every *cow at that which is* before her;
and ye shall cast *them* into the palace,
saith the LORD.
4 Come to Beth-el, and transgress; at
Gilgal multiply transgression; and
bring your sacrifices every morning,
and your tithes after three years:
5 And offer a sacrifice of thanksgiving with leaven, and proclaim *and* publish the free offerings: for this liketh
you, O ye children of Israel, saith the
Lord GOD.
6 And I also have given you cleanness
of teeth in all your cities, and want of
bread in all your places: yet have ye not
returned unto me, saith the LORD.
7 And also I have withholden the rain
from you, when *there were* yet three
months to the harvest: and I caused it
to rain upon one city, and caused it not
to rain upon another city: one piece
was rained upon, and the piece whereupon it rained not withered.
8 So two *or* three cities wandered
unto one city, to drink water; but they
were not satisfied: yet have ye not
returned unto me, saith the LORD.

9 I have smitten you with blasting and mildew: when your gardens and your vineyards and your fig trees and your olive trees increased, the palmerworm devoured *them*: yet have ye not returned unto me, saith the LORD.

10 I have sent among you the pestilence after the manner of Egypt: your young men have I slain with the sword, and have taken away your horses; and I have made the stink of your camps to come up unto your nostrils: yet have ye not returned unto me, saith the LORD.

11 I have overthrown *some* of you, as God overthrew Sodom and Gomorrah, and ye were as a firebrand plucked out of the burning: yet have ye not returned unto me, saith the LORD.

12 Therefore thus will I do unto thee, O Israel: *and* because I will do this unto thee, prepare to meet thy God, O Israel.

13 For, lo, he that formeth the mountains, and createth the wind, and declareth unto man what *is* his thought, that maketh the morning darkness, and treadeth upon the high places of the earth, The LORD, The God of hosts, *is* his name.

5 Hear ye this word which I take up against you, *even* a lamentation, O house of Israel.

2 The virgin of Israel is fallen; she shall no more rise: she is forsaken upon her land; *there is* none to raise her up.

3 For thus saith the Lord GOD; The city that went out *by* a thousand shall leave an hundred, and that which went forth *by* an hundred shall leave ten, to the house of Israel.

4 For thus saith the LORD unto the house of Israel, Seek ye me, and ye shall live:

5 But seek not Beth-el, nor enter into Gilgal, and pass not to Beer-sheba: for Gilgal shall surely go into captivity, and Beth-el shall come to nought.

6 Seek the LORD, and ye shall live; lest he break out like fire in the house of Joseph, and devour *it*, and *there be* none to quench *it* in Beth-el.

7 Ye who turn judgment to wormwood, and leave off righteousness in the earth,

8 *Seek him* that maketh the seven stars and Orion, and turneth the shadow of death into the morning, and maketh the day dark with night: that calleth for the waters of the sea, and poureth them out upon the face of the earth: The LORD *is* his name:

9 That strengtheneth the spoiled against the strong, so that the spoiled shall come against the fortress.

10 They hate him that rebuketh in the gate, and they abhor him that speaketh uprightly.

11 Forasmuch therefore as your treading *is* upon the poor, and ye take from him burdens of wheat: ye have built houses of hewn stone, but ye shall not dwell in them; ye have planted pleasant vineyards, but ye shall not drink wine of them.

12 For I know your manifold transgressions and your mighty sins: they afflict the just, they take a bribe, and they turn aside the poor in the gate *from their right*.

13 Therefore the prudent shall keep silence in that time; for it *is* an evil time.

14 Seek good, and not evil, that ye may live: and so the LORD, the God of hosts, shall be with you, as ye have spoken.

15 Hate the evil, and love the good, and establish judgment in the gate: it may be that the LORD God of hosts will be gracious unto the remnant of Joseph.

16 Therefore the LORD, the God of hosts, the Lord, saith thus; Wailing *shall be* in all streets; and they shall say in all the highways, Alas! alas! and they shall call the husbandman to mourning, and such as are skilful of lamentation to wailing.

17 And in all vineyards *shall be* wailing: for I will pass through thee, saith the LORD.

18 Woe unto you that desire the day of the LORD! to what end *is* it for you? the day of the LORD *is* darkness, and not light.

19 As if a man did flee from a lion, and a bear met him; or went into the house, and leaned his hand on the wall, and a serpent bit him.

20 *Shall* not the day of the LORD *be* darkness, and not light? even very dark, and no brightness in it?

21 I hate, I despise your feast days, and I will not smell in your solemn assemblies.

22 Though ye offer me burnt offerings and your meat offerings, I will not accept *them*: neither will I regard the peace offerings of your fat beasts.

23 Take thou away from me the noise of thy songs; for I will not hear the melody of thy viols.

24 But let judgment run down as waters, and righteousness as a mighty stream.

25 Have ye offered unto me sacrifices and offerings in the wilderness forty years, O house of Israel?

26 But ye have borne the tabernacle of your Moloch and Chiun your images, the star of your god, which ye made to yourselves.

27 Therefore will I cause you to go into captivity beyond Damascus, saith the LORD, whose name *is* The God of hosts.

6 Woe to them *that are* at ease in Zion, and trust in the mountain of Samaria, *which are* named chief of the nations, to whom the house of Israel came!

2 Pass ye unto Calneh, and see; and from thence go ye to Hamath the great: then go down to Gath of the Philistines: *be they* better than these kingdoms? or their border greater than your border?

3 Ye that put far away the evil day, and cause the seat of violence to come near;

4 That lie upon beds of ivory, and stretch themselves upon their couches, and eat the lambs out of the flock, and the calves out of the midst of the stall;

5 That chant to the sound of the viol, *and* invent to themselves instruments of musick, like David;

6 That drink wine in bowls, and anoint themselves with the chief ointments: but they are not grieved for the affliction of Joseph.

7 Therefore now shall they go captive with the first that go captive, and the banquet of them that stretched themselves shall be removed.

8 The Lord GOD hath sworn by himself, saith the LORD the God of hosts, I abhor the excellency of Jacob, and hate his palaces: therefore will I deliver up the city with all that is therein.

9 And it shall come to pass, if there remain ten men in one house, that they shall die.

10 And a man's uncle shall take him up, and he that burneth him, to bring out the bones out of the house, and shall say unto him that *is* by the sides of the house, *Is there* yet *any* with thee? and he shall say, No. Then shall he say, Hold thy tongue: for we may not make mention of the name of the LORD.

11 For, behold, the LORD commandeth, and he will smite the great house with breaches, and the little house with clefts.

12 Shall horses run upon the rock? will *one* plow *there* with oxen? for ye have turned judgment into gall, and the fruit of righteousness into hemlock:

13 Ye which rejoice in a thing of nought, which say, Have we not taken to us horns by our own strength?

14 But, behold, I will raise up against you a nation, O house of Israel, saith the LORD the God of hosts; and they shall afflict you from the entering in of Hemath unto the river of the wilderness.

7 Thus hath the Lord GOD shewed unto me; and, behold, he formed grasshoppers in the beginning of the shooting up of the latter growth; and, lo, *it was* the latter growth after the king's mowings.

2 And it came to pass, *that* when they had made an end of eating the grass of the land, then I said, O Lord GOD, forgive, I beseech thee: by whom shall Jacob arise? for he *is* small.

3 The LORD repented for this: It shall not be, saith the LORD.

4 Thus hath the Lord GOD shewed unto me: and, behold, the Lord GOD called to contend by fire, and it devoured the great deep, and did eat up a part.

5 Then said I, O Lord GOD, cease, I beseech thee: by whom shall Jacob arise? for he *is* small.

6 The LORD repented for this: This also shall not be, saith the Lord GOD.

7 Thus he shewed me: and, behold, the Lord stood upon a wall *made* by a plumbline, with a plumbline in his hand.

8 And the LORD said unto me, Amos, what seest thou? And I said, A plumbline. Then said the Lord, Behold, I will set a plumbline in the midst of my people Israel: I will not again pass by them any more:

9 And the high places of Isaac shall be desolate, and the sanctuaries of Israel shall be laid waste; and I will rise against the house of Jeroboam with the sword.

10 Then Amaziah the priest of Beth-el sent to Jeroboam king of Israel, saying, Amos hath conspired against thee in the midst of the house of Israel: the land is not able to bear all his words.

11 For thus Amos saith, Jeroboam shall die by the sword, and Israel shall surely be led away captive out of their own land.

12 Also Amaziah said unto Amos, O thou seer, go, flee thee away into the land of Judah, and there eat bread, and prophesy there:

13 But prophesy not again any more at Beth-el: for it *is* the king's chapel, and it *is* the king's court.

14 Then answered Amos, and said to Amaziah, I *was* no prophet, neither *was* I a prophet's son; but I *was* an herdman, and a gatherer of sycomore fruit:

15 And the LORD took me as I followed the flock, and the LORD said unto me, Go, prophesy unto my people Israel.

16 Now therefore hear thou the word of the LORD: Thou sayest, Prophesy not against Israel, and drop not *thy word* against the house of Isaac.

17 Therefore thus saith the LORD; Thy wife shall be an harlot in the city, and thy sons and thy daughters shall fall by the sword, and thy land shall be divided by line; and thou shalt die in a polluted land: and Israel shall surely go into captivity forth of his land.

8 Thus hath the Lord GOD shewed unto me: and behold a basket of summer fruit.

2 And he said, Amos, what seest thou? And I said, A basket of summer fruit. Then said the LORD unto me, The end is come upon my people of Israel; I will not again pass by them any more.

3 And the songs of the temple shall be howlings in that day, saith the Lord GOD: *there shall be* many dead bodies in every place; they shall cast *them* forth with silence.

4 Hear this, O ye that swallow up the needy, even to make the poor of the land to fail,

5 Saying, When will the new moon be gone, that we may sell corn? and the sabbath, that we may set forth wheat, making the ephah small, and the shekel great, and falsifying the balances by deceit?

6 That we may buy the poor for silver, and the needy for a pair of shoes; *yea*, and sell the refuse of the wheat?

7 The LORD hath sworn by the excellency of Jacob, Surely I will never forget any of their works.

8 Shall not the land tremble for this, and every one mourn that dwelleth therein? and it shall rise up wholly as a flood; and it shall be cast out and drowned, as *by* the flood of Egypt.

9 And it shall come to pass in that day, saith the Lord GOD, that I will cause the sun to go down at noon, and I will darken the earth in the clear day:

10 And I will turn your feasts into mourning, and all your songs into lamentation; and I will bring up sackcloth upon all loins, and baldness upon every head; and I will make it as the mourning of an only *son*, and the end thereof as a bitter day.

11 Behold, the days come, saith the Lord GOD, that I will send a famine in the land, not a famine of bread, nor a thirst for water, but of hearing the words of the LORD:

12 And they shall wander from sea to sea, and from the north even to the east, they shall run to and fro to seek the word of the LORD, and shall not find *it*.

13 In that day shall the fair virgins and young men faint for thirst.

14 They that swear by the sin of Samaria, and say, Thy god, O Dan, liveth; and, The manner of Beer-sheba liveth; even they shall fall, and never rise up again.

9 I saw the Lord standing upon the altar: and he said, Smite the lintel of the door, that the posts may shake: and cut them in the head, all of them; and I will slay the last of them with the sword: he that fleeth of them shall not flee away, and he that escapeth of them shall not be delivered.

2 Though they dig into hell, thence shall mine hand take them; though they climb up to heaven, thence will I bring them down:

3 And though they hide themselves in the top of Carmel, I will search and take them out thence; and though they be hid from my sight in the bottom of the sea, thence will I command the serpent, and he shall bite them:

4 And though they go into captivity before their enemies, thence will I command the sword, and it shall slay them: and I will set mine eyes upon them for evil, and not for good.

5 And the Lord GOD of hosts *is* he that toucheth the land, and it shall melt, and all that dwell therein shall mourn: and it shall rise up wholly like a flood; and shall be drowned, as *by* the flood of Egypt.

6 *It is* he that buildeth his stories in the heaven, and hath founded his troop in the earth; he that calleth for the waters of the sea, and poureth them out upon the face of the earth: The LORD *is* his name.

7 *Are* ye not as children of the Ethiopians unto me, O children of Israel? saith the LORD. Have not I brought up Israel out of the land of Egypt? and the Philistines from Caphtor, and the Syrians from Kir?

8 Behold, the eyes of the Lord GOD *are* upon the sinful kingdom, and I will destroy it from off the face of the earth; saving that I will not utterly destroy the house of Jacob, saith the LORD.

9 For, lo, I will command, and I will sift the house of Israel among all nations, like as *corn* is sifted in a sieve, yet shall not the least grain fall upon the earth.

10 All the sinners of my people shall die by the sword, which say, The evil shall not overtake nor prevent us.

11 In that day will I raise up the tabernacle of David that is fallen, and close up the breaches thereof; and I will raise up his ruins, and I will build it as in the days of old:

12 That they may possess the remnant of Edom, and of all the heathen, which are called by my name, saith the LORD that doeth this.

13 Behold, the days come, saith the LORD, that the plowman shall overtake the reaper, and the treader of grapes him that soweth seed; and the mountains shall drop sweet wine, and all the hills shall melt.

14 And I will bring again the captivity of my people of Israel, and they shall build the waste cities, and inhabit *them*; and they shall plant vineyards, and drink the wine thereof; they shall also make gardens, and eat the fruit of them.

15 And I will plant them upon their land, and they shall no more be pulled up out of their land which I have given them, saith the LORD thy God.

THE BOOK OF

OBADIAH

1 The vision of Obadiah. Thus saith the LORD GOD concerning Edom; We have heard a rumour from the LORD, and an ambassador is sent among the heathen, Arise ye, and let us rise up against her in battle.

2 Behold, I have made thee small among the heathen: thou art greatly despised.

3 The pride of thine heart hath deceived thee, thou that dwellest in the clefts of the rock, whose habitation *is* high; that saith in his heart, Who shall bring me down to the ground?

4 Though thou exalt *thyself* as the eagle, and though thou set thy nest among the stars, thence will I bring thee down, saith the LORD.

5 If thieves came to thee, if robbers by night, (how art thou cut off!) would they not have stolen till they had enough? if the grapegatherers came to thee, would they not leave *some* grapes?

6 How are *the things* of Esau searched out! *how* are his hidden things sought up!

7 All the men of thy confederacy have brought thee *even* to the border: the men that were at peace with thee have deceived thee, *and* prevailed against thee; *they that eat* thy bread have laid a wound under thee: *there is* none understanding in him.

8 Shall I not in that day, saith the LORD, even destroy the wise *men* out of Edom, and understanding out of the mount of Esau?

9 And thy mighty *men*, O Teman, shall be dismayed, to the end that every one of the mount of Esau may be cut off by slaughter.

10 For *thy* violence against thy brother Jacob shame shall cover thee, and thou shalt be cut off for ever.

11 In the day that thou stoodest on the other side, in the day that the strangers carried away captive his forces, and foreigners entered into his gates, and cast lots upon Jerusalem, even thou *wast* as one of them.

12 But thou shouldest not have looked on the day of thy brother in the day that he became a stranger; neither shouldest thou have rejoiced over the children of Judah in the day of their destruction; neither shouldest thou have spoken proudly in the day of distress.

13 Thou shouldest not have entered into the gate of my people in the day of their calamity; yea, thou shouldest not have looked on their affliction in the day of their calamity, nor have laid *hands* on their substance in the day of their calamity;

14 Neither shouldest thou have stood in the crossway, to cut off those of his that did escape; neither shouldest thou have delivered up those of his that did remain in the day of distress.

15 For the day of the LORD *is* near upon all the heathen: as thou hast done, it shall be done unto thee: thy reward shall return upon thine own head.

16 For as ye have drunk upon my holy mountain, *so* shall all the heathen drink continually, yea, they shall drink, and they shall swallow down, and they shall be as though they had not been.

17 But upon mount Zion shall be deliverance, and there shall be holiness; and the house of Jacob shall possess their possessions.

18 And the house of Jacob shall be a fire, and the house of Joseph a flame, and the house of Esau for stubble, and they shall kindle in them, and devour them; and there shall not be *any* remaining of the house of Esau; for the LORD hath spoken *it*.

19 And *they of* the south shall possess the mount of Esau; and *they of* the plain the Philistines: and they shall possess the fields of Ephraim, and the fields of Samaria: and Benjamin *shall possess* Gilead.

20 And the captivity of this host of the children of Israel *shall possess* that of the Canaanites, *even* unto Zarephath; and the captivity of Jerusalem, which *is* in Sepharad, shall possess the cities of the south.

21 And saviours shall come up on mount Zion to judge the mount of Esau; and the kingdom shall be the LORD's.

THE BOOK OF JONAH

1 Now the word of the LORD came unto Jonah the son of Amittai, saying,

2 Arise, go to Nineveh, that great city, and cry against it; for their wickedness is come up before me.

3 But Jonah rose up to flee unto Tarshish from the presence of the LORD, and went down to Joppa; and he found a ship going to Tarshish: so he paid the fare thereof, and went down into it, to go with them unto Tarshish from the presence of the LORD.

4 But the LORD sent out a great wind into the sea, and there was a mighty tempest in the sea, so that the ship was like to be broken.

5 Then the mariners were afraid, and cried every man unto his god, and cast forth the wares that *were* in the ship into the sea, to lighten *it* of them. But Jonah was gone down into the sides of the ship; and he lay, and was fast asleep.

6 So the shipmaster came to him, and said unto him, What meanest thou, O sleeper? arise, call upon thy God, if so be that God will think upon us, that we perish not.

7 And they said every one to his fellow, Come, and let us cast lots, that we may know for whose cause this evil *is* upon us. So they cast lots, and the lot fell upon Jonah.

8 Then said they unto him, Tell us, we pray thee, for whose cause this evil *is* upon us; What *is* thine occupation? and whence comest thou? what *is* thy country? and of what people *art* thou?

9 And he said unto them, I *am* an Hebrew; and I fear the LORD, the God of

heaven, which hath made the sea and the dry *land*.

10 Then were the men exceedingly afraid, and said unto him, Why hast thou done this? For the men knew that he fled from the presence of the LORD, because he had told them.

11 Then said they unto him, What shall we do unto thee, that the sea may be calm unto us? for the sea wrought, and was tempestuous.

12 And he said unto them, Take me up, and cast me forth into the sea; so shall the sea be calm unto you: for I know that for my sake this great tempest *is* upon you.

13 Nevertheless the men rowed hard to bring *it* to the land; but they could not: for the sea wrought, and was tempestuous against them.

14 Wherefore they cried unto the LORD, and said, We beseech thee, O LORD, we beseech thee, let us not perish for this man's life, and lay not upon us innocent blood: for thou, O LORD, hast done as it pleased thee.

15 So they took up Jonah, and cast him forth into the sea: and the sea ceased from her raging.

16 Then the men feared the LORD exceedingly, and offered a sacrifice unto the LORD, and made vows.

17 Now the LORD had prepared a great fish to swallow up Jonah. And Jonah was in the belly of the fish three days and three nights.

2 Then Jonah prayed unto the LORD his God out of the fish's belly,

2 And said, I cried by reason of mine affliction unto the LORD, and he heard me; out of the belly of hell cried I, *and* thou heardest my voice.

3 For thou hadst cast me into the deep, in the midst of the seas; and the floods compassed me about: all thy billows and thy waves passed over me.

4 Then I said, I am cast out of thy sight; yet I will look again toward thy holy temple.

5 The waters compassed me about, *even* to the soul: the depth closed me round about, the weeds were wrapped about my head.

6 I went down to the bottoms of the mountains; the earth with her bars *was* about me for ever: yet hast thou brought up my life from corruption, O LORD my God.

7 When my soul fainted within me I remembered the LORD: and my prayer came in unto thee, into thine holy temple.

8 They that observe lying vanities forsake their own mercy.

9 But I will sacrifice unto thee with the voice of thanksgiving; I will pay *that* that I have vowed. Salvation *is* of the LORD.

10 And the LORD spake unto the fish, and it vomited out Jonah upon the dry *land*.

3 And the word of the LORD came unto Jonah the second time, saying,

2 Arise, go unto Nineveh, that great city, and preach unto it the preaching that I bid thee.

3 So Jonah arose, and went unto Nineveh, according to the word of the LORD. Now Nineveh was an exceeding great city of three days' journey.

4 And Jonah began to enter into the city a day's journey, and he cried, and said, Yet forty days, and Nineveh shall be overthrown.

5 So the people of Nineveh believed God, and proclaimed a fast, and put on sackcloth, from the greatest of them even to the least of them.

6 For word came unto the king of Nineveh, and he arose from his throne, and he laid his robe from him, and covered *him* with sackcloth, and sat in ashes.

7 And he caused *it* to be proclaimed and published through Nineveh by the decree of the king and his nobles, saying, Let neither man nor beast, herd nor flock, taste any thing: let them not feed, nor drink water:

8 But let man and beast be covered with sackcloth, and cry mightily unto God: yea, let them turn every one from his evil way, and from the violence that *is* in their hands.

9 Who can tell *if* God will turn and repent, and turn away from his fierce anger, that we perish not?

10 And God saw their works, that they turned from their evil way; and God repented of the evil, that he had said that he would do unto them; and he did *it* not.

4 But it displeased Jonah exceedingly, and he was very angry.

2 And he prayed unto the LORD, and said, I pray thee, O LORD, *was* not this my saying, when I was yet in my country? Therefore I fled before unto Tarshish: for I knew that thou *art* a gracious God, and merciful, slow to anger, and of great kindness, and repentest thee of the evil.

3 Therefore now, O LORD, take, I beseech thee, my life from me; for *it is* better for me to die than to live.

4 Then said the LORD, Doest thou well to be angry?

5 So Jonah went out of the city, and sat on the east side of the city, and there made him a booth, and sat under it in the shadow, till he might see what would become of the city.

6 And the LORD God prepared a gourd, and made *it* to come up over Jonah, that it might be a shadow over his head, to deliver him from his grief. So Jonah was exceeding glad of the gourd.

7 But God prepared a worm when the morning rose the next day, and it smote the gourd that it withered.

8 And it came to pass, when the sun did arise, that God prepared a vehement east wind; and the sun beat upon the head of Jonah, that he fainted, and wished in himself to die, and said, *It is* better for me to die than to live.

9 And God said to Jonah, Doest thou well to be angry for the gourd? And he said, I do well to be angry, *even* unto death.

10 Then said the LORD, Thou hast had pity on the gourd, for the which thou hast not laboured, neither madest it grow; which came up in a night, and perished in a night:

11 And should not I spare Nineveh, that great city, wherein are more than sixscore thousand persons that cannot discern between their right hand and their left hand; and *also* much cattle?

THE BOOK OF
MICAH

1 The word of the LORD that came to
Micah the Morasthite in the days of
Jotham, Ahaz, *and* Hezekiah, kings of
Judah, which he saw concerning
Samaria and Jerusalem.
2 Hear, all ye people; hearken, O
earth, and all that therein is: and let the
Lord GOD be witness against you, the
Lord from his holy temple.
3 For, behold, the LORD cometh forth
out of his place, and will come down,
and tread upon the high places of the
earth.
4 And the mountains shall be molten
under him, and the valleys shall be
cleft, as wax before the fire, *and* as the
waters *that are* poured down a steep
place.
5 For the transgression of Jacob *is* all
this, and for the sins of the house of
Israel. What *is* the transgression of
Jacob? *is it* not Samaria? and what *are*
the high places of Judah? *are they* not
Jerusalem?
6 Therefore I will make Samaria as an
heap of the field, *and* as plantings of a
vineyard: and I will pour down the
stones thereof into the valley, and I will
discover the foundations thereof.
7 And all the graven images thereof
shall be beaten to pieces, and all the
hires thereof shall be burned with the
fire, and all the idols thereof will I lay
desolate: for she gathered *it* of the hire
of an harlot, and they shall return to
the hire of an harlot.
8 Therefore I will wail and howl, I will
go stripped and naked: I will make a
wailing like the dragons, and mourning
as the owls.
9 For her wound *is* incurable; for it is
come unto Judah; he is come unto the
gate of my people, *even* to Jerusalem.
10 Declare ye *it* not at Gath, weep ye
not at all: in the house of Aphrah roll
thyself in the dust.
11 Pass ye away, thou inhabitant of
Saphir, having thy shame naked: the
inhabitant of Zaanan came not forth in
the mourning of Beth-ezel; he shall
receive of you his standing.
12 For the inhabitant of Maroth waited carefully for good: but evil came
down from the LORD unto the gate of
Jerusalem.
13 O thou inhabitant of Lachish, bind
the chariot to the swift beast: she *is* the
beginning of the sin to the daughter of
Zion: for the transgressions of Israel
were found in thee.
14 Therefore shalt thou give presents
to Moresheth-gath: the houses of
Achzib *shall be* a lie to the kings of
Israel.
15 Yet will I bring an heir unto thee,
O inhabitant of Mareshah: he shall
come unto Adullam the glory of Israel.
16 Make thee bald, and poll thee for
thy delicate children; enlarge thy baldness as the eagle; for they are gone into
captivity from thee.

2 Woe to them that devise iniquity,
and work evil upon their beds!
when the morning is light, they practise
it, because it is in the power of their
hand.
2 And they covet fields, and take
them by violence; and houses, and take
them away: so they oppress a man and
his house, even a man and his heritage.

3 Therefore thus saith the LORD;
Behold, against this family do I devise
an evil, from which ye shall not remove
your necks; neither shall ye go haugh-
tily: for this time *is* evil.
4 In that day shall *one* take up a parable against you, and lament with a
doleful lamentation, *and* say, We be
utterly spoiled: he hath changed the
portion of my people: how hath he
removed *it* from me! turning away he
hath divided our fields.
5 Therefore thou shalt have none that
shall cast a cord by lot in the congregation of the LORD.
6 Prophesy ye not, *say they to them*
that prophesy: they shall not prophesy
to them, *that* they shall not take shame.
7 O *thou that art* named the house of
Jacob, is the spirit of the LORD straitened? *are* these his doings? do not my
words do good to him that walketh
uprightly?
8 Even of late my people is risen up
as an enemy: ye pull off the robe with
the garment from them that pass by
securely as men averse from war.
9 The women of my people have ye
cast out from their pleasant houses;
from their children have ye taken away
my glory for ever.
10 Arise ye, and depart; for this *is* not
your rest: because it is polluted, it shall
destroy *you*, even with a sore destruction.
11 If a man walking in the spirit and
falsehood do lie, *saying*, I will prophesy
unto thee of wine and of strong drink;
he shall even be the prophet of this
people.
12 I will surely assemble, O Jacob, all
of thee; I will surely gather the remnant of Israel; I will put them together
as the sheep of Bozrah, as the flock in
the midst of their fold: they shall make
great noise by reason of *the multitude*
of men.
13 The breaker is come up before
them: they have broken up, and have
passed through the gate, and are gone
out by it: and their king shall pass
before them, and the LORD on the head
of them.

3 And I said, Hear, I pray you, O
heads of Jacob, and ye princes of
the house of Israel; *Is it* not for you to
know judgment?
2 Who hate the good, and love the
evil; who pluck off their skin from off
them, and their flesh from off their
bones;
3 Who also eat the flesh of my people,
and flay their skin from off them; and
they break their bones, and chop them
in pieces, as for the pot, and as flesh
within the caldron.
4 Then shall they cry unto the LORD,
but he will not hear them: he will even
hide his face from them at that time, as
they have behaved themselves ill in
their doings.
5 Thus saith the LORD concerning the
prophets that make my people err, that
bite with their teeth, and cry, Peace;
and he that putteth not into their
mouths, they even prepare war against
him.
6 Therefore night *shall be* unto you,
that ye shall not have a vision; and it
shall be dark unto you, that ye shall not
divine; and the sun shall go down over
the prophets, and the day shall be dark
over them.
7 Then shall the seers be ashamed,
and the diviners confounded: yea, they
shall all cover their lips; for *there is* no
answer of God.

8 But truly I am full of power by the spirit of the LORD, and of judgment, and of might, to declare unto Jacob his transgression, and to Israel his sin.

9 Hear this, I pray you, ye heads of the house of Jacob, and princes of the house of Israel, that abhor judgment, and pervert all equity.

10 They build up Zion with blood, and Jerusalem with iniquity.

11 The heads thereof judge for reward, and the priests thereof teach for hire, and the prophets thereof divine for money: yet will they lean upon the LORD, and say, *Is* not the LORD among us? none evil can come upon us.

12 Therefore shall Zion for your sake be plowed *as* a field, and Jerusalem shall become heaps, and the mountain of the house as the high places of the forest.

4 But in the last days it shall come to pass, *that* the mountain of the house of the LORD shall be established in the top of the mountains, and it shall be exalted above the hills; and people shall flow unto it.

2 And many nations shall come, and say, Come, and let us go up to the mountain of the LORD, and to the house of the God of Jacob; and he will teach us of his ways, and we will walk in his paths: for the law shall go forth of Zion, and the word of the LORD from Jerusalem.

3 And he shall judge among many people, and rebuke strong nations afar off; and they shall beat their swords into plowshares, and their spears into pruninghooks: nation shall not lift up a sword against nation, neither shall they learn war any more.

4 But they shall sit every man under his vine and under his fig tree; and none shall make *them* afraid: for the mouth of the LORD of hosts hath spoken *it*.

5 For all people will walk every one in the name of his god, and we will walk in the name of the LORD our God for ever and ever.

6 In that day, saith the LORD, will I assemble her that halteth, and I will gather her that is driven out, and her that I have afflicted;

7 And I will make her that halted a remnant, and her that was cast far off a strong nation: and the LORD shall reign over them in mount Zion from henceforth, even for ever.

8 And thou, O tower of the flock, the strong hold of the daughter of Zion, unto thee shall it come, even the first dominion; the kingdom shall come to the daughter of Jerusalem.

9 Now why dost thou cry out aloud? *is there* no king in thee? is thy counsellor perished? for pangs have taken thee as a woman in travail.

10 Be in pain, and labour to bring forth, O daughter of Zion, like a woman in travail: for now shalt thou go forth out of the city, and thou shalt dwell in the field, and thou shalt go *even* to Babylon; there shalt thou be delivered; there the LORD shall redeem thee from the hand of thine enemies.

11 Now also many nations are gathered against thee, that say, Let her be defiled, and let our eye look upon Zion.

12 But they know not the thoughts of the LORD, neither understand they his counsel: for he shall gather them as the sheaves into the floor.

13 Arise and thresh, O daughter of
Zion: for I will make thine horn iron,
and I will make thy hoofs brass: and
thou shalt beat in pieces many people:
and I will consecrate their gain unto
the Lord, and their substance unto the
Lord of the whole earth.

5 Now gather thyself in troops, O
daughter of troops: he hath laid
siege against us: they shall smite the
judge of Israel with a rod upon the
cheek.
2 But thou, Beth-lehem Ephratah,
though thou be little among the thousands of Judah, *yet* out of thee shall he
come forth unto me *that is* to be ruler
in Israel; whose goings forth *have been*
from of old, from everlasting.
3 Therefore will he give them up,
until the time *that* she which travaileth
hath brought forth: then the remnant
of his brethren shall return unto the
children of Israel.
4 And he shall stand and feed in the
strength of the Lord, in the majesty of
the name of the Lord his God; and they
shall abide: for now shall he be great
unto the ends of the earth.
5 And this *man* shall be the peace,
when the Assyrian shall come into our
land: and when he shall tread in our
palaces, then shall we raise against him
seven shepherds, and eight principal
men.
6 And they shall waste the land of
Assyria with the sword, and the land of
Nimrod in the entrances thereof: thus
shall he deliver *us* from the Assyrian,
when he cometh into our land, and
when he treadeth within our borders.
7 And the remnant of Jacob shall be
in the midst of many people as a dew
from the Lord, as the showers upon the
grass, that tarrieth not for man, nor
waiteth for the sons of men.
8 And the remnant of Jacob shall be
among the Gentiles in the midst of
many people as a lion among the beasts
of the forest, as a young lion among the
flocks of sheep: who, if he go through,
both treadeth down, and teareth in
pieces, and none can deliver.
9 Thine hand shall be lifted up upon
thine adversaries, and all thine enemies shall be cut off.
10 And it shall come to pass in that
day, saith the Lord, that I will cut off
thy horses out of the midst of thee, and
I will destroy thy chariots:
11 And I will cut off the cities of thy
land, and throw down all thy strong
holds:
12 And I will cut off witchcrafts out of
thine hand; and thou shalt have no
more soothsayers:
13 Thy graven images also will I cut
off, and thy standing images out of the
midst of thee; and thou shalt no more
worship the work of thine hands.
14 And I will pluck up thy groves out
of the midst of thee: so will I destroy
thy cities.
15 And I will execute vengeance in
anger and fury upon the heathen, such
as they have not heard.

6 Hear ye now what the Lord saith;
Arise, contend thou before the
mountains, and let the hills hear thy
voice.
2 Hear ye, O mountains, the Lord's
controversy, and ye strong foundations
of the earth: for the Lord hath a controversy with his people, and he will plead
with Israel.
3 O my people, what have I done unto
thee? and wherein have I wearied
thee? testify against me.

4 For I brought thee up out of the
land of Egypt, and redeemed thee out
of the house of servants; and I sent
before thee Moses, Aaron, and Miriam.
5 O my people, remember now what
Balak king of Moab consulted, and
what Balaam the son of Beor answered
him from Shittim unto Gilgal; that ye
may know the righteousness of the
LORD.
6 Wherewith shall I come before the
LORD, *and* bow myself before the high
God? shall I come before him with
burnt offerings, with calves of a year
old?
7 Will the LORD be pleased with thousands of rams, *or* with ten thousands of
rivers of oil? shall I give my firstborn
for my transgression, the fruit of my
body *for* the sin of my soul?
8 He hath shewed thee, O man, what
is good; and what doth the LORD require
of thee, but to do justly, and to love
mercy, and to walk humbly with thy
God?
9 The LORD's voice crieth unto the
city, and *the man of* wisdom shall see
thy name: hear ye the rod, and who
hath appointed it.
10 Are there yet the treasures of wickedness in the house of the wicked, and
the scant measure *that is* abominable?
11 Shall I count *them* pure with the
wicked balances, and with the bag of
deceitful weights?
12 For the rich men thereof are full of
violence, and the inhabitants thereof
have spoken lies, and their tongue *is*
deceitful in their mouth.
13 Therefore also will I make *thee*
sick in smiting thee, in making *thee*
desolate because of thy sins.
14 Thou shalt eat, but not be satisfied;
and thy casting down *shall be* in the
midst of thee; and thou shalt take hold,
but shalt not deliver; and *that* which
thou deliverest will I give up to the
sword.
15 Thou shalt sow, but thou shalt not
reap; thou shalt tread the olives, but
thou shalt not anoint thee with oil; and
sweet wine, but shalt not drink wine.
16 For the statutes of Omri are kept,
and all the works of the house of Ahab,
and ye walk in their counsels; that I
should make thee a desolation, and the
inhabitants thereof an hissing: therefore ye shall bear the reproach of my
people.

7 Woe is me! for I am as when they
have gathered the summer fruits, as
the grapegleanings of the vintage:
there is no cluster to eat: my soul
desired the firstripe fruit.
2 The good *man* is perished out of the
earth: and *there is* none upright among
men: they all lie in wait for blood; they
hunt every man his brother with a net.
3 That they may do evil with both
hands earnestly, the prince asketh, and
the judge *asketh* for a reward; and the
great *man*, he uttereth his mischievous
desire: so they wrap it up.
4 The best of them *is* as a brier: the
most upright *is sharper* than a thorn
hedge: the day of thy watchmen *and*
thy visitation cometh; now shall be
their perplexity.
5 Trust ye not in a friend, put ye not
confidence in a guide: keep the doors
of thy mouth from her that lieth in thy
bosom.
6 For the son dishonoureth the father,
the daughter riseth up against her
mother, the daughter in law against her
mother in law; a man's enemies *are* the
men of his own house.

7 Therefore I will look unto the LORD;
I will wait for the God of my salvation:
my God will hear me.
8 Rejoice not against me, O mine
enemy: when I fall, I shall arise; when I
sit in darkness, the LORD *shall be* a light
unto me.
9 I will bear the indignation of the
LORD, because I have sinned against
him, until he plead my cause, and execute judgment for me: he will bring me
forth to the light, *and* I shall behold his
righteousness.
10 Then *she that is* mine enemy shall
see *it*, and shame shall cover her which
said unto me, Where is the LORD thy
God? mine eyes shall behold her: now
shall she be trodden down as the mire
of the streets.
11 *In* the day that thy walls are to be
built, *in* that day shall the decree be far
removed.
12 *In* that day *also* he shall come even
to thee from Assyria, and *from* the fortified cities, and from the fortress even
to the river, and from sea to sea, and
from mountain to mountain.
13 Notwithstanding the land shall be
desolate because of them that dwell
therein, for the fruit of their doings.
14 Feed thy people with thy rod, the
flock of thine heritage, which dwell
solitarily *in* the wood, in the midst of
Carmel: let them feed *in* Bashan and
Gilead, as in the days of old.
15 According to the days of thy coming out of the land of Egypt will I shew
unto him marvellous *things*.
16 The nations shall see and be confounded at all their might: they shall
lay *their* hand upon *their* mouth, their
ears shall be deaf.
17 They shall lick the dust like a serpent, they shall move out of their holes
like worms of the earth: they shall be
afraid of the LORD our God, and shall
fear because of thee.
18 Who *is* a God like unto thee, that
pardoneth iniquity, and passeth by the
transgression of the remnant of his
heritage? he retaineth not his anger for
ever, because he delighteth *in* mercy.
19 He will turn again, he will have
compassion upon us; he will subdue
our iniquities; and thou wilt cast all
their sins into the depths of the sea.
20 Thou wilt perform the truth to
Jacob, *and* the mercy to Abraham,
which thou hast sworn unto our fathers
from the days of old.

THE BOOK OF
NAHUM

1 The burden of Nineveh. The book of the vision of Nahum the Elkoshite.

2 God *is* jealous, and the LORD revengeth; the LORD revengeth, and *is* furious; the LORD will take vengeance on his adversaries, and he reserveth *wrath* for his enemies.

3 The LORD *is* slow to anger, and great in power, and will not at all acquit *the wicked*: the LORD hath his way in the whirlwind and in the storm, and the clouds *are* the dust of his feet.

4 He rebuketh the sea, and maketh it dry, and drieth up all the rivers: Bashan languisheth, and Carmel, and the flower of Lebanon languisheth.

5 The mountains quake at him, and the hills melt, and the earth is burned at his presence, yea, the world, and all that dwell therein.

6 Who can stand before his indignation? and who can abide in the fierceness of his anger? his fury is poured out like fire, and the rocks are thrown down by him.

7 The LORD *is* good, a strong hold in the day of trouble; and he knoweth them that trust in him.

8 But with an overrunning flood he will make an utter end of the place thereof, and darkness shall pursue his enemies.

9 What do ye imagine against the LORD? he will make an utter end: affliction shall not rise up the second time.

10 For while *they be* folden together *as* thorns, and while they are drunken *as* drunkards, they shall be devoured as stubble fully dry.

11 There is *one* come out of thee, that imagineth evil against the LORD, a wicked counsellor.

12 Thus saith the LORD; Though *they be* quiet, and likewise many, yet thus shall they be cut down, when he shall pass through. Though I have afflicted thee, I will afflict thee no more.

13 For now will I break his yoke from off thee, and will burst thy bonds in sunder.

14 And the LORD hath given a commandment concerning thee, *that* no more of thy name be sown: out of the house of thy gods will I cut off the graven image and the molten image: I will make thy grave; for thou art vile.

15 Behold upon the mountains the feet of him that bringeth good tidings, that publisheth peace! O Judah, keep thy solemn feasts, perform thy vows: for the wicked shall no more pass through thee; he is utterly cut off.

2 He that dasheth in pieces is come up before thy face: keep the munition, watch the way, make *thy* loins strong, fortify *thy* power mightily.

2 For the LORD hath turned away the excellency of Jacob, as the excellency of Israel: for the emptiers have emptied them out, and marred their vine branches.

3 The shield of his mighty men is made red, the valiant men *are* in scarlet: the chariots *shall be* with flaming torches in the day of his preparation, and the fir trees shall be terribly shaken.

4 The chariots shall rage in the
streets, they shall justle one against
another in the broad ways: they shall
seem like torches, they shall run like
the lightnings.
5 He shall recount his worthies: they
shall stumble in their walk; they shall
make haste to the wall thereof, and the
defence shall be prepared.
6 The gates of the rivers shall be
opened, and the palace shall be dissolved.
7 And Huzzab shall be led away captive, she shall be brought up, and her
maids shall lead *her* as with the voice
of doves, tabering upon their breasts.
8 But Nineveh *is* of old like a pool of
water: yet they shall flee away. Stand,
stand, *shall they cry*; but none shall
look back.
9 Take ye the spoil of silver, take the
spoil of gold: for *there is* none end of
the store *and* glory out of all the pleasant furniture.
10 She is empty, and void, and waste:
and the heart melteth, and the knees
smite together, and much pain *is* in all
loins, and the faces of them all gather
blackness.
11 Where *is* the dwelling of the lions,
and the feedingplace of the young
lions, where the lion, *even* the old lion,
walked, *and* the lion's whelp, and none
made *them* afraid?
12 The lion did tear in pieces enough
for his whelps, and strangled for his
lionesses, and filled his holes with prey,
and his dens with ravin.
13 Behold, I *am* against thee, saith
the LORD of hosts, and I will burn her
chariots in the smoke, and the sword
shall devour thy young lions: and I will
cut off thy prey from the earth, and the
voice of thy messengers shall no more
be heard.

3 Woe to the bloody city! it *is* all full
of lies *and* robbery; the prey
departeth not;
2 The noise of a whip, and the noise of
the rattling of the wheels, and of the
pransing horses, and of the jumping
chariots.
3 The horseman lifteth up both the
bright sword and the glittering spear:
and *there is* a multitude of slain, and a
great number of carcases; and *there is*
none end of *their* corpses; they stumble
upon their corpses:
4 Because of the multitude of the
whoredoms of the wellfavoured harlot,
the mistress of witchcrafts, that selleth
nations through her whoredoms, and
families through her witchcrafts.
5 Behold, I *am* against thee, saith the
LORD of hosts; and I will discover thy
skirts upon thy face, and I will shew the
nations thy nakedness, and the kingdoms thy shame.
6 And I will cast abominable filth
upon thee, and make thee vile, and will
set thee as a gazingstock.
7 And it shall come to pass, *that* all
they that look upon thee shall flee from
thee, and say, Nineveh is laid waste:
who will bemoan her? whence shall I
seek comforters for thee?
8 Art thou better than populous No,
that was situate among the rivers, *that*
had the waters round about it, whose
rampart *was* the sea, *and* her wall *was*
from the sea?
9 Ethiopia and Egypt *were* her
strength, and *it was* infinite; Put and
Lubim were thy helpers.
10 Yet *was* she carried away, she went
into captivity: her young children also
were dashed in pieces at the top of all

the streets: and they cast lots for her
honourable men, and all her great men
were bound in chains.
11 Thou also shalt be drunken: thou
shalt be hid, thou also shalt seek
strength because of the enemy.
12 All thy strong holds *shall be like*
fig trees with the firstripe figs: if they
be shaken, they shall even fall into the
mouth of the eater.
13 Behold, thy people in the midst of
thee *are* women: the gates of thy land
shall be set wide open unto thine enemies: the fire shall devour thy bars.
14 Draw thee waters for the siege,
fortify thy strong holds: go into clay,
and tread the morter, make strong the
brickkiln.
15 There shall the fire devour thee;
the sword shall cut thee off, it shall eat
thee up like the cankerworm: make
thyself many as the cankerworm, make
thyself many as the locusts.
16 Thou hast multiplied thy merchants above the stars of heaven: the
cankerworm spoileth, and flieth away.
17 Thy crowned *are* as the locusts,
and thy captains as the great grasshoppers, which camp in the hedges in the
cold day, *but* when the sun ariseth they
flee away, and their place is not known
where they *are*.
18 Thy shepherds slumber, O king of
Assyria: thy nobles shall dwell *in the*
dust: thy people is scattered upon the
mountains, and no man gathereth
them.
19 *There is* no healing of thy bruise;
thy wound is grievous: all that hear the
bruit of thee shall clap the hands over
thee: for upon whom hath not thy wickedness passed continually?

THE BOOK OF HABAKKUK

1 The burden which Habakkuk the
prophet did see.
2 O LORD, how long shall I cry, and
thou wilt not hear! *even* cry out unto
thee *of* violence, and thou wilt not save!
3 Why dost thou shew me iniquity,
and cause *me* to behold grievance? for
spoiling and violence *are* before me:
and there are *that* raise up strife and
contention.
4 Therefore the law is slacked, and
judgment doth never go forth: for the
wicked doth compass about the
righteous; therefore wrong judgment
proceedeth.
5 Behold ye among the heathen, and
regard, and wonder marvellously: for I
will work a work in your days, *which* ye
will not believe, though it be told *you*.
6 For, lo, I raise up the Chaldeans,
that bitter and hasty nation, which
shall march through the breadth of the
land, to possess the dwellingplaces *that*
are not theirs.
7 They *are* terrible and dreadful:
their judgment and their dignity shall
proceed of themselves.
8 Their horses also are swifter than
the leopards, and are more fierce than
the evening wolves: and their horse-

men shall spread themselves, and their
horsemen shall come from far; they
shall fly as the eagle *that* hasteth to
eat.
9 They shall come all for violence:
their faces shall sup up *as* the east
wind, and they shall gather the captivity as the sand.
10 And they shall scoff at the kings,
and the princes shall be a scorn unto
them: they shall deride every strong
hold; for they shall heap dust, and take
it.
11 Then shall *his* mind change, and
he shall pass over, and offend, *imputing* this his power unto his god.
12 *Art* thou not from everlasting, O
LORD my God, mine Holy One? we shall
not die. O LORD, thou hast ordained
them for judgment; and, O mighty God,
thou hast established them for correction.
13 *Thou art* of purer eyes than to
behold evil, and canst not look on iniquity: wherefore lookest thou upon them
that deal treacherously, *and* holdest thy
tongue when the wicked devoureth *the
man that is* more righteous than he?
14 And makest men as the fishes of
the sea, as the creeping things, *that
have* no ruler over them?
15 They take up all of them with the
angle, they catch them in their net, and
gather them in their drag: therefore
they rejoice and are glad.
16 Therefore they sacrifice unto their
net, and burn incense unto their drag;
because by them their portion *is* fat,
and their meat plenteous.
17 Shall they therefore empty their
net, and not spare continually to slay
the nations?

2 I will stand upon my watch, and set
me upon the tower, and will watch
to see what he will say unto me, and
what I shall answer when I am reproved.
2 And the LORD answered me, and
said, Write the vision, and make *it*
plain upon tables, that he may run that
readeth it.
3 For the vision *is* yet for an appointed time, but at the end it shall speak,
and not lie: though it tarry, wait for it;
because it will surely come, it will not
tarry.
4 Behold, his soul *which* is lifted up is
not upright in him: but the just shall
live by his faith.
5 Yea also, because he transgresseth
by wine, *he is* a proud man, neither
keepeth at home, who enlargeth his
desire as hell, and *is* as death, and cannot be satisfied, but gathereth unto him
all nations, and heapeth unto him all
people:
6 Shall not all these take up a parable
against him, and a taunting proverb
against him, and say, Woe to him that
increaseth *that which is* not his! how
long? and to him that ladeth himself
with thick clay!
7 Shall they not rise up suddenly that
shall bite thee, and awake that shall
vex thee, and thou shalt be for booties
unto them?
8 Because thou hast spoiled many
nations, all the remnant of the people
shall spoil thee; because of men's
blood, and *for* the violence of the land,
of the city, and of all that dwell therein.
9 Woe to him that coveteth an evil
covetousness to his house, that he may
set his nest on high, that he may be
delivered from the power of evil!
10 Thou hast consulted shame to thy
house by cutting off many people, and
hast sinned *against* thy soul.

11 For the stone shall cry out of the wall, and the beam out of the timber shall answer it.

12 Woe to him that buildeth a town with blood, and stablisheth a city by iniquity!

13 Behold, *is it* not of the LORD of hosts that the people shall labour in the very fire, and the people shall weary themselves for very vanity?

14 For the earth shall be filled with the knowledge of the glory of the LORD, as the waters cover the sea.

15 Woe unto him that giveth his neighbour drink, that puttest thy bottle to *him*, and makest *him* drunken also, that thou mayest look on their nakedness!

16 Thou art filled with shame for glory: drink thou also, and let thy foreskin be uncovered: the cup of the LORD's right hand shall be turned unto thee, and shameful spewing *shall be* on thy glory.

17 For the violence of Lebanon shall cover thee, and the spoil of beasts, *which* made them afraid, because of men's blood, and for the violence of the land, of the city, and of all that dwell therein.

18 What profiteth the graven image that the maker thereof hath graven it; the molten image, and a teacher of lies, that the maker of his work trusteth therein, to make dumb idols?

19 Woe unto him that saith to the wood, Awake; to the dumb stone, Arise, it shall teach! Behold, it *is* laid over with gold and silver, and *there is* no breath at all in the midst of it.

20 But the LORD *is* in his holy temple: let all the earth keep silence before him.

3 A prayer of Habakkuk the prophet upon Shigionoth.

2 O LORD, I have heard thy speech, *and* was afraid: O LORD, revive thy work in the midst of the years, in the midst of the years make known; in wrath remember mercy.

3 God came from Teman, and the Holy One from mount Paran. Selah. His glory covered the heavens, and the earth was full of his praise.

4 And *his* brightness was as the light; he had horns *coming* out of his hand: and there *was* the hiding of his power.

5 Before him went the pestilence, and burning coals went forth at his feet.

6 He stood, and measured the earth: he beheld, and drove asunder the nations; and the everlasting mountains were scattered, the perpetual hills did bow: his ways *are* everlasting.

7 I saw the tents of Cushan in affliction: *and* the curtains of the land of Midian did tremble.

8 Was the LORD displeased against the rivers? *was* thine anger against the rivers? *was* thy wrath against the sea, that thou didst ride upon thine horses *and* thy chariots of salvation?

9 Thy bow was made quite naked, *according* to the oaths of the tribes, *even thy* word. Selah. Thou didst cleave the earth with rivers.

10 The mountains saw thee, *and* they trembled: the overflowing of the water passed by: the deep uttered his voice, *and* lifted up his hands on high.

11 The sun *and* moon stood still in their habitation: at the light of thine arrows they went, *and* at the shining of thy glittering spear.

12 Thou didst march through the land in indignation, thou didst thresh the heathen in anger.

13 Thou wentest forth for the salvation of thy people, *even* for salvation with thine anointed; thou woundedst the head out of the house of the wicked, by discovering the foundation unto the neck. Selah.

14 Thou didst strike through with his staves the head of his villages: they came out as a whirlwind to scatter me: their rejoicing *was* as to devour the poor secretly.

15 Thou didst walk through the sea with thine horses, *through* the heap of great waters.

16 When I heard, my belly trembled; my lips quivered at the voice: rottenness entered into my bones, and I trembled in myself, that I might rest in the day of trouble: when he cometh up unto the people, he will invade them with his troops.

17 Although the fig tree shall not blossom, neither *shall* fruit *be* in the vines; the labour of the olive shall fail, and the fields shall yield no meat; the flock shall be cut off from the fold, and *there shall be* no herd in the stalls:

18 Yet I will rejoice in the LORD, I will joy in the God of my salvation.

19 The LORD God *is* my strength, and he will make my feet like hinds' *feet*, and he will make me to walk upon mine high places. To the chief singer on my stringed instruments.

THE BOOK OF ZEPHANIAH

1 The word of the LORD which came unto Zephaniah the son of Cushi, the son of Gedaliah, the son of Amariah, the son of Hizkiah, in the days of Josiah the son of Amon, king of Judah.

2 I will utterly consume all *things* from off the land, saith the LORD.

3 I will consume man and beast; I will consume the fowls of the heaven, and the fishes of the sea, and the stumblingblocks with the wicked; and I will cut off man from off the land, saith the LORD.

4 I will also stretch out mine hand upon Judah, and upon all the inhabitants of Jerusalem; and I will cut off the remnant of Baal from this place, *and* the name of the Chemarims with the priests;

5 And them that worship the host of heaven upon the housetops; and them that worship *and* that swear by the LORD, and that swear by Malcham;

6 And them that are turned back from the LORD; and *those* that have not sought the LORD, nor enquired for him.

7 Hold thy peace at the presence of the Lord GOD: for the day of the LORD *is* at hand: for the LORD hath prepared a sacrifice, he hath bid his guests.

8 And it shall come to pass in the day of the LORD's sacrifice, that I will punish the princes, and the king's children, and all such as are clothed with strange apparel.

9 In the same day also will I punish all those that leap on the threshold, which

fill their masters' houses with violence
and deceit.
10 And it shall come to pass in that
day, saith the LORD, *that there shall be*
the noise of a cry from the fish gate,
and an howling from the second, and a
great crashing from the hills.
11 Howl, ye inhabitants of Maktesh,
for all the merchant people are cut
down; all they that bear silver are cut
off.
12 And it shall come to pass at that
time, *that* I will search Jerusalem with
candles, and punish the men that are
settled on their lees: that say in their
heart, The LORD will not do good, neither will he do evil.
13 Therefore their goods shall become a booty, and their houses a desolation: they shall also build houses, but
not inhabit *them*; and they shall plant
vineyards, but not drink the wine thereof.
14 The great day of the LORD *is* near,
it is near, and hasteth greatly, *even* the
voice of the day of the LORD: the mighty
man shall cry there bitterly.
15 That day *is* a day of wrath, a day of
trouble and distress, a day of wasteness
and desolation, a day of darkness and
gloominess, a day of clouds and thick
darkness,
16 A day of the trumpet and alarm
against the fenced cities, and against
the high towers.
17 And I will bring distress upon men,
that they shall walk like blind men,
because they have sinned against the
LORD: and their blood shall be poured
out as dust, and their flesh as the dung.
18 Neither their silver nor their gold
shall be able to deliver them in the day
of the LORD's wrath; but the whole land
shall be devoured by the fire of his
jealousy: for he shall make even a
speedy riddance of all them that dwell
in the land.

2 Gather yourselves together, yea,
gather together, O nation not desired;
2 Before the decree bring forth, *before*
the day pass as the chaff, before the
fierce anger of the LORD come upon
you, before the day of the LORD's anger
come upon you.
3 Seek ye the LORD, all ye meek of the
earth, which have wrought his judgment; seek righteousness, seek meekness: it may be ye shall be hid in the
day of the LORD's anger.
4 For Gaza shall be forsaken, and
Ashkelon a desolation: they shall drive
out Ashdod at the noon day, and Ekron
shall be rooted up.
5 Woe unto the inhabitants of the sea
coast, the nation of the Cherethites! the
word of the LORD *is* against you; O
Canaan, the land of the Philistines, I
will even destroy thee, that there shall
be no inhabitant.
6 And the sea coast shall be dwellings
and cottages for shepherds, and folds
for flocks.
7 And the coast shall be for the remnant of the house of Judah; they shall
feed thereupon: in the houses of
Ashkelon shall they lie down in the
evening: for the LORD their God shall
visit them, and turn away their captivity.
8 I have heard the reproach of Moab,
and the revilings of the children of
Ammon, whereby they have reproached
my people, and magnified *themselves*
against their border.
9 Therefore *as* I live, saith the LORD of
hosts, the God of Israel, Surely Moab
shall be as Sodom, and the children of

Ammon as Gomorrah, *even* the breed-
ing of nettles, and saltpits, and a perpetual desolation: the residue of my
people shall spoil them, and the remnant of my people shall possess them.
10 This shall they have for their pride,
because they have reproached and
magnified *themselves* against the people of the LORD of hosts.
11 The LORD *will be* terrible unto
them: for he will famish all the gods of
the earth; and *men* shall worship him,
every one from his place, *even* all the
isles of the heathen.
12 Ye Ethiopians also, ye *shall be*
slain by my sword.
13 And he will stretch out his hand
against the north, and destroy Assyria;
and will make Nineveh a desolation,
and dry like a wilderness.
14 And flocks shall lie down in the
midst of her, all the beasts of the
nations: both the cormorant and the
bittern shall lodge in the upper lintels
of it; *their* voice shall sing in the windows; desolation *shall be* in the thresholds: for he shall uncover the cedar
work.
15 This *is* the rejoicing city that dwelt
carelessly, that said in her heart, I *am*,
and *there is* none beside me: how is she
become a desolation, a place for beasts
to lie down in! every one that passeth
by her shall hiss, *and* wag his hand.

3 Woe to her that is filthy and
polluted, to the oppressing city!
2 She obeyed not the voice; she received not correction; she trusted not
in the LORD; she drew not near to her
God.
3 Her princes within her *are* roaring
lions; her judges *are* evening wolves;
they gnaw not the bones till the morrow.
4 Her prophets *are* light *and* treacherous persons: her priests have polluted
the sanctuary, they have done violence
to the law.
5 The just LORD *is* in the midst thereof; he will not do iniquity: every morning doth he bring his judgment to light,
he faileth not; but the unjust knoweth
no shame.
6 I have cut off the nations: their towers are desolate; I made their streets
waste, that none passeth by: their cities
are destroyed, so that there is no man,
that there is none inhabitant.
7 I said, Surely thou wilt fear me, thou
wilt receive instruction; so their dwelling should not be cut off, howsoever I
punished them: but they rose early, *and*
corrupted all their doings.
8 Therefore wait ye upon me, saith
the LORD, until the day that I rise up to
the prey: for my determination *is* to
gather the nations, that I may assemble
the kingdoms, to pour upon them mine
indignation, *even* all my fierce anger:
for all the earth shall be devoured with
the fire of my jealousy.
9 For then will I turn to the people a
pure language, that they may all call
upon the name of the LORD, to serve
him with one consent.
10 From beyond the rivers of Ethiopia
my suppliants, *even* the daughter of my
dispersed, shall bring mine offering.
11 In that day shalt thou not be
ashamed for all thy doings, wherein
thou hast transgressed against me: for
then I will take away out of the midst of
thee them that rejoice in thy pride, and
thou shalt no more be haughty because
of my holy mountain.

12 I will also leave in the midst of thee an afflicted and poor people, and they shall trust in the name of the LORD.

13 The remnant of Israel shall not do iniquity, nor speak lies; neither shall a deceitful tongue be found in their mouth: for they shall feed and lie down, and none shall make *them* afraid.

14 Sing, O daughter of Zion; shout, O Israel; be glad and rejoice with all the heart, O daughter of Jerusalem.

15 The LORD hath taken away thy judgments, he hath cast out thine enemy: the king of Israel, *even* the LORD, *is* in the midst of thee: thou shalt not see evil any more.

16 In that day it shall be said to Jerusalem, Fear thou not: *and to* Zion, Let not thine hands be slack.

17 The LORD thy God in the midst of thee *is* mighty; he will save, he will rejoice over thee with joy; he will rest in his love, he will joy over thee with singing.

18 I will gather *them that are* sorrowful for the solemn assembly, *who* are of thee, *to whom* the reproach of it *was* a burden.

19 Behold, at that time I will undo all that afflict thee: and I will save her that halteth, and gather her that was driven out; and I will get them praise and fame in every land where they have been put to shame.

20 At that time will I bring you *again*, even in the time that I gather you: for I will make you a name and a praise among all people of the earth, when I turn back your captivity before your eyes, saith the LORD.

THE BOOK OF HAGGAI

1 In the second year of Darius the king, in the sixth month, in the first day of the month, came the word of the LORD by Haggai the prophet unto Zerubbabel the son of Shealtiel, governor of Judah, and to Joshua the son of Josedech, the high priest, saying,

2 Thus speaketh the LORD of hosts, saying, This people say, The time is not come, the time that the LORD's house should be built.

3 Then came the word of the LORD by Haggai the prophet, saying,

4 *Is it* time for you, O ye, to dwell in your cieled houses, and this house *lie* waste?

5 Now therefore thus saith the LORD of hosts; Consider your ways.

6 Ye have sown much, and bring in little; ye eat, but ye have not enough; ye drink, but ye are not filled with drink; ye clothe you, but there is none warm; and he that earneth wages earneth wages *to put it* into a bag with holes.

7 Thus saith the LORD of hosts; Consider your ways.

8 Go up to the mountain, and bring wood, and build the house; and I will take pleasure in it, and I will be glorified, saith the LORD.

9 Ye looked for much, and, lo, *it came* to little; and when ye brought *it* home, I did blow upon it. Why? saith the LORD of hosts. Because of mine house that *is* waste, and ye run every man unto his own house.

10 Therefore the heaven over you is stayed from dew, and the earth is stayed *from* her fruit.

11 And I called for a drought upon the land, and upon the mountains, and upon the corn, and upon the new wine, and upon the oil, and upon *that* which the ground bringeth forth, and upon men, and upon cattle, and upon all the labour of the hands.

12 Then Zerubbabel the son of Shealtiel, and Joshua the son of Josedech, the high priest, with all the remnant of the people, obeyed the voice of the LORD their God, and the words of Haggai the prophet, as the LORD their God had sent him, and the people did fear before the LORD.

13 Then spake Haggai the LORD's messenger in the LORD's message unto the people, saying, I *am* with you, saith the LORD.

14 And the LORD stirred up the spirit of Zerubbabel the son of Shealtiel, governor of Judah, and the spirit of Joshua the son of Josedech, the high priest, and the spirit of all the remnant of the people; and they came and did work in the house of the LORD of hosts, their God,

15 In the four and twentieth day of the sixth month, in the second year of Darius the king.

2 In the seventh *month*, in the one and twentieth *day* of the month, came the word of the LORD by the prophet Haggai, saying,

2 Speak now to Zerubbabel the son of Shealtiel, governor of Judah, and to Joshua the son of Josedech, the high priest, and to the residue of the people, saying,

3 Who *is* left among you that saw this house in her first glory? and how do ye see it now? *is it* not in your eyes in comparison of it as nothing?

4 Yet now be strong, O Zerubbabel, saith the LORD; and be strong, O Joshua, son of Josedech, the high priest; and be strong, all ye people of the land, saith the LORD, and work: for I *am* with you, saith the LORD of hosts:

5 *According to* the word that I covenanted with you when ye came out of Egypt, so my spirit remaineth among you: fear ye not.

6 For thus saith the LORD of hosts; Yet once, it *is* a little while, and I will shake the heavens, and the earth, and the sea, and the dry *land*;

7 And I will shake all nations, and the desire of all nations shall come: and I will fill this house with glory, saith the LORD of hosts.

8 The silver *is* mine, and the gold *is* mine, saith the LORD of hosts.

9 The glory of this latter house shall be greater than of the former, saith the LORD of hosts: and in this place will I give peace, saith the LORD of hosts.

10 In the four and twentieth *day* of the ninth *month*, in the second year of Darius, came the word of the LORD by Haggai the prophet, saying,

11 Thus saith the LORD of hosts; Ask now the priests *concerning* the law, saying,

12 If one bear holy flesh in the skirt of his garment, and with his skirt do touch bread, or pottage, or wine, or oil, or any

meat, shall it be holy? And the priests
answered and said, No.
13 Then said Haggai, If *one that is*
unclean by a dead body touch any of
these, shall it be unclean? And the
priests answered and said, It shall be
unclean.
14 Then answered Haggai, and said,
So *is* this people, and so *is* this nation
before me, saith the LORD; and so *is*
every work of their hands; and that
which they offer there *is* unclean.
15 And now, I pray you, consider from
this day and upward, from before a
stone was laid upon a stone in the
temple of the LORD:
16 Since those *days* were, when *one*
came to an heap of twenty *measures*,
there were *but* ten: when *one* came to
the pressfat for to draw out fifty *vessels*
out of the press, there were *but* twenty.
17 I smote you with blasting and with
mildew and with hail in all the labours
of your hands; yet ye *turned* not to me,
saith the LORD.
18 Consider now from this day and
upward, from the four and twentieth
day of the ninth *month, even* from the
day that the foundation of the LORD's
temple was laid, consider *it*.
19 Is the seed yet in the barn? yea, as
yet the vine, and the fig tree, and the
pomegranate, and the olive tree, hath
not brought forth: from this day will I
bless *you*.
20 And again the word of the LORD
came unto Haggai in the four and twentieth *day* of the month, saying,
21 Speak to Zerubbabel, governor of
Judah, saying, I will shake the heavens
and the earth;
22 And I will overthrow the throne of
kingdoms, and I will destroy the
strength of the kingdoms of the heathen; and I will overthrow the chariots,
and those that ride in them; and the
horses and their riders shall come
down, every one by the sword of his
brother.
23 In that day, saith the LORD of hosts,
will I take thee, O Zerubbabel, my servant, the son of Shealtiel, saith the
LORD, and will make thee as a signet:
for I have chosen thee, saith the LORD
of hosts.

THE BOOK OF ZECHARIAH

1 In the eighth month, in the second
year of Darius, came the word of
the LORD unto Zechariah, the son of
Berechiah, the son of Iddo the prophet,
saying,
2 The LORD hath been sore displeased
with your fathers.
3 Therefore say thou unto them, Thus
saith the LORD of hosts; Turn ye unto
me, saith the LORD of hosts, and I will
turn unto you, saith the LORD of hosts.
4 Be ye not as your fathers, unto
whom the former prophets have cried,
saying, Thus saith the LORD of hosts;
Turn ye now from your evil ways, and
from your evil doings: but they did not
hear, nor hearken unto me, saith the
LORD.

5 Your fathers, where *are* they? and
the prophets, do they live for ever?
6 But my words and my statutes,
which I commanded my servants the
prophets, did they not take hold of your
fathers? and they returned and said,
Like as the LORD of hosts thought to do
unto us, according to our ways, and
according to our doings, so hath he
dealt with us.
7 Upon the four and twentieth day of
the eleventh month, which *is* the month
Sebat, in the second year of Darius,
came the word of the LORD unto
Zechariah, the son of Berechiah, the
son of Iddo the prophet, saying,
8 I saw by night, and behold a man
riding upon a red horse, and he stood
among the myrtle trees that *were* in the
bottom; and behind him *were there* red
horses, speckled, and white.
9 Then said I, O my lord, what *are*
these? And the angel that talked with
me said unto me, I will shew thee what
these *be*.
10 And the man that stood among the
myrtle trees answered and said, These
are they whom the LORD hath sent to
walk to and fro through the earth.
11 And they answered the angel of
the LORD that stood among the myrtle
trees, and said, We have walked to and
fro through the earth, and, behold, all
the earth sitteth still, and is at rest.
12 Then the angel of the LORD answered and said, O LORD of hosts, how
long wilt thou not have mercy on
Jerusalem and on the cities of Judah,
against which thou hast had indignation these threescore and ten years?
13 And the LORD answered the angel
that talked with me *with* good words
and comfortable words.
14 So the angel that communed with
me said unto me, Cry thou, saying, Thus
saith the LORD of hosts; I am jealous for
Jerusalem and for Zion with a great
jealousy.
15 And I am very sore displeased with
the heathen *that are* at ease: for I was
but a little displeased, and they helped
forward the affliction.
16 Therefore thus saith the LORD; I
am returned to Jerusalem with mercies: my house shall be built in it, saith
the LORD of hosts, and a line shall be
stretched forth upon Jerusalem.
17 Cry yet, saying, Thus saith the
LORD of hosts; My cities through prosperity shall yet be spread abroad; and
the LORD shall yet comfort Zion, and
shall yet choose Jerusalem.
18 Then lifted I up mine eyes, and
saw, and behold four horns.
19 And I said unto the angel that
talked with me, What *be* these? And he
answered me, These *are* the horns
which have scattered Judah, Israel, and
Jerusalem.
20 And the LORD shewed me four
carpenters.
21 Then said I, What come these to
do? And he spake, saying, These *are* the
horns which have scattered Judah, so
that no man did lift up his head: but
these are come to fray them, to cast out
the horns of the Gentiles, which lifted
up *their* horn over the land of Judah to
scatter it.

2 I lifted up mine eyes again, and
looked, and behold a man with a
measuring line in his hand.
2 Then said I, Whither goest thou?
And he said unto me, To measure
Jerusalem, to see what *is* the breadth
thereof, and what *is* the length thereof.

3 And, behold, the angel that talked with me went forth, and another angel went out to meet him,

4 And said unto him, Run, speak to this young man, saying, Jerusalem shall be inhabited *as* towns without walls for the multitude of men and cattle therein:

5 For I, saith the LORD, will be unto her a wall of fire round about, and will be the glory in the midst of her.

6 Ho, ho, *come forth*, and flee from the land of the north, saith the LORD: for I have spread you abroad as the four winds of the heaven, saith the LORD.

7 Deliver thyself, O Zion, that dwellest *with* the daughter of Babylon.

8 For thus saith the LORD of hosts; After the glory hath he sent me unto the nations which spoiled you: for he that toucheth you toucheth the apple of his eye.

9 For, behold, I will shake mine hand upon them, and they shall be a spoil to their servants: and ye shall know that the LORD of hosts hath sent me.

10 Sing and rejoice, O daughter of Zion: for, lo, I come, and I will dwell in the midst of thee, saith the LORD.

11 And many nations shall be joined to the LORD in that day, and shall be my people: and I will dwell in the midst of thee, and thou shalt know that the LORD of hosts hath sent me unto thee.

12 And the LORD shall inherit Judah his portion in the holy land, and shall choose Jerusalem again.

13 Be silent, O all flesh, before the LORD: for he is raised up out of his holy habitation.

3 And he shewed me Joshua the high priest standing before the angel of the LORD, and Satan standing at his right hand to resist him.

2 And the LORD said unto Satan, The LORD rebuke thee, O Satan; even the LORD that hath chosen Jerusalem rebuke thee: *is* not this a brand plucked out of the fire?

3 Now Joshua was clothed with filthy garments, and stood before the angel.

4 And he answered and spake unto those that stood before him, saying, Take away the filthy garments from him. And unto him he said, Behold, I have caused thine iniquity to pass from thee, and I will clothe thee with change of raiment.

5 And I said, Let them set a fair mitre upon his head. So they set a fair mitre upon his head, and clothed him with garments. And the angel of the LORD stood by.

6 And the angel of the LORD protested unto Joshua, saying,

7 Thus saith the LORD of hosts; If thou wilt walk in my ways, and if thou wilt keep my charge, then thou shalt also judge my house, and shalt also keep my courts, and I will give thee places to walk among these that stand by.

8 Hear now, O Joshua the high priest, thou, and thy fellows that sit before thee: for they *are* men wondered at: for, behold, I will bring forth my servant the BRANCH.

9 For behold the stone that I have laid before Joshua; upon one stone *shall be* seven eyes: behold, I will engrave the graving thereof, saith the LORD of hosts, and I will remove the iniquity of that land in one day.

10 In that day, saith the LORD of hosts, shall ye call every man his neighbour under the vine and under the fig tree.

4 And the angel that talked with me came again, and waked me, as a man that is wakened out of his sleep,

2 And said unto me, What seest thou? And I said, I have looked, and behold a candlestick all *of* gold, with a bowl upon the top of it, and his seven lamps thereon, and seven pipes to the seven lamps, which *are* upon the top thereof:

3 And two olive trees by it, one upon the right *side* of the bowl, and the other upon the left *side* thereof.

4 So I answered and spake to the angel that talked with me, saying, What *are* these, my lord?

5 Then the angel that talked with me answered and said unto me, Knowest thou not what these be? And I said, No, my lord.

6 Then he answered and spake unto me, saying, This *is* the word of the LORD unto Zerubbabel, saying, Not by might, nor by power, but by my spirit, saith the LORD of hosts.

7 Who *art* thou, O great mountain? before Zerubbabel *thou shalt become* a plain: and he shall bring forth the headstone *thereof with* shoutings, *crying*, Grace, grace unto it.

8 Moreover the word of the LORD came unto me, saying,

9 The hands of Zerubbabel have laid the foundation of this house; his hands shall also finish it; and thou shalt know that the LORD of hosts hath sent me unto you.

10 For who hath despised the day of small things? for they shall rejoice, and shall see the plummet in the hand of Zerubbabel *with* those seven; they *are* the eyes of the LORD, which run to and fro through the whole earth.

11 Then answered I, and said unto him, What *are* these two olive trees upon the right *side* of the candlestick and upon the left *side* thereof?

12 And I answered again, and said unto him, What *be these* two olive branches which through the two golden pipes empty the golden *oil* out of themselves?

13 And he answered me and said, Knowest thou not what these *be*? And I said, No, my lord.

14 Then said he, These *are* the two anointed ones, that stand by the Lord of the whole earth.

5 Then I turned, and lifted up mine eyes, and looked, and behold a flying roll.

2 And he said unto me, What seest thou? And I answered, I see a flying roll; the length thereof *is* twenty cubits, and the breadth thereof ten cubits.

3 Then said he unto me, This *is* the curse that goeth forth over the face of the whole earth: for every one that stealeth shall be cut off *as* on this side according to it; and every one that sweareth shall be cut off *as* on that side according to it.

4 I will bring it forth, saith the LORD of hosts, and it shall enter into the house of the thief, and into the house of him that sweareth falsely by my name: and it shall remain in the midst of his house, and shall consume it with the timber thereof and the stones thereof.

5 Then the angel that talked with me went forth, and said unto me, Lift up now thine eyes, and see what *is* this that goeth forth.

6 And I said, What *is* it? And he said, This *is* an ephah that goeth forth. He said moreover, This *is* their resemblance through all the earth.

7 And, behold, there was lifted up a talent of lead: and this *is* a woman that sitteth in the midst of the ephah.

8 And he said, This *is* wickedness. And he cast it into the midst of the ephah; and he cast the weight of lead upon the mouth thereof.

9 Then lifted I up mine eyes, and looked, and, behold, there came out two women, and the wind *was* in their wings; for they had wings like the wings of a stork: and they lifted up the ephah between the earth and the heaven.

10 Then said I to the angel that talked with me, Whither do these bear the ephah?

11 And he said unto me, To build it an house in the land of Shinar: and it shall be established, and set there upon her own base.

6 And I turned, and lifted up mine eyes, and looked, and, behold, there came four chariots out from between two mountains; and the mountains *were* mountains of brass.

2 In the first chariot *were* red horses; and in the second chariot black horses;

3 And in the third chariot white horses; and in the fourth chariot grisled and bay horses.

4 Then I answered and said unto the angel that talked with me, What *are* these, my lord?

5 And the angel answered and said unto me, These *are* the four spirits of the heavens, which go forth from standing before the Lord of all the earth.

6 The black horses which *are* therein go forth into the north country; and the white go forth after them; and the grisled go forth toward the south country.

7 And the bay went forth, and sought to go that they might walk to and fro through the earth: and he said, Get you hence, walk to and fro through the earth. So they walked to and fro through the earth.

8 Then cried he upon me, and spake unto me, saying, Behold, these that go toward the north country have quieted my spirit in the north country.

9 And the word of the LORD came unto me, saying,

10 Take of *them of* the captivity, *even* of Heldai, of Tobijah, and of Jedaiah, which are come from Babylon, and come thou the same day, and go into the house of Josiah the son of Zephaniah;

11 Then take silver and gold, and make crowns, and set *them* upon the head of Joshua the son of Josedech, the high priest;

12 And speak unto him, saying, Thus speaketh the LORD of hosts, saying, Behold the man whose name *is* The BRANCH; and he shall grow up out of his place, and he shall build the temple of the LORD:

13 Even he shall build the temple of the LORD; and he shall bear the glory, and shall sit and rule upon his throne; and he shall be a priest upon his throne: and the counsel of peace shall be between them both.

14 And the crowns shall be to Helem, and to Tobijah, and to Jedaiah, and to Hen the son of Zephaniah, for a memorial in the temple of the LORD.

15 And they *that are* far off shall come and build in the temple of the LORD, and ye shall know that the LORD of hosts hath sent me unto you. And *this* shall come to pass, if ye will diligently obey the voice of the LORD your God.

7 And it came to pass in the fourth year of king Darius, *that* the word of the LORD came unto Zechariah in the

fourth *day* of the ninth month, *even* in
Chisleu;
2 When they had sent unto the house
of God Sherezer and Regemmelech,
and their men, to pray before the LORD,
3 *And* to speak unto the priests which
were in the house of the LORD of hosts,
and to the prophets, saying, Should I
weep in the fifth month, separating
myself, as I have done these so many
years?
4 Then came the word of the LORD of
hosts unto me, saying,
5 Speak unto all the people of the
land, and to the priests, saying, When
ye fasted and mourned in the fifth and
seventh *month*, even those seventy
years, did ye at all fast unto me, *even* to
me?
6 And when ye did eat, and when ye
did drink, did not ye eat *for yourselves*,
and drink *for yourselves*?
7 *Should ye* not *hear* the words which
the LORD hath cried by the former
prophets, when Jerusalem was inhabited and in prosperity, and the cities
thereof round about her, when *men*
inhabited the south and the plain?
8 And the word of the LORD came
unto Zechariah, saying,
9 Thus speaketh the LORD of hosts,
saying, Execute true judgment, and
shew mercy and compassions every
man to his brother:
10 And oppress not the widow, nor
the fatherless, the stranger, nor the
poor; and let none of you imagine evil
against his brother in your heart.
11 But they refused to hearken, and
pulled away the shoulder, and stopped
their ears, that they should not hear.
12 Yea, they made their hearts *as* an
adamant stone, lest they should hear
the law, and the words which the LORD
of hosts hath sent in his spirit by the
former prophets: therefore came a
great wrath from the LORD of hosts.
13 Therefore it is come to pass, *that*
as he cried, and they would not hear; so
they cried, and I would not hear, saith
the LORD of hosts:
14 But I scattered them with a whirlwind among all the nations whom they
knew not. Thus the land was desolate
after them, that no man passed through
nor returned: for they laid the pleasant
land desolate.

8 Again the word of the LORD of hosts
came *to me*, saying,
2 Thus saith the LORD of hosts; I was
jealous for Zion with great jealousy,
and I was jealous for her with great
fury.
3 Thus saith the LORD; I am returned
unto Zion, and will dwell in the midst of
Jerusalem: and Jerusalem shall be
called a city of truth; and the mountain
of the LORD of hosts the holy mountain.
4 Thus saith the LORD of hosts; There
shall yet old men and old women dwell
in the streets of Jerusalem, and every
man with his staff in his hand for very
age.
5 And the streets of the city shall be
full of boys and girls playing in the
streets thereof.
6 Thus saith the LORD of hosts; If it be
marvellous in the eyes of the remnant
of this people in these days, should it
also be marvellous in mine eyes? saith
the LORD of hosts.
7 Thus saith the LORD of hosts;
Behold, I will save my people from the
east country, and from the west country;
8 And I will bring them, and they
shall dwell in the midst of Jerusalem:
and they shall be my people, and I will

be their God, in truth and in righteousness.
9 Thus saith the LORD of hosts; Let
your hands be strong, ye that hear in
these days these words by the mouth of
the prophets, which *were* in the day
that the foundation of the house of the
LORD of hosts was laid, that the temple
might be built.
10 For before these days there was no
hire for man, nor any hire for beast;
neither *was there any* peace to him
that went out or came in because of the
affliction: for I set all men every one
against his neighbour.
11 But now I *will* not *be* unto the residue of this people as in the former
days, saith the LORD of hosts.
12 For the seed *shall be* prosperous;
the vine shall give her fruit, and the
ground shall give her increase, and the
heavens shall give their dew; and I will
cause the remnant of this people to possess all these *things*.
13 And it shall come to pass, *that* as
ye were a curse among the heathen, O
house of Judah, and house of Israel; so
will I save you, and ye shall be a blessing: fear not, *but* let your hands be
strong.
14 For thus saith the LORD of hosts; As
I thought to punish you, when your
fathers provoked me to wrath, saith the
LORD of hosts, and I repented not:
15 So again have I thought in these
days to do well unto Jerusalem and to
the house of Judah: fear ye not.
16 These *are* the things that ye shall
do; Speak ye every man the truth to his
neighbour; execute the judgment of
truth and peace in your gates:
17 And let none of you imagine evil in
your hearts against his neighbour; and
love no false oath: for all these *are*
things that I hate, saith the LORD.
18 And the word of the LORD of hosts
came unto me, saying,
19 Thus saith the LORD of hosts; The
fast of the fourth *month*, and the fast of
the fifth, and the fast of the seventh,
and the fast of the tenth, shall be to the
house of Judah joy and gladness, and
cheerful feasts; therefore love the truth
and peace.
20 Thus saith the LORD of hosts; *It*
shall yet *come to pass*, that there shall
come people, and the inhabitants of
many cities:
21 And the inhabitants of one *city*
shall go to another, saying, Let us go
speedily to pray before the LORD, and to
seek the LORD of hosts: I will go also.
22 Yea, many people and strong
nations shall come to seek the LORD of
hosts in Jerusalem, and to pray before
the LORD.
23 Thus saith the LORD of hosts; In
those days *it shall come to pass*, that
ten men shall take hold out of all languages of the nations, even shall take
hold of the skirt of him that is a Jew,
saying, We will go with you: for we have
heard *that* God *is* with you.

9 The burden of the word of the LORD
in the land of Hadrach, and
Damascus *shall be* the rest thereof:
when the eyes of man, as of all the
tribes of Israel, *shall be* toward the
LORD.
2 And Hamath also shall border
thereby; Tyrus, and Zidon, though it be
very wise.
3 And Tyrus did build herself a strong
hold, and heaped up silver as the dust,
and fine gold as the mire of the streets.

4 Behold, the Lord will cast her out,
and he will smite her power in the sea;
and she shall be devoured with fire.
5 Ashkelon shall see *it*, and fear;
Gaza also *shall see it*, and be very sorrowful, and Ekron; for her expectation
shall be ashamed; and the king shall
perish from Gaza, and Ashkelon shall
not be inhabited.
6 And a bastard shall dwell in Ashdod,
and I will cut off the pride of the
Philistines.
7 And I will take away his blood out of
his mouth, and his abominations from
between his teeth: but he that
remaineth, even he, *shall be* for our
God, and he shall be as a governor in
Judah, and Ekron as a Jebusite.
8 And I will encamp about mine
house because of the army, because of
him that passeth by, and because of
him that returneth: and no oppressor
shall pass through them any more: for
now have I seen with mine eyes.
9 Rejoice greatly, O daughter of Zion;
shout, O daughter of Jerusalem:
behold, thy King cometh unto thee: he
is just, and having salvation; lowly, and
riding upon an ass, and upon a colt the
foal of an ass.
10 And I will cut off the chariot from
Ephraim, and the horse from Jerusalem,
and the battle bow shall be cut off: and
he shall speak peace unto the heathen:
and his dominion *shall be* from sea
even to sea, and from the river *even* to
the ends of the earth.
11 As for thee also, by the blood of thy
covenant I have sent forth thy prisoners
out of the pit wherein *is* no water.
12 Turn you to the strong hold, ye
prisoners of hope: even to day do I
declare *that* I will render double unto
thee;
13 When I have bent Judah for me,
filled the bow with Ephraim, and raised
up thy sons, O Zion, against thy sons, O
Greece, and made thee as the sword of
a mighty man.
14 And the LORD shall be seen over
them, and his arrow shall go forth as
the lightning: and the Lord GOD shall
blow the trumpet, and shall go with
whirlwinds of the south.
15 The LORD of hosts shall defend
them; and they shall devour, and subdue with sling stones; and they shall
drink, *and* make a noise as through
wine; and they shall be filled like
bowls, *and* as the corners of the altar.
16 And the LORD their God shall save
them in that day as the flock of his
people: for *they shall be as* the stones
of a crown, lifted up as an ensign upon
his land.
17 For how great *is* his goodness, and
how great *is* his beauty! corn shall
make the young men cheerful, and new
wine the maids.

10 Ask ye of the LORD rain in the
time of the latter rain; *so* the
LORD shall make bright clouds, and give
them showers of rain, to every one grass
in the field.
2 For the idols have spoken vanity,
and the diviners have seen a lie, and
have told false dreams; they comfort in
vain: therefore they went their way as a
flock, they were troubled, because
there was no shepherd.
3 Mine anger was kindled against the
shepherds, and I punished the goats:
for the LORD of hosts hath visited his
flock the house of Judah, and hath
made them as his goodly horse in the
battle.

4 Out of him came forth the corner, out of him the nail, out of him the battle bow, out of him every oppressor together.

5 And they shall be as mighty *men*, which tread down *their enemies* in the mire of the streets in the battle: and they shall fight, because the LORD *is* with them, and the riders on horses shall be confounded.

6 And I will strengthen the house of Judah, and I will save the house of Joseph, and I will bring them again to place them; for I have mercy upon them: and they shall be as though I had not cast them off: for I *am* the LORD their God, and will hear them.

7 And *they of* Ephraim shall be like a mighty *man*, and their heart shall rejoice as through wine: yea, their children shall see *it*, and be glad; their heart shall rejoice in the LORD.

8 I will hiss for them, and gather them; for I have redeemed them: and they shall increase as they have increased.

9 And I will sow them among the people: and they shall remember me in far countries; and they shall live with their children, and turn again.

10 I will bring them again also out of the land of Egypt, and gather them out of Assyria; and I will bring them into the land of Gilead and Lebanon; and *place* shall not be found for them.

11 And he shall pass through the sea with affliction, and shall smite the waves in the sea, and all the deeps of the river shall dry up: and the pride of Assyria shall be brought down, and the sceptre of Egypt shall depart away.

12 And I will strengthen them in the LORD; and they shall walk up and down in his name, saith the LORD.

11 Open thy doors, O Lebanon, that the fire may devour thy cedars.

2 Howl, fir tree; for the cedar is fallen; because the mighty are spoiled: howl, O ye oaks of Bashan; for the forest of the vintage is come down.

3 *There is* a voice of the howling of the shepherds; for their glory is spoiled: a voice of the roaring of young lions; for the pride of Jordan is spoiled.

4 Thus saith the LORD my God; Feed the flock of the slaughter;

5 Whose possessors slay them, and hold themselves not guilty: and they that sell them say, Blessed *be* the LORD; for I am rich: and their own shepherds pity them not.

6 For I will no more pity the inhabitants of the land, saith the LORD: but, lo, I will deliver the men every one into his neighbour's hand, and into the hand of his king: and they shall smite the land, and out of their hand I will not deliver *them*.

7 And I will feed the flock of slaughter, *even* you, O poor of the flock. And I took unto me two staves; the one I called Beauty, and the other I called Bands; and I fed the flock.

8 Three shepherds also I cut off in one month; and my soul lothed them, and their soul also abhorred me.

9 Then said I, I will not feed you: that that dieth, let it die; and that that is to be cut off, let it be cut off; and let the rest eat every one the flesh of another.

10 And I took my staff, *even* Beauty, and cut it asunder, that I might break my covenant which I had made with all the people.

11 And it was broken in that day: and so the poor of the flock that waited upon me knew that it *was* the word of the LORD.

12 And I said unto them, If ye think good, give *me* my price; and if not, forbear. So they weighed for my price thirty *pieces* of silver.

13 And the LORD said unto me, Cast it unto the potter: a goodly price that I was prised at of them. And I took the thirty *pieces* of silver, and cast them to the potter in the house of the LORD.

14 Then I cut asunder mine other staff, *even* Bands, that I might break the brotherhood between Judah and Israel.

15 And the LORD said unto me, Take unto thee yet the instruments of a foolish shepherd.

16 For, lo, I will raise up a shepherd in the land, *which* shall not visit those that be cut off, neither shall seek the young one, nor heal that that is broken, nor feed that that standeth still: but he shall eat the flesh of the fat, and tear their claws in pieces.

17 Woe to the idol shepherd that leaveth the flock! the sword *shall be* upon his arm, and upon his right eye: his arm shall be clean dried up, and his right eye shall be utterly darkened.

12 The burden of the word of the LORD for Israel, saith the LORD, which stretcheth forth the heavens, and layeth the foundation of the earth, and formeth the spirit of man within him.

2 Behold, I will make Jerusalem a cup of trembling unto all the people round about, when they shall be in the siege both against Judah *and* against Jerusalem.

3 And in that day will I make Jerusalem a burdensome stone for all people: all that burden themselves with it shall be cut in pieces, though all the people of the earth be gathered together against it.

4 In that day, saith the LORD, I will smite every horse with astonishment, and his rider with madness: and I will open mine eyes upon the house of Judah, and will smite every horse of the people with blindness.

5 And the governors of Judah shall say in their heart, The inhabitants of Jerusalem *shall be* my strength in the LORD of hosts their God.

6 In that day will I make the governors of Judah like an hearth of fire among the wood, and like a torch of fire in a sheaf; and they shall devour all the people round about, on the right hand and on the left: and Jerusalem shall be inhabited again in her own place, *even* in Jerusalem.

7 The LORD also shall save the tents of Judah first, that the glory of the house of David and the glory of the inhabitants of Jerusalem do not magnify *themselves* against Judah.

8 In that day shall the LORD defend the inhabitants of Jerusalem; and he that is feeble among them at that day shall be as David; and the house of David *shall be* as God, as the angel of the LORD before them.

9 And it shall come to pass in that day, *that* I will seek to destroy all the nations that come against Jerusalem.

10 And I will pour upon the house of David, and upon the inhabitants of Jerusalem, the spirit of grace and of supplications: and they shall look upon me whom they have pierced, and they shall mourn for him, as one mourneth for *his* only *son*, and shall be in bitterness for him, as one that is in bitterness for *his* firstborn.

11 In that day shall there be a great
mourning in Jerusalem, as the mourning of Hadadrimmon in the valley of
Megiddon.
12 And the land shall mourn, every
family apart; the family of the house of
David apart, and their wives apart; the
family of the house of Nathan apart,
and their wives apart;
13 The family of the house of Levi
apart, and their wives apart; the family
of Shimei apart, and their wives apart;
14 All the families that remain, every
family apart, and their wives apart.

13 In that day there shall be a fountain opened to the house of
David and to the inhabitants of
Jerusalem for sin and for uncleanness.
2 And it shall come to pass in that day,
saith the LORD of hosts, *that* I will cut
off the names of the idols out of the
land, and they shall no more be remembered: and also I will cause the prophets and the unclean spirit to pass out of
the land.
3 And it shall come to pass, *that* when
any shall yet prophesy, then his father
and his mother that begat him shall say
unto him, Thou shalt not live; for thou
speakest lies in the name of the LORD:
and his father and his mother that
begat him shall thrust him through
when he prophesieth.
4 And it shall come to pass in that day,
that the prophets shall be ashamed
every one of his vision, when he hath
prophesied; neither shall they wear a
rough garment to deceive:
5 But he shall say, I *am* no prophet, I
am an husbandman; for man taught me
to keep cattle from my youth.
6 And *one* shall say unto him, What
are these wounds in thine hands? Then
he shall answer, *Those* with which I was
wounded *in* the house of my friends.
7 Awake, O sword, against my shepherd, and against the man *that is* my
fellow, saith the LORD of hosts: smite
the shepherd, and the sheep shall be
scattered: and I will turn mine hand
upon the little ones.
8 And it shall come to pass, *that* in all
the land, saith the LORD, two parts
therein shall be cut off *and* die; but the
third shall be left therein.
9 And I will bring the third part
through the fire, and will refine them
as silver is refined, and will try them as
gold is tried: they shall call on my
name, and I will hear them: I will say, It
is my people: and they shall say, The
LORD *is* my God.

14 Behold, the day of the LORD
cometh, and thy spoil shall be
divided in the midst of thee.
2 For I will gather all nations against
Jerusalem to battle; and the city shall
be taken, and the houses rifled, and the
women ravished; and half of the city
shall go forth into captivity, and the
residue of the people shall not be cut
off from the city.
3 Then shall the LORD go forth, and
fight against those nations, as when he
fought in the day of battle.
4 And his feet shall stand in that day
upon the mount of Olives, which *is*
before Jerusalem on the east, and the
mount of Olives shall cleave in the
midst thereof toward the east and
toward the west, *and there shall be* a
very great valley; and half of the mountain shall remove toward the north, and
half of it toward the south.
5 And ye shall flee *to* the valley of the
mountains; for the valley of the mountains shall reach unto Azal: yea, ye shall

flee, like as ye fled from before the earthquake in the days of Uzziah king of Judah: and the LORD my God shall come, *and* all the saints with thee.

6 And it shall come to pass in that day, *that* the light shall not be clear, *nor* dark:

7 But it shall be one day which shall be known to the LORD, not day, nor night: but it shall come to pass, *that* at evening time it shall be light.

8 And it shall be in that day, *that* living waters shall go out from Jerusalem; half of them toward the former sea, and half of them toward the hinder sea: in summer and in winter shall it be.

9 And the LORD shall be king over all the earth: in that day shall there be one LORD, and his name one.

10 All the land shall be turned as a plain from Geba to Rimmon south of Jerusalem: and it shall be lifted up, and inhabited in her place, from Benjamin's gate unto the place of the first gate, unto the corner gate, and *from* the tower of Hananeel unto the king's winepresses.

11 And *men* shall dwell in it, and there shall be no more utter destruction; but Jerusalem shall be safely inhabited.

12 And this shall be the plague wherewith the LORD will smite all the people that have fought against Jerusalem; Their flesh shall consume away while they stand upon their feet, and their eyes shall consume away in their holes, and their tongue shall consume away in their mouth.

13 And it shall come to pass in that day, *that* a great tumult from the LORD shall be among them; and they shall lay hold every one on the hand of his neighbour, and his hand shall rise up against the hand of his neighbour.

14 And Judah also shall fight at Jerusalem; and the wealth of all the heathen round about shall be gathered together, gold, and silver, and apparel, in great abundance.

15 And so shall be the plague of the horse, of the mule, of the camel, and of the ass, and of all the beasts that shall be in these tents, as this plague.

16 And it shall come to pass, *that* every one that is left of all the nations which came against Jerusalem shall even go up from year to year to worship the King, the LORD of hosts, and to keep the feast of tabernacles.

17 And it shall be, *that* whoso will not come up of *all* the families of the earth unto Jerusalem to worship the King, the LORD of hosts, even upon them shall be no rain.

18 And if the family of Egypt go not up, and come not, that *have* no *rain*; there shall be the plague, wherewith the LORD will smite the heathen that come not up to keep the feast of tabernacles.

19 This shall be the punishment of Egypt, and the punishment of all nations that come not up to keep the feast of tabernacles.

20 In that day shall there be upon the bells of the horses, HOLINESS UNTO THE LORD; and the pots in the LORD's house shall be like the bowls before the altar.

21 Yea, every pot in Jerusalem and in Judah shall be holiness unto the LORD of hosts: and all they that sacrifice shall come and take of them, and seethe therein: and in that day there shall be no more the Canaanite in the house of the LORD of hosts.

THE BOOK OF
MALACHI

1 The burden of the word of the LORD
to Israel by Malachi.
2 I have loved you, saith the LORD. Yet
ye say, Wherein hast thou loved us?
Was not Esau Jacob's brother? saith
the LORD: yet I loved Jacob,
3 And I hated Esau, and laid his
mountains and his heritage waste for
the dragons of the wilderness.
4 Whereas Edom saith, We are impoverished, but we will return and build
the desolate places; thus saith the LORD
of hosts, They shall build, but I will
throw down; and they shall call them,
The border of wickedness, and, The
people against whom the LORD hath
indignation for ever.
5 And your eyes shall see, and ye shall
say, The LORD will be magnified from
the border of Israel.
6 A son honoureth *his* father, and a
servant his master: if then I *be* a father,
where *is* mine honour? and if I *be* a
master, where *is* my fear? saith the
LORD of hosts unto you, O priests, that
despise my name. And ye say, Wherein
have we despised thy name?
7 Ye offer polluted bread upon mine
altar; and ye say, Wherein have we polluted thee? In that ye say, The table of
the LORD *is* contemptible.
8 And if ye offer the blind for sacrifice, *is it* not evil? and if ye offer the
lame and sick, *is it* not evil? offer it now
unto thy governor; will he be pleased
with thee, or accept thy person? saith
the LORD of hosts.
9 And now, I pray you, beseech God
that he will be gracious unto us: this
hath been by your means: will he
regard your persons? saith the LORD of
hosts.
10 Who *is there* even among you that
would shut the doors *for nought*? neither do ye kindle *fire* on mine altar for
nought. I have no pleasure in you, saith
the LORD of hosts, neither will I accept
an offering at your hand.
11 For from the rising of the sun even
unto the going down of the same my
name *shall be* great among the
Gentiles; and in every place incense
shall be offered unto my name, and a
pure offering: for my name *shall be*
great among the heathen, saith the
LORD of hosts.
12 But ye have profaned it, in that ye
say, The table of the LORD *is* polluted;
and the fruit thereof, *even* his meat, *is*
contemptible.
13 Ye said also, Behold, what a weariness *is it*! and ye have snuffed at it,
saith the LORD of hosts; and ye brought
that which was torn, and the lame, and
the sick; thus ye brought an offering:
should I accept this of your hand? saith
the LORD.
14 But cursed *be* the deceiver, which
hath in his flock a male, and voweth,
and sacrificeth unto the Lord a corrupt
thing: for I *am* a great King, saith the
LORD of hosts, and my name *is* dreadful
among the heathen.

2 And now, O ye priests, this commandment *is* for you.
2 If ye will not hear, and if ye will not
lay *it* to heart, to give glory unto my
name, saith the LORD of hosts, I will
even send a curse upon you, and I will
curse your blessings: yea, I have cursed

them already, because ye do not lay *it* to heart.

3 Behold, I will corrupt your seed, and spread dung upon your faces, *even* the dung of your solemn feasts; and *one* shall take you away with it.

4 And ye shall know that I have sent this commandment unto you, that my covenant might be with Levi, saith the LORD of hosts.

5 My covenant was with him of life and peace; and I gave them to him *for* the fear wherewith he feared me, and was afraid before my name.

6 The law of truth was in his mouth, and iniquity was not found in his lips: he walked with me in peace and equity, and did turn many away from iniquity.

7 For the priest's lips should keep knowledge, and they should seek the law at his mouth: for he *is* the messenger of the LORD of hosts.

8 But ye are departed out of the way; ye have caused many to stumble at the law; ye have corrupted the covenant of Levi, saith the LORD of hosts.

9 Therefore have I also made you contemptible and base before all the people, according as ye have not kept my ways, but have been partial in the law.

10 Have we not all one father? hath not one God created us? why do we deal treacherously every man against his brother, by profaning the covenant of our fathers?

11 Judah hath dealt treacherously, and an abomination is committed in Israel and in Jerusalem; for Judah hath profaned the holiness of the LORD which he loved, and hath married the daughter of a strange god.

12 The LORD will cut off the man that doeth this, the master and the scholar, out of the tabernacles of Jacob, and him that offereth an offering unto the LORD of hosts.

13 And this have ye done again, covering the altar of the LORD with tears, with weeping, and with crying out, insomuch that he regardeth not the offering any more, or receiveth *it* with good will at your hand.

14 Yet ye say, Wherefore? Because the LORD hath been witness between thee and the wife of thy youth, against whom thou hast dealt treacherously: yet *is* she thy companion, and the wife of thy covenant.

15 And did not he make one? Yet had he the residue of the spirit. And wherefore one? That he might seek a godly seed. Therefore take heed to your spirit, and let none deal treacherously against the wife of his youth.

16 For the LORD, the God of Israel, saith that he hateth putting away: for *one* covereth violence with his garment, saith the LORD of hosts: therefore take heed to your spirit, that ye deal not treacherously.

17 Ye have wearied the LORD with your words. Yet ye say, Wherein have we wearied *him*? When ye say, Every one that doeth evil *is* good in the sight of the LORD, and he delighteth in them; or, Where *is* the God of judgment?

3 Behold, I will send my messenger, and he shall prepare the way before me: and the Lord, whom ye seek, shall suddenly come to his temple, even the messenger of the covenant, whom ye delight in: behold, he shall come, saith the LORD of hosts.

2 But who may abide the day of his coming? and who shall stand when he appeareth? for he *is* like a refiner's fire, and like fullers' soap:

3 And he shall sit *as* a refiner and purifier of silver: and he shall purify the sons of Levi, and purge them as gold and silver, that they may offer unto the LORD an offering in righteousness.

4 Then shall the offering of Judah and Jerusalem be pleasant unto the LORD, as in the days of old, and as in former years.

5 And I will come near to you to judgment; and I will be a swift witness against the sorcerers, and against the adulterers, and against false swearers, and against those that oppress the hireling in *his* wages, the widow, and the fatherless, and that turn aside the stranger *from his right*, and fear not me, saith the LORD of hosts.

6 For I *am* the LORD, I change not; therefore ye sons of Jacob are not consumed.

7 Even from the days of your fathers ye are gone away from mine ordinances, and have not kept *them*. Return unto me, and I will return unto you, saith the LORD of hosts. But ye said, Wherein shall we return?

8 Will a man rob God? Yet ye have robbed me. But ye say, Wherein have we robbed thee? In tithes and offerings.

9 Ye *are* cursed with a curse: for ye have robbed me, *even* this whole nation.

10 Bring ye all the tithes into the storehouse, that there may be meat in mine house, and prove me now herewith, saith the LORD of hosts, if I will not open you the windows of heaven, and pour you out a blessing, that *there shall* not *be room* enough *to receive it*.

11 And I will rebuke the devourer for your sakes, and he shall not destroy the fruits of your ground; neither shall your vine cast her fruit before the time in the field, saith the LORD of hosts.

12 And all nations shall call you blessed: for ye shall be a delightsome land, saith the LORD of hosts.

13 Your words have been stout against me, saith the LORD. Yet ye say, What have we spoken *so much* against thee?

14 Ye have said, It *is* vain to serve God: and what profit *is it* that we have kept his ordinance, and that we have walked mournfully before the LORD of hosts?

15 And now we call the proud happy; yea, they that work wickedness are set up; yea, *they that* tempt God are even delivered.

16 Then they that feared the LORD spake often one to another: and the LORD hearkened, and heard *it*, and a book of remembrance was written before him for them that feared the LORD, and that thought upon his name.

17 And they shall be mine, saith the LORD of hosts, in that day when I make up my jewels; and I will spare them, as a man spareth his own son that serveth him.

18 Then shall ye return, and discern between the righteous and the wicked, between him that serveth God and him that serveth him not.

4 For, behold, the day cometh, that shall burn as an oven; and all the proud, yea, and all that do wickedly, shall be stubble: and the day that cometh shall burn them up, saith the LORD of hosts, that it shall leave them neither root nor branch.

THE GOSPEL ACCORDING TO

SAINT MATTHEW

1 The book of the generation of Jesus Christ, the son of David, the son of Abraham.

2 Abraham begat Isaac; and Isaac begat Jacob; and Jacob begat Judas and his brethren;

3 And Judas begat Phares and Zara of Thamar; and Phares begat Esrom; and Esrom begat Aram;

4 And Aram begat Aminadab; and Aminadab begat Naasson; and Naasson begat Salmon;

5 And Salmon begat Booz of Rachab; and Booz begat Obed of Ruth; and Obed begat Jesse;

6 And Jesse begat David the king; and David the king begat Solomon of her *that had been the wife* of Urias;

7 And Solomon begat Roboam; and Roboam begat Abia; and Abia begat Asa;

8 And Asa begat Josaphat; and Josaphat begat Joram; and Joram begat Ozias;

9 And Ozias begat Joatham; and Joatham begat Achaz; and Achaz begat Ezekias;

10 And Ezekias begat Manasses; and Manasses begat Amon; and Amon begat Josias;

11 And Josias begat Jechonias and his brethren, about the time they were carried away to Babylon:

12 And after they were brought to Babylon, Jechonias begat Salathiel; and Salathiel begat Zorobabel;

13 And Zorobabel begat Abiud; and Abiud begat Eliakim; and Eliakim begat Azor;

14 And Azor begat Sadoc; and Sadoc begat Achim; and Achim begat Eliud;

15 And Eliud begat Eleazar; and Eleazar begat Matthan; and Matthan begat Jacob;

16 And Jacob begat Joseph the husband of Mary, of whom was born Jesus, who is called Christ.

17 So all the generations from Abraham to David *are* fourteen generations; and from David until the carrying away into Babylon *are* fourteen generations; and from the carrying away into Babylon unto Christ *are* fourteen generations.

18 Now the birth of Jesus Christ was on this wise: When as his mother Mary was espoused to Joseph, before they came together, she was found with child of the Holy Ghost.

19 Then Joseph her husband, being a just *man*, and not willing to make her a publick example, was minded to put her away privily.

20 But while he thought on these things, behold, the angel of the Lord appeared unto him in a dream, saying, Joseph, thou son of David, fear not to take unto thee Mary thy wife: for that which is conceived in her is of the Holy Ghost.

21 And she shall bring forth a son, and thou shalt call his name JESUS: for he shall save his people from their sins.

22 Now all this was done, that it might be fulfilled which was spoken of the Lord by the prophet, saying,

23 Behold, a virgin shall be with child, and shall bring forth a son, and they

shall call his name Emmanuel, which
being interpreted is, God with us.
24 Then Joseph being raised from
sleep did as the angel of the Lord had
bidden him, and took unto him his wife:
25 And knew her not till she had
brought forth her firstborn son: and he
called his name JESUS.

2 Now when Jesus was born in
Bethlehem of Judaea in the days of
Herod the king, behold, there came
wise men from the east to Jerusalem,
2 Saying, Where is he that is born
King of the Jews? for we have seen his
star in the east, and are come to worship him.
3 When Herod the king had heard
these things, he was troubled, and all
Jerusalem with him.
4 And when he had gathered all the
chief priests and scribes of the people
together, he demanded of them where
Christ should be born.
5 And they said unto him, In Bethlehem of Judaea: for thus it is written by
the prophet,
6 And thou Bethlehem, *in* the land of
Juda, art not the least among the
princes of Juda: for out of thee shall
come a Governor, that shall rule my
people Israel.
7 Then Herod, when he had privily
called the wise men, enquired of them
diligently what time the star appeared.
8 And he sent them to Bethlehem,
and said, Go and search diligently for
the young child; and when ye have
found *him*, bring me word again, that I
may come and worship him also.
9 When they had heard the king, they
departed; and, lo, the star, which they
saw in the east, went before them, till it
came and stood over where the young
child was.
10 When they saw the star, they
rejoiced with exceeding great joy.
11 And when they were come into the
house, they saw the young child with
Mary his mother, and fell down, and
worshipped him: and when they had
opened their treasures, they presented
unto him gifts; gold, and frankincense,
and myrrh.
12 And being warned of God in a
dream that they should not return to
Herod, they departed into their own
country another way.
13 And when they were departed,
behold, the angel of the Lord appeareth
to Joseph in a dream, saying, Arise, and
take the young child and his mother,
and flee into Egypt, and be thou there
until I bring thee word: for Herod will
seek the young child to destroy him.
14 When he arose, he took the young
child and his mother by night, and
departed into Egypt:
15 And was there until the death of
Herod: that it might be fulfilled which
was spoken of the Lord by the prophet,
saying, Out of Egypt have I called my
son.
16 Then Herod, when he saw that he
was mocked of the wise men, was
exceeding wroth, and sent forth, and
slew all the children that were in
Bethlehem, and in all the coasts thereof, from two years old and under,
according to the time which he had
diligently enquired of the wise men.
17 Then was fulfilled that which was
spoken by Jeremy the prophet, saying,
18 In Rama was there a voice heard,
lamentation, and weeping, and great
mourning, Rachel weeping *for* her children, and would not be comforted,
because they are not.

19 But when Herod was dead, behold,
an angel of the Lord appeareth in a
dream to Joseph in Egypt,
20 Saying, Arise, and take the young
child and his mother, and go into the
land of Israel: for they are dead which
sought the young child's life.
21 And he arose, and took the young
child and his mother, and came into the
land of Israel.
22 But when he heard that Archelaus
did reign in Judaea in the room of his
father Herod, he was afraid to go
thither: notwithstanding, being warned
of God in a dream, he turned aside into
the parts of Galilee:
23 And he came and dwelt in a city
called Nazareth: that it might be fulfilled which was spoken by the prophets, He shall be called a Nazarene.

3 In those days came John the Baptist, preaching in the wilderness of
Judaea,
2 And saying, Repent ye: for the kingdom of heaven is at hand.
3 For this is he that was spoken of by
the prophet Esaias, saying, The voice of
one crying in the wilderness, Prepare
ye the way of the Lord, make his paths
straight.
4 And the same John had his raiment
of camel's hair, and a leathern girdle
about his loins; and his meat was
locusts and wild honey.
5 Then went out to him Jerusalem,
and all Judaea, and all the region round
about Jordan,
6 And were baptized of him in Jordan,
confessing their sins.
7 But when he saw many of the
Pharisees and Sadducees come to his
baptism, he said unto them, O generation of vipers, who hath warned you to
flee from the wrath to come?
8 Bring forth therefore fruits meet for
repentance:
9 And think not to say within yourselves, We have Abraham to *our* father:
for I say unto you, that God is able of
these stones to raise up children unto
Abraham.
10 And now also the axe is laid unto
the root of the trees: therefore every
tree which bringeth not forth good fruit
is hewn down, and cast into the fire.
11 I indeed baptize you with water
unto repentance: but he that cometh
after me is mightier than I, whose shoes
I am not worthy to bear: he shall baptize you with the Holy Ghost, and *with*
fire:
12 Whose fan *is* in his hand, and he
will throughly purge his floor, and
gather his wheat into the garner; but
he will burn up the chaff with unquenchable fire.
13 Then cometh Jesus from Galilee to
Jordan unto John, to be baptized of
him.
14 But John forbad him, saying, I have
need to be baptized of thee, and comest
thou to me?
15 And Jesus answering said unto
him, Suffer *it to be so* now: for thus it
becometh us to fulfil all righteousness.
Then he suffered him.
16 And Jesus, when he was baptized,
went up straightway out of the water:
and, lo, the heavens were opened unto
him, and he saw the Spirit of God
descending like a dove, and lighting
upon him:
17 And lo a voice from heaven, saying,
This is my beloved Son, in whom I am
well pleased.

4 Then was Jesus led up of the Spirit
into the wilderness to be tempted
of the devil.

2 And when he had fasted forty days
and forty nights, he was afterward an
hungred.
3 And when the tempter came to him,
he said, If thou be the Son of God, command that these stones be made bread.
4 But he answered and said, It is written, Man shall not live by bread alone,
but by every word that proceedeth out
of the mouth of God.
5 Then the devil taketh him up into
the holy city, and setteth him on a pinnacle of the temple,
6 And saith unto him, If thou be the
Son of God, cast thyself down: for it is
written, He shall give his angels charge
concerning thee: and in *their* hands
they shall bear thee up, lest at any time
thou dash thy foot against a stone.
7 Jesus said unto him, It is written
again, Thou shalt not tempt the Lord
thy God.
8 Again, the devil taketh him up into
an exceeding high mountain, and
sheweth him all the kingdoms of the
world, and the glory of them;
9 And saith unto him, All these things
will I give thee, if thou wilt fall down
and worship me.
10 Then saith Jesus unto him, Get
thee hence, Satan: for it is written,
Thou shalt worship the Lord thy God,
and him only shalt thou serve.
11 Then the devil leaveth him, and,
behold, angels came and ministered
unto him.
12 Now when Jesus had heard that
John was cast into prison, he departed
into Galilee;
13 And leaving Nazareth, he came
and dwelt in Capernaum, which is upon
the sea coast, in the borders of Zabulon
and Nephthalim:
14 That it might be fulfilled which
was spoken by Esaias the prophet, saying,
15 The land of Zabulon, and the land
of Nephthalim, *by* the way of the sea,
beyond Jordan, Galilee of the Gentiles;
16 The people which sat in darkness
saw great light; and to them which sat
in the region and shadow of death light
is sprung up.
17 From that time Jesus began to
preach, and to say, Repent: for the kingdom of heaven is at hand.
18 And Jesus, walking by the sea of
Galilee, saw two brethren, Simon called
Peter, and Andrew his brother, casting a
net into the sea: for they were fishers.
19 And he saith unto them, Follow
me, and I will make you fishers of men.
20 And they straightway left *their*
nets, and followed him.
21 And going on from thence, he saw
other two brethren, James *the son* of
Zebedee, and John his brother, in a ship
with Zebedee their father, mending
their nets; and he called them.
22 And they immediately left the ship
and their father, and followed him.
23 And Jesus went about all Galilee,
teaching in their synagogues, and
preaching the gospel of the kingdom,
and healing all manner of sickness and
all manner of disease among the people.
24 And his fame went throughout all
Syria: and they brought unto him all
sick people that were taken with divers
diseases and torments, and those which
were possessed with devils, and those
which were lunatick, and those that
had the palsy; and he healed them.
25 And there followed him great multitudes of people from Galilee, and
from Decapolis, and *from* Jerusalem,

and *from* Judaea, and *from* beyond Jordan.

5 And seeing the multitudes, he went up into a mountain: and when he was set, his disciples came unto him:

2 And he opened his mouth, and taught them, saying,

3 Blessed *are* the poor in spirit: for theirs is the kingdom of heaven.

4 Blessed *are* they that mourn: for they shall be comforted.

5 Blessed *are* the meek: for they shall inherit the earth.

6 Blessed *are* they which do hunger and thirst after righteousness: for they shall be filled.

7 Blessed *are* the merciful: for they shall obtain mercy.

8 Blessed *are* the pure in heart: for they shall see God.

9 Blessed *are* the peacemakers: for they shall be called the children of God.

10 Blessed *are* they which are persecuted for righteousness' sake: for theirs is the kingdom of heaven.

11 Blessed are ye, when *men* shall revile you, and persecute *you*, and shall say all manner of evil against you falsely, for my sake.

12 Rejoice, and be exceeding glad: for great *is* your reward in heaven: for so persecuted they the prophets which were before you.

13 Ye are the salt of the earth: but if the salt have lost his savour, wherewith shall it be salted? it is thenceforth good for nothing, but to be cast out, and to be trodden under foot of men.

14 Ye are the light of the world. A city that is set on an hill cannot be hid.

15 Neither do men light a candle, and put it under a bushel, but on a candlestick; and it giveth light unto all that are in the house.

16 Let your light so shine before men, that they may see your good works, and glorify your Father which is in heaven.

17 Think not that I am come to destroy the law, or the prophets: I am not come to destroy, but to fulfil.

18 For verily I say unto you, Till heaven and earth pass, one jot or one tittle shall in no wise pass from the law, till all be fulfilled.

19 Whosoever therefore shall break one of these least commandments, and shall teach men so, he shall be called the least in the kingdom of heaven: but whosoever shall do and teach *them*, the same shall be called great in the kingdom of heaven.

20 For I say unto you, That except your righteousness shall exceed *the righteousness* of the scribes and Pharisees, ye shall in no case enter into the kingdom of heaven.

21 Ye have heard that it was said by them of old time, Thou shalt not kill; and whosoever shall kill shall be in danger of the judgment:

22 But I say unto you, That whosoever is angry with his brother without a cause shall be in danger of the judgment: and whosoever shall say to his brother, Raca, shall be in danger of the council: but whosoever shall say, Thou fool, shall be in danger of hell fire.

23 Therefore if thou bring thy gift to the altar, and there rememberest that thy brother hath ought against thee;

24 Leave there thy gift before the altar, and go thy way; first be reconciled to thy brother, and then come and offer thy gift.

25 Agree with thine adversary quickly, whiles thou art in the way with him; lest at any time the adversary deliver thee to the judge, and the judge deliver

thee to the officer, and thou be cast into
prison.
26 Verily I say unto thee, Thou shalt
by no means come out thence, till thou
hast paid the uttermost farthing.
27 Ye have heard that it was said by
them of old time, Thou shalt not commit adultery:
28 But I say unto you, That whosoever
looketh on a woman to lust after her
hath committed adultery with her
already in his heart.
29 And if thy right eye offend thee,
pluck it out, and cast *it* from thee: for it
is profitable for thee that one of thy
members should perish, and not *that*
thy whole body should be cast into hell.
30 And if thy right hand offend thee,
cut it off, and cast *it* from thee: for it is
profitable for thee that one of thy members should perish, and not *that* thy
whole body should be cast into hell.
31 It hath been said, Whosoever shall
put away his wife, let him give her a
writing of divorcement:
32 But I say unto you, That whosoever
shall put away his wife, saving for the
cause of fornication, causeth her to
commit adultery: and whosoever shall
marry her that is divorced committeth
adultery.
33 Again, ye have heard that it hath
been said by them of old time, Thou
shalt not forswear thyself, but shalt
perform unto the Lord thine oaths:
34 But I say unto you, Swear not at all;
neither by heaven; for it is God's throne:
35 Nor by the earth; for it is his footstool: neither by Jerusalem; for it is the
city of the great King.
36 Neither shalt thou swear by thy
head, because thou canst not make one
hair white or black.
37 But let your communication be,
Yea, yea; Nay, nay: for whatsoever is
more than these cometh of evil.
38 Ye have heard that it hath been
said, An eye for an eye, and a tooth for
a tooth:
39 But I say unto you, That ye resist
not evil: but whosoever shall smite thee
on thy right cheek, turn to him the
other also.
40 And if any man will sue thee at the
law, and take away thy coat, let him
have *thy* cloke also.
41 And whosoever shall compel thee
to go a mile, go with him twain.
42 Give to him that asketh thee, and
from him that would borrow of thee
turn not thou away.
43 Ye have heard that it hath been
said, Thou shalt love thy neighbour, and
hate thine enemy.
44 But I say unto you, Love your enemies, bless them that curse you, do
good to them that hate you, and pray
for them which despitefully use you,
and persecute you;
45 That ye may be the children of
your Father which is in heaven: for he
maketh his sun to rise on the evil and
on the good, and sendeth rain on the
just and on the unjust.
46 For if ye love them which love you,
what reward have ye? do not even the
publicans the same?
47 And if ye salute your brethren
only, what do ye more *than others*? do
not even the publicans so?
48 Be ye therefore perfect, even as
your Father which is in heaven is perfect.

6 Take heed that ye do not your alms
before men, to be seen of them:
otherwise ye have no reward of your
Father which is in heaven.

2 Therefore when thou doest *thine*
alms, do not sound a trumpet before
thee, as the hypocrites do in the synagogues and in the streets, that they may
have glory of men. Verily I say unto you,
They have their reward.
3 But when thou doest alms, let not
thy left hand know what thy right hand
doeth:
4 That thine alms may be in secret:
and thy Father which seeth in secret
himself shall reward thee openly.
5 And when thou prayest, thou shalt
not be as the hypocrites *are*: for they
love to pray standing in the synagogues
and in the corners of the streets, that
they may be seen of men. Verily I say
unto you, They have their reward.
6 But thou, when thou prayest, enter
into thy closet, and when thou hast shut
thy door, pray to thy Father which is in
secret; and thy Father which seeth in
secret shall reward thee openly.
7 But when ye pray, use not vain rep-
etitions, as the heathen *do*: for they
think that they shall be heard for their
much speaking.
8 Be not ye therefore like unto them:
for your Father knoweth what things ye
have need of, before ye ask him.
9 After this manner therefore pray ye:
Our Father which art in heaven,
Hallowed be thy name.
10 Thy kingdom come. Thy will be
done in earth, as *it is* in heaven.
11 Give us this day our daily bread.
12 And forgive us our debts, as we
forgive our debtors.
13 And lead us not into temptation,
but deliver us from evil: For thine is the
kingdom, and the power, and the glory,
for ever. Amen.
14 For if ye forgive men their trespasses, your heavenly Father will also
forgive you:
15 But if ye forgive not men their
trespasses, neither will your Father
forgive your trespasses.
16 Moreover when ye fast, be not, as
the hypocrites, of a sad countenance:
for they disfigure their faces, that they
may appear unto men to fast. Verily I
say unto you, They have their reward.
17 But thou, when thou fastest, anoint
thine head, and wash thy face;
18 That thou appear not unto men to
fast, but unto thy Father which is in
secret: and thy Father, which seeth in
secret, shall reward thee openly.
19 Lay not up for yourselves treasures
upon earth, where moth and rust doth
corrupt, and where thieves break
through and steal:
20 But lay up for yourselves treasures
in heaven, where neither moth nor rust
doth corrupt, and where thieves do not
break through nor steal:
21 For where your treasure is, there
will your heart be also.
22 The light of the body is the eye: if
therefore thine eye be single, thy whole
body shall be full of light.
23 But if thine eye be evil, thy whole
body shall be full of darkness. If therefore the light that is in thee be darkness, how great *is* that darkness!
24 No man can serve two masters: for
either he will hate the one, and love the
other; or else he will hold to the one,
and despise the other. Ye cannot serve
God and mammon.
25 Therefore I say unto you, Take no
thought for your life, what ye shall eat,
or what ye shall drink; nor yet for your
body, what ye shall put on. Is not the

life more than meat, and the body than raiment?

26 Behold the fowls of the air: for they sow not, neither do they reap, nor gather into barns; yet your heavenly Father feedeth them. Are ye not much better than they?

27 Which of you by taking thought can add one cubit unto his stature?

28 And why take ye thought for raiment? Consider the lilies of the field, how they grow; they toil not, neither do they spin:

29 And yet I say unto you, That even Solomon in all his glory was not arrayed like one of these.

30 Wherefore, if God so clothe the grass of the field, which to day is, and to morrow is cast into the oven, *shall he* not much more *clothe* you, O ye of little faith?

31 Therefore take no thought, saying, What shall we eat? or, What shall we drink? or, Wherewithal shall we be clothed?

32 (For after all these things do the Gentiles seek:) for your heavenly Father knoweth that ye have need of all these things.

33 But seek ye first the kingdom of God, and his righteousness; and all these things shall be added unto you.

34 Take therefore no thought for the morrow: for the morrow shall take thought for the things of itself. Sufficient unto the day *is* the evil thereof.

7 Judge not, that ye be not judged.
2 For with what judgment ye judge, ye shall be judged: and with what measure ye mete, it shall be measured to you again.

3 And why beholdest thou the mote that is in thy brother's eye, but considerest not the beam that is in thine own eye?

4 Or how wilt thou say to thy brother, Let me pull out the mote out of thine eye; and, behold, a beam *is* in thine own eye?

5 Thou hypocrite, first cast out the beam out of thine own eye; and then shalt thou see clearly to cast out the mote out of thy brother's eye.

6 Give not that which is holy unto the dogs, neither cast ye your pearls before swine, lest they trample them under their feet, and turn again and rend you.

7 Ask, and it shall be given you; seek, and ye shall find; knock, and it shall be opened unto you:

8 For every one that asketh receiveth; and he that seeketh findeth; and to him that knocketh it shall be opened.

9 Or what man is there of you, whom if his son ask bread, will he give him a stone?

10 Or if he ask a fish, will he give him a serpent?

11 If ye then, being evil, know how to give good gifts unto your children, how much more shall your Father which is in heaven give good things to them that ask him?

12 Therefore all things whatsoever ye would that men should do to you, do ye even so to them: for this is the law and the prophets.

13 Enter ye in at the strait gate: for wide *is* the gate, and broad *is* the way, that leadeth to destruction, and many there be which go in thereat:

14 Because strait *is* the gate, and narrow *is* the way, which leadeth unto life, and few there be that find it.

15 Beware of false prophets, which come to you in sheep's clothing, but inwardly they are ravening wolves.

16 Ye shall know them by their fruits. Do men gather grapes of thorns, or figs of thistles?

17 Even so every good tree bringeth forth good fruit; but a corrupt tree bringeth forth evil fruit.

18 A good tree cannot bring forth evil fruit, neither *can* a corrupt tree bring forth good fruit.

19 Every tree that bringeth not forth good fruit is hewn down, and cast into the fire.

20 Wherefore by their fruits ye shall know them.

21 Not every one that saith unto me, Lord, Lord, shall enter into the kingdom of heaven; but he that doeth the will of my Father which is in heaven.

22 Many will say to me in that day, Lord, Lord, have we not prophesied in thy name? and in thy name have cast out devils? and in thy name done many wonderful works?

23 And then will I profess unto them, I never knew you: depart from me, ye that work iniquity.

24 Therefore whosoever heareth these sayings of mine, and doeth them, I will liken him unto a wise man, which built his house upon a rock:

25 And the rain descended, and the floods came, and the winds blew, and beat upon that house; and it fell not: for it was founded upon a rock.

26 And every one that heareth these sayings of mine, and doeth them not, shall be likened unto a foolish man, which built his house upon the sand:

27 And the rain descended, and the floods came, and the winds blew, and beat upon that house; and it fell: and great was the fall of it.

28 And it came to pass, when Jesus had ended these sayings, the people were astonished at his doctrine:

29 For he taught them as *one* having authority, and not as the scribes.

8 When he was come down from the mountain, great multitudes followed him.

2 And, behold, there came a leper and worshipped him, saying, Lord, if thou wilt, thou canst make me clean.

3 And Jesus put forth *his* hand, and touched him, saying, I will; be thou clean. And immediately his leprosy was cleansed.

4 And Jesus saith unto him, See thou tell no man; but go thy way, shew thyself to the priest, and offer the gift that Moses commanded, for a testimony unto them.

5 And when Jesus was entered into Capernaum, there came unto him a centurion, beseeching him,

6 And saying, Lord, my servant lieth at home sick of the palsy, grievously tormented.

7 And Jesus saith unto him, I will come and heal him.

8 The centurion answered and said, Lord, I am not worthy that thou shouldest come under my roof: but speak the word only, and my servant shall be healed.

9 For I am a man under authority, having soldiers under me: and I say to this *man*, Go, and he goeth; and to another, Come, and he cometh; and to my servant, Do this, and he doeth *it*.

10 When Jesus heard *it*, he marvelled, and said to them that followed, Verily I say unto you, I have not found so great faith, no, not in Israel.

11 And I say unto you, That many
shall come from the east and west, and
shall sit down with Abraham, and Isaac,
and Jacob, in the kingdom of heaven.
12 But the children of the kingdom
shall be cast out into outer darkness:
there shall be weeping and gnashing of
teeth.
13 And Jesus said unto the centurion,
Go thy way; and as thou hast believed,
so be it done unto thee. And his servant
was healed in the selfsame hour.
14 And when Jesus was come into
Peter's house, he saw his wife's mother
laid, and sick of a fever.
15 And he touched her hand, and the
fever left her: and she arose, and ministered unto them.
16 When the even was come, they
brought unto him many that were possessed with devils: and he cast out the
spirits with *his* word, and healed all
that were sick:
17 That it might be fulfilled which
was spoken by Esaias the prophet, saying, Himself took our infirmities, and
bare *our* sicknesses.
18 Now when Jesus saw great multitudes about him, he gave commandment to depart unto the other side.
19 And a certain scribe came, and
said unto him, Master, I will follow thee
whithersoever thou goest.
20 And Jesus saith unto him, The
foxes have holes, and the birds of the
air *have* nests; but the Son of man hath
not where to lay *his* head.
21 And another of his disciples said
unto him, Lord, suffer me first to go and
bury my father.
22 But Jesus said unto him, Follow
me; and let the dead bury their dead.
23 And when he was entered into a
ship, his disciples followed him.
24 And, behold, there arose a great
tempest in the sea, insomuch that the
ship was covered with the waves: but he
was asleep.
25 And his disciples came to *him*, and
awoke him, saying, Lord, save us: we
perish.
26 And he saith unto them, Why are
ye fearful, O ye of little faith? Then he
arose, and rebuked the winds and the
sea; and there was a great calm.
27 But the men marvelled, saying,
What manner of man is this, that even
the winds and the sea obey him!
28 And when he was come to the
other side into the country of the
Gergesenes, there met him two possessed with devils, coming out of the
tombs, exceeding fierce, so that no man
might pass by that way.
29 And, behold, they cried out, saying,
What have we to do with thee, Jesus,
thou Son of God? art thou come hither
to torment us before the time?
30 And there was a good way off from
them an herd of many swine feeding.
31 So the devils besought him, saying,
If thou cast us out, suffer us to go away
into the herd of swine.
32 And he said unto them, Go. And
when they were come out, they went
into the herd of swine: and, behold, the
whole herd of swine ran violently down
a steep place into the sea, and perished
in the waters.
33 And they that kept them fled, and
went their ways into the city, and told
every thing, and what was befallen to
the possessed of the devils.
34 And, behold, the whole city came
out to meet Jesus: and when they saw
him, they besought *him* that he would
depart out of their coasts.

9 And he entered into a ship, and passed over, and came into his own city.

2 And, behold, they brought to him a man sick of the palsy, lying on a bed: and Jesus seeing their faith said unto the sick of the palsy; Son, be of good cheer; thy sins be forgiven thee.

3 And, behold, certain of the scribes said within themselves, This *man* blasphemeth.

4 And Jesus knowing their thoughts said, Wherefore think ye evil in your hearts?

5 For whether is easier, to say, *Thy* sins be forgiven thee; or to say, Arise, and walk?

6 But that ye may know that the Son of man hath power on earth to forgive sins, (then saith he to the sick of the palsy,) Arise, take up thy bed, and go unto thine house.

7 And he arose, and departed to his house.

8 But when the multitudes saw *it*, they marvelled, and glorified God, which had given such power unto men.

9 And as Jesus passed forth from thence, he saw a man, named Matthew, sitting at the receipt of custom: and he saith unto him, Follow me. And he arose, and followed him.

10 And it came to pass, as Jesus sat at meat in the house, behold, many publicans and sinners came and sat down with him and his disciples.

11 And when the Pharisees saw *it*, they said unto his disciples, Why eateth your Master with publicans and sinners?

12 But when Jesus heard *that*, he said unto them, They that be whole need not a physician, but they that are sick.

13 But go ye and learn what *that* meaneth, I will have mercy, and not sacrifice: for I am not come to call the righteous, but sinners to repentance.

14 Then came to him the disciples of John, saying, Why do we and the Pharisees fast oft, but thy disciples fast not?

15 And Jesus said unto them, Can the children of the bridechamber mourn, as long as the bridegroom is with them? but the days will come, when the bridegroom shall be taken from them, and then shall they fast.

16 No man putteth a piece of new cloth unto an old garment, for that which is put in to fill it up taketh from the garment, and the rent is made worse.

17 Neither do men put new wine into old bottles: else the bottles break, and the wine runneth out, and the bottles perish: but they put new wine into new bottles, and both are preserved.

18 While he spake these things unto them, behold, there came a certain ruler, and worshipped him, saying, My daughter is even now dead: but come and lay thy hand upon her, and she shall live.

19 And Jesus arose, and followed him, and *so did* his disciples.

20 And, behold, a woman, which was diseased with an issue of blood twelve years, came behind *him*, and touched the hem of his garment:

21 For she said within herself, If I may but touch his garment, I shall be whole.

22 But Jesus turned him about, and when he saw her, he said, Daughter, be of good comfort; thy faith hath made thee whole. And the woman was made whole from that hour.

23 And when Jesus came into the
ruler's house, and saw the minstrels
and the people making a noise,
24 He said unto them, Give place: for
the maid is not dead, but sleepeth. And
they laughed him to scorn.
25 But when the people were put
forth, he went in, and took her by the
hand, and the maid arose.
26 And the fame hereof went abroad
into all that land.
27 And when Jesus departed thence,
two blind men followed him, crying,
and saying, *Thou* Son of David, have
mercy on us.
28 And when he was come into the
house, the blind men came to him: and
Jesus saith unto them, Believe ye that I
am able to do this? They said unto him,
Yea, Lord.
29 Then touched he their eyes, saying,
According to your faith be it unto you.
30 And their eyes were opened; and
Jesus straitly charged them, saying, See
that no man know *it*.
31 But they, when they were departed, spread abroad his fame in all that
country.
32 As they went out, behold, they
brought to him a dumb man possessed
with a devil.
33 And when the devil was cast out,
the dumb spake: and the multitudes
marvelled, saying, It was never so seen
in Israel.
34 But the Pharisees said, He casteth
out devils through the prince of the
devils.
35 And Jesus went about all the cities
and villages, teaching in their synagogues, and preaching the gospel of the
kingdom, and healing every sickness
and every disease among the people.
36 But when he saw the multitudes,
he was moved with compassion on
them, because they fainted, and were
scattered abroad, as sheep having no
shepherd.
37 Then saith he unto his disciples,
The harvest truly *is* plenteous, but the
labourers *are* few;
38 Pray ye therefore the Lord of the
harvest, that he will send forth labourers into his harvest.

10 And when he had called unto
him his twelve disciples, he gave
them power *against* unclean spirits, to
cast them out, and to heal all manner of
sickness and all manner of disease.
2 Now the names of the twelve apostles are these; The first, Simon, who is
called Peter, and Andrew his brother;
James *the son* of Zebedee, and John his
brother;
3 Philip, and Bartholomew; Thomas,
and Matthew the publican; James *the
son* of Alphaeus, and Lebbaeus, whose
surname was Thaddaeus;
4 Simon the Canaanite, and Judas
Iscariot, who also betrayed him.
5 These twelve Jesus sent forth, and
commanded them, saying, Go not into
the way of the Gentiles, and into *any*
city of the Samaritans enter ye not:
6 But go rather to the lost sheep of
the house of Israel.
7 And as ye go, preach, saying, The
kingdom of heaven is at hand.
8 Heal the sick, cleanse the lepers,
raise the dead, cast out devils: freely ye
have received, freely give.
9 Provide neither gold, nor silver, nor
brass in your purses,
10 Nor scrip for *your* journey, neither
two coats, neither shoes, nor yet staves:
for the workman is worthy of his meat.

11 And into whatsoever city or town
ye shall enter, enquire who in it is worthy; and there abide till ye go thence.
12 And when ye come into an house,
salute it.
13 And if the house be worthy, let
your peace come upon it: but if it be not
worthy, let your peace return to you.
14 And whosoever shall not receive
you, nor hear your words, when ye
depart out of that house or city, shake
off the dust of your feet.
15 Verily I say unto you, It shall be
more tolerable for the land of Sodom
and Gomorrha in the day of judgment,
than for that city.
16 Behold, I send you forth as sheep
in the midst of wolves: be ye therefore
wise as serpents, and harmless as
doves.
17 But beware of men: for they will
deliver you up to the councils, and they
will scourge you in their synagogues;
18 And ye shall be brought before
governors and kings for my sake, for
a testimony against them and the
Gentiles.
19 But when they deliver you up, take
no thought how or what ye shall speak:
for it shall be given you in that same
hour what ye shall speak.
20 For it is not ye that speak, but the
Spirit of your Father which speaketh in
you.
21 And the brother shall deliver up
the brother to death, and the father the
child: and the children shall rise up
against *their* parents, and cause them
to be put to death.
22 And ye shall be hated of all *men*
for my name's sake: but he that
endureth to the end shall be saved.
23 But when they persecute you in
this city, flee ye into another: for verily
I say unto you, Ye shall not have gone
over the cities of Israel, till the Son of
man be come.
24 The disciple is not above *his* master, nor the servant above his lord.
25 It is enough for the disciple that he
be as his master, and the servant as his
lord. If they have called the master of
the house Beelzebub, how much more
shall they call them of his household?
26 Fear them not therefore: for there
is nothing covered, that shall not be
revealed; and hid, that shall not be
known.
27 What I tell you in darkness, *that*
speak ye in light: and what ye hear in
the ear, *that* preach ye upon the housetops.
28 And fear not them which kill the
body, but are not able to kill the soul:
but rather fear him which is able to
destroy both soul and body in hell.
29 Are not two sparrows sold for a
farthing? and one of them shall not fall
on the ground without your Father.
30 But the very hairs of your head are
all numbered.
31 Fear ye not therefore, ye are of
more value than many sparrows.
32 Whosoever therefore shall confess
me before men, him will I confess also
before my Father which is in heaven.
33 But whosoever shall deny me
before men, him will I also deny before
my Father which is in heaven.
34 Think not that I am come to send
peace on earth: I came not to send
peace, but a sword.
35 For I am come to set a man at vari-
ance against his father, and the daughter against her mother, and the daughter in law against her mother in law.
36 And a man's foes *shall be* they of
his own household.

37 He that loveth father or mother more than me is not worthy of me: and he that loveth son or daughter more than me is not worthy of me.

38 And he that taketh not his cross, and followeth after me, is not worthy of me.

39 He that findeth his life shall lose it: and he that loseth his life for my sake shall find it.

40 He that receiveth you receiveth me, and he that receiveth me receiveth him that sent me.

41 He that receiveth a prophet in the name of a prophet shall receive a prophet's reward; and he that receiveth a righteous man in the name of a righteous man shall receive a righteous man's reward.

42 And whosoever shall give to drink unto one of these little ones a cup of cold *water* only in the name of a disciple, verily I say unto you, he shall in no wise lose his reward.

11 And it came to pass, when Jesus had made an end of commanding his twelve disciples, he departed thence to teach and to preach in their cities.

2 Now when John had heard in the prison the works of Christ, he sent two of his disciples,

3 And said unto him, Art thou he that should come, or do we look for another?

4 Jesus answered and said unto them, Go and shew John again those things which ye do hear and see:

5 The blind receive their sight, and the lame walk, the lepers are cleansed, and the deaf hear, the dead are raised up, and the poor have the gospel preached to them.

6 And blessed is *he*, whosoever shall not be offended in me.

7 And as they departed, Jesus began to say unto the multitudes concerning John, What went ye out into the wilderness to see? A reed shaken with the wind?

8 But what went ye out for to see? A man clothed in soft raiment? behold, they that wear soft *clothing* are in kings' houses.

9 But what went ye out for to see? A prophet? yea, I say unto you, and more than a prophet.

10 For this is *he*, of whom it is written, Behold, I send my messenger before thy face, which shall prepare thy way before thee.

11 Verily I say unto you, Among them that are born of women there hath not risen a greater than John the Baptist: notwithstanding he that is least in the kingdom of heaven is greater than he.

12 And from the days of John the Baptist until now the kingdom of heaven suffereth violence, and the violent take it by force.

13 For all the prophets and the law prophesied until John.

14 And if ye will receive *it*, this is Elias, which was for to come.

15 He that hath ears to hear, let him hear.

16 But whereunto shall I liken this generation? It is like unto children sitting in the markets, and calling unto their fellows,

17 And saying, We have piped unto you, and ye have not danced; we have mourned unto you, and ye have not lamented.

18 For John came neither eating nor drinking, and they say, He hath a devil.

19 The Son of man came eating and
drinking, and they say, Behold a man
gluttonous, and a winebibber, a friend
of publicans and sinners. But wisdom is
justified of her children.
20 Then began he to upbraid the cities wherein most of his mighty works
were done, because they repented not:
21 Woe unto thee, Chorazin! woe unto
thee, Bethsaida! for if the mighty
works, which were done in you, had
been done in Tyre and Sidon, they
would have repented long ago in sackcloth and ashes.
22 But I say unto you, It shall be more
tolerable for Tyre and Sidon at the day
of judgment, than for you.
23 And thou, Capernaum, which art
exalted unto heaven, shalt be brought
down to hell: for if the mighty works,
which have been done in thee, had
been done in Sodom, it would have
remained until this day.
24 But I say unto you, That it shall be
more tolerable for the land of Sodom in
the day of judgment, than for thee.
25 At that time Jesus answered and
said, I thank thee, O Father, Lord of
heaven and earth, because thou hast
hid these things from the wise and
prudent, and hast revealed them unto
babes.
26 Even so, Father: for so it seemed
good in thy sight.
27 All things are delivered unto me of
my Father: and no man knoweth the
Son, but the Father; neither knoweth
any man the Father, save the Son, and
he to whomsoever the Son will reveal
him.
28 Come unto me, all *ye* that labour
and are heavy laden, and I will give you
rest.
29 Take my yoke upon you, and learn
of me; for I am meek and lowly in heart:
and ye shall find rest unto your souls.
30 For my yoke *is* easy, and my burden is light.

12 At that time Jesus went on the
sabbath day through the corn;
and his disciples were an hungred, and
began to pluck the ears of corn, and to
eat.
2 But when the Pharisees saw *it*, they
said unto him, Behold, thy disciples do
that which is not lawful to do upon the
sabbath day.
3 But he said unto them, Have ye not
read what David did, when he was an
hungred, and they that were with him;
4 How he entered into the house of
God, and did eat the shewbread, which
was not lawful for him to eat, neither
for them which were with him, but only
for the priests?
5 Or have ye not read in the law, how
that on the sabbath days the priests in
the temple profane the sabbath, and
are blameless?
6 But I say unto you, That in this place
is *one* greater than the temple.
7 But if ye had known what *this*
meaneth, I will have mercy, and not
sacrifice, ye would not have condemned
the guiltless.
8 For the Son of man is Lord even of
the sabbath day.
9 And when he was departed thence,
he went into their synagogue:
10 And, behold, there was a man
which had *his* hand withered. And they
asked him, saying, Is it lawful to heal on
the sabbath days? that they might
accuse him.
11 And he said unto them, What man
shall there be among you, that shall
have one sheep, and if it fall into a pit

on the sabbath day, will he not lay hold on it, and lift *it* out?

12 How much then is a man better than a sheep? Wherefore it is lawful to do well on the sabbath days.

13 Then saith he to the man, Stretch forth thine hand. And he stretched *it* forth; and it was restored whole, like as the other.

14 Then the Pharisees went out, and held a council against him, how they might destroy him.

15 But when Jesus knew *it*, he withdrew himself from thence: and great multitudes followed him, and he healed them all;

16 And charged them that they should not make him known:

17 That it might be fulfilled which was spoken by Esaias the prophet, saying,

18 Behold my servant, whom I have chosen; my beloved, in whom my soul is well pleased: I will put my spirit upon him, and he shall shew judgment to the Gentiles.

19 He shall not strive, nor cry; neither shall any man hear his voice in the streets.

20 A bruised reed shall he not break, and smoking flax shall he not quench, till he send forth judgment unto victory.

21 And in his name shall the Gentiles trust.

22 Then was brought unto him one possessed with a devil, blind, and dumb: and he healed him, insomuch that the blind and dumb both spake and saw.

23 And all the people were amazed, and said, Is not this the son of David?

24 But when the Pharisees heard *it*, they said, This *fellow* doth not cast out devils, but by Beelzebub the prince of the devils.

25 And Jesus knew their thoughts, and said unto them, Every kingdom divided against itself is brought to desolation; and every city or house divided against itself shall not stand:

26 And if Satan cast out Satan, he is divided against himself; how shall then his kingdom stand?

27 And if I by Beelzebub cast out devils, by whom do your children cast *them* out? therefore they shall be your judges.

28 But if I cast out devils by the Spirit of God, then the kingdom of God is come unto you.

29 Or else how can one enter into a strong man's house, and spoil his goods, except he first bind the strong man? and then he will spoil his house.

30 He that is not with me is against me; and he that gathereth not with me scattereth abroad.

31 Wherefore I say unto you, All manner of sin and blasphemy shall be forgiven unto men: but the blasphemy *against* the *Holy* Ghost shall not be forgiven unto men.

32 And whosoever speaketh a word against the Son of man, it shall be forgiven him: but whosoever speaketh against the Holy Ghost, it shall not be forgiven him, neither in this world, neither in the *world* to come.

33 Either make the tree good, and his fruit good; or else make the tree corrupt, and his fruit corrupt: for the tree is known by *his* fruit.

34 O generation of vipers, how can ye, being evil, speak good things? for out of the abundance of the heart the mouth speaketh.

35 A good man out of the good treasure of the heart bringeth forth good
things: and an evil man out of the evil
treasure bringeth forth evil things.
36 But I say unto you, That every idle
word that men shall speak, they shall
give account thereof in the day of judgment.
37 For by thy words thou shalt be
justified, and by thy words thou shalt
be condemned.
38 Then certain of the scribes and of
the Pharisees answered, saying, Master,
we would see a sign from thee.
39 But he answered and said unto
them, An evil and adulterous generation seeketh after a sign; and there
shall no sign be given to it, but the sign
of the prophet Jonas:
40 For as Jonas was three days and
three nights in the whale's belly; so
shall the Son of man be three days and
three nights in the heart of the earth.
41 The men of Nineveh shall rise in
judgment with this generation, and
shall condemn it: because they repented at the preaching of Jonas; and,
behold, a greater than Jonas *is* here.
42 The queen of the south shall rise
up in the judgment with this generation, and shall condemn it: for she came
from the uttermost parts of the earth to
hear the wisdom of Solomon; and,
behold, a greater than Solomon *is* here.
43 When the unclean spirit is gone
out of a man, he walketh through dry
places, seeking rest, and findeth none.
44 Then he saith, I will return into my
house from whence I came out; and
when he is come, he findeth *it* empty,
swept, and garnished.
45 Then goeth he, and taketh with
himself seven other spirits more wicked than himself, and they enter in and
dwell there: and the last *state* of that
man is worse than the first. Even so
shall it be also unto this wicked generation.
46 While he yet talked to the people,
behold, *his* mother and his brethren
stood without, desiring to speak with
him.
47 Then one said unto him, Behold,
thy mother and thy brethren stand
without, desiring to speak with thee.
48 But he answered and said unto him
that told him, Who is my mother? and
who are my brethren?
49 And he stretched forth his hand
toward his disciples, and said, Behold
my mother and my brethren!
50 For whosoever shall do the will of
my Father which is in heaven, the same
is my brother, and sister, and mother.

13 The same day went Jesus out of
the house, and sat by the sea
side.
2 And great multitudes were gathered together unto him, so that he went
into a ship, and sat; and the whole
multitude stood on the shore.
3 And he spake many things unto
them in parables, saying, Behold, a
sower went forth to sow;
4 And when he sowed, some *seeds* fell
by the way side, and the fowls came
and devoured them up:
5 Some fell upon stony places, where
they had not much earth: and forthwith
they sprung up, because they had no
deepness of earth:
6 And when the sun was up, they were
scorched; and because they had no
root, they withered away.
7 And some fell among thorns; and
the thorns sprung up, and choked
them:

8 But other fell into good ground, and brought forth fruit, some an hundredfold, some sixtyfold, some thirtyfold.

9 Who hath ears to hear, let him hear.

10 And the disciples came, and said unto him, Why speakest thou unto them in parables?

11 He answered and said unto them, Because it is given unto you to know the mysteries of the kingdom of heaven, but to them it is not given.

12 For whosoever hath, to him shall be given, and he shall have more abundance: but whosoever hath not, from him shall be taken away even that he hath.

13 Therefore speak I to them in parables: because they seeing see not; and hearing they hear not, neither do they understand.

14 And in them is fulfilled the prophecy of Esaias, which saith, By hearing ye shall hear, and shall not understand; and seeing ye shall see, and shall not perceive:

15 For this people's heart is waxed gross, and *their* ears are dull of hearing, and their eyes they have closed; lest at any time they should see with *their* eyes, and hear with *their* ears, and should understand with *their* heart, and should be converted, and I should heal them.

16 But blessed *are* your eyes, for they see: and your ears, for they hear.

17 For verily I say unto you, That many prophets and righteous *men* have desired to see *those things* which ye see, and have not seen *them*; and to hear *those things* which ye hear, and have not heard *them*.

18 Hear ye therefore the parable of the sower.

19 When any one heareth the word of the kingdom, and understandeth *it* not, then cometh the wicked *one*, and catcheth away that which was sown in his heart. This is he which received seed by the way side.

20 But he that received the seed into stony places, the same is he that heareth the word, and anon with joy receiveth it;

21 Yet hath he not root in himself, but dureth for a while: for when tribulation or persecution ariseth because of the word, by and by he is offended.

22 He also that received seed among the thorns is he that heareth the word; and the care of this world, and the deceitfulness of riches, choke the word, and he becometh unfruitful.

23 But he that received seed into the good ground is he that heareth the word, and understandeth *it*; which also beareth fruit, and bringeth forth, some an hundredfold, some sixty, some thirty.

24 Another parable put he forth unto them, saying, The kingdom of heaven is likened unto a man which sowed good seed in his field:

25 But while men slept, his enemy came and sowed tares among the wheat, and went his way.

26 But when the blade was sprung up, and brought forth fruit, then appeared the tares also.

27 So the servants of the householder came and said unto him, Sir, didst not thou sow good seed in thy field? from whence then hath it tares?

28 He said unto them, An enemy hath done this. The servants said unto him, Wilt thou then that we go and gather them up?

29 But he said, Nay; lest while ye
gather up the tares, ye root up also the
wheat with them.
30 Let both grow together until the
harvest: and in the time of harvest I will
say to the reapers, Gather ye together
first the tares, and bind them in bundles to burn them: but gather the
wheat into my barn.
31 Another parable put he forth unto
them, saying, The kingdom of heaven is
like to a grain of mustard seed, which a
man took, and sowed in his field:
32 Which indeed is the least of all
seeds: but when it is grown, it is the
greatest among herbs, and becometh a
tree, so that the birds of the air come
and lodge in the branches thereof.
33 Another parable spake he unto
them; The kingdom of heaven is like
unto leaven, which a woman took, and
hid in three measures of meal, till the
whole was leavened.
34 All these things spake Jesus unto
the multitude in parables; and without
a parable spake he not unto them:
35 That it might be fulfilled which
was spoken by the prophet, saying, I
will open my mouth in parables; I will
utter things which have been kept
secret from the foundation of the world.
36 Then Jesus sent the multitude
away, and went into the house: and his
disciples came unto him, saying,
Declare unto us the parable of the tares
of the field.
37 He answered and said unto them,
He that soweth the good seed is the Son
of man;
38 The field is the world; the good
seed are the children of the kingdom;
but the tares are the children of the
wicked *one*;
39 The enemy that sowed them is the
devil; the harvest is the end of the
world; and the reapers are the angels.
40 As therefore the tares are gathered
and burned in the fire; so shall it be in
the end of this world.
41 The Son of man shall send forth his
angels, and they shall gather out of his
kingdom all things that offend, and
them which do iniquity;
42 And shall cast them into a furnace
of fire: there shall be wailing and
gnashing of teeth.
43 Then shall the righteous shine
forth as the sun in the kingdom of their
Father. Who hath ears to hear, let him
hear.
44 Again, the kingdom of heaven is
like unto treasure hid in a field; the
which when a man hath found, he
hideth, and for joy thereof goeth and
selleth all that he hath, and buyeth that
field.
45 Again, the kingdom of heaven is
like unto a merchant man, seeking
goodly pearls:
46 Who, when he had found one pearl
of great price, went and sold all that he
had, and bought it.
47 Again, the kingdom of heaven is
like unto a net, that was cast into the
sea, and gathered of every kind:
48 Which, when it was full, they drew
to shore, and sat down, and gathered
the good into vessels, but cast the bad
away.
49 So shall it be at the end of the
world: the angels shall come forth, and
sever the wicked from among the just,
50 And shall cast them into the furnace of fire: there shall be wailing and
gnashing of teeth.

51 Jesus saith unto them, Have ye understood all these things? They say unto him, Yea, Lord.

52 Then said he unto them, Therefore every scribe *which is* instructed unto the kingdom of heaven is like unto a man *that is* an householder, which bringeth forth out of his treasure *things* new and old.

53 And it came to pass, *that* when Jesus had finished these parables, he departed thence.

54 And when he was come into his own country, he taught them in their synagogue, insomuch that they were astonished, and said, Whence hath this *man* this wisdom, and *these* mighty works?

55 Is not this the carpenter's son? is not his mother called Mary? and his brethren, James, and Joses, and Simon, and Judas?

56 And his sisters, are they not all with us? Whence then hath this *man* all these things?

57 And they were offended in him. But Jesus said unto them, A prophet is not without honour, save in his own country, and in his own house.

58 And he did not many mighty works there because of their unbelief.

14

At that time Herod the tetrarch heard of the fame of Jesus,

2 And said unto his servants, This is John the Baptist; he is risen from the dead; and therefore mighty works do shew forth themselves in him.

3 For Herod had laid hold on John, and bound him, and put *him* in prison for Herodias' sake, his brother Philip's wife.

4 For John said unto him, It is not lawful for thee to have her.

5 And when he would have put him to death, he feared the multitude, because they counted him as a prophet.

6 But when Herod's birthday was kept, the daughter of Herodias danced before them, and pleased Herod.

7 Whereupon he promised with an oath to give her whatsoever she would ask.

8 And she, being before instructed of her mother, said, Give me here John Baptist's head in a charger.

9 And the king was sorry: nevertheless for the oath's sake, and them which sat with him at meat, he commanded *it* to be given *her*.

10 And he sent, and beheaded John in the prison.

11 And his head was brought in a charger, and given to the damsel: and she brought *it* to her mother.

12 And his disciples came, and took up the body, and buried it, and went and told Jesus.

13 When Jesus heard *of it*, he departed thence by ship into a desert place apart: and when the people had heard *thereof*, they followed him on foot out of the cities.

14 And Jesus went forth, and saw a great multitude, and was moved with compassion toward them, and he healed their sick.

15 And when it was evening, his disciples came to him, saying, This is a desert place, and the time is now past; send the multitude away, that they may go into the villages, and buy themselves victuals.

16 But Jesus said unto them, They need not depart; give ye them to eat.

17 And they say unto him, We have here but five loaves, and two fishes.

18 He said, Bring them hither to me.

19 And he commanded the multitude to sit down on the grass, and took the five loaves, and the two fishes, and looking up to heaven, he blessed, and brake, and gave the loaves to *his* disciples, and the disciples to the multitude.

20 And they did all eat, and were filled: and they took up of the fragments that remained twelve baskets full.

21 And they that had eaten were about five thousand men, beside women and children.

22 And straightway Jesus constrained his disciples to get into a ship, and to go before him unto the other side, while he sent the multitudes away.

23 And when he had sent the multitudes away, he went up into a mountain apart to pray: and when the evening was come, he was there alone.

24 But the ship was now in the midst of the sea, tossed with waves: for the wind was contrary.

25 And in the fourth watch of the night Jesus went unto them, walking on the sea.

26 And when the disciples saw him walking on the sea, they were troubled, saying, It is a spirit; and they cried out for fear.

27 But straightway Jesus spake unto them, saying, Be of good cheer; it is I; be not afraid.

28 And Peter answered him and said, Lord, if it be thou, bid me come unto thee on the water.

29 And he said, Come. And when Peter was come down out of the ship, he walked on the water, to go to Jesus.

30 But when he saw the wind boisterous, he was afraid; and beginning to sink, he cried, saying, Lord, save me.

31 And immediately Jesus stretched forth *his* hand, and caught him, and said unto him, O thou of little faith, wherefore didst thou doubt?

32 And when they were come into the ship, the wind ceased.

33 Then they that were in the ship came and worshipped him, saying, Of a truth thou art the Son of God.

34 And when they were gone over, they came into the land of Gennesaret.

35 And when the men of that place had knowledge of him, they sent out into all that country round about, and brought unto him all that were diseased;

36 And besought him that they might only touch the hem of his garment: and as many as touched were made perfectly whole.

15 Then came to Jesus scribes and Pharisees, which were of Jerusalem, saying,

2 Why do thy disciples transgress the tradition of the elders? for they wash not their hands when they eat bread.

3 But he answered and said unto them, Why do ye also transgress the commandment of God by your tradition?

4 For God commanded, saying, Honour thy father and mother: and, He that curseth father or mother, let him die the death.

5 But ye say, Whosoever shall say to *his* father or *his* mother, *It is* a gift, by whatsoever thou mightest be profited by me;

6 And honour not his father or his mother, *he shall be free*. Thus have ye made the commandment of God of none effect by your tradition.

7 *Ye* hypocrites, well did Esaias prophesy of you, saying,

8 This people draweth nigh unto me
with their mouth, and honoureth me
with *their* lips; but their heart is far
from me.
9 But in vain they do worship me,
teaching *for* doctrines the commandments of men.
10 And he called the multitude, and
said unto them, Hear, and understand:
11 Not that which goeth into the
mouth defileth a man; but that which
cometh out of the mouth, this defileth
a man.
12 Then came his disciples, and said
unto him, Knowest thou that the
Pharisees were offended, after they
heard this saying?
13 But he answered and said, Every
plant, which my heavenly Father hath
not planted, shall be rooted up.
14 Let them alone: they be blind leaders of the blind. And if the blind lead
the blind, both shall fall into the ditch.
15 Then answered Peter and said
unto him, Declare unto us this parable.
16 And Jesus said, Are ye also yet
without understanding?
17 Do not ye yet understand, that
whatsoever entereth in at the mouth
goeth into the belly, and is cast out into
the draught?
18 But those things which proceed
out of the mouth come forth from the
heart; and they defile the man.
19 For out of the heart proceed evil
thoughts, murders, adulteries, fornications, thefts, false witness, blasphemies:
20 These are *the things* which defile a
man: but to eat with unwashen hands
defileth not a man.
21 Then Jesus went thence, and
departed into the coasts of Tyre and
Sidon.
22 And, behold, a woman of Canaan
came out of the same coasts, and cried
unto him, saying, Have mercy on me, O
Lord, *thou* Son of David; my daughter
is grievously vexed with a devil.
23 But he answered her not a word.
And his disciples came and besought
him, saying, Send her away; for she crieth after us.
24 But he answered and said, I am not
sent but unto the lost sheep of the
house of Israel.
25 Then came she and worshipped
him, saying, Lord, help me.
26 But he answered and said, It is not
meet to take the children's bread, and
to cast *it* to dogs.
27 And she said, Truth, Lord: yet the
dogs eat of the crumbs which fall from
their masters' table.
28 Then Jesus answered and said
unto her, O woman, great *is* thy faith: be
it unto thee even as thou wilt. And her
daughter was made whole from that
very hour.
29 And Jesus departed from thence,
and came nigh unto the sea of Galilee;
and went up into a mountain, and sat
down there.
30 And great multitudes came unto
him, having with them *those that were*
lame, blind, dumb, maimed, and many
others, and cast them down at Jesus'
feet; and he healed them:
31 Insomuch that the multitude wondered, when they saw the dumb to
speak, the maimed to be whole, the
lame to walk, and the blind to see: and
they glorified the God of Israel.
32 Then Jesus called his disciples
unto him, and said, I have compassion
on the multitude, because they continue with me now three days, and have

nothing to eat: and I will not send them
away fasting, lest they faint in the way.
33 And his disciples say unto him,
Whence should we have so much bread
in the wilderness, as to fill so great a
multitude?
34 And Jesus saith unto them, How
many loaves have ye? And they said,
Seven, and a few little fishes.
35 And he commanded the multitude
to sit down on the ground.
36 And he took the seven loaves and
the fishes, and gave thanks, and brake
them, and gave to his disciples, and the
disciples to the multitude.
37 And they did all eat, and were
filled: and they took up of the broken
meat that was left seven baskets full.
38 And they that did eat were four
thousand men, beside women and children.
39 And he sent away the multitude,
and took ship, and came into the coasts
of Magdala.

16 The Pharisees also with the
Sadducees came, and tempting
desired him that he would shew them a
sign from heaven.
2 He answered and said unto them,
When it is evening, ye say, *It will be* fair
weather: for the sky is red.
3 And in the morning, *It will be* foul
weather to day: for the sky is red and
lowring. O *ye* hypocrites, ye can discern
the face of the sky; but can ye not *discern* the signs of the times?
4 A wicked and adulterous generation seeketh after a sign; and there
shall no sign be given unto it, but the
sign of the prophet Jonas. And he left
them, and departed.
5 And when his disciples were come
to the other side, they had forgotten to
take bread.
6 Then Jesus said unto them, Take
heed and beware of the leaven of the
Pharisees and of the Sadducees.
7 And they reasoned among themselves, saying, *It is* because we have
taken no bread.
8 *Which* when Jesus perceived, he
said unto them, O ye of little faith, why
reason ye among yourselves, because
ye have brought no bread?
9 Do ye not yet understand, neither
remember the five loaves of the five
thousand, and how many baskets ye
took up?
10 Neither the seven loaves of the
four thousand, and how many baskets
ye took up?
11 How is it that ye do not understand
that I spake *it* not to you concerning
bread, that ye should beware of the
leaven of the Pharisees and of the
Sadducees?
12 Then understood they how that he
bade *them* not beware of the leaven of
bread, but of the doctrine of the
Pharisees and of the Sadducees.
13 When Jesus came into the coasts
of Caesarea Philippi, he asked his disciples, saying, Whom do men say that I
the Son of man am?
14 And they said, Some *say that thou
art* John the Baptist: some, Elias; and
others, Jeremias, or one of the prophets.
15 He saith unto them, But whom say
ye that I am?
16 And Simon Peter answered and
said, Thou art the Christ, the Son of the
living God.
17 And Jesus answered and said unto
him, Blessed art thou, Simon Bar-jona:
for flesh and blood hath not revealed *it*
unto thee, but my Father which is in
heaven.

18 And I say also unto thee, That thou art Peter, and upon this rock I will build my church; and the gates of hell shall not prevail against it.

19 And I will give unto thee the keys of the kingdom of heaven: and whatsoever thou shalt bind on earth shall be bound in heaven: and whatsoever thou shalt loose on earth shall be loosed in heaven.

20 Then charged he his disciples that they should tell no man that he was Jesus the Christ.

21 From that time forth began Jesus to shew unto his disciples, how that he must go unto Jerusalem, and suffer many things of the elders and chief priests and scribes, and be killed, and be raised again the third day.

22 Then Peter took him, and began to rebuke him, saying, Be it far from thee, Lord: this shall not be unto thee.

23 But he turned, and said unto Peter, Get thee behind me, Satan: thou art an offence unto me: for thou savourest not the things that be of God, but those that be of men.

24 Then said Jesus unto his disciples, If any *man* will come after me, let him deny himself, and take up his cross, and follow me.

25 For whosoever will save his life shall lose it: and whosoever will lose his life for my sake shall find it.

26 For what is a man profited, if he shall gain the whole world, and lose his own soul? or what shall a man give in exchange for his soul?

27 For the Son of man shall come in the glory of his Father with his angels; and then he shall reward every man according to his works.

28 Verily I say unto you, There be some standing here, which shall not taste of death, till they see the Son of man coming in his kingdom.

17

And after six days Jesus taketh Peter, James, and John his brother, and bringeth them up into an high mountain apart,

2 And was transfigured before them: and his face did shine as the sun, and his raiment was white as the light.

3 And, behold, there appeared unto them Moses and Elias talking with him.

4 Then answered Peter, and said unto Jesus, Lord, it is good for us to be here: if thou wilt, let us make here three tabernacles; one for thee, and one for Moses, and one for Elias.

5 While he yet spake, behold, a bright cloud overshadowed them: and behold a voice out of the cloud, which said, This is my beloved Son, in whom I am well pleased; hear ye him.

6 And when the disciples heard *it*, they fell on their face, and were sore afraid.

7 And Jesus came and touched them, and said, Arise, and be not afraid.

8 And when they had lifted up their eyes, they saw no man, save Jesus only.

9 And as they came down from the mountain, Jesus charged them, saying, Tell the vision to no man, until the Son of man be risen again from the dead.

10 And his disciples asked him, saying, Why then say the scribes that Elias must first come?

11 And Jesus answered and said unto them, Elias truly shall first come, and restore all things.

12 But I say unto you, That Elias is come already, and they knew him not, but have done unto him whatsoever

they listed. Likewise shall also the Son
of man suffer of them.
13 Then the disciples understood that
he spake unto them of John the Baptist.
14 And when they were come to the
multitude, there came to him a *certain*
man, kneeling down to him, and saying,
15 Lord, have mercy on my son: for he
is lunatick, and sore vexed: for ofttimes
he falleth into the fire, and oft into the
water.
16 And I brought him to thy disciples,
and they could not cure him.
17 Then Jesus answered and said, O
faithless and perverse generation, how
long shall I be with you? how long shall
I suffer you? bring him hither to me.
18 And Jesus rebuked the devil; and
he departed out of him: and the child
was cured from that very hour.
19 Then came the disciples to Jesus
apart, and said, Why could not we cast
him out?
20 And Jesus said unto them, Because
of your unbelief: for verily I say unto
you, If ye have faith as a grain of mustard seed, ye shall say unto this mountain, Remove hence to yonder place;
and it shall remove; and nothing shall
be impossible unto you.
21 Howbeit this kind goeth not out
but by prayer and fasting.
22 And while they abode in Galilee,
Jesus said unto them, The Son of man
shall be betrayed into the hands of
men:
23 And they shall kill him, and the
third day he shall be raised again. And
they were exceeding sorry.
24 And when they were come to
Capernaum, they that received tribute
money came to Peter, and said, Doth
not your master pay tribute?
25 He saith, Yes. And when he was
come into the house, Jesus prevented
him, saying, What thinkest thou,
Simon? of whom do the kings of the
earth take custom or tribute? of their
own children, or of strangers?
26 Peter saith unto him, Of strangers.
Jesus saith unto him, Then are the children free.
27 Notwithstanding, lest we should
offend them, go thou to the sea, and
cast an hook, and take up the fish that
first cometh up; and when thou hast
opened his mouth, thou shalt find a
piece of money: that take, and give
unto them for me and thee.

18 At the same time came the disciples unto Jesus, saying, Who is
the greatest in the kingdom of heaven?
2 And Jesus called a little child unto
him, and set him in the midst of them,
3 And said, Verily I say unto you,
Except ye be converted, and become as
little children, ye shall not enter into
the kingdom of heaven.
4 Whosoever therefore shall humble
himself as this little child, the same is
greatest in the kingdom of heaven.
5 And whoso shall receive one such
little child in my name receiveth me.
6 But whoso shall offend one of these
little ones which believe in me, it were
better for him that a millstone were
hanged about his neck, and *that* he
were drowned in the depth of the sea.
7 Woe unto the world because of
offences! for it must needs be that
offences come; but woe to that man by
whom the offence cometh!
8 Wherefore if thy hand or thy foot
offend thee, cut them off, and cast
them from thee: it is better for thee to
enter into life halt or maimed, rather

than having two hands or two feet to be cast into everlasting fire.

9 And if thine eye offend thee, pluck it out, and cast *it* from thee: it is better for thee to enter into life with one eye, rather than having two eyes to be cast into hell fire.

10 Take heed that ye despise not one of these little ones; for I say unto you, That in heaven their angels do always behold the face of my Father which is in heaven.

11 For the Son of man is come to save that which was lost.

12 How think ye? if a man have an hundred sheep, and one of them be gone astray, doth he not leave the ninety and nine, and goeth into the mountains, and seeketh that which is gone astray?

13 And if so be that he find it, verily I say unto you, he rejoiceth more of that *sheep*, than of the ninety and nine which went not astray.

14 Even so it is not the will of your Father which is in heaven, that one of these little ones should perish.

15 Moreover if thy brother shall trespass against thee, go and tell him his fault between thee and him alone: if he shall hear thee, thou hast gained thy brother.

16 But if he will not hear *thee, then* take with thee one or two more, that in the mouth of two or three witnesses every word may be established.

17 And if he shall neglect to hear them, tell *it* unto the church: but if he neglect to hear the church, let him be unto thee as an heathen man and a publican.

18 Verily I say unto you, Whatsoever ye shall bind on earth shall be bound in heaven: and whatsoever ye shall loose on earth shall be loosed in heaven.

19 Again I say unto you, That if two of you shall agree on earth as touching any thing that they shall ask, it shall be done for them of my Father which is in heaven.

20 For where two or three are gathered together in my name, there am I in the midst of them.

21 Then came Peter to him, and said, Lord, how oft shall my brother sin against me, and I forgive him? till seven times?

22 Jesus saith unto him, I say not unto thee, Until seven times: but, Until seventy times seven.

23 Therefore is the kingdom of heaven likened unto a certain king, which would take account of his servants.

24 And when he had begun to reckon, one was brought unto him, which owed him ten thousand talents.

25 But forasmuch as he had not to pay, his lord commanded him to be sold, and his wife, and children, and all that he had, and payment to be made.

26 The servant therefore fell down, and worshipped him, saying, Lord, have patience with me, and I will pay thee all.

27 Then the lord of that servant was moved with compassion, and loosed him, and forgave him the debt.

28 But the same servant went out, and found one of his fellowservants, which owed him an hundred pence: and he laid hands on him, and took *him* by the throat, saying, Pay me that thou owest.

29 And his fellowservant fell down at his feet, and besought him, saying, Have patience with me, and I will pay thee all.

30 And he would not: but went and
cast him into prison, till he should pay
the debt.
31 So when his fellowservants saw
what was done, they were very sorry,
and came and told unto their lord all
that was done.
32 Then his lord, after that he had
called him, said unto him, O thou
wicked servant, I forgave thee all that
debt, because thou desiredst me:
33 Shouldest not thou also have had
compassion on thy fellowservant, even
as I had pity on thee?
34 And his lord was wroth, and delivered him to the tormentors, till he
should pay all that was due unto him.
35 So likewise shall my heavenly
Father do also unto you, if ye from your
hearts forgive not every one his brother
their trespasses.

19 And it came to pass, *that* when
Jesus had finished these sayings,
he departed from Galilee, and came
into the coasts of Judaea beyond Jordan;
2 And great multitudes followed him;
and he healed them there.
3 The Pharisees also came unto him,
tempting him, and saying unto him, Is it
lawful for a man to put away his wife
for every cause?
4 And he answered and said unto
them, Have ye not read, that he which
made *them* at the beginning made
them male and female,
5 And said, For this cause shall a man
leave father and mother, and shall
cleave to his wife: and they twain shall
be one flesh?
6 Wherefore they are no more twain,
but one flesh. What therefore God hath
joined together, let not man put
asunder.
7 They say unto him, Why did Moses
then command to give a writing of
divorcement, and to put her away?
8 He saith unto them, Moses because
of the hardness of your hearts suffered
you to put away your wives: but from
the beginning it was not so.
9 And I say unto you, Whosoever shall
put away his wife, except *it be* for fornication, and shall marry another, committeth adultery: and whoso marrieth
her which is put away doth commit
adultery.
10 His disciples say unto him, If the
case of the man be so with *his* wife, it is
not good to marry.
11 But he said unto them, All *men*
cannot receive this saying, save *they* to
whom it is given.
12 For there are some eunuchs, which
were so born from *their* mother's
womb: and there are some eunuchs,
which were made eunuchs of men: and
there be eunuchs, which have made
themselves eunuchs for the kingdom of
heaven's sake. He that is able to receive
it, let him receive *it*.
13 Then were there brought unto him
little children, that he should put *his*
hands on them, and pray: and the disciples rebuked them.
14 But Jesus said, Suffer little children, and forbid them not, to come unto
me: for of such is the kingdom of heav-
en.
15 And he laid *his* hands on them,
and departed thence.
16 And, behold, one came and said
unto him, Good Master, what good
thing shall I do, that I may have eternal
life?

17 And he said unto him, Why callest
thou me good? *there is* none good but
one, *that is*, God: but if thou wilt enter
into life, keep the commandments.
18 He saith unto him, Which? Jesus
said, Thou shalt do no murder, Thou
shalt not commit adultery, Thou shalt
not steal, Thou shalt not bear false witness,
19 Honour thy father and *thy* mother:
and, Thou shalt love thy neighbour as
thyself.
20 The young man saith unto him, All
these things have I kept from my youth
up: what lack I yet?
21 Jesus said unto him, If thou wilt be
perfect, go *and* sell that thou hast, and
give to the poor, and thou shalt have
treasure in heaven: and come *and* follow me.
22 But when the young man heard
that saying, he went away sorrowful: for
he had great possessions.
23 Then said Jesus unto his disciples,
Verily I say unto you, That a rich man
shall hardly enter into the kingdom of
heaven.
24 And again I say unto you, It is easier for a camel to go through the eye of
a needle, than for a rich man to enter
into the kingdom of God.
25 When his disciples heard *it*, they
were exceedingly amazed, saying, Who
then can be saved?
26 But Jesus beheld *them*, and said
unto them, With men this is impossible;
but with God all things are possible.
27 Then answered Peter and said
unto him, Behold, we have forsaken all,
and followed thee; what shall we have
therefore?
28 And Jesus said unto them, Verily I
say unto you, That ye which have followed me, in the regeneration when the
Son of man shall sit in the throne of his
glory, ye also shall sit upon twelve
thrones, judging the twelve tribes of
Israel.
29 And every one that hath forsaken
houses, or brethren, or sisters, or father,
or mother, or wife, or children, or lands,
for my name's sake, shall receive an
hundredfold, and shall inherit everlasting life.
30 But many *that are* first shall be
last; and the last *shall be* first.

20 For the kingdom of heaven is like
unto a man *that is* an householder, which went out early in the
morning to hire labourers into his vineyard.
2 And when he had agreed with the
labourers for a penny a day, he sent
them into his vineyard.
3 And he went out about the third
hour, and saw others standing idle in
the marketplace,
4 And said unto them; Go ye also into
the vineyard, and whatsoever is right I
will give you. And they went their way.
5 Again he went out about the sixth
and ninth hour, and did likewise.
6 And about the eleventh hour he
went out, and found others standing
idle, and saith unto them, Why stand ye
here all the day idle?
7 They say unto him, Because no man
hath hired us. He saith unto them, Go
ye also into the vineyard; and whatsoever is right, *that* shall ye receive.
8 So when even was come, the lord of
the vineyard saith unto his steward,
Call the labourers, and give them *their*
hire, beginning from the last unto the
first.
9 And when they came that *were*
hired about the eleventh hour, they
received every man a penny.

10 But when the first came, they supposed that they should have received more; and they likewise received every man a penny.

11 And when they had received *it*, they murmured against the goodman of the house,

12 Saying, These last have wrought *but* one hour, and thou hast made them equal unto us, which have borne the burden and heat of the day.

13 But he answered one of them, and said, Friend, I do thee no wrong: didst not thou agree with me for a penny?

14 Take *that* thine *is*, and go thy way: I will give unto this last, even as unto thee.

15 Is it not lawful for me to do what I will with mine own? Is thine eye evil, because I am good?

16 So the last shall be first, and the first last: for many be called, but few chosen.

17 And Jesus going up to Jerusalem took the twelve disciples apart in the way, and said unto them,

18 Behold, we go up to Jerusalem; and the Son of man shall be betrayed unto the chief priests and unto the scribes, and they shall condemn him to death,

19 And shall deliver him to the Gentiles to mock, and to scourge, and to crucify *him*: and the third day he shall rise again.

20 Then came to him the mother of Zebedee's children with her sons, worshipping *him*, and desiring a certain thing of him.

21 And he said unto her, What wilt thou? She saith unto him, Grant that these my two sons may sit, the one on thy right hand, and the other on the left, in thy kingdom.

22 But Jesus answered and said, Ye know not what ye ask. Are ye able to drink of the cup that I shall drink of, and to be baptized with the baptism that I am baptized with? They say unto him, We are able.

23 And he saith unto them, Ye shall drink indeed of my cup, and be baptized with the baptism that I am baptized with: but to sit on my right hand, and on my left, is not mine to give, but *it shall be given to them* for whom it is prepared of my Father.

24 And when the ten heard *it*, they were moved with indignation against the two brethren.

25 But Jesus called them *unto him*, and said, Ye know that the princes of the Gentiles exercise dominion over them, and they that are great exercise authority upon them.

26 But it shall not be so among you: but whosoever will be great among you, let him be your minister;

27 And whosoever will be chief among you, let him be your servant:

28 Even as the Son of man came not to be ministered unto, but to minister, and to give his life a ransom for many.

29 And as they departed from Jericho, a great multitude followed him.

30 And, behold, two blind men sitting by the way side, when they heard that Jesus passed by, cried out, saying, Have mercy on us, O Lord, *thou* Son of David.

31 And the multitude rebuked them, because they should hold their peace: but they cried the more, saying, Have mercy on us, O Lord, *thou* Son of David.

32 And Jesus stood still, and called them, and said, What will ye that I shall do unto you?

33 They say unto him, Lord, that our eyes may be opened.

34 So Jesus had compassion *on them*,
and touched their eyes: and immediately their eyes received sight, and they
followed him.

21 And when they drew nigh unto
Jerusalem, and were come to
Bethphage, unto the mount of Olives,
then sent Jesus two disciples,
2 Saying unto them, Go into the village over against you, and straightway
ye shall find an ass tied, and a colt with
her: loose *them*, and bring *them* unto
me.
3 And if any *man* say ought unto you,
ye shall say, The Lord hath need of
them; and straightway he will send
them.
4 All this was done, that it might be
fulfilled which was spoken by the
prophet, saying,
5 Tell ye the daughter of Sion, Behold,
thy King cometh unto thee, meek, and
sitting upon an ass, and a colt the foal
of an ass.
6 And the disciples went, and did as
Jesus commanded them,
7 And brought the ass, and the colt,
and put on them their clothes, and they
set *him* thereon.
8 And a very great multitude spread
their garments in the way; others cut
down branches from the trees, and
strawed *them* in the way.
9 And the multitudes that went
before, and that followed, cried, saying,
Hosanna to the Son of David: Blessed *is*
he that cometh in the name of the Lord;
Hosanna in the highest.
10 And when he was come into
Jerusalem, all the city was moved, saying, Who is this?
11 And the multitude said, This is
Jesus the prophet of Nazareth of
Galilee.
12 And Jesus went into the temple of
God, and cast out all them that sold and
bought in the temple, and overthrew
the tables of the moneychangers, and
the seats of them that sold doves,
13 And said unto them, It is written,
My house shall be called the house of
prayer; but ye have made it a den of
thieves.
14 And the blind and the lame came
to him in the temple; and he healed
them.
15 And when the chief priests and
scribes saw the wonderful things that
he did, and the children crying in the
temple, and saying, Hosanna to the Son
of David; they were sore displeased,
16 And said unto him, Hearest thou
what these say? And Jesus saith unto
them, Yea; have ye never read, Out of
the mouth of babes and sucklings thou
hast perfected praise?
17 And he left them, and went out of
the city into Bethany; and he lodged
there.
18 Now in the morning as he returned
into the city, he hungered.
19 And when he saw a fig tree in the
way, he came to it, and found nothing
thereon, but leaves only, and said unto
it, Let no fruit grow on thee henceforward for ever. And presently the fig tree
withered away.
20 And when the disciples saw *it*,
they marvelled, saying, How soon is the
fig tree withered away!
21 Jesus answered and said unto
them, Verily I say unto you, If ye have
faith, and doubt not, ye shall not only
do this *which is done* to the fig tree, but
also if ye shall say unto this mountain,
Be thou removed, and be thou cast into
the sea; it shall be done.

22 And all things, whatsoever ye shall
ask in prayer, believing, ye shall receive.
23 And when he was come into the
temple, the chief priests and the elders
of the people came unto him as he was
teaching, and said, By what authority
doest thou these things? and who gave
thee this authority?
24 And Jesus answered and said unto
them, I also will ask you one thing,
which if ye tell me, I in like wise will
tell you by what authority I do these
things.
25 The baptism of John, whence was
it? from heaven, or of men? And they
reasoned with themselves, saying, If we
shall say, From heaven; he will say unto
us, Why did ye not then believe him?
26 But if we shall say, Of men; we fear
the people; for all hold John as a
prophet.
27 And they answered Jesus, and
said, We cannot tell. And he said unto
them, Neither tell I you by what authority I do these things.
28 But what think ye? A *certain* man
had two sons; and he came to the first,
and said, Son, go work to day in my
vineyard.
29 He answered and said, I will not:
but afterward he repented, and went.
30 And he came to the second, and
said likewise. And he answered and
said, I *go*, sir: and went not.
31 Whether of them twain did the will
of *his* father? They say unto him, The
first. Jesus saith unto them, Verily I say
unto you, That the publicans and the
harlots go into the kingdom of God
before you.
32 For John came unto you in the way
of righteousness, and ye believed him
not: but the publicans and the harlots
believed him: and ye, when ye had seen
it, repented not afterward, that ye
might believe him.
33 Hear another parable: There was a
certain householder, which planted a
vineyard, and hedged it round about,
and digged a winepress in it, and built
a tower, and let it out to husbandmen,
and went into a far country:
34 And when the time of the fruit
drew near, he sent his servants to the
husbandmen, that they might receive
the fruits of it.
35 And the husbandmen took his servants, and beat one, and killed another,
and stoned another.
36 Again, he sent other servants more
than the first: and they did unto them
likewise.
37 But last of all he sent unto them
his son, saying, They will reverence my
son.
38 But when the husbandmen saw the
son, they said among themselves, This
is the heir; come, let us kill him, and let
us seize on his inheritance.
39 And they caught him, and cast *him*
out of the vineyard, and slew *him*.
40 When the lord therefore of the
vineyard cometh, what will he do unto
those husbandmen?
41 They say unto him, He will miser-
ably destroy those wicked men, and
will let out *his* vineyard unto other
husbandmen, which shall render him
the fruits in their seasons.
42 Jesus saith unto them, Did ye
never read in the scriptures, The stone
which the builders rejected, the same
is become the head of the corner: this
is the Lord's doing, and it is marvellous
in our eyes?

43 Therefore say I unto you, The kingdom of God shall be taken from you, and given to a nation bringing forth the fruits thereof.

44 And whosoever shall fall on this stone shall be broken: but on whomsoever it shall fall, it will grind him to powder.

45 And when the chief priests and Pharisees had heard his parables, they perceived that he spake of them.

46 But when they sought to lay hands on him, they feared the multitude, because they took him for a prophet.

22 And Jesus answered and spake unto them again by parables, and said,

2 The kingdom of heaven is like unto a certain king, which made a marriage for his son,

3 And sent forth his servants to call them that were bidden to the wedding: and they would not come.

4 Again, he sent forth other servants, saying, Tell them which are bidden, Behold, I have prepared my dinner: my oxen and *my* fatlings *are* killed, and all things *are* ready: come unto the marriage.

5 But they made light of *it*, and went their ways, one to his farm, another to his merchandise:

6 And the remnant took his servants, and entreated *them* spitefully, and slew *them*.

7 But when the king heard *thereof*, he was wroth: and he sent forth his armies, and destroyed those murderers, and burned up their city.

8 Then saith he to his servants, The wedding is ready, but they which were bidden were not worthy.

9 Go ye therefore into the highways, and as many as ye shall find, bid to the marriage.

10 So those servants went out into the highways, and gathered together all as many as they found, both bad and good: and the wedding was furnished with guests.

11 And when the king came in to see the guests, he saw there a man which had not on a wedding garment:

12 And he saith unto him, Friend, how camest thou in hither not having a wedding garment? And he was speechless.

13 Then said the king to the servants, Bind him hand and foot, and take him away, and cast *him* into outer darkness; there shall be weeping and gnashing of teeth.

14 For many are called, but few *are* chosen.

15 Then went the Pharisees, and took counsel how they might entangle him in *his* talk.

16 And they sent out unto him their disciples with the Herodians, saying, Master, we know that thou art true, and teachest the way of God in truth, neither carest thou for any *man*: for thou regardest not the person of men.

17 Tell us therefore, What thinkest thou? Is it lawful to give tribute unto Caesar, or not?

18 But Jesus perceived their wickedness, and said, Why tempt ye me, *ye* hypocrites?

19 Shew me the tribute money. And they brought unto him a penny.

20 And he saith unto them, Whose *is* this image and superscription?

21 They say unto him, Caesar's. Then saith he unto them, Render therefore unto Caesar the things which are

Caesar's; and unto God the things that are God's.

22 When they had heard *these words*, they marvelled, and left him, and went their way.

23 The same day came to him the Sadducees, which say that there is no resurrection, and asked him,

24 Saying, Master, Moses said, If a man die, having no children, his brother shall marry his wife, and raise up seed unto his brother.

25 Now there were with us seven brethren: and the first, when he had married a wife, deceased, and, having no issue, left his wife unto his brother:

26 Likewise the second also, and the third, unto the seventh.

27 And last of all the woman died also.

28 Therefore in the resurrection whose wife shall she be of the seven? for they all had her.

29 Jesus answered and said unto them, Ye do err, not knowing the scriptures, nor the power of God.

30 For in the resurrection they neither marry, nor are given in marriage, but are as the angels of God in heaven.

31 But as touching the resurrection of the dead, have ye not read that which was spoken unto you by God, saying,

32 I am the God of Abraham, and the God of Isaac, and the God of Jacob? God is not the God of the dead, but of the living.

33 And when the multitude heard *this*, they were astonished at his doctrine.

34 But when the Pharisees had heard that he had put the Sadducees to silence, they were gathered together.

35 Then one of them, *which was* a lawyer, asked *him a question*, tempting him, and saying,

36 Master, which *is* the great commandment in the law?

37 Jesus said unto him, Thou shalt love the Lord thy God with all thy heart, and with all thy soul, and with all thy mind.

38 This is the first and great commandment.

39 And the second *is* like unto it, Thou shalt love thy neighbour as thyself.

40 On these two commandments hang all the law and the prophets.

41 While the Pharisees were gathered together, Jesus asked them,

42 Saying, What think ye of Christ? whose son is he? They say unto him, *The Son* of David.

43 He saith unto them, How then doth David in spirit call him Lord, saying,

44 The LORD said unto my Lord, Sit thou on my right hand, till I make thine enemies thy footstool?

45 If David then call him Lord, how is he his son?

46 And no man was able to answer him a word, neither durst any *man* from that day forth ask him any more *questions*.

23 Then spake Jesus to the multitude, and to his disciples,

2 Saying, The scribes and the Pharisees sit in Moses' seat:

3 All therefore whatsoever they bid you observe, *that* observe and do; but do not ye after their works: for they say, and do not.

4 For they bind heavy burdens and grievous to be borne, and lay *them* on men's shoulders; but they *themselves*

will not move them with one of their fingers.

5 But all their works they do for to be seen of men: they make broad their phylacteries, and enlarge the borders of their garments,

6 And love the uppermost rooms at feasts, and the chief seats in the synagogues,

7 And greetings in the markets, and to be called of men, Rabbi, Rabbi.

8 But be not ye called Rabbi: for one is your Master, *even* Christ; and all ye are brethren.

9 And call no *man* your father upon the earth: for one is your Father, which is in heaven.

10 Neither be ye called masters: for one is your Master, *even* Christ.

11 But he that is greatest among you shall be your servant.

12 And whosoever shall exalt himself shall be abased; and he that shall humble himself shall be exalted.

13 But woe unto you, scribes and Pharisees, hypocrites! for ye shut up the kingdom of heaven against men: for ye neither go in *yourselves*, neither suffer ye them that are entering to go in.

14 Woe unto you, scribes and Pharisees, hypocrites! for ye devour widows' houses, and for a pretence make long prayer: therefore ye shall receive the greater damnation.

15 Woe unto you, scribes and Pharisees, hypocrites! for ye compass sea and land to make one proselyte, and when he is made, ye make him twofold more the child of hell than yourselves.

16 Woe unto you, *ye* blind guides, which say, Whosoever shall swear by the temple, it is nothing; but whosoever shall swear by the gold of the temple, he is a debtor!

17 Ye fools and blind: for whether is greater, the gold, or the temple that sanctifieth the gold?

18 And, Whosoever shall swear by the altar, it is nothing; but whosoever sweareth by the gift that is upon it, he is guilty.

19 Ye fools and blind: for whether *is* greater, the gift, or the altar that sanctifieth the gift?

20 Whoso therefore shall swear by the altar, sweareth by it, and by all things thereon.

21 And whoso shall swear by the temple, sweareth by it, and by him that dwelleth therein.

22 And he that shall swear by heaven, sweareth by the throne of God, and by him that sitteth thereon.

23 Woe unto you, scribes and Pharisees, hypocrites! for ye pay tithe of mint and anise and cummin, and have omitted the weightier *matters* of the law, judgment, mercy, and faith: these ought ye to have done, and not to leave the other undone.

24 Ye blind guides, which strain at a gnat, and swallow a camel.

25 Woe unto you, scribes and Pharisees, hypocrites! for ye make clean the outside of the cup and of the platter, but within they are full of extortion and excess.

26 *Thou* blind Pharisee, cleanse first that *which is* within the cup and platter, that the outside of them may be clean also.

27 Woe unto you, scribes and Pharisees, hypocrites! for ye are like unto whited sepulchres, which indeed appear beautiful outward, but are within full of dead *men's* bones, and of all uncleanness.

28 Even so ye also outwardly appear
righteous unto men, but within ye are
full of hypocrisy and iniquity.
29 Woe unto you, scribes and Pharisees, hypocrites! because ye build the
tombs of the prophets, and garnish the
sepulchres of the righteous,
30 And say, If we had been in the days
of our fathers, we would not have been
partakers with them in the blood of the
prophets.
31 Wherefore ye be witnesses unto
yourselves, that ye are the children of
them which killed the prophets.
32 Fill ye up then the measure of your
fathers.
33 *Ye* serpents, *ye* generation of
vipers, how can ye escape the damnation of hell?
34 Wherefore, behold, I send unto you
prophets, and wise men, and scribes:
and *some* of them ye shall kill and crucify; and *some* of them shall ye scourge
in your synagogues, and persecute
them from city to city:
35 That upon you may come all the
righteous blood shed upon the earth,
from the blood of righteous Abel unto
the blood of Zacharias son of Barachias,
whom ye slew between the temple and
the altar.
36 Verily I say unto you, All these
things shall come upon this generation.
37 O Jerusalem, Jerusalem, *thou* that
killest the prophets, and stonest them
which are sent unto thee, how often
would I have gathered thy children
together, even as a hen gathereth her
chickens under *her* wings, and ye would
not!
38 Behold, your house is left unto you
desolate.
39 For I say unto you, Ye shall not see
me henceforth, till ye shall say, Blessed
is he that cometh in the name of the
Lord.

24

24 And Jesus went out, and departed from the temple: and his disciples came to *him* for to shew him the
buildings of the temple.
2 And Jesus said unto them, See ye
not all these things? verily I say unto
you, There shall not be left here one
stone upon another, that shall not be
thrown down.
3 And as he sat upon the mount of
Olives, the disciples came unto him
privately, saying, Tell us, when shall
these things be? and what *shall be* the
sign of thy coming, and of the end of
the world?
4 And Jesus answered and said unto
them, Take heed that no man deceive
you.
5 For many shall come in my name,
saying, I am Christ; and shall deceive
many.
6 And ye shall hear of wars and
rumours of wars: see that ye be not
troubled: for all *these things* must
come to pass, but the end is not yet.
7 For nation shall rise against nation,
and kingdom against kingdom: and
there shall be famines, and pestilences,
and earthquakes, in divers places.
8 All these *are* the beginning of sorrows.
9 Then shall they deliver you up to be
afflicted, and shall kill you: and ye shall
be hated of all nations for my name's
sake.
10 And then shall many be offended,
and shall betray one another, and shall
hate one another.
11 And many false prophets shall rise,
and shall deceive many.
12 And because iniquity shall abound,
the love of many shall wax cold.

13 But he that shall endure unto the
end, the same shall be saved.
14 And this gospel of the kingdom
shall be preached in all the world for a
witness unto all nations; and then shall
the end come.
15 When ye therefore shall see the
abomination of desolation, spoken of
by Daniel the prophet, stand in the holy
place, (whoso readeth, let him understand:)
16 Then let them which be in Judaea
flee into the mountains:
17 Let him which is on the housetop
not come down to take any thing out of
his house:
18 Neither let him which is in the
field return back to take his clothes.
19 And woe unto them that are with
child, and to them that give suck in
those days!
20 But pray ye that your flight be not
in the winter, neither on the sabbath
day:
21 For then shall be great tribulation,
such as was not since the beginning of
the world to this time, no, nor ever shall
be.
22 And except those days should be
shortened, there should no flesh be
saved: but for the elect's sake those
days shall be shortened.
23 Then if any man shall say unto you,
Lo, here *is* Christ, or there; believe *it*
not.
24 For there shall arise false Christs,
and false prophets, and shall shew
great signs and wonders; insomuch
that, if *it were* possible, they shall
deceive the very elect.
25 Behold, I have told you before.
26 Wherefore if they shall say unto
you, Behold, he is in the desert; go not
forth: behold, *he is* in the secret chambers; believe *it* not.
27 For as the lightning cometh out of
the east, and shineth even unto the
west; so shall also the coming of the
Son of man be.
28 For wheresoever the carcase is,
there will the eagles be gathered
together.
29 Immediately after the tribulation
of those days shall the sun be darkened, and the moon shall not give her
light, and the stars shall fall from
heaven, and the powers of the heavens
shall be shaken:
30 And then shall appear the sign of
the Son of man in heaven: and then
shall all the tribes of the earth mourn,
and they shall see the Son of man coming in the clouds of heaven with power
and great glory.
31 And he shall send his angels with a
great sound of a trumpet, and they
shall gather together his elect from the
four winds, from one end of heaven to
the other.
32 Now learn a parable of the fig tree;
When his branch is yet tender, and
putteth forth leaves, ye know that summer *is* nigh:
33 So likewise ye, when ye shall see
all these things, know that it is near,
even at the doors.
34 Verily I say unto you, This generation shall not pass, till all these things
be fulfilled.
35 Heaven and earth shall pass away,
but my words shall not pass away.
36 But of that day and hour knoweth
no *man*, no, not the angels of heaven,
but my Father only.
37 But as the days of Noe *were*, so
shall also the coming of the Son of man
be.

38 For as in the days that were before
the flood they were eating and drinking, marrying and giving in marriage,
until the day that Noe entered into the
ark,
39 And knew not until the flood
came, and took them all away; so shall
also the coming of the Son of man be.
40 Then shall two be in the field; the
one shall be taken, and the other left.
41 Two *women shall be* grinding at
the mill; the one shall be taken, and the
other left.
42 Watch therefore: for ye know not
what hour your Lord doth come.
43 But know this, that if the goodman
of the house had known in what watch
the thief would come, he would have
watched, and would not have suffered
his house to be broken up.
44 Therefore be ye also ready: for in
such an hour as ye think not the Son of
man cometh.
45 Who then is a faithful and wise
servant, whom his lord hath made ruler
over his household, to give them meat
in due season?
46 Blessed *is* that servant, whom his
lord when he cometh shall find so
doing.
47 Verily I say unto you, That he shall
make him ruler over all his goods.
48 But and if that evil servant shall
say in his heart, My lord delayeth his
coming;
49 And shall begin to smite *his* fellowservants, and to eat and drink with
the drunken;
50 The lord of that servant shall come
in a day when he looketh not for *him*,
and in an hour that he is not aware of,
51 And shall cut him asunder, and
appoint *him* his portion with the hypocrites: there shall be weeping and
gnashing of teeth.

25 Then shall the kingdom of heav-
en be likened unto ten virgins,
which took their lamps, and went forth
to meet the bridegroom.
2 And five of them were wise, and five
were foolish.
3 They that *were* foolish took their
lamps, and took no oil with them:
4 But the wise took oil in their vessels
with their lamps.
5 While the bridegroom tarried, they
all slumbered and slept.
6 And at midnight there was a cry
made, Behold, the bridegroom cometh;
go ye out to meet him.
7 Then all those virgins arose, and
trimmed their lamps.
8 And the foolish said unto the wise,
Give us of your oil; for our lamps are
gone out.
9 But the wise answered, saying, *Not
so*; lest there be not enough for us and
you: but go ye rather to them that sell,
and buy for yourselves.
10 And while they went to buy, the
bridegroom came; and they that were
ready went in with him to the marriage:
and the door was shut.
11 Afterward came also the other virgins, saying, Lord, Lord, open to us.
12 But he answered and said, Verily I
say unto you, I know you not.
13 Watch therefore, for ye know neither the day nor the hour wherein the
Son of man cometh.
14 For *the kingdom of heaven is* as a
man travelling into a far country, *who*
called his own servants, and delivered
unto them his goods.
15 And unto one he gave five talents,
to another two, and to another one; to

every man according to his several ability; and straightway took his journey.
16 Then he that had received the five
talents went and traded with the same,
and made *them* other five talents.
17 And likewise he that *had received*
two, he also gained other two.
18 But he that had received one went
and digged in the earth, and hid his
lord's money.
19 After a long time the lord of those
servants cometh, and reckoneth with
them.
20 And so he that had received five
talents came and brought other five
talents, saying, Lord, thou deliveredst
unto me five talents: behold, I have
gained beside them five talents more.
21 His lord said unto him, Well done,
thou good and faithful servant: thou
hast been faithful over a few things, I
will make thee ruler over many things:
enter thou into the joy of thy lord.
22 He also that had received two talents came and said, Lord, thou deliveredst unto me two talents: behold, I
have gained two other talents beside
them.
23 His lord said unto him, Well done,
good and faithful servant; thou hast
been faithful over a few things, I will
make thee ruler over many things:
enter thou into the joy of thy lord.
24 Then he which had received the
one talent came and said, Lord, I knew
thee that thou art an hard man, reaping
where thou hast not sown, and gathering where thou hast not strawed:
25 And I was afraid, and went and hid
thy talent in the earth: lo, *there* thou
hast *that is* thine.
26 His lord answered and said unto
him, *Thou* wicked and slothful servant,
thou knewest that I reap where I sowed
not, and gather where I have not
strawed:
27 Thou oughtest therefore to have
put my money to the exchangers, and
then at my coming I should have
received mine own with usury.
28 Take therefore the talent from
him, and give *it* unto him which hath
ten talents.
29 For unto every one that hath shall
be given, and he shall have abundance:
but from him that hath not shall be
taken away even that which he hath.
30 And cast ye the unprofitable servant into outer darkness: there shall be
weeping and gnashing of teeth.
31 When the Son of man shall come in
his glory, and all the holy angels with
him, then shall he sit upon the throne
of his glory:
32 And before him shall be gathered
all nations: and he shall separate them
one from another, as a shepherd divideth *his* sheep from the goats:
33 And he shall set the sheep on his
right hand, but the goats on the left.
34 Then shall the King say unto them
on his right hand, Come, ye blessed of
my Father, inherit the kingdom prepared for you from the foundation of
the world:
35 For I was an hungred, and ye gave
me meat: I was thirsty, and ye gave me
drink: I was a stranger, and ye took me
in:
36 Naked, and ye clothed me: I was
sick, and ye visited me: I was in prison,
and ye came unto me.
37 Then shall the righteous answer
him, saying, Lord, when saw we thee an
hungred, and fed *thee*? or thirsty, and
gave *thee* drink?

38 When saw we thee a stranger, and
took *thee* in? or naked, and clothed
thee?
39 Or when saw we thee sick, or in
prison, and came unto thee?
40 And the King shall answer and say
unto them, Verily I say unto you,
Inasmuch as ye have done *it* unto one
of the least of these my brethren, ye
have done *it* unto me.
41 Then shall he say also unto them
on the left hand, Depart from me, ye
cursed, into everlasting fire, prepared
for the devil and his angels:
42 For I was an hungred, and ye gave
me no meat: I was thirsty, and ye gave
me no drink:
43 I was a stranger, and ye took me
not in: naked, and ye clothed me not:
sick, and in prison, and ye visited me
not.
44 Then shall they also answer him,
saying, Lord, when saw we thee an hungred, or athirst, or a stranger, or naked,
or sick, or in prison, and did not minister unto thee?
45 Then shall he answer them, saying,
Verily I say unto you, Inasmuch as ye
did *it* not to one of the least of these, ye
did *it* not to me.
46 And these shall go away into everlasting punishment: but the righteous
into life eternal.

26 And it came to pass, when Jesus
had finished all these sayings, he
said unto his disciples,
2 Ye know that after two days is *the
feast of* the passover, and the Son of
man is betrayed to be crucified.
3 Then assembled together the chief
priests, and the scribes, and the elders
of the people, unto the palace of the
high priest, who was called Caiaphas,
4 And consulted that they might take
Jesus by subtilty, and kill *him*.
5 But they said, Not on the feast *day*,
lest there be an uproar among the
people.
6 Now when Jesus was in Bethany, in
the house of Simon the leper,
7 There came unto him a woman having an alabaster box of very precious
ointment, and poured it on his head, as
he sat *at meat*.
8 But when his disciples saw *it*, they
had indignation, saying, To what purpose *is* this waste?
9 For this ointment might have been
sold for much, and given to the poor.
10 When Jesus understood *it*, he said
unto them, Why trouble ye the woman?
for she hath wrought a good work upon
me.
11 For ye have the poor always with
you; but me ye have not always.
12 For in that she hath poured this
ointment on my body, she did *it* for my
burial.
13 Verily I say unto you, Wheresoever
this gospel shall be preached in the
whole world, *there* shall also this, that
this woman hath done, be told for a
memorial of her.
14 Then one of the twelve, called
Judas Iscariot, went unto the chief
priests,
15 And said *unto them*, What will ye
give me, and I will deliver him unto
you? And they covenanted with him for
thirty pieces of silver.
16 And from that time he sought
opportunity to betray him.
17 Now the first *day* of the *feast of*
unleavened bread the disciples came to
Jesus, saying unto him, Where wilt thou
that we prepare for thee to eat the
passover?

18 And he said, Go into the city to such a man, and say unto him, The Master saith, My time is at hand; I will keep the passover at thy house with my disciples.

19 And the disciples did as Jesus had appointed them; and they made ready the passover.

20 Now when the even was come, he sat down with the twelve.

21 And as they did eat, he said, Verily I say unto you, that one of you shall betray me.

22 And they were exceeding sorrowful, and began every one of them to say unto him, Lord, is it I?

23 And he answered and said, He that dippeth *his* hand with me in the dish, the same shall betray me.

24 The Son of man goeth as it is written of him: but woe unto that man by whom the Son of man is betrayed! it had been good for that man if he had not been born.

25 Then Judas, which betrayed him, answered and said, Master, is it I? He said unto him, Thou hast said.

26 And as they were eating, Jesus took bread, and blessed *it*, and brake *it*, and gave *it* to the disciples, and said, Take, eat; this is my body.

27 And he took the cup, and gave thanks, and gave *it* to them, saying, Drink ye all of it;

28 For this is my blood of the new testament, which is shed for many for the remission of sins.

29 But I say unto you, I will not drink henceforth of this fruit of the vine, until that day when I drink it new with you in my Father's kingdom.

30 And when they had sung an hymn, they went out into the mount of Olives.

31 Then saith Jesus unto them, All ye shall be offended because of me this night: for it is written, I will smite the shepherd, and the sheep of the flock shall be scattered abroad.

32 But after I am risen again, I will go before you into Galilee.

33 Peter answered and said unto him, Though all *men* shall be offended because of thee, *yet* will I never be offended.

34 Jesus said unto him, Verily I say unto thee, That this night, before the cock crow, thou shalt deny me thrice.

35 Peter said unto him, Though I should die with thee, yet will I not deny thee. Likewise also said all the disciples.

36 Then cometh Jesus with them unto a place called Gethsemane, and saith unto the disciples, Sit ye here, while I go and pray yonder.

37 And he took with him Peter and the two sons of Zebedee, and began to be sorrowful and very heavy.

38 Then saith he unto them, My soul is exceeding sorrowful, even unto death: tarry ye here, and watch with me.

39 And he went a little further, and fell on his face, and prayed, saying, O my Father, if it be possible, let this cup pass from me: nevertheless not as I will, but as thou *wilt*.

40 And he cometh unto the disciples, and findeth them asleep, and saith unto Peter, What, could ye not watch with me one hour?

41 Watch and pray, that ye enter not into temptation: the spirit indeed *is* willing, but the flesh *is* weak.

42 He went away again the second time, and prayed, saying, O my Father,

if this cup may not pass away from me, except I drink it, thy will be done.
43 And he came and found them asleep again: for their eyes were heavy.
44 And he left them, and went away again, and prayed the third time, saying the same words.
45 Then cometh he to his disciples, and saith unto them, Sleep on now, and take *your* rest: behold, the hour is at hand, and the Son of man is betrayed into the hands of sinners.
46 Rise, let us be going: behold, he is at hand that doth betray me.
47 And while he yet spake, lo, Judas, one of the twelve, came, and with him a great multitude with swords and staves, from the chief priests and elders of the people.
48 Now he that betrayed him gave them a sign, saying, Whomsoever I shall kiss, that same is he: hold him fast.
49 And forthwith he came to Jesus, and said, Hail, master; and kissed him.
50 And Jesus said unto him, Friend, wherefore art thou come? Then came they, and laid hands on Jesus, and took him.
51 And, behold, one of them which were with Jesus stretched out *his* hand, and drew his sword, and struck a servant of the high priest's, and smote off his ear.
52 Then said Jesus unto him, Put up again thy sword into his place: for all they that take the sword shall perish with the sword.
53 Thinkest thou that I cannot now pray to my Father, and he shall presently give me more than twelve legions of angels?
54 But how then shall the scriptures be fulfilled, that thus it must be?
55 In that same hour said Jesus to the multitudes, Are ye come out as against a thief with swords and staves for to take me? I sat daily with you teaching in the temple, and ye laid no hold on me.
56 But all this was done, that the scriptures of the prophets might be fulfilled. Then all the disciples forsook him, and fled.
57 And they that had laid hold on Jesus led *him* away to Caiaphas the high priest, where the scribes and the elders were assembled.
58 But Peter followed him afar off unto the high priest's palace, and went in, and sat with the servants, to see the end.
59 Now the chief priests, and elders, and all the council, sought false witness against Jesus, to put him to death;
60 But found none: yea, though many false witnesses came, *yet* found they none. At the last came two false witnesses,
61 And said, This *fellow* said, I am able to destroy the temple of God, and to build it in three days.
62 And the high priest arose, and said unto him, Answerest thou nothing? what *is it which* these witness against thee?
63 But Jesus held his peace. And the high priest answered and said unto him, I adjure thee by the living God, that thou tell us whether thou be the Christ, the Son of God.
64 Jesus saith unto him, Thou hast said: nevertheless I say unto you, Hereafter shall ye see the Son of man sitting on the right hand of power, and coming in the clouds of heaven.
65 Then the high priest rent his clothes, saying, He hath spoken blas-

phemy; what further need have we of
witnesses? behold, now ye have heard
his blasphemy.
66 What think ye? They answered and
said, He is guilty of death.
67 Then did they spit in his face, and
buffeted him; and others smote *him*
with the palms of their hands,
68 Saying, Prophesy unto us, thou
Christ, Who is he that smote thee?
69 Now Peter sat without in the palace: and a damsel came unto him, saying, Thou also wast with Jesus of
Galilee.
70 But he denied before *them* all, saying, I know not what thou sayest.
71 And when he was gone out into the
porch, another *maid* saw him, and said
unto them that were there, This *fellow*
was also with Jesus of Nazareth.
72 And again he denied with an oath,
I do not know the man.
73 And after a while came unto *him*
they that stood by, and said to Peter,
Surely thou also art *one* of them; for thy
speech bewrayeth thee.
74 Then began he to curse and to
swear, *saying*, I know not the man. And
immediately the cock crew.
75 And Peter remembered the word
of Jesus, which said unto him, Before
the cock crow, thou shalt deny me
thrice. And he went out, and wept bitterly.

27 When the morning was come, all
the chief priests and elders of the
people took counsel against Jesus to
put him to death:
2 And when they had bound him,
they led *him* away, and delivered him
to Pontius Pilate the governor.
3 Then Judas, which had betrayed
him, when he saw that he was condemned, repented himself, and brought
again the thirty pieces of silver to the
chief priests and elders,
4 Saying, I have sinned in that I have
betrayed the innocent blood. And they
said, What *is that* to us? see thou *to*
that.
5 And he cast down the pieces of silver in the temple, and departed, and
went and hanged himself.
6 And the chief priests took the silver
pieces, and said, It is not lawful for to
put them into the treasury, because it is
the price of blood.
7 And they took counsel, and bought
with them the potter's field, to bury
strangers in.
8 Wherefore that field was called, The
field of blood, unto this day.
9 Then was fulfilled that which was
spoken by Jeremy the prophet, saying,
And they took the thirty pieces of silver, the price of him that was valued,
whom they of the children of Israel did
value;
10 And gave them for the potter's
field, as the Lord appointed me.
11 And Jesus stood before the governor: and the governor asked him, saying, Art thou the King of the Jews? And
Jesus said unto him, Thou sayest.
12 And when he was accused of the
chief priests and elders, he answered
nothing.
13 Then said Pilate unto him, Hearest
thou not how many things they witness
against thee?
14 And he answered him to never a
word; insomuch that the governor marvelled greatly.
15 Now at *that* feast the governor was
wont to release unto the people a prisoner, whom they would.
16 And they had then a notable prisoner, called Barabbas.

17 Therefore when they were gathered together, Pilate said unto them,
Whom will ye that I release unto you?
Barabbas, or Jesus which is called
Christ?
18 For he knew that for envy they had
delivered him.
19 When he was set down on the judgment seat, his wife sent unto him, saying, Have thou nothing to do with that
just man: for I have suffered many
things this day in a dream because of
him.
20 But the chief priests and elders
persuaded the multitude that they
should ask Barabbas, and destroy Jesus.
21 The governor answered and said
unto them, Whether of the twain will ye
that I release unto you? They said,
Barabbas.
22 Pilate saith unto them, What shall
I do then with Jesus which is called
Christ? *They* all say unto him, Let him
be crucified.
23 And the governor said, Why, what
evil hath he done? But they cried out
the more, saying, Let him be crucified.
24 When Pilate saw that he could
prevail nothing, but *that* rather a
tumult was made, he took water, and
washed *his* hands before the multitude,
saying, I am innocent of the blood of
this just person: see ye *to it*.
25 Then answered all the people, and
said, His blood *be* on us, and on our
children.
26 Then released he Barabbas unto
them: and when he had scourged Jesus,
he delivered *him* to be crucified.
27 Then the soldiers of the governor
took Jesus into the common hall, and
gathered unto him the whole band *of
soldiers*.
28 And they stripped him, and put on
him a scarlet robe.
29 And when they had platted a
crown of thorns, they put *it* upon his
head, and a reed in his right hand: and
they bowed the knee before him, and
mocked him, saying, Hail, King of the
Jews!
30 And they spit upon him, and took
the reed, and smote him on the head.
31 And after that they had mocked
him, they took the robe off from him,
and put his own raiment on him, and
led him away to crucify *him*.
32 And as they came out, they found
a man of Cyrene, Simon by name: him
they compelled to bear his cross.
33 And when they were come unto a
place called Golgotha, that is to say, a
place of a skull,
34 They gave him vinegar to drink
mingled with gall: and when he had
tasted *thereof*, he would not drink.
35 And they crucified him, and parted his garments, casting lots: that it
might be fulfilled which was spoken by
the prophet, They parted my garments
among them, and upon my vesture did
they cast lots.
36 And sitting down they watched
him there;
37 And set up over his head his accusation written, THIS IS JESUS THE
KING OF THE JEWS.
38 Then were there two thieves crucified with him, one on the right hand,
and another on the left.
39 And they that passed by reviled
him, wagging their heads,
40 And saying, Thou that destroyest
the temple, and buildest *it* in three
days, save thyself. If thou be the Son of
God, come down from the cross.

41 Likewise also the chief priests
mocking *him*, with the scribes and
elders, said,
42 He saved others; himself he cannot
save. If he be the King of Israel, let him
now come down from the cross, and we
will believe him.
43 He trusted in God; let him deliver
him now, if he will have him: for he said,
I am the Son of God.
44 The thieves also, which were crucified with him, cast the same in his
teeth.
45 Now from the sixth hour there was
darkness over all the land unto the
ninth hour.
46 And about the ninth hour Jesus
cried with a loud voice, saying, Eli, Eli,
lama sabachthani? that is to say, My
God, my God, why hast thou forsaken
me?
47 Some of them that stood there,
when they heard *that*, said, This *man*
calleth for Elias.
48 And straightway one of them ran,
and took a spunge, and filled *it* with
vinegar, and put *it* on a reed, and gave
him to drink.
49 The rest said, Let be, let us see
whether Elias will come to save him.
50 Jesus, when he had cried again
with a loud voice, yielded up the ghost.
51 And, behold, the veil of the temple
was rent in twain from the top to the
bottom; and the earth did quake, and
the rocks rent;
52 And the graves were opened; and
many bodies of the saints which slept
arose,
53 And came out of the graves after
his resurrection, and went into the holy
city, and appeared unto many.
54 Now when the centurion, and they
that were with him, watching Jesus,
saw the earthquake, and those things
that were done, they feared greatly, saying, Truly this was the Son of God.
55 And many women were there
beholding afar off, which followed
Jesus from Galilee, ministering unto
him:
56 Among which was Mary Magdalene, and Mary the mother of James
and Joses, and the mother of Zebedee's
children.
57 When the even was come, there
came a rich man of Arimathaea, named
Joseph, who also himself was Jesus'
disciple:
58 He went to Pilate, and begged the
body of Jesus. Then Pilate commanded
the body to be delivered.
59 And when Joseph had taken the
body, he wrapped it in a clean linen
cloth,
60 And laid it in his own new tomb,
which he had hewn out in the rock: and
he rolled a great stone to the door of
the sepulchre, and departed.
61 And there was Mary Magdalene,
and the other Mary, sitting over against
the sepulchre.
62 Now the next day, that followed
the day of the preparation, the chief
priests and Pharisees came together
unto Pilate,
63 Saying, Sir, we remember that that
deceiver said, while he was yet alive,
After three days I will rise again.
64 Command therefore that the
sepulchre be made sure until the third
day, lest his disciples come by night,
and steal him away, and say unto the
people, He is risen from the dead: so
the last error shall be worse than the
first.

65 Pilate said unto them, Ye have a
watch: go your way, make *it* as sure as
ye can.
66 So they went, and made the sepulchre sure, sealing the stone, and setting
a watch.

28 In the end of the sabbath, as it
began to dawn toward the first
day of the week, came Mary Magdalene
and the other Mary to see the sepulchre.
2 And, behold, there was a great
earthquake: for the angel of the Lord
descended from heaven, and came and
rolled back the stone from the door,
and sat upon it.
3 His countenance was like lightning,
and his raiment white as snow:
4 And for fear of him the keepers did
shake, and became as dead *men*.
5 And the angel answered and said
unto the women, Fear not ye: for I know
that ye seek Jesus, which was crucified.
6 He is not here: for he is risen, as he
said. Come, see the place where the
Lord lay.
7 And go quickly, and tell his disciples
that he is risen from the dead; and,
behold, he goeth before you into
Galilee; there shall ye see him: lo, I
have told you.
8 And they departed quickly from the
sepulchre with fear and great joy; and
did run to bring his disciples word.
9 And as they went to tell his disciples, behold, Jesus met them, saying,
All hail. And they came and held him
by the feet, and worshipped him.
10 Then said Jesus unto them, Be not
afraid: go tell my brethren that they go
into Galilee, and there shall they see
me.
11 Now when they were going, behold,
some of the watch came into the city,
and shewed unto the chief priests all
the things that were done.
12 And when they were assembled
with the elders, and had taken counsel,
they gave large money unto the soldiers,
13 Saying, Say ye, His disciples came
by night, and stole him *away* while we
slept.
14 And if this come to the governor's
ears, we will persuade him, and secure
you.
15 So they took the money, and did as
they were taught: and this saying is
commonly reported among the Jews
until this day.
16 Then the eleven disciples went
away into Galilee, into a mountain
where Jesus had appointed them.
17 And when they saw him, they worshipped him: but some doubted.
18 And Jesus came and spake unto
them, saying, All power is given unto
me in heaven and in earth.
19 Go ye therefore, and teach all
nations, baptizing them in the name of
the Father, and of the Son, and of the
Holy Ghost:
20 Teaching them to observe all
things whatsoever I have commanded
you: and, lo, I am with you alway, *even*
unto the end of the world. Amen.

THE GOSPEL ACCORDING TO
SAINT MARK

1 The beginning of the gospel of Jesus Christ, the Son of God;
2 As it is written in the prophets, Behold, I send my messenger before thy face, which shall prepare thy way before thee.
3 The voice of one crying in the wilderness, Prepare ye the way of the Lord, make his paths straight.
4 John did baptize in the wilderness, and preach the baptism of repentance for the remission of sins.
5 And there went out unto him all the land of Judaea, and they of Jerusalem, and were all baptized of him in the river of Jordan, confessing their sins.
6 And John was clothed with camel's hair, and with a girdle of a skin about his loins; and he did eat locusts and wild honey;
7 And preached, saying, There cometh one mightier than I after me, the latchet of whose shoes I am not worthy to stoop down and unloose.
8 I indeed have baptized you with water: but he shall baptize you with the Holy Ghost.
9 And it came to pass in those days, that Jesus came from Nazareth of Galilee, and was baptized of John in Jordan.
10 And straightway coming up out of the water, he saw the heavens opened, and the Spirit like a dove descending upon him:
11 And there came a voice from heaven, *saying*, Thou art my beloved Son, in whom I am well pleased.
12 And immediately the Spirit driveth him into the wilderness.
13 And he was there in the wilderness forty days, tempted of Satan; and was with the wild beasts; and the angels ministered unto him.
14 Now after that John was put in prison, Jesus came into Galilee, preaching the gospel of the kingdom of God,
15 And saying, The time is fulfilled, and the kingdom of God is at hand: repent ye, and believe the gospel.
16 Now as he walked by the sea of Galilee, he saw Simon and Andrew his brother casting a net into the sea: for they were fishers.
17 And Jesus said unto them, Come ye after me, and I will make you to become fishers of men.
18 And straightway they forsook their nets, and followed him.
19 And when he had gone a little further thence, he saw James the *son* of Zebedee, and John his brother, who also were in the ship mending their nets.
20 And straightway he called them: and they left their father Zebedee in the ship with the hired servants, and went after him.
21 And they went into Capernaum; and straightway on the sabbath day he entered into the synagogue, and taught.
22 And they were astonished at his doctrine: for he taught them as one that had authority, and not as the scribes.
23 And there was in their synagogue a man with an unclean spirit; and he cried out,
24 Saying, Let *us* alone; what have we to do with thee, thou Jesus of Nazareth?

art thou come to destroy us? I know
thee who thou art, the Holy One of God.
25 And Jesus rebuked him, saying,
Hold thy peace, and come out of him.
26 And when the unclean spirit had
torn him, and cried with a loud voice,
he came out of him.
27 And they were all amazed, insomuch that they questioned among
themselves, saying, What thing is this?
what new doctrine *is* this? for with
authority commandeth he even the
unclean spirits, and they do obey him.
28 And immediately his fame spread
abroad throughout all the region round
about Galilee.
29 And forthwith, when they were
come out of the synagogue, they
entered into the house of Simon and
Andrew, with James and John.
30 But Simon's wife's mother lay sick
of a fever, and anon they tell him of her.
31 And he came and took her by the
hand, and lifted her up; and immediately the fever left her, and she ministered unto them.
32 And at even, when the sun did set,
they brought unto him all that were
diseased, and them that were possessed with devils.
33 And all the city was gathered
together at the door.
34 And he healed many that were
sick of divers diseases, and cast out
many devils; and suffered not the devils to speak, because they knew him.
35 And in the morning, rising up a
great while before day, he went out, and
departed into a solitary place, and
there prayed.
36 And Simon and they that were
with him followed after him.
37 And when they had found him,
they said unto him, All *men* seek for
thee.
38 And he said unto them, Let us go
into the next towns, that I may preach
there also: for therefore came I forth.
39 And he preached in their synagogues throughout all Galilee, and cast
out devils.
40 And there came a leper to him,
beseeching him, and kneeling down to
him, and saying unto him, If thou wilt,
thou canst make me clean.
41 And Jesus, moved with compassion, put forth *his* hand, and touched
him, and saith unto him, I will; be thou
clean.
42 And as soon as he had spoken,
immediately the leprosy departed from
him, and he was cleansed.
43 And he straitly charged him, and
forthwith sent him away;
44 And saith unto him, See thou say
nothing to any man: but go thy way,
shew thyself to the priest, and offer for
thy cleansing those things which Moses
commanded, for a testimony unto
them.
45 But he went out, and began to
publish *it* much, and to blaze abroad
the matter, insomuch that Jesus could
no more openly enter into the city, but
was without in desert places: and they
came to him from every quarter.

2 And again he entered into Capernaum after *some* days; and it was
noised that he was in the house.
2 And straightway many were gathered together, insomuch that there was
no room to receive *them*, no, not so
much as about the door: and he
preached the word unto them.

3 And they come unto him, bringing one sick of the palsy, which was borne of four.

4 And when they could not come nigh unto him for the press, they uncovered the roof where he was: and when they had broken *it* up, they let down the bed wherein the sick of the palsy lay.

5 When Jesus saw their faith, he said unto the sick of the palsy, Son, thy sins be forgiven thee.

6 But there were certain of the scribes sitting there, and reasoning in their hearts,

7 Why doth this *man* thus speak blasphemies? who can forgive sins but God only?

8 And immediately when Jesus perceived in his spirit that they so reasoned within themselves, he said unto them, Why reason ye these things in your hearts?

9 Whether is it easier to say to the sick of the palsy, *Thy* sins be forgiven thee; or to say, Arise, and take up thy bed, and walk?

10 But that ye may know that the Son of man hath power on earth to forgive sins, (he saith to the sick of the palsy,)

11 I say unto thee, Arise, and take up thy bed, and go thy way into thine house.

12 And immediately he arose, took up the bed, and went forth before them all; insomuch that they were all amazed, and glorified God, saying, We never saw it on this fashion.

13 And he went forth again by the sea side; and all the multitude resorted unto him, and he taught them.

14 And as he passed by, he saw Levi the *son* of Alphaeus sitting at the receipt of custom, and said unto him, Follow me. And he arose and followed him.

15 And it came to pass, that, as Jesus sat at meat in his house, many publicans and sinners sat also together with Jesus and his disciples: for there were many, and they followed him.

16 And when the scribes and Pharisees saw him eat with publicans and sinners, they said unto his disciples, How is it that he eateth and drinketh with publicans and sinners?

17 When Jesus heard *it*, he saith unto them, They that are whole have no need of the physician, but they that are sick: I came not to call the righteous, but sinners to repentance.

18 And the disciples of John and of the Pharisees used to fast: and they come and say unto him, Why do the disciples of John and of the Pharisees fast, but thy disciples fast not?

19 And Jesus said unto them, Can the children of the bridechamber fast, while the bridegroom is with them? as long as they have the bridegroom with them, they cannot fast.

20 But the days will come, when the bridegroom shall be taken away from them, and then shall they fast in those days.

21 No man also seweth a piece of new cloth on an old garment: else the new piece that filled it up taketh away from the old, and the rent is made worse.

22 And no man putteth new wine into old bottles: else the new wine doth burst the bottles, and the wine is spilled, and the bottles will be marred: but new wine must be put into new bottles.

23 And it came to pass, that he went through the corn fields on the sabbath

day; and his disciples began, as they
went, to pluck the ears of corn.
24 And the Pharisees said unto him,
Behold, why do they on the sabbath day
that which is not lawful?
25 And he said unto them, Have ye
never read what David did, when he
had need, and was an hungred, he, and
they that were with him?
26 How he went into the house of God
in the days of Abiathar the high priest,
and did eat the shewbread, which is not
lawful to eat but for the priests, and
gave also to them which were with him?
27 And he said unto them, The sabbath was made for man, and not man
for the sabbath:
28 Therefore the Son of man is Lord
also of the sabbath.

3 And he entered again into the
synagogue; and there was a man
there which had a withered hand.
2 And they watched him, whether he
would heal him on the sabbath day;
that they might accuse him.
3 And he saith unto the man which
had the withered hand, Stand forth.
4 And he saith unto them, Is it lawful
to do good on the sabbath days, or to do
evil? to save life, or to kill? But they
held their peace.
5 And when he had looked round
about on them with anger, being
grieved for the hardness of their hearts,
he saith unto the man, Stretch forth
thine hand. And he stretched *it* out:
and his hand was restored whole as the
other.
6 And the Pharisees went forth, and
straightway took counsel with the
Herodians against him, how they might
destroy him.
7 But Jesus withdrew himself with his
disciples to the sea: and a great multitude from Galilee followed him, and
from Judaea,
8 And from Jerusalem, and from
Idumaea, and *from* beyond Jordan; and
they about Tyre and Sidon, a great multitude, when they had heard what great
things he did, came unto him.
9 And he spake to his disciples, that a
small ship should wait on him because
of the multitude, lest they should
throng him.
10 For he had healed many; insomuch
that they pressed upon him for to touch
him, as many as had plagues.
11 And unclean spirits, when they
saw him, fell down before him, and
cried, saying, Thou art the Son of God.
12 And he straitly charged them that
they should not make him known.
13 And he goeth up into a mountain,
and calleth *unto him* whom he would:
and they came unto him.
14 And he ordained twelve, that they
should be with him, and that he might
send them forth to preach,
15 And to have power to heal sicknesses, and to cast out devils:
16 And Simon he surnamed Peter;
17 And James the *son* of Zebedee,
and John the brother of James; and he
surnamed them Boanerges, which is,
The sons of thunder:
18 And Andrew, and Philip, and
Bartholomew, and Matthew, and
Thomas, and James the *son* of
Alphaeus, and Thaddaeus, and Simon
the Canaanite,
19 And Judas Iscariot, which also
betrayed him: and they went into an
house.
20 And the multitude cometh together again, so that they could not so much
as eat bread.

21 And when his friends heard *of it*, they went out to lay hold on him: for they said, He is beside himself.

22 And the scribes which came down from Jerusalem said, He hath Beelzebub, and by the prince of the devils casteth he out devils.

23 And he called them *unto him*, and said unto them in parables, How can Satan cast out Satan?

24 And if a kingdom be divided against itself, that kingdom cannot stand.

25 And if a house be divided against itself, that house cannot stand.

26 And if Satan rise up against himself, and be divided, he cannot stand, but hath an end.

27 No man can enter into a strong man's house, and spoil his goods, except he will first bind the strong man; and then he will spoil his house.

28 Verily I say unto you, All sins shall be forgiven unto the sons of men, and blasphemies wherewith soever they shall blaspheme:

29 But he that shall blaspheme against the Holy Ghost hath never forgiveness, but is in danger of eternal damnation:

30 Because they said, He hath an unclean spirit.

31 There came then his brethren and his mother, and, standing without, sent unto him, calling him.

32 And the multitude sat about him, and they said unto him, Behold, thy mother and thy brethren without seek for thee.

33 And he answered them, saying, Who is my mother, or my brethren?

34 And he looked round about on them which sat about him, and said, Behold my mother and my brethren!

35 For whosoever shall do the will of God, the same is my brother, and my sister, and mother.

4 And he began again to teach by the sea side: and there was gathered unto him a great multitude, so that he entered into a ship, and sat in the sea; and the whole multitude was by the sea on the land.

2 And he taught them many things by parables, and said unto them in his doctrine,

3 Hearken; Behold, there went out a sower to sow:

4 And it came to pass, as he sowed, some fell by the way side, and the fowls of the air came and devoured it up.

5 And some fell on stony ground, where it had not much earth; and immediately it sprang up, because it had no depth of earth:

6 But when the sun was up, it was scorched; and because it had no root, it withered away.

7 And some fell among thorns, and the thorns grew up, and choked it, and it yielded no fruit.

8 And other fell on good ground, and did yield fruit that sprang up and increased; and brought forth, some thirty, and some sixty, and some an hundred.

9 And he said unto them, He that hath ears to hear, let him hear.

10 And when he was alone, they that were about him with the twelve asked of him the parable.

11 And he said unto them, Unto you it is given to know the mystery of the kingdom of God: but unto them that are without, all *these* things are done in parables:

12 That seeing they may see, and not perceive; and hearing they may hear,

and not understand; lest at any time
they should be converted, and *their*
sins should be forgiven them.
13 And he said unto them, Know ye
not this parable? and how then will ye
know all parables?
14 The sower soweth the word.
15 And these are they by the way
side, where the word is sown; but when
they have heard, Satan cometh immediately, and taketh away the word that
was sown in their hearts.
16 And these are they likewise which
are sown on stony ground; who, when
they have heard the word, immediately
receive it with gladness;
17 And have no root in themselves,
and so endure but for a time: afterward,
when affliction or persecution ariseth
for the word's sake, immediately they
are offended.
18 And these are they which are sown
among thorns; such as hear the word,
19 And the cares of this world, and
the deceitfulness of riches, and the
lusts of other things entering in, choke
the word, and it becometh unfruitful.
20 And these are they which are sown
on good ground; such as hear the word,
and receive *it*, and bring forth fruit,
some thirtyfold, some sixty, and some
an hundred.
21 And he said unto them, Is a candle
brought to be put under a bushel, or
under a bed? and not to be set on a
candlestick?
22 For there is nothing hid, which
shall not be manifested; neither was
any thing kept secret, but that it should
come abroad.
23 If any man have ears to hear, let
him hear.
24 And he said unto them, Take heed
what ye hear: with what measure ye
mete, it shall be measured to you: and
unto you that hear shall more be given.
25 For he that hath, to him shall be
given: and he that hath not, from him
shall be taken even that which he hath.
26 And he said, So is the kingdom of
God, as if a man should cast seed into
the ground;
27 And should sleep, and rise night
and day, and the seed should spring
and grow up, he knoweth not how.
28 For the earth bringeth forth fruit
of herself; first the blade, then the ear,
after that the full corn in the ear.
29 But when the fruit is brought forth,
immediately he putteth in the sickle,
because the harvest is come.
30 And he said, Whereunto shall we
liken the kingdom of God? or with what
comparison shall we compare it?
31 *It is* like a grain of mustard seed,
which, when it is sown in the earth, is
less than all the seeds that be in the
earth:
32 But when it is sown, it groweth up,
and becometh greater than all herbs,
and shooteth out great branches; so
that the fowls of the air may lodge
under the shadow of it.
33 And with many such parables
spake he the word unto them, as they
were able to hear *it*.
34 But without a parable spake he not
unto them: and when they were alone,
he expounded all things to his disciples.
35 And the same day, when the even
was come, he saith unto them, Let us
pass over unto the other side.
36 And when they had sent away the
multitude, they took him even as he
was in the ship. And there were also
with him other little ships.

37 And there arose a great storm of wind, and the waves beat into the ship, so that it was now full.

38 And he was in the hinder part of the ship, asleep on a pillow: and they awake him, and say unto him, Master, carest thou not that we perish?

39 And he arose, and rebuked the wind, and said unto the sea, Peace, be still. And the wind ceased, and there was a great calm.

40 And he said unto them, Why are ye so fearful? how is it that ye have no faith?

41 And they feared exceedingly, and said one to another, What manner of man is this, that even the wind and the sea obey him?

5

And they came over unto the other side of the sea, into the country of the Gadarenes.

2 And when he was come out of the ship, immediately there met him out of the tombs a man with an unclean spirit,

3 Who had *his* dwelling among the tombs; and no man could bind him, no, not with chains:

4 Because that he had been often bound with fetters and chains, and the chains had been plucked asunder by him, and the fetters broken in pieces: neither could any *man* tame him.

5 And always, night and day, he was in the mountains, and in the tombs, crying, and cutting himself with stones.

6 But when he saw Jesus afar off, he ran and worshipped him,

7 And cried with a loud voice, and said, What have I to do with thee, Jesus, *thou* Son of the most high God? I adjure thee by God, that thou torment me not.

8 For he said unto him, Come out of the man, *thou* unclean spirit.

9 And he asked him, What *is* thy name? And he answered, saying, My name *is* Legion: for we are many.

10 And he besought him much that he would not send them away out of the country.

11 Now there was there nigh unto the mountains a great herd of swine feeding.

12 And all the devils besought him, saying, Send us into the swine, that we may enter into them.

13 And forthwith Jesus gave them leave. And the unclean spirits went out, and entered into the swine: and the herd ran violently down a steep place into the sea, (they were about two thousand;) and were choked in the sea.

14 And they that fed the swine fled, and told *it* in the city, and in the country. And they went out to see what it was that was done.

15 And they come to Jesus, and see him that was possessed with the devil, and had the legion, sitting, and clothed, and in his right mind: and they were afraid.

16 And they that saw *it* told them how it befell to him that was possessed with the devil, and *also* concerning the swine.

17 And they began to pray him to depart out of their coasts.

18 And when he was come into the ship, he that had been possessed with the devil prayed him that he might be with him.

19 Howbeit Jesus suffered him not, but saith unto him, Go home to thy friends, and tell them how great things the Lord hath done for thee, and hath had compassion on thee.

20 And he departed, and began to publish in Decapolis how great things

Jesus had done for him: and all *men*
did marvel.
21 And when Jesus was passed over
again by ship unto the other side, much
people gathered unto him: and he was
nigh unto the sea.
22 And, behold, there cometh one of
the rulers of the synagogue, Jairus by
name; and when he saw him, he fell at
his feet,
23 And besought him greatly, saying,
My little daughter lieth at the point of
death: *I pray thee*, come and lay thy
hands on her, that she may be healed;
and she shall live.
24 And *Jesus* went with him; and
much people followed him, and
thronged him.
25 And a certain woman, which had
an issue of blood twelve years,
26 And had suffered many things of
many physicians, and had spent all that
she had, and was nothing bettered, but
rather grew worse,
27 When she had heard of Jesus,
came in the press behind, and touched
his garment.
28 For she said, If I may touch but his
clothes, I shall be whole.
29 And straightway the fountain of
her blood was dried up; and she felt in
her body that she was healed of that
plague.
30 And Jesus, immediately knowing
in himself that virtue had gone out of
him, turned him about in the press, and
said, Who touched my clothes?
31 And his disciples said unto him,
Thou seest the multitude thronging
thee, and sayest thou, Who touched
me?
32 And he looked round about to see
her that had done this thing.
33 But the woman fearing and trembling,
knowing what was done in her,
came and fell down before him, and
told him all the truth.
34 And he said unto her, Daughter,
thy faith hath made thee whole; go in
peace, and be whole of thy plague.
35 While he yet spake, there came
from the ruler of the synagogue's *house*
certain which said, Thy daughter is
dead: why troublest thou the Master
any further?
36 As soon as Jesus heard the word
that was spoken, he saith unto the ruler
of the synagogue, Be not afraid, only
believe.
37 And he suffered no man to follow
him, save Peter, and James, and John
the brother of James.
38 And he cometh to the house of the
ruler of the synagogue, and seeth the
tumult, and them that wept and wailed
greatly.
39 And when he was come in, he saith
unto them, Why make ye this ado, and
weep? the damsel is not dead, but
sleepeth.
40 And they laughed him to scorn.
But when he had put them all out, he
taketh the father and the mother of the
damsel, and them that were with him,
and entereth in where the damsel was
lying.
41 And he took the damsel by the
hand, and said unto her, Talitha cumi;
which is, being interpreted, Damsel, I
say unto thee, arise.

42 And straightway the damsel arose, and walked; for she was *of the age* of twelve years. And they were astonished with a great astonishment.
43 And he charged them straitly that no man should know it; and commanded that something should be given her to eat.

6 And he went out from thence, and came into his own country; and his disciples follow him.
2 And when the sabbath day was come, he began to teach in the synagogue: and many hearing *him* were astonished, saying, From whence hath this *man* these things? and what wisdom *is* this which is given unto him, that even such mighty works are wrought by his hands?
3 Is not this the carpenter, the son of Mary, the brother of James, and Joses, and of Juda, and Simon? and are not his sisters here with us? And they were offended at him.
4 But Jesus said unto them, A prophet is not without honour, but in his own country, and among his own kin, and in his own house.
5 And he could there do no mighty work, save that he laid his hands upon a few sick folk, and healed *them*.
6 And he marvelled because of their unbelief. And he went round about the villages, teaching.
7 And he called *unto him* the twelve, and began to send them forth by two and two; and gave them power over unclean spirits;
8 And commanded them that they should take nothing for *their* journey, save a staff only; no scrip, no bread, no money in *their* purse:
9 But *be* shod with sandals; and not put on two coats.
10 And he said unto them, In what place soever ye enter into an house, there abide till ye depart from that place.
11 And whosoever shall not receive you, nor hear you, when ye depart thence, shake off the dust under your feet for a testimony against them. Verily I say unto you, It shall be more tolerable for Sodom and Gomorrha in the day of judgment, than for that city.
12 And they went out, and preached that men should repent.
13 And they cast out many devils, and anointed with oil many that were sick, and healed *them*.
14 And king Herod heard *of him*; (for his name was spread abroad:) and he said, That John the Baptist was risen from the dead, and therefore mighty works do shew forth themselves in him.
15 Others said, That it is Elias. And others said, That it is a prophet, or as one of the prophets.
16 But when Herod heard *thereof*, he said, It is John, whom I beheaded: he is risen from the dead.
17 For Herod himself had sent forth and laid hold upon John, and bound him in prison for Herodias' sake, his brother Philip's wife: for he had married her.
18 For John had said unto Herod, It is not lawful for thee to have thy brother's wife.
19 Therefore Herodias had a quarrel against him, and would have killed him; but she could not:
20 For Herod feared John, knowing that he was a just man and an holy, and observed him; and when he heard him, he did many things, and heard him gladly.

21 And when a convenient day was
come, that Herod on his birthday made
a supper to his lords, high captains, and
chief *estates* of Galilee;
22 And when the daughter of the said
Herodias came in, and danced, and
pleased Herod and them that sat with
him, the king said unto the damsel, Ask
of me whatsoever thou wilt, and I will
give *it* thee.
23 And he sware unto her, Whatsoever
thou shalt ask of me, I will give *it* thee,
unto the half of my kingdom.
24 And she went forth, and said unto
her mother, What shall I ask? And she
said, The head of John the Baptist.
25 And she came in straightway with
haste unto the king, and asked, saying,
I will that thou give me by and by in a
charger the head of John the Baptist.
26 And the king was exceeding sorry;
yet for his oath's sake, and for their
sakes which sat with him, he would not
reject her.
27 And immediately the king sent an
executioner, and commanded his head
to be brought: and he went and beheaded him in the prison,
28 And brought his head in a charger,
and gave it to the damsel: and the damsel gave it to her mother.
29 And when his disciples heard *of it*,
they came and took up his corpse, and
laid it in a tomb.
30 And the apostles gathered themselves together unto Jesus, and told
him all things, both what they had
done, and what they had taught.
31 And he said unto them, Come ye
yourselves apart into a desert place,
and rest a while: for there were many
coming and going, and they had no lei-
sure so much as to eat.
32 And they departed into a desert
place by ship privately.
33 And the people saw them departing, and many knew him, and ran afoot
thither out of all cities, and outwent
them, and came together unto him.
34 And Jesus, when he came out, saw
much people, and was moved with compassion toward them, because they
were as sheep not having a shepherd:
and he began to teach them many
things.
35 And when the day was now far
spent, his disciples came unto him, and
said, This is a desert place, and now the
time *is* far passed:
36 Send them away, that they may go
into the country round about, and into
the villages, and buy themselves bread:
for they have nothing to eat.
37 He answered and said unto them,
Give ye them to eat. And they say unto
him, Shall we go and buy two hundred
pennyworth of bread, and give them to
eat?
38 He saith unto them, How many
loaves have ye? go and see. And when
they knew, they say, Five, and two fishes.
39 And he commanded them to make
all sit down by companies upon the
green grass.
40 And they sat down in ranks, by
hundreds, and by fifties.
41 And when he had taken the five
loaves and the two fishes, he looked up
to heaven, and blessed, and brake the
loaves, and gave *them* to his disciples
to set before them; and the two fishes
divided he among them all.
42 And they did all eat, and were
filled.
43 And they took up twelve baskets
full of the fragments, and of the fishes.

44 And they that did eat of the loaves
were about five thousand men.
45 And straightway he constrained
his disciples to get into the ship, and to
go to the other side before unto
Bethsaida, while he sent away the people.
46 And when he had sent them away,
he departed into a mountain to pray.
47 And when even was come, the ship
was in the midst of the sea, and he
alone on the land.
48 And he saw them toiling in rowing;
for the wind was contrary unto them:
and about the fourth watch of the night
he cometh unto them, walking upon
the sea, and would have passed by
them.
49 But when they saw him walking
upon the sea, they supposed it had
been a spirit, and cried out:
50 For they all saw him, and were
troubled. And immediately he talked
with them, and saith unto them, Be of
good cheer: it is I; be not afraid.
51 And he went up unto them into the
ship; and the wind ceased: and they
were sore amazed in themselves beyond measure, and wondered.
52 For they considered not *the mira-*
cle of the loaves: for their heart was
hardened.
53 And when they had passed over,
they came into the land of Gennesaret,
and drew to the shore.
54 And when they were come out of
the ship, straightway they knew him,
55 And ran through that whole region
round about, and began to carry about
in beds those that were sick, where
they heard he was.
56 And whithersoever he entered,
into villages, or cities, or country, they
laid the sick in the streets, and besought
him that they might touch if it were but
the border of his garment: and as many
as touched him were made whole.

7 Then came together unto him the
Pharisees, and certain of the
scribes, which came from Jerusalem.
2 And when they saw some of his disciples eat bread with defiled, that is to
say, with unwashen, hands, they found
fault.
3 For the Pharisees, and all the Jews,
except they wash *their* hands oft, eat
not, holding the tradition of the elders.
4 And *when they come* from the market, except they wash, they eat not. And
many other things there be, which they
have received to hold, *as* the washing of
cups, and pots, brasen vessels, and of
tables.
5 Then the Pharisees and scribes
asked him, Why walk not thy disciples
according to the tradition of the elders,
but eat bread with unwashen hands?
6 He answered and said unto them,
Well hath Esaias prophesied of you
hypocrites, as it is written, This people
honoureth me with *their* lips, but their
heart is far from me.
7 Howbeit in vain do they worship
me, teaching *for* doctrines the commandments of men.
8 For laying aside the commandment
of God, ye hold the tradition of men, *as*
the washing of pots and cups: and many
other such like things ye do.
9 And he said unto them, Full well ye
reject the commandment of God, that
ye may keep your own tradition.
10 For Moses said, Honour thy father
and thy mother; and, Whoso curseth
father or mother, let him die the death:

11 But ye say, If a man shall say to his father or mother, *It is* Corban, that is to say, a gift, by whatsoever thou mightest be profited by me; *he shall be free.*

12 And ye suffer him no more to do ought for his father or his mother;

13 Making the word of God of none effect through your tradition, which ye have delivered: and many such like things do ye.

14 And when he had called all the people *unto him*, he said unto them, Hearken unto me every one *of you*, and understand:

15 There is nothing from without a man, that entering into him can defile him: but the things which come out of him, those are they that defile the man.

16 If any man have ears to hear, let him hear.

17 And when he was entered into the house from the people, his disciples asked him concerning the parable.

18 And he saith unto them, Are ye so without understanding also? Do ye not perceive, that whatsoever thing from without entereth into the man, *it* cannot defile him;

19 Because it entereth not into his heart, but into the belly, and goeth out into the draught, purging all meats?

20 And he said, That which cometh out of the man, that defileth the man.

21 For from within, out of the heart of men, proceed evil thoughts, adulteries, fornications, murders,

22 Thefts, covetousness, wickedness, deceit, lasciviousness, an evil eye, blasphemy, pride, foolishness:

23 All these evil things come from within, and defile the man.

24 And from thence he arose, and went into the borders of Tyre and Sidon, and entered into an house, and would have no man know *it*: but he could not be hid.

25 For a *certain* woman, whose young daughter had an unclean spirit, heard of him, and came and fell at his feet:

26 The woman was a Greek, a Syrophenician by nation; and she besought him that he would cast forth the devil out of her daughter.

27 But Jesus said unto her, Let the children first be filled: for it is not meet to take the children's bread, and to cast *it* unto the dogs.

28 And she answered and said unto him, Yes, Lord: yet the dogs under the table eat of the children's crumbs.

29 And he said unto her, For this saying go thy way; the devil is gone out of thy daughter.

30 And when she was come to her house, she found the devil gone out, and her daughter laid upon the bed.

31 And again, departing from the coasts of Tyre and Sidon, he came unto the sea of Galilee, through the midst of the coasts of Decapolis.

32 And they bring unto him one that was deaf, and had an impediment in his speech; and they beseech him to put his hand upon him.

33 And he took him aside from the multitude, and put his fingers into his ears, and he spit, and touched his tongue;

34 And looking up to heaven, he sighed, and saith unto him, Ephphatha, that is, Be opened.

35 And straightway his ears were opened, and the string of his tongue was loosed, and he spake plain.

36 And he charged them that they should tell no man: but the more he charged them, so much the more a great deal they published *it*;

37 And were beyond measure astonished, saying, He hath done all things well: he maketh both the deaf to hear, and the dumb to speak.

8 In those days the multitude being very great, and having nothing to eat, Jesus called his disciples *unto him*, and saith unto them,

2 I have compassion on the multitude, because they have now been with me three days, and have nothing to eat:

3 And if I send them away fasting to their own houses, they will faint by the way: for divers of them came from far.

4 And his disciples answered him, From whence can a man satisfy these *men* with bread here in the wilderness?

5 And he asked them, How many loaves have ye? And they said, Seven.

6 And he commanded the people to sit down on the ground: and he took the seven loaves, and gave thanks, and brake, and gave to his disciples to set before *them*; and they did set *them* before the people.

7 And they had a few small fishes: and he blessed, and commanded to set them also before *them*.

8 So they did eat, and were filled: and they took up of the broken *meat* that was left seven baskets.

9 And they that had eaten were about four thousand: and he sent them away.

10 And straightway he entered into a ship with his disciples, and came into the parts of Dalmanutha.

11 And the Pharisees came forth, and began to question with him, seeking of him a sign from heaven, tempting him.

12 And he sighed deeply in his spirit, and saith, Why doth this generation seek after a sign? verily I say unto you, There shall no sign be given unto this generation.

13 And he left them, and entering into the ship again departed to the other side.

14 Now *the disciples* had forgotten to take bread, neither had they in the ship with them more than one loaf.

15 And he charged them, saying, Take heed, beware of the leaven of the Pharisees, and *of* the leaven of Herod.

16 And they reasoned among themselves, saying, *It is* because we have no bread.

17 And when Jesus knew *it*, he saith unto them, Why reason ye, because ye have no bread? perceive ye not yet, neither understand? have ye your heart yet hardened?

18 Having eyes, see ye not? and having ears, hear ye not? and do ye not remember?

19 When I brake the five loaves among five thousand, how many baskets full of fragments took ye up? They say unto him, Twelve.

20 And when the seven among four thousand, how many baskets full of fragments took ye up? And they said, Seven.

21 And he said unto them, How is it that ye do not understand?

22 And he cometh to Bethsaida; and they bring a blind man unto him, and besought him to touch him.

23 And he took the blind man by the hand, and led him out of the town; and when he had spit on his eyes, and put his hands upon him, he asked him if he saw ought.

24 And he looked up, and said, I see men as trees, walking.

25 After that he put *his* hands again upon his eyes, and made him look up: and he was restored, and saw every man clearly.

26 And he sent him away to his house, saying, Neither go into the town, nor tell *it* to any in the town.

27 And Jesus went out, and his disciples, into the towns of Caesarea Philippi: and by the way he asked his disciples, saying unto them, Whom do men say that I am?

28 And they answered, John the Baptist: but some *say*, Elias; and others, One of the prophets.

29 And he saith unto them, But whom say ye that I am? And Peter answereth and saith unto him, Thou art the Christ.

30 And he charged them that they should tell no man of him.

31 And he began to teach them, that the Son of man must suffer many things, and be rejected of the elders, and *of* the chief priests, and scribes, and be killed, and after three days rise again.

32 And he spake that saying openly. And Peter took him, and began to rebuke him.

33 But when he had turned about and looked on his disciples, he rebuked Peter, saying, Get thee behind me, Satan: for thou savourest not the things that be of God, but the things that be of men.

34 And when he had called the people *unto him* with his disciples also, he said unto them, Whosoever will come after me, let him deny himself, and take up his cross, and follow me.

35 For whosoever will save his life shall lose it; but whosoever shall lose his life for my sake and the gospel's, the same shall save it.

36 For what shall it profit a man, if he shall gain the whole world, and lose his own soul?

37 Or what shall a man give in exchange for his soul?

38 Whosoever therefore shall be ashamed of me and of my words in this adulterous and sinful generation; of him also shall the Son of man be ashamed, when he cometh in the glory of his Father with the holy angels.

9 And he said unto them, Verily I say unto you, That there be some of them that stand here, which shall not taste of death, till they have seen the kingdom of God come with power.

2 And after six days Jesus taketh *with him* Peter, and James, and John, and leadeth them up into an high mountain apart by themselves: and he was transfigured before them.

3 And his raiment became shining, exceeding white as snow; so as no fuller on earth can white them.

4 And there appeared unto them Elias with Moses: and they were talking with Jesus.

5 And Peter answered and said to Jesus, Master, it is good for us to be here: and let us make three tabernacles; one for thee, and one for Moses, and one for Elias.

6 For he wist not what to say; for they were sore afraid.

7 And there was a cloud that overshadowed them: and a voice came out of the cloud, saying, This is my beloved Son: hear him.

8 And suddenly, when they had looked round about, they saw no man any more, save Jesus only with themselves.

9 And as they came down from the mountain, he charged them that they should tell no man what things they had seen, till the Son of man were risen from the dead.

10 And they kept that saying with themselves, questioning one with another what the rising from the dead should mean.

11 And they asked him, saying, Why say the scribes that Elias must first come?

12 And he answered and told them, Elias verily cometh first, and restoreth all things; and how it is written of the Son of man, that he must suffer many things, and be set at nought.

13 But I say unto you, That Elias is indeed come, and they have done unto him whatsoever they listed, as it is written of him.

14 And when he came to *his* disciples, he saw a great multitude about them, and the scribes questioning with them.

15 And straightway all the people, when they beheld him, were greatly amazed, and running to *him* saluted him.

16 And he asked the scribes, What question ye with them?

17 And one of the multitude answered and said, Master, I have brought unto thee my son, which hath a dumb spirit;

18 And wheresoever he taketh him, he teareth him: and he foameth, and gnasheth with his teeth, and pineth away: and I spake to thy disciples that they should cast him out; and they could not.

19 He answereth him, and saith, O faithless generation, how long shall I be with you? how long shall I suffer you? bring him unto me.

20 And they brought him unto him: and when he saw him, straightway the spirit tare him; and he fell on the ground, and wallowed foaming.

21 And he asked his father, How long is it ago since this came unto him? And he said, Of a child.

22 And ofttimes it hath cast him into the fire, and into the waters, to destroy him: but if thou canst do any thing, have compassion on us, and help us.

23 Jesus said unto him, If thou canst believe, all things *are* possible to him that believeth.

24 And straightway the father of the child cried out, and said with tears, Lord, I believe; help thou mine unbelief.

25 When Jesus saw that the people came running together, he rebuked the foul spirit, saying unto him, *Thou* dumb and deaf spirit, I charge thee, come out of him, and enter no more into him.

26 And *the spirit* cried, and rent him sore, and came out of him: and he was as one dead; insomuch that many said, He is dead.

27 But Jesus took him by the hand, and lifted him up; and he arose.

28 And when he was come into the house, his disciples asked him privately, Why could not we cast him out?

29 And he said unto them, This kind can come forth by nothing, but by prayer and fasting.

30 And they departed thence, and passed through Galilee; and he would not that any man should know *it*.

31 For he taught his disciples, and said unto them, The Son of man is delivered into the hands of men, and they shall kill him; and after that he is killed, he shall rise the third day.

32 But they understood not that saying, and were afraid to ask him.

33 And he came to Capernaum: and being in the house he asked them,

What was it that ye disputed among
yourselves by the way?
34 But they held their peace: for by
the way they had disputed among
themselves, who *should be* the greatest.
35 And he sat down, and called the
twelve, and saith unto them, If any man
desire to be first, *the same* shall be last
of all, and servant of all.
36 And he took a child, and set him in
the midst of them: and when he had
taken him in his arms, he said unto
them,
37 Whosoever shall receive one of
such children in my name, receiveth
me: and whosoever shall receive me,
receiveth not me, but him that sent me.
38 And John answered him, saying,
Master, we saw one casting out devils in
thy name, and he followeth not us: and
we forbad him, because he followeth
not us.
39 But Jesus said, Forbid him not: for
there is no man which shall do a miracle in my name, that can lightly speak
evil of me.
40 For he that is not against us is on
our part.
41 For whosoever shall give you a cup
of water to drink in my name, because
ye belong to Christ, verily I say unto
you, he shall not lose his reward.
42 And whosoever shall offend one of
these little ones that believe in me, it is
better for him that a millstone were
hanged about his neck, and he were
cast into the sea.
43 And if thy hand offend thee, cut it
off: it is better for thee to enter into life
maimed, than having two hands to go
into hell, into the fire that never shall
be quenched:
44 Where their worm dieth not, and
the fire is not quenched.
45 And if thy foot offend thee, cut it
off: it is better for thee to enter halt
into life, than having two feet to be cast
into hell, into the fire that never shall
be quenched:
46 Where their worm dieth not, and
the fire is not quenched.
47 And if thine eye offend thee, pluck
it out: it is better for thee to enter into
the kingdom of God with one eye, than
having two eyes to be cast into hell fire:
48 Where their worm dieth not, and
the fire is not quenched.
49 For every one shall be salted with
fire, and every sacrifice shall be salted
with salt.
50 Salt *is* good: but if the salt have
lost his saltness, wherewith will ye season it? Have salt in yourselves, and
have peace one with another.

10 And he arose from thence, and
cometh into the coasts of Judaea
by the farther side of Jordan: and the
people resort unto him again; and, as
he was wont, he taught them again.
2 And the Pharisees came to him, and
asked him, Is it lawful for a man to put
away *his* wife? tempting him.
3 And he answered and said unto
them, What did Moses command you?
4 And they said, Moses suffered to
write a bill of divorcement, and to put
her away.
5 And Jesus answered and said unto
them, For the hardness of your heart he
wrote you this precept.
6 But from the beginning of the creation God made them male and female.
7 For this cause shall a man leave his
father and mother, and cleave to his
wife;
8 And they twain shall be one flesh:
so then they are no more twain, but one
flesh.

9 What therefore God hath joined together, let not man put asunder.

10 And in the house his disciples asked him again of the same *matter*.

11 And he saith unto them, Whosoever shall put away his wife, and marry another, committeth adultery against her.

12 And if a woman shall put away her husband, and be married to another, she committeth adultery.

13 And they brought young children to him, that he should touch them: and *his* disciples rebuked those that brought *them*.

14 But when Jesus saw *it*, he was much displeased, and said unto them, Suffer the little children to come unto me, and forbid them not: for of such is the kingdom of God.

15 Verily I say unto you, Whosoever shall not receive the kingdom of God as a little child, he shall not enter therein.

16 And he took them up in his arms, put *his* hands upon them, and blessed them.

17 And when he was gone forth into the way, there came one running, and kneeled to him, and asked him, Good Master, what shall I do that I may inherit eternal life?

18 And Jesus said unto him, Why callest thou me good? *there is* none good but one, *that is*, God.

19 Thou knowest the commandments, Do not commit adultery, Do not kill, Do not steal, Do not bear false witness, Defraud not, Honour thy father and mother.

20 And he answered and said unto him, Master, all these have I observed from my youth.

21 Then Jesus beholding him loved him, and said unto him, One thing thou lackest: go thy way, sell whatsoever thou hast, and give to the poor, and thou shalt have treasure in heaven: and come, take up the cross, and follow me.

22 And he was sad at that saying, and went away grieved: for he had great possessions.

23 And Jesus looked round about, and saith unto his disciples, How hardly shall they that have riches enter into the kingdom of God!

24 And the disciples were astonished at his words. But Jesus answereth again, and saith unto them, Children, how hard is it for them that trust in riches to enter into the kingdom of God!

25 It is easier for a camel to go through the eye of a needle, than for a rich man to enter into the kingdom of God.

26 And they were astonished out of measure, saying among themselves, Who then can be saved?

27 And Jesus looking upon them saith, With men *it is* impossible, but not with God: for with God all things are possible.

28 Then Peter began to say unto him, Lo, we have left all, and have followed thee.

29 And Jesus answered and said, Verily I say unto you, There is no man that hath left house, or brethren, or sisters, or father, or mother, or wife, or children, or lands, for my sake, and the gospel's,

30 But he shall receive an hundredfold now in this time, houses, and brethren, and sisters, and mothers, and children, and lands, with persecutions; and in the world to come eternal life.

31 But many *that are* first shall be
last; and the last first.
32 And they were in the way going up
to Jerusalem; and Jesus went before
them: and they were amazed; and as
they followed, they were afraid. And he
took again the twelve, and began to tell
them what things should happen unto
him,
33 *Saying*, Behold, we go up to
Jerusalem; and the Son of man shall be
delivered unto the chief priests, and
unto the scribes; and they shall condemn him to death, and shall deliver
him to the Gentiles:
34 And they shall mock him, and shall
scourge him, and shall spit upon him,
and shall kill him: and the third day he
shall rise again.
35 And James and John, the sons of
Zebedee, come unto him, saying,
Master, we would that thou shouldest
do for us whatsoever we shall desire.
36 And he said unto them, What
would ye that I should do for you?
37 They said unto him, Grant unto us
that we may sit, one on thy right hand,
and the other on thy left hand, in thy
glory.
38 But Jesus said unto them, Ye know
not what ye ask: can ye drink of the cup
that I drink of? and be baptized with
the baptism that I am baptized with?
39 And they said unto him, We can.
And Jesus said unto them, Ye shall
indeed drink of the cup that I drink of;
and with the baptism that I am baptized withal shall ye be baptized:
40 But to sit on my right hand and on
my left hand is not mine to give; but *it
shall be given to them* for whom it is
prepared.
41 And when the ten heard *it*, they
began to be much displeased with
James and John.
42 But Jesus called them *to him*, and
saith unto them, Ye know that they
which are accounted to rule over the
Gentiles exercise lordship over them;
and their great ones exercise authority
upon them.
43 But so shall it not be among you:
but whosoever will be great among you,
shall be your minister:
44 And whosoever of you will be the
chiefest, shall be servant of all.
45 For even the Son of man came not
to be ministered unto, but to minister,
and to give his life a ransom for many.
46 And they came to Jericho: and as
he went out of Jericho with his disciples and a great number of people,
blind Bartimaeus, the son of Timaeus,
sat by the highway side begging.
47 And when he heard that it was
Jesus of Nazareth, he began to cry out,
and say, Jesus, *thou* Son of David, have
mercy on me.
48 And many charged him that he
should hold his peace: but he cried the
more a great deal, *Thou* Son of David,
have mercy on me.
49 And Jesus stood still, and commanded him to be called. And they call
the blind man, saying unto him, Be of
good comfort, rise; he calleth thee.
50 And he, casting away his garment,
rose, and came to Jesus.
51 And Jesus answered and said unto
him, What wilt thou that I should do
unto thee? The blind man said unto
him, Lord, that I might receive my
sight.

52 And Jesus said unto him, Go thy
way; thy faith hath made thee whole.
And immediately he received his sight,
and followed Jesus in the way.

11 And when they came nigh to
Jerusalem, unto Bethphage and
Bethany, at the mount of Olives, he
sendeth forth two of his disciples,
2 And saith unto them, Go your way
into the village over against you: and as
soon as ye be entered into it, ye shall
find a colt tied, whereon never man sat;
loose him, and bring *him*.
3 And if any man say unto you, Why
do ye this? say ye that the Lord hath
need of him; and straightway he will
send him hither.
4 And they went their way, and found
the colt tied by the door without in a
place where two ways met; and they
loose him.
5 And certain of them that stood
there said unto them, What do ye, loosing the colt?
6 And they said unto them even as
Jesus had commanded: and they let
them go.
7 And they brought the colt to Jesus,
and cast their garments on him; and he
sat upon him.
8 And many spread their garments in
the way: and others cut down branches
off the trees, and strawed *them* in the
way.
9 And they that went before, and they
that followed, cried, saying, Hosanna;
Blessed *is* he that cometh in the name
of the Lord:
10 Blessed *be* the kingdom of our
father David, that cometh in the name
of the Lord: Hosanna in the highest.
11 And Jesus entered into Jerusalem,
and into the temple: and when he had
looked round about upon all things,
and now the eventide was come, he
went out unto Bethany with the twelve.
12 And on the morrow, when they
were come from Bethany, he was hungry:
13 And seeing a fig tree afar off having leaves, he came, if haply he might
find any thing thereon: and when he
came to it, he found nothing but leaves;
for the time of figs was not *yet*.
14 And Jesus answered and said unto
it, No man eat fruit of thee hereafter
for ever. And his disciples heard *it*.
15 And they come to Jerusalem: and
Jesus went into the temple, and began
to cast out them that sold and bought in
the temple, and overthrew the tables of
the moneychangers, and the seats of
them that sold doves;
16 And would not suffer that any man
should carry *any* vessel through the
temple.
17 And he taught, saying unto them,
Is it not written, My house shall be
called of all nations the house of
prayer? but ye have made it a den of
thieves.
18 And the scribes and chief priests
heard *it*, and sought how they might
destroy him: for they feared him,
because all the people was astonished
at his doctrine.
19 And when even was come, he went
out of the city.
20 And in the morning, as they passed
by, they saw the fig tree dried up from
the roots.
21 And Peter calling to remembrance
saith unto him, Master, behold, the fig
tree which thou cursedst is withered
away.
22 And Jesus answering saith unto
them, Have faith in God.

23 For verily I say unto you, That whosoever shall say unto this mountain, Be thou removed, and be thou cast into the sea; and shall not doubt in his heart, but shall believe that those things which he saith shall come to pass; he shall have whatsoever he saith.

24 Therefore I say unto you, What things soever ye desire, when ye pray, believe that ye receive *them*, and ye shall have *them*.

25 And when ye stand praying, forgive, if ye have ought against any: that your Father also which is in heaven may forgive you your trespasses.

26 But if ye do not forgive, neither will your Father which is in heaven forgive your trespasses.

27 And they come again to Jerusalem: and as he was walking in the temple, there come to him the chief priests, and the scribes, and the elders,

28 And say unto him, By what authority doest thou these things? and who gave thee this authority to do these things?

29 And Jesus answered and said unto them, I will also ask of you one question, and answer me, and I will tell you by what authority I do these things.

30 The baptism of John, was *it* from heaven, or of men? answer me.

31 And they reasoned with themselves, saying, If we shall say, From heaven; he will say, Why then did ye not believe him?

32 But if we shall say, Of men; they feared the people: for all *men* counted John, that he was a prophet indeed.

33 And they answered and said unto Jesus, We cannot tell. And Jesus answering saith unto them, Neither do I tell you by what authority I do these things.

12 And he began to speak unto them by parables. A *certain* man planted a vineyard, and set an hedge about *it*, and digged *a place for* the winefat, and built a tower, and let it out to husbandmen, and went into a far country.

2 And at the season he sent to the husbandmen a servant, that he might receive from the husbandmen of the fruit of the vineyard.

3 And they caught *him*, and beat him, and sent *him* away empty.

4 And again he sent unto them another servant; and at him they cast stones, and wounded *him* in the head, and sent *him* away shamefully handled.

5 And again he sent another; and him they killed, and many others; beating some, and killing some.

6 Having yet therefore one son, his wellbeloved, he sent him also last unto them, saying, They will reverence my son.

7 But those husbandmen said among themselves, This is the heir; come, let us kill him, and the inheritance shall be ours.

8 And they took him, and killed *him*, and cast *him* out of the vineyard.

9 What shall therefore the lord of the vineyard do? he will come and destroy the husbandmen, and will give the vineyard unto others.

10 And have ye not read this scripture; The stone which the builders rejected is become the head of the corner:

11 This was the Lord's doing, and it is marvellous in our eyes?

12 And they sought to lay hold on him, but feared the people: for they knew that he had spoken the parable

against them: and they left him, and
went their way.
13 And they send unto him certain of
the Pharisees and of the Herodians, to
catch him in *his* words.
14 And when they were come, they
say unto him, Master, we know that
thou art true, and carest for no man: for
thou regardest not the person of men,
but teachest the way of God in truth: Is
it lawful to give tribute to Caesar, or
not?
15 Shall we give, or shall we not give?
But he, knowing their hypocrisy, said
unto them, Why tempt ye me? bring me
a penny, that I may see *it*.
16 And they brought *it*. And he saith
unto them, Whose *is* this image and
superscription? And they said unto
him, Caesar's.
17 And Jesus answering said unto
them, Render to Caesar the things that
are Caesar's, and to God the things that
are God's. And they marvelled at him.
18 Then come unto him the Sadducees, which say there is no resurrection;
and they asked him, saying,
19 Master, Moses wrote unto us, If a
man's brother die, and leave *his* wife
behind him, and leave no children, that
his brother should take his wife, and
raise up seed unto his brother.
20 Now there were seven brethren:
and the first took a wife, and dying left
no seed.
21 And the second took her, and died,
neither left he any seed: and the third
likewise.
22 And the seven had her, and left no
seed: last of all the woman died also.
23 In the resurrection therefore,
when they shall rise, whose wife shall
she be of them? for the seven had her
to wife.
24 And Jesus answering said unto
them, Do ye not therefore err, because
ye know not the scriptures, neither the
power of God?
25 For when they shall rise from the
dead, they neither marry, nor are given
in marriage; but are as the angels
which are in heaven.
26 And as touching the dead, that
they rise: have ye not read in the book
of Moses, how in the bush God spake
unto him, saying, I *am* the God of
Abraham, and the God of Isaac, and the
God of Jacob?
27 He is not the God of the dead, but
the God of the living: ye therefore do
greatly err.
28 And one of the scribes came, and
having heard them reasoning together,
and perceiving that he had answered
them well, asked him, Which is the first
commandment of all?
29 And Jesus answered him, The first
of all the commandments *is*, Hear, O
Israel; The Lord our God is one Lord:
30 And thou shalt love the Lord thy
God with all thy heart, and with all thy
soul, and with all thy mind, and with all
thy strength: this *is* the first commandment.
31 And the second *is* like, *namely*
this, Thou shalt love thy neighbour as
thyself. There is none other commandment greater than these.
32 And the scribe said unto him, Well,
Master, thou hast said the truth: for
there is one God; and there is none
other but he:
33 And to love him with all the heart,
and with all the understanding, and
with all the soul, and with all the
strength, and to love *his* neighbour as
himself, is more than all whole burnt
offerings and sacrifices.

34 And when Jesus saw that he answered discreetly, he said unto him, Thou art not far from the kingdom of God. And no man after that durst ask him *any question*.

35 And Jesus answered and said, while he taught in the temple, How say the scribes that Christ is the Son of David?

36 For David himself said by the Holy Ghost, The LORD said to my Lord, Sit thou on my right hand, till I make thine enemies thy footstool.

37 David therefore himself calleth him Lord; and whence is he *then* his son? And the common people heard him gladly.

38 And he said unto them in his doctrine, Beware of the scribes, which love to go in long clothing, and *love* salutations in the marketplaces,

39 And the chief seats in the synagogues, and the uppermost rooms at feasts:

40 Which devour widows' houses, and for a pretence make long prayers: these shall receive greater damnation.

41 And Jesus sat over against the treasury, and beheld how the people cast money into the treasury: and many that were rich cast in much.

42 And there came a certain poor widow, and she threw in two mites, which make a farthing.

43 And he called *unto him* his disciples, and saith unto them, Verily I say unto you, That this poor widow hath cast more in, than all they which have cast into the treasury:

44 For all *they* did cast in of their abundance; but she of her want did cast in all that she had, *even* all her living.

13 And as he went out of the temple, one of his disciples saith unto him, Master, see what manner of stones and what buildings *are here*!

2 And Jesus answering said unto him, Seest thou these great buildings? there shall not be left one stone upon another, that shall not be thrown down.

3 And as he sat upon the mount of Olives over against the temple, Peter and James and John and Andrew asked him privately,

4 Tell us, when shall these things be? and what *shall be* the sign when all these things shall be fulfilled?

5 And Jesus answering them began to say, Take heed lest any *man* deceive you:

6 For many shall come in my name, saying, I am *Christ*; and shall deceive many.

7 And when ye shall hear of wars and rumours of wars, be ye not troubled: for *such things* must needs be; but the end *shall* not *be* yet.

8 For nation shall rise against nation, and kingdom against kingdom: and there shall be earthquakes in divers places, and there shall be famines and troubles: these *are* the beginnings of sorrows.

9 But take heed to yourselves: for they shall deliver you up to councils; and in the synagogues ye shall be beaten: and ye shall be brought before rulers and kings for my sake, for a testimony against them.

10 And the gospel must first be published among all nations.

11 But when they shall lead *you*, and deliver you up, take no thought beforehand what ye shall speak, neither do ye premeditate: but whatsoever shall be given you in that hour, that speak ye:

for it is not ye that speak, but the Holy
Ghost.
12 Now the brother shall betray the
brother to death, and the father the
son; and children shall rise up against
their parents, and shall cause them to
be put to death.
13 And ye shall be hated of all *men*
for my name's sake: but he that shall
endure unto the end, the same shall be
saved.
14 But when ye shall see the abomination of desolation, spoken of by Daniel
the prophet, standing where it ought
not, (let him that readeth understand,)
then let them that be in Judaea flee to
the mountains:
15 And let him that is on the housetop not go down into the house, neither
enter *therein*, to take any thing out of
his house:
16 And let him that is in the field not
turn back again for to take up his garment.
17 But woe to them that are with
child, and to them that give suck in
those days!
18 And pray ye that your flight be not
in the winter.
19 For *in* those days shall be affliction, such as was not from the beginning of the creation which God created
unto this time, neither shall be.
20 And except that the Lord had
shortened those days, no flesh should
be saved: but for the elect's sake, whom
he hath chosen, he hath shortened the
days.
21 And then if any man shall say to
you, Lo, here *is* Christ; or, lo, *he is* there;
believe *him* not:
22 For false Christs and false prophets shall rise, and shall shew signs and
wonders, to seduce, if *it were* possible,
even the elect.
23 But take ye heed: behold, I have
foretold you all things.
24 But in those days, after that tribulation, the sun shall be darkened, and
the moon shall not give her light,
25 And the stars of heaven shall fall,
and the powers that are in heaven shall
be shaken.
26 And then shall they see the Son of
man coming in the clouds with great
power and glory.
27 And then shall he send his angels,
and shall gather together his elect from
the four winds, from the uttermost part
of the earth to the uttermost part of
heaven.
28 Now learn a parable of the fig tree;
When her branch is yet tender, and
putteth forth leaves, ye know that summer is near:
29 So ye in like manner, when ye shall
see these things come to pass, know
that it is nigh, *even* at the doors.
30 Verily I say unto you, that this generation shall not pass, till all these
things be done.
31 Heaven and earth shall pass away:
but my words shall not pass away.
32 But of that day and *that* hour
knoweth no man, no, not the angels
which are in heaven, neither the Son,
but the Father.
33 Take ye heed, watch and pray: for
ye know not when the time is.
34 *For the Son of man is* as a man
taking a far journey, who left his house,
and gave authority to his servants, and
to every man his work, and commanded
the porter to watch.

35 Watch ye therefore: for ye know not when the master of the house cometh, at even, or at midnight, or at the cockcrowing, or in the morning:

36 Lest coming suddenly he find you sleeping.

37 And what I say unto you I say unto all, Watch.

14

After two days was *the feast of* the passover, and of unleavened bread: and the chief priests and the scribes sought how they might take him by craft, and put *him* to death.

2 But they said, Not on the feast *day*, lest there be an uproar of the people.

3 And being in Bethany in the house of Simon the leper, as he sat at meat, there came a woman having an alabaster box of ointment of spikenard very precious; and she brake the box, and poured *it* on his head.

4 And there were some that had indignation within themselves, and said, Why was this waste of the ointment made?

5 For it might have been sold for more than three hundred pence, and have been given to the poor. And they murmured against her.

6 And Jesus said, Let her alone; why trouble ye her? she hath wrought a good work on me.

7 For ye have the poor with you always, and whensoever ye will ye may do them good: but me ye have not always.

8 She hath done what she could: she is come aforehand to anoint my body to the burying.

9 Verily I say unto you, Wheresoever this gospel shall be preached throughout the whole world, *this* also that she hath done shall be spoken of for a memorial of her.

10 And Judas Iscariot, one of the twelve, went unto the chief priests, to betray him unto them.

11 And when they heard *it*, they were glad, and promised to give him money. And he sought how he might conveniently betray him.

12 And the first day of unleavened bread, when they killed the passover, his disciples said unto him, Where wilt thou that we go and prepare that thou mayest eat the passover?

13 And he sendeth forth two of his disciples, and saith unto them, Go ye into the city, and there shall meet you a man bearing a pitcher of water: follow him.

14 And wheresoever he shall go in, say ye to the goodman of the house, The Master saith, Where is the guestchamber, where I shall eat the passover with my disciples?

15 And he will shew you a large upper room furnished *and* prepared: there make ready for us.

16 And his disciples went forth, and came into the city, and found as he had said unto them: and they made ready the passover.

17 And in the evening he cometh with the twelve.

18 And as they sat and did eat, Jesus said, Verily I say unto you, One of you which eateth with me shall betray me.

19 And they began to be sorrowful, and to say unto him one by one, *Is* it I? and another *said, Is* it I?

20 And he answered and said unto them, *It is* one of the twelve, that dippeth with me in the dish.

21 The Son of man indeed goeth, as it is written of him: but woe to that man by whom the Son of man is betrayed!

good were it for that man if he had never been born.

22 And as they did eat, Jesus took bread, and blessed, and brake *it*, and gave to them, and said, Take, eat: this is my body.

23 And he took the cup, and when he had given thanks, he gave *it* to them: and they all drank of it.

24 And he said unto them, This is my blood of the new testament, which is shed for many.

25 Verily I say unto you, I will drink no more of the fruit of the vine, until that day that I drink it new in the kingdom of God.

26 And when they had sung an hymn, they went out into the mount of Olives.

27 And Jesus saith unto them, All ye shall be offended because of me this night: for it is written, I will smite the shepherd, and the sheep shall be scattered.

28 But after that I am risen, I will go before you into Galilee.

29 But Peter said unto him, Although all shall be offended, yet *will* not I.

30 And Jesus saith unto him, Verily I say unto thee, That this day, *even* in this night, before the cock crow twice, thou shalt deny me thrice.

31 But he spake the more vehemently, If I should die with thee, I will not deny thee in any wise. Likewise also said they all.

32 And they came to a place which was named Gethsemane: and he saith to his disciples, Sit ye here, while I shall pray.

33 And he taketh with him Peter and James and John, and began to be sore amazed, and to be very heavy;

34 And saith unto them, My soul is exceeding sorrowful unto death: tarry ye here, and watch.

35 And he went forward a little, and fell on the ground, and prayed that, if it were possible, the hour might pass from him.

36 And he said, Abba, Father, all things *are* possible unto thee; take away this cup from me: nevertheless not what I will, but what thou wilt.

37 And he cometh, and findeth them sleeping, and saith unto Peter, Simon, sleepest thou? couldest not thou watch one hour?

38 Watch ye and pray, lest ye enter into temptation. The spirit truly *is* ready, but the flesh *is* weak.

39 And again he went away, and prayed, and spake the same words.

40 And when he returned, he found them asleep again, (for their eyes were heavy,) neither wist they what to answer him.

41 And he cometh the third time, and saith unto them, Sleep on now, and take *your* rest: it is enough, the hour is come; behold, the Son of man is betrayed into the hands of sinners.

42 Rise up, let us go; lo, he that betrayeth me is at hand.

43 And immediately, while he yet spake, cometh Judas, one of the twelve, and with him a great multitude with swords and staves, from the chief priests and the scribes and the elders.

44 And he that betrayed him had given them a token, saying, Whomsoever I shall kiss, that same is he; take him, and lead *him* away safely.

45 And as soon as he was come, he goeth straightway to him, and saith, Master, master; and kissed him.

46 And they laid their hands on him, and took him.

47 And one of them that stood by drew a sword, and smote a servant of the high priest, and cut off his ear.

48 And Jesus answered and said unto them, Are ye come out, as against a thief, with swords and *with* staves to take me?

49 I was daily with you in the temple teaching, and ye took me not: but the scriptures must be fulfilled.

50 And they all forsook him, and fled.

51 And there followed him a certain young man, having a linen cloth cast about *his* naked *body*; and the young men laid hold on him:

52 And he left the linen cloth, and fled from them naked.

53 And they led Jesus away to the high priest: and with him were assembled all the chief priests and the elders and the scribes.

54 And Peter followed him afar off, even into the palace of the high priest: and he sat with the servants, and warmed himself at the fire.

55 And the chief priests and all the council sought for witness against Jesus to put him to death; and found none.

56 For many bare false witness against him, but their witness agreed not together.

57 And there arose certain, and bare false witness against him, saying,

58 We heard him say, I will destroy this temple that is made with hands, and within three days I will build another made without hands.

59 But neither so did their witness agree together.

60 And the high priest stood up in the midst, and asked Jesus, saying, Answerest thou nothing? what *is it which* these witness against thee?

61 But he held his peace, and answered nothing. Again the high priest asked him, and said unto him, Art thou the Christ, the Son of the Blessed?

62 And Jesus said, I am: and ye shall see the Son of man sitting on the right hand of power, and coming in the clouds of heaven.

63 Then the high priest rent his clothes, and saith, What need we any further witnesses?

64 Ye have heard the blasphemy: what think ye? And they all condemned him to be guilty of death.

65 And some began to spit on him, and to cover his face, and to buffet him, and to say unto him, Prophesy: and the servants did strike him with the palms of their hands.

66 And as Peter was beneath in the palace, there cometh one of the maids of the high priest:

67 And when she saw Peter warming himself, she looked upon him, and said, And thou also wast with Jesus of Nazareth.

68 But he denied, saying, I know not, neither understand I what thou sayest. And he went out into the porch; and the cock crew.

69 And a maid saw him again, and began to say to them that stood by, This is *one* of them.

70 And he denied it again. And a little after, they that stood by said again to Peter, Surely thou art *one* of them: for thou art a Galilaean, and thy speech agreeth *thereto*.

71 But he began to curse and to swear,
saying, I know not this man of whom ye
speak.
72 And the second time the cock crew.
And Peter called to mind the word that
Jesus said unto him, Before the cock
crow twice, thou shalt deny me thrice.
And when he thought thereon, he wept.

15 And straightway in the morning
the chief priests held a consulta-
tion with the elders and scribes and the
whole council, and bound Jesus, and
carried *him* away, and delivered *him* to
Pilate.
2 And Pilate asked him, Art thou the
King of the Jews? And he answering
said unto him, Thou sayest *it*.
3 And the chief priests accused him
of many things: but he answered nothing.
4 And Pilate asked him again, saying,
Answerest thou nothing? behold how
many things they witness against thee.
5 But Jesus yet answered nothing; so
that Pilate marvelled.
6 Now at *that* feast he released unto
them one prisoner, whomsoever they
desired.
7 And there was *one* named Barabbas,
which lay bound with them that had
made insurrection with him, who had
committed murder in the insurrection.
8 And the multitude crying aloud
began to desire *him to do* as he had
ever done unto them.
9 But Pilate answered them, saying,
Will ye that I release unto you the King
of the Jews?
10 For he knew that the chief priests
had delivered him for envy.
11 But the chief priests moved the
people, that he should rather release
Barabbas unto them.
12 And Pilate answered and said
again unto them, What will ye then that
I shall do *unto him* whom ye call the
King of the Jews?
13 And they cried out again, Crucify
him.
14 Then Pilate said unto them, Why,
what evil hath he done? And they cried
out the more exceedingly, Crucify him.
15 And *so* Pilate, willing to content
the people, released Barabbas unto
them, and delivered Jesus, when he
had scourged *him*, to be crucified.
16 And the soldiers led him away into
the hall, called Praetorium; and they
call together the whole band.
17 And they clothed him with purple,
and platted a crown of thorns, and put
it about his *head*,
18 And began to salute him, Hail,
King of the Jews!
19 And they smote him on the head
with a reed, and did spit upon him, and
bowing *their* knees worshipped him.
20 And when they had mocked him,
they took off the purple from him, and
put his own clothes on him, and led him
out to crucify him.
21 And they compel one Simon a
Cyrenian, who passed by, coming out of
the country, the father of Alexander
and Rufus, to bear his cross.
22 And they bring him unto the place
Golgotha, which is, being interpreted,
The place of a skull.
23 And they gave him to drink wine
mingled with myrrh: but he received *it*
not.
24 And when they had crucified him,
they parted his garments, casting lots
upon them, what every man should
take.
25 And it was the third hour, and they
crucified him.

26 And the superscription of his accusation was written over, THE KING OF THE JEWS.

27 And with him they crucify two thieves; the one on his right hand, and the other on his left.

28 And the scripture was fulfilled, which saith, And he was numbered with the transgressors.

29 And they that passed by railed on him, wagging their heads, and saying, Ah, thou that destroyest the temple, and buildest *it* in three days,

30 Save thyself, and come down from the cross.

31 Likewise also the chief priests mocking said among themselves with the scribes, He saved others; himself he cannot save.

32 Let Christ the King of Israel descend now from the cross, that we may see and believe. And they that were crucified with him reviled him.

33 And when the sixth hour was come, there was darkness over the whole land until the ninth hour.

34 And at the ninth hour Jesus cried with a loud voice, saying, Eloi, Eloi, lama sabachthani? which is, being interpreted, My God, my God, why hast thou forsaken me?

35 And some of them that stood by, when they heard *it*, said, Behold, he calleth Elias.

36 And one ran and filled a spunge full of vinegar, and put *it* on a reed, and gave him to drink, saying, Let alone; let us see whether Elias will come to take him down.

37 And Jesus cried with a loud voice, and gave up the ghost.

38 And the veil of the temple was rent in twain from the top to the bottom.

39 And when the centurion, which stood over against him, saw that he so cried out, and gave up the ghost, he said, Truly this man was the Son of God.

40 There were also women looking on afar off: among whom was Mary Magdalene, and Mary the mother of James the less and of Joses, and Salome;

41 (Who also, when he was in Galilee, followed him, and ministered unto him;) and many other women which came up with him unto Jerusalem.

42 And now when the even was come, because it was the preparation, that is, the day before the sabbath,

43 Joseph of Arimathaea, an honourable counsellor, which also waited for the kingdom of God, came, and went in boldly unto Pilate, and craved the body of Jesus.

44 And Pilate marvelled if he were already dead: and calling *unto him* the centurion, he asked him whether he had been any while dead.

45 And when he knew *it* of the centurion, he gave the body to Joseph.

46 And he bought fine linen, and took him down, and wrapped him in the linen, and laid him in a sepulchre which was hewn out of a rock, and rolled a stone unto the door of the sepulchre.

47 And Mary Magdalene and Mary *the mother* of Joses beheld where he was laid.

16 And when the sabbath was past, Mary Magdalene, and Mary the *mother* of James, and Salome, had bought sweet spices, that they might come and anoint him.

2 And very early in the morning the first *day* of the week, they came unto the sepulchre at the rising of the sun.

3 And they said among themselves,
Who shall roll us away the stone from
the door of the sepulchre?
4 And when they looked, they saw
that the stone was rolled away: for it
was very great.
5 And entering into the sepulchre,
they saw a young man sitting on the
right side, clothed in a long white garment; and they were affrighted.
6 And he saith unto them, Be not
affrighted: Ye seek Jesus of Nazareth,
which was crucified: he is risen; he is
not here: behold the place where they
laid him.
7 But go your way, tell his disciples
and Peter that he goeth before you into
Galilee: there shall ye see him, as he
said unto you.
8 And they went out quickly, and fled
from the sepulchre; for they trembled
and were amazed: neither said they any
thing to any *man*; for they were afraid.
9 Now when *Jesus* was risen early the
first *day* of the week, he appeared first
to Mary Magdalene, out of whom he
had cast seven devils.
10 *And* she went and told them that
had been with him, as they mourned
and wept.
11 And they, when they had heard
that he was alive, and had been seen of
her, believed not.
12 After that he appeared in another
form unto two of them, as they walked,
and went into the country.
13 And they went and told *it* unto the
residue: neither believed they them.
14 Afterward he appeared unto the
eleven as they sat at meat, and upbraid-
ed them with their unbelief and hardness of heart, because they believed
not them which had seen him after he
was risen.
15 And he said unto them, Go ye into
all the world, and preach the gospel to
every creature.
16 He that believeth and is baptized
shall be saved; but he that believeth
not shall be damned.
17 And these signs shall follow them
that believe; In my name shall they cast
out devils; they shall speak with new
tongues;
18 They shall take up serpents; and if
they drink any deadly thing, it shall not
hurt them; they shall lay hands on the
sick, and they shall recover.
19 So then after the Lord had spoken
unto them, he was received up into
heaven, and sat on the right hand of
God.
20 And they went forth, and preached
every where, the Lord working with
them, and confirming the word with
signs following. Amen.

THE GOSPEL ACCORDING TO

SAINT LUKE

1 Forasmuch as many have taken in hand to set forth in order a declaration of those things which are most surely believed among us,

2 Even as they delivered them unto us, which from the beginning were eyewitnesses, and ministers of the word;

3 It seemed good to me also, having had perfect understanding of all things from the very first, to write unto thee in order, most excellent Theophilus,

4 That thou mightest know the certainty of those things, wherein thou hast been instructed.

5 There was in the days of Herod, the king of Judaea, a certain priest named Zacharias, of the course of Abia: and his wife *was* of the daughters of Aaron, and her name *was* Elisabeth.

6 And they were both righteous before God, walking in all the commandments and ordinances of the Lord blameless.

7 And they had no child, because that Elisabeth was barren, and they both were *now* well stricken in years.

8 And it came to pass, that while he executed the priest's office before God in the order of his course,

9 According to the custom of the priest's office, his lot was to burn incense when he went into the temple of the Lord.

10 And the whole multitude of the people were praying without at the time of incense.

11 And there appeared unto him an angel of the Lord standing on the right side of the altar of incense.

12 And when Zacharias saw *him*, he was troubled, and fear fell upon him.

13 But the angel said unto him, Fear not, Zacharias: for thy prayer is heard; and thy wife Elisabeth shall bear thee a son, and thou shalt call his name John.

14 And thou shalt have joy and gladness; and many shall rejoice at his birth.

15 For he shall be great in the sight of the Lord, and shall drink neither wine nor strong drink; and he shall be filled with the Holy Ghost, even from his mother's womb.

16 And many of the children of Israel shall he turn to the Lord their God.

17 And he shall go before him in the spirit and power of Elias, to turn the hearts of the fathers to the children, and the disobedient to the wisdom of the just; to make ready a people prepared for the Lord.

18 And Zacharias said unto the angel, Whereby shall I know this? for I am an old man, and my wife well stricken in years.

19 And the angel answering said unto him, I am Gabriel, that stand in the presence of God; and am sent to speak unto thee, and to shew thee these glad tidings.

20 And, behold, thou shalt be dumb, and not able to speak, until the day that these things shall be performed, because thou believest not my words, which shall be fulfilled in their season.

21 And the people waited for Zacharias, and marvelled that he tarried so long in the temple.

22 And when he came out, he could
not speak unto them: and they perceived that he had seen a vision in the
temple: for he beckoned unto them,
and remained speechless.
23 And it came to pass, that, as soon
as the days of his ministration were
accomplished, he departed to his own
house.
24 And after those days his wife
Elisabeth conceived, and hid herself
five months, saying,
25 Thus hath the Lord dealt with me
in the days wherein he looked on *me*, to
take away my reproach among men.
26 And in the sixth month the angel
Gabriel was sent from God unto a city
of Galilee, named Nazareth,
27 To a virgin espoused to a man
whose name was Joseph, of the house
of David; and the virgin's name *was*
Mary.
28 And the angel came in unto her,
and said, Hail, *thou that art* highly
favoured, the Lord *is* with thee: blessed
art thou among women.
29 And when she saw *him*, she was
troubled at his saying, and cast in her
mind what manner of salutation this
should be.
30 And the angel said unto her, Fear
not, Mary: for thou hast found favour
with God.
31 And, behold, thou shalt conceive in
thy womb, and bring forth a son, and
shalt call his name JESUS.
32 He shall be great, and shall be
called the Son of the Highest: and the
Lord God shall give unto him the
throne of his father David:
33 And he shall reign over the house
of Jacob for ever; and of his kingdom
there shall be no end.
34 Then said Mary unto the angel,
How shall this be, seeing I know not a
man?
35 And the angel answered and said
unto her, The Holy Ghost shall come
upon thee, and the power of the
Highest shall overshadow thee: therefore also that holy thing which shall be
born of thee shall be called the Son of
God.
36 And, behold, thy cousin Elisabeth,
she hath also conceived a son in her old
age: and this is the sixth month with
her, who was called barren.
37 For with God nothing shall be
impossible.
38 And Mary said, Behold the handmaid of the Lord; be it unto me according to thy word. And the angel departed from her.
39 And Mary arose in those days, and
went into the hill country with haste,
into a city of Juda;
40 And entered into the house of
Zacharias, and saluted Elisabeth.
41 And it came to pass, that, when
Elisabeth heard the salutation of Mary,
the babe leaped in her womb; and
Elisabeth was filled with the Holy
Ghost:
42 And she spake out with a loud
voice, and said, Blessed *art* thou among
women, and blessed *is* the fruit of thy
womb.
43 And whence *is* this to me, that the
mother of my Lord should come to me?
44 For, lo, as soon as the voice of thy
salutation sounded in mine ears, the
babe leaped in my womb for joy.
45 And blessed *is* she that believed:
for there shall be a performance of
those things which were told her from
the Lord.

46 And Mary said, My soul doth magnify the Lord,
47 And my spirit hath rejoiced in God my Saviour.
48 For he hath regarded the low estate of his handmaiden: for, behold, from henceforth all generations shall call me blessed.
49 For he that is mighty hath done to me great things; and holy *is* his name.
50 And his mercy *is* on them that fear him from generation to generation.
51 He hath shewed strength with his arm; he hath scattered the proud in the imagination of their hearts.
52 He hath put down the mighty from *their* seats, and exalted them of low degree.
53 He hath filled the hungry with good things; and the rich he hath sent empty away.
54 He hath holpen his servant Israel, in remembrance of *his* mercy;
55 As he spake to our fathers, to Abraham, and to his seed for ever.
56 And Mary abode with her about three months, and returned to her own house.
57 Now Elisabeth's full time came that she should be delivered; and she brought forth a son.
58 And her neighbours and her cousins heard how the Lord had shewed great mercy upon her; and they rejoiced with her.
59 And it came to pass, that on the eighth day they came to circumcise the child; and they called him Zacharias, after the name of his father.
60 And his mother answered and said, Not *so*; but he shall be called John.
61 And they said unto her, There is none of thy kindred that is called by this name.
62 And they made signs to his father, how he would have him called.
63 And he asked for a writing table, and wrote, saying, His name is John. And they marvelled all.
64 And his mouth was opened immediately, and his tongue *loosed*, and he spake, and praised God.
65 And fear came on all that dwelt round about them: and all these sayings were noised abroad throughout all the hill country of Judaea.
66 And all they that heard *them* laid *them* up in their hearts, saying, What manner of child shall this be! And the hand of the Lord was with him.
67 And his father Zacharias was filled with the Holy Ghost, and prophesied, saying,
68 Blessed *be* the Lord God of Israel; for he hath visited and redeemed his people,
69 And hath raised up an horn of salvation for us in the house of his servant David;
70 As he spake by the mouth of his holy prophets, which have been since the world began:
71 That we should be saved from our enemies, and from the hand of all that hate us;
72 To perform the mercy *promised* to our fathers, and to remember his holy covenant;
73 The oath which he sware to our father Abraham,
74 That he would grant unto us, that we being delivered out of the hand of our enemies might serve him without fear,
75 In holiness and righteousness before him, all the days of our life.
76 And thou, child, shalt be called the prophet of the Highest: for thou shalt

go before the face of the Lord to prepare his ways;
77 To give knowledge of salvation
unto his people by the remission of
their sins,
78 Through the tender mercy of our
God; whereby the dayspring from on
high hath visited us,
79 To give light to them that sit in
darkness and *in* the shadow of death,
to guide our feet into the way of peace.
80 And the child grew, and waxed
strong in spirit, and was in the deserts
till the day of his shewing unto Israel.

2 And it came to pass in those days,
that there went out a decree from
Caesar Augustus, that all the world
should be taxed.
2 (*And* this taxing was first made
when Cyrenius was governor of Syria.)
3 And all went to be taxed, every one
into his own city.
4 And Joseph also went up from
Galilee, out of the city of Nazareth, into
Judaea, unto the city of David, which is
called Bethlehem; (because he was of
the house and lineage of David:)
5 To be taxed with Mary his espoused
wife, being great with child.
6 And so it was, that, while they were
there, the days were accomplished that
she should be delivered.
7 And she brought forth her firstborn
son, and wrapped him in swaddling
clothes, and laid him in a manger;
because there was no room for them in
the inn.
8 And there were in the same country
shepherds abiding in the field, keeping
watch over their flock by night.
9 And, lo, the angel of the Lord came
upon them, and the glory of the Lord
shone round about them: and they were
sore afraid.
10 And the angel said unto them,
Fear not: for, behold, I bring you good
tidings of great joy, which shall be to all
people.
11 For unto you is born this day in the
city of David a Saviour, which is Christ
the Lord.
12 And this *shall be* a sign unto you;
Ye shall find the babe wrapped in swaddling clothes, lying in a manger.
13 And suddenly there was with the
angel a multitude of the heavenly host
praising God, and saying,
14 Glory to God in the highest, and on
earth peace, good will toward men.
15 And it came to pass, as the angels
were gone away from them into heaven,
the shepherds said one to another, Let
us now go even unto Bethlehem, and
see this thing which is come to pass,
which the Lord hath made known unto
us.
16 And they came with haste, and
found Mary, and Joseph, and the babe
lying in a manger.
17 And when they had seen *it*, they
made known abroad the saying which
was told them concerning this child.
18 And all they that heard *it* wondered at those things which were told
them by the shepherds.
19 But Mary kept all these things, and
pondered *them* in her heart.
20 And the shepherds returned, glorifying and praising God for all the
things that they had heard and seen, as
it was told unto them.
21 And when eight days were accomplished for the circumcising of the
child, his name was called JESUS,
which was so named of the angel before
he was conceived in the womb.
22 And when the days of her purification according to the law of Moses were

accomplished, they brought him to
Jerusalem, to present *him* to the Lord;
23 (As it is written in the law of the
Lord, Every male that openeth the
womb shall be called holy to the Lord;)
24 And to offer a sacrifice according
to that which is said in the law of the
Lord, A pair of turtledoves, or two
young pigeons.
25 And, behold, there was a man in
Jerusalem, whose name *was* Simeon;
and the same man *was* just and devout,
waiting for the consolation of Israel:
and the Holy Ghost was upon him.
26 And it was revealed unto him by
the Holy Ghost, that he should not see
death, before he had seen the Lord's
Christ.
27 And he came by the Spirit into the
temple: and when the parents brought
in the child Jesus, to do for him after
the custom of the law,
28 Then took he him up in his arms,
and blessed God, and said,
29 Lord, now lettest thou thy servant
depart in peace, according to thy word:
30 For mine eyes have seen thy salvation,
31 Which thou hast prepared before
the face of all people;
32 A light to lighten the Gentiles, and
the glory of thy people Israel.
33 And Joseph and his mother marvelled at those things which were spoken of him.
34 And Simeon blessed them, and
said unto Mary his mother, Behold, this
child is set for the fall and rising again
of many in Israel; and for a sign which
shall be spoken against;
35 (Yea, a sword shall pierce through
thy own soul also,) that the thoughts of
many hearts may be revealed.
36 And there was one Anna, a prophetess, the daughter of Phanuel, of the
tribe of Aser: she was of a great age,
and had lived with an husband seven
years from her virginity;
37 And she *was* a widow of about
fourscore and four years, which departed not from the temple, but served *God*
with fastings and prayers night and day.
38 And she coming in that instant
gave thanks likewise unto the Lord,
and spake of him to all them that
looked for redemption in Jerusalem.
39 And when they had performed all
things according to the law of the Lord,
they returned into Galilee, to their own
city Nazareth.
40 And the child grew, and waxed
strong in spirit, filled with wisdom: and
the grace of God was upon him.
41 Now his parents went to Jerusalem
every year at the feast of the passover.
42 And when he was twelve years old,
they went up to Jerusalem after the
custom of the feast.
43 And when they had fulfilled the
days, as they returned, the child Jesus
tarried behind in Jerusalem; and
Joseph and his mother knew not *of it*.
44 But they, supposing him to have
been in the company, went a day's journey; and they sought him among *their*
kinsfolk and acquaintance.
45 And when they found him not,
they turned back again to Jerusalem,
seeking him.
46 And it came to pass, that after
three days they found him in the temple, sitting in the midst of the doctors,
both hearing them, and asking them
questions.
47 And all that heard him were astonished at his understanding and answers.

48 And when they saw him, they were
amazed: and his mother said unto him,
Son, why hast thou thus dealt with us?
behold, thy father and I have sought
thee sorrowing.
49 And he said unto them, How is it
that ye sought me? wist ye not that I
must be about my Father's business?
50 And they understood not the saying which he spake unto them.
51 And he went down with them, and
came to Nazareth, and was subject unto
them: but his mother kept all these sayings in her heart.
52 And Jesus increased in wisdom
and stature, and in favour with God and
man.

3 Now in the fifteenth year of the
reign of Tiberius Caesar, Pontius
Pilate being governor of Judaea, and
Herod being tetrarch of Galilee, and his
brother Philip tetrarch of Ituraea and
of the region of Trachonitis, and
Lysanias the tetrarch of Abilene,
2 Annas and Caiaphas being the high
priests, the word of God came unto
John the son of Zacharias in the wilderness.
3 And he came into all the country
about Jordan, preaching the baptism of
repentance for the remission of sins;
4 As it is written in the book of the
words of Esaias the prophet, saying,
The voice of one crying in the wilderness, Prepare ye the way of the Lord,
make his paths straight.
5 Every valley shall be filled, and
every mountain and hill shall be
brought low; and the crooked shall be
made straight, and the rough ways *shall*
be made smooth;
6 And all flesh shall see the salvation
of God.
7 Then said he to the multitude that
came forth to be baptized of him, O
generation of vipers, who hath warned
you to flee from the wrath to come?
8 Bring forth therefore fruits worthy
of repentance, and begin not to say
within yourselves, We have Abraham to
our father: for I say unto you, That God
is able of these stones to raise up children unto Abraham.
9 And now also the axe is laid unto
the root of the trees: every tree therefore which bringeth not forth good fruit
is hewn down, and cast into the fire.
10 And the people asked him, saying,
What shall we do then?
11 He answereth and saith unto them,
He that hath two coats, let him impart
to him that hath none; and he that hath
meat, let him do likewise.
12 Then came also publicans to be
baptized, and said unto him, Master,
what shall we do?
13 And he said unto them, Exact no
more than that which is appointed you.
14 And the soldiers likewise demanded of him, saying, And what shall we
do? And he said unto them, Do violence
to no man, neither accuse *any* falsely;
and be content with your wages.
15 And as the people were in expectation, and all men mused in their hearts
of John, whether he were the Christ, or
not;
16 John answered, saying unto *them*
all, I indeed baptize you with water; but
one mightier than I cometh, the latchet
of whose shoes I am not worthy to
unloose: he shall baptize you with the
Holy Ghost and with fire:

17 Whose fan *is* in his hand, and he
will throughly purge his floor, and will
gather the wheat into his garner; but
the chaff he will burn with fire
unquenchable.
18 And many other things in his
exhortation preached he unto the people.
19 But Herod the tetrarch, being
reproved by him for Herodias his brother Philip's wife, and for all the evils
which Herod had done,
20 Added yet this above all, that he
shut up John in prison.
21 Now when all the people were
baptized, it came to pass, that Jesus
also being baptized, and praying, the
heaven was opened,
22 And the Holy Ghost descended in
a bodily shape like a dove upon him,
and a voice came from heaven, which
said, Thou art my beloved Son; in thee I
am well pleased.
23 And Jesus himself began to be
about thirty years of age, being (as was
supposed) the son of Joseph, which was
the son of Heli,
24 Which was *the son* of Matthat,
which was *the son* of Levi, which was
the son of Melchi, which was *the son* of
Janna, which was *the son* of Joseph,
25 Which was *the son* of Mattathias,
which was *the son* of Amos, which was
the son of Naum, which was *the son* of
Esli, which was *the son* of Nagge,
26 Which was *the son* of Maath, which
was *the son* of Mattathias, which was
the son of Semei, which was *the son* of
Joseph, which was *the son* of Juda,
27 Which was *the son* of Joanna,
which was *the son* of Rhesa, which was
the son of Zorobabel, which was *the son*
of Salathiel, which was *the son* of Neri,
28 Which was *the son* of Melchi,
which was *the son* of Addi, which was
the son of Cosam, which was *the son* of
Elmodam, which was *the son* of Er,
29 Which was *the son* of Jose, which
was *the son* of Eliezer, which was *the
son* of Jorim, which was *the son* of
Matthat, which was *the son* of Levi,
30 Which was *the son* of Simeon,
which was *the son* of Juda, which was
the son of Joseph, which was *the son* of
Jonan, which was *the son* of Eliakim,
31 Which was *the son* of Melea, which
was *the son* of Menan, which was *the
son* of Mattatha, which was *the son* of
Nathan, which was *the son* of David,
32 Which was *the son* of Jesse, which
was *the son* of Obed, which was *the son*
of Booz, which was *the son* of Salmon,
which was *the son* of Naasson,
33 Which was *the son* of Aminadab,
which was *the son* of Aram, which was
the son of Esrom, which was *the son* of
Phares, which was *the son* of Juda,
34 Which was *the son* of Jacob, which
was *the son* of Isaac, which was *the son*
of Abraham, which was *the son* of
Thara, which was *the son* of Nachor,
35 Which was *the son* of Saruch,
which was *the son* of Ragau, which was
the son of Phalec, which was *the son* of
Heber, which was *the son* of Sala,
36 Which was *the son* of Cainan,
which was *the son* of Arphaxad, which
was *the son* of Sem, which was *the son*
of Noe, which was *the son* of Lamech,
37 Which was *the son* of Mathusala,
which was *the son* of Enoch, which was
the son of Jared, which was *the son* of
Maleleel, which was *the son* of Cainan,
38 Which was *the son* of Enos, which
was *the son* of Seth, which was *the son*
of Adam, which was *the son* of God.

4 And Jesus being full of the Holy
Ghost returned from Jordan, and
was led by the Spirit into the wilderness,
2 Being forty days tempted of the
devil. And in those days he did eat
nothing: and when they were ended, he
afterward hungered.
3 And the devil said unto him, If thou
be the Son of God, command this stone
that it be made bread.
4 And Jesus answered him, saying, It
is written, That man shall not live by
bread alone, but by every word of God.
5 And the devil, taking him up into an
high mountain, shewed unto him all the
kingdoms of the world in a moment of
time.
6 And the devil said unto him, All this
power will I give thee, and the glory of
them: for that is delivered unto me; and
to whomsoever I will I give it.
7 If thou therefore wilt worship me,
all shall be thine.
8 And Jesus answered and said unto
him, Get thee behind me, Satan: for it
is written, Thou shalt worship the Lord
thy God, and him only shalt thou serve.
9 And he brought him to Jerusalem,
and set him on a pinnacle of the temple, and said unto him, If thou be the
Son of God, cast thyself down from
hence:
10 For it is written, He shall give his
angels charge over thee, to keep thee:
11 And in *their* hands they shall bear
thee up, lest at any time thou dash thy
foot against a stone.
12 And Jesus answering said unto
him, It is said, Thou shalt not tempt the
Lord thy God.
13 And when the devil had ended all
the temptation, he departed from him
for a season.
14 And Jesus returned in the power
of the Spirit into Galilee: and there
went out a fame of him through all the
region round about.
15 And he taught in their synagogues,
being glorified of all.
16 And he came to Nazareth, where
he had been brought up: and, as his
custom was, he went into the synagogue on the sabbath day, and stood up
for to read.
17 And there was delivered unto him
the book of the prophet Esaias. And
when he had opened the book, he
found the place where it was written,
18 The Spirit of the Lord *is* upon me,
because he hath anointed me to preach
the gospel to the poor; he hath sent me
to heal the brokenhearted, to preach
deliverance to the captives, and recovering of sight to the blind, to set at liberty them that are bruised,
19 To preach the acceptable year of
the Lord.
20 And he closed the book, and he
gave *it* again to the minister, and sat
down. And the eyes of all them that
were in the synagogue were fastened
on him.
21 And he began to say unto them,
This day is this scripture fulfilled in
your ears.
22 And all bare him witness, and wondered at the gracious words which proceeded out of his mouth. And they said,
Is not this Joseph's son?
23 And he said unto them, Ye will
surely say unto me this proverb,
Physician, heal thyself: whatsoever we
have heard done in Capernaum, do also
here in thy country.
24 And he said, Verily I say unto you,
No prophet is accepted in his own country.

25 But I tell you of a truth, many widows were in Israel in the days of Elias,
when the heaven was shut up three
years and six months, when great famine was throughout all the land;
26 But unto none of them was Elias
sent, save unto Sarepta, *a city* of Sidon,
unto a woman *that was* a widow.
27 And many lepers were in Israel in
the time of Eliseus the prophet; and
none of them was cleansed, saving
Naaman the Syrian.
28 And all they in the synagogue,
when they heard these things, were
filled with wrath,
29 And rose up, and thrust him out of
the city, and led him unto the brow of
the hill whereon their city was built,
that they might cast him down headlong.
30 But he passing through the midst
of them went his way,
31 And came down to Capernaum, a
city of Galilee, and taught them on the
sabbath days.
32 And they were astonished at his
doctrine: for his word was with power.
33 And in the synagogue there was a
man, which had a spirit of an unclean
devil, and cried out with a loud voice,
34 Saying, Let *us* alone; what have we
to do with thee, *thou* Jesus of Nazareth?
art thou come to destroy us? I know
thee who thou art; the Holy One of
God.
35 And Jesus rebuked him, saying,
Hold thy peace, and come out of him.
And when the devil had thrown him in
the midst, he came out of him, and hurt
him not.
36 And they were all amazed, and
spake among themselves, saying, What
a word *is* this! for with authority and
power he commandeth the unclean
spirits, and they come out.
37 And the fame of him went out into
every place of the country round about.
38 And he arose out of the synagogue,
and entered into Simon's house. And
Simon's wife's mother was taken with a
great fever; and they besought him for
her.
39 And he stood over her, and rebuked
the fever; and it left her: and immediately she arose and ministered unto
them.
40 Now when the sun was setting, all
they that had any sick with divers diseases brought them unto him; and he
laid his hands on every one of them,
and healed them.
41 And devils also came out of many,
crying out, and saying, Thou art Christ
the Son of God. And he rebuking *them*
suffered them not to speak: for they
knew that he was Christ.
42 And when it was day, he departed
and went into a desert place: and the
people sought him, and came unto him,
and stayed him, that he should not
depart from them.
43 And he said unto them, I must
preach the kingdom of God to other
cities also: for therefore am I sent.
44 And he preached in the synagogues of Galilee.

5 And it came to pass, that, as the
people pressed upon him to hear
the word of God, he stood by the lake of
Gennesaret,
2 And saw two ships standing by the
lake: but the fishermen were gone out
of them, and were washing *their* nets.
3 And he entered into one of the
ships, which was Simon's, and prayed
him that he would thrust out a little

from the land. And he sat down, and
taught the people out of the ship.
4 Now when he had left speaking, he
said unto Simon, Launch out into the
deep, and let down your nets for a
draught.
5 And Simon answering said unto
him, Master, we have toiled all the
night, and have taken nothing: nevertheless at thy word I will let down the
net.
6 And when they had this done, they
inclosed a great multitude of fishes:
and their net brake.
7 And they beckoned unto *their* part-
ners, which were in the other ship, that
they should come and help them. And
they came, and filled both the ships, so
that they began to sink.
8 When Simon Peter saw *it*, he fell
down at Jesus' knees, saying, Depart
from me; for I am a sinful man, O Lord.
9 For he was astonished, and all that
were with him, at the draught of the
fishes which they had taken:
10 And so *was* also James, and John,
the sons of Zebedee, which were part-
ners with Simon. And Jesus said unto
Simon, Fear not; from henceforth thou
shalt catch men.
11 And when they had brought their
ships to land, they forsook all, and followed him.
12 And it came to pass, when he was
in a certain city, behold a man full of
leprosy: who seeing Jesus fell on *his*
face, and besought him, saying, Lord, if
thou wilt, thou canst make me clean.
13 And he put forth *his* hand, and
touched him, saying, I will: be thou
clean. And immediately the leprosy
departed from him.
14 And he charged him to tell no man:
but go, and shew thyself to the priest,
and offer for thy cleansing, according
as Moses commanded, for a testimony
unto them.
15 But so much the more went there a
fame abroad of him: and great multitudes came together to hear, and to be
healed by him of their infirmities.
16 And he withdrew himself into the
wilderness, and prayed.
17 And it came to pass on a certain
day, as he was teaching, that there were
Pharisees and doctors of the law sitting
by, which were come out of every town
of Galilee, and Judaea, and Jerusalem:
and the power of the Lord was *present*
to heal them.
18 And, behold, men brought in a bed
a man which was taken with a palsy:
and they sought *means* to bring him in,
and to lay *him* before him.
19 And when they could not find by
what *way* they might bring him in
because of the multitude, they went
upon the housetop, and let him down
through the tiling with *his* couch into
the midst before Jesus.
20 And when he saw their faith, he
said unto him, Man, thy sins are forgiv-
en thee.
21 And the scribes and the Pharisees
began to reason, saying, Who is this
which speaketh blasphemies? Who can
forgive sins, but God alone?
22 But when Jesus perceived their
thoughts, he answering said unto them,
What reason ye in your hearts?
23 Whether is easier, to say, Thy sins
be forgiven thee; or to say, Rise up and
walk?
24 But that ye may know that the Son
of man hath power upon earth to forgive sins, (he said unto the sick of the
palsy,) I say unto thee, Arise, and take
up thy couch, and go into thine house.

25 And immediately he rose up
before them, and took up that whereon
he lay, and departed to his own house,
glorifying God.
26 And they were all amazed, and
they glorified God, and were filled with
fear, saying, We have seen strange
things to day.
27 And after these things he went
forth, and saw a publican, named Levi,
sitting at the receipt of custom: and he
said unto him, Follow me.
28 And he left all, rose up, and followed him.
29 And Levi made him a great feast in
his own house: and there was a great
company of publicans and of others
that sat down with them.
30 But their scribes and Pharisees
murmured against his disciples, saying,
Why do ye eat and drink with publicans
and sinners?
31 And Jesus answering said unto
them, They that are whole need not a
physician; but they that are sick.
32 I came not to call the righteous,
but sinners to repentance.
33 And they said unto him, Why do
the disciples of John fast often, and
make prayers, and likewise *the disciples* of the Pharisees; but thine eat and
drink?
34 And he said unto them, Can ye
make the children of the bridechamber
fast, while the bridegroom is with
them?
35 But the days will come, when the
bridegroom shall be taken away from
them, and then shall they fast in those
days.
36 And he spake also a parable unto
them; No man putteth a piece of a new
garment upon an old; if otherwise, then
both the new maketh a rent, and the
piece that was *taken* out of the new
agreeth not with the old.
37 And no man putteth new wine into
old bottles; else the new wine will burst
the bottles, and be spilled, and the
bottles shall perish.
38 But new wine must be put into new
bottles; and both are preserved.
39 No man also having drunk old
wine straightway desireth new: for he
saith, The old is better.

6 And it came to pass on the second
sabbath after the first, that he went
through the corn fields; and his disciples plucked the ears of corn, and did
eat, rubbing *them* in *their* hands.
2 And certain of the Pharisees said
unto them, Why do ye that which is not
lawful to do on the sabbath days?
3 And Jesus answering them said,
Have ye not read so much as this, what
David did, when himself was an hungred, and they which were with him;
4 How he went into the house of God,
and did take and eat the shewbread,
and gave also to them that were with
him; which it is not lawful to eat but for
the priests alone?
5 And he said unto them, That the
Son of man is Lord also of the sabbath.
6 And it came to pass also on another
sabbath, that he entered into the synagogue and taught: and there was a man
whose right hand was withered.
7 And the scribes and Pharisees
watched him, whether he would heal
on the sabbath day; that they might
find an accusation against him.
8 But he knew their thoughts, and
said to the man which had the withered
hand, Rise up, and stand forth in the
midst. And he arose and stood forth.
9 Then said Jesus unto them, I will
ask you one thing; Is it lawful on the

sabbath days to do good, or to do evil? to save life, or to destroy *it*?
10 And looking round about upon them all, he said unto the man, Stretch forth thy hand. And he did so: and his hand was restored whole as the other.
11 And they were filled with madness; and communed one with another what they might do to Jesus.
12 And it came to pass in those days, that he went out into a mountain to pray, and continued all night in prayer to God.
13 And when it was day, he called *unto him* his disciples: and of them he chose twelve, whom also he named apostles;
14 Simon, (whom he also named Peter,) and Andrew his brother, James and John, Philip and Bartholomew,
15 Matthew and Thomas, James the *son* of Alphaeus, and Simon called Zelotes,
16 And Judas *the brother* of James, and Judas Iscariot, which also was the traitor.
17 And he came down with them, and stood in the plain, and the company of his disciples, and a great multitude of people out of all Judaea and Jerusalem, and from the sea coast of Tyre and Sidon, which came to hear him, and to be healed of their diseases;
18 And they that were vexed with unclean spirits: and they were healed.
19 And the whole multitude sought to touch him: for there went virtue out of him, and healed *them* all.
20 And he lifted up his eyes on his disciples, and said, Blessed *be ye* poor: for yours is the kingdom of God.
21 Blessed *are ye* that hunger now: for ye shall be filled. Blessed *are ye* that weep now: for ye shall laugh.
22 Blessed are ye, when men shall hate you, and when they shall separate you *from their company*, and shall reproach *you*, and cast out your name as evil, for the Son of man's sake.
23 Rejoice ye in that day, and leap for joy: for, behold, your reward *is* great in heaven: for in the like manner did their fathers unto the prophets.
24 But woe unto you that are rich! for ye have received your consolation.
25 Woe unto you that are full! for ye shall hunger. Woe unto you that laugh now! for ye shall mourn and weep.
26 Woe unto you, when all men shall speak well of you! for so did their fathers to the false prophets.
27 But I say unto you which hear, Love your enemies, do good to them which hate you,
28 Bless them that curse you, and pray for them which despitefully use you.
29 And unto him that smiteth thee on the *one* cheek offer also the other; and him that taketh away thy cloke forbid not *to take thy* coat also.
30 Give to every man that asketh of thee; and of him that taketh away thy goods ask *them* not again.
31 And as ye would that men should do to you, do ye also to them likewise.
32 For if ye love them which love you, what thank have ye? for sinners also love those that love them.
33 And if ye do good to them which do good to you, what thank have ye? for sinners also do even the same.
34 And if ye lend *to them* of whom ye hope to receive, what thank have ye? for sinners also lend to sinners, to receive as much again.
35 But love ye your enemies, and do good, and lend, hoping for nothing

again; and your reward shall be great, and ye shall be the children of the Highest: for he is kind unto the unthankful and *to* the evil.

36 Be ye therefore merciful, as your Father also is merciful.

37 Judge not, and ye shall not be judged: condemn not, and ye shall not be condemned: forgive, and ye shall be forgiven:

38 Give, and it shall be given unto you; good measure, pressed down, and shaken together, and running over, shall men give into your bosom. For with the same measure that ye mete withal it shall be measured to you again.

39 And he spake a parable unto them, Can the blind lead the blind? shall they not both fall into the ditch?

40 The disciple is not above his master: but every one that is perfect shall be as his master.

41 And why beholdest thou the mote that is in thy brother's eye, but perceivest not the beam that is in thine own eye?

42 Either how canst thou say to thy brother, Brother, let me pull out the mote that is in thine eye, when thou thyself beholdest not the beam that is in thine own eye? Thou hypocrite, cast out first the beam out of thine own eye, and then shalt thou see clearly to pull out the mote that is in thy brother's eye.

43 For a good tree bringeth not forth corrupt fruit; neither doth a corrupt tree bring forth good fruit.

44 For every tree is known by his own fruit. For of thorns men do not gather figs, nor of a bramble bush gather they grapes.

45 A good man out of the good treasure of his heart bringeth forth that which is good; and an evil man out of the evil treasure of his heart bringeth forth that which is evil: for of the abundance of the heart his mouth speaketh.

46 And why call ye me, Lord, Lord, and do not the things which I say?

47 Whosoever cometh to me, and heareth my sayings, and doeth them, I will shew you to whom he is like:

48 He is like a man which built an house, and digged deep, and laid the foundation on a rock: and when the flood arose, the stream beat vehemently upon that house, and could not shake it: for it was founded upon a rock.

49 But he that heareth, and doeth not, is like a man that without a foundation built an house upon the earth; against which the stream did beat vehemently, and immediately it fell; and the ruin of that house was great.

7 Now when he had ended all his sayings in the audience of the people, he entered into Capernaum.

2 And a certain centurion's servant, who was dear unto him, was sick, and ready to die.

3 And when he heard of Jesus, he sent unto him the elders of the Jews, beseeching him that he would come and heal his servant.

4 And when they came to Jesus, they besought him instantly, saying, That he was worthy for whom he should do this:

5 For he loveth our nation, and he hath built us a synagogue.

6 Then Jesus went with them. And when he was now not far from the house, the centurion sent friends to him, saying unto him, Lord, trouble not thyself: for I am not worthy that thou shouldest enter under my roof:

7 Wherefore neither thought I myself
worthy to come unto thee: but say in a
word, and my servant shall be healed.
8 For I also am a man set under
authority, having under me soldiers,
and I say unto one, Go, and he goeth;
and to another, Come, and he cometh;
and to my servant, Do this, and he
doeth *it*.
9 When Jesus heard these things, he
marvelled at him, and turned him
about, and said unto the people that
followed him, I say unto you, I have not
found so great faith, no, not in Israel.
10 And they that were sent, returning
to the house, found the servant whole
that had been sick.
11 And it came to pass the day after,
that he went into a city called Nain;
and many of his disciples went with
him, and much people.
12 Now when he came nigh to the
gate of the city, behold, there was a
dead man carried out, the only son of
his mother, and she was a widow: and
much people of the city was with her.
13 And when the Lord saw her, he
had compassion on her, and said unto
her, Weep not.
14 And he came and touched the bier:
and they that bare *him* stood still. And
he said, Young man, I say unto thee,
Arise.
15 And he that was dead sat up, and
began to speak. And he delivered him
to his mother.
16 And there came a fear on all: and
they glorified God, saying, That a great
prophet is risen up among us; and, That
God hath visited his people.
17 And this rumour of him went forth
throughout all Judaea, and throughout
all the region round about.

18 And the disciples of John shewed
him of all these things.
19 And John calling *unto him* two of
his disciples sent *them* to Jesus, saying,
Art thou he that should come? or look
we for another?
20 When the men were come unto
him, they said, John Baptist hath sent
us unto thee, saying, Art thou he that
should come? or look we for another?
21 And in that same hour he cured
many of *their* infirmities and plagues,
and of evil spirits; and unto many *that*
were blind he gave sight.
22 Then Jesus answering said unto
them, Go your way, and tell John what
things ye have seen and heard; how
that the blind see, the lame walk, the
lepers are cleansed, the deaf hear, the
dead are raised, to the poor the gospel
is preached.
23 And blessed is *he*, whosoever shall
not be offended in me.
24 And when the messengers of John
were departed, he began to speak unto
the people concerning John, What went
ye out into the wilderness for to see? A
reed shaken with the wind?
25 But what went ye out for to see? A
man clothed in soft raiment? Behold,
they which are gorgeously apparelled,
and live delicately, are in kings' courts.
26 But what went ye out for to see? A
prophet? Yea, I say unto you, and much
more than a prophet.
27 This is *he*, of whom it is written,
Behold, I send my messenger before
thy face, which shall prepare thy way
before thee.
28 For I say unto you, Among those
that are born of women there is not a
greater prophet than John the Baptist:
but he that is least in the kingdom of
God is greater than he.

29 And all the people that heard *him*,
and the publicans, justified God, being
baptized with the baptism of John.
30 But the Pharisees and lawyers
rejected the counsel of God against
themselves, being not baptized of him.
31 And the Lord said, Whereunto
then shall I liken the men of this generation? and to what are they like?
32 They are like unto children sitting
in the marketplace, and calling one to
another, and saying, We have piped
unto you, and ye have not danced; we
have mourned to you, and ye have not
wept.
33 For John the Baptist came neither
eating bread nor drinking wine; and ye
say, He hath a devil.
34 The Son of man is come eating and
drinking; and ye say, Behold a gluttonous man, and a winebibber, a friend of
publicans and sinners!
35 But wisdom is justified of all her
children.
36 And one of the Pharisees desired
him that he would eat with him. And he
went into the Pharisee's house, and sat
down to meat.
37 And, behold, a woman in the city,
which was a sinner, when she knew that
Jesus sat at meat in the Pharisee's
house, brought an alabaster box of ointment,
38 And stood at his feet behind *him*
weeping, and began to wash his feet
with tears, and did wipe *them* with the
hairs of her head, and kissed his feet,
and anointed *them* with the ointment.
39 Now when the Pharisee which had
bidden him saw *it*, he spake within
himself, saying, This man, if he were a
prophet, would have known who and
what manner of woman *this is* that
toucheth him: for she is a sinner.

40 And Jesus answering said unto
him, Simon, I have somewhat to say
unto thee. And he saith, Master, say on.
41 There was a certain creditor which
had two debtors: the one owed five
hundred pence, and the other fifty.
42 And when they had nothing to pay,
he frankly forgave them both. Tell me
therefore, which of them will love him
most?
43 Simon answered and said, I suppose that *he*, to whom he forgave most.
And he said unto him, Thou hast rightly
judged.
44 And he turned to the woman, and
said unto Simon, Seest thou this
woman? I entered into thine house,
thou gavest me no water for my feet:
but she hath washed my feet with tears,
and wiped *them* with the hairs of her
head.
45 Thou gavest me no kiss: but this
woman since the time I came in hath
not ceased to kiss my feet.
46 My head with oil thou didst not
anoint: but this woman hath anointed
my feet with ointment.
47 Wherefore I say unto thee, Her
sins, which are many, are forgiven; for
she loved much: but to whom little is
forgiven, *the same* loveth little.
48 And he said unto her, Thy sins are
forgiven.
49 And they that sat at meat with him
began to say within themselves, Who is
this that forgiveth sins also?
50 And he said to the woman, Thy
faith hath saved thee; go in peace.

8 And it came to pass afterward, that
he went throughout every city and
village, preaching and shewing the glad
tidings of the kingdom of God: and the
twelve *were* with him,

2 And certain women, which had
been healed of evil spirits and infirmities, Mary called Magdalene, out of
whom went seven devils,
3 And Joanna the wife of Chuza
Herod's steward, and Susanna, and
many others, which ministered unto
him of their substance.
4 And when much people were gathered together, and were come to him
out of every city, he spake by a parable:
5 A sower went out to sow his seed:
and as he sowed, some fell by the way
side; and it was trodden down, and the
fowls of the air devoured it.
6 And some fell upon a rock; and as
soon as it was sprung up, it withered
away, because it lacked moisture.
7 And some fell among thorns; and
the thorns sprang up with it, and
choked it.
8 And other fell on good ground, and
sprang up, and bare fruit an hundredfold. And when he had said these
things, he cried, He that hath ears to
hear, let him hear.
9 And his disciples asked him, saying,
What might this parable be?
10 And he said, Unto you it is given to
know the mysteries of the kingdom of
God: but to others in parables; that seeing they might not see, and hearing
they might not understand.
11 Now the parable is this: The seed is
the word of God.
12 Those by the way side are they that
hear; then cometh the devil, and taketh
away the word out of their hearts, lest
they should believe and be saved.
13 They on the rock *are they*, which,
when they hear, receive the word with
joy; and these have no root, which for a
while believe, and in time of temptation fall away.
14 And that which fell among thorns
are they, which, when they have heard,
go forth, and are choked with cares and
riches and pleasures of *this* life, and
bring no fruit to perfection.
15 But that on the good ground are
they, which in an honest and good
heart, having heard the word, keep *it*,
and bring forth fruit with patience.
16 No man, when he hath lighted a
candle, covereth it with a vessel, or
putteth *it* under a bed; but setteth *it* on
a candlestick, that they which enter in
may see the light.
17 For nothing is secret, that shall not
be made manifest; neither *any thing*
hid, that shall not be known and come
abroad.
18 Take heed therefore how ye hear:
for whosoever hath, to him shall be
given; and whosoever hath not, from
him shall be taken even that which he
seemeth to have.
19 Then came to him *his* mother and
his brethren, and could not come at
him for the press.
20 And it was told him *by certain*
which said, Thy mother and thy brethren stand without, desiring to see thee.
21 And he answered and said unto
them, My mother and my brethren are
these which hear the word of God, and
do it.
22 Now it came to pass on a certain
day, that he went into a ship with his
disciples: and he said unto them, Let us
go over unto the other side of the lake.
And they launched forth.
23 But as they sailed he fell asleep:
and there came down a storm of wind
on the lake; and they were filled *with
water*, and were in jeopardy.
24 And they came to him, and awoke
him, saying, Master, master, we perish.

Then he arose, and rebuked the wind
and the raging of the water: and they
ceased, and there was a calm.
25 And he said unto them, Where is
your faith? And they being afraid wondered, saying one to another, What
manner of man is this! for he commandeth even the winds and water, and
they obey him.
26 And they arrived at the country of
the Gadarenes, which is over against
Galilee.
27 And when he went forth to land,
there met him out of the city a certain
man, which had devils long time, and
ware no clothes, neither abode in *any*
house, but in the tombs.
28 When he saw Jesus, he cried out,
and fell down before him, and with a
loud voice said, What have I to do with
thee, Jesus, *thou* Son of God most high?
I beseech thee, torment me not.
29 (For he had commanded the
unclean spirit to come out of the man.
For oftentimes it had caught him: and
he was kept bound with chains and in
fetters; and he brake the bands, and
was driven of the devil into the wilderness.)
30 And Jesus asked him, saying, What
is thy name? And he said, Legion:
because many devils were entered into
him.
31 And they besought him that he
would not command them to go out
into the deep.
32 And there was there an herd of
many swine feeding on the mountain:
and they besought him that he would
suffer them to enter into them. And he
suffered them.
33 Then went the devils out of the
man, and entered into the swine: and
the herd ran violently down a steep
place into the lake, and were choked.
34 When they that fed *them* saw what
was done, they fled, and went and told
it in the city and in the country.
35 Then they went out to see what
was done; and came to Jesus, and found
the man, out of whom the devils were
departed, sitting at the feet of Jesus,
clothed, and in his right mind: and they
were afraid.
36 They also which saw *it* told them
by what means he that was possessed
of the devils was healed.
37 Then the whole multitude of the
country of the Gadarenes round about
besought him to depart from them; for
they were taken with great fear: and he
went up into the ship, and returned
back again.
38 Now the man out of whom the
devils were departed besought him
that he might be with him: but Jesus
sent him away, saying,
39 Return to thine own house, and
shew how great things God hath done
unto thee. And he went his way, and
published throughout the whole city
how great things Jesus had done unto
him.
40 And it came to pass, that, when
Jesus was returned, the people *gladly*
received him: for they were all waiting
for him.
41 And, behold, there came a man
named Jairus, and he was a ruler of the
synagogue: and he fell down at Jesus'
feet, and besought him that he would
come into his house:
42 For he had one only daughter,
about twelve years of age, and she lay a
dying. But as he went the people
thronged him.

43 And a woman having an issue of
blood twelve years, which had spent all
her living upon physicians, neither
could be healed of any,
44 Came behind *him*, and touched
the border of his garment: and immediately her issue of blood stanched.
45 And Jesus said, Who touched me?
When all denied, Peter and they that
were with him said, Master, the multitude throng thee and press *thee*, and
sayest thou, Who touched me?
46 And Jesus said, Somebody hath
touched me: for I perceive that virtue is
gone out of me.
47 And when the woman saw that she
was not hid, she came trembling, and
falling down before him, she declared
unto him before all the people for what
cause she had touched him, and how
she was healed immediately.
48 And he said unto her, Daughter, be
of good comfort: thy faith hath made
thee whole; go in peace.
49 While he yet spake, there cometh
one from the ruler of the synagogue's
house, saying to him, Thy daughter is
dead; trouble not the Master.
50 But when Jesus heard *it*, he
answered him, saying, Fear not: believe
only, and she shall be made whole.
51 And when he came into the house,
he suffered no man to go in, save Peter,
and James, and John, and the father
and the mother of the maiden.
52 And all wept, and bewailed her:
but he said, Weep not; she is not dead,
but sleepeth.
53 And they laughed him to scorn,
knowing that she was dead.
54 And he put them all out, and took
her by the hand, and called, saying,
Maid, arise.
55 And her spirit came again, and she
arose straightway: and he commanded
to give her meat.
56 And her parents were astonished:
but he charged them that they should
tell no man what was done.

9 Then he called his twelve disciples
together, and gave them power and
authority over all devils, and to cure
diseases.
2 And he sent them to preach the
kingdom of God, and to heal the sick.
3 And he said unto them, Take nothing for *your* journey, neither staves, nor
scrip, neither bread, neither money;
neither have two coats apiece.
4 And whatsoever house ye enter
into, there abide, and thence depart.
5 And whosoever will not receive you,
when ye go out of that city, shake off
the very dust from your feet for a testimony against them.
6 And they departed, and went
through the towns, preaching the gospel, and healing every where.
7 Now Herod the tetrarch heard of all
that was done by him: and he was perplexed, because that it was said of
some, that John was risen from the
dead;
8 And of some, that Elias had appeared; and of others, that one of the
old prophets was risen again.
9 And Herod said, John have I
beheaded: but who is this, of whom I
hear such things? And he desired to see
him.
10 And the apostles, when they were
returned, told him all that they had
done. And he took them, and went
aside privately into a desert place
belonging to the city called Bethsaida.
11 And the people, when they knew
it, followed him: and he received them,

and spake unto them of the kingdom of God, and healed them that had need of healing.

12 And when the day began to wear away, then came the twelve, and said unto him, Send the multitude away, that they may go into the towns and country round about, and lodge, and get victuals: for we are here in a desert place.

13 But he said unto them, Give ye them to eat. And they said, We have no more but five loaves and two fishes; except we should go and buy meat for all this people.

14 For they were about five thousand men. And he said to his disciples, Make them sit down by fifties in a company.

15 And they did so, and made them all sit down.

16 Then he took the five loaves and the two fishes, and looking up to heaven, he blessed them, and brake, and gave to the disciples to set before the multitude.

17 And they did eat, and were all filled: and there was taken up of fragments that remained to them twelve baskets.

18 And it came to pass, as he was alone praying, his disciples were with him: and he asked them, saying, Whom say the people that I am?

19 They answering said, John the Baptist; but some *say*, Elias; and others *say*, that one of the old prophets is risen again.

20 He said unto them, But whom say ye that I am? Peter answering said, The Christ of God.

21 And he straitly charged them, and commanded *them* to tell no man that thing;

22 Saying, The Son of man must suffer many things, and be rejected of the elders and chief priests and scribes, and be slain, and be raised the third day.

23 And he said to *them* all, If any *man* will come after me, let him deny himself, and take up his cross daily, and follow me.

24 For whosoever will save his life shall lose it: but whosoever will lose his life for my sake, the same shall save it.

25 For what is a man advantaged, if he gain the whole world, and lose himself, or be cast away?

26 For whosoever shall be ashamed of me and of my words, of him shall the Son of man be ashamed, when he shall come in his own glory, and *in his* Father's, and of the holy angels.

27 But I tell you of a truth, there be some standing here, which shall not taste of death, till they see the kingdom of God.

28 And it came to pass about an eight days after these sayings, he took Peter and John and James, and went up into a mountain to pray.

29 And as he prayed, the fashion of his countenance was altered, and his raiment *was* white *and* glistering.

30 And, behold, there talked with him two men, which were Moses and Elias:

31 Who appeared in glory, and spake of his decease which he should accomplish at Jerusalem.

32 But Peter and they that were with him were heavy with sleep: and when they were awake, they saw his glory, and the two men that stood with him.

33 And it came to pass, as they departed from him, Peter said unto Jesus, Master, it is good for us to be here: and let us make three taberna-

cles; one for thee, and one for Moses, and one for Elias: not knowing what he said.

34 While he thus spake, there came a cloud, and overshadowed them: and they feared as they entered into the cloud.

35 And there came a voice out of the cloud, saying, This is my beloved Son: hear him.

36 And when the voice was past, Jesus was found alone. And they kept *it* close, and told no man in those days any of those things which they had seen.

37 And it came to pass, that on the next day, when they were come down from the hill, much people met him.

38 And, behold, a man of the company cried out, saying, Master, I beseech thee, look upon my son: for he is mine only child.

39 And, lo, a spirit taketh him, and he suddenly crieth out; and it teareth him that he foameth again, and bruising him hardly departeth from him.

40 And I besought thy disciples to cast him out; and they could not.

41 And Jesus answering said, O faithless and perverse generation, how long shall I be with you, and suffer you? Bring thy son hither.

42 And as he was yet a coming, the devil threw him down, and tare *him*. And Jesus rebuked the unclean spirit, and healed the child, and delivered him again to his father.

43 And they were all amazed at the mighty power of God. But while they wondered every one at all things which Jesus did, he said unto his disciples,

44 Let these sayings sink down into your ears: for the Son of man shall be delivered into the hands of men.

45 But they understood not this saying, and it was hid from them, that they perceived it not: and they feared to ask him of that saying.

46 Then there arose a reasoning among them, which of them should be greatest.

47 And Jesus, perceiving the thought of their heart, took a child, and set him by him,

48 And said unto them, Whosoever shall receive this child in my name receiveth me: and whosoever shall receive me receiveth him that sent me: for he that is least among you all, the same shall be great.

49 And John answered and said, Master, we saw one casting out devils in thy name; and we forbad him, because he followeth not with us.

50 And Jesus said unto him, Forbid *him* not: for he that is not against us is for us.

51 And it came to pass, when the time was come that he should be received up, he stedfastly set his face to go to Jerusalem,

52 And sent messengers before his face: and they went, and entered into a village of the Samaritans, to make ready for him.

53 And they did not receive him, because his face was as though he would go to Jerusalem.

54 And when his disciples James and John saw *this*, they said, Lord, wilt thou that we command fire to come down from heaven, and consume them, even as Elias did?

55 But he turned, and rebuked them, and said, Ye know not what manner of spirit ye are of.

56 For the Son of man is not come to
destroy men's lives, but to save *them*.
And they went to another village.
57 And it came to pass, that, as they
went in the way, a certain *man* said
unto him, Lord, I will follow thee whithersoever thou goest.
58 And Jesus said unto him, Foxes
have holes, and birds of the air *have*
nests; but the Son of man hath not
where to lay *his* head.
59 And he said unto another, Follow
me. But he said, Lord, suffer me first to
go and bury my father.
60 Jesus said unto him, Let the dead
bury their dead: but go thou and preach
the kingdom of God.
61 And another also said, Lord, I will
follow thee; but let me first go bid them
farewell, which are at home at my
house.
62 And Jesus said unto him, No man,
having put his hand to the plough, and
looking back, is fit for the kingdom of
God.

10 After these things the Lord
appointed other seventy also,
and sent them two and two before his
face into every city and place, whither
he himself would come.
2 Therefore said he unto them, The
harvest truly *is* great, but the labourers
are few: pray ye therefore the Lord of
the harvest, that he would send forth
labourers into his harvest.
3 Go your ways: behold, I send you
forth as lambs among wolves.
4 Carry neither purse, nor scrip, nor
shoes: and salute no man by the way.
5 And into whatsoever house ye enter,
first say, Peace *be* to this house.
6 And if the son of peace be there,
your peace shall rest upon it: if not, it
shall turn to you again.
7 And in the same house remain, eating and drinking such things as they
give: for the labourer is worthy of his
hire. Go not from house to house.
8 And into whatsoever city ye enter,
and they receive you, eat such things as
are set before you:
9 And heal the sick that are therein,
and say unto them, The kingdom of God
is come nigh unto you.
10 But into whatsoever city ye enter,
and they receive you not, go your ways
out into the streets of the same, and say,
11 Even the very dust of your city,
which cleaveth on us, we do wipe off
against you: notwithstanding be ye sure
of this, that the kingdom of God is come
nigh unto you.
12 But I say unto you, that it shall be
more tolerable in that day for Sodom,
than for that city.
13 Woe unto thee, Chorazin! woe unto
thee, Bethsaida! for if the mighty works
had been done in Tyre and Sidon, which
have been done in you, they had a great
while ago repented, sitting in sackcloth
and ashes.
14 But it shall be more tolerable for
Tyre and Sidon at the judgment, than
for you.
15 And thou, Capernaum, which art
exalted to heaven, shalt be thrust down
to hell.
16 He that heareth you heareth me;
and he that despiseth you despiseth
me; and he that despiseth me despiseth
him that sent me.
17 And the seventy returned again
with joy, saying, Lord, even the devils
are subject unto us through thy name.
18 And he said unto them, I beheld
Satan as lightning fall from heaven.
19 Behold, I give unto you power to
tread on serpents and scorpions, and

over all the power of the enemy: and
nothing shall by any means hurt you.
20 Notwithstanding in this rejoice
not, that the spirits are subject unto
you; but rather rejoice, because your
names are written in heaven.
21 In that hour Jesus rejoiced in spirit, and said, I thank thee, O Father, Lord
of heaven and earth, that thou hast hid
these things from the wise and prudent, and hast revealed them unto
babes: even so, Father; for so it seemed
good in thy sight.
22 All things are delivered to me of
my Father: and no man knoweth who
the Son is, but the Father; and who the
Father is, but the Son, and *he* to whom
the Son will reveal *him*.
23 And he turned him unto *his* disciples, and said privately, Blessed *are* the
eyes which see the things that ye see:
24 For I tell you, that many prophets
and kings have desired to see those
things which ye see, and have not seen
them; and to hear those things which
ye hear, and have not heard *them*.
25 And, behold, a certain lawyer
stood up, and tempted him, saying,
Master, what shall I do to inherit eternal life?
26 He said unto him, What is written
in the law? how readest thou?
27 And he answering said, Thou shalt
love the Lord thy God with all thy
heart, and with all thy soul, and with all
thy strength, and with all thy mind; and
thy neighbour as thyself.
28 And he said unto him, Thou hast
answered right: this do, and thou shalt
live.
29 But he, willing to justify himself,
said unto Jesus, And who is my neighbour?
30 And Jesus answering said, A certain *man* went down from Jerusalem to
Jericho, and fell among thieves, which
stripped him of his raiment, and
wounded *him*, and departed, leaving
him half dead.
31 And by chance there came down a
certain priest that way: and when he
saw him, he passed by on the other
side.
32 And likewise a Levite, when he
was at the place, came and looked *on
him*, and passed by on the other side.
33 But a certain Samaritan, as he
journeyed, came where he was: and
when he saw him, he had compassion
on him,
34 And went to *him*, and bound up
his wounds, pouring in oil and wine,
and set him on his own beast, and
brought him to an inn, and took care of
him.
35 And on the morrow when he
departed, he took out two pence, and
gave *them* to the host, and said unto
him, Take care of him; and whatsoever
thou spendest more, when I come
again, I will repay thee.
36 Which now of these three, thinkest
thou, was neighbour unto him that fell
among the thieves?
37 And he said, He that shewed
mercy on him. Then said Jesus unto
him, Go, and do thou likewise.
38 Now it came to pass, as they went,
that he entered into a certain village:
and a certain woman named Martha
received him into her house.
39 And she had a sister called Mary,
which also sat at Jesus' feet, and heard
his word.
40 But Martha was cumbered about
much serving, and came to him, and
said, Lord, dost thou not care that my

sister hath left me to serve alone? bid
her therefore that she help me.
41 And Jesus answered and said unto
her, Martha, Martha, thou art careful
and troubled about many things:
42 But one thing is needful: and Mary
hath chosen that good part, which shall
not be taken away from her.

11 And it came to pass, that, as he
was praying in a certain place,
when he ceased, one of his disciples
said unto him, Lord, teach us to pray, as
John also taught his disciples.
2 And he said unto them, When ye
pray, say, Our Father which art in heav-
en, Hallowed be thy name. Thy kingdom come. Thy will be done, as in
heaven, so in earth.
3 Give us day by day our daily bread.
4 And forgive us our sins; for we also
forgive every one that is indebted to us.
And lead us not into temptation; but
deliver us from evil.
5 And he said unto them, Which of
you shall have a friend, and shall go
unto him at midnight, and say unto
him, Friend, lend me three loaves;
6 For a friend of mine in his journey
is come to me, and I have nothing to set
before him?
7 And he from within shall answer
and say, Trouble me not: the door is now
shut, and my children are with me in
bed; I cannot rise and give thee.
8 I say unto you, Though he will not
rise and give him, because he is his
friend, yet because of his importunity
he will rise and give him as many as he
needeth.
9 And I say unto you, Ask, and it shall
be given you; seek, and ye shall find;
knock, and it shall be opened unto you.
10 For every one that asketh
receiveth; and he that seeketh findeth;
and to him that knocketh it shall be
opened.
11 If a son shall ask bread of any of
you that is a father, will he give him a
stone? or if *he ask* a fish, will he for a
fish give him a serpent?
12 Or if he shall ask an egg, will he
offer him a scorpion?
13 If ye then, being evil, know how to
give good gifts unto your children: how
much more shall *your* heavenly Father
give the Holy Spirit to them that ask
him?
14 And he was casting out a devil, and
it was dumb. And it came to pass, when
the devil was gone out, the dumb
spake; and the people wondered.
15 But some of them said, He casteth
out devils through Beelzebub the chief
of the devils.
16 And others, tempting *him*, sought
of him a sign from heaven.
17 But he, knowing their thoughts,
said unto them, Every kingdom divided
against itself is brought to desolation;
and a house *divided* against a house
falleth.
18 If Satan also be divided against
himself, how shall his kingdom stand?
because ye say that I cast out devils
through Beelzebub.
19 And if I by Beelzebub cast out
devils, by whom do your sons cast *them*
out? therefore shall they be your judges.
20 But if I with the finger of God cast
out devils, no doubt the kingdom of
God is come upon you.
21 When a strong man armed keepeth his palace, his goods are in peace:
22 But when a stronger than he shall
come upon him, and overcome him, he
taketh from him all his armour wherein
he trusted, and divideth his spoils.

23 He that is not with me is against
me: and he that gathereth not with me
scattereth.
24 When the unclean spirit is gone
out of a man, he walketh through dry
places, seeking rest; and finding none,
he saith, I will return unto my house
whence I came out.
25 And when he cometh, he findeth *it*
swept and garnished.
26 Then goeth he, and taketh *to him*
seven other spirits more wicked than
himself; and they enter in, and dwell
there: and the last *state* of that man is
worse than the first.
27 And it came to pass, as he spake
these things, a certain woman of the
company lifted up her voice, and said
unto him, Blessed *is* the womb that
bare thee, and the paps which thou
hast sucked.
28 But he said, Yea rather, blessed *are*
they that hear the word of God, and
keep it.
29 And when the people were gathered thick together, he began to say,
This is an evil generation: they seek a
sign; and there shall no sign be given it,
but the sign of Jonas the prophet.
30 For as Jonas was a sign unto the
Ninevites, so shall also the Son of man
be to this generation.
31 The queen of the south shall rise
up in the judgment with the men of
this generation, and condemn them: for
she came from the utmost parts of the
earth to hear the wisdom of Solomon;
and, behold, a greater than Solomon *is*
here.
32 The men of Nineve shall rise up in
the judgment with this generation, and
shall condemn it: for they repented at
the preaching of Jonas; and, behold, a
greater than Jonas *is* here.
33 No man, when he hath lighted a
candle, putteth *it* in a secret place,
neither under a bushel, but on a candlestick, that they which come in may
see the light.
34 The light of the body is the eye:
therefore when thine eye is single, thy
whole body also is full of light; but
when *thine eye* is evil, thy body also *is*
full of darkness.
35 Take heed therefore that the light
which is in thee be not darkness.
36 If thy whole body therefore *be* full
of light, having no part dark, the whole
shall be full of light, as when the bright
shining of a candle doth give thee light.
37 And as he spake, a certain Pharisee
besought him to dine with him: and he
went in, and sat down to meat.
38 And when the Pharisee saw *it*, he
marvelled that he had not first washed
before dinner.
39 And the Lord said unto him, Now
do ye Pharisees make clean the outside
of the cup and the platter; but your
inward part is full of ravening and wickedness.
40 *Ye* fools, did not he that made that
which is without make that which is
within also?
41 But rather give alms of such things
as ye have; and, behold, all things are
clean unto you.
42 But woe unto you, Pharisees! for ye
tithe mint and rue and all manner of
herbs, and pass over judgment and the
love of God: these ought ye to have
done, and not to leave the other undone.
43 Woe unto you, Pharisees! for ye
love the uppermost seats in the synagogues, and greetings in the markets.

44 Woe unto you, scribes and Pharisees, hypocrites! for ye are as graves which appear not, and the men that walk over *them* are not aware *of them*.

45 Then answered one of the lawyers, and said unto him, Master, thus saying thou reproachest us also.

46 And he said, Woe unto you also, *ye* lawyers! for ye lade men with burdens grievous to be borne, and ye yourselves touch not the burdens with one of your fingers.

47 Woe unto you! for ye build the sepulchres of the prophets, and your fathers killed them.

48 Truly ye bear witness that ye allow the deeds of your fathers: for they indeed killed them, and ye build their sepulchres.

49 Therefore also said the wisdom of God, I will send them prophets and apostles, and *some* of them they shall slay and persecute:

50 That the blood of all the prophets, which was shed from the foundation of the world, may be required of this generation;

51 From the blood of Abel unto the blood of Zacharias, which perished between the altar and the temple: verily I say unto you, It shall be required of this generation.

52 Woe unto you, lawyers! for ye have taken away the key of knowledge: ye entered not in yourselves, and them that were entering in ye hindered.

53 And as he said these things unto them, the scribes and the Pharisees began to urge *him* vehemently, and to provoke him to speak of many things:

54 Laying wait for him, and seeking to catch something out of his mouth, that they might accuse him.

12

In the mean time, when there were gathered together an innumerable multitude of people, insomuch that they trode one upon another, he began to say unto his disciples first of all, Beware ye of the leaven of the Pharisees, which is hypocrisy.

2 For there is nothing covered, that shall not be revealed; neither hid, that shall not be known.

3 Therefore whatsoever ye have spoken in darkness shall be heard in the light; and that which ye have spoken in the ear in closets shall be proclaimed upon the housetops.

4 And I say unto you my friends, Be not afraid of them that kill the body, and after that have no more that they can do.

5 But I will forewarn you whom ye shall fear: Fear him, which after he hath killed hath power to cast into hell; yea, I say unto you, Fear him.

6 Are not five sparrows sold for two farthings, and not one of them is forgotten before God?

7 But even the very hairs of your head are all numbered. Fear not therefore: ye are of more value than many sparrows.

8 Also I say unto you, Whosoever shall confess me before men, him shall the Son of man also confess before the angels of God:

9 But he that denieth me before men shall be denied before the angels of God.

10 And whosoever shall speak a word against the Son of man, it shall be forgiven him: but unto him that blasphemeth against the Holy Ghost it shall not be forgiven.

11 And when they bring you unto the synagogues, and *unto* magistrates, and

powers, take ye no thought how or what
thing ye shall answer, or what ye shall
say:
12 For the Holy Ghost shall teach you
in the same hour what ye ought to say.
13 And one of the company said unto
him, Master, speak to my brother, that
he divide the inheritance with me.
14 And he said unto him, Man, who
made me a judge or a divider over you?
15 And he said unto them, Take heed,
and beware of covetousness: for a man's
life consisteth not in the abundance of
the things which he possesseth.
16 And he spake a parable unto them,
saying, The ground of a certain rich
man brought forth plentifully:
17 And he thought within himself,
saying, What shall I do, because I have
no room where to bestow my fruits?
18 And he said, This will I do: I will
pull down my barns, and build greater;
and there will I bestow all my fruits and
my goods.
19 And I will say to my soul, Soul,
thou hast much goods laid up for many
years; take thine ease, eat, drink, *and*
be merry.
20 But God said unto him, *Thou* fool,
this night thy soul shall be required of
thee: then whose shall those things be,
which thou hast provided?
21 So *is* he that layeth up treasure for
himself, and is not rich toward God.
22 And he said unto his disciples,
Therefore I say unto you, Take no
thought for your life, what ye shall eat;
neither for the body, what ye shall put
on.
23 The life is more than meat, and the
body *is more* than raiment.
24 Consider the ravens: for they neither sow nor reap; which neither have
storehouse nor barn; and God feedeth
them: how much more are ye better
than the fowls?
25 And which of you with taking
thought can add to his stature one
cubit?
26 If ye then be not able to do that
thing which is least, why take ye
thought for the rest?
27 Consider the lilies how they grow:
they toil not, they spin not; and yet I say
unto you, that Solomon in all his glory
was not arrayed like one of these.
28 If then God so clothe the grass,
which is to day in the field, and to morrow is cast into the oven; how much
more *will he clothe* you, O ye of little
faith?
29 And seek not ye what ye shall eat,
or what ye shall drink, neither be ye of
doubtful mind.
30 For all these things do the nations
of the world seek after: and your Father
knoweth that ye have need of these
things.
31 But rather seek ye the kingdom of
God; and all these things shall be
added unto you.
32 Fear not, little flock; for it is your
Father's good pleasure to give you the
kingdom.
33 Sell that ye have, and give alms;
provide yourselves bags which wax not
old, a treasure in the heavens that faileth not, where no thief approacheth,
neither moth corrupteth.
34 For where your treasure is, there
will your heart be also.
35 Let your loins be girded about, and
your lights burning;
36 And ye yourselves like unto men
that wait for their lord, when he will
return from the wedding; that when he
cometh and knocketh, they may open
unto him immediately.

37 Blessed *are* those servants, whom the lord when he cometh shall find watching: verily I say unto you, that he shall gird himself, and make them to sit down to meat, and will come forth and serve them.
38 And if he shall come in the second watch, or come in the third watch, and find *them* so, blessed are those servants.
39 And this know, that if the goodman of the house had known what hour the thief would come, he would have watched, and not have suffered his house to be broken through.
40 Be ye therefore ready also: for the Son of man cometh at an hour when ye think not.
41 Then Peter said unto him, Lord, speakest thou this parable unto us, or even to all?
42 And the Lord said, Who then is that faithful and wise steward, whom *his* lord shall make ruler over his household, to give *them their* portion of meat in due season?
43 Blessed *is* that servant, whom his lord when he cometh shall find so doing.
44 Of a truth I say unto you, that he will make him ruler over all that he hath.
45 But and if that servant say in his heart, My lord delayeth his coming; and shall begin to beat the menservants and maidens, and to eat and drink, and to be drunken;
46 The lord of that servant will come in a day when he looketh not for *him*, and at an hour when he is not aware, and will cut him in sunder, and will appoint him his portion with the unbelievers.
47 And that servant, which knew his lord's will, and prepared not *himself*, neither did according to his will, shall be beaten with many *stripes*.
48 But he that knew not, and did commit things worthy of stripes, shall be beaten with few *stripes*. For unto whomsoever much is given, of him shall be much required: and to whom men have committed much, of him they will ask the more.
49 I am come to send fire on the earth; and what will I, if it be already kindled?
50 But I have a baptism to be baptized with; and how am I straitened till it be accomplished!
51 Suppose ye that I am come to give peace on earth? I tell you, Nay; but rather division:
52 For from henceforth there shall be five in one house divided, three against two, and two against three.
53 The father shall be divided against the son, and the son against the father; the mother against the daughter, and the daughter against the mother; the mother in law against her daughter in law, and the daughter in law against her mother in law.
54 And he said also to the people, When ye see a cloud rise out of the west, straightway ye say, There cometh a shower; and so it is.
55 And when *ye see* the south wind blow, ye say, There will be heat; and it cometh to pass.
56 Ye hypocrites, ye can discern the face of the sky and of the earth; but how is it that ye do not discern this time?
57 Yea, and why even of yourselves judge ye not what is right?

58 When thou goest with thine adversary to the magistrate, *as thou art* in
the way, give diligence that thou mayest be delivered from him; lest he hale
thee to the judge, and the judge deliver
thee to the officer, and the officer cast
thee into prison.
59 I tell thee, thou shalt not depart
thence, till thou hast paid the very last
mite.

13

13 There were present at that season some that told him of the
Galilaeans, whose blood Pilate had
mingled with their sacrifices.
2 And Jesus answering said unto
them, Suppose ye that these Galilaeans
were sinners above all the Galilaeans,
because they suffered such things?
3 I tell you, Nay: but, except ye repent,
ye shall all likewise perish.
4 Or those eighteen, upon whom the
tower in Siloam fell, and slew them,
think ye that they were sinners above
all men that dwelt in Jerusalem?
5 I tell you, Nay: but, except ye repent,
ye shall all likewise perish.
6 He spake also this parable; A certain *man* had a fig tree planted in his
vineyard; and he came and sought fruit
thereon, and found none.
7 Then said he unto the dresser of his
vineyard, Behold, these three years I
come seeking fruit on this fig tree, and
find none: cut it down; why cumbereth
it the ground?
8 And he answering said unto him,
Lord, let it alone this year also, till I
shall dig about it, and dung *it*:
9 And if it bear fruit, *well*: and if not,
then after that thou shalt cut it down.
10 And he was teaching in one of the
synagogues on the sabbath.
11 And, behold, there was a woman
which had a spirit of infirmity eighteen
years, and was bowed together, and
could in no wise lift up *herself*.
12 And when Jesus saw her, he called
her to him, and said unto her, Woman,
thou art loosed from thine infirmity.
13 And he laid *his* hands on her: and
immediately she was made straight,
and glorified God.
14 And the ruler of the synagogue
answered with indignation, because
that Jesus had healed on the sabbath
day, and said unto the people, There are
six days in which men ought to work: in
them therefore come and be healed,
and not on the sabbath day.
15 The Lord then answered him, and
said, *Thou* hypocrite, doth not each one
of you on the sabbath loose his ox or *his*
ass from the stall, and lead *him* away to
watering?
16 And ought not this woman, being a
daughter of Abraham, whom Satan
hath bound, lo, these eighteen years, be
loosed from this bond on the sabbath
day?
17 And when he had said these
things, all his adversaries were
ashamed: and all the people rejoiced
for all the glorious things that were
done by him.
18 Then said he, Unto what is the
kingdom of God like? and whereunto
shall I resemble it?
19 It is like a grain of mustard seed,
which a man took, and cast into his
garden; and it grew, and waxed a great
tree; and the fowls of the air lodged in
the branches of it.
20 And again he said, Whereunto
shall I liken the kingdom of God?
21 It is like leaven, which a woman
took and hid in three measures of meal,
till the whole was leavened.

22 And he went through the cities
and villages, teaching, and journeying
toward Jerusalem.
23 Then said one unto him, Lord, are
there few that be saved? And he said
unto them,
24 Strive to enter in at the strait gate:
for many, I say unto you, will seek to
enter in, and shall not be able.
25 When once the master of the
house is risen up, and hath shut to the
door, and ye begin to stand without,
and to knock at the door, saying, Lord,
Lord, open unto us; and he shall answer
and say unto you, I know you not
whence ye are:
26 Then shall ye begin to say, We have
eaten and drunk in thy presence, and
thou hast taught in our streets.
27 But he shall say, I tell you, I know
you not whence ye are; depart from me,
all *ye* workers of iniquity.
28 There shall be weeping and gnashing of teeth, when ye shall see Abraham,
and Isaac, and Jacob, and all the prophets, in the kingdom of God, and you
yourselves thrust out.
29 And they shall come from the east,
and *from* the west, and from the north,
and *from* the south, and shall sit down
in the kingdom of God.
30 And, behold, there are last which
shall be first, and there are first which
shall be last.
31 The same day there came certain
of the Pharisees, saying unto him, Get
thee out, and depart hence: for Herod
will kill thee.
32 And he said unto them, Go ye, and
tell that fox, Behold, I cast out devils,
and I do cures to day and to morrow,
and the third *day* I shall be perfected.
33 Nevertheless I must walk to day,
and to morrow, and the *day* following:
for it cannot be that a prophet perish
out of Jerusalem.
34 O Jerusalem, Jerusalem, which
killest the prophets, and stonest them
that are sent unto thee; how often
would I have gathered thy children
together, as a hen *doth gather* her
brood under *her* wings, and ye would
not!
35 Behold, your house is left unto you
desolate: and verily I say unto you, Ye
shall not see me, until *the time* come
when ye shall say, Blessed *is* he that
cometh in the name of the Lord.

14 And it came to pass, as he went
into the house of one of the chief
Pharisees to eat bread on the sabbath
day, that they watched him.
2 And, behold, there was a certain
man before him which had the dropsy.
3 And Jesus answering spake unto
the lawyers and Pharisees, saying, Is it
lawful to heal on the sabbath day?
4 And they held their peace. And he
took *him*, and healed him, and let him
go;
5 And answered them, saying, Which
of you shall have an ass or an ox fallen
into a pit, and will not straightway pull
him out on the sabbath day?
6 And they could not answer him
again to these things.
7 And he put forth a parable to those
which were bidden, when he marked
how they chose out the chief rooms;
saying unto them,
8 When thou art bidden of any *man*
to a wedding, sit not down in the highest room; lest a more honourable man
than thou be bidden of him;
9 And he that bade thee and him
come and say to thee, Give this man
place; and thou begin with shame to
take the lowest room.

10 But when thou art bidden, go and
sit down in the lowest room; that when
he that bade thee cometh, he may say
unto thee, Friend, go up higher: then
shalt thou have worship in the presence
of them that sit at meat with thee.
11 For whosoever exalteth himself
shall be abased; and he that humbleth
himself shall be exalted.
12 Then said he also to him that bade
him, When thou makest a dinner or a
supper, call not thy friends, nor thy
brethren, neither thy kinsmen, nor *thy*
rich neighbours; lest they also bid thee
again, and a recompence be made thee.
13 But when thou makest a feast, call
the poor, the maimed, the lame, the
blind:
14 And thou shalt be blessed; for they
cannot recompense thee: for thou shalt
be recompensed at the resurrection of
the just.
15 And when one of them that sat at
meat with him heard these things, he
said unto him, Blessed *is* he that shall
eat bread in the kingdom of God.
16 Then said he unto him, A certain
man made a great supper, and bade
many:
17 And sent his servant at supper
time to say to them that were bidden,
Come; for all things are now ready.
18 And they all with one *consent*
began to make excuse. The first said
unto him, I have bought a piece of
ground, and I must needs go and see it:
I pray thee have me excused.
19 And another said, I have bought
five yoke of oxen, and I go to prove
them: I pray thee have me excused.
20 And another said, I have married a
wife, and therefore I cannot come.
21 So that servant came, and shewed
his lord these things. Then the master
of the house being angry said to his
servant, Go out quickly into the streets
and lanes of the city, and bring in hither the poor, and the maimed, and the
halt, and the blind.
22 And the servant said, Lord, it is
done as thou hast commanded, and yet
there is room.
23 And the lord said unto the servant,
Go out into the highways and hedges,
and compel *them* to come in, that my
house may be filled.
24 For I say unto you, That none of
those men which were bidden shall
taste of my supper.
25 And there went great multitudes
with him: and he turned, and said unto
them,
26 If any *man* come to me, and hate
not his father, and mother, and wife,
and children, and brethren, and sisters,
yea, and his own life also, he cannot be
my disciple.
27 And whosoever doth not bear his
cross, and come after me, cannot be my
disciple.
28 For which of you, intending to
build a tower, sitteth not down first, and
counteth the cost, whether he have *sufficient* to finish *it*?
29 Lest haply, after he hath laid the
foundation, and is not able to finish *it*,
all that behold *it* begin to mock him,
30 Saying, This man began to build,
and was not able to finish.
31 Or what king, going to make war
against another king, sitteth not down
first, and consulteth whether he be
able with ten thousand to meet him
that cometh against him with twenty
thousand?
32 Or else, while the other is yet a
great way off, he sendeth an ambassage, and desireth conditions of peace.

33 So likewise, whosoever he be of you that forsaketh not all that he hath, he cannot be my disciple.

34 Salt *is* good: but if the salt have lost his savour, wherewith shall it be seasoned?

35 It is neither fit for the land, nor yet for the dunghill; *but* men cast it out. He that hath ears to hear, let him hear.

15

Then drew near unto him all the publicans and sinners for to hear him.

2 And the Pharisees and scribes murmured, saying, This man receiveth sinners, and eateth with them.

3 And he spake this parable unto them, saying,

4 What man of you, having an hundred sheep, if he lose one of them, doth not leave the ninety and nine in the wilderness, and go after that which is lost, until he find it?

5 And when he hath found *it*, he layeth *it* on his shoulders, rejoicing.

6 And when he cometh home, he calleth together *his* friends and neighbours, saying unto them, Rejoice with me; for I have found my sheep which was lost.

7 I say unto you, that likewise joy shall be in heaven over one sinner that repenteth, more than over ninety and nine just persons, which need no repentance.

8 Either what woman having ten pieces of silver, if she lose one piece, doth not light a candle, and sweep the house, and seek diligently till she find *it*?

9 And when she hath found *it*, she calleth *her* friends and *her* neighbours together, saying, Rejoice with me; for I have found the piece which I had lost.

10 Likewise, I say unto you, there is joy in the presence of the angels of God over one sinner that repenteth.

11 And he said, A certain man had two sons:

12 And the younger of them said to *his* father, Father, give me the portion of goods that falleth *to me*. And he divided unto them *his* living.

13 And not many days after the younger son gathered all together, and took his journey into a far country, and there wasted his substance with riotous living.

14 And when he had spent all, there arose a mighty famine in that land; and he began to be in want.

15 And he went and joined himself to a citizen of that country; and he sent him into his fields to feed swine.

16 And he would fain have filled his belly with the husks that the swine did eat: and no man gave unto him.

17 And when he came to himself, he said, How many hired servants of my father's have bread enough and to spare, and I perish with hunger!

18 I will arise and go to my father, and will say unto him, Father, I have sinned against heaven, and before thee,

19 And am no more worthy to be called thy son: make me as one of thy hired servants.

20 And he arose, and came to his father. But when he was yet a great way off, his father saw him, and had compassion, and ran, and fell on his neck, and kissed him.

21 And the son said unto him, Father, I have sinned against heaven, and in thy sight, and am no more worthy to be called thy son.

22 But the father said to his servants, Bring forth the best robe, and put *it* on him; and put a ring on his hand, and shoes on *his* feet:

23 And bring hither the fatted calf, and kill *it*; and let us eat, and be merry:

24 For this my son was dead, and is alive again; he was lost, and is found. And they began to be merry.

25 Now his elder son was in the field: and as he came and drew nigh to the house, he heard musick and dancing.

26 And he called one of the servants, and asked what these things meant.

27 And he said unto him, Thy brother is come; and thy father hath killed the fatted calf, because he hath received him safe and sound.

28 And he was angry, and would not go in: therefore came his father out, and intreated him.

29 And he answering said to *his* father, Lo, these many years do I serve thee, neither transgressed I at any time thy commandment: and yet thou never gavest me a kid, that I might make merry with my friends:

30 But as soon as this thy son was come, which hath devoured thy living with harlots, thou hast killed for him the fatted calf.

31 And he said unto him, Son, thou art ever with me, and all that I have is thine.

32 It was meet that we should make merry, and be glad: for this thy brother was dead, and is alive again; and was lost, and is found.

16 And he said also unto his disciples, There was a certain rich man, which had a steward; and the same was accused unto him that he had wasted his goods.

2 And he called him, and said unto him, How is it that I hear this of thee? give an account of thy stewardship; for thou mayest be no longer steward.

3 Then the steward said within himself, What shall I do? for my lord taketh away from me the stewardship: I cannot dig; to beg I am ashamed.

4 I am resolved what to do, that, when I am put out of the stewardship, they may receive me into their houses.

5 So he called every one of his lord's debtors *unto him*, and said unto the first, How much owest thou unto my lord?

6 And he said, An hundred measures of oil. And he said unto him, Take thy bill, and sit down quickly, and write fifty.

7 Then said he to another, And how much owest thou? And he said, An hundred measures of wheat. And he said unto him, Take thy bill, and write fourscore.

8 And the lord commended the unjust steward, because he had done wisely: for the children of this world are in their generation wiser than the children of light.

9 And I say unto you, Make to yourselves friends of the mammon of unrighteousness; that, when ye fail, they may receive you into everlasting habitations.

10 He that is faithful in that which is least is faithful also in much: and he that is unjust in the least is unjust also in much.

11 If therefore ye have not been faithful in the unrighteous mammon, who will commit to your trust the true *riches*?

12 And if ye have not been faithful in that which is another man's, who shall give you that which is your own?

13 No servant can serve two masters:
for either he will hate the one, and love
the other; or else he will hold to the
one, and despise the other. Ye cannot
serve God and mammon.
14 And the Pharisees also, who were
covetous, heard all these things: and
they derided him.
15 And he said unto them, Ye are they
which justify yourselves before men;
but God knoweth your hearts: for that
which is highly esteemed among men is
abomination in the sight of God.
16 The law and the prophets *were*
until John: since that time the kingdom
of God is preached, and every man
presseth into it.
17 And it is easier for heaven and
earth to pass, than one tittle of the law
to fail.
18 Whosoever putteth away his wife,
and marrieth another, committeth
adultery: and whosoever marrieth her
that is put away from *her* husband committeth adultery.
19 There was a certain rich man,
which was clothed in purple and fine
linen, and fared sumptuously every
day:
20 And there was a certain beggar
named Lazarus, which was laid at his
gate, full of sores,
21 And desiring to be fed with the
crumbs which fell from the rich man's
table: moreover the dogs came and
licked his sores.
22 And it came to pass, that the beggar died, and was carried by the angels
into Abraham's bosom: the rich man
also died, and was buried;
23 And in hell he lift up his eyes,
being in torments, and seeth Abraham
afar off, and Lazarus in his bosom.
24 And he cried and said, Father
Abraham, have mercy on me, and send
Lazarus, that he may dip the tip of his
finger in water, and cool my tongue; for
I am tormented in this flame.
25 But Abraham said, Son, remember
that thou in thy lifetime receivedst thy
good things, and likewise Lazarus evil
things: but now he is comforted, and
thou art tormented.
26 And beside all this, between us
and you there is a great gulf fixed: so
that they which would pass from hence
to you cannot; neither can they pass to
us, that *would come* from thence.
27 Then he said, I pray thee therefore,
father, that thou wouldest send him to
my father's house:
28 For I have five brethren; that he
may testify unto them, lest they also
come into this place of torment.
29 Abraham saith unto him, They
have Moses and the prophets; let them
hear them.
30 And he said, Nay, father Abraham:
but if one went unto them from the
dead, they will repent.
31 And he said unto him, If they hear
not Moses and the prophets, neither
will they be persuaded, though one
rose from the dead.

17 Then said he unto the disciples,
It is impossible but that offences
will come: but woe *unto him*, through
whom they come!
2 It were better for him that a millstone were hanged about his neck, and
he cast into the sea, than that he should
offend one of these little ones.
3 Take heed to yourselves: If thy
brother trespass against thee, rebuke
him; and if he repent, forgive him.
4 And if he trespass against thee
seven times in a day, and seven times in

a day turn again to thee, saying, I repent; thou shalt forgive him.

5 And the apostles said unto the Lord, Increase our faith.

6 And the Lord said, If ye had faith as a grain of mustard seed, ye might say unto this sycamine tree, Be thou plucked up by the root, and be thou planted in the sea; and it should obey you.

7 But which of you, having a servant plowing or feeding cattle, will say unto him by and by, when he is come from the field, Go and sit down to meat?

8 And will not rather say unto him, Make ready wherewith I may sup, and gird thyself, and serve me, till I have eaten and drunken; and afterward thou shalt eat and drink?

9 Doth he thank that servant because he did the things that were commanded him? I trow not.

10 So likewise ye, when ye shall have done all those things which are commanded you, say, We are unprofitable servants: we have done that which was our duty to do.

11 And it came to pass, as he went to Jerusalem, that he passed through the midst of Samaria and Galilee.

12 And as he entered into a certain village, there met him ten men that were lepers, which stood afar off:

13 And they lifted up *their* voices, and said, Jesus, Master, have mercy on us.

14 And when he saw *them*, he said unto them, Go shew yourselves unto the priests. And it came to pass, that, as they went, they were cleansed.

15 And one of them, when he saw that he was healed, turned back, and with a loud voice glorified God,

16 And fell down on *his* face at his feet, giving him thanks: and he was a Samaritan.

17 And Jesus answering said, Were there not ten cleansed? but where *are* the nine?

18 There are not found that returned to give glory to God, save this stranger.

19 And he said unto him, Arise, go thy way: thy faith hath made thee whole.

20 And when he was demanded of the Pharisees, when the kingdom of God should come, he answered them and said, The kingdom of God cometh not with observation:

21 Neither shall they say, Lo here! or, lo there! for, behold, the kingdom of God is within you.

22 And he said unto the disciples, The days will come, when ye shall desire to see one of the days of the Son of man, and ye shall not see *it*.

23 And they shall say to you, See here; or, see there: go not after *them*, nor follow *them*.

24 For as the lightning, that lighteneth out of the one *part* under heaven, shineth unto the other *part* under heaven; so shall also the Son of man be in his day.

25 But first must he suffer many things, and be rejected of this generation.

26 And as it was in the days of Noe, so shall it be also in the days of the Son of man.

27 They did eat, they drank, they married wives, they were given in marriage, until the day that Noe entered into the ark, and the flood came, and destroyed them all.

28 Likewise also as it was in the days of Lot; they did eat, they drank, they

bought, they sold, they planted, they
builded;
29 But the same day that Lot went out
of Sodom it rained fire and brimstone
from heaven, and destroyed *them* all.
30 Even thus shall it be in the day
when the Son of man is revealed.
31 In that day, he which shall be upon
the housetop, and his stuff in the house,
let him not come down to take it away:
and he that is in the field, let him likewise not return back.
32 Remember Lot's wife.
33 Whosoever shall seek to save his
life shall lose it; and whosoever shall
lose his life shall preserve it.
34 I tell you, in that night there shall
be two *men* in one bed; the one shall be
taken, and the other shall be left.
35 Two *women* shall be grinding
together; the one shall be taken, and
the other left.
36 Two *men* shall be in the field; the
one shall be taken, and the other left.
37 And they answered and said unto
him, Where, Lord? And he said unto
them, Wheresoever the body *is*, thither
will the eagles be gathered together.

18 And he spake a parable unto
them *to this end*, that men ought
always to pray, and not to faint;
2 Saying, There was in a city a judge,
which feared not God, neither regarded
man:
3 And there was a widow in that city;
and she came unto him, saying, Avenge
me of mine adversary.
4 And he would not for a while: but
afterward he said within himself,
Though I fear not God, nor regard man;
5 Yet because this widow troubleth
me, I will avenge her, lest by her continual coming she weary me.
6 And the Lord said, Hear what the
unjust judge saith.
7 And shall not God avenge his own
elect, which cry day and night unto
him, though he bear long with them?
8 I tell you that he will avenge them
speedily. Nevertheless when the Son of
man cometh, shall he find faith on the
earth?
9 And he spake this parable unto
certain which trusted in themselves
that they were righteous, and despised
others:
10 Two men went up into the temple
to pray; the one a Pharisee, and the
other a publican.
11 The Pharisee stood and prayed
thus with himself, God, I thank thee,
that I am not as other men *are*, extortioners, unjust, adulterers, or even as
this publican.
12 I fast twice in the week, I give
tithes of all that I possess.
13 And the publican, standing afar
off, would not lift up so much as *his*
eyes unto heaven, but smote upon his
breast, saying, God be merciful to me a
sinner.
14 I tell you, this man went down to
his house justified *rather* than the
other: for every one that exalteth himself shall be abased; and he that humbleth himself shall be exalted.
15 And they brought unto him also
infants, that he would touch them: but
when *his* disciples saw *it*, they rebuked
them.
16 But Jesus called them *unto him*,
and said, Suffer little children to come
unto me, and forbid them not: for of
such is the kingdom of God.

17 Verily I say unto you, Whosoever shall not receive the kingdom of God as a little child shall in no wise enter therein.

18 And a certain ruler asked him, saying, Good Master, what shall I do to inherit eternal life?

19 And Jesus said unto him, Why callest thou me good? none *is* good, save one, *that is*, God.

20 Thou knowest the commandments, Do not commit adultery, Do not kill, Do not steal, Do not bear false witness, Honour thy father and thy mother.

21 And he said, All these have I kept from my youth up.

22 Now when Jesus heard these things, he said unto him, Yet lackest thou one thing: sell all that thou hast, and distribute unto the poor, and thou shalt have treasure in heaven: and come, follow me.

23 And when he heard this, he was very sorrowful: for he was very rich.

24 And when Jesus saw that he was very sorrowful, he said, How hardly shall they that have riches enter into the kingdom of God!

25 For it is easier for a camel to go through a needle's eye, than for a rich man to enter into the kingdom of God.

26 And they that heard *it* said, Who then can be saved?

27 And he said, The things which are impossible with men are possible with God.

28 Then Peter said, Lo, we have left all, and followed thee.

29 And he said unto them, Verily I say unto you, There is no man that hath left house, or parents, or brethren, or wife, or children, for the kingdom of God's sake,

30 Who shall not receive manifold more in this present time, and in the world to come life everlasting.

31 Then he took *unto him* the twelve, and said unto them, Behold, we go up to Jerusalem, and all things that are written by the prophets concerning the Son of man shall be accomplished.

32 For he shall be delivered unto the Gentiles, and shall be mocked, and spitefully entreated, and spitted on:

33 And they shall scourge *him*, and put him to death: and the third day he shall rise again.

34 And they understood none of these things: and this saying was hid from them, neither knew they the things which were spoken.

35 And it came to pass, that as he was come nigh unto Jericho, a certain blind man sat by the way side begging:

36 And hearing the multitude pass by, he asked what it meant.

37 And they told him, that Jesus of Nazareth passeth by.

38 And he cried, saying, Jesus, *thou* Son of David, have mercy on me.

39 And they which went before rebuked him, that he should hold his peace: but he cried so much the more, *Thou* Son of David, have mercy on me.

40 And Jesus stood, and commanded him to be brought unto him: and when he was come near, he asked him,

41 Saying, What wilt thou that I shall do unto thee? And he said, Lord, that I may receive my sight.

42 And Jesus said unto him, Receive thy sight: thy faith hath saved thee.

43 And immediately he received his sight, and followed him, glorifying God: and all the people, when they saw *it*, gave praise unto God.

19 And *Jesus* entered and passed
through Jericho.
2 And, behold, *there was* a man
named Zacchaeus, which was the chief
among the publicans, and he was rich.
3 And he sought to see Jesus who he
was; and could not for the press, because he was little of stature.
4 And he ran before, and climbed up
into a sycomore tree to see him: for he
was to pass that *way*.
5 And when Jesus came to the place,
he looked up, and saw him, and said
unto him, Zacchaeus, make haste, and
come down; for to day I must abide at
thy house.
6 And he made haste, and came
down, and received him joyfully.
7 And when they saw *it*, they all murmured, saying, That he was gone to be
guest with a man that is a sinner.
8 And Zacchaeus stood, and said unto
the Lord; Behold, Lord, the half of my
goods I give to the poor; and if I have
taken any thing from any man by false
accusation, I restore *him* fourfold.
9 And Jesus said unto him, This day is
salvation come to this house, forsomuch
as he also is a son of Abraham.
10 For the Son of man is come to seek
and to save that which was lost.
11 And as they heard these things, he
added and spake a parable, because he
was nigh to Jerusalem, and because
they thought that the kingdom of God
should immediately appear.
12 He said therefore, A certain nobleman went into a far country to receive
for himself a kingdom, and to return.
13 And he called his ten servants, and
delivered them ten pounds, and said
unto them, Occupy till I come.
14 But his citizens hated him, and
sent a message after him, saying, We
will not have this *man* to reign over us.
15 And it came to pass, that when he
was returned, having received the kingdom, then he commanded these servants to be called unto him, to whom he
had given the money, that he might
know how much every man had gained
by trading.
16 Then came the first, saying, Lord,
thy pound hath gained ten pounds.
17 And he said unto him, Well, thou
good servant: because thou hast been
faithful in a very little, have thou
authority over ten cities.
18 And the second came, saying,
Lord, thy pound hath gained five
pounds.
19 And he said likewise to him, Be
thou also over five cities.
20 And another came, saying, Lord,
behold, *here is* thy pound, which I have
kept laid up in a napkin:
21 For I feared thee, because thou art
an austere man: thou takest up that
thou layedst not down, and reapest that
thou didst not sow.
22 And he saith unto him, Out of
thine own mouth will I judge thee, *thou*
wicked servant. Thou knewest that I
was an austere man, taking up that I
laid not down, and reaping that I did
not sow:
23 Wherefore then gavest not thou
my money into the bank, that at my
coming I might have required mine
own with usury?
24 And he said unto them that stood
by, Take from him the pound, and give
it to him that hath ten pounds.
25 (And they said unto him, Lord, he
hath ten pounds.)

26 For I say unto you, That unto every
one which hath shall be given; and
from him that hath not, even that he
hath shall be taken away from him.
27 But those mine enemies, which
would not that I should reign over
them, bring hither, and slay *them*
before me.
28 And when he had thus spoken, he
went before, ascending up to Jerusalem.
29 And it came to pass, when he was
come nigh to Bethphage and Bethany,
at the mount called *the mount* of
Olives, he sent two of his disciples,
30 Saying, Go ye into the village over
against *you*; in the which at your entering ye shall find a colt tied, whereon yet
never man sat: loose him, and bring
him hither.
31 And if any man ask you, Why do ye
loose *him*? thus shall ye say unto him,
Because the Lord hath need of him.
32 And they that were sent went their
way, and found even as he had said
unto them.
33 And as they were loosing the colt,
the owners thereof said unto them,
Why loose ye the colt?
34 And they said, The Lord hath need
of him.
35 And they brought him to Jesus:
and they cast their garments upon the
colt, and they set Jesus thereon.
36 And as he went, they spread their
clothes in the way.
37 And when he was come nigh, even
now at the descent of the mount of
Olives, the whole multitude of the disciples began to rejoice and praise God
with a loud voice for all the mighty
works that they had seen;
38 Saying, Blessed *be* the King that
cometh in the name of the Lord: peace
in heaven, and glory in the highest.
39 And some of the Pharisees from
among the multitude said unto him,
Master, rebuke thy disciples.
40 And he answered and said unto
them, I tell you that, if these should
hold their peace, the stones would
immediately cry out.
41 And when he was come near, he
beheld the city, and wept over it,
42 Saying, If thou hadst known, even
thou, at least in this thy day, the things
which belong unto thy peace! but now
they are hid from thine eyes.
43 For the days shall come upon thee,
that thine enemies shall cast a trench
about thee, and compass thee round,
and keep thee in on every side,
44 And shall lay thee even with the
ground, and thy children within thee;
and they shall not leave in thee one
stone upon another; because thou
knewest not the time of thy visitation.
45 And he went into the temple, and
began to cast out them that sold therein, and them that bought;
46 Saying unto them, It is written, My
house is the house of prayer: but ye
have made it a den of thieves.
47 And he taught daily in the temple.
But the chief priests and the scribes
and the chief of the people sought to
destroy him,
48 And could not find what they
might do: for all the people were very
attentive to hear him.

20 And it came to pass, that on one
of those days, as he taught the
people in the temple, and preached the
gospel, the chief priests and the scribes
came upon him with the elders,
2 And spake unto him, saying, Tell us,
by what authority doest thou these
things? or who is he that gave thee this
authority?

3 And he answered and said unto them, I will also ask you one thing; and answer me:

4 The baptism of John, was it from heaven, or of men?

5 And they reasoned with themselves, saying, If we shall say, From heaven; he will say, Why then believed ye him not?

6 But and if we say, Of men; all the people will stone us: for they be persuaded that John was a prophet.

7 And they answered, that they could not tell whence *it was*.

8 And Jesus said unto them, Neither tell I you by what authority I do these things.

9 Then began he to speak to the people this parable; A certain man planted a vineyard, and let it forth to husbandmen, and went into a far country for a long time.

10 And at the season he sent a servant to the husbandmen, that they should give him of the fruit of the vineyard: but the husbandmen beat him, and sent *him* away empty.

11 And again he sent another servant: and they beat him also, and entreated *him* shamefully, and sent *him* away empty.

12 And again he sent a third: and they wounded him also, and cast *him* out.

13 Then said the lord of the vineyard, What shall I do? I will send my beloved son: it may be they will reverence *him* when they see him.

14 But when the husbandmen saw him, they reasoned among themselves, saying, This is the heir: come, let us kill him, that the inheritance may be ours.

15 So they cast him out of the vineyard, and killed *him*. What therefore shall the lord of the vineyard do unto them?

16 He shall come and destroy these husbandmen, and shall give the vineyard to others. And when they heard *it*, they said, God forbid.

17 And he beheld them, and said, What is this then that is written, The stone which the builders rejected, the same is become the head of the corner?

18 Whosoever shall fall upon that stone shall be broken; but on whomsoever it shall fall, it will grind him to powder.

19 And the chief priests and the scribes the same hour sought to lay hands on him; and they feared the people: for they perceived that he had spoken this parable against them.

20 And they watched *him*, and sent forth spies, which should feign themselves just men, that they might take hold of his words, that so they might deliver him unto the power and authority of the governor.

21 And they asked him, saying, Master, we know that thou sayest and teachest rightly, neither acceptest thou the person *of any*, but teachest the way of God truly:

22 Is it lawful for us to give tribute unto Caesar, or no?

23 But he perceived their craftiness, and said unto them, Why tempt ye me?

24 Shew me a penny. Whose image and superscription hath it? They answered and said, Caesar's.

25 And he said unto them, Render therefore unto Caesar the things which be Caesar's, and unto God the things which be God's.

26 And they could not take hold of his words before the people: and they marvelled at his answer, and held their peace.

27 Then came to *him* certain of the
Sadducees, which deny that there is
any resurrection; and they asked him,
28 Saying, Master, Moses wrote unto
us, If any man's brother die, having a
wife, and he die without children, that
his brother should take his wife, and
raise up seed unto his brother.
29 There were therefore seven brethren: and the first took a wife, and died
without children.
30 And the second took her to wife,
and he died childless.
31 And the third took her; and in like
manner the seven also: and they left no
children, and died.
32 Last of all the woman died also.
33 Therefore in the resurrection
whose wife of them is she? for seven
had her to wife.
34 And Jesus answering said unto
them, The children of this world marry,
and are given in marriage:
35 But they which shall be accounted
worthy to obtain that world, and the
resurrection from the dead, neither
marry, nor are given in marriage:
36 Neither can they die any more: for
they are equal unto the angels; and are
the children of God, being the children
of the resurrection.
37 Now that the dead are raised, even
Moses shewed at the bush, when he
calleth the Lord the God of Abraham,
and the God of Isaac, and the God of
Jacob.
38 For he is not a God of the dead, but
of the living: for all live unto him.
39 Then certain of the scribes answering said, Master, thou hast well said.
40 And after that they durst not ask
him any *question at all*.
41 And he said unto them, How say
they that Christ is David's son?
42 And David himself saith in the
book of Psalms, The LORD said unto my
Lord, Sit thou on my right hand,
43 Till I make thine enemies thy footstool.
44 David therefore calleth him Lord,
how is he then his son?
45 Then in the audience of all the
people he said unto his disciples,
46 Beware of the scribes, which desire
to walk in long robes, and love greetings in the markets, and the highest
seats in the synagogues, and the chief
rooms at feasts;
47 Which devour widows' houses, and
for a shew make long prayers: the same
shall receive greater damnation.

21 And he looked up, and saw the
rich men casting their gifts into
the treasury.
2 And he saw also a certain poor
widow casting in thither two mites.
3 And he said, Of a truth I say unto
you, that this poor widow hath cast in
more than they all:
4 For all these have of their abundance cast in unto the offerings of God:
but she of her penury hath cast in all
the living that she had.
5 And as some spake of the temple,
how it was adorned with goodly stones
and gifts, he said,
6 *As for* these things which ye behold,
the days will come, in the which there
shall not be left one stone upon another, that shall not be thrown down.
7 And they asked him, saying, Master,
but when shall these things be? and
what sign *will there be* when these
things shall come to pass?
8 And he said, Take heed that ye be
not deceived: for many shall come in
my name, saying, I am *Christ*; and the

time draweth near: go ye not therefore
after them.
9 But when ye shall hear of wars and
commotions, be not terrified: for these
things must first come to pass; but the
end *is* not by and by.
10 Then said he unto them, Nation
shall rise against nation, and kingdom
against kingdom:
11 And great earthquakes shall be in
divers places, and famines, and pestilences; and fearful sights and great
signs shall there be from heaven.
12 But before all these, they shall lay
their hands on you, and persecute *you*,
delivering *you* up to the synagogues,
and into prisons, being brought before
kings and rulers for my name's sake.
13 And it shall turn to you for a testimony.
14 Settle *it* therefore in your hearts,
not to meditate before what ye shall
answer:
15 For I will give you a mouth and
wisdom, which all your adversaries
shall not be able to gainsay nor resist.
16 And ye shall be betrayed both by
parents, and brethren, and kinsfolks,
and friends; and *some* of you shall they
cause to be put to death.
17 And ye shall be hated of all *men*
for my name's sake.
18 But there shall not an hair of your
head perish.
19 In your patience possess ye your
souls.
20 And when ye shall see Jerusalem
compassed with armies, then know that
the desolation thereof is nigh.
21 Then let them which are in Judaea
flee to the mountains; and let them
which are in the midst of it depart out;
and let not them that are in the countries enter thereinto.
22 For these be the days of vengeance, that all things which are written may be fulfilled.
23 But woe unto them that are with
child, and to them that give suck, in
those days! for there shall be great distress in the land, and wrath upon this
people.
24 And they shall fall by the edge of
the sword, and shall be led away captive into all nations: and Jerusalem
shall be trodden down of the Gentiles,
until the times of the Gentiles be fulfilled.
25 And there shall be signs in the sun,
and in the moon, and in the stars; and
upon the earth distress of nations, with
perplexity; the sea and the waves roaring;
26 Men's hearts failing them for fear,
and for looking after those things
which are coming on the earth: for the
powers of heaven shall be shaken.
27 And then shall they see the Son of
man coming in a cloud with power and
great glory.
28 And when these things begin to
come to pass, then look up, and lift up
your heads; for your redemption draweth nigh.
29 And he spake to them a parable;
Behold the fig tree, and all the trees;
30 When they now shoot forth, ye see
and know of your own selves that summer is now nigh at hand.
31 So likewise ye, when ye see these
things come to pass, know ye that the
kingdom of God is nigh at hand.
32 Verily I say unto you, This generation shall not pass away, till all be fulfilled.
33 Heaven and earth shall pass away:
but my words shall not pass away.

34 And take heed to yourselves, lest at any time your hearts be overcharged with surfeiting, and drunkenness, and cares of this life, and *so* that day come upon you unawares.

35 For as a snare shall it come on all them that dwell on the face of the whole earth.

36 Watch ye therefore, and pray always, that ye may be accounted worthy to escape all these things that shall come to pass, and to stand before the Son of man.

37 And in the day time he was teaching in the temple; and at night he went out, and abode in the mount that is called *the mount* of Olives.

38 And all the people came early in the morning to him in the temple, for to hear him.

22 Now the feast of unleavened bread drew nigh, which is called the Passover.

2 And the chief priests and scribes sought how they might kill him; for they feared the people.

3 Then entered Satan into Judas surnamed Iscariot, being of the number of the twelve.

4 And he went his way, and communed with the chief priests and captains, how he might betray him unto them.

5 And they were glad, and covenanted to give him money.

6 And he promised, and sought opportunity to betray him unto them in the absence of the multitude.

7 Then came the day of unleavened bread, when the passover must be killed.

8 And he sent Peter and John, saying, Go and prepare us the passover, that we may eat.

9 And they said unto him, Where wilt thou that we prepare?

10 And he said unto them, Behold, when ye are entered into the city, there shall a man meet you, bearing a pitcher of water; follow him into the house where he entereth in.

11 And ye shall say unto the goodman of the house, The Master saith unto thee, Where is the guestchamber, where I shall eat the passover with my disciples?

12 And he shall shew you a large upper room furnished: there make ready.

13 And they went, and found as he had said unto them: and they made ready the passover.

14 And when the hour was come, he sat down, and the twelve apostles with him.

15 And he said unto them, With desire I have desired to eat this passover with you before I suffer:

16 For I say unto you, I will not any more eat thereof, until it be fulfilled in the kingdom of God.

17 And he took the cup, and gave thanks, and said, Take this, and divide *it* among yourselves:

18 For I say unto you, I will not drink of the fruit of the vine, until the kingdom of God shall come.

19 And he took bread, and gave thanks, and brake *it*, and gave unto them, saying, This is my body which is given for you: this do in remembrance of me.

20 Likewise also the cup after supper, saying, This cup *is* the new testament in my blood, which is shed for you.

21 But, behold, the hand of him that betrayeth me *is* with me on the table.

22 And truly the Son of man goeth, as
it was determined: but woe unto that
man by whom he is betrayed!
23 And they began to enquire among
themselves, which of them it was that
should do this thing.
24 And there was also a strife among
them, which of them should be accounted the greatest.
25 And he said unto them, The kings
of the Gentiles exercise lordship over
them; and they that exercise authority
upon them are called benefactors.
26 But ye *shall* not *be* so: but he that
is greatest among you, let him be as the
younger; and he that is chief, as he that
doth serve.
27 For whether *is* greater, he that
sitteth at meat, or he that serveth? *is*
not he that sitteth at meat? but I am
among you as he that serveth.
28 Ye are they which have continued
with me in my temptations.
29 And I appoint unto you a kingdom,
as my Father hath appointed unto me;
30 That ye may eat and drink at my
table in my kingdom, and sit on thrones
judging the twelve tribes of Israel.
31 And the Lord said, Simon, Simon,
behold, Satan hath desired *to have* you,
that he may sift *you* as wheat:
32 But I have prayed for thee, that thy
faith fail not: and when thou art converted, strengthen thy brethren.
33 And he said unto him, Lord, I am
ready to go with thee, both into prison,
and to death.
34 And he said, I tell thee, Peter, the
cock shall not crow this day, before that
thou shalt thrice deny that thou knowest me.
35 And he said unto them, When I
sent you without purse, and scrip, and
shoes, lacked ye any thing? And they
said, Nothing.
36 Then said he unto them, But now,
he that hath a purse, let him take *it*,
and likewise *his* scrip: and he that hath
no sword, let him sell his garment, and
buy one.
37 For I say unto you, that this that is
written must yet be accomplished in
me, And he was reckoned among the
transgressors: for the things concerning
me have an end.
38 And they said, Lord, behold, here
are two swords. And he said unto them,
It is enough.
39 And he came out, and went, as he
was wont, to the mount of Olives; and
his disciples also followed him.
40 And when he was at the place, he
said unto them, Pray that ye enter not
into temptation.
41 And he was withdrawn from them
about a stone's cast, and kneeled down,
and prayed,
42 Saying, Father, if thou be willing,
remove this cup from me: nevertheless
not my will, but thine, be done.
43 And there appeared an angel unto
him from heaven, strengthening him.
44 And being in an agony he prayed
more earnestly: and his sweat was as it
were great drops of blood falling down
to the ground.
45 And when he rose up from prayer,
and was come to his disciples, he found
them sleeping for sorrow,
46 And said unto them, Why sleep ye?
rise and pray, lest ye enter into temptation.
47 And while he yet spake, behold a
multitude, and he that was called
Judas, one of the twelve, went before
them, and drew near unto Jesus to kiss
him.

48 But Jesus said unto him, Judas, betrayest thou the Son of man with a kiss?

49 When they which were about him saw what would follow, they said unto him, Lord, shall we smite with the sword?

50 And one of them smote the servant of the high priest, and cut off his right ear.

51 And Jesus answered and said, Suffer ye thus far. And he touched his ear, and healed him.

52 Then Jesus said unto the chief priests, and captains of the temple, and the elders, which were come to him, Be ye come out, as against a thief, with swords and staves?

53 When I was daily with you in the temple, ye stretched forth no hands against me: but this is your hour, and the power of darkness.

54 Then took they him, and led *him*, and brought him into the high priest's house. And Peter followed afar off.

55 And when they had kindled a fire in the midst of the hall, and were set down together, Peter sat down among them.

56 But a certain maid beheld him as he sat by the fire, and earnestly looked upon him, and said, This man was also with him.

57 And he denied him, saying, Woman, I know him not.

58 And after a little while another saw him, and said, Thou art also of them. And Peter said, Man, I am not.

59 And about the space of one hour after another confidently affirmed, saying, Of a truth this *fellow* also was with him: for he is a Galilaean.

60 And Peter said, Man, I know not what thou sayest. And immediately, while he yet spake, the cock crew.

61 And the Lord turned, and looked upon Peter. And Peter remembered the word of the Lord, how he had said unto him, Before the cock crow, thou shalt deny me thrice.

62 And Peter went out, and wept bitterly.

63 And the men that held Jesus mocked him, and smote *him*.

64 And when they had blindfolded him, they struck him on the face, and asked him, saying, Prophesy, who is it that smote thee?

65 And many other things blasphemously spake they against him.

66 And as soon as it was day, the elders of the people and the chief priests and the scribes came together, and led him into their council, saying,

67 Art thou the Christ? tell us. And he said unto them, If I tell you, ye will not believe:

68 And if I also ask *you*, ye will not answer me, nor let *me* go.

69 Hereafter shall the Son of man sit on the right hand of the power of God.

70 Then said they all, Art thou then the Son of God? And he said unto them, Ye say that I am.

71 And they said, What need we any further witness? for we ourselves have heard of his own mouth.

23

And the whole multitude of them arose, and led him unto Pilate.

2 And they began to accuse him, saying, We found this *fellow* perverting the nation, and forbidding to give tribute to Caesar, saying that he himself is Christ a King.

3 And Pilate asked him, saying, Art
thou the King of the Jews? And he
answered him and said, Thou sayest *it*.
4 Then said Pilate to the chief priests
and *to* the people, I find no fault in this
man.
5 And they were the more fierce, saying,
He stirreth up the people, teaching
throughout all Jewry, beginning from
Galilee to this place.
6 When Pilate heard of Galilee, he
asked whether the man were a
Galilaean.
7 And as soon as he knew that he
belonged unto Herod's jurisdiction, he
sent him to Herod, who himself also
was at Jerusalem at that time.
8 And when Herod saw Jesus, he was
exceeding glad: for he was desirous to
see him of a long *season*, because he
had heard many things of him; and he
hoped to have seen some miracle done
by him.
9 Then he questioned with him in
many words; but he answered him nothing.
10 And the chief priests and scribes
stood and vehemently accused him.
11 And Herod with his men of war set
him at nought, and mocked *him*, and
arrayed him in a gorgeous robe, and
sent him again to Pilate.
12 And the same day Pilate and
Herod were made friends together: for
before they were at enmity between
themselves.
13 And Pilate, when he had called
together the chief priests and the rulers
and the people,
14 Said unto them, Ye have brought
this man unto me, as one that perverteth
the people: and, behold, I, having
examined *him* before you, have found
no fault in this man touching those
things whereof ye accuse him:
15 No, nor yet Herod: for I sent you to
him; and, lo, nothing worthy of death is
done unto him.
16 I will therefore chastise him, and
release *him*.
17 (For of necessity he must release
one unto them at the feast.)
18 And they cried out all at once, saying,
Away with this *man*, and release
unto us Barabbas:
19 (Who for a certain sedition made
in the city, and for murder, was cast into
prison.)
20 Pilate therefore, willing to release
Jesus, spake again to them.
21 But they cried, saying, Crucify
him, crucify him.
22 And he said unto them the third
time, Why, what evil hath he done? I
have found no cause of death in him: I
will therefore chastise him, and let *him*
go.
23 And they were instant with loud
voices, requiring that he might be crucified.
And the voices of them and of
the chief priests prevailed.
24 And Pilate gave sentence that it
should be as they required.
25 And he released unto them him
that for sedition and murder was cast
into prison, whom they had desired;
but he delivered Jesus to their will.
26 And as they led him away, they laid
hold upon one Simon, a Cyrenian, coming
out of the country, and on him they
laid the cross, that he might bear *it*
after Jesus.
27 And there followed him a great
company of people, and of women,
which also bewailed and lamented him.
28 But Jesus turning unto them said,
Daughters of Jerusalem, weep not for

me, but weep for yourselves, and for
your children.
29 For, behold, the days are coming, in
the which they shall say, Blessed *are*
the barren, and the wombs that never
bare, and the paps which never gave
suck.
30 Then shall they begin to say to the
mountains, Fall on us; and to the hills,
Cover us.
31 For if they do these things in a
green tree, what shall be done in the
dry?
32 And there were also two other,
malefactors, led with him to be put to
death.
33 And when they were come to the
place, which is called Calvary, there
they crucified him, and the malefactors, one on the right hand, and the
other on the left.
34 Then said Jesus, Father, forgive
them; for they know not what they do.
And they parted his raiment, and cast
lots.
35 And the people stood beholding.
And the rulers also with them derided
him, saying, He saved others; let him
save himself, if he be Christ, the chosen
of God.
36 And the soldiers also mocked him,
coming to him, and offering him vinegar,
37 And saying, If thou be the king of
the Jews, save thyself.
38 And a superscription also was written over him in letters of Greek, and
Latin, and Hebrew, THIS IS THE KING
OF THE JEWS.
39 And one of the malefactors which
were hanged railed on him, saying, If
thou be Christ, save thyself and us.
40 But the other answering rebuked
him, saying, Dost not thou fear God,
seeing thou art in the same condemnation?
41 And we indeed justly; for we
receive the due reward of our deeds:
but this man hath done nothing amiss.
42 And he said unto Jesus, Lord,
remember me when thou comest into
thy kingdom.
43 And Jesus said unto him, Verily I
say unto thee, To day shalt thou be with
me in paradise.
44 And it was about the sixth hour,
and there was a darkness over all the
earth until the ninth hour.
45 And the sun was darkened, and
the veil of the temple was rent in the
midst.
46 And when Jesus had cried with a
loud voice, he said, Father, into thy
hands I commend my spirit: and having
said thus, he gave up the ghost.
47 Now when the centurion saw what
was done, he glorified God, saying,
Certainly this was a righteous man.
48 And all the people that came
together to that sight, beholding the
things which were done, smote their
breasts, and returned.
49 And all his acquaintance, and the
women that followed him from Galilee,
stood afar off, beholding these things.
50 And, behold, *there was* a man
named Joseph, a counsellor; *and he
was* a good man, and a just:
51 (The same had not consented to
the counsel and deed of them;) *he was*
of Arimathaea, a city of the Jews: who
also himself waited for the kingdom of
God.
52 This *man* went unto Pilate, and
begged the body of Jesus.
53 And he took it down, and wrapped
it in linen, and laid it in a sepulchre

that was hewn in stone, wherein never
man before was laid.
54 And that day was the preparation,
and the sabbath drew on.
55 And the women also, which came
with him from Galilee, followed after,
and beheld the sepulchre, and how his
body was laid.
56 And they returned, and prepared
spices and ointments; and rested the
sabbath day according to the commandment.

24 Now upon the first *day* of the
week, very early in the morning,
they came unto the sepulchre, bringing
the spices which they had prepared,
and certain *others* with them.
2 And they found the stone rolled
away from the sepulchre.
3 And they entered in, and found not
the body of the Lord Jesus.
4 And it came to pass, as they were
much perplexed thereabout, behold,
two men stood by them in shining garments:
5 And as they were afraid, and bowed
down *their* faces to the earth, they said
unto them, Why seek ye the living
among the dead?
6 He is not here, but is risen: remember how he spake unto you when he
was yet in Galilee,
7 Saying, The Son of man must be
delivered into the hands of sinful men,
and be crucified, and the third day rise
again.
8 And they remembered his words,
9 And returned from the sepulchre,
and told all these things unto the elev-
en, and to all the rest.
10 It was Mary Magdalene, and
Joanna, and Mary *the mother* of James,
and other *women that were* with them,
which told these things unto the apostles.
11 And their words seemed to them
as idle tales, and they believed them
not.
12 Then arose Peter, and ran unto the
sepulchre; and stooping down, he
beheld the linen clothes laid by themselves, and departed, wondering in
himself at that which was come to pass.
13 And, behold, two of them went
that same day to a village called
Emmaus, which was from Jerusalem
about threescore furlongs.
14 And they talked together of all
these things which had happened.
15 And it came to pass, that, while
they communed *together* and reasoned,
Jesus himself drew near, and went with
them.
16 But their eyes were holden that
they should not know him.
17 And he said unto them, What manner of communications *are* these that
ye have one to another, as ye walk, and
are sad?
18 And the one of them, whose name
was Cleopas, answering said unto him,
Art thou only a stranger in Jerusalem,
and hast not known the things which
are come to pass there in these days?
19 And he said unto them, What
things? And they said unto him,
Concerning Jesus of Nazareth, which
was a prophet mighty in deed and word
before God and all the people:
20 And how the chief priests and our
rulers delivered him to be condemned
to death, and have crucified him.
21 But we trusted that it had been he
which should have redeemed Israel:
and beside all this, to day is the third
day since these things were done.

22 Yea, and certain women also of our company made us astonished, which were early at the sepulchre;

23 And when they found not his body, they came, saying, that they had also seen a vision of angels, which said that he was alive.

24 And certain of them which were with us went to the sepulchre, and found *it* even so as the women had said: but him they saw not.

25 Then he said unto them, O fools, and slow of heart to believe all that the prophets have spoken:

26 Ought not Christ to have suffered these things, and to enter into his glory?

27 And beginning at Moses and all the prophets, he expounded unto them in all the scriptures the things concerning himself.

28 And they drew nigh unto the village, whither they went: and he made as though he would have gone further.

29 But they constrained him, saying, Abide with us: for it is toward evening, and the day is far spent. And he went in to tarry with them.

30 And it came to pass, as he sat at meat with them, he took bread, and blessed *it*, and brake, and gave to them.

31 And their eyes were opened, and they knew him; and he vanished out of their sight.

32 And they said one to another, Did not our heart burn within us, while he talked with us by the way, and while he opened to us the scriptures?

33 And they rose up the same hour, and returned to Jerusalem, and found the eleven gathered together, and them that were with them,

34 Saying, The Lord is risen indeed, and hath appeared to Simon.

35 And they told what things *were done* in the way, and how he was known of them in breaking of bread.

36 And as they thus spake, Jesus himself stood in the midst of them, and saith unto them, Peace *be* unto you.

37 But they were terrified and affrighted, and supposed that they had seen a spirit.

38 And he said unto them, Why are ye troubled? and why do thoughts arise in your hearts?

39 Behold my hands and my feet, that it is I myself: handle me, and see; for a spirit hath not flesh and bones, as ye see me have.

40 And when he had thus spoken, he shewed them *his* hands and *his* feet.

41 And while they yet believed not for joy, and wondered, he said unto them, Have ye here any meat?

42 And they gave him a piece of a broiled fish, and of an honeycomb.

43 And he took *it*, and did eat before them.

44 And he said unto them, These *are* the words which I spake unto you, while I was yet with you, that all things must be fulfilled, which were written in the law of Moses, and *in* the prophets, and *in* the psalms, concerning me.

45 Then opened he their understanding, that they might understand the scriptures,

46 And said unto them, Thus it is written, and thus it behoved Christ to suffer, and to rise from the dead the third day:

47 And that repentance and remission of sins should be preached in his name among all nations, beginning at Jerusalem.

48 And ye are witnesses of these things.

49 And, behold, I send the promise of
my Father upon you: but tarry ye in the
city of Jerusalem, until ye be endued
with power from on high.
50 And he led them out as far as to
Bethany, and he lifted up his hands,
and blessed them.
51 And it came to pass, while he
blessed them, he was parted from
them, and carried up into heaven.
52 And they worshipped him, and
returned to Jerusalem with great joy:
53 And were continually in the temple, praising and blessing God. Amen.

THE GOSPEL ACCORDING TO SAINT JOHN

1 In the beginning was the Word, and
the Word was with God, and the
Word was God.
2 The same was in the beginning with
God.
3 All things were made by him; and
without him was not any thing made
that was made.
4 In him was life; and the life was the
light of men.
5 And the light shineth in darkness;
and the darkness comprehended it not.
6 There was a man sent from God,
whose name *was* John.
7 The same came for a witness, to
bear witness of the Light, that all *men*
through him might believe.
8 He was not that Light, but *was sent*
to bear witness of that Light.
9 *That* was the true Light, which lighteth every man that cometh into the
world.
10 He was in the world, and the world
was made by him, and the world knew
him not.
11 He came unto his own, and his own
received him not.
12 But as many as received him, to
them gave he power to become the sons
of God, *even* to them that believe on his
name:
13 Which were born, not of blood, nor
of the will of the flesh, nor of the will of
man, but of God.
14 And the Word was made flesh, and
dwelt among us, (and we beheld his
glory, the glory as of the only begotten
of the Father,) full of grace and truth.
15 John bare witness of him, and
cried, saying, This was he of whom I
spake, He that cometh after me is preferred before me: for he was before me.
16 And of his fulness have all we
received, and grace for grace.
17 For the law was given by Moses,
but grace and truth came by Jesus
Christ.
18 No man hath seen God at any time;
the only begotten Son, which is in the
bosom of the Father, he hath declared
him.
19 And this is the record of John,
when the Jews sent priests and Levites
from Jerusalem to ask him, Who art
thou?
20 And he confessed, and denied not;
but confessed, I am not the Christ.

21 And they asked him, What then?
Art thou Elias? And he saith, I am not.
Art thou that prophet? And he
answered, No.
22 Then said they unto him, Who art
thou? that we may give an answer to
them that sent us. What sayest thou of
thyself?
23 He said, I *am* the voice of one crying in the wilderness, Make straight the
way of the Lord, as said the prophet
Esaias.
24 And they which were sent were of
the Pharisees.
25 And they asked him, and said unto
him, Why baptizest thou then, if thou
be not that Christ, nor Elias, neither
that prophet?
26 John answered them, saying, I baptize with water: but there standeth one
among you, whom ye know not;
27 He it is, who coming after me is
preferred before me, whose shoe's
latchet I am not worthy to unloose.
28 These things were done in
Bethabara beyond Jordan, where John
was baptizing.
29 The next day John seeth Jesus
coming unto him, and saith, Behold the
Lamb of God, which taketh away the
sin of the world.
30 This is he of whom I said, After me
cometh a man which is preferred
before me: for he was before me.
31 And I knew him not: but that he
should be made manifest to Israel,
therefore am I come baptizing with
water.
32 And John bare record, saying, I
saw the Spirit descending from heaven
like a dove, and it abode upon him.
33 And I knew him not: but he that
sent me to baptize with water, the same
said unto me, Upon whom thou shalt
see the Spirit descending, and remaining on him, the same is he which baptizeth with the Holy Ghost.
34 And I saw, and bare record that
this is the Son of God.
35 Again the next day after John
stood, and two of his disciples;
36 And looking upon Jesus as he
walked, he saith, Behold the Lamb of
God!
37 And the two disciples heard him
speak, and they followed Jesus.
38 Then Jesus turned, and saw them
following, and saith unto them, What
seek ye? They said unto him, Rabbi,
(which is to say, being interpreted,
Master,) where dwellest thou?
39 He saith unto them, Come and see.
They came and saw where he dwelt,
and abode with him that day: for it was
about the tenth hour.
40 One of the two which heard John
speak, and followed him, was Andrew,
Simon Peter's brother.
41 He first findeth his own brother
Simon, and saith unto him, We have
found the Messias, which is, being
interpreted, the Christ.
42 And he brought him to Jesus. And
when Jesus beheld him, he said, Thou
art Simon the son of Jona: thou shalt be
called Cephas, which is by interpretation, A stone.
43 The day following Jesus would go
forth into Galilee, and findeth Philip,
and saith unto him, Follow me.
44 Now Philip was of Bethsaida, the
city of Andrew and Peter.
45 Philip findeth Nathanael, and
saith unto him, We have found him, of
whom Moses in the law, and the prophets, did write, Jesus of Nazareth, the
son of Joseph.

46 And Nathanael said unto him, Can there any good thing come out of Nazareth? Philip saith unto him, Come and see.

47 Jesus saw Nathanael coming to him, and saith of him, Behold an Israelite indeed, in whom is no guile!

48 Nathanael saith unto him, Whence knowest thou me? Jesus answered and said unto him, Before that Philip called thee, when thou wast under the fig tree, I saw thee.

49 Nathanael answered and saith unto him, Rabbi, thou art the Son of God; thou art the King of Israel.

50 Jesus answered and said unto him, Because I said unto thee, I saw thee under the fig tree, believest thou? thou shalt see greater things than these.

51 And he saith unto him, Verily, verily, I say unto you, Hereafter ye shall see heaven open, and the angels of God ascending and descending upon the Son of man.

2 And the third day there was a marriage in Cana of Galilee; and the mother of Jesus was there:

2 And both Jesus was called, and his disciples, to the marriage.

3 And when they wanted wine, the mother of Jesus saith unto him, They have no wine.

4 Jesus saith unto her, Woman, what have I to do with thee? mine hour is not yet come.

5 His mother saith unto the servants, Whatsoever he saith unto you, do *it*.

6 And there were set there six waterpots of stone, after the manner of the purifying of the Jews, containing two or three firkins apiece.

7 Jesus saith unto them, Fill the waterpots with water. And they filled them up to the brim.

8 And he saith unto them, Draw out now, and bear unto the governor of the feast. And they bare *it*.

9 When the ruler of the feast had tasted the water that was made wine, and knew not whence it was: (but the servants which drew the water knew;) the governor of the feast called the bridegroom,

10 And saith unto him, Every man at the beginning doth set forth good wine; and when men have well drunk, then that which is worse: *but* thou hast kept the good wine until now.

11 This beginning of miracles did Jesus in Cana of Galilee, and manifested forth his glory; and his disciples believed on him.

12 After this he went down to Capernaum, he, and his mother, and his brethren, and his disciples: and they continued there not many days.

13 And the Jews' passover was at hand, and Jesus went up to Jerusalem,

14 And found in the temple those that sold oxen and sheep and doves, and the changers of money sitting:

15 And when he had made a scourge of small cords, he drove them all out of the temple, and the sheep, and the oxen; and poured out the changers' money, and overthrew the tables;

16 And said unto them that sold doves, Take these things hence; make not my Father's house an house of merchandise.

17 And his disciples remembered that it was written, The zeal of thine house hath eaten me up.

18 Then answered the Jews and said unto him, What sign shewest thou unto us, seeing that thou doest these things?

19 Jesus answered and said unto them, Destroy this temple, and in three days I will raise it up.

20 Then said the Jews, Forty and six years was this temple in building, and wilt thou rear it up in three days?

21 But he spake of the temple of his body.

22 When therefore he was risen from the dead, his disciples remembered that he had said this unto them; and they believed the scripture, and the word which Jesus had said.

23 Now when he was in Jerusalem at the passover, in the feast *day*, many believed in his name, when they saw the miracles which he did.

24 But Jesus did not commit himself unto them, because he knew all *men*,

25 And needed not that any should testify of man: for he knew what was in man.

3 There was a man of the Pharisees, named Nicodemus, a ruler of the Jews:

2 The same came to Jesus by night, and said unto him, Rabbi, we know that thou art a teacher come from God: for no man can do these miracles that thou doest, except God be with him.

3 Jesus answered and said unto him, Verily, verily, I say unto thee, Except a man be born again, he cannot see the kingdom of God.

4 Nicodemus saith unto him, How can a man be born when he is old? can he enter the second time into his mother's womb, and be born?

5 Jesus answered, Verily, verily, I say unto thee, Except a man be born of water and *of* the Spirit, he cannot enter into the kingdom of God.

6 That which is born of the flesh is flesh; and that which is born of the Spirit is spirit.

7 Marvel not that I said unto thee, Ye must be born again.

8 The wind bloweth where it listeth, and thou hearest the sound thereof, but canst not tell whence it cometh, and whither it goeth: so is every one that is born of the Spirit.

9 Nicodemus answered and said unto him, How can these things be?

10 Jesus answered and said unto him, Art thou a master of Israel, and knowest not these things?

11 Verily, verily, I say unto thee, We speak that we do know, and testify that we have seen; and ye receive not our witness.

12 If I have told you earthly things, and ye believe not, how shall ye believe, if I tell you *of* heavenly things?

13 And no man hath ascended up to heaven, but he that came down from heaven, *even* the Son of man which is in heaven.

14 And as Moses lifted up the serpent in the wilderness, even so must the Son of man be lifted up:

15 That whosoever believeth in him should not perish, but have eternal life.

16 For God so loved the world, that he gave his only begotten Son, that whosoever believeth in him should not perish, but have everlasting life.

17 For God sent not his Son into the world to condemn the world; but that the world through him might be saved.

18 He that believeth on him is not condemned: but he that believeth not is condemned already, because he hath not believed in the name of the only begotten Son of God.

19 And this is the condemnation, that light is come into the world, and men loved darkness rather than light, because their deeds were evil.

20 For every one that doeth evil hateth the light, neither cometh to the light, lest his deeds should be reproved.

21 But he that doeth truth cometh to the light, that his deeds may be made manifest, that they are wrought in God.

22 After these things came Jesus and his disciples into the land of Judaea; and there he tarried with them, and baptized.

23 And John also was baptizing in Aenon near to Salim, because there was much water there: and they came, and were baptized.

24 For John was not yet cast into prison.

25 Then there arose a question between *some* of John's disciples and the Jews about purifying.

26 And they came unto John, and said unto him, Rabbi, he that was with thee beyond Jordan, to whom thou barest witness, behold, the same baptizeth, and all *men* come to him.

27 John answered and said, A man can receive nothing, except it be given him from heaven.

28 Ye yourselves bear me witness, that I said, I am not the Christ, but that I am sent before him.

29 He that hath the bride is the bridegroom: but the friend of the bridegroom, which standeth and heareth him, rejoiceth greatly because of the bridegroom's voice: this my joy therefore is fulfilled.

30 He must increase, but I *must* decrease.

31 He that cometh from above is above all: he that is of the earth is earthly, and speaketh of the earth: he that cometh from heaven is above all.

32 And what he hath seen and heard, that he testifieth; and no man receiveth his testimony.

33 He that hath received his testimony hath set to his seal that God is true.

34 For he whom God hath sent speaketh the words of God: for God giveth not the Spirit by measure *unto him*.

35 The Father loveth the Son, and hath given all things into his hand.

36 He that believeth on the Son hath everlasting life: and he that believeth not the Son shall not see life; but the wrath of God abideth on him.

4 When therefore the Lord knew how the Pharisees had heard that Jesus made and baptized more disciples than John,

2 (Though Jesus himself baptized not, but his disciples,)

3 He left Judaea, and departed again into Galilee.

4 And he must needs go through Samaria.

5 Then cometh he to a city of Samaria, which is called Sychar, near to the parcel of ground that Jacob gave to his son Joseph.

6 Now Jacob's well was there. Jesus therefore, being wearied with *his* journey, sat thus on the well: *and* it was about the sixth hour.

7 There cometh a woman of Samaria to draw water: Jesus saith unto her, Give me to drink.

8 (For his disciples were gone away unto the city to buy meat.)

9 Then saith the woman of Samaria unto him, How is it that thou, being a Jew, askest drink of me, which am a woman of Samaria? for the Jews have no dealings with the Samaritans.

10 Jesus answered and said unto her, If thou knewest the gift of God, and who it is that saith to thee, Give me to drink; thou wouldest have asked of him, and he would have given thee living water.

11 The woman saith unto him, Sir, thou hast nothing to draw with, and the well is deep: from whence then hast thou that living water?

12 Art thou greater than our father Jacob, which gave us the well, and drank thereof himself, and his children, and his cattle?

13 Jesus answered and said unto her, Whosoever drinketh of this water shall thirst again:

14 But whosoever drinketh of the water that I shall give him shall never thirst; but the water that I shall give him shall be in him a well of water springing up into everlasting life.

15 The woman saith unto him, Sir, give me this water, that I thirst not, neither come hither to draw.

16 Jesus saith unto her, Go, call thy husband, and come hither.

17 The woman answered and said, I have no husband. Jesus said unto her, Thou hast well said, I have no husband:

18 For thou hast had five husbands; and he whom thou now hast is not thy husband: in that saidst thou truly.

19 The woman saith unto him, Sir, I perceive that thou art a prophet.

20 Our fathers worshipped in this mountain; and ye say, that in Jerusalem is the place where men ought to worship.

21 Jesus saith unto her, Woman, believe me, the hour cometh, when ye shall neither in this mountain, nor yet at Jerusalem, worship the Father.

22 Ye worship ye know not what: we know what we worship: for salvation is of the Jews.

23 But the hour cometh, and now is, when the true worshippers shall worship the Father in spirit and in truth: for the Father seeketh such to worship him.

24 God *is* a Spirit: and they that worship him must worship *him* in spirit and in truth.

25 The woman saith unto him, I know that Messias cometh, which is called Christ: when he is come, he will tell us all things.

26 Jesus saith unto her, I that speak unto thee am *he*.

27 And upon this came his disciples, and marvelled that he talked with the woman: yet no man said, What seekest thou? or, Why talkest thou with her?

28 The woman then left her waterpot, and went her way into the city, and saith to the men,

29 Come, see a man, which told me all things that ever I did: is not this the Christ?

30 Then they went out of the city, and came unto him.

31 In the mean while his disciples prayed him, saying, Master, eat.

32 But he said unto them, I have meat to eat that ye know not of.

33 Therefore said the disciples one to another, Hath any man brought him *ought* to eat?

34 Jesus saith unto them, My meat is to do the will of him that sent me, and to finish his work.

35 Say not ye, There are yet four months, and *then* cometh harvest? behold, I say unto you, Lift up your eyes, and look on the fields; for they are white already to harvest.

36 And he that reapeth receiveth wages, and gathereth fruit unto life eternal: that both he that soweth and he that reapeth may rejoice together.

37 And herein is that saying true, One soweth, and another reapeth.

38 I sent you to reap that whereon ye bestowed no labour: other men laboured, and ye are entered into their labours.

39 And many of the Samaritans of that city believed on him for the saying of the woman, which testified, He told me all that ever I did.

40 So when the Samaritans were come unto him, they besought him that he would tarry with them: and he abode there two days.

41 And many more believed because of his own word;

42 And said unto the woman, Now we believe, not because of thy saying: for we have heard *him* ourselves, and know that this is indeed the Christ, the Saviour of the world.

43 Now after two days he departed thence, and went into Galilee.

44 For Jesus himself testified, that a prophet hath no honour in his own country.

45 Then when he was come into Galilee, the Galilaeans received him, having seen all the things that he did at Jerusalem at the feast: for they also went unto the feast.

46 So Jesus came again into Cana of Galilee, where he made the water wine. And there was a certain nobleman, whose son was sick at Capernaum.

47 When he heard that Jesus was come out of Judaea into Galilee, he went unto him, and besought him that he would come down, and heal his son: for he was at the point of death.

48 Then said Jesus unto him, Except ye see signs and wonders, ye will not believe.

49 The nobleman saith unto him, Sir, come down ere my child die.

50 Jesus saith unto him, Go thy way; thy son liveth. And the man believed the word that Jesus had spoken unto him, and he went his way.

51 And as he was now going down, his servants met him, and told *him*, saying, Thy son liveth.

52 Then enquired he of them the hour when he began to amend. And they said unto him, Yesterday at the seventh hour the fever left him.

53 So the father knew that *it was* at the same hour, in the which Jesus said unto him, Thy son liveth: and himself believed, and his whole house.

54 This *is* again the second miracle *that* Jesus did, when he was come out of Judaea into Galilee.

5 After this there was a feast of the Jews; and Jesus went up to Jerusalem.

2 Now there is at Jerusalem by the sheep *market* a pool, which is called in the Hebrew tongue Bethesda, having five porches.

3 In these lay a great multitude of impotent folk, of blind, halt, withered, waiting for the moving of the water.

4 For an angel went down at a certain season into the pool, and troubled the water: whosoever then first after the troubling of the water stepped in was made whole of whatsoever disease he had.

5 And a certain man was there, which had an infirmity thirty and eight years.

6 When Jesus saw him lie, and knew that he had been now a long time *in*

that case, he saith unto him, Wilt thou be made whole?

7 The impotent man answered him, Sir, I have no man, when the water is troubled, to put me into the pool: but while I am coming, another steppeth down before me.

8 Jesus saith unto him, Rise, take up thy bed, and walk.

9 And immediately the man was made whole, and took up his bed, and walked: and on the same day was the sabbath.

10 The Jews therefore said unto him that was cured, It is the sabbath day: it is not lawful for thee to carry *thy* bed.

11 He answered them, He that made me whole, the same said unto me, Take up thy bed, and walk.

12 Then asked they him, What man is that which said unto thee, Take up thy bed, and walk?

13 And he that was healed wist not who it was: for Jesus had conveyed himself away, a multitude being in *that* place.

14 Afterward Jesus findeth him in the temple, and said unto him, Behold, thou art made whole: sin no more, lest a worse thing come unto thee.

15 The man departed, and told the Jews that it was Jesus, which had made him whole.

16 And therefore did the Jews persecute Jesus, and sought to slay him, because he had done these things on the sabbath day.

17 But Jesus answered them, My Father worketh hitherto, and I work.

18 Therefore the Jews sought the more to kill him, because he not only had broken the sabbath, but said also that God was his Father, making himself equal with God.

19 Then answered Jesus and said unto them, Verily, verily, I say unto you, The Son can do nothing of himself, but what he seeth the Father do: for what things soever he doeth, these also doeth the Son likewise.

20 For the Father loveth the Son, and sheweth him all things that himself doeth: and he will shew him greater works than these, that ye may marvel.

21 For as the Father raiseth up the dead, and quickeneth *them*; even so the Son quickeneth whom he will.

22 For the Father judgeth no man, but hath committed all judgment unto the Son:

23 That all *men* should honour the Son, even as they honour the Father. He that honoureth not the Son honoureth not the Father which hath sent him.

24 Verily, verily, I say unto you, He that heareth my word, and believeth on him that sent me, hath everlasting life, and shall not come into condemnation; but is passed from death unto life.

25 Verily, verily, I say unto you, The hour is coming, and now is, when the dead shall hear the voice of the Son of God: and they that hear shall live.

26 For as the Father hath life in himself; so hath he given to the Son to have life in himself;

27 And hath given him authority to execute judgment also, because he is the Son of man.

28 Marvel not at this: for the hour is coming, in the which all that are in the graves shall hear his voice,

29 And shall come forth; they that have done good, unto the resurrection of life; and they that have done evil, unto the resurrection of damnation.

30 I can of mine own self do nothing: as I hear, I judge: and my judgment is

just; because I seek not mine own will, but the will of the Father which hath sent me.

31 If I bear witness of myself, my witness is not true.

32 There is another that beareth witness of me; and I know that the witness which he witnesseth of me is true.

33 Ye sent unto John, and he bare witness unto the truth.

34 But I receive not testimony from man: but these things I say, that ye might be saved.

35 He was a burning and a shining light: and ye were willing for a season to rejoice in his light.

36 But I have greater witness than *that* of John: for the works which the Father hath given me to finish, the same works that I do, bear witness of me, that the Father hath sent me.

37 And the Father himself, which hath sent me, hath borne witness of me. Ye have neither heard his voice at any time, nor seen his shape.

38 And ye have not his word abiding in you: for whom he hath sent, him ye believe not.

39 Search the scriptures; for in them ye think ye have eternal life: and they are they which testify of me.

40 And ye will not come to me, that ye might have life.

41 I receive not honour from men.

42 But I know you, that ye have not the love of God in you.

43 I am come in my Father's name, and ye receive me not: if another shall come in his own name, him ye will receive.

44 How can ye believe, which receive honour one of another, and seek not the honour that *cometh* from God only?

45 Do not think that I will accuse you to the Father: there is *one* that accuseth you, *even* Moses, in whom ye trust.

46 For had ye believed Moses, ye would have believed me: for he wrote of me.

47 But if ye believe not his writings, how shall ye believe my words?

6 After these things Jesus went over the sea of Galilee, which is *the sea* of Tiberias.

2 And a great multitude followed him, because they saw his miracles which he did on them that were diseased.

3 And Jesus went up into a mountain, and there he sat with his disciples.

4 And the passover, a feast of the Jews, was nigh.

5 When Jesus then lifted up *his* eyes, and saw a great company come unto him, he saith unto Philip, Whence shall we buy bread, that these may eat?

6 And this he said to prove him: for he himself knew what he would do.

7 Philip answered him, Two hundred pennyworth of bread is not sufficient for them, that every one of them may take a little.

8 One of his disciples, Andrew, Simon Peter's brother, saith unto him,

9 There is a lad here, which hath five barley loaves, and two small fishes: but what are they among so many?

10 And Jesus said, Make the men sit down. Now there was much grass in the place. So the men sat down, in number about five thousand.

11 And Jesus took the loaves; and when he had given thanks, he distributed to the disciples, and the disciples to them that were set down; and likewise of the fishes as much as they would.

12 When they were filled, he said
unto his disciples, Gather up the fragments that remain, that nothing be lost.
13 Therefore they gathered *them*
together, and filled twelve baskets with
the fragments of the five barley loaves,
which remained over and above unto
them that had eaten.
14 Then those men, when they had
seen the miracle that Jesus did, said,
This is of a truth that prophet that
should come into the world.
15 When Jesus therefore perceived
that they would come and take him by
force, to make him a king, he departed
again into a mountain himself alone.
16 And when even was *now* come, his
disciples went down unto the sea,
17 And entered into a ship, and went
over the sea toward Capernaum. And it
was now dark, and Jesus was not come
to them.
18 And the sea arose by reason of a
great wind that blew.
19 So when they had rowed about five
and twenty or thirty furlongs, they see
Jesus walking on the sea, and drawing
nigh unto the ship: and they were
afraid.
20 But he saith unto them, It is I; be
not afraid.
21 Then they willingly received him
into the ship: and immediately the ship
was at the land whither they went.
22 The day following, when the people which stood on the other side of the
sea saw that there was none other boat
there, save that one whereinto his disciples were entered, and that Jesus
went not with his disciples into the
boat, but *that* his disciples were gone
away alone;
23 (Howbeit there came other boats
from Tiberias nigh unto the place
where they did eat bread, after that the
Lord had given thanks:)
24 When the people therefore saw
that Jesus was not there, neither his
disciples, they also took shipping, and
came to Capernaum, seeking for Jesus.
25 And when they had found him on
the other side of the sea, they said unto
him, Rabbi, when camest thou hither?
26 Jesus answered them and said,
Verily, verily, I say unto you, Ye seek
me, not because ye saw the miracles,
but because ye did eat of the loaves,
and were filled.
27 Labour not for the meat which
perisheth, but for that meat which
endureth unto everlasting life, which
the Son of man shall give unto you: for
him hath God the Father sealed.
28 Then said they unto him, What
shall we do, that we might work the
works of God?
29 Jesus answered and said unto
them, This is the work of God, that ye
believe on him whom he hath sent.
30 They said therefore unto him,
What sign shewest thou then, that we
may see, and believe thee? what dost
thou work?
31 Our fathers did eat manna in the
desert; as it is written, He gave them
bread from heaven to eat.
32 Then Jesus said unto them, Verily,
verily, I say unto you, Moses gave you
not that bread from heaven; but my
Father giveth you the true bread from
heaven.
33 For the bread of God is he which
cometh down from heaven, and giveth
life unto the world.
34 Then said they unto him, Lord,
evermore give us this bread.
35 And Jesus said unto them, I am the
bread of life: he that cometh to me

shall never hunger; and he that believeth on me shall never thirst.
36 But I said unto you, That ye also
have seen me, and believe not.
37 All that the Father giveth me shall
come to me; and him that cometh to me
I will in no wise cast out.
38 For I came down from heaven, not
to do mine own will, but the will of him
that sent me.
39 And this is the Father's will which
hath sent me, that of all which he hath
given me I should lose nothing, but
should raise it up again at the last day.
40 And this is the will of him that sent
me, that every one which seeth the Son,
and believeth on him, may have everlasting life: and I will raise him up at
the last day.
41 The Jews then murmured at him,
because he said, I am the bread which
came down from heaven.
42 And they said, Is not this Jesus, the
son of Joseph, whose father and mother
we know? how is it then that he saith, I
came down from heaven?
43 Jesus therefore answered and said
unto them, Murmur not among yourselves.
44 No man can come to me, except
the Father which hath sent me draw
him: and I will raise him up at the last
day.
45 It is written in the prophets, And
they shall be all taught of God. Every
man therefore that hath heard, and
hath learned of the Father, cometh
unto me.
46 Not that any man hath seen the
Father, save he which is of God, he hath
seen the Father.
47 Verily, verily, I say unto you, He
that believeth on me hath everlasting
life.
48 I am that bread of life.
49 Your fathers did eat manna in the
wilderness, and are dead.
50 This is the bread which cometh
down from heaven, that a man may eat
thereof, and not die.
51 I am the living bread which came
down from heaven: if any man eat of
this bread, he shall live for ever: and
the bread that I will give is my flesh,
which I will give for the life of the
world.
52 The Jews therefore strove among
themselves, saying, How can this man
give us *his* flesh to eat?
53 Then Jesus said unto them, Verily,
verily, I say unto you, Except ye eat the
flesh of the Son of man, and drink his
blood, ye have no life in you.
54 Whoso eateth my flesh, and drinketh my blood, hath eternal life; and I
will raise him up at the last day.
55 For my flesh is meat indeed, and
my blood is drink indeed.
56 He that eateth my flesh, and drinketh my blood, dwelleth in me, and I in
him.
57 As the living Father hath sent me,
and I live by the Father: so he that
eateth me, even he shall live by me.
58 This is that bread which came
down from heaven: not as your fathers
did eat manna, and are dead: he that
eateth of this bread shall live for ever.
59 These things said he in the synagogue, as he taught in Capernaum.
60 Many therefore of his disciples,
when they had heard *this*, said, This is
an hard saying; who can hear it?
61 When Jesus knew in himself that
his disciples murmured at it, he said
unto them, Doth this offend you?
62 *What* and if ye shall see the Son of
man ascend up where he was before?

63 It is the spirit that quickeneth; the flesh profiteth nothing: the words that I speak unto you, *they* are spirit, and *they* are life.

64 But there are some of you that believe not. For Jesus knew from the beginning who they were that believed not, and who should betray him.

65 And he said, Therefore said I unto you, that no man can come unto me, except it were given unto him of my Father.

66 From that *time* many of his disciples went back, and walked no more with him.

67 Then said Jesus unto the twelve, Will ye also go away?

68 Then Simon Peter answered him, Lord, to whom shall we go? thou hast the words of eternal life.

69 And we believe and are sure that thou art that Christ, the Son of the living God.

70 Jesus answered them, Have not I chosen you twelve, and one of you is a devil?

71 He spake of Judas Iscariot *the son* of Simon: for he it was that should betray him, being one of the twelve.

7 After these things Jesus walked in Galilee: for he would not walk in Jewry, because the Jews sought to kill him.

2 Now the Jews' feast of tabernacles was at hand.

3 His brethren therefore said unto him, Depart hence, and go into Judaea, that thy disciples also may see the works that thou doest.

4 For *there is* no man *that* doeth any thing in secret, and he himself seeketh to be known openly. If thou do these things, shew thyself to the world.

5 For neither did his brethren believe in him.

6 Then Jesus said unto them, My time is not yet come: but your time is alway ready.

7 The world cannot hate you; but me it hateth, because I testify of it, that the works thereof are evil.

8 Go ye up unto this feast: I go not up yet unto this feast; for my time is not yet full come.

9 When he had said these words unto them, he abode *still* in Galilee.

10 But when his brethren were gone up, then went he also up unto the feast, not openly, but as it were in secret.

11 Then the Jews sought him at the feast, and said, Where is he?

12 And there was much murmuring among the people concerning him: for some said, He is a good man: others said, Nay; but he deceiveth the people.

13 Howbeit no man spake openly of him for fear of the Jews.

14 Now about the midst of the feast Jesus went up into the temple, and taught.

15 And the Jews marvelled, saying, How knoweth this man letters, having never learned?

16 Jesus answered them, and said, My doctrine is not mine, but his that sent me.

17 If any man will do his will, he shall know of the doctrine, whether it be of God, or *whether* I speak of myself.

18 He that speaketh of himself seeketh his own glory: but he that seeketh his glory that sent him, the same is true, and no unrighteousness is in him.

19 Did not Moses give you the law, and *yet* none of you keepeth the law? Why go ye about to kill me?

20 The people answered and said, Thou hast a devil: who goeth about to kill thee?

21 Jesus answered and said unto them, I have done one work, and ye all marvel.

22 Moses therefore gave unto you circumcision; (not because it is of Moses, but of the fathers;) and ye on the sabbath day circumcise a man.

23 If a man on the sabbath day receive circumcision, that the law of Moses should not be broken; are ye angry at me, because I have made a man every whit whole on the sabbath day?

24 Judge not according to the appearance, but judge righteous judgment.

25 Then said some of them of Jerusalem, Is not this he, whom they seek to kill?

26 But, lo, he speaketh boldly, and they say nothing unto him. Do the rulers know indeed that this is the very Christ?

27 Howbeit we know this man whence he is: but when Christ cometh, no man knoweth whence he is.

28 Then cried Jesus in the temple as he taught, saying, Ye both know me, and ye know whence I am: and I am not come of myself, but he that sent me is true, whom ye know not.

29 But I know him: for I am from him, and he hath sent me.

30 Then they sought to take him: but no man laid hands on him, because his hour was not yet come.

31 And many of the people believed on him, and said, When Christ cometh, will he do more miracles than these which this *man* hath done?

32 The Pharisees heard that the people murmured such things concerning him; and the Pharisees and the chief priests sent officers to take him.

33 Then said Jesus unto them, Yet a little while am I with you, and *then* I go unto him that sent me.

34 Ye shall seek me, and shall not find *me*: and where I am, *thither* ye cannot come.

35 Then said the Jews among themselves, Whither will he go, that we shall not find him? will he go unto the dispersed among the Gentiles, and teach the Gentiles?

36 What *manner of* saying is this that he said, Ye shall seek me, and shall not find *me*: and where I am, *thither* ye cannot come?

37 In the last day, that great *day* of the feast, Jesus stood and cried, saying, If any man thirst, let him come unto me, and drink.

38 He that believeth on me, as the scripture hath said, out of his belly shall flow rivers of living water.

39 (But this spake he of the Spirit, which they that believe on him should receive: for the Holy Ghost was not yet *given*; because that Jesus was not yet glorified.)

40 Many of the people therefore, when they heard this saying, said, Of a truth this is the Prophet.

41 Others said, This is the Christ. But some said, Shall Christ come out of Galilee?

42 Hath not the scripture said, That Christ cometh of the seed of David, and out of the town of Bethlehem, where David was?

43 So there was a division among the people because of him.

44 And some of them would have taken him; but no man laid hands on him.

45 Then came the officers to the chief
priests and Pharisees; and they said
unto them, Why have ye not brought
him?
46 The officers answered, Never man
spake like this man.
47 Then answered them the Pharisees, Are ye also deceived?
48 Have any of the rulers or of the
Pharisees believed on him?
49 But this people who knoweth not
the law are cursed.
50 Nicodemus saith unto them, (he
that came to Jesus by night, being one
of them,)
51 Doth our law judge *any* man,
before it hear him, and know what he
doeth?
52 They answered and said unto him,
Art thou also of Galilee? Search, and
look: for out of Galilee ariseth no
prophet.
53 And every man went unto his own
house.

8 Jesus went unto the mount of
Olives.
2 And early in the morning he came
again into the temple, and all the people came unto him; and he sat down,
and taught them.
3 And the scribes and Pharisees
brought unto him a woman taken in
adultery; and when they had set her in
the midst,
4 They say unto him, Master, this
woman was taken in adultery, in the
very act.
5 Now Moses in the law commanded
us, that such should be stoned: but
what sayest thou?
6 This they said, tempting him, that
they might have to accuse him. But
Jesus stooped down, and with *his* finger wrote on the ground, *as though he
heard them not*.
7 So when they continued asking him,
he lifted up himself, and said unto
them, He that is without sin among you,
let him first cast a stone at her.
8 And again he stooped down, and
wrote on the ground.
9 And they which heard *it*, being con-
victed by *their own* conscience, went
out one by one, beginning at the eldest,
even unto the last: and Jesus was left
alone, and the woman standing in the
midst.
10 When Jesus had lifted up himself,
and saw none but the woman, he said
unto her, Woman, where are those thine
accusers? hath no man condemned
thee?
11 She said, No man, Lord. And Jesus
said unto her, Neither do I condemn
thee: go, and sin no more.
12 Then spake Jesus again unto them,
saying, I am the light of the world: he
that followeth me shall not walk in
darkness, but shall have the light of
life.
13 The Pharisees therefore said unto
him, Thou bearest record of thyself; thy
record is not true.
14 Jesus answered and said unto
them, Though I bear record of myself,
yet my record is true: for I know
whence I came, and whither I go; but ye
cannot tell whence I come, and whither
I go.
15 Ye judge after the flesh; I judge no
man.
16 And yet if I judge, my judgment is
true: for I am not alone, but I and the
Father that sent me.
17 It is also written in your law, that
the testimony of two men is true.

18 I am one that bear witness of
myself, and the Father that sent me
beareth witness of me.
19 Then said they unto him, Where is
thy Father? Jesus answered, Ye neither
know me, nor my Father: if ye had
known me, ye should have known my
Father also.
20 These words spake Jesus in the
treasury, as he taught in the temple:
and no man laid hands on him; for his
hour was not yet come.
21 Then said Jesus again unto them, I
go my way, and ye shall seek me, and
shall die in your sins: whither I go, ye
cannot come.
22 Then said the Jews, Will he kill
himself? because he saith, Whither I go,
ye cannot come.
23 And he said unto them, Ye are
from beneath; I am from above: ye are
of this world; I am not of this world.
24 I said therefore unto you, that ye
shall die in your sins: for if ye believe
not that I am *he*, ye shall die in your
sins.
25 Then said they unto him, Who art
thou? And Jesus saith unto them, Even
the same that I said unto you from the
beginning.
26 I have many things to say and to
judge of you: but he that sent me is
true; and I speak to the world those
things which I have heard of him.
27 They understood not that he spake
to them of the Father.
28 Then said Jesus unto them, When
ye have lifted up the Son of man, then
shall ye know that I am *he*, and *that* I
do nothing of myself; but as my Father
hath taught me, I speak these things.
29 And he that sent me is with me:
the Father hath not left me alone; for I
do always those things that please him.
30 As he spake these words, many
believed on him.
31 Then said Jesus to those Jews
which believed on him, If ye continue
in my word, *then* are ye my disciples
indeed;
32 And ye shall know the truth, and
the truth shall make you free.
33 They answered him, We be
Abraham's seed, and were never in
bondage to any man: how sayest thou,
Ye shall be made free?
34 Jesus answered them, Verily, verily,
I say unto you, Whosoever committeth
sin is the servant of sin.
35 And the servant abideth not in the
house for ever: *but* the Son abideth
ever.
36 If the Son therefore shall make you
free, ye shall be free indeed.
37 I know that ye are Abraham's seed;
but ye seek to kill me, because my word
hath no place in you.
38 I speak that which I have seen with
my Father: and ye do that which ye
have seen with your father.
39 They answered and said unto him,
Abraham is our father. Jesus saith unto
them, If ye were Abraham's children, ye
would do the works of Abraham.
40 But now ye seek to kill me, a man
that hath told you the truth, which I
have heard of God: this did not
Abraham.
41 Ye do the deeds of your father.
Then said they to him, We be not born
of fornication; we have one Father, *even*
God.
42 Jesus said unto them, If God were
your Father, ye would love me: for I
proceeded forth and came from God;
neither came I of myself, but he sent
me.

43 Why do ye not understand my
speech? *even* because ye cannot hear
my word.
44 Ye are of *your* father the devil, and
the lusts of your father ye will do. He
was a murderer from the beginning,
and abode not in the truth, because
there is no truth in him. When he speaketh a lie, he speaketh of his own: for
he is a liar, and the father of it.
45 And because I tell *you* the truth,
ye believe me not.
46 Which of you convinceth me of
sin? And if I say the truth, why do ye
not believe me?
47 He that is of God heareth God's
words: ye therefore hear *them* not,
because ye are not of God.
48 Then answered the Jews, and said
unto him, Say we not well that thou art
a Samaritan, and hast a devil?
49 Jesus answered, I have not a devil;
but I honour my Father, and ye do dishonour me.
50 And I seek not mine own glory:
there is one that seeketh and judgeth.
51 Verily, verily, I say unto you, If a
man keep my saying, he shall never see
death.
52 Then said the Jews unto him, Now
we know that thou hast a devil.
Abraham is dead, and the prophets;
and thou sayest, If a man keep my saying, he shall never taste of death.
53 Art thou greater than our father
Abraham, which is dead? and the
prophets are dead: whom makest thou
thyself?
54 Jesus answered, If I honour myself,
my honour is nothing: it is my Father
that honoureth me; of whom ye say,
that he is your God:
55 Yet ye have not known him; but I
know him: and if I should say, I know
him not, I shall be a liar like unto you:
but I know him, and keep his saying.
56 Your father Abraham rejoiced to
see my day: and he saw *it*, and was glad.
57 Then said the Jews unto him, Thou
art not yet fifty years old, and hast thou
seen Abraham?
58 Jesus said unto them, Verily, verily,
I say unto you, Before Abraham was, I
am.
59 Then took they up stones to cast at
him: but Jesus hid himself, and went
out of the temple, going through the
midst of them, and so passed by.

9 And as *Jesus* passed by, he saw a
man which was blind from *his* birth.
2 And his disciples asked him, saying,
Master, who did sin, this man, or his
parents, that he was born blind?
3 Jesus answered, Neither hath this
man sinned, nor his parents: but that
the works of God should be made
manifest in him.
4 I must work the works of him that
sent me, while it is day: the night
cometh, when no man can work.
5 As long as I am in the world, I am
the light of the world.
6 When he had thus spoken, he spat
on the ground, and made clay of the
spittle, and he anointed the eyes of the
blind man with the clay,
7 And said unto him, Go, wash in the
pool of Siloam, (which is by interpretation, Sent.) He went his way therefore,
and washed, and came seeing.
8 The neighbours therefore, and they
which before had seen him that he was
blind, said, Is not this he that sat and
begged?
9 Some said, This is he: others *said*,
He is like him: *but* he said, I am *he*.
10 Therefore said they unto him, How
were thine eyes opened?

11 He answered and said, A man that
is called Jesus made clay, and anointed
mine eyes, and said unto me, Go to the
pool of Siloam, and wash: and I went
and washed, and I received sight.
12 Then said they unto him, Where is
he? He said, I know not.
13 They brought to the Pharisees him
that aforetime was blind.
14 And it was the sabbath day when
Jesus made the clay, and opened his
eyes.
15 Then again the Pharisees also
asked him how he had received his
sight. He said unto them, He put clay
upon mine eyes, and I washed, and do
see.
16 Therefore said some of the Pharisees, This man is not of God, because he
keepeth not the sabbath day. Others
said, How can a man that is a sinner do
such miracles? And there was a division
among them.
17 They say unto the blind man again,
What sayest thou of him, that he hath
opened thine eyes? He said, He is a
prophet.
18 But the Jews did not believe concerning him, that he had been blind,
and received his sight, until they called
the parents of him that had received
his sight.
19 And they asked them, saying, Is
this your son, who ye say was born
blind? how then doth he now see?
20 His parents answered them and
said, We know that this is our son, and
that he was born blind:
21 But by what means he now seeth,
we know not; or who hath opened his
eyes, we know not: he is of age; ask him:
he shall speak for himself.
22 These *words* spake his parents,
because they feared the Jews: for the
Jews had agreed already, that if any
man did confess that he was Christ, he
should be put out of the synagogue.
23 Therefore said his parents, He is of
age; ask him.
24 Then again called they the man
that was blind, and said unto him, Give
God the praise: we know that this man
is a sinner.
25 He answered and said, Whether he
be a sinner *or no*, I know not: one thing
I know, that, whereas I was blind, now I
see.
26 Then said they to him again, What
did he to thee? how opened he thine
eyes?
27 He answered them, I have told you
already, and ye did not hear: wherefore
would ye hear *it* again? will ye also be
his disciples?
28 Then they reviled him, and said,
Thou art his disciple; but we are Moses'
disciples.
29 We know that God spake unto
Moses: *as for* this *fellow*, we know not
from whence he is.
30 The man answered and said unto
them, Why herein is a marvellous thing,
that ye know not from whence he is,
and *yet* he hath opened mine eyes.
31 Now we know that God heareth
not sinners: but if any man be a worshipper of God, and doeth his will, him
he heareth.
32 Since the world began was it not
heard that any man opened the eyes of
one that was born blind.
33 If this man were not of God, he
could do nothing.
34 They answered and said unto him,
Thou wast altogether born in sins, and
dost thou teach us? And they cast him
out.

35 Jesus heard that they had cast him
out; and when he had found him, he
said unto him, Dost thou believe on the
Son of God?
36 He answered and said, Who is he,
Lord, that I might believe on him?
37 And Jesus said unto him, Thou
hast both seen him, and it is he that
talketh with thee.
38 And he said, Lord, I believe. And
he worshipped him.
39 And Jesus said, For judgment I am
come into this world, that they which
see not might see; and that they which
see might be made blind.
40 And *some* of the Pharisees which
were with him heard these words, and
said unto him, Are we blind also?
41 Jesus said unto them, If ye were
blind, ye should have no sin: but now ye
say, We see; therefore your sin remaineth.

10 Verily, verily, I say unto you, He
that entereth not by the door
into the sheepfold, but climbeth up
some other way, the same is a thief and
a robber.
2 But he that entereth in by the door
is the shepherd of the sheep.
3 To him the porter openeth; and the
sheep hear his voice: and he calleth his
own sheep by name, and leadeth them
out.
4 And when he putteth forth his own
sheep, he goeth before them, and the
sheep follow him: for they know his
voice.
5 And a stranger will they not follow,
but will flee from him: for they know
not the voice of strangers.
6 This parable spake Jesus unto them:
but they understood not what things
they were which he spake unto them.
7 Then said Jesus unto them again,
Verily, verily, I say unto you, I am the
door of the sheep.
8 All that ever came before me are
thieves and robbers: but the sheep did
not hear them.
9 I am the door: by me if any man
enter in, he shall be saved, and shall go
in and out, and find pasture.
10 The thief cometh not, but for to
steal, and to kill, and to destroy: I am
come that they might have life, and
that they might have *it* more abundantly.
11 I am the good shepherd: the good
shepherd giveth his life for the sheep.
12 But he that is an hireling, and not
the shepherd, whose own the sheep are
not, seeth the wolf coming, and leaveth
the sheep, and fleeth: and the wolf
catcheth them, and scattereth the
sheep.
13 The hireling fleeth, because he is
an hireling, and careth not for the
sheep.
14 I am the good shepherd, and know
my *sheep*, and am known of mine.
15 As the Father knoweth me, even so
know I the Father: and I lay down my
life for the sheep.
16 And other sheep I have, which are
not of this fold: them also I must bring,
and they shall hear my voice; and there
shall be one fold, *and* one shepherd.
17 Therefore doth my Father love me,
because I lay down my life, that I might
take it again.
18 No man taketh it from me, but I lay
it down of myself. I have power to lay it
down, and I have power to take it again.
This commandment have I received of
my Father.
19 There was a division therefore
again among the Jews for these sayings.

20 And many of them said, He hath a devil, and is mad; why hear ye him?

21 Others said, These are not the words of him that hath a devil. Can a devil open the eyes of the blind?

22 And it was at Jerusalem the feast of the dedication, and it was winter.

23 And Jesus walked in the temple in Solomon's porch.

24 Then came the Jews round about him, and said unto him, How long dost thou make us to doubt? If thou be the Christ, tell us plainly.

25 Jesus answered them, I told you, and ye believed not: the works that I do in my Father's name, they bear witness of me.

26 But ye believe not, because ye are not of my sheep, as I said unto you.

27 My sheep hear my voice, and I know them, and they follow me:

28 And I give unto them eternal life; and they shall never perish, neither shall any *man* pluck them out of my hand.

29 My Father, which gave *them* me, is greater than all; and no *man* is able to pluck *them* out of my Father's hand.

30 I and *my* Father are one.

31 Then the Jews took up stones again to stone him.

32 Jesus answered them, Many good works have I shewed you from my Father; for which of those works do ye stone me?

33 The Jews answered him, saying, For a good work we stone thee not; but for blasphemy; and because that thou, being a man, makest thyself God.

34 Jesus answered them, Is it not written in your law, I said, Ye are gods?

35 If he called them gods, unto whom the word of God came, and the scripture cannot be broken;

36 Say ye of him, whom the Father hath sanctified, and sent into the world, Thou blasphemest; because I said, I am the Son of God?

37 If I do not the works of my Father, believe me not.

38 But if I do, though ye believe not me, believe the works: that ye may know, and believe, that the Father *is* in me, and I in him.

39 Therefore they sought again to take him: but he escaped out of their hand,

40 And went away again beyond Jordan into the place where John at first baptized; and there he abode.

41 And many resorted unto him, and said, John did no miracle: but all things that John spake of this man were true.

42 And many believed on him there.

11 Now a certain *man* was sick, *named* Lazarus, of Bethany, the town of Mary and her sister Martha.

2 (It was *that* Mary which anointed the Lord with ointment, and wiped his feet with her hair, whose brother Lazarus was sick.)

3 Therefore his sisters sent unto him, saying, Lord, behold, he whom thou lovest is sick.

4 When Jesus heard *that*, he said, This sickness is not unto death, but for the glory of God, that the Son of God might be glorified thereby.

5 Now Jesus loved Martha, and her sister, and Lazarus.

6 When he had heard therefore that he was sick, he abode two days still in the same place where he was.

7 Then after that saith he to *his* disciples, Let us go into Judaea again.

8 *His* disciples say unto him, Master, the Jews of late sought to stone thee; and goest thou thither again?

9 Jesus answered, Are there not
twelve hours in the day? If any man
walk in the day, he stumbleth not,
because he seeth the light of this world.
10 But if a man walk in the night, he
stumbleth, because there is no light in
him.
11 These things said he: and after
that he saith unto them, Our friend
Lazarus sleepeth; but I go, that I may
awake him out of sleep.
12 Then said his disciples, Lord, if he
sleep, he shall do well.
13 Howbeit Jesus spake of his death:
but they thought that he had spoken of
taking of rest in sleep.
14 Then said Jesus unto them plainly,
Lazarus is dead.
15 And I am glad for your sakes that I
was not there, to the intent ye may
believe; nevertheless let us go unto
him.
16 Then said Thomas, which is called
Didymus, unto his fellowdisciples, Let
us also go, that we may die with him.
17 Then when Jesus came, he found
that he had *lain* in the grave four days
already.
18 Now Bethany was nigh unto
Jerusalem, about fifteen furlongs off:
19 And many of the Jews came to
Martha and Mary, to comfort them
concerning their brother.
20 Then Martha, as soon as she heard
that Jesus was coming, went and met
him: but Mary sat *still* in the house.
21 Then said Martha unto Jesus,
Lord, if thou hadst been here, my
brother had not died.
22 But I know, that even now, whatsoever thou wilt ask of God, God will give
it thee.
23 Jesus saith unto her, Thy brother
shall rise again.
24 Martha saith unto him, I know that
he shall rise again in the resurrection
at the last day.
25 Jesus said unto her, I am the resurrection, and the life: he that believeth
in me, though he were dead, yet shall
he live:
26 And whosoever liveth and believeth in me shall never die. Believest
thou this?
27 She saith unto him, Yea, Lord: I
believe that thou art the Christ, the Son
of God, which should come into the
world.
28 And when she had so said, she
went her way, and called Mary her sister secretly, saying, The Master is come,
and calleth for thee.
29 As soon as she heard *that*, she
arose quickly, and came unto him.
30 Now Jesus was not yet come into
the town, but was in that place where
Martha met him.
31 The Jews then which were with
her in the house, and comforted her,
when they saw Mary, that she rose up
hastily and went out, followed her, saying, She goeth unto the grave to weep
there.
32 Then when Mary was come where
Jesus was, and saw him, she fell down
at his feet, saying unto him, Lord, if
thou hadst been here, my brother had
not died.
33 When Jesus therefore saw her
weeping, and the Jews also weeping
which came with her, he groaned in the
spirit, and was troubled,
34 And said, Where have ye laid him?
They said unto him, Lord, come and
see.
35 Jesus wept.
36 Then said the Jews, Behold how he
loved him!

37 And some of them said, Could not this man, which opened the eyes of the blind, have caused that even this man should not have died?

38 Jesus therefore again groaning in himself cometh to the grave. It was a cave, and a stone lay upon it.

39 Jesus said, Take ye away the stone. Martha, the sister of him that was dead, saith unto him, Lord, by this time he stinketh: for he hath been *dead* four days.

40 Jesus saith unto her, Said I not unto thee, that, if thou wouldest believe, thou shouldest see the glory of God?

41 Then they took away the stone *from the place* where the dead was laid. And Jesus lifted up *his* eyes, and said, Father, I thank thee that thou hast heard me.

42 And I knew that thou hearest me always: but because of the people which stand by I said *it*, that they may believe that thou hast sent me.

43 And when he thus had spoken, he cried with a loud voice, Lazarus, come forth.

44 And he that was dead came forth, bound hand and foot with graveclothes: and his face was bound about with a napkin. Jesus saith unto them, Loose him, and let him go.

45 Then many of the Jews which came to Mary, and had seen the things which Jesus did, believed on him.

46 But some of them went their ways to the Pharisees, and told them what things Jesus had done.

47 Then gathered the chief priests and the Pharisees a council, and said, What do we? for this man doeth many miracles.

48 If we let him thus alone, all *men* will believe on him: and the Romans shall come and take away both our place and nation.

49 And one of them, *named* Caiaphas, being the high priest that same year, said unto them, Ye know nothing at all,

50 Nor consider that it is expedient for us, that one man should die for the people, and that the whole nation perish not.

51 And this spake he not of himself: but being high priest that year, he prophesied that Jesus should die for that nation;

52 And not for that nation only, but that also he should gather together in one the children of God that were scattered abroad.

53 Then from that day forth they took counsel together for to put him to death.

54 Jesus therefore walked no more openly among the Jews; but went thence unto a country near to the wilderness, into a city called Ephraim, and there continued with his disciples.

55 And the Jews' passover was nigh at hand: and many went out of the country up to Jerusalem before the passover, to purify themselves.

56 Then sought they for Jesus, and spake among themselves, as they stood in the temple, What think ye, that he will not come to the feast?

57 Now both the chief priests and the Pharisees had given a commandment, that, if any man knew where he were, he should shew *it*, that they might take him.

12 Then Jesus six days before the passover came to Bethany, where Lazarus was which had been dead, whom he raised from the dead.

2 There they made him a supper; and Martha served: but Lazarus was one of them that sat at the table with him.
3 Then took Mary a pound of ointment of spikenard, very costly, and anointed the feet of Jesus, and wiped his feet with her hair: and the house was filled with the odour of the ointment.
4 Then saith one of his disciples, Judas Iscariot, Simon's *son*, which should betray him,
5 Why was not this ointment sold for three hundred pence, and given to the poor?
6 This he said, not that he cared for the poor; but because he was a thief, and had the bag, and bare what was put therein.
7 Then said Jesus, Let her alone: against the day of my burying hath she kept this.
8 For the poor always ye have with you; but me ye have not always.
9 Much people of the Jews therefore knew that he was there: and they came not for Jesus' sake only, but that they might see Lazarus also, whom he had raised from the dead.
10 But the chief priests consulted that they might put Lazarus also to death;
11 Because that by reason of him many of the Jews went away, and believed on Jesus.
12 On the next day much people that were come to the feast, when they heard that Jesus was coming to Jerusalem,
13 Took branches of palm trees, and went forth to meet him, and cried, Hosanna: Blessed *is* the King of Israel that cometh in the name of the Lord.
14 And Jesus, when he had found a young ass, sat thereon; as it is written,
15 Fear not, daughter of Sion: behold, thy King cometh, sitting on an ass's colt.
16 These things understood not his disciples at the first: but when Jesus was glorified, then remembered they that these things were written of him, and *that* they had done these things unto him.
17 The people therefore that was with him when he called Lazarus out of his grave, and raised him from the dead, bare record.
18 For this cause the people also met him, for that they heard that he had done this miracle.
19 The Pharisees therefore said among themselves, Perceive ye how ye prevail nothing? behold, the world is gone after him.
20 And there were certain Greeks among them that came up to worship at the feast:
21 The same came therefore to Philip, which was of Bethsaida of Galilee, and desired him, saying, Sir, we would see Jesus.
22 Philip cometh and telleth Andrew: and again Andrew and Philip tell Jesus.
23 And Jesus answered them, saying, The hour is come, that the Son of man should be glorified.
24 Verily, verily, I say unto you, Except a corn of wheat fall into the ground and die, it abideth alone: but if it die, it bringeth forth much fruit.
25 He that loveth his life shall lose it; and he that hateth his life in this world shall keep it unto life eternal.
26 If any man serve me, let him follow me; and where I am, there shall also my servant be: if any man serve me, him will *my* Father honour.

27 Now is my soul troubled; and what
shall I say? Father, save me from this
hour: but for this cause came I unto this
hour.
28 Father, glorify thy name. Then
came there a voice from heaven, *saying*, I have both glorified *it*, and will
glorify *it* again.
29 The people therefore, that stood
by, and heard *it*, said that it thundered:
others said, An angel spake to him.
30 Jesus answered and said, This
voice came not because of me, but for
your sakes.
31 Now is the judgment of this world:
now shall the prince of this world be
cast out.
32 And I, if I be lifted up from the
earth, will draw all *men* unto me.
33 This he said, signifying what death
he should die.
34 The people answered him, We have
heard out of the law that Christ abideth
for ever: and how sayest thou, The Son
of man must be lifted up? who is this
Son of man?
35 Then Jesus said unto them, Yet a
little while is the light with you. Walk
while ye have the light, lest darkness
come upon you: for he that walketh in
darkness knoweth not whither he
goeth.
36 While ye have light, believe in the
light, that ye may be the children of
light. These things spake Jesus, and
departed, and did hide himself from
them.
37 But though he had done so many
miracles before them, yet they believed
not on him:
38 That the saying of Esaias the
prophet might be fulfilled, which he
spake, Lord, who hath believed our
report? and to whom hath the arm of
the Lord been revealed?
39 Therefore they could not believe,
because that Esaias said again,
40 He hath blinded their eyes, and
hardened their heart; that they should
not see with *their* eyes, nor understand
with *their* heart, and be converted, and
I should heal them.
41 These things said Esaias, when he
saw his glory, and spake of him.
42 Nevertheless among the chief rulers also many believed on him; but
because of the Pharisees they did not
confess *him*, lest they should be put out
of the synagogue:
43 For they loved the praise of men
more than the praise of God.
44 Jesus cried and said, He that
believeth on me, believeth not on me,
but on him that sent me.
45 And he that seeth me seeth him
that sent me.
46 I am come a light into the world,
that whosoever believeth on me should
not abide in darkness.
47 And if any man hear my words,
and believe not, I judge him not: for I
came not to judge the world, but to
save the world.
48 He that rejecteth me, and receiveth not my words, hath one that
judgeth him: the word that I have spoken, the same shall judge him in the
last day.
49 For I have not spoken of myself;
but the Father which sent me, he gave
me a commandment, what I should say,
and what I should speak.
50 And I know that his commandment is life everlasting: whatsoever I
speak therefore, even as the Father
said unto me, so I speak.

13 Now before the feast of the passover, when Jesus knew that his hour was come that he should depart out of this world unto the Father, having loved his own which were in the world, he loved them unto the end.

2 And supper being ended, the devil having now put into the heart of Judas Iscariot, Simon's *son*, to betray him;

3 Jesus knowing that the Father had given all things into his hands, and that he was come from God, and went to God;

4 He riseth from supper, and laid aside his garments; and took a towel, and girded himself.

5 After that he poureth water into a bason, and began to wash the disciples' feet, and to wipe *them* with the towel wherewith he was girded.

6 Then cometh he to Simon Peter: and Peter saith unto him, Lord, dost thou wash my feet?

7 Jesus answered and said unto him, What I do thou knowest not now; but thou shalt know hereafter.

8 Peter saith unto him, Thou shalt never wash my feet. Jesus answered him, If I wash thee not, thou hast no part with me.

9 Simon Peter saith unto him, Lord, not my feet only, but also *my* hands and *my* head.

10 Jesus saith to him, He that is washed needeth not save to wash *his* feet, but is clean every whit: and ye are clean, but not all.

11 For he knew who should betray him; therefore said he, Ye are not all clean.

12 So after he had washed their feet, and had taken his garments, and was set down again, he said unto them, Know ye what I have done to you?

13 Ye call me Master and Lord: and ye say well; for *so* I am.

14 If I then, *your* Lord and Master, have washed your feet; ye also ought to wash one another's feet.

15 For I have given you an example, that ye should do as I have done to you.

16 Verily, verily, I say unto you, The servant is not greater than his lord; neither he that is sent greater than he that sent him.

17 If ye know these things, happy are ye if ye do them.

18 I speak not of you all: I know whom I have chosen: but that the scripture may be fulfilled, He that eateth bread with me hath lifted up his heel against me.

19 Now I tell you before it come, that, when it is come to pass, ye may believe that I am *he*.

20 Verily, verily, I say unto you, He that receiveth whomsoever I send receiveth me; and he that receiveth me receiveth him that sent me.

21 When Jesus had thus said, he was troubled in spirit, and testified, and said, Verily, verily, I say unto you, that one of you shall betray me.

22 Then the disciples looked one on another, doubting of whom he spake.

23 Now there was leaning on Jesus' bosom one of his disciples, whom Jesus loved.

24 Simon Peter therefore beckoned to him, that he should ask who it should be of whom he spake.

25 He then lying on Jesus' breast saith unto him, Lord, who is it?

26 Jesus answered, He it is, to whom I shall give a sop, when I have dipped *it*. And when he had dipped the sop, he gave *it* to Judas Iscariot, *the son* of Simon.

27 And after the sop Satan entered
into him. Then said Jesus unto him,
That thou doest, do quickly.
28 Now no man at the table knew for
what intent he spake this unto him.
29 For some *of them* thought, because
Judas had the bag, that Jesus had said
unto him, Buy *those things* that we
have need of against the feast; or, that
he should give something to the poor.
30 He then having received the sop
went immediately out: and it was night.
31 Therefore, when he was gone out,
Jesus said, Now is the Son of man glorified, and God is glorified in him.
32 If God be glorified in him, God
shall also glorify him in himself, and
shall straightway glorify him.
33 Little children, yet a little while I
am with you. Ye shall seek me: and as I
said unto the Jews, Whither I go, ye cannot come; so now I say to you.
34 A new commandment I give unto
you, That ye love one another; as I have
loved you, that ye also love one another.
35 By this shall all *men* know that ye
are my disciples, if ye have love one to
another.
36 Simon Peter said unto him, Lord,
whither goest thou? Jesus answered
him, Whither I go, thou canst not follow
me now; but thou shalt follow me afterwards.
37 Peter said unto him, Lord, why cannot I follow thee now? I will lay down
my life for thy sake.
38 Jesus answered him, Wilt thou lay
down thy life for my sake? Verily, verily,
I say unto thee, The cock shall not crow,
till thou hast denied me thrice.

14 Let not your heart be troubled:
ye believe in God, believe also in
me.
2 In my Father's house are many man-
sions: if *it were* not *so*, I would have told
you. I go to prepare a place for you.
3 And if I go and prepare a place for
you, I will come again, and receive you
unto myself; that where I am, *there* ye
may be also.
4 And whither I go ye know, and the
way ye know.
5 Thomas saith unto him, Lord, we
know not whither thou goest; and how
can we know the way?
6 Jesus saith unto him, I am the way,
the truth, and the life: no man cometh
unto the Father, but by me.
7 If ye had known me, ye should have
known my Father also: and from henceforth ye know him, and have seen him.
8 Philip saith unto him, Lord, shew us
the Father, and it sufficeth us.
9 Jesus saith unto him, Have I been so
long time with you, and yet hast thou
not known me, Philip? he that hath
seen me hath seen the Father; and how
sayest thou *then*, Shew us the Father?
10 Believest thou not that I am in the
Father, and the Father in me? the words
that I speak unto you I speak not of
myself: but the Father that dwelleth in
me, he doeth the works.
11 Believe me that I *am* in the Father,
and the Father in me: or else believe
me for the very works' sake.
12 Verily, verily, I say unto you, He
that believeth on me, the works that I
do shall he do also; and greater *works*
than these shall he do; because I go
unto my Father.
13 And whatsoever ye shall ask in my
name, that will I do, that the Father
may be glorified in the Son.

14 If ye shall ask any thing in my
name, I will do *it*.
15 If ye love me, keep my commandments.
16 And I will pray the Father, and he
shall give you another Comforter, that
he may abide with you for ever;
17 *Even* the Spirit of truth; whom the
world cannot receive, because it seeth
him not, neither knoweth him: but ye
know him; for he dwelleth with you,
and shall be in you.
18 I will not leave you comfortless: I
will come to you.
19 Yet a little while, and the world
seeth me no more; but ye see me:
because I live, ye shall live also.
20 At that day ye shall know that I *am*
in my Father, and ye in me, and I in you.
21 He that hath my commandments,
and keepeth them, he it is that loveth
me: and he that loveth me shall be
loved of my Father, and I will love him,
and will manifest myself to him.
22 Judas saith unto him, not Iscariot,
Lord, how is it that thou wilt manifest
thyself unto us, and not unto the world?
23 Jesus answered and said unto him,
If a man love me, he will keep my
words: and my Father will love him, and
we will come unto him, and make our
abode with him.
24 He that loveth me not keepeth not
my sayings: and the word which ye hear
is not mine, but the Father's which sent
me.
25 These things have I spoken unto
you, being *yet* present with you.
26 But the Comforter, *which is* the
Holy Ghost, whom the Father will send
in my name, he shall teach you all
things, and bring all things to your
remembrance, whatsoever I have said
unto you.
27 Peace I leave with you, my peace I
give unto you: not as the world giveth,
give I unto you. Let not your heart be
troubled, neither let it be afraid.
28 Ye have heard how I said unto you,
I go away, and come *again* unto you. If
ye loved me, ye would rejoice, because
I said, I go unto the Father: for my
Father is greater than I.
29 And now I have told you before it
come to pass, that, when it is come to
pass, ye might believe.
30 Hereafter I will not talk much with
you: for the prince of this world cometh,
and hath nothing in me.
31 But that the world may know that I
love the Father; and as the Father gave
me commandment, even so I do. Arise,
let us go hence.

15 I am the true vine, and my Father
is the husbandman.
2 Every branch in me that beareth
not fruit he taketh away: and every
branch that beareth fruit, he purgeth
it, that it may bring forth more fruit.
3 Now ye are clean through the word
which I have spoken unto you.
4 Abide in me, and I in you. As the
branch cannot bear fruit of itself,
except it abide in the vine; no more can
ye, except ye abide in me.
5 I am the vine, ye *are* the branches:
He that abideth in me, and I in him, the
same bringeth forth much fruit: for
without me ye can do nothing.
6 If a man abide not in me, he is cast
forth as a branch, and is withered; and
men gather them, and cast *them* into
the fire, and they are burned.
7 If ye abide in me, and my words
abide in you, ye shall ask what ye will,
and it shall be done unto you.

8 Herein is my Father glorified, that
ye bear much fruit; so shall ye be my
disciples.
9 As the Father hath loved me, so
have I loved you: continue ye in my
love.
10 If ye keep my commandments, ye
shall abide in my love; even as I have
kept my Father's commandments, and
abide in his love.
11 These things have I spoken unto
you, that my joy might remain in you,
and *that* your joy might be full.
12 This is my commandment, That ye
love one another, as I have loved you.
13 Greater love hath no man than
this, that a man lay down his life for his
friends.
14 Ye are my friends, if ye do whatsoever I command you.
15 Henceforth I call you not servants;
for the servant knoweth not what his
lord doeth: but I have called you
friends; for all things that I have heard
of my Father I have made known unto
you.
16 Ye have not chosen me, but I have
chosen you, and ordained you, that ye
should go and bring forth fruit, and
that your fruit should remain: that
whatsoever ye shall ask of the Father in
my name, he may give it you.
17 These things I command you, that
ye love one another.
18 If the world hate you, ye know that
it hated me before *it hated* you.
19 If ye were of the world, the world
would love his own: but because ye are
not of the world, but I have chosen you
out of the world, therefore the world
hateth you.
20 Remember the word that I said
unto you, The servant is not greater
than his lord. If they have persecuted
me, they will also persecute you; if they
have kept my saying, they will keep
yours also.
21 But all these things will they do
unto you for my name's sake, because
they know not him that sent me.
22 If I had not come and spoken unto
them, they had not had sin: but now
they have no cloke for their sin.
23 He that hateth me hateth my
Father also.
24 If I had not done among them the
works which none other man did, they
had not had sin: but now have they
both seen and hated both me and my
Father.
25 But *this cometh to pass*, that the
word might be fulfilled that is written
in their law, They hated me without a
cause.
26 But when the Comforter is come,
whom I will send unto you from the
Father, *even* the Spirit of truth, which
proceedeth from the Father, he shall
testify of me:
27 And ye also shall bear witness,
because ye have been with me from the
beginning.

16 These things have I spoken unto
you, that ye should not be offended.
2 They shall put you out of the synagogues: yea, the time cometh, that
whosoever killeth you will think that
he doeth God service.
3 And these things will they do unto
you, because they have not known the
Father, nor me.
4 But these things have I told you,
that when the time shall come, ye may
remember that I told you of them. And
these things I said not unto you at the
beginning, because I was with you.

5 But now I go my way to him that
sent me; and none of you asketh me,
Whither goest thou?
6 But because I have said these things
unto you, sorrow hath filled your heart.
7 Nevertheless I tell you the truth; It
is expedient for you that I go away: for
if I go not away, the Comforter will not
come unto you; but if I depart, I will
send him unto you.
8 And when he is come, he will
reprove the world of sin, and of righteousness, and of judgment:
9 Of sin, because they believe not on
me;
10 Of righteousness, because I go to
my Father, and ye see me no more;
11 Of judgment, because the prince
of this world is judged.
12 I have yet many things to say unto
you, but ye cannot bear them now.
13 Howbeit when he, the Spirit of
truth, is come, he will guide you into all
truth: for he shall not speak of himself;
but whatsoever he shall hear, *that* shall
he speak: and he will shew you things
to come.
14 He shall glorify me: for he shall
receive of mine, and shall shew *it* unto
you.
15 All things that the Father hath are
mine: therefore said I, that he shall
take of mine, and shall shew *it* unto
you.
16 A little while, and ye shall not see
me: and again, a little while, and ye
shall see me, because I go to the Father.
17 Then said *some* of his disciples
among themselves, What is this that he
saith unto us, A little while, and ye shall
not see me: and again, a little while,
and ye shall see me: and, Because I go
to the Father?
18 They said therefore, What is this
that he saith, A little while? we cannot
tell what he saith.
19 Now Jesus knew that they were
desirous to ask him, and said unto
them, Do ye enquire among yourselves
of that I said, A little while, and ye shall
not see me: and again, a little while,
and ye shall see me?
20 Verily, verily, I say unto you, That
ye shall weep and lament, but the
world shall rejoice: and ye shall be sorrowful, but your sorrow shall be turned
into joy.
21 A woman when she is in travail
hath sorrow, because her hour is come:
but as soon as she is delivered of the
child, she remembereth no more the
anguish, for joy that a man is born into
the world.
22 And ye now therefore have sorrow:
but I will see you again, and your heart
shall rejoice, and your joy no man
taketh from you.
23 And in that day ye shall ask me
nothing. Verily, verily, I say unto you,
Whatsoever ye shall ask the Father in
my name, he will give *it* you.
24 Hitherto have ye asked nothing in
my name: ask, and ye shall receive, that
your joy may be full.
25 These things have I spoken unto
you in proverbs: but the time cometh,
when I shall no more speak unto you in
proverbs, but I shall shew you plainly of
the Father.
26 At that day ye shall ask in my
name: and I say not unto you, that I will
pray the Father for you:
27 For the Father himself loveth you,
because ye have loved me, and have
believed that I came out from God.

28 I came forth from the Father, and
am come into the world: again, I leave
the world, and go to the Father.
29 His disciples said unto him, Lo,
now speakest thou plainly, and speakest no proverb.
30 Now are we sure that thou knowest
all things, and needest not that any
man should ask thee: by this we believe
that thou camest forth from God.
31 Jesus answered them, Do ye now
believe?
32 Behold, the hour cometh, yea, is
now come, that ye shall be scattered,
every man to his own, and shall leave
me alone: and yet I am not alone,
because the Father is with me.
33 These things I have spoken unto
you, that in me ye might have peace. In
the world ye shall have tribulation: but
be of good cheer; I have overcome the
world.

17 These words spake Jesus, and
lifted up his eyes to heaven, and
said, Father, the hour is come; glorify
thy Son, that thy Son also may glorify
thee:
2 As thou hast given him power over
all flesh, that he should give eternal life
to as many as thou hast given him.
3 And this is life eternal, that they
might know thee the only true God, and
Jesus Christ, whom thou hast sent.
4 I have glorified thee on the earth: I
have finished the work which thou
gavest me to do.
5 And now, O Father, glorify thou me
with thine own self with the glory
which I had with thee before the world
was.
6 I have manifested thy name unto
the men which thou gavest me out of
the world: thine they were, and thou
gavest them me; and they have kept thy
word.
7 Now they have known that all things
whatsoever thou hast given me are of
thee.
8 For I have given unto them the
words which thou gavest me; and they
have received *them*, and have known
surely that I came out from thee, and
they have believed that thou didst send
me.
9 I pray for them: I pray not for the
world, but for them which thou hast
given me; for they are thine.
10 And all mine are thine, and thine
are mine; and I am glorified in them.
11 And now I am no more in the
world, but these are in the world, and I
come to thee. Holy Father, keep through
thine own name those whom thou hast
given me, that they may be one, as we
are.
12 While I was with them in the
world, I kept them in thy name: those
that thou gavest me I have kept, and
none of them is lost, but the son of
perdition; that the scripture might be
fulfilled.
13 And now come I to thee; and these
things I speak in the world, that they
might have my joy fulfilled in themselves.
14 I have given them thy word; and
the world hath hated them, because
they are not of the world, even as I am
not of the world.
15 I pray not that thou shouldest take
them out of the world, but that thou
shouldest keep them from the evil.
16 They are not of the world, even as
I am not of the world.
17 Sanctify them through thy truth:
thy word is truth.

18 As thou hast sent me into the world, even so have I also sent them into the world.

19 And for their sakes I sanctify myself, that they also might be sanctified through the truth.

20 Neither pray I for these alone, but for them also which shall believe on me through their word;

21 That they all may be one; as thou, Father, *art* in me, and I in thee, that they also may be one in us: that the world may believe that thou hast sent me.

22 And the glory which thou gavest me I have given them; that they may be one, even as we are one:

23 I in them, and thou in me, that they may be made perfect in one; and that the world may know that thou hast sent me, and hast loved them, as thou hast loved me.

24 Father, I will that they also, whom thou hast given me, be with me where I am; that they may behold my glory, which thou hast given me: for thou lovedst me before the foundation of the world.

25 O righteous Father, the world hath not known thee: but I have known thee, and these have known that thou hast sent me.

26 And I have declared unto them thy name, and will declare *it*: that the love wherewith thou hast loved me may be in them, and I in them.

18 When Jesus had spoken these words, he went forth with his disciples over the brook Cedron, where was a garden, into the which he entered, and his disciples.

2 And Judas also, which betrayed him, knew the place: for Jesus ofttimes resorted thither with his disciples.

3 Judas then, having received a band *of men* and officers from the chief priests and Pharisees, cometh thither with lanterns and torches and weapons.

4 Jesus therefore, knowing all things that should come upon him, went forth, and said unto them, Whom seek ye?

5 They answered him, Jesus of Nazareth. Jesus saith unto them, I am *he*. And Judas also, which betrayed him, stood with them.

6 As soon then as he had said unto them, I am *he*, they went backward, and fell to the ground.

7 Then asked he them again, Whom seek ye? And they said, Jesus of Nazareth.

8 Jesus answered, I have told you that I am *he*: if therefore ye seek me, let these go their way:

9 That the saying might be fulfilled, which he spake, Of them which thou gavest me have I lost none.

10 Then Simon Peter having a sword drew it, and smote the high priest's servant, and cut off his right ear. The servant's name was Malchus.

11 Then said Jesus unto Peter, Put up thy sword into the sheath: the cup which my Father hath given me, shall I not drink it?

12 Then the band and the captain and officers of the Jews took Jesus, and bound him,

13 And led him away to Annas first; for he was father in law to Caiaphas, which was the high priest that same year.

14 Now Caiaphas was he, which gave counsel to the Jews, that it was expedient that one man should die for the people.

15 And Simon Peter followed Jesus, and *so did* another disciple: that disci-

ple was known unto the high priest, and went in with Jesus into the palace of the high priest.

16 But Peter stood at the door without. Then went out that other disciple, which was known unto the high priest, and spake unto her that kept the door, and brought in Peter.

17 Then saith the damsel that kept the door unto Peter, Art not thou also *one* of this man's disciples? He saith, I am not.

18 And the servants and officers stood there, who had made a fire of coals; for it was cold: and they warmed themselves: and Peter stood with them, and warmed himself.

19 The high priest then asked Jesus of his disciples, and of his doctrine.

20 Jesus answered him, I spake openly to the world; I ever taught in the synagogue, and in the temple, whither the Jews always resort; and in secret have I said nothing.

21 Why askest thou me? ask them which heard me, what I have said unto them: behold, they know what I said.

22 And when he had thus spoken, one of the officers which stood by struck Jesus with the palm of his hand, saying, Answerest thou the high priest so?

23 Jesus answered him, If I have spoken evil, bear witness of the evil: but if well, why smitest thou me?

24 Now Annas had sent him bound unto Caiaphas the high priest.

25 And Simon Peter stood and warmed himself. They said therefore unto him, Art not thou also *one* of his disciples? He denied *it*, and said, I am not.

26 One of the servants of the high priest, being *his* kinsman whose ear Peter cut off, saith, Did not I see thee in the garden with him?

27 Peter then denied again: and immediately the cock crew.

28 Then led they Jesus from Caiaphas unto the hall of judgment: and it was early; and they themselves went not into the judgment hall, lest they should be defiled; but that they might eat the passover.

29 Pilate then went out unto them, and said, What accusation bring ye against this man?

30 They answered and said unto him, If he were not a malefactor, we would not have delivered him up unto thee.

31 Then said Pilate unto them, Take ye him, and judge him according to your law. The Jews therefore said unto him, It is not lawful for us to put any man to death:

32 That the saying of Jesus might be fulfilled, which he spake, signifying what death he should die.

33 Then Pilate entered into the judgment hall again, and called Jesus, and said unto him, Art thou the King of the Jews?

34 Jesus answered him, Sayest thou this thing of thyself, or did others tell it thee of me?

35 Pilate answered, Am I a Jew? Thine own nation and the chief priests have delivered thee unto me: what hast thou done?

36 Jesus answered, My kingdom is not of this world: if my kingdom were of this world, then would my servants fight, that I should not be delivered to the Jews: but now is my kingdom not from hence.

37 Pilate therefore said unto him, Art thou a king then? Jesus answered, Thou sayest that I am a king. To this end was

I born, and for this cause came I into the world, that I should bear witness unto the truth. Every one that is of the truth heareth my voice.
38 Pilate saith unto him, What is truth? And when he had said this, he went out again unto the Jews, and saith unto them, I find in him no fault *at all*.
39 But ye have a custom, that I should release unto you one at the passover: will ye therefore that I release unto you the King of the Jews?
40 Then cried they all again, saying, Not this man, but Barabbas. Now Barabbas was a robber.

19 Then Pilate therefore took Jesus, and scourged *him*.
2 And the soldiers platted a crown of thorns, and put *it* on his head, and they put on him a purple robe,
3 And said, Hail, King of the Jews! and they smote him with their hands.
4 Pilate therefore went forth again, and saith unto them, Behold, I bring him forth to you, that ye may know that I find no fault in him.
5 Then came Jesus forth, wearing the crown of thorns, and the purple robe. And *Pilate* saith unto them, Behold the man!
6 When the chief priests therefore and officers saw him, they cried out, saying, Crucify *him*, crucify *him*. Pilate saith unto them, Take ye him, and crucify *him*: for I find no fault in him.
7 The Jews answered him, We have a law, and by our law he ought to die, because he made himself the Son of God.
8 When Pilate therefore heard that saying, he was the more afraid;
9 And went again into the judgment hall, and saith unto Jesus, Whence art thou? But Jesus gave him no answer.
10 Then saith Pilate unto him, Speakest thou not unto me? knowest thou not that I have power to crucify thee, and have power to release thee?
11 Jesus answered, Thou couldest have no power *at all* against me, except it were given thee from above: therefore he that delivered me unto thee hath the greater sin.
12 And from thenceforth Pilate sought to release him: but the Jews cried out, saying, If thou let this man go, thou art not Caesar's friend: whosoever maketh himself a king speaketh against Caesar.
13 When Pilate therefore heard that saying, he brought Jesus forth, and sat down in the judgment seat in a place that is called the Pavement, but in the Hebrew, Gabbatha.
14 And it was the preparation of the passover, and about the sixth hour: and he saith unto the Jews, Behold your King!
15 But they cried out, Away with *him*, away with *him*, crucify him. Pilate saith unto them, Shall I crucify your King? The chief priests answered, We have no king but Caesar.
16 Then delivered he him therefore unto them to be crucified. And they took Jesus, and led *him* away.
17 And he bearing his cross went forth into a place called *the place* of a skull, which is called in the Hebrew Golgotha:
18 Where they crucified him, and two other with him, on either side one, and Jesus in the midst.
19 And Pilate wrote a title, and put *it* on the cross. And the writing was, JESUS OF NAZARETH THE KING OF THE JEWS.

20 This title then read many of the
Jews: for the place where Jesus was
crucified was nigh to the city: and it
was written in Hebrew, *and* Greek, *and*
Latin.
21 Then said the chief priests of the
Jews to Pilate, Write not, The King of
the Jews; but that he said, I am King of
the Jews.
22 Pilate answered, What I have written I have written.
23 Then the soldiers, when they had
crucified Jesus, took his garments, and
made four parts, to every soldier a part;
and also *his* coat: now the coat was
without seam, woven from the top
throughout.
24 They said therefore among themselves, Let us not rend it, but cast lots
for it, whose it shall be: that the scripture might be fulfilled, which saith,
They parted my raiment among them,
and for my vesture they did cast lots.
These things therefore the soldiers did.
25 Now there stood by the cross of
Jesus his mother, and his mother's sister, Mary the *wife* of Cleophas, and
Mary Magdalene.
26 When Jesus therefore saw his
mother, and the disciple standing by,
whom he loved, he saith unto his mother, Woman, behold thy son!
27 Then saith he to the disciple,
Behold thy mother! And from that hour
that disciple took her unto his own
home.
28 After this, Jesus knowing that all
things were now accomplished, that the
scripture might be fulfilled, saith, I
thirst.
29 Now there was set a vessel full of
vinegar: and they filled a spunge with
vinegar, and put *it* upon hyssop, and
put *it* to his mouth.
30 When Jesus therefore had received
the vinegar, he said, It is finished: and
he bowed his head, and gave up the
ghost.
31 The Jews therefore, because it was
the preparation, that the bodies should
not remain upon the cross on the sabbath day, (for that sabbath day was an
high day,) besought Pilate that their
legs might be broken, and *that* they
might be taken away.
32 Then came the soldiers, and brake
the legs of the first, and of the other
which was crucified with him.
33 But when they came to Jesus, and
saw that he was dead already, they
brake not his legs:
34 But one of the soldiers with a spear
pierced his side, and forthwith came
there out blood and water.
35 And he that saw *it* bare record, and
his record is true: and he knoweth that
he saith true, that ye might believe.
36 For these things were done, that
the scripture should be fulfilled, A
bone of him shall not be broken.
37 And again another scripture saith,
They shall look on him whom they
pierced.
38 And after this Joseph of Arimathaea, being a disciple of Jesus, but
secretly for fear of the Jews, besought
Pilate that he might take away the
body of Jesus: and Pilate gave *him*
leave. He came therefore, and took the
body of Jesus.
39 And there came also Nicodemus,
which at the first came to Jesus by
night, and brought a mixture of myrrh
and aloes, about an hundred pound
weight.

40 Then took they the body of Jesus,
and wound it in linen clothes with the
spices, as the manner of the Jews is to
bury.
41 Now in the place where he was
crucified there was a garden; and in the
garden a new sepulchre, wherein was
never man yet laid.
42 There laid they Jesus therefore
because of the Jews' preparation *day*;
for the sepulchre was nigh at hand.

20 The first *day* of the week cometh
Mary Magdalene early, when it
was yet dark, unto the sepulchre, and
seeth the stone taken away from the
sepulchre.
2 Then she runneth, and cometh to
Simon Peter, and to the other disciple,
whom Jesus loved, and saith unto them,
They have taken away the Lord out of
the sepulchre, and we know not where
they have laid him.
3 Peter therefore went forth, and that
other disciple, and came to the sepulchre.
4 So they ran both together: and the
other disciple did outrun Peter, and
came first to the sepulchre.
5 And he stooping down, *and looking
in*, saw the linen clothes lying; yet went
he not in.
6 Then cometh Simon Peter following
him, and went into the sepulchre, and
seeth the linen clothes lie,
7 And the napkin, that was about his
head, not lying with the linen clothes,
but wrapped together in a place by
itself.
8 Then went in also that other disciple, which came first to the sepulchre,
and he saw, and believed.
9 For as yet they knew not the scripture, that he must rise again from the
dead.
10 Then the disciples went away
again unto their own home.
11 But Mary stood without at the sepulchre weeping: and as she wept, she
stooped down, *and looked* into the sepulchre,
12 And seeth two angels in white sitting, the one at the head, and the other
at the feet, where the body of Jesus had
lain.
13 And they say unto her, Woman,
why weepest thou? She saith unto
them, Because they have taken away
my Lord, and I know not where they
have laid him.
14 And when she had thus said, she
turned herself back, and saw Jesus
standing, and knew not that it was
Jesus.
15 Jesus saith unto her, Woman, why
weepest thou? whom seekest thou?
She, supposing him to be the gardener,
saith unto him, Sir, if thou have borne
him hence, tell me where thou hast laid
him, and I will take him away.
16 Jesus saith unto her, Mary. She
turned herself, and saith unto him,
Rabboni; which is to say, Master.
17 Jesus saith unto her, Touch me not;
for I am not yet ascended to my Father:
but go to my brethren, and say unto
them, I ascend unto my Father, and
your Father; and *to* my God, and your
God.
18 Mary Magdalene came and told
the disciples that she had seen the
Lord, and *that* he had spoken these
things unto her.
19 Then the same day at evening,
being the first *day* of the week, when
the doors were shut where the disciples
were assembled for fear of the Jews,
came Jesus and stood in the midst, and
saith unto them, Peace *be* unto you.

20 And when he had so said, he
shewed unto them *his* hands and his
side. Then were the disciples glad,
when they saw the Lord.
21 Then said Jesus to them again,
Peace *be* unto you: as *my* Father hath
sent me, even so send I you.
22 And when he had said this, he
breathed on *them*, and saith unto them,
Receive ye the Holy Ghost:
23 Whose soever sins ye remit, they
are remitted unto them; *and* whose
soever *sins* ye retain, they are retained.
24 But Thomas, one of the twelve,
called Didymus, was not with them
when Jesus came.
25 The other disciples therefore said
unto him, We have seen the Lord. But
he said unto them, Except I shall see in
his hands the print of the nails, and put
my finger into the print of the nails,
and thrust my hand into his side, I will
not believe.
26 And after eight days again his disciples were within, and Thomas with
them: *then* came Jesus, the doors being
shut, and stood in the midst, and said,
Peace *be* unto you.
27 Then saith he to Thomas, Reach
hither thy finger, and behold my hands;
and reach hither thy hand, and thrust *it*
into my side: and be not faithless, but
believing.
28 And Thomas answered and said
unto him, My Lord and my God.
29 Jesus saith unto him, Thomas,
because thou hast seen me, thou hast
believed: blessed *are* they that have not
seen, and *yet* have believed.
30 And many other signs truly did
Jesus in the presence of his disciples,
which are not written in this book:
31 But these are written, that ye
might believe that Jesus is the Christ,
the Son of God; and that believing ye
might have life through his name.

21 After these things Jesus shewed
himself again to the disciples at
the sea of Tiberias; and on this wise
shewed he *himself*.
2 There were together Simon Peter,
and Thomas called Didymus, and
Nathanael of Cana in Galilee, and the
sons of Zebedee, and two other of his
disciples.
3 Simon Peter saith unto them, I go a
fishing. They say unto him, We also go
with thee. They went forth, and entered
into a ship immediately; and that night
they caught nothing.
4 But when the morning was now
come, Jesus stood on the shore: but the
disciples knew not that it was Jesus.
5 Then Jesus saith unto them, Children, have ye any meat? They answered
him, No.
6 And he said unto them, Cast the net
on the right side of the ship, and ye
shall find. They cast therefore, and now
they were not able to draw it for the
multitude of fishes.
7 Therefore that disciple whom Jesus
loved saith unto Peter, It is the Lord.
Now when Simon Peter heard that it
was the Lord, he girt *his* fisher's coat
unto him, (for he was naked,) and did
cast himself into the sea.
8 And the other disciples came in a
little ship; (for they were not far from
land, but as it were two hundred
cubits,) dragging the net with fishes.
9 As soon then as they were come to
land, they saw a fire of coals there, and
fish laid thereon, and bread.
10 Jesus saith unto them, Bring of the
fish which ye have now caught.

11 Simon Peter went up, and drew the net to land full of great fishes, an hundred and fifty and three: and for all there were so many, yet was not the net broken.

12 Jesus saith unto them, Come *and* dine. And none of the disciples durst ask him, Who art thou? knowing that it was the Lord.

13 Jesus then cometh, and taketh bread, and giveth them, and fish likewise.

14 This is now the third time that Jesus shewed himself to his disciples, after that he was risen from the dead.

15 So when they had dined, Jesus saith to Simon Peter, Simon, *son* of Jonas, lovest thou me more than these? He saith unto him, Yea, Lord; thou knowest that I love thee. He saith unto him, Feed my lambs.

16 He saith to him again the second time, Simon, *son* of Jonas, lovest thou me? He saith unto him, Yea, Lord; thou knowest that I love thee. He saith unto him, Feed my sheep.

17 He saith unto him the third time, Simon, *son* of Jonas, lovest thou me? Peter was grieved because he said unto him the third time, Lovest thou me? And he said unto him, Lord, thou knowest all things; thou knowest that I love thee. Jesus saith unto him, Feed my sheep.

18 Verily, verily, I say unto thee, When thou wast young, thou girdedst thyself, and walkedst whither thou wouldest: but when thou shalt be old, thou shalt stretch forth thy hands, and another shall gird thee, and carry *thee* whither thou wouldest not.

19 This spake he, signifying by what death he should glorify God. And when he had spoken this, he saith unto him, Follow me.

20 Then Peter, turning about, seeth the disciple whom Jesus loved following; which also leaned on his breast at supper, and said, Lord, which is he that betrayeth thee?

21 Peter seeing him saith to Jesus, Lord, and what *shall* this man *do*?

22 Jesus saith unto him, If I will that he tarry till I come, what *is that* to thee? follow thou me.

23 Then went this saying abroad among the brethren, that that disciple should not die: yet Jesus said not unto him, He shall not die; but, If I will that he tarry till I come, what *is that* to thee?

24 This is the disciple which testifieth of these things, and wrote these things: and we know that his testimony is true.

25 And there are also many other things which Jesus did, the which, if they should be written every one, I suppose that even the world itself could not contain the books that should be written. Amen.

THE

ACTS

OF THE APOSTLES

1

1 The former treatise have I made, O Theophilus, of all that Jesus began both to do and teach,

2 Until the day in which he was taken up, after that he through the Holy Ghost had given commandments unto the apostles whom he had chosen:

3 To whom also he shewed himself alive after his passion by many infallible proofs, being seen of them forty days, and speaking of the things pertaining to the kingdom of God:

4 And, being assembled together with *them*, commanded them that they should not depart from Jerusalem, but wait for the promise of the Father, which, *saith he*, ye have heard of me.

5 For John truly baptized with water; but ye shall be baptized with the Holy Ghost not many days hence.

6 When they therefore were come together, they asked of him, saying, Lord, wilt thou at this time restore again the kingdom to Israel?

7 And he said unto them, It is not for you to know the times or the seasons, which the Father hath put in his own power.

8 But ye shall receive power, after that the Holy Ghost is come upon you: and ye shall be witnesses unto me both in Jerusalem, and in all Judaea, and in Samaria, and unto the uttermost part of the earth.

9 And when he had spoken these things, while they beheld, he was taken up; and a cloud received him out of their sight.

10 And while they looked stedfastly toward heaven as he went up, behold, two men stood by them in white apparel;

11 Which also said, Ye men of Galilee, why stand ye gazing up into heaven? this same Jesus, which is taken up from you into heaven, shall so come in like manner as ye have seen him go into heaven.

12 Then returned they unto Jerusalem from the mount called Olivet, which is from Jerusalem a sabbath day's journey.

13 And when they were come in, they went up into an upper room, where abode both Peter, and James, and John, and Andrew, Philip, and Thomas, Bartholomew, and Matthew, James *the son* of Alphaeus, and Simon Zelotes, and Judas *the brother* of James.

14 These all continued with one accord in prayer and supplication, with the women, and Mary the mother of Jesus, and with his brethren.

15 And in those days Peter stood up in the midst of the disciples, and said, (the number of names together were about an hundred and twenty,)

16 Men *and* brethren, this scripture must needs have been fulfilled, which the Holy Ghost by the mouth of David spake before concerning Judas, which was guide to them that took Jesus.

17 For he was numbered with us, and had obtained part of this ministry.

18 Now this man purchased a field with the reward of iniquity; and falling headlong, he burst asunder in the midst, and all his bowels gushed out.

19 And it was known unto all the
dwellers at Jerusalem; insomuch as
that field is called in their proper
tongue, Aceldama, that is to say, The
field of blood.
20 For it is written in the book of
Psalms, Let his habitation be desolate,
and let no man dwell therein: and his
bishoprick let another take.
21 Wherefore of these men which
have companied with us all the time
that the Lord Jesus went in and out
among us,
22 Beginning from the baptism of
John, unto that same day that he was
taken up from us, must one be ordained
to be a witness with us of his resurrection.
23 And they appointed two, Joseph
called Barsabas, who was surnamed
Justus, and Matthias.
24 And they prayed, and said, Thou,
Lord, which knowest the hearts of all
men, shew whether of these two thou
hast chosen,
25 That he may take part of this ministry and apostleship, from which Judas
by transgression fell, that he might go
to his own place.
26 And they gave forth their lots; and
the lot fell upon Matthias; and he was
numbered with the eleven apostles.

2 And when the day of Pentecost was
fully come, they were all with one
accord in one place.
2 And suddenly there came a sound
from heaven as of a rushing mighty
wind, and it filled all the house where
they were sitting.
3 And there appeared unto them cloven tongues like as of fire, and it sat
upon each of them.
4 And they were all filled with the
Holy Ghost, and began to speak with
other tongues, as the Spirit gave them
utterance.
5 And there were dwelling at Jerusalem Jews, devout men, out of every
nation under heaven.
6 Now when this was noised abroad,
the multitude came together, and were
confounded, because that every man
heard them speak in his own language.
7 And they were all amazed and marvelled, saying one to another, Behold,
are not all these which speak Galilaeans?
8 And how hear we every man in our
own tongue, wherein we were born?
9 Parthians, and Medes, and Elamites,
and the dwellers in Mesopotamia, and
in Judaea, and Cappadocia, in Pontus,
and Asia,
10 Phrygia, and Pamphylia, in Egypt,
and in the parts of Libya about Cyrene,
and strangers of Rome, Jews and proselytes,
11 Cretes and Arabians, we do hear
them speak in our tongues the wonderful works of God.
12 And they were all amazed, and
were in doubt, saying one to another,
What meaneth this?
13 Others mocking said, These men
are full of new wine.
14 But Peter, standing up with the
eleven, lifted up his voice, and said
unto them, Ye men of Judaea, and all *ye*
that dwell at Jerusalem, be this known
unto you, and hearken to my words:
15 For these are not drunken, as ye
suppose, seeing it is *but* the third hour
of the day.
16 But this is that which was spoken
by the prophet Joel;

17 And it shall come to pass in the
last days, saith God, I will pour out of
my Spirit upon all flesh: and your sons
and your daughters shall prophesy, and
your young men shall see visions, and
your old men shall dream dreams:
18 And on my servants and on my
handmaidens I will pour out in those
days of my Spirit; and they shall prophesy:
19 And I will shew wonders in heaven
above, and signs in the earth beneath;
blood, and fire, and vapour of smoke:
20 The sun shall be turned into darkness, and the moon into blood, before
that great and notable day of the Lord
come:
21 And it shall come to pass, *that*
whosoever shall call on the name of the
Lord shall be saved.
22 Ye men of Israel, hear these words;
Jesus of Nazareth, a man approved of
God among you by miracles and wonders and signs, which God did by him in
the midst of you, as ye yourselves also
know:
23 Him, being delivered by the deter-
minate counsel and foreknowledge of
God, ye have taken, and by wicked
hands have crucified and slain:
24 Whom God hath raised up, having
loosed the pains of death: because it
was not possible that he should be
holden of it.
25 For David speaketh concerning
him, I foresaw the Lord always before
my face, for he is on my right hand, that
I should not be moved:
26 Therefore did my heart rejoice,
and my tongue was glad; moreover also
my flesh shall rest in hope:
27 Because thou wilt not leave my
soul in hell, neither wilt thou suffer
thine Holy One to see corruption.
28 Thou hast made known to me the
ways of life; thou shalt make me full of
joy with thy countenance.
29 Men *and* brethren, let me freely
speak unto you of the patriarch David,
that he is both dead and buried, and his
sepulchre is with us unto this day.
30 Therefore being a prophet, and
knowing that God had sworn with an
oath to him, that of the fruit of his loins,
according to the flesh, he would raise
up Christ to sit on his throne;
31 He seeing this before spake of the
resurrection of Christ, that his soul was
not left in hell, neither his flesh did see
corruption.
32 This Jesus hath God raised up,
whereof we all are witnesses.
33 Therefore being by the right hand
of God exalted, and having received of
the Father the promise of the Holy
Ghost, he hath shed forth this, which ye
now see and hear.
34 For David is not ascended into the
heavens: but he saith himself, The LORD
said unto my Lord, Sit thou on my right
hand,
35 Until I make thy foes thy footstool.
36 Therefore let all the house of Israel
know assuredly, that God hath made
that same Jesus, whom ye have crucified, both Lord and Christ.
37 Now when they heard *this*, they
were pricked in their heart, and said
unto Peter and to the rest of the apostles, Men *and* brethren, what shall we
do?
38 Then Peter said unto them, Repent, and be baptized every one of you
in the name of Jesus Christ for the
remission of sins, and ye shall receive
the gift of the Holy Ghost.

39 For the promise is unto you, and to
your children, and to all that are afar
off, *even* as many as the Lord our God
shall call.
40 And with many other words did he
testify and exhort, saying, Save yourselves from this untoward generation.
41 Then they that gladly received his
word were baptized: and the same day
there were added *unto them* about
three thousand souls.
42 And they continued stedfastly in
the apostles' doctrine and fellowship,
and in breaking of bread, and in
prayers.
43 And fear came upon every soul:
and many wonders and signs were done
by the apostles.
44 And all that believed were together, and had all things common;
45 And sold their possessions and
goods, and parted them to all *men*, as
every man had need.
46 And they, continuing daily with
one accord in the temple, and breaking
bread from house to house, did eat
their meat with gladness and singleness of heart,
47 Praising God, and having favour
with all the people. And the Lord
added to the church daily such as
should be saved.

3 Now Peter and John went up
together into the temple at the
hour of prayer, *being* the ninth *hour*.
2 And a certain man lame from his
mother's womb was carried, whom they
laid daily at the gate of the temple
which is called Beautiful, to ask alms of
them that entered into the temple;
3 Who seeing Peter and John about to
go into the temple asked an alms.
4 And Peter, fastening his eyes upon
him with John, said, Look on us.
5 And he gave heed unto them,
expecting to receive something of
them.
6 Then Peter said, Silver and gold
have I none; but such as I have give I
thee: In the name of Jesus Christ of
Nazareth rise up and walk.
7 And he took him by the right hand,
and lifted *him* up: and immediately his
feet and ankle bones received strength.
8 And he leaping up stood, and
walked, and entered with them into the
temple, walking, and leaping, and
praising God.
9 And all the people saw him walking
and praising God:
10 And they knew that it was he
which sat for alms at the Beautiful gate
of the temple: and they were filled with
wonder and amazement at that which
had happened unto him.
11 And as the lame man which was
healed held Peter and John, all the
people ran together unto them in the
porch that is called Solomon's, greatly
wondering.
12 And when Peter saw *it*, he
answered unto the people, Ye men of
Israel, why marvel ye at this? or why
look ye so earnestly on us, as though by
our own power or holiness we had
made this man to walk?
13 The God of Abraham, and of Isaac,
and of Jacob, the God of our fathers,
hath glorified his Son Jesus; whom ye
delivered up, and denied him in the
presence of Pilate, when he was determined to let *him* go.
14 But ye denied the Holy One and
the Just, and desired a murderer to be
granted unto you;
15 And killed the Prince of life, whom
God hath raised from the dead; whereof we are witnesses.

16 And his name through faith in his
name hath made this man strong,
whom ye see and know: yea, the faith
which is by him hath given him this
perfect soundness in the presence of
you all.
17 And now, brethren, I wot that
through ignorance ye did *it*, as *did* also
your rulers.
18 But those things, which God before
had shewed by the mouth of all his
prophets, that Christ should suffer, he
hath so fulfilled.
19 Repent ye therefore, and be converted, that your sins may be blotted
out, when the times of refreshing shall
come from the presence of the Lord;
20 And he shall send Jesus Christ,
which before was preached unto you:
21 Whom the heaven must receive
until the times of restitution of all
things, which God hath spoken by the
mouth of all his holy prophets since the
world began.
22 For Moses truly said unto the
fathers, A prophet shall the Lord your
God raise up unto you of your brethren,
like unto me; him shall ye hear in all
things whatsoever he shall say unto
you.
23 And it shall come to pass, *that*
every soul, which will not hear that
prophet, shall be destroyed from among
the people.
24 Yea, and all the prophets from
Samuel and those that follow after, as
many as have spoken, have likewise
foretold of these days.
25 Ye are the children of the prophets, and of the covenant which God
made with our fathers, saying unto
Abraham, And in thy seed shall all the
kindreds of the earth be blessed.
26 Unto you first God, having raised
up his Son Jesus, sent him to bless you,
in turning away every one of you from
his iniquities.

4 And as they spake unto the people,
the priests, and the captain of the
temple, and the Sadducees, came upon
them,
2 Being grieved that they taught the
people, and preached through Jesus
the resurrection from the dead.
3 And they laid hands on them, and
put *them* in hold unto the next day: for
it was now eventide.
4 Howbeit many of them which heard
the word believed; and the number of
the men was about five thousand.
5 And it came to pass on the morrow,
that their rulers, and elders, and
scribes,
6 And Annas the high priest, and
Caiaphas, and John, and Alexander,
and as many as were of the kindred of
the high priest, were gathered together
at Jerusalem.
7 And when they had set them in the
midst, they asked, By what power, or by
what name, have ye done this?
8 Then Peter, filled with the Holy
Ghost, said unto them, Ye rulers of the
people, and elders of Israel,
9 If we this day be examined of the
good deed done to the impotent man,
by what means he is made whole;
10 Be it known unto you all, and to all
the people of Israel, that by the name
of Jesus Christ of Nazareth, whom ye
crucified, whom God raised from the
dead, *even* by him doth this man stand
here before you whole.
11 This is the stone which was set at
nought of you builders, which is
become the head of the corner.

12 Neither is there salvation in any
other: for there is none other name
under heaven given among men, whereby we must be saved.
13 Now when they saw the boldness
of Peter and John, and perceived that
they were unlearned and ignorant men,
they marvelled; and they took knowledge of them, that they had been with
Jesus.
14 And beholding the man which was
healed standing with them, they could
say nothing against it.
15 But when they had commanded
them to go aside out of the council,
they conferred among themselves,
16 Saying, What shall we do to these
men? for that indeed a notable miracle
hath been done by them *is* manifest to
all them that dwell in Jerusalem; and
we cannot deny *it*.
17 But that it spread no further
among the people, let us straitly threat-
en them, that they speak henceforth to
no man in this name.
18 And they called them, and commanded them not to speak at all nor
teach in the name of Jesus.
19 But Peter and John answered and
said unto them, Whether it be right in
the sight of God to hearken unto you
more than unto God, judge ye.
20 For we cannot but speak the things
which we have seen and heard.
21 So when they had further threatened them, they let them go, finding
nothing how they might punish them,
because of the people: for all *men* glorified God for that which was done.
22 For the man was above forty years
old, on whom this miracle of healing
was shewed.
23 And being let go, they went to
their own company, and reported all
that the chief priests and elders had
said unto them.
24 And when they heard that, they
lifted up their voice to God with one
accord, and said, Lord, thou *art* God,
which hast made heaven, and earth,
and the sea, and all that in them is:
25 Who by the mouth of thy servant
David hast said, Why did the heathen
rage, and the people imagine vain
things?
26 The kings of the earth stood up,
and the rulers were gathered together
against the Lord, and against his Christ.
27 For of a truth against thy holy child
Jesus, whom thou hast anointed, both
Herod, and Pontius Pilate, with the
Gentiles, and the people of Israel, were
gathered together,
28 For to do whatsoever thy hand and
thy counsel determined before to be
done.
29 And now, Lord, behold their threat-
enings: and grant unto thy servants,
that with all boldness they may speak
thy word,
30 By stretching forth thine hand to
heal; and that signs and wonders may
be done by the name of thy holy child
Jesus.
31 And when they had prayed, the
place was shaken where they were
assembled together; and they were all
filled with the Holy Ghost, and they
spake the word of God with boldness.
32 And the multitude of them that
believed were of one heart and of one
soul: neither said any *of them* that
ought of the things which he possessed
was his own; but they had all things
common.

33 And with great power gave the apostles witness of the resurrection of the Lord Jesus: and great grace was upon them all.

34 Neither was there any among them that lacked: for as many as were possessors of lands or houses sold them, and brought the prices of the things that were sold,

35 And laid *them* down at the apostles' feet: and distribution was made unto every man according as he had need.

36 And Joses, who by the apostles was surnamed Barnabas, (which is, being interpreted, The son of consolation,) a Levite, *and* of the country of Cyprus,

37 Having land, sold *it*, and brought the money, and laid *it* at the apostles' feet.

5 But a certain man named Ananias, with Sapphira his wife, sold a possession,

2 And kept back *part* of the price, his wife also being privy *to it*, and brought a certain part, and laid *it* at the apostles' feet.

3 But Peter said, Ananias, why hath Satan filled thine heart to lie to the Holy Ghost, and to keep back *part* of the price of the land?

4 Whiles it remained, was it not thine own? and after it was sold, was it not in thine own power? why hast thou conceived this thing in thine heart? thou hast not lied unto men, but unto God.

5 And Ananias hearing these words fell down, and gave up the ghost: and great fear came on all them that heard these things.

6 And the young men arose, wound him up, and carried *him* out, and buried *him*.

7 And it was about the space of three hours after, when his wife, not knowing what was done, came in.

8 And Peter answered unto her, Tell me whether ye sold the land for so much? And she said, Yea, for so much.

9 Then Peter said unto her, How is it that ye have agreed together to tempt the Spirit of the Lord? behold, the feet of them which have buried thy husband *are* at the door, and shall carry thee out.

10 Then fell she down straightway at his feet, and yielded up the ghost: and the young men came in, and found her dead, and, carrying *her* forth, buried *her* by her husband.

11 And great fear came upon all the church, and upon as many as heard these things.

12 And by the hands of the apostles were many signs and wonders wrought among the people; (and they were all with one accord in Solomon's porch.

13 And of the rest durst no man join himself to them: but the people magnified them.

14 And believers were the more added to the Lord, multitudes both of men and women.)

15 Insomuch that they brought forth the sick into the streets, and laid *them* on beds and couches, that at the least the shadow of Peter passing by might overshadow some of them.

16 There came also a multitude *out* of the cities round about unto Jerusalem, bringing sick folks, and them which were vexed with unclean spirits: and they were healed every one.

17 Then the high priest rose up, and all they that were with him, (which is the sect of the Sadducees,) and were filled with indignation,

18 And laid their hands on the apostles, and put them in the common prison.
19 But the angel of the Lord by night opened the prison doors, and brought them forth, and said,
20 Go, stand and speak in the temple to the people all the words of this life.
21 And when they heard *that*, they entered into the temple early in the morning, and taught. But the high priest came, and they that were with him, and called the council together, and all the senate of the children of Israel, and sent to the prison to have them brought.
22 But when the officers came, and found them not in the prison, they returned, and told,
23 Saying, The prison truly found we shut with all safety, and the keepers standing without before the doors: but when we had opened, we found no man within.
24 Now when the high priest and the captain of the temple and the chief priests heard these things, they doubted of them whereunto this would grow.
25 Then came one and told them, saying, Behold, the men whom ye put in prison are standing in the temple, and teaching the people.
26 Then went the captain with the officers, and brought them without violence: for they feared the people, lest they should have been stoned.
27 And when they had brought them, they set *them* before the council: and the high priest asked them,
28 Saying, Did not we straitly command you that ye should not teach in this name? and, behold, ye have filled Jerusalem with your doctrine, and intend to bring this man's blood upon us.
29 Then Peter and the *other* apostles answered and said, We ought to obey God rather than men.
30 The God of our fathers raised up Jesus, whom ye slew and hanged on a tree.
31 Him hath God exalted with his right hand *to be* a Prince and a Saviour, for to give repentance to Israel, and forgiveness of sins.
32 And we are his witnesses of these things; and *so is* also the Holy Ghost, whom God hath given to them that obey him.
33 When they heard *that*, they were cut *to the heart*, and took counsel to slay them.
34 Then stood there up one in the council, a Pharisee, named Gamaliel, a doctor of the law, had in reputation among all the people, and commanded to put the apostles forth a little space;
35 And said unto them, Ye men of Israel, take heed to yourselves what ye intend to do as touching these men.
36 For before these days rose up Theudas, boasting himself to be somebody; to whom a number of men, about four hundred, joined themselves: who was slain; and all, as many as obeyed him, were scattered, and brought to nought.
37 After this man rose up Judas of Galilee in the days of the taxing, and drew away much people after him: he also perished; and all, *even* as many as obeyed him, were dispersed.
38 And now I say unto you, Refrain from these men, and let them alone: for if this counsel or this work be of men, it will come to nought:

39 But if it be of God, ye cannot overthrow it; lest haply ye be found even to
fight against God.
40 And to him they agreed: and when
they had called the apostles, and beat-
en *them*, they commanded that they
should not speak in the name of Jesus,
and let them go.
41 And they departed from the presence of the council, rejoicing that they
were counted worthy to suffer shame
for his name.
42 And daily in the temple, and in
every house, they ceased not to teach
and preach Jesus Christ.

6 And in those days, when the number of the disciples was multiplied,
there arose a murmuring of the Grecians against the Hebrews, because
their widows were neglected in the
daily ministration.
2 Then the twelve called the multitude of the disciples *unto them*, and
said, It is not reason that we should
leave the word of God, and serve tables.
3 Wherefore, brethren, look ye out
among you seven men of honest report,
full of the Holy Ghost and wisdom,
whom we may appoint over this business.
4 But we will give ourselves continually to prayer, and to the ministry of the
word.
5 And the saying pleased the whole
multitude: and they chose Stephen, a
man full of faith and of the Holy Ghost,
and Philip, and Prochorus, and Nicanor,
and Timon, and Parmenas, and Nicolas
a proselyte of Antioch:
6 Whom they set before the apostles:
and when they had prayed, they laid
their hands on them.
7 And the word of God increased; and
the number of the disciples multiplied
in Jerusalem greatly; and a great company of the priests were obedient to
the faith.
8 And Stephen, full of faith and
power, did great wonders and miracles
among the people.
9 Then there arose certain of the
synagogue, which is called *the synagogue* of the Libertines, and Cyrenians,
and Alexandrians, and of them of
Cilicia and of Asia, disputing with
Stephen.
10 And they were not able to resist
the wisdom and the spirit by which he
spake.
11 Then they suborned men, which
said, We have heard him speak blasphemous words against Moses, and *against*
God.
12 And they stirred up the people,
and the elders, and the scribes, and
came upon *him*, and caught him, and
brought *him* to the council,
13 And set up false witnesses, which
said, This man ceaseth not to speak
blasphemous words against this holy
place, and the law:
14 For we have heard him say, that
this Jesus of Nazareth shall destroy this
place, and shall change the customs
which Moses delivered us.
15 And all that sat in the council,
looking stedfastly on him, saw his face
as it had been the face of an angel.

7 Then said the high priest, Are these
things so?
2 And he said, Men, brethren, and
fathers, hearken; The God of glory
appeared unto our father Abraham,
when he was in Mesopotamia, before
he dwelt in Charran,

3 And said unto him, Get thee out of thy country, and from thy kindred, and come into the land which I shall shew thee.

4 Then came he out of the land of the Chaldaeans, and dwelt in Charran: and from thence, when his father was dead, he removed him into this land, wherein ye now dwell.

5 And he gave him none inheritance in it, no, not *so much as* to set his foot on: yet he promised that he would give it to him for a possession, and to his seed after him, when *as yet* he had no child.

6 And God spake on this wise, That his seed should sojourn in a strange land; and that they should bring them into bondage, and entreat *them* evil four hundred years.

7 And the nation to whom they shall be in bondage will I judge, said God: and after that shall they come forth, and serve me in this place.

8 And he gave him the covenant of circumcision: and so *Abraham* begat Isaac, and circumcised him the eighth day; and Isaac *begat* Jacob; and Jacob *begat* the twelve patriarchs.

9 And the patriarchs, moved with envy, sold Joseph into Egypt: but God was with him,

10 And delivered him out of all his afflictions, and gave him favour and wisdom in the sight of Pharaoh king of Egypt; and he made him governor over Egypt and all his house.

11 Now there came a dearth over all the land of Egypt and Chanaan, and great affliction: and our fathers found no sustenance.

12 But when Jacob heard that there was corn in Egypt, he sent out our fathers first.

13 And at the second *time* Joseph was made known to his brethren; and Joseph's kindred was made known unto Pharaoh.

14 Then sent Joseph, and called his father Jacob to *him*, and all his kindred, threescore and fifteen souls.

15 So Jacob went down into Egypt, and died, he, and our fathers,

16 And were carried over into Sychem, and laid in the sepulchre that Abraham bought for a sum of money of the sons of Emmor *the father* of Sychem.

17 But when the time of the promise drew nigh, which God had sworn to Abraham, the people grew and multiplied in Egypt,

18 Till another king arose, which knew not Joseph.

19 The same dealt subtilly with our kindred, and evil entreated our fathers, so that they cast out their young children, to the end they might not live.

20 In which time Moses was born, and was exceeding fair, and nourished up in his father's house three months:

21 And when he was cast out, Pharaoh's daughter took him up, and nourished him for her own son.

22 And Moses was learned in all the wisdom of the Egyptians, and was mighty in words and in deeds.

23 And when he was full forty years old, it came into his heart to visit his brethren the children of Israel.

24 And seeing one *of them* suffer wrong, he defended *him*, and avenged him that was oppressed, and smote the Egyptian:

25 For he supposed his brethren would have understood how that God by his hand would deliver them: but they understood not.

26 And the next day he shewed himself unto them as they strove, and would have set them at one again, saying, Sirs, ye are brethren; why do ye wrong one to another?
27 But he that did his neighbour wrong thrust him away, saying, Who made thee a ruler and a judge over us?
28 Wilt thou kill me, as thou diddest the Egyptian yesterday?
29 Then fled Moses at this saying, and was a stranger in the land of Madian, where he begat two sons.
30 And when forty years were expired, there appeared to him in the wilderness of mount Sina an angel of the Lord in a flame of fire in a bush.
31 When Moses saw *it*, he wondered at the sight: and as he drew near to behold *it*, the voice of the Lord came unto him,
32 *Saying*, I *am* the God of thy fathers, the God of Abraham, and the God of Isaac, and the God of Jacob. Then Moses trembled, and durst not behold.
33 Then said the Lord to him, Put off thy shoes from thy feet: for the place where thou standest is holy ground.
34 I have seen, I have seen the affliction of my people which is in Egypt, and I have heard their groaning, and am come down to deliver them. And now come, I will send thee into Egypt.
35 This Moses whom they refused, saying, Who made thee a ruler and a judge? the same did God send *to be* a ruler and a deliverer by the hand of the angel which appeared to him in the bush.
36 He brought them out, after that he had shewed wonders and signs in the land of Egypt, and in the Red sea, and in the wilderness forty years.
37 This is that Moses, which said unto the children of Israel, A prophet shall the Lord your God raise up unto you of your brethren, like unto me; him shall ye hear.
38 This is he, that was in the church in the wilderness with the angel which spake to him in the mount Sina, and *with* our fathers: who received the lively oracles to give unto us:
39 To whom our fathers would not obey, but thrust *him* from them, and in their hearts turned back again into Egypt,
40 Saying unto Aaron, Make us gods to go before us: for *as for* this Moses, which brought us out of the land of Egypt, we wot not what is become of him.
41 And they made a calf in those days, and offered sacrifice unto the idol, and rejoiced in the works of their own hands.
42 Then God turned, and gave them up to worship the host of heaven; as it is written in the book of the prophets, O ye house of Israel, have ye offered to me slain beasts and sacrifices *by the space of* forty years in the wilderness?
43 Yea, ye took up the tabernacle of Moloch, and the star of your god Remphan, figures which ye made to worship them: and I will carry you away beyond Babylon.
44 Our fathers had the tabernacle of witness in the wilderness, as he had appointed, speaking unto Moses, that he should make it according to the fashion that he had seen.
45 Which also our fathers that came after brought in with Jesus into the possession of the Gentiles, whom God drave out before the face of our fathers, unto the days of David;

46 Who found favour before God, and
desired to find a tabernacle for the God
of Jacob.
47 But Solomon built him an house.
48 Howbeit the most High dwelleth
not in temples made with hands; as
saith the prophet,
49 Heaven *is* my throne, and earth *is*
my footstool: what house will ye build
me? saith the Lord: or what *is* the place
of my rest?
50 Hath not my hand made all these
things?
51 Ye stiffnecked and uncircumcised
in heart and ears, ye do always resist
the Holy Ghost: as your fathers *did*, so
do ye.
52 Which of the prophets have not
your fathers persecuted? and they have
slain them which shewed before of the
coming of the Just One; of whom ye
have been now the betrayers and murderers:
53 Who have received the law by the
disposition of angels, and have not kept
it.
54 When they heard these things,
they were cut to the heart, and they
gnashed on him with *their* teeth.
55 But he, being full of the Holy
Ghost, looked up stedfastly into heav-
en, and saw the glory of God, and Jesus
standing on the right hand of God,
56 And said, Behold, I see the heavens
opened, and the Son of man standing
on the right hand of God.
57 Then they cried out with a loud
voice, and stopped their ears, and ran
upon him with one accord,
58 And cast *him* out of the city, and
stoned *him*: and the witnesses laid
down their clothes at a young man's
feet, whose name was Saul.
59 And they stoned Stephen, calling
upon *God*, and saying, Lord Jesus,
receive my spirit.
60 And he kneeled down, and cried
with a loud voice, Lord, lay not this sin
to their charge. And when he had said
this, he fell asleep.

8 And Saul was consenting unto his
death. And at that time there was a
great persecution against the church
which was at Jerusalem; and they were
all scattered abroad throughout the
regions of Judaea and Samaria, except
the apostles.
2 And devout men carried Stephen *to
his burial*, and made great lamentation
over him.
3 As for Saul, he made havock of the
church, entering into every house, and
haling men and women committed
them to prison.
4 Therefore they that were scattered
abroad went every where preaching the
word.
5 Then Philip went down to the city of
Samaria, and preached Christ unto
them.
6 And the people with one accord
gave heed unto those things which
Philip spake, hearing and seeing the
miracles which he did.
7 For unclean spirits, crying with loud
voice, came out of many that were possessed *with them*: and many taken
with palsies, and that were lame, were
healed.
8 And there was great joy in that city.
9 But there was a certain man, called
Simon, which beforetime in the same
city used sorcery, and bewitched the
people of Samaria, giving out that himself was some great one:

10 To whom they all gave heed, from
the least to the greatest, saying, This
man is the great power of God.
11 And to him they had regard,
because that of long time he had
bewitched them with sorceries.
12 But when they believed Philip
preaching the things concerning the
kingdom of God, and the name of Jesus
Christ, they were baptized, both men
and women.
13 Then Simon himself believed also:
and when he was baptized, he continued with Philip, and wondered, beholding the miracles and signs which were
done.
14 Now when the apostles which were
at Jerusalem heard that Samaria had
received the word of God, they sent
unto them Peter and John:
15 Who, when they were come down,
prayed for them, that they might
receive the Holy Ghost:
16 (For as yet he was fallen upon none
of them: only they were baptized in the
name of the Lord Jesus.)
17 Then laid they *their* hands on
them, and they received the Holy
Ghost.
18 And when Simon saw that through
laying on of the apostles' hands the
Holy Ghost was given, he offered them
money,
19 Saying, Give me also this power,
that on whomsoever I lay hands, he
may receive the Holy Ghost.
20 But Peter said unto him, Thy
money perish with thee, because thou
hast thought that the gift of God may
be purchased with money.
21 Thou hast neither part nor lot in
this matter: for thy heart is not right in
the sight of God.
22 Repent therefore of this thy wickedness, and pray God, if perhaps the
thought of thine heart may be forgiven
thee.
23 For I perceive that thou art in the
gall of bitterness, and *in* the bond of
iniquity.
24 Then answered Simon, and said,
Pray ye to the Lord for me, that none of
these things which ye have spoken
come upon me.
25 And they, when they had testified
and preached the word of the Lord,
returned to Jerusalem, and preached
the gospel in many villages of the
Samaritans.
26 And the angel of the Lord spake
unto Philip, saying, Arise, and go
toward the south unto the way that
goeth down from Jerusalem unto Gaza,
which is desert.
27 And he arose and went: and,
behold, a man of Ethiopia, an eunuch of
great authority under Candace queen
of the Ethiopians, who had the charge
of all her treasure, and had come to
Jerusalem for to worship,
28 Was returning, and sitting in his
chariot read Esaias the prophet.
29 Then the Spirit said unto Philip,
Go near, and join thyself to this chariot.
30 And Philip ran thither to *him*, and
heard him read the prophet Esaias, and
said, Understandest thou what thou
readest?
31 And he said, How can I, except
some man should guide me? And he
desired Philip that he would come up
and sit with him.
32 The place of the scripture which
he read was this, He was led as a sheep
to the slaughter; and like a lamb dumb
before his shearer, so opened he not his
mouth:

33 In his humiliation his judgment
was taken away: and who shall declare
his generation? for his life is taken
from the earth.
34 And the eunuch answered Philip,
and said, I pray thee, of whom speaketh
the prophet this? of himself, or of some
other man?
35 Then Philip opened his mouth, and
began at the same scripture, and
preached unto him Jesus.
36 And as they went on *their* way,
they came unto a certain water: and
the eunuch said, See, *here is* water;
what doth hinder me to be baptized?
37 And Philip said, If thou believest
with all thine heart, thou mayest. And
he answered and said, I believe that
Jesus Christ is the Son of God.
38 And he commanded the chariot to
stand still: and they went down both
into the water, both Philip and the
eunuch; and he baptized him.
39 And when they were come up out
of the water, the Spirit of the Lord
caught away Philip, that the eunuch
saw him no more: and he went on his
way rejoicing.
40 But Philip was found at Azotus:
and passing through he preached in all
the cities, till he came to Caesarea.

9 And Saul, yet breathing out threat-
enings and slaughter against the
disciples of the Lord, went unto the
high priest,
2 And desired of him letters to
Damascus to the synagogues, that if he
found any of this way, whether they
were men or women, he might bring
them bound unto Jerusalem.
3 And as he journeyed, he came near
Damascus: and suddenly there shined
round about him a light from heaven:
4 And he fell to the earth, and heard
a voice saying unto him, Saul, Saul, why
persecutest thou me?
5 And he said, Who art thou, Lord?
And the Lord said, I am Jesus whom
thou persecutest: *it is* hard for thee to
kick against the pricks.
6 And he trembling and astonished
said, Lord, what wilt thou have me to
do? And the Lord *said* unto him, Arise,
and go into the city, and it shall be told
thee what thou must do.
7 And the men which journeyed with
him stood speechless, hearing a voice,
but seeing no man.
8 And Saul arose from the earth; and
when his eyes were opened, he saw no
man: but they led him by the hand, and
brought *him* into Damascus.
9 And he was three days without
sight, and neither did eat nor drink.
10 And there was a certain disciple at
Damascus, named Ananias; and to him
said the Lord in a vision, Ananias. And
he said, Behold, I *am here*, Lord.
11 And the Lord *said* unto him, Arise,
and go into the street which is called
Straight, and enquire in the house of
Judas for *one* called Saul, of Tarsus: for,
behold, he prayeth,
12 And hath seen in a vision a man
named Ananias coming in, and putting
his hand on him, that he might receive
his sight.
13 Then Ananias answered, Lord, I
have heard by many of this man, how
much evil he hath done to thy saints at
Jerusalem:
14 And here he hath authority from
the chief priests to bind all that call on
thy name.

15 But the Lord said unto him, Go thy
way: for he is a chosen vessel unto me,
to bear my name before the Gentiles,
and kings, and the children of Israel:
16 For I will shew him how great
things he must suffer for my name's
sake.
17 And Ananias went his way, and
entered into the house; and putting his
hands on him said, Brother Saul, the
Lord, *even* Jesus, that appeared unto
thee in the way as thou camest, hath
sent me, that thou mightest receive thy
sight, and be filled with the Holy Ghost.
18 And immediately there fell from
his eyes as it had been scales: and he
received sight forthwith, and arose, and
was baptized.
19 And when he had received meat,
he was strengthened. Then was Saul
certain days with the disciples which
were at Damascus.
20 And straightway he preached
Christ in the synagogues, that he is the
Son of God.
21 But all that heard *him* were
amazed, and said; Is not this he that
destroyed them which called on this
name in Jerusalem, and came hither
for that intent, that he might bring
them bound unto the chief priests?
22 But Saul increased the more in
strength, and confounded the Jews
which dwelt at Damascus, proving that
this is very Christ.
23 And after that many days were
fulfilled, the Jews took counsel to kill
him:
24 But their laying await was known
of Saul. And they watched the gates
day and night to kill him.
25 Then the disciples took him by
night, and let *him* down by the wall in
a basket.
26 And when Saul was come to Jerusalem, he assayed to join himself to the
disciples: but they were all afraid of
him, and believed not that he was a
disciple.
27 But Barnabas took him, and
brought *him* to the apostles, and declared unto them how he had seen the
Lord in the way, and that he had spoken
to him, and how he had preached boldly at Damascus in the name of Jesus.
28 And he was with them coming in
and going out at Jerusalem.
29 And he spake boldly in the name
of the Lord Jesus, and disputed against
the Grecians: but they went about to
slay him.
30 *Which* when the brethren knew,
they brought him down to Caesarea,
and sent him forth to Tarsus.
31 Then had the churches rest
throughout all Judaea and Galilee and
Samaria, and were edified; and walking
in the fear of the Lord, and in the comfort of the Holy Ghost, were multiplied.
32 And it came to pass, as Peter
passed throughout all *quarters*, he
came down also to the saints which
dwelt at Lydda.
33 And there he found a certain man
named Aeneas, which had kept his bed
eight years, and was sick of the palsy.
34 And Peter said unto him, Aeneas,
Jesus Christ maketh thee whole: arise,
and make thy bed. And he arose immediately.
35 And all that dwelt at Lydda and
Saron saw him, and turned to the Lord.
36 Now there was at Joppa a certain
disciple named Tabitha, which by interpretation is called Dorcas: this woman
was full of good works and almsdeeds
which she did.

37 And it came to pass in those days,
that she was sick, and died: whom when
they had washed, they laid *her* in an
upper chamber.
38 And forasmuch as Lydda was nigh
to Joppa, and the disciples had heard
that Peter was there, they sent unto
him two men, desiring *him* that he
would not delay to come to them.
39 Then Peter arose and went with
them. When he was come, they brought
him into the upper chamber: and all
the widows stood by him weeping, and
shewing the coats and garments which
Dorcas made, while she was with them.
40 But Peter put them all forth, and
kneeled down, and prayed; and turning
him to the body said, Tabitha, arise.
And she opened her eyes: and when
she saw Peter, she sat up.
41 And he gave her *his* hand, and
lifted her up, and when he had called
the saints and widows, presented her
alive.
42 And it was known throughout all
Joppa; and many believed in the Lord.
43 And it came to pass, that he tarried many days in Joppa with one
Simon a tanner.

10 There was a certain man in
Caesarea called Cornelius, a centurion of the band called the Italian
band,
2 *A* devout *man*, and one that feared
God with all his house, which gave
much alms to the people, and prayed to
God alway.
3 He saw in a vision evidently about
the ninth hour of the day an angel of
God coming in to him, and saying unto
him, Cornelius.
4 And when he looked on him, he was
afraid, and said, What is it, Lord? And
he said unto him, Thy prayers and thine
alms are come up for a memorial
before God.
5 And now send men to Joppa, and
call for *one* Simon, whose surname is
Peter:
6 He lodgeth with one Simon a tanner, whose house is by the sea side: he
shall tell thee what thou oughtest to do.
7 And when the angel which spake
unto Cornelius was departed, he called
two of his household servants, and a
devout soldier of them that waited on
him continually;
8 And when he had declared all *these*
things unto them, he sent them to
Joppa.
9 On the morrow, as they went on
their journey, and drew nigh unto the
city, Peter went up upon the housetop
to pray about the sixth hour:
10 And he became very hungry, and
would have eaten: but while they made
ready, he fell into a trance,
11 And saw heaven opened, and a
certain vessel descending unto him, as
it had been a great sheet knit at the
four corners, and let down to the earth:
12 Wherein were all manner of fourfooted beasts of the earth, and wild
beasts, and creeping things, and fowls
of the air.
13 And there came a voice to him,
Rise, Peter; kill, and eat.
14 But Peter said, Not so, Lord; for I
have never eaten any thing that is common or unclean.
15 And the voice *spake* unto him
again the second time, What God hath
cleansed, *that* call not thou common.
16 This was done thrice: and the vessel was received up again into heaven.
17 Now while Peter doubted in himself what this vision which he had seen
should mean, behold, the men which

were sent from Cornelius had made
enquiry for Simon's house, and stood
before the gate,
18 And called, and asked whether
Simon, which was surnamed Peter,
were lodged there.
19 While Peter thought on the vision,
the Spirit said unto him, Behold, three
men seek thee.
20 Arise therefore, and get thee
down, and go with them, doubting nothing:
for I have sent them.
21 Then Peter went down to the men
which were sent unto him from
Cornelius; and said, Behold, I am he
whom ye seek: what *is* the cause wherefore
ye are come?
22 And they said, Cornelius the centurion,
a just man, and one that feareth
God, and of good report among all the
nation of the Jews, was warned from
God by an holy angel to send for thee
into his house, and to hear words of
thee.
23 Then called he them in, and lodged
them. And on the morrow Peter went
away with them, and certain brethren
from Joppa accompanied him.
24 And the morrow after they entered
into Caesarea. And Cornelius waited
for them, and had called together his
kinsmen and near friends.
25 And as Peter was coming in,
Cornelius met him, and fell down at his
feet, and worshipped *him*.
26 But Peter took him up, saying,
Stand up; I myself also am a man.
27 And as he talked with him, he
went in, and found many that were
come together.
28 And he said unto them, Ye know
how that it is an unlawful thing for a
man that is a Jew to keep company, or
come unto one of another nation; but
God hath shewed me that I should not
call any man common or unclean.
29 Therefore came I *unto you* without
gainsaying, as soon as I was sent for:
I ask therefore for what intent ye have
sent for me?
30 And Cornelius said, Four days ago
I was fasting until this hour; and at the
ninth hour I prayed in my house, and,
behold, a man stood before me in
bright clothing,
31 And said, Cornelius, thy prayer is
heard, and thine alms are had in
remembrance in the sight of God.
32 Send therefore to Joppa, and call
hither Simon, whose surname is Peter;
he is lodged in the house of *one* Simon
a tanner by the sea side: who, when he
cometh, shall speak unto thee.
33 Immediately therefore I sent to
thee; and thou hast well done that thou
art come. Now therefore are we all here
present before God, to hear all things
that are commanded thee of God.
34 Then Peter opened *his* mouth, and
said, Of a truth I perceive that God is no
respecter of persons:
35 But in every nation he that feareth
him, and worketh righteousness, is
accepted with him.
36 The word which *God* sent unto the
children of Israel, preaching peace by
Jesus Christ: (he is Lord of all:)
37 That word, *I say*, ye know, which
was published throughout all Judaea,
and began from Galilee, after the baptism
which John preached;
38 How God anointed Jesus of
Nazareth with the Holy Ghost and with
power: who went about doing good, and
healing all that were oppressed of the
devil; for God was with him.

39 And we are witnesses of all things
which he did both in the land of the
Jews, and in Jerusalem; whom they
slew and hanged on a tree:
40 Him God raised up the third day,
and shewed him openly;
41 Not to all the people, but unto witnesses chosen before of God, *even* to us,
who did eat and drink with him after
he rose from the dead.
42 And he commanded us to preach
unto the people, and to testify that it is
he which was ordained of God *to be* the
Judge of quick and dead.
43 To him give all the prophets witness, that through his name whosoever
believeth in him shall receive remission
of sins.
44 While Peter yet spake these words,
the Holy Ghost fell on all them which
heard the word.
45 And they of the circumcision
which believed were astonished, as
many as came with Peter, because that
on the Gentiles also was poured out the
gift of the Holy Ghost.
46 For they heard them speak with
tongues, and magnify God. Then
answered Peter,
47 Can any man forbid water, that
these should not be baptized, which
have received the Holy Ghost as well as
we?
48 And he commanded them to be
baptized in the name of the Lord. Then
prayed they him to tarry certain days.

11 And the apostles and brethren
that were in Judaea heard that
the Gentiles had also received the word
of God.
2 And when Peter was come up to
Jerusalem, they that were of the circumcision contended with him,
3 Saying, Thou wentest in to men
uncircumcised, and didst eat with
them.
4 But Peter rehearsed *the matter*
from the beginning, and expounded *it*
by order unto them, saying,
5 I was in the city of Joppa praying:
and in a trance I saw a vision, A certain
vessel descend, as it had been a great
sheet, let down from heaven by four
corners; and it came even to me:
6 Upon the which when I had fastened mine eyes, I considered, and saw
fourfooted beasts of the earth, and wild
beasts, and creeping things, and fowls
of the air.
7 And I heard a voice saying unto me,
Arise, Peter; slay and eat.
8 But I said, Not so, Lord: for nothing
common or unclean hath at any time
entered into my mouth.
9 But the voice answered me again
from heaven, What God hath cleansed,
that call not thou common.
10 And this was done three times: and
all were drawn up again into heaven.
11 And, behold, immediately there
were three men already come unto the
house where I was, sent from Caesarea
unto me.
12 And the Spirit bade me go with
them, nothing doubting. Moreover
these six brethren accompanied me,
and we entered into the man's house:
13 And he shewed us how he had seen
an angel in his house, which stood and
said unto him, Send men to Joppa, and
call for Simon, whose surname is Peter;
14 Who shall tell thee words, whereby
thou and all thy house shall be saved.
15 And as I began to speak, the Holy
Ghost fell on them, as on us at the
beginning.

16 Then remembered I the word of
the Lord, how that he said, John indeed
baptized with water; but ye shall be
baptized with the Holy Ghost.
17 Forasmuch then as God gave them
the like gift as *he did* unto us, who
believed on the Lord Jesus Christ; what
was I, that I could withstand God?
18 When they heard these things,
they held their peace, and glorified
God, saying, Then hath God also to the
Gentiles granted repentance unto life.
19 Now they which were scattered
abroad upon the persecution that arose
about Stephen travelled as far as
Phenice, and Cyprus, and Antioch,
preaching the word to none but unto
the Jews only.
20 And some of them were men of
Cyprus and Cyrene, which, when they
were come to Antioch, spake unto the
Grecians, preaching the Lord Jesus.
21 And the hand of the Lord was with
them: and a great number believed,
and turned unto the Lord.
22 Then tidings of these things came
unto the ears of the church which was
in Jerusalem: and they sent forth
Barnabas, that he should go as far as
Antioch.
23 Who, when he came, and had seen
the grace of God, was glad, and exhorted them all, that with purpose of heart
they would cleave unto the Lord.
24 For he was a good man, and full of
the Holy Ghost and of faith: and much
people was added unto the Lord.
25 Then departed Barnabas to Tarsus,
for to seek Saul:
26 And when he had found him, he
brought him unto Antioch. And it came
to pass, that a whole year they assembled themselves with the church, and
taught much people. And the disciples
were called Christians first in Antioch.
27 And in these days came prophets
from Jerusalem unto Antioch.
28 And there stood up one of them
named Agabus, and signified by the
Spirit that there should be great dearth
throughout all the world: which came
to pass in the days of Claudius Caesar.
29 Then the disciples, every man
according to his ability, determined to
send relief unto the brethren which
dwelt in Judaea:
30 Which also they did, and sent it to
the elders by the hands of Barnabas
and Saul.

12 Now about that time Herod the
king stretched forth *his* hands to
vex certain of the church.
2 And he killed James the brother of
John with the sword.
3 And because he saw it pleased the
Jews, he proceeded further to take
Peter also. (Then were the days of
unleavened bread.)
4 And when he had apprehended
him, he put *him* in prison, and delivered *him* to four quaternions of soldiers to keep him; intending after
Easter to bring him forth to the people.
5 Peter therefore was kept in prison:
but prayer was made without ceasing of
the church unto God for him.
6 And when Herod would have
brought him forth, the same night
Peter was sleeping between two soldiers, bound with two chains: and the
keepers before the door kept the prison.
7 And, behold, the angel of the Lord
came upon *him*, and a light shined in
the prison: and he smote Peter on the
side, and raised him up, saying, Arise

up quickly. And his chains fell off from
his hands.
8 And the angel said unto him, Gird
thyself, and bind on thy sandals. And so
he did. And he saith unto him, Cast thy
garment about thee, and follow me.
9 And he went out, and followed him;
and wist not that it was true which was
done by the angel; but thought he saw
a vision.
10 When they were past the first and
the second ward, they came unto the
iron gate that leadeth unto the city;
which opened to them of his own
accord: and they went out, and passed
on through one street; and forthwith
the angel departed from him.
11 And when Peter was come to himself, he said, Now I know of a surety,
that the Lord hath sent his angel, and
hath delivered me out of the hand of
Herod, and *from* all the expectation of
the people of the Jews.
12 And when he had considered *the*
thing, he came to the house of Mary
the mother of John, whose surname
was Mark; where many were gathered
together praying.
13 And as Peter knocked at the door
of the gate, a damsel came to hearken,
named Rhoda.
14 And when she knew Peter's voice,
she opened not the gate for gladness,
but ran in, and told how Peter stood
before the gate.
15 And they said unto her, Thou art
mad. But she constantly affirmed that
it was even so. Then said they, It is his
angel.
16 But Peter continued knocking: and
when they had opened *the door*, and
saw him, they were astonished.
17 But he, beckoning unto them with
the hand to hold their peace, declared
unto them how the Lord had brought
him out of the prison. And he said, Go
shew these things unto James, and to
the brethren. And he departed, and
went into another place.
18 Now as soon as it was day, there
was no small stir among the soldiers,
what was become of Peter.
19 And when Herod had sought for
him, and found him not, he examined
the keepers, and commanded that *they*
should be put to death. And he went
down from Judaea to Caesarea, and
there abode.
20 And Herod was highly displeased
with them of Tyre and Sidon: but they
came with one accord to him, and, having made Blastus the king's chamberlain their friend, desired peace;
because their country was nourished
by the king's *country*.
21 And upon a set day Herod, arrayed
in royal apparel, sat upon his throne,
and made an oration unto them.
22 And the people gave a shout, *say-*
ing, It is the voice of a god, and not of
a man.
23 And immediately the angel of the
Lord smote him, because he gave not
God the glory: and he was eaten of
worms, and gave up the ghost.
24 But the word of God grew and multiplied.
25 And Barnabas and Saul returned
from Jerusalem, when they had fulfilled *their* ministry, and took with
them John, whose surname was Mark.

13 Now there were in the church
that was at Antioch certain
prophets and teachers; as Barnabas,
and Simeon that was called Niger, and
Lucius of Cyrene, and Manaen, which
had been brought up with Herod the
tetrarch, and Saul.

2 As they ministered to the Lord, and fasted, the Holy Ghost said, Separate me Barnabas and Saul for the work whereunto I have called them.

3 And when they had fasted and prayed, and laid *their* hands on them, they sent *them* away.

4 So they, being sent forth by the Holy Ghost, departed unto Seleucia; and from thence they sailed to Cyprus.

5 And when they were at Salamis, they preached the word of God in the synagogues of the Jews: and they had also John to *their* minister.

6 And when they had gone through the isle unto Paphos, they found a certain sorcerer, a false prophet, a Jew, whose name *was* Bar-jesus:

7 Which was with the deputy of the country, Sergius Paulus, a prudent man; who called for Barnabas and Saul, and desired to hear the word of God.

8 But Elymas the sorcerer (for so is his name by interpretation) withstood them, seeking to turn away the deputy from the faith.

9 Then Saul, (who also *is called* Paul,) filled with the Holy Ghost, set his eyes on him,

10 And said, O full of all subtilty and all mischief, *thou* child of the devil, *thou* enemy of all righteousness, wilt thou not cease to pervert the right ways of the Lord?

11 And now, behold, the hand of the Lord *is* upon thee, and thou shalt be blind, not seeing the sun for a season. And immediately there fell on him a mist and a darkness; and he went about seeking some to lead him by the hand.

12 Then the deputy, when he saw what was done, believed, being astonished at the doctrine of the Lord.

13 Now when Paul and his company loosed from Paphos, they came to Perga in Pamphylia: and John departing from them returned to Jerusalem.

14 But when they departed from Perga, they came to Antioch in Pisidia, and went into the synagogue on the sabbath day, and sat down.

15 And after the reading of the law and the prophets the rulers of the synagogue sent unto them, saying, *Ye* men *and* brethren, if ye have any word of exhortation for the people, say on.

16 Then Paul stood up, and beckoning with *his* hand said, Men of Israel, and ye that fear God, give audience.

17 The God of this people of Israel chose our fathers, and exalted the people when they dwelt as strangers in the land of Egypt, and with an high arm brought he them out of it.

18 And about the time of forty years suffered he their manners in the wilderness.

19 And when he had destroyed seven nations in the land of Chanaan, he divided their land to them by lot.

20 And after that he gave *unto them* judges about the space of four hundred and fifty years, until Samuel the prophet.

21 And afterward they desired a king: and God gave unto them Saul the son of Cis, a man of the tribe of Benjamin, by the space of forty years.

22 And when he had removed him, he raised up unto them David to be their king; to whom also he gave testimony, and said, I have found David the *son* of Jesse, a man after mine own heart, which shall fulfil all my will.

23 Of this man's seed hath God according to *his* promise raised unto Israel a Saviour, Jesus:

24 When John had first preached
before his coming the baptism of
repentance to all the people of Israel.
25 And as John fulfilled his course, he
said, Whom think ye that I am? I am not
he. But, behold, there cometh one after
me, whose shoes of *his* feet I am not
worthy to loose.
26 Men *and* brethren, children of the
stock of Abraham, and whosoever
among you feareth God, to you is the
word of this salvation sent.
27 For they that dwell at Jerusalem,
and their rulers, because they knew
him not, nor yet the voices of the prophets which are read every sabbath day,
they have fulfilled *them* in condemning *him*.
28 And though they found no cause of
death *in him*, yet desired they Pilate
that he should be slain.
29 And when they had fulfilled all
that was written of him, they took *him*
down from the tree, and laid *him* in a
sepulchre.
30 But God raised him from the dead:
31 And he was seen many days of
them which came up with him from
Galilee to Jerusalem, who are his witnesses unto the people.
32 And we declare unto you glad tidings, how that the promise which was
made unto the fathers,
33 God hath fulfilled the same unto
us their children, in that he hath raised
up Jesus again; as it is also written in
the second psalm, Thou art my Son, this
day have I begotten thee.
34 And as concerning that he raised
him up from the dead, *now* no more to
return to corruption, he said on this
wise, I will give you the sure mercies of
David.
35 Wherefore he saith also in another
psalm, Thou shalt not suffer thine Holy
One to see corruption.
36 For David, after he had served his
own generation by the will of God, fell
on sleep, and was laid unto his fathers,
and saw corruption:
37 But he, whom God raised again,
saw no corruption.
38 Be it known unto you therefore,
men *and* brethren, that through this
man is preached unto you the forgiveness of sins:
39 And by him all that believe are
justified from all things, from which ye
could not be justified by the law of
Moses.
40 Beware therefore, lest that come
upon you, which is spoken of in the
prophets;
41 Behold, ye despisers, and wonder,
and perish: for I work a work in your
days, a work which ye shall in no wise
believe, though a man declare it unto
you.
42 And when the Jews were gone out
of the synagogue, the Gentiles besought
that these words might be preached to
them the next sabbath.
43 Now when the congregation was
broken up, many of the Jews and religious proselytes followed Paul and
Barnabas: who, speaking to them, persuaded them to continue in the grace of
God.
44 And the next sabbath day came
almost the whole city together to hear
the word of God.
45 But when the Jews saw the multitudes, they were filled with envy, and
spake against those things which were
spoken by Paul, contradicting and blas-
pheming.

46 Then Paul and Barnabas waxed bold, and said, It was necessary that the word of God should first have been spoken to you: but seeing ye put it from you, and judge yourselves unworthy of everlasting life, lo, we turn to the Gentiles.

47 For so hath the Lord commanded us, *saying*, I have set thee to be a light of the Gentiles, that thou shouldest be for salvation unto the ends of the earth.

48 And when the Gentiles heard this, they were glad, and glorified the word of the Lord: and as many as were ordained to eternal life believed.

49 And the word of the Lord was published throughout all the region.

50 But the Jews stirred up the devout and honourable women, and the chief men of the city, and raised persecution against Paul and Barnabas, and expelled them out of their coasts.

51 But they shook off the dust of their feet against them, and came unto Iconium.

52 And the disciples were filled with joy, and with the Holy Ghost.

14 And it came to pass in Iconium, that they went both together into the synagogue of the Jews, and so spake, that a great multitude both of the Jews and also of the Greeks believed.

2 But the unbelieving Jews stirred up the Gentiles, and made their minds evil affected against the brethren.

3 Long time therefore abode they speaking boldly in the Lord, which gave testimony unto the word of his grace, and granted signs and wonders to be done by their hands.

4 But the multitude of the city was divided: and part held with the Jews, and part with the apostles.

5 And when there was an assault made both of the Gentiles, and also of the Jews with their rulers, to use *them* despitefully, and to stone them,

6 They were ware of *it*, and fled unto Lystra and Derbe, cities of Lycaonia, and unto the region that lieth round about:

7 And there they preached the gospel.

8 And there sat a certain man at Lystra, impotent in his feet, being a cripple from his mother's womb, who never had walked:

9 The same heard Paul speak: who stedfastly beholding him, and perceiving that he had faith to be healed,

10 Said with a loud voice, Stand upright on thy feet. And he leaped and walked.

11 And when the people saw what Paul had done, they lifted up their voices, saying in the speech of Lycaonia, The gods are come down to us in the likeness of men.

12 And they called Barnabas, Jupiter; and Paul, Mercurius, because he was the chief speaker.

13 Then the priest of Jupiter, which was before their city, brought oxen and garlands unto the gates, and would have done sacrifice with the people.

14 *Which* when the apostles, Barnabas and Paul, heard *of*, they rent their clothes, and ran in among the people, crying out,

15 And saying, Sirs, why do ye these things? We also are men of like passions with you, and preach unto you that ye should turn from these vanities unto the living God, which made heaven, and earth, and the sea, and all things that are therein:

16 Who in times past suffered all nations to walk in their own ways.

17 Nevertheless he left not himself without witness, in that he did good, and gave us rain from heaven, and fruitful seasons, filling our hearts with food and gladness.

18 And with these sayings scarce restrained they the people, that they had not done sacrifice unto them.

19 And there came thither *certain* Jews from Antioch and Iconium, who persuaded the people, and, having stoned Paul, drew *him* out of the city, supposing he had been dead.

20 Howbeit, as the disciples stood round about him, he rose up, and came into the city: and the next day he departed with Barnabas to Derbe.

21 And when they had preached the gospel to that city, and had taught many, they returned again to Lystra, and *to* Iconium, and Antioch,

22 Confirming the souls of the disciples, *and* exhorting them to continue in the faith, and that we must through much tribulation enter into the kingdom of God.

23 And when they had ordained them elders in every church, and had prayed with fasting, they commended them to the Lord, on whom they believed.

24 And after they had passed throughout Pisidia, they came to Pamphylia.

25 And when they had preached the word in Perga, they went down into Attalia:

26 And thence sailed to Antioch, from whence they had been recommended to the grace of God for the work which they fulfilled.

27 And when they were come, and had gathered the church together, they rehearsed all that God had done with them, and how he had opened the door of faith unto the Gentiles.

28 And there they abode long time with the disciples.

15 And certain men which came down from Judaea taught the brethren, *and said*, Except ye be circumcised after the manner of Moses, ye cannot be saved.

2 When therefore Paul and Barnabas had no small dissension and disputation with them, they determined that Paul and Barnabas, and certain other of them, should go up to Jerusalem unto the apostles and elders about this question.

3 And being brought on their way by the church, they passed through Phenice and Samaria, declaring the conversion of the Gentiles: and they caused great joy unto all the brethren.

4 And when they were come to Jerusalem, they were received of the church, and *of* the apostles and elders, and they declared all things that God had done with them.

5 But there rose up certain of the sect of the Pharisees which believed, saying, That it was needful to circumcise them, and to command *them* to keep the law of Moses.

6 And the apostles and elders came together for to consider of this matter.

7 And when there had been much disputing, Peter rose up, and said unto them, Men *and* brethren, ye know how that a good while ago God made choice among us, that the Gentiles by my mouth should hear the word of the gospel, and believe.

8 And God, which knoweth the hearts, bare them witness, giving them the Holy Ghost, even as *he did* unto us;

9 And put no difference between us and them, purifying their hearts by faith.

10 Now therefore why tempt ye God, to put a yoke upon the neck of the disciples, which neither our fathers nor we were able to bear?

11 But we believe that through the grace of the Lord Jesus Christ we shall be saved, even as they.

12 Then all the multitude kept silence, and gave audience to Barnabas and Paul, declaring what miracles and wonders God had wrought among the Gentiles by them.

13 And after they had held their peace, James answered, saying, Men *and* brethren, hearken unto me:

14 Simeon hath declared how God at the first did visit the Gentiles, to take out of them a people for his name.

15 And to this agree the words of the prophets; as it is written,

16 After this I will return, and will build again the tabernacle of David, which is fallen down; and I will build again the ruins thereof, and I will set it up:

17 That the residue of men might seek after the Lord, and all the Gentiles, upon whom my name is called, saith the Lord, who doeth all these things.

18 Known unto God are all his works from the beginning of the world.

19 Wherefore my sentence is, that we trouble not them, which from among the Gentiles are turned to God:

20 But that we write unto them, that they abstain from pollutions of idols, and *from* fornication, and *from* things strangled, and *from* blood.

21 For Moses of old time hath in every city them that preach him, being read in the synagogues every sabbath day.

22 Then pleased it the apostles and elders, with the whole church, to send chosen men of their own company to Antioch with Paul and Barnabas; *namely*, Judas surnamed Barsabas, and Silas, chief men among the brethren:

23 And they wrote *letters* by them after this manner; The apostles and elders and brethren *send* greeting unto the brethren which are of the Gentiles in Antioch and Syria and Cilicia:

24 Forasmuch as we have heard, that certain which went out from us have troubled you with words, subverting your souls, saying, *Ye must* be circumcised, and keep the law: to whom we gave no *such* commandment:

25 It seemed good unto us, being assembled with one accord, to send chosen men unto you with our beloved Barnabas and Paul,

26 Men that have hazarded their lives for the name of our Lord Jesus Christ.

27 We have sent therefore Judas and Silas, who shall also tell *you* the same things by mouth.

28 For it seemed good to the Holy Ghost, and to us, to lay upon you no greater burden than these necessary things;

29 That ye abstain from meats offered to idols, and from blood, and from things strangled, and from fornication: from which if ye keep yourselves, ye shall do well. Fare ye well.

30 So when they were dismissed, they came to Antioch: and when they had gathered the multitude together, they delivered the epistle:

31 *Which* when they had read, they rejoiced for the consolation.

32 And Judas and Silas, being prophets also themselves, exhorted the brethren with many words, and confirmed
them.
33 And after they had tarried *there* a
space, they were let go in peace from
the brethren unto the apostles.
34 Notwithstanding it pleased Silas to
abide there still.
35 Paul also and Barnabas continued
in Antioch, teaching and preaching the
word of the Lord, with many others
also.
36 And some days after Paul said
unto Barnabas, Let us go again and
visit our brethren in every city where
we have preached the word of the Lord,
and see how they do.
37 And Barnabas determined to take
with them John, whose surname was
Mark.
38 But Paul thought not good to take
him with them, who departed from
them from Pamphylia, and went not
with them to the work.
39 And the contention was so sharp
between them, that they departed
asunder one from the other: and so
Barnabas took Mark, and sailed unto
Cyprus;
40 And Paul chose Silas, and departed, being recommended by the brethren unto the grace of God.
41 And he went through Syria and
Cilicia, confirming the churches.

16 Then came he to Derbe and
Lystra: and, behold, a certain
disciple was there, named Timotheus,
the son of a certain woman, which was
a Jewess, and believed; but his father
was a Greek:
2 Which was well reported of by the
brethren that were at Lystra and
Iconium.
3 Him would Paul have to go forth
with him; and took and circumcised
him because of the Jews which were in
those quarters: for they knew all that
his father was a Greek.
4 And as they went through the cities,
they delivered them the decrees for to
keep, that were ordained of the apostles and elders which were at Jerusalem.
5 And so were the churches established in the faith, and increased in
number daily.
6 Now when they had gone throughout Phrygia and the region of Galatia,
and were forbidden of the Holy Ghost
to preach the word in Asia,
7 After they were come to Mysia, they
assayed to go into Bithynia: but the
Spirit suffered them not.
8 And they passing by Mysia came
down to Troas.
9 And a vision appeared to Paul in
the night; There stood a man of Macedonia, and prayed him, saying, Come
over into Macedonia, and help us.
10 And after he had seen the vision,
immediately we endeavoured to go into
Macedonia, assuredly gathering that
the Lord had called us for to preach the
gospel unto them.
11 Therefore loosing from Troas, we
came with a straight course to Sam-
othracia, and the next *day* to Neapolis;
12 And from thence to Philippi, which
is the chief city of that part of
Macedonia, *and* a colony: and we were
in that city abiding certain days.
13 And on the sabbath we went out of
the city by a river side, where prayer
was wont to be made; and we sat down,
and spake unto the women which
resorted *thither*.
14 And a certain woman named
Lydia, a seller of purple, of the city of

Thyatira, which worshipped God, heard
us: whose heart the Lord opened, that
she attended unto the things which
were spoken of Paul.
15 And when she was baptized, and
her household, she besought *us*, saying,
If ye have judged me to be faithful to
the Lord, come into my house, and
abide *there*. And she constrained us.
16 And it came to pass, as we went to
prayer, a certain damsel possessed with
a spirit of divination met us, which
brought her masters much gain by
soothsaying:
17 The same followed Paul and us,
and cried, saying, These men are the
servants of the most high God, which
shew unto us the way of salvation.
18 And this did she many days. But
Paul, being grieved, turned and said to
the spirit, I command thee in the name
of Jesus Christ to come out of her. And
he came out the same hour.
19 And when her masters saw that
the hope of their gains was gone, they
caught Paul and Silas, and drew *them*
into the marketplace unto the rulers,
20 And brought them to the magistrates, saying, These men, being Jews,
do exceedingly trouble our city,
21 And teach customs, which are not
lawful for us to receive, neither to
observe, being Romans.
22 And the multitude rose up together against them: and the magistrates
rent off their clothes, and commanded
to beat *them*.
23 And when they had laid many
stripes upon them, they cast *them* into
prison, charging the jailor to keep them
safely:
24 Who, having received such a
charge, thrust them into the inner prison, and made their feet fast in the
stocks.
25 And at midnight Paul and Silas
prayed, and sang praises unto God: and
the prisoners heard them.
26 And suddenly there was a great
earthquake, so that the foundations of
the prison were shaken: and immediately all the doors were opened, and
every one's bands were loosed.
27 And the keeper of the prison
awaking out of his sleep, and seeing the
prison doors open, he drew out his
sword, and would have killed himself,
supposing that the prisoners had been
fled.
28 But Paul cried with a loud voice,
saying, Do thyself no harm: for we are
all here.
29 Then he called for a light, and
sprang in, and came trembling, and fell
down before Paul and Silas,
30 And brought them out, and said,
Sirs, what must I do to be saved?
31 And they said, Believe on the Lord
Jesus Christ, and thou shalt be saved,
and thy house.
32 And they spake unto him the word
of the Lord, and to all that were in his
house.
33 And he took them the same hour
of the night, and washed *their* stripes;
and was baptized, he and all his,
straightway.
34 And when he had brought them
into his house, he set meat before them,
and rejoiced, believing in God with all
his house.
35 And when it was day, the magistrates sent the serjeants, saying, Let
those men go.
36 And the keeper of the prison told
this saying to Paul, The magistrates

have sent to let you go: now therefore depart, and go in peace.

37 But Paul said unto them, They have beaten us openly uncondemned, being Romans, and have cast *us* into prison; and now do they thrust us out privily? nay verily; but let them come themselves and fetch us out.

38 And the serjeants told these words unto the magistrates: and they feared, when they heard that they were Romans.

39 And they came and besought them, and brought *them* out, and desired *them* to depart out of the city.

40 And they went out of the prison, and entered into *the house of* Lydia: and when they had seen the brethren, they comforted them, and departed.

17 Now when they had passed through Amphipolis and Apollonia, they came to Thessalonica, where was a synagogue of the Jews:

2 And Paul, as his manner was, went in unto them, and three sabbath days reasoned with them out of the scriptures,

3 Opening and alleging, that Christ must needs have suffered, and risen again from the dead; and that this Jesus, whom I preach unto you, is Christ.

4 And some of them believed, and consorted with Paul and Silas; and of the devout Greeks a great multitude, and of the chief women not a few.

5 But the Jews which believed not, moved with envy, took unto them certain lewd fellows of the baser sort, and gathered a company, and set all the city on an uproar, and assaulted the house of Jason, and sought to bring them out to the people.

6 And when they found them not, they drew Jason and certain brethren unto the rulers of the city, crying, These that have turned the world upside down are come hither also;

7 Whom Jason hath received: and these all do contrary to the decrees of Caesar, saying that there is another king, *one* Jesus.

8 And they troubled the people and the rulers of the city, when they heard these things.

9 And when they had taken security of Jason, and of the other, they let them go.

10 And the brethren immediately sent away Paul and Silas by night unto Berea: who coming *thither* went into the synagogue of the Jews.

11 These were more noble than those in Thessalonica, in that they received the word with all readiness of mind, and searched the scriptures daily, whether those things were so.

12 Therefore many of them believed; also of honourable women which were Greeks, and of men, not a few.

13 But when the Jews of Thessalonica had knowledge that the word of God was preached of Paul at Berea, they came thither also, and stirred up the people.

14 And then immediately the brethren sent away Paul to go as it were to the sea: but Silas and Timotheus abode there still.

15 And they that conducted Paul brought him unto Athens: and receiving a commandment unto Silas and Timotheus for to come to him with all speed, they departed.

16 Now while Paul waited for them at Athens, his spirit was stirred in him, when he saw the city wholly given to idolatry.

17 Therefore disputed he in the synagogue with the Jews, and with the devout persons, and in the market daily with them that met with him.

18 Then certain philosophers of the Epicureans, and of the Stoicks, encountered him. And some said, What will this babbler say? other some, He seemeth to be a setter forth of strange gods: because he preached unto them Jesus, and the resurrection.

19 And they took him, and brought him unto Areopagus, saying, May we know what this new doctrine, whereof thou speakest, *is*?

20 For thou bringest certain strange things to our ears: we would know therefore what these things mean.

21 (For all the Athenians and strangers which were there spent their time in nothing else, but either to tell, or to hear some new thing.)

22 Then Paul stood in the midst of Mars' hill, and said, *Ye* men of Athens, I perceive that in all things ye are too superstitious.

23 For as I passed by, and beheld your devotions, I found an altar with this inscription, TO THE UNKNOWN GOD. Whom therefore ye ignorantly worship, him declare I unto you.

24 God that made the world and all things therein, seeing that he is Lord of heaven and earth, dwelleth not in temples made with hands;

25 Neither is worshipped with men's hands, as though he needed any thing, seeing he giveth to all life, and breath, and all things;

26 And hath made of one blood all nations of men for to dwell on all the face of the earth, and hath determined the times before appointed, and the bounds of their habitation;

27 That they should seek the Lord, if haply they might feel after him, and find him, though he be not far from every one of us:

28 For in him we live, and move, and have our being; as certain also of your own poets have said, For we are also his offspring.

29 Forasmuch then as we are the offspring of God, we ought not to think that the Godhead is like unto gold, or silver, or stone, graven by art and man's device.

30 And the times of this ignorance God winked at; but now commandeth all men every where to repent:

31 Because he hath appointed a day, in the which he will judge the world in righteousness by *that* man whom he hath ordained; *whereof* he hath given assurance unto all *men*, in that he hath raised him from the dead.

32 And when they heard of the resurrection of the dead, some mocked: and others said, We will hear thee again of this *matter*.

33 So Paul departed from among them.

34 Howbeit certain men clave unto him, and believed: among the which *was* Dionysius the Areopagite, and a woman named Damaris, and others with them.

18 After these things Paul departed from Athens, and came to Corinth;

2 And found a certain Jew named Aquila, born in Pontus, lately come from Italy, with his wife Priscilla; (because that Claudius had commanded all Jews to depart from Rome:) and came unto them.

3 And because he was of the same
craft, he abode with them, and wrought:
for by their occupation they were tent-
makers.
4 And he reasoned in the synagogue
every sabbath, and persuaded the Jews
and the Greeks.
5 And when Silas and Timotheus
were come from Macedonia, Paul was
pressed in the spirit, and testified to
the Jews *that* Jesus *was* Christ.
6 And when they opposed themselves, and blasphemed, he shook *his*
raiment, and said unto them, Your
blood *be* upon your own heads; I *am*
clean: from henceforth I will go unto
the Gentiles.
7 And he departed thence, and
entered into a certain *man's* house,
named Justus, *one* that worshipped
God, whose house joined hard to the
synagogue.
8 And Crispus, the chief ruler of the
synagogue, believed on the Lord with
all his house; and many of the
Corinthians hearing believed, and were
baptized.
9 Then spake the Lord to Paul in the
night by a vision, Be not afraid, but
speak, and hold not thy peace:
10 For I am with thee, and no man
shall set on thee to hurt thee: for I have
much people in this city.
11 And he continued *there* a year and
six months, teaching the word of God
among them.
12 And when Gallio was the deputy of
Achaia, the Jews made insurrection
with one accord against Paul, and
brought him to the judgment seat,
13 Saying, This *fellow* persuadeth
men to worship God contrary to the law.
14 And when Paul was now about to
open *his* mouth, Gallio said unto the
Jews, If it were a matter of wrong or
wicked lewdness, O *ye* Jews, reason
would that I should bear with you:
15 But if it be a question of words and
names, and *of* your law, look ye *to it*; for
I will be no judge of such *matters*.
16 And he drave them from the judgment seat.
17 Then all the Greeks took Sosthenes, the chief ruler of the syngogue,
and beat *him* before the judgment
seat. And Gallio cared for none of those
things.
18 And Paul *after this* tarried *there*
yet a good while, and then took his
leave of the brethren, and sailed thence
into Syria, and with him Priscilla and
Aquila; having shorn *his* head in
Cenchrea: for he had a vow.
19 And he came to Ephesus, and left
them there: but he himself entered into
the synagogue, and reasoned with the
Jews.
20 When they desired *him* to tarry
longer time with them, he consented
not;
21 But bade them farewell, saying, I
must by all means keep this feast that
cometh in Jerusalem: but I will return
again unto you, if God will. And he
sailed from Ephesus.
22 And when he had landed at
Caesarea, and gone up, and saluted the
church, he went down to Antioch.
23 And after he had spent some time
there, he departed, and went over *all*
the country of Galatia and Phrygia in
order, strengthening all the disciples.
24 And a certain Jew named Apollos,
born at Alexandria, an eloquent man,
and mighty in the scriptures, came to
Ephesus.
25 This man was instructed in the way
of the Lord; and being fervent in the

spirit, he spake and taught diligently the things of the Lord, knowing only the baptism of John.

26 And he began to speak boldly in the synagogue: whom when Aquila and Priscilla had heard, they took him unto *them*, and expounded unto him the way of God more perfectly.

27 And when he was disposed to pass into Achaia, the brethren wrote, exhorting the disciples to receive him: who, when he was come, helped them much which had believed through grace:

28 For he mightily convinced the Jews, *and that* publickly, shewing by the scriptures that Jesus was Christ.

19 And it came to pass, that, while Apollos was at Corinth, Paul having passed through the upper coasts came to Ephesus: and finding certain disciples,

2 He said unto them, Have ye received the Holy Ghost since ye believed? And they said unto him, We have not so much as heard whether there be any Holy Ghost.

3 And he said unto them, Unto what then were ye baptized? And they said, Unto John's baptism.

4 Then said Paul, John verily baptized with the baptism of repentance, saying unto the people, that they should believe on him which should come after him, that is, on Christ Jesus.

5 When they heard *this*, they were baptized in the name of the Lord Jesus.

6 And when Paul had laid *his* hands upon them, the Holy Ghost came on them; and they spake with tongues, and prophesied.

7 And all the men were about twelve.

8 And he went into the synagogue, and spake boldly for the space of three months, disputing and persuading the things concerning the kingdom of God.

9 But when divers were hardened, and believed not, but spake evil of that way before the multitude, he departed from them, and separated the disciples, disputing daily in the school of one Tyrannus.

10 And this continued by the space of two years; so that all they which dwelt in Asia heard the word of the Lord Jesus, both Jews and Greeks.

11 And God wrought special miracles by the hands of Paul:

12 So that from his body were brought unto the sick handkerchiefs or aprons, and the diseases departed from them, and the evil spirits went out of them.

13 Then certain of the vagabond Jews, exorcists, took upon them to call over them which had evil spirits the name of the Lord Jesus, saying, We adjure you by Jesus whom Paul preacheth.

14 And there were seven sons of *one* Sceva, a Jew, *and* chief of the priests, which did so.

15 And the evil spirit answered and said, Jesus I know, and Paul I know; but who are ye?

16 And the man in whom the evil spirit was leaped on them, and overcame them, and prevailed against them, so that they fled out of that house naked and wounded.

17 And this was known to all the Jews and Greeks also dwelling at Ephesus; and fear fell on them all, and the name of the Lord Jesus was magnified.

18 And many that believed came, and confessed, and shewed their deeds.

19 Many of them also which used curious arts brought their books together, and burned them before all

men: and they counted the price of
them, and found *it* fifty thousand *pieces*
of silver.
20 So mightily grew the word of God
and prevailed.
21 After these things were ended,
Paul purposed in the spirit, when he
had passed through Macedonia and
Achaia, to go to Jerusalem, saying,
After I have been there, I must also see
Rome.
22 So he sent into Macedonia two of
them that ministered unto him, Timotheus and Erastus; but he himself
stayed in Asia for a season.
23 And the same time there arose no
small stir about that way.
24 For a certain *man* named Demetrius, a silversmith, which made silver
shrines for Diana, brought no small
gain unto the craftsmen;
25 Whom he called together with the
workmen of like occupation, and said,
Sirs, ye know that by this craft we have
our wealth.
26 Moreover ye see and hear, that not
alone at Ephesus, but almost throughout all Asia, this Paul hath persuaded
and turned away much people, saying
that they be no gods, which are made
with hands:
27 So that not only this our craft is in
danger to be set at nought; but also
that the temple of the great goddess
Diana should be despised, and her
magnificence should be destroyed,
whom all Asia and the world worshippeth.
28 And when they heard *these sayings*, they were full of wrath, and cried
out, saying, Great *is* Diana of the
Ephesians.
29 And the whole city was filled with
confusion: and having caught Gaius
and Aristarchus, men of Macedonia,
Paul's companions in travel, they
rushed with one accord into the theatre.
30 And when Paul would have entered in unto the people, the disciples
suffered him not.
31 And certain of the chief of Asia,
which were his friends, sent unto him,
desiring *him* that he would not adventure himself into the theatre.
32 Some therefore cried one thing,
and some another: for the assembly
was confused; and the more part knew
not wherefore they were come together.
33 And they drew Alexander out of
the multitude, the Jews putting him
forward. And Alexander beckoned with
the hand, and would have made his
defence unto the people.
34 But when they knew that he was a
Jew, all with one voice about the space
of two hours cried out, Great *is* Diana of
the Ephesians.
35 And when the townclerk had
appeased the people, he said, *Ye* men
of Ephesus, what man is there that
knoweth not how that the city of the
Ephesians is a worshipper of the great
goddess Diana, and of the *image* which
fell down from Jupiter?
36 Seeing then that these things cannot be spoken against, ye ought to be
quiet, and to do nothing rashly.
37 For ye have brought hither these
men, which are neither robbers of
churches, nor yet blasphemers of your
goddess.
38 Wherefore if Demetrius, and the
craftsmen which are with him, have a
matter against any man, the law is
open, and there are deputies: let them
implead one another.

39 But if ye enquire any thing concerning other matters, it shall be determined in a lawful assembly.
40 For we are in danger to be called in
question for this day's uproar, there
being no cause whereby we may give an
account of this concourse.
41 And when he had thus spoken, he
dismissed the assembly.

20 And after the uproar was ceased,
Paul called unto *him* the disciples, and embraced *them*, and departed for to go into Macedonia.
2 And when he had gone over those
parts, and had given them much exhortation, he came into Greece,
3 And *there* abode three months. And
when the Jews laid wait for him, as he
was about to sail into Syria, he purposed to return through Macedonia.
4 And there accompanied him into
Asia Sopater of Berea; and of the
Thessalonians, Aristarchus and
Secundus; and Gaius of Derbe, and
Timotheus; and of Asia, Tychicus and
Trophimus.
5 These going before tarried for us at
Troas.
6 And we sailed away from Philippi
after the days of unleavened bread, and
came unto them to Troas in five days;
where we abode seven days.
7 And upon the first *day* of the week,
when the disciples came together to
break bread, Paul preached unto them,
ready to depart on the morrow; and
continued his speech until midnight.
8 And there were many lights in the
upper chamber, where they were gathered together.
9 And there sat in a window a certain
young man named Eutychus, being
fallen into a deep sleep: and as Paul
was long preaching, he sunk down with
sleep, and fell down from the third loft,
and was taken up dead.
10 And Paul went down, and fell on
him, and embracing *him* said, Trouble
not yourselves; for his life is in him.
11 When he therefore was come up
again, and had broken bread, and
eaten, and talked a long while, even till
break of day, so he departed.
12 And they brought the young man
alive, and were not a little comforted.
13 And we went before to ship, and
sailed unto Assos, there intending to
take in Paul: for so had he appointed,
minding himself to go afoot.
14 And when he met with us at Assos,
we took him in, and came to Mitylene.
15 And we sailed thence, and came
the next *day* over against Chios; and
the next *day* we arrived at Samos, and
tarried at Trogyllium; and the next *day*
we came to Miletus.
16 For Paul had determined to sail by
Ephesus, because he would not spend
the time in Asia: for he hasted, if it
were possible for him, to be at
Jerusalem the day of Pentecost.
17 And from Miletus he sent to
Ephesus, and called the elders of the
church.
18 And when they were come to him,
he said unto them, Ye know, from the
first day that I came into Asia, after
what manner I have been with you at
all seasons,
19 Serving the Lord with all humility
of mind, and with many tears, and
temptations, which befell me by the
lying in wait of the Jews:
20 *And* how I kept back nothing that
was profitable *unto you*, but have
shewed you, and have taught you publickly, and from house to house,

21 Testifying both to the Jews, and
also to the Greeks, repentance toward
God, and faith toward our Lord Jesus
Christ.
22 And now, behold, I go bound in the
spirit unto Jerusalem, not knowing the
things that shall befall me there:
23 Save that the Holy Ghost witnesseth in every city, saying that bonds and
afflictions abide me.
24 But none of these things move me,
neither count I my life dear unto
myself, so that I might finish my course
with joy, and the ministry, which I have
received of the Lord Jesus, to testify
the gospel of the grace of God.
25 And now, behold, I know that ye
all, among whom I have gone preaching
the kingdom of God, shall see my face
no more.
26 Wherefore I take you to record this
day, that I *am* pure from the blood of all
men.
27 For I have not shunned to declare
unto you all the counsel of God.
28 Take heed therefore unto yourselves, and to all the flock, over the
which the Holy Ghost hath made you
overseers, to feed the church of God,
which he hath purchased with his own
blood.
29 For I know this, that after my
departing shall grievous wolves enter
in among you, not sparing the flock.
30 Also of your own selves shall men
arise, speaking perverse things, to draw
away disciples after them.
31 Therefore watch, and remember,
that by the space of three years I
ceased not to warn every one night and
day with tears.
32 And now, brethren, I commend you
to God, and to the word of his grace,
which is able to build you up, and to
give you an inheritance among all them
which are sanctified.
33 I have coveted no man's silver, or
gold, or apparel.
34 Yea, ye yourselves know, that these
hands have ministered unto my necessities, and to them that were with me.
35 I have shewed you all things, how
that so labouring ye ought to support
the weak, and to remember the words
of the Lord Jesus, how he said, It is
more blessed to give than to receive.
36 And when he had thus spoken, he
kneeled down, and prayed with them
all.
37 And they all wept sore, and fell on
Paul's neck, and kissed him,
38 Sorrowing most of all for the words
which he spake, that they should see
his face no more. And they accompanied him unto the ship.

21 And it came to pass, that after we
were gotten from them, and had
launched, we came with a straight
course unto Coos, and the *day* following unto Rhodes, and from thence unto
Patara:
2 And finding a ship sailing over unto
Phenicia, we went aboard, and set
forth.
3 Now when we had discovered
Cyprus, we left it on the left hand, and
sailed into Syria, and landed at Tyre:
for there the ship was to unlade her
burden.
4 And finding disciples, we tarried
there seven days: who said to Paul
through the Spirit, that he should not
go up to Jerusalem.
5 And when we had accomplished
those days, we departed and went our
way; and they all brought us on our way,
with wives and children, till *we were*

out of the city: and we kneeled down on
the shore, and prayed.
6 And when we had taken our leave
one of another, we took ship; and they
returned home again.
7 And when we had finished *our*
course from Tyre, we came to Ptolemais,
and saluted the brethren, and abode
with them one day.
8 And the next *day* we that were of
Paul's company departed, and came
unto Caesarea: and we entered into the
house of Philip the evangelist, which
was *one* of the seven; and abode with
him.
9 And the same man had four daughters, virgins, which did prophesy.
10 And as we tarried *there* many
days, there came down from Judaea a
certain prophet, named Agabus.
11 And when he was come unto us, he
took Paul's girdle, and bound his own
hands and feet, and said, Thus saith the
Holy Ghost, So shall the Jews at
Jerusalem bind the man that owneth
this girdle, and shall deliver *him* into
the hands of the Gentiles.
12 And when we heard these things,
both we, and they of that place,
besought him not to go up to Jerusalem.
13 Then Paul answered, What mean
ye to weep and to break mine heart?
for I am ready not to be bound only, but
also to die at Jerusalem for the name of
the Lord Jesus.
14 And when he would not be persuaded, we ceased, saying, The will of
the Lord be done.
15 And after those days we took up
our carriages, and went up to
Jerusalem.
16 There went with us also *certain* of
the disciples of Caesarea, and brought
with them one Mnason of Cyprus, an
old disciple, with whom we should
lodge.
17 And when we were come to Jerusalem, the brethren received us gladly.
18 And the *day* following Paul went
in with us unto James; and all the
elders were present.
19 And when he had saluted them, he
declared particularly what things God
had wrought among the Gentiles by his
ministry.
20 And when they heard *it*, they glorified the Lord, and said unto him, Thou
seest, brother, how many thousands of
Jews there are which believe; and they
are all zealous of the law:
21 And they are informed of thee,
that thou teachest all the Jews which
are among the Gentiles to forsake
Moses, saying that they ought not to
circumcise *their* children, neither to
walk after the customs.
22 What is it therefore? the multitude
must needs come together: for they will
hear that thou art come.
23 Do therefore this that we say to
thee: We have four men which have a
vow on them;
24 Them take, and purify thyself with
them, and be at charges with them, that
they may shave *their* heads: and all
may know that those things, whereof
they were informed concerning thee,
are nothing; but *that* thou thyself also
walkest orderly, and keepest the law.
25 As touching the Gentiles which
believe, we have written *and* concluded
that they observe no such thing, save
only that they keep themselves from
things offered to idols, and from blood,
and from strangled, and from fornication.
26 Then Paul took the men, and the
next day purifying himself with them

entered into the temple, to signify the
accomplishment of the days of purification, until that an offering should be
offered for every one of them.
27 And when the seven days were
almost ended, the Jews which were of
Asia, when they saw him in the temple,
stirred up all the people, and laid
hands on him,
28 Crying out, Men of Israel, help:
This is the man, that teacheth all *men*
every where against the people, and
the law, and this place: and further
brought Greeks also into the temple,
and hath polluted this holy place.
29 (For they had seen before with him
in the city Trophimus an Ephesian,
whom they supposed that Paul had
brought into the temple.)
30 And all the city was moved, and
the people ran together: and they took
Paul, and drew him out of the temple:
and forthwith the doors were shut.
31 And as they went about to kill him,
tidings came unto the chief captain of
the band, that all Jerusalem was in an
uproar.
32 Who immediately took soldiers
and centurions, and ran down unto
them: and when they saw the chief
captain and the soldiers, they left beating of Paul.
33 Then the chief captain came near,
and took him, and commanded *him* to
be bound with two chains; and demanded who he was, and what he had done.
34 And some cried one thing, some
another, among the multitude: and
when he could not know the certainty
for the tumult, he commanded him to
be carried into the castle.
35 And when he came upon the stairs,
so it was, that he was borne of the soldiers for the violence of the people.
36 For the multitude of the people
followed after, crying, Away with him.
37 And as Paul was to be led into the
castle, he said unto the chief captain,
May I speak unto thee? Who said, Canst
thou speak Greek?
38 Art not thou that Egyptian, which
before these days madest an uproar,
and leddest out into the wilderness
four thousand men that were murderers?
39 But Paul said, I am a man *which*
am a Jew of Tarsus, *a city* in Cilicia, a
citizen of no mean city: and, I beseech
thee, suffer me to speak unto the people.
40 And when he had given him
licence, Paul stood on the stairs, and
beckoned with the hand unto the people. And when there was made a great
silence, he spake unto *them* in the
Hebrew tongue, saying,

22 Men, brethren, and fathers, hear
ye my defence *which I make* now
unto you.
2 (And when they heard that he
spake in the Hebrew tongue to them,
they kept the more silence: and he
saith,)
3 I am verily a man *which am* a Jew,
born in Tarsus, *a city* in Cilicia, yet
brought up in this city at the feet of
Gamaliel, *and* taught according to the
perfect manner of the law of the
fathers, and was zealous toward God, as
ye all are this day.
4 And I persecuted this way unto the
death, binding and delivering into prisons both men and women.
5 As also the high priest doth bear me
witness, and all the estate of the elders:
from whom also I received letters unto
the brethren, and went to Damascus, to

bring them which were there bound unto Jerusalem, for to be punished.
6 And it came to pass, that, as I made my journey, and was come nigh unto Damascus about noon, suddenly there shone from heaven a great light round about me.
7 And I fell unto the ground, and heard a voice saying unto me, Saul, Saul, why persecutest thou me?
8 And I answered, Who art thou, Lord? And he said unto me, I am Jesus of Nazareth, whom thou persecutest.
9 And they that were with me saw indeed the light, and were afraid; but they heard not the voice of him that spake to me.
10 And I said, What shall I do, Lord? And the Lord said unto me, Arise, and go into Damascus; and there it shall be told thee of all things which are appointed for thee to do.
11 And when I could not see for the glory of that light, being led by the hand of them that were with me, I came into Damascus.
12 And one Ananias, a devout man according to the law, having a good report of all the Jews which dwelt *there*,
13 Came unto me, and stood, and said unto me, Brother Saul, receive thy sight. And the same hour I looked up upon him.
14 And he said, The God of our fathers hath chosen thee, that thou shouldest know his will, and see that Just One, and shouldest hear the voice of his mouth.
15 For thou shalt be his witness unto all men of what thou hast seen and heard.
16 And now why tarriest thou? arise, and be baptized, and wash away thy sins, calling on the name of the Lord.
17 And it came to pass, that, when I was come again to Jerusalem, even while I prayed in the temple, I was in a trance;
18 And saw him saying unto me, Make haste, and get thee quickly out of Jerusalem: for they will not receive thy testimony concerning me.
19 And I said, Lord, they know that I imprisoned and beat in every synagogue them that believed on thee:
20 And when the blood of thy martyr Stephen was shed, I also was standing by, and consenting unto his death, and kept the raiment of them that slew him.
21 And he said unto me, Depart: for I will send thee far hence unto the Gentiles.
22 And they gave him audience unto this word, and *then* lifted up their voices, and said, Away with such a *fellow* from the earth: for it is not fit that he should live.
23 And as they cried out, and cast off *their* clothes, and threw dust into the air,
24 The chief captain commanded him to be brought into the castle, and bade that he should be examined by scourging; that he might know wherefore they cried so against him.
25 And as they bound him with thongs, Paul said unto the centurion that stood by, Is it lawful for you to scourge a man that is a Roman, and uncondemned?
26 When the centurion heard *that*, he went and told the chief captain, saying, Take heed what thou doest: for this man is a Roman.

27 Then the chief captain came, and said unto him, Tell me, art thou a Roman? He said, Yea.

28 And the chief captain answered, With a great sum obtained I this freedom. And Paul said, But I was *free* born.

29 Then straightway they departed from him which should have examined him: and the chief captain also was afraid, after he knew that he was a Roman, and because he had bound him.

30 On the morrow, because he would have known the certainty wherefore he was accused of the Jews, he loosed him from *his* bands, and commanded the chief priests and all their council to appear, and brought Paul down, and set him before them.

23 And Paul, earnestly beholding the council, said, Men *and* brethren, I have lived in all good conscience before God until this day.

2 And the high priest Ananias commanded them that stood by him to smite him on the mouth.

3 Then said Paul unto him, God shall smite thee, *thou* whited wall: for sittest thou to judge me after the law, and commandest me to be smitten contrary to the law?

4 And they that stood by said, Revilest thou God's high priest?

5 Then said Paul, I wist not, brethren, that he was the high priest: for it is written, Thou shalt not speak evil of the ruler of thy people.

6 But when Paul perceived that the one part were Sadducees, and the other Pharisees, he cried out in the council, Men *and* brethren, I am a Pharisee, the son of a Pharisee: of the hope and resurrection of the dead I am called in question.

7 And when he had so said, there arose a dissension between the Pharisees and the Sadducees: and the multitude was divided.

8 For the Sadducees say that there is no resurrection, neither angel, nor spirit: but the Pharisees confess both.

9 And there arose a great cry: and the scribes *that were* of the Pharisees' part arose, and strove, saying, We find no evil in this man: but if a spirit or an angel hath spoken to him, let us not fight against God.

10 And when there arose a great dissension, the chief captain, fearing lest Paul should have been pulled in pieces of them, commanded the soldiers to go down, and to take him by force from among them, and to bring *him* into the castle.

11 And the night following the Lord stood by him, and said, Be of good cheer, Paul: for as thou hast testified of me in Jerusalem, so must thou bear witness also at Rome.

12 And when it was day, certain of the Jews banded together, and bound themselves under a curse, saying that they would neither eat nor drink till they had killed Paul.

13 And they were more than forty which had made this conspiracy.

14 And they came to the chief priests and elders, and said, We have bound ourselves under a great curse, that we will eat nothing until we have slain Paul.

15 Now therefore ye with the council signify to the chief captain that he bring him down unto you to morrow, as though ye would enquire something more perfectly concerning him: and we, or ever he come near, are ready to kill him.

16 And when Paul's sister's son heard
of their lying in wait, he went and
entered into the castle, and told Paul.
17 Then Paul called one of the centurions unto *him*, and said, Bring this
young man unto the chief captain: for
he hath a certain thing to tell him.
18 So he took him, and brought *him*
to the chief captain, and said, Paul the
prisoner called me unto *him*, and
prayed me to bring this young man
unto thee, who hath something to say
unto thee.
19 Then the chief captain took him by
the hand, and went *with him* aside
privately, and asked *him*, What is that
thou hast to tell me?
20 And he said, The Jews have agreed
to desire thee that thou wouldest bring
down Paul to morrow into the council,
as though they would enquire somewhat of him more perfectly.
21 But do not thou yield unto them:
for there lie in wait for him of them
more than forty men, which have bound
themselves with an oath, that they will
neither eat nor drink till they have
killed him: and now are they ready,
looking for a promise from thee.
22 So the chief captain *then* let the
young man depart, and charged *him*,
See thou tell no man that thou hast
shewed these things to me.
23 And he called unto *him* two centurions, saying, Make ready two hundred
soldiers to go to Caesarea, and horsemen threescore and ten, and spearmen
two hundred, at the third hour of the
night;
24 And provide *them* beasts, that
they may set Paul on, and bring *him*
safe unto Felix the governor.
25 And he wrote a letter after this
manner:
26 Claudius Lysias unto the most
excellent governor Felix *sendeth* greeting.
27 This man was taken of the Jews,
and should have been killed of them:
then came I with an army, and rescued
him, having understood that he was a
Roman.
28 And when I would have known the
cause wherefore they accused him, I
brought him forth into their council:
29 Whom I perceived to be accused of
questions of their law, but to have nothing laid to his charge worthy of death or
of bonds.
30 And when it was told me how that
the Jews laid wait for the man, I sent
straightway to thee, and gave commandment to his accusers also to say
before thee what *they had* against him.
Farewell.
31 Then the soldiers, as it was commanded them, took Paul, and brought
him by night to Antipatris.
32 On the morrow they left the horsemen to go with him, and returned to the
castle:
33 Who, when they came to Caesarea,
and delivered the epistle to the governor, presented Paul also before him.
34 And when the governor had read
the letter, he asked of what province he
was. And when he understood that *he
was* of Cilicia;
35 I will hear thee, said he, when
thine accusers are also come. And he
commanded him to be kept in Herod's
judgment hall.

24 And after five days Ananias the
high priest descended with the
elders, and *with* a certain orator *named*
Tertullus, who informed the governor
against Paul.

2 And when he was called forth,
Tertullus began to accuse *him*, saying,
Seeing that by thee we enjoy great
quietness, and that very worthy deeds
are done unto this nation by thy provi-
dence,
3 We accept *it* always, and in all
places, most noble Felix, with all thank-
fulness.
4 Notwithstanding, that I be not further tedious unto thee, I pray thee that
thou wouldest hear us of thy clemency
a few words.
5 For we have found this man *a* pesti-
lent *fellow*, and a mover of sedition
among all the Jews throughout the
world, and a ringleader of the sect of
the Nazarenes:
6 Who also hath gone about to profane the temple: whom we took, and
would have judged according to our
law.
7 But the chief captain Lysias came
upon us, and with great violence took
him away out of our hands,
8 Commanding his accusers to come
unto thee: by examining of whom thyself mayest take knowledge of all these
things, whereof we accuse him.
9 And the Jews also assented, saying
that these things were so.
10 Then Paul, after that the governor
had beckoned unto him to speak,
answered, Forasmuch as I know that
thou hast been of many years a judge
unto this nation, I do the more cheer-
fully answer for myself:
11 Because that thou mayest understand, that there are yet but twelve
days since I went up to Jerusalem for to
worship.
12 And they neither found me in the
temple disputing with any man, neither
raising up the people, neither in the
synagogues, nor in the city:
13 Neither can they prove the things
whereof they now accuse me.
14 But this I confess unto thee, that
after the way which they call heresy, so
worship I the God of my fathers, believing all things which are written in the
law and in the prophets:
15 And have hope toward God, which
they themselves also allow, that there
shall be a resurrection of the dead,
both of the just and unjust.
16 And herein do I exercise myself, to
have always a conscience void of
offence toward God, and *toward* men.
17 Now after many years I came to
bring alms to my nation, and offerings.
18 Whereupon certain Jews from
Asia found me purified in the temple,
neither with multitude, nor with
tumult.
19 Who ought to have been here
before thee, and object, if they had
ought against me.
20 Or else let these same *here* say, if
they have found any evil doing in me,
while I stood before the council,
21 Except it be for this one voice, that
I cried standing among them, Touching
the resurrection of the dead I am called
in question by you this day.
22 And when Felix heard these
things, having more perfect knowledge
of *that* way, he deferred them, and said,
When Lysias the chief captain shall
come down, I will know the uttermost
of your matter.
23 And he commanded a centurion to
keep Paul, and to let *him* have liberty,
and that he should forbid none of his
acquaintance to minister or come unto
him.

24 And after certain days, when Felix
came with his wife Drusilla, which was
a Jewess, he sent for Paul, and heard
him concerning the faith in Christ.
25 And as he reasoned of righteousness, temperance, and judgment to
come, Felix trembled, and answered,
Go thy way for this time; when I have a
convenient season, I will call for thee.
26 He hoped also that money should
have been given him of Paul, that he
might loose him: wherefore he sent for
him the oftener, and communed with
him.
27 But after two years Porcius Festus
came into Felix' room: and Felix, willing to shew the Jews a pleasure, left
Paul bound.

25 Now when Festus was come into
the province, after three days he
ascended from Caesarea to Jerusalem.
2 Then the high priest and the chief
of the Jews informed him against Paul,
and besought him,
3 And desired favour against him,
that he would send for him to Jerusalem, laying wait in the way to kill
him.
4 But Festus answered, that Paul
should be kept at Caesarea, and that he
himself would depart shortly *thither*.
5 Let them therefore, said he, which
among you are able, go down with *me*,
and accuse this man, if there be any
wickedness in him.
6 And when he had tarried among
them more than ten days, he went
down unto Caesarea; and the next day
sitting on the judgment seat commanded Paul to be brought.
7 And when he was come, the Jews
which came down from Jerusalem
stood round about, and laid many and
grievous complaints against Paul,
which they could not prove.
8 While he answered for himself,
Neither against the law of the Jews,
neither against the temple, nor yet
against Caesar, have I offended any
thing at all.
9 But Festus, willing to do the Jews a
pleasure, answered Paul, and said, Wilt
thou go up to Jerusalem, and there be
judged of these things before me?
10 Then said Paul, I stand at Caesar's
judgment seat, where I ought to be
judged: to the Jews have I done no
wrong, as thou very well knowest.
11 For if I be an offender, or have
committed any thing worthy of death, I
refuse not to die: but if there be none of
these things whereof these accuse me,
no man may deliver me unto them. I
appeal unto Caesar.
12 Then Festus, when he had conferred with the council, answered, Hast
thou appealed unto Caesar? unto
Caesar shalt thou go.
13 And after certain days king
Agrippa and Bernice came unto
Caesarea to salute Festus.
14 And when they had been there
many days, Festus declared Paul's
cause unto the king, saying, There is a
certain man left in bonds by Felix:
15 About whom, when I was at
Jerusalem, the chief priests and the
elders of the Jews informed *me*, desiring *to have* judgment against him.
16 To whom I answered, It is not the
manner of the Romans to deliver any
man to die, before that he which is
accused have the accusers face to face,
and have licence to answer for himself
concerning the crime laid against him.

17 Therefore, when they were come
hither, without any delay on the morrow I sat on the judgment seat, and
commanded the man to be brought
forth.
18 Against whom when the accusers
stood up, they brought none accusation
of such things as I supposed:
19 But had certain questions against
him of their own superstition, and of
one Jesus, which was dead, whom Paul
affirmed to be alive.
20 And because I doubted of such
manner of questions, I asked *him*
whether he would go to Jerusalem, and
there be judged of these matters.
21 But when Paul had appealed to be
reserved unto the hearing of Augustus,
I commanded him to be kept till I
might send him to Caesar.
22 Then Agrippa said unto Festus, I
would also hear the man myself. To
morrow, said he, thou shalt hear him.
23 And on the morrow, when Agrippa
was come, and Bernice, with great
pomp, and was entered into the place
of hearing, with the chief captains, and
principal men of the city, at Festus'
commandment Paul was brought forth.
24 And Festus said, King Agrippa,
and all men which are here present
with us, ye see this man, about whom
all the multitude of the Jews have dealt
with me, both at Jerusalem, and *also*
here, crying that he ought not to live
any longer.
25 But when I found that he had committed nothing worthy of death, and
that he himself hath appealed to
Augustus, I have determined to send
him.
26 Of whom I have no certain thing to
write unto my lord. Wherefore I have
brought him forth before you, and specially before thee, O king Agrippa, that,
after examination had, I might have
somewhat to write.
27 For it seemeth to me unreasonable
to send a prisoner, and not withal to
signify the crimes *laid* against him.

26 Then Agrippa said unto Paul,
Thou art permitted to speak for
thyself. Then Paul stretched forth the
hand, and answered for himself:
2 I think myself happy, king Agrippa,
because I shall answer for myself this
day before thee touching all the things
whereof I am accused of the Jews:
3 Especially *because I know* thee to
be expert in all customs and questions
which are among the Jews: wherefore I
beseech thee to hear me patiently.
4 My manner of life from my youth,
which was at the first among mine own
nation at Jerusalem, know all the Jews;
5 Which knew me from the beginning, if they would testify, that after the
most straitest sect of our religion I lived
a Pharisee.
6 And now I stand and am judged for
the hope of the promise made of God
unto our fathers:
7 Unto which *promise* our twelve
tribes, instantly serving *God* day and
night, hope to come. For which hope's
sake, king Agrippa, I am accused of the
Jews.
8 Why should it be thought a thing
incredible with you, that God should
raise the dead?
9 I verily thought with myself, that I
ought to do many things contrary to the
name of Jesus of Nazareth.
10 Which thing I also did in Jerusalem:
and many of the saints did I shut up in
prison, having received authority from
the chief priests; and when they were

put to death, I gave my voice against
them.
11 And I punished them oft in every
synagogue, and compelled *them* to
blaspheme; and being exceedingly
mad against them, I persecuted *them*
even unto strange cities.
12 Whereupon as I went to Damascus
with authority and commission from
the chief priests,
13 At midday, O king, I saw in the way
a light from heaven, above the brightness
of the sun, shining round about me
and them which journeyed with me.
14 And when we were all fallen to the
earth, I heard a voice speaking unto
me, and saying in the Hebrew tongue,
Saul, Saul, why persecutest thou me? *it
is* hard for thee to kick against the
pricks.
15 And I said, Who art thou, Lord?
And he said, I am Jesus whom thou
persecutest.
16 But rise, and stand upon thy feet:
for I have appeared unto thee for this
purpose, to make thee a minister and a
witness both of these things which thou
hast seen, and of those things in the
which I will appear unto thee;
17 Delivering thee from the people,
and *from* the Gentiles, unto whom now
I send thee,
18 To open their eyes, *and* to turn
them from darkness to light, and *from*
the power of Satan unto God, that they
may receive forgiveness of sins, and
inheritance among them which are
sanctified by faith that is in me.
19 Whereupon, O king Agrippa, I was
not disobedient unto the heavenly
vision:
20 But shewed first unto them of
Damascus, and at Jerusalem, and
throughout all the coasts of Judaea,
and *then* to the Gentiles, that they
should repent and turn to God, and do
works meet for repentance.
21 For these causes the Jews caught
me in the temple, and went about to
kill *me*.
22 Having therefore obtained help of
God, I continue unto this day, witnessing
both to small and great, saying none
other things than those which the
prophets and Moses did say should
come:
23 That Christ should suffer, *and* that
he should be the first that should rise
from the dead, and should shew light
unto the people, and to the Gentiles.
24 And as he thus spake for himself,
Festus said with a loud voice, Paul, thou
art beside thyself; much learning doth
make thee mad.
25 But he said, I am not mad, most
noble Festus; but speak forth the words
of truth and soberness.
26 For the king knoweth of these
things, before whom also I speak freely:
for I am persuaded that none of these
things are hidden from him; for this
thing was not done in a corner.
27 King Agrippa, believest thou the
prophets? I know that thou believest.
28 Then Agrippa said unto Paul,
Almost thou persuadest me to be a
Christian.
29 And Paul said, I would to God, that
not only thou, but also all that hear me
this day, were both almost, and altogether
such as I am, except these
bonds.
30 And when he had thus spoken, the
king rose up, and the governor, and
Bernice, and they that sat with them:

31 And when they were gone aside, they talked between themselves, saying, This man doeth nothing worthy of death or of bonds.

32 Then said Agrippa unto Festus, This man might have been set at liberty, if he had not appealed unto Caesar.

27 And when it was determined that we should sail into Italy, they delivered Paul and certain other prisoners unto *one* named Julius, a centurion of Augustus' band.

2 And entering into a ship of Adramyttium, we launched, meaning to sail by the coasts of Asia; *one* Aristarchus, a Macedonian of Thessalonica, being with us.

3 And the next *day* we touched at Sidon. And Julius courteously entreated Paul, and gave *him* liberty to go unto his friends to refresh himself.

4 And when we had launched from thence, we sailed under Cyprus, because the winds were contrary.

5 And when we had sailed over the sea of Cilicia and Pamphylia, we came to Myra, *a city* of Lycia.

6 And there the centurion found a ship of Alexandria sailing into Italy; and he put us therein.

7 And when we had sailed slowly many days, and scarce were come over against Cnidus, the wind not suffering us, we sailed under Crete, over against Salmone;

8 And, hardly passing it, came unto a place which is called The fair havens; nigh whereunto was the city *of* Lasea.

9 Now when much time was spent, and when sailing was now dangerous, because the fast was now already past, Paul admonished *them*,

10 And said unto them, Sirs, I perceive that this voyage will be with hurt and much damage, not only of the lading and ship, but also of our lives.

11 Nevertheless the centurion believed the master and the owner of the ship, more than those things which were spoken by Paul.

12 And because the haven was not commodious to winter in, the more part advised to depart thence also, if by any means they might attain to Phenice, *and there* to winter; *which is* an haven of Crete, and lieth toward the south west and north west.

13 And when the south wind blew softly, supposing that they had obtained *their* purpose, loosing *thence*, they sailed close by Crete.

14 But not long after there arose against it a tempestuous wind, called Euroclydon.

15 And when the ship was caught, and could not bear up into the wind, we let *her* drive.

16 And running under a certain island which is called Clauda, we had much work to come by the boat:

17 Which when they had taken up, they used helps, undergirding the ship; and, fearing lest they should fall into the quicksands, strake sail, and so were driven.

18 And we being exceedingly tossed with a tempest, the next *day* they lightened the ship;

19 And the third *day* we cast out with our own hands the tackling of the ship.

20 And when neither sun nor stars in many days appeared, and no small tempest lay on *us*, all hope that we should be saved was then taken away.

21 But after long abstinence Paul stood forth in the midst of them, and said, Sirs, ye should have hearkened unto me, and not have loosed from

Crete, and to have gained this harm
and loss.
22 And now I exhort you to be of good
cheer: for there shall be no loss of *any*
man's life among you, but of the ship.
23 For there stood by me this night
the angel of God, whose I am, and
whom I serve,
24 Saying, Fear not, Paul; thou must
be brought before Caesar: and, lo, God
hath given thee all them that sail with
thee.
25 Wherefore, sirs, be of good cheer:
for I believe God, that it shall be even
as it was told me.
26 Howbeit we must be cast upon a
certain island.
27 But when the fourteenth night was
come, as we were driven up and down
in Adria, about midnight the shipmen
deemed that they drew near to some
country;
28 And sounded, and found *it* twenty
fathoms: and when they had gone a little further, they sounded again, and
found *it* fifteen fathoms.
29 Then fearing lest we should have
fallen upon rocks, they cast four
anchors out of the stern, and wished for
the day.
30 And as the shipmen were about to
flee out of the ship, when they had let
down the boat into the sea, under
colour as though they would have cast
anchors out of the foreship,
31 Paul said to the centurion and to
the soldiers, Except these abide in the
ship, ye cannot be saved.
32 Then the soldiers cut off the ropes
of the boat, and let her fall off.
33 And while the day was coming on,
Paul besought *them* all to take meat,
saying, This day is the fourteenth day
that ye have tarried and continued fasting, having taken nothing.
34 Wherefore I pray you to take *some*
meat: for this is for your health: for
there shall not an hair fall from the
head of any of you.
35 And when he had thus spoken, he
took bread, and gave thanks to God in
presence of them all: and when he had
broken *it*, he began to eat.
36 Then were they all of good cheer,
and they also took *some* meat.
37 And we were in all in the ship two
hundred threescore and sixteen souls.
38 And when they had eaten enough,
they lightened the ship, and cast out
the wheat into the sea.
39 And when it was day, they knew
not the land: but they discovered a
certain creek with a shore, into the
which they were minded, if it were possible, to thrust in the ship.
40 And when they had taken up the
anchors, they committed *themselves*
unto the sea, and loosed the rudder
bands, and hoised up the mainsail to
the wind, and made toward shore.
41 And falling into a place where two
seas met, they ran the ship aground;
and the forepart stuck fast, and
remained unmoveable, but the hinder
part was broken with the violence of
the waves.
42 And the soldiers' counsel was to
kill the prisoners, lest any of them
should swim out, and escape.
43 But the centurion, willing to save
Paul, kept them from *their* purpose;
and commanded that they which could
swim should cast *themselves* first *into*
the sea, and get to land:

44 And the rest, some on boards, and
some on *broken pieces* of the ship. And
so it came to pass, that they escaped all
safe to land.

28 And when they were escaped,
then they knew that the island
was called Melita.
2 And the barbarous people shewed
us no little kindness: for they kindled a
fire, and received us every one, because
of the present rain, and because of the
cold.
3 And when Paul had gathered a
bundle of sticks, and laid *them* on the
fire, there came a viper out of the heat,
and fastened on his hand.
4 And when the barbarians saw the
venomous beast hang on his hand, they
said among themselves, No doubt this
man is a murderer, whom, though he
hath escaped the sea, yet vengeance
suffereth not to live.
5 And he shook off the beast into the
fire, and felt no harm.
6 Howbeit they looked when he
should have swollen, or fallen down
dead suddenly: but after they had
looked a great while, and saw no harm
come to him, they changed their minds,
and said that he was a god.
7 In the same quarters were possessions of the chief man of the island,
whose name was Publius; who received
us, and lodged us three days courteously.
8 And it came to pass, that the father
of Publius lay sick of a fever and of a
bloody flux: to whom Paul entered in,
and prayed, and laid his hands on him,
and healed him.
9 So when this was done, others also,
which had diseases in the island, came,
and were healed:
10 Who also honoured us with many
honours; and when we departed, they
laded *us* with such things as were necessary.
11 And after three months we departed in a ship of Alexandria, which had
wintered in the isle, whose sign was
Castor and Pollux.
12 And landing at Syracuse, we tarried *there* three days.
13 And from thence we fetched a
compass, and came to Rhegium: and
after one day the south wind blew, and
we came the next day to Puteoli:
14 Where we found brethren, and
were desired to tarry with them seven
days: and so we went toward Rome.
15 And from thence, when the brethren heard of us, they came to meet us as
far as Appii forum, and The three taverns: whom when Paul saw, he thanked
God, and took courage.
16 And when we came to Rome, the
centurion delivered the prisoners to
the captain of the guard: but Paul was
suffered to dwell by himself with a soldier that kept him.
17 And it came to pass, that after
three days Paul called the chief of the
Jews together: and when they were
come together, he said unto them, Men
and brethren, though I have committed
nothing against the people, or customs
of our fathers, yet was I delivered prisoner from Jerusalem into the hands of
the Romans.
18 Who, when they had examined me,
would have let *me* go, because there
was no cause of death in me.
19 But when the Jews spake against
it, I was constrained to appeal unto
Caesar; not that I had ought to accuse
my nation of.

20 For this cause therefore have I
called for you, to see *you*, and to speak
with *you*: because that for the hope of
Israel I am bound with this chain.
21 And they said unto him, We neither received letters out of Judaea
concerning thee, neither any of the
brethren that came shewed or spake
any harm of thee.
22 But we desire to hear of thee what
thou thinkest: for as concerning this
sect, we know that every where it is
spoken against.
23 And when they had appointed him
a day, there came many to him into *his*
lodging; to whom he expounded and
testified the kingdom of God, persuading them concerning Jesus, both out of
the law of Moses, and *out of* the prophets, from morning till evening.
24 And some believed the things
which were spoken, and some believed
not.
25 And when they agreed not among
themselves, they departed, after that
Paul had spoken one word, Well spake
the Holy Ghost by Esaias the prophet
unto our fathers,
26 Saying, Go unto this people, and
say, Hearing ye shall hear, and shall not
understand; and seeing ye shall see,
and not perceive:
27 For the heart of this people is
waxed gross, and their ears are dull of
hearing, and their eyes have they
closed; lest they should see with *their*
eyes, and hear with *their* ears, and
understand with *their* heart, and
should be converted, and I should heal
them.
28 Be it known therefore unto you,
that the salvation of God is sent unto
the Gentiles, and *that* they will hear it.
29 And when he had said these words,
the Jews departed, and had great reasoning among themselves.
30 And Paul dwelt two whole years in
his own hired house, and received all
that came in unto him,
31 Preaching the kingdom of God,
and teaching those things which concern the Lord Jesus Christ, with all
confidence, no man forbidding him.

THE EPISTLE OF PAUL THE APOSTLE
TO THE

ROMANS

1 Paul, a servant of Jesus Christ, called *to be* an apostle, separated unto the gospel of God,

2 (Which he had promised afore by his prophets in the holy scriptures,)

3 Concerning his Son Jesus Christ our Lord, which was made of the seed of David according to the flesh;

4 And declared *to be* the Son of God with power, according to the spirit of holiness, by the resurrection from the dead:

5 By whom we have received grace and apostleship, for obedience to the faith among all nations, for his name:

6 Among whom are ye also the called of Jesus Christ:

7 To all that be in Rome, beloved of God, called *to be* saints: Grace to you and peace from God our Father, and the Lord Jesus Christ.

8 First, I thank my God through Jesus Christ for you all, that your faith is spoken of throughout the whole world.

9 For God is my witness, whom I serve with my spirit in the gospel of his Son, that without ceasing I make mention of you always in my prayers;

10 Making request, if by any means now at length I might have a prosperous journey by the will of God to come unto you.

11 For I long to see you, that I may impart unto you some spiritual gift, to the end ye may be established;

12 That is, that I may be comforted together with you by the mutual faith both of you and me.

13 Now I would not have you ignorant, brethren, that oftentimes I purposed to come unto you, (but was let hitherto,) that I might have some fruit among you also, even as among other Gentiles.

14 I am debtor both to the Greeks, and to the Barbarians; both to the wise, and to the unwise.

15 So, as much as in me is, I am ready to preach the gospel to you that are at Rome also.

16 For I am not ashamed of the gospel of Christ: for it is the power of God unto salvation to every one that believeth; to the Jew first, and also to the Greek.

17 For therein is the righteousness of God revealed from faith to faith: as it is written, The just shall live by faith.

18 For the wrath of God is revealed from heaven against all ungodliness and unrighteousness of men, who hold the truth in unrighteousness;

19 Because that which may be known of God is manifest in them; for God hath shewed *it* unto them.

20 For the invisible things of him from the creation of the world are clearly seen, being understood by the things that are made, *even* his eternal power and Godhead; so that they are without excuse:

21 Because that, when they knew God, they glorified *him* not as God, neither were thankful; but became vain in their imaginations, and their foolish heart was darkened.

22 Professing themselves to be wise, they became fools,

23 And changed the glory of the uncorruptible God into an image made like to corruptible man, and to birds,

and fourfooted beasts, and creeping
things.
24 Wherefore God also gave them up
to uncleanness through the lusts of
their own hearts, to dishonour their
own bodies between themselves:
25 Who changed the truth of God into
a lie, and worshipped and served the
creature more than the Creator, who is
blessed for ever. Amen.
26 For this cause God gave them up
unto vile affections: for even their
women did change the natural use into
that which is against nature:
27 And likewise also the men, leaving
the natural use of the woman, burned
in their lust one toward another; men
with men working that which is
unseemly, and receiving in themselves
that recompence of their error which
was meet.
28 And even as they did not like to
retain God in *their* knowledge, God
gave them over to a reprobate mind, to
do those things which are not convenient;
29 Being filled with all unrighteousness, fornication, wickedness, covetousness, maliciousness; full of envy, murder, debate, deceit, malignity; whisper-
ers,
30 Backbiters, haters of God, despiteful, proud, boasters, inventors of evil
things, disobedient to parents,
31 Without understanding, covenant-
breakers, without natural affection,
implacable, unmerciful:
32 Who knowing the judgment of
God, that they which commit such
things are worthy of death, not only do
the same, but have pleasure in them
that do them.

2 Therefore thou art inexcusable, O
man, whosoever thou art that
judgest: for wherein thou judgest
another, thou condemnest thyself; for
thou that judgest doest the same
things.
2 But we are sure that the judgment
of God is according to truth against
them which commit such things.
3 And thinkest thou this, O man, that
judgest them which do such things, and
doest the same, that thou shalt escape
the judgment of God?
4 Or despisest thou the riches of his
goodness and forbearance and longsuffering; not knowing that the goodness
of God leadeth thee to repentance?
5 But after thy hardness and impeni-
tent heart treasurest up unto thyself
wrath against the day of wrath and
revelation of the righteous judgment of
God;
6 Who will render to every man
according to his deeds:
7 To them who by patient continuance in well doing seek for glory and
honour and immortality, eternal life:
8 But unto them that are contentious,
and do not obey the truth, but obey unrighteousness, indignation and wrath,
9 Tribulation and anguish, upon
every soul of man that doeth evil, of the
Jew first, and also of the Gentile;
10 But glory, honour, and peace, to
every man that worketh good, to the
Jew first, and also to the Gentile:
11 For there is no respect of persons
with God.
12 For as many as have sinned without law shall also perish without law:
and as many as have sinned in the law
shall be judged by the law;

13 (For not the hearers of the law *are* just before God, but the doers of the law shall be justified.

14 For when the Gentiles, which have not the law, do by nature the things contained in the law, these, having not the law, are a law unto themselves:

15 Which shew the work of the law written in their hearts, their conscience also bearing witness, and *their* thoughts the mean while accusing or else excusing one another;)

16 In the day when God shall judge the secrets of men by Jesus Christ according to my gospel.

17 Behold, thou art called a Jew, and restest in the law, and makest thy boast of God,

18 And knowest *his* will, and approvest the things that are more excellent, being instructed out of the law;

19 And art confident that thou thyself art a guide of the blind, a light of them which are in darkness,

20 An instructor of the foolish, a teacher of babes, which hast the form of knowledge and of the truth in the law.

21 Thou therefore which teachest another, teachest thou not thyself? thou that preachest a man should not steal, dost thou steal?

22 Thou that sayest a man should not commit adultery, dost thou commit adultery? thou that abhorrest idols, dost thou commit sacrilege?

23 Thou that makest thy boast of the law, through breaking the law dishonourest thou God?

24 For the name of God is blasphemed among the Gentiles through you, as it is written.

25 For circumcision verily profiteth, if thou keep the law: but if thou be a breaker of the law, thy circumcision is made uncircumcision.

26 Therefore if the uncircumcision keep the righteousness of the law, shall not his uncircumcision be counted for circumcision?

27 And shall not uncircumcision which is by nature, if it fulfil the law, judge thee, who by the letter and circumcision dost transgress the law?

28 For he is not a Jew, which is one outwardly; neither *is that* circumcision, which is outward in the flesh:

29 But he *is* a Jew, which is one inwardly; and circumcision *is that* of the heart, in the spirit, *and* not in the letter; whose praise *is* not of men, but of God.

3

What advantage then hath the Jew? or what profit *is there* of circumcision?

2 Much every way: chiefly, because that unto them were committed the oracles of God.

3 For what if some did not believe? shall their unbelief make the faith of God without effect?

4 God forbid: yea, let God be true, but every man a liar; as it is written, That thou mightest be justified in thy sayings, and mightest overcome when thou art judged.

5 But if our unrighteousness commend the righteousness of God, what shall we say? *Is* God unrighteous who taketh vengeance? (I speak as a man)

6 God forbid: for then how shall God judge the world?

7 For if the truth of God hath more abounded through my lie unto his glory; why yet am I also judged as a sinner?

8 And not *rather*, (as we be slander-
ously reported, and as some affirm that
we say,) Let us do evil, that good may
come? whose damnation is just.
9 What then? are we better *than*
they? No, in no wise: for we have before
proved both Jews and Gentiles, that
they are all under sin;
10 As it is written, There is none righteous, no, not one:
11 There is none that understandeth,
there is none that seeketh after God.
12 They are all gone out of the way,
they are together become unprofitable;
there is none that doeth good, no, not
one.
13 Their throat *is* an open sepulchre;
with their tongues they have used
deceit; the poison of asps *is* under their
lips:
14 Whose mouth *is* full of cursing and
bitterness:
15 Their feet *are* swift to shed blood:
16 Destruction and misery *are* in
their ways:
17 And the way of peace have they
not known:
18 There is no fear of God before
their eyes.
19 Now we know that what things
soever the law saith, it saith to them
who are under the law: that every
mouth may be stopped, and all the
world may become guilty before God.
20 Therefore by the deeds of the law
there shall no flesh be justified in his
sight: for by the law *is* the knowledge of
sin.
21 But now the righteousness of God
without the law is manifested, being
witnessed by the law and the prophets;
22 Even the righteousness of God
which is by faith of Jesus Christ unto
all and upon all them that believe: for
there is no difference:
23 For all have sinned, and come
short of the glory of God;
24 Being justified freely by his grace
through the redemption that is in
Christ Jesus:
25 Whom God hath set forth *to be* a
propitiation through faith in his blood,
to declare his righteousness for the
remission of sins that are past, through
the forbearance of God;
26 To declare, *I say*, at this time his
righteousness: that he might be just,
and the justifier of him which believeth
in Jesus.
27 Where *is* boasting then? It is
excluded. By what law? of works? Nay:
but by the law of faith.
28 Therefore we conclude that a man
is justified by faith without the deeds
of the law.
29 *Is he* the God of the Jews only? *is*
he not also of the Gentiles? Yes, of the
Gentiles also:
30 Seeing *it is* one God, which shall
justify the circumcision by faith, and
uncircumcision through faith.
31 Do we then make void the law
through faith? God forbid: yea, we
establish the law.

4 What shall we say then that Abraham our father, as pertaining to the
flesh, hath found?
2 For if Abraham were justified by
works, he hath *whereof* to glory; but not
before God.
3 For what saith the scripture?
Abraham believed God, and it was
counted unto him for righteousness.
4 Now to him that worketh is the
reward not reckoned of grace, but of
debt.

5 But to him that worketh not, but believeth on him that justifieth the ungodly, his faith is counted for righteousness.

6 Even as David also describeth the blessedness of the man, unto whom God imputeth righteousness without works,

7 *Saying*, Blessed *are* they whose iniquities are forgiven, and whose sins are covered.

8 Blessed *is* the man to whom the Lord will not impute sin.

9 *Cometh* this blessedness then upon the circumcision *only*, or upon the uncircumcision also? for we say that faith was reckoned to Abraham for righteousness.

10 How was it then reckoned? when he was in circumcision, or in uncircumcision? Not in circumcision, but in uncircumcision.

11 And he received the sign of circumcision, a seal of the righteousness of the faith which *he had yet* being uncircumcised: that he might be the father of all them that believe, though they be not circumcised; that righteousness might be imputed unto them also:

12 And the father of circumcision to them who are not of the circumcision only, but who also walk in the steps of that faith of our father Abraham, which *he had* being *yet* uncircumcised.

13 For the promise, that he should be the heir of the world, *was* not to Abraham, or to his seed, through the law, but through the righteousness of faith.

14 For if they which are of the law *be* heirs, faith is made void, and the promise made of none effect:

15 Because the law worketh wrath: for where no law is, *there is* no transgression.

16 Therefore *it is* of faith, that *it might be* by grace; to the end the promise might be sure to all the seed; not to that only which is of the law, but to that also which is of the faith of Abraham; who is the father of us all,

17 (As it is written, I have made thee a father of many nations,) before him whom he believed, *even* God, who quickeneth the dead, and calleth those things which be not as though they were.

18 Who against hope believed in hope, that he might become the father of many nations, according to that which was spoken, So shall thy seed be.

19 And being not weak in faith, he considered not his own body now dead, when he was about an hundred years old, neither yet the deadness of Sara's womb:

20 He staggered not at the promise of God through unbelief; but was strong in faith, giving glory to God;

21 And being fully persuaded that, what he had promised, he was able also to perform.

22 And therefore it was imputed to him for righteousness.

23 Now it was not written for his sake alone, that it was imputed to him;

24 But for us also, to whom it shall be imputed, if we believe on him that raised up Jesus our Lord from the dead;

25 Who was delivered for our offences, and was raised again for our justification.

5 Therefore being justified by faith, we have peace with God through our Lord Jesus Christ:

2 By whom also we have access by faith into this grace wherein we stand, and rejoice in hope of the glory of God.

3 And not only *so*, but we glory in tribulations also: knowing that tribulation worketh patience;

4 And patience, experience; and experience, hope:

5 And hope maketh not ashamed; because the love of God is shed abroad in our hearts by the Holy Ghost which is given unto us.

6 For when we were yet without strength, in due time Christ died for the ungodly.

7 For scarcely for a righteous man will one die: yet peradventure for a good man some would even dare to die.

8 But God commendeth his love toward us, in that, while we were yet sinners, Christ died for us.

9 Much more then, being now justified by his blood, we shall be saved from wrath through him.

10 For if, when we were enemies, we were reconciled to God by the death of his Son, much more, being reconciled, we shall be saved by his life.

11 And not only *so*, but we also joy in God through our Lord Jesus Christ, by whom we have now received the atonement.

12 Wherefore, as by one man sin entered into the world, and death by sin; and so death passed upon all men, for that all have sinned:

13 (For until the law sin was in the world: but sin is not imputed when there is no law.

14 Nevertheless death reigned from Adam to Moses, even over them that had not sinned after the similitude of Adam's transgression, who is the figure of him that was to come.

15 But not as the offence, so also *is* the free gift. For if through the offence of one many be dead, much more the grace of God, and the gift by grace, *which is* by one man, Jesus Christ, hath abounded unto many.

16 And not as *it was* by one that sinned, *so is* the gift: for the judgment *was* by one to condemnation, but the free gift *is* of many offences unto justification.

17 For if by one man's offence death reigned by one; much more they which receive abundance of grace and of the gift of righteousness shall reign in life by one, Jesus Christ.)

18 Therefore as by the offence of one *judgment came* upon all men to condemnation; even so by the righteousness of one *the free gift came* upon all men unto justification of life.

19 For as by one man's disobedience many were made sinners, so by the obedience of one shall many be made righteous.

20 Moreover the law entered, that the offence might abound. But where sin abounded, grace did much more abound:

21 That as sin hath reigned unto death, even so might grace reign through righteousness unto eternal life by Jesus Christ our Lord.

6 What shall we say then? Shall we continue in sin, that grace may abound?

2 God forbid. How shall we, that are dead to sin, live any longer therein?

3 Know ye not, that so many of us as were baptized into Jesus Christ were baptized into his death?

4 Therefore we are buried with him by baptism into death: that like as Christ was raised up from the dead by

the glory of the Father, even so we also should walk in newness of life.
5 For if we have been planted together in the likeness of his death, we shall be also *in the likeness* of *his* resurrection:
6 Knowing this, that our old man is crucified with *him*, that the body of sin might be destroyed, that henceforth we should not serve sin.
7 For he that is dead is freed from sin.
8 Now if we be dead with Christ, we believe that we shall also live with him:
9 Knowing that Christ being raised from the dead dieth no more; death hath no more dominion over him.
10 For in that he died, he died unto sin once: but in that he liveth, he liveth unto God.
11 Likewise reckon ye also yourselves to be dead indeed unto sin, but alive unto God through Jesus Christ our Lord.
12 Let not sin therefore reign in your mortal body, that ye should obey it in the lusts thereof.
13 Neither yield ye your members *as* instruments of unrighteousness unto sin: but yield yourselves unto God, as those that are alive from the dead, and your members *as* instruments of righteousness unto God.
14 For sin shall not have dominion over you: for ye are not under the law, but under grace.
15 What then? shall we sin, because we are not under the law, but under grace? God forbid.
16 Know ye not, that to whom ye yield yourselves servants to obey, his servants ye are to whom ye obey; whether of sin unto death, or of obedience unto righteousness?
17 But God be thanked, that ye were the servants of sin, but ye have obeyed from the heart that form of doctrine which was delivered you.
18 Being then made free from sin, ye became the servants of righteousness.
19 I speak after the manner of men because of the infirmity of your flesh: for as ye have yielded your members servants to uncleanness and to iniquity unto iniquity; even so now yield your members servants to righteousness unto holiness.
20 For when ye were the servants of sin, ye were free from righteousness.
21 What fruit had ye then in those things whereof ye are now ashamed? for the end of those things *is* death.
22 But now being made free from sin, and become servants to God, ye have your fruit unto holiness, and the end everlasting life.
23 For the wages of sin *is* death; but the gift of God *is* eternal life through Jesus Christ our Lord.

7 Know ye not, brethren, (for I speak to them that know the law,) how that the law hath dominion over a man as long as he liveth?
2 For the woman which hath an husband is bound by the law to *her* husband so long as he liveth; but if the husband be dead, she is loosed from the law of *her* husband.
3 So then if, while *her* husband liveth, she be married to another man, she shall be called an adulteress: but if her husband be dead, she is free from that law; so that she is no adulteress, though she be married to another man.
4 Wherefore, my brethren, ye also are become dead to the law by the body of Christ; that ye should be married to another, *even* to him who is raised from

the dead, that we should bring forth
fruit unto God.
5 For when we were in the flesh, the
motions of sins, which were by the law,
did work in our members to bring forth
fruit unto death.
6 But now we are delivered from the
law, that being dead wherein we were
held; that we should serve in newness
of spirit, and not *in* the oldness of the
letter.
7 What shall we say then? *Is* the law
sin? God forbid. Nay, I had not known
sin, but by the law: for I had not known
lust, except the law had said, Thou shalt
not covet.
8 But sin, taking occasion by the commandment, wrought in me all manner
of concupiscence. For without the law
sin *was* dead.
9 For I was alive without the law once:
but when the commandment came, sin
revived, and I died.
10 And the commandment, which
was ordained to life, I found *to be* unto
death.
11 For sin, taking occasion by the
commandment, deceived me, and by it
slew *me*.
12 Wherefore the law *is* holy, and the
commandment holy, and just, and good.
13 Was then that which is good made
death unto me? God forbid. But sin,
that it might appear sin, working death
in me by that which is good; that sin by
the commandment might become exceeding sinful.
14 For we know that the law is spiritual: but I am carnal, sold under sin.
15 For that which I do I allow not: for
what I would, that do I not; but what I
hate, that do I.
16 If then I do that which I would not,
I consent unto the law that *it is* good.
17 Now then it is no more I that do it,
but sin that dwelleth in me.
18 For I know that in me (that is, in
my flesh,) dwelleth no good thing: for
to will is present with me; but *how* to
perform that which is good I find not.
19 For the good that I would I do not:
but the evil which I would not, that I do.
20 Now if I do that I would not, it is no
more I that do it, but sin that dwelleth
in me.
21 I find then a law, that, when I
would do good, evil is present with me.
22 For I delight in the law of God
after the inward man:
23 But I see another law in my members, warring against the law of my
mind, and bringing me into captivity to
the law of sin which is in my members.
24 O wretched man that I am! who
shall deliver me from the body of this
death?
25 I thank God through Jesus Christ
our Lord. So then with the mind I
myself serve the law of God; but with
the flesh the law of sin.

8 *There is* therefore now no condemnation to them which are in Christ
Jesus, who walk not after the flesh, but
after the Spirit.
2 For the law of the Spirit of life in
Christ Jesus hath made me free from
the law of sin and death.
3 For what the law could not do, in
that it was weak through the flesh, God
sending his own Son in the likeness of
sinful flesh, and for sin, condemned sin
in the flesh:
4 That the righteousness of the law
might be fulfilled in us, who walk not
after the flesh, but after the Spirit.
5 For they that are after the flesh do
mind the things of the flesh; but they

that are after the Spirit the things of the Spirit.

6 For to be carnally minded *is* death; but to be spiritually minded *is* life and peace.

7 Because the carnal mind *is* enmity against God: for it is not subject to the law of God, neither indeed can be.

8 So then they that are in the flesh cannot please God.

9 But ye are not in the flesh, but in the Spirit, if so be that the Spirit of God dwell in you. Now if any man have not the Spirit of Christ, he is none of his.

10 And if Christ *be* in you, the body *is* dead because of sin; but the Spirit *is* life because of righteousness.

11 But if the Spirit of him that raised up Jesus from the dead dwell in you, he that raised up Christ from the dead shall also quicken your mortal bodies by his Spirit that dwelleth in you.

12 Therefore, brethren, we are debtors, not to the flesh, to live after the flesh.

13 For if ye live after the flesh, ye shall die: but if ye through the Spirit do mortify the deeds of the body, ye shall live.

14 For as many as are led by the Spirit of God, they are the sons of God.

15 For ye have not received the spirit of bondage again to fear; but ye have received the Spirit of adoption, whereby we cry, Abba, Father.

16 The Spirit itself beareth witness with our spirit, that we are the children of God:

17 And if children, then heirs; heirs of God, and joint-heirs with Christ; if so be that we suffer with *him*, that we may be also glorified together.

18 For I reckon that the sufferings of this present time *are* not worthy *to be compared* with the glory which shall be revealed in us.

19 For the earnest expectation of the creature waiteth for the manifestation of the sons of God.

20 For the creature was made subject to vanity, not willingly, but by reason of him who hath subjected *the same* in hope,

21 Because the creature itself also shall be delivered from the bondage of corruption into the glorious liberty of the children of God.

22 For we know that the whole creation groaneth and travaileth in pain together until now.

23 And not only *they*, but ourselves also, which have the firstfruits of the Spirit, even we ourselves groan within ourselves, waiting for the adoption, *to wit*, the redemption of our body.

24 For we are saved by hope: but hope that is seen is not hope: for what a man seeth, why doth he yet hope for?

25 But if we hope for that we see not, *then* do we with patience wait for *it*.

26 Likewise the Spirit also helpeth our infirmities: for we know not what we should pray for as we ought: but the Spirit itself maketh intercession for us with groanings which cannot be uttered.

27 And he that searcheth the hearts knoweth what *is* the mind of the Spirit, because he maketh intercession for the saints according to *the will of* God.

28 And we know that all things work together for good to them that love God, to them who are the called according to *his* purpose.

29 For whom he did foreknow, he also did predestinate *to be* conformed to the image of his Son, that he might be the firstborn among many brethren.

30 Moreover whom he did predestinate, them he also called: and whom he called, them he also justified: and whom he justified, them he also glorified.

31 What shall we then say to these things? If God *be* for us, who *can be* against us?

32 He that spared not his own Son, but delivered him up for us all, how shall he not with him also freely give us all things?

33 Who shall lay any thing to the charge of God's elect? *It is* God that justifieth.

34 Who *is* he that condemneth? *It is* Christ that died, yea rather, that is risen again, who is even at the right hand of God, who also maketh intercession for us.

35 Who shall separate us from the love of Christ? *shall* tribulation, or distress, or persecution, or famine, or nakedness, or peril, or sword?

36 As it is written, For thy sake we are killed all the day long; we are accounted as sheep for the slaughter.

37 Nay, in all these things we are more than conquerors through him that loved us.

38 For I am persuaded, that neither death, nor life, nor angels, nor principalities, nor powers, nor things present, nor things to come,

39 Nor height, nor depth, nor any other creature, shall be able to separate us from the love of God, which is in Christ Jesus our Lord.

9 I say the truth in Christ, I lie not, my conscience also bearing me witness in the Holy Ghost,

2 That I have great heaviness and continual sorrow in my heart.

3 For I could wish that myself were accursed from Christ for my brethren, my kinsmen according to the flesh:

4 Who are Israelites; to whom *pertaineth* the adoption, and the glory, and the covenants, and the giving of the law, and the service *of God*, and the promises;

5 Whose *are* the fathers, and of whom as concerning the flesh Christ *came*, who is over all, God blessed for ever. Amen.

6 Not as though the word of God hath taken none effect. For they *are* not all Israel, which are of Israel:

7 Neither, because they are the seed of Abraham, *are they* all children: but, In Isaac shall thy seed be called.

8 That is, They which are the children of the flesh, these *are* not the children of God: but the children of the promise are counted for the seed.

9 For this *is* the word of promise, At this time will I come, and Sara shall have a son.

10 And not only *this*; but when Rebecca also had conceived by one, *even* by our father Isaac;

11 (For *the children* being not yet born, neither having done any good or evil, that the purpose of God according to election might stand, not of works, but of him that calleth;)

12 It was said unto her, The elder shall serve the younger.

13 As it is written, Jacob have I loved, but Esau have I hated.

14 What shall we say then? *Is there* unrighteousness with God? God forbid.

15 For he saith to Moses, I will have mercy on whom I will have mercy, and I will have compassion on whom I will have compassion.

16 So then *it is* not of him that willeth, nor of him that runneth, but of God that sheweth mercy.

17 For the scripture saith unto Pharaoh, Even for this same purpose have I raised thee up, that I might shew my power in thee, and that my name might be declared throughout all the earth.

18 Therefore hath he mercy on whom he will *have mercy*, and whom he will he hardeneth.

19 Thou wilt say then unto me, Why doth he yet find fault? For who hath resisted his will?

20 Nay but, O man, who art thou that repliest against God? Shall the thing formed say to him that formed *it*, Why hast thou made me thus?

21 Hath not the potter power over the clay, of the same lump to make one vessel unto honour, and another unto dishonour?

22 *What* if God, willing to shew *his* wrath, and to make his power known, endured with much longsuffering the vessels of wrath fitted to destruction:

23 And that he might make known the riches of his glory on the vessels of mercy, which he had afore prepared unto glory,

24 Even us, whom he hath called, not of the Jews only, but also of the Gentiles?

25 As he saith also in Osee, I will call them my people, which were not my people; and her beloved, which was not beloved.

26 And it shall come to pass, *that* in the place where it was said unto them, Ye *are* not my people; there shall they be called the children of the living God.

27 Esaias also crieth concerning Israel, Though the number of the children of Israel be as the sand [illegible] a remnant shall be saved:

28 For he will finish the work, and cut *it* short in righteousness: because a short work will the Lord make upon the earth.

29 And as Esaias said before, Except the Lord of Sabaoth had left us a seed, we had been as Sodoma, and been made like unto Gomorrha.

30 What shall we say then? That the Gentiles, which followed not after righteousness, have attained to righteousness, even the righteousness which is of faith.

31 But Israel, which followed after the law of righteousness, hath not attained to the law of righteousness.

32 Wherefore? Because *they sought it* not by faith, but as it were by the works of the law. For they stumbled at that stumblingstone;

33 As it is written, Behold, I lay in Sion a stumblingstone and rock of offence: and whosoever believeth on him shall not be ashamed.

10 Brethren, my heart's desire and prayer to God for Israel is, that they might be saved.

2 For I bear them record that they have a zeal of God, but not according to knowledge.

3 For they being ignorant of God's righteousness, and going about to establish their own righteousness, have not submitted themselves unto the righteousness of God.

4 For Christ *is* the end of the law for righteousness to every one that believeth.

5 For Moses describeth the righteousness which is of the law, That the man which doeth those things shall live by them.

6 But the righteousness which is of
faith speaketh on this wise, Say not in
thine heart, Who shall ascend into
heaven? (that is, to bring Christ down
from above:)
7 Or, Who shall descend into the
deep? (that is, to bring up Christ again
from the dead.)
8 But what saith it? The word is nigh
thee, *even* in thy mouth, and in thy
heart: that is, the word of faith, which
we preach;
9 That if thou shalt confess with thy
mouth the Lord Jesus, and shalt believe
in thine heart that God hath raised him
from the dead, thou shalt be saved.
10 For with the heart man believeth
unto righteousness; and with the mouth
confession is made unto salvation.
11 For the scripture saith, Whosoever
believeth on him shall not be ashamed.
12 For there is no difference between
the Jew and the Greek: for the same
Lord over all is rich unto all that call
upon him.
13 For whosoever shall call upon the
name of the Lord shall be saved.
14 How then shall they call on him in
whom they have not believed? and how
shall they believe in him of whom they
have not heard? and how shall they
hear without a preacher?
15 And how shall they preach, except
they be sent? as it is written, How beautiful are the feet of them that preach
the gospel of peace, and bring glad
tidings of good things!
16 But they have not all obeyed the
gospel. For Esaias saith, Lord, who hath
believed our report?
17 So then faith *cometh* by hearing,
and hearing by the word of God.
18 But I say, Have they not heard? Yes
verily, their sound went into all the
earth, and their words unto the ends of
the world.
19 But I say, Did not Israel know? First
Moses saith, I will provoke you to jealousy by *them that are* no people, *and*
by a foolish nation I will anger you.
20 But Esaias is very bold, and saith, I
was found of them that sought me not;
I was made manifest unto them that
asked not after me.
21 But to Israel he saith, All day long
I have stretched forth my hands unto a
disobedient and gainsaying people.

11 I say then, Hath God cast away
his people? God forbid. For I also
am an Israelite, of the seed of Abraham,
of the tribe of Benjamin.
2 God hath not cast away his people
which he foreknew. Wot ye not what the
scripture saith of Elias? how he maketh
intercession to God against Israel, saying,
3 Lord, they have killed thy prophets,
and digged down thine altars; and I am
left alone, and they seek my life.
4 But what saith the answer of God
unto him? I have reserved to myself
seven thousand men, who have not
bowed the knee to *the image of* Baal.
5 Even so then at this present time
also there is a remnant according to the
election of grace.
6 And if by grace, then *is it* no more
of works: otherwise grace is no more
grace. But if *it be* of works, then is it no
more grace: otherwise work is no more
work.
7 What then? Israel hath not obtained
that which he seeketh for; but the election hath obtained it, and the rest were
blinded.
8 (According as it is written, God hath
given them the spirit of slumber, eyes

that they should not see, and ears that they should not hear;) unto this day.

9 And David saith, Let their table be made a snare, and a trap, and a stumblingblock, and a recompence unto them:

10 Let their eyes be darkened, that they may not see, and bow down their back alway.

11 I say then, Have they stumbled that they should fall? God forbid: but *rather* through their fall salvation *is come* unto the Gentiles, for to provoke them to jealousy.

12 Now if the fall of them *be* the riches of the world, and the diminishing of them the riches of the Gentiles; how much more their fulness?

13 For I speak to you Gentiles, inasmuch as I am the apostle of the Gentiles, I magnify mine office:

14 If by any means I may provoke to emulation *them which are* my flesh, and might save some of them.

15 For if the casting away of them *be* the reconciling of the world, what *shall* the receiving *of them be*, but life from the dead?

16 For if the firstfruit *be* holy, the lump *is* also *holy*: and if the root *be* holy, so *are* the branches.

17 And if some of the branches be broken off, and thou, being a wild olive tree, wert graffed in among them, and with them partakest of the root and fatness of the olive tree;

18 Boast not against the branches. But if thou boast, thou bearest not the root, but the root thee.

19 Thou wilt say then, The branches were broken off, that I might be graffed in.

20 Well; because of unbelief they were broken off, and thou standest by faith. Be not highminded, but fear:

21 For if God spared not the natural branches, *take heed* lest he also spare not thee.

22 Behold therefore the goodness and severity of God: on them which fell, severity; but toward thee, goodness, if thou continue in *his* goodness: otherwise thou also shalt be cut off.

23 And they also, if they abide not still in unbelief, shall be graffed in: for God is able to graff them in again.

24 For if thou wert cut out of the olive tree which is wild by nature, and wert graffed contrary to nature into a good olive tree: how much more shall these, which be the natural *branches*, be graffed into their own olive tree?

25 For I would not, brethren, that ye should be ignorant of this mystery, lest ye should be wise in your own conceits; that blindness in part is happened to Israel, until the fulness of the Gentiles be come in.

26 And so all Israel shall be saved: as it is written, There shall come out of Sion the Deliverer, and shall turn away ungodliness from Jacob:

27 For this *is* my covenant unto them, when I shall take away their sins.

28 As concerning the gospel, *they are* enemies for your sakes: but as touching the election, *they are* beloved for the fathers' sakes.

29 For the gifts and calling of God *are* without repentance.

30 For as ye in times past have not believed God, yet have now obtained mercy through their unbelief:

31 Even so have these also now not believed, that through your mercy they also may obtain mercy.

32 For God hath concluded them all
in unbelief, that he might have mercy
upon all.
33 O the depth of the riches both of
the wisdom and knowledge of God!
how unsearchable *are* his judgments,
and his ways past finding out!
34 For who hath known the mind of
the Lord? or who hath been his counsellor?
35 Or who hath first given to him, and
it shall be recompensed unto him
again?
36 For of him, and through him, and
to him, *are* all things: to whom *be* glory
for ever. Amen.

12 I beseech you therefore, brethren, by the mercies of God, that
ye present your bodies a living sacrifice, holy, acceptable unto God, *which
is* your reasonable service.
2 And be not conformed to this world:
but be ye transformed by the renewing
of your mind, that ye may prove what *is*
that good, and acceptable, and perfect,
will of God.
3 For I say, through the grace given
unto me, to every man that is among
you, not to think *of himself* more highly
than he ought to think; but to think
soberly, according as God hath dealt to
every man the measure of faith.
4 For as we have many members in
one body, and all members have not the
same office:
5 So we, *being* many, are one body in
Christ, and every one members one of
another.
6 Having then gifts differing according to the grace that is given to us,
whether prophecy, *let us prophesy*
according to the proportion of faith;
7 Or ministry, *let us wait* on *our* ministering: or he that teacheth, on teaching;
8 Or he that exhorteth, on exhortation: he that giveth, *let him do it* with
simplicity; he that ruleth, with diligence; he that sheweth mercy, with
cheerfulness.
9 *Let* love be without dissimulation.
Abhor that which is evil; cleave to that
which is good.
10 *Be* kindly affectioned one to another with brotherly love; in honour preferring one another;
11 Not slothful in business; fervent in
spirit; serving the Lord;
12 Rejoicing in hope; patient in tribulation; continuing instant in prayer;
13 Distributing to the necessity of
saints; given to hospitality.
14 Bless them which persecute you:
bless, and curse not.
15 Rejoice with them that do rejoice,
and weep with them that weep.
16 *Be* of the same mind one toward
another. Mind not high things, but con-
descend to men of low estate. Be not
wise in your own conceits.
17 Recompense to no man evil for
evil. Provide things honest in the sight
of all men.
18 If it be possible, as much as lieth in
you, live peaceably with all men.
19 Dearly beloved, avenge not yourselves, but *rather* give place unto
wrath: for it is written, Vengeance *is*
mine; I will repay, saith the Lord.
20 Therefore if thine enemy hunger,
feed him; if he thirst, give him drink:
for in so doing thou shalt heap coals of
fire on his head.
21 Be not overcome of evil, but overcome evil with good.

13 Let every soul be subject unto the higher powers. For there is no power but of God: the powers that be are ordained of God.

2 Whosoever therefore resisteth the power, resisteth the ordinance of God: and they that resist shall receive to themselves damnation.

3 For rulers are not a terror to good works, but to the evil. Wilt thou then not be afraid of the power? do that which is good, and thou shalt have praise of the same:

4 For he is the minister of God to thee for good. But if thou do that which is evil, be afraid; for he beareth not the sword in vain: for he is the minister of God, a revenger to *execute* wrath upon him that doeth evil.

5 Wherefore *ye* must needs be subject, not only for wrath, but also for conscience sake.

6 For for this cause pay ye tribute also: for they are God's ministers, attending continually upon this very thing.

7 Render therefore to all their dues: tribute to whom tribute *is due*; custom to whom custom; fear to whom fear; honour to whom honour.

8 Owe no man any thing, but to love one another: for he that loveth another hath fulfilled the law.

9 For this, Thou shalt not commit adultery, Thou shalt not kill, Thou shalt not steal, Thou shalt not bear false witness, Thou shalt not covet; and if *there be* any other commandment, it is briefly comprehended in this saying, namely, Thou shalt love thy neighbour as thyself.

10 Love worketh no ill to his neighbour: therefore love *is* the fulfilling of the law.

11 And that, knowing the time, that now *it is* high time to awake out of sleep: for now *is* our salvation nearer than when we believed.

12 The night is far spent, the day is at hand: let us therefore cast off the works of darkness, and let us put on the armour of light.

13 Let us walk honestly, as in the day; not in rioting and drunkenness, not in chambering and wantonness, not in strife and envying.

14 But put ye on the Lord Jesus Christ, and make not provision for the flesh, to *fulfil* the lusts *thereof*.

14 Him that is weak in the faith receive ye, *but* not to doubtful disputations.

2 For one believeth that he may eat all things: another, who is weak, eateth herbs.

3 Let not him that eateth despise him that eateth not; and let not him which eateth not judge him that eateth: for God hath received him.

4 Who art thou that judgest another man's servant? to his own master he standeth or falleth. Yea, he shall be holden up: for God is able to make him stand.

5 One man esteemeth one day above another: another esteemeth every day *alike*. Let every man be fully persuaded in his own mind.

6 He that regardeth the day, regardeth *it* unto the Lord; and he that regardeth not the day, to the Lord he doth not regard *it*. He that eateth, eateth to the Lord, for he giveth God thanks; and he that eateth not, to the Lord he eateth not, and giveth God thanks.

7 For none of us liveth to himself, and no man dieth to himself.

8 For whether we live, we live unto the Lord; and whether we die, we die unto the Lord: whether we live therefore, or die, we are the Lord's.

9 For to this end Christ both died, and rose, and revived, that he might be Lord both of the dead and living.

10 But why dost thou judge thy brother? or why dost thou set at nought thy brother? for we shall all stand before the judgment seat of Christ.

11 For it is written, *As* I live, saith the Lord, every knee shall bow to me, and every tongue shall confess to God.

12 So then every one of us shall give account of himself to God.

13 Let us not therefore judge one another any more: but judge this rather, that no man put a stumblingblock or an occasion to fall in *his* brother's way.

14 I know, and am persuaded by the Lord Jesus, that *there is* nothing unclean of itself: but to him that esteemeth any thing to be unclean, to him *it is* unclean.

15 But if thy brother be grieved with *thy* meat, now walkest thou not charitably. Destroy not him with thy meat, for whom Christ died.

16 Let not then your good be evil spoken of:

17 For the kingdom of God is not meat and drink; but righteousness, and peace, and joy in the Holy Ghost.

18 For he that in these things serveth Christ *is* acceptable to God, and approved of men.

19 Let us therefore follow after the things which make for peace, and things wherewith one may edify another.

20 For meat destroy not the work of God. All things indeed *are* pure; but *it is* evil for that man who eateth with offence.

21 *It is* good neither to eat flesh, nor to drink wine, nor *any thing* whereby thy brother stumbleth, or is offended, or is made weak.

22 Hast thou faith? have *it* to thyself before God. Happy *is* he that condemneth not himself in that thing which he alloweth.

23 And he that doubteth is damned if he eat, because *he eateth* not of faith: for whatsoever *is* not of faith is sin.

15 We then that are strong ought to bear the infirmities of the weak, and not to please ourselves.

2 Let every one of us please *his* neighbour for *his* good to edification.

3 For even Christ pleased not himself; but, as it is written, The reproaches of them that reproached thee fell on me.

4 For whatsoever things were written aforetime were written for our learning, that we through patience and comfort of the scriptures might have hope.

5 Now the God of patience and consolation grant you to be likeminded one toward another according to Christ Jesus:

6 That ye may with one mind *and* one mouth glorify God, even the Father of our Lord Jesus Christ.

7 Wherefore receive ye one another, as Christ also received us to the glory of God.

8 Now I say that Jesus Christ was a minister of the circumcision for the truth of God, to confirm the promises *made* unto the fathers:

9 And that the Gentiles might glorify God for *his* mercy; as it is written, For this cause I will confess to thee among the Gentiles, and sing unto thy name.

10 And again he saith, Rejoice, ye Gentiles, with his people.

11 And again, Praise the Lord, all ye Gentiles; and laud him, all ye people.

12 And again, Esaias saith, There shall be a root of Jesse, and he that shall rise to reign over the Gentiles; in him shall the Gentiles trust.

13 Now the God of hope fill you with all joy and peace in believing, that ye may abound in hope, through the power of the Holy Ghost.

14 And I myself also am persuaded of you, my brethren, that ye also are full of goodness, filled with all knowledge, able also to admonish one another.

15 Nevertheless, brethren, I have written the more boldly unto you in some sort, as putting you in mind, because of the grace that is given to me of God,

16 That I should be the minister of Jesus Christ to the Gentiles, ministering the gospel of God, that the offering up of the Gentiles might be acceptable, being sanctified by the Holy Ghost.

17 I have therefore whereof I may glory through Jesus Christ in those things which pertain to God.

18 For I will not dare to speak of any of those things which Christ hath not wrought by me, to make the Gentiles obedient, by word and deed,

19 Through mighty signs and wonders, by the power of the Spirit of God; so that from Jerusalem, and round about unto Illyricum, I have fully preached the gospel of Christ.

20 Yea, so have I strived to preach the gospel, not where Christ was named, lest I should build upon another man's foundation:

21 But as it is written, To whom he was not spoken of, they shall see: and they that have not heard shall understand.

22 For which cause also I have been much hindered from coming to you.

23 But now having no more place in these parts, and having a great desire these many years to come unto you;

24 Whensoever I take my journey into Spain, I will come to you: for I trust to see you in my journey, and to be brought on my way thitherward by you, if first I be somewhat filled with your *company*.

25 But now I go unto Jerusalem to minister unto the saints.

26 For it hath pleased them of Macedonia and Achaia to make a certain contribution for the poor saints which are at Jerusalem.

27 It hath pleased them verily; and their debtors they are. For if the Gentiles have been made partakers of their spiritual things, their duty is also to minister unto them in carnal things.

28 When therefore I have performed this, and have sealed to them this fruit, I will come by you into Spain.

29 And I am sure that, when I come unto you, I shall come in the fulness of the blessing of the gospel of Christ.

30 Now I beseech you, brethren, for the Lord Jesus Christ's sake, and for the love of the Spirit, that ye strive together with me in *your* prayers to God for me;

31 That I may be delivered from them that do not believe in Judaea; and that my service which *I have* for Jerusalem may be accepted of the saints;

32 That I may come unto you with joy by the will of God, and may with you be refreshed.

33 Now the God of peace *be* with you all. Amen.

16 I commend unto you Phebe our
sister, which is a servant of the
church which is at Cenchrea:
2 That ye receive her in the Lord, as
becometh saints, and that ye assist her
in whatsoever business she hath need
of you: for she hath been a succourer of
many, and of myself also.
3 Greet Priscilla and Aquila my helpers in Christ Jesus:
4 Who have for my life laid down
their own necks: unto whom not only I
give thanks, but also all the churches of
the Gentiles.
5 Likewise *greet* the church that is in
their house. Salute my wellbeloved
Epaenetus, who is the firstfruits of
Achaia unto Christ.
6 Greet Mary, who bestowed much
labour on us.
7 Salute Andronicus and Junia, my
kinsmen, and my fellowprisoners, who
are of note among the apostles, who
also were in Christ before me.
8 Greet Amplias my beloved in the
Lord.
9 Salute Urbane, our helper in Christ,
and Stachys my beloved.
10 Salute Apelles approved in Christ.
Salute them which are of Aristobulus'
household.
11 Salute Herodion my kinsman.
Greet them that be of the *household* of
Narcissus, which are in the Lord.
12 Salute Tryphena and Tryphosa,
who labour in the Lord. Salute the
beloved Persis, which laboured much in
the Lord.
13 Salute Rufus chosen in the Lord,
and his mother and mine.
14 Salute Asyncritus, Phlegon, Her-
mas, Patrobas, Hermes, and the brethren which are with them.
15 Salute Philologus, and Julia,
Nereus, and his sister, and Olympas,
and all the saints which are with them.
16 Salute one another with an holy
kiss. The churches of Christ salute you.
17 Now I beseech you, brethren, mark
them which cause divisions and offences contrary to the doctrine which ye
have learned; and avoid them.
18 For they that are such serve not
our Lord Jesus Christ, but their own
belly; and by good words and fair
speeches deceive the hearts of the
simple.
19 For your obedience is come abroad
unto all *men*. I am glad therefore on
your behalf: but yet I would have you
wise unto that which is good, and simple concerning evil.
20 And the God of peace shall bruise
Satan under your feet shortly. The
grace of our Lord Jesus Christ *be* with
you. Amen.
21 Timotheus my workfellow, and
Lucius, and Jason, and Sosipater, my
kinsmen, salute you.
22 I Tertius, who wrote *this* epistle,
salute you in the Lord.
23 Gaius mine host, and of the whole
church, saluteth you. Erastus the chamberlain of the city saluteth you, and
Quartus a brother.
24 The grace of our Lord Jesus Christ
be with you all. Amen.
25 Now to him that is of power to stablish you according to my gospel, and
the preaching of Jesus Christ, according to the revelation of the mystery,
which was kept secret since the world
began,
26 But now is made manifest, and by
the scriptures of the prophets, according to the commandment of the everlasting God, made known to all nations
for the obedience of faith:
27 To God only wise, *be* glory through
Jesus Christ for ever. Amen.

THE FIRST EPISTLE OF PAUL THE APOSTLE TO THE CORINTHIANS

1

1 Paul, called *to be* an apostle of Jesus Christ through the will of God, and Sosthenes *our* brother,

2 Unto the church of God which is at Corinth, to them that are sanctified in Christ Jesus, called *to be* saints, with all that in every place call upon the name of Jesus Christ our Lord, both theirs and ours:

3 Grace *be* unto you, and peace, from God our Father, and *from* the Lord Jesus Christ.

4 I thank my God always on your behalf, for the grace of God which is given you by Jesus Christ;

5 That in every thing ye are enriched by him, in all utterance, and *in* all knowledge;

6 Even as the testimony of Christ was confirmed in you:

7 So that ye come behind in no gift; waiting for the coming of our Lord Jesus Christ:

8 Who shall also confirm you unto the end, *that ye may be* blameless in the day of our Lord Jesus Christ.

9 God *is* faithful, by whom ye were called unto the fellowship of his Son Jesus Christ our Lord.

10 Now I beseech you, brethren, by the name of our Lord Jesus Christ, that ye all speak the same thing, and *that* there be no divisions among you; but *that* ye be perfectly joined together in the same mind and in the same judgment.

11 For it hath been declared unto me of you, my brethren, by them *which are of the house* of Chloe, that there are contentions among you.

12 Now this I say, that every one of you saith, I am of Paul; and I of Apollos; and I of Cephas; and I of Christ.

13 Is Christ divided? was Paul crucified for you? or were ye baptized in the name of Paul?

14 I thank God that I baptized none of you, but Crispus and Gaius;

15 Lest any should say that I had baptized in mine own name.

16 And I baptized also the household of Stephanas: besides, I know not whether I baptized any other.

17 For Christ sent me not to baptize, but to preach the gospel: not with wisdom of words, lest the cross of Christ should be made of none effect.

18 For the preaching of the cross is to them that perish foolishness; but unto us which are saved it is the power of God.

19 For it is written, I will destroy the wisdom of the wise, and will bring to nothing the understanding of the prudent.

20 Where *is* the wise? where *is* the scribe? where *is* the disputer of this world? hath not God made foolish the wisdom of this world?

21 For after that in the wisdom of God the world by wisdom knew not God, it pleased God by the foolishness of preaching to save them that believe.

22 For the Jews require a sign, and the Greeks seek after wisdom:

23 But we preach Christ crucified, unto the Jews a stumblingblock, and unto the Greeks foolishness;

24 But unto them which are called,
both Jews and Greeks, Christ the power
of God, and the wisdom of God.
25 Because the foolishness of God is
wiser than men; and the weakness of
God is stronger than men.
26 For ye see your calling, brethren,
how that not many wise men after the
flesh, not many mighty, not many noble,
are called:
27 But God hath chosen the foolish
things of the world to confound the
wise; and God hath chosen the weak
things of the world to confound the
things which are mighty;
28 And base things of the world, and
things which are despised, hath God
chosen, *yea*, and things which are not,
to bring to nought things that are:
29 That no flesh should glory in his
presence.
30 But of him are ye in Christ Jesus,
who of God is made unto us wisdom,
and righteousness, and sanctification,
and redemption:
31 That, according as it is written, He
that glorieth, let him glory in the Lord.

2 And I, brethren, when I came to
you, came not with excellency of
speech or of wisdom, declaring unto
you the testimony of God.
2 For I determined not to know any
thing among you, save Jesus Christ, and
him crucified.
3 And I was with you in weakness,
and in fear, and in much trembling.
4 And my speech and my preaching
was not with enticing words of man's
wisdom, but in demonstration of the
Spirit and of power:
5 That your faith should not stand in
the wisdom of men, but in the power of
God.
6 Howbeit we speak wisdom among
them that are perfect: yet not the wisdom of this world, nor of the princes of
this world, that come to nought:
7 But we speak the wisdom of God in
a mystery, *even* the hidden *wisdom*,
which God ordained before the world
unto our glory:
8 Which none of the princes of this
world knew: for had they known *it*, they
would not have crucified the Lord of
glory.
9 But as it is written, Eye hath not
seen, nor ear heard, neither have
entered into the heart of man, the
things which God hath prepared for
them that love him.
10 But God hath revealed *them* unto
us by his Spirit: for the Spirit searcheth
all things, yea, the deep things of God.
11 For what man knoweth the things
of a man, save the spirit of man which
is in him? even so the things of God
knoweth no man, but the Spirit of God.
12 Now we have received, not the
spirit of the world, but the spirit which
is of God; that we might know the
things that are freely given to us of
God.
13 Which things also we speak, not in
the words which man's wisdom teacheth, but which the Holy Ghost teacheth;
comparing spiritual things with spiritual.
14 But the natural man receiveth not
the things of the Spirit of God: for they
are foolishness unto him: neither can
he know *them*, because they are spiritually discerned.
15 But he that is spiritual judgeth all
things, yet he himself is judged of no
man.

16 For who hath known the mind of the Lord, that he may instruct him? But we have the mind of Christ.

3 And I, brethren, could not speak unto you as unto spiritual, but as unto carnal, *even* as unto babes in Christ.

2 I have fed you with milk, and not with meat: for hitherto ye were not able *to bear it*, neither yet now are ye able.

3 For ye are yet carnal: for whereas *there is* among you envying, and strife, and divisions, are ye not carnal, and walk as men?

4 For while one saith, I am of Paul; and another, I *am* of Apollos; are ye not carnal?

5 Who then is Paul, and who *is* Apollos, but ministers by whom ye believed, even as the Lord gave to every man?

6 I have planted, Apollos watered; but God gave the increase.

7 So then neither is he that planteth any thing, neither he that watereth; but God that giveth the increase.

8 Now he that planteth and he that watereth are one: and every man shall receive his own reward according to his own labour.

9 For we are labourers together with God: ye are God's husbandry, *ye are* God's building.

10 According to the grace of God which is given unto me, as a wise masterbuilder, I have laid the foundation, and another buildeth thereon. But let every man take heed how he buildeth thereupon.

11 For other foundation can no man lay than that is laid, which is Jesus Christ.

12 Now if any man build upon this foundation gold, silver, precious stones, wood, hay, stubble;

13 Every man's work shall be made manifest: for the day shall declare it, because it shall be revealed by fire; and the fire shall try every man's work of what sort it is.

14 If any man's work abide which he hath built thereupon, he shall receive a reward.

15 If any man's work shall be burned, he shall suffer loss: but he himself shall be saved; yet so as by fire.

16 Know ye not that ye are the temple of God, and *that* the Spirit of God dwelleth in you?

17 If any man defile the temple of God, him shall God destroy; for the temple of God is holy, which *temple* ye are.

18 Let no man deceive himself. If any man among you seemeth to be wise in this world, let him become a fool, that he may be wise.

19 For the wisdom of this world is foolishness with God. For it is written, He taketh the wise in their own craftiness.

20 And again, The Lord knoweth the thoughts of the wise, that they are vain.

21 Therefore let no man glory in men. For all things are yours;

22 Whether Paul, or Apollos, or Cephas, or the world, or life, or death, or things present, or things to come; all are yours;

23 And ye are Christ's; and Christ *is* God's.

4 Let a man so account of us, as of the ministers of Christ, and stewards of the mysteries of God.

2 Moreover it is required in stewards, that a man be found faithful.

3 But with me it is a very small thing
that I should be judged of you, or of
man's judgment: yea, I judge not mine
own self.
4 For I know nothing by myself; yet
am I not hereby justified: but he that
judgeth me is the Lord.
5 Therefore judge nothing before the
time, until the Lord come, who both
will bring to light the hidden things of
darkness, and will make manifest the
counsels of the hearts: and then shall
every man have praise of God.
6 And these things, brethren, I have
in a figure transferred to myself and *to*
Apollos for your sakes; that ye might
learn in us not to think *of men* above
that which is written, that no one of you
be puffed up for one against another.
7 For who maketh thee to differ *from
another*? and what hast thou that thou
didst not receive? now if thou didst
receive *it*, why dost thou glory, as if
thou hadst not received *it*?
8 Now ye are full, now ye are rich, ye
have reigned as kings without us: and I
would to God ye did reign, that we also
might reign with you.
9 For I think that God hath set forth
us the apostles last, as it were appointed to death: for we are made a specta-
cle unto the world, and to angels, and to
men.
10 We *are* fools for Christ's sake, but
ye *are* wise in Christ; we *are* weak, but
ye *are* strong; ye *are* honourable, but we
are despised.
11 Even unto this present hour we
both hunger, and thirst, and are naked,
and are buffeted, and have no certain
dwellingplace;
12 And labour, working with our own
hands: being reviled, we bless; being
persecuted, we suffer it:
13 Being defamed, we intreat: we are
made as the filth of the world, *and are*
the offscouring of all things unto this
day.
14 I write not these things to shame
you, but as my beloved sons I warn *you*.
15 For though ye have ten thousand
instructors in Christ, yet *have ye* not
many fathers: for in Christ Jesus I have
begotten you through the gospel.
16 Wherefore I beseech you, be ye followers of me.
17 For this cause have I sent unto you
Timotheus, who is my beloved son, and
faithful in the Lord, who shall bring you
into remembrance of my ways which be
in Christ, as I teach every where in
every church.
18 Now some are puffed up, as though
I would not come to you.
19 But I will come to you shortly, if the
Lord will, and will know, not the speech
of them which are puffed up, but the
power.
20 For the kingdom of God *is* not in
word, but in power.
21 What will ye? shall I come unto
you with a rod, or in love, and *in* the
spirit of meekness?

5 It is reported commonly *that there
is* fornication among you, and such
fornication as is not so much as named
among the Gentiles, that one should
have his father's wife.
2 And ye are puffed up, and have not
rather mourned, that he that hath done
this deed might be taken away from
among you.
3 For I verily, as absent in body, but
present in spirit, have judged already,
as though I were present, *concerning*
him that hath so done this deed,
4 In the name of our Lord Jesus
Christ, when ye are gathered together,

and my spirit, with the power of our
Lord Jesus Christ,
5 To deliver such an one unto Satan
for the destruction of the flesh, that the
spirit may be saved in the day of the
Lord Jesus.
6 Your glorying *is* not good. Know ye
not that a little leaven leaveneth the
whole lump?
7 Purge out therefore the old leaven,
that ye may be a new lump, as ye are
unleavened. For even Christ our passover is sacrificed for us:
8 Therefore let us keep the feast, not
with old leaven, neither with the leaven
of malice and wickedness; but with the
unleavened *bread* of sincerity and
truth.
9 I wrote unto you in an epistle not to
company with fornicators:
10 Yet not altogether with the fornicators of this world, or with the covetous, or extortioners, or with idolaters;
for then must ye needs go out of the
world.
11 But now I have written unto you
not to keep company, if any man that is
called a brother be a fornicator, or covetous, or an idolater, or a railer, or a
drunkard, or an extortioner; with such
an one no not to eat.
12 For what have I to do to judge
them also that are without? do not ye
judge them that are within?
13 But them that are without God
judgeth. Therefore put away from
among yourselves that wicked person.

6 Dare any of you, having a matter
against another, go to law before
the unjust, and not before the saints?
2 Do ye not know that the saints shall
judge the world? and if the world shall
be judged by you, are ye unworthy to
judge the smallest matters?
3 Know ye not that we shall judge
angels? how much more things that
pertain to this life?
4 If then ye have judgments of things
pertaining to this life, set them to judge
who are least esteemed in the church.
5 I speak to your shame. Is it so, that
there is not a wise man among you? no,
not one that shall be able to judge
between his brethren?
6 But brother goeth to law with brother, and that before the unbelievers.
7 Now therefore there is utterly a
fault among you, because ye go to law
one with another. Why do ye not rather
take wrong? why do ye not rather *suffer
yourselves to* be defrauded?
8 Nay, ye do wrong, and defraud, and
that *your* brethren.
9 Know ye not that the unrighteous
shall not inherit the kingdom of God?
Be not deceived: neither fornicators,
nor idolaters, nor adulterers, nor effem-
inate, nor abusers of themselves with
mankind,
10 Nor thieves, nor covetous, nor
drunkards, nor revilers, nor extortioners, shall inherit the kingdom of God.
11 And such were some of you: but ye
are washed, but ye are sanctified, but
ye are justified in the name of the Lord
Jesus, and by the Spirit of our God.
12 All things are lawful unto me, but
all things are not expedient: all things
are lawful for me, but I will not be
brought under the power of any.
13 Meats for the belly, and the belly
for meats: but God shall destroy both it
and them. Now the body *is* not for fornication, but for the Lord; and the Lord
for the body.
14 And God hath both raised up the
Lord, and will also raise up us by his
own power.

15 Know ye not that your bodies are the members of Christ? shall I then take the members of Christ, and make *them* the members of an harlot? God forbid.

16 What? know ye not that he which is joined to an harlot is one body? for two, saith he, shall be one flesh.

17 But he that is joined unto the Lord is one spirit.

18 Flee fornication. Every sin that a man doeth is without the body; but he that committeth fornication sinneth against his own body.

19 What? know ye not that your body is the temple of the Holy Ghost *which is* in you, which ye have of God, and ye are not your own?

20 For ye are bought with a price: therefore glorify God in your body, and in your spirit, which are God's.

7 Now concerning the things whereof ye wrote unto me: *It is* good for a man not to touch a woman.

2 Nevertheless, *to avoid* fornication, let every man have his own wife, and let every woman have her own husband.

3 Let the husband render unto the wife due benevolence: and likewise also the wife unto the husband.

4 The wife hath not power of her own body, but the husband: and likewise also the husband hath not power of his own body, but the wife.

5 Defraud ye not one the other, except *it be* with consent for a time, that ye may give yourselves to fasting and prayer; and come together again, that Satan tempt you not for your incontinency.

6 But I speak this by permission, *and* not of commandment.

7 For I would that all men were even as I myself. But every man hath his proper gift of God, one after this manner, and another after that.

8 I say therefore to the unmarried and widows, It is good for them if they abide even as I.

9 But if they cannot contain, let them marry: for it is better to marry than to burn.

10 And unto the married I command, *yet* not I, but the Lord, Let not the wife depart from *her* husband:

11 But and if she depart, let her remain unmarried, or be reconciled to *her* husband: and let not the husband put away *his* wife.

12 But to the rest speak I, not the Lord: If any brother hath a wife that believeth not, and she be pleased to dwell with him, let him not put her away.

13 And the woman which hath an husband that believeth not, and if he be pleased to dwell with her, let her not leave him.

14 For the unbelieving husband is sanctified by the wife, and the unbelieving wife is sanctified by the husband: else were your children unclean; but now are they holy.

15 But if the unbelieving depart, let him depart. A brother or a sister is not under bondage in such *cases*: but God hath called us to peace.

16 For what knowest thou, O wife, whether thou shalt save *thy* husband? or how knowest thou, O man, whether thou shalt save *thy* wife?

17 But as God hath distributed to every man, as the Lord hath called every one, so let him walk. And so ordain I in all churches.

18 Is any man called being circumcised? let him not become uncircumcised. Is any called in uncircumcision?
let him not be circumcised.
19 Circumcision is nothing, and uncircumcision is nothing, but the keeping
of the commandments of God.
20 Let every man abide in the same
calling wherein he was called.
21 Art thou called *being* a servant?
care not for it: but if thou mayest be
made free, use *it* rather.
22 For he that is called in the Lord,
being a servant, is the Lord's freeman:
likewise also he that is called, *being*
free, is Christ's servant.
23 Ye are bought with a price; be not
ye the servants of men.
24 Brethren, let every man, wherein
he is called, therein abide with God.
25 Now concerning virgins I have no
commandment of the Lord: yet I give
my judgment, as one that hath obtained
mercy of the Lord to be faithful.
26 I suppose therefore that this is
good for the present distress, *I say*, that
it is good for a man so to be.
27 Art thou bound unto a wife? seek
not to be loosed. Art thou loosed from a
wife? seek not a wife.
28 But and if thou marry, thou hast
not sinned; and if a virgin marry, she
hath not sinned. Nevertheless such
shall have trouble in the flesh: but I
spare you.
29 But this I say, brethren, the time *is*
short: it remaineth, that both they that
have wives be as though they had none;
30 And they that weep, as though
they wept not; and they that rejoice, as
though they rejoiced not; and they that
buy, as though they possessed not;
31 And they that use this world, as not
abusing *it*: for the fashion of this world
passeth away.
32 But I would have you without carefulness. He that is unmarried careth for
the things that belong to the Lord, how
he may please the Lord:
33 But he that is married careth for
the things that are of the world, how he
may please *his* wife.
34 There is difference *also* between a
wife and a virgin. The unmarried
woman careth for the things of the
Lord, that she may be holy both in body
and in spirit: but she that is married
careth for the things of the world, how
she may please *her* husband.
35 And this I speak for your own
profit; not that I may cast a snare upon
you, but for that which is comely, and
that ye may attend upon the Lord without distraction.
36 But if any man think that he beha-
veth himself uncomely toward his virgin, if she pass the flower of *her* age,
and need so require, let him do what he
will, he sinneth not: let them marry.
37 Nevertheless he that standeth
stedfast in his heart, having no necessity, but hath power over his own will,
and hath so decreed in his heart that he
will keep his virgin, doeth well.
38 So then he that giveth *her* in marriage doeth well; but he that giveth *her*
not in marriage doeth better.
39 The wife is bound by the law as
long as her husband liveth; but if her
husband be dead, she is at liberty to be
married to whom she will; only in the
Lord.
40 But she is happier if she so abide,
after my judgment: and I think also
that I have the Spirit of God.

8 Now as touching things offered
unto idols, we know that we all have
knowledge. Knowledge puffeth up, but
charity edifieth.
2 And if any man think that he
knoweth any thing, he knoweth nothing
yet as he ought to know.
3 But if any man love God, the same is
known of him.
4 As concerning therefore the eating
of those things that are offered in sacrifice unto idols, we know that an idol *is*
nothing in the world, and that *there is*
none other God but one.
5 For though there be that are called
gods, whether in heaven or in earth, (as
there be gods many, and lords many,)
6 But to us *there is but* one God, the
Father, of whom *are* all things, and we
in him; and one Lord Jesus Christ, by
whom *are* all things, and we by him.
7 Howbeit *there is* not in every man
that knowledge: for some with conscience of the idol unto this hour eat *it*
as a thing offered unto an idol; and
their conscience being weak is defiled.
8 But meat commendeth us not to
God: for neither, if we eat, are we the
better; neither, if we eat not, are we the
worse.
9 But take heed lest by any means
this liberty of yours become a stumblingblock to them that are weak.
10 For if any man see thee which hast
knowledge sit at meat in the idol's
temple, shall not the conscience of him
which is weak be emboldened to eat
those things which are offered to idols;
11 And through thy knowledge shall
the weak brother perish, for whom
Christ died?
12 But when ye sin so against the
brethren, and wound their weak conscience, ye sin against Christ.
13 Wherefore, if meat make my brother to offend, I will eat no flesh while the
world standeth, lest I make my brother
to offend.

9 Am I not an apostle? am I not free?
have I not seen Jesus Christ our
Lord? are not ye my work in the Lord?
2 If I be not an apostle unto others,
yet doubtless I am to you: for the seal of
mine apostleship are ye in the Lord.
3 Mine answer to them that do examine me is this,
4 Have we not power to eat and to
drink?
5 Have we not power to lead about a
sister, a wife, as well as other apostles,
and *as* the brethren of the Lord, and
Cephas?
6 Or I only and Barnabas, have not we
power to forbear working?
7 Who goeth a warfare any time at his
own charges? who planteth a vineyard,
and eateth not of the fruit thereof? or
who feedeth a flock, and eateth not of
the milk of the flock?
8 Say I these things as a man? or saith
not the law the same also?
9 For it is written in the law of Moses,
Thou shalt not muzzle the mouth of the
ox that treadeth out the corn. Doth God
take care for oxen?
10 Or saith he *it* altogether for our
sakes? For our sakes, no doubt, *this* is
written: that he that ploweth should
plow in hope; and that he that thresheth
in hope should be partaker of his hope.
11 If we have sown unto you spiritual
things, *is it* a great thing if we shall
reap your carnal things?
12 If others be partakers of *this*
power over you, *are* not we rather?
Nevertheless we have not used this
power; but suffer all things, lest we
should hinder the gospel of Christ.

13 Do ye not know that they which
minister about holy things live *of the
things* of the temple? and they which
wait at the altar are partakers with the
altar?
14 Even so hath the Lord ordained
that they which preach the gospel
should live of the gospel.
15 But I have used none of these
things: neither have I written these
things, that it should be so done unto
me: for *it were* better for me to die,
than that any man should make my
glorying void.
16 For though I preach the gospel, I
have nothing to glory of: for necessity is
laid upon me; yea, woe is unto me, if I
preach not the gospel!
17 For if I do this thing willingly, I
have a reward: but if against my will, a
dispensation *of the gospel* is committed
unto me.
18 What is my reward then? *Verily*
that, when I preach the gospel, I may
make the gospel of Christ without
charge, that I abuse not my power in
the gospel.
19 For though I be free from all *men*,
yet have I made myself servant unto all,
that I might gain the more.
20 And unto the Jews I became as a
Jew, that I might gain the Jews; to them
that are under the law, as under the law,
that I might gain them that are under
the law;
21 To them that are without law, as
without law, (being not without law to
God, but under the law to Christ,) that
I might gain them that are without law.
22 To the weak became I as weak,
that I might gain the weak: I am made
all things to all *men*, that I might by all
means save some.
23 And this I do for the gospel's sake,
that I might be partaker thereof with
you.
24 Know ye not that they which run in
a race run all, but one receiveth the
prize? So run, that ye may obtain.
25 And every man that striveth for
the mastery is temperate in all things.
Now they *do it* to obtain a corruptible
crown; but we an incorruptible.
26 I therefore so run, not as uncer-
tainly; so fight I, not as one that beateth
the air:
27 But I keep under my body, and
bring *it* into subjection: lest that by any
means, when I have preached to others,
I myself should be a castaway.

10 Moreover, brethren, I would not
that ye should be ignorant, how
that all our fathers were under the
cloud, and all passed through the sea;
2 And were all baptized unto Moses
in the cloud and in the sea;
3 And did all eat the same spiritual
meat;
4 And did all drink the same spiritual
drink: for they drank of that spiritual
Rock that followed them: and that
Rock was Christ.
5 But with many of them God was not
well pleased: for they were overthrown
in the wilderness.
6 Now these things were our exam-
ples, to the intent we should not lust
after evil things, as they also lusted.
7 Neither be ye idolaters, as *were*
some of them; as it is written, The people sat down to eat and drink, and rose
up to play.
8 Neither let us commit fornication,
as some of them committed, and fell in
one day three and twenty thousand.

9 Neither let us tempt Christ, as some of them also tempted, and were destroyed of serpents.

10 Neither murmur ye, as some of them also murmured, and were destroyed of the destroyer.

11 Now all these things happened unto them for ensamples: and they are written for our admonition, upon whom the ends of the world are come.

12 Wherefore let him that thinketh he standeth take heed lest he fall.

13 There hath no temptation taken you but such as is common to man: but God *is* faithful, who will not suffer you to be tempted above that ye are able; but will with the temptation also make a way to escape, that ye may be able to bear *it*.

14 Wherefore, my dearly beloved, flee from idolatry.

15 I speak as to wise men; judge ye what I say.

16 The cup of blessing which we bless, is it not the communion of the blood of Christ? The bread which we break, is it not the communion of the body of Christ?

17 For we *being* many are one bread, *and* one body: for we are all partakers of that one bread.

18 Behold Israel after the flesh: are not they which eat of the sacrifices partakers of the altar?

19 What say I then? that the idol is any thing, or that which is offered in sacrifice to idols is any thing?

20 But I *say*, that the things which the Gentiles sacrifice, they sacrifice to devils, and not to God: and I would not that ye should have fellowship with devils.

21 Ye cannot drink the cup of the Lord, and the cup of devils: ye cannot be partakers of the Lord's table, and of the table of devils.

22 Do we provoke the Lord to jealousy? are we stronger than he?

23 All things are lawful for me, but all things are not expedient: all things are lawful for me, but all things edify not.

24 Let no man seek his own, but every man another's *wealth*.

25 Whatsoever is sold in the shambles, *that* eat, asking no question for conscience sake:

26 For the earth *is* the Lord's, and the fulness thereof.

27 If any of them that believe not bid you *to a feast*, and ye be disposed to go; whatsoever is set before you, eat, asking no question for conscience sake.

28 But if any man say unto you, This is offered in sacrifice unto idols, eat not for his sake that shewed it, and for conscience sake: for the earth *is* the Lord's, and the fulness thereof:

29 Conscience, I say, not thine own, but of the other: for why is my liberty judged of another *man's* conscience?

30 For if I by grace be a partaker, why am I evil spoken of for that for which I give thanks?

31 Whether therefore ye eat, or drink, or whatsoever ye do, do all to the glory of God.

32 Give none offence, neither to the Jews, nor to the Gentiles, nor to the church of God:

33 Even as I please all *men* in all *things*, not seeking mine own profit, but the *profit* of many, that they may be saved.

11 Be ye followers of me, even as I also *am* of Christ.

2 Now I praise you, brethren, that ye remember me in all things, and keep

the ordinances, as I delivered *them* to
you.
3 But I would have you know, that the
head of every man is Christ; and the
head of the woman *is* the man; and the
head of Christ *is* God.
4 Every man praying or prophesying,
having *his* head covered, dishonoureth
his head.
5 But every woman that prayeth or
prophesieth with *her* head uncovered
dishonoureth her head: for that is even
all one as if she were shaven.
6 For if the woman be not covered, let
her also be shorn: but if it be a shame
for a woman to be shorn or shaven, let
her be covered.
7 For a man indeed ought not to cover
his head, forasmuch as he is the image
and glory of God: but the woman is the
glory of the man.
8 For the man is not of the woman;
but the woman of the man.
9 Neither was the man created for the
woman; but the woman for the man.
10 For this cause ought the woman to
have power on *her* head because of the
angels.
11 Nevertheless neither is the man
without the woman, neither the woman
without the man, in the Lord.
12 For as the woman *is* of the man,
even so *is* the man also by the woman;
but all things of God.
13 Judge in yourselves: is it comely
that a woman pray unto God uncovered?
14 Doth not even nature itself teach
you, that, if a man have long hair, it is a
shame unto him?
15 But if a woman have long hair, it is
a glory to her: for *her* hair is given her
for a covering.
16 But if any man seem to be contentious, we have no such custom, neither
the churches of God.
17 Now in this that I declare *unto you*
I praise *you* not, that ye come together
not for the better, but for the worse.
18 For first of all, when ye come
together in the church, I hear that there
be divisions among you; and I partly
believe it.
19 For there must be also heresies
among you, that they which are
approved may be made manifest
among you.
20 When ye come together therefore
into one place, *this* is not to eat the
Lord's supper.
21 For in eating every one taketh
before *other* his own supper: and one is
hungry, and another is drunken.
22 What? have ye not houses to eat
and to drink in? or despise ye the
church of God, and shame them that
have not? What shall I say to you? shall
I praise you in this? I praise *you* not.
23 For I have received of the Lord
that which also I delivered unto you,
That the Lord Jesus the *same* night in
which he was betrayed took bread:
24 And when he had given thanks, he
brake *it*, and said, Take, eat: this is my
body, which is broken for you: this do in
remembrance of me.
25 After the same manner also *he*
took the cup, when he had supped, saying, This cup is the new testament in
my blood: this do ye, as oft as ye drink
it, in remembrance of me.
26 For as often as ye eat this bread,
and drink this cup, ye do shew the
Lord's death till he come.
27 Wherefore whosoever shall eat
this bread, and drink *this* cup of the

Lord, unworthily, shall be guilty of the
body and blood of the Lord.
28 But let a man examine himself,
and so let him eat of *that* bread, and
drink of *that* cup.
29 For he that eateth and drinketh
unworthily, eateth and drinketh damnation to himself, not discerning the
Lord's body.
30 For this cause many *are* weak and
sickly among you, and many sleep.
31 For if we would judge ourselves,
we should not be judged.
32 But when we are judged, we are
chastened of the Lord, that we should
not be condemned with the world.
33 Wherefore, my brethren, when ye
come together to eat, tarry one for
another.
34 And if any man hunger, let him eat
at home; that ye come not together
unto condemnation. And the rest will I
set in order when I come.

12 Now concerning spiritual *gifts*,
brethren, I would not have you
ignorant.
2 Ye know that ye were Gentiles, carried away unto these dumb idols, even
as ye were led.
3 Wherefore I give you to understand,
that no man speaking by the Spirit of
God calleth Jesus accursed: and *that*
no man can say that Jesus is the Lord,
but by the Holy Ghost.
4 Now there are diversities of gifts,
but the same Spirit.
5 And there are differences of admin-
istrations, but the same Lord.
6 And there are diversities of opera-
tions, but it is the same God which
worketh all in all.
7 But the manifestation of the Spirit
is given to every man to profit withal.
8 For to one is given by the Spirit the
word of wisdom; to another the word of
knowledge by the same Spirit;
9 To another faith by the same Spirit;
to another the gifts of healing by the
same Spirit;
10 To another the working of miracles; to another prophecy; to another
discerning of spirits; to another *divers*
kinds of tongues; to another the interpretation of tongues:
11 But all these worketh that one and
the selfsame Spirit, dividing to every
man severally as he will.
12 For as the body is one, and hath
many members, and all the members of
that one body, being many, are one
body: so also *is* Christ.
13 For by one Spirit are we all baptized into one body, whether *we be*
Jews or Gentiles, whether *we be* bond
or free; and have been all made to
drink into one Spirit.
14 For the body is not one member,
but many.
15 If the foot shall say, Because I am
not the hand, I am not of the body; is it
therefore not of the body?
16 And if the ear shall say, Because I
am not the eye, I am not of the body; is
it therefore not of the body?
17 If the whole body *were* an eye,
where *were* the hearing? If the whole
were hearing, where *were* the smelling?
18 But now hath God set the members
every one of them in the body, as it hath
pleased him.
19 And if they were all one member,
where *were* the body?
20 But now *are they* many members,
yet but one body.

21 And the eye cannot say unto the hand, I have no need of thee: nor again the head to the feet, I have no need of you.

22 Nay, much more those members of the body, which seem to be more feeble, are necessary:

23 And those *members* of the body, which we think to be less honourable, upon these we bestow more abundant honour; and our uncomely *parts* have more abundant comeliness.

24 For our comely *parts* have no need: but God hath tempered the body together, having given more abundant honour to that *part* which lacked:

25 That there should be no schism in the body; but *that* the members should have the same care one for another.

26 And whether one member suffer, all the members suffer with it; or one member be honoured, all the members rejoice with it.

27 Now ye are the body of Christ, and members in particular.

28 And God hath set some in the church, first apostles, secondarily prophets, thirdly teachers, after that miracles, then gifts of healings, helps, governments, diversities of tongues.

29 *Are* all apostles? *are* all prophets? *are* all teachers? *are* all workers of miracles?

30 Have all the gifts of healing? do all speak with tongues? do all interpret?

31 But covet earnestly the best gifts: and yet shew I unto you a more excellent way.

13 Though I speak with the tongues of men and of angels, and have not charity, I am become *as* sounding brass, or a tinkling cymbal.

2 And though I have *the gift of* prophecy, and understand all mysteries, and all knowledge; and though I have all faith, so that I could remove mountains, and have not charity, I am nothing.

3 And though I bestow all my goods to feed *the poor*, and though I give my body to be burned, and have not charity, it profiteth me nothing.

4 Charity suffereth long, *and* is kind; charity envieth not; charity vaunteth not itself, is not puffed up,

5 Doth not behave itself unseemly, seeketh not her own, is not easily provoked, thinketh no evil;

6 Rejoiceth not in iniquity, but rejoiceth in the truth;

7 Beareth all things, believeth all things, hopeth all things, endureth all things.

8 Charity never faileth: but whether *there be* prophecies, they shall fail; whether *there be* tongues, they shall cease; whether *there be* knowledge, it shall vanish away.

9 For we know in part, and we prophesy in part.

10 But when that which is perfect is come, then that which is in part shall be done away.

11 When I was a child, I spake as a child, I understood as a child, I thought as a child: but when I became a man, I put away childish things.

12 For now we see through a glass, darkly; but then face to face: now I know in part; but then shall I know even as also I am known.

13 And now abideth faith, hope, charity, these three; but the greatest of these *is* charity.

14 Follow after charity, and desire spiritual *gifts*, but rather that ye may prophesy.

2 For he that speaketh in an *unknown* tongue speaketh not unto men, but

unto God: for no man understandeth
him; howbeit in the spirit he speaketh
mysteries.
3 But he that prophesieth speaketh
unto men *to* edification, and exhortation, and comfort.
4 He that speaketh in an *unknown*
tongue edifieth himself; but he that
prophesieth edifieth the church.
5 I would that ye all spake with
tongues, but rather that ye prophesied:
for greater *is* he that prophesieth than
he that speaketh with tongues, except
he interpret, that the church may
receive edifying.
6 Now, brethren, if I come unto you
speaking with tongues, what shall I
profit you, except I shall speak to you
either by revelation, or by knowledge,
or by prophesying, or by doctrine?
7 And even things without life giving
sound, whether pipe or harp, except
they give a distinction in the sounds,
how shall it be known what is piped or
harped?
8 For if the trumpet give an uncertain
sound, who shall prepare himself to the
battle?
9 So likewise ye, except ye utter by
the tongue words easy to be understood, how shall it be known what is
spoken? for ye shall speak into the air.
10 There are, it may be, so many kinds
of voices in the world, and none of them
is without signification.
11 Therefore if I know not the meaning of the voice, I shall be unto him that
speaketh a barbarian, and he that speaketh *shall be* a barbarian unto me.
12 Even so ye, forasmuch as ye are
zealous of spiritual *gifts*, seek that ye
may excel to the edifying of the church.
13 Wherefore let him that speaketh in
an *unknown* tongue pray that he may
interpret.
14 For if I pray in an *unknown* tongue,
my spirit prayeth, but my understanding is unfruitful.
15 What is it then? I will pray with the
spirit, and I will pray with the understanding also: I will sing with the spirit,
and I will sing with the understanding
also.
16 Else when thou shalt bless with
the spirit, how shall he that occupieth
the room of the unlearned say Amen at
thy giving of thanks, seeing he understandeth not what thou sayest?
17 For thou verily givest thanks well,
but the other is not edified.
18 I thank my God, I speak with
tongues more than ye all:
19 Yet in the church I had rather
speak five words with my understanding, that *by my voice* I might teach
others also, than ten thousand words in
an *unknown* tongue.
20 Brethren, be not children in understanding: howbeit in malice be ye children, but in understanding be men.
21 In the law it is written, With *men of*
other tongues and other lips will I
speak unto this people; and yet for all
that will they not hear me, saith the
Lord.
22 Wherefore tongues are for a sign,
not to them that believe, but to them
that believe not: but prophesying *serveth* not for them that believe not, but
for them which believe.
23 If therefore the whole church be
come together into one place, and all
speak with tongues, and there come in
those that are unlearned, or unbelievers, will they not say that ye are mad?

24 But if all prophesy, and there come
in one that believeth not, or *one*
unlearned, he is convinced of all, he is
judged of all:
25 And thus are the secrets of his
heart made manifest; and so falling
down on *his* face he will worship God,
and report that God is in you of a truth.
26 How is it then, brethren? when ye
come together, every one of you hath a
psalm, hath a doctrine, hath a tongue,
hath a revelation, hath an interpretation. Let all things be done unto edifying.
27 If any man speak in an *unknown*
tongue, *let it be* by two, or at the most
by three, and *that* by course; and let
one interpret.
28 But if there be no interpreter, let
him keep silence in the church; and let
him speak to himself, and to God.
29 Let the prophets speak two or
three, and let the other judge.
30 If *any thing* be revealed to another that sitteth by, let the first hold his
peace.
31 For ye may all prophesy one by
one, that all may learn, and all may be
comforted.
32 And the spirits of the prophets are
subject to the prophets.
33 For God is not *the author* of confusion, but of peace, as in all churches of
the saints.
34 Let your women keep silence in
the churches: for it is not permitted
unto them to speak; but *they are commanded* to be under obedience, as also
saith the law.
35 And if they will learn any thing, let
them ask their husbands at home: for it
is a shame for women to speak in the
church.
36 What? came the word of God out
from you? or came it unto you only?
37 If any man think himself to be a
prophet, or spiritual, let him acknowledge that the things that I write unto
you are the commandments of the
Lord.
38 But if any man be ignorant, let him
be ignorant.
39 Wherefore, brethren, covet to prophesy, and forbid not to speak with
tongues.
40 Let all things be done decently
and in order.

15 Moreover, brethren, I declare
unto you the gospel which I
preached unto you, which also ye have
received, and wherein ye stand;
2 By which also ye are saved, if ye
keep in memory what I preached unto
you, unless ye have believed in vain.
3 For I delivered unto you first of all
that which I also received, how that
Christ died for our sins according to the
scriptures;
4 And that he was buried, and that he
rose again the third day according to
the scriptures:
5 And that he was seen of Cephas,
then of the twelve:
6 After that, he was seen of above five
hundred brethren at once; of whom the
greater part remain unto this present,
but some are fallen asleep.
7 After that, he was seen of James;
then of all the apostles.
8 And last of all he was seen of me
also, as of one born out of due time.
9 For I am the least of the apostles,
that am not meet to be called an apostle, because I persecuted the church of
God.
10 But by the grace of God I am what
I am: and his grace which *was bestowed*

upon me was not in vain; but I laboured
more abundantly than they all: yet not
I, but the grace of God which was with
me.
11 Therefore whether *it were* I or
they, so we preach, and so ye believed.
12 Now if Christ be preached that he
rose from the dead, how say some
among you that there is no resurrection
of the dead?
13 But if there be no resurrection of
the dead, then is Christ not risen:
14 And if Christ be not risen, then *is*
our preaching vain, and your faith *is*
also vain.
15 Yea, and we are found false witnesses of God; because we have testified of God that he raised up Christ:
whom he raised not up, if so be that the
dead rise not.
16 For if the dead rise not, then is not
Christ raised:
17 And if Christ be not raised, your
faith *is* vain; ye are yet in your sins.
18 Then they also which are fallen
asleep in Christ are perished.
19 If in this life only we have hope in
Christ, we are of all men most miserable.
20 But now is Christ risen from the
dead, *and* become the firstfruits of
them that slept.
21 For since by man *came* death, by
man *came* also the resurrection of the
dead.
22 For as in Adam all die, even so in
Christ shall all be made alive.
23 But every man in his own order:
Christ the firstfruits; afterward they
that are Christ's at his coming.
24 Then *cometh* the end, when he
shall have delivered up the kingdom to
God, even the Father; when he shall
have put down all rule and all authority
and power.
25 For he must reign, till he hath put
all enemies under his feet.
26 The last enemy *that* shall be
destroyed *is* death.
27 For he hath put all things under
his feet. But when he saith all things
are put under *him, it is* manifest that
he is excepted, which did put all things
under him.
28 And when all things shall be subdued unto him, then shall the Son also
himself be subject unto him that put all
things under him, that God may be all
in all.
29 Else what shall they do which are
baptized for the dead, if the dead rise
not at all? why are they then baptized
for the dead?
30 And why stand we in jeopardy
every hour?
31 I protest by your rejoicing which I
have in Christ Jesus our Lord, I die
daily.
32 If after the manner of men I have
fought with beasts at Ephesus, what
advantageth it me, if the dead rise not?
let us eat and drink; for to morrow we
die.
33 Be not deceived: evil communications corrupt good manners.
34 Awake to righteousness, and sin
not; for some have not the knowledge
of God: I speak *this* to your shame.
35 But some *man* will say, How are
the dead raised up? and with what
body do they come?
36 *Thou* fool, that which thou sowest
is not quickened, except it die:
37 And that which thou sowest, thou
sowest not that body that shall be, but
bare grain, it may chance of wheat, or
of some other *grain*:

38 But God giveth it a body as it hath
pleased him, and to every seed his own
body.
39 All flesh *is* not the same flesh: but
there is one *kind of* flesh of men,
another flesh of beasts, another of
fishes, *and* another of birds.
40 *There are* also celestial bodies, and
bodies terrestrial: but the glory of the
celestial *is* one, and the *glory* of the
terrestrial *is* another.
41 *There is* one glory of the sun, and
another glory of the moon, and another
glory of the stars: for *one* star differeth
from *another* star in glory.
42 So also *is* the resurrection of the
dead. It is sown in corruption; it is
raised in incorruption:
43 It is sown in dishonour; it is raised
in glory: it is sown in weakness; it is
raised in power:
44 It is sown a natural body; it is
raised a spiritual body. There is a natural body, and there is a spiritual body.
45 And so it is written, The first man
Adam was made a living soul; the last
Adam *was made* a quickening spirit.
46 Howbeit that *was* not first which is
spiritual, but that which is natural; and
afterward that which is spiritual.
47 The first man *is* of the earth,
earthy: the second man *is* the Lord
from heaven.
48 As *is* the earthy, such *are* they also
that are earthy: and as *is* the heavenly,
such *are* they also that are heavenly.
49 And as we have borne the image of
the earthy, we shall also bear the image
of the heavenly.
50 Now this I say, brethren, that flesh
and blood cannot inherit the kingdom
of God; neither doth corruption inherit
incorruption.
51 Behold, I shew you a mystery; We
shall not all sleep, but we shall all be
changed,
52 In a moment, in the twinkling of an
eye, at the last trump: for the trumpet
shall sound, and the dead shall be
raised incorruptible, and we shall be
changed.
53 For this corruptible must put on
incorruption, and this mortal *must* put
on immortality.
54 So when this corruptible shall
have put on incorruption, and this mortal shall have put on immortality, then
shall be brought to pass the saying that
is written, Death is swallowed up in victory.
55 O death, where *is* thy sting? O
grave, where *is* thy victory?
56 The sting of death *is* sin; and the
strength of sin *is* the law.
57 But thanks *be* to God, which giveth
us the victory through our Lord Jesus
Christ.
58 Therefore, my beloved brethren,
be ye stedfast, unmoveable, always
abounding in the work of the Lord, forasmuch as ye know that your labour is
not in vain in the Lord.

16 Now concerning the collection
for the saints, as I have given
order to the churches of Galatia, even
so do ye.
2 Upon the first *day* of the week let
every one of you lay by him in store, as
God hath prospered him, that there be
no gatherings when I come.
3 And when I come, whomsoever ye
shall approve by *your* letters, them will
I send to bring your liberality unto
Jerusalem.
4 And if it be meet that I go also, they
shall go with me.

5 Now I will come unto you, when I
shall pass through Macedonia: for I do
pass through Macedonia.
6 And it may be that I will abide, yea,
and winter with you, that ye may bring
me on my journey whithersoever I go.
7 For I will not see you now by the
way; but I trust to tarry a while with
you, if the Lord permit.
8 But I will tarry at Ephesus until
Pentecost.
9 For a great door and effectual is
opened unto me, and *there are* many
adversaries.
10 Now if Timotheus come, see that
he may be with you without fear: for he
worketh the work of the Lord, as I also
do.
11 Let no man therefore despise him:
but conduct him forth in peace, that he
may come unto me: for I look for him
with the brethren.
12 As touching *our* brother Apollos, I
greatly desired him to come unto you
with the brethren: but his will was not
at all to come at this time; but he will
come when he shall have convenient
time.
13 Watch ye, stand fast in the faith,
quit you like men, be strong.
14 Let all your things be done with
charity.
15 I beseech you, brethren, (ye know
the house of Stephanas, that it is the
firstfruits of Achaia, and *that* they have
addicted themselves to the ministry of
the saints,)
16 That ye submit yourselves unto
such, and to every one that helpeth
with *us*, and laboureth.
17 I am glad of the coming of Stephanas and Fortunatus and Achaicus: for
that which was lacking on your part
they have supplied.
18 For they have refreshed my spirit
and yours: therefore acknowledge ye
them that are such.
19 The churches of Asia salute you.
Aquila and Priscilla salute you much in
the Lord, with the church that is in
their house.
20 All the brethren greet you. Greet
ye one another with an holy kiss.
21 The salutation of *me* Paul with
mine own hand.
22 If any man love not the Lord Jesus
Christ, let him be Anathema Maran-
atha.
23 The grace of our Lord Jesus Christ
be with you.
24 My love *be* with you all in Christ
Jesus. Amen.

THE SECOND EPISTLE OF PAUL THE APOSTLE
TO THE

CORINTHIANS

1 Paul, an apostle of Jesus Christ by
the will of God, and Timothy *our*
brother, unto the church of God which
is at Corinth, with all the saints which
are in all Achaia:
2 Grace *be* to you and peace from God
our Father, and *from* the Lord Jesus
Christ.
3 Blessed *be* God, even the Father of
our Lord Jesus Christ, the Father of
mercies, and the God of all comfort;
4 Who comforteth us in all our tribulation, that we may be able to comfort
them which are in any trouble, by the
comfort wherewith we ourselves are
comforted of God.
5 For as the sufferings of Christ
abound in us, so our consolation also
aboundeth by Christ.
6 And whether we be afflicted, *it is*
for your consolation and salvation,
which is effectual in the enduring of
the same sufferings which we also suffer: or whether we be comforted, *it is*
for your consolation and salvation.
7 And our hope of you *is* stedfast,
knowing, that as ye are partakers of the
sufferings, so *shall ye be* also of the
consolation.
8 For we would not, brethren, have
you ignorant of our trouble which came
to us in Asia, that we were pressed out
of measure, above strength, insomuch
that we despaired even of life:
9 But we had the sentence of death in
ourselves, that we should not trust in
ourselves, but in God which raiseth the
dead:
10 Who delivered us from so great a
death, and doth deliver: in whom we
trust that he will yet deliver *us*;
11 Ye also helping together by prayer
for us, that for the gift *bestowed* upon
us by the means of many persons
thanks may be given by many on our
behalf.
12 For our rejoicing is this, the testimony of our conscience, that in simplicity and godly sincerity, not with fleshly
wisdom, but by the grace of God, we
have had our conversation in the world,
and more abundantly to you-ward.
13 For we write none other things
unto you, than what ye read or acknowledge; and I trust ye shall acknowledge
even to the end;
14 As also ye have acknowledged us
in part, that we are your rejoicing, even
as ye also *are* ours in the day of the
Lord Jesus.
15 And in this confidence I was minded to come unto you before, that ye
might have a second benefit;
16 And to pass by you into Macedonia,
and to come again out of Macedonia
unto you, and of you to be brought on
my way toward Judaea.
17 When I therefore was thus minded,
did I use lightness? or the things that I
purpose, do I purpose according to the
flesh, that with me there should be yea
yea, and nay nay?
18 But *as* God *is* true, our word toward
you was not yea and nay.
19 For the Son of God, Jesus Christ,
who was preached among you by us,
even by me and Silvanus and Timotheus,

was not yea and nay, but in him was yea.

20 For all the promises of God in him *are* yea, and in him Amen, unto the glory of God by us.

21 Now he which stablisheth us with you in Christ, and hath anointed us, *is* God;

22 Who hath also sealed us, and given the earnest of the Spirit in our hearts.

23 Moreover I call God for a record upon my soul, that to spare you I came not as yet unto Corinth.

24 Not for that we have dominion over your faith, but are helpers of your joy: for by faith ye stand.

2 But I determined this with myself, that I would not come again to you in heaviness.

2 For if I make you sorry, who is he then that maketh me glad, but the same which is made sorry by me?

3 And I wrote this same unto you, lest, when I came, I should have sorrow from them of whom I ought to rejoice; having confidence in you all, that my joy is *the joy* of you all.

4 For out of much affliction and anguish of heart I wrote unto you with many tears; not that ye should be grieved, but that ye might know the love which I have more abundantly unto you.

5 But if any have caused grief, he hath not grieved me, but in part: that I may not overcharge you all.

6 Sufficient to such a man *is* this punishment, which *was inflicted* of many.

7 So that contrariwise ye *ought* rather to forgive *him*, and comfort *him*, lest perhaps such a one should be swallowed up with overmuch sorrow.

8 Wherefore I beseech you that ye would confirm *your* love toward him.

9 For to this end also did I write, that I might know the proof of you, whether ye be obedient in all things.

10 To whom ye forgive any thing, I *forgive* also: for if I forgave any thing, to whom I forgave *it*, for your sakes *forgave I it* in the person of Christ;

11 Lest Satan should get an advantage of us: for we are not ignorant of his devices.

12 Furthermore, when I came to Troas to *preach* Christ's gospel, and a door was opened unto me of the Lord,

13 I had no rest in my spirit, because I found not Titus my brother: but taking my leave of them, I went from thence into Macedonia.

14 Now thanks *be* unto God, which always causeth us to triumph in Christ, and maketh manifest the savour of his knowledge by us in every place.

15 For we are unto God a sweet savour of Christ, in them that are saved, and in them that perish:

16 To the one *we are* the savour of death unto death; and to the other the savour of life unto life. And who *is* sufficient for these things?

17 For we are not as many, which corrupt the word of God: but as of sincerity, but as of God, in the sight of God speak we in Christ.

3 Do we begin again to commend ourselves? or need we, as some *others*, epistles of commendation to you, or *letters* of commendation from you?

2 Ye are our epistle written in our hearts, known and read of all men:

3 *Forasmuch as ye are* manifestly declared to be the epistle of Christ ministered by us, written not with ink, but with the Spirit of the living God; not in tables of stone, but in fleshy tables of the heart.

4 And such trust have we through Christ to God-ward:

5 Not that we are sufficient of ourselves to think any thing as of ourselves; but our sufficiency *is* of God;

6 Who also hath made us able ministers of the new testament; not of the letter, but of the spirit: for the letter killeth, but the spirit giveth life.

7 But if the ministration of death, written *and* engraven in stones, was glorious, so that the children of Israel could not stedfastly behold the face of Moses for the glory of his countenance; which *glory* was to be done away:

8 How shall not the ministration of the spirit be rather glorious?

9 For if the ministration of condemnation *be* glory, much more doth the ministration of righteousness exceed in glory.

10 For even that which was made glorious had no glory in this respect, by reason of the glory that excelleth.

11 For if that which is done away *was* glorious, much more that which remaineth *is* glorious.

12 Seeing then that we have such hope, we use great plainness of speech:

13 And not as Moses, *which* put a vail over his face, that the children of Israel could not stedfastly look to the end of that which is abolished:

14 But their minds were blinded: for until this day remaineth the same vail untaken away in the reading of the old testament; which *vail* is done away in Christ.

15 But even unto this day, when Moses is read, the vail is upon their heart.

16 Nevertheless when it shall turn to the Lord, the vail shall be taken away.

17 Now the Lord is that Spirit: and where the Spirit of the Lord *is*, there *is* liberty.

18 But we all, with open face beholding as in a glass the glory of the Lord, are changed into the same image from glory to glory, *even* as by the Spirit of the Lord.

4 Therefore seeing we have this ministry, as we have received mercy, we faint not;

2 But have renounced the hidden things of dishonesty, not walking in craftiness, nor handling the word of God deceitfully; but by manifestation of the truth commending ourselves to every man's conscience in the sight of God.

3 But if our gospel be hid, it is hid to them that are lost:

4 In whom the god of this world hath blinded the minds of them which believe not, lest the light of the glorious gospel of Christ, who is the image of God, should shine unto them.

5 For we preach not ourselves, but Christ Jesus the Lord; and ourselves your servants for Jesus' sake.

6 For God, who commanded the light to shine out of darkness, hath shined in our hearts, to *give* the light of the knowledge of the glory of God in the face of Jesus Christ.

7 But we have this treasure in earthen vessels, that the excellency of the power may be of God, and not of us.

8 *We are* troubled on every side, yet not distressed; *we are* perplexed, but not in despair;

9 Persecuted, but not forsaken; cast down, but not destroyed;

10 Always bearing about in the body the dying of the Lord Jesus, that the life also of Jesus might be made manifest in our body.

11 For we which live are alway delivered unto death for Jesus' sake, that the life also of Jesus might be made manifest in our mortal flesh.

12 So then death worketh in us, but life in you.

13 We having the same spirit of faith, according as it is written, I believed, and therefore have I spoken; we also believe, and therefore speak;

14 Knowing that he which raised up the Lord Jesus shall raise up us also by Jesus, and shall present *us* with you.

15 For all things *are* for your sakes, that the abundant grace might through the thanksgiving of many redound to the glory of God.

16 For which cause we faint not; but though our outward man perish, yet the inward *man* is renewed day by day.

17 For our light affliction, which is but for a moment, worketh for us a far more exceeding *and* eternal weight of glory;

18 While we look not at the things which are seen, but at the things which are not seen: for the things which are seen *are* temporal; but the things which are not seen *are* eternal.

5 For we know that if our earthly house of *this* tabernacle were dissolved, we have a building of God, an house not made with hands, eternal in the heavens.

2 For in this we groan, earnestly desiring to be clothed upon with our house which is from heaven:

3 If so be that being clothed we shall not be found naked.

4 For we that are in *this* tabernacle do groan, being burdened: not for that we would be unclothed, but clothed upon, that mortality might be swallowed up of life.

5 Now he that hath wrought us for the selfsame thing *is* God, who also hath given unto us the earnest of the Spirit.

6 Therefore *we are* always confident, knowing that, whilst we are at home in the body, we are absent from the Lord:

7 (For we walk by faith, not by sight:)

8 We are confident, *I say*, and willing rather to be absent from the body, and to be present with the Lord.

9 Wherefore we labour, that, whether present or absent, we may be accepted of him.

10 For we must all appear before the judgment seat of Christ; that every one may receive the things *done* in *his* body, according to that he hath done, whether *it be* good or bad.

11 Knowing therefore the terror of the Lord, we persuade men; but we are made manifest unto God; and I trust also are made manifest in your consciences.

12 For we commend not ourselves again unto you, but give you occasion to glory on our behalf, that ye may have somewhat to *answer* them which glory in appearance, and not in heart.

13 For whether we be beside ourselves, *it is* to God: or whether we be sober, *it is* for your cause.

14 For the love of Christ constraineth us; because we thus judge, that if one died for all, then were all dead:

15 And *that* he died for all, that they which live should not henceforth live unto themselves, but unto him which died for them, and rose again.

16 Wherefore henceforth know we no man after the flesh: yea, though we have known Christ after the flesh, yet now henceforth know we *him* no more.

17 Therefore if any man *be* in Christ, *he is* a new creature: old things are passed away; behold, all things are become new.

18 And all things *are* of God, who hath reconciled us to himself by Jesus Christ, and hath given to us the ministry of reconciliation;

19 To wit, that God was in Christ, reconciling the world unto himself, not imputing their trespasses unto them; and hath committed unto us the word of reconciliation.

20 Now then we are ambassadors for Christ, as though God did beseech *you* by us: we pray *you* in Christ's stead, be ye reconciled to God.

21 For he hath made him *to be* sin for us, who knew no sin; that we might be made the righteousness of God in him.

6 We then, *as* workers together *with him*, beseech *you* also that ye receive not the grace of God in vain.

2 (For he saith, I have heard thee in a time accepted, and in the day of salvation have I succoured thee: behold, now *is* the accepted time; behold, now *is* the day of salvation.)

3 Giving no offence in any thing, that the ministry be not blamed:

4 But in all *things* approving ourselves as the ministers of God, in much patience, in afflictions, in necessities, in distresses,

5 In stripes, in imprisonments, in tumults, in labours, in watchings, in fastings;

6 By pureness, by knowledge, by longsuffering, by kindness, by the Holy Ghost, by love unfeigned,

7 By the word of truth, by the power of God, by the armour of righteousness on the right hand and on the left,

8 By honour and dishonour, by evil report and good report: as deceivers, and *yet* true;

9 As unknown, and *yet* well known; as dying, and, behold, we live; as chastened, and not killed;

10 As sorrowful, yet alway rejoicing; as poor, yet making many rich; as having nothing, and *yet* possessing all things.

11 O *ye* Corinthians, our mouth is open unto you, our heart is enlarged.

12 Ye are not straitened in us, but ye are straitened in your own bowels.

13 Now for a recompence in the same, (I speak as unto *my* children,) be ye also enlarged.

14 Be ye not unequally yoked together with unbelievers: for what fellowship hath righteousness with unrighteousness? and what communion hath light with darkness?

15 And what concord hath Christ with Belial? or what part hath he that believeth with an infidel?

16 And what agreement hath the temple of God with idols? for ye are the temple of the living God; as God hath said, I will dwell in them, and walk in *them*; and I will be their God, and they shall be my people.

17 Wherefore come out from among them, and be ye separate, saith the Lord, and touch not the unclean *thing*; and I will receive you,

18 And will be a Father unto you, and ye shall be my sons and daughters, saith the Lord Almighty.

7 Having therefore these promises,
dearly beloved, let us cleanse
ourselves from all filthiness of the flesh
and spirit, perfecting holiness in the
fear of God.
2 Receive us; we have wronged no
man, we have corrupted no man, we
have defrauded no man.
3 I speak not *this* to condemn *you*: for
I have said before, that ye are in our
hearts to die and live with *you*.
4 Great *is* my boldness of speech
toward you, great *is* my glorying of you:
I am filled with comfort, I am exceeding joyful in all our tribulation.
5 For, when we were come into
Macedonia, our flesh had no rest, but
we were troubled on every side; without *were* fightings, within *were* fears.
6 Nevertheless God, that comforteth
those that are cast down, comforted us
by the coming of Titus;
7 And not by his coming only, but by
the consolation wherewith he was comforted in you, when he told us your
earnest desire, your mourning, your
fervent mind toward me; so that I
rejoiced the more.
8 For though I made you sorry with a
letter, I do not repent, though I did
repent: for I perceive that the same
epistle hath made you sorry, though *it*
were but for a season.
9 Now I rejoice, not that ye were
made sorry, but that ye sorrowed to
repentance: for ye were made sorry
after a godly manner, that ye might
receive damage by us in nothing.
10 For godly sorrow worketh repentance to salvation not to be repented of:
but the sorrow of the world worketh
death.
11 For behold this selfsame thing,
that ye sorrowed after a godly sort,
what carefulness it wrought in you, yea,
what clearing of yourselves, yea, *what*
indignation, yea, *what* fear, yea, *what*
vehement desire, yea, *what* zeal, yea,
what revenge! In all *things* ye have
approved yourselves to be clear in this
matter.
12 Wherefore, though I wrote unto
you, *I did it* not for his cause that had
done the wrong, nor for his cause that
suffered wrong, but that our care for
you in the sight of God might appear
unto you.
13 Therefore we were comforted in
your comfort: yea, and exceedingly the
more joyed we for the joy of Titus,
because his spirit was refreshed by you
all.
14 For if I have boasted any thing to
him of you, I am not ashamed; but as we
spake all things to you in truth, even so
our boasting, which *I made* before
Titus, is found a truth.
15 And his inward affection is more
abundant toward you, whilst he remembereth the obedience of you all, how
with fear and trembling ye received
him.
16 I rejoice therefore that I have confidence in you in all *things*.

8 Moreover, brethren, we do you to
wit of the grace of God bestowed on
the churches of Macedonia;
2 How that in a great trial of affliction
the abundance of their joy and their
deep poverty abounded unto the riches
of their liberality.
3 For to *their* power, I bear record,
yea, and beyond *their* power *they were*
willing of themselves;
4 Praying us with much intreaty that
we would receive the gift, and *take*
upon us the fellowship of the ministering to the saints.

5 And *this they did*, not as we hoped, but first gave their own selves to the Lord, and unto us by the will of God.

6 Insomuch that we desired Titus, that as he had begun, so he would also finish in you the same grace also.

7 Therefore, as ye abound in every *thing, in* faith, and utterance, and knowledge, and *in* all diligence, and *in* your love to us, *see* that ye abound in this grace also.

8 I speak not by commandment, but by occasion of the forwardness of others, and to prove the sincerity of your love.

9 For ye know the grace of our Lord Jesus Christ, that, though he was rich, yet for your sakes he became poor, that ye through his poverty might be rich.

10 And herein I give *my* advice: for this is expedient for you, who have begun before, not only to do, but also to be forward a year ago.

11 Now therefore perform the doing *of it*; that as *there was* a readiness to will, so *there may be* a performance also out of that which ye have.

12 For if there be first a willing mind, *it is* accepted according to that a man hath, *and* not according to that he hath not.

13 For *I mean* not that other men be eased, and ye burdened:

14 But by an equality, *that* now at this time your abundance *may be a supply* for their want, that their abundance also may be *a supply* for your want: that there may be equality:

15 As it is written, He that *had gathered* much had nothing over; and he that *had gathered* little had no lack.

16 But thanks *be* to God, which put the same earnest care into the heart of Titus for you.

17 For indeed he accepted the exhortation; but being more forward, of his own accord he went unto you.

18 And we have sent with him the brother, whose praise *is* in the gospel throughout all the churches;

19 And not *that* only, but who was also chosen of the churches to travel with us with this grace, which is administered by us to the glory of the same Lord, and *declaration of* your ready mind:

20 Avoiding this, that no man should blame us in this abundance which is administered by us:

21 Providing for honest things, not only in the sight of the Lord, but also in the sight of men.

22 And we have sent with them our brother, whom we have oftentimes proved diligent in many things, but now much more diligent, upon the great confidence which *I have* in you.

23 Whether *any do enquire* of Titus, *he is* my partner and fellowhelper concerning you: or our brethren *be enquired of, they are* the messengers of the churches, *and* the glory of Christ.

24 Wherefore shew ye to them, and before the churches, the proof of your love, and of our boasting on your behalf.

9 For as touching the ministering to the saints, it is superfluous for me to write to you:

2 For I know the forwardness of your mind, for which I boast of you to them of Macedonia, that Achaia was ready a year ago; and your zeal hath provoked very many.

3 Yet have I sent the brethren, lest our boasting of you should be in vain in this behalf; that, as I said, ye may be ready:

4 Lest haply if they of Macedonia
come with me, and find you unpre-
pared, we (that we say not, ye) should
be ashamed in this same confident
boasting.
5 Therefore I thought it necessary to
exhort the brethren, that they would go
before unto you, and make up beforehand your bounty, whereof ye had
notice before, that the same might be
ready, as *a matter of* bounty, and not as
of covetousness.
6 But this *I say*, He which soweth
sparingly shall reap also sparingly; and
he which soweth bountifully shall reap
also bountifully.
7 Every man according as he purpos-
eth in his heart, *so let him give*; not
grudgingly, or of necessity: for God
loveth a cheerful giver.
8 And God *is* able to make all grace
abound toward you; that ye, always having all sufficiency in all *things*, may
abound to every good work:
9 (As it is written, He hath dispersed
abroad; he hath given to the poor: his
righteousness remaineth for ever.
10 Now he that ministereth seed to
the sower both minister bread for *your*
food, and multiply your seed sown, and
increase the fruits of your righteousness;)
11 Being enriched in every thing to all
bountifulness, which causeth through
us thanksgiving to God.
12 For the administration of this service not only supplieth the want of the
saints, but is abundant also by many
thanksgivings unto God;
13 Whiles by the experiment of this
ministration they glorify God for your
professed subjection unto the gospel of
Christ, and for *your* liberal distribution
unto them, and unto all *men*;
14 And by their prayer for you, which
long after you for the exceeding grace
of God in you.
15 Thanks *be* unto God for his
unspeakable gift.

10 Now I Paul myself beseech you
by the meekness and gentleness
of Christ, who in presence *am* base
among you, but being absent am bold
toward you:
2 But I beseech *you*, that I may not be
bold when I am present with that confidence, wherewith I think to be bold
against some, which think of us as if we
walked according to the flesh.
3 For though we walk in the flesh, we
do not war after the flesh:
4 (For the weapons of our warfare *are*
not carnal, but mighty through God to
the pulling down of strong holds;)
5 Casting down imaginations, and
every high thing that exalteth itself
against the knowledge of God, and
bringing into captivity every thought to
the obedience of Christ;
6 And having in a readiness to
revenge all disobedience, when your
obedience is fulfilled.
7 Do ye look on things after the outward appearance? If any man trust to
himself that he is Christ's, let him of
himself think this again, that, as he *is*
Christ's, even so *are* we Christ's.
8 For though I should boast somewhat
more of our authority, which the Lord
hath given us for edification, and not
for your destruction, I should not be
ashamed:
9 That I may not seem as if I would
terrify you by letters.
10 For *his* letters, say they, *are*
weighty and powerful; but *his* bodily
presence *is* weak, and *his* speech contemptible.

11 Let such an one think this, that,
such as we are in word by letters when
we are absent, such *will we be* also in
deed when we are present.
12 For we dare not make ourselves of
the number, or compare ourselves with
some that commend themselves: but
they measuring themselves by themselves, and comparing themselves
among themselves, are not wise.
13 But we will not boast of things
without *our* measure, but according to
the measure of the rule which God hath
distributed to us, a measure to reach
even unto you.
14 For we stretch not ourselves
beyond *our measure*, as though we
reached not unto you: for we are come
as far as to you also in *preaching* the
gospel of Christ:
15 Not boasting of things without *our*
measure, *that is*, of other men's labours;
but having hope, when your faith is
increased, that we shall be enlarged by
you according to our rule abundantly,
16 To preach the gospel in the *regions*
beyond you, *and* not to boast in another
man's line of things made ready to our
hand.
17 But he that glorieth, let him glory
in the Lord.
18 For not he that commendeth himself is approved, but whom the Lord
commendeth.

11 Would to God ye could bear with
me a little in *my* folly: and
indeed bear with me.
2 For I am jealous over you with godly
jealousy: for I have espoused you to one
husband, that I may present *you as* a
chaste virgin to Christ.
3 But I fear, lest by any means, as the
serpent beguiled Eve through his subtilty, so your minds should be corrupted
from the simplicity that is in Christ.
4 For if he that cometh preacheth
another Jesus, whom we have not
preached, or *if* ye receive another spirit, which ye have not received, or another gospel, which ye have not accepted,
ye might well bear with *him*.
5 For I suppose I was not a whit
behind the very chiefest apostles.
6 But though *I be* rude in speech, yet
not in knowledge; but we have been
throughly made manifest among you in
all things.
7 Have I committed an offence in
abasing myself that ye might be exalted, because I have preached to you the
gospel of God freely?
8 I robbed other churches, taking
wages *of them*, to do you service.
9 And when I was present with you,
and wanted, I was chargeable to no
man: for that which was lacking to me
the brethren which came from
Macedonia supplied: and in all *things* I
have kept myself from being burdensome unto you, and *so* will I keep
myself.
10 As the truth of Christ is in me, no
man shall stop me of this boasting in
the regions of Achaia.
11 Wherefore? because I love you
not? God knoweth.
12 But what I do, that I will do, that I
may cut off occasion from them which
desire occasion; that wherein they
glory, they may be found even as we.
13 For such *are* false apostles, deceitful workers, transforming themselves
into the apostles of Christ.
14 And no marvel; for Satan himself
is transformed into an angel of light.
15 Therefore *it is* no great thing if his
ministers also be transformed as the

ministers of righteousness; whose end shall be according to their works.

16 I say again, Let no man think me a fool; if otherwise, yet as a fool receive me, that I may boast myself a little.

17 That which I speak, I speak *it* not after the Lord, but as it were foolishly, in this confidence of boasting.

18 Seeing that many glory after the flesh, I will glory also.

19 For ye suffer fools gladly, seeing ye *yourselves* are wise.

20 For ye suffer, if a man bring you into bondage, if a man devour *you*, if a man take *of you*, if a man exalt himself, if a man smite you on the face.

21 I speak as concerning reproach, as though we had been weak. Howbeit whereinsoever any is bold, (I speak foolishly,) I am bold also.

22 Are they Hebrews? so *am* I. Are they Israelites? so *am* I. Are they the seed of Abraham? so *am* I.

23 Are they ministers of Christ? (I speak as a fool) I *am* more; in labours more abundant, in stripes above measure, in prisons more frequent, in deaths oft.

24 Of the Jews five times received I forty *stripes* save one.

25 Thrice was I beaten with rods, once was I stoned, thrice I suffered shipwreck, a night and a day I have been in the deep;

26 *In* journeyings often, *in* perils of waters, *in* perils of robbers, *in* perils by *mine own* countrymen, *in* perils by the heathen, *in* perils in the city, *in* perils in the wilderness, *in* perils in the sea, *in* perils among false brethren;

27 In weariness and painfulness, in watchings often, in hunger and thirst, in fastings often, in cold and nakedness.

28 Beside those things that are without, that which cometh upon me daily, the care of all the churches.

29 Who is weak, and I am not weak? who is offended, and I burn not?

30 If I must needs glory, I will glory of the things which concern mine infirmities.

31 The God and Father of our Lord Jesus Christ, which is blessed for evermore, knoweth that I lie not.

32 In Damascus the governor under Aretas the king kept the city of the Damascenes with a garrison, desirous to apprehend me:

33 And through a window in a basket was I let down by the wall, and escaped his hands.

12 It is not expedient for me doubtless to glory. I will come to visions and revelations of the Lord.

2 I knew a man in Christ above fourteen years ago, (whether in the body, I cannot tell; or whether out of the body, I cannot tell: God knoweth;) such an one caught up to the third heaven.

3 And I knew such a man, (whether in the body, or out of the body, I cannot tell: God knoweth;)

4 How that he was caught up into paradise, and heard unspeakable words, which it is not lawful for a man to utter.

5 Of such an one will I glory: yet of myself I will not glory, but in mine infirmities.

6 For though I would desire to glory, I shall not be a fool; for I will say the truth: but *now* I forbear, lest any man should think of me above that which he seeth me *to be*, or *that* he heareth of me.

7 And lest I should be exalted above
measure through the abundance of the
revelations, there was given to me a
thorn in the flesh, the messenger of
Satan to buffet me, lest I should be
exalted above measure.
8 For this thing I besought the Lord
thrice, that it might depart from me.
9 And he said unto me, My grace is
sufficient for thee: for my strength is
made perfect in weakness. Most gladly
therefore will I rather glory in my infirmities, that the power of Christ may
rest upon me.
10 Therefore I take pleasure in infirmities, in reproaches, in necessities, in
persecutions, in distresses for Christ's
sake: for when I am weak, then am I
strong.
11 I am become a fool in glorying; ye
have compelled me: for I ought to have
been commended of you: for in nothing
am I behind the very chiefest apostles,
though I be nothing.
12 Truly the signs of an apostle were
wrought among you in all patience, in
signs, and wonders, and mighty deeds.
13 For what is it wherein ye were
inferior to other churches, except *it be*
that I myself was not burdensome to
you? forgive me this wrong.
14 Behold, the third time I am ready
to come to you; and I will not be burdensome to you: for I seek not yours,
but you: for the children ought not to
lay up for the parents, but the parents
for the children.
15 And I will very gladly spend and
be spent for you; though the more
abundantly I love you, the less I be
loved.
16 But be it so, I did not burden you:
nevertheless, being crafty, I caught you
with guile.
17 Did I make a gain of you by any of
them whom I sent unto you?
18 I desired Titus, and with *him* I sent
a brother. Did Titus make a gain of you?
walked we not in the same spirit?
walked we not in the same steps?
19 Again, think ye that we excuse
ourselves unto you? we speak before
God in Christ: but *we do* all things,
dearly beloved, for your edifying.
20 For I fear, lest, when I come, I shall
not find you such as I would, and *that* I
shall be found unto you such as ye
would not: lest *there be* debates, envyings, wraths, strifes, backbitings, whis-
perings, swellings, tumults:
21 *And* lest, when I come again, my
God will humble me among you, and
that I shall bewail many which have
sinned already, and have not repented
of the uncleanness and fornication and
lasciviousness which they have committed.

13 This *is* the third *time* I am coming to you. In the mouth of two or
three witnesses shall every word be
established.
2 I told you before, and foretell you, as
if I were present, the second time; and
being absent now I write to them which
heretofore have sinned, and to all other,
that, if I come again, I will not spare:
3 Since ye seek a proof of Christ
speaking in me, which to you-ward is
not weak, but is mighty in you.
4 For though he was crucified through
weakness, yet he liveth by the power of
God. For we also are weak in him, but
we shall live with him by the power of
God toward you.
5 Examine yourselves, whether ye be
in the faith; prove your own selves.
Know ye not your own selves, how that

Jesus Christ is in you, except ye be
reprobates?
6 But I trust that ye shall know that
we are not reprobates.
7 Now I pray to God that ye do no evil;
not that we should appear approved,
but that ye should do that which is honest, though we be as reprobates.
8 For we can do nothing against the
truth, but for the truth.
9 For we are glad, when we are weak,
and ye are strong: and this also we wish,
even your perfection.
10 Therefore I write these things
being absent, lest being present I
should use sharpness, according to the
power which the Lord hath given me to
edification, and not to destruction.
11 Finally, brethren, farewell. Be perfect, be of good comfort, be of one
mind, live in peace; and the God of love
and peace shall be with you.
12 Greet one another with an holy
kiss.
13 All the saints salute you.
14 The grace of the Lord Jesus Christ,
and the love of God, and the communion of the Holy Ghost, *be* with you all.
Amen.

THE EPISTLE OF PAUL THE APOSTLE

TO THE

GALATIANS

1 Paul, an apostle, (not of men,
neither by man, but by Jesus Christ,
and God the Father, who raised him
from the dead;)
2 And all the brethren which are with
me, unto the churches of Galatia:
3 Grace *be* to you and peace from God
the Father, and *from* our Lord Jesus
Christ,
4 Who gave himself for our sins, that
he might deliver us from this present
evil world, according to the will of God
and our Father:
5 To whom *be* glory for ever and ever.
Amen.
6 I marvel that ye are so soon removed
from him that called you into the grace
of Christ unto another gospel:
7 Which is not another; but there be
some that trouble you, and would pervert the gospel of Christ.
8 But though we, or an angel from
heaven, preach any other gospel unto
you than that which we have preached
unto you, let him be accursed.
9 As we said before, so say I now
again, If any *man* preach any other
gospel unto you than that ye have
received, let him be accursed.
10 For do I now persuade men, or
God? or do I seek to please men? for if
I yet pleased men, I should not be the
servant of Christ.
11 But I certify you, brethren, that the
gospel which was preached of me is not
after man.
12 For I neither received it of man,
neither was I taught *it*, but by the revelation of Jesus Christ.
13 For ye have heard of my conversation in time past in the Jews' religion,
how that beyond measure I persecuted
the church of God, and wasted it:

14 And profited in the Jews' religion
above many my equals in mine own
nation, being more exceedingly zealous
of the traditions of my fathers.
15 But when it pleased God, who separated me from my mother's womb, and
called *me* by his grace,
16 To reveal his Son in me, that I
might preach him among the heathen;
immediately I conferred not with flesh
and blood:
17 Neither went I up to Jerusalem to
them which were apostles before me;
but I went into Arabia, and returned
again unto Damascus.
18 Then after three years I went up to
Jerusalem to see Peter, and abode with
him fifteen days.
19 But other of the apostles saw I
none, save James the Lord's brother.
20 Now the things which I write unto
you, behold, before God, I lie not.
21 Afterwards I came into the regions
of Syria and Cilicia;
22 And was unknown by face unto the
churches of Judaea which were in
Christ:
23 But they had heard only, That he
which persecuted us in times past now
preacheth the faith which once he
destroyed.
24 And they glorified God in me.

2 Then fourteen years after I went up
again to Jerusalem with Barnabas,
and took Titus with *me* also.
2 And I went up by revelation, and
communicated unto them that gospel
which I preach among the Gentiles, but
privately to them which were of reputation, lest by any means I should run, or
had run, in vain.
3 But neither Titus, who was with me,
being a Greek, was compelled to be
circumcised:
4 And that because of false brethren
unawares brought in, who came in privily to spy out our liberty which we have
in Christ Jesus, that they might bring
us into bondage:
5 To whom we gave place by subjection, no, not for an hour; that the truth
of the gospel might continue with you.
6 But of these who seemed to be
somewhat, (whatsoever they were, it
maketh no matter to me: God accepteth no man's person:) for they who
seemed *to be somewhat* in conference
added nothing to me:
7 But contrariwise, when they saw
that the gospel of the uncircumcision
was committed unto me, as *the gospel*
of the circumcision *was* unto Peter;
8 (For he that wrought effectually in
Peter to the apostleship of the circumcision, the same was mighty in me
toward the Gentiles:)
9 And when James, Cephas, and
John, who seemed to be pillars, perceived the grace that was given unto
me, they gave to me and Barnabas the
right hands of fellowship; that we
should go unto the heathen, and they
unto the circumcision.
10 Only *they would* that we should
remember the poor; the same which I
also was forward to do.
11 But when Peter was come to
Antioch, I withstood him to the face,
because he was to be blamed.
12 For before that certain came from
James, he did eat with the Gentiles: but
when they were come, he withdrew and
separated himself, fearing them which
were of the circumcision.
13 And the other Jews dissembled
likewise with him; insomuch that
Barnabas also was carried away with
their dissimulation.

14 But when I saw that they walked
not uprightly according to the truth of
the gospel, I said unto Peter before
them all, If thou, being a Jew, livest
after the manner of Gentiles, and not
as do the Jews, why compellest thou
the Gentiles to live as do the Jews?
15 We *who are* Jews by nature, and
not sinners of the Gentiles,
16 Knowing that a man is not justified by the works of the law, but by the
faith of Jesus Christ, even we have
believed in Jesus Christ, that we might
be justified by the faith of Christ, and
not by the works of the law: for by the
works of the law shall no flesh be justified.
17 But if, while we seek to be justified
by Christ, we ourselves also are found
sinners, *is* therefore Christ the minister
of sin? God forbid.
18 For if I build again the things
which I destroyed, I make myself a
transgressor.
19 For I through the law am dead to
the law, that I might live unto God.
20 I am crucified with Christ: nevertheless I live; yet not I, but Christ liveth
in me: and the life which I now live in
the flesh I live by the faith of the Son of
God, who loved me, and gave himself
for me.
21 I do not frustrate the grace of God:
for if righteousness *come* by the law,
then Christ is dead in vain.

3 O foolish Galatians, who hath
bewitched you, that ye should not
obey the truth, before whose eyes Jesus
Christ hath been evidently set forth,
crucified among you?
2 This only would I learn of you,
Received ye the Spirit by the works of
the law, or by the hearing of faith?
3 Are ye so foolish? having begun in
the Spirit, are ye now made perfect by
the flesh?
4 Have ye suffered so many things in
vain? if *it be* yet in vain.
5 He therefore that ministereth to
you the Spirit, and worketh miracles
among you, *doeth he it* by the works of
the law, or by the hearing of faith?
6 Even as Abraham believed God,
and it was accounted to him for righteousness.
7 Know ye therefore that they which
are of faith, the same are the children
of Abraham.
8 And the scripture, foreseeing that
God would justify the heathen through
faith, preached before the gospel unto
Abraham, *saying*, In thee shall all
nations be blessed.
9 So then they which be of faith are
blessed with faithful Abraham.
10 For as many as are of the works of
the law are under the curse: for it is
written, Cursed *is* every one that continueth not in all things which are written in the book of the law to do them.
11 But that no man is justified by the
law in the sight of God, *it is* evident: for,
The just shall live by faith.
12 And the law is not of faith: but, The
man that doeth them shall live in them.
13 Christ hath redeemed us from the
curse of the law, being made a curse for
us: for it is written, Cursed *is* every one
that hangeth on a tree:
14 That the blessing of Abraham
might come on the Gentiles through
Jesus Christ; that we might receive the
promise of the Spirit through faith.
15 Brethren, I speak after the manner
of men; Though *it be* but a man's covenant, yet *if it be* confirmed, no man
disannulleth, or addeth thereto.

16 Now to Abraham and his seed
were the promises made. He saith not,
And to seeds, as of many; but as of one,
And to thy seed, which is Christ.
17 And this I say, *that* the covenant,
that was confirmed before of God in
Christ, the law, which was four hundred
and thirty years after, cannot disannul,
that it should make the promise of
none effect.
18 For if the inheritance *be* of the law,
it is no more of promise: but God gave
it to Abraham by promise.
19 Wherefore then *serveth* the law? It
was added because of transgressions,
till the seed should come to whom the
promise was made; *and it was* ordained
by angels in the hand of a mediator.
20 Now a mediator is not *a mediator*
of one, but God is one.
21 *Is* the law then against the promises of God? God forbid: for if there had
been a law given which could have
given life, verily righteousness should
have been by the law.
22 But the scripture hath concluded
all under sin, that the promise by faith
of Jesus Christ might be given to them
that believe.
23 But before faith came, we were
kept under the law, shut up unto the
faith which should afterwards be revealed.
24 Wherefore the law was our schoolmaster *to bring us* unto Christ, that we
might be justified by faith.
25 But after that faith is come, we are
no longer under a schoolmaster.
26 For ye are all the children of God
by faith in Christ Jesus.
27 For as many of you as have been
baptized into Christ have put on Christ.
28 There is neither Jew nor Greek,
there is neither bond nor free, there is
neither male nor female: for ye are all
one in Christ Jesus.
29 And if ye *be* Christ's, then are ye
Abraham's seed, and heirs according to
the promise.

4 Now I say, *That* the heir, as long as
he is a child, differeth nothing from
a servant, though he be lord of all;
2 But is under tutors and governors
until the time appointed of the father.
3 Even so we, when we were children,
were in bondage under the elements of
the world:
4 But when the fulness of the time
was come, God sent forth his Son, made
of a woman, made under the law,
5 To redeem them that were under
the law, that we might receive the adoption of sons.
6 And because ye are sons, God hath
sent forth the Spirit of his Son into your
hearts, crying, Abba, Father.
7 Wherefore thou art no more a servant, but a son; and if a son, then an
heir of God through Christ.
8 Howbeit then, when ye knew not
God, ye did service unto them which by
nature are no gods.
9 But now, after that ye have known
God, or rather are known of God, how
turn ye again to the weak and beggarly
elements, whereunto ye desire again to
be in bondage?
10 Ye observe days, and months, and
times, and years.
11 I am afraid of you, lest I have
bestowed upon you labour in vain.
12 Brethren, I beseech you, be as I
am; for I *am* as ye *are*: ye have not
injured me at all.
13 Ye know how through infirmity of
the flesh I preached the gospel unto
you at the first.

14 And my temptation which was in
my flesh ye despised not, nor rejected;
but received me as an angel of God,
even as Christ Jesus.
15 Where is then the blessedness ye
spake of? for I bear you record, that, if
it had been possible, ye would have
plucked out your own eyes, and have
given them to me.
16 Am I therefore become your enemy, because I tell you the truth?
17 They zealously affect you, *but* not
well; yea, they would exclude you, that
ye might affect them.
18 But *it is* good to be zealously
affected always in *a* good *thing*, and
not only when I am present with you.
19 My little children, of whom I travail in birth again until Christ be
formed in you,
20 I desire to be present with you now,
and to change my voice; for I stand in
doubt of you.
21 Tell me, ye that desire to be under
the law, do ye not hear the law?
22 For it is written, that Abraham had
two sons, the one by a bondmaid, the
other by a freewoman.
23 But he *who was* of the bondwoman
was born after the flesh; but he of the
freewoman *was* by promise.
24 Which things are an allegory: for
these are the two covenants; the one
from the mount Sinai, which gendereth
to bondage, which is Agar.
25 For this Agar is mount Sinai in
Arabia, and answereth to Jerusalem
which now is, and is in bondage with
her children.
26 But Jerusalem which is above is
free, which is the mother of us all.
27 For it is written, Rejoice, *thou* barren that bearest not; break forth and
cry, thou that travailest not: for the
desolate hath many more children than
she which hath an husband.
28 Now we, brethren, as Isaac was, are
the children of promise.
29 But as then he that was born after
the flesh persecuted him *that was born*
after the Spirit, even so *it is* now.
30 Nevertheless what saith the scripture? Cast out the bondwoman and her
son: for the son of the bondwoman shall
not be heir with the son of the freewoman.
31 So then, brethren, we are not children of the bondwoman, but of the free.

5 Stand fast therefore in the liberty
wherewith Christ hath made us
free, and be not entangled again with
the yoke of bondage.
2 Behold, I Paul say unto you, that if
ye be circumcised, Christ shall profit
you nothing.
3 For I testify again to every man that
is circumcised, that he is a debtor to do
the whole law.
4 Christ is become of no effect unto
you, whosoever of you are justified by
the law; ye are fallen from grace.
5 For we through the Spirit wait for
the hope of righteousness by faith.
6 For in Jesus Christ neither circumcision availeth any thing, nor uncircumcision; but faith which worketh by love.
7 Ye did run well; who did hinder you
that ye should not obey the truth?
8 This persuasion *cometh* not of him
that calleth you.
9 A little leaven leaveneth the whole
lump.
10 I have confidence in you through
the Lord, that ye will be none otherwise
minded: but he that troubleth you shall
bear his judgment, whosoever he be.

11 And I, brethren, if I yet preach circumcision, why do I yet suffer persecution? then is the offence of the cross
ceased.
12 I would they were even cut off
which trouble you.
13 For, brethren, ye have been called
unto liberty; only *use* not liberty for an
occasion to the flesh, but by love serve
one another.
14 For all the law is fulfilled in one
word, *even* in this; Thou shalt love thy
neighbour as thyself.
15 But if ye bite and devour one
another, take heed that ye be not consumed one of another.
16 *This* I say then, Walk in the Spirit,
and ye shall not fulfil the lust of the
flesh.
17 For the flesh lusteth against the
Spirit, and the Spirit against the flesh:
and these are contrary the one to the
other: so that ye cannot do the things
that ye would.
18 But if ye be led of the Spirit, ye are
not under the law.
19 Now the works of the flesh are
manifest, which are *these*; Adultery,
fornication, uncleanness, lasciviousness,
20 Idolatry, witchcraft, hatred, vari-
ance, emulations, wrath, strife, sedi-
tions, heresies,
21 Envyings, murders, drunkenness,
revellings, and such like: of the which I
tell you before, as I have also told *you*
in time past, that they which do such
things shall not inherit the kingdom of
God.
22 But the fruit of the Spirit is love,
joy, peace, longsuffering, gentleness,
goodness, faith,
23 Meekness, temperance: against
such there is no law.
24 And they that are Christ's have
crucified the flesh with the affections
and lusts.
25 If we live in the Spirit, let us also
walk in the Spirit.
26 Let us not be desirous of vain glory,
provoking one another, envying one
another.

6 Brethren, if a man be overtaken in
a fault, ye which are spiritual,
restore such an one in the spirit of
meekness; considering thyself, lest
thou also be tempted.
2 Bear ye one another's burdens, and
so fulfil the law of Christ.
3 For if a man think himself to be
something, when he is nothing, he
deceiveth himself.
4 But let every man prove his own
work, and then shall he have rejoicing
in himself alone, and not in another.
5 For every man shall bear his own
burden.
6 Let him that is taught in the word
communicate unto him that teacheth in
all good things.
7 Be not deceived; God is not mocked:
for whatsoever a man soweth, that shall
he also reap.
8 For he that soweth to his flesh shall
of the flesh reap corruption; but he that
soweth to the Spirit shall of the Spirit
reap life everlasting.
9 And let us not be weary in well
doing: for in due season we shall reap,
if we faint not.
10 As we have therefore opportunity,
let us do good unto all *men*, especially
unto them who are of the household of
faith.
11 Ye see how large a letter I have
written unto you with mine own hand.
12 As many as desire to make a fair
shew in the flesh, they constrain you to

be circumcised; only lest they should suffer persecution for the cross of Christ.

13 For neither they themselves who are circumcised keep the law; but desire to have you circumcised, that they may glory in your flesh.

14 But God forbid that I should glory, save in the cross of our Lord Jesus Christ, by whom the world is crucified unto me, and I unto the world.

15 For in Christ Jesus neither circumcision availeth any thing, nor uncircumcision, but a new creature.

16 And as many as walk according to this rule, peace *be* on them, and mercy, and upon the Israel of God.

17 From henceforth let no man trouble me: for I bear in my body the marks of the Lord Jesus.

18 Brethren, the grace of our Lord Jesus Christ *be* with your spirit. Amen.

THE EPISTLE OF PAUL THE APOSTLE
TO THE

EPHESIANS

1 Paul, an apostle of Jesus Christ by the will of God, to the saints which are at Ephesus, and to the faithful in Christ Jesus:

2 Grace *be* to you, and peace, from God our Father, and *from* the Lord Jesus Christ.

3 Blessed *be* the God and Father of our Lord Jesus Christ, who hath blessed us with all spiritual blessings in heavenly *places* in Christ:

4 According as he hath chosen us in him before the foundation of the world, that we should be holy and without blame before him in love:

5 Having predestinated us unto the adoption of children by Jesus Christ to himself, according to the good pleasure of his will,

6 To the praise of the glory of his grace, wherein he hath made us accepted in the beloved.

7 In whom we have redemption through his blood, the forgiveness of sins, according to the riches of his grace;

8 Wherein he hath abounded toward us in all wisdom and prudence;

9 Having made known unto us the mystery of his will, according to his good pleasure which he hath purposed in himself:

10 That in the dispensation of the fulness of times he might gather together in one all things in Christ, both which are in heaven, and which are on earth; *even* in him:

11 In whom also we have obtained an inheritance, being predestinated according to the purpose of him who worketh all things after the counsel of his own will:

12 That we should be to the praise of his glory, who first trusted in Christ.

13 In whom ye also *trusted*, after that ye heard the word of truth, the gospel of your salvation: in whom also after that ye believed, ye were sealed with that holy Spirit of promise,

14 Which is the earnest of our inheritance until the redemption of the purchased possession, unto the praise of his glory.
15 Wherefore I also, after I heard of your faith in the Lord Jesus, and love unto all the saints,
16 Cease not to give thanks for you, making mention of you in my prayers;
17 That the God of our Lord Jesus Christ, the Father of glory, may give unto you the spirit of wisdom and revelation in the knowledge of him:
18 The eyes of your understanding being enlightened; that ye may know what is the hope of his calling, and what the riches of the glory of his inheritance in the saints,
19 And what *is* the exceeding greatness of his power to us-ward who believe, according to the working of his mighty power,
20 Which he wrought in Christ, when he raised him from the dead, and set *him* at his own right hand in the heavenly *places*,
21 Far above all principality, and power, and might, and dominion, and every name that is named, not only in this world, but also in that which is to come:
22 And hath put all *things* under his feet, and gave him *to be* the head over all *things* to the church,
23 Which is his body, the fulness of him that filleth all in all.

2 And you *hath he quickened*, who were dead in trespasses and sins;
2 Wherein in time past ye walked according to the course of this world, according to the prince of the power of the air, the spirit that now worketh in the children of disobedience:
3 Among whom also we all had our conversation in times past in the lusts of our flesh, fulfilling the desires of the flesh and of the mind; and were by nature the children of wrath, even as others.
4 But God, who is rich in mercy, for his great love wherewith he loved us,
5 Even when we were dead in sins, hath quickened us together with Christ, (by grace ye are saved;)
6 And hath raised *us* up together, and made *us* sit together in heavenly *places* in Christ Jesus:
7 That in the ages to come he might shew the exceeding riches of his grace in *his* kindness toward us through Christ Jesus.
8 For by grace are ye saved through faith; and that not of yourselves: *it is* the gift of God:
9 Not of works, lest any man should boast.
10 For we are his workmanship, created in Christ Jesus unto good works, which God hath before ordained that we should walk in them.
11 Wherefore remember, that ye *being* in time past Gentiles in the flesh, who are called Uncircumcision by that which is called the Circumcision in the flesh made by hands;
12 That at that time ye were without Christ, being aliens from the commonwealth of Israel, and strangers from the covenants of promise, having no hope, and without God in the world:
13 But now in Christ Jesus ye who sometimes were far off are made nigh by the blood of Christ.
14 For he is our peace, who hath made both one, and hath broken down the middle wall of partition *between us*;

15 Having abolished in his flesh the
enmity, *even* the law of commandments
contained in ordinances; for to make in
himself of twain one new man, *so* making peace;
16 And that he might reconcile both
unto God in one body by the cross, having slain the enmity thereby:
17 And came and preached peace to
you which were afar off, and to them
that were nigh.
18 For through him we both have
access by one Spirit unto the Father.
19 Now therefore ye are no more
strangers and foreigners, but fellowciti-
zens with the saints, and of the household of God;
20 And are built upon the foundation
of the apostles and prophets, Jesus
Christ himself being the chief corner
stone;
21 In whom all the building fitly
framed together groweth unto an holy
temple in the Lord:
22 In whom ye also are builded
together for an habitation of God
through the Spirit.

3 For this cause I Paul, the prisoner of
Jesus Christ for you Gentiles,
2 If ye have heard of the dispensation
of the grace of God which is given me to
you-ward:
3 How that by revelation he made
known unto me the mystery; (as I wrote
afore in few words,
4 Whereby, when ye read, ye may
understand my knowledge in the mystery of Christ)
5 Which in other ages was not made
known unto the sons of men, as it is
now revealed unto his holy apostles
and prophets by the Spirit;
6 That the Gentiles should be fellow-
heirs, and of the same body, and partakers of his promise in Christ by the gospel:
7 Whereof I was made a minister,
according to the gift of the grace of God
given unto me by the effectual working
of his power.
8 Unto me, who am less than the least
of all saints, is this grace given, that I
should preach among the Gentiles the
unsearchable riches of Christ;
9 And to make all *men* see what *is* the
fellowship of the mystery, which from
the beginning of the world hath been
hid in God, who created all things by
Jesus Christ:
10 To the intent that now unto the
principalities and powers in heavenly
places might be known by the church
the manifold wisdom of God,
11 According to the eternal purpose
which he purposed in Christ Jesus our
Lord:
12 In whom we have boldness and
access with confidence by the faith of
him.
13 Wherefore I desire that ye faint
not at my tribulations for you, which is
your glory.
14 For this cause I bow my knees unto
the Father of our Lord Jesus Christ,
15 Of whom the whole family in heav-
en and earth is named,
16 That he would grant you, according to the riches of his glory, to be
strengthened with might by his Spirit
in the inner man;
17 That Christ may dwell in your
hearts by faith; that ye, being rooted
and grounded in love,
18 May be able to comprehend with
all saints what *is* the breadth, and
length, and depth, and height;
19 And to know the love of Christ,
which passeth knowledge, that ye

might be filled with all the fulness of God.

20 Now unto him that is able to do exceeding abundantly above all that we ask or think, according to the power that worketh in us,

21 Unto him *be* glory in the church by Christ Jesus throughout all ages, world without end. Amen.

4 I therefore, the prisoner of the Lord, beseech you that ye walk worthy of the vocation wherewith ye are called,

2 With all lowliness and meekness, with longsuffering, forbearing one another in love;

3 Endeavouring to keep the unity of the Spirit in the bond of peace.

4 *There is* one body, and one Spirit, even as ye are called in one hope of your calling;

5 One Lord, one faith, one baptism,

6 One God and Father of all, who *is* above all, and through all, and in you all.

7 But unto every one of us is given grace according to the measure of the gift of Christ.

8 Wherefore he saith, When he ascended up on high, he led captivity captive, and gave gifts unto men.

9 (Now that he ascended, what is it but that he also descended first into the lower parts of the earth?

10 He that descended is the same also that ascended up far above all heavens, that he might fill all things.)

11 And he gave some, apostles; and some, prophets; and some, evangelists; and some, pastors and teachers;

12 For the perfecting of the saints, for the work of the ministry, for the edifying of the body of Christ:

13 Till we all come in the unity of the faith, and of the knowledge of the Son of God, unto a perfect man, unto the measure of the stature of the fulness of Christ:

14 That we *henceforth* be no more children, tossed to and fro, and carried about with every wind of doctrine, by the sleight of men, *and* cunning craftiness, whereby they lie in wait to deceive;

15 But speaking the truth in love, may grow up into him in all things, which is the head, *even* Christ:

16 From whom the whole body fitly joined together and compacted by that which every joint supplieth, according to the effectual working in the measure of every part, maketh increase of the body unto the edifying of itself in love.

17 This I say therefore, and testify in the Lord, that ye henceforth walk not as other Gentiles walk, in the vanity of their mind,

18 Having the understanding darkened, being alienated from the life of God through the ignorance that is in them, because of the blindness of their heart:

19 Who being past feeling have given themselves over unto lasciviousness, to work all uncleanness with greediness.

20 But ye have not so learned Christ;

21 If so be that ye have heard him, and have been taught by him, as the truth is in Jesus:

22 That ye put off concerning the former conversation the old man, which is corrupt according to the deceitful lusts;

23 And be renewed in the spirit of your mind;

24 And that ye put on the new man,
which after God is created in righteousness and true holiness.
25 Wherefore putting away lying,
speak every man truth with his neighbour: for we are members one of
another.
26 Be ye angry, and sin not: let not the
sun go down upon your wrath:
27 Neither give place to the devil.
28 Let him that stole steal no more:
but rather let him labour, working with
his hands the thing which is good, that
he may have to give to him that
needeth.
29 Let no corrupt communication proceed out of your mouth, but that which
is good to the use of edifying, that it
may minister grace unto the hearers.
30 And grieve not the holy Spirit of
God, whereby ye are sealed unto the
day of redemption.
31 Let all bitterness, and wrath, and
anger, and clamour, and evil speaking,
be put away from you, with all malice:
32 And be ye kind one to another,
tenderhearted, forgiving one another,
even as God for Christ's sake hath forgiven you.

5 Be ye therefore followers of God, as
dear children;
2 And walk in love, as Christ also hath
loved us, and hath given himself for us
an offering and a sacrifice to God for a
sweetsmelling savour.
3 But fornication, and all uncleanness, or covetousness, let it not be once
named among you, as becometh saints;
4 Neither filthiness, nor foolish talking, nor jesting, which are not convenient: but rather giving of thanks.
5 For this ye know, that no whoremon-
ger, nor unclean person, nor covetous
man, who is an idolater, hath any
inheritance in the kingdom of Christ
and of God.
6 Let no man deceive you with vain
words: for because of these things
cometh the wrath of God upon the children of disobedience.
7 Be not ye therefore partakers with
them.
8 For ye were sometimes darkness,
but now *are ye* light in the Lord: walk
as children of light:
9 (For the fruit of the Spirit *is* in all
goodness and righteousness and truth;)
10 Proving what is acceptable unto
the Lord.
11 And have no fellowship with the
unfruitful works of darkness, but rather reprove *them*.
12 For it is a shame even to speak of
those things which are done of them in
secret.
13 But all things that are reproved are
made manifest by the light: for whatsoever doth make manifest is light.
14 Wherefore he saith, Awake thou
that sleepest, and arise from the dead,
and Christ shall give thee light.
15 See then that ye walk circum-
spectly, not as fools, but as wise,
16 Redeeming the time, because the
days are evil.
17 Wherefore be ye not unwise, but
understanding what the will of the
Lord *is*.
18 And be not drunk with wine,
wherein is excess; but be filled with the
Spirit;
19 Speaking to yourselves in psalms
and hymns and spiritual songs, singing
and making melody in your heart to the
Lord;
20 Giving thanks always for all things
unto God and the Father in the name of
our Lord Jesus Christ;

21 Submitting yourselves one to another in the fear of God.

22 Wives, submit yourselves unto your own husbands, as unto the Lord.

23 For the husband is the head of the wife, even as Christ is the head of the church: and he is the saviour of the body.

24 Therefore as the church is subject unto Christ, so *let* the wives *be* to their own husbands in every thing.

25 Husbands, love your wives, even as Christ also loved the church, and gave himself for it;

26 That he might sanctify and cleanse it with the washing of water by the word,

27 That he might present it to himself a glorious church, not having spot, or wrinkle, or any such thing; but that it should be holy and without blemish.

28 So ought men to love their wives as their own bodies. He that loveth his wife loveth himself.

29 For no man ever yet hated his own flesh; but nourisheth and cherisheth it, even as the Lord the church:

30 For we are members of his body, of his flesh, and of his bones.

31 For this cause shall a man leave his father and mother, and shall be joined unto his wife, and they two shall be one flesh.

32 This is a great mystery: but I speak concerning Christ and the church.

33 Nevertheless let every one of you in particular so love his wife even as himself; and the wife *see* that she reverence *her* husband.

6

Children, obey your parents in the Lord: for this is right.

2 Honour thy father and mother; (which is the first commandment with promise;)

3 That it may be well with thee, and thou mayest live long on the earth.

4 And, ye fathers, provoke not your children to wrath: but bring them up in the nurture and admonition of the Lord.

5 Servants, be obedient to them that are *your* masters according to the flesh, with fear and trembling, in singleness of your heart, as unto Christ;

6 Not with eyeservice, as menpleasers; but as the servants of Christ, doing the will of God from the heart;

7 With good will doing service, as to the Lord, and not to men:

8 Knowing that whatsoever good thing any man doeth, the same shall he receive of the Lord, whether *he be* bond or free.

9 And, ye masters, do the same things unto them, forbearing threatening: knowing that your Master also is in heaven; neither is there respect of persons with him.

10 Finally, my brethren, be strong in the Lord, and in the power of his might.

11 Put on the whole armour of God, that ye may be able to stand against the wiles of the devil.

12 For we wrestle not against flesh and blood, but against principalities, against powers, against the rulers of the darkness of this world, against spiritual wickedness in high *places*.

13 Wherefore take unto you the whole armour of God, that ye may be able to withstand in the evil day, and having done all, to stand.

14 Stand therefore, having your loins girt about with truth, and having on the breastplate of righteousness;

15 And your feet shod with the preparation of the gospel of peace;

16 Above all, taking the shield of
faith, wherewith ye shall be able to
quench all the fiery darts of the wicked.
17 And take the helmet of salvation,
and the sword of the Spirit, which is the
word of God:
18 Praying always with all prayer and
supplication in the Spirit, and watching
thereunto with all perseverance and
supplication for all saints;
19 And for me, that utterance may be
given unto me, that I may open my
mouth boldly, to make known the mystery of the gospel,
20 For which I am an ambassador in
bonds: that therein I may speak boldly,
as I ought to speak.
21 But that ye also may know my
affairs, *and* how I do, Tychicus, a beloved brother and faithful minister in
the Lord, shall make known to you all
things:
22 Whom I have sent unto you for the
same purpose, that ye might know our
affairs, and *that* he might comfort your
hearts.
23 Peace *be* to the brethren, and love
with faith, from God the Father and the
Lord Jesus Christ.
24 Grace *be* with all them that love
our Lord Jesus Christ in sincerity.
Amen.

THE EPISTLE OF PAUL THE APOSTLE

TO THE

PHILIPPIANS

1 Paul and Timotheus, the servants of
Jesus Christ, to all the saints in
Christ Jesus which are at Philippi, with
the bishops and deacons:
2 Grace *be* unto you, and peace, from
God our Father, and *from* the Lord
Jesus Christ.
3 I thank my God upon every remembrance of you,
4 Always in every prayer of mine for
you all making request with joy,
5 For your fellowship in the gospel
from the first day until now;
6 Being confident of this very thing,
that he which hath begun a good work
in you will perform *it* until the day of
Jesus Christ:
7 Even as it is meet for me to think
this of you all, because I have you in my
heart; inasmuch as both in my bonds,
and in the defence and confirmation of
the gospel, ye all are partakers of my
grace.
8 For God is my record, how greatly I
long after you all in the bowels of Jesus
Christ.
9 And this I pray, that your love may
abound yet more and more in knowledge and *in* all judgment;
10 That ye may approve things that
are excellent; that ye may be sincere
and without offence till the day of
Christ;
11 Being filled with the fruits of righteousness, which are by Jesus Christ,
unto the glory and praise of God.
12 But I would ye should understand,
brethren, that the things *which happened* unto me have fallen out rather
unto the furtherance of the gospel;

13 So that my bonds in Christ are manifest in all the palace, and in all other *places*;

14 And many of the brethren in the Lord, waxing confident by my bonds, are much more bold to speak the word without fear.

15 Some indeed preach Christ even of envy and strife; and some also of good will:

16 The one preach Christ of contention, not sincerely, supposing to add affliction to my bonds:

17 But the other of love, knowing that I am set for the defence of the gospel.

18 What then? notwithstanding, every way, whether in pretence, or in truth, Christ is preached; and I therein do rejoice, yea, and will rejoice.

19 For I know that this shall turn to my salvation through your prayer, and the supply of the Spirit of Jesus Christ,

20 According to my earnest expectation and *my* hope, that in nothing I shall be ashamed, but *that* with all boldness, as always, *so* now also Christ shall be magnified in my body, whether *it be* by life, or by death.

21 For to me to live *is* Christ, and to die *is* gain.

22 But if I live in the flesh, this *is* the fruit of my labour: yet what I shall choose I wot not.

23 For I am in a strait betwixt two, having a desire to depart, and to be with Christ; which is far better:

24 Nevertheless to abide in the flesh *is* more needful for you.

25 And having this confidence, I know that I shall abide and continue with you all for your furtherance and joy of faith;

26 That your rejoicing may be more abundant in Jesus Christ for me by my coming to you again.

27 Only let your conversation be as it becometh the gospel of Christ: that whether I come and see you, or else be absent, I may hear of your affairs, that ye stand fast in one spirit, with one mind striving together for the faith of the gospel;

28 And in nothing terrified by your adversaries: which is to them an evident token of perdition, but to you of salvation, and that of God.

29 For unto you it is given in the behalf of Christ, not only to believe on him, but also to suffer for his sake;

30 Having the same conflict which ye saw in me, and now hear *to be* in me.

2 If *there be* therefore any consolation in Christ, if any comfort of love, if any fellowship of the Spirit, if any bowels and mercies,

2 Fulfil ye my joy, that ye be likeminded, having the same love, *being* of one accord, of one mind.

3 *Let* nothing *be done* through strife or vainglory; but in lowliness of mind let each esteem other better than themselves.

4 Look not every man on his own things, but every man also on the things of others.

5 Let this mind be in you, which was also in Christ Jesus:

6 Who, being in the form of God, thought it not robbery to be equal with God:

7 But made himself of no reputation, and took upon him the form of a servant, and was made in the likeness of men:

8 And being found in fashion as a
man, he humbled himself, and became
obedient unto death, even the death of
the cross.
9 Wherefore God also hath highly
exalted him, and given him a name
which is above every name:
10 That at the name of Jesus every
knee should bow, of *things* in heaven,
and *things* in earth, and *things* under
the earth;
11 And *that* every tongue should confess that Jesus Christ *is* Lord, to the
glory of God the Father.
12 Wherefore, my beloved, as ye have
always obeyed, not as in my presence
only, but now much more in my absence,
work out your own salvation with fear
and trembling.
13 For it is God which worketh in you
both to will and to do of *his* good pleasure.
14 Do all things without murmurings
and disputings:
15 That ye may be blameless and
harmless, the sons of God, without
rebuke, in the midst of a crooked and
perverse nation, among whom ye shine
as lights in the world;
16 Holding forth the word of life; that
I may rejoice in the day of Christ, that I
have not run in vain, neither laboured
in vain.
17 Yea, and if I be offered upon the
sacrifice and service of your faith, I joy,
and rejoice with you all.
18 For the same cause also do ye joy,
and rejoice with me.
19 But I trust in the Lord Jesus to
send Timotheus shortly unto you, that I
also may be of good comfort, when I
know your state.
20 For I have no man likeminded, who
will naturally care for your state.
21 For all seek their own, not the
things which are Jesus Christ's.
22 But ye know the proof of him, that,
as a son with the father, he hath served
with me in the gospel.
23 Him therefore I hope to send presently, so soon as I shall see how it will
go with me.
24 But I trust in the Lord that I also
myself shall come shortly.
25 Yet I supposed it necessary to send
to you Epaphroditus, my brother, and
companion in labour, and fellowsoldier,
but your messenger, and he that ministered to my wants.
26 For he longed after you all, and
was full of heaviness, because that ye
had heard that he had been sick.
27 For indeed he was sick nigh unto
death: but God had mercy on him; and
not on him only, but on me also, lest I
should have sorrow upon sorrow.
28 I sent him therefore the more carefully, that, when ye see him again, ye
may rejoice, and that I may be the less
sorrowful.
29 Receive him therefore in the Lord
with all gladness; and hold such in reputation:
30 Because for the work of Christ he
was nigh unto death, not regarding his
life, to supply your lack of service
toward me.

3 Finally, my brethren, rejoice in the
Lord. To write the same things to
you, to me indeed *is* not grievous, but
for you *it is* safe.
2 Beware of dogs, beware of evil workers, beware of the concision.
3 For we are the circumcision, which
worship God in the spirit, and rejoice in
Christ Jesus, and have no confidence in
the flesh.

4 Though I might also have confidence in the flesh. If any other man thinketh that he hath whereof he might trust in the flesh, I more:

5 Circumcised the eighth day, of the stock of Israel, *of* the tribe of Benjamin, an Hebrew of the Hebrews; as touching the law, a Pharisee;

6 Concerning zeal, persecuting the church; touching the righteousness which is in the law, blameless.

7 But what things were gain to me, those I counted loss for Christ.

8 Yea doubtless, and I count all things *but* loss for the excellency of the knowledge of Christ Jesus my Lord: for whom I have suffered the loss of all things, and do count them *but* dung, that I may win Christ,

9 And be found in him, not having mine own righteousness, which is of the law, but that which is through the faith of Christ, the righteousness which is of God by faith:

10 That I may know him, and the power of his resurrection, and the fellowship of his sufferings, being made conformable unto his death;

11 If by any means I might attain unto the resurrection of the dead.

12 Not as though I had already attained, either were already perfect: but I follow after, if that I may apprehend that for which also I am apprehended of Christ Jesus.

13 Brethren, I count not myself to have apprehended: but *this* one thing *I do*, forgetting those things which are behind, and reaching forth unto those things which are before,

14 I press toward the mark for the prize of the high calling of God in Christ Jesus.

15 Let us therefore, as many as be perfect, be thus minded: and if in any thing ye be otherwise minded, God shall reveal even this unto you.

16 Nevertheless, whereto we have already attained, let us walk by the same rule, let us mind the same thing.

17 Brethren, be followers together of me, and mark them which walk so as ye have us for an ensample.

18 (For many walk, of whom I have told you often, and now tell you even weeping, *that they are* the enemies of the cross of Christ:

19 Whose end *is* destruction, whose God *is their* belly, and *whose* glory *is* in their shame, who mind earthly things.)

20 For our conversation is in heaven; from whence also we look for the Saviour, the Lord Jesus Christ:

21 Who shall change our vile body, that it may be fashioned like unto his glorious body, according to the working whereby he is able even to subdue all things unto himself.

4 Therefore, my brethren dearly beloved and longed for, my joy and crown, so stand fast in the Lord, *my* dearly beloved.

2 I beseech Euodias, and beseech Syntyche, that they be of the same mind in the Lord.

3 And I intreat thee also, true yokefellow, help those women which laboured with me in the gospel, with Clement also, and *with* other my fellowlabourers, whose names *are* in the book of life.

4 Rejoice in the Lord always: *and* again I say, Rejoice.

5 Let your moderation be known unto all men. The Lord *is* at hand.

6 Be careful for nothing; but in every
thing by prayer and supplication with
thanksgiving let your requests be made
known unto God.
7 And the peace of God, which passeth all understanding, shall keep your
hearts and minds through Christ Jesus.
8 Finally, brethren, whatsoever things
are true, whatsoever things *are* honest,
whatsoever things *are* just, whatsoever
things *are* pure, whatsoever things *are*
lovely, whatsoever things *are* of good
report; if *there be* any virtue, and if
there be any praise, think on these
things.
9 Those things, which ye have both
learned, and received, and heard, and
seen in me, do: and the God of peace
shall be with you.
10 But I rejoiced in the Lord greatly,
that now at the last your care of me
hath flourished again; wherein ye were
also careful, but ye lacked opportunity.
11 Not that I speak in respect of want:
for I have learned, in whatsoever state
I am, *therewith* to be content.
12 I know both how to be abased, and
I know how to abound: every where and
in all things I am instructed both to be
full and to be hungry, both to abound
and to suffer need.
13 I can do all things through Christ
which strengtheneth me.
14 Notwithstanding ye have well
done, that ye did communicate with my
affliction.
15 Now ye Philippians know also, that
in the beginning of the gospel, when I
departed from Macedonia, no church
communicated with me as concerning
giving and receiving, but ye only.
16 For even in Thessalonica ye sent
once and again unto my necessity.
17 Not because I desire a gift: but I
desire fruit that may abound to your
account.
18 But I have all, and abound: I am
full, having received of Epaphroditus
the things *which were sent* from you,
an odour of a sweet smell, a sacrifice
acceptable, wellpleasing to God.
19 But my God shall supply all your
need according to his riches in glory by
Christ Jesus.
20 Now unto God and our Father *be*
glory for ever and ever. Amen.
21 Salute every saint in Christ Jesus.
The brethren which are with me greet
you.
22 All the saints salute you, chiefly
they that are of Caesar's household.
23 The grace of our Lord Jesus Christ
be with you all. Amen.

THE EPISTLE OF PAUL THE APOSTLE

TO THE

COLOSSIANS

1 Paul, an apostle of Jesus Christ by the will of God, and Timotheus *our* brother,

2 To the saints and faithful brethren in Christ which are at Colosse: Grace *be* unto you, and peace, from God our Father and the Lord Jesus Christ.

3 We give thanks to God and the Father of our Lord Jesus Christ, praying always for you,

4 Since we heard of your faith in Christ Jesus, and of the love *which ye have* to all the saints,

5 For the hope which is laid up for you in heaven, whereof ye heard before in the word of the truth of the gospel;

6 Which is come unto you, as *it is* in all the world; and bringeth forth fruit, as *it doth* also in you, since the day ye heard *of it*, and knew the grace of God in truth:

7 As ye also learned of Epaphras our dear fellowservant, who is for you a faithful minister of Christ;

8 Who also declared unto us your love in the Spirit.

9 For this cause we also, since the day we heard *it*, do not cease to pray for you, and to desire that ye might be filled with the knowledge of his will in all wisdom and spiritual understanding;

10 That ye might walk worthy of the Lord unto all pleasing, being fruitful in every good work, and increasing in the knowledge of God;

11 Strengthened with all might, according to his glorious power, unto all patience and longsuffering with joyfulness;

12 Giving thanks unto the Father, which hath made us meet to be partakers of the inheritance of the saints in light:

13 Who hath delivered us from the power of darkness, and hath translated *us* into the kingdom of his dear Son:

14 In whom we have redemption through his blood, *even* the forgiveness of sins:

15 Who is the image of the invisible God, the firstborn of every creature:

16 For by him were all things created, that are in heaven, and that are in earth, visible and invisible, whether *they be* thrones, or dominions, or principalities, or powers: all things were created by him, and for him:

17 And he is before all things, and by him all things consist.

18 And he is the head of the body, the church: who is the beginning, the firstborn from the dead; that in all *things* he might have the preeminence.

19 For it pleased *the Father* that in him should all fulness dwell;

20 And, having made peace through the blood of his cross, by him to reconcile all things unto himself; by him, *I say*, whether *they be* things in earth, or things in heaven.

21 And you, that were sometime alienated and enemies in *your* mind by wicked works, yet now hath he reconciled

22 In the body of his flesh through death, to present you holy and unblameable and unreproveable in his sight:

23 If ye continue in the faith grounded and settled, and *be* not moved away

from the hope of the gospel, which ye
have heard, *and* which was preached to
every creature which is under heaven;
whereof I Paul am made a minister;
24 Who now rejoice in my sufferings
for you, and fill up that which is behind
of the afflictions of Christ in my flesh
for his body's sake, which is the church:
25 Whereof I am made a minister,
according to the dispensation of God
which is given to me for you, to fulfil
the word of God;
26 *Even* the mystery which hath been
hid from ages and from generations,
but now is made manifest to his saints:
27 To whom God would make known
what *is* the riches of the glory of this
mystery among the Gentiles; which is
Christ in you, the hope of glory:
28 Whom we preach, warning every
man, and teaching every man in all
wisdom; that we may present every
man perfect in Christ Jesus:
29 Whereunto I also labour, striving
according to his working, which worketh in me mightily.

2 For I would that ye knew what great
conflict I have for you, and *for* them
at Laodicea, and *for* as many as have
not seen my face in the flesh;
2 That their hearts might be comforted, being knit together in love, and
unto all riches of the full assurance of
understanding, to the acknowledge-
ment of the mystery of God, and of the
Father, and of Christ;
3 In whom are hid all the treasures of
wisdom and knowledge.
4 And this I say, lest any man should
beguile you with enticing words.
5 For though I be absent in the flesh,
yet am I with you in the spirit, joying
and beholding your order, and the stedfastness of your faith in Christ.
6 As ye have therefore received Christ
Jesus the Lord, *so* walk ye in him:
7 Rooted and built up in him, and
stablished in the faith, as ye have been
taught, abounding therein with thanksgiving.
8 Beware lest any man spoil you
through philosophy and vain deceit,
after the tradition of men, after the
rudiments of the world, and not after
Christ.
9 For in him dwelleth all the fulness
of the Godhead bodily.
10 And ye are complete in him, which
is the head of all principality and
power:
11 In whom also ye are circumcised
with the circumcision made without
hands, in putting off the body of the
sins of the flesh by the circumcision of
Christ:
12 Buried with him in baptism,
wherein also ye are risen with *him*
through the faith of the operation of
God, who hath raised him from the
dead.
13 And you, being dead in your sins
and the uncircumcision of your flesh,
hath he quickened together with him,
having forgiven you all trespasses;
14 Blotting out the handwriting of
ordinances that was against us, which
was contrary to us, and took it out of
the way, nailing it to his cross;
15 *And* having spoiled principalities
and powers, he made a shew of them
openly, triumphing over them in it.
16 Let no man therefore judge you in
meat, or in drink, or in respect of an
holyday, or of the new moon, or of the
sabbath *days*:
17 Which are a shadow of things to
come; but the body *is* of Christ.

18 Let no man beguile you of your reward in a voluntary humility and worshipping of angels, intruding into those things which he hath not seen, vainly puffed up by his fleshly mind,

19 And not holding the Head, from which all the body by joints and bands having nourishment ministered, and knit together, increaseth with the increase of God.

20 Wherefore if ye be dead with Christ from the rudiments of the world, why, as though living in the world, are ye subject to ordinances,

21 (Touch not; taste not; handle not;

22 Which all are to perish with the using;) after the commandments and doctrines of men?

23 Which things have indeed a shew of wisdom in will worship, and humility, and neglecting of the body; not in any honour to the satisfying of the flesh.

3 If ye then be risen with Christ, seek those things which are above, where Christ sitteth on the right hand of God.

2 Set your affection on things above, not on things on the earth.

3 For ye are dead, and your life is hid with Christ in God.

4 When Christ, *who is* our life, shall appear, then shall ye also appear with him in glory.

5 Mortify therefore your members which are upon the earth; fornication, uncleanness, inordinate affection, evil concupiscence, and covetousness, which is idolatry:

6 For which things' sake the wrath of God cometh on the children of disobedience:

7 In the which ye also walked some time, when ye lived in them.

8 But now ye also put off all these; anger, wrath, malice, blasphemy, filthy communication out of your mouth.

9 Lie not one to another, seeing that ye have put off the old man with his deeds;

10 And have put on the new *man*, which is renewed in knowledge after the image of him that created him:

11 Where there is neither Greek nor Jew, circumcision nor uncircumcision, Barbarian, Scythian, bond *nor* free: but Christ *is* all, and in all.

12 Put on therefore, as the elect of God, holy and beloved, bowels of mercies, kindness, humbleness of mind, meekness, longsuffering;

13 Forbearing one another, and forgiving one another, if any man have a quarrel against any: even as Christ forgave you, so also *do* ye.

14 And above all these things *put on* charity, which is the bond of perfectness.

15 And let the peace of God rule in your hearts, to the which also ye are called in one body; and be ye thankful.

16 Let the word of Christ dwell in you richly in all wisdom; teaching and admonishing one another in psalms and hymns and spiritual songs, singing with grace in your hearts to the Lord.

17 And whatsoever ye do in word or deed, *do* all in the name of the Lord Jesus, giving thanks to God and the Father by him.

18 Wives, submit yourselves unto your own husbands, as it is fit in the Lord.

19 Husbands, love *your* wives, and be not bitter against them.

20 Children, obey *your* parents in all things: for this is well pleasing unto the Lord.

21 Fathers, provoke not your children
to anger, lest they be discouraged.
22 Servants, obey in all things *your*
masters according to the flesh; not with
eyeservice, as menpleasers; but in singleness of heart, fearing God:
23 And whatsoever ye do, do *it* heart-
ily, as to the Lord, and not unto men;
24 Knowing that of the Lord ye shall
receive the reward of the inheritance:
for ye serve the Lord Christ.
25 But he that doeth wrong shall
receive for the wrong which he hath
done: and there is no respect of persons.

4 Masters, give unto *your* servants
that which is just and equal; knowing that ye also have a Master in heav-
en.
2 Continue in prayer, and watch in the
same with thanksgiving;
3 Withal praying also for us, that God
would open unto us a door of utterance,
to speak the mystery of Christ, for
which I am also in bonds:
4 That I may make it manifest, as I
ought to speak.
5 Walk in wisdom toward them that
are without, redeeming the time.
6 Let your speech *be* alway with
grace, seasoned with salt, that ye may
know how ye ought to answer every
man.
7 All my state shall Tychicus declare
unto you, *who is* a beloved brother, and
a faithful minister and fellowservant in
the Lord:
8 Whom I have sent unto you for the
same purpose, that he might know your
estate, and comfort your hearts;
9 With Onesimus, a faithful and beloved brother, who is *one* of you. They
shall make known unto you all things
which *are done* here.
10 Aristarchus my fellowprisoner
saluteth you, and Marcus, sister's son to
Barnabas, (touching whom ye received
commandments: if he come unto you,
receive him;)
11 And Jesus, which is called Justus,
who are of the circumcision. These only
are my fellowworkers unto the kingdom of God, which have been a comfort
unto me.
12 Epaphras, who is *one* of you, a servant of Christ, saluteth you, always
labouring fervently for you in prayers,
that ye may stand perfect and complete in all the will of God.
13 For I bear him record, that he hath
a great zeal for you, and them *that are*
in Laodicea, and them in Hierapolis.
14 Luke, the beloved physician, and
Demas, greet you.
15 Salute the brethren which are in
Laodicea, and Nymphas, and the
church which is in his house.
16 And when this epistle is read
among you, cause that it be read also in
the church of the Laodiceans; and that
ye likewise read the *epistle* from
Laodicea.
17 And say to Archippus, Take heed to
the ministry which thou hast received
in the Lord, that thou fulfil it.
18 The salutation by the hand of me
Paul. Remember my bonds. Grace *be*
with you. Amen.

THE FIRST EPISTLE OF PAUL THE APOSTLE

TO THE

THESSALONIANS

1 Paul, and Silvanus, and Timotheus,
unto the church of the Thessalonians
which is in God the Father and *in* the
Lord Jesus Christ: Grace *be* unto you,
and peace, from God our Father, and
the Lord Jesus Christ.
2 We give thanks to God always for
you all, making mention of you in our
prayers;
3 Remembering without ceasing your
work of faith, and labour of love, and
patience of hope in our Lord Jesus
Christ, in the sight of God and our
Father;
4 Knowing, brethren beloved, your
election of God.
5 For our gospel came not unto you in
word only, but also in power, and in the
Holy Ghost, and in much assurance; as
ye know what manner of men we were
among you for your sake.
6 And ye became followers of us, and
of the Lord, having received the word
in much affliction, with joy of the Holy
Ghost:
7 So that ye were ensamples to all
that believe in Macedonia and Achaia.
8 For from you sounded out the word
of the Lord not only in Macedonia and
Achaia, but also in every place your
faith to God-ward is spread abroad; so
that we need not to speak any thing.
9 For they themselves shew of us
what manner of entering in we had
unto you, and how ye turned to God
from idols to serve the living and true
God;
10 And to wait for his Son from heav-
en, whom he raised from the dead, *even*
Jesus, which delivered us from the
wrath to come.

2 For yourselves, brethren, know our
entrance in unto you, that it was not
in vain:
2 But even after that we had suffered
before, and were shamefully entreated,
as ye know, at Philippi, we were bold in
our God to speak unto you the gospel of
God with much contention.
3 For our exhortation *was* not of
deceit, nor of uncleanness, nor in guile:
4 But as we were allowed of God to be
put in trust with the gospel, even so we
speak; not as pleasing men, but God,
which trieth our hearts.
5 For neither at any time used we flattering words, as ye know, nor a cloke of
covetousness; God *is* witness:
6 Nor of men sought we glory, neither
of you, nor *yet* of others, when we
might have been burdensome, as the
apostles of Christ.
7 But we were gentle among you, even
as a nurse cherisheth her children:
8 So being affectionately desirous of
you, we were willing to have imparted
unto you, not the gospel of God only,
but also our own souls, because ye were
dear unto us.
9 For ye remember, brethren, our
labour and travail: for labouring night
and day, because we would not be
chargeable unto any of you, we
preached unto you the gospel of God.

10 Ye *are* witnesses, and God *also*,
how holily and justly and unblameably
we behaved ourselves among you that
believe:
11 As ye know how we exhorted and
comforted and charged every one of
you, as a father *doth* his children,
12 That ye would walk worthy of God,
who hath called you unto his kingdom
and glory.
13 For this cause also thank we God
without ceasing, because, when ye
received the word of God which ye
heard of us, ye received *it* not *as* the
word of men, but as it is in truth, the
word of God, which effectually worketh
also in you that believe.
14 For ye, brethren, became followers
of the churches of God which in Judaea
are in Christ Jesus: for ye also have suffered like things of your own countrymen, even as they *have* of the Jews:
15 Who both killed the Lord Jesus,
and their own prophets, and have persecuted us; and they please not God,
and are contrary to all men:
16 Forbidding us to speak to the
Gentiles that they might be saved, to
fill up their sins alway: for the wrath is
come upon them to the uttermost.
17 But we, brethren, being taken from
you for a short time in presence, not in
heart, endeavoured the more abundantly to see your face with great
desire.
18 Wherefore we would have come
unto you, even I Paul, once and again;
but Satan hindered us.
19 For what *is* our hope, or joy, or
crown of rejoicing? *Are* not even ye in
the presence of our Lord Jesus Christ
at his coming?
20 For ye are our glory and joy.

3 Wherefore when we could no longer
forbear, we thought it good to be
left at Athens alone;
2 And sent Timotheus, our brother,
and minister of God, and our fellowlabourer in the gospel of Christ, to establish you, and to comfort you concerning
your faith:
3 That no man should be moved by
these afflictions: for yourselves know
that we are appointed thereunto.
4 For verily, when we were with you,
we told you before that we should suffer tribulation; even as it came to pass,
and ye know.
5 For this cause, when I could no longer forbear, I sent to know your faith,
lest by some means the tempter have
tempted you, and our labour be in vain.
6 But now when Timotheus came
from you unto us, and brought us good
tidings of your faith and charity, and
that ye have good remembrance of us
always, desiring greatly to see us, as we
also *to see* you:
7 Therefore, brethren, we were comforted over you in all our affliction and
distress by your faith:
8 For now we live, if ye stand fast in
the Lord.
9 For what thanks can we render to
God again for you, for all the joy wherewith we joy for your sakes before our
God;
10 Night and day praying exceedingly
that we might see your face, and might
perfect that which is lacking in your
faith?
11 Now God himself and our Father,
and our Lord Jesus Christ, direct our
way unto you.

12 And the Lord make you to increase
and abound in love one toward another,
and toward all *men*, even as we *do*
toward you:
13 To the end he may stablish your
hearts unblameable in holiness before
God, even our Father, at the coming of
our Lord Jesus Christ with all his
saints.

4 Furthermore then we beseech you,
brethren, and exhort *you* by the
Lord Jesus, that as ye have received of
us how ye ought to walk and to please
God, *so* ye would abound more and
more.
2 For ye know what commandments
we gave you by the Lord Jesus.
3 For this is the will of God, *even* your
sanctification, that ye should abstain
from fornication:
4 That every one of you should know
how to possess his vessel in sanctification and honour;
5 Not in the lust of concupiscence,
even as the Gentiles which know not
God:
6 That no *man* go beyond and defraud
his brother in *any* matter: because that
the Lord *is* the avenger of all such, as
we also have forewarned you and testified.
7 For God hath not called us unto
uncleanness, but unto holiness.
8 He therefore that despiseth, despiseth not man, but God, who hath also
given unto us his holy Spirit.
9 But as touching brotherly love ye
need not that I write unto you: for ye
yourselves are taught of God to love
one another.
10 And indeed ye do it toward all the
brethren which are in all Macedonia:
but we beseech you, brethren, that ye
increase more and more;
11 And that ye study to be quiet, and
to do your own business, and to work
with your own hands, as we commanded you;
12 That ye may walk honestly toward
them that are without, and *that* ye may
have lack of nothing.
13 But I would not have you to be
ignorant, brethren, concerning them
which are asleep, that ye sorrow not,
even as others which have no hope.
14 For if we believe that Jesus died
and rose again, even so them also which
sleep in Jesus will God bring with him.
15 For this we say unto you by the
word of the Lord, that we which are
alive *and* remain unto the coming of
the Lord shall not prevent them which
are asleep.
16 For the Lord himself shall descend
from heaven with a shout, with the
voice of the archangel, and with the
trump of God: and the dead in Christ
shall rise first:
17 Then we which are alive *and*
remain shall be caught up together
with them in the clouds, to meet the
Lord in the air: and so shall we ever be
with the Lord.
18 Wherefore comfort one another
with these words.

5 But of the times and the seasons,
brethren, ye have no need that I
write unto you.
2 For yourselves know perfectly that
the day of the Lord so cometh as a thief
in the night.
3 For when they shall say, Peace and
safety; then sudden destruction cometh
upon them, as travail upon a woman
with child; and they shall not escape.
4 But ye, brethren, are not in darkness, that that day should overtake you
as a thief.

5 Ye are all the children of light, and
the children of the day: we are not of
the night, nor of darkness.
6 Therefore let us not sleep, as *do* others; but let us watch and be sober.
7 For they that sleep sleep in the
night; and they that be drunken are
drunken in the night.
8 But let us, who are of the day, be
sober, putting on the breastplate of
faith and love; and for an helmet, the
hope of salvation.
9 For God hath not appointed us to
wrath, but to obtain salvation by our
Lord Jesus Christ,
10 Who died for us, that, whether we
wake or sleep, we should live together
with him.
11 Wherefore comfort yourselves together, and edify one another, even as
also ye do.
12 And we beseech you, brethren, to
know them which labour among you,
and are over you in the Lord, and
admonish you;
13 And to esteem them very highly in
love for their work's sake. *And* be at
peace among yourselves.
14 Now we exhort you, brethren, warn
them that are unruly, comfort the fee-
bleminded, support the weak, be
patient toward all *men*.
15 See that none render evil for evil
unto any *man*; but ever follow that
which is good, both among yourselves,
and to all *men*.
16 Rejoice evermore.
17 Pray without ceasing.
18 In every thing give thanks: for this
is the will of God in Christ Jesus concerning you.
19 Quench not the Spirit.
20 Despise not prophesyings.
21 Prove all things; hold fast that
which is good.
22 Abstain from all appearance of
evil.
23 And the very God of peace sanctify
you wholly; and *I pray God* your whole
spirit and soul and body be preserved
blameless unto the coming of our Lord
Jesus Christ.
24 Faithful *is* he that calleth you, who
also will do *it*.
25 Brethren, pray for us.
26 Greet all the brethren with an holy
kiss.
27 I charge you by the Lord that this
epistle be read unto all the holy brethren.
28 The grace of our Lord Jesus Christ
be with you. Amen.

THE SECOND EPISTLE OF PAUL THE APOSTLE
TO THE

THESSALONIANS

1 Paul, and Silvanus, and Timotheus, unto the church of the Thessalonians in God our Father and the Lord Jesus Christ:

2 Grace unto you, and peace, from God our Father and the Lord Jesus Christ.

3 We are bound to thank God always for you, brethren, as it is meet, because that your faith groweth exceedingly, and the charity of every one of you all toward each other aboundeth;

4 So that we ourselves glory in you in the churches of God for your patience and faith in all your persecutions and tribulations that ye endure:

5 *Which is* a manifest token of the righteous judgment of God, that ye may be counted worthy of the kingdom of God, for which ye also suffer:

6 Seeing *it is* a righteous thing with God to recompense tribulation to them that trouble you;

7 And to you who are troubled rest with us, when the Lord Jesus shall be revealed from heaven with his mighty angels,

8 In flaming fire taking vengeance on them that know not God, and that obey not the gospel of our Lord Jesus Christ:

9 Who shall be punished with everlasting destruction from the presence of the Lord, and from the glory of his power;

10 When he shall come to be glorified in his saints, and to be admired in all them that believe (because our testimony among you was believed) in that day.

11 Wherefore also we pray always for you, that our God would count you worthy of *this* calling, and fulfil all the good pleasure of *his* goodness, and the work of faith with power:

12 That the name of our Lord Jesus Christ may be glorified in you, and ye in him, according to the grace of our God and the Lord Jesus Christ.

2 Now we beseech you, brethren, by the coming of our Lord Jesus Christ, and *by* our gathering together unto him,

2 That ye be not soon shaken in mind, or be troubled, neither by spirit, nor by word, nor by letter as from us, as that the day of Christ is at hand.

3 Let no man deceive you by any means: for *that day shall not come,* except there come a falling away first, and that man of sin be revealed, the son of perdition;

4 Who opposeth and exalteth himself above all that is called God, or that is worshipped; so that he as God sitteth in the temple of God, shewing himself that he is God.

5 Remember ye not, that, when I was yet with you, I told you these things?

6 And now ye know what withholdeth that he might be revealed in his time.

7 For the mystery of iniquity doth already work: only he who now letteth *will let,* until he be taken out of the way.

8 And then shall that Wicked be revealed, whom the Lord shall consume with the spirit of his mouth, and shall destroy with the brightness of his coming:

9 *Even him*, whose coming is after
the working of Satan with all power
and signs and lying wonders,
10 And with all deceivableness of
unrighteousness in them that perish;
because they received not the love of
the truth, that they might be saved.
11 And for this cause God shall send
them strong delusion, that they should
believe a lie:
12 That they all might be damned
who believed not the truth, but had
pleasure in unrighteousness.
13 But we are bound to give thanks
alway to God for you, brethren beloved
of the Lord, because God hath from the
beginning chosen you to salvation
through sanctification of the Spirit and
belief of the truth:
14 Whereunto he called you by our
gospel, to the obtaining of the glory of
our Lord Jesus Christ.
15 Therefore, brethren, stand fast,
and hold the traditions which ye have
been taught, whether by word, or our
epistle.
16 Now our Lord Jesus Christ himself,
and God, even our Father, which hath
loved us, and hath given *us* everlasting
consolation and good hope through
grace,
17 Comfort your hearts, and stablish
you in every good word and work.

3 Finally, brethren, pray for us, that
the word of the Lord may have *free*
course, and be glorified, even as *it is*
with you:
2 And that we may be delivered from
unreasonable and wicked men: for all
men have not faith.
3 But the Lord is faithful, who shall
stablish you, and keep *you* from evil.
4 And we have confidence in the Lord
touching you, that ye both do and will
do the things which we command you.
5 And the Lord direct your hearts into
the love of God, and into the patient
waiting for Christ.
6 Now we command you, brethren, in
the name of our Lord Jesus Christ, that
ye withdraw yourselves from every
brother that walketh disorderly, and
not after the tradition which he received of us.
7 For yourselves know how ye ought
to follow us: for we behaved not ourselves disorderly among you;
8 Neither did we eat any man's bread
for nought; but wrought with labour
and travail night and day, that we might
not be chargeable to any of you:
9 Not because we have not power, but
to make ourselves an ensample unto
you to follow us.
10 For even when we were with you,
this we commanded you, that if any
would not work, neither should he eat.
11 For we hear that there are some
which walk among you disorderly,
working not at all, but are busybodies.
12 Now them that are such we command and exhort by our Lord Jesus
Christ, that with quietness they work,
and eat their own bread.
13 But ye, brethren, be not weary in
well doing.
14 And if any man obey not our word
by this epistle, note that man, and have
no company with him, that he may be
ashamed.
15 Yet count *him* not as an enemy,
but admonish *him* as a brother.
16 Now the Lord of peace himself
give you peace always by all means. The
Lord *be* with you all.
17 The salutation of Paul with mine
own hand, which is the token in every
epistle: so I write.
18 The grace of our Lord Jesus Christ
be with you all. Amen.

THE FIRST EPISTLE OF PAUL THE APOSTLE
TO
TIMOTHY

1 Paul, an apostle of Jesus Christ by
the commandment of God our
Saviour, and Lord Jesus Christ, *which is*
our hope;
2 Unto Timothy, *my* own son in the
faith: Grace, mercy, *and* peace, from
God our Father and Jesus Christ our
Lord.
3 As I besought thee to abide still at
Ephesus, when I went into Macedonia,
that thou mightest charge some that
they teach no other doctrine,
4 Neither give heed to fables and endless genealogies, which minister questions, rather than godly edifying which
is in faith: *so do*.
5 Now the end of the commandment
is charity out of a pure heart, and *of* a
good conscience, and *of* faith unfeigned:
6 From which some having swerved
have turned aside unto vain jangling;
7 Desiring to be teachers of the law;
understanding neither what they say,
nor whereof they affirm.
8 But we know that the law *is* good, if
a man use it lawfully;
9 Knowing this, that the law is not
made for a righteous man, but for the
lawless and disobedient, for the ungodly and for sinners, for unholy and profane, for murderers of fathers and murderers of mothers, for manslayers,
10 For whoremongers, for them that
defile themselves with mankind, for
menstealers, for liars, for perjured persons, and if there be any other thing
that is contrary to sound doctrine;
11 According to the glorious gospel of
the blessed God, which was committed
to my trust.
12 And I thank Christ Jesus our Lord,
who hath enabled me, for that he
counted me faithful, putting me into
the ministry;
13 Who was before a blasphemer, and
a persecutor, and injurious: but I
obtained mercy, because I did *it* ignorantly in unbelief.
14 And the grace of our Lord was
exceeding abundant with faith and
love which is in Christ Jesus.
15 This *is* a faithful saying, and worthy of all acceptation, that Christ Jesus
came into the world to save sinners; of
whom I am chief.
16 Howbeit for this cause I obtained
mercy, that in me first Jesus Christ
might shew forth all longsuffering, for a
pattern to them which should hereafter
believe on him to life everlasting.
17 Now unto the King eternal, immor-
tal, invisible, the only wise God, *be*
honour and glory for ever and ever.
Amen.
18 This charge I commit unto thee,
son Timothy, according to the prophecies which went before on thee, that
thou by them mightest war a good
warfare;
19 Holding faith, and a good conscience; which some having put away
concerning faith have made shipwreck;
20 Of whom is Hymenaeus and Alexander; whom I have delivered unto
Satan, that they may learn not to blaspheme.

2 I exhort therefore, that, first of all,
supplications, prayers, interces-
sions, *and* giving of thanks, be made for
all men;

2 For kings, and *for* all that are in authority; that we may lead a quiet and peaceable life in all godliness and honesty.

3 For this *is* good and acceptable in the sight of God our Saviour;

4 Who will have all men to be saved, and to come unto the knowledge of the truth.

5 For *there is* one God, and one mediator between God and men, the man Christ Jesus;

6 Who gave himself a ransom for all, to be testified in due time.

7 Whereunto I am ordained a preacher, and an apostle, (I speak the truth in Christ, *and* lie not;) a teacher of the Gentiles in faith and verity.

8 I will therefore that men pray every where, lifting up holy hands, without wrath and doubting.

9 In like manner also, that women adorn themselves in modest apparel, with shamefacedness and sobriety; not with broided hair, or gold, or pearls, or costly array;

10 But (which becometh women professing godliness) with good works.

11 Let the woman learn in silence with all subjection.

12 But I suffer not a woman to teach, nor to usurp authority over the man, but to be in silence.

13 For Adam was first formed, then Eve.

14 And Adam was not deceived, but the woman being deceived was in the transgression.

15 Notwithstanding she shall be saved in childbearing, if they continue in faith and charity and holiness with sobriety.

3 This *is* a true saying, If a man desire the office of a bishop, he desireth a good work.

2 A bishop then must be blameless, the husband of one wife, vigilant, sober, of good behaviour, given to hospitality, apt to teach;

3 Not given to wine, no striker, not greedy of filthy lucre; but patient, not a brawler, not covetous;

4 One that ruleth well his own house, having his children in subjection with all gravity;

5 (For if a man know not how to rule his own house, how shall he take care of the church of God?)

6 Not a novice, lest being lifted up with pride he fall into the condemnation of the devil.

7 Moreover he must have a good report of them which are without; lest he fall into reproach and the snare of the devil.

8 Likewise *must* the deacons *be* grave, not doubletongued, not given to much wine, not greedy of filthy lucre;

9 Holding the mystery of the faith in a pure conscience.

10 And let these also first be proved; then let them use the office of a deacon, being *found* blameless.

11 Even so *must their* wives *be* grave, not slanderers, sober, faithful in all things.

12 Let the deacons be the husbands of one wife, ruling their children and their own houses well.

13 For they that have used the office of a deacon well purchase to themselves a good degree, and great boldness in the faith which is in Christ Jesus.

14 These things write I unto thee, hoping to come unto thee shortly:

15 But if I tarry long, that thou mayest
know how thou oughtest to behave
thyself in the house of God, which is the
church of the living God, the pillar and
ground of the truth.
16 And without controversy great is
the mystery of godliness: God was
manifest in the flesh, justified in the
Spirit, seen of angels, preached unto
the Gentiles, believed on in the world,
received up into glory.

4 Now the Spirit speaketh expressly,
that in the latter times some shall
depart from the faith, giving heed to
seducing spirits, and doctrines of devils;
2 Speaking lies in hypocrisy; having
their conscience seared with a hot iron;
3 Forbidding to marry, *and commanding* to abstain from meats, which
God hath created to be received with
thanksgiving of them which believe
and know the truth.
4 For every creature of God *is* good,
and nothing to be refused, if it be
received with thanksgiving:
5 For it is sanctified by the word of
God and prayer.
6 If thou put the brethren in remembrance of these things, thou shalt be a
good minister of Jesus Christ, nourished up in the words of faith and of
good doctrine, whereunto thou hast
attained.
7 But refuse profane and old wives'
fables, and exercise thyself *rather* unto
godliness.
8 For bodily exercise profiteth little:
but godliness is profitable unto all
things, having promise of the life that
now is, and of that which is to come.
9 This *is* a faithful saying and worthy
of all acceptation.
10 For therefore we both labour and
suffer reproach, because we trust in the
living God, who is the Saviour of all
men, specially of those that believe.
11 These things command and teach.
12 Let no man despise thy youth; but
be thou an example of the believers, in
word, in conversation, in charity, in
spirit, in faith, in purity.
13 Till I come, give attendance to
reading, to exhortation, to doctrine.
14 Neglect not the gift that is in thee,
which was given thee by prophecy, with
the laying on of the hands of the presbytery.
15 Meditate upon these things; give
thyself wholly to them; that thy profiting may appear to all.
16 Take heed unto thyself, and unto
the doctrine; continue in them: for in
doing this thou shalt both save thyself,
and them that hear thee.

5 Rebuke not an elder, but intreat
him as a father; *and* the younger
men as brethren;
2 The elder women as mothers; the
younger as sisters, with all purity.
3 Honour widows that are widows
indeed.
4 But if any widow have children or
nephews, let them learn first to shew
piety at home, and to requite their
parents: for that is good and acceptable
before God.
5 Now she that is a widow indeed, and
desolate, trusteth in God, and continueth in supplications and prayers night
and day.
6 But she that liveth in pleasure is
dead while she liveth.
7 And these things give in charge,
that they may be blameless.

8 But if any provide not for his own, and specially for those of his own house, he hath denied the faith, and is worse than an infidel.

9 Let not a widow be taken into the number under threescore years old, having been the wife of one man,

10 Well reported of for good works; if she have brought up children, if she have lodged strangers, if she have washed the saints' feet, if she have relieved the afflicted, if she have diligently followed every good work.

11 But the younger widows refuse: for when they have begun to wax wanton against Christ, they will marry;

12 Having damnation, because they have cast off their first faith.

13 And withal they learn *to be* idle, wandering about from house to house; and not only idle, but tattlers also and busybodies, speaking things which they ought not.

14 I will therefore that the younger women marry, bear children, guide the house, give none occasion to the adversary to speak reproachfully.

15 For some are already turned aside after Satan.

16 If any man or woman that believeth have widows, let them relieve them, and let not the church be charged; that it may relieve them that are widows indeed.

17 Let the elders that rule well be counted worthy of double honour, especially they who labour in the word and doctrine.

18 For the scripture saith, Thou shalt not muzzle the ox that treadeth out the corn. And, The labourer *is* worthy of his reward.

19 Against an elder receive not an accusation, but before two or three witnesses.

20 Them that sin rebuke before all, that others also may fear.

21 I charge *thee* before God, and the Lord Jesus Christ, and the elect angels, that thou observe these things without preferring one before another, doing nothing by partiality.

22 Lay hands suddenly on no man, neither be partaker of other men's sins: keep thyself pure.

23 Drink no longer water, but use a little wine for thy stomach's sake and thine often infirmities.

24 Some men's sins are open beforehand, going before to judgment; and some *men* they follow after.

25 Likewise also the good works *of some* are manifest beforehand; and they that are otherwise cannot be hid.

6 Let as many servants as are under the yoke count their own masters worthy of all honour, that the name of God and *his* doctrine be not blasphemed.

2 And they that have believing masters, let them not despise *them*, because they are brethren; but rather do *them* service, because they are faithful and beloved, partakers of the benefit. These things teach and exhort.

3 If any man teach otherwise, and consent not to wholesome words, *even* the words of our Lord Jesus Christ, and to the doctrine which is according to godliness;

4 He is proud, knowing nothing, but doting about questions and strifes of words, whereof cometh envy, strife, railings, evil surmisings,

5 Perverse disputings of men of corrupt minds, and destitute of the truth, supposing that gain is godliness: from such withdraw thyself.

6 But godliness with contentment is great gain.

7 For we brought nothing into *this* world, *and it is* certain we can carry nothing out.

8 And having food and raiment let us be therewith content.

9 But they that will be rich fall into temptation and a snare, and *into* many foolish and hurtful lusts, which drown men in destruction and perdition.

10 For the love of money is the root of all evil: which while some coveted after, they have erred from the faith, and pierced themselves through with many sorrows.

11 But thou, O man of God, flee these things; and follow after righteousness, godliness, faith, love, patience, meekness.

12 Fight the good fight of faith, lay hold on eternal life, whereunto thou art also called, and hast professed a good profession before many witnesses.

13 I give thee charge in the sight of God, who quickeneth all things, and *before* Christ Jesus, who before Pontius Pilate witnessed a good confession;

14 That thou keep *this* commandment without spot, unrebukeable, until the appearing of our Lord Jesus Christ:

15 Which in his times he shall shew, *who is* the blessed and only Potentate, the King of kings, and Lord of lords;

16 Who only hath immortality, dwelling in the light which no man can approach unto; whom no man hath seen, nor can see: to whom *be* honour and power everlasting. Amen.

17 Charge them that are rich in this world, that they be not highminded, nor trust in uncertain riches, but in the living God, who giveth us richly all things to enjoy;

18 That they do good, that they be rich in good works, ready to distribute, willing to communicate;

19 Laying up in store for themselves a good foundation against the time to come, that they may lay hold on eternal life.

20 O Timothy, keep that which is committed to thy trust, avoiding profane *and* vain babblings, and oppositions of science falsely so called:

21 Which some professing have erred concerning the faith. Grace *be* with thee. Amen.

THE SECOND EPISTLE OF PAUL THE APOSTLE
TO

TIMOTHY

1 Paul, an apostle of Jesus Christ by
the will of God, according to the
promise of life which is in Christ Jesus,
2 To Timothy, *my* dearly beloved son:
Grace, mercy, *and* peace, from God the
Father and Christ Jesus our Lord.
3 I thank God, whom I serve from *my*
forefathers with pure conscience, that
without ceasing I have remembrance of
thee in my prayers night and day;
4 Greatly desiring to see thee, being
mindful of thy tears, that I may be
filled with joy;
5 When I call to remembrance the
unfeigned faith that is in thee, which
dwelt first in thy grandmother Lois,
and thy mother Eunice; and I am persuaded that in thee also.
6 Wherefore I put thee in remembrance that thou stir up the gift of God,
which is in thee by the putting on of my
hands.
7 For God hath not given us the spirit
of fear; but of power, and of love, and of
a sound mind.
8 Be not thou therefore ashamed of
the testimony of our Lord, nor of me his
prisoner: but be thou partaker of the
afflictions of the gospel according to
the power of God;
9 Who hath saved us, and called *us*
with an holy calling, not according to
our works, but according to his own
purpose and grace, which was given us
in Christ Jesus before the world began,
10 But is now made manifest by the
appearing of our Saviour Jesus Christ,
who hath abolished death, and hath
brought life and immortality to light
through the gospel:
11 Whereunto I am appointed a
preacher, and an apostle, and a teacher
of the Gentiles.
12 For the which cause I also suffer
these things: nevertheless I am not
ashamed: for I know whom I have
believed, and am persuaded that he is
able to keep that which I have committed unto him against that day.
13 Hold fast the form of sound words,
which thou hast heard of me, in faith
and love which is in Christ Jesus.
14 That good thing which was committed unto thee keep by the Holy
Ghost which dwelleth in us.
15 This thou knowest, that all they
which are in Asia be turned away from
me; of whom are Phygellus and Her-
mogenes.
16 The Lord give mercy unto the
house of Onesiphorus; for he oft refreshed me, and was not ashamed of my
chain:
17 But, when he was in Rome, he
sought me out very diligently, and
found *me*.
18 The Lord grant unto him that he
may find mercy of the Lord in that day:
and in how many things he ministered
unto me at Ephesus, thou knowest very
well.

2 Thou therefore, my son, be strong in
the grace that is in Christ Jesus.
2 And the things that thou hast heard
of me among many witnesses, the same
commit thou to faithful men, who shall
be able to teach others also.
3 Thou therefore endure hardness, as
a good soldier of Jesus Christ.

4 No man that warreth entangleth himself with the affairs of *this* life; that he may please him who hath chosen him to be a soldier.

5 And if a man also strive for masteries, *yet* is he not crowned, except he strive lawfully.

6 The husbandman that laboureth must be first partaker of the fruits.

7 Consider what I say; and the Lord give thee understanding in all things.

8 Remember that Jesus Christ of the seed of David was raised from the dead according to my gospel:

9 Wherein I suffer trouble, as an evil doer, *even* unto bonds; but the word of God is not bound.

10 Therefore I endure all things for the elect's sakes, that they may also obtain the salvation which is in Christ Jesus with eternal glory.

11 *It is* a faithful saying: For if we be dead with *him*, we shall also live with *him*:

12 If we suffer, we shall also reign with *him*: if we deny *him*, he also will deny us:

13 If we believe not, *yet* he abideth faithful: he cannot deny himself.

14 Of these things put *them* in remembrance, charging *them* before the Lord that they strive not about words to no profit, *but* to the subverting of the hearers.

15 Study to shew thyself approved unto God, a workman that needeth not to be ashamed, rightly dividing the word of truth.

16 But shun profane *and* vain babblings: for they will increase unto more ungodliness.

17 And their word will eat as doth a canker: of whom is Hymenaeus and Philetus;

18 Who concerning the truth have erred, saying that the resurrection is past already; and overthrow the faith of some.

19 Nevertheless the foundation of God standeth sure, having this seal, The Lord knoweth them that are his. And, Let every one that nameth the name of Christ depart from iniquity.

20 But in a great house there are not only vessels of gold and of silver, but also of wood and of earth; and some to honour, and some to dishonour.

21 If a man therefore purge himself from these, he shall be a vessel unto honour, sanctified, and meet for the master's use, *and* prepared unto every good work.

22 Flee also youthful lusts: but follow righteousness, faith, charity, peace, with them that call on the Lord out of a pure heart.

23 But foolish and unlearned questions avoid, knowing that they do gender strifes.

24 And the servant of the Lord must not strive; but be gentle unto all *men*, apt to teach, patient,

25 In meekness instructing those that oppose themselves; if God peradventure will give them repentance to the acknowledging of the truth;

26 And *that* they may recover themselves out of the snare of the devil, who are taken captive by him at his will.

3 This know also, that in the last days perilous times shall come.

2 For men shall be lovers of their own selves, covetous, boasters, proud, blasphemers, disobedient to parents, unthankful, unholy,

3 Without natural affection, trucebreakers, false accusers, incontinent, fierce, despisers of those that are good,

4 Traitors, heady, highminded, lovers
of pleasures more than lovers of God;
5 Having a form of godliness, but
denying the power thereof: from such
turn away.
6 For of this sort are they which creep
into houses, and lead captive silly
women laden with sins, led away with
divers lusts,
7 Ever learning, and never able to
come to the knowledge of the truth.
8 Now as Jannes and Jambres withstood Moses, so do these also resist the
truth: men of corrupt minds, reprobate
concerning the faith.
9 But they shall proceed no further:
for their folly shall be manifest unto all
men, as theirs also was.
10 But thou hast fully known my doctrine, manner of life, purpose, faith,
longsuffering, charity, patience,
11 Persecutions, afflictions, which
came unto me at Antioch, at Iconium,
at Lystra; what persecutions I endured:
but out of *them* all the Lord delivered
me.
12 Yea, and all that will live godly in
Christ Jesus shall suffer persecution.
13 But evil men and seducers shall
wax worse and worse, deceiving, and
being deceived.
14 But continue thou in the things
which thou hast learned and hast been
assured of, knowing of whom thou hast
learned *them*;
15 And that from a child thou hast
known the holy scriptures, which are
able to make thee wise unto salvation
through faith which is in Christ Jesus.
16 All scripture *is* given by inspiration of God, and *is* profitable for doctrine, for reproof, for correction, for
instruction in righteousness:
17 That the man of God may be perfect, throughly furnished unto all good
works.

4 I charge *thee* therefore before God,
and the Lord Jesus Christ, who
shall judge the quick and the dead at
his appearing and his kingdom;
2 Preach the word; be instant in season, out of season; reprove, rebuke,
exhort with all longsuffering and doctrine.
3 For the time will come when they
will not endure sound doctrine; but
after their own lusts shall they heap to
themselves teachers, having itching
ears;
4 And they shall turn away *their* ears
from the truth, and shall be turned
unto fables.
5 But watch thou in all things, endure
afflictions, do the work of an evangelist,
make full proof of thy ministry.
6 For I am now ready to be offered,
and the time of my departure is at
hand.
7 I have fought a good fight, I have
finished *my* course, I have kept the
faith:
8 Henceforth there is laid up for me a
crown of righteousness, which the Lord,
the righteous judge, shall give me at
that day: and not to me only, but unto
all them also that love his appearing.
9 Do thy diligence to come shortly
unto me:
10 For Demas hath forsaken me, having loved this present world, and is
departed unto Thessalonica; Crescens
to Galatia, Titus unto Dalmatia.
11 Only Luke is with me. Take Mark,
and bring him with thee: for he is profitable to me for the ministry.
12 And Tychicus have I sent to
Ephesus.

13 The cloke that I left at Troas with Carpus, when thou comest, bring *with thee*, and the books, *but* especially the parchments.

14 Alexander the coppersmith did me much evil: the Lord reward him according to his works:

15 Of whom be thou ware also; for he hath greatly withstood our words.

16 At my first answer no man stood with me, but all *men* forsook me: *I pray God* that it may not be laid to their charge.

17 Notwithstanding the Lord stood with me, and strengthened me; that by me the preaching might be fully known, and *that* all the Gentiles might hear: and I was delivered out of the mouth of the lion.

18 And the Lord shall deliver me from every evil work, and will preserve *me* unto his heavenly kingdom: to whom *be* glory for ever and ever. Amen.

19 Salute Prisca and Aquila, and the household of Onesiphorus.

20 Erastus abode at Corinth: but Trophimus have I left at Miletum sick.

21 Do thy diligence to come before winter. Eubulus greeteth thee, and Pudens, and Linus, and Claudia, and all the brethren.

22 The Lord Jesus Christ *be* with thy spirit. Grace *be* with you. Amen.

THE EPISTLE OF PAUL THE APOSTLE TO

TITUS

1 Paul, a servant of God, and an apostle of Jesus Christ, according to the faith of God's elect, and the acknowledging of the truth which is after godliness;

2 In hope of eternal life, which God, that cannot lie, promised before the world began;

3 But hath in due times manifested his word through preaching, which is committed unto me according to the commandment of God our Saviour;

4 To Titus, *mine* own son after the common faith: Grace, mercy, *and* peace, from God the Father and the Lord Jesus Christ our Saviour.

5 For this cause left I thee in Crete, that thou shouldest set in order the things that are wanting, and ordain elders in every city, as I had appointed thee:

6 If any be blameless, the husband of one wife, having faithful children not accused of riot or unruly.

7 For a bishop must be blameless, as the steward of God; not selfwilled, not soon angry, not given to wine, no striker, not given to filthy lucre;

8 But a lover of hospitality, a lover of good men, sober, just, holy, temperate;

9 Holding fast the faithful word as he hath been taught, that he may be able by sound doctrine both to exhort and to convince the gainsayers.

10 For there are many unruly and vain talkers and deceivers, specially they of the circumcision:

11 Whose mouths must be stopped, who subvert whole houses, teaching things which they ought not, for filthy lucre's sake.

12 One of themselves, *even* a prophet of their own, said, The Cretians *are* alway liars, evil beasts, slow bellies.

13 This witness is true. Wherefore rebuke them sharply, that they may be sound in the faith;

14 Not giving heed to Jewish fables, and commandments of men, that turn from the truth.

15 Unto the pure all things *are* pure: but unto them that are defiled and unbelieving *is* nothing pure; but even their mind and conscience is defiled.

16 They profess that they know God; but in works they deny *him*, being abominable, and disobedient, and unto every good work reprobate.

2 But speak thou the things which become sound doctrine:

2 That the aged men be sober, grave, temperate, sound in faith, in charity, in patience.

3 The aged women likewise, that *they be* in behaviour as becometh holiness, not false accusers, not given to much wine, teachers of good things;

4 That they may teach the young women to be sober, to love their husbands, to love their children,

5 *To be* discreet, chaste, keepers at home, good, obedient to their own husbands, that the word of God be not blasphemed.

6 Young men likewise exhort to be sober minded.

7 In all things shewing thyself a pattern of good works: in doctrine *shewing* uncorruptness, gravity, sincerity,

8 Sound speech, that cannot be condemned; that he that is of the contrary part may be ashamed, having no evil thing to say of you.

9 *Exhort* servants to be obedient unto their own masters, *and* to please *them* well in all *things*; not answering again;

10 Not purloining, but shewing all good fidelity; that they may adorn the doctrine of God our Saviour in all things.

11 For the grace of God that bringeth salvation hath appeared to all men,

12 Teaching us that, denying ungodliness and worldly lusts, we should live soberly, righteously, and godly, in this present world;

13 Looking for that blessed hope, and the glorious appearing of the great God and our Saviour Jesus Christ;

14 Who gave himself for us, that he might redeem us from all iniquity, and purify unto himself a peculiar people, zealous of good works.

15 These things speak, and exhort, and rebuke with all authority. Let no man despise thee.

3 Put them in mind to be subject to principalities and powers, to obey magistrates, to be ready to every good work,

2 To speak evil of no man, to be no brawlers, *but* gentle, shewing all meekness unto all men.

3 For we ourselves also were sometimes foolish, disobedient, deceived, serving divers lusts and pleasures, living in malice and envy, hateful, *and* hating one another.

4 But after that the kindness and love of God our Saviour toward man appeared,

5 Not by works of righteousness which we have done, but according to his mercy he saved us, by the washing of regeneration, and renewing of the Holy Ghost;

6 Which he shed on us abundantly
through Jesus Christ our Saviour;
7 That being justified by his grace, we
should be made heirs according to the
hope of eternal life.
8 *This is* a faithful saying, and these
things I will that thou affirm constantly,
that they which have believed in God
might be careful to maintain good
works. These things are good and profitable unto men.
9 But avoid foolish questions, and
genealogies, and contentions, and strivings about the law; for they are unprofitable and vain.
10 A man that is an heretick after the
first and second admonition reject;
11 Knowing that he that is such is
subverted, and sinneth, being condemned of himself.
12 When I shall send Artemas unto
thee, or Tychicus, be diligent to come
unto me to Nicopolis: for I have determined there to winter.
13 Bring Zenas the lawyer and
Apollos on their journey diligently, that
nothing be wanting unto them.
14 And let ours also learn to maintain
good works for necessary uses, that
they be not unfruitful.
15 All that are with me salute thee.
Greet them that love us in the faith.
Grace *be* with you all. Amen.

THE EPISTLE OF PAUL THE APOSTLE TO

PHILEMON

1 Paul, a prisoner of Jesus Christ, and
Timothy *our* brother, unto Philemon
our dearly beloved, and fellowlabourer,
2 And to *our* beloved Apphia, and
Archippus our fellowsoldier, and to the
church in thy house:
3 Grace to you, and peace, from God
our Father and the Lord Jesus Christ.
4 I thank my God, making mention of
thee always in my prayers,
5 Hearing of thy love and faith, which
thou hast toward the Lord Jesus, and
toward all saints;
6 That the communication of thy faith
may become effectual by the acknowledging of every good thing which is in
you in Christ Jesus.
7 For we have great joy and consolation in thy love, because the bowels
of the saints are refreshed by thee,
brother.
8 Wherefore, though I might be much
bold in Christ to enjoin thee that which
is convenient,
9 Yet for love's sake I rather beseech
thee, being such an one as Paul the
aged, and now also a prisoner of Jesus
Christ.
10 I beseech thee for my son
Onesimus, whom I have begotten in my
bonds:
11 Which in time past was to thee
unprofitable, but now profitable to
thee and to me:
12 Whom I have sent again: thou
therefore receive him, that is, mine own
bowels:
13 Whom I would have retained with
me, that in thy stead he might have
ministered unto me in the bonds of the
gospel:

14 But without thy mind would I do nothing; that thy benefit should not be as it were of necessity, but willingly.

15 For perhaps he therefore departed for a season, that thou shouldest receive him for ever;

16 Not now as a servant, but above a servant, a brother beloved, specially to me, but how much more unto thee, both in the flesh, and in the Lord?

17 If thou count me therefore a partner, receive him as myself.

18 If he hath wronged thee, or oweth *thee* ought, put that on mine account;

19 I Paul have written *it* with mine own hand, I will repay *it*: albeit I do not say to thee how thou owest unto me even thine own self besides.

20 Yea, brother, let me have joy of thee in the Lord: refresh my bowels in the Lord.

21 Having confidence in thy obedience I wrote unto thee, knowing that thou wilt also do more than I say.

22 But withal prepare me also a lodging: for I trust that through your prayers I shall be given unto you.

23 There salute thee Epaphras, my fellowprisoner in Christ Jesus;

24 Marcus, Aristarchus, Demas, Lucas, my fellowlabourers.

25 The grace of our Lord Jesus Christ *be* with your spirit. Amen.

THE EPISTLE OF PAUL THE APOSTLE
TO THE

HEBREWS

1 God, who at sundry times and in divers manners spake in time past unto the fathers by the prophets,

2 Hath in these last days spoken unto us by *his* Son, whom he hath appointed heir of all things, by whom also he made the worlds;

3 Who being the brightness of *his* glory, and the express image of his person, and upholding all things by the word of his power, when he had by himself purged our sins, sat down on the right hand of the Majesty on high;

4 Being made so much better than the angels, as he hath by inheritance obtained a more excellent name than they.

5 For unto which of the angels said he at any time, Thou art my Son, this day have I begotten thee? And again, I will be to him a Father, and he shall be to me a Son?

6 And again, when he bringeth in the firstbegotten into the world, he saith, And let all the angels of God worship him.

7 And of the angels he saith, Who maketh his angels spirits, and his ministers a flame of fire.

8 But unto the Son *he saith*, Thy throne, O God, *is* for ever and ever: a sceptre of righteousness *is* the sceptre of thy kingdom.

9 Thou hast loved righteousness, and hated iniquity; therefore God, *even* thy God, hath anointed thee with the oil of gladness above thy fellows.

10 And, Thou, Lord, in the beginning hast laid the foundation of the earth; and the heavens are the works of thine hands:

11 They shall perish; but thou remainest; and they all shall wax old as doth a garment;

12 And as a vesture shalt thou fold them up, and they shall be changed: but thou art the same, and thy years shall not fail.

13 But to which of the angels said he at any time, Sit on my right hand, until I make thine enemies thy footstool?

14 Are they not all ministering spirits, sent forth to minister for them who shall be heirs of salvation?

2 Therefore we ought to give the more earnest heed to the things which we have heard, lest at any time we should let *them* slip.

2 For if the word spoken by angels was stedfast, and every transgression and disobedience received a just recompence of reward;

3 How shall we escape, if we neglect so great salvation; which at the first began to be spoken by the Lord, and was confirmed unto us by them that heard *him*;

4 God also bearing *them* witness, both with signs and wonders, and with divers miracles, and gifts of the Holy Ghost, according to his own will?

5 For unto the angels hath he not put in subjection the world to come, whereof we speak.

6 But one in a certain place testified, saying, What is man, that thou art mindful of him? or the son of man, that thou visitest him?

7 Thou madest him a little lower than the angels; thou crownedst him with glory and honour, and didst set him over the works of thy hands:

8 Thou hast put all things in subjection under his feet. For in that he put all in subjection under him, he left nothing *that is* not put under him. But now we see not yet all things put under him.

9 But we see Jesus, who was made a little lower than the angels for the suffering of death, crowned with glory and honour; that he by the grace of God should taste death for every man.

10 For it became him, for whom *are* all things, and by whom *are* all things, in bringing many sons unto glory, to make the captain of their salvation perfect through sufferings.

11 For both he that sanctifieth and they who are sanctified *are* all of one: for which cause he is not ashamed to call them brethren,

12 Saying, I will declare thy name unto my brethren, in the midst of the church will I sing praise unto thee.

13 And again, I will put my trust in him. And again, Behold I and the children which God hath given me.

14 Forasmuch then as the children are partakers of flesh and blood, he also himself likewise took part of the same; that through death he might destroy him that had the power of death, that is, the devil;

15 And deliver them who through fear of death were all their lifetime subject to bondage.

16 For verily he took not on *him the nature of* angels; but he took on *him* the seed of Abraham.

17 Wherefore in all things it behoved him to be made like unto *his* brethren,

that he might be a merciful and faithful
high priest in things *pertaining* to God,
to make reconciliation for the sins of
the people.
18 For in that he himself hath suffered being tempted, he is able to succour them that are tempted.

3 Wherefore, holy brethren, partakers
of the heavenly calling, consider
the Apostle and High Priest of our
profession, Christ Jesus;
2 Who was faithful to him that appointed him, as also Moses *was faithful*
in all his house.
3 For this *man* was counted worthy of
more glory than Moses, inasmuch as he
who hath builded the house hath more
honour than the house.
4 For every house is builded by some
man; but he that built all things *is* God.
5 And Moses verily *was* faithful in all
his house, as a servant, for a testimony
of those things which were to be spoken after;
6 But Christ as a son over his own
house; whose house are we, if we hold
fast the confidence and the rejoicing of
the hope firm unto the end.
7 Wherefore (as the Holy Ghost saith,
To day if ye will hear his voice,
8 Harden not your hearts, as in the
provocation, in the day of temptation in
the wilderness:
9 When your fathers tempted me,
proved me, and saw my works forty
years.
10 Wherefore I was grieved with that
generation, and said, They do alway err
in *their* heart; and they have not known
my ways.
11 So I sware in my wrath, They shall
not enter into my rest.)
12 Take heed, brethren, lest there be
in any of you an evil heart of unbelief,
in departing from the living God.
13 But exhort one another daily, while
it is called To day; lest any of you be
hardened through the deceitfulness of
sin.
14 For we are made partakers of
Christ, if we hold the beginning of our
confidence stedfast unto the end;
15 While it is said, To day if ye will
hear his voice, harden not your hearts,
as in the provocation.
16 For some, when they had heard,
did provoke: howbeit not all that came
out of Egypt by Moses.
17 But with whom was he grieved
forty years? *was it* not with them that
had sinned, whose carcases fell in the
wilderness?
18 And to whom sware he that they
should not enter into his rest, but to
them that believed not?
19 So we see that they could not enter
in because of unbelief.

4 Let us therefore fear, lest, a promise
being left *us* of entering into his
rest, any of you should seem to come
short of it.
2 For unto us was the gospel preached,
as well as unto them: but the word
preached did not profit them, not being
mixed with faith in them that heard *it*.
3 For we which have believed do
enter into rest, as he said, As I have
sworn in my wrath, if they shall enter
into my rest: although the works were
finished from the foundation of the
world.
4 For he spake in a certain place of
the seventh *day* on this wise, And God
did rest the seventh day from all his
works.

5 And in this *place* again, If they shall
enter into my rest.
6 Seeing therefore it remaineth that
some must enter therein, and they to
whom it was first preached entered not
in because of unbelief:
7 Again, he limiteth a certain day, saying in David, To day, after so long a
time; as it is said, To day if ye will hear
his voice, harden not your hearts.
8 For if Jesus had given them rest,
then would he not afterward have spoken of another day.
9 There remaineth therefore a rest to
the people of God.
10 For he that is entered into his rest,
he also hath ceased from his own
works, as God *did* from his.
11 Let us labour therefore to enter
into that rest, lest any man fall after the
same example of unbelief.
12 For the word of God *is* quick, and
powerful, and sharper than any twoedged sword, piercing even to the dividing asunder of soul and spirit, and of
the joints and marrow, and *is* a dis-
cerner of the thoughts and intents of
the heart.
13 Neither is there any creature that
is not manifest in his sight: but all
things *are* naked and opened unto the
eyes of him with whom we have to do.
14 Seeing then that we have a great
high priest, that is passed into the heavens, Jesus the Son of God, let us hold
fast *our* profession.
15 For we have not an high priest
which cannot be touched with the feeling of our infirmities; but was in all
points tempted like as *we are, yet* without sin.
16 Let us therefore come boldly unto
the throne of grace, that we may obtain
mercy, and find grace to help in time of
need.

5 For every high priest taken from
among men is ordained for men in
things *pertaining* to God, that he may
offer both gifts and sacrifices for sins:
2 Who can have compassion on the
ignorant, and on them that are out of
the way; for that he himself also is compassed with infirmity.
3 And by reason hereof he ought, as
for the people, so also for himself, to
offer for sins.
4 And no man taketh this honour
unto himself, but he that is called of
God, as *was* Aaron.
5 So also Christ glorified not himself
to be made an high priest; but he that
said unto him, Thou art my Son, to day
have I begotten thee.
6 As he saith also in another *place*,
Thou *art* a priest for ever after the
order of Melchisedec.
7 Who in the days of his flesh, when
he had offered up prayers and supplications with strong crying and tears unto
him that was able to save him from
death, and was heard in that he feared;
8 Though he were a Son, yet learned
he obedience by the things which he
suffered;
9 And being made perfect, he became
the author of eternal salvation unto all
them that obey him;
10 Called of God an high priest after
the order of Melchisedec.
11 Of whom we have many things to
say, and hard to be uttered, seeing ye
are dull of hearing.
12 For when for the time ye ought to
be teachers, ye have need that one
teach you again which *be* the first prin-

ciples of the oracles of God; and are become such as have need of milk, and not of strong meat.

13 For every one that useth milk *is* unskilful in the word of righteousness: for he is a babe.

14 But strong meat belongeth to them that are of full age, *even* those who by reason of use have their senses exercised to discern both good and evil.

6

Therefore leaving the principles of the doctrine of Christ, let us go on unto perfection; not laying again the foundation of repentance from dead works, and of faith toward God,

2 Of the doctrine of baptisms, and of laying on of hands, and of resurrection of the dead, and of eternal judgment.

3 And this will we do, if God permit.

4 For *it is* impossible for those who were once enlightened, and have tasted of the heavenly gift, and were made partakers of the Holy Ghost,

5 And have tasted the good word of God, and the powers of the world to come,

6 If they shall fall away, to renew them again unto repentance; seeing they crucify to themselves the Son of God afresh, and put *him* to an open shame.

7 For the earth which drinketh in the rain that cometh oft upon it, and bringeth forth herbs meet for them by whom it is dressed, receiveth blessing from God:

8 But that which beareth thorns and briers *is* rejected, and *is* nigh unto cursing; whose end *is* to be burned.

9 But, beloved, we are persuaded better things of you, and things that accompany salvation, though we thus speak.

10 For God *is* not unrighteous to forget your work and labour of love, which ye have shewed toward his name, in that ye have ministered to the saints, and do minister.

11 And we desire that every one of you do shew the same diligence to the full assurance of hope unto the end:

12 That ye be not slothful, but followers of them who through faith and patience inherit the promises.

13 For when God made promise to Abraham, because he could swear by no greater, he sware by himself,

14 Saying, Surely blessing I will bless thee, and multiplying I will multiply thee.

15 And so, after he had patiently endured, he obtained the promise.

16 For men verily swear by the greater: and an oath for confirmation *is* to them an end of all strife.

17 Wherein God, willing more abundantly to shew unto the heirs of promise the immutability of his counsel, confirmed *it* by an oath:

18 That by two immutable things, in which *it was* impossible for God to lie, we might have a strong consolation, who have fled for refuge to lay hold upon the hope set before us:

19 Which *hope* we have as an anchor of the soul, both sure and stedfast, and which entereth into that within the veil;

20 Whither the forerunner is for us entered, *even* Jesus, made an high priest for ever after the order of Melchisedec.

7

For this Melchisedec, king of Salem, priest of the most high God, who met Abraham returning from the slaughter of the kings, and blessed him;

2 To whom also Abraham gave a tenth part of all; first being by interpretation King of righteousness, and after that also King of Salem, which is, King of peace;

3 Without father, without mother, without descent, having neither beginning of days, nor end of life; but made like unto the Son of God; abideth a priest continually.

4 Now consider how great this man *was*, unto whom even the patriarch Abraham gave the tenth of the spoils.

5 And verily they that are of the sons of Levi, who receive the office of the priesthood, have a commandment to take tithes of the people according to the law, that is, of their brethren, though they come out of the loins of Abraham:

6 But he whose descent is not counted from them received tithes of Abraham, and blessed him that had the promises.

7 And without all contradiction the less is blessed of the better.

8 And here men that die receive tithes; but there he *receiveth them*, of whom it is witnessed that he liveth.

9 And as I may so say, Levi also, who receiveth tithes, payed tithes in Abraham.

10 For he was yet in the loins of his father, when Melchisedec met him.

11 If therefore perfection were by the Levitical priesthood, (for under it the people received the law,) what further need *was there* that another priest should rise after the order of Melchisedec, and not be called after the order of Aaron?

12 For the priesthood being changed, there is made of necessity a change also of the law.

13 For he of whom these things are spoken pertaineth to another tribe, of which no man gave attendance at the altar.

14 For *it is* evident that our Lord sprang out of Juda; of which tribe Moses spake nothing concerning priesthood.

15 And it is yet far more evident: for that after the similitude of Melchisedec there ariseth another priest,

16 Who is made, not after the law of a carnal commandment, but after the power of an endless life.

17 For he testifieth, Thou *art* a priest for ever after the order of Melchisedec.

18 For there is verily a disannulling of the commandment going before for the weakness and unprofitableness thereof.

19 For the law made nothing perfect, but the bringing in of a better hope *did*; by the which we draw nigh unto God.

20 And inasmuch as not without an oath *he was made priest*:

21 (For those priests were made without an oath; but this with an oath by him that said unto him, The Lord sware and will not repent, Thou *art* a priest for ever after the order of Melchisedec:)

22 By so much was Jesus made a surety of a better testament.

23 And they truly were many priests, because they were not suffered to continue by reason of death:

24 But this *man*, because he continueth ever, hath an unchangeable priesthood.

25 Wherefore he is able also to save them to the uttermost that come unto God by him, seeing he ever liveth to make intercession for them.

26 For such an high priest became us, *who is* holy, harmless, undefiled, separate from sinners, and made higher than the heavens;

27 Who needeth not daily, as those high priests, to offer up sacrifice, first for his own sins, and then for the people's: for this he did once, when he offered up himself.

28 For the law maketh men high priests which have infirmity; but the word of the oath, which was since the law, *maketh* the Son, who is consecrated for evermore.

8 Now of the things which we have spoken *this is* the sum: We have such an high priest, who is set on the right hand of the throne of the Majesty in the heavens;

2 A minister of the sanctuary, and of the true tabernacle, which the Lord pitched, and not man.

3 For every high priest is ordained to offer gifts and sacrifices: wherefore *it is* of necessity that this man have somewhat also to offer.

4 For if he were on earth, he should not be a priest, seeing that there are priests that offer gifts according to the law:

5 Who serve unto the example and shadow of heavenly things, as Moses was admonished of God when he was about to make the tabernacle: for, See, saith he, *that* thou make all things according to the pattern shewed to thee in the mount.

6 But now hath he obtained a more excellent ministry, by how much also he is the mediator of a better covenant, which was established upon better promises.

7 For if that first *covenant* had been faultless, then should no place have been sought for the second.

8 For finding fault with them, he saith, Behold, the days come, saith the Lord, when I will make a new covenant with the house of Israel and with the house of Judah:

9 Not according to the covenant that I made with their fathers in the day when I took them by the hand to lead them out of the land of Egypt; because they continued not in my covenant, and I regarded them not, saith the Lord.

10 For this *is* the covenant that I will make with the house of Israel after those days, saith the Lord; I will put my laws into their mind, and write them in their hearts: and I will be to them a God, and they shall be to me a people:

11 And they shall not teach every man his neighbour, and every man his brother, saying, Know the Lord: for all shall know me, from the least to the greatest.

12 For I will be merciful to their unrighteousness, and their sins and their iniquities will I remember no more.

13 In that he saith, A new *covenant*, he hath made the first old. Now that which decayeth and waxeth old *is* ready to vanish away.

9 Then verily the first *covenant* had also ordinances of divine service, and a worldly sanctuary.

2 For there was a tabernacle made; the first, wherein *was* the candlestick, and the table, and the shewbread; which is called the sanctuary.

3 And after the second veil, the tabernacle which is called the Holiest of all;

4 Which had the golden censer, and the ark of the covenant overlaid round about with gold, wherein *was* the gold-

en pot that had manna, and Aaron's rod
that budded, and the tables of the covenant;
5 And over it the cherubims of glory
shadowing the mercyseat; of which we
cannot now speak particularly.
6 Now when these things were thus
ordained, the priests went always into
the first tabernacle, accomplishing the
service *of God*.
7 But into the second *went* the high
priest alone once every year, not without blood, which he offered for himself,
and *for* the errors of the people:
8 The Holy Ghost this signifying, that
the way into the holiest of all was not
yet made manifest, while as the first
tabernacle was yet standing:
9 Which *was* a figure for the time
then present, in which were offered
both gifts and sacrifices, that could not
make him that did the service perfect,
as pertaining to the conscience;
10 *Which stood* only in meats and
drinks, and divers washings, and carnal
ordinances, imposed *on them* until the
time of reformation.
11 But Christ being come an high
priest of good things to come, by a
greater and more perfect tabernacle,
not made with hands, that is to say, not
of this building;
12 Neither by the blood of goats and
calves, but by his own blood he entered
in once into the holy place, having
obtained eternal redemption *for us*.
13 For if the blood of bulls and of
goats, and the ashes of an heifer sprinkling the unclean, sanctifieth to the
purifying of the flesh:
14 How much more shall the blood of
Christ, who through the eternal Spirit
offered himself without spot to God,
purge your conscience from dead works
to serve the living God?
15 And for this cause he is the mediator of the new testament, that by means
of death, for the redemption of the
transgressions *that were* under the first
testament, they which are called might
receive the promise of eternal inheritance.
16 For where a testament *is*, there
must also of necessity be the death of
the testator.
17 For a testament *is* of force after
men are dead: otherwise it is of no
strength at all while the testator liveth.
18 Whereupon neither the first *testament* was dedicated without blood.
19 For when Moses had spoken every
precept to all the people according to
the law, he took the blood of calves and
of goats, with water, and scarlet wool,
and hyssop, and sprinkled both the
book, and all the people,
20 Saying, This *is* the blood of the
testament which God hath enjoined
unto you.
21 Moreover he sprinkled with blood
both the tabernacle, and all the vessels
of the ministry.
22 And almost all things are by the
law purged with blood; and without
shedding of blood is no remission.
23 *It was* therefore necessary that the
patterns of things in the heavens
should be purified with these; but the
heavenly things themselves with better
sacrifices than these.
24 For Christ is not entered into the
holy places made with hands, *which
are* the figures of the true; but into
heaven itself, now to appear in the presence of God for us:

25 Nor yet that he should offer himself often, as the high priest entereth
into the holy place every year with
blood of others;
26 For then must he often have suffered since the foundation of the world:
but now once in the end of the world
hath he appeared to put away sin by
the sacrifice of himself.
27 And as it is appointed unto men
once to die, but after this the judgment:
28 So Christ was once offered to bear
the sins of many; and unto them that
look for him shall he appear the second
time without sin unto salvation.

10 For the law having a shadow of
good things to come, *and* not the
very image of the things, can never
with those sacrifices which they offered
year by year continually make the com-
ers thereunto perfect.
2 For then would they not have
ceased to be offered? because that the
worshippers once purged should have
had no more conscience of sins.
3 But in those *sacrifices there is* a
remembrance again *made* of sins every
year.
4 For *it is* not possible that the blood
of bulls and of goats should take away
sins.
5 Wherefore when he cometh into the
world, he saith, Sacrifice and offering
thou wouldest not, but a body hast thou
prepared me:
6 In burnt offerings and *sacrifices* for
sin thou hast had no pleasure.
7 Then said I, Lo, I come (in the volume of the book it is written of me,) to
do thy will, O God.
8 Above when he said, Sacrifice and
offering and burnt offerings and *offering* for sin thou wouldest not, neither
hadst pleasure *therein*; which are offered by the law;
9 Then said he, Lo, I come to do thy
will, O God. He taketh away the first,
that he may establish the second.
10 By the which will we are sanctified
through the offering of the body of
Jesus Christ once *for all*.
11 And every priest standeth daily
ministering and offering oftentimes
the same sacrifices, which can never
take away sins:
12 But this man, after he had offered
one sacrifice for sins for ever, sat down
on the right hand of God;
13 From henceforth expecting till his
enemies be made his footstool.
14 For by one offering he hath perfected for ever them that are sanctified.
15 *Whereof* the Holy Ghost also is a
witness to us: for after that he had said
before,
16 This *is* the covenant that I will
make with them after those days, saith
the Lord, I will put my laws into their
hearts, and in their minds will I write
them;
17 And their sins and iniquities will I
remember no more.
18 Now where remission of these *is*,
there is no more offering for sin.
19 Having therefore, brethren, boldness to enter into the holiest by the
blood of Jesus,
20 By a new and living way, which he
hath consecrated for us, through the
veil, that is to say, his flesh;
21 And *having* an high priest over the
house of God;
22 Let us draw near with a true heart
in full assurance of faith, having our
hearts sprinkled from an evil

conscience, and our bodies washed with pure water.

23 Let us hold fast the profession of *our* faith without wavering; (for he *is* faithful that promised;)

24 And let us consider one another to provoke unto love and to good works:

25 Not forsaking the assembling of ourselves together, as the manner of some *is*; but exhorting *one another*: and so much the more, as ye see the day approaching.

26 For if we sin wilfully after that we have received the knowledge of the truth, there remaineth no more sacrifice for sins,

27 But a certain fearful looking for of judgment and fiery indignation, which shall devour the adversaries.

28 He that despised Moses' law died without mercy under two or three witnesses:

29 Of how much sorer punishment, suppose ye, shall he be thought worthy, who hath trodden under foot the Son of God, and hath counted the blood of the covenant, wherewith he was sanctified, an unholy thing, and hath done despite unto the Spirit of grace?

30 For we know him that hath said, Vengeance *belongeth* unto me, I will recompense, saith the Lord. And again, The Lord shall judge his people.

31 *It is* a fearful thing to fall into the hands of the living God.

32 But call to remembrance the former days, in which, after ye were illuminated, ye endured a great fight of afflictions;

33 Partly, whilst ye were made a gazingstock both by reproaches and afflictions; and partly, whilst ye became companions of them that were so used.

34 For ye had compassion of me in my bonds, and took joyfully the spoiling of your goods, knowing in yourselves that ye have in heaven a better and an enduring substance.

35 Cast not away therefore your confidence, which hath great recompence of reward.

36 For ye have need of patience, that, after ye have done the will of God, ye might receive the promise.

37 For yet a little while, and he that shall come will come, and will not tarry.

38 Now the just shall live by faith: but if *any man* draw back, my soul shall have no pleasure in him.

39 But we are not of them who draw back unto perdition; but of them that believe to the saving of the soul.

11 Now faith is the substance of things hoped for, the evidence of things not seen.

2 For by it the elders obtained a good report.

3 Through faith we understand that the worlds were framed by the word of God, so that things which are seen were not made of things which do appear.

4 By faith Abel offered unto God a more excellent sacrifice than Cain, by which he obtained witness that he was righteous, God testifying of his gifts: and by it he being dead yet speaketh.

5 By faith Enoch was translated that he should not see death; and was not found, because God had translated him: for before his translation he had this testimony, that he pleased God.

6 But without faith *it is* impossible to please *him*: for he that cometh to God must believe that he is, and *that* he is a rewarder of them that diligently seek him.

7 By faith Noah, being warned of God
of things not seen as yet, moved with
fear, prepared an ark to the saving of
his house; by the which he condemned
the world, and became heir of the righteousness which is by faith.

8 By faith Abraham, when he was
called to go out into a place which he
should after receive for an inheritance,
obeyed; and he went out, not knowing
whither he went.

9 By faith he sojourned in the land of
promise, as *in* a strange country, dwelling in tabernacles with Isaac and Jacob,
the heirs with him of the same promise:

10 For he looked for a city which hath
foundations, whose builder and maker
is God.

11 Through faith also Sara herself
received strength to conceive seed, and
was delivered of a child when she was
past age, because she judged him faithful who had promised.

12 Therefore sprang there even of
one, and him as good as dead, *so many*
as the stars of the sky in multitude, and
as the sand which is by the sea shore
innumerable.

13 These all died in faith, not having
received the promises, but having seen
them afar off, and were persuaded of
them, and embraced *them*, and confessed that they were strangers and
pilgrims on the earth.

14 For they that say such things
declare plainly that they seek a country.

15 And truly, if they had been mindful of that *country* from whence they
came out, they might have had opportunity to have returned.

16 But now they desire a better *country*, that is, an heavenly: wherefore God
is not ashamed to be called their God:
for he hath prepared for them a city.

17 By faith Abraham, when he was
tried, offered up Isaac: and he that had
received the promises offered up his
only begotten *son*,

18 Of whom it was said, That in Isaac
shall thy seed be called:

19 Accounting that God *was* able to
raise *him* up, even from the dead; from
whence also he received him in a figure.

20 By faith Isaac blessed Jacob and
Esau concerning things to come.

21 By faith Jacob, when he was a
dying, blessed both the sons of Joseph;
and worshipped, *leaning* upon the top
of his staff.

22 By faith Joseph, when he died,
made mention of the departing of the
children of Israel; and gave commandment concerning his bones.

23 By faith Moses, when he was born,
was hid three months of his parents,
because they saw *he was* a proper
child; and they were not afraid of the
king's commandment.

24 By faith Moses, when he was come
to years, refused to be called the son of
Pharaoh's daughter;

25 Choosing rather to suffer affliction
with the people of God, than to enjoy
the pleasures of sin for a season;

26 Esteeming the reproach of Christ
greater riches than the treasures in
Egypt: for he had respect unto the recompence of the reward.

27 By faith he forsook Egypt, not fearing the wrath of the king: for he
endured, as seeing him who is invisible.

28 Through faith he kept the passover, and the sprinkling of blood, lest he that destroyed the firstborn should touch them.

29 By faith they passed through the Red sea as by dry *land*: which the Egyptians assaying to do were drowned.

30 By faith the walls of Jericho fell down, after they were compassed about seven days.

31 By faith the harlot Rahab perished not with them that believed not, when she had received the spies with peace.

32 And what shall I more say? for the time would fail me to tell of Gedeon, and *of* Barak, and *of* Samson, and *of* Jephthae; *of* David also, and Samuel, and *of* the prophets:

33 Who through faith subdued kingdoms, wrought righteousness, obtained promises, stopped the mouths of lions,

34 Quenched the violence of fire, escaped the edge of the sword, out of weakness were made strong, waxed valiant in fight, turned to flight the armies of the aliens.

35 Women received their dead raised to life again: and others were tortured, not accepting deliverance; that they might obtain a better resurrection:

36 And others had trial of *cruel* mockings and scourgings, yea, moreover of bonds and imprisonment:

37 They were stoned, they were sawn asunder, were tempted, were slain with the sword: they wandered about in sheepskins and goatskins; being destitute, afflicted, tormented;

38 (Of whom the world was not worthy:) they wandered in deserts, and *in* mountains, and *in* dens and caves of the earth.

39 And these all, having obtained a good report through faith, received not the promise:

40 God having provided some better thing for us, that they without us should not be made perfect.

12 Wherefore seeing we also are compassed about with so great a cloud of witnesses, let us lay aside every weight, and the sin which doth so easily beset *us*, and let us run with patience the race that is set before us,

2 Looking unto Jesus the author and finisher of *our* faith; who for the joy that was set before him endured the cross, despising the shame, and is set down at the right hand of the throne of God.

3 For consider him that endured such contradiction of sinners against himself, lest ye be wearied and faint in your minds.

4 Ye have not yet resisted unto blood, striving against sin.

5 And ye have forgotten the exhortation which speaketh unto you as unto children, My son, despise not thou the chastening of the Lord, nor faint when thou art rebuked of him:

6 For whom the Lord loveth he chasteneth, and scourgeth every son whom he receiveth.

7 If ye endure chastening, God dealeth with you as with sons; for what son is he whom the father chasteneth not?

8 But if ye be without chastisement, whereof all are partakers, then are ye bastards, and not sons.

9 Furthermore we have had fathers of our flesh which corrected *us*, and we gave *them* reverence: shall we not much rather be in subjection unto the Father of spirits, and live?

10 For they verily for a few days chastened *us* after their own pleasure; but
he for *our* profit, that *we* might be partakers of his holiness.
11 Now no chastening for the present
seemeth to be joyous, but grievous:
nevertheless afterward it yieldeth the
peaceable fruit of righteousness unto
them which are exercised thereby.
12 Wherefore lift up the hands which
hang down, and the feeble knees;
13 And make straight paths for your
feet, lest that which is lame be turned
out of the way; but let it rather be
healed.
14 Follow peace with all *men*, and
holiness, without which no man shall
see the Lord:
15 Looking diligently lest any man
fail of the grace of God; lest any root of
bitterness springing up trouble *you*,
and thereby many be defiled;
16 Lest there *be* any fornicator, or
profane person, as Esau, who for one
morsel of meat sold his birthright.
17 For ye know how that afterward,
when he would have inherited the
blessing, he was rejected: for he found
no place of repentance, though he
sought it carefully with tears.
18 For ye are not come unto the
mount that might be touched, and that
burned with fire, nor unto blackness,
and darkness, and tempest,
19 And the sound of a trumpet, and
the voice of words; which *voice* they
that heard intreated that the word
should not be spoken to them any
more:
20 (For they could not endure that
which was commanded, And if so much
as a beast touch the mountain, it shall
be stoned, or thrust through with a
dart:
21 And so terrible was the sight, *that*
Moses said, I exceedingly fear and
quake:)
22 But ye are come unto mount Sion,
and unto the city of the living God, the
heavenly Jerusalem, and to an innumerable company of angels,
23 To the general assembly and
church of the firstborn, which are written in heaven, and to God the Judge of
all, and to the spirits of just men made
perfect,
24 And to Jesus the mediator of the
new covenant, and to the blood of
sprinkling, that speaketh better things
than *that of* Abel.
25 See that ye refuse not him that
speaketh. For if they escaped not who
refused him that spake on earth, much
more *shall not* we *escape*, if we turn
away from him that *speaketh* from
heaven:
26 Whose voice then shook the earth:
but now he hath promised, saying, Yet
once more I shake not the earth only,
but also heaven.
27 And this *word*, Yet once more, sig-
nifieth the removing of those things
that are shaken, as of things that are
made, that those things which cannot
be shaken may remain.
28 Wherefore we receiving a kingdom
which cannot be moved, let us have
grace, whereby we may serve God
acceptably with reverence and godly
fear:
29 For our God *is* a consuming fire.

13 Let brotherly love continue.
2 Be not forgetful to entertain
strangers: for thereby some have enter-
tained angels unawares.
3 Remember them that are in bonds,
as bound with them; *and* them which

suffer adversity, as being yourselves
also in the body.
4 Marriage *is* honourable in all, and
the bed undefiled: but whoremongers
and adulterers God will judge.
5 *Let your* conversation *be* without
covetousness; *and be* content with such
things as ye have: for he hath said, I will
never leave thee, nor forsake thee.
6 So that we may boldly say, The Lord
is my helper, and I will not fear what
man shall do unto me.
7 Remember them which have the
rule over you, who have spoken unto
you the word of God: whose faith follow,
considering the end of *their* conversation.
8 Jesus Christ the same yesterday,
and to day, and for ever.
9 Be not carried about with divers
and strange doctrines. For *it is* a good
thing that the heart be established with
grace; not with meats, which have not
profited them that have been occupied
therein.
10 We have an altar, whereof they
have no right to eat which serve the
tabernacle.
11 For the bodies of those beasts,
whose blood is brought into the sanctuary by the high priest for sin, are
burned without the camp.
12 Wherefore Jesus also, that he
might sanctify the people with his own
blood, suffered without the gate.
13 Let us go forth therefore unto him
without the camp, bearing his reproach.
14 For here have we no continuing
city, but we seek one to come.
15 By him therefore let us offer the
sacrifice of praise to God continually,
that is, the fruit of *our* lips giving
thanks to his name.
16 But to do good and to communicate forget not: for with such sacrifices
God is well pleased.
17 Obey them that have the rule over
you, and submit yourselves: for they
watch for your souls, as they that must
give account, that they may do it with
joy, and not with grief: for that *is*
unprofitable for you.
18 Pray for us: for we trust we have a
good conscience, in all things willing to
live honestly.
19 But I beseech *you* the rather to do
this, that I may be restored to you the
sooner.
20 Now the God of peace, that
brought again from the dead our Lord
Jesus, that great shepherd of the sheep,
through the blood of the everlasting
covenant,
21 Make you perfect in every good
work to do his will, working in you that
which is wellpleasing in his sight,
through Jesus Christ; to whom *be* glory
for ever and ever. Amen.
22 And I beseech you, brethren, suffer the word of exhortation: for I have
written a letter unto you in few words.
23 Know ye that *our* brother Timothy
is set at liberty; with whom, if he come
shortly, I will see you.
24 Salute all them that have the rule
over you, and all the saints. They of
Italy salute you.
25 Grace *be* with you all. Amen.

THE GENERAL EPISTLE OF
JAMES

1 James, a servant of God and of the
Lord Jesus Christ, to the twelve
tribes which are scattered abroad,
greeting.
2 My brethren, count it all joy when
ye fall into divers temptations;
3 Knowing *this*, that the trying of
your faith worketh patience.
4 But let patience have *her* perfect
work, that ye may be perfect and
entire, wanting nothing.
5 If any of you lack wisdom, let him
ask of God, that giveth to all *men* liberally, and upbraideth not; and it shall be
given him.
6 But let him ask in faith, nothing
wavering. For he that wavereth is like a
wave of the sea driven with the wind
and tossed.
7 For let not that man think that he
shall receive any thing of the Lord.
8 A double minded man *is* unstable in
all his ways.
9 Let the brother of low degree
rejoice in that he is exalted:
10 But the rich, in that he is made low:
because as the flower of the grass he
shall pass away.
11 For the sun is no sooner risen with
a burning heat, but it withereth the
grass, and the flower thereof falleth,
and the grace of the fashion of it perisheth: so also shall the rich man fade
away in his ways.
12 Blessed *is* the man that endureth
temptation: for when he is tried, he
shall receive the crown of life, which
the Lord hath promised to them that
love him.
13 Let no man say when he is tempted, I am tempted of God: for God cannot be tempted with evil, neither
tempteth he any man:
14 But every man is tempted, when he
is drawn away of his own lust, and
enticed.
15 Then when lust hath conceived, it
bringeth forth sin: and sin, when it is
finished, bringeth forth death.
16 Do not err, my beloved brethren.
17 Every good gift and every perfect
gift is from above, and cometh down
from the Father of lights, with whom is
no variableness, neither shadow of
turning.
18 Of his own will begat he us with
the word of truth, that we should be a
kind of firstfruits of his creatures.
19 Wherefore, my beloved brethren,
let every man be swift to hear, slow to
speak, slow to wrath:
20 For the wrath of man worketh not
the righteousness of God.
21 Wherefore lay apart all filthiness
and superfluity of naughtiness, and
receive with meekness the engrafted
word, which is able to save your souls.
22 But be ye doers of the word, and
not hearers only, deceiving your own
selves.
23 For if any be a hearer of the word,
and not a doer, he is like unto a man
beholding his natural face in a glass:
24 For he beholdeth himself, and
goeth his way, and straightway forgetteth what manner of man he was.
25 But whoso looketh into the perfect
law of liberty, and continueth *therein*,
he being not a forgetful hearer, but a

doer of the work, this man shall be blessed in his deed.

26 If any man among you seem to be religious, and bridleth not his tongue, but deceiveth his own heart, this man's religion *is* vain.

27 Pure religion and undefiled before God and the Father is this, To visit the fatherless and widows in their affliction, *and* to keep himself unspotted from the world.

2 My brethren, have not the faith of our Lord Jesus Christ, *the Lord* of glory, with respect of persons.

2 For if there come unto your assembly a man with a gold ring, in goodly apparel, and there come in also a poor man in vile raiment;

3 And ye have respect to him that weareth the gay clothing, and say unto him, Sit thou here in a good place; and say to the poor, Stand thou there, or sit here under my footstool:

4 Are ye not then partial in yourselves, and are become judges of evil thoughts?

5 Hearken, my beloved brethren, Hath not God chosen the poor of this world rich in faith, and heirs of the kingdom which he hath promised to them that love him?

6 But ye have despised the poor. Do not rich men oppress you, and draw you before the judgment seats?

7 Do not they blaspheme that worthy name by the which ye are called?

8 If ye fulfil the royal law according to the scripture, Thou shalt love thy neighbour as thyself, ye do well:

9 But if ye have respect to persons, ye commit sin, and are convinced of the law as transgressors.

10 For whosoever shall keep the whole law, and yet offend in one *point*, he is guilty of all.

11 For he that said, Do not commit adultery, said also, Do not kill. Now if thou commit no adultery, yet if thou kill, thou art become a transgressor of the law.

12 So speak ye, and so do, as they that shall be judged by the law of liberty.

13 For he shall have judgment without mercy, that hath shewed no mercy; and mercy rejoiceth against judgment.

14 What *doth it* profit, my brethren, though a man say he hath faith, and have not works? can faith save him?

15 If a brother or sister be naked, and destitute of daily food,

16 And one of you say unto them, Depart in peace, be *ye* warmed and filled; notwithstanding ye give them not those things which are needful to the body; what *doth it* profit?

17 Even so faith, if it hath not works, is dead, being alone.

18 Yea, a man may say, Thou hast faith, and I have works: shew me thy faith without thy works, and I will shew thee my faith by my works.

19 Thou believest that there is one God; thou doest well: the devils also believe, and tremble.

20 But wilt thou know, O vain man, that faith without works is dead?

21 Was not Abraham our father justified by works, when he had offered Isaac his son upon the altar?

22 Seest thou how faith wrought with his works, and by works was faith made perfect?

23 And the scripture was fulfilled which saith, Abraham believed God, and it was imputed unto him for righ-

teousness: and he was called the Friend
of God.
24 Ye see then how that by works a
man is justified, and not by faith only.
25 Likewise also was not Rahab the
harlot justified by works, when she had
received the messengers, and had sent
them out another way?
26 For as the body without the spirit
is dead, so faith without works is dead
also.

3 My brethren, be not many masters,
knowing that we shall receive the
greater condemnation.
2 For in many things we offend all. If
any man offend not in word, the same *is*
a perfect man, *and* able also to bridle
the whole body.
3 Behold, we put bits in the horses'
mouths, that they may obey us; and we
turn about their whole body.
4 Behold also the ships, which though
they be so great, and *are* driven of
fierce winds, yet are they turned about
with a very small helm, whithersoever
the governor listeth.
5 Even so the tongue is a little member, and boasteth great things. Behold,
how great a matter a little fire kindleth!
6 And the tongue *is* a fire, a world of
iniquity: so is the tongue among our
members, that it defileth the whole
body, and setteth on fire the course of
nature; and it is set on fire of hell.
7 For every kind of beasts, and of
birds, and of serpents, and of things in
the sea, is tamed, and hath been tamed
of mankind:
8 But the tongue can no man tame; *it*
is an unruly evil, full of deadly poison.
9 Therewith bless we God, even the
Father; and therewith curse we men,
which are made after the similitude of
God.
10 Out of the same mouth proceedeth
blessing and cursing. My brethren,
these things ought not so to be.
11 Doth a fountain send forth at the
same place sweet *water* and bitter?
12 Can the fig tree, my brethren, bear
olive berries? either a vine, figs? so *can*
no fountain both yield salt water and
fresh.
13 Who *is* a wise man and endued
with knowledge among you? let him
shew out of a good conversation his
works with meekness of wisdom.
14 But if ye have bitter envying and
strife in your hearts, glory not, and lie
not against the truth.
15 This wisdom descendeth not from
above, but *is* earthly, sensual, devilish.
16 For where envying and strife *is*,
there *is* confusion and every evil work.
17 But the wisdom that is from above
is first pure, then peaceable, gentle,
and easy to be intreated, full of mercy
and good fruits, without partiality, and
without hypocrisy.
18 And the fruit of righteousness is
sown in peace of them that make
peace.

4 From whence *come* wars and
fightings among you? *come they*
not hence, *even* of your lusts that war in
your members?
2 Ye lust, and have not: ye kill, and
desire to have, and cannot obtain: ye
fight and war, yet ye have not, because
ye ask not.
3 Ye ask, and receive not, because ye
ask amiss, that ye may consume *it* upon
your lusts.
4 Ye adulterers and adulteresses,
know ye not that the friendship of the
world is enmity with God? whosoever

therefore will be a friend of the world
is the enemy of God.
5 Do ye think that the scripture saith
in vain, The spirit that dwelleth in us
lusteth to envy?
6 But he giveth more grace. Wherefore
he saith, God resisteth the proud, but
giveth grace unto the humble.
7 Submit yourselves therefore to God.
Resist the devil, and he will flee from
you.
8 Draw nigh to God, and he will draw
nigh to you. Cleanse *your* hands, *ye* sinners; and purify *your* hearts, *ye* double
minded.
9 Be afflicted, and mourn, and weep:
let your laughter be turned to mourning, and *your* joy to heaviness.
10 Humble yourselves in the sight of
the Lord, and he shall lift you up.
11 Speak not evil one of another,
brethren. He that speaketh evil of *his*
brother, and judgeth his brother, speaketh evil of the law, and judgeth the
law: but if thou judge the law, thou art
not a doer of the law, but a judge.
12 There is one lawgiver, who is able
to save and to destroy: who art thou
that judgest another?
13 Go to now, ye that say, To day or to
morrow we will go into such a city, and
continue there a year, and buy and sell,
and get gain:
14 Whereas ye know not what *shall be*
on the morrow. For what *is* your life? It
is even a vapour, that appeareth for a
little time, and then vanisheth away.
15 For that ye *ought* to say, If the Lord
will, we shall live, and do this, or that.
16 But now ye rejoice in your boast-
ings: all such rejoicing is evil.
17 Therefore to him that knoweth to
do good, and doeth *it* not, to him it is
sin.

5 Go to now, *ye* rich men, weep and
howl for your miseries that shall
come upon *you*.
2 Your riches are corrupted, and your
garments are motheaten.
3 Your gold and silver is cankered;
and the rust of them shall be a witness
against you, and shall eat your flesh as
it were fire. Ye have heaped treasure
together for the last days.
4 Behold, the hire of the labourers
who have reaped down your fields,
which is of you kept back by fraud, crieth: and the cries of them which have
reaped are entered into the ears of the
Lord of sabaoth.
5 Ye have lived in pleasure on the
earth, and been wanton; ye have nourished your hearts, as in a day of slaughter.
6 Ye have condemned *and* killed the
just; *and* he doth not resist you.
7 Be patient therefore, brethren, unto
the coming of the Lord. Behold, the
husbandman waiteth for the precious
fruit of the earth, and hath long
patience for it, until he receive the
early and latter rain.
8 Be ye also patient; stablish your
hearts: for the coming of the Lord
draweth nigh.
9 Grudge not one against another,
brethren, lest ye be condemned: behold, the judge standeth before the
door.
10 Take, my brethren, the prophets,
who have spoken in the name of the
Lord, for an example of suffering affliction, and of patience.
11 Behold, we count them happy
which endure. Ye have heard of the
patience of Job, and have seen the end
of the Lord; that the Lord is very pitiful,
and of tender mercy.

12 But above all things, my brethren, swear not, neither by heaven, neither by the earth, neither by any other oath: but let your yea be yea; and *your* nay, nay; lest ye fall into condemnation.

13 Is any among you afflicted? let him pray. Is any merry? let him sing psalms.

14 Is any sick among you? let him call for the elders of the church; and let them pray over him, anointing him with oil in the name of the Lord:

15 And the prayer of faith shall save the sick, and the Lord shall raise him up; and if he have committed sins, they shall be forgiven him.

16 Confess *your* faults one to another, and pray one for another, that ye may be healed. The effectual fervent prayer of a righteous man availeth much.

17 Elias was a man subject to like passions as we are, and he prayed earnestly that it might not rain: and it rained not on the earth by the space of three years and six months.

18 And he prayed again, and the heaven gave rain, and the earth brought forth her fruit.

19 Brethren, if any of you do err from the truth, and one convert him;

20 Let him know, that he which converteth the sinner from the error of his way shall save a soul from death, and shall hide a multitude of sins.

THE FIRST EPISTLE GENERAL OF

PETER

1 Peter, an apostle of Jesus Christ, to the strangers scattered throughout Pontus, Galatia, Cappadocia, Asia, and Bithynia,

2 Elect according to the foreknowledge of God the Father, through sanctification of the Spirit, unto obedience and sprinkling of the blood of Jesus Christ: Grace unto you, and peace, be multiplied.

3 Blessed *be* the God and Father of our Lord Jesus Christ, which according to his abundant mercy hath begotten us again unto a lively hope by the resurrection of Jesus Christ from the dead,

4 To an inheritance incorruptible, and undefiled, and that fadeth not away, reserved in heaven for you,

5 Who are kept by the power of God through faith unto salvation ready to be revealed in the last time.

6 Wherein ye greatly rejoice, though now for a season, if need be, ye are in heaviness through manifold temptations:

7 That the trial of your faith, being much more precious than of gold that perisheth, though it be tried with fire, might be found unto praise and honour and glory at the appearing of Jesus Christ:

8 Whom having not seen, ye love; in whom, though now ye see *him* not, yet believing, ye rejoice with joy unspeakable and full of glory:

9 Receiving the end of your faith, *even* the salvation of *your* souls.

10 Of which salvation the prophets
have enquired and searched diligently,
who prophesied of the grace *that*
should come unto you:
11 Searching what, or what manner of
time the Spirit of Christ which was in
them did signify, when it testified
beforehand the sufferings of Christ,
and the glory that should follow.
12 Unto whom it was revealed, that
not unto themselves, but unto us they
did minister the things, which are now
reported unto you by them that have
preached the gospel unto you with the
Holy Ghost sent down from heaven;
which things the angels desire to look
into.
13 Wherefore gird up the loins of your
mind, be sober, and hope to the end for
the grace that is to be brought unto you
at the revelation of Jesus Christ;
14 As obedient children, not fashion-
ing yourselves according to the former
lusts in your ignorance:
15 But as he which hath called you is
holy, so be ye holy in all manner of
conversation;
16 Because it is written, Be ye holy;
for I am holy.
17 And if ye call on the Father, who
without respect of persons judgeth
according to every man's work, pass the
time of your sojourning *here* in fear:
18 Forasmuch as ye know that ye
were not redeemed with corruptible
things, *as* silver and gold, from your
vain conversation *received* by tradition
from your fathers;
19 But with the precious blood of
Christ, as of a lamb without blemish
and without spot:
20 Who verily was foreordained before the foundation of the world, but
was manifest in these last times for you,
21 Who by him do believe in God, that
raised him up from the dead, and gave
him glory; that your faith and hope
might be in God.
22 Seeing ye have purified your souls
in obeying the truth through the Spirit
unto unfeigned love of the brethren, *see*
that ye love one another with a pure
heart fervently:
23 Being born again, not of corruptible seed, but of incorruptible, by the
word of God, which liveth and abideth
for ever.
24 For all flesh *is* as grass, and all the
glory of man as the flower of grass. The
grass withereth, and the flower thereof
falleth away:
25 But the word of the Lord endureth
for ever. And this is the word which by
the gospel is preached unto you.

2 Wherefore laying aside all malice,
and all guile, and hypocrisies, and
envies, and all evil speakings,
2 As newborn babes, desire the sincere milk of the word, that ye may grow
thereby:
3 If so be ye have tasted that the Lord
is gracious.
4 To whom coming, *as unto* a living
stone, disallowed indeed of men, but
chosen of God, *and* precious,
5 Ye also, as lively stones, are built up
a spiritual house, an holy priesthood, to
offer up spiritual sacrifices, acceptable
to God by Jesus Christ.
6 Wherefore also it is contained in the
scripture, Behold, I lay in Sion a chief
corner stone, elect, precious: and he
that believeth on him shall not be confounded.
7 Unto you therefore which believe *he*
is precious: but unto them which be
disobedient, the stone which the build-

ers disallowed, the same is made the
head of the corner,
8 And a stone of stumbling, and a
rock of offence, *even to them* which
stumble at the word, being disobedient:
whereunto also they were appointed.
9 But ye *are* a chosen generation, a
royal priesthood, an holy nation, a
peculiar people; that ye should shew
forth the praises of him who hath
called you out of darkness into his marvellous light:
10 Which in time past *were* not a
people, but *are* now the people of God:
which had not obtained mercy, but now
have obtained mercy.
11 Dearly beloved, I beseech *you* as
strangers and pilgrims, abstain from
fleshly lusts, which war against the
soul;
12 Having your conversation honest
among the Gentiles: that, whereas they
speak against you as evildoers, they
may by *your* good works, which they
shall behold, glorify God in the day of
visitation.
13 Submit yourselves to every ordinance of man for the Lord's sake:
whether it be to the king, as supreme;
14 Or unto governors, as unto them
that are sent by him for the punishment of evildoers, and for the praise of
them that do well.
15 For so is the will of God, that with
well doing ye may put to silence the
ignorance of foolish men:
16 As free, and not using *your* liberty
for a cloke of maliciousness, but as the
servants of God.
17 Honour all *men*. Love the brotherhood. Fear God. Honour the king.
18 Servants, *be* subject to *your* masters with all fear; not only to the good
and gentle, but also to the froward.
19 For this *is* thankworthy, if a man
for conscience toward God endure
grief, suffering wrongfully.
20 For what glory *is it*, if, when ye be
buffeted for your faults, ye shall take it
patiently? but if, when ye do well, and
suffer *for it*, ye take it patiently, this *is*
acceptable with God.
21 For even hereunto were ye called:
because Christ also suffered for us,
leaving us an example, that ye should
follow his steps:
22 Who did no sin, neither was guile
found in his mouth:
23 Who, when he was reviled, reviled
not again; when he suffered, he threatened not; but committed *himself* to
him that judgeth righteously:
24 Who his own self bare our sins in
his own body on the tree, that we, being
dead to sins, should live unto righteousness: by whose stripes ye were healed.
25 For ye were as sheep going astray;
but are now returned unto the Shepherd and Bishop of your souls.

3 Likewise, ye wives, *be* in subjection
to your own husbands; that, if any
obey not the word, they also may without the word be won by the conversation of the wives;
2 While they behold your chaste conversation *coupled* with fear.
3 Whose adorning let it not be that
outward *adorning* of plaiting the hair,
and of wearing of gold, or of putting on
of apparel;
4 But *let it be* the hidden man of the
heart, in that which is not corruptible,
even the ornament of a meek and quiet
spirit, which is in the sight of God of
great price.
5 For after this manner in the old
time the holy women also, who trusted

in God, adorned themselves, being in
subjection unto their own husbands:
6 Even as Sara obeyed Abraham, calling him lord: whose daughters ye are,
as long as ye do well, and are not afraid
with any amazement.
7 Likewise, ye husbands, dwell with
them according to knowledge, giving
honour unto the wife, as unto the
weaker vessel, and as being heirs
together of the grace of life; that your
prayers be not hindered.
8 Finally, *be ye* all of one mind, having
compassion one of another, love as
brethren, *be* pitiful, *be* courteous:
9 Not rendering evil for evil, or railing
for railing: but contrariwise blessing;
knowing that ye are thereunto called,
that ye should inherit a blessing.
10 For he that will love life, and see
good days, let him refrain his tongue
from evil, and his lips that they speak
no guile:
11 Let him eschew evil, and do good;
let him seek peace, and ensue it.
12 For the eyes of the Lord *are* over
the righteous, and his ears *are open*
unto their prayers: but the face of the
Lord *is* against them that do evil.
13 And who *is* he that will harm you,
if ye be followers of that which is good?
14 But and if ye suffer for righteousness' sake, happy *are ye*: and be not
afraid of their terror, neither be troubled;
15 But sanctify the Lord God in your
hearts: and *be* ready always to *give* an
answer to every man that asketh you a
reason of the hope that is in you with
meekness and fear:
16 Having a good conscience; that,
whereas they speak evil of you, as of
evildoers, they may be ashamed that
falsely accuse your good conversation
in Christ.
17 For *it is* better, if the will of God be
so, that ye suffer for well doing, than for
evil doing.
18 For Christ also hath once suffered
for sins, the just for the unjust, that he
might bring us to God, being put to
death in the flesh, but quickened by
the Spirit:
19 By which also he went and
preached unto the spirits in prison;
20 Which sometime were disobedient, when once the longsuffering of
God waited in the days of Noah, while
the ark was a preparing, wherein few,
that is, eight souls were saved by water.
21 The like figure whereunto *even*
baptism doth also now save us (not the
putting away of the filth of the flesh,
but the answer of a good conscience
toward God,) by the resurrection of
Jesus Christ:
22 Who is gone into heaven, and is on
the right hand of God; angels and
authorities and powers being made
subject unto him.

4 Forasmuch then as Christ hath suffered for us in the flesh, arm yourselves likewise with the same mind: for
he that hath suffered in the flesh hath
ceased from sin;
2 That he no longer should live the
rest of *his* time in the flesh to the lusts
of men, but to the will of God.
3 For the time past of *our* life may
suffice us to have wrought the will of
the Gentiles, when we walked in lasciviousness, lusts, excess of wine, revellings, banquetings, and abominable
idolatries:
4 Wherein they think it strange that
ye run not with *them* to the same
excess of riot, speaking evil of *you*:

5 Who shall give account to him that is ready to judge the quick and the dead.

6 For for this cause was the gospel preached also to them that are dead, that they might be judged according to men in the flesh, but live according to God in the spirit.

7 But the end of all things is at hand: be ye therefore sober, and watch unto prayer.

8 And above all things have fervent charity among yourselves: for charity shall cover the multitude of sins.

9 Use hospitality one to another without grudging.

10 As every man hath received the gift, *even so* minister the same one to another, as good stewards of the manifold grace of God.

11 If any man speak, *let him speak* as the oracles of God; if any man minister, *let him do it* as of the ability which God giveth: that God in all things may be glorified through Jesus Christ, to whom be praise and dominion for ever and ever. Amen.

12 Beloved, think it not strange concerning the fiery trial which is to try you, as though some strange thing happened unto you:

13 But rejoice, inasmuch as ye are partakers of Christ's sufferings; that, when his glory shall be revealed, ye may be glad also with exceeding joy.

14 If ye be reproached for the name of Christ, happy *are ye*; for the spirit of glory and of God resteth upon you: on their part he is evil spoken of, but on your part he is glorified.

15 But let none of you suffer as a murderer, or *as* a thief, or *as* an evildoer, or as a busybody in other men's matters.

16 Yet if *any man suffer* as a Christian, let him not be ashamed; but let him glorify God on this behalf.

17 For the time *is come* that judgment must begin at the house of God: and if *it* first *begin* at us, what shall the end *be* of them that obey not the gospel of God?

18 And if the righteous scarcely be saved, where shall the ungodly and the sinner appear?

19 Wherefore let them that suffer according to the will of God commit the keeping of their souls *to him* in well doing, as unto a faithful Creator.

5 The elders which are among you I exhort, who am also an elder, and a witness of the sufferings of Christ, and also a partaker of the glory that shall be revealed:

2 Feed the flock of God which is among you, taking the oversight *thereof*, not by constraint, but willingly; not for filthy lucre, but of a ready mind;

3 Neither as being lords over *God's* heritage, but being ensamples to the flock.

4 And when the chief Shepherd shall appear, ye shall receive a crown of glory that fadeth not away.

5 Likewise, ye younger, submit yourselves unto the elder. Yea, all *of you* be subject one to another, and be clothed with humility: for God resisteth the proud, and giveth grace to the humble.

6 Humble yourselves therefore under the mighty hand of God, that he may exalt you in due time:

7 Casting all your care upon him; for he careth for you.

8 Be sober, be vigilant; because your adversary the devil, as a roaring lion, walketh about, seeking whom he may devour:

9 Whom resist stedfast in the faith, knowing that the same afflictions are accomplished in your brethren that are in the world.

10 But the God of all grace, who hath called us unto his eternal glory by Christ Jesus, after that ye have suffered a while, make you perfect, stablish, strengthen, settle *you*.

11 To him *be* glory and dominion for ever and ever. Amen.

12 By Silvanus, a faithful brother unto you, as I suppose, I have written briefly, exhorting, and testifying that this is the true grace of God wherein ye stand.

13 The *church that is* at Babylon, elected together with *you*, saluteth you; and *so doth* Marcus my son.

14 Greet ye one another with a kiss of charity. Peace *be* with you all that are in Christ Jesus. Amen.

THE SECOND EPISTLE GENERAL OF PETER

1 Simon Peter, a servant and an apostle of Jesus Christ, to them that have obtained like precious faith with us through the righteousness of God and our Saviour Jesus Christ:

2 Grace and peace be multiplied unto you through the knowledge of God, and of Jesus our Lord,

3 According as his divine power hath given unto us all things that *pertain* unto life and godliness, through the knowledge of him that hath called us to glory and virtue:

4 Whereby are given unto us exceeding great and precious promises: that by these ye might be partakers of the divine nature, having escaped the corruption that is in the world through lust.

5 And beside this, giving all diligence, add to your faith virtue; and to virtue knowledge;

6 And to knowledge temperance; and to temperance patience; and to patience godliness;

7 And to godliness brotherly kindness; and to brotherly kindness charity.

8 For if these things be in you, and abound, they make *you that ye shall* neither *be* barren nor unfruitful in the knowledge of our Lord Jesus Christ.

9 But he that lacketh these things is blind, and cannot see afar off, and hath forgotten that he was purged from his old sins.

10 Wherefore the rather, brethren, give diligence to make your calling and election sure: for if ye do these things, ye shall never fall:

11 For so an entrance shall be ministered unto you abundantly into the everlasting kingdom of our Lord and Saviour Jesus Christ.

12 Wherefore I will not be negligent to put you always in remembrance of these things, though ye know *them*, and be established in the present truth.

13 Yea, I think it meet, as long as I am in this tabernacle, to stir you up by putting *you* in remembrance;

14 Knowing that shortly I must put off
this my tabernacle, even as our Lord
Jesus Christ hath shewed me.
15 Moreover I will endeavour that ye
may be able after my decease to have
these things always in remembrance.
16 For we have not followed cunning-
ly devised fables, when we made known
unto you the power and coming of our
Lord Jesus Christ, but were eyewitnesses of his majesty.
17 For he received from God the
Father honour and glory, when there
came such a voice to him from the
excellent glory, This is my beloved Son,
in whom I am well pleased.
18 And this voice which came from
heaven we heard, when we were with
him in the holy mount.
19 We have also a more sure word of
prophecy; whereunto ye do well that ye
take heed, as unto a light that shineth
in a dark place, until the day dawn, and
the day star arise in your hearts:
20 Knowing this first, that no prophecy of the scripture is of any private
interpretation.
21 For the prophecy came not in old
time by the will of man: but holy men
of God spake *as they were* moved by
the Holy Ghost.

2 But there were false prophets also
among the people, even as there
shall be false teachers among you, who
privily shall bring in damnable heresies, even denying the Lord that bought
them, and bring upon themselves swift
destruction.
2 And many shall follow their perni-
cious ways; by reason of whom the way
of truth shall be evil spoken of.
3 And through covetousness shall
they with feigned words make merchandise of you: whose judgment now
of a long time lingereth not, and their
damnation slumbereth not.
4 For if God spared not the angels
that sinned, but cast *them* down to hell,
and delivered *them* into chains of darkness, to be reserved unto judgment;
5 And spared not the old world, but
saved Noah the eighth *person*, a preacher of righteousness, bringing in the
flood upon the world of the ungodly;
6 And turning the cities of Sodom and
Gomorrha into ashes condemned *them*
with an overthrow, making *them* an
ensample unto those that after should
live ungodly;
7 And delivered just Lot, vexed with
the filthy conversation of the wicked:
8 (For that righteous man dwelling
among them, in seeing and hearing,
vexed *his* righteous soul from day to
day with *their* unlawful deeds;)
9 The Lord knoweth how to deliver
the godly out of temptations, and to
reserve the unjust unto the day of judgment to be punished:
10 But chiefly them that walk after
the flesh in the lust of uncleanness, and
despise government. Presumptuous *are
they*, selfwilled, they are not afraid to
speak evil of dignities.
11 Whereas angels, which are greater
in power and might, bring not railing
accusation against them before the
Lord.
12 But these, as natural brute beasts,
made to be taken and destroyed, speak
evil of the things that they understand
not; and shall utterly perish in their
own corruption;
13 And shall receive the reward of
unrighteousness, *as* they that count it
pleasure to riot in the day time. Spots
they are and blemishes, sporting them-

selves with their own deceivings while
they feast with you;
14 Having eyes full of adultery, and
that cannot cease from sin; beguiling
unstable souls: an heart they have exercised with covetous practices; cursed
children:
15 Which have forsaken the right way,
and are gone astray, following the way
of Balaam *the son* of Bosor, who loved
the wages of unrighteousness;
16 But was rebuked for his iniquity:
the dumb ass speaking with man's
voice forbad the madness of the
prophet.
17 These are wells without water,
clouds that are carried with a tempest;
to whom the mist of darkness is
reserved for ever.
18 For when they speak great swelling *words* of vanity, they allure through
the lusts of the flesh, *through much*
wantonness, those that were clean
escaped from them who live in error.
19 While they promise them liberty,
they themselves are the servants of corruption: for of whom a man is overcome, of the same is he brought in
bondage.
20 For if after they have escaped the
pollutions of the world through the
knowledge of the Lord and Saviour
Jesus Christ, they are again entangled
therein, and overcome, the latter end is
worse with them than the beginning.
21 For it had been better for them not
to have known the way of righteousness, than, after they have known *it*, to
turn from the holy commandment
delivered unto them.
22 But it is happened unto them
according to the true proverb, The dog
is turned to his own vomit again; and
the sow that was washed to her wallowing in the mire.

3 This second epistle, beloved, I now
write unto you; in *both* which I stir
up your pure minds by way of remembrance:
2 That ye may be mindful of the
words which were spoken before by the
holy prophets, and of the commandment of us the apostles of the Lord and
Saviour:
3 Knowing this first, that there shall
come in the last days scoffers, walking
after their own lusts,
4 And saying, Where is the promise of
his coming? for since the fathers fell
asleep, all things continue as *they were*
from the beginning of the creation.
5 For this they willingly are ignorant
of, that by the word of God the heavens
were of old, and the earth standing out
of the water and in the water:
6 Whereby the world that then was,
being overflowed with water, perished:
7 But the heavens and the earth,
which are now, by the same word are
kept in store, reserved unto fire against
the day of judgment and perdition of
ungodly men.
8 But, beloved, be not ignorant of this
one thing, that one day *is* with the Lord
as a thousand years, and a thousand
years as one day.
9 The Lord is not slack concerning his
promise, as some men count slackness;
but is longsuffering to us-ward, not willing that any should perish, but that all
should come to repentance.
10 But the day of the Lord will come
as a thief in the night; in the which the
heavens shall pass away with a great
noise, and the elements shall melt with
fervent heat, the earth also and the

works that are therein shall be burned up.

11 *Seeing* then *that* all these things shall be dissolved, what manner *of persons* ought ye to be in *all* holy conversation and godliness,

12 Looking for and hasting unto the coming of the day of God, wherein the heavens being on fire shall be dissolved, and the elements shall melt with fervent heat?

13 Nevertheless we, according to his promise, look for new heavens and a new earth, wherein dwelleth righteousness.

14 Wherefore, beloved, seeing that ye look for such things, be diligent that ye may be found of him in peace, without spot, and blameless.

15 And account *that* the longsuffering of our Lord *is* salvation; even as our beloved brother Paul also according to the wisdom given unto him hath written unto you;

16 As also in all *his* epistles, speaking in them of these things; in which are some things hard to be understood, which they that are unlearned and unstable wrest, as *they do* also the other scriptures, unto their own destruction.

17 Ye therefore, beloved, seeing ye know *these things* before, beware lest ye also, being led away with the error of the wicked, fall from your own stedfastness.

18 But grow in grace, and *in* the knowledge of our Lord and Saviour Jesus Christ. To him *be* glory both now and for ever. Amen.

THE FIRST EPISTLE GENERAL OF JOHN

1 That which was from the beginning, which we have heard, which we have seen with our eyes, which we have looked upon, and our hands have handled, of the Word of life;

2 (For the life was manifested, and we have seen *it*, and bear witness, and shew unto you that eternal life, which was with the Father, and was manifested unto us;)

3 That which we have seen and heard declare we unto you, that ye also may have fellowship with us: and truly our fellowship *is* with the Father, and with his Son Jesus Christ.

4 And these things write we unto you, that your joy may be full.

5 This then is the message which we have heard of him, and declare unto you, that God is light, and in him is no darkness at all.

6 If we say that we have fellowship with him, and walk in darkness, we lie, and do not the truth:

7 But if we walk in the light, as he is in the light, we have fellowship one with another, and the blood of Jesus Christ his Son cleanseth us from all sin.

8 If we say that we have no sin, we deceive ourselves, and the truth is not in us.

9 If we confess our sins, he is faithful and just to forgive us *our* sins, and to cleanse us from all unrighteousness.

10 If we say that we have not sinned,
we make him a liar, and his word is not
in us.

2

My little children, these things
write I unto you, that ye sin not.
And if any man sin, we have an
advocate with the Father, Jesus Christ
the righteous:

2 And he is the propitiation for our
sins: and not for ours only, but also for
the sins of the whole world.

3 And hereby we do know that we
know him, if we keep his commandments.

4 He that saith, I know him, and keepeth not his commandments, is a liar,
and the truth is not in him.

5 But whoso keepeth his word, in him
verily is the love of God perfected:
hereby know we that we are in him.

6 He that saith he abideth in him
ought himself also so to walk, even as
he walked.

7 Brethren, I write no new commandment unto you, but an old commandment which ye had from the beginning.
The old commandment is the word
which ye have heard from the beginning.

8 Again, a new commandment I write
unto you, which thing is true in him and
in you: because the darkness is past,
and the true light now shineth.

9 He that saith he is in the light, and
hateth his brother, is in darkness even
until now.

10 He that loveth his brother abideth
in the light, and there is none occasion
of stumbling in him.

11 But he that hateth his brother is in
darkness, and walketh in darkness, and
knoweth not whither he goeth, because
that darkness hath blinded his eyes.

12 I write unto you, little children,
because your sins are forgiven you for
his name's sake.

13 I write unto you, fathers, because
ye have known him *that is* from the
beginning. I write unto you, young men,
because ye have overcome the wicked
one. I write unto you, little children,
because ye have known the Father.

14 I have written unto you, fathers,
because ye have known him *that is*
from the beginning. I have written unto
you, young men, because ye are strong,
and the word of God abideth in you,
and ye have overcome the wicked one.

15 Love not the world, neither the
things *that are* in the world. If any man
love the world, the love of the Father is
not in him.

16 For all that *is* in the world, the lust
of the flesh, and the lust of the eyes,
and the pride of life, is not of the
Father, but is of the world.

17 And the world passeth away, and
the lust thereof: but he that doeth the
will of God abideth for ever.

18 Little children, it is the last time:
and as ye have heard that antichrist
shall come, even now are there many
antichrists; whereby we know that it is
the last time.

19 They went out from us, but they
were not of us; for if they had been of
us, they would *no doubt* have continued with us: but *they went out*, that
they might be made manifest that they
were not all of us.

20 But ye have an unction from the
Holy One, and ye know all things.

21 I have not written unto you
because ye know not the truth, but
because ye know it, and that no lie is of
the truth.

22 Who is a liar but he that denieth that Jesus is the Christ? He is antichrist, that denieth the Father and the Son.

23 Whosoever denieth the Son, the same hath not the Father: *(but) he that acknowledgeth the Son hath the Father also.*

24 Let that therefore abide in you, which ye have heard from the beginning. If that which ye have heard from the beginning shall remain in you, ye also shall continue in the Son, and in the Father.

25 And this is the promise that he hath promised us, *even* eternal life.

26 These *things* have I written unto you concerning them that seduce you.

27 But the anointing which ye have received of him abideth in you, and ye need not that any man teach you: but as the same anointing teacheth you of all things, and is truth, and is no lie, and even as it hath taught you, ye shall abide in him.

28 And now, little children, abide in him; that, when he shall appear, we may have confidence, and not be ashamed before him at his coming.

29 If ye know that he is righteous, ye know that every one that doeth righteousness is born of him.

3 Behold, what manner of love the Father hath bestowed upon us, that we should be called the sons of God: therefore the world knoweth us not, because it knew him not.

2 Beloved, now are we the sons of God, and it doth not yet appear what we shall be: but we know that, when he shall appear, we shall be like him; for we shall see him as he is.

3 And every man that hath this hope in him purifieth himself, even as he is pure.

4 Whosoever committeth sin transgresseth also the law: for sin is the transgression of the law.

5 And ye know that he was manifested to take away our sins; and in him is no sin.

6 Whosoever abideth in him sinneth not: whosoever sinneth hath not seen him, neither known him.

7 Little children, let no man deceive you: he that doeth righteousness is righteous, even as he is righteous.

8 He that committeth sin is of the devil; for the devil sinneth from the beginning. For this purpose the Son of God was manifested, that he might destroy the works of the devil.

9 Whosoever is born of God doth not commit sin; for his seed remaineth in him: and he cannot sin, because he is born of God.

10 In this the children of God are manifest, and the children of the devil: whosoever doeth not righteousness is not of God, neither he that loveth not his brother.

11 For this is the message that ye heard from the beginning, that we should love one another.

12 Not as Cain, *who* was of that wicked one, and slew his brother. And wherefore slew he him? Because his own works were evil, and his brother's righteous.

13 Marvel not, my brethren, if the world hate you.

14 We know that we have passed from death unto life, because we love the brethren. He that loveth not *his* brother abideth in death.

15 Whosoever hateth his brother is a murderer: and ye know that no murderer hath eternal life abiding in him.

16 Hereby perceive we the love *of God*, because he laid down his life for us: and we ought to lay down *our* lives for the brethren.

17 But whoso hath this world's good, and seeth his brother have need, and shutteth up his bowels *of compassion* from him, how dwelleth the love of God in him?

18 My little children, let us not love in word, neither in tongue; but in deed and in truth.

19 And hereby we know that we are of the truth, and shall assure our hearts before him.

20 For if our heart condemn us, God is greater than our heart, and knoweth all things.

21 Beloved, if our heart condemn us not, *then* have we confidence toward God.

22 And whatsoever we ask, we receive of him, because we keep his commandments, and do those things that are pleasing in his sight.

23 And this is his commandment, That we should believe on the name of his Son Jesus Christ, and love one another, as he gave us commandment.

24 And he that keepeth his commandments dwelleth in him, and he in him. And hereby we know that he abideth in us, by the Spirit which he hath given us.

4 Beloved, believe not every spirit, but try the spirits whether they are of God: because many false prophets are gone out into the world.

2 Hereby know ye the Spirit of God: Every spirit that confesseth that Jesus Christ is come in the flesh is of God:

3 And every spirit that confesseth not that Jesus Christ is come in the flesh is not of God: and this is that *spirit* of antichrist, whereof ye have heard that it should come; and even now already is it in the world.

4 Ye are of God, little children, and have overcome them: because greater is he that is in you, than he that is in the world.

5 They are of the world: therefore speak they of the world, and the world heareth them.

6 We are of God: he that knoweth God heareth us; he that is not of God heareth not us. Hereby know we the spirit of truth, and the spirit of error.

7 Beloved, let us love one another: for love is of God; and every one that loveth is born of God, and knoweth God.

8 He that loveth not knoweth not God; for God is love.

9 In this was manifested the love of God toward us, because that God sent his only begotten Son into the world, that we might live through him.

10 Herein is love, not that we loved God, but that he loved us, and sent his Son *to be* the propitiation for our sins.

11 Beloved, if God so loved us, we ought also to love one another.

12 No man hath seen God at any time. If we love one another, God dwelleth in us, and his love is perfected in us.

13 Hereby know we that we dwell in him, and he in us, because he hath given us of his Spirit.

14 And we have seen and do testify that the Father sent the Son *to be* the Saviour of the world.

15 Whosoever shall confess that Jesus is the Son of God, God dwelleth in him, and he in God.

16 And we have known and believed
the love that God hath to us. God is
love; and he that dwelleth in love dwelleth in God, and God in him.
17 Herein is our love made perfect,
that we may have boldness in the day of
judgment: because as he is, so are we in
this world.
18 There is no fear in love; but perfect
love casteth out fear: because fear hath
torment. He that feareth is not made
perfect in love.
19 We love him, because he first loved
us.
20 If a man say, I love God, and hateth
his brother, he is a liar: for he that
loveth not his brother whom he hath
seen, how can he love God whom he
hath not seen?
21 And this commandment have we
from him, That he who loveth God love
his brother also.

5 Whosoever believeth that Jesus is
the Christ is born of God: and every
one that loveth him that begat loveth
him also that is begotten of him.
2 By this we know that we love the
children of God, when we love God, and
keep his commandments.
3 For this is the love of God, that we
keep his commandments: and his commandments are not grievous.
4 For whatsoever is born of God overcometh the world: and this is the victory that overcometh the world, *even* our
faith.
5 Who is he that overcometh the
world, but he that believeth that Jesus
is the Son of God?
6 This is he that came by water and
blood, *even* Jesus Christ; not by water
only, but by water and blood. And it is
the Spirit that beareth witness, because
the Spirit is truth.
7 For there are three that bear record
in heaven, the Father, the Word, and the
Holy Ghost: and these three are one.
8 And there are three that bear witness in earth, the Spirit, and the water,
and the blood: and these three agree in
one.
9 If we receive the witness of men, the
witness of God is greater: for this is the
witness of God which he hath testified
of his Son.
10 He that believeth on the Son of
God hath the witness in himself: he
that believeth not God hath made him
a liar; because he believeth not the
record that God gave of his Son.
11 And this is the record, that God
hath given to us eternal life, and this
life is in his Son.
12 He that hath the Son hath life; *and*
he that hath not the Son of God hath
not life.
13 These things have I written unto
you that believe on the name of the Son
of God; that ye may know that ye have
eternal life, and that ye may believe on
the name of the Son of God.
14 And this is the confidence that we
have in him, that, if we ask any thing
according to his will, he heareth us:
15 And if we know that he hear us,
whatsoever we ask, we know that we
have the petitions that we desired of
him.
16 If any man see his brother sin a sin
which is not unto death, he shall ask,
and he shall give him life for them that
sin not unto death. There is a sin unto
death: I do not say that he shall pray for
it.
17 All unrighteousness is sin: and
there is a sin not unto death.
18 We know that whosoever is born of
God sinneth not; but he that is begotten

of God keepeth himself, and that
wicked one toucheth him not.
19 *And* we know that we are of God,
and the whole world lieth in wickedness.
20 And we know that the Son of God
is come, and hath given us an understanding, that we may know him that is
true, and we are in him that is true,
even in his Son Jesus Christ. This is the
true God, and eternal life.
21 Little children, keep yourselves
from idols. Amen.

THE SECOND EPISTLE OF JOHN

1 The elder unto the elect lady and
her children, whom I love in the
truth; and not I only, but also all they
that have known the truth;
2 For the truth's sake, which dwelleth
in us, and shall be with us for ever.
3 Grace be with you, mercy, *and*
peace, from God the Father, and from
the Lord Jesus Christ, the Son of the
Father, in truth and love.
4 I rejoiced greatly that I found of thy
children walking in truth, as we have
received a commandment from the
Father.
5 And now I beseech thee, lady, not as
though I wrote a new commandment
unto thee, but that which we had from
the beginning, that we love one another.
6 And this is love, that we walk after
his commandments. This is the commandment, That, as ye have heard from
the beginning, ye should walk in it.
7 For many deceivers are entered into
the world, who confess not that Jesus
Christ is come in the flesh. This is a
deceiver and an antichrist.
8 Look to yourselves, that we lose not
those things which we have wrought,
but that we receive a full reward.
9 Whosoever transgresseth, and abideth not in the doctrine of Christ, hath
not God. He that abideth in the doctrine of Christ, he hath both the Father
and the Son.
10 If there come any unto you, and
bring not this doctrine, receive him not
into *your* house, neither bid him God
speed:
11 For he that biddeth him God speed
is partaker of his evil deeds.
12 Having many things to write unto
you, I would not *write* with paper and
ink: but I trust to come unto you, and
speak face to face, that our joy may be
full.
13 The children of thy elect sister
greet thee. Amen.

THE THIRD EPISTLE OF
JOHN

1 The elder unto the wellbeloved
Gaius, whom I love in the truth.
2 Beloved, I wish above all things that
thou mayest prosper and be in health,
even as thy soul prospereth.
3 For I rejoiced greatly, when the
brethren came and testified of the
truth that is in thee, even as thou walkest in the truth.
4 I have no greater joy than to hear
that my children walk in truth.
5 Beloved, thou doest faithfully whatsoever thou doest to the brethren, and
to strangers;
6 Which have borne witness of thy
charity before the church: whom if thou
bring forward on their journey after a
godly sort, thou shalt do well:
7 Because that for his name's sake
they went forth, taking nothing of the
Gentiles.
8 We therefore ought to receive such,
that we might be fellowhelpers to the
truth.
9 I wrote unto the church: but
Diotrephes, who loveth to have the
preeminence among them, receiveth us
not.
10 Wherefore, if I come, I will remember his deeds which he doeth, prating
against us with malicious words: and
not content therewith, neither doth he
himself receive the brethren, and for-
biddeth them that would, and casteth
them out of the church.
11 Beloved, follow not that which is
evil, but that which is good. He that
doeth good is of God: but he that doeth
evil hath not seen God.
12 Demetrius hath good report of all
men, and of the truth itself: yea, and we
also bear record; and ye know that our
record is true.
13 I had many things to write, but I
will not with ink and pen write unto
thee:
14 But I trust I shall shortly see thee,
and we shall speak face to face. Peace
be to thee. *Our* friends salute thee.
Greet the friends by name.

THE GENERAL EPISTLE OF
JUDE

1 Jude, the servant of Jesus Christ,
and brother of James, to them that
are sanctified by God the Father, and
preserved in Jesus Christ, *and* called:
2 Mercy unto you, and peace, and
love, be multiplied.
3 Beloved, when I gave all diligence to
write unto you of the common salvation, it was needful for me to write unto
you, and exhort *you* that ye should
earnestly contend for the faith which
was once delivered unto the saints.
4 For there are certain men crept in
unawares, who were before of old
ordained to this condemnation, ungodly men, turning the grace of our God

into lasciviousness, and denying the
only Lord God, and our Lord Jesus
Christ.
5 I will therefore put you in remembrance, though ye once knew this, how
that the Lord, having saved the people
out of the land of Egypt, afterward
destroyed them that believed not.
6 And the angels which kept not their
first estate, but left their own habitation, he hath reserved in everlasting
chains under darkness unto the judgment of the great day.
7 Even as Sodom and Gomorrha, and
the cities about them in like manner,
giving themselves over to fornication,
and going after strange flesh, are set
forth for an example, suffering the
vengeance of eternal fire.
8 Likewise also these *filthy* dreamers
defile the flesh, despise dominion, and
speak evil of dignities.
9 Yet Michael the archangel, when
contending with the devil he disputed
about the body of Moses, durst not
bring against him a railing accusation,
but said, The Lord rebuke thee.
10 But these speak evil of those
things which they know not: but what
they know naturally, as brute beasts, in
those things they corrupt themselves.
11 Woe unto them! for they have gone
in the way of Cain, and ran greedily
after the error of Balaam for reward,
and perished in the gainsaying of Core.
12 These are spots in your feasts of
charity, when they feast with you, feeding themselves without fear: clouds
they are without water, carried about
of winds; trees whose fruit withereth,
without fruit, twice dead, plucked up
by the roots;
13 Raging waves of the sea, foaming
out their own shame; wandering stars,
to whom is reserved the blackness of
darkness for ever.
14 And Enoch also, the seventh from
Adam, prophesied of these, saying,
Behold, the Lord cometh with ten thousands of his saints,
15 To execute judgment upon all, and
to convince all that are ungodly among
them of all their ungodly deeds which
they have ungodly committed, and of
all their hard *speeches* which ungodly
sinners have spoken against him.
16 These are murmurers, complain-
ers, walking after their own lusts; and
their mouth speaketh great swelling
words, having men's persons in admiration because of advantage.
17 But, beloved, remember ye the
words which were spoken before of the
apostles of our Lord Jesus Christ;
18 How that they told you there
should be mockers in the last time, who
should walk after their own ungodly
lusts.
19 These be they who separate themselves, sensual, having not the Spirit.
20 But ye, beloved, building up yourselves on your most holy faith, praying
in the Holy Ghost,
21 Keep yourselves in the love of God,
looking for the mercy of our Lord Jesus
Christ unto eternal life.
22 And of some have compassion,
making a difference:
23 And others save with fear, pulling
them out of the fire; hating even the
garment spotted by the flesh.
24 Now unto him that is able to keep
you from falling, and to present *you*
faultless before the presence of his
glory with exceeding joy,
25 To the only wise God our Saviour,
be glory and majesty, dominion and
power, both now and ever. Amen.

THE REVELATION OF SAINT JOHN THE DIVINE

1 The Revelation of Jesus Christ,
which God gave unto him, to shew
unto his servants things which must
shortly come to pass; and he sent and
signified *it* by his angel unto his servant
John:
2 Who bare record of the word of God,
and of the testimony of Jesus Christ,
and of all things that he saw.
3 Blessed *is* he that readeth, and they
that hear the words of this prophecy,
and keep those things which are written therein: for the time *is* at hand.
4 John to the seven churches which
are in Asia: Grace *be* unto you, and
peace, from him which is, and which
was, and which is to come; and from the
seven Spirits which are before his
throne;
5 And from Jesus Christ, *who is* the
faithful witness, *and* the first begotten
of the dead, and the prince of the kings
of the earth. Unto him that loved us,
and washed us from our sins in his own
blood,
6 And hath made us kings and priests
unto God and his Father; to him *be*
glory and dominion for ever and ever.
Amen.
7 Behold, he cometh with clouds; and
every eye shall see him, and they *also*
which pierced him: and all kindreds of
the earth shall wail because of him.
Even so, Amen.
8 I am Alpha and Omega, the beginning and the ending, saith the Lord,
which is, and which was, and which is to
come, the Almighty.
9 I John, who also am your brother,
and companion in tribulation, and in
the kingdom and patience of Jesus
Christ, was in the isle that is called
Patmos, for the word of God, and for the
testimony of Jesus Christ.
10 I was in the Spirit on the Lord's
day, and heard behind me a great voice,
as of a trumpet,
11 Saying, I am Alpha and Omega, the
first and the last: and, What thou seest,
write in a book, and send *it* unto the
seven churches which are in Asia; unto
Ephesus, and unto Smyrna, and unto
Pergamos, and unto Thyatira, and unto
Sardis, and unto Philadelphia, and unto
Laodicea.
12 And I turned to see the voice that
spake with me. And being turned, I saw
seven golden candlesticks;
13 And in the midst of the seven candlesticks *one* like unto the Son of man,
clothed with a garment down to the
foot, and girt about the paps with a
golden girdle.
14 His head and *his* hairs *were* white
like wool, as white as snow; and his eyes
were as a flame of fire;
15 And his feet like unto fine brass, as
if they burned in a furnace; and his
voice as the sound of many waters.
16 And he had in his right hand seven
stars: and out of his mouth went a sharp
twoedged sword: and his countenance
was as the sun shineth in his strength.
17 And when I saw him, I fell at his
feet as dead. And he laid his right hand
upon me, saying unto me, Fear not; I am
the first and the last:
18 I *am* he that liveth, and was dead;
and, behold, I am alive for evermore,

Amen; and have the keys of hell and of
death.
19 Write the things which thou hast
seen, and the things which are, and the
things which shall be hereafter;
20 The mystery of the seven stars
which thou sawest in my right hand,
and the seven golden candlesticks. The
seven stars are the angels of the seven
churches: and the seven candlesticks
which thou sawest are the seven
churches.

2 Unto the angel of the church of
Ephesus write; These things saith
he that holdeth the seven stars in his
right hand, who walketh in the midst of
the seven golden candlesticks;
2 I know thy works, and thy labour,
and thy patience, and how thou canst
not bear them which are evil: and thou
hast tried them which say they are
apostles, and are not, and hast found
them liars:
3 And hast borne, and hast patience,
and for my name's sake hast laboured,
and hast not fainted.
4 Nevertheless I have *somewhat*
against thee, because thou hast left thy
first love.
5 Remember therefore from whence
thou art fallen, and repent, and do the
first works; or else I will come unto
thee quickly, and will remove thy candlestick out of his place, except thou
repent.
6 But this thou hast, that thou hatest
the deeds of the Nicolaitans, which I
also hate.
7 He that hath an ear, let him hear
what the Spirit saith unto the churches;
To him that overcometh will I give to
eat of the tree of life, which is in the
midst of the paradise of God.
8 And unto the angel of the church in
Smyrna write; These things saith the
first and the last, which was dead, and
is alive;
9 I know thy works, and tribulation,
and poverty, (but thou art rich) and *I
know* the blasphemy of them which say
they are Jews, and are not, but *are* the
synagogue of Satan.
10 Fear none of those things which
thou shalt suffer: behold, the devil shall
cast *some* of you into prison, that ye
may be tried; and ye shall have tribulation ten days: be thou faithful unto
death, and I will give thee a crown of
life.
11 He that hath an ear, let him hear
what the Spirit saith unto the churches;
He that overcometh shall not be hurt of
the second death.
12 And to the angel of the church in
Pergamos write; These things saith he
which hath the sharp sword with two
edges;
13 I know thy works, and where thou
dwellest, *even* where Satan's seat *is*:
and thou holdest fast my name, and
hast not denied my faith, even in those
days wherein Antipas *was* my faithful
martyr, who was slain among you,
where Satan dwelleth.
14 But I have a few things against
thee, because thou hast there them
that hold the doctrine of Balaam, who
taught Balac to cast a stumblingblock
before the children of Israel, to eat
things sacrificed unto idols, and to commit fornication.
15 So hast thou also them that hold
the doctrine of the Nicolaitans, which
thing I hate.
16 Repent; or else I will come unto
thee quickly, and will fight against
them with the sword of my mouth.

17 He that hath an ear, let him hear
what the Spirit saith unto the churches;
To him that overcometh will I give to
eat of the hidden manna, and will give
him a white stone, and in the stone a
new name written, which no man
knoweth saving he that receiveth *it*.
18 And unto the angel of the church
in Thyatira write; These things saith the
Son of God, who hath his eyes like unto
a flame of fire, and his feet *are* like fine
brass;
19 I know thy works, and charity, and
service, and faith, and thy patience,
and thy works; and the last *to be* more
than the first.
20 Notwithstanding I have a few
things against thee, because thou suf-
ferest that woman Jezebel, which calleth herself a prophetess, to teach and
to seduce my servants to commit fornication, and to eat things sacrificed unto
idols.
21 And I gave her space to repent of
her fornication; and she repented not.
22 Behold, I will cast her into a bed,
and them that commit adultery with
her into great tribulation, except they
repent of their deeds.
23 And I will kill her children with
death; and all the churches shall know
that I am he which searcheth the reins
and hearts: and I will give unto every
one of you according to your works.
24 But unto you I say, and unto the
rest in Thyatira, as many as have not
this doctrine, and which have not
known the depths of Satan, as they
speak; I will put upon you none other
burden.
25 But that which ye have *already*
hold fast till I come.
26 And he that overcometh, and keepeth my works unto the end, to him will
I give power over the nations:
27 And he shall rule them with a rod
of iron; as the vessels of a potter shall
they be broken to shivers: even as I
received of my Father.
28 And I will give him the morning
star.
29 He that hath an ear, let him hear
what the Spirit saith unto the churches.

3 And unto the angel of the church in
Sardis write; These things saith he
that hath the seven Spirits of God, and
the seven stars; I know thy works, that
thou hast a name that thou livest, and
art dead.
2 Be watchful, and strengthen the
things which remain, that are ready to
die: for I have not found thy works perfect before God.
3 Remember therefore how thou hast
received and heard, and hold fast, and
repent. If therefore thou shalt not
watch, I will come on thee as a thief,
and thou shalt not know what hour I
will come upon thee.
4 Thou hast a few names even in
Sardis which have not defiled their garments; and they shall walk with me in
white: for they are worthy.
5 He that overcometh, the same shall
be clothed in white raiment; and I will
not blot out his name out of the book of
life, but I will confess his name before
my Father, and before his angels.
6 He that hath an ear, let him hear
what the Spirit saith unto the churches.
7 And to the angel of the church in
Philadelphia write; These things saith
he that is holy, he that is true, he that
hath the key of David, he that openeth,
and no man shutteth; and shutteth, and
no man openeth;

8 I know thy works: behold, I have set before thee an open door, and no man can shut it: for thou hast a little strength, and hast kept my word, and hast not denied my name.

9 Behold, I will make them of the synagogue of Satan, which say they are Jews, and are not, but do lie; behold, I will make them to come and worship before thy feet, and to know that I have loved thee.

10 Because thou hast kept the word of my patience, I also will keep thee from the hour of temptation, which shall come upon all the world, to try them that dwell upon the earth.

11 Behold, I come quickly: hold that fast which thou hast, that no man take thy crown.

12 Him that overcometh will I make a pillar in the temple of my God, and he shall go no more out: and I will write upon him the name of my God, and the name of the city of my God, *which is* new Jerusalem, which cometh down out of heaven from my God: and *I will write upon him* my new name.

13 He that hath an ear, let him hear what the Spirit saith unto the churches.

14 And unto the angel of the church of the Laodiceans write; These things saith the Amen, the faithful and true witness, the beginning of the creation of God;

15 I know thy works, that thou art neither cold nor hot: I would thou wert cold or hot.

16 So then because thou art lukewarm, and neither cold nor hot, I will spue thee out of my mouth.

17 Because thou sayest, I am rich, and increased with goods, and have need of nothing; and knowest not that thou art wretched, and miserable, and poor, and blind, and naked:

18 I counsel thee to buy of me gold tried in the fire, that thou mayest be rich; and white raiment, that thou mayest be clothed, and *that* the shame of thy nakedness do not appear; and anoint thine eyes with eyesalve, that thou mayest see.

19 As many as I love, I rebuke and chasten: be zealous therefore, and repent.

20 Behold, I stand at the door, and knock: if any man hear my voice, and open the door, I will come in to him, and will sup with him, and he with me.

21 To him that overcometh will I grant to sit with me in my throne, even as I also overcame, and am set down with my Father in his throne.

22 He that hath an ear, let him hear what the Spirit saith unto the churches.

4 After this I looked, and, behold, a door *was* opened in heaven: and the first voice which I heard *was* as it were of a trumpet talking with me; which said, Come up hither, and I will shew thee things which must be hereafter.

2 And immediately I was in the spirit: and, behold, a throne was set in heaven, and *one* sat on the throne.

3 And he that sat was to look upon like a jasper and a sardine stone: and *there was* a rainbow round about the throne, in sight like unto an emerald.

4 And round about the throne *were* four and twenty seats: and upon the seats I saw four and twenty elders sitting, clothed in white raiment; and they had on their heads crowns of gold.

5 And out of the throne proceeded lightnings and thunderings and voices: and *there were* seven lamps of fire

burning before the throne, which are
the seven Spirits of God.
6 And before the throne *there was* a
sea of glass like unto crystal: and in the
midst of the throne, and round about
the throne, *were* four beasts full of eyes
before and behind.
7 And the first beast *was* like a lion,
and the second beast like a calf, and
the third beast had a face as a man, and
the fourth beast *was* like a flying eagle.
8 And the four beasts had each of
them six wings about *him*; and *they*
were full of eyes within: and they rest
not day and night, saying, Holy, holy,
holy, Lord God Almighty, which was,
and is, and is to come.
9 And when those beasts give glory
and honour and thanks to him that sat
on the throne, who liveth for ever and
ever,
10 The four and twenty elders fall
down before him that sat on the throne,
and worship him that liveth for ever
and ever, and cast their crowns before
the throne, saying,
11 Thou art worthy, O Lord, to receive
glory and honour and power: for thou
hast created all things, and for thy pleasure they are and were created.

5 And I saw in the right hand of him
that sat on the throne a book
written within and on the backside,
sealed with seven seals.
2 And I saw a strong angel proclaiming with a loud voice, Who is worthy to
open the book, and to loose the seals
thereof?
3 And no man in heaven, nor in earth,
neither under the earth, was able to
open the book, neither to look thereon.
4 And I wept much, because no man
was found worthy to open and to read
the book, neither to look thereon.
5 And one of the elders saith unto me,
Weep not: behold, the Lion of the tribe
of Juda, the Root of David, hath prevailed to open the book, and to loose
the seven seals thereof.
6 And I beheld, and, lo, in the midst of
the throne and of the four beasts, and
in the midst of the elders, stood a Lamb
as it had been slain, having seven horns
and seven eyes, which are the seven
Spirits of God sent forth into all the
earth.
7 And he came and took the book out
of the right hand of him that sat upon
the throne.
8 And when he had taken the book,
the four beasts and four *and* twenty
elders fell down before the Lamb, having every one of them harps, and gold-
en vials full of odours, which are the
prayers of saints.
9 And they sung a new song, saying,
Thou art worthy to take the book, and
to open the seals thereof: for thou wast
slain, and hast redeemed us to God by
thy blood out of every kindred, and
tongue, and people, and nation;
10 And hast made us unto our God
kings and priests: and we shall reign on
the earth.
11 And I beheld, and I heard the voice
of many angels round about the throne
and the beasts and the elders: and the
number of them was ten thousand
times ten thousand, and thousands of
thousands;
12 Saying with a loud voice, Worthy is
the Lamb that was slain to receive
power, and riches, and wisdom, and
strength, and honour, and glory, and
blessing.
13 And every creature which is in
heaven, and on the earth, and under
the earth, and such as are in the sea,

and all that are in them, heard I saying,
Blessing, and honour, and glory, and
power, *be* unto him that sitteth upon
the throne, and unto the Lamb for ever
and ever.
14 And the four beasts said, Amen.
And the four *and* twenty elders fell
down and worshipped him that liveth
for ever and ever.

6 And I saw when the Lamb opened
one of the seals, and I heard, as it
were the noise of thunder, one of the
four beasts saying, Come and see.
2 And I saw, and behold a white
horse: and he that sat on him had a
bow; and a crown was given unto him:
and he went forth conquering, and to
conquer.
3 And when he had opened the second seal, I heard the second beast say,
Come and see.
4 And there went out another horse
that was red: and *power* was given to
him that sat thereon to take peace from
the earth, and that they should kill one
another: and there was given unto him
a great sword.
5 And when he had opened the third
seal, I heard the third beast say, Come
and see. And I beheld, and lo a black
horse; and he that sat on him had a pair
of balances in his hand.
6 And I heard a voice in the midst of
the four beasts say, A measure of wheat
for a penny, and three measures of barley for a penny; and *see* thou hurt not
the oil and the wine.
7 And when he had opened the fourth
seal, I heard the voice of the fourth
beast say, Come and see.
8 And I looked, and behold a pale
horse: and his name that sat on him was
Death, and Hell followed with him. And
power was given unto them over the
fourth part of the earth, to kill with
sword, and with hunger, and with death,
and with the beasts of the earth.
9 And when he had opened the fifth
seal, I saw under the altar the souls of
them that were slain for the word of
God, and for the testimony which they
held:
10 And they cried with a loud voice,
saying, How long, O Lord, holy and true,
dost thou not judge and avenge our
blood on them that dwell on the earth?
11 And white robes were given unto
every one of them; and it was said unto
them, that they should rest yet for a
little season, until their fellowservants
also and their brethren, that should be
killed as they *were*, should be fulfilled.
12 And I beheld when he had opened
the sixth seal, and, lo, there was a great
earthquake; and the sun became black
as sackcloth of hair, and the moon
became as blood;
13 And the stars of heaven fell unto
the earth, even as a fig tree casteth her
untimely figs, when she is shaken of a
mighty wind.
14 And the heaven departed as a
scroll when it is rolled together; and
every mountain and island were moved
out of their places.
15 And the kings of the earth, and the
great men, and the rich men, and the
chief captains, and the mighty men,
and every bondman, and every free
man, hid themselves in the dens and in
the rocks of the mountains;
16 And said to the mountains and
rocks, Fall on us, and hide us from the
face of him that sitteth on the throne,
and from the wrath of the Lamb:
17 For the great day of his wrath is
come; and who shall be able to stand?

7 And after these things I saw four
angels standing on the four corners
of the earth, holding the four winds of
the earth, that the wind should not
blow on the earth, nor on the sea, nor
on any tree.
2 And I saw another angel ascending
from the east, having the seal of the
living God: and he cried with a loud
voice to the four angels, to whom it was
given to hurt the earth and the sea,
3 Saying, Hurt not the earth, neither
the sea, nor the trees, till we have
sealed the servants of our God in their
foreheads.
4 And I heard the number of them
which were sealed: *and there were*
sealed an hundred *and* forty *and* four
thousand of all the tribes of the children of Israel.
5 Of the tribe of Juda *were* sealed
twelve thousand. Of the tribe of
Reuben *were* sealed twelve thousand.
Of the tribe of Gad *were* sealed twelve
thousand.
6 Of the tribe of Aser *were* sealed
twelve thousand. Of the tribe of
Nepthalim *were* sealed twelve thousand. Of the tribe of Manasses *were*
sealed twelve thousand.
7 Of the tribe of Simeon *were* sealed
twelve thousand. Of the tribe of Levi
were sealed twelve thousand. Of the
tribe of Issachar *were* sealed twelve
thousand.
8 Of the tribe of Zabulon *were* sealed
twelve thousand. Of the tribe of Joseph
were sealed twelve thousand. Of the
tribe of Benjamin *were* sealed twelve
thousand.
9 After this I beheld, and, lo, a great
multitude, which no man could number, of all nations, and kindreds, and
people, and tongues, stood before the
throne, and before the Lamb, clothed
with white robes, and palms in their
hands;
10 And cried with a loud voice, saying, Salvation to our God which sitteth
upon the throne, and unto the Lamb.
11 And all the angels stood round
about the throne, and *about* the elders
and the four beasts, and fell before the
throne on their faces, and worshipped
God,
12 Saying, Amen: Blessing, and glory,
and wisdom, and thanksgiving, and
honour, and power, and might, *be* unto
our God for ever and ever. Amen.
13 And one of the elders answered,
saying unto me, What are these which
are arrayed in white robes? and whence
came they?
14 And I said unto him, Sir, thou
knowest. And he said to me, These are
they which came out of great tribulation, and have washed their robes, and
made them white in the blood of the
Lamb.
15 Therefore are they before the
throne of God, and serve him day and
night in his temple: and he that sitteth
on the throne shall dwell among them.
16 They shall hunger no more, neither thirst any more; neither shall the
sun light on them, nor any heat.
17 For the Lamb which is in the midst
of the throne shall feed them, and shall
lead them unto living fountains of
waters: and God shall wipe away all
tears from their eyes.

8 And when he had opened the
seventh seal, there was silence in
heaven about the space of half an hour.
2 And I saw the seven angels which
stood before God; and to them were
given seven trumpets.

3 And another angel came and stood at the altar, having a golden censer; and there was given unto him much incense, that he should offer *it* with the prayers of all saints upon the golden altar which was before the throne.

4 And the smoke of the incense, *which came* with the prayers of the saints, ascended up before God out of the angel's hand.

5 And the angel took the censer, and filled it with fire of the altar, and cast *it* into the earth: and there were voices, and thunderings, and lightnings, and an earthquake.

6 And the seven angels which had the seven trumpets prepared themselves to sound.

7 The first angel sounded, and there followed hail and fire mingled with blood, and they were cast upon the earth: and the third part of trees was burnt up, and all green grass was burnt up.

8 And the second angel sounded, and as it were a great mountain burning with fire was cast into the sea: and the third part of the sea became blood;

9 And the third part of the creatures which were in the sea, and had life, died; and the third part of the ships were destroyed.

10 And the third angel sounded, and there fell a great star from heaven, burning as it were a lamp, and it fell upon the third part of the rivers, and upon the fountains of waters;

11 And the name of the star is called Wormwood: and the third part of the waters became wormwood; and many men died of the waters, because they were made bitter.

12 And the fourth angel sounded, and the third part of the sun was smitten, and the third part of the moon, and the third part of the stars; so as the third part of them was darkened, and the day shone not for a third part of it, and the night likewise.

13 And I beheld, and heard an angel flying through the midst of heaven, saying with a loud voice, Woe, woe, woe, to the inhabiters of the earth by reason of the other voices of the trumpet of the three angels, which are yet to sound!

9 And the fifth angel sounded, and I saw a star fall from heaven unto the earth: and to him was given the key of the bottomless pit.

2 And he opened the bottomless pit; and there arose a smoke out of the pit, as the smoke of a great furnace; and the sun and the air were darkened by reason of the smoke of the pit.

3 And there came out of the smoke locusts upon the earth: and unto them was given power, as the scorpions of the earth have power.

4 And it was commanded them that they should not hurt the grass of the earth, neither any green thing, neither any tree; but only those men which have not the seal of God in their foreheads.

5 And to them it was given that they should not kill them, but that they should be tormented five months: and their torment *was* as the torment of a scorpion, when he striketh a man.

6 And in those days shall men seek death, and shall not find it; and shall desire to die, and death shall flee from them.

7 And the shapes of the locusts *were* like unto horses prepared unto battle; and on their heads *were* as it were crowns like gold, and their faces *were* as the faces of men.

8 And they had hair as the hair of
women, and their teeth were as *the
teeth* of lions.
9 And they had breastplates, as it
were breastplates of iron; and the
sound of their wings *was* as the sound
of chariots of many horses running to
battle.
10 And they had tails like unto scorpions, and there were stings in their tails:
and their power *was* to hurt men five
months.
11 And they had a king over them,
which is the angel of the bottomless
pit, whose name in the Hebrew tongue
is Abaddon, but in the Greek tongue
hath *his* name Apollyon.
12 One woe is past; *and*, behold, there
come two woes more hereafter.
13 And the sixth angel sounded, and I
heard a voice from the four horns of the
golden altar which is before God,
14 Saying to the sixth angel which
had the trumpet, Loose the four angels
which are bound in the great river
Euphrates.
15 And the four angels were loosed,
which were prepared for an hour, and a
day, and a month, and a year, for to slay
the third part of men.
16 And the number of the army of the
horsemen *were* two hundred thousand
thousand: and I heard the number of
them.
17 And thus I saw the horses in the
vision, and them that sat on them, having breastplates of fire, and of jacinth,
and brimstone: and the heads of the
horses *were* as the heads of lions; and
out of their mouths issued fire and
smoke and brimstone.
18 By these three was the third part
of men killed, by the fire, and by the
smoke, and by the brimstone, which
issued out of their mouths.
19 For their power is in their mouth,
and in their tails: for their tails *were*
like unto serpents, and had heads, and
with them they do hurt.
20 And the rest of the men which
were not killed by these plagues yet
repented not of the works of their
hands, that they should not worship
devils, and idols of gold, and silver, and
brass, and stone, and of wood: which
neither can see, nor hear, nor walk:
21 Neither repented they of their
murders, nor of their sorceries, nor of
their fornication, nor of their thefts.

10 And I saw another mighty angel
come down from heaven, clothed
with a cloud: and a rainbow *was* upon
his head, and his face *was* as it were the
sun, and his feet as pillars of fire:
2 And he had in his hand a little book
open: and he set his right foot upon the
sea, and *his* left *foot* on the earth,
3 And cried with a loud voice, as
when a lion roareth: and when he had
cried, seven thunders uttered their
voices.
4 And when the seven thunders had
uttered their voices, I was about to
write: and I heard a voice from heaven
saying unto me, Seal up those things
which the seven thunders uttered, and
write them not.
5 And the angel which I saw stand
upon the sea and upon the earth lifted
up his hand to heaven,
6 And sware by him that liveth for
ever and ever, who created heaven, and
the things that therein are, and the
earth, and the things that therein are,
and the sea, and the things which are
therein, that there should be time no
longer:

7 But in the days of the voice of the
seventh angel, when he shall begin to
sound, the mystery of God should be
finished, as he hath declared to his
servants the prophets.
8 And the voice which I heard from
heaven spake unto me again, and said,
Go *and* take the little book which is
open in the hand of the angel which
standeth upon the sea and upon the
earth.
9 And I went unto the angel, and said
unto him, Give me the little book. And
he said unto me, Take *it*, and eat it up;
and it shall make thy belly bitter, but it
shall be in thy mouth sweet as honey.
10 And I took the little book out of
the angel's hand, and ate it up; and it
was in my mouth sweet as honey: and
as soon as I had eaten it, my belly was
bitter.
11 And he said unto me, Thou must
prophesy again before many peoples,
and nations, and tongues, and kings.

11 And there was given me a reed
like unto a rod: and the angel
stood, saying, Rise, and measure the
temple of God, and the altar, and them
that worship therein.
2 But the court which is without the
temple leave out, and measure it not;
for it is given unto the Gentiles: and the
holy city shall they tread under foot
forty *and* two months.
3 And I will give *power* unto my two
witnesses, and they shall prophesy a
thousand two hundred *and* threescore
days, clothed in sackcloth.
4 These are the two olive trees, and
the two candlesticks standing before
the God of the earth.
5 And if any man will hurt them, fire
proceedeth out of their mouth, and
devoureth their enemies: and if any
man will hurt them, he must in this
manner be killed.
6 These have power to shut heaven,
that it rain not in the days of their
prophecy: and have power over waters
to turn them to blood, and to smite the
earth with all plagues, as often as they
will.
7 And when they shall have finished
their testimony, the beast that ascendeth out of the bottomless pit shall
make war against them, and shall overcome them, and kill them.
8 And their dead bodies *shall lie* in
the street of the great city, which spiritually is called Sodom and Egypt,
where also our Lord was crucified.
9 And they of the people and kindreds and tongues and nations shall
see their dead bodies three days and an
half, and shall not suffer their dead
bodies to be put in graves.
10 And they that dwell upon the
earth shall rejoice over them, and make
merry, and shall send gifts one to
another; because these two prophets
tormented them that dwelt on the
earth.
11 And after three days and an half
the Spirit of life from God entered into
them, and they stood upon their feet;
and great fear fell upon them which
saw them.
12 And they heard a great voice from
heaven saying unto them, Come up
hither. And they ascended up to heaven
in a cloud; and their enemies beheld
them.
13 And the same hour was there a
great earthquake, and the tenth part of
the city fell, and in the earthquake
were slain of men seven thousand: and
the remnant were affrighted, and gave
glory to the God of heaven.

14 The second woe is past; *and*,
behold, the third woe cometh quickly.
15 And the seventh angel sounded;
and there were great voices in heaven,
saying, The kingdoms of this world are
become *the kingdoms* of our Lord, and
of his Christ; and he shall reign for ever
and ever.
16 And the four and twenty elders,
which sat before God on their seats, fell
upon their faces, and worshipped God,
17 Saying, We give thee thanks, O
Lord God Almighty, which art, and
wast, and art to come; because thou
hast taken to thee thy great power, and
hast reigned.
18 And the nations were angry, and
thy wrath is come, and the time of the
dead, that they should be judged, and
that thou shouldest give reward unto
thy servants the prophets, and to the
saints, and them that fear thy name,
small and great; and shouldest destroy
them which destroy the earth.
19 And the temple of God was opened
in heaven, and there was seen in his
temple the ark of his testament: and
there were lightnings, and voices, and
thunderings, and an earthquake, and
great hail.

12

12 And there appeared a great wonder in heaven; a woman clothed
with the sun, and the moon under her
feet, and upon her head a crown of
twelve stars:
2 And she being with child cried, travailing in birth, and pained to be delivered.
3 And there appeared another wonder in heaven; and behold a great red
dragon, having seven heads and ten
horns, and seven crowns upon his
heads.
4 And his tail drew the third part of
the stars of heaven, and did cast them
to the earth: and the dragon stood
before the woman which was ready to
be delivered, for to devour her child as
soon as it was born.
5 And she brought forth a man child,
who was to rule all nations with a rod of
iron: and her child was caught up unto
God, and *to* his throne.
6 And the woman fled into the wilderness, where she hath a place prepared
of God, that they should feed her there
a thousand two hundred *and* threescore days.
7 And there was war in heaven:
Michael and his angels fought against
the dragon; and the dragon fought and
his angels,
8 And prevailed not; neither was their
place found any more in heaven.
9 And the great dragon was cast out,
that old serpent, called the Devil, and
Satan, which deceiveth the whole
world: he was cast out into the earth,
and his angels were cast out with him.
10 And I heard a loud voice saying in
heaven, Now is come salvation, and
strength, and the kingdom of our God,
and the power of his Christ: for the
accuser of our brethren is cast down,
which accused them before our God
day and night.
11 And they overcame him by the
blood of the Lamb, and by the word of
their testimony; and they loved not
their lives unto the death.
12 Therefore rejoice, *ye* heavens, and
ye that dwell in them. Woe to the inhabiters of the earth and of the sea! for the
devil is come down unto you, having
great wrath, because he knoweth that
he hath but a short time.

13 And when the dragon saw that he
was cast unto the earth, he persecuted
the woman which brought forth the
man *child*.
14 And to the woman were given two
wings of a great eagle, that she might
fly into the wilderness, into her place,
where she is nourished for a time, and
times, and half a time, from the face of
the serpent.
15 And the serpent cast out of his
mouth water as a flood after the
woman, that he might cause her to be
carried away of the flood.
16 And the earth helped the woman,
and the earth opened her mouth, and
swallowed up the flood which the dragon cast out of his mouth.
17 And the dragon was wroth with the
woman, and went to make war with the
remnant of her seed, which keep the
commandments of God, and have the
testimony of Jesus Christ.

13 And I stood upon the sand of the
sea, and saw a beast rise up out
of the sea, having seven heads and ten
horns, and upon his horns ten crowns,
and upon his heads the name of blasphemy.
2 And the beast which I saw was like
unto a leopard, and his feet were as *the*
feet of a bear, and his mouth as the
mouth of a lion: and the dragon gave
him his power, and his seat, and great
authority.
3 And I saw one of his heads as it
were wounded to death; and his deadly
wound was healed: and all the world
wondered after the beast.
4 And they worshipped the dragon
which gave power unto the beast: and
they worshipped the beast, saying, Who
is like unto the beast? who is able to
make war with him?
5 And there was given unto him a
mouth speaking great things and blasphemies; and power was given unto
him to continue forty *and* two months.
6 And he opened his mouth in blasphemy against God, to blaspheme his
name, and his tabernacle, and them
that dwell in heaven.
7 And it was given unto him to make
war with the saints, and to overcome
them: and power was given him over all
kindreds, and tongues, and nations.
8 And all that dwell upon the earth
shall worship him, whose names are not
written in the book of life of the Lamb
slain from the foundation of the world.
9 If any man have an ear, let him hear.
10 He that leadeth into captivity shall
go into captivity: he that killeth with
the sword must be killed with the
sword. Here is the patience and the
faith of the saints.
11 And I beheld another beast coming up out of the earth; and he had two
horns like a lamb, and he spake as a
dragon.
12 And he exerciseth all the power of
the first beast before him, and causeth
the earth and them which dwell therein
to worship the first beast, whose deadly
wound was healed.
13 And he doeth great wonders, so
that he maketh fire come down from
heaven on the earth in the sight of men,
14 And deceiveth them that dwell on
the earth by *the means of* those miracles which he had power to do in the
sight of the beast; saying to them that
dwell on the earth, that they should
make an image to the beast, which had
the wound by a sword, and did live.
15 And he had power to give life unto
the image of the beast, that the image
of the beast should both speak, and

cause that as many as would not worship the image of the beast should be
killed.
16 And he causeth all, both small and
great, rich and poor, free and bond, to
receive a mark in their right hand, or in
their foreheads:
17 And that no man might buy or sell,
save he that had the mark, or the name
of the beast, or the number of his name.
18 Here is wisdom. Let him that hath
understanding count the number of the
beast: for it is the number of a man; and
his number *is* Six hundred threescore
and six.

14 And I looked, and, lo, a Lamb
stood on the mount Sion, and
with him an hundred forty *and* four
thousand, having his Father's name
written in their foreheads.
2 And I heard a voice from heaven, as
the voice of many waters, and as the
voice of a great thunder: and I heard
the voice of harpers harping with their
harps:
3 And they sung as it were a new song
before the throne, and before the four
beasts, and the elders: and no man
could learn that song but the hundred
and forty *and* four thousand, which
were redeemed from the earth.
4 These are they which were not
defiled with women; for they are virgins. These are they which follow the
Lamb whithersoever he goeth. These
were redeemed from among men, *being*
the firstfruits unto God and to the
Lamb.
5 And in their mouth was found no
guile: for they are without fault before
the throne of God.
6 And I saw another angel fly in the
midst of heaven, having the everlasting
gospel to preach unto them that dwell
on the earth, and to every nation, and
kindred, and tongue, and people,
7 Saying with a loud voice, Fear God,
and give glory to him; for the hour of
his judgment is come: and worship him
that made heaven, and earth, and the
sea, and the fountains of waters.
8 And there followed another angel,
saying, Babylon is fallen, is fallen, that
great city, because she made all nations
drink of the wine of the wrath of her
fornication.
9 And the third angel followed them,
saying with a loud voice, If any man
worship the beast and his image, and
receive *his* mark in his forehead, or in
his hand,
10 The same shall drink of the wine of
the wrath of God, which is poured out
without mixture into the cup of his
indignation; and he shall be tormented
with fire and brimstone in the presence
of the holy angels, and in the presence
of the Lamb:
11 And the smoke of their torment
ascendeth up for ever and ever: and
they have no rest day nor night, who
worship the beast and his image, and
whosoever receiveth the mark of his
name.
12 Here is the patience of the saints:
here *are* they that keep the commandments of God, and the faith of Jesus.
13 And I heard a voice from heaven
saying unto me, Write, Blessed *are* the
dead which die in the Lord from henceforth: Yea, saith the Spirit, that they
may rest from their labours; and their
works do follow them.
14 And I looked, and behold a white
cloud, and upon the cloud *one* sat like
unto the Son of man, having on his
head a golden crown, and in his hand a
sharp sickle.

15 And another angel came out of the temple, crying with a loud voice to him that sat on the cloud, Thrust in thy sickle, and reap: for the time is come for thee to reap; for the harvest of the earth is ripe.

16 And he that sat on the cloud thrust in his sickle on the earth; and the earth was reaped.

17 And another angel came out of the temple which is in heaven, he also having a sharp sickle.

18 And another angel came out from the altar, which had power over fire; and cried with a loud cry to him that had the sharp sickle, saying, Thrust in thy sharp sickle, and gather the clusters of the vine of the earth; for her grapes are fully ripe.

19 And the angel thrust in his sickle into the earth, and gathered the vine of the earth, and cast *it* into the great winepress of the wrath of God.

20 And the winepress was trodden without the city, and blood came out of the winepress, even unto the horse bridles, by the space of a thousand *and* six hundred furlongs.

15 And I saw another sign in heaven, great and marvellous, seven angels having the seven last plagues; for in them is filled up the wrath of God.

2 And I saw as it were a sea of glass mingled with fire: and them that had gotten the victory over the beast, and over his image, and over his mark, *and* over the number of his name, stand on the sea of glass, having the harps of God.

3 And they sing the song of Moses the servant of God, and the song of the Lamb, saying, Great and marvellous *are* thy works, Lord God Almighty; just and true *are* thy ways, thou King of saints.

4 Who shall not fear thee, O Lord, and glorify thy name? for *thou* only *art* holy: for all nations shall come and worship before thee; for thy judgments are made manifest.

5 And after that I looked, and, behold, the temple of the tabernacle of the testimony in heaven was opened:

6 And the seven angels came out of the temple, having the seven plagues, clothed in pure and white linen, and having their breasts girded with golden girdles.

7 And one of the four beasts gave unto the seven angels seven golden vials full of the wrath of God, who liveth for ever and ever.

8 And the temple was filled with smoke from the glory of God, and from his power; and no man was able to enter into the temple, till the seven plagues of the seven angels were fulfilled.

16 And I heard a great voice out of the temple saying to the seven angels, Go your ways, and pour out the vials of the wrath of God upon the earth.

2 And the first went, and poured out his vial upon the earth; and there fell a noisome and grievous sore upon the men which had the mark of the beast, and *upon* them which worshipped his image.

3 And the second angel poured out his vial upon the sea; and it became as the blood of a dead *man*: and every living soul died in the sea.

4 And the third angel poured out his vial upon the rivers and fountains of waters; and they became blood.

5 And I heard the angel of the waters
say, Thou art righteous, O Lord, which
art, and wast, and shalt be, because
thou hast judged thus.
6 For they have shed the blood of
saints and prophets, and thou hast
given them blood to drink; for they are
worthy.
7 And I heard another out of the altar
say, Even so, Lord God Almighty, true
and righteous *are* thy judgments.
8 And the fourth angel poured out his
vial upon the sun; and power was given
unto him to scorch men with fire.
9 And men were scorched with great
heat, and blasphemed the name of
God, which hath power over these
plagues: and they repented not to give
him glory.
10 And the fifth angel poured out his
vial upon the seat of the beast; and his
kingdom was full of darkness; and they
gnawed their tongues for pain,
11 And blasphemed the God of heav-
en because of their pains and their
sores, and repented not of their deeds.
12 And the sixth angel poured out his
vial upon the great river Euphrates;
and the water thereof was dried up,
that the way of the kings of the east
might be prepared.
13 And I saw three unclean spirits
like frogs *come* out of the mouth of the
dragon, and out of the mouth of the
beast, and out of the mouth of the false
prophet.
14 For they are the spirits of devils,
working miracles, *which* go forth unto
the kings of the earth and of the whole
world, to gather them to the battle of
that great day of God Almighty.
15 Behold, I come as a thief. Blessed *is*
he that watcheth, and keepeth his garments, lest he walk naked, and they see
his shame.
16 And he gathered them together
into a place called in the Hebrew
tongue Armageddon.
17 And the seventh angel poured out
his vial into the air; and there came a
great voice out of the temple of heaven,
from the throne, saying, It is done.
18 And there were voices, and thunders, and lightnings; and there was a
great earthquake, such as was not since
men were upon the earth, so mighty an
earthquake, *and* so great.
19 And the great city was divided into
three parts, and the cities of the nations
fell: and great Babylon came in remembrance before God, to give unto her the
cup of the wine of the fierceness of his
wrath.
20 And every island fled away, and
the mountains were not found.
21 And there fell upon men a great
hail out of heaven, *every stone* about
the weight of a talent: and men blasphemed God because of the plague of
the hail; for the plague thereof was
exceeding great.

17 And there came one of the seven
angels which had the seven vials,
and talked with me, saying unto me,
Come hither; I will shew unto thee the
judgment of the great whore that
sitteth upon many waters:
2 With whom the kings of the earth
have committed fornication, and the
inhabitants of the earth have been
made drunk with the wine of her fornication.
3 So he carried me away in the spirit
into the wilderness: and I saw a woman
sit upon a scarlet coloured beast, full of

names of blasphemy, having seven heads and ten horns.

4 And the woman was arrayed in purple and scarlet colour, and decked with gold and precious stones and pearls, having a golden cup in her hand full of abominations and filthiness of her fornication:

5 And upon her forehead *was* a name written, MYSTERY, BABYLON THE GREAT, THE MOTHER OF HARLOTS AND ABOMINATIONS OF THE EARTH.

6 And I saw the woman drunken with the blood of the saints, and with the blood of the martyrs of Jesus: and when I saw her, I wondered with great admiration.

7 And the angel said unto me, Wherefore didst thou marvel? I will tell thee the mystery of the woman, and of the beast that carrieth her, which hath the seven heads and ten horns.

8 The beast that thou sawest was, and is not; and shall ascend out of the bottomless pit, and go into perdition: and they that dwell on the earth shall wonder, whose names were not written in the book of life from the foundation of the world, when they behold the beast that was, and is not, and yet is.

9 And here *is* the mind which hath wisdom. The seven heads are seven mountains, on which the woman sitteth.

10 And there are seven kings: five are fallen, and one is, *and* the other is not yet come; and when he cometh, he must continue a short space.

11 And the beast that was, and is not, even he is the eighth, and is of the seven, and goeth into perdition.

12 And the ten horns which thou sawest are ten kings, which have received no kingdom as yet; but receive power as kings one hour with the beast.

13 These have one mind, and shall give their power and strength unto the beast.

14 These shall make war with the Lamb, and the Lamb shall overcome them: for he is Lord of lords, and King of kings: and they that are with him *are* called, and chosen, and faithful.

15 And he saith unto me, The waters which thou sawest, where the whore sitteth, are peoples, and multitudes, and nations, and tongues.

16 And the ten horns which thou sawest upon the beast, these shall hate the whore, and shall make her desolate and naked, and shall eat her flesh, and burn her with fire.

17 For God hath put in their hearts to fulfil his will, and to agree, and give their kingdom unto the beast, until the words of God shall be fulfilled.

18 And the woman which thou sawest is that great city, which reigneth over the kings of the earth.

18 And after these things I saw another angel come down from heaven, having great power; and the earth was lightened with his glory.

2 And he cried mightily with a strong voice, saying, Babylon the great is fallen, is fallen, and is become the habitation of devils, and the hold of every foul spirit, and a cage of every unclean and hateful bird.

3 For all nations have drunk of the wine of the wrath of her fornication, and the kings of the earth have committed fornication with her, and the merchants of the earth are waxed rich through the abundance of her delicacies.

4 And I heard another voice from heaven, saying, Come out of her, my people, that ye be not partakers of her sins, and that ye receive not of her plagues.

5 For her sins have reached unto heaven, and God hath remembered her iniquities.

6 Reward her even as she rewarded you, and double unto her double according to her works: in the cup which she hath filled fill to her double.

7 How much she hath glorified herself, and lived deliciously, so much torment and sorrow give her: for she saith in her heart, I sit a queen, and am no widow, and shall see no sorrow.

8 Therefore shall her plagues come in one day, death, and mourning, and famine; and she shall be utterly burned with fire: for strong *is* the Lord God who judgeth her.

9 And the kings of the earth, who have committed fornication and lived deliciously with her, shall bewail her, and lament for her, when they shall see the smoke of her burning,

10 Standing afar off for the fear of her torment, saying, Alas, alas, that great city Babylon, that mighty city! for in one hour is thy judgment come.

11 And the merchants of the earth shall weep and mourn over her; for no man buyeth their merchandise any more:

12 The merchandise of gold, and silver, and precious stones, and of pearls, and fine linen, and purple, and silk, and scarlet, and all thyine wood, and all manner vessels of ivory, and all manner vessels of most precious wood, and of brass, and iron, and marble,

13 And cinnamon, and odours, and ointments, and frankincense, and wine, and oil, and fine flour, and wheat, and beasts, and sheep, and horses, and chariots, and slaves, and souls of men.

14 And the fruits that thy soul lusted after are departed from thee, and all things which were dainty and goodly are departed from thee, and thou shalt find them no more at all.

15 The merchants of these things, which were made rich by her, shall stand afar off for the fear of her torment, weeping and wailing,

16 And saying, Alas, alas, that great city, that was clothed in fine linen, and purple, and scarlet, and decked with gold, and precious stones, and pearls!

17 For in one hour so great riches is come to nought. And every shipmaster, and all the company in ships, and sailors, and as many as trade by sea, stood afar off,

18 And cried when they saw the smoke of her burning, saying, What *city* *is* like unto this great city!

19 And they cast dust on their heads, and cried, weeping and wailing, saying, Alas, alas, that great city, wherein were made rich all that had ships in the sea by reason of her costliness! for in one hour is she made desolate.

20 Rejoice over her, *thou* heaven, and *ye* holy apostles and prophets; for God hath avenged you on her.

21 And a mighty angel took up a stone like a great millstone, and cast *it* into the sea, saying, Thus with violence shall that great city Babylon be thrown down, and shall be found no more at all.

22 And the voice of harpers, and musicians, and of pipers, and trumpeters, shall be heard no more at all in thee; and no craftsman, of whatsoever craft *he be*, shall be found any more in

thee; and the sound of a millstone shall
be heard no more at all in thee;
23 And the light of a candle shall
shine no more at all in thee; and the
voice of the bridegroom and of the
bride shall be heard no more at all in
thee: for thy merchants were the great
men of the earth; for by thy sorceries
were all nations deceived.
24 And in her was found the blood of
prophets, and of saints, and of all that
were slain upon the earth.

19 And after these things I heard a
great voice of much people in
heaven, saying, Alleluia; Salvation, and
glory, and honour, and power, unto the
Lord our God:
2 For true and righteous *are* his judgments: for he hath judged the great
whore, which did corrupt the earth
with her fornication, and hath avenged
the blood of his servants at her hand.
3 And again they said, Alleluia. And
her smoke rose up for ever and ever.
4 And the four and twenty elders and
the four beasts fell down and worshipped God that sat on the throne,
saying, Amen; Alleluia.
5 And a voice came out of the throne,
saying, Praise our God, all ye his servants, and ye that fear him, both small
and great.
6 And I heard as it were the voice of a
great multitude, and as the voice of
many waters, and as the voice of mighty
thunderings, saying, Alleluia: for the
Lord God omnipotent reigneth.
7 Let us be glad and rejoice, and give
honour to him: for the marriage of the
Lamb is come, and his wife hath made
herself ready.
8 And to her was granted that she
should be arrayed in fine linen, clean
and white: for the fine linen is the righteousness of saints.
9 And he saith unto me, Write,
Blessed *are* they which are called unto
the marriage supper of the Lamb. And
he saith unto me, These are the true
sayings of God.
10 And I fell at his feet to worship
him. And he said unto me, See *thou do
it* not: I am thy fellowservant, and of
thy brethren that have the testimony of
Jesus: worship God: for the testimony
of Jesus is the spirit of prophecy.
11 And I saw heaven opened, and
behold a white horse; and he that sat
upon him *was* called Faithful and True,
and in righteousness he doth judge and
make war.
12 His eyes *were* as a flame of fire,
and on his head *were* many crowns; and
he had a name written, that no man
knew, but he himself.
13 And he *was* clothed with a vesture
dipped in blood: and his name is called
The Word of God.
14 And the armies *which were* in
heaven followed him upon white horses, clothed in fine linen, white and
clean.
15 And out of his mouth goeth a sharp
sword, that with it he should smite the
nations: and he shall rule them with a
rod of iron: and he treadeth the winepress of the fierceness and wrath of
Almighty God.
16 And he hath on *his* vesture and on
his thigh a name written, KING OF
KINGS, AND LORD OF LORDS.
17 And I saw an angel standing in the
sun; and he cried with a loud voice, saying to all the fowls that fly in the midst
of heaven, Come and gather yourselves
together unto the supper of the great
God;

18 That ye may eat the flesh of kings,
and the flesh of captains, and the flesh
of mighty men, and the flesh of horses,
and of them that sit on them, and the
flesh of all *men, both* free and bond,
both small and great.
19 And I saw the beast, and the kings
of the earth, and their armies, gathered
together to make war against him that
sat on the horse, and against his army.
20 And the beast was taken, and with
him the false prophet that wrought
miracles before him, with which he
deceived them that had received the
mark of the beast, and them that worshipped his image. These both were
cast alive into a lake of fire burning
with brimstone.
21 And the remnant were slain with
the sword of him that sat upon the
horse, which *sword* proceeded out of
his mouth: and all the fowls were filled
with their flesh.

20 And I saw an angel come down
from heaven, having the key of
the bottomless pit and a great chain in
his hand.
2 And he laid hold on the dragon, that
old serpent, which is the Devil, and
Satan, and bound him a thousand
years,
3 And cast him into the bottomless
pit, and shut him up, and set a seal
upon him, that he should deceive the
nations no more, till the thousand years
should be fulfilled: and after that he
must be loosed a little season.
4 And I saw thrones, and they sat
upon them, and judgment was given
unto them: and *I saw* the souls of them
that were beheaded for the witness of
Jesus, and for the word of God, and
which had not worshipped the beast,
neither his image, neither had received
his mark upon their foreheads, or in
their hands; and they lived and reigned
with Christ a thousand years.
5 But the rest of the dead lived not
again until the thousand years were
finished. This *is* the first resurrection.
6 Blessed and holy *is* he that hath
part in the first resurrection: on such
the second death hath no power, but
they shall be priests of God and of
Christ, and shall reign with him a thousand years.
7 And when the thousand years are
expired, Satan shall be loosed out of his
prison,
8 And shall go out to deceive the
nations which are in the four quarters
of the earth, Gog and Magog, to gather
them together to battle: the number of
whom *is* as the sand of the sea.
9 And they went up on the breadth of
the earth, and compassed the camp of
the saints about, and the beloved city:
and fire came down from God out of
heaven, and devoured them.
10 And the devil that deceived them
was cast into the lake of fire and brimstone, where the beast and the false
prophet *are*, and shall be tormented
day and night for ever and ever.
11 And I saw a great white throne,
and him that sat on it, from whose face
the earth and the heaven fled away;
and there was found no place for them.
12 And I saw the dead, small and
great, stand before God; and the books
were opened: and another book was
opened, which is *the book* of life: and
the dead were judged out of those
things which were written in the books,
according to their works.
13 And the sea gave up the dead
which were in it; and death and hell
delivered up the dead which were in

them: and they were judged every man according to their works.

14 And death and hell were cast into the lake of fire. This is the second death.

15 And whosoever was not found written in the book of life was cast into the lake of fire.

21

And I saw a new heaven and a new earth: for the first heaven and the first earth were passed away; and there was no more sea.

2 And I John saw the holy city, new Jerusalem, coming down from God out of heaven, prepared as a bride adorned for her husband.

3 And I heard a great voice out of heaven saying, Behold, the tabernacle of God *is* with men, and he will dwell with them, and they shall be his people, and God himself shall be with them, *and be* their God.

4 And God shall wipe away all tears from their eyes; and there shall be no more death, neither sorrow, nor crying, neither shall there be any more pain: for the former things are passed away.

5 And he that sat upon the throne said, Behold, I make all things new. And he said unto me, Write: for these words are true and faithful.

6 And he said unto me, It is done. I am Alpha and Omega, the beginning and the end. I will give unto him that is athirst of the fountain of the water of life freely.

7 He that overcometh shall inherit all things; and I will be his God, and he shall be my son.

8 But the fearful, and unbelieving, and the abominable, and murderers, and whoremongers, and sorcerers, and idolaters, and all liars, shall have their part in the lake which burneth with fire and brimstone: which is the second death.

9 And there came unto me one of the seven angels which had the seven vials full of the seven last plagues, and talked with me, saying, Come hither, I will shew thee the bride, the Lamb's wife.

10 And he carried me away in the spirit to a great and high mountain, and shewed me that great city, the holy Jerusalem, descending out of heaven from God,

11 Having the glory of God: and her light *was* like unto a stone most precious, even like a jasper stone, clear as crystal;

12 And had a wall great and high, *and* had twelve gates, and at the gates twelve angels, and names written thereon, which are *the names* of the twelve tribes of the children of Israel:

13 On the east three gates; on the north three gates; on the south three gates; and on the west three gates.

14 And the wall of the city had twelve foundations, and in them the names of the twelve apostles of the Lamb.

15 And he that talked with me had a golden reed to measure the city, and the gates thereof, and the wall thereof.

16 And the city lieth foursquare, and the length is as large as the breadth: and he measured the city with the reed, twelve thousand furlongs. The length and the breadth and the height of it are equal.

17 And he measured the wall thereof, an hundred *and* forty *and* four cubits, *according to* the measure of a man, that is, of the angel.

18 And the building of the wall of it was *of* jasper: and the city *was* pure gold, like unto clear glass.

19 And the foundations of the wall of
the city *were* garnished with all manner of precious stones. The first foundation *was* jasper; the second, sapphire;
the third, a chalcedony; the fourth, an
emerald;
20 The fifth, sardonyx; the sixth, sardius; the seventh, chrysolite; the eighth,
beryl; the ninth, a topaz; the tenth, a
chrysoprasus; the eleventh, a jacinth;
the twelfth, an amethyst.
21 And the twelve gates *were* twelve
pearls; every several gate was of one
pearl: and the street of the city *was*
pure gold, as it were transparent glass.
22 And I saw no temple therein: for
the Lord God Almighty and the Lamb
are the temple of it.
23 And the city had no need of the
sun, neither of the moon, to shine in it:
for the glory of God did lighten it, and
the Lamb *is* the light thereof.
24 And the nations of them which are
saved shall walk in the light of it: and
the kings of the earth do bring their
glory and honour into it.
25 And the gates of it shall not be
shut at all by day: for there shall be no
night there.
26 And they shall bring the glory and
honour of the nations into it.
27 And there shall in no wise enter
into it any thing that defileth, neither
whatsoever worketh abomination, or
maketh a lie: but they which are written in the Lamb's book of life.

22 And he shewed me a pure river
of water of life, clear as crystal,
proceeding out of the throne of God
and of the Lamb.
2 In the midst of the street of it, and
on either side of the river, *was there* the
tree of life, which bare twelve *manner
of* fruits, *and* yielded her fruit every
month: and the leaves of the tree *were*
for the healing of the nations.
3 And there shall be no more curse:
but the throne of God and of the Lamb
shall be in it; and his servants shall
serve him:
4 And they shall see his face; and his
name *shall be* in their foreheads.
5 And there shall be no night there;
and they need no candle, neither light
of the sun; for the Lord God giveth
them light: and they shall reign for ever
and ever.
6 And he said unto me, These sayings
are faithful and true: and the Lord God
of the holy prophets sent his angel to
shew unto his servants the things which
must shortly be done.
7 Behold, I come quickly: blessed *is*
he that keepeth the sayings of the
prophecy of this book.
8 And I John saw these things, and
heard *them*. And when I had heard and
seen, I fell down to worship before the
feet of the angel which shewed me
these things.
9 Then saith he unto me, See *thou do
it* not: for I am thy fellowservant, and of
thy brethren the prophets, and of them
which keep the sayings of this book:
worship God.
10 And he saith unto me, Seal not the
sayings of the prophecy of this book: for
the time is at hand.
11 He that is unjust, let him be unjust
still: and he which is filthy, let him be
filthy still: and he that is righteous, let
him be righteous still: and he that is
holy, let him be holy still.
12 And, behold, I come quickly; and
my reward *is* with me, to give every
man according as his work shall be.
13 I am Alpha and Omega, the beginning and the end, the first and the last.

14 Blessed *are* they that do his commandments, that they may have right to the tree of life, and may enter in through the gates into the city.
15 For without *are* dogs, and sorcerers, and whoremongers, and murderers, and idolaters, and whosoever loveth and maketh a lie.
16 I Jesus have sent mine angel to testify unto you these things in the churches. I am the root and the offspring of David, *and* the bright and morning star.
17 And the Spirit and the bride say, Come. And let him that heareth say, Come. And let him that is athirst come. And whosoever will, let him take the water of life freely.

18 For I testify unto every man that heareth the words of the prophecy of this book, If any man shall add unto these things, God shall add unto him the plagues that are written in this book:
19 And if any man shall take away from the words of the book of this prophecy, God shall take away his part out of the book of life, and out of the holy city, and *from* the things which are written in this book.
20 He which testifieth these things saith, Surely I come quickly. Amen. Even so, come, Lord Jesus.
21 The grace of our Lord Jesus Christ *be* with you all. Amen.

VERSE FINDER

WHEN YOU NEED:

ACCEPTANCE
John 17:9–14
Romans 8:1
1 Corinthians 1:30
Ephesians 1:3–6

ASSURANCE
Isaiah 26:19
Matthew 17:20
John 5:24
Colossians 1:27
1 John 5:13

BLESSINGS
John 13:12–17
Galatians 3:9–14
Ephesians 1:3

CARING
Psalm 146:9
Matthew 6:30
1 Corinthians 8:3
1 Peter 5:7

COMFORT
Psalm 10:17
Psalm 94:19
Isaiah 61:1
Haggai 1:13
2 Corinthians 1:4–7

COMPASSION
Psalm 51:1
Isaiah 30:18
Isaiah 49:13
Mark 6:34

CONFIDENCE
Psalm 118:8–9
Jeremiah 17:7
1 Thessalonians 5:8
Hebrews 6:18
1 John 5:14

CONTENTMENT
Genesis 3:1–7
Philippians 4:10–14
1 Timothy 6:6
Hebrews 13:5

COURAGE
Joshua 1:9
Psalm 27:14
Hebrews 6:18
1 John 2:28

DECISIVENESS
Psalm 119:105
Proverbs 15:7
James 1:2–8

DISCERNMENT
Psalm 119:125
Acts 17:11
1 Corinthians 12:3

EMPLOYMENT
Genesis 31:42
Psalm 37:4
Ephesians 6:6–7

ENCOURAGEMENT
Psalm 138:3
Isaiah 40:31
Romans 15:4
1 Thessalonians 4:18

ENDURANCE/PERSEVERANCE
Matthew 10:22
Romans 5:3–4
2 Corinthians 6:4
James 1:12

FAITH
Romans 3:27–31
Ephesians 6:16
Hebrews 12:1–2
1 Peter 1:7

FORGIVENESS
Isaiah 1:18
Ezekiel 36:25
Acts 13:38–39
Hebrews 9:22
1 John 1:8–9

GOD
Nehemiah 9:31
Psalm 62:6
Romans 8:15
Hebrews 4:16
1 John 4:16

GOD'S PRESENCE
Psalm 16:8
Isaiah 41:10
Matthew 28:20
John 14:15–21

GOD'S WILL
Psalm 143:10
Mark 14:36
Romans 12:2
Hebrews 10:36
1 Peter 2:15

GRACE
Romans 6:14
2 Corinthians 4:15
Ephesians 2:8
Hebrews 4:16
1 Peter 5:12

GUIDANCE
Exodus 15:13
Psalm 25:4–5
Psalm 43:3
Proverbs 13:13–14

HEALING/RECOVERY
2 Kings 20:1–7
Psalm 6:1–3
Matthew 9:6
2 Corinthians 12:7–10

HOPE
Psalm 130:5
Acts 1:11
2 Thessalonians 2:16–17
Hebrews 10:23
Revelation 21:1–5

HUMILITY
Philippians 2:3–4
Titus 3:2
1 Peter 5:5
1 Peter 5:6

INTEGRITY
Psalm 101:2
Psalm 119:1
Proverbs 2:7
Titus 2:7

JOY
Psalm 16:11
Psalm 19:8
Psalm 30:5
John 16:20–24
Galatians 5:22–23

LIGHT
Psalm 27:1
Psalm 119:105
Isaiah 42:16
Ephesians 5:8

LOVE
John 3:16
John 13:34
Romans 8:35–39
Romans 13:8–10
1 Corinthians 13:4–7
Galatians 5:22–23
1 John 4:16

MERCY
1 Timothy 1:16
Hebrews 4:16
1 Peter 1:3
Jude 22–23

PATIENCE
Romans 15:5
Galatians 5:22–23
Ephesians 4:2
James 5:10–11

PEACE
John 14:27
Romans 5:1
Galatians 5:22–23
Philippians 4:6–7

PERSPECTIVE
Genesis 50:20
Psalm 51:4
Luke 18:27
Romans 8:28
Romans 8:35–39

POWER
Acts 1:8
Hebrews 1:3
Hebrews 4:12
James 5:16

PRAYER
Psalm 40:13
Psalm 116:1
Luke 18:9–14
John 16:23–24
James 4:3

PRIORITIES
Proverbs 3:1–6
Proverbs 4:7
Matthew 6:33
Mark 12:29–31

PROTECTION
Psalm 32:7
Psalm 91:1-4
Proverbs 19:23
Daniel 3:16-18
1 Peter 1:5

PROVISION
Deuteronomy 10:18
Matthew 6:25-34
Luke 11:3
2 Thessalonians 3:10-12

PURPOSE
Psalm 57:2
Proverbs 19:21
Romans 8:28
2 Timothy 2:21

RESTORATION
Psalm 6:1-5
Psalm 51:12
Psalm 119:93
1 Peter 5:10

SELF-CONTROL
Galatians 5:22-23
Titus 2:12
2 Peter 1:6

SELF-ESTEEM/SELF-WORTH
Psalm 8:3-5
Psalm 139:1-6
Luke 12:7
John 3:16

STRENGTH
Exodus 15:2
Deuteronomy 11:8
Isaiah 40:31
2 Thessalonians 2:16-17
1 Peter 4:11

TRUTH
John 14:6
John 17:17
Colossians 1:5-6, 23
2 Timothy 2:19

WISDOM
Proverbs 2:6-22
Proverbs 9:10
Colossians 2:2-3
James 1:5

WHEN YOU FEEL:

AFRAID
2 Chronicles 20:15
Psalm 23
Psalm 27:1
John 14:27

ANGRY
Proverbs 14:29
Proverbs 15:1
Matthew 5:22
Ephesians 4:26-27

ASHAMED
Psalm 51:1-4
Psalm 119:46
Matthew 10:32-33
Romans 1:16-17

BITTER
Luke 15:11-32
Ephesians 4:31-32
Hebrews 12:14-17

BORED
Psalm 34:1
Galatians 5:13
1 Thessalonians 5:17

BROKENHEARTED
Psalm 34:18
Psalm 147:3
Isaiah 61:1

BURNED OUT
Exodus 18:13-26
Isaiah 40:31
Matthew 11:28-30
Mark 6:31-32

CRITICIZED
Proverbs 13:18
Proverbs 15:31-32
Ecclesiastes 7:5
Titus 2:8
James 4:11

DEPRESSED
1 Kings 19:1-9
Psalm 42:5-11
Psalm 130
Isaiah 61:3

DISAPPOINTED
Proverbs 23:18
Romans 5:4-5
1 Peter 2:6

DISCOURAGED
Deuteronomy 31:8
2 Corinthians 7:6
Galatians 6:9
Hebrews 12:5-6

DOUBTFUL
Matthew 17:14-20
Luke 7:18-23
John 20:24-29
James 1:5-8

ENVIOUS **(SEE JEALOUS)**

GRIEF/SORROW
2 Samuel 1:1-12
Nehemiah 1:1-11
Psalm 23
Psalm 31:10, 14
John 11:33-35
John 16:33
1 Peter 5:7

GUILTY
Romans 3:21-31
Romans 8:1-17
1 John 3:18-24

HURT
Isaiah 11:9
Luke 6:28
1 Thessalonians 3:1-8

INSECURE
Exodus 3:7-4:17
Numbers 13:25-30
1 Peter 4:10-11

INTIMIDATED
Genesis 15:1
Psalm 27:1
Psalm 46:1-3
Acts 4:31

JEALOUS
1 Corinthians 13:4
James 3:13-18
1 Peter 2:1

LONELY
1 Kings 19:1-18
Psalm 68:6
John 16:5-15
Hebrews 10:25
Hebrews 13:5

REBELLIOUS
1 Samuel 15:22-23
Proverbs 27:12
Titus 1:10

REJECTED
Psalm 27:9-10
Psalm 77:1-12
Jeremiah 33:25
Mark 6:1-6

SAD
1 Samuel 1:15-18
Nehemiah 8:10-12
Psalm 42:5-11
Romans 12:15

STRESSED
Exodus 18:13-26
Psalm 62:1-8
Matthew 11:28-30
Mark 6:31-32

TEMPTED
Matthew 4:1-11
Mark 14:38
1 Corinthians 10:13
Hebrews 2:18

THANKFUL
1 Chronicles 16:8
Colossians 3:15-17
1 Timothy 4:4
James 5:13

WEAK
Psalm 73:26
2 Corinthians 12:8-10
2 Corinthians 13:3-4
Philippians 3:21

WORRIED
Matthew 6:25-34
Luke 10:38-42
Philippians 4:6-9
1 Peter 5:7

WHAT THE BIBLE SAYS ABOUT:

ABORTION
Genesis 1:26
Psalm 139:13–16
Jeremiah 1:5
Mark 9:36–37

ABUSE
Psalm 12:5
Matthew 26:67–68
Ephesians 5:21–6:4

ACCOUNTABILITY
Matthew 12:36
Luke 17:3
1 Corinthians 3:8
2 Corinthians 5:10

ADULTERY
Exodus 20:14
Leviticus 20:10
2 Samuel 11
Proverbs 5:15–23
Romans 13:9
1 Corinthians 6:9–11
Hebrews 13:4

AGING
Psalm 92:12–15
Proverbs 16:31
Proverbs 20:29
Titus 2:1–8

ALCOHOL
Proverbs 20:1
Proverbs 23:29–35
Romans 13:13–14
Galatians 5:19–21

ANGELS
Exodus 14:19
Psalm 103:21
Daniel 4:17
Daniel 6:22
Daniel 10:12–13
Zechariah 1:9–14
Hebrews 1:14

APPEARANCE
1 Samuel 16:7
Proverbs 19:22
1 Timothy 2:9–10
1 Peter 3:3–4

ARGUMENTS
Proverbs 15:1
Proverbs 20:3
Proverbs 26:17
Ephesians 4:26

ASTROLOGY
Deuteronomy 4:19
Job 9:9
Isaiah 45:12
Jeremiah 10:2

ATTITUDES
Genesis 4:6–7
Numbers 14:1–4
Habakkuk 3:17–19
Philippians 1:20–25

AUTHORITY
Matthew 28:18–20
Acts 4:2–12
Romans 13:1–5
2 Corinthians 2:17

BELIEF
John 20:25–29
Romans 4:20–24
Romans 10:9–10
James 2:14–24

BIBLE
Psalm 119:99
1 Corinthians 2:12–16
Ephesians 6:17
2 Timothy 3:16
1 Peter 2:2

CHARACTER
Psalm 105:16–22
Matthew 5:43–48
Romans 5:3–4
James 1:2–4

CHURCH
Matthew 16:18
Ephesians 2:21
Ephesians 4:11–12
Hebrews 10:25

CONFESSION
Psalm 66:16–20
James 5:16
1 John 1:8–10

CONSCIENCE
Proverbs 28:13–18
Romans 9:1
1 Timothy 1:19
Hebrews 10:22

CONSEQUENCES
Genesis 3
Proverbs 27:12
Galatians 6:7–8

CREATION
Genesis 1:27
Genesis 1:31
Psalm 19:1
Psalm 89:11
Revelation 21:1–4

CRITICISM
Proverbs 27:6
Matthew 7:3–5
Luke 17:3–4
1 Corinthians 13:4–5

CULTS
2 Corinthians 11:3–4
Ephesians 4:14–15
1 Timothy 6:3–5
2 Peter 2:1

DEATH
Psalm 23:4
Romans 5:15
1 Corinthians 15:51–58
Hebrews 9:27–28

DEVIL
2 Corinthians 11:14
Ephesians 6:11–12
1 Peter 5:8–9
Revelation 12:10–12

DISCIPLINING CHILDREN
Proverbs 13:24
Proverbs 19:18
Proverbs 29:15
Ephesians 6:4

DISCRIMINATION
Leviticus 19:15
Malachi 3:5
Galatians 3:28
James 2:1–4

DISHONESTY
Leviticus 19:35–36
Deuteronomy 19:14
Proverbs 12:22

DIVORCE
Genesis 2:21–24
Malachi 2:15–16
Matthew 19:3–11
1 Corinthians 7:10–16

DRINKING (SEE ALCOHOL)

EMOTIONS
Genesis 4:2–8
Ezra 3
Proverbs 4:23
Galatians 5:1–17

ETERNAL LIFE
Matthew 25:46
John 3:16
2 Corinthians 5:1–10
1 John 5:11–12

EVIL
Job 4:8
Romans 1:24–28
Ephesians 4:22
Ephesians 6:12
Revelation 21:4

EVOLUTION
Genesis 1
Genesis 5:1–2
Job 38:4
Psalm 8:3–9
Psalm 33:4–11

FAMILY
Exodus 10:2
Deuteronomy 6:6–7
Ephesians 5:21–6:4
1 Timothy 3:5

FOUL LANGUAGE
Proverbs 4:24
Ephesians 5:4
Colossians 4:6
1 Timothy 4:12

FREEDOM
John 8:36
Romans 5:21
Galatians 5:1

FRIENDSHIP
Proverbs 16:28
Proverbs 17:17
Proverbs 27:6, 9
John 15:15

FUTURE
Deuteronomy 5:29
Jeremiah 29:11
Jeremiah 31:17
1 Corinthians 2:9

GIVING
Exodus 35:22
Ezra 2:68–69
Acts 2:44–45
1 John 3:17

GOD'S ACCEPTANCE
Romans 3:27–30
Romans 5:15–16
Romans 15:7
Hebrews 12:6

GOSSIP
Exodus 23:1
Proverbs 11:13
Proverbs 16:28
1 Timothy 5:13

GREED
Proverbs 1:15–19
Ephesians 5:3–5
Colossians 3:5

HEAVEN
Isaiah 66:1
Daniel 7:27
John 14:2–3
Revelation 21
Revelation 21:3–4

HELL
Matthew 25:41–46
Romans 1:18–32
Revelation 20:11–15

HOMOSEXUALITY
Leviticus 18:22
Romans 1:26–27
1 Corinthians 6:9–11

HONESTY (SEE INTEGRITY)

HOSPITALITY
Luke 10:7
Romans 12:13
Hebrews 13:2

HYPOCRISY
Matthew 6:1–16
Matthew 23:1–36
1 Peter 2:1

INTEGRITY
Psalm 101:3–8
Psalm 119:1
Proverbs 10:9
Proverbs 20:7

JUDGMENTALISM
Isaiah 11:3–5
Matthew 7:1–5
1 Corinthians 5:12–13
James 5:9

JUSTICE
Deuteronomy 16:19–20
Psalm 75:2
Isaiah 42:3
Daniel 9:14
Romans 2:1–4

KINDNESS
Ephesians 4:32
1 Thessalonians 5:15
2 Timothy 2:24

LAZINESS
Proverbs 6:6–11
1 Thessalonians 5:14
2 Thessalonians 3:10

LEADERSHIP
1 Chronicles 12:18
Proverbs 28:2
Luke 22:25–26
Romans 12:8

LEGALISM
Mark 7:6–9
Galatians 4:8–12
Colossians 2:16–23

MARRIAGE
Genesis 2:23–24
Matthew 19:4–8
Ephesians 5:21–26
Hebrews 13:4

MATERIALISM
Psalm 119:37
Matthew 6:19–21
Matthew 10:41–42
Mark 4:18–19
1 John 2:16

MONEY
Matthew 6:19–24
Mark 10:23
1 Timothy 6:10
1 Timothy 6:17–18

MUSIC
Exodus 15:1
Psalm 81:1–2
Colossians 3:16

OCCULT
Deuteronomy 18:10–14
2 Chronicles 33:6
Isaiah 47:9
Revelation 21:8

PAIN
Psalm 41:3
Hebrews 4:15–16
Hebrews 13:3
Revelation 21:4

PARENTING
Deuteronomy 6:6–7
Proverbs 1:8
Proverbs 22:6
Ephesians 6:4

PRAYER
Psalm 5:1–3
Psalm 138:3
Colossians 4:2
Hebrews 4:14–16

PREJUDICE
Luke 10:25–37
Ephesians 2:14
Colossians 3:11
James 2:1–9

PRIDE
Proverbs 16:5
Proverbs 16:18
Mark 7:20–23
Luke 18:9–14

PROCRASTINATION
Joshua 24:15
Habakkuk 2:3
Luke 14:16–24
2 Corinthians 6:2

PURITY
Psalm 119:9
1 Corinthians 1:30
2 Timothy 2:21
1 John 3:2–3

QUESTIONS
Job 42:1–3
Luke 7:18–23
Luke 21:12–15
1 Peter 3:15

REPENTANCE
2 Kings 22:19
Luke 13:5
2 Corinthians 7:10
2 Peter 3:9

REPUTATION
Deuteronomy 4:1–14
Ruth 2:1–13
Proverbs 3:3–4
Proverbs 22:1

RESPECT
Exodus 3:5
Leviticus 19:3
Romans 13:1–7
Ephesians 5:33
1 Peter 2:17

RESURRECTION
Matthew 28:5–10
John 5:24–30
John 6:38–40
1 Corinthians 15:12–21
1 Corinthians 15:51–53

REST
Exodus 20:8–10
Matthew 11:28–29
Mark 6:31
Hebrews 4:9–11

REVENGE
Leviticus 19:18
Nahum 1:2
Romans 12:19

SALVATION
Acts 2:21
Acts 4:12
Romans 10:8–10
Ephesians 2:8–9

SATAN **(SEE DEVIL)**

SECOND COMING
Matthew 24:36
1 Thessalonians 4:13–14
1 Thessalonians 4:17
1 Thessalonians 5:2–6

SERVING OTHERS
Matthew 8:14–15
Matthew 20:28
Matthew 23:11–12
Luke 22:24–27
John 13:1–17

SEX
Genesis 2:24
Matthew 5:28
1 Corinthians 6:18
1 Thessalonians 4:3–5

SICKNESS
Psalm 41
Matthew 25:34–40
James 5:14–15

SIN
Genesis 3:17
Romans 3:23
Romans 6:23
James 4:17
1 John 1:9

SINGLENESS
Matthew 19:12
1 Corinthians 7:6–7
1 Corinthians 7:32–35

SUBMISSION
1 Corinthians 11:11–12
Ephesians 5:21–33
Hebrews 12:9

SUCCESS
Proverbs 16:3
Mark 9:33–37
2 Corinthians 3:5

SUFFERING
John 9:2–3
John 16:33
Hebrews 2:18
James 1:2–4
1 Peter 4:12–16

SUICIDE
1 Chronicles 10
Psalm 40:1–3
Jeremiah 29:11
Ephesians 1:15–21

SWEARING (SEE FOUL LANGUAGE)

WOMEN
Genesis 1:26–27
Proverbs 31:10–30
Galatians 3:28

WORK
Genesis 2:1–3
Exodus 35:30–36:1
Ruth 2:7
John 3:27
Ephesians 6:6–7

WORSHIP
Psalm 24:6
Psalm 150
Mark 7:7
John 4:21–24
Philippians 3:3

ONE–YEAR READING PLAN

READ THROUGH THE ENTIRE BIBLE IN ONE YEAR

- ❑ January 1 .... Genesis 1:1–3:24
- ❑ January 2 .... Genesis 4:1–5:32
- ❑ January 3 .... Genesis 6:1–8:22
- ❑ January 4 .... Genesis 9:1–11:32
- ❑ January 5 .... Genesis 12:1–14:24
- ❑ January 6 .... Genesis 15:1–17:27
- ❑ January 7 .... Genesis 18:1–20:18
- ❑ January 8 .... Genesis 21:1–23:20
- ❑ January 9 .... Genesis 24:1–28:9
- ❑ January 10 .... Genesis 28:10–30:43
- ❑ January 11 .... Genesis 31:1–36:43
- ❑ January 12 .... Genesis 37:1–41:57
- ❑ January 13 .... Genesis 42:1–45:28
- ❑ January 14 .... Genesis 46:1–50:26
- ❑ January 15 .... Exodus 1:1–4:31
- ❑ January 16 .... Exodus 5:1–7:13
- ❑ January 17 .... Exodus 7:14–12:30
- ❑ January 18 .... Exodus 12:31–18:27
- ❑ January 19 .... Exodus 19:1–24:18
- ❑ January 20 .... Exodus 25:1–31:18
- ❑ January 21 .... Exodus 32:1–34:35
- ❑ January 22 .... Exodus 35:1–40:38
- ❑ January 23 .... Leviticus 1:1–7:38
- ❑ January 24 .... Leviticus 8:1–10:20
- ❑ January 25 .... Leviticus 11:1–17:16
- ❑ January 26 .... Leviticus 18:1–22:33
- ❑ January 27 .... Leviticus 23:1–25:55
- ❑ January 28 .... Leviticus 26:1–27:34
- ❑ January 29 .... Numbers 1:1–4:49
- ❑ January 30 .... Numbers 5:1–10:10
- ❑ January 31 .... Numbers 10:11–14:45
- ❑ February 1 .... Numbers 15:1–21:35
- ❑ February 2 .... Numbers 22:1–25:18
- ❑ February 3 .... Numbers 26:1–31:54
- ❑ February 4 .... Numbers 32:1–34:29
- ❑ February 5 .... Numbers 35:1–36:13
- ❑ February 6 .... Deuteronomy 1:1–5:33
- ❑ February 7 .... Deuteronomy 6:1–11:32
- ❑ February 8 .... Deuteronomy 12:1–16:17
- ❑ February 9 .... Deuteronomy 16:18–20:20
- ❑ February 10 .... Deuteronomy 21:1–26:19
- ❑ February 11 .... Deuteronomy 27:1–30:20
- ❑ February 12 .... Deuteronomy 31:1–34:12
- ❑ February 13 .... Joshua 1:1–5:12
- ❑ February 14 .... Joshua 5:13–8:35
- ❑ February 15 .... Joshua 9:1–12:24
- ❑ February 16 .... Joshua 13:1–19:51
- ❑ February 17 .... Joshua 20:1–24:33
- ❑ February 18 .... Judges 1:1–3:6
- ❑ February 19 .... Judges 3:7–8:35
- ❑ February 20 .... Judges 9:1–12:15
- ❑ February 21 .... Judges 13:1–16:31
- ❑ February 22 .... Judges 17:1–21:25
- ❑ February 23 .... Ruth 1:1–4:22
- ❑ February 24 .... 1 Samuel 1:1–3:21
- ❑ February 25 .... 1 Samuel 4:1–7:17
- ❑ February 26 .... 1 Samuel 8:1–12:25
- ❑ February 27 .... 1 Samuel 13:1–15:35
- ❑ February 28 .... 1 Samuel 16:1–17:58
- ❑ March 1 .... 1 Samuel 18:1–20:42
- ❑ March 2 .... 1 Samuel 21:1–26:25
- ❑ March 3 .... 1 Samuel 27:1–31:13
- ❑ March 4 .... 2 Samuel 1:1–4:12
- ❑ March 5 .... 2 Samuel 5:1–7:29
- ❑ March 6 .... 2 Samuel 8:1–10:19
- ❑ March 7 .... 2 Samuel 11:1–12:31
- ❑ March 8 .... 2 Samuel 13:1–14:33
- ❑ March 9 .... 2 Samuel 15:1–20:26
- ❑ March 10 .... 2 Samuel 21:1–24:25
- ❑ March 11 .... 1 Kings 1:1–4:34
- ❑ March 12 .... 1 Kings 5:1–8:66
- ❑ March 13 .... 1 Kings 9:1–11:43
- ❑ March 14 .... 1 Kings 12:1–16:34
- ❑ March 15 .... 1 Kings 17:1–19:21

- ❑ March 16 .... 1 Kings 20:1–22:53
- ❑ March 17 .... 2 Kings 1:1–8:15
- ❑ March 18 .... 2 Kings 8:16–10:36
- ❑ March 19 .... 2 Kings 11:1–13:25
- ❑ March 20 .... 2 Kings 14:1–17:41
- ❑ March 21 .... 2 Kings 18:1–21:26
- ❑ March 22 .... 2 Kings 22:1–25:30
- ❑ March 23 .... 1 Chronicles 1:1–9:44
- ❑ March 24 .... 1 Chronicles 10:1–12:40
- ❑ March 25 .... 1 Chronicles 13:1–17:27
- ❑ March 26 .... 1 Chronicles 18:1–22:1
- ❑ March 27 .... 1 Chronicles 22:2–27:34
- ❑ March 28 .... 1 Chronicles 28:1–29:30
- ❑ March 29 .... 2 Chronicles 1:1–5:1
- ❑ March 30 .... 2 Chronicles 5:2–9:31
- ❑ March 31 .... 2 Chronicles 10:1–14:1
- ❑ April 1 .... 2 Chronicles 14:2–16:14
- ❑ April 2 .... 2 Chronicles 17:1–20:37
- ❑ April 3 .... 2 Chronicles 21:1–24:27
- ❑ April 4 .... 2 Chronicles 25:1–28:27
- ❑ April 5 .... 2 Chronicles 29:1–32:33
- ❑ April 6 .... 2 Chronicles 33:1–35:27
- ❑ April 7 .... 2 Chronicles 36:1–23
- ❑ April 8 .... Ezra 1:1–2:70
- ❑ April 9 .... Ezra 3:1–6:22
- ❑ April 10 .... Ezra 7:1–8:36
- ❑ April 11 .... Ezra 9:1–10:44
- ❑ April 12 .... Nehemiah 1:1–2:10
- ❑ April 13 .... Nehemiah 2:11–3:32
- ❑ April 14 .... Nehemiah 4:1–7:73
- ❑ April 15 .... Nehemiah 8:1–10:39
- ❑ April 16 .... Nehemiah 11:1–13:31
- ❑ April 17 .... Esther 1:1–2:23
- ❑ April 18 .... Esther 3:1–4:17
- ❑ April 19 .... Esther 5:1–10:3
- ❑ April 20 .... Job 1:1–2:13
- ❑ April 21 .... Job 3:1–14:22
- ❑ April 22 .... Job 15:1–21:34
- ❑ April 23 .... Job 22:1–31:40
- ❑ April 24 .... Job 32:1–37:24
- ❑ April 25 .... Job 38:1–41:34
- ❑ April 26 .... Job 42:1–17
- ❑ April 27 .... Psalms 1:1–4:8
- ❑ April 28 .... Psalms 5:1–8:9
- ❑ April 29 .... Psalms 9:1–12:8
- ❑ April 30 .... Psalms 13:1–16:11
- ❑ May 1 .... Psalms 17:1–20:9
- ❑ May 2 .... Psalms 21:1–24:10
- ❑ May 3 .... Psalms 25:1–28:9
- ❑ May 4 .... Psalms 29:1–32:11
- ❑ May 5 .... Psalms 33:1–36:12
- ❑ May 6 .... Psalms 37:1–41:13
- ❑ May 7 .... Psalms 42:1–45:17
- ❑ May 8 .... Psalms 46:1–49:20
- ❑ May 9 .... Psalms 50:1–53:6
- ❑ May 10 .... Psalms 54:1–56:13
- ❑ May 11 .... Psalms 57:1–59:17
- ❑ May 12 .... Psalms 60:1–62:12
- ❑ May 13 .... Psalms 63:1–65:13
- ❑ May 14 .... Psalms 66:1–68:35
- ❑ May 15 .... Psalms 69:1–72:20
- ❑ May 16 .... Psalms 73:1–75:10
- ❑ May 17 .... Psalms 76:1–78:72
- ❑ May 18 .... Psalms 79:1–81:16
- ❑ May 19 .... Psalms 82:1–84:12
- ❑ May 20 .... Psalms 85:1–89:52
- ❑ May 21 .... Psalms 90:1–92:15
- ❑ May 22 .... Psalms 93:1–95:11
- ❑ May 23 .... Psalms 96:1–98:9
- ❑ May 24 .... Psalms 99:1–101:8
- ❑ May 25 .... Psalms 102:1–104:35
- ❑ May 26 .... Psalms 105:1–106:48
- ❑ May 27 .... Psalms 107:1–109:31
- ❑ May 28 .... Psalms 110:1–112:10
- ❑ May 29 .... Psalms 113:1–115:18
- ❑ May 30 .... Psalms 116:1–118:29
- ❑ May 31 .... Psalm 119:1–176
- ❑ June 1 .... Psalms 120:1–124:8
- ❑ June 2 .... Psalms 125:1–129:8
- ❑ June 3 .... Psalms 130:1–134:3

- ❑ June 4 .... Psalms 135:1-137:9
- ❑ June 5 .... Psalms 138:1-140:13
- ❑ June 6 .... Psalms 141:1-144:15
- ❑ June 7 .... Psalms 145:1-150:6
- ❑ June 8 .... Proverbs 1:1-33
- ❑ June 9 .... Proverbs 2:1-22
- ❑ June 10 .... Proverbs 3:1-35
- ❑ June 11 .... Proverbs 4:1-27
- ❑ June 12 .... Proverbs 5:1-23
- ❑ June 13 .... Proverbs 6:1-35
- ❑ June 14 .... Proverbs 7:1-27
- ❑ June 15 .... Proverbs 8:1-36
- ❑ June 16 .... Proverbs 9:1-18
- ❑ June 17 .... Proverbs 10:1-32
- ❑ June 18 .... Proverbs 11:1-31
- ❑ June 19 .... Proverbs 12:1-28
- ❑ June 20 .... Proverbs 13:1-25
- ❑ June 21 .... Proverbs 14:1-35
- ❑ June 22 .... Proverbs 15:1-33
- ❑ June 23 .... Proverbs 16:1-33
- ❑ June 24 .... Proverbs 17:1-28
- ❑ June 25 .... Proverbs 18:1-24
- ❑ June 26 .... Proverbs 19:1-29
- ❑ June 27 .... Proverbs 20:1-30
- ❑ June 28 .... Proverbs 21:1-31
- ❑ June 29 .... Proverbs 22:1-29
- ❑ June 30 .... Proverbs 23:1-35
- ❑ July 1 .... Proverbs 24:1-34
- ❑ July 2 .... Proverbs 25:1-28
- ❑ July 3 .... Proverbs 26:1-28
- ❑ July 4 .... Proverbs 27:1-27
- ❑ July 5 .... Proverbs 28:1-28
- ❑ July 6 .... Proverbs 29:1-27
- ❑ July 7 .... Proverbs 30:1-33
- ❑ July 8 .... Proverbs 31:1-31
- ❑ July 9 .... Ecclesiastes 1:1-2:26
- ❑ July 10 .... Ecclesiastes 3:1-5:20
- ❑ July 11 .... Ecclesiastes 6:1-8:17
- ❑ July 12 .... Ecclesiastes 9:1-12:14
- ❑ July 13 .... Song of Songs 1:1-8:14
- ❑ July 14 .... Isaiah 1:1-6:13
- ❑ July 15 .... Isaiah 7:1-12:6
- ❑ July 16 .... Isaiah 13:1-18:7
- ❑ July 17 .... Isaiah 19:1-23:18
- ❑ July 18 .... Isaiah 24:1-27:13
- ❑ July 19 .... Isaiah 28:1-31:9
- ❑ July 20 .... Isaiah 32:1-35:10
- ❑ July 21 .... Isaiah 36:1-39:8
- ❑ July 22 .... Isaiah 40:1-48:22
- ❑ July 23 .... Isaiah 49:1-52:12
- ❑ July 24 .... Isaiah 52:13-55:13
- ❑ July 25 .... Isaiah 56:1-59:21
- ❑ July 26 .... Isaiah 60:1-66:24
- ❑ July 27 .... Jeremiah 1:1-6:30
- ❑ July 28 .... Jeremiah 7:1-10:25
- ❑ July 29 .... Jeremiah 11:1-15:21
- ❑ July 30 .... Jeremiah 16:1-20:18
- ❑ July 31 .... Jeremiah 21:1-24:10
- ❑ August 1 .... Jeremiah 25:1-29:32
- ❑ August 2 .... Jeremiah 30:1-33:26
- ❑ August 3 .... Jeremiah 34:1-38:28
- ❑ August 4 .... Jeremiah 39:1-45:5
- ❑ August 5 .... Jeremiah 46:1-52:34
- ❑ August 6 .... Lamentations 1:1-5:22
- ❑ August 7 .... Ezekiel 1:1-3:27
- ❑ August 8 .... Ezekiel 4:1-11:25
- ❑ August 9 .... Ezekiel 12:1-17:24
- ❑ August 10 .... Ezekiel 18:1-24:27
- ❑ August 11 .... Ezekiel 25:1-32:32
- ❑ August 12 .... Ezekiel 33:1-39:29
- ❑ August 13 .... Ezekiel 40:1-48:35
- ❑ August 14 .... Daniel 1:1-3:30
- ❑ August 15 .... Daniel 4:1-6:28
- ❑ August 16 .... Daniel 7:1-12:13
- ❑ August 17 .... Hosea 1:1-3:5
- ❑ August 18 .... Hosea 4:1-5:15
- ❑ August 19 .... Hosea 6:1-10:10
- ❑ August 20 .... Hosea 10:11-14:9
- ❑ August 21 .... Joel 1:1-2:27
- ❑ August 22 .... Joel 2:28-3:21

❑ August 23............................Amos 1:1-2:16
❑ August 24............................Amos 3:1-6:14
❑ August 25............................Amos 7:1-9:15
❑ August 26.........................Obadiah 1:1-21
❑ August 27.......................... Jonah 1:1-2:10
❑ August 28.......................... Jonah 3:1-4:11
❑ August 29..........................Micah 1:1-3:12
❑ August 30..........................Micah 4:1-5:15
❑ August 31..........................Micah 6:1-7:20
❑ September 1 ....Nahum 1:1-3:19
❑ September 2 .... Habakkuk 1:1-3:19
❑ September 3 ....Zephaniah 1:1-3:20
❑ September 4 ....Haggai 1:1-2:23
❑ September 5 .... Zechariah 1:1-8:23
❑ September 6 .... Zechariah 9:1-14:21
❑ September 7 ....Malachi 1:1-4:6
❑ September 8 .... Matthew 1:1-4:25
❑ September 9 .... Matthew 5:1-48
❑ September 10 .... Matthew 6:1-34
❑ September 11 .... Matthew 7:1-29
❑ September 12 .... Matthew 8:1-10:42
❑ September 13 .... Matthew 11:1-13:53
❑ September 14 .... Matthew 13:54-15:39
❑ September 15 .... Matthew 16:1-18:35
❑ September 16 .... Matthew 19:1-20:34
❑ September 17 .... Matthew 21:1-23:39
❑ September 18 .... Matthew 24:1-25:46
❑ September 19 .... Matthew 26:1-28:20
❑ September 20 ....Mark 1:1-3:35
❑ September 21 ....Mark 4:1-7:23
❑ September 22 ....Mark 7:24-9:1
❑ September 23 ....Mark 9:2-10:52
❑ September 24 ....Mark 11:1-12:44
❑ September 25 ....Mark 13:1-37
❑ September 26 ....Mark 14:1-16:20
❑ September 27 .... Luke 1:1-4:13
❑ September 28 .... Luke 4:14-6:49
❑ September 29 .... Luke 7:1-9:50
❑ September 30 .... Luke 9:51-10:42
❑ October 1 .... Luke 11:1-54
❑ October 2.............................. Luke 12:1-59
❑ October 3......................... Luke 13:1-14:35
❑ October 4......................... Luke 15:1-16:31
❑ October 5......................... Luke 17:1-19:27
❑ October 6...................... Luke 19:28-21:38
❑ October 7.............................. Luke 22:1-71
❑ October 8.............................. Luke 23:1-56
❑ October 9.............................. Luke 24:1-53
❑ October 10............................ John 1:1-2:12
❑ October 11........................ John 2:13-3:36
❑ October 12............................... John 4:1-42
❑ October 13........................ John 4:43-6:71
❑ October 14.......................... John 7:1-10:42
❑ October 15........................ John 11:1-12:50
❑ October 16........................ John 13:1-14:31
❑ October 17........................ John 15:1-17:26
❑ October 18........................ John 18:1-19:42
❑ October 19........................ John 20:1-21:25
❑ October 20............................ Acts 1:1-4:37
❑ October 21.............................. Acts 5:1-8:3
❑ October 22.......................... Acts 8:4-12:24
❑ October 23...................... Acts 12:25-15:35
❑ October 24...................... Acts 15:36-18:14
❑ October 25...................... Acts 18:15-21:14
❑ October 26...................... Acts 21:15-28:31
❑ October 27......................Romans 1:1-3:20
❑ October 28....................Romans 3:21-5:21
❑ October 29......................Romans 6:1-8:39
❑ October 30....................Romans 9:1-11:36
❑ October 31..................Romans 12:1-16:27
❑ November 1......... 1 Corinthians 1:1-4:21
❑ November 2......... 1 Corinthians 5:1-6:20
❑ November 3............ 1 Corinthians 7:1-40
❑ November 4......... 1 Corinthians 8:1-11:1
❑ November 5..... 1 Corinthians 11:2-14:40
❑ November 6..... 1 Corinthians 15:1-16:24
❑ November 7......... 2 Corinthians 1:1-2:11
❑ November 8....... 2 Corinthians 2:12-7:16
❑ November 9......... 2 Corinthians 8:1-9:15
❑ November 10... 2 Corinthians 10:1-13:14

- ❑ November 11 .... Galatians 1:1–2:21
- ❑ November 12 .... Galatians 3:1–4:31
- ❑ November 13 .... Galatians 5:1–6:18
- ❑ November 14 .... Ephesians 1:1–3:21
- ❑ November 15 .... Ephesians 4:1–6:24
- ❑ November 16 .... Philippians 1:1–30
- ❑ November 17 .... Philippians 2:1–30
- ❑ November 18 .... Philippians 3:1–21
- ❑ November 19 .... Philippians 4:1–23
- ❑ November 20 .... Colossians 1:1–2:23
- ❑ November 21 .... Colossians 3:1–4:18
- ❑ November 22 ... 1 Thessalonians 1:1–3:13
- ❑ November 23 ... 1 Thessalonians 4:1–5:28
- ❑ November 24 ... 2 Thessalonians 1:1–2:17
- ❑ November 25 ...... 2 Thessalonians 3:1–18
- ❑ November 26 .... 1 Timothy 1:1–17
- ❑ November 27 .... 1 Timothy 1:18–3:16
- ❑ November 28 .... 1 Timothy 4:1–6:21
- ❑ November 29 .... 2 Timothy 1:1–2:26
- ❑ November 30 .... 2 Timothy 3:1–4:22
- ❑ December 1 .... Titus 1:1–16
- ❑ December 2 .... Titus 2:1–15
- ❑ December 3 .... Titus 3:1–15
- ❑ December 4 .... Philemon 1:1–25
- ❑ December 5 .... Hebrews 1:1–2:18
- ❑ December 6 .... Hebrews 3:1–4:13
- ❑ December 7 .... Hebrews 4:14–7:28
- ❑ December 8 .... Hebrews 8:1–10:23
- ❑ December 9 .... Hebrews 10:24–13:25
- ❑ December 10 .... James 1:1–27
- ❑ December 11 .... James 2:1–3:12
- ❑ December 12 .... James 3:13–5:20
- ❑ December 13 .... 1 Peter 1:1–2:12
- ❑ December 14 .... 1 Peter 2:13–4:19
- ❑ December 15 .... 1 Peter 5:1–14
- ❑ December 16 .... 2 Peter 1:1–21
- ❑ December 17 .... 2 Peter 2:1–22
- ❑ December 18 .... 2 Peter 3:1–18
- ❑ December 19 .... 1 John 1:1–2:27
- ❑ December 20 .... 1 John 2:28–4:21
- ❑ December 21 .... 1 John 5:1–21
- ❑ December 22 .... 2 John 1:1–3 John 1:14
- ❑ December 23 .... Jude 1:1–25
- ❑ December 24 .... Revelation 1:1–3:22
- ❑ December 25 .... Revelation 4:1–5:14
- ❑ December 26 .... Revelation 6:1–8:6
- ❑ December 27 .... Revelation 8:7–11:19
- ❑ December 28 .... Revelation 12:1–14:20
- ❑ December 29 .... Revelation 15:1–16:21
- ❑ December 30 .... Revelation 17:1–20:15
- ❑ December 31 .... Revelation 21:1–22:21

CONCORDANCE

AARON
called for Moses and *A* — **Ex. 8:8**
prophetess, the sister of *A* — **Ex. 15:20**
And *A* shall burn thereon — **Ex. 30:7**
A shall make an atonement — **Ex. 30:10**
Speak unto *A* thy brother — **Lev. 16:2**
when *A* and his sons — **Num. 4:15**
to Moses, and to *A* — **Num. 13:26**
LORD spake unto *A* — **Num. 18:20**

ABOMINATION
every ***a*** to the LORD — **Deut. 12:31**
Chemosh, the ***a*** of Moab — **1 Kin. 11:7**
incense is an ***a*** unto — **Is. 1:13**
whatsoever worketh ***a*** — **Rev. 21:27**

ABOMINATIONS
and with all thine ***a*** — **Ezek. 5:11**
committed in all their ***a*** — **Ezek. 6:9**
thee for all thine ***a*** — **Ezek. 7:8**
man cast away the ***a*** — **Ezek. 20:8**
overspreading of ***a*** — **Dan. 9:27**

ABRAHAM
A fell upon his face — **Gen. 17:17**
I sware unto *A* thy — **Gen. 26:3**
LORD God of *A* thy father — **Gen. 28:13**
father, the God of *A* — **Ex. 3:6**
fathers, the God of *A* — **Ex. 3:15**
Remember *A*, Isaac — **Ex. 32:13**
the seed of *A*, Isaac — **Jer. 33:26**
unto our father *A* — **Acts 7:2**

AFRAID
Egypt, which thou wast ***a*** — **Deut. 28:60**
fear not, nor be ***a*** — **Deut. 31:6**
not ***a***, neither be thou — **Josh. 1:9**
whom shall I be ***a*** — **Ps. 27:1**
trust, and not be ***a*** — **Is. 12:2**
And they shall be ***a*** — **Is. 13:8**

ALTAR
there builded he an ***a*** — **Gen. 12:7**
there he builded an ***a*** — **Gen. 12:8**
and built there an ***a*** — **Gen. 13:18**
horns of the ***a*** of sweet — **Lev. 4:7**
his fat upon the ***a*** — **Lev. 4:26**
mine ***a***, to burn incense — **1 Sam. 2:28**
accepted upon mine ***a*** — **Is. 56:7**
the porch and the ***a*** — **Ezek. 8:16**

ANGEL
a of his presence saved — **Is. 63:9**
And the ***a*** answered — **Luke 1:35**
unto the ***a*** of the church — **Rev. 3:1**
to the ***a*** of the church — **Rev. 3:7**
unto the ***a*** of the church — **Rev. 3:14**
The first ***a*** sounded — **Rev. 8:7**
And the seventh ***a*** sounded — **Rev. 11:15**
Jesus have sent mine ***a*** — **Rev. 22:16**

ANGELS
Father with his ***a*** — **Matt. 16:27**
the devil and his ***a*** — **Matt. 25:41**
Spirit, seen of ***a*** — **1 Tim. 3:16**
innumerable company of ***a*** — **Heb. 12:22**
presence of the holy ***a*** — **Rev. 14:10**

ANGER
overthrew in his ***a*** — **Deut. 29:23**
have provoked me to ***a*** — **Deut. 32:21**
a of the LORD was hot — **Judg. 2:14**
to provoke him to ***a*** — **2 Kin. 17:17**
the ***a*** of the LORD kindled — **Is. 5:25**
to accomplish my ***a*** — **Ezek. 20:8**
merciful, slow to ***a*** — **Joel 2:13**
retaineth not his ***a*** — **Mic. 7:18**

ANOINTED
horn of oil, and ***a*** — **1 Sam. 16:13**
God, thy God, hath ***a*** — **Ps. 45:7**
LORD to his ***a***, to Cyrus — **Is. 45:1**
LORD hath ***a*** me to preach — **Is. 61:1**

APPEARED
the LORD ***a*** unto Abram — **Gen. 12:7**
the LORD ***a*** to Abram — **Gen. 17:1**
And the LORD ***a*** unto — **Gen. 18:1**
The God of glory ***a*** — **Acts 7:2**

APPOINTED
the time ***a*** I will return — **Gen. 18:14**
thee, in the time ***a*** — **Ex. 23:15**
a feasts my soul hateth — **Is. 1:14**
Son, whom he hath ***a*** — **Heb. 1:2**

ARISE
after thee shall any ***a*** — **1 Kin. 3:12**
Kings shall see and ***a*** — **Is. 49:7**
trouble they will say, *A* — **Jer. 2:27**
a, and be baptized — **Acts 22:16**

ARK
upon the ***a*** of the testimony — **Ex. 25:22**
which is upon the ***a*** — **Lev. 16:2**
his face before the ***a*** — **Josh. 7:6**
fear, prepared an ***a*** — **Heb. 11:7**

ARM
greatness of thine ***a*** — **Ex. 15:16**
the lambs with his ***a*** — **Is. 40:11**
made bare his holy ***a*** — **Is. 52:10**
and stretched out ***a*** — **Jer. 32:17**

ASHAMED

said, O my God, I am ***a***	**Ezra 9:6**
a and brought to confusion	**Ps. 35:26**
not be ***a*** that wait	**Is. 49:23**
not thou therefore ***a***	**2 Tim. 1:8**
nevertheless I am not ***a***	**2 Tim. 1:12**

ASSYRIA

Tiglathpileser king of ***A***	**2 Kin. 15:29**
Hoshea the king of ***A***	**2 Kin. 17:6**
king of ***A*** sent Tartan	**2 Kin. 18:17**
shall be left, from ***A***	**Is. 11:11**
perish in the land of ***A***	**Is. 27:13**

BABYLON

out to the king of ***B***	**2 Kin. 24:12**
B, and the king's mother	**2 Kin. 24:15**
and brought him to ***B***	**2 Chr. 36:10**
Go ye forth of ***B***, flee	**Is. 48:20**
Nebuchad-rezzar king of ***B***	**Jer. 21:7**
hand of the king of ***B***	**Jer. 21:10**
Nebuchad-rezzar the king of ***B***	**Jer. 25:9**
the king of ***B*** slew	**Jer. 39:6**

BARE

The LORD hath made ***b***	**Is. 52:10**
and he ***b*** the sin of	**Is. 53:12**
he ***b*** them, and carried	**Is. 63:9**
tree of life, which ***b***	**Rev. 22:2**

BEAR

shalt not avenge, nor ***b***	**Lev. 19:18**
Kohath shall come to ***b***	**Num. 4:15**
which she shall ***b***	**Deut. 28:57**
conceive, and ***b*** a son	**Is. 7:14**
he shall ***b*** their iniquities	**Is. 53:11**
falsely, and the priests ***b***	**Jer. 5:31**
vessel unto me, to ***b***	**Acts 9:15**
b witness, and shew	**1 John 1:2**

BEAST

Egypt, both man and ***b***	**Ex. 12:12**
night, who worship the ***b***	**Rev. 14:11**
And the ***b*** was taken	**Rev. 19:20**
not worshipped the ***b***	**Rev. 20:4**
b and the false prophet	**Rev. 20:10**

BEASTS

drank, and their ***b***	**Num. 20:11**
air, and unto the ***b***	**Deut. 28:26**
the wild ***b*** of the islands	**Is. 13:22**
idols were upon the ***b***	**Is. 46:1**
heaven, and for the ***b***	**Jer. 7:33**
heaven, and for the ***b***	**Jer. 16:4**
b, and in the midst	**Rev. 5:6**

BEGINNING

all nations, ***b*** at Jerusalem	**Luke 24:47**
murderer from the ***b***	**John 8:44**
b, which we have heard	**1 John 1:1**
Alpha and Omega, the ***b***	**Rev. 1:8**

BLESS

b thee, and make thy	**Gen. 12:2**
b them that ***b*** thee	**Gen. 12:3**
blessing I will ***b*** thee	**Gen. 22:17**
thee, and will ***b*** thee	**Gen. 26:3**
b all the work of thine	**Deut. 28:12**

BLESSED

of the earth be ***b***	**Gen. 12:3**
of the earth be ***b***	**Gen. 22:18**
of the earth be ***b***	**Gen. 26:4**
LORD thy God hath ***b***	**Deut. 12:7**
right hand, Come, ye ***b***	**Matt. 25:34**
B be the Lord God of	**Luke 1:68**
b hope, and the glorious	**Titus 2:13**
B is the man that endureth	**James 1:12**

BLOOD

Whoso sheddeth man's ***b***	**Gen. 9:6**
shall put some of the ***b***	**Lev. 4:7**
hands are full of ***b***	**Is. 1:15**
LORD is filled with ***b***	**Is. 34:6**
and the moon into ***b***	**Joel 2:31**
purchased with his own ***b***	**Acts 20:28**
shall the ***b*** of Christ	**Heb. 9:14**
sins in his own ***b***	**Rev. 1:5**

BODY

the fruit of thy ***b***	**Deut. 28:18**
fruit of thine own ***b***	**Deut. 28:53**
transgression, the fruit of my ***b***	**Mic. 6:7**
them which kill the ***b***	**Matt. 10:28**
baptized into one ***b***	**1 Cor. 12:13**
things done in his ***b***	**2 Cor. 5:10**
the head of the ***b***	**Col. 1:18**
our sins in his own ***b***	**1 Pet. 2:24**

BOOK

this ***b***, that thou mayest	**Deut. 28:58**
found written in the ***b***	**Dan. 12:1**
seest, write in a ***b***	**Rev. 1:11**
b of life, but I will	**Rev. 3:5**
b of life of the Lamb	**Rev. 13:8**

BORN

Shall a child be ***b***	**Gen. 17:17**
be a stranger, or ***b***	**Ex. 12:19**
Behold, a son shall be ***b***	**1 Chr. 22:9**
unto us a child is ***b***	**Is. 9:6**
thing which shall be ***b***	**Luke 1:35**
man which am a Jew, ***b***	**Acts 22:3**

BOW

Thou shalt not ***b*** down	**Ex. 20:5**
shall ***b*** down to thee	**Is. 49:23**
Lud, that draw the ***b***	**Is. 66:19**
appearance of the ***b***	**Ezek. 1:28**

BREAD

face shalt thou eat ***b***	**Gen. 3:19**
fire, and unleavened ***b***	**Ex. 12:8**
ye eat unleavened ***b***	**Ex. 12:15**
feast of unleavened ***b***	**Ex. 23:15**
eat ***b***, nor drink water	**Ex. 34:28**
be on the ***b*** for a memorial	**Lev. 24:7**
feast of unleavened ***b***	**Deut. 16:16**
eat of my ***b***, hath lifted	**Ps. 41:9**

BREAK

Thou shalt ***b*** them with	**Ps. 2:9**
b down the wall thereof	**Is. 5:5**
wilderness shall waters ***b***	**Is. 35:6**
and ***b*** forth into singing	**Is. 49:13**
pluck up, and to ***b***	**Jer. 31:28**
b in pieces and consume	**Dan. 2:44**

BRETHREN

the midst of his ***b***	**1 Sam. 16:13**
of these my ***b***, ye have	**Matt. 25:40**
firstborn among many ***b***	**Rom. 8:29**
beseech you therefore, ***b***	**Rom. 12:1**
we command you, ***b***	**2 Thess. 3:6**
Wherefore, my beloved ***b***	**James 1:19**
b, Hath not God chosen	**James 2:5**
unfeigned love of the ***b***	**1 Pet. 1:22**

BROKEN

And the city was ***b***	**2 Kin. 25:4**
thou hast ***b*** the yoke	**Is. 9:4**
withered, they shall be ***b***	**Is. 27:11**
out cisterns, ***b*** cisterns	**Jer. 2:13**
time I have ***b*** thy yoke	**Jer. 2:20**
daughter of my people is ***b***	**Jer. 14:17**
confounded, Merodach is ***b***	**Jer. 50:2**
captives, because I am ***b***	**Ezek. 6:9**

BROTHER

evil toward his ***b***	**Deut. 28:54**
made Zedekiah his ***b***	**2 Chr. 36:10**
trust ye not in any ***b***	**Jer. 9:4**
and every man his ***b***	**Jer. 31:34**
he did pursue his ***b***	**Amos 1:11**
is angry with his ***b***	**Matt. 5:22**
Zelotes, and Judas the ***b***	**Acts 1:13**
b that walketh disorderly	**2 Thess. 3:6**

BROUGHT

he ***b*** him forth abroad	**Gen. 15:5**
thy God, which have ***b***	**Ex. 20:2**
gods, O Israel, which ***b***	**1 Kin. 12:28**
Nebuchadnezzar sent, and ***b***	**2 Chr. 36:10**
b upon them the king	**2 Chr. 36:17**
he is ***b*** as a lamb to	**Is. 53:7**
And he ***b*** me into the	**Ezek. 8:16**
city in Cilicia, yet ***b***	**Acts 22:3**

BUILD

thou shalt ***b*** an house	**Deut. 28:30**
He shall ***b*** an house	**2 Sam. 7:13**
Solomon ***b*** an high place	**1 Kin. 11:7**
to throw down, to ***b***	**Jer. 1:10**
restore and to ***b*** Jerusalem	**Dan. 9:25**

BUILT

b for Pharaoh treasure	**Ex. 1:11**
also ***b*** them high places	**1 Kin. 14:23**
the street shall be ***b***	**Dan. 9:25**
b houses of hewn stone	**Amos 5:11**
are ***b*** upon the foundation	**Eph. 2:20**
lively stones, are ***b***	**1 Pet. 2:5**

BULLOCK

hath sinned, a young ***b***	**Lev. 4:3**
the blood of the ***b***	**Lev. 4:7**
the skin of the ***b***	**Lev. 4:11**
whole ***b*** shall he carry	**Lev. 4:12**

BURN

morning ye shall ***b***	**Ex. 12:10**
are poured out, and ***b***	**Lev. 4:12**
children of Israel did ***b***	**2 Kin. 18:4**
and it shall ***b***, and	**Jer. 7:20**
Babylon, and he shall ***b***	**Jer. 21:10**
Chaldeans, and they shall ***b***	**Jer. 38:18**
own mouth, to ***b*** incense	**Jer. 44:17**
cometh, that shall ***b***	**Mal. 4:1**

BURNED

thou shalt not be ***b***	**Is. 43:2**
Chaldeans ***b*** the king's	**Jer. 39:8**
And ***b*** the house of	**Jer. 52:13**
earth is ***b*** at his presence	**Nah. 1:5**
brass, as if they ***b***	**Rev. 1:15**

BURNT

altar of the ***b*** offering	**Lev. 4:7**
out shall he be ***b***	**Lev. 4:12**
bring your ***b*** offerings	**Deut. 12:6**
your ***b*** offerings, and	**Deut. 12:11**
great delight in ***b***	**1 Sam. 15:22**
And he ***b*** the house	**2 Kin. 25:9**
their ***b*** offerings and	**Is. 56:7**
your ***b*** offerings are	**Jer. 6:20**

CALL

I ***c*** heaven and earth	**Deut. 4:26**
c upon me in the day	**Ps. 50:15**
them that ***c*** upon thee	**Ps. 86:5**
c upon me, but I will	**Prov. 1:28**
a son, and shall ***c***	**Is. 7:14**
the city that men ***c***	**Lam. 2:15**
c on my name, and I	**Zech. 13:9**
son, and thou shalt ***c***	**Matt. 1:21**

DARKNESS

blind gropeth in ***d***	**Deut. 28:29**
the land, behold ***d***	**Is. 5:30**
shall be turned into ***d***	**Joel 2:31**
to turn them from ***d***	**Acts 26:18**
hidden things of ***d***	**1 Cor. 4:5**
called you out of ***d***	**1 Pet. 2:9**

DAUGHTER

thy son, nor thy ***d***	**Ex. 20:10**
thy ***d*** thou shalt not	**Deut. 7:3**
wife Jezebel the ***d***	**1 Kin. 16:31**
make his son or his ***d***	**2 Kin. 23:10**
virgin ***d*** of my people	**Jer. 14:17**
head at the ***d*** of Jerusalem	**Lam. 2:15**
Rejoice greatly, O ***d***	**Zech. 9:9**
D, be of good comfort	**Matt. 9:22**

DAUGHTERS

escaped, and his ***d***	**Num. 21:29**
Thy sons and thy ***d***	**Deut. 28:32**
shalt beget sons and ***d***	**Deut. 28:41**
sons and of thy ***d***	**Deut. 28:53**
their sons and their ***d***	**2 Kin. 17:17**
your sons and your ***d***	**Joel 2:28**

DAVID

D from that day forward	**1 Sam. 16:13**
upon the throne of ***D***	**Is. 9:7**
sure mercies of ***D***	**Is. 55:3**
I will raise unto ***D***	**Jer. 23:5**
LORD their God, and ***D***	**Hos. 3:5**
upon the house of ***D***	**Zech. 12:10**
throne of his father ***D***	**Luke 1:32**
hath the key of ***D***	**Rev. 3:7**

DAY

d the LORD made a covenant	**Gen. 15:18**
first ***d*** ye shall put	**Ex. 12:15**
seventh ***d*** is the sabbath	**Ex. 20:10**
d have I begotten thee	**Ps. 2:7**
call upon me in the ***d***	**Ps. 50:15**
to pass in that ***d***	**Is. 11:11**
I have this ***d*** set thee	**Jer. 1:10**
behold, the ***d*** cometh	**Mal. 4:1**

DAYS

d shall ye eat unleavened	**Ex. 12:15**
that thy ***d*** may be long	**Ex. 20:12**
thee all the ***d*** of thy	**Josh. 1:5**
And when thy ***d*** be fulfilled	**2 Sam. 7:12**
shall prolong his ***d***	**Is. 53:10**
d come, saith the LORD	**Jer. 23:5**
d Judah shall be saved	**Jer. 23:6**
in the ***d*** of these kings	**Dan. 2:44**

DEAD

supposing he had been ***d***	**Acts 14:19**
conscience from ***d*** works	**Heb. 9:14**
the ***d*** our Lord Jesus	**Heb. 13:20**
Christ from the ***d***	**1 Pet. 1:3**
begotten of the ***d***	**Rev. 1:5**
fell at his feet as ***d***	**Rev. 1:17**
liveth, and was ***d***	**Rev. 1:18**
livest, and art ***d***	**Rev. 3:1**

DEATH

out his soul unto ***d***	**Is. 53:12**
loosed the pains of ***d***	**Acts 2:24**
wages of sin is ***d***	**Rom. 6:23**
d he might destroy	**Heb. 2:14**
God, being put to ***d***	**1 Pet. 3:18**
keys of hell and of ***d***	**Rev. 1:18**
d and hell were cast	**Rev. 20:14**
which is the second ***d***	**Rev. 21:8**

DEFILED

after wizards, to be ***d***	**Lev. 19:31**
And he ***d*** Topheth, which	**2 Kin. 23:10**
sanctuary, they have ***d***	**Ps. 74:7**
thou hast ***d*** my sanctuary	**Ezek. 5:11**

DELIVER

I am come down to ***d***	**Ex. 3:8**
LORD thy God shall ***d***	**Deut. 7:2**
can ***d*** out of my hand	**Deut. 32:39**
d thee, and thou shalt	**Ps. 50:15**
have I no power to ***d***	**Is. 50:2**
LORD, I will ***d*** Zedekiah	**Jer. 21:7**
And I will ***d*** them to	**Jer. 24:9**
midst of Babylon, and ***d***	**Jer. 51:6**

DELIVERED

against Israel, and he ***d***	**Judg. 2:14**
children of Israel, who ***d***	**Judg. 3:9**
and the LORD ***d*** Chushanrishathaim	**Judg. 3:10**
people shall be ***d***	**Dan. 12:1**
All things are ***d*** unto	**Matt. 11:27**
d him to Pontius Pilate	**Matt. 27:2**
being ***d*** by the determinate	**Acts 2:23**
Who was ***d*** for our offences	**Rom. 4:25**

DEPART

sceptre shall not ***d***	**Gen. 49:10**
my mercy shall not ***d***	**2 Sam. 7:15**
on the left hand, ***D***	**Matt. 25:41**
d out of this world	**John 13:1**

DESOLATE

your land shall be ***d***	**Lev. 26:33**
cry in their ***d*** houses	**Is. 13:22**
any more be termed ***D***	**Is. 62:4**
to make thy land ***d***	**Jer. 4:7**
make their land ***d***	**Jer. 18:16**
and I will make it ***d***	**Ezek. 25:13**
he shall make it ***d***	**Dan. 9:27**

DESTROY
them, and utterly ***d*** **Deut. 7:2**
rejoice over you to ***d*** **Deut. 28:63**
d in all my holy mountain **Is. 11:9**
pull down, and to ***d*** **Jer. 1:10**
and will utterly ***d*** **Jer. 25:9**
shed blood, and to ***d*** **Ezek. 22:27**
come shall ***d*** the city **Dan. 9:26**
through death he might ***d*** **Heb. 2:14**

DESTROYED
shall utterly be ***d*** **Deut. 4:26**
d, and until thou perish **Deut. 28:20**
thee, until thou be ***d*** **Deut. 28:24**
neck, until he have ***d*** **Deut. 28:48**
land, until thou be ***d*** **Deut. 28:51**
which shall never be ***d*** **Dan. 2:44**

DESTRUCTION
into the pit of ***d*** **Ps. 55:23**
raise up a cry of ***d*** **Is. 15:5**
the earth, for the ***d*** **Lam. 2:11**
then sudden ***d*** cometh **1 Thess. 5:3**

DIE
that he ***d*** not **Lev. 16:2**
thing, lest they ***d*** **Num. 4:15**
surely ***d*** in the wilderness **Num. 26:65**
thou diest, will I ***d*** **Ruth 1:17**
a man that shall ***d*** **Is. 51:12**
d of grievous deaths **Jer. 16:4**
part of thee shall ***d*** **Ezek. 5:12**
it, though he shall ***d*** **Ezek. 12:13**

DIED
but Er and Onan ***d*** in **Gen. 46:12**
the king of Egypt ***d*** **Ex. 2:23**
devoured them, and they ***d*** **Lev. 10:2**
hanged himself, and ***d*** **2 Sam. 17:23**
These all ***d*** in faith **Heb. 11:13**

DOOR
on the upper ***d*** post **Ex. 12:7**
offering, which is at the ***d*** **Lev. 4:7**
three keepers of the ***d*** **2 Kin. 25:18**
Jerusalem, to the ***d*** **Ezek. 8:3**
and, behold, at the ***d*** **Ezek. 8:16**

DRINK
that the people may ***d*** **Ex. 17:6**
eat bread, nor ***d*** water **Ex. 34:28**
but shalt neither ***d*** **Deut. 28:39**
a mocker, strong ***d*** **Prov. 20:1**
and through strong ***d*** **Is. 28:7**
plant vineyards, and ***d*** **Amos 9:14**
been all made to ***d*** **1 Cor. 12:13**
shall ***d*** of the wine **Rev. 14:10**

DUST
formed man of the ***d*** **Gen. 2:7**
for ***d*** thou art, and **Gen. 3:19**
seed shall be as the ***d*** **Gen. 28:14**
land powder and ***d*** **Deut. 28:24**
earth, and lick up the ***d*** **Is. 49:23**

DWELL
sware to make you ***d*** **Num. 14:30**
cause his name to ***d*** **Deut. 12:11**
and thou shalt not ***d*** **Deut. 28:30**
I ***d*** in the high and **Is. 57:15**
Israel shall ***d*** safely **Jer. 23:6**
ye shall ***d*** in the land **Jer. 35:15**
shall ***d*** in the land **Ezek. 37:25**
that ***d*** upon the earth **Rev. 13:8**

DWELT
came unto Haran, and ***d*** **Gen. 11:31**
and Israel ***d*** in all **Num. 21:25**
and ***d*** among the people **Judg. 1:16**
it be ***d*** in from generation **Is. 13:20**
your fathers have ***d*** **Ezek. 37:25**
was made flesh, and ***d*** **John 1:14**

EAR
and give ***e***, O earth **Is. 1:2**
Incline your ***e***, and **Is. 55:3**
not inclined your ***e*** **Jer. 35:15**
He that hath an ***e*** **Rev. 2:7**

EARS
fat, and make their ***e*** **Is. 6:10**
they cry in mine ***e*** **Ezek. 8:18**
uncircumcised in heart and ***e*** **Acts 7:51**
e of the Lord of sabaoth **James 5:4**

EARTH
for all the ***e*** is mine **Ex. 19:5**
the face of the ***e*** **Deut. 7:6**
kingdoms of the ***e*** **Deut. 28:25**
end of the ***e***, as swift **Deut. 28:49**
the one end of the ***e*** **Deut. 28:64**
unto the end of the ***e*** **Is. 49:6**
and justice in the ***e*** **Jer. 23:5**
in heaven and in ***e*** **Matt. 28:18**

EAST
west, and to the ***e*** **Gen. 28:14**
back by a strong ***e*** **Ex. 14:21**
children of the ***e*** **Judg. 6:3**
thy seed from the ***e*** **Is. 43:5**
faces toward the ***e*** **Ezek. 8:16**

EAT
thy face shalt thou ***e*** **Gen. 3:19**
they shall ***e*** the flesh **Ex. 12:8**
days shall ye ***e*** unleavened **Ex. 12:15**
And there ye shall ***e*** **Deut. 12:7**
thou knowest not ***e*** **Deut. 28:33**
e the fruit of thy **Deut. 28:51**
e of my bread, hath **Ps. 41:9**
overcometh will I give to ***e*** **Rev. 2:7**

FALL
Fear and dread shall *f* **Ex. 15:16**
shall *f* when none pursueth **Lev. 26:36**
Your carcases shall *f* **Num. 14:29**
their host shall *f* **Is. 34:4**
f by the sword round **Ezek. 5:12**
And the slain shall *f* **Ezek. 6:7**
they of Dedan shall *f* **Ezek. 25:13**
and the stars shall *f* **Matt. 24:29**

FALSE
a *f* vision and divination **Jer. 14:14**
adulterers, and against *f* **Mal. 3:5**
because many *f* prophets **1 John 4:1**
f prophet that wrought **Rev. 19:20**
beast and the *f* prophet **Rev. 20:10**

FAMINE
for the *f*, to the *f* **Jer. 15:2**
the sword, and by *f* **Jer. 16:4**
sword, and from the *f* **Jer. 21:7**
pestilence, and with *f* **Ezek. 5:12**

FAT
that ye eat neither *f* **Lev. 3:17**
But Jeshurun waxed *f* **Deut. 32:15**
hearken than the *f* **1 Sam. 15:22**
heart of this people *f* **Is. 6:10**
blood, it is made *f* **Is. 34:6**

FATHER
F, The Prince of Peace **Is. 9:6**
the glory of his *F* **Matt. 16:27**
the *F*, and of the Son **Matt. 28:19**
throne of his *f* David **Luke 1:32**
begotten of the *F* **John 1:14**
of the *F*, he hath declared **John 1:18**
Ye are of your *f* the **John 8:44**
cometh unto the *F* **John 14:6**

FATHERS
the iniquity of the *f* **Ex. 20:5**
neither thou nor thy *f* **Deut. 28:36**
neither thou nor thy *f* **Deut. 28:64**
shalt sleep with thy *f* **2 Sam. 7:12**
LORD God of their *f* **2 Chr. 36:15**
shall be thy nursing *f* **Is. 49:23**
servant, wherein your *f* **Ezek. 37:25**
of the law of the *f* **Acts 22:3**

FEAR
F and dread shall fall **Ex. 15:16**
that thou mayest *f* **Deut. 28:58**
F thou not **Is. 41:10**
F not, thou worm Jacob **Is. 41:14**
and shall *f* the LORD **Hos. 3:5**
and *f* not me, saith **Mal. 3:5**
moved with *f*, prepared **Heb. 11:7**
me, saying unto me, *F* **Rev. 1:17**

FEAST
ye shall keep it a *f* **Ex. 12:14**
Thou shalt keep the *f* **Ex. 23:15**
f of harvest, the firstfruits **Ex. 23:16**
f of unleavened bread **Deut. 16:16**

FEED
He shall *f* his flock **Is. 40:11**
their own land, and *f* **Ezek. 34:13**
f them, even my servant **Ezek. 34:23**
f the church of God **Acts 20:28**

FEET
his *f*, until Shiloh **Gen. 49:10**
your shoes on your *f* **Ex. 12:11**
f, and toward her children **Deut. 28:57**
the dust of thy *f* **Is. 49:23**
darkness, and before your *f* **Jer. 13:16**
city at the *f* of Gamaliel **Acts 22:3**
Satan under your *f* **Rom. 16:20**
him, I fell at his *f* **Rev. 1:17**

FELL
they *f* upon their faces **Num. 16:22**
his clothes, and *f* **Josh. 7:6**
when I saw it, I *f* **Ezek. 1:28**
and *f* on his face **Matt. 26:39**
when I saw him, I *f* **Rev. 1:17**
cities of the nations *f* **Rev. 16:19**

FIELD
hast sown in the *f* **Ex. 23:16**
the trees of the *f* **Lev. 26:4**
shalt thou be in the *f* **Deut. 28:16**
the *f*, and shalt gather **Deut. 28:38**
of the fuller's *f* **2 Kin. 18:17**
the trees of the *f* **Jer. 7:20**

FILLED
f Jerusalem with innocent **2 Kin. 24:4**
then the house was *f* **2 Chr. 5:13**
sword of the LORD is *f* **Is. 34:6**
f with the Holy Ghost **Luke 1:15**
f with the Holy Ghost **Acts 2:4**
f with envy, and spake **Acts 13:45**
but be *f* with the Spirit **Eph. 5:18**

FIRE
night, roast with *f* **Ex. 12:8**
pass through the *f* **Lev. 18:21**
pass through the *f* **2 Kin. 17:17**
part through the *f* **Zech. 13:9**
everlasting *f*, prepared **Matt. 25:41**
be tormented with *f* **Rev. 14:10**
alive into a lake of *f* **Rev. 19:20**
which burneth with *f* **Rev. 21:8**

FIRSTBORN

f in the land of Egypt	**Ex. 12:12**
the *f*, whatsoever openeth	**Ex. 13:2**
bitterness for his *f*	**Zech. 12:10**
the *f* among many brethren	**Rom. 8:29**

FLEE

and ye shall *f* when	**Lev. 26:17**
them, and *f* seven ways	**Deut. 28:25**
f unto Zoar, an heifer	**Is. 15:5**
of Babylon, *f* ye from	**Is. 48:20**

FLESH

eat the *f* in that night	**Ex. 12:8**
f, shall one man sin	**Num. 16:22**
of the *f* of his children	**Deut. 28:55**
spirit upon all *f*	**Joel 2:28**
the Word was made *f*	**John 1:14**
manifest in the *f*	**1 Tim. 3:16**
to death in the *f*	**1 Pet. 3:18**
the filth of the *f*	**1 Pet. 3:21**

FLOCK

f of Jethro his father	**Ex. 3:1**
leadest Joseph like a *f*	**Ps. 80:1**
feed his *f* like a shepherd	**Is. 40:11**
yourselves, and to all the *f*	**Acts 20:28**

FOUND

leaven *f* in your houses	**Ex. 12:19**
seek him, he will be *f*	**1 Chr. 28:9**
seek him, he will be *f*	**2 Chr. 15:2**
he could not be *f*	**Ps. 37:36**
gladness shall be *f*	**Is. 51:3**
f written in the book	**Dan. 12:1**
f in fashion as a man	**Phil. 2:8**
f written in the book	**Rev. 20:15**

FRUIT

The *f* of thy land	**Deut. 28:33**
olive shall cast his *f*	**Deut. 28:40**
eat the *f* of thy cattle	**Deut. 28:51**
thou shalt eat the *f*	**Deut. 28:53**
they shall eat the *f*	**Is. 3:10**
to the *f* of his doings	**Jer. 17:10**
to the *f* of his doings	**Jer. 32:19**
and bringeth forth *f*	**Col. 1:6**

FULL

f line to keep alive	**2 Sam. 8:2**
O Lord, art a God *f*	**Ps. 86:15**
hands are *f* of blood	**Is. 1:15**
earth is *f* of his glory	**Is. 6:3**
the earth shall be *f*	**Is. 11:9**
f of grace and truth	**John 1:14**
I am *f*, having received	**Phil. 4:18**
a true heart in *f* assurance	**Heb. 10:22**

FURY

LORD the cup of his *f*	**Is. 51:17**
will I also deal in *f*	**Ezek. 8:18**
will pour out my *f*	**Ezek. 20:8**
would pour out my *f*	**Ezek. 20:13**
his *f* is poured out	**Nah. 1:6**

GATE

shall possess the *g*	**Gen. 22:17**
the *g* between two walls	**2 Kin. 25:4**
builded the sheep *g*	**Neh. 3:1**
above the *g* of Ephraim	**Neh. 12:39**
door of the inner *g*	**Ezek. 8:3**

GATES

that is within thy *g*	**Ex. 20:10**
stranger that is in thy *g*	**Deut. 14:21**
thy *g*, until thy high	**Deut. 28:52**
thee in all thy *g*	**Deut. 28:55**
distress thee in thy *g*	**Deut. 28:57**
him the two leaved *g*	**Is. 45:1**

GATHER

vineyard, and shalt not *g*	**Deut. 28:30**
field, and shalt *g*	**Deut. 28:38**
wine, nor *g* the grapes	**Deut. 28:39**
outcasts of Israel, and *g*	**Is. 11:12**
he shall *g* the lambs	**Is. 40:11**
captivity, and I will *g*	**Jer. 29:14**
g the shields	**Jer. 51:11**
from the people, and *g*	**Ezek. 34:13**

GATHERED

year, when thou hast *g*	**Ex. 23:16**
Sihon *g* all his people	**Num. 21:23**
congregation was *g*	**Judg. 20:1**
g out the stones thereof	**Is. 5:2**
nations shall be *g*	**Jer. 3:17**
children of Israel be *g*	**Hos. 1:11**

GAVE

And he *g* unto Moses	**Ex. 31:18**
he *g* them all into	**2 Chr. 36:17**
I *g* my back to the	**Is. 50:6**
Hamath, where he *g*	**Jer. 39:5**
received him, to them *g*	**John 1:12**
the world, that he *g*	**John 3:16**
tongues, as the Spirit *g*	**Acts 2:4**
Who *g* himself for us	**Titus 2:14**

GENERATIONS

after thee in their *g*	**Gen. 17:7**
throughout your *g*	**Ex. 12:14**
commandments to a thousand *g*	**Deut. 7:9**
ancient days, in the *g*	**Is. 51:9**

GENTILES

judgment to the *G*	**Is. 42:1**
the *G*, that thou mayest	**Is. 49:6**
destroyer of the *G*	**Jer. 4:7**
before the *G*, and kings	**Acts 9:15**
hath God also to the *G*	**Acts 11:18**
whether we be Jews or *G*	**1 Cor. 12:13**
preached unto the *G*	**1 Tim. 3:16**
is given unto the *G*	**Rev. 11:2**

GHOST

and of the Holy *G*	**Matt. 28:19**
Holy *G*, whom the Father	**John 14:26**
after that the Holy *G*	**Acts 1:8**
filled with the Holy *G*	**Acts 2:4**
gift of the Holy *G*	**Acts 2:38**
Nazareth with the Holy *G*	**Acts 10:38**
the Holy *G* hath made	**Acts 20:28**
renewing of the Holy *G*	**Titus 3:5**

GIVE

Unto thy seed will I *g*	**Gen. 12:7**
And I will *g* unto thee	**Gen. 17:8**
Lord himself shall *g*	**Is. 7:14**
I will also *g* thee	**Is. 49:6**
the reins, even to *g*	**Jer. 17:10**
to *g* his life a ransom	**Matt. 20:28**
the Lord God shall *g*	**Luke 1:32**
I *g* to eat of the tree	**Rev. 2:7**

GIVETH

LORD thy God *g* thee	**Ex. 20:12**
LORD thy God *g* thee	**Deut. 4:40**
g breath unto the people	**Is. 42:5**
g wisdom unto the wise	**Dan. 2:21**
killeth, but the spirit *g*	**2 Cor. 3:6**
the living God, who *g*	**1 Tim. 6:17**
that *g* to all men liberally	**James 1:5**

GLORY

the LORD, and shalt *g*	**Is. 41:16**
the likeness of the *g*	**Ezek. 1:28**
in the *g* of his Father	**Matt. 16:27**
beheld his *g*, the *g*	**John 1:14**
to whom be *g* for ever	**Rom. 11:36**
God, be honour and *g*	**1 Tim. 1:17**
received up into *g*	**1 Tim. 3:16**
brightness of his *g*	**Heb. 1:3**

GOD

for I the LORD thy *G*	**Ex. 20:5**
LORD your *G* shall choose	**Deut. 12:5**
the messengers of *G*	**2 Chr. 36:16**
Counsellor, The mighty *G*	**Is. 9:6**
Spirit of the Lord *G*	**Is. 61:1**
No man hath seen *G*	**John 1:18**
G so loved the world	**John 3:16**
and a sacrifice to *G*	**Eph. 5:2**

GODS

g of Egypt I will execute	**Ex. 12:12**
LORD, among the *g*	**Ex. 15:11**
your God is God of *g*	**Deut. 10:17**
thou serve other *g*	**Deut. 28:36**
shalt serve other *g*	**Deut. 28:64**
behold thy *g*, O Israel	**1 Kin. 12:28**
worshipped other *g*	**Jer. 22:9**
after other *g* to serve	**Jer. 35:15**

GOLD

linen, and put a *g*	**Gen. 41:42**
made two calves of *g*	**1 Kin. 12:28**
g which Solomon king	**2 Kin. 24:13**
silver and their *g*	**Is. 60:9**
the carbuncle, and *g*	**Ezek. 28:13**
and have a chain of *g*	**Dan. 5:7**
gods of silver, and *g*	**Dan. 5:23**
will try them as *g*	**Zech. 13:9**

GOOD

land unto a *g* land	**Ex. 3:8**
shall he not make it *g*	**Num. 23:19**
anointed me to preach *g*	**Is. 61:1**
for *g*, saith the LORD	**Jer. 21:10**
thee, O man, what is *g*	**Mic. 6:8**
people, zealous of *g*	**Titus 2:14**
g gift and every perfect	**James 1:17**
the answer of a *g* conscience	**1 Pet. 3:21**

GOSPEL

and preaching the *g*	**Matt. 4:23**
separated unto the *g*	**Rom. 1:1**
my spirit in the *g*	**Rom. 1:9**
to my *g*, and the preaching	**Rom. 16:25**
light of the glorious *g*	**2 Cor. 4:4**
g, which ye have heard	**Col. 1:23**

GRACE

Jerusalem, the spirit of *g*	**Zech. 12:10**
full of *g* and truth	**John 1:14**
G to you and peace	**Rom. 1:7**
the *g* of our Lord Jesus	**2 Cor. 8:9**
The *g* of the Lord Jesus	**2 Cor. 13:14**
and knew the *g* of God	**Col. 1:6**
G unto you, and peace	**1 Pet. 1:2**
G be unto you, and	**Rev. 1:4**

GREAT

make of thee a *g* nation	**Gen. 12:2**
Egypt unto the *g* river	**Gen. 15:18**
lords, a *g* God, a mighty	**Deut. 10:17**
portion with the *g*	**Is. 53:12**
anger, and of *g* kindness	**Joel 2:13**
g, and shall be called	**Luke 1:32**
without controversy *g*	**1 Tim. 3:16**
the *g* God and our Saviour	**Titus 2:13**

GROUND

the dust of the ***g*** Gen. 2:7
return unto the ***g*** Gen. 3:19
not again curse the ***g*** Gen. 8:21
thy name to the ***g*** Ps. 74:7
floods upon the dry ***g*** Is. 44:3
root out of a dry ***g*** Is. 53:2
the fruit of the ***g*** Jer. 7:20

HAND

deliver them out of the ***h*** Ex. 3:8
a timbrel in her ***h*** Ex. 15:20
h, until I make thine Ps. 110:1
shall prosper in his ***h*** Is. 53:10
I will turn mine ***h*** Zech. 13:7
right ***h***, Come, ye blessed Matt. 25:34
on the left ***h***, Depart Matt. 25:41
right ***h*** of the Majesty Heb. 1:3

HANDS

delivered them into the ***h*** Judg. 2:14
the work of thy ***h*** Ps. 102:25
h, I will hide mine Is. 1:15
the reward of his ***h*** Is. 3:11
planting, the work of my ***h*** Is. 60:21
pass by clap their ***h*** Lam. 2:15
looked upon, and our ***h*** 1 John 1:1
foreheads, or in their ***h*** Rev. 20:4

HAST

thou ***h*** obeyed my voice Gen. 22:18
which thou ***h*** purchased Ex. 15:16
labours, which thou ***h*** Ex. 23:16
doings, whereby thou ***h*** Deut. 28:20
h drunk at the hand Is. 51:17
thou ***h*** stricken them Jer. 5:3
behold, thou ***h*** made Jer. 32:17
saith unto him, Thou ***h*** Matt. 26:64

HEAD

bruise thy ***h***, and thou Gen. 3:15
thy ***h*** shall be brass Deut. 28:23
unto the top of thy ***h*** Deut. 28:35
the ***h***, and thou shalt Deut. 28:44
poured it upon his ***h*** 1 Sam. 10:1
lip, they shake the ***h*** Ps. 22:7
astonished, and wag his ***h*** Jer. 18:16
hiss and wag their ***h*** Lam. 2:15

HEAR

him, ***H*** ye me, Asa 2 Chr. 15:2
prayers, I will not ***h*** Is. 1:15
with their eyes, and ***h*** Is. 6:10
h, and your soul shall Is. 55:3
voice, yet will I not ***h*** Ezek. 8:18
name, and I will ***h*** Zech. 13:9
h ye him Matt. 17:5
hath an ear, let him ***h*** Rev. 2:7

HEARD

h their cry by reason Ex. 3:7
they ***h*** that the LORD Ex. 4:31
the LORD, and he ***h*** Ps. 120:1
have not ***h*** my fame Is. 66:19
face, and I ***h*** a voice Ezek. 1:28
When they ***h*** these things Acts 11:18
gospel, which ye have ***h*** Col. 1:23
beginning, which we have ***h*** 1 John 1:1

HEARKEN

thou wilt diligently ***h*** Ex. 15:26
if thou wilt not ***h*** Deut. 28:15
h than the fat of rams 1 Sam. 15:22
deceive you, neither ***h*** Jer. 29:8
me, and would not ***h*** Ezek. 20:8
H, my beloved brethren James 2:5

HEART

with gladness of ***h*** Deut. 28:47
LORD looketh on the ***h*** 1 Sam. 16:7
him with a perfect ***h*** 1 Chr. 28:9
h of this people fat Is. 6:10
and to revive the ***h*** Is. 57:15
deceit of their ***h*** Jer. 14:14
LORD search the ***h*** Jer. 17:10
And rend your ***h***, and Joel 2:13

HEARTS

faintness into their ***h*** Lev. 26:36
LORD with all your ***h*** 1 Sam. 7:3
LORD searcheth all ***h*** 1 Chr. 28:9
write it in their ***h*** Jer. 31:33
counsels of the ***h*** 1 Cor. 4:5
stablish your ***h*** unblameable 1 Thess. 3:13
faith, having our ***h*** Heb. 10:22

HEATHEN

scatter you among the ***h*** Lev. 26:33
number among the ***h*** Deut. 4:27
shall give thee the ***h*** Ps. 2:8
didst drive out the ***h*** Ps. 44:2
hast cast out the ***h*** Ps. 80:8
polluted before the ***h*** Ezek. 20:9
h, which ye have profaned Ezek. 36:23
the ***h***, saith the LORD Mal. 1:11

HEAVEN

the stars of the ***h*** Gen. 22:17
LORD's throne is in ***h*** Ps. 11:4
for the fowls of ***h*** Jer. 16:4
God of ***h*** set up a kingdom Dan. 2:44
lo a voice from ***h*** Matt. 3:17
in the clouds of ***h*** Matt. 26:64
me in ***h*** and in earth Matt. 28:18
God out of ***h***, prepared Rev. 21:2

HEAVENS
h are the work of thy **Ps. 102:25**
Hear, O ***h***, and give **Is. 1:2**
darkened in the ***h*** thereof **Is. 5:30**
dissolved, and the ***h*** **Is. 34:4**
that created the ***h*** **Is. 42:5**
stretcheth forth the ***h*** **Is. 44:24**
lo, the ***h*** were opened **Matt. 3:16**
the powers of the ***h*** **Matt. 24:29**

HID
I ***h*** not my face from **Is. 50:6**
h as it were our faces **Is. 53:3**
wrath I ***h*** my face from **Is. 54:8**
are not ***h*** from my face **Jer. 16:17**

HIDE
h it not from me **Josh. 7:19**
apple of the eye, ***h*** **Ps. 17:8**
hands, I will ***h*** mine **Is. 1:15**
will even ***h*** his face **Mic. 3:4**

HIGH
Solomon build an ***h*** **1 Kin. 11:7**
salvation, and my ***h*** **Ps. 18:2**
JEHOVAH, art the most ***h*** **Ps. 83:18**
to Dibon, the ***h*** places **Is. 15:2**
saith the ***h*** and lofty **Is. 57:15**
Mind not ***h*** things **Rom. 12:16**
of the Majesty on ***h*** **Heb. 1:3**
we have not an ***h*** priest **Heb. 4:15**

HOLD
trembling shall take ***h*** **Ex. 15:15**
h not thy peace at **Ps. 39:12**
sorrows shall take ***h*** **Is. 13:8**
cisterns, that can ***h*** **Jer. 2:13**
I cannot ***h*** my peace **Jer. 4:19**
take ***h*** of your fathers **Zech. 1:6**
h the doctrine of Balaam **Rev. 2:14**

HOLY
priests, and an ***h*** nation **Ex. 19:6**
For thou art an ***h*** people **Deut. 7:6**
set my king upon my ***h*** **Ps. 2:6**
Son, and of the ***H*** Ghost **Matt. 28:19**
filled with the ***H*** Ghost **Acts 2:4**
receive the gift of the ***H*** **Acts 2:38**
the ***H*** Ghost hath made **Acts 20:28**
royal priesthood, an ***h*** **1 Pet. 2:9**

HONOUR
H thy father and thy **Ex. 20:12**
with their lips do ***h*** **Is. 29:13**
only wise God, be ***h*** **1 Tim. 1:17**
be ***h*** and power everlasting **1 Tim. 6:16**
crowned with glory and ***h*** **Heb. 2:9**

HOPE
promise, having no ***h*** **Eph. 2:12**
moved away from the ***h*** **Col. 1:23**
love, and patience of ***h*** **1 Thess. 1:3**
In ***h*** of eternal life **Titus 1:2**
for that blessed ***h*** **Titus 2:13**

HORSES
shall not multiply ***h*** **Deut. 17:16**
chariots, and some in ***h*** **Ps. 20:7**
stay on ***h***, and trust **Is. 31:1**
Their ***h*** also are swifter **Hab. 1:8**

HOST
said, This is God's ***h*** **Gen. 32:2**
and upon all his ***h*** **Ex. 14:4**
the ***h*** of heaven, shouldest **Deut. 4:19**
h of heaven, and served **2 Kin. 17:16**
Hezekiah with a great ***h*** **2 Kin. 18:17**
And all the ***h*** of heaven **Is. 34:4**

HOSTS
zeal of the LORD of ***h*** **Is. 9:7**
redeemer the LORD of ***h*** **Is. 44:6**
saith the LORD of ***h*** **Jer. 49:7**
saith the LORD of ***h*** **Zech. 13:7**
messenger of the LORD of ***h*** **Mal. 2:7**
saith the LORD of ***h*** **Mal. 3:1**
saith the LORD of ***h*** **Mal. 3:5**
saith the LORD of ***h*** **Mal. 4:1**

HOUR
whole from that ***h*** **Matt. 9:22**
him, because his ***h*** **John 7:30**
Jesus knew that his ***h*** **John 13:1**
h was there a great **Rev. 11:13**

HOUSE
Egypt, out of the ***h*** **Ex. 20:2**
He shall build an ***h*** **2 Sam. 7:13**
thine ***h*** and thy kingdom **2 Sam. 7:16**
treasures of the ***h*** **2 Kin. 24:13**
mountain of the LORD's ***h*** **Is. 2:2**
will make with the ***h*** **Jer. 31:33**
will pour upon the ***h*** **Zech. 12:10**
shall reign over the ***h*** **Luke 1:33**

HOUSES
leaven out of your ***h*** **Ex. 12:15**
house, and all the ***h*** **2 Kin. 25:9**
desolate ***h***, and dragons **Is. 13:22**
and all the ***h*** of Jerusalem **Jer. 52:13**

HUNDRED
him that is an ***h*** years **Gen. 17:17**
upward, for six ***h*** thousand **Ex. 38:26**
you shall chase an ***h*** **Lev. 26:8**
h horsemen, and twenty **2 Sam. 8:4**
Obadiah took an ***h*** prophets **1 Kin. 18:4**
two ***h*** and ninety days **Dan. 12:11**

IDOLS
Nebo stoopeth, their *i* **Is. 46:1**
her *i* are confounded **Jer. 50:2**
whoring after their *i* **Ezek. 6:9**
forsake the *i* of Egypt **Ezek. 20:8**
your *i*, will I cleanse **Ezek. 36:25**
in sacrifice unto *i* **1 Cor. 8:4**
temple of God with *i* **2 Cor. 6:16**

IMAGE
i of God made he man **Gen. 9:6**
i of God, should shine **2 Cor. 4:4**
glory, and the express *i* **Heb. 1:3**
i, and whosoever receiveth **Rev. 14:11**
that worshipped his *i* **Rev. 19:20**

INCENSE
the altar of sweet *i* **Lev. 4:7**
of Israel did burn *i* **2 Kin. 18:4**
cometh there to me *i* **Jer. 6:20**
own mouth, to burn *i* **Jer. 44:17**
place *i* shall be offered **Mal. 1:11**

INHABITANTS
will deliver the *i* **Ex. 23:31**
have withdrawn the *i* **Deut. 13:13**
the *i* of the land faint **Josh. 2:9**
i of Dor and her towns **Josh. 17:11**
Tishbite, who was of the *i* **1 Kin. 17:1**
land, and against the *i* **Jer. 25:9**
David, and upon the *i* **Zech. 12:10**

INHERITANCE
is the lot of his *i* **Deut. 32:9**
captain over his *i* **1 Sam. 10:1**
heathen for thine *i* **Ps. 2:8**
an *i* unto your fathers **Jer. 3:18**
is the rod of his *i* **Jer. 10:16**
forgiveness of sins, and *i* **Acts 26:18**
have obtained an *i* **Eph. 1:11**

INIQUITY
God, visiting the *i* **Ex. 20:5**
truth and without *i* **Deut. 32:4**
commit *i*, I will chasten **2 Sam. 7:14**
hath laid on him the *i* **Is. 53:6**
i, and I will remember **Jer. 31:34**
reconciliation for *i* **Dan. 9:24**
thee, that pardoneth *i* **Mic. 7:18**
redeem us from all *i* **Titus 2:14**

ISAAC
father, and the God of *I* **Gen. 28:13**
Abraham, the God of *I* **Ex. 3:15**
Remember Abraham, *I* **Ex. 32:13**
seed of Abraham, *I* **Jer. 33:26**

ISRAEL
be cut off from *I* **Ex. 12:15**
the children of *I* **Ex. 19:6**
from reigning over *I* **1 Sam. 16:1**
behold thy gods, O *I* **1 Kin. 12:28**
LORD the King of *I* **Is. 44:6**
the preserved of *I* **Is. 49:6**
and *I* shall dwell safely **Jer. 23:6**
is to be ruler in *I* **Mic. 5:2**

JACOB
And *J* called the name **Gen. 32:30**
And *J* rent his clothes **Gen. 37:34**
house of the God of *J* **Is. 2:3**
Fear not, thou worm *J* **Is. 41:14**
redeemed his servant *J* **Is. 48:20**
up the tribes of *J* **Is. 49:6**
I have given unto *J* **Ezek. 37:25**
over the house of *J* **Luke 1:33**

JERUSALEM
you to go up to *J* **1 Kin. 12:28**
beautiful garments, O *J* **Is. 52:1**
all the houses of *J* **Jer. 52:13**
shout, O daughter of *J* **Zech. 9:9**
J, the spirit of grace **Zech. 12:10**
go unto *J*, and suffer **Matt. 16:21**
nations, beginning at *J* **Luke 24:47**
holy city, new *J*, coming **Rev. 21:2**

JESUS
J went about all Galilee **Matt. 4:23**
And *J* came and spake **Matt. 28:18**
J saith unto him, I **John 14:6**
J Christ for the remission **Acts 2:38**
Father, and the Lord *J* **Rom. 1:7**
are ye in Christ *J* **1 Cor. 1:30**
God and our Saviour *J* **Titus 2:13**
And from *J* Christ **Rev. 1:5**

JEWS
J, came Jesus and stood **John 20:19**
the *J* saw the multitudes **Acts 13:45**
came thither certain *J* **Acts 14:19**
J that Jesus was Christ **Acts 18:5**
Testifying both to the *J* **Acts 20:21**
body, whether we be *J* **1 Cor. 12:13**

JOHN
day *J* seeth Jesus coming **John 1:29**
Peter, and James, and *J* **Acts 1:13**
J to the seven churches **Rev. 1:4**
I *J* saw the holy city **Rev. 21:2**

JOSEPH
drew and lifted up *J* **Gen. 37:28**
the LORD was with *J* **Gen. 39:2**
And *J* was the governor **Gen. 42:6**
thou that leadest *J* **Ps. 80:1**

JOSHUA

and *J* the son of Nun	**Num. 14:30**
And *J* rent his clothes	**Josh. 7:6**
commandment of the LORD to *J*	**Josh. 15:13**
to *J* the son of Josedech	**Hag. 1:1**
Hear now, O *J* the high	**Zech. 3:8**

JOY

for situation, the *j*	**Ps. 48:2**
rejoice even with *j*	**Is. 35:2**
j and gladness shall	**Is. 51:3**
ashes, the oil of *j*	**Is. 61:3**
The voice of *j*, and	**Jer. 33:11**
perfection of beauty, The *j*	**Lam. 2:15**
the *j* that was set	**Heb. 12:2**

JUDAH

And the sons of *J*	**Gen. 46:12**
not depart from *J*	**Gen. 49:10**
Jehoiachin the king of *J*	**2 Kin. 24:12**
me, Asa, and all *J*	**2 Chr. 15:2**
Zedekiah king of *J*	**Jer. 21:7**
days *J* shall be saved	**Jer. 23:6**
all the nobles of *J*	**Jer. 39:6**
the thousands of *J*	**Mic. 5:2**

JUDGE

the *J* of all the earth	**Gen. 18:25**
LORD shall *j* his people	**Deut. 32:36**
cometh to *j* the earth	**Ps. 96:13**
relieve the oppressed, *j*	**Is. 1:17**
they *j* not the fatherless	**Is. 1:23**
j the poor, and reprove	**Is. 11:4**
The heads thereof *j*	**Mic. 3:11**
Therefore *j* nothing	**1 Cor. 4:5**

JUDGMENT

Egypt I will execute *j*	**Ex. 12:12**
shalt not wrest *j*	**Deut. 16:19**
all his ways are *j*	**Deut. 32:4**
establish it with *j*	**Is. 9:7**
shall bring forth *j*	**Is. 42:1**
prison and from *j*	**Is. 53:8**
execute *j* and justice	**Jer. 23:5**
come near to you to *j*	**Mal. 3:5**

JUDGMENTS

arm, and with great *j*	**Ex. 6:6**
statutes, and my *j*	**Lev. 18:5**
sinned against thy *j*	**Neh. 9:29**
they despised my *j*	**Ezek. 20:13**
walk in my *j*, and observe	**Ezek. 37:24**
j, and his ways past	**Rom. 11:33**

KING

bring thee, and thy *k*	**Deut. 28:36**
the *k* took counsel	**1 Kin. 12:28**
Yet have I set my *k*	**Ps. 2:6**
saith the LORD the *K*	**Is. 44:6**
righteous Branch, and a *K*	**Jer. 23:5**
k of Babylon, my servant	**Jer. 25:9**
behold, thy *K* cometh	**Zech. 9:9**
Then shall the *K* say	**Matt. 25:34**

KINGDOM

be unto me a *k* of priests	**Ex. 19:6**
will establish his *k*	**2 Sam. 7:12**
the throne of his *k*	**2 Sam. 7:13**
David, and upon his *k*	**Is. 9:7**
heaven set up a *k*	**Dan. 2:44**
the gospel of the *k*	**Matt. 4:23**
Father, inherit the *k*	**Matt. 25:34**
and of his *k* there	**Luke 1:33**

KINGS

loose the loins of *k*	**Is. 45:1**
servant of rulers, *K*	**Is. 49:7**
k shall be thy nursing	**Is. 49:23**
k of the land of Uz	**Jer. 25:20**
the days of these *k*	**Dan. 2:44**
the Gentiles, and *k*	**Acts 9:15**
the prince of the *k*	**Rev. 1:5**
lords, and King of *k*	**Rev. 17:14**

KNEW

thee in the belly I *k*	**Jer. 1:5**
passover, when Jesus *k*	**John 13:1**
be sin for us, who *k*	**2 Cor. 5:21**
k the grace of God	**Col. 1:6**

KNOWETH

the proud he *k* afar	**Ps. 138:6**
and no man *k* the Son	**Matt. 11:27**
walketh in darkness *k*	**John 12:35**
him not, neither *k*	**John 14:17**
written, which no man *k*	**Rev. 2:17**

KNOWLEDGE

shall be full of the *k*	**Is. 11:9**
by his *k* shall my righteous	**Is. 53:11**
unto the wise, and *k*	**Dan. 2:21**
lips should keep *k*	**Mal. 2:7**
wisdom and *k* of God	**Rom. 11:33**
mysteries, and all *k*	**1 Cor. 13:2**

LAID

Dibon, and we have *l*	**Num. 21:30**
hast thou *l* the foundation	**Ps. 102:25**
for it is *l* waste	**Is. 23:1**
and the LORD hath *l*	**Is. 53:6**
thy cities shall be *l*	**Jer. 4:7**
had prayed, they *l*	**Acts 6:6**
Henceforth there is *l*	**2 Tim. 4:8**
he *l* his right hand	**Rev. 1:17**

LAMB
he is brought as a *l* — **Is. 53:7**
saith, Behold the *L* — **John 1:29**
L which is in the midst — **Rev. 7:17**
book of life of the *L* — **Rev. 13:8**
presence of the *L* — **Rev. 14:10**
make war with the *L* — **Rev. 17:14**

LAND
will I give this *l* — **Gen. 12:7**
have I given this *l* — **Gen. 15:18**
l unto a good *l* and — **Ex. 3:8**
brought thee out of the *l* — **Ex. 20:2**
l which the LORD thy — **Ex. 20:12**
The fruit of thy *l* — **Deut. 28:33**
thee up out of the *l* — **1 Kin. 12:28**
them against this *l* — **Jer. 25:9**

LAW
Jethro his father in *l* — **Ex. 3:1**
the words of this *l* — **Deut. 28:58**
l, which Moses my servant — **Josh. 1:7**
the *l*, and the word — **Is. 2:3**
LORD, I will put my *l* — **Jer. 31:33**
seek the *l* at his mouth — **Mal. 2:7**
perfect manner of the *l* — **Acts 22:3**
woman, made under the *l* — **Gal. 4:4**

LAY
that I may *l* my hand — **Ex. 7:4**
flesh, and fasted, and *l* — **1 Kin. 21:27**
And I will *l* it waste — **Is. 5:6**
l their hand upon Edom — **Is. 11:14**
Lord GOD, Behold, I *l* — **Is. 28:16**
pray thee, come and *l* — **Mark 5:23**
and I *l* down my life — **John 10:15**

LIE
man, that he should *l* — **Num. 23:19**
another man shall *l* — **Deut. 28:30**
and I *l* even among — **Ps. 57:4**
speaketh a *l*, he speaketh — **John 8:44**
God, that cannot *l* — **Titus 1:2**
abomination, or maketh a *l* — **Rev. 21:27**

LIFE
nostrils the breath of *l* — **Gen. 2:7**
the days of thy *l* — **Josh. 1:5**
minister, and to give his *l* — **Matt. 20:28**
have everlasting *l* — **John 3:16**
the truth, and the *l* — **John 14:6**
the spirit giveth *l* — **2 Cor. 3:6**
(For the *l* was manifested — **1 John 1:2**
eat of the tree of *l* — **Rev. 2:7**

LIFT
thou *l* up thine eyes — **Deut. 4:19**
ashamed and blush to *l* — **Ezra 9:6**
he will *l* up an ensign — **Is. 5:26**
L up your eyes to the — **Is. 51:6**
aloud, spare not, *l* — **Is. 58:1**

LIFTED
And Lot *l* up his eyes — **Gen. 13:10**
Moses *l* up his hand — **Num. 20:11**
they *l* up their voice — **2 Chr. 5:13**
of my bread, hath *l* — **Ps. 41:9**
every one that is *l* — **Is. 2:12**
and the spirit *l* me — **Ezek. 8:3**
Because thine heart is *l* — **Ezek. 28:2**

LIGHT
l thing that thou shouldest — **Is. 49:6**
shall not give her *l* — **Matt. 24:29**
life was the *l* of men — **John 1:4**
from darkness to *l* — **Acts 26:18**
bring to *l* the hidden — **1 Cor. 4:5**
l of the glorious gospel — **2 Cor. 4:4**
immortality, dwelling in the *l* — **1 Tim. 6:16**
into his marvellous *l* — **1 Pet. 2:9**

LIVE
man do, he shall *l* — **Lev. 18:5**
man do, he shall *l* — **Neh. 9:29**
deceitful men shall not *l* — **Ps. 55:23**
your soul shall *l* — **Is. 55:3**
as I *l*, saith the Lord — **Ezek. 5:11**
do, he shall even *l* — **Ezek. 20:13**
Syriack, O king, *l* — **Dan. 2:4**
as I *l*, saith the LORD — **Zeph. 2:9**

LIVING
man became a *l* soul — **Gen. 2:7**
every thing *l*, as I — **Gen. 8:21**
sight shall no man *l* — **Ps. 143:2**
the land of the *l* — **Is. 53:8**
the fountain of *l* waters — **Jer. 2:13**
true God, he is the *l* — **Jer. 10:10**
present your bodies a *l* — **Rom. 12:1**
works to serve the *l* — **Heb. 9:14**

LONG
that thy days may be *l* — **Ex. 20:12**
them all the day *l* — **Deut. 28:32**
great plagues, and of *l* — **Deut. 28:59**
How *l* wilt thou mourn — **1 Sam. 16:1**
said I, Lord, how *l* — **Is. 6:11**
How *l*, O Lord, holy — **Rev. 6:10**

LORD
L appeared unto Abram — **Gen. 12:7**
day the *L* made a covenant — **Gen. 15:18**
for I the *L* thy God — **Ex. 20:5**
L your God shall choose — **Deut. 12:5**
L shall scatter thee — **Deut. 28:64**
zeal of the *L* of hosts — **Is. 9:7**
saith the *L*, that I — **Jer. 23:5**
called, THE *L* OUR RIGHTEOUSNESS — **Jer. 23:6**

LOVE
thou shalt *l* thy neighbour Lev. 19:18
his *l* and in his pity Is. 63:9
and my people *l* to Jer. 5:31
justly, and to *l* mercy Mic. 6:8
And walk in *l*, as Christ Eph. 5:2
promised to them that *l* James 1:12
promised to them that *l* James 2:5
is *l*, not that we loved 1 John 4:10

LOVED
For God so *l* the world John 3:16
Christ also hath *l* Eph. 5:2
love, not that we *l* 1 John 4:10
that *l* us, and washed Rev. 1:5

MADE
day the LORD *m* a covenant Gen. 15:18
and *m* the sea dry land Ex. 14:21
forsook God which *m* Deut. 32:15
m two calves of gold 1 Kin. 12:28
sin of many, and *m* Is. 53:12
the Word was *m* flesh John 1:14
the Holy Ghost hath *m* Acts 20:28
Jesus, who of God is *m* 1 Cor. 1:30

MAKE
shall he not *m* it good Num. 23:19
thou shalt *m* no covenant Deut. 7:2
I *m* thine enemies thy Ps. 110:1
yea, when ye *m* many Is. 1:15
thou shalt *m* his soul Is. 53:10
and I will *m* an everlasting Is. 55:3
destroy them, and *m* Jer. 25:9
to *m* an end of sins Dan. 9:24

MAKETH
He *m* wars to cease Ps. 46:9
m the clouds his chariot Ps. 104:3
wise son *m* a glad father Prov. 10:1
LORD that *m* all things Is. 44:24
worketh abomination, or *m* Rev. 21:27

MAN
God is not a *m*, that Num. 23:19
any *m* be able to stand Josh. 1:5
even to give every *m* Jer. 17:10
shepherd, and against the *m* Zech. 13:7
For the Son of *m* shall Matt. 16:27
Even as the Son of *m* Matt. 20:28
No *m* hath seen God John 1:18
m cometh unto the Father John 14:6

MANNER
m, to slay the righteous Gen. 18:25
any *m* of creeping thing Lev. 11:44
eateth any *m* of blood Lev. 17:10
kingdom, and healing all *m* Matt. 4:23
perfect *m* of the law Acts 22:3
bare twelve *m* of fruits Rev. 22:2

MAYEST
thou *m* prolong thy Deut. 4:40
book, that thou *m* fear Deut. 28:58
courageous, that thou *m* Josh. 1:7
Gentiles, that thou *m* Is. 49:6

MEAT
remnant of the *m* offering Lev. 2:3
theirs, every *m* offering Num. 18:9
carcase shall be *m* Deut. 28:26
this people shall be *m* Jer. 7:33
carcases shall be *m* Jer. 16:4
bodies shall be for *m* Jer. 34:20

MEN
with the rod of *m* 2 Sam. 7:14
the children of *m* Ps. 11:4
m may know that thou Ps. 83:18
worm Jacob, and ye *m* Is. 41:14
and rejected of *m* Is. 53:3
houses of the great *m* Jer. 52:13
the city that *m* call Lam. 2:15
old *m* shall dream dreams Joel 2:28

MERCY
thee from above the *m* Ex. 25:22
with them, nor shew *m* Deut. 7:2
and plenteous in *m* Ps. 86:15
them shall have *m* Prov. 28:13
and he will have *m* Is. 55:7
have pity, nor have *m* Jer. 21:7
justly, and to love *m* Mic. 6:8
he delighteth in *m* Mic. 7:18

MIDST
anointed him in the *m* 1 Sam. 16:13
were torn in the *m* Is. 5:25
diviners, that be in the *m* Jer. 29:8
be consumed in the *m* Ezek. 5:12
shall fall in the *m* Ezek. 6:7
m of the land of Egypt Ezek. 20:8
princes in the *m* thereof Ezek. 22:27
life, which is in the *m* Rev. 2:7

MIGHTY
a *m* hand, and redeemed Deut. 7:8
lords, a great God, a *m* Deut. 10:17
all the *m* men of valour 2 Kin. 24:14
officers, and the *m* 2 Kin. 24:15
Wonderful, Counsellor, The *m* Is. 9:6
let the *m* man glory Jer. 9:23
Great in counsel, and *m* Jer. 32:19
heart of the *m* men Jer. 49:22

MINE
all the earth is *m* Ex. 19:5
Yea, *m* own familiar Ps. 41:9
hands, I will hide *m* Is. 1:15
m elect, in whom my Is. 42:1
transgressions for *m* Is. 43:25
accepted upon *m* altar Is. 56:7
m eye shall not spare Ezek. 8:18
and I will turn *m* hand Zech. 13:7

MINISTER

ministered unto, but to ***m***	**Matt. 20:28**
I Paul am made a ***m***	**Col. 1:23**
spirits, sent forth to ***m***	**Heb. 1:14**
if any man ***m***, let him	**1 Pet. 4:11**

MOAB

mighty men of ***M***, trembling	**Ex. 15:15**
hath consumed Ar of ***M***	**Num. 21:28**
Woe to thee, ***M***	**Num. 21:29**
he smote ***M***, and measured	**2 Sam. 8:2**
the abomination of ***M***	**1 Kin. 11:7**
M shall howl over Nebo	**Is. 15:2**
shall cry out for ***M***	**Is. 15:5**
of Israel, Surely ***M***	**Zeph. 2:9**

MONTH

day of the same ***m***	**Ex. 12:6**
first ***m***, on the fourteenth	**Ex. 12:18**
appointed of the ***m***	**Ex. 23:15**
Observe the ***m*** of Abib	**Deut. 16:1**
king, in the sixth ***m***	**Hag. 1:1**
her fruit every ***m***	**Rev. 22:2**

MOON

the sun, and the ***m***	**Deut. 4:19**
going forth, and the ***m***	**Is. 13:10**
darkness, and the ***m***	**Joel 2:31**
darkened, and the ***m***	**Matt. 24:29**

MORNING

remain until the ***m***	**Ex. 12:10**
third day in the ***m***	**Ex. 19:16**
sweet incense every ***m***	**Ex. 30:7**
night until the ***m***	**Lev. 19:13**
In the ***m*** thou shalt	**Deut. 28:67**
he wakeneth ***m*** by ***m***	**Is. 50:4**
the bright and ***m*** star	**Rev. 22:16**

MOSES

Now ***M*** kept the flock	**Ex. 3:1**
And ***M*** stretched out	**Ex. 14:21**
M did so in the sight	**Ex. 17:6**
And he gave unto ***M***	**Ex. 31:18**
M lifted up his hand	**Num. 20:11**
I was with ***M***, so I	**Josh. 1:5**
law, which ***M*** my servant	**Josh. 1:7**
offer the gift that ***M***	**Matt. 8:4**

MOTHER

thy father and thy ***m***	**Ex. 20:12**
Babylon, he, and his ***m***	**2 Kin. 24:12**
Babylon, and the king's ***m***	**2 Kin. 24:15**
heaviness of his ***m***	**Prov. 10:1**
thy father and thy ***m***	**Matt. 19:19**
women, and Mary the ***m***	**Acts 1:14**

MOUNT

thick cloud upon the ***m***	**Ex. 19:16**
upon ***m*** Sinai, two tables	**Ex. 31:18**
shined forth from ***m***	**Deut. 33:2**
whole earth, is ***m*** Zion	**Ps. 48:2**
sit also upon the ***m***	**Is. 14:13**
LORD in the holy ***m***	**Is. 27:13**
in ***m*** Zion from henceforth	**Mic. 4:7**
ye are come unto ***m***	**Heb. 12:22**

MOUNTAIN

m of God, even to Horeb	**Ex. 3:1**
m of the LORD's house	**Is. 2:2**
to the ***m*** of the LORD	**Is. 2:3**
destroy in all my holy ***m***	**Is. 11:9**
bring to my holy ***m***	**Is. 56:7**
in Zion, my holy ***m***	**Joel 3:17**

MOUNTAINS

Before the ***m*** were brought	**Ps. 90:2**
in the top of the ***m***	**Is. 2:2**
singing, ye ***m***, O forest	**Is. 44:23**
into singing, O ***m***	**Is. 49:13**
stumble upon the dark ***m***	**Jer. 13:16**
feed them upon the ***m***	**Ezek. 34:13**
The ***m*** quake at him	**Nah. 1:5**
that I could remove ***m***	**1 Cor. 13:2**

MOUTH

with the rod of his ***m***	**Is. 11:4**
m, and with their lips	**Is. 29:13**
he opened not his ***m***	**Is. 53:7**
own ***m***, to burn incense	**Jer. 44:17**
m they shew much love	**Ezek. 33:31**
the trumpet to thy ***m***	**Hos. 8:1**
seek the law at his ***m***	**Mal. 2:7**
m went a sharp twoedged	**Rev. 1:16**

MULTITUDE

stars of heaven for ***m***	**Deut. 28:62**
the sea shore in ***m***	**1 Sam. 13:5**
gone with the ***m***, I	**Ps. 42:4**
m of thy tender mercies	**Ps. 51:1**
to the ***m*** of his mercies	**Ps. 106:45**
m, and take her spoil	**Ezek. 29:19**
man is mad, for the ***m***	**Hos. 9:7**

NATION

of thee a great ***n***	**Gen. 12:2**
priests, and an holy ***n***	**Ex. 19:6**
a ***n*** which thou knowest	**Deut. 28:33**
over thee, unto a ***n***	**Deut. 28:36**
LORD shall bring a ***n***	**Deut. 28:49**
A ***n*** of fierce countenance	**Deut. 28:50**
n abhorreth, to a servant	**Is. 49:7**
priesthood, an holy ***n***	**1 Pet. 2:9**

NATIONS

n of the earth be blessed	**Gen. 22:18**
byword, among all ***n***	**Deut. 28:37**
n shalt thou find no	**Deut. 28:65**
the kindreds of the ***n***	**Ps. 22:27**
and all ***n*** shall flow	**Is. 2:2**
set thee over the ***n***	**Jer. 1:10**
all these ***n*** round about	**Jer. 25:9**
and teach all ***n***, baptizing	**Matt. 28:19**

NEIGHBOUR

thou shalt love thy ***n***	**Lev. 19:18**
hath given it to a ***n***	**1 Sam. 15:28**
his ***n***, and trust ye	**Jer. 9:4**
more every man his ***n***	**Jer. 31:34**

NIGHT

flesh in that ***n***, roast	**Ex. 12:8**
land of Egypt this ***n***	**Ex. 12:12**
east wind all that ***n***	**Ex. 14:21**
men of war fled by ***n***	**2 Kin. 25:4**
run down with tears ***n***	**Jer. 14:17**
came to Jesus by ***n***	**John 3:2**
no rest day nor ***n***	**Rev. 14:11**
tormented day and ***n***	**Rev. 20:10**

NORTH

the sides of the ***n***	**Ps. 48:2**
the sides of the ***n***	**Is. 14:13**
the ***n***, saith the LORD	**Jer. 25:9**
looketh toward the ***n***	**Ezek. 8:3**

NUMBER

if thou be able to ***n***	**Gen. 15:5**
n, from twenty years	**Num. 14:29**
shall be left few in ***n***	**Deut. 4:27**
shall be left few in ***n***	**Deut. 28:62**
marvellous things without ***n***	**Job 5:9**

OFFER

But ye shall ***o*** an offering	**Lev. 23:8**
Seven days ye shall ***o***	**Lev. 23:36**
children of Israel ***o***	**Num. 18:19**
fire which ye shall ***o***	**Num. 28:3**
O unto God thanksgiving	**Ps. 50:14**
Sheba and Seba shall ***o***	**Ps. 72:10**
priest, and ***o*** the gift	**Matt. 8:4**
holy priesthood, to ***o***	**1 Pet. 2:5**

OFFERED

incense shall be ***o***	**Mal. 1:11**
those things that are ***o***	**1 Cor. 8:4**
without blood, which he ***o***	**Heb. 9:7**
the eternal Spirit ***o***	**Heb. 9:14**

OFFERING

shekel shall be the ***o***	**Ex. 30:13**
altar of the burnt ***o***	**Lev. 4:7**
even an ***o*** made by fire	**Lev. 24:7**
is the ***o*** made by fire	**Num. 28:3**
tithes, and the heave ***o***	**Deut. 12:11**
make his soul an ***o***	**Is. 53:10**
name, and a pure ***o***	**Mal. 1:11**
for us an ***o*** and a sacrifice	**Eph. 5:2**

OFFERINGS

heave ***o*** of the holy	**Num. 18:19**
bring your burnt ***o***	**Deut. 12:6**
burnt ***o***, and your sacrifices	**Deut. 12:11**
delight in burnt ***o***	**1 Sam. 15:22**
burnt ***o*** and their sacrifices	**Is. 56:7**
burnt ***o*** are not acceptable	**Jer. 6:20**
to pour out drink ***o***	**Jer. 44:17**

OIL

thyself with the ***o***	**Deut. 28:40**
either corn, wine, or ***o***	**Deut. 28:51**
Samuel took a vial of ***o***	**1 Sam. 10:1**
thine horn with ***o***	**1 Sam. 16:1**
horn of ***o***, and anointed	**1 Sam. 16:13**
anointed thee with the ***o***	**Ps. 45:7**
beauty for ashes, the ***o***	**Is. 61:3**

OPEN

LORD shall ***o*** unto thee	**Deut. 28:12**
loins of kings, to ***o***	**Is. 45:1**
for thine eyes are ***o***	**Jer. 32:19**
To ***o*** their eyes, and	**Acts 26:18**

OPENED

afflicted, yet he ***o***	**Is. 53:7**
and the books were ***o***	**Dan. 7:10**
the heavens were ***o***	**Matt. 3:16**
Then Peter ***o*** his mouth	**Acts 10:34**
temple of God was ***o***	**Rev. 11:19**

PART

p of thee shall die	**Ezek. 5:12**
will bring the third ***p***	**Zech. 13:9**
unto the uttermost ***p***	**Acts 1:8**
now I know in ***p***	**1 Cor. 13:12**
their ***p*** in the lake	**Rev. 21:8**

PASS

For I will ***p*** through	**Ex. 12:12**
let any of thy seed ***p***	**Lev. 18:21**
to ***p***, if thou wilt	**Deut. 28:15**
their daughters to ***p***	**2 Kin. 17:17**
to ***p*** in the last days	**Is. 2:2**
come to ***p*** in that day	**Is. 11:11**
p by clap their hands	**Lam. 2:15**
p afterward, that I	**Joel 2:28**

PASSED

And the LORD ***p*** by before	**Ex. 34:6**
and the people ***p*** over	**Josh. 3:16**
he ***p*** away, and, lo	**Ps. 37:36**
old things are ***p*** away	**2 Cor. 5:17**

PAUL

P and Barnabas waxed	**Acts 13:46**
having stoned ***P***, drew	**Acts 14:19**
Macedonia, ***P*** was pressed	**Acts 18:5**
P, a servant of Jesus	**Rom. 1:1**
whereof I ***P*** am made	**Col. 1:23**

PEACE

Father, The Prince of ***P***	Is. 9:6
his government and ***p***	Is. 9:7
chastisement of our ***p***	Is. 53:5
held their ***p***, and glorified	Acts 11:18
p from God our Father	Rom. 1:7
Follow ***p*** with all men	Heb. 12:14
Grace unto you, and ***p***	1 Pet. 1:2
be unto you, and ***p***	Rev. 1:4

PEOPLE

gathering of the ***p***	Gen. 49:10
unto me above all ***p***	Ex. 19:5
thou art an holy ***p***	Deut. 7:6
scatter thee among all ***p***	Deut. 28:64
arose against his ***p***	2 Chr. 36:16
disease among the ***p***	Matt. 4:23
a peculiar ***p***, zealous	Titus 2:14
nation, a peculiar ***p***	1 Pet. 2:9

PERFECT

me, and be thou ***p***	Gen. 17:1
Rock, his work is ***p***	Deut. 32:4
serve him with a ***p***	1 Chr. 28:9
man was ***p*** and upright	Job 1:1
good gift and every ***p***	James 1:17

PERISH

shall soon utterly ***p***	Deut. 4:26
destroyed, and until thou ***p***	Deut. 28:20
thee until thou ***p***	Deut. 28:22
be angry, and ye ***p***	Ps. 2:12
not ***p***, but have everlasting	John 3:16

PHARAOH

P took off his ring	Gen. 41:42
they built for ***P*** treasure	Ex. 1:11
P, which I have put	Ex. 4:21
P also called the wise	Ex. 7:11
hand of ***P*** king of Egypt	Deut. 7:8
wise counsellors of ***P***	Is. 19:11

PHILISTINES

unto the sea of the ***P***	Ex. 23:31
five lords of the ***P***	Josh. 13:3
the hand of the ***P***	1 Sam. 7:3
the land of the ***P***	Jer. 25:20

PIECES

groves, and brake in ***p***	2 Kin. 18:4
house, and cut in ***p***	2 Kin. 24:13
shalt dash them in ***p***	Ps. 2:9
Merodach is broken in ***p***	Jer. 50:2
break in ***p*** and consume	Dan. 2:44
shall be dashed in ***p***	Hos. 13:16

PIT

the ***p***, and sold Joseph	Gen. 37:28
go down into the ***p***	Ps. 28:1
into the ***p*** of destruction	Ps. 55:23
the sides of the ***p***	Is. 14:15

PLACE

unto the ***p*** of the Canaanites	Ex. 3:8
the ***p*** which the LORD	Deut. 12:5
be a ***p*** which the LORD	Deut. 12:11
LORD thy God in the ***p***	Deut. 16:16
Solomon build an high ***p***	1 Kin. 11:7
on his dwelling ***p***	2 Chr. 36:15
the high and holy ***p***	Is. 57:15
his ***p*** to make thy land	Jer. 4:7

PLACES

lords of the high ***p***	Num. 21:28
ride on the high ***p***	Deut. 32:13
Dibon, the high ***p***	Is. 15:2
comfort all her waste ***p***	Is. 51:3
shall weep in secret ***p***	Jer. 13:17
p whither I shall drive	Jer. 24:9
all the inhabited ***p***	Ezek. 34:13
wickedness in high ***p***	Eph. 6:12

PLAIN

and beheld all the ***p***	Gen. 13:10
p, even the salt sea	Josh. 3:16
the way toward the ***p***	2 Kin. 25:4
a ***p*** from Geba to Rimmon	Zech. 14:10

POOR

hath pity upon the ***p***	Prov. 19:17
judge the ***p***, and reprove	Is. 11:4
strength to the ***p***	Is. 25:4
children, and of the ***p***	Jer. 40:7
treading is upon the ***p***	Amos 5:11
the gospel to the ***p***	Luke 4:18
sakes he became ***p***	2 Cor. 8:9
not God chosen the ***p***	James 2:5

POSSESS

and thy seed shall ***p***	Gen. 22:17
go over Jordan to ***p***	Deut. 4:26
whither thou goest to ***p***	Deut. 28:21
whither thou goest to ***p***	Deut. 28:63

POUR

shall ***p*** all the blood	Lev. 4:7
For I will ***p*** water	Is. 44:3
afterward, that I will ***p***	Joel 2:28
I will ***p*** upon the house	Zech. 12:10

POURED

where the ashes are ***p***	Lev. 4:12
vial of oil, and ***p***	1 Sam. 10:1
he hath ***p*** out his soul	Is. 53:12
of God, which is ***p***	Rev. 14:10

POWER

or have I no ***p*** to deliver	Is. 50:2
hand of ***p***, and coming	Matt. 26:64
them, saying, All ***p***	Matt. 28:18
ye shall receive ***p***	Acts 1:8
p of Satan unto God	Acts 26:18
that is of ***p*** to stablish	Rom. 16:25
be honour and ***p*** everlasting	1 Tim. 6:16
the word of his ***p***	Heb. 1:3

PRAISE
voice of joy and ***p*** **Ps. 42:4**
mourning, the garment of ***p*** **Is. 61:3**
P the LORD of hosts **Jer. 33:11**
whose ***p*** is not of men **Rom. 2:29**
man have ***p*** of God **1 Cor. 4:5**
sacrifice of ***p*** to God **Heb. 13:15**
Christ, to whom be ***p*** **1 Pet. 4:11**

PRAY
a little water, I ***p*** **Gen. 18:4**
Achan, My son, give, I ***p*** **Josh. 7:19**
LORD thy God, and ***p*** **1 Kin. 13:6**
said, I ***p*** thee, O LORD **Jon. 4:2**
and I ***p*** God your whole **1 Thess. 5:23**
say that he shall ***p*** **1 John 5:16**

PRAYER
the ***p*** which thy servant **1 Kin. 8:29**
Hear my ***p***, O LORD **Ps. 39:12**
joyful in my house of ***p*** **Is. 56:7**
Praying always with all ***p*** **Eph. 6:18**

PRESENCE
be moved at his ***p*** **Is. 19:1**
angel of his ***p*** saved **Is. 63:9**
burned at his ***p***, yea **Nah. 1:5**
the ***p*** of the holy angels **Rev. 14:10**

PRIEST
father in law, the ***p*** **Ex. 3:1**
And the ***p*** shall put **Lev. 4:7**
the ***p*** and the prophet **Is. 28:7**
the ***p***, the son of Buzi **Ezek. 1:3**
Josedech, the high ***p*** **Hag. 1:1**
shew thyself to the ***p*** **Matt. 8:4**
have not an high ***p*** **Heb. 4:15**
second went the high ***p*** **Heb. 9:7**

PRIESTS
of ***p***, and an holy nation **Ex. 19:6**
Abiathar, were the ***p*** **2 Sam. 8:17**
places, and made ***p*** **1 Kin. 12:31**
and the ***p*** bear rule **Jer. 5:31**
captivity with his ***p*** **Jer. 48:7**
Her ***p*** have violated **Ezek. 22:26**
reward, and the ***p*** thereof **Mic. 3:11**
elders and chief ***p*** **Matt. 16:21**

PRINCE
everlasting Father, The ***P*** **Is. 9:6**
David shall be their ***p*** **Ezek. 37:25**
the people of the ***p*** **Dan. 9:26**
the dead, and the ***p*** **Rev. 1:5**

PRINCES
servants, and his ***p*** **2 Kin. 24:12**
Jerusalem, and all the ***p*** **2 Kin. 24:14**
Thy ***p*** are rebellious **Is. 1:23**
shall see and arise, ***p*** **Is. 49:7**
king of Babylon's ***p*** **Jer. 38:18**
his priests and his ***p*** **Jer. 48:7**
p in the midst thereof **Ezek. 22:27**

PROPHESY
The prophets ***p*** falsely **Jer. 5:31**
The prophets ***p*** lies **Jer. 14:14**
Wherefore dost thou ***p*** **Jer. 32:3**
daughters shall ***p*** **Joel 2:28**

PROPHET
be a ***p*** among you, I **Num. 12:6**
called a ***P*** was beforetime **1 Sam. 9:9**
the priest and the ***p*** **Is. 28:7**
p is a fool, the spiritual **Hos. 9:7**
LORD by Haggai the ***p*** **Hag. 1:1**
send you Elijah the ***p*** **Mal. 4:5**
the false ***p*** that wrought **Rev. 19:20**
beast and the false ***p*** **Rev. 20:10**

PROPHETS
and misused his ***p*** **2 Chr. 36:16**
backs, and slew thy ***p*** **Neh. 9:26**
The ***p*** prophesy falsely **Jer. 5:31**
The ***p*** prophesy lies **Jer. 14:14**
your ***p*** and your diviners **Jer. 29:8**
servants the ***p***, rising **Jer. 35:15**
hire, and the ***p*** thereof **Mic. 3:11**
my servants the ***p*** **Zech. 1:6**

PURE
a row, upon the ***p*** table **Lev. 24:6**
thou shalt put ***p*** frankincense **Lev. 24:7**
my name, and a ***p*** offering **Mal. 1:11**
bodies washed with ***p*** **Heb. 10:22**

RAISED
the LORD hath ***r*** up **Jer. 51:11**
be killed, and be ***r*** **Matt. 16:21**
Whom God hath ***r*** up **Acts 2:24**
offences, and was ***r*** **Rom. 4:25**

RECEIVE
have refused to ***r*** correction **Jer. 5:3**
But ye shall ***r*** power **Acts 1:8**
sins, and ye shall ***r*** **Acts 2:38**
r forgiveness of sins **Acts 26:18**
one may ***r*** the things **2 Cor. 5:10**
r the crown of life **James 1:12**

RECEIVED
he was ***r*** up into heaven **Mark 16:19**
as ***r*** him, to them gave **John 1:12**
tradition which he ***r*** **2 Thess. 3:6**
world, ***r*** up into glory **1 Tim. 3:16**
r the mark of the beast **Rev. 19:20**
image, neither had ***r*** **Rev. 20:4**

REDEEMED
mighty hand, and ***r*** **Deut. 7:8**
ye, The LORD hath ***r*** **Is. 48:20**
and in his pity he ***r*** **Is. 63:9**
hath visited and ***r*** **Luke 1:68**

REIGN
that hate you shall *r* **Lev. 26:17**
eighth year of his *r* **2 Kin. 24:12**
King shall *r* and prosper **Jer. 23:5**
shall *r* over the house **Luke 1:33**

REJOICE
God, and ye shall *r* **Deut. 12:7**
so the LORD will *r* **Deut. 28:63**
glad and *r* in his salvation **Is. 25:9**
blossom abundantly, and *r* **Is. 35:2**
and thou shalt *r* in **Is. 41:16**
I will greatly *r* in **Is. 61:10**
R greatly, O daughter **Zech. 9:9**
Who now *r* in my sufferings **Col. 1:24**

REMEMBER
people, *R* this day **Ex. 13:3**
world shall *r* and turn **Ps. 22:27**
R, O LORD, the children **Ps. 137:7**
will not *r* thy sins **Is. 43:25**
iniquity, and I will *r* **Jer. 31:34**
escape of you shall *r* **Ezek. 6:9**

REMNANT
Bashan remained of the *r* **Deut. 3:11**
bosom, and toward the *r* **Deut. 28:54**
r of the house of Jeroboam **1 Kin. 14:10**
time to recover the *r* **Is. 11:11**
and Ekron, and the *r* **Jer. 25:20**
transgression of the *r* **Mic. 7:18**

REPROACH
and taketh away the *r* **1 Sam. 17:26**
become a *r* to our neighbours **Ps. 79:4**
their hurt, to be a *r* **Jer. 24:9**
r, a waste, and a curse **Jer. 49:13**

REST
of thy foot have *r* **Deut. 28:65**
his *r* shall be glorious **Is. 11:10**
the place of my *r* **Is. 66:1**
cause my fury to *r* **Ezek. 5:13**
and ye shall find *r* **Matt. 11:29**
have no *r* day nor night **Rev. 14:11**

RETURN
bread, till thou *r* **Gen. 3:19**
appointed I will *r* **Gen. 18:14**
people to *r* to Egypt **Deut. 17:16**
him *r* unto the LORD **Is. 55:7**
have refused to *r* **Jer. 5:3**
For I will cause to *r* **Jer. 33:11**
R ye now every man **Jer. 35:15**
children of Israel *r* **Hos. 3:5**

RETURNED
the waters *r*, and covered **Ex. 14:28**
Jews *r* out of all places **Jer. 40:12**
and they *r* and said **Zech. 1:6**
I am *r* unto Zion, and **Zech. 8:3**

RIGHTEOUS
manner, to slay the *r* **Gen. 18:25**
the words of the *r* **Ex. 23:8**
the words of the *r* **Deut. 16:19**
Say ye to the *r*, that **Is. 3:10**
my *r* servant justify **Is. 53:11**
raise unto David a *r* **Jer. 23:5**
the *r* into life eternal **Matt. 25:46**
Jesus Christ the *r* **1 John 2:1**

RIGHTEOUSNESS
Thou lovest *r*, and **Ps. 45:7**
with *r* shall he judge **Is. 11:4**
called trees of *r* **Is. 61:3**
robe of *r*, as a bridegroom **Is. 61:10**
called, THE LORD OUR *R* **Jer. 23:6**
bring in everlasting *r* **Dan. 9:24**
of God, and his *r* **Matt. 6:33**
unto us wisdom, and *r* **1 Cor. 1:30**

RIVER
this land, from the *r* **Gen. 15:18**
of Hamath unto the *r* **1 Kin. 8:65**
Habor by the *r* of Gozan **2 Kin. 17:6**
north country by the *r* **Jer. 46:10**
Chaldeans by the *r* **Ezek. 1:3**
the waters of the *r* **Dan. 12:7**
either side of the *r* **Rev. 22:2**

ROCK
thee there upon the *r* **Ex. 17:6**
R, his work is perfect **Deut. 32:4**
lightly esteemed the *R* **Deut. 32:15**
The LORD is my *r*, and **Ps. 18:2**
faces harder than a *r* **Jer. 5:3**

ROD
r he smote the rock **Num. 20:11**
chasten him with the *r* **2 Sam. 7:14**
break them with a *r* **Ps. 2:9**
the earth with the *r* **Is. 11:4**

ROUND
of their enemies *r* **Judg. 2:14**
against the city *r* **2 Kin. 25:4**
from all his enemies *r* **1 Chr. 22:9**
to them that are *r* **Ps. 79:4**
all these nations *r* **Jer. 25:9**
of the brightness *r* **Ezek. 1:28**
fall by the sword *r* **Ezek. 5:12**
her a wall of fire *r* **Zech. 2:5**

SABBATH
Remember the *s* day **Ex. 20:8**
s of the LORD thy God **Ex. 20:10**
LORD blessed the *s* **Ex. 20:11**
Every *s* he shall set **Lev. 24:8**

SACRIFICE	
obey is better than *s*	**1 Sam. 15:22**
LORD hath a *s* in Bozrah	**Is. 34:6**
bring the *s* of praise	**Jer. 33:11**
the *s* and the oblation	**Dan. 9:27**
a living *s*, holy, acceptable	**Rom. 12:1**
offered in *s* unto idols	**1 Cor. 8:4**
a *s* to God for a sweetsmelling	**Eph. 5:2**
sweet smell, a *s* acceptable	**Phil. 4:18**

SACRIFICES	
offerings, and your *s*	**Deut. 12:6**
offerings, and your *s*	**Deut. 12:11**
burnt offerings and *s*	**1 Sam. 15:22**
offerings and their *s*	**Is. 56:7**

SAINTS	
ten thousands of *s*	**Deut. 33:2**
the people of the *s*	**Dan. 7:27**
God, called to be *s*	**Rom. 1:7**
supplication for all *s*	**Eph. 6:18**
Christ with all his *s*	**1 Thess. 3:13**

SAKE	
any more for man's *s*	**Gen. 8:21**
transgressions for mine own *s*	**Is. 43:25**
Christ's *s* hath forgiven	**Eph. 4:32**
flesh for his body's *s*	**Col. 1:24**

SALVATION	
the Rock of his *s*	**Deut. 32:15**
my *s*, and my high tower	**Ps. 18:2**
Behold, God is my *s*	**Is. 12:2**
and rejoice in his *s*	**Is. 25:9**
thou mayest be my *s*	**Is. 49:6**
garments of *s*, he hath	**Is. 61:10**
just, and having *s*	**Zech. 9:9**
shall be heirs of *s*	**Heb. 1:14**

SANCTIFIED	
I *s* thee, and I ordained	**Jer. 1:5**
when I shall be *s*	**Ezek. 36:23**
which are *s* by faith	**Acts 26:18**
washed, but ye are *s*	**1 Cor. 6:11**

SANCTIFY	
S unto me all the firstborn	**Ex. 13:2**
ye shall therefore *s*	**Lev. 11:44**
And I will *s* my great	**Ezek. 36:23**
he might *s* and cleanse	**Eph. 5:26**

SANCTUARY	
the shekel of the *s*	**Ex. 30:13**
of covering the *s*	**Num. 4:15**
the house of their *s*	**2 Chr. 36:17**
cast fire into thy *s*	**Ps. 74:7**
the city and the *s*	**Dan. 9:26**

SAT	
of the LORD, and *s*	**Ezek. 20:1**
into heaven, and *s*	**Mark 16:19**
purged our sins, *s*	**Heb. 1:3**
thrones, and they *s*	**Rev. 20:4**

SAUL	
wilt thou mourn for *S*	**1 Sam. 16:1**
it from *S*, whom I put	**2 Sam. 7:15**
As for *S*, he made havock	**Acts 8:3**
the tetrarch, and *S*	**Acts 13:1**

SAVE	
dwell therein, *s* Caleb	**Num. 14:30**
no man shall *s* thee	**Deut. 28:29**
remained, *s* the poorest	**2 Kin. 24:14**
did their own arm *s*	**Ps. 44:3**
him, and he will *s*	**Is. 25:9**
he shall *s* his people	**Matt. 1:21**
any man the Father, *s*	**Matt. 11:27**
baptism doth also now *s*	**1 Pet. 3:21**

SAVED	
and we shall be *s*	**Ps. 80:7**
angel of his presence *s*	**Is. 63:9**
days Judah shall be *s*	**Jer. 23:6**
the end shall be *s*	**Matt. 10:22**
through him might be *s*	**John 3:17**
according to his mercy he *s*	**Titus 3:5**

SCATTERED	
out his arrows, and *s*	**Ps. 18:14**
Israel is a *s* sheep	**Jer. 50:17**
the sheep shall be *s*	**Zech. 13:7**
were *s* abroad, as sheep	**Matt. 9:36**

SEA	
the fish of the *s*	**Gen. 1:26**
is upon the *s* shore	**Gen. 22:17**
his hand over the *s*	**Ex. 14:21**
heaven and earth, the *s*	**Ex. 20:11**
the *s* of the plain	**Josh. 3:16**
waters cover the *s*	**Is. 11:9**
the islands of the *s*	**Is. 11:11**
I dry up the *s*, I make	**Is. 50:2**

SEED	
woman, and between thy *s*	**Gen. 3:15**
Unto thy *s* will I give	**Gen. 12:7**
Unto thy *s* have I given	**Gen. 15:18**
thee, and to thy *s*	**Gen. 17:8**
will multiply thy *s*	**Gen. 22:17**
let any of thy *s* pass	**Lev. 18:21**
I will set up thy *s*	**2 Sam. 7:12**
his *s*, he shall prolong	**Is. 53:10**

SEEK
ye *s*, and thither thou — Deut. 12:5
if thou *s* him, he will — 1 Chr. 28:9
and if ye *s* him, he — 2 Chr. 15:2
s judgment, relieve — Is. 1:17
Israel return, and *s* — Hos. 3:5
s the law at his mouth — Mal. 2:7
the Lord, whom ye *s* — Mal. 3:1
s ye first the kingdom — Matt. 6:33

SEND
LORD shall *s* upon thee — Deut. 28:20
which the LORD shall *s* — Deut. 28:48
I will *s* thee to Jesse — 1 Sam. 16:1
Behold, I will *s* and — Jer. 25:9
Behold, I will *s* my — Mal. 3:1
whom the Father will *s* — John 14:26
come, whom I will *s* — John 15:26
write in a book, and *s* — Rev. 1:11

SERVANT
law, which Moses my *s* — Josh. 1:7
Behold my *s*, whom I — Is. 42:1
hath redeemed his *s* — Is. 48:20
thou shouldest be my *s* — Is. 49:6
nation abhorreth, to a *s* — Is. 49:7
my righteous *s* justify — Is. 53:11
king of Babylon, my *s* — Jer. 25:9
Paul, a *s* of Jesus — Rom. 1:1

SERVANTS
his *s*, when he seeth — Deut. 32:36
Moabites became David's *s* — 2 Sam. 8:2
Edom became David's *s* — 2 Sam. 8:14
which he spake by his *s* — 2 Kin. 24:2
mother, and his *s* — 2 Kin. 24:12
of Judah, and his *s* — Jer. 21:7
s the prophets, rising — Jer. 35:15
which I commanded my *s* — Zech. 1:6

SERVE
thyself to them, nor *s* — Ex. 20:5
worship them, and *s* — Deut. 4:19
there shalt thou *s* — Deut. 28:36
shalt thou *s* thine — Deut. 28:48
there thou shalt *s* — Deut. 28:64
of thy father, and *s* — 1 Chr. 28:9
my witness, whom I *s* — Rom. 1:9
from dead works to *s* — Heb. 9:14

SET
the camp is to *s* forward — Num. 4:15
thou shalt *s* over thee — Deut. 28:36
thy fathers, I will *s* — 2 Sam. 7:12
Yet have I *s* my king — Ps. 2:6
Lord shall *s* his hand — Is. 11:11
I have this day *s* thee — Jer. 1:10
the God of heaven *s* — Dan. 2:44
the joy that was *s* — Heb. 12:2

SEVENTH
day until the *s* day — Ex. 12:15
the *s* day is the sabbath — Ex. 20:10
and rested the *s* day — Ex. 20:11
And the *s* angel sounded — Rev. 11:15

SHADOW
yea, in the *s* of thy — Ps. 57:1
from the storm, a *s* — Is. 25:4
dry place, as the *s* — Is. 32:2
variableness, neither *s* — James 1:17

SHAME
them be clothed with *s* — Ps. 35:26
uncovered, to the *s* — Is. 20:4
face from *s* and spitting — Is. 50:6
cross, despising the *s* — Heb. 12:2

SHED
shall his blood be *s* — Gen. 9:6
ravening the prey, to *s* — Ezek. 22:27
testament, which is *s* — Matt. 26:28
Holy Ghost, he hath *s* — Acts 2:33

SHEEP
thy *s* shall be given — Deut. 28:31
or flocks of thy *s* — Deut. 28:51
his people, and the *s* — Ps. 100:3
like *s* have gone astray — Is. 53:6
slaughter, and as a *s* — Is. 53:7
shepherd, and the *s* — Zech. 13:7
scattered abroad, as *s* — Matt. 9:36
shepherd of the *s* — Heb. 13:20

SHEPHERD
his flock like a *s* — Is. 40:11
I will set up one *s* — Ezek. 34:23
all shall have one *s* — Ezek. 37:24
sword, against my *s* — Zech. 13:7

SHEW
covenant with them, nor *s* — Deut. 7:2
s favour to the young — Deut. 28:50
mouth they *s* much love — Ezek. 33:31
dream, and we will *s* — Dan. 2:4
but go thy way, *s* thyself — Matt. 8:4
forth began Jesus to *s* — Matt. 16:21
that ye should *s* forth — 1 Pet. 2:9
bear witness, and *s* — 1 John 1:2

SHUT
is none *s* up, or left — Deut. 32:36
s up and left in Israel — 1 Kin. 14:10
their ears heavy, and *s* — Is. 6:10
gates shall not be *s* — Is. 45:1

SIDE
strike it on the two *s* — Ex. 12:7
Hinnom unto the south *s* — Josh. 15:8
many, fear on every *s* — Jer. 20:10
either *s* of the river — Rev. 22:2

SIGHT
Moses did so in the *s* **Ex. 17:6**
shalt be mad for the *s* **Deut. 28:34**
the *s* of thine eyes **Deut. 28:67**
wickedness in the *s* **1 Kin. 21:25**
s of the LORD, to provoke **2 Kin. 17:17**
in thy *s* shall no man **Ps. 143:2**
and recovering of *s* **Luke 4:18**
Jesus Christ, in the *s* **1 Thess. 1:3**

SIGN
be upon thee for a *s* **Deut. 28:46**
shall give you a *s* **Is. 7:14**
And I will set a *s* **Is. 66:19**
s of the Son of man **Matt. 24:30**

SILVER
twenty pieces of *s* **Gen. 37:28**
sons from far, their *s* **Is. 60:9**
praised the gods of *s* **Dan. 5:23**
over with gold and *s* **Hab. 2:19**
their *s* nor their gold **Zeph. 1:18**
will refine them as *s* **Zech. 13:9**
and purifier of *s* **Mal. 3:3**

SIN
transgression and *s* **Ex. 34:7**
man *s*, and wilt thou **Num. 16:22**
an offering for *s* **Is. 53:10**
and he bare the *s* of **Is. 53:12**
will remember their *s* **Jer. 31:34**
which taketh away the *s* **John 1:29**
hath made him to be *s* **2 Cor. 5:21**
are, yet without *s* **Heb. 4:15**

SINNED
hath *s*, a young bullock **Lev. 4:3**
your sins which ye *s* **Deut. 9:18**
but *s* against thy judgments **Neh. 9:29**
God, because we have *s* **Dan. 9:11**

SINS
that covereth his *s* **Prov. 28:13**
your *s* be as scarlet **Is. 1:18**
not remember thy *s* **Is. 43:25**
to make an end of *s* **Dan. 9:24**
s, and ye shall receive **Acts 2:38**
purged our *s*, sat down **Heb. 1:3**
once suffered for *s* **1 Pet. 3:18**
washed us from our *s* **Rev. 1:5**

SIT
unto my Lord, *S* thou **Ps. 110:1**
I will *s* also upon **Is. 14:13**
said, I am a God, I *s* **Ezek. 28:2**
cometh, and they *s* **Ezek. 33:31**

SLAIN
you, and ye shall be *s* **Lev. 26:17**
and the *s* of the LORD **Is. 66:16**
And the *s* shall fall **Ezek. 6:7**
life of the Lamb *s* **Rev. 13:8**

SLAY
manner, to *s* the righteous **Gen. 18:25**
innocent and righteous *s* **Ex. 23:7**
his lips shall he *s* **Is. 11:4**
he shall *s* the dragon **Is. 27:1**

SLEW
s the sons of Zedekiah **2 Kin. 25:7**
who *s* their young men **2 Chr. 36:17**
backs, and *s* thy prophets **Neh. 9:26**
the king of Babylon *s* **Jer. 39:6**

SMITE
this night, and will *s* **Ex. 12:12**
thou shalt *s* them **Deut. 7:2**
The LORD will *s* thee **Deut. 28:27**
he shall *s* the earth **Is. 11:4**
s the shepherd, and **Zech. 13:7**

SMOTE
his rod he *s* the rock **Num. 20:11**
And Israel *s* him with **Num. 21:24**
he *s* Moab, and measured **2 Sam. 8:2**
David *s* also Hadadezer **2 Sam. 8:3**
And *s* all the firstborn **Ps. 78:51**
s him with the palms **Matt. 26:67**

SOLOMON
time *S* held a feast **1 Kin. 8:65**
S build an high place **1 Kin. 11:7**
vessels of gold which *S* **2 Kin. 24:13**
And thou, *S* my son **1 Chr. 28:9**
The proverbs of *S* **Prov. 10:1**

SON
neither the *s* of man **Num. 23:19**
conceive, and bear a *s* **Is. 7:14**
is born, unto us a *s* **Is. 9:6**
For the *S* of man shall **Matt. 16:27**
Father, and of the *S* **Matt. 28:19**
shall be called the *S* **Luke 1:32**
the only begotten *S* **John 1:18**
begotten *S*, that whosoever **John 3:16**

SONS
And the *s* of Judah **Gen. 46:12**
s have made an end **Num. 4:15**
Thy *s* and thy daughters **Deut. 28:32**
Thou shalt beget *s* **Deut. 28:41**
a king among his *s* **1 Sam. 16:1**
they caused their *s* **2 Kin. 17:17**
Babylon slew the *s* **Jer. 39:6**
your *s* and your daughters **Joel 2:28**

SOUL
became a living *s* **Gen. 2:7**
seventh day, that *s* **Ex. 12:15**
elect, in whom my *s* **Is. 42:1**
thou shalt make his *s* **Is. 53:10**
the travail of his *s* **Is. 53:11**
hath poured out his *s* **Is. 53:12**
hear, and your *s* shall **Is. 55:3**
rejoice in the LORD, my *s* **Is. 61:10**

SOULS
blood, and to destroy *s* Ezek. 22:27
find rest unto your *s* Matt. 11:29
Confirming the *s* of Acts 14:22
and I saw the *s* of Rev. 20:4

SPIRIT
I have put my *s* upon Is. 42:1
The *S* of the Lord GOD Is. 61:1
will pour out my *s* Joel 2:28
s of grace and of supplications Zech. 12:10
tongues, as the *S* gave Acts 2:4
justified in the *S* 1 Tim. 3:16
quickened by the *S* 1 Pet. 3:18
hear what the *S* saith Rev. 2:7

STAND
Behold, I will *s* before Ex. 17:6
any man be able to *s* Josh. 1:5
could not any longer *s* Judg. 2:14
liveth, before whom I *s* 1 Kin. 17:1
Jesse, which shall *s* Is. 11:10
awake, *s* up, O Jerusalem Is. 51:17
kingdoms, and it shall *s* Dan. 2:44
time shall Michael *s* Dan. 12:1

STARS
heaven, and tell the *s* Gen. 15:5
multiply thy seed as the *s* Gen. 22:17
to multiply as the *s* Gen. 26:4
s shall fall from heaven Matt. 24:29

STATUTES
keep my *s*, and my judgments Lev. 18:5
his *s*, and his commandments Deut. 4:40
s which I command thee Deut. 28:15
walked not in my *s* Ezek. 20:13
judgments, and observe my *s* Ezek. 37:24
and my *s*, which I commanded Zech. 1:6

STONE
be as still as a *s* Ex. 15:16
testimony, tables of *s* Ex. 31:18
other gods, wood and *s* Deut. 28:36
known, even wood and *s* Deut. 28:64
The *s* which the builders Ps. 118:22
a *s*, a tried *s*, a precious Is. 28:16
the chief corner *s* Eph. 2:20
And a *s* of stumbling 1 Pet. 2:8

STONES
hail *s* and coals of Ps. 18:13
s thereof, and planted Is. 5:2
committed adultery with *s* Jer. 3:9
these *s* be made bread Matt. 4:3
as lively *s*, are built 1 Pet. 2:5

STOOD
behold, the LORD *s* Gen. 28:13
from above *s* and rose Josh. 3:16
spake to the men that *s* 1 Sam. 17:26
came and *s* by the conduit 2 Kin. 18:17
s still in the prison Neh. 12:39
times ten thousand *s* Dan. 7:10
Jews, came Jesus and *s* John 20:19
midst of the elders, *s* Rev. 5:6

STRANGER
wherein thou art a *s* Gen. 17:8
s, or born in the land Ex. 12:19
thy cattle, nor thy *s* Ex. 20:10
s that is within thee Deut. 28:43
for I am a *s* with thee Ps. 39:12
that turn aside the *s* Mal. 3:5

STRENGTH
by *s* of hand the LORD Ex. 13:3
By *s* of hand the LORD Ex. 13:14
s, in whom I will trust Ps. 18:2
the LORD is the *s* of Ps. 27:1
made not God his *s* Ps. 52:7
LORD JEHOVAH is my *s* Is. 12:2
put on thy *s*, O Zion Is. 52:1
sun shineth in his *s* Rev. 1:16

STRONG
back by a *s* east wind Ex. 14:21
children of Ammon was *s* Num. 21:24
s and of a good courage Deut. 31:6
thou *s* and very courageous Josh. 1:7
Wine is a mocker, *s* Prov. 20:1
wine, and through *s* Is. 28:7
because they are very *s* Is. 31:1
the spoil with the *s* Is. 53:12

SUN
when thou seest the *s* Deut. 4:19
the *s* shall be darkened Is. 13:10
they worshipped the *s* Ezek. 8:16
the *s* and the moon Joel 2:10
The *s* shall be turned Joel 2:31
the rising of the *s* Mal. 1:11
those days shall the *s* Matt. 24:29

SURELY
LORD said, I have *s* Ex. 3:7
s be a snare unto thee Ex. 23:33
s die in the wilderness Num. 26:65
S the princes of Zoan Is. 19:11
S he hath borne our Is. 53:4
S the least of the Jer. 49:20
S, because thou hast Ezek. 5:11
God of Israel, *S* Moab Zeph. 2:9

SWEET

LORD smelled a *s* savour	**Gen. 8:21**
horns of the altar of *s*	**Lev. 4:7**
Sheba, and the *s* cane	**Jer. 6:20**
an odour of a *s* smell	**Phil. 4:18**

SWORD

the edge of the *s*	**Num. 21:24**
burning, and with the *s*	**Deut. 28:22**
young men with the *s*	**2 Chr. 36:17**
s of the LORD is filled	**Is. 34:6**
consumed by the *s*	**Jer. 16:4**
pestilence, from the *s*	**Jer. 21:7**
fall by the *s* round	**Ezek. 5:12**
Awake, O *s*, against	**Zech. 13:7**

TABERNACLE

in the *t* of the congregation	**Lev. 4:7**
the court of the *t*	**Lev. 6:16**
Aaron went into the *t*	**Lev. 9:23**
And I will set my *t*	**Lev. 26:11**
pitch round about the *t*	**Num. 1:53**
of Kohath in the *t*	**Num. 4:15**
tarried long upon the *t*	**Num. 9:19**
Shiloh, and set up the *t*	**Josh. 18:1**

TEACH

will *t* us of his ways	**Is. 2:3**
t no more every man	**Jer. 31:34**
the priests thereof *t*	**Mic. 3:11**
t all nations, baptizing	**Matt. 28:19**
shall *t* you all things	**John 14:26**

TEMPLE

Israel had made in the *t*	**2 Kin. 24:13**
LORD is in his holy *t*	**Ps. 11:4**
vengeance of his *t*	**Jer. 51:11**
at the door of the *t*	**Ezek. 8:16**
suddenly come to his *t*	**Mal. 3:1**
agreement hath the *t*	**2 Cor. 6:16**
t leave out, and measure	**Rev. 11:2**

TEN

covenant, the *t* commandments	**Ex. 34:28**
t thousands of saints	**Deut. 33:2**
men of valour, even *t*	**2 Kin. 24:14**
t thousand times *t*	**Dan. 7:10**

THINE

thou settest *t* hand	**Deut. 28:20**
smitten before *t* enemies	**Deut. 28:25**
shalt thou serve *t*	**Deut. 28:48**
fill *t* horn with oil	**1 Sam. 16:1**
t house and thy kingdom	**2 Sam. 7:16**
I make *t* enemies thy	**Ps. 110:1**
blessing upon *t* offspring	**Is. 44:3**
O LORD, are not *t* eyes	**Jer. 5:3**

THOUSAND

put ten *t* to flight	**Lev. 26:8**
commandments to a *t*	**Deut. 7:9**
a *t*, and two put ten	**Deut. 32:30**
Syrians of Zoba, twenty *t*	**2 Sam. 10:6**
valour, even ten *t*	**2 Kin. 24:14**
t thousands ministered	**Dan. 7:10**
reigned with Christ a *t*	**Rev. 20:4**

THRONE

will stablish the *t*	**2 Sam. 7:13**
thy *t* shall be established	**2 Sam. 7:16**
temple, the LORD's *t*	**Ps. 11:4**
Thy *t*, O God, is for	**Ps. 45:6**
no end, upon the *t*	**Is. 9:7**
t of his father David	**Luke 1:32**
hand of the *t* of God	**Heb. 12:2**
which are before his *t*	**Rev. 1:4**

TIME

the *t* appointed I will	**Gen. 18:14**
commanded thee, in the *t*	**Ex. 23:15**
t to recover the remnant	**Is. 11:11**
t shall Michael stand	**Dan. 12:1**
t forth began Jesus	**Matt. 16:21**
seen God at any *t*	**John 1:18**
the *t*, until the Lord	**1 Cor. 4:5**
the fulness of the *t*	**Gal. 4:4**

TIMES

Three *t* in a year shall	**Deut. 16:16**
fire, and observed *t*	**2 Kin. 21:6**
And he changeth the *t*	**Dan. 2:21**
ten thousand *t* ten	**Dan. 7:10**
to change *t* and laws	**Dan. 7:25**
even in troublous *t*	**Dan. 9:25**
a time, *t*, and an half	**Dan. 12:7**

TONGUE

t thou shalt not understand	**Deut. 28:49**
t cleaveth to my jaws	**Ps. 22:15**
their *t* a sharp sword	**Ps. 57:4**
the *t* of the dumb sing	**Is. 35:6**

TREE

under every green *t*	**1 Kin. 14:23**
fig from the fig *t*	**Is. 34:4**
forest, and every *t*	**Is. 44:23**
green *t* thou wanderest	**Jer. 2:20**
that hangeth on a *t*	**Gal. 3:13**
give to eat of the *t*	**Rev. 2:7**
t of life, which bare	**Rev. 22:2**

TREES

shalt have olive *t*	**Deut. 28:40**
All thy *t* and fruit	**Deut. 28:42**
be called *t* of righteousness	**Is. 61:3**
beast, and upon the *t*	**Jer. 7:20**

TROUBLE
me in the day of *t* — **Ps. 50:15**
they are a *t* unto me — **Is. 1:14**
the time of their *t* — **Jer. 2:27**
shall be a time of *t* — **Dan. 12:1**

TRUE
the LORD is the *t* God — **Jer. 10:10**
a *t* heart in full assurance — **Heb. 10:22**
know him that is *t* — **1 John 5:20**
holy, he that is *t* — **Rev. 3:7**

TRUST
strength, in whom I will *t* — **Ps. 18:2**
I will *t*, and not be — **Is. 12:2**
stay on horses, and *t* — **Is. 31:1**
neighbour, and *t* ye — **Jer. 9:4**
t in uncertain riches — **1 Tim. 6:17**

TRUTH
a God of *t* and without — **Deut. 32:4**
plenteous in mercy and *t* — **Ps. 86:15**
people with his *t* — **Ps. 96:13**
thine eyes upon the *t* — **Jer. 5:3**
full of grace and *t* — **John 1:14**
abode not in the *t* — **John 8:44**
the *t*, and the life — **John 14:6**
even the Spirit of *t* — **John 15:26**

TURN
t not from it to the — **Josh. 1:7**
testified against them to *t* — **Neh. 9:26**
shall remember and *t* — **Ps. 22:27**
your garments, and *t* — **Joel 2:13**
and I will *t* mine hand — **Zech. 13:7**
fatherless, and that *t* — **Mal. 3:5**
everlasting life, lo, we *t* — **Acts 13:46**
their eyes, and to *t* — **Acts 26:18**

TURNED
his anger is not *t* — **Is. 5:25**
we have *t* every one — **Is. 53:6**
was *t* to be their enemy — **Is. 63:10**
they have *t* their back — **Jer. 2:27**
mine heart is *t* within — **Hos. 11:8**
The sun shall be *t* — **Joel 2:31**
But Jesus *t* him about — **Matt. 9:22**

TWENTY
(a shekel is *t* gerahs — **Ex. 30:13**
number, from *t* years — **Num. 14:29**
Zoba, *t* thousand footmen — **2 Sam. 10:6**
t men, with their backs — **Ezek. 8:16**

UNCLEAN
his clothes, and be *u* — **Lev. 11:25**
in water, and be *u* — **Lev. 15:5**
I am a man of *u* lips — **Is. 6:5**
uncircumcised and the *u* — **Is. 52:1**
difference between the *u* — **Ezek. 22:26**

UNDERSTANDING
thee a wise and an *u* — **1 Kin. 3:12**
is a people of no *u* — **Is. 27:11**
to them that know *u* — **Dan. 2:21**
not children in *u* — **1 Cor. 14:20**
hath given us an *u* — **1 John 5:20**

UTTERLY
ye shall soon *u* perish — **Deut. 4:26**
shalt smite them, and *u* — **Deut. 7:2**
brother will *u* supplant — **Jer. 9:4**
round about, and will *u* — **Jer. 25:9**

VAIN
Bring no more *v* oblations — **Is. 1:13**
In *v* have I smitten — **Jer. 2:30**
deceive you with *v* — **Eph. 5:6**
philosophy and *v* deceit — **Col. 2:8**

VALLEY
v of the son of Hinnom — **Josh. 15:8**
Topheth, which is in the *v* — **2 Kin. 23:10**
walk through the *v* — **Ps. 23:4**
v of the son of Hinnom — **Jer. 7:31**
the cities of the *v* — **Jer. 32:44**

VENGEANCE
time of the LORD's *v* — **Jer. 51:6**
is the *v* of the LORD — **Jer. 51:11**
is written, *V* is mine — **Rom. 12:19**
flaming fire taking *v* — **2 Thess. 1:8**

VERILY
Jesus said unto them, *V* — **Matt. 19:28**
say unto them, *V* I — **Matt. 25:40**
V, *v*, I say unto you — **John 5:24**
I am *v* a man which — **Acts 22:3**

VISION
in a *v*, and will speak — **Num. 12:6**
err in *v*, they stumble — **Is. 28:7**
you a false *v* and divination — **Jer. 14:14**
seal up the *v* and prophecy — **Dan. 9:24**

VOICE
thou hast obeyed my *v* — **Gen. 22:18**
if ye will obey my *v* — **Ex. 19:5**
v of the LORD thy God — **Deut. 28:15**
a *v* of singing declare — **Is. 48:20**
thanksgiving, and the *v* — **Is. 51:3**
ears with a loud *v* — **Ezek. 8:18**
And lo a *v* from heaven — **Matt. 3:17**
and behold a *v* out — **Matt. 17:5**

WAIT
W on the LORD — **Ps. 27:14**
not be ashamed that *w* — **Is. 49:23**
Surely the isles shall *w* — **Is. 60:9**
we will *w* upon thee — **Jer. 14:22**

WISDOM
man glory in his *w* Jer. 9:23
Is *w* no more in Teman Jer. 49:7
giveth *w* unto the wise Dan. 2:21
riches both of the *w* Rom. 11:33
is made unto us *w* 1 Cor. 1:30
any of you lack *w* James 1:5

WISE
gift blindeth the *w* Ex. 23:8
the eyes of the *w* Deut. 16:19
thee a *w* and an understanding 1 Kin. 3:12
deceived thereby is not *w* Prov. 20:1
wisdom unto the *w* Dan. 2:21
not *w* in your own conceits Rom. 12:16
only *w* God, be honour 1 Tim. 1:17
shall in no *w* enter Rev. 21:27

WITNESS
heaven and earth to *w* Deut. 4:26
I will be a swift *w* Mal. 3:5
God is my *w*, whom I Rom. 1:9
shalt not bear false *w* Rom. 13:9
and bear *w*, and shew 1 John 1:2
is the faithful *w* Rev. 1:5
beheaded for the *w* Rev. 20:4

WOE
W to thee, Moab Num. 21:29
W unto the wicked Is. 3:11
Then said I, *W* is me Is. 6:5
W to them that go down Is. 31:1

WOMAN
between thee and the *w* Gen. 3:15
tender and delicate *w* Deut. 28:56
slay both man and *w* 1 Sam. 15:3
pain as a *w* that travaileth Is. 13:8
as the heart of a *w* Jer. 49:22
And the *w* was made Matt. 9:22
Son, made of a *w*, made Gal. 4:4
as travail upon a *w* 1 Thess. 5:3

WOMEN
and all the *w* went Ex. 15:20
the *w* come, and set Is. 27:11
pieces, and their *w* Hos. 13:16
w, and Mary the mother Acts 1:14
haling men and *w* committed Acts 8:3

WORD
according to my *w* 1 Kin. 17:1
the law, and the *w* Is. 2:3
The *w* of the LORD came Ezek. 1:3
w of the LORD by Haggai Hag. 1:1
beginning was the *W* John 1:1
the *W* was made flesh John 1:14
all things by the *w* Heb. 1:3
have handled, of the *W* 1 John 1:1

WORDS
the *w* which thou shalt Ex. 19:6
and perverteth the *w* Ex. 23:8
wise, and pervert the *w* Deut. 16:19
observe to do all the *w* Deut. 28:58
and despised his *w* 2 Chr. 36:16
hath confirmed his *w* Dan. 9:12
But my *w* and my statutes Zech. 1:6
deceive you with vain *w* Eph. 5:6

WORK
labour, and do all thy *w* Ex. 20:9
w, thou, nor thy son Ex. 20:10
shall do no servile *w* Lev. 23:36
the *w* of thine hand Deut. 28:12
Rock, his *w* is perfect Deut. 32:4
sell himself to *w* wickedness 1 Kin. 21:25
are the *w* of thy hands Ps. 102:25
counsel, and mighty in *w* Jer. 32:19

WORKS
righteous in all his *w* Dan. 9:14
according to his *w* Matt. 16:27
me, he doeth the *w* John 14:10
good *w*, which God hath Eph. 2:10
zealous of good *w* Titus 2:14
Not by *w* of righteousness Titus 3:5
conscience from dead *w* Heb. 9:14
may by your good *w* 1 Pet. 2:12

WORLD
All the ends of the *w* Ps. 22:27
foundation of the *w* Matt. 25:34
away the sin of the *w* John 1:29
God so loved the *w* John 3:16
secret since the *w* Rom. 16:25
the god of this *w* hath 2 Cor. 4:4
believed on in the *w* 1 Tim. 3:16
poor of this *w* rich James 2:5

WORSHIP
shouldest be driven to *w* Deut. 4:19
the nations shall *w* Ps. 22:27
princes also shall *w* Is. 49:7
upon the earth shall *w* Rev. 13:8
day nor night, who *w* Rev. 14:11

WORSHIPPED
their heads and *w* Ex. 4:31
served Baal, and *w* 1 Kin. 16:31
and they *w* the sun Ezek. 8:16
beast, and them that *w* Rev. 19:20

WRATH
anger, and in his *w* Deut. 29:23
the *w* of the LORD arose 2 Chr. 36:16
when his *w* is kindled Ps. 2:12
w the earth shall tremble Jer. 10:10
but the *w* of God abideth John 3:36
things cometh the *w* Eph. 5:6
to speak, slow to *w* James 1:19
wine of the *w* of God Rev. 14:10

WRITTEN

tables of stone, *w*	**Ex. 31:18**
this law that are *w*	**Deut. 28:58**
be found *w* in the book	**Dan. 12:1**
is *w*, Thou shalt worship	**Matt. 4:10**
w, Vengeance is mine	**Rom. 12:19**
w in the book of life	**Rev. 13:8**
whosoever was not found *w*	**Rev. 20:15**
w in the Lamb's book	**Rev. 21:27**

YEAR

y, when thou hast gathered	**Ex. 23:16**
y without spot day	**Num. 28:3**
a *y* shall all thy males	**Deut. 16:16**
In the ninth *y* of Hoshea	**2 Kin. 17:6**
eighth *y* of his reign	**2 Kin. 24:12**
y was expired, king	**2 Chr. 36:10**
y of Darius the king	**Hag. 1:1**
y, not without blood	**Heb. 9:7**

YEARS

Abram was ninety *y*	**Gen. 17:1**
numbered, from twenty *y*	**Ex. 38:26**
number, from twenty *y*	**Num. 14:29**
thee these forty *y*	**Deut. 8:2**
dew nor rain these *y*	**1 Kin. 17:1**
an heifer of three *y*	**Is. 15:5**
seventy *y* be accomplished	**Jer. 29:10**
Christ a thousand *y*	**Rev. 20:4**

YOUNG

hath sinned, a *y* bullock	**Lev. 4:3**
shew favour to the *y*	**Deut. 28:50**
her *y* one that cometh	**Deut. 28:57**
Chaldees, who slew their *y*	**2 Chr. 36:17**
Ethiopians captives, *y*	**Is. 20:4**
those that are with *y*	**Is. 40:11**
dream dreams, your *y*	**Joel 2:28**
forest, as a *y* lion	**Mic. 5:8**

ZEDEKIAH

the LORD, and made *Z*	**2 Chr. 36:10**
I will deliver *Z* king	**Jer. 21:7**
overtook *Z* in the plains	**Jer. 39:5**
slew the sons of *Z*	**Jer. 39:6**

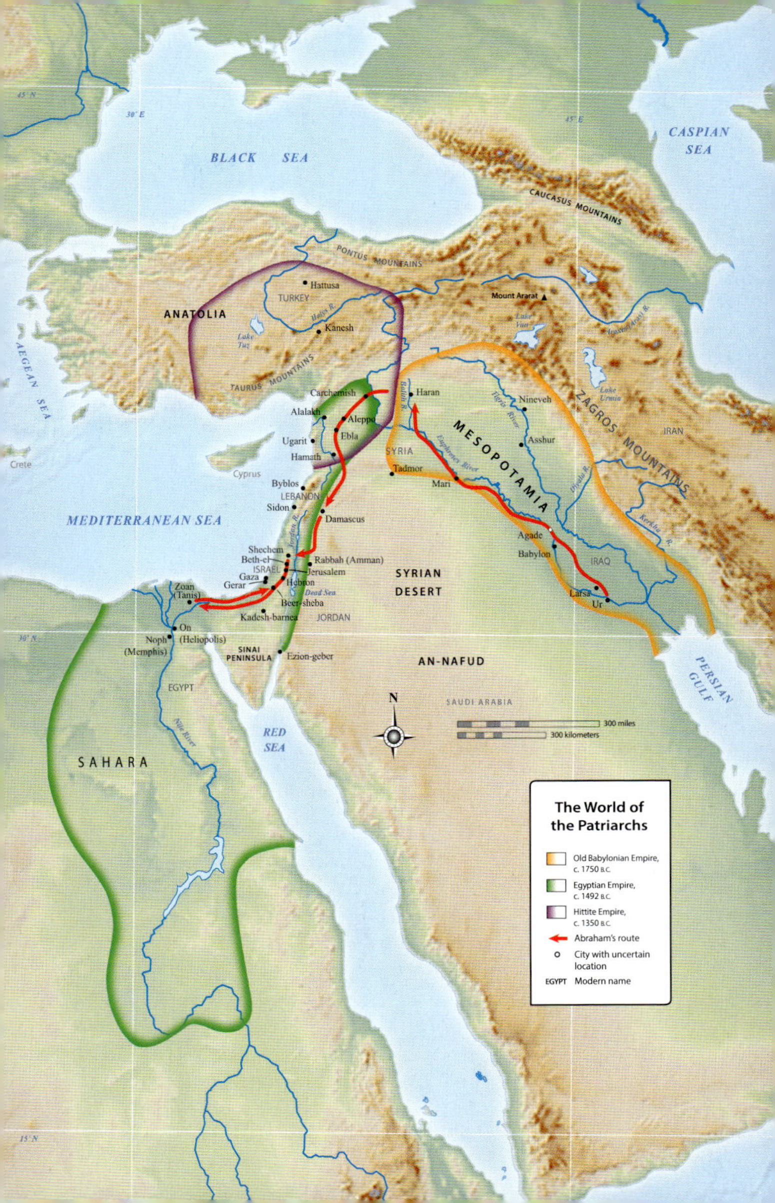

The World of the Patriarchs
Old Babylonian Empire, c. 1750 B.C.
Egyptian Empire, c. 1492 B.C.
Hittite Empire, c. 1350 B.C.
Abraham's route
City with uncertain location
EGYPT Modern name
BLACK SEA
CASPIAN SEA
CAUCASUS MOUNTAINS
PONTUS MOUNTAINS
ANATOLIA
TURKEY
Hattusa
Kanesh
Halys R.
Lake Tuz
TAURUS MOUNTAINS
Mount Ararat
Lake Van
Araxes/Aras R.
Lake Urmia
ZAGROS MOUNTAINS
IRAN
AEGEAN SEA
Crete
Cyprus
MEDITERRANEAN SEA
Carchemish
Haran
Balih R.
Nineveh
Tigris River
Asshur
Alalakh
Aleppo
Ebla
Ugarit
Hamath
SYRIA
Tadmor
Mari
Euphrates River
MESOPOTAMIA
Diyala R.
Kerkha R.
Byblos
LEBANON
Sidon
Damascus
Jordan R.
Agade
Babylon
IRAQ
Larsa
Ur
Shechem
Beth-el
ISRAEL
Jerusalem
Rabbah (Amman)
Gaza
Gerar
Hebron
Dead Sea
Beer-sheba
Zoan (Tanis)
Kadesh-barnea
JORDAN
SYRIAN DESERT
On (Heliopolis)
Noph (Memphis)
SINAI PENINSULA
Ezion-geber
AN-NAFUD
EGYPT
Nile River
SAUDI ARABIA
PERSIAN GULF
RED SEA
SAHARA
N
300 miles
300 kilometers
45° N
30° E
45° E
30° N
15° N

The Exodus from Egypt
Traditional route
Alternate routes of Red Sea crossing
City
City with uncertain location
Mountain
50 miles
50 kilometers
32° E
34° E
32° N
30° N
28° N
MEDITERRANEAN SEA
Sea of Galilee
AMMON
Jordan R.
Mount Nebo
CANAAN
Dead Sea
MOAB
Kadesh-barnea
Zoar
WILDERNESS OF ZIN
Punon
EDOM
Sile
Raamses
GOSHEN
Succoth
Pithom
Lake Timsah
Great Bitter Lake
Little Bitter Lake
EGYPT
On (Heliopolis)
Noph (Memphis)
WILDERNESS OF PARAN
SINAI
Ezion-geber
WILDERNESS OF SIN
Gulf of Suez
Rephidim
Mount Sinai (Jebel Musa)
Gulf of Aqaba
MIDIAN
N
Nile River
RED SEA

The Conquest of Canaan
City
City with uncertain location
Route from Kadesh-barnea
Advance through Canaan and beyond
Battle
City attacked
City burned
City left unconquered
1. The Israelites cross the Jordan River, camp at Gilgal, then attack and conquer Jericho (Joshua 1-6).
2. The Israelites conquer Ai after an initial defeat (Joshua 7-8).
3. The Israelites are tricked into a treaty with Gibeon. They then defeat five Amorite kings in the valley of Aijalon, where the sun stands still (Joshua 9-10).
4. The Israelites attack and conquer the northern kings and burn the city of Hazor (Joshua 11).
MEDITERRANEAN SEA
PHOENICIA
GALILEE
SAMARIA
GILEAD
AMMON
MOAB
35° E
35°30' E
36° E
33°N
32°30'N
32°N
31°30'N
N
Tyre
Litani River
Dan
Kedesh
Lake Huleh
Hazor
Achzib
Merom
Acco
Beth-anath
Capernaum
Sea of Galilee
Achshaph
Yarmuk River
Megiddo
Kishon River
Dor
Edrei
Ramoth-gilead
Taanach
Beth-shean
Dothan
Ibleam
Jabesh-gilead
Jordan River
Samaria
Mount Ebal
Wadi Far'a
Mount Gerizim
Shechem
Mahanaim
Jabbok River
Shiloh
Jazer
Beth-el
Ai
Gilgal
Rabbath (Amman)
Gezer
Aijalon
Gibeon
Jericho
Abel-shittim
Heshbon
Mount Nebo
Ashdod
Ekron
Beth-shemish
Jerusalem
Medeba
Jarmuth
Gath
Bethlehem
Libnah
Mareshah
Lachish
Jahaz
Eglon
Hebron
Makkedah
En-gedi
Aroer
Debir
Dead Sea
Arnon River
Arad
Beer-sheba
Hormah
20 miles
20 kilometers

The Allotments to the Twelve Tribes
City
City of refuge
City with uncertain location
34° 30' E
35° E
35° 30' E
36° E
33°N
32°30'N
32°N
31°30'N
31°N
MEDITERRANEAN SEA
N
Litani River
Tyre
Ijon
Dan
ARAM (Syria)
ASHER
NAPHTALI
Rehob
Abdon
Kedesh
Hazor
Lake Huleh
Merom
EAST MANASSEH
Mishal
Nahalal
Rimmon
Helkath
ZEBULUN
Sea of Galilee
Hammath
Golan
Ashtaroth
Daberath
Yarmuk River
Jokneam
Megiddo
Kishon River
ISSACHAR
Dor
Jarmuth
Edrei
Taanach
Ramoth-gilead
Beth-shean
Ibleam
Jabesh-gilead
WEST MANASSEH
Samaria
Wadi Faria
Jordan River
Mount Ebal
Shechem
Mount Gerizim
Jabbok River
Mahanaim
Gath-rimmon
Joppa
Shiloh
GAD
EPHRAIM
Jazer
AMMON
DAN
Rabbah (Amman)
Eltekah
Beth-horon
Gezer
Bethel
Gibeon
Gilgal
Geba
Gibbethon
Aijalon
BENJAMIN
Jericho
Abel-shittim
Heshbon
Mount Nebo
Bezer
Beth-shemesh
Jerusalem
Medeba
Bethlehem
Ashkelon
Libnah
REUBEN
Lachish
Hebron
Dead Sea
Eglon
Jahaz
Gaza
JUDAH
Juttah
Aroer
Debir
En-gedi
Eshtemoa
Arnon River
Gerar
MOAB
Ashan
Beer-sheba
Hormah
SIMEON
20 miles
20 kilometers
Zered Brook
EDOM

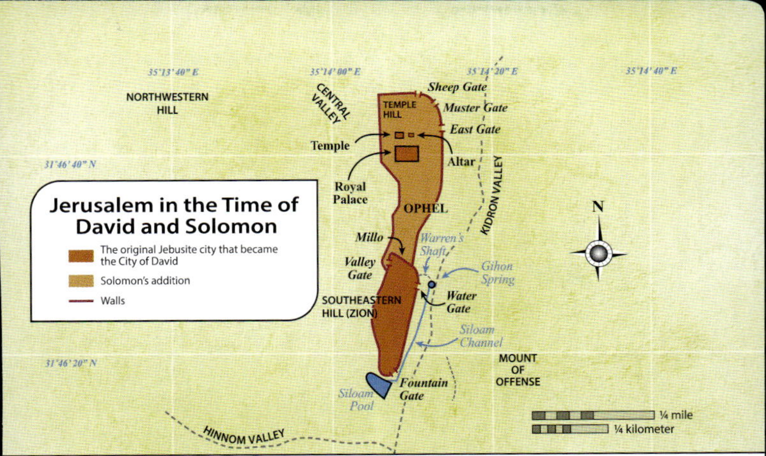

Jerusalem in the Time of David and Solomon

- The original Jebusite city that became the City of David
- Solomon's addition
- Walls

35°13′40″ E
35°14′00″ E
35°14′20″ E
35°14′40″ E
31°46′40″ N
31°46′20″ N
NORTHWESTERN HILL
CENTRAL VALLEY
Sheep Gate
TEMPLE HILL
Muster Gate
East Gate
Temple
Altar
Royal Palace
OPHEL
KIDRON VALLEY
Millo
Warren's Shaft
Valley Gate
Gihon Spring
SOUTHEASTERN HILL (ZION)
Water Gate
Siloam Channel
MOUNT OF OFFENSE
Siloam Pool
Fountain Gate
HINNOM VALLEY
N
¼ mile
¼ kilometer

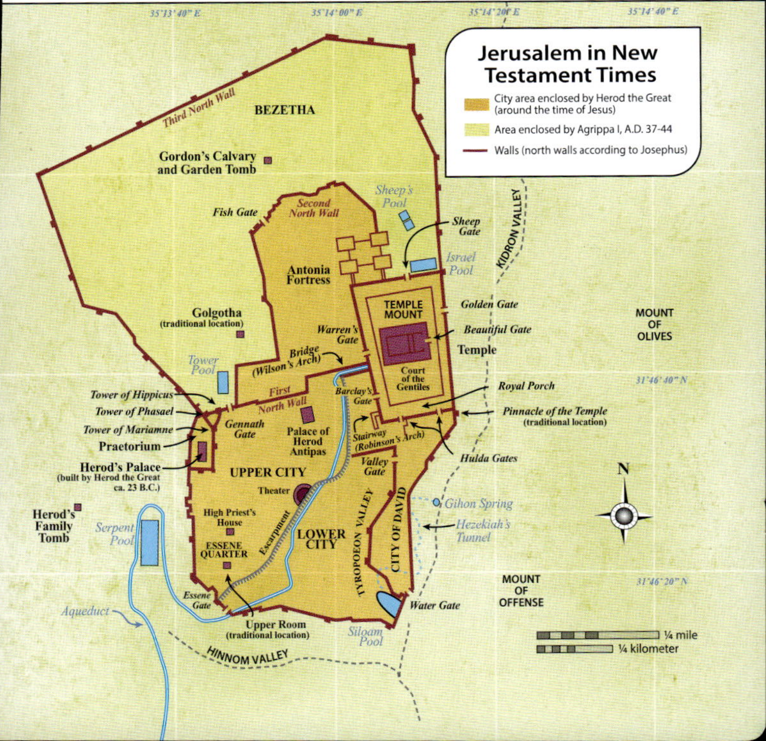

Jerusalem in New Testament Times

- City area enclosed by Herod the Great (around the time of Jesus)
- Area enclosed by Agrippa I, A.D. 37-44
- Walls (north walls according to Josephus)

35°13′40″ E
35°14′00″ E
35°14′20″ E
35°14′40″ E
31°46′40″ N
31°46′20″ N
Third North Wall
BEZETHA
Gordon's Calvary and Garden Tomb
Fish Gate
Second North Wall
Sheep's Pool
Sheep Gate
Israel Pool
KIDRON VALLEY
Antonia Fortress
TEMPLE MOUNT
Golden Gate
Golgotha (traditional location)
Warren's Gate
Beautiful Gate
Temple
MOUNT OF OLIVES
Tower Pool
Bridge (Wilson's Arch)
Court of the Gentiles
Royal Porch
Tower of Hippicus
First North Wall
Barclay's Gate
Tower of Phasael
Pinnacle of the Temple (traditional location)
Tower of Mariamne
Gennath Gate
Palace of Herod Antipas
Stairway (Robinson's Arch)
Praetorium
Hulda Gates
Herod's Palace (built by Herod the Great ca. 23 B.C.)
Valley Gate
UPPER CITY
Theater
Gihon Spring
Herod's Family Tomb
High Priest's House
Serpent Pool
Hezekiah's Tunnel
Escarpment
LOWER CITY
TYROPOEON VALLEY
CITY OF DAVID
ESSENE QUARTER
MOUNT OF OFFENSE
Essene Gate
Aqueduct
Water Gate
Upper Room (traditional location)
Siloam Pool
HINNOM VALLEY
N
¼ mile
¼ kilometer

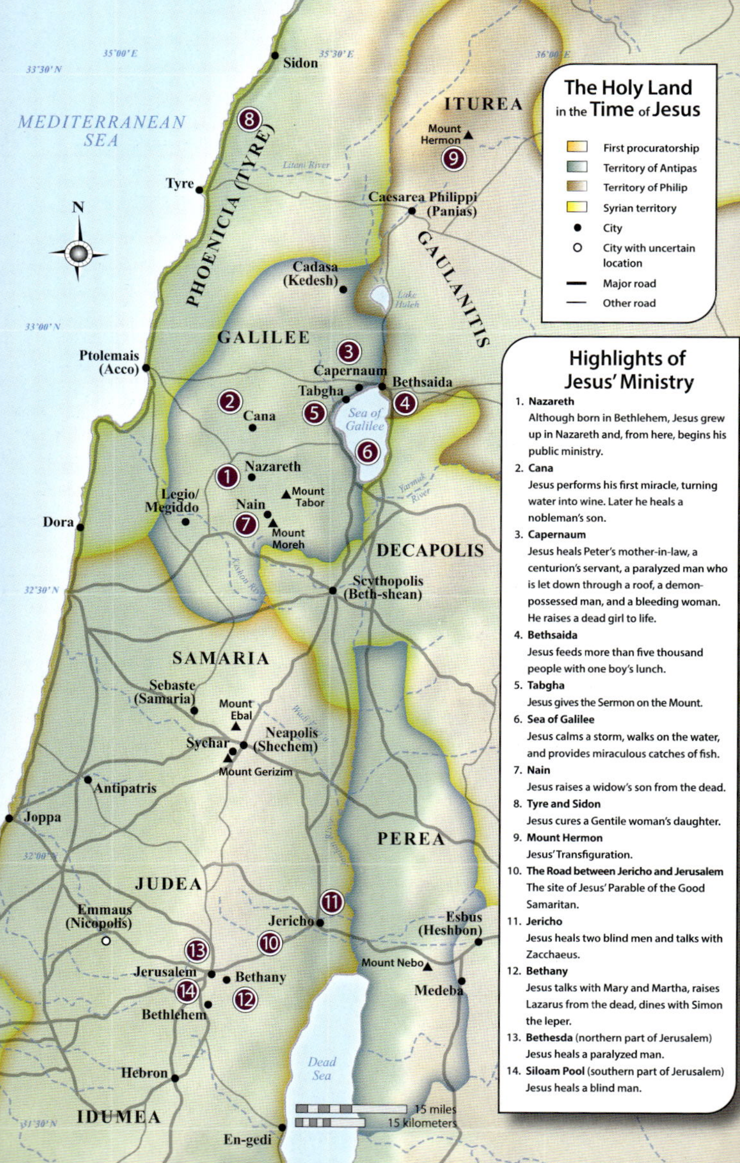

Highlights of Jesus' Ministry

1. **Nazareth**
   Although born in Bethlehem, Jesus grew up in Nazareth and, from here, begins his public ministry.
2. **Cana**
   Jesus performs his first miracle, turning water into wine. Later he heals a nobleman's son.
3. **Capernaum**
   Jesus heals Peter's mother-in-law, a centurion's servant, a paralyzed man who is let down through a roof, a demon-possessed man, and a bleeding woman. He raises a dead girl to life.
4. **Bethsaida**
   Jesus feeds more than five thousand people with one boy's lunch.
5. **Tabgha**
   Jesus gives the Sermon on the Mount.
6. **Sea of Galilee**
   Jesus calms a storm, walks on the water, and provides miraculous catches of fish.
7. **Nain**
   Jesus raises a widow's son from the dead.
8. **Tyre and Sidon**
   Jesus cures a Gentile woman's daughter.
9. **Mount Hermon**
   Jesus' Transfiguration.
10. **The Road between Jericho and Jerusalem**
    The site of Jesus' Parable of the Good Samaritan.
11. **Jericho**
    Jesus heals two blind men and talks with Zacchaeus.
12. **Bethany**
    Jesus talks with Mary and Martha, raises Lazarus from the dead, dines with Simon the leper.
13. **Bethesda** (northern part of Jerusalem)
    Jesus heals a paralyzed man.
14. **Siloam Pool** (southern part of Jerusalem)
    Jesus heals a blind man.

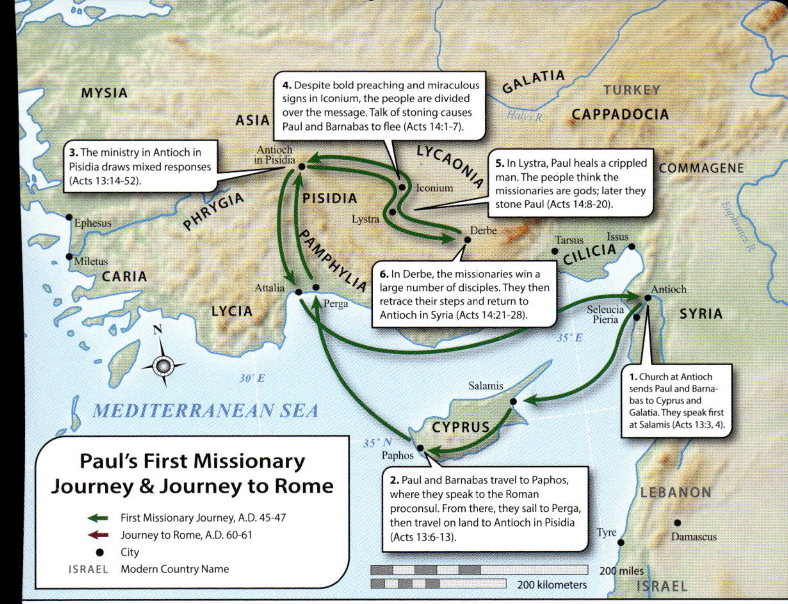

Paul's First Missionary Journey & Journey to Rome

First Missionary Journey, A.D. 45-47
Journey to Rome, A.D. 60-61
City
ISRAEL Modern Country Name

200 miles
200 kilometers

1. Church at Antioch sends Paul and Barnabas to Cyprus and Galatia. They speak first at Salamis (Acts 13:3, 4).

2. Paul and Barnabas travel to Paphos, where they speak to the Roman proconsul. From there, they sail to Perga, then travel on land to Antioch in Pisidia (Acts 13:6-13).

3. The ministry in Antioch in Pisidia draws mixed responses (Acts 13:14-52).

4. Despite bold preaching and miraculous signs in Iconium, the people are divided over the message. Talk of stoning causes Paul and Barnabas to flee (Acts 14:1-7).

5. In Lystra, Paul heals a crippled man. The people think the missionaries are gods; later they stone Paul (Acts 14:8-20).

6. In Derbe, the missionaries win a large number of disciples. They then retrace their steps and return to Antioch in Syria (Acts 14:21-28).

MYSIA
ASIA
GALATIA
TURKEY
CAPPADOCIA
Halys R.
LYCAONIA
COMMAGENE
Antioch in Pisidia
Iconium
PHRYGIA
PISIDIA
Lystra
Ephesus
Derbe
Euphrates R.
Miletus
PAMPHYLIA
Tarsus
Issus
CILICIA
CARIA
Attalia
Perga
Antioch
LYCIA
Seleucia Pieria
SYRIA
35° E
N
30° E
Salamis
MEDITERRANEAN SEA
CYPRUS
35° N
Paphos
LEBANON
Tyre
Damascus
ISRAEL

1. At his trial before Festus, Paul appeals to Caesar (Acts 25:10-12). Paul and other prisoners are put on board a ship sailing for Italy. They sail to Crete (Acts 27:1-8).

2. The weather changes and wind forces the ship away from Crete and across the sea where it drifts for two weeks (Acts 27:9-38).

3. The ship runs aground on the island of Malta, but all on board are safe. Paul is bitten by a snake but survives, then he heals the father of a Roman official (Acts 27:39-28:10).

4. After three months, they leave Malta, then make several stops. At Three Taverns, some believers meet Paul to encourage him (Acts 28:11-15).

5. In Rome, Paul lives under house arrest. He speaks to many and writes letters to the churches (Acts 28:16-31).

BLACK SEA
N
ITALIA
ROME
Three Taverns
Appii Forum
Puteoli
THRACE
Byzantium
BITHYNIA AND PONTUS
TURKEY
GALATIA
CAPPADOCIA
Halys R.
EPIRUS
MYSIA
TYRRHENIAN SEA
IONIAN SEA
GREECE
AEGEAN SEA
ASIA
LYCAONIA
COMMAGENE
LYDIA
PHRYGIA
Antioch in Pisidia
PISIDIA
Iconium
Delphi
Ephesus
Tarsus
Issus
Euphrates R.
Corinth
Athens
CARIA
Antioch
ACHAIA
Miletus
PAMPHYLIA
CILICIA
SICILY
Rhegium
MEDITERRANEAN
Sparta
Cnidus
LYCIA
Myra
SYRIA
Syracuse
CYPRUS
LEBANON
MALTA
CRETE
SEA
Phoenix
Fair Havens
Sidon
Damascus
Tyre
Caesarea
30°E
25°E
ISRAEL
Jerusalem
Dead Sea
JUDEA
JORDAN
NABATEA
200 miles
200 kilometers
EGYPT
Nile R.
RED SEA

BLACK SEA
2C. Lydia and the jailer are converted in Philippi. The missionaries go to Thessalonica and Berea (Acts 16:11–17:14).
3D. Paul speaks in Troas and raises Eutychus from the dead (Acts 20:6-12).
3B. In Ephesus, Paul ministers for three years (Acts 18:23–19:41).
2B. Paul chooses Silas and they revisit cities in Galatia. In Lystra, Timothy joins them. Paul receives the Macedonian call (Acts 15:36–16:10).
3C. Paul stays in Greece for three months (Acts 20:1-5).
2D. In Athens, Paul speaks about the "unknown God" (Acts 17:15-34).
2E. After time in Corinth, Paul sails to Ephesus and then heads back to Antioch (Acts 18:1-22).
3E. Paul says farewell to the Ephesian elders (Acts 20:13-38).
2A and 3A. Paul begins both journeys from Antioch in Syria.
3F. Paul is arrested in Jerusalem, put on trial, has his life threatened, spends two years in prison in Caesarea, and appeals to have his case heard by Caesar (Acts 21–26).
THRACE
MACEDONIA
BITHYNIA AND PONTUS
TURKEY
CAPPADOCIA
GALATIA
MYSIA
ASIA
LYDIA
PHRYGIA
PISIDIA
GREECE
ACHAIA
CARIA
LYCIA
PAMPHYLIA
CILICIA
SYRIA
LEBANON
JORDAN
JUDEA
ISRAEL
EGYPT
LIBYA
CYRENAICA
AEGEAN SEA
MEDITERRANEAN SEA
RED SEA
Dead Sea
Philippi
Amphipolis
Thessalonica
Neapolis
Apollonia
Berea
Mount Olympus
Troas
Byzantium
Delphi
Corinth
Athens
Cenchreae
Sparta
Ephesus
Miletus
Cnidus
Rhodes
Patara
Antioch in Pisidia
Iconium
Lystra
Derbe
Tarsus
Issus
Antioch
Cyprus
Tyre
Damascus
Ptolemais
Caesarea
Jerusalem
Alexandria
Cyrene
Halys R.
Euphrates R.
Jordan R.
Nile R.
30° E
35° E
40° E
35° N
N
200 miles
200 kilometers
Paul's Second and Third Missionary Journeys
Second Missionary Journey, A.D. 49-52
Third Missionary Journey, A.D. 53-58
City
Mountain
ISRAEL Modern Country Name